DOD'S
PARLIAMENTARY
COMPANION
2001

Dod's Parliamentary Companion 2001

168th Year

1832

Dod's Parliamentary Companion published since 1832

©182nd edition Vacher Dod Publishing Limited 2000

Published by
Vacher Dod Publishing Ltd
PO Box 3700
Westminster
London SW1P 4WU

Tel: 020 7828 7256
Fax: 020 7828 7269
E-mail: politics@vacherdod.co.uk
Website: www.politicallinks.co.uk

ISBN 0 905702 30 1   ISSN 0070-7007

Database typesetting by Vacher Dod Publishing Limited

Printed in Great Britain by The Cromwell Press, Trowbridge, Wiltshire

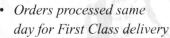

CONTENTS

FOREWORD

HOUSE OF COMMONS
LONDON SW1A 0AA

Dod's Parliamentary Companion is the essential handbook for those who seek accurate information on the detailed workings of Parliament.

Recent years have brought many changes: some, such as the beginning of reform of the House of Lords and the creation of the devolved assemblies have been seismic, in the change which they have wrought – with further implications yet to be felt. Others, such as the election of many more women to Parliament and progress in modernising the procedures of the House of Commons, are a more quiet revolution, bringing about change but in a less obtrusive way.

Parliament has always changed and evolved while remaining at the heart of our democracy. *Dod's* helps to chronicle those changes and guide those who follow them.

Margaret Beckett

Rt Hon Margaret Beckett MP
President of the Council and Leader of the House of Commons

Parliamentary Notes

The Speakership

The most dramatic event of the parliamentary year happened just two weeks before the beginning of the summer recess. On 12 July Betty Boothroyd announced to the Commons that she was to resign as Speaker, with effect from the last day of the summer recess, 22 October. On 21 July the House debated a motion of thanks to Madam Speaker, moved by the Prime Minister. The Speaker's standing as a national figure, and the high regard in which she was held within the House, were reflected in the warmth of the tributes paid to her inside and outside Parliament.

In her valedictory speech, Betty Boothroyd reflected on the disillusionment and cynicism about politics that she found to be growing in society at large, and urged the House to take steps to improve its effectiveness in holding the government to account.

It has long been held that Speakers should resign well before a general election to enable a cohort of MPs to elect someone they know and to give the new Speaker a chance to 'bed in'. Miss Boothroyd is the first in recent times to have done so. However, the three-month notice meant that there was an extended summer campaign in the polite competition to succeed her. Even before the House rose for the summer at least half a dozen members had expressed an interest in standing.

By the week before the election, the field had apparently grown to 13: the three deputy Speakers, Sir Alan Haselhurst, Michael Lord and Michael Martin; Alan Beith, John Butterfill, Sir Patrick Cormack, Menzies Campbell, David Clark, Gwyneth Dunwoody, John McWilliam, Richard Shepherd, Nicholas Winterton and Sir George Young (who resigned from the Conservative front bench to stand). There is no formal means for declaring a candidacy, so normally these names would have remained speculative. However, the unprecedentedly large field had alerted backbenchers to the fact that the procedure for the election (which is by motion and amendment rather than ballot) was ill-suited to anything other than a two-horse race. There was no time to reform the standing orders before the summer break.

When the Commons reassembled on 23 October to elect its new Speaker, there was a concerted effort, led by Tony Benn and supported from all quarters of the House, to hold a preliminary ballot to reduce the field to two. The Father of the House, Sir Edward Heath, declined to do so and the election went ahead in accordance with the traditional procedures.

However, in a slight departure from precedent, Sir Edward announced the order in which he proposed to call the 12 candidates (John Butterfill had withdrawn), starting with Michael Martin. Every succeeding amendment to propose an alternative name was defeated, with Sir George Young emerging as the runner-up with 241 votes to 317. No other candidate secured more than 200 votes.

Eventually, after over six hours' debate and divisions, Mr Martin was elected by 370 votes to 8, with most Conservative members abstaining. That is unlikely to be the end of the matter; it is evident that most Members will expect there to be an inquiry into the procedures for election of a Speaker before the general election, after which Mr Martin will need to seek re-election.

By-elections

By-elections have been called for 23 November to fill the Westminster seats of Labour's Audrey Wise, who died on 2 September, Donald Dewar, who died on 11 October and Betty Boothroyd, who resigned her seat once she had been replaced as Speaker. The constituencies are respectively Preston, Glasgow Anniesland and West Bromwich West.

The by-election for Donald Dewar's Scottish Parliament seat for the same constituency is to be held on the same day. Labour is expected to retain all the seats.

There may be a by-election in Falkirk West, held by Dennis Canavan, who was expelled from the Labour Party for standing against the official party candidate in the Scottish Parliament elections (in which he was successful). Mr Canavan had announced his intention of resigning his Westminster seat by the end of October, but at the beginning of November was reported to be negotiating with the Labour Party on being re-instated in the party and staying in his House of Commons seat.

At a by-election on 3 February for the Commons constituency of Ceredigion Simon Thomas held the seat for Plaid Cymru. The vacancy had been created by the resignation of Cynog Dafis to concentrate on his duties in the National Assembly for Wales. Labour, which had come second in the seat at the general election, only made fourth place.

A by-election was held on 4 May in Romsey to replace the Conservative member, Michael Colvin, who died in a fire at his home in February. The Liberal Democrat candidate, Sandra Gidley, captured the seat, converting Michael Colvin's majority of over 8000 in May 1997 to one of over 3000 for her party. This defeat took some of the shine off the Conservatives' otherwise good results in the English local elections on the same day. The Labour vote was cut severely, with its candidate losing his deposit.

In the Tottenham by-election – following the death of Bernie Grant – on 22 June, David Lammy, who had only just been elected to the GLA in May, held the seat easily for Labour.

In the South Antrim by-election on 21 September, called to fill the vacancy created by the death of UUP MP Clifford Forsythe, the DUP candidate William McCrea was returned. This was interpreted by some as a blow to the authority of David Trimble as leader of the Ulster Unionist Party.

The Lords
The House of Lords has made many of the parliamentary headlines this year. In January the Wakeham Commission published its report on reform of the second chamber. It proposed a chamber of around 550 members, of whom between 65 and 195 would be elected by proportional representation, for terms of up to 15 years (either at the time of general elections or European Parliament elections).

The Commission proposed three alternative methods of election, but all were based on representation for the regions of England and for Scotland, Wales and Northern Ireland. It recommended that the remaining members of the chamber should be appointed by an independent appointments commission, with a duty to 'create a second chamber which was broadly representative of British society'.

These appointed members would also serve for fixed terms of around 15 years. The appointments commission would be required to secure an 'independent' element of around 20 per cent, and to secure a balance among the politically affiliated appointees reflecting the votes cast at the most recent general election. On the powers of the second chamber the Wakeham Commission proposed only minor changes to the status quo, though it made some detailed recommendations for expanding and defining the scrutiny functions of the reformed House.

The Royal Commission's proposals received mixed reviews. The proposals were debated in the Commons on 19 June, when the Leader of that House, Margaret Beckett, told the House that the government was 'minded to accept the broad outlines of the Royal Commission report . . .' and reaffirmed the intention of setting up a joint committee of the two Houses 'to examine the parliamentary aspects' of the Commission's proposals – implicitly confirming the government's previously stated position that the joint committee would not be given a remit to re-examine questions of the composition of the reformed Chamber. Another, and permanent, joint committee is expected to be established soon – the Joint Committee on Human Rights, which was adumbrated in the Human Rights Act which came into effect on 2 October.

Meanwhile the 'transitional' House of Lords, consisting of the life peers and 92 hereditary peers (elected by their peers), defeated the government quite frequently. On 21 January it rejected the Home Secretary's proposals to restrict the right to trial by jury in England and Wales by 222 votes to 126. On 7 February, by 210 to 165, it defeated the government's proposal to repeal the notorious 'Section 28' provisions relating to 'promotion' of homosexuality. And on 22 February, exercising one of its few unilateral powers in an unprecedented move, the Lords voted down proposed government regulations on the conduct of the Greater London Assembly elections in a dispute over the distribution of election addresses by candidates in the mayoral elections.

In October the Lords rejected for a second time the proposals (presented in a new form) to restrict jury trial. This bill too is likely to be re-presented by the Commons under Parliament Act procedures next session.

In its turn, the Commons sent the bill equalising the age of consent for homosexual and heterosexual acts once again to the Lords, following its rejection by the Upper House in the previous session. This time, under the terms of the Parliament Acts, the Lords will not be able to prevent the bill becoming law.

The Lords has also pre-empted some of the recommendations of the Royal Commission. A private peer's bill, promoted by Lord Kingsland, was passed by the House on 7 July. The Life Peerages (Appointments Commission) Bill makes the Appointments Commission a statutory body and transfers to it the right of nomination from the prime minister. The bill has no chance of being passed by the Commons.

Thirty-three new 'working Peers' were created in March, the majority of them taking the Labour Whip to rebalance the composition of the House in the government's favour (though as the Lords' voting record attests, the government is still far from enjoying an assured majority). On 17 July the Lords agreed to establish a Constitutional Committee, which will 'examine the constitutional implications' of bills and 'keep under review the operation of the constitution'.

The Commons

In the Commons the Government has had to contend with a number of challenges from its own backbenchers over some key elements of its legislative programme, in particular the Freedom of Information Bill and the proposals for private sector participation in the national air traffic control system.

The new 'parallel chamber' of the Commons has been operating in Westminster Hall on Tuesdays, Wednesdays and Thursdays since the beginning of December 1999. The new forum deals mainly with private Members' business and debates on select committee reports. It does not vote, and so deals only with uncontroversial business. This is the latest innovation proposed by the Commons' Modernisation Committee to have been implemented.

That Committee has been fairly quiet over the year, and the pace of procedural innovation seems, at least until the general election, to have slowed. However, in July the Committee published a report proposing a number of radical changes in the programming of legislation and the voting patterns of the House – introducing a concept of 'deferred divisions'. Whether these proposals will be implemented, without the co-operation of the official opposition, remains to be seen.

The Conservative Party's own Commission on parliamentary reform, under the chairmanship of Professor Lord Norton of Louth, produced a report in July. It was wide-ranging in its proposals. William Hague promised to use it as a 'route map' for reform under a future Conservative government. Like the Liberal Democrats, the Norton report proposes a staged reduction in the size of the Commons (the Liberal Democrats proposing 450 members).

The Opposition continued to press for some measure of legislative 'devolution' to England. The government continues to resist, but on 11 April the Commons agreed to a new standing order paving the way to the revivification of the Standing Committee on Regional Affairs (a kind of English Grand Committee), which has been dormant since 1978. On 28 June the Labour former minister, Frank Field, proposed a ten-minute rule bill which would have restricted the right of Scottish and Northern Ireland MPs to vote on matters not 'reserved' to the UK government. It was defeated by 190 to 131.

The Liaison Committee of the Commons (the committee whose membership comprises the chairmen of all the other select committees of the House) published one of its rare reports at the beginning of March entitled *Shifting the Balance: Select Committees and the Executive*. The report contained a number of moderately radical proposals for strengthening the powers and resources of the Commons' select committee system. On 18 May the government published its response to these proposals, which was distinctly negative. The Liaison Committee described it as 'both disappointing and surprising'.

Determined to pursue their agenda of reform, the Committee summoned the Leader of the House, Margaret Beckett, to explain the government's response in oral evidence on 10 July, and followed this with a further report, combatively entitled *Independence or Control?*, published at the end of July. They disputed the government's justifications for its negative stance, expressing the view that 'the government has missed an opportunity of reforms which would have been greatly to its credit . . . expressions of support for increasing the effectiveness of select committees are not matched by things that might make a real difference – not even by select committees at Westminster having some of the powers which the government has been happy to see in Edinburgh, Cardiff and Belfast'.

The Procedure Committee also published a report recommending wide-ranging changes to the way in which the House deals with delegated legislation. Taken together with the Procedure Committee's earlier report on the reform of financial procedure and the Liaison committee's proposals, these reports represent a fairly radical agenda for change for the Commons.

July saw the usual seasonal rush of ministerial statements in the Commons on major policy initiatives. The Chancellor of the Exchequer unveiled his next three-year spending programme 'Spending Review 2000' on 18 July, promising very substantial increases in public spending. This was followed by a series of further statements on major policy initiatives including transport, defence and the National Health Service. The statement on the NHS was made by the Prime Minister, the last in a series of unusually frequent appearances by him in the House in July on subjects as diverse as the civil list, the Queen Mother's 100th birthday, the government's annual report and the Speaker's retirement.

The Government

At the end of January Peter Kilfoyle resigned as Parliamentary Under Secretary at the Ministry of Defence. He was replaced by Dr Lewis Moonie.

There was no summer reshuffle, although Minister for the Cabinet Office, Mo Mowlam, announced her intention of leaving the Commons at the general election.

The Opposition

On 2 February William Hague appointed Michael Portillo as his shadow Chancellor of the Exchequer, less than three months after the latter's return to the Commons at the Kensington and Chelsea by-election. Francis Maude was moved from shadow Chancellor to replace John Maples as shadow Foreign Secretary, and Archie Norman replaced John Redwood in the shadow environment and transport post.

There have been minor reshuffles since, including Angela Browning's promotion to shadow Leader of the House following Sir George Young's resignation to stand for Speaker.

Devolved Parliaments and Assemblies

Scottish Parliament

All other events were overshadowed by the death of Scotland's First Minister, Donald Dewar, in October.

Following Mr Dewar's death Minister for Lifelong Learning, Henry McLeish was elected interim First Minister on 21 October. He polled 44 votes to Scottish Finance Minister Jim McConnell's 36 votes in a ballot of Scotland's senior Labour politicians. A full election by all Scottish Labour Party members and affiliated trade union members will be held in December.

The official opposition in the Scottish Parliament also had to find a new leader after the unexpected resignation by Alex Salmond, who had led the SNP for 10 years – a period he declared to have been his planned tenure. After a fairly hard-fought contest John Swinney, his deputy, was elected his successor at the party conference in September.

The most controversial issues faced by the Scottish Parliament in its first 12 months were the repeal of the Scottish equivalent of 'Section 28' relating to 'promotion' of homosexuality, and the still rumbling scandal over the shambolic administration of this year's 'Higher' exams. At least, in its battles over Section 28, the Scottish Executive does not have a House of Lords to contend with. The ongoing construction of the new parliamentary building also ran into predictable accusations of inefficiency and extravagance.

The Executive in Edinburgh was also forced to back down in Parliament over a private member's bill to abolish warrant sales, an assertion of backbench power rarely seen at Westminster.

National Assembly for Wales

The First Secretary in Wales and leader of the minority administration, Alun Michael, resigned in February in anticipation of losing a motion of no confidence in the National Assembly. He was replaced by Rhodri Morgan, whom Mr Michael had defeated in a close run battle for leadership of the Welsh Labour Party in 1999. The new Welsh First Secretary conducted his first reshuffle when he replaced his Agriculture Secretary, Christine Gwyther, in July.

His second was forced on him by his surprise decision, announced in October, to form a coalition Executive with the Liberal Democrats.

Following an overwhelming vote to join the ruling Labour minority, the Liberal Democrats gained two seats in the Assembly cabinet: Liberal Democrat leader Mike German became Deputy First Minister and Minister for Economic Development and Jenny Randerson was made Minister of Culture and Sports. Rhodri Morgan took the opportunity to undertake a substantial reshuffle of people and portfolios and redesignated all cabinet members Ministers rather than Secretaries.

The official opposition in the National Assembly, Plaid Cymru, elected a new leader at its annual conference, Ieuan Wyn Jones, to succeed Dafydd Wigley, who had unexpectedly resigned.

Northern Ireland Assembly

The First Minister in Northern Ireland, David Trimble, has also been having a difficult year. The hopes surrounding the setting up of a new devolved executive in Northern Ireland in November 1999 were dealt a blow when the Secretary of State suspended its operation and that of the Northern Ireland Assembly on 5 February. The crisis was brought about by disagreements over the progress of decommissioning of paramilitary weapons. Direct rule from Westminster was reintroduced temporarily.

The Northern Ireland Assembly and its executive remained in suspension for three months. The original deadline for weapons decommissioning in the Good Friday Agreement had been 22 May. A deal was eventually done, which Mr Trimble managed narrowly to get approved by his party executive, which allowed the four-party Executive Committee and Assembly to begin operating once more at the end of that month, despite the policy of non-co-operation by Ian Paisley's Democratic Unionist Party. This included rotating their two cabinet posts, regional development and social development, between their members periodically.

There was a deteriorating security situation during the 'marching season' in July and August, and the implementation of the Patten proposals for the reform of the Royal Ulster Constabulary are also proving difficult to implement.

Greater London Assembly

So far the battle for the new Greater London Mayor and Assembly before the elections has proved by far the most exciting aspect of the new body's activities. At the elections on 4 May Ken Livingstone MP, standing against the official Labour Party candidate Frank Dobson MP, won a convincing victory as Mayor, although run an unexpectedly close second by Steve Norris, the Conservative candidate.

The Assembly elections (a combination of first-past-the-post and proportional top-up seats) resulted in 9 seats to Labour (6 first-past-the-post and 3 top-up), 9 to the Conservatives (8 first-past-the-post and 1 top-up), 4 to the Liberal Democrats (all top-up) and 3 to the Greens (all top-up). The Greater London Assembly and the Mayor became fully operational on 3 July.

New Session

A considerable backlog of unfinished bills had built up by the end of July, partly as a result of the Lords' new found willingness to defy the government. This meant the Lords had to return from their summer break on 27 September, the earliest date in recent memory, and in its turn the Commons delayed their return until 23 October. The Commons have had to deal with a large volume of legislation coming back from the Lords in the so-called 'spill-over' period, which means that the State Opening and Queen's Speech were delayed until very much later than is customary.

Parliamentary Summary, Legislation and Party Conferences 1999-2000

1999-2000 SESSION

The Queen's Speech

Her Majesty the Queen, accompanied by HRH the Duke of Edinburgh, went in state to the Palace of Westminster and opened the new Session of Parliament on 17 November, 1999. The following is the text of the Queen's speech.

My Lords and Members of the House of Commons
This is my Government's third legislative programme. It aims to build on my Government's programme of reform as they seek to modernise the country and its institutions to meet the challenges of the new Millennium.

My Government's aim is to promote fairness and enterprise, providing people with real opportunities to liberate their potential. They will focus on continued modernising of our economy, the promotion of enterprise, reform of the welfare system, protection of the public, and the development of a safe transport system.

The central economic objectives of my Government are high and stable levels of economic growth and employment. More people are in work in Britain today than ever before, with employment up by 700,000, and long term unemployment has halved.

My Government are helping people back into work. The New Deal has helped 145,000 young people into employment.

My Government have introduced a national minimum wage and a new 10p starting rate of tax. They have reformed National Insurance and from next April will cut the basic rate of income tax. The new Working Families Tax Credit, introduced in October, is raising incomes of working families.

My Government will continue to manage the public finances prudently, in accordance with the Code for Fiscal Stability and the two fiscal rules.

The new system of monetary policy-making ensures that interest rate decisions are taken in the best long-term interests of the economy. As a result, long-term interest rates are around their lowest level for almost thirty years. Inflation is historically low and expected to meet my Government's target of 2½ per cent.

My Government will continue to work with others to promote economic reform in Europe. They will work for more open markets, greater economic growth and new job creation.

To prepare Britain as a dynamic, knowledge-based economy my Government will introduce a Bill to promote electronic commerce and electronic government, improving our ability to compete in the digital marketplace.

Financial services lie at the heart of a modern economy. The financial services industry accounts for 7 per cent of our national income, employing over 1 million people. With the new Financial Services Authority, my Government are determined to maintain and advance the UK's position, and the Bill introduced last Session will be carried over to this.

As part of my Government's drive to address inappropriate and over-complex regulation, legislation will be introduced to increase the effectiveness of the power to remove regulatory burdens.

My Government will introduce a Bill to enable the Post Office to improve its services and to compete more effectively in UK and overseas markets.

To put the consumer first, cut prices and make utility regulation more transparent and accountable, a Bill will be introduced to modernise the utility regulation system.

Legislation will be introduced to assist the rescue of viable businesses in short term difficulties, and improve the procedure for disqualifying unfit company directors.

My Government believe a stronger and fairer society strengthens our economy. They will continue to give young people and the long-term unemployed the opportunity to learn new skills and fulfil their potential.

Education remains my Government's number one priority. My Government will continue to implement policies to reward good teaching, reduce infant class sizes, and continue the drive to build on the improvements in literacy and numeracy already achieved.

Having focused change upon primary and secondary education, a Bill will now be introduced to establish a new Learning and Skills Council to improve standards for Post 16 education and training.

As part of my Government's drive against social exclusion, a Bill will be introduced to improve the help available to young people leaving local authority care.

To build on my Government's modernisation of the welfare system, a Bill will be introduced to reform child support so that money gets to children more speedily and effectively. It will introduce further pension reforms, including the State Second Pension which will give more help to low earners, carers and long term disabled people with broken work records. And it will reinforce people's obligations to society by linking benefit entitlement to compliance with community sentences.

Legislation will be introduced to improve the education of children with Special Educational Needs. My Government are determined to promote fairness of opportunity for disabled people building on the establishment of a Disability Rights Commission.

Members of the House of Commons
Estimates for the public service will be laid before you.

My Lords and Members of the House of Commons
My Government's ten year programme of modernisation for health and social care will provide faster, more convenient services to help improve the country's health.

As part of this programme, a Bill will be introduced to improve standards and stamp out abuse in social services, in private and voluntary healthcare, and in childcare.

My Government are determined to reduce crime and improve public protection. A Bill will be introduced to extend the use of mandatory drug testing in the criminal justice system. It will reform the probation services in England and Wales, create a new Children and Family Court Advisory Service, and prevent unsuitable people from working with children.

A Bill will be introduced to give the courts themselves the power to decide whether certain defendants should be tried by jury or by magistrates.

The Bill to equalise the age of consent, and strengthen the protection of young people from abuse of trust, will be re-introduced.

My Government are determined to combat terrorism. A Bill will be introduced to modernise and make permanent the powers available to respond to all forms of terrorism.

A Bill will be introduced to ensure that the interception of communications, and the use of other intrusive techniques, continues to be regulated for the protection both of the rights of individuals and of society as a whole.

The report into the murder of Stephen Lawrence raised profound issues for our multiracial society. A Bill will be introduced which will make it unlawful for public bodies to racially discriminate, implementing one of the report's key recommendations.

A Bill will be introduced to give people greater access to the countryside and to improve protection for wildlife. And my Government will continue their leading role in protecting the global climate.

My Government are committed to creating a modern integrated and safe transport system, providing more choice for the travelling public. Following the recent tragedy at Paddington my Government will ensure that rail safety is a top priority. A Bill will be re-introduced to establish a Strategic Rail Authority. It will contain measures to improve bus services and reduce road congestion. It will include measures for National Air Traffic Services to separate safety regulation from operational matters, and deliver major investment in the next generation technology.

My Government will bring forward a Bill to introduce the latest accounting methods to improve value for money in Whitehall and generate more investment in public infrastructure and front line services.

A Bill will be brought forward to allow firms to incorporate with limited liability whilst organising themselves as partnerships.

A Bill will be introduced to modernise the powers and duties of trustees.

My Lords and Members of the House of Commons
In Northern Ireland, my Government will continue to work closely with the political parties and the Irish Government to secure the full implementation of the Good Friday Agreement. A Bill will be presented to implement proposals from the Independent Commission on Policing, following the completion of consultation.

My Government are committed to making devolution in Scotland and Wales work and to continue the process of decentralising Government in the interests of all the people in the United Kingdom.

A Bill will be introduced to set up an Electoral Commission to regulate the funding and spending of political parties and organisations. My Government will also bring forward a Bill to reform our electoral procedures to make it easier for people to participate in elections.

My Government are committed to further long-term reform of the House of Lords and will look forward to the recommendations of the Royal Commission on the Reform of the House of Lords.

A Bill will be brought forward to reform local government to make it more innovative and accountable.

My Government will introduce a Bill on Freedom of Information. It will give everyone the right of access to information held across the public sector for the first time.

My Government will continue to provide greater openness by publishing legislation in draft for public scrutiny. This will include Bills enabling the United Kingdom to ratify the International Criminal Court, promoting more efficient water use and leasehold reform as well as commonhold for flat owners.

Other measures will be laid before you.

The Duke of Edinburgh and I look forward to receiving a State Visit by Her Majesty Queen Margrethe of Denmark and Prince Henrik in February next year.

We also look forward to our visit to Australia in March.

My Government will work towards a new partnership between Britain and the Overseas Territories. They will take forward the offer of British Citizenship to the people of the Territories.

My Government will take a leading role with our partners to shape the future development of the European Union. They will promote the enlargement of the Union, support co-operation in the fight against cross-border crime and work to improve the effectiveness of the European Union's Foreign and Security Policy and its development programmes.

My Government will ensure that NATO remains the foundation of Britain's defence and security. They will seek to continue the work of adapting the Alliance to meet the challenges and opportunities of the new century.

A Bill will be introduced to reform aspects of the armed forces' system for administering discipline.

My Government will seek to modernise the United Nations. They will work to make the Security Council more effective and more representative.

Over the coming year, which is the 10th anniversary of the United Nations Convention on the Rights of the Child, my Government will build on their work to strengthen protection for children. My Government will take further measures to meet its target of abolishing child poverty in 20 years. It will play an active part in the Council of Europe Conference against Racism.

My Government believe this is a substantial programme of work, addressing their priorities and helping the country to meet the challenges of the new millennium.

My Lords and Members of the House of Commons

I pray that the blessing of Almighty God may rest upon your counsels.

Dr Jack Cunningham moved the Loyal Address in reply, speaking of the delights of his con-stituency, Copeland in the Lake District, and the benefits that the Government was bringing to his constituents. Ivan Lewis seconded the motion.

The Leader of the Opposition, William Hague, in a speech full of humour poked fun at the Deputy Prime Minister, likening him to an ageing Soviet leader in times past who gradually had his powers removed. He then accused the Prime Minister of finding it difficult to tell the truth. Tony Blair responded by saying that: 'New Labour was working', though 'the Conservatives would reverse the work we have done'. For the Liberal Democrats Charles Kennedy said the Speech was disappointing and a Government with so large a majority should be more ambitious.

On *18 November* the debate focused on the environment, transport and the countryside, with John Prescott denying that the Government was anti-motorist and Michael Heseltine supporting the Government's plans for elected mayors as a way of encouraging people of the 'right calibre' to enter local government, though he and others ridiculed the contortions going on within the Labour party over its choice of candidate for mayor of London.

On Friday *19 November* the House debated trade, industry and social security. On Monday *22 November* Peter Mandelson made a Statement on political progress in Northern Ireland; in this he announced his intention to call a meeting of the Assembly the following week, and – assuming ministers were nominated to the new Executive – transfer of powers would take place immediately afterwards. The Conservatives expressed support; John Major said this was a 'justifiable gamble' which he 'wholly supported'. For the Democratic Unionists John Taylor said this was a 'jump into the dark', but David Trimble of the Ulster Unionists said: 'we have a basis on which we can proceed to both devolution and decommissioning'.

MPs then debated foreign affairs and defence with Robin Cook, Foreign Secretary, saying that the good health of the Atlantic alliance had been demonstrated during the Kosovo conflict, and criticising the Russians for the scale of the military conflict in Chechnya. John Maples for the Opposition said the Government's handling of European affairs had been characterised by sur-render. Donald Anderson, the Labour back bench chairman of the Foreign Affairs select committee, said that he was concerned that the foreign affairs content of the Speech 'appeared to be an afterthought'.

On *23 November* the debate dealt with home affairs, education and employment. From the Conservative front bench Ann Widdecombe accused Jack Straw of topping the year's league of incompetence with 'all his ministerial bungles'.

On *24 November* at prime minister's question time the two party leaders clashed sharply, disagreeing on whether tax was rising or falling, a theme continued in the debate that day, which concerned the economy. The Queen's Speech debate concluded with a Conservative amendment being defeated by 149 votes to 381.

In the House of Lords the four-day debate on the Speech ended on *24 November* with the Conservative opposition pressing their amendment to the Loyal Address to a division; this deplored 'the incoherence and lack of vision' of the proposed legislation. Baroness Jay questioned the procedure, asking: 'what is the point of making a political point to a constitutional monarch?' Despite their three-line whip the Conservatives were defeated by 168 votes to 164 in the new 670-strong House.

On *25 November* the House of Commons held its annual debate on reports from the Public Accounts Committee, and then on *26 November* debated Government support for the arts on a motion for the adjournment. Peers debated two reports from their European Communities Committee on *25 November*.

On Monday *29 November* Jack Straw, Home Secretary, made a Statement on the Government's crime reduction strategy in which he said recorded crime had risen at an annual rate of around 5 per cent throughout the century, but had fallen by 19 per cent over the past five years. Some police forces had been much more successful in reducing crime than others, as figures published that day indicated. Tough prison sentences, many more CCT cameras and an expansion of the DNA database were all planned. Michael Howard said that nearly all the proposals announced built on measures that he had introduced as Home Secretary before 1997.

The House then debated the **Electronic Communications Bill** at second reading, voting by 128 to 319 against an Opposition amendment which said that the Bill introduced a 'completely unnecessary element of regulation in the supervision of electronic commerce'. On Tuesday *30 November* Dr Phyllis Starkey introduced the first ever debate in the Commons parallel Chamber in Westminster Hall. Her subject was Palestinian refugees, and this was followed by debates on RAF Fairford, children and tobacco products and pensions mis-selling in a three-hour sitting, to be repeated experimentally on three days a week.

Later Nick Brown, Minister for Agriculture, Fisheries and Food, announced the lifting of the ban on beef on the bone, to the evident pleasure of many MPs. Jack Straw then introduced the second reading of the **Representation of the People Bill**, which he said was concerned with modernising electoral procedures. An Opposition amendment criticising the Government for haste on the Bill and seeking more consultation was defeated by 143 votes to 332.

DECEMBER

On *1 December* the Prime Minister announced that the Queen had made the Order devolving power to the Northern Ireland Assembly from midnight. Chris Smith then made a Statement about Wembley Stadium in which he cast serious doubt about the viability of the new stadium design for international athletics events. The debate that followed was on the European Union in advance of the Helsinki summit. Robin Cook said that widening the Union and making its institutions more effective were the Government's aims, but for the Opposition John Maples said this Government had 'given away a great deal and got nothing in return, not even goodwill'. In Westminster Hall that morning Paddy Ashdown had made his first ever speech as a back bencher; in this he was sharply critical of policy towards the Balkans, saying that having fought a war there we were now in danger of losing the peace. Peers debated the countryside on a motion moved by Earl Ferrers, who began his speech by saying that hereditary peers who are in the House have more legitimacy than anyone else: 'we have been elected. Everyone else has been appointed'. Replying, Lord Haskel said he was not sure of the legitimacy of the electoral college which elected Earl Ferrers!

On *2 December* MPs debated the report of the Royal Commission on long-term care, while in the Upper House Lord Forsyth of Drumlean moved an address seeking leave to introduce a Bill to amend the Act of Settlement to allow a Roman Catholic, or someone married to a Catholic, to ascend the Throne. Lord St John of Fawsley opposed the motion, arguing that it was in part incorrect, and on division it was defeated by 14 votes to 65. Peers then debated at second reading the **Criminal Justice (Mode of Trial) Bill** with many peers expressing strong criticism of the Bill.

On Monday *6 December* Jack Straw made a Statement on increases in fees for passports, saying these were necessary in order to fund an investment programme to speed up processing applications, but Ann Widdecombe said his announcement would convince 'the average applicant that the spirit of Ebenezer Scrooge lives on in the Home Office'. MPs then debated the **Government Resources and Accounts Bill** which the Conservatives opposed with an amendment which said that it gave 'unfettered discretion to the Treasury'; their amendment was defeated by 140 votes to 327.

Jack Straw was in action again when on *7 December* he introduced the second reading of the **Freedom of Information Bill.** This would for the first time, he said, give the public the right to know, and it would transform the culture in which government operated. Other speakers were critical of the restrictions and exceptions contained within the Bill. Robert Maclennan for the Liberal Democrats said he was baffled and mystified by the extent to which the draft Bill had been watered down. Dr Tony Wright, Labour chairman of the Public Administration select committee, said this was a historic Bill which had already been improved since it was first published in draft form, but it was capable of further improvement.

Peers debated enlargement of the EU that day, and then on the following day, *8 December*, peers debated the state of British universities. In the Commons this was the 1st Opposition day with debate on a Conservative motion condemning the Government for its mishandling of the future of the London Underground. One of the morning debates in Westminster Hall concerned the scrutiny of European legislation, and indicated that difficulties still arose over the precise practical remit of varying committees engaged in this area.

The following day, *9 December*, the first Government-initiated debate in Westminster Hall took place, on the subject of the White Paper on modernising government. The debate in the main chamber that day was on the World Trade Organisation following its recent Seattle conference, with Stephen Byers, Secretary of State for Trade and Industry, saying that Britain would be pressing for the modernisation and reform of the WTO after the collapse of the Seattle talks. Prior to that Nick Brown made a Statement on the refusal by the French Government to lift its ban on British beef, which was greeted with anger around the House, with Conservative members criticising the Government for failing to take a tougher line at an earlier stage. In the Lords peers voted by 122 to 76 to allow former members of the House certain privileges, including the right to sit on the steps of the throne, at least for an experimental period. However, given that no car parking privileges were included, Lord Boston of Faversham, Lord Chairman of Committees, didn't foresee much demand for the use of 'club rights'.

In a Statement on Monday *13 December* on the recent Helsinki summit the Prime Minister said 'the main issue was the enlargement of the European Union, which the Government strongly supported'; he went on to say that in addition to the six countries with whom negotiations had already commenced, the European Council decided to open negotiations with six more. On Russia he said that 'business as usual was not possible while human rights were being comprehensively abused in Chechnya'. William Hague in response said 'Labour in Europe is not working' and accused the Government of being 'experts in tactical ineptitude'.

The House then debated fisheries in advance of the December quota fixing meeting of the European Council. A Conservative amendment to the Government motion calling for the devolution of power to national, regional and local levels was defeated by 131 votes to 347. During the debate the Father of the House, Sir Edward Heath, revealed that he had once caught over 146 lb of cod in a single day, a national record! He went on to say that when he negotiated British entry to the Community his Government had secured a 12-mile fishing limit exclusive to our fishermen; that was what had been asked for and it had been renewed up to at least 2002, though it was now necessary to limit catches. He criticised the Conservative amendment, saying it led him to conclude that the party leadership now wished to leave the Community. Later 15 back bench members had the opportunity to pursue varied constituency matters in the recess adjournment debate.

In the upper House Lord Peyton of Yeovil asked about staff working at 10 Downing Street, and was told the number had risen by half – to 199 – since the election; Lord Lipsey, drawing on his own experience as a former employee there, commented: 'the amazing thing about No 10 is not that the staff is so big, but that it is so small'.

On *14 December* the Commons debated the **Terrorism Bill** which would repeal but in part re-enact the Prevention of Terrorism Act. Introducing the measure Jack Straw, Home Secretary, said it would be used in situations where demonstrations turned ugly, but some of his back bench colleagues suggested the Bill could lead to the outlawing of campaigning groups such as Greenpeace, and that Mr Straw himself had undergone a 'Damascene conversion' since his time in opposition when he had opposed the Prevention of Terrorism Act.

Ann Widdecombe said the Conservatives would not oppose the Bill, but the Liberal Democrats forced a division on a motion seeking to refer the Bill to a Special Standing Committee; this was lost by 47 votes to 262. Peers debated the **Race Relations (Amendment) Bill** at second reading that day.

At prime minister's questions on *15 December* William Hague took up the theme that 1999 was supposed to be the year of delivery for the Government, but as far as police numbers, hospital waiting lists and tax levels were concerned this had not been so; he suggested Tony Blair's new year resolution should be 'to keep the promises he has been breaking over the past year'. Margaret Beckett, Lord President of the Council, made a Statement on preparations for the millennium bug problems, saying that over £400 million had been spent making sure that computers in government departments were Year 2000 compliant, and that a special official unit would monitor any difficulties over the new year period.

The House then debated the **Representation of the People Bill** in committee, with Simon Hughes arguing that the voting age should be reduced from 18 to 16, the age at which people were 'old enough to marry, have children, fight, work and pay tax'. Mike O'Brien, Parliamentary Under-Secretary at the Home Office, asked Mr Hughes to withdraw his amendment and allow the matter to be considered by the Home Affairs select committee, but Mr Hughes declined, whereupon the amendment was defeated by 434 votes to 36. The continued applicability of the Salisbury Convention exercised the minds of peers at question time in their House, with the Leader of the House, Baroness Jay, saying that 'the convention had nothing to do with the strength of the parties in either House and everything to do with the relationship between the two Houses'.

Lord Denham, former Tory Chief Whip in the House, said that Labour had taken a 'lot of convincing' that the convention applied to them when they were in opposition, and Lord Hooson from the Liberal Democrat benches said the conditions that necessitated the convention coming into being still existed, but Lord Strathclyde, Conservative leader in the House, said the time had come to re-examine the convention. The following day, *16 December*, the argument over whether taxes were rising or falling led to further sharp exchanges at Treasury question time in the Commons.

Later Jack Straw made a Statement saying he would study the ruling of the European Court of Human Rights concerning the trial of the two children convicted of murdering the two-year-old boy, James Bulger, but that the judgement had not overturned the guilty verdict or in any way exonerated the two youths.

Later the House debated select committee reports on this the first Estimates Day. Gwyneth Dunwoody, chairman of the Transport committee, said the Government had responded complacently to a report made by her committee on aviation safety. A report from the Scottish Affairs committee on inward and outward investment was also debated. The House of Lords debated the **Armed Forces Discipline Bill** in committee that day, following which the House adjourned

for the Christmas recess, with the customary short speeches of reflection and thanks being made from all sides. The Chief Whip, Lord Carter, welcomed Lord Craig of Radley as the new Convenor of the Cross Bench peers following the retirement of Lord Weatherill from this role.

On Monday *20 December* Mr John Prescott introduced the second reading of the **Transport Bill,** a wide-ranging measure authorising congestion taxes, creating a Strategic Rail Authority 'to plug the loopholes in the last Government's rail legislation', and privatising in part the national air traffic control services. Among back bench speakers was the former Labour transport minister, Gavin Strang, who argued that air traffic control should not be privatised. The Bill was given a second reading by 358 votes to 163.

On *21 December* MPs heard from George Foulkes, Parliamentary Under-Secretary for International Development, about British help to the people of Venezuela following the recent floods which Mr Foulkes said had directly affected at least 150,000 people. Jack Straw then made a Statement about millennium preparations, emphasising police readiness to cope with large scale celebrations in city centres. Following this the House debated public expenditure on a government motion, to which the Conservative Opposition put down an amendment focusing on the increased 'burden of taxation'. The amendment was defeated by 125 votes to 306. The House then rose for the Christmas recess.

JANUARY

The Commons returned from the Christmas recess on Monday *10 January* with Shaun Woodward, the member for Witney, sitting on the Labour benches for the first time.

The Home Secretary, Jack Straw, introduced the second reading debate on the **Political Parties, Elections and Referendums Bill**, describing the Bill as 'an important milestone in the development of our democratic institutions', explaining that at its heart was the need 'to ensure that the funding of political parties is open and transparent'.

For the Conservatives Sir George Young said that his party supported the recommendations made by Lord Neill and therefore would not obstruct the Bill, though they disagreed with the Government where the Bill departed from the Neill Committee recommendations. For the Liberal Democrats Robert Maclennan also said he agreed with the underlying purpose of the Bill, though he thought it had not gone quite far enough. The Bill was given an unopposed second reading.

In the House of Lords, Lord Colville of Culross initiated a short debate on the need to ensure that secondary legislation complies with the new Human Rights Act.

On *11 January* MPs debated the **Child Support, Pensions and Social Security Bill** at second reading, with an Opposition amendment deploring the Bill's complexity and arguing that it represented a missed opportunity being rejected by 180 votes to 340, after which the Bill was given a second reading by 338 votes to 43.

At prime minister's question time on *12 January* William Hague attacked the Government for not having prepared better for the flu epidemic, with Tony Blair in response acknowledging that Britain lacked sufficient doctors and nurses.

In the Lords that day Lord Carrington initiated a six-hour debate on the international situation in which four former foreign secretaries and three former chancellors took part.

The following day, *13 January*, peers expressed disquiet at the failure of the House to re-establish their select committee on Monetary Policy in the new session of parliament.

Monday *17 January* was an Opposition Day, assigned to the Liberal Democrats who chose to attack the Government for its treatment of pensioners, with their spokesman Steve Webb describing the recent 75p increase in the pension as an insult. Peers debated the **Learning and Skills Bill** at second reading that day.

The 3rd Opposition Day was taken on *18 January* with Liam Fox from the Conservative front bench making a strident attack on government handling of the National Health Service, saying ministers were 'blinded by dogma', but for the government Alan Milburn blamed 'years of neglect' for the problems recently aggravated by the flu crisis; the Opposition motion was defeated by 183 votes to 328. A second motion on Government running costs was then debated and defeated by 179 votes to 331.

On *19 January* MPs debated the **Representation of the People Bill** at report stage, with the Leader of the House, Margaret Beckett, announcing at 10 pm that in view of the slow progress on the Bill, an allocation of time order would be introduced the next day, and remaining stages of the Bill would then be taken.

The following day, *20 January*, the House of Lords debated the **Criminal Justice (Mode of Trial) Bill** in committee, with a cross-party amendment preserving the right to jury trial for offences such as grievous bodily harm, forgery, violent disorder, affray and theft being carried against the Government by 222 votes to 126.

The Leader of the House immediately announced that the Government would abandon that Bill (which had been introduced into the Lords) and bring in a No 2 Bill in the Commons later that same session, thus preserving the ability of the Commons if necessary to over-ride the House of Lords through use of the Parliament Acts. From the Liberal Democrat benches Lord Rodgers of Quarry Bank said ministers should take more time to reflect before making decisions about what to do next, but Baroness Jay said the Government had won the argument though it had lost the vote.

On Monday *24 January* Mike O'Brien, Parliamentary Under Secretary at the Home Office, introduced the second reading debate on the **Disqualifications Bill**, which he explained would allow members of either the Irish Dáil or the Irish Senate to become members of the British Parliament or any devolved legislature within the UK. For the Opposition Ann Widdecombe said the Bill built on what had already been achieved in Northern Ireland, and though the Conservative party would not oppose it, they would seek to amend it in committee. The Bill was given a second reading by 300 votes to 17.

The following day MPs commenced the further stages of the Bill shortly before 6 pm and continued through the night and until 7.30 pm the next day, *26 January*, before the Bill was given its third reading by 326 votes to 141.

Because the House was in continuous session for over 26 hours, business scheduled for Wednesday, including prime minister's question time on this Tony Blair's 1000th day in office, was lost. For the Conservatives Sir Patrick Cormack said that this was the most inept handling of government business he had seen in 30 years in the House, while Andrew Mackay, shadow Northern Ireland Secretary, said the Government was trying to bulldoze the Bill through the House. In particular MPs pressed amendments seeking to link the changes brought in by the Bill to the implementation of the Belfast Agreement on decommissioning.

Peers debated nursing education and practice on *26 January* on a motion moved by Baroness McFarlane of Llandaff, while on *27 January* MPs debated the **Financial Services and Markets Bill** at report stage.

On Friday *28 January*, Ann Winterton introduced her **Medical Treatment (Prevention of Euthanasia) Bill**, saying she was worried about the 'slide towards acceptance of the practice of euthanasia', but her Bill was vigorously opposed by some MPs, with GP Dr Peter Brand, a Liberal Democrat, claiming that he could have been branded a multiple murderer under it. The Bill was approved at second reading by 113 votes to 2.

On Monday *31 January* Stephen Byers, Trade and Industry Secretary, introduced the second reading debate on the **Utilities Bill** saying that the Bill would 'modernise and reform the utilities markets and deliver efficiency and fairness' and result in savings for high electricity users.

For the Opposition Angela Browning said the Bill would increase regulation and intervention by government, add to industry costs, and impair transparency and accountability in the regulatory framework. After the Opposition amendment had been defeated by 136 votes to 343, the Bill was given an unopposed second reading.

In the Lords Baroness Jay announced that PricewaterhouseCoopers had been contracted by the government to assist in identifying suitable candidates for membership of the Appointments Commission to be established to select new cross bench members of the House.

Both Houses heard a Statement on *1 February* from the Secretary of State for Health, Alan Milburn, announcing an inquiry following the conviction of a doctor on 15 charges of murder; the chairman of the Health Select Committee, David Hinchliffe, wanted the inquiry to evaluate the role of coroners in identifying trends in reported deaths.

FEBRUARY

At prime minister's question time on *2 February* all party leaders expressed their horror at the attack made the previous Friday by a constituent on the member for Cheltenham, Nigel Jones, in which one of his party members had been killed. Later William Hague accused the Prime Minister of making Britain 'a soft touch for asylum seekers', but Tony Blair said the Government had simply been 'clearing up the mess' that the previous government had left.

Asylum and immigration were then the subject of debate on this the 4th Opposition Day, which began with the Home Secretary apologising for an administrative blunder which had resulted in the wrong government response to the motion being tabled. As a result the Speaker had selected an amendment put down by the Liberal Democrats, which was critical of both the other parties. This was defeated by 38 votes to 147 after which the Conservative motion was defeated by 145 votes to 362. A second Opposition motion on development policy was then debated and defeated by 173 votes to 321.

A motion to appoint Eric Forth a member of the House of Commons Commission in place of Sir Peter Lloyd was resisted by Labour back benchers and Liberal Democrats and defeated by 108 votes to 87.

Peers debated the National Health Service that day, with Baroness Cumberlege, who initiated the debate, arguing for a new insurance premium to boost funding. MPs debated the annual Police Grant Report on *3 February*, which was approved on division by 271 votes to 156, following which the Local Government Finance Report was debated and approved by 266 votes to 146.

Earlier that day, at Treasury question time, the new Opposition front bench spokesman, Michael Portillo, accused Labour of raising taxes faster than in any other industrialised country in the world, a charge which the Chancellor attempted vigorously to refute.

On Friday *4 February* the **Carers and Disabled Children Bill**, introduced by Tom Pendry, was debated and given an unopposed second reading.

On Monday *8 February*, when the House of Lords debated the **Local Government Bill** in committee, the Bishop of Blackburn moved but then withdrew an amendment concerned with sex education, following which Baroness Young moved an amendment to retain Section 28 (the 'promotion of homosexuality') which was carried against the Government by 210 votes to 165.

On the same day in the Commons Paul Boateng, Minister of State at the Home Office, announced the Government's intention to reintroduce under Parliament Act procedure the Sexual Offences (Amendment) Bill which had been passed by that House the previous session, but rejected by the House of Lords.

Peter Mandelson, Secretary of State for Northern Ireland, introduced the **Northern Ireland Bill** on *8 February* which allowed for a pause in the operation of the devolved political institutions of the province consequent upon the lack of progress in relation to decommissioning. Second reading was approved by 352 votes to 11 with the committee stage and third reading following immediately.

Peers debated the Bill at second reading the following day, *9 February*, with Lord Fitt saying the IRA had given nothing in return for what the government had done, which included allowing 300 convicted murderers back on to the streets of Northern Ireland.

Meanwhile in the Commons Tony Blair first expressed his confidence in Alun Michael as First Secretary of the National Assembly for Wales, then moments later was asked by William Hague why he did this given that Mr Michael had resigned a few minutes earlier. In his reply the Prime Minister referred to the 'fun and games down at the Assembly' and accused the Conservatives of getting into bed with the Nationalists and together trying to be the wreckers of devolution.

MPs then completed work on the **Financial Services and Markets Bill** which was given a third reading by 340 votes to 128.

When the **Sexual Offences (Amendment) Bill** was debated and approved at second reading on *10 February* John Bercow began his speech by saying: 'I have changed my mind on this subject, and I owe it to myself, the House and my constituents to explain why. The words "I was wrong" do not readily trip off my tongue, but that is what I believe.'

He now supported the Bill which reduced the age of consent for males from 18 to 16, and which was approved by 263 votes to 102. Peers completed remaining stages of the **Northern Ireland Bill** that day, before working until after midnight on the committee stage of the **Learning and Skills Bill**.

On Friday *11 February* MPs debated and approved at second reading Paul Truswell's **Licensing (Young Persons) Bill**.

On Monday *14 February* John Prescott, Secretary of State for the Environment, Transport and the Regions, made a Statement to the Commons on the outcome of Lord Justice Clarke's inquiry into safety on the Thames and the circumstances surrounding the *Marchioness* disaster in 1989, announcing that a judicial inquiry would now be appointed. Archie Norman in response drew attention to the fact that the *Bowbelle* (which sank the *Marchioness*) had been involved in half of the 18 collisions on the Thames in the previous 20 years, and that there was still no restriction on 'drink-driving' on the river.

MPs then considered the **Political Parties, Elections and Referendums Bill** in committee, while peers dealt with the **Representation of the People Bill** in committee that day.

On *15 February* Paul Murphy, Secretary of State for Wales, made a Statement on the Waterhouse inquiry into child abuse in north Wales which he said catalogued 'deeds of appalling mistreatment and wickedness, of sexual, physical and emotional abuse, and of the total abuse of trust'.

The **Postal Services Bill** was then debated and approved at second reading by 331 votes to 155, after which the House debated the rules for elections for the London Mayor and Assembly, with the Government being heavily criticised for refusing to allow free mailings for mayoral candidates before approving the relevant Order by 262 votes to 168.

At prime minister's question time on *17 February* William Hague accused the Prime Minister of being 'all mouth and no delivery', citing especially figures on NHS waiting lists, crime and asylum seekers.

MPs then continued debate on the **Political Parties, Elections and Referendums Bill** in committee. At question time in the upper House Lord Russell asked: 'Whether a legitimate revising chamber should occasionally be able to revise legislation in ways the House of Commons would not have wished?' In her reply the Leader of the House, Baroness Jay, said that

ultimate authority had to rest with the Commons, but Lord Russell responded that if the will of the Commons was always to prevail then there would be no need for a revising chamber. Later he introduced a debate on the Rowntree report on poverty and social exclusion.

On *17 February* MPs held a three-hour adjournment debate in Westminster Hall on the subject of Africa, introduced by the Minister of State at the Foreign Office, Peter Hain, who said that AIDS was killing many more people in Africa – 5,500 a day – than war.

In the main chamber MPs debated and approved at second reading by 276 votes to 131 the **Armed Forces Discipline Bill**.

Monday *21 February* was the 5th Opposition Day with first a motion condemning the Government for failing to meet its manifesto commitment to spend a higher proportion of national income on education being debated and defeated by 123 votes to 300, before a motion deploring the 'fact that Government interference in the Millennium Dome had rendered it a source of national embarrassment' was also debated and defeated by 141 votes to 275.

Peers debated the **Financial Services and Markets Bill** at second reading, and then the extent to which devolution to Wales was fulfilling government objectives.

On Tuesday *22 February* the Commons debated the Defence White Paper, before rising for a 'half-term recess' until the following Monday.

Meanwhile the House of Lords debated the rules for elections to the Greater London Authority. Lord Mackay of Ardbecknish, from the Opposition front bench, moved an amendment declining to approve the Government's draft order until a freepost delivery for candidates was included; this amendment was approved by 215 votes to 150. After this a Prayer was carried to annul the Greater London Authority Elections Order by 206 votes to 143, with Lord Goodhart from the Liberal Democrat benches saying that the Government had 'forfeited the right to preach about democracy' because of the Labour Party's own record on candidate selection, and that in defence of democracy the House of Lords should not 'be a poodle but a rottweiler'.

The following day, *23 February*, the House of Lords debated the number and nature of task forces and similar bodies created since May 1997 on a motion moved by Lord Smith of Clifton.

When MPs returned on Monday *28 February* tributes were paid to Michael Colvin who with his wife had died in a fire at his home over the previous weekend.

In the resumed debate on the Defence White Paper, many speakers referred to the speech Mr Colvin had made during the first day of the defence debate the previous week. Alice Mahon moved an amendment declining to approve a policy 'which has been used to make war upon innocent civilians in Iraq and Yugoslavia . . . without any explicit authorisation by the House of Commons . . .'. This was rejected by 12 votes to 340, after which the White Paper was approved by 348 votes to 149.

Earlier the House had heard a Statement from the Secretary of State for International Development, Clare Short, saying that Britain had already provided £2.2 million in aid for Mozambique following the disastrous floods there, and that the UK stood ready to provide further assistance.

On *29 February* MPs sat through the night dealing with the **Government Resources and Accounts Bill** at report stage, eventually completing third reading at 7.44 am.

In the Lords during the report stage of the **Representation of the People Bill** Lord Bassam of Brighton, Parliamentary Under-Secretary at the Home Office, announced that the Government now accepted the principle that there should be a free mailshot for the London mayoral election, though he added that ministers wanted a low cost mailshot with minimum risk of abuse by frivolous candidates.

In an answer to a written question in the House of Lords that day, the Government Chief Whip, Lord Carter, said that in the first two sessions of the 1997 parliament only one out of 58 changes to legislation resulting from government defeats had been wholly accepted by the Commons, while 46 had been directly reversed.

MARCH

On *1 March* MPs debated a report from their Committee on Standards and Privileges and agreed a recommendation that Teresa Gorman should be suspended from the House for one month for having deceived parliament in respect of her business interests.

A Liberal Democrat motion on tax cuts and public services was then debated on this the first part of the 6th Opposition Day. For the Liberal Democrats Matthew Taylor said the Government were failing to meet their election pledges on spending; the motion was defeated by 39 votes to 280.

The House of Lords that day debated a motion moved by Lord Elton 'calling attention to the case for policies towards asylum seekers that are both effective and humane'. On *2 March* Jack Straw, Home Secretary, said in a Statement that General Pinochet had that day been allowed to

leave the country and return to Chile. The response from MPs indicated a degree of frustration on all sides of the House, with some very angry at the General's release and others expressing their anger once again at his initial arrest.

MPs also heard from Stephen Byers, Secretary of State for Trade and Industry, that the provisions relating to telecoms and water were being removed from the Utilities Bill then before parliament; this was, he said, a result of listening to the representations made by the telecoms operators. From the Opposition front bench Angela Browning said that her party had warned the minister at second reading, and consistently in committee on the Bill, that it was flawed and that it was now a shambles and should be withdrawn.

Later MPs debated Welsh Affairs, with the Secretary of State for Wales, Paul Murphy, saying that at least half a dozen bills with considerable Welsh sections were currently going through the House, and therefore despite devolution it was necessary for MPs to represent Wales at Westminster.

On Friday *3 March* MPs debated and approved at second reading the **Health Service Commissioners (Amendment) Bill** introduced by Sir Geoffrey Johnson Smith, the purpose of which (he said) was to close a loophole in the previous Act 'which allows general practitioners and others involved in health matters to retire to avoid investigation by the health service ombudsman'. The Bill was given an unopposed second reading, after which Stephen O'Brien's **Food Labelling Bill** was debated for over two hours but not allowed a second reading.

Baroness Hogg introduced a debate in the upper House on a report from the Science and Technology Committee on non-food crops, which concluded in less than two hours allowing the House to rise soon after 1 pm.

On Monday *6 March* Jack Straw, Home Secretary, introduced the **Regulation of Investigatory Powers Bill** which he said would ensure for the first time that the use of interception techniques was properly regulated by law and externally supervised. The Bill took account of changes in technology, such as the huge growth in e-mails, and sought to secure a better balance between law enforcement and individual rights.

From the Opposition front bench Ann Widdecombe said she was broadly supportive of the Bill, but would seek amendments on matters of detail, as did Simon Hughes from the Liberal Democrat front bench, who said that the balance struck in the Bill between the individual and the state required adjustment. The Bill was given an unopposed second reading.

In the upper House Lord Bassam for the Home Office moved amendments during the third reading of the **Representation of the People Bill** providing for a free mailing for London mayoral candidates in the form of a booklet containing two sides of A5 paper from all candidates. This was generally welcomed by peers, with Lord Goodhart saying it reflected considerable credit both on the House and eventually on the Government. Lord Bassam commented that in negotiating the details of this arrangement he had learned 'a great deal about the direct mailing industry'!

After passing the Bill, the House debated and approved the Greater London Authority Elections (Expenses) Order 2000 which specified the expenditure limits for mayoral and assembly candidates, parties and independent candidates campaigning expenses.

The next day, *7 March*, peers debated the Wakeham report on reform of their House. Baroness Jay, Leader of the House, said that the Government broadly agreed with the report but said any elected element should be small, but said more time was needed to consider the 132 recommendations made by the Commission.

Lord Strathclyde, Conservative party leader in the House, said the real problem was that the Government did not know what it wanted. When Lord Rodgers from the Liberal Democrat benches said that his party had been offered more peerages providing they 'behaved' themselves in the voting lobbies, he was challenged to produce the evidence, which he said he would place in the Library of the House providing the government ministers concerned gave their agreement.

In the Commons that day the Labour back bencher Robert Marshall-Andrews moved an amendment at second reading to the **Criminal Justice (Mode of Trial)(No 2) Bill** declining to give the Bill a second reading because it 'fails properly to safeguard or maintain the right to trial by jury in "either-way" offences which may result in serious punishment and loss of livelihood'. The amendment was rejected by 214 votes to 315 with 29 Labour back benchers voting against the Government, after which the Bill was approved at second reading by 315 votes to 188.

8 March was the 7th Opposition Day, with first a motion condemning the Government's handling of the National Health Service being debated and defeated by 179 votes to 307. Following this a motion on small business was also debated and defeated by 159 votes to 309.

The House then debated a guillotine motion for dealing with Lords amendments to the **Representation of the People Bill**; John Greenway commented that most of the amendments made by the Lords had first been tabled in the Commons, and went on: 'If the Government believe that this House should have supremacy over the other place, when will the House make its own amendments to legislation, rather than relying on the other place to do it?'

Richard Shepherd said that 35 bills had already been guillotined by the Labour Government, and that in his 20 years in the House he had seen 'the gradual squeezing by a jealous, self-aggrandising Executive of the freedom to debate and properly discuss the issues'. The guillotine motion was approved by 260 votes to 134, after a debate which took most of the two hours allowed for completing work on the Bill, leaving most of the amendments undebated by the House. Peers debated defence on *8 March*.

An amendment resisted by the Government to allow local councils to keep the committee system rather than be obliged to introduce elected mayors or cabinet style local government was moved during the third reading of the **Local Government Bill**, and accepted by 144 votes to 82.

MPs debated and gave an unopposed second reading to the **Race Relations (Amendment) Bill** that day, while in Westminster Hall Margaret Hodge, a junior education and employment minister, introduced a three-hour debate on the 'work-life balance', which she said was about trying to change the culture throughout society to produce a better balance, not just for women but for men too.

On Friday *10 March* MPs debated and approved for second reading by 143 votes to 0 the **Warm Homes and Energy Conservation Bill**.

On Monday *13 March* Jack Straw, Home Secretary, made a Statement indicating how he proposed to respond to the judgement of the European Court of Human Rights in the James Bulger case concerning court procedures in dealing with children charged with murder.

MPs then considered the **Political Parties and Referendums Bill** at report stage dealing with amendments to extend the role of the proposed Electoral Commission. An Opposition amendment to preclude the Commission using its funds to promote public awareness of the institutions of the EU was defeated by 110 votes to 308.

Peers debated the **Learning and Skills Bill** at report stage that day, continuing with the same Bill the following day, *14 March*, when the Government suffered defeat by 166 votes to 161 on an amendment moved by Baroness Blatch which removed the possibility of quinquennial parental ballots being held to decide future admissions policies to remaining grammar schools.

MPs that day completed work on the **Political Parties and Referendums Bill** which was given an unopposed third reading, with Sir George Young from the Opposition front bench saying: 'The Bill has a key role to play in cleaning up British politics by setting out a framework with clear rules, with an independent umpire and greater transparency.'

At prime minister's question time on *15 March* William Hague attacked the Government for increasing taxes contrary to their election pledges, but Tony Blair ridiculed the Opposition, especially the charge that raising taxes was 'immoral'.

In answer to a private notice question David Blunkett, Secretary of State for Education and Employment, said the Government would seek to reverse the defeat suffered the previous night in the House of Lords concerning the status of grammar schools.

Later the House debated the **Terrorism Bill** which was given a third reading at 1.50 am by 210 votes to 1, the dissenter being the back bench Labour MP Paul Flynn, with two of his colleagues, John McDonnell and Jeremy Corbyn, acting as tellers.

On *16 March* in the upper House Lord Lamont asked about a proposal from the European Commission that some MEPs should be elected on European lists presented to voters throughout the EU; in reply Baroness Scotland of Asthal, Foreign Office minister, said the Government saw little merit in this proposal, and that it had not attracted any serious support from other member states.

This was the 8th Opposition Day in the Commons, with the first debate on a motion noting with concern that the Government's 'response to the humanitarian crisis in Mozambique was hampered by indecision and delay'; this was defeated by 125 votes to 310. Then a motion on the future of Rover was debated and defeated by 149 votes to 275.

In Westminster Hall a debate on QUANGOs was initiated by Tony Wright based on a report from the select committee of which he was chairman, that on Public Administration.

On Friday *17 March* the Minister of State at the Department of Health, John Hutton, initiated a debate on the adjournment on the subject of improving safeguards for children, while peers spent some five hours debating Lord Pearson of Rannoch's **European Union (Implications of Withdrawl) Bill** which, he said, would require 'the Treasury to set up an independent committee of inquiry into what life might be like outside the European Union for our economy, defence and constitution'. The Bill was given an unopposed second reading.

On Monday *20 March* the Commons debated the **Countryside and Rights of Way Bill** at second reading. Introducing this Michael Meacher, Minister for the Environment, said the Bill would grant a right of access for the first time to approximately one-ninth of the total land in the country, as well as increasing protection for Sites of Special Scientific Interest.

For the Opposition Archie Norman said the Bill put forward heavy handed proposals for open access, and would be disastrous for farmers and landowners. From the Labour back benches Gordon Prentice said amendments would be tabled to make the Bill a vehicle for banning fox hunting. After an Opposition amendment had been defeated by 138 votes to 334, the Bill was given an unopposed second reading.

Budget day was on *21 March*. The Chancellor made his Statement in less than an hour, saying that in 1999 the British economy had grown by 2 per cent and that the forecast for 2000 was for growth of 2.75 to 3.25 per cent. Among Gordon Brown's proposals were substantial spending increases in health and education; adjustment of vehicle excise duty to favour environmentally friendly cars; inflation-only increases on beer and wine with no increase on spirits; and he confirmed a cut of 1p in the standard rate of income tax to 'the lowest basic rate for 70 years'.

In his immediate response William Hague said this was 'the stealth Chancellor who taxes more and delivers less', and that one of his favourite tricks was 'the constant re-announcement of Government spending'.

Charles Kennedy, Leader of the Liberal Democrats, said the Chancellor's prudence had a purpose: 'spending for a second term'. Barry Jones described the budget as 'clever, cautious and compassionate'.

The following day, *22 March*, the Prime Minister made a Statement on modernisation of the National Health Service in which he said the Government had come up with the money for a 'step-change' in the health service, including a £2 billion cash injection this year, and now he wanted to challenge those who worked in the health service to ensure it was reformed and the money spent to best possible effect.

In a scathing reply William Hague said: 'if all the clichés and the waffle that one could express about the health service had been swept into a heap, the result would be remarkably similar to the Prime Minister's statement'.

The House then continued with the debate on the budget both that day and the next, *23 March*. On that latter day peers three times defeated the Government during the third reading debate on the **Learning and Skills Bill**; first an amendment removing the restriction on the new

Learning and Skills Council from funding more expensive courses for the over-16s was carried by 173 votes to 127; then an amendment to ensure that the new youth and careers service did not harm existing information, advice and guidance services was carried by 157 to 142; finally by 190 to 175 peers supported a series of changes put forward by Baroness Young to the proposed statutory guidance for schools on sex and relationships.

On Friday 24 March MPs debated Anthony Steen's **Urban Regeneration and Countryside Protection Bill** but after five hours the debate was adjourned.

On Monday 27 March the Prime Minister made a Statement on the meeting of the European Council in Lisbon at the end of the previous week. This had he said marked 'a sea change in European economic thinking' pointing Europe away from 'heavy-handed intervention and regulation towards a new approach based on enterprise, innovation and competition'.

In his response William Hague said it was time the Prime Minister realised that 'soundbites, pious pledges and rhetoric will have to be backed up by action'. MPs then continued debate on the budget, eventually concluding with votes on a series of resolutions at midnight.

The **Criminal Justice and Court Services Bill** was debated and given an unopposed second reading by MPs on 28 March, while in the House of Lords the Government suffered a further defeat when peers voted 162 to 132 for an opposition amendment to the **Care Standards Bill**; this was designed to ensure that private hospitals and NHS hospitals were subject to inspection and regulation by a single body.

In answer to a written question, David Blunkett, Secretary of State for Education and Employment, said the Government accepted the recommendation of the Quigley Committee that students from England, Wales and Northern Ireland at Scottish universities should have their tuition fees paid for their fourth year.

The following day, 29 March, Baroness Blatch complained at the obscure manner in which this announcement had been made, saying that it completely vindicated the stand taken by the House of Lords on the issue of the 'Scottish anomaly'.

At question time in the Commons on 29 March Clare Short, Secretary of State for International Development, acknowledged that the situation in Zimbabwe had become very serious, but said this was not a reason to cancel Britain's assistance to the country.

William Hague attacked the Prime Minister over the Government's handling of the proposed sale of Rover by BMW and the implications for the Longbridge plant.

Lord Dean of Harptree introduced a debate that day on 'the case for a power of delay on statutory instruments', a proposal that won much support from peers, though not from the Government minister Lord Falconer, who argued that the House had the power to make Government think again by various procedural means.

On 30 March MPs debated the **Learning and Skills Bill** with a Conservative amendment critical of the Bill being defeated by 119 votes to 280, after which the Bill was given an unopposed second reading.

Meanwhile in Westminster Hall Bowen Wells introduced a three-hour debate on women and development, the subject of a recent report by the select committee on international development.

APRIL

A further private notice question on Rover was dealt with in the Commons on Monday 3 April, with Angela Browning from the Conservative front bench accusing Stephen Byers, Secretary of State, of a 'cover-up' and 'incompetence and negligence', with Mr Byers arguing that he had established a task force to advise him on the best way for the Government to respond, and he had committed £129 million to support its recommendations.

Later the House debated the **Child Support, Pensions and Social Security Bill** at report stage, with over 40 Labour back benchers joining forces with Liberal Democrats voting to restore the link between pensions and earnings. The Bill was eventually given an unopposed third reading at 1 am.

Peers debated the **Political Parties, Elections and Referendums Bill** at second reading, with Lord Neill of Bladen, chairman of the Committee on Standards in Public Life, and three other members of the committee contributing. Lord Neill said some countries exemplified the fact that good statutes 'are useless unless there is a general will to comply with their provisions', and that his committee had encountered a great deal of public cynicism; 'it is not enough for an institution or for a set of rules to be very good; we need to be aware of what the public think is happening on the ground'.

On 4 April the **Freedom of Information Bill** was considered on report, with Tony Wright, chairman of the Select Committee on Public Administration, and former minister Mark Fisher leading a group of around 30 other Labour back benchers in voting against the Government on amendments designed to diminish the power of ministers to withhold information.

On *5 April* the Speaker in answer to a point of order raised by Peter Ainsworth said that the launch of a government sports strategy at a press conference that morning without any parallel announcement in Parliament was 'totally unacceptable to me and to the House'. She called on ministers to review procedures across Whitehall to ensure such events did not happen again.

At prime minister's question time William Hague focused on the way Stephen Byers, Secretary of State for Trade and Industry, had handled BMW over the sale of Rover and the 'doctoring' of statements that had gone on.

Later the House continued work on the **Freedom of Information Bill** with over 30 Labour back benchers voting against the Government on amendments concerned with limiting non-disclosure of information. At third reading Jack Straw, Home Secretary, said the Bill had 'genuinely been improved' as a result of proceedings in the House, not least over the previous two days; Tony Wright said that this historic piece of legislation was worth celebrating, even though the Bill still had flaws and defects, some of which had been corrected, and that the 'third Reading is not the end of the story'.

For the Liberal Democrats Robert Maclennan said 'backward moves had been a depressing feature of the process', and that though definite improvements had been made while the Bill was before the House many more were still required 'if the Bill is to fulfil the hopes' that had been expressed in the original government white paper.

The second part of the 6th Opposition Day was taken on *6 April* with a debate on the Patten Report on Policing in Northern Ireland introduced by David Trimble, Leader of the Official Ulster Unionists, calling for the postponement of the implementation of the report; this was defeated by 118 votes to 264.

At the commencement of business on Friday *7 April* Andrew Dismore moved that the House should sit in private; his motion was defeated by 30 votes to 0, but since fewer than 40 MPs had voted the business under consideration, Iain Duncan Smith's private member's bill was 'stood over' until the next sitting of the House, and debate immediately began on the next private member's bill down for consideration, Ken Livingstone's **Wild Mammals (Hunting with Dogs) Bill**. However, at 2.15 pm only 74 MPs were present to support the closure, resulting in the debate being adjourned without the Bill gaining its second reading.

On Monday *10 April* Jack Staw, Home Secretary, made a Statement introducing a White Paper on licensing reform which indicated Government plans to allow for 24-hour opening of pubs, and proposed the transfer of licensing powers from magistrates to local authorities.

MPs then debated the **Nuclear Safeguards Bill**, the second reading of which was approved by 215 votes to 7, following which another division took place before debate began at 10.13 pm on the second reading of the **Television Licenses Bill**. Introducing this, Chris Smith, Secretary of State for Culture, Media and Sport, said it was necessary in order to ensure that free television licences for households containing someone over the age of 75 could be administered as cheaply as possible; the debate concluded at 1 am with the Bill approved without a division.

The following day, *11 April*, the second reading debate of the **Local Government Bill** took place, with Hilary Armstrong, the Minister for Local Government and the Regions, saying it would return local government to the heart of local communities, but Archie Norman said this was an extravagant claim, and he criticised the way the Bill had been 'cobbled together' with over 400 amendments having been made to it in the Lords. An Opposition amendment was rejected by 130 votes to 342.

Following this at 10.30 pm MPs began a debate on a government motion to establish a Standing Committee on Regional Affairs to deal with England; Sir George Young said he was pleased the Government now recognised that 'post-devolution there are some unresolved questions relating to England', but he argued that this particular proposal was not the best way forward because the proposed committee would not fit well with existing committees; nor would it be an adequate response to the problems posed by devolution, nor indeed did the proposal fit well with the Government's own agenda. The motion to establish the committee was approved by 187 votes to 130.

Peers debated the **Sexual Offences (Amendment) Bill** at second reading, with the Government declaring its determination to see this measure enacted, while Baroness Young declared the use of Parliament Act procedures on a conscience bill a 'parliamentary disgrace'. After a passionate five-hour debate the Bill was given an unopposed second reading, thereby preventing it from going immediately for Royal Assent under Parliament Act procedure.

Five baronesses were then the only participants in a short Lords debate concerned with participation in the Euro-Mediterranean Forum of Women Parliamentarians.

At prime minister's question time on *12 April* Andrew Mackinlay from the Labour back benches asked Tony Blair if he would use his authority to ensure an early vote took place to implement the recent report from the Liaison

Committee allowing more freedom in the choice of select committee members, and saying 'goodbye to the parliamentary choreographers'; the Prime Minister in his reply merely said a response would be made in due course.

This was the 9th Opposition Day with Angela Browning initiating a debate on rural post offices, which ended in a government amendment being accepted by 310 votes to 167, following which a debate on asylum seekers had a similar result, 312 votes to 169.

On 13 April in Westminster Hall MPs held a three-hour debate on disabled people based on a report from the Select Committee on Education and Employment, with Margaret Hodge who had been co-chairman of the committee when it commenced work replying to the debate for the Government, saying that she felt 'like a poacher turned gamekeeper', but that the report made her job easier because it contained much meat with which she agreed.

On Friday 14 April peers debated a **Life Peerages (Appointments Commission) Bill** which sought to place the selection of life peers on a statutory basis. In support of the Bill Lord Strathclyde said; 'We cannot go on with a Prime Minister creating a peer, on average, every five days or so and not expect people to ask some questions', but the Government warned that this was a complex process, and emphasised that some steps had been taken to ensure the independence of the process.

Stephen Byers, Secretary of State for Trade and Industry, made a Statement on 17 April on energy policy in which he announced the Government were prepared to make up to £100 million available through state aid to the coal industry.

The House then debated the **Finance Bill** at second reading, with an Opposition amendment declaring that the Bill imposed more complex regulations, introduced further taxes and failed to reverse the increasing burden of taxation. This was defeated by 136 votes to 342.

Peers debated the **Child Support, Pensions and Social Security Bill**, at second reading.

On 18 April MPs dealt with the **Postal Services Bill** at report stage, with the Minister, Stephen Byers, responding to a petition signed by over three million people calling for more to be done to help people who live in the country.

On 19 April William Hague asked the Prime Minister to confirm that 'in the financial year just ended, the Government spent £633 million more on the cost of administering Whitehall than even they had planned', but Tony Blair in response said 'in real terms the costs of government are falling and are less than they were in the last year of the previous government'.

The **Utilities Bill** was then debated at report and third reading. Peers debated globalisation on a motion from Lord Borrie.

On 20 April MPs debated various topics on a motion for the adjournment before the House rose at 1 pm for the Easter recess. Peers likewise rose that day after debating the **Freedom of Information Bill** at second reading.

MAY

On Tuesday 2 May when MPs returned to Westminster they heard a Statement from Jack Straw about the 'violence and disorder associated with the so-called anti-capitalist demonstrations over the bank holiday weekend', during which 'vandals desecrated the Cenotaph and defaced the statue of Sir Winston Churchill' with 97 people arrested in London. In response Ann Widdecombe called for all those charged with offences to face exemplary sentences.

Peers debated the **Postal Services Bill** at second reading, while the Commons debated the **Finance Bill** in committee both that day and the next day.

On 3 May Robin Cook, Foreign Secretary, made a Statement to MPs on Zimbabwe, saying the Government would refuse all new licence applications for the export of arms and military equipment, and that the EU was the 'natural and right place' for Britain to start mobilising the international community to react to the Zimbabwean situation. For the Opposition Francis Maude said the process of 'suspending the Mugabe regime from the Commonwealth' should begin.

At prime minister's question time William Hague attacked the Government for its 'utter weakness on law and order', but Tony Blair reminded the House that under the previous Conservative government crime had doubled.

Meanwhile the House of Lords debated essential local services on a motion moved by Lord Rodgers of Quarry Bank, Leader of the Liberal Democrat peers.

On 4 May MPs debated defence, with Tom King suggesting that the timing of the debate (when many MPs were absent because of the local elections) reinforced the image of a party that did not take defence seriously.

In the upper House Baroness Jay answered a private notice question giving details about the House of Lords Appointments Commission, repeating details given in a parliamentary written answer that day by the Prime Minister. Peers then debated the **Utilities Bill** at second reading.

On Friday 5 May the Commons spent all day dealing with the **Carers and Disabled Children Bill** at report stage, before according the Bill an unopposed third reading.

On Monday *8 May* MPs heard two Statements. In the first Peter Mandelson said he intended to bring forward an Order to restore the Northern Ireland Assembly and its Executive in the light of declarations made by the IRA over the weekend.

Robin Cook then announced evacuation plans for British nationals in Sierra Leone in the light of serious disorder there, but he assured the House that Britain would not abandon its commitment to the country and would 'continue to take the lead at the UN and elsewhere to restore the peace process'.

The House then debated the **Regulation of Investigatory Powers Bill** at report stage. Various Opposition amendments were rejected on division, and then at third reading Oliver Heald from the Conservative front bench moved an amendment saying that the Bill failed 'to give crimefighters the powers they need, imposed unspecified and potentially costly burdens on internet service providers without adequate protection against over-regulation', but this was defeated by 139 votes to 330.

MPs heard another Statement from Stephen Byers on Rover-BMW on *9 May* in which the Trade and Industry Secretary said that he was pleased with the outcome of negotiations that had resulted in BMW agreeing to sell Rover to the Phoenix consortium.

The House then debated the **Transport Bill** at report stage, the key issue being the Government's plans to privatise in part the air traffic control system. Gwynneth Dunwoody, chairman of the Transport Select Committee, led over 40 Labour MPs into the opposition lobby, and with others abstaining the Government majority fell to 60 in one division (248 to 308), despite a passionate plea from the deputy prime minister, John Prescott, who argued that safety would not be compromised. At one point in his speech he refused to take an intervention from the Conservative John Redwood, saying that he was 'dealing with the real opposition', which was clearly coming from the benches behind him. The former Labour Transport minister Gavin Strang said no other country in the world had privatised their air traffic control network.

The following day, *10 May*, MPs completed work on this Bill, which was given a third reading by 304 votes to 109.

In a Westminster Hall debate that morning Ann Clwyd called for Government regulation of cosmetic surgery, while in another debate Nick St Aubyn promoted the Year-out Programme for school leavers.

At prime minister's question time William Hague said the Government ought to listen to people who had worked in industry because 'not a single senior member of the Government has ever worked in business', but the Prime Minister drew attention to the Conservative record in the 'early 1990s when 1 million jobs were lost, output fell by 7 per cent and investment by 28 per cent'.

Peers that day debated a motion moved by Lord Peston calling attention to the case for a review of the workings of the House of Lords in the 21st century. He argued that the 'best way to embarrass the executive is by informed exposure of their failings; not knockabout rough stuff'.

Baroness Jay said she thought it would be difficult to achieve the ambition of having one-third of the membership women unless working practices changed, but Lord Rodgers said that if back benchers spent too much time with their families they would be rather less of a nuisance to the Government than they should be. Lord Cranborne said newcomers to parliament almost always confused efficiency with effectiveness. Lord Bragg said working peers really needed better facilities.

Following this debate Lord Rees-Mogg moved that 'the House asserts its responsibility for the conduct of its own affairs', explaining that he believed a sub-committee of the Committee of Privileges should investigate the register of peers' interests rather than the Neill Committee. After debate an amendment welcoming the proposed inquiry by the Neill Committee, while still asserting the right of the House ultimately to be responsible for the conduct of its own affairs was accepted by 111 votes to 3.

On *11 May* in the Commons a Government motion on the Common Agricultural Policy was debated with an Opposition amendment calling on the Government to address with urgency the crisis in the countryside being rejected by 123 votes to 257.

On Friday *12 May* MPs spent the day debating the **Licensing (Young Persons) Bill** without completing the passage of the Bill, while the House of Lords spent the day debating defence.

On Monday *15 May* Geoff Hoon, Secretary of State for Defence, said there was no question of British troops being drawn into a civil war in Sierra Leone, but Iain Duncan Smith for the Opposition said the Government was being 'less than frank' about Britain's role.

Peers debated the **Child Support, Pensions and Social Security Bill** in committee that day, with the Government suffering a defeat when the House voted in support of an amendment to allow people with an occupational pension to contribute at the same time to a stakeholder pension; only 11 peers were present to support the Government when the division took pace at 11.20 pm with 22 peers going into the opposition lobby.

In the Commons the 10th Opposition Day was taken on *16 May* with Conservative motions on UK manufacturing and enterprise and then the future of the teaching profession being defeated by 173 to 377 and 158 to 309 respectively.

In Westminster Hall that morning Tony Benn initiated a debate calling for 'legislation to inaugurate a Socialist Commonwealth founded upon the common ownership of land and capital, production for use and not for profit, and equality of opportunity for every citizen'. Several speeches supported Mr Benn, while others expressed gratitude for the opportunity to debate political philosophy and not simply details of policy.

Replying to the debate the Economic Secretary to the Treasury, Melanie Johnson said: 'Passion and principle are important, but they should be directed towards practical changes that are beneficial to people' and she concluded that the Government was 'moving forward in the right direction'.

Both Houses also that day approved two orders dealing with Northern Ireland, one concerned with flag flying, and the other extending the amnesty for handing in weapons. Speaking on the flags order Lord Hylton said that the fewer flags of any kind flown in the Province the better, while Baroness Blatch said flying the flag of one's own sovereign country is a basic human right.

On *17 May* the House of Lords debated law and order on a motion moved by Lord Tebbit who said that faced with a ten-fold increase in crime in the last 40 years 'the forces against crime have not surrendered – but they have conceded ground to criminality and disorder'. In his reply to the debate he described it as having been 'remarkably short of political partisanship, until the Minister read his departmental political rant'.

In the Commons that day both William Hague and Charles Kennedy attacked the Prime Minister for signs of inconsistency within his Government on the question of UK entry to the single currency.

On *18 May* the **Care Standards Bill** was debated at second reading in the Commons with an Opposition amendment describing the Bill as unnecessarily bureaucratic and intrusive being defeated by 120 votes to 274.

In the Lords that day peers twice defeated the Government during proceedings on the third reading of the **Financial Services and Markets Bill** over the protection to be afforded to the Takeover Panel from a possible hostile bid from the Financial Services Authority.

On Friday *19 May* MPs completed work on the **Health Service Commissioners (Amendment) Bill** promoted by Sir Geoffrey Johnson Smith.

On Monday *22 May* backbench Labour MPs were sharply critical at question time of the Home Secretary for his decision to allow Mike Tyson, the boxer and convicted rapist, a visa to enter the country.

When MPs debated guillotine motions on four government bills, Tess Kingham, who had at the weekend announced her departure from the Commons, spoke of being 'kept up all night by silly games that have very little to do with scrutinising legislation'. Sir Patrick Cormack responded by saying that 'she had failed to understand what being a Member of Parliament is all about. . . . She treats this as a job that should involve fixed hours, clocking on and off. We are here as servants of the people who sent us here, and we are expected to debate at length important issues.'

The House then dealt with the **Nuclear Safeguards Bill**, the **Sea Fishing Grants (Charges) Bill**, the **Royal Parks Trading Bill** and the **Television Licences (Disclosure of Information) Bill** all under guillotines, all given third readings before the House rose at 2.24 am.

Peers that day again defeated the Government when they voted 143 to 117 in support of an amendment to the **Child Support, Pensions and Social Security Bill** ensuring that war widows who remarry or co-habit would keep their pensions from the armed forces.

On *23 May* Paddy Tipping, Parliamentary Secretary at the Privy Council Office, introduced a motion to provide MPs with insurance against legal costs incurred in defending themselves against actions brought against them for carrying out their public duties. This was prompted by the fact that Peter Luff had incurred legal costs of over £2000 having an action deemed frivolous by the courts struck out, the action being one for damages brought by a constituent.

The House also that day debated and approved at second reading without divisions the **Limited Liability Partnerships Bill** and the **Crown Prosecution Service Inspectorate Bill**.

The 11th Opposition Day was on *24 May* with, first, a motion on crime being moved by Ann Widdecombe, who said that the Government had betrayed the electorate, betrayed the general public and broken one of the major promises made by the Labour Party; they had turned around the first sustained fall in crime since the second world war, and 'we are now faced with a rising crime rate'. Jack Straw, Home Secretary, said that while crime had come down towards the end of the Conservative Government, the overall Tory record was clear – 'much more crime and many more criminals getting away with it'. The Conservative motion was defeated by 138 votes to 358. After this a motion on transport was debated and this too was defeated by 130 votes to 349.

At prime minister's question time that day the deputy prime minister, John Prescott, said Tony Blair had been 'working throughout the night on exhausting domestic matters', and went on: 'I am sure that the country and the House will wish to join me in expressing warm congratulations to my right hon friend, his wife and family on the birth of baby Leo'.

Peers that day held two debates, the first on the merging of the London and Frankfurt stock exchanges, and the second on the 'continuing need for a professional civil service'.

On *25 May* MPs raised various issues on the adjournment debate which took place before the House rose for the Whitsun recess.

Peers gave the **Regulation of Investigatory Powers Bill** a second reading debate that day, with Lord Cope from the Opposition front bench saying he and his colleagues would try to toughen the Bill in some respects, while in others they were concerned at its vague and rather open-ended approach.

JUNE

On Monday *5 June* MPs debated a guillotine motion for the **Financial Services Bill**, with Richard Shepherd pointing out that this allowed only five minutes per major change made in the House of Lords, with almost 700 amendments in all to consider, but Melanie Johnson, speaking as a Treasury minister, said that mostly the amendments were technical and many had cross-party support. The guillotine was agreed by 244 votes to 126.

Conservatives then criticised the Government's refusal to accept Lords amendments safeguarding the position of the Takeover Panel. The **Transport Bill** was debated at second reading in the House of Lords that day, with peers from all sides indicating their opposition to the part-privatisation of National Air Traffic Services.

On *6 June* MPs debated the **Police (Northern Ireland) Bill** implementing the Patten Commission Report, which would according to Peter Mandelson, Secretary of State for Northern Ireland, 'provide as good a model for policing as can be found anywhere in the world'.

From the Opposition front bench Andrew MacKay moved an amendment calling for the 'proud title and insignia of the Royal Ulster Constabulary' to be retained, while Kevin McNamara said that if the Bill went through unchanged it would 'not carry the confidence of the nationalist community'. The Opposition amendment was defeated by 142 votes to 342, following which the Bill was approved by 329 votes to 14.

At prime minister's question time William Hague focused on the recent remarks made by the Chancellor concerning university entrance suggesting that these 'had reignited class war and plunged the Government into a complete shambles', but Tony Blair in reply said children from independent schools are 25 times more likely to enter a top university than those from state schools.

This was the 12th Opposition Day with two Liberal Democrat motions being debated, the first saying that the Chancellor had been 'simplistic and divisive in attacking the admissions procedure of Oxford University', but also regretting the 'lack of action by the Government to promote freedom and opportunity for all the people of the UK'; this was defeated by 41 votes to 249. The second motion dealt with Britain's strategic interests, calling for collective action through the UN and NATO; this was defeated by 40 votes to 229. Peers debated housing in the south east, and then coastal erosion.

The next day, *8 June*, was the 13th Opposition Day, with Conservative motions, first on pensions, and second on genetically modified crops being debated and defeated by 121 to 301 and 144 to 267 respectively.

Friday *9 June* saw the Commons completion of work on the **Licensing (Young Persons) Bill**.

On Monday *12 June* Jack Straw, Home Secretary, made a Statement on the Burns Committee report on hunting with dogs published that day. This dealt with factual questions in relation to hunting which Mr Straw summarised, before concluding his statement by saying that the Government would introduce a bill early in the next session which would allow the House on a free vote to decide between various legislative options about the future of hunting. From the Opposition front bench David Liddington said the introduction of such a bill was 'a distraction from the issues that really matter to the people we represent'.

When the Statement was repeated in the Lords, Baroness Mallalieu from the Labour back benches said that her family, her neighbours and some of her best friends would be imprisoned when the Bill became law if 'we continued to behave as we do now'.

MPs then debated the **Criminal Justice and Court Services Bill** at report before the Bill was given an unopposed third reading. The House of Lords considered Commons amendments to the **Financial Services Bill** that day, with Lord Alexander of Weedon moving a further amendment seeking as he put it to 'preserve the well-established, effective current system under which the Takeover Panel does its work'.

Lord McIntosh of Haringey, speaking for the Government, said that this further debate was already ping-ponging between the two Houses, but Lord Alexander said that Lord MacIntosh's reply indicated a lack of comprehension, and that the arguments put to the Government had resulted in a 'dialogue of the deaf'. On division the amendment was defeated by 183 votes to 188, giving the Government a narrow victory. Peers spent the remainder of the day debating the **Regulatory and Investigatory Powers Bill** in committee.

On *13 June* Teresa Gorman initiated a Westminster Hall debate on the Committee on Standards and Privileges which had recently sentenced her to a month's suspension from the House. She argued that the Committee had become too political, and was open to manipulation by disgruntled people from outside the House.

MPs then debated both that day and the next, *14 June*, the **Countryside and Rights of Way Bill** at report stage with Conservatives seeking to amend the Bill to limit in various ways the rights of access it created, for example to prohibit roaming one hour after sunset to one hour before sunrise, but the Government sticking to its view won the divisions; the Opposition amendment declining to give the Bill a third reading was defeated by 130 votes to 323.

At prime minister's question time on *14 June* William Hague quoted from leaked memos written by Labour party advisers as well as from back bench Labour MPs, critical of Tony Blair as 'being all spin and presentation', concluding 'the Prime Minister started with every political advantage, and now he has squandered that advantage with spin, gimmick and a failure to deliver'. Mr Blair in response read out some comments from Conservative Party focus groups describing Mr Hague as 'false', 'pathetic' and a 'complete waste of time'.

On that day in the Lords peers debated higher education with a string of former vice-chancellors, heads of colleges and professors offering their thoughts, and in general warning the Government that things could not continue as they are.

On *15 June* peers debated the **Television Licences (Disclosure of Information) Bill** at second reading, while MPs debated European affairs in advance of the European Summit.

The following day, *16 June*, the Commons did not sit, but the Lords debated a report from their select committee on the EU charter of fundamental rights.

On Monday *19 June* MPs heard from the Minister for Housing and Planning, Nick Raynsford, about the failure of the national air

traffic services computer systems the previous weekend, which had left many thousands of air travellers with disrupted holiday plans.

Then Jack Straw made a Statement about the discovery in Dover of 58 people dead in the back of a lorry, a 'terrible tragedy' which he said 'must serve as a stark warning to others who might be tempted to place their fate in the hands of organised traffickers'. This was followed by another Statement from Mr Straw concerning violence 'by so-called England supporters at the Euro 2000 football championships in Brussels and Charleroi in Belgium'.

MPs then debated the report of the Royal Commission on House of Lords reform. The Leader of the House, Margaret Beckett, said the Government were minded to accept the broad outlines of the report: 'we believe that there is a role for a clearly subordinate second chamber, primarily in the legislative process'. Sir George Young from the Conservative front bench said: 'the real contest today is not between the Lords and the Commons, but between Parliament and the Executive. In that battle the Houses are not rivals, but partners'.

For the Liberal Democrats Robert Maclennan said: 'This chamber's pre-eminence is not threatened by the creation of a second effective Chamber of parliament that does what this Chamber has not done, cannot do or would prefer to be done elsewhere', and he went on to describe the report as full of internal contradictions, incoherent and deeply disappointing. Kenneth Clarke said that a 'directly elected upper House is the only one that will have full political legitimacy and the necessary clout properly to hold the modern Executive to account'.

Other Conservatives expressed the view that the reformed second chamber should contain no elected members at all, and Labour back benchers were similarly divided, with Paddy Tipping, minister at the Privy Council Office, concluding the debate for the Government by saying: 'It is fair to say that there is unanimity neither between parties nor within them'.

The 14th Opposition Day took place on *20 June*, with first a motion on football hooliganism moved by Ann Widdecombe being debated and defeated 132 to 363, and then a motion on Government economic policy, moved by Archie Norman, being defeated after debate by 175 votes to 326.

In Westminster Hall Valerie Davey opened a debate on the Okinawa G7 summit with several MPs from all parties pressing the Government to seek faster progress to relieve third world heavily indebted countries.

On *21 June* the Prime Minister made a Statement on the recent European Council meeting held in Feira in Portugal which he described as having been a success for 'Europe and the United Kingdom', especially with progress made on the problem of cross-border tax evasion. William Hague in his response pointed to the absence of mention of the single currency, and again pressed Tony Blair to say exactly where the Government stood on this, to which Mr Blair replied that unlike the Conservatives who would not even allow the public a say on the issue, the Government was committed to a referendum.

MPs then debated the **Children (Leaving Care) Bill** before this was given an unopposed second reading.

The following day, *22 June*, the Commons debated the security and intelligence services, while peers discussed the **Child Support, Pensions and Social Security Bill** at report stage, with an amendment to restore the earnings link for pensions being voted on at 11.20 pm, and defeated by 84 votes to 6; during the debate Baroness Castle said the path being taken by the Government would eventually lead to the disappearance of the basic state pension.

On Friday *23 June* MPs debated the policing of London on a motion for the adjournment, while peers debated a report from their Select Committee entitled 'A European Food Authority', before debating at second reading the **Carers and Disabled Children Bill**.

MPs heard a Statement on *26 June* on the human genome project which Patricia Hewitt, the Minister for Small Business and E-Commerce, described as 'an enormous scientific achievement . . . which will be of benefit to all humanity'.

The **Crown Prosecution Service Inspectorate Bill** was then dealt with at report and third reading, with the House rising before 6 pm. Peers that day debated the **Countryside and Rights of Way Bill** at second reading with some 45 speeches being made in an eight-hour debate, including a maiden speech from Lord Brittan of Spennithorne, former EU Commissioner.

Summing up for the Government Lord Whitty said: 'This has been an interesting debate. We have heard a great many opinions. Everyone has claimed that there is a great deal of consensus, but there also seem to be some fundamental problems. . . . So I am sure the Committee and subsequent stages will be interesting'.

The following day, *27 June*, peers debated the **Child Support, Pensions and Social Security Bill** at report stage, with the Government suffering two defeats, first when Lord Higgins moved an amendment to alter the presumption about

misleading information given by the DSS so that it would be easier for widows and widowers to prove they had been misled over inherited rights under the SERPS scheme; this was carried by 166 votes to 135.

Then Lord Windlesham moved an amendment to require court confirmation of any cuts in benefits where claimants had persistently failed to comply with a community service order, rather than allowing such cuts to be made without any court intervention; this was carried by 170 votes to 116. Supporting Lord Windlesham was the Bishop of Lincoln who described benefit cuts made at the 'diktat' of the DSS as morally objectionable.

MPs completed work on the **Learning and Skills Bill** which received an unopposed third reading that day.

At prime minister's question time William Hague attacked the Government for its stealth tax increases, saying that petrol had gone up far faster than pensions, but Tony Blair said it was the Conservatives who had introduced the fuel duty escalator.

Earlier at Welsh question time the Secretary of State for Wales was asked about the previous day's vote by the National Assembly in favour of having an option to decide about hunting in Wales; he responded by saying that the decision would be made at Westminster.

MPs then completed report and third reading on both the **Limited Liability Partnerships Bill** and the **Fur Farming (Prohibition) Bill**.

In Westminster Hall that day MPs debated the growing evidence of the threat to health posed by organophosphates, following which David Davis, chairman of the Public Accounts Committee initiated a debate on fraud in the European Union.

The 15th Opposition Day was on *29 June*, with Liam Fox from the Conservative front bench initiating a debate on priorities within the NHS in which he accused the Government of bullying, secrecy and manipulation, and said the Tories wanted to take the politics out of healthcare. In response Alan Milburn, Secretary of State for Health, pointed to increased numbers of doctors and nurses and reduced waiting lists as evidence of achievement under Labour. The Opposition motion was defeated by 122 votes to 278.

In Westminster Hall that day MPs debated sanctions based on a report from the International Development select committee. The House of Lords considered the **Regulation of Investigatory Powers Bill** in committee on *28 June* then the **Postal Services Bill** on report on *29 June*, and then debated a select committee report on EU proposals to combat discrimination on Friday *30 June* when the House of Commons did not sit.

JULY

Monday *3 July* was taken as the 16th Opposition Day. First Ann Widdecombe moved a motion condemning the Government for giving early release to so many prisoners, saying the Prime Minister was far more interested in grabbing a quick headline than in the substance of policy; 'the Government swagger and they posture; the Prime Minister grins and he spins. The rhetoric of the Government is as vainglorious as any action that they take is vacuous'. Jack Straw rebutted her analysis, and said the Government was getting on top of crime. The Conservative motion was defeated by 137 votes to 319.

After this Andrew Lansley introduced a debate on the Government's response – or lack of it – to the Neill Committee report on ministers and special advisers, saying that these now cost the taxpayer £4.3 million a year, and that the Government had treated the Committee on Standards in Public Life with arrogant disdain. Tony Wright offered a careful rebuttal of the Conservative motion, quoting extensively from the Neill Committee report, while Martin Bell said that behaving better was the most obvious way of increasing public trust. The Conservative motion was defeated by 165 votes to 295.

In answer to a written question that day Baroness Jay said that it was the Government's intention to establish a joint committee to consider the parliamentary implications of the Wakeham report on Lords reform 'as soon as possible after the summer recess'.

On *4 July* the Prime Minister made a Statement on the civil list, explaining that this would remain over the next 10 years at the same figure as the past 10, namely £7.9 million, though some expenditure would be transferred to other headings. In questions following this Statement some MPs expressed regret at past opaqueness in regard to royal finances, which they felt had only partially been lifted, while others indicated that they felt more open debate on the future of the monarchy ought to take place in the House of Commons.

Jack Straw then made a Statement indicating his intention to bring forward legislation quickly to try to curb football hooliganism, but Simon Hughes from the Liberal Democrat benches said that some of the proposals being made went far beyond conventional impositions on the rights of citizens.

The House then agreed a timetable motion to deal with remaining stages of the **Local Government Bill**, with the Opposition supporting the guillotine. Richard Shepherd once more deplored this, saying it was the 35th bill in this Parliament to which the guillotine had been applied. Ewan Harris initiated a short debate in

Westminster Hall that morning on widening access to Oxford University.

At prime minister's question time on *5 July* Wiliam Hague mocked the proposal put forward by Tony Blair for on the spot fines of £100 for drunken and violent thugs.

Later when the **Local Government Bill** was further debated an Opposition attempt to block the repeal of 'Section 28' – banning the promotion of a homosexual lifestyle – was defeated by 133 votes to 305.

In Westminster Hall Geoffrey Clifton-Brown initiated a 90-minute debate on the cost of changeover to the Euro.

The 2nd Estimates Day was on *6 July*, with first a debate on HM Customs and Excise based on a report from the Treasury select committee, then a debate on the provision of medical services to the Benefits Agency, based on a Social Security select committee report. Introducing the latter, Archy Kirkwood said that Parliament does not take enough time to revisit some earlier policy decisions taken in primary legislation.

On Friday *7 July* Jack Straw, Home Secretary, introduced a debate on the adjournment on the Burns Report on hunting with dogs.

On Monday *10 July* MPs considered Lords Amendments to the **Terrorism Bill**, while peers examined the **Transport Bill** in committee.

Tributes were paid to the Queen Mother on *11 July* from all party leaders on the occasion of her forthcoming 100th birthday, though some newspapers commented on how sparsely attended the House was, especially on the Labour benches, for this occasion.

The **Police (Northern Ireland) Bill** was then further considered on report, before being approved at third reading by 307 votes to 16. Peers debated the **Utilities Bill** at third reading with the Government being defeated by 136 votes to 133 on an amendment requiring the new gas and electricity regulator to try to secure a diverse and viable long term energy supply.

The following day, *12 July*, the Speaker made a Statement announcing that she intended to relinquish the office of Speaker immediately before the House returns from the Summer recess. The Leader of the House, Margaret Beckett, said that it was very obvious that MPs heard the Statement with great regret.

Also that day the Government suffered three further defeats in the House of Lords; first peers voted by 124 to 122 for an amendment to the **Government Resources and Accounts Bill** giving the National Audit Office greater rights of access to the accounts of QUANGOs. Then during the report stage on the **Regulation of Investigatory Powers Bill** Lord Cope from the Conservative front bench moved that an advisory board on the technical requirements and financial consequences of the intercept system should be set up to advise the commissioner; this was carried by 155 votes to 130.

Lord Astor, also from the Conservative front bench moved that the Government should be required (rather than simply allowed) to contribute to the costs falling on industry for the installation of an intercept system; this was carried by 131 votes to 119. The Commons then debated the **Care Standards Bill** on report, before approving the Bill at third reading at 2.40 am.

In presenting the Government's annual report on *13 July* the Prime Minister said that inflation was down to 2.2 per cent, an inherited £28 billion deficit had been turned into a £16 billion surplus, real take home pay was up 8 per cent since May 1997, and one million new jobs had been created.

In response William Hague quoted from reports made in previous years, and then ridiculed the Prime Minister for living in a fantasy world 'in which the Dome is a great success, everyone wants to abolish Section 28, everyone wants to adopt the Euro and everyone believes the figures produced by the Chancellor'.

This was the 17th Opposition Day and the Conservatives used it for William Hague to introduce a debate on Parliament and the Executive with a motion regretting the accelerated loss of power and influence from parliament since 1997, and calling for reforms to reassert the authority of the House. John Major said that the House and back bench MPs must have more power to end the perception that government is an elective dictatorship; he accepted that he should have done more about that himself when prime minister.

Many speakers quoted from the Commission under Lord Norton whose report had recently been issued, but Margaret Beckett claimed that many of the reforms recommended by Lord Norton were already being implemented. The Opposition motion was predictably defeated – by 165 votes to 304. The House then debated the **Football (Disorder) Bill** which was approved at second reading by 206 votes to 6 shortly after 1 am.

On *14 July* peers debated a report from their European Union Committee on the World Trade Organisation.

On Monday *17 July* MPs heard a Statement from Estelle Morris saying that the Government intended to go ahead with the performance related pay scheme for teachers which the High Court had ruled unlawful because of the manner of its introduction.

A guillotine was then introduced on the **Football (Disorder) Bill** which then completed all its remaining Commons stages shortly before 3 am the next morning.

The Chancellor, Gordon Brown, made a Statement on *18 July* introducing public spending allocations for 2001 to 2004; he said: 'sustained and sustainable improvement in our public finances makes possible a sustained and sustainable improvement in our public services', with education getting an extra £12 billion and health an extra £13 billion. Michael Portillo for the Conservative opposition said that the Government had become big spenders rather than wise spenders, and that the Chancellor only had this 'election war chest because he had taken £5 billion out of the people's pension funds'.

The House then debated the **Finance Bill** on report, continuing with this on *19 July* before the Bill gained its third reading by 310 votes to 170.

At prime minister's question time on that day the subject of public spending remained very much to the fore. In the Lords the **Child Support, Pensions and Social Security Bill** was debated at third reading, with the Government accepting that cuts in benefits should not be made without court confirmation.

On *20 July* MPs held a day's debate on public expenditure on a motion for the adjournment.

On Friday *21 July* MPs completed remaining stages of the **Warm Homes and Energy Conservation Bill** and the **Protection of Animals (Amendment) Bill**.

On Monday *24 July* MPs heard a Statement from the Prime Minister on the G8 Summit in Okinawa. A wide range of subjects had been discussed, including debt relief, trade, AIDS, access to the internet, drugs, genetically modified food, and environmental damage. William Hague said there was a feeling that 'world leaders had blown it', and in particular progress on debt relief had been very limited. He questioned Tony Blair about reports that £500 million had been spent on the Summit itself, but Mr Blair responded that the hospitality and cost were matters for the Japanese Government.

The House then heard a Statement on defence spending, before considering Lords' amendments to the **Child Support, Pensions and Social Security Bill**, and the **Government Resources and Accounts Bill**, with Government defeats in the Lords on these Bills being reversed by MPs.

In the upper House that day peers considered Commons amendments to the **Local Government Bill**, with the Commons reversal of the Lords amendment allowing local councils to opt to retain the committee system being accepted, though not without resistance led by Lord Dixon-Smith, who moved for the rejection of the relevant Commons amendment, but his motion was lost by 169 votes to 221.

Later Baroness Young once again led resistance to the Government motion to accept the will of the Commons in deleting from the Bill the clause retaining Section 28; she argued that this was a matter of fighting for the protection of children, and her motion was carried by 270 votes to 228. (With 498 peers voting and an attendance that day of 567 out of a total House of 697, this was the largest turnout since the expulsion from the House of most hereditary peers.) Peers then turned to the **Football (Disorder) Bill** which they debated all night, rising at 5.12 am.

At the commencement of business on the following day, *25 July*, the Government moved for the suspension of Standing Orders to allow for the Bill to be taken through its remaining stages, but Lord Marlesford opposed this, arguing that it was inimical to the proper scrutiny of the Bill; peers did not even have Hansard for the last five hours of the previous day's debate, which had in effect taken place that morning. Conservative front benchers had agreed the timetable with the Government, and did not take part in the vote, but the Government were still defeated on Lord Marlesford's amendment by 143 votes to 124.

Later during report stage proceedings on the Bill the Government was again defeated (by 174 votes to 136) on an amendment moved by Lord Cope reducing the time specified in the so-called sunset provisions within the Bill. Third reading of the **Football (Disorder) Bill** was taken the following day, *26 July*.

Meanwhile in the Commons on *25 July* MPs debated a guillotine motion on the **Criminal Justice (Mode of Trial)(No2) Bill** which was accepted by 306 votes to 180, with proceedings on this Bill concluding five hours later when the third reading was approved by 282 votes to 199.

On *27 July* Tony Blair introducing a motion of thanks to Betty Boothroyd, saying she had been an outstanding Speaker who had greatly enhanced the reputation of her office; other party leaders and senior MPs joined in the tributes. Miss Boothroyd herself in her farewell remarks said: 'The level of cynicism about Parliament and the accompanying alienation of many of the young from the democratic process is troubling,' and she continued: 'Let's make a start by remembering that the function of parliament is to hold the Executive to account. It is in Parliament in the first instance that ministers must explain and justify their policies.'

In the upper House that day the Lord Chairman of Committees, Lord Boston of Faversham, came under strong pressure from back bench peers over the proposal from the Offices Committee to appoint an outside consultant at a fee of £70,000 to conduct a review of the management and committee structure of the House. After two hours of argument on the floor of the House he agreed to withdraw this recommendation.

Late that evening during debate on the second reading of the **Disqualification Bill** Lord Cranborne and Lord Lamont called a division, which they lost by 13 votes to 2, but as fewer than 30 peers had voted, the debate was adjourned.

This Bill was then given its second reading the following day, *28 July*, with the House also taking all stages of the **Finance Bill** that day too, before rising for the Summer recess, as did the House of Commons after various issues had been debated on the adjournment.

Public Legislation 1999–2000

(Attaining Royal Assent by 31 July 2000)

*   legislation introduced by a private member whose name follows the title of the Act.
†   consolidation bill.
HL legislation introduced into the House of Lords.
Dates are day of Royal Assent.

Appropriation Act 2000 (20 July 2000)
[Introduced as the Consolidated Fund (Appropriation) Bill]
Prescribes how expenditure is appropriated in order to finance specific public services.

Armed Forces (Discipline Act) *HL* (25 May 2000)
Revises and updates procedures for military discipline to ensure these are compliant with the Human Rights Act 1998; alters custody rules and establishes independent judicial officers to decide on custody before trial; establishes a new summary appeal court to which a new right of appeal may be made; alters the time within which an election to trial by court-martial trial may be made.

Care Standards Act 2000 *HL* (28 July 2000)
Establishes in England the National Care Standards Commission to regulate organisations providing care services, and a General Social Care Council to oversee the training and registration of social care workers, with parallel bodies for Wales; makes new provision for the regulation of childminding services; provides for a children's rights director for England and a children's commissioner for Wales.

*Carers and Disabled Children Act 2000 *Tom Pendry* (20 July 2000)
Makes new provision in England and Wales for carers aged 16 or over who provide substantial care for an adult; amends the Community Care (Direct Payments) Act 1996 to extend local authority power to make direct payments to carers aged 16 or over; amends the Children Act 1989 in regard to assessment of the ability to provide care for a disabled child; extends the option of direct payment to those providing such care, including payments to disabled children between the ages of 16 and 18.

*Census (Amendment) Act 2000 *HL Lord Weatherill* (28 July 2000)
Amends the Census Act 1920 to allow for the asking of a voluntary question on religion in the 2001 Census in England and Wales.

Child Support, Pensions, and Social Security Act 2000 (28 July 2000)
Amends the law relating to child support; creates a new simpler formula for calculating child support and removes many of the existing exemptions for paying child support; creates new powers designed to ensure parents liable to pay support do in fact do so, including disqualification from driving; amends the law relating to occupational and personal pensions and war pensions; introduces the State Second Pension in replacement of SERPS; extends the powers of the Occupational Pensions Regulatory Authority, and revises the framework within which the Pensions Ombudsman operates; amends the law relating to social security benefits and social security administration; amends the law relating to national insurance contributions; and for connected purposes.

Consolidated Fund (No 2) Act 1999 (20 December 1999)
Gives parliamentary authority for sums to be issued out of the Consolidated Fund to meet the Government's expenditure requirements.

Consolidated Fund Act 2000 (21 March 2000)
Gives parliamentary authority for sums to be issued out of the Consolidated Fund to meet the Government's expenditure requirements.

Crown Prosecution Service Inspectorate Act 2000 *HL* (28 July 2000)
Makes the Crown Prosecution Service inspectorate a statutory body.

Electronic Communications Act 2000 (25 May 2000)
Provides statutory back-up for self-regulation within the field of electronic commerce; implements the EU Electronic Signatures Directive and confirms the legal admissibility of electronic signatures; provides for a revision in the procedure for modification of licences for telecommunications operators.

Finance Act 2000 (28 July 2000)
Makes various changes in personal tax and benefits, including a cut in the basic rate of income tax to 22p; makes changes to the tax regime for business, in particular by adjustments in capital gains tax, development tax credits and capital allowances; makes provision for changes in the tax treatment of international business operations; varies the rate of landfill tax and clarifies liabilities; adjusts tax to provide incentives for energy saving in domestic heating; alters the tax limits in relation to charitable giving and seeks to improve the tax system for charities.

Financial Services and Markets Act 2000 (14 June 2000)
Makes provision regarding the regulation of financial services and markets; provides for the transfer of certain statutory functions in relation to building societies, friendly societies, industrial and provident societies and certain other mutual societies; and for connected purposes.

Football Disorder Act 2000 (28 July 2000)
Introduces a new banning order combining aspects of both domestic and international football banning orders; makes new requirements regarding the surrender of passports; introduces summary powers allowing police constables to issue notices preventing citizens leaving the country and providing for the surrender of passports.

Government Resources and Accounts Act 2000 (28 July 2000)
Amends existing legislation to allow for the introduction of resource accounting and budgeting to the whole of the public sector ('Whole of Government Accounts'); empowers the Treasury to expend funds on the establishment of a new body to carry on private-public partnership business ('Partnerships UK').

Learning and Skills Act 2000 *HL* (28 July 2000)
Establishes the Learning and Skills Council for England and the National Council for Education and Training for Wales to be responsible for planning, funding, and management of post-16 education and training excluding higher education; makes new arrangements for the independent inspection of post-16 education and training by the Adult Learning Inspectorate and OFSTED in England, with parallel arrangements for Wales; makes other varied provisions in relation to funding and regulation of post-16 education; makes provision for individual learning accounts throughout the UK.

Limited Liability Partnerships Act 2000 *HL* (28 July 2000)
Creates a new form of corporate entity, the limited liability partnership, combining features of limited companies and partnerships, and available on a voluntary basis to any undertaking consisting of two or more people within Britain.

LEGISLATION

Local Government Act 2000 *HL* (28 July 2000)
Enables local authorities to make new executive arrangements separating executive and scrutiny functions within local government, including provision for altered electoral arrangements, possible referendums and executive mayors; empowers local authorities to promote the economic, social and environmental well-being of their area; makes provision for a new framework within which local authorities will plan and commission welfare services for vulnerable people.

Northern Ireland Act 2000 (2 February 2000)
Provides for the suspension of the Northern Ireland Assembly and Executive, and makes various consequential provisions in relation to the restoration of devolved government.

Nuclear Safeguards Act 2000 *HL* (25 May 2000)
Makes changes to UK law to enable the Government to fulfil obligations under the new Additional Protocol to the UK's Safeguards Agreement, including powers enabling the Secretary of State to require people to give him information and to authorise entry to premises to obtain information.

Postal Services Act 2000 (28 July 2000)
Establishes the Postal Services Commission with duties and powers to protect the interests of postal service users, in particular by promoting competition in postal markets wherever this is appropriate and consistent with the universal service obligation at a uniform tariff; replaces the Post Office Users' National Council with the Consumer Council for Postal Services; provides for the conversion of the Post Office from a statutory corporation to a public limited company, with ownership remaining with the Crown.

†Powers of Criminal Courts (Sentencing) Act 2000 *HL* (25 May 2000)
Consolidates all major legislation regarding the powers of courts in sentencing.

Regulation of Investigatory Powers Act 2000 (28 July 2000)
Creates a statutory framework for the interception of communications, the use of surveillance and access to encrypted data by various investigatory agencies including the police, replacing and adding to earlier non-statutory codes of guidance.

Representation of the People Act 2000 (9 March 2000)
Makes provision for the introduction of a system of rolling electoral registration in place of registration by reference to an annual qualifying date; makes various provisions to facilitate the registration of certain groups, including the homeless; makes provision for electors to opt out of inclusion in the version of the electoral register made available for sale, while allowing rights of access to the full register to certain institutions such as credit reference agencies; makes provision for postal votes on demand; enables local authorities to run pilot schemes to try out innovative electoral procedures, such as electronic voting; makes provision to assist electors with disabilities; creates a new offence of making false statements with regard to names and addresses of candidates on nomination papers.

Royal Parks (Trading) Act 2000 (28 July 2000)
Makes provision about certain offences under Section 2 of the Parks Regulation (Amendment) Act 1926.

Sea Fishing Grants (Charges) Act 2000 (28 July 2000)
Gives retrospective statutory authority to charges made by the Sea Fish Industry Authority for handling applications for fishing vessel grants before 1996.

Television Licenses (Disclosure of Information) Act 2000 (20 July 2000)
Gives the Secretary of State the legal authority to require the disclosure of information of a prescribed kind to the BBC and to certain third parties providing services for the BBC in connection with the provision of television licences to persons over the age of 75.

Terrorism Act 2000 (20 July 2000)
Provides a statutory definition of terrorism; gives the Secretary of State new powers to proscribe organisations involved in international or domestic terrorism; creates a new power to seize terrorist cash at borders; renews and extends various counter-terrorist powers; creates a new system for detention under independent judicial authority; allows for the removal of temporary provisions in relation to Northern Ireland; requires that an annual report on the operation of the Act be placed before parliament.

Utilities Act 2000 (28 July 2000)
Amends existing law relating to the regulation of the privatised gas and electricity markets; creates a new Gas and Electricity Markets Authority, with a primary duty to protect the interests of consumers through the promotion of competition; establishes new consumer councils for these industries with wider powers; allows the Secretary of State to issue guidance on social and environmental objectives to the regulatory authority; provides for new monetary penalties on utilities in breach of licence conditions.

Departmental Select Committee Reports 1999–2000

excluding special reports
(reports published before 20 October 2000)

AGRICULTURE
1st   The Current Crisis in the Livestock Industry, *HC 94*
2nd   The Marketing of Milk, *HC 36*
3rd   The Segregation of Genetically Modified Foods, *HC 71*
4th   Environmental Regulation and Farming, *HC 212*
5th   The Government's Proposals for Organophosphate Sheep Dips, *HC 425*
6th   The Implications for UK Agriculture and EU Agricultural Policy of Trade
       Liberalisation and the WTO Round, *HC 246*
7th   Horticulture Research International, *HC 484*
8th   Genetically Modified Organisms and Seed Segregation, *HC 812*
9th   MAFF/Intervention Board Departmental Report 2000, *HC 610*
10th Regional Service Centres, *HC 509*

CULTURE, MEDIA AND SPORT
1st   Countdown to the Millennium, *HC 24*
2nd   The Future of Professional Rugby, *HC 99*
3rd   The Funding of the BBC, *HC 25*
4th   Wembley National Stadium, *HC 164*
5th   Whatever Happened to News at Ten? *HC 289*
6th   Public Libraries, *HC 241*
7th   Cultural Property: Return and Illicit Trade, *HC 371*
8th   Marking the Millennium in the United Kingdom, *HC 578*
9th   Report and Accounts for the BBC, *HC 719*

DEFENCE
1st   The OCCAR Convention, *HC 69*
2nd   Ministry of Defence Annual Reporting Cycle, *HC 158*
3rd   Annual Reports for 1997 and 1998 on Strategic Export Councils, *HC 225*
4th   Armed Forces Discipline Bill [Lords], *HC 253*
5th   The Defence Geographic and Imagery Intelligence Agency, *HC 100*
6th   The Appointment of the New Chief Scientific Adviser, *HC 318*
7th   Gulf Veterans' Illness, *HC 125*
8th   European Security and Defence, *HC 264*
9th   The Future of DERA, *HC 462*
10th Major Procurement Projects, *HC 528*
11th Strategic Export Controls: Further Report and Parliamentary Prior Scrutiny, *HC 467*
12th The Adaptation of the Treaty on Conventional Forces in Europe, *HC 295*
13th Iraqi No-Fly Zones, *HC 453*

EDUCATION AND EMPLOYMENT
1st   School Meals, *HC 96*
2nd   Visit to the USA: Raising Educational Standards and the Role of the
       Private Sector, *HC 290*
3rd   The Draft Part-Time Employees (Prevention of Laws Favourable Treatment)
       Regulations 2000, *HC 297*
4th   Employability and Jobs: Is there a Jobs Gap? *HC 60*
5th   Work Permits for Overseas Footballers, *HC 218*
6th   Standards and Quality in Education: The Annual Report of Her Majesty's Chief
       Inspector of Schools 1998–99, *HC 345*
7th   The Role of Private Sector Organisations in Public Education, *HC 118*
8th   New Deal for Young People: Two Years On, *HC 510*

ENVIRONMENT, TRANSPORT AND REGIONAL AFFAIRS

FOREIGN AFFAIRS

HEALTH

HOME AFFAIRS

INTERNATIONAL DEVELOPMENT

DEPARTMENTAL SELECT COMMITTEE REPORTS

NORTHERN IRELAND AFFAIRS

PUBLIC ADMINISTRATION

SCIENCE AND TECHNOLOGY

SCOTTISH AFFAIRS

SOCIAL SECURITY

TRADE AND INDUSTRY

Visit the Vacher Dod Website...

www.Politicallinks.co.uk

Political information and biographies updated daily

- TODAY'S BUSINESS
- THIS WEEK'S BUSINESS
- PROGRESS OF GOVERNMENT BILLS
- SELECT COMMITTEES
- DIARY
- HOUSE OF COMMONS
- HOUSE OF LORDS
- SCOTTISH PARLIAMENT

- NATIONAL ASSEMBLY FOR WALES
- NORTHERN IRELAND ASSEMBLY
- GREATER LONDON ASSEMBLY
- EUROPEAN UNION
- GENERAL ELECTION
- STOP PRESS

Dod *on* Line

AN UP-TO-THE-MINUTE POLITICAL DATABASE UPDATED AS EVENTS HAPPEN...

Dod's Parliamentary Companion and **Vacher's** have created the most comprehensive political database live on the Net with up-to-the-minute changes.

Click on 'STOP PRESS' to check political events which affect the database – as they happen.

Westminster, Scotland, Wales, Northern Ireland, Europe, the GLA, and the Civil Service.

Arrange an immediate free online trial by phone or Email

Contact Oliver Cox on 020 7828 7256 or Email: olivercox@vacherdod.co.uk

Vacher Dod Publishing Limited
PO Box 3700, Westminster, London SW1P 4WU
Tel: 020 7828 7256   Fax: 020 7828 7269
Email: olivercox@vacherdod.co.uk
Website: www.politicallinks.co.uk

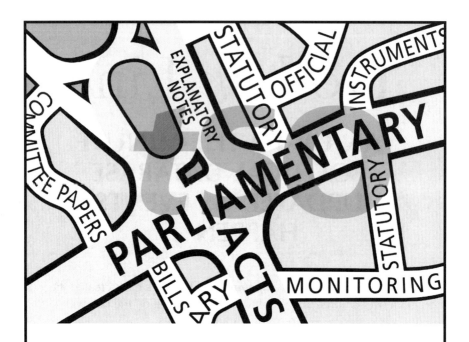

The quickest route to Parliament

The Stationery Office: The official source for parliamentary publications

---

Parliamentary Hotline
0845 7023 474

www.the**StationeryOffice**.com

PARLIAMENT

State of parties (October 2000)

Labour	414
Conservative	162
Liberal Democrats	47
Ulster Unionist Party	9
Scottish National Party	6
Plaid Cymru	4
Social Democratic and Labour	3
Democratic Unionist Party	3
Independents	3
MP for Falkirk West	1
United Kingdom Unionist Party	1
Sinn Fein (Seats not taken)	2
Speaker	1
Total seats	659*

(Includes the three Deputy Speakers)

*By-elections pending due to deaths of Labour MPs for Preston Audrey Wise and for Glasgow Anniesland Donald Dewar and resignation of Speaker Betty Boothroyd

Constituencies by country and party

For alphabetical list see polling results on page 352.

ENGLAND – 528 Members
By-elections pending in Preston and West Bromwich West

LABOUR (328 Members)
(*Labour/Co-operative)

Amber Valley	Judy Mallaber
Ashfield	Geoffrey Hoon
Ashton under Lyne	Robert Sheldon
Barking	Margaret Hodge
Barnsley Central	Eric Illsley
Barnsley East and Mexborough	Jeffrey Ennis
Barnsley West and Penistone	Michael Clapham
Barrow and Furness	John Hutton
Basildon	Angela Smith*
Bassetlaw	Joe Ashton
Batley and Spen	Mike Wood
Battersea	Martin Linton
Bedford	Patrick Hall
Bethnal Green and Bow	Oona King
Bexleyheath and Crayford	Nigel Beard
Birkenhead	Frank Field
Birmingham Edgbaston	Gisela Stuart
Birmingham Erdington	Robin Corbett
Birmingham Hall Green	Stephen McCabe
Birmingham Hodge Hill	Terry Davis
Birmingham Ladywood	Clare Short
Birmingham Northfield	Richard Burden
Birmingham Perry Barr	Jeffrey Rooker
Birmingham Selly Oak	Lynne Jones
Birmingham Sparkbrook and Small Heath	Roger Godsiff
Birmingham Yardley	Estelle Morris
Bishop Auckland	Derek Foster
Blackburn	Jack Straw
Blackpool North and Fleetwood	Joan Humble
Blackpool South	Gordon Marsden
Blaydon	John McWilliam
Blyth Valley	Ronnie Campbell
Bolsover	Dennis Skinner
Bolton North East	David Crausby
Bolton South East	Brian Iddon
Bolton West	Ruth Kelly
Bootle	Joe Benton
Bradford North	Terence Rooney
Bradford South	Gerry Sutcliffe
Bradford West	Marsha Singh
Braintree	Alan Hurst
Brent North	Barry Gardiner
Brent South	Paul Boateng
Brentford and Isleworth	Ann Keen
Brigg and Goole	Ian Cawsey
Brighton Kemptown	Des Turner
Brighton Pavilion	David Lepper*
Bristol East	Jean Corston
Bristol North West	Doug Naysmith*
Bristol South	Dawn Primarolo
Bristol West	Valerie Davey
Broxtowe	Nicholas Palmer
Burnley	Peter Pike
Burton	Janet Dean
Bury North	David Chaytor
Bury South	Ivan Lewis
Calder Valley	Christine McCafferty
Camberwell and Peckham	Harriet Harman
Cambridge	Anne Campbell
Cannock Chase	Tony Wright
Carlisle	Eric Martlew
Castle Point	Christine Butler
Chatham and Aylesford	Jonathan Shaw
Chesterfield	Tony Benn
Chorley	Lindsay Hoyle
City of Chester	Christine Russell
City of Durham	Gerry Steinberg
City of York	Hugh Bayley
Cleethorpes	Shona McIsaac
Colne Valley	Kali Mountford
Copeland	Jack Cunningham
Corby	Phil Hope*
Coventry North East	Bob Ainsworth
Coventry North West	Geoffrey Robinson
Coventry South	James Cunningham
Crawley	Laura Moffatt
Crewe and Nantwich	Gwyneth Dunwoody
Crosby	Claire Curtis-Thomas
Croydon Central	Geraint Davies
Croydon North	Malcolm Wicks
Dagenham	Judith Church
Darlington	Alan Milburn
Dartford	Howard Stoate
Denton and Reddish	Andrew Bennett
Derby North	Bob Laxton
Derby South	Margaret Beckett
Dewsbury	Ann Taylor
Don Valley	Caroline Flint
Doncaster Central	Rosie Winterton

Doncaster North	Kevin Hughes
Dover	Gwyn Prosser
Dudley North	Ross Cranston
Dudley South	Ian Pearson
Dulwich and West Norwood	Tessa Jowell
Durham North	Giles Radice
Ealing North	Stephen Pound
Ealing Southall	Piara Khabra
Ealing, Acton and Shepherd's Bush	Clive Soley
Easington	John Cummings
East Ham	Stephen Timms
Eccles	Ian Stewart
Edmonton	Andrew Love*
Ellesmere Port and Neston	Andrew Miller
Elmet	Colin Burgon
Eltham	Clive Efford
Enfield North	Joan Ryan
Enfield Southgate	Stephen Twigg
Erewash	Elizabeth Blackman
Erith and Thamesmead	John Austin
Exeter	Ben Bradshaw
Falmouth and Camborne	Candy Atherton
Feltham and Heston	Alan Keen*
Finchley and Golders Green	Rudi Vis
Forest of Dean	Diana Organ
Gateshead East and Washington West	Joyce Quin
Gedling	Vernon Coaker
Gillingham	Paul Clark
Gloucester	Tess Kingham
Gravesham	Chris Pond
Great Grimsby	Austin Mitchell
Great Yarmouth	Anthony Wright
Greenwich and Woolwich	Nick Raynsford
Hackney North and Stoke Newington	Diane Abbott
Hackney South and Shoreditch	Brian Sedgemore
Halesowen and Rowley Regis	Sylvia Heal
Halifax	Alice Mahon
Halton	Derek Twigg
Hammersmith and Fulham	Iain Coleman
Hampstead and Highgate	Glenda Jackson
Harlow	Bill Rammell
Harrow East	Tony McNulty
Harrow West	Gareth R Thomas
Hartlepool	Peter Mandelson
Harwich	Ivan Henderson
Hastings and Rye	Michael Jabez Foster
Hayes and Harlington	John McDonnell
Hemel Hempstead	Tony McWalter*
Hemsworth	Jon Trickett
Hendon	Andrew Dismore
Heywood and Middleton	Jim Dobbin*
High Peak	Tom Levitt
Holborn and St Pancras	Frank Dobson
Hornchurch	John Cryer
Hornsey and Wood Green	Barbara Roche
Houghton and Washington East	Fraser Kemp
Hove	Ivor Caplin
Huddersfield	Barry Sheerman*
Hull East	John Prescott
Hull North	Kevin McNamara
Hull West and Hessle	Alan Johnson
Hyndburn	Greg Pope
Ilford North	Linda Perham
Ilford South	Mike Gapes*
Ipswich	Jamie Cann
Islington North	Jeremy Corbyn
Islington South and Finsbury	Chris Smith
Jarrow	Stephen Hepburn
Keighley	Ann Cryer
Kettering	Philip Sawford
Kingswood	Roger Berry
Knowsley North and Sefton East	George Howarth
Knowsley South	Edward O'Hara
Lancaster and Wyre	Hilton Dawson
Leeds Central	Hilary Benn
Leeds East	George Mudie
Leeds North East	Fabian Hamilton
Leeds North West	Harold Best
Leeds West	John Battle
Leicester East	Keith Vaz
Leicester South	James Marshall
Leicester West	Patricia Hewitt
Leigh	Lawrence Cunliffe
Leominster	Peter Temple-Morris
Lewisham East	Bridget Prentice
Lewisham West	Jim Dowd
Lewisham, Deptford	Joan Ruddock
Leyton and Wanstead	Harry Cohen
Lincoln	Gillian Merron
Liverpool Garston	Maria Eagle
Liverpool Riverside	Louise Ellman*
Liverpool Walton	Peter Kilfoyle
Liverpool Wavertree	Jane Kennedy
Liverpool West Derby	Robert Wareing
Loughborough	Andrew Reed*
Luton North	Kelvin Hopkins
Luton South	Margaret Moran
Makerfield	Ian McCartney

Manchester Blackley	Graham Stringer
Manchester Central	Tony Lloyd
Manchester Gorton	Gerald Kaufman
Manchester Withington	Keith Bradley
Mansfield	Alan Meale
Medway	Robert Marshall-Andrews
Middlesbrough	Stuart Bell
Middlesbrough South and East Cleveland	Ashok Kumar
Milton Keynes North East	Brian White
Milton Keynes South West	Phyllis Starkey
Mitcham and Morden	Siobhain McDonagh
Morecambe and Lunesdale	Geraldine Smith
Morley and Rothwell	John Gunnell
Newark	Fiona Jones
Newcastle upon Tyne Central	Jim Cousins
Newcastle upon Tyne East and Wallsend	Nick Brown
Newcastle upon Tyne North	Doug Henderson
Newcastle-under-Lyme	Llin Golding
Normanton	William O'Brien
North East Derbyshire	Harry Barnes
North Swindon	Michael Wills
North Tyneside	Stephen Byers
North Warwickshire	Mike O'Brien
North West Durham	Hilary Armstrong
North West Leicestershire	David Taylor*
North West Norfolk	George Turner
Northampton North	Sally Keeble
Northampton South	Tony Clarke
Norwich North	Ian Gibson
Norwich South	Charles Clarke
Nottingham East	John Heppell
Nottingham North	Graham Allen
Nottingham South	Alan Simpson
Nuneaton	Bill Olner
Oldham East and Saddleworth	Philip Woolas
Oldham West and Royton	Michael Meacher
Oxford East	Andrew Smith
Pendle	Gordon Prentice
Peterborough	Helen Brinton
Plymouth Devonport	David Jamieson
Plymouth Sutton	Linda Gilroy*
Pontefract and Castleford	Yvette Cooper
Poplar and Canning Town	Jim Fitzpatrick
Portsmouth North	Syd Rapson
Preston	by-election pending
Pudsey	Paul Truswell
Putney	Tony Colman
Reading East	Jane Griffiths
Reading West	Martin Salter
Redcar	Marjorie Mowlam
Redditch	Jacqui Smith
Regent's Park and Kensington North	Karen Buck
Rochdale	Lorna Fitzsimons
Romford	Eileen Gordon
Rossendale and Darwen	Janet Anderson
Rother Valley	Kevin Barron
Rotherham	Denis MacShane
Rugby and Kenilworth	Andy King
Salford	Hazel Blears
Scarborough and Whitby	Lawrie Quinn
Scunthorpe	Elliot Morley
Sedgefield	Tony Blair
Selby	John Grogan
Sheffield Attercliffe	Clive Betts
Sheffield Brightside	David Blunkett
Sheffield Central	Richard Caborn
Sheffield Heeley	Bill Michie
Sheffield Hillsborough	Helen Jackson
Sherwood	Paddy Tipping
Shipley	Christopher Leslie
Shrewsbury and Atcham	Paul Marsden
Sittingbourne and Sheppey	Derek Wyatt
Slough	Fiona Mactaggart
South Derbyshire	Mark Todd
South Ribble	David Borrow
South Shields	David Clark
South Swindon	Julia Drown
South Thanet	Stephen Ladyman
Southampton Itchen	John Denham
Southampton Test	Alan Whitehead
St Albans	Kerry Pollard
St Helens North	David Watts
St Helens South	Gerry Bermingham
Stafford	David Kidney
Staffordshire Moorlands	Charlotte Atkins
Stalybridge and Hyde	Tom Pendry
Stevenage	Barbara Follett
Stockport	Ann Coffey
Stockton North	Frank Cook
Stockton South	Dari Taylor
Stoke-on-Trent Central	Mark Fisher
Stoke-on-Trent North	Joan Walley
Stoke-on-Trent South	George Stevenson
Stourbridge	Debra Shipley
Streatham	Keith Hill
Stretford and Urmston	Beverley Hughes

Stroud	David Drew*
Sunderland North	William Etherington
Sunderland South	Chris Mullin
Tamworth	Brian Jenkins
Telford	Bruce Grocott
Thurrock	Andrew Mackinlay
Tooting	Tom Cox
Tottenham	David Lammy
Tyne Bridge	David Clelland
Tynemouth	Alan Campbell
Upminster	Keith Darvill
Vauxhall	Kate Hoey
Wakefield	David Hinchliffe
Wallasey	Angela Eagle
Walsall North	David Winnick
Walsall South	Bruce George
Walthamstow	Neil Gerrard
Wansbeck	Denis Murphy
Wansdyke	Dan Norris
Warley	John Spellar
Warrington North	Helen Jones
Warrington South	Helen Southworth
Warwick and Leamington	James Plaskitt
Watford	Claire Ward
Waveney	Bob Blizzard
Weaver Vale	Mike Hall
Wellingborough	Paul Stinchcombe
Welwyn Hatfield	Melanie Johnson
Wentworth	John Healey
West Bromwich East	Peter Snape
West Bromwich West	by-election pending
West Ham	Tony Banks
West Lancashire	Colin Pickthall
Wigan	Neil Turner
Wimbledon	Roger Casale
Wirral South	Ben Chapman
Wirral West	Stephen Hesford
Witney	Shaun Woodward
Wolverhampton North East	Ken Purchase*
Wolverhampton South East	Dennis Turner*
Wolverhampton South West	Jenny Jones
Worcester	Michael John Foster
Workington	Dale Campbell-Savours
Worsley	Terry Lewis
The Wrekin	Peter Bradley
Wyre Forest	David Lock
Wythenshawe and Sale East	Paul Goggins

CONSERVATIVE (162 Members)

Aldershot	Gerald Howarth
Aldridge-Brownhills	Richard Shepherd
Altrincham and Sale West	Graham Brady
Arundel and South Downs	Howard Flight
Ashford	Damian Green
Aylesbury	David Lidington
Banbury	Tony Baldry
Basingstoke	Andrew Hunter
Beaconsfield	Dominic Grieve
Beckenham	Jacqui Lait
Beverley and Holderness	James Cran
Bexhill and Battle	Charles Wardle
Billericay	Teresa Gorman
Blaby	Andrew Robathan
Bognor Regis and Littlehampton	Nick Gibb
Boston and Skegness	Sir Richard Body
Bosworth	David Tredinnick
Bournemouth East	David Atkinson
Bournemouth West	John Butterfill
Bracknell	Andrew Mackay
Brentwood and Ongar	Eric Pickles
Bridgwater	Tom King
Bromley and Chislehurst	Eric Forth
Bromsgrove	Julie Kirkbride
Broxbourne	Marion Roe
Buckingham	John Bercow
Bury St Edmunds	David Ruffley
Canterbury	Julian Brazier
Central Suffolk and North Ipswich	Michael Lord
Charnwood	Stephen Dorrell
Cheadle	Stephen Day
Chelmsford West	Simon Burns
Chesham and Amersham	Cheryl Gillan
Chichester	Andrew Tyrie
Chingford and Woodford Green	Iain Duncan Smith
Chipping Barnet	Sydney Chapman
Christchurch	Christopher Chope
Cities of London and Westminster	Peter Brooke
Congleton	Ann Winterton
Cotswold	Geoffrey Clifton-Brown
Croydon South	Richard Ottaway
Daventry	Timothy Boswell
Devizes	Michael Ancram
East Devon	Peter Emery
East Hampshire	Michael Mates
East Surrey	Peter Ainsworth
East Worthing and Shoreham	Tim Loughton
Eastbourne	Nigel Waterson
Eddisbury	Stephen O'Brien

Epping Forest	Eleanor Laing	North West Hampshire	Sir George Young
Epsom and Ewell	Sir Archie Hamilton	North Wiltshire	James Gray
		Old Bexley and Sidcup	Sir Edward Heath
Esher and Walton	Ian Taylor	Orpington	John Horam
Fareham	Sir Peter Lloyd	Penrith and The Border	David Maclean
Faversham and Mid Kent	Andrew Rowe	Poole	Robert Syms
Folkestone and Hythe	Michael Howard	Rayleigh	Michael Clark
Fylde	Michael Jack	Reigate	Crispin Blunt
Gainsborough	Edward Leigh	Ribble Valley	Nigel Evans
Gosport	Peter Viggers	Richmond (Yorkshire)	William Hague
Grantham and Stamford	Quentin Davies	Rochford and Southend	
Guildford	Nicholas St Aubyn	East	Sir Teddy Taylor
		Ruislip Northwood	John Wilkinson
Haltemprice and Howden	David Davis	Runnymede and	
Harborough	Edward Garnier	Weybridge	Philip Hammond
Havant	David Willetts	Rushcliffe	Kenneth Clarke
Henley	Michael Heseltine	Rutland and Melton	Alan Duncan
Hertford and Stortford	Bowen Wells	Ryedale	John Greenway
Hertsmere	James Clappison	Saffron Walden	Sir Alan Haselhurst
Hexham	Peter Atkinson		
Hitchin and Harpenden	Peter Lilley	Salisbury	Robert Key
Horsham	Francis Maude	Sevenoaks	Michael Fallon
Huntingdon	John Major	Skipton and Ripon	David Curry
Kensington and Chelsea	Michael Portillo	Sleaford and North	
Lichfield	Michael Fabricant	Hykeham	Douglas Hogg
Louth and Horncastle	Sir Peter Tapsell	Solihull	John M Taylor
Ludlow	Christopher Gill	South Cambridgeshire	Andrew Lansley
Macclesfield	Nicholas Winterton	South Dorset	Ian Bruce
		South East	
Maidenhead	Theresa May	Cambridgeshire	James Paice
Maidstone and The Weald	Ann Widdecombe	South Holland and	
Maldon and Chelmsford		The Deepings	John Hayes
East	John Whittingdale	South Norfolk	John MacGregor
Meriden	Caroline Spelman	South Staffordshire	Sir Patrick Cormack
Mid Bedfordshire	Jonathan Sayeed		
Mid Dorset and Poole		South Suffolk	Tim Yeo
North	Christopher Fraser	South West Bedfordshire	Sir David Madel
Mid Norfolk	Keith Simpson	South West Devon	Gary Streeter
Mid Sussex	Nicholas Soames	South West Hertfordshire	Richard Page
Mid Worcestershire	Peter Luff	South West Norfolk	Gillian Shephard
Mole Valley	Sir Paul Beresford	South West Surrey	Virginia Bottomley
New Forest East	Julian Lewis		
New Forest West	Desmond Swayne	Southend West	David Amess
North Dorset	Robert Walter	Spelthorne	David Wilshire
North East Bedfordshire	Sir Nicholas Lyell	Stone	William Cash
North East		Stratford-on-Avon	John Maples
Cambridgeshire	Malcolm Moss	Suffolk Coastal	John Gummer
North East Hampshire	James Arbuthnot	Surrey Heath	Nick Hawkins
North East Hertfordshire	Oliver Heald	Sutton Coldfield	Sir Norman Fowler
North Essex	Bernard Jenkin		
North Norfolk	David Prior	Teignbridge	Patrick Nicholls
North Shropshire	Owen Paterson	Tewkesbury	Laurence Robertson
North Thanet	Roger Gale		
North West		Tiverton and Honiton	Angela Browning
Cambridgeshire	Sir Brian Mawhinney	Tonbridge and Malling	Sir John Stanley
		Totnes	Anthony Steen

Tunbridge Wells	Archie Norman
Uxbridge	John Randall
Vale of York	Anne McIntosh
Wantage	Robert Jackson
Wealden	Sir Geoffrey Johnson Smith
Wells	David Heathcoat-Amory
West Derbyshire	Patrick McLoughlin
West Dorset	Oliver Letwin
West Suffolk	Richard Spring
West Worcestershire	Sir Michael Spicer
Westbury	David Faber
Westmorland and Lonsdale	Tim Collins
Windsor	Michael Trend
Woking	Humfrey Malins
Wokingham	John Redwood
Woodspring	Liam Fox
Worthing West	Peter Bottomley
Wycombe	Sir Raymond Whitney
Yorkshire East	John Townend

LIBERAL DEMOCRAT (35 Members)

Bath	Don Foster
Berwick-upon-Tweed	Alan Beith
Carshalton and Wallington	Tom Brake
Cheltenham	Nigel Jones
Colchester	Bob Russell
Eastleigh	David Chidgey
Harrogate and Knaresborough	Phil Willis
Hazel Grove	Andrew Stunell
Hereford	Paul Keetch
Isle of Wight	Peter Brand
Kingston and Surbiton	Edward Davey
Lewes	Norman Baker
Newbury	David Rendel
North Cornwall	Paul Tyler
North Devon	Nick Harvey
North Southwark and Bermondsey	Simon Hughes
Northavon	Steve Webb
Oxford West and Abingdon	Evan Harris
Portsmouth South	Mike Hancock
Richmond Park	Jennifer Tonge
Romsey	Sandra Gidley
Sheffield Hallam	Richard Allan
Somerton and Frome	David Heath
South East Cornwall	Colin Breed
Southport	Ronnie Fearn
St Ives	Andrew George

Sutton and Cheam	Paul Burstow
Taunton	Jackie Ballard
Torbay	Adrian Sanders
Torridge and West Devon	John Burnett
Truro and St Austell	Matthew Taylor
Twickenham	Vincent Cable
Weston-Super-Mare	Brian Cotter
Winchester	Mark Oaten
Yeovil	Paddy Ashdown

INDEPENDENT (2 Members)

Brent East	Ken Livingstone
Tatton	Martin Bell

THE SPEAKER

Glasgow Springburn	Michael Martin

SCOTLAND – 72 Members
By-election pending in Glasgow Anniesland

LABOUR (53 Members)
(*Labour/Co-operative)

Aberdeen Central	Frank Doran
Aberdeen North	Malcolm Savidge
Aberdeen South	Anne Begg
Airdrie and Shotts	Helen Liddell
Ayr	Sandra Osborne
Carrick, Cumnock and Doon Valley	George Foulkes*
Central Fife	Henry McLeish
Clydebank and Milngavie	Tony Worthington
Clydesdale	Jimmy Hood
Coatbridge and Chryston	Tom Clarke
Cumbernauld and Kilsyth	Rosemary McKenna
Cunninghame North	Brian Wilson
Cunninghame South	Brian Donohoe
Dumbarton	John McFall*
Dumfries	Russell Brown
Dundee East	John McAllion
Dundee West	Ernie Ross
Dunfermline East	Gordon Brown
Dunfermline West	Rachel Squire
East Kilbride	Adam Ingram
East Lothian	John Home Robertson
Eastwood	Jim Murphy
Edinburgh Central	Alistair Darling
Edinburgh East and Musselburgh	Gavin Strang
Edinburgh North and Leith	Malcolm Chisholm
Edinburgh Pentlands	Lynda Clark

Edinburgh South — Nigel Griffiths
Falkirk East — Michael Connarty
Glasgow Anniesland — by-election pending
Glasgow Baillieston — James Wray
Glasgow Cathcart — John Maxton
Glasgow Govan — Mohammed Sarwar
Glasgow Kelvin — George Galloway
Glasgow Maryhill — Maria Fyfe
Glasgow Pollok — Ian Davidson*
Glasgow Rutherglen — Thomas McAvoy*
Glasgow Shettleston — David Marshall
Greenock and Inverclyde — Norman Godman
Hamilton North and Bellshill — John Reid
Hamilton South — Bill Tynan
Inverness East, Nairn and Lochaber — David Stewart
Kilmarnock and Loudoun — Desmond Browne
Kirkcaldy — Lewis Moonie*
Linlithgow — Tam Dalyell
Livingston — Robin Cook
Midlothian — Eric Clarke
Motherwell and Wishaw — Frank Roy
Ochil — Martin O'Neill
Paisley North — Irene Adams
Paisley South — Douglas Alexander
Stirling — Anne McGuire
Strathkelvin and Bearsden — Sam Galbraith
Western Isles — Calum MacDonald

LIBERAL DEMOCRAT (10 Members)

Argyll and Bute — Ray Michie
Caithness, Sutherland and Easter Ross — Robert Maclennan
Edinburgh West — Donald Gorrie
Gordon — Malcolm Bruce
North East Fife — Menzies Campbell
Orkney and Shetland — James Wallace
Ross, Skye and Inverness West — Charles Kennedy
Roxburgh and Berwickshire — Archy Kirkwood
Tweeddale, Ettrick and Lauderdale — Michael Moore
West Aberdeenshire and Kincardine — Robert Smith

SCOTTISH NATIONAL PARTY (6 Members)

Angus — Andrew Welsh
Banff and Buchan — Alex Salmond
Galloway and Upper Nithsdale — Alasdair Morgan
Moray — Margaret Ewing
North Tayside — John Swinney
Perth — Roseanna Cunningham

INDEPENDENT

West Renfrewshire — Tommy Graham

MP FOR FALKIRK WEST

Falkirk West — Dennis Canavan

WALES – 40 Members

LABOUR (34 Members)

Aberavon — Sir John Morris
Alyn and Deeside — Barry Jones
Blaenau Gwent — Llewellyn Smith
Bridgend — Win Griffiths
Caerphilly — Ron Davies
Cardiff Central — Jon Owen Jones*
Cardiff North — Julie Morgan
Cardiff South and Penarth — Alun Michael*
Cardiff West — Rhodri Morgan
Carmarthen East and Dinefwr — Alan Williams
Carmarthen West and South Pembrokeshire — Nick Ainger
Clwyd South — Martyn Jones
Clwyd West — Gareth Thomas
Conwy — Betty Williams
Cynon Valley — Ann Clwyd
Delyn — David Hanson
Gower — Martin Caton
Islwyn — Don Touhig*
Llanelli — Denzil Davies
Merthyr Tydfil and Rhymney — Edward Rowlands
Monmouth — Huw Edwards
Neath — Peter Hain
Newport East — Alan Howarth
Newport West — Paul Flynn
Ogmore — Sir Raymond Powell
Pontypridd — Kim Howells
Preseli Pembrokeshire — Jackie Lawrence
Rhondda — Allan Rogers

Swansea East	Donald Anderson
Swansea West	Alan Williams
Torfaen	Paul Murphy
Vale of Clwyd	Chris Ruane
Vale of Glamorgan	John Smith
Wrexham	John Marek

PLAID CYMRU (4 Members)

Caernarfon	Dafydd Wigley
Ceredigion	Simon Thomas
Meirionnydd Nant Conwy	Elfyn Llwyd
Ynys Môn	Ieuan Wyn Jones

LIBERAL DEMOCRAT (2 Members)

Brecon and Radnorshire	Richard Livsey
Montgomeryshire	Lembit Öpik

NORTHERN IRELAND – 18 Members

ULSTER UNIONIST PARTY (9 Members)

Belfast North	Cecil Walker
Belfast South	Martin Smyth
East Antrim	Roy Beggs
East Londonderry	William Ross
Fermanagh and South Tyrone	Ken Maginnis
Lagan Valley	Jeffrey Donaldson
Strangford	John D Taylor
Upper Bann	David Trimble
West Tyrone	William Thompson

SOCIAL DEMOCRATIC AND LABOUR PARTY (3 Members)

Foyle	John Hume
Newry and Armagh	Seamus Mallon
South Down	Edward McGrady

DEMOCRATIC UNIONIST PARTY (3 Members)

Belfast East	Peter Robinson
North Antrim	Ian Paisley
South Antrim	William McCrea

SINN FEIN (2 Members)

Belfast West	Gerry Adams
Mid Ulster	Martin McGuinness

UK UNIONIST PARTY (1 Members)

North Down	Robert McCartney

MEMBERS' BIOGRAPHIES

A

DIANE ABBOTT Hackney North and Stoke Newington *Lab majority 15,627*

Born 27 September 1953; Daughter of late Reginald Abbott, welder, and late Mrs Julie Abbott, psychiatric nurse; Educated Harrow County Girls' Grammar School; Newnham College, Cambridge (BA history 1976); Married 1991, David Thompson (1 son) (marriage dissolved 1993). Administration trainee, Home Office 1976–78; Race relations officer, National Council for Civil Liberties 1978–80; Journalist, Thames Television 1980–82, TV AM 1982–84, freelance 1984–85; Principal press officer, Lambeth Council 1986–87; Equality Officer, ACTT 1985–86. Westminster City Councillor 1982–86; Member Greater London Assembly advisory cabinet for women and equality 2000–. **House of Commons:** Member for Hackney North and Stoke Newington since June 1987; *Select Committees:* Member: Treasury and Civil Service 1989–97, Entry Clearance Sub-Committee 1997–98; Member: Foreign Affairs 1997–. Member, Labour Party National Executive Committee 1994–. First black female MP. *Address:* Diane Abbott, MP, House of Commons, London, SW1A 0AA *Tel:* 020 7219 5062.

GERRY ADAMS Belfast West *SF majority 7,909*

Born 6 October 1948; Son of Gerard Adams; Educated St Mary's Christian Brothers' School, Belfast; Married 1971, Colette McArdle (1 son). Bartender; Founder member of the civil rights movement. **House of Commons:** Member for Belfast West 1983–92, and since May 1, 1997; Member, Northern Ireland Assembly 1981; Vice-President, Sinn Fein 1978–83, President 1983–; Member: Northern Ireland Forum 1996, new Northern Ireland Assembly for Belfast West 1998–. Member, PEN; *Publications: Before the Dawn, An Irish Voice, A Pathway to Peace, The Politics of Irish Freedom and Selected Writings, Falls Memories, Cage Eleven, The Street and Other Stories;* Thorr Peace Prize 1996; *Sportsclubs:* Naomh Eoig; *Recreations:* Gaelic sports, Irish traditional music. *Address:* Gerry Adams Esq, MP, House of Commons, London, SW1A 0AA *Tel:* 020 7219 3000. *Constituency:* 53 Falls Road, Belfast BT12 4PD.

IRENE ADAMS Paisley North *Lab majority 12,814*

Born 27 December 1947; Educated Stanley Green High School, Paisley; Married February 24, 1968, Allen Adams (MP 1979–90, died 1990) (1 son 2 daughters). Councillor: Paisley Town Council 1970, Renfrew District Council 1974–78, Strathclyde Regional Council 1979–84; JP. **House of Commons:** Member for Paisley North since November 29, 1990 by-election; *Select Committees:* Member: Catering 1991–95; Member: Scottish Affairs 1997–, Chairmen's Panel 1998–. *Recreations:* Reading, walking. *Address:* Mrs Irene Adams, JP, MP, House of Commons, London, SW1A 0AA *Tel:* 020 7219 3564. *Constituency:* 10 Forbes Place, Paisley, PA1 1UT *Tel:* 0141–887 5949 *Fax:* 0141–887 8025 *E-mail:* contact@ireneadams-mp.new.labour.org.uk.

NICK AINGER   Carmarthen West and South Pembrokeshire   *Lab majority 9,621*

Born 24 October 1949; Son of Richard John Wilkinson and Marjorie Isabel, née Dye; Educated Netherthorpe Grammar School, Staveley, Derbyshire; Married 1976, Sally Robinson (1 daughter). Marine and Port Services Ltd., Pembroke Dock 1977–92; Branch secretary, TGWU. Councillor, Dyfed County Council 1981–93; Vice-Chair, Dyfed County Council Labour Group 1989–92. **House of Commons:** Member for Pembroke 1992–97, and for Carmarthen West and South Pembrokeshire since May 1, 1997; PPS to Secretaries of State for Wales: Ron Davies 1997–98, Alun Michael 1998–99, Paul Murphy 1999–; *Select Committees:* Member: Broadcasting 1992–94, Welsh Affairs 1993–97. Member: Amnesty International, RSPB; Member, Dyfed Wildlife Trust. *Address:* Nick Ainger Esq, MP, House of Commons, London, SW1A 0AA *Tel:* 020 7219 4004 *Fax:* 020 7219 2690. *Constituency:* Ferry Lane Works, Ferry Lane, Pembroke Dock, Dyfed, SA71 4RE *Tel:* 01646 684404 *Fax:* 01646 682954 *E-mail:* aingern@parliament.uk.

PETER AINSWORTH   East Surrey   *Con majority 15,093*

Born 16 November 1956; Son of late Lieutenant-Commander Michael Lionel Yeoward Ainsworth and Patricia Mary (née Bedford); Educated Ludgrove School; Bradfield College; Lincoln College, Oxford (MA English literature and language 1979); Married 1981, Claire Burnett (1 son 2 daughters). Research assistant to Sir John Stewart-Clark MEP 1979–81; Investment analyst, Laing & Cruickshank 1981–85; S G Warburg Securities 1985–1992: Investment analyst 1985–87, Corporate finance 1987–92, Director 1990–92. Councillor, London Borough of Wandsworth 1986–94; Chair, Conservative Group on the Council 1990–92; Deputy Chair, Policy and Finance Committee. **House of Commons:** Member for East Surrey since April 9, 1992; Assistant Government Whip 1996–97; Opposition Deputy Chief Whip 1997–98; PPS: to Jonathan Aitken as Chief Secretary to the Treasury 1994–95, to Virginia Bottomley as Secretary of State for National Heritage 1995–96; Member, Shadow Cabinet 1998–; Shadow Secretary of State for Culture, Media and Sport 1998–; *Select Committees:* Member: Consolidation Bills Joint Committee 1993–96, Environment 1993–94, Public Service 1993–96, Selection 1997–98. *Special Interests:* Economic Policy, Environment. Member, The Bow Group 1983–. Secretary, Conservative and Unionist Agents' Superannuation Fund 1993–; *Country Life* Country MP of the Year 1994; *Green* Magazine Campaigning MP of the Year 1994; *Clubs:* MCC; *Recreations:* Family, music, gardening. *Address:* Peter Ainsworth Esq, MP, House of Commons, London, SW1A 0AA *Tel:* 020 7219 5078 *Fax:* 020 7219 2527. *Constituency:* 2 Hoskins Road, Oxted, Surrey, RH8 9HT *Tel:* 01883 715782 *Fax:* 01883 730576 *E-mail:* kyprianouc@parliament.uk.

BOB AINSWORTH   Coventry North East   *Lab majority 22,569*

Born 19 June 1952; Son of late Stanley and Pearl Ainsworth; Educated Foxford Comprehensive School, Coventry; Married June 22, 1974, Gloria, daughter of Denis and Jean Sandall (2 daughters). Sheet metal worker; fitter with Jaguar Cars, Coventry 1971–91; MSF: Shop steward 1974, Senior steward and secretary of joint shop stewards 1980–91, Union Branch President 1983–87. Councillor, Coventry City Council 1984–93, Deputy Leader 1988–91, Chairman, Finance Committee 1989–92. **House of Commons:** Member for Coventry North East since April 9, 1992; Opposition Whip 1995–97; Government Whip (Lord Commissioner of HM Treasury) (Environment, Transport and the Regions: West Midlands) 1997–; *Special Interests:* Industry, Environment, Tax; France, India, Pakistan, USA. *Clubs:* Bell Green Working Men's; *Sportsclubs:* Broad Street Rugby Football Old Boys'; *Recreations:* Walking, chess, reading, cycling. *Address:* Robert Ainsworth Esq, MP, House of Commons, London, SW1A 0AA *Tel:* 020 7219 4047. *Constituency:* 2nd Floor, 107 New Union Street, Coventry CV1 2NT *Tel:* 024 7622 6707 *Fax:* 024 7622 6707 *E-mail:* robert.ainsworth@hm-treasury.gov.uk.

DOUGLAS ALEXANDER   Paisley South   *Lab majority 2,731*

Born 26 October 1967; Son of Rev. Douglas N. Alexander and Dr. Joyce O. Alexander; Educated Park Mains High School, Erskine, Renfrewshire; Lester B. Pearson College, Vancouver, Canada; Edinburgh University (MA 1990, LLB 1993, Diploma in Legal Practice 1994); University of Pennsylvania, USA. Parliamentary researcher for Gordon Brown MP 1990–91; Solicitor: Brodies W.S. 1994–96, Digby Brown 1996–97; Member, TGWU. **House of Commons:** Contested Perth and Kinross 1995 by-election and Perth 1997 general election. Member for Paisley South since by-election November 6, 1997; *Special Interests:* Constitutional Reform, Economic Policy, Employment Policy. General election campaign co-ordinator 1999–. Member, Muir Society; Rector's Assessor, Edinburgh University 1993–96; *Publications:* Co-author *New Scotland, New Britain*, 1999; Notary Public; *Recreations:* Running, angling. *Address:* Douglas Alexander Esq, MP, House of Commons, London, SW1A 0AA *Tel:* 020 7219 1345. *Constituency:* 19 Sir James Clark Building, Abbey Mill Business Centre, Paisley, PA1 1TJ *Tel:* 0141–561 0333 *Fax:* 0141–561 0334.

RICHARD ALLAN   Sheffield Hallam   *LD majority 8,271*

Born 11 February 1966; Son of John Allan, retired, and Elizabeth Allan, doctor's receptionist; Educated Oundle School, Northants; Pembroke College, Cambridge (BA archaeology and anthropology 1988); Bristol Polytechnic (MSc information technology 1990); Married May 25, 1991, Louise, daughter of Robin and Pat Netley (1 daughter). Field archaeologist in: Britain, France and Netherlands 1984–85, Ecuador 1988–89; Computer manager: Avon FHSA 1991–95, FHS 1995–97. Councillor, Avon County Council 1993–95, Deputy Group Leader of Liberal Democrats; Councillor, Bath City Council 1994–95. **House of Commons:** Member for Sheffield Hallam since May 1, 1997; Spokesman for Home and Legal Affairs: Community Relations and Urban Affairs 1997–99, Immigration 1998–99, Home Affairs 1999–, Education and Employment (employment and information technology) 1999–; *Select Committees:* Member: Home Affairs 1997–98; Member: Finance and Services 1998–; Chairman: Information 1998–; Member: Liaison 1998–. *Special Interests:* Information Technology, Heritage, Home Affairs, Education; Latin America especially Ecuador, USA. Member, World Development Movement; Board Member, Parliamentary Office of Science and Technology (POST) 1997–; Board Member, Sheffield City Trust 1999–; *Recreations:* Visiting sites of natural beauty and historical interest, flying kites, walking. *Address:* Richard Allan Esq, MP, House of Commons, London, SW1A 0AA *Tel:* 020 7219 1104 *Fax:* 020 7219 0971. *Constituency:* Belmayne House, 99 Clarkehouse Road, Sheffield, S10 2LN *Tel:* 0114–249 4774 *Fax:* 0114–249 4775 *E-mail:* allanr@parliament.uk.

GRAHAM ALLEN   Nottingham North   *Lab majority 18,801*

Born 11 January 1953; Son of Bill and Edna Allen; Educated Forest Fields Grammar School, Nottingham; City of London Polytechnic (BA politics and economics); Leeds University (MA political sociology); Married Allyson (1 daughter). Warehouseman 1974; Labour Party research officer 1979–83; Local government officer 1983–84; National co-ordinator, Political Fund ballots 1984–86; GMBATU research and education officer 1986–87. **House of Commons:** Member for Nottingham North since June 1987; Government Whip 1997–: (Lord Commissioner of HM Treasury) 1997–98; (Vice-Chamberlain of HM Household) (HM Treasury; East Midlands) 1998–; Shadow Minister for: Social Security 1991–92, Constitutional Affairs 1992–94, Media and Broadcasting 1994–95, Transport 1995–96, Environment 1996–97; *Select Committees:* Member: Public Accounts 1988–91. *Special Interests:* Economic Policy, Democratic Renewal; USA. *Publications: Reinventing Democracy*, 1995; *Clubs:* Basford Hall Miners Welfare; *Sportsclubs:* Secretary, Lords and Commons Cricket XI; Member, Dunkirk Cricket; *Recreations:* Cricket, walking, cooking, oil painting. *Address:* Graham Allen Esq, MP, House of Commons, London, SW1A 0AA *Tel:* 020 7219 3000 *Tel (Constituency):* 0115–979 2344.

DAVID AMESS   Southend West   *Con majority 2,615*

Born 26 March 1952; Son of late James Amess and of Maud Amess; Educated St Bonaventure's Grammar School; Bournemouth College of Technology (BSc economics 1974); Married September 10, 1983, Julia, daughter of Graham and Faith Arnold (1 son 4 daughters). Junior school teacher 1970–71; Underwriter, Leslie Godwin Agency 1974–76; Accountancy personnel 1976–79; Senior consultant, Executemps Company Agency 1979–81; Chair: Accountancy Solutions 1987–90, Accountancy Group 1990–96. Redbridge Council: Councillor 1982–86, Vice-Chair, Housing Committee 1982–85. **House of Commons:** Contested Newham North West 1979 general election. Member for Basildon 1983–97, and for Southend West since May 1, 1997; PPS to Parliamentary under secretaries, DHSS: Edwina Currie 1987–88, Lord Skelmersdale 1988, to Michael Portillo: as Minister of State Department of Transport 1988–90, at Department of Environment 1990–92, as Chief Secretary to the Treasury 1992–94, as Secretary of State for Employment 1994–95, for Defence 1995–97; Sponsored: Horses and Ponies Bill 1984–85, Members of Parliament (Minimum Age) Bill 1984–85, Horses, Ponies and Donkeys Bill 1987–88, Abortion (Right of Conscience) (Amendment) Bill 1988–89, British Nationality (Hon. Citizenship) Bill 1988–89, Adoption (Amendment) Bill 1989–90, Dogs Bill 1989–90, Pet Animals (Amendment) Bill 1990–91, Protection Against Cruel Tethering Act 1988, Human Fertilisation (Choice) Bill 1992–93, Voluntary Personal Security Cards Bill 1992–93, Football Matches (Violent and Disorderly Conduct) Bill 1992–93, Newly Qualified Drivers Bill 1993–94, Coercion in Family Planning (Prohibition) Bill 1994–95, Freezing of Human Embryos Bill 1995–96, Abortion (Amendment) Bill 1996–97, Reform of Quarantine Regulations Bill 1997–98, Voluntary Personal Security Cards Bill 1997–98; *Select Committees:* Member: Broadcasting 1994–97; Member: Health 1998–. *Special Interests:* Health, Education, Transport, Environment, Pro-Life Movement; USA, European Union, Middle East, Far East, Pacific Basin. Hon. Secretary, Conservative Friends of Israel 1998–. Founder Member, Wallenberg Appeal Foundation; President, 1912 Club 1996–; *Publications: The Basildon Experience*, 1995; Freeman, City of London; *Clubs:* Carlton, St Stephen's Constitutional; *Sportsclubs:* Kingswood Squash and Racketball; *Recreations:* Socialising, reading, writing, sports, modern music, keeping animals, gardening. *Address:* David Amess Esq, MP, House of Commons, London, SW1A 0AA *Tel:* 020 7219 6387 *Fax:* 020 7219 2245. *Constituency:* Iveagh Hall, 67 Leigh Road, Leigh-on-Sea, Essex *Tel:* 01702 472391 *Fax:* 01702 480677 *E-mail:* amessd@parliament.uk.

MICHAEL ANCRAM   Devizes   *Con majority 9,782*

Born 7 July 1945; Son of 12th Marquess of Lothian, KCVO, DL; Educated Ampleforth; Christ Church, Oxford (BA history 1966, MA); Edinburgh University (LLB 1968); Married June 7, 1975, Lady Jane Fitzalan-Howard, daughter of 16th Duke of Norfolk, KG, PC, GCVO, GBE, TD, and of late Lavinia, Duchess of Norfolk, LG, CBE (2 daughters). Advocate, Scottish Bar 1970, QC(Scot) 1996. DL, Roxburgh, Ettrick and Lauderdale 1990–. **House of Commons:** Contested West Lothian 1970 general election. Member for Berwickshire and East Lothian February–October 1974, and Edinburgh South 1979–87 and for Devizes since April 9, 1992; Frontbench Spokesman on Constitutional Affairs, with overall responsibility for Scottish and Welsh issues 1997–98; Parliamentary Under-Secretary of State, Scottish Office 1983–87; Northern Ireland Office: Parliamentary Under-Secretary of State 1993–94, Minister of State 1994–97; Member, Shadow Cabinet 1997–; *Select Committees:* Member: Public Accounts 1992–93. *Special Interests:* Housing, Defence, Agriculture. Chair, Conservative Party in Scotland 1980–83; Deputy Chair, Conservative Party June–October 1998, Chair October 1998–. Member, Board of Scottish Homes 1988–90; Heir to the marquessate; PC 1996; *Recreations:* Skiing, photography, folksinging. *Address:* Rt Hon Michael Ancram, QC, DL, MP (Earl of Ancram), House of Commons, London, SW1A 0AA *Tel:* 020 7219 4435. *Constituency:* 116 High Street, Marlborough, Wiltshire, SN8 1LZ *Tel:* 01672 512675 *E-mail:* ancramm@parliament.uk.

DONALD ANDERSON   Swansea East   *Lab majority 25,569*

Born 17 June 1939; Son of late David Robert Anderson, fitter and Eva Anderson (née Mathias); Educated Swansea Grammar School; University College, Swansea (BA modern history and politics 1960); Inner Temple (barrister 1969); Married September 28, 1963, Dr Dorothy Mary, eldest daughter of Rev. Frank Trotman (3 sons). HM Diplomatic Service 1960–64; Lecturer in US and comparative government, University College of Wales, Swansea 1964–66; Called to the Bar, Inner Temple 1969; Barrister, South Eastern Circuit 1970–97; RMT Sponsored. Councillor, Royal Borough of Kensington and Chelsea 1970–75. **House of Commons:** Member for Monmouth 1966–70, and for Swansea East since October 1974; Opposition Front Bench Spokesman on: Foreign and Commonwealth Affairs 1983–92, Defence, Disarmament and Arms Control 1993–94; PPS: to Minister of Defence (Administration) 1969–70, to Attorney General 1974–79, Shadow Solicitor General 1994–95; *Select Committees:* Member: Home Affairs 1994–95, Chairmen's Panel 1995–99, Entry Clearance Sub-Committee 1997–98; Chairman: Foreign Affairs 1997–; Member: Liaison 1997–. *Special Interests:* Foreign Affairs, Housing Law, Transport, Wales, Environment. Vice-Chair, Welsh Labour Group 1969–70, Chair 1977–78. President, Gower Society 1976–78; Chair, Parliamentary Campaign for the Homeless and Rootless (CHAR) 1984–90; Vice-President, Institute of Environmental Health Officers 1984–95; Senior Vice-President, Association of European Parliamentarians for Africa 1984–97; President, Swansea Male Choir; Vice-President, Morriston Orpheus Choir; Member, HAFOD Brotherhood; Director, Campaign for a Political Europe 1966–67; Member, Executive Committee, Commonwealth Parliamentary Association (CPA) UK Branch 1983–, Vice-Chair 1987–88, Treasurer 1990–93, Special Representative 1989–90, Chair 1997–2000; Vice-Chair, IPU 1985–88, Treasurer 1988–90 and 1993–95; Member, UK Delegation to North Atlantic Assembly 1992–, Leader 1997–; Member, Organisation for Security and Co-operation in Europe 1997–, Leader UK delegation 1997–98; Executive Committee Member, IPU British Group; Commander's Cross, Order of Merit, Federal Republic of Germany 1986; Hon. Fellow, University College of Wales, Swansea 1985–; Visiting Parliamentary Fellow, St Antony's College, Oxford 1999–; Freeman, City of Swansea 2000;*Sportsclubs:* Bonymaen RFC; *Recreations:* Walking, Church work. *Address:* Donald Anderson Esq, MP, House of Commons, London, SW1A 0AA *Tel:* 020 7219 3425 *E-mail:* trotmang@parliament.uk.

JANET ANDERSON   Rossendale and Darwen   *Lab majority 10,949*

Born 6 December 1949; Daughter of late Tom Anderson, Labour Party agent, and late Ethel Pearson; Educated Kingsfield Comprehensive School, Bristol; Polytechnic of Central London (Diploma in bi-lingual business studies); University of Nantes; Married 1972, Vincent William Humphreys (2 sons 1 daughter) (divorced). Secretary, *The Scotsman* and *The Sunday Times* 1971–74. **House of Commons:** Contested Rossendale and Darwen 1987 general election. Member for Rossendale and Darwen since April 9, 1992; Opposition Spokeswoman on Women 1996–97; Opposition Whip 1995–96; Government Whip 1997–98; Personal assistant: to Barbara Castle as MP and MEP 1974–81, to Jack Straw MP 1981–87; PPS to Margaret Beckett as Deputy Leader of the Labour Party 1992–93; Parliamentary Labour Party Representative, House of Commons Commission 1993–94; Parliamentary Under-Secretary of State, Department for Culture, Media and Sport (Minister for Tourism, Film and Broadcasting) 1998–; *Select Committees:* Member: Home Affairs 1994–95, Accommodation and Works 1997–98. *Special Interests:* Footwear, Textile Industries, Quotas for Women, Health, Constitution/Constitutional Issues, Employment Rights and Protection, Home Affairs, Culture, Media and Sport; France, Cyprus, Italy. Parliamentary Labour Party Campaign Organiser 1988–90; Vice-Chair, Labour Campaign for Electoral Reform; Steering Committee Member, Labour Women's Network; Secretary, Tribune Group 1993–96. Northern regional organiser, Shopping Hours Reform Council 1991–92; Hon. adviser, Emily's List UK; Member, Parliamentary Panel, Royal College of Nursing 1992–97; President, East Lancashire Environment Business Association; Vice-President, Association of District Councils; Fellow, Royal Society for the Arts; *Clubs:* Rosemount Working Men's, Stacksteads; *Recreations:* Playing the piano, listening to opera. *Address:* Janet Anderson, MP, House of Commons, London, SW1A 0AA *Tel:* 020 7219 6629 *Fax:* 020 7219 2148. *Constituency:* 23 Bolton Road, Darwen, Lancashire, BB3 1DF *Fax:* 01254 762077 *E-mail:* andersonj@parliament.uk; janet.anderson@culture.gov.uk *Website:* www.culture.gov.uk.

JAMES ARBUTHNOT   North East Hampshire   *Con majority 14,398*

Born 4 August 1952; Son of late Sir John Sinclair-Wemyss Arbuthnot, 1st Bt, MBE, TD, MP for Dover 1950–64 and Lady Arbuthnot; Educated Wellesley House, Broadstairs; Eton; Trinity College, Cambridge (BA law 1974); Married September 6, 1984, Emma Broadbent (1 son 3 daughters). Called to the Bar, Inner Temple 1975 and Lincoln's Inn 1977. Councillor, Royal Borough of Kensington and Chelsea 1978–87. **House of Commons:** Contested Cynon Valley 1983 general election and 1984 by-election. Member for Wanstead and Woodford 1987–97 and for North East Hampshire since May 1, 1997; Assistant Government Whip 1992–94; Opposition Chief Whip 1997–; PPS: to Archie Hamilton as Minister of State for the Armed Forces 1988–90, to Peter Lilley as Secretary of State for Trade and Industry 1990–92; Parliamentary Under-Secretary of State, Department of Social Security 1994–95; Minister of State for Procurement, Ministry of Defence 1995–97; Member, Shadow Cabinet 1997–; *Special Interests:* Tax, Defence, Foreign Affairs, Law. Branch Chair, Putney Conservative Association 1975–77; Joint Deputy Chair, Chelsea Conservative Association 1980–82; President, Cynon Valley Conservative Association 1983–92. Heir presumptive to baronetcy; PC 1998; *Clubs:* Buck's; *Recreations:* Playing guitar, skiing. *Address:* Rt Hon James Arbuthnot, MP, House of Commons, London, SW1A 0AA *Tel:* 020 7219 4649. *Constituency:* North East Hampshire Conservative Association, 14a Butts Road, Alton, Hampshire, GU34 1ND *Tel:* 01420 84122 *Fax:* 01420 84925.

HILARY ARMSTRONG   North West Durham   *Lab majority 24,754*

Born 30 November 1945; Daughter of late Ernest Armstrong, MP for Durham North West 1966–87, and of Hannah Armstrong; Educated Monkwearmouth Comprehensive School, Sunderland; West Ham College of Technology; Birmingham University (BSc sociology; Diploma in social work); Married October 17, 1992, Dr Paul Corrigan. VSO teaching in Kenya 1967–69; Social worker, Newcastle Social Services 1970–73; Community worker, Southwick Neighbourhood Action Project 1973–75; Lecturer in community and youth work, Sunderland Polytechnic 1975–86; Secretary/Researcher for Ernest Armstrong MP (father) 1986–87; Chair, ASTMS Northern Division Council 1981–88. Councillor, Durham County Council 1985–88. **House of Commons:** Member for North West Durham since June 1987; Opposition Spokesperson on: Education 1988–92, Treasury and Economic Affairs 1994–95, The Environment and London 1995–97; PPS to John Smith, as Leader of the Opposition 1992–94; Minister of State, Department of the Environment, Transport and the Regions 1999–, (Minister for Local Government and Housing 1997–99, for Local Government and Regions 1999–); *Select Committees:* Member: Education 1998. *Special Interests:* Regional Development, World Development, Education, Environment; Central Africa, Kenya, South Africa, Tanzania, Uganda. Member, Labour Party National Executive Committee 1992–94, 1996–. NCH Action for Children: Member NCH Board 1985–91, Vice-president 1991–97; Member, UNICEF National Committee 1995–97; Vice-Chair, The British Council 1994–97; PC 1999; *Recreations:* Theatre, reading. *Address:* Rt Hon Hilary Armstrong, MP, House of Commons, London, SW1A 0AA *Tel:* 020 7219 5076. *Constituency:* North House, 17 North Terrace, Crook, Co Durham, DL15 9AZ *Tel:* 01388 767065 *Fax:* 01388 767923 *E-mail:* hilary-armstrong@detr.gsi.gov.uk.

SIR PADDY ASHDOWN   Yeovil   *LD majority 11,403*

Born 27 February 1941; Son of late Lieutenant Colonel John W. R. D. Ashdown; Educated Bedford School; Married February 10, 1961, Mary Jane Donne Courtenay (1 son 1 daughter). Royal Marines Officer (Captain) 1959–72 with Commando Units in Far East, Middle East and Belfast; Commanded Unit of Special Boat Service in Far East; Studied Chinese (Mandarin) at Hong Kong Language School 1967–70; 1st Class Interpreter, Chinese; First Secretary, UK Mission (Foreign Office) to UN in Geneva 1971–76; Westland Helicopters, Yeovil 1976–78; Morlands, Yeovil 1978–81; Youth Officer, Dorset County Council 1981–83. **House of Commons:** Contested Yeovil 1979 general election; Member for Yeovil since June 1983; Liberal Spokesman on Trade and

Industry 1985–87; Alliance Spokesman on Education and Science 1987; Liberal Spokesman on Education and Science 1987–88; Spokesman on Northern Ireland 1988–92; Leader: Social and Liberal Democrats 1988–89, Liberal Democrats 1988–99; *Select Committees:* Member: Science and Technology 2000–. *Special Interests:* Youth Affairs, Foreign Affairs, Defence, Industry, New Technology; Bosnia, China, Hong Kong, Balkans. *Publications: Citizens' Britain: A Radical Agenda for the 1990s*, 1989; *Beyond Westminster: Finding Hope in Britain,* 1992; PC 1989; KBE 2000; *Clubs:* National Liberal; *Recreations:* Gardening, classical music, hill walking, wine making. *Address:* Rt Hon Sir Paddy Ashdown, KBE, MP, House of Commons, London, SW1A 0AA *Tel:* 020 7219 1430 *Fax:* 020 7219 3367. *Constituency:* Yeovil Liberal Club, 94 Middle Street, Yeovil, Somerset, BA20 1LT *Tel:* 01935 423284 *Fax:* 01935 433652 *E-mail:* paddyashdown@cix.compulink.co.uk.

JOE ASHTON   Bassetlaw   *Lab majority 17,460*

Born 9 October 1933; Son of late Arthur Ashton, steelsmelter; Educated High Storrs Grammar School; Rotherham Technical College; Married December 24, 1957, Margaret, daughter of George Lee (1 daughter). RAF national service 1954–56 inc Suez Campaign; Engineering apprentice 1949–54; Journalist, author; Columnist for: *Labour Weekly* 1973–80, *Sheffield Star* 1970–75, 1979–80, *Daily Star* 1979–87, *Sunday People* 1987–88, *Plus Magazine* 1988–89; Director, Sheffield Wednesday FC 1990–99, Vice-President 1999–2000; AEU shop steward 1950s; Member, MSF. City Councillor and Chief Whip in Sheffield 1962–68. **House of Commons:** Member for Bassetlaw since October 1968 by-election; Opposition Front Bench Spokesman on Energy 1979–81; Government Whip 1977–78; PPS to Anthony Wedgwood Benn as Secretary of State for Industry, for Energy 1974–76; Introduced Doctor Assisted Dying Bill (10 Minute Rule Bill) December 1987; *Select Committees:* Member: Home Affairs 1987–92, National Heritage 1992–97, Modernisation of the House of Commons 1997–98. *Special Interests:* Media, Trade Unions, National Lottery, Tourism, Labour Party, Elections; USA. Chair, East Midlands Group of Labour MPs 1972–75. *Publications: Grassroots* (novel, later a radio play), 1977; *A Majority of One* (stage play); *Red Rose Blues* (memoirs), 2000; Columnist of the Year, Granada's *What the Papers Say* 1984; *Sportsclubs:* Director, Sheffield Wednesday Football Club 1990–99; *Recreations:* Football, films, travel, do-it-yourself. *Address:* Joseph Ashton Esq, MP, House of Commons, London, SW1A 0AA *Tel:* 020 7219 4453 *Fax:* 020 7219 0708. *Constituency:* 57 Church Walk, Worksop, Nottinghamshire *Tel:* 0114–230 7175.

CANDY ATHERTON   Falmouth and Camborne   *Lab majority 2,688*

Born 21 September 1955; Daughter of late Denis Gordon Atherton, journalist, and Pamela Osborne, hairdresser/salon owner/ Former Mayoress of Falmouth; Educated Convent of Sacred Hearts, Surrey; Midhurst Grammar School, Sussex; Polytechnic of North London (BA applied social studies 1985). Researcher for Jo Richardson MP and Judith Hart MP 1981; Probation officer 1975; Launched women's magazine *Everywoman* 1985; Press officer, Labour Party; Journalist for broadsheet newspapers; Member: UNISON, NUJ. Councillor, London Borough of Islington 1986–92, Mayor 1989–90; Member, Islington Health Authority 1986–90. **House of Commons:** Contested Chesham and Amersham 1992 general election. Member for Falmouth and Camborne since May 1, 1997; *Select Committees:* Member: Education and Employment 1997–, Employment Sub-Committee 1997–. *Special Interests:* Environment, Disabled/Disability, Health; South Africa. Vice-Chair: South and West Group of Labour MPs 1997–99, South West Regional Group of Labour MPs 1999–. *Publications: Housing in Camden, Hackney and Islington,* 1975; Freeman, City of London 1989; *Clubs:* Falmouth Labour; *Sportsclubs:* Falmouth Golf Club; *Recreations:* Gliding, gig racing, ornithology. *Address:* Candy Atherton, MP, House of Commons, London, SW1A 0AA *Tel:* 020 7219 4094 *Fax:* 020 7219 0982. *Constituency:* 4 Webber Hill, Falmouth, Cornwall, TR11 2BU *Tel:* 01326 314440 *Fax:* 01326 314415 *E-mail:* atherton@parliament.uk.

CHARLOTTE ATKINS   Staffordshire Moorlands   *Lab majority 10,049*

Born 24 September 1950; Daughter of Ronald and Jessie Atkins; Educated Colchester County High School, Essex; London School of Economics (BSc economics); London University (MA area studies); Married 1990, Gus Brain (1 daughter). Assistant community relations officer, Luton CRC 1974–76; Research officer/head of research, UCATT 1976–80; Research/political officer, AUEW (TASS) 1980–84; Press officer/parliamentary officer, COHSE/UNISON 1984–97; Member: UNISON, NUJ. Councillor, London Borough of Wandsworth 1982–86, Chief Whip and Deputy Leader of Labour Group. **House of Commons:** Contested Eastbourne 1990 by-election. Member for Staffordshire Moorlands since May 1, 1997; *Select Committees:* Member: Education and Employment 1997–, Education Sub-Committee 1997–, Selection 1997–. *Special Interests:* Civil Liberties, Education, Employment, Health, Agriculture. Member: National Policy Forum to 1998, National Women's Committee to 1998. Member, Liberty; *Publications:* Various articles in *Chartist* on parliamentary and equality issues; co-author *How to Select or Reselect Your MP; Recreations:* Family activities, theatre, keeping fit, cycling, conservation. *Address:* Charlotte Atkins, MP, House of Commons, London, SW1A 0AA *Tel:* 020 7219 3591 *Tel (Constituency):* 01782 866666 *Fax (Constituency):* 01782 866666.

DAVID ATKINSON   Bournemouth East   *Con majority 4,346*

Born 24 March 1940; Son of late Arthur Joseph Atkinson and of Joan Margaret Atkinson; Educated St George's College, Weybridge; Southend College of Technology; College of Automobile and Aeronautical Engineering, Chelsea (Diplomas in automobile engineering and motor trade management 1972); Married February 10, 1968, Susan Nicola Pilsworth (1 son 1 daughter). Director: Chalkwell Motor Co Ltd 1963–72, David Graham Studios Ltd (printing, marketing, artwork, design) 1973–77. Councillor: Southend County Borough Council 1969–72, Essex County Council 1973–78. **House of Commons:** Contested Newham North West February 1974 and Basildon October 1974 general elections. Member for Bournemouth East since November 1977 by-election; PPS to Paul Channon: as Minister of State for the Civil Service 1979–81, as Minister for the Arts 1981–83, as Minister of State for Trade 1983–86, as Secretary of State for Trade and Industry 1986–87; Author Licensing (Occasional Permissions) Act 1983; *Select Committees:* Member: Science and Technology 1997–98. *Special Interests:* Human Rights, Small Businesses, Mental Health, Foreign Affairs, Arts, Heritage, Space Technology; Russia, former USSR. Chair, National Young Conservatives 1970–71. National Chair/President, Christian Solidarity International (UK) 1979–97; UK Representative on the Council of Europe and Western Europe Union 1979–86 and 1987–, Leader, Conservative delegation 1997–, Chair, European Democratic Group 1998–; Chair, Council of Europe Committee for Non-Member Countries 1991–95; Chair, Western European Union Committee on Technology and Aerospace 2000–; *Recreations:* Art and architecture, mountaineering. *Address:* David Atkinson Esq, MP, House of Commons, London, SW1A 0AA *Tel:* 020 7219 3598 *Fax:* 020 7219 3847. *Constituency:* Bournemouth East Conservative Association, Haviland Road, Boscombe, Bournemouth, BH1 4JW *Tel:* 01202 397047 *E-mail:* atkinsond@parliament.uk.

PETER ATKINSON   Hexham   *Con majority 222*

Born 19 January 1943; Son of Major Douglas Atkinson and of Amy Atkinson; Educated Cheltenham College; Married April 7, 1976, Brione Darley (2 daughters). Journalist: various weekly newspapers, freelance news agency 1961–68; *The Journal*, Newcastle upon Tyne 1968–72; reporter, later news editor *The Evening Standard* 1972–82; Director of public affairs, British Field Sports Society 1983–92. Councillor, London Borough of Wandsworth 1978–82; Member, Wandsworth Health Authority 1982–89; Councillor, Suffolk County Council 1989–92. **House of Commons:** Member for Hexham since April 9, 1992; Opposition Whip: Agriculture; Scotland 1999–2000; Environment, Transport and the Regions; Scotland 2000–; PPS: to Jeremy Hanley as Minister of State for the Armed Forces 1994, as Minister without Portfolio and Chair Conservative Party 1994–95,

to Jeremy Hanley and Sir Nicholas Bonsor as Ministers of State, Foreign and Commonwealth Office 1995–96, to Lord Parkinson, as Chair Conservative Party 1997–99; *Select Committees:* Member: European Legislation 1992–97, Scottish Affairs 1992–97, Deregulation 1995–97, Chairmen's Panel 1997–99; Member: Court of Referees 1997–, Scottish Affairs 1997–. *Special Interests:* Agriculture, Industry; Overseas Territories, Eastern Europe, USA. *Clubs:* Albert Edward (Hexham), Northern Counties (Newcastle upon Tyne), Turf; *Sportsclubs:* Tynedale Rugby; *Recreations:* Shooting, gardening, racing. *Address:* Peter Atkinson Esq, MP, House of Commons, London, SW1A 0AA *Tel:* 020 7219 3000 *Fax:* 020 7219 2775. *Constituency:* Hexham Conservative Association, Beaumont Street, Hexham, Northumberland NE46 3AS *Tel:* 01434 603777 *E-mail:* hexham@conservative.freeserve.co.uk.

JOHN AUSTIN   Erith and Thamesmead
Lab majority 17,424

Born 21 August 1944; Son of late Stanley Austin, electrician, and late Ellen Austin; Educated Glyn Grammar School, Epsom; Goldsmiths' College, London (Certificate in Community and Youth Work 1972); Bristol University (MA policy studies 1990); Married October 6, 1965, Linda Walker (divorced 1988) (2 sons 1 daughter). Medical laboratory technician 1961–63; Labour Party organiser/agent 1963–70; Social/community worker, London Borough of Bexley 1972–74; Director, Bexley Council for Racial Equality 1974–92; Member, MSF; Chair, MSF Parliamentary Group 1998–2000. Councillor, London Borough of Greenwich 1970–94: Chair, Social Services Committee 1974–78, Deputy Leader 1981–82, Leader 1982–87, Mayor 1987–88, 1988–89. **House of Commons:** Contested Woolwich 1987, as John Austin-Walker. Member for Woolwich 1992–97, and for Erith and Thamesmead since May 1, 1997 (contested as John Austin-Walker); *Select Committees:* Member: Health 1994–97; Member: Health 1997–, Unopposed Bills (Panel) 1998–. *Special Interests:* Health, Social Services, Mental Health, Equal Opportunity, Environment, Foreign Affairs; Eastern Europe, Ireland, Kurdistan, Middle East. Member, Labour Friends of Bosnia 1994–; Chair, Socialist Campaign Group of MPs 1994–97; Joint Vice-Chair, London Regional Group of Labour MPs 1996–98, 1999 Treasurer, Labour First Past the Post Group 1997–. Chairman, Greenwich MIND 1978–82; Chairman, Greenwich Community Health Council 1976–80; National Chairman, Association of Community Health Councils for England and Wales 1980–82; Vice-Chairman: Association of London Authorities (ALA) 1983–87, London Strategic Policy Unit 1985–87; Chairman: London Boroughs Emergency Planning Information Committee 1985–87, London Ecology Unit 1985–87; Member, Political Committee CWS (Retail South East) 1987–93; Environment spokesperson for ALA 1992–94; Member, Executive Committee Inter-Parliamentary Union British Group 1996–; Vice-Chair, International Executive Parliamentary Association for Euro-Arab Co-operation 1997–; Co-Chair, Council for the Advancement of Arab British Understanding 1998–; Member, Executive Committee, Commonwealth Parliamentary Association UK Branch 1999–; Trustee (unpaid): The Adolescent and Children's Trust, Greenwich MIND; Unpaid Director: London Marathon Charitable Trust, Grossness Engines Trust; *Clubs:* St Patrick's Social (Plumstead), Northumberland Heath Working Men's (Erith), Woolwich Catholic; *Recreations:* Gardening, cookery, running (including marathons). *Address:* John Austin Esq, MP, House of Commons, London, SW1A 0AA *Tel:* 020 7219 5195 *Fax:* 020 7219 2706. *Constituency:* 315 Bexley Road, Erith, Kent, DA8 3EX *E-mail:* austinj@parliament.uk *Website:* www.john-austin-mp.org.uk.

B

NORMAN BAKER   Lewes   LD majority 1,300

Born 26 July 1957; Educated Royal Liberty School, Gidea Park; Royal Holloway College, London University (BA German 1978). Regional director, Our Price Records 1978–83; English as a foreign language teacher/lecturer 1985–97; Lib Dem environment campaigner, House of Commons 1989–90. Councillor: Lewes District Council 1987–99, Leader 1991–97, East Sussex County Council 1989–97. **House of Commons:** Contested Lewes 1992 general election. Member for Lewes since May 1, 1997; Spokesman for Environment and Transport: Genetic modification and environment 1997–99, environment 1997–99, Animal welfare 1997–, the Millennium Dome 1998–, Transport 1998–99, Consumer Affairs and Broadcasting 1999–; *Select Committees:* Member: Environmental Audit 1997–2000, European Legislation 1997–98; Member: Broadcasting 2000–; *Special Interests:* Civil Liberties, Environment, Oppressed Minority Races; Tibet, Sweden; Member, European Standing Committee C 2000–. Member: Greenpeace, Amnesty International, Free Tibet, Liberty; *Publications:* Various environmental texts; *Recreations:* Walking, music. *Address:* Norman Baker MP, House of Commons, London, SW1A 0AA *Tel:* 020 7219 5138 *Fax:* 020 7219 0445. *Constituency:* 204 High Street, Lewes, East Sussex, BN7 2NS *Tel:* 01273 480281 *Fax:* 01273 480287 *E-mail:* bakern@parliament.uk.

TONY BALDRY   Banbury   Con majority 4,737

Born 10 July 1950; Son of Peter Baldry, consultant physician, and Oina, née Paterson; Educated Leighton Park School, Reading; Sussex University (BA, social science 1972, LLB 1973); Lincoln's Inn (barrister 1975); Married May 19, 1979, Catherine Weir (1 son 1 daughter) (marriage dissolved 1996). TA Officer 1971–83; Honorary Colonel RLC (TA); barrister specialising in construction and international arbitration; construction industry. **House of Commons:** Contested Thurrock 1979 general election. Member for Banbury since June 1983; PA to Margaret Thatcher 1974 general election, served in her private office March-October 1975; PPS: to Lynda Chalker as Minister of State, FCO 1985–87, to John Wakeham, as Lord Privy Seal 1987–88, as Leader of the House 1987–89, as Lord President of The Council 1988–89, as Secretary of State for Energy 1989–90; Parliamentary Under-Secretary of State: Department of Energy 1990, Department of Environment 1990–94, Foreign and Commonwealth Office 1994–95; Minister of State, Ministry of Agriculture, Fisheries and Food 1995–97; *Select Committees:* Member: Trade and Industry 1997–. *Special Interests:* Employment Policy, Youth Affairs, Legal Affairs, Overseas Aid, European Union, Childcare; Asia, Africa, Caribbean, North America. Chair, Conservative Parliamentary Mainstream Group 1997. Vice-President, National Children's Homes 1981–83; Deputy Chair, Conservative Group for Europe 1981–83; Executive Committee Member, IPU British Group 1997–; Liveryman: Merchant Taylors Company, Stationers and Newspaper Makers Company, Arbitrators Company; Robert Schumann Silver Medal 1978; *Clubs:* Carlton, Farmers'; *Recreations:* Walking, gardening, beagling. *Address:* Tony Baldry Esq, MP, House of Commons, London, SW1A 0AA *Tel:* 020 7219 4491 *Fax:* 020 7219 5826. *Constituency:* 16a North Bar, Banbury, Oxfordshire, OX16 0TS *Tel:* 01295 262341 *Fax:* 01295 263140 *E-mail:* baldryt@parliament.uk.

JACKIE BALLARD   Taunton   LD majority 2,443

Born 4 January 1953; Daughter of late Alexander Mackenzie and Daisy Mackenzie; Educated Monmouth School for Girls; London School of Economics (BSc social psychology); Yeovil College (FE Teachers' Certificate); Married October 11, 1975, Derek Ballard (marriage dissolved 1989) (1 daughter). Social worker, London Borough of Waltham Forest 1974–76; FE Lecturer in psychology, communication, information technology 1981–93; Council support officer, Association of Liberal Democratic Councillors 1993–97. South Somerset District Council: Councillor 1987–91, Deputy Leader 1988–90, Leader 1990–91; Somerset Council Council: Councillor 1993–97, Deputy Leader 1993–95. **House of Commons:**

Contested Taunton 1992. Member for Taunton since May 1, 1997; Spokeswoman for: Local Government and Housing (Local Council Liaison) 1997–99, Women and Childcare 1997–99, Education and Employment (Employment and Childcare) 1999–2000, Home Affairs 2000–; *Select Committees:* Member: Catering 1997–99; Member: European Standing Committee A 1998–2000, European Standing Committee B 2000–. *Special Interests:* Environment, Youth Affairs, Civil Liberties, Local Government. Member: Liberal Democrat Federal Policy Committee 1990–95, Liberal Democrat Federal Executive 1997–. Member: Friends of the Earth, National Trust, League Against Cruel Sports; *Sportsclubs:* Taunton School Sports Club; *Recreations:* Swimming, working out in the gym, gardening, music. *Address:* Jackie Ballard, MP, House of Commons, London, SW1A 0AA *Tel:* 020 7219 6247 *Fax:* 020 7219 3962. *Constituency:* 10 Belvedere Road, Taunton, Devon, TA1 1BW *Tel:* 01823 337874 *Fax:* 01823 323075 *E-mail:* jackieballard@cix.compulink.co.uk.

TONY BANKS   West Ham   *Lab majority 19,494*

Born 8 April 1943; Son of Albert Banks; Educated State schools; York University (BA); LSE; Married Sally Jones. Head of research, AUEW 1969–75; Assistant general secretary, Association of Broadcasting Staff 1976–83. Councillor, GLC 1970–77, 1981–86, Chairman 1985–86. **House of Commons:** Contested East Grinstead 1970, Newcastle North October 1974 and Watford 1979 general elections. Member for Newham North West 1983–97, and for West Ham since May 1, 1997; Opposition Spokesman on Social Security 1990–91; Opposition Front Bench Spokesman on: Transport 1992–93, Environment 1992–93; Political adviser to Judith Hart as Minister for Overseas Development 1975; Parliamentary Under-Secretary of State, Department of National Heritage/Department for Culture, Media and Sport (Minister for Sport) 1997–99; Resigned July 1999 reshuffle; *Select Committees:* Member: Procedure 1989–97; Member: Procedure 1999–. *Special Interests:* Economics, Local Government, Media, Arts, Animal Welfare; Europe, Lithuania, Nicaragua, Panama, USA. Chair, London Group Labour MPs 1987–91. Member, Council of Europe, WEU 1989–91; Representative, UK Delegation to Council of Europe and Western Europe Union; *Recreations:* Soccer, trade union history. *Address:* Tony Banks Esq, MP, House of Commons, London, SW1A 0AA *Tel:* 020 7219 3522. *Constituency:* 306 High Street, Stratford, London, E15 1AJ *Tel:* 020 8555 0036.

HARRY BARNES   North East Derbyshire   *Lab majority 18,321*

Born 22 July 1936; Son of late Joseph and Betsy Barnes; Educated Easington Colliery Secondary Modern School; Ryhope Grammar School; Ruskin College, Oxford (Diploma in economics and political science 1962); Hull University (BA philosophy and political studies 1965); Married September 14, 1963, Elizabeth Ann, daughter of late Richard and Evelyn Stephenson (1 son 1 daughter). RAF national service 1954–56; Railway clerk 1952–54, 1956–60; Adult student 1960–65; Lecturer: in British government North Notts College of Further Education 1965–66, in political studies and industrial relations Sheffield University 1966–87; Member, National Administrative Council of Independent Labour Publications 1977–80, 1982–85; Director, Mature Matriculation Courses 1984–87 (Sheffield University). **House of Commons:** Member for North East Derbyshire since June 1987; *Select Committees:* Member: European Legislation 1989–97, Members' Interests 1990–92; Member: Northern Ireland Affairs 1997–. *Special Interests:* Education, Industrial Relations, Local Government, European Union, Energy, Environment, Northern Ireland, Electoral Registration; Ireland, Malta, Africa. Vice-Chair, East Midland Group of Labour MPs 1991–95; Campaign Officer, Central Regional Group, Labour MPs 1993–95; Hon. Treasurer: Central Region Group of Labour MPs 1997–99, East Midlands Regional Group of Labour MPs 1999–. Member, Standing Committees on: Poll Tax 1988, Employment and Football 1989, Student Loans 1990; Member, Standing Committee A on European Legislation 1990–97; Member, Standing Committees on: Northern Ireland Emergency Provisions 1991, Transport and Works 1992, Further and Higher Education 1992; Associate Member, British-Irish Parliamentary Body 1992–97, Full Member 1997–. *Address:* Harry Barnes Esq, MP, House of Commons, London, SW1A 0AA *Tel:* 020 7219 4521 *Fax:* 020 7219 2381 *Tel (Constituency):* 01246 412588.

KEVIN BARRON   Rother Valley   *Lab majority 23,485*

Born 26 October 1946; Son of Richard Barron, retired; Educated Maltby Hall Secondary Modern; Ruskin College, Oxford; Married June 7, 1969, Carol McGrath (1 son 2 daughters). National Coal Board 1962–83. **House of Commons:** Member for Rother Valley since June 1983; Opposition Spokesman on: Energy 1988–92, Employment 1993–95, Health 1995–97; PPS to Neil Kinnock as Leader of the Opposition 1985–87; *Select Committees:* Member: Environment 1992–93. *Special Interests:* Energy, Environment, Home Affairs; Bulgaria. Member, area and local Labour Party; Chairman, Yorkshire Regional Group of Labour MPs 1987–. Member, General Medical Council 1999–; *Recreations:* Local history, family life, football, fly fishing. *Address:* Kevin Barron Esq, MP, House of Commons, London, SW1A 0AA *Tel:* 020 7219 4432 *Tel (Constituency):* 01909 568611.

JOHN BATTLE   Leeds West   *Lab majority 19,771*

Born 26 April 1951; Son of John Battle, electrical engineer, and late Audrey Battle; Educated St Michael's College; Upholland College; Leeds University (BA); Married April 12, 1977, Mary Meenan (1 son 2 daughters). Research assistant 1979–83; National co-ordinator, Church Action on Poverty 1983–87. Councillor, Leeds City Council 1980–87. **House of Commons:** Contested Leeds North West 1983 general election. Member for Leeds West since June 1987; Opposition Front Bench Spokesman on the Environment (Shadow Minister of Housing and Planning) 1992–94; Labour Whip 1990; Shadow Minister for Housing 1993–94, Science and Technology 1994–95, Energy 1995–97; Minister of State: Department of Trade and Industry 1997–99, Foreign and Commonwealth Office 1999–; *Select Committees:* Member: Environment 1991–92. *Special Interests:* Poverty and Wealth at Home and Abroad, Housing, Economic Policy, International Development, Science, Engineering and Technology; South Korea, Latin America. Joint Chair, British Trade International Board 2000–; *Recreations:* Folk music, poetry. *Address:* John Battle Esq, MP, House of Commons, London, SW1A 0AA *Tel:* 020 7219 3000. *Constituency:* 2a Conference Place, Leeds, West Yorkshire, LS12 3DZ *Tel:* 0113–231 0258 *Fax:* 0113–279 5850 *E-mail:* johnbattlemp@dial.pipex.com.

HUGH BAYLEY   City of York   *Lab majority 20,523*

Born 9 January 1952; Son of Michael Bayley, architect, and Pauline Bayley; Educated Haileybury; Bristol University (BSc politics 1974); York University (BPhil Southern African studies 1976); Married December 22, 1984, Fenella, daughter of Joseph Jeffers (1 son 1 daughter). District officer, then National officer NALGO 1975–82; General secretary, International Broadcasting Trust 1982–86; York University: lecturer in social policy 1986–98; Research fellow in health economics 1987–92; TGWU 1975–82, BECTU 1982–92, RMT 1992–. Councillor, Camden Borough Council 1980–86; York Health Authority 1988–90. **House of Commons:** Contested York 1987 general election. Member for York 1992–97, and for City of York since May 1, 1997; PPS to Frank Dobson as Secretary of State for Health 1997–99; Parliamentary Under-Secretary of State, Department of Social Security 1999–; *Select Committees:* Member: Health 1992–97. *Special Interests:* Health, Economic Policy, Environment, International Development, Defence, Media, Electoral Reform; Africa. Member, Executive Committee: Inter-Parliamentary Union – UK Branch 1997–99, Commonwealth Parliamentary Association – UK Branch 1997–99; Member, UK Delegation to the North Atlantic Assembly 1997–99; *Publications: The Nation's Health*, 1995; *Recreations:* Family life. *Address:* Hugh Bayley Esq, MP, House of Commons, London, SW1A 0AA *Tel:* 020 7219 5100 *Fax:* 020 7219 4293. *Constituency:* 59 Holgate Road, York, YO2 4AA *Tel:* 01904 623713 *Fax:* 01904 623260 *E-mail:* dellaganal@parliament.uk.

NIGEL BEARD   Bexleyheath and Crayford   *Lab majority 3,415*

Born 10 October 1936; Son of late Albert Leonard Beard, and late Irene Bowes; Educated Castleford Grammar School; University College, London (BSc physics 1958); Married 1969, Jennifer Cotton (1 son 1 daughter). Central Policy Staff, MoD 1961–73; Chief planner, GLC 1973–74; Head, London Docklands Development Organisation 1974–79; Manager, innovation and new business development, ICI 1979–93; Group research and development manager, Zeneca 1993–; Member, GMB. Member, SW Thames Regional Health Authority 1978–86; and Member Royal Marsden Hospital Board 1980–88. **House of Commons:** Contested Woking 1979, Portsmouth North 1983, Erith and Crayford 1992 general elections. Member for Bexleyheath and Crayford since May 1, 1997; *Select Committees:* Member: Unopposed Bills (Panel) 1998–, Treasury Sub-Committee 2000–, Treasury 2000–. *Special Interests:* Defence, Foreign Affairs, Economy (Industrial Renewal), Technology, Inner Cities; France. Member: Labour Party Southern Region Executive 1981–95, Labour Party National Constitutional Committee 1994–98, Fabian Society. Board Member, Institute of Cancer Research 1986–88; Comprehensive School Governor 1974–1991; Member, Ecclesiastical Committee; *Publications: Use of Linear Programming in Planning and Analysis,* 1971; FRSA; *Clubs:* Athenaeum; *Recreations:* Reading, walking, classical music, modern art. *Address:* Nigel Beard Esq, MP, House of Commons, London, SW1A 0AA *Tel:* 020 7219 5061 *Fax:* 020 7219 2708. *Constituency:* 50 Peareswood Road, Sladegreen, Erith, Kent, DA8 2HP *Tel:* 01322 332261 *Fax:* 01322 332279 *E-mail:* nigel.beard@ge02.poptel.org.uk *Website:* www.mymp.org.uk/nigelbeard.

MARGARET BECKETT   Derby South   *Lab majority 16,106*

Born 15 January 1943; Daughter of late Cyril Jackson, carpenter and Winifred Jackson, teacher; Educated Notre Dame High School, Manchester and Norwich; Manchester College of Science and Technology; John Dalton Polytechnic; Married July 7, 1979, Lionel Arthur, son of Arthur Beckett (2 stepsons). Student apprentice in metallurgy, AEI Manchester 1961–66; Experimental officer, Department of Metallurgy, Manchester University 1966–70; Industrial policy researcher, Labour Party 1970–74; Principal researcher, Granada Television 1979–83; Political adviser, Ministry of Overseas Development 1974; Member: T&GWU 1964–, NUJ, BECTU. **House of Commons:** Contested Lincoln February 1974 general election. Member for Lincoln October 1974–79, and for Derby South since June 1983; Assistant Government Whip 1975–76; PPS to Judith Hart as Minister of Overseas Development 1974–75; Parliamentary Under-Secretary of State, Department of Education and Science 1976–79; Shadow Minister, Social Security 1984–89; Shadow Chief Secretary to the Treasury 1989–92; Shadow Leader, House of Commons and Campaign Co-ordinator 1992–94; Deputy Leader, Labour Party and Opposition 1992–94; Leader of Opposition May-July 1994; Shadow Secretary of State for Health 1994–95; Shadow President of the Board of Trade 1995–97; President of the Board of Trade and Secretary of State for Trade and Industry 1997–98; President of the Council and Leader of the House of Commons 1998–; *Select Committees:* Chairman: Modernisation of the House of Commons 1998–. *Special Interests:* Industry. Secretary, Traders Council and Labour Party 1968–70; Member: Labour Party National Executive Committee 1980–81, 1985–86, 1988–97, Fabian Society, Tribune Group, Socialist Education Committee, Labour Women's Action Committee, Derby Co-Op Party, Socialist Environment and Resources Association. Member: CND, Amnesty International, Anti-Apartheid Movement; *Publications: The Need For Consumer Protection,* 1972; *The National Enterprise Board; The Nationalisation of Shipbuilding, Ship Repair and Marine Engineering; Relevant sections of Labour's Programme,* 1972/73; *Renewing the NHS,* 1995; *Vision for Growth – A New Industrial Strategy for Britain,* 1996; PC 1993; *Recreations:* Cooking, reading, caravanning. *Address:* Rt Hon Margaret Beckett, MP, House of Commons, London, SW1A 0AA *Tel:* 020 7219 3000.

ANNE BEGG   Aberdeen South   *Lab majority 3,365*

Born 6 December 1955; Daughter of David Begg, MBE, retired orthotist, and Margaret Catherine Begg, retired nurse; Educated Damacre Primary School; Brechin High School; Aberdeen University (MA history and politics); Aberdeen College of Education (Secondary Teaching Certificate 1978). English and history teacher, Webster's High School, Kirriemuir 1978–88; English teacher, Arbroath Academy 1988–97; Member: Educational Institute of Scotland 1978–, EIS National Council 1990–95. **House of Commons:** Member for Aberdeen South since May 1, 1997; *Select Committees:* Member: Scottish Affairs 1997–. *Special Interests:* Education, Scottish Affairs, Health, Disabled/Disability, Arts, Broadcasting.
Member, Labour Party National Executive Committee 1998–99. Patron: PHAB Scotland, Scottish Motor Neuron Society, Angus Special Playscheme; Elected Member, General Teaching Council for Scotland 1994–97; Disabled Scot of the Year 1988; *Recreations:* Reading, cinema, theatre, public speaking. *Address:* Anne Begg, MP, House of Commons, London, SW1A 0AA *Tel:* 020 7219 2140 *Fax:* 020 7219 1264. *Constituency:* 166 Market Street, Aberdeen, AB11 5PP *Tel:* 01224 252704 *Fax:* 01224 252705 *E-mail:* begga@parliament.uk.

ROY BEGGS   East Antrim   *UUP majority 6,389*

Born 20 February 1936; Son of John Beggs; Educated Ballyclare High School; Stranmillis Training College (DipEd); Married 1959, Wilma Lorimer (2 sons 2 daughters). Assistant teacher, science department 1957–78; Vice-Principal, Larne High School 1978–83. Councillor, Larne Borough Council 1973–; Mayor of Larne 1978–83; Member, Northern Ireland Assembly 1982–86. **House of Commons:** Member for East Antrim since June 1983; Former Spokesman for Education, Employment and National Heritage; Spokesman for: Education and Employment, for Community Relations and Culture, Media and Sport 1997–2000, Education and Employment 2000–; UUP Chief Whip 2000–; Shadow Leader of the House 2000–; *Select Committees:* Member: Northern
Ireland Affairs 1997–; Member, House of Commons Public Accounts Commission 1983–. *Special Interests:* Education, Employment, National Heritage. Member, North Eastern Education and Library Board 1973–, Vice-Chairman 1981–; President, Northern Ireland Association of Education and Library Boards 1984–; *Recreations:* Fishing. *Address:* Roy Beggs Esq, MP, House of Commons, London, SW1A 0AA *Tel:* 020 7219 6305 *Fax:* 020 7219 3889.

ALAN BEITH   Berwick-upon-Tweed   *LD majority 8,042*

Born 20 April 1943; Son of late James Beith, foreman packer, and Joan Beith; Educated King's School, Macclesfield; Balliol College; Nuffield College, Oxford (BLitt, MA philosophy, politics and economics 1964); Married September 1, 1965, Barbara Jean Ward (died 1998) (1 son deceased 1 daughter). Politics lecturer, Newcastle University 1966–73; Parliamentary Adviser, Association of University Teachers. Councillor: Hexham RDC 1969–74, Tynedale DC 1974–75. **House of Commons:** Contested Berwick-upon-Tweed 1970 general election. Member for Berwick-upon-Tweed since 1973 by-election; Liberal Spokesman on Foreign Affairs 1985–87; Alliance Spokesman on Foreign Affairs 1987; Liberal Treasury
Spokesman 1987; SLD Treasury Spokesman 1988–89; Liberal Democrat: Treasury Spokesman 1989–94, Home Affairs Spokesman 1994–95, Spokesman for Police, Prison and Security Matters 1995–97, Spokesman for Home and Legal Affairs (Home Affairs) 1997–99; Chief Whip, Liberal Party 1976–87; *Select Committees:* Member: House of Commons Commission 1979–97, Treasury and Civil Service 1987–94; Member: Procedure 2000–. *Special Interests:* Parliamentary and Constitutional Affairs, Architectural and Artistic Heritage; Canada, Scandinavia, Zimbabwe. Deputy Leader: Liberal Party 1985–88, Liberal Democrat Parliamentary Party 1992–. Member, Intelligence and Security Committee 1994–; Representative, Council of Europe Assembly 1976–84; Member, Western

European Union Assembly 1976–84; Trustee, Historic Chapels Trust; *Publications:* co-author *Case for Liberal Party and Alliance*, 1983; *Faith and Politics*, 1987; PC 1992; Hon. DCL, Newcastle University 1998; *Clubs:* National Liberal; *Recreations:* Music, walking, boating. *Address:* Rt Hon Alan Beith, MP, House of Commons, London, SW1A 0AA *Tel:* 020 7219 3540 *Fax:* 020 7219 5890. *Constituency:* 5 Paikes Street, Alnwick, Northumberland, NE66 1HX *Tel:* 01665 602901 *Fax:* 01665 605700 *E-mail:* berwicklibdems@cix.compulink.co.uk; cheeseman@parliament.uk.

MARTIN BELL   Tatton   *Ind majority 11,077*

Born 31 August 1938; Son of late Adrian Hanbury Bell; Educated Taverham Hall Preparatory School; The Leys School, Cambridge; King's College, Cambridge (MA English 1962); Married 1st, 1971, Nelly Lucienne Gourdon (2 daughters) (marriage dissolved); married 2nd, 1985, Rebecca Sobel (marriage dissolved 1993); married 3rd, July 17, 1998, Fiona, daughter of Robert Goddard. Army national service 1957–59; BBC TV News: reporter 1965–77, diplomatic correspondent 1977–78, chief Washington correspondent 1978–89, Berlin correspondent 1989–93, East European correspondent 1993–94, foreign affairs correspondent 1994–97. **House of Commons:** Member for Tatton since May 1, 1997; *Select Committees:* Member: Standards and Privileges 1997–. *Special Interests:* Standards in Public Life, Foreign Affairs, Welfare of Armed Services Families. Vice-President, Hope and Homes for Children; Member, Ecclesiastical Committee; *Publications: In Harm's Way*, 1995; *An Accidental MP*, 2000; OBE 1992; Royal Television Society, Reporter of the Year 1977; TV Journalist of the Year 1992; Four honorary degrees; *Recreations:* Swimming. *Address:* Martin Bell Esq, OBE, MP, House of Commons, London, SW1A 0AA *Tel:* 020 7219 4010. *Constituency:* 9–11 Princess Street, Knutsford, Cheshire, WA16 6BV *Tel:* 01565 652882 *E-mail:* pricemah@parliament.uk.

STUART BELL   Middlesbrough   *Lab majority 25,018*

Born 16 May 1938; Son of late Ernest Bell, pitman; Educated Hookergate Grammar School; Council of Legal Education, Gray's Inn; Married 1st, July 16, 1960, Margaret Bruce (1 son 1 daughter), married 2nd, June 6, 1980, Margaret Allan (1 son). Barrister, called to the Bar, Gray's Inn 1970; Previously: colliery clerk, newspaper reporter, typist novelist; Conseil Juridique and International Lawyer Paris 1970–77; Member, General Municipal Boilermakers and Allied Trades Union. Councillor, Newcastle City Council 1980–83, Member: Finance, Health and Environment, Arts and Education Committee, Association of Metropolitan Authorities, Education Committee, Council of Local Education Authorities, Newcastle Area Health Authority (teaching). **House of Commons:** Contested Hexham 1979. Member for Middlesbrough since June 1983; Opposition Front Bench Spokesman on: Northern Ireland 1984–87, Trade and Industry 1992–97; PPS to Roy Hattersley as Deputy Leader of Opposition 1983–84; Second Church Estates Commissioner 1997–; *Select Committees:* Chairman: Finance and Services 2000–; Member: Liaison 2000–. *Special Interests:* Economic Policy, European Union, Irish Affairs; Europe, USA, France. Member: Fabian Society, Society of Labour Lawyers. Founder member, British Irish Inter-Parliamentary Body 1990; Executive Member, British Group, Inter-Parliamentary Union 1992–95, Vice-Chairman 1992–95; *Publications: Paris 69*; *Days That Used to Be*; *When Salem Came to the Boro*; *The Children Act 1989 (annotated)*; *Fabian Tract: How to Abolish the Lords*; *Legal Tract: United States Customs Valuation*; *Raising the Standard: The Case for First Past the Post*; *Where Jenkins Went Wrong: A Further Case for First Past the Post*; *Clubs:* Beefsteak; *Recreations:* Writing short stories, novels and feature articles. *Address:* Stuart Bell Esq, MP, House of Commons, London, SW1A 0AA *Tel:* 020 7219 3000.

Visit the Vacher Dod Website . . .

www.politicallinks.co.uk

HILARY BENN   Leeds Central   *Lab majority 2,293*

Born 26 November 1953; Son of Tony Benn, MP (*qv*) and Caroline Middleton De Camp; Educated Holland Park Comprehensive School; Sussex University (BA Russian and East European studies 1974); Married 1973 Rosalind Retey (died 1979); married 1982, Sally Christina Clark (3 sons, 1 daughter). Research officer and latterly head of policy and communications, MSF 1975–97; Special Adviser to David Blunkett, as Secretary of State for Education and Employment 1997–99; Member: MSF, GMB; Trustee, Unions 21. London Borough of Ealing: Councillor 1979–99, Deputy Leader 1986–90, Chair, Education Committee 1986–90. **House of Commons:** Contested Ealing North 1983 and 1987 general elections. Member for Leeds Central since June 10, 1999 by-election; *Select Committees:* Member: Environment, Transport and Regional Affairs 1999–, Environment Sub-Committee 1999–. *Special Interests:* Education, Employment, Trade Unions, Environment, Urban Policy, Home Affairs. Member, Association of Metropolitan Authorities Education Committee 1986–90; Chair, Association of London Authorities Education Committee 1989–90; *Recreations:* Football, gardening, hillwalking. *Address:* Hilary Benn Esq, MP, House of Commons, London, SW1A 0AA *Tel:* 020 7219 5770 *Fax:* 020 7219 2639. *Constituency:* 2 Blenheim Terrace, Leeds, LS2 9JG *Tel:* 0113–244 1097 *Fax:* 0113–234 1176 *E-mail:* bennh@parliament.uk.

TONY BENN   Chesterfield   *Lab majority 5,775*

Born 3 April 1925; Second son of late William Wedgwood Benn, Former Secretary of State and Labour MP for North Aberdeen and Gorton, and later created Viscount Stansgate; Educated Westminster; New College, Oxford (MA); Married June 17, 1949, Caroline Middleton, daughter of late James Milton De Camp (3 sons 1 daughter). Pilot Officer, RAFVR 1945, Later Sub-Lieutenant (A) RNVR; BBC producer North American service 1949–50; Member: TGWU, NUJ; Hon. Member: NUM, GMBATU, SOGAT. **House of Commons:** Member for Bristol South-East 1950–60. Re-elected May 1961; unseated by Election Court, July 1961; Member for Bristol South-East 1963–1983, and for Chesterfield since 1 March 1984 by-election; Spokesman on: RAF 1957–58, Transport 1959–60; Opposition Spokesman on Trade and Industry 1970; Postmaster General 1964–66; Minister of Technology July 1966–70; Minister of Power October 1969–70; Secretary of State for: Industry and Minister of Posts and Telecommunications 1974–75, Energy 1975–79; *Select Committees:* Member: Privileges 1984–97. *Special Interests:* International Affairs, Industrial Policy, Labour History, Socialism, Constitution, Democracy, Technology; Europe, USA. Member, Labour Party National Executive Committee 1959–94; Chair, Labour Party 1971–72; President, Socialist Campaign Group of Labour MPs 1990–. Succeeded his father to the Viscountcy 1960, but disclaimed his peerage for life 1963; Member, Inter-Parliamentary Union; President, EEC Energy Council of Ministers 1977; *Publications: Regeneration of Britain*, 1964; *Arguments for Socialism*, 1979; *Arguments for Democracy*, 1981; *Parliament, People and Power*, 1982; *The Sizewell Syndrome*, 1984; *Writing on the Wall*, editor 1984; *Out of the Wilderness, Diaries 1963–67*, 1987; *Fighting Back*, 1988; *Office without Power, Diaries 1968–72*, 1988; *Against the Tide, Diaries 1973–76*, 1989; *Conflicts of Interest, Diaries 1977–80*, 1990; *The End of an Era, Diaries 1980–90*, 1992; *Years of Hope, Diaries 1940–62*, 1994; *Common Sense*, 1993; *Speaking Up in Parliament*, (video) 1993; *Benn Diaries 1940–90*, 1995; *Westminster Behind Closed Doors*, (video) 1995; *Benn Diaries 1 & 2* – BBC Radio Collection; *Benn Diaries 1940–90* – on cassettes; *Writings on the Wall* – cassettes 1996; *New Labour in Focus*, (video) 1999 *Tony Benn Speaks*, (video) 1999; PC 1964; Backbencher of the Year 1990; Channel 4 and House Award for Speechmaker of the Year 1999; Five honorary doctorates from British and American universities. *Address:* Rt Hon Tony Benn, MP, House of Commons, London, SW1A 0AA *Tel:* 020 7219 6448. *Constituency:* Labour Club, 113 Saltergate, Chesterfield, S40 1NF *Tel:* 01246 2390779 *E-mail:* 106267.2444@compuserve.com.

ANDREW BENNETT   Denton and Reddish   *Lab majority 20,311*

Born 9 March 1939; Educated Birmingham University (BSocSc); Married 1961, Gillian Lawley (2 sons 1 daughter). Geography teacher 1960–74; Member, National Union of Teachers. Councillor, Oldham Borough Council 1964–74. **House of Commons:** Contested Knutsford 1970 general election. Member for Stockport North February 1974–83 and Denton and Reddish since 1983; Opposition Front Bench Spokesman on Education 1983–88; *Select Committees:* Member: Social Security and Sittings of the House of Commons 1991–92, Environment 1992–97; Chairman: Joint and Select Committees on Statutory Instruments 1994–97; Member: Liaison 1994–97, Standing Orders Committee 1994–96; Chairman: Environment 1995–97; Chairman (Environment): Environment, Transport and Regional Affairs 1997–98; Chairman (Environment): Environment, Transport and Regional Affairs 1997–; Chairman: Environment Sub-Committee 1997–; Member: Transport Sub-Committee 1997–, Joint Committee on Statutory Instruments 1997–, Liaison 1997–. *Recreations:* Photography, walking, climbing. *Address:* Andrew Bennett Esq, MP, House of Commons, London, SW1A 0AA *Tel:* 020 7219 4155. *Constituency:* Town Hall, Market Place, Denton, Greater Manchester, M34 2AP *Tel:* 0161–320 1504 *Fax:* 0161–320 1503 *E-mail:* bennett.andrew@pop3.poptel.org.uk *Website:* http://www.poptel.org.uk/andrew.bennett/index.html.

JOE BENTON   Bootle   *Lab majority 28,421*

Born 28 September 1933; Son of late Thomas and Agnes Benton; Educated St Monica's Primary and Secondary School; Bootle Technical College; Married March 30, 1959, Doris Wynne (4 daughters). Joined RAF 1955, National Service; Apprentice fitter and turner 1949; Formerly with Pacific Steam Navigation Company as personnel manager; Girobank 1982–90. Sefton Borough Council: Councillor 1970–90, Leader, Labour Group 1985–90, Former education spokesman; JP, Bootle bench 1969. **House of Commons:** Member for Bootle since by-election November 8, 1990; Opposition Whip 1994–97; *Select Committees:* Member: Energy 1991–92, Speaker's Panel of Chairmen 1992–94, Education and Employment 1997–99, Education Sub-Committee 1997, Chairmen's Panel 1998; Member: Parliamentary Privilege (Joint Committee) 1997–, Chairman's Panel 1998–. *Special Interests:* Education, Housing, Local Government. Chairman of Governors, Hugh Baird College of Technology; Working knowledge of Spanish; Member, Institute of Linguists; Affiliate Member, Institute of Personnel Management; *Recreations:* Reading, listening to classical music, squash, swimming. *Address:* Joseph Benton Esq, JP, MP, House of Commons, London, SW1A 0AA *Tel:* 020 7219 6973. *Constituency:* 23A Oxford Road, Bootle, Liverpool, L20 9HJ *Tel:* 0151–933 8432 *Fax:* 0151–933 4746.

JOHN BERCOW   Buckingham   *Con majority 12,386*

Born 19 January 1963; Son of Brenda, née Bailey, and late Charles Bercow; Educated Finchley Manorhill School; Essex University (BA government 1985). Credit analyst, Hambros Bank 1987–88; Public affairs consultant, Rowland Sallingbury Casey, Public Affairs Arm of Saatchi & Saatchi 1988–95; Board director, Rowland Company 1994–95; Special adviser: to Jonathan Aitken as Chief Secretary to the Treasury 1995, to Virginia Bottomley as Secretary of State for National Heritage 1995–96. Lambeth Borough Council: Councillor, 1986–90, Deputy Leader, Conservative Opposition 1987–89. **House of Commons:** Contested Motherwell South 1987 and Bristol South 1992 general elections. Member for Buckingham since May 1, 1997; Opposition Frontbench Spokesman for: Education and Employment 1999–2000, Home Affairs 2000–; *Select Committees:* Member: Welsh Affairs 1997–98, Trade and Industry 1998–99. *Special Interests:* Education, Economic Policy, Small Businesses, Britain: EU relations; Israel, USA, Far East. Chair, University of Essex Conservative Association 1984–85; National Chair, Federation of Conservative Students 1986–87; Vice-Chair, Conservative Collegiate Forum 1987. Co-Director, Advanced Speaking and Campaigning Course; Executive Member, 1922 Committee 1998–99; *Publications: Turning Scotland Around,* 1987; *Faster Moves Forward for Scotland,* 1987; *Recreations:* Tennis, squash, golf, reading, swimming, music. *Address:* John Bercow Esq, MP, House of Commons, London, SW1A 0AA *Tel:* 020 7219 3462. *Constituency:* Buckingham Constituency Conservative Association, Buckingham Road, Winslow, Buckingham, MK18 3DY *Tel:* 01296 714240 *Fax:* 01296 714273.

SIR PAUL BERESFORD Mole Valley *Con majority 10,221*

Born 6 April 1946; Son of Raymond and Joan Beresford; Educated Waimea College, Richmond, Nelson, New Zealand; Otago University, Dunedin, New Zealand; Married Julie Haynes (3 sons 1 daughter). Dental surgeon. Councillor, Wandsworth Borough Council 1978–94, Leader 1983–92. **House of Commons:** Member for Croydon Central 1992–97, and for Mole Valley since May 1, 1997; Parliamentary Under-Secretary of State, Department of the Environment 1994–97; *Select Committees:* Member: Education 1992–94; Member: Procedure 1997–. *Special Interests:* Inner Cities, Housing, Education; Fiji, New Zealand, Samoa, Australia. Knighted 1990; BDS; *Recreations:* DIY, reading. *Address:* Sir Paul Beresford, MP, House of Commons, London, SW1A 0AA *Tel:* 020 7219 3000. *Constituency:* Mole Valley Conservative Association, 86 South Street, Dorking, Surrey, RH4 2E2 *Tel:* 01306 883 312 *Fax:* 01306 885 194.

GERRY BERMINGHAM St Helens South *Lab majority 23,739*

Born 20 August 1940; Son of late Dr Patrick Xavier Bermingham; Educated Cotton College, North Staffordshire; Wellingborough Grammar School; Sheffield University (LLB 1963); Married 1998, Jilly Foster (3 sons, 2 by 1st marriage). Admitted Solicitor 1967; Barrister, Gray's Inn, called to the Bar 1985; Vice-Chair, GMB Parliamentary Group1997–; Various positions in APEX. Councillor, Sheffield City Council 1975–79, 1980–82. **House of Commons:** Contested South East Derbyshire 1979 general election. Member for St Helens South since June 1983; *Select Committees:* Member: Catering 1999–. *Special Interests:* Home Affairs, Penal Reform, Energy Conservation, Investment; Europe, USA. Member: SERA, NCCL, Campaign for Criminal Justice; *Sportsclubs:* Vice-President, Sheffield Tigers RUFC; *Recreations:* Music, theatre, sport. *Address:* Gerald Bermingham Esq, MP, House of Commons, London, SW1A 0AA *Tel:* 020 7219 3502 *Fax:* 020 7219 2684. *Constituency:* Anne Ward House, 2 Milk Street, St Helens, Merseyside, WA10 1PX *Tel:* 01744 623418 *Fax:* 01744 811826.

DR ROGER BERRY Kingswood *Lab majority 14,253*

Born 4 July 1948; Son of Sydney and Mary Joyce Berry; Educated Dalton County Junior School; Huddersfield New College; Bristol and Sussex Universities (BSc economics 1970; DPhil economics 1977); Married 1996, Alison Delyth. Temporary lecturer in economics, School of African and Asian Studies, London 1973–74; Associate fellow, Institute of Development Studies, Sussex University 1973–74; Lecturer in economics: University of Papua New Guinea 1974–78, Bristol University 1978–92; Member, MSF 1988: chair parliamentary group 1997–98; Member, AUT 1978–. Avon County Council: Councillor 1981–92, Chair, Finance and Administration Committee 1983–86, Deputy Leader 1985–86, Leader, Labour Group 1986–92. **House of Commons:** Contested Weston-Super-Mare 1983 and Kingswood 1987 general elections. Member for Kingswood since April 9, 1992; *Select Committees:* Member: Deregulation 1994–95, Trade and Industry 1995–97; Member: Trade and Industry 1997–. *Special Interests:* Economic Policy, Disabled/Disability, Third World, Local Government; India, USA, Ireland, Papua New Guinea. Chair: South and West Group of Labour MPs 1997–99, South West Regional Group of Labour MPs 1999–. Trustee: Snowdon Award Scheme; Vice-President, Disabled Drivers' Association; Patron: Artsline, Circomedia; Director, Tribune Publications Ltd; *Publications:* Numerous journal and newspaper articles and pamphlets; Highland Park/Spectator Backbencher of the Year 1994; *Clubs:* Kingswood Labour; *Recreations:* Travel, food, cooking, gardening, reading. *Address:* Dr Roger Berry, MP, House of Commons, London, SW1A 0AA *Tel:* 020 7219 4106. *Constituency:* 2 Nelson Court, Nelson Road, Staple Hill, Bristol, BS16 5EY *Tel:* 0117–956 1837 *Fax:* 0117–970 1363 *E-mail:* berryr@parliament.uk.

HAROLD BEST   Leeds North West   *Lab majority 3,844*

Born 18 December 1937; Son of Fred and Marie Best; Educated Meanwood County School; Technical College; Married 1960, Mary Glyn (2 sons 2 daughters). Apprentice 1953–58; Contracting electrician 1958–66; Full-time trade union official 1966–78; Principal electrical technician Leeds Education Authority –1997; Activist and full-time official. Councillor, West Yorkshire County Council 1981–86; Deputy Chair, West Yorkshire Police Authority 1982–86. **House of Commons:** Member for Leeds North West since May 1, 1997; *Select Committees:* Member: Joint Committee on Statutory Instruments 1999–; Member, European Standing Committee A 1998. Chair, North West Leeds Constituency Labour Party 1992–95. National Executive Committee Member, National Council for Civil Liberties 1994; Member: Amnesty International, Liberty National Executive Committee; Governor, two Leeds Schools; Chair, Headingley Network Community Group; Founder Member, Campaign Against Racial Discrimination, Leeds. *Address:* Harold Best Esq, MP, House of Commons, London, SW1A 0AA *Tel:* 020 7219 6999 *Fax:* 020 7219 6979. *Constituency:* 7 Iveson Approach, Leeds, LS16 6LJ *Tel:* 0113–261 0002 *Fax:* 0113–261 0199.

CLIVE BETTS   Sheffield Attercliffe   *Lab majority 21,818*

Born 13 January 1950; Son of late Harold and Nellie Betts; Educated King Edward VII School, Sheffield; Pembroke College, Cambridge (BA economics and politics). Economist, Trades Union Congress 1971–73; Local government economist: Derbyshire County Council 1973–74, South Yorkshire County Council 1974–86, Rotherham Borough Council 1986–91; Member, TGWU. Sheffield City Council: Councillor 1976–92, Chairman: Housing Committee 1980–86, Finance Committee 1986–88, Deputy Leader 1986–87, Leader 1987–92. **House of Commons:** Contested Sheffield Hallam October 1974 and Louth 1979 general elections. Member for Sheffield Attercliffe since April 9, 1992; Opposition Whip 1996–97; Assistant Government Whip 1997–98; Government Whip (Lord Commissioner of HM Treasury) (Education and Employment; Committee Whip: Eastern) 1998–; *Select Committees:* Member: Treasury and Civil Service 1995–96, Treasury 1996–97; Member: Selection 1997–. *Special Interests:* Economic Policy, Local Government, Housing; Europe. Joined Labour Party 1969; Member, Labour Leader's Campaign Team with responsibility for Environment and Local Government 1995–96; Member, Labour Housing Group. Member, Anti-Apartheid Movement; Past Patron, National Association for Therapeutic Education; Patron: Mosborough Township Youth Project, British Deaf Sports Council; President, Mosborough Citizens' Advice Bureau; Past Vice-President, Energy from Waste Association; Vice-Chairman, Association of Metropolitan Authorities 1988–91; Chairman, AMA Housing Committee 1985–89; Vice-President, AMA; Chairman, South Yorkshire Pensions Authority 1989–92; *Recreations:* Supporting Sheffield Wednesday FC, playing squash, cricket, walking, real ale, scuba diving. *Address:* Clive Betts Esq, MP, House of Commons, London, SW1A 0AA *Tel:* 020 7219 3588 *Fax:* 020 7219 2289. *Constituency:* 2nd Floor, Barkers Pool House, Burgess Street, Sheffield, S1 2HH *Tel:* 0114–273 4444 *Fax:* 0114–273 9666 *E-mail:* bettsc@parliament.uk.

ELIZABETH BLACKMAN   Erewash   *Lab majority 9,135*

Born 26 September 1949; Educated Carlisle County High School for Girls; Prince Henry's Grammar School, Otley; Clifton College, Nottingham (BEd); Married Derek Blackman (separated) (1 son 1 daughter). Head, Upper School, Bramcote Park Comprehensive, Nottingham; Member, NASUWT. Deputy Leader, Broxtowe Borough Council. **House of Commons:** Member for Erewash since May 1, 1997; *Select Committees:* Member: Treasury 1997–, Treasury Sub-Committee 1998–. *Special Interests:* Education, Job Re-Training, Local Community, Economic Regeneration, Crime. Member: Co-operative Party, Fabian Society. *Publications: Parliamentary Portions*, recipe book 1998; *Recreations:* Family, music, reading. *Address:* Elizabeth Blackman, MP, House of Commons, London, SW1A 0AA *Tel:* 020 7219 2397 *Fax:* 020 7219 4837. *Constituency:* 23 Barratt Lane, Attenborough, Nottingham, NG9 6AG *Tel:* 0115–922 4380 *Fax:* 0115–943 1860.

TONY BLAIR   Sedgefield   *Lab majority 25,143*

Born 6 May 1953; Son of Leo Charles Lynton Blair and late Hazel Elisabeth Blair; Educated Durham Choristers School; Fettes College, Edinburgh; St John's College, Oxford (MA law 1974); Married 1980, Cherie Booth (3 sons 1 daughter). Called to the Bar, Lincoln's Inn 1976; Barrister specialising in trade union and industrial law 1976–83; Sponsored until March 1996 by Transport and General Workers' Union. **House of Commons:** Contested Beaconsfield by-election May 1982. Member for Sedgefield since June, 1983; Opposition Front Bench Spokesman on: Treasury and Economic Affairs 1984–87, Trade and Industry 1987–88; Shadow Secretary of State for Energy 1988–89, Employment 1989–92, Shadow Home Secretary 1992 94; Leader, Labour Party 1994–; Leader of the Opposition 1994–97; Prime Minister, First Lord of the Treasury and Minister for the Civil Service May 1997–. Vice-President, Federation of Economic Development Authorities (FEDA); Vice-President, Federation of Economic Development Authorities (FEDA); *Publications: New Britain: My Vision of a Young Country*, 1996; PC 1994; Charlemagne Prize 1999; Hon. DCL, Northumbria University 1995. *Address:* Rt Hon Tony Blair, MP, House of Commons, London, SW1A 0AA *Tel:* 020 7219 5676. *Constituency:* Myrobella, Farfield Terrace, Trindon Colliery, Co Durham *Tel:* 01429 882202 *Website:* http://www.number–10.gov.uk.

HAZEL BLEARS   Salford   *Lab majority 17,069*

Born 14 May 1956; Daughter of Arthur and Dorothy Blears; Educated Wardley Grammar School; Eccles VIth Form College; Trent Polytechnic; Chester College of Law (BA law 1977); Married October 21, 1989, Michael Halsall. Trainee solicitor, Salford Council 1978–80; Private practice solicitor 1980–81; Solicitor: Rossendale Council 1981–83, Wigan Council 1983–85; Principal solicitor, Manchester City Council 1985–; Branch Secretary, UNISON 1981–85; Member, TGWU. Councillor, Salford City Council 1984–92. **House of Commons:** Contested Tatton 1987, Bury South 1992 general elections. Member for Salford since May 1, 1997; PPS to Alan Milburn: as Minister of State, Department of Health 1998, as Chief Secretary, HM Treasury January–October 1999; *Select Committees:* Member: European Legislation 1997–98. *Special Interests:* Employment, Health, Arts, Urban Regeneration. Vice-Chair, North West Regional Group of Labour MPs 1997–98, Chair 1998–99; Member: North West Executive 1997–99, National Policy Forum 1997–, Leadership Campaign Team 1997–98; Labour Party Development Co-ordinator and Deputy to Ian McCartney. Chair, Salford Community Health Council; Vice-Chair, Pendleton College Governors; Trustee: Working Class Movement Library, National Museum Labour History, Imperial Society of Teachers of Dancing; *Recreations:* Dance, motorcycling. *Address:* Hazel Anne Blears, MP, House of Commons, London, SW1A 0AA *Tel:* 020 7219 6595 *Fax:* 020 7219 0949. *Constituency:* Jubilee House, 51 The Crescent, Salford, Greater Manchester, M51 4WX *Tel:* 0161–925 0705 *Fax:* 0161–743 9173 *E-mail:* blearsh@parl.uk.

BOB BLIZZARD   Waveney   *Lab majority 12,093*

Born 31 May 1950; Son of Arthur Blizzard, signwriter, and late Joan Blizzard; Educated Culford School, Bury St Edmunds; Birmingham University (BA 1971); Married 1978, Lyn, daughter of Walter and Val Chance (1 son 1 daughter). Teacher: Gravesend Secondary School 1973–75, Head of English, Bexley Secondary School, 1976–86, Head of English, Gorleston Secondary School, 1986–97; Member, NUT. Waveney District Council: Councillor 1987–97, Leader 1991–97; Vice-Chair, SCEALA 1995–97. **House of Commons:** Member for Waveney since May 1, 1997; PPS to Baroness Hayman as Minister of State, Ministry of Agriculture, Fisheries and Food 1999–; *Select Committees:* Member: Environmental Audit 1997–2000. *Special Interests:* Employment, Health, Local Government, Education, Agriculture; Canada, USA, Europe, Asia. *Recreations:* Walking, skiing, listening to jazz. *Address:* Bob Blizzard Esq, MP, House of Commons, London, SW1A 0AA *Tel:* 020 7219 3880 *Fax:* 020 7219 3980. *Constituency:* 27 Milton Road East, Lowestoft, Suffolk, NR32 1NT *Tel:* 01502 513913 *Fax:* 01502 580694.

DAVID BLUNKETT   Sheffield Brightside   Lab majority 19,954

Born 6 June 1947; Son of late Arthur and Doris Blunkett; Educated Sheffield School for the Blind; Royal Normal College for the Blind; Shrewsbury Technical College; Sheffield Richmond College of Further Education (day release and evening courses); Sheffield University (BA political theory and institutions 1972); Huddersfield College of Education (PGCE 1973); Married July 18, 1970, Ruth Gwynneth Mitchell (3 sons) (marriage dissolved 1990). Office work, East Midlands Gas Board 1967–69; Tutor in industrial relations and politics, Barnsley College of Technology 1973–81; Shop steward GMB EMGB 1967–69; member, NATFHE 1973–87; member, UNISON 1973–. Councillor, Sheffield City Council 1970–1988, Chair, Social Services Committee 1976–80, Seconded as Leader 1980–87; Councillor, South Yorkshire County Council 1973–77. **House of Commons:** Contested Sheffield Hallam February 1974 general election. Member for Sheffield Brightside since June 1987; Opposition Spokesman on Environment (Local Government) 1988–92; Shadow Secretary of State for: Health 1992–94, Education 1994–95, Education and Employment 1995–97; Secretary of State for Education and Employment 1997–; *Special Interests:* Local Government, Education, Economic and Democratic Planning. Member, Labour Party National Executive Committee 1983–98; Labour Party: Vice-Chair 1992–93, Chair 1993–94. *Publications: Building from the Bottom*, 1983; *Democracy in Crisis – the Town Halls Respond*, 1987; *On a Clear Day –* (autobiography), 1995; PC 1997; *Recreations:* Walking, sailing, music, poetry. *Address:* Rt Hon David Blunkett, MP, House of Commons, London, SW1A 0AA *Tel:* 020 7219 4043 *Fax:* 020 7219 5903. *Constituency:* 4th Floor, Palatine Chambers, Pinstone Street, Sheffield, S1 2HN *Tel:* 0114–273 5987 *Fax:* 0114–278 0384.

CRISPIN BLUNT   Reigate   Con majority 7,741

Born 15 July 1960; Son of Major-General Peter Blunt and Adrienne Blunt; Educated Wellington College; Royal Military Academy, Sandhurst; University College, Durham University (BA politics 1984); Cranfield Institute of Technology (MBA 1991); Married September 15, 1990, Victoria, daughter of Kenneth Jenkins (1 son 1 daughter). Army Officer 1979–90; Regimental duty 13th/18th Royal Hussars (QMO) in England, Germany and Cyprus; District Agent, Forum of Private Business 1991–92; Political Consultant, Politics International 1993; Special Adviser to Malcolm Rifkind: as Secretary of State for Defence 1993–95, as Foreign Secretary 1995–97. **House of Commons:** Contested West Bromwich East 1992 general election. Member for Reigate since May 1, 1997; *Select Committees:* Member: Defence 1997–2000; Member: Environment, Transport and Regional Affairs 2000–, Environment Sub-Committee 2000–. *Special Interests:* Economic Policy, Defence, Foreign Affairs, Environment. *Clubs:* Redhill Constitutional, Royal Automobile; *Sportsclubs:* Fantasians Cricket, Reigate Priory Cavaliers; *Recreations:* Cricket. *Address:* Crispin Blunt Esq, MP, House of Commons, London, SW1A 0AA *Tel:* 020 7219 3454. *Constituency:* Reigate Conservative Association, 18 Warwick Road, Redhill, Surrey, RH1 1BU *Tel:* 01737 765411 *Fax:* 01737 765411 *E-mail:* crispinbluntmp@parliament.uk.

PAUL BOATENG   Brent South   Lab majority 19,691

Born 14 June 1951; Son of Kwaku Boateng, barrister, and Eleanor Boateng, teacher; Educated Achimota; Accra Academy; Apsley Grammar School, Ghana; Bristol University (LLB); College of Law; Married November 20, 1980, Janet Olivia Alleyne (2 sons 3 daughters). Solicitor 1975; Barrister-at-law. Member GLC 1981–86: Chair, Police Committee 1981–86, Vice-Chair, Ethnic Minority Committee 1981–86. **House of Commons:** Contested Hertfordshire West 1983 general election. Member for Brent South since June 1987; Opposition Front Bench Spokesman on: Treasury and Economic Affairs 1989–92, Lord Chancellor's Department 1992–97; Parliamentary Under-Secretary of State, Department of Health 1997–98; Home Office: Minister of State (Minister for Criminal Policy) 1998–99, Minister of State and Deputy Home Secretary 1999–;

Special Interests: Home Affairs, Housing, Inner Cities, Overseas Aid and Development, Environment; Africa, Caribbean, USA, Southern Africa. Member: Labour Party NEC sub committee Human Rights 1979–83, Labour Party Joint Committee on Crime and Policing 1984–86. Chairman: Afro-Caribbean Education Resource Project 1978–84, Westminster Community Relations Council 1979–81; Legal Adviser, Scrap Sus Campaign 1977–81; Vice-President, Waltham Forest Community Relations Council 1981–; Home Office Advisory Council on Race Relations 1981–86; World Council of Churches Commission on programme to combat racism 1984–91; Vice-Moderator 1984–91; Police Training Council 1981–85; Executive NCCL 1980–86; Governor, Police Staff College Bramshill 1981–84; Board of English National Opera 1984–97; *Publications:* (contributor) *Reclaiming the Ground*; *Introduction to Sense and Sensibility: The Complete Jane Austen*; PC 1999; *Recreations:* Family, swimming, opera. *Address:* Rt Hon Paul Boateng, MP, House of Commons, London, SW1A 0AA *Tel:* 020 7219 6816.

SIR RICHARD BODY Boston and Skegness	*Con majority 647*

Born 18 May 1927; Son of Lieutenant-Colonel B. R. Body; Educated Reading School; Inns of Court School of Law; Married 1959, Marion Graham (1 son 1 daughter). RAFVR (India Command) 1945–48; Called to the Bar by the Middle Temple 1949; Farmer; Editor, *World Review* 1996–; Branch Secretary, AScW 1950–52; Delegate to Holborn Trades Council 1950–53. **House of Commons:** Contested Rotherham 1950, Abertillery 1950 and Leek 1951 general elections. Member for Billericay 1955–59, for Holland with Boston 1966–97, and for Boston and Skegness since May 1, 1997; *Select Committees:* Member: Environmental Audit 1999–. *Special Interests:* Agriculture, Environment, European Union, Third World; Europe, Australia and New Zealand. Chair, Society for Individual Freedom (1984–95); President, Campaign for an Independent Britain 1994–; Joint Chair, Council of the Get Britain Out Referendum Campaign, 1975; Chair of Trustees, Centre for European Studies 1989–; President, Disabled and Able Bodies Sports Inititative (DABSI) 1999–; *Publications: The Architect and the Law*, 1954; contributor *Destiny or Delusion*, 1971; co-editor *Freedom and Stability in the World Economy*, 1976; *Agriculture: the Triumph and the Shame*, 1982; *Farming in the Clouds*, 1984; *Red or Green for Farmers and the Rest of Us)*, 1987; *Europe of Many Circles*, 1990; *Our Food, Our Land*, 1991; Knighted 1986; *Clubs:* Carlton, Reform, Athenaeum. *Address:* Sir Richard Body, MP, House of Commons, London, SW1A 0AA *Tel:* 020 7219 4100. *Constituency:* 5 Church Close, Boston, PE21 6NT *Tel:* 01205 355884.

DAVID BORROW   South Ribble   *Lab majority 5,084*

Born 2 August 1952; Son of James Borrow, retired training officer, and Nancy Borrow, secretary; Educated Mirfield Grammar School, Mirfield; Lanchester Polytechnic (BA economics 1973); Single. Clerk to Merseyside Valuation Tribunal 1983–97; Member, UNISON; Former Branch Vice-Chair. Councillor, Preston Borough Council 1987–98, Leader 1992–94, 1995–97. **House of Commons:** Contested Wyre 1992 general election. Member for South Ribble since May 1, 1997; *Select Committees:* Member: Agriculture 1999–. *Special Interests:* Regional Development, Local Government Finance, Aerospace; Southern Africa; Member: European Standing Committee A 1998, European Standing Committee C 1999–. Member: Fabian Society, Co-operative Party. President, Society of Clerks 1990–92 and 1996–97; *Clubs:* Lostock Hall Labour. *Address:* David Borrow Esq, MP, House of Commons, London, SW1A 0AA *Tel:* 020 7219 4126 *Fax:* 020 7219 4126. *Constituency:* Crescent House, 2–6 Sandy Lane, Leyland, Lancashire, PR5 1CB *Tel:* 01772 454727 *Fax:* 01772 422982 *E-mail:* david.borrow@labour.co.uk.

TIMOTHY BOSWELL   Daventry   *Con majority 7,378*

Born 2 December 1942; Son of late Eric Boswell and Joan Boswell; Educated Marlborough College; New College, Oxford (MA classics 1965, Diploma in agricultural economics 1966); Married August 2, 1969, Helen Delahay, daughter of late Revd Arthur Rees (3 daughters). Conservative Research Department 1966–73; Head, Economic Section 1970–73; Farmer 1974–87; Leicestershire, Northamptonshire and Rutland County Branch of NFU, County Chairman 1983; Part-time Special Adviser to Minister of Agriculture 1984–86. **House of Commons:** Contested Rugby February 1974 general election. Member for Daventry since June 1987; Opposition Front Bench Spokesman for: the Treasury June-December 1997, Trade and Industry December 1997–99; Education and Employment (people with disabilities) 1999–; Assistant Government Whip 1990–92; Government Whip 1992; PPS to Peter Lilley as Financial Secretary to Treasury 1989–90; Parliamentary Under-Secretary of State, Department for Education 1992–95; Parliamentary Secretary, Ministry of Agriculture, Fisheries and Food 1995–97; *Special Interests:* Agriculture, Finance and Taxation, European Union; Europe. Daventry Constituency Conservative Association Treasurer 1976–79, Chairman 1979–83. Council of Perry Foundation 1967–90, President 1984–90; Member, Agricultural and Food Research Council 1988–90; *Clubs:* Farmers'; *Recreations:* Shooting. *Address:* Timothy Boswell Esq, MP, House of Commons, London, SW1A 0AA *Tel:* 020 7219 3520 *Fax:* 020 7219 4919. *Constituency:* Lloyds Bank Chambers, North Street, Daventry, Northamptonshire, NN11 5PN *Tel:* 01327 703192 *Fax:* 01327 310263.

PETER BOTTOMLEY   Worthing West   *Con majority 7,713*

Born 20 July 1944; Son of Sir James Bottomley, KCMG, HM Diplomatic Service; Educated Comprehensive School, Washington DC; Westminster; Trinity College, Cambridge (MA); Married 1967, Virginia Garnett (now MP – qv) (1 son 2 daughters). Industrial sales, industrial relations, industrial economics; Member, TGWU. **House of Commons:** Contested Greenwich, Woolwich West February and October 1974 general election. Member for Greenwich, Woolwich West by-election 1975–83, for Eltham 1983–97, and for Worthing West since May 1, 1997; PPS: to Cranley Onslow as Minister of State, Foreign and Commonwealth Office 1982–83, to Norman Fowler as Secretary of State for Health and Social Security 1983–84; Parliamentary Under-Secretary of State: at Department of Employment 1984–86, at Department of Transport (Minister for Roads and Traffic) 1986–89, at Northern Ireland Office (Agriculture, Environment) 1989–90; PPS to Peter Brooke as Secretary of State for Northern Ireland September-November 1990; *Select Committees:* Member: Transport 1992–97; Member: Standards and Privileges 1997–,

Unopposed Bills (Panel) 1997–. *Special Interests:* Southern Africa, El Salvador, USA. Former President, Conservative Trade Unionists. Chairman, Family Forum 1980–82; Hon. President, The Water Companies Association; Chairman, Church of England Children's Society 1982–84; Member, Council of NACRO; RIIA; Trustee, Christian Aid 1978–84; Fellow, Industry and Parliament Trust; Court Member, Drapers' Company; Gold Medal, Institute of the Motor Industry 1988; Former Fellow, Institute of Personnel Management; Fellow, Institute of Road Safety Officers; *Sportsclubs:* Former Parliamentary swimming and occasional dinghy sailing champion. *Address:* Peter Bottomley Esq, MP, House of Commons, London, SW1A 0AA *Tel:* 020 7219 6505. *Constituency:* Haverfield House, Union Place, Worthing, West Sussex, BN11 1LG *Tel:* 01903 235168.

VIRGINIA BOTTOMLEY   South West Surrey   Con majority 2,694

Born 12 March 1948; Daughter of late W. John Garnett CBE; Educated Putney High School; Essex University (BA sociology); London School of Economics (MSc social work and administration); Married 1967, Peter Bottomley (now MP – qv) (1 son 2 daughters). Researcher, Child Poverty Action Group 1971–73; Psychiatric social worker in South London, Social Policy Tutor 1973–74; Director, Mid Southern Water Company 1987–88. Magistrate in Inner London Juvenile Courts 1975–84; Chairman, Lambeth Juvenile Court 1980–84. **House of Commons:** Contested Isle of Wight in 1983 general election. Member for South West Surrey since May 3, 1984 by-election; PPS: to Chris Patten, as Minister of State, Department of Education and Science 1985–86, as Minister of State (Minister for Overseas Development), FCO 1986–87, to Sir Geoffrey Howe as Secretary of State for Foreign and Commonwealth Affairs 1987–88; Parliamentary Under-Secretary of State, Department of Environment 1988–89; Minister of State, Department of Health 1989–92; Secretary of State for: Health 1992–95, National Heritage 1995–97; *Select Committees:* Member: Foreign Affairs 1997–99, Entry Clearance Sub-Committee 1997–98. Governor, London School of Economics 1985–; Vice-President, Carers' National Association 1990–; Governor, Ditchley Foundation 1991–; Member, Medical Research Council 1987–88; Chair, Millennium Commission 1995–97; Government Co-Chair, Women's National Commission 1991–92; Vice-Chair, British Council Board 1997–; Fellow, Industry and Parliament Trust; PC 1992; Honorary LLD (University of Portsmouth); Freeman, City of London 1988. *Address:* Rt Hon Virginia Bottomley, MP, House of Commons, London, SW1A 0AA *Tel:* 020 7219 6499 *Fax:* 020 7219 6279. *Constituency:* 2 Royal Parade, Tilford Road, Hindhead, Surrey, GU26 6TD *Tel:* 01428 604526 *Fax:* 01428 667498.

KEITH BRADLEY   Manchester Withington   Lab majority 18,581

Born 17 May 1950; Son of late John Bradley and Mrs Beatrice Harris; Educated Bishop Vesey's Grammar School; Manchester Polytechnic; York University (BA, MPhil, DipAcct); Married May 16, 1987, Rhona Ann Graham (2 sons 1 daughter). Charles Impey and Co, chartered accountants 1969–73; Research officer, Manchester City Council Housing Department 1978–81; Secretary, Stockport Community Health Council 1981–87; Member: MSF, UNISON. Councillor, Manchester City Council 1983–88, Chair, Environment and Consumer Services Committee 1984–88; Formerly City Council Director: Manchester Ship Canal Co, Manchester Airport plc. **House of Commons:** Member for Manchester Withington since June 1987; Opposition Spokesman on: Social Security 1991–96, Transport 1996–97; Deputy Chief Whip (Treasurer of HM Household) 1998–; Parliamentary Under-Secretary of State, Department of Social Security 1997–98; *Select Committees:* Member: Agriculture 1989–92; Member: Accommodation and Works 1998–, Finance and Services 1999–, Selection 1999–. *Special Interests:* Local Government, Housing, Health, Pensions, Poverty. Member, Co-op Party. *Recreations:* All sports, theatre, cinema. *Address:* Keith Bradley Esq, MP, House of Commons, London, SW1A 0AA *Tel:* 020 7219 2279 *Fax:* 020 7219 5901. *Constituency:* Investment House, 425 Wilmslow Road, Withington, Manchester, M20 4AF *Tel:* 0161–446 2047 *Fax:* 0161–445 5543 *E-mail:* keith.bradley@hm-treasury.gov.uk.

PETER BRADLEY   The Wrekin   *Lab majority 3,025*

Born 12 April 1953; Son of Fred and Trudie Bradley; Educated Abingdon; Sussex University (BA American studies 1975); Partner, Annie Hart (twin son and daughter); Research director, Centre for Contemporary Studies 1979–85; Director, Good Relations 1985–93; Managing director, Millbank Consultants Ltd 1993–97; Member, MSF, GMB. Councillor, Westminster City Council 1986–96, Deputy Leader, Labour Group 1990–96. **House of Commons:** Member for The Wrekin since May 1, 1997; *Select Committees:* Member: Public Administration 1997–99. *Special Interests:* Economic Policy, Transport, Education, Health, Housing, Rural Affairs. Chair, Rural Group of Labour MPs. Patron, Friends of Searchlight; Vice-President, UK Local Authority Forum of World Heritage Sites; *Publications:* Various research and press articles; *Sportsclubs:* Warwickshire County Cricket Club; *Recreations:* Playing cricket, watching football (especially Aston Villa) and rugby, walking. *Address:* Peter Bradley Esq, MP, House of Commons, London, SW1A 0AA *Tel:* 020 7219 4112 *Fax:* 020 7219 0536. *Constituency:* Wrekin Labour Party, 9A Queen Street, Wellington, Telford, Shropshire, TF1 1EH *Tel:* 01952 240010 *Fax:* 01952 240455 *E-mail:* taylorc@parliament.uk.

BEN BRADSHAW   Exeter   *Lab majority 11,705*

Born 30 August 1960; Son of late Canon Peter Bradshaw and late Daphne Bradshaw, teacher; Educated Thorpe St Andrew School, Norwich; Sussex University (BA German 1982); Freidburg University, Germany; Award-winning BBC Reporter and Presenter; BBC Berlin correspondent during fall of Berlin Wall 1989–91; Reporter for 'World At One' and 'World This Weekend' on BBC Radio 4 1991–97; Member, NUJ. **House of Commons:** Member for Exeter since May 1, 1997; Introduced Pesticides Act (Private Member's Bill) 1998; *Select Committees:* Member: European Legislation 1998; Member: European Scrutiny 1998–. *Special Interests:* Foreign Affairs, Environment and Transport, Modernisation of Parliament; Europe – particularly Germany and Italy, USA. Secretary, Labour Movement for Europe, Member: Labour Campaign for Electoral Reform, SERA, Christian Socialist Movement. *Publications:* Numerous for the BBC on domestic and foreign affairs; Argos Consumer Journalist of the Year 1989; Anglo-German Foundation Journalist of the Year 1990; Sony News Reporter Award 1993; Norfolk County Scholar; *Clubs:* Whipton Labour, Exeter; *Recreations:* Cycling, walking, cooking, music. *Address:* Benjamin Bradshaw Esq, MP, House of Commons, London, SW1A 0AA *Tel:* 020 7219 6597 *Fax:* 020 7219 0950. *Constituency:* Labour HQ, 26B Clifton Hill, Exeter, Devon, EX1 2DJ *Tel:* 01392 424464 *Fax:* 01392 425630 *E-mail:* bradshawb@parliament.uk.

GRAHAM BRADY   Altrincham and Sale West   *Con majority 1,505*

Born 20 May 1967; Son of John Brady, accountant, and Maureen Brady, née Birch, medical secretary; Educated Altrincham Grammar School; Durham University (BA law 1989); Married 1992, Victoria Lowther (1 son, 1 daughter). Shandwick PLC PR consultancy 1989–90; Centre for Policy Studies 1990–92; Public affairs director, The Waterfront Partnership PR and strategic public affairs consultancy 1992–97. **House of Commons:** Member for Altrincham and Sale West since May 1, 1997; Opposition Whip 2000–; Parliamentary Private Secretary to Michael Ancram as Conservative Party Chairman 1999–2000; *Select Committees:* Member: Education and Employment 1997–, Employment Sub-Committee 1997–. *Special Interests:* European Union, Employment, Education, Foreign Affairs, Health; Commonwealth, Far East, British Overseas Territories. Chairman, Durham University Conservative Association 1987–88; National Union Executive Committee 1988; Chairman, Northern Area Conservative Collegiate Forum 1987–89; Vice-Chairman, East Berkshire Conservative Association 1993–95. School governor 1991–93; Vice-President, Greater Altrincham Chamber of Trade Commerce and Industry 1997–; Executive Member, 1922 Committee 1998–; *Publications: Towards an Employees' Charter – and Away From Collective Bargaining* (Centre for Policy Studies), 1991; *Recreations:* Family, gardening, reading. *Address:* Graham Brady Esq, MP, House of Commons, London, SW1A 0AA *Tel:* 020 7219 4604. *Constituency:* Altrincham and Sale West Conservative Association, Thatcher House, Delahays Farm, Green Lane, Timperley, Cheshire, WA15 8QW *Tel:* 0161–904 8828 *Fax:* 0161–904 8868 *E-mail:* crowthers@parliament.uk.

TOM BRAKE   Carshalton and Wallington   *LD majority 2,267*

Born 6 May 1962; Son of Michael and Judy Brake; Educated Lycee International, St Germain-en-Laye, France; Imperial College, London (BSc physics 1983); Married August 23, 1998, Candida Goulden (1 daughter). Principal Consultant (IT), Cap Gemini. Councillor: London Borough of Hackney 1988–90, London Borough of Sutton 1994–98. **House of Commons:** Contested Carshalton and Wallington 1992 general election. Member for Carshalton and Wallington since May 1, 1997; Spokesman for: Environment, Transport in London and Air Transport 1997–99, Environment, Transport, the Regions, Social Justice and London Transport 1999–; London Whip 2000–; *Select Committees:* Member: Transport Sub-Committee 1999–2000; Member: Environment, Transport and Regional Affairs 1997–, Environment Sub-Committee 1997–. *Special Interests:* Environment, Transport; France, Portugal, Russia. Member: Oxfam, Amnesty International, Greenpeace; *Recreations:* Sport, film, eating. *Address:* Tom Brake Esq, MP, House of Commons, London, SW1A 0AA *Tel:* 020 7219 6491 *Fax:* 020 7219 6491. *Constituency:* 6 Station Approach, Gordon Road, Carshalton, Surrey, SM5 3RF *Tel:* 020 8255 8155 *Fax:* 020 8395 4453 *E-mail:* cwlibs@cix.co.uk.

DR PETER BRAND   Isle of Wight   *LD majority 6,406*

Born 16 May 1947; Son of late Louis H. Brand and late Ans, née Fredericks; Educated Thornbury Grammar School; Birmingham University; Married 1972, Jane Vivienne Attlee (2 sons). Junior hospital posts, Kent and Dorset 1971–73; General practice 1973–76; Member, BMA: Former ARM Representative, Local Secretary, Local Chairman. County Councillor, Isle of Wight 1985–95; Councillor, Isle of Wight (Unitary Authority) 1995–97. **House of Commons:** Contested Isle of Wight 1992 general election. Member for Isle of Wight since May 1, 1997; Spokesman for: Health (Public Health, Health Promotion, Family and Ethical Issues, Voluntary and Independent Sector, PFI) 1997–99, Health (Public Health) 1999–2000, Health 2000–; *Select Committees:* Member: Health 1997–. *Special Interests:* Health, Social Services, Isle of Wight; Europe. Chairman, Islecare 1993–96; Governor, special needs schools; Patron: Medina Park Residents Association, IW Prosthetic Users Group, IW Gilten Market, Don Mills Variety Club, IW Group of Crohn's Disease and Ulcerative Colitis, ASCSA (Adult Survivors of Child Sexual Abuse); Member, Council of Europe –2000; Member, National Trust; MRCS; LRCP; DORCOG; MRCGP; *Clubs:* National Liberal; *Sportsclubs:* Five yachting/sailing clubs; *Recreations:* Boating, maintenance of an ancient house, food and wine. *Address:* Dr Peter Brand, MP, House of Commons, London, SW1A 0AA *Tel:* 020 7219 4404 *Fax:* 020 7219 2165. *Constituency:* 30 Quay Street, Newport, Isle of Wight, PO30 5BA *Tel:* 01983 524427 *Fax:* 01983 525819 *E-mail:* islandmp@cix.co.uk *Website:* http://www.the-commons.com/peter-brand.

JULIAN BRAZIER   Canterbury   *Con majority 3,964*

Born 24 July 1953; Son of Lieutenant Colonel Peter Hendy Brazier, retired, and Patricia Audrey Helen, née Stubbs; Educated Dragon School; Wellington College, Berks; Brasenose College, Oxford (Scholarship MA mathematics); London Business School; Married July 21, 1984, Katherine Elizabeth Blagden (3 sons). TA 1972–82, 1989–92; Charter Consolidated Ltd 1975–84, economic research 1975–77, corporate finance 1977–81 and Secretary, executive committee of the Board 1981–84; Management Consultant, H B Maynard International 1984–87. **House of Commons:** Contested Berwick-upon-Tweed 1983 general election. Member for Canterbury since June 1987; PPS to Gillian Shephard: as Minister of State, Treasury 1990–92; as Secretary of State for Employment 1992–93; *Select Committees:* Member: Defence 1997–. *Special Interests:* Defence, Economics, Law and Order, Family, Countryside; Middle East, South Africa, USA, Australia, Russia. President, Conservative Family Campaign. *Publications:* Co-author *Not Fit to Fight: The Cultural Subversion of the Armed Forces in Britain and America*, Social Affairs Unit 1999 Ten pamphlets on defence, social and economic issues (with Bow Group, Centre for Policy Studies and Conservative 2000); Highland Park/*The Spectator* Backbencher of the Year (jointly) 1996; Territorial Decoration 1993; *Recreations:* Cross-country running, science, philosophy. *Address:* Julian Brazier Esq, TD, MP, House of Commons, London, SW1A 0AA *Tel:* 020 7219 3000. *Constituency:* c/o 9 Hawks Lane, Canterbury, Kent *Tel:* 01227 65332 *Website:* www.julianbrazier.co.uk.

COLIN BREED   South East Cornwall   *LD majority 6,480*

Born 4 May 1947; Son of late Alfred and late Edith Violet Breed; Educated Torquay Boys Grammar School; Married July 6, 1968, Janet, daughter of Ronald and Leonora Courtiour (1 son 1 daughter). Manager, Midland Bank plc 1964–81; Managing director, Dartington and Co plc 1981–91; Director, Gemini Abrasives Ltd 1991–96. Councillor, Caradon District Council 1982–92; Mayor of Saltash 1989–90, 1995–96. **House of Commons:** Member for South East Cornwall since May 1, 1997; Spokesman for: Competition and Consumer Affairs 1997–99, Competition 1999; Principal Spokesman for Agriculture, Rural Affairs and Fisheries 1999–; *Select Committees:* Member: European Legislation 1998; Member: European Scrutiny 1998–. *Special Interests:* Cornwall. Member, General Medical Council 1999–; Executive Committee Member, Council for Advancement of Arab-British Understanding; Chair, Princes Trust Volunteers (Devon); ACIB; *Sportsclubs:* St Mellion Golf and Country Club; *Recreations:* Watching sport, golf. *Address:* Colin Breed Esq, MP, House of Commons, London, SW1A 0AA *Tel:* 020 7219 2588 *Fax:* 020 7219 5905. *Constituency:* Barras Street, Liskeard, Cornwall, PL14 6AD *Tel:* 01579 342150 *Fax:* 01579 347019 *E-mail:* colinbreedmp@compuserve.com.

HELEN BRINTON   Peterborough   *Lab majority 7,323*

Born 23 December 1954; Daughter of Phyllis May Dyche, ex infant headmistress, and George Henry Dyche, ex junior teacher; Educated Spondon Park Grammar, Derby; Bristol University (BA English literature, MA medieval literature, PGCE); Divorced (1 son 1 daughter). Assistant teacher of English, Katharine Lady Berkeley Comprehensive 1979–82; 2nd Department, Harrogate College 1983–88; Lecturer, North Thanet FIE College 1992–1993; Year Head, Rochester Grammar For Girls 1993–97; Student Rep, NUT 1978–79; Member: NUT 1979–, TGWU 1989–; School Rep, NUT 1994–97. **House of Commons:** Member for Peterborough since May 1, 1997; *Select Committees:* Member: Environmental Audit 1997–, Unopposed Bills (Panel) 1998–. *Special Interests:* Environment, Home Affairs, Health. Member: Fabian Society 1988–97, Co-op Party 1988–97; Has held many posts in Labour Party and Co-operative Party; Kent county election organiser 1993. Volunteer: ASBAH, MIND-NCVO Parliamentary Secondment Scheme, Parliamentary Police Scheme; Member, Standing Committees on: Crime and Disorder Bill 1997–98, Water Bill 1999, Finance Bill 1999, Financial Services and Markets Bill 1999, Countryside and Rights of Way Bill 2000; *Publications:* Articles in: *Co-op Members News, Tribune, Fabian News, New Statesman & Society, Progress, Labour Weekly* Green Government; *Recreations:* Reading, modern film. *Address:* Mrs Helen Brinton, MP, House of Commons, London, SW1A 0AA *Tel:* 020 7219 4469. *Constituency:* Unity Hall, Northfield Road, Peterborough *Tel:* 01733 347979 *Fax:* 01733 897500.

PETER BROOKE   Cities of London and Westminster   *Con majority 4,881*

Born 3 March 1934; Son of Baroness Brooke of Ystradfellte, DBE and late Lord Brooke of Cumnor, PC, CH; Educated Marlborough College; Balliol College, Oxford (MA mods and greats 1957); Harvard Business School (MBA 1959); Married 1st, Joan Margaret Smith (died 1985) (3 sons and 1 son deceased), married 2nd, January 25, 1991, Lindsay Allinson. Royal Engineers; Research Associate, IMEDE, Lausanne 1960–61; Swiss Correspondent, *Financial Times* 1960–61; Spencer Stuart Management Consultants 1961–79, served in: New York 1969–71, Brussels 1971–72, Chair 1974–79. **House of Commons:** Member for City of London and Westminster South 1977–97, and for Cities of London and Westminster since May 1, 1997; Government Whip 1979–83; Parliamentary Under-Secretary of State, Department of Education and Science 1983–85; HM Treasury: Minister of State 1985–87, Paymaster General 1987–89; Secretary of State for: Northern Ireland 1989–92, National Heritage 1992–94; *Select Committees:* Chairman: Northern Ireland Affairs 1997–; Member: Liaison 1998–. Chair, Conservative Party 1987–89. Council, London University 1995–;

President, British Antique Dealers Association 1995–; Trustee, Wordsworth Trust 1975–; Member, Drapers' Company; PC 1988; CH 1992; Commonwealth Fund Fellow, Harvard; Senior Fellow, Royal College of Art 1987; Presentation Fellow, King's College, London 1989; Honorary fellowship and doctorate; *Clubs:* Beefsteak, Brooks's, City Livery, MCC, St George's (Hanover Sq) Conservative; *Sportsclubs:* I Zingari, MCC; *Recreations:* Churches, conservation, cricket. *Address:* Rt Hon Peter Brooke, CH, MP, House of Commons, London, SW1A 0AA *Tel:* 020 7219 5041 *Fax:* 020 7219 0254 *Tel (Constituency):* 020 7730 8181 *Fax (Constituency):* 020 7730 4520.

GORDON BROWN   Dunfermline East   *Lab majority 18,751*

Born 20 February 1951; Son of late Rev. Dr John Brown; Educated Kirkcaldy High School; Edinburgh University (MA 1972, PhD 1982); Married August 3, 2000, Sarah Macaulay. Edinburgh University: Rector 1972–75, Temporary lecturer 1975–76; Lecturer in politics, Glasgow College of Technology 1976–80; Journalist, then editor, Scottish Television current affairs department 1980–83; Member, TGWU. **House of Commons:** Member for Dunfermline East since June, 1983; Opposition Front Bench Spokesman on Trade and Industry 1985–87; Shadow Spokesman for Trade and Industry 1989–92; Shadow Chief Secretary to The Treasury 1987–89; Shadow Chancellor of the Exchequer 1992–97; Chancellor of the Exchequer 1997–; *Special Interests:* Economic and Employment Policy, Health, Social Security, Scotland. Member, Scottish Executive Labour Party 1977–83; Chairman, Labour Party in Scotland 1983–84; Former Member, Labour Party National Executive Committee; Head, General Election Campaign (Strategy) 1999–. Joint Hon Treasurer (ex-officio), Commonwealth Parliamentary Association (CPA) UK Branch 1997–99, Joint Hon Secretary 1999–; *Publications:* Co-editor *Values, Visions and Voices: An Anthology of Socialism*; Co-author *John Smith: Life and Soul of the Party*; *Maxton*; *Where There is Greed*; PC 1996; *The Spectator*/Highland Park Parliamentarian of the Year 1997; Channel 4 and *The House* Magazine Speechmaker of the Year 1999; *Recreations:* Tennis, football, reading, writing. *Address:* Rt Hon Gordon Brown, MP, House of Commons, London, SW1A 0AA *Tel:* 020 7270 3000. *Constituency:* 318–324 High Street, Cowdenbeath, Fife, KY4 9QS *Tel:* 01383 611702 *Fax:* 01383 611703.

NICK BROWN   Newcastle upon Tyne East and Wallsend   *Lab majority 23,811*

Born 13 June 1950; Educated Tunbridge Wells Technical High School; Manchester University (BA 1971). Proctor and Gamble advertising department; Legal adviser for northern region of GMBATU 1978–83. Councillor, Newcastle upon Tyne City Council 1980–83. **House of Commons:** Member for Newcastle upon Tyne East 1983–97, and for Newcastle upon Tyne East and Wallsend since May 1, 1997; Opposition Front Bench Spokesman on: Legal Affairs 1985–92, Treasury and Economic Affairs 1988–94; Opposition Spokesman on Health 1994–95; Opposition Deputy Chief Whip 1995–97; Government Chief Whip (Parliamentary Secretary, HM Treasury) 1997–98; Deputy to Margaret Beckett as Shadow Leader of the Commons 1992–94; Minister of Agriculture, Fisheries and Food 1998–; *Select Committees:* Member: Broadcasting 1994–95, Selection 1996–97. *Special Interests:* Australia, China, Japan, New Zealand, USA. PC 1997. *Address:* Rt Hon Nicholas Brown, MP, House of Commons, London, SW1A 0AA *Tel:* 020 7219 3000.

RUSSELL BROWN   Dumfries   *Lab majority 9,643*

Born 17 September 1951; Son of late Howard Russell Brown and Muriel Brown; Educated Annan Academy; Married March 3, 1973, Christine Calvert (2 daughters). production supervisor ICI 1974–97; Member, TGWU 1974–: Branch Secretary and Branch Chair 1979–85. Councillor: Dumfries and Galloway Regional Council 1986–96, Annandale and Eskdale District Council 1988–96, Dumfries and Galloway Unitary Council 1995–97; Member, Dumfries and Galloway Tourist Board 1996–97. **House of Commons:** Member for Dumfries since May 1, 1997; *Select Committees:* Member: European Legislation 1997–98, European Legislation 1997–98, European Scrutiny 1998–99; Member: Deregulation 1999–, Scottish Affairs 1999–.

Special Interests: Employment Legislation, Welfare State; European Union. Chair, Local Community Education Project 1991–97; *Recreations:* Sport. *Address:* Russell Brown Esq, MP, House of Commons, London, SW1A 0AA *Tel:* 020 7219 4429 *Fax:* 020 7219 0922. *Constituency:* Loreburn Chambers, 11 Great King Street, Dumfries, DG1 1BA *Tel:* 01387 247902 *Fax:* 01387 247903 *E-mail:* russell@brownmp.new.labour.org.uk.

DESMOND BROWNE   Kilmarnock and Loudoun   Lab majority 7,256

Born 22 March 1952; Son of late Peter Browne, process worker, and of Maureen Browne, catering manageress; Educated Saint Michael's Academy, Kilwinning; Glasgow University (LLB); Married July 7, 1983, Maura Taylor (2 sons). Qualified as Solicitor 1976; Called to Scottish Bar 1993. **House of Commons:** Contested Argyll and Bute 1992 general election. Member for Kilmarnock and Loudoun since May 1, 1997; PPS to Donald Dewar as Secretary of State for Scotland 1998–99, to Adam Ingram as Minister of State, Northern Ireland Office 2000–; *Select Committees:* Member: Northern Ireland Affairs 1997–98, Public Administration 1999–2000. *Special Interests:* Legal Affairs, Human Rights, Disabled/Disability, Education, Northern Ireland, Constitutional Affairs, International Affairs; France, South Africa, Colombia. Secretary, Scottish Labour Party Working Party on Prison System 1988–. Council Member, Law Society of Scotland 1988–91; Member, Scottish Council For Civil Liberties 1976–; Chair: Children's Rights Group 1981–86, Scottish Child Law Centre 1988–; *Publications:* Briefing Paper for MPs on Criminal Justice (Scotland) Bill 1980; Report for Lord MacAulay's Working Party on the Prison System 1990; *Recreations:* Hill-walking, football, swimming, reading, computing. *Address:* Desmond Browne Esq, MP, House of Commons, London, SW1A 0AA *Tel:* 020 7219 4501 *Fax:* 020 7219 2423. *Constituency:* 24 Portland Road, Kilmarnock, KA1 2BS *Tel:* 01563 539439 *Fax:* 01563 572815 *E-mail:* browned@parliament.uk.

ANGELA BROWNING   Tiverton and Honiton   Con majority 1,653

Born 4 December 1946; Daughter of late Thomas and of Linda Pearson; Educated Reading College of Technology; Bournemouth College of Technology; Married January 6, 1968, David Browning (2 sons). Teacher home economics, Adult Education 1968–74; Auxiliary nurse 1976–77; Self-employed consultant, manufacturing industry 1977–85; Management consultant specialising in training, corporate communications and finance 1985–94; Director, Small Business Bureau 1985–94; Chairman, Women Into Business 1988–92; Member, Department of Employment Advisory Committee for Women's Employment 1989–92. **House of Commons:** Contested Crewe and Nantwich 1987 general election. Member for Tiverton 1992–97, and for Tiverton and Honiton since May 1, 1997; Opposition Spokeswoman on Education and Employment (Education and Disability) 1997–98; PPS to Michael Forsyth as Minister of State, Department of Employment 1993–94; Parliamentary Secretary, Ministry of Agriculture, Fisheries and Food 1994–97; Member, Shadow Cabinet 1999–; Shadow Secretary of State for Trade and Industry 1999–2000; Shadow Leader of the House 2000–; *Select Committees:* Member: Agriculture 1992–93. *Special Interests:* Small Businesses, Education (Special Needs), Mental Health, Learning Disabilities. Has held various offices in Conservative Party in Devon. Member, National Autistic Society, Special Councillor 1993–; National Vice-President, Alzheimers Disease Society 1997–; Co-Chair, The Women's National Commission 1995–97; Vice-President, Institute of Sales and Marketing Management 1997–; Fellow, Institute of Sales and Marketing Management; *Recreations:* Theatre, supporting family of keen oarsmen, member of Thomas Hardy Society. *Address:* Mrs Angela Browning, MP, House of Commons, London, SW1A 0AA *Tel:* 020 7219 3000 *Tel (Constituency):* 01404 822103 *Website:* http://www.abrowning.demon.co.uk.

Visit the Vacher Dod Website . . .
www.politicallinks.co.uk

IAN BRUCE   South Dorset   *Con majority 77*

Born 14 March 1947; Son of late Henry Bruce, factory manager, and Ellen Flora, née Bingham, retired building society clerk; Educated Chelmsford Technical High School; Bradford University (electronics); Mid-Essex Technical College (HNC electronics); Married September 6, 1969, Hazel, daughter of late Edward Sidney and Kathleen Marjorie Roberts (1 son 3 daughters). Marconi: Student apprentice 1965–68, Work study engineer 1968–69; Method study engineer, Pye Unicam, 1969–70; Work study officer, J. Sainsbury, 1970–72; BEPI (part of Pye Group): Work study manager 1972–73, Production manager 1970–74; Sinclair: Product manager 1973–75, Works manager 1975, Sales manager 1975; Owner, employment agency and consultancy group 1975–; contested Yorkshire West 1984 European Parliament election. **House of Commons:** Contested Burnley 1983 general election. Member for South Dorset since June 1987; PPS to Parliamentary Under-Secretaries of State, Department of Social Security 1993–94; *Select Committees:* Member: Employment 1990–92, Science and Technology 1995–97; Member: Information 1997–. *Special Interests:* Employment, Energy, Defence, Information Technology, Tourism, Trade and Industry; Bahamas, Canada, Europe, Guatemala, Indonesia, USA, Zambia, Finland, Nepal, Cayman Islands, former USSR and Eastern Bloc. President, Conservative Technology Forum 1997–. Member, Institute of Management Services; Chair, EURIM; Vice-Chair, European Infomatics Market Group 1994–2000; Chair, 2000–; *Sportsclubs:* Weymouth Boardsailing Club, House of Commons Yacht Club; *Recreations:* Badminton, camping, writing, sailing, gardening, scouting, squash, wind surfing. *Address:* Ian Bruce Esq, MP, House of Commons, London, SW1A 0AA *Tel:* 020 7219 5086 *Fax:* 020 7219 6151 *Tel (Constituency):* 01305 833320 *Fax (Constituency):* 01305 833320 *E-mail:* brucei@parliament.uk.

MALCOLM BRUCE   Gordon   *LD majority 6,997*

Born 17 November 1944; Son of David Bruce, former agricultural merchant and hotelier, retired; Educated Wrekin College; St Andrews University; Strathclyde University (MA economics and political science, MSc marketing); CPE and Inns of Court School of Law; Married 1st, September 13, 1969, Jane Wilson (marriage dissolved 1992) (1 son 1 daughter); married 2nd, May 23, 1998, Rosemary Vetterlein (1 daughter). Trainee journalist, Liverpool Post 1966–67; Boots section buyer 1968–69; Research and information officer, NE Scotland Development Authority 1971–75; Director, Noroil Publishing House (UK) Ltd. 1975–81; Joint editor/publisher, Aberdeen Petroleum Publishing 1981–84; Member, NUJ. **House of Commons:** Contested Angus North and Mearns October 1974, Aberdeenshire West 1979 general elections. Member for Gordon since June 1983; Liberal Spokesman for Energy 1985–87; Scottish Liberal Spokesman for Education 1986–87; Alliance Spokesman for Employment 1987; Liberal Spokesman for Trade and Industry 1987–88; SLD Spokesman for Natural Resources (energy and conservation) 1988–89; Liberal Democrat Spokesman for: The Environment and Natural Resources 1989–90, Scottish Affairs 1990–92, Trade and Industry 1992–94, The Treasury 1994–99; Chair, Liberal Democrat Parliamentary Party 1999–; *Select Committees:* Member: Scottish Affairs 1990–92, Trade and Industry 1992–94, Treasury and Civil Service 1994–97, Treasury 1997–99; Member: Standards and Privileges 1999–. *Special Interests:* Energy, Gas Industry, Oil Industry, Industrial Policy, Trade Policy, Deaf Children, Scottish Home Rule and Federalism. Leader: Scottish Social and Liberal Democrats 1988–89, Liberal Democrats 1989–92. Vice-President, National Deaf Children's Society, President, Grampian Branch; Rector, Dundee University 1986–89; Vice-President, Federation of Economic Development Authorities (FEDA); Member, UK Delegation Parliamentary Assembly of the Council of Europe/Western European Union 2000–; *Recreations:* Golf, cycling, walking, theatre and music. *Address:* Malcolm Bruce Esq, MP, House of Commons, London, SW1A 0AA *Tel:* 020 7219 6233 *Fax:* 020 7219 2334. *Constituency:* 17b North Street, Inverurie, Aberdeenshire, AB51 4RJ *Tel:* 01467 623413 *Fax:* 01467 624994 *E-mail:* gordonlibdems@cix.co.uk.

KAREN BUCK   Regent's Park and Kensington North   *Lab majority 14,657*

Born 30 August 1958; Educated Chelmsford High School; LSE (BSc Econ, MSc Econ, MA social policy and administration); Partner, Barrie Taylor (1 son). Research and development worker, Outset (charity specialising in employment for disabled people) 1979–83; London Borough of Hackney: specialist officer developing services/employment for disabled people 1983–86, public health officer 1986–87; Labour Party Policy Directorate (Health) 1987–92; Labour Party Campaign Strategy Co-ordinator 1992–99; Former Member: ASTMS, NALGO; Member, TGWU. Councillor, Westminster City Council 1990–97; Member: Health Authority (late 1980s), Urban Regeneration Board. **House of Commons:** Member for Regent's Park and Kensington North since May 1, 1997; *Select Committees:* Member: Social Security 1997–, Selection 1999–. *Special Interests:* Housing, Urban Regeneration, Health Care, Welfare, Children. Chair, Constituency Labour Party; Chair, London Regional Group of Labour MPs 1999–. Member, Queen's Park Single Regeneration Budget Board; *Recreations:* Music: rock, soul, jazz, opera. *Address:* Karen Buck, MP, House of Commons, London, SW1A 0AA *Tel:* 020 7219 3533 *Tel (Constituency):* 020 8968 7999 *Fax (Constituency):* 020 8960 0150.

RICHARD BURDEN   Birmingham Northfield   *Lab majority 11,443*

Born 1 September 1954; Son of Kenneth Rodney Burden, engineer, and of late Pauline Burden, secretary; Educated Wallasey Technical Grammar School; Bramhall Comprehensive School; St John's College of Further Education, Manchester; York University (BA politics 1978); Warwick University (MA industrial relations 1979); Partner, Jane Slowey. President, York University Students' Union 1976–77; NALGO: Branch Organiser, North Yorkshire 1979–81, West Midlands District Officer 1981–92; Member, TGWU 1979–; Sponsored by TGWU 1989–96. **House of Commons:** Contested Meriden 1987 general election. Member for Birmingham Northfield since April 9, 1992; PPS to Jeffrey Rooker: as Minister of State and Deputy Minister, Ministry of Agriculture, Fisheries and Food (Minister for Food Safety) 1997–99, as Minister of State, Department of Social Security (Minister for Pensions) 1999–; *Special Interests:* Motor Industry, Water Industry, Middle East, Poverty, Health, Employment Rights and Protection, Constitution, Electoral Reform; Europe, Middle East. Founder member, Bedale Labour Party 1980; Member, Labour Middle East Council, Vice-Chair 1994–95; Member, Co-operative Party; Chair, Labour Campaign for Electoral Reform 1996–98, Vice-Chair 1998–; Member, Fabian Society. Member: CND, SERA; Co-chair, Parliamentary Advisory Council on Transport Safety (PACTS) 1995–98; Director, Northfield Community Development Association; Founded Joint Action for Water Services (Jaws) 1985 to oppose water privatisation, Secretary 1985–90; *Publications: Tap Dancing – Water, The Environment and Privatisation,* 1988; *Clubs:* Kingshurst Labour, Austin Sports and Social, Austin Branch British Legion; *Sportsclubs:* 750 Motor, Historic Sports Car Club; *Recreations:* Cinema, motor racing. *Address:* Richard Burden Esq, MP, House of Commons, London, SW1A 0AA *Tel:* 020 7219 3000 *Fax:* 020 7219 2170 *Tel (Constituency):* 0121–475 9295 *Fax (Constituency):* 0121–476 2400 *E-mail:* burdenr@parliament.uk.

COLIN BURGON   Elmet   *Lab majority 8,779*

Born 22 April 1948; Son of Thomas Burgon, tailoring worker, and Winifred Burgon, school secretary; Educated St Charles School, Leeds; St Michael's College, Leeds; City of Leeds and Carnegie College; Divorced (1 daughter). Teacher; Local government policy and research officer. **House of Commons:** Contested Elmet 1987 and 1992 general elections. Member for Elmet since May 1, 1997; *Select Committees:* Member: Joint Committee on Statutory Instruments 1997–99; Member: Accommodation and Works 1999–, Procedure 1999–, Northern Ireland Affairs 2000–. *Special Interests:* Youth Affairs, Planning Policy; USA, France, Italy, Spain. Former Secretary, Elmet Constituency Labour Party; Former Chair, Leeds Euro Constituency Labour Party. Member: Amnesty International, Friends of the Earth; Member, CPRE; *Recreations:* Football (Leeds United), walking, the countryside, history (military and American Civil War). *Address:* Colin Burgon Esq, MP, House of Commons, London, SW1A 0AA *Tel:* 020 7219 6487 *Tel (Constituency):* 0113–287 5198 *Fax (Constituency):* 0113–287 5958.

JOHN BURNETT   Torridge and West Devon   LD majority 1,957

Born 19 September 1945; Son of late Lt-Col Aubone Burnett, OBE, and Joan Burnett (née Bolt); Educated Ampleforth College; Royal Marines Commando Training Centre; Britannia Royal Naval College, Dartmouth; College of Law, London; Married October 9, 1971, Elizabeth Sherwood, née de la Mare (2 sons 2 daughters). Royal Marines 1964–70: Troop Commander, 42 Commando in Borneo and Singapore, Troop Commander and Company Second-in-Command, 40 Commando in Far East and Middle East; Member, NFU. **House of Commons:** Contested Torridge and West Devon 1987 general election. Member for Torridge and West Devon since May 1, 1997; Spokesman for Home and Legal Affairs: (Legal Affairs) 1997–, (Legal Affairs and Attorney General, Solicitor General, Lord Chancellor) 1999; *Special Interests:* Economic Policy, Defence, Agriculture. Member: Law Society, Devon and Exeter Law Society, Law Society's Revenue (Tax) Law Committee 1984–96, Council of Devon Cattle Breeders' Association, Royal Marine Association, Royal British Legion; *Recreations:* Breeding Devon cattle, walking, sport. *Address:* John Burnett Esq, MP, House of Commons, London, SW1A 0AA *Tel:* 020 7219 5132. *Constituency:* Liberal Democrats, 21–25 St James Street, Okehampton, Devon, EX20 1DH *Tel:* 01837 55881 *Fax:* 01837 55694.

SIMON BURNS   Chelmsford West   Con majority 6,691

Born 6 September 1952; Son of late Major B. S. Burns MC and Mrs Anthony Nash; Educated Christ the King School, Accra; Stamford School; Worcester College, Oxford (BA 1975 history); Married September 22, 1982, Emma Clifford (1 son 1 daughter) (divorced). Assistant to Sally Oppenheim, MP 1975–81; Director and company secretary, What to Buy for Business Ltd 1981–83; Conference organiser, Institute of Directors 1983–87. **House of Commons:** Contested Alyn and Deeside 1983 general election. Member for Chelmsford 1987–97, and for Chelmsford West since May 1, 1997; Opposition Front Bench Spokesman for: Social Security 1997-August 1998, Environment, Transport and the Regions (Planning, Housing and Construction) August 1998–99; Assistant Government Whip 1994–95; Government Whip 1995–96; PPS: to Timothy Eggar as Minister of State: at Department of Employment 1989–90, at Department of Education and Science 1990–92, at Department of Trade and Industry 1992–93; to Gillian Shephard as Minister of Agriculture, Fisheries and Food 1993–94; Parliamentary Under-Secretary of State, Department of Health 1996–97; *Select Committees:* Member: Health 1999–. *Special Interests:* Employment, Foreign Affairs; USA. President, Chelmsford Osteoporosis Society; Executive Member, 1922 Committee 1999, Treasurer 1999–; *Clubs:* Essex; *Recreations:* Photography, American politics, reading. *Address:* Simon Burns Esq, MP, House of Commons, London, SW1A 0AA *Tel:* 020 7219 4052. *Constituency:* 88 Rectory Lane, Chelmsford, CH2 0AA *Tel:* 01245 352872.

PAUL BURSTOW   Sutton and Cheam   LD majority 2,097

Born 13 May 1962; Son of Brian Burstow, tailor, and Sheila Burstow; Educated Glastonbury High School For Boys; Carshalton College of Further Education; South Bank Polytechnic (BA business studies); Married Mary Kemm. Political Secretary, Association of Liberal Democrat Councillors 1996–97. Councillor, London Borough of Sutton 1986–, Chair, Environment Services 1988–96, Deputy Leader 1994–99. **House of Commons:** Contested Sutton and Cheam 1992 general election. Member for Sutton and Cheam since May 1, 1997; Spokesman for: Disabled People 1997–98, Local Government (Social Services and Community Care) 1997–99, Local Government (Team Leader) 1997–99, Older People 1999–; *Special Interests:* Environment, Disabled/Disability, Community Safety, Ageing. Former Member: SDP/Liberal Alliance, London Regional Liberal Democrat Executive; Member, Federal Policy Committee 1988–90. *Clubs:* National Liberal; *Recreations:* Cooking, reading, cycling, walking, keeping fit. *Address:* Paul Burstow Esq, MP, House of Commons, London, SW1A 0AA *Tel:* 020 7219 1196. *Constituency:* 312–314 High Street, Sutton, Surrey, SM1 1PR *Tel:* 020 8288 6555 *Fax:* 020 8288 6550 *Website:* www.burstowmp.org.uk.

CHRISTINE BUTLER Castle Point — *Lab majority 1,116*

Born 14 December 1943; Daughter of late Cecil and Gertrude Smith; Educated Nelson Grammar School; Middlesex Polytechnic (BA); Married 1964, Robert Butler (3 sons). Pharmaceutical Industry; NHS; Visual arts; Member, MSF. Former County Councillor; Former Chair, Essex Co-operative Development Agency. **House of Commons:** Member for Castle Point since May 1, 1997; *Select Committees:* Member: Environment, Transport and Regional Affairs 1997–, Environment Sub-Committee 1997–. *Special Interests:* Local Government, Environment, Employment, Education. Member: Co-operative Party, Fabian Society, SERA. Former School Governor; *Recreations:* Walking, music, art. *Address:* Christine Butler, MP, House of Commons, London, SW1A 0AA *Tel:* 020 7219 6955. *Constituency:* Labour Hall, Lionel Road, Canvey Island, Essex *Tel:* 01268 684722.

JOHN BUTTERFILL Bournemouth West — *Con majority 5,710*

Born 14 February 1941; Son of late George Thomas, Lloyd's broker, and late Elsie Amelia Butterfill (née Watts), Bank of England executive; Educated Caterham School; College of Estate Management (London); Married October 2, 1965, Pamela Ross (1 son 3 daughters). Valuer, Jones Lang Wootton 1962–64; Senior Executive, Hammerson Group 1964–69; Director, Audley Properties Ltd (Bovis Group) 1969–71; Managing Director, St Paul's Securities Group 1971–76; Senior Partner, Curchod & Co. Chartered Surveyors 1977–92; President, European Property Associates 1977–; Director: ISLEF Building and Construction Ltd 1985–91, Pavilion Services Group 1992–94. **House of Commons:** Contested Croydon North West by-election 1981. Member for Bournemouth West since June 1983; PPS: to Cecil Parkinson: as Secretary of State for Energy 1988–89, as Secretary of State for Transport 1989–90, to Dr Brian Mawhinney as Minister of State, Northern Ireland Office 1991–92; *Select Committees:* Member: Trade and Industry 1992–97; Member: Chairmen's Panel 1997–, Court of Referees 1997–, Trade and Industry 1997–, Unopposed Bills (Panel) 1997–. *Special Interests:* Trade and Industry, Tourism, Foreign Affairs, Environment, Housing, Health; France, Germany, Scandinavia, Israel. Chair: Conservative Group for Europe 1989–92, Conservative Party Rules Committee 1997–; Vice-Chair, 1922 Committee 1997–; Member, Conservative Party Constitutional Committee 1998–; Vice-Chair, Conservative Friends of Israel. Member, Council of Management PDSA 1990–; Founder Chairman, Guildford/Freiburg Town Twinning Association; Joint Vice-Chairman, 1922 Committee 1997–; Fellow, Royal Institution of Chartered Surveyors 1974; *Clubs:* Carlton; *Recreations:* Skiing, tennis, riding, bridge, music. *Address:* John Butterfill Esq, MP, House of Commons, London, SW1A 0AA *Tel:* 020 7219 6383. *Constituency:* 135 Hankinson Road, Bournemouth, Dorset, BH9 1HR *Tel:* 01202 776607 *Fax:* 01202 521481.

STEPHEN BYERS North Tyneside — *Lab majority 26,643*

Born 13 April 1953; Son of late Robert Byers, chief technician, RAF; Educated Chester City Grammar School; Chester College of Further Education; Liverpool Polytechnic (LLB). Senior lecturer in law, Newcastle Polytechnic 1977–92. North Tyneside Council: Councillor 1980–92, Chair, Education Committee 1982–85, Deputy Leader of the Council 1985–92. **House of Commons:** Contested Hexham 1983 general election. Member for Wallsend 1992–97, and for North Tyneside since May 1, 1997; Opposition Spokesman on Education and Employment 1995–97; Opposition Whip 1994–95; Minister of State, Department for Education and Employment (Minister for School Standards) 1997–98; Chief Secretary, HM Treasury July-December 1998; Secretary of State for Trade and Industry December 1998–; *Select Committees:* Member: Home Affairs 1993–94. *Special Interests:* Education, Treasury, Home Affairs, Trade and Industry, Local Government. Member, Business and Technician Education Council 1985–89; Chair, Association of Metropolitan Authorities Education Committee 1990–92; Leader, Council of Local Education Authorities 1990–92; Chair, National Employers' Organisation for Teachers 1990–92; PC 1998; Fellow, Royal Society of Arts; *Recreations:* Cinema, travel, theatre, walking. *Address:* Rt Hon Stephen Byers, MP, House of Commons, London, SW1A 0AA *Tel:* 020 7219 4085. *Constituency:* 7 Palmersville, Great Lime Road, Forest Hall, Newcastle upon Tyne, NE12 9HW *Tel:* 0191–268 9111 *Fax:* 0191–268 9777 *E-mail:* tlo.byers@tlo.dti.gov.uk.

C

DR VINCENT CABLE   Twickenham   *LD majority 4,281*

Born 9 May 1943; Son of late Leonard Cable and of Edith Cable; Educated Nunthorpe Grammar School, York; Fitzwilliam College, Cambridge (President of Union) (BA natural science and economics 1966); Glasgow University (PhD international economics 1973); Married July 21, 1968, Dr Olympia Rebelo (2 sons 1 daughter). Finance officer, Kenya Treasury 1966–68; Economics lecturer, Glasgow University 1968–74; Diplomatic Service 1974–76; Adviser to World Commission on Environment and Development (Brundtland Commission) 1975–77; Deputy Director, Overseas Development Institute 1976–83; Special Adviser to John Smith as Secretary of State for Trade 1979; Special Adviser, Commonwealth Secretariat 1983–90; Group Planning, Shell 1990–95; Head, Economics Programme, Chatham House 1993–95; Chief Economist, Shell International 1995–97. Councillor (Labour), Glasgow City Council 1971–74. **House of Commons:** Contested Glasgow Hillhead (Labour) 1970, York (SDP/Alliance) 1983 and 1987, Twickenham (Liberal Democrat) 1992 general elections. Member for Twickenham since May 1, 1997; A Spokesman for the Treasury (EMU and The City) 1997–99; Principal Spokesman for Trade and Industry 1999–; *Select Committees:* Member: Treasury 1998–99, Treasury Sub-Committee 1998–99. *Special Interests:* European Union, Trade and Industry, Economic Policy, Foreign Affairs, Energy, Environment; India, Russia, China, Nigeria, Kenya; Member, European Standing Committee B 1998–2000. Member: HACAN (Aircraft Noise), Hospital Alert, Charter 88; *Publications:* Wide variety of books and pamphlets including: *Protectionism and Industrial Decline*, 1983, *Globalisation and Global Governance*, 1999; Journalism for the *Independent*; Visiting fellow, Nuffield College, Oxford; Special professor of economics, Nottingham University 1999; Research fellow, international economics, Royal Institute of International Affairs; *Clubs:* Lensbury (Shell); *Recreations:* Ballroom and Latin dancing, classical music, cinema, walking. *Address:* Dr Vincent Cable, MP, House of Commons, London, SW1A 0AA *Tel:* 020 7219 1106 *Fax:* 020 7219 1191. *Constituency:* 164c Heath Road, Twickenham, TW1 4BN *Tel:* 020 8892 0215 *Fax:* 020 8892 0218 *E-mail:* vincentcable@cix.co.uk.

RICHARD CABORN   Sheffield Central   *Lab majority 16,906*

Born 6 October 1943; Son of late George Caborn; Educated Hurlfield Comprehensive School; Granville College; Sheffield Polytechnic (engineering); Married May 21, 1966, Margaret Hayes (1 son 1 daughter). Skilled engineer 1964–1979; MEP for Sheffield District 1979–84; Convenor of shop stewards AEEU. **House of Commons:** Member for Sheffield Central since June, 1983; Opposition Spokesperson on: Trade and Industry 1988–90, with special responsibility for Regional Policy 1990–92, National Competitiveness and Regulation 1995–97; Minister of State: Department of the Environment, Transport and the Regions (Minister for the Regions, Regeneration and Planning) 1997–99, Department of Trade and Industry (Minister for Trade) 1999–; *Select Committees:* Member: Liaison 1992–95; Chairman: Trade and Industry 1992–95. *Special Interests:* European Union, Trade Unions, Steel Industry; South Africa. Chair, Sheffield District Labour Party, served on Education Committee. Vice-President, Sheffield Trades Council 1968–79; Member, BBC Advisory Council 1975–78; Joint Chair, British Trade International Board 2000–; Chair, European Parliament British Labour Party Group 1979–84; PC 1999; *Recreations:* Golf. *Address:* Rt Hon Richard Caborn, MP, House of Commons, London, SW1A 0AA *Tel:* 020 7219 4211/6259 *Fax:* 020 7219 4866. *Constituency:* 2nd Floor, Barkers Pool House, Burgess Street, Sheffield, S1 2HF *Tel:* 0114–273 7947 *Fax:* 0114–275 3944 *E-mail:* tlo.caborn@tlo.dti.gov.uk.

Visit the Vacher Dod Website . . .

www.politicallinks.co.uk

ALAN CAMPBELL   Tynemouth   *Lab majority 11,273*

Born 8 July 1957; Educated Blackfyne Secondary School, Consett; Lancaster University (BA politics); Leeds University (PGCE); Newcastle Polytechnic (MA history); Married Jayne Lamont (1 son 1 daughter). Whitley Bay High School 1980–89; Hirst High School, Ashington, Northumberland: Teacher 1989–97, Head of Sixth Form, Head of Department; Member, NAS/UWT. **House of Commons:** Member for Tynemouth since May 1, 1997; *Select Committees:* Member: Public Accounts 1997–. *Special Interests:* Education, Constitutional Reform. Branch Secretary, Chair, Agent; Tynemouth Constituency Labour Party: Secretary, Campaign Co-ordinator; Hon. Secretary and Hon. Treasurer, Northern Group of Labour MPs 1999–. *Recreations:* Family. *Address:* Alan Campbell Esq, MP, House of Commons, London, SW1A 0AA *Tel:* 020 7219 6619. *Constituency:* 99 Howard Street, North Shields, Tyne and Wear, NE30 2NA *Tel:* 0191-257 1927 *Fax:* 0191-257 6537 *E-mail:* alan-campbellmp@office-mail.co.uk.

ANNE CAMPBELL   Cambridge   *Lab majority 14,137*

Born 6 April 1940; Daughter of late Frank Lucas, NHS clerical worker, and late Susan Lucas; Educated Penistone Grammar School; Newnham College, Cambridge (MA mathematics 1962); Married August 10, 1963, Dr Archie Campbell (1 son 2 daughters). Assistant Maths teacher: Herts and Essex High School, Bishops Stortford 1962–64, Girls' Grammar School, Cambridge 1964–65; Various part-time teaching posts 1965–70; Lecturer, then senior lecturer in statistics, Cambridgeshire College of Arts and Technology 1970–83; Head, Statistics and Data Processing, National Institute of Agricultural Botany, Cambridge 1983–92; Member, MSF. Councillor, Cambridgeshire County Council 1985–89. **House of Commons:** Member for Cambridge since April 9, 1992; PPS: to Ministers of State, Department of Trade and Industry: John Battle 1997–99, to Patricia Hewitt (Minister for Small Business and E-Commerce) 1999–; *Select Committees:* Member: Science and Technology 1992–97. *Special Interests:* Education, Science Policy, Environment. Chair: South and East Group of Labour MPs 1997–99, Eastern Regional Group of Labour MPs 1999. Member, Greenpeace; Vice-Chair, Parliamentary Office of Science and Technology 1994–98; *Publications: Calculations for Commercial Students,* 1972; Fellow: Institute of Statisticians 1987, Royal Statistical Society 1987, Royal Society of Arts 1992; *Recreations:* Gardening, tennis, mountain walking, skiing. *Address:* Mrs Anne Campbell, MP, House of Commons, London, SW1A 0AA *Tel:* 020 7219 5089 *Fax:* 020 7219 2264. *Constituency:* Alex Wood Hall, Norfolk Street, Cambridge, CB1 2LD *Tel:* 01223 506500 *Fax:* 01223 311315 *E-mail:* anne.campbell.mp@dial.pipex.com.

MENZIES CAMPBELL   North East Fife   *LD majority 10,356*

Born 22 May 1941; Son of late George and Elizabeth Campbell; Educated Hillhead High School, Glasgow; Glasgow University (MA 1962, LLB 1965); Stanford University, California; Married June 13, 1970, Elspeth Mary, daughter of Major General R. E. Urquhart, CB, DSO. Called to the Bar (Scotland) 1968; QC (Scotland) 1982; Competed: 1964 (Tokyo) Olympics, 1966 Commonwealth Games (Jamaica); UK Athletics Team Captain 1965–66; UK 100 metres record holder 1967–74; Chair, Royal Lyceum Theatre Company, Edinburgh 1984–87. **House of Commons:** Contested Greenock and Port Glasgow February and October 1974, East Fife 1979, North East Fife 1983 general elections. Member for North East Fife since June 1987; Liberal Spokesman for Arts, Broadcasting and Sport 1987–88; SLD Spokesman for Defence, Sport 1988–89; Liberal Democrat Spokesman for: Defence and Disarmament, Sport 1989–94, Foreign Affairs and Defence, Sport 1994–97, Foreign Affairs (Defence and Europe) 1997–99, Scotland (Legal Affairs, Lord Advocate) 1998–99; Principal Spokesman for Foreign Affairs and Defence 1999–; *Select Committees:* Member: Trade and Industry 1990–92, Defence 1992–97, Defence 1997–99. *Special Interests:* Defence, Foreign

Affairs, Legal Affairs, Sport, Arts; Middle East, North America. Chair, Scottish Liberal Party 1975–77. Member, Board of the British Council 1998–; Member: North Atlantic Assembly 1989–, UK Delegation, Parliamentary Assembly of OSCE 1992–97, 1999–; CBE 1987; PC 1999; Highland Park/*The Spectator* Member to Watch 1996; *Clubs:* Reform; *Recreations:* All sports, theatre, music. *Address:* Rt Hon Menzies Campbell, CBE, QC, MP, House of Commons, London, SW1A 0AA *Tel:* 020 7219 4446 *Fax:* 020 7219 0559. *Constituency:* 16 Millbank, Cupar, Fife *Tel:* 01334 656361 *Fax:* 01334 654045 *E-mail:* nefifelibdem@cix.co.uk.

RONNIE CAMPBELL   Blyth Valley   Lab majority 17,736

Born 14 August 1943; Son of Ronnie and Edna Campbell; Educated Ridley High School, Blyth; Married June 17, 1967, Deidre McHale (5 sons (2 twins) 1 daughter). Miner 1958–86; NUM Lodge Secretary, Bates Colliery, Blyth 1982–86; NUM Sponsored MP. Councillor: Blyth Borough Council 1969–74, Blyth Valley Council 1974–88. **House of Commons:** Member for Blyth Valley since June 1987; *Select Committees:* Member: Parliamentary Commissioner for Administration 1987–97; Member: Public Administration 1997–. Chair, Northern Regional Group of Labour MPs 1999–. *Recreations:* Furniture restoration, stamp collecting, antiques. *Address:* Ronnie Campbell Esq, MP, House of Commons, London, SW1A 0AA *Tel:* 020 7219 4216 *Fax:* 020 7219 4358. *Constituency:* 42 Renwick Road, Blyth, Northumberland, NE24 2LQ *Tel:* 01670 363050 *Fax:* 01670 363050 *E-mail:* ronnie@campbellmp.abelgratis.com.

DALE CAMPBELL-SAVOURS   Workington   Lab majority 19,656

Born 23 August 1943; Son of late John Lawrence; Educated Keswick School; The Sorbonne, Paris; Married 1970, Gudrun Kristin Runolfsdottir (3 sons). Former Company director; Member: Transport & General Workers Union, UNISON Trade Union. Councillor, Ramsbottom Urban District Council 1972–74. **House of Commons:** Contested Darwen February and October 1974 general elections, Workington 1976 by-election. Member for Workington since May 1979; Opposition Spokesman on Development and Co-operation 1991–92; Opposition Front Bench Spokesman on Food, Agriculture and Rural Affairs 1992–94; *Select Committees:* Member: Agriculture 1994–96, Standards and Privileges 1995–97; Member: Standards and Privileges 1997–. *Special Interests:* Investigative Political and Social Work, Ending Privilege in Education and Health, Application of Industrial Democracy, Marketing; former Soviet Union, USA, Italy. *Publications: The Case for the Supplementary Vote,* 1990; *The Case for The University of the Lakes,* 1995; *Recreations:* Angling, travelling. *Address:* Dale Campbell-Savours Esq, MP, House of Commons, London, SW1A 0AA *Tel:* 020 7219 3513 *Tel (Constituency):* 017687 74747.

DENNIS CANAVAN   Falkirk West   Lab* majority 13,783

Born 8 August 1942; Educated St Columba's High School, Cowdenbeath; Edinburgh University (BSc, DipEd). Principal teacher of mathematics, St Modan's High School, Stirling 1970–74; Assistant head, Holy Rood High School, Edinburgh 1974; MSP for Falkirk West constituency since May 6, 1999; Chair, Parliamentary Branch of Educational Institute of Scotland; Member, UNISON. District Councillor 1973–74; Labour Group Leader, Stirling District Council 1974. **House of Commons:** Member for Stirlingshire West October 1974–83, and for Falkirk West since June 1983 (*Labour whip withdrawn 1999); *Select Committees:* Member: Foreign Affairs 1982–97, International Development 1997–99. *Special Interests:* Foreign Affairs, Health Service, Education, British-Irish Relations, Disarmament, Sport; Ireland, Middle East, Southern Africa. *Clubs:* Camelon Labour, Bannockburn Miners' Welfare; *Recreations:* Hill-climbing, swimming, running, angling, football spectating (former Scottish Universities' football international). *Address:* Dennis Canavan Esq, MP, MSP, House of Commons, London, SW1A 0AA *Tel:* 020 7219 4127 *Fax:* 020 7219 2513. *Constituency:* 37 Church Walk, Denny, Stirlingshire, FK6 6DF *Tel:* 01324 825922 *Fax:* 01324 823972 *E-mail:* dennis.canavan.msp@scottish.parliament.uk.

JAMIE CANN   Ipswich   *Lab majority 10,436*

Born 28 June 1946; Son of Charles Cann, steel mill manager, and Brenda Cann, shopkeeper; Educated Barton-on-Humber Grammar School; Married May 26, 1970, Rosemary Lovitt (2 sons). Handford Hall Primary School, Ipswich: School teacher 1967–92, Deputy Head Teacher. Ipswich Borough Council: Councillor 1973–92, Leader, Labour Group 1976–91, Leader of the Council 1979–91; Member, Ipswich Port Authority 1986–94. **House of Commons:** Member for Ipswich since April 9, 1992; *Select Committees:* Member: Defence 1997–. *Special Interests:* British Constitution, Electoral Reform, Education, Tax, Social Issues, Defence, Environment; Former Soviet Union, Greece, Hong Kong, USA, Cyprus, Gibraltar. Fellow, Armed Forces Trust (Navy); *Recreations:* Watching sport, squash, badminton, snooker, history, reading, walking. *Address:* Jamie Cann Esq, MP, House of Commons, London, SW1A 0AA *Tel:* 020 7219 4171. *Constituency:* 33 Silent Street, Ipswich, Suffolk, IP1 1TF *Tel:* 01473 281559 *Fax:* 01473 217489.

IVOR CAPLIN   Hove   *Lab majority 3,959*

Born 8 November 1958; Son of late Leonard Caplin, chartered accountant, and of Alma Caplin, market researcher; Educated King Edward's School, Witley; Brighton College of Technology (National Certificate in Business Studies 1979); Married Maureen, daughter of Michael J. Whelan, retired, and of late Joan Ross (2 sons 1 daughter). Legal and General Assurance Society Ltd 1978–97, Former quality manager, sales and marketing; Member, MSF. Councillor, Hove 1991–97; Leader 1995–97; Councillor, Brighton and Hove Council 1996–98, and Deputy Leader 1996–98. **House of Commons:** Member for Hove since May 1, 1997; PPS to Margaret Beckett as President of the Council and Leader of the House of Commons 1998–; *Select Committees:* Member: Broadcasting 1997–98, Broadcasting 1999–2000; Member: Modernisation of the House of Commons 1998–. *Special Interests:* Finance, Heritage, Pensions, Sport, Arts, Local Government, Animal Welfare. Chair, Hove Constituency Labour Party 1986–92; Member: Co-operative Party, Labour Friends of Israel. Member, League Against Cruel Sports; Trustee, Old Market Trust, Hove; *Sportsclubs:* Vice-President, Lewes Priory Cricket Club, Brighton and Hove Cricket Club; *Recreations:* Football (Brighton and Hove Albion FC), music, cricket, eating out. *Address:* Ivor Caplin Esq, MP, House of Commons, London, SW1A 0AA *Tel:* 020 7219 2146 *Fax:* 020 7219 0259. *Constituency:* Parliamentary Office, Town Hall, Norton Road, Hove, East Sussex, BN3 4AH *Tel:* 01273 292933 *Fax:* 01273 291054 *E-mail:* caplini@parliament.uk.

ROGER CASALE   Wimbledon   *Lab majority 2,990*

Born 22 May 1960; Son of Edward and Jean Casale; Educated King's College, Wimbledon; Hurstpierpoint College, Sussex; Brasenose College, Oxford (BA philosophy, politics, economics 1982); Johns Hopkins, Bologna (MA international affairs 1994); Married August 30, 1997, Fernanda Miucci (1 daughter). Head, Training Institute 1984–91; Policy adviser to office of John Prescott and Tony Blair 1995–97; University lecturer in European studies, Greenwich 1994–97; Member, GMB. **House of Commons:** Member for Wimbledon since May 1, 1997; *Select Committees:* Member: European Legislation 1997–98; Member: European Scrutiny 1999–. *Special Interests:* Foreign Affairs, Treasury; Italy. Member: Fabian Society, Labour Movement in Europe. *Recreations:* Spending time with family and friends. *Address:* Roger Casale Esq, MP, House of Commons, London, SW1A 0AA *Tel:* 020 7219 4565 *Fax:* 020 7219 0789. *Constituency:* Wimbledon Community Association, 28 St George's Road, Wimbledon, London, SW19 4DP *Tel:* 020 8540 1012 *Fax:* 020 8540 1018.

WILLIAM CASH Stone
Con majority 3,818

Born 10 May 1940; Son of Paul Cash, MC (killed in action, 1944); Educated Stonyhurst College; Lincoln College, Oxford (MA); Married October 16, 1965, Bridget Mary Lee (2 sons 1 daughter). Solicitor, William Cash & Company. **House of Commons:** Member for Stafford 1984–97, and for Stone since May 1, 1997; *Select Committees:* Member: European Legislation 1985–97, European Legislation 1997–98; Member: European Scrutiny 1998–. *Special Interests:* European Union, Trade and Industry, Media, Small Businesses, Heritage; East Africa, Europe. Chair, Friends of Bruges Group in the House of Commons 1989–. Vice-President, Conservative Small Business Bureau; Member, Standing Committees on: Financial Services 1985–86, Banking 1986–87; Founder and Chair, The European Foundation; *Publications: Against a Federal Europe,* 1991; *Europe – The Crunch,* 1992; *Clubs:* Beefsteak, Carlton, Vincent's (Oxford); *Sportsclubs:* Secretary, Lords and Commons Cricket Club 1988–92; *Recreations:* Local history, cricket, jazz. *Address:* William Cash Esq, MP, House of Commons, London, SW1A 0AA *Tel:* 020 7219 3431.

MARTIN CATON Gower
Lab majority 13,007

Born 15 June 1951; Son of William John Caton and Pauline Joan Caton, shop-keepers; Educated Newport (Essex) Grammar School; Norfolk School of Agriculture; Aberystwyth College of Further Education (National Certificate in Agriculture, Higher National Certificate in Applied Biology); Married September 20, 1996, Bethan Evans (2 step daughters). Member, GMB; Former Section Treasurer/Membership Secretary, IPCS. Councillor: Mumbles Community Council 1986–90, Swansea City Council 1988–95, City and County of Swansea 1995–97. **House of Commons:** Member for Gower since May 1, 1997; *Select Committees:* Member: Welsh Affairs 1997–. *Special Interests:* Environment, Planning, Education, European Union. Member: Socialist Environmental Resources Association, Socialist Health Association. Member, CND Cymru; *Recreations:* Reading, walking, theatre, thinking about gardening. *Address:* Martin Caton Esq, MP, House of Commons, London, SW1A 0AA *Tel:* 020 7219 5111 *Fax:* 020 7219 0905. *Constituency:* 26 Pontardulais Road, Gorseinon, Swansea, SA4 4FE *Tel:* 01792 892100 *Fax:* 01792 892375 *E-mail:* martin.caton@politics.demon.co.uk.

IAN CAWSEY Brigg and Goole
Lab majority 6,389

Born 14 April 1960; Son of Arthur Henry Cawsey and Edith Morrison Cawsey; Educated Wintringham School; Married July 19, 1987, Linda Mary Kirman (1 son 2 daughters). Computing/IT work Imperial Foods and Seven Seas Health Care 1977–87 Personal assistant to Elliot Morley, MP 1987–97; Member: ISTL, GMB. Councillor, Humberside County Council 1989–96; Chair, Humberside Police Authority 1993–97; Leader, North Lincolnshire Council 1995–97. **House of Commons:** Member for Brigg and Goole since May 1, 1997; *Select Committees:* Member: Home Affairs 1999–. *Special Interests:* Police, Local Government, Animal Welfare; Poland. Member Fabian Society. Member, Scunthorpe Hospitals Broadcasting Organisation; Vice-President: Federation of Economic Development Authorities (FEDA), Broughton Ex-Servicemen's Association; *Clubs:* Kinsley Labour, Ashby Mill Road; *Recreations:* Football, playing in local 60s band 'The Moggies'. *Address:* Ian Cawsey Esq, MP, House of Commons, London, SW1A 0AA *Tel:* 020 7219 5237. *Constituency:* 7 Market Place, Brigg, North Lincolnshire, DN20 8ES, The Courtyard, Boothferry Road, Goole, DN14 6AE *Tel:* 01652 651327, 01405 767744 *Fax:* 01652 657132, 01405 767733 *E-mail:* ianmp@btclick.com.

BEN CHAPMAN Wirral South — *Lab majority 7,004*

Born 8 July 1940; Son of John Hartley and Elsie Vera Chapman; Educated Appleby Grammar School, Westmorland; Divorced (3 daughters); married 2nd, July 10, 1999, Maureen Ann. Pilot Officer, RAFVR 1959–61; Civil Servant: Ministry of Pensions and National Insurance 1958–62, Ministry of Aviation/ BAA 1962–67, Rochdale Committee of Inquiry into Shipping 1967–70, Board of Trade 1970–74; First Secretary (Commercial) High Commission, Dar es Salaam, Tanzania 1974–78; First Secretary (Economic), High Commission, Accra, Ghana 1978–81; Assistant Secretary, Department of Trade and Industry 1981–87; Commercial Counsellor, Peking Embassy 1987–90; DTI North West: Director Merseyside and Deputy Regional Director 1991–93, Director Trade and Industry and Regional Director 1993–95; Director: On the Waterfront (Manchester) Ltd 1995–96, China Business Links Ltd 1995–97; Founder Consultant, Ben Chapman Associates 1995–97; Former Member, FDA; Member: UNISON, MSF. **House of Commons:** Member for Wirral South since February 27, 1997 by-election; PPS to Richard Caborn: as Minister of State, Department of the Environment, Transport and the Regions (Minister for the Regions, Regeneration and Planning) 1997–99, as Minister of State, Department of Trade and Industry 1999–; *Special Interests:* Economic Development, Regional Development, Trade and Industry, Foreign Affairs; China, Pacific Rim, Turkey. Director, Wirral Chamber of Commerce 1995–96; Council of Management, Lake District Summer Music Ltd 1996–97; Fellow, Industry and Parliament Trust elect; *Recreations:* Opera, theatre, music, reading, walking. *Address:* Ben Chapman Esq, MP, House of Commons, London, SW1A 0AA *Tel:* 020 7219 1143 *Fax:* 020 7219 1179. *Constituency:* 32 Bebington Road, New Ferry, Merseyside, CH62 5BQ *Tel:* 0151–643 8797 *Fax:* 0151–643 8546 *E-mail:* chapmanb@parliament.uk.

SYDNEY CHAPMAN Chipping Barnet — *Con majority 1,035*

Born 17 October 1935; Son of late W. Dobson Chapman; Educated Rugby School; Manchester University (DipArch 1958, DipTP 1961); Married 1976, Claire McNab (2 sons 1 daughter) (marriage dissolved). Architect, Planner, Lecturer and occasional Journalist; Director (Information), British Property Federation 1976–79. **House of Commons:** Contested Stalybridge and Hyde 1964 general election. Member for Birmingham Handsworth 1970–74, and for Chipping Barnet since May 1979; Assistant Government Whip 1988–90; Government Whip 1990–95; PPS: to Health and Social Security Ministers 1973–74; to Norman Fowler as Secretary of State for: Transport 1979–81, Social Services 1981–83; *Select Committees:* Member: Administration 1992–95, Accommodation and Works 1994–97, Public Service 1995–97; Chairman: Accommodation and Works 1997–; Member: Finance and Services 1997–, Liaison 1997–. *Special Interests:* Environment, Architectural Heritage, Conservation, Construction Industry, Inner Cities, Arboriculture; Belize, Seychelles. National Chair, Young Conservatives 1964–66; Senior Vice-Chair, North Western Area Conservatives and Unionist Associations 1966–70. Arboricultural Association: Vice-President 1973–83, President 1983–89; Instigator, National Tree Year 1973; Vice-President, RIBA 1974–75, Member of Council 1972–76; Vice-Chair, United and Cecil Club 1979–; President, London Green Belt Council 1984–89; Formerly Vice-Chair, Wildlife Link; Vice-President, Tree Council; Hon. Associate, British Veterinary Association; Former Vice-President, National Housing and Town Planning Council; Member, Sherlock Holmes Society of London; Formerly Member, Foreign Office Property Advisory Panel; Executive Member, 1922 Committee 1997–; Member, UK Delegation to Council of Europe and Western Europe Union; HM The Queen's Silver Jubilee Medal 1977; Knighted 1995; RIBA; FRTPI; FRSA; Hon. FRICS; Hon. MLI; Hon. FBEng; Hon. FFB; Hon. FIAS; *Clubs:* United and Cecil. *Address:* Sir Sydney Chapman, MP, House of Commons, London, SW1A 0AA *Tel:* 020 7219 4542 *Fax:* 020 7219 2694. *Constituency:* Chipping Barnet Conservative Association, 163 High Street, Barnet, Hertfordshire, EN5 5SU *Tel:* 020 8449 7345 *Fax:* 020 8449 7346.

DAVID CHAYTOR Bury North   *Lab majority 7,866*

Born 3 August 1949; Educated Bury Grammar School; London University (BA 1970, MPhil 1979); Leeds University (PGCE 1976); Married (1 son 2 daughters). Various lecturing posts 1973–82; Senior staff tutor, Manchester College of Adult Education 1983–90; Head, Department of Continuing Education, Manchester College of Arts and Technology 1990–97; Member, TGWU. Councillor, Calderdale Council 1982–97, Chair: Education Committee, Highways Committee, Economic Development Committee. **House of Commons:** Contested Calder Valley 1987 and 1992 general elections. Member for Bury North since May 1, 1997; *Select Committees:* Member: Deregulation 1997–, Environmental Audit 2000–. *Special Interests:* Environment, Education, Foreign Policy and International Development, Transport; France, Albania, USA, Kazakhstan. Member, European Standing Committee A 1998–; *Clubs:* Rochdale Labour; *Recreations:* Walking, cycling, restoration of old buildings. *Address:* David Chaytor Esq, MP, House of Commons, London, SW1A 0AA *Tel:* 020 7219 6625 *Fax:* 020 7219 0952. *Constituency:* Bury North Constituency Labour Party, 65A The Rock, Bury, Lancashire, BL9 0NB *Tel:* 0161–764 2023 *Fax:* 0161–763 3410 *E-mail:* hollandj@parliament.uk.

DAVID CHIDGEY Eastleigh   *LD majority 754*

Born 9 July 1942; Son of Major Cyril and Winifred Chidgey; Educated Brune Park County High School, Gosport; Portsmouth Polytechnic (Dip CivilEng, CEng); Portsmouth Naval College; Married February 6, 1965, April Carolyn Idris-Jones (1 son 2 daughters). Consulting civil engineer; Senior Engineer, Hampshire County Council 1964–73; Coordinating Engineer, Brian Colquhoun and Partners 1973–78; Worked on projects in Guinea (West Africa) and South East Asia 1978–87; Managing Director, Brian Colquhoun and Partners – Ireland 1981–87; Chief Consultant to Dublin Transport Authority 1988–; Associate Partner 1988–93; Associate Director, Thorburn Colquhoun 1994. Winchester City Council: Councillor, Alresford 1987–91, Spokesman for: Health and Works 1987–90, Amenities 1987–89, Director, Direct Works Organisation 1990–91; contested Hampshire Central European Parliament (SLD) 1988 by-election and 1989 election. **House of Commons:** Contested Eastleigh (Lib Dem) 1992 general election. Member for Eastleigh since June 9, 1994 by-election; Spokesman for: Employment 1994–95, Transport 1995–97, Trade and Industry 1997–99; *Select Committees:* Member: Accommodation and Works 1998–, Foreign Affairs 1999–. *Special Interests:* Manufacturing, Transport, Engineering Services, Foriegn Affairs; French speaking Africa, Pacific Rim, Middle East, Eastern Europe. Regional Chair, Hampshire and Wight Liberal Democrats 1992–94. Joint Founder and President, Association of Liberal Democrat Engineers and Applied Scientists; Member: Association of Liberal District Councillors, Council for the Protection of Rural England, President, NSPCC Eastleigh Branch; Member: National Trust, The Tramman Trust; Member, Worshipful Company of Carmen; FICE; FIHT; FIEI; MCIT; AConsEI; Companion, Royal Aeronautical Society; Companion, Institute of Mechanical Engineers; *Clubs:* National Liberal; *Sportsclubs:* Hampshire County Cricket; *Recreations:* Reading, golf, tennis. *Address:* David Chidgey Esq, MP, House of Commons, London, SW1A 0AA *Tel:* 020 7219 4298 *Fax:* 020 7219 2810. *Constituency:* 113 Leigh Road, Eastleigh, Hampshire, SO50 9DS *Tel:* 023 8062 0007 *Fax:* 023 8061 8245 *E-mail:* chidgeyd@parliament.uk.

MALCOLM CHISHOLM   Edinburgh North and Leith   *Lab majority 10,978*

Born 7 March 1949; Son of George and Olive Chisholm; Educated George Watson's College; Edinburgh University (MA, DipEd); Married 1975, Janet Broomfield (2 sons 1 daughter). Teacher; MSP for Edinburgh North and Leith constituency since May 6, 1999; Member, Educational Institute of Scotland. **House of Commons:** Member for Edinburgh Leith 1992–97, and for Edinburgh North and Leith since May 1, 1997; Opposition Spokesman on Scotland 1996–97; Opposition Whip January-June 1996; Parliamentary Under-Secretary of State, Scottish Office May-December 1997; *Special Interests:* Economic Policy, Health, Childcare, Housing. *Recreations:* Reading, cinema, theatre. *Address:* Malcolm Chisholm Esq, MP, MSP, House of Commons, London, SW1A 0AA *Tel:* 020 7219 4613. *Constituency:* 274 Leith Walk, Edinburgh *Tel:* 0131–555 3636 *Fax:* 0131–555 3737 *E-mail:* lamonta@parliament.uk.

CHRISTOPHER CHOPE   Christchurch   *Con majority 2,165*

Born 19 May 1947; Son of late Judge Robert Chope and of Pamela Chope, née Durell; Educated St Andrew's School, Eastbourne; Marlborough College; St Andrew's University (LLB 1970); Married April 20, 1987, Christine Mary Hutchinson (1 son 1 daughter). Barrister, Inner Temple 1972; Consultant, Ernst and Young 1992–98. Councillor, London Borough Wandsworth 1974–83, Chair, Housing Committee 1978–79, Leader of the Council 1979–83. **House of Commons:** Member for Southampton Itchen 1983–92, and for Christchurch since May 1, 1997; Opposition Front Bench Spokesman for: the Environment, Transport and the Regions 1997–98, Trade and Industry 1998–99; PPS to Peter Brooke, as Minister of State, HM Treasury 1986; Parliamentary Under-Secretary of State: at Department of the Environment 1986–90, at Department of Transport (Minister for Roads and Traffic) 1990–92; *Select Committees:* Member: Trade and Industry 1999–. Member, Executive Committee, Society of Conservative Lawyers 1983–86; Vice-Chair, Conservative Party 1997–98. Member: Health and Safety Commission 1992–97, Local Government Commission for England 1994–95; OBE 1982. *Address:* Christopher Chope Esq, OBE, MP, House of Commons, London, SW1A 0AA *Tel:* 020 7219 5808. *Constituency:* 18a Bargates, Christchurch, Dorset.

JUDITH CHURCH   Dagenham   *Lab majority 17,054*

Born 19 September 1953; Daughter of late Edmund Church, and of Helen Church; Educated St Bernard's Convent School, Slough; Leeds University (BSc maths and philosophy 1975); Huddersfield Polytechnic (Postgraduate Certificate in Education (Technical Education) 1978); Aston University (Postgraduate Diploma in Occupational Health and Safety 1981); Thames Valley University (Postgraduate Diploma in Management Studies 1984); (2 sons). Maths teacher in West Africa with Voluntary Service Overseas 1975–77; Technical Officer, GAF UK 1978–79; Process research, Mars UK 1979–80; HM Factory Inspector 1980–86; National Health and Safety Officer for MSF 1986–94; First woman to be elected in union section of Labour Party National Executive Committee 1992. **House of Commons:** Contested Stevenage 1992 general election; Member for Dagenham since June 9, 1994 by-election; *Select Committees:* Member: Deregulation 1995–97. *Special Interests:* Breast Cancer. Chair, Hornsey and Wood Green CLP 1988–89; Joint Chair, Labour Party Economic Policy Commission 1992–94; Member, Labour Party National Executive Committee 1992–94; Member, Fabian Society. *Recreations:* Reading, keeping fit. *Address:* Judith Church, MP, House of Commons, London, SW1A 0AA *Tel:* 020 7219 6000 *Fax:* 020 7219 0076 *Tel (Constituency):* 01279 757147 *Fax (Constituency):* 01279 757147 *E-mail:* dewdneyk@parliament.uk.

MICHAEL CLAPHAM   Barnsley West and Penistone   *Lab majority 17,267*

Born 15 May 1943; Son of late Thomas Clapham; Educated Gawber Junior and Infant; Darton Secondary Modern School; Barnsley Technical College; Leeds Polytechnic (BSc 1973); Leeds University (PGCE 1974); Bradford University (MPhil 1990); Married December 4, 1965, Yvonne Hallsworth (1 son 1 daughter). Miner 1958–70; Lecturer trade union studies, Whitwood FE College, Castleford 1974–77; Deputy Head, Comp Dept, Yorkshire Area NUM 1977–83; Head, Industrial Relations NUM 1983–92; NUM: Member, Claims Officer 1977–83, Head, Industrial Relations Department 1983–; Member, UCATT 1997–. Chair, Barnsley Crime Prevention Partnership 1995–, Chair, Barnsley MAP– Anti-Racist Strategy Body. **House of Commons:** Member for Barnsley West and Penistone since April 9, 1992; PPS to Alan Milburn, as Minister of State, Department of Health May-December 1997; *Select Committees:* Member: Trade and Industry 1992–97. *Special Interests:* Coal Industry, Energy, Employment, Health; Tibet, Nepal, South Africa. Member, Co-operative Party; Secretary, Higham Labour Party Branch 1981–83; Treasurer, Barnsley West and Penistone Constituency Labour Party 1983–92; Chair, Dodworth Labour Party Branch 1984–86. *Recreations:* Walking, gardening, reading. *Address:* Michael Clapham Esq, MP, House of Commons, London, SW1A 0AA *Tel:* 020 7219 2907 *Fax:* 020 7219 5015. *Constituency:* 18 Regent Street, Barnsley, South Yorkshire, S70 2HG *Tel:* 01226 731244 *Fax:* 01226 779429 *E-mail:* claphamm@parliament.uk; mclapham@constoffice.fsnet.co.uk.

JAMES CLAPPISON   Hertsmere   *Con majority 3,075*

Born 14 September 1956; Son of late Leonard Clappison, farmer, and of Dorothy Clappison; Educated St Peter's School, York; The Queen's College, Oxford (BA philosophy, politics and economics 1978); Married July 6, 1984, Helen Margherita, daughter of Alan and Dorothy Carter (1 son 3 daughters). Barrister 1981–; contested Yorkshire South 1989 European Parliament election. **House of Commons:** Contested Barnsley East 1987 general election, Bootle May and November 1990 by-elections. Member for Hertsmere since April 9, 1992; Opposition Front Bench Spokesman for: Home Affairs (Crime, Immigration and Asylums) 1997–99, Education and Employment 1999–; PPS to Baroness Blatch: as Minister of State, Department for Education 1992–94, Home Office 1994–95; Parliamentary Under-Secretary of State, Department of the Environment 1995–97; *Select Committees:* Member: Health 1992–94, Members' Interests 1994–95. *Special Interests:* Home Affairs, Economic Policy, Health, Education; Israel. *Clubs:* United Oxford and Cambridge University, Carlton; *Recreations:* Bridge, walking. *Address:* James Clappison Esq, MP, House of Commons, London, SW1A 0AA *Tel:* 020 7219 5027. *Constituency:* 11 Stanhope Road, St Albans, Hertfordshire, AL1 5BH *Tel:* 01727 850661 *Fax:* 01727 868579 *E-mail:* clappisonj@parliament.uk.

DAVID CLARK   South Shields   *Lab majority 22,153*

Born 19 October 1939; Son of George Clark; Educated Windermere Grammar School; Manchester University (BA economics 1963, MSc 1965) Sheffield University (PhD 1978); Married March 24, 1970, Christine, daughter of Ronald Kirkby (1 daughter). Forester 1956–57; Laboratory worker in textile mill 1957–59; Student Teacher, Salford 1959–60; President, University of Manchester Union 1963–64; Lecturer in Public Administration, Salford University 1965–70; Member, UNISON. **House of Commons:** Contested Manchester Withington Division 1966 general election. Member for Colne Valley 1970–74, and for South Shields since May 1979; Front Bench Spokesman on: Agriculture, Fisheries and Food 1972–74, Defence 1980–81, The Environment 1981–87, Food, Agricultural and Rural Affairs 1987–92, Defence, disarmament and arms control 1992–97; Chancellor of the Duchy of Lancaster 1997–98; *Special Interests:* Open Spaces; New Zealand, Scandinavia. Chair, Atlantic Council of the UK; Member, UK Delegation of the North Atlantic Assembly 1980–97, 1998–; Executive Member, National Trust 1980–94; Trustee: Vindolanda Trust 1983–, History of Parliament Trust 1986–;

Publications: Industrial Manager, 1966; *Colne Valley: Radicalism to Socialism,* 1981; *Victor Grayson: Labour's Lost Leader,* 1985; *We do not want The Earth,* 1992; PC 1997; Borough of South Tyneside 1999; *Recreations:* Gardening, fell-walking, reading, watching football. *Address:* Rt Hon Dr David Clark, MP, House of Commons, London, SW1A 0AA *Tel:* 020 7219 4028. *Constituency:* Ede House, 143 Westoe Road, South Shields, Tyne and Wear, NE33 3PD *Tel:* 0191–456 0762 *Fax:* 0191–454 0364 *E-mail:* david-clarkmp@lineone.net.

DR LYNDA CLARK   Edinburgh Pentlands — *Lab majority 4,862*

Born 26 February 1949; Educated Queens College, St Andrews University (LLB 1970); Edinburgh University (PhD 1975). Dundee University: part-time tutor 1971–73, lecturer in jurisprudence 1973–76; Advocate, Scots Bar 1977–89; QC 1989; Called to the English Bar 1990; Governing member Inner Temple 2000. **House of Commons:** Contested North East Fife 1992 general election. Member for Edinburgh Pentlands since May 1, 1997; Advocate General for Scotland 1999–; *Select Committees:* Member: Public Administration 1997–99. *Special Interests:* Constitutional Reform, Legal System, Health, Higher Education, Pensions. Member: Scottish Legal Aid Board, Edinburgh University Court. *Address:* Dr Lynda Clark, QC, MP, House of Commons, London, SW1A 0AA *Tel:* 020 7219 4492. *Constituency:* The Reception Block, Princess Margaret Rose Hospital, 41/43 Frogston Road West, Edinburgh, EH10 7ED *Tel:* 0131–536 4834 *E-mail:* scottishsecretary@scotland.gov.uk *Website:* www.scottishsecretary.gov.uk.

DR MICHAEL CLARK   Rayleigh — *Con majority 10,684*

Born 8 August 1935; Son of late Mervyn Clark; Educated King Edward VI Grammar School, East Retford; King's College, London (BSc chemistry); University of Minnesota; St John's College, Cambridge (PhD); Married July 26, 1958, Valerie Ethel Harbord (1 son 1 daughter). Fulbright Scholarship to USA 1956; Industrial chemist: ICI and Smiths Industries 1960–69; Management consultant 1969–94. **House of Commons:** Contested Ilkeston, Derbyshire 1979 general election. Member for Rochford 1983–97, and for Rayleigh since May 1, 1997; *Select Committees:* Member: Energy 1983–92; Chairman: Energy 1989–92; Member: Liaison 1989–92, Trade and Industry 1992–94; Member: Chairmen's Panel 1997–; Chairman: Science and Technology 1997–; Member: Liaison 1998–. *Special Interests:* Energy, Manufacturing, Science and Technology, Animal Welfare; Russia, Venezuela, Turkey, Cyprus, Argentina. Cambridgeshire Conservative Association: Treasurer 1975–78, Vice-Chair 1978–80, Chair 1980–83; Member, Eastern Area Executive Council 1980–84. Melbourn Village College: Governor 1974–82, Chairman of Governors 1977–80; Board of Parliamentary Office of Science and Technology 1988–, Chair 1993–98; Executive Member, 1922 Committee 1997–; Executive Inter Parliamentary Union: Member 1987–95, Chair 1990–93; *Publications: The History of Rochford Hall*; Gold Medal, Coal Research Council 1992; Fellow, King's College, London; Fellow: King's College, London 1987, Royal Society of Chemistry 1988; Companion, Institute of Energy 1991; *Clubs:* Rayleigh Conservative; *Sportsclubs:* Rochford Hundred Golf; *Recreations:* Gardening, DIY, golf. *Address:* Dr Michael Clark, MP, House of Commons, London, SW1A 0AA *Tel:* 020 7219 4016 *Fax:* 020 7219 3548. *Constituency:* Conservative Office, 25 Bellingham Lane, Rayleigh, Essex, SS6 7ED *Tel:* 01268 742044 *Fax:* 01268 741833.

PAUL CLARK   Gillingham   *Lab majority 1,980*

Born 29 April 1957; Son of Gordon Thomas Clark, retired journalist, and of Sheila Gladys Clark, Councillor, former Mayor of Gillingham; Educated Gillingham Grammar School; Keele University (BA economics and politics 1980); University of Derby (DMS 1997); Married November 29, 1980 Julie Hendrick (1 son 1 daughter). Centre manager, Trades Union Congress, National Education Centre 1986–97; AEEU: researcher, President's researcher, education officer 1980–86; Member: TUC, AEU (Gillingham Branch). Councillor, Gillingham Borough Council 1982–90, Labour Group Leader 1988–90, Board Member of Thames Gateway Kent Partnership 2000–. **House of Commons:** Contested Gillingham 1992 general election. Member for Gillingham since May 1, 1997; Joint PPS to Lord Irvine of Lairg as Lord Chancellor 1999–; *Special Interests:* Education, Transport, Environment; Europe, including East Europe. Member: European Standing Committee A 1998, European Standing Committee B 1998–2000; *Clubs:* Anchorians Association; *Recreations:* Historic buildings, reading. *Address:* Paul Clark Esq, MP, House of Commons, London, SW1A 0AA *Tel:* 020 7219 5207 *Fax:* 020 7219 2545. *Constituency:* 62A Watling Street, Gillingham, Kent, ME7 2YN *Tel:* 01634 574261 *Fax:* 01634 574276 *E-mail:* clarkp@parliament.uk.

CHARLES CLARKE   Norwich South   *Lab majority 14,239*

Born 21 September 1950; Son of late Sir Richard Clarke, KCB, and Lady Brenda Clarke; Educated Highgate School, London; King's College, Cambridge (BA maths and economics); Married October 1984, Carol Pearson (2 sons). Part-time adult education maths lecturer, City Literary Institute 1981–83; Organiser, Community Challenge Conference, Gulbenkian Fund 1981–82; Researcher to Neil Kinnock, MP 1981–83; Chief of Staff to Neil Kinnock, MP 1983–92; Chief Executive, Quality Public Affairs 1992–97; Sabbatical President, Cambridge Students' Union 1971–72; Member, National Union of Students' Executive, President 1975–77. Councillor, London Borough of Hackney 1980–86, Chair, Housing Committee, Vice-Chair, Economic Development. **House of Commons:** Member for Norwich South since May 1, 1997; Parliamentary Under-Secretary of State (School Standards), Department for Education and Employment 1998–99; Minister of State, Home Office 1999–; *Select Committees:* Member: Treasury 1997–98, Treasury Sub-Committee 1998. Organiser, Hackney People In Partnership 1978–80; *Clubs:* Norwich Labour; *Recreations:* Chess, reading, walking. *Address:* Charles Clarke Esq, MP, House of Commons, London, SW1A 0AA *Tel:* 020 7219 1194 *Fax:* 020 7219 0526. *Constituency:* Norwich Labour Party, 59 Bethel Street, Norwich, NR2 1NL *Tel:* 01603 661144 *Fax:* 01603 663502.

ERIC CLARKE   Midlothian   *Lab majority 9,870*

Born 9 April 1933; Son of late Ernest Clarke, railway guard, and late Annie Clarke, laundress; Educated St Cuthbert's; Holy Cross Academy; W. M. Ramsey Technical College, Edinburgh; Esk Valley College, Midlothian (Certificate for General Education – Mining Qualification Board); Married September 10, 1955, June, daughter of late Richard Hewat, boiler fireman (2 sons 1 daughter). Roslin Colliery 1949–52; Faceman, Lingerwood Colliery 1952–67; Trainer, supervisor, repairer, Bilstonglen Colliery 1967–77; General Secretary, Scottish Area NUM 1977–89. County and Regional Councillor 1962–78. **House of Commons:** Member for Midlothian since April 9, 1992; Opposition Scottish and Defence Whip 1994–97; *Select Committees:* Member: Scottish Affairs 1992–94; Chairman: Broadcasting 1997–99; Member: Finance and Services 1997–, Scottish Affairs 1997–, Liaison 1998–; Chairman: Broadcasting 2000–. *Special Interests:* Coal Industry, Scottish Affairs, Foreign Affairs; Cyprus, Middle East, Vietnam, Nepal. Member, Scottish Mining Museum Trust; Honorary Citizen, Morphu, Cyprus; *Clubs:* Mayfield Labour, Morris Workingmen's, Danderhall Miners' Welfare; *Recreations:* Trout angling, carpentry, gardening, watching football. *Address:* Eric Clarke Esq, MP, House of Commons, London, SW1A 0AA *Tel:* 020 7219 6373 *Fax:* 020 7219 2117. *Constituency:* PO Box 11, 95 High Street, Dalkeith, Midlothian, EH22 1AX *Tel:* 0131–654 1585 *Fax:* 0131–654 1586.

KENNETH CLARKE   Rushcliffe   *Con majority 5,055*

Born 2 July 1940; Son of late Kenneth Clarke, watchmaker and jeweller, and Doris Clarke; Educated Nottingham High School; Gonville and Caius College, Cambridge (BA, LLB) (President, Cambridge Union 1963); Married November 7, 1964, Gillian Mary Edwards (1 son 1 daughter). Called to the Bar 1963; Member, Midland Circuit, practising from Birmingham; QC 1980; Chairman, Alliance UniChem 1997–; Director, Foreign & Colonial Investment Trust 1997–; Deputy Chairman, British American Tobacco 1998–; Director, Independent News and Media (UK). **House of Commons:** Contested Mansfield Notts 1964 and 1966 general elections. Member for Rushcliffe since June 1970; Opposition Spokesman on: Social Services 1974–76, Industry 1976–79; Assistant Government Whip 1972–74; Government Whip for Europe 1973–74; Lord Commissioner of the Treasury January-March 1974; PPS to Solicitor General 1971–72; Parliamentary Secretary, Ministry of Transport 1979–80; Parliamentary Under-Secretary of State, Department of Transport 1980–82; Minister for Health 1982–85; Paymaster General and Employment Minister 1985–87; Chancellor, Duchy of Lancaster (Minister of Trade and Industry) 1987–88; Secretary of State for: Health 1988–90, Education and Science 1990–92; Home Secretary 1992–93, Chancellor of the Exchequer 1993–97; Contested Leadership of the Conservative Party June 1997. Chair: Cambridge University Conservative Association 1961, Federation Conservative Students 1963–65. Liveryman, The Clockmakers Company; Hon. LLD: Nottingham University 1989, Huddersfield University 1992, Nottingham Trent University 1995; Honorary Fellow, Gonville and Caius College, Cambridge; *Clubs:* Garrick. *Address:* Rt Hon Kenneth Clarke, QC, MP, House of Commons, London, SW1A 0AA *Tel:* 020 7219 5189 *Fax:* 020 7219 4841. *Constituency:* Rushcliffe House, 17/19 Rectory Road, West Bridgford, Nottingham, NG2 6BE *Tel:* 0115–981 7224 *Fax:* 0115–981 7273 *E-mail:* clarkek@parliament.uk.

TOM CLARKE   Coatbridge and Chryston   *Lab majority 19,295*

Born 10 January 1941; Son of late James Clarke; Educated Columba High School, Coatbridge; Scottish College of Commerce. Assistant Director, Scottish Council for Educational Technology (Scottish Film Council); Member, GMB. Councillor: Coatbridge Town Council 1964–74, Monklands District Council 1974–82; Provost of Monklands 1974–82; JP 1972; President, Convention of Scottish Local Authorities 1978–80. **House of Commons:** Member for Coatbridge and Airdrie by-election 1982–83, for Monklands West 1983–97, and for Coatbridge and Chryston since May 1, 1997; Principal Opposition Spokesman on Development and Co-operation 1993–94; Author and Sponsor Disabled Persons (Services, Representation and Consultation) Act 1986; Shadow Minister for UK Personal Social Services 1987–92; Shadow Secretary of State for Scotland 1992–93, for International Development 1994–95; Shadow Minister for Disabled People's Rights 1995–97; Minister of State (Film and Tourism), Department of National Heritage/for Culture, Media and Sport 1997–98; *Special Interests:* Film Industry, Foreign Affairs, Civil Service, Local Government; Central America, Philippines, Africa, Asia, Eastern Europe, USA. Director, Award-winning amateur film *Give Us A Goal*; Fellow, Industry and Parliament Trust; CBE 1980; PC 1997; *Sportsclubs:* Coatbridge Municipal Golf; *Recreations:* Films, walking, reading, astrology. *Address:* Rt Hon Thomas Clarke, CBE, JP, MP, House of Commons, London, SW1A 0AA *Tel:* 020 7219 6997 *Fax:* 020 7219 6094 *Tel (Constituency):* 01236 600800 *Fax (Constituency):* 01236 600808.

TONY CLARKE   Northampton South   *Lab majority 744*

Born 6 September 1963; Son of Walter Arthur Clarke, engineer, and Joan Ada Iris Clarke; Educated Lings Upper School, Northampton; Institute of Training and Development; Institute of Safety and Health; Married Carole Chalmers (1 son 1 daughter). Social Work Trainer, Northamptonshire County Council; Currently Disability Training Officer; sponsored MP for CWU. Councillor, Northampton Borough Council 1991–99; Chair, Environment Services. **House of Commons:** Member for Northampton South since May 1, 1997; *Select Committees:* Member: Joint Committee on Consolidation of Bills Etc 1997–, Northern Ireland Affairs 1999–. *Special Interests:* Environment, Leisure, Constitution, Sport, Local Government; Europe. Member, East Midlands Sports Council; *Sportsclubs:* Director, Northampton Town FC; *Recreations:* Football. *Address:* Tony Clarke Esq, MP, House of Commons, London, SW1A 0AA *Tel:* 020 7219 4465 *Fax:* 020 7219 0526. *Constituency:* 1 St Giles Terrace, Northampton, NN1 2BN *Tel:* 01604 250044 *Fax:* 01604 250055 *E-mail:* tonyclarkemp@lineone.com.

DAVID CLELLAND   Tyne Bridge   *Lab majority 22,906*

Born 27 June 1943; Son of Archibald Clelland; Educated Kelvin Grove Boys School; Gateshead Technical College; Hebburn Technical College; Married March 31, 1965, Maureen, daughter of William Potts (2 daughters) (separated). Electrical Fitter 1964–81; Local Government Association Secretary 1981–86; AEEU: Member, 35 years, Shop Steward, 14 years. Chair, Gateshead Council Recreation Committee 1976–84; Secretary, Association of Councillors 1981–86; Vice-Chair, Gateshead Health Authority 1982–84; Leader, Gateshead Council 1984–86. **House of Commons:** Member for Tyne Bridge since December 5, 1985 by-election; Opposition Whip 1995–97; Assistant Government Whip (Defence, International Development: North-East) 1997–; *Special Interests:* Local Government, Home Affairs, Transport, Environment, Employment, Energy. Hon. Secretary and Hon. Treasurer, Northern Group of Labour MPs –1998, Vice-Chair 1999. *Recreations:* Golf, music. *Address:* David Clelland Esq, MP, House of Commons, London, SW1A 0AA *Tel:* 020 7219 3669. *Constituency:* 19 Ravensworth Road, Dunston, Gateshead, Tyne and Wear, NE11 9AB *Tel:* 01914 200300 *Fax:* 01914 200301 *E-mail:* david.clelland@hm-treasury.gov.uk.

GEOFFREY CLIFTON-BROWN   Cotswold   *Con majority 11,965*

Born 23 March 1953; Son of Robert and Elizabeth Clifton-Brown; Educated Eton; Royal Agricultural College, Cirencester; Married 1979, Alexandra Peto-Shepherd (1 son 1 daughter). Graduate estate surveyor, Property Services Agency, Dorchester 1975; Investment surveyor, Jones Lang Wootton 1975–79; Managing Director, own farming business in Norfolk 1979–. **House of Commons:** Member for Cirencester and Tewkesbury 1992–97, and for Cotswold since May 1, 1997; An Opposition Whip: (Agriculture; Education and Employment: Scotland) 1999, (Education and Employment; Defence; Culture, Media and Sport) 1999–2000, (Education and Employment; Defence; Agriculture) 2000–; PPS to Douglas Hogg as Minister of Agriculture, Fisheries and Food 1995–97; *Select Committees:* Member: Environment 1992–97, Public Accounts 1997–99; Member: Broadcasting 2000–. *Special Interests:* Economy and Taxation, Foreign Affairs, Environment, Agriculture; Brazil, France, Italy, Kashmir, Hong Kong. Chair, North Norfolk Constituency Association 1986–91. Vice-Chair: Charities Property Association 1993–, Small Business Bureau 1995–; Member: Eastern Area Executive and Agricultural Committees 1986–91; Liveryman, The Worshipful Company of Farmers; *Publications: Privatisation of the State Pension – Secure Funded Provision for all,* 1996; ARICS; Freeman, City of London; *Clubs:* Carlton, Farmers'; *Recreations:* Fishing, other rural pursuits. *Address:* Geoffrey Clifton-Brown Esq, ARICS, MP, House of Commons, London, SW1A 0AA *Tel:* 020 7219 5147 *Fax:* 020 7219 2550. *Constituency:* 7 Rodney Road, Cheltenham, Gloucestershire, GL50 1HX *Tel:* 01242 514551 *Fax:* 01242 514949 *E-mail:* gcb@gcbmp.demon.co.uk.

ANN CLWYD   Cynon Valley — Lab majority 19,755

Born 21 March 1937; Daughter of Gwilym and Elizabeth Lewis; Educated Holywell Grammar School; The Queen's School, Chester; University College of Wales, Bangor; Married 1963, Owen Roberts. Journalist; Broadcaster; MEP for Mid and West Wales 1979–84. **House of Commons:** Contested Denbigh 1970 and Gloucester October 1974 general elections. Member for Cynon Valley since by-election May 3, 1984; Opposition Spokesman on: Employment 1993–94, Foreign Affairs 1994–95; Shadow Minister of Education and Women's Rights 1987–88; Shadow Secretary of State for: International Development 1989–92, Wales July-November 1992, National Heritage 1992–93; Assistant to John Prescott as Deputy Leader of Labour Party 1994–95; *Select Committees:* Member: International Development 1997–. *Special Interests:* Iraq, Turkey, Iran, Russia, South East Asia. Member, Labour Party National Executive Committee 1983–84; Chair, Tribune Group 1986–87. Member, Arts Council 1975–79; Vice-Chair, Welsh Arts Council 1975–79; Royal Commission on NHS 1976–79; Inter-Parliamentary Union: Executive committee member, British Group, Member, Human Rights Group; Hon. Fellow, University of North Wales. *Address:* Ann Clwyd, MP, House of Commons, London, SW1A 0AA *Tel:* 020 7219 6609. *Constituency:* 6 Dean Court, Aberdare, CF44 7BN *Tel:* 01685 871394 *E-mail:* annclwyd@parliament.uk.

VERNON COAKER   Gedling — Lab majority 3,802

Born 17 June 1953; Son of Edwin Coaker; Educated Drayton Manor Grammar School, London; Warwick University (BA); Trent Polytechnic (PGCE); Married December 23, 1978, Jacqueline Heaton (1 son 1 daughter). Teaching; Member, NUT. Councillor, Rushcliffe Borough Council 1983–97. **House of Commons:** Member for Gedling since May 1, 1997; PPS to Stephen Timms: as Minister of State, Department of Social Security 1999, as Financial Secretary, HM Treasury 1999–; *Select Committees:* Member: Social Security 1998–99; Member, European Standing Committee B 1998. *Special Interests:* Environment, Education, Welfare Reform, Foreign Policy; France, Kosovo, Macedonia. Member: League Against Cruel Sports, Friends of the Earth; *Recreations:* Sport, walking. *Address:* Vernon Coaker Esq, MP, House of Commons, SW1A 0AA *Tel:* 020 7219 6627. *Constituency:* 2A Parkyn Road, Daybrook, Nottingham, NG5 6BG *Tel:* 0115–920 4224 *Fax:* 0115–920 4500 *E-mail:* coakerv@parliament.uk.

ANN COFFEY   Stockport — Lab majority 18,912

Born 31 August 1946; Daughter of late John Brown, MBE, Flight-Lieutenant, RAF, and of Marie Brown, nurse; Educated Nairn Academy; Bodmin and Bushey Grammar Schools; Polytechnic of South Bank, London (BSc sociology 1967); Walsall College of Education (Postgraduate Certificate in Education 1971); Manchester University (MSc psychiatric social work 1977); Married 1973, marriage dissolved 1989 (1 daughter). Trainee Social Worker, Walsall Social Services 1971–72; Social Worker: Birmingham 1972–73, Gwynedd 1973–74, Wolverhampton 1974–75, Stockport 1977–82, Cheshire 1982–88; Team Leader, Fostering, Oldham Social Services 1988–92; Member, USDAW. Stockport Metropolitan Borough Council: Councillor 1984–92, Leader of Labour Group 1988–92; Member, District Health Authority 1986–90. **House of Commons:** Contested Cheadle 1987 general election. Member for Stockport since April 9, 1992; Opposition Spokeswoman on Health 1996–97; Opposition Whip 1995–96; Joint PPS to Tony Blair as Prime Minister 1997–98; PPS to Alistair Darling as Secretary of State for Social Security 1998–; *Select Committees:* Member: Trade and Industry 1993–95; Member: Modernisation of the House of Commons 2000–. *Special Interests:* Trade and Industry, Health, Personal Social Services, Voluntary Organisations. *Recreations:* Photography, drawing, cinema, swimming, reading. *Address:* Ann Coffey, MP, House of Commons, London, SW1A 0AA *Tel:* 020 7219 4546 *Fax:* 020 7219 0770 *Tel (Constituency):* 0161–491 0615 *Fax (Constituency):* 0161–491 0338 *E-mail:* coffeya@parliament.uk.

HARRY COHEN   Leyton and Wanstead   *Lab majority 15,186*

Born 10 December 1949; Son of Emanuel and Anne Cohen; Educated George Gascoigne Secondary Modern; East Ham Technical College (part-time) Chartered Institute of Public Finance and Accountancy 1974; Birkbeck College, London University (MSc politics and administration 1995); Married 1978, Ellen Hussain (1 stepson 1 stepdaughter 1 foster son). Accountant and auditor, London Borough of Waltham Forest, Hackney and Haringey; Auditor, NALGO; Member, UNISON. Waltham Forest Borough Council: Councillor 1972–83, Chair, Planning Committee 1972–83, Secretary, Labour Group 1972–83; Member, Waltham Forest Area Health Authority 1972–83. **House of Commons:** Member for Leyton 1983–97, and for Leyton and Wanstead since May 1, 1997; *Select Committees:* Member: Defence 1997–. *Special Interests:* Defence, Equality issues, Health, Transport, Ecology and Conservation, Animal Rights; Middle East, Central Europe, Eastern Europe, India, Pakistan, Bangladesh, Tibet. Vice-President, The Royal College of Midwives; Member, UK Delegation to North Atlantic Assembly 1992–; Chair, Sub-Committee for Economic Co-operation and Convergence with Central and Eastern Europe; Reserve, UK delegation to Organisation for Security and Co-operation in Europe 1997–; Member, CIPFA 1974. *Address:* Harry Cohen Esq, MP, House of Commons, London, SW1A 0AA *Tel:* 020 7219 6376/4137 *Fax:* 020 7219 0438. *Constituency:* 91 Chesterfield Road, Leyton, London, E10 6CN *E-mail:* cohenh@parliament.uk.

IAIN COLEMAN   Hammersmith and Fulham   *Lab majority 3,842*

Born 18 January 1958; Educated Tonbridge School; Married Sally Powell (1 son). Senior administrative officer, London Borough of Islington; Member, MSF. Councillor, Hammersmith and Fulham 1986–97, Leader 1991–96, Mayor 1996–97. **House of Commons:** Member for Hammersmith and Fulham since May 1, 1997; *Select Committees:* Member: Deregulation 1997–99. *Special Interests:* Housing, Sport, Asylum and Immigration; Ireland, France. Vice-Chair, London Regional Group of Labour MPs 1999–. Vice-Chair, Association of London Authorities 1993–95; *Sportsclubs:* Arsenal FC; *Recreations:* Football, opera. *Address:* Iain Coleman Esq, MP, House of Commons, London, SW1A 0AA *Tel:* 020 7381 5074 *Fax:* 020 7386 5415. *Constituency:* 28 Greyhound Road, London, W6 8NX *Tel:* 020 7381 5074 *Fax:* 020 7386 5415 *E-mail:* jacksona@parliament.uk.

TIM COLLINS   Westmorland and Lonsdale   *Con majority 4,521*

Born 7 May 1964; Son of late William Collins, and of Diana Collins; Educated Chigwell School, Essex; London School of Economics (BSc 1985); King's College, London (MA 1986); Married July 26, 1997, Clare Benson. Conservative Research Department 1986–89; Special Adviser: to David Hunt and Michael Howard as Secretaries of State for the Environment 1989–90, to Michael Howard as Employment Secretary 1990–92; Press Secretary to the Prime Minister 1992; Director of Communications, Conservative Party 1992–95; Member, Prime Minister's Policy Unit, Downing Street 1995; Media Consultant to Conservative Party Chairman 1995–97; Senior Strategy Consultant, WCT Ltd 1995–97. **House of Commons:** Member for Westmorland and Lonsdale since May 1, 1997; Opposition Whip (Social Security, Trade and Industry) 1998–99; Senior Vice-Chairman, Conservative Party 1999–; *Select Committees:* Member: Agriculture 1997–98; Member: Information 1998–. *Special Interests:* Defence, Media, Tourism, Constitution, Agriculture, European Union, Economic Policy, Employment, Northern Ireland; USA, Germany, Australia. Ex-officio Member, National Union Executive Committee 1992–95. CBE 1996; *Recreations:* Literature, cinema, heritage. *Address:* Tim Collins Esq, CBE, MP, House of Commons, London, SW1A 0AA *Tel:* 020 7219 3378. *Constituency:* 112 Highgate, Kendal, Cumbria, LA9 4HE *Tel:* 01539 721010 *Fax:* 01539 733039 *E-mail:* listening@timcollins.co.uk *Website:* www.timcollins.co.uk.

TONY COLMAN   Putney   *Lab majority 2,976*

Born 24 July 1943; Son of late William and Beatrice Colman; Educated Paston Grammar School, North Walsham, Norfolk; Magdalene College, Cambridge (MA history 1964); Married November 2, 1989, Juliet Owen (2 sons plus 1 stepson 1 stepdaughter and 3 sons 1 daughter from previous marriages). Unilever (United Africa Company) 1964–69; Associated Fisheries Ltd 1969–71; Burton Group 1969–90, Main Board Director 1981–90; Director, London First Centre Ltd 1994–; Member, GMB. Councillor, London Borough of Merton 1990–98, Leader of Council 1991–97. **House of Commons:** Contested South West Hertfordshire 1979 general election. Member for Putney since May 1, 1997; PPS to Adam Ingram as Minister of State, Northern Ireland Office 1998–2000; *Select Committees:* Member: Treasury 1997–98; Member: International Development 2000–. *Special Interests:* Agenda 21, Private Finance Initiative, Pension Funds. Member: Labour Finance and Industry Group 1973–, Labour Party Enquiry into Education and Training in Europe 1991–93. Chair, Low Pay Unit 1990–98; Member, Prices Commission 1977–79; Vice-Chair, Association of London Authorities 1991–95; Director, London Arts Board 1994–98; Chair: UK Standing Committee Local Authority Pensions 1994–98, Public Private Partnership Program 1995–98; Director, CCLA 1995–98; Chair, Wimbledon Theatre Trust 1991–97; Industrial Fellow, Kingston University; FRSA 1983; Freeman, City of London 1997; *Clubs:* Reform, Winchester (Putney); *Recreations:* Swimming, theatre. *Address:* Tony Colman Esq, MP, House of Commons, London, SW1A 0AA *Tel:* 020 7219 2843 *Fax:* 020 7219 1137. *Constituency:* 35 Felsham Road, London, SW15 1AY *Tel:* 020 8788 8961 *Fax:* 020 8785 2053.

MICHAEL CONNARTY   Falkirk East   *Lab majority 13,385*

Born 3 September 1947; Son of late Patrick Connarty, electrician, and Elizabeth, née Plunkett; Educated St Patrick's High School, Coatbridge; Stirling University (BA economics 1972); Glasgow University; Jordanhill College of Education (DCE 1975); Married August 9, 1969, Margaret Doran (1 son 1 daughter). President, Student Association, Stirling University 1970–71; Teacher of children with special needs 1976–92; Chair, Stirling Economic Development Co. 1987–90; Member: TGWU, EIS. Stirling District Council: Councillor 1977–90, Council leader 1980–90; JP 1977–90. **House of Commons:** Contested Stirling 1983 and 1987 general elections. Member for Falkirk East since April 9, 1992; PPS to Tom Clarke, as Minister of State, Department for Culture, Media and Sport (Film and Tourism) 1997–98; *Select Committees:* Member: European Directives Committee A (Agriculture, Environment, Health and Safety) 1993–97, Select Committee on Parliamentary Commissioner for Administration 1995–97; Member: Information 1997–, European Scrutiny 1998–. *Special Interests:* Economy and Enterprise, Local Government, European Union, Industry, Skills and Training, Youth Affairs, Students, Crime, Drug Abuse; Middle East, Central America. Member, Labour Party Scottish Executive Committee 1981–82, 1983–92; Chair, LP Scottish Local Government Committee 1988–90; Member, LP Local Government Committee (UK) 1989–91; Vice-Chair, COSLA Labour Group 1988–90; Chair, Stirlingshire Co-operative Party 1990–92; Vice-Chair, Scottish Group of Labour MPs 1996–98, Chair 1998–99. Loch Lomond, Trossachs and Stirling Tourist Board: Financial Controller 1981–84, Member 1981–90; Member, Socialist Education Association 1978–; Central EIS President 1983–84; National Council EIS 1984–85; Rector, Stirling University 1983–84; Vice-Chair, Scottish Medical Aid for Palestinians 1988–95; Board Member, Parliamentary Office of Science and Technology (POST) 1997–; Life Member: International Parliamentary Union 1992–, Commonwealth Parliamentary Association 1992–; *Recreations:* Family, music (jazz and classical), reading, walking. *Address:* Michael Connarty Esq, MP, House of Commons, London, SW1A 0AA *Tel:* 020 7219 5071 *Fax:* 020 7219 2541. *Constituency:* 47 Bo'Ness Road, Grangemouth, FK3 8AN *Tel:* 01324 474832 *Fax:* 01324 666811 *E-mail:* mc003@post.almac.co.uk *Website:* www.mconnartymp.org.uk.

FRANK COOK   Stockton North   *Lab majority 21,357*

Born 3 November 1935; Son of late James Cook; Educated Corby School, Sunderland; De La Salle College, Manchester; Institute of Education, Leeds; Married March 30, 1959, Patricia Lundrigan (divorced) (1 son 3 daughters). Previously: Schoolmaster, Gravedigger, Butlins Redcoat, Barman, Brewery hand, Gardener, Postman, Steel works transport manager; Construction, planning, field, cost engineer, project manager; Member and Sponsored by MSF. **House of Commons:** Member for Stockton North since June 1983; Opposition Whip 1987–92; Deputy Speaker, Westminster Hall 1999–; *Select Committees:* Member: Procedure 1989–92, Defence 1992–97; Member: Chairmen's Panel 1997–. *Special Interests:* Engineering, Peace and Disarmament, Alternative Energy, Expatriate Workers, Pensioners' Rights, Education, Ecology, Race Relations, Landmine Victim Support, Landmine Eradication Measures, Child Protection and Safety, Shooters' Rights; North Korea, South Korea, Turkey, Laos. Trustee and Director, Lucy Faithfull Foundation (for rehabilitation of paedophiles); Member: NATO – Parliamentary Assembly 1987–, Vice-President 1998–; Organisation for Security and Co-operation in Europe Parliamentary Body 1991–; Fellow: Industry and Parliament Trust, Parliamentary Armed Services Trust; *Recreations:* Singing, climbing, fell-walking, swimming. *Address:* Francis Cook Esq, MP, House of Commons, London, SW1A 0AA *Tel:* 020 7219 4527 *Fax:* 020 7219 4303. *Constituency:* c/o The Health Centre, Queensway, Billingham, Teesside, TS23 2LA *Tel:* 01642 643288 *Fax:* 01642 803271 *E-mail:* cookf@parliament.uk.

ROBIN COOK   Livingston   *Lab majority 11,747*

Born 28 February 1946; Son of late Peter Cook; Educated Aberdeen Grammar School; Edinburgh University (MA English literature); Married 1st, September 15, 1969, Margaret Whitmore, medical consultant (2 sons) (marriage dissolved 1998); married 2nd, April 9, 1998, Gaynor Regan, née Wellings. Tutor-organiser, Workers' Educational Association 1970–74. Edinburgh Town Council: Councillor 1971–74, Chairman, Edinburgh Housing Committee 1973–74. **House of Commons:** Contested Edinburgh North 1970 general election. Member for Edinburgh Central 1974–83, and for Livingston since June 1983; Opposition Front Bench Spokesman on: Treasury and Economic Affairs 1980–83, European and Community Affairs 1983–84; Spokesman on the City 1986–87; Shadow Secretary of State for: Health and Social Security 1987–92, Trade and Industry 1992–94, Foreign and Commonwealth Affairs 1994–97; Chair, Parliamentary Labour Party 1997; Secretary of State for Foreign and Commonwealth Affairs 1997–; *Special Interests:* Welfare, Environment, Defence. Chair, Scottish Association of Labour Student Organisations 1966–67; Secretary, Edinburgh City Labour Party 1970–72; Labour Party Campaign Co-ordinator 1984–86; Former Member, Labour Party National Executive Committee. Member, Executive Committee, Commonwealth Parliamentary Association (CPA) UK Branch 1999–; PC 1996; *The Spectator* Parliamentarian of the Year 1991, Debater of the Year 1996; *Recreations:* Reading, eating and talking. *Address:* Rt Hon Robin Cook, MP, House of Commons, London, SW1A 0AA *Tel:* 020 7219 1500.

YVETTE COOPER   Pontefract and Castleford   *Lab majority 25,725*

Born 20 March 1969; Daughter of Tony and June Cooper; Educated Eggars Comprehensive; Balliol College, Oxford (BA philosophy, politics and economics); Harvard University (Kennedy Scholar 1991); London School of Economics (MSc economics); Married January 10, 1998, Ed Balls (1 daughter). Economic researcher for John Smith MP 1990–92; Domestic policy specialist, Bill Clinton presidential campaign 1992; Policy adviser to Labour Treasury teams 1992–94; Economic columnist/Leader writer, *The Independent* 1995–97; Member, GMB. **House of Commons:** Member for Pontefract and Castleford since May 1, 1997; Parliamentary Under-Secretary of State, Department of Health (Minister for Public Health) 1999–; *Select Committees:* Member: Education and Employment 1997–99, Employment Sub-Committee 1997–99. *Special Interests:* Unemployment, Coal Industry; USA. *Recreations:* Swimming, painting, watching soap operas. *Address:* Yvette Cooper, MP, House of Commons, London, SW1A 0AA *Tel:* 020 7219 5080 *Fax:* 020 7219 0912. *Constituency:* 2 Wesley Street, Castleford, West Yorkshire, WF10 1AE *Tel:* 01977 553388 *Fax:* 01977 553388 *E-mail:* coopery@parliament.uk.

ROBIN CORBETT   Birmingham Erdington   *Lab majority 12,657*

Born 22 December 1933; Son of late Thomas Corbett, foundry worker; Educated Holly Lodge Grammar School, Smethwick, Staffordshire; Married May 1970, Val Hudson, daughter of Fred Jonas (1 son 2 daughters). National Service RAF 1951–53; Journalist; Assistant editor, *Farmers Weekly* 1968–70; Editorial staff development executive, ICP Magazines 1970–73; Senior labour adviser, IPC Magazines 1973–74; Communications consultant 1979–83; Member, National Executive Council, National Union of Journalists 1964–69. **House of Commons:** Member for Hemel Hempstead 1974–79, and for Birmingham Erdington since June 1983; Opposition Front Bench Deputy Spokesman on Home Affairs 1987–92; Opposition Front Bench Spokesman on: National Heritage, Broadcasting and Press 1992–94, Disabled People's Rights 1994–95; West Midlands Labour Whip 1984–87; *Select Committees:* Member: Agriculture 1995–97; Chairman: Home Affairs 1997–99; Chairman: Home Affairs 1997–; Member: Liaison 1999–. *Special Interests:* Home Affairs, Police, Civil Liberties, Motor Industry, Manufacturing, Disabled/Disability, Children's Rights, Alternative Energy, Environment, Agriculture, Animal Welfare, Press; Australia, Cyprus, India, New Zealand, South Africa, Egypt. Member, Parliamentary Labour Party Campaign Unit 1984–85. Chair, Farm Animal Welfare Co-ordinating Executive 1975–87; Member, Committee for the Reform of Animal Experiments; Director, Rehab UK 1998–; Fellow, Industry and Parliament Trust; *Publications: Can I Count on Your Support?* (for Save the Children Fund, with wife), 1986; *Tales from the Campaign Trail* (co-author, for Save the Children Fund); *Clubs:* Castle Vale Residents', Forget-Me-Not; *Recreations:* Collecting bric-a-brac, walking. *Address:* Robin Corbett Esq, MP, House of Commons, London, SW1A 0AA *Tel:* 020 7219 3420 *Fax:* 020 7219 2461. *Constituency:* Regent House, 50a Reservoir Road, Erdington, Birmingham, B23 6DG *Tel:* 0121–373 1147 *Fax:* 0121–382 6347.

JEREMY CORBYN   Islington North   *Lab majority 19,955*

Born 26 May 1949; Son of David Benjamin and Naomi Loveday Jocelyn Corbyn; Educated Adams Grammar School, Newport, Shropshire; (3 sons). Former full-time organiser, National Union of Public Employees; Also worked for Tailor and Garment workers and AUEW; NUPE sponsored MP. Haringey Borough Council: Chair: Community Development 1975–78, Public Works 1978–79, Planning 1980–81. **House of Commons:** Member for Islington North since June 1983; *Select Committees:* Member: Social Security 1991–97. *Special Interests:* People of Islington, Defence, Welfare State, Health Service, Campaigning for Socialism in the Community and against Racism, Anti-Imperialism and Internationalism, Safe Transport Systems in Cities, Environment, Irish Affairs, Liberation Islington Local Agenda 21. *Recreations:* Running, railways. *Address:* Jeremy Corbyn Esq, MP, House of Commons, London, SW1A 0AA *Tel:* 020 7219 3545 *Tel (Constituency):* 020 7263 9450.

SIR PATRICK CORMACK   South Staffordshire   *Con majority 7,821*

Born 18 May 1939; Son of late Thomas C. Cormack, local government officer; Educated St James' Choir School; Havelock School, Grimsby; Hull University (BA 1961); Married August 18, 1967, Kathleen Mary McDonald (2 sons). Industrial Consultant; Second master, St James' Choir School, Grimsby 1961–66; Training and education officer, Ross Group Ltd. 1966–67; Assistant housemaster, Wrekin College, Shropshire 1967–69; Head of history, Brewood Grammar School, Staffordshire 1969–70; Associate editor, *Time and Tide* 1977–79; Company director Historic House Hotels 1980–88, Aitken Dott 1984–90; Editor, *The House Magazine* 1983–; Visiting lecturer, University of Texas 1984; Visiting Parliamentary Fellowship, St Anthony's College, Oxford 1994; Visiting senior lecturer, Hull University 1994–; International President, *First* magazine 1994–; Governor, English Speaking Union 1999–. **House of Commons:** Contested Bolsover 1964 and Grimsby 1966 general elections. Member for Cannock division 1970–74, for South-West Staffordshire 1974–83 and for South Staffordshire since June 1983; Spokesman on Constitutional Affairs 1997–2000;

PPS to the Joint Parliamentary Secretaries, Department of Health and Social Security 1970–73; Deputy to the Shadow Leader of the House of Commons 1997–2000; *Select Committees:* Member: House of Commons Services 1979–92, Speaker's Panel of Chairmen 1983–97; Chairman: House of Commons Works of Art 1987–97; Member: Chairmen's Panel 1997–98, Modernisation of the House of Commons 1997–98; Member: Accommodation and Works 1987–, Parliamentary Privilege (Joint Committee) 1997–. *Special Interests:* Arts, Heritage, Defence and NATO, Parliamentary History, Education, Electoral Reform, Industrial Relations, Human Rights; Bosnia, former Soviet Union, Croatia, Finland, Netherlands, Lithuania, USA. Member, Council of Historical Association 1963–66; Founder and Vice-Chairman, Heritage in Danger 1974–97; Member, Historic Buildings Council 1979–84; Chairman, Council for Independent Education from 1980–95; Member: Royal Commission on Historical Manuscripts 1981–, General Synod of the Church of England 1995–; Member: Institute of Journalists 1979–89, Royal Commission on Historical Manuscripts 1981–, Lord Chancellor's Advisory Committee on Public Records 1982–87; Vice-Chair, De Burght Conference; Member, Council for Peace in the Balkans 1992–; Member, Executive Committee, Commonwealth Parliamentary Association (CPA) UK Branch 1997–99; Joint Vice-Chair 1999–; Trustee, Historic Churches Preservation Trust 1973–; Member, Council of Winston Churchill Memorial Trust 1983–93; Trustee, Museum of Garden History 1980–2000; President, Staffordshire Historic Churches Trust 1998–; Member, Worshipful Company of Glaziers; *Publications: Heritage in Danger,* 1976; *Right Turn,* 1978; *Westminster: Palace and Parliament,* 1981; *Castles of Britain* 1982; *Wilberforce – The Nation's Conscience,* 1983; *English Cathedrals 1984*; Hon. Citizen of Texas 1985; Knighted 1995; Commander of the Order of the Lion (Finland) 1998; Fellow, Society of Antiquaries 1978, Vice-President 1994–98; Freeman, City of London 1980; *Clubs:* Athenaeum; *Recreations:* Walking, talking, fighting Philistines. *Address:* Sir Patrick Cormack, FSA, MP, House of Commons, London, SW1A 0AA *Tel:* 020 7219 5514. *Constituency:* The Firs, Codsall, Staffordshire, WV8 1BX *Tel:* 01902 844985 *Fax:* 01902 844949.

JEAN CORSTON   Bristol East   *Lab majority 16,159*

Born 5 May 1942; Daughter of Laurie Parkin, trade union official, and late Eileen Parkin; Educated Yeovil Girls' High School; London School of Economics (LLB 1989); Inns of Court School of Law 1989–90; Open University; Married 1st, September 23, 1961, Christopher Corston (1 son 1 daughter); married 2nd, January 4, 1985, Professor Peter Townsend. Barrister; Member, TGWU. **House of Commons:** Member for Bristol East since April 9, 1992; PPS to David Blunkett as Secretary of State for Education and Employment 1997–; *Select Committees:* Member: Agriculture 1992–95, Home Affairs 1995–97. *Special Interests:* Employment Law, Legal Reform, Women's Rights, Disabled/Disability; India, Kenya, USA. Organiser, Taunton Labour Party 1974–76; South West Region Labour Party: Assistant regional organiser 1976–81, Regional organiser 1981–85; Assistant national agent, The Labour Party, London 1985–86; Secretary, Labour Party Annual Conference Arrangements 1985–86; Deputy Chair, PLP 1997–98, 1999–2000. Associate Member, British-Irish Inter-Parliamentary Body; Member, Executive Committee, Commonwealth Parliamentary Association (CPA) UK Branch 1999–; Chair, Commonwealth Women Parliamentarians 2000–; *Recreations:* Gardening, reading, walking. *Address:* Jean Corston, MP, House of Commons, London, SW1A 0AA *Tel:* 020 7219 4575 *Fax:* 020 7219 4878. *Constituency:* PO Box 1105, Bristol, BS99 2DP *Tel:* 0117–939 9901 *Fax:* 0117–939 9902.

BRIAN COTTER   Weston-Super-Mare   *LD majority 1,274*

Born 24 August 1938; Son of late Michael Joseph and late Mary Cotter; Educated Downside School; London Polytechnic (business studies); Married February 1963, Eyleen Patricia Wade (2 sons 1 daughter). Plasticable Ltd 1990–: Sales manager, Managing director. Councillor, Woking Borough Council 1986–90. **House of Commons:** Contested Weston-Super-Mare 1992 general election. Member for Weston-Super-Mare since May 1, 1997; Spokesman for Trade and Industry: (Small Business and Millennium Bug) 1997–99, (Small Business) 1999–; *Select Committees:* Member: Deregulation 1997–. *Special Interests:* Business, Tourism, Disabled/Disability, Youth Affairs. Member: Lib Dem Parliamentary Association, ASLDC, Green Liberal Democrat Association. *Clubs:* National Liberal; *Recreations:* Reading, walking, gardening, films. *Address:* Brian Cotter Esq, MP, House of Commons, SW1A 0AA *Tel:* 020 7219 5127 *Fax:* 020 7219 2277. *Constituency:* 8a Alexandra Parade, Weston-super-Mare, North Somerset, BS23 1QT *Tel:* 01934 419200 *Fax:* 01934 419300 *E-mail:* briancottermp@liberty.compulink.co.uk.

JIM COUSINS   Newcastle upon Tyne Central   *Lab majority 16,480*

Born 23 February 1944; Son of late Charles John Cousins, printing trade worker, and late Grace Ellen Cousins; Educated New College, Oxford; London School of Economics; Married Anne Elizabeth (2 sons, 1 stepson, 1 stepdaughter). Industrial relations and research worker in industry 1967–72; Research worker, urban affairs and city labour markets 1972–82; Lecturer, Sunderland Polytechnic 1982–87. Councillor, Wallsend Borough Council 1969–73; Tyne and Wear County Council: Councillor 1973–86, Deputy leader 1981–86. **House of Commons:** Member for Newcastle upon Tyne Central since June 1987; Opposition Front Bench Spokesman on: Trade and Industry 1992–94, Foreign and Commonwealth Affairs 1994–95; *Select Committees:* Member: Trade and Industry 1989–92, Public Service 1995–97; Member: Treasury 1997–, Treasury Sub-Committee 1998–. *Special Interests:* Health, Science, Arms Control; Czechoslovakia, Ethiopia, Iran, Central Asian Republics. Chair, Northern Group of Labour MPs 1997–. *Recreations:* Composting. *Address:* Jim Cousins Esq, MP, House of Commons, London, SW1A 0AA *Tel:* 020 7219 4204 *Fax:* 020 7219 6290. *Constituency:* 1st Floor, 21 Portland Terrace, Newcastle upon Tyne, NE2 1QQ *Tel:* 0191–281 9888 *Fax:* 0191–281 3383 *E-mail:* jcousins@globalnet.co.uk.

TOM COX   Tooting   *Lab majority 15,011*

Born 19 January 1930; Educated state schools; London School of Economics. Electrical Worker. Former Alderman, Fulham Borough Council. **House of Commons:** Contested Stroud 1966 general election. Member for Wandsworth Central 1970–74, and for Tooting since 1974; Assistant Whip 1974–77; Lord Commissioner of the Treasury 1977–79. Member, UK Delegation of the Council of Europe and Western European Union; Representative, UK Delegation to Organisation for Security and Co-operation in Europe; Executive Committee Member, IPU British Group; Member, Executive Committee, Commonwealth Parliamentary Association (CPA) UK Branch 1999–. *Address:* Thomas Cox Esq, MP, House of Commons, London, SW1A 0AA *Tel:* 020 7219 5034.

JAMES CRAN   Beverley and Holderness   *Con majority 1,211*

Born 28 January 1944; Son of late James and Jane Macdonald-Cran; Educated Ruthrieston School, Aberdeen (Dux Medallion Winner); King's College, Aberdeen University (MA politics, philosophy and economics 1968); Married April 7, 1973, Penelope Barbara, daughter of Richard and Barbara Wilson (1 daughter). Conservative Research Department 1970–71; Secretary and Chief Executive, National Association of Pension Funds 1971–79; CBI: Northern Director 1979–84, West Midlands Director 1984–87. Councillor, London Borough of Sutton 1974–79, Chair, Health and Housing Committee. **House of Commons:** Contested Glasgow Shettleston October 1974 and Gordon 1983 general elections. Member for Beverley 1987–97, and for Beverley and Holderness since May 1, 1997; Opposition Whip (Home Office, Northern Ireland: Northern and Yorkshire) 1997–98; Opposition Whip for Northern Ireland and Pairing Whip 1998–; PPS to Sir Patrick Mayhew as Secretary of State for Northern Ireland 1995–96; *Select Committees:* Member: Trade and Industry 1987–92, Northern Ireland Affairs 1994–95, Administration 1997–98, Selection 1998; Member: Selection 1998–. *Special Interests:* Trade and Industry, Pensions, Regional Policy, European Union, Irish Affairs, Economic Policy; Canada, Europe, Hong Kong, Taiwan, USA, Mexico, China, New Zealand. Member of Court: Birmingham University 1984–87, Hull University 1987–; Treasurer, European Research Group 1994–97; Fellow, Armed Forces Parliamentary Scheme 1992; Council Member, Pensions Trustee Forum 1992–95; Fellow, Industry and Parliament Trust 1994; OStJ; *Recreations:* Travelling, reading biographies and autobiographies, military history. *Address:* James Cran Esq, MP, House of Commons, London, SW1A 0AA *Tel:* 020 7219 4445 *Fax:* 020 7219 2271. *Constituency:* 9 Cross Street, Beverley, East Yorkshire, HU17 9AX *Tel:* 01482 881316 *Fax:* 01482 861667 *E-mail:* cranp@parliament.uk.

ROSS CRANSTON   Dudley North — *Lab majority 9,457*

Born 23 July 1948; Educated University of Queensland (BA 1969, LLB 1970); Harvard Law School (LLM 1973); Oxford (DPhil 1976, DCL 1998); Divorced. Barrister, Gray's Inn 1976; Professor of law, London University: Queen Mary College 1986–91, London School of Economics 1992–97; Practising barrister, Gray's Inn; Assistant Recorder 1991–97; Recorder 1997–98; QC 1998–; Visiting Professor of Law, LSE 1997–; Member: GMB, AUT. **House of Commons:** Contested Richmond, Yorkshire 1992 general election. Member for Dudley North since May 1, 1997; Solicitor General 1998–; *Select Committees:* Member: Home Affairs 1997–98, Home Affairs 1998. *Special Interests:* Home Affairs, Legal Affairs, Treasury. President, Society of Public Teachers of Law 1992–93; Consultant to Woolf Inquiry into Access to Justice 1994–96; Consultant (1988–97) to: UNCTAD, Commonwealth Secretariat, World Bank, IMF; Chair, Trustees of Public Concern at Work (The Whistleblowers Charity) 1996–97; *Publications: Regulating Business,* 1979; *Legal Foundations of the Welfare State,* 1985; *Legal Ethics and Professional Responsibility,* editor 1995; *Principles of Banking Law,* 1997; *Cranston's Consumers and the Law,* 3rd edition 2000. *Address:* Ross Cranston Esq, QC, MP, House of Commons, London, SW1A 0AA *Tel:* 020 7219 4195 *Fax:* 020 7219 2726. *Constituency:* Holloway Chambers, 28 Priory Street, Dudley, West Midlands, DY1 1EZ *Tel:* 01384 233100 *Fax:* 01384 233 099.

DAVID CRAUSBY   Bolton North East — *Lab majority 12,669*

Born 17 June 1946; Son of late Thomas Crausby, factory worker/club steward, and of Kathleen Crausby, cotton worker; Educated Derby Grammar School, Bury; Bury Technical College; Married September 4, 1965, Enid Noon (2 sons). Shop steward/works convenor, AEEU; Full-time works convenor 1978–97. Councillor, Bury Council 1979–92, Chair of Housing 1985–92. **House of Commons:** Contested Bury North 1987 and Bolton North East 1992 general elections. Member for Bolton North East since May 1, 1997; *Select Committees:* Member: Administration 1997–, Social Security 1999–. *Special Interests:* Industrial Relations, Pensions, Housing. Member, European Standing Committee C 1999–. *Address:* David Crausby Esq, MP, House of Commons, London, SW1A 0AA *Tel:* 020 7219 4092 *Fax:* 020 7219 3713. *Constituency:* 60 St George's Road, Bolton, Greater Manchester *Tel:* 01204 523574 *Fax:* 01204 523574.

ANN CRYER   Keighley — *Lab majority 7,132*

Born 14 December 1939; Daughter of late Allen and Margaret Ann Place; Educated St John's Church of England Primary School; Spring Bank Secondary Modern, Darwen; Bolton Technical College; Keighley Technical College (part-time); Married August 3, 1963, Bob Cryer, MP for Keighley and Bradford South (died 1994) (1 son John Cryer, MP (*qv*) 1 daughter). Clerk: ICI Ltd 1955–60, GPO 1960–64; Personal assistant, Bob Cryer, MP, MEP 1974–94; Member, TGWU. Member, Darwen Borough Council 1962–65; JP, Bradford Bench, appointed 1996. **House of Commons:** Member for Keighley since May 1, 1997; *Special Interests:* Early Years Education, Health, Railways, Planning, Immigration, Human Rights of Asian, United Kingdom women – campaigned against Forced Marriages; South Africa, Pakistan, Afghanistan, Palestine. Member, Co-operative Party 1965–; Chair, PLP CND Group. Former governor: Shipley Church of England First School, Frizinghall First School; President, Keighley and Worth Valley Railway Preservation Society; Member: Friends of the Earth, CND, Brontë Society; Member: Social Security Appeal Tribunal 1987–96, Keighley Business Forum; Delegate, Parliamentary Assembly of the Council of Europe 1997–; Member: Legal Affairs on Human Rights Committee 1997–, CPA 1998–, Equal Opportunities Committee 1998–, Culture and Education Committee 2000–, Heritage sub Committee 2000–; Contributor to Canon Collins' Educational Trust for South Africa; Vice-President: Keighley Bus Museum, Friends of the Settle to Carlisle Railway; *Publications:* Compiled *Boldness Be My Friend: Remembering Bob Cryer,* 1996; *Recreations:* Gardening, theatre, cinema, time with my six grandchildren, walking. *Address:* Mrs Ann Cryer, MP, House of Commons, London, SW1A 0AA *Tel:* 020 7219 6649. *Constituency:* Bob Cryer House, 35 Devonshire Street, Keighley, West Yorkshire, BD21 2BH *Tel:* 01535 210083 *Fax:* 01535 210085.

JOHN CRYER   Hornchurch   *Lab majority 5,680*

Born 11 April 1964; Son of late Bob Cryer, MP and of Ann Cryer, MP (*qv*); Educated Oakbank School, Keighley; Hatfield Polytechnic (BA literature and history 1985); London College of Printing (Postgraduate Certificate in Print Journalism 1988); Married 1994, Narinder Bains (2 sons 1 daughter). Journalist with: *Tribune* 1992–96, *Morning Star* 1989–92; Freelance Journalist with: *Labour Briefing* (editor), *Guardian*, *GMPU Journal*, *T&G Record*; Lloyd's of London Publications; Member: TGWU 1986–, NUJ 1988–, UCATT 1997–. **House of Commons:** Member for Hornchurch since May 1, 1997; *Select Committees:* Member: Deregulation 1997–. *Special Interests:* Employment, Social Security, Education, Further and Higher Education, European Union, Health, Economic Policy, Industry, Coal Industry, Transport; Australia, India. Member, Executive of Labour Euro Safeguards Committee; Press officer, For Defend Clause Four Campaign 1995; Member, Co-operative Party. Member: CND, Amnesty International, Transport on Water, Tibet Support Group, Keighley and Worth Valley Railway, RAF Hornchurch Association; Patron, St Frances Hospice; *Publications:* Co-author with Ann Cryer, *Boldness be my Friend: Remembering Bob Cryer MP*, 1996; Many articles mainly in political publications; *Sportsclubs:* Member: House of Commons Cricket Club, House of Commons Rugby Club; *Recreations:* Swimming, reading, sport, old cars, cinema. *Address:* John Cryer Esq, MP, House of Commons, London, SW1A 0AA *Tel:* 020 7219 6988/1134 *Fax:* 020 7219 1183. *Constituency:* 11 Park Lane, Hornchurch, Essex *Tel:* 01708 742674 *Fax:* 01708 735576.

JOHN CUMMINGS   Easington   *Lab majority 30,012*

Born 6 July 1943; Son of late George and Mary Cummings, née Cain; Educated Murton Council Infant, Junior, Senior Schools; Easington and Durham Technical Colleges 1958–62. Murton Colliery 1958–87, Colliery Electrician and Secretary 1967–87; Sponsored by NUM; Trustee NUM 1986–2000. Councillor, Easington Rural District Council 1970–73; Easington District Council: Councillor 1973–87, Chair 1975–76, Leader 1979–87; Member: Northumbrian Water Authority 1977–83, Peterlee and Aycliffe Development Corporation 1980–87. **House of Commons:** Member for Easington since June 1987; Opposition Whip (Northern and Overseas Development) 1994–97; *Select Committees:* Member: Environment, Transport and Regional Affairs 1997–, Environment Sub-Committee 1997–. *Special Interests:* Energy, Environment, Coal Industry; Eastern Europe, Middle East, China. Chair, Northern Regional Group of Labour MPs 1999–. Vice-Chair, Coalfield Communities Campaign 1985–87; Member: Council of Europe 1992–, Western European Union 1992–; *Recreations:* Jack Russell terriers, walking, travel. *Address:* John Cummings Esq, MP, House of Commons, London, SW1A 0AA *Tel:* 020 7219 5122. *Constituency:* Seaton Holme, Easington Village, County Durham, SR8 3BS *Tel:* 01915 273773.

LAWRENCE CUNLIFFE   Leigh   *Lab majority 24,496*

Born 25 March 1929; Educated St. Edmund's Roman Catholic School, Worsley, Manchester; Ruskin College, Oxford (economics, industrial relations); Married April 11, 1950, Winifred Haslem (marriage dissolved 1983) (3 sons 2 daughters). Engineer, NCB 1949–79. Councillor: Farnworth Borough Council 1960–74, Bolton Metropolitan District Council 1974–79; Magistrate 1967–79. **House of Commons:** Contested Rochdale October 1972 by-election and February 1974 general election. Member for Leigh since May, 1979; Opposition Whip 1981–87; *Special Interests:* Energy, Industry, Aerospace, Aviation. Deputy Leader, UK Delegation to Council of Europe and Western Europe Union; *Recreations:* Cricket, football, swimming. *Address:* Lawrence Cunliffe Esq, MP, House of Commons, London, SW1A 0AA *Tel:* 020 7219 4185.

DR JACK CUNNINGHAM   Copeland   *Lab majority 11,996*

Born 4 August 1939; Son of Andrew and Freda Cunningham; Educated Jarrow Grammar School; Bede College, Durham University (BSc chemistry 1962, PhD 1966); Married 1964, Maureen Appleby (1 son 2 daughters). Research fellow, Durham University 1966–68; Full-time Officer, GMWU 1969–70. DL, Cumbria 1991. **House of Commons:** Member for Whitehaven 1970–83, and for Copeland since June 1983; Opposition Front Bench Spokesman on Industry 1979–83; PPS to James Callaghan as Foreign Secretary and Prime Minister 1974–76; Parliamentary Under-Secretary for Energy 1976–79; Shadow Environment Secretary 1983–89; Shadow Leader, House of Commons and Campaigns Co-ordinator 1989–92; Shadow Secretary of State for: Foreign and Commonwealth Affairs 1992–94, Trade and Industry 1994–95, National Heritage 1995–97; Minister of Agriculture, Fisheries and Food 1997–98; Minister for the Cabinet Office, and Chancellor of the Duchy of Lancaster 1998–99; Commissioner, Millennium Commission 1998–99; *Select Committees:* Member: Privileges 1989–95. *Special Interests:* Regional Policy, Environment, Foreign Affairs, Industry; China, Japan, South Africa, Europe, USA. Fellow, Industry and Parliament Trust; PC 1993; *Recreations:* Fell-walking, gardening, music, reading, fishing, theatre. *Address:* Rt Hon Dr Jack Cunningham, DL, MP, House of Commons, London, SW1A 0AA *Tel:* 020 7219 3000. *Constituency:* Copeland CLP, 3 Carter Lane, Whitehaven, Cumbria *Tel:* 01946 62024.

JAMES CUNNINGHAM   Coventry South   *Lab majority 10,953*

Born 4 February 1941; Son of Adam and Elizabeth Cunningham; Educated Columbia High School, Coatbridge; Tillycoultry College, Ruskin Courses (Labour Movement, Industrial Law); Married March 1, 1985, Marion Douglas, daughter of Frank and Nancy Podmore (1 son 1 stepson 1 daughter 1 stepdaughter). Engineer Rolls Royce 1965–88; MSF Shop steward 1968–88. Coventry City Council: Councillor 1972–92, Chair, Consumer Services Committee 1975–77, Vice-Chair: Finance Committee 1975–77, 1979–82, 1985–88, Leisure Committee 1975–77, Chair 1979–82, Vice-Chair, Transportation and Highways Committee 1983–85, Chief Whip, Labour Group 1985–87, Deputy Leader of the Council 1987–88, Leader of the Council 1988–92. **House of Commons:** Member for Coventry South East 1992–97, and for Coventry South since May 1, 1997; *Select Committees:* Member: Home Affairs 1993–97; Member: Trade and Industry 1997–, Chairmen's Panel 1998–. *Special Interests:* Economic Policy, European Union, Industrial Relations, Health Service; USA, Eastern Europe, Russia. Coventry South East CLP: Secretary 1976–77, Chair 1977–79. *Recreations:* Walking, reading, historical buildings. *Address:* James Cunningham Esq, MP, House of Commons, London, SW1A 0AA *Tel:* 020 7219 6362 *Fax:* 020 7219 6362. *Constituency:* 2nd Floor, 107 New Union Street, Coventry, CV1 2NT *Tel:* 024 7655 3159 *Fax:* 024 7655 3159.

ROSEANNA CUNNINGHAM   Perth   *SNP majority 3,141*

Born 27 July 1951; Daughter of late Hugh Cunningham, and of Catherine Cunningham; Educated University of Western Australia (Degree in politics); Edinburgh University (MA law); Aberdeen University (Diploma in legal practice). SNP Research Department 1977–79; Solicitor: Dumbarton District Council 1983–86, Glasgow District Council 1986–89; Private practice solicitor 1989–; Called as Advocate 1990; MSP for Perth constituency since May 6, 1999; SNP Principal Shadow Spokesperson for Justice 1999–, Equality and Land Reform 1999–2000; Deputy Leader SNP and SNP Spokesperson for Justice 2000–; Former convenor and shop steward for NALGO Member, NUJ. **House of Commons:** Contested Perth and Kinross 1992 general election. Member for Perth and Kinross May 25, 1995 by-election –1997, and for Perth since May 1, 1997; SNP Spokeswoman for: Home Affairs 1995–, Environment and Land Reform, Arts and Broadcasting 1997–, Employment 1998, Women's Issues 1998–; *Special Interests:* Constitution, Land; Former Member, European Standing Committee B. Member SNP national executive; Deputy Leader SNP 2000–. *Recreations:* Martial Art Aikido, reading – especially science fiction, cinema. *Address:* Roseanna Cunningham, MP, MSP, House of Commons, London, SW1A 0AA *Tel:* 020 7219 3000. *Constituency:* 51 York Place, Perth, PH2 8EH *Tel:* 01738 444002 *Fax:* 01738 444602 *E-mail:* rcmp.perth@snp.org.uk; roseanna.cunningham.msp@scottish.parliament.uk.

DAVID CURRY   Skipton and Ripon
Con majority 11,620

Born 13 June 1944; Son of Thomas Harold and late Florence Joan Curry (née Tyerman); Educated Ripon Grammar School; Corpus Christi College, Oxford (BA modern history 1966); Kennedy School of Government, Harvard University; Married July 24, 1971, Anne Helene Maude, daughter of late Yahn Roullet and Madelaine Chambaud (1 son twin daughters). Newspaper Reporter, *Newcastle Journal* 1966–70; *Financial Times* 1970–79: world trade editor, international companies editor, Brussels correspondent, Paris correspondent; Freelance journalist. Vice-President, Local Government Association; Board Member British Association for Central and Eastern Europe; MEP for Essex North East 1979–89; Conservative Spokesman, Budget Committee 1984–89.

House of Commons: Contested Morpeth February and October 1974 general elections. Member for Skipton and Ripon since June 1987; Ministry of Agriculture, Fisheries and Food: Parliamentary Secretary 1989–92, Minister of State 1992–93; Minister of State, Department of the Environment for: Local Government and Planning 1993–94, Local Government, Housing and Urban Regeneration 1994–97; Shadow Minister of Agriculture, Fisheries and Food June-November 1997; *Select Committees:* Member: Agriculture 1998–2000; Member: Public Accounts 1999–; Chairman: Agriculture 2000–; Member: Liaison 2000–. *Special Interests:* Agriculture, Foreign Affairs, Urban Issues and Local Government. General rapporteur, EEC Budget for 1987; Director, British Association for Central and Eastern Europe; *Publications: The Conservative Tradition in Europe*, 1998; *Lobbying Government*, 1999; *The Sorcerer's apprentice: Government and Globalisation*, 2000; PC 1996; *Recreations:* Vegetable gardening, sailing. *Address:* Rt Hon David Curry, MP, House of Commons, London, SW1A 0AA *Tel:* 020 7219 5164. *Constituency:* 19 Otley Street, Skipton, North Yorks, BD23 1DY *Tel:* 01756 792092 *Fax:* 01756 798742 *E-mail:* currydm@parliament.uk.

CLAIRE CURTIS-THOMAS   Crosby
Lab majority 7,182

Born 30 April 1958; Daughter of Joyce Curtis-Thomas; Educated Mynyddbach Comprehensive School For Girls, Swansea; University College of Wales, Cardiff (BSc mechanical engineering); Aston University (MBA business administration); Staffordshire University (PhD technology 1999); Married Michael Lewis (1 son 2 daughters). Chartered engineer; Head, strategic planning, Birmingham City Council; Shell Chemicals: Head, environmental affairs, Head, Distribution UK Ltd; Dean, Faculty of Business and Engineering, University of Wales College, Newport; Member, TGWU. Councillor, Crewe and Nantwich Borough Council 1995–97. **House of Commons:** Member for Crosby since May 1, 1997 (Contested the seat as Claire Curtis-Tansley); *Select Committees:* Member: Science and Technology 1997–. *Special Interests:* Economic Policy, Trade and Industry, Education, Foreign Affairs; USA, Pan-Pacific Nations, Malaysia, China, Africa. Member: Co-operative Party, Fabian Society, Labour Women's Network; Membership Secretary, Rossett and Marford Labour Party; Secretary, Eddisbury Constituency Labour Party. Member: Soroptimist International, Amnesty International, Women's Engineering Society, National Trust; Adviser, Control Division, Institution of Electrical Engineers; Changed surname from Curtis-Tansley May 1997; Member, two Education Trusts to promote science and engineering to the public (Founder and Chair of one, Founder and President of the other); Senator, Engineering Council; Committee Member, Institution of Mechanical Engineering; CEng; FIMechE; Hon. FRICS; Hon PhD; *Recreations:* Family. *Address:* Claire Curtis-Thomas, MP, House of Commons, London, SW1A 0AA *Tel:* 020 7219 4193. *Constituency:* The Minster, 16 Beach Lawn, Waterloo, Liverpool, L22 8QA *Tel:* 0151–928 7250 *Fax:* 0151–928 9325 *E-mail:* curtisthomasc@parliament.uk.

D

Born 9 August 1932; Son of late Gordon Dalyell, Indian Civil Servant and late Eleanor Dalyell; Educated Edinburgh Academy, Harecroft; Eton College; King's College, Cambridge (MA 1956); Moray House, Edinburgh; Married December 1963, Kathleen, only daughter of late Lord Wheatley, Lord Justice Clerk of Scotland (1 son 1 daughter). National service, Royal Scots Greys 1950–52; Teacher Bo'ness Academy 1956–60; Deputy director of studies, BI ship-school, Dunera, 1961–62; Member: EIS, RMT **House of Commons:** Contested Roxburgh, Selkirk, Peebles 1959 general election. Member for West Lothian 1962–83, and for Linlithgow since June 1983; Opposition Front Bench Spokesman on Science 1980–82; PPS to Richard Crossman as Minister of Housing, Leader of the House of Commons and Secretary of State for Social Services 1964–65, 1967–70; MEP 1975–79; *Special Interests:* Science Policy, Central Economic Issues, Wildlife and Countryside Legislation, Kidney Transplantation, Rainforest Issues; Brazil, Burma, Indonesia, Libya, Zaire, Iran, Iraq, Peru. Vice-Chair, Parliamentary Labour Party 1974–76; Member, Labour Party National Executive Committee 1985–86. Member, Socialist Bureau of the Parliamentary and Budget Committee 1975; Vice-Chair, Control Committee on Budgets of European Parliament 1976–79; *Publications:* Case for Ship-Schools; Ship-School; Devolution: End of Britain, 1977; One Man's Falklands, 1982; A Science Policy for Britain, 1983; Thatcher's Torpedo, 1983; Misrule, 1987; Dick Crossman: a portrait, 1989; Hon. DSc, Edinburgh University 1994; Hon. Doctorate, City University, London 1998; *Recreations:* Squash, tennis, hill-walking. *Address:* Tam Dalyell Esq, MP, House of Commons, London, SW1A 0AA *Tel:* 020 7219 3427. *Constituency:* The Binns, Linlithgow, West Lothian, EH49 7NA *Tel:* 01506 834255.

Born 28 November 1953; Educated Loretto School; Aberdeen University (LLB); Married November 12, 1986, Margaret McQueen Vaughan (1 son 1 daughter). Solicitor 1978–82; Advocate 1984–. Lothian Regional Council: Councillor 1982–87, Chair, Lothian Region Transport Committee 1986–87. **House of Commons:** Member for Edinburgh Central since June 1987; Opposition Spokesman on Home Affairs 1988–92; Opposition Front Bench Spokesman on Treasury, Economic Affairs and the City 1992–96; Shadow Chief Secretary to the Treasury 1996–97; Sponsored Solicitors (Scotland) Act 1988 (Private Member's Bill); Chief Secretary to the Treasury 1997–98; Secretary of State for Social Security 1998–; *Special Interests:* Transport, Education, Health, Economic Policy, Constitution. Member, Labour Party's Economic Commission 1994–97. PC 1997. *Address:* Rt Hon Alistair Darling, MP, House of Commons, London, SW1A 0AA *Tel:* 020 7219 4584. *Constituency:* 15A Stafford Street, Edinburgh, EH3 7BU *Tel:* 0131–476 2552 *Fax:* 0131–467 3574.

Born 28 May 1948; Son of late Ernest Arthur James, dockworker, and of late Ellen Darvill; Educated Norlington Secondary Modern, Leyton; Central London Polytechnic; College of Law, Chester; Married 1971 Julia de Saran (2 sons 1 daughter). Solicitor 1982–; Member, TGWU. **House of Commons:** Member for Upminster since May 1, 1997; *Select Committees:* Member: Procedure 1997–. *Special Interests:* Environment, Education, Housing, Planning; Member, European Standing Committee C 1999–. Member: Co-operative Society, Fabian Society, Society of Labour Lawyers. Governor: Gaynes School (Upminster) 1983–, Havering Sixth Form College 1990–, Kingswood School Harold Hill 1999–; *Sportsclubs:* Cranston Park Lawn Tennis (Upminster); *Recreations:* Sport, tennis, badminton, gardening. *Address:* Keith Darvill Esq, MP, House of Commons, London, SW1A 0AA *Tel:* 020 7219 5106 *Fax:* 020 7219 5106. *Constituency:* 171 Howard Road, Upminster, Essex, RN14 2UQ *Tel:* 01708 222687 *E-mail:* darvillek@parliament.uk.

EDWARD DAVEY   Kingston and Surbiton   *LD majority 56*

Born 25 December 1965; Son of late John George Davey, solicitor, and of late Nina Joan Davey (née Stanbrook), teacher; Educated Nottingham High School; Jesus College, Oxford (College President) (BA); Birkbeck College, London (MSc economics). Senior economics adviser to Liberal Democrat MPs 1989–93; Management consultant, Omega Partners 1993; Director, Omega Partners Postal. **House of Commons:** Member for Kingston and Surbiton since May 1, 1997; Spokesman for: the Treasury (Public Spending and Taxation) 1997–99, Economy 1999–; London Whip until 2000; *Select Committees:* Member: Procedure 1997–2000; Member: Treasury 1999–, Treasury Sub-Committee 1999–. *Special Interests:* Tax, Macro Economics, European Monetary Union, Employment, Environment; Latin America. Chair, Costing Group (costing all policies for manifesto) 1992 and 1997 general elections; Member, Federal Policy Committee 1994–95; Liberal Democrat Policy Group (Economics, Tax and Benefits and Transport); Member, Association of Liberal Democrat Councillors. Royal Humane Society Honourable Testimonial; Chief Constable London Transport Police Commendation; *Recreations:* Cinema, music, walking, squash, swimming. *Address:* Edward Davey Esq, MP, House of Commons, London, SW1A 0AA *Tel:* 020 7219 3512 *Fax:* 020 7219 0250. *Constituency:* Liberal Democrats, 23A Victoria Road, Surbiton, Surrey, KT6 4JZ *Tel:* 020 8288 0161 *Fax:* 020 8288 1090 *E-mail:* daveye@parliament.uk.

VALERIE DAVEY   Bristol West   *Lab majority 1,493*

Born 16 April 1940; Educated Birmingham University (MA); London University (PGCE); Married August 1966, Graham Davey (1 son 2 daughters). Teacher, Wolverhampton; Teacher, Tanzania; Part-time Teacher, Further Education College; Member, NUT. Avon County Council: Councillor 1981–96, Leader, Labour Group 1992–96; Former Member, Avon Health Authority. **House of Commons:** Member for Bristol West since May 1, 1997; *Select Committees:* Member: Education and Employment 1997–, Education Sub-Committee 1997–. *Special Interests:* Education, Health, Local Government, International Aid and Development; East Africa (especially Tanzania), Cyprus. Member: Bristol University Court (formerly Member of Council), Amnesty International, ACTSA, Macular Disease Society; *Recreations:* Walking, gardens, reading, making marmalade. *Address:* Mrs Valerie Davey, MP, House of Commons, London, SW1A 0AA *Tel:* 020 7219 3576 *Fax:* 020 7219 3658. *Constituency:* PO Box 1947, Bristol, BS99 2UG *Tel:* 0117–907 7464 *Fax:* 0117–907 7465 *E-mail:* valdavey@labourbriswest.demon.co.uk.

IAN DAVIDSON   Glasgow Pollok   *Lab/Co-op majority 13,791*

Born 8 September 1950; Son of Graham Davidson and Elizabeth Crowe; Educated Jedburgh Grammar School; Galashiels Academy; Edinburgh University (MA Hons); Jordanhill College; Married 1978, Morag Christine Anne Mackinnon (1 son 1 daughter). Sabbatical Chair, National Organisation of Labour Students 1973–74; President, Students' Association, Jordanhill College 1975–76; Researcher for Janey Buchan, MEP 1978–85; Community Service Volunteers 1985–92; Chair, MSF Parliamentary Group, Secretary, Trade Union Group. Strathclyde Regional Council: Councillor 1978–92, Chair, Education Committee 1986–92. **House of Commons:** Member for Glasgow Govan 1992–97, and for Glasgow Pollok since May 1, 1997; *Select Committees:* Member: Selection 1997–99; Member: Public Accounts 1997–. *Special Interests:* Local Government, Education, Commonwealth, Third World, Local Economic Development, Defence, Co-operative Movement; Africa, Europe, Scandinavia, The Commonwealth, USA, Japan, Germany, British Overseas Territories. Chair, Kelvingrove Constituency Labour Party; Executive: Glasgow Labour Party, Strathclyde Regional Labour Party; Member, Co-operative Party; Secretary: Tribune Group, Trade Union Group of Labour MPs; Chair, Co-operative Parliamentary Group. Chair, COSLA Education Committee 1990–92; Chairman, COSLA Education Committee 1990–92; *Recreations:* Sport, distance running, swimming, family. *Address:* Ian Davidson Esq, MP, House of Commons, London, SW1A 0AA *Tel:* 020 7219 3610 *Fax:* 020 7219 2238. *Constituency:* 1829 Paisley Road West, Glasgow, G52 3SS *Tel:* 0141–883 8338 *Fax:* 0141–883 4116.

DENZIL DAVIES Llanelli   *Lab majority 16,039*

Born 9 October 1938; Educated Carmarthen Grammar School; Pembroke College, Oxford University (BA law 1962); Married 1963, Mary Ann Finlay (divorced 1988) (1 son 1 daughter). Lectured at Chicago 1963 and Leeds 1964 Universities; Called to Bar, Gray's Inn 1964. **House of Commons:** Member for Llanelli since June 18, 1970; Opposition Front Bench Spokesman on: The Treasury and Economic Affairs 1979–80, Foreign and Commonwealth Affairs 1980–81, Defence and Disarmament 1981–1983; Deputy Spokesman on Defence and Disarmament 1983–84; Chief Opposition Spokesman 1984–88; PPS to Secretary of State for Wales 1974–76; Minister of State, HM Treasury 1975–79; *Select Committees:* Member: Public Accounts 1992–97. *Special Interests:* Foreign Affairs, Treasury, Wales. PC 1978. *Address:* Rt Hon Denzil Davies, MP, House of Commons, London, SW1A 0AA *Tel:* 020 7219 5197 *Tel (Constituency):* 01554 756374.

GERAINT DAVIES Croydon Central   *Lab majority 3,897*

Born 3 May 1960; Son of David Thomas Morgan Davies, senior civil servant, and of Betty Ferrer Davies; Educated Llanishen Comprehensive, Cardiff; JCR President, Jesus College, Oxford (BA philosophy, politics and economics 1982); Married September 7, 1991, Dr Vanessa Catherine Fry (2 daughters). Group Product Manager, Unilever 1982; Former Marketing Manager, Colgate Palmolive Ltd; Managing Partner, Pure Crete 1989; Member, GMB. Councillor, Croydon Council 1986–97: Chair, Housing Committee 1994–96, Leader of Council 1996–97. **House of Commons:** Contested Croydon South 1987 and Croydon Central 1992 general elections. Member for Croydon Central since May 1, 1997; *Select Committees:* Member: Public Accounts 1997–. *Special Interests:* Treasury, Trade and Industry, Environment, Transport and the Regions; Wales, Crete. Chair, Labour Finance and Industry Group 1998–. Chair, London Boroughs Association Housing Committee 1996–97; *Clubs:* Ruskin House; *Recreations:* Family. *Address:* Geraint Davies Esq, MP, House of Commons, London, SW1A 0AA *Tel:* 020 7219 4599 *Fax:* 020 7219 5962. *Constituency:* PO Box 679, Croydon, CR9 1UQ *E-mail:* geraintdaviesmp@parliament.uk.

QUENTIN DAVIES Grantham and Stamford   *Con majority 2,692*

Born 29 May 1944; Son of late Dr M I Davies, general practitioner, and of Thelma Davies; Educated Dragon School, Oxford; Leighton Park; Gonville and Caius College, Cambridge (BA history 1966); Harvard University, USA; Married April 9, 1983, Chantal Tamplin (2 sons). HM Diplomatic Service 1967–74: 3rd Secretary, FCO 1967–69, 2nd Secretary, Moscow 1969–72, 1st Secretary, FCO 1972–74; Manager then assistant director, Morgan Grenfell & Co Ltd 1974–78; Director General and President, Morgan Grenfell France 1978–81; Director, Morgan Grenfell Co Ltd and certain group subsidiaries 1981–87, Consultant 1987–93; Consultant, National Westminster Securities plc 1993–; Director: Dewe Rogerson International 1987–94, Société Genérale d'Entreprises 1999–2000, Vinci 2000–. **House of Commons:** Contested Birmingham Ladywood 1977 by-election. Member for Stamford and Spalding 1987–97, and for Grantham and Stamford since May 1, 1997; Opposition Spokesman for: Social Security 1998–99, the Treasury 1999–2000, Defence 2000–; PPS to Angela Rumbold as Minister of State at: Department of Education and Science 1988–90, Home Office 1990–91; Shadow Minister for Pensions 1998–99; Shadow Paymaster General 1999–2000; *Select Committees:* Member: Treasury and Civil Service 1992–97, Standards and Privileges 1995–97, European Legislation 1997–98, Standards and Privileges 1997–98, Treasury 1997–98, European Scrutiny 1998. *Special Interests:* Trade and Industry, Finance and Economics, Agriculture, Health, Welfare, Pensions; Other EU, USA, Russia. Member of Executive Committee, Council for Economic Policy Research; Executive Member, IPU (British Branch); Liveryman, Goldsmiths' Company; *Publications: Britain and Europe: A Conservative View*, 1996; *Clubs:* Beefsteak, Brooks's, Travellers', Crankham Conservative; *Recreations:* Reading, riding, walking, skiing, travel. *Address:* Quentin Davies Esq, MP, House of Commons, London, SW1A 0AA *Tel:* 020 7219 5518 *Fax:* 020 7219 2963. *Constituency:* Agent: Mrs Janice Thurston, Conservative Office, North Street, Bourne, Lincolnshire *Tel:* 01778 421498 *Fax:* 01778 394443.

RON DAVIES   Caerphilly   Lab majority 25,839

Born 6 August 1946; Son of late Ronald Davies, fitter; Educated Bassaleg Grammar School; Portsmouth Polytechnic; University College of Wales, Cardiff; Married December 24, 1981, Christina Elizabeth Rees (1 daughter). School-teacher 1968–70; Tutor-organiser, Workers' Educational Association 1970–74; Further education advisor, Mid-Glamorgan LEA 1974–83; AM for Caerphilly constituency since May 6, 1999. Councillor: Bedwas and Machen UDC and Rhymney Valley DC 1969–84. **House of Commons:** Member for Caerphilly since June 1983; Opposition Spokesman on: Agriculture and Rural Affairs 1987–92, Food 1989–92; Opposition Whip 1985–87; Shadow Minister of Agriculture, Fisheries and Food July-November 1992; Shadow Secretary of State for Wales 1992–97; Secretary of State for Wales 1997–98; *Special Interests:* Regional Policy, Agriculture, Adult Education, Low Pay, Poverty, Environment, Conservation. Member: Council of The Royal Society for the Protection of Birds 1993–, Highest Order Gorsedd of Bards, National Eisteddfod of Wales 1998; PC 1997; *Recreations:* Sport (rugby and squash), walking, gardening, nature study. *Address:* Rt Hon Ron Davies, MP, AM, House of Commons, London, SW1A 0AA *Tel:* 020 7219 3552. *Constituency:* Council Offices, Newport Road, Bedwas, Caerphilly, CF83 8YB *Tel:* 029 2085 2477 *Fax:* 029 2986 6022 *E-mail:* ron.davies@wales.gsi.gov.uk.

DAVID DAVIS   Haltemprice and Howden   Con majority 7,514

Born 23 December 1948; Son of late Ronald and Elizabeth Davis; Educated Bec Grammar School; Warwick University (BSc molecular science, computing science 1971); London Business School (MSc business studies 1973); Harvard Business School (AMP 1985); Married July 28, 1973, Doreen Cook (1 son 2 daughters). Joined Tate & Lyle 1974; Finance director, Manbré & Garton 1976–80; Managing director, Tate & Lyle Transport 1980–82; President, Redpath-Labatt joint venture 1982–84; Strategic planning director, Tate & Lyle 1984–87; Non-Executive director, Tate & Lyle 1987–90. **House of Commons:** Member for Boothferry 1987–97, and for Haltemprice and Howden since May 1, 1997; Assistant Government Whip 1990–93; PPS to Francis Maude as Financial Secretary to Treasury 1988–90; Parliamentary Secretary, Office of Public Service and Science 1993–94; Minister of State, Foreign and Commonwealth Office 1994–97; *Select Committees:* Chairman: Public Accounts 1997–; Member: Liaison 1998–. *Special Interests:* Health, Law and Order, Industry, Agriculture. Member, Public Accounts Commission 1997–; *Publications: The BBC Viewer's Guide to Parliament, How to Turn Round a Company;* PC 1997; *Recreations:* Mountaineering, flying light aircraft, writing. *Address:* Rt Hon David Davis, MP, House of Commons, London, SW1A 0AA *Tel:* 020 7219 4183. *Constituency:* Spaldington Court, Spaldington, Goole, East Yorkshire, DN14 7NG *Tel:* 01430 430365.

TERRY DAVIS   Birmingham Hodge Hill   Lab majority 14,200

Born 5 January 1938; Son of late Gordon and Gladys Davis; Educated King Edward VI Grammar School, Stourbridge; University College, London (LLB 1960); University of Michigan, USA (MBA 1962); Married 1963, Anne Cooper (1 son 1 daughter). Company executive 1962–71; Manager in motor industry 1974–79; Member, MSF. Councillor, Yeovil Rural District Council 1967–68. **House of Commons:** Contested Bromsgrove 1970 and October 1974 general elections. Member for Bromsgrove by-election 1971-February 74. Contested Birmingham Stechford 1977 by-election. Member for Birmingham Stechford 1979–83, for Birmingham Hodge Hill since June 1983; Opposition Front Bench Spokesman on: NHS 1980–83, Treasury and Economic Affairs 1983–86, Trade and Industry 1986–87; Labour Whip for West Midlands 1979–80; *Select Committees:* Member: Public Accounts 1987–94. *Special Interests:* Europe, USA. Member, Socialist Health Association;

Member, Advisory Council on Public Records 1989–94; Member, British Delegation to Council of Europe Assembly and Western European Union Assembly 1992–; Leader, Labour Delegation 1995–; Chair: Economic Affairs and Development Committee, Council of Europe Assembly 1995–98, Rules Committee, Western European Union Assembly 1995–96; Leader, UK Delegation 1997–; Vice-President: Western European Union Assembly 1997–, Council of Europe Assembly 1998–; Executive Committee Member, IPU British Group 1998–; PC 1999. *Address:* Rt Hon Terry Davis Esq, MP, House of Commons, London, SW1A 0AA *Tel:* 020 7219 4509 *Fax:* 020 7219 6221 *Tel (Constituency):* 0121–747 9500 *Fax (Constituency):* 0121–747 9504.

HILTON DAWSON   Lancaster and Wyre   *Lab majority 1,295*

Born 30 September 1953; Son of late Harry Dawson, teacher, and Sally Dawson, teacher; Educated Ashington Grammar School, Northumberland; Warwick University (BA philosophy, politics 1975); Lancaster University (Diploma in social work 1982); Married August 11, 1973, Susan Williams (2 daughters). Social work manager 1983–97: Children's Homes, Fostering and Adoption, Day Care; Member, UNISON. Councillor, Lancaster City Council 1987–97. **House of Commons:** Member for Lancaster and Wyre since May 1, 1997; *Select Committees:* Member: Administration 1997–. *Special Interests:* Community Politics, Children's Rights, Poverty, Jobs, Health, Development. *Recreations:* Keeping fit, family. *Address:* Hilton Dawson Esq, MP, House of Commons, London, SW1A 0AA *Tel:* 020 7219 4207 *Fax:* 020 7219 4207. *Constituency:* 15A Moor Lane, Lancaster, LA1 1QD *Tel:* 01524 380057 *E-mail:* dawsonth@msn.com.

STEPHEN DAY   Cheadle   *Con majority 3,189*

Born 30 October 1948; Son of late Francis Day, engineer and shop assistant and Mrs Annie Day; Educated Otley Secondary Modern School; Park Lane College of Further Education; Leeds Polytechnic (HNC/HND business); Married 2nd, 1982, Frances Booth (separated 1997)(1 son by 1st marriage). William Sinclair and Sons: Sales clerk 1965–70, Assistant sales manager 1970–77; Sales representative: Larkfield Printing Co. 1977–80, A. H. Leach and Co. 1980–84; Sales executive: PPL Chromacopy 1984–86, Chromagene 1986–87; Parliamentary Consultant to NALGO Section of UNISON 1990–96. Councillor: Otley Town Council 1975–76, 1979–83, Leeds City Council 1975–80. **House of Commons:** Contested Bradford West 1983 general election. Member for Cheadle since June 1987; Opposition Whip: Environment, Transport and the Regions, Agriculture: Greater London and North West 1997–98, Constitutional Affairs, Education and Employment 1998–99, Home Office, Culture, Media and Sport 1999, Health; Private Members' Bills; Defence 1999, Home Office; Private Members' Bills; Cabinet Office 1999–; Sponsored Motor Vehicles (wearing of rear seat belts by children) Act 1988 (Private Member's Bill); *Select Committees:* Member: Social Security 1991–97, Catering 1997–98, Environment, Transport and Regional Affairs 1997 (May-Nov), Transport 1997–98; Member: Administration 2000–. *Special Interests:* Transport, Israel, Constitution; Cyprus, Israel. Vice-Chair, Association of Conservative Clubs (ACC), Chair 1999–. Vice-President: Stockport Chamber of Commerce, Stockport Heart Foundation Hon. Member, Bromhall and Woodford Rotary Club; Vice-Chair, Commonwealth Parliamentary Association (CPA) UK Branch 1996–97, Executive Committee Member 1993–; Patron, Humane Research Trust; *Recreations:* Music, films, Roman history. *Address:* Stephen Day Esq, MP, House of Commons, London, SW1A 0AA *Tel:* 020 7219 6200. *Constituency:* Conservative Offices, Mellor Road, Cheadle Hulme, Cheadle, Cheshire, SK8 5AT *Tel:* 0161–486 6875.

JANET DEAN   Burton   *Lab majority 6,330*

Born 28 January 1949; Daughter of late Harry and late Mary Gibson; Educated Winsford Verdin Grammar School; Married August 3, 1968, Alan Dean (deceased) (2 daughters). Bank clerk 1965–69; Clerk 1969–70. Member, Health Authority 1981–90; Staffordshire County Council: Councillor 1981–97, Vice-Chair, Highways 1985–93, Vice-Chair, Social Services 1993–96; Councillor: East Staffordshire Borough Council 1991–97, Uttoxeter Town Council 1995–97; Mayor, East Staffordshire Borough Council 1996–97. **House of Commons:** Member for Burton since May 1, 1997; *Select Committees:* Member: Catering 1997–, Home Affairs 1999–. *Special Interests:* Health, Social Services, Education, Transport, Housing, Home Affairs; Member, European Standing Committee A 1998–. School Governor 1979–97; Member: Uttoxeter General Charities, Arthritis and Rheumatism Council (Uttoxeter Branch), Crime Prevention Panel, Lupus UK; Chair, Burton Breweries Charitable Trust; *Recreations:* Dress-making, reading. *Address:* Mrs Janet Dean, MP, House of Commons, London, SW1A 0AA *Tel:* 020 7219 6320 *Fax:* 020 7219 3010. *Constituency:* Suite 13, First Floor, Cross Street Business Centre, Cross Street, Burton upon Trent, DE14 1EF *Tel:* 01283 509166 *Fax:* 01283 569964 *E-mail:* mcgirrc@parliament.uk.

JOHN DENHAM   Southampton Itchen   *Lab majority 14,209*

Born 15 July 1953; Son of Edward and Beryl Denham; Educated Woodroffe Comprehensive School, Lyme Regis; Southampton University (President, Student's Union 1976–77); Married October 6, 1979, Ruth Eleanore Dixon (1 son 1 daughter) (separated). Advice worker, Energy Advice Agency, Durham 1977–78; Transport campaigner, Friends of the Earth 1978–79; Head of Youth Affairs, British Youth Council 1979–83; Campaigner, War on Want 1984–88; Consultant to various voluntary organisations 1988–. Hampshire County Council: Councillor 1981–89, Spokesperson on Education; Southampton City Council: Councillor 1989–92, Former Chairman, Housing Committee. **House of Commons:** Member for Southampton Itchen since April 9, 1992; Opposition Spokesman on Social Security 1995–97; Department of Social Security: Parliamentary Under-Secretary of State 1997–98, Minister of State 1998–99; Minister of State, Department of Health 1999–; *Select Committees:* Member: Environment 1993–95. *Special Interests:* Development, Housing, Education, Pensions and Personal Financial Services; Latin America, Philippines. PC 2000; *Recreations:* Cricket, cooking, walking, family. *Address:* Rt Hon John Denham Esq, MP, House of Commons, London, SW1A 0AA *Tel:* 020 7219 4515. *Constituency:* 32 Henry Road, Southampton, SO1 3HA *Tel:* 023 8070 5656 *Fax:* 023 8077 0094.

ANDREW DISMORE Hendon — *Lab majority 6,155*

Born 2 September 1954; Son of late Ian Dismore, hotelier, and Brenda Dismore; Educated Bridlington Grammar School; Warwick University (LLB 1975); London School of Economics (LLM 1976); Guildford College of Law 1978. Education Department, GMWU 1976–78; Solicitor: Robin Thomson and Partners 1978–95, Russell Jones and Walker 1995–; Member, GMB. Councillor, Westminster City Council 1982–97, Leader, Labour Group 1990–97. **House of Commons:** Member for Hendon since May 1, 1997; *Select Committees:* Member: Accommodation and Works 1997–99; Member: Social Security 1998–. *Special Interests:* Health, Civil Justice, Rights of Victims of Accidents and Crime; Greece, Cyprus, Israel. London, Member, Labour Friends of Israel. Member Executive Committee, Association of Personal Injury Lawyers; *Publications:* Various legal journals and articles; *Recreations:* Art, opera, travel, gardening. *Address:* Andrew Dismore Esq, MP, House of Commons, London, SW1A 0AA *Tel:* 020 7219 4026 *Fax:* 020 7219 1279. *Constituency:* Red Rose Shop, 63 Watling Avenue, Burnt Oak, Edgware, HA8 0LD *Tel:* 020 8952 5779 *Fax:* 020 8952 5771 *E-mail:* andrewdismoremp@parliament.uk.

JIM DOBBIN Heywood and Middleton — *Lab majority 17,542*

Born 26 May 1941; Son of William Dobbin, miner, and Catherine Dobbin, née McCabe, mill worker; Educated St Columba's High, Cowdenbeath; St Andrew's High, Kirkcaldy; Napier College, Edinburgh (bacteriology, virology 1970); Married 1964, Pat Russell (2 sons 2 daughters). Microbiologist, NHS 1966–94; Member, MSF. Councillor, Rochdale Metropolitan Borough Council 1983–92, 1994–97; Chairman of Housing 1986–90, Leader of Labour Group 1994–96, Deputy Leader 1990–92, Leader of Council 1996–97. **House of Commons:** Contested Bury North 1992 general election. Member for Heywood and Middleton since May 1, 1997; *Select Committees:* Member: European Legislation 1998, European Legislation 1998; Member: European Scrutiny 1998–. *Special Interests:* Local Government, Health, Housing; Member, European Standing Committee A 1998–. Chair, Rochdale District Labour Party 1980–81: Executive Member, Rochdale Constituency Labour Party 1986–87; Hon Treasurer, North West Regional Group of Labour MPs 1999–. Chair, Neighbourhood Services; Amnesty International; *Recreations:* Walking, football. *Address:* Jim Dobbin Esq, MP, House of Commons, London, SW1A 0AA *Tel:* 020 7219 4530 *Fax:* 020 7219 2696. *Constituency:* 45 York Street, Heywood, Lancashire, OL10 4NN *Tel:* 01706 361135 *Fax:* 01706 361137.

FRANK DOBSON Holborn and St Pancras — *Lab majority 17,903*

Born 15 March 1940; Son of late James William Dobson, railwayman, and late Irene Dobson; Educated Archbishop Holgate's Grammar School, York; London School of Economics; Married February 18, 1967, Janet Mary Alker (1 daughter 2 sons). Worked at HQ of: CEGB 1962–70, Electricity Council 1970–75; Assistant Secretary, Office of Local Ombudsman 1975–79; NUR sponsored MP. Camden Borough Council: Councillor 1971–76, Leader of the Council 1973–75. **House of Commons:** Member for Holborn and St Pancras since May 1979; Opposition Front Bench Spokesman on Education 1982–83; Principal Opposition Front Bench Spokesman on: Energy 1989–92, Employment 1992–93, Transport and London 1993–94, Environment and London 1994–97; Shadow Health Minister 1983–87; Shadow Leader, House of Commons and Campaigns Co-ordinator 1987–89; Secretary of State for Health 1997–99. Governor, London School of Economics and Political Science 1986–; PC 1997. *Address:* Rt Hon Frank Dobson, MP, House of Commons, London, SW1A 0AA *Tel:* 020 7219 5040.

JEFFREY DONALDSON   Lagan Valley   *UUP majority 16,925*

Born 7 December 1962; Son of James and Sarah Anne Donaldson; Educated Kilkeel High School; Castlereagh College; Married June 26, 1987, Eleanor, daughter of late Gilbert and Kathleen Cousins (2 daughters). Ulster Defence Regiment 1980–85; Agent to Enoch Powell, MP 1983–84; Personal assistant to Sir James Molyneaux, MP 1984–85; Principal, Financial Services and Estate Agency Business 1986–96; Former Member, AEEU. **House of Commons:** Member for Lagan Valley since May 1, 1997; Spokesman for: Trade and Industry 1997–2000, Environment, Transport and the Regions 2000–; Member, Northern Ireland Assembly 1985–86; Member, Northern Ireland Forum 1996–98; *Select Committees:* Member: Northern Ireland Affairs 1997–2000; Member: Environment, Transport and Regional Affairs 2000–, Transport Sub-Committee 2000–. *Special Interests:* Northern Ireland, Christian Values, Trade and Industry, Constitution; USA, South Africa, Israel. Honorary Secretary, Ulster Unionist Council 1988–2000, Vice-President 2000–. Member: Evangelical Alliance, CARE, Tear Fund; *Recreations:* Hill-walking, reading, church. *Address:* Jeffrey Donaldson Esq, MP, House of Commons, London, SW1A 0AA *Tel:* 020 7219 3407 *Fax:* 020 7219 0696. *Constituency:* 2 Sackville Street, Wallace Avenue, Lisburn, Co Antrim, BT27 4AB *Tel:* 028 9266 8001 *Fax:* 028 9267 1845 *E-mail:* mckeem@parliament.uk.

BRIAN DONOHOE   Cunninghame South   *Lab majority 14,869*

Born 10 September 1948; Son of late George and Catherine Donohoe; Educated Patna and Loudoun Montgomery primary schools; Irvine Royal Academy; Kilmarnock Technical College (National certificate engineering 1972); Married July 16, 1973, Christine, daughter of Raymond Pawson (2 sons). Apprentice engineer, Ailsa Shipyard 1965–70; Hunterston Nuclear Power Station 1977; ICI Organics Division, draughtsman 1977–81; NALGO District Officer 1981–; Convenor, Political and Education Committee TASS 1969–81; Secretary, Irvine Trades Council 1973–82. Chair: Cunninghame Industrial Development Committee 1975–85, North Ayrshire and Arran Local Health Council 1977–79. **House of Commons:** Member for Cunninghame South since April 9, 1992; *Select Committees:* Member: Transport 1993–97; Member: Environment, Transport and Regional Affairs 1997–, Environment Sub-Committee 1997–, Transport Sub-Committee 1997–. *Special Interests:* Health, Local Government, Transport; Singapore, Indonesia, Malaysia, USA. Treasurer, Cunninghame South Constituency Labour Party 1983–91; Chair, Scottish Group of Labour MPs 1997–98. *Recreations:* Gardening. *Address:* Brian Donohoe Esq, MP, House of Commons, London, SW1A 0AA *Tel:* 020 7219 6230 *Fax:* 020 7219 5388. *Constituency:* 17 Townhead, Irvine, Strathclyde, KA12 0BL *Tel:* 01294 276844 *Fax:* 01294 313463.

FRANK DORAN   Aberdeen Central   *Lab majority 10,801*

Born 13 April 1949; Son of Francis Anthony and Betty Hedges Doran; Educated Ainslie Park Secondary School; Leith Academy; Dundee University (LLB 1975); Married February 4, 1967, Patricia Ann Govan (separated) (2 sons). Solicitor 1977–88; Member, GMB 1983–; Contested North-East Scotland 1984 European Parliament election. **House of Commons:** Member for Aberdeen South 1987–92, and for Aberdeen Central since May 1, 1997; Opposition Spokesman on Energy 1988–92; PPS to Ian McCartney, MP: as Minister of State, Department of Trade and Industry (Competitiveness) 1997–99, as Minister of State, Cabinet Office 1999–; *Special Interests:* Energy, Childcare, Family, Mental Health, Employment. Founder Member, Scottish Legal Action Group 1974; Chair, Dundee Association for Mental Health 1979–82; *Clubs:* Aberdeen Trades Council; *Recreations:* Cinema, art, football, sport. *Address:* Frank Doran Esq, MP, House of Commons, London, SW1A 0AA *Tel:* 020 7219 3481. *Constituency:* 166 Market Street, Aberdeen, AB11 5PP *Tel:* 01224 252715 *Fax:* 01224 252716 *E-mail:* doranf@parliament.uk.

STEPHEN DORRELL   Charnwood   Con majority 5,900

Born 25 March 1952; Son of late Philip Dorrell, Company Director; Educated Uppingham School; Brasenose College, Oxford (BA); Married September 1980, Penelope Anne Taylor (3 sons). Director, family industrial clothing firm 1975–87. **House of Commons:** Contested Kingston-upon-Hull East October 1974 general election. Member for Loughborough 1979–97, and for Charnwood since May 1, 1997; Assistant Government Whip 1987–88; Government Whip (Lord Commissioner of the Treasury) 1988–90; PPS to Secretary of State for Energy 1983–87; Parliamentary Under-Secretary of State, Department of Health 1990–92; Financial Secretary, HM Treasury 1992–94, Secretary of State for: National Heritage 1994–1995, Health 1995–97; Member, Shadow Cabinet 1997–98; Shadow Secretary of State for Education and Employment 1997–98; *Select Committees:* Honorary Member: Public Accounts 1992–94. *Special Interests:* Economics, Foreign Affairs. Chairman, Millennium Commission 1994–95; PC 1994; *Recreations:* Reading, theatre. *Address:* Rt Hon Stephen Dorrell, MP, House of Commons, London, SW1A 0AA *Tel:* 020 7219 4472 *Fax:* 020 7219 5838. *Constituency:* 19A The Nook, Anstey, Leicester, LE7 7AZ *Tel:* 0116–236 6898 *Fax:* 0116–236 6902.

JIM DOWD   Lewisham West   Lab majority 14,317

Born 5 March 1951; Son of late James and Elfriede Dowd; Educated Sedgehill Comprehensive School, London; London Nautical School. Apprentice telephone engineer, GPO (now BT) 1967–72; Station manager, Heron Petrol Stations Ltd. 1972–73; Telecommunications engineer, Plessey Company (now GPT) 1973–; Member: POEU 1967–72, MSF (ASTMS) 1973–. London Borough of Lewisham: Councillor 1974–94, Deputy Leader 1984–86, Chair, Finance Committee, Deputy Mayor 1987, 1990, Mayor 1992; Member, Lewisham and North Southwark District Health Authority. **House of Commons:** Contested Beckenham 1983 and Lewisham West 1987 general elections. Member for Lewisham West since April 9, 1992; Opposition Spokesman on Northern Ireland 1995–97; Opposition Whip for London 1993–95; Government Whip (Lord Commissioner of HM Treasury) (Culture, Media and Sport, Northern Ireland, London Bill: London) 1997–; *Special Interests:* Health Service, Transport, Economic Policy, Industrial Policy, Environment, Housing, Animal Welfare, Human Rights. Member: Greenpeace, CND, International Fund for Animal Welfare, RSPB, WWFFN, Cats Protection League; Member, National Trust; *Recreations:* Music, reading, theatre, Cornwall. *Address:* Jim Dowd Esq, MP, House of Commons, London, SW1A 0AA *Tel:* 020 7219 4617 *Fax:* 020 7219 2686. *Constituency:* 43 Sunderland Road, Forest Hill, London, SE23 2PS *Tel:* 020 8699 2001 *Fax:* 020 8291 5607 *E-mail:* contact@jim-dowd-mp.new.labour.org.uk.

DAVID DREW   Stroud   Lab/Co-op majority 2,910

Born 13 April 1952; Son of Ronald Montague Drew, company accountant, and late Maisie Joan Drew, hospital administrator; Educated Kingsfield School, Gloucestershire; Nottingham University (BA economics 1974); Birmingham University (PGCE 1976); Bristol Polytechnic (MA historical studies 1988); University of the West of England (MEd 1994); Married 1990, Anne Baker (2 sons 2 daughters). Teacher, various schools in Warwickshire, Hertfordshire and Gloucestershire 1976–86; Lecturer, Bristol Polytechnic/University of the West of England 1986–97; Member, NAS/UWT 1976–86, Branch secretary 1984–86; Member, NATFHE 1986–; Member, UNISON, then NUPE 1990–. Councillor: Stevenage Borough Council 1981–82, Stroud District Council 1987–95, Stonehouse Town Council 1987–, Gloucestershire County Council 1993–97. **House of Commons:** Contested Stroud 1992 general election. Member for Stroud since May 1, 1997; *Select Committees:* Member: Modernisation of the House of Commons 1998–99; Member: Procedure 1997–, Agriculture 1999–. *Special Interests:* Housing, Poverty, Planning, Environment, Education, Agriculture, Rural Issues; South Africa. Member: Co-op Party 1980–, Christian Socialist Movement, Socialist Educational Association, Labour Party Rural Revival, Labour Campaign for Electoral Reform;

Treasurer, Gloucestershire County Labour Party 1987–93; Secretary, Stroud Constituency Labour Party 1992–93. Member: Friends of the Earth, SERA, Greenpeace, ACTSA, Age Concern, Care and Repair, South Stroud Small Business Club, St Cyr's Ministry Team, Charter 88, NHS Support Federation; Governor, Maidenhill School; Spent 20–25 days with MoD on "work experience" 1999; *Publications:* Various IT related materials; *Sportsclubs:* Bristol Rugby Football Club, Forest Green FC; *Recreations:* Reading, watching rugby, football. *Address:* David Drew Esq, MP, House of Commons, London, SW1A 0AA *Tel:* 020 7219 6479 *Fax:* 020 7219 0910. *Constituency:* 5A Lansdown, Stroud, Gloucestershire, G5 1BB *Tel:* 01453 764355 *Fax:* 01453 753756 *E-mail:* drewd@parliament.uk.

JULIA DROWN   South Swindon   *Lab majority 5,645*

Born 23 August 1962; Daughter of David Drown, picture restorer, and Audrey Drown (née Harris), nurse; Educated Hampstead Comprehensive; University College, Oxford (BA politics and economics 1985); Married 1999, Bill Child (1 son 1 daughter deceased). NHS accountancy trainee, Oxfordshire 1985–88; Unit accountant, Learning Disabilities, Oxfordshire 1989–90; Director, finance, contracts and information, Radcliffe Infirmary 1990–96; Member: UNISON (formerly NALGO), TGWU. Councillor, Oxfordshire County Council 1989–96, Labour Spokesperson/Deputy Spokesperson on Social Services 1990–96, Vice-Chair, Labour Group 1994–95; Director/Chair, Oxfordshire Co-operative Development Agency 1994–95. **House of Commons:** Member for South Swindon since May 1, 1997; *Select Committees:* Member: Health 1997–99. *Special Interests:* Health Service, Social Services, World Development, Co-operative Movement. Member: Co-operative Party 1992–, Labour Women's Network 1996–. School Governor 1989–96; Member: World Development Movement, Amnesty International, Friends of the Earth, Greenpeace; Trust Board Member, Radcliffe Infirmary NHS Trust 1993–96; Member, Chartered Institute of Public Finance and Accountancy (CIPFA) 1988; *Recreations:* Family, music, walking. *Address:* Julia Drown, MP, House of Commons, London, SW1A 0AA *Tel:* 020 7219 2392 *Fax:* 020 7219 0266. *Constituency:* 13 Bath Road, Swindon, Wiltshire, SN1 4AS *Tel:* 01793 615444 *Fax:* 01793 644752 *E-mail:* juliadrownmp@parliament.uk.

ALAN DUNCAN   Rutland and Melton   *Con majority 8,836*

Born 31 March 1957; Son of late Wing-Commander James Duncan, OBE, and Anne Duncan (née Carter); Educated Beechwood Park School, St Albans; Merchant Taylors' School, Northwood; St John's College, Oxford (President, Oxford Union 1979); Harvard University (Kennedy Scholar). Formerly graduate trainee, Shell International Petroleum; Oil trader and adviser to governments and companies on oil supply, shipping and refining 1989–. **House of Commons:** Contested Barnsley West and Penistone 1987 general election. Member for Rutland and Melton since April 9, 1992; Opposition Front Bench Spokesman for: Health 1998–99, Trade and Industry 1999–; PPS to Dr. Brian Mawhinney: as Minister of State, Department of Health 1993–94, as Chairman, Conservative Party 1995–97; PPS to William Hague as Leader of the Conservative Party 1997–98; *Select Committees:* Member: Social Security 1992–95. *Special Interests:* International Trade and Finance, Social Security. Vice-Chair, Conservative Party 1997–98. *Publications:* Co-author: (CPC pamphlet) *Bearing the Standard: Themes for a Fourth Term*, 1991, *Who Benefits? Reinventing Social Security, An End to Illusions*, 1993, *Saturn's Children: How the State Devours Liberty, Prosperity and Virtue*, 1995; *Beware Blair*, 1997; Freeman, City of London; *Recreations:* Shooting, Stalking, Fishing. *Address:* Alan Duncan Esq, MP, House of Commons, London, SW1A 0AA *Tel:* 020 7219 5204 *Tel (Constituency):* 01664 566444 *Fax (Constituency):* 01664 566555.

Visit the Vacher Dod Website . . .
www.politicallinks.co.uk

IAIN DUNCAN SMITH   Chingford and Woodford Green   *Con majority 5,714*

Born 9 April 1954; Son of late Group Captain W. G. G. Duncan Smith, DSO, DFC, and Pamela, née Summers; Educated HMS Conway (Cadet School); University of Perugia, Italy; RMA Sandhurst; Dunchurch College of Management; Married 1982, Hon. Elizabeth Wynne Fremantle, daughter of Commander 5th Baron Cottesloe (2 sons 2 daughters). Commissioned, Scots Guards 1975; ADC to Major-General Sir John Acland, KCB, CBE, Commander of Commonwealth Monitoring Force in Zimbabwe 1979–81; GEC Marconi 1981; Director: Bellwing Property 1988–89, Jane's Information Group 1989–92. **House of Commons:** Contested Bradford West 1987 general election. Member for Chingford 1992–97, and for Chingford and Woodford Green since May 1, 1997; Member, Shadow Cabinet 1997–; Shadow Secretary of State for: Social Security 1997–99, Defence 1999–; *Select Committees:* Member: Administration 1993–97, Health 1993–95, Standards and Privileges 1995–97. *Special Interests:* Finance, Small Businesses, Transport, Defence, Environment; India, Italy, Sri Lanka, USA. Vice-Chair, Fulham Conservative Association 1991. *Publications:* Co-author *Who Benefits? Reinventing Social Security; Game, Set and Match?* (Maastricht); *Facing the Future* (Defence and Foreign and Commonwealth Affairs); *1994 and Beyond; A Response to Chancellor Kohl;* Freeman, City of London 1993; *Recreations:* Cricket, rugby, tennis, sport in general, painting, theatre, family. *Address:* Iain Duncan Smith Esq, MP, House of Commons, London, SW1A 0AA *Tel:* 020 7219 3574. *Constituency:* 20A Station Road, Chingford, London, E4 7BE *Tel:* 020 8524 4344.

GWYNETH DUNWOODY   Crewe and Nantwich   *Lab majority 15,798*

Born 12 December 1930; Daughter of late Morgan Phillips, sometime General Secretary of the Labour Party and late Baroness Phillips; Married May 28, 1954, Dr. John Elliott Orr Dunwoody (marriage dissolved 1975) (2 sons 1 daughter). Director, Film Production Association of GB 1970–74. **House of Commons:** Contested Exeter 1964 general election. Member for Exeter 1966–70, for Crewe February 1974–83, and for Crewe and Nantwich since June 1983; Opposition Front Bench Spokesman on: Foreign and Commonwealth Affairs 1979–80, NHS 1980–83, Parliamentary Campaigning and Information 1983–84; Opposition Spokesman on Transport 1984–85; Parliamentary Secretary to Board of Trade 1967–70; MEP 1975–79; *Select Committees:* Member: Chairmen's Panel 1997–; Chairman (Transport): Environment, Transport and Regional Affairs 1997–; Member: Environment Sub-Committee 1997–; Chairman: Transport Sub-Committee 1997–; Member: Liaison 1997–. *Special Interests:* Transport, Health Service, Arts; Botswana, Central Africa, East Africa, Middle East. Labour Friends of Israel: Former Chair, President 1993–95, Life President 1995–. Patron, BRAKE 1995–; Vice-President, Socialist International Women; Vice-Chairman, European Parliament Social Affairs Committee; *Recreations:* Reading, listening to music. *Address:* Hon Gwyneth Dunwoody, MP, House of Commons, London, SW1A 0AA *Tel:* 020 7219 3490 *Fax:* 020 7219 6046. *Constituency:* 154 Nantwich Road, Crewe, CW2 6BG *Tel:* 01270 589132 *Fax:* 01270 589135.

E

ANGELA EAGLE   Wallasey   *Lab majority 19,074*

Born 17 February 1961; Daughter of André Eagle, printworker, and late Shirley Eagle, dressmaker and student; Educated Formby High School; St John's College, Oxford (BA philosophy, politics and economics). COHSE 1984–: first as a researcher, then as National Press Officer, currently as Parliamentary Liaison Officer; Member: COHSE, NUJ. **House of Commons:** Member for Wallasey since April 9, 1992; Opposition Whip 1996–97; Parliamentary Under-Secretary of State: Department of the Environment, Transport and the Regions (Minister for Green Issues and Regeneration) 1997–98, Department of Social Security 1998–; *Select Committees:* Member: Members' Interests 1992–97, Employment 1994–96, Public Accounts 1995–97. *Special Interests:* Economic Policy, Health Service, Politics of Sport. Active at branch, women's section, general committee levels in Crosby Constituency 1978–80; Chairman: Oxford University Fabian Club 1980–83, National Conference of Labour Women 1991. Member, British Film Institute; *Publications:* Columnist and regular contributor to *Tribune*; *Recreations:* Chess, cricket, cinema. *Address:* Angela Eagle, MP, House of Commons, London, SW1A 0AA *Tel:* 020 7219 4074 *Tel (Constituency):* 0151–637 1979 *E-mail:* eaglea@parliament.uk *Website:* http://www2.poptel.org.uk/angela.eagle.mp.

MARIA EAGLE   Liverpool Garston   *Lab majority 18,417*

Born 17 February 1961; Daughter of André Eagle, printworker, and late Shirley Eagle, dressmaker and student; Educated St Peter's Church of England Primary School, Formby; Formby High School (Comprehensive); Pembroke College, Oxford (BA philosophy, politics and economics 1983); College of Law, London (Common Professional Exam, Law Society Finals 1990). Voluntary sector 1983–90; Articles of clerkship, Brian Thompson & Partners, Liverpool 1990–92; Goldsmith Williams, Liverpool 1992–95; Senior Solicitor, Steven Irving & Co, Liverpool 1994–97; Member GMB. **House of Commons:** Contested Crosby 1992 general election. Member for Liverpool Garston since May 1, 1997; PPS to John Hutton as Minister of State, Department of Health 1999–; *Select Committees:* Member: Public Accounts 1997–99. *Special Interests:* Transport, Housing, Employment; Nicaragua, USA, Australia. Campaigns organiser Crosby 1993–96; Campaigns organiser, Press officer, Merseyside West Euro Constituency Labour Party 1983–84; Constituency Labour Party secretary, Press officer, political education officer 1983–85. Played cricket for Lancashire as a Junior; Played chess for England and Lancashire; *Publications:* Co-author *High Time or High Tide for Labour Women*; *Recreations:* Cinema, chess, cricket. *Address:* Maria Eagle, MP, House of Commons, London, SW1A 0AA *Tel:* 020 7219 5288 *Fax:* 020 7219 1157. *Constituency:* Unit House, Speke Boulevard, Liverpool, L24 9HZ *Tel:* 0151–448 1167 *Fax:* 0151–448 0976 *E-mail:* eaglem@parliament.uk.

HUW EDWARDS   Monmouth   *Lab majority 4,178*

Born 12 April 1953; Son of Rev Dr Ifor and Esme Edwards; Educated Eastfields High School, Mitcham, Surrey; Manchester Polytechnic (BA social science 1976); York University (MA social policy 1978, MPhil 1984); Single. Lecturer in social policy, Brighton Polytechnic/University 1988–97; Research consultant, Low Pay Unit 1988–97; Tutor, Open University 1988–89, 1993–96. **House of Commons:** Member for Monmouth 1991 by-election–1992, and from May 1, 1997; *Select Committees:* Member: Modernisation of the House of Commons 1997–98; Member: Welsh Affairs 1997–. *Special Interests:* Health, Housing, Education, Wales, Constitutional Reform, Low Pay and Social Inequality; Wales, Japan. Member, Fabian Society; Chair, Welsh Group of Labour MPs 2000–01. Member: Amnesty International (Monmouth), One World Action, Shelter (Cymru), Gwalia Male Choir (London), London Welsh Association; Member, Gwent Wildlife Trust;

Publications: Low Pay in South Wales, 1989; *Wales in the 1990s – Land of Low Pay*, 1995; Plus articles in new review of Low Pay Unit; *Clubs:* London Welsh Association; *Sportsclubs:* London Welsh AFC, Preston Park CC, Lords and Commons Cricket XI, Lords and Commons Rugby Football, Lords and Commons Skiing, Parliamentary Football; Vice President Monmouth Rugby; *Recreations:* Playing football, cricket, rugby, squash, skiing. *Address:* Huw Edwards Esq, MP, House of Commons, London, SW1A 0AA *Tel:* 020 7219 3489 *Fax:* 020 7219 3949. *Constituency:* Constituency Office, 7 Agincourt Street, Monmouth, Monmouthshire, NP5 3DZ *Tel:* 01600 713537 *Fax:* 01600 712847 *E-mail:* edwardsh@parliament.uk.

CLIVE EFFORD   Eltham   *Lab majority 10,182*

Born 10 July 1958; Son of Stanley Efford, retired civil servant; Educated Walworth Comprehensive School; Married Gillian Vallius (3 daughters). Worked in family-owned jewellery shop till 1987; Taxi driver 1987–97; Member, T&GWU. Councillor, London Borough of Greenwich 1989–, Chair, Social Services, Chief Whip, Labour Group 1990–91. **House of Commons:** Contested Eltham 1992 General Election. Member for Eltham since May 1, 1997; *Select Committees:* Member: Procedure 1997–, Standing Orders 1999–. *Special Interests:* Welfare State, Health, Transport, Education, Environment, Local Government. Founder, Job Club 1980; *Recreations:* Football (FA Coaches Club), Millwall. *Address:* Clive Efford Esq, MP, House of Commons, London, SW1A 0AA *Tel:* 020 7219 4057. *Constituency:* Westmount Road, Eltham, London, SE9.

LOUISE ELLMAN   Liverpool Riverside   *Lab majority 21,799*

Born 14 November 1945; Daughter of late Harold and Anne Rosenberg; Educated Manchester High School for Girls; Hull University (BA 1967); York University (MPhil 1972); Married July 16, 1967, Geoffrey Ellman (1 son 1 daughter). Member, T&GWU. Councillor, Lancashire County Council 1970–97, Leader, County Labour Group 1977–97, Leader of Council 1981–97; Councillor, West Lancashire District Council 1974–87; Vice-Chair, Lancashire Enterprise 1982–97; Founder Chair, Northwest Regional Association 1991–92, Vice-Chair 1996–97. **House of Commons:** Member for Liverpool Riverside since May 1, 1997; *Select Committees:* Member: Environment, Transport and Regional Affairs 1997–, Environment Sub-Committee 1997–. *Special Interests:* Public Services, Regional Economic Development, Devolution, Health, Europe, Environment, Transport, Local Government. Member, Co-op Party. *Address:* Mrs Louise Ellman, MP, House of Commons, London, SW1A 0AA *Tel:* 020 7219 5210 *Fax:* 020 7219 2592. *Constituency:* First Floor, Threlfall Building, Trueman Street, Liverpool, L3 2EX *Tel:* 0151–236 2969 *Fax:* 0151–236 4301.

PETER EMERY   East Devon   *Con majority 7,489*

Born 27 February 1926; Educated Scotch Plains, New Jersey, USA; Oriel College, Oxford (MA); Married 1st, July 1954, Elizabeth Nicholson (marriage dissolved) (1 son 1 daughter); married 2nd, December 15, 1972, Elizabeth Monnington (1 son 1 daughter). RAF 1943–47, RAFVR 1942–72; Director, Institute of Purchasing and Supply 1961–72; Secretary General, European Federation of Purchasing 1962–72; Chair, Consultative Council of Professional Management Organisations 1967–72; Director: Phillips Petroleum UK 1964–72, Property Growth Assurance 1969–72; Chairman: Shenley Trust Services Ltd 1972–94, The Winglaw Group 1984–; Member, ASLEF 1952–57. Councillor, Hornsey Borough Council 1951–59; Chair, Housing Committee 1953–57; Deputy Mayor 1957. **House of Commons:** Contested Poplar 1951 and Lincoln 1955 general election. Member for Reading 1959–66, for Honiton 1967–97, and for East Devon since May 1, 1997; Opposition Front Bench Spokesman on Trade, Treasury and Economic Affairs 1965–66; PPS: to David Ormsby-Gore as Minister of State, Foreign Office 1960–63, to Joe Godber as Secretary of State for War 1963, to Minister of Labour 1963–64; Parliamentary Under-Secretary of State for: Industry 1972, Industry and Consumer Affairs 1973–74, Energy 1974; *Select Committees:* Member: Procedure 1976–97; Chairman: Procedure 1983–92; Member: Science and Technology 1985–2000, Liaison 1992–97; Chairman: Procedure 1993–97; Member: Foreign Affairs 1997–, Modernisation of the House of

Commons 1997–. *Special Interests:* Trade and Industry, Purchasing and Supply, Commonwealth, Parliamentary Procedure, Foreign Affairs, Defence, Space; USA, Europe, Africa, Japan, The Commonwealth. Joint Founder, Bow Group 1951; Chair, Conservative West Country Members. Member, Asthma Research Council 1968–89; Chairman, National Asthma Campaign 1989–; Secretary, 1922 Committee 1964–66, Treasurer 1997–2000; Delegate, Council of Europe and Western European Union 1964–66, 1970–72; North Atlantic Assembly: Member 1983–, Officer, Science Committee 1988–, Vice-President, Science and Technology Committee, Vice-Chair 1990, President 1991–95; OSCE Assembly: Member 1970–, Member 1992–, Treasurer 1992–; Member, Advisory Board of the United States Center for Strategic and International Studies; Knighted 1982; PC 1993; FInstPS (now FCIPS); Freeman, City of: Reading, Pennsylvania, USA, Houston, Texas, USA; *Clubs:* Carlton, Leander; *Sportsclubs:* Captain, House of Commons Bridge Team 1984–; Member: Middlesex County Cricket Club, Camberley Heath Golf Club; *Recreations:* Skiing, tennis, golf, gardening, bridge, watching cricket. *Address:* Rt Hon Sir Peter Emery, MP, House of Commons, London, SW1A 0AA *Tel:* 020 7219 4044 *Fax:* 020 7219 3021. *Constituency:* 45 Imperial Rd, Exmouth, Devon *Tel:* 01460 220309.

JEFFREY ENNIS   Barnsley East and Mexborough   *Lab majority 26,763*

Born 13 November 1952; Son of William, retired miner, and Jean Ennis; Educated Hemsworth Grammar School; Redland College, Bristol (CertEd, BEd 1975); Married 1980, Margaret Angela, daughter of Martin and Margaret Knight (3 sons). Raw materials inspector, Lyons Bakery 1975–76; Primary teacher: Wolverhampton 1976–78, Hillsborough Primary School, Sheffield 1979–96; Member, TU 1975–; Representative, NASUWT at Hillsborough Primary 1979–96; Member, TGWU 1997–. Councillor, Barnsley Council 1980–96; Councillor, Barnsley Metropolitan Borough Council 1980–96, Deputy Leader 1988–95, Leader 1995–96; Chair, South Yorkshire Fire and Civil Defence Authority 1995–96. **House of Commons:** Member for Barnsley East from December 12, 1996 by-election–1997, and for Barnsley East and Mexborough since May 1, 1997; PPS to Tessa Jowell: as Minister for Public Health, Department of Health 1997–99, as Minister of State, Department for Education and Employment (Minister for Employment, Welfare to Work and Equal Opportunities) 1999–; *Special Interests:* Local Government, Environment, Education, Regeneration, Fire Service; Germany, Ukraine. Chair: Barnsley Economic Regeneration Forum, Barnsley City Challenge, Barnsley Partnership Ltd; Board member, Dearne Valley Partnership; Board director, Barnsley and Doncaster and Training and Enterprise Council; *Recreations:* Family activities, hill walking, sport, music, swimming, caravanning. *Address:* Jeffrey Ennis Esq, MP, House of Commons, London, SW1A 0AA *Tel:* 020 7219 5008 *Fax:* 020 7219 2728. *Constituency:* Dearne Town Hall, Bolton-on-Dearne, Rotherham, South Yorkshire, S63 9EJ *Tel:* 01226 775080 *Fax:* 01226 775080 *E-mail:* ennisj@parliament.uk.

WILLIAM ETHERINGTON   Sunderland North   *Lab majority 19,697*

Born 17 July 1941; Educated Redby Infant and Junior School; Monkwearmouth Grammar School; Married April 3, 1963, Irene Holton (2 daughters). Apprentice fitter, Austin & Pickersgill Shipyard 1957–63; Fitter, Dawdon Colliery 1963–83; Full-time official, NUM 1983–92; Member: AEU 1957–, NUM 1963–, National Executive Committee of NUM 1986–88, 1995–; Trustee, Mineworkers' Pension Scheme 1985–87; Representative, North Regional TUC 1985–92; NUM delegate, TUC 1990–91; Vice-President, North East Area NUM 1988–92. **House of Commons:** Member for Sunderland North since April 9, 1992; *Select Committees:* Member: Members' Interests 1994–95, Catering 1995–97, Parliamentary Commissioner for Administration 1996–97; Member: Court of Referees 1997–. *Special Interests:* Trades Union Legislation, Employment, Adult Education, Human Rights, Education, Equal Opportunity, Health Service, Homelessness, Disabled/Disability, Animal Welfare. Held various posts in the Labour Party including local ward treasurer 1978–87; GMC delegate 1978–87; CLP Executive Committee member 1981–87. Member, UK Delegation to Council of Europe and Western Europe Union 1997–; *Clubs:* Kelloe Working Men's, Durham City Working Men's; *Recreations:* Fell walking, motorcycling, watching soccer, local, industrial and transport history, reading. *Address:* William Etherington Esq, MP, House of Commons, London, SW1A 0AA *Tel:* 020 7219 4603 *Fax:* 020 7219 4603. *Constituency:* 7 Bridge House, Bridge Street, Sunderland, SR1 1TE *Tel:* 0191–564 2489 *Fax:* 0191–564 2486.

NIGEL EVANS   Ribble Valley   *Con majority 6,640*

Born 10 November 1957; Son of late Albert Evans, and of Betty Evans; Educated Dynevor School; University College of Wales, Swansea (BA politics 1979). Management family retail newsagent and convenience store 1979–90. West Glamorgan County Council: Councillor 1985–91, Deputy Leader, Conservative Group 1990–91. **House of Commons:** Contested Swansea West 1987 general election, Pontypridd 1989 by-election, Ribble Valley 1991 by-election. Member for Ribble Valley since April 9, 1992; Opposition Front Bench Spokesman for: Constitutional Affairs (Scotland and Wales) 1997–99, Constitutional Affairs (Wales) 1999–; PPS: to David Hunt: as Secretary of State for Employment 1993–94, as Chancellor of the Duchy of Lancaster 1994–95; to Tony Baldry as Minister of State, Ministry of Agriculture, Fisheries and Food 1995–96; to William Hague as Secretary of State for Wales 1996–97; *Select Committees:* Member: Transport 1993, Public Service 1995–97. *Special Interests:* Education, Small Businesses, US Elections, Local Government, Defence, Agriculture, International Politics, Europe, Telecommunications; Caribbean, Central America, Europe, USA, Asia, Far East. Chair, Conservative Welsh Parliamentary Candidates Policy Group 1990; President, Conservative North West Parliamentary Candidates Group 1991; Secretary, North West Conservative MPs 1992–; Vice-Chair (Wales), Conservative Party 1999–. Has worked on three US presidential elections in New York, Florida and California; *Clubs:* Carlton, Stringfellows, I.O.D. *Recreations:* Tennis, swimming, running, theatre, cinema, arts. *Address:* Nigel Evans Esq, MP, House of Commons, London, SW1A 0AA *Tel:* 020 7219 4165 *Fax:* 0870 131 3711. *Constituency:* 9 Railway View, Clitheroe, Lancashire, BB7 2HA *Tel:* 01200 425939 *Fax:* 01200 422904 *E-mail:* nigelmp@hotmail.com *Website:* www.nigelmp.com.

MARGARET EWING   Moray   *SNP majority 5,566*

Born 1 September 1945; Daughter of late John McAdam, farmworker, and late Mrs Peggie McAdam; Educated Biggar High School; Glasgow University (MA English and history 1968); Strathclyde University (BA economic history 1973); Jordanhill College of Education (Secondary School Teachers Certificate 1968); Married November 30, 1983, Fergus Stewart Ewing, son of Stewart Ewing, former MP and Winifred Ewing MEP, Highlands and Islands. Secondary school teacher 1968–74; Principal teacher, remedial education 1972–74; Freelance journalist 1979–81; Co-ordinator, West of Scotland Certificate in Social Service Scheme 1981–87; MSP for Moray constituency since May 6, 1999. **House of Commons:** Member for Dunbartonshire East (as Margaret Bain) 1974–79. Contested Strathkelvin/Bearsden 1983 general election. Member for Moray since June 1987; Spokeswoman for Europe and Foreign Affairs, Defence, Health, Highlands and Islands, Gaelic; *Select Committees:* Member: European Legislation 1992–97, European Legislation 1997–98; Member: European Scrutiny 1998–. *Special Interests:* Education, Social Services, European Union, Foreign Affairs; Baltic States, Europe. Member, SNP NEC 1974–80, Vice-President 1981–83, Senior Vice-Convenor 1983–87; SNP Parliamentary Leader 1987–. *Recreations:* Arts, gardening. *Address:* Mrs Margaret Ewing, MP, MSP, House of Commons, London, SW1A 0AA *Tel:* 020 7219 5230 *Fax:* 020 7219 2797. *Constituency:* Mrs Marian Hoare, 7 Dunbar Street, Lossiemouth, Moray, IV31 6AG *Tel:* 01343 812222 *Fax:* 01343 813221 *E-mail:* margaret.ewing.msp@scottish.parliament.uk.

F

DAVID FABER   Westbury   *Con majority 6,068*

Born 7 July 1961; Son of Julian Faber and Lady Caroline Faber, daughter of 1st Earl of Stockton; Educated Eton; Balliol College, Oxford (BA/MA French and Spanish 1984); Married 1st, October 15, 1988, Sally Gilbert (marriage dissolved 1996) (1 son); married 2nd, November 20, 1998, Sophie, daughter of Martyn Hedley. Conservative Research Assistant, House of Commons 1984–85; Conservative Central Office, including personal assistant to Jeffrey Archer as Deputy Chair 1985–87; Founding director, Sterling Marketing Ltd, marketing consultants 1987–. **House of Commons:** Contested Stockton North 1987 general election. Member for Westbury since April 9, 1992; Opposition Spokesman on Foreign and Commonwealth Affairs 1997–98; PPS: to Baroness Chalker of Wallasey as Minister for Overseas Development 1994–95, to Stephen Dorrell as Secretary of State for Health 1995–97; *Select Committees:* Member: Social Security 1992–97; Member: Culture, Media and Sport 1998–. *Special Interests:* Education, Foreign Affairs, Drug Abuse, Alcohol Abuse and Under-age Drinking, Rural Affairs. Ward Chairman, Cities of London and Westminster Conservative Association 1986–87. *Publications:* Co-author, *Bearing the Standard – Themes for a Fourth Term,* 1991; *Clubs:* Vincent's (Oxford), MCC (Committee Member 1997–), Queen's; *Sportsclubs:* Royal St George's Golf, Sunningdale Golf; *Recreations:* Cricket, golf, squash, watching Chelsea Football Club. *Address:* David Faber Esq, MP, House of Commons, London, SW1A 0AA *Tel:* 020 7219 5215. *Constituency:* Lovemead House, Roundstone Street, Trowbridge, Wiltshire, BA14 8DG *Tel:* 01225 752141.

MICHAEL FABRICANT   Lichfield   *Con majority 238*

Born 12 June 1950; Son of late Isaac Nathan Fabricant, and of Helena Fabricant, née Freed; Educated state schools; Loughborough University (BSc economics and law 1973); Sussex University (MSc systems and econometrics 1974); Oxford University; London University; University of Southern California, Los Angeles, USA (PhD economics 1978). Economist and founder director, leading broadcast and communications group, manufacturing and commissioning electronics equipment to radio stations in over 50 countries 1980–91; Adviser, Home Office on broadcasting matters; Former radio broadcaster and journalist; Has been an adviser to foreign governments on the establishment and management of radio stations, including the Russian Federation; Has lived and worked extensively in Europe, Africa, the Far East, and former Soviet Union. **House of Commons:** Contested South Shields 1987 general election. Member for Mid-Staffordshire 1992–97, and for Lichfield since May 1, 1997; PPS to Michael Jack as Financial Secretary to the Treasury 1996–97; *Select Committees:* Member: European Legislation Scrutiny Committee B (Trade) 1992–97, National Heritage 1993–96, Culture, Media and Sport 1997–98, Culture, Media and Sport 1997–99; Member: Catering 1999–, Home Affairs 1999–. *Special Interests:* Trade and Industry, Foreign Affairs, Broadcasting; Russia, Israel, USA, Australia, Eastern Europe. Former Chair, Brighton Pavilion Conservative Association; Member, Conservative Way Forward; Associate Member, European Research Group. Member, Council of the Institution of Electrical Engineers 1996–; Presented Bills to strengthen economic and political ties between UK, United States, Canada, Australia and New Zealand; Promoted legislation to encourage the flying of the Union Jack; Member: Inter-Parliamentary Union, Commonwealth Parliamentary Association; CEng; FIEE; *Clubs:* Rottingdean (Sussex); *Recreations:* Reading, music, fell-walking, skiing and listening to the Omnibus Edition of The Archers. *Address:* Michael Fabricant Esq, MP, House of Commons, London, SW1A 0AA *Tel:* 020 7219 5022 *Tel (Constituency):* 01543 419650.

MICHAEL FALLON   Sevenoaks   Con majority 10,461

Born 14 May 1952; Son of late Martin Fallon, OBE, FRICS, and Hazel Fallon; Educated Epsom College, Surrey; St Andrews University (MA classics and ancient history 1974); Married September 27, 1986, Wendy Elisabeth Payne (2 sons). European Educational Research Trust 1974–75; Conservative Research Department 1975–79 (seconded to Opposition Whips Office, House of Lords 1975–77, EEC Desk Officer 1977–79); Secretary, Lord Home's Committee on Future of the House of Lords 1977–78; Joint Managing Director, European Consultants Ltd 1979–81; Assistant to Baroness Elles 1979–83; Director, Quality Care Homes plc 1992–97; Chief Executive, Quality Care Developments Ltd 1996 97; Director of other companies. **House of Commons:** Contested Darlington by-election March 1983. Member for Darlington 1983–92, and for Sevenoaks since May 1, 1997; Front Bench Spokesman on: Trade and Industry June-December 1997, the Treasury December 1997–98; Assistant Government Whip 1988–90; Government Whip (Lord Commissioner of HM Treasury) May-July 1990; PPS to Cecil Parkinson as Secretary of State for Energy 1987–88; Parliamentary Under-Secretary of State, Department of Education and Science 1990–92; *Select Committees:* Member: Treasury 1999–, Treasury Sub-Committee 1999–. *Special Interests:* Constitution, Public Sector, Education. Non-Executive Director, International Care and Relief; Member: Higher Education Funding Council 1992–97, Deregulation Task Force 1994–97, Advisory Council, Social Market Foundation 1994–; *Publications: Brighter Schools*, Social Market Foundation 1993. *Address:* Michael Fallon Esq, MP, House of Commons, London, SW1A 0AA *Tel:* 020 7219 6482. *Constituency:* 113 St John's Hill, Sevenoaks, TN13 3PF *Tel:* 01732 452261.

RONNIE FEARN   Southport   LD majority 6,160

Born 6 February 1931; Son of late James Fearn and late Martha Ellen Fearn; Educated Norwood School; King George V Grammar School; Married June 11, 1955, Joyce Dugan (1 son 1 daughter). Two years service in Royal Navy; Banking, Royal Bank of Scotland 1947–87; Member, Association of Liberal Democrat Trade Unionists. Councillor and Leader of Lib Dem Group: Southport Borough Council 1963–74, Merseyside Metropolitan County Council 1974–86; Councillor, Sefton Metropolitan Borough Council 1974–. **House of Commons:** Member for Southport: Liberal 1987–88, Liberal Democrat 1988–92. Contested Southport 1992 general election. Member for Southport since May 1, 1997; Liberal Democrat Spokesman for: Health, Tourism, Housing, Transport 1989–92, National Heritage, Constitution and Civil Service (Tourism) 1997, Culture, Media, Sport and Civil Service (Tourism) 1997–99, Culture, Media and Sport (Tourism) 1999–; Deputy Whip 1988–90; *Select Committees:* Member: Culture, Media and Sport 1997–. *Special Interests:* Tourism, Health, Transport, Leisure, Local Government. Voluntary Youth Leader in Southport for 21 years; President, Local Carers' Association; Local President, Sue Rider Association; Member: All Souls' Dramatic Club, Southport Offshore Lifeboat; Hon. Member, LIFE; President, Southport M.E. Society; Member, Sefton Sports Council; Member: IPU, CPA; OBE 1985; Fellow, Chartered Institute of Bankers; *Sportsclubs:* Southport and Waterloo Athletic Club; *Recreations:* Amateur dramatics, badminton, athletics, community work. *Address:* Ronnie Fearn Esq, OBE, MP, House of Commons, London, SW1A 0AA *Tel:* 020 7219 5116 *Fax:* 020 7219 2331. *Constituency:* Liberal Democrat Headquarters, 35 Shakespeare Street, Southport, Merseyside, PR8 5AB *Tel:* 01704 533555 *Fax:* 01704 533535 *E-mail:* southportldp@cix.co.uk; fearnr@parliament.uk.

Dod *on* Line
An Electronic Directory without rival . . .
MPs' biographies and photographs available with daily updates *via* the internet
For a *free* trial, call Oliver Cox on 020 7828 7256

FRANK FIELD   Birkenhead   *Lab majority 21,843*

Born 16 July 1942; Son of late Walter Field; Educated St Clement Danes Grammar School; Hull University. Teacher in further education 1964–69; Director: Child Poverty Action Group 1969–79, Low Pay Unit 1974–80. Councillor, Hounslow Borough Council 1964–68. **House of Commons:** Contested Buckinghamshire South 1966 general election. Member for Birkenhead since May 1979; Opposition Front Bench Spokesman on Education 1980–81; Minister of State, Department of Social Security (Welfare Reform) 1997–98; *Select Committees:* Chairman: Social Security 1990–97. *Special Interests:* Poverty and Income Redistribution, Ecclesiastical Matters; Poland. *Publications:* Publications on low pay, poverty and social issues since 1971; PC 1997. *Address:* Rt Hon Frank Field, MP, House of Commons, London, SW1A 0AA *Tel:* 020 7219 5193 *Fax:* 020 7219 0601 *E-mail:* hendeyj@parliament.uk.

MARK FISHER   Stoke-on-Trent Central   *Lab majority 19,924*

Born 29 October 1944; Son of late Sir Nigel Fisher, MC, MP 1950–83 and late Lady Gloria Flower; Educated Eton College; Trinity College, Cambridge (MA); Married December 16, 1971, Ingrid Hunt (marriage dissolved 1999) (2 sons 2 daughters). Documentary film producer and scriptwriter 1966–75; Principal, The Tattenhall Centre of Education 1975–83; Member: NUT, MU. Staffordshire County Council: Councillor 1981–85, Chair, Libraries Committee 1981–83. **House of Commons:** Contested Leek 1979 general election. Member for Stoke-on-Trent Central since June 1983; Spokesperson on Arts and Media 1987–92; Front Bench Spokesperson on: The Citizen's Charter 1992–93, National Heritage 1993–97; Opposition Whip 1985–86; Parliamentary Under-Secretary of State: Department of National Heritage 1997, Department for Culture, Media and Sport 1997–98; *Select Committees:* Member: Treasury and Civil Service 1983–85. *Special Interests:* Urban Policies, Freedom of Information, Human Rights, Overseas Aid and Development, Broadcasting, Press, Cultural Policy, Arts; Hong Kong, Kashmir, Pakistan, Central Asia, Indonesia. Deputy Pro-Chancellor, Keele University 1989–97; Member, BBC General Advisory Council 1987–97; Member of Council, Policy Studies Institute 1989–97; Member, Museums and Galleries Commission 1998–2000; Museums and Galleries Commission 1999–; Trustee: National Benevolent Fund for the Aged 1986–97, Education Extra 1992–97, Britten Pears Foundation 1998–; *Publications:* City Centres, City Cultures, 1988; *Whose Cities?* (editor) 1991; *A New London,* 1992; Hon. FRIBA 1992; Hon. Fellow, Royal College of Art 1993. *Address:* Mark Fisher Esq, MP, House of Commons, London, SW1A 0AA *Tel:* 020 7219 4502 *Fax:* 020 7219 4894. *Constituency:* 83 Marsh Street, Hanley, Stoke-on-Trent, ST1 5HN *Tel:* 01782 284009 *Fax:* 01782 283119 *E-mail:* markfishermp@parliament.uk.

JIM FITZPATRICK   Poplar and Canning Town   *Lab majority 18,915*

Born 4 April 1952; Son of James and Jean Fitzpatrick; Educated Holyrood Senior Secondary, Glasgow; Married July 12, 1980, Jane Lowe (1 son 1 daughter). Trainee, Tytrak Ltd, Glasgow 1970–73; Driver, Mintex Ltd, London 1973–74; Firefighter, London Fire Brigade 1974–97; Member, National Executive Council, Fire Brigades Union. **House of Commons:** Member for Poplar and Canning Town since May 1, 1997; PPS to Alan Milburn as Secretary of State for Health 1999–; *Special Interests:* Anti-Poverty, Regeneration, Anti-Racism, Fire. Barking Constituency Labour Party: Voluntary Agent 1986–91, Chair 1989–90; Member, London Labour Executive 1988–; Chair, Greater London Labour Party 1991–; Hon. Treasurer, London Regional Group of Labour MPs 1999–. Parent Governor, Eastbury Comprehensive School; Member: War on Want, Amnesty International, Greenpeace, Labour Animal Welfare Society; Fire Brigade Long Service and Good Conduct Medal (20 years) 1994; *Sportsclubs:* West Ham United FC; *Recreations:* Golf, cycling, reading, TV/film, football. *Address:* Jim Fitzpatrick Esq, MP, House of Commons, London, SW1A 0AA *Tel:* 020 7219 5085/6215 *Fax:* 020 7219 2776. *Constituency:* c/o Trussler Hall, Grundy Street, London E14 *Tel:* 020 7536 0562 *Fax:* 020 7536 0572 *E-mail:* fitzpatrickj@parliament.uk.

LORNA FITZSIMONS   Rochdale   *Lab majority 4,545*

Born 6 August 1967; Daughter of Derek Fitzsimons and Barbara Jean Fitzsimons (née Taylor); Educated St James's Church of England, Wardle; Wardle High School, Rochdale; Rochdale College of Art and Design; Loughborough College of Art and Design (BA textile design); Married April 8, 2000, Stephen Benedict Cooney (1 stepdaughter). Director: NUS Services 1990–94; Endsleigh Insurance 1992–94; Political consultant (associate director), The Rowland Company 1994–97; National Union of Students: Part-time executive member 1989–90; Vice-President, Education 1990–92; President 1992–94; Member, MSF. **House of Commons:** Member for Rochdale since May 1, 1997; *Select Committees:* Member: Procedure 1997–, Modernisation of the House of Commons 1999–. *Special Interests:* Education, Modernisation of Parliament, Health; USA, Italy, South Africa, Vietnam, Kashmir, Pakistan, Bangladesh. Member: Labour Campaign for Electoral Reform, Labour NEC Youth Committee 1990–94, LCC Executive 1994–97; Fabian Society, Labour Friends of Israel. Governor: Wardle High School 1982–83, Loughborough College of Art and Design 1988–89, Sheffield Hallam University 1995–96; Hansard Society 2000–; Member, Further Education Funding Council Quality Committee 1993–94; Registered with The Sheffield Institute for Dyslexia; Chair, The European Students Forum 1992–93; Parliamentary Vice-Chair, Council for Education in the Commonwealth 1997–; Patron, Real Lancashire; Institute of Public Relations Young Communicator of the Year Award, 1996; *Recreations:* Music, walking, cooking, cinema. *Address:* Lorna Fitzsimons, MP, House of Commons, London, SW1A 0AA *Tel:* 020 7219 3433. *Constituency:* 81 Durham Street, Rochdale, Greater Manchester, OL11 1LR *Tel:* 01706 644911 *Fax:* 01706 759826 *E-mail:* fitzsimonsl@parliament.uk.

HOWARD FLIGHT   Arundel and South Downs   *Con majority 14,035*

Born 16 June 1948; Son of late Bernard Thomas Flight and late Doris Mildred Emerson Flight; Educated Brentwood School, Essex; Magdalene College, Cambridge (MA Economics 1969); University of Michigan, USA (MBA 1971); Married June 16, 1973, Christabel Diana Beatrice Norbury (1 son 3 daughters). Investment adviser, N M Rothschild 1971–73; Manager: Cayzer Ltd 1973–77, Wardley Ltd (HSBC) Hong Kong 1977–78; Hong Kong Bank, Merchant Banking Division, Bombay, India 1978–79; Director, investment division, Guinness Mahon 1979–86; Joint managing director, Guinness Flight Global Asset Management Ltd 1986–97; Chair, Investec Guinness Flight Asset Management 1998–; ACM Enchanced European Bonds Trust 2000–; Buyers' Guide 2000–. **House of Commons:** Contested Southwark (Bermondsey) February and October 1974 general elections. Member for Arundel and South Downs since May 1, 1997; Shadow Economic Secretary to the Treasury 1999–; *Select Committees:* Member: Environment, Transport and Regional Affairs 1997–98, Environment 1997–98, Social Security 1998–99. *Special Interests:* Tax, Economic Policy, Farming, Charities, PFI, Venture Capital, EMU; India, South-East Asia, USA, China. Chair, Cambridge University Conservative Association 1968–69; Vice-Chair, Federation of Conservative Students 1969. President, Magdalene College Association, Cambridge; Member, Tax Consultative Committee to HM Treasury 1988–92; Power Exchange Scholar 1969–71; Trustee, Elgar Foundation; Governor/Trustee Brentwood School; Liveryman, Carpenters' Company; *Publications: All You Need to Know About Exchange Rates* 1988; FRSA; Freeman, City of London 1999; *Clubs:* Carlton; *Sportsclubs:* Marden (Skiing); *Recreations:* Skiing, classical music, antique collecting, gardening. *Address:* Howard Flight Esq, MP, House of Commons, London, SW1A 0AA *Tel:* 020 7219 3461 *Fax:* 020 7219 2455. *Constituency:* The Old Town Hall, Steyning, West Sussex, BN44 3YE *Tel:* 01903 816886/879787 *Fax:* 01903 816880 *E-mail:* flighth@parliament.uk *Website:* http://www.the-flight-site.org/.

CAROLINE FLINT   Don Valley   *Lab majority 14,659*

Born 20 September 1961; Daughter of late Wendy Flint (née Beasley), clerical/ shop employee; Educated Twickenham Girls School; Richmond Tertiary College; University of East Anglia (BA American history/literature and film studies); Marriage dissolved; partner, Phil Cole (1 son 1 daughter 1 stepson). Management trainee, GLC/ILEA 1984–85; Policy officer, ILEA 1985–87; Head, Women's Unit, NUS 1988–89; Equal opportunities officer, Lambeth Council 1989–91; Welfare and staff development officer, Lambeth Council 1991–93; Senior researcher/Political officer, GMB Trade Union 1994–97; Member, GMB; Former Shop Steward: NALGO at GLC/LEA, GMB at Lambeth Council. **House of Commons:** Member for Don Valley since May 1, 1997; Joint PPS to the Ministers of State, Foreign and Commonwealth Office 1999–; *Select Committees:* Member: Education and Employment 1997–99, Education Sub-Committee 1997–99. *Special Interests:* Employment, Education and Training, Childcare, Welfare to Work, Family Friendly Employment, Crime/Anti-Social Behaviour, House of Commons Modernisation. National Women's Officer, Labour Students 1983–85; Executive Member, Labour Co-ordinating Committee 1984–85; Chair, Brentford and Isleworth Constituency Labour Party 1991–95; Branch Chair, Branch Secretary and GC Delegate; Facilitator, Labour National Policy Forums 1994–97; Associate Editor, *Renewal* 1995–; Member, Fabian Society; Member, Trade Union Group of Labour MPs. Member, Working For Childcare 1989–99, Chair 1991–95; Board member, Sure Start Denaby Main Partnership 2000–; Member, GMB Group of MPs; Labour Party adviser to the Police Federation of England and Wales 1999; Member, Inter-Parliamentary Union 1997–; *Recreations:* Cinema, tennis, being with my family and friends. *Address:* Caroline Flint, MP, House of Commons, London, SW1A 0AA *Tel:* 020 7219 4407 *Fax:* 020 7219 1277. *Constituency:* Room 10, 7 North Bridge Road, Doncaster, South Yorkshire, DN5 9AA *Tel:* 01302 366778 *Fax:* 01302 328833 *E-mail:* flintc@parliament.uk *Website:* www.carolineflint.co.uk.

PAUL FLYNN   Newport West   *Lab majority 14,537*

Born 9 February 1935; Son of late James and late Kathleen Flynn; Educated St Illtyd's College, Cardiff; University College of Wales, Cardiff; Married 2nd, January 31, 1985, Samantha Cumpstone (1 stepson, 1 stepdaughter and 1 son and 1 daughter (deceased) from previous marriage). Chemist, steel industry 1962–83; Broadcaster, Gwent Community Radio 1983–84; Research officer for Llewellyn Smith, as Labour MEP for South Wales 1984–87. Councillor: Newport Council 1972–81, Gwent County Council 1974–83. **House of Commons:** Contested Denbigh October 1974 general election. Member for Newport West since June 1987; Opposition Spokesman on: Health and Social Security 1988–89, Social Security 1989–90; *Select Committees:* Member: Transport 1992–97, Welsh Affairs 1997–98. *Special Interests:* Health, Medicinal and Illegal Drugs, Social Security, Pensions, Animal Welfare, Devolution in Wales and Welsh Language, Parliamentary and Constitutional Reform; Baltic States, Eastern Europe, Hungary, Romania, Israel. Secretary, Welsh Group of Labour MPs 1997–. Board member, Parliamentary Office of Science and Technology (POST) 1997–; Member, UK Delegation to Council of Europe and Western European Union 1997–; *Publications: Commons Knowledge. How to be a Backbencher,* 1997; *Baglu Mlaen (Staggering Forward),* 1998; *Dragons Led by Poodles,* 1999; Campaign for Freedom of Information Award 1991; Highland Park/*The Spectator* Backbencher of the Year (jointly) 1996; *New Statesman* Best Website of an Elected Representative 2000–; *Recreations:* Local history, photography. *Address:* Paul Flynn Esq, MP, House of Commons, London, SW1A 0AA *Tel:* 020 7219 3478 *Fax:* 020 7219 2433 *Tel (Constituency):* 01633 262348 *E-mail:* info@paulflynnmp.co.uk *Website:* www.paulflynnmp.co.uk.

Visit the Vacher Dod Website . . .
www.politicallinks.co.uk

BARBARA FOLLETT   Stevenage   *Lab majority 11,582*

Born 25 December 1942; Daughter of late William Vernon and Charlotte Hubbard; Educated Sandford School, Addis Ababa, Ethiopia; Ellerslie Girls' High School, Cape Town; University of Cape Town; Open University; London School of Economics (BSc econ); Married 1st, 1963, Richard Turner (2 daughters); married 2nd, Gerald Stonestreet; married 3rd, Les Broer (1 son); married 4th, Kenneth Martin Follett (1 stepson 1 stepdaughter). Part-time salesperson 1960–62; Ledger clerk, Barclays Bank of South Africa 1962–63; EFL teacher, Berlitz School of Languages 1964–66; Joint manager, fruit farm 1966–70; Acting regional secretary, South African Institute of Race Relations 1970–71; Regional manager, Kupugani 1971 74; National health education director, Kupugani 1975–78; Lecturer and assistant course organiser Centre for International Briefing 1980–84; Lecturer in cross-cultural communications 1985–87; Research associate, Institute of Public Policy Research 1993–96, Visiting Fellow 1993–; Director, EMILY's List UK 1993–; Founding Patron, EQ 2000–; Member, MSF. **House of Commons:** Contested Woking 1983, Epsom and Ewell 1987 general elections. Member for Stevenage since May 1, 1997; *Select Committees:* Member: International Development 1997–. *Special Interests:* Economic and Industrial Policy, Gender, Race Relations, Overseas Aid and Development, International Development, Trade and Industry, Housing, Film Industry; Africa, France. Member: Fabian Society, SERA; Chair, Eastern Regional Group of Labour MPs 1999–. Member: ACTSA, Charter 88, CPAG, FOE, Greenpeace, LCER, Liberty, OWA, Fawcett Society, NAWO; Head, South African Women's Movement for Peace 1976–78; Governor: Heath End Comprehensive 1981–84, Ashburnham School 1986–87, Bousefield School 1986–87, Nobel School Stevenage; RSA; *Recreations:* Reading, Scrabble, photography, film, theatre and Star Trek. *Address:* Barbara Follett, MP, House of Commons, London, SW1A 0AA *Tel:* 020 7219 2649 *Fax:* 020 7219 1158. *Constituency:* Stevenage Labour Party, 4 Popple Way, Stevenage, Herts, SG1 3TG *Tel:* 01438 222800 *Fax:* 01438 222292 *E-mail:* barbara@barbara-follett.org.uk *Website:* www.poptel.org.uk/barbara.follett.

ERIC FORTH   Bromley and Chislehurst   *Con majority 11,118*

Born 9 September 1944; Son of late William Forth and Aileen Forth; Educated Jordanhill College School, Glasgow; Glasgow University (MA) politics and economics); Married 1st, March 11, 1967, Linda St Clair (marriage dissolved 1994) (2 daughters) married 2nd, 1994, Mrs Carroll Goff (1 stepson). Manager, industry (Ford, Rank Xerox). Councillor, Brentwood Urban District Council 1968–72; MEP for Birmingham North 1979–84. **House of Commons:** Contested Barking February and October 1974 general elections. Member for Mid Worcestershire 1983–97, and for Bromley and Chislehurst since May 1, 1997; Joint Parliamentary Under-Secretary of State for Industry and Consumer Affairs, Department of Trade and Industry 1988–90; Joint Parliamentary Under-Secretary of State, Department of Employment 1990–92; Department for Education: Parliamentary Under-Secretary of State for Schools 1992–94, Minister of State 1994–95; Minister of State, Department for Education and Employment 1995–97; *Select Committees:* Member: Procedure 1999–, Standards and Privileges 1999–. *Special Interests:* Economic Policy, European Union, USA; Canada, USA, Australia, New Zealand. PC 1997; Channel 4 and *The House* Magazine Opposition Politician of the Year 1999; *Clubs:* Bromley Conservative; *Recreations:* Cinema, political biographies. *Address:* Rt Hon Eric Forth, MP, House of Commons, London, SW1A 0AA *Tel:* 020 7219 6344. *Constituency:* Bromley and Chislehurst Conservative Association, 5 White Horse Hill, Chislehurst, Kent, BR7 6DG *Tel:* 020 8295 2639 *E-mail:* forthe@parliament.uk.

Dod *on* Line
An Electronic Directory without rival . . .
MPs' biographies and photographs available with daily updates *via* the internet
For a *free* trial, call Oliver Cox on 020 7828 7256

DEREK FOSTER   Bishop Auckland   *Lab majority 21,064*

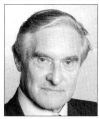

Born 25 June 1937; Son of Joseph Foster, Shipyard worker; Educated Bede Grammar School, Sunderland; Oxford University (BA philosophy, politics and economics 1960); Married October 21, 1972, Florence Anne Bulmer (3 sons 1 daughter). Ten years marketing in the private sector; Youth and community 1970–73; Further education organiser 1973–74; Assistant director of education, Sunderland Borough Council 1974–79. Councillor, Sunderland County Borough Council 1972–74; Tyne and Wear County Council: Councillor 1973–77, Chair: Economic Development Committee 1974–76, North of England Development Council 1974–76. **House of Commons:** Member for Bishop Auckland since May 1979; Opposition Front Bench Spokesman on Social Security 1982–83; Principal Opposition Spokesman for the Duchy of Lancaster 1995–97; Opposition Whip 1981–82; Opposition Chief Whip 1985–95; PPS to Neil Kinnock as Leader of Opposition 1983–85; Member, Shadow Cabinet 1985–97; Shadow Chancellor of the Duchy of Lancaster 1995–97; *Select Committees:* Chairman (Employment): Education and Employment 1997–; Member: Education Sub-Committee 1997–; Chairman: Employment Sub-Committee 1997–; Member: Liaison 1997–. *Special Interests:* Youth Affairs, Education and Training, Regional Policy, Socialist Enterprise, Transport, Economics, Finance; USA, Japan. Ex-Officio Member, Labour Party National Executive Committee 1985–95; Member: Fabian Society, Christian Socialists Society; Chair, Labour Manufacturing Industry Group. Uniformed Member, Salvation Army; Vice-Chair, Youthaid 1979–83; Vice-Chair, Youth Affairs Lobby 1984–86; Hon. President, British Youth Council 1984–86; Vice-President, Christian Socialist Movement 1985–; Member: Ecclesiastical Committee 1997–, National Advisory Board of the Salvation Army 1995–, Advisory Committee for the Registration of Political Parties 1998; Chair: Pioneering Care Partnership 1997–, North Regional Information Society Initiative 1997–2000, National Prayer Breakfast 1998; Non-Executive Director, Northern Informatics 1998–; Chair, Regional Electronics Economy Project 2000–; Fellow, Industry and Parliament Trust; Trustee, Auckland Castle; *Publications:* Articles in: *Guardian* newspaper, *Overview*; PC 1993; *Sportsclubs:* Durham County Cricket; *Recreations:* Brass Bands, Male Voice Choirs, Cricket, Soccer. *Address:* Rt Hon Derek Foster, MP, House of Commons, London, SW1A 0AA *Tel:* 020 7219 3582/6500 *Fax:* 020 7219 2711. *Constituency:* Hackworth House, Byerley Road, Shildon, Co Durham, DL4 1HN *Tel:* 01388 777175 *Fax:* 01388 777175.

DON FOSTER   Bath   *LD majority 9,319*

Born 31 March 1947; Educated Lancaster Royal Grammar School; Keele University (BSc physics and psychology 1969, CEd 1969); Bath University (MEd 1981); Married December 31, 1968, Victoria Jane Dorcas Pettegree (1 son 1 daughter). Science teacher, Sevenoaks School, Kent 1969–75; Science project director, Resources for Learning Development Unit, Avon LEA 1975–80; Education lecturer, Bristol University 1980–89; Managing consultant, Pannell Kerr Forster 1989–92. Avon County Council: Councillor, Cabot Ward, Bristol 1981–89, Chair, Education Committee 1987–89. **House of Commons:** Contested (Liberal/Alliance) Bristol East 1987 general election. Member for Bath since April 9, 1992; Spokesman for: Education 1992–95, Education and Employment 1995–97; Nursery Education and Schools 1997–99, Labour Market Statistics 1997–99; Principal Spokesman for Environment, Transport, the Regions and Social Justice 1999–; *Select Committees:* Member: Education and Employment 1996–99, Education Sub-Committee 1997–99 *Special Interests:* Education, Local Government; Africa, Israel, Central Europe. President, Liberal Democrat Youth and Students 1993–95. Vice-Chair, National Campaign for Nursery Education 1993–99, President 1999–; President, British Association for Early Childhood Education 1998–; Executive, Association of County Councils 1985–89; Joint Hon. President, British Youth Council 1992–99; Vice-Chair, British Association for Central and Eastern Europe 1994–97; Trustee, Open School and Education Extra 1993–99; *Publications: Resource-based Learning in Science*, 1979; *Science With Gas*, 1981; Co-author: *Aspects of Science*, 1984, *Reading About Science*, 1984, *Nuffield Science*, 1986; Numerous educational and political articles and pamphlets; Hon. Fellow, Bath College of High Education 1995; CPhys; MInstP; *Clubs:* National Liberal; *Recreations:* Classical music, travel, sport. *Address:* Don Foster Esq, MP, House of Commons, London, SW1A 0AA *Tel:* 020 7219 5001 *Fax:* 020 7219 2695. *Constituency:* 31 James Street West, Bath, BA1 2BT *Tel:* 01225 338973 *Fax:* 01225 463630 *E-mail:* fosterd@parliament.uk.

MICHAEL JABEZ FOSTER   Hastings and Rye   *Lab majority 2,560*

Born 26 February 1946; Son of Dorothy Foster; Educated Hastings Secondary; Hastings Grammar School; Leicester University (LLM); Married September 13, 1969, Rosemary Kemp (2 sons). Litigation Clerk 1963–72; Solicitor 1980–98; Member and Legal Adviser to GMB. Councillor: Hastings County Borough Council 1971–74, Hastings Borough Council 1973–79, 1983–87, East Sussex County Council 1973–77, 1981–97; Former Member: Sussex Police Authority, East Sussex Health Authority; DL, East Sussex. **House of Commons:** Contested Hastings February and October 1974 and 1979 general elections. Member for Hastings and Rye since May 1, 1997; PPS: to Attorneys General John Morris 1999 and Lord Williams of Mostyn 1999–, and to Ross Cranston as Solicitor General 1999–; *Select Committees:* Member: Social Security 1998–99; Member: Standards and Privileges 1997–. *Special Interests:* Health and Poverty, Animal Welfare, Tax, Employment Law; Member, European Standing Committee A. Member: Society of Labour Lawyers, Christian Socialist Movement, Fabian Society. Member, The Child Poverty Action Group; Member, Methodist Church, 1998–, Law Society, Chartered Institute of Arbitrators; Member, National Trust; ASCAb; *Sportsclubs:* Amherst Tennis Club; *Recreations:* Lawn Tennis, Table Tennis. *Address:* Michael Jabez Foster Esq, DL, MP (Hastings and Rye), House of Commons, London, SW1A 0AA *Tel:* 020 7219 3613 *Fax:* 020 7219 1393. *Constituency:* Ellen Draper Centre, 84 Bohemia Road, St Leonards on Sea, East Sussex, TN37 6RN *Tel:* 01424 460070 *Fax:* 01424 460072 *E-mail:* mp@1066.net.

MICHAEL JOHN FOSTER   Worcester   *Lab majority 7,425*

Born 14 March 1963; Son of Brian William Foster, retired car worker, and Edna Foster, retired teacher; Educated Great Wyrley High School, Staffordshire; Wolverhampton Polytechnic (BA economics 1984); Wolverhampton University (PGCE 1995); Married September 28, 1985, Shauna Ogle (1 son 2 daughters). Financial planning and control department, Jaguar Cars Ltd: Financial analyst 1984–5, Senior analyst 1985–87, Manager 1989–91; Lecturer in accountancy, Worcester College of Technology 1991–97; Shop steward, TGWU 1986–88; Member, GMB, NATFHE. **House of Commons:** Member for Worcester since May 1, 1997; Introduced Private Members' Bill to Ban Hunting With Dogs 1998; On School Crossing Patrols 2000, since incorporated into Transport Bill; *Select Committees:* Member: Education and Employment 1999–, Education Sub-Committee 1999–. *Special Interests:* Trade and Industry, Education and Training, Hunting With Dogs. Agent, Mid Worcester 1992; Secretary, Constituency Labour Party, Worcester 1992–95. Patron: Maggs Day Centre for Homeless People, Worcester Barn Owls Society; President, Worcester City Blind Group; Associate of Chartered Institute of Management Accountants (ACMA); *Sportsclubs:* Worcestershire County Cricket Club, House of Commons Soccer and Cricket Teams; *Recreations:* Sport. *Address:* Michael John Foster Esq, MP (Worcester), House of Commons, London, SW1A 0AA *Tel:* 020 7219 6379 *Fax:* 020 7219 6379. *Constituency:* 2a The Avenue, The Cross, Worcester, WR1 3QA *Tel:* 01905 26504 *E-mail:* fosterm@parliament.uk.

GEORGE FOULKES   Carrick, Cumnock and Doon Valley   *Lab/Co-op majority 21,062*

Born 21 January 1942; Son of late George Foulkes, engineer and Jessie Foulkes; Educated Keith Grammar School, Banff; Haberdashers' Aske's School; Edinburgh University (BSc psychology 1964); Married July 4, 1970, Elizabeth Anna Hope (2 sons 1 daughter). President, Scottish Union of Students 1964–6; Director, ELEC 1966–68; Scottish organiser, European Movement 1968–69; Director, Enterprise Youth 1969–73; Director, Age Concern Scotland 1973–79; Member, GMB. Councillor: Edinburgh Corporation 1970–75, Lothian Regional Council 1974–79; Chair: Lothian Region Education Committee 1974–79, Education Committee of Convention of Scottish Local Authorities 1975–78; JP, Edinburgh 1975. **House of Commons:** Contested Edinburgh West 1970 and Edinburgh Pentlands October 1974 general elections. Member for South Ayrshire 1979–83 and for Carrick, Cumnock and Doon Valley since June 1983; Opposition Front Bench

Spokesman on: Europe 1983–85, Foreign and Commonwealth Affairs 1985–92, Defence, Disarmament and Arms Control 1992–93, Overseas Development 1994–97; Parliamentary Under-Secretary of State, Department of International Development 1997–; *Select Committees:* Member: Foreign Affairs 1980–83. *Special Interests:* International Development, Foreign Affairs, Devolution, Social Services, Tax Havens, Education, Aerospace, Aviation, Energy, Human Rights, Defence; Latin America, Canada, Netherlands, Eastern Europe. Chair, Labour Campaign for a Scottish Parliament–1997; Member, Co-operative Party. Member, Board of St Cuthbert's Co-op Association 1975–79; President, Edinburgh University SRC 1963–64; Rector's Assessor, University of Edinburgh 1968–71; Director, The Co-operative Press 1990–97; Chairman, The John Wheatley Centre 1990–97; Delegate, Parliamentary Assemblies of the Council of Europe and Western European Union 1979–80; Vice-Chair: UK-Netherlands Group of Inter-Parliamentary Union–1997, UK-Canadian Group of Commonwealth Parliamentary Association–1997; Treasurer, Anglo-Spanish Group of Inter-Parliamentary Union to 1997; Member: Executive UK Branch of Commonwealth Parliamentary Association 1989–97, Executive British Section of Inter-Parliamentary Union 1989–97; Member, Commonwealth Parliamentary Association; *Publications:* Editor, *80 Years On* (History of Edinburgh University SRC); Chapters in: *Scotland – A Claim of Right, Football and the Commons People*; Wilberforce Medal 1999; *Clubs:* Edinburgh University Staff; *Recreations:* Boating, season ticket holder and shareholder Heart of Midlothian FC. *Address:* George Foulkes Esq, MP, House of Commons, London, SW1A 0AA *Tel:* 020 7219 3474 *Fax:* 020 7219 6492. *Constituency:* South Wing, Skerrington Farm, Glaisnock Road, Netherthird, Cumnock, KA18 3BU *Tel:* 01290 422990 *Fax:* 01290 424973 *Website:* www.dfid.gov.uk.

SIR NORMAN FOWLER   Sutton Coldfield   *Con majority 14,885*

Born 2 February 1938; Son of late N. F. Fowler and Katherine Fowler; Educated King Edward VI School, Chelmsford; Trinity Hall, Cambridge (MA); Married May 29, 1979, Mrs Fiona Poole, née Donald (2 daughters). National Service, Essex Regiment 1956–58; *The Times*: Special Correspondent 1961–66, Home Affairs Correspondent 1966–70. **House of Commons:** Member for Nottingham South 1970–74, and for Sutton Coldfield since February 1974; Opposition Spokesman on Home Affairs 1974–75; Chief Opposition Spokesman on: Social Services 1975–76, Transport 1976–79; PPS to Secretary for Northern Ireland 1972–74; Minister of Transport 1979–81; Secretary of State for: Transport January-September 1981, Social Services 1981–87, Employment 1987–90; Member, Shadow Cabinet 1997–99; Shadow Secretary of State for: the Environment, Transport and the Regions 1997–98, the Home Department 1998–99. Chair, Cambridge University Conservative Association 1960; Editorial Board, *Crossbow* 1962–70; Council Member, Bow Group 1967–69; Vice-Chair, North Kensington Conservative Association 1967–68; Chair: East Midlands Conservative Political Centre 1970–73, Conservative Party 1992–94. *Publications: After the Riots*, 1979; *Ministers Decide*, 1991; PC 1979; Knighted 1990. *Address:* Rt Hon Sir Norman Fowler, MP, House of Commons, London, SW1A 0AA *Tel:* 020 7219 3525 *Fax:* 020 7219 2412. *Constituency:* 36 High Street, Sutton Coldfield, B72 1UP *Tel:* 0121–354 2229 *Fax:* 0121–321 1762.

DR LIAM FOX   Woodspring   *Con majority 7,734*

Born 22 September 1961; Son of William Fox, teacher, and Catherine Fox; Educated St Bride's High School, East Kilbride; Glasgow University (MB, ChB 1983, MROGP 1989). General practitioner; Divisional surgeon, St John's Ambulance. **House of Commons:** Contested Roxburgh and Berwickshire 1987 general election. Member for Woodspring since April 9, 1992; Opposition Spokesman for Constitutional Affairs, Scotland and Wales 1997–98; Front Bench Spokesman for Constitutional Affairs, with overall responsibility for Scottish and Welsh issues 1998–99; Assistant Government Whip 1994–95; Government Whip 1995–96; PPS to Michael Howard as Home Secretary 1993–94; Parliamentary Under-Secretary of State, Foreign and Commonwealth Office 1996–97; Member, Shadow Cabinet 1998–; Shadow Secretary of State for Health 1999–; *Select Committees:* Member: Scottish Affairs 1992–93. *Special Interests:* Health, Economic Policy, Foreign Affairs. Chair, West of Scotland Young Conservatives 1983; National Vice-Chair, Scottish Young Conservatives 1983–84; Secretary, West Country Conservative Members' Committee 1992–93.

Member, Central Committee, Families for Defence 1987–89; President, Glasgow University Club 1982–83; Guest of US State Department, involving study of drug abuse problems in USA, and Republican Party campaigning techniques 1985; *Publications: Making Unionism Positive*, 1988; *Review of Health Reforms* (House of Commons Magazine), 1989; World Debating Competition, Toronto (Individual speaking prize) 1982; Best Speaker's Trophy, Glasgow University 1983; *Recreations:* Tennis, swimming, cinema, theatre. *Address:* Dr Liam Fox, MP, House of Commons, London, SW1A 0AA *Tel:* 020 7219 4086 *Fax:* 020 7219 2617. *Constituency:* 71 High Street, Nailsea, North Somerset, BS48 1AW *Tel:* 01275 790090 *Fax:* 01275 790091.

CHRISTOPHER FRASER   Mid Dorset and Poole North   *Con majority 681*

Born 25 October 1962; Educated Harrow College; University of Westminster (BA); Married 1987, Lisa Margaret Norman (1 son 1 daughter). Chairman, International Communications Group of Companies. Councillor, Three Rivers District Council 1992–96. **House of Commons:** Member for Mid Dorset and Poole North since May 1, 1997; PPS to Lord Strathclyde, as Shadow Leader of the House of Lords 1999–; *Select Committees:* Member: Culture, Media and Sport 1997–. *Special Interests:* Small Business and Enterprise, Arts, Media, Voluntary Organisations, Constitution, Foreign Affairs, Local Government, Rural Affairs, Tourism/Leisure Industry; SE Asia, Europe, USA, Canada, China, Australia. Member, The Society of Dorset Men; LEA-appointed School Governor 1992–96; Director, Small Business Bureau; Patron, Firm Link, Business Forum, Dorset; Appeals Chairman, Pramacare Charity, Dorset; Member, County Committee, Holton Lee Charity, Dorset; Member, Institute of Directors; Member: Inter-Parliamentary Union 1997–, Commonwealth Parliamentary Association 1997–; Freeman, City of London; *Clubs:* Carlton, Athenaeum; *Recreations:* Golf, sailing, skiing, riding. *Address:* Christopher Fraser Esq, MP, House of Commons, London, SW1A 0AA *Tel:* 020 7219 6569 *Fax:* 020 7219 4499. *Constituency:* 38 Sandbanks Road, Poole, Dorset, BH14 8BX *Tel:* 01202 718080 *E-mail:* fraserc@parliament.uk.

MARIA FYFE   Glasgow Maryhill   *Lab majority 14,264*

Born 25 November 1938; Daughter of late James and Margaret O'Neill, née Lacey; Educated Notre Dame High School, Glasgow; Strathclyde University (BA economic history); Married April 4, 1964, James Fyfe (deceased) (2 sons). Secretary, Scottish Gas Board; Mature student 1970–75; Senior lecturer, Trade Union Studies Unit, Central College of Commerce, Glasgow 1978–87. Glasgow District Council: Councillor 1980–87, Vice-Convenor, Finance 1980–84, Convenor, Personnel 1984–87. **House of Commons:** Member for Glasgow Maryhill since June 1987; Opposition Spokesperson on: Women 1988–91, Scottish Health and Social Services 1992–94, Scottish Education and Social Work 1994–95; *Special Interests:* Local Government, Trade Unions, Employment Law, Women's Rights; Central America, Guyana, Nicaragua, Palestine, Ireland. Member, Labour Party Scottish Executive 1982–88; Chair, Local Government Committee 1985–87. Member: UK Delegation to Council of Europe and Western Europe Union, Chair, Labour Group 1997–; British-Irish Parliamentary Body 1998–; *Clubs:* Keir Hardie; *Recreations:* Reading, music, walking. *Address:* Mrs Maria Fyfe, MP, House of Commons, London, SW1A 0AA *Tel:* 020 7219 4430 *Fax:* 020 7219 4885. *Constituency:* c/o Maryhill Public Library, 1508 Maryhill Road, Glasgow, G20 9AB *Tel:* 0141–945 1495 *Fax:* 0141–945 1846 *E-mail:* mariafyfe@parliament.uk.

Dod *on* Line
An Electronic Directory without rival . . .
MPs' biographies and photographs available with daily updates *via* the internet

For a *free* trial, call Oliver Cox on 020 7828 7256

G

SAM GALBRAITH   Strathkelvin and Bearsden   *Lab majority 16,292*

Born 18 October 1945; Son of late Sam and Cathie Galbraith; Educated Greenock High School; Glasgow University (BSc 1968, MB ChB 1971, MD 1977); Married 1987 (3 daughters). Neurosurgeon. **House of Commons:** Member for Strathkelvin and Bearsden since June 1987; Opposition Spokesperson on: Health 1988–92, Scotland 1988–92, Opposition Front Bench Spokesperson on Employment 1992–93; Parliamentary Under-Secretary of State, Scottish Office (Minister for Health and the Arts) 1997–99. **Scottish Parliament:** MSP for Strathkelvin and Bearsden constituency since May 6, 1999; Minister for Children and Education 1999–. *Publications: An Introduction to Neurosurgery,* 1983; FRCS Glas. 1975. *Address:* Sam Galbraith Esq, MP, MSP, House of Commons, London, SW1A 0AA *Tel:* 020 7219 4079. *Constituency:* 110A Maxwell Avenue, Bearsden, Glasgow, G61 1HU *Tel:* 0141–942 9662 *Fax:* 0141–942 9658 *E-mail:* sam.galbraith.msp@scottish.parliament.uk.

ROGER GALE   North Thanet   *Con majority 2,766*

Born 20 August 1943; Son of Richard Byrne Gale, solicitor, and Phyllis Mary Gale, née Rowell; Educated Hardye's School, Dorchester; Guildhall School of Music and Drama (LGSM&D 1963); Married 1st, 1964, Wendy Bowman (marriage dissolved 1967), married 2nd, 1971, Susan Linda Sampson (marriage dissolved 1980) (1 daughter), married 3rd, 1980, Susan Gabrielle Marks (2 sons). Freelance broadcaster 1963–; Programme director, Radio Scotland 1965; Personal assistant to general manager, Universal Films 1971–72; Freelance reporter, BBC Radio London 1972–73; Producer: Radio 1 *Newsbeat,* BBC Radio 4 *Today* 1973–76; Director, BBC Children's Television 1976–79; Senior producer, Children's Television, Thames TV; Editor, Teenage Unit; Producer special projects, Thames TV 1979–83; Member: NUJ, Equity, BECTU. **House of Commons:** Contested Birmingham Northfield by-election 1982. Member for North Thanet since June 1983; PPS to Ministers of State for the Armed Forces: Archibald Hamilton 1992–93, Jeremy Hanley 1993–94; *Select Committees:* Member: Home Affairs 1990–92; Member: Broadcasting 1997–, Chairmen's Panel 1997–. *Special Interests:* Education, Animal Welfare, Media, Broadcasting, Tourism, Leisure Industry, Licensed Trade; Cyprus, Cuba, Tunisia, Mongolia. Fellow, Parliament and Armed Forces Fellowship; Inaugural Fellowship, Police and Parliamentary Fellowship 1995; Hon. Associate, British Veterinary Association; Delegate, Council of Europe 1987–89; Member, Delegation of Council of Europe, Western European Union 1987–89; Fellow, Industry and Parliament Trust; LGSM&D; Freeman, City of London; *Clubs:* Farmer's; *Sportsclubs:* Kent County Cricket, Royal Temple Yacht; *Recreations:* Swimming, sailing. *Address:* Roger Gale Esq, MP, House of Commons, London, SW1A 0AA *Tel:* 020 7219 4087 *Fax:* 020 7219 6828. *Constituency:* The Old Forge, 215a Canterbury Road, Birchington, Kent, CT7 9AH *Tel:* 01843 848588 *Fax:* 01843 844856.

GEORGE GALLOWAY   Glasgow Kelvin   *Lab majority 9,665*

Born 16 August 1954; Son of George, engineer, and Sheila, née Reilly, factory worker; Educated Charleston Primary; Harris Academy; Married 1st December 20, 1979, Elaine Fyffe (marriage dissolved 1999) (1 daughter); married 2nd Dr Amireh Abu-Zayyad. General labourer, Garden Works, Dundee 1972; Production worker, Michelin Tyres 1973; Labour organiser 1977–83; General secretary, War on Want 1983–87; Member, TGWU 1974–99; Sponsored by TGWU 1987–96. **House of Commons:** Member for Glasgow Hillhead 1987–97, and for Glasgow Kelvin since May 1, 1997; *Select Committees:* Member: Broadcasting 1997–99, Broadcasting 2000. *Special Interests:* Foreign Affairs, Defence, Scotland. Labour Party organiser, Dundee East and West Constituencies 1977–83; Chair, Scottish Labour Party 1980–81. General Secretary, War on Want 1983–87;

Publications: Downfall: The Ceausescus and the Romanian Revolution (jointly) 1989; Hilal-i-Quaid-Azam, the highest civil award in Pakistan for services to the restoration of democracy in Pakistan 1990; Hilal-i-Pakistan for services to the people of Kashmir 1996; Kashmir Centres Europe Kashmir Award for work, efforts, support and services to the Kashmir cause 1998; *Clubs:* Groucho; *Recreations:* Football, sport, films, music. *Address:* George Galloway Esq, MP, House of Commons, London, SW1A 0AA *Tel:* 020 7219 3000 *Fax:* 020 7219 2879. *Constituency:* 8a Parkgrove Terrace, Glasgow, G3 7ST *Tel:* 0141–357 2073 *Fax:* 0141–357 2073 *E-mail:* gallowayg@parliament.uk.

MIKE GAPES   Ilford South   *Lab/Co-op majority 14,200*

Born 4 September 1952; Son of Frank Gapes, retired postal worker, and Emily Gapes, retired office worker; Educated Buckhurst Hill County High School; Fitzwilliam College, Cambridge (MA economics); Middlesex Polytechnic, Enfield (Diploma in industrial relations); Married September 4, 1992, Frances Smith (3 daughters). Voluntary Service Overseas (VSO) Teacher, Swaziland 1971–72; Secretary, Cambridge Students' Union 1973–74; National Organisation of Labour Students: Vice-Chair 1975–76, Chair 1976–77; National student organiser, The Labour Party 1977–80; Research officer, Labour Party International Department 1980–88; Senior international officer, The Labour Party 1988–92; Member, TGWU. **House of Commons:** Contested Ilford North 1983 general election. Member for Ilford South since April 9, 1992; PPS to Paul Murphy as Minister of State, Northern Ireland Office 1997–99; *Select Committees:* Member: Foreign Affairs 1992–97; Member: Defence 1999–. *Special Interests:* Defence, International Affairs, European Union, Economic Policy, Education. Member, The Co-operative Party; Deputy Chair, Parliamentary Labour Friends of Israel 1997–. President, Redbridge United Chinese Association, Trustee Parkside Community Association 1999–, Council Member Voluntary Service Overseas 1997– President, Valentines Park Conservationists, Vice-President, Redbridge Chamber of Commerce; Vice-President, Council of European National Youth Committees 1977–79; Council Member: Royal Institute of International Affairs 1996–99; *Publications:* Contributor to several books and pamphlets; Fabian Society pamphlet: *After the Cold War*, 1990; *Sportsclubs:* Vice-President, Ilford Football Club; West Ham United Supporters' Club; *Recreations:* My family and when I get time watching football at West Ham, blues and jazz music. *Address:* Mike Gapes Esq, MP, House of Commons, London, SW1A 0AA *Tel:* 020 7219 6485 *Fax:* 020 7219 0978 *E-mail:* gapesm@parliament.uk.

BARRY GARDINER   Brent North   *Lab majority 4,019*

Born 10 March 1957; Son of late John Flannegan Gardiner, general manager, Kelvin Hall, and of late Sylvia Strachan, doctor; Educated Glasgow High School; Haileybury College; St Andrews (MA): Harvard University (J. F. Kennedy Scholarship 1983); Cambridge University (research 1984–87); Married Caroline Smith (3 sons 1 daughter). Occasional Lecturer, The Academy of National Economy, Moscow; Partner, Mediterranean Average Adjusting Co; Member: MSF, GMB. Cambridge City Council: Councillor 1988–94, Chair of Finance, Mayor 1992–93. **House of Commons:** Member for Brent North since May 1, 1997; *Select Committees:* Member: Procedure 1997–, Broadcasting 1998–, Public Accounts 1999–. *Special Interests:* Economic Policy, Trade and Industry, Education, Foreign Affairs; India, Sri Lanka, Russia, Georgia. Member, Labour Finance and Industry Group; Chair, Labour Friends of India. Member, Amnesty International; Member, Shipwrights' Company; *Publications:* Various articles relating to shipping and maritime affairs; Articles on Political Philosophy in the *Philosophical Quarterly*; ACII; Freeman, City of London; *Clubs:* Royal Overseas League; *Recreations:* Walking, music, reading philosophy, bird-watching. *Address:* Barry Gardiner Esq, MP, House of Commons, London, SW1A 0AA *Tel:* 020 7219 4046 *Fax:* 020 7219 2495.

EDWARD GARNIER   Harborough   *Con majority 6,524*

Born 26 October 1952; Son of late Colonel William d'Arcy Garnier, and Hon. Mrs Garnier; Educated Wellington College; Jesus College, Oxford 1971–74 (BA modern history 1974, MA); College of Law, London; Married April 17, 1982, Anna Caroline Mellows (2 sons 1 daughter). Barrister; Called to the Bar, Middle Temple 1976; QC 1995. **House of Commons:** Contested Hemsworth 1987 general election. Member for Harborough since April 9, 1992; PPS: to Ministers of State, Foreign and Commonwealth Office, Alastair Goodlad 1994–95, David Davis 1994–95; to Sir Nicholas Lyell Attorney-General and Sir Derek Spencer as Solicitor-General 1995–, to Roger Freeman as Chancellor of the Duchy of Lancaster 1996–97; Shadow Minister, Lord Chancellor's Department 1997–99; Shadow Attorney General 1999–; *Select Committees:* Member: Home Affairs 1992–95. *Special Interests:* Agriculture, Defence, Foreign Affairs, Education. Treasurer, Macleod Group of Conservative MPs 1995–97; Member, Society of Conservative Lawyers. Secretary, Foreign Affairs Forum 1988–92, Vice-Chairman 1992–; Director, Great Britain-China Centre 1998–; *Publications:* Co-author *Bearing the Standard: Themes for a Fourth Term*, 1991; *Facing the Future*, 1993; Contributor to *Halsbury's Laws of England*, 4th edition 1985; Visiting Parliamentary Fellow, St Anthony's College, Oxford 1996–97; *Clubs:* Pratt's, Vincent's (Oxford); *Recreations:* Shooting, cricket, tennis, skiing, opera, biographical research. *Address:* Edward Garnier Esq, QC, MP, House of Commons, London, SW1A 0AA *Tel:* 020 7219 6524. *Constituency:* 24 Nelson Street, Market Harborough, Leicestershire, LE16 9AY *Tel:* 01858 464146 *Fax:* 01858 410013 *E-mail:* garniere@parliament.uk.

ANDREW GEORGE   St Ives   *LD majority 7,170*

Born 2 December 1958; Son of Reginald Hugh George, horticulturist, and Diana May (née Petherick), teacher and musician; Educated Helston Grammar School; Sussex University (BA); University College, Oxford (MSc); Married July 4, 1987, Jill Elizabeth Marshall (1 son 1 daughter). Charity Worker. **House of Commons:** Contested St Ives 1992 general election. Member for St Ives since May 1, 1997; Spokesman for: Agriculture, Fisheries, Food and Rural Affairs (Fisheries) 1997–99, Social Security (Disabilities) 1999–; Fisheries 2000–; *Select Committees:* Member: Agriculture 1997–99. *Special Interests:* Third World, Cornwall, Economic Development, Housing, Fishing, Agriculture, Social Exclusion, Devolution, Small Nations, Anti-Racism, Domestic Violence, Immigration, Environment, Minority Groups; All Small Nations. *Publications: Cornwall at the Crossroads*, 1989; Plus other publications and articles; *Recreations:* Cricket, football, rugby, tennis, swimming, writing, walking, Cornish culture, cycling, gardening, drawing. *Address:* Andrew George Esq, MP, House of Commons, London, SW1A 0AA *Tel:* 020 7219 4588 *Fax:* 020 7219 5572. *Constituency:* Knights Yard, Belgravia Street, Penzance, Cornwall, TR18 2EL *Tel:* 01736 860020 *Fax:* 01736 332866 *E-mail:* mcguffiea@parliament.uk.

BRUCE GEORGE   Walsall South   *Lab majority 11,312*

Born 1 June 1942; Son of late Edgar Lewis George and late Phyllis George; Educated Mountain Ash Grammar School; University of Wales (BA); Warwick University (MA); Married July 1992, Lisa Toelle. Assistant lecturer in politics, Glamorgan College of Technology 1964–66; Lecturer in politics, Manchester Polytechnic 1968–70; Senior lecturer in politics, Birmingham Polytechnic 1970–74; Visiting lecturer, Essex University 1983; Former tutor, Open University. **House of Commons:** Contested Southport 1970 general election. Member for Walsall South since February 1974; *Select Committees:* Chairman: Defence 1997–; Member: Liaison 1997–. *Special Interests:* Defence, International Affairs, Housing, Health, Social Services, Private Security. Member: RIIA, RUSI, International Institute of Strategic Studies, American Society for Industrial Security (UK); Patron: Institute of Security Management, Sister Dora Hospice Appeal Ltd, Hon. Adviser, Royal British Legion 1997; Councillor, Council for Arms Control; Chair, Mediterranean Special Group;

Former Chair, Political Committee, North Atlantic Assembly; Parliamentary Assembly of Organisation for Security and Co-operation in Europe: Chair, General (First) Committee on Political Affairs and Security 1994–, Leader, UK Delegation 1997–, Vice-President 1999; Fellow, Industry and Parliament Trust; *Publications:* Numerous books and articles on defence and Foreign affairs; Editor, *Jane's NATO Handbook 1990–91*; Hon. Fellow, Warwick University; *Sportsclubs:* Founder, House of Commons Football Club; *Recreations:* Reading, supports Walsall Football Club. *Address:* Bruce George Esq, MP, House of Commons, London, SW1A 0AA *Tel:* 020 7219 4049/6610 *Fax:* 020 7219 3823. *Constituency:* 34 Bridge Street, Walsall, West Midlands, WS1 1HQ *Tel:* 01922 724960 *Fax:* 01922 621844.

NEIL GERRARD   Walthamstow   *Lab majority 17,149*

Born 3 July 1942; Son of late Francis and Emma Gerrard, primary school teachers; Educated Manchester Grammar School; Wadham College, Oxford (BA natural science 1964); Chelsea College, London (MED 1973); Polytechnic of South Bank (DPSE 1983); Married 1968, Marian Fitzgerald (marriage dissolved 1983) (2 sons). Teacher, Queen Elizabeth's School, Barnet 1965–68; Lecturer, Hackney College 1968–92; Member: NATFHE, GMB. London Borough of Waltham Forest: Councillor 1973–90, Leader, Labour Group 1983–90, Leader of Council 1986–90. **House of Commons:** Contested Chingford 1979 general election. Member for Walthamstow since April 9, 1992; PPS to: Dawn Primarolo as Financial Secretary, HM Treasury May-December 1997; *Select Committees:* Member: Deregulation 1995–97, Environment 1995–97; Member: Information 1997–, Environmental Audit 1999–. *Special Interests:* Housing, Planning, Race Relations, Foreign Affairs, HIV/AIDS, Refugees/Asylum, Criminal Justice, Disabled/Disability; Middle East, Sri Lanka, Kashmir, India. Member, PLP Civil Liberties Group. Former Board Member, SHAC; Board Member, Theatre Royal, Stratford, East London; Board of Trustees Leyton Orient Community Sports Programme; *Recreations:* Theatre, cinema, reading, music, sport. *Address:* Neil Gerrard Esq, MP, House of Commons, London, SW1A 0AA *Tel:* 020 7219 6368 *Fax:* 020 7219 4899. *Constituency:* 23 Orford Road, Walthamstow, London, E17 9NL *Tel:* 020 8521 1223 *Fax:* 020 8521 1223 *E-mail:* gerrardn@parliament.uk.

NICK GIBB   Bognor Regis and Littlehampton   *Con majority 7,321*

Born 3 September 1960; Son of late John McLean Gibb, civil engineer, and Eileen Mavern Gibb, retired schoolteacher; Educated Maidstone Boys' Grammar School; Roundhay School, Leeds; Thornes House School, Wakefield; Durham University (BA law 1981). Chartered accountant, specialising in taxation, KPMG, London 1984–97. **House of Commons:** Contested Stoke-on-Trent Central 1992 general election and Rotherham by-election 1994. Member for Bognor Regis and Littlehampton since May 1, 1997; Opposition Front Bench Spokesman for: the Treasury December 1998–99, Trade and Industry (Energy, Regulation, Company Law, Competition) 1999–; *Select Committees:* Member: Social Security 1997–98, Treasury 1998, Treasury Sub-Committee 1998. *Special Interests:* Economics, Tax, Education, Social Security; USA, Israel. *Publications: Maintaining Momentum*, Pamphlet on Tax Reform 1992; *Bucking the Market*, Pamphlet Opposing Membership of ERM 1990; *Duty to Repeal*, Pamphlet Calling for Abolition of Stamp Duty 1989; *Simplifying Taxes*, Pamphlet on Tax Reform 1987; Member, Institute of Chartered Accountants in England and Wales; ACA; *Recreations:* Long-distance running, skiing. *Address:* Nick Gibb Esq, MP, House of Commons, London, SW1A 0AA *Tel:* 020 7219 6374 *Fax:* 020 7219 1395. *Constituency:* 4 The Precinct, West Meads, Bognor Regis, West Sussex, PO21 5SB *Tel:* 01243 826410 *Fax:* 01243 842076.

DR IAN GIBSON   Norwich North   *Lab majority 9,470*

Born 26 September 1938; Son of late William and Winifred Gibson; Educated Dumfries Academy; Edinburgh University (BSc genetics 1962, PhD); Married March 1974, Elizabeth Frances Lubbock (2 daughters). University of East Anglia: lecturer 1965–71, senior lecturer 1971–97, dean of biology 1991–97; National Executive Committee, ASTMS/MSF 1972–96. **House of Commons:** Contested Norwich North 1992. Member for Norwich North since May 1, 1997; *Select Committees:* Member: Science and Technology 1997–. *Special Interests:* Science, Technology, Health, Environment. Chair, MSF Parliamentary Group. MIBiol; FIBiol; *Sportsclubs:* Football Supporters' Association; *Recreations:* Football. *Address:* Dr Ian Gibson, MP, House of Commons, London, SW1A 0AA *Tel:* 020 7219 4419 *Fax:* 020 7219 2799. *Constituency:* Norwich Labour Centre, 59 Bethel Street, Norwich, NR1 1NL *Tel:* 01603 661144 *Fax:* 01603 663502 *E-mail:* padillaa@parliament.uk.

SANDRA GIDLEY   Romsey   *LD majority 3,311*

Born 26 March 1957; Educated Eggars Grammar School, Alton, Hampshire; Afcent International, Brunssum, Netherlands; Windsor Girls School, Hamm, West Germany; Bath University (BPharm 1978); married 1979, William Arthur Gidley (1 daughter 1 son). pharmacist, Badham Chemists 1979–80; pharmacy manager, G K Chemists 1980–81; locum pharmacist 1982–92; pharmacy manager, supermarkets 1992–2000. Councillor, Test Valley Borough Council 1995–2000: mayor Romsey Town 1997–98. **House of Commons:** Member for Romsey since May 4, 2000; *Special Interests:* health, education. MRPharmS 1979; *Recreations:* photography, travel, theatre, badminton. *Address:* Sandra Gidley, MP, House of Commons, London, SW1A 0AA *Tel:* 020 7219 5986 *Fax:* 020 7219 2324. *Constituency:* 74 The Hundred, Romsey, Hampshire, SO51 8BX *Tel:* 01794 514900 *Fax:* 01794 512538 *E-mail:* gidleys@parliament.uk.

CHRISTOPHER GILL   Ludlow   *Con majority 5,909*

Born 28 October 1936; Educated Shrewsbury School; Married July 2, 1960, Patricia Greenway (1 son 2 daughters). RNVR 1952, RN 1955–57, Reserve Decoration 1971; Chairman, family farming, meat processing and wholesaling business F. A. Gill Ltd. Wolverhampton Borough Council: Councillor 1965–72, Chair, Public Works Committee 1967–69; Chair, Local Education Authority 1969–70. **House of Commons:** Member for Ludlow since June 1987. Conservative Whip withdrawn November 1994, restored April 1995; *Select Committees:* Member: Agriculture 1989–95, Welsh Affairs 1995–97. *Special Interests:* Agriculture, Fisheries, European Union; Europe; Member, European Standing Committee A 1998–. President, Midlands West European Conservative Council 1983–84. Formerly Council member, Wolverhampton Chamber of Commerce; Executive Member, 1922 Committee 1997–2000; Member: Council of Europe 1997–99, Western European Union Assemblies 1997–99; Liveryman, Worshipful Company of Butchers; *Publications: In Their Own Words*; Freeman, City of London; *Clubs:* Carlton; *Recreations:* Walking, golf, sailing, skiing, DIY. *Address:* Christopher Gill Esq, MP, House of Commons, London, SW1A 0AA *Tel:* 020 7219 5101 *Tel (Constituency):* 01746 861267 *Fax (Constituency):* 01746 861267.

CHERYL GILLAN   Chesham and Amersham   *Con majority 13,859*

Born 21 April 1952; Daughter of late Adam Mitchell Gillan, company director, and late Mona Gillan; Educated Cheltenham Ladies' College; College of Law; Chartered Institute of Marketing; Married December 7, 1985, John Coates Leeming. International Management Group 1977–84; Director, British Film Year 1984–86; Senior marketing consultant, Ernst and Young 1986–91; Marketing director, Kidsons Impey 1991–93; Contested Greater Manchester Central 1989 European Parliament election. **House of Commons:** Member for Chesham and Amersham since April 9, 1992; Opposition Spokesman for: Trade and Industry 1997–98, Foreign and Commonwealth Affairs 1998–, International Development 1998–; PPS to Viscount Cranborne, as Leader of the House of Lords and Lord Privy Seal 1994–95; Parliamentary Under-Secretary of State, Department of Education and Employment 1995–97; *Select Committees:* Member: Science and Technology 1992–95, Procedure 1994–95. *Special Interests:* Industry, Space, International Affairs, Defence; Former Soviet Union, Europe, Hungary, Poland, USA, Japan, Pacific Rim. Chairman, Bow Group 1987–88; Member, Highflyers' Conservative Group. Member, Executive Committee, Commonwealth Parliamentary Association (CPA) UK Branch 1998–; Member, Worshipful Company of Marketors; FCIM; Freeman, City of London; *Clubs:* RAC; *Recreations:* Golf, music, gardening. *Address:* Cheryl Gillan, MP, House of Commons, London, SW1A 0AA *Tel:* 020 7219 4061.

LINDA GILROY   Plymouth Sutton   *Lab/Co-op majority 9,440*

Born 19 July 1949; Daughter of William and Gwendolen Jarvie; Educated Maynards, Exeter; Stirling High School; Edinburgh University (MA history 1971); Strathclyde University (postgraduate diploma, secretarial studies 1972); Married March 10, 1986, Bernard Gilroy. Deputy director, Age Concern, Scotland 1972–79; Regional manager, Gas Consumers' Council 1979–96; Member, TGWU; Contested Devon and East Plymouth 1994 European Parliament election. **House of Commons:** Contested South-East Cornwall 1992 general election. Member for Plymouth Sutton since May 1, 1997; *Select Committees:* Member: European Legislation 1997–98, European Scrutiny 1998. *Special Interests:* Pensioners' Rights, Trade and Industry, Energy, Utility Regulation; Turkey, Poland, New Zealand, Australia, America, Tanzania. *Recreations:* Theatre, swimming, walking. *Address:* Linda Gilroy, MP, House of Commons, London, SW1A 0AA *Tel:* 020 7219 3000.

DR NORMAN GODMAN   Greenock and Inverclyde   *Lab majority 13,040*

Born 19 April 1938; Son of late Wilfrid Godman, fisherman and late Isabella Godman, fishergirl; Educated Westbourne Street Boys' School, Hull; Hull University (BA); Heriot-Watt University (PhD 1982); Married, Patricia. National Service with the Royal Military Police; Shipwright; Teacher, Scottish Further and Higher Education. **House of Commons:** Contested Aberdeen South 1979 general election. Member for Greenock and Port Glasgow 1983–97, and for Greenock and Inverclyde since May 1, 1997; Opposition Spokesman on: Fisheries 1988–89, Agriculture and Rural Affairs 1988–89; *Select Committees:* Member: European Legislation 1990–95; Member: Foreign Affairs 1997–. *Special Interests:* Foreign Affairs, Human Rights, Law Reform, Incomes Policies. Amnesty International; National Trust for Scotland; United Nations Association; Fellow, Industry and Parliament Trust; *Recreations:* Hill-walking, reading, going to concerts, cinema and theatre, fishing, allotment. *Address:* Dr Norman Godman, MP, House of Commons, London, SW1A 0AA *Tel:* 020 7219 4441.

Visit the Vacher Dod Website . . .

www.politicallinks.co.uk

ROGER GODSIFF   Birmingham Sparkbrook and Small Heath   *Lab majority 19,526*

Born 28 June 1946; Son of late George Godsiff, chargehand/fitter, and of Gladys Godsiff; Educated Catford Comprehensive School, London; Married 1977, Julia Brenda Morris (1 son 1 daughter). Banking 1965–70; Political Officer, APEX 1970–88; Senior research officer, GMB 1988–91; Member of and sponsored by GMB. London Borough of Lewisham: Councillor 1971–90, Labour Chief Whip 1974–77, Mayor 1977. **House of Commons:** Contested Birmingham Yardley 1983 general election. Member for Birmingham Small Heath 1992–97, and for Birmingham Sparkbrook and Small Heath since May 1, 1997; *Special Interests:* European Union, Foreign Affairs, Industrial Relations, Sport, Recreation, Immigration Policy; Indian Sub-Continent, America, Middle East, Asia. Joined Labour Party 1966; Member, Co-operative Party. Member, Executive Committee, IPU 1999–; *Sportsclubs:* Member, Charlton Athletic Supporters Club; *Recreations:* Sport in general, particularly football, member of Charlton Athletic Supporters' Club. *Address:* Roger Godsiff Esq, MP, House of Commons, London, SW1A 0AA *Tel:* 020 7219 5191 *Fax:* 020 7219 2221. *Constituency:* 15D Lloyd Street, Small Heath, Birmingham, B10 0LH *Tel:* 0121–772 2383 *Fax:* 0121–772 2383.

PAUL GOGGINS   Wythenshawe and Sale East   *Lab majority 15,019*

Born 16 June 1953; Son of John Goggins and late Rita Goggins; Educated St Bede's, Manchester 1964–71; Ushaw College, Durham 1971–73; Birmingham Polytechnic (Certificate in Residential Care of Children and Young People 1976); Manchester Polytechnic (Certificate of Qualification in Social Work 1982); Married August 20, 1977, Wyn Bartley (2 sons 1 daughter). Child care worker, Liverpool Catholic Social Services 1974–75; Officer-in-Charge, Local Authority Children's Home, Wigan 1976–84; Project director, NCH Action For Children, Salford 1984–89; National director, Church Action On Poverty 1989–97; Shop Steward; Member, TGWU. Councillor, Salford City Council 1990–98. **House of Commons:** Member for Wythenshawe and Sale East since May 1, 1997; PPS to John Denham as Minister of State: Department of Social Security 1998–99, Department of Health 1999–; *Select Committees:* Member: Social Security 1997–98. *Special Interests:* UK Poverty, Unemployment, Housing, Transport, Global Poverty, Democratic Renewal, Community Regeneration. Associate Member, CAFOD Board; Patron, Trafford Crossroads; Hon. President, Wythenshawe Mobile; Director, Campus Ventures Ltd; *Recreations:* Watching Manchester City football team, walking, singing. *Address:* Paul Goggins Esq, MP, House of Commons, London, SW1A 0AA *Tel:* 020 7219 5865. *Constituency:* 2/10 Alderman Downward House, Civic Centre, Wythenshawe, Manchester, M22 5RF *Tel:* 0161–499 7900 *Fax:* 0161–499 7911 *E-mail:* gogginsp@parliament.uk.

LLIN GOLDING   Newcastle-under-Lyme   *Lab majority 17,206*

Born 21 March 1933; Daughter of late Ness Edwards, MP; Educated Caerphilly Girls Grammar School; Married 1st, 1957, Dr Roland Lewis (1 son 2 daughters), married 2nd, August 8, 1980, John Golding, MP (died 1999). Member, Society of Radiographers 1953–; Secretary and assistant to second husband, when an MP; Former NUPE Branch Secretary. Member, North Staffs District Health Authority 1983–87. **House of Commons:** Member for Newcastle-under-Lyme since by-election July 17, 1986; Opposition Whip 1987–92; Member of Opposition team on: Social Security 1992–93, Children and Families 1993–95, Food, Agriculture and Rural Affairs 1995–97; *Select Committees:* Member: Broadcasting the House of Commons 1990–92; Member: Culture, Media and Sport 1997–, Standing Orders 1998–. *Special Interests:* Health Service, Trade Unions, Children. Secretary, Newcastle Staffs and District Trades Council 1976–86; Former Member, District Manpower Services Committee; Member: BBC Advisory Committee 1989–92, Commonwealth War Graves Commission 1992–; Trustee (unpaid): NSPCC 1988–, Second Chance 1988–, SAFE; Executive Committee Member, IPU British Group; *Recreations:* Fishing. *Address:* Llin Golding, MP, House of Commons, London, SW1A 0AA *Tel:* 020 7219 4209 *Fax:* 020 7219 2395. *Constituency:* 6 Lancaster Avenue, Newcastle-under-Lyme, Staffordshire, ST5 1DR *Tel:* 01782 636200 *Fax:* 01782 614336.

EILEEN GORDON   Romford   *Lab majority 649*

Born 22 October 1946; Daughter of late Charles Leatt and late Margaret Rose Leatt; Educated Harold Hill Grammar School; Shoreditch Comprehensive; Westminster College of Education (Oxford) (Cert Ed); Married Tony Gordon (1 son 1 daughter). Former Teacher; Caseworker/Assistant to Tony Banks MP 1990–97; Member, TGWU. **House of Commons:** Contested Romford 1992. Member for Romford since May 1, 1997; *Select Committees:* Member: Broadcasting 1997–, Health 1999–. *Special Interests:* Education, Health, Housing, Equal Opportunities. Member: Co-operative Party, Greater London Party Regional Executive 1993–98; Member, European Standing Committee B 1998–. Former Member, Community Health Council; Member: YMCA, League Against Cruel Sports; School Governor; Campaigned to save services at Oldchurch Hospital 1987–97; *Recreations:* Cinema, family, keeping fit, socialising. *Address:* Eileen Gordon, MP, House of Commons, London, SW1A 0AA *Tel:* 020 7219 4413 *Fax:* 020 7219 2779. *Constituency:* Saffron House, 273 South Street, Romford, Essex, RM1 2BE *Tel:* 01708 764020 *Fax:* 01708 732728.

TERESA GORMAN   Billericay   *Con majority 1,356*

Born 30 September 1931; Educated Fulham County School; London University (BSc zoology, botany; Brighton College of Education (DipEd); Married. Teacher; Entrepreneur; Writer. Westminster City Council: Councillor 1982–86, Vice-Chair: Housing, Social Services, General Purposes Committees, Whip. **House of Commons:** Contested (Independent) Lambeth, Streatham as Teresa Moore October 1974 general election. Member for Billericay since June 1987; Sponsored first ever Women into Politics exhibition and festival in House of Commons July 1993; *Select Committees:* Member: Environment, Transport and Regional Affairs 1998–, Deregulation 1999–, Transport Sub-Committee 1999–. *Special Interests:* Free Trade, Individual Freedom, Women's Issues, Environment; Southern Africa, USA, Australia, SE Asia. Conservative Women's National Committee 1983–88. Chair, Alliance of Small Firms and Self Employed People 1973–87; Founder Chair, Amarant Trust, a charity to raise awareness of HRT 1985–92; *Publications:* Papers for: Centre for Policy Studies, Institute of Economic Affairs, Adam Smith Institute; *The Amarant Book of HRT*, 1988; *Chickengate*, 1992; *The Bastards*, 1993; *Enterprise Culture*; *Worried to Death*; *Business Still Burdened*; *Not a Penny More*, 1994; FLS; *Recreations:* Natural history, travel. *Address:* Mrs Teresa Gorman, MP, House of Commons, London, SW1A 0AA *Tel:* 020 7219 6521 *Fax:* 020 7219 6856 *Tel (Constituency):* 01375 892683 *Fax (Constituency):* 01375 892683 *E-mail:* gormant@parliament.uk.

DONALD GORRIE   Edinburgh West   *LD majority 7,253*

Born 2 April 1933; Son of late Robert MacLagan Gorrie, DSc, and late Sydney Grace Easterbrook Gorrie; Educated Oundle School; Corpus Christi College, Oxford (MA modern history); Married August 24, 1957, Astrid Margaret Salvesen (2 sons). Second Lieutenant, Royal Artillery 1951–53; Schoolmaster, Gordonstoun School 1957–60; Director of Physical Education, Marlborough College 1960–66; Research at Edinburgh University (Scottish History), Adult Education Lecturer 1966–69; Director of Research, then Director of Administration, Scottish Liberal Party 1969–75; Started Small Business 1976–79; Full-Time Councillor 1980–97; MSP for Central Scotland region since May 6, 1999. Councillor, Edinburgh Town Council 1971–75; Councillor/Group Leader: Lothian Regional Council 1974–96, Edinburgh District Council 1980–96, City of Edinburgh Council 1995–97. **House of Commons:** Member for Edinburgh West since May 1, 1997; Spokesman for Scotland: Education 1997–99, Housing 1997–99, Local Government 1997–99, Youth 1997–99, Sport 1997–99; Liberal Democrat Whip 1997–99; *Special Interests:* Local Government, Education, Youth Affairs, Sport, Arts. Former Convenor: Edinburgh City Youth Cafes, Diverse Attractions; Former Director/Committee Member: Edinburgh International Festival, Royal Lyceum Theatre, Queen's Hall, Edinburgh, Lothian Youth Clubs, Castle Rock Housing Association; OBE 1984;

Scottish Parliament Backbencher of the Year 1999; *Clubs:* Scottish Liberal; *Sportsclubs:* Honorary President: Corstorphine Amateur Athletic Club, Salvesen Boys' Club; Member: City of Edinburgh Athletic Club, Achilles Club; *Recreations:* Reading, music, theatre, ruins, sight-seeing. *Address:* Donald Gorrie Esq, OBE, DL, JP, MP, MSP, House of Commons, London, SW1A 0AA *Tel:* 020 7219 4104. *Constituency:* West Edinburgh Liberal Democrats, 11 Drum Brae Avenue, Edinburgh, EH12 8TE *Tel:* 0131–339 0339 *Fax:* 0131–476 7101 *E-mail:* gorried@parliament.uk; donald.gorrie.msp@scottish.parliament.uk.

TOMMY GRAHAM   West Renfrewshire   *Lab majority 7,979**

Born 5 December 1943; Son of late William Graham, factory assembler, and Mrs Elizabeth Whitehead; Educated Crookston Castle Secondary, Pollock; Stow College of Engineering, Glasgow, day release 1959–65; Married Joan Bagley (2 sons). Machine and tool engineer; Served apprenticeship with Mathew Wylies; Rolls-Royce 1965–78; Office Manager, Robertson and Ross, Solicitors 1982–87; AEUU; Sponsored by USDAW. Former Community Councillor, Linwood West; District Councillor, Renfrew District Council before re-organisation; Former Regional Councillor, Strathclyde. **House of Commons:** Member for Renfrew West and Inverclyde 1987–97, and for West Renfrewshire since May 1, 1997. *Labour Whip withdrawn September 1998, now sits as Independent; *Select Committees:* Member: Catering 1997–98. *Special Interests:* Social Security, Foreign Affairs, Elderly, Disabled/Disability, Unemployment, Urban Funding. Chairman, Linwood Tenants Association; *Recreations:* Walking, ornithology, family, reading, music, photography. *Address:* Tommy Graham Esq, MP, House of Commons, London, SW1A 0AA *Tel:* 020 7219 4063. *Constituency:* 17 Murray Street, Paisley, Renfrewshire, PA3 1QW *Tel:* 0141–889 1736 *Fax:* 0141–848 9902.

JAMES GRAY   North Wiltshire   *Con majority 3,475*

Born 7 November 1954; Son of late Very Revd John R. Gray and Dr Sheila Gray; Educated Glasgow High School; Glasgow University (MA history 1975); Christ Church, Oxford (history thesis 1975–77); Married July 11, 1980, Sarah Ann Beale (2 sons 1 daughter). Honourable Artillery Company (TA) 1978–84; Management trainee, P & O 1977–78; Broker, senior broker then department manager, Anderson Hughes & Co Ltd (Shipbrokers) 1978–84; Member, The Baltic Exchange 1978–92, Pro Bono Member 1997–; Managing director, GNI Freight Futures Ltd, Senior Manager, GNI Ltd (Futures Brokers) 1984–1992; Director: Baltic Futures Exchange 1989–91, Westminster Strategy 1995–96. **House of Commons:** Contested Ross, Cromarty and Skye 1992 general election. Member for North Wiltshire since May 1, 1997; Special Adviser to Michael Howard, John Gummer as Secretaries of State for Environment 1991–95; *Select Committees:* Member: Environment, Transport and Regional Affairs 1997–, Environment Sub-Committee 1997–, Transport Sub-Committee 1997–. *Special Interests:* Housing, Local Government, Countryside, Agriculture, Defence, Scotland, Environment; America, China, Mongolia. Deputy Chair, Wandsworth Tooting Conservative Association 1994–96. Governor, Hearnville Primary School, Balham 1989–92; Governor, Chestnut Grove Secondary School, Balham 1993–96; Vice-President, HAC Saddle Club; Consultant, British Horse Industry Confederation 1995–; Member: Armed Forces Parliamentary Scheme (Army) 1998, Post Graduate Scheme 2000–; Member, Honourable Artillery Company; *Publications: Financial Risk Management in the Shipping Industry,* 1985; *Futures and Options for Shipping,* 1987 (Winner of Lloyds of London Book Prize); *Shipping Futures,* 1990; Freeman, City of London 1978–; *Clubs:* Chippenham Constitutional President 2000–; Wootton Bassett Conservative; *Sportsclubs:* Member, Royal Artillery Foxhounds; *Recreations:* Riding Horses. *Address:* James Gray Esq, MP, House of Commons, London, SW1A 0AA *Tel:* 020 7219 6237 *Fax:* 020 7219 1169. *Constituency:* North Wilts Conservative Association, 8 St Mary Street, Chippenham, Wiltshire, SN15 3JJ *Tel:* 01249 652851 *Fax:* 01249 448582 *E-mail:* jamesgray.mp@parliament.uk.

DAMIAN GREEN   Ashford   Con majority 5,345

Born 17 January 1956; Son of Howard and late Audrey Green; Educated Reading School; Balliol College, Oxford (BA philosophy, politics and economics 1977, MA); President, Oxford Union 1997; Married 1988, Alicia, daughter of late Judge Jeffreys Collinson and Gwendolen Collinson-Stokes (2 daughters). Financial journalist, BBC Radio 1978–82; Business producer, Channel 4 News 1982–84; News editor, business news, *The Times* 1984–85; Business editor, Channel 4 News, 1985–87; Programme presenter and city editor, *Business Daily* 1987–92; Special Adviser, Prime Minister's Policy Unit 1992–94; Public Affairs Consultant (Self-employed) 1995–97. **House of Commons:** Contested Brent East 1992 general election. Member for Ashford since 1997; Opposition Front Bench Spokesman for: Education and Employment 1998–99, Environment, Transport and the Regions 1999–; *Select Committees:* Member: Culture, Media and Sport 1997–98, Procedure 1997–98. *Special Interests:* Economic Policy, Foreign Affairs, Media, Education, Employment, Rural Affairs; France. Vice-President, Tory Reform Group 1997–; Vice-Chair, Conservative Parliamentary Mainstream Group 1997–. Director, European Media Forum; Member, SPUC; Trustee, Community Development Foundations; *Publications: ITN Budget Fact Book,* 1984–85–86; *A Better BBC,* 1990; *The Cross-Media Revolution,* 1995; *Communities in the Countryside,* 1996; *Regulating the Media in the Digital Age,* 1997; *21st Century Conservatism,* 1998; *The Four Failures of the New Deal,* 1999; *Clubs:* Carlton; *Sportsclubs:* Fowlers FC, MCC; *Recreations:* Football, cricket, opera, cinema. *Address:* Damian Green Esq, MP, House of Commons, London, SW1A 0AA *Tel:* 020 7219 3518. *Constituency:* c/o Hardy House, The Street, Bethenden, Ashford, Kent, TN26 3AG *Tel:* 01233 820454 *Fax:* 01233 820111 *E-mail:* greend@parliament.uk.

JOHN GREENWAY   Ryedale   Con majority 5,058

Born 15 February 1946; Son of Bill and Kathleen Greenway; Educated Sir John Deane's Grammar School, Northwich; Hendon Police College; London College of Law; Married August 24, 1974, Sylvia Ann Gant (2 sons 1 daughter). Metropolitan Police Officer, stationed West End Central 1965–69; Insurance Co. representative 1970–72; Insurance broker and financial consultant 1973–; Financial journalist: *Post Magazine, Insurance Weekly.* North Yorkshire County Council: Councillor 1985–87, Education and Schools Committees, Vice-Chairman, North Yorkshire Police Committee. **House of Commons:** Member for Ryedale since June 1987; Opposition Spokesman for: Home Affairs (Police, Criminal Policy, Constitution, Data Protection, Electoral Policy, Gambling and Licensing) 1997–2000, Culture, Media and Sport 2000–; PPS to Baroness Trumpington, as Minister of State, Ministry of Agriculture, Fisheries and Food 1991–92; *Select Committees:* Member: Home Affairs 1987–97. *Special Interests:* Law and Order, Personal Finance, Agriculture, Broadcasting, Sales Promotion and Marketing. Former Governor, York Theatre Royal; Member, Standing Committees 1997–98 to Consider: Data Protection Bill, Registration of Political Parties Bill, Special Immigration Appeals Commissioners Bill; Member, Executive, 1922 Committee 1997; *Sportsclubs:* President, York City FC; *Recreations:* Opera, music, wine, travel. *Address:* John Greenway Esq, MP, House of Commons, London, SW1A 0AA *Tel:* 020 7219 6397 *Fax:* 020 7219 6059. *Constituency:* 109 Tower Street, Old Malton, North Yorkshire, YO17 0HD *Tel:* 01653 692023 *Fax:* 01653 696108 *E-mail:* greenwayj@parliament.uk.

Dod *on* Line
An Electronic Directory without rival ...

MPs' biographies and photographs
available with daily updates *via* the internet

For a *free* trial, call Oliver Cox on 020 7828 7256

DOMINIC GRIEVE Beaconsfield *Con majority 13,987*

Born 24 May 1956; Son of late W. P. Grieve, MP 1964–83, and of late Evelyn Grieve, née Mijouain; Educated Westminster School; Magdalen College, Oxford (BA modern history, 1978, MA 1989); Central London Polytechnic (Diploma in law 1980); Married October 6, 1990, Caroline Hutton (2 sons and 1 son deceased). Territorial Army 1981–83. Councillor, London Borough of Hammersmith and Fulham 1982–86. **House of Commons:** Contested Norwood 1987 general election. Member for Beaconsfield since May 1, 1997; Opposition Front Bench Spokesman for Constitutional Affairs (Scotland) 1999–; *Select Committees:* Member: Environmental Audit 1997–, Joint Committee on Statutory Instruments 1997–. *Special Interests:* Law and Order, Environment, Defence, Foreign Affairs, European Union, Constitution; France, Luxembourg. President, Oxford University Conservative Association 1997; Chair, Research Committee, Society of Conservative Lawyers 1992–95. Vice-Chair/Director, Hammersmith and Fulham MIND 1986–89; Lay visitor to police stations 1990–96; Member Council of: Franco-British Society, Luxembourg Society; Member, London Diocesan Synod of Church of England 1994–2000; Deputy Churchwarden; Member: National Trust, John Muir Trust; *Clubs:* Carlton; *Recreations:* Mountaineering, skiing, fell-walking, travel, architecture and art. *Address:* Dominic Grieve Esq, MP, House of Commons, London, SW1A 0AA *Tel:* 020 7219 3000. *Constituency:* Disraeli House, 12 Aylesbury End, Beaconsfield, Buckinghamshire, HP9 1LW *Tel:* 01494 673745 *Fax:* 01494 670428 *E-mail:* gricvcd@parliament.uk.

JANE GRIFFITHS Reading East *Lab majority 3,795*

Born 17 April 1954; Daughter of late John Griffiths, advertising agent, and of Pat Griffiths; Educated Cedars Grammar School, Leighton Buzzard; Durham University (BA Russian 1975); Married 1999, Andrew Tattersall (1 son 1 daughter from previous marriage). Linguist, GCHQ 1977–84; Asia Editor, BBC Monitoring 1984–97; Member, NUJ. Councillor, Reading Borough Council 1989–99. **House of Commons:** Member for Reading East since May 1, 1997; *Select Committees:* Member: Public Accounts 1997–99. *Special Interests:* Transport, Environment; Korea, Japan, Mongolia. Branch Chair 1990–92. Member, Transport 2000; Member, European Standing Committee B 1998–; Government Resources and Accounts Standing Committee; Licensing (Young Persons) Standing Committee; Member, Ectopic Pregnancy Trust; *Publications:* Co-author *Bushido* 1988; *Recreations:* Cycling, urban living. *Address:* Jane Griffiths, MP, House of Commons, London, SW1A 0AA *Tel:* 020 7219 4122 *Fax:* 020 7219 0719. *Constituency:* St Giles House, 10 Church Street, Reading, Berkshire, RG1 2SD *Tel:* 0118–957 3756 *Fax:* 0118–958 0949 *E-mail:* info@janegriffithsmp.org.

NIGEL GRIFFITHS Edinburgh South *Lab majority 11,452*

Born 20 May 1955; Son of late Lionel Griffiths and of Elizabeth Griffiths; Educated Hawick High School; Edinburgh University (MA 1977); Moray House College of Education (1978); Married 1979, Sally, daughter of Hugh and Sally McLaughlin. City of Edinburgh District Council: Councillor 1980–87, Chair: Housing Committee, Decentralisation Committee 1986–87; Member: Edinburgh Festival Council 1984–87, Edinburgh Health Council 1982–87; Executive Member, Edinburgh Council of Social Service 1984–87. **House of Commons:** Member for Edinburgh South since June, 1987; Opposition Spokesman on Trade and Industry Specialising in International Trade and Consumer Affairs 1989–97; Opposition Whip 1987–89; Parliamentary Under-Secretary of State, Department of Trade and Industry (Competition and Consumer Affairs) 1997–98; *Select Committees:* Member: Procedure 1999–, Public Accounts 1999–. *Special Interests:* Education, Housing, Health, Social Services, Disabled/Disability, Scotland, Arts, Economic Policy. President, EU Labour Club 1976–77. Rights Adviser, Mental Handicap Pressure Group 1979–87; Member, Wester Hailes School Council 1981; Member: War on Want, SEAD, Amnesty International, Anti-apartheid,

Friends of the Earth; Secretary, Lothian Devolution Campaign 1978; Executive Member, Scottish Constitutional Convention 1988–90; Vice-President, Institute of Trading Standards Administration 1994–; Member, National Trust; *Publications: Guide to Council Housing in Edinburgh,* 1981; *Council Housing on the Point of Collapse,* 1982; *Welfare Rights Survey,* 1981; *Welfare Rights Guide,* 1982, 1983, 1984, 1985, 1986; *Rights Guide for Mentally Handicapped People,* 1988; *Recreations:* Travel, live entertainment, badminton, hill-walking and rock-climbing, architecture, reading, politics. *Address:* Nigel Griffiths Esq, JP, MP, House of Commons, London, SW1A 0AA *Tel:* 020 7219 2424. *Constituency:* 31 Minto Street, Edinburgh, EH9 2BT *Tel:* 0131–662 4520 *E-mail:* nigelgriffithsmp@parliament.uk; www.griffithsmp.co.uk.

WIN GRIFFITHS   Bridgend   *Lab majority 15,248*

Born 11 February 1943; Son of late Evan George Griffiths and late Rachel Elizabeth Griffiths; Educated Brecon Boys' Grammar School; University College of Wales, Cardiff (BA 1965, DipEd); Married August 22, 1966, Elizabeth Ceri Gravell (1 son 1 daughter). Teacher: secondary school, Tanzania 1966–68, George Dixon Boys' Grammar School 1969–70, Barry Boys' Comprehensive School 1970–76; Head of history department, Cowbridge Comprehensive School 1976–79; Member, TGWU (ACTS). Vale of Glamorgan Borough Council: Councillor and Chair, Leisure Services Committee 1973–76; Member, St Andrew's Major Community Council 1974–79. **House of Commons:** Member for Bridgend since June 1987; Opposition Spokesman on: The Environment 1990–92, Education 1992–94, Welsh Affairs 1994–97; MEP for South Wales 1979–89; Vice-President, European Parliament 1984–87; Parliamentary Under-Secretary of State, Welsh Office 1997–98; *Special Interests:* Education, European Union, Disabled/Disability, Overseas Aid and Development, Animal Welfare; European Union, Tanzania, South Africa. Member, Court of Governors, University College, Cardiff 1981–97; Convention drawing up EU Charter of Fundamental Rights – representative of the House of Commons, December 1999–; *Recreations:* Reading, erstwhile runner, cultivating pot plants. *Address:* Win Griffiths Esq, MP, House of Commons, London, SW1A 0AA *Tel:* 020 7219 4461 *Fax:* 020 7219 6052. *Constituency:* 47 Nolton Street, Bridgend, CF31 3AA *Tel:* 01656 645432 *Fax:* 01656 767551 *E-mail:* westwoodc@parliament.uk.

BRUCE GROCOTT   Telford   *Lab majority 11,290*

Born 1 November 1940; Son of Reginald Grocott and late Helen Grocott; Educated Hemel Hempstead Grammar School; Leicester University; Manchester University (BA politics, MA economics); Married July 17, 1965, Sally Ridgway (2 sons). Administration officer, LCC 1963–64; Tutor in politics, Manchester University 1964–65; Lecturer then senior lecturer in politics, Birmingham Polytechnic 1965–72; Principal lecturer, North Staffs Polytechnic 1972–74; Presenter then producer, Central Television 1979–87; Member: NUJ, BECTU. Councillor, Bromsgrove Urban District Council 1971–74. **House of Commons:** Contested South West Hertfordshire 1970, Lichfield and Tamworth February 1974 general elections. Member for Lichfield and Tamworth October 1974–79. Contested Lichfield and Tamworth 1979, The Wrekin 1983 general elections. Member for The Wrekin 1987–97, and for Telford since May 1, 1997; Opposition Front Bench Spokesman on Foreign and Commonwealth Affairs 1992–93; PPS to John Silkin: as Minister for Planning and Local Government 1975–76, as Minister of Agriculture 1976–78; Deputy Shadow Leader of the House and Deputy Campaigns Co-ordinator 1987–92; PPS to Tony Blair: as Leader of the Labour Party 1994–, as Prime Minister 1997–; *Select Committees:* Member: Broadcasting the House of Commons 1988–93, National Heritage 1993–94. *Special Interests:* Foreign Affairs, Media, Health Service, Machinery of Government; South Africa, The Commonwealth. *Clubs:* Trench Labour; *Recreations:* Football, steam railways, fiction writing, all sport. *Address:* Bruce Grocott Esq, MP, House of Commons, London, SW1A 0AA *Tel:* 020 7219 5058 *Fax:* 020 7219 5136. *Constituency:* Suite 1, Matthew Webb House, High Street, Dawley, Telford, Shropshire, TF4 2EX *Tel:* 01952 507747 *Fax:* 01952 506064.

JOHN GROGAN Selby
Lab majority 3,836

Born 24 February 1961; Son of John Martin Grogan and late Maureen Grogan; Educated St Michael's College, Leeds; St John's College, Oxford (BA modern history and economics 1982). Self-employed conference organiser 1996–97; communications co-ordinator, Leeds City Council 1987–94; Labour Party press officer, European Parliament, Brussels 1995; Member, GMB; Contested York European Parliament election 1989. **House of Commons:** Contested Selby 1987, 1992 general elections. Member for Selby since May 1, 1997; *Select Committees:* Member: Northern Ireland Affairs 1997–. *Special Interests:* Local Government, European Union, Economic Policy, Broadcasting, Sport, Liquor Licensing Reform; Ukraine, Mongolia, Australia, New Zealand. Member: Fabian Society, Institute of Public Policy Research. *Recreations:* Football, running, cinema. *Address:* John Grogan Esq, MP, House of Commons, London, SW1A 0AA *Tel:* 020 7219 4403. *Constituency:* 58 Gowthorpe, Selby, North Yorkshire, YO8 4ET *Tel:* 01757 291152 *Fax:* 01757 291153 *E-mail:* sexton@johngroganmp.y-net.com.

JOHN GUMMER Suffolk Coastal
Con majority 3,254

Born 26 November 1939; Son of late Canon Selwyn Gummer; Educated King's School, Rochester; Selwyn College, Cambridge (BA history 1961, MA 1971) (President of the Union 1962); Married 1977, Penelope Jane Gardner (2 sons 2 daughters). Former chair, Siemssen Hunter Ltd; Since leaving office – Chair, Sancroft International Ltd (environment consultants); Chair, Valpak Ltd; Director, Vivendi UK Ltd; Chair, International Commission on Sustainable Consumption; Chair, Marine Stewardship Council. Councillor, ILEA 1967–70. **House of Commons:** Contested Greenwich 1964 and 1966 general elections. Member for Lewisham West 1970–74, for Eye 1979–83, and for Suffolk Coastal since June 1983; Assistant Government Whip January 1981; Government Whip 1981–83; PPS: to Minister of Agriculture, Fisheries and Food 1971–72, to Secretary of State for Social Services 1979–81; Parliamentary Under-Secretary of State, Department of Employment 1983; Minister of State, Department of Employment 1983–84; Paymaster General 1984–85; Minister of State, Ministry of Agriculture, Fisheries and Food 1985–88; Minister for Local Government 1988–89; Minister of Agriculture, Fisheries and Food 1989–93; Secretary of State for the Environment 1993–97; *Special Interests:* Europe, Environment. Chair, Cambridge University Conservative Association 1961; Conservative Party: Vice-Chair 1972–74, Chair 1983–85; Chair, Conservative Group for Europe 1997–. Member, General Synod of Church of England for St Edmundsbury and Ipswich Diocese 1978–92; *Publications: When the Coloured People Come; The Permissive Society;* Co-author *The Christian Calendar; Faith in Politics* 1987; PC 1985. *Address:* Rt Hon John Gummer, MP, House of Commons, London, SW1A 0AA *Tel:* 020 7219 4591 *Fax:* 020 7219 5906. *Constituency:* Suffolk Coastal Conservative Association, National Hall, Sun Lane, Woodbridge, Suffolk, IP12 1EG *Tel:* 01394 380001 *Fax:* 01394 382570 *E-mail:* gummerj@parliament.uk.

JOHN GUNNELL Morley and Rothwell
Lab majority 14,750

Born 1 October 1933; Son of late William and Norah Gunnell; Educated King Edward's School, Birmingham; Leeds University (BSc 1955); Married October 8, 1955, Jean Louise Lacey (3 sons 1 daughter). Hospital porter, St Bartholomew's Hospital, London 1955–57; Leeds Modern School: science teacher 1959–62, head of science, United Nations International School, New York 1962–70; lecturer, Centre for Studies in Science Education, Leeds University 1970–88; Yorkshire Enterprise Ltd: Chairman 1982–90, 1995–6, Vice-Chairman 1990–95; Member, GMB 1955–. West Yorkshire Metropolitan County Council: Councillor 1977–86, Leader of the Council 1981–86; Yorkshire and Humberside Development Association: Chairman 1981–93, Hon. President 1993–; North of England Regional Consortium: Chair 1982–92, Hon. President 1992–;

Leeds City Council: Councillor 1986–92, Chair, Social Services Committee 1990–92; Member: Leeds Healthcare 1990–92, Leeds Development Corporation 1988–92. **House of Commons:** Contested Leeds North East February and October 1974 general elections. Member for Leeds South and Morley 1992–97, and for Morley and Rothwell since May 1, 1997; *Select Committees:* Member: Broadcasting 1992–97, Public Service 1995–97; Member: Health 1997–. *Special Interests:* Industry, Venture Capital, Investment, Regional Development, Health, Social Services; Middle East, Belize. Non-Executive Director, Opera North 1982–; Member, Audit Commission 1983–90; Director, Leeds Theatre Trust (West Yorkshire Playhouse) 1986–93; Member: South Leeds Groundwork Trust, National Coal Mining Museum for England; *Sportsclubs:* Warwickshire CC, Yorkshire CC; *Recreations:* Watching cricket and soccer, music, opera, photography. *Address:* John Gunnell Esq, MP, House of Commons, London, SW1A 0AA *Tel:* 020 7219 4549 *Fax:* 020 7219 2552. *Constituency:* Morley Town Hall, Leeds, LS27 9DY *Tel:* 0113 247 7138 *Fax:* 0113–247 7190 *E-mail:* gunnelljz@parliament.uk.

H

WILLIAM HAGUE   Richmond (Yorkshire)   *Con majority 10,051*

Born 26 March 1961; Son of Nigel and Stella Hague; Educated Wath-on-Dearne Comprehensive School; Magdalen College, Oxford (President, Oxford Union 1981); INSEAD Business School, France; Married December 19, 1997, Ffion, daughter of Emyr and Myra Jenkins. Shell UK 1982–83; McKinsey and Company 1983–88; Political adviser to Sir Geoffrey Howe as Chancellor of the Exchequer and Leon Brittan as Chief Secretary to the Treasury 1983. **House of Commons:** Contested Wentworth 1987 general election. Member for Richmond, Yorks. since February 23, 1989 by-election; PPS to Norman Lamont as Chancellor of the Exchequer 1990–93; Department of Social Security: Joint Parliamentary Under-Secretary of State, 1993–94, Minister of State, (Minister for Social Security and Disabled People) 1994–95; Secretary of State for Wales 1995–97; Leader of the Opposition 1997–; *Special Interests:* Agriculture, Economic Policy. President, Oxford University Conservative Association 1981; Leader, Conservative Party June 1997–. PC 1995; *The Spectator*/Highland Park Parliamentarian of the Year 1998; *Clubs:* Beefsteak, Carlton, Buck's; *Recreations:* Walking, swimming. *Address:* Rt Hon William Hague, MP, House of Commons, London, SW1A 0AA *Tel:* 020 7219 4553. *Constituency:* c/o 67 High Street, Northallerton, North Yorkshire, DL7 8EG *Tel:* 01609 779093 *Fax:* 01609 778172 *E-mail:* whague@conservative-party.org.uk.

PETER HAIN   Neath   *Lab majority 26,741*

Born 16 February 1950; Son of Walter and Adelaine Hain; Educated Pretoria Boys High School, South Africa; Emanuel School, Wandsworth, London; Queen Mary College, London University (BSc economics); Sussex University (MPhil); Married February 8, 1975, Patricia Western (separated) (2 sons). Head of research, Union of Communication Workers 1976–91; Member, GMB. Health Authority Member 1981–87. **House of Commons:** Contested Putney 1983 and 1987 general elections. Member for Neath since by-election April 4, 1991; Opposition Spokesman on Employment 1996–97; Opposition Whip 1995–96; Parliamentary Under-Secretary of State, Welsh Office 1997–99; Minister of State, Foreign and Commonwealth Office 1999–; *Special Interests:* Post Office, Telecommunications, Reform of Government, Economic Policy; Southern Africa. Leader, Young Liberals 1971–73; Member: Co-op, Fabians. Leader, Stop the Seventy Tour 1969–70; Anti-Nazi League 1977–79; Member: CND, Anti-Apartheid Movement; School Governor 1981–90; Tribune Newspaper Board of Directors; *Publications:* 13 books including *Ayes to the Left: A future for socialism*, 1995; *Clubs:* Royal British Legion, Resolven; *Sportsclubs:* Resolven Rugby, Ynysygerwn Cricket; *Recreations:* Rugby, soccer, cricket, motor racing, rock and folk music. *Address:* Peter Hain Esq, MP, House of Commons, London, SW1A 0AA *Tel:* 020 7219 3925 *Fax:* 020 7219 3816. *Constituency:* 14 The Parade, Neath, SA11 1RA *Tel:* 01639 630152 *Fax:* 01639 641196 *E-mail:* hains@parliament.uk.

MIKE HALL   Weaver Vale   Lab majority 13,448

Born 20 September 1952; Son of late Thomas Hall, maintenance engineer, and of late Veronica Hall, mail order clerk; Educated St Mary's Primary School, Ashton-under-Lyne; St Damian's Secondary Modern School; Padgate College of Higher Education (Teacher's Certificate 1977); North Cheshire College (BEd 1987); University College of Wales, Bangor (Diploma in Education 1989); Married August 2, 1975, Lesley Gosling (1 son). Scientific assistant, chemical industry 1969–73; Teacher of history and physical education, Bolton LEA 1977–85; Support teacher, Halton Community Assessment Team 1985–92. Warrington Borough Council: Councillor 1979–93; Chair: Environmental Health Committee 1981–84, Finance Sub-Committee 1984–85, Policy and Resources Committee 1985–92; Council Leader 1985–92. **House of Commons:** Member for Warrington South 1992–97, and for Weaver Vale since May 1, 1997; Assistant Government Whip (Home Affairs, North West) 1998–; PPS to Ann Taylor as Leader of the House and President of the Council 1997–98; *Select Committees:* Member: Public Accounts Committee 1992–97, Modernisation of the House of Commons 1997–98; Member: Administration 1999–. *Special Interests:* Poverty, Education, Local Government, Home Affairs. *Sportsclubs:* Lymm Lawn Tennis and Croquet; *Recreations:* Tennis, walking, cooking, reading. *Address:* Michael Hall Esq, MP, House of Commons, London, SW1A 0AA *Tel:* 020 7219 3000. *Constituency:* Room 17, Castle Park, Frodsham, Cheshire, WA6 6UJ *Tel:* 01928 735000 *Fax:* 01928 735250 *E-mail:* michael.hall@geo2.poptel.org.uk; michael.hall@hm-treasury.gov.uk.

PATRICK HALL   Bedford   Lab majority 8,300

Born 20 October 1951; Educated Bedford Modern School; Birmingham University; Oxford Polytechnic. Local government planning officer; Bedford Town Centre co-ordinator; Member, NALGO. Councillor, Bedfordshire County Council 1989–97; Member, North Bedfordshire Community Health Council. **House of Commons:** Contested North Bedfordshire 1992 general election. Member for Bedford since May 1, 1997; *Select Committees:* Member: Joint Committee on Consolidation of Bills Etc 1997–, European Scrutiny 1999–. Hon. Secretary, Eastern Regional Group of Labour MPs 1999–. Chair, Bedford Door to Door Dial-a-Ride 1989–; Governor, Beauchamp Middle School; Member, Chartered Institute of Public Finance and Accountancy; *Recreations:* Squash, gardens. *Address:* Patrick Hall Esq, MP, House of Commons, London, SW1A 0AA *Tel:* 020 7219 3605. *Constituency:* 5 Mill Street, Bedford *Tel:* 01234 262699 *Fax:* 01234 272921.

SIR ARCHIE HAMILTON   Epsom and Ewell   Con majority 11,525

Born 30 December 1941; Son of late 3rd Baron Hamilton of Dalzell, GCVO, MC; Educated Eton; Married December 14, 1968, Anne Napier (3 daughters). Coldstream Guards 1960–62, Lieutenant. Councillor, Royal Borough of Kensington and Chelsea 1968–71. **House of Commons:** Contested Dagenham February and October 1974 general elections. Member for Epsom and Ewell since by-election April 27, 1978; Assistant Government Whip 1982–84; Government Whip 1984–86; PPS to David Howell: as Secretary of State for Energy 1979–81, as Secretary of State for Transport 1981–82; Parliamentary Under-Secretary of State for Defence Procurement 1986–87; PPS to Margaret Thatcher, as Prime Minister 1987–88; Minister of State for the Armed Forces, Ministry of Defence 1988–93; *Select Committees:* Member: Members' Interests 1995, Standards and Privileges 1995–97, Standards in Public Life 1995. *Special Interests:* Finance, Tax, Economic Policy, Trade and Industry, Defence. Governor, Westminster Foundation for Democracy 1993–97; Member, Committee on Intelligence and Security 1994–97; Executive Member, 1922 Committee 1995–97, Chair 1997–; Member, Conservative Ethics and Integrity Committee 1999–; PC 1991; Knighted 1994. *Address:* Rt Hon Sir Archibald Hamilton, MP, House of Commons, London, SW1A 0AA *Tel:* 020 7219 5109 *Fax:* 020 7219 2429. *Constituency:* 212 Barnet Wood Lane, Ashford, Surrey, KT21 2DB *Tel:* 01372 277066.

FABIAN HAMILTON   Leeds North East   *Lab majority 6,959*

Born 12 April 1955; Son of late Mario Uziell-Hamilton, solicitor, and Adrianne Uziell-Hamilton (Her Honour Judge Uziell-Hamilton); Educated Brentwood School, Brentwood, Essex; York University (BA); Married April 17, 1980, Rosemary Ratcliffe (1 son 2 daughters). Taxi driver 1978–79; graphic designer 1979–94; consultant and dealer, Apple Macintosh computer systems 1994–97; Member: SLADE 1978–82, NGA 1982–91, GPMU 1991–. Councillor, Leeds City Council 1987–98, Chair: Race Equality Committee 1988–94, Economic Development Committee 1994–96, Education Committee 1996–97. **House of Commons:** Contested Leeds North East 1992 general election; *Select Committees:* Member. Administration 1997–. *Special Interests:* Education, Economic Development and Small Business, Anti-Racism, International Development, Alternative Fuels; Middle East, Europe, Southern Africa, Caribbean and Indian sub-continent, Cyprus; Member, European Standing Committee B 1998–. Member: Co-op Party, Labour Friends of Israel. School Governor; Member: Anti-Apartheid Movement, Poale Zion; Member, National Heart Research Fund; *Recreations:* Film, theatre, opera, music. *Address:* Fabian Hamilton Esq, MP, House of Commons, London, SW1A 0AA *Tel:* 020 7219 3493 *Fax:* 020 7219 4945. *Constituency:* 6 Queenshill Approach, Leeds, LS17 6AY *Tel:* 0113–237 0022 *Fax:* 0113–237 0404 *E-mail:* fabian.mp@hamilton.go-serif.net.

PHILIP HAMMOND   Runnymede and Weybridge   *Con majority 9,875*

Born 4 December 1955; Son of Bernard Lawrence Hammond, AMICE, retired civil engineer and local government officer; Educated Shenfield School, Brentwood, Essex; University College, Oxford (MA politics, philosophy and economics); Married June 29, 1991, Susan Carolyn Williams-Walker (2 daughters 1 son). Assistant to Chair then marketing manager, Speywood Laboratories Ltd 1977–81; Director, Speywood Medical Ltd 1981–83; Established and ran medical equipment distribution agency 1983–94; Director, Castlemead Ltd 1984–; Director, various medical equipment manufacturing companies 1983–96; Partner, CMA Consultants 1993–95; Director, Castlemead Homes Ltd 1994–; Consultant to Government of Malawi 1995–97. **House of Commons:** Contested Newham North East by-election 1994. Member for Runnymede and Weybridge since May 1, 1997; Opposition Spokesman for Health and Social Services 1998–; *Select Committees:* Member: Environment, Transport and Regional Affairs 1998, Transport 1998; Member: Unopposed Bills (Panel) 1997–. *Special Interests:* Economic Policy, International Trade, European Union, Defence, Social Security, Transport, Housing and Planning, Energy, Health; Latin America, Germany, Italy, Southern and Eastern Africa; Member, European Standing Committee B 1997–1998. East Lewisham Conservative Association: Executive Council Member 1982–89, Chair 1989–96; Member, Greater London Area Executive Council 1989–96; Vice-Chair, Greenwich and Lewisham Conservative Action Group 1993–94. *Clubs:* Carlton; *Recreations:* Travel, cinema, walking. *Address:* Philip Hammond Esq, MP, House of Commons, London, SW1A 0AA *Tel:* 020 7219 4055 *Fax:* 020 7219 5851. *Constituency:* 74A Church Street, Weybridge, Surrey, KT13 8DL *Tel:* 01932 s851239 *Fax:* 01932 854305 *E-mail:* hammondp@parliament.uk.

MIKE HANCOCK   Portsmouth South   *LD majority 4,327*

Born 9 April 1946; Son of Thomas William Hancock and Margaret Eva Hancock (née Cole); Married 1967, Jacqueline Elliott (1 son 1 daughter). Director, BBC Daytime Club; District Officer for Hampshire, Isle of Wight and Channel Islands Mencap 1989–; Former Shop Steward and Convenor; Member, Engineering Union. Councillor, Portsmouth City Council 1971, Fratton Ward 1973–, Leader, Liberal Democrat Group 1989–97, Chair, Planning and Economic Development Committee; Councillor, Hampshire County Council 1973–97, Leader of the Opposition 1977–81, 1989–93, Leader 1993–97; Contested (Liberal Democrat) Wight and Hampshire South European Parliamentary election 1994. **House of Commons:** Contested Portsmouth South (SDP) 1983, (SDP/Alliance) 1987 general elections. Member (SDP) for Portsmouth South 1984–87. Member for Portsmouth South since May 1, 1997; Spokesman for: Foreign Affairs, Defence and Europe (Defence) 1997–99; Environment, Transport, the Regions and Social Justice (Planning) 2000–;

Select Committees: Member: Public Administration 1997–99; Member: Defence 1999–. *Special Interests:* European Democracy, Defence, Sport. Member: Labour Party 1968–81, Social Democrat Party 1981–87, Liberal Democrat Party 1987–. Chairman, Southern Branch, NSPCC 1989–; Vice-Chairman, Portsmouth Docks 1992–; Council of Europe, Western European Union, NATO; Trustee, Royal Marine Museum; CBE 1992. *Address:* Mike Hancock Esq, CBE, MP, House of Commons, London, SW1A 0AA *Tel:* 020 7219 5180 *Fax:* 020 7219 2496. *Constituency:* 1A Albert Road, Southsea, Hampshire, PO5 2SE *Tel:* 023 9286 1055 *Fax:* 023 9283 0530 *E-mail:* portsmouthldp@cix.co.uk.

DAVID HANSON Delyn   Lab majority 12,693

Born 5 July 1957; Son of Brian Hanson, retired fork lift driver and Glenda Hanson, retired wages clerk; Educated Verdin Comprehensive School, Winsford, Cheshire; Hull University (BA 1978, Certificate of Education 1980); Married September 6, 1986, Margaret, daughter of late Ronald Mitchell and of May Mitchell (1 son 2 daughters). Vice-President, Hull University Students' Union 1978–79; Trainee, Co-operative Union 1980–81; Manager, Plymouth Co-operative 1981–82; Various posts with The Spastics Society 1982–89; Director, Re-Solv (The Society for the Prevention of Solvent Abuse) 1989–92. Councillor: Vale Royal Borough Council 1983–91, Northwich Town Council 1987–91; Vale Royal Borough Council: Chair, Economic Development Committee 1988–89, Labour Leader 1989–91; Contested Cheshire West 1984 European Parliament election. **House of Commons:** Contested Eddisbury 1983 and Delyn 1987 general elections. Member for Delyn since April 9, 1992; Assistant Government Whip 1998–99; PPS to Alastair Darling as Chief Secretary to the Treasury 1997–98; Parliamentary Under-Secretary of State, Wales Office 1999–; *Select Committees:* Member: Welsh Affairs 1992–95, Public Service 1995–97. *Special Interests:* Foreign Affairs, Health, Heritage, Local Government, Solvent Abuse, Treasury; South Africa, Cyprus. Member, Leadership Campaign Team 1994–97. *Recreations:* Football, cinema, family. *Address:* David Hanson Esq, MP, House of Commons, London, SW1A 0AA *Tel:* 020 7219 5064 *Fax:* 020 7219 2671. *Constituency:* 64 Chester Street, Flint, Flintshire, CH6 5DH *Tel:* 01352 763159 *Fax:* 01352 730140 *E-mail:* hansond@parliament.uk.

HARRIET HARMAN Camberwell and Peckham   Lab majority 16,351

Born 30 July 1950; Daughter of late John Bishop Harman, and of Anna Harman; Educated St Paul's Girls' School; York University (BA politics 1998); Married 1982, Jack Dromey (2 sons 1 daughter). Legal officer, National Council for Civil Liberties 1978–82. **House of Commons:** Member for Peckham 1982–1997, and for Camberwell and Peckham since May 1, 1997; Spokesperson on Health 1987–92; Shadow Minister, Social Services 1984, 1985–87; Shadow Chief Secretary to the Treasury 1992–94; Shadow Secretary of State for: Employment 1994–95, Health 1995–96; Social Security 1996–97; Secretary of State for Social Security and Minister for Women 1997–98; *Special Interests:* Women, Social Services, Provision for under 5's. Member, Labour Party National Executive Committee 1993–. Chair, Childcare Commission 1999–; PC 1997. *Address:* Rt Hon Harriet Harman, MP, House of Commons, London, SW1A 0AA *Tel:* 020 7219 4218 *Fax:* 020 7219 4877 *E-mail:* harmanh@parliament.uk.

Dod *on* Line
An Electronic Directory without rival ...
MPs' biographies and photographs available with daily updates *via* the internet

For a *free* trial, call Oliver Cox on 020 7828 7256

EVAN HARRIS   Oxford West and Abingdon   *LD majority 6,285*

Born 21 October 1965; Son of Prof Frank Harris, CBE, Dean of Medicine, Leicester University, and Brenda Harris, formerly scientific officer; Educated Liverpool Blue Coat Secondary School; Wadham College, Oxford (BA physiology, Diploma in medical sociology 1988); Oxford University Medical School (BM, BCh 1991); Divorced. NHS Hospital Doctor 1991–94; Public Health Registrar (Hon) 1994–97; Place of Work Representative, BMA 1992–94; BMA National Council 1994–97; Junior Doctors Committee Executive 1995–97. **House of Commons:** Member for Oxford West and Abingdon since May 1, 1997; Spokesman for: Health (NHS Staff, Organisation and Planning) 1997–99, Higher Education, Science and Women's Issues 1999–; *Select Committees:* Member: Education and Employment 1999–, Education Sub-Committee 1999–. *Special Interests:* Health, Civil Liberties, Voting Systems, Asylum Issues, Science, Medical Ethics; Israel, South Africa, USA; Member, European Standing Committee C 1999–. Member: SDP 1985, Oxford West and Abingdon SDP and Lib Dem Executive Committee 1986–97, Green Liberal Democrats 1995–; Hon. President, Lib Dems for Gay and Lesbian Rights 2000–. Member: Oxford Asylum Welcome, OXAIDS, Liberty, Amnesty International, English Bridge Union, British Chess Federation; Member: Central Oxford Research Ethics Committee 1995–98, Oxford Diocesan Board of Social Responsibility 1998–, BMA Ethics Committee 1999–; *Publications:* Various contributions and articles to medical journals; ESU Scholarship to Harvard High School 1984; Open Scholarship to Wadham College 1985; *Clubs:* National Liberal; *Recreations:* TV, Squash, Bridge. *Address:* Dr Evan Harris, MP, House of Commons, London, SW1A 0AA *Tel:* 020 7219 3614 *Fax:* 020 7219 2346. *Constituency:* The Old Jam Factory, 27 Park End Street, Oxford, OX1 1HU *Tel:* 01865 245584 *Fax:* 01865 245589 *E-mail:* harrise@parliament.uk.

NICK HARVEY   North Devon   *LD majority 6,181*

Born 3 August 1961; Son of Frederick Harvey, civil servant, and Christine Harvey, teacher; Educated Queen's College, Taunton; Middlesex Polytechnic (BA business studies 1983). President, Middlesex Polytechnic Students' Union 1981–82; Communications and marketing executive: Profile PR Ltd 1984–86, Dewe Rogerson Ltd 1986–91; Communications Consultant 1989–92. **House of Commons:** Contested Enfield Southgate (Liberal/Alliance) 1987 general election. Member for North Devon since April 9, 1992; Liberal Democrat Spokesman for: Transport 1992–94, Trade and Industry 1994–97, Constitution (English Regions) 1997–99; Principal Spokesman for Health 1999–; *Select Committees:* Member: Trade and Industry 1994–95. *Special Interests:* Economics, European Union, Health. National Vice-Chair, Union of Liberal Students 1981–82; Chair of Candidates Committee 1993–98; Liberal Democrat Chair of Campaigns and Communications 1994–99. Vice-President, Federation of Economic Development Authorities (FEDA) 2000–; *Recreations:* Travel, football, walking, music. *Address:* Nick Harvey Esq, MP, House of Commons, London, SW1A 0AA *Tel:* 020 7219 6232. *Constituency:* 9 Cross Street, Barnstaple, North Devon, EX31 1BA *Tel:* 01271 328631 *Fax:* 01271 345664 *E-mail:* harveyn@parliament.uk.

SIR ALAN HASELHURST   Saffron Walden   *Con majority 10,573*

Born 23 June 1937; Son of late John Haselhurst; Educated King Edward VI School, Birmingham; Cheltenham College; Oriel College, Oxford; Married April 16, 1977, Angela Margaret Bailey (2 sons 1 daughter). Secretary, Treasurer, Librarian, Oxford Union Society 1959–60. **House of Commons:** Member for Middleton and Prestwich 1970-February 1974, and for Saffron Walden from July 7, 1977 by-election; PPS to Mark Carlisle as Secretary of State, Education and Science 1979–81; Chair, Ways and Means and Deputy Speaker 1997–; *Select Committees:* Member: European Legislation 1982–97, Catering 1991–97, Transport 1992–97; Chairman of Ways and Means: Chairmen's Panel 1997–, Court of Referees 1997–, Unopposed Bills (Panel) 1997–, Standing Orders 1998–. *Special Interests:* Education, Aerospace, Aviation, Youth Affairs, European Union, Agriculture, Community Development. President, Oxford University Conservative

Association 1958; National Chair, Young Conservative Movement 1966–68; Deputy Chair, Conservative Group for Europe 1982–85. Chair, Commonwealth Youth Exchange Council 1978–81; Chair of Trustees, Community Projects Foundation 1986–97; Fellow, Industry and Parliament Trust 1979; *Publications: Occasionally Cricket*; Knighted 1995; PC 1999; *Clubs:* MCC; *Sportsclubs:* Essex County Cricket Club, Executive Committee Member 1996–; *Recreations:* Hi-fi, watching cricket, gardening. *Address:* Rt Hon Sir Alan Haselhurst, MP, House of Commons, London, SW1A 0AA *Tel:* 020 7219 5214 *Fax:* 020 7219 5600. *Constituency:* The Old Armoury, Saffron Walden, Essex, CB10 1JN *Tel:* 01799 506349 *Fax:* 01799 522349 *E-mail:* haselhursta@parliament.uk.

NICK HAWKINS Surrey Heath — *Con majority 16,287*

Born 27 March 1957; Son of Dr Arthur Ernest and Patricia Jean Hawkins, née Papworth; Educated Bedford Modern School; Lincoln College, Oxford (MA Jurisprudence 1978); Middle Temple, Inns of Court School of Law 1979; Married July 21, 1979, Angela Margaret Turner (separated 1999) (2 sons 1 daughter). Barrister, Birmingham and Northampton 1979–86; Consultant 1986–87; Company legal adviser, Access (The Joint Credit Card Co. Ltd) 1987–89; Group legal adviser, Lloyds Abbey Life plc 1989–92; Member, NATSOPA 1976–77. **House of Commons:** Contested Huddersfield 1987 general election. Member for Blackpool South 1992–97, and for Surrey Heath since May 1, 1997; Opposition Front Bench Spokesman for: Lord Chancellor's Department 1999–, Home Affairs 2000–; Government Whip, Armed Forces Bill Committee 1996; PPS: to James Arbuthnot and Nicholas Soames, Ministers of State, Ministry of Defence 1995–96, to Virginia Bottomley as Secretary of State for National Heritage 1996–97; Political aide, to Gillian Shepherd as Shadow Leader of the House and as Shadow Secretary of State, Department of the Environment, Transport and the Regions 1997–99; *Select Committees:* Member: Transport 1992–95, Home Affairs 1998–99. *Special Interests:* Defence, Home Affairs, Law and Order, Trade and Industry, Finance, Insurance, Financial Services, Environment, Transport, Education, Tourism, Sport, Small Businesses; Numerous. Vice-Chair, Rochford Constituency Conservative Association, Essex 1988–91; Bow Group 1990–92, Research Secretary 1990–91, Campaign Director 1991–92, Chair 1992–93. Area Chair, Business Support Group, Marie Curie Cancer Care; Sponsor, Parliamentary Events, Association of Medical Research Charities; Founder Patron, Knight foundation for Cystic Fibrosis; NSPCC; Hon. Major, Armed Forces Parliamentary Scheme 1997–98; Government Whip on Armed Forces Bill Select Committee 1996; Chair, International Committee, Bar Association for Commerce, Finance and Industry 1989–92; Member, International Practice Committee, Bar Council 1989–91; Co-Sponsor, Event for Coopers' Company 1999; *Publications:* Co-author *1992 – The Single Market in Insurance*, 1990; Author *Competitive Sport in Schools*, 1994; *Televising Sport – Responding to Debate*, 1996; *Bringing Order to the Law*, 1997 Various articles on transport history and employment/legal matters; Eastern Area CPC Public Speaking Competition Winner 1990; *Sportsclubs:* Surrey CCC, Lords Taverners; *Recreations:* Cricket, theatre, music, other sports including swimming, rugby union, soccer. *Address:* Nick Hawkins Esq, MP, House of Commons, London, SW1A 0AA *Tel:* 020 7219 6329 *Fax:* 020 7219 2693. *Constituency:* Curzon House, Church Road, Windlesham, Surrey, GU20 6BH *Tel:* 01276 472468 *Fax:* 01276 476110.

JOHN HAYES South Holland and The Deepings — *Con majority 7,991*

Born 23 June 1958; Son of Henry John Hayes and late Lily Hayes; Educated Colfe's Grammar School, London; Nottingham University (BA politics, PGCE history/English); Married July 1997, Susan Hopwell. IT company 1983–, executive director until 1997, non-executive director 1997–. Councillor, Nottinghamshire County Council 1985–98, Conservative Spokesman on Education 1997–98, Former Chair, County Conservative Group's Campaigns Committee. **House of Commons:** Contested Derby North East 1987, 1992 general elections. Member for South Holland and The Deepings since May 1, 1997; Opposition Frontbench Spokesman for Education and Employment 2000–; *Select Committees:* Member: Agriculture 1997–99, Education and Employment 1998–99, Education and Employment 1999–2000, Education Sub-Committee 1999–2000.

Special Interests: Education, Parties and Elections and Campaigning, Political Ideas and Philosophy, Local Government, Agriculture, Commerce, Industry, Welfare of Elderly and Disabled; England, Italy, USA, Spain. Former Chair: YC Branches, Nottingham University Conservative Association; Vice-Chair, Conservative Party 1999–2000. Member: British Field Sports Society, SPUC; Member, National Trust; *Publications:* Numerous articles and pamphlets; *Clubs:* Carlton, Spalding; *Recreations:* The arts, many sports, gardening, good food and wine. *Address:* John Hayes Esq, MP, House of Commons, London, SW1A 0AA *Tel:* 020 7219 3453. *Constituency:* The Manor House, 11 Broad Street, Spalding, Lincolnshire, PE11 1TB *Tel:* 01775 713905 *Fax:* 01775 713905.

SYLVIA HEAL   Halesowen and Rowley Regis   *Lab majority 10,337*

Born 20 July 1942; Daughter of late John Lloyd Fox, steelworker, and Ruby Fox; Educated Elfed Secondary Modern School, Buckley, North Wales; Coleg Harlech, University College of Wales, Swansea (BSc Econ 1968); Married July 31, 1965, Keith Heal (1 son 1 daughter). Medical records clerk 1957–63; Social worker: Department of Employment 1968–70, Rehabilitation Centre 1980–90; National officer, Carers National Association 1992–97; Member, GMB. JP. **House of Commons:** Member for Mid Staffordshire 1990 by-election–1992. Member for Halesowen and Rowley Regis since May 1, 1997; Shadow Minister of Health 1991–92; Deputy Shadow Minister for Women 1991–92; PPS to Secretaries of State for Defence: Lord Robertson of Port Ellen 1997–99, Geoffrey Hoon 1999–2000; First Deputy Chair of Ways and Means and Deputy Speaker 2000–; *Select Committees:* Education and Science 1990–91. *Special Interests:* Health Education, Equal Opportunities (Disability/Women). Council Member, ASA 1992–97; Member: Action for South Africa (ACTSA), One World Action; *Clubs:* London-Welsh Association, Rowley and Blackheath Labour Club; *Recreations:* Walking, gardening, listening to male voice choirs. *Address:* Mrs Sylvia Heal, MP, House of Commons, London, SW1A 0AA *Tel:* 020 7219 2317 *Fax:* 020 7219 0956. *Constituency:* Municipal Buildings, Barrs Road, Cradley Heath, West Midlands, B64 7JX *Tel:* 0121–569 4646 *Fax:* 0121–569 4647.

OLIVER HEALD   North East Hertfordshire   *Con majority 3,088*

Born 15 December 1954; Son of J. A. Heald; Educated Reading School; Pembroke College, Cambridge (MA); Married August 15, 1979, Christine Whittle (1 son 2 daughters). Barrister, Middle Temple 1977–. **House of Commons:** Contested Southwark and Bermondsey 1987 general election. Member for North Hertfordshire 1992–97, and for North East Hertfordshire since May 1, 1997; Opposition Frontbench Spokesman for Home Affairs 2000–; Opposition Whip 1997–2000; PPS: to Sir Peter Lloyd as Minister of State, Home Office 1994, to William Waldegrave as Minister of Agriculture, Fisheries and Food 1994–95; Parliamentary Under-Secretary of State, Department of Social Security 1995–97; Sponsored Private Member's Bill: Insurance Companies (Reserves) Act 1995; *Select Committees:* Member: Employment 1992–94, Administration 1998–2000. *Special Interests:* Industrial Relations, Environment, Law and Order, Pensions. Chair, North Hertfordshire Conservative Association 1984–86; Vice-President, Southwark and Bermondsey Conservative Association 1988–93, President 1993–98, Patron 1998–. *Recreations:* Sport, family. *Address:* Oliver Heald Esq, MP, House of Commons, London, SW1A 0AA *Tel:* 020 7219 4505 *Tel (Constituency):* 01763 247640 *E-mail:* healdo@parliament.uk.

Visit the Vacher Dod Website ...

www.politicallinks.co.uk

JOHN HEALEY Wentworth — *Lab majority 23,959*

Born 13 February 1960; Son of Aidan Healey, prison service, and Jean Healey, teacher; Educated Lady Lumley's Comprehensive School, Pickering; St Peter's School, York; Christ's College, Cambridge (BA 1982); Married October 25, 1993, Jackie, daughter of Leon and Jean Bate (1 son). Journalist/deputy editor, *The House Magazine* 1983–84; Disability campaigner for three national charities 1984–90; Tutor, Open University Business School 1989–92; Campaigns manager, Issue Communications 1990–92; Head of communications, MSF Union 1992–94; Campaigns and communications director, TUC 1994–97; Member: NUJ, GMB. **House of Commons:** Contested Ryedale 1992 general election. Member for Wentworth since May 1, 1997; PPS to Gordon Brown as Chancellor of the Exchequer 1999–; *Select Committees:* Member: Education and Employment 1997–99, Employment Sub-Committee 1997–99. *Special Interests:* Employment, Trade Unions, Economic Regeneration, Industrial Relations, Disabled/Disability, Local Government Finance. Member: Child Poverty Action Group, Amnesty International Liberty World Development Movement; *Recreations:* Family. *Address:* John Healey Esq, MP, House of Commons, London, SW1A 0AA *Tel:* 020 7219 5170/2448 *Fax:* 020 7219 2451. *Constituency:* 79 High Street, Wath-upon-Deane, Rotherham, South Yorkshire, S63 7QB *Tel:* 01709 875665 *Fax:* 01709 874207 *E-mail:* healeyj@parliament.uk.

DAVID HEATH Somerton and Frome — *LD majority 130*

Born 16 March 1954; Son of Eric and Pamela Heath; Educated Millfield School, Street; St John's College, Oxford (MA physiological sciences); City University (ophthalmic optics); Married May 1987, Caroline Netherton (1 son 1 daughter). Qualified optician in practice 1979–85; Parliamentary consultant, Worldwide Fund for Nature 1990–91; Consultant to various NGOs/Charities; Member, Audit Commission 1995–97. Councillor, Somerset County Council 1985–97, Leader of Council 1985–89; Chairman, Avon and Somerset Police Authority 1993–96. **House of Commons:** Contested Somerton and Frome 1992 general election. Member for Somerton and Frome since May 1, 1997; Spokesman for: Foreign Affairs 1997–99, Agriculture, Rural Affairs and Fisheries 1999–; *Select Committees:* Member: Foreign Affairs 1997–99, Foreign Affairs 1997–98, Entry Clearance Sub-Committee 1998. *Special Interests:* Education, Local Government, Rural Affairs, Environment, Home Affairs; Europe, France. Member: Liberal Party National Executive 1988–89, Liberal Democrats Federal Executive 1990–92, 1993–95. Member, Witham Friary Friendly Society; Vice-Chair: Association of County Councils 1994–97, Committee of Local Police Authorities 1993–97; Member, Audit Commission 1994–97; Member: Council of Local Authorities and Regions of Europe 1993–97, Parliamentary Assembly of the Organisation for Security and Co-operation in Europe (OSCE) 1997–; CBE 1989; FRSA; FADO; *Clubs:* National Liberal; *Recreations:* Cricket, rugby football, until recently pig breeding. *Address:* David Heath Esq, CBE, MP, House of Commons, London, SW1A 0AA *Tel:* 020 7219 6245 *Fax:* 020 7219 5939. *Constituency:* 14 Catherine Hill, Frome, Somerset, BA11 1B7 *Tel:* 01373 473618 *Fax:* 01373 455152 *E-mail:* davidheath@davidheath.co.uk.

SIR EDWARD HEATH Old Bexley and Sidcup — *Con majority 3,569*

Born 9 July 1916; Son of late William George Heath; Educated Chatham House, Kent; Balliol College, Oxford (MA) (President, Oxford Union 1939). Served with Royal Artillery overseas 1940–46 (Mentioned in Despatches); Cmnd 2 Regt Honorable Artillery Company 1947–51; Master Gunner within the Tower of London 1951–54. **House of Commons:** Member for Bexley 1950–74, for Bexley Sidcup 1974–83 and for Old Bexley and Sidcup since June 1983; Opposition Whip February 1951; Government Whip November 1951; Joint Deputy Government Chief Whip May 1952; Deputy Government Chief Whip 1953–55; Government Chief Whip 1955–59; Minister of Labour 1959–60; Lord Privy Seal 1960–63; Secretary of State for Industry, Trade and Regional Development, and President of the Board of Trade 1963–64; Leader of the Opposition 1965–70, 1974–75; Prime Minister, First Lord of the Treasury and Minister for the Civil Service 1970–74;

Responsible in 1971 for successfully completing the negotiations for Britain's entry into the EEC; Father of the House of Commons 1992–; *Special Interests:* European Union, Economic Policy, Arts. President, Oxford University Conservative Association 1937; Chair, Federation of University Conservative Associations 1938; Leader, Conservative Party 1965–75. Patron of many charities and voluntary organisations, nationally and within Old Bexley and Sidcup; International Adviser, Praemium Imperiale (Japan); *Publications: One Nation: A Tory Approach to Social Problems,* 1950; *Old World New Horizons,* 1970; *Sailing: A Course in My Life,* 1975; *Music: A Joy for Life,* 1976, second edition 1997; *Travels: People and Places in My Life,* 1977; *Carols: The Joy of Christmas,* 1977; *The Course of My Life,* (autobiography) 1998; MBE 1946; PC 1955; KG 1992; Charlemagne Prize 1963; Channel 4 and House Award for Political Book of the Year 1999; Various honorary degrees; *Clubs:* Royal Yacht Squadron (Cowes), Buck's, Pratt's, Carlton; *Recreations:* Sailing, music, travel. *Address:* Rt Hon Sir Edward Heath, KG, MBE, MP, House of Commons, London, SW1A 0AA *Tel:* 020 7219 5559 *Fax:* 020 7219 5919 *Tel (Constituency):* 020 8300 3471 *Fax (Constituency):* 020 8300 9270.

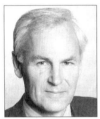

DAVID HEATHCOAT-AMORY Wells	*Con majority 528*

Born 21 March 1949; Son of late Brigadier Roderick Heathcoat-Amory, MC; Educated Eton College; Christ Church College, Oxford (MA philosophy, politics and economics); Married February 4, 1978, Linda Adams (2 sons 1 daughter). Qualified as chartered accountant 1974; Assistant finance director, British Technology Group 1980–83. **House of Commons:** Contested Brent South 1979 general election. Member for Wells since June 1983; Assistant Government Whip 1988–89; Government Whip July-October 1989; Deputy Chief Whip 1992–93; PPS: to Norman Lamont as Financial Secretary to the Treasury 1985–87, to Douglas Hurd as Home Secretary 1987–88; Parliamentary Under-Secretary of State: at Department of Environment 1989–90, at Department of Energy 1990–92; Minister of State, Foreign and Commonwealth Office 1993–94; Paymaster General 1994–96; Member, Shadow Cabinet 1997–; Shadow Chief Secretary to the Treasury 1997–2000; Shadow Secretary of State for Trade and Industry 2000–; *Select Committees:* Member: Broadcasting 1992–93, Finance and Services 1992–93. *Special Interests:* Industrial Policy, Agriculture, Forestry, Arms Control, Energy, European Union. Treasurer, West Country Group of Conservative MPs 1983–85. PC 1996; FCA 1980; *Recreations:* Fishing, shooting, music. *Address:* Rt Hon David Heathcoat-Amory, MP, House of Commons, London, SW1A 0AA *Tel:* 020 7219 3543 *Tel (Constituency):* 01749 673146.

DOUG HENDERSON Newcastle upon Tyne North	*Lab majority 19,332*

Born 9 June 1949; Son of John Henderson, railwayman, and Joy Henderson; Educated Waid Academy, Fife; Central College, Glasgow; Strathclyde University, Glasgow; Married September 27, 1974, Janet Graham (separated) (1 son). Apprentice, Rolls-Royce, Glasgow 1966–68; British Rail clerk, London 1969; Research Officer GMWU, Glasgow 1973; Scottish organiser GMB 1975–85, Organiser Newcastle 1985–87. **House of Commons:** Member for Newcastle upon Tyne North since June 1987; Opposition Spokesman on: Trade and Industry 1988–92, The Environment (Local Government) 1992–94, Citizen's Charter 1994–95, Home Affairs 1995–97; Minister of State (Europe), Foreign and Commonwealth Office 1997–98; Minister of State for the Armed Forces, Ministry of Defence 1998–99; *Special Interests:* Economic Policy, Industrial Policy, Employment Policy; former Soviet Union, USA. *Clubs:* Lemington Labour, Newburn Memorial, Dinnington; *Sportsclubs:* Elswick Harriers, Cambuslang Harriers; *Recreations:* Athletics, mountaineering, cross-country skiing. *Address:* Douglas Henderson Esq, MP, House of Commons, London, SW1A 0AA *Tel:* 020 7219 5017 *Tel (Constituency):* 0191–286 2024.

IVAN HENDERSON Harwich   Lab majority 1,216

Born 7 June 1958; Stepson of late Michael Bloice, son of Margaret Bloice; Educated Sir Anthony Deane Comprehensive; Trade Union Courses – Political/Health and Safety; Married 1st (1 son 1 daughter), married 2nd, June 13, 1992, Jo'Anne Atkinson. Former Dock Operative, Harwich International Port; Union organiser, Docks; Member, NUR/RMT: Shop steward 1984, Executive officer 1991–94, Member, Political and Transport Committee, Former President, RMT Anglia District Council. Councillor: Harwich Town Council 1986–97, Harwich District Council 1995–97. **House of Commons:** Member for Harwich since May 1, 1997; *Select Committees:* Member: Joint Committee on Statutory Instruments 1999–.

Special Interests: Transport, Employment, Health; Member, European Standing Committee C 1999–; Member: Young Socialists, Executive Member, Harwich Constituency Labour Party; Member, Co-operative Party. Member, PHAB (Harwich); President, Clacton and District Chamber of Trade & Commerce; Member: Trade's Council – Harwich Hospital Review Committee; Worked with International Transport Federation; European Works Council; *Sportsclubs:* Harwich and Parkeston Football Club; Vice-President, Harwich and Dovercourt Cricket Club; *Recreations:* Football, golf, sailing. *Address:* Ivan Henderson Esq, MP, House of Commons, London, SW1A 0AA *Tel:* 020 7219 3434. *Constituency:* Kingsway House, 21 Kingsway, Dovercourt, Essex, CO12 3AB *Tel:* 01255 552859 *Fax:* 01255 556771 *E-mail:* ivanhenderson@houseofcommons.fsnet.co.uk.

STEPHEN HEPBURN Jarrow   Lab majority 21,933

Born 6 December 1959; Son of Peter and Margaret Hepburn; Educated Springfield Comprehensive, Jarrow; Newcastle University (BA). Member, UCATT. Councillor, South Tyneside Council 1985–, Deputy Leader 1990–; Chair, Tyne & Wear Pensions 1989–. **House of Commons:** Member for Jarrow since May 1, 1997; *Select Committees:* Member: Administration 1997–, Defence 1999–. *Recreations:* Soccer, music, art. *Address:* Stephen Hepburn Esq, MP, House of Commons, London, SW1A 0AA *Tel:* 020 7219 4134. *Constituency:* 35 Park Road, Jarrow, Tyne & Wear, NE32 5JL *Tel:* 0191–420 0648.

JOHN HEPPELL Nottingham East   Lab majority 15,419

Born 3 November 1948; Son of late Robert Heppell, miner, and late Helen Heppell; Educated Rutherford Grammar School; South East Northumberland Technical College; Ashington Technical College; Married 1974, Eileen Golding (2 sons 1 daughter). Fitter: NCB 1964–70 and for number of firms in Nottingham area 1970–75; British Rail: Diesel fitter 1975–78, Workshop supervisor 1978–89; Member, RMT (previously NUR). Councillor, Nottinghamshire County Council 1981–93; Assistant Whip 1982; Vice-Chair, Environment Committee 1983; Chair: East Midlands Airport 1985, Resources Committee 1986, Deputy Leader, Nottinghamshire County Council 1989–92; Former Chair, Equal Opportunities Committee; Former Chair, Greater Nottingham LRT Board; Former Vice-Chair, Policy Committee. **House of Commons:** Member for Nottingham East since April 9, 1992; PPS to: Lord Richard as Lord Privy Seal and Leader of the House of Lords 1997–98, John Prescott as Deputy Prime Minister and Secretary of State for the Environment, Transport and the Regions 1998–; *Special Interests:* Equal Opportunity, Transport, Local Government; India, Pakistan, Cyprus. *Recreations:* Walking, reading. *Address:* John Heppell Esq, MP, House of Commons, London, SW1A 0AA *Tel:* 020 7219 4095 *Fax:* 020 7219 2969. *Constituency:* 1 Talbot Street, Nottingham, NG1 5GQ *Tel:* 0115–956 0450 *Fax:* 0115–956 0445 *E-mail:* tanvirj@parliament.uk.

MICHAEL HESELTINE   Henley   Con majority 11,167

Born 21 March 1933; Son of late Colonel R. D. Heseltine; Educated Shrewsbury School; Pembroke College, Oxford (President of the Union); Married 1962, Anne Williams (1 son 2 daughters). Chairman: Haymarket Press (Magazine Publishers) 1964–70, Haymarket Publishing Group 1999–. **House of Commons:** Contested Gower 1959 and Coventry North 1964 general elections. Member for Tavistock 1966–74, and for Henley from February 1974; Opposition Spokesman for: Industry 1974–76, The Environment 1976–79; Parliamentary Secretary, Ministry of Transport June-October 1970; Parliamentary Under-Secretary of State, Department of the Environment October 1970–72; Minister for Aerospace and Shipping, DTI 1972–74; Secretary of State for: the Environment 1979–83, Defence 1983–86; Contested Leadership of the Conservative Party November 1990; Secretary of State for the Environment 1990–92; President of the Board of Trade and Secretary of State for Trade and Industry 1992–95; Deputy Prime Minister and First Secretary of State 1995–97. Chair, Conservative Mainstream Group. Member, The Millennium Commission 1994–; Chairman, Anglo/Chinese Forum 1998–; *Publications: Where There's a Will* 1987; *The Challenge of Europe: Can Britain Win?* 1989; *Life in the Jungle – the autobiography* 2000; CH 1997; PC 1979; Hon. Fellow, Pembroke College 1986; Hon. LLD, Liverpool University 1990; *Clubs:* Carlton. *Address:* Rt Hon Michael Heseltine, CH, MP, House of Commons, London, SW1A 0AA *Tel:* 020 7219 5167.

STEPHEN HESFORD   Wirral West   Lab majority 2,738

Born 27 May 1957; Son of Bernard and Nellie Hesford; Educated Urmston Grammar School; Bradford University (BSc social science 1978); Central London Polytechnic (LLM 1980); Married Elizabeth Anne Henshall (2 sons). Barrister 1981–97; Assistant to Joan Lestor, MP 1992–93; Branch Equal Opportunities Officer, GMB. Vice-Chair, North Manchester Community Health Council. **House of Commons:** Contested Suffolk South 1992 general election. Member for Wirral West since May 1, 1997; *Select Committees:* Member: Deregulation 1997–98, Northern Ireland Affairs 1998–99; Member: Health 1999–. *Special Interests:* Economic Policy, Health, Social Services, Pensions, Education; France; Member, European Standing Committee C 1999–. Member, Fabian Society; NEC Member, Socialist Health Association. Member: Greenpeace, Amnesty International, Child Poverty Action Group; Fellow: Royal Institue of Public Health and Hygiene, Society of Public Health; *Sportsclubs:* Life Member, Lancashire Cricket Club; *Recreations:* Sport, music, reading. *Address:* Stephen Hesford Esq, MP, House of Commons, London, SW1A 0AA *Tel:* 020 7219 6227 *Fax:* 020 7219 4953. *Constituency:* 140 Ford Road, Upton, Wirral, Merseyside, CH49 0TQ *Tel:* 0151–522 0531 *Fax:* 0151–522 0558 *E-mail:* hesfords@parliament.uk.

PATRICIA HEWITT   Leicester West   Lab majority 12,864

Born 2 December 1948; Daughter of Sir Lenox Hewitt, OBE and Lady Hope Hewitt; Educated Canberra Girls' Grammar School; Newnham College, Cambridge (MA); Nuffield College, Oxford (MA); Married 1981, William Jack Birtles (1 son 1 daughter). Public relations officer, Age Concern 1971–73; National Council for Civil Liberties: Women's rights officer 1973–74, General Secretary 1974–83; To Neil Kinnock as Leader of the Opposition: Press secretary 1983–87, Policy co-ordinator 1987–89; Deputy director, Institute for Public Policy Research 1989–94; Director of research, Andersen Consulting 1994–97; Member, MSF. **House of Commons:** Contested Leicester East 1983 general election. Member for Leicester West since May 1, 1997; Economic Secretary, HM Treasury 1998–99; Minister of State, Department of Trade and Industry (Minister for Small Business and E-Commerce) 1999–; *Select Committees:* Member: Social Security 1997–98, Social Security 1998. *Special Interests:* Social Security, Employment, Family, Information Technology; Australia, South Africa, India. Member: Labour Women's Advisory Committee 1976–82, Labour Campaign for Social Justice, Fabian Society. Governor, Kentish Town Primary School 1993–96;

Member: CPAG, Liberty; Member, Secretary of State's Advisory Committee on the Employment of Women 1976–83; Vice-Chair: Commission on Social Justice 1992–94, British Council Board 1997–98; Advisory Board, International Human Rights League; Trustee, Institute for Public Policy Research 1995–98; *Publications:* Numerous, including books, pamphlets and articles for academic, specialist and popular journals. Also regular contributor on radio and television programmes; Fellow, Royal Society for the Arts; *Recreations:* Gardening, music, theatre. *Address:* Patricia Hewitt, MP, House of Commons, London, SW1A 0AA. *Constituency:* Janner House, Woodgate, Leicester, LE3 5GH *Tel:* 0116–251 6160 *Fax:* 0116–251 0482 *E-mail:* hewittph@parliament.uk; tlo.hewitt@tlo.dti.gov.uk.

KEITH HILL   Streatham   *Lab majority 18,423*

Born 28 July 1943; Son of Ernest Hill, printer, and Ida Hill, textile machine operative; Educated City of Leicester Grammar School; Corpus Christi College, Oxford (MA); University College of Wales, Aberystwyth (DipEd (Wales)); Married May 19, 1972, Lesley Ann Doktor. Research assistant in politics, Leicester University 1966–68; Belgian government scholar, Brussels 1968–69; Lecturer in politics, Strathclyde University 1969–73; Research officer, Labour Party International Department 1974–76; Political liaison officer, National Union of Rail, Maritime and Transport Workers (formerly NUR) 1976–92. **House of Commons:** Contested Blaby 1979 general election. Member for Streatham since April 9, 1992; Assistant Government Whip 1998–99; Department of the Environment, Transport and the Regions: PPS to Hilary Armstrong, as Minister of State (Minister for Local Government and Housing) 1997–98, Parliamentary Under-Secretary of State 1999–; *Select Committees:* Member: Transport 1992–97. *Special Interests:* Transport, European Union, Environment; Europe, Africa. London Campaigner, Leadership Campaigns Team 1995; Hon. Secretary, London Group of Labour MPs 1997–98; Chair, Labour Movement in Europe 1997–98. *Publications: Belgium* in *European Political Parties* 1969; *Belgium: Political Change in A Segmented Society* in *Electoral Behaviour* 1974; *Recreations:* Walking, books, films, music. *Address:* Keith Hill Esq, MP, House of Commons, London, SW1A 0AA *Tel:* 020 7219 6980 *Fax:* 020 7219 2565 *E-mail:* hillk@parliament.uk.

DAVID HINCHLIFFE   Wakefield   *Lab majority 14,604*

Born 14 October 1948; Son of late Robert Hinchliffe, leading railman, and late Muriel Hinchliffe; Educated Lawefield Lane Primary School; Cathedral Secondary School, Wakefield; Wakefield Technical College; Leeds Polytechnic (CQSW 1971); Bradford University (MA social work and community work 1978); Married July 17, 1982, Julia North (1 son 1 daughter). Social worker, Leeds 1968–79; Social work tutor, Kirklees MDC 1980–87. Councillor: Wakefield City Council 1971–74, Wakefield Metropolitan District Council 1979–88. **House of Commons:** Member for Wakefield since June 1987; Opposition Front Bench Spokesman on Health (Shadow Minister for Personal Social Services and Community Care) 1992–95; *Select Committees:* Member: Health 1990–92; Chairman: Health 1997–; Member: Liaison 1997–. *Special Interests:* Health Service, Social Services. *Sportsclubs:* Vice-President, Wakefield Trinity RLFC; *Recreations:* Rugby League, researching family history, inland waterways. *Address:* David Hinchliffe Esq, MP, House of Commons, London, SW1A 0AA *Tel:* 020 7219 4447. *Constituency:* 6 Rishworth Street, Wakefield, WF1 3BY *Tel:* 01924 290590 *Fax:* 01924 290690.

Dod *on* Line
An Electronic Directory without rival . . .
MPs' biographies and photographs available with daily updates *via* the internet

For a *free* trial, call Oliver Cox on 020 7828 7256

MARGARET HODGE   Barking   *Lab majority 15,896*

Born 8 September 1944; Daughter of Hans and Lisbeth Oppenheimer; Educated Bromley High School; Oxford High School; London School of Economics (BSc economics 1966); Married 1st, 1968, Andrew Watson (marriage dissolved 1978) (1 son 1 daughter), married 2nd, 1978, Henry Hodge, OBE (2 daughters). Teaching and market research 1966–73; Senior consultant, Price Waterhouse 1992–94; Member, TGWU. Councillor, London Borough of Islington 1973–94, Chair, Housing Committee 1975–79, Deputy Leader of Council 1981–82, Leader 1982–92. **House of Commons:** Member for Barking since June 9, 1994 by-election; Parliamentary Under-Secretary of State (Employment and Equal Opportunities), Department for Education and Employment 1998–; *Select Committees:* Member: Deregulation 1996–97, Education and Employment 1996–97; Chairman (Education): Education and Employment 1997–98; Joint Chairman: Education and Employment 1997–98; Chairman: Education Sub-Committee 1997–98; Chairman (Education): Education Sub-Committee 1997–98; Member: Employment Sub-Committee 1997–98, Liaison 1997–98. *Special Interests:* Education, Local Government, Housing, Inner Cities, Democratic Reform, London Government. Member, Labour Party Local Government Committee 1983–92; Chair, London Group of Labour MPs 1995–98; Vice-Chair, Fabians 1997–98. Member, Home Office Advisory Committee on Race Relations 1988–92; Director: University College, Middlesex Hospitals; Governor, London School of Economics 1990–; Chair, Association of London Authorities 1984–92; Vice-Chair, AMA 1991–92; *Publications: Quality, Equality and Democracy; Beyond the Town Hall;* Fabian pamphlet on London Government, *Not Just the Flower Show;* Contributed chapters to a number of books as well as articles in numerous journals and newspapers; MBE 1978; Hon. Fellow, University of North London; Hon. DCL, City 1993; *Recreations:* Family, opera, piano, travel, cooking. *Address:* Margaret Hodge, MBE, MP, House of Commons, London, SW1A 0AA *Tel:* 020 7219 6666 *Tel (Constituency):* 020 8594 1333 *Fax (Constituency):* 020 8594 1131 *E-mail:* haywoodmw@parliament.uk.

KATE HOEY   Vauxhall   *Lab majority 18,660*

Born 21 June 1946; Daughter of Thomas and Letitia Hoey; Educated Belfast Royal Academy; Ulster College of Physical Education (teaching diploma); City of London College, London (BSc economics). Senior lecturer, Kingsway College 1976–85; Educational adviser to Arsenal Football Club 1985–89; Member, GMB. Councillor: Hackney Borough Council 1978–82, Southwark Borough Council 1988–89. **House of Commons:** Contested Dulwich 1983 and 1987 general elections. Member for Vauxhall since June 15, 1989 by-election; Member, Opposition team on Citizen's Charter and Women 1992–93; PPS to Frank Field as Minister of State, Department of Social Security 1997–98; Parliamentary Under-Secretary of State: Home Office (Metropolitan Police, European Union, Judicial Co-operation) 1998–99, Department for Culture, Media and Sport (Minister for Sport) 1999–; *Select Committees:* Member: Broadcasting 1991–97, Social Security 1994–97. *Special Interests:* Environment, Sport, Foreign Affairs, Dog Control, Housing; Angola, Bosnia. *Publications:* Occasional articles on sport in the press; *The Spectator*/Highland Park Debater of the Year Award 1998; University of Ulster Distinguished Graduate 2000; *Sportsclubs:* Member, Surrey County Cricket Club. *Address:* Kate Hoey, MP, House of Commons, London, SW1A 0AA *Tel:* 020 7219 5803 *Fax:* 020 7219 5989 *Website:* www.culture.gov.uk.

Dod *on* Line
An Electronic Directory without rival ...

MPs' biographies and photographs
available with daily updates *via* the internet

For a *free* trial, call Oliver Cox on 020 7828 7256

DOUGLAS HOGG   Sleaford and North Hykeham   *Con majority 5,123*

Born 5 February 1945; Son of Baron Hailsham of St Marylebone (*qv*), former Lord Chancellor; Educated Eton; Christ Church, Oxford (MA history 1968) (President, Oxford Union); Married 1968, Hon. Sarah Boyd-Carpenter (cr. Baroness Hogg, 1995) (*qv*) daughter of late Baron Boyd-Carpenter (1 son 1 daughter). Called to the Bar, Lincoln's Inn 1968 (Kennedy Law Scholar); QC 1990. **House of Commons:** Member for Grantham 1979–97, and for Sleaford and North Hykeham since May 1, 1997; Government Whip 1983–84; PPS to Leon Brittan Chief as Secretary to the Treasury 1982–86; Parliamentary Under-Secretary, Home Office 1986–89; Minister of State at: Department of Trade and Industry (Minister for Industry and Enterprise) 1989–90, Foreign and Commonwealth Office 1990–95; Minister of Agriculture, Fisheries and Food 1995–97; *Select Committees:* Member: Home Affairs 1997–98. QC 1990; PC 1992. *Address:* Rt Hon Douglas Hogg QC, MP, House of Commons, London, SW1A 0AA *Tel:* 020 7219 3444/3484 *Fax:* 020 7219 4123. *Constituency:* Sleaford and North Hykeham Conservative Association, The Old Forge, Main Street, Leadenham, Lincolnshire, LN5 0PE *Tel:* 01400 272187 *Fax:* 01400 272189 *E-mail:* hoggd@parliament.uk; edwardsa@parliament.uk.

JOHN HOME ROBERTSON   East Lothian   *Lab majority 14,221*

Born 5 December 1948; Son of late Lieutenant-Colonel J. W. Home Robertson; Educated Ampleforth; West of Scotland Agricultural College; Married 1977, Catherine Brewster (2 sons). Farmer; MSP for East Lothian constituency since May 6, 1999. Councillor, Berwickshire District Council 1974–78; Member, Borders Health Board 1975–78. **House of Commons:** Member for Berwick and East Lothian 1978–83, and for East Lothian since June 1983; Opposition Front Bench Spokesman on: Agriculture 1984–87, Scottish Affairs 1987–88, Agricultural and Rural Affairs 1988–90; Opposition Scottish Whip 1983–84; PPS to Dr Jack Cunningham: as Minister of Agriculture, Fisheries and Food 1997–98, as Minister for the Cabinet Office and Chancellor of the Duchy of Lancaster 1998–99; *Select Committees:* Member: Defence 1990–97. *Special Interests:* Scottish Affairs, Defence, Rural Affairs; Ireland, Bosnia. Chair, Scottish Group of Labour MPs 1982–83. Member, Edinburgh District Aid to Bosnia; Holds Heavy Goods Vehicle Driver's Licence; Member, Armed Forces Parliamentary Scheme 1996; British-Irish Parliamentary Body 1990–; Member: The Paxton Trust, East Lothian Community Development Trust. *Address:* John Home Robertson Esq, MP, MSP, House of Commons, London, SW1A 0AA *Tel:* 020 7219 4135. *Constituency:* Town House, High Street, Dunbar, East Lothian, EH42 1ER *Tel:* 01368 861679.

JIMMY HOOD   Clydesdale   *Lab majority 13,809*

Born 16 May 1948; Son of William Hood, retired miner, and Bridget Hood; Educated Lesmahagow Higher Grade School, Coatbridge; Nottingham University; Married January 28, 1967, Marion Stewart, daughter of Ronald and late Rose McCleary (1 son 1 daughter). Mining engineer 1964–87; Member, NUM 1964–: Official 1973–87, Leader of Nottinghamshire striking miners in 1984–85 national miners' strike; Member, AEEU 1996–. Councillor, Newark and Sherwood District Council 1979–87. **House of Commons:** Member for Clydesdale since June 1987; *Select Committees:* Member: European Legislation 1987–97; Chairman: European Legislation 1992–98; Member: Liaison 1992–97; Member: Chairmen's Panel 1997–, Defence 1997–, Liaison 1997–; Chairman: European Scrutiny 1998–. *Special Interests:* Health Service, Home Affairs, Agriculture, Environment, Energy, Housing, Education, Alcohol Abuse and Under-age Drinking, European Union, Defence. Convenor, Scottish Parliamentary Group of Labour MPs; Member, Co-operative Party. Fellow, Industry and Parliament Trust; Armed Forces Parliamentary Scheme; *Clubs:* Lesmahagow Miners; *Recreations:* Gardening, reading, writing. *Address:* James Hood Esq, MP, House of Commons, London, SW1A 0AA *Tel:* 020 7219 4585 *Fax:* 020 7219 5872. *Constituency:* c/o Council Offices, South Vennel, Lanark, ML11 7JT *Tel:* 01555 673177 *Fax:* 01555 673188 *E-mail:* hoodj@parliament.uk.

GEOFFREY HOON   Ashfield   *Lab majority 22,728*

Born 6 December 1953; Son of Ernest and June Hoon; Educated Nottingham High School; Jesus College, Cambridge (BA law 1976, MA); Married April 4, 1981, Elaine Anne Dumelow (1 son 2 daughters). Lecturer in law, Leeds University 1976–82; Visiting professor of law, University of Louisville, USA 1980–81; Practising barrister 1982–84; MEP for Derbyshire 1984–94. **House of Commons:** Member for Ashfield since April 9, 1992; Opposition Spokesman on Trade and Industry 1995–97; Opposition Whip 1994–95; Lord Chancellor's Department: Parliamentary Secretary 1997–98, Minister of State 1998–99; Minister of State, Foreign and Commonwealth Office 1999; Secretary of State for Defence 1999–; *Special Interests:* Economic Policy, European Union, Constitution, Defence; Europe, USA. Chair, European Parliament Delegation for relations with: China 1986–89, United States 1989–93; PC 1999; *Recreations:* Sport, particularly squash, football and running, cinema, music. *Address:* Rt Hon Geoffrey Hoon, MP, House of Commons, London, SW1A 0AA *Tel:* 020 7219 3477. *Constituency:* 8 Station Street, Kirkby-in-Ashfield, Nottinghamshire, NG17 7AR *Tel:* 01623 720399 *Fax:* 01623 720399 *E-mail:* public@ministers.mod.uk.

PHIL HOPE   Corby   *Lab majority 11,860*

Born 19 April 1955; Son of A. G. (Bob) Hope, former police commander, and Grace Hope; Educated Wandsworth Comprehensive, London; St Luke's College, Exeter University (BEd 1978); Married July 25, 1980, Allison Butt (1 son 1 daughter). Secondary school teacher, Kettering School for Boys 1978–79; Youth policy adviser, National Council for Voluntary Organisations 1979–82; Head, Young Volunteer Resources Unit, National Youth Bureau 1982–85; Management/community work consultant, Framework 1985–97; Director, Framework in Print Publishing Co-operative; Member, NUT 1978–79; Member, MSF 1979–. Councillor, Kettering Borough Council 1983–87, Deputy Leader, Labour Group 1986–87; Councillor, Northamptonshire County Council 1993–97, Chair, Equal Opportunities Sub-Committee 1993–97, Chair, Labour Group 1993–97. **House of Commons:** Contested Kettering 1992 general election. Member for Corby since May 1, 1997; PPS to Nick Raynsford as Minister of State, Department of the Environment, Transport and the Regions 1999–; *Select Committees:* Member: Public Accounts 1997–98; Member: Selection 1999–. *Special Interests:* Equal Opportunity, Youth Affairs. National Adviser on Youth Policy 1982–87; Member, Co-operative Party 1982–; Delegate to National Conference; Member, Labour Party Leadership Campaign Team 1997–99. Member, Corby MIND; President: Corby Accommodation Project, Thrapston Volunteer Centre; Member: Wine Society Co-operative, Midlands Co-operative Society; Member: National Advisory Group on Personal, Social and Health Education (DfEE), Development Awareness Working Group (DfID); Member, Commonwealth Parliamentary Association 1997–; *Publications:* Author/Co-Author of many publications including: *Making the Best Use of Consultants*, 1993; *Education for Parenthood*, 1994; *Analysis and Action on Youth Health*, 1995; *Performance Appraisal*, 1995; *Sportsclubs:* Corby Tennis Centre; *Recreations:* Juggling, computing, gardening, tennis. *Address:* Phil Hope Esq, MP, House of Commons, London, SW1A 0AA *Tel:* 020 7219 4075 *Fax:* 020 7219 2673. *Constituency:* 2nd Floor, Chisholm House, Queen's Square, Corby, Northamptonshire, NN17 1PD *Tel:* 01536 443325 *Fax:* 01536 269462 *E-mail:* taylors@parliament.uk.

KELVIN HOPKINS   Luton North   *Lab majority 9,626*

Born 22 August 1941; Son of late Professor Harold Horace Hopkins, FRS, physicist and mathematician, and Joan Avery Frost, medical secretary; Educated Queen Elizabeth's Grammar School, High Barnet; Nottingham University (BA politics, economics and mathematics with statistics); Married August 21, 1965, Patricia Langley (1 son 1 daughter). TUC Economic Department 1969–70, 1973–77; Policy and research officer, NALGO/UNISON 1977–94; Member, GMB; Delegate, Luton Trades Union Council. Councillor, Luton Borough 1972–76. **House of Commons:** Contested Luton North 1983 general election. Member for Luton North since May 1, 1997; *Select Committees:* Member: Broadcasting 1999–. *Special Interests:* Economic

Policy, Employment, Transport, The Arts; France, Sweden; Member, European Standing Committee B 1998–. Vice-Chair, Central Region Labour Party 1995–96. Governor, Luton Sixth Form College; Chair of Governors, Luton College of Higher Education 1985–89; Member: Mary Seacole House, Luton, Wine Society, Hon. Vice-President, UK Carrom Federation; *Publications:* Various NALGO publications; Hon. Fellow, Luton University 1993; *Clubs:* Luton Socialist, Lansdowne (Luton); *Sportsclubs:* Luton Town Football Club, UK Carrom Federation; *Recreations:* Music, photography, sailing on the Norfolk Broads. *Address:* Kelvin Hopkins Esq, MP, House of Commons, London, SW1A 0AA *Tel:* 020 7219 6670 *Fax:* 020 7219 0957. *Constituency:* 3 Union Street, Luton, Bedfordshire, LU1 3AN *Tel:* 01582 488208 *Fax:* 01582 480990.

JOHN HORAM   Orpington   *Con majority 2,952*

Born 7 March 1939; Son of Sydney and Catherine Horam; Educated Silcoates School, Wakefield; St Catharine's College, Cambridge (MA economics 1960); Married 2nd, 1987, Judith Jackson (2 sons from previous marriage). Market research officer, Rowntree & Co. 1960–62; Leader and feature writer: *Financial Times* 1962–65, *The Economist* 1965–68; Managing director: Commodities Research Unit Ltd 1968–70, 1983–87, CRU Holdings Ltd. 1988–92; Deputy chair, CRU International Ltd 1992–95, 1997–. **House of Commons:** Contested (Labour) Folkestone and Hythe 1966 general election. Member for Gateshead West 1970–83 (Labour 1970–81, SDP 1981–83). Contested Newcastle upon Tyne Central (SDP/Alliance) 1983 general election. Member for Orpington since April 9, 1992; Labour Spokesman on Economic Affairs 1979–81; SDP Spokesman 1981–83; Parliamentary Under-Secretary of State, Department of Transport 1976–79; Parliamentary Secretary, Office of Public Service July-November 1995; Parliamentary Under-Secretary of State, Department of Health 1995–97; *Select Committees:* Member: Public Accounts Committee 1992–95; Chairman: Environmental Audit 1997–; Member: Liaison 1997–. *Special Interests:* Economic Policy, Transport, Health, Tax, London. *Publications:*   *Making Britain Competitive,* 1993; *Clubs:* Orpington Conservative; *Recreations:* Opera, ballet, gardening, walking. *Address:* John Horam Esq, MP, House of Commons, London, SW1A 0AA *Tel:* 020 7219 6328.

MICHAEL HOWARD   Folkestone and Hythe   *Con majority 6,332*

Born 7 July 1941; Son of late Bernard and Hilda Howard; Educated Llanelli Grammar School; Peterhouse, Cambridge (MA, LLB); Married 1975, Sandra Paul (1 son 1 daughter and 1 step-son). Called to the Bar, Inner Temple 1964; QC 1982; Junior Counsel to the Crown 1980–82. **House of Commons:** Contested Liverpool Edge Hill 1966 and 1970 general elections. Member for Folkestone and Hythe since June 1983; PPS to Sir Patrick Mayhew as Solicitor-General 1984–85; Parliamentary Under-Secretary of State, Trade and Industry 1985–87; Minister for: Local Government 1987–88, Water and Planning 1988–89, Housing and Planning 1989–90; Secretary of State for: Employment 1990–92, The Environment 1992–93, The Home Department 1993–97; Contested Leadership of the Conservative Party June 1997; Member, Shadow Cabinet 1997–99; Shadow Secretary of State for Foreign and Commonwealth Affairs 1997–99; *Special Interests:* Home Affairs, Employment, Trade Union Law Reform. Chair: Bow Group 1970, Coningsby Club 1972–73. PC 1990; *Clubs:* Carlton; *Recreations:* Football and baseball. *Address:* Rt Hon Michael Howard, QC, MP, House of Commons, London, SW1A 0AA *Tel:* 020 7219 5493 *Fax:* 020 7219 5322. *Constituency:* Folkestone and Hythe Conservative Association, 4 Westcliff Gardens, Folkestone, Kent, CT20 1SP *Tel:* 01303 253524 *Fax:* 01303 251061 *E-mail:* howardm@parliament.uk.

Visit the Vacher Dod Website . . .

www.politicallinks.co.uk

ALAN HOWARTH   Newport East   *Lab majority 13,523*

Born 11 June 1944; Son of late T. E. B. Howarth, MC, TD, and Margaret Howarth (née Teakle); Educated Rugby School; King's College, Cambridge; Married September 23, 1967, Gillie Chance (marriage dissolved 1996) (2 sons 2 daughters). Senior research assistant to Field-Marshal Montgomery on *A History of Warfare* 1965–67; Assistant master, Westminster School 1968–74; Member, GMB. **House of Commons:** Member for Stratford-on-Avon (Conservative – June 1983 to Oct 1995, Labour – Oct 1995 to May 1997), and for Newport East since May 1, 1997; Assistant Government Whip, 1987–88; Government Whip 1988–89; PPS to Sir Rhodes Boyson as Minister of State, Northern Ireland Office and Department of Environment 1985–87; Parliamentary Under-Secretary of State, Department for Education and Science 1989–92; Resigned from the Conservative Party and joined the Labour Party, October 1995; Parliamentary Under-Secretary of State: Department for Education and Employment (Employment and Equal Opportunities) 1997–98, Department for Culture, Media and Sport (Minister for the Arts) 1998–; *Select Committees:* Member: National Heritage 1992–93, Social Security 1996–97. *Special Interests:* Economic Policy, Employment, Education, Charities and the Voluntary Sector, Social Security, The Arts. Personal assistant to Chair Conservative Party 1975–79; Director, Conservative Research Department 1979–81; Vice-Chair, Conservative Party 1980–81. *Publications:* Co-author of *Changing Charity*, 1984; *Montgomery at Close Quarters*, 1986; *Save Our Schools*, 1986; *The Arts: The Next Move Forward*, 1987; CBE 1982; PC 2000; *Recreations:* Books, arts, running. *Address:* Rt Hon Alan Howarth Esq, CBE, MP, House of Commons, London, SW1A 0AA *Tel:* 020 7219 3000. *Constituency:* Ringland Labour Club, Ringland, Newport, Gwent, NP19 9PS *Tel:* 01633 277910/273111 *E-mail:* alan.howarth@culture.gov.uk *Website:* www.culture.gov.uk.

GEORGE HOWARTH   Knowsley North and Sefton East   *Lab majority 26,147*

Born 29 June 1949; Educated Schools in Huyton; Liverpool Polytechnic (BA social sciences); Married 1977, Julie Rodgers (2 sons 1 daughter). Engineering apprentice 1966–70; Engineer 1970–75; Teacher 1975–80; Co-operative Development Services 1980–82; Chief executive Walm Co-operative Centre 1982–86; AEU; Chief executive, Wales TUC sponsored co-op. centre, Cardiff 1984–86. Councillor, Huyton Urban District Council 1971–75; Knowsley Borough Council: Councillor 1975–86, Deputy Leader 1982–83. **House of Commons:** Member Knowsley North November 13, 1986 by-election–1997, and for Knowsley North and Sefton East since May 1, 1997; Opposition Spokesman on: the Environment 1989–92; Environmental Protection 1993–94; Home Affairs 1994–97; Parliamentary Under-Secretary of State: Home Office (Minister for Fire and Emergency Planning, Liquor, Drugs and Elections) 1997–99, Northern Ireland Office 1999–; *Special Interests:* Housing, Environment. Chair, Knowsley South Labour Party 1981–85; Secretary, Knowsley Borough District Labour Party 1977–80; Member, North West Region Executive, Labour Party 1981–84. *Recreations:* Coarse fishing, family, reading. *Address:* George Howarth Esq, MP, House of Commons, London, SW1A 0AA *Tel:* 020 7219 6902. *Constituency:* 149 Cherryfield Drive, Kirkby, Merseyside, L32 8SE *Tel:* 0151–546 9918 *Fax:* 0151–546 9918 *E-mail:* georgehowarthmp@hotmail.com.

GERALD HOWARTH   Aldershot   *Con majority 6,621*

Born 12 September 1947; Son of Mary and late James Howarth, retired company director; Educated Haileybury and ISC Junior School, Windsor; Bloxham School, Banbury (Scholar); Southampton University (BA English 1969); Married 1973, Elizabeth Squibb (2 sons 1 daughter). Commissioned RAFVR 1968; Assistant manager, loan syndication Bank of America International Ltd 1971–77; European Arab Bank 1977–81: Manager and personal assistant to group managing director 1979, Manager, loan syndications 1980; Loan syndication manager responsible for arranging project and other loans in Africa, Middle East and South America, Standard Chartered Bank plc 1981–83; Joint managing director, Taskforce Communications 1993–95; Member, National Union of Seamen 1966. London Borough Council of Hounslow: Councillor 1982–82, Shadow Vice-Chair, Environmental Planning Committee, Member, Finance and General Purposes Committee.

House of Commons: Member for Cannock and Burntwood 1983–92, and for Aldershot since May 1, 1997; PPS to Michael Spicer: as Parliamentary Under-Secretary of State, at Department of Energy 1987–90, as Minister of State, Department of the Environment (Minister for Housing and Construction) 1990; to Sir George Young as Minister of State, Department of the Environment 1990–91, to Margaret Thatcher, MP December 1991-April 1992; *Select Committees:* Member: Home Affairs 1997–. *Special Interests:* Aerospace, Aviation, Defence, Media, Education, Privatisation; Germany, Russia, South Africa, Chile, Pakistan. Member, Greater London Area CPC Advisory Committee; Vice-Chair, City Conservative Forum 1981–84; Founder Member, No Turning Back Group. General Secretary, Society for Individual Freedom 1969–71; Director, Freedom Under Law; Britannia Airways Parliamentary Pilot of the Year 1988; Executive Member, 1922 Committee 2000–; Fellow, Industry and Parliament Trust; *Publications:* Co-author *No Turning Back*, 1985, and further publications by the Group; *Clubs:* Aldershot Conservative; *Recreations:* Flying, squash, tennis, DIY, family. *Address:* Gerald Howarth Esq, MP, House of Commons, London, SW1A 0AA *Tel:* 020 7219 5650 *Fax:* 020 7219 1198. *Constituency:* Conservative Club, Victoria Road, Aldershot, Hampshire, GU11 1JX *Tel:* 01252 323637 *Fax:* 01252 323637.

DR KIM HOWELLS   Pontypridd — *Lab majority 23,129*

Born 27 November 1946; Son of late Glanville Howells and of Glenys Howells; Educated Mountain Ash Grammar School; Hornsey College of Art; Cambridge CAT (BA 1974); Warwick University (PhD 1979); Married September 22, 1983, Eirlys Davies (2 sons 1 daughter). Research officer, Coalfield History Project, University College of Wales, Swansea 1979–82; Freelance radio and television presenter and writer 1986–89; Research officer and newspaper editor, NUM South Wales Area 1982–89. **House of Commons:** Member for Pontypridd since February 23, 1989 by-election; Opposition Spokesman on: Development and Co-operation 1993–94, Foreign Affairs 1994, Home Affairs 1994–95, Trade and Industry 1995–97; Parliamentary Under-Secretary of State: Department for Education and Employment (Life-long Learning) 1997–98, Department of Trade and Industry 1998– (Consumer and Corporate Affairs 1999–2000, Competition and Consumer Affairs 2000–); *Select Committees:* Member: Welsh Affairs 1989–90, Environment 1990–92, Public Accounts 1993–94. *Special Interests:* Energy, Environment, Foreign Affairs, Transnational Broadcasting, Arts, Intellectual Property; Germany, Italy, Latin America, Switzerland, USA, South Africa, Austria, Romania. President: Arthritis Care, Pontypridd, Taff Ely Drugs Support Group; Vice-President, Travol Pontypridd; Patron, Dragon Swimming Club for Disabled; Member, British Mountaineering Council; *Publications:* Various, on 20th century industrial history and economics and politics of energy; Honorary Doctorate, Anglia Polytechnic University 1998; *Sportsclubs:* Llantwit Fadre Cricket, Hopkinstown Cricket, Pontypridd Rugby Football, Pontypridd Cricket Club, British Mountaineering Council; *Recreations:* Literature, films, jazz, mountain climbing, art, cycling. *Address:* Dr Kim Howells, MP, House of Commons, London, SW1A 0AA *Tel:* 020 7219 5813. *Constituency:* 16 Tyfica Road, Pontypridd, Mid Glamorgan, CF37 2DA *Tel:* 01443 402551 *Fax:* 01443 485628 *E-mail:* tlo.howells@tlo.dti.gov.uk.

LINDSAY HOYLE   Chorley — *Lab majority 9,870*

Born 10 June 1957; Son of Baron Hoyle (*qv*) and late Pauline Hoyle; Educated Anderton County Primary; Lords College, Bolton; Horwich FE; Bolton TIC (City & Guilds Construction); Married Catherine Swindley (2 daughters). Company director; Shop steward; Member, MSF. Councillor, Adlington Town Council; Councillor, Chorley Borough Council 1980–98; Chair, Economic Development, Deputy Leader 1994–97; Mayor of Chorley 1997–98. **House of Commons:** Member for Chorley since May 1, 1997; *Select Committees:* Member: Catering 1997–, Trade and Industry 1998–. *Special Interests:* Trade and Industry, Sport, Defence; Gibraltar, Falkland Islands, British Overseas Territories. Member: Royal Lancashire Agricultural Society, Adlington Cricket Club, Chorley Cricket Club; Former Chairman, Chorley Rugby League; Armed Forces Parliamentary Scheme (Royal Marines) 1998–; Member, Cuerdon Valley Trust; *Recreations:* Cricket. *Address:* Hon Lindsay Hoyle, MP, House of Commons, London, SW1A 0AA *Tel:* 020 7219 1135 *Fax:* 020 7219 3831. *Constituency:* 35–39 Market Street, Chorley, Lancashire, PR7 2SW *Tel:* 01257 483887.

BEVERLEY HUGHES   Stretford and Urmston   *Lab majority 13,640*

Born 30 March 1950; Daughter of late Norman Hughes and Doris Hughes; Educated Ellesmere Port Girls' Grammar School; Manchester University; Liverpool University (BSc, MSc); Married March 31, 1973, Thomas McDonald (1 son 2 daughters). Trainee probation officer, Merseyside 1971; Probation officer, Merseyside 1972; Manchester University: Research associate 1976; Lecturer 1981, Senior lecturer and head of department 1993–97; Director: G-Mex Ltd, Modesole Ltd, Midas. Trafford Metropolitan Borough Council: Councillor 1986, Labour Group Deputy Leader 1990, Labour Group Leader 1992, Council Leader 1995; Director: Trafford Park Development Corporation, Manchester Airport plc. **House of Commons:** Member for Stretford and Urmston since May 1, 1997; PPS to Hilary Armstrong as Minister of State, Department of the Environment, Transport and the Regions (Minister for Local Government and Housing) 1998–99; Parliamentary Under-Secretary of State, Department of the Environment, Transport and the Regions 1999–; *Select Committees:* Member: Home Affairs 1997–98. *Special Interests:* Economic Regeneration, Investment, Local Government, Health and Community Care, Family, Regional Development, Education, Criminal Justice, Child Protection and Safety. Chair, Age Concern, Trafford 1986–92; *Publications: Older People and Community Care: Critical Theory and Practice,* 1995; Numerous academic and professional publications; *Recreations:* Jazz, fell-walking. *Address:* Beverley Hughes, MP, House of Commons, London, SW1A 0AA *Tel:* 020 7219 3802 *Fax:* 020 7219 2961 *Tel (Constituency):* 0161–749 9120 *Fax (Constituency):* 0161–749 9121 *E-mail:* beverley_hughes@detr.gsi.gov.uk.

KEVIN HUGHES   Doncaster North   *Lab majority 21,937*

Born 15 December 1952; Son of Leonard Hughes, retired coal miner, and Annie Hughes, retired school assistant; Educated local schools; Sheffield University, Department of Extra Mural Studies (industrial relations, trade union history, economics and politics); Married August 26, 1972, Lynda Saunders (1 son 1 daughter). Coal miner 1970–90; Branch delegate, Brodsworth NUM 1981–90; Member, Yorkshire NUM Executive Committee 1983–87. Councillor, Doncaster Borough Council 1986–92; Chair, Social Services Committee 1987–92. **House of Commons:** Member for Doncaster North since April 9, 1992; Opposition Whip 1996–97; Assistant Government Whip (social security: Yorkshire West) 1997–; *Select Committees:* Member: European Legislation 1994–96. *Special Interests:* Social Services, Childcare, Elderly. Secretary/Agent: Don Valley CLP 1980–83 Doncaster North 1983–89. Hon. President, DIAL (Doncaster); Fellow, Industry and Parliament Trust 1995; *Clubs:* Doncaster Trades and Labour, Skellow Grange Workingmen's; *Recreations:* Golf, walking, listening to opera. *Address:* Kevin Hughes Esq, MP, House of Commons, London, SW1A 0AA *Tel:* 020 7219 4107 *Fax:* 020 7219 2521 *Tel (Constituency):* 01302 873974 *Fax (Constituency):* 01302 876176 *E-mail:* kevin.hughes@hm-treasury.gov.uk.

SIMON HUGHES   North Southwark and Bermondsey   *LD majority 3,387*

Born 17 May 1951; Son of late James Henry Hughes and of Sylvia Hughes (née Ward); Educated Llandaff Cathedral School, Cardiff; Christ College, Brecon; Selwyn College Cambridge (BA, MA); Inns of Court School of Law; College of Europe, Bruges (Certificate in Higher European Studies). Barrister Called to the Bar, Inner Temple 1974; In practice 1978–. GLC candidate 1981; Southwark Borough Council candidate 1982. **House of Commons:** Member for Southwark and Bermondsey by-election February 1983–97, and for North Southwark and Bermondsey since May 1, 1997; Liberal Spokesman for the Environment 1983–88; Alliance Spokesman for Health January-June 1987; Liberal Democrat Spokesman for: Education, Science and Training 1989–92, Environment and Natural Resources 1992–94, Urban Affairs and Young People 1994–97, The Church of England 1988–97, Health and Social Welfare 1995–97, Health (Future of NHS) 1997–99; Principal Spokesman for Home and Legal Affairs 1999–; Liberal Democrat Deputy Whip 1989–99; *Select Committees:* Member: Ecclesiastical Committee 1987–97, Accommodation and Works 1992–97.

Special Interests: Human Rights, Civil Liberties, Youth Affairs, Social Issues, Housing, Environment; South Africa. President, National League of Young Liberals 1986–92, Vice-President, Liberal Democrat Youth and Students 1983–86, President 1992–; Vice-Chair, Southwark and Bermondsey Liberal Association 1981–83; Former Chair, Liberal Party's Home Affairs Panel; Member, Association of Liberal Lawyers. Trainee, EEC Brussels 1976; Trainee and member Secretariat, Directorate and Commission on Human Rights, Council of Europe, Strasbourg 1976–77; *Publications:* Co-author *Human Rights in Western Europe – The Next 30 Years,* 1981; *The Prosecutorial Process in England and Wales,* 1981; *Across the Divide – Liberal Values for Defence and Disarmament,* 1986; *Pathways to Power,* 1992; *Clubs:* Redriff (Rotherhithe); *Recreations:* Music, theatre, history, sport (Millwall and Hereford FCs; Glamorgan CCC and Wales RFU), the countryside and open air. *Address:* Simon Hughes Esq, MP, House of Commons, London, SW1A 0AA *Tel:* 020 7219 6256.

JOAN HUMBLE   Blackpool North and Fleetwood   *Lab majority 8,946*

Born 3 March 1951; Daughter of Jova Piplica and Darinka Piplica; Educated Greenhead Grammar School, Keighley; Lancaster University (BA history 1972); Married January 22, 1972, Paul Humble (2 daughters). Civil servant, Department of Health and Social Security and Inland Revenue 1972–77; Housewife 1977–85; Member, TGWU. Councillor, Lancashire County Council 1985–97, Chair, Lancashire Social Services 1990–97; JP, Preston Bench. **House of Commons:** Member for Blackpool North and Fleetwood since May 1, 1997; *Select Committees:* Member: Social Security 1998–. *Special Interests:* Social Services, Education, Economic Regeneration; Member, European Standing Committee A 1998. Member: Co-operative Party, Christian Socialist Movement; Hon. Secretary, North West Regional Group of Labour MPs 1999–. School Governor 1982–97; *Recreations:* Reading, gardening, cooking. *Address:* Mrs Joan Humble, MP, House of Commons, London, SW1A 0AA *Tel:* 020 7219 5025 *Fax:* 020 7219 2755. *Constituency:* 216 Lord Street, Fleetwood, Lancashire, FY7 6SW *Tel:* 01253 877346 *Fax:* 01253 777236 *E-mail:* sue@humblemp-freeserve.co.uk.

JOHN HUME   Foyle   *SDLP majority 13,664*

Born 18 January 1937; Son of Samuel Hume; Educated Rosemount Primary School; St Columb's College, Derry; St Patrick's College, Maynooth (MA); Married 1960, Patricia Hone (2 sons 3 daughters). Teacher; President, Credit Union League of Ireland 1964–68; Associate Fellow, Centre for International Affairs, Harvard 1976; Research Fellow in European Studies, Trinity College, Dublin 1976–77; MP for Foyle, Northern Ireland Parliament 1969–72; Member (SDLP) for Londonderry: Northern Ireland Assembly 1973–75, Minister of Commerce Northern Ireland 1974; Northern Ireland Constitutional Convention 1975–76, MEP for Northern Ireland 1979–; Northern Ireland Assembly 1982–86; Member: New Ireland Forum 1983–84, Northern Ireland Forum 1996–98, New Northern Ireland Assembly 1998–; Member, SIPTU (Services, Industrial, Professional and Technical Union). **House of Commons:** Member for Foyle since June 1983; *Special Interests:* European Union, Third World, Poverty, Credit Unions, Northern Ireland; Belgium, Europe, France, USA. SDLP: Founder Member, Deputy Leader 1970–79, Leader 1979–. *Publications: Personal Views – Politics, Peace and Reconciliation in Ireland,* 1996; Numerous awards internationally, especially for human rights, including recently European of the Year Award; International Human Rights Award 1996; Global Citizens Award 1998; The Nobel Peace Prize (jointly) 1998; Martin Luther King Award 1999; 13 honorary doctorates from British, Irish, French and American universities; Freeman, City of Londonderry 2000. *Address:* John Hume Esq, MP, House of Commons, London, SW1A 0AA *Tel:* 020 7219 3000. *Constituency:* 5 Bayview Terrace, Derry, BT48 7EE *Tel:* 028 7126 5340 *Fax:* 028 7136 3423.

ANDREW HUNTER   Basingstoke   *Con majority 2,397*

Born 8 January 1943; Son of late Squadron-Leader Roger Hunter, DFC and late Winifred Mary née Nelson; Educated St George's School, Harpenden; Durham University (BA theology 1996, MA history 1968); Jesus College, Cambridge (Diploma in education 1967); Westcott House, Cambridge; Married March 24, 1972, Janet Bourne (1 son 1 daughter). TAVR 1973–83; Manufacturing industry 1968–71; Assistant master, Harrow School 1971–83. **House of Commons:** Contested Southampton Itchen 1979 general election. Member for Basingstoke since 1983; PPS to Lord Elton, Minister of State, Department of Environment 1985–86; Sponsored Private Members' Bills: Control of Smoke Pollution Act 1989, Timeshare Act 1992, Noise and Statutory Nuisance (Amendment) Act 1993, Dogs (Fouling of Land) Act 1996 Road Traffic (Vehicle Testing Act) 1999; *Select Committees:* Member: Environment 1986–92, Agriculture 1993–94; Member: Northern Ireland Affairs 1994–. *Special Interests:* Ireland, Southern Africa. Vice-President, National Prayer Book Society 1987–; Member: National Farmers' Union, Countryside Alliance; Honorary Member, Society of the Sealed Knot 1990–; Member, 1922 Executive Committee 1997–98; *Clubs:* St Stephen's Constitutional, Pratt's, Carlton; *Recreations:* Horse riding, watching cricket and rugby football. *Address:* Andrew Hunter Esq, MP, House of Commons, London, SW1A 0AA *Tel:* 020 7219 5216. *Constituency:* Basingstoke Conservative Association, 149D Pack Lane, Basingstoke.

ALAN HURST   Braintree   *Lab majority 1,451*

Born 2 September 1945; Son of late George Hurst; Educated Westcliff High School; Liverpool University (BA history); Married 1976, Hilary Burch (2 sons 1 daughter). Partner, Law Firm. Councillor, Southend Borough Council 1968–96, Labour Group Leader 1990–95; Deputy Leader 1994–95, Councillor, Essex County Council 1993–98. **House of Commons:** Member for Braintree since May 1, 1997; *Select Committees:* Member: Agriculture 1997–. *Special Interests:* Employment, Housing, Conservation, Agriculture. Member, Law Society; Former President, Southend Law Society; *Recreations:* Bird watching, local history. *Address:* Alan Hurst Esq, MP, House of Commons, London, SW1A 0AA *Tel:* 020 7219 4068. *Constituency:* The Labour Hall, Collingwood Road, Witham, Essex, CM8 2EE *Tel:* 01376 520128 *Fax:* 01376 517709.

JOHN HUTTON   Barrow and Furness   *Lab majority 14,497*

Born 6 May 1955; Son of late George Hutton, salesman and general labourer, and Rosemary Hutton, orthoptist; Educated Westcliff High School, Southend; Magdalen College, Oxford (BA 1976, BCL 1978); Married April 28, 1978, Rosemary Caroline Little (marriage dissolved 1993) (3 sons 1 daughter and 1 son deceased). Research associate, Templeton College, Oxford 1980–81; Senior law lecturer, Newcastle Polytechnic 1981–92; Contested Cumbria and North Lancashire 1989 European Parliament election. **House of Commons:** Contested Penrith and the Border 1987 general election. Member for Barrow and Furness since April 9, 1992; PPS to Margaret Beckett: as President of the Board of Trade and Secretary of State for Trade and Industry 1997–98, as President of the Council and Leader of the House of Commons 1998; Department of Health: Parliamentary Under-Secretary of State 1998–99, Minister of State 1999–; *Select Committees:* Member: Home Affairs 1994–97. *Special Interests:* Defence, Industry, Welfare State, Health. *Clubs:* Cemetery Cottages Workingmen's (Barrow-in-Furness); *Recreations:* Cricket, swimming. *Address:* John Hutton Esq, MP, House of Commons, London, SW1A 0AA *Tel:* 020 7219 6228. *Constituency:* 22 Hartington Street, Barrow-in-Furness, Cumbria, LA14 5SL *Tel:* 01229 431204 *Fax:* 01229 432016; email: mcsorleyt@parliament.uk *E-mail:* huttonj@parliament.uk.

I

Born 5 July 1940; Son of late John Iddon and late Violet Iddon; Educated Tarleton Church of England Primary School; Christ Church Boys' School, Southport; Southport Technical College; Hull University (BSc chemistry 1961, PhD organic chemistry 1964, DSc 1981); Married May 15, 1965, Merrilyn-Ann Muncaster (marriage dissolved 1989); (2 daughters) married 2nd, September 16, 1995, Eileen Harrison, née Barker (2 stepsons). Durham University: temporary lecturer 1964–65, senior demonstrator 1965–66 in organic chemistry; Salford University: lecturer 1966–78, senior lecturer 1978–86, reader 1986–97 in organic chemistry; Member, Association of University Teachers. Councillor, Bolton Metropolitan District Council 1977–98, Hon. Alderman 1998–, Housing Committee: Vice-Chair, 1980–82, Chair, 1986–96. **House of Commons:** Member for Bolton South East since May 1, 1997; *Select Committees:* Member: Environmental Audit 1997–2000; Member: Science and Technology 2000–. *Special Interests:* Housing, Science, Engineering and Technology, Health, Education (FE in particular); Europe, Africa, India, Middle East. Member: North West Group of the Labour Party, Arts For Labour, Co-operative Party, Labour Middle East Council, Labour Friends of Remploy, Labour Housing Group, Labour PLP Keep The Link Group. Member, Amnesty International; Local patron, Kids Club Network (Bolton-Bury Branch); National patron, Society of Registration Officers; Patron, Bully Free Zone Programme; Member: IPU, CPA; *Publications:* two books, research papers, research communications, major reviews, articles in magazines and a number of papers presented orally at conferences; FRSC; CChem; *Clubs:* Member, Bradford Ward Labour; Honorary Membership, Derby Ward Labour; *Recreations:* Philately, gardening, cricket (spectator). *Address:* Dr Brian Iddon, MP, House of Commons, London, SW1A 0AA *Tel:* 020 7219 4064 *Fax:* 020 7219 2653. *Constituency:* 60 St Georges Road, Bolton, BL1 2DD *Tel:* 01204 371202 *Fax:* 01204 371374 *E-mail:* iddonb@parliament.uk.

Born 9 April 1955; Son of John and Maud Illsley; Educated Barnsley Holgate Grammar School; Leeds University (LLB 1977); Married September 16, 1978, Dawn Webb (2 daughters). Yorkshire Area NUM: Compensation officer 1978–81, Assistant head of general department 1981–84, Head of general department and chief administration officer 1984–87. **House of Commons:** Member for Barnsley Central since June 1987; Opposition Spokesman on: Health 1994–95, Local Government 1995, Northern Ireland 1995–97; Labour Whip 1991–94; *Select Committees:* Member: Procedure 1991–97; Chairman: Entry Clearance Sub-Committee 1997–98; Member: Foreign Affairs 1997–, Procedure 1997–. *Special Interests:* Trade Unions, Mining, Energy, Social Security, Glass Industry; Australia, France. Secretary, Barnsley Constituency Labour Party 1981–83, Treasurer 1980–81; Secretary and election agent, Yorkshire South European Labour Party 1984–86; Member, Mining Group of MPs 1987–97; Hon. Treasurer, Yorkshire Regional Group of Labour MP 1997–. Patron, Barnsley Alzheimer's Disease Society; Member, Executive Committee: IPU 1997–, Commonwealth Parliamentary Association (CPA) UK Branch 1997–; *Recreations:* Gymnasium. *Address:* Eric Illsley Esq, MP, House of Commons, London, SW1A 0AA *Tel:* 020 7219 3501 *Fax:* 020 7219 4863. *Constituency:* 18 Regent Street, Barnsley, S70 2HG *Tel:* 01226 730692 *Fax:* 01226 779429 *E-mail:* illsleye@parliament.uk.

ADAM INGRAM   East Kilbride   Lab majority 17,384

Born 1 February 1947; Son of Bert Ingram, fitter, and Louisa Ingram; Educated Cranhill Senior Secondary School; Married March 20, 1970, Maureen McMahon. Computer programmer/systems analyst 1967–77; Full-time trade union official 1977–87; Full-time union official, NALGO 1977–87; Member of Parliament supported by TGWU 1987–. District Councillor, East Kilbride 1980–87, Leader 1984–87; Member, COSLA Policy Committee 1984–87. **House of Commons:** Contested Strathkelvin and Bearsden 1983 general election. Member for East Kilbride since June 1987; Opposition Spokesman on: Social Security 1993–95 Trade and Industry 1995–97; Opposition Whip for Scottish Affairs and Treasury Matters 1988–89; PPS to Neil Kinnock as Leader of the Opposition 1988–92; Minister of State, Northern Ireland Office 1997–; *Select Committees:* Member: Trade and Industry 1992–93. *Special Interests:* Energy, Local Government, Aerospace. Chair, East Kilbride Constituency Labour Party 1981–85. PC 1999; *Recreations:* Fishing, cooking, reading. *Address:* Rt Hon Adam Ingram, MP, House of Commons, London, SW1A 0AA *Tel:* 020 7219 4093. *Constituency:* 17 Weaver Place, East Kilbride, Lanarkshire, G75 8SH *Tel:* 01355 235343 *Fax:* 01355 265252 *E-mail:* adam_ingram@compuserve.com.

J

MICHAEL JACK   Fylde   Con majority 8,963

Born 17 September 1946; Son of late Ralph Jack and Florence Edith Jack; Educated Bradford Grammar School; Bradford Technical College; Leicester University (BA economics, MPhil transport economics); Married December 1976, Alison Jane Musgrave (2 sons). Proctor and Gamble 1971–75; PA to Lord Rayner 1975–76; Marks and Spencer 1975–80; Director, L. O. Jeffs Ltd 1981–87. Member, Mersey Regional Health Authority 1984–87. **House of Commons:** Contested Newcastle Central February 1974. Member for Fylde since June 1987; Opposition Spokesman on Health June-November 1997; PA to James Prior, MP 1979 general election; PPS to John Gummer: as Minister for Local Government 1988–89, as Minister of Agriculture, Fisheries and Food 1989–90; Joint Parliamentary Under-Secretary of State for Social Security 1990–92; Minister of State at: Home Office 1992–93, Ministry of Agriculture, Fisheries and Food 1993–95; Financial Secretary, HM Treasury 1995–97; Member, Shadow Cabinet 1997–98; Shadow Minister of Agriculture, Fisheries and Food November 1997-August 1998; *Select Committees:* Member: Agriculture 1999–. *Special Interests:* Health, Nuclear Industry, Horticulture, Sheltered Housing, Aerospace, Transport, Agriculture; China, USA, Italy; Member, European Standing Committee C 1999–. National Chair, Young Conservatives 1976. Member, Eastern Electricity Consultative Council 1979; Member, Tax Law Rewrite Committee 1999–; Executive Member, 1922 Committee 2000–; PC 1997; Freeman, City of London; *Recreations:* Boule, motorsport, dinghy sailing, growing vegetables. *Address:* Rt Hon Michael Jack, MP, House of Commons, London, SW1A 0AA *Tel:* 020 7219 4454. *Constituency:* Fylde Conservative Association, 26 Hastings Place, Lytham *Tel:* 01253 796169 *Fax:* 01253 796170.

GLENDA JACKSON   Hampstead and Highgate   Lab majority 13,284

Born 9 May 1936; Daughter of Harry and Joan Jackson; Educated West Kirby County Grammar School for Girls; RADA; Married 1958, Roy Hodges (marriage dissolved 1976) (1 son). Actress: Plays include: *The Idiot* 1962, *Love's Labour's Lost*, *Hamlet* 1965, *Three Sisters* 1967, *Hedda Gabler* 1975; Films include: *Women in Love*, *Mary, Queen of Scots*, *A Touch of Class*; Television includes *Elizabeth R* 1971; Member, Royal Shakespeare Company 1963–67, 1979–80. Member, Greater London Assembly advisory cabinet for homelessness 2000–. **House of Commons:** Member for Hampstead and Highgate since April 9, 1992; Opposition Spokeswoman on Transport 1996–97; Parliamentary Under-Secretary of State, Department of the Environment, Transport and the Regions 1997–99; Resigned in July 1999 reshuffle; *Special Interests:* Overseas Aid and Development, Housing, Environment. Member: Anti-Apartheid Movement, Amnesty International, Has campaigned for: Oxfam, Shelter, Friends of the Earth; President, The National Toy Libraries Association; CBE 1978; Best film actress awards: Variety Clubs of Great Britain 1971, 1975, 1978, NY Film critics 1971, Oscar 1971, 1974; *Recreations:* Cooking, gardening, reading Jane Austen. *Address:* Glenda Jackson, CBE, MP, House of Commons, London, SW1A 0AA *Tel:* 020 7219 4008 *Fax:* 020 7219 2112.

HELEN JACKSON   Sheffield Hillsborough   Lab majority 16,451

Born 19 May 1939; Daughter of late Stanley Price, further education adviser, and late Katherine Price, health visitor; Educated Berkhamsted School for Girls; St Hilda's College, Oxford (BA modern history 1960, MA); C. F. Mott College of Education (Postgraduate teaching certificate 1972); Married 1960, Keith Jackson (marriage dissolved 1998) (2 sons 1 daughter). Assistant librarian, The Queen's College, Oxford 1960–61; Assistant teacher, City of Stoke-on-Trent 1961–62; Teacher: Lancashire Education Authority 1972–74, Sheffield Education Authority 1974–80. Councillor: Huyton Urban District Council 1973–74, Sheffield City Council 1980–91; Chairman: Public Works Committee 1981–83, Employment and Economic Development Committee 1983–91, Sheffield Economic Regeneration Committee 1987–91; Board Member: Sheffield Partnerships Ltd 1988–91, Sheffield Science Park 1988–91, Sheffield Development Corporation 1989–90; Founder Member and Chair, Centre for Local Economic Strategies. **House of Commons:** Member for Sheffield Hillsborough since April 9, 1992; PPS to Secretaries of State for Northern Ireland: Marjorie Mowlam 1997–99, Peter Mandelson 1999–; *Select Committees:* Member: Environment 1992–97; Member: Modernisation of the House of Commons 1997–. *Special Interests:* Environment, Women's Issues, Northern Ireland; Southern Africa. Member: Labour Party National Policy Forum 1998–, Labour Party National Executive Committee 1999–. Child Care; Voluntary work as playgroup organiser; School governor; Occasional research work for Liverpool Council Social Services 1962–70; UK representative to AWEPA 1997–; *Recreations:* Walking, music. *Address:* Helen Jackson, MP, House of Commons, London, SW1A 0AA *Tel:* 020 7219 4587 *Fax:* 020 7219 2442. *Constituency:* Hillsborough Library, Middlewood Road, Sheffield, S6 4HD *Tel:* 0114–232 2439 *Fax:* 0114–285 5808 *E-mail:* jacksonh@parliament.uk.

ROBERT JACKSON   Wantage   Con majority 6,089

Born 24 September 1946; Son of late Maurice Henry Jackson; Educated Falcon College, Rhodesia; St Edmund Hall, Oxford; All Souls College, Oxford (MA) (President, Oxford Union 1967); Married 1975, Caroline Frances Harvey (MEP 1994–) (1 son deceased). MEP for Upper Thames 1979–83. Councillor, Oxford City Council 1969–71. **House of Commons:** Contested Manchester Central October 1974 general election. Member for Wantage since June 1983; Political adviser: to Willie Whitelaw as Secretary of State for Employment 1973–74, to Sir Christopher Soames as EC Commissioner 1974–76; Chef de Cabinet to Basil De Ferranti, as President of EEC Economic and Social Committee 1976–78; Special Adviser to Lord Soames as Governor of Rhodesia 1980; Parliamentary Under-Secretary of State: at Department of Education and Science 1987–90, at Department of Employment 1990–92; Parliamentary Secretary, Office of Public Service and Science 1992–93;

Select Committees: Member: Science and Technology 1999–. *Special Interests:* European Union, Agriculture, Science, Foreign Affairs. Treasurer, Conservative Parliamentary Mainstream Group 2000–. EP Rapporteur on EEC Budget 1983; Member, UK Delegation Parliamentary Assembly of the Council of Europe and Assembly of Western European Union 2000–; *Publications: The Round Table: The Commonwealth Journal of International Affairs,* 1970–74; *South Asian Crisis, Pakistan, Bangladesh,* 1974; *The European Parliament: a Guide for Direct Elections,* 1978; Editor: *International Affairs,* 1979–80; Fellow, All Souls College, Oxford 1968–75; *Recreations:* Walking, gardening, singing. *Address:* Robert Jackson Esq, MP, House of Commons, London, SW1A 0AA *Tel:* 020 7219 4557 *Fax:* 020 7219 0480. *Constituency:* Orchard House, Portway, Wantage, Oxfordshire, OX13 5HR *Tel:* 01235 769090 *Fax:* 01235 224833 *E-mail:* jacksonr@parliament.uk.

DAVID JAMIESON   Plymouth Devonport   Lab majority 19,067

Born 18 May 1947; Son of late Frank Jamieson, engineer, and of Eileen Jamieson; Educated Tudor Grange Grammar School, Solihull; St Peter's College, Birmingham; Open University (BA social science and education management); Married December 11, 1971, Patricia Hofton (2 sons 1 daughter). Assistant teacher, mathematics, Riland-Bedford School, Sutton Coldfield 1970–76; Head of mathematics, Crown Hills Community College, Leicester 1976–81; Senior vice-principal, The John Kitto Community College, Plymouth 1981–92. Solihull Borough Council: Councillor 1970–74, Vice-Chairman, Housing Committee 1973–74. **House of Commons:** Contested Birmingham Hall Green February 1974 and Plymouth Drake 1987 general elections. Member for Plymouth Devonport since April 9, 1992; Assistant Government Whip 1997–98; Government Whip (Lord Commissioner of HM Treasury) (Health: South East and South West) 1998–; Promoted as Private Member's Bill: Activity Centres (Young Persons' Safety) Act 1995; *Select Committees:* Member: Education 1992–96, Education and Employment 1996–97; Member: Accommodation and Works 1998–. *Special Interests:* Education. *Recreations:* Music, classic cars, gardening. *Address:* David Jamieson Esq, MP, House of Commons, London, SW1A 0AA *Tel:* 020 7219 6252 *Fax:* 020 7219 2388 *Tel (Constituency):* 01752 704677 *Fax (Constituency):* 01752 704677 *E-mail:* williamsde@parliament.uk.

BERNARD JENKIN   North Essex   Con majority 5,476

Born 9 April 1959; Son of Rt Hon. Baron Jenkin of Roding (*qv*); Educated Highgate School; William Ellis School; Corpus Christi College, Cambridge (BA English literature 1982) (President, Cambridge Union Society 1982); Married 1988, Anne Strutt (2 sons). Previously employed by: Ford Motor Co Ltd and 3i plc; Manager, Legal and General Ventures Ltd 1989–92; Adviser, Legal and General Group plc 1992–95. Chairman, Matching Parish Council 1985–87. **House of Commons:** Contested Glasgow Central 1987 general election. Member for North Colchester 1992–97, and for North Essex since May 1, 1997; Opposition Spokesman for: Constitutional Affairs, Scotland and Wales 1997–98, Environment, Transport and the Regions (Roads and Environment) 1998; Political Adviser to Leon Brittan MP 1986–88; PPS to Michael Forsyth as Secretary of State for Scotland 1995–97; Shadow Minister for Transport 1998–; Member, Shadow Cabinet 1999–; *Select Committees:* Member: Social Security 1993–97. *Special Interests:* Economic Policy, Trade, European Union, Defence, Foreign Affairs; USA, New Zealand, Singapore, Chile, France, Germany; Member, European Standing Committee B 1992–97. Governor, Central Foundation Girls' School ILEA 1985–89; Governor, London Goodenough Trust for Overseas Graduates 1992–; *Publications:* Co-author *Who Benefits: Reinventing Social Security,* 1993; *A Conservative Europe: 1994 and beyond,* 1994; *Fairer Business Rates,* 1996; *Clubs:* Colchester Conservative; *Recreations:* Sailing, music (especially opera), fishing, family, DIY. *Address:* Hon. Bernard Jenkin, MP, House of Commons, London, SW1A 0AA *Tel:* 020 7219 4029 *Fax:* 020 7219 5963. *Constituency:* North Essex Conservative Association, 167B London Road, Stanway, Colchester, Essex, CO3 5PB *Tel:* 01206 717900 *Fax:* 01206 717909 *E-mail:* jenkinb@parliament.uk.

BRIAN JENKINS   Tamworth   *Lab majority 7,496*

Born 19 September 1942; Son of late Hiram and Gladys Jenkins; Educated Kingsbury High School, Tamworth; Coventry College; Coleg Harlech; London School of Economics (BSc econ); Wolverhampton Polytechnic (PGCE); Married October 12, 1963, Joan Dix (1 son 1 daughter). Instrument mechanic, CEGB 1961–68; Industrial engineer, Jaguar Cars 1968–73; Percy Lane 1973–75; Student 1975–81; College lecturer: Isle of Man College 1981–83, Tamworth College 1983–96. Councillor, Tamworth Borough Council, Mayor 1993–94. **House of Commons:** Contested South East Staffordshire 1992 general election. Member for South East Staffordshire by-election April 11, 1996–97, and for Tamworth since May 1, 1997; PPS: to Joyce Quin, as Minister of State, Home Office (Minister for Prisons, Probation and Europe) 1997–98, to Joyce Quin, Derek Fatchett and Tony Lloyd as Ministers of State, Foreign and Commonwealth Office 1998–99, to Joyce Quin, Geoff Hoon and Tony Lloyd as Ministers of State, Foreign and Commonwealth Office 1999, to Joyce Quin, as Minister of State and Deputy Minister, Ministry of Agriculture, Fisheries and Food 1999–; *Select Committees:* Member: Unopposed Bills (Panel) 1997–, Standing Orders 1998–. *Special Interests:* Trade and Industry, Training, Housing; Europe, North America. School governor; *Clubs:* Tamworth Royal British Legion; *Recreations:* Music, reading, watching sport. *Address:* Brian Jenkins Esq, MP, House of Commons, London, SW1A 0AA *Tel:* 020 7219 3000. *Constituency:* 11 Albert Road, Tamworth, Staffordshire, B79 7JN *Tel:* 01827 311957 *Fax:* 01827 311958.

ALAN JOHNSON   Hull West and Hessle   *Lab majority 15,525*

Born 17 May 1950; Son of Stephen Arthur and late Lillian May Johnson; Educated Sloane Grammar School, Chelsea; Married 1st, 1968, Judith Cox (divorced) (1 son 2 daughters); married 2nd, August 3, 1991, Laura Jane Patient (1 son). Postman 1968; Local Officer, Slough UCW 1974–81; Union of Communication Workers: Branch Official 1976, Executive Council 1981–, National Officer 1987–93, General Secretary 1993–95; Member, General Council, TUC 1993–95; Executive Member, Postal, Telegraph and Telephone International 1993–97; Director, Unity Bank Trust plc 1993–97; Joint General Secretary, Communication Workers Union 1995–97; Member, CWU. **House of Commons:** Member for Hull West and Hessle since May 1, 1997; PPS to Dawn Primarolo: as Financial Secretary, HM Treasury 1997–99, as Paymaster General, HM Treasury 1999; Parliamentary Under-Secretary of State, Department of Trade and Industry (Competitiveness) 1999–; *Select Committees:* Member: Trade and Industry 1997–98. *Special Interests:* Education, Electoral Reform, Employment Law, Post Office. Member: Eton and Slough Labour Party GMC 1976–87, Southern Regional Executive of Labour Party 1981–87, Member, Labour Party National Executive Committee 1995–97, Labour Campaign for Electoral Reform. Governor, Ruskin College; Member, World Executive, Postal, Telegraph and Telephone International (PTTI) 1993–97; *Recreations:* Tennis, cooking, reading, Radio 4, music. *Address:* Alan Johnson Esq, MP, House of Commons, London, SW1A 0AA *Tel:* 020 7219 5227 *Fax:* 020 7219 5856. *Constituency:* Goodwin Resource Centre, Icehouse Road, Hull, HU3 2HQ *Tel:* 01482 219691 *Fax:* 01482 219691 *E-mail:* eked@parliament.uk; tlo.johnson@tlo.dti.gov.uk.

MELANIE JOHNSON Welwyn Hatfield — *Lab majority 5,595*

Born 5 February 1955; Daughter of David Johnson, retired civil engineer, and Angela Johnson, retired pharmacist; Educated Clifton High School, Bristol; University College, London (BA philosophy and ancient Greek 1976); King's College, Cambridge (Postgraduate research); Partner, William Jordan (twin daughters 1 son). Member relations officer, Cambridge Co-op 1981–88; Retail administration manager, Cambridge Co-op 1988–90; Assistant general manager, quality assurance, Cambridge FHSA 1990–92; Schools inspector, OFSTED 1993–97; Member, UNISON. Councillor, Cambridgeshire County Council 1981–97; JP 1994–; Contested Cambridgeshire 1994 European Parliament election. **House of Commons:** Member for Welwyn Hatfield since May 1, 1997; HM Treasury: PPS to Barbara Roche as Financial Secretary 1999, Economic Secretary 1999–; *Select Committees:* Member: Public Administration 1997–98, Home Affairs 1998–99. *Special Interests:* Business, Employment, Education, Health, Child Protection and Safety. Vice-Chair, Eastern Regional Group of Labour MPs 1999. School governor; *Recreations:* Family, gardening, a wide range of classical and rock music, films. *Address:* Miss Melanie Johnson, MP, House of Commons, London, SW1A 0AA *Tel:* 020 7219 4119 *Fax:* 020 7219 0942. *Constituency:* 2 Queensway House, Hatfield, Herts, AL10 0LW *Tel:* 01707 262920 *Fax:* 01707 262834 *E-mail:* melaniej@netcomuk.co.uk.

SIR GEOFFREY JOHNSON SMITH Wealden — *Con majority 14,204*

Born 16 April 1924; Son of late J. Johnson Smith; Educated Charterhouse; Lincoln College, Oxford (BA philosophy, politics and economics 1949); Married July 21, 1951, Jeanne Pomeroy (2 sons 1 daughter). Army Service 1942–47, Captain, RA; Information officer, British Consulate-General, San Francisco 1950–52; Member, production staff, Talks Department, BBC TV 1953–54; Interviewer-reporter, BBC TV 1954–59. LCC Councillor, Putney 1955–58; DL, East Sussex 1986. **House of Commons:** Member for Holborn and St Pancras South 1959–64, for East Grinstead 1965–83 and for Wealden since June 1983; Opposition Whip February-July 1965; PPS: to John Rodgers as Parliamentary Secretary, Board of Trade 1960–62, to Niall Macpherson as Minister of Pensions 1962–63; Under-Secretary of State for Defence (Army) 1971–72; Parliamentary Secretary, Civil Service Department 1972–74; *Select Committees:* Chairman: House of Commons Members' Interests 1980–95; Member: Liaison 1992–96, Standards and Privileges 1994–96. *Special Interests:* Defence, Media, Agriculture, Health; USA. Vice-Chair, Conservative Party 1965–71. Member, IBA General Advisory Council 1976–80; Patron, Wealden Mencap 1980–; Executive Member, 1922 Committee 1979–88, Joint Vice-Chairman 1988–; UK Delegate, North Atlantic Assembly 1980–; Chair, Military Committee, North Atlantic Assembly 1985–89; Leader, UK Delegation 1987–97, Treasurer 1996–; Representative, UK Delegation to Organisation for Security and Co-operation in Europe 1992–; Member: Thames Salmon Trust 1988–, Salmon and Trout Trust 1996–; Trustee, Handicapped Anglers Trust; President, London Youth Trust; Knighted 1982; PC 1996; FRSA; Freeman, City of London 1980; *Clubs:* Travellers'; *Recreations:* Angling, visiting country houses and gardens. *Address:* Rt Hon Sir Geoffrey Johnson Smith, DL, MP, House of Commons, London, SW1A 0AA *Tel:* 020 7219 4158 *Fax:* 020 7219 5333.

BARRY JONES Alyn and Deeside — *Lab majority 16,403*

Born 26 June 1937; Son of late Stephen Jones, steelworker, and late Grace Jones; Educated Hawarden Grammar School; University College of North Wales, Bangor; Married Janet Davies (1 son). Head of English department, Deeside Secondary School, Flintshire; Regional officer, National Union of Teachers. **House of Commons:** Contested Northwich, Cheshire 1966 general election; member for East Flint 1970–83, and for Alyn and Deeside since June 1983; Opposition Front Bench Spokesman on Employment 1980–83; PPS to Denis Healey 1972–74; Parliamentary Under-Secretary of State for Wales 1974–79; Member, Shadow Cabinet 1983–92; *Select Committees:* Member: Chairmen's Panel 1993–. *Special Interests:* Unemployment, Regional Policy, Education; Germany, France. Former Member, Executive of Labour Party, Wales. Governor: National Museum of Wales, National Library of Wales; Life Member, Liverpool Royal Philharmonic Society;

Friend of: The Royal Academy, The Tate Gallery, National Trust, Museums and Galleries of Merseyside; Member, Prime Minister's Intelligence and Security Committee 1994–97, 1997–; Vice-President, Federation of Economic Development Authorities; Member, Delegation of Council of Europe and Western European Union 1971–74; PC 1999; *Recreations:* Soccer, cricket, tennis. *Address:* Rt Hon Barry Jones, MP, House of Commons, London, SW1A 0AA *Tel:* 020 7219 3000 *Fax:* 020 7219 4027. *Constituency:* 6 Cross Tree Close, Hawarden, Deeside, Clwyd, CH5 3PX *Tel:* 01244 543373 *Fax:* 01244 543373.

FIONA JONES   Newark   *Lab majority 3,016*

Born 27 February 1957; Daughter of late Frederick and Alicia Hamilton; Educated Mary Help of Christians Convent, Liverpool and North London; (Degree course in Media and Communications); Married 1982, Chris Jones (2 sons). Journalism; Member, NUJ: Chair, Lincolnshire Branch 1990. Councillor, West Lindsey 1990–94. **House of Commons:** Member for Newark since May 1, 1997. Disqualified after conviction for election fraud March 1999. Reinstated after conviction quashed April 1999; *Select Committees:* Member: Agriculture 1999–2000. *Special Interests:* Employment, Crime, Health; Cyprus, Isle of Man. *Address:* Fiona Jones, MP, House of Commons, London, SW1A 0AA *Tel:* 020 7219 3445. *Constituency:* 25 Castlegate, Newark, Notts *Tel:* 01636 605530 *Fax:* 01636 612150 *E-mail:* jones@newlab.u-net.com *Website:* www.newlab.u-net.com.

HELEN JONES   Warrington North   *Lab majority 19,527*

Born 24 December 1954; Daughter of late Robert Edward Jones and of Mary Scanlan; Educated St Werburgh's Primary School; Ursuline Convent, Chester; University College, London (BA); Chester College; Liverpool University (MEd); Manchester Metropolitan University; Married July 23, 1988, Michael Vobe (1 son). Teacher of English; Development officer, MIND; Justice and peace officer, Liverpool Archdiocese; Solicitor; MSF: Labour Party Liaison Officer, North West Coast Region, Former Member: National Women's Committee, National Appeals Panel. Councillor, Chester City Council 1984–91; Contested Lancashire Central 1984 European Parliament election. **House of Commons:** Contested Shropshire North 1983 general election, Ellesmere Port and Neston 1987 general election. Member for Warrington North since May 1, 1997; *Select Committees:* Member: Catering 1997–98, Public Administration 1998–2000; Member: Education and Employment 1999–, Education Sub-Committee 1999–, Standing Orders 1999–, Unopposed Bills (Panel) 1999–.*Special Interests:* Education. *Recreations:* Gardening, reading, cooking. *Address:* Helen Jones, MP, House of Commons, London, SW1A 0AA *Tel:* 020 7219 4048. *Constituency:* Gilbert Wakefield House, 67 Bewsey Street, Warrington, WA2 7JQ *Tel:* 01925 232480 *Fax:* 01925 232239 *E-mail:* jonesh@parliament.uk.

IEUAN WYN JONES   Ynys Môn   *PC majority 2,481*

Born 22 May 1949; Educated Pontardawe Grammar School, Glamorgan; Bala Comprehensive, Meirionnydd; Liverpool Polytechnic; London University (LLB 1970); Married August 17, 1974, Eirian Llwyd (2 sons 1 daughter). Qualified as Solicitor 1973 Partner in Solicitors' firm 1974–87. Contested North Wales 1979 European Parliament election. **House of Commons:** Contested West Denbigh October 1974 and 1979 general elections, Ynys Môn 1983 general election. Member for Ynys Môn since June 1987; Spokesman for: Agriculture 1987–, Health 1987–2000, Europe, Housing, Home Affairs, Local Government, Tourism, Northern Ireland 1987–97, Foreign Affairs, Defence 1997–2000; Plaid Cymru Whip 1991–95; Sponsored Hearing Aid Council (Amendment) Act 1989 (Private Member's Bill); *Select Committees:* Member: Welsh Affairs 1989–98, Agriculture 1992–97. **National Assembly for Wales:** AM for Ynys Môn constituency since May 6, 1999; Shadow First Secretary and Shadow Secretary for Finance 2000–. *Special Interests:* Agriculture, Transport, Elderly, Education and Industry Links, European Union; Scandinavia. Plaid Cymru: National Vice-Chair 1975–79, National Chair 1980–82, 1990–92, President 2000–. President, North Wales Relate; Member, Industry and Parliament Trust; *Publications: Europe: The Challenge Facing Wales,* 1996; *Biography of Thomas Gee,* 1998; *Recreations:* Sport, walking, reading. *Address:* Ieuan Wyn Jones Esq, MP, AM, House of Commons, London, SW1A 0AA *Tel:* 020 7219 3439 *Fax:* 020 7219 3705. *Constituency:* 45 Stryd-y-Bont, Llangefni, Ynys Môn, LL77 7PN *Tel:* 01248 723599 *Fax:* 01248 722868.

JENNY JONES   Wolverhampton South West   *Lab majority 5,118*

Born 8 February 1948; Educated Bradford University (BA); Birmingham University (MSocSci); Wolverhampton University (CITD). Social worker; Business adviser/Training manager; Member, MSF. **House of Commons:** Member for Wolverhampton South West since May 1, 1997; *Select Committees:* Member: European Legislation 1997–98; Member: European Scrutiny 1998–. *Special Interests:* Economic Development, Environment, Human Rights. Constituency Labour Party: Membership Secretary, Secretary, Vice-Chair, Chair. Member, UK Delegation to Council of Europe and Western European Union 1997–; *Recreations:* Swimming, gardening, keeping cats, craftwork. *Address:* Jenny Jones, MP, House of Commons, London, SW1A 0AA *Tel:* 020 7219 4105 *Fax:* 020 7219 4105. *Constituency:* 57 Victoria Street, Wolverhampton, West Midlands, WV1 3NX *Tel:* 01902 714911 *Fax:* 01902 712580.

JON OWEN JONES   Cardiff Central   *Lab/Co-op majority 7,923*

Born 19 April 1954; Son of Gwynfor Owen Jones, retired optical salesman and former miner, and Dorothy Jones, retired teacher; Educated Ysgol Gyfun Rhydfelin; University of East Anglia (BSc 1975); University College of Wales, Cardiff (PGCE 1976); Married February 11, 1989, Allison Mary Clement (2 sons 1 daughter). Teacher of biology and science in comprehensive schools 1977–92; President: Caerphilly NUT 1983, Mid Glamorgan NUT 1984. Cardiff City Council: Councillor 1987–92, Vice-Chair, Finance Committee 1987–91, Chair, Economic Development Committee 1990–92. **House of Commons:** Contested Cardiff Central in 1987 general election. Member for Cardiff Central since April 9, 1992; Opposition Welsh/Agricultural Whip 1993–97; Transport Whip 1994–97; Government Whip 1997–98; Parliamentary Under-Secretary of State, Welsh Office 1998–99; *Select Committees:* Member: Welsh Affairs 1992–93; Chairman: Information 1997–98; Member: Information 1998; Member: Environmental Audit 1999–. *Special Interests:* Environment, Wales, Education. Secretary, Cardiff Central Labour Party 1984–85; Member, Co-operative Party. Chair, Campaign for Welsh Assembly 1988–91; *Clubs:* Roath Labour; *Recreations:* Walking, cooking, natural history, watching rugby, family, golf. *Address:* Jon Owen Jones Esq, MP, House of Commons, London, SW1A 0AA *Tel:* 020 7219 4531 *Fax:* 020 7219 2698. *Constituency:* 50A Crwys Road, Cathays, Cardiff, CF24 4NN *Tel:* 029 2063 5811 *Fax:* 029 2063 5814 *E-mail:* jon@jonowen99.freeserve.co.uk.

DR LYNNE JONES   Birmingham Selly Oak   *Lab majority 14,088*

Born 26 April 1951; Daughter of late Stanley Stockton and of Jean Stockton; Educated Birmingham University (BSc, PhD); (2 sons). Research fellow, Birmingham University 1972–86; Housing association manager 1987–92; Member, MSF. Birmingham City Councillor 1980–94, Chair, Housing Committee 1984–87. **House of Commons:** Member for Birmingham Selly Oak since April 9, 1992; *Select Committees:* Member: Science and Technology 1992–97; Member: Science and Technology 1997–. *Special Interests:* Economic Policy, Science, Social Security, Housing. Member: Liberty, Greenpeace, CND; *Recreations:* Family. *Address:* Dr Lynne Jones, MP, House of Commons, London, SW1A 0AA *Tel:* 020 7219 3000 *Fax:* 020 7219 3870 *Tel (Constituency):* 0121–486 2808 *Fax (Constituency):* 0121–486 2808 *E-mail:* jonesl@parliament.uk.

MARTYN JONES   Clwyd South   *Lab majority 13,810*

Born 1 March 1947; Son of Vernon, engine driver, and Violet Jones; Educated Grove Park Grammar School, Wrexham; Liverpool College of Commerce; Liverpool Polytechnic (CIBiol); Trent Polytechnic (MIBiol); Married January 5, 1974, Rhona Bellis (marriage dissolved 1991) (1 son 1 daughter). Microbiologist, Wrexham Lager Beer Co. 1969-June 1987; Member, TGWU 1974–; Vice-Chair, TGWU Parliamentary Group 2000–01. Councillor, Clwyd County Council 1981–89. **House of Commons:** Member for Clwyd South West 1987–97, and for Clwyd South since May 1, 1997; Opposition Front Bench Spokesman on Food, Agricultural and Rural Affairs 1994–95; Labour Whip 1988–92; *Select Committees:* Member: Agriculture 1988–94, Speaker's Panel of Chairmen 1993–94, Agriculture 1996–97; Member: Liaison 1997–; Chairman: Welsh Affairs 1997–. *Special Interests:* Science, Ecology, Agriculture; Spain, USA, Wales. Chair, Clwyd County Party 1979–81; Member: Christian Socialist Movement, Socialist Environment and Resources Association, Fabian Society. Member, SERA; Council Member: Royal College of Veterinary Surgeons, National Rifle Association; Vice-President, Federation of Economic Development Authorities (FEDA); *Recreations:* Backpacking, first aid, target shooting. *Address:* Martyn Jones Esq, MP, House of Commons, London, SW1A 0AA *Tel:* 020 7219 3417 *Fax:* 020 7219 6090. *Constituency:* Foundry Buildings, Gutter Hill, Johnstown, Wrexham, LL14 1LU *Tel:* 01978 845938 *Fax:* 01978 843392.

NIGEL JONES   Cheltenham   *LD majority 6,645*

Born 30 March 1948; Son of late A. J. Jones, and of Nora Jones; Educated Prince Henry's Grammar School, Evesham; Married May 21, 1981, Katy Grinnell (1 son twin daughters). Clerk; Computer operator, Westminster Bank 1965–67; Computer programmer, ICL Computers 1967–70; Systems analyst, Vehicle and General Insurance 1970–71; Systems programmer, Atkins Computing 1971; Systems designer; Consultant; Project manager, ICL Computers 1971–92. Councillor, Gloucestershire County Council 1989–93. **House of Commons:** Contested Cheltenham 1979 general election. Member for Cheltenham since April 9, 1992; Liberal Democrat Spokesman for: England, Local Government and Housing 1992–93, Science and Technology 1993–, Consumer Affairs 1995–97, National Heritage, Constitution and Civil Service (Sport) 1997, Culture, Media, Sport, and Civil Service (Sport) 1997–99, Trade and Industry (Science and Technology) 1997–99, International Development 1999–; *Select Committees:* Member: Broadcasting 1994–97, Standards and Privileges 1995–97, Science and Technology 1997–2000; Member: International Development 1999–. *Special Interests:* Trade and Industry, Transport, Restructuring of Defence Industries, Information Technology, Sport, International Development; Middle East, Africa. Member, Executive Committee: Inter-Parliamentary Union British Group 1997–, Commonwealth Parliamentary Association UK Branch 1999–, Governing Body British Association for Central and Eastern Europe 1996–; *Clubs:* National Liberal; *Sportsclubs:* Gloucestershire County Cricket Club, Cheltenham Town FC Season Ticket Holder; *Recreations:* Watching Swindon Town and Cheltenham Town Football Club, playing cricket, gardening. *Address:* Nigel Jones Esq, MP, House of Commons, London, SW1A 0AA *Tel:* 020 7219 4415 *Fax:* 020 7219 2537. *Constituency:* 16 Hewlett Road, Cheltenham, Gloucestershire, GL52 6AA *Tel:* 01242 224889 *Fax:* 01242 256658 *E-mail:* nigeljonesmp@cix.co.uk.

TESSA JOWELL   Dulwich and West Norwood   *Lab majority 16,769*

Born 17 September 1947; Daughter of Dr. Kenneth Palmer, and of Rosemary Palmer, radiographer; Educated St Margaret's School, Aberdeen; Aberdeen (MA), Edinburgh University; Goldsmith's College, London University; Married 1st, 1970, Roger Jowell (marriage dissolved 1977), married 2nd, March 17, 1979, David Mills (1 son 1 daughter, 3 stepchildren). Child care officer, London Borough of Lambeth 1969–71; Psychiatric social worker, Maudsley Hospital 1972–74; Assistant director, MIND 1974–86; Director: Community care special action project, Birmingham 1987–90, Joseph Rowntree Foundation, Community Care Programme 1990–92; Senior visiting research fellow: Policy Studies Institute 1987–90, King's Fund Institute 1990–92.

Councillor, London Borough of Camden 1971–86; Vice-Chair, then Chair, Social Services Committee of Association of Metropolitan Authorities 1978–86; Mental Health Act Commission 1985–90.**House of Commons:** Contested Ilford North 1978 by-election and 1979 general election. Member for Dulwich 1992–97, and for Dulwich and West Norwood since May 1, 1997; Frontbench Opposition Spokesperson on: Women 1995–96, Health 1994–95, 1996–97; Opposition Whip 1994–95; Minister of State: Department of Health (Minister for Public Health) 1997–99, Department for Education and Employment (Minister for Employment, Welfare to Work and Equal Opportunities) 1999–; *Select Committees:* Member: Health 1992–94. *Special Interests:* Community Care, Human Rights, Constitutional Reform. Governor, National Institute for Social Work 1985–97; Member: Central Council for Training and Education in Social Work 1983–89; PC 1998; Visiting Fellow, Nuffield College, Oxford.*Address:* Rt Hon Tessa Jowell, MP, House of Commons, London, SW1A 0AA *Tel:* 020 7219 3409 *Fax:* 020 7219 2702 *E-mail:* jowellt@parliament.uk.

K

GERALD KAUFMAN   Manchester Gorton   *Lab majority 17,342*

Born 21 June 1930; Son of Louis Kaufman; Educated Leeds Council Schools; Leeds Grammar School; The Queen's College, Oxford (MA). Assistant general secretary, Fabian Society 1954–55; Political staff, *Daily Mirror* 1955–64; Political correspondent, *New Statesman* 1964–65; Parliamentary press liaison officer, Labour Party 1965–70; Member, GMB. **House of Commons:** Contested Bromley 1955 and Gillingham 1959 general elections. Member for Ardwick 1970–1983, and for Manchester Gorton since 1983; Opposition Front Bench Spokesman on the Environment 1979–80; Parliamentary Under-Secretary of State for the Environment 1974–75; Parliamentary Under-Secretary, Department of Industry 1975; Minister of State, Department of Industry 1975–79; Shadow Environment Secretary 1980–83; Shadow Home Secretary 1983–87; Shadow Foreign Secretary 1987–92; *Select Committees:* Member: Liaison 1992–97; Chairman: National Heritage 1992–97; Chairman: Culture, Media and Sport 1997–; Member: Liaison 1997–. Member: Labour Party National Executive 1991–92, Fabian Society. Member, Poale Zion; Member, Royal Commission on Lords Reform February 1999–; *Publications: To Build the Promised Land; How to Be a Minister; Inside the Promised Land; My Life in the Silver Screen; How to Be a Minister* (updated and revised edition); Co-author, *How to Live Under Labour;* Editor: *The Left; Renewal;* PC 1978; Hilal-i-Pakistan 1999; *Sportsclubs:* Member, East Levenshulme Cricket Club; *Recreations:* Cinema, theatre, opera, concerts, travel. *Address:* Rt Hon Gerald Kaufman, MP, House of Commons, London, SW1A 0AA *Tel:* 020 7219 5145 *Fax:* 020 7219 6825 *Tel (Constituency):* 0161–248 0073 *Fax (Constituency):* 0161–248 0073.

SALLY KEEBLE   Northampton North   *Lab majority 10,000*

Born 13 October 1951; Daughter of Sir Curtis Keeble, GCMG, and Lady Keeble; Educated Cheltenham Ladies' College; St Hugh's College, Oxford (BA theology 1973); University of South Africa (BA sociology 1981); Married June 9, 1990, Andrew Hilary Porter (1 son 1 daughter). Journalist: *Daily News,* Durban, South Africa 1973–79, *Birmingham Post* 1978–83; Press officer, Labour Headquarters 1983–84; Assistant director, External Relations, ILEA 1984–86; Head of communications, GMB 1986–90; Public affairs consultant 1995–97; Member: National Union of Journalists, GMB. Councillor, Southwark Council 1986–94, Leader 1990–93. **House of Commons:** Member for Northampton North since May 1, 1997; PPS to Hilary Armstrong as Minister of State, Department of the Environment, Transport and the Regions (Minister for Local Government and Regions) 1999–; *Select Committees:* Member: Agriculture 1997–99. *Special Interests:* Economic Policy, Home Affairs, Education, Local Government, Financial Services; North Africa, South Africa, USA. Chair, Northampton Rail Users' Group; Hon. Secretary, Friends of the Lakes;

Publications: Citizens Look At Congress Profiles, 1971; *Flat Broke,* 1984; *Collectors Corner,* 1986; *Feminism, Infertility and New Reproductive Technologies,* 1994; *Conceiving Your Baby, How Medicine Can Help,* 1995; Honorary Fellow, South Bank University; *Recreations:* Antiques, walking, writing. *Address:* Sally Keeble, MP, House of Commons, London, SW1A 0AA *Tel:* 020 7219 4039 *Fax:* 020 7219 2642. *Constituency:* Unit 5, Barratt Building, Kingsthorpe Road, Northampton, NN2 6EZ *Tel:* 01604 27803 *Fax:* 01604 27805 *E-mail:* keebles@parliament.uk.

ALAN KEEN   Feltham and Heston   *Lab/Co-op majority 15,273*

Born 25 November 1937; Son of late Jack and Gladys Keen; Educated St William Turner's School, Redcar, Cleveland; Married June 1980, Ann Fox (qv as Ann Keen MP) (2 sons 1 daughter). Part-time tactical scout (assessing opposition tactics) Middlesbrough FC; Miscellaneous positions in private industry and commerce, mainly in the fire protection industry; Systems analyst; Accountant and manager 1963–92; Member, GMB. Councillor, London Borough of Hounslow 1986–90. **House of Commons:** Member for Feltham and Heston since April 9, 1992; *Select Committees:* Member: Deregulation 1995–96, Education 1995–96; Member: Culture, Media and Sport 1997–. *Special Interests:* Commerce, Industry, Foreign Affairs, Development, Democracy, Defence, Sport, Culture. Co-operative Party MP; Secretary, Labour First Past the Post Group. *Clubs:* Feltham Labour, Heston Catholic Social, Hanworth British Legion; *Sportsclubs:* Secretary, Lords and Commons Cricket; *Recreations:* Playing and listening to music, Association football, athletics. *Address:* Alan Keen Esq, MP, House of Commons, London, SW1A 0AA *Tel:* 020 7219 2819 *Fax:* 020 7219 2233. *Constituency:* Labour Party, Manor Place, Feltham, Middlesex, TW14 9BT *Tel:* 020 8890 4489 *Fax:* 020 8893 2606.

ANN KEEN   Brentford and Isleworth   *Lab majority 14,424*

Born 26 November 1948; Daughter of late John Fox, and of Ruby Fox; Educated Elfed Secondary Modern, Clwyd; Surrey University (PGCEA); Married June 1980, Alan Keen (now MP – qv) (2 sons 1 daughter). Registered Nurse; Former Head, Faculty of Advanced Nursing, Queen Charlotte's College, Hammersmith; General Secretary, Community and District Nursing Association; Member, GMB. **House of Commons:** Contested Brentford and Isleworth 1987 and 1992 general elections. Member for Brentford and Isleworth since May 1, 1997; PPS to Frank Dobson as Secretary of State for Health 1999; *Select Committees:* Member: Health 1997–99. *Special Interests:* Health; South Africa, Cyprus. Hon. Professor of Nursing, Thames Valley University; *Clubs:* Ewloe Social and Working Men's; *Sportsclubs:* Nurse/Physiotherapist, the House of Commons' Football Team; *Recreations:* Theatre, music, football, vegetarian cookery. *Address:* Mrs Ann Keen, MP, House of Commons, London, SW1A 0AA *Tel:* 020 7219 2819. *Constituency:* Brentford and Isleworth Labour Party, 367 Chiswick High Road, London, W4 4AG *Tel:* 020 8995 7289 *Fax:* 020 8742 1004.

PAUL KEETCH   Hereford   *LD majority 6,648*

Born 21 May 1961; Son of late John Norton, engineer, and late Agnes (née Hughes); Educated Hereford High School for Boys; Hereford Sixth Form College; Married December 21, 1991, Claire Elizabeth Baker (1 son). Self-employed business consultant 1979–95; Non-executive director, London Computer Company 1996–. Councillor, Hereford City Council 1983–86. **House of Commons:** Member for Hereford since May 1, 1997; Spokesman for: Health 1997, Education and Employment (Employment and Training) 1997–99, Defence 1999–; *Select Committees:* Member: Education and Employment 1997–99, Education 1997–99, Employment Sub-Committee 1997–99, Catering 1998–99; Member: Environmental Audit 2000–. *Special Interests:* National Heritage, Defence, Foreign Affairs; Former Soviet Union, Eastern Bloc countries, Eastern Europe.

Joined Liberal Party 1975. Member: National Development Board, British Dyslexia Association 1993–; OSCE Observer, Albanian Elections 1996; Adviser, Lithuanian Local and National Elections 1995, 1996; Member, Council of The Electoral Reform Society; *Clubs:* Hereford Liberal, Herefordshire Farmers', National Liberal; *Sportsclubs:* Herefordshire County Cricket Club; *Recreations:* Cricket (watching), swimming, entertaining friends at home, country walks with my wife and son.*Address:* Paul Keetch Esq, MP, House of Commons, London, SW1A 0AA *Tel:* 020 7219 5163 *Fax:* 020 7219 1184. *Constituency:* 39 Widemarsh Street, Hereford, HR4 9EA *Tel:* 01432 341483 *Fax:* 01432 378111 *E-mail:* paulkeetch@cix.co.uk.

RUTH KELLY   Bolton West   *Lab majority 7,072*

Born 9 May 1968; Daughter of Bernard James Kelly, pharmacist, and Gertrude Anne Kelly, teacher; Educated Sutton High School; Westminster School; Queen's College, Oxford (BA philosophy, politics and economics 1989); London School of Economics (MSc economics 1992); Married June 1, 1996, Derek John Gadd (1 son 1 daughter). Economics writer, *The Guardian* 1990–94; Deputy head, Inflation Report Division, Bank of England 1994–97; Member, MSF. **House of Commons:** Member for Bolton West since May 1, 1997; PPS to Nick Brown as Minister of Agriculture, Fisheries and Food 1998–; *Select Committees:* Member: Treasury 1997–98, Treasury Sub-Committee 1998. *Special Interests:* Economic Policy, Europe, Social Policy, Welfare Reform, Employment Policy, Parental Leave; France, Spain. Bethnal Green and Stepney/Bow Constituency Labour Party: Treasurer 1994–96, Ward Secretary 1994–96. Tower Hamlets Anti-Racist Committee; Member, Research Panel, Employment Policy Institute; Member, Council of Management, National Institute for Economic and Social Research; Member, Royal Economic Society Council; *Publications:* Various Pamphlets on Finance and Taxation; *Recreations:* Walking, writing. *Address:* Ruth Kelly, MP, House of Commons, London, SW1A 0AA *Tel:* 020 7219 3496. *Constituency:* Labour Party, 60 St George's Road, Bolton, Lancashire, BL1 2DD *Tel:* 01204 523920 *Fax:* 01204 371246 *E-mail:* kellyr@parliament.uk.

FRASER KEMP   Houghton and Washington East   *Lab majority 26,555*

Born 1 September 1958; Son of William and Mary Kemp; Educated Washington Comprehensive; Married July 1, 1989, Patricia Mary Byrne (2 sons 1 daughter). Civil servant 1975–81; Full-time Labour Party organiser, Leicester 1981–84; Assistant regional organiser, East Midlands 1984–86; Regional secretary, West Midlands 1986–94; National Labour Party general election co-ordinator 1994–96; Full-time branch secretary CPSA 1975–80; Member: GMB, AEEU. **House of Commons:** Member for Houghton and Washington East since May 1, 1997; *Select Committees:* Member: Public Administration 1997–99, Selection 1997–99. *Special Interests:* Technology, Motor Industry; Australia. Secretary: National Annual Labour Party Conference Arrangements Committee 1993–96, Labour's National General Election Planning Group 1994–96; Secretary, Labour's NEC Campaigns and Elections Committee 1995–96. Vice-chair, Herrington Burn YMCA; Honorary president, Northguard Roman Research and Living History Society; Member, Russell Foster Tyne & Wear Sports Foundation; Honorary member, North East Chamber of Commerce; President, Washington MIND; Patron, The Friends of Houghton Parish Church Trust; Member, Beamish Development Trust (North of England Open Air Museum); *Clubs:* Usworth and District Workmens and Institute (Washington); Hetton; *Sportsclubs:* Member, Houghton and Peterlee Athletics Club; *Recreations:* Reading, cinema. *Address:* Fraser Kemp Esq, MP, House of Commons, London, SW1A 0AA *Tel:* 020 7219 5181 *Fax:* 020 7219 2536. *Constituency:* 14 Nesham Place, Church Street, Houghton-Le-Spring, Tyne and Wear, DH5 8AG *Tel:* 0191–584 9266 *Fax:* 0191–584 8329.

Visit the Vacher Dod Website . . .
www.politicallinks.co.uk

CHARLES KENNEDY Ross, Skye and Inverness West *LD majority 4,019*

Born 25 November 1959; Son of Ian Kennedy, crofter and Mary MacVarish MacEachen; Educated Lochaber High School, Fort William; Glasgow University (MA politics, philosophy and English 1982); Indiana University (1982–83). President, Glasgow University Union 1980–81; Winner, British Observer Mace Debating Tournament 1982; Journalist with BBC Highland, at Inverness 1982. **House of Commons:** Member for Ross, Cromarty and Skye 1983–97, and for Ross, Skye and Inverness West since May 1, 1997; Alliance Spokesman for Social Security 1987; SDP Spokesman for: Scotland and Social Security 1987–88, Trade and Industry 1988–89; Liberal Democrat Spokesman for: Health 1989–92, European Union Affairs 1992–97, Agriculture, Fisheries, Food and Rural Affairs 1997–99; Leader, Liberal Democrat Party 1999–; *Select Committees:* Member: Standards and Privileges 1997–99. *Special Interests:* Scotland, Social Policy, Broadcasting, European Union. Chair, Glasgow University Social Democratic Club 1979–80; President, Liberal Democrat Party 1990–94; Deputy Convenor, Foreign Affairs, Defence and Overseas Development Committee 1994–. Associate Member, Scottish Crofters Union; PC 1999; *The Spectator* Member to Watch Award 1989; Channel 4 and *The House* Magazine, Political Humourist of the Year Award 1999; *Clubs:* National Liberal; *Recreations:* Reading, writing, music, swimming, golf, journalism, broadcasting. *Address:* Rt Hon Charles Kennedy, MP, House of Commons, London, SW1A 0AA *Tel:* 020 7219 6226 *Fax:* 020 7219 4881. *Constituency:* 1a Montague Row, Inverness, IV3 5DX *Tel:* 01463 714377 *Fax:* 01463 714380 *E-mail:* rossldp@cix.co.uk.

JANE KENNEDY Liverpool Wavertree *Lab majority 19,701*

Born 4 May 1958; Daughter of Clifford Hodgson, engineer, and of Barbara Hodgson; Educated Haughton School, Darlington; Queen Elizabeth Sixth Form College; Liverpool University; Married December 14, 1977, Malcolm Kennedy (marriage dissolved 1998) (2 sons). Residential child care officer, Liverpool City Council (LCC) 1979–83; Care assistant, LCC Social Services 1983–88; Branch Secretary, NUPE 1983–88, Area Organiser 1988–92. **House of Commons:** Member for Liverpool Broadgreen 1992–97, and for Liverpool Wavertree since May 1, 1997; Opposition Whip 1995–97; Assistant Government Whip 1997–98; Government Whip 1998–99; Parliamentary Secretary, Lord Chancellor's Department 1999–; *Select Committees:* Member: Social Security 1992–94, Administration 1997–99. *Special Interests:* Local Government, Public Services, Social Security, Foreign Affairs; Middle East and South East Asia. Chair, Labour Friends of Israel 1997–. Member, Governing Body: Liverpool Polytechnic 1986–88, Oldham Sixth Form College 1990–92; Member: Ramblers' Association, Youth Hostelling Association; Fellow, Industry and Parliament Trust; *Recreations:* Walking, training Belgian Shepherd dogs, horse-riding. *Address:* Jane Kennedy, MP, House of Commons, London, SW1A 0AA *Tel:* 020 7219 4523 *Fax:* 020 7219 4880. *Constituency:* 1st Floor, Threlfall Building, Trueman Street, Liverpool, L3 2EX *Tel:* 0151–236 1117 *Fax:* 0151–236 0067.

ROBERT KEY Salisbury *Con majority 6,276*

Born 22 April 1945; Son of late Rt Rev. Maurice Key, former Bishop of Truro; Educated Salisbury Cathedral School; Sherborne School; Clare College, Cambridge (MA, CertEd); Married 1968, Susan Priscilla Bright, daughter of Very Revd Thurstan Irvine (1 son 2 daughters). Assistant master: Loretto School, Edinburgh 1967–69, Harrow School (Economics Department) 1969–83; Vice-Chair, Wembley Branch ASTMS 1975–80. **House of Commons:** Contested Camden, Holborn and St Pancras South 1979 general election. Member for Salisbury since June 1983; Opposition Spokesman for Defence 1997–; Political Secretary to Edward Heath 1984–85; PPS: to Alick Buchanan-Smith as Minister of State for Energy 1985–87, to Christopher Patten: as Minister for Overseas Development 1987–89, as Secretary of State for the Environment 1989–90; Parliamentary Under-Secretary of State: at Department of the Environment 1990–92, at Department of National Heritage 1992–93 at Department of Transport (Minister for Roads and Traffic) 1993–94;

Select Committees: Member: Health 1994–95, Defence 1995–97. *Special Interests:* Education, Arts, Foreign Affairs, Defence, Agriculture. Treasurer, Conservative Candidates' Association 1976–79; Chair, Harrow Central Conservative Association 1980–82; Vice-Chair, London Central Euro-Constituency 1980–82; Member: Conservative Party National Advisory Committee on Education 1979–82, Executive Committee National Union of Conservative Party 1980–83. Chair, Governors of School at Great Ormond Street Children's Hospital 1976–79; Governor, Sir William Collins Comprehensive School 1976–79; Member of Council, Gap Activity Projects 1970–82; Member: UK National Commission for UNESCO 1984–85, Medical Research Council 1989–90; Member, Executive Council, Inter Parliamentary Union British Branch 1986–90; Chair, Council for Education in the Commonwealth 1985–87; Substitute, UK Delegation to Council of Europe and Western Europe Union 1996–97; Founding Chairman, the Alice Trust for Autistic Children 1977–80; *Publications: Reforming our Schools*, 1988; Hon. Fellow, College of Preceptors 1989–; *Recreations:* Singing, cooking, countryside. *Address:* Robert Key Esq, MP, House of Commons, London, SW1A 0AA *Tel:* 020 7219 6501 *E-mail:* rob@robertkey.com.

Born 20 November 1924; Educated Punjab University (BA social services, BEd); Whitelands College, Putney (Diploma in Teaching); Married Beulah Marian. Served Indian Armed Corps 1942–46; Clerical work, British Oxygen 1964–66; Teacher, ILEA 1968–80; Community worker 1981–91; Member, MSF. Councillor, London Borough of Ealing 1978–82; JP 1977–. **House of Commons:** Member for Ealing Southall since April 9, 1992; *Select Committees:* Member: Members' Interests 1994–97; Member: International Development 1997–. *Special Interests:* Employment, Education, Race Relations, European Union, International Development; India. Chair, Indian Workers' Association, Southall, Middlesex; *Recreations:* Reading, watching football. *Address:* Piara S. Khabra Esq, JP, MP, House of Commons, London, SW1A 0AA *Tel:* 020 7219 5010 *Fax:* 020 7219 5699 *Tel (Constituency):* 020 8992 5614.

Born 21 March 1955; Son of Neil Bernard Kidney, retired clerk, and late Doris Kidney; Educated Longton High School; Sixth Form College, Stoke-on-Trent; Bristol University (LLB); Married September 9, 1979, Elaine (1 son 1 daughter). Solicitor: Hanley, Stoke-on-Trent 1977–79, Stafford 1979–97; Member, MSF. Councillor: Checkley Parish Council 1983–87, Stafford Borough Council 1987–97. **House of Commons:** Member for Stafford since May 1, 1997; *Select Committees:* Member: Treasury 1998–, Treasury Sub-Committee 1998–. *Special Interests:* Children, Housing; Britain. Member, Society of Labour Lawyers. Member: Bethany Project for Homeless, ASIST (Citizen Advocacy), British Agencies for Adoption and Fostering, Law Society; *Recreations:* Chess, bridge. *Address:* David Kidney Esq, MP, House of Commons, London, SW1A 0AA *Tel:* 020 7219 6472 *Fax:* 020 7219 0919. *Constituency:* Labour Rooms, Meyrick Road, Stafford, ST17 4DG *Tel:* 01785 224444/250356 *Fax:* 01785 250357 *E-mail:* kidneyd@parliament.uk.

Born 9 June 1946; Son of late Edward and Ellen Kilfoyle; Educated St Edward's College, Liverpool; Durham University; Christ's College, Liverpool; Married July 27, 1968, Bernadette Slater (2 sons 3 daughters). Labourer 1965–70, 1973–75; Student 1970–73; Teacher 1975–85. **House of Commons:** Member for Liverpool Walton since July 4, 1991 by-election; Opposition Spokesman on: Education 1994–96, Education and Employment 1996–97; Opposition Whip 1992–94; Parliamentary Secretary: Office of Public Service 1997–98, Cabinet Office 1998–99; Parliamentary Under-Secretary of State, Ministry of Defence 1999–2000; *Special Interests:* Foreign Affairs, Commonwealth, Employment, Education; Australia, Latin America, The Commonwealth. Labour Party organiser 1986–91. *Recreations:* Reading, music, spectator sport. *Address:* Peter Kilfoyle Esq, MP, House of Commons, London, SW1A 0AA *Tel:* 020 7219 2591. *Constituency:* 4 Christopher Street, Liverpool, L4 4JX *Tel:* 0151–298 1148 *Fax:* 0151–298 1149 *E-mail:* kilfoylep@parliament.uk.

ANDY KING   Rugby and Kenilworth   *Lab majority 495*

Born 14 September 1948; Son of late Charles King, labourer, and of late Mary King; Educated St John the Baptist School, Uddingston; Coatbridge Technical College; Missionary Institute, London; Hatfield Polytechnic; Stevenage College; Nene College, Northants (CQSW, CMS); Married 1975, Semma Ahmet (1 daughter). Former: Labourer, Postal officer, Apprentice motor vehicle mechanic; Social work manager, Northamptonshire County Council 1989–; Member, UNISON. Member, Warwickshire Police Authority 1989–97; Councillor, Warwickshire County Council 1989–98, Chair, Social Services Committee 1993–96; Councillor, Rugby Borough Council 1995–98. **House of Commons:** Member for Rugby and Kenilworth since May 1, 1997; *Select Committees:* Member: Deregulation 1999–, Social Security 1999–. *Special Interests:* Health, Law and Order, Social Services, Home Affairs; Ethiopia, New Zealand, Brazil, Turkey, Australia, China. Member, Co-operative Party; Treasurer, Rugby and Kenilworth Constituency Labour Party 1984–88. Member, British Association of Social Workers; Vice-Chair, Rugby Parkinsons Disease Society; *Sportsclubs:* Rugby Golf Club; President, Rugby Town Junior FC; *Recreations:* Golf, football, dominoes, theatre. *Address:* Andy King Esq, MP, House of Commons, London, SW1A 0AA *Tel:* 020 7219 6229. *Constituency:* 12 Regent Place, Rugby, Warwickshire, CU21 2PN *Tel:* 01788 575504 *Fax:* 01788 575506 *E-mail:* kinga@parliament.uk.

OONA KING   Bethnal Green and Bow   *Lab majority 11,285*

Born 22 October 1967; Daughter of Preston King, professor of political science, and of Hazel King, teacher; Educated Haverstock Comprehensive Secondary School; York University (BA politics 1990); Berkeley-University of California (Scholarship); Married July 15, 1994, Tiberio Santomarco. Researcher, Socialist Group, European Parliament 1990; Political assistant to Glyn Ford MEP, as Leader, EPLP 1991–93; John Smith's Labour Party leadership campaign team 1992; Freelance speech-writer/ghost writer 1993–94; Political assistant to Glenys Kinnock MEP 1994–95; Trade Union Organiser, GMB Southern Region 1995–97; Southern Region Equality Officer, GMB. **House of Commons:** Member for Bethnal Green and Bow since May 1, 1997; *Select Committees:* Member: International Development 1997–. *Special Interests:* Race Relations, Employment, Education, Health, Development, Gender Equality, Housing, Europe, Electoral Reform; Bangladesh, Nicaragua, USA, Italy, France, South Africa, Rwanda and Great Lakes Region (Africa). Member, Fabian Society; Joint Vice-Chair, London Regional Group of Labour MPs 1997–; Committee Member, Labour Campaign for Electoral Reform. Member: Oxfam, Campaign for Pension Fund Democracy, Amnesty International, Jewish Council for Racial Equality (J-Core), One World Action, UNICEF; Member, 1990 Trust, Toynbee Hall; Vice-Chair, British Council 1999–; *Recreations:* Music, cinema. *Address:* Oona King, MP, House of Commons, London, SW1A 0AA *Tel:* 020 7219 5020 *Fax:* 020 7219 2798 *E-mail:* silverv@parliament.uk.

TOM KING   Bridgwater   *Con majority 1,796*

Born 13 June 1933; Educated Rugby; Emmanuel College, Cambridge (MA); Married January 20, 1960, Jane Tilney (1 son 1 daughter). Army national service 1952–53; service in East Africa; E. S. and A. Robinson Ltd, Bristol 1956–69, Divisional General Manager 1964–69; Chair, Sale, Tilney & Co. Ltd 1971–79. **House of Commons:** Member for Bridgwater since March 12, 1970 by-election; Opposition Front Bench Spokesman for Industry 1975–76; Shadow Spokesman for Energy 1976–79; PPS to Christopher Chataway: as Minister of Posts and Telecommunications 1970–72, as Minister for Industrial Development 1972–74; Minister for Local Government and Environmental Services 1979–83; Secretary of State for: Environment January-June 1983, Transport June-October 1983, Employment 1983–85, Northern Ireland 1985–89, Defence 1989–92; *Select Committees:* Member: Standards in Public Life 1994–97. *Special Interests:* Asia, Europe, USA. Chair, Intelligence and Security Committee 1994–; PC 1979; CH 1992; *Recreations:* Cricket, skiing. *Address:* Rt Hon Tom King, CH, MP, House of Commons, London, SW1A 0AA *Tel:* 020 7219 4566 *Fax:* 020 7219 0612 *Tel (Constituency):* 01278 423110 *Fax (Constituency):* 01278 431034 *E-mail:* tomkingmp@parliament.uk.

TESS KINGHAM   Gloucester   *Lab majority 8,259*

Born 4 May 1963; Daughter of Roy Thomas Kingham, deeds clerk, and Patricia Ribbian, née Murphy; Educated Dartford Girls Grammar School; Royal Holloway College, London University (BA German with Italian 1984); University of East Anglia (PGCE modern languages); Married October 26, 1991, Mark Luetchford (1 daughter, twin son and daughter). Liaison officer, Norfolk, British Trust for Conservation Volunteers 1984–85; National appeals director, War on Want 1985–90; Marketing and communications director, Blue Cross 1990–92; Editor, Youth Express 1992–94; Communications manager, Oxfam 1994–96; Communications director, War on Want 1996–97; Member: TGWU; Contested Cotswolds 1994 European Parliament election. **House of Commons:** Member for Gloucester since May 1, 1997; *Select Committees:* Member: International Development 1997–. *Special Interests:* European Union, Foreign Affairs, Overseas Aid and Development; Central America, Southern Africa, Russia, Germany, Albania. Member: Oxford, Swindon and Gloucester Cooperative Society, Co-op Party, Labour Women's Network; Vice-Chair, Campaign Group of Labour MPs. Council Member, Overseas Development Institute (ODI); Member, Egypt Exploration Society; Nicaragua Solidarity Campaign; Western Sahara Campaign; Patron, Gloucester Family Support; President, Mozambique Angola Committee; President, Mozambique Angola Committee; Member: Inter-Parliamentary Union (IPU), Commonwealth Parliamentary Association (CPA); *Clubs:* Royal Commonwealth Club; *Recreations:* Modern music (not classical), art and dance, archaeology, Egyptology, walking, food, international travel, enjoying my family (husband, children and dog). *Address:* Tess Kingham, MP, House of Commons, London, SW1A 0AA *Tel:* 020 7219 4611. *Constituency:* Gloucester Labour Party, Transport House, 1 Pullman Court, Gloucester GL1 3ND *Tel:* 01452 311870 *Fax:* 01452 311874 *E-mail:* hnewton@parliament.uk.

JULIE KIRKBRIDE   Bromsgrove   *Con majority 4,895*

Born 5 June 1960; Daughter of late Henry Raymond Kirkbride and Barbara Kirkbride (née Bancroft); Educated Highlands School, Halifax; Girton College, Cambridge (BA economics and history 1981, MA); Graduate School of Journalism, University of California 1982–83; Married 1997, Andrew Mackay, MP (*qv*) (1 son). Researcher, Yorkshire Television 1983–86; Producer, BBC News and Current Affairs 1986–89; ITN 1989–92; Political correspondent, *Daily Telegraph* 1992–96; Social affairs editor, *Sunday Telegraph* 1996. **House of Commons:** Member for Bromsgrove since May 1, 1997; *Select Committees:* Member: Social Security 1997–99; Member: Catering 1998–, Culture, Media and Sport 1999–. *Special Interests:* Tax, European Union, Social Security, Law and Order, Health. Vice-President, The Cambridge Union Society 1981. International Republican Institute Lecturer in Romania 1995; Member, Executive Committee, Commonwealth Parliamentary Association (CPA) UK Branch 1999–; Rotary Foundation Scholar 1982–83; *Recreations:* Walking, opera. *Address:* Julie Kirkbride, MP, House of Commons, London, SW1A 0AA *Tel:* 020 7219 6417. *Constituency:* Conservative Association, 37 Worcester Road, Bromsgrove, Worcestershire *Tel:* 01527 872135.

ARCHY KIRKWOOD   Roxburgh and Berwickshire   *LD majority 7,906*

Born 22 April 1946; Son of David Kirkwood; Educated Cranhill School; Heriot-Watt University (BSc pharmacy 1971); Married December 30, 1972, Rosemary Chester (1 son 1 daughter). Solicitor; Notary Public. **House of Commons:** Member for Roxburgh and Berwickshire since June 1983; Liberal Spokesman on: Health, Social Services and Social Security 1985–87; Alliance Spokesman on Overseas Development 1987; Liberal Spokesman on Scotland 1987–88; Convenor and Spokesman on Welfare and Social Security 1989–94; Liberal Democrat Shadow Leader of the House 1994–97; Spokesman on Community Care 1994–97; Liberal Democrat Deputy Chief Whip 1989–92, Chief Whip 1992–97; Aide to David Steel 1971–75, 1977–78; Sponsored: Access to Personal Files Act 1987 (Private Member's Bill), Access to Medical Reports Act 1988 (Private Member's Bill); *Select Committees:* Member: Finance and Services 1992–97, Liaison 1992–97, Selection 1992–97; Member: Court of Referees 1997–, Liaison 1997–; Chairman: Social Security 1997–.

Special Interests: Freedom of Information, Health, Social Security, Human Rights. Social and Liberal Democrat Convenor on Welfare, Health and Education 1988–89. Member, House of Commons Commission 1997–; Joseph Rowntree Reform Trust: Trustee 1985–, Chair 1999–; *Publications:* Co-author *Long Term Care – a Framework for Reform;* Rowntree Political Fellow 1971; *Recreations:* Music, photography. *Address:* Archy Kirkwood Esq, MP, House of Commons, London, SW1A 0AA *Tel:* 020 7219 6523 *Fax:* 020 7219 6437 *E-mail:* kirkwooda@parliament.uk.

DR ASHOK KUMAR   Middlesbrough South and East Cleveland   *Lab majority 10,607*

Born 28 May 1956; Educated Rykenld School for Boys; Derby and District College of Art and Technology; Aston University (BSc chemical engineering 1978, MSc process analysis and development 1980, PhD fluid mechanics 1982). Research fellow, Imperial College, London 1982–85; Research scientist, British Steel 1985–97; Member: Association of University Teachers 1982–84, Steel and Industrial Managers' Union 1984–. Councillor, Middlesbrough Borough Council 1987–97. **House of Commons:** Member for Langbaurgh 1991 by-election – 1992, and for Middlesbrough South and East Cleveland since May 1, 1997; *Select Committees:* Member: Science and Technology 1997–, Deregulation 1999–. *Special Interests:* Trade and Industry, Education, Local Government; Japan, USA, India, Korea, Kazakhstan, Bahrain. Member: Middlesbrough Law Centre 1985–95, Institution of Chemical Engineers, Institute of Energy; Board Member, Parliamentary Office of Science and Technology (POST) 1997–; Vice-President, Federation of Economic Development Authorities (FEDA) 1997–; *Publications:* Articles in scientific and mathematical journals; *Sportsclubs:* Marton Cricket Club; *Recreations:* Listening to music, reading history and philosophy books, playing badminton and cricket. *Address:* Dr Ashok Kumar, MP, House of Commons, London, SW1A 0AA *Tel:* 020 7219 4460. *Constituency:* 6–8 Wilson Street, Guisborough, Cleveland, TS14 6NA *Tel:* 01287 610878 *Fax:* 01287 631894 *E-mail:* ashokkumarmp@parliament.uk.

L

DR STEPHEN LADYMAN   South Thanet   *Lab majority 2,878*

Born 6 November 1952; Son of Frank Ladyman, engineer, and of Winifred Ladyman; Educated Birkenhead Institute; Liverpool Polytechnic (BSc applied biology); Strathclyde University (PhD for research into isotopic abundances in soil development); Married Janet Baker (1 daughter 2 stepsons 1 stepdaughter). Computer manager, Pfizer Central Research; Member, GMB. Councillor, Thanet District Council 1995–99, Chair, Labour Group 1995–97, Chair, Finance Committee 1995–97. **House of Commons:** Contested Wantage 1987 general election. Member for South Thanet since May 1, 1997; *Select Committees:* Member: Environment, Transport and Regional Affairs 1999–, Transport Sub-Committee 2000–. *Special Interests:* Environment, Economics, Industry, Science and Technology, Research; Member: European Standing Committee B 1998, European Standing Committee C 1999–. Former Chair, Thanet South Constituency Labour Party; Member, Fabian Society. *Sportsclubs:* Manager, Under 15s Ramsgate Football Club; *Recreations:* Football, family, golf. *Address:* Dr Stephen Ladyman, MP, House of Commons, London, SW1A 0AA *Tel:* 020 7219 6946. *Constituency:* Willson Hall, Willsons Road, Ramsgate, Kent, CT11 9LZ *Tel:* 01843 852696 *Fax:* 01843 852689 *E-mail:* ladymans@parliament.uk.

ELEANOR LAING   Epping Forest   *Con majority 5,252*

Born 1 February 1958; Daughter of late Matthew Pritchard and Betty Pritchard (née McFarlane); Educated St Columba's School, Kilmacolm, Renfrewshire; Edinburgh University (BA, LLB) (First Woman President of Union); Married June 25, 1983, Alan, son of Alan and Margaret Laing. Practised Law in Edinburgh, City of London and Industry; Special Adviser to John MacGregor: as Secretary of State for Education 1989–90, as Leader of the House of Commons 1990–92, as Secretary of State for Transport 1992–94. **House of Commons:** Contested Paisley North 1987 general election. Member for Epping Forest since May 1, 1997; Opposition Frontbench Spokesman for Constitutional Affairs (Scotland) 2000–; Opposition Whip: (Constitutional, Education and Employment) 1999, (Social Security, Trade and Industry) 1999, (International Development; Trade and Industry; Wales) 1999–2000; *Select Committees:* Member: Education and Employment 1997–98, Employment Sub-Committee 1997–98, Environment, Transport and Regional Affairs 1998–99, Transport Sub-Committee 1998–99. *Special Interests:* Education, Transport, Economic Policy, Constitution, Devolution; Australia, Gibraltar, USA, New Zealand. *Recreations:* Theatre, music, golf. *Address:* Mrs Eleanor Laing, MP, House of Commons, London, SW1A 0AA *Tel:* 020 7219 4203 *Fax:* 020 7219 0980. *Constituency:* Thatcher House, 4 Meadow Road, Loughton, Essex, G10 4HX *Tel:* 020 8508 6608 *Fax:* 020 8508 8099.

JACQUI LAIT   Beckenham   *Con majority 1,227*

Born 16 December 1947; Daughter of late Graham Lait and of Margaret Lait; Educated Paisley Grammar School; Strathclyde University (BA business 1967); Married June 1, 1974, Peter Jones. Public relations, Jute Industries Ltd 1968–70 Visnews Ltd 1970–74 Government Information Service 1974–79 Parliamentary adviser, Chemical Industries Association 1980–84 Parliamentary consultant – own business 1984–92. Chair, City and East London Family Health Services Authority 1987–91; Contested Strathclyde West 1984 European Parliament election. **House of Commons:** Contested 1985 Tyne Bridge by-election. Member for Hastings and Rye 1992–97, and for Beckenham since November 20, 1997 by-election; Opposition Front Bench Spokeswoman for Social Security 2000–; Assistant Government Whip 1996–97; Opposition Whip 1999–2000; PPS: to Parliamentary Under-Secretaries of State, Department of Social Security 1994–95, to William Hague as Secretary of State for Wales 1995–96; *Select Committees:* Member: Health 1992–93, Scottish Affairs 1994–95, Catering 1998–99, Science and Technology 1998–99; Member: Deregulation 1997–. *Special Interests:* Trade and Industry, European Union, Health; Australia, Europe, South Africa, USA. First woman in the Conservative Whips Office 1996–97; Executive Member, 1922 Committee 1998–99; Chair, British Section, European Union of Women 1990–92; Trustee, National Missing Persons Helpline; *Recreations:* Walking, swimming, theatre, food and wine. *Address:* Mrs Jacqui Lait, MP, House of Commons, London, SW1A 0AA *Tel:* 020 7219 4551 *Fax:* 020 7219 0141 *E-mail:* jacquilaitmp@parliament.uk.

DAVID LAMMY   Tottenham   *Labour majority 5,646*

Born 19 July 1972; Educated King's School, Peterborough; law, School of Oriental and African Studies, London University, London (LLB 1993), Harvard Law School, USA (LLM 1997)). Barrister, 3 Serjeants Inn, Philip Naughton QC 1994–96; Attorney, Howard Rice Nemerovsky Canada Falk & Rabkin 1997–98; Barrister, D J Freeman 1998–2000; member MSF. Member Greater London Assembly 2000. **House of Commons:** Member for Tottenham since by-election June 22, 2000; *Special Interests:* Treasury (regeneration), Arts and Culture, Education, International development; USA, Caribbean, Latin America, Brazil, Africa. Member, Fabian Society. worked part-time as a vol-unteer for the Free Representation Unit while at University; Member, Christian Socialist Movement; Archbishops' Council (new Executive Board, Church of England); *Recreations:* Film, live music, Spurs FC. *Address:* David Lammy Esq, MP, House of Commons, London, SW1A 0AA *Tel:* 020 7219 0767 *Fax:* 020 7219 0357 *E-mail:* lammyd@parliament.uk.

ANDREW LANSLEY   South Cambridgeshire   *Con majority 8,712*

Born 11 December 1956; Son of Thomas Lansley, OBE, and Irene Lansley; Educated Brentwood School; Exeter University (BA politics 1979); Married November 30, 1985, Marilyn Biggs (separated 1997) (3 daughters). Department of Industry (Department of Trade and Industry 1984–87) 1979–87; Private secretary to Secretary of State, at Department of Trade and Industry 1984–85; Principal Private Secretary, to Norman Tebbit as Chancellor of the Duchy of Lancaster 1985–87; Policy director, British Chambers of Commerce 1987–89; Deputy director-general, British Chambers of Commerce 1989–90; Director, Conservative Research Department 1990–95; Director, Public Policy Unit 1995–97. Vice-President, Local Government Association. **House of Commons:** Member for South Cambridgeshire since May 1, 1997; Member, Shadow Cabinet 1999–; Shadow Minister for the Cabinet Office and Policy Renewal 1999–, Shadow Chancellor of the Duchy of Lancaster 1999–; *Select Committees:* Member: Health 1997–98. *Special Interests:* Trade and Industry, Economic Policy, Small Businesses, Health, Local Government, Police, Film Industry; USA, Japan, Egypt, Israel, France, Germany, South Africa. A Vice-Chairman, Conservative Party (with responsibility for Policy Renewal) 1998–99. Member, National Union Executive Committee 1990–95; Patron: Cambridgeshire Small Business Group, International Centre for Child Studies; *Publications: A Private Route*, 1988; Co-author *Conservatives and the Constitution*, 1997; CBE 1996; *Recreations:* Spending time with my children, films, biography, history, cricket. *Address:* Andrew Lansley Esq, CBE, MP, House of Commons, London, SW1A 0AA *Tel:* 020 7219 6416 *Fax:* 020 7219 6835. *Constituency:* 153 St Neots Road, Harwick, Cambridge, CB3 7QJ *Tel:* 01954 212707 *Fax:* 01954 212707 *E-mail:* lansleya@parliament.uk.

JACKIE LAWRENCE   Preseli Pembrokeshire   *Lab majority 8,736*

Born 9 August 1948; Daughter of the late Sidney and Rita Beale; Educated Upperthorpe School, Darlington, County Durham; Upperthorpe College; Open University; Married David Lawrence (2 sons 1 daughter). Assistant to Nick Ainger, MP; TSB Bank plc; Member, TGWU. Leader, Labour Group, Pembrokeshire County Council 1995–97; Councillor, Dyfed County Council 1993–96; Member, Dyfed Powys Police Authority 1994–97; Member, Pembrokeshire Coast National Park Committee 1993–95. **House of Commons:** Member for Preseli Pembrokeshire since May 1, 1997; *Select Committees:* Member: Welsh Affairs 1997–99. Election Agent, Pembroke County Constituency 1992; Secretary, Pembroke Constituency Labour Party 1992–95; Chair, Pembroke Constituency Labour Party 1995–96; Hon. Treasurer, Welsh Regional Group of Labour MPs 1999, Hon. Secretary 1999–. Member: RSPB, West Wales Naturalists Trust, Amnesty International, War on Want; *Recreations:* Walking. *Address:* Jackie Lawrence, MP, House of Commons, London, SW1A 0AA *Tel:* 020 7219 2757. *Constituency:* Fulke Street, Milford Haven, Pembrokeshire, SA73 2HH *Tel:* 01646 697969 *Fax:* 01646 698830 *E-mail:* lawrencej@parliament.uk.

BOB LAXTON   Derby North   *Lab majority 10,615*

Born 7 September 1944; Son of Alan and Elsie Laxton; Educated Woodlands Secondary School; Derby College of Art and Technology; Divorced (1 son). TU branch officer, Communication Workers' Union; Telecommunications engineer, BT plc 1961–; Member, Communication Workers' Union. Derby City Council: Councillor 1979–97, Council Leader 1986–88, 1994–97; Chair, East Midlands LGA to 1997. **House of Commons:** Member for Derby North since May 1, 1997; *Select Committees:* Member: Trade and Industry 1997–. *Special Interests:* Local Government; Germany. Labour Party Conference Debate, Local Government 1995; *Recreations:* Hill walking. *Address:* Bob Laxton Esq, MP, House of Commons, London, SW1A 0AA *Tel:* 020 7219 4096 *Fax:* 020 7219 2329. *Constituency:* 1st Floor, Abbots Hill Chamber, Gower Street, Derby, DE1 1SD *Tel:* 01332 206699 *Fax:* 01332 206444 *E-mail:* laxtonb@parliament.uk.

EDWARD LEIGH   Gainsborough   *Con majority 6,826*

Born 20 July 1950; Son of late Sir Neville Leigh, KCVO, former Clerk to the Privy Council; Educated Oratory School, Berkshire; French Lycee, London; Durham University (BA history 1972) (President of Union); Married July 25, 1984, Mary Goodman (3 sons 3 daughters). Member: Conservative Research Department 1973–75, Private Office of Margaret Thatcher as Leader of the Opposition 1976–77; Barrister, Inner Temple 1977. Councillor: Richmond Borough Council 1974–78, GLC 1977–81. **House of Commons:** Contested Teesside, Middlesbrough October 1974 general election. Member for Gainsborough and Horncastle 1983–97, and for Gainsborough since May 1, 1997; PPS to John Patten Minister of State, Home Office 1990; Parliamentary Under-Secretary of State, Department of Trade and Industry 1990–93; *Select Committees:* Member: Social Security 1995–97, Agriculture 1996–97, Deregulation 1997; Member: Social Security 1997–, Public Accounts 2000–. *Special Interests:* Defence, Foreign Affairs, Agriculture. Former Chairman, Durham University Conservative Association. Chair, National Council for Civil Defence; Director, Coalition For Peace Through Security 1981–83; Fellow, Industry and Parliament Trust; *Publications: Right Thinking*, 1982; *Onwards from Bruges*, 1989; *Choice and Responsibility – The Enabling State*, 1990; Knight of Honour and Devotion of the Sovereign Military Order of Malta; *Recreations:* Walking, reading. *Address:* Edward Leigh Esq, MP, House of Commons, London, SW1A 0AA *Tel:* 020 7219 6480. *Constituency:* 23 Queen Street, Market Rasen, Lincolnshire *Tel:* 01673 844501.

DAVID LEPPER   Brighton Pavilion   *Lab/Co-op majority 13,181*

Born 15 September 1945; Son of late Harry Lepper, lorry driver, and Maggie Lepper; Educated Gainsborough Secondary Modern, Richmond; Wimbledon Secondary School; Kent University (BA English and American literature); Sussex University (PGCE, postgraduate certificate in media education); Polytechnic of Central London (postgraduate diploma in film); Married 1966, Jeane Stroud (1 son 1 daughter). Secondary school teacher 1969–96; Member, NUT 1969–. Councillor, Brighton Council 1980–97, Council Leader 1986, Mayor 1993–94. **House of Commons:** Contested Brighton Pavilion 1992 general election. Member for Brighton Pavilion since May 1, 1997; *Select Committees:* Member: Broadcasting 1997–, Public Administration 1999–. *Special Interests:* Cultural Industries, Media, Multimedia, Community Regeneration, Consumer Issues, Animal Welfare, Leasehold Reform, Town Centre Issues, Cyprus; France, Italy, Japan, Cyprus; Member, European Standing Committee B 1998–. Member: Fabian Society, Socialist Education Association, Socialist Health Association, SERA, Labour Animal Welfare Society. Board Member, Alzheimers and Related Dementia Sufferers Society, Brighton (ARDIS); Member: Alzheimers Disease Society, Brighton MENCAP; Patron: Brighton Age Concern, Brighton Cares; Member: CPA 1997–, IPU; Trustee: Brighton Youth Orchestra, Lighthouse Media; *Publications: John Wayne*, 1986; Contributor to British Film Institute publications and other film journalism; Fellow, Sussex University; Fellow, University of Sussex Society; *Clubs:* Brighton Trades and Labour; *Recreations:* Music, cinema, reading fiction and poetry, watching professional cycling. *Address:* David Lepper Esq, MP, House of Commons, London, SW1A 0AA *Tel:* 020 7219 4421 *Fax:* 020 7219 5814. *Constituency:* John Saunders House, 179 Preston Road, Brighton, East Sussex, BN1 6AG *Tel:* 01273 551532 *Fax:* 01273 550617.

CHRISTOPHER LESLIE   Shipley   *Lab majority 2,996*

Born 28 June 1972; Educated Bingley Grammar School; Leeds University (BA 1994, MA industrial and labour studies 1996). Office administrator 1994–96; Political research assistant 1996–97; Member: TGWU, GMB. Councillor, Bradford City Council 1994–98. **House of Commons:** Member for Shipley since May 1, 1997; PPS to Lord Falconer as Minister of State, Cabinet Office 1998–; *Select Committees:* Member: Public Accounts 1997–98. *Special Interests:* Industrial Policy, Economic Policy, Environment, Local Government. *Recreations:* Travel, tennis, cinema, opera, art. *Address:* Christopher Leslie Esq, MP, House of Commons, London, SW1A 0AA *Tel:* 020 7219 4424 *Fax:* 020 7219 2832. *Constituency:* 33 Saltaire Road, Shipley, BD18 3HH *Tel:* 01274–401300 *Fax:* 01274–401313 *E-mail:* lesliec@parliament.uk.

OLIVER LETWIN   West Dorset   *Con majority 1,840*

Born 19 May 1956; Son of Professor William Letwin and late Dr Shirley Robin Letwin; Educated Eton College; Trinity College, Cambridge (BA, MA, PhD); London Business School; Married September 15, 1984, Isabel Grace Davidson (1 son 1 daughter). Visiting fellow (Procter Fellow), Princeton University, USA 1980–81; Research fellow, Darwin College, Cambridge 1981–82; Special adviser to Sir Keith Joseph as Secretary of State for Education 1982–83; Special adviser, Prime Minister's Policy Unit 1983–86; N. M. Rothschild & Son, Merchant Bank 1986–: Manager 1986, Assistant Director 1987, Director 1991–. **House of Commons:** Contested Hackney North 1987, Hampstead and Highgate 1992 general elections. Member for West Dorset since May 1, 1997; Opposition Front Bench Spokesman for: Constitutional Affairs, Scotland and Wales 1998–99, the Treasury 1999–2000; Shadow Chief Secretary to the Treasury 2000–; *Select Committees:* Member: Deregulation 1998–99. *Special Interests:* Microeconomic Policy, Employment, Education; Eastern Europe, Africa; Member, European Standing Committee B 1998. Member: Conservative Disability Group, Conservative Green Initiative. Member, Tony Green Initiative; Patron, Joseph Weld Hospice; *Publications: Ethics, Emotion and the Unity of the Self,* 1985; *Aims of Schooling,* 1986; *Privatising the World,* 1989; *Drift to Union,* 1989; *The Purpose of Politics,* 1999; Plus Articles and Reviews in learned and popular journals; Fellow, Royal Society of Arts; *Clubs:* St Stephen's Constitutional; Carlyle; *Recreations:* Ski-ing, sailing, tennis, reading, writing books. *Address:* Oliver Letwin Esq, MP, House of Commons, London, SW1A 0AA *Tel:* 020 7219 4192 *Fax:* 020 7219 0805. *Constituency:* Chapel House, Dorchester Road, Maiden Newton, Dorset, DT2 0BG *Tel:* 01300 321188 *Fax:* 01300 321233.

TOM LEVITT   High Peak   *Lab majority 8,791*

Born 10 April 1954; Son of John and Joan Levitt; Educated Westwood High School, Leek; Lancaster University (BSc biological sciences 1975); Oxford University (PGCE 1976); Married March, 1983, Teresa Sledziewski (1 daughter). Teacher: Wiltshire County Council 1976–79, Gloucestershire County Council 1980–91; Supply teacher, Staffordshire County Council 1991–95; Sensory awareness trainer 1993–97; Consultant, Access for People With Sensory Impairments 1993–97; Member, NUT 1975–; School representative, NUT 1977–79, 1984–90; Local association president, NUT 1985; County division president, NUT 1988; Member: NUPE 1988–94, GMB 1995–. Councillor: Cirencester Town 1983–87, Stroud District 1990–92, Derbyshire County 1993–97, Vice-Chair, Education 1994–95; Contested Cotswolds 1989 European Parliament election. **House of Commons:** Contested Stroud 1987 general election, High Peak 1992 general election. Member for High Peak since May 1, 1997; PPS to Barbara Roche as Minister of State, Home Office 1999–; *Select Committees:* Member: Standards and Privileges 1997–. *Special Interests:* Disabled/Disability, Education, Local Government, Quarrying; Western Europe, Poland. Member, SERA. Member: Place (Educational Charity); Friends of Buxton Museum; British Deaf Association; League Against Cruel Sports; Friends of the Earth; Amnesty International; SEA; *Publications:* Local Government Management Board: *Sound Policies,* 1994, *Sound Practice,* 1995, *Clear Access,* 1996; *Sportsclubs:* Tideswell Cricket Club; *Recreations:* Cricket, walking, theatre. *Address:* Tom Levitt Esq, MP, House of Commons, London, SW1A 0AA *Tel:* 020 7219 6599 *Fax:* 020 7219 0935. *Constituency:* 20 Hardwick Street, Buxton, Derbyshire, SK17 6DH *Tel:* 01298 71111 *Fax:* 01298 71522 *E-mail:* tomlevittmp@parliament.uk *Website:* www.cel.co.uk/labour/tom.

IVAN LEWIS   Bury South   Lab majority 12,381

Born 4 March 1967; Son of Joe and Gloria Lewis; Educated William Hulme Grammar School; Stand College; Bury Further Education College; Married June 3, 1990, Juliette Fox (2 sons). Coordinator, Contact Community Care Group 1986–89; Community care manager, Jewish Social Services 1989–92; Chief executive, Manchester Jewish Federation 1992–97; Member, MSF. Councillor, Bury Metropolitan Borough Council 1990–98; Chairman, Social Services Committee 1991–95. **House of Commons:** Member for Bury South since May 1, 1997; PPS to Stephen Byers as Secretary of State for Trade and Industry 1999–; *Select Committees:* Member: Deregulation 1997–99, Health 1999. *Special Interests:* Health, Crime, Education; Israel, USA. Chair, Bury South Labour Party 1991–96; Vice-Chair, Labour Friends of Israel 1997–. Chair, Bury MENCAP 1989–92; Member, Bury Carers Partnership Management Committee; Founder Member, Coordinator and Chair, Contact Community Care Group 1986–92; Trustee, Holocaust Educational Trust; *Recreations:* Keen supporter of Manchester City FC. *Address:* Ivan Lewis Esq, MP, House of Commons, London, SW1A 0AA *Tel:* 020 7219 6404 *Fax:* 020 7219 6866. *Constituency:* 513 Bury New Road, Prestwich, Manchester, M25 3JA *Tel:* 0161–773 5500 *Fax:* 0161–773 7959 *E-mail:* heneghanp@parliament.uk; burysouthclp@hotmail.com.

DR JULIAN LEWIS   New Forest East   Con majority 5,215

Born 26 September 1951; Son of Samuel Lewis and late Hilda Lewis; Educated Dynevor Grammar School, Swansea; Balliol College, Oxford (MA philosophy and politics 1977); St Antony's College, Oxford (DPhil strategic studies 1981). Seaman, HM Royal Naval Reserve 1979–82; Doctoral research (strategic studies) 1975–77, 1978–81; Secretary, Campaign for Representative Democracy 1977–78; Research director and director, Coalition for Peace Through Security 1981–85; Director, Policy Research Associates 1985–; Deputy director, Conservative Research Department 1990–96. **House of Commons:** Contested Swansea West 1983 general election. Member for New Forest East since May 1, 1997; *Select Committees:* Member: Welsh Affairs 1998–, Defence 2000–. *Special Interests:* Defence, Security, Foreign Affairs, Europe, Media, Education, Mental Health; Western Europe, Central and Eastern Europe, Russia. Treasurer, Oxford University Conservative Association 1971; Secretary, Oxford Union 1972; Honorary Vice-President, Greater London and West London Young Conservatives 1980s. Member: RNLI, Medical Charities; Joint organiser of campaign against militant infiltration of the Labour Party 1977–78; Trustee, British Military Powerboat Trust; *Publications: Changing Direction: British Military Planning for Post-War Strategic Defence, 1942–1947,* 1988; *Who's Left? An Index of Labour MPs and Left-Wing Causes, 1985–1992,* 1992; *Labour's CND Cover-Up,* 1992; *The Liberal Democrats: The Character of Their Politics,* 1993; *What's Liberal? Liberal Democrat Quotations and Facts,* 1996; *Clubs:* Athenaeum, Totton Conservative; *Recreations:* History, fiction, films, music, photography. *Address:* Dr Julian Lewis, MP, House of Commons, London, SW1A 0AA *Tel:* 023 8081 4817 (Parliamentary Office). *Constituency:* New Forest East Conservative Association, 3 The Parade, Southampton Road, Cadnam, Hampshire, SO40 2NG *Tel:* 023 8081 4905 *Fax:* 023 8081 4906 *Website:* www.julianlewis.net.

TERRY LEWIS   Worsley   Lab majority 17,741

Born 29 December 1935; Son of Andrew Lewis, dockworker; Educated Our Lady of Mount Carmel School, Salford; Technical College; Married 1958, Audrey Clarke (1 son and 1 son deceased). RAMC 1954–56; Local Government 1976–84; Personnel Officer 1979–83; Sponsored by TGWU. Deputy leader, Bolton Borough Council 1980–83; Chair, Education Committee 1981–83. **House of Commons:** Member for Worsley since June 1983; *Select Committees:* Member: Environment 1991–92, Members' Interests 1992–97; Member: Standards and Privileges 1997–. *Special Interests:* Local Government, Employment. *Recreations:* Football spectating. *Address:* Terry Lewis Esq, MP, House of Commons, London, SW1A 0AA *Tel:* 020 7219 3479. *Constituency:* Emlyn Hall, Emlyn Street, Worsley, Greater Manchester, M28 3JZ *Tel:* 0161–703 8017 *Fax:* 0161–703 8346 *E-mail:* terry-lewismp@btinternet.com.

HELEN LIDDELL   Airdrie and Shotts   *Lab majority 15,412*

Born 6 December 1950; Daughter of Hugh and Bridget Reilly; Educated St Patrick's High School, Coatbridge; Strathclyde University (BA economics 1972); Married 1972, Dr Alistair Liddell (1 son 1 daughter). Economics correspondent, BBC Scotland 1976–77; General secretary, Labour Party in Scotland 1977–88; Director, personnel and public affairs, Scottish Daily Record and Sunday Mail (1986) Ltd 1988–92; Chief executive, Business Venture Programme 1993–94; Scottish TUC: Head of economics department 1971–75, Assistant secretary 1975–76. **House of Commons:** Contested Fife East October 1974 general election. Member for Monklands East from June 30, 1994 by-election–1997, and for Airdrie and Shotts since May 1, 1997; Opposition Spokeswoman on Scotland 1995–97; Economic Secretary, HM Treasury 1997–98; Minister of State: Scottish Office (Minister for Education) 1998–99, Department of the Environment, Transport and the Regions (Minister for Transport) 1999, Department of Trade and Industry (Minister for Energy and Competitiveness in Europe) 1999–; *Special Interests:* Media, Scottish Affairs, Economic Policy, Trade and Industry; USA, Europe, Russia. Chair, Independent Review into the future of the Scottish Symphony Orchestra and Orchestra of Scottish Opera 1993–94; Vice-Chair, Rehab Scotland 1990–92; Chair, UN5O: Scotland 1994; *Publications: Elite*, 1990; PC 1998; *Recreations:* Cooking, hill-walking, music, writing. *Address:* Rt Hon Helen Liddell, MP, House of Commons, London, SW1A 0AA *Tel:* 020 7219 6507 *Fax:* 020 7219 3390. *Constituency:* 115 Graham Street, Airdrie, Lanarkshire, ML6 6DE *Tel:* 01236 748777 *Fax:* 01236 748666 *E-mail:* tlo.liddell@tlo.dti.gov.uk.

DAVID LIDINGTON   Aylesbury   *Con majority 8,419*

Born 30 June 1956; Son of Roy and Rosa Lidington; Educated Haberdashers' Aske's School, Elstree; Sidney Sussex College, Cambridge (MA history, PhD); Married August 5, 1989, Helen Parry (4 sons). British Petroleum 1983–86; Rio Tinto Zinc 1986–87; Special Adviser to Douglas Hurd: at Home Office 1987–89, at Foreign and Commonwealth Office 1989–90; Senior Consultant, The Public Policy Unit 1991–92. **House of Commons:** Contested Vauxhall 1987 general election. Member for Aylesbury since April 9, 1992; Opposition Front Bench Spokesman for Home Affairs 1999–; PPS: to Michael Howard as Home Secretary 1994–97, to William Hague as Leader of the Opposition 1997–99; *Select Committees:* Member: Education 1992–96. *Special Interests:* Home Office, Foreign Office, Education; Europe, Hong Kong. Various offices in: Cambridge University (Chairman), Enfield North Conservative Association. *Clubs:* Aylesbury Conservative; *Recreations:* History, choral singing, reading. *Address:* David Lidington Esq, MP, House of Commons, London, SW1A 0AA *Tel:* 020 7219 3000 *Fax:* 020 7219 2564. *Constituency:* 100 Walton Street, Aylesbury, Buckinghamshire, HP21 7QP *Tel:* 01296 482102 *Fax:* 01296 398481 *E-mail:* richardsmall@aylesbury.tory.org.uk.

PETER LILLEY   Hitchin and Harpenden   *Con majority 6,671*

Born 23 August 1943; Son of Arnold and Lillian (née Elliott) Lilley; Educated Dulwich College; Clare College, Cambridge (BA natural sciences and economic sciences 1965); Married May 24, 1979, Gail Ansell. Director: Great Western Resources Ltd 1985–87; Greenwell Montague Stockbrokers 1986–87 (Head, oil investment department); Investment adviser on North Sea oil and other energy industries 1972–84; Economic adviser on underdeveloped countries 1966–72; Consultant director, Conservative Research Department 1979–83. **House of Commons:** Contested Haringey, Tottenham October 1974 general election. Member for St Albans 1983–97, and for Hitchin and Harpenden since May 1, 1997; Joint PPS: to Lord Bellwin, as Minister of State for Local Government, Department of the Environment and William Waldegrave as Parliamentary Under-Secretary of State, Department of Environment June-November 1984, to Nigel Lawson, as Chancellor of the Exchequer 1984–87; Economic Secretary to the Treasury 1987–89; Financial Secretary to the Treasury 1989–90; Secretary of State for: Trade and Industry 1990–92, Social Security 1992–97;

Contested Leadership of the Conservative Party June 1997; Member, Shadow Cabinet 1997–99; Shadow Chancellor of the Exchequer 1997–98; Deputy Leader of the Opposition (with overall responsibility for development of party policy) 1998–99; *Special Interests:* Economic Policy, European Union, Education, Race Relations; France. Chair, Bow Group 1973–75. PC 1990; *Clubs:* Carlton. *Address:* Rt Hon Peter Lilley, MP, House of Commons, London, SW1A 0AA *Tel:* 020 7219 4577 *Fax:* 020 7219 3840 *Tel (Constituency):* 01582 834 344 *E-mail:* lilleyp@parliament.uk.

MARTIN LINTON   Battersea   *Lab majority 5,360*

Born 11 August 1944; Son of Sydney Linton and late Karin Linton; Educated Limpsfield Primary School, Surrey; Christ's Hospital, Sussex; Pembroke College, Oxford (MA Philosophy, Politics and Economics); Université de Lyon; Married 1975, Kathy (died 1995) (2 daughters). Journalist on:*Daily Mail* 1966–71, *Financial Times* 1971, *Labour Weekly* 1971–79, *Daily Star* 1980–81, *The Guardian* 1981–97; Former member, NUJ; Member, GMB. Councillor, London Borough of Wandsworth 1971–82, Chairman, Recreation Committee 1971–77. **House of Commons:** Member for Battersea since May 1, 1997; *Select Committees:* Member: Home Affairs 1997–. *Special Interests:* Housing, Education, Political Finance, Media Influence, Voting Systems; Sweden. Joined Labour Party 1968; Former Chairman, Constituency Labour Party. President, Battersea Arts Centre; Treasurer, British Swedish Parliamentary Association; *Publications: Get Me Out Of Here,* 1980; *The Swedish Road to Socialism,* 1984; *Labour Can Still Win,* 1988; *The Guardian Guide to the House of Commons,* (editor) 1992; *What's wrong with first-past-the-post?,* 1993; *Money and Votes,* 1994; *Was It The Sun Wot Won It?,* 1995; Editor, *Guardian Election Guide,* 1997; *Making Votes Count,* 1998; *Recreations:* Playing music, watching football. *Address:* Martin Linton Esq, MP, House of Commons, London, SW1A 0AA *Tel:* 020 7219 4619 *Fax:* 020 7219 5728. *Constituency:* 177 Lavender Hill, London, SW11 5TE *Tel:* 020 7207 3060 *Fax:* 020 7207 3063 *E-mail:* lintonm@parliament.uk.

KEN LIVINGSTONE   Brent East   *Lab majority 15,882**

Born 17 June 1945; Son of late Robert Moffat Livingstone and late Ethel Ada Livingstone; Educated Tulse Hill Comprehensive; Philippa Fawcett College of Education (Teaching Certificate); Married 1973, Christine Pamela Chapman (marriage dissolved 1982). Cancer research worker 1962–70; Teacher Training College 1970–73; Member: MSF 1969–75, TGWU 1977–. Lambeth Council: Councillor 1971–78, Vice-Chair, Housing Committee 1971–73; Camden Council: Councillor 1978–82, Chair, Housing Committee 1978–80, Councillor, GLC 1973–86: Chair, Ethnic Minorities Committee and Council Leader 1981–86; Mayor of London 2000–. **House of Commons:** Contested Camden, Hampstead 1979 general election. *Labour Member for Brent East June 1987-April 2000, Independent Member since April 2000; *Select Committees:* Member: Northern Ireland Affairs 1997–99. *Special Interests:* Economic Policy, Democratising Britain, Northern Ireland; Former Soviet Union, Tibet, USA. Member, Labour Party National Executive Committee 1987–89, 1997–98. Elected to Council, The Zoological Society of London 1994, Vice-President 1996–98; *Publications: If voting changed anything, they'd abolish it,* 1987; *Livingstone's Labour: A Programme for the Nineties,* 1989; *Recreations:* Films, science-fiction, walking, gardening. *Address:* Ken Livingstone Esq, MP, House of Commons, London, SW1A 0AA *Tel:* 020 7219 6941 *Fax:* 020 7219 1202 *E-mail:* 105277.3653@compuserve.com *Website:* http://www.poptel.org.uk/ken-livingstone/.

RICHARD LIVSEY Brecon and Radnorshire — LD majority 5,097

Born 2 May 1935; Son of late Arthur Norman and Lilian Maisie Livsey; Educated Talgarth County Primary School; Bedales; Seal Hayne Agricultural College (NDA); Reading University (MSc); Married April 3, 1964, Irene Earsman (2 sons 1 daughter). Agricultural development officer, ICI 1961–67; Farm manager, Blairdrummond Estate, Perthshire 1967–71; Senior lecturer in farm management, Welsh Agricultural College, Llanbadarn Fawr, Aberystwyth 1971–85. **House of Commons:** Contested (Liberal) Perth and East Perthshire 1970, Pembroke 1979, Brecon and Radnor 1983 general elections. Member for Brecon and Radnor from July 4, 1985 by-election to 1992 (Liberal 1985–88, Lib Dem 1988–92), and for Brecon and Radnorshire since May 1, 1997; Spokesman on: Agriculture 1985–87, Welsh Affairs 1987–92; Principal Spokesman for Wales 1997–; *Select Committees:* Member: Welsh Affairs 1997–. *Special Interests:* Agriculture. Leader, Welsh Liberal Democrats 1988–92, 1997–; Member, Constitution Reform Strategy Committee 1997–. CBE 1994; *Recreations:* Cricket, fishing, cycling. *Address:* Richard Livsey Esq, CBE, MP, House of Commons, London, SW1A 0AA *Tel:* 020 7219 3000. *Constituency:* 99 The Street, Brecon, Powys, LD3 7LS *Tel:* 01874 625 739 *Fax:* 01874 625 635.

TONY LLOYD Manchester Central — Lab majority 19,682

Born 25 February 1950; Son of late Sydney Lloyd, Lithographic printer; Educated Stretford Grammar School; Nottingham University; Manchester Business School; Married September 21, 1974, Judith Ann Tear (1 son 3 daughters). University lecturer. Councillor, Trafford District Council 1979–84. **House of Commons:** Member for Stretford 1983–97, and for Manchester Central since May 1, 1997; Opposition Spokesman on: Transport 1988–89, Employment 1988–92, 1993–94, Education (responsible for co-ordinating policies on education and training) 1992–94, The Environment and London 1994–95, Foreign and Commonwealth Affairs 1995–97; Minister of State, Foreign and Commonwealth Office 1997–99; *Special Interests:* Civil Liberties, Disarmament, Immigration Policy, Race Relations, Industrial Policy, Human Rights, Overseas Aid and Development; Former Soviet Union, Guatemala, Japan, Poland. Member, UK Delegation Parliamentary Assembly of the Council of Europe/Western European Union 2000–; *Recreations:* Family. *Address:* Anthony Lloyd Esq, MP, House of Commons, London, SW1A 0AA *Tel:* 020 7219 4442.

SIR PETER LLOYD Fareham — Con majority 10,358

Born 12 November 1937; Son of late David Lloyd, JP; Educated Tonbridge School; Pembroke College, Cambridge; Married October 14, 1967, Hilary Creighton (1 son 1 daughter). Marketing manager, United Biscuits Ltd until 1979. **House of Commons:** Contested Nottingham West February and October 1974 general elections. Member for Fareham since May 1979; Assistant Government Whip 1984–86; Government Whip 1986–88; PPS: to Adam Butler as Minister of State for Northern Ireland 1981–82, to Sir Keith Joseph as Secretary of State for Education and Science July 1983–84, Parliamentary Under Secretary of State: Department of Social Security 1988–89; Home Office: Parliamentary Under Secretary 1989–92, Minister of State 1992–94; *Select Committees:* Member: Public Service 1995–97, Treasury 1997–99; Chairman: Treasury Sub-Committee 1998–99; Member: Treasury Sub-Committee 1999. Chair, Bow Group 1972–73; Editor, Crossbow 1974–76. Chair, New Bridge; Council Member, Howard League for Penal Reform; Member, House of Commons Commission 1997–; Joint Chair, Council for the Advancement of Arab British Understanding 1997–; PC 1994; Knighted 1995; *Clubs:* Players Theatre. *Address:* Rt Hon Sir Peter Lloyd, MP, House of Commons, London, SW1A 0AA *Tel:* 020 7219 4442.

ELFYN LLWYD   Meirionnydd Nant Conwy   *PC majority 6,805*

Born 26 September 1951; Son of late Huw Meirion Hughes, and of Hefina Hughes; Educated Ysgol Dyffryn Conwy, Llanrwst Grammar School; University College of Wales, Aberystwyth (BA 1972); College of Law, Chester (LLB Wales); Married July 27, 1974, Eleri Llwyd, daughter of Huw Lloyd Edwards (1 son 1 daughter). Solicitor until 1997; President, Gwynedd Law Society 1990–91; Barrister 1997–. **House of Commons:** Member for Meirionnydd Nant Conwy since April 9, 1992; Spokesman for: Transport, Treasury and Economy, Trade and Industry, Social Security, Disability; Northern Ireland 1997–99, Spokesman for: Housing 1997–, Local Government 1997–, Tourism 1997–, Home Affairs 1999–; Plaid Cymru Parliamentary Whip 1995–; Leader, Plaid Cymru Parliamentary Party 2000–; *Select Committees:* Member: Welsh Affairs 1992–97; Member: Welsh Affairs 1998–. *Special Interests:* Civil Liberties, Agriculture, Tourism, Home Affairs; Spain, Scotland, USA, Wales, Greece. Member, Plaid Cymru Policy Cabinet 1994–, Parliamentary Leader 1997–. Council member, NSPCC Wales; Member, Parliamentary Panel UNICEF; Hon member, Gorsedd of Bards 1998; Council member, University of Wales, Aberystwyth; Chair, Dolgellau Hatchery Trust; *Sportsclubs:* President: Estimaner Angling Association, Betws-y-Coed Football Club, Llanuwchllyn Football Club, Bala Rugby Club; Vice-President, Dolgellau Old Grammarians' Rugby Club; *Recreations:* Pigeon breeding, choral singing, rugby, fishing, cycling. *Address:* Elfyn Llwyd Esq, MP, House of Commons, London, SW1A 0AA *Tel:* 020 7219 3555. *Constituency:* Adeiladau Glyndwr, Heol Glyndwr, Dolgellau, Gwynedd, LL40 1BD *Tel:* 01341 422661 *Fax:* 01341 423990.

DAVID LOCK   Wyre Forest   *Lab majority 6,946*

Born 2 May 1960; Son of John, research engineer, and Jeanette Lock, nurse; Educated Esher Grammar School; Woking Sixth Form College; Jesus College, Cambridge (MA theology 1982); Central London Polytechnic (Diploma in law 1984); Gray's Inn (Wilson Scholar 1985) (Barrister); Married April 8, 1985, Bernadette Gregory (1 son 2 daughters). Management trainee, GEC; Barrister 1985–97; Member, MSF. Councillor, Wychavon District Council 1995–97, Chair: Amenities and Economic Development Committee, Wychavon Leisure Management Board. **House of Commons:** Member for Wyre Forest since May 1, 1997; PPS: Lord Chancellor's Department 1997–98, to Lord Irvine of Lairg as Lord Chancellor 1998–99; Parliamentary Secretary 1999–; *Select Committees:* Member: Deregulation 1997–98. *Special Interests:* Economics, Employment, Human Rights, Legal Issues; Switzerland, USA, France. Member, Society of Labour Lawyers. *Publications:* Various legal publications; Contributor to *Beyond 2002: Long-term Policies for Labour*, ed. Martin Linton, MP; Wilson Scholar 1985; *Recreations:* Family, cycling, friends, squash, running. *Address:* David Lock Esq, MP, House of Commons, London, SW1A 0AA *Tel:* 020 7219 4652 *Fax:* 020 7219 6193. *Constituency:* Lowland House, Green Street, Kidderminster, Worcestershire, DY10 1GJ *Tel:* 01562 827007 *Fax:* 01562 751007 *E-mail:* lock@parliament.uk.

MICHAEL LORD   Central Suffolk and North Ipswich   *Con majority 3,538*

Born 17 October 1938; Son of late John Lord, schoolmaster; Educated William Hulme's Grammar School; Christ's College, Cambridge (MA agriculture 1962); Married 1965, Jennifer Margaret Childs (1 son 1 daughter). Farmer and taught agriculture 1962–66; Director, Power Line Maintenance Ltd 1966–68; Founded Lords Tree Services Ltd 1968; Aboricultural Consultant 1983. North Bedfordshire Borough Council: Former Councillor, Chair, Policy Commission 1974–77; Bedfordshire County Council: Former Councillor, Chair, Further Education Committee 1981–83. **House of Commons:** Contested Manchester Gorton 1979 general election. Member for Central Suffolk 1983–97, and for Central Suffolk and North Ipswich since May 1, 1997; PPS to: John MacGregor, as Minister of Agriculture, Fisheries and Food 1984–85, as Chief Secretary to the Treasury 1985–87; Second Deputy Chairman, Ways and Means 1997–; *Select Committees:* Member: Parliamentary Commissioner for Administration 1990–97; Second Deputy Chairman of Ways and Means: Chairmen's Panel 1997–, Court of Referees 1997–, Standing Orders 1998–. *Special Interests:* Agriculture, Forestry,

Environment. Vice-President, The Arboricultural Association, President 1989–95; Hon. Secretary, Parliamentary Golfing Society (Captain); Cambridge Rugby Blue; Parliamentary delegate, The Council of Europe and the Western European Union 1987–91; Member, Executive Committee, Inter Parliamentary Union (IPU) British Group 1995–97; FArbA; *Recreations:* Golf, sailing, gardening. *Address:* Michael Lord Esq, MP, House of Commons, London, SW1A 0AA *Tel:* 020 7219 5055. *Constituency:* Central Suffolk and North Ipswich Conservative Association, 19 The Business Centre, Earl Soham, Woodbridge, Suffolk, IP13 7SA *Tel:* 01728 685148.

TIM LOUGHTON   East Worthing and Shoreham   Con majority 5,098

Born 30 May 1962; Son of Reverend Michael Loughton and Pamela Dorothy Loughton; Educated The Priory School, Lewes, Sussex; Warwick University (BA classical civilisation 1983); Clare College, Cambridge (Research Mesopotamian archaeology 1983–84); Married July 25, 1992, Elizabeth Juliet MacLauchlan (1 son 2 daughters). Fund manager, Fleming Private Asset Management, City of London 1984–, Director 1992–2000. **House of Commons:** Contested Sheffield Brightside 1992 general election. Member for East Worthing and Shoreham since May 1, 1997; Opposition Spokesman for Environment, Transport and the Regions 2000–; *Select Committees:* Member: Environmental Audit 1997–. *Special Interests:* Finance, Foreign Affairs, Home Affairs, Drugs, Education (Special Needs), Environmental Taxation, Environment and Housing, Disabilities; Latin America, Middle East, Indian sub-continent; Member: Burns committee Financial Services and Markets Bill 1999; Standing committee Financial Services and Markets Bill 1999–; Standing committee Local Government Bill 2000–; European Standing committee C 1999–2000. Chair, Lewes Young Conservatives 1978; Vice-Chair: Sussex Young Conservatives 1979, Lewes Constituency Conservative Association 1979, South East Area Young Conservatives 1980; Secretary, Warwick University Conservative Association 1981–82; Member, Cambridge University Conservative Association 1983–84; Member, Bow Group 1985–92; Vice-Chair, Battersea Conservative Association 1990–91; Member, London Area Conservative Executive Committee 1993–; Life Vice-President, Sheffield Brightside Constituency Association 1993–; Deputy Chair, Battersea Constituency Conservative Association 1994–; Executive Committee Member, Selsdon Group 1994–; Member, Carlton Club Political Committee 1994–; Chair, Conservative Disability Group 1998. Member: Sussex Archaeological Society, Society of Sussex Downsmen, RNLI, RSPCA, British Museum Society, Centre for Policy Studies, Institute of Economic Affairs, Worldwide Fund for Nature, Tibet Action (UK), Court of Sussex University; Patron: League of Friends of Worthing Hospital, St Barnabas Hospice, Worthing, Patron, Worthing Hockey Club; President Adur Art Club; General election PA to Tim Eggar, MP 1987; Member, Linking Agriculture and Farming (LEAF); Vice-President, Worthing United Nations Association; Lecturer, English Wine and Stock Exchange; Member: Royal Institute International Affairs, CPA, IPU; Vice-Chair, Shoreham Old Town Hall Trust; MSi(Dip); *Clubs:* Carlton; *Sportsclubs:* Captain, Fleming's Hockey Team; Patron, Worthing Hockey; *Recreations:* Skiing, tennis, hockey, wine, archaeology. *Address:* Timothy Loughton Esq, MP, House of Commons, London, SW1A 0AA *Tel:* 020 7219 4471 *Fax:* 020 7219 0461. *Constituency:* Haverfield House, 4 Union Place, Worthing, West Sussex, BN11 1LG *Tel:* 01903 235168 *Fax:* 01903 219755 *E-mail:* loughtont@parliament.uk.

ANDREW LOVE   Edmonton   Lab/Co-op majority 13,472

Born 21 March 1949; Son of late James Love and Olive Love; Educated Greenock High School; Strathclyde University (BSc); Association of Chartered Institute of Secretaries; Married March 12, 1983, Ruth Rosenthal. Parliamentary Officer, Co-operative Party; Member (former branch chairman), TGWU; Former National Executive Member, NACO. Councillor, London Borough of Haringey 1980–86. **House of Commons:** Contested Edmonton 1992 general election. Member for Edmonton since May 1, 1997; *Select Committees:* Member: Public Accounts 1997–, Deregulation 1999–. *Special Interests:* Housing, Regeneration, Health; France, Cyprus. Chair: Hornsey and Wood Green Labour Party 1987–89, Policy Committee, Greater London Labour Party 1990–94, Co-operative Parliamentary Group 1999–. Former member, NETRHA; Former vice-chair, North London FE College; Member, St Pancras Housing Association; Vice-Patron, Helen Rollason Cancer Appeal 1999–; Trustee, ICOF; ACIS; *Sportsclubs:* Muswell Hill Golf Club; *Recreations:* History, opera, cinema. *Address:* Andrew Love Esq, MP, House of Commons, London, SW1A 0AA *Tel:* 020 7219 5497 *Fax:* 020 7219 6623. *Constituency:* Broad House, 205 Fore Street, Edmonton, London, N18 2TZ *Tel:* 020 8803 0574 *Fax:* 020 8807 1673 *E-mail:* lovea@parliament.uk.

PETER LUFF   Mid Worcestershire   *Con majority 9,412*

Born 18 February 1955; Son of late Thomas Luff, master printer, and late Joyce Luff; Educated Windsor Grammar School; Corpus Christi College, Cambridge (BA economics 1976, MA); Married May 8, 1982, Julia Jenks (1 son 1 daughter). Research assistant to Peter Walker, MP 1977–80; Head of private office to Edward Heath, MP 1980–82; Company secretary, family stationery business, Luff & Sons Ltd to 1987; Account director, director and managing director, Good Relations Public Affairs Ltd 1982–87; Assistant managing director, Good Relations Ltd 1990–92; Senior consultant, Lowe Bell Communications 1989–90. **House of Commons:** Contested Holborn and St Pancras 1987 general election. Member for Worcester 1992–97, and for Mid Worcestershire since May 1, 1997; Opposition Whip 2000–; PPS: to Tim Eggar as Minister of State, Department of Trade and Industry 1993–96, to Lord Mackay of Clashfern as Lord Chancellor 1996–97, to Ann Widdecombe as Minister for Prisons, Home Office 1996–97; *Select Committees:* Member: Welsh Affairs 1992–97, Transport 1993, Consolidation Etc Joint Bills Committee 1995–97, Public Service 1996–97; Chairman: Agriculture 1997–2000; Member: Liaison 1997–2000. *Special Interests:* Railways, Trade and Industry, Rural Affairs, Performing Arts, International Development; Hong Kong, Falkland Islands, Israel, India, Mongolia. Patron, Conservative Students 1995–98; Vice-President, Severn Valley Railway 1997–; Member, Joseph Rowntree Inquiry into Planning for Housing 1992–94; Member, Armed Forces Parliamentary Scheme (Royal Navy) 1996; *Publications: Supporting Excellence – Funding Dance and Drama Students* (Bow Group), 1995; Fellow, Institute of Public Relations; *Clubs:* Royal Automobile; *Sportsclubs:* Worcestershire County Cricket; *Recreations:* Steam railways, theatre, photography. *Address:* Peter Luff Esq, MP, House of Commons, London, SW1A 0AA *Tel (Constituency):* 01905 763952 *Fax (Constituency):* 01905 763952 *E-mail:* luffpj@parliament.uk.

SIR NICHOLAS LYELL   North East Bedfordshire   *Con majority 5,883*

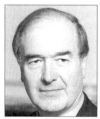

Born 6 December 1938; Son of late Hon. Mr. Justice Lyell (Sir Maurice Legat); Educated Stowe School; Christ Church, Oxford (BA modern history); College of Law; Married September 2, 1967, Susanna Mary Fletcher (2 sons 2 daughters). National Service, Royal Artillery (commissioned) 1957–59; Walter Runciman & Co. (Shipping) Newcastle upon Tyne 1962–64; Called to The Bar 1965; Private practice at the bar in commercial and employment law 1965–86, 1997–; QC 1980; Bencher, Inner Temple 1986. **House of Commons:** Contested Lambeth Central October 1974 general election. Member for Hemel Hempstead 1979–83, for Mid Bedfordshire 1983–97, and for North East Bedfordshire since May 1, 1997; PPS to Sir Michael Havers as Attorney General 1979–86; Parliamentary Under-Secretary of State DHSS 1986–87; Solicitor General 1987–92; Attorney General 1992–97; Shadow Attorney General 1997–99; *Select Committees:* Member: Privileges 1994–96. *Special Interests:* Home Affairs, Employment, Defence, Penal Affairs and Policy, Environment. Executive Chair, Society of Conservative Lawyers 1985–86, 1997–. Member, Salters' Company; Knighted 1987; PC 1990; *Clubs:* Brooks's, Pratt's, Beefsteak; *Recreations:* Gardening, shooting, drawing. *Address:* Rt Hon Sir Nicholas Lyell, QC, MP, House of Commons, London, SW1A 0AA *Tel:* 020 7219 6631. *Constituency:* Biggleswade Conservative Club, St Andrews Street, Biggleswade, Bedfordshire, SG18 1YB *Tel:* 01767 313385 *Fax:* 01767 316697 *E-mail:* lyelln@parliament.uk.

M

Born 13 February 1948; Son of late Joseph and Norah McAllion; Educated St Augustine's Secondary School, Glasgow; St Andrews University (MA, BEd); Married October 9, 1971, Dr Susan Jean Godlonton (2 sons). School teacher: St Saviour's High School, Dundee 1973–78; Balgowan School 1978–82; Research Assistant to Bob McTaggart, MP for Glasgow Central 1982–86; MSP for Dundee East constituency since May 6, 1999. Regional councillor, Tayside 1984–87; Convenor, Tayside Regional Council 1986–87. **House of Commons:** Member for Dundee East since June 1987; Opposition Spokesman on Scotland 1994–96; *Select Committees:* Member: Energy 1992, Scottish Affairs 1997–99. *Special Interests:* Employment, Industry, Education, Housing; Cuba, Cyprus, Czechoslovakia, USA. Member, Campaign Group 1997–. Member, Shelter (Scotland) Advisory Board; *Recreations:* Football, reading, watching ice-hockey. *Address:* John McAllion Esq, MP, MSP, House of Commons, London, SW1A 0AA *Tel:* 020 7219 5048 *Fax:* 020 7219 5834. *Constituency:* 18B Marketgait, Dundee, DD1 1QR *Tel:* 01382 207000 *Fax:* 01382 221280.

Born 14 December 1943; Son of late Edward McAvoy, steelworker, and late Frances McLaughlin McAvoy; Educated St Columbkilles Primary and Junior Secondary Schools; Married December 14, 1968, Eleanor Kerr (4 sons). Former Shop Steward, AEU. Chair, Rutherglen Community Council 1980; Strathclyde regional councillor for Rutherglen and Toryglen 1982–87. **House of Commons:** Member for Glasgow Rutherglen since June 1987; Opposition Whip 1991–93, 1996–97; Government Whip Comptroller of HM Household (Pairing Whip) 1997–; *Select Committees:* Member: Northern Ireland Affairs 1994–96; Member: Finance and Services 1997–. *Special Interests:* Social Services; Ireland, USA. Member, Co-operative Party. Chair: Fernhill Tenants Association, Rutherglen Federation of Tenants Associations. *Address:* Thomas McAvoy Esq, MP, House of Commons, London, SW1A 0AA *Tel:* 020 7219 3000. *Constituency:* 9 Douglas Avenue, Rutherglen, Lanarkshire, G73 4RA *Tel:* 0141–634 8083 *E-mail:* thomas.mcavoy@hm-treasury.gov.uk.

Born 4 August 1955; Son of James and Margaret McCabe; Educated Port Glasgow, Senior Secondary; Moray House College, Edinburgh (Diploma in Social Studies 1977, Certificate Qualification Social Work 1977); Bradford University (MA social work 1986); Married August 2, 1991, Lorraine Lea Clendon (1 son 1 daughter). Social work; Education adviser; Central Council for Education in Social Work 1991–97; Member, MSF; Shop steward, NALGO 1978–82. Birmingham City Council: Councillor 1990–98, Chair, Transportation Committee 1993–96. **House of Commons:** Member for Birmingham Hall Green since May 1, 1997; *Select Committees:* Member: Deregulation 1997–99; Member: Northern Ireland Affairs 1998–. *Special Interests:* Community Care, Transport, Economic Issues, Police. School Governor; *Sportsclubs:* Local Cricket Club; *Recreations:* Reading, football, hill walking. *Address:* Stephen McCabe Esq, MP, House of Commons, London, SW1A 0AA *Tel:* 020 7219 4842/3509 *Fax:* 020 7219 0367. *Constituency:* c/o The Labour Party, 14–16 Bristol Street, Birmingham *Tel:* 0121–622 6761 *Fax:* 0121–666 7322 *E-mail:* mccabes@parliament.uk.

CHRISTINE McCAFFERTY   Calder Valley   *Lab majority 6,255*

Born 14 October 1945; Daughter of late John and late Dorothy Livesley; Educated Whalley Range Grammar School For Girls, Manchester; Footscray High School, Melbourne, Australia; Married 1st, Michael McCafferty (1 son), married 2nd, David Tarlo. Welfare worker (Disabled), CHS Manchester 1963–70; Education welfare officer, Manchester Education Committee 1970–72; Registrar of marriages, Bury Registration District 1978–80; Project worker, Calderdale Well Woman Centre 1989–96; Member: NALGO 1967–81, MSF 1994–. Calderdale MBC: Councillor 1991–97, Chair, woman's advisory group 1991–93, disabilities advisory group 1991–93, adoption panel 1992–96; Member: Independent Education Appeals Panel 1991–97, Independent Advisory Panel 1991–97, Calderdale District Council 1991–, Hebden Royd Town Council 1991–95; Chair/Spokesperson, social services 1993–96; Executive of North Region Association for the Blind 1993–96; Member: West Yorkshire Police Authority 1994–97, West Yorkshire Police Complaints Committee 1994–97; Chair: Brighouse Police Community Forum 1994–97, Sowerby Bridge Police Community Forum 1994–97; Advisory Board, Queen Mary and Westfield College Public Policy Seminars. **House of Commons:** Member for Calder Valley since May 1, 1997; *Select Committees:* Member: Procedure 1997–99. *Special Interests:* Health, Social Services; Gambia, India, Australia. Member, Co-op Party 1990–. Member: Calderdale Well Women Centre, Redwater Arts; Governor/press officer, Central St School 1988–92; Founder member/chair, Calderdale Domestic Violence Forum 1989–97; Governor, Luddenden Dene School 1993–95; West Yorkshire Lay Prison Visitor 1994–; Founder member/chair, Calderdale Valley Cancer Support Group; Director, Royd Regeneration Ltd; Trustee, Trades Club Building Hebden Bridge; Member, Political Advisory Committee, Environmental Industries Commission; Parliamentary Member, Council of Europe 1999; Member: Social Health and Family Committee, Sub Committee for Children; Parliamentary Member, Western European Union 1999–; Member, Rules and Procedures Committee; Trustee, Trades Club Building, Hebden Bridge 1992–; Director, Royd Regeneration Ltd 1996–; *Recreations:* Swimming, reading, caravanning. *Address:* Christine McCafferty, MP, House of Commons, London, SW1A 0AA *Tel:* 020 7219 5026 *Fax:* 020 7219 7269. *Constituency:* 15 Heptonstall Road, Hebden Bridge, West Yorkshire, HX4 6AZ *Tel:* 01422 843713 *Fax:* 01422 846713 *E-mail:* mccafferty@btinternet.com.

IAN McCARTNEY   Makerfield   *Lab majority 26,177*

Born 25 April 1951; Son of Hugh McCartney, Labour MP; Educated State Schools; Married 1st (1 son deceased 2 daughters) (marriage dissolved), married 2nd, December 28, 1988, Mrs Ann Parkes, née Kevan. Secretary to Roger Stott MP until 1987; TGWU: Branch secretary 1968, Shop steward 1970; Former chair, TGWU Parliamentary Group. Wigan Borough Councillor 1982–87. **House of Commons:** Member for Makerfield since June 1987; Opposition Front Bench Spokesperson on: National Health Service 1992–94, Employment 1994–96, Education and Employment (Chief Employment Spokesperson) 1996–97; Minister of State: Department of Trade and Industry 1997–99, Cabinet Office 1999–; *Select Committees:* Member: Social Security 1991–92. *Special Interests:* Local Government, Fire Service, Civil Defence, Health and Safety at Work, Health Service, Social Services, Employment; Australia. Labour Party full-time officer 1973; Member, Labour Party National Executive Committee 1996–; Member, PLP General Election Campaign (Country) 1999–; Vice-Chair, Labour Party National Policy Forum; Member, Labour Party Joint Policy Commission. Chair, Children's Wheelchair Fund; Vice-President, BARLA (British Amateur Rugby League Association); PC 1999; *Clubs:* Platt Bridge Labour; *Recreations:* Wigan Rugby League. *Address:* Rt Hon Ian McCartney, MP, House of Commons, London, SW1A 0AA *Tel:* 020 7219 4503. *Constituency:* 1st Floor, Gerrard Winstanley House, Crawford Street, Wigan, Greater Manchester, WN1 1NJ *Tel:* 01942 824029 *Fax:* 01942 828171 *E-mail:* mccartney@cabinet-office.gov.uk *Website:* http://www.cabinet-office.gov.uk.

ROBERT McCARTNEY   North Down   *UKU majority 1,449*

Born 24 April 1936; Son of late William and Elizabeth McCartney; Educated Grosvenor Grammar School, Belfast; Queen's University, Belfast (LLB 1958); Married June 22, 1960, Maureen Ann Bingham (1 son 3 daughters). Solicitor, Supreme Court of Justice, Northern Ireland 1962; Called to the Bar of Northern Ireland 1968; QC 1975; Member: Northern Ireland Assembly for North Down 1982–86, Northern Ireland Forum 1996–98, New Northern Ireland Assembly 1998–. **House of Commons:** Contested North Down 1983 and 1987 general elections. Member for North Down since June 15, 1995 by-election; *Special Interests:* Northern Ireland's Constitutional future. Leader, United Kingdom Unionist Party. *Publications: Liberty and Authority in Ireland,* 1985; *McCartney Report on Consent,* 1997; *McCartney Report on Framework Documents,* 1997; *Recreations:* Reading political and military history, walking, all sport generally, particularly rugby. *Address:* Robert McCartney Esq, QC, MP, House of Commons, London, SW1A 0AA *Tel:* 020 7219 6590 *Fax:* 020 7219 0371. *Constituency:* 10 Hamilton Road, Bangor, Co Down, BT20 4LE *Tel:* 028 9127 2994 *Fax:* 028 9146 5037 *E-mail:* contactus@ukunionists.freeserve.co.uk *Website:* http://www.welcome.to/ukup.

WILLIAM McCREA   South Antrim   *DUP majority 822*

Born 6 August 1948; Son of Robert Thomas McCrea, farmer; Educated Cookstown Grammar School; Theological College; Married June 25, 1971, Anne Shirley McKnight (2 sons 3 daughters). Gospel recording artist; Holder of Silver, Gold and Platinum discs for record sales; Civil servant, NI Department of Health and Social Services 1966; Minister, Magherafelt Free Presbyterian Church 1968–; Member: Northern Ireland Assembly 1982–86, Northern Ireland Forum for Political Dialogue 1996–98, new Northern Ireland Assembly 1998–: Chair, Environmental Departmental Committee 1999–. Magherafelt District Council: Councillor 1973–, Mayor 1977–81; Vice-President, Local Authorities Northern Ireland 1980–81; Board Member, Northern Ireland Housing Executive 1981. **House of Commons:** Member for Ulster Mid 1983–97, for South Antrim since September 21, 2000 by-election; Party Spokesman on: Education 1987–88, Health and Social Services 1988–, Security 1992–; DUP Whip 1987–; *Special Interests:* Agriculture, Health, Law and Order, The Elderly. Vice-President, Local Authorities NI 1980–81; Board Member, Northern Ireland Housing Executive 1981; *Publications: In His Pathway* (biography); Hon. Doctorate Degree of Divinity 1989; *Recreations:* Horse riding. *Address:* Rev Dr William McCrea MP MLA, House of Commons, London, SW1A 0AA *Tel:* 020 7219 3000. *Constituency:* 10 Highfield Road, Magherafelt, Co Londonderry, BT45 5JD *Tel:* 028 7963 1965 *Fax:* 028 7930 0701 *E-mail:* williammccrea.dup@talk21.com.

SIOBHAIN McDONAGH   Mitcham and Morden   *Lab majority 13,741*

Born 20 February 1960; Daughter of Cummin and Breda McDonagh, retired builder and nurse; Educated Holy Cross Convent; Essex University. Clerical officer, DHSS 1981–83; Housing Benefits assistant 1983–84; Receptionist, Homeless Persons Unit, London Borough of Wandsworth 1984–86; Housing adviser 1986–88; Development co-ordinator, Battersea Church Housing Trust 1988–97. Councillor, London Borough of Merton 1982–1997, Chair, Housing Committee 1990–95. **House of Commons:** Contested Mitcham and Morden 1987 and 1992 general elections. Member for Mitcham and Morden since May 1, 1997; *Select Committees:* Member: Social Security 1997–98. *Special Interests:* Housing, Benefits, Private/Public Sector Partnership, Welfare Reform. Former Governor, Liberty Middle School and Tamworth Manor High School, Mitcham; Member: South Mitcham Community Centre, Colliers Wood Community Centre, Grenfell Housing Association, Merton MIND; Vice-President QUIT (smoking cessation charity); Made first Conference Speech aged 23; *Recreations:* Shopping, clothes, music. *Address:* Siobhain McDonagh, MP, House of Commons, London, SW1A 0AA *Tel:* 020 7219 4678 *Fax:* 020 7219 2697. *Constituency:* 1 Crown Road, Morden, Surrey, SM4 5DD *Tel:* 020 8542 4835 *Fax:* 020 8544 0377 *E-mail:* siobhainmcdonagh@hotmail.com *Website:* www.siobhainmcdonagh.org.uk.

158   HOUSE OF COMMONS

CALUM MacDONALD   Western Isles   *Lab majority 3,576*

Born 7 May 1956; Son of Malcolm MacDonald, crofter and weaver and
Donella MacDonald; Educated Bayble School; Nicholson Institute,
Stornoway; Edinburgh University; University of California (PhD). Former
teaching fellow in political philosophy, University of California at Los
Angeles. **House of Commons:** Member for Western Isles since June 1987;
PPS to Donald Dewar as Secretary of State for Scotland May-December
1997; Parliamentary Under-Secretary of State, Scottish Office (Minister for
Housing, Transport and European Affairs) December 1997–99; *Select
Committees:* Member: Agriculture 1987–92. *Special Interests:* Former Soviet
Union, Europe, USA. *Address:* Calum MacDonald Esq, MP, House of
Commons, London, SW1A 0AA *Tel:* 020 7219 3000. *Constituency:* 4 South Beach Street, Stornoway,
Isle of Lewis *Tel:* 01851 704684.

JOHN McDONNELL   Hayes and Harlington   *Lab majority 14,291*

Born 8 September 1951; Son of late Robert and Elsie McDonnell; Educated
Great Yarmouth Grammar School; Brunel University; Birkbeck College,
London University (BSc government and politics, MSc politics and sociology);
Married 1995, Cynthia Nunes (1 son 2 daughters). Shopfloor production
worker 1968–73; Assistant head, social insurance department, National Union
of Mineworkers 1977–78; Researcher, TUC 1978–82; Head of policy unit,
London Borough of Camden 1985–87; Chief Executive: Association of London
Authorities 1987–95, Association of London Government 1995–; Former Shop
Steward, UNISON. GLC Councillor 1981–86: Chair Finance Committee,
Deputy Leader. **House of Commons:** Member for Hayes and Harlington
since May 1, 1997; *Select Committees:* Member: Deregulation 1999–, Unopposed Bills (Panel) 1999–.
Special Interests: Economics, Local Government, Irish Affairs, Environment; Ireland, Kenya, Gambia,
Tanzania. Member: Greater London Labour Party Regional Executive, National Policy Forum Labour
Party, Labour Party Animal Welfare Society, Labour Party Committee on Ireland, Labour Party CND;
Chair, Labour Party Irish Society. Member: Liberty, Action for South Africa, Hayes and Harlington
Community Centre, League Against Cruel Sports; Member, Friends of Ireland – Coalition in support
of Belfast Agreement; Chair, Britain and Ireland Human Rights Centre; Member, London Wildlife
Trust; *Publications:* Editor, *Labour Herald; Clubs:* Member: Hayes Irish Society, Hayes and
Harlington Workingmens, Hayes and Harlington History Society; *Sportsclubs:* Hillingdon Outdoor
Activities Centre; Wayfarer Sailing Association; Vice-President, Hayes Football Club; *Recreations:*
Sailing, football, cycling, gardening, theatre, cinema. *Address:* John McDonnell Esq, MP, House of
Commons, London, SW1A 0AA *Tel:* 020 7219 6908 *Fax:* 020 7219 0927. *Constituency:* Hayes and
Harlington Labour Party Shop, 65 Station Road, Hayes, Middlesex *Tel:* 020 8569 0010 *Fax:* 020 8569 0109
E-mail: mcdonnellj@parliament.uk.

JOHN McFALL   Dumbarton   *Lab majority 10,883*

Born 4 October 1944; Son of late John and Jean McFall; Educated Paisley
College of Technology; Strathclyde University (BSc chemistry, MBA); Open
University (BA education). School teacher. **House of Commons:** Member
for Dumbarton since June 1987; Opposition Front Bench Spokesman on
Scottish Affairs (with responsibilities for Industry, Economic Affairs,
Employment and Training, Home Affairs, Transport and Roads, Agriculture,
Fisheries and Forestry) 1992–97; Opposition Whip 1989–91; Government
Whip 1997–98; Parliamentary Under-Secretary of State, Northern Ireland
Office 1998– (Minister for Education, Training and Employment, Health and
Community Relations 1998–99, for Economy and Education 1999–2000);
Select Committees: Member: Public Administration 2000–. *Special Interests:* Defence, Education,
Economic Policy, Co-operative Development; Latin America, Middle East, Romania. Member, Co-oper-
ative Party. *Recreations:* Jogging, golf, reading. *Address:* John McFall Esq, MP, House of Commons,
London, SW1A 0AA *Tel:* 020 7219 3521. *Constituency:* 125 College Street, Dumbarton, G82 1NH.

EDWARD McGRADY   South Down   SDLP majority 9,933

Born 3 June 1935; Son of late Michael and Lilian McGrady; Educated St Patrick's High School, Downpatrick; Married November 7, 1959, Patricia Swail (2 sons 1 daughter). Partner, M B McGrady & Co., Chartered Accountants. Downpatrick Urban District Council: Councillor 1961–73, Chair 1964–73; Down District Council: Councillor 1973–89, Chair 1975. **House of Commons:** Contested South Down 1979 and 1983 general elections and 1986 by-election. Member for South Down since June 1987; Spokesman on: Housing, Local Government, Environment; Chief Whip, SDLP 1979–; Member: Northern Ireland Assembly 1973, Minister for Co-ordination 1974, Northern Ireland Assembly 1982–86, Northern Ireland Forum 1996–98,
Northern Ireland Assembly 1998–; *Select Committees:* Member: Northern Ireland Affairs 1997–. *Special Interests:* Northern Ireland, Constitutional issues; Ireland, USA. Founder Member and First Chairman, SDLP 1970–72. Fellow, Institute Chartered Accountants; *Recreations:* Walking, gardening. *Address:* Edward McGrady Esq, MP, House of Commons, London, SW1A 0AA *Tel:* 020 7219 4481. *Constituency:* 32 Saul Street, Downpatrick, County Down, BT30 6NQ *Tel:* 028 4461 2882 *Fax:* 028 4461 9574 *E-mail:* e.mcgrady@sdlp.ie.

JOHN MacGREGOR   South Norfolk   Con majority 7,378

Born 14 February 1937; Son of late Dr N. S. R. MacGregor; Educated Merchiston Castle School, Edinburgh; St Andrews University (MA economics and history 1959); King's College, London University (LLB 1962); Married September 22, 1962, Jean Mary Elizabeth Dungey (1 son 2 daughters). Administrator, London University 1961–62; Editorial staff, *New Society* 1962–63; Special assistant to Sir Alec Douglas-Home, MP 1963–64; Head of private office of Edward Heath, MP 1965–68; Business executive in the City 1968–79; Director: Hill Samuel Registrars Ltd 1971–79, Hill Samuel & Co. Ltd 1973–79; Deputy Chair, Hill Samuel & Co. Ltd 1994–96; Director: Associated British Foods 1994–, Slough Estates 1995–, Unigate 1996–; Director, Friends
Provident 1998–. **House of Commons:** Member for South Norfolk since February 1974; Conservative Opposition Whip 1977–79; Government Whip 1979–81; Parliamentary Under-Secretary of State for Industry 1981–83; Minister of State, Ministry of Agriculture, Fisheries and Food 1983–85; Chief Secretary to the Treasury 1985–87; Minister of Agriculture, Fisheries and Food 1987–89; Secretary of State for Education and Science 1989–90; Lord President of the Council and Leader of the House of Commons 1990–92; Secretary of State for Transport 1992–94; *Select Committees:* Member: Privileges 1990–92, Standards and Privileges 1996–97. *Special Interests:* Economic and Financial Matters, Agriculture, Education, Industry, Housing, Countryside; Europe, USA, Australia and New Zealand, Japan. Chair: Young Conservative External Relations Committee 1959–62, Bow Group 1961–62; First President, Conservative and Christian Democratic Youth Community 1965. Member: Council of King's College, London 1996–, Inner Magic Circle; Member, Council of Institute of Directors 1995–; Vice-President, Association of County Councils 1995–97; Member, Committee on Standards in Public Life 1997–; Deputy Chairman, Governing Bodies Association 1998–; Trustee, Foundation of Business Responsibilities; OBE 1971; PC 1985; Fellow, King's College, London; Hon. LLD, Westminster University; *Recreations:* Music, gardening, travel, conjuring. *Address:* Rt Hon John MacGregor, OBE, MP, House of Commons, London, SW1A 0AA *Tel:* 020 7219 4439 *Fax:* 020 7219 0323. *Constituency:* Grasmere, Denmark Street, Diss, Norfolk, IP22 3LE *Tel:* 01379 642097 *Fax:* 01379 650765.

MARTIN McGUINNESS   Mid Ulster   SF majority 1,883

Born 23 May 1950; Educated Christian Brothers' Technical College. Sinn Fein Chief negotiator mid–1980s–; Member, Northern Ireland Assembly 1982, 1998–; Sinn Fein representative to the Dublin Forum for Peace and Reconciliation 1994–95; Minister for Education, Northern Ireland Assembly 1999–. **House of Commons:** Contested Foyle 1983, 1987 and 1992 general elections. Member for Mid Ulster since May 1, 1997; *Special Interests:* South Africa. *Recreations:* Cooking, walking, reading, fly fishing. *Address:* Martin McGuinness Esq, MP, House of Commons, London, SW1A 0AA *Tel:* 020 7219 3000. *Constituency:* 32 Burn Road, Cookstown, Co Tyrone, BT80 8DN *Tel:* 028 8676 5850 *Fax:* 028 8676 6734 *E-mail:* midulstersf@ireland.com.

ANNE McGUIRE   Stirling   Lab majority 6,411

Born 26 May 1949; Daughter of late Albert Long, railway signalman, and late Agnes Long, shop worker; Educated Our Lady of St Francis Secondary School, Glasgow; Glasgow University (MA Politics with History); Notre Dame College of Education (Diploma in Secondary Education); Married February 12, 1972, Len McGuire (1 son 1 daughter). Teacher; Development Worker/Senior Manager, Voluntary Sector; Depute Director, Scottish Council for Voluntary Organisations; National Executive, GMB 1987–91. Councillor, Strathclyde Regional Council 1980–82. **House of Commons:** Member for Stirling since May 1, 1997; Assistant Government Whip (Scotland, Agriculture: Scotland) 1998–; PPS to Donald Dewar as Secretary of State for Scotland December 1997–98; *Select Committees:* Member: European Legislation 1997–98. *Special Interests:* European Union, Rural Development, Urban Regeneration; USA, Germany. Member: Labour Party Scottish Executive 1984–; Chair, Labour Party Scotland 1992–93. Board Member, John Wheatly Centre; *Recreations:* Learning Gaelic, reading, walking. *Address:* Mrs Anne McGuire, MP, House of Commons, London, SW1A 0AA *Tel:* 020 7219 5014 *Fax:* 020 7219 2503. *Constituency:* 22 Viewfield Street, Stirling, FK8 1UA *Tel:* 01786 446515 *Fax:* 01786 446513 *E-mail:* mcguirea@parliament.uk.

ANNE McINTOSH   Vale of York   Con majority 9,721

Born 20 September 1954; Daughter of Dr Alastair McIntosh, retired medical practitioner, and Mrs Grethe-Lise McIntosh; Educated Harrogate College; Edinburgh University (LLB 1977); Århus University, Denmark (European Law); Married September 19, 1992, John Harvey. Trainee, EEC Competition Directorate 1978; Legal adviser, Didier and Associates, Brussels 1979–80; Apprentice, Scottish Bar, Edinburgh 1980–82; Admitted to Faculty of Advocates June 1982; Advocate, practising with Community Law Office, Brussels 1982–83; Adviser, European Democratic Group, principally on Transport, Youth Education, Culture, Tourism, Relations with Scandinavia, Austria and Yugoslavia 1983–89; MEP for Essex North East 1989–94, and for Essex North and Suffolk South 1994–99: Assistant Whip, European Democratic Group 1989–92, Member, Committee on Transport and Tourism 1989–99, Substitute, Committee on Legal Affairs and Citizens' Rights 1989–99, Conservative Spokesman on Transport and Tourism 1992–99, Member, European People's Party 1992–99, Bureau Member 1994–97, Rapporteur on Air Transport, relations with third world countries and Trans-European Road Networks, EU Competition Policy, Air Transport Safety, Substitute, Committee on Women's Rights 1994–99, Member, Delegation to EU-Poland Joint Parliamentary Committee 1994–99. **House of Commons:** Contested Workington, Cumbria 1987 general election. Member of Parliament for Vale of York since May 1, 1997; *Select Committees:* Member: Environment, Transport and Regional Affairs 1999–, Transport Sub-Committee 1999–. *Special Interests:* Transport, Legal Affairs, Animal Welfare; Eastern Europe, Scandinavia; Member, European Standing Committee C 1999–. President, Yorkshire First – Enterprise in Yorkshire; Co-Chair, European Transport Safety Council; President, Anglia Enterprise in Europe; Fellow, Industry and Parliament Trust 1995; *Recreations:* Swimming, walking, cinema. *Address:* Anne McIntosh, MP, House of Commons, London, SW1A 0AA *Tel:* 020 7219 0972 *Fax:* 020 7219 0972. *Constituency:* Vale of York Conservative Association, Thirsk Conservative Club, Westgate, Thirsk, North Yorkshire, YO7 1QS *Tel:* 01845 527240 *Fax:* 01845 527507.

SHONA McISAAC   Cleethorpes   *Lab majority 9,176*

Born 3 April 1960; Daughter of Angus McIsaac, retired chief petty officer, and Isa, née Nicol, school dinner lady; Educated SHAPE School, Belgium; Barne Barton Secondary Modern, Plymouth; Stoke Damerel High, Plymouth; Durham University (BSc geography 1981); Married April 2, 1994, Peter John Keith. Senior sub-editor, *Chat*; Deputy chief-sub-editor, *Bella*; Chief sub-editor, *Woman*; Freelance food writer; Member, NUJ. Councillor, London Borough of Wandsworth 1990–98. **House of Commons:** Member for Cleethorpes since May 1, 1997; *Select Committees:* Member: Standards and Privileges 1997–. *Special Interests:* Finance, Tax, Benefits, Economic Policy. Member, Northern Ireland Grand Committee; *Publications:* Various non-political work-related publications; *Recreations:* Football, food, travel, cycling, archaeology of the UK, soap operas. *Address:* Shona McIsaac, MP, House of Commons, London, SW1A 0AA *Tel:* 020 7219 5801 *Fax:* 020 7219 3047. *Constituency:* Immingham Resource Centre, Margaret Street, Immingham, Lincolnshire, DN40 1LE *Tel:* 01469 574324 *Fax:* 01469 510842.

ANDREW MACKAY   Bracknell   *Con majority 10,387*

Born 27 August 1949; Son of late Robert and Olive Mackay; Educated Solihull School; Married 1st, 1974, Diana Joy Kinchin (1 son 1 daughter) (divorced 1996); married 2nd, 1997, Julie Kirkbride, MP (*qv*) (1 son). Consultant to various public companies. **House of Commons:** Member for Birmingham Stechford 1977 by-election–1979. Member for Berkshire East 1983–97, and for Bracknell since May 1, 1997; Assistant Government Whip 1992–93; Government Whip 1993–96; Deputy Chief Whip 1996–97; PPS to Tom King as Secretary of State: for Northern Ireland 1986–89, for Defence 1989–92; Sponsored Licensing (Retail Sales) Act 1988 (Private Member's Bill); Member, Shadow Cabinet 1997–; Shadow Secretary of State for Northern Ireland 1997–; *Select Committees:* Member: Procedure 1994–95, Selection 1994–97. *Special Interests:* Foreign Affairs, Industry, Environment. Chair, Solihull Young Conservative 1971–74; Vice-Chair, Solihull Conservative Association 1971–74; Member, Conservative Party National Executive 1979–82. Chair, *Britain in Europe* Meriden Branch 1975 (Referendum); PC 1998; *Recreations:* Golf, squash, tennis, good food, travel. *Address:* Rt Hon Andrew Mackay, MP, House of Commons, London, SW1A 0AA *Tel:* 020 7219 2989.

ROSEMARY McKENNA   Cumbernauld and Kilsyth   *Lab majority 11,128*

Born 8 May 1941; Daughter of late Cornelius Harvey, publican, and late Mary Susan Crossan; Educated St Augustine's Comprehensive, Glasgow; Notre Dame College of Education (Diploma in Primary Education 1974); Married September 28, 1963, James Stephen McKenna (3 sons 1 daughter). Member: Educational Institute of Scotland, GMB. Councillor, Cumbernauld and Kilsyth District Council 1984–96, Leader and Convenor of Policy and Resources 1984–88, Provost 1988–92, Leader 1992–94; Member: Cumbernauld Development Corporation 1985–97, Scottish Enterprise 1993–96, 1996–. **House of Commons:** Member for Cumbernauld and Kilsyth since May 1, 1997; Joint PPS to Ministers of State, Foreign and Commonwealth Office 1999–; *Select Committees:* Member: Joint Committee on Statutory Instruments 1997–99, Scottish Affairs 1997–98, Catering 1998–99, European Legislation 1998, European Scrutiny 1998–99. *Special Interests:* Constitutional Reform, Democratic Renewal and Inclusive Politics; France, USA. Chair, Constituency Party 1979–85; Member, Scottish Executive and National Local Government Committee 1994–98. Chair, SLIC (Scottish Libraries and Information Council) 1998–; Member, Convention of Scottish Local Authorities 1984–, Vice-President 1992–94, President 1994–96; Member, EU Committee of the Regions 1993–97; Chair, Ad-Hoc Committee on Equality Issues until 1997; Chair, Scotland Europa 1994–96; Chair, UK and European Standing Committees of Women Elected Members of the Council of European Municipalities and Regions 1995–98; Cumbernauld Theatre Trust 1984–95; CBE; *Recreations:* Reading. *Address:* Mrs Rosemary McKenna, CBE, MP, House of Commons, London, SW1A 0AA *Tel:* 020 7219 4003 *Fax:* 020 7219 6492. *Constituency:* Lennox House, Lennox Road, Cumbernauld Road, Strathclyde, G67 1LL *Tel:* 01236 457788 *Fax:* 01236 457313 *E-mail:* mckennar@parliament.uk.

ANDREW MACKINLAY   Thurrock   *Lab majority 17,256*

Born 24 April 1949; Educated Salesian College, Chertsey, Surrey; (DMA); Married October 21, 1972, Ruth Segar (2 sons 1 daughter). Local government officer with Surrey County Council 1965–75; NALGO Official 1975–92; Former NALGO District Officer; Member, TGWU. Councillor, London Borough of Kingston upon Thames 1971–78. **House of Commons:** Contested Kingston-upon-Thames, Surbiton February and October 1974, Croydon Central 1983 and Peterborough 1987 general elections; London South and Surrey East 1984 European Parliament election. Member for Thurrock since April 9, 1992; Opposition Whip 1993–94; *Select Committees:* Member: Transport 1992–97; Member: Foreign Affairs 1997–, Unopposed Bills (Panel) 1997–. *Special Interests:* Constitution, Devolution, Electoral Reform, Police, Ports Industry, River Thames, Transport, Channel Islands, Isle of Man, Irish Affairs, Elderly, Environment; Poland, Belgium, France, Baltic States, Czech/Slovak Republics, Hungary, Falkland Islands, Gibraltar, USA. Vice-Chair, South and East Group of Labour MPs 1997–. Armed Forces Parliamentary Scheme (Royal Marines) 1997–98; Member, Parliamentary Delegation to OSCE; Member, Executive Committee, Commonwealth Parliamentary Association (CPA) UK Branch 1999–; Associate Member, Chartered Institute of Secretaries and Administrators; *Clubs:* Chadwell Workingmens'; *Sportsclubs:* Patron, Tilbury Football Club; *Recreations:* Visiting and studying First World War battlefields in France and Belgium, collecting Labour and Trade Union ephemera and memorabilia; non-league soccer. *Address:* Andrew Mackinlay Esq, MP, House of Commons, London, SW1A 0AA *Tel:* 020 7219 3000 *Tel (Constituency):* 01375 850359.

DAVID MACLEAN   Penrith and The Border   *Con majority 10,233*

Born 16 May 1953; Educated Fortrose Academy; Aberdeen University; Married 1977. **House of Commons:** Member for Penrith and The Border since July 1983 by-election; Assistant Government Whip 1987–89; Government Whip 1988–89; Parliamentary Secretary, Ministry of Agriculture, Fisheries and Food 1989–92; Minister of State: at Department of the Environment 1992–93, at Home Office 1993–97. PC 1995. *Address:* Rt Hon David Maclean, MP, House of Commons, London, SW1A 0AA *Tel:* 020 7219 6494 *Tel (Constituency):* 01697 478519.

HENRY McLEISH   Central Fife   *Lab majority 13,713*

Born 15 June 1948; Educated Buckhaven High School, Fife; Herriot Watt University, Edinburgh (BA urban planning 1973); Married 1st, March 16, 1968, Margaret Thomson Drysdale (died 1995) (1 son 1 daughter); married 2nd, May 1, 1998, Julie Fulton. Planning officer, Glenrothes Development Corporation 1973–74; Research officer, Edinburgh Social Work Department 1974–75; Planning and employment officer, Dunfermline District Council 1975–85; Employment co-ordinator 1985–87; Part-time lecturer, Heriot Watt University 1973–87; Part-time consultant on Employment Matters 1984–87; Member, UNISON. Chair, Planning Committee, Kirkcaldy District Council 1974–77; Chair, Education Committee, Fife Regional Council 1978–82, Leader of Council 1982–87. **House of Commons:** Contested North East Fife 1979 general election. Member for Central Fife since June 1987; Opposition Spokesman on: Scotland 1988–89, 1992–94, Employment 1989–92, Transport 1994–95, Health 1995–96, Social Security 1996–97; Minister of State, Scottish Office: (Minister for Health, Devolution and Transport) 1997–98, (Minister for Home Affairs, Devolution and Local Government) 1998–99. **Scottish Parliament:** MSP for Central Fife constituency since May 6, 1999; Minister for Enterprise and Lifelong Learning 1999–2000; First Minister 2000–. *Special Interests:* Employment, Trade and Industry, Energy, Local Government, Health; China, France, Germany, USA, former USSR. Fellow, Industry and Parliament Trust 1993. PC 2000. *Recreations:* Reading, sport, travel, history. *Address:* Rt Hon Henry McLeish, MP, MSP, House of Commons, London, SW1A 0AA. *Constituency:* Unit 14A Hanover Court, North Street, Glenrothes, Fife, KY7 5SB *Tel:* 01592 755540 *Fax:* 01592 610325 *E-mail:* h.b.mcleish@btinternet.com.

ROBERT MACLENNAN   Caithness, Sutherland and Easter Ross   *LD majority 2,259*

Born 26 June 1936; Son of late Sir Hector Maclennan; Educated Glasgow Academy; Balliol College, Oxford (MA); Trinity College, Cambridge (LLB); Columbia University, New York; Married August 1968, Mrs Helen Noyes (1 son 1 daughter and 1 stepson). Barrister. **House of Commons:** Member for Caithness and Sutherland, firstly as Labour, then as SDP and as a Liberal Democrat 1966–97, and for Caithness, Sutherland and Easter Ross since May 1, 1997; Additional Opposition Spokesman for: Scottish Affairs 1970–71, Defence 1971–72; Opposition Front Bench Spokesman for Foreign and Commonwealth Affairs 1980–81; SDP Spokesman for: Agriculture, Fisheries and Food 1981–87, Home and Legal Affairs 1983–87, Northern Ireland 1983–87, Scotland (jointly) 1982–87; Alliance Spokesman for Agriculture and Fisheries and Food 1987; Former Liberal Democrat Spokesman for: Home Affairs and National Heritage 1988–94, National Heritage; Spokesman for: Constitutional Affairs (Arts and Broadcasting) 1994–97, Constitution 1997–99, Culture, Media and Sport and Civil Service, Arts and Broadcasting 1997–99; Principal Liberal Democrat Spokesman for Constitutional Affairs and Culture 1999–; PPS to: George Thomson, as Minister without Portfolio 1967–69, as Chancellor of the Duchy of Lancaster 1969–70; Parliamentary Under-Secretary of State, Department of Prices and Consumer Protection 1974–79; Resigned the Labour Party and joined the Social Democrats 1981; *Select Committees:* Member: Public Accounts 1979–99. *Special Interests:* Constitutional Reform, European Union, Energy, Rural Affairs, Arts; Norway, Sweden, Denmark, USA. Leader, SDP 1987–88; President, Liberal Democrat Party 1994–98. Council member: Foundation for Management Education, Cancer Research Council, Association of British Orchestras; PC 1997; *Clubs:* Brooks's; *Recreations:* Theatre, music, visual arts. *Address:* Rt Hon Robert Maclennan, MP, House of Commons, London, SW1A 0AA *Tel:* 020 7219 6553 *Fax:* 020 7219 4846 *Tel (Constituency):* 01847 893750 (Caithness) 01408 633837 (Sutherland) *E-mail:* bobmaclennan@cix.compulink.co.uk.

PATRICK McLOUGHLIN   West Derbyshire   *Con majority 4,885*

Born 30 November 1957; Son of Patrick Alphonsos McLoughlin; Educated Cardinal Griffin Comprehensive School, Cannock; Staffordshire College of Agriculture; Married August 18, 1984, Lynne Patricia Newman (1 son 1 daughter). Agricultural worker 1974–79; Various positions with National Coal Board 1979–86. Councillor: Cannock Chase District Council 1980–87, Staffordshire County Council 1981–87. **House of Commons:** Contested Wolverhampton South East 1983 general election. Member for West Derbyshire since May 8, 1986 By-election; Assistant Government Whip 1995–96; Government Whip 1996–97; Opposition Pairing Whip 1997–98; Opposition Deputy Chief Whip 1998–; PPS: to Angela Rumbold as Minister of State, Department of Education 1987–88, to Lord Young of Graffham, as Secretary of State for Trade and Industry 1988–89; Parliamentary Under-Secretary of State, Department of Transport (Minister for Aviation and Shipping) 1989–92; Joint Parliamentary Under-Secretary of State, Department of Employment 1992–93; Parliamentary Under-Secretary of State for Trade and Technology, Department of Trade and Industry 1993–94; *Select Committees:* Member: Broadcasting 1994–95, National Heritage 1994–95; Member: Selection 1997–, Finance and Services 1998–. *Special Interests:* Agriculture, Education. National Vice-Chair, Young Conservatives 1982–84. *Address:* Patrick McLoughlin Esq, MP, House of Commons, London, SW1A 0AA *Tel:* 020 7219 3511 *Tel (Constituency):* 01332 558125 *Fax (Constituency):* 01332 558125 *E-mail:* patrick.mcloughlin@talk21.com.

Visit the Vacher Dod Website . . .

www.politicallinks.co.uk

KEVIN McNAMARA   Hull North   Lab majority 19,705

Born 5 September 1934; Son of late Patrick McNamara; Educated St Mary's College, Crosby; Hull University; Married August 4, 1960, Nora Jones (4 sons 1 daughter). Lecturer in Law; Secretary, Parliamentary Group TGWU. **House of Commons:** Contested Bridlington 1964 general election. Member for Kingston-upon-Hull North 1966–74, for Kingston-upon-Hull Central February 1974–83, and for Hull North since June 1983; Opposition Spokesman for Defence (Armed Forces) 1983–87; Principal Spokesperson on Northern Ireland 1987–94; Opposition Spokesperson on the Civil Service 1994–95; *Special Interests:* Northern Ireland; Ireland. Secretary, National Association of Labour Student Organisations 1956–57. Formerly Member, British Delegation, Council of Europe; Member, UK Delegation, North Atlantic Assembly 1984–88; Substitute, UK Delegation to Council of Europe and Western Europe Union; *Recreations:* Family, reading, walking. *Address:* Kevin McNamara Esq, MP, House of Commons, London, SW1A 0AA *Tel:* 020 7219 5194.

TONY McNULTY   Harrow East   Lab majority 9,734

Born 3 November 1958; Son of James Anthony McNulty, self-employed builder, and of Eileen McNulty; Educated Salvatorian College; Stanmore Sixth Form College; Liverpool University (BA political theory and institutions 1981); Virginia Polytechnic Institute and State University, USA (MA political science 1982). Lecturer, Business School, Polytechnic/University of North London 1983–97; Member: NUPE 1983–90, NATPHE 1983–97. Councillor, London Borough of Harrow 1986–97, Deputy Leader, Labour Group 1990–95, Leader 1995–97. **House of Commons:** Contested Harrow East 1992 general election. Member for Harrow East since May 1, 1997; Assistant Government Whip (Foreign Affairs: London) 1999–; PPS to David Blunkett as Secretary of State for Education and Employment with responsibility for post–16 provision 1997–99; *Special Interests:* Education, Health, Local Government, Regeneration, London; Ireland, France, Germany. Member: Socialist Educational Association, Fabian Society; Co-founder, Labour Friends of India; Member, Labour Friends of Israel. *Publications:* Various academic papers; *Clubs:* Wealdstone CIU; *Recreations:* Reading, theatre, rugby, cinema, football, gaelic games. *Address:* Tony McNulty Esq, MP, House of Commons, London, SW1A 0AA *Tel:* 020 7219 4108 *Fax:* 020 7219 2417. *Constituency:* 18 Byron Road, Wealdstone, Harrow, HA3 7ST *Tel:* 020 8427 2100 *Fax:* 020 8424 2319 *E-mail:* mcnultyt@parliament.uk.

DR DENIS MacSHANE   Rotherham   Lab majority 21,469

Born 21 May 1948; Educated Merton College, Oxford (MA modern history); London University (PhD international economics); Married 1987, Nathalie Pham (1 son 4 daughters). BBC producer 1969–77; Policy director, International Metal Workers' Federation 1980–92; Director, European Policy Institute 1992–94; President, National Union of Journalists 1978–79. **House of Commons:** Contested Solihull October 1974 general election. Member for Rotherham since May 5, 1994 By-Election; PPS: to Joyce Quin, Derek Fatchett and Tony Lloyd as Ministers of State, Foreign and Commonwealth Office 1997–99, to Geoff Hoon as Minister of State, Foreign and Commonwealth Office 1999; Joint PPS to Ministers of State, Foreign and Commonwealth Office 1999–; *Select Committees:* Member: Deregulation 1996–97. *Special Interests:* International Economics, European Union, Manufacturing; Europe, East and South East Asia. *Publications:* Several books on international politics; *Clubs:* East Dene Working Men's; *Recreations:* Family, walking. *Address:* Dr Denis MacShane, MP, House of Commons, London, SW1A 0AA *Tel:* 020 7219 4060 *Fax:* 020 7219 6888 *Tel (Constituency):* 01709 837577 *Fax (Constituency):* 01709 835622.

FIONA MACTAGGART   Slough   Lab majority 13,071

Born 12 September 1953; Daughter of late Sir Ian Mactaggart and of late Rosemary Belhaven; Educated London University: King's College (BA English), Goldsmiths' College (Postgraduate Teaching Certificate), Institute of Education (MA). Vice-President, National Secretary, National Union of Students 1978–81; General Secretary, Joint Council for the Welfare of Immigrants 1982–86; Primary school teacher 1987–92; Lecturer in primary education, Institute of Education 1992–97; Former Member: TGWU, NUJ, ASTMS; Member: NUT 1987–92, AUT 1992–1997, GMB 1997–. London Borough of Wandsworth: Councillor, Shaftesbury Ward 1986–90, Leader, Labour Group 1988–90. **House of Commons:** Member for Slough since May 1, 1997; PPS to Chris Smith as Secretary of State for Culture, Media and Sport 1997–; *Select Committees:* Member: Public Administration 1997–98. *Special Interests:* Human Rights, Civil Liberties, Home Affairs, Education, the Arts. Member, Fabian Society. Chair, Liberty 1994–96, Editorial Board, Renewal; *Recreations:* Walking, talking, reading, the arts. *Address:* Fiona Mactaggart, MP, House of Commons, London, SW1A 0AA *Tel:* 020 7219 3416 *Fax:* 020 7219 0989. *Constituency:* 29 Church Street, Slough, Berkshire, SL1 1PL *Tel:* 01753 518161 *Fax:* 01753 550293 *E-mail:* fionamac@netcomuk.co.uk.

TONY McWALTER   Hemel Hempstead   Lab majority 3,636

Born 20 March 1945; Son of late Joe McWalter, painter/decorator, and late Ann McWalter; Educated St Benedict's, Ealing; University College of Wales, Aberystwyth (BSc pure maths 1967, BSc philosophy 1968); McMaster University, Canada (MA philosophy 1968); University College, Oxford (BPhil philosophy 1971, MLitt 1983); Married March 30, 1991, Karen Omer (1 son 2 daughters). School teacher, Cardinal Wiseman Secondary School 1963–64; Long-distance lorry driver, E. H. Paterson Ltd 1964–67; Teaching Fellow, McMaster University, Canada 1968–69; Lecturer: Thames Polytechnic 1972–74, Hatfield Polytechnic/University of Hertfordshire 1974–; Member, TGWU; Branch Chair, NATFHE 1979–87; Polytechnics Panel, NATFHE 1984–89. Councillor, North Hertfordshire District Council 1979–83; Contested Hertfordshire 1984 and Bedfordshire South 1989 European Parliament elections. **House of Commons:** Contested St Albans 1987 and North Luton 1992 general elections. Member for Hemel Hempstead since May 1, 1997; *Select Committees:* Member: Northern Ireland Affairs 1997–2000. *Special Interests:* Local Government, Green Issues, Political Philosophy, Science and Technology; Ireland, Canada, USA. Member: The Samaritans 1971–81, Greenpeace, Friends of the Earth, Compassion in World Farming, Amnesty International, World Development Movement, CND; School Governor 1983–93; *Publications:* Co-editor *Kant and His Influence*, 1990; *Recreations:* Club tennis, family pursuits, contract bridge, philosophy, theatre, the Arts. *Address:* Tony McWalter Esq, MP, House of Commons, London, SW1A 0AA *Tel:* 020 7219 4547. *Constituency:* 5A Marlowes, Hemel Hempstead, Hertfordshire, AL1 1LA *Tel:* 01442 251251 *Fax:* 01442 241268 *E-mail:* tony.mcwalter@geo2.poptel.org.uk.

JOHN McWILLIAM   Blaydon   Lab majority 16,605

Born 16 May 1941; Son of late Alexander McWilliam, post office engineer; Educated Leith Academy; Heriot-Watt College; Napier College of Science and Technology; Married 1st, February 2, 1965, Lesley Catling (2 daughters); married 2nd, March 31, 1994, Mary McLoughlin (divorced 1997); married 3rd, March 1998, Helena Lovegreen. Telecommunications engineer; Former Branch Secretary and Regional Council Member, CWU. Councillor, Edinburgh City Council 1970–75; City Treasurer, Edinburgh 1974–75; Member: Commission for Local Authority Accounts, Scotland 1974–78; Scottish Council for Technical Education 1994–98. **House of Commons:** Member for Blaydon since May 1979; Opposition Whip 1984–87; Deputy Shadow Leader of the House 1983–84; Assistant to Opposition Chief Whip 1984–87; Deputy Speaker (Westminster Hall) 1999–;

Select Committees: Member: Defence 1987–97, Speaker's Panel of Chairmen 1987–97, Defence 1997–99, Liaison 1997–99; Member: Chairmen's Panel 1997–; Chairman: Selection 1997–; Member: Liaison 2000–. *Special Interests:* Defence, Technology, Education; Canada, Former Yugoslavia, New Zealand, USA, former Eastern Europe. Vice-Chair, Pitcom 1987–; *Recreations:* Reading, angling, listening to music. *Address:* John McWilliam Esq, MP, House of Commons, London, SW1A 0AA *Tel:* 020 7219 4020 *Fax:* 020 7219 6536. *Constituency:* 15 Shibdon Road, Blaydon on Tyne, NE21 5AF *Tel:* 0191–414 2488 *Fax:* 0191–414 8036.

SIR DAVID MADEL   South West Bedfordshire   *Con majority 132*

Born 6 August 1938; Son of late William Madel; Educated Uppingham School; Keble College, Oxford (MA 1965); Married October 16, 1971, Susan Catherine Carew (1 son 1 daughter). Graduate management trainee 1963–64; Advertising executive, Thomson Organisation 1964–70. **House of Commons:** Contested Erith and Crayford November 1965 by-election and 1966 general election. Member for South Bedfordshire 1970–83, and for South West Bedfordshire since June 1983; Opposition Whip: Education and Employment, Defence: Wessex 1997–98, Foreign and Commonwealth Office, International Development, Health 1998–99; PPS to service ministers at Ministry of Defence 1973–74; *Select Committees:* Member: European Legislation 1983–97, Administration 1992–95, Transport 1995–97, Chairmen's Panel 1997; Member: Chairmen's Panel 1999–, Foreign Affairs 1999–. *Special Interests:* Education, Employment. Member, Executive, 1922 Committee 1997; Fellow, Industry and Parliament Trust; Knighted 1994; *Clubs:* Carlton. *Address:* Sir David Madel, MP, House of Commons, London, SW1A 0AA *Tel:* 020 7219 3000 *Fax:* 020 7219 5540. *Constituency:* 6c Princes Street, Dunstable, Bedfordshire *Tel:* 01582 662821.

KEN MAGINNIS   Fermanagh and South Tyrone   *UUP majority 13,688*

Born 21 January 1938; Son of late Gilbert and Margaret Maginnis, née Wiggins; Educated Royal School, Dungannon; Stranmillis Teacher Training College, Belfast 1958; Married July 14, 1961, Joy Stewart (2 sons 2 daughters). 8 Battalion, Ulster Defence Regiment (Substantive Major) 1970–81; Teacher: Cookstown Secondary School 1959–60, Drumglass Primary School, Dungannon 1960–66; Principal, Pomeroy Primary School 1966–82. Dungannon District Council: Councillor 1981–93, Member, Southern Health and Social Services Council 1989–93, Chair, Finance and Personnel Committee. **House of Commons:** Contested Fermanagh and South Tyrone by-election August 1981. Member for Fermanagh and South Tyrone since June 1983. Resigned December 1985 in protest against the Anglo-Irish Agreement. Re-elected at by-election January 23, 1986; Spokesman for: Defence and Home Office 1997–2000, Defence, Trade and Industry 2000–; Member: Northern Ireland Assembly 1982, Northern Ireland Forum 1996–98; *Select Committees:* Member: Northern Ireland Affairs 1994–97. *Special Interests:* Terrorism and Internal Security, Defence; Brazil, Northern Cyprus. Vice-President, Ulster Unionist Council. Chair, Moygashel Regeneration Group; Director, Fermanagh Business Initiative (FBI); Chair, Police Rehabilitation and Retraining Trust (RUC). *Address:* Ken Maginnis Esq, MP, House of Commons, London, SW1A 0AA *Tel:* 020 7219 5234. *Constituency:* 20 Brooke Street, Dungannon, BT71 7AN *Tel:* 028 8772 3265 *Fax:* 028 8772 5569 *E-mail:* maginnisk@parliament.uk.

ALICE MAHON Halifax
Lab majority 11,212

Born 28 September 1937; Daughter of late Thomas Edward Reginald Bottomley, bus driver, and late Edna Bottomley; Educated Local Grammar School; Bradford University (BA social policy and administration 1979); Married 1st (divorced) (2 sons), married 2nd, Tony Mahon. Worked in NHS; Nursing auxiliary for 10 years; Higher education 1980; Taught trade union studies at Bradford College 1980–87; Activist with NUPE (now UNISON). Calderdale Borough Councillor 1982–87. **House of Commons:** Member for Halifax since June 1987; PPS to Chris Smith as Secretary of State: for National Heritage 1997, for Culture, Media and Sport to December 1997; *Select Committees:* Member: Health 1991–97. *Special Interests:* Health, Employment, Local Government, Trade Unions, Defence; Balkans, Russia. UK Delegate, North Atlantic Assembly 1992–; *Recreations:* Family. *Address:* Mrs Alice Mahon, MP, House of Commons, London, SW1A 0AA *Tel:* 020 7219 4464 *Fax:* 020 7219 2450. *Constituency:* 2 West Parade, Halifax, West Yorkshire, HX1 2TA *Tel:* 01422 251800 *Fax:* 01422 251888 *E-mail:* mahona@parliament.com.

JOHN MAJOR Huntingdon
Con majority 18,140

Born 29 March 1943; Son of late Thomas Major and Gwendolyn Minny Coates; Educated Rutlish School, Merton; Married October 1970, Norma Christina Elizabeth Johnson (1 son 1 daughter). Executive, Standard Chartered Bank 1965–81; Director, Warden Housing Association 1974–82; Chairman, European Advisory Board, UK-based Emerson Electric 1999–; Non-Executive Director, Mayflower Corporation plc 2000–. London Borough of Lambeth: Councillor 1968–71, Chairman, Housing Committee 1970–71. **House of Commons:** Contested Camden, St Pancras North February and October 1974 General Elections. Member for Huntingdonshire 1979–83, and for Huntingdon since June 1983; Government Whip 1983–85; PPS to Timothy Raison and Patrick Mayhew as Ministers of State, Home Office 1981–83; Parliamentary Under-Secretary of State for Social Security 1985–86; Minister of State for Social Security and the Disabled 1986–87; Chief Secretary of HM Treasury 1987–89; Secretary of State for Foreign and Commonwealth Affairs July-October 1989; Chancellor of the Exchequer 1989–90; Prime Minister, First Lord of the Treasury and Minister of the Civil Service 1990–97; Leader of the Opposition May-June 1997; *Special Interests:* Finance, Local Government, Agriculture, Race Relations, Social Policy, Housing, Northern Ireland, Constitution. Brixton Conservative Association: Various offices 1960–69, Chairman 1970–71; Leader, Conservative and Unionist Party 1990–97. President, National Asthma Campaign; Patron, Child of Achievement Awards; Chair: The Westminster Woodland 1998–, European Advisory Council, Emerson Electric Company 1999–; Member: European Advisory Board, The Carlyle Group 1998–, Board of Advisers, Baker Institute, Houston 1998–; Member: International Board of Governors, Peres Center for Peace, Israel 1997–, InterAction Council, Tokyo 1998–; *Publications: John Major, The Autobiography,* 1999; PC 1987; CH 1999; *The Spectator* Parliamentarian of the Year Award 1999; Politico's Book of 1999 Award, Channel 4 and *The House* Magazine; *Clubs:* Carlton, MCC; *Sportsclubs:* President, Surrey CCC 2000–; *Recreations:* Reading, watching opera, cricket, football and rugby. *Address:* Rt Hon John Major, CH, MP, House of Commons, London, SW1A 0AA *Tel:* 020 7219 5916. *Constituency:* Huntingdon Constituency Conservative Association, 8 Stukeley Road, Huntingdon, PE18 6XG *Tel:* 01480 453062.

HUMFREY MALINS Woking
Con majority 5,678

Born 31 July 1945; Son of Rev P. Malins and late Lilian Joan Malins; Educated St John's School, Leatherhead; Brasenose College, Oxford (MA jurisprudence 1967); Married July 21, 1979, Lynda Petman (1 son 1 daughter). Deputy Metropolitan Stipendiary Magistrate 1992–97; Recorder of the Crown Court 1996–. Mole Valley District Council: Member 1973–82, Chairman, Housing Committee 1980–81. **House of Commons:** Contested Liverpool Toxteth February and October 1974, East Lewisham 1979 general elections. Member for Croydon North West 1983–92, and for Woking since May 1, 1997; PPS: to Tim Renton as Minister of State, Home Office 1987–89, to Virginia Bottomley as Minister of State, Department of Health 1989–92;

Select Committees: Member: Home Affairs 1997–, Chairmen's Panel 1998–. *Special Interests:* Penal Affairs and Policy, Criminal Law Reform, European Union, Sport. Conservative Back Bench Legal Committee: Secretary 1983–86, Vice-Chair 1986–87. Chair, Trustees Immigration Advisory Service 1993–96; CBE 1997; *Clubs:* Vincents, Oxford, Walton Heath Golf, Richmond RFC; *Recreations:* Rugby, golf, gardening, family. *Address:* Humfrey Malins Esq, CBE, MP, House of Commons, London, SW1A 0AA *Tel:* 020 7219 4169. *Constituency:* Woking Constituency Conservative Association, Churchill House, Chobham Road, Woking, Surrey, GU21 4AA *Tel:* 01483 773384 *Fax:* 01483 770060.

JUDY MALLABER   Amber Valley   *Lab majority 11,613*

Born 10 July 1951; Daughter of late Kenneth Mallaber, librarian, and of late Margaret Joyce Mallaber, librarian; Educated North London Collegiate School; St Anne's College, Oxford (BA). Research officer, National Union of Public Employees 1975–85; Local government information unit 1985–96, Director 1987–95; Member, UNISON; Research Officer, NUPE 1975–85. **House of Commons:** Member for Amber Valley since May 1, 1997; *Select Committees:* Member: Education and Employment 1997–, Employment Sub-Committee 1997–. *Special Interests:* Economic Policy, Local Government, Education, Equal Opportunity, Employment. Labour Party posts include: Constituency Chair, Greater London Labour Party Regional Executive; Chair, Labour Research Department 1991–94. Member: Action for Southern Africa, Liberty, Friends of the Earth, Amnesty; Advisory Council Member, Northern College for Adult Education, Barnsley; *Clubs:* Anvil, Ironville; *Recreations:* Cinema, theatre, reading, family and friends. *Address:* Judy Mallaber, MP, House of Commons, London, SW1A 0AA *Tel:* 020 7219 3428. *Constituency:* Prospect House, Nottingham Road, Ripley, Derbyshire, DE5 3AZ *Tel:* 01773 512792 *Fax:* 01773 742393.

SEAMUS MALLON   Newry and Armagh   *SDLP majority 4,889*

Born 17 August 1936; Son of late Francis and Jane Mallon; Educated Abbey Grammar School, Newry; St Joseph's College of Education, Belfast; Married June 22, 1966, Gertrude Cush (1 daughter). Headmaster, St James Primary School, Markethill 1960–73; Member: Northern Ireland Assembly 1973–74, Northern Ireland Convention 1975–76, Irish Senate 1982, New Ireland Forum 1983–84, Northern Ireland Forum 1996–98, new Northern Ireland Assembly 1998–; Deputy First Minister, Northern Ireland Assembly 1998–. Councillor, Armagh District Council 1973–86. **House of Commons:** Contested Newry and Armagh, June 1983 general election. Member for Newry and Armagh since by-election January 23, 1986; Spokesman on Justice 1978–; *Select Committees:* Member: Agriculture 1987–92. *Special Interests:* Justice, Social Services; Australia, USA. Party Deputy Leader 1979–. Member, British-Irish Inter-Parliamentary Body 1986–; *Publications: Adam's Children;* Regular contributor to *Tribune; Sportsclubs:* Member, House of Commons Golf Society; *Recreations:* Angling, horse racing. *Address:* Seamus Mallon Esq, MP, House of Commons, London, SW1A 0AA *Tel:* 020 7219 3000. *Constituency:* 2 Bridge Street, Newry, County Down, BT35 8AE *Tel:* 028 3026 7933 *Fax:* 028 3026 7828.

PETER MANDELSON   Hartlepool   *Lab majority 17,508*

Born 21 October 1953; Son of late George Mandelson, and of Hon. Mary Joyce Morrison, daughter of late Baron Morrison of Lambeth; Educated Hendon County Grammar School; St Catherine's College, Oxford (BA philosophy, politics and economics). Producer LWT 1982–85; Director of Campaigns and Communications, Labour Party 1985–90; Industrial consultant, SRU Group 1990–92; Economic Department TUC 1977–78. Councillor, London Borough of Lambeth 1979–82. **House of Commons:** Member for Hartlepool since April 9, 1992; Opposition Spokesman on: The Duchy of Lancaster with responsibility for the Civil Service 1995–96, Election Planning 1996–97; Opposition Whip 1994–95; Minister without Portfolio, Cabinet Office 1997–98; Secretary of State for Trade and Industry July–December 1998, for Northern Ireland 1999–; *Special Interests:* Europe, USA.

Chair, PLP General Election Campaign (Planning) 1999–. Chairman, British Youth Council 1978–80; Vice-President, Federation of Economic Development Authorities (FEDA); Vice-Chairman, British Council 1999–; *Publications: Youth Employment: causes and cures*, 1977; *Broadcasting and Youth*, 1980; Co-author *The Blair Revolution – Can New Labour Deliver*, 1996; PC 1998; *Recreations:* Walking and the countryside, swimming. *Address:* Rt Hon Peter Mandelson, MP, House of Commons, London, SW1A 0AA *Tel:* 020 7219 2632 *Tel (Constituency):* 01429 264956 *Fax (Constituency):* 01429 264956.

JOHN MAPLES   Stratford-on-Avon   Con majority 14,106

Born 22 April 1943; Educated Marlborough College; Cambridge University (BA law 1964, MA); Harvard Business School; Married 1986, Jane Corbin (1 son 1 daughter). Barrister at Law 1965–; Called to Bar 1965. **House of Commons:** Member for Lewisham West 1983–92, and for Stratford-upon-Avon since May 1, 1997; PPS to Norman Lamont as Chief Secretary to the Treasury 1987–90; Economic Secretary, Treasury 1990–92; Member, Shadow Cabinet 1997–2000; Shadow Secretary of State for: Health 1997–98, Defence 1998–99, Foreign and Commonwealth Affairs 1999–2000; *Special Interests:* Foreign Affairs, Health, Economy. Deputy Chair, Conservative Party 1994–95. Joint Vice-Chair, British-American Parliamentary International Group 1999–. *Address:* John Maples Esq, MP, House of Commons, London, SW1A 0AA *Tel:* 020 7219 5495 *Fax:* 020 7219 2829. *Constituency:* 3 Trinity Street, Stratford upon Avon, CV37 6BL *Tel:* 01789 292723 *Fax:* 01789 415866 *E-mail:* maplesj@parliament.uk.

DR JOHN MAREK   Wrexham   Lab majority 11,762

Born 24 December 1940; Son of late John Marek; Educated Chatham House Grammar School; King's College, London (BSc, PhD); Married 1964, Anne Pritchard. Lecturer in Applied Mathematics, University College of Wales 1966–83. Councillor, Ceredigion District Council 1979–83; Chairman, Finance Committee 1982–83. **House of Commons:** Contested Ludlow October 1974 general election. Member for Wrexham since June 1983; Opposition Front Bench Spokesman on: Health 1985–87, Treasury and Civil Service matters 1987–92; *Select Committees:* Member: Catering 1997–. **National Assembly for Wales:** AM for Wrexham constituency since May 6, 1999; Deputy Presiding Officer 2000–. *Special Interests:* Transport, Economic Policy; Gibraltar, Hong Kong, Korea, Mauritius, St Helena. Secretary, Aberystwyth Labour Party 1971–79; Chair, Dyfed County Labour Party 1978–80. Member, Executive Committee, Commonwealth Parliamentary Association (CPA) UK Branch 1987–; Member, Executive Committee, Commonwealth Parliamentary Association (CPA) 1997–; Fellow, Industry and Parliament Trust. *Address:* Dr John Marek, MP, AM, House of Commons, London, SW1A 0AA. *Constituency:* 67 Regent Street, Wrexham, LL11 1PG *Tel:* 01978 364334 *Fax:* 01978 364334 *E-mail:* john.marek@wales.gsi.gov.uk.

GORDON MARSDEN   Blackpool South   Lab majority 11,616

Born 28 November 1953; Son of George Henry Marsden and Joyce Marsden; Educated Stockport Grammar School; New College, Oxford (MA history); London University; Harvard University. Open University tutor/associate lecturer, arts faculty 1977–97; Public relations consultant 1980–85; Chief public affairs adviser to English Heritage 1984–85; Editor, *History Today* 1985–97; Constituency posts in Hazel Grove, Oxford, London and Brighton; Member, GMB/APEX. **House of Commons:** Contested Blackpool South 1992. Member for Blackpool South since May 1, 1997; *Select Committees:* Member: Deregulation 1997–99; Member: Education and Employment 1998–, Education Sub-Committee 1998–. *Special Interests:* Heritage, Education, International Affairs, Social Issues, Disabled/Disability; USA, Russia, Caribbean, Eastern Europe. Joined Labour Party 1971; Joined Fabian Society 1975; Former Chairman, Young Fabians; Vice-Chair Fabian Society, Chair, Research and and Public Committee 1998–. Member, Association of British Editors; Editor, *New Socialist* 1989–90; Judge, Ford Conservation Awards UK 1990–97; Board Member, Institute of Historical Research 1996–;

President, British Resorts Association 1998–; Member, National Trust; Trustee, Dartmouth Street Trust; Board, History Today Trust 1999–; *Publications: Victorian Values* (ed.) 1990; Contributor to *The History Debate*, 1990; *Victorian Values*, 2nd edition 1998; *Low Cost Socialism*, 1997; Gibbs Prize in History 1975; Kennedy Scholar, Harvard 1978–79; *Recreations:* Theatre, early music and medieval culture, swimming, watching cricket, heritage sites, architecture. *Address:* Gordon Marsden Esq, MP, House of Commons, London, SW1A 0AA *Tel:* 020 7219 4166 *Fax:* 020 7219 1262. *Constituency:* 132 Highfield Road, Blackpool, Lancashire, FY4 2JP *Tel:* 01253 344143.

PAUL MARSDEN   Shrewsbury and Atcham   *Lab majority 1,670*

Born 18 March 1968; Son of late Tom Marsden and of Audrey Marsden; Educated Helsby High School; Mid-Cheshire College of Further Education (National Diploma in Building Studies 1986); Teesside Polytechnic 1990; Open University (Professional Certificate in Management, Professional Diploma in Management 1995); Newcastle College (Diploma in Business Excellence 2000); Married May 14, 1994, Shelly Somerville (2 sons). Quality manager: Taylor Woodrow Group 1990–94, Natwest Bank 1994–96, Mitel Telecom 1996–97; Member, CWU. **House of Commons:** Member for Shrewsbury and Atcham since May 1, 1997; *Select Committees:* Member: Agriculture 1997–. *Special Interests:* Health, Agriculture, Rural Affairs, Environment, Education, Economy; USA, Europe. Personal assistant to Parliamentary candidate in Cheshire 1987; Key organiser for Parliamentary candidate in Halifax 1992; Campaign manager/social secretary, Teesside Labour Party 1986–90; Branch secretary/GC delegate, Huddersfield CLP 1990–91; Member, National Executive Committee, Young Fabians 1990; Chair/secretary, several local Labour Party Branches. Member: English Heritage, Shropshire Chamber of Commerce, Training and Enterprise; Vice-President: Offa's Dyke Association, Heart of Wales Line Travellers Association; Member: Institute of Management, Health Bill Standing Committee 1999; Member, Commonwealth Parliamentary Association; Member, Shropshire Wildlife Trust; MIMgt; *Recreations:* Marathon running, reading, cinema, being with my family. *Address:* Paul Marsden Esq, MP, House of Commons, London, SW1A 0AA *Tel:* 020 7219 6913 *Fax:* 020 7219 0963. *Constituency:* Talbot House, Market Street, Shrewsbury, SY1 1LG *Tel:* 01743 341422 *Fax:* 01743 341261 *E-mail:* marsdenp@parliament.uk.

DAVID MARSHALL   Glasgow Shettleston   *Lab majority 15,868*

Born 7 May 1941; Educated Woodside Senior Secondary School, Glasgow; Larbert High School; Denny High School; Falkirk High School; Married, Christina (2 sons 1 daughter). Former transport worker; Shop steward; Member, TGWU 1960–; Chairman, TGWU Group of 33 MPs 1987–88. Councillor, Glasgow Corporation 1972–75; Strathclyde Regional Council: Councillor 1974–79, Chair, Manpower Committee; Former Chair, Manpower Committee of Convention of Scottish Local Authorities; Former Member, Local Authorities Conditions of Service Advisory Board. **House of Commons:** Member for Glasgow Shettleston since May 1979; Put Private Member's Bill, The Solvent Abuse (Scotland) Act through Parliament, May 1983; *Select Committees:* Member: Transport 1985–96, Liaison 1987–92; Chairman: Transport 1987–92; Member: Scottish Affairs 1994–97; Member: Liaison 1997–; Chairman: Scottish Affairs 1997–; Member: Unopposed Bills (Panel) 1997–. *Special Interests:* Transport, Third World, Scottish Affairs, Drug Abuse, Solvent Abuse, Pensioners' Rights. Former Labour Party Organiser, Glasgow; Hon. Secretary, Scottish Group of Labour MPs 1981–97; Hon. Secretary and Hon. Treasurer, Scottish Group of Labour MPs 1997–. Co-Chair, PACTS 1991–; Chair, Inter-Parliamentary Union (IPU) British Group; Member, Executive Committee, Commonwealth Parliamentary Association (CPA) UK Branch 1997–99, Joint Vice-Chair 1999–; *Recreations:* Gardening, music. *Address:* David Marshall Esq, MP, House of Commons, London, SW1A 0AA *Tel:* 020 7219 3000.

JAMES MARSHALL   Leicester South   *Lab majority 16,493*

Born 13 March 1941; Son of late Fred Marshall and Mrs Lilian Marshall; Educated Sheffield City Grammar School; Leeds University (PhD 1968); Married 1st, June 9, 1962, Shirley Ellis (marriage dissolved) (1 son 1 daughter), married 2nd, July 15, 1986, Sue Carter. Research scientist, Wool Industries Research Association 1963–67; Lecturer, Leicester Polytechnic 1968–74. Councillor, Leeds City 1965–68; Leicester City Council: Councillor 1971–76, Chair, Finance Committee 1972–74, Leader 1974. **House of Commons:** Contested the Harborough division of Leicestershire 1970 and Leicester South February 1974 general elections. Member for Leicester South October 1974–83 and since June 1987; Opposition Spokesman on: Home Affairs 1982–83, Northern Ireland 1988–92; Assistant Government Whip 1977–79; *Select Committees:* Member: European Legislation 1997–98; Member: European Scrutiny 1998–. *Special Interests:* Housing, Education, Local Government. Labour Leader, Association of District Councils 1974; Member, British Delegation to the Council of Europe and WEU. *Address:* James Marshall Esq, MP, House of Commons, London, SW1A 0AA *Tel:* 020 7219 5187. *Constituency:* 57 Regent Road, Leicester, CE1 6BF *Tel:* 0116–254 6900 *Fax:* 0116–255 3651.

ROBERT MARSHALL-ANDREWS   Medway   *Lab majority 5,354*

Born 10 April 1944; Son of late Robin and late Eileen Marshall; Educated Mill Hill School; Bristol University (LLB); Married 1968, Gillian Diana Elliott (1 son 1 daughter). Called to the Bar, Gray's Inn 1967, QC 1987, Bencher 1996; Recorder of the Crown Court 1982; Occasional novelist. **House of Commons:** Contested Richmond 1974 and Medway 1992. Member for Medway since May 1, 1997; *Select Committees:* Member: Joint Committee on Consolidation of Bills Etc 1997–. *Special Interests:* Economic Policy, Environment; East Africa, USA. Member, Society of Labour Lawyers. Former Head Governor, Grey Court School; Trustee: George Adamson Wildlife Trust 1988–, Geffreye Museum 1990–; *Publications: Palace of Wisdom,* 1989/1990; *Sportsclubs:* Vice-President, Old Millhillians Rugby; *Recreations:* Theatre, reading, watching rugby, writing, walking, travel. *Address:* Robert Marshall-Andrews Esq, QC, MP, House of Commons, London, SW1A 0AA *Tel:* 020 7219 6920 *Fax:* 020 7219 2933. *Constituency:* Moat House, 1 Castle Hill, Rochester, Kent, ME1 1QQ *Tel:* 01634 814687 *Fax:* 01634 831294 *E-mail:* marshallandrewsr@parliament.uk.

MICHAEL MARTIN   Glasgow Springburn   *Lab majority 17,326*

Born 3 July 1945; Son of Michael Martin, merchant seaman and Mary McNeil, school cleaner; Educated St Patrick's Boys' School, Glasgow; Married 1966, Mary McLay (1 son 1 daughter). Metal worker, Rolls-Royce Engineering; Full-time trades union official; Trade union organiser, NUPE; Member, AEEU (Craft Sector); Sponsored as MP by AEEU. Councillor: Glasgow Corporation 1973–75, Glasgow District Council 1975–79. **House of Commons:** Member for Glasgow Springburn since May 1979; PPS to Denis Healey as Deputy Leader of the Labour Party 1980–83; Deputy Speaker 1997–2000; Speaker 2000–; *Select Committees:* Chairman: Scottish Grand Committee 1987–97; Member: Speaker's Panel of Chairmen 1987–97; Chairman: Administration 1992–97, Liaison 1993–97; First Deputy Chairman of Ways and Means: Chairmen's Panel 1987–2000, Court of Referees 1997–2000, Unopposed Bills (Panel) 1997–2000, Standing Orders 1998–2000. *Special Interests:* Trade and Industry, Drug Abuse, Industrial Relations, Women's Rights, Care of the Elderly, Human Rights; Italy, Canada, USA. PC 2000; Fellow, Industry and Parliament Trust. *Recreations:* Hillwalking, folk music, local history, playing the Highland Pipes and member of the College of Piping. *Address:* Rt Hon Michael Martin, MP, House of Commons, London, SW1A 0AA *Tel:* 020 7219 1651.

ERIC MARTLEW   Carlisle   *Lab majority 12,390*

Born 3 January 1949; Son of late George and Mary Jane Martlew; Educated Harraby School, Carlisle; Carlisle College; Married December 19, 1970, Elsie Barbara Duggan. Nestlé Co. 1966–87: Laboratory technician, Personnel manager. Councillor, Carlisle County Borough Council 1972–74; Cumbria County Council: Councillor 1973–88, Chair 1983–85; Member, Cumbria Health Authority; East Cumbria Health Authority: Member 1975–88, Chairman 1977–79. **House of Commons:** Member for Carlisle since June 1987; Opposition Front Bench Spokesman on Defence, Disarmament and Arms Control with special responsibilities for the RAF 1992–95; Opposition Whip 1995–97; PPS: to Dr David Clark as Chancellor of the Duchy of Lancaster 1997–98, to Baroness Jay of Paddington as Lord Privy Seal, Leader of the Lords and Minister for Women 1998–; *Special Interests:* Transport, Health, Social Services, Agriculture, Defence. *Recreations:* Photography, fell-walking, horse-racing, watching rugby league. *Address:* Eric Martlew Esq, MP, House of Commons, London, SW1A 0AA *Tel:* 020 7219 4114 *Fax:* 020 7219 6898. *Constituency:* 3 Chatsworth Square, Carlisle, Cumbria, CA1 1HB *Tel:* 01228 511395 *Fax:* 01228 819798.

MICHAEL MATES   East Hampshire   *Con majority 11,590*

Born 9 June 1934; Son of Claude John Mates; Educated Blundell's School; King's College, Cambridge; Married 1st, 1959, Mary Rosamund Paton (marriage dissolved 1980) (2 sons 2 daughters), married 2nd, May 26, 1982, Rosellen Bett (marriage dissolved 1995) (1 daughter). Joined Army 1954; 2nd Lieutenant RUR 1955; Queen's Dragoon Guards, RAC 1961, Major 1967, Lieutenant-Colonel 1973, Resigned commission 1974. **House of Commons:** Member for Petersfield October 1974–83, East Hampshire since June 1983; Minister of State, Northern Ireland Office 1992–93; *Select Committees:* Chairman: Defence 1987–92. *Special Interests:* Defence, Northern Ireland, Home Affairs. Member, Committee on Intelligence and Security 1994–; Secretary, 1922 Committee 1987–88, Joint Secretary 1997–; UK Delegate, North Atlantic Assembly; Liveryman, Farriers' Company 1975, Master 1986–87; *Clubs:* MCC, Garrick; *Recreations:* Music. *Address:* Michael Mates Esq, MP, House of Commons, London, SW1A 0AA *Tel:* 020 7219 5166 *Fax:* 020 7219 4884. *Constituency:* 14A Butts Road, Alton, Hampshire *Tel:* 01420 84122.

FRANCIS MAUDE   Horsham   *Con majority 14,862*

Born 4 July 1953; Son of late Baron Maude of Stratford-upon-Avon, PC (Life Peer), author and journalist, and late Lady Maude; Educated Abingdon School; Corpus Christi, Cambridge (MA history 1976) (Hulse Prize and Avory Studentship); College of Law (Forster Boulton Prize and Inner Temple Law Scholarship 1977); Married 1984, Christina Jane Hadfield (2 sons 3 daughters). Called to Bar, Inner Temple 1977; Practising barrister 1977–85; Head of global privatisation, Saloman Bros International 1992–93; Managing Director, global privatisation, Morgan Stanley & Co Ltd 1993–97; Chairman, Deregulation Task Force 1993–97; Non-executive Director: Asda Group plc 1993–99, Benfield Reinsurance Ltd 1994–99, Gartmore Shared Equity Trust 1997–99, Benfield Greig plc 1999–, Businesses for Sale Company plc 2000–. Councillor, Westminster City Council 1978–84. **House of Commons:** Member for North Warwickshire 1983–92, and for Horsham since May 1, 1997; Government Whip 1985–87; PPS to Peter Morrison, as Minister of State for Employment 1984; Minister for Corporate and Consumer Affairs, Department of Trade and Industry 1987–89; Minister of State, Foreign and Commonwealth Office 1989–90; Financial Secretary to the Treasury 1990–92; Member, Shadow Cabinet 1997–; Shadow Secretary of State: for National Heritage 1997, for Culture, Media and Sport 1997–98; Shadow Chancellor of the Exchequer 1998–2000; Shadow Secretary of State for Foreign and Commonwealth Affairs 2000–; *Select Committees:* Member: Public Accounts 1990–92. Chairman, Governors of Abingdon School 1994–; Member, Executive, 1922 Committee 1997; PC 1992; *Recreations:* Skiing, reading, opera. *Address:* Rt Hon Francis Maude, MP, House of Commons, London, SW1A 0AA *Tel:* 020 7219 2494 *Fax:* 020 7219 0638. *Constituency:* Gough House, Madeira Avenue, Horsham, West Sussex, RH12 1AB *Tel:* 01403 242000 *Fax:* 01403 210600.

SIR BRIAN MAWHINNEY   North West Cambridgeshire   *Con majority 7,754*

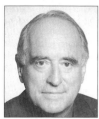

Born 26 July 1940; Son of Frederick Stanley Arnot and Coralie Jean Mawhinney; Educated Royal Belfast Academical Institution; Queen's University, Belfast (BSc physics 1963); Michigan University, USA (MSc radiation biology 1964); London University (PhD radiation biology 1968); Married August 27, 1965, Betty Louise Oja (2 sons 1 daughter). Assistant professor of radiation research, Iowa University, USA 1968–1970; Lecturer (subsequently senior lecturer), Royal Free Hospital School of Medicine 1970–84; Life Member, AUT. **House of Commons:** Contested Teeside Stockton October 1974 general election. Member for Peterborough 1979–97, and for North West Cambridgeshire since May 1, 1997; PPS: to Barney Hayhoe as Minister of State at the Treasury 1982–84; to Tom King: as Secretary of State for Employment 1983–85, for Northern Ireland 1984–86; Northern Ireland Office: Parliamentary Under-Secretary of State 1986–90, Minister of State, 1990–92; Minister of State, Department of Health 1992–94; Secretary of State for Transport 1994–95; Minister without Portfolio 1995–97; Member, Shadow Cabinet 1997–98: Shadow Home Secretary 1997–98; *Special Interests:* Health, Northern Ireland, Anglo-American Relations, Trade and Industry; Middle East, USA. National President, Conservative Trade Unionists 1987–90; Chair, Conservative Party 1995–97. Member: National Council, National Society for Cancer Relief 1981–85, General Synod 1985–90; President, Peterborough Association for the Blind; Member, Medical Research Council 1979–83; Fellow, Industry and Parliament Trust; *Publications:* Co-author *Conflict and Christianity in Northern Ireland* 1972; *In the Firing Line – Politics, Faith, Power and Forgiveness,* 1999; PC 1994; Kt 1997; *Sportsclubs:* Member, Etton Furze Golf Club; *Recreations:* Sport, reading. *Address:* Rt Hon Sir Brian Mawhinney, MP, House of Commons, London, SW1A 0AA *Tel:* 020 7219 6205. *Constituency:* 18 Peterborough Road, Wansford, Cambridgeshire, PE6 6JN *Tel:* 01780 783869; 01733 261868 *Fax:* 01780 783770; 01733 266887.

JOHN MAXTON   Glasgow Cathcart   *Lab majority 12,245*

Born 5 May 1936; Son of late John Maxton, agricultural economist, and late Jenny Maxton; Educated Lord William's Grammar School, Thame; University College, Oxford (BA modern history 1960, DipEd 1961); Married July 9, 1970, Christine Waine (3 sons). Lecturer in social studies, Hamilton College 1970–79; Member: MSF, Educational Institute of Scotland. **House of Commons:** Member for Glasgow Cathcart since May 1979; Opposition Front Bench Spokesman on Scotland 1985–92; Scottish and Treasury Whip 1985; *Select Committees:* Member: National Heritage 1992–97, Speaker's Panel of Chairmen 1994–97; Member: Chairmen's Panel 1997–, Culture, Media and Sport 1997–. *Special Interests:* Scotland, Devolution, Housing, Sport, The Arts; Spain. Member: Association of Lecturers in Colleges of Education, Socialist Educational Association, CND, Scottish Council for Civil Liberties; Member, Scottish Civil Liberties Trust; Council Member, National Trust for Scotland; *Recreations:* Listening to Jazz, running, fitness, holiday golf on the Isle of Arran. *Address:* John Maxton Esq, MP, House of Commons, London, SW1A 0AA *Tel:* 020 7219 4550. *Constituency:* Labour Club, Barlia Drive, Castlemilk, Glasgow *E-mail:* maxtonj@parliament.uk.

THERESA MAY   Maidenhead   *Con majority 11,981*

Born 1 October 1956; Daughter of late Rev Hubert Brasier and late Zaidee Brasier; Educated Wheatley Park Comprehensive School; St Hugh's, Oxford University (BA geography 1977, MA); Married September 6, 1980, Philip John May. Senior adviser, International Affairs at Association for Payment Clearing Services 1985–97. Councillor, London Borough of Merton 1986–94. **House of Commons:** Contested North-West Durham 1992 general election, Barking 1994 by-election. Member for Maidenhead since May 1, 1997; Opposition Spokeswoman for Education and Employment (schools, disabled people and women) 1998–99; Shadow Cabinet Spokeswoman for Women's Issues 1999–; Member, Shadow Cabinet 1999–; Shadow Secretary of State for Education and Employment 1999–; *Select Committees:* Member: Education and Employment 1997–98, Education Sub-Committee 1997–99. *Special Interests:* Education, Disabled/Disability, Europe. Fellow, Royal Geographical Society; *Clubs:* Lady Associate, Carlton, Maidenhead Conservative; *Recreations:* Walking, cooking. *Address:* Mrs Theresa May, MP, House of Commons, London, SW1A 0AA *Tel:* 020 7219 5206 *Fax:* 020 7219 1145. *Constituency:* Maidenhead Conservative Association, 2 Castle End Farm, Ruscombe, Berkshire, RG10 9XQ *Tel:* 0118 934 5433 *Fax:* 0118 934 5288 *E-mail:* mayt@parliament.uk.

MICHAEL MEACHER   Oldham West and Royton   *Lab majority 16,201*

Born 4 November 1939; Son of late George H. Meacher; Educated Berkhamsted School, Hertfordshire; New College, Oxford (BA Greats 1962); Married 1st, August 11, 1962, Molly Christine Reid (divorced 1987) (2 sons 2 daughters), married 2nd, May 28, 1988, Lucianne Sawyer, née Craven. Secretary, Danilo Dolci Trust 1964; Sembal research fellow in social gerontology, Essex University 1965–66; Lecturer in social administration: York University 1966–69, London School of Economics 1970; Visiting professor to Department of Sociology, Surrey University 1980–86; Member, UNISON. **House of Commons:** Contested Colchester 1966 general election and Oldham West 1968 by-election. Member for Oldham West 1970–97, and for Oldham West and Royton since May 1, 1997; Principal Opposition Front Bench Spokesman on: Health and Social Security 1983–87, Employment 1987–89, Social Security 1989–92, Overseas Development and Co-operation 1992–93, Citizen's Charter and Science 1993–94, Transport 1994–95, Education and Employment 1995–96, Environmental Protection 1996–97; Parliamentary Under-Secretary of State: Department of Industry 1974–75, Department of Health and Social Security 1975–76, Department of Trade 1976–79; Member, Shadow Cabinet 1983–97; Minister of State, Department of the Environment, Transport and the Regions (Minister for the Environment) 1997–; *Select Committees:* Member: Environmental Audit 1998; Ex-officio member: Environmental Audit 1997–. *Special Interests:* Economics and Social Policy, Redistribution of Income and Wealth, Industrial Democracy, Civil Liberties, Housing. Candidate for Deputy Leadership, Labour Party 1983; Member, Labour Party National Executive Committee 1983–89. Fellow, Industry and Parliament Trust; *Publications: The Care of Old People,* Fabian Society 1969; *Taken For A Ride: Special Residential Homes for the Elderly Mentally Infirm* 1972; *A Study of Separatism in Social Policy,* 1972; *Socialism with a Human Face – the Political Economy in the 1980s,* 1982; *Diffusing Power – The key to Socialist Revival,* 1992; Numerous articles and pamphlets on social and economic policy; PC 1997; *Recreations:* Sport, music, reading. *Address:* Rt Hon Michael Meacher, MP, House of Commons, London, SW1A 0AA *Tel:* 020 7219 4532/6461 *Fax:* 020 7219 5945. *Constituency:* 110 Union Street, Oldham, OL1 1DU *Tel:* 0161–626 5779 *Fax:* 0161–626 8572 *E-mail:* michael-meacher@detr.gsi.gov.uk.

Visit the Vacher Dod Website . . .
www.politicallinks.co.uk

ALAN MEALE   Mansfield   *Lab majority 20,518*

Born 31 July 1949; Son of late Albert Henry Meale, and of Elizabeth Meale; Educated St Joseph Roman Catholic School, Bishop Auckland; Durham University; Ruskin College, Oxford; Sheffield Hallam University; Married March 10, 1983, Diana Gilhespy. Author; editor; development officer; researcher for MPs Barbara Castle, Tony Benn, Dennis Skinner, Albert Booth; Parliamentary and political adviser to Michael Meacher as Principal Opposition Front Bench Spokesman on Health and Social Security 1984–87; National employment development officer, NACRO 1977–80; Assistant to Ray Buckton, General Secretary of ASLEF 1979–84; Sponsored by MSF. Former Deputy Leader, Local Authority. **House of Commons:** Member for Mansfield since June 1987; Opposition Whip 1992–94; PPS to John Prescott: as Deputy Leader of the Labour Party 1994–97, as Deputy Prime Minister and Secretary of State for the Environment, Transport and the Regions 1997–98; Parliamentary Under-Secretary of State, Department of the Environment, Transport and the Regions 1998–99; *Select Committees:* : European Legislation 1988–90; Member: Home Affairs 1990–92, Court of Referees 1997–98; Member: Court of Referees 1999–. *Special Interests:* Home Affairs, Transport, Health, Social Security, Drug Abuse, Human Rights, Environment, Poverty, Sport, Unemployment, Media, Music; Cyprus. Chair, PLP East Midlands and Central Groups 1988–95; Former Vice-Chair, PLP Employment Committee; Member, Co-operative Party. Parliamentary Representative, SSAFA 1990–94; Member, War Pensions Board 1990–; Author; Vice-President, NAPP; Parliamentary Representative, SSAFA (Armed Forces Social Welfare Organisation) 1989–95 Member, War Pensions Board 1989–97; Chair, British Cyprus Committee; Vice-Chair, Parliamentary Ukraine Committee; Fellow and Postgraduate Fellow of the Industry and Parliament Trust; Founder, Former Chair, Executive Member, Parliamentary Beer Industries Committee; Treasurer, CPA Cyprus Group (British Section); Former Executive Member: Commonwealth Parliamentary Association (CPA), Inter-Parliamentary Union (IPU); Member, UK Delegation Parliamentary Assembly of the Council of Europe/Western European Union 2000–; Fellow and Postgraduate Fellow, Industry and Parliament Trust; Honorary Citizenship: of Cyprus, of Mansfield, Ohio (USA); Honorary Senatorship of Louisiana (USA); Freeman, State of Louisiana, USA; Freeman, City of: Mansfield, Ohio, USA; Morphou, Cyprus; *Recreations:* Reading, writing, arts, politics, sports, Mansfield Football Club, Cyprus. *Address:* Alan Meale Esq, MP, House of Commons, London, SW1A 0AA *Tel:* 020 7219 4159. *Constituency:* 5 Clumber Street, Mansfied, Nottinghamshire, NG18 1NT *Tel:* 01623 660531 *Fax:* 01623 420495 *E-mail:* alan.meale@geo2.poptel.org.uk.

GILLIAN MERRON   Lincoln   *Lab majority 11,130*

Born 12 April 1959; Educated Wanstead High School; Lancaster University (BSc management sciences). Business development adviser; Local government officer; Lay representative and official, National Union of Public Employees (now UNISON); Senior officer for Lincolnshire, UNISON; Member, UNISON. **House of Commons:** Member for Lincoln since May 1, 1997; Sponsored, Football Sponsorship Levy Bill 1997; PPS to Ministers of State, Ministry of Defence: Doug Henderson, MP (Minister for the Armed Forces) 1998–99, Baroness Symons of Vernham Dean (Minister for Defence Procurement) 1999–; *Select Committees:* Member: Trade and Industry 1997–98. *Special Interests:* Economy, Employment, Low Pay, Business. Constituency and Regional Labour Party Officer; Member, Co-operative Party; Vice-Chair, Central Region Group of Labour MPs 1997–99; Board Member, Westminster Foundation for Democracy; Chair, East Midlands Regional Group of Labour MPs 1999–. Member: Amnesty International, Cats Protection League, Action for Southern Africa (formerly Anti Apartheid), Greenpeace, National Campaign for Nursery Education; Co-ordinated the Shadow Cabinet Central Region Campaign in General and European Elections; Campaigner on health, human rights and privatisation of Public utilities; Member, Armed Forces Parliamentary Scheme (RAF) 1997–98; Member, Standing Committee on: National Minimum Wage Bill, Northern Ireland Arms Decommissioning, Local Authority Tendering, New Northern Ireland Assembly (Elections) Order 1998–; Fellow-Elect, Industry and Parliament Trust; *Recreations:* Football, walking, films. *Address:* Gillian Merron, MP, House of Commons, London, SW1A 0AA *Tel:* 020 7219 4031 *Fax:* 020 7219 0489. *Constituency:* Grafton House, 32 Newland, Lincoln, LN1 1XJ *Tel:* 01522 888688 *Fax:* 01522 888686 *E-mail:* merrong@parliament.uk.

ALUN MICHAEL   Cardiff South and Penarth   *Lab/Co-op majority 13,881*

Born 22 August 1943; Son of late Leslie Michael and of Elizabeth Michael; Educated Colwyn Bay Grammar School; Keele University (BA); Married July 23, 1966, Mary Crawley (2 sons 3 daughters). Journalist, *South Wales Echo* 1966–72; Youth Worker, Cardiff City Council 1972–74; Youth and Community Worker, South Glamorgan CC 1974–87; AM for Mid and West Wales region 1999–2000; Member, GMB; Former Member: TGWU, CYWU; Branch Secretary, National Union of Journalists 1967–70; General Secretary, Welsh Association of FE and Youth Service Officers 1973–75. JP, Cardiff 1972–; Chair, Cardiff Juvenile Bench 1986–87; Cardiff City Council: Councillor 1973–89, Past Chair: Finance Committee, Planning Committee, Economic Development Committee 1987–89. **House of Commons:** Member for Cardiff South and Penarth since June 1987; Opposition Front Bench Spokesman on: Welsh Affairs 1988–92, Home Affairs 1992–97; The Voluntary Sector 1994–97; Opposition Whip 1987–88; Minister of State, Home Office (Minister for Criminal Policy also responsible for Police and the Voluntary Sector) 1997–98; Secretary of State for Wales 1998–99. **National Assembly for Wales:** AM for Mid and West Wales region 1999–2000; Labour Leader 1999–2000; First Secretary 1999–2000. *Special Interests:* Local Government, Housing, Youth Work, Juvenile Justice, Voluntary Sector, Community Development, Economic Development, Co-operative Development, Political Philosophy; Germany, South Africa, Israel, Canada, Somalia, USA, Japan. Former Chair, Co-operative Group of MPs; Member, National Executive, Co-operative Party (representing Wales); Member, Christian Socialist Movement. National Vice-President, Youth Hostels Association; Member of Board, Crime Concern 1993–97; Member: Commonwealth Parliamentary Association (CPA) (delegation to South Africa and Canada), Inter-Parliamentary Association (IPA); *Publications:* Contributor, *Restoring Faith in Politics*, 1966, *Challenges to a Challenging Faith*, 1995; Editor, *Tough on Crime and Tough on the Causes of Crime*, 1997, *Building the Future Together*, 1997; PC 1998; *Recreations:* Long-distance walking, running, reading, opera, music. *Address:* Rt Hon Alun Michael, JP, MP, House of Commons, London, SW1A 0AA *Tel:* 020 7219 5980 *Fax:* 020 7219 5930. *Constituency:* PO Box 453, Cardiff, CF11 9YN *Tel:* 029 2022 3533 *Fax:* 029 2022 9936/9947 *E-mail:* alunmichaelmp@parliament.uk.

BILL MICHIE   Sheffield Heeley   *Lab majority 17,078*

Born 24 November 1935; Son of late Arthur Michie, engineer, and late Violet Michie; Educated Abbeydale Secondary School, Sheffield; Sheffield Polytechnic (electrical engineering); Married May 1, 1987, Judith (2 sons, 1 stepson, 1 stepdaughter). RAF national service 1957–59; Electrician 1952–61; Laboratory technician 1961–81; Chair, AEEU Members Parliamentary Group. Councillor: Sheffield City Council 1970–84, South Yorkshire County Council 1974–86; Sheffield City Council, Chairman: Planning 1974–81, Employment 1981–83. **House of Commons:** Member for Sheffield Heeley since June 1983; *Select Committees:* Member: Members' Interests 1992–96, Privileges 1994–96; Member: Parliamentary Privilege (Joint Committee) 1997–. *Special Interests:* Industry, Local Government, Social Security. Member, Co-operative Party. Chairman, AEEU Members Parliamentary Group; *Clubs:* WMC Affiliated; *Recreations:* Darts, soccer. *Address:* Bill Michie Esq, MP, House of Commons, London, SW1A 0AA *Tel:* 020 7219 4140. *Constituency:* Barkers Pool House, Burgess Street, Sheffield, S1 2HF *Tel:* 0114–270 1181 *Fax:* 0114–276 9874 *E-mail:* michieb@parliament.uk.

RAY MICHIE   Argyll and Bute   *LD majority 6,081*

Born 4 February 1934; Daughter of late Lord and Lady Bannerman of Kildonan; Educated Aberdeen High School for Girls; Lansdowne House, Edinburgh; Edinburgh College of Speech Therapy (MCST 1955); Married May 11, 1957, Dr Iain Michie FRCP (3 daughters). Area speech therapist, Argyll and Clyde Health Board 1977–87; Member: Scottish National Farmers Union, Scottish Crofters Union. **House of Commons:** Contested Argyll 1979, Argyll and Bute 1983 general elections. Member for Argyll and Bute since June 1987; Liberal Spokeswoman for Transport and Rural Development 1987–88; Liberal Democrat Spokeswoman for: Women's Issues 1988–94, Scotland 1988–, (Scottish Team) for Agriculture, Community Care, Rural Affairs and

National Heritage 1997–99; *Select Committees:* Member: Scottish Affairs 1992–97; Member: Chairmen's Panel 1997–. *Special Interests:* Constitutional Reform, Home Rule for Scotland, Farming, Crofting, Gaelic language, Health Education, Fishing; Political Institutions in the EU. Vice-Chair, Scottish Liberal Party 1976–78; Chair, Scottish Liberal Democrats 1992–93; Deputy Leader, Scottish Liberal Democrats 1997–99. Vice-President, Royal College of Speech and Language Therapists; Hon. President, CFA (Clyde Fishermens Association); Member: An Comunn Gaidhealach, Scottish Constitutional Convention; Hon. Associate, National Council of Women of GB; *Clubs:* National Liberal; *Recreations:* Golf, swimming, gardening, watching rugby. *Address:* Mrs Ray Michie, MP, House of Commons, SW1A 0AA *Tel:* 020 7219 4140. *Constituency:* 5 Stafford Street, Oban, Argyll, PA34 5NJ *Tel:* 01631 563551 *Fax:* 01631 565736; Email: margaret.wills@virgin.net *E-mail:* medinam@parliament.uk.

ALAN MILBURN Darlington Lab majority 16,025

Born 27 January 1958; Son of Evelyn Metcalfe, former NHS secretary; Educated John Marlay School, Newcastle; Stokesley Comprehensive School; Lancaster University (BA history); Newcastle University; Partner, Ruth Briel (2 sons). Senior business development officer, North Tyneside Council 1990–92; Co-ordinator, Trade Union Studies Information Unit, Newcastle 1984–90; Co-ordinator, Sunderland Shipyards Campaign 1988–89; President, North East Region, MSF Union 1990–92. **House of Commons:** Member for Darlington since April 9, 1992; Opposition Spokesman on: Health 1995–96, Treasury and Economic Affairs (Shadow Economic Secretary) 1996–97; Minister of State, Department of Health 1997–98; Chief Secretary, HM Treasury December 1998–99; Secretary of State for Health 1999–; *Select Committees:* Member: Public Accounts 1994–95. *Special Interests:* Economic Policy, Industry, Regional Policy, Crime, Health. Chair, Newcastle Central Constituency Labour Party 1988–90; Member, Northern Region Labour Party Executive Committee 1990–92. *Publications: Jobs and Industry, the North Can Make It,* 1986; *Plan for the North,* 1987; *The Case for Regional Government,* 1989; PC 1998; *Recreations:* Cricket, football, music, cinema. *Address:* Rt Hon Alan Milburn, MP, House of Commons, London, SW1A 0AA *Tel:* 020 7219 3000. *Constituency:* 123 Victoria Road, Darlington, County Durham, DL1 5JH *Tel:* 01325 380366.

ANDREW MILLER Ellesmere Port and Neston Lab majority 16,036

Born 23 March 1949; Son of late Ernest and Daphne Miller; Educated Hayling Island Secondary School; Highbury Technical College; London School of Economics (diploma in industrial relations 1977); Married Frances Ewan (2 sons 1 daughter). Technician, Portsmouth Polytechnic, analyst in geology 1967–76; Regional official, MSF (formerly ASTMS) 1977–92. **House of Commons:** Member for Ellesmere Port and Neston since April 9, 1992; *Select Committees:* Member: Information 1992–97, Science and Technology 1992–97; Member: Information 1997–. *Special Interests:* Industry, Economic Policy, Science and Technology, Communications and Information Technology, Occupational Pensions; Europe, China, USA. Member: Labour Party, NW Regional Executive Committee 1984–92; President, Computing for Labour 1993–; Chair: Leadership Campaign Team 1997–98, North West Group of Labour MPs 1997–98; Member, Scientists for Labour 1997–. Patron: Road Peace, Chester Childbirth Trust, Parents Against Drug Abuse; *Sportsclubs:* Vice-President: Alvanley Cricket Club, Chester and Ellesmere Port Athletics Club; *Recreations:* Walking, photography, tennis, cricket. *Address:* Andrew Miller Esq, MP, House of Commons, London, SW1A 0AA *Tel:* 020 7219 3580 *Fax:* 020 7219 3796. *Constituency:* Whitby Hall Lodge, Stanney Lane, Ellesmere Port, Cheshire, CH65 6QY *Tel:* 0151–357 3019 *Fax:* 0151–356 8226 *E-mail:* millera@parliament.uk.

AUSTIN MITCHELL Great Grimsby   *Lab majority 16,244*

Born 19 September 1934; Son of Richard Vernon Mitchell, Dyer; Educated Woodbottom Council School; Bingley Grammar School; Manchester University; Nuffield College, Oxford (BA, MA, DPhil); Married 1st, Patricia Dorothea Jackson (divorced) (2 daughters), married 2nd, Linda Mary McDougall (1 son 1 daughter). Lecturer in history, Otago University, Dunedin, New Zealand 1959–63; Senior lecturer in politics, University of Canterbury, Christchurch, NZ 1963–67; Official fellow, Nuffield College, Oxford 1967–69; Journalist: Yorkshire Television 1969–71, BBC 1972, Yorkshire Television 1973–77; Political commentator, Sky Television's Target programme 1989–98; Associate editor, *The House Magazine.* **House of Commons:** Member for Grimsby 1977–83 and for Great Grimsby since June 1983; Front Bench Spokesman, Trade and Industry 1988–89; Former Opposition Whip; PPS to John Fraser as Minister of State for Prices and Consumer Protection 1977–79; *Select Committees:* Member: Agriculture 1997–. *Special Interests:* Economics, Media, Fishing, Agriculture, Poverty, Accountancy, Legal Reform, European Union, Electoral Reform, Constitutional Reform; Canada, Iceland, New Zealand, France, Germany, China, Hong Kong, Nigeria. Member, Executive Council Fabian Society; Vice-Chair: Labour Campaign for Electoral Reform, Labour Euro-Safeguards Campaign; Chair, Labour Economic Policy Group. Vice-Chair, Hansard Society; Member: Hairdressing Council, Advisory Council, National Fishing Heritage Centre, Public Accounts Commission 1997–; Vice-President, Federation of Economic Development Authorities (FEDA); President, Debating Group; Member, Royal Institute of International Affairs; Joint Secretary, Esperanto Parliamentary Group; Fellow, Industry and Parliament Trust; *Publications: New Zealand Politics in Action 1962;* Government by Party, 1966; *Whigs in Opposition, 1815–30,* 1969; *Politics and People in New Zealand,* 1970; *Half Gallon Quarter Acre Pavlova – Paradise,* 1974; *Can Labour Win Again,* 1979; *Yes Maggie there is an Alternative*; *Westminster Man,* 1982; *The Case for Labour,* 1983; *Four Years in the Death of the Labour Party,* 1983; *Yorkshire Jokes* 1988; *Teach Thissen Tyke* 1988; *Britain, Beyond the Blue Horizon,* 1989; *Competitive Socialism,* 1989; *Election '45,* 1995; *Accounting for Change,* 1993; *Corporate Governance Matters,* 1996; *The Common Fisheries Policy, End or Mend?,* 1996; Co-author *Last Time: Labour's Lessons from the Sixties* 1997; *Farewell My Lords,* 1999; Co-author *Parliament in Pictures* 1999; *Recreations:* Photography, contemplating exercise. *Address:* Austin Mitchell Esq, MP, House of Commons, London, SW1A 0AA *Tel:* 020 7219 4559 *Fax:* 020 7219 4843. *Constituency:* 15 New Cartergate, Grimsby, NE Lincs, DN31 1RB *Tel:* 01472 342145 *Fax:* 01472 251484 *E-mail:* austin@austinmitchell.co.uk.

LAURA MOFFATT Crawley   *Lab majority 11,707*

Born 9 April 1954; Daughter of Stanley and Barbara Field; Educated Hazelwick School, Crawley; Crawley College of Technology; Married November 1, 1975, Colin Moffatt (3 sons). State Registered Nurse, Crawley Hospital; Member, UNISON. Crawley Borough Council: Councillor 1984–96, Mayor 1989–90, Chair, Environmental Services 1987–96. **House of Commons:** Member for Crawley since May 1, 1997; *Select Committees:* Member: Defence 1997–. *Special Interests:* Health, Housing, Aerospace, Aviation, Defence, AIDS, Drug Abuse. Member, Lioness Club; Director, Furniaid (registered charity to provide furniture for needy); President, Relate; *Recreations:* Family, friends, walking, pets, swimming. *Address:* Mrs Laura Moffatt, MP, House of Commons, London, SW1A 0AA *Tel:* 020 7219 3619 *Fax:* 020 7219 3619. *Constituency:* 6 The Broadway, Crawley, West Sussex, RH10 1DS *Tel:* 01293 526005 *Fax:* 01293 526005 *E-mail:* clewerd@parliament.uk.

Visit the Vacher Dod Website . . .
www.politicallinks.co.uk

LEWIS MOONIE   Kirkcaldy   Lab/Co-op majority 10,710

Born 25 February 1947; Son of late George Moonie, retired accountant, and of Eva Moonie; Educated Grove Academy, Dundee; St Andrews University (MB, ChB 1970); Edinburgh University (DPM 1975, MRCPsych 1979, MSc Community Medicine 1981, MFCM 1984); Married December 28, 1971, Sheila Ann Burt (2 sons). Registrar training in psychiatry 1973–75; Full-time research clinical pharmacologist and medical adviser in pharmaceutical industry in Netherlands, Switzerland and Edinburgh 1975–80; Trainee Community Medicine, Fife Health Board 1980–84; Community Medicine specialist, Fife Health Board 1984–87. Councillor, Fife Regional Council 1982–86. **House of Commons:** Member for Kirkcaldy since June 1987; Opposition Front Bench Spokesman on: Technology, Trade and Industry 1989–92, Science and Technology 1992–94, Trade and Industry 1994–95, Broadcasting and Telecommunications 1995–97; Parliamentary Under-Secretary of State, Ministry of Defence 2000–; *Select Committees:* Member: Public Accounts Commission 1995–97; Chairman: Finance and Services 1997–2000; Member: Liaison 1997–2000, Treasury 1998–2000, Treasury Sub-Committee 1998–2000. *Special Interests:* Industry, Technology, Economic Policy, Defence. Member, Co-operative Party. Member, House of Commons Commission 1997–2000; *Recreations:* A wide variety of sporting and recreational activities. *Address:* Dr Lewis Moonie, MP, House of Commons, London, SW1A 0AA *Tel:* 020 7219 4097 *Tel (Constituency):* 01592 564115.

MICHAEL MOORE   Tweeddale, Ettrick and Lauderdale   LD majority 1,489

Born 3 June 1965; Son of Reverend W. Haisley Moore, Church of Scotland minister, and Jill Moore, physiotherapist; Educated Strathallan School; Jedburgh Grammar School; Edinburgh University (MA politics and modern history 1987); Single. Research assistant to Archy Kirkwood, MP 1987–88; Coopers and Lybrand, Edinburgh 1988–97; Manager, Corporate Finance Practice 1993–97. **House of Commons:** Member for Tweeddale, Ettrick and Lauderdale since May 1, 1997; Spokesman for: Scotland (Industry, Employment, Health and Environment) 1997–99, Environment, Transport, the Regions and Social Justice (Transport) 1999–; *Select Committees:* Member: Scottish Affairs 1997–99. *Special Interests:* Business, Employment, Housing. Campaign Chairman, 1999 Scottish Elections; Parliamentary Group Convenor 2000–. Member, Amnesty International; Scottish Spokesman on Business and Employment 1995–99; Liberal Democrat Party Conference, Debate on Economy 1995; Institute of Chartered Accountants of Scotland 1991; *Recreations:* Rugby, hill-walking, music, films. *Address:* Michael Moore Esq, MP, House of Commons, London, SW1A 0AA *Tel:* 020 7219 2236. *Constituency:* Tweeddale, Ettrick and Lauderdale Liberal Democrats, 46 High Street, Innerleithen, Borders, EH44 6HF *Tel:* 01896 831011 *Fax:* 01896 831437 *E-mail:* michaelmoore@cix.compulink.co.uk.

MARGARET MORAN   Luton South   Lab majority 11,319

Born 24 April 1955; Daughter of late Patrick (Jack) Moran, caretaker and of Mary, née Murphy, home care worker; Educated St Ursula's, South London; St Mary's, Strawberry Hill, Twickenham; Birmingham University (BSocSc 1978). Director, Housing Association; Housing, local government, social services and education; Former national president, NALGO Housing Association Branch. Councillor, London Borough of Lewisham 1984–97, Leader 1993–95, Chair, Housing Committee (6 years). **House of Commons:** Contested Carshalton and Wallington 1992. Member for Luton South since May 1, 1997; PPS to Gavin Strang as Minister of State (in Cabinet), Department of the Environment, Transport and the Regions (Minister for Transport) 1997–98, to Dr Mo Mowlam as Minister for the Cabinet Office 1999–; *Select Committees:* Member: Northern Ireland Affairs 1998, Public Administration 1999–2000. *Special Interests:* Economy and Employment, Welfare, Housing and Urban Regeneration, Childcare, E-Issues; Northern Ireland, Kashmir, Spain, Bangladesh, Ireland.

Member: Labour National Policy Forum, Labour Women's Network, Labour Housing Group. Patron, Homes for Homeless People; Vice-Chair: Association of London Local Authorities, Association of Metropolitan Authorities; Chair, AMA Housing Committee; *Recreations:* Visiting historic sites, rambling, cinema. *Address:* Margaret Moran, MP, House of Commons, London, SW1A 0AA *Tel:* 020 7219 5049 *Fax:* 020 7219 5094. *Constituency:* 3 Union Street, Luton, Bedfordshire *Tel:* 01582 731882 *Fax:* 01582 731885 *E-mail:* moranm@parliament.uk *Website:* http://www.margaretmoran.org.

ALASDAIR MORGAN   Galloway and Upper Nithsdale   *SNP majority 5,624*

Born 21 April 1945; Son of late Alexander Morgan, insurance superintendent, and Emily Morgan; Educated Breadalbane Academy, Aberfeldy; Glasgow University (MA mathematics and political economy 1968); Open University (BA 1989); Married August 28, 1969, Anne Gilfillan (2 daughters). MSP for Galloway and Upper Nithsdale since May 6, 1999. **House of Commons:** Member for Galloway and Upper Nithsdale since May 1, 1997; Spokesman for Employment, Trade and Industry (including tourism and small businesses), Energy, Forestry, Transport 1997–99; SNP Chief Whip 1999–; *Select Committees:* Member: Trade and Industry 1997–. *Special Interests:* European Union, Transport, Rural Affairs. SNP: National Treasurer 1983–90, Senior Vice-Convenor 1990–91, Election Director 1992, National Secretary 1992–97, Vice-President 1997–. *Recreations:* Hill-walking. *Address:* Alasdair Morgan Esq, MP, MSP, House of Commons, London, SW1A 0AA *Tel:* 020 7219 3472 *Fax:* 020 7219 1235. *Constituency:* 106a High Street, Dalbeattie, Kirkcudbrightshire, DG5 4HB *Tel:* 01556 611956 *Fax:* 01556 613240 *E-mail:* morganal@parliament.uk.

JULIE MORGAN   Cardiff North   *Lab majority 8,126*

Born 2 November 1944; Daughter of late Jack Edwards and Grace Edwards; Educated Dinas Powys Primary School; Howell's School, Llandaff, Cardiff; King's College, London University (BA); Manchester University; Cardiff University (Postgraduate Diploma in Social Administration, CQSW); Married April 22, 1967, Rhodri Morgan (now MP – *qv*) (1 son 2 daughters). Principal officer and development officer, West Glamorgan County Council 1983–87; Senior social worker, Barry Social Services 1985–87; Assistant director, Child Care, Barnados 1987–; Member, TGWU. Councillor: South Glamorgan Council 1985–96, Cardiff Council 1996; Member, Probation Committee. **House of Commons:** Contested Cardiff North 1992 General Election. Member for Cardiff North since May 1, 1997; *Select Committees:* Member: Welsh Affairs 1997–. *Special Interests:* Equal Opportunity, Social Services, Childcare; Nicaragua. Hon. Treasurer: Welsh Regional Group of Labour MPs 1999–, Parliamentary Labour Party Women's Group. Chair of Governors, Albany Road School; Member: Welsh Refugee Council, Race Equality Council, Nicaragua Solidarity Campaign; Permanent Waves, Women's Arts Association; *Recreations:* Swimming, walking. *Address:* Mrs Julie Morgan, MP, House of Commons, London, SW1A 0AA *Tel:* 020 7219 6960 *Fax:* 020 7219 0960. *Constituency:* Cardiff North Constituency Office, 17 Plasnewydd, Whitchurch, Cardiff, CF14 1NR *Tel:* 029 2052 2913 *Fax:* 029 2061 3662.

RHODRI MORGAN   Cardiff West   *Lab majority 15,628*

Born 29 September 1939; Son of late Thomas John Morgan, Vice-Principal of University College, Swansea, and Huana Morgan; Educated Whitchurch Grammar School, Cardiff; St John's College, Oxford University (BA philosophy, politics and economics 1961); Harvard University; Graduate School of Arts and Sciences (MA government 1963); Married April 22, 1967, Julie Edwards (*qv* as Julie Morgan MP) (1 son 2 daughters). Tutor, Organiser Workers' Educational Association 1963–65; Research Officer: Cardiff City Planning Department 1965–66; Welsh Office 1967–71; Economic Adviser, Department of Trade and Industry 1972–74; Industrial Development Officer, South Glamorgan County Council 1974–80; Head, European Commission Press and Information Office for Wales 1980–87; Member, TGWU. **House of Commons:** Member for Cardiff West since June 1987; Opposition Front Bench Spokesman on Energy 1988–92, on Welsh Affairs 1992–97; *Select Committees:* Member: Energy 1987–88, Members' Interests 1987–88, Liaison 1997–99;

Chairman: Public Administration 1997–99. **National Assembly for Wales:** AM for Cardiff West constituency since May 6, 1999; Economic Development Secretary 1999–2000; Labour Leader 2000–; First Secretary 2000–. *Special Interests:* Industrial Policy, Regional Policy, Wild Life Conservation (Especially Bird and Marine), Health; USA, France, Germany. Chair, Welsh Regional Group of Labour MPs 1999. Founder Member, Wales Co-operative Centre 1985; *Publications: Cardiff – Half and Half a Capital,* 1994; PC 2000; *Clubs:* Canton Labour, Grange, Riverside Labour; *Sportsclubs:* Fairwater Rugby; Secretary, Lords and Commons Tennis Club; *Recreations:* Running, wood-carving, watching rugby and athletics. *Address:* Rt Hon Rhodri Morgan, MP, AM, House of Commons, London, SW1A 0AA *Tel:* 020 7219 3498/2510 *Fax:* 020 7219 6838. *Constituency:* Transport House, 1 Cathedral Road, Cardiff, CF1 9SD *Tel:* 029 2022 3207/ 3370 *Fax:* 029 2023 0422.

| ELLIOT MORLEY   Scunthorpe | *Lab majority 14,173* |

Born 6 July 1952; Son of Anthony Morley and late Margaret Morley; Educated St Margaret's High School, Liverpool; Hull College of Education (BEd); Married September 1975, Patricia Hunt (1 son 1 daughter). Teacher; Former President, Hull Teachers Association. Hull City Council: Councillor 1979–86, Chair, City Transport Committee 1981–85, Former deputy traffic commissioner, NE Region; Member, NIJC of Municipal Bus Industries; Executive member, Federation of Public Passenger Employers 1981–86. **House of Commons:** Contested Beverley 1983 general election. Member for Glanford and Scunthorpe 1987–97, and for Scunthorpe since May 1, 1997; Opposition Spokesman on Food, Agriculture and Rural Affairs with special responsibility for animal welfare 1989–97; Parliamentary Secretary, Ministry of Agriculture, Fisheries and Food (Minister for Fisheries and the Countryside) 1997–; *Select Committees:* Member: Agriculture 1987–89. *Special Interests:* Education, Public Transport, Local Government, Green Issues, Countryside; Africa, Cyprus. Parliamentary Convenor, Socialist Environmental Resources Association 1989–91. Council member, RSPB; Vice-President, Wildlife Link; President, South Humber and North Lincolnshire RSPCA; Vice-President, Steel Action; Vice-President: Federation of Economic Development Authorities (FEDA), Association of Drainage Authorities, Wildlife and Countryside Link; Council Member, British Trust for Ornithology; Trustee, Birds of the Humber Trust; Hon. Fellow, Lincolnshire and Humberside University; *Recreations:* Ornithology, travel. *Address:* Elliot Morley Esq, MP, House of Commons, London, SW1A 0AA *Tel:* 020 7219 3569. *Constituency:* Kinsley Labour Club, Cole Street, Scunthorpe, Lincolnshire, DN15 6QS *Tel:* 01724 842000 *Fax:* 01724 281734 *E-mail:* emorleymp@aol.com; parlsecc@sec.maff.gov.uk.

| ESTELLE MORRIS   Birmingham Yardley | *Lab majority 5,315* |

Born 17 June 1952; Daughter of Rt Hon. Charles Morris, DL, and of Pauline Morris; Educated Whalley Range High School; Coventry College of Education (BEd). Teacher, Sidney Stringer School and Community College 1974–92. Councillor, Warwick District Council 1979–91; Leader, Labour Group 1982–89. **House of Commons:** Member for Birmingham Yardley since April 9, 1992; Opposition Spokeswoman on Education and Employment 1995–97; Opposition Whip 1994–95; Department for Education and Employment: Parliamentary Under-Secretary of State, (School Standards) 1997–98, Minister of State (Minister for School Standards) 1998–; *Special Interests:* Education and Training, Housing, Local Government. PC 1999. *Address:* Rt Hon Estelle Morris, MP, House of Commons, London, SW1A 0AA *Tel:* 020 7219 6450 *Tel (Constituency):* 0121–789 7356 *Fax (Constituency):* 0121–789 9754 *E-mail:* estelle@morrisrthon.freeserve.co.uk.

Dod *on* Line
An Electronic Directory without rival . . .

MPs' biographies and photographs available with daily updates *via* the internet

For a *free* trial, call Oliver Cox on 020 7828 7256

SIR JOHN MORRIS   Aberavon   *Lab majority 21,571*

Born 5 November 1931; Son of late D W Morris and M O A Lewis; Educated Ardwyn School, Aberystwyth; University College of Wales, Aberystwyth; Gonville and Caius College, Cambridge (LLM); Married 1959, Margaret Lewis (3 daughters). Commissioned Welch Regiment and served Royal Welsh Fusiliers; Called to the Bar, Gray's Inn 1954; QC 1973; Recorder of Crown Court 1982–97; Member, GMB. **House of Commons:** Member for Aberavon since 1959; Former Principal Opposition Front Bench Spokesman on Legal Affairs; Parliamentary Secretary to the Ministry of Power 1964–1966; Joint Parliamentary Secretary Ministry of Transport 1966–1968; Minister of Defence for Equipment 1968–70; Secretary of State for Wales 1974–79; Opposition Attorney General 1979–81, 1983–97; Attorney General 1997–99; *Select Committees:* Member: Privileges 1994–97. Chair, National Road Safety Advisory Council 1967–68; Chair, Joint Review of British Railways 1966–67; Committee Member, Implementation of Nolan Report 1997; Member: UK Delegation Consultative Assemblies Council of Europe and WEU 1963–64, 1982–83, UK Delegates North Atlantic Assembly 1970; PC 1970; Knighted 1999; Hon. LLD, University of Wales; Hon. Fellow: University College, Aberystwyth, Trinity College, Carmarthen, University College, Swansea; *Sportsclubs:* Vice-President, Aberavon RFC. *Address:* Rt Hon Sir John Morris, QC, MP, House of Commons, London, SW1A 0AA *Tel:* 020 7219 3470 *Fax:* 020 7219 5999. *Constituency:* 22 Depot Road, Cwmaron, Port Talbot, West Glamorgan *Tel:* 01639 896807 *Fax:* 01639 891725.

MALCOLM MOSS   North East Cambridgeshire   *Con majority 5,101*

Born 6 March 1943; Son of late Norman Moss and Annie Moss, née Gay; Educated Audenshaw Grammar School; St John's College, Cambridge (BA 1965, MA 1967); Married 1st, December 28, 1965, Vivien Lorraine Peake (died 1997) (2 daughters); married 2nd, May 12, 2000, Sonya Alexandra McFarlin, née Evans. Blundell's School: Assistant master 1966–68, Head of Department, geography and economics 1968–70; Barwick Associates Ltd: Insurance consultant 1971–72, General manager 1972–74; Mandrake Associates Ltd: Founder and director 1974–94, Managing director 1986–88; Chairman: Mandrake Group plc 1986–88, Mandrake Associates Ltd 1988–93. Wisbech Town Councillor 1979–87; Fenland District Councillor 1983–87; Cambridgeshire County Councillor 1985–87. **House of Commons:** Member for North East Cambridgeshire since June 1987; Opposition Front Bench Spokesman for: Northern Ireland November 1997–1999; Agriculture, Fisheries and Food 1999–; Opposition Whip 1997; PPS: to Tristan Garel-Jones as Minister of State, Foreign and Commonwealth Office 1991–93, to Sir Patrick Mayhew as Secretary of State for Northern Ireland 1993–94; Parliamentary Under-Secretary of State, Northern Ireland Office 1994–97; *Select Committees:* Member: Energy 1989–91. *Special Interests:* Energy, Education, Housing, Small Businesses, Financial Services, Rural Development; France, Switzerland, USA. Trustee, Angles Theatre and Arts Centre, Wisbech; Larmor Award, St John's College; *Sportsclubs:* Member, Lords and Commons: Ski Club, Tennis Club; *Recreations:* Amateur dramatics, gardening, skiing, tennis. *Address:* Malcolm Moss Esq, MP, House of Commons, London, SW1A 0AA *Tel:* 020 7219 6933 *Fax:* 020 7219 6840. *Constituency:* 111 High Street, March, Cambridgeshire, PE15 9LH *Tel:* 01354 656541 *Fax:* 01354 660417 *E-mail:* mossm@parliament.uk.

KALI MOUNTFORD   Colne Valley   *Lab majority 4,840*

Born 12 January 1954; Educated Crewe Grammar School for Girls; Crewe and Alsager College (DipHE) (BA philosophy, psychology, sociology 1988); (1 son 1 daughter). Member, CPSA 1975–97: Shop steward 1983–95, Branch secretary 1985–90, Regional secretary 1987–92, Department Employment Whitley Council Secretary 1988–95, Branch chair 1990–92, Trades Council Executive 1990–95. Councillor, Sheffield City Council 1992–96: Vice-Chair, Economic Development 1992–94, Chair, Personnel 1994–95, Deputy Chair, Finance 1995, Chair, Finance 1995–96. **House of Commons:** Member for Colne Valley since May 1, 1997; *Select Committees:* Member: Social Security 1998–99. *Special Interests:* Social Security, Employment, Textiles, Agriculture. Member, Labour Party (Sheffield Brightside): General Management Committee 1985–95,

Women's Officer 1989–91, Euro Constituency Vice-Chair 1989–91, Campaign Co-ordinator 1992, Recruitment Officer 1992–93. Member: Sheffield Co-ordinating Committee Against Unemployment 1992–94, National Centre for Popular Music 1994–95; Vice-Chair: CAB 1998–, Victim Support 1998–; President, Mehfal-E-Niswan 2000–; Member, Sheffield Race Equality Council 1993–95. *Address:* Kali Mountford, MP, House of Commons, London, SW1A 0AA *Tel:* 020 7219 4507. *Constituency:* 1043 Manchester Road, Linthwaite, Huddersfield, HD7 5LS *Tel:* 01484 319876 *Fax:* 01484 319878.

DR MARJORIE MOWLAM   Redcar   *Lab majority 21,667*

Born 18 September 1949; Daughter of late Frank William Mowlam and late Bettina Mary Mowlam; Educated Coundon Court Comprehensive School, Coventry; Durham University (BA social anthropology); Iowa University, USA (MA, PhD 1978); Married June 24, 1995, Peter Jon Norton. Lecturer, Newcastle University 1979–83; Senior administrator, Northern College, Barnsley 1984–87; Member, TGWU. **House of Commons:** Member for Redcar since June 1987; Opposition Spokesperson on: Northern Ireland 1988–89, Trade and Industry specialising in City affairs 1989–92; Principal Opposition Spokesperson on: Citizen's Charter and Women's Affairs 1992–93, National Heritage 1993–94, Northern Ireland 1994–96; Member Shadow Cabinet 1992–97: Shadow Secretary of State for Northern Ireland 1996–97; Secretary of State for Northern Ireland 1997–99; Minister for the Cabinet Office and Chancellor of the Duchy of Lancaster 1999–. Member, Labour Party National Executive Committee 1995–. Vice-President, The Big Issue Foundation; PC 1997; Channel 4 and House Award for Major Political Achievement 1999; *Irish America* magazine Special Peace Award 2000; Honorary degrees Teesside, Durham and Coventry Universities; Freeman: City of Sheffield, City of Coventry, Borough of Redcar and Cleveland; *Recreations:* Swimming, walking, travelling, jigsaws. *Address:* Rt Hon Dr Marjorie Mowlam, MP, House of Commons, London, SW1A 0AA *Tel:* 020 7219 5066. *Constituency:* PO Box 77, Redcar, Cleveland, TS10 1YF *Tel:* 01642 490404 *Fax:* 01642 489260 *E-mail:* mmowlam@cabinet-office.x.gsi.gov.uk.

GEORGE MUDIE   Leeds East   *Lab majority 17,466*

Born 6 February 1945; Educated Local state schools; Married (2 children). Trade Union Official. Former Leader, Leeds City Council. **House of Commons:** Member for Leeds East since April 9, 1992; Opposition Whip 1994–97; Pairing and Accommodation Whip 1995–97; Deputy Chief Whip (Treasurer of HM Household) 1997–98; Parliamentary Under-Secretary of State (Lifelong Learning), Department for Education and Employment 1998–99; *Select Committees:* Member: Accommodation and Works 1992–98, Public Accounts 1994–95, Selection 1995–97, Finance and Services 1997–98, Selection 1997–98, Finance and Services 1998–99, Selection 1998–99. *Clubs:* Harehills Labour; *Recreations:* Watching football. *Address:* George Mudie Esq, MP, House of Commons, London, SW1A 0AA *Tel:* 020 7219 5889.

CHRIS MULLIN   Sunderland South   *Lab majority 19,638*

Born 12 December 1947; Son of Leslie and Teresa Mullin; Educated St Joseph's College, Ipswich; Hull University (LLB 1969); Married April 14, 1987, Nguyen Thi Ngoc (2 daughters). Author; Journalist; travelled extensively in China, Vietnam and India; BBC World Service 1974–78; *Tribune* 1978–84, editor 1982–84; Member: NUJ, MSF. **House of Commons:** Contested Devon North 1970, Kingston Upon Thames February 1974 general elections. Member for Sunderland South since June 1987; Parliamentary Under-Secretary of State, Department of the Environment, Transport and the Regions 1999–; *Select Committees:* Member: Home Affairs 1992–97; Chairman: Home Affairs 1997–99; Member: Liaison 1997–99. *Special Interests:* Home Affairs, Media Ownership, Justice; Cambodia, Tibet, Vietnam. *Publications:* How to Select or Reselect your MP, 1981; *The Tibetans*, 1981; *A Very British Coup*, 1982; *Error of Judgement*, 1986; *The Last Man Out of Saigon*, 1986; *The Year of the Fire Monkey*, 1991; Channel 4 and House Award for Questioner of the Year 1999; Hon. LLD, City University, London; *Recreations:* Walking, gardening. *Address:* Chris Mullin Esq, MP, House of Commons, London, SW1A 0AA *Tel:* 020 7219 4343. *Constituency:* 3 The Esplanade, Sunderland, Tyne and Wear, SR2 7BQ *Tel:* Sunderland Office: 0191–567 2848 *Fax:* 0191–510 1063 *E-mail:* chris_mullin@detr.gsi.gov.uk.

DENIS MURPHY   Wansbeck   *Lab majority 22,367*

Born 2 November 1948; Son of late John Murphy and of Josephine Murphy; Educated St Cuthberts Grammar School, Newcastle upon Tyne; Northumberland College; Married September 1969, Nancy Moffat (separated) (1 son 1 daughter). Apprentice electrician 1965–69; Underground electrician, Ellington Colliery 1969–94; Member, National Union of Mineworkers (Craft Section) 1965–; General Secretary, Northumberland Colliery Mechanics Association 1989–97. Wansbeck District Council: Councillor 1990–97, Chair of Planning, Leader of Council 1994–97. **House of Commons:** Member for Wansbeck since May 1, 1997; *Select Committees:* Member: Deregulation 1998–. *Special Interests:* Economic Development, Planning Transport. Member, Labour Party 1974–. Chair, Board of Governors, Northumberland Aged Mineworkers Homes Association; *Recreations:* Cycling, walking. *Address:* Denis Murphy Esq, MP, House of Commons, London, SW1A 0AA *Tel:* 020 7219 6474. *Constituency:* 94 Station Road, Ashington, Northumberland, NE63 8RN *Tel:* 01670 523100 *Fax:* 01670 813208.

JIM MURPHY   Eastwood   *Lab majority 3,236*

Born 23 August 1967; Son of Jim Murphy, pipe-fitter, and Anne Murphy, secretary; Educated Bellarmine Secondary School, Glasgow; Milnerton High School, Cape Town; Strathclyde University; Married Claire Cook (1 daughter). Director, Endsleigh Insurance 1994–96; Project Manager, Scottish Labour Party 1996–97; President: NUS (Scotland) 1992–94, NUS 1994–96; Member, GMB. **House of Commons:** Member for Eastwood since May 1, 1997; *Select Committees:* Member: Public Accounts 1999–. *Special Interests:* Economy, International Affairs, Defence, Consumer Issues, Sport; Southern Africa, Israel. Vice-Chair, Labour Friends of Israel 1997–; Member, Co-operative Party. *Publications: The House of Lords – An Abuse of Power,* 1998; Fellow, Royal Society of Arts; *Sportsclubs:* Bonnington Golf; *Recreations:* Football, travelling in Scotland, cinema, horse-racing, golf. *Address:* Jim Murphy Esq, MP, House of Commons, London, SW1A 0AA *Tel:* 020 7219 4615 *Fax:* 020 7219 5657. *Constituency:* Millworks, 28 Field Road, Busby, Strathclyde, G76 8SE *Tel:* 0141–644 3330 *Fax:* 0141–644 4771.

PAUL MURPHY   Torfaen   *Lab majority 24,536*

Born 25 November 1948; Son of late Ronald and late Marjorie Murphy; Educated St Francis School, Abersychan; West Monmouth School, Pontypool; Oriel College, Oxford (MA). Management trainee, CWS 1970–71; Lecturer in government, Ebbw Vale College of Further Education 1971–87. Torfaen Borough Council: Councillor 1973–87, Chair, Finance Committee 1976–86. **House of Commons:** Contested Wells 1979 general election. Member for Torfaen since June 1987; Opposition Spokesman on: Welsh Affairs 1988–94, Northern Ireland 1994–95, Foreign Affairs 1995, Defence, Disarmament and Arms Control 1995–97; Minister of State, Northern Ireland Office (Minister for Political Development) 1997–99; Secretary of State for Wales 1999–; *Special Interests:* Local Government, Wales, Education, Housing, Foreign Affairs. Secretary, Torfaen Constituency Labour Party 1971–87; Former Chair, Welsh Group of Labour MPs. Former school and college governor; Former Treasurer, Anglo-Austrian Society; Member, Royal Institute of International Affairs 1997–; Knight of St Gregory (Papal Award); PC 1999; *Recreations:* Classical music, cooking. *Address:* Rt Hon Paul Murphy, MP, House of Commons, London, SW1A 0AA *Tel:* 020 7219 3463. *Constituency:* 73 Upper Trosnant Street, Pontypool, Torfaen *Tel:* 01495 750078 *Fax:* 01495 752584.

N

DR DOUG NAYSMITH   Bristol North West   *Lab majority 11,382*

Born 1 April 1941; Son of late James Naysmith and late Ina Vass; Educated Musselburgh Burgh School; George Heriots School, Edinburgh; Heriot Watt University (biology); Edinburgh University (BSc zoology 1965, PhD surgical science 1970); Married September 3, 1966, Caroline Hill (separated) (1 son 1 daughter). Research assistant, Edinburgh University 1966–69; Post-doctoral fellow, Yale University 1969–70; Research immunologist, Beecham Research Laboratories 1970–72; Bristol University: Research associate, Fellow, lecturer in immunology, Pathology Department 1972–92, Administrator, Registrar's Office 1992–97; Past President and Secretary, Bristol AUT. Bristol City Council: Councillor 1981–98, Past Chair: Docks Committee, Health and Environmental Services Committee, Health Policy Committee, Past Labour Group Whip; Past member, Avon FPC; Past member, Bristol CHC. **House of Commons:** Member for Bristol North West since May 1, 1997; *Select Committees:* Member: Deregulation 1998–, Social Security 1999–. *Special Interests:* Health, Co-operative Development, Local Government, International Development, Science, Higher Education. Chair, Bristol District Labour Party; President, Socialist Health Association; National Vice-President, Socialist Health Association. Member: Citizens Advice Bureau, CND, WDM; Member, Wildlife Trust; Trustee, Jenner Trust; *Publications:* Various scientific papers and book chapters; FRSM; FIBiol; *Recreations:* Music, theatre, films, preserving paddle steamers. *Address:* Dr Doug Naysmith, MP, House of Commons, London, SW1A 0AA *Tel:* 020 7219 4187 *Fax:* 020 7219 2602. *Constituency:* Unit 7, Greenway Business Centre, Doncaster Road, Bristol, BS10 5PY *Tel:* 0117-950 2385 *Fax:* 0117-950 5302 *E-mail:* naysmithd@parliament.uk.

PATRICK NICHOLLS   Teignbridge   *Con majority 281*

Born 14 November 1948; Son of late Douglas Charles Martyn Nicholls, Solicitor; Educated Redrice School, Andover; College of Law, Guildford; Married July 3, 1976, Bridget Elizabeth Fergus, née Owens (1 son 2 daughters). Qualified as solicitor 1974; Partner with firm of solicitors in Exeter 1976–; PA to Peter Emery, MP, in 1979 general election; Steward, British Boxing Board of Control 1985–87. Councillor, East Devon District Council 1980–84. **House of Commons:** Member for Teignbridge since June 1983; Opposition Spokesman for: National Heritage 1997, Culture, Media and Sport June-November 1997, Health November 1997–98; Opposition Spokesman for Agriculture, Fisheries and Food 1998–1999; PPS: to David Mellor as Parliamentary Under-Secretary of State, Home Office, and assisting Lord Elton at the Home Office 1984–86, to John Selwyn Gummer as Minister of State, Ministry of Agriculture 1986–87; Parliamentary Under-Secretary of State: at Department of Employment 1987–90, at Department of Environment July-Oct 1990; *Select Committees:* Member: Social Security 1990–93, Deregulation 1995–97; Member: Education and Employment 2000–, Employment Sub-Committee 2000–. *Special Interests:* Constitution, EU, Home Affairs, Defence, Construction Industry, Retail Industry; Indonesia, Malaysia, Venezuela, Bahrain. Secretary, West Country MPs' Group 1984–97; Vice-Chair, Conservative Party 1993–94 Founder Member, Westminster Foundation for Democracy. Board Member, Westminster Foundation for Democracy 1992–93; Member, Standing Committees on: Police and Criminal Evidence Bill, Video Cassettes Bill; Member, North Atlantic Assembly Delegation 1992–97; Freeman, City of London; *Clubs:* Carlton; *Recreations:* Skiing, historical research, theatre, opera. *Address:* Patrick Nicholls Esq, MP, House of Commons, London, SW1A 0AA *Tel:* 020 7219 4077 *Fax:* 020 7219 4957. *Constituency:* Unit D, Minerva Way, Brunel Road, Newton Abbot, Devon, TQ12 4JP *Tel:* 01392 204031 *Fax:* 01626 204033.

ARCHIE NORMAN   Tunbridge Wells   *Con majority 7,506*

Born 1 May 1954; Son of Dr Archie Norman, physician, and Aleida Elisabeth Norman; Educated Charterhouse; Harvard Business School; Emmanuel College, Cambridge (Exhibitioner); University of Minnesota, Minneapolis (MBA, MA economics); Married 1983, Vanessa Mary Peet (1 daughter). Citibank NA 1975–77; Partner, McKinsey & Co Inc 1979–86; Group finance director, Kingfisher plc 1986–91; Non-executive director: British Rail 1992–94, Railtrack plc 1994–2000, Geest plc 1988–91; Chief executive, Asda Group plc 1991–96; Chair, Asda Group plc 1996–99. **House of Commons:** Member for Tunbridge Wells since May 1, 1997; Opposition Front Bench Spokesman for Europe 1999–2000; Member, Shadow Cabinet 2000–; Shadow Secretary of State for Environment, Transport and the Regions 2000–; *Special Interests:* Business, Transport, Agriculture, Countryside. Chair: Cambridge University Conservative Association 1975, East Region Federation of Conservative Students 1975; Council Member, Federation of Conservative Students 1975–76; Patron, North East Bow Group 1990–96; President, West Yorkshire (Conservative) Businessmen's Association 1990–96; Vice-Chair, Conservative Party (with responsibility for organisation) 1997–98, Chief executive and Deputy chair 1998–99; DTI Deregulation Taskforce 1994–; ACISE Government Committee on Business and the Environment 1995–96; Member, Council of the Industrial Society; Fellow, Marketing Society; Hon. Degree, Leeds Metropolitan University; *Sportsclubs:* Vanderbuilt Tennis Club; *Recreations:* Farming, music, opera, tennis, football. *Address:* Archie Norman Esq, MP, House of Commons, London, SW1A 0AA *Tel:* 020 7219 5156 *Fax:* 020 7219 6050. *Constituency:* 84 London Road, Tunbridge Wells, Kent, TN1 1EA *Tel:* 01892 522581 *Fax:* 01892 522582.

DAN NORRIS   Wansdyke   *Lab majority 4,799*

Born 28 January 1960; Son of David Norris and June Norris (née Allen); Educated State schools; Sussex University (MSW). Former child protection officer; Member, GMB. Councillor: Bristol City Council 1989–92, 1995–97, Avon County Council 1994–96. **House of Commons:** Member for Wansdyke since May 1, 1997; *Special Interests:* Freedom of Information, Child Protection and Safety, Animal Welfare. Member: Co-op Party, Labour Leader's Campaign Team with responsibility for Health 1998–99, General Election Campaign Team with responsibility for campaigning against the Liberal Democrats 1999–. *Publications:* Various publications on prevention and reduction of violence; Hon. Fellow, School of Cultural and Community Studies, Sussex University; *Clubs:* Radstock Working Men's; *Recreations:* Photography. *Address:* Dan Norris Esq, MP, House of Commons, London, SW1A 0AA *Tel:* 020 7219 6395 *Tel (Constituency):* 0117–985 4856 *E-mail:* norrisd@parliament.uk.

O

MARK OATEN   Winchester   *LD majority 21,556*

Born 8 March 1964; Son of Ivor and Audrey Oaten; Educated Queen's Comprehensive School, Watford; Hatfield Polytechnic (BA history, Diploma in International Public Relations); Married September 1992, Belinda, daughter of Bob Fordham (2 daughters). Managing Director, Westminster Communications Ltd; Director, Oasis Radio. Councillor, Watford Borough Council 1986–94, Liberal Democrat Group Leader. **House of Commons:** Contested Watford 1992 general election. Member for Winchester since May 1, 1997. (The two-vote victory was declared invalid and a by-election held in November); Spokesman for: Social Security and Welfare (Disabled People) 1997–99, Foreign Affairs and Defence (Foreign Affairs) 1999–2000,

Foreign Affairs and Defence (Europe) 2000–; PPS to Charles Kennedy as Leader of the Liberal Democrat Party 1999–; *Select Committees:* Member: Public Administration 1999–. Member, European Standing Committee C 1999–2000; *Recreations:* Gardening, swimming. *Address:* Mark Oaten Esq, MP, House of Commons, London, SW1A 0AA *Tel:* 020 7219 5152 *Fax:* 020 7219 2389. *Constituency:* 45 Southgate Street, Winchester, Hampshire, SO23 4EH *Tel:* 01962 868800 *E-mail:* oatenm@parliament.uk.

MIKE O'BRIEN   North Warwickshire   *Lab majority 14,767*

Born 19 June 1954; Son of Timothy O'Brien, railwayman, and Mary O'Brien (née Toomey); Educated St George's School; Blessed Edward Oldcorne School; North Staffs Polytechnic (BA history and politics, PGCE); Married July 11, 1987, Alison Joy Munro (2 daughters). Trainee solicitor 1977–80; Teacher training 1980–81; Lecturer in Law, Colchester College of Further and Higher Education 1981–87; In practice as solicitor 1987–92; Branch Secretary, NATFHE 1989–90. **House of Commons:** Contested Ruislip Northwood 1983 and North Warwickshire 1987 general elections. Member for North Warwickshire since April 9, 1992; Opposition Spokesman on Treasury and Economic Affairs 1995–96; Shadow Economic Secretary to the Treasury 1996–97; Parliamentary Under-Secretary of State, Home Office 1997–; *Select Committees:* Member: Home Affairs 1992–93, Treasury and Civil Service 1993–95. *Special Interests:* Housing, Environment, West Midlands Industry, Police, Criminal Law, Coal Industry; CIS, Eastern Europe, USA. Parliamentary Adviser to the Police Federation of England and Wales 1993–96; *Clubs:* Bedworth Ex Servicemen's, Woodend Workingmen's; *Recreations:* Cinema and spending time with family. *Address:* Michael O'Brien Esq, MP, House of Commons, London, SW1A 0AA *Tel:* 020 7219 3000. *Constituency:* 2 Croft House, Croft Fields, Bedworth, Nuneaton, Warwickshire, CV12 8QT *Tel:* 024 7631 5084.

STEPHEN O'BRIEN   Eddisbury   *Con majority 1,606*

Born 1 April 1957; Son of David and Rothy O'Brien; Educated Loretto School, Mombasa, Kenya; Handbridge School, Chester; Heronwater School, Abergele, N Wales; Sedbergh School, Cumbria; Emmanuel College, Cambridge (law 1979, MA); College of Law, Chester (MA 1980); Married August 30, 1986, Gemma Townshend (2 sons 1 daughter). Articles, Freshfields (Solicitors, City of London) 1981–83, Senior Managing Solicitor 1983–88; Redland plc 1988–98: Group secretary and director, Strategy and Corporate Affairs, Director of UK and overseas operations, Member, Group Executive Committee, Deputy chair, Redland Tile and Brick (Northern Ireland 1995–98), Executive Director, Redland Clay Tile (Mexico1994–98); International business consultant 1998–. **House of Commons:** Member for Eddisbury since July 22, 1999; Private Members' Bill, Food Labelling 1999–2000; Backbench representative, Shadow Foreign Affairs team; *Select Committees:* Member: Education and Employment 1999–, Education Sub-Committee 1999–; Member: Standing Committee, Freedom of Information Bill 1999–, Standing Committee, Limited Liability Partnerships Bill 2000–. *Special Interests:* Economy, Trade and Industry, Agriculture and the Rural Economy, Housing, Infrastructure, Transport, Northern Ireland, Foreign Affairs, Education; Ireland, East African countries, Australia, New Zealand, Mexico, USA. Chair, Chichester Conservative Association 1998–99; Executive committee member, Westminster Candidates Association 1998–99; Special adviser, Conservative Business Liaison Unit (construction sector) 1998–; Member, National Membership Committee of the Conservative Party 1999–. Non-executive director, Cambridge University Careers Service 1992–99; Founder Member, Brazil-UK Joint Business Council 1994–; Council of Members, Scottish Business in the Community 1995–98; Elected Member, CBI South East Regional Council 1995–98; Chairman, Public and Parliamentary Affairs Committee BMP (National Council of Building Materials Producers) 1995–99; FCIS; *Clubs:* Carlton, Institute of Chartered Secretaries and Administrators, Law Society, Winsford Constitutional and Conservative; *Recreations:* Music (piano), fell-walking, golf. *Address:* Stephen O'Brien Esq, MP, House of Commons, London, SW1A 0AA *Tel:* 020 7219 4996 *Fax:* 020 7219 0584. *Constituency:* Eddisbury Conservative Association, 4 Church Walk, High Street, Tarporley, Cheshire, CW6 0AJ *Tel:* 01829 733243 *Fax:* 01829 733243 *E-mail:* wegodae@parliament.uk.

WILLIAM O'BRIEN   Normanton   *Lab majority 15,893*

Born 25 January 1929; Educated State schools; Leeds University; Married Jean Scofield (3 daughters). Coalminer 1946–83; Member, NUM 1945–. Councillor: Knottingly Urban District Council 1952–85, West Riding County Council 1964–74; Member, Yorkshire Water Authority 1973–83; Wakefield Council: Councillor 1973–83, Former Deputy Leader, Chairman, Finance and General Purposes Committee; JP, Wakefield Division. **House of Commons:** Member for Normanton since June 1983; Opposition Front Bench Spokesman on: Environment (Local Government) 1988–92, Northern Ireland 1992–96; *Select Committees:* Member: Environment, Transport and Regional Affairs 1997–, Transport Sub-Committee 1997–, Chairmen's Panel 1998–, Standing Orders 1998–. *Special Interests:* Local Government, Water Industry, Energy. Member, Public Accounts Commission 1997–; Executive Committee Member, IPU British Group; Fellow, Industry and Parliament Trust; *Recreations:* Reading, organising. *Address:* William O'Brien Esq, MP, House of Commons, London, SW1A 0AA *Tel:* 020 7219 6464 *Fax:* 020 7219 0301 *Tel (Constituency):* 01977 709868; 01924 826225 *Fax (Constituency):* 01977 599830; 01924 826225.

EDWARD O'HARA   Knowsley South   *Lab majority 30,708*

Born 1 October 1937; Son of late Robert and Clara O'Hara, née Davies; Educated Liverpool Collegiate School; Magdalen College, Oxford (MA literae humaniores 1962); Married September 11, 1962, Lillian Hopkins (2 sons 1 daughter). Lecturer in higher education: C.F. Mott College 1970–75, City of Liverpool College of Higher Education 1975–85, Liverpool Polytechnic 1985–90. Councillor, Knowsley Borough Council 1975–90. **House of Commons:** Member for Knowsley South since September 27, 1990 by-election; *Select Committees:* Member: Education 1992–96, Speaker's Panel of Chairmen 1993–97, Education and Employment 1996–97; Member: Chairmen's Panel 1997–. *Special Interests:* Local Government, Regional Development, European Union, Education, Housing, Emergency Planning, Animal Welfare, Ageing Issues; CIS, Cyprus, Germany, Greece, Japan, USA. Member: Socialist Education Association, Co-operative Party, Fabian Society. Member: Merseyside Arts Association 1976–79, Board of management, Royal Liverpool Philharmonic Society 1987–90, Board of management, National Foundation for Educational Research 1987–90; Chairman of governors, Cartbridge School 1976–; Governor, Knowsley Community College 1991–; Corresponding fellow, Foundation for Hellenic Culture 1993–; Vice-President, *TS Iron Duke* (Huyton) 1994–; President, Knowsley South Juniors Football Club 1997–; Merseyside delegate to Régions Européenes de Tradition Industrielle 1989–90, Permanent Committee, Assembly of European Regions 1989–90, Member, Labour Movement in Europe 1990–, Council of Europe 1997–; Patron, Marilyn Houlton MND Trust 1991–; Community Development Foundation: Trustee 1992–, Chair 1997–; Vice-Chair, National Wild Flower Centre Development Trust 1996–; *Recreations:* Theatre, literature, music (classical, jazz, folk – especially Rembetiko), watching soccer, Greek language and culture. *Address:* Edward O'Hara Esq, MP, House of Commons, London, SW1A 0AA *Tel:* 020 7219 5232 *Fax:* 020 7219 4952 *Tel (Constituency):* 0151 489 8021 *Fax (Constituency):* 0151 449 3873.

BILL OLNER   Nuneaton   *Lab majority 13,540*

Born 9 May 1942; Son of late C. William Olner, coalminer, and late Lillian Olner; Educated Atherstone Secondary Modern School; North Warwickshire Technical College (City and Guilds Mechanical Engineering); Married March 10, 1962, Gillian Everitt. Engineer; Apprenticed with Armstrong Siddeley Motors; Skilled machinist, Rolls Royce, Coventry 1957–92; Member, AEU and branch secretary 1972–. Nuneaton Borough Council: Councillor 1971–92, Chair, Planning Committee 1974–76, Deputy Leader 1980–82, Leader 1982–87, Chair, Policy and Resources Committee 1982–86, Mayor 1987–88, Chair, Environmental Health Committee 1990–92. **House of Commons:** Member for Nuneaton since April 9, 1992; *Select Committees:* Member: Environment 1995–97, Standing Orders 1998–99; Member: Environment, Transport and Regional Affairs 1997–,

Environment Sub-Committee 1997–, Transport Sub-Committee 1997–, Chairmen's Panel 1998–. *Special Interests:* Engineering, Local Government; France, USA, China, Ghana, Australia. Chair, various school governing bodies; Joint Vice-Chair, Executive Committee, Commonwealth Parliamentary Association (CPA) UK Branch 1995–99, Member, 1999–; Freeman, City of Coventry; *Recreations:* Local Hospice Movement, walking, current affairs, television. *Address:* William Olner Esq, MP, House of Commons, London, SW1A 0AA *Tel:* 020 7219 4154. *Constituency:* 171 Queen's Road, Nuneaton, Warwickshire, CV11 5NB *Tel:* 024 7664 2222 *Fax:* 024 7664 2223.

MARTIN O'NEILL   Ochil   *Lab majority 4,652*

Born 6 January 1945; Son of John O'Neill, fitter and turner; Educated Trinity Academy, Edinburgh; Heriot Watt University (BA economics); Moray House College of Education, Edinburgh; Married July 21, 1973, Elaine Marjorie Samuel (2 sons). Insurance Clerk 1963–67; President, Scottish Union of Students 1970–71. **House of Commons:** Contested Edinburgh North October 1974 general election. Member for Stirlingshire East and Clackmannan 1979–83, for Clackmannan 1983–97, and for Ochil since May 1, 1997; Opposition Front Bench Spokesman on: Scotland 1980–84, Defence and Disarmament and Arms Control 1984–88; Principal Opposition Front Bench Spokesman on Defence 1988–92; Opposition Front Bench Spokesman on Trade and Industry (Energy) 1992–95; *Select Committees:* Chairman: Trade and Industry 1995–97; Chairman: Trade and Industry 1995–; Member: Liaison 1997–. *Special Interests:* Education, Defence, Trade and Industry; Argentina. Labour Party Member since 1963; Held most Party positions in Constituency and Local Government Organisations. *Recreations:* Cinema, jazz. *Address:* Martin O'Neill Esq, MP, House of Commons, London, SW1A 0AA *Tel:* 020 7219 5059. *Constituency:* 19 Mar Street, Alloa, FK10 1HR *Tel:* 01259 721536 *Fax:* 01259 216716 *E-mail:* cartere@parliament.uk.

LEMBIT ÖPIK   Montgomeryshire   *LD majority 6,303*

Born 2 March 1965; Son of Dr Uno Öpik and Liivi Öpik; Educated Royal Belfast Academical Institution; Bristol University (BA philosophy 1987) (President Union 1985–86). Procter and Gamble Ltd: Brand assistant/ Assistant brand manager 1988–91, Corporate Training and Organisation Development Manager 1991–96, Global Human Resources Training Manager 1996–; President, National Union of Students Executive 1987–88. Councillor, Newcastle upon Tyne City Council 1992; Contested Northumbria 1994 European Parliament election. **House of Commons:** Contested Newcastle Central 1992 general election. Member for Montgomeryshire since May 1, 1997; Spokesman for: Northern Ireland 1997–99, Welsh Affairs 1997–99, Young People 1997–99, Home and Legal Affairs (Northern Ireland and Youth) 1999–; *Select Committees:* Member: Agriculture 1999–. *Special Interests:* Public Transport, Education and Youth, Aerospace; Eastern Europe, China, Fiji. Member, Federal Executive Committee of Liberal Democrats 1991–; Welsh Vice-President, Liberal Democrat Federal Party 1999–. President: Shropshire Astronomical Society; Clive Motorcycle Club; Member, Welsh Grand Committee 1997–; *Recreations:* Aviation, military history, astronomy, films. *Address:* Lembit Öpik Esq, MP, House of Commons, London, SW1A 0AA *Tel:* 020 7219 1144 *Fax:* 020 7219 2210. *Constituency:* Montgomeryshire Liberal Democrats, 3 Park Street, Newtown, Powys, SY16 1EE *Tel:* 01686 625527 *Fax:* 01686 628891 *E-mail:* fionahall@cix.compulink.co.uk (political officer).

Dod *on* Line
An Electronic Directory without rival . . .

MPs' biographies and photographs
available with daily updates *via* the internet

For a *free* trial, call Oliver Cox on 020 7828 7256

DIANA ORGAN   Forest of Dean   *Lab majority 6,343*

Born 21 February 1952; Daughter of Jack, company director, and Vera Pugh, voluntary organiser; Educated Edgbaston Church of England College for Girls, Birmingham; St Hugh's College, Oxford (BA geography 1973); Bath University School of Education (PGCE 1974); Bristol Polytechnic (Diploma in Special Education 1981); Married August 9, 1975, Richard Thomas Organ (2 daughters). Assistant teacher special needs 1974–77; Deputy head teacher, St Germans, Cornwall 1977–79; Head of special needs unit, Somerset 1979–82; Supply special school, Somerset 1982–88; Assistant English teacher, Somerset 1988–92; Political researcher, Oxfordshire County Council 1992–95; Member: NUT, NUPE (now UNISON); Contested Somerset and Dorset West 1989 European Parliament election. **House of Commons:** Contested Gloucestershire West 1992 general election. Member for Forest of Dean since May 1, 1997; *Select Committees:* Member: Agriculture 1997–99, Joint Committee on Statutory Instruments 1997–99; Member: Culture, Media and Sport 1999–. *Special Interests:* Education, Transport, Rural Affairs; India, Tibet, China, Mongolia. Joined Labour Party 1970–73; Rejoined 1982–; Secretary, Constituency Labour Party; Member: South-West Women's Committee, South-West Regional Executive, Labour REC 1990–92, 300 Group, Co-op Party. Member, Amnesty International; School governor; Political Board Member, TV South West; Labour Party Conference Debates: Nuclear Energy 1990, Defence 1992, Transport 1993, Education 1994, Rural issues 1995; *Recreations:* Swimming, sailing, tennis, gardening, cinema. *Address:* Mrs Diana Organ, MP, House of Commons, London, SW1A 0AA *Tel:* 020 7219 5498 *Fax:* 020 7219 6860. *Constituency:* St Annals House, Bellevue Centre, Cinderford, Gloucestershire, GL14 1AB *Tel:* 01594 826835 *Fax:* 01594 827892 *E-mail:* lapingtona@parliament.uk.

SANDRA OSBORNE   Ayr   *Lab majority 6,543*

Born 23 February 1956; Daughter of Thomas Clark, labourer, and Isabella Clark, shop worker, meat factory worker, cleaner and laundry worker; Educated Camphill Senior Secondary, Paisley; Anniesland College; Jordanhill College; Strathclyde University (Diploma in Community Education, Diploma in Equality and Discrimination, MSc Equality and Discrimination); Married February 20, 1982, Alastair Osborne (2 daughters). Member, APEX; Former Branch Secretary, TGWU. Councillor, Kyle and Carrick District Council 1990–95; South Ayrshire Council: Councillor 1994–97, Convenor, Community Services (Housing and Social Work) –1997. **House of Commons:** Member for Ayr since May 1, 1997; PPS to Brian Wilson as Minister of State for Scotland 1999–; *Select Committees:* Member: Information 1997–2000, Scottish Affairs 1998–99. *Special Interests:* Women's Issues, Housing, Poverty; All countries. Vice-Chair, Scottish Regional Group of Labour MPs 1998–99, Chair 1999–. Women's Aid; *Recreations:* Reading and television. *Address:* Mrs Sandra Osborne, MP, House of Commons, London, SW1A 0AA *Tel:* 020 7219 6402. *Constituency:* Room 1009, Aviation House, Glasgow Prestwick International Airport, Prestwick, Strathclyde, KA9 2PL *Tel:* 01292 476650 *Fax:* 01292 478540.

RICHARD OTTAWAY   Croydon South   *Con majority 11,930*

Born 24 May 1945; Son of late Professor Christopher Ottaway and of Grace Ottaway; Educated Backwell School, Somerset; Bristol University (LLB 1974); Married June 5, 1982, Nicola Kisch. Officer in the Royal Navy 1961–70, Serving on: HMSs Beechampton, Nubian and Eagle 1967–70; Admitted solicitor 1977, specialising in international, maritime and commercial law; Partner, William A. Crump & Son 1981–87; Director, Coastal States Petroleum (UK) Ltd 1988–95. **House of Commons:** Member for Nottingham North 1983–87. Contested Nottingham North 1987 General Election. Member for Croydon South since April 9, 1992; Opposition Spokesman for: Local Government and London 1997–99, Defence 1999–2000; Treasury 2000–; Government Whip 1995–97; Opposition Whip June-November 1997; PPS: to Ministers of State, Foreign and Commonwealth Office 1985–87, to Michael Heseltine: as President of the Board of Trade and Secretary

of State for Trade and Industry 1992–95, as Deputy Prime Minister and First Secretary of State 1995; Vice-Chair, Conservative Party (with responsibility for local government) 1998–99; *Select Committees:* Member: Procedure 1996–97. *Special Interests:* Defence, Industry, Commerce, World Population. *Publications:* Papers on international and maritime law, global pollution, debt and international fraud; *Recreations:* Yacht racing, jazz, skiing. *Address:* Richard Ottaway Esq, MP, House of Commons, London, SW1A 0AA *Tel:* 020 7219 6392 *Fax:* 020 7219 2256 *E-mail:* ottawayrgj@parliament.uk.

P

RICHARD PAGE   South West Hertfordshire   *Con majority 10,021*

Born 22 February 1941; Son of late Victor Charles Page; Educated Hurstpierpoint College; Luton Technical College; Married October 3, 1964, Madeleine Ann Brown (1 son 1 daughter). Chair, Page Holdings Ltd 1985–95, 1997–. Councillor, Banstead Urban District Council 1968–71. **House of Commons:** Contested Workington February and October 1974 general elections. Member for Workington November 1976 by-election -May 1979. Member for South West Hertfordshire since December 1979; Opposition Spokesman on Trade and Industry 2000–; PPS to John Biffen as Leader of the House 1982–87; Parliamentary Under-Secretary of State, Department of Trade and Industry 1995–97; *Select Committees:* Member: Public Accounts 1987–95, Public Accounts 1997–2000. *Special Interests:* Small Businesses, Horses, Scientific Research and Development, Trade and Industry; Middle East, Eastern Europe. Chair, International Office CCO 1998–2000. Governor, Rickmansworth Masonic School for Girls 1984–95; Hon. National Treasurer, Leukaemia Research Fund 1987–95; Member, Investment Committee LRF 1997–; Liveryman, The Pattenmakers Company 1979–; Freeman, City of London; *Recreations:* Shooting. *Address:* Richard Page Esq, MP, House of Commons, London, SW1A 0AA *Tel:* 020 7219 5032 *Fax:* 020 7219 2775. *Constituency:* SW Herts Conservative Association, c/o Holstein Friesan Society, Scots Hill, Rickmansworth, Hertfordshire *Tel:* 01923 771781 *Fax:* 01923 779471.

JAMES PAICE   South East Cambridgeshire   *Con majority 9,349*

Born 24 April 1949; Son of late Edward Paice and of Winifred Paice; Educated Framlingham College; Writtle Agricultural College; Married January 6, 1973, Ava Patterson (2 sons). Farm manager 1970–73; Farmer and contractor 1973–79; Training manager, later general manager, Framlingham Management and Training Services Ltd 1979–87, Non-executive director, 1987–89; Director, United Framlingham Farmers Ltd 1989–94. Chair, Suffolk Coastal District Council 1982–83. **House of Commons:** Contested Caernarvon 1979 general election. Member for South East Cambridgeshire since June 1987; Opposition Spokesman for Agriculture, Fisheries and Food 1997–; PPS: to Baroness Trumpington, as Minister of State, Ministry of Agriculture, Fisheries and Food 1989–90, to John Selwyn Gummer: as Minister of Agriculture, Fisheries and Food 1990–93, as Secretary of State for the Environment 1993–94; Parliamentary Under-Secretary of State: Department of Employment 1994–95, Department for Education and Employment 1995–97; *Special Interests:* Small Businesses, Employment Promotion, Agriculture, Rural Affairs, Training, Waste Management; Europe, New Zealand. UK delegate, EEC Council of Young Farmers 1974–78; Fellow, Writtle University College; *Recreations:* Windsurfing, shooting. *Address:* James Paice Esq, MP, House of Commons, London, SW1A 0AA *Tel:* 020 7219 4101. *Constituency:* 153 St Neots Road, Hardwick, Cambridge, CB3 7QJ *Tel:* 01954 211450 *E-mail:* paicejet@parliament.uk.

REV IAN PAISLEY   North Antrim   *DUP majority 10,574*

Born 6 April 1926; Son of late Rev. J. Kyle Paisley; Educated Ballymena Model School; Ballymena Technical High School; South Wales Bible College; Reformed Presbyterian Theological College, Belfast; Married 1956, Eileen Emily Cassells (2 twin sons 3 daughters). Ordained 1946; Minister, Martyrs Memorial Free Presbyterian Church 1946–; Moderator, Free Presbyterian Church of Ulster 1951–; Founded *Protestant Telegraph* 1966; Member, Northern Ireland Assembly 1973–74; Co-Chairman, World Congress of Fundamentalists 1978; MEP for Northern Ireland 1979–; Elected to second Northern Ireland Assembly 1982; MP (Protestant Unionist) for Bannside, Co. Antrim, Parliament of Northern Ireland (Stormont) 1970 72; Leader of Opposition 1972; Member: Northern Ireland Forum 1996–98, Northern Ireland Assembly 1998–. **House of Commons:** Member for North Antrim since June 1970; Spokesman for Constitutional Affairs; *Special Interests:* Foreign Affairs, Religious Affairs, Constitution. Leader (co-founder), Democratic Unionist Party 1971–. President, Whitefield College of the Bible, Laurencetown 1980; Member, Constitutional Convention 1975–76; Member: Rex Committee, Political Committee, European Parliament; *Publications:* Author of several publications; *Recreations:* History, Antiquarian book collecting. *Address:* Rev Ian Paisley, MP, House of Commons, London, SW1A 0AA *Tel:* 020 7219 3000. *Constituency:* 256 Ravenhill Road, Belfast, BT6 8GJ.

DR NICHOLAS PALMER   Broxtowe   *Lab majority 5,575*

Born 5 February 1950; Son of late Reginald Palmer and of Irina Palmer; Educated International Schools, Vienna and Copenhagen; Copenhagen University (mathemactics and computing 1967–72); Birkbeck College, London University (PhD mathematics 1975); Married February 5, 2000 Fiona Hunter. Head of internet services, Novartis, Switzerland 1997–; Health and safety officer, MSF Brighton 1975–76; Contested East Sussex and South Kent 1995 European Parliament election. **House of Commons:** Contested Chelsea 1983 general election. Member for Broxtowe since May 1, 1997; *Select Committees:* Member: Administration 1998–, European Scrutiny 1998–, Northern Ireland Affairs 1999–. *Special Interests:* Training, Tax, Development, Animal Welfare; Scandinavia, Switzerland; Member, European Standing Committee B 1998–. National Executive Member, Labour Animal Welfare Society 1999–; Vice-chair, World Government Group 2000–. Member: Compassion in World Farming, World Development Movement, Cats Protection League (Patron), United Nations Association; Former Member, Danish and Swiss Social Democrats; Worked on Draft Swiss Social Democrat Economic Programme; *Publications: The Comprehensive Guide to Board Wargaming*, 1977; *The Best of Board Wargaming*, 1980; *Beyond the Arcade*, 1984; *Parliamentary Portions*, 1998; *Recreations:* Postal games. *Address:* Dr Nicholas Palmer, MP, House of Commons, London, SW1A 0AA *Tel:* 020 7219 2397 *Fax:* 020 7219 4837. *Constituency:* 23 Barratt Lane, Attenborough, Nottingham, NG9 6AD *Tel:* 0115–943 0721 *Fax:* 0115–943 1860 *E-mail:* 76276.2147@compuserve.com.

OWEN PATERSON   North Shropshire   *Con majority 2,195*

Born 24 June 1956; Son of Alfred Dobell Paterson; Educated Radley College; Corpus Christi College, Cambridge (MA history 1978); Married January 26, 1980, Hon. Rose Ridley (2 sons 1 daughter). Managing director, British Leather Co Ltd 1993–99. **House of Commons:** Contested Wrexham 1992 general election. Member for North Shropshire since May 1, 1997; Opposition Whip (International Development; Trade and Industry; Wales) 2000–; *Select Committees:* Member: Welsh Affairs 1997–, European Scrutiny 1999–, Agriculture 2000–. *Special Interests:* Trade, Industry, Agriculture, Foreign Affairs; Western and Eastern Europe, USA, China, India; Member, European Standing Committee A 1998–. Member: 92 Group 1997–, Conservative Friends of Israel 1997–, Conservative Way Forward 1997–, Conservative 2000 1997–; Vice-President, Conservatives Against a Federal Europe 1998–, Member, No Turning Back Group 1998–. Director, Orthopaedic Institute Ltd, Oswestry; President, Ellesmere Cadet Force; Member, Countryside Alliance;

Member: Institute of Directors, Welsh Grand Committee 1998–2000; Executive Member, 1922 Committee 2000–; President, Cotance (European Tanners' Confederation) 1996–98, Vice-President 1998–; Member: World League For Freedom and Democracy 1997–, Inter-Parliamentary Union 1997–, Commonwealth Parliamentary Association 1997–; Member, Advisory Board, European Foundation 1998–; Liveryman, Leathersellers' Company; *Sportsclubs:* Patron, Oswestry Cricket Club; Member, Shropshire Cricket Club; *Recreations:* Travel, racing, hunting. *Address:* Owen Paterson Esq, MP, House of Commons, London, SW1A 0AA *Tel:* 020 7219 5185 *Fax:* 020 7219 3955. *Constituency:* 35 Willow Street, Oswestry, Shropshire, SY11 1AQ *Tel:* 01691 653596 *Fax:* 01691 671309 *E-mail:* owenpatersonmp@parliament.uk.

IAN PEARSON   Dudley South   *Lab majority 13,027*

Born 5 April 1959; Educated Brierley Hill Grammar School; Balliol College, Oxford (BA philosophy, politics and economics); Warwick University (MA industrial relations, PhD industrial and business studies); Married Annette Pearson (2 daughters 1 son). Deputy Director, Urban Trust 1987–88; Business and economic development consultant 1988–99; Joint chief executive, The West Midlands Enterprise Board 1989–94; Member, TGWU. Councillor, Dudley Borough Council 1984–87. **House of Commons:** Member for Dudley West December 15, 1994 by-election–1997, and for Dudley South since May 1, 1997; PPS to Geoffrey Robinson as Paymaster General, HM Treasury 1997–98; *Select Committees:* Member: Deregulation 1996–97, Treasury 1996–97; Member: Education and Employment 1999–, Employment Sub-Committee 1999–. *Special Interests:* Economic and Industrial Policy, Regional Economic Development; Central and Eastern Europe, Latin and South America, Far East. Local Government Policy Research Officer for the Labour Party 1985–87. Patron, Black Country Headway and Wordsley Kidney Patients Association; Chairman, Redhouse Cone Trust; *Publications: Universities and Innovation: Meeting the Challenge* 2000; Visiting Fellow, Warwick University; *Sportsclubs:* Stourbridge RFC, West Bromwich Albion FC; *Recreations:* Playing rugby, literature, architecture. *Address:* Ian Pearson Esq, MP, House of Commons, London, SW1A 0AA *Tel:* 020 7219 6462 *Fax:* 020 7219 0390. *Constituency:* 139 High Street, Brierley Hill, West Midlands, DY5 3BU *Tel:* 01384 482123 *Fax:* 01384 482209 *E-mail:* pearsoni@parliament.uk.

TOM PENDRY   Stalybridge and Hyde   *Lab majority 14,806*

Born 10 June 1934; Son of late Leonard E. Pendry; Educated St Augustine's School, Ramsgate; Plater Hall, Oxford University; Married February 19, 1966, Moira Ann Smith (separated 1983) (1 son 1 daughter). Steward, British Boxing Board of Control 1999–. Councillor, Paddington Council 1962–65. **House of Commons:** Member for Stalybridge and Hyde since 1970; Opposition Front Bench Spokesman on: Northern Ireland 1979–82, Regional Affairs and Devolution 1982–92, National Heritage (Sport and Tourism) 1992–97; Opposition Whip 1971–74; Government Whip 1974–77 (resigned 1977); Under-Secretary of State Northern Ireland 1978–79; *Special Interests:* Industrial Relations, Housing, Sport, Recreation, Finance, Social Security, Environment. Chair, Derby Labour Party 1966. Middleweight Colonial champion, Hong Kong 1957; Boxed for Oxford University 1957–59; President, Stalybridge Public Band; Member, Council of Europe and Western European Union 1973–75; Fellow, Industry and Parliament Trust; Chair, Football Foundation; Member, Tameside Sports Trust; Freeman, Borough of Tameside (Lord Mottram of Longendale); *Clubs:* Wig and Pen, Vincent's; *Sportsclubs:* Lord's Taverners; *Recreations:* Watching all sport, meeting sportspersons. *Address:* Tom Pendry Esq, MP, House of Commons, London, SW1A 0AA *Tel:* 020 7219 5011. *Constituency:* Hyde Town Hall, Market Street, Hyde, Cheshire, SK15 2RG *Tel:* 0161–367 8077 *E-mail:* pendryt@parliament.uk.

Visit the Vacher Dod Website . . .
www.politicallinks.co.uk

LINDA PERHAM   Ilford North   *Lab majority 3,224*

Born 29 June 1947; Daughter of George Sidney Conroy and Edith, née Overton; Educated Mary Datchelor Girls' School, Camberwell, London, SE5; Leicester University (BA Classics 1969); Ealing Technical College (Postgraduate Diploma of the Library Association 1970); Married April 9 1972, Raymond Perham (2 daughters). Library assistant, London Borough of Southwark 1966; Information officer, GLC Research Library 1970–72; City of London Polytechnic: Archives librarian 1972–76, Staff development Librarian 1976–78; Cataloguer, Fawcett Library 1981–92; Bibliographical librarian, Epping Forest College 1992–97; Local organiser, GLC Staff Association 1970–78; Chair, Joint Union Committee, City of London Polytechnic 1975–78; Member, UNISON (NALGO) 1985–. Member, Redbridge Community Health Council 1984–88; JP 1990–; London Borough of Redbridge: Former Councillor, Mayor 1994–95, Chair, Highways Committee 1995–96, Leisure Committee 1996–97. **House of Commons:** Contested Ilford North 1995 by-election. Member for Ilford North since May 1, 1997; *Select Committees:* Member: Accommodation and Works 1997–, Trade and Industry 1998–. *Special Interests:* Leisure, Environment, Education, Transport, Age Discrimination; Italy, Greece, Spain, Cyprus, USA, Israel, Saudi Arabia. Constituency Secretary, Ilford North Labour Party 1987–91; Member: Socialist Educational Association; Labour Friends of Israel. Patron, Haven House Foundation (Children's Hospice Project); Postnatal support organiser, National Childbirth Trust 1979–85; *Publications: Directory of GLC Library Resources,* 1970, 2nd ed 1971; *Greater London Council Publications 1965–71,* 1972; *Libraries of London,* 1973; *How To Find Out In French,* 1977; ALA; *Recreations:* Art, cinema, theatre, organising quizzes. *Address:* Linda Perham, MP, House of Commons, London, SW1A 0AA *Tel:* 020 7219 5853 *Fax:* 020 7219 1161. *Constituency:* Coventry House, 3 Coventry Road, Ilford, Essex, IG1 4GR *Tel:* 020 8554 3789 *Fax:* 020 8518 0594 *E-mail:* lindaperhammp@parliament.uk *Website:* www.the-commons.com/linda-perham.

ERIC PICKLES   Brentwood and Ongar   *Con majority 9,690*

Born 20 April 1952; Educated Greenhead Grammar School; Leeds Polytechnic; Married September 1976, Irene. Bradford Metropolitan District Council: Councillor 1979–91, Chairman: Social Services Committee 1982–84, Education Committee 1984–86, Leader of Conservative Group 1987–91; Member, Yorkshire Regional Health Authority 1982–90. **House of Commons:** Member for Brentwood and Ongar since April 9, 1992; Opposition Spokesman for Social Security 1998–; *Select Committees:* Member: Environment 1992–93, Transport 1995–97, Environment, Transport and Regional Affairs 1997–98, Transport Sub-Committee 1997–98. *Special Interests:* Housing, Health, Social Services, Local Government; Eastern Europe, India, Poland, USA. Member, Conservative Party National Union Executive Committee 1975–97; National Chairman, Young Conservatives 1980–81; Member, Conservative Party National Local Government Advisory Committee 1985–; Local Government Editor, Newsline 1990–; Deputy Leader, Conservative Group on Association of Metropolitan Authorities 1989–91; Vice-Chairman, Conservative Party 1993–97. Chairman, National Local Government Advisory Committee 1992–; Member, One Nation Forum 1987–91; *Clubs:* Carlton; *Recreations:* Films, opera, serious walking. *Address:* Eric Pickles Esq, MP, House of Commons, London, SW1A 0AA *Tel:* 020 7219 4428. *Constituency:* 19 Crown Street, Brentwood, Essex *Tel:* 01277 210725 *Fax:* 01277 202221.

COLIN PICKTHALL West Lancashire
Lab majority 17,119

Born 13 September 1944; Son of Francis and Edith Pickthall; Educated Ulverston Grammar School; University College of Wales, Bangor (BA 1966); Lancaster University (MA 1968); Married 1973, Judith Ann Tranter (2 daughters). Assistant master, Ruffwood Comprehensive School, Kirkby, Liverpool 1967–70; Lecturer in English, head of modern European cultural studies, Edge Hill College, Ormskirk, Lancashire 1970–92; Member, USDAW; Chair, USDAW MPs Group. Councillor, Ormskirk, Lancashire County Council 1989–92. **House of Commons:** Contested West Lancashire 1987 general election; Member for West Lancashire since April 9, 1992; PPS to: Alun Michael as Minister of State, Home Office (Minister for Criminal Policy) 1997–98, Jack Straw as Home Secretary 1999–; *Select Committees:* Member: Agriculture 1992–97. *Special Interests:* Home Affairs, Agriculture and Rural Affairs, Education; Canada, France. Hon. Secretary, North West Group of Labour MPs 1997–99. President, West Lancashire Arthritis Care; *Clubs:* Skelmersdale Labour; *Sportsclubs:* Dalton-in-Furness Cricket; *Recreations:* Fell-walking, cricket, Shakespeare, gardening, literature. *Address:* Colin Pickthall Esq, MP, House of Commons, London, SW1A 0AA *Tel:* 020 7219 5011 *Fax:* 020 7219 2354. *Constituency:* 127 Burscough Street, Ormskirk, Lancashire, L39 2EP *Tel:* 01695 570094 *Fax:* 01695 570094 *E-mail:* colin@colinpickthallmp.labour.org.uk.

PETER PIKE Burnley
Lab majority 17,062

Born 26 June 1937; Son of late Leslie Henry Pike; Educated Hinchley Wood County Secondary School; Kingston Technical College (evening classes); Married December 8, 1962, Sheila Lillian Bull (2 daughters). Royal Marines, national service 1956–58; Clerk: Midland Bank 1958–62, Twinings Tea 1962–63; Labour Party organiser 1963–73; Final Inspector, Mullards (Simonstone) Ltd 1973–83; Shop Steward, GMB 1976–83. Councillor, Merton and Morden Urban District Council 1962–63; Burnley Borough Council: Councillor 1976–84, Group Leader 1980–83. **House of Commons:** Member for Burnley since June 1983; Opposition Front Bench Spokesperson on: Rural Affairs 1990–92, Environment (Housing) 1992–94; *Select Committees:* Member: Deregulation 1995–97, Procedure 1995–97; Chair: Deregulation 1997–; Member: Liaison 1997–, Modernisation of the House of Commons 1997–. *Special Interests:* Local Government, Energy, Employment, Trade and Industry, Pensions, Health Service, Environment; Bangladesh, Brazil, India, Pakistan, Romania, Southern Africa. Member, Executive Committee, Commonwealth Parliamentary Association (CPA) UK Branch 1999–; *Clubs:* Byerden House Socialist; *Recreations:* Burnley Football Club supporter, member of National Trust. *Address:* Peter Pike Esq, MP, House of Commons, London, SW1A 0AA *Tel:* 020 7219 3514 *Fax:* 020 7219 3872. *Constituency:* 2 Victoria Street, Burnley, Lancashire, BB11 1DD *Tel:* 01282 450840 *Fax:* 01282 839623 *E-mail:* peterpikemp@parliament.uk.

JAMES PLASKITT Warwick and Leamington
Lab majority 3,398

Born 23 June 1954; Son of late Ronald Edmund Plaskitt, and Phyllis Irene Plaskitt; Educated Pilgrim School, Bedford; University College, Oxford (MA philosophy, politics and economics 1976, MPhil). Lecturer, University College 1977–78, Christ Church 1984–87, Oxford; Business analyst, Brunel University 1981–84; Member, MSF. Councillor, Oxfordshire County Council 1985–97, Leader 1990–96. **House of Commons:** Contested Witney 1992 general election. Member for Warwick and Leamington since May 1, 1997; *Select Committees:* : Financial Services (Joint Committee) 1998–99; Member: Joint Committee on Consolidation of Bills Etc 1997–, Treasury 1999–, Treasury Sub-Committee 1999–. *Special Interests:* Constitution, European Union, Education, Local Government, Welfare Reform, Economic Policy; All EU, USA. Member, Standing Committee on Finance Bill 1998; *Publications:* Contributor, *Beyond 2002 – A Programme for Labour's Second Term*, 1999. *Address:* James Plaskitt Esq, MP, House of Commons, London, SW1A 0AA *Tel:* 020 7219 6207 *Fax:* 020 7219 4993. *Constituency:* First Floor, 2A Leam Terrace, Leamington Spa, Warwickshire, CV31 1BB *Tel:* 01926 831151 *Fax:* 01926 831151 *E-mail:* plaskittj@parliament.uk.

KERRY POLLARD   St Albans   *Lab majority 4,459*

Born 27 April 1944; Son of late Patrick Joseph Pollard, and Iris Betty Pollard; Thornleigh Grammar School, Bolton; Open University (BA industrial relations and urban regeneration); Married March 19, 1966, Maralyn Murphy (5 sons 2 daughters). Process/development engineer, British Gas 1960–92; Co-ordinator, Homes for Homeless People 1992–; Director, Cherry Tree Housing Association 1992–97; Member: UNISON, MSF. Councillor: Hertfordshire County Council 1989, St Albans District Council 1982, 1992–94; JP 1984. **House of Commons:** Member for St Albans since May 1, 1997; *Special Interests:* Housing, Social Services; Ireland, Morocco, Bangladesh. Vice-Chair, Eastern Regional Group of Labour MPs 1999–. President, St Albans Community Forum; Director, Open Door Trust; *Recreations:* Relaxing with my family. *Address:* Kerry Pollard Esq, MP, House of Commons, London, SW1A 0AA *Tel:* 020 7219 4537. *Constituency:* 28 Alma Road, St Albans, Hertfordshire, AL1 3BW *Tel:* 01727 761031 *Fax:* 01727 761032 *E-mail:* kpollard@stalbansclp.u-net.com.

CHRIS POND   Gravesham   *Lab majority 5,779*

Born 25 September 1952; Son of late Charles Richard and late Doris Violet Pond; Educated Minchenden School, Southgate; Sussex University (BA economics 1974); Married December, 1990, Carole Tongue (divorced 1999) (1 daughter). Research assistant (economics) Birkbeck College, London 1974–75; Research officer, Low Pay Unit 1975–79; Lecturer in economics, Civil Service College 1979–80; Visiting lecturer in economics, University of Kent 1981–82; Visiting professor/Research fellow, University of Surrey 1984–86; Consultant, Open University 1987–88, 1991–92; 'Expert' DGV European Commission 1996; Member, TGWU. **House of Commons:** Contested Welwyn-Hatfield 1987 general election. Member for Gravesham since May 1, 1997; PPS to Dawn Primarolo as Paymaster General, HM Treasury 1999–; *Select Committees:* Member: Social Security 1997–99. *Special Interests:* Employment, Social Policy, Poverty; European Union, USA, Eastern Europe, India (Punjab). Member, Editorial Board, Charity Magazine; Former Member, Management Committees of Unemployment Unit and Child Poverty Action Group; Chair, Low Pay Unit (unpaid) 1998–; European Commission; *Publications: Inflation and Low Incomes*, 1975; *Trade Unions and Taxation*, 1976; *To Him Who Hath*, 1977; *The Poverty Trap: a study in statistical sources*, 1978; *Taxing Wealth Inequalities*, 1980; *Taxation & Social Policy*, 1981; *Low Pay: Labour's Response*, 1983; *The Changing Distribution of Income, Wealth & Poverty, in Restructuring Britain*, 1989; *Beyond 2001* Plus numerous contributions to other publications, together with articles published in magazines and newspapers; Hon. Visiting Professor, Middlesex University; Fellow, Royal Society of Arts 1994–95; *Clubs:* Royal Academy; *Sportsclubs:* Former Member, London Road Runners' Club (ten marathons); Gravesend Road Runners and Athletics Club; *Recreations:* Running, reading. *Address:* Chris Pond Esq, MP, House of Commons, London, SW1A 0AA *Tel:* 020 7219 6493 *Fax:* 020 7219 0946. *Constituency:* 24 Overcliffe, Gravesend, Kent, DA11 0EH *Tel:* 01474 354725 *Fax:* 01474 351679 *E-mail:* cpond@parliament.uk.

GREG POPE   Hyndburn   *Lab majority 11,448*

Born 29 August 1960; Son of late Samuel Pope, ambulance officer, and of Sheila Pope; Educated St Mary's College Roman Catholic Grammar School, Blackburn; Hull University (BA Hons Politics); Married August 2, 1985, Catherine Fallon (2 sons 1 daughter). Vice-President, Hull University Students Union 1981–82; Co-ordinator, Blackburn Trade Union Centre for the unemployed 1983–85; Paperworker, Star newspaper, Blackburn 1985–87; Local government officer, Lancashire County Council 1987–92. Councillor: Hyndburn Borough Council 1984–88, Blackburn Borough Council 1989–91. **House of Commons:** Contested Ribble Valley 1987 general election. Member for Hyndburn since April 9, 1992; Opposition Whip 1995–97; Assistant Government Whip 1997–99; Government Whip (Lord Commissioner of HM Treasury) (Trade and Industry: North-West) 1999–; *Select Committees:* Member: Education 1994–95. *Special Interests:* Education, Housing, Foreign Affairs. *Clubs:* Accrington Old Band (CIU); *Recreations:* Walking, chess, music. *Address:* Gregory Pope Esq, MP, House of Commons, London, SW1A 0AA *Tel:* 020 7219 5842 *Fax:* 020 7219 0685. *Constituency:* 149 Blackburn Road, Accrington, Lancs, BB5 0AA *Tel:* 01254 382283 *Fax:* 01254 392438 *E-mail:* popegj@parliament.uk.

MICHAEL PORTILLO   Kensington and Chelsea   *Con majority 6,706*

Born 26 May 1953; Son of late Luis Gabriel Portillo, and of Cora Blyth; Educated Harrow County School for Boys; Peterhouse College, Cambridge (MA history 1975); Married February 12, 1982, Carolyn Claire Eadie. Conservative Research Department 1976–79; Special adviser to David Howell, MP, as Secretary of State for Energy 1979–81; Oil industry consultant 1981–83; Special adviser to: Cecil Parkinson, MP, as Secretary of State for Trade and Industry 1983, Nigel Lawson, MP, as Chancellor of the Exchequer 1983–84; Presenter: *Portillo's Progress* Channel 4 1998, BBC TV programme in series *Great Railway Journeys* 1999, BBC Radio programme *The Legacy of Division* 2000. **House of Commons:** Contested Birmingham Perry Barr June 1983. Member for Enfield Southgate 1984–97, for Kensington and Chelsea since November 25, 1999 by-election; Government Whip October 1986–87; PPS to Secretary of State for Transport 1986; Parliamentary Under-Secretary of State DHSS 1987–88; Minister of State: at Department of Transport 1988–90, at Department of Environment (Minister for Local Government and Inner Cities) 1990–92; Chief Secretary to HM Treasury 1992–94; Secretary of State for: Employment 1994–95, Defence 1995–97; Member, Shadow Cabinet 2000–; Shadow Chancellor of the Exchequer 2000–. PC 1992. *Address:* Rt Hon Michael Portillo, MP, House of Commons, London, SW1A 0AA *Tel:* 020 7219 3000.

STEPHEN POUND   Ealing North   *Lab majority 9,160*

Born 3 July 1948; Son of Pelham Pound, journalist, and Dominica Pound, teacher; Educated Hertford Grammar School; London School of Economics (Diploma in industrial relations, BSc economics) (Sabbatical President of Union 1981–82); Married June 1976, Maggie Griffiths (1 son 1 daughter). Seaman 1964–66; 'Bus Conductor 1966–68; Hospital Porter 1969–79; Student 1979–84; Housing Officer 1984–97; Branch Secretary, 640 Middlesex Branch, COHSE 1975–79; Branch Officer, T&GWU (ACTS) 1990–96. Councillor, London Borough of Ealing 1982–98, Mayor 1995–96. **House of Commons:** Member for Ealing North since May 1, 1997; *Select Committees:* Member: Broadcasting 1997–, Northern Ireland 1999–. *Special Interests:* Housing, Transport; Ireland. Director, Hanwell Community Centre; Trustee, Charity of Wm Hobbayne (Hanwell); *Clubs:* St Joseph's Catholic Social, Hanwell; *Sportsclubs:* Fulham FC Supporters Club; *Recreations:* Watching football, playing cricket, snooker, jazz, gardening, collecting comics. *Address:* Stephen Pound Esq, MP, House of Commons, London, SW1A 0AA *Tel:* 020 7219 1140 *Fax:* 020 7219 5982.

SIR RAYMOND POWELL   Ogmore   *Lab majority 24,447*

Born 19 June 1928; Son of late Albert Ernest Powell, miner; Educated Pentre Grammar School; National Council of Labour Colleges; London School of Economics; Married January 28, 1950, Marion Grace Evans (1 son 1 daughter). Fireman with British Rail 1946–51; Shop assistant 1951–56; Own business 1956–66; Administration officer, PMSB 1969–74; Senior administration officer (Morgannwg Division), Welsh Water Authority 1974–79; Member, USDAW for over 50 years; Has held most branch positions; Sponsored by USDAW 1979–. Councillor, Ogmore Borough Council 1973–79. **House of Commons:** Member for Ogmore since May 1979; Opposition Whip 1984–95, Pairing Whip 1987–95, Accommodation Whip 1987–95; *Select Committees:* Chairman: Accommodation and Works 1988–97; Member: Liaison 1993–95, Selection 1995; Member: Accommodation and Works 1997–. *Special Interests:* Coal Industry, Steel Industry, CND, Childcare, Grandparents' Rights, Marketing, Keep Sunday Special, Sunday Trading, Sunday Drinking, Licensing Hours Pubs-Clubs, Parliamentary Buildings/Accommodation/Preservation; Cyprus (Greek), Bulgaria, America, Switzerland, Canada. Secretary, Ogmore Constituency Labour Party; Chair, Wales Labour Party 1977; Chair, South Wales Euro Constituency Labour Party 1978–; Hon. Secretary: Welsh Parliamentary Party, Welsh Parliamentary Labour Party 1982–92; Member, Co-operative Party Fabian Group. Chair, Community Activities and Training in Ogmore Charity Organisation 1980–90; Member, Co-op Society, Bridgend; Member, Keep Sunday Special Committee; Fellow, Industry and Parliament Trust; Knighted 1996; *Clubs:* Ogmore Labour Party; *Sportsclubs:* Life President, Ogmore Constituency Labour Party Sports; *Recreations:* Gardening, sports. *Address:* Sir Raymond Powell, MP, House of Commons, London, SW1A 0AA *Tel:* 020 7219 4030. *Constituency:* 14 Blackmill Road, Bryncethin, Bridgend, Mid Glamorgan *Tel:* 01656 721300 *Fax:* 01656 729662.

BRIDGET PRENTICE   Lewisham East   *Lab majority 12,127*

Born 28 December 1952; Daughter of late James Corr, joiner, and of Bridget Corr, clerical worker; Educated Our Lady and St Francis School, Glasgow; Glasgow University (MA English literature and modern history); London University (PGCE); South Bank University (LLB); Married December 20, 1975, Gordon Prentice (now MP – *qv*) (divorced 2000). Rector's assessor, Glasgow University 1972–73; London Oratory School: Teacher 1974–86, Head of careers 1984–86; Head of careers, John Archer School 1986–88. London Borough of Hammersmith and Fulham: Councillor 1986–92, Chair: Public Services Committee 1987–90, Labour Group 1986–89; JP 1985–. **House of Commons:** Contested Croydon Central 1987 general election. Member for Lewisham East since April 9, 1992; Opposition Whip 1995–97; Assistant Government Whip 1997–98; PPS to Brian Wilson as Minister of State, Department of Trade and Industry (Minister for Trade) 1998–99; Joint PPS to the Lord Irvine of Lairg as Lord Chancellor 1999–; *Select Committees:* Member: Parliamentary Commissioner for Administration 1992–96. *Special Interests:* Education, Training, Constitutional Reform, Human Rights, Home Affairs; South Africa, USA. Chair, Fulham Constituency Labour Party 1982–85; Leadership Campaign Team Co-ordinator 1995–96. *Recreations:* Reading, music, crosswords, gardening, two cats, badminton (qualified coach), football. *Address:* Bridget Prentice, MP, House of Commons, London, SW1A 0AA *Tel:* 020 7219 3000 *Fax:* 020 7219 5581. *Constituency:* 149 Lee High Road, London, SE13 5PF *Tel:* 020 8852 3995 *Fax:* 020 8852 2386 *E-mail:* prenticeb@parliament.uk.

GORDON PRENTICE   Pendle   *Lab majority 10,824*

Born 28 January 1951; Son of late William Prentice, and of Esther Prentice; Educated George Heriot's School, Edinburgh; Glasgow University (MA politics and economics 1972); Married December 20, 1975, Bridget Corr (now MP as Bridget Prentice – *qv*) (divorced 2000). Labour Party Policy Directorate 1982–92; Labour Party Local Government Officer 1985–92; Member, TGWU. London Borough of Hammersmith and Fulham: Councillor 1982–90, Deputy Leader, Labour Group 1982–84, Leader 1984–88. **House of Commons:** Member for Pendle since April 9, 1992; PPS to Gavin Strang as Minister of State (in Cabinet), Department of the Environment, Transport and the Regions (Minister for Transport) May-December 1997; *Select Committees:* Member: Statutory Instruments 1993–97, Deregulation 1995–97, Agriculture 1996–97; Member: Modernisation of the House of Commons 1999–. *Special Interests:* countryside, agriculture, manufacturing industry, poverty and low pay, regional policy. Executive Committee Member, Inter-Parliamentary Union (IPU) British Group; *Recreations:* Cooking, hillwalking. *Address:* Gordon Prentice Esq, MP, House of Commons, London, SW1A 0AA *Tel:* 020 7219 4011. *Constituency:* 33 Carr Road, Nelson, BB9 7JS *Tel:* 01282 695471 *Fax:* 01282 614097 *E-mail:* gordonprentice@compuserve.com, www.gordonpricemp.com.

JOHN PRESCOTT   Hull East   *Lab majority 23,318*

Born 31 May 1938; Son of John Herbert Prescott, railway controller; Educated Ellesmere Port Secondary Modern School; Ruskin College, Oxford; Hull University; Married November 11, 1961, Pauline Tilston (2 sons). Steward in the Merchant Navy 1955–63; TU Official, National Union of Seamen 1968–70. **House of Commons:** Contested Southport 1966 general election. Member for Kingston-upon-Hull East June 18, 1970–83 and for Hull East 1983–; Opposition Front Bench Spokesman on: Transport 1979–81, Regional Affairs and Devolution 1981–83; Labour Party Spokesman on Transport 1983–84; Opposition Front Bench Spokesman on: Employment 1984–87, Energy 1987–88, Transport 1988–93, Employment 1993–94; PPS to Peter Shore as Secretary of State for Trade 1974–76; Member, Shadow Cabinet 1983–97; Deputy Prime Minister and Secretary of State for the Environment, Transport and the Regions 1997–. Deputy Leader, Labour Party 1994–; Member, National Executive Committee of the Labour Party; Deputy Leader, Labour Party National Executive Committee 1997–. Member, Council of Europe 1972–75; Delegate, EEC Parliamentary 1975; Leader, Labour Party Delegation to European Parliament 1976–79; PC 1994; *Recreations:* Jazz, theatre, music, aqua diving. *Address:* Rt Hon John Prescott, MP, House of Commons, London, SW1A 0AA *Tel:* 020 7219 5030 *E-mail:* john-prescott@detr.gsi.gov.uk *Website:* http://www.detr.gov.uk.

DAWN PRIMAROLO   Bristol South   *Lab majority 19,328*

Born 2 May 1954; Educated Thomas Bennett Comprehensive School, Crawley; Bristol Polytechnic (BA social science 1984); Bristol University; Married 1st, October 7, 1972 (divorced) (1 son), married 2nd, November 29, 1990, Thomas Ian Ducat. Secretary 1972–73; Secretary and advice worker, Law Centre, East London; Secretary, Avon County Council 1975–78; Voluntary work 1978–81; Mature student 1981–87. Councillor, Avon County Council 1985–87. **House of Commons:** Member for Bristol South since June 1987; Opposition Front Bench Spokesperson on: Health 1992–94, Treasury and Economic Affairs 1994–97; HM Treasury: Financial Secretary 1997–99, Paymaster General 1999–; *Select Committees:* Member: Members' Interests 1990–92, Public Accounts 1997–98. *Special Interests:* Education, Housing, Women's Rights, Social Security, Health, Economic Policy. *Address:* Dawn Primarolo, MP, House of Commons, London, SW1A 0AA *Tel: Fax:* 020 7219 2276. *Constituency:* PO Box 1002, Bristol, BS99 1WH *Tel:* 0117–909 0063 *Fax:* 0117–909 0064 *E-mail:* dawn.primarolo@hm-treasury.gov.uk.

DAVID PRIOR   North Norfolk   *Con majority 1,293*

Born 3 December 1954; Son of The Rt Hon. Baron Prior (*qv*) and Lady Prior; Educated Charterhouse; Cambridge (MA law); Married February 14, 1987, Caroline Holmes (1 son 1 daughter). Lehman Brothers and Lazard Freres, Investment Banks 1977–80; British Steel Corporation, last job Commercial Director 1980–87; Investor and Manager of various industrial businesses. **House of Commons:** Member for North Norfolk since May 1, 1997; *Select Committees:* Member: Trade and Industry 1997–98. *Special Interests:* City, Trade and Industry, Employment, Education, Agriculture; Asia, USA. Chair, Mid Norfolk Conservative Association 1995–96; Vice-Chair, Conservative Party (with responsibility for Organisation) 1998, Deputy Chief Executive 1998–99; Deputy Chair and Chief Executive, Conservative Party 1999–. *Clubs:* RAC; *Recreations:* Gardening, sport. *Address:* Hon David Prior, MP, House of Commons, London, SW1A 0AA. *Constituency:* North Norfolk Conservative Association, 8 Louden Road, Norfolk, NR27 9EF *Tel:* 01263 510240 *Fax:* 01263 513473 *E-mail:* priordgl@parliament.uk.

GWYN PROSSER   Dover   *Lab majority 11,739*

Born 27 April 1943; Son of late Glyn Prosser and of Doreen Prosser; Educated Dunvant Secondary Modern; Swansea Technical School; Swansea College of Technology (National Diploma, Mechanical Engineering, First Class Certificate of Competency, Marine Engineering); Married April 6, 1972, Rhoda McLeod (1 son 2 daughters). Merchant Navy cadet engineer 1960–64; Seagoing engineer, BP 1964–67, Blue Funnel 1967–71; Chief engineer, BR Shipping 1971–74; Test and guarantee engineer, Kincaid of Greenock 1974–77; Port engineer, Aramco, Saudi Arabia 1977–78; Chief engineer: Anscar 1978–79, Sealink Ferries at Dover 1979–92; Social survey interviewer, Civil Service 1993–96; Former member, NUMAST NEC; Political officer, MSF, South East Kent. Councillor, Dover District Council 1987–97; Kent County Council: Councillor 1989–97, Co-Chair, Economic Development and President, European Affairs 1993–97. **House of Commons:** Member for Dover since May 1, 1997; *Select Committees:* Member: Information 2000–. *Special Interests:* Transport, Shipping, Economic Development, Environment, Asylum and Immigration Policy; Hungary. Director, East Kent Women's Refuge; Member, Greenpeace; Organising opposition, Channel Tunnel Bill; Member, Parliamentary Assembly of: Council of Europe 1997–, Western European Union 1997–; Trustee, Numerous Local Charities; MIMarE; CEng; *Recreations:* Hill walking, swimming, awaiting revival of Welsh rugby. *Address:* Gwyn Prosser Esq, MP, House of Commons, London, SW1A 0AA *Tel:* 020 7219 3704. *Constituency:* 26 Coombe Valley Road, Dover, Kent, CT17 0EP *Tel:* 01304 214484 *Fax:* 01304 214486 *E-mail:* prosserg@parliament.uk.

KEN PURCHASE   Wolverhampton North East   *Lab/Co-op majority 12,987*

Born 8 January 1939; Son of late Albert Purchase, diecaster, and late Rebecca Purchase, cleaner; Educated Springfield Secondary Modern School; Wolverhampton Polytechnic (BA social science); Married August 20, 1960, Brenda Sanders (2 daughters). Apprentice toolmaker, foundry industry 1956–60; Experimental component development, aerospace industry 1960–68; Toolroom machinist, motor industry 1968–76; Property division, Telford Development Corporation 1977–80; Housing Department, Walsall Metropolitan Borough Council 1981–82; Business Development Adviser, Black Country CDA Ltd 1982–92; Member, TGWU (ACTSS). Councillor: Wolverhampton County Borough Council 1970–74; Wolverhampton Metropolitan Borough Council 1973–90; Member: Wolverhampton Health Authority 1978–82, 1985–87, 1988–90, Wolverhampton Community Health Council 1990–92. **House of Commons:** Contested Wolverhampton North East 1987 general election. Member for Wolverhampton North East since April 9, 1992; PPS to Robin Cook as Foreign Secretary 1997–; *Select Committees:* Member: Trade and Industry 1993–97. *Special Interests:* Trade and Industry, Health, Education. Sponsored by Co-operative Party. *Recreations:* Listening to jazz. *Address:* Kenneth Purchase Esq, MP, House of Commons, London, SW1A 0AA *Tel:* 020 7219 3602 *Fax:* 020 7219 2110. *Constituency:* 492a Stafford Road, Wolverhampton, WV10 6AN *Tel:* 01902 397698 *Fax:* 01902 397538 *E-mail:* ken.purchase@cwcom.net.

Q

JOYCE QUIN   Gateshead East and Washington West   *Lab majority 24,950*

Born 26 November 1944; Daughter of late Basil Godfrey Quin, schoolmaster, and late Ida Quin, née Ritson, teacher; Educated Whitley Bay Grammar School; Newcastle University (BA French 1967); LSE (MSc international relations 1969). Lecturer in French, Bath University 1972–76; Tutor and lecturer in French and politics, Durham University 1976–79; MEP for Tyne and Wear 1979–89; Member, TGWU. **House of Commons:** Member for Gateshead East 1987–97, and for Gateshead East and Washington West since May 1, 1997; Opposition Spokesperson on Trade and Industry 1989–92; Opposition Front Bench Spokesperson on: Employment 1992–93, Foreign and Commonwealth Affairs 1993–97; Minister of State: Home Office 1997–98, Foreign and Commonwealth Office 1998–99; Minister of State and Deputy Minister, Ministry of Agriculture, Fisheries and Food 1999–; *Special Interests:* European Policy, Industrial Policy, Regional Policy; Australia, Europe, New Zealand, USA. Research officer, International Department, Labour Party HQ 1969–72. PC 1998; Hon. Fellow: Sunderland Polytechnic 1986, St Mary's College, University of Durham 1996; *Recreations:* North-East local history, walking, music, reading, cycling, playing Northumbrian pipes. *Address:* Rt Hon Joyce Quin, MP, House of Commons, London, SW1A 0AA *Tel:* 020 7219 4009. *Constituency:* Design Works, William Street, Felling, Gateshead, Tyne & Wear, NE10 0JP *Tel:* 0191–469 6006 *Fax:* 0191–469 6009.

LAWRIE QUINN   Scarborough and Whitby   *Lab majority 5,124*

Born 25 December 1956; Son of late Jimmy and Sheila Quinn; Educated Pennine Way Schools, Carlisle; Harraby School, Carlisle; Hatfield Polytechnic (BSc civil engineering); Married April 10, 1982, Ann. Railway civil engineer and planning development engineer, Railtrack London NE; Chair/Secretary, TSSA. Councillor, North Yorkshire County Council 1989–93, Member: Highways Committee, Policy and Resources Committee, Planning Committee. **House of Commons:** Member for Scarborough and Whitby since May 1, 1997; *Special Interests:* Transport, Devolution, Constitution, Health and Safety at Work, Tourism, Deep Sea Fishing Industry, Regional Assemblies; Member, European Standing Committee A 1998–. Member: Fabian Society,

Labour Campaigning for Electoral Reform, SERA; Member, North and Yorks Labour Executive 1993–97; Chair, City of York CLP 1994–97. Member: Governing Board, York Sixth Form College 1989–93, Permanent Way Institution, Hon. Life Member, Civil Engineering Trainees, Transport 2000; MICE; CEng; *Clubs:* York Speakers; *Recreations:* Reading, history, cooking, theatre, avid internet user, long-distance supporter of Carlisle United, train travel around Europe. *Address:* Lawrie Quinn Esq, MP, House of Commons, London, SW1A 0AA *Tel:* 020 7219 4170 *Fax:* 020 7219 2477. *Constituency:* 53 Westborough, Scarborough, North Yorkshire, YO11 1TU *Tel:* 01723 507000 *Fax:* 01723 507008 *E-mail:* quinnl@parliament.uk.

R

GILES RADICE   Durham North   *Lab majority 26,299*

Born 4 October 1936; Educated Winchester; Magdalen College, Oxford; Married March 4, 1971, Lisanne Koch. Head of research department GMWU 1966–73. **House of Commons:** Contested Chippenham 1964 and 1966 general elections. Member for Chester-le-Street by-election 1973–83 and for Durham North since June 1983; Opposition Front Bench Spokesman on: Foreign Affairs 1981, Employment 1982–83, Education 1983–87; PPS to Shirley Williams as Secretary of State for Education and Science 1978–1979; *Select Committees:* Member: Treasury and Civil Service 1987–96, Public Service 1995–97, Liaison 1996–97; Chairman: Public Service 1996–97; Member: Liaison 1997–; Chairman: Treasury 1997–; Member: Treasury Sub-Committee 1998–. *Special Interests:* Economic and European Affairs, Labour Party Policy Revision; Eastern Europe, Europe, Poland, Germany, India. Chairman, British Association for Central and Eastern Europe 1997–; *Publications: Democratic Socialism,* 1965; *More Power to People,* 1968; Co-author *Will Thorne,* 1974; *The Industrial Democrats,* 1978; Co-author *Socialists in the Recession: a Survey of European Socialism,* 1986; *Labour's Path to Power: the New Revisionism,* 1989; *Offshore – Britain and the European Idea,* 1992; *The New Germans,* 1995; *What Needs to Change* Editor 1996; PC 1999; *Recreations:* Reading, tennis, gardening. *Address:* Rt Hon Giles Radice, MP, House of Commons, London, SW1A 0AA *Tel:* 020 7219 4194. *Constituency:* Station Master's House, Station Lane, Chester-le-Street, Co Durham, DH3 3DU *Tel:* 0191–387 1107 *Fax:* 0191–387 1107.

BILL RAMMELL   Harlow   *Lab majority 10,514*

Born 10 October 1959; Son of William Ernest and Joan Elizabeth Rammell; Educated Burnt Mill Comprehensive, Harlow; University College of Wales, Cardiff (BA French and politics 1982); Married January 1, 1983, Beryl Jarhall (1 son 1 daughter). President, Cardiff University SU 1982–83; Management trainee, British Rail 1983–84; Regional officer, NUS 1984–87; Head of youth services, Basildon Council 1987–89; General manager, Kings College, London SU 1980–94; Senior university business manager, London University 1994–; Member, MSF. Councillor, Harlow Council 1985–97; Former Member, Local Government Information Unit. **House of Commons:** Member for Harlow since May 1, 1997; *Select Committees:* Member: Education and Employment 1997–99, European Legislation 1997–98, European Scrutiny 1998–2000; Member: European Scrutiny 2000–. *Special Interests:* Education, Housing, Economic Policy, Europe, Media, Sport, Electoral Reform; France, Sweden, USA, Germany, Hungary, Netherlands; Member, European Standing Committee B 1998–. Former Chair, CLP; Chair, Labour Movement for Europe 1999–. Member, Community Health Council; Chair, Community Safety Group; *Recreations:* Family, friends, sport, reading. *Address:* Bill Rammell Esq, MP, House of Commons, London, SW1A 0AA *Tel:* 020 7219 2828 *Fax:* 020 7219 2804. *Constituency:* 1 Adams House, The High, Harlow, Essex, CM20 1BE *Tel:* 01279 439706 *Website:* www.rammell.freeserve.co.uk.

JOHN RANDALL   Uxbridge   *Con majority 3,766*

Born 5 August 1955; Son of late Alec Albert Randall, company director, and of Joyce Margaret Randall (née Gore); Educated Rutland House School, Hillingdon; Merchant Taylors School, Moor Park; School of Slavonic and East European Studies, London University (BA Serbo-Croat 1979); Married October 25, 1986, Katherine Frances Gray (2 sons 1 daughter). Randall's of Uxbridge: Sales assistant, Buyer, Director 1980–, Managing director 1988–; Tour leader, Birdquest Holidays and Limosa Holidays as specialist ornithologist 1986–. **House of Commons:** Member for Uxbridge since July 31, 1997 by-election; Opposition Whip (Social Security; Culture, Media and Sport) 2000–; *Select Committees:* Member: Environment, Transport and Regional Affairs 1998–2000, Environment Sub-Committee 1998–2000; Member: Deregulation 1997–. *Special Interests:* Environment, Trade and Industry, Foreign Affairs. Hon. Treasurer, Uxbridge Conservative Association 1994, Chairman 1994–97. Chair: Uxbridge Retailers' Association to 1997, Cowley Residents' Association to 1997; Member: Uxbridge Town Centre Steering Committee to 1997, Royal Society for the Protection of Birds, British Ornithologists Union; *Clubs:* Uxbridge Conservative; *Sportsclubs:* Vice-President: Uxbridge Cricket Club, Uxbridge Rugby Football Club; *Recreations:* Local history, ornithology, theatre, opera, travel, music (plays piano), Uxbridge FC supporter. *Address:* John Randall Esq, MP, House of Commons, London, SW1A 0AA *Tel:* 020 7219 3400 *Fax:* 020 7219 2590. *Constituency:* 36 Harefield Road, Uxbridge, Middlesex, UB8 1PH *Tel:* 01895 239465 *Fax:* 01895 253105 *E-mail:* randallj@parliament.com.

SYD RAPSON   Portsmouth North   *Lab majority 4,323*

Born 17 April 1942; Son of late Sidney Rapson and of Doris Rapson, née Fisher, adopted by Lily and Sidney Rapson (grandparents); Educated Southsea and Paulsgrove Secondary Modern; Portsmouth Dockyard College (City and Guilds); National Council of Labour Colleges; Married March 17, 1967, Phyllis Edna Williams (1 son 1 daughter). Ministry of Defence: apprentice aircraft fitter, MoD 1958–63; aircraft fitter 1963–96; industrial technician 1997; AEEU: Shop steward 1965–97, Convenor 1979–97, National delegate, District president. Councillor, Portsmouth City Council 1971–99; Lord Mayor 1990–91, Deputy Leader 1994–95; Councillor, Hampshire County Council 1973–77; Hon Alderman, Portsmouth City Council 1999–. **House of Commons:** Contested Portsmouth South 1992. Member for Portsmouth North since May 1, 1997; *Select Committees:* Member: Accommodation and Works 1997–, Unopposed Bills (Panel) 1998–. *Special Interests:* Leisure, Economic Development, Defence, Local Government; America, Germany, Australia. Member, Co-operative Party; Joined Labour Party 1968; Chair, Portsmouth South Constituency 1970–71; Member, Parliamentary Armed Forces Scheme (Royal Marines) 1998–99. Member: Britain Australia Society Portsmouth Branch 1984–, Portsmouth/Sydney Sister Link Committee 1984–, Vice-President, Portsmouth/Duisburg Friendship Committee 1991–, Portsmouth Haifa Friendship Committee 1991–, Council of Europe, Parliamentary Assembly 1998–, Council of Europe Science and Technology Committee 1998–, Western European Union 1998–, Western European Union Defence Committee 1998–; Former non-executive member, Portsmouth Healthcare NHS Trust; *Publications: New Missions for European Armed Forces and their Collective Capabilities Required for their Implementation* Western European Union Document 1987; BEM 1984; Imperial Service Medal 1998; Freeman, City of London; *Sportsclubs:* Former President, Portsmouth Athletic Club 1991–96; *Recreations:* Swimming, gardening. *Address:* Syd Rapson Esq, BEM, MP, House of Commons, London, SW1A 0AA *Tel:* 020 7219 6351/6248 *Fax:* 020 7219 0915. *Constituency:* Portsmouth North Labour Party HQ, 1 Holbrook Road, Landport, Portsmouth, Hampshire, PO1 1JB *Tel:* 023 9235 0035 *Fax:* 023 9234 0451.

NICK RAYNSFORD — Greenwich and Woolwich — *Lab majority 18,128*

Born 28 January 1945; Son of late Wyvill and Patricia Raynsford; Educated Repton School; Sidney Sussex College, Cambridge (BA history 1966, MA); Chelsea School of Art (diploma in art and design 1972); Married 1968, Anne Jelley (3 daughters). Director, SHAC, the London Housing Aid Centre 1976–86. London Borough of Hammersmith and Fulham: Councillor 1971–75. **House of Commons:** Member for Fulham 1986 by-election –1987. Member for Greenwich 1992–97, and for Greenwich and Woolwich since May 1, 1997; Opposition Spokesman on: Transport and London 1993–94, Housing, Construction and London 1994–97; Former PPS to Roy Hattersley; Department of the Environment, Transport and the Regions 1997–: Parliamentary Under-Secretary of State 1997–99, Minister of State (Minister for Housing and Planning) 1999–; *Select Committees:* Member: Environment 1992–93. *Special Interests:* Housing, Social Policy, Transport, Environment; Europe. *Publications: A Guide to Housing Benefit,* 1982; Contributor to journals including *Building, Housing* and *New Statesman; Recreations:* Photography, walking, golf. *Address:* Nick Raynsford Esq, MP, House of Commons, London, SW1A 0AA *Tel:* 020 7219 2773 *Fax:* 020 7219 2619. *Constituency:* 32 Woolwich Road, London, SE10 0JU *Tel:* 020 7219 5895 *Fax:* 020 7219 2619 *E-mail:* seabeckaj@parliament.uk; nick-raynsford@detr.gsi.gov.uk.

JOHN REDWOOD — Wokingham — *Con majority 9,365*

Born 15 June 1951; Son of William and Amy Redwood (née Champion); Educated Kent College, Canterbury; Magdalen College, Oxford (MA 1971); St Antony's College, Oxford (DPhil 1975); Married April 1974, Gail Felicity Chippington (1 son 1 daughter). Fellow, All Souls College, Oxford 1972–87; Tutor and lecturer 1972–73; Investment analyst, Robert Fleming & Co. 1974–77; N. M. Rothschild: Bank clerk 1977–78, Manager 1978–79, Assistant director 1979–80, Director, investment division 1980–83, Overseas corporate finance director and head of international (non-UK) privatisation 1986–87; Norcros plc: Non-executive director 1985–87, Chair 1987–89; Chair, Mabey Securities 1999–; Visiting professor Middlesex University Business School 2000–. Councillor, Oxfordshire County Council 1973–77. **House of Commons:** Contested Southwark Peckham 1982 general election. Member for Wokingham since June 1987; Parliamentary Under-Secretary of State for Corporate Affairs, Department of Trade and Industry 1989–90; Minister of State 1990–92; Minister of State, Department of the Environment (Minister for Local Government) 1992–93; Secretary of State for Wales 1993–95; Contested Leadership of the Conservative Party 1995 and 1997; Member, Shadow Cabinet 1997–2000; Shadow Secretary of State for: Trade and Industry 1997–99, Environment, Transport and the Regions 1999–2000; *Special Interests:* British Business, Popular Capitalism; USA. Chair, Conservative Parliamentary Campaigns Unit 2000–. Governor, Oxford Polytechnic 1973–77; Governor of various schools in West Oxfordshire and Inner London 1973–82; Adviser, Treasury and Civil Service Select Committee 1981; Head, Prime Minister's policy unit 1983–85; *Publications: Reason, Ridicule and Religion,* 1976; *Public Enterprise in Crisis,* 1980; *Going for Broke,* 1984; *Popular Capitalism,* 1987; *The Global Marketplace,* 1993; *Our Currency, Our Country,* 1997; Several books and articles, especially on wider ownership and popular capitalism; *The Death of Britain,* 1999; PC 1993; *Sportsclubs:* Lords and Commons Cricket; *Recreations:* Village cricket, water sports. *Address:* Rt Hon John Redwood, MP, House of Commons, London, SW1A 0AA *Tel:* 020 7219 3000. *Constituency:* 30 Rose Street, Wokingham, Berkshire, RG40 3SU *Tel:* 01734 629501 *E-mail:* redwoodj@parliament.uk.

ANDREW REED   Loughborough   *Lab majority 5,712*

Born 17 September 1964; Son of James Donald Reed and Margaret Ann Reed; Educated Riverside Junior, Birstall, Leicestershire; Stonehill High School, Birstall, Leicestershire; Longslade Community College, Birstall, Leicestershire; Leicester Polytechnic (BA public administration 1997); Married August 29, 1992, Sarah Elizabeth Chester. Parliamentary assistant to Keith Vaz MP 1987–88; Urban regeneration, Leicester City Council 1988–90; Leicestershire County Council: economic development unit 1990–94, European affairs adviser 1994–97; NALGO 1988–: Unison 1990–, Steward, Convenor, Executive, Leicestershire County Council, Conference Delegate, Service Conditions Officer. Councillor: Birstall Parish Council 1987–92, Charnwood Borough Council 1995–97, Chair, Economic Development 1995–97; Vice-Chair, Loughborough Town Partnership 1995–97; Board Member, Business Link Loughborough 1995–99. **House of Commons:** Contested Loughborough 1992 general election. Member for Loughborough since May 1, 1997; *Special Interests:* Economic Regeneration, Unemployment, Lifelong Learning, Education, Vocational Training, Sport, International Development, Co-operatives; South Africa, Germany. Loughborough Constituency Labour Party: Chair 1988–92, Regional executive 1993–94; Member, East Midlands PLP; Vice-Chair, East Midlands Regional Group of Labour MPs 1999–. *Clubs:* Loughborough Labour; *Sportsclubs:* Leicester Rugby Football Club, Birstall Rugby Football Club (player), Sileby Tennis Club, Leicester PVC Volleyball Club; *Recreations:* Rugby, tennis, volleyball, any sport. *Address:* Andrew Reed Esq, MP, House of Commons, London, SW1A 0AA *Tel:* 020 7219 3529 *Fax:* 020 7219 2405. *Constituency:* Unity House, Fennel Street, Loughborough, Leceistershire, LE11 1UQ *Tel:* 01509 261226 *Fax:* 01509 230579 *E-mail:* andy@andyreedmp.org.uk.

DR JOHN REID   Hamilton North and Bellshill   *Lab majority 17,067*

Born 8 May 1947; Son of late Thomas Reid, postman, and of Mary Reid, factory worker; Educated St Patrick's Senior Secondary School, Coatbridge; Stirling University (MA history, PhD economic history); Married 1969, Cathie McGowan (died 1998) (2 sons). Scottish research officer, Labour Party 1979–83; Adviser to Neil Kinnock as Leader of the Labour Party 1983–85; Scottish organiser, Trade Unionists for Labour 1985–87; Member, TGWU. **House of Commons:** Member for Motherwell North 1987–97, and for Hamilton North and Bellshill since May 1, 1997; Deputy Shadow Spokesman on Children 1989–90; Opposition Spokesman on Defence, Disarmament and Arms Control 1990–97; Shadow Deputy Secretary of State for Defence 1995–97; Minister of State, Ministry of Defence (Minister for the Armed Forces) 1997–98; Minister of State, Department of the Environment, Transport and the Regions (Minister for Transport) 1998–99; Secretary of State for Scotland 1999–; *Special Interests:* Foreign Affairs, Defence, Economy. Fellow, Armed Services Parliamentary Scheme 1990–; PC 1998; *Recreations:* Football, crosswords. *Address:* Rt Hon Dr John Reid, MP, House of Commons, London, SW1A 0AA *Tel:* 020 7219 4118. *Constituency:* Parliamentary Office, Montrose House, 154 Montrose Crescent, Hamilton, ML3 6LL *Tel:* 01698 454672 *Fax:* 01698 424732 *E-mail:* scottishsecretary@scotland.gov.uk *Website:* www.scottishsecretary.gov.uk.

DAVID RENDEL   Newbury   *LD majority 8,517*

Born 15 April 1949; Son of late Alexander Rendel, CBE and of Elizabeth Rendel; Educated Eton; Magdalen College and St Cross College, Oxford (BA physics and philosophy); Married September 7, 1974, Dr Susan Taylor (3 sons). Volunteer teacher in Cameroon and Uganda, Voluntary Service Overseas; Operational research analyst, Shell International 1974–76; Financial analyst, British Gas 1976–77; Various analytical and management posts (finance and computing), Esso Petroleum 1977–90. Councillor: Newbury District Council 1987–95, St John's Ward 1987–91, Craven Ward 1991–95; Chairman: Finance and Property Sub-Committee 1991–92, Recreation and Amenities Committee 1992–93. **House of Commons:** Contested Hammersmith Fulham 1979, Fulham 1983,

Newbury 1987 and 1992 general elections. Member for Newbury since May 6, 1993 by-election; Spokesman for: Housing 1993–94, Local Government in England 1993–97, Local Government and Housing 1997, Social Security and Welfare 1997–99; *Select Committees:* Member: Accommodation and Works 1997–98; Member: Public Accounts 1999–. Member: Association of Liberal Democrat Councillors, Liberal Democrat Parliamentary Candidates Association, Green Liberal Democrats. Member, Oxford Boat Race crew 1974; *Recreations:* Family, sport, music, travel. *Address:* David Rendel Esq, MP, House of Commons, London, SW1A 0AA *Tel:* 020 7219 3495 *Fax:* 020 7219 2941. *Constituency:* Kendrick House, Wharf Street, Newbury, Berkshire, RG14 5AP *Tel:* 01635 581048 *Fax:* 01635 581049.

ANDREW ROBATHAN   Blaby   Con majority 6,474

Born 17 July 1951; Son of Douglas and Sheena Robathan (née Gimson); Educated Merchant Taylors' School, Northwood; Oriel College, Oxford (BA modern history 1973, MA); RMA, Sandhurst; Married December 20, 1991, Rachael Maunder (1 son 1 daughter). Regular Army Officer, Coldstream Guards 1974–89; Rejoined Army for Gulf War January-April 1991; BP 1991–92. Councillor, London Borough of Hammersmith and Fulham 1990–92. **House of Commons:** Member for Blaby since April 9, 1992; PPS to Iain Sproat, as Minister of State, Department of National Heritage 1995–97; *Select Committees:* Member: Employment 1992–94; Member: International Development 1997–. *Special Interests:* Environment, Transport, Defence, Northern Ireland; Caucasus, Africa. Freeman, Merchant Taylors Company; Freeman, City of London; *Recreations:* Mountain walking, skiing, wild life, shooting. *Address:* Andrew Robathan Esq, MP, House of Commons, London, SW1A 0AA *Tel:* 020 7219 3550. *Constituency:* Blaby Conservative Association, 35 Lutterworth Road, Blaby, Leicestershire, LE8 4DW *Tel:* 0116–277 9992 *Fax:* 0116–278 6664.

LAURENCE ROBERTSON   Tewkesbury   Con majority 9,234

Born 29 March 1958; Son of James Robertson, former colliery electrician, and Jean Robertson (née Larkin); Educated St James' Church of England Secondary School; Farnworth Grammar School; Bolton Institute of Higher Education (Management Services Diploma); Married May 6, 1989, Susan Lees (2 stepdaughters). Warehouse assistant 1976–77; Work study engineer 1977–83; Industrial management consultant 1983–89; Factory owner 1987–88; Charity fundraising, public relations and special events consultant 1988–. **House of Commons:** Contested Makerfield 1987, Ashfield 1992 general elections. Member for Tewkesbury since May 1, 1997; *Select Committees:* Member: Environmental Audit 1997–99; Member: Joint Committee on Consolidation of Bills Etc 1997–, European Scrutiny 1999–, Social Security 1999–. *Special Interests:* Constitution, European Policy, Education, Economic Policy, Law and Order, Countryside; UK, USA, Switzerland, Mexico. Former Member, Conservative 2000 Foundation; Member, Conservative Way Forward; Vice-Chair, Association of Conservative Clubs (ACC) 1997–. Member, Freedom Association; Executive Member, 1922 Committee 1999–; *Publications: Europe: the Case Against Integration,* 1991; *The Right Way Ahead,* 1995; *Recreations:* Sport (completed 6 marathons), reading, writing, countryside. *Address:* Laurence Robertson Esq, MP, House of Commons, London, SW1A 0AA *Tel:* 020 7219 3000 *Fax:* 020 7219 2325. *Constituency:* Tewkesbury Conservative Association, Lloyds Bank Chambers, Abbey Terrace, Winchcombe, Gloucestershire, GL54 5LL *Tel:* 01242 602388 *Fax:* 01242 604364.

GEOFFREY ROBINSON   Coventry North West   *Lab majority 16,601*

Born 25 May 1938; Son of late Robert Norman Robinson and late Dorothy Jane Robinson; Educated Emanuel School, London; Clare College, Cambridge; Yale University, USA; Married 1967, Marie Elena Giorgio (1 son 1 daughter). Labour Party research assistant 1965–68; Senior executive, Industrial Reorganisation Corporation 1968–70; Financial controller, British Leyland 1970–72; Managing director, Leyland Innocenti 1972–73; Chief executive, Jaguar Cars Coventry 1974–75; Chief executive (unpaid), Triumph Motorcycles (Meriden) Ltd 1978–80; Director, West Midlands Enterprise Board 1982–85; Chief executive, TransTec plc 1986–97. **House of Commons:** Member for Coventry North West since March 1976 by-election; Opposition Front Bench Spokesman on: Science 1982–83, Trade and Industry and Regional Affairs 1983–87; Paymaster General, HM Treasury 1997–98; *Special Interests:* Regional Policy, Industry, Economic Policy, New Technology; France, Germany, Italy, USA. *Recreations:* Motorcars, gardens, architecture. *Address:* Geoffrey Robinson Esq, MP, House of Commons, London, SW1A 0AA *Tel:* 020 7219 4504 *Fax:* 020 7219 0984. *Constituency:* Transport House, Short Street, Coventry, CV1 2LS *Tel:* 024 7625 7870 *Fax:* 024 7625 7813.

PETER ROBINSON   Belfast East   *DUP majority 6,754*

Born 29 December 1948; Son of late David McCrea Robinson and of Sheila Robinson; Educated Annadale Grammar School; Castlereagh College of Further Education; Married July 25, 1970, Iris Collins (2 sons 1 daughter). Estate Agent; Member, Northern Ireland Assembly 1982–86; Deputy Leader, Democratic Unionist Party: resigned 1987, re-elected 1988; Member: Northern Ireland Forum 1996–98, new Northern Ireland Assembly 1998–; Minister for Regional Development, Northern Ireland Assembly 1999–. Castlereagh Borough Council: Councillor 1977–, Alderman 1977, Deputy Mayor 1978, Mayor 1986. **House of Commons:** Member for Belfast East since May 1979 (resigned seat December 1985 in protest against Anglo-Irish Agreement; re-elected January 1986); Spokesman for Constitutional Affairs; *Select Committees:* Member: Northern Ireland Affairs 1994–97; Member: Northern Ireland Affairs 1997–. *Special Interests:* Housing, Shipbuilding, Community Care, Aerospace, Aviation, International Terrorism. Foundation Member, Ulster Democratic Unionist Party, Deputy Leader 1979–; Secretary, Central Executive Committee 1974–79; General Secretary 1975. Member, NI Sports Council; *Publications: The North Answers Back; Capital Punishment for Capital Crime; Savagery and Suffering; Self-inflicted; Ulster the Prey; Ulster – The facts; Carson Man of Action; A War to be Won; It's Londonderry; Ulster in Peril; Give me Liberty; Hands off the UDR; Their cry was 'No Surrender'; IRA-Sinn Fein; The Union under Fire; Recreations:* Golf, bowling, breeding Koi carp. *Address:* Peter Robinson Esq, MP, House of Commons, London, SW1A 0AA *Tel:* 020 7219 3506 *Fax:* 020 7219 5854. *Constituency:* Strandtown Hall, 96 Belmont Avenue, Belfast, BT19 1NG *Tel:* 028 9047 3111 *Fax:* 028 9047 1797 *E-mail:* info@dup.org.uk.

BARBARA ROCHE   Hornsey and Wood Green   *Lab majority 20,499*

Born 13 April 1954; Daughter of Barnet and Hannah Margolis; Educated Comprehensive school; Lady Margaret Hall, Oxford University (BA); Married August 1, 1977, Patrick Roche (1 daughter). Barrister, called to the Bar 1977. **House of Commons:** Contested Surrey South West by-election 1984 and Hornsey and Wood Green 1987 general election. Member for Hornsey and Wood Green since April 9, 1992; Opposition Spokeswoman on Trade and Industry 1995–97; Opposition Whip 1994–95; PPS to Margaret Beckett as deputy leader of Labour Party 1993–94; Parliamentary Under-Secretary of State, Department of Trade and Industry 1997–99; Financial Secretary, HM Treasury 1999; Minister of State, Home Office 1999–; *Select Committees:* Member: Home Affairs 1992–94, Public Accounts 1999. *Special Interests:* Home Affairs, Legal Reform, Environment; Cyprus, Israel. *Clubs:* Wood Green Labour; *Recreations:* Theatre, family. *Address:* Barbara Roche, MP, House of Commons, London, SW1A 0AA *Tel:* 020 7219 3411.

MARION ROE   Broxbourne   *Con majority 6,653*

Born 15 July 1936; Daughter of late William and Grace Keyte (née Bocking); Educated Bromley High School; Croydon High School; English School of Languages, Vevey, Switzerland; Married March 15, 1958, James Kenneth Roe (1 son 2 daughters). Member, South East Thames Regional Health Authority 1980–83; Councillor, London Borough of Bromley 1975–78; GLC Councillor, Ilford North 1977–86: served on every Committee of the Council; GLC Representative, General Services Committee of the Association of Metropolitan Authorities 1978–81; UK Representative, Conference of Local and Regional Authorities of Europe 1978–81. **House of Commons:** Contested Barking 1979 general election. Member for Broxbourne since June 1983; Promoted: Prohibition of Female Circumcision Act 1985 (Private Member's Bill); PPS to: David Mitchell as Parliamentary Under-Secretary of State for Transport 1985–86, as Minister of State for Transport 1986, John Moore, as Secretary of State for Transport 1986–87; Parliamentary Under-Secretary of State, Department of Environment 1987–88; *Select Committees:* Member: Procedure 1990–92, Administration 1991–97, Sittings of the House 1991–92; Chairman: Health 1992–97; Member: Liaison 1992–97; Chairman: Administration 1997–; Member: Chairmen's Panel 1997–, Finance and Services 1997–, Liaison 1997–. *Special Interests:* Health, Social Security, Horticulture, Environment; Angola, Canada, Seychelles, South Africa, USA. Vice-President, Greater London Young Conservative Group 3 1977–80; Member, Conservative Women's National Committee Working Party on Women; Numerous Conservative Party Organisations. Patron, UN Development Fund for Women 1985–87; Vice-President, Women's Nationwide Cancer Control Campaign 1985–; Member: Greater London Area Local Government Advisory Committee 1978–82, BBC's General Advisory Council 1986–87; Numerous organisations concerned primarily with women, health and horticulture; Member, Department of Employment's Advisory Committee on Women's Employment 1989–92; Executive Member, 1922 Committee 1992–94, Joint Secretary 1997–; Vice-President, Association of District Councils 1994–; Member, Armed Forces Parliamentary Scheme 1998; Chair, Conservative House of Commons Benevolent Fund 1998–99; Parliamentary Consultant to the Horticultural Trades Association 1990–95; UK Representative on Commonwealth Observer Group Monitoring Elections in the Seychelles and Angola 1992–; Substitute Member, UK Delegation to Parliamentary Assemblies of Council of Europe and WEU 1989–92; Member, Executive Committee: Commonwealth Parliamentary Association (CPA) UK Branch 1997–, British Group of the Inter-Parliamentary Union (IPU) 1997–, A Vice-Chairman 1998–; Fellow, Industry and Parliament Trust 1990; Managing Trustee, Parliamentary Contributory Pension Fund 1990–97; Freeman, Worshipful Company of Gardeners 1990, Liveryman 1993; *Publications: The Labour Left in London – A Blueprint for a Socialist Britain,* CPC 1985; FRSA 1990; Hon. Member, Institute of Horticulture 1993; Hon. Fellowship, Professional Business and Technical Management 1995; Freeman, City of London 1981; *Recreations:* Ballet and opera. *Address:* Mrs Marion Roe, MP, House of Commons, London, SW1A 0AA *Tel:* 020 7219 3528. *Constituency:* Broxbourne Parliamentary Conservative Association, 16 High Street, Hoddesdon, Hertfordshire, EN11 8ET *Tel:* 01992 479972 *Fax:* 01992 479973.

ALLAN ROGERS   Rhondda   *Lab majority 24,931*

Born 24 October 1932; Son of late John Henry Rogers, coalminer; Educated Gelligaer Primary School; Bargoed Secondary School; University College of Wales, Swansea (BSc geology 1956); Married April 9, 1955, Ceridwen James (1 son 3 daughters). Army national service 1951–53; Geologist: UK, Canada, USA, Australia, Africa; District secretary, Workers' Educational Association for South Wales; MEP for South East Wales 1979–84; COHSE/UNISON sponsored. District Councillor 1965–71; County Councillor 1970–80. **House of Commons:** Member for Rhondda since June 1983; Opposition Spokesman on: Defence and Disarmament and Arms Control 1987–92, Foreign and Commonwealth Affairs 1992–94; *Select Committees:* Member: Welsh Public Accounts, European Scrutiny 2000. *Special Interests:* European Union, Health, Education, Environment, Defence, Energy; Asia, Falkland Islands, Hong Kong, Japan, USA, Canada, Scandinavia.

Chair, Polytechnic of Wales 1973–80; Member, Committee on Intelligence and Security 1994–; Vice-President, Federation of Economic Development Authorities (FEDA); European Parliament: Vice-President 1979–82, Secretary and Whip, British Labour Group 1979–84; Treasurer, Inter-Parliamentary Union (IPU) British Group 1995–97, Vice-Chair 1998–; International President, Parliamentarians for Global Action 1999–; Associate professor, Glamorgan University; Fellow, Geological Society; *Clubs:* Treorchy Workmens, Penygraig Labour; *Sportsclubs:* Treorchy RFC; *Recreations:* All sports. *Address:* Allan Rogers Esq, MP, House of Commons, London, SW1A 0AA *Tel:* 020 7219 3560 *Tel (Constituency):* 01443 682925.

JEFFREY ROOKER   Birmingham Perry Barr   *Lab majority 18,957*

Born 5 June 1941; Educated Handsworth Technical College; Warwick University; Aston University; Married 1972, Angela. Production manager, Rola Celestion Ltd 1967–70; Lecturer, Lanchester Polytechnic, Coventry 1972–74. Member, Birmingham Education Committee 1972–74. **House of Commons:** Member for Birmingham Perry Barr since February 1974; Opposition Front Bench Spokesman on: Social Services 1979–80, Social Security 1980–83, Treasury and Economic Affairs 1983–84, Environment 1984–88, Community Care and Social Services 1990–92, Education 1992–93; PPS to the Government Law Officers 1977; Shadow Deputy Leader, House of Commons 1994–97; Minister of State and Deputy Minister, Ministry of Agriculture, Fisheries and Food (Minister for Food Safety) 1997–99; Minister of State, Department of Social Security 1999–. Member of Council, Institution of Production Engineers 1975–80; PC 1999. *Address:* Rt Hon Jeffrey Rooker Esq, MP, House of Commons, London, SW1A 0AA *Tel:* 020 7219 4153.

TERENCE ROONEY   Bradford North   *Lab majority 12,770*

Born 11 November 1950; Son of Eric and Frances Rooney; Educated Buttershaw Comprehensive School; Bradford College; Married 1969, Susanne Chapman (1 son 2 daughters). Commercial insurance broker; Welfare rights worker. Bradford City Council: Councillor 1983–91, Chair, Labour Group 1988–91, Deputy Leader 1990–91. **House of Commons:** Member for Bradford North since November 8, 1990 by-election; PPS to Michael Meacher, as Minister of State, Department of the Environment, Transport and the Regions (Minister for the Environment) 1997–; *Select Committees:* Member: Broadcasting 1991–97. *Special Interests:* Public Sector Housing, Poverty, Industrial Relations; Pakistan, India, Bangladesh. Campaign co-ordinator, Bradford West Labour Party in 1983 general election campaign; Hon. secretary, Yorkshire Regional Group of Labour MPs 1997–. Member: Low Pay Unit, Unemployment Unit; Trustee, Brierley Community Association; *Recreations:* Crosswords, football, tennis. *Address:* Terence Rooney Esq, MP, House of Commons, London, SW1A 0AA *Tel:* 020 7219 6407. *Constituency:* 76 Kirkgate, Bradford, West Yorkshire, BD1 1SZ *Tel:* 01274 777821 *Fax:* 01274 777817.

ERNIE ROSS   Dundee West   *Lab majority 11,859*

Born 27 July 1942; Educated St John's Junior Secondary School; Married (2 sons 1 daughter). Quality control engineer, Timex Ltd 1970–79; Member, MSF. **House of Commons:** Member for Dundee West since May 1979; *Select Committees:* Member: Education and Employment 1996–97, Standards and Privileges 1996–97, Foreign Affairs 1997–99; Member: Court of Referees 1997–, Standing Orders 1997–. *Special Interests:* Social Services, Defence, Industry, Employment, Education; Bangladesh, Former Soviet Union, Cuba, Cyprus, Latin America, Middle East, South Africa, USA. UK Delegation to Organisation for Security and Co-operation in Europe; *Recreations:* Football, cricket. *Address:* Ernie Ross Esq, MP, House of Commons, London, SW1A 0AA *Tel:* 020 7219 3480 *Fax:* 020 7219 2359. *Constituency:* 18B Marketgait, Dundee, DD1 1QR *Tel:* 01382 207000 *Fax:* 01382 221280 *E-mail:* rossm@parliament.uk.

WILLIAM ROSS   East Londonderry   UUP majority 3,794

Born 4 February 1936; Son of late Leslie Alexander Ross and late Mabel Ross; Educated Dungiven Primary School; Northwest College of Agriculture; Married July 20, 1974, Christine Haslett (3 sons 1 daughter). Farmer. **House of Commons:** Member for Londonderry February 1974–83 and for East Londonderry since June 1983; Spokesman for: Agriculture and Fisheries 1992–97, the Treasury and Civil Service 1997–2000, Home Affairs, Cabinet Office, Treasury 2000–; Former UUP Whip; *Select Committees:* Member: Joint Committee on Statutory Instruments 1992–97, Deregulation 1995–97; Member: Administration 1997–, Deregulation 1997–, Joint Committee on Statutory Instruments 1997–. *Special Interests:* Disabled/Disability, Housing, Local Government, Defence, Firearms Legislation, Marketing; Australia, Canada, New Zealand, South Africa; Member, European Standing Committee B 1998–. Secretary: Mid-Londonderry Unionist Party (Northern Ireland Constituency) 1964–74, Londonderry Constituency Unionist Party 1964–74. *Clubs:* Northern Counties Londonderry; *Recreations:* Angling, shooting. *Address:* William Ross Esq, MP, House of Commons, London, SW1A 0AA *Tel:* 020 7219 3571. *Constituency:* Turmeel, Dungiven, County Londonderry, BT47 4SL *Fax:* 028 7174 2291.

ANDREW ROWE   Faversham and Mid Kent   Con majority 4,173

Born 11 September 1935; Son of late John Douglas Rowe; Educated Eton College; Merton College, Oxford (MA); Married 1st, 1960, Alison Boyd (divorced 1975) (1 son); 2nd, November 1983, Sheila Leslie Finkle (2 step-daughters). Sub-Lieutenant, RNVR 1954–56; Assistant master, Eton College 1959–62; Principal, Scottish Office 1962–67; Lecturer, Edinburgh University 1967–74; Consultant to Voluntary Service Unit 1973–74; Editor, *Small Business* 1980; Consultant in Government Affairs 1979–83. **House of Commons:** Member for Mid Kent 1983–97, and for Faversham and Mid Kent since May 1, 1997; PPS to Ministers of State, Department of Trade and Industry: Richard Needham 1992–95, Earl Ferrers 1994–95; *Select Committees:* Member: Health 1991–92, Public Accounts 1995–97; Member: International Development 1997–. *Special Interests:* Small Businesses, Employment, Conservation, Voluntary Organisations; China, Europe, Hong Kong, India, Nepal. Director, Community Affairs, Conservative Central Office 1975–79; Member: Tory Reform Group, Mainstream Group, Positive European Group. Member, NSPCC; President: Kent Engineering Society, North Downs Rail Concern; Member, Swann Committee 1979–84; Formerly Chair, Parliamentary Panel on Personal Social Services; Founder/Chair, JC 2000 The Millennium Arts Festival for Schools 1997–2000; Founder/Trustee and Co-Chair, UK Youth Parliament 1999–; Formerly Member, UK delegation to Council of Europe; Trustee: Community Service Volunteers, NSPCC; *Publications: Democracy Renewed; Somewhere to Start;* and other pamphlets; *Recreations:* Photography, fishing, reading, theatre. *Address:* Andrew Rowe Esq, MP, House of Commons, London, SW1A 0AA *Tel:* 020 7219 3536 *Fax:* 020 7219 3826. *Constituency:* 8 Faversham Road, Lenham, Maidstone, Kent *Tel:* 01622 850574.

EDWARD ROWLANDS   Merthyr Tydfil and Rhymney   Lab majority 27,086

Born 23 January 1940; Son of William Samuel Rowlands, Clerk of Works; Educated Rhondda Grammar School; Wirral Grammar, Cheshire; King's College, London (BA history 1962); Married 1968, Janice Williams (2 sons 1 daughter). Research student 1962; Research assistant, History of Parliament Trust 1963–65; Lecturer: Modern History and Government, Welsh CAT 1965–, Law Department, LSC 1972–74. **House of Commons:** Member for Cardiff North 1966–70, for Merthyr Tydfil by-election 1972–83 and for Merthyr Tydfil and Rhymney since June 1983; Opposition Front Bench Spokesman on: Foreign and Commonwealth Affairs 1979–1980, Energy December 1980–87; Parliamentary Under-Secretary of State: Welsh Office October 1969–70, 1974–75, Foreign and Commonwealth Office 1975–76; Minister of State for Foreign and Commonwealth Affairs 1976–79; *Select Committees:* Member: Foreign Affairs 1987–97; Member: Foreign Affairs 1997–.

Special Interests: Energy, Overseas Aid, Disabled/Disability, Education, Publishing; Europe, Mozambique, Uganda. Judge, Booker McConnel Novel of the Year Competition 1984; Fellow, Industry and Parliament Trust; Chairman, History of Parliamentary Trust 1993–; *Publications: Robert Harley's Parliamentary Apprenticeship 1690–1695,* (British Library Journal 1989); *Robert Harley and the Battle for Power in Radnorshire 1690–1693,* (Welsh History Review 1990). *Address:* Edward Rowlands Esq, MP, House of Commons, London, SW1A 0AA *Tel:* 020 7219 4480.

FRANK ROY   Motherwell and Wishaw   *Lab majority 12,791*

Born 29 August 1958; Son of late James Roy, settler manager, and Esther McMahon, home-help; Educated St Joseph's High School, Motherwell; Our Lady's High School, Motherwell; Motherwell College (HNC marketing 1994); Glasgow Caledonian University (BA consumer and management studies 1994); Married September 17, 1977, to Ellen Foy (1 son 1 daughter). Ravenscraig Steelworker 1977–91; Personal assistant to Helen Liddell, MP 1994–97; Member, GMB; Shop steward, ISTC 1983–90. **House of Commons:** Member for Motherwell and Wishaw since May 1, 1997; PPS: to Helen Liddell as Minister of State, Scottish Office (Minister for Education) 1998–99, to Dr John Reid as Secretary of State for Scotland 1999–; *Select Committees:* Member: Social Security 1997–98. *Special Interests:* Employment Law, Social Welfare Issues; Europe, USA. Parliamentary Election Agent to Dr Jeremy Bray 1987–92; Vice-President, Federation of Economic Development Authorities (FEDA); *Recreations:* Football, reading, music. *Address:* Frank Roy Esq, MP, House of Commons, London, SW1A 0AA *Tel:* 020 7219 6467. *Constituency:* Constituency Office, 265 Main Street, Wishaw, Lanarkshire, ML2 7NE *Tel:* 01698 303040 *Fax:* 01698 303060 *E-mail:* scottishsecretary@scotland.gov.uk *Website:* www.scottishsecretary.gov.uk; royf@parliament.uk.

CHRIS RUANE   Vale of Clwyd   *Lab majority 8,955*

Born 18 July 1958; Son of late Michael Ruane, labourer, and Esther Ruane; Educated Ysgol Mair RC, Rhyl Primary; Blessed Edward Jones Comprehensive, Rhyl; University College of Wales, Aberystwyth (BSc economics 1979); Liverpool University (PGCE 1980); Married February 14, 1994, Gill Roberts (2 daughters). Primary school teacher 1982–97, Deputy head 1991–97; National Union of Teachers: School Rep 1982–97, President, West Clwyd 1991, Vale of Clwyd 1997. Councillor, Rhyl Town Council 1988–99. **House of Commons:** Contested Clwyd North West 1992 general election. Member for Vale of Clwyd since May 1, 1997; *Select Committees:* Member: Welsh Affairs 1999–. *Special Interests:* Anti-Poverty, Human Rights, Education, Environment. Labour Group of Seaside MPs; Rural Group of Labour MPs. Member: Welfare Benefits Shop Management Committee, Steering Group forming Vale of Clwyd Credit Union; Founder Member: Rhyl Anti Apartheid 1987, Rhyl and District Amnesty International Group 1991, Rhyl Environmental Association 1988, President; *Recreations:* Cooking, walking, reading, humour, family. *Address:* Chris Ruane Esq, MP, House of Commons, London, SW1A 0AA *Tel:* 020 7219 6378 *Fax:* 020 7219 6090. *Constituency:* 45–57 Kinmel Street, Rhyl, Clwyd, LL18 1AG *Tel:* 01745 354626 *Fax:* 01745 334827 *E-mail:* ruanec@parliament.uk.

JOAN RUDDOCK   Lewisham, Deptford   *Lab majority 18,878*

Born 28 December 1943; Daughter of late Kenneth Anthony and Eileen Anthony; Educated Pontypool Grammar School for Girls; Imperial College, London University (BSc); Married July 3, 1963, Keith Ruddock (separated 1990, died 1996). Director: research and publications, Shelter, National Campaign for Homeless 1968–73; Oxford Housing Aid Centre 1973–77; Special programmes officer (MSC) for unemployed young people, Berkshire County Council 1977–79; Manager, Citizens Advice Bureau, Reading 1979–86. **House of Commons:** Contested Newbury 1979 general election. Member for Lewisham Deptford since June 1987; Opposition Transport Spokesperson 1989–92; Opposition Front Bench Spokesperson on: Home Affairs 1992–94,

Environmental Protection 1994–97; Private Members' Bill on flytipping – Control of Pollution Act (amendment) 1989; Parliamentary Under-Secretary of State for Women 1997–98; Promoted: Ten Minute Rule Bill 1999, Prophylactic Mastectomy Registry Presentation Bill 1999, Organic Food and Farming Targets Bill 1999; *Special Interests:* Foreign Affairs, Transport, Environment, Women. Chairperson, CND 1981–85; Member, British Delegation to Council of Europe and Western European Union 1988–89; Hon. Fellow: Goldsmith's College, London University; Laban Centre, London; ARCS (1965); *Recreations:* Travel, music, gardening. *Address:* Joan Ruddock, MP, House of Commons, London, SW1A 0AA *Tel:* 020 7219 6206 *Fax:* 020 7219 6045 *E-mail:* alexanderh@parliament.uk.

DAVID RUFFLEY   Bury St Edmunds   *Con majority 368*

Born 18 April 1962; Son of Jack Laurie Ruffley solicitor and Yvonne Grace, née Harris; Educated Bolton Boys' School; Queens' College, Cambridge (BA law 1985). Clifford Chance Solicitors, London 1985–91; Special adviser to Ken Clarke, MP as: Secretary of State for Education and Science 1991–92, Home Secretary 1992–93, Chancellor of the Exchequer 1993–96; Strategic Economic Consultant to the Conservative Party 1996–97; Vice-President, Small Business Bureau 1996–. **House of Commons:** Member for Bury St Edmunds since May 1, 1997; *Select Committees:* Member: Public Administration 1997–99; Member: Treasury 1998–, Treasury Sub-Committee 1999–. *Special Interests:* Treasury, Home Affairs, Education; USA, China, France. Member, The Britain Club. Patron, Bury St Edmunds Constitutional Club; Patron, West Suffolk Voluntary Association for the Blind; Unpaid adviser: to Grant Maintained Schools Foundation 1991–96, to 'Catch 'em Young' young offenders project 1992; *Clubs:* Athenaeum; *Sportsclubs:* Patron, Bury St Edmunds and District Football League; Stowmarket FC, The Suffolk Golf and Country Club; *Recreations:* Football, cinema, golf, thinking. *Address:* David Ruffley Esq, MP, House of Commons, London, SW1A 0AA *Tel:* 020 7219 2880 *Fax:* 020 7219 3998. *Constituency:* 3 Woolhall Street, Bury St Edmunds, Suffolk, IP33 1LA *Tel:* 01284 754072 *Fax:* 01284 763515 *E-mail:* davidruffleymp@parliament.uk.

BOB RUSSELL   Colchester   *LD majority 1,581*

Born 31 March 1946; Son of late Ewart Russell and late Muriel Russell (née Sawdy); Educated St Helena Secondary Boys, Colchester; North-East Essex Technical College (Proficiency Certificate, National Council for the Training of Journalists 1966); Married April 1, 1967, Audrey Blandon (twin sons 1 daughter, 1 daughter deceased). Trainee reporter, *Essex County Standard* and *Colchester Gazette* 1963–66; News editor, *Braintree and Witham Times* 1966–68; Editor, *Maldon and Burnham Standard* 1968–69; Sub-editor: London *Evening News* 1969–72, London *Evening Standard* 1972–73; Press officer, BT Eastern Region 1973–85; Publicity information officer, Essex University 1986–97; Branch secretary, North-Essex, National Union of Journalists 1967–68. Councillor, Colchester Borough Council 1971, Mayor 1986–87, Council Leader 1987–91. **House of Commons:** Member for Colchester since May 1, 1997; Spokesman for: Home and Legal Affairs (Immigration) 1997–99, Sport 1999–; North, Midlands and Wales Whip 1999–; *Select Committees:* Member: Home Affairs 1998–, Catering 2000–. *Special Interests:* Environment, Local Government, Sport, Transport, Animal Welfare; St Helena. Member: Labour Party 1966, SDP May 1981, Liberal Democrats since formation. Member: Oxfam, Colchester and East Essex Co-operative Society; Journalists Prize, NEETC 1965; *Sportsclubs:* Colchester United Football Club; *Recreations:* Local history, walking, camping, watching Colchester Utd FC. *Address:* Bob Russell Esq, MP, House of Commons, London, SW1A 0AA *Tel:* 020 7219 5150 *Fax:* 020 7219 2365. *Constituency:* Corporate House, Queen Street, Colchester, CO1 2PG *Tel:* 01206 710172 *Fax:* 01206 710184.

CHRISTINE RUSSELL   City of Chester   *Lab majority 10,553*

Born 25 March 1945; Daughter of late John Alfred William Carr, farmer, and Phyllis Carr; Educated Spalding High School; London School of Librarianship; Polytechnic of North West London (Professional Librarianship Qualification, ALA 1970); Married 30 July 1971, Dr James Russell (divorced 1991) (1 son 1 daughter). Librarian: London Borough of Camden 1967–70, Glasgow University 1970–71, Dunbartonshire County Council 1971–73; Personal assistant to: Lyndon Harrison, MEP 1989–91, Brian Simpson, MEP 1992–94; Co-ordinator of Advocacy Project, MIND 1994–97; Member, GMB. JP 1980–; Chester City Council: Councillor 1980–97, Chair, Development Committee 1990–97. **House of Commons:** Member for City of Chester since May 1, 1997; *Select Committees:* Member: Environmental Audit 1999–. *Special Interests:* Transport, Environment, Education, Urban Regeneration, Arts; South Africa, Romania, Portugal, South America, Eastern Europe. Chester Constituency Labour Party: Agent 1986–95, Chair/President 1989–92. President, Chester Womens Hostel Association; Elected member, Citizens Advice Bureau; Chair, Chester Film Society and Festival; Member, Magistrates Association; Among other broadcasts, On The Record: General Election 1992; ALA, JP; *Recreations:* Cinema, football, walking, art and architecture, travel. *Address:* Mrs Christine Russell, MP, House of Commons, London, SW1A 0AA *Tel:* 020 7219 6398 *Fax:* 020 7219 0943. *Constituency:* York House, York Street, Chester, CH1 3LR *Tel:* 01244 400174 *Fax:* 01244 400487 *E-mail:* russellcm@parliament.uk.

JOAN RYAN   Enfield North   *Lab majority 6,822*

Born 8 September 1955; Daughter of Michael Joseph and Dolores Marie Ryan, née Joyce; Educated St Josephs Secondary School, Notre Dame High School; City of Liverpool College (BA history, sociology 1979); Polytechnic of the South Bank (MSc sociology 1981); Married 2nd, Martin Hegarty (1 son 1 daughter). Member: NUT, MSF. Councillor, Barnet Council 1990–98, Deputy Leader 1994–98, Chair, Policy and Resources Committee 1994. **House of Commons:** Member for Enfield North since May 1, 1997; PPS to Andrew Smith: as Minister of State, Department for Education and Employment (Minister for Employment, Welfare to Work and Equal Opportunities) 1998–99, as Chief Secretary to the Treasury 1999–; *Special Interests:* Jobs, Investment, Health Service, Local Government, Employment, Regeneration, Health; Cyprus, Ireland, Israel. Member, Labour Party 1984–; Chair: Finchley Constituency Labour Party 1992–96, London North European Constituency 1994–97; Hon. Secretary, London Regional Group of Labour MPs 1999–. School Govenor: Lea Valley High School, Chase Side Primary School; Vice-President, Brimsdown Sports and Social Club; Trustee, Riders For Health; Patron, Enfield Lock Village Fair; *Recreations:* Swimming, reading, music, visiting historic buildings. *Address:* Joan Ryan, MP, House of Commons, London, SW1A 0AA *Tel:* 020 7219 6502 *Fax:* 020 7219 2335. *Constituency:* 180 High Street, Enfield, EN3 4EU *Tel:* 020 8805 9470 *Fax:* 020 8373 0455 *E-mail:* joan-ryanmp@hotmail.com.

S

NICHOLAS ST AUBYN   Guildford   Con majority 4,791

Born 19 November 1955; Son of Piers and late Mary St Aubyn; Educated Eton College; Trinity College, Oxford (BA philosophy, politics and economics 1977, MA); Married April 26, 1980, Jane Mary Brooks (2 sons, 3 daughters). Investment Banking: Loan officer, Morgan Guaranty 1977–81; Head of London office, Morgan Futures 1981–84; Head of Morgan Guaranty's sterling and arbitrage swaps desk 1984–86; Vice-President: Kleinwort Benson Cross Finance 1986–87, American International Group's Financial Products Division 1987–89; Chair: Gemini Ltd 1989–93, Fitzroy Joinery Ltd 1993–. Councillor, Westminster City Council 1982–86. **House of Commons:** Contested Truro 1987 by-election, 1987, 1992 general elections. Member for Guildford since May 1, 1997; *Select Committees:* Member: Employment Sub-Committee 1999–2000; Member: Education and Employment 1997–, Education Sub-Committee 1997–, Unopposed Bills (Panel) 1997–. *Special Interests:* Economic Policy, Education, Small Businesses, Planning, Housing; USA, South Africa. Member, Bow Group. *Clubs:* Guildford County, Brooks'; *Recreations:* Swimming, riding, shooting, walking, children. *Address:* Nicholas St Aubyn Esq, MP, House of Commons, London, SW1A 0AA *Tel:* 020 7219 3000. *Constituency:* Conservative Association, 63 Woodbridge Road, Guildford, Surrey, GU1 4RD *Tel:* 01483 575151 *Fax:* 01483 562855.

ALEX SALMOND   Banff and Buchan   SNP majority 12,845

Born 31 December 1954; Son of Robert and Mary Salmond; Educated Linlithgow Academy; St Andrew's University (MA economics and history); Married May 6, 1981, Moira French McGlashan. Assistant agriculture and fisheries economist, Department of Agriculture and Fisheries (Scotland) 1978–80; Assistant economist, Royal Bank of Scotland 1980–82; Oil economist 1982–87; Economist 1984–87; MSP for Banff and Buchan constituency since May 6, 1999. **House of Commons:** Member for Banff and Buchan since June 1987; Parliamentary Spokesperson for: Constitution, Economy, Trade and Industry, Fishing 1992–97, Constitution and Fishing 1997–2000; *Special Interests:* Fishing, Agriculture, Energy, Third World, Scottish Economy; Europe. SNP National Executive: Member 1981–, Vice-chair 1985–87, Deputy Leader 1987, Senior Vice-convener 1988–90, National convener 1990–2000. Hon. Vice-President, Scottish Centre for Economic and Social Research; *Recreations:* Golf, reading, football. *Address:* Alex Salmond Esq, MP, MSP, House of Commons, London, SW1A 0AA *Tel:* 020 7219 4500. *Constituency:* 17 Maiden Street, Peterhead, Aberdeenshire, AB42 1EE *Tel:* 01779 470444 *Fax:* 01779 474460 *E-mail:* asmp.peterhead@snp.org.

MARTIN SALTER   Reading West   Lab majority 2,997

Born 19 April 1954; Son of Raymond and Naomi Salter; Educated Grammar school; Sussex University; Partner Natalie O'Toole. Co-ordinator, Reading Centre for the Unemployed 1986–86; Regional manager, Co-operative Home Services housing association 1987–96; Member, TGWU; Former shop steward: TGWU, UCATT. Reading Borough Council: Councillor 1984–96, Chair Leisure Committee 1986–88, Deputy Leader 1987–96. **House of Commons:** Contested Reading East 1987 general election. Member for Reading West since May 1, 1997; *Select Committees:* Member: Northern Ireland Affairs 1997–99. *Special Interests:* Environment, Local Government, Housing, Northern Ireland, Human Rights; India, Pakistan, Ireland. Member, Co-operative Party; Organiser, Network of Labour Councils in South 1987–94; Joint Vice-Chair, South and West Group of Labour MPs 1997–98; Chair, South East Regional Group of Labour MPs 1998–; Representative, South East PLP Campaign Team 1999–. Member: Greenpeace, Open Spaces Society, Amnesty International, Angling Conservation Association, Green Lanes Environmental Action Movement; Patron, Cystinosis Foundation; Secretary, Punjab Human Rights Sub Group; *Publications:* Various articles in national and local press, Fabian Review and Punch; *Sportsclubs:* Reading and District Angling Association and other Fishing Clubs; *Recreations:* Angling, walking, football. *Address:* Martin Salter Esq, MP, House of Commons, London, SW1A 0AA *Tel:* 020 7219 2416 *Fax:* 020 7219 2749. *Constituency:* 413 Oxford Road, Reading, Berkshire, RG30 1HA *Tel:* 0118–954 6782 *Fax:* 0118–954 6784 *E-mail:* salterm@parliament.uk.

Born 25 April 1959; Son of John Sanders, insurance official, and of Helen, nurse; Educated Torquay Boys' Grammar School; Married Alison Nortcliffe. Parliamentary officer, Liberal Democrat Whips' Office 1989–90; Association of Liberal Democrat Councillors 1990–92; Policy officer, National Council for Voluntary Organisations 1992–93; Worked for Paddy Ashdown, MP and Party Leader 1992–93, organised his tour of Britain 1993; Southern Association of Voluntary Action Groups for Europe 1993–97. Councillor, Torbay Borough Council 1984–86; Contested Devon and East Plymouth 1994 European Parliament election. **House of Commons:** Contested Torbay 1992 general election. Member for Torbay since May 1, 1997; Spokesman for: Housing 1997–99, Environment, Transport, the Regions and Social Justice 1999–; South and South West Regional Whip 1997–; *Select Committees:* Member: Joint Committee on Consolidation of Bills Etc 1997–. *Special Interests:* Local Government, Voluntary Sector, Tourism; USA. Vice-President, National League of Young Liberals 1985; Political secretary, Devon and Cornwall Regional Liberal Party 1983–84; Information officer, Association of Liberal Councillors 1986–89. Member: Paignton Preservation Society, British Diabetic Association; Director (non-pecuniary), Southern Association of Voluntary Action Groups; Member: CPA, IPU; *Clubs:* Paignton Club; *Recreations:* Football. *Address:* Adrian Sanders Esq, MP, House of Commons, London, SW1A 0AA *Tel:* 020 7219 6304 *Fax:* 020 7219 3963. *Constituency:* 69 Belgrave Road, Torquay, Devon, TQ2 5HZ *Tel:* 01803 200036 *Fax:* 01803 200031 *E-mail:* asanders@cix.co.uk.

Born 18 August 1952; Educated University of Faisalabad, Pakistan (BA political science); Married Perveen Sarwar (3 sons, 1 daughter). Director, United Wholesale Ltd; Member, GMB. Councillor: Glasgow District Council 1992–95, Glasgow City Council 1995–. **House of Commons:** Member for Glasgow Govan since May 1, 1997; *Select Committees:* Member: Scottish Affairs 1999–. *Special Interests:* Housing, Employment, Economic Policy, Devolution, International Affairs, International Development, British Shipbuilding, Pensioners' Rights, Senior Citizens; Pakistan, Middle East, Developing World. Member: Scottish Labour Executive 1994–, Scottish Labour Gala Fund-raising Dinner Organising Committee; Constituency Labour Party: Former Branch Chair, Membership Secretary, Trades Union Liaison Officer. Scottish Conference, Racism Debate 1994; BBC Scotland, Frontline Scotland 1995; BBC Newsnight 1995; Several appearances Reporting Scotland 1995–96; *Recreations:* Family and friends, charitable work, abseiling. *Address:* Mohammed Sarwar Esq, MP, House of Commons, London, SW1A 0AA *Tel:* 020 7219 3000. *Constituency:* 247 Paisley Road West, Glasgow, G51 1NE *Tel:* 0141–427 5250 *Fax:* 0141–427 5938 *E-mail:* msarwar@govanlabour.fsnet.co.uk.

Born 9 May 1946; Son of late David Gordon Madgwick Savidge and late Jean Kirkpatrick, née Kemp Savidge; Educated Wallington County Grammar School For Boys, Surrey; Aberdeen University (MA 1970); Aberdeen College of Education (Teaching Certificate 1972). Clerk 1970–71; Secondary school teacher Nottingham and Scotland 1970–97: Maths teacher, Kincorth Academy, Aberdeen 1973–97; Educational Institute of Scotland: National Executive 1982–84, National Council 1980–86, 1989–90; Member, Transport and General Workers Union. Aberdeen City Council: Councillor 1980–96, Vice-Chair, Labour Group 1980–88, Libraries Convenor 1984–87, 1988–94, Finance Convenor and Deputy Leader of the Council 1994–96; JP 1984–96. **House of Commons:** Contested Kincardine and Deeside 1991 by-election, 1992 general election. Member for Aberdeen North since May 1, 1997; *Select Committees:* Member: Environmental Audit 1997–. *Special Interests:* International Affairs, Foreign Affairs, Defence, Non-Proliferation and Disarmament, Scotland,

Constitution, Northern Ireland, International Development. Member: Scottish Executive of the Labour Party 1993–94, Co-op Party. Governor: Aberdeen College of Education 1980–87, Robert Gordon Institute of Technology 1980–88; Member: Scientists For Global Responsibility, Amnesty International; Member, United Nations Association; Hon. Fellow, Robert Gordon University, Aberdeen 1997; *Recreations:* Exploring life, spectator sport, crosswords and puzzles, reading, real ale, the Arts, heraldry. *Address:* Malcolm Savidge Esq, MP, House of Commons, London, SW1A 0AA *Tel:* 020 7219 3570 *Fax:* 020 7219 2398. *Constituency:* Aberdeen Constituency Office, 166 Market Street, Aberdeen, AB11 5PP *Tel:* 01224 252708 *Fax:* 01224 252712 *E-mail:* savidgem@parliament.uk, msavidgemp@aol.com.

PHILIP SAWFORD   Kettering   *Lab majority 189*

Born 26 June 1950; Son of John William Sawford and Audrey Kathleen Sawford; Educated Kettering Grammar School; Ruskin College, Oxford (Diploma 1982); Leicester University (BA 1985); Married May 1, 1971, Rosemary Stokes (2 sons). Apprentice carpenter/joiner, Moulton; British Steel Corporation, Corby 1977–80; Wellingborough Community Relations Council 1985–; Training partnership, Wellingborough 1985–97; Member, GMB. Councillor, Desborough Town Council 1977–97, Chair 1985; Councillor, Kettering Borough Council 1979–83, 1986–97, Leader 1991–97. **House of Commons:** GMB supported candidate. Contested Wellingborough 1992 general election. Member for Kettering since May 1, 1997; *Select Committees:* Member: Information 1997–, Environmental Audit 2000–. *Special Interests:* Education, Employment; France. Branch secretary, District party chair, political education organiser, Constituency vice-chair, Annual conference delegate and various other capacities 1971–97; Member, Co-operative Party. Member, Institute of Personnel and Development; MIPD; *Recreations:* Playing guitar, music, reading. *Address:* Philip Sawford Esq, MP, House of Commons, London, SW1A 0AA *Tel:* 020 7219 6213 *Fax:* 020 7219 6174. *Constituency:* 1A Headlands, Kettering, Northamptonshire, NN15 7ER *Tel:* 01536 411900 *Fax:* 01536 410742 *E-mail:* sawfordp@parliament.uk.

JONATHAN SAYEED   Mid Bedfordshire   *Con majority 7,090*

Born 20 March 1948; Son of late M M Sayeed, chartered electrical engineer, and L S Sayeed; Educated Britannia Royal Naval College, Dartmouth; Royal Naval Engineering College, Manadon, Plymouth; Married October 18, 1980, Nicola Anne Power (2 sons). Royal Navy and Royal Naval Reserve 1964–74; Founder director, Wade Emerson & Co Ltd 1974–82; Chair and chief executive, Calmady Insurance Services Ltd 1982–83; Chair, Ranelagh Ltd 1992–96; Non-executive, director Love Lane Investments Ltd (Holding Company) 1992–96; Chair, Training Division Corporate Services Group plc 1996–97. **House of Commons:** Member for Bristol East 1983–92, for Mid Bedfordshire since May 1, 1997; PPS to Lord Belstead as Paymaster General 1991–92; *Select Committees:* Member: Broadcasting 1997–. President, Bristol East Conservative Association. *Clubs:* Carlton; *Recreations:* Golf, sailing, tennis, skiing, flying, classical music, books, architecture. *Address:* Jonathan Sayeed Esq, MP, House of Commons, London, SW1A 0AA *Tel:* 020 7219 2355 *Fax:* 020 7219 1294. *Constituency:* Mid-Bedfordshire Conservative Association, St Michaels Close, High Street, Shefford, Bedfordshire, SG17 5DD *Tel:* 01462 811992 *Fax:* 01462 811010.

BRIAN SEDGEMORE   Hackney South and Shoreditch   *Lab majority 14,980*

Born 17 March 1937; Son of late Charles John Sedgemore; Educated State Schools; Oxford University (MA, Diploma in Public and Social Administration); Married December 19, 1966, Audrey Reece (divorced) (1 son). RAF national service 1956–58; Principal, Ministry of Housing and Local Government 1962–66; Private secretary to Robert Mellish as Parliamentary Secretary to Minister of Housing 1964–66; Barrister 1966–74; Granada TV 1979–83; Member, NUJ. Councillor, Wandsworth Council 1971–74, Chair, Community Relations 1971–74. **House of Commons:** Member for Luton West February 1974–79 and for Hackney South and Shoreditch since June 1983; PPS to Tony Benn as Secretary of State for Energy 1977–79; *Select Committees:* Member: Treasury and Civil Service 1987–96, Treasury 1996–97; Member: Treasury 1997–, Treasury Sub-Committee 1998–. *Special Interests:* Economic Policy; Europe, USA. Member: Fabian Society, Co-operative Party. Member: World Development Movement, London Brook; Chair, East London Committee, Sanctuary Housing Association; Member, Defence of Literature and Arts; Member, Writers Guild of Great Britain; *Publications:* Contributor to *Tribune*; *The How and Why of Socialism*, 1977; *Mr Secretary of State* (fiction), 1979; *The Secret Constitution*, 1980; *Power Failure* (fiction), 1985; *Big Bang 2000*, 1986; *Pitless Pursuit* (fiction), 1994; *Insider's Guide to Parliament*, 1995; *Sportsclubs:* Vice-President, Esher RFC, Stockwood Park RFC; *Recreations:* Music, sleeping on the grass. *Address:* Brian Sedgemore Esq, MP, House of Commons, London, SW1A 0AA *Tel:* 020 7219 3410 *Fax:* 020 7219 5969. *Constituency:* 17 Sutton Square, Urswick Road, Hackney, London, E9 6EQ *Tel:* 020 8533 1305 *Fax:* 020 7533 3392 *E-mail:* sedgemoreb@parliament.uk.

JONATHAN SHAW   Chatham and Aylesford   *Lab majority 2,790*

Born 3 June 1966; Son of Alan James Shaw and Les Percival; Educated Vinters Boys School, Maidstone; West Kent College of FE (Diploma in Social Care); Bromley College (Certificate in Social Services 1990); Married Sue Gurmin (1 son 1 daughter). Social worker, Kent Council; Member, UNISON. Councillor, Rochester 1993–98, Chair, Community Development Committee 1995. **House of Commons:** Member for Chatham and Aylesford since May 1, 1997; *Select Committees:* Member: Environmental Audit 1997–. *Special Interests:* Community Development, Economic Development, Housing, Welfare. Member, Fabian Society. *Recreations:* All music especially folk music, reading, walking, family. *Address:* Jonathan Shaw Esq, MP, House of Commons, London, SW1A 0AA *Tel:* 020 7219 6919 *Fax:* 020 7219 0938. *Constituency:* 5a New Road Avenue, Chatham, Kent, ME4 6BB *Tel:* 01634 811573 *Fax:* 01634 811006 *E-mail:* shawj@parliament.uk.

BARRY SHEERMAN   Huddersfield   *Lab/Co-op majority 15,848*

Born 17 August 1940; Son of late Albert William and Florence Sheerman; Educated Hampton Grammar School; Kingston Technical College; London School of Economics (BSc economics); London University (MSc); Married August 28, 1965, Pamela Elizabeth Brenchley (1 son 3 daughters). University Lecturer 1966–79; Member, AUT, MSF. **House of Commons:** Contested Taunton October 1974 general election. Member for Huddersfield East 1979–83. Member for Huddersfield since June 1983; Opposition Front Bench Spokesman on: Employment and Education 1983–88, Home Affairs 1988–92, Disabled People's Rights 1992–94; Shadow Minister for: Education and Employment 1983–87, Home Affairs deputy to Roy Hattersley 1987–92, Disability 1992–94; *Select Committees:* Chairman (Education): Education and Employment 1999–; Chairman: Education Sub-Committee 1999–; Member: Liaison 1999–, Employment Sub-Committee 2000–. *Special Interests:* Trade, Industry, Finance, Further and Higher Education, Economy; European Union, South America, USA. Member, Co-operative Party; Chair, Labour Forum for Criminal Justice. Chair: Parliamentary Advisory Council on Transport Safety 1981–, Urban Mines 1995–, Networking for Industry 1995–; Governor, LSE 1995–; Chair, Cross-Party Advisory Group on Preparation for EMU 1998–; Vice-Chair, Joint Pre-Legislative Committee Investigating the Financial Services and Markets Bill 1998–;

Chair and Interparliamentary Director, Democracy International; Chair, Interparle (Parliamentary Communication Across Europe); Chair, National Educational Research and Development Trust; Fellow, Industry and Parliament Trust; Director and Trustee, National Childrens Centre; *Publications: Harold Laski: A Life on the Left*, (jointly) 1993; FRSA, FRGS; *Sportsclubs:* Member, Millbank Leisure; *Recreations:* Walking, biography, films. *Address:* Barry Sheerman Esq, MP, House of Commons, London, SW1A 0AA *Tel:* 020 7219 5037 *Fax:* 020 7219 2404. *Constituency:* Labour Party, 6 Cross Church Street, Huddersfield, West Yorkshire, HD1 2PT *Tel:* 01484 451382 *Fax:* 01484 451334 *E-mail:* barry.sheerman@virgin.net; sheerman.const@btconnect-com.

ROBERT SHELDON   Ashton under Lyne
Lab majority 22,965

Born 13 September 1923; Educated Elementary; Grammar; Technical schools; London University (External graduate, Whitworth Scholar); Married 1st, 1945, Eileen Shamash (died 1969) (1 son 1 daughter), married 2nd, 1971, Mary Shield. Qualified Engineer. **House of Commons:** Contested Manchester Withington 1959 general election. Member for Ashton under Lyne since October 15, 1964; Opposition Front Bench Spokesman on Civil Service, Treasury Matters and Machinery of Government 1970–74; Deputy Opposition Front Bench Spokesman on Treasury and Economic Affairs 1981–83; Minister of State: Department of Civil Service 1974, HM Treasury 1974–1975; Financial Secretary to HM Treasury 1975–79; *Select Committees:* Chairman: Public Accounts 1983–97; Chairman: Liaison 1997–, Standards and Privileges 1997–. *Special Interests:* Economy, Treasury. Chair, Northwest Group Labour MPs 1970–74. Chair, Public Accounts Commission 1997–; PC 1977. *Address:* Rt Hon Robert Sheldon, MP, House of Commons, London, SW1A 0AA *Tel:* 020 7219 3618. *Constituency:* 27 Darley Avenue, Manchester, M20 2ZD *Tel:* 0161–799 6060 *Fax:* 0161–799 0001 *E-mail:* sheldonr@parliament.uk.

GILLIAN SHEPHARD   South West Norfolk
Con majority 2,464

Born 22 January 1940; Daughter of Reginald and Bertha Watts; Educated North Walsham Girls' High School; St Hilda's College, Oxford (MA); Married December 27, 1975, Thomas Shephard (2 stepsons). Education Officer and Schools Inspector, Norfolk County Council 1963–75; Anglia TV 1975–77. Norfolk County Council: Councillor 1977–89, Deputy Leader 1982–87, Chair: Social Services Committee 1978–83, West Norfolk Health Authority 1981–85, Education Committee 1983–85, Norwich Health Authority 1985–87. **House of Commons:** Member for South West Norfolk since June 1987; PPS to Peter Lilley as Economic Secretary to the Treasury 1988–89; Parliamentary Under-Secretary of State, Department of Social Security 1989–90; Minister of State, HM Treasury 1990–92; Secretary of State for Employment 1992–93; Minister of Agriculture, Fisheries and Food 1993–94; Secretary of State for: Education 1994–95; Education and Employment 1995–97; Shadow Leader of the House of Commons 1997–98; Shadow Chancellor of the Duchy of Lancaster 1997–98; Shadow Secretary of State for the Environment, Transport and the Regions 1998–99; *Select Committees:* Member: Modernisation of the House of Commons 1997–98. *Special Interests:* Health, Education, Penal Affairs and Policy, European Union; France, Latin America. Joint Deputy Chairman, Conservative Party 1991–92. Government Co-Chairman, Women's National Commission 1990; Member, House of Commons Commission 1997–; *Publications: Reforming Local Government* 1999; *Shephard's Watch* 2000; PC 1992; Hon. Fellow, St Hilda's College, Oxford 1991; *Recreations:* Music, gardening, France. *Address:* Rt Hon Gillian Shephard, MP, House of Commons, London, SW1A 0AA *Tel:* 020 7219 2898. *Constituency:* 17A Lynn Road, Downham Market, Norfolk, PE38 4NJ *Tel:* 01366 385072 *E-mail:* foxl@parliament.uk.

Visit the Vacher Dod Website . . .
www.politicallinks.co.uk

RICHARD SHEPHERD   Aldridge-Brownhills   *Con majority 2,526*

Born 6 December 1942; Son of late Alfred Shepherd and Davida Sophia (neé Wallace); Educated London School of Economics; John Hopkins School of Advanced International Studies (MSc economics). Director, retail food business in London Underwriter, Lloyd's 1974–94. **House of Commons:** Contested Nottingham East February 1974 general election. Member for Aldridge-Brownhills since May 1979; Personal assistant to Edward Taylor, MP (Glasgow Cathcart) October 1974 general election; Introduced four Private Member's Bills: The Crown Immunity Bill 1986, Protection of Official Information Bill 1988, The Referendum Bill 1992, Public Interest Disclosure Bill; *Select Committees:* Member: Public Administration 1997–2000; Member: Modernisation of the House of Commons 1997–. Co-Chair, Campaign for Freedom of Information; Member, South East Economic Planning Council 1970–74; The Spectator's Award as: Backbencher of the Year 1987, Parliamentarian of the Year 1995; Campaign for Freedom of Information 1988; *Clubs:* Carlton, Beefsteak, Chelsea Arts. *Address:* Richard Shepherd Esq, MP, House of Commons, London, SW1A 0AA *Tel:* 020 7219 3000 *Tel (Constituency):* 01922 451449 *Fax (Constituency):* 01922 451449.

DEBRA SHIPLEY   Stourbridge   *Lab majority 5,645*

Born 22 June 1957; Educated Kidderminster High School; Kidderminster College; Oxford Polytechnic (BA history of art and anthropology 1980); London University (MA history of art and architecture 1990). Writer and Lecturer; Member, GMB. **House of Commons:** Member for Stourbridge since May 1, 1997; Initiated Private Member's Bill for Protection of Children Act 1999; *Select Committees:* Member: Social Security 1999. *Special Interests:* Children, Elderly; Mongolia, Portugal. Board Member, Opportunities For Volunteering; Member, Amnesty; Patron, Headway Blackcountry; Member, Co-op; Member; Western European Union Defence Committee 1998–99, Council of Europe 1998–99; *Publications:* 17 books; FRSA; *Recreations:* Walking, cooking/eating. *Address:* Debra Shipley, MP, House of Commons, London, SW1A 0AA *Tel:* 020 7219 3053 *Tel (Constituency):* 01384 374356 *Fax (Constituency):* 01384 370111.

CLARE SHORT   Birmingham Ladywood   *Lab majority 23,082*

Born 15 February 1946; Daughter of late Frank and Joan Short; Educated St Francis JI School, Handsworth; St Paul's Grammar, Birmingham; Keele University; Leeds University (BA political science 1968); Married 1st, September 17, 1964, Andrew Moss (divorced 1971) (1 son); married 2nd, 1982, Alex Lyon, MP 1966–83 (died 1993). Civil servant, Home Office 1970–75; Director: AFFOR – Community organisation concerned with race and urban deprivation in Handsworth 1976–77, Youth Aid 1979–83, Unemployment unit 1981–83; Member, Unison. **House of Commons:** Member for Birmingham Ladywood since June 1983; Spokesperson on Employment 1985–88; Opposition Spokesperson on Social Security 1989–91; Opposition Front Bench Spokesperson on: Environmental Protection 1992–93, Women 1993–95; Principal Opposition Spokesperson on Transport 1995–96; Shadow Minister for Overseas Development 1996–97; Vice-Chair, Parliamentary Labour Party 1997–99; Secretary of State for International Development 1997–; *Special Interests:* Unemployment, Race Relations, Immigration Policy, Low Pay, Home Affairs, Northern Ireland, Women. Member, Labour Party National Executive Committee 1988–98. Chair, Human Rights Committee of Socialist International 1996–98; PC 1997; *Recreations:* Swimming, family, friends. *Address:* Rt Hon Clare Short, MP, House of Commons, London, SW1A 0AA *Tel:* 020 7219 4148 *Fax:* 020 7219 2586 *Tel (Constituency):* 020 7219 4264 *E-mail:* shortc@parliament.uk *Website:* www.dfid.gov.uk.

ALAN SIMPSON   Nottingham South   *Lab majority 13,364*

Born 20 September 1948; Son of Reg and Marjorie Simpson; Educated Bootle Grammar School; Nottingham Polytechnic (BSc economics); Divorced (2 sons 1 daughter). President, Students' Union, Nottingham Polytechnic 1969–70; Assistant General Secretary, Nottingham Council of Voluntary Service 1970–74; set up first pilot project for the national non-custodial treatment of offenders programme 1971–74; Community worker, Inner city anti-vandalism project 1974–78; Research Officer, Nottingham Racial Equality Council 1979–92; Member, UNISON. **House of Commons:** Contested Nottingham South in 1987 general election. Member for Nottingham South since April 9, 1992; *Special Interests:* Environment, Economics, Disarmament. Secretary, Socialist Campaign of Labour MPs 1995–; Board Member, Tribune Newspaper 1996–. Member: CND Oxfam; *Publications:* Author of books on: common security, community development, housing, employment, policing policies, Europe, racism; 1999 Green Ribbon Award, Environment Back Bencher of the Year; *Recreations:* Sport (lifelong supporter of Everton FC), vegetarian cooking, music (eclectic taste), reading. *Address:* Alan Simpson Esq, MP, House of Commons, London, SW1A 0AA *Tel:* 020 7219 3000. *Constituency:* 1 Talbot Street, Nottingham, NG1 5GQ *Tel:* 0115–956 0460 *Fax:* 0115–956 0445 *E-mail:* simpsona@parliament.uk.

KEITH SIMPSON   Mid Norfolk   *Con majority 1,336*

Born 29 March 1949; Son of Harry Simpson and Jean Betty, née Day; Educated Thorpe Grammar School, Norfolk; Hull University (BA); King's College, University of London; Married August 4, 1984, Pepita Hollingsworth (1 son). University of London OTC 1970–72; Senior lecturer in war studies, RMA Sandhurst 1973–86; Head of foreign affairs and defence section, Conservative Research Department 1987–88; Special adviser to George Younger and Tom King as Secretaries of State for Defence 1988–90; Director, Cranfield Security Studies Institute, Cranfield University 1991–97. **House of Commons:** Contested Plymouth Devonport 1992 general election. Member for Mid Norfolk since May 1, 1997; Opposition Spokesman for Defence 1998–99; Opposition Whip: (Home Office; Culture, Media and Sport: Wales) 1999, (Treasury; Health) 1999–; *Select Committees:* Member: Catering 1998. *Special Interests:* Foreign Affairs, Defence, Education, Farming, Countryside; USA, Germany, France, Poland; Member, European Standing Committee A 1998. National Vice-Chair, Federation of Conservative Students 1971–72. Member: International Institute for Strategic Studies, Royal United Services Institute for Defence Studies, British Field Sports Society, British Commission for Military History; Council Member, SSAFA 1997–; *Publications: The Old Contemptibles*, 1981; Joint Editor *A Nations in Arms*, 1985; *History of the German Army*, 1985; Editor *The War the Infantry Knew 1914–1919*, 1986; *Clubs:* Norfolk; *Recreations:* Walking dogs, reading, visiting restaurants, cinema, collecting and consuming malt whiskies, observing ambitious people. *Address:* Keith Simpson Esq, MP, House of Commons, London, SW1A 0AA *Tel:* 020 7219 4059 *Fax:* 020 7219 0975. *Constituency:* Mid Norfolk Conservative Association, The Stable, Church Farm, Attlebridge, Norwich, Norfolk NR9 5ST *Tel:* 01603 261594 *Fax:* 01603 261794 *E-mail:* keithsimpsonmp@parliament.uk.

MARSHA SINGH   Bradford West   *Lab majority 3,877*

Born 11 October 1954; Son of Harbans Singh and late Kartar Kaur; Educated Belle Vue Boys Upper School; Loughborough University (BA languages, politics and economics of modern Europe 1976); Married 1971, Sital Kaur (1 son 1 daughter). Senior development manager, Bradford Community Health 1990–97; Member, UNISON. **House of Commons:** Member for Bradford West since May 1, 1997; *Select Committees:* Member: Home Affairs 1997–. *Special Interests:* European Union, Health, Education. Chair: Bradford West Labour Party 1986–91, 1996–97, District Labour Party 1992. *Recreations:* Chess, bridge, reading. *Address:* Marsha Singh Esq, MP, House of Commons, London, SW1A 0AA *Tel:* 020 7219 4625 *Fax:* 020 7219 0965. *Constituency:* Bradford West Constituency Office, 2nd Floor, 76 Kirkgate, Bradford, West Yorkshire, BD1 1SZ *Tel:* 01274 402220 *E-mail:* singhmp@parliament.uk.

DENNIS SKINNER   Bolsover   *Lab majority 27,149*

Born 11 February 1932; Son of Edward Skinner; Educated Tupton Hall Grammar School; Ruskin College, Oxford; Married March 12, 1960, Mary Parker (1 son 2 daughters). Miner 1949–70; President, Derbyshire Miners 1966–70. Clay Cross UDC 1960–70; County Councillor, Derbyshire 1964–70; Former President, Derbyshire UDC Association. **House of Commons:** Member for Bolsover since 1970; *Special Interests:* Inland Waterways, Energy, Economic Policy, Environment, Anti-Common Market, Third World. President, North East Derbyshire Constituency Labour Party 1968–71; Member, Labour Party National Executive Committee 1978–92, 1994–98, 1999–; Vice-Chair, Labour Party 1987–88, Chair 1988–89. Former Member, Scarsdale Valuation Panel, *Recreations:* Cycling, tennis, athletics (watching). *Address:* Dennis Skinner Esq, MP, House of Commons, London, SW1A 0AA *Tel:* 020 7219 3000 *Fax:* 020 7219 0028. *Constituency:* 1 Elmhurst Close, South Normanton, Derbyshire *Tel:* 01773 581027.

ANDREW SMITH   Oxford East   *Lab majority 16,665*

Born 1 February 1951; Son of late David E. C. Smith and Georgina H. J. Smith; Educated Reading Grammar School; St John's College, Oxford (BA, BPhil); Married March 26, 1976, Valerie Labert (1 son). Member relations officer, Oxford and Swindon Co-op Society 1979–87; Member, Union of Oxford Shop, Distributive and Allied Workers. Oxford City Councillor 1976–87; Chairman: Recreation and Amenities Committee 1980–83, Planning Committee 1985–87. **House of Commons:** Contested Oxford East 1983. Member for Oxford East since June 1987; Opposition Spokesman on Education 1988–92; Opposition Frontbench Spokesman on Treasury and Economic Affairs 1992–96; Shadow Chief Secretary to the Treasury 1994–96; Shadow Secretary of State for Transport 1996–97; Minister of State, Department for Education and Employment (Minister for Employment, Welfare to Work and Equal Opportunities) 1997–99; Chief Secretary to the Treasury 1999–; *Select Committees:* : Health and Social Services 1987–88. *Special Interests:* Car Industry, Education, Retail Industry, Transport, Employment; Europe. Member, Labour Party Economy Policy Commission. Chair of governors, Oxford Polytechnic/Oxford Brookes University 1987–93; PC 1997; Hon. Doctorate, Oxford Brookes University; *Clubs:* Blackbird Leys Community Association. *Address:* Rt Hon Andrew Smith, MP, House of Commons, London, SW1A 0AA *Tel:* 020 7219 4512 *Fax:* 020 7219 2965. *Constituency:* 4 Flaxfield Road, Blackbird Leys, Oxford, OX4 5QD *Tel:* 01865 772893 *Fax:* 01865 715990 *Website:* www.andrewsmithmp.org.uk.

ANGELA SMITH   Basildon   *Lab/Co-op majority 13,280*

Born 7 January 1959; Daughter of Patrick Evans, factory worker, and Emily, née Russell, supervisor of church pre-school; Educated Chalvedon Comprehensive, Basildon; Leicester Polytechnic (BA public administration); Married December 16, 1978, Nigel Smith. Trainee accountant, London Borough of Newham 1982–83; League Against Cruel Sports, finally head of political and public relations 1983–95; Research assistant to Alun Michael, MP 1995–97; Member: TGWU, AEEU. Essex County Council: Councillor 1989–97, Chief Whip 1993–96, Lead Spokesperson, Fire and Public Protection Committee 1993–96. **House of Commons:** Contested Southend West 1987 general election. Member for Basildon since May 1, 1997; PPS to Paul Boateng as Minister of State, Home Office 1999–; *Special Interests:* Home Affairs, Animal Welfare, International Development, Employment Rights and Protection. Voluntary Representative for Traidcraft; Patron: Basildon Home Start, Basildon Co-op Development Agency, Basildon Women's Refuge, Vange United Boys FC; Board Member, Cuba Initiative. *Address:* Angela Smith, MP, House of Commons, London, SW1A 0AA *Tel:* 020 7219 6273 *Fax:* 020 7219 0926. *Constituency:* 1A Southend Road, Stanford le Hope, Essex, SS17 0PQ *Tel:* 01375 645770 *Fax:* 01375 645771 *E-mail:* flackk@parliament.uk.

Born 24 July 1951; Son of Colin Smith, civil servant and Gladys Smith, teacher; Educated George Watson's College, Edinburgh; Pembroke College, Cambridge (BA, PhD) (President, Cambridge Union 1972); Harvard University (Kennedy Scholar). Worked for: The Housing Corporation 1976–77, Shaftesbury Society Housing Association 1977–80, Society for Co-operative Dwellings 1980–83; Branch Secretary, ASTMS 1977–80, Branch Chairman 1980–83. Islington Borough Council: Councillor 1978–83, Chief Whip 1978–79, Chair of Housing 1981–83. **House of Commons:** Contested Epsom and Ewell 1979 general election. Member for Islington South and Finsbury since June 1983; London Labour Whip 1986–87; Shadow Treasury Minister 1987–92; Shadow Secretary of State for: Environmental Protection 1992–94, National Heritage 1994–95, Social Security 1995–96, Health 1996–97; Sponsored Environment and Safety Information Act 1988 (Private Member's Bill); Secretary of State: for National Heritage May-July 1997, for Culture, Media and Sport July 1997–; *Select Committees:* Environment 1983–86. *Special Interests:* Heritage, Housing, Local Government, Foreign Affairs, Environment, Civil Liberties, Criminal Justice, Economic Policy, Social Security, Health; Cyprus, Europe, Hong Kong, USA, Australia. Secretary, Tribune Group 1984–88, Chair 1988–89; Chair, Labour Campaign for Criminal Justice 1985–88; Chair, Board of *Tribune* newspaper 1990–93; Member, Executive of Fabian Society 1990–97, Vice-Chair 1995–96, Chair 1996–97; President, SERA 1992–; Chair, Board of New Century Magazine 1993–96. Member: Shelter Board 1986–92, Executive of National Council for Civil Liberties 1986–88; Board Member, Sadlers Wells Theatre 1986–92, Governor 1992–97; Vice-President, Wildlife Link 1986–90; Co-opted Member, Council for National Parks 1980–89; Trustee, John Muir Trust 1991–97; Executive Committee, National Trust 1995–97; *Publications:* Fabian Society: *National Parks*, 1977; Fabian Society: *New Questions for Socialism*, 1996; *Creative Britain*, 1998; PC 1997; *Recreations:* Mountaineering, literature, theatre, music. *Address:* Rt Hon Chris Smith, MP, House of Commons, London, SW1A 0AA *Tel:* 020 7219 5119 *Fax:* 020 7219 5820. *Constituency:* 65 Barnsbury Street, London, N1 *Tel:* 020 7607 8373 *E-mail:* chris.smith@culture.gov.uk *Website:* www.culture.gov.uk.

Born 29 August 1961; Daughter of John and Ann Smith; Educated Morecambe High School; Lancaster and Morecambe College (Diploma business studies). Postal officer 1980–97; Member, Communication Workers Union 1980–: positions including area representative. Councillor, Lancaster City Council 1991–97. **House of Commons:** Member for Morecambe and Lunesdale since May 1, 1997; *Select Committees:* Member: Deregulation 1997–99. *Special Interests:* Economic Regeneration, Tourism, Public/Private Partnerships; Ireland, Eastern Europe; Member, European Standing Committee C 1999–. Various positions including constituency secretary. UK substitute delegate, Council of Europe 1999–; *Recreations:* Playing chess, walking and campaigning. *Address:* Geraldine Smith, MP, House of Commons, London, SW1A 0AA *Tel:* 020 7219 5816. *Constituency:* Morecambe and Lunesdale CLP, Labour Party Offices, 26–28 Victoria Street, Morecambe, Lancashire, LA4 4AJ *Tel:* 01524 411367 *Fax:* 01524 411369.

Dod *on* Line
An Electronic Directory without rival ...
MPs' biographies and photographs
available with daily updates *via* the internet
For a *free* trial, call Oliver Cox on 020 7828 7256

JACQUI SMITH   Redditch   *Lab majority 6,125*

Born 3 November 1962; Daughter of Michael L. Smith, headteacher, and Jill Smith, retired teacher; Educated Dyson Perrins High School, Malvern, Worcs; Hertford College, Oxford University (BA philosophy, politics and economics); Worcester College of Higher Education (PGCE); Married 1987, Richard Timney (2 sons). Teacher, Economics, Arrow Vale High School, Redditch 1986–88; Teacher, Worcester Sixth Form College 1988–90; Head of Economics, GNVQ Co-ordinator, Haybridge High School, Hagley 1990–97; Member: NUT, GMB. Councillor, Redditch Borough Council 1991–97. **House of Commons:** Member for Redditch since May 1, 1997; Parliamentary Under-Secretary of State, Department for Education and Employment 1999–; *Select Committees:* Member: Treasury 1998–99, Treasury Sub-Committee 1998–99. *Special Interests:* Industry, Education and Training, Economic Policy. Member, British East-West Centre; Member, Worcester Nature Conservation Trust; *Recreations:* Family, football, theatre. *Address:* Jacqui Smith, MP, House of Commons, London, SW1A 0AA *Tel:* 020 7219 5845 *Fax:* 020 7219 4815 *Tel (Constituency):* 01527 585863 *Fax (Constituency):* 01527 585863 *E-mail:* smithjj@parliament.uk.

JOHN SMITH   Vale of Glamorgan   *Lab majority 10,532*

Born 17 March 1951; Son of John and Margaret Smith; Educated Fairfield Primary School, Penarth; Penarth Grammar School; Gwent College of Higher Education; University College of Wales, Cardiff (BSc economics); Married April 10, 1971, Kathleen Mulvaney (2 sons 1 daughter). RAF 1967–71; Carpenter and joiner, Vale Borough Council 1971–76; Mature student 1976–81; University tutor (UCC) 1981–85; Senior lecturer in business studies 1985–89; Campaign manager, Gwent Image Partnership, chief executive 1992–; Member: MSF 1970–, TASS, NATFHE, AUT, NUPE, UCATT. Vale of Glamorgan Borough Council: Councillor 1979–91, Opposition Finance and Housing Spokesperson 1979–87, Labour Group Secretary 1981–83, Labour Group Leader 1983–88. **House of Commons:** Contested Vale of Glamorgan 1987 general election. Member for Vale of Glamorgan 1989–92 and since May 1, 1997; PPS to Roy Hattersley as Deputy Leader of Labour Party 1989–92; Contributed to: Trade Union Bill, Armed Forces Bill, Barry Old Harbour Bill, Seat Belt Regulation; PPS to Dr John Reid: as Minister of State, Ministry of Defence (Minister for the Armed Forces) 1997–98, Department of the Environment, Transport and the Regions (Minister of Transport) 1998–99; *Select Committees:* Member: Welsh Affairs 1990–92; Member: Welsh Affairs 2000–. *Special Interests:* Economic Development, Industrial Relations, Transport Safety, Defence. Chair, Young Socialists 1967–94; Member: Vale of Glamorgan CLP 1972–, Welsh Executive 1985–89, 1996–; Chair, Wales Labour Party 1988–89; Member, National Policy Forum 1996; Former Vice-Chair, Welsh Parliamentary Labour Party; Vice-Chair, Welsh Regional Group of Labour MPs 1999, Chair 1999–. Chair, Anti-Apartheid Movement (ACTSA); Hon. Vice-President: Imperial Cancer Foundation, Rail Users Federation, Local Arthritis Care; President, Local Leisure and Community Centre; Team Manager, Valley and Vale Arts; Chair, Parliamentary Advisory Council on Transport Safety 1989–92; Member: Commonwealth Parliamentary Association (CPA), UK Delegation to North Atlantic Assembly; *Recreations:* Reading, walking, camping, boating. *Address:* John Smith Esq, MP, House of Commons, London, SW1A 0AA *Tel:* 020 7219 3589. *Constituency:* 115 High Street, Barry *Tel:* 01446 743769 *Fax:* 01446 743769 *E-mail:* smithj@parliament.uk.

Dod *on* Line
An Electronic Directory without rival ...
MPs' biographies and photographs available with daily updates *via* the internet
For a *free* trial, call Oliver Cox on 020 7828 7256

LLEWELLYN SMITH   Blaenau Gwent   *Lab majority 28,035*

Born 16 April 1944; Son of late Ernest Smith, and of Cissie Smith; Educated Greenfields Secondary Modern School; Colleg Harlech; Cardiff University (Bsc, MSc); Married December 13, 1969, Pamela Williams (2 sons 1 daughter). Labourer; computer operator; tutor-organiser, Worker's Educational Association; MEP for South East Wales 1984–94; Member, TGWU. **House of Commons:** Member for Blaenau Gwent since April 9, 1992; *Special Interests:* Cuba. Member: CND, Socialist Education Association; Vice-President, Anti-Apartheid Wales; *Publications:* Co-author: *Bombing Ahead With Disarmament*, 1990, *The Politics of Poverty*, 1993. *Address:* Llewellyn Smith Esq, MP, House of Commons, London, SW1A 0AA *Tel:* 020 7219 3000. *Constituency:* 23 Beaufort Street, Brynmawr, Gwent, NP3 4AQ *Tel:* 01495 313345.

ROBERT SMITH   West Aberdeenshire and Kincardine   *LD majority 2,662*

Born 15 April 1958; Son of late Sir (William) Gordon Smith, Bt, VRD, and of Diana Lady Smith; Educated Merchant Taylors' School, Northwood; Aberdeen University (BSc); Married August 13, 1993, Fiona Anne Cormack, MD (3 daughters). Family estate manager until 1997. Councillor, Aberdeenshire Council 1995–97; JP 1997. **House of Commons:** Contested (SDP/Liberal Alliance) Aberdeen North 1987 general election. Member for West Aberdeenshire and Kincardine since May 1, 1997; Spokesman for Scotland 1999–; Liberal Democrat Regional Whip (Scotland) 1999–; *Select Committees:* Member: Catering 1999–2000; Member: Scottish Affairs 1999–. *Special Interests:* Electoral Reform; Member, European Standing Committee A 2000–. General Council Assessor, Aberdeen University 1994–98; Director, Grampian Transport Museum 1995–97; Vice-Convenor, Grampian Joint Police Board 1995–97; Member, Electoral Reform Society; *Clubs:* Royal Yacht Squadron, Royal Thames Yacht; *Recreations:* Hill-walking, sailing. *Address:* Sir Robert Smith, Bt, MP, House of Commons, London, SW1A 0AA *Tel:* 020 7219 4930 *Fax:* 020 7219 0907. *Constituency:* 6 Dee Street, Banchory, Kincardineshire, AB31 5ST *Tel:* 01330 820330 *Fax:* 01330 820106 *E-mail:* bobsmith@cix.co.uk.

REV MARTIN SMYTH   Belfast South   *UUP majority 4,600*

Born 15 June 1931; Son of late James Smyth, JP; Educated Methodist College, Belfast; Magee University College, Londonderry; Trinity College, Dublin (BA general arts 1953); Presbyterian College, Dublin 1955; San Francisco Theological Seminary (BD 1961); Married 1957, Kathleen Johnston (2 daughters and 1 daughter deceased). Assistant Minister, Finaghy Presbyterian Church, Belfast 1953–57; Minister: Raffrey Church 1957–63, Alexandra Presbyterian Church 1963–82. **House of Commons:** Member for Belfast South since by-election March 1982; Party Spokesman for: Health and Social Services 1992–97, Health and Family Policy 1997–2000, Health, Social Security, Youth and Women's Issues 2000–; Chief Whip 1996–2000; Member, Northern Ireland Constitutional Convention 1975; Northern Ireland Assembly: Member for Belfast South 1982–86; Chair, Health and Social Services Committee 1983–84, Finance and Personnel Committee 1984–86; Sponsored Disabled Persons (Northern Ireland) Act, 1989 (Private Member's Bill); Contested Ulster Unionist Party Leadership March 2000; *Select Committees:* Member: Health 1990–97. *Special Interests:* World Protestantism, Health, Social Services, Education, Foreign Affairs, Human Rights, Transport; Brazil, Canada, Malawi, Morocco, New Zealand, Taiwan, USA, India, Australia. Chair, Ulster Unionist Executive Committee 1972–74; Vice-President, Ulster Unionist Council 1974–2000, Honorary Secretary 2000–. Grand Master: Grand Orange Lodge of Ireland 1972–96, Grand Orange Council of the World 1973–82; Chairman, Belfast No. 1 School Management Committee 1972–80; President, Orange Council of the World 1985–88; Member, Executive Committee: IPU (UK Branch) 1985–92, 1994–, Commonwealth Parliamentary Association (CPA) UK Branch 1989–; Fellow, Industry and Parliament Trust; *Publications:* Editor *Faith For Today*, 1961; Pamphlets: *In Defence of Ulster*; *The Battle for Northern Ireland*; *A Federated People*; *Till Death Us Do Part*; *Why Presbyterian?*; *Recreations:* Travel, photography, reading. *Address:* Rev Martin Smyth, MP, House of Commons, London, SW1A 0AA *Tel:* 020 7219 4098 *Fax:* 020 7219 2347. *Constituency:* 117 Cregagh Road, Belfast, BT6 0LA *Tel:* 028 9045 7009 *Fax:* 028 9045 0837 *E-mail:* mckeem@parliament.uk.

PETER SNAPE   West Bromwich East   *Lab majority 13,584*

Born 12 February 1942; Son of late Thomas Snape, Railway Chargeman; Educated St. Joseph's School, Stockport; Married 1963, Winifred Grimshaw (divorced 1980) (2 daughters). Army service 1960–66; British Railways/Rail: Railwayman 1957–60, Goods guard 1966–70, Controller 1970–74. Bredbury and Romiley Urban District Council: Councillor 1971–74, Chair, Finance Committee 1972–74. **House of Commons:** Member for West Bromwich East since February 1974; Opposition Front Bench Spokesman on: Defence 1979–82, Home Affairs 1982–83, Transport 1983–92; Government Whip 1975–79; *Special Interests:* Transport; Hungary, Iraq. Chair, West Midlands Regional Group of Labour MPs 1984–. *Recreations:* Golf, soccer. *Address:* Peter Snape Esq, MP, House of Commons, London, SW1A 0AA *Tel:* 020 7219 5149 *Fax:* 020 7219 5847. *Constituency:* Town Hall, High Street, West Bromwich, West Midlands, B70 8DK *Tel:* 0121–525 4408 *Fax:* 0121–525 4643.

NICHOLAS SOAMES   Mid Sussex   *Con majority 6,854*

Born 12 February 1948; Son of late Baron and Lady Soames; Educated Eton College; Married 1st, June 4, 1981, Catherine Weatherall (divorced 1988) (1 son), married 2nd, December 21, 1993, Serena Smith (1 daughter). Lieutenant, 11th Hussars 1967–70; Equerry to HRH The Prince of Wales, KG 1970–72; Stockbroker 1972–74; PA to: Sir James Goldsmith 1974–76, US Senator Mark Hatfield 1976–78; Assistant director, Sedgwick Group 1979–81. **House of Commons:** Contested Dumbartonshire Central 1979 general election. Member for Crawley 1983–97, and for Mid Sussex since May 1, 1997; PPS: to John Gummer as Minister of State for Employment and Chairman of the Conservative Party 1984–86; to Nicholas Ridley as Secretary of State for the Environment 1987–89; Joint Parliamentary Secretary, Ministry of Agriculture, Fisheries and Food 1992–94; Minister of State for the Armed Forces, Ministry of Defence 1994–97; *Select Committees:* Member: Public Administration 1999. *Special Interests:* Defence, Foreign Affairs, Trade and Industry, Aerospace, Aviation, Agriculture and Countryside matters. Executive member, 1922 Committee 2000–; *Clubs:* White's, Turf, Pratts; *Recreations:* Country pursuits. *Address:* Hon Nicholas Soames, MP, House of Commons, London, SW1A 0AA *Tel:* 020 7219 4184 *Tel (Constituency):* 01444 452590.

CLIVE SOLEY   Ealing, Acton and Shepherd's Bush   *Lab majority 15,647*

Born 7 May 1939; Educated Downshall Secondary Modern, Ilford; Newbattle Abbey Adult Education College; Strathclyde University (BA politics and psychology 1968); Southampton University (Diploma applied social studies 1970); (1 son 1 daughter). Probation officer and senior probation officer, Inner London Probation Service 1970–79. **House of Commons:** Member for Hammersmith North 1979–83, for Hammersmith 1983–97, and for Ealing, Acton and Shepherds Bush since May 1, 1997; Opposition Spokesman on: Northern Ireland 1982–85, Home Affairs 1985–87, Housing and Local Government 1987–89, Housing and Planning 1989–92; *Select Committees:* Member: Northern Ireland Affairs 1994–97; Chairman: Northern Ireland Affairs 1995–97; Member: Modernisation of the House of Commons 1997–. *Special Interests:* Environment, Housing, Penal Affairs and Policy, Civil Liberties, Northern Ireland; China, South East Asia. Chair: Labour Campaign for Criminal Justice 1983–97, Parliamentary Labour Party 1997–; Member, Labour Party National Executive Committee 1998–; Chair, London Selection Board for Labour candidate for Mayor 1999–. Chair, Alcohol Education Centre –1984; Member of several House of Commons Committees including: Prevention of Terrorism Bill 1983–84, Criminal Justice Bill 1987–99, Housing Bill 1987–88, Local Government and Housing Bill 1988–89, Planning and Compensation Bill 1990–91, Freedom and Responsibility of the Press 1992–93; International Observer at: first National Elections in Mongolia 1990, Peruvian General Election 1995; Fellow, Industry and Parliament Trust; *Publications:* Chapter: The Politics of the Family in *Rewriting the Sexual Contract*; co-author, *Regulating the Press* 2000; *Recreations:* Walking, photography, scuba diving. *Address:* Clive Soley Esq, MP, House of Commons, London, SW1A 0AA *Tel:* 020 7219 5490 *Fax:* 020 7219 5974. *Constituency:* Ruskin Hall, 16 Church Road, London, W3 8PP *Tel:* 020 8992 5614 *Fax:* 020 8752 1200 *E-mail:* macleodn@parliament.uk.

HELEN SOUTHWORTH   Warrington South   *Lab majority 10,807*

Born 13 November 1956; Educated Larkhill Convent School; Lancaster University (BA); Married Edmund Southworth (1 son). Director, Age Concern (St Helens); Non-executive director, St Helens and Knowsley Health Authority; Representative on the Community Health Council for 8 years; Member, MSF. Councillor, St Helens Borough Council 1994–98, Chair, Leisure Committee 1994–96; Non-executive Member, St Helens and Knowsley Health Authority. **House of Commons:** Contested Wirral South general election 1992. Member for Warrington South since May 1, 1997; *Select Committees:* Member: Procedure 1997–99; Member: Trade and Industry 1998–. *Special Interests:* Health, Housing, Democracy, Small Businesses; Denmark, Sweden, Finland. Governor, Age Concern; Director, Grosvenor Housing Association; Council Member, St Helen's College; Member, Sankey Canal Restoration Society; Trustee, History of Parliament Trust; *Publications:* Co-author, *National Standards for Day Care Provision*; *Recreations:* Family, gardening, painting, walking the dog. *Address:* Helen Southworth, MP, House of Commons, London, SW1A 0AA *Tel:* 020 7219 3568 *Fax:* 020 7219 2115. *Constituency:* 33 Cairo Street, Warrington, WA1 1EH *Tel:* 01925 240002 *Fax:* 01925 632614 *E-mail:* southworthh@parliament.uk.

JOHN SPELLAR   Warley   *Lab majority 15,451*

Born 5 August 1947; Son of late William David Spellar, and of Phyllis Kathleen Spellar; Educated Dulwich College, London; St Edmund's Hall, Oxford (BA philosophy, politics and economics 1969); Married 1981, Anne Rosalind Wilmot (1 daughter). National Officer, Electrical, Electronic, Tele-communication and Plumbing Union 1969–97. **House of Commons:** Contested Bromley 1970 general election. Member for Birmingham Northfield from October 28, 1982 by-election to June 1983. Contested Birmingham Northfield 1987 general election. Member for Warley West 1992–97, and for Warley since May 1, 1997; Opposition Spokesman on: Northern Ireland 1994–95, Defence, Disarmament and Arms Control 1995–97; Opposition Whip 1992–94; Ministry of Defence: Parliamentary Under-Secretary of State 1997–99, Minister of State for the Armed Forces 1999–; *Special Interests:* Energy, Industry (Electronics), Motor Industry, Construction Industry; Australia, Israel, USA. *Clubs:* Rowley Regis and Blackheath Labour; *Recreations:* Gardening. *Address:* John Spellar Esq, MP, House of Commons, London, SW1A 0AA *Tel:* 020 7219 5800 *E-mail:* spellarj@parliament.uk.

CAROLINE SPELMAN   Meriden   *Con majority 582*

Born 4 May 1958; Daughter of Marshall Cormack and late Helen Margaret, née Greenfield; Educated Herts and Essex Grammar School for Girls; Queen Mary College, London University (BA European studies 1980); Married April 25, 1987, Mark Spelman (2 sons 1 daughter). Sugar Beet commodity secretary, National Farmers Union 1981–84; Deputy director, International Confederation of European Beetgrowers, Paris 1984–89; Research fellow, Centre for European Agricultural Studies 1989–93; Director, Spelman, Cormack and Associates, Food and Biotechnology Consultancy 1989–. **House of Commons:** Contested Bassetlaw 1992 general election. Member for Meriden since May 1, 1997; Opposition Front Bench Spokeswoman for Women's Issues 1999–; Opposition Whip (Agriculture; Environment, Transport and the Regions) 1998–99; *Select Committees:* Member: Science and Technology 1997–98. *Special Interests:* Health, Trade and Industry, Environment, Agriculture; France, Germany, Brazil, South Africa. Board Member, Parliamentary Office of Science and Technology (POST) 1997–; Trustee: Snowdon Awards Scheme for Disabled, Oxford Kilburn Club for Deprived Inner City Kids; *Publications: A Green and Pleasant Land*, Bow Group Paper; *Sportsclubs:* Member: Hampton in Arden Hockey Club, Knowle and Dorridge Tennis Club, Lords and Commons Ski Club, Lords and Commons Tennis Club; *Recreations:* Tennis, skiing, cooking, gardening. *Address:* Caroline Spelman, MP, House of Commons, London, SW1A 0AA *Tel:* 020 7219 4189 *Fax:* 020 7219 0378. *Constituency:* 2 Manor Road, Solihull, West Midlands, B91 2BH *Tel:* 0121–711 2955 *Fax:* 0121–711 2955 *E-mail:* spelmanc@parliament.uk.

SIR MICHAEL SPICER   West Worcestershire   *Con majority 3,846*

Born 22 January 1943; Son of late Brigadier L. H. Spicer; Educated Sacre Coeur, Vienna; Gaunts House Preparatory School; Wellington College; Emmanuel College, Cambridge (MA economics); Married April 7, 1967, Patricia Ann Hunter (1 son 2 daughters). Director, Conservative Systems Research Centre 1968–70, Managing director, Economic Models Limited 1970–80. **House of Commons:** Contested Easington 1966 and 1970 general elections. Member for South Worcestershire 1974–97, and for West Worcestershire since May 1, 1997; PPS to Sally Oppenheim as Minister for Trade and Consumer Affairs 1979–81; Parliamentary Under-Secretary of State for Transport 1984–87; Aviation Minister 1985–87; Parliamentary Under-Secretary of State, Department of Energy 1987–90; Minister of State, Housing and Planning, Department of Environment 1990; *Select Committees:* Chairman: Treasury Sub-Committee 1999; Member: Treasury 1997–; Chairman: Treasury Sub-Committee 1999–. Vice-Chair, Conservative Party 1981–83; Deputy Chair 1983–84. Governor, Wellington College 1992–; Chair: European Research Group; Member, Executive, 1922 Committee 1997–98; Joint chair, Congress of Democracy; *Publications: A Treaty Too Far: A New Policy For Europe*, 1992; *The Challenge from the East: The Rebirth of the West*, 1996; Six novels; Knighted 1996; *Clubs:* Pratts, Garrick; *Recreations:* Tennis, writing novels, painting. *Address:* Sir Michael Spicer, MP, House of Commons, London, SW1A 0AA *Tel:* 020 7219 3491. *Constituency:* 209a Worcester Road, Malvern Link, Malvern, Worcestershire, WR14 1SP *Tel:* 01684 573469 *Fax:* 01684 575280.

RICHARD SPRING   West Suffolk   *Con majority 1,867*

Born 24 September 1946; Son of late H. J. A. Spring and of late Marjorie Watson-Morris; Educated Rondebosch, Cape; University of Cape Town; Magdalene College, Cambridge; Married December 13, 1979, Hon. Jane Henniker-Major (divorced 1993) (1 son 1 daughter). Merrill Lynch Ltd 1971–86, Vice-President 1976–86; Deputy managing director, Hutton International Associates 1986–88; Executive director, Shearson Lehman Hutton 1988–90; Managing director, Xerox Furman Selz 1990–92. **House of Commons:** Contested Ashton-under-Lyne 1983 general election. Member for Bury St Edmunds 1992–97, and for West Suffolk since May 1, 1997; Opposition Spokesman for: Culture, Media and Sport November 1997–2000, Foreign and Commonwealth Affairs 2000–; PPS: to Sir Patrick Mayhew as Secretary of State for Northern Ireland 1994–95, to Tim Eggar, as Minister for Trade and Industry 1995–96, to Nicholas Soames and James Arbuthnot as Ministers of State, Ministry of Defence 1996–97; *Select Committees:* Member: Employment 1992–94, Health 1995–96, Northern Ireland Affairs 1995–97, Deregulation 1997. *Special Interests:* Spain, South Africa, USA, Estonia. Various offices in Westminster Conservative Association 1976–87, including CPC Chair 1990; Vice-Chair, Conservative Industrial Fund 1993–96. Deputy-Chairman, Small Business Bureau 1992–; *Clubs:* Boodle's; *Recreations:* Country pursuits, tennis, swimming. *Address:* Richard Spring Esq, MP, House of Commons, London, SW1A 0AA *Tel:* 020 7219 4062. *Constituency:* 4a Exeter Road, Newmarket, Suffolk, CB8 8LT *Tel:* 01638 669391 *Fax:* 01638 669410.

RACHEL SQUIRE   Dunfermline West   *Lab majority 12,354*

Born 13 July 1954; Daughter of Louise Anne Squire; Educated Godolphin and Latymer Girls' School; Durham University (BA anthropology 1975); Birmingham University (CQSW 1978); Married July 6, 1984, Allan Lee Mason. Social worker, Birmingham City Council 1975–81; Area officer, NUPE: Liverpool 1981–82, Ayrshire 1982–83, Renfrewshire 1983–85, All of Scotland Education Officer 1985–92; Trade Union Official 1981–92; Member, UNISON. **House of Commons:** Member for Dunfermline West since April 9, 1992; PPS to Ministers of State, Department for Education and Employment: Stephen Byers 1997–98, Estelle Morris 1998–; *Select Committees:* Member: Procedure 1992–97, European Legislation 1994–97, Modernisation of the House of Commons 1997–99. *Special Interests:* Defence, Health Service, Community Care, Foreign Affairs;

Scandinavia, Europe, Former Eastern Bloc. Head, Scottish Labour Party's Task Force on Community Care 1993–97; Member, Labour Movement in Europe; Chair, Scottish Policy Forum, Labour Party 1998–. Member: Amnesty International, WEA, Council for British Archaeology, Council for Scotland Archaeology, Historic Scotland, Camping and Caravanning Club; Labour Representative, Commission on Future of Scotland's Voluntary Sector; Fellow, Industry and Parliament Trust (BAe); Member, National Trust (Scotland); Fellow (Navy), Armed Forces Parliamentary Scheme 1993–94; *Recreations:* Archaeology, reading. *Address:* Rachel Squire, MP, House of Commons, London, SW1A 0AA *Tel:* 020 7219 5144. *Constituency:* 10–14 Douglas Street, Dunfermline, KY12 7EB *Tel:* 01383 622889 *Fax:* 01383 623500.

SIR JOHN STANLEY   Tonbridge and Malling   *Con majority 10,230*

Born 19 January 1942; Educated Repton School; Lincoln College, Oxford; Married December 21, 1968, Susan Giles (1 son 1 daughter 1 son deceased). Conservative Research Department 1967–68; Research Associate, Institute for Strategic Studies 1968–69; Rio Tinto-Zinc Corp. Ltd 1969–79. **House of Commons:** Contested Newton 1970 general election. Member for Tonbridge and Malling since February 1974; PPS to Margaret Thatcher as Leader of the Opposition 1976–79; Minister for Housing and Construction 1979–83; Minister for the Armed Forces 1983–87; Minister of State, Northern Ireland Office 1987–88; *Select Committees:* Member: Foreign Affairs 1992–97, Entry Clearance Sub-Committee 1997–98; Member: Foreign Affairs 1997–. Member, Executive Committee, Commonwealth Parliamentary Association (CPA) UK Branch 1999–; Trustee, ActionAid; PC 1984; Knighted 1988; *Recreations:* Music and the arts, sailing. *Address:* Rt Hon Sir John Stanley, MP, House of Commons, London, SW1A 0AA *Tel:* 020 7219 3000.

DR PHYLLIS STARKEY   Milton Keynes South West   *Lab majority 10,292*

Born 4 January 1947; Daughter of Dr John Williams, food chemist, and late Catherine Hooson Williams; Educated Perse School for Girls, Cambridge; Lady Margaret Hall, Oxford (BA biochemistry 1970); Clare Hall, Cambridge (PhD 1974); Married September 6, 1969, Hugh Walton Starkey (2 daughters). Research scientist: Strangeways Laboratory, Cambridge 1974–81, Sir William Dunn School of Pathology, Oxford 1981–84; University lecturer in obstetrics, Oxford University and fellow, Somerville College 1984–93; Science policy administrator, Biotechnology and Biological Sciences Research Council 1993–97; Parliamentary fellow, St Antony's College, Oxford 1997–98; Member: AUT 1974–93, MSF 1992–, PTC 1993–97. Oxford City Council: Councillor 1983–97, Leader 1990–93, Chair of Transport 1985–88, Chair of Finance 1988–90, 1993–96. **House of Commons:** Member for Milton Keynes South West since May 1, 1997; *Select Committees:* Member: Modernisation of the House of Commons 1997–99; Member: Foreign Affairs 1999–. *Special Interests:* Science, Health, Environmentally Sustainable Transport, Local Government and Devolution, Foreign Affairs, Middle East; Palestine, France, North Africa. Vice-Chair, South East Regional Group of Labour MPs 1998–. Chair, Local Government Information Unit 1992–97; Representative of Labour Councillors on National Policy Forum 1995–97; Board Member, Parliamentary Office of Science and Technology (POST) 1997–; *Publications:* Seventy scientific papers 1977–96; K M Stott Prize, Newnham College, Cambridge 1974; *Recreations:* Gardening, cinema, walking, family. *Address:* Dr Phyllis Starkey, MP, House of Commons, London, SW1A 0AA *Tel:* 020 7219 0456/6427 *Fax:* 020 7219 6865. *Constituency:* The Labour Hall, Newport Road, New Bradwell, Milton Keynes, MK13 0AA *Tel:* 01908 225522 *Fax:* 01908 312297 *E-mail:* starkey@miltonkeynes-sw.demon.co.uk.

Visit the Vacher Dod Website . . .
www.politicallinks.co.uk

ANTHONY STEEN   Totnes   *Con majority 877*

Born 22 July 1939; Son of late Stephen Steen; Educated Westminster School; London University; Married 1966, Carolyn Padfield (1 son 1 daughter). Called to the Bar 1962; Barrister, Gray's Inn; Youth leader and social worker; Founder, Task Force (Young helping the old) with Government grant 1964, First Director 1964–68; As community worker initiated Young Volunteer Force, Government Urban Development Foundation, First Director 1968–74; Lecturer in law, Ghana High Commission and Council of Legal Education 1964–67; Ministry of Defence Court Martials Defence Counsel; Adviser to Federal and Provincial Canadian Governments on unemployment and youth problems 1970–71. **House of Commons:** Member for Liverpool Wavertree 1974–83, for South Hams 1983–97, and for Totnes since May 1, 1997; PPS to Peter Brooke as Secretary of State for National Heritage 1992–94; *Select Committees:* Member: Environment 1989–92, House of Commons Catering 1991–95, European Legislation 1997–98, European Legislation 1998; Member: Deregulation 1997–, European Scrutiny 1998–. *Special Interests:* Environment, Urban Regeneration, Community Care, Youth Affairs, Conservation, Heritage, Fishing, Agriculture, Deregulation; Middle East. Appointed by the Prime Minister to generate new activity amongst MPs in constituency work 1994; Conservative Central Office Co-ordinator for Critical Seats 1982–87; Joint National Chairman, Impact 80s Campaign 1980–82; Chair, Minority Party Unit 1999–. Founder of two national charities; Vice-President: International Centre for Child Studies, Association of District Councils, Malborough with South Huish Horticultural Society; Advisory tutor to the School of Environment, Polytechnic of Central London 1982–83; Patron, Kidscape; Member, Council for Christians and Jews; Trustee of: Education Extra, Dartington Summer Arts Foundation; *Publications: New Life for Old Cities,* 1981; *Tested Ideas for Political Success,* 1983; *Public Land Utilisation Management Schemes (PLUMS),* 1988; *Clubs:* Royal North Cape, Royal Automobile; *Sportsclubs:* Lords and Commons Cycle, Lords and Commons Tennis; *Recreations:* Piano playing, cycling, swimming, tennis, tree-hugging. *Address:* Anthony D. Steen Esq, MP, House of Commons, London, SW1A 0AA *Tel:* 020 7219 3000. *Constituency:* TCCA, Station Road, Totnes, Devon, TQ9 5HW *Tel:* 01803 866064 *Fax:* 01803 867236 *E-mail:* steena@parliament.uk.

GERRY STEINBERG   City of Durham   *Lab majority 22,504*

Born 20 April 1945; Son of late Harry and Esther Steinberg; Educated Whinney Hill Secondary Modern School; Durham Johnston Grammar School; Sheffield College of Education (Teachers Certificate); Newcastle Polytechnic (Certificate Education of Backward Children); Married August 25, 1969, Margaret Thornton (1 son 1 daughter). Teacher, Hexham Camp School 1966–69; Elemore Hall 1969–75, Deputy head 1975–79; Head teacher, Whitworth House School 1979–87; Member: TGWU, NUT. Councillor, Durham City Council 1976–87. **House of Commons:** Member for City of Durham since June 1987; *Select Committees:* Member: Education 1987–96, Education and Employment 1997–98, Education Sub-Committee 1997–98; Member: Catering 1998–, Public Accounts 1998–. *Special Interests:* Education, Local Government, Animal Welfare. Secretary, Durham CLP and Agent to Dr Mark Hughes, MP 1973–83; Secretary, Durham City Labour Group 1981–87; Vice-Chair, Northern Group of Labour MPs 1997–98, Chair 1998–. *Clubs:* Sherburn Village Workman's, Brandon Village Workman's, Crossgate Workman's, Neville's Cross Workman's, New Durham Workman's; *Recreations:* All sport, supporting Sunderland AFC. *Address:* Gerald Steinberg Esq, MP, House of Commons, London, SW1A 0AA *Tel:* 020 7219 6909. *Constituency:* 32 Claypath, Durham, DH1 1RH *Tel:* 0191–386 0166 *Fax:* 0191–383 0047.

GEORGE STEVENSON   Stoke-on-Trent South   *Lab majority 18,303*

Born 30 August 1938; Son of Harold and Elsie Stevenson; Educated Queensberry Road Secondary Modern School; Married 1st, June 14, 1958, Doreen June Parkes (died 1989) (2 sons 1 daughter), married 2nd, June 1, 1991, Pauline Margaret Barber. Pottery industry 1953–57; Mining industry 1957–66; MEP for Staffordshire East 1984–94: Chair, British Labour Group 1987–88; TGWU Shop steward 1968; Chair, 5/24 Branch TGWU 1975–83. Deputy Leader, Stoke-on-Trent City Council 1972–83, Chair, Highways Committee; Deputy Leader, Staffordshire County Council 1981–85, Former Chair, Social Services and Establishment Committees. **House of Commons:** Member for Stoke-on-Trent South since April 9, 1992; *Select Committees:* Member: Agriculture 1992–96, European Legislation 1996–97, Chairmen's Panel 1998; Member: Environment, Transport and Regional Affairs 1997–, Transport Sub-Committee 1997–, Chairmen's Panel 1998–. *Special Interests:* Transport, Energy, Agriculture, Human Rights, Education; India, Kashmir, Pakistan, Sri Lanka, Tibet, South Asia; Member: European Standing Committee B 1998, European Standing Committee A 1998–. Member: Amnesty International, ACTSA; Vice-President, Federation of Economic Development Authorities (FEDA); *Recreations:* Walking, travel, reading. *Address:* George Stevenson Esq, MP, House of Commons, London, SW1A 0AA *Tel:* 020 7219 5012 *Fax:* 020 7219 2688. *Constituency:* 2A Stanton Road, Meir, Stoke-on-Trent, Staffs, ST3 6DD *Tel:* 01782 593393 *Fax:* 01782 593430 *E-mail:* stevensonp@parliament.uk.

DAVID STEWART   Inverness East, Nairn and Lochaber   *Lab majority 2,339*

Born 5 May 1956; Son of John Stewart, retired postal executive, and Alice Stewart; Educated Inverness High School; Paisley College (BA 1978); Stirling University (Postgraduate diploma in social work and CQSW 1981); Open University Business School (Prof Dip Mgt 1996); Married August 6, 1982, Linda MacDonald (1 son 1 daughter 1 son deceased). Social worker and social work manager 1980–97; Member, UNISON. Councillor: Nithsdale Council, Dumfries 1984–86, Inverness District Council 1988–96. **House of Commons:** Contested Inverness, Nairn and Lochaber 1987 and 1992 general elections. Member for Inverness East, Nairn and Lochaber since May 1, 1997; *Select Committees:* Member: Scottish Affairs 1997–99. *Special Interests:* Rural Affairs, Local Government, Health, International Development, Social Security; USA, Italy. Member, Scottish Executive Labour Party 1985–95. Governor, Eden Court Theatre 1992–96; Trustee: Bacnain House Inverness, Scottish Cot Death Trust; Member, Interparliamentary Union; *Sportsclubs:* Inverness Caledonian Thistle Football Club; *Recreations:* Football, films, fitness, American political biographies. *Address:* David Stewart Esq, MP, House of Commons, London, SW1A 0AA *Tel:* 020 7219 3586 *Fax:* 020 7219 5687. *Constituency:* Queensgate Business Centre, 1/3 Fraser Street, Inverness, IV1 1DY *Tel:* 01463 237441 *Fax:* 01463 237661 *E-mail:* stewartd@parliament.uk, *Website:* www.davidstewartmp.co.uk.

IAN STEWART   Eccles   *Lab majority 21,916*

Born 28 August 1950; Son of John and Helen; Educated Calder St Secondary, Blantyre; Alfred Turner Secondary Modern, Irlam, nr Manchester; Stretford Technical College 1966–69; Manchester Metropolitan University (MPhil Management of Change in progress); Married August 9, 1968, Merilyn Holding (2 sons 1 daughter). Regional full-time officer, Transport and General Workers Union for 20 years; Member, Transport and General Workers 1966–. **House of Commons:** Member for Eccles since May 1, 1997; *Select Committees:* Member: Deregulation 1997–, Information 1998–. *Special Interests:* Employment, Education and Training, Economics, Trade and Industry, Investment, Regional Development, Information Technology, Democracy, International Affairs; EU, Central and Eastern Europe, China, USA, Commonwealth. Member: International Society of Industrial Relations, UK Society of Industrial Tutors, Manchester Industrial Relations Society; Founder, European Foundation for Social Partnership and Continuing Training Initiatives; Secretary, House of Commons Football Team; Member: Society of International Industrial Relations,

UK China Forum (Industry Group); Executive Member, Great Britain-China Centre; *Publications: Youth Unemployment and Government Training Strategies*, 1981; Visiting fellow, Salford University; *Recreations:* Tai-Chi, painting, research into philosophical religious and life systems, scientific and medical developments. *Address:* Ian Stewart Esq, MP, House of Commons, London, SW1A 0AA *Tel:* 020 7219 6175 *Fax:* 020 7219 0903. *Constituency:* Eccles Parliamentary Office, Eccles Town Hall, Church Street, Eccles, Greater Manchester, M30 0EL *Tel:* 0161–707 4688 *Fax:* 0161–789 8065 *E-mail:* ianstewartmp@parliament.uk.

PAUL STINCHCOMBE   Wellingborough   Lab majority 187

Born 25 April 1962; Son of Lionel and Pauline Stinchcombe; Educated High Wycombe Royal Grammar School; Trinity College, Cambridge (BA law, MA); Harvard Law School, USA (LLM); Married July 7, 1990, Suzanne Gardiner (2 sons 1 daughter). Barrister, specialising in environmental law and judicial review; Member: GMB, MSF. London Borough of Camden: Councillor 1990–94, Chair Labour Group 1992–94; Member, Board of Management: Arlington House 1990–91, Central London Law Centre 1990–94, Member, Board of Trustees, Prison Reform Trust, Member, Council of Justice. **House of Commons:** Member for Wellingborough since May 1, 1997; *Select Committees:* Member: Procedure 1997–99; Member: Home Affairs 1998–. *Special Interests:* Environment, Civil Liberties, Home Affairs; Kenya, India, Philippines. Member: Christian Socialist Movement, Society of Labour Lawyers; Labour Planning and Environment Group: Executive Committee Member 1997–2000, Chair 2000–. Member: Friends of the Earth, Liberty; *Publications: Law Reform For All*, 1996; Senior Scholar, Trinity College, Cambridge; Frank Knox Fellow, Harvard Law School; *Recreations:* Football, cricket, golf. *Address:* Paul Stinchcombe Esq, MP, House of Commons, London, SW1A 0AA *Tel:* 020 7219 4066. *Constituency:* Queen Anne House, 29 High Street, Wellingborough, Northamptonshire, NN8 4JZ *Tel:* 01933 279022 *Fax:* 01933 279029.

DR HOWARD STOATE   Dartford   Lab majority 4,328

Born 14 April 1954; Son of Alvan Stoate, retired engineer, and Maisie Stoate, retired teacher; Educated Kingston Grammar School; Kings College, London University (MSc, DRCOG); Married September 22, 1979, Deborah Dunkerley (2 sons). Junior hospital doctor 1977–81; GP, Bexley Heath 1982–; GP tutor, Queen Mary's Hospital, Sidcup 1989–; Chair, Bexley Ethics Research Committee 1995–97; Member: MPU, MSF. Councillor, Dartford Borough Council 1990–99, Chair, Finance and Corporate Business 1995–99. **House of Commons:** Member for Dartford since May 1, 1997; *Select Committees:* Member: Health 1997–. *Special Interests:* Health, Education, Environment; Spain. Vice-Chair, DCLP 1984–91; Chair, LP Branch 1985–97; Vice-Chair, Dartford Fabian Society. Governor, Dartford Grammar School 1996–; Vice-Chair, Regional Graduate Education Board 1997–; Member, British Medical Association; *Publications:* Many medical publications, particularly on health screening; MBBS Msc FRCGP; *Sportsclubs:* Emsworth Sailing Club; *Recreations:* Running, sailing, reading, music. *Address:* Dr Howard Stoate, MP, House of Commons, London, SW1A 0AA *Tel:* 020 7219 4571 *Fax:* 020 7219 6820. *Constituency:* Civic Centre, Home Gardens, Dartford, Kent, DA1 1DR *Tel:* 01322 343234 *Fax:* 01322 343235 *E-mail:* stoateh@parliament.co.uk.

GAVIN STRANG   Edinburgh East and Musselburgh   Lab majority 14,530

Born 10 July 1943; Son of James S. Strang, tenant farmer; Educated Morrison's Academy; Edinburgh University (BSc 1964); Churchill College, Cambridge University (DipAgriSci); Edinburgh University (PhD); Married August 1973, Bettina Morrison, née Smith (1 son, 2 stepsons). Member, Tayside Economic Planning Consultative Group 1966–68; Scientist, Agricultural Research Council 1968–70; Member, TGWU. **House of Commons:** Member for Edinburgh East 1970–97, and for Edinburgh East and Musselburgh since May 1, 1997; Opposition Front Bench Spokesman on: Agriculture 1979–82, Employment 1987–89, Food, Agriculture and Rural Affairs 1992–97; Parliamentary Under-Secretary of State for Energy February-October 1974;

Parliamentary Secretary to Ministry of Agriculture 1974–79; Minister of State (in Cabinet), Department of the Environment, Transport and the Regions (Minister for Transport) 1997–98; *Select Committees:* Member: Agriculture, Science and Technology, Scottish Affairs. *Special Interests:* Agriculture, Transport, Fisheries, AIDS; Europe. PC 1997; *Recreations:* Swimming, golf, watching football, walking in the countryside. *Address:* Rt Hon Gavin Strang, MP, House of Commons, London, SW1A 0AA *Tel:* 020 7219 3000. *Constituency:* 54 Portobello High Street, Edinburgh, EH15 1DA *Tel:* 0131–669 6002 *E-mail:* strangg@parliament.uk.

JACK STRAW Blackburn — *Lab majority 14,451*

Born 3 August 1946; Son of Walter Arthur Straw; Educated Brentwood School; Leeds University (LLB 1967); Inns of Court School of Law 1972; Married November 10, 1978, Alice Perkins (1 son 1 daughter). President, National Union of Students 1969–71; Called to the Bar, Inner Temple 1972; Special adviser: to Barbara Castle, MP as Secretary of State for Social Services 1974–76, to Peter Shore, MP as Secretary of State for the Environment 1976–77; Member, staff of Granada Television *World in Action* 1977–79; Elected Master of Bench of the Inner Temple 1997; Member, GMB. Councillor, Islington Borough Council 1971–74; ILEA: Member 1971–74, Deputy Leader 1973. **House of Commons:** Contested Tonbridge and Malling February 1974 general election. Member for Blackburn since May 1979; Opposition Front Bench Spokesman on: Treasury and Economic Affairs 1980–83, Environment 1983–87; Shadow Education Secretary 1987–92; Shadow Environment Secretary 1992–94; Shadow Home Secretary 1994–97; Home Secretary 1997–; *Special Interests:* Education, Tax, Economic Policy, Local Government, Police, European Union. Member, Labour Party National Executive Committee 1994–95. Member of Council, Lancaster University 1989–92; Governor: Blackburn College 1990–, Pimlico School 1994–, Chair 1995–98; Joint Vice-Chair, British-American Parliamentary International Group 1999–; *Publications: Policy and Ideology*, 1993; PC 1997; Visiting fellow, Nuffield College, Oxford 1990–98; Hon. LLD, Leeds University 1999; Fellow, Royal Statistical Society 1995–; *Sportsclubs:* Vice-President, Blackburn Rovers FC 1998; *Recreations:* Cooking, walking, music, watching Blackburn Rovers. *Address:* Rt Hon Jack Straw, MP, House of Commons, London, SW1A 0AA *Tel:* 020 7219 3000. *Constituency:* Richmond Chambers, Richmond Road, Blackburn, BB1 7AS *Tel:* 01254 52317 *Fax:* 01254 682213.

GARY STREETER South West Devon — *Con majority 7,397*

Born 2 October 1955; Son of Kenneth and Shirley Streeter; Educated Tiverton Grammar School; King's College, London (LLB); Married July 15, 1978, Janet Vanessa Stevens (1 son 1 daughter). Solicitor; Partner, Foot and Bowden, Plymouth 1984–98, specialist in company and employment law. Plymouth City Council: Councillor 1986–92, Chairman, Housing Committee 1989–91. **House of Commons:** Member for Plymouth Sutton 1992–97, and for South West Devon since May 1, 1997; Opposition Spokesman on: Foreign Affairs 1997–98, Europe 1997–98; Assistant Government Whip 1995–96; PPS: to Sir Derek Spencer as Solicitor General 1993–95, to Sir Nicholas Lyell as Attorney-General 1994–95; Parliamentary Secretary, Lord Chancellor's Department 1996–97; Shadow Secretary of State for International Development 1998–; *Select Committees:* Member: Environment 1992–93. *Special Interests:* Law and Order, Family Moral and Social Issues, Developing World. *Recreations:* Watching cricket and rugby, family. *Address:* Gary Streeter Esq, MP, House of Commons, London, SW1A 0AA *Tel:* 020 7219 4070 *Fax:* 020 7219 2414 *Tel (Constituency):* 01752 335666 *Fax (Constituency):* 01752 338401 *E-mail:* garystreeter@compuserve.com.

Visit the Vacher Dod Website . . .
www.politicallinks.co.uk

GRAHAM STRINGER   Manchester Blackley   *Lab majority 19,588*

Born 17 February 1950; Son of late Albert Stringer, railway clerk, and Brenda Stringer, shop assistant; Educated Moston Brook High School; Sheffield University (BSc chemistry 1971); Married Kathryn. Analytical chemist; Chair of Board, Manchester Airport plc 1996–97; Branch officer and shop steward, MSF. Councillor, Manchester City Council 1979–98, Leader 1984–96. **House of Commons:** Member for Manchester Blackley since May 1, 1997; Parliamentary Secretary, Cabinet Office 1999–; *Select Committees:* Member: Environment, Transport and Regional Affairs 1997–99, Transport Sub-Committee 1997–99. Hon. RNCM; *Sportsclubs:* Member: Manchester Tennis and Racquet Club, Cheetham Hill Cricket Club. *Address:* Graham Stringer Esq, MP, House of Commons, London, SW1A 0AA *Tel:* 020 7219 6055 *Tel (Constituency):* 0161–202 6600 *Fax (Constituency):* 0161–202 6626 *E-mail:* gstringer@cabinet-office.x.gsi.gov.uk.

GISELA STUART   Birmingham Edgbaston   *Lab majority 4,842*

Born 26 November 1955; Daughter of late Martin Gschaider and Liane Krompholz; Educated Realschule Vilsbiburg; Manchester Polytechnic; London University (LLB); Married 1980, Robert Scott Stuart (divorced 2000) (2 sons). Deputy Director, London Book Fair 1983; Translator; Lawyer and lecturer, Worcester College of Technology and Birmingham University 1992–1997. **House of Commons:** Member for Birmingham Edgbaston since May 1, 1997; PPS to Paul Boateng as Minister of State, Home Office 1998–99; Parliamentary Under-Secretary of State, Department of Health 1999–; *Select Committees:* Member: Social Security 1997–98. *Special Interests:* Manufacturing, Pension Law. *Address:* Gisela Stuart, MP, House of Commons, London, SW1A 0AA *Tel:* 020 7219 5051. *Constituency:* 7 Tudor Eaves, Harborne Park Road, Birmingham, B17 0DE *Tel:* 0121–428 5011 *Fax:* 0121–428 5073.

ANDREW STUNELL   Hazel Grove   *LD majority 11,814*

Born 24 November 1942; Son of late Robert George Stunell and Trixie Stunell; Educated Surbiton Grammar School; Manchester University; Liverpool Polytechnic (RIBA Part III); Married July 29, 1967, Gillian Chorley (3 sons 2 daughters). Architectural assistant: CWS Manchester 1965–67, Runcorn New Town 1967–81; Freelance architectural assistant 1981–85; Various posts including political secretary, Association of Liberal Democrat Councillors (ALDC) 1985–87, Head of Service 1989–96; Member, NALGO: New Towns Whitley Council 1977–81. Councillor: Chester City Council 1979–90, Cheshire County Council 1981–91, Stockport Metropolitan Borough Council 1994–. **House of Commons:** Contested City of Chester 1979, 1983, 1987, Hazel Grove 1992 general elections. Member for Hazel Grove since May 1, 1997; Spokesman for: Environment and Transport 1997–98, Energy 1997–; Deputy Chief Whip 1997–; *Select Committees:* Member: Broadcasting 1997–2000; Member: Modernisation of the House of Commons 1997–, Procedure 1997–, Unopposed Bills (Panel) 1997–, Standing Orders 1998–. *Special Interests:* Local Democracy, Third World, Race Relations, Energy, Climate Change. Various local and national party offices 1977–. Member: United Nations Association 1959–, Romiley Methodist Church; President, Goyt Valley Rail Users Association; Vice-Chair, Association of County Councils 1985–90; Vice-President, Local Government Association 1997–; *Publications: Life In The Balance,* 1986; *Budgeting For Real,* 1984, 2nd edition 1994, 3rd edition 1999; *Thriving In The Balance,* 1995; *Open Active & Effective,* 1995; *Local Democracy Guaranteed,* 1996; *Energy – Clean and Green to 2050,* 1999; OBE 1995; *Recreations:* Theoretical astronomy, camping, table tennis. *Address:* Andrew Stunell Esq, OBE, MP, House of Commons, London, SW1A 0AA *Tel:* 020 7219 5223 *Fax:* 020 7219 2302. *Constituency:* Liberal Democrat HQ, 68A Compstall Road, Romiley, Stockport, Greater Manchester, SK6 4DE *Tel:* 0161–406 7070 *Fax:* 0161–494 2425.

GERRY SUTCLIFFE   Bradford South   *Lab majority 12,936*

Born 13 May 1953; Son of Henry and Margaret Sutcliffe; Educated Cardinal Hinsley Grammar School, Bradford; Married October 14, 1972, Maria Holgate (3 sons). Salesperson 1969–72; Display advertising, *Bradford Telegraph and Argus* 1972–75; Field printers, Bradford 1975–80; Deputy Branch Secretary, SOGAT/GPMU 1980–94; Member: Yorkshire and Humberside Trade Union Friends of Labour, Regional TUC. Bradford City Council: Councillor 1982–94, Leader 1992–94. **House of Commons:** Member for Bradford South since by-election June 9, 1994; Assistant Government Whip (Cabinet office: Yorkshire South) 1999–; PPS to Harriet Harman as Secretary of State for Social Security and Minister for Women 1997–98; PPS to Stephen Byers: as Chief Secretary, HM Treasury July-December 1998, as Secretary of State for Trade and Industry 1999; *Select Committees:* Member: Public Accounts 1996–98, Unopposed Bills (Panel) 1997–99. *Special Interests:* Employment, Local Government; Pakistan, Bangladesh, India, European Union. Member, Regional Labour Party Executive; Vice-Chair, Yorkshire Regional Group of Labour MPs 1997–. School governor; Director: Bradford TEC, Yorkshire Enterprise Ltd; Member: Friends of the Earth, Amnesty International; *Recreations:* Sport, music. *Address:* Gerry Sutcliffe Esq, MP, House of Commons, London, SW1A 0AA *Tel:* 020 7219 3247. *Constituency:* 3rd Floor, 76 Kirkgate, Bradford BD1 1SZ *Tel:* 01274 400007 *Fax:* 01274 400020 *E-mail:* sutcliffeg@parliament.uk.

DESMOND SWAYNE   New Forest West   *Con majority 11,332*

Born 20 August 1956; Son of George Joseph Swayne and Elisabeth McAlister Swayne, née Gibson; Educated Drumley House, Ayrshire; Bedford School; St Mary's College, St Andrews University (MA theology); Married August 8, 1987, Moira Cecily Teek (1 son 2 daughters). Major, Territorial Army; Schoolmaster, 'A' Level Economics: Charterhouse 1980–81, Wrekin College 1982–87; Manager, Risk Management Systems, Royal Bank of Scotland 1988–96. **House of Commons:** Contested Pontypridd 1987, West Bromwich West 1992 general elections. Member for New Forest West since May 1, 1997; *Select Committees:* Member: Scottish Affairs 1997–, Social Security 1999–. Member, British Field Sports Society; *Clubs:* Cavalry and Guards; *Sportsclubs:* Serpentine Swimming Club; *Recreations:* Territorial Army. *Address:* Desmond Swayne Esq, MP, House of Commons, London, SW1A 0AA *Tel:* 020 7219 3544. *Constituency:* 4 Cliff Crescent, Marine Drive, Barton-on-Sea, New Milton, Hampshire, BH25 7EB *Tel:* 023 8081 4554 *Fax:* 023 8081 2019.

JOHN SWINNEY   North Tayside   *SNP majority 4,160*

Born 13 April 1964; Son of Kenneth Swinney, garage manager, and Nancy Swinney; Educated Forrester High School, Edinburgh; Edinburgh University (MA politics 1986); Married November 30, 1991, Lorna Ann King (1 son 1 daughter) (separated 1998). Managing consultant, Development Options Ltd 1987–92; Strategic planning principal, Scottish Amicable 1992–97. **House of Commons:** Member for North Tayside since May 1, 1997; Spokesman for Economy, Social Security and Agriculture 1997–; *Special Interests:* Economic Policy, Housing, Enterprise, Further and Higher Education; Eastern Europe; Member European Standing Committee C 1999. SNP: National secretary 1986–92, Vice-convenor publicity 1992–97, Treasury spokesperson 1995–99, Senior vice-convenor 1998–2000, National convenor 2000–. *Recreations:* Hill-walking, reading, music. *Address:* John Swinney Esq, MP, MSP, House of Commons, London, SW1A 0AA *Tel:* 020 7219 6581 *Fax:* 020 7219 3960. *Constituency:* 35 Perth Street, Blairgowrie, PH10 6DL *Tel:* 01250 876576 *Fax:* 01250 876991 *E-mail:* jsmp.blairg@snp.org.uk; john.swinney.msp@scottish.parliament.uk.

ROBERT SYMS Poole — *Con majority 5,298*

Born 15 August 1956; Son of Raymond Syms, builder, and Mary Syms, teacher; Educated Colston's School, Bristol; Married 1st 1991, Nicola Guy (divorced 1999); married 2nd 2000, Fiona Mcllersh (1 daughter). Managing director, family building, plant hire and property group, based in Chippenham, Wiltshire. Councillor: North Wiltshire District Council 1983–87, Wiltshire County Council 1985–97; Member, Wessex Regional Health Authority 1988–90. **House of Commons:** Contested Walsall North 1992 general election. Member for Poole since May 1, 1997; Opposition Front Bench Spokesman for Environment, Transport and Regions 1999–; PPS to Michael Ancram as Chair Conservative Party 1999–2000; *Select Committees:* Member: Procedure 1998–99; Member: Health 1997–. *Special Interests:* Economic Policy, Constitution, Local Government; USA, most of English speaking world. North Wiltshire Conservative Association: Treasurer 1982–84, Deputy Chair 1983–84, Chair 1984–86. Member, North Wiltshire Enterprise Agency 1986–90; Member, Calne Development Project Trust 1986–97; *Recreations:* Reading, music. *Address:* Robert Syms Esq, MP, House of Commons, London, SW1A 0AA *Tel:* 020 7219 4601. *Constituency:* Poole Conservative Association, 38 Sandbanks Road, Poole, Dorset, BH14 8BX *Tel:* 01202 739922 *Fax:* 01202 739944.

T

SIR PETER TAPSELL Louth and Horncastle — *Con majority 6,900*

Born 1 February 1930; Son of late Eustace Tapsell and late Jessie Tapsell (née Hannay); Educated Tonbridge School; Merton College, Oxford (BA modern history 1953, MA); Diploma in Economics 1954; Married 1st, 1963, Hon. Cecilia Hawke, daughter of 9th Baron Hawke (divorced 1971) (1 son), married 2nd, 1974, Gabrielle Mahieu. Army national service 1948–50; Life member, 6th Squadron RAF (non-flying); Conservative Research Department 1954–57; Personal assistant to Sir Anthony Eden MP during 1955 general election campaign; Member, London Stock Exchange 1957–90; Adviser to central banks and international companies 1960–; Partner, James Capel and Co 1960–90. **House of Commons:** Contested Wednesbury February 1957 by-election. Member for Nottingham West 1959–64, for Horncastle 1966–83, for Lindsey East 1983–97, and for Louth and Horncastle since May 1, 1997; Opposition Front Bench Spokesman on: Foreign and Commonwealth Affairs 1976–77, Treasury and Economic Affairs 1977–78; *Special Interests:* Foreign Affairs, Economics and Finance. Council Member, Institute of Fiscal Studies; Vice-President, Tennyson Society; Member, Trilateral Commission 1979–98; Hon Deputy Chair, Mitsubishi Trust Oxford Foundation; Brunei Dato 1971; Knighted 1985; Spectator Backbencher of the Year 1993; Honorary Postmaster, Merton College, Oxford 1953; Honorary Fellow, Merton College, Oxford 1989; *Clubs:* Athenaeum, Carlton, Hurlingham; *Recreations:* Overseas travel, walking, reading, history. *Address:* Sir Peter Tapsell, MP, House of Commons, London, SW1A 0AA *Tel:* 020 7219 4409. *Constituency:* Cannon Street House, Cannon Street, Louth, Lincolnshire *Tel:* 01507 603713 *Fax:* 01507 602154.

ANN TAYLOR Dewsbury — *Lab majority 8,323*

Born 2 July 1947; Daughter of late John Walker and Doreen Bowling; Educated Bolton School; Bradford and Sheffield Universities; Married October 28, 1966, David Taylor (1 son 1 daughter). Part-time tutor, Open University; Monitoring officer, Housing Corporation 1985–87; Member: Association of University Teachers GMB. Holmfirth UDC 1972–74. **House of Commons:** Contested Bolton West February 1974 general election. Member for Bolton West October 1974–83, contested Bolton North East 1983 general election. Member for Dewsbury since June 1987; Opposition Front Bench Spokesman on: Education 1979–81, Housing 1981–83, Home Office 1987–88, Environment 1988–92; Citizen's Charter 1994–95; Government Whip 1977–79; Government Chief Whip

(Parliamentary Secretary, HM Treasury) 1998–; PPS: to Fred Mulley as Secretary of State for Education and Science 1975–76, as Secretary of State for Defence 1976–77; Shadow Secretary of State for Education 1992–94; Shadow Chancellor of the Duchy of Lancaster 1994–95; Shadow Leader of the House 1994–97; President of the Council and Leader of the House of Commons 1997–98; *Select Committees:* Member: Standards and Privileges 1995–97; Chairman: Modernisation of the House of Commons 1997–98; Member: Parliamentary Privilege (Joint Committee) 1997–. *Special Interests:* Education, Housing, Health, Home Office. Member: House of Commons Commission 1994–98, Public Accounts Commission 1997–98; *Publications: Choosing Our Future – Practical Politics of the Environment,* 1992; PC 1997; Hon. Fellow, Birkbeck College, London University; Hon. Doctorate, Bradford University. *Address:* Rt Hon Ann Taylor, MP, House of Commons, London, SW1A 0AA *Tel:* 020 7219 4400. *Constituency:* Dewsbury Business and Media Centre, Wellington Road East, Dewsbury, West Yorkshire, WF13 1HF *Tel:* 01924 324999 *Fax:* 01924 324998.

DARI TAYLOR   Stockton South   *Lab majority 11,585*

Born 13 December 1944; Daughter of late Daniel Jones, MP for Burnley 1959–83, and late Phyllis Jones; Educated Ynyshir Girls' School; Burnley Municipal College; Nottingham University (BA); Durham University (MA); Married July 18, 1970, David E Taylor (1 daughter). Assistant lecturer, Basford College of Further Education 1970; Lecturer, Westbridgeford College of Further Education; Lecturer (PT), North Tyneside College of Further Education 1986; General Municipal and Boilermakers: Research Support 1990, Regional Education Officer, Northern Region 1993; Regional/Local Representative NATFHE; Member, General Municipal and Boilermakers (GMB); Trade Union Support and Information Unit. Councillor, Sunderland Metropolitan Council 1986–97. **House of Commons:** Member for Stockton South since May 1, 1997; *Select Committees:* Member: Defence 1997–99. *Special Interests:* Economic Policy, Industry, Education, Housing; Europe, Africa, USA. Vice-Chair, Labour Women's Committee; Leadership Campaign Team. Member, Domestic Violence Multi-Agency; Supporter: NSPCC, NSPCA, Children's Society; *Recreations:* Choral singing, walking, travelling. *Address:* Dari Taylor, MP, House of Commons, London, SW1A 0AA *Tel:* 020 7219 4608. *Constituency:* The Old Town Hall, Mandale Road, Thornaby on Tees, TS17 6AW *Tel:* 01642 604546 *Fax:* 01642 608395.

DAVID TAYLOR   North West Leicestershire   *Lab majority 13,219*

Born 22 August 1946; Son of late Leslie Taylor, civil servant, and Eileen Mary Taylor, retired postal worker; Educated Ashby-de-la-Zouch Boys Grammar School; Leicester Polytechnic; Lanchester Polytechnic (Chartered Public Finance Accountant 1970); Open University (BA maths and computing 1974); Married September 13, 1969, Pamela Caunt (4 daughters 1 son deceased). Accountant and Computer Manager, Leicestershire County Council 1977–97; Department steward and auditor, NALGO (now UNISON) 1985–97. Councillor, North West Leicestershire District Council 1981–87, 1992–95; Councillor, Heather Parish Council 1987–, Chair 1996–97; JP, Ashby-de-la-Zouch 1985. **House of Commons:** Contested North West Leicestershire 1992 general election. Member for North West Leicestershire since May 1, 1997; *Select Committees:* Sub-Committee Staff: Environment Sub-Committee –; Member: Modernisation of the House of Commons 1999–. *Special Interests:* Housing, Low Pay, Rural Affairs, Environment, Safer Communities (Crime), CCTV; France. Member, Labour Campaign for Electoral Reform. Member: CPRE, Greenpeace; Member, Chartered Institute of Public Finance and Accountancy (Prize Winner in Accountancy Final Exams); *Clubs:* Ibstock Working Mens; Coalville Labour, Hugglescote; *Sportsclubs:* President, Heather Sparkenhoe Cricket Club; *Recreations:* Running, Cycling. *Address:* David Taylor Esq, MP, House of Commons, London, SW1A 0AA *Tel:* 020 7219 4567 *Fax:* 020 7219 6808. *Constituency:* Labour Office, 17 Hotel Street, Coalville, Leicestershire, LE67 3EQ *Tel:* 01530 814372 *Fax:* 01530 813833 *E-mail:* taylordl@parliament.uk.

IAN TAYLOR   Esher and Walton   Con majority 14,528

Born 18 April 1945; Son of late Horace Stanley Taylor and late Beryl Harper; Educated Whitley Abbey School, Coventry; Keele University (BA economics, politics and modern history 1967); LSE (research scholar); Married 1974, Hon. Carole Alport (2 sons). Director, Mathercourt Securities Ltd 1980–91; Corporate Finance Consultant; Director of technology companies 1997–. **House of Commons:** Contested Coventry South East 1974 general election. Member for Esher 1987–97, and for Esher and Walton since May 1, 1997; Opposition Spokesman on Northern Ireland June-November 1997; PPS to William Waldegrave as: Minister of State, Foreign and Commonwealth Office 1988–90, as Secretary of State for Health 1990 92, as Chancellor of the Duchy of Lancaster, Minister for Public Services and Science 1992–94; Parliamentary Under Secretary of State, Department of Trade and Industry (Minister for Science and Technology) 1994–97; *Select Committees:* Member: Foreign Affairs 1987–89; Member: Science and Technology 1998–. *Special Interests:* European Union, Economy, Science and Technology; Former Soviet Union, France, Germany, Middle East, Scandinavia, USA. National Chair, Federation of Conservative Students 1968–69; Chair, European Union of Christian Democratic and Conservative Students 1969–70; Member, Conservative National Union Executive and other national committees 1966–75, 1990–95; National Chair, Conservative Group for Europe 1985–88; Vice-Chair, Association of Conservative Clubs 1988–92; Chair, Conservative Foreign and Commonwealth Council 1990–95. Chair, Commonwealth Youth Exchange Council 1980–84, Vice-President 1984–; Patron, UK Centre for European Education 1991–94; Governor, Westminster Foundation for Democracy 1992–94; Member, Royal Society for International Affairs; Governor, Research into Ageing 1997–; Council Member, Anglo-German Foundation 1999–; Governor for British Association for Central and Eastern Europe 1997–2000; Member, Finance Bill Standing Committees 1987–94; Board Member, Parliamentary Office of Science and Technology (POST) 1997–; Council Member, Parliamentary Information Technology Committee; Director, EURIM (European Informatics Market) 1999–; Vice-Chair, European Movement; Trustee, Painshill Park Trust 1998–; Worshipful Company of Information Technologists 1998–; *Publications: Fair Shares for all the Workers,* 1988; *Releasing the Community Spirit – The Active Citizen,* 1990; *A Community of Employee Shareholders,* 1992; *The Positive Europe,* 1993; *Escaping the Protectionist Trap,* 1995; *Net-Working,* 1996; *Conservative Tradition in Europe,* 1996; *Science, Government and Society,* 1998; MBE 1974; Associate, Institute of Investment Management and Research 1972–; *Clubs:* Carlton, Molesey Working Men's, Walton Conservative, IOD; *Recreations:* Country walks, shooting, cigars. *Address:* Ian Taylor Esq, MBE, MP, House of Commons, London, SW1A 0AA *Tel:* 020 7219 5221 *Fax:* 020 7219 5492. *Constituency:* 74A Church Street, Weybridge, Surrey, KT13 8DL *Tel:* 01932 843314 *Fax:* 01932 854246 *E-mail:* taylori@parliament.uk *Website:* http://www.political.co.uk/iantaylor.

JOHN D TAYLOR   Strangford   UUP majority 5,852

Born 24 December 1937; Son of late George David Taylor, architect, and late Georgina Taylor (née Baird); Educated Royal School, Armagh; Queen's University, Belfast (BSc Applied science and technology 1950); Eastern Mediterranean University (PLA international relations 1999); Married December 30, 1970, Mary Frances Todd (1 son 5 daughters). Company director; Chairman, Alpha Newspaper Group; MP (South Tyrone) Stormont 1965–73; Parliamentary Secretary, Ministry of Home Affairs, Northern Ireland 1969–70; Minister of State, Home Affairs 1970–72; Member: for Fermanagh and South Tyrone, Northern Ireland Assembly 1973–75, for North Down, Northern Ireland Constitutional Convention 1976–77, for North Down, Northern Ireland Assembly 1982–86; MEP (Northern Ireland) 1979–89; Northern Ireland Forum 1996–98; New Northern Ireland Assembly 1998–. Leader, Ulster Unionists in Castlereagh Borough Council 1989–94. **House of Commons:** Member for Strangford since June 1983; Spokesman for: Trade and Industry 1992–97, Foreign and Commonwealth Affairs 1997–; *Select Committees:* Member: Northern Ireland Affairs 1994–97. *Special Interests:* Irish Politics, European Union, Regional Policy, Agriculture; Asia, Cyprus, Gibraltar, Ireland, Turkey, Taiwan. Chair: Queen's University Conservative and Unionist Association 1959–60, Ulster Young Unionist Council 1961–62; Hon. Secretary, Ulster Unionist Party 1994–96, Deputy Leader 1995–. Chair, Gosford Housing Association; Member, Board of

Charles Sheils Charity Homes; Governor, The Royal School, Armagh; Member for Northern Ireland, European Parliament 1979–89; Member: Council of Europe 1998–, Western European Union 1998–; *Publications: Ulster – The Economic Facts*; PC (Northern Ireland) 1970; AMICEI; AMInstHE; *Clubs:* Farmers (London), County (Armagh); *Sportsclubs:* Ards Football Club; *Recreations:* Antiques, Irish Art, Travelling, Horticulture. *Address:* Rt Hon John David Taylor, MP, House of Commons, London, SW1A 0AA *Tel:* 020 7931 7211 *Fax:* 020 7219 4536. *Constituency:* 6 William Street, Newtownards, BT23 4AE *Tel:* 028 9181 4123 *Fax:* 028 9181 4123.

JOHN M TAYLOR   Solihull   *Con majority 11,397*

Born 19 August 1941; Son of late Wilfred and Eileen Martha Taylor; Educated Bromsgrove School; College of Law. Senior Partner, John Taylor & Co., Solicitors; MEP for Midlands East 1979–84. Councillor, Solihull County Borough Council 1971–74; West Midlands County Council: Councillor 1973–86, Leader of Opposition 1975–77, Leader of Council 1977–79; Member, West Midland Economic Planning Council 1977–79. **House of Commons:** Contested Dudley East February and October 1974 general elections. Member for Solihull since June 1983; Opposition Front Bench Spokesman on Northern Ireland 1999–; Assistant Government Whip 1988–89; Government Whip 1989–92; Opposition Whip 1997–99; PPS to Kenneth Clarke: as Chancellor of the Duchy of Lancaster and Minister for, Trade and Industry 1987–88; Parliamentary Secretary, Lord Chancellor's Department 1992–95; Parliamentary Under-Secretary of State, Department of Trade and Industry 1995–97; *Special Interests:* Environment, European Union, Care of Ancient Monuments, Legal Affairs, Trade and Industry; USA. Member, Conservative Friends of Israel. Chair, Solihull Business Enterprise; President, Shirley Citizens' Advice Bureau; President, Oakenshaw Association; Founder chair, Solihull Institute for Medical Training and Research; Life member, English Heritage; Shoreline (Life) member, RNLI; Association of Metropolitan Authorities: Deputy Chair 1978–79, Vice-President 1979–; European Parliament 1979–84: Group Budget Spokesman 1979–81, Group Deputy Chair 1981–82, Council of Europe and WEU 1997–; Life Member, National Trust; *Clubs:* Carlton, MCC; *Sportsclubs:* Bromsgrove Martlets Cricket Club, Hampton-in-Arden Cricket Club, Olton Cricket Club, Olton Golf Club, Warwickshire County Cricket Club; *Recreations:* Fellowship, cricket, golf, reading. *Address:* John M Taylor Esq, MP, House of Commons, London, SW1A 0AA *Tel:* 020 7219 4146 *Fax:* 020 7219 1243. *Constituency:* Northampton House, Poplar Road, Solihull, West Midlands, B91 3AW *Tel:* 0121–704 3071 *Fax:* 0121–705 6388.

MATTHEW TAYLOR   Truro and St Austell   *LD majority 12,501*

Born 3 January 1963; Son of Ken and Jill Taylor; Educated Treliske School, Truro; University College School, London; Lady Margaret Hall, Oxford. President, Oxford University Student Union 1985–86; Economic researcher to David Penhaligan, MP 1986. **House of Commons:** Member for Truro March 12, 1987 by-election –1997 and for Truro and St Austell since May 1, 1997; Liberal Spokesman for Energy 1987–88; Liberal Democrat Spokesman for: England (Local Government, Housing and Transport) 1988–89, Trade and Industry 1989–90, Education 1990–92, Citizen's Charter 1992–94; Principal Spokesman for: Environment 1994–97, the Environment and Transport 1997–99, Economy 1999–; *Select Committees:* Member: Broadcasting 1992–94, Environment 1995–97, Environmental Audit 1997. Chair, Liberal Democrat Campaigns and Communications 1989–95. *Address:* Matthew Taylor Esq, MP, House of Commons, London, SW1A 0AA *Tel:* 020 7219 6686. *Constituency:* Liberal Democrats, 10 South Street, St Austell, Cornwall, PL25 5BH *E-mail:* frigerioa@parliament.uk.

Visit the Vacher Dod Website . . .
www.politicallinks.co.uk

SIR TEDDY TAYLOR   Rochford and Southend East   *Con majority 4,225*

Born 18 April 1937; Son of late Edward Taylor; Educated The High School of Glasgow; Glasgow University (MA economics and politics 1958); Married December 12, 1970, Sheila Duncan (2 sons 1 daughter). Commercial editorial staff, *Glasgow Herald* October 1958-April 1959; Industrial relations officer, Clyde Shipbuilders' Association 1959–1964. Councillor, Glasgow Town Council 1959–64. **House of Commons:** Contested Glasgow Springburn 1959 general election. Member for Glasgow Cathcart 1964–79, for Southend East from March 15, 1980 by-election–1997, and for Rochford and Southend East since May 1, 1997; Shadow Spokesman on: Trade 1977, Scottish Affairs 1977–79; Parliamentary Under-Secretary of State, Scottish Office 1970–71 (resigned over Government decision to join EC) and 1974; *Select Committees:* Member: Treasury 1997–, Treasury Sub-Committee 1998–. *Special Interests:* Temperance Movement, Common Market, Home Affairs, Environment; Libya, Pakistan. *Publications: Hearts of Stone* (novel), 1970; Knighted 1991; *Recreations:* Golf, chess, history. *Address:* Sir Teddy Taylor, MP, House of Commons, London, SW1A 0AA *Tel:* 020 7219 3000. *Constituency:* Suite 1, Strand House, 742 Southchurch Road, Southend, Essex, SS1 2PS *Tel:* 01702 600460 *Fax:* 01702 600460 *E-mail:* dayea@parliament.uk.

PETER TEMPLE-MORRIS   Leominster   *Con majority 8,835**

Born 12 February 1938; Son of late His Hon. Sir Owen Temple-Morris, QC; Educated Malvern College; St. Catharine's College, Cambridge (MA); Married July 25, 1964, Tahere, daughter of His Excellency Senator Khozeime Alam, of Tehran (2 sons 2 daughters). Barrister, Inner Temple 1962; Solicitor 1989–; Member, GMB. **House of Commons:** Contested Newport 1964 and 1966, Norwood Lambeth 1970 general elections. *Conservative Member for Leominster February 1974-October 1997, Independent Member October 1997-June 1998, Labour Member since October 1998; PPS to Norman Fowler as Minister of Transport 1979; *Select Committees:* Member: Consolidation Bills (Joint Committee) 1991–92. *Special Interests:* Foreign Affairs, Irish Affairs, European Union, Constitutional and Legal Affairs; Europe, Hong Kong, Iran, Ireland, Middle East, Russia, USA, South Africa. Chair: Cambridge University Conservative Association 1961, Bow Group Standing Committee on Home Affairs 1975–80, Society of Conservative Lawyers, Executive Committee 1995–97. Member, Cambridge Afro-Asian Expedition 1961; Chair, Afghanistan Support Committee 1981–82; Member, Academic Council, Wilton Park (FCO) 1990–97; Iran Society Council: Member 1968–80, President 1995–; Chevalier du Tastevin (Chat. de Vougeot) 1988–; Chair, Lords and Commons Solicitors Group 1992–; Jurade De St Emilion 1999–; Executive British Branch of Inter-Parliamentary Union: Member 1977–97, Chair 1982–85, Member, Parliamentary Delegation to United Nations 1980, 1984; Hon. Vice-President, United Nations Association 1987–; Founding Co-Chair, British-Irish Parliamentary Body 1990–97, Member 1997–; Vice-Chair, GB-Russia and Eastern Europe Centre 1993–98; Member, Executive, Commonwealth Parliamentary Association 1994–98; Fellow, Industry and Parliament Trust; Trustee, Eveson Trust; Liveryman, Barbers Companies; *Publications: Motoring Justice,* 1979, plus various articles on foreign affairs and Ireland; Honorary Citizen: New Orleans, Havana, Cuba; Hon. Member, National Party of Australia, Queensland; *Clubs:* Cardiff and County (Cardiff); *Recreations:* Wine and food, travel, family relaxation. *Address:* Peter Temple-Morris Esq, MP, House of Commons, London, SW1A 0AA *Tel:* 020 7219 4181 *Fax:* 020 7219 3801. *Constituency:* 6 West Street, Leominster, Herefordshire, HR6 8ES *Tel:* 01568 616759 *Fax:* 01568 613857 *E-mail:* templemorrist@parliament.uk.

GARETH THOMAS   Clwyd West   Lab majority 1,848

Born 25 September 1954; Educated Rock Ferry High School, Birkenhead; University College of Wales, Aberystwyth (LLB 1976); Council of Legal Education, London 1977; Married December 5, 1987, Sioned Wyn Jones (1 daughter 1 son). Insurance industry in UK and overseas; Formerly loss adjuster: Toplis and Harding Guardian Royal Exchange; Barrister 1986–: Oriel Chambers, Liverpool 1986–99, Arden Chambers, London 1999–, Grays Inn; Member, MSF. Councillor, Flintshire County Council 1995–97. **House of Commons:** Member for Clwyd West since May 1, 1997; *Select Committees:* Member: Welsh Affairs 1997–2000; Member: Social Security 1999–. *Special Interests:* Constitutional Reform, Human Rights, Social Security, Legal Affairs including criminal justice and policing, Agriculture; West Indies, South America. Member: Society of Labour Lawyers, SERA, Fabian Society, Campaign for Electoral Reform. Member: Amnesty International, Oxfam, Local Credit Union, Country Landowners Association Legal and Parliamentary Committee; North Wales Campaign Co-ordinator for Labour Party in 1997 Welsh Referendum; ACII; *Recreations:* Rugby, walking, family, theatre. *Address:* Gareth Thomas Esq, MP (Clwyd West), House of Commons, London, SW1A 0AA *Tel:* 020 7219 3516/2003 *Fax:* 020 7219 1263. *Constituency:* 23a Abergele Road, Colwyn Bay, LL29 7RS *Tel:* 01492 531154 *Fax:* 01492 535731 *E-mail:* thomasg@parliament.uk.

GARETH RICHARD THOMAS   Harrow West   Lab majority 1,240

Born 15 July 1967; Educated Hatch End High School; Lowlands College; University College of Wales, Aberystwyth; King's College, London (BSc economics, MA); University of Greenwich (PGCE). Member, AEEU. Councillor, Harrow 1990–98, Labour Group Whip 1997–98. **House of Commons:** Member for Harrow West since May 1, 1997; PPS to Charles Clarke as Minister of State, Home Office 1999–; *Select Committees:* Member: Environmental Audit 1997–99. *Special Interests:* Health, Social Services, Environment, Renewable Energy; Europe. Member: Fabian Society, SERA; Chair, Co-operative Party 2000–. Vice-Chair, Association of Local Government Social Services Committee; *Clubs:* United Services Club, Pinner; *Recreations:* Canoeing, running, theatre. *Address:* Gareth R Thomas Esq, MP (Harrow West), House of Commons, London, SW1A 0AA *Tel:* 020 7219 6436. *Constituency:* 132 Blenheim Road, West Harrow, Middlesex, HA2 7AA *Tel:* 020 8861 1300.

SIMON THOMAS   Ceredigion   PC majority 4,948

Born 28 December 1963; Educated Aberdare Boys Grammar/Comprehensive School; University College of Wales, Aberystwyth (BA Welsh 1985); College of Librarianship, Aberystwyth (post-graduate diploma 1988); Married Gwen (1 son 1 daughter). Assistant curator National Library of Wales 1986–92; policy and research officer Taff-Ely borough council 1992–94; Rural development manager Jigso rural regeneration agency 1994–2000. Councillor, Ceredigion County Council 1999–2000. **House of Commons:** Member for Ceredigion since By-election February 3, 2000; Plaid Cymru Spokesman for Environment and the Regions; Transport; Education and Employment; International Development; Culture, Media and Sport; Energy 2000–; *Select Committees:* Member: Environmental Audit 2000–. Director for Policy and Research, Plaid Cymru's National Executive 1995–98. *Address:* Simon Thomas Esq, MP, House of Commons, London, SW1A 0AA *Tel:* 020 7219 5021. *Constituency:* 8 Water Street, Aberaeron, Ceredigion, SA46 0DG *Tel:* 01545 571688 *Fax:* 01545 571567 *E-mail:* thomassi@parliament.uk.

WILLIAM THOMPSON   West Tyrone   UUP majority 1,161

Born 26 October 1939; Educated Omagh Academy Grammar School; Married July 26, 1962, Violet Joyce Armstrong (1 son 2 daughters). Tyrone County Council 1957–66; Radio and TV retailer, 1966–. Councillor, Omagh District Council 1981–93. **House of Commons:** Member for West Tyrone since May 1, 1997; Ulster Unionist Spokesman for Agriculture and Local Government 2000–; Member: NI Assembly 1973–74, NI Convention 1975–76, NI Assembly 1982–84; *Select Committees:* Member: Northern Ireland Affairs 2000–. Member, European Standing Committee A 1998–; *Recreations:* Golf, chess, political biography. *Address:* William Thompson Esq, MP, House of Commons, London, SW1A 0AA *Tel:* 020 7219 3553 *Fax:* 020 7219 2347. *Constituency:* Donaghanie Post Office, 156 Donaghanie Road, Beragh, Co Tyrone, Northern Ireland, BT79 0XE *Tel:* 028 8224 5568 *Fax:* 028 8224 5742 *E-mail:* 100552.1524@compuserve.com.

STEPHEN TIMMS   East Ham   Lab majority 19,358

Born 29 July 1955; Son of late Ronald James Timms, engineer, and of Margaret Joyce Timms, retired school teacher; Educated Farnborough Grammar School, Hampshire; Emmanuel College, Cambridge (MA mathematics 1977, MPhil operational research 1978); Married July 26, 1986, Hui-Leng Lim. Computer and telecommunications industry; Logica Ltd 1978–86; Ovum Ltd 1986–94; Member, MSF. Little Ilford Ward, London Borough of Newham: Councillor 1984–97, Leader of the Council 1990–94, Former Chair, Economic Development Committee, Chair, Planning Committee 1987–90; Board Member, East London Partnership 1990–; Stratford Development Partnership 1992–94. **House of Commons:** Member for Newham North East from June 9, 1994 by-election–1997, and for East Ham since May 1, 1997; PPS to Andrew Smith as Minister of State, Department for Education and Employment 1997–98; Joint PPS to Marjorie Mowlam, as Secretary of State for Northern Ireland 1998; Parliamentary Under-Secretary of State, Department of Social Security 1998–99, Minister of State 1999; Financial Secretary, HM Treasury 1999–; *Select Committees:* Member: Treasury 1996–97; Member: Public Accounts 1999–. *Special Interests:* Economic Policy, Urban Regeneration, Telecommunications, Employment, Christian Socialism. Joint Vice-Chair, Christian Socialist Movement 1995–98. *Address:* Stephen Timms Esq, MP, House of Commons, London, SW1A 0AA *Tel:* 020 7219 3000 *Fax:* 020 7219 2949 *E-mail:* 100746.2456@compuserve.com.

PADDY TIPPING   Sherwood   Lab majority 16,812

Born 24 October 1949; Son of late Ernest Tipping, newsagent, and late Margaret Tipping, clerk; Educated Hipperholme Grammar School; Nottingham University (BA philosophy 1972, MA applied social science 1978); Married January 8, 1970, Irene Margaret, daughter of Bert and Ida Quinn (2 daughters). Social worker, Nottingham and Nottinghamshire 1972–79; Project Leader, Church of England Children's Society, Nottingham 1979–83; Member, UNISON. Councillor, Nottinghamshire County Council 1981–93; Director: Nottinghamshire Co-operative Development Agency 1983–93, Nottingham Development Enterprise 1987–93. **House of Commons:** Contested Rushcliffe 1987 general election. Member for Sherwood since April 9, 1992; PPS to Jack Straw as Home Secretary 1997–99; Parliamentary Secretary, Privy Council Office 1999–; *Select Committees:* Member: Parliamentary Commissioner for Administration 1996–97. *Special Interests:* Local Government, Energy, Education, Police, Workers' Co-operatives; Former Soviet Union. Member, Co-operative Party; Chair: Central Region Group of Labour MPs 1997–, East Midlands Group of Labour MPs until 1999. Vice-President, The Ramblers' Association; Member: Industry and Parliament Trust, Armed Forces Parliamentary Trust; *Clubs:* Clipstone Miners' Welfare; *Recreations:* Family, gardening, running. *Address:* Paddy Tipping Esq, MP, House of Commons, London, SW1A 0AA *Tel:* 020 7219 5044 *Fax:* 020 7219 3641. *Constituency:* Sherwood Parliamentary Office, 1st Floor, Council Offices, Watnall Road, Hucknall, Nottinghamshire, NG15 7LA *Tel:* 0115–964 0314 *Fax:* 0115–968 1639.

MARK TODD   South Derbyshire   *Lab majority 13,967*

Born 29 December 1954; Son of Matthew and Viv Todd; Educated Sherborne School; Emmanuel College, Cambridge (BA history 1976); Married February 3, 1979, Sarah Margaret Dawson (1 son). Longman Group, latterly Addison Wesley Longman 1977–96: Managing Director: Longman Industry and Public Service Management 1988–92, Longman Carter Mill 1990–92, Director: Information Technology 1992–94, Operations 1994–96; ASTMS (now MSF), union chairman at employers. Cambridge City Council 1980–92: Deputy Leader 1982–87, Leader of Council 1987–90. **House of Commons:** Member for South Derbyshire since May 1, 1997; *Select Committees:* Member: Agriculture 1997–. *Special Interests:* Business, Economics, Local Government, Environment, Agriculture; Europe, Third World. Member: Greenpeace, Royal Society of Arts and Manufacture; Director, Cambridge and District Co-operative Society 1986–89; FRSA; *Recreations:* Reading, cinema. *Address:* Mark Todd Esq, MP, House of Commons, London, SW1A 0AA *Tel:* 020 7219 3549 *Fax:* 020 7219 2495. *Constituency:* 37 Market Street, Church Gresley, Swadlincote, Derbyshire, DE11 9PR *Tel:* 01283 551573 *Fax:* 01283 551573 *E-mail:* toddm@parliament.uk.

DR JENNIFER TONGE   Richmond Park   *LD majority 2,951*

Born 19 February 1941; Daughter of late Sidney Smith, school teacher, and late Violet Smith, school teacher; Educated Dudley Girls' High School 1957–59; University College Hospital, London (MB, BS 1964); Married May 23, 1964, Keith Tonge (2 sons 1 daughter). General practice/family planning 1968–78; Senior medical officer, Women's Services (Ealing) 1980–85; Manager, Community Health Services (Ealing) 1992–96; SW Thames Representative, BMA Public and Community Health Committee. Councillor, London Borough of Richmond-on-Thames 1981–90, Chair, Social Services 1981–86. **House of Commons:** Contested Richmond and Barnes 1992 general election. Member for Richmond Park since May 1, 1997; Spokeswoman for: Foreign Affairs and Defence and Europe (International Development) 1997–99, International Development 1999–; *Select Committees:* Member: International Development 1997–99. *Special Interests:* Health, Environment, Social Services, International Development; Africa, India, Pakistan, Tibet, Indonesia. Chair, Richmond and Barnes Liberal Party 1978–80. Chair, Governors of Waldegrave School 1981–86; Member: RSPB, Amnesty International, Action For South Africa, Karuna Trust, Project Hope (UK); Member, Standing Committee on Asian Development Bank 1997–; Member, Parliamentary Assembly Organisation for Security and Co-operation in Europe; Trustee, Off the Record, Richmond; School – James Smellie Gold Medal; MFFP; MFCH; Visiting Parliamentary Fellow, St Anthony's College, Oxford 1999–2000; *Recreations:* Birdwatching. *Address:* Dr Jennifer Tonge, MP, House of Commons, London, SW1A 0AA *Tel:* 020 7219 4596 *Fax:* 020 7219 4596. *Constituency:* Aaron House, 6 Bardolph Road, Richmond, Surrey, TW9 2LS *Tel:* 020 8332 7919 *Fax:* 020 8332 7919 *E-mail:* tonge@cix.compulink.co.uk.

DON TOUHIG   Islwyn   *Lab/Co-op majority 23,931*

Born 5 December 1947; Son of late Michael and Catherine Touhig; Educated St Francis School, Abersychan; Mid Gwent College; Married September 21, 1968, Jennifer Hughes (2 sons 2 daughters). Journalist 1968–76; Editor, Free Press of Monmouthshire 1976–90; General manager and editor in chief, Free Press Group of Newspapers 1988–92; General manager (business development), Bailey Group 1992–93, Bailey Print 1993–95; Member, TGWU. Councillor, Gwent County Council 1973–; Chair, Finance Committee 1995–. **House of Commons:** Contested Richmond and Barnes 1992 general election. Member for Islwyn since February 16, 1995 by-election; Assistant Government Whip (Wales) 1999–; Public Interest Disclosure (Private Member's Bill) 1995; PPS to Gordon Brown as Chancellor of the Exchequer 1997–99; *Select Committees:* Member: Welsh Affairs 1996–97. *Special Interests:* Treasury, Employment, Health, Education, Local Government. Hon. Secretary, Welsh Regional Group of Labour MPs 1995–99;

Member, European Standing Committee B 1995–96; Member, Labour Leadership Campaign Team (responsible for Devolution in Wales) 1996–97; Member, Co-operative Party; Chair, Co-operative Parliamentary Group 1999. Past President, South Wales Newspaper Society; Member: MENSA, MENCAP. Amnesty International, St David's Foundation, Credit Union; President: Home Start, Islwyn Drug and Alcohol Project, National Old Age Pensioners Association of Wales, Caerphilly County Borough Access Group; Member, Medical Council on Alcoholism; Papal Knight of the Order of St Sylvester; *Recreations:* Reading, cooking for family and friends, music, walking.*Address:* Don Touhig Esq, MP, House of Commons, London, SW1A 0AA *Tel:* 020 7219 6435 *Fax:* 020 7219 2070. *Constituency:* The Institute, Crumlin, Gwent, NP11 4QD *Tel:* 01495 244699 *Fax:* 01495 245109.

JOHN TOWNEND   Yorkshire East   Con majority 3,337

Born 12 June 1934; Son of late Charles Townend and Dorothy Townend; Educated Hymers College, Hull; Married May 4, 1963, Jennifer Lawson (2 sons 2 daughters). Served RAF 1957–59, Commissioned Pilot Officer; Articled clerk in chartered accountancy 1951–57; Joined family business as company secretary and finance director 1959, managing director 1961–79, Chair 1977–; Chair, Yorkshire and Humberside Wine and Spirit Merchants' Association 1975–76; Underwriter, Lloyd's 1977. Humberside County Council: Chair, Humber Bridge Board 1969–71, Leader, Conservative Group 1973–77, Councillor 1973–79, Leader of the Council 1977–79, Chair, Policy Committee 1977–79. **House of Commons:** Contested Kingston-upon-Hull North 1970 general election. Member for Bridlington 1979–97, and for Yorkshire East since May 1, 1997; PPS to Sir Hugh Rossi, MP, as Minister of Pensions and Disabled 1981–83; *Select Committees:* Member: Treasury and Civil Service 1983–92; Member: Public Administration 1999–. *Special Interests:* Treasury, Tax, Small Businesses, Employment, Europe; France, South Africa, USA, Southern Africa. Member: Conservative National Advisory Committee on Local Government, Chair, 92 Group, 1996–97, 1997–. Member, Policy Committee of the ACC 1977–79; Member, Executive 1922 Committee 1996–97, 1997–98; Vice-Chair, British Council; Member, Council of Europe and Western European Union 1992–; Executive Committee Member, Inter-Parliamentary Union British Group; Fellow, Industry and Parliament Trust; Liveryman: Woolmen's Company, Distillers Company; Plender Prize in CA Finals; FCA; *Clubs:* Carlton; *Recreations:* Swimming, tennis. *Address:* John Townend Esq, MP, House of Commons, London, SW1A 0AA *Tel:* 020 7219 3000 *Fax:* 020 7219 2723. *Constituency:* Conservative Club, 3 Tennyson Avenue, Bridlington, East Yorkshire, YO15 2EU *Tel:* 01262 674072 *Fax:* 01262 401231.

DAVID TREDINNICK   Bosworth   Con majority 1,027

Born 19 January 1950; Son of Stephen Victor Tredinnick and Evelyn Mabel, née Wates; Educated Eton; Mons Officer Cadet School; Graduate School of Business; Cape Town University (MBA); St John's College, Oxford (MLitt); Married July 7, 1983, Rebecca Shott (1 son 1 daughter). 2nd Lieutenant Grenadier Guards 1968–71; Trainee, E. B. Savory Milln & Co. (Stockbrokers) 1972–73; Account executive, Quadrant Int. 1974; Salesman, Kalle Infotech UK 1976; Sales manager, Word Right Word Processing 1977–78; Consultant, Baird Communications NY 1978–79; Marketing manager, QI Europe Ltd 1979–81; Manager, Malden Mitcham Properties 1981–87. **House of Commons:** Contested Cardiff South and Penarth 1983 general election. Member for Bosworth since June 1987; PPS to Rt Hon. Sir Wyn Roberts, MP, as Minister of State, Welsh Office 1991–94; *Select Committees:* Chairman: Joint Committee on Statutory Instruments 1997–; Member: Liaison 1997–. *Special Interests:* Foreign Affairs, Trade and Industry, Defence, Home Affairs, Police, Public Order, Employment, Environment; Eastern Europe. Chair, British Atlantic Group of Young Politicians 1989–91; *Recreations:* Golf, skiing, tennis, windsurfing, sailing, shooting. *Address:* David Tredinnick Esq, MP, House of Commons, London, SW1A 0AA *Tel:* 020 7219 3000 *Fax:* 020 7219 4901. *Constituency:* Bosworth Conservative Association, 10a Priory Walk, Hinckley, Leicestershire, LE10 1HU *Tel:* 01455 635741 *Fax:* 01455 612023 *E-mail:* tredinnickd@parliament.uk.

MICHAEL TREND Windsor — *Con majority 9,917*

Born 19 April 1952; Son of late Rt Hon. Baron Trend, GCB, CVO and Patricia Charlotte Shaw; Educated Westminster School; Oriel College, Oxford (MA Oxon); Married 1987, Jill Kershaw (1 son 2 daughters). Journalist; Editor; Broadcaster; Chief leader writer, *Daily Telegraph* 1990–92. **House of Commons:** Contested North East London 1989 European Parliament election. Member for Windsor and Maidenhead 1992–97, and for Windsor since May 1, 1997; Opposition Front Bench Spokesman for: Foreign and Commonwealth Affairs 1998–99, Social Security 1999–2000; PPS: to Tim Yeo as Minister of State, Department of Environment 1993–94, to Brian Mawhinney: as Minister of State, Department of Health 1992–94, as Secretary of State for Transport 1994–95; *Select Committees:* Member: Health 1992–93; Member: Public Administration 2000–. *Special Interests:* Education, Health, Defence, Foreign Affairs. Deputy Chair, Conservative Party 1995–98; Head of Conservative Party International Office 2000–. CBE 1997; *Recreations:* Hill walking, cricket, playing the organ. *Address:* Hon Michael Trend, CBE, MP, House of Commons, London, SW1A 0AA *Tel:* 020 7219 3000. *Constituency:* 87 St Leonards Road, Windsor, Berkshire, SL4 3BZ *Tel:* 01753 678693 *Fax:* 01753 832774.

JON TRICKETT Hemsworth — *Lab majority 23,992*

Born 2 July 1950; Son of Laurence and Rose Trickett; Educated Roundhay School, Leeds; Hull University (BA politics); Leeds University (MA political sociology); Married October 31, 1993, Sarah Balfour (1 son 2 daughters). Plumber/builder 1974–86; Member, GMB Union. Leeds City Council: Councillor 1984–96, Chair: Finance Committee 1985–88, Housing Committee 1988–89, Leader of the Council 1989–96. **House of Commons:** Member for Hemsworth since February 1, 1996 By-election; PPS to Peter Mandelson: as Minister without Portfolio 1997–98, as Secretary of State for Trade and Industry July-December 1998; *Select Committees:* Member: Unopposed Bills (Panel) 1997–. *Special Interests:* Economic Policy, Finance, Industry, Sport; Middle East, France, USA. *Clubs:* British Cycling Federation; *Sportsclubs:* Member: British Cycling Federation, West Riding Sailing Club; Hon Life Member, Cyclists' Touring Club; *Recreations:* Cycle racing, windsurfing. *Address:* Jon Trickett Esq, MP, House of Commons, London, SW1A 0AA *Tel:* 020 7219 5074 *Fax:* 020 7219 2133. *Constituency:* 18 Market Street, Hemsworth, Dorset, WF9 5LB *Tel:* 01977 722290 *Fax:* 01977 722290.

DAVID TRIMBLE Upper Bann — *UUP majority 9,252*

Born 15 October 1944; Son of late William and Ivy Trimble; Educated Bangor Grammar School; Queen's University, Belfast (LLB); Married 1978, Daphne Orr (2 sons 2 daughters). Queen's University, Belfast: Lecturer in Law 1968–77, Senior Lecturer 1977–90; Member, South Belfast, Northern Ireland Constitutional Convention 1975–76; Elected to the Northern Ireland Forum 1996–98; Elected to the Northern Ireland Assembly 1998–; First Minister, Northern Ireland Assembly 1998–. **House of Commons:** Member for Upper Bann since May 17, 1990 by-election; UUP Spokesman on Constitutional Affairs. Chair, Lagan Valley Unionist Association 1985–90; Leader, Ulster Unionist Party 1995–. Chair, Ulster Society 1985–90; PC 1998; Nobel Peace Prize (jointly) 1998; Channel 4 and *The House* Magazine, Major Political Achievement 1999; *Recreations:* Music, reading. *Address:* Rt Hon David Trimble, MP, House of Commons, London, SW1A 0AA *Tel:* 020 7219 3000. *Constituency:* 2 Queen Street, Lurgan, BT66 8BQ *Tel:* 028 3832 8088 *Fax:* 028 3832 2343.

PAUL TRUSWELL   Pudsey   *Lab majority 6,207*

Born 17 November 1955; Son of John Truswell, retired foundryman, and Olive Truswell, retired cleaner; Educated Firth Park Comprehensive School; Leeds University (BA); Married Suzanne Evans (2 sons). Journalist, Yorkshire Post Newspapers 1977–88; Local government officer, Wakefield MDC 1988–; Member: UNISON, NUJ. Councillor, Leeds City Council 1982–97; Member: Leeds Eastern Health Authority 1982–90, Leeds Community Health Council 1990–92, Leeds Family Health Services Authority 1992–96. **House of Commons:** Member for Pudsey since May 1, 1997; *Select Committees:* Member: Environmental Audit 1997–99. *Special Interests:* Health, Social Services, Environment. *Clubs:* Civil Service, Hawkshill Social (Guiseley); *Recreations:* Cinema, Cricket, Tennis, Badminton, Photography. *Address:* Paul Truswell Esq, MP, House of Commons, London, SW1A 0AA *Tel:* 020 7219 3504 *Fax:* 020 7219 2252. *Constituency:* 10A Greenside, Pudsey, West Yorkshire, LS28 8PU *Tel:* 0113–229 3553 *Fax:* 0113–229 3800.

DENNIS TURNER   Wolverhampton South East   *Lab/Co-op majority 15,182*

Born 26 August 1942; Son of late Thomas Herbert and Mary Elizabeth Turner; Educated Stonefield Secondary School, Bilston; Bilston College of Further Education; Married June 19, 1976, Patricia Narroway (1 son 1 daughter). Director, Springvale Co-operative, sports, social and leisure centre 1981–; Former Chair, Midlands Iron and Steel Trades Confederation Conference. Former Director, Black Country Co-operative Development Agency; Councillor: Wolverhampton Borough Council 1966–86, West Midlands County Council 1973–86; Chair: Wolverhampton Social Services Committee 1973–79, Higher Education Committee 1974–81, Economic Development Committee 1979–84, Theatre Committee 1980–82, Deputy Leader 1980–86, Housing Committee 1985–86. **House of Commons:** Contested Halesowen and Stourbridge February and October 1974 general elections. Member for Wolverhampton South East since June 1987; Opposition Whip 1992–97; PPS to Clare Short as Secretary of State for International Development 1997–; *Select Committees:* Education 1988–94; Chairman: Catering 1997–; Member: Court of Referees 1997–, Finance and Services 1997–, Liaison 1998–. *Special Interests:* Education, Social Services, Housing; South Africa, The Commonwealth, British Overseas Territories. Member, Co-operative Party; Vice-Chair, West Midlands Regional Group of Labour MPs 1997–; Chair, Parliamentary Labour Party Local Government Group 1997–. President: Bilston Community Association, Wolverhampton Deaf Children's Society; Vice-President: Wolverhampton MENCAP, Wolverhampton Race Equality Council; Member, Executive Committee: IPU (British Branch); Commonwealth Parliamentary Association (CPA) UK Branch 1999–, Vice-Chair; Trustee-Secretary, Bradley Old People's Trust; *Clubs:* New Springvale Sports and Social (Bilston); *Recreations:* Tasting traditional ales, all card games. *Address:* Dennis Turner Esq, MP, House of Commons, London, SW1A 0AA *Tel:* 020 7219 4210. *Constituency:* Springvale House, Millfields Road, Bilston, West Midlands, WV14 0QS *Tel:* 01902 492364 *Website:* www.dfid.gov.uk.

DR DES TURNER   Brighton Kemptown   *Lab majority 3,534*

Born 17 July 1939; Son of late Stanley M. M. Turner and of Elsie Turner; Educated Luton Grammar School; Imperial College, London (BSc, MSc); University College, London (PhD); Brighton Polytechnic (PGCE); Married 2nd, September 20, 1997 Lynne Rogers (1 daughter from previous marriage). Medical researcher; Teacher; Partner in independent brewery; Past Member: AUT, TGWU, NUT; Member, MSF. Councillor: East Sussex County Council 1985–96, Brighton Borough Council 1994–96, Brighton and Hove Unitary Council 1996–98. **House of Commons:** Contested Mid-Sussex 1979 general election. Member for Brighton Kemptown since May 1, 1997; *Select Committees:* Member: Science and Technology 1997–. *Special Interests:* Health, Social Services, Employment, Disability, Housing, Science Policy and Animal Welfare; Europe. Member: Age Concern, East Sussex, Shelter, LACS, CFAW, Terence Higgins Trust, Brighton Housing Trust, Brighton and Hove ME Group; Parliamentary Observer: Albanian Elections 1997,

Bosnian Elections 1998; Member, Brighton Housing Trust; *Publications:* Research papers and reviews; R. D. Lawrence Memorial Fellow, British Diabetic Association 1970–72; ARCS; *Sportsclubs:* Polytechnic Fencing Club, Brighton Marina Yacht Club; *Recreations:* Sailing, fencing. *Address:* Dr Des Turner, MP, House of Commons, London, SW1A 0AA *Tel:* 020 7219 4024. *Constituency:* 179 Preston Road, Brighton, BN1 6AG *Tel:* 01273 330610 *Fax:* 01273 500966 *E-mail:* turnerd@parliament.uk.

DR GEORGE TURNER   North West Norfolk — *Lab majority 1,339*

Born 9 August 1940; Son of late George Turner and late Jane Turner; Educated Laxton Grammar School, Oundle; Imperial College, London (BSc); Gonville and Caius, Cambridge (PhD physics 1967); Married Lesley Duggan (2 daughters 1 stepson 1 stepdaughter). Head, electrical engineering, University of East Anglia; Member, AUT. Councillor, Norfolk County Council 1977–97, Group Leader 1985–90, Chair, Education 1992–97; Former Member, Norfolk Police Authority. **House of Commons:** Contested North West Norfolk 1992 general election. Member for North West Norfolk since May 1, 1997; *Select Committees:* Member: Public Administration 2000; Member: Joint Committee on Consolidation of Bills Etc 1997–, Agriculture 2000–. *Special Interests:* Education, Trade and Industry. School Governor; Board Member, Kings Lyn Festival; *Recreations:* Poetry, travelling, theatre, cinema, keeping fit, swimming. *Address:* Dr George Turner, MP, House of Commons, London, SW1A 0AA *Tel:* 020 7219 4618. *Constituency:* 78 Chapel Street, Kings Lynn, Norfolk, PE30 1EF *Fax:* 01553 666112 *E-mail:* mp@nwnorfolk.demon.co.uk.

NEIL TURNER   Wigan — *Lab majority 6,729*

Born 16 September 1945; Educated Carlisle Grammar School; Married March 26, 1971, Susan (1 son). Quantity surveyor, Fairclough Builders (later AMEC) 1967–94; Operations manager, North Shropshire District Council 1995–97; Member, MSF. Councillor, Wigan County Borough Council 1972–74; Wigan Metropolitan Borough Council: Councillor 1975–2000, Vice-Chair, Highways and Works Committee 1978–80, Chair 1980–97, Chair, Best Value Review Panel 1998–99. **House of Commons:** Contested Oswestry 1970 general election. Member for Wigan since September 23, 1999 By-election; *Select Committees:* Member: Public Administration 2000–. *Special Interests:* Local Government, Housing. Former Member, Sale Young Socialists. Vice-Chair, Public Services Committee, Association of Metropolitan Authorities 1987–95, Chair 1995–97; Vice-Chair, Local Government Association Quality Panel 1997–98, Chair 1998–99; *Recreations:* Keen follower of Wigan Rugby League Club. *Address:* Neil Turner Esq, MP, House of Commons, London, SW1A 0AA *Tel:* 020 7219 3000. *Constituency:* Gerrard Winstanley House, Crawford Street, Wigan, Greater Manchester, WN1 1NG *Tel:* 01942 242047 *Fax:* 01942 828008 *E-mail:* gerrard@labour.u-net.com.

DEREK TWIGG   Halton — *Lab majority 23,650*

Born 9 July 1959; Son of Kenneth and Irene Twigg; Educated Bankfield High School, Widnes; Halton College of Further Education; Married January 23, 1988, Mary Cassidy (1 son 1 daughter). Civil servant, Department for Education and Employment 1975–96; Political consultant 1996–; Trade Union Member for over 20 years; Branch secretary, Branch chair 1978–84. Councillor, Cheshire County Council 1981–85; Halton Borough Council: Councillor 1983–97, Chair of Housing 1988–93, Chair of Finance 1993–96, Education Spokesperson 1996–97. **House of Commons:** Member for Halton since May 1, 1997; PPS to Helen Liddell: as Minister of State, Department of the Environment, Transport and the Regions (Minister for Transport) 1999, as Minister of State, Department of Trade and Industry (Minister for Energy and Competitiveness in Europe) 1999–; *Select Committees:* Member: Public Accounts 1998–99. *Special Interests:* Finance, Education, Health and Poverty, Housing; Greece. Vice-Chair, North West Regional Group of Labour MPs 1998–99, Chair 1999–; Member, European Standing Committee B 1997–98. Member, Halton Community Health Council; *Recreations:* Liverpool Football Club, various sporting activities, walking, reading history. *Address:* Derek Twigg Esq, MP, House of Commons, London, SW1A 0AA *Tel:* 020 7219 3554 *Fax:* 020 7219 2115. *Constituency:* 76 Victoria Road, Widnes, Cheshire, WA8 7RA *Tel:* 0151–424 7030 *Fax:* 0151–495 3800 *E-mail:* derek.twigg@virgin.net.

STEPHEN TWIGG   Enfield Southgate   *Lab majority 1,433*

Born 25 December 1966; Son of Ian David Twigg and late Jean Barbara Twigg; Educated Southgate Comprehensive; Balliol College, Oxford (BA politics and economics 1988). Former President, National Union of Students; Former Parliamentary Officer: Amnesty International UK, NCVO; Former Research Assistant to Margaret Hodge, MP for Barking; Former Political Consultant, Rowland Sallingbury Casey; General Secretary, Fabian Society 1996–97; Member, MSF. Councillor, London Borough of Islington 1990–97, Chief Whip 1994–96, Deputy Leader 1996. **House of Commons:** Member for Enfield Southgate since May 1, 1997; *Select Committees:* Member: Modernisation of the House of Commons 1998–2000; Member: Education and Employment 1999–, Employment Sub-Committee 1999–. *Special Interests:* Education, Electoral Reform, Local Government, Foreign Affairs; Israel; Cyprus. Member, Co-operative Party; Executive Member, Fabian Society; Chair, Labour Campaign for Electoral Reform; Chair, Labour Friends of Israel; Hon. Treasurer, London Group of Labour MPs 1997–. Member: Amnesty International, Stonewall, League Against Cruel Sports; Director, Crime Concern; Governor: Merryhills Primary School, Southgate School; Patron, The Richmond and Kingston AIDS Project; Member, Holocaust Educational Trust; *Publications:* Co-author *The Cross We Bear: Electoral Reform in Local Government*, 1997; *Clubs:* National Liberal; *Sportsclubs:* Southgate Cricket. *Address:* Stephen Twigg Esq, MP, House of Commons, London, SW1A 0AA *Tel:* 020 7219 6554 *Fax:* 020 7219 0948 *E-mail:* twiggs@parliament.uk.

PAUL TYLER   North Cornwall   *LD majority 13,847*

Born 29 October 1941; Son of Oliver and Grace Tyler; Educated Sherborne School; Exeter College, Oxford (BA modern history 1963, MA); Married 1970, Nicola Mary Ingram (1 son 1 daughter). Director, public affairs, Royal Institute of British Architects 1972–73; Board member, Shelter: National Campaign for the Homeless 1975–76; Managing director, Cornwall Courier Newspaper Group 1976–81; Public affairs division, Good Relations plc: Executive director 1982–84, Chief executive 1984–86, Chair 1986–87; Senior consultant, Public Affairs 1987–92; Director, Western Approaches Public Relations Ltd 1987–92. Councillor, Devon County Council 1964–70; Member, Devon and Cornwall Police Authority 1965–70; Vice-Chair, Dartmoor National Park Committee 1965–70; Contested (SLD) Cornwall and Plymouth 1989 European Parliament election. **House of Commons:** Contested (Liberal) Totnes 1966 and Bodmin 1970 general elections. Member for Bodmin February-October 1974. Contested Bodmin 1979 general election and Beaconsfield 1982 by-election. Member (Liberal Democrat) for North Cornwall since April 9, 1992; Spokesman for: Agriculture, Tourism, Transport and Rural Affairs 1992–95, Agriculture and Rural Affairs 1995–97, Food 1997–99; Chief Whip and Shadow Leader of the House 1997–; *Select Committees:* Member: Procedure 1992–97, Procedure 1997–98; Member: Finance and Services 1997–, Modernisation of the House of Commons 1997–, Parliamentary Privilege (Joint Committee) 1997–, Selection 1997–. *Special Interests:* Tourism, Rural Affairs. Chair: Devon and Cornwall Region Liberal Party 1981–82, Liberal Party National Executive Committee 1983–86; Campaign adviser to David Steel, MP in 1983 and 1987 general elections. Vice-President: British Resorts Association, Youth Hostels Association, Action for Communities in Rural England; Chair, CPRE Working Party on the future of the village 1974–81; Vice-President, Federation of Economic Development Authorities (FEDA); Vice-President, British Trust for Conservation Volunteers; *Publications:* Co-author *Power to the Provinces*, 1968; *A New Deal for Rural Britain*, 1978; *Country Lives, Country Landscapes*, 1996; CBE 1985; *Clubs:* Launceston and District Liberal Democrat; *Recreations:* Sailing, gardening, walking. *Address:* Paul Tyler Esq, CBE, MP, House of Commons, London, SW1A 0AA *Tel:* 020 7219 6355. *Constituency:* Church Stile, Launceston, Cornwall, PL15 8AT *Tel:* 01566 777123 *Fax:* 01566 772122.

Visit the Vacher Dod Website ...
www.politicallinks.co.uk

BILL TYNAN   Hamilton South   *Lab majority 556*

Born 18 August 1940; Son of late James and Mary Tynan; Educated St Mungo's Academy, Glasgow; Stow College (mechanical engineering); Married July 11, 1964, Elizabeth Mathieson (3 daughters). Press toolmaker; full-time union official: district secretary, regional office and political officer 1988–; AEEU 1966–: Shop steward, convenor, local and national posts; Scottish Political Secretary; Treasurer, Scottish Trade Union Labour Liaison Committee. **House of Commons:** Member for Hamilton South since September 23, 1999 by-election; *Select Committees:* Member: Scottish Affairs 1999–. *Special Interests:* Employment Law, Social Security, Equal Opportunities, Social Inclusion. Member: Labour Party 1969–: Constituency and Scottish Labour Party posts; Labour's Scottish Policy Forum. *Recreations:* Golf, swimming, cycling, watching football, diy, gardening. *Address:* Bill Tynan, Esq, MP, House of Commons, London, SW1A 0AA *Tel:* 020 7219 6285 *Fax:* 020 7219 6285. *Constituency:* 154 Montrose Crescent, Hamilton, South Lanarkshire, ML3 6LL *Tel:* 01698 454925 *Fax:* 01698 454926 *E-mail:* tynanb@parliament.uk; hamiltonsouth@bill-tynan-mp.com.

ANDREW TYRIE   Chichester   *Con majority 9,734*

Born 15 January 1957; Son of the late Derek and Patricia Tyrie; Educated Felstead School, Essex; Trinity College, Oxford (BA philosophy, politics and economics 1979 MA); College of Europe, Bruges; Wolfson College, Cambridge (MPhil). Group head office, British Petroleum 1981–83; Adviser to Chancellors of the Exchequer: Nigel Lawson 1986–89, John Major 1989–90, Fellow, Nuffield College, Oxford 1990–91; Senior economist, European Bank for Reconstruction and Development 1992–97. **House of Commons:** Contested Houghton and Washington 1992 general election. Member for Chichester since May 1, 1997; *Select Committees:* Member: Joint Committee on Consolidation of Bills Etc 1997–, Public Administration 1997–. *Special Interests:* European Union, Economic Policy. Member, Public Accounts Commission 1997–; Member, Inter-Parliamentary Union; *Publications:* Various works on economic and monetary union in Europe and other European issues; *The Prospects for Public Spending,* 1996; Co-author *Reforming the Lords: a Conservative Approach,* 1998; *Sense on EMU,* 1998; *Leviathan at Large: The New Regulator for the Financial Markets,* 2000; *Mr Blair's Poodle: An Agenda for Reviving the House of Commons,* 2000; *Clubs:* MCC, RAC, Chichester Yacht Club; *Recreations:* Golf. *Address:* Andrew Tyrie Esq, MP, House of Commons, London, SW1A 0AA *Tel:* 020 7219 6371 *Fax:* 020 7219 0625. *Constituency:* Chichester Conservative Association, 145 St Pancras, Chichester, West Sussex, PO19 4LH *Tel:* 01243 783519 *Fax:* 01243 536848 *E-mail:* marsha@parliament.uk.

V

KEITH VAZ   Leicester East   *Lab majority 18,422*

Born 26 November 1956; Son of Merlyn Verona Vaz, mother and teacher; Educated St Joseph's Convent, Aden; Latymer Upper School, Hammersmith; Gonville and Caius College, Cambridge (BA 1979, MA 1987, MCFI 1988); College of Law, London; Married April 3, 1993, Maria Fernandes (1 son, 1 daughter). Articled clerk, Richmond Council 1980–82; Solicitor 1982; Senior solicitor, Islington LBC 1982–85; Solicitor: Highfields and Belgrave Law Centre 1985–87, North Leicester Advice Centre 1986–87; Member, UNISON 1985–. **House of Commons:** Contested Richmond and Barnes 1983 general election. Contested Surrey West European Parliament election 1984. Member for Leicester East since June 1987; Opposition Front Bench Spokesman on: The Environment 1992–97; PPS to: John Morris as Attorney General 1997–99, Solicitors General Lord Falconer of Thoroton 1997–98, Ross Cranston 1998–99; Parliamentary Secretary, Lord Chancellor's Department 1999; Minister of State, Foreign and Commonwealth Office (Minister for Europe) 1999–;

Select Committees: Member: Home Affairs 1987–92. *Special Interests:* Education, Legal Services, Local Government, Race Relations, Urban Policies; India, Pakistan, Yemen, Bangladesh, Oman. Chair: Labour Party Race Action Group 1983–, Unison Group 1990–; Tribune Group: Vice-chair 1992, Treasurer 1994; Labour Party Regional Executive 1994–96. President, Leicester and South Leicestershire RSPCA 1988–99; Patron, Gingerbread 1990–; National Advisory Committee, Crime Concern; Chair, City 2020 Urban Policy Commission 1993–; Patron, Asian Business Club 1998–; President: Asian Business Network 1998–, National Organisation of Asian Businesses; Patron, Asian Doners Appeal 2000–; Several local organisations; Member, Standing Committees on: Immigration Bill 1987–88, Legal Aid Bill 1988, Children's Bill 1988–89, Football Spectators Bill 1989, National Health Service and Community Care Bill 1989–90, Courts and Legal Services Bill 1990, Armed Forces Bill 1990–91, Promoter, Race Relations Remedies Act 1994; Governor, Commonwealth Institute 1998–99; Board Member, The British Council 1999–; Member, Executive Committee Inter-Parliamentary Union 1993–94; *Publications:* Co-author *Law Reform Now,* 1996; *Clubs:* Safari (Leicester). *Address:* Keith Vaz Esq, MP, House of Commons, London, SW1A 0AA *Tel:* 020 7219 4605 *Fax:* 020 7219 5743.

PETER VIGGERS   Gosport   *Con majority 6,258*

Born 13 March 1938; Son of late John Sidney Viggers; Educated Portsmouth Grammar School; Trinity Hall, Cambridge (history and law 1961, MA); College of Law, Guildford 1967; Married December 7, 1968, Dr Jennifer Mary McMillan (2 sons 1 daughter). National service RAF pilot 1956–58; Territorial Army Officer 1962–67; Solicitor 1967; Chair and director of companies in banking, oil, hotels, textiles, pharmaceuticals, venture capital 1970–79; Member, Council of Lloyd's of London 1992–95; Chair: Tracer Petroleum Corporation 1996–98, Lloyd's Pension Fund 1996–; Director, Emerald Energy plc 1998–. **House of Commons:** Member for Gosport since February 1974; PPS: to Sir Ian Percival as Solicitor General 1979–83, to Peter Rees as Chief Secretary to the Treasury 1983–85; Parliamentary Under-Secretary of State (Industry Minister), Northern Ireland Office 1986–89; *Select Committees:* Member: Defence 1992–97, Armed Forces Bill 1996; Member: Defence 2000–. *Special Interests:* Finance, Trade and Industry, Defence; China, Japan, South East Asia, USA; Member, European Standing Committee A 1998–. Chair, Cambridge University Conservative Association 1960. RNLI: National Committee 1979–, Vice-President 1989–; Chairman, Governors of St Vincent College, Gosport 1993–97; Executive Member, 1922 Committee 1997–; UK Delegate, North Atlantic Assembly 1981–86, 1992–; Chair, Sub-Committee on Central and Eastern Europe 1999–; Fellow, Industry and Parliament Trust; *Sportsclubs:* Member, House of Commons Yacht Club: Commodore 1982–83, Admiral 1997–99; *Recreations:* Beagling, opera, travel. *Address:* Peter Viggers Esq, MP, House of Commons, London, SW1A 0AA *Tel:* 020 7219 5081 *Fax:* 020 7219 3985. *Constituency:* 167 Stoke Road, Gosport, Hampshire.

RUDI VIS   Finchley and Golders Green   *Lab majority 3,189*

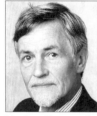

Born 4 April 1941; Son of late Laurens Vis, insurance broker, and late Helena Vis; Educated High School, Alkmaar, The Netherlands; University of Maryland, USA (BSc economics 1970); London School of Economics (MSc economics 1972); Brunel University (PhD economics 1976); Married Joan Hanin (divorced) (1 son); partner, Jacqueline Suffling (twin sons). Dutch Armed Services 1960–64; Principal lecturer, economics, North East London Polytechnic/University of East London 1971–97; Member: NATFHE 1971–94, MSF 1994–. Councillor, London Borough of Barnet 1986–98. **House of Commons:** Member for Finchley and Golders Green since May 1, 1997; *Special Interests:* Finance, European Union, Economics, Defence, Elderly; Member, European Standing Committee A 1998–. Member: Co-op Party 1971–, SERA 1986–, Labour Movement in Europe 1997–, Labour Friends of Israel 1997–, Labour Friends of India 1997–, European Movement 1999–. Member: CND 1971–, Friends of the Earth 1978–, Friends of Cyprus 1997–, UNA 1998–; Member, Finchley Society 1998–; Member: Council of Europe, Western European Union; Member: College Farm Finchley, Hendon Youth Club; Hon. Doctorate, Schiller International University; *Recreations:* Walking through London. *Address:* Dr Rudi Vis, MP, House of Commons, London, SW1A 0AA *Tel:* 020 7219 4562 *Fax:* 020 7219 0565. *Constituency:* Labour Party Constituency Office, 38 Church Lane, London N2 8DT *Tel:* 020 8883 0411 *Fax:* 020 8883 0411.

W

Born 17 December 1924; Son of late Alfred George Walker, police constable; Educated Methodist College, Belfast; Married July 1953, Joan Verrant (2 sons). James P. Corry & Co. Ltd., Belfast timber merchants 1941–83; Joinery sales manager 1951–83. Councillor, Belfast City Council 1976–83; Member, Belfast Education and Library Board 1976–83; JP 1966. **House of Commons:** Contested Belfast North 1979 general election. Member for Belfast North since June, 1983; Spokesman for Culture, Media and Sport 1999–; *Special Interests:* Housing, Local Government, Fishing, Industry, Conservation, Timber, Irish Affairs, Elderly; Cyprus, South Africa, USA. *Sportsclubs:* Down Cruising, Magheramorne Sailing; *Recreations:* Sailing, angling, gardening. *Address:* Cecil Walker Esq, JP, MP, House of Commons, London, SW1A 0AA *Tel:* 020 7219 6307 *Fax:* 020 7219 2347. *Constituency:* 20 Old Park Road, Belfast, BT14 6FR *Tel:* 028 9083 3463 *Fax:* 028 9084 4697 *E-mail:* cecil.walker@virgin.net.

Born 25 August 1954; Educated Annan Academy, Dumfriesshire; Downing College, Cambridge (MA); Edinburgh University (LLB); Married July 9, 1983, Rosemary Janet Fraser (2 daughters). Called to the Scottish Bar 1979; QC (Scot) 1997; Contested South Scotland 1979 European Parliament election. Member, Scottish Office Consultative Steering Group on the Scottish Parliament 1998. **House of Commons:** Contested Dumfries 1979 general election. Member for Orkney and Shetland since June 1983; Liberal Parliamentary Spokesman for: Energy 1983–85, Fishing 1985–87, Defence 1985–88; Alliance Spokesman for Transport 1987; Liberal Democrat Spokesman for: Employment and Fishing 1988–92, Scotland and Fishing 1992–94, Scotland, Energy, Fisheries and Maritime Transport 1994–97; Principal Spokesman for Scotland 1997–; Deputy Whip 1985–87; Chief Whip, Parliamentary Liberal Party 1987–88; First Chief Whip, Social and Liberal Democrats 1988; Liberal Democrat Chief Whip 1988–92; *Select Committees:* Member: Selection 1987–92, Procedure 1988–92. **Scottish Parliament:** MSP for Orkney constituency since May 6, 1999; Deputy First Minister and Minister for Justice 1999–. *Special Interests:* Constitutional Reform, Scottish Home Rule and Federalism, Scottish Law, Rural Development, Energy Conservation, Fishing, Shipping, Amnesty International. Chair, Edinburgh University Liberal Club 1976–77; Member, Scottish Liberal Party Executive 1976–85; Vice-Chair (Policy), Scottish Liberal Party 1982–85; Hon. President, Scottish Young Liberals 1984–85; Leader, Scottish Liberal Democrats 1992–; PC 2000; Joint recipient Saltire Society's Andrew Fletcher Award for Services to Scotland 1998; *Clubs:* Caledonian, Scottish Liberal; *Recreations:* Golf, travel, novice horse-riding. *Address:* Rt Hon James Wallace, QC, MP, MSP, House of Commons, London, SW1A 0AA *Tel:* 020 7219 6254 *Fax:* 020 7219 1162. *Constituency:* 39 Junction Road, Kirkwall, Orkney; Albert Buildings, Lerwick, Shetland *Tel:* 01856 876541 (Orkney) *Fax:* 01856 876162 (Orkney) *E-mail:* jim.wallace@zetnet.co.uk; jimwallace@cix.compulink.co.uk.

Born 23 January 1949; Daughter of late Arthur and late Mary Emma Walley; Educated Biddulph Grammar School; Hull University; University College of Wales, Swansea; Married August 3, 1981, Jan Ostrowski (2 sons). Alcoholics Recovery Project 1970–73; Local government officer: Swansea City Council 1974–78, Wandsworth Council 1978–79; NACRO development officer 1979–82; Member, UNISON. Lambeth Council: Formerly Councillor, Chair, Health and Consumer Services Committee. **House of Commons:** Member for Stoke-on-Trent North since June 1987; Opposition Spokesperson on: Environmental Protection and Development 1988–90, Transport 1990–95; *Select Committees:* Member: Trade and Industry 1995–97, Trade and Industry 1997–98; Member: Environmental Audit 1997–. *Special Interests:* Environment, Health; Eastern Europe.

Member: SERA, SEA. Vice-President, Institute Environmental Health Officers; President: West Midlands Home and Water Safety Council, City of Stoke on Trent Primary School Sports Association; Member, Armed Forces Parliamentary Scheme (RAF); *Clubs:* Newchapel Sports and Social Institute, Fegg Hayes Sports and Social; *Recreations:* Walking, swimming, music. *Address:* Joan Walley, MP, House of Commons, London, SW1A 0AA *Tel:* 020 7219 3000 *Fax:* 020 7219 4397. *Constituency:* Unit 5, Burslem Enterprise Centre, Moorland Road, Burslem, Stoke-on-Trent, ST6 1JN *Tel:* 01782 577900 *Fax:* 01782 836462.

ROBERT WALTER North Dorset — *Con majority 2,746*

Born 30 May 1948; Educated Lord Weymouth School, Warminster; Aston University, Birmingham (BSc 1971); Widower (2 sons 1 daughter). Farmer; Sheep farm, South Devon; Director and Vice-President, Aubrey G. Langston and Co 1986–; Former member, London Stock Exchange; Visiting lecturer in East-West trade, University of Westminster. **House of Commons:** Contested Bedwelty 1979. Member for North Dorset since May 1, 1997; Opposition Front Bench Spokesman for Constitutional Affairs (Wales) 1999–; *Select Committees:* Member: Health 1997–99, European Scrutiny 1999; Member: Unopposed Bills (Panel) 1997–. *Special Interests:* European Union, Environment, East-West Trade; Member, European Standing Committee B 1998–. Chair: Aston University Conservative Association 1967–69, Westbury Constituency Young Conservative 1973–76, Conservative Foreign Affairs Forum 1986–88, Member: Carlton Club Political Committee 1991–, National Union Executive Committee 1992–95, Conservative Foreign and Commonwealth Council; Chair, Conservative Group for Europe 1992–95, currently Vice-President. Founder Chair, Wiltshire Europe Society; Member: National Farmers Union, National Sheep Association, Royal Agricultural Society of England; Former Chairman, European Democrat Forum; Liveryman, Worshipful Company of Needlemakers 1983; Freeman, City of London 1983. *Address:* Robert Walter Esq, MP, House of Commons, London, SW1A 0AA *Tel:* 020 7219 6981 *Fax:* 020 7219 2608. *Constituency:* The Stables, White Cliff Gardens, Blandford Forum, Dorset, DT11 7BU *Tel:* 01258 452420 *Fax:* 01258 454231 *E-mail:* walterr@parliament.uk.

CLAIRE WARD Watford — *Lab majority 5,792*

Born 9 May 1972; Daughter of Frank and Catherine Ward; Educated Loreto College, St Albans, Hertfordshire; University of Hertfordshire (LLB); Brunel University (MA Britain and the European Union); College of Law, London. Part-time clerical and secretarial work 1985–95; Trainee Solicitor 1995–98; Solicitor 1998–; Member, TGWU 1987–; Winner: South East TUC Mike Perkins Memorial Award for Young Trade Unionists 1989, TGWU National Youth Award 1990; Delegate, TGWU Biennial Delegate Conference 1991. Councillor, Elstree and Boreham Wood Town Council 1994–97, Mayor 1996–97, Former Vice-Chair, Leisure and Entertainments Committee. **House of Commons:** Member for Watford since May 1, 1997; *Select Committees:* Member: Culture, Media and Sport 1997–. *Special Interests:* Transport, Education, Employment, Home Affairs, Culture, Media, Sport; St Lucia. Member, Co-operative Party and CRS Ltd 1987–; Youth Representative, Labour Party National Executive Committee 1991–95; Chair: Boreham Wood Branch Labour Party 1991–97, Hertsmere Constituency Labour Party 1992–96; Member, Central Region Executive Committee 1993; Member: London Region CRS Political Committee 1993–, Co-operative Party Parliamentary Panel 1994–95; Member, Labour Party National Policy Commissions on: Democracy and Citizenship 1992–95, Social Policy 1992–95, Equalities 1992–95, Environment 1992–95; Member: Fabian Society, Society of Labour Lawyers. Youngest Woman MP; *Clubs:* Reform; *Recreations:* Cinema, reading, restaurants, Watford Football Club. *Address:* Claire Ward, MP, House of Commons, London, SW1A 0AA *Tel:* 020 7219 4910 *Fax:* 020 7219 0468 *E-mail:* wardc@parliament.uk.

CHARLES WARDLE   Bexhill and Battle   Con majority 11,100

Born 23 August 1939; Son of late Frederick Maclean Wardle and Constance (née Roach); Educated Tonbridge School; Lincoln College, Oxford; Harvard Business School; Married August 29, 1964, Lesley Ann Wells (1 daughter). Assistant to the President, American Express Co., New York 1966–69; Merchant banking, London 1969–72; Benjamin Priest Group: Director 1972–74, Managing director 1974–77, Chair 1977–84. **House of Commons:** Member for Bexhill and Battle since June 1983; PPS: to Minister for Health 1984, to Secretary of State for Social Services 1984–87, to Ian Lang as Secretary of State for Scotland 1991–92; Parliamentary Under-Secretary of State, Home Office 1992–94; Parliamentary Under-Secretary of State for Industry and Energy, Department of Trade and Industry 1994–95; *Select Committees:* Member: Public Accounts 1996–97; Member: Public Accounts 2000–. *Special Interests:* Industry, Employment, Economic Policy, Immigration, Police. Chair, One Nation Forum 1989–90. Member: CBI Council 1980–84, CBI West Midlands Regional Council, Commercial and Economic Committee, Engineering and Employers' Federation 1980–83, Midlands Committee, Institute of Directors 1980–83; *Recreations:* Books, sport, travel. *Address:* Charles Wardle Esq, MP, House of Commons, London, SW1A 0AA *Tel:* 020 7219 3426. *Constituency:* Bexhill and Battle Conservative Association, 6a Amherst Road, Bexhill-on-Sea, TN39 1QJ *Tel:* 01424 219117 *Fax:* 01424 218367 *E-mail:* charles@wardlecharles.tory.org.uk.

ROBERT WAREING   Liverpool West Derby   Lab majority 25,965

Born 20 August 1930; Son of late Robert and Florence Patricia Wareing; Educated Ranworth Square Council School, Liverpool; Alsop High School, Liverpool; Bolton College of Education (Teacher's Certificate 1957); External student, London University (BSc economics 1956); Married August 16, 1962, Betty Coward (died 1989). RAF 1948–50; Local government officer, Liverpool Corporation 1946–48, 1950–56; Lecturer: Brooklyn Technical College 1957–59, Wigan and District Mining and Technical College 1959–63, Liverpool College of Commerce 1963–64, Liverpool City Institute of Further Education 1964–72; Principal lecturer/deputy head adult education, Central Liverpool College of FE 1972–83; Member, MSF. Merseyside County Council: Councillor 1981–86, Chairman, Economic Development Committee 1981–83, Chief Whip, Labour Group 1981–83. **House of Commons:** Contested Berwick-upon-Tweed 1970 general election and Liverpool Edge Hill 1979 by-election and general election of 1979. Member for Liverpool, West Derby since June 1983; Assistant Opposition Whip 1987–92; *Select Committees:* Member: Foreign Affairs 1992–97. *Special Interests:* Economic and Foreign Affairs, Regional Economic Policy, Disabled/Disability, NHS Tranquillisers Addiction, Motor Industry, Airports Policy; Russia, Yugoslavia, Germany, Latin America, Eastern Europe, Far East. President, Liverpool District Labour Party 1972–73, 1974–81. Council Member, British-Russian Centre; Member, Hansard Society; Vice-President, AMA 1984–97; *Clubs:* Dovecot Labour (Liverpool); *Recreations:* Watching soccer, concert-going, ballet, motoring, travel. *Address:* Robert Wareing Esq, MP, House of Commons, London, SW1A 0AA *Tel:* 020 7219 3482 *Fax:* 020 7219 6187. *Constituency:* 74a Mill Lane, Liverpool, L12 *Tel:* 0151–256 9111 *Fax:* 0151–226 0285.

NIGEL WATERSON   Eastbourne   Con majority 1,994

Born 12 October 1950; Son of late James Waterson and Katherine Mahon; Educated Leeds Grammar School; The Queen's College, Oxford (BA law 1971, MA); Married 1st, 1979, Gisela Guettler (divorced), married 2nd, 1989, Bernadette Anne O'Halloran (divorced), married 3rd, 1999, Dr Barbara Judge. Solicitor; Barrister; Founder and senior partner of law firm, Waterson Hicks; Research assistant to Sally Oppenheim, MP 1972–73. Councillor, London Borough of Hammersmith and Fulham 1974–78. **House of Commons:** Contested Islington South and Finsbury 1979 general election. Member for Eastbourne since April 9, 1992; Opposition Front Bench Spokesman for Local Government and Housing 1999–; Opposition Whip: Social Security, Health, Legal, Lord Chancellor; Eastern 1997–98, Home Office, Culture, Media and Sport 1998–99;

PPS to: Gerry Malone as Minister of State, Department of Health 1995–96, Michael Heseltine as Deputy Prime Minister 1996–97; *Select Committees:* Member: Joint Committee on Statutory Instruments 1992–97, National Heritage 1995–96. *Special Interests:* Health, Foreign Affairs, Tourism, Shipping, Shipbuilding, Energy. President, Oxford University Conservative Association 1970; Chair, Bow Group 1986–87; Chair: Hammersmith Conservative Association 1987–90, Hammersmith and Fulham Joint Management Committee 1988–90; Member, CPC Advisory Committee 1986–90; Hon. Patron, Bow Group 1993–95. School governor 1986–88; Member, Management Committee of Stonham Housing Association Hostel for Ex-Offenders 1988–90; Vice-Chair, Eastbourne Branch of BLESMA; Member: IPU, CPA; *Clubs:* Carlton, Eastbourne Constitutional, Coningsby,; *Sportsclubs:* Guards' Polo, Sussex County Cricket Club; *Recreations:* Sailing, polo, reading, music. *Address:* Nigel Waterson Esq, MP, House of Commons, London, SW1A 0AA *Tel:* 020 7219 4576 *Fax:* 020 7219 2561. *Constituency:* Eastbourne Conservative Association, 7A Hyde Gardens, Eastbourne, East Sussex, BN21 4PN *Tel.* 01323 720776 *Fax:* 01323 410994 *E-mail:* nigelwatersonmp@parliament.uk.

DAVID WATTS   St Helens North   Lab majority 23,417

Born 26 August 1951; Educated Seel Road Secondary Modern School; Married 1972, Avril Davies (2 sons). Research assistant to Angela Eagle, MP 1992–93 and John Evans, MP 1993–97; Shop Steward, United Biscuits. St Helens MBC: Councillor 1979–97, Deputy Leader 1990–93, Leader 1993–97; Chair: Education Development Committee 1979–83, Economic Development Committee 1983–90. **House of Commons:** Member for St Helens North since May 1, 1997; PPS to John Spellar as Minister of State for the Armed Forces, Ministry of Defence 1999–; *Select Committees:* Member: Finance and Services 1997–. *Special Interests:* Regional Policy, Education, Training. Vice-Chair, North West Regional Group of Labour MPs 1999–. Vice-Chair, Association of Metropolitan Authorities; UK President, Euro Group of Industrial Regions 1989–93; *Recreations:* Watching football and rugby, reading. *Address:* David Watts Esq, MP, House of Commons, London, SW1A 0AA *Tel:* 020 7219 6325. *Constituency:* Ann Ward House, 1 Milk Street, St Helens, Merseyside, WA10 1PX *Tel:* 01744 623416 *Fax:* 01744 623417.

PROF STEVE WEBB   Northavon   LD majority 2,137

Born 18 July 1965; Son of Brian and Patricia Webb; Educated Dartmouth High School, Birmingham; Hertford College, Oxford (BA philosophy, politics and economics); Married July 10, 1993, Helen Edwards (1 daughter 1 son). Researcher then programme director, Institute for Fiscal Studies 1986–95; Professor of social policy, University of Bath 1995–. **House of Commons:** Member for Northavon since May 1, 1997; Spokesman for Social Security and Welfare (Pensions) 1997–99; Principal Spokesman for Social Security 1999–; *Special Interests:* Social Issues, Welfare, Third World. Member: Liberal Democrat Tax and Benefits Working Group, Liberal Democrat Costings Group. Member: Oxfam, Amnesty International, World Development Movement; Member, Commission on Social Justice; Specialist Adviser to Social Security Select Committee; *Publications:* Include: *Beyond The Welfare State*, 1990, Co-author *For Richer, For Poorer*, 1994, *Inequality in the UK*, 1997; *Recreations:* Football (West Bromwich Albion FC), cricket, music (play oboe, piano and organ), reading. *Address:* Prof Steve Webb Esq, MP, House of Commons, London, SW1A 0AA *Tel:* 020 7219 3000.

BOWEN WELLS   Hertford and Stortford   *Con majority 6,885*

Born 4 August 1935; Son of late Reginald Laird Wells, chartered accountant, and Agnes Mary Wells (née Hunter); Educated St Paul's School, Barnes; Exeter University (BA political history and government); Regent Street Polytechnic (Diploma in Business Management); Married October 25, 1975, Rennie Heyde (2 sons). National Service, Royal Navy 1954–56; Schoolmaster 1956–57; Sales Trainee, British Aluminium Co. 1957–58; Exeter University, President of Guild of Students 1958–61; Senior Executive, in charge of subsidiary and associated Development Finance Companies of Commonwealth Development Corporation 1961–73; Director, Outward Bound School, Aberdovey 1979–92; Governor, Institute of Development Studies, Sussex University 1981–92. **House of Commons:** Member for Hertford and Stevenage 1979–83 and for Hertford and Stortford since June 1983; Assistant Government Whip 1994–95; Government Whip (Lord Commissioner of HM Treasury) 1995–97; PPS: to Minister of State for Employment June 1982–83, to Roger Freeman as Minister for Public Transport, to Earl of Caithness as Minister for Aviation and Shipping 1992–94; *Select Committees:* Member: European Legislation 1981–92, Foreign Affairs 1990–92; Member: Chairmen's Panel 1997–; Chairman: International Development 1997–; Member: Liaison 1997–. *Special Interests:* Foreign Affairs, Overseas Aid and Development, Trade and Industry, United Nations, Treasury; Africa, Caribbean, Central America, Europe, Hong Kong, West Indies. Chairman, Westminster for Europe 1975; Executive Member, 1922 Committee 1997–; Treasurer, International CPA and of UK Branch; Member, CPA Executive 1984–; Fellow and Trustee, Industry and Parliament Trust; *Publications: Managing Third World Debt; Growing out of Debt; Recreations:* Swimming, walking, sailing, gardening, cooking, music. *Address:* Bowen Wells Esq, MP, House of Commons, London, SW1A 0AA *Tel:* 020 7219 5154.

ANDREW WELSH   Angus   *SNP majority 10,189*

Born 19 April 1944; Son of late William and late Agnes (née Paton) Welsh; Educated Govan High School; Glasgow University (MA modern history and politics 1970, DipEd 1971); Married 1971, Sheena Margaret Cannon (1 daughter). Teacher; Senior lecturer in business studies and public administration; MSP for Angus constituency since May 6, 1999; Member: EIS, SHFEA. Stirling District Councillor 1974; Provost, Angus District Council 1984–87. **House of Commons:** Contested Dumbartonshire Central February 1974 general election. Member for Angus South October 1974–79. Contested Angus East 1983 general election. Member for Angus East 1987–97, and for Angus since May 1, 1997; SNP Parliamentary Spokesman for: Housing 1974–79, 1987–97, 1997–, Agriculture 1974–79, 1987–97, Self Employed and Small Businesses 1975–79, Local Government 1987–97, 1997–, Education 1997–; SNP Chief Whip 1977–79, 1987–99; *Select Committees:* Member: Members' Interests 1990–92, Scottish Affairs 1992–97; Member: Chairmen's Panel 1997–, Scottish Affairs 1997–. *Special Interests:* Local Government, Environment; China, France. Prayer Breakfast for Scotland; *Recreations:* Music, football. *Address:* Andrew Welsh Esq, MP, MSP, House of Commons, London, SW1A 0AA *Tel:* 020 7219 6921 *Fax:* 020 7219 6716. *Constituency:* The Scottish Parliament Office, 31 Market Place, Arbroath, Angus, DD11 1HR *Tel:* 01241 439369 *Fax:* 01241 871561 *E-mail:* andrew.welsh.msp@scottish.parliament.uk.

BRIAN WHITE   Milton Keynes North East   *Lab majority 240*

Born 5 May 1957; Son of William Edward White and Elinor White; Educated Methodist College, Belfast; Married Leena Lindholm (2 stepsons). Civil servant, HM Customs and Excise; IT consultant; Systems analyst, Abbey National; Member, MSF. Councillor, Milton Keynes Borough Council 1987–97, former Deputy Leader; Councillor, Buckinghamshire County Council 1994–97. **House of Commons:** Member for Milton Keynes North East since May 1, 1997; *Select Committees:* Member: Joint Committee on Consolidation of Bills Etc 1997–, Deregulation 1999–, Joint Committee on Statutory Instruments 1999–, Public Administration 1999–. *Special Interests:* Environment, Transport, Economic Policy, European Union, International Trade,

Information Technology, Animal Welfare, Third World Debt, Modernising Government. Member, Milton Keynes Energy Association; Agent, Milton Keynes South West General Election 1992; Local Government Association: Member, Policy and Strategy Committee, Chair, Planning Committee, Secretary, Labour Group; *Recreations:* Reading, ten-pin bowling. *Address:* Brian White Esq, MP, House of Commons, London, SW1A 0AA *Tel:* 020 7219 3435 *Fax:* 020 7219 2887. *Constituency:* Labour Hall, Newport Road, New Bradwell, Milton Keynes, Buckinghamshire, MK13 0AA *Tel:* 01908 313933 *Fax:* 01908 313960 *E-mail:* whitebar@parliament.uk.

DR ALAN WHITEHEAD   Southampton Test   *Lab majority 13,684*

Born 15 September 1950; Educated Isleworth Grammar School, Isleworth, Middlesex; Southampton University (BA, PhD); Married December 1, 1979, Sophie Wronska (1 son 1 daughter). Director, Outset 1979–83, Deputy 1976–79; Director, BIIT 1983–92; Professor of Public Policy, Southampton Institute 1992–97; Member, UNISON (formerly NUPE). Councillor, Southampton City Council 1980–92, Leader 1984–92. **House of Commons:** Contested Southampton Test 1983, 1987, 1992 general elections. Member for Southampton Test since May 1, 1997; Joint PPS to David Blunkett as Secretary of State for Education and Employment 1999–; PPS to Baroness Blackstone as Minister for Education and Employment 1999–; *Select Committees:* Member: Environment, Transport and Regional Affairs 1997–99, Environment Sub-Committee 1997–99. *Special Interests:* Environment, Local and Regional Government, Further and Higher Education, Constitutional Affairs, Transport; Poland, France. Member, Labour Party National Policy Forum 1999–. Governor, Cantell School, Southampton; Director/Board Member, Southampton Environment Centre; Vice-President, Local Government Association 1998–; Director/Board Member, Mayflower Theatre Trust; Director, Southampton Environment Centre; *Publications:* Various chapters, articles and papers including: Co-author *TUPE – the EU's Revenge on the Iron Lady*, 1994; *Spain, European Regions and City States*, 1995; *Rational Actors and Irrational Structures*, 1995; *Local Government Finance – Accountancy or Accountability?*, 1995; Joint editor, *Beyond 2002: Long-Term Policies for Labour*; Visiting Professor, Southampton Institute 1997–; Senior Research Fellow, Southampton University 1998–; *Recreations:* Football (playing and watching), writing, tennis. *Address:* Dr Alan Whitehead, MP, House of Commons, London, SW1A 0AA *Tel:* 020 7219 6338 *Fax:* 020 7219 0918. *Constituency:* Southampton Labour Party, 20–22 Southampton Street, Southampton, SO15 1ED *Tel:* 023 8023 1942 *Fax:* 023 8023 1943 *E-mail:* whiteheada@parliament.uk *Website:* www.alan-whitehead.org.uk.

SIR RAYMOND WHITNEY   Wycombe   *Con majority 2,370*

Born 28 November 1930; Son of late George William Whitney, hotel keeper; Educated Wellingborough School; Royal Military Academy, Sandhurst 1950; London University (BA oriental studies 1959); Hong Kong University 1960; Australian National University (Postgraduate studies 1963); Married March 31, 1956, Sheila Margot Beswick, daughter of Walter Henry Prince (2 sons). Army service 1951–64: service in Italy, Germany, Korea, seconded to Australian Army 1960–63; Diplomatic Service, Peking and Argentina 1964; Deputy High Commissioner, Bangladesh 1973–76; Head, Information Research Department, Overseas Information Department, Foreign and Commonwealth Office 1976–78. **House of Commons:** Member for Wycombe since April 1978 by-election; PPS to Treasury Minister 1979–80; Parliamentary Under-Secretary of State: Foreign and Commonwealth Office 1983–84, Department of Social Security 1984–85, Department of Health 1985–86; *Special Interests:* European Union, Foreign Affairs, Defence, Economic Policy, Health; Bangladesh, China, Europe, Hong Kong, Latin America, Taiwan; Member, European Standing Committee B 1998–. Chair, The Positive European Group 1993–. Chair, Mountbatten Community Trust; Executive Member, 1922 Committee 1997–; *Publications: National Health Crisis. A Modern Solution; Time to Return to Euro-Sanity; Europe: In or Out?* Co-author with Michael Welsh; OBE 1968; Knighted 1997; *Sportsclubs:* Windlesham Golf Club; *Recreations:* Golf, bridge, theatre. *Address:* Sir Raymond Whitney, OBE, House of Commons, London, SW1A 0AA *Tel:* 020 7219 5099 *Fax:* 020 7219 4614. *Constituency:* 150A West Wycombe Road, High Wycombe, Buckinghamshire, HP12 3AE *Tel:* 01494 521777 *Fax:* 01494 510042 *E-mail:* whitneyr@parliament.uk.

JOHN WHITTINGDALE   Maldon and Chelmsford East   *Con majority 10,039*

Born 16 October 1959; Son of late John Whittingdale and of Margaret Whittingdale; Educated Sandroyd School, Wiltshire; Winchester College; University College, London (BSc economics 1982); Married 1990, Ancilla Murfitt (1 son 1 daughter). Head, political section, Conservative research department 1982–84; Special adviser to Secretary of State for Trade and Industry 1984–87; Manager, N. M. Rothschild & Sons 1987; Political secretary to Margaret Thatcher as Prime Minister 1988–90; Private secretary to Margaret Thatcher 1990–92. **House of Commons:** Member for South Colchester and Maldon 1992–97, and for Maldon and Chelmsford East since May 1, 1997; Front Bench Spokesman for the Treasury (Tax, VAT and Duties; EU Budget and other EU Issues) 1998–99; Opposition Whip 1997–98; PPS to Eric Forth: as Minister of State for Education 1994–95, as Minister of State for Education and Employment 1994–96; Parliamentary private secretary to William Hague as Leader of the Opposition 1999–; *Select Committees:* Member: Health 1993–97, Information 1997–98. *Special Interests:* Broadcasting and Media; Israel, USA. *Publications: New Policies for the Media*, 1995; OBE 1990; *Clubs:* Essex; *Recreations:* Cinema, music. *Address:* John Whittingdale Esq, OBE, MP, House of Commons, London, SW1A 0AA *Tel:* 020 7219 3557 *Fax:* 020 7219 2522. *Constituency:* Maldon and East Chelmsford Conservative Association, 120B High Street, Maldon, Essex, CM9 5ET *Tel:* 01621 855663 *E-mail:* jwhittingdale.mp@email.tory.org.uk.

MALCOLM WICKS   Croydon North   *Lab majority 18,398*

Born 1 July 1947; Son of Arthur Wicks and of late Daisy Wicks; Educated Elizabeth College, Guernsey; North West London Polytechnic; London School of Economics (BSc Sociology); Married September 7, 1968, Margaret Baron (1 son 2 daughters). Fellow, Department of Social Administration, York University 1968–70; Research worker, Centre for Environmental Studies 1970–72; Lecturer in social administration, Brunel University 1970–74; Social policy analyst, Urban Deprivation Unit, Home Office 1974–77; Lecturer in social policy, Civil Service College 1977–78; Research director and secretary, Study Commission on the Family 1978–83; Director, Family Policy Studies Centre 1983–92; Co-director, European Family and Social Policy Unit 1992–. **House of Commons:** Contested Croydon North West 1987 general election. Member for Croydon North West 1992–97, and for Croydon North since May 1, 1997; Opposition Spokesman on Social Security 1995–97; Parliamentary Under-Secretary of State (Lifelong Learning), Department for Education and Employment 1999–; *Select Committees:* Member: Social Security 1994–96, Social Security 1997–98; Chairman (Education): Education and Employment 1998–99; Chairman: Education Sub-Committee 1998–99; Member: Liaison 1998–99. *Special Interests:* Social Policy, Welfare State, Education; Australia, Europe, New Zealand. Member, European Institute of Social Security; Trustee, National Energy Foundation; *Publications:* Several publications and articles on social policy and welfare including: *Old and Cold: hypothermia and social policy*, 1978; *Government and Urban Poverty*, 1983 (co-author); *A Future for All: do we need a welfare state?* 1987; *Family Change and Future Policy*, 1990 (co-author); *A New Agenda* (jointly) IPPR, 1993; *Clubs:* Ruskin House Labour (Croydon); *Recreations:* Music, walking, gardening, very occasional white water rafting. *Address:* Malcolm Wicks Esq, MP, House of Commons, London, SW1A 0AA *Tel:* 020 7219 4554 *Fax:* 020 7219 2795. *Constituency:* 84 High Street, Thornton Heath, Surrey, CR7 8LF *Tel:* 020 8665 1214 *Fax:* 020 8683 0179.

ANN WIDDECOMBE   Maidstone and The Weald   *Con majority 9,603*

Born 4 October 1947; Daughter of late James Murray Widdecombe CB, OBE, retired Director General in Ministry of Defence, and of Rita Widdecombe; Educated Royal Naval School, Singapore; La Sainte Union Convent, Bath; Birmingham University (BA Latin); Lady Margaret Hall, Oxford (BA philosophy, politics and economics, MA). With Unilever in Marketing 1973–75; Senior Administrator, London University 1975–1987. Councillor, Runnymede District Council 1976–78. **House of Commons:** Contested Burnley 1979, Plymouth Devonport 1983 general elections. Member for Maidstone 1987–97, and for Maidstone and The Weald since May 1, 1997; Introduced Abortion Amendment Bill 1988–89; PPS to Tristan Garel-Jones as Minister of State, Foreign and Commonwealth Office 1990; Joint Parliamentary Under-Secretary of State, Department of Social Security 1990–93; Department of Employment: Joint Parliamentary Under-Secretary of State 1993–94, Minister of State 1994–95; Minister of State, Home Office 1995–97; Member, Shadow Cabinet 1998–; Shadow Secretary of State for Health 1998–99; Shadow Home Secretary 1999–; *Select Committees:* Member: Health and Social Security 1989–90, Standards and Privileges 1997, Chairmen's Panel 1998. *Special Interests:* Abortion, Health, Defence, Prisons. Vice-Chairman, National Association of Conservative Graduates 1974–76. Founding Member and Vice-Chair, Women and Families for Defence; National Patron, *Life*; Member, SPUC; Member, Gas Consumers Council 1984–86; *Publications:* Various publications including *A Layman's Guide to Defence*, 1984; *Outspoken and Inspired*, 1999; *This Spring*, 1999; *The Clematis Tree*, 2000; PC 1997; Highland Park/*The Spectator* Minister of the Year 1996; Talk Radio, Straight Talker of the Year 1997; *Recreations:* Reading, researching Charles II's escape. *Address:* Rt Hon Ann Widdecombe, MP, House of Commons, London, SW1A 0AA *Tel:* 020 7219 5091. *Constituency:* Kloof Cottage, Sutton Valence, Maidstone, Kent *Tel:* 01622 843868 *Fax:* Home: 01622 844330, Office: 01622 752463.

DAFYDD WIGLEY   Caernarfon   *PC majority 7,949*

Born 1 April 1943; Son of Elfyn Edward and Myfanwy Wigley; Educated Caernarfon Grammar School; Rydal School, Colwyn Bay; Manchester University (BSc physics 1964); Married August 26, 1967, Elinor, daughter of late Emrys Bennett Owen (1 son 1 daughter, and 2 sons deceased). Finance staff, Ford Motor Co. 1964–67; Chief cost accountant and financial planning manager, Mars Ltd. 1967–71; Financial controller, Hoover Ltd., Merthyr Plant 1971–74; Chair, Alpha-Dyffryn Ltd (Electronics) 1987–91; Former Member, ASTMS. Councillor, Merthyr Tydfil County Borough Council 1972–74; Contested North Wales 1994 European Parliament election. **House of Commons:** Contested Merioneth 1970 general election. Member for Caernarfon since February 1974; Spokesman for Constitutional Affairs 1997–2000; Plaid Cymru Whip 1987–91; Sponsor, 1981 Disabled Persons Act; *Select Committees:* Member: Public Accounts 1997–98. **National Assembly for Wales:** AM for Caernarfon constituency since May 6, 1999; Shadow First Secretary and Shadow Secretary for Finance 1999–2000. *Special Interests:* Industry, Employment, Disabled/Disability, European Regional Issues, Minority Languages; Argentina, Ireland, USA, Slovenia. President, Plaid Cymru 1981–84, 1991–2000. Vice-President, Wales Council for the Disabled; President, Spastic Society for Wales 1985–90; Member, Mencap Profound Mental Handicap Study Committee 1987–97; Vice-President, Mencap in Wales 1990–; President, Epilepsy Wales 1998–; Vice-President, Federation of Economic Development Authorities (FEDA); *Publications:* Co-author *An Economic Plan for Wales*, 1970; *Agenda i'r iaith*, 1988; Report *Tourism in Wales*, 1987; *O Ddifri*, 1992; *Dal Ati*, 1993; *A Democratic Wales in an United Europe*, 1994; *A Fair Choice for Wales*, 1996; PC 1997; National Federation of the Blind Grimshaw Memorial Award 1981; *Sportsclubs:* Member, Caernarfon Town Football Club; *Recreations:* Football, tennis, swimming, chess. *Address:* Rt Hon Dafydd Wigley, MP, AM, House of Commons, London, SW1A 0AA *Tel:* 020 7219 4182 *Fax:* 020 7219 3705. *Constituency:* 8 Stryd y Castell, Caernarfon, Gwynedd, LL55 1SE *Tel:* 01286 672076 *Fax:* 01286 672003 *E-mail:* wigleyd@parliament.uk.

JOHN WILKINSON   Ruislip Northwood   *Con majority 7,794*

Born 23 September 1940; Son of late Denys Wilkinson, schoolmaster, and late Gillian, née Nairn, university lecturer; Educated Eton College (King's Scholar); RAF College, Cranwell; Churchill College, Cambridge (BA history 1965); University of Aix/Marseilles (Diploma) 1961; Married 1st, July 5, 1969, Paula Adey (divorced 1987) (1 daughter), married 2nd, July 25, 1987, Cecilia Lyon (1 son). Commissioned into RAF from Cranwell 1961; Qualified French interpreter in RAF 1961; Flying instructor: No. 8 FTS 1962; Trooper, 21 SAS Regiment (Artists') TA 1963–65; Qualified flying instructor, RAF College, Cranwell 1966–67; ADC to Commander, 2nd Allied Tactical Air Force, Germany 1967; Head of university department, Conservative Central Office 1967–68; Aviation specialist, Conservative Research Department 1969; Senior administration officer (Anglo/French Jaguar Project), Preston Division BAC 1969–70; Correspondence tutor, Open University 1970–71; Chief flying instructor, Skywork Ltd, Stansted 1974–75; Sales manager, Brooklands Aviation 1975; Personal assistant to Chairman, BAC 1976–77; Sales manager, Executive Air Services 1978–79. **House of Commons:** Member for Bradford West 1970-February 1974. Contested Bradford West October 1974 general election. Member for Ruislip Northwood since May 1979; PPS: to Minister of State for Industry 1979–80, to John Nott as Secretary of State for Defence 1981–82; Whip withdrawn over European Communities Finance Bill 1994–1995; *Select Committees:* Armed Forces Bill (Special Select Committee) 1990–91. *Special Interests:* International Affairs, Defence, Aerospace, Aviation, European Union, Industry; Latin America, Baltic States, Ukraine, Philippines and ASEAN States, Bosnia; Member, European Standing Committee B 1998–. Chair, Anglo/Asian Conservative Society 1979–82. Chair: European Freedom Council 1982–90; Horn of Africa Council 1984–88; Commonwealth War Graves Commissioner 1997–; President, London Green Belt Council 1997–; Delegate, Council of Europe and WEU 1979–90; Chair: Aerospace Committee, WEU 1986–89, Space Sub-Committee, Council of Europe 1984–88; Member, UK Delegation Parliamentary Assembly of the Council of Europe/Western European Union 2000–; Fellow, Industry and Parliament Trust 1993; *Publications:* Co-author *The Uncertain Ally,* 1982; *British Defence: A Blueprint for Reform,* 1987; Hilal-i-Quaid-i-Azam (HQA) Pakistan 1989; Cross of Land of Mary (Estonia) 1999; Companion, Royal Aeronautical Society; *Recreations:* Cross country skiing, hill-walking. *Address:* John Wilkinson Esq, MP, House of Commons, London, SW1A 0AA *Tel:* 020 7219 6317 *Tel (Constituency):* 01923 822876.

DAVID WILLETTS   Havant   *Con majority 3,729*

Born 9 March 1956; Son of John and Hilary Willetts; Educated King Edward's School, Birmingham; Christ Church, Oxford (BA philosophy, politics and economics 1978); Married 1986, Hon. Sarah Butterfield (1 son 1 daughter). HM Treasury 1978–84; Private secretary to Financial Secretary 1981–82; Principal, Monetary Policy Division 1982–84; Prime Minister's Downing Street Policy Unit 1984–86; Director of Studies, Centre for Policy Studies 1987–92; Consultant director, Conservative Research Department 1987–92; Director: Retirement Security Ltd 1988–94, Electra Corporate Ventures Ltd 1988–94. Member: Lambeth and Lewisham Family Practitioners' Committee 1987–90, Parkside Health Authority 1988–90, Social Security Advisory Committee 1989–92. **House of Commons:** Member for Havant since April 9, 1992; Opposition Spokesman on Education and Employment (Employment) 1997–98; Assistant Government Whip 1994–95; Government Whip July-November 1995; PPS to Sir Norman Fowler as Chairman of Conservative Party 1993–94; Parliamentary Secretary, Office of Public Service 1995–96; Paymaster General, Office of Public Service July-December 1996; Shadow Secretary of State for: Education and Employment 1998–99, Social Security 1999–; *Select Committees:* Member: Social Security 1992–93. *Special Interests:* Economic Policy, Health, Social Security, Education; Japan, USA, Germany. Chair, Conservative Research Department 1997. *Publications: Modern Conservatism,* 1992; *Civic Conservatism,* 1994; *Blair's Gurus,* 1996; *Why Vote Conservative,* 1997; *Welfare to Work,* 1998; *After the Landslide,* 1999; *Clubs:* Athenaeum, Hurlingham; *Recreations:* Swimming, reading. *Address:* David Willetts Esq, MP, House of Commons, London, SW1A 0AA *Tel:* 020 7219 4570 *Fax:* 020 7219 2567. *Constituency:* c/o Havant Conservative Association, Homewell House, 22 Homewell, Havant, Hampshire PO9 1EE *Tel:* 023 9247 5066 *E-mail:* willettsd@parliament.uk.

ALAN JOHN WILLIAMS   Swansea West   *Lab majority 14,459*

Born 14 October 1930; Son of Emlyn Williams, coal miner; Educated Cardiff High School; Cardiff College of Technology (BSc economics, London 1954); University College, Oxford (BA philosophy, politics and economics); Married June 1957, Patricia Rees (2 sons 1 daughter). Lecturer in economics, Welsh College of Advanced Technology; Member, Association of Teachers at Technical Institutes, affiliated to NUT 1958–; Member, Transport Salaried Staff Association (TSSA). **House of Commons:** Contested Poole 1959 general election. Member for Swansea West since October 15, 1964; Opposition Spokesman on: Industry 1970–71, Higher Education 1971–72, Consumer Affairs 1973–74; Opposition Front Bench Spokesman on: Wales 1979 80, Industry and Consumer Affairs 1979–87, The Civil Service 1980–83; PPS to Edward Short as Postmaster General 1966–67; Joint Parliamentary Secretary, Ministry of Technology 1969–70; Parliamentary Under-Secretary of State, Department of Economic Affairs 1967–69; Minister of State for: Prices and Consumer Protection 1974–76, Industry 1976–79; Shadow Secretary of State for Wales 1987–88; Deputy Shadow Leader of the House and Campaigns Co-ordinator 1983–89; *Select Committees:* Member: Public Accounts 1990–97, Privileges 1994–97; Member: Parliamentary Privilege (Joint Committee) 1997–, Public Accounts 1997–, Standards and Privileges 1997–. *Special Interests:* Regional Policy, Industrial Policy, Job-Creating Strategies, Micro-Technology. Member: Fabian Society, Co-operative Party; Chair, Welsh Parliamentary Labour Group 1966–67. Member: Lord Chancellor's Advisory Council on Committee Records 1995–, Public Accounts Commission 1997–; Council of Europe and Western European 1966–67; Chair, Welsh Branch of British-Russia Centre 1995–; Member, North Atlantic Alliance 1997–; Joint Hon. Treasurer, British-American Parliamentary International Group 1999–; PC January 1977; Freeman, City of Swansea; *Clubs:* Clyne Golf; *Recreations:* Golf. *Address:* Rt Hon Alan John Williams, MP (Swansea West), House of Commons, London, SW1A 0AA *Tel:* 020 7219 3449 *Fax:* 020 7219 6943. *Constituency:* Alexandra House, 10th Floor, Alexandra Road, Swansea *Fax:* 01792 655097 *E-mail:* batchelore@parliament.uk.

DR ALAN WYNNE WILLIAMS   Carmarthen East and Dinefwr   *Lab majority 3,450*

Born 21 December 1945; Son of late Tom Williams and late Mary Williams; Educated Carmarthen Grammar School; Jesus College, Oxford (BA chemistry 1966, DPhil 1969); Married September 4, 1973, Marian Williams. Lecturer in environmental science, Trinity College, Carmarthen 1971–87. **House of Commons:** Member for Carmarthen 1987–97, and for Carmarthen East and Dinefwr since May 1, 1997; *Select Committees:* Member: Welsh Affairs 1987–91, Science and Technology 1992–97; Member: Science and Technology 2000–. *Special Interests:* Agriculture, Environmental Protection, Trade and Industry, Economics. Secretary, Carmarthen Constituency Labour Party 1981–84, Election Agent 1983. *Recreations:* Reading, television, watching sport. *Address:* Dr Alan Wynne Williams, MP (Carmarthen East & Dinefwr), House of Commons, London, SW1A 0AA *Tel:* 020 7219 3000. *Constituency:* 33 Wind Street, Ammanford, Carmarthenshire, SA18 3DN *Tel:* 01269 593809 *Fax:* 01269 597271.

BETTY WILLIAMS   Conwy   *Lab majority 1,596*

Born 31 July 1944; Daughter of late Griffith Williams and of Elizabeth Williams; Educated Ysgol Dyffryn Nantlle, Penygroes; Normal College, Bangor (BA); Evan Glyn Williams (2 sons). Secretarial; Freelance journalist/media researcher; Member, T&GWU. Councillor: Parish/Community 1967–83, District Council 1970–91, County Council 1976–93; Mayor, Arfon Borough Council 1990–91; Former Member: Gwynedd Health Authority, Snowdonia National Park Committee (Northern). **House of Commons:** Contested Caernarfon 1983, Conwy 1987 and 1992 general elections. Member for Conwy since May 1, 1997; *Select Committees:* Member: Welsh Affairs 1997–. *Special Interests:* Social Services, Health, Health Education, Environmental Health, Consumer Issues, Education (Special Needs), Railways. Chair, Governors of Special School in Caernarfon; Former Governor: Normal College, Bangor, Gwynedd Technical College;

Former Chair, National Eisteddfod Local Finance Committee; Chair: Victims' Support, Arfon Carers' Committee; Christian Aid Organiser; Member, Gas Consumers' Council for Wales; Deacon, Seion C Talysarn; Hon Fellow University of Wales, Bangor 2000; HTV Student of the Year; National Eisteddfod Prize for video production; John Evans Memorial Prize; *Recreations:* Eisteddfodau, opera, hymn singing festivals, sheep dog trials. *Address:* Betty Williams, MP, House of Commons, London, SW1A 0AA *Tel:* 020 7219 5052 *Fax:* 020 7219 2759 *E-mail:* bettywilliamsmp@parliament.uk.

PHIL WILLIS   Harrogate and Knaresborough — *LD majority 6,236*

Born 30 November 1941; Son of late George Willis, postman, and of late Norah, nurse; Educated Burnley Grammar School; City of Leeds and Carnegie College (Cert Ed 1963); Birmingham University (BPhil education 1978); Married Heather Sellars (1 son 1 daughter). Head teacher, Ormesby School, Cleveland 1978–82; Head teacher, John Smeaton Community High School, Leeds 1983–97; Member, Secondary Heads Association. Harrogate Borough Council: Councillor 1988–, First Liberal Democrat Leader 1990–97; North Yorkshire County Council: Councillor 1993–97, Deputy Group Leader 1993–97. **House of Commons:** Member for Harrogate and Knaresborough since May 1, 1997; Spokesman for Education and Employment (Further, Higher and Adult Education) 1997–99; Principal Spokesman for Education and Employment 1999–; North, Midlands and Wales Whip 1997–99; *Select Committees:* Member: Education Sub-Committee 1999–2000; Member: Education and Employment 1999–. *Special Interests:* Inclusive Education, Health, Local Government, Northern Ireland, Gibraltar; Ireland. Member, Association of Liberal Democrat Councillors. Member: Charter 88, Friends of the Earth, Amnesty International; *Sportsclubs:* Leeds United Football Club; *Recreations:* Theatre, music, dance (especially ballet), football (Leeds United). *Address:* Phil Willis Esq, MP, House of Commons, London, SW1A 0AA *Tel:* 020 7219 3846 *Fax:* 020 7219 0971. *Constituency:* Ashdown House, Station Parade, Harrogate, North Yorkshire, HG1 5BR *Tel:* 01423 528888 *Fax:* 01423 505700 *E-mail:* johnfox@cix.co.uk.

MICHAEL WILLS   North Swindon — *Lab majority 7,688*

Born 20 May 1952; Son of late Stephen Wills and Elizabeth Wills; Educated Haberdashers Aske's, Elstree; Clare College, Cambridge (BA); Married January 19, 1984, Jill Freeman (3 sons 2 daughters). Third secretary later second secretary, HM Diplomatic Service 1976–80; Researcher, later producer, London Weekend Television 1980–84; Director, Juniper Productions 1984–97; Member, TGWU. **House of Commons:** Member for North Swindon since May 1, 1997; Parliamentary Under-Secretary of State: Department of Trade and Industry (Minister for Small Firms, Trade and Industry) 1999, Department for Education and Employment 1999–. Chair, Non-Ministerial Cross-Party Advisory Group on Preparation for the EMU 1998–. *Address:* Michael Wills Esq, MP, House of Commons, London, SW1A 0AA *Tel:* 020 7219 3000. *Constituency:* People's Centre, Beech Avenue, Swindon, SN2 1JT *Tel:* 01793 481016 *Fax:* 01793 524483 *E-mail:* tlo.wills@tlo.dti.gov.uk.

DAVID WILSHIRE   Spelthorne — *Con majority 3,473*

Born 16 September 1943; Educated Kingswood School, Bath; Fitzwilliam College, Cambridge (BA geography 1965, MA); Married 1967, Margaret Weeks (separated 2000) (1 son, and 1 daughter deceased). Built up own group of small businesses; Worked for MEPs 1979–85; Partner, Western Political Research Services 1979–2000; Co-director, political management programme, Brunel University 1985–90; Partner, Moorlands Research Services 2000–. Formerly Parish, District and County Councillor; Leader, Wansdyke District Council (Avon) 1981–87. **House of Commons:** Member for Spelthorne since June 1987; PPS: to Alan Clark as Minister for Defence Procurement 1991–92, to Peter Lloyd as Minister of State, Home Office 1992–94; *Select Committees:* Member: Northern Ireland Affairs 1994–97, Entry Clearance Sub-Committee 1997–98;

Member: Foreign Affairs 1997–. *Special Interests:* Foreign Affairs, Aviation, Local Government, Political Process, Northern Ireland. Member, British-Irish Inter-Parliamentary Body 1990–; Substitute Member, Assembly of Council of Europe 1997–; Treasurer, IPU British Branch 1997–; Vice-Chair, CPA UK Branch 1998–99; *Publications: Scene from the Hill; Recreations:* Gardening, wine and cider-making. *Address:* David Wilshire Esq, MP, House of Commons, London, SW1A 0AA *Tel:* 020 7219 3534. *Constituency:* 55 Cherry Orchard, Staines, Middx, TW8 2DQ *Tel:* 01784 450822.

BRIAN WILSON   Cunninghame North   *Lab majority 11,039*

Born 13 December 1948; Son of late John Forrest Wilson and Marion MacIntyre; Educated Dunoon Grammar School; Dundee University; University College, Cardiff (MA); Married December 11, 1981, Joni Buchanan (2 sons 1 daughter). Journalist; Founding Editor and Publisher, *West Highland Free Press* 1972–97; Contributor to: *The Guardian, Glasgow Herald.* **House of Commons:** Contested Ross and Cromarty October 1974, Inverness 1979 and Western Isles 1983 general elections. Member for Cunninghame North since June 1987; Opposition Spokesman on: Scotland 1988–92, Citizen's Charter and Women July-November 1992, Transport November 1992–94, Trade and Industry 1994–95, Transport 1995–96, Election Planning 1996–97; Minister of State: Scottish Office (Minister for Education and Industry) 1997–98, Department of Trade and Industry (Minister for Trade) 1998–99; Minister of State, Scotland Office 1999–. *Publications: Celtic: A Century with Honour,* 1988; First winner, Nicholas Tomalin Memorial Award for outstanding journalism; *Spectator* Parliamentarian of the Year 'New Member' Award 1990; FRSA (Scot); *Clubs:* Garnock Labour; *Sportsclubs:* Kilbirnie Place Golf. *Address:* Brian Wilson Esq, MP, House of Commons, London, SW1A 0AA *Tel:* 020 7219 3000. *Constituency:* 37 Main Street, Kilbirnie, Ayrshire, KA25 7BX *Tel:* 01505 682847 *Fax:* 01505 684648 *E-mail:* scottishsecretary@scotland.gov.uk *Website:* www.scottishsecretary.gov.uk.

DAVID WINNICK   Walsall North   *Lab majority 12,588*

Born 26 June 1933; Son of late E. G. and Rose Winnick; Educated Secondary school; London School of Economics; Married September 23, 1968, Bengisu Rona (marriage dissolved). Association of Professional, Executive, Clerical & Computer Staff (APEX): Member of Executive Council 1978–88, Vice-President 1983–88. Councillor: Willesden Borough Council 1959–64, Brent Borough Council 1964–66. **House of Commons:** Contested Harwich 1964 general election. Member for Croydon South 1966–70. Contested Croydon Central October 1974 general election and Walsall North 1976 by-election. Member for Walsall North since May 1979; *Select Committees:* Member: Procedure 1989–97; Member: Home Affairs 1997–. Chair, United Kingdom Immigrants Advisory Service 1984–; British Co-Chair, British-Irish Inter-Parliamentary Body 1997–. *Address:* David Winnick Esq, MP, House of Commons, London, SW1A 0AA *Tel:* 020 7219 5003 *Fax:* 020 7219 0257 *Tel (Constituency):* 01922 495629.

ANN WINTERTON   Congleton   *Con majority 6,130*

Born 6 March 1941; Daughter of late Joseph Robert Hodgson and Ellen Jane Hodgson; Educated Erdington Grammar School for Girls; Married 1960, Nicholas Winterton (now MP – *qv*) (2 sons 1 daughter). **House of Commons:** Member for Congleton since June, 1983; Opposition Frontbench Spokeswoman on National Drug Strategy 1998–; *Select Committees:* Member: Agriculture 1987–97, Chairmen's Panel 1992–98; Member: Unopposed Bills (Panel) 1997–. *Special Interests:* Textile Industries, Pharmaceutical and Chemical Industries, Agriculture, Transport, Think British Campaign; Austria, Namibia, South Africa, USA. Member, West Midlands Conservative Women's Advisory Committee 1969–71. Vice-President: Townswomen's Guilds, East Cheshire and St Luke's Hospices; Patron: East Cheshire NSPCC, VISYON; President, Congleton Division of the St. John Ambulance; Joint Master, South Staffordshire Hunt 1959–64; Fellow, Industry and Parliament Trust; *Recreations:* Cinema, theatre, music, tennis, riding, skiing. *Address:* Mrs Ann Winterton, MP, House of Commons, London, SW1A 0AA *Tel:* 020 7219 3585. *Constituency:* Riverside, Mountbatten Way, Congleton, Cheshire, CW12 1DY *Tel:* 01260 278866 *Fax:* 01260 271212.

NICHOLAS WINTERTON   Macclesfield   *Con majority 8,654*

Born 31 March 1938; Son of late Norman Harry Winterton; Educated Bilton Grange Preparatory School; Rugby School; Married 1960, Ann (now MP – *qv*) Hodgson (2 sons 1 daughter). Army national service 1957–59; Sales executive trainee, Shell-Mex BP Ltd 1959–60; Sales and general manager, Stevens & Hodgson Ltd 1960–71. Warwickshire County Council: Councillor 1967–72, Chair, County Youth Service Sub-Committee 1969–72, Deputy Chair, Education Committee 1970–72. **House of Commons:** Contested Newcastle-under-Lyme October 1969 by-election and 1970 general election. Member for Macclesfield since by-election Sept 30, 1971; Deputy Speaker of the House of Commons 1999–; *Select Committees:* Chairman: Health 1991–92; Member: Liaison 1997–98; Member: Chairmen's Panel 1997–, Modernisation of the House of Commons 1997–; Chairman: Procedure 1997–; Member: Liaison 1998–, Standing Orders 1998–. *Special Interests:* Local Government, Health Service, Sport, Recreation, Paper Industries, Textile Industries, Foreign Affairs, Media, Pharmaceutical and Chemical Industries; South Africa, Indonesia, Taiwan, USA, Denmark, Sweden, Austria, Namibia. Patron, International Centre for Child Care Studies; Chair, Zimbabwe Rhodesia Relief Fund; President: Macclesfield Riding for the Disabled Branch, Macclesfield Handicapped Social Club, Macclesfield Branch of RNLI, Friends of Pallotti Day Care Centre, Rossendale Trust; Vice-President: Macclesfield Branch Multiple Sclerosis Society, Macclesfield and District Council for Voluntary Service, Macclesfield Division of St John Ambulance Brigade, East Cheshire Hospice; Chair, Executive Committee of Anglo/Austrian Society 1999–2000; Hon. Vice-President: National Association of Master Bakers, Confectioners and Caterers, The Royal College of Midwives; Executive Member, 1922 Committee 1997–; Vice-President, National Association of Local Councils; Member of Council, League for Exchange of Commonwealth Teachers 1979–92; Member, Executive Committee, Commonwealth Parliamentary Association (CPA) UK Branch 1997–; Fellow, Industry and Parliament Trust; Past Upper Bailiff and Member of the Court of Assistants, Worshipful Company of Weavers; Freeman, City of London; *Clubs:* Cavalry and Guards, Lighthouse, Old Boys and Park Green Macclesfield; *Sportsclubs:* Bollington Bowling Club; Bollington Cricket Club; Macclesfield Cricket Club; Macclesfield Hockey Club; New Century Bowman; Prince Albert Angling Society; *Recreations:* Squash, tennis, swimming, jogging, skiing. *Address:* Nicholas Winterton Esq, MP, House of Commons, London, SW1A 0AA *Tel:* 020 7219 3000. *Constituency:* Macclesfield Conservative and Unionist Association, West Bank Road, Macclesfield, Cheshire, SK10 3DU *Tel:* 01625 422848 *Fax:* 01625 617066.

ROSIE WINTERTON   Doncaster Central   *Lab majority 17,856*

Born 10 August 1958; Daughter of Gordon Winterton, teacher, and late Valerie Winterton, teacher; Educated Doncaster Grammar School; Hull University (BA history 1979). Constituency personal assistant to John Prescott, MP 1980–86; Parliamentary officer: Southwark Council 1986–88; Royal College of Nursing 1988–90; Managing Director, Connect Public Affairs 1990–94; Head of private office of John Prescott, MP, Deputy Leader of the Labour Party 1994–97; Former Branch Officer, TGWU; Member: NUJ, TGWU. **House of Commons:** Member for Doncaster Central since May 1, 1997; *Special Interests:* Regional Policy, Employment, Transport, Housing, Home Affairs. Member, Labour Party Strategic Campaign Committee; Representative, PLP on the National Policy Forum of the Labour Party. Member, Amnesty International; Leader, Leadership Campaign Team 1998–99; Chair, Transport and General Workers' Parliamentary Group 1998–99; Former Member, Standing Committees: Local Government Finance (Supplementary Credit Approvals) Bill, Regional Development Agencies Bill; Member Standing Committees: Transport Bill January 2000, Finance Bill April 2000; Intelligence and Security Committee January 2000–; *Clubs:* Doncaster Trades and Labour, Intake Social, Doncaster Catholic; *Recreations:* Sailing, reading. *Address:* Rosie Winterton, MP, House of Commons, London, SW1A 0AA *Tel:* 020 7219 0925/6357 *Fax:* 020 7219 4581. *Constituency:* Guildhall Advice Centre, Old Guildhall Yard, Doncaster, South Yorkshire, DN1 1QW *Tel:* 01302 735241 *Fax:* 01302 735242 *E-mail:* wintertonr@parliament.uk.

MIKE WOOD · Batley and Spen   *Lab majority 6,141*

Born 3 March 1946; Son of late Rowland L. Wood, foundry worker, and Laura M. Wood, retired cleaner; Educated Nantwich and Acton Grammar School, Nantwich, Cheshire; Salisbury/Wells Theological College (Cert Theol 1974); Leeds University (CQSW 1981); Leeds Metropolitan University (BA history and politics 1989); Married July 24, 1999 Christine O'Leary (2 stepdaughters; 1 son 1 daughter from previous marriage). Probation officer, social worker, community worker 1965–97; Trade Unionist since 1962; Member: UNISON, GMB. Kirklees Metropolitan District Council: Councillor 1980–88, Deputy Leader of Council 1986–87. **House of Commons:** Contested Hexham 1987 general election. Member for Batley and Spen since May 1, 1997; *Select Committees:* Member: Broadcasting 1997–98. *Special Interests:* Poverty, Housing, Transport, Environmental Issues and World Development; France, Indian Sub-continent. Member, Labour Friends of India. Former Director, Housing Charity; *Publications: Probation Hostel Directory*, 1980; *Recreations:* Sport, music, ornithology, walking. *Address:* Mike Wood Esq, MP, House of Commons, London, SW1A 0AA *Tel:* 020 7219 4125. *Constituency:* Tom Myer's House, 9 Cross Crown Street, Cleckheaton, West Yorkshire, BD19 3HW *Tel:* 01274 335233 *Fax:* 01274 335235 *E-mail:* mike.wood@geo2.pop.org.uk, www.mikewood.org.uk.

SHAUN WOODWARD · Witney   *Con majority 7,028**

Born 26 October 1958; Son of Dennis George Woodward and Joan Lillian, née Nunn; Educated Bristol Grammar School; Jesus College, Cambridge (MA English literature); Married May 2, 1987, Camilla Davan Sainsbury, daughter of Rt Hon. Sir Timothy Sainsbury (1 son 3 daughters). BBC TV News and Current Affairs 1982–98; Director of communications, Conservative Party 1991–92. **House of Commons:** *Conservative Member for Witney May 1, 1997-December 1999, Labour Member since December 1999; Opposition Front Bench Spokesman for Environment, Transport and the Regions 1999; *Select Committees:* Member: Broadcasting 1997–99, European Legislation 1997–99, European Scrutiny 1998–99, Foreign Affairs 1999; Member: Broadcasting 2000–. *Special Interests:* Finance, Environment, Education, Culture; USA, France, Germany, Italy, China and Australia. Director: English National Opera, Marine Stewardship Council; Member, Foundation Board, RSC; Trustee, Childline; *Publications:* Co-author: *Tranquilisers*,1983, *Ben: The Story of Ben Hardwick*, 1984, *Drugwatch*, 1985; Visiting professor, Queen Mary and Westfield College, London University; Visiting fellow, John F. Kennedy School of Government, Harvard University; *Recreations:* Opera, tennis, reading, gardening, architecture. *Address:* Shaun Woodward Esq, MP, House of Commons, London, SW1A 0AA *Tel:* 020 7219 2680 *Fax:* 020 7219 0979 *E-mail:* seelyr@parliament.uk.

PHILIP WOOLAS · Oldham East and Saddleworth   *Lab majority 3,389*

Born 11 December 1959; Son of Dennis and Maureen Woolas; Educated Nelson Grammar School; Walton Lane High School; Nelson and Colne College; Manchester University (BA philosophy); Married June 25, 1988, Tracey Allen (1 son). President, National Union of Students 1984–86; BBC Newsnight producer 1988–90; Channel 4 News producer 1990; Head of communication, GMB 1991–97; Member, GMB. **House of Commons:** Contested Littleborough and Saddleworth by-election 1995. Member for Oldham East and Saddleworth since May 1, 1997; PPS to Lord Macdonald of Tradeston, as Minister of State for Transport, Department of the Environment, Transport and the Regions (Minister for Transport) 1999–; *Special Interests:* Employment, Economics, Media, Trade and Industry; Kashmir and Jammu. Chair, Tribune Newspaper 1997– Deputy Leader, Leadership Campaign Team 1997–99. RTS Award for Political Coverage 1990; *Clubs:* Groucho; *Sportsclubs:* Lancashire County Cricket Club, Manchester United Football Club; *Recreations:* Photography. *Address:* Philip Woolas Esq, MP, House of Commons, London, SW1A 0AA *Tel:* 020 7219 1149 *Fax:* 020 7219 0992. *Constituency:* Textile House, 110 Union Street, Oldham, Lancashire *Tel:* 0161-624 4248.

TONY WORTHINGTON   Clydebank and Milngavie   *Lab majority 13,320*

Born 11 October 1941; Son of late Malcolm and Monica Worthington; Educated City School, Lincoln; York and Durham Universities; London School of Economics (BA 1966); Glasgow University (MEd); Married 1966, Angela Oliver (1 son 1 daughter). Lecturer: HM Borstal, Dover 1962–66, Monkwearmouth College of F.E., Sunderland 1967–71, Jordanhill College of Education 1971–87. Clydebank North: Regional Councillor 1974–87, Chair, Finance Committee 1986–87. **House of Commons:** Member for Clydebank and Milngavie since June 1987; Opposition Spokesman for Scotland on: Education, Employment, Training and Social Work 1989–92, Development and Co-operation 1992–93; Opposition Spokesman on: Foreign and Commonwealth Affairs 1993–94, Northern Ireland 1995–97; Parliamentary Under-Secretary of State, Northern Ireland Office 1997–98; *Select Committees:* Member: Home Affairs 1987–88; Member: International Development 1999–. *Special Interests:* International Development, Employment; Africa, Middle East, Eastern Europe. *Recreations:* Gardening. *Address:* Tony Worthington Esq, MP, House of Commons, London, SW1A 0AA *Tel:* 020 7219 3507 *Fax:* 020 7219 3507. *Constituency:* 24 Cleddans Crescent, Handgate, Clydebank, Dunbartonshire, G81 5NW *Tel:* 01389 873195 *Fax:* 01389 873195 *E-mail:* worthingtont@parliament.uk.

JAMES WRAY   Glasgow Baillieston   *Lab majority 14,840*

Born 28 April 1938; Son of late Harold Wray and the late Elizabeth Wray; Educated St Bonaventure's, Gorbals; Married (2 sons 2 daughters). Member of Committee, TGWU. Strathclyde Regional Councillor, Gorbals for 1976–88; Councillor, Glasgow Corporation Mile-End Ward 1972–75. **House of Commons:** Member for Glasgow Provan 1987–97, and for Glasgow Baillieston since May 1, 1997; *Special Interests:* Social Services, Education, Foreign Affairs. Parliamentary Agent for the late Frank McElhone, former Labour MP for Gorbals division of Glasgow 1969–74 and Queens Park division 1974–82; Former Parliamentary election agent for late Robert McTaggart, Labour MP for Glasgow Central. Leader: Anti-Dampness campaign, Anti-Eviction campaign, Anti-Fluoridation campaign, Gorbals rent strike; Substitute, UK Delegation to Council of Europe and Western Europe Union; *Sportsclubs:* Hon. President, Scottish Pro-Amateur Ex-Boxers Association; President: Kelvin Amateur Boxing Club, Strathclyde Community Boxers Club; *Recreations:* Boxing. *Address:* James Wray Esq, MP, House of Commons, London, SW1A 0AA *Tel:* 020 7219 4606.

ANTHONY DAVID WRIGHT   Great Yarmouth   *Lab majority 8,668*

Born 12 August 1954; Son of late Arthur Wright and of Jean Wright; Educated Secondary modern school; Married August 13, 1988, Barbara Fleming (1 son 1 daughter 1 stepdaughter). Engineering apprentice 1970–74; Engineer 1974–83; Labour Party organiser/agent 1983–97; Member: AEEU, GMB. Great Yarmouth Borough Council: Councillor 1980–82, 1986–98, Leader of Council 1996–97. **House of Commons:** Member for Great Yarmouth since May 1, 1997; *Select Committees:* Member: Public Administration 2000–. *Special Interests:* Local Government, Trade and Industry; Cyprus. Member, European Standing Committee C 1999–. *Address:* Anthony David Wright Esq, MP (Great Yarmouth), House of Commons, London, SW1A 0AA *Tel:* 020 7219 4832 *Fax:* 020 7219 2304. *Constituency:* 21 Euston Road, Great Yarmouth, Norfolk, NR30 1DZ *Tel:* 01493 332291 *Fax:* 01493 332189 *E-mail:* wrighta@parliament.uk.

Visit the Vacher Dod Website . . .
www.politicallinks.co.uk

DR TONY WAYLAND WRIGHT   Cannock Chase   *Lab majority 14,478*

Born 11 March 1948; Son of Frank and Maud Wright; Educated Desborough Primary School; Kettering Grammar School; London School of Economics (BSc economics 1970); Harvard University (Kennedy Scholar 1970–71); Balliol College, Oxford (DPhil 1973); Married July 21, 1973, Moira Elynwy Phillips (3 sons and 1 son deceased). Lecturer in politics, University College of North Wales, Bangor 1973–75; School of Continuing Studies, Birmingham University: Lecturer, Senior lecturer, Reader in politics 1975–92. Chair, South Birmingham Community Health Council 1983–85. **House of Commons:** Contested Kidderminster 1979 general election. Member for Cannock and Burntwood 1992–97, and for Cannock Chase since May 1, 1997, PPS to the Lord Irvine of Lairg, as Lord Chancellor 1997–98; *Select Committees:* Member: Parliamentary Commissioner for Administration 1992–96, Public Service 1995–97; Member: Liaison 1999–; Chairman: Public Administration 1999–. *Special Interests:* Education, Health, Environment, Constitution. Executive Member, Fabian Society. Parent Governor, St Laurence Church Schools, Northfield, Birmingham 1989–92; Co-Chair, Campaign for Freedom of Information 1997–99; *Publications:* Include: *G. D. H. Cole and Socialist Democracy*, 1979; *Local Radio and Local Democracy*, 1982; *British Socialism*, 1983; *Socialisms: Theories and Practices*, 1986; *R. H. Tawney*, 1987; *Matters of Death and Life: A Study of Bereavement Support in Hospitals*, 1988; *Consuming Public Services*, 1990 (editor); *Contemporary Political Ideologies*, 1993 (editor); *Subjects and Citizens*, 1993; *Socialisms: Old and New*, 1996; *The People's Party*, 1997; *Who Can I Complain To?*, 1997; *Why Vote Labour?*, 1997; Joint Editor, *The Political Quarterly*; *The New Social Democracy*, 1999 (joint editor); *The British Political Process*, 2000 (editor); *The English Question*, 2000 (joint editor); Hon professor, Birmingham University 1999–; *Recreations:* Tennis, football, secondhand bookshops, walking, gardening. *Address:* Dr Anthony Wayland Wright, MP (Cannock Chase), House of Commons, London, SW1A 0AA *Tel:* 020 7219 5029/5583 *Fax:* 020 7219 2665. *Constituency:* 6A Hallcourt Crescent, Cannock, Staffordshire, WS11 3AB *Tel:* 01543 467810 *Fax:* 01543 467811 *E-mail:* wrightt@parliament.uk.

DEREK WYATT   Sittingbourne and Sheppey   *Lab majority 1,929*

Born 4 December 1949; Son of late Reginald and Margaret Wyatt; Educated Westcliff County High School; Colchester Royal Grammar School; St Luke's College, Exeter (Certificate of Education 1971); Open University (BA art and architecture 1978); St Catherine's College, Oxford (research 1981–82); Married Joanna Willett (1 daughter 1 son). Director and a Publisher, William Heinemann 1986–88; Head of Programmes, Wire TV 1994–95; Director, Computer Channel, BSkyB 1995–97; Member, NUJ. Councillor, London Borough of Haringey 1994–96, Chair, Alexandra Palace and Parks 1994–96. **House of Commons:** Member for Sittingbourne and Sheppey since May 1, 1997; *Select Committees:* Member: Culture, Media and Sport 1997–. *Special Interests:* Venture Capital, Sport, Internet Strategy, British Council, Foreign Affairs, Urban Parks, National Grid for Learning, Swiss Banking, Media; Southern Africa, Middle East, China. Chair, Kent Labour MPs Group. Member: RSPB, Charter 88, ANC, Amnesty International; Founded the Women's Sports Foundation 1986; Executive Member, European Media Forum; Founder, World Internet Forum, London 13–15 November 2000; Major Stanley's, Oxford University 1993–; Fellow, Industry and Parliament Trust (Motorola) 1998–; Parliament Charitable Trust (Raleigh International) 1999–; *Publications:* 5 books to date including: *Wisecracks From The Movies*, 1987, *Rugby DisUnion*, 1995; United Nations Commendation (Apartheid in Sport) 1987; FRSA; *Clubs:* RAC, Vincents (Oxford); *Sportsclubs:* Charlton Athletic FC, Penguin International RFC (Executive); Played Rugby for Oxford University, Barbarians and England; *Recreations:* Reading, sport, writing, travel, jazz. *Address:* Derek Wyatt, MP, House of Commons, London, SW1A 0AA *Tel:* 020 7219 3000. *Constituency:* 29 Park Road, Sittingbourne, Kent, ME10 1DR *Tel:* 01795 477277 *Fax:* 01795 477277 *E-mail:* wyattd@parliament.uk *Website:* www.derekwyattmp.co.uk.

Y

TIM YEO   South Suffolk   *Con majority 4,175*

Born 20 March 1945; Son of late Dr Kenneth John Yeo; Educated Charterhouse; Emmanuel College, Cambridge (MA history); Married March 30, 1970, Diane Helen Pickard (1 son 1 daughter). Assistant treasurer, Bankers Trust Company 1970–73; Director: Worcester Engineering Co. Ltd 1975–86, The Spastics Society 1980–83. **House of Commons:** Contested Bedwelty February 1974 general election. Member for South Suffolk since June 1983; Opposition Spokesman on Environment, Transport and the Regions (Local Government, Regions, Planning and Housing) 1997–98; PPS to Douglas Hurd: as Home Secretary 1988–89, as Foreign and Commonwealth Secretary 1989–90; Joint Parliamentary Under-Secretary of State at: Department of the Environment 1990–92, Department of Health 1992–93; Minister of State for Environment and Countryside, Department of the Environment 1993–94; Shadow Minister of Agriculture, Fisheries and Food 1998–; *Select Committees:* Member: Employment 1994–96, Treasury 1996–97. *Special Interests:* Health, Economic Policy, Unemployment, Charity Reform, Rural Affairs. Vice-Chair, Conservative Party (with responsibility for Local Government) 1998. Chair, Charities VAT Reform Group 1981–88; President, Charities Tax Reform Group 1988–90; Vice-President, International Voluntary Service 1984; Chair, Tadworth Court Trust 1984–91; Trustee, Tanzania Development Trust 1980–97; Fellow, Industry and Parliament Trust; *Clubs:* Royal St George's (Sandwich); *Sportsclubs:* Captain, Parliamentary Golfing Society 1991–95; *Recreations:* Golf, skiing. *Address:* Timothy Yeo Esq, MP, House of Commons, London, SW1A 0AA *Tel:* 020 7219 6366 *Fax:* 020 7219 4857. *Constituency:* 7 Queen Street, Hadleigh, Suffolk, IP7 5DA *Tel:* 01473 823435 *E-mail:* timyeomp@parliament.uk.

SIR GEORGE YOUNG   North West Hampshire   *Con majority 11,551*

Born 16 July 1941; Son of Sir George Young, 5th Bt, CMG, and Elizabeth Young, née Knatchbull-Hugessen; Educated Eton; Christ Church, Oxford (BA philosophy, politics and economics 1963, MA); Surrey University (MPhil); Married July 11, 1964, Aurelia Nemon-Stuart (2 sons 2 daughters). Economic adviser, Post Office 1969–74. Councillor, London Borough of Lambeth 1968–71; GLC Councillor for Ealing 1970–73; Chair, Acton Housing Association 1972–79. **House of Commons:** Member for Ealing Acton 1974–97, and for North West Hampshire since May 1, 1997; Opposition Whip 1976–79; Government Whip July–November 1990; Parliamentary Under-Secretary of State at: Department of Health and Social Services 1979–81, Department of Environment 1981–86; Department of Environment: Minister for Housing and Planning 1990–93, Minister for Housing, Inner Cities and Construction 1993–94; Financial Secretary, HM Treasury 1994–95; Secretary of State for Transport 1995–97; Member, Shadow Cabinet 1997–; Shadow Secretary of State for Defence 1997–98; Shadow Leader of the House of Commons 1998–99; Shadow Chancellor of the Duchy of Lancaster 1998–99; Shadow Leader of the House of Commons and Constitutional Affairs 1999–2000; *Select Committees:* Member: Public Accounts 1994–95; Member: Modernisation of the House of Commons 1998–. *Special Interests:* Housing, Disabled/Disability, Health Education. 6th Baronet, created 1813, succeeded his father 1960; Trustee, Guinness Trust 1986–90; *Publications: Tourism – Blessing or Blight,* 1970; PC 1993; *Recreations:* Bicycling, opera. *Address:* Rt Hon Sir George Young, Bt, MP, House of Commons, London, SW1A 0AA *Tel:* 020 7219 6665 *Fax:* 020 7219 2566. *Constituency:* 2 Church Close, Andover, Hampshire, SP10 1DP *Tel:* 01264 401401 *Fax:* 01264 391155 *E-mail:* sir-george-young@nwh-tories.org.uk, www.nwh-tories.org.uk-/george-young.

Women members

ABBOTT Diane
ADAMS Irene
ANDERSON Janet
ARMSTRONG Hilary
ATHERTON Candy
ATKINS Charlotte
BALLARD Jackie
BECKETT Margaret
BEGG Anne
BLACKMAN Elizabeth
BLEARS Hazel
BOOTHROYD Betty
BOTTOMLEY Virginia
BRINTON Helen
BROWNING Angela
BUCK Karen
BUTLER Christine
CAMPBELL Anne
CHURCH Judith
CLARK Dr Lynda
CLWYD Ann
COFFEY Ann
COOPER Yvette
CORSTON Jean
CRYER Ann
CUNNINGHAM Roseanna
CURTIS-THOMAS Claire
DAVEY Valerie
DEAN Janet
DROWN Julia
DUNWOODY Hon Mrs Gwyneth
EAGLE Angela
EAGLE Maria
ELLMAN Louise
EWING Margaret
FITZSIMONS Lorna
FLINT Caroline
FOLLETT Barbara
FYFE Maria
GIDLEY Sandra
GILLAN Cheryl
GILROY Linda
GOLDING Llin
GORDON Eileen
GORMAN Teresa
GRIFFITHS Jane
HARMAN Harriet
HEAL Sylvia
HEWITT Patricia
HODGE Margaret
HOEY Kate
HUGHES Beverley
HUMBLE Joan
JACKSON Glenda

JACKSON Helen
JOHNSON Melanie
JONES Fiona
JONES Helen
JONES Jenny
JONES Dr Lynne
JOWELL Tessa
KEEBLE Sally
KEEN Ann
KELLY Ruth
KENNEDY Jane
KING Oona
KINGHAM Tess
KIRKBRIDE Julie
LAING Eleanor
LAIT Jacqui
LAWRENCE Jackie
LIDDELL Helen
McCAFFERTY Christine
McDONAGH Siobhain
McGUIRE Anne
McINTOSH Anne
McISAAC Shona
McKENNA Rosemary
MACTAGGART Fiona
MAHON Alice
MALLABER Judy
MAY Theresa
MERRON Gillian
MICHIE Ray
MOFFATT Laura
MORAN Margaret
MORGAN Julie
MORRIS Estelle
MOUNTFORD Kali
MOWLAM Dr Marjorie
ORGAN Diana
OSBORNE Sandra
PERHAM Linda
PRENTICE Bridget
PRIMAROLO Dawn
QUIN Joyce
ROCHE Barbara
ROE Marion
RUDDOCK Joan
RUSSELL Christine
RYAN Joan
SHEPHARD Gillian
SHIPLEY Debra
SHORT Clare
SMITH Angela
SMITH Geraldine
SMITH Jacqui
SOUTHWORTH Helen

SPELMAN Caroline
SQUIRE Rachel
STARKEY Dr Phyllis
STUART Gisela
TAYLOR Ann
TAYLOR Daria
TONGE Dr Jennifer

WALLEY Joan
WARD Claire
WIDDECOMBE Ann
WILLIAMS Betty
WINTERTON Ann
WINTERTON Rosie

The 300 Group

PO Box 166, Horsham RH13 7YS Tel: 01403 733797 Fax: 01403 734432

The 300 Group is an all party campaign for more women in Parliament, Local Government and all areas of public life. Its members are women and men from all walks of life across the country. It encourages and trains women to seek and hold public office and to participate in public decision making processes at all levels.

Chair: Rhian Chilcott
Finance Director: Sara Phillp
Directors: Carolyn Hilder, Ann Swain

MPs who are members of other assemblies

Gerry Adams	Northern Ireland Assembly
Malcolm Chisolm	Scottish Parliament
Roseanna Cunningham	Scottish Parliament
Ron Davies	National Assembly for Wales
Margaret Ewing	Scottish Parliament
Sam Galbraith	Scottish Parliament
Donald Gorrie	Scottish Parliament
John Home Robertson	Scottish Parliament
John Hume	Northern Ireland Assembly, European Parliament
Ieuan Wyn Jones	National Assembly for Wales
John McAllion	Scottish Parliament
Robert McCartney	Northern Ireland Assembly
William McCrea	Northern Ireland Assembly
Edward McGrady	Northern Ireland Assembly
Martin McGuinness	Northern Ireland Assembly
Henry McLeish	Scottish Parliament
Seamus Mallon	Northern Ireland Assembly
John Marek	National Assembly for Wales
Alun Michael	National Assembly for Wales
Alasdair Morgan	Scottish Parliament
Rhodri Morgan	National Assembly for Wales
Ian Paisley	Northern Ireland Assembly, European Parliament
Peter Robinson	Northern Ireland Assembly
Alex Salmond	Scottish Parliament
John Swinney	Scottish Parliament
John Taylor	Northern Ireland Assembly
David Trimble	Northern Ireland Assembly
Jim Wallace	Scottish Parliament
Andrew Welsh	Scottish Parliament
Dafydd Wigley	National Assembly for Wales

MPs' Political Interests

The interests listed are supplied to Dod by MPs themselves.

Abortion
Widdecombe, Ann *(Con)*

Accountancy
Mitchell, Austin *(Lab)*

Aerospace
Borrow, David *(Lab)*
Cunliffe, Lawrence *(Lab)*
Foulkes, George *(Lab/Co-op)*
Haselhurst, Sir Alan *(Con)*
Howarth, Gerald *(Con)*
Ingram, Adam *(Lab)*
Jack, Michael *(Con)*
Moffatt, Laura *(Lab)*
Öpik, Lembit *(Lib Dem)*
Robinson, Peter *(DUP)*
Soames, Nicholas *(Con)*
Wilkinson, John *(Con)*

Age Discrimination
Burstow, Paul *(Lib Dem)*
O'Hara, Edward *(Lab)*
Perham, Linda *(Lab)*

Agenda 21
Colman, Tony *(Lab)*

Agriculture
Ancram, Michael *(Con)*
Atkins, Charlotte *(Lab)*
Atkinson, Peter *(Con)*
Blizzard, Bob *(Lab)*
Body, Sir Richard *(Con)*
Boswell, Timothy *(Con)*
Burnett, John *(Lib Dem)*
Clifton-Brown, Geoffrey
   (Con)
Collins, Tim *(Con)*
Corbett, Robin *(Lab)*
Curry, David *(Con)*
Davies, Quentin *(Con)*
Davies, Ron *(Lab)*
Davis, David *(Con)*
Drew, David *(Lab/Co-op)*
Evans, Nigel *(Con)*
Flight, Howard *(Con)*
Garnier, Edward *(Con)*
George, Andrew *(Lib Dem)*
Gill, Christopher *(Con)*

Gray, James *(Con)*
Greenway, John *(Con)*
Hague, William *(Con)*
Haselhurst, Sir Alan *(Con)*
Hayes, John *(Con)*
Heathcoat-Amory, David
   (Con)
Hood, Jimmy *(Lab)*
Hurst, Alan *(Lab)*
Jack, Michael *(Con)*
Jackson, Robert *(Con)*
Johnson Smith, Sir Geoffrey
   (Con)
Jones, Ieuan Wyn *(PC)*
Jones, Martyn *(Lab)*
Key, Robert *(Con)*
Leigh, Edward *(Con)*
Livsey, Richard *(Lib Dem)*
Llwyd, Elfyn *(PC)*
Lord, Michael *(Con)*
McCrea, William *(DUP)*
MacGregor, John *(Con)*
McLoughlin, Patrick *(Con)*
Major, John *(Con)*
Marsden, Paul *(Lab)*
Martlew, Eric *(Lab)*
Michie, Ray *(Lib Dem)*
Mitchell, Austin *(Lab)*
Mountford, Kali *(Lab)*
Norman, Archie *(Con)*
O'Brien, Stephen *(Con)*
Paice, James *(Con)*
Paterson, Owen *(Con)*
Pickthall, Colin *(Lab)*
Prentice, Gordon *(Lab)*
Prior, David *(Con)*
Salmond, Alex *(SNP)*
Simpson, Keith *(Con)*
Soames, Nicholas *(Con)*
Spelman, Caroline *(Con)*
Steen, Anthony *(Con)*
Stevenson, George *(Lab)*
Strang, Gavin *(Lab)*
Taylor, John D *(UUP)*
Thomas, Gareth *(Lab)*
   (Clwyd West)
Todd, Mark *(Lab)*
Williams, Dr Alan Wynne
   (Lab)
Winterton, Ann *(Con)*

AIDS
Gerrard, Neil *(Lab)*
Moffatt, Laura *(Lab)*
Strang, Gavin *(Lab)*

Airports
Wareing, Robert *(Lab)*

**Alcohol Abuse and
   Under-age Drinking**
Faber, David *(Con)*
Hood, Jimmy *(Lab)*

Amnesty International
Wallace, James *(Lib Dem)*

Ancient Monuments
Taylor, John M *(Con)*

Anglo-American Relations
Mawhinney, Sir Brian *(Con)*

Animal Welfare
Banks, Tony *(Lab)*
Caplin, Ivor *(Lab)*
Cawsey, Ian *(Lab)*
Clark, Dr Michael *(Con)*
Cohen, Harry *(Lab)*
Corbett, Robin *(Lab)*
Dowd, Jim *(Lab)*
Etherington, William *(Lab)*
Flynn, Paul *(Lab)*
Foster, Michael Jabez *(Lab)*
Gale, Roger *(Con)*
Griffiths, Win *(Lab)*
Lepper, David *(Lab/Co-op)*
McIntosh, Anne *(Con)*
Norris, Dan *(Lab)*
O'Hara, Edward *(Lab)*
Palmer, Dr Nicholas *(Lab)*
Russell, Bob *(Lib Dem)*
Smith, Angela
   (Lab/Co-op)
Steinberg, Gerry *(Lab)*
White, Brian *(Lab)*

Anti-Imperialism
Corbyn, Jeremy *(Lab)*

Arboriculture
Chapman, Sydney *(Con)*

Architecture
Beith, Alan *(Lib Dem)*
Chapman, Sydney *(Con)*

Arms Control
Cousins, Jim *(Lab)*
Heathcoat-Amory, David
(Con)

Arts
Atkinson, David *(Con)*
Banks, Tony *(Lab)*
Begg, Anne *(Lab)*
Beith, Alan *(Lib Dem)*
Blears, Hazel *(Lab)*
Campbell, Menzies *(Lib Dem)*
Caplin, Ivor *(Lab)*
Cormack, Sir Patrick *(Con)*
Dunwoody, Gwyneth *(Lab)*
Fisher, Mark *(Lab)*
Fraser, Christopher *(Con)*
Gorrie, Donald *(Lib Dem)*
Griffiths, Nigel *(Lab)*
Heath, Sir Edward *(Con)*
Hopkins, Kelvin *(Lab)*
Howarth, Alan *(Lab)*
Howells, Dr Kim *(Lab)*
Key, Robert *(Con)*
Lammy, David *(Lab)*
Maclennan, Robert *(Lib Dem)*
Mactaggart, Fiona *(Lab)*
Maxton, John *(Lab)*
Russell, Christine *(Lab)*

Asylum
Coleman, Iain *(Lab)*
Gerrard, Neil *(Lab)*
Harris, Evan *(Lib Dem)*
Prosser, Gwyn *(Lab)*

Aviation
Cunliffe, Lawrence *(Lab)*
Foulkes, George *(Lab/Co-op)*
Haselhurst, Sir Alan *(Con)*
Howarth, Gerald *(Con)*
Moffatt, Laura *(Lab)*
Robinson, Peter *(DUP)*
Soames, Nicholas *(Con)*
Wilkinson, John *(Con)*
Wilshire, David *(Con)*

Benefits
McDonagh, Siobhain *(Lab)*
McIsaac, Shona *(Lab)*

Breast Cancer
Church, Judith *(Lab)*

British Council
Wyatt, Derek *(Lab)*

Broadcasting
Begg, Anne *(Lab)*
Fabricant, Michael *(Con)*
Fisher, Mark *(Lab)*
Gale, Roger *(Con)*
Greenway, John *(Con)*
Grogan, John *(Lab)*
Howells, Dr Kim *(Lab)*
Kennedy, Charles *(Lib Dem)*
Whittingdale, John *(Con)*

Business
Cotter, Brian *(Lib Dem)*
Johnson, Melanie *(Lab)*
Merron, Gillian *(Lab)*
Moore, Michael *(Lib Dem)*
Norman, Archie *(Con)*
Redwood, John *(Con)*
Todd, Mark *(Lab)*

Capitalism
Redwood, John *(Con)*

Car Industry
Smith, Andrew *(Lab)*

CCTV
Taylor, David *(Lab/Co-op)*

Channel Islands
Mackinlay, Andrew *(Lab)*

Charities
Flight, Howard *(Con)*
Howarth, Alan *(Lab)*

Charity Reform
Yeo, Tim *(Con)*

Child Protection
Cook, Frank *(Lab)*
Hughes, Beverley *(Lab)*
Johnson, Melanie *(Lab)*
Norris, Dan *(Lab)*

Childcare
Baldry, Tony *(Con)*
Chisholm, Malcolm *(Lab)*
Doran, Frank *(Lab)*
Flint, Caroline *(Lab)*
Hughes, Kevin *(Lab)*
Moran, Margaret *(Lab)*
Morgan, Julie *(Lab)*
Powell, Sir Raymond *(Lab)*

Children
Buck, Karen *(Lab)*
Corbett, Robin *(Lab)*
Dawson, Hilton *(Lab)*
Golding, Llin *(Lab)*
Kidney, David *(Lab)*
Shipley, Debra *(Lab)*

Christian Socialism
Timms, Stephen *(Lab)*

Christian Values
Donaldson, Jeffrey *(UUP)*

City
Prior, David *(Con)*

Civil Defence
McCartney, Ian *(Lab)*

Civil Justice
Dismore, Andrew *(Lab)*

Civil Liberties
Atkins, Charlotte *(Lab)*
Baker, Norman *(Lib Dem)*
Ballard, Jackie *(Lib Dem)*
Corbett, Robin *(Lab)*
Harris, Evan *(Lib Dem)*
Hughes, Simon *(Lib Dem)*
Lloyd, Tony *(Lab)*
Llwyd, Elfyn *(PC)*
Mactaggart, Fiona *(Lab)*
Meacher, Michael *(Lab)*
Smith, Chris *(Lab)*
Soley, Clive *(Lab)*
Stinchcombe, Paul *(Lab)*

Civil Service
Clarke, Tom *(Lab)*

Climate Change
Stunell, Andrew *(Lib Dem)*

CND
Powell, Sir Raymond *(Lab)*

Co-operative Movement
Davidson, Ian *(Lab/Co-op)*
Drown, Julia *(Lab)*
McFall, John *(Lab/Co-op)*
Michael, Alun *(Lab/Co-op)*
Naysmith, Dr Doug
(Lab/Co-op)
Reed, Andrew
(Lab/Co-op)

Coal Industry
Clapham, Michael *(Lab)*
Clarke, Eric *(Lab)*
Cooper, Yvette *(Lab)*
Cryer, John *(Lab)*
Cummings, John *(Lab)*
O'Brien, Mike *(Lab)*
Powell, Sir Raymond *(Lab)*

Commerce
Hayes, John *(Con)*
Keen, Alan *(Lab/Co-op)*
Ottaway, Richard *(Con)*

Commonwealth
Davidson, Ian
  (Lab/Co-op)
Emery, Peter *(Con)*
Kilfoyle, Peter *(Lab)*

Communications
Miller, Andrew *(Lab)*

Community Care
Dawson, Hilton *(Lab)*
Hughes, Beverley *(Lab)*
Jowell, Tessa *(Lab)*
McCabe, Stephen *(Lab)*
Robinson, Peter *(DUP)*
Squire, Rachel *(Lab)*
Steen, Anthony *(Con)*

Community Development
Haselhurst, Sir Alan *(Con)*
Michael, Alun
  (Lab/Co-op)
Shaw, Jonathan *(Lab)*

Community Regeneration
Goggins, Paul *(Lab)*
Lepper, David
  (Lab/Co-op)

Community Safety
Burstow, Paul *(Lib Dem)*

Conservation
Chapman, Sydney *(Con)*
Cohen, Harry *(Lab)*
Dalyell, Tam *(Lab)*
Davies, Ron *(Lab)*
Hurst, Alan *(Lab)*
Morgan, Rhodri *(Lab)*
Rowe, Andrew *(Con)*
Steen, Anthony *(Con)*
Walker, Cecil *(UUP)*

Constitution
Anderson, Janet *(Lab)*
Benn, Tony *(Lab)*
Brown, Desmond *(Lab)*
Burden, Richard *(Lab)*
Cann, Jamie *(Lab)*
Clarke, Tony *(Lab)*
Collins, Tim *(Con)*
Cunningham, Roseanna
  (SNP)
Darling, Alistair *(Lab)*
Day, Stephen *(Con)*
Donaldson, Jeffrey *(UUP)*
Fallon, Michael *(Con)*
Fraser, Christopher *(Con)*
Grieve, Dominic *(Con)*
Hoon, Geoffrey *(Lab)*
Laing, Eleanor *(Con)*
McGrady, Edward *(SDLP)*
Mackinlay, Andrew *(Lab)*
Major, John *(Con)*
Nicholls, Patrick *(Con)*
Paisley, Rev Ian *(DUP)*
Plaskitt, James *(Lab)*
Quinn, Lawrie *(Lab)*
Robertson, Laurence *(Con)*
Savidge, Malcolm *(Lab)*
Syms, Robert *(Con)*
Temple-Morris, Peter *(Lab)*
Whitehead, Dr Alan *(Lab)*
Wright, Dr Tony *(Lab)*

Constitutional Reform
Alexander, Douglas *(Lab)*
Campbell, Alan *(Lab)*
Clark, Dr Lynda *(Lab)*
Edwards, Huw *(Lab)*
Jowell, Tessa *(Lab)*
McKenna, Rosemary *(Lab)*
Maclennan, Robert
  (Lib Dem)
Michie, Ray *(Lib Dem)*
Mitchell, Austin *(Lab)*
Prentice, Bridget *(Lab)*
Thomas, Gareth *(Lab)*
Wallace, James *(Lib Dem)*

Construction Industry
Chapman, Sydney *(Con)*
Nicholls, Patrick *(Con)*
Spellar, John *(Lab)*

Consumer Issues
Lepper, David *(Lab/Co-op)*
Murphy, Jim *(Lab)*
Williams, Betty *(Lab)*

Cornwall
Breed, Colin *(Lib Dem)*
George, Andrew *(Lib Dem)*

Countryside
Brazier, Julian *(Con)*
Dalyell, Tam *(Lab)*
Gray, James *(Con)*
MacGregor, John *(Con)*
Morgan, Rhodri *(Lab)*
Morley, Elliot *(Lab)*
Norman, Archie *(Con)*
Prentice, Gordon *(Lab)*
Robertson, Laurence *(Con)*
Simpson, Keith *(Con)*
Soames, Nicholas *(Con)*

Credit Unions
Hume, John *(SDLP)*

Crime
Blackman, Elizabeth *(Lab)*
Connarty, Michael *(Lab)*
Flint, Caroline *(Lab)*
Jones, Fiona *(Lab)*
Lewis, Ivan *(Lab)*
Milburn, Alan *(Lab)*
Taylor, David
  (Lab/Co-op)

Criminal Justice
Gerrard, Neil *(Lab)*
Hughes, Beverley *(Lab)*
Smith, Chris *(Lab)*

Criminal Law
Malins, Humfrey *(Con)*
O'Brien, Mike *(Lab)*

Crofting
Michie, Ray *(Lib Dem)*

Culture
Anderson, Janet *(Lab)*
Fisher, Mark *(Lab)*
Keen, Alan *(Lab/Co-op)*
Lammy, David *(Lab)*
Lepper, David *(Lab/Co-op)*
Ward, Claire *(Lab)*
Woodward, Shaun *(Lab)*

Cyprus
Lepper, David *(Lab/Co-op)*

Deaf Children
Bruce, Malcolm *(Lib Dem)*

Defence

Ancram, Michael *(Con)*
Arbuthnot, James *(Con)*
Ashdown, Sir Paddy
   (Lib Dem)
Bayley, Hugh *(Lab)*
Beard, Nigel *(Lab)*
Blunt, Crispin *(Con)*
Brazier, Julian *(Con)*
Bruce, Ian *(Con)*
Burnett, John *(Lib Dem)*
Campbell, Menzies
   (Lib Dem)
Cann, Jamie *(Lab)*
Cohen, Harry *(Lab)*
Collins, Tim *(Con)*
Cook, Robin *(Lab)*
Corbyn, Jeremy *(Lab)*
Cormack, Sir Patrick *(Con)*
Davidson, Ian *(Lab/Co-op)*
Duncan Smith, Iain *(Con)*
Emery, Peter *(Con)*
Evans, Nigel *(Con)*
Foulkes, George
   (Lab/Co-op)
Galloway, George *(Lab)*
Gapes, Mike *(Lab/Co-op)*
Garnier, Edward *(Con)*
George, Bruce *(Lab)*
Gillan, Cheryl *(Con)*
Gray, James *(Con)*
Grieve, Dominic *(Con)*
Hamilton, Sir Archie *(Con)*
Hammond, Philip *(Con)*
Hancock, Mike *(Lib Dem)*
Hawkins, Nick *(Con)*
Home Robertson, John
   (Lab)
Hood, Jimmy *(Lab)*
Hoon, Geoffrey *(Lab)*
Howarth, Gerald *(Con)*
Hoyle, Lindsay *(Lab)*
Hutton, John *(Lab)*
Jenkin, Bernard *(Con)*
Johnson Smith, Sir Geoffrey
   (Con)
Keen, Alan *(Lab/Co-op)*
Keetch, Paul *(Lib Dem)*
Key, Robert *(Con)*
Leigh, Edward *(Con)*
Lewis, Dr Julian *(Con)*
Lyell, Sir Nicholas *(Con)*
McFall, John *(Lab/Co-op)*
McWilliam, John *(Lab)*
Maginnis, Ken *(UUP)*
Mahon, Alice *(Lab)*

Martlew, Eric *(Lab)*
Mates, Michael *(Con)*
Moffatt, Laura *(Lab)*
Moonie, Lewis *(Lab/Co-op)*
Murphy, Jim *(Lab)*
Nicholls, Patrick *(Con)*
O'Neill, Martin *(Lab)*
Ottaway, Richard *(Con)*
Rapson, Syd *(Lab)*
Reid, Dr John *(Lab)*
Robathan, Andrew *(Con)*
Rogers, Allan *(Lab)*
Ross, Ernie *(Lab)*
Ross, William *(UUP)*
Savidge, Malcolm *(Lab)*
Simpson, Keith *(Con)*
Smith, John *(Lab)*
Soames, Nicholas *(Con)*
Squire, Rachel *(Lab)*
Tredinnick, David *(Con)*
Trend, Michael *(Con)*
Viggers, Peter *(Con)*
Vis, Rudi *(Lab)*
Whitney, Sir Raymond *(Con)*
Widdecombe, Ann *(Con)*
Wilkinson, John *(Con)*

Democracy

Allen, Graham *(Lab)*
Benn, Tony *(Lab)*
Goggins, Paul *(Lab)*
Hodge, Margaret *(Lab)*
Keen, Alan *(Lab/Co-op)*
Livingstone, Ken
   (Independent)
McKenna, Rosemary
   (Lab)
Southworth, Helen *(Lab)*
Stewart, Ian *(Lab)*

Deregulation

Steen, Anthony *(Con)*

Development

Dawson, Hilton *(Lab)*
Denham, John *(Lab)*
Keen, Alan *(Lab/Co-op)*
King, Oona *(Lab)*
Palmer, Dr Nicholas *(Lab)*

Devolution

Ellman, Louise *(Lab/Co-op)*
Foulkes, George
   (Lab/Co-op)
George, Andrew *(Lib Dem)*
Laing, Eleanor *(Con)*

Mackinlay, Andrew *(Lab)*
Maxton, John *(Lab)*
Quinn, Lawrie *(Lab)*
Sarwar, Mohammed *(Lab)*

Devolution in Wales

Flynn, Paul *(Lab)*

Disabled

Atherton, Candy *(Lab)*
Begg, Anne *(Lab)*
Berry, Dr Roger *(Lab)*
Browne, Desmond *(Lab)*
Burstow, Paul *(Lib Dem)*
Corbett, Robin *(Lab)*
Corston, Jean *(Lab)*
Cotter, Brian *(Lib Dem)*
Etherington, William
   (Lab)
Gerrard, Neil *(Lab)*
Graham, Tommy
   (Independent)
Griffiths, Nigel *(Lab)*
Griffiths, Win *(Lab)*
Hayes, John *(Con)*
Heal, Sylvia *(Lab)*
Healey, John *(Lab)*
Levitt, Tom *(Lab)*
Loughton, Tim *(Con)*
Marsden, Gordon *(Lab)*
May, Theresa *(Con)*
Ross, William *(UUP)*
Rowlands, Edward *(Lab)*
Turner, Dr Des *(Lab)*
Wareing, Robert *(Lab)*
Wigley, Dafydd *(PC)*
Young, Sir George *(Con)*

Disarmament

Cook, Frank *(Lab)*
Lloyd, Tony *(Lab)*
Simpson, Alan *(Lab)*

Dog Control

Hoey, Kate *(Lab)*

Domestic Violence

George, Andrew *(Lib Dem)*

Drug Abuse

Connarty, Michael *(Lab)*
Faber, David *(Con)*
Loughton, Tim *(Con)*
Marshall, David *(Lab)*
Martin, Michael *(Lab)*
Meale, Alan *(Lab)*
Moffatt, Laura *(Lab)*

E-Issues
Moran, Margaret *(Lab)*
Wyatt, Derek *(Lab)*

Ecclesiastical Matters
Field, Frank *(Lab)*

Economic Development
Chapman, Ben *(Lab)*
George, Andrew *(Lib Dem)*
Hamilton, Fabian *(Lab)*
Jones, Jenny *(Lab)*
Michael, Alun *(Lab/Co-op)*
Murphy, Denis *(Lab)*
Prosser, Gwyn *(Lab)*
Rapson, Syd *(Lab)*
Shaw, Jonathan *(Lab)*
Smith, John *(Lab)*

Economic Policy
Ainsworth, Peter *(Con)*
Alexander, Douglas *(Lab)*
Allen, Graham *(Lab)*
Banks, Tony *(Lab)*
Battle, John *(Lab)*
Bayley, Hugh *(Lab)*
Beard, Nigel *(Lab)*
Bell, Stuart *(Lab)*
Bercow, John *(Con)*
Berry, Dr Roger *(Lab)*
Betts, Clive *(Lab)*
Blunkett, David *(Lab)*
Blunt, Crispin *(Con)*
Bradley, Peter *(Lab)*
Brazier, Julian *(Con)*
Brown, Gordon *(Lab)*
Burnett, John *(Lib Dem)*
Cable, Dr Vincent
   (Lib Dem)
Chisholm, Malcolm *(Lab)*
Clappison, James *(Con)*
Clifton-Brown, Geoffrey
   (Con)
Collins, Tim *(Con)*
Connarty, Michael *(Lab)*
Cran, James *(Con)*
Cryer, John *(Lab)*
Cunningham, James *(Lab)*
Curtis-Thomas, Claire *(Lab)*
Darling, Alistair *(Lab)*
Dalyell, Tam *(Lab)*
Davies, Quentin *(Con)*
Davy, Edward *(Lib Dem)*
Dorrell, Stephen *(Con)*
Dowd, Jim *(Lab)*
Eagle, Angela *(Lab)*

Flight, Howard *(Con)*
Follett, Barbara *(Lab)*
Forth, Eric *(Con)*
Foster, Derek *(Lab)*
Fox, Dr Liam *(Con)*
Gapes, Mike *(Lab/Co-op)*
Gardiner, Barry *(Lab)*
Gibb, Nick *(Con)*
Green, Damian *(Con)*
Griffiths, Nigel *(Lab)*
Grogan, John *(Lab)*
Hague, William *(Con)*
Hain, Peter *(Lab)*
Hamilton, Sir Archie *(Con)*
Hammond, Philip *(Con)*
Harvey, Nick *(Lib Dem)*
Heath, Sir Edward *(Con)*
Henderson, Doug *(Lab)*
Hesford, Stephen *(Lab)*
Hoon, Geoffrey *(Lab)*
Hopkins, Kelvin *(Lab)*
Horam, John *(Con)*
Howarth, Alan *(Lab)*
Jenkin, Bernard *(Con)*
Jones, Dr Lynne *(Lab)*
Keeble, Sally *(Lab)*
Kelly, Ruth *(Lab)*
Ladyman, Dr Stephen *(Lab)*
Laing, Eleanor *(Con)*
Lansley, Andrew *(Con)*
Leslie, Christopher *(Lab)*
Letwin, Oliver *(Con)*
Liddell, Helen *(Lab)*
Lilley, Peter *(Con)*
Livingstone, Ken
   (Independent)
Lock, David *(Lab)*
McCabe, Stephen *(Lab)*
McDonnell, John *(Lab)*
McFall, John *(Lab/Co-op)*
MacGregor, John *(Con)*
McIsaac, Shona *(Lab)*
Mallaber, Judy *(Lab)*
Maples, John *(Con)*
Marek, Dr John *(Lab)*
Marsden, Paul *(Lab)*
Marshall-Andrews, Robert
   (Lab)
Meacher, Michael *(Lab)*
Merron, Gillian *(Lab)*
Milburn, Alan *(Lab)*
Miller, Andrew *(Lab)*
Mitchell, Austin *(Lab)*
Moonie, Lewis *(Lab/Co-op)*
Moran, Margaret *(Lab)*
Murphy, Jim *(Lab)*

O'Brien, Stephen *(Con)*
Pearson, Ian *(Lab)*
Plaskitt, James *(Lab)*
Primarolo, Dawn *(Lab)*
Radice, Giles *(Lab)*
Rammell, Bill *(Lab)*
Reid, Dr John *(Lab)*
Robertson, Laurence *(Con)*
Robinson, Geoffrey *(Lab)*
St Aubyn, Nicholas *(Con)*
Sarwar, Mohammed *(Lab)*
Sedgemore, Brian *(Lab)*
Sheerman, Barry
   (Lab/Co-op)
Sheldon, Robert *(Lab)*
Simpson, Alan *(Lab)*
Skinner, Dennis *(Lab)*
Smith, Chris *(Lab)*
Smith, Jacqui *(Lab)*
Stewart, Ian *(Lab)*
Straw, Jack *(Lab)*
Swinney, John *(SNP)*
Syms, Robert *(Con)*
Tapsell, Sir Peter *(Con)*
Taylor, Dari *(Lab)*
Taylor, Ian *(Con)*
Timms, Stephen *(Lab)*
Todd, Mark *(Lab)*
Trickett, Jon *(Lab)*
Tyrie, Andrew *(Con)*
Vis, Rudi *(Lab)*
Wardle, Charles *(Con)*
Wareing, Robert *(Lab)*
White, Brian *(Lab)*
Whitney, Sir Raymond *(Con)*
Willetts, David *(Con)*
Williams, Dr Alan Wynne
   (Lab)
Woolas, Philip *(Lab)*
Yeo, Tim *(Con)*

Economic Regeneration
Blackman, Elizabeth *(Lab)*
Healey, John *(Lab)*
Hughes, Beverley *(Lab)*
Humble, Joan *(Lab)*
Reed, Andrew *(Lab/Co-op)*
Smith, Geraldine *(Lab)*

Education
Allan, Richard *(Lib Dem)*
Amess, David *(Con)*
Armstrong, Hilary *(Lab)*
Atkins, Charlotte *(Lab)*
Barnes, Harry *(Lab)*
Begg, Anne *(Lab)*

Beggs, Roy *(UUP)*
Benn, Hilary *(Lab)*
Benton, Joe *(Lab)*
Bercow, John *(Con)*
Beresford, Sir Paul *(Con)*
Blackman, Elizabeth *(Lab)*
Blizzard, Bob *(Lab)*
Blunkett, David *(Lab)*
Bradley, Peter *(Lab)*
Brady, Graham *(Con)*
Browne, Desmond *(Lab)*
Butler, Christine *(Lab)*
Byers, Stephen *(Lab)*
Campbell, Alan *(Lab)*
Campbell, Anne *(Lab)*
Campbell-Savours, Dale
    (Lab)
Cann, Jamie *(Lab)*
Caton, Martin *(Lab)*
Chaytor, David *(Lab)*
Clappison, James *(Con)*
Clark, Paul *(Lab)*
Coaker, Vernon *(Lab)*
Cook, Frank *(Lab)*
Cormack, Sir Patrick *(Con)*
Cryer, John *(Lab)*
Curtis-Thomas, Claire
    (Lab)
Darling, Alistair *(Lab)*
Darvill, Keith *(Lab)*
Davey, Valerie *(Lab)*
Davidson, Ian *(Lab/Co-op)*
Dean, Janet *(Lab)*
Denham, John *(Lab)*
Drew, David *(Lab/Co-op)*
Edwards, Huw *(Lab)*
Efford, Clive *(Lab)*
Ennis, Jeffrey *(Lab)*
Etherington, William *(Lab)*
Evans, Nigel *(Con)*
Ewing, Margaret *(SNP)*
Faber, David *(Con)*
Fallon, Michael *(Con)*
Fitzsimons, Lorna *(Lab)*
Flint, Caroline *(Lab)*
Foster, Derek *(Lab)*
Foster, Don *(Lib Dem)*
Foster, Michael John *(Lab)*
Foulkes, George
    (Lab/Co-op)
Gale, Roger *(Con)*
Gapes, Mike *(Lab/Co-op)*
Gardiner, Barry *(Lab)*
Garnier, Edward *(Con)*
Gibb, Nick *(Con)*
Gidley, Sandra *(Lib Dem)*

Gordon, Eileen *(Lab)*
Gorrie, Donald *(Lib Dem)*
Green, Damian *(Con)*
Griffiths, Nigel *(Lab)*
Griffiths, Win *(Lab)*
Hall, Mike *(Lab)*
Hamilton, Fabian *(Lab)*
Haselhurst, Sir Alan *(Con)*
Hawkins, Nick *(Con)*
Hayes, John *(Con)*
Heath, David *(Lib Dem)*
Hesford, Stephen *(Lab)*
Hodge, Margaret *(Lab)*
Hood, Jimmy *(Lab)*
Howarth, Alan *(Lab)*
Howarth, Gerald *(Con)*
Hughes, Beverley *(Lab)*
Humble, Joan *(Lab)*
Jamieson, David *(Lab)*
Johnson, Alan *(Lab)*
Johnson, Melanie *(Lab)*
Jones, Barry *(Lab)*
Jones, Helen *(Lab)*
Jones, Ieuan Wyn *(PC)*
Jones, Jon Owen
    (Lab/Co-op)
Keeble, Sally *(Lab)*
Key, Robert *(Con)*
Khabra, Piara *(Lab)*
Kilfoyle, Peter *(Lab)*
King, Oona *(Lab)*
Kumar, Dr Ashok *(Lab)*
Laing, Eleanor *(Con)*
Lammy, David *(Lab)*
Letwin, Oliver *(Con)*
Levitt, Tom *(Lab)*
Lewis, Ivan *(Lab)*
Lewis, Dr Julian *(Con)*
Lidington, David *(Con)*
Lilley, Peter *(Con)*
Linton, Martin *(Lab)*
McAllion, John *(Lab)*
McFall, John *(Lab/Co-op)*
MacGregor, John *(Con)*
McLoughlin, Patrick *(Con)*
McNulty, Tony *(Lab)*
Mactaggart, Fiona *(Lab)*
McWilliam, John *(Lab)*
Madel, Sir David *(Con)*
Mallaber, Judy *(Lab)*
Marsden, Gordon *(Lab)*
Marsden, Paul *(Lab)*
Marshall, James *(Lab)*
May, Theresa *(Con)*
Morley, Elliot *(Lab)*
Morris, Estelle *(Lab)*

Moss, Malcolm *(Con)*
Murphy, Paul *(Lab)*
O'Brien, Stephen *(Con)*
O'Hara, Edward *(Lab)*
O'Neill, Martin *(Lab)*
Öpik, Lembit *(Lib Dem)*
Organ, Diana *(Lab)*
Perham, Linda *(Lab)*
Pickthall, Colin *(Lab)*
Plaskitt, James *(Lab)*
Pope, Greg *(Lab)*
Prentice, Bridget *(Lab)*
Primarolo, Dawn *(Lab)*
Prior, David *(Con)*
Purchase, Ken *(Lab/Co-op)*
Rammell, Bill *(Lab)*
Reed, Andrew *(Lab/Co-op)*
Robertson, Laurence
    (Con)
Rogers, Allan *(Lab)*
Ross, Ernie *(Lab)*
Rowlands, Edward *(Lab)*
Ruane, Chris *(Lab)*
Ruffley, David *(Con)*
Russell, Christine *(Lab)*
St Aubyn, Nicholas *(Con)*
Sawford, Philip *(Lab)*
Shephard, Gillian *(Con)*
Simpson, Keith *(Con)*
Singh, Marsha *(Lab)*
Smith, Andrew *(Lab)*
Smith, Jacqui *(Lab)*
Smyth, Rev Martin *(UUP)*
Steinberg, Gerry *(Lab)*
Stevenson, George *(Lab)*
Stewart, Ian *(Lab)*
Stoate, Dr Howard *(Lab)*
Straw, Jack *(Lab)*
Taylor, Ann *(Lab)*
Taylor, Dari *(Lab)*
Tipping, Paddy *(Lab)*
Touhig, Don *(Lab/Co-op)*
Trend, Michael *(Con)*
Turner, Dennis *(Lab/Co-op)*
Turner, Dr George *(Lab)*
Twigg, Derek *(Lab)*
Twigg, Stephen *(Lab)*
Vaz, Keith *(Lab)*
Ward, Claire *(Lab)*
Watts, David *(Lab)*
Wicks, Malcolm *(Lab)*
Willetts, David *(Con)*
Willis, Phil *(Lib Dem)*
Woodward, Shaun *(Lab)*
Wray, James *(Lab)*
Wright, Dr Tony *(Lab)*

Education (Adult)
Davies, Ron *(Lab)*
Etherington, William *(Lab)*

Education (Early Years)
Cryer, Ann *(Lab)*

Education (Further and Higher)
Clark, Dr Lynda *(Lab)*
Cryer, John *(Lab)*
Iddon, Dr Brian *(Lab)*
Naysmith, Dr Doug *(Lab/Co-op)*
Sheerman, Barry *(Lab/Co-op)*
Swinney, John *(SNP)*
Whitehead, Dr Alan *(Lab)*

Education (Special Needs)
Browning, Angela *(Con)*
Loughton, Tim *(Con)*
Williams, Betty *(Lab)*

Elderly
Graham, Tommy *(Independent)*
Hayes, John *(Con)*
Hughes, Kevin *(Lab)*
Jones, Ieuan Wyn *(PC)*
McCrea, William *(DUP)*
Mackinlay, Andrew *(Lab)*
Martin, Michael *(Lab)*
Sarwar, Mohammed *(Lab)*
Shipley, Debra *(Lab)*
Vis, Rudi *(Lab)*
Walker, Cecil *(UUP)*

Elections
Ashton, Joe *(Lab)*

Electoral Reform
Bayley, Hugh *(Lab)*
Burden, Richard *(Lab)*
Cann, Jamie *(Lab)*
Cormack, Sir Patrick *(Con)*
Johnson, Alan *(Lab)*
King, Oona *(Lab)*
Mackinlay, Andrew *(Lab)*
Mitchell, Austin *(Lab)*
Rammell, Bill *(Lab)*
Smith, Robert *(Lib Dem)*
Twigg, Stephen *(Lab)*

Electoral Registration
Barnes, Harry *(Lab)*

Emergency Planning
O'Hara, Edward *(Lab)*

Employment
Alexander, Douglas *(Lab)*
Atkins, Charlotte *(Lab)*
Baldry, Tony *(Con)*
Beggs, Roy *(UUP)*
Benn, Hilary *(Lab)*
Blears, Hazel *(Lab)*
Blizzard, Bob *(Lab)*
Brady, Graham *(Con)*
Brown, Gordon *(Lab)*
Bruce, Ian *(Con)*
Burns, Simon *(Con)*
Butler, Christine *(Lab)*
Clapham, Michael *(Lab)*
Clelland, David *(Lab)*
Collins, Tim *(Con)*
Cryer, John *(Lab)*
Davey, Edward *(Lib Dem)*
Dawson, Hilton *(Lab)*
Doran, Frank *(Lab)*
Eagle, Maria *(Lab)*
Etherington, William *(Lab)*
Flint, Caroline *(Lab)*
Green, Damian *(Con)*
Healey, John *(Lab)*
Henderson, Doug *(Lab)*
Henderson, Ivan *(Lab)*
Hewitt, Patricia *(Lab)*
Hopkins, Kelvin *(Lab)*
Howard, Michael *(Con)*
Howarth, Alan *(Lab)*
Hurst, Alan *(Lab)*
Johnson, Melanie *(Lab)*
Jones, Fiona *(Lab)*
Kelly, Ruth *(Lab)*
Khabra, Piara *(Lab)*
Kilfoyle, Peter *(Lab)*
King, Oona *(Lab)*
Letwin, Oliver *(Con)*
Lewis, Terry *(Lab)*
Lock, David *(Lab)*
Lyell, Sir Nicholas *(Con)*
McAllion, John *(Lab)*
McCartney, Ian *(Lab)*
McLeish, Henry *(Lab)*
Madel, Sir David *(Con)*
Mahon, Alice *(Lab)*
Mallaber, Judy *(Lab)*
Merron, Gillian *(Lab)*
Moore, Michael *(Lib Dem)*
Moran, Margaret *(Lab)*
Mountford, Kali *(Lab)*
Paice, James *(Con)*

Pike, Peter *(Lab)*
Pond, Chris *(Lab)*
Prior, David *(Con)*
Ross, Ernie *(Lab)*
Rowe, Andrew *(Con)*
Ryan, Joan *(Lab)*
Sarwar, Mohammed *(Lab)*
Sawford, Philip *(Lab)*
Smith, Andrew *(Lab)*
Stewart, Ian *(Lab)*
Sutcliffe, Gerry *(Lab)*
Timms, Stephen *(Lab)*
Touhig, Don *(Lab/Co-op)*
Townend, John *(Con)*
Tredinnick, David *(Con)*
Turner, Dr Des *(Lab)*
Ward, Claire *(Lab)*
Wardle, Charles *(Con)*
Wigley, Dafydd *(PC)*
Williams, Alan John *(Lab)*
Winterton, Rosie *(Lab)*
Woolas, Philip *(Lab)*
Worthington, Tony *(Lab)*

Employment Law
Anderson, Janet *(Lab)*
Brown, Russell *(Lab)*
Burden, Richard *(Lab)*
Corston, Jean *(Lab)*
Foster, Michael Jabez *(Lab)*
Fyfe, Maria *(Lab)*
Johnson, Alan *(Lab)*
Roy, Frank *(Lab)*
Smith, Angela *(Lab/Co-op)*
Tynan, Bill *(Lab)*

Employment (Retraining)
Blackman, Elizabeth *(Lab)*

Energy
Barnes, Harry *(Lab)*
Barron, Kevin *(Lab)*
Bermingham, Gerry *(Lab)*
Bruce, Ian *(Con)*
Bruce, Malcolm *(Lib Dem)*
Cable, Dr Vincent *(Lib Dem)*
Clapham, Michael *(Lab)*
Clark, Dr Michael *(Con)*
Clelland, David *(Lab)*
Cook, Frank *(Lab)*
Corbett, Robin *(Lab)*
Cummings, John *(Lab)*
Cunliffe, Lawrence *(Lab)*
Doran, Frank *(Lab)*
Foulkes, George *(Lab/Co-op)*

Gilroy, Linda *(Lab/Co-op)*
Hamilton, Fabian *(Lab)*
Hammond, Philip *(Con)*
Heathcoat-Amory, David
(Con)
Hood, Jimmy *(Lab)*
Howells, Dr Kim *(Lab)*
Illsley, Eric *(Lab)*
Ingram, Adam *(Lab)*
McLeish, Henry *(Lab)*
Maclennan, Robert
(Lib Dem)
Moss, Malcolm *(Con)*
O'Brien, William *(Lab)*
Pike, Peter *(Lab)*
Rogers, Allan *(Lab)*
Rowlands, Edward *(Lab)*
Salmond, Alex *(SNP)*
Skinner, Dennis *(Lab)*
Spellar, John *(Lab)*
Stevenson, George *(Lab)*
Stunell, Andrew *(Lib Dem)*
Tipping, Paddy *(Lab)*
Wallace, James *(Lib Dem)*
Waterson, Nigel *(Con)*

Engineering
Battle, John *(Lab)*
Chidgey, David *(Lib Dem)*
Cook, Frank *(Lab)*
Iddon, Dr Brian *(Lab)*
Olner, Bill *(Lab)*

Enterprise
Connarty, Michael *(Lab)*
Swinney, John *(SNP)*

Environment
Ainsworth, Peter *(Con)*
Ainsworth, Bob *(Lab)*
Amess, David *(Con)*
Anderson, Donald *(Lab)*
Armstrong, Hilary *(Lab)*
Atherton, Candy *(Lab)*
Austin, John *(Lab)*
Baker, Norman *(Lib Dem)*
Ballard, Jackie *(Lib Dem)*
Barnes, Harry *(Lab)*
Barron, Kevin *(Lab)*
Bayley, Hugh *(Lab)*
Benn, Hilary *(Lab)*
Blunt, Crispin *(Con)*
Boateng, Paul *(Lab)*
Body, Sir Richard *(Con)*
Bradshaw, Ben *(Lab)*
Brake, Tom *(Lib Dem)*

Brinton, Helen *(Lab)*
Burstow, Paul *(Lib Dem)*
Butler, Christine *(Lab)*
Butterfill, John *(Con)*
Cable, Dr Vincent *(Lib Dem)*
Campbell, Anne *(Lab)*
Cann, Jamie *(Lab)*
Caton, Martin *(Lab)*
Chapman, Sydney *(Con)*
Chaytor, David *(Lab)*
Clark, Paul *(Lab)*
Clarke, Tony *(Lab)*
Clelland, David *(Lab)*
Clifton-Brown, Geoffrey
(Con)
Coaker, Vernon *(Lab)*
Cohen, Harry *(Lab)*
Cook, Frank *(Lab)*
Cook, Robin *(Lab)*
Corbett, Robin *(Lab)*
Corbyn, Jeremy *(Lab)*
Cummings, John *(Lab)*
Cunningham, Dr Jack *(Lab)*
Darvill, Keith *(Lab)*
Davey, Edward *(Lib Dem)*
Davies, Geraint *(Lab)*
Davies, Ron *(Lab)*
Dowd, Jim *(Lab)*
Drew, David *(Lab/Co-op)*
Duncan Smith, Iain *(Con)*
Efford, Clive *(Lab)*
Ellman, Louise *(Lab/Co-op)*
Ennis, Jeffrey *(Lab)*
George, Andrew *(Lib Dem)*
Gibson, Dr Ian *(Lab)*
Gorman, Teresa *(Con)*
Gray, James *(Con)*
Grieve, Dominic *(Con)*
Griffiths, Jane *(Lab)*
Gummer, John *(Con)*
Hawkins, Nick *(Con)*
Heald, Oliver *(Con)*
Heath, David *(Lib Dem)*
Hill, Keith *(Lab)*
Hoey, Kate *(Lab)*
Hood, Jimmy *(Lab)*
Howarth, George *(Lab)*
Howells, Dr Kim *(Lab)*
Hughes, Simon *(Lib Dem)*
Jackson, Glenda *(Lab)*
Jackson, Helen *(Lab)*
Jones, Jenny *(Lab)*
Jones, Jon Owen
(Lab/Co-op)
Jones, Martyn *(Lab)*
Ladyman, Dr Stephen *(Lab)*

Leslie, Christopher *(Lab)*
Lord, Michael *(Con)*
Loughton, Tim *(Con)*
Lyell, Sir Nicholas *(Con)*
McDonnell, John *(Lab)*
Mackay, Andrew *(Con)*
Mackinlay, Andrew *(Lab)*
McWalter, Tony *(Lab)*
Marsden, Paul *(Lab/Co-op)*
Marshall-Andrews, Robert
(Lab)
Meale, Alan *(Lab)*
Morley, Elliot *(Lab)*
O'Brien, Mike *(Lab)*
Pendry, Tom *(Lab)*
Perham, Linda *(Lab)*
Pike, Peter *(Lab)*
Prosser, Gwyn *(Lab)*
Randall, John *(Con)*
Raynsford, Nick *(Lab)*
Robathan, Andrew *(Con)*
Roche, Barbara *(Lab)*
Roe, Marion *(Con)*
Rogers, Allan *(Lab)*
Ruane, Chris *(Lab)*
Ruddock, Joan *(Lab)*
Russell, Bob *(Lib Dem)*
Russell, Christine *(Lab)*
Salter, Martin *(Lab)*
Simpson, Alan *(Lab)*
Skinner, Dennis *(Lab)*
Smith, Chris *(Lab)*
Soley, Clive *(Lab)*
Spelman, Caroline *(Con)*
Steen, Anthony *(Con)*
Stinchcombe, Paul *(Lab)*
Stoate, Dr Howard *(Lab)*
Taylor, David *(Lab/Co-op)*
Taylor, John M *(Con)*
Taylor, Sir Teddy *(Con)*
Thomas, Gareth Richard *(Lab)*
Todd, Mark *(Lab)*
Tonge, Dr Jennifer *(Lib Dem)*
Tredinnick, David *(Con)*
Truswell, Paul *(Lab)*
Walley, Joan *(Lab)*
Walter, Robert *(Con)*
Welsh, Andrew *(SNP)*
White, Brian *(Lab)*
Whitehead, Dr Alan *(Lab)*
Wood, Mike *(Lab)*
Woodward, Shaun *(Lab)*
Wright, Dr Tony *(Lab)*

Environmental Health
Williams, Betty *(Lab)*

Environmental Protection
Williams, Dr Alan Wynne *(Lab)*

Environmental Taxation
Loughton, Tim *(Con)*

Environmentally Sustainable Transport
Starkey, Dr Phyllis *(Lab)*

Equal Opportunities
Austin, John *(Lab)*
Cohen, Harry *(Lab)*
Etherington, William *(Lab)*
Gordon, Eileen *(Lab)*
Heal, Sylvia *(Lab)*
Heppell, John *(Lab)*
Hope, Phil *(Lab/Co-op)*
Mallaber, Judy *(Lab)*
Morgan, Julie *(Lab)*
Tynan, Bill *(Lab)*

European Democracy
Hancock, Mike *(Lib Dem)*

European Monetary Union
Davey, Edward *(Lib Dem)*
Flight, Howard *(Con)*

European Regional Issues
Wigley, Dafydd *(PC)*

European Union
Baldry, Tony *(Con)*
Barnes, Harry *(Lab)*
Bell, Stuart *(Lab)*
Bercow, John *(Con)*
Body, Sir Richard *(Con)*
Boswell, Timothy *(Con)*
Brady, Graham *(Con)*
Cable, Dr Vincent *(Lib Dem)*
Caborn, Richard *(Lab)*
Cash, William *(Con)*
Caton, Martin *(Lab)*
Collins, Tim *(Con)*
Connarty, Michael *(Lab)*
Cran, James *(Con)*
Cryer, John *(Lab)*
Cunningham, James *(Lab)*
Ellman, Louise *(Lab/Co-op)*
Evans, Nigel *(Con)*
Ewing, Margaret *(SNP)*
Forth, Eric *(Con)*
Gapes, Mike *(Lab/Co-op)*

Gill, Christopher *(Con)*
Godsiff, Roger *(Lab)*
Grieve, Dominic *(Con)*
Griffiths, Win *(Lab)*
Grogan, John *(Lab)*
Gummer, John *(Con)*
Hammond, Philip *(Con)*
Harvey, Nick *(Lib Dem)*
Haselhurst, Sir Alan *(Con)*
Heath, Sir Edward *(Con)*
Heathcoat-Amory, David *(Con)*
Hill, Keith *(Lab)*
Hood, Jimmy *(Lab)*
Hoon, Geoffrey *(Lab)*
Hume, John *(SDLP)*
Jackson, Robert *(Con)*
Jenkin, Bernard *(Con)*
Jones, Ieuan Wyn *(PC)*
Kelly, Ruth *(Lab)*
Kennedy, Charles *(Lib Dem)*
Khabra, Piara *(Lab)*
King, Oona *(Lab)*
Kingham, Tess *(Lab)*
Kirkbride, Julie *(Con)*
Lait, Jacqui *(Con)*
Lewis, Dr Julian *(Con)*
Lilley, Peter *(Con)*
McGuire, Anne *(Lab)*
Maclennan, Robert *(Lib Dem)*
MacShane, Dr Denis *(Lab)*
Malins, Humfrey *(Con)*
May, Theresa *(Con)*
Mitchell, Austin *(Lab)*
Morgan, Alasdair *(SNP)*
Nicholls, Patrick *(Con)*
O'Hara, Edward *(Lab)*
Plaskitt, James *(Lab)*
Quin, Joyce *(Lab)*
Radice, Giles *(Lab)*
Rammell, Bill *(Lab)*
Robertson, Laurence *(Lab)*
Rogers, Allan *(Lab)*
Shephard, Gillian *(Con)*
Singh, Marsha *(Lab)*
Skinner, Dennis *(Lab)*
Straw, Jack *(Lab)*
Taylor, Ian *(Con)*
Taylor, John D *(UUP)*
Taylor, John M *(Con)*
Taylor, Sir Teddy *(Con)*
Temple-Morris, Peter *(Lab)*
Townend, John *(Con)*
Tyrie, Andrew *(Con)*
Vis, Rudi *(Lab)*

Walter, Robert *(Con)*
White, Brian *(Lab)*
Whitney, Sir Raymond *(Con)*
Wilkinson, John *(Con)*

Expatriate Workers
Cook, Frank *(Lab)*

Family
Brazier, Julian *(Con)*
Doran, Frank *(Lab)*
Hewitt, Patricia *(Lab)*
Hughes, Beverley *(Lab)*
Streeter, Gary *(Con)*

Family Friendly Employment
Flint, Caroline *(Lab)*

Film Industry
Clarke, Tom *(Lab)*
Follett, Barbara *(Lab)*
Lansley, Andrew *(Con)*

Finance
Boswell, Tim *(Con)*
Caplin, Ivor *(Lab)*
Davies, Quentin *(Con)*
Duncan, Alan *(Con)*
Duncan Smith, Iain *(Con)*
Foster, Derek *(Lab)*
Hamilton, Sir Archie *(Con)*
Hawkins, Nick *(Con)*
Loughton, Tim *(Con)*
MacGregor, John *(Con)*
McIsaac, Shona *(Lab)*
Major, John *(Con)*
Pendry, Tom *(Lab)*
Sheerman, Barry *(Lab/Co-op)*
Tapsell, Sir Peter *(Con)*
Trickett, Jon *(Lab)*
Twigg, Derek *(Lab)*
Viggers, Peter *(Con)*
Vis, Rudi *(Lab)*
Woodward, Shaun *(Lab)*

Financial Services
Denham, John *(Lab)*
Hawkins, Nick *(Con)*
Keeble, Sally *(Lab)*
Moss, Malcolm *(Con)*

Fire Service
Ennis, Jeffrey *(Lab)*
Fitzpatrick, Jim *(Lab)*
McCartney, Ian *(Lab)*

Firearms Legislation
Ross, William *(UUP)*

Fishing
Gill, Christopher *(Con)*
George, Andrew *(Lib Dem)*
Michie, Ray *(Lib Dem)*
Mitchell, Austin *(Lab)*
Quinn, Laurie *(Lab)*
Salmond, Alex *(SNP)*
Steen, Anthony *(Con)*
Strang, Gavin *(Lab)*
Walker, Cecil *(UUP)*
Wallace, James *(Lib Dem)*

Footwear
Anderson, Janet *(Lab)*

Foreign Affairs
Anderson, Donald *(Lab)*
Arbuthnot, James *(Con)*
Ashdown, Sir Paddy
   (Lib Dem)
Atkinson, David *(Con)*
Austin, John *(Lab)*
Beard, Nigel *(Lab)*
Bell, Martin *(Independent)*
Blunt, Crispin *(Con)*
Bradshaw, Ben *(Lab)*
Brady, Graham *(Con)*
Burns, Simon *(Con)*
Butterfill, John *(Con)*
Cable, Dr Vincent *(Lib Dem)*
Campbell, Menzies
   (Lib Dem)
Casale, Roger *(Lab)*
Chapman, Ben *(Lab)*
Chaytor, David *(Lab)*
Chidgey, David *(Lib Dem)*
Clarke, Eric *(Lab)*
Clarke, Tom *(Lab)*
Clifton-Brown, Geoffrey
   (Con)
Coaker, Vernon *(Lab)*
Cunningham, Dr Jack *(Lab)*
Curry, David *(Con)*
Curtis-Thomas, Claire *(Lab)*
Davies, Denzil *(Lab)*
Dorrell, Stephen *(Con)*
Emery, Peter *(Con)*
Ewing, Margaret *(SNP)*
Faber, David *(Con)*
Fabricant, Michael *(Con)*
Foulkes, George
   (Lab/Co-op)
Fox, Dr Liam *(Con)*

Fraser, Christopher *(Con)*
Galloway, George *(Lab)*
Gardiner, Barry *(Lab)*
Garnier, Edward *(Con)*
Gerrard, Neil *(Lab)*
Godman, Dr Norman *(Lab)*
Godsiff, Roger *(Lab)*
Graham, Tommy
   (Independent)
Green, Damian *(Con)*
Grieve, Dominic *(Con)*
Grocott, Bruce *(Lab)*
Hanson, David *(Lab)*
Hoey, Kate *(Lab)*
Howells, Dr Kim *(Lab)*
Jackson, Robert *(Con)*
Jenkin, Bernard *(Con)*
Keen, Alan *(Lab/Co-op)*
Keetch, Paul *(Lib Dem)*
Kennedy, Jane *(Lab)*
Key, Robert *(Con)*
Kilfoyle, Peter *(Lab)*
Kingham, Tess *(Lab)*
Leigh, Edward *(Con)*
Lewis, Dr Julian *(Con)*
Lidington, David *(Con)*
Loughton, Tim *(Con)*
Mackay, Andrew *(Con)*
Maples, John *(Con)*
Murphy, Paul *(Lab)*
O'Brien, Stephen *(Con)*
Paisley, Rev Ian *(DUP)*
Paterson, Owen *(Con)*
Pope, Greg *(Lab)*
Randall, John *(Con)*
Reid, Dr John *(Lab)*
Ruddock, Joan *(Lab)*
Savidge, Malcolm *(Lab)*
Simpson, Keith *(Con)*
Smith, Chris *(Lab)*
Smyth, Rev Martin *(UUP)*
Soames, Nicholas *(Con)*
Squire, Rachel *(Lab)*
Starkey, Dr Phyllis *(Lab)*
Tapsell, Sir Peter *(Con)*
Temple-Morris, Peter
   (Lab)
Tredinnick, David *(Con)*
Trend, Michael *(Con)*
Twigg, Stephen *(Lab)*
Wareing, Robert *(Lab)*
Waterson, Nigel *(Con)*
Wells, Bowen *(Con)*
Whitney, Sir Raymond
   (Con)
Wilshire, David *(Con)*

Winterton, Nicholas *(Con)*
Wray, James *(Lab)*
Wyatt, Derek *(Lab)*

Forestry
Heathcoat-Amory, David
   (Con)
Lord, Michael *(Con)*

Freedom of Information
Fisher, Mark *(Lab)*
Kirkwood, Archy *(Lib Dem)*
Norris, Dan *(Lab)*

Gaelic Language
Michie, Ray *(Lib Dem)*

Gas Industry
Bruce, Malcolm *(Lib Dem)*

Gender Equality
Follett, Barbara *(Lab)*
King, Oona *(Lab)*

Gibraltar
Willis, Phil *(Lib Dem)*

Glass Industry
Illsley, Eric *(Lab)*

Grandparents' Rights
Powell, Sir Raymond *(Lab)*

Government
Grocott, Bruce *(Lab)*

Health
Amess, David *(Con)*
Anderson, Janet *(Lab)*
Atherton, Candy *(Lab)*
Atkins, Charlotte *(Lab)*
Austin, John *(Lab)*
Bayley, Hugh *(Lab)*
Begg, Anne *(Lab)*
Blears, Hazel *(Lab)*
Blizzard, Bob *(Lab)*
Bradley, Keith *(Lab)*
Bradley, Peter *(Lab)*
Brady, Graham *(Con)*
Brand, Dr Peter *(Lib Dem)*
Brinton, Helen *(Lab)*
Brown, Gordon *(Lab)*
Buck, Karen *(Lab)*
Burden, Richard *(Lab)*
Butterfill, John *(Con)*
Campbell-Savours, Dale *(Lab)*

Health *continued*
Chisholm, Malcolm *(Lab)*
Clapham, Michael *(Lab)*
Clappison, James *(Con)*
Clark, Dr Lynda *(Lab)*
Coffey, Ann *(Lab)*
Cohen, Harry *(Lab)*
Cousins, Jim *(Lab)*
Cryer, Ann *(Lab)*
Cryer, John *(Lab)*
Darling, Alistair *(Lab)*
Davey, Valerie *(Lab)*
Davies, Quentin *(Con)*
Davis, David *(Con)*
Dawson, Hilton *(Lab)*
Dean, Janet *(Lab)*
Dismore, Andrew *(Lab)*
Dobbin, Jim *(Lab/Co-op)*
Donohoe, Brian *(Lab)*
Edwards, Huw *(Lab)*
Efford, Clive *(Lab)*
Ellman, Louise *(Lab/Co-op)*
Fearn, Ronnie *(Lib Dem)*
Fitzsimons, Lorna *(Lab)*
Foster, Michael Jabez *(Lab)*
Flynn, Paul *(Lab)*
Fox, Dr Liam *(Con)*
George, Bruce *(Lab)*
Gibson, Dr Ian *(Lab)*
Gidley, Sandra *(Lib Dem)*
Gordon, Eileen *(Lab)*
Griffiths, Nigel *(Lab)*
Gunnell, John *(Lab)*
Hammond, Philip *(Con)*
Hanson, David *(Lab)*
Harris, Evan *(Lib Dem)*
Harvey, Nick *(Lib Dem)*
Henderson, Ivan *(Lab)*
Hesford, Stephen *(Lab)*
Horam, John *(Con)*
Hughes, Beverley *(Lab)*
Hutton, John *(Lab)*
Iddon, Dr Brian *(Lab)*
Jack, Michael *(Con)*
Johnson, Melanie *(Lab)*
Johnson Smith, Sir Geoffrey
    (Con)
Jones, Fiona *(Lab)*
Keen, Ann *(Lab)*
King, Andy *(Lab)*
King, Oona *(Lab)*
Kirkbride, Julie *(Con)*
Kirkwood, Archy *(Lib Dem)*
Lait, Jacqui *(Con)*
Lansley, Andrew *(Con)*
Lewis, Ivan *(Lab)*

Love, Andrew *(Lab/Co-op)*
McCafferty, Christine *(Lab)*
McCrea, William *(DUP)*
McLeish, Henry *(Lab)*
McNulty, Tony *(Lab)*
Mahon, Alice *(Lab)*
Maples, John *(Con)*
Marsden, Paul *(Lab)*
Martlew, Eric *(Lab)*
Mawhinney, Sir Brian *(Con)*
Meale, Alan *(Lab)*
Milburn, Alan *(Lab)*
Moffatt, Laura *(Lab)*
Morgan, Rhodri *(Lab)*
Naysmith, Dr Doug
    (Lab/Co-op)
Pickles, Eric *(Con)*
Primarolo, Dawn *(Lab)*
Purchase, Ken *(Lab/Co-op)*
Roe, Marion *(Con)*
Rogers, Allan *(Lab)*
Ryan, Joan *(Lab)*
Shephard, Gillian *(Con)*
Singh, Marsha *(Lab)*
Smith, Chris *(Lab)*
Smyth, Rev Martin *(UUP)*
Southworth, Helen *(Lab)*
Spelman, Caroline *(Con)*
Starkey, Dr Phyllis *(Lab)*
Stewart, David *(Lab)*
Stoate, Dr Howard *(Lab)*
Taylor, Ann *(Lab)*
Thomas, Gareth Richard *(Lab)*
Tonge, Dr Jennifer *(Lib Dem)*
Touhig, Don *(Lab/Co-op)*
Trend, Michael *(Con)*
Truswell, Paul *(Lab)*
Turner, Dr Des *(Lab)*
Twigg, Derek *(Lab)*
Walley, Joan *(Lab)*
Waterson, Nigel *(Con)*
Whitney, Sir Raymond *(Con)*
Widdecombe, Ann *(Con)*
Willetts, David *(Con)*
Williams, Betty *(Lab)*
Willis, Phil *(Lib Dem)*
Wright, Dr Tony *(Lab)*
Yeo, Tim *(Con)*

Health and Safety at Work
McCartney, Ian *(Lab)*
Quinn, Lawrie *(Lab)*

Health Education
Heal, Sylvia *(Lab)*
Michie, Ray *(Lib Dem)*

Williams, Betty *(Lab)*
Young, Sir George *(Con)*

Health Service
Corbyn, Jeremy *(Lab)*
Cunningham, James *(Lab)*
Dowd, Jim *(Lab)*
Drown, Julia *(Lab)*
Dunwoody, Gwyneth
    (Lab)
Eagle, Angela *(Lab)*
Etherington, William *(Lab)*
Golding, Llin *(Lab)*
Grocott, Bruce *(Lab)*
Hinchliffe, David *(Lab)*
Hood, Jimmy *(Lab)*
McCartney, Ian *(Lab)*
Pike, Peter *(Lab)*
Ryan, Joan *(Lab)*
Squire, Rachel *(Lab)*
Winterton, Nicholas *(Con)*

Heritage
Allan, Richard *(Lib Dem)*
Atkinson, David *(Con)*
Beggs, Roy *(UUP)*
Caplin, Ivor *(Lab)*
Cash, William *(Con)*
Cormack, Sir Patrick
    (Con)
Hanson, David *(Lab)*
Keetch, Paul *(Lib Dem)*
Marsden, Gordon *(Lab)*
Smith, Chris *(Lab)*
Steen, Anthony *(Con)*

Home Affairs
Allan, Richard *(Lib Dem)*
Anderson, Janet *(Lab)*
Barron, Kevin *(Lab)*
Benn, Hilary *(Lab)*
Bermingham, Gerry *(Lab)*
Boateng, Paul *(Lab)*
Brinton, Helen *(Lab)*
Byers, Stephen *(Lab)*
Clappison, James *(Con)*
Clelland, David *(Lab)*
Corbett, Robin *(Lab)*
Cranston, Ross *(Lab)*
Dean, Janet *(Lab)*
Hall, Mike *(Lab)*
Hawkins, Nick *(Con)*
Heath, David *(Lib Dem)*
Hood, Jimmy *(Lab)*
Howard, Michael *(Con)*
Keeble, Sally *(Lab)*

King, Andy *(Lab)*
Lidington, David *(Con)*
Llwyd, Elfyn *(PC)*
Loughton, Tim *(Con)*
Lyell, Sir Nicholas *(Con)*
Mactaggart, Fiona *(Lab)*
Mates, Michael *(Con)*
Meale, Alan *(Lab)*
Mullin, Chris *(Lab)*
Nicholls, Patrick *(Con)*
Pickthall, Colin *(Lab)*
Prentice, Bridget *(Lab)*
Roche, Barbara *(Lab)*
Ruffley, David *(Con)*
Short, Clare *(Lab)*
Smith, Angela *(Lab/Co-op)*
Stinchcombe, Paul *(Lab)*
Taylor, Ann *(Lab)*
Taylor, Sir Teddy *(Con)*
Tredinnick, David *(Con)*
Ward, Claire *(Lab)*
Winterton, Rosie *(Lab)*

Homelessness
Etherington, William *(Lab)*

Horses
Page, Richard *(Con)*

Horticulture
Jack, Michael *(Con)*
Roe, Marion *(Con)*

Housing
Ancram, Michael *(Con)*
Battle, John *(Lab)*
Benton, Joe *(Lab)*
Beresford, Sir Paul *(Con)*
Betts, Clive *(Lab)*
Boateng, Paul *(Lab)*
Bradley, Keith *(Lab)*
Bradley, Peter *(Lab)*
Buck, Karen *(Lab)*
Butterfill, John *(Con)*
Chisholm, Malcolm *(Lab)*
Coleman, Iain *(Lab)*
Crausby, David *(Lab)*
Darvill, Keith *(Lab)*
Dean, Janet *(Lab)*
Denham, John *(Lab)*
Dobbin, Jim *(Lab/Co-op)*
Dowd, Jim *(Lab)*
Drew, David *(Lab/Co-op)*
Eagle, Maria *(Lab)*
Edwards, Huw *(Lab)*
Follett, Barbara *(Lab)*

George, Andrew *(Lib Dem)*
George, Bruce *(Lab)*
Gerrard, Neil *(Lab)*
Goggins, Paul *(Lab)*
Gordon, Eileen *(Lab)*
Gray, James *(Con)*
Griffiths, Nigel *(Lab)*
Hammond, Philip *(Con)*
Hodge, Margaret *(Lab)*
Hoey, Kate *(Lab)*
Hood, Jimmy *(Lab)*
Howarth, George *(Lab)*
Hughes, Simon *(Lib Dem)*
Hurst, Alan *(Lab)*
Iddon, Dr Brian *(Lab)*
Jackson, Glenda *(Lab)*
Jenkins, Brian *(Lab)*
Jones, Dr Lynne *(Lab)*
Kidney, David *(Lab)*
King, Oona *(Lab)*
Linton, Martin *(Lab)*
Love, Andrew *(Lab/Co-op)*
Loughton, Tim *(Con)*
McAllion, John *(Lab)*
McDonagh, Siobhain *(Lab)*
MacGregor, John *(Con)*
Major, John *(Con)*
Marshall, James *(Lab)*
Maxton, John *(Lab)*
Meacher, Michael *(Lab)*
Michael, Alun *(Lab/Co-op)*
Moffatt, Laura *(Lab)*
Moore, Michael *(Lib Dem)*
Moran, Margaret *(Lab)*
Morris, Estelle *(Lab)*
Moss, Malcolm *(Con)*
Murphy, Paul *(Lab)*
O'Brien, Mike *(Lab)*
O'Brien, Stephen *(Con)*
O'Hara, Edward *(Lab)*
Osborne, Sandra *(Lab)*
Pendry, Tom *(Lab)*
Pickles, Eric *(Con)*
Pollard, Kerry *(Lab)*
Pope, Greg *(Lab)*
Pound, Stephen *(Lab)*
Primarolo, Dawn *(Lab)*
Rammell, Bill *(Lab)*
Raynsford, Nick *(Lab)*
Robinson, Peter *(DUP)*
Rooney, Terence *(Lab)*
Ross, William *(UUP)*
St Aubyn, Nicholas *(Con)*
Salter, Martin *(Lab)*
Sarwar, Mohammed *(Lab)*
Shaw, Jonathan *(Lab)*

Smith, Chris *(Lab)*
Soley, Clive *(Lab)*
Southworth, Helen *(Lab)*
Swinney, John *(SNP)*
Taylor, Ann *(Lab)*
Taylor, Dari *(Lab)*
Taylor, David *(Lab/Co-op)*
Turner, Dennis *(Lab/Co-op)*
Turner, Dr Des *(Lab)*
Turner, Neil *(Lab)*
Twigg, Derek *(Lab)*
Walker, Cecil *(UUP)*
Winterton, Rosie *(Lab)*
Wood, Mike *(Lab)*
Young, Sir George *(Con)*

Housing Law
Anderson, Donald *(Lab)*

Housing (Sheltered)
Jack, Michael *(Con)*

Human Rights
Atkinson, David *(Con)*
Browne, Desmond *(Lab)*
Cormack, Sir Patrick *(Con)*
Cryer, Ann *(Lab)*
Dowd, Jim *(Lab)*
Etherington, William *(Lab)*
Fisher, Mark *(Lab)*
Foulkes, George *(Lab/Co-op)*
Godman, Dr Norman *(Lab)*
Hughes, Simon *(Lib Dem)*
Jones, Jenny *(Lab)*
Jowell, Tessa *(Lab)*
Kirkwood, Archy *(Lib Dem)*
Lloyd, Tony *(Lab)*
Lock, David *(Lab)*
Mactaggart, Fiona *(Lab)*
Martin, Michael *(Lab)*
Meale, Alan *(Lab)*
Prentice, Bridget *(Lab)*
Ruane, Chris *(Lab)*
Salter, Martin *(Lab)*
Smyth, Rev Martin *(UUP)*
Stevenson, George *(Lab)*
Thomas, Gareth *(Lab)*

Hunting With Dogs
Foster, Michael John *(Lab)*

Immigration
Coleman, Iain *(Lab)*
Cryer, Ann *(Lab)*
George, Andrew *(Lib Dem)*
Godsiff, Roger *(Lab)*

Immigration *continued*
Lloyd, Tony *(Lab)*
Prosser, Gwyn *(Lab)*
Short, Clare *(Lab)*
Wardle, Charles *(Con)*

Incomes Redistribution
Field, Frank *(Lab)*

Incomes Policies
Godman, Dr Norman *(Lab)*

Individual Freedom
Gorman, Teresa *(Con)*

Industrial Relations
Barnes, Harry *(Lab)*
Campbell-Savours, Dale
    (Lab)
Cormack, Sir Patrick *(Con)*
Crausby, David *(Lab)*
Cunningham, James *(Lab)*
Godsiff, Roger *(Lab)*
Heald, Oliver *(Con)*
Healey, John *(Lab)*
Martin, Michael *(Lab)*
Meacher, Michael *(Lab)*
Pendry, Tom *(Lab)*
Rooney, Terence *(Lab)*
Smith, John *(Lab)*

Industry
Ainsworth, Bob *(Lab)*
Ashdown, Sir Paddy
    (Lib Dem)
Atkinson, Peter *(Con)*
Beckett, Margaret *(Lab)*
Benn, Tony *(Lab)*
Bruce, Malcolm *(Lib Dem)*
Connarty, Michael *(Lab)*
Cryer, John *(Lab)*
Cunliffe, Lawrence *(Lab)*
Cunningham, Dr Jack *(Lab)*
Davis, David *(Con)*
Dowd, Jim *(Lab)*
Follett, Barbara *(Lab)*
Gillan, Cheryl *(Con)*
Gunnell, John *(Lab)*
Hayes, John *(Con)*
Heathcoat-Amory, David
    (Con)
Henderson, Doug *(Lab)*
Hutton, John *(Lab)*
Jones, Ieuan Wyn *(PC)*
Keen, Alan *(Lab/Co-op)*
Ladyman, Dr Stephen *(Lab)*

Leslie, Christopher *(Lab)*
Lloyd, Tony *(Lab)*
McAllion, John *(Lab)*
MacGregor, John *(Con)*
Mackay, Andrew *(Con)*
Michie, Bill *(Lab)*
Milburn, Alan *(Lab)*
Miller, Andrew *(Lab)*
Moonie, Lewis *(Lab/Co-op)*
Morgan, Rhodri *(Lab)*
Ottaway, Richard *(Con)*
Paterson, Owen *(Con)*
Pearson, Ian *(Lab)*
Quin, Joyce *(Lab)*
Robinson, Geoffrey *(Lab)*
Ross, Ernie *(Lab)*
Sheerman, Barry *(Lab/Co-op)*
Smith, Jacqui *(Lab)*
Taylor, Dari *(Lab)*
Trickett, Jon *(Lab)*
Walker, Cecil *(UUP)*
Wardle, Charles *(Con)*
Wigley, Dafydd *(PC)*
Wilkinson, John *(Con)*
Williams, Alan John *(Lab)*

Industry (Electronics)
Spellar, John *(Lab)*

Information Technology
Allan, Richard *(Lib Dem)*
Bruce, Ian *(Con)*
Hewitt, Patricia *(Lab)*
Jones, Nigel *(Lib Dem)*
Miller, Andrew *(Lab)*
Stewart, Ian *(Lab)*
White, Brian *(Lab)*

Infrastructure
O'Brien, Stephen *(Con)*

Inland Waterways
Skinner, Dennis *(Lab)*

Inner Cities
Beard, Nigel *(Lab)*
Beresford, Sir Paul *(Con)*
Boateng, Paul *(Lab)*
Chapman, Sydney *(Con)*
Hodge, Margaret *(Lab)*

Insurance
Hawkins, Nick *(Con)*

Intellectual Property
Howells, Dr Kim *(Lab)*

International Affairs
Benn, Tony *(Lab)*
Browne, Desmond *(Lab)*
Corbyn, Jeremy *(Lab)*
Evans, Nigel *(Con)*
Gapes, Mike *(Lab/Co-op)*
George, Bruce *(Lab)*
Gillan, Cheryl *(Con)*
Marsden, Gordon *(Lab)*
Murphy, Jim *(Lab)*
Sarwar, Mohammed *(Lab)*
Savidge, Malcolm *(Lab)*
Stewart, Ian *(Lab)*
Wilkinson, John *(Con)*

International Development
Battle, John *(Lab)*
Bayley, Hugh *(Lab)*
Chaytor, David *(Lib Dem)*
Davey, Valerie *(Lab)*
Follett, Barbara *(Lab)*
Foulkes, George *(Lab/Co-op)*
Hamilton, Fabian *(Lab)*
Jones, Nigel *(Lib Dem)*
Khabra, Piara *(Lab)*
Lammy, David *(Lab)*
Luff, Peter *(Con)*
Naysmith, Dr Doug
    (Lab/Co-op)
Reed, Andrew *(Lab/Co-op)*
Sarwar, Mohammed *(Lab)*
Savidge, Malcolm *(Lab)*
Smith, Angela *(Lab/Co-op)*
Stewart, David *(Lab)*
Tonge, Dr Jennifer *(Lib Dem)*
Worthington, Tony *(Lab)*

International Economics
MacShane, Dr Denis *(Lab)*

International Terrorism
Robinson, Peter *(DUP)*

**Investigative Political and
    Social Work**
Campbell-Savours, Dale *(Lab)*

Investment
Bermingham, Gerry *(Lab)*
Gunnell, John *(Lab)*
Hughes, Beverley *(Lab)*
Ryan, Joan *(Lab)*
Stewart, Ian *(Lab)*

Irish Affairs
Bell, Stuart *(Lab)*

Corbyn, Jeremy *(Lab)*
Cran, James *(Con)*
McDonnell, John *(Lab)*
Mackinlay, Andrew *(Lab)*
Taylor, John D *(UUP)*
Temple-Morris, Peter
    (Lab)
Walker, Cecil *(UUP)*

Isle of Man
Mackinlay, Andrew *(Lab)*

Isle of Wight
Brand, Dr Peter *(Lib Dem)*

Israel
Day, Stephen *(Con)*

Justice
Mallon, Seamus *(SDLP)*
Mullin, Chris *(Lab)*

Justice (Juvenile)
Michael, Alun *(Lab/Co-op)*

Keep Sunday Special
Powell, Sir Raymond *(Lab)*

Kidney Transplantation
Dalyell, Tam *(Lab)*

Labour Party
Ashton, Joe *(Lab)*
Benn, Tony *(Lab)*

**Labour Party Policy
    Revision**
Radice, Giles *(Lab)*

Land
Cunningham, Roseanna
    (SNP)

**Landmine Eradication
    Measures**
Cook, Frank *(Lab)*

Law and Order
Arbuthnot, James *(Con)*
Brazier, Julian *(Con)*
Davis, David *(Con)*
Greenway, John *(Con)*
Grieve, Dominic *(Con)*
Hawkins, Nick *(Con)*
Heald, Oliver *(Con)*
King, Andy *(Lab)*

Kirkbride, Julie *(Con)*
McCrea, William *(DUP)*
Robertson, Laurence *(Con)*
Streeter, Gary *(Con)*

Law Reform
Corston, Jean *(Lab)*
Godman, Dr Norman *(Lab)*
Mitchell, Austin *(Lab)*
Roche, Barbara *(Lab)*

Learning Disabilities
Browning, Angela *(Con)*

Leasehold Reform
Lepper, David *(Lab/Co-op)*

Legal Affairs
Baldry, Tony *(Con)*
Browne, Desmond *(Lab)*
Campbell, Menzies
    (Lib Dem)
Clark, Dr Lynda *(Lab)*
Cranston, Ross *(Lab)*
Lock, David *(Lab)*
McIntosh, Anne *(Con)*
Taylor, John M *(Con)*
Temple-Morris, Peter *(Lab)*
Thomas, Gareth *(Lab)*

Legal Services
Vaz, Keith *(Lab)*

Leisure
Clarke, Tony *(Lab)*
Fearn, Ronnie *(Lib Dem)*
Fraser, Christopher *(Con)*
Gale, Roger *(Con)*
Perham, Linda *(Lab)*
Rapson, Syd *(Lab)*

**Liberation Islington Local
    Agenda 21**
Corbyn, Jeremy *(Lab)*

Licensed Trade
Gale, Roger *(Con)*
Grogan, John *(Lab)*
Powell, Sir Raymond *(Lab)*

Lifelong Learning
Reed, Andrew
    (Lab/Co-op)

Local Community
Blackman, Elizabeth *(Lab)*

Local Democracy
Stunell, Andrew *(Lib Dem)*

**Local Economic
    Development**
Davidson, Ian *(Lab/Co-op)*

Local Government
Ballard, Jackie *(Lib Dem)*
Banks, Tony *(Lab)*
Barnes, Harry *(Lab)*
Benton, Joe *(Lab)*
Berry, Dr Roger *(Lab)*
Betts, Clive *(Lab)*
Blizzard, Bob *(Lab)*
Blunkett, David *(Lab)*
Bradley, Keith *(Lab)*
Butler, Christine *(Lab)*
Byers, Stephen *(Lab)*
Caplin, Ivor *(Lab)*
Cawsey, Ian *(Lab)*
Clarke, Tom *(Lab)*
Clarke, Tony *(Lab)*
Clelland, David *(Lab)*
Connarty, Michael *(Lab)*
Curry, David *(Con)*
Davey, Valerie *(Lab)*
Davidson, Ian *(Lab/Co-op)*
Dobbin, Jim *(Lab/Co-op)*
Donohoe, Brian *(Lab)*
Efford, Clive *(Lab)*
Ellman, Louise *(Lab/Co-op)*
Ennis, Jeffrey *(Lab)*
Evans, Nigel *(Con)*
Fearn, Ronnie *(Lib Dem)*
Foster, Don *(Lib Dem)*
Fraser, Christopher *(Con)*
Fyfe, Maria *(Lab)*
Gorrie, Donald *(Lib Dem)*
Gray, James *(Con)*
Grogan, John *(Lab)*
Hall, Mike *(Lab)*
Hanson, David *(Lab)*
Hayes, John *(Con)*
Heath, David *(Lib Dem)*
Heppell, John *(Lab)*
Hodge, Margaret *(Lab)*
Hughes, Beverley *(Lab)*
Ingram, Adam *(Lab)*
Keeble, Sally *(Lab)*
Kennedy, Jane *(Lab)*
Kumar, Dr Ashok *(Lab)*
Lansley, Andrew *(Con)*
Laxton, Bob *(Lab)*
Leslie, Christopher *(Lab)*
Levitt, Tom *(Lab)*

Local Government *continued*
Lewis, Terry *(Lab)*
McCartney, Ian *(Lab)*
McDonnell, John *(Lab)*
McLeish, Henry *(Lab)*
McNulty, Tony *(Lab)*
McWalter, Tony *(Lab/Co-op)*
Mahon, Alice *(Lab)*
Major, John *(Con)*
Mallaber, Judy *(Lab)*
Marshall, James *(Lab)*
Michael, Alun *(Lab/Co-op)*
Michie, Bill *(Lab)*
Morley, Elliot *(Lab)*
Morris, Estelle *(Lab)*
Murphy, Paul *(Lab)*
Naysmith, Dr Doug
   (Lab/Co-op)
O'Brien, William *(Lab)*
O'Hara, Edward *(Lab)*
Olner, Bill *(Lab)*
Pickles, Eric *(Con)*
Pike, Peter *(Lab)*
Plaskitt, James *(Lab)*
Rapson, Syd *(Lab)*
Ross, William *(UUP)*
Russell, Bob *(Lib Dem)*
Ryan, Joan *(Lab)*
Salter, Martin *(Lab)*
Sanders, Adrian *(Lib Dem)*
Smith, Chris *(Lab)*
Steinberg, Gerry *(Lab)*
Stewart, David *(Lab)*
Straw, Jack *(Lab)*
Sutcliffe, Gerry *(Lab)*
Syms, Robert *(Con)*
Tipping, Paddy *(Lab)*
Todd, Mark *(Lab)*
Touhig, Don *(Lab/Co-op)*
Turner, Neil *(Lab)*
Twigg, Stephen *(Lab)*
Vaz, Keith *(Lab)*
Walker, Cecil *(UUP)*
Welsh, Andrew *(SNP)*
Whitehead, Dr Alan *(Lab)*
Willis, Phil *(Lib Dem)*
Wilshire, David *(Con)*
Winterton, Nicholas *(Con)*
Wright, Anthony David *(Lab)*

**Local Government and
   Devolution**
Starkey, Dr Phyllis *(Lab)*

Local Government Finance
Borrow, David *(Lab)*
Healey, John *(Lab)*

London
Hodge, Margaret *(Lab)*
Horam, John *(Con)*
McNulty, Tony *(Lab)*

Low Pay
Davies, Ron *(Lab)*
Edwards, Huw *(Lab)*
Merron, Gillian *(Lab)*
Prentice, Gordon *(Lab)*
Short, Clare *(Lab)*
Taylor, David *(Lab/Co-op)*

Manufacturing
Chidgey, David *(Lib Dem)*
Clark, Dr Michael *(Con)*
Corbett, Robin *(Lab)*
MacShane, Dr Denis *(Lab)*
Prentice, Gordon *(Lab)*
Stuart, Gisela *(Lab)*

Marketing
Campbell-Savours, Dale *(Lab)*
Greenway, John *(Con)*
Powell, Sir Raymond *(Lab)*
Ross, William *(UUP)*

Media
Anderson, Janet *(Lab)*
Ashton, Joe *(Lab)*
Banks, Tony *(Lab)*
Bayley, Hugh *(Lab)*
Cash, William *(Con)*
Collins, Tim *(Con)*
Fraser, Christopher *(Con)*
Gale, Roger *(Con)*
Green, Damian *(Con)*
Grocott, Bruce *(Lab)*
Howarth, Gerald *(Con)*
Johnson Smith, Sir Geoffrey
   (Con)
Lepper, David *(Lab/Co-op)*
Lewis, Dr Julian *(Con)*
Liddell, Helen *(Lab)*
Linton, Martin *(Lab)*
Meale, Alan *(Lab)*
Mitchell, Austin *(Lab)*
Rammell, Bill *(Lab)*
Ward, Claire *(Lab)*
Whittingdale, John *(Con)*
Winterton, Nicholas *(Con)*
Woolas, Philip *(Lab)*
Wyatt, Derek *(Lab)*

Media Ownership
Mullin, Chris *(Lab)*

Medical Ethics
Harris, Evan *(Lib Dem)*

**Medicinal and Illegal
   Drugs**
Flynn, Paul *(Lab)*

Mental Health
Atkinson, David *(Con)*
Austin, John *(Lab)*
Browning, Angela *(Con)*
Doran, Frank *(Lab)*
Lewis, Dr Julian *(Con)*

Micro-Technology
Williams, Alan John *(Lab)*

Middle East
Burden, Richard *(Lab)*
Starkey, Dr Phyllis *(Lab)*

Mining
Illsley, Eric *(Lab)*

Minority Groups
George, Andrew *(Lib Dem)*

Minority Languages
Wigley, Dafydd *(PC)*

Modernisation of Parliament
Bradshaw, Ben *(Lab)*
Fitzsimons, Lorna *(Lab)*
Flint, Caroline *(Lab)*

Modernising Government
White, Brian *(Lab)*

Motor Industry
Burden, Richard *(Lab)*
Corbett, Robin *(Lab)*
Kemp, Fraser *(Lab)*
Spellar, John *(Lab)*
Wareing, Robert *(Lab)*

Music
Meale, Alan *(Lab)*

National Grid for Learning
Wyatt, Derek *(Lab)*

National Lottery
Ashton, Joe *(Lab)*

NATO
Cormack, Sir Patrick *(Con)*

New Technology
Ashdown, Sir Paddy
(Lib Dem)
Robinson, Geoffrey (Lab)

NHS Tranquillisers
Addiction
Wareing, Robert (Lab)

Non-Proliferation and
Disarmament
Savidge, Malcolm (Lab)

Northern Ireland
Barnes, Harry (Lab)
Browne, Desmond (Lab)
Collins, Tim (Con)
Donaldson, Jeffrey (UUP)
Hume, John (SDLP)
Jackson, Helen (Lab)
Livingstone, Ken
(Independent)
McCartney, Robert (UKU)
McGrady, Edward (SDLP)
McNamara, Kevin (Lab)
Major, John (Con)
Mates, Michael (Con)
Mawhinney, Sir Brian
(Con)
O'Brien, Stephen (Con)
Robathan, Andrew (Con)
Salter, Martin (Lab)
Savidge, Malcolm (Lab)
Short, Clare (Lab)
Soley, Clive (Lab)
Willis, Phil (Lib Dem)
Wilshire, David (Con)

Nuclear Industry
Jack, Michael (Con)

Oil Industry
Bruce, Malcolm (Lib Dem)

Open Spaces
Clark, David (Lab)

Oppressed Minority Races
Baker, Norman (Lib Dem)

Overseas Aid
Baldry, Tony (Con)
Boateng, Paul (Lab)
Fisher, Mark (Lab)
Follett, Barbara (Lab)
Griffiths, Win (Lab)

Jackson, Glenda (Lab)
Kingham, Tess (Lab)
Lloyd, Tony (Lab)
Rowlands, Edward (Lab)
Wells, Bowen (Con)

Paper Industries
Winterton, Nicholas (Con)

Parental Leave
Kelly, Ruth (Lab)

Parliamentary and
Constitutional Affairs
Beith, Alan (Lib Dem)
Flynn, Paul (Lab)

Parliamentary Buildings/
Accommodation/
Preservation
Powell, Sir Raymond (Lab)

Parliamentary History
Cormack, Sir Patrick (Con)

Parliamentary Procedure
Emery, Peter (Con)

Parties and Elections and
Campaigning
Hayes, John (Con)

Peace and Disarmament
Cook, Frank (Lab)

Penal Affairs
Bermingham, Gerry (Lab)
Lyell, Sir Nicholas (Con)
Malins, Humfrey (Con)
Shephard, Gillian (Con)
Soley, Clive (Lab)
Widdecombe, Ann (Con)

Pension Funds
Colman, Tony (Lab)

Pensioners' Rights
Cook, Frank (Lab)
Gilroy, Linda (Lab/Co-op)
Marshall, David (Lab)
Sarwar, Mohammed (Lab)

Pensions
Bradley, Keith (Lab)
Caplin, Ivor (Lab)
Clark, Dr Lynda (Lab)

Cran, James (Con)
Crausby, David (Lab)
Davies, Quentin (Con)
Flynn, Paul (Lab)
Heald, Oliver (Con)
Hesford, Stephen (Lab)
Miller, Andrew (Lab)
Pike, Peter (Lab)
Stuart, Gisela (Lab)

Performing Arts
Luff, Peter (Con)

Personal Finance
Greenway, John (Con)

Pharmaceutical and
Chemical Industries
Winterton, Ann (Con)
Winterton, Nicholas (Con)

Planning
Burgon, Colin (Lab)
Caton, Martin (Lab)
Cryer, Ann (Lab)
Darvill, Keith (Lab)
Drew, David (Lab/Co-op)
Gerrard, Neil (Lab)
Hammond, Philip (Con)
St Aubyn, Nicholas (Con)

Police
Cawsey, Ian (Lab)
Corbett, Robin (Lab)
Lansley, Andrew (Con)
McCabe, Stephen (Lab)
Mackinlay, Andrew (Lab)
O'Brien, Mike (Lab)
Straw, Jack (Lab)
Tipping, Paddy (Lab)
Tredinnick, David (Con)
Wardle, Charles (Con)

Political Biography
Thompson, William (UUP)

Political Finance
Linton, Martin (Lab)

Political Philosophy
Hayes, John (Con)
McWalter, Tony (Lab/Co-op)
Michael, Alun (Lab/Co-op)

Political Process
Wilshire, David (Con)

Ports Industry
Mackinlay, Andrew *(Lab)*

Post Office
Hain, Peter *(Lab)*
Johnson, Alan *(Lab)*

Poverty
Battle, John *(Lab)*
Bradley, Keith *(Lab)*
Burden, Richard *(Lab)*
Davies, Ron *(Lab)*
Dawson, Hilton *(Lab)*
Drew, David
    (Lab/Co-op)
Field, Frank *(Lab)*
Fitzpatrick, Jim *(Lab)*
Foster, Michael Jabez
    (Lab)
Goggins, Paul *(Lab)*
Hall, Mike *(Lab)*
Hume, John *(SDLP)*
Meale, Alan *(Lab)*
Mitchell, Austin *(Lab)*
Osborne, Sandra *(Lab)*
Pond, Chris *(Lab)*
Prentice, Gordon *(Lab)*
Rooney, Terence *(Lab)*
Ruane, Chris *(Lab)*
Twigg, Derek *(Lab)*
Wood, Mike *(Lab)*

Press
Corbett, Robin *(Lab)*
Fisher, Mark *(Lab)*

Private Finance Initiative
Colman, Tony *(Lab)*
Flight, Howard *(Con)*

**Private/Public Sector
    Partnership**
McDonagh, Siobhain *(Lab)*
Smith, Geraldine *(Lab)*

Privatisation
Howarth, Gerald *(Con)*

Pro-Life Movement
Amess, David *(Con)*

Provision for under 5s
Harman, Harriet *(Lab)*

Public Order
Tredinnick, David *(Con)*

Public Sector
Fallon, Michael *(Con)*

Public Services
Ellman, Louise *(Lab/Co-op)*
Kennedy, Jane *(Lab)*

Publishing
Rowlands, Edward *(Lab)*

Purchasing and Supply
Emery, Peter *(Con)*

Quarrying
Levitt, Tom *(Lab)*

Quotas for Women
Anderson, Janet *(Lab)*

Race Relations
Cook, Frank *(Lab)*
Corbyn, Jeremy *(Lab)*
Fitzpatrick, Jim *(Lab)*
Follett, Barbara *(Lab)*
George, Andrew *(Lib Dem)*
Gerrard, Neil *(Lab)*
Hamilton, Fabian *(Lab)*
Khabra, Piara *(Lab)*
King, Oona *(Lab)*
Lilley, Peter *(Con)*
Lloyd, Tony *(Lab)*
Major, John *(Con)*
Short, Clare *(Lab)*
Stunell, Andrew
    (Lib Dem)
Vaz, Keith *(Lab)*

Railways
Cryer, Ann *(Lab)*
Luff, Peter *(Con)*
Williams, Betty *(Lab)*

Rainforest Issues
Dalyell, Tam *(Lab)*

Recreation
Godsiff, Roger *(Lab)*
Pendry, Tom *(Lab)*
Winterton, Nicholas *(Con)*

**Redistribution of Income
    and Wealth**
Meacher, Michael *(Lab)*

Reform of Government
Hain, Peter *(Lab)*

Regeneration
Ennis, Jeffrey *(Lab)*
Fitzpatrick, Jim *(Lab)*
Love, Andrew *(Lab/Co-op)*
McNulty, Tony *(Lab)*
Ryan, Joan *(Lab)*

Regional Assemblies
Quinn, Lawrie *(Lab)*

Regional Economic Policy
Ellman, Louise
    (Lab/Co-op)
Pearson, Ian *(Lab)*
Wareing, Robert *(Lab)*

Regional Policy
Armstrong, Hilary *(Lab)*
Borrow, David *(Lab)*
Chapman, Ben *(Lab)*
Cran, James *(Con)*
Cunningham, Dr Jack *(Lab)*
Davies, Ron *(Lab)*
Foster, Derek *(Lab)*
Gunnell, John *(Lab)*
Hughes, Beverley *(Lab)*
Jones, Barry *(Lab)*
Milburn, Alan *(Lab)*
Morgan, Rhodri *(Lab)*
O'Hara, Edward *(Lab)*
Prentice, Gordon *(Lab)*
Quin, Joyce *(Lab)*
Robinson, Geoffrey *(Lab)*
Stewart, Ian *(Lab)*
Taylor, John D *(UUP)*
Watts, David *(Lab)*
Williams, Alan John *(Lab)*
Winterton, Rosie *(Lab)*

Religious Affairs
Paisley, Rev Ian *(DUP)*

Renewable Energy
Thomas, Gareth Richard
    (Lab)

Research
Ladyman, Dr Stephen *(Lab)*

**Restructuring of Defence
    Industries**
Jones, Nigel *(Lib Dem)*

Retail Industry
Nicholls, Patrick *(Con)*
Smith, Andrew *(Lab)*

Rights of Victims of Accidents and Crime
Dismore, Andrew *(Lab)*

River Thames
Mackinlay, Andrew *(Lab)*

Rural Affairs
Bradley, Peter *(Lab)*
Drew, David *(Lab/Co-op)*
Faber, David *(Con)*
Fraser, Christopher *(Con)*
Green, Damian *(Con)*
Heath, David *(Lib Dem)*
Home Robertson, John
    (Lab)
Luff, Peter *(Con)*
McGuire, Anne *(Lab)*
Maclennan, Robert
    (Lib Dem)
Marsden, Paul *(Lab)*
Morgan, Alasdair *(SNP)*
Moss, Malcolm *(Con)*
O'Brien, Stephen *(Con)*
Organ, Diana *(Lab)*
Paice, James *(Con)*
Pickthall, Colin *(Lab)*
Stewart, David *(Lab)*
Taylor, David *(Lab/Co-op)*
Tyler, Paul *(Lib Dem)*
Wallace, James *(Lib Dem)*
Yeo, Tim *(Con)*

Science
Battle, John *(Lab)*
Campbell, Anne *(Lab)*
Cousins, Jim *(Lab)*
Dalyell, Tam *(Lab)*
Gibson, Dr Ian *(Lab)*
Harris, Evan *(Lib Dem)*
Iddon, Dr Brian *(Lab)*
Jackson, Robert *(Con)*
Jones, Dr Lynne *(Lab)*
Jones, Martyn *(Lab)*
Naysmith, Dr Doug
    (Lab/Co-op)
Starkey, Dr Phyllis *(Lab)*

Science and Technology
Clark, Dr Michael *(Con)*
Ladyman, Dr Stephen
    (Lab)
McWalter, Tony
    (Lab/Co-op)
Miller, Andrew *(Lab)*
Taylor, Ian *(Con)*

Science Policy and Animal Welfare
Turner, Dr Des *(Lab)*

Scientific Research and Development
Page, Richard *(Con)*

Scotland
Begg, Anne *(Lab)*
Brown, Gordon *(Lab)*
Clarke, Eric *(Lab)*
Galloway, George *(Lab)*
Gray, James *(Con)*
Griffiths, Nigel *(Lab)*
Home Robertson, John *(Lab)*
Kennedy, Charles
    (Lib Dem)
Liddell, Helen *(Lab)*
Marshall, David *(Lab)*
Maxton, John *(Lab)*
Savidge, Malcolm *(Lab)*

Scottish Economy
Salmond, Alex *(SNP)*

Scottish Home Rule and Federalism
Bruce, Malcolm *(Lib Dem)*
Michie, Ray *(Lib Dem)*
Wallace, James *(Lib Dem)*

Scottish Law
Wallace, James *(Lib Dem)*

Security
Lewis, Dr Julian *(Con)*

Security (Private)
George, Bruce *(Lab)*

Shipbuilding
Robinson, Peter *(DUP)*
Sarwar, Mohammed *(Lab)*
Waterson, Nigel *(Con)*

Shipping
Prosser, Gwyn *(Lab)*
Wallace, James *(Lib Dem)*
Waterson, Nigel *(Con)*

Shooters' Rights
Cook, Frank *(Lab)*

Small Businesses
Atkinson, David *(Con)*

Bercow, John *(Con)*
Browning, Angela *(Con)*
Cash, William *(Con)*
Duncan Smith, Iain *(Con)*
Evans, Nigel *(Con)*
Fraser, Christopher *(Con)*
Hamilton, Fabian *(Lab)*
Hawkins, Nick *(Con)*
Lansley, Andrew *(Con)*
Moss, Malcolm *(Con)*
Page, Richard *(Con)*
Paice, James *(Con)*
Rowe, Andrew *(Con)*
St Aubyn, Nicholas *(Con)*
Southworth, Helen *(Lab)*
Townend, John *(Con)*

Small Nations
George, Andrew *(Lib Dem)*

Social Exclusion/Inclusion
George, Andrew *(Lib Dem)*
Tynan, Bill *(Lab)*

Social Policy
Cann, Jamie *(Lab)*
Hughes, Simon *(Lib Dem)*
Kelly, Ruth *(Lab)*
Kennedy, Charles *(Lib Dem)*
Major, John *(Con)*
Marsden, Gordon *(Lab)*
Meacher, Michael *(Lab)*
Pond, Chris *(Lab)*
Raynsford, Nick *(Lab)*
Roy, Frank *(Lab)*
Streeter, Gary *(Con)*
Webb, Prof Steve *(Lib Dem)*
Wicks, Malcolm *(Lab)*

Social Security
Austin, John *(Lab)*
Brand, Dr Peter *(Lib Dem)*
Brown, Gordon *(Lab)*
Coffey, Ann *(Lab)*
Cryer, John *(Lab)*
Dean, Janet *(Lab)*
Drown, Julia *(Lab)*
Duncan, Alan *(Con)*
Ewing, Margaret *(SNP)*
Flynn, Paul *(Lab)*
Foulkes, George
    (Lab/Co-op)
George, Bruce *(Lab)*
Gibb, Nick *(Con)*
Graham, Tommy
    (Independent)

Social Security *continued*
Griffiths, Nigel *(Lab)*
Gunnell, John *(Lab)*
Hammond, Philip *(Con)*
Harman, Harriet *(Lab)*
Hesford, Stephen *(Lab)*
Hewitt, Patricia *(Lab)*
Hinchliffe, David *(Lab)*
Howarth, Alan *(Lab)*
Hughes, Kevin *(Lab)*
Humble, Joan *(Lab)*
Illsley, Eric *(Lab)*
Jones, Dr Lynne *(Lab)*
Kennedy, Jane *(Lab)*
King, Andy *(Lab)*
Kirkbride, Julie *(Con)*
Kirkwood, Archy *(Lib Dem)*
McAvoy, Thomas
    (Lab/Co-op)
McCafferty, Christine *(Lab)*
McCartney, Ian *(Lab)*
Mallon, Seamus *(SDLP)*
Martlew, Eric *(Lab)*
Meale, Alan *(Lab)*
Michie, Bill *(Lab)*
Morgan, Julie *(Lab)*
Mountford, Kali *(Lab)*
Pendry, Tom *(Lab)*
Pickles, Eric *(Con)*
Pollard, Kerry *(Lab)*
Primarolo, Dawn *(Lab)*
Roe, Marion *(Con)*
Ross, Ernie *(Lab)*
Smith, Chris *(Lab)*
Smyth, Rev Martin *(UUP)*
Stewart, David *(Lab)*
Thomas, Gareth *(Lab)*
Thomas, Gareth Richard
    (Lab)
Tonge, Dr Jennifer *(Lib Dem)*
Truswell, Paul *(Lab)*
Turner, Dennis *(Lab/Co-op)*
Turner, Dr Des *(Lab)*
Tynan, Bill *(Lab)*
Willetts, David *(Con)*
Williams, Betty *(Lab)*
Wray, James *(Lab)*

Socialism
Benn, Tony *(Lab)*
Corbyn, Jeremy *(Lab)*
Foster, Derek *(Lab)*

Solvent Abuse
Hanson, David *(Lab)*
Marshall, David *(Lab)*

South Africa
McGuinness, Martin
    (Sinn Fein)

Space
Atkinson, David *(Con)*
Emery, Peter *(Con)*
Gillan, Cheryl *(Con)*

Sport
Anderson, Janet *(Lab)*
Campbell, Menzies
    (Lib Dem)
Caplin, Ivor *(Lab)*
Clarke, Tony *(Lab)*
Coleman, Iain *(Lab)*
Eagle, Angela *(Lab)*
Godsiff, Roger *(Lab)*
Gorrie, Donald *(Lib Dem)*
Grogan, John *(Lab)*
Hancock, Mike *(Lib Dem)*
Hawkins, Nick *(Con)*
Hoey, Kate *(Lab)*
Hoyle, Lindsay *(Lab)*
Jones, Nigel *(Lib Dem)*
Keen, Alan *(Lab/Co-op)*
Malins, Humfrey *(Con)*
Maxton, John *(Lab)*
Meale, Alan *(Lab)*
Murphy, Jim *(Lab)*
Pendry, Tom *(Lab)*
Rammell, Bill *(Lab)*
Reed, Andrew
    (Lab/Co-op)
Russell, Bob *(Lib Dem)*
Trickett, Jon *(Lab)*
Ward, Claire *(Lab)*
Winterton, Nicholas
    (Con)
Wyatt, Derek *(Lab)*

Standards in Public Life
Bell, Martin *(Independent)*

Steel Industry
Caborn, Richard *(Lab)*
Powell, Sir Raymond *(Lab)*

Students
Connarty, Michael *(Lab)*

Sunday Drinking
Powell, Sir Raymond *(Lab)*

Sunday Trading
Powell, Sir Raymond *(Lab)*

Swiss Banking
Wyatt, Derek *(Lab)*

Tax
Ainsworth, Bob *(Lab)*
Arbuthnot, James *(Con)*
Boswell, Tim *(Con)*
Cann, Jamie *(Lab)*
Clifton-Brown, Geoffrey
    (Con)
Davey, Edward *(Lib Dem)*
Flight, Howard *(Con)*
Foster, Michael Jabez *(Lab)*
Gibb, Nick *(Con)*
Hamilton, Sir Archie *(Con)*
Horam, John *(Con)*
Kirkbride, Julie *(Con)*
McIsaac, Shona *(Lab)*
Palmer, Dr Nicholas *(Lab)*
Straw, Jack *(Lab)*
Townend, John *(Con)*

Tax Havens
Foulkes, George *(Lab/Co-op)*

Technology
Battle, John *(Lab)*
Beard, Nigel *(Lab)*
Benn, Tony *(Lab)*
Gibson, Dr Ian *(Lab)*
Iddon, Dr Brian *(Lab)*
Kemp, Fraser *(Lab)*
McWilliam, John *(Lab)*
Moonie, Lewis
    (Lab/Co-op)

Telecommunications
Evans, Nigel *(Con)*
Hain, Peter *(Lab)*
Timms, Stephen *(Lab)*

Temperance Movement
Taylor, Sir Teddy *(Con)*

**Terrorism and Internal
    Security**
Maginnis, Ken *(UUP)*

Textile Industries
Anderson, Janet *(Lab)*
Mountford, Kali *(Lab)*
Winterton, Ann *(Con)*
Winterton, Nicholas *(Con)*

Think British Campaign
Winterton, Ann *(Con)*

Third World
Berry, Dr Roger *(Lab)*
Body, Sir Richard *(Con)*
Davidson, Ian *(Lab/Co-op)*
George, Andrew *(Lib Dem)*
Hume, John *(SDLP)*
Marshall, David *(Lab)*
Salmond, Alex *(SNP)*
Skinner, Dennis *(Lab)*
Streeter, Gary *(Con)*
Stunell, Andrew *(Lib Dem)*
Webb, Prof Steve
   (Lib Dem)

Third World Debt
White, Brian *(Lab)*

Timber
Walker, Cecil *(UUP)*

Tourism
Ashton, Joe *(Lab)*
Bruce, Ian *(Con)*
Butterfill, John *(Con)*
Collins, Tim *(Con)*
Cotter, Brian *(Lib Dem)*
Fearn, Ronnie *(Lib Dem)*
Fraser, Christopher *(Con)*
Gale, Roger *(Con)*
Hawkins, Nick *(Con)*
Llwyd, Elfyn *(PC)*
Quinn, Lawrie *(Lab)*
Sanders, Adrian *(Lib Dem)*
Smith, Geraldine *(Lab)*
Tyler, Paul *(Lib Dem)*
Waterson, Nigel *(Con)*

Town Centres
Lepper, David *(Lab/Co-op)*

Trade and Industry
Bruce, Ian *(Con)*
Bruce, Malcolm *(Lib Dem)*
Butterfill, John *(Con)*
Byers, Stephen *(Lab)*
Cable, Dr Vincent
   (Lib Dem)
Cash, William *(Con)*
Chapman, Ben *(Lab)*
Coffey, Ann *(Lab)*
Cran, James *(Con)*
Curtis-Thomas, Claire *(Lab)*
Davies, Geraint *(Lab)*
Davies, Quentin *(Con)*
Donaldson, Jeffrey *(UUP)*
Duncan, Alan *(Con)*

Emery, Peter *(Con)*
Fabricant, Michael *(Con)*
Follett, Barbara *(Lab)*
Foster, Michael John *(Lab)*
Gardiner, Barry *(Lab)*
Gilroy, Linda *(Lab/Co-op)*
Gorman, Teresa *(Con)*
Hamilton, Sir Archie *(Con)*
Hammond, Philip *(Con)*
Hawkins, Nick *(Con)*
Hoyle, Lindsay *(Lab)*
Jenkin, Bernard *(Con)*
Jenkins, Brian *(Lab)*
Jones, Nigel *(Lib Dem)*
Kumar, Dr Ashok *(Lab)*
Lait, Jacqui *(Con)*
Lansley, Andrew *(Con)*
Liddell, Helen *(Lab)*
Luff, Peter *(Con)*
McLeish, Henry *(Lab)*
Martin, Michael *(Lab)*
Mawhinney, Sir Brian *(Con)*
O'Brien, Stephen *(Con)*
O'Neill, Martin *(Lab)*
Page, Richard *(Con)*
Paterson, Owen *(Con)*
Pike, Peter *(Lab)*
Prior, David *(Con)*
Purchase, Ken *(Lab/Co-op)*
Randall, John *(Con)*
Sheerman, Barry
   (Lab/Co-op)
Soames, Nicholas *(Con)*
Spelman, Caroline *(Con)*
Stewart, Ian *(Lab)*
Taylor, John M *(Con)*
Tredinnick, David *(Con)*
Turner, Dr George *(Lab)*
Viggers, Peter *(Con)*
Walter, Robert *(Con)*
Wells, Bowen *(Con)*
White, Brian *(Lab)*
Williams, Dr Alan Wynne
   (Lab)
Woolas, Philip *(Lab)*
Wright, Anthony David *(Lab)*

Trade Unions
Ashton, Joe *(Lab)*
Benn, Hilary *(Lab)*
Caborn, Richard *(Lab)*
Fyfe, Maria *(Lab)*
Golding, Llin *(Lab)*
Healey, John *(Lab)*
Illsley, Eric *(Lab)*
Mahon, Alice *(Lab)*

Trades Union Legislation
Etherington, William *(Lab)*
Howard, Michael *(Con)*

Training
Connarty,. Michael *(Lab)*
Flint, Caroline *(Lab)*
Foster, Derek *(Lab)*
Foster, Michael John *(Lab)*
Jenkins, Brian *(Lab)*
Morris, Estelle *(Lab)*
Paice, James *(Con)*
Palmer, Dr Nicholas *(Lab)*
Prentice, Bridget *(Lab)*
Smith, Jacqui *(Lab)*
Stewart, Ian *(Lab)*
Watts, David *(Lab)*

Transport
Amess, David *(Con)*
Anderson, Donald *(Lab)*
Bradley, Peter *(Lab)*
Bradshaw, Ben *(Lab)*
Brake, Tom *(Lib Dem)*
Chaytor, David *(Lab)*
Chidgey, David *(Lib Dem)*
Clark, Paul *(Lab)*
Clelland, David *(Lab)*
Cohen, Harry *(Lab)*
Cryer, John *(Lab)*
Darling, Alistair *(Lab)*
Davies, Geraint *(Lab)*
Day, Stephen *(Con)*
Dean, Janet *(Lab)*
Donohoe, Brian *(Lab)*
Dowd, Jim *(Lab)*
Duncan Smith, Iain *(Con)*
Dunwoody, Gwyneth *(Lab)*
Eagle, Maria *(Lab)*
Efford, Clive *(Lab)*
Ellman, Louise
   (Lab/Co-op)
Fearn, Ronnie *(Lib Dem)*
Foster, Derek *(Lab)*
Goggins, Paul *(Lab)*
Griffiths, Jane *(Lab)*
Hammond, Philip *(Con)*
Hawkins, Nick *(Con)*
Henderson, Ivan *(Lab)*
Heppell, John *(Lab)*
Hill, Keith *(Lab)*
Hopkins, Kelvin *(Lab)*
Horam, John *(Con)*
Jack, Michael *(Con)*
Jones, Ieuan Wyn *(PC)*
Jones, Nigel *(Lib Dem)*

Transport *continued*
Laing, Eleanor *(Con)*
McCabe, Stephen *(Lab)*
McIntosh, Anne *(Con)*
Mackinlay, Andrew *(Lab)*
Marek, Dr John *(Lab)*
Marshall, David *(Lab)*
Martlew, Eric *(Lab)*
Meale, Alan *(Lab)*
Morgan, Alasdair *(SNP)*
Morley, Elliot *(Lab)*
Murphy, Denis *(Lab)*
Norman, Archie *(Con)*
O'Brien, Stephen *(Con)*
Öpik, Lembit *(Lib Dem)*
Organ, Diana *(Lab)*
Perham, Linda *(Lab)*
Pound, Stephen *(Lab)*
Prosser, Gwyn *(Lab)*
Quinn, Lawrie *(Lab)*
Raynsford, Nick *(Lab)*
Robathan, Andrew *(Con)*
Ruddock, Joan *(Lab)*
Russell, Bob *(Lib Dem)*
Russell, Christine *(Lab)*
Smith, Andrew *(Lab)*
Smyth, Rev Martin
 (UUP)
Snape, Peter *(Lab)*
Stevenson, George *(Lab)*
Strang, Gavin *(Lab)*
Ward, Claire *(Lab)*
White, Brian *(Lab)*
Whitehead, Dr Alan *(Lab)*
Winterton, Ann *(Con)*
Winterton, Rosie *(Lab)*
Wood, Mike *(Lab)*

**Transport (Environmentally
 Sustainable)**
Starkey, Dr Phyllis *(Lab)*

Transport Safety
Corbyn, Jeremy *(Lab)*
Smith, John *(Lab)*

Treasury
Byers, Stephen *(Lab)*
Casale, Roger *(Lab)*
Cranston, Ross *(Lab)*
Davies, Denzil *(Lab)*
Davies, Geraint *(Lab)*
Hanson, David *(Lab)*
Lammy, David *(Lab)*
Ruffley, David *(Con)*
Sheldon, Robert *(Lab)*

Touhig, Don *(Lab/Co-op)*
Townend, John *(Con)*
Wells, Bowen *(Con)*

Unemployment
Cooper, Yvette *(Lab)*
Goggins, Paul *(Lab)*
Graham, Tommy
 (Independent)
Jones, Barry *(Lab)*
Meale, Alan *(Lab)*
Reed, Andrew
 (Lab/Co-op)
Short, Clare *(Lab)*
Yeo, Tim *(Con)*

**United Kingdom Women –
 Campaigned Against
 Forced Marriages**
Cryer, Ann *(Lab)*

United Nations
Wells, Bowen *(Con)*

Urban Funding
Graham, Tommy
 (Independent)

Urban Parks
Wyatt, Derek *(Lab)*

Urban Policy
Benn, Hilary *(Lab)*
Curry, David *(Con)*
Fisher, Mark *(Lab)*
Vaz, Keith *(Lab)*

Urban Regeneration
Blears, Hazel *(Lab)*
Buck, Karen *(Lab)*
McGuire, Anne *(Lab)*
Moran, Margaret *(Lab)*
Russell, Christine *(Lab)*
Steen, Anthony *(Con)*
Timms, Stephen *(Lab)*

USA Elections
Evans, Nigel *(Con)*

USA
Forth, Eric *(Con)*

Utility Regulation
Gilroy, Linda
 (Lab/Co-op)

Venture Capital
Flight, Howard *(Con)*
Gunnell, John *(Lab)*
Wyatt, Derek *(Lab)*

Vocational Training
Reed, Andrew *(Lab/Co-op)*

Voluntary Organisations
Coffey, Ann *(Lab)*
Fraser, Christopher *(Con)*
Howarth, Alan *(Lab)*
Michael, Alun *(Lab/Co-op)*
Rowe, Andrew *(Con)*
Sanders, Adrian *(Lib Dem)*

Voting Systems
Harris, Evan *(Lib Dem)*
Linton, Martin *(Lab)*

Wales
Anderson, Donald *(Lab)*
Davies, Denzil *(Lab)*
Edwards, Huw *(Lab)*
Jones, Jon Owen *(Lab/Co-op)*
Murphy, Paul *(Lab)*

Waste Management
Paice, James *(Con)*

Water Industry
Burden, Richard *(Lab)*
O'Brien, William *(Lab)*

Welfare
Buck, Karen *(Lab)*
Coaker, Vernon *(Lab)*
Cook, Robin *(Lab)*
Davies, Quentin *(Con)*
Kelly, Ruth *(Lab)*
McDonagh, Siobhain *(Lab)*
Moran, Margaret *(Lab)*
Plaskitt, James *(Lab)*
Shaw, Jonathan *(Lab)*
Webb, Prof Steve *(Lib Dem)*

**Welfare of Armed Services
 Families**
Bell, Martin *(Independent)*

Welfare State
Brown, Russell *(Lab)*
Corbyn, Jeremy *(Lab)*
Efford, Clive *(Lab)*
Hutton, John *(Lab)*
Wicks, Malcolm *(Lab)*

Welfare to Work
Flint, Caroline *(Lab)*

Welsh Language
Flynn, Paul *(Lab)*

West Midlands Industry
O'Brien, Mike *(Lab)*

Wildlife
Dalyell, Tam *(Lab)*
Morgan, Rhodri *(Lab)*

Women
Gorman, Teresa *(Con)*
Harman, Harriet *(Lab)*
Jackson, Helen *(Lab)*
Osborne, Sandra *(Lab)*
Ruddock, Joan *(Lab)*
Short, Clare *(Lab)*

Women's Rights
Corston, Jean *(Lab)*
Fyfe, Maria *(Lab)*
Martin, Michael *(Lab)*
Primarolo, Dawn *(Lab)*

Workers' Co-operatives
Tipping, Paddy *(Lab)*

World Development
Armstrong, Hilary *(Lab)*
Drown, Julia *(Lab)*
Wood, Mike *(Lab)*

World Population
Ottaway, Richard *(Con)*

World Protestantism
Smyth, Rev Martin *(UUP)*

Youth Affairs
Ashdown, Sir Paddy
  (Lib Dem)
Baldry, Tony *(Con)*
Ballard, Jackie
  (Lib Dem)
Burgon, Colin *(Lab)*
Connarty, Michael *(Lab)*
Cotter, Brian *(Lib Dem)*
Foster, Derek *(Lab)*
Gorrie, Donald *(Lib Dem)*
Haselhurst, Sir Alan *(Con)*
Hope, Phil *(Lab/Co-op)*
Hughes, Simon *(Lib Dem)*
Michael, Alun
  (Lab/Co-op)
Öpik, Lembit *(Lib Dem)*
Steen, Anthony *(Con)*

THE GOVERNMENT

The Cabinet

Prime Minister, First Lord of the Treasury and Minister for the Civil Service	Rt Hon **Tony Blair** MP
Deputy Prime Minister and Secretary of State for the Environment, Transport and the Regions	Rt Hon **John Prescott** MP
Chancellor of the Exchequer	Rt Hon **Gordon Brown** MP
Secretary of State for Foreign and Commonwealth Affairs	Rt Hon **Robin Cook** MP
Lord Chancellor	Rt Hon **Lord Irvine of Lairg** QC
Secretary of State for the Home Department	Rt Hon **Jack Straw** MP
Secretary of State for Education and Employment	Rt Hon **David Blunkett** MP
President of the Council and Leader of the House of Commons	Rt Hon **Margaret Beckett** MP
Parliamentary Secretary, Treasury and Chief Whip	Rt Hon **Ann Taylor** MP
Secretary of State for Culture, Media and Sport	Rt Hon **Chris Smith** MP
Minister for the Cabinet Office and Chancellor of the Duchy of Lancaster	Rt Hon Dr **Marjorie Mowlam** MP
Secretary of State for International Development	Rt Hon **Clare Short** MP
Secretary of State for Social Security	Rt Hon **Alistair Darling** MP
Minister of Agriculture, Fisheries and Food	Rt Hon **Nick Brown** MP
Leader of the House of Lords and Minister for Women*	Rt Hon **Baroness Jay of Paddington**
Secretary of State for Trade and Industry	Rt Hon **Stephen Byers** MP
Secretary of State for Health	Rt Hon **Alan Milburn** MP
Secretary of State for Scotland	Rt Hon Dr **John Reid** MP
Secretary of State for Wales	Rt Hon **Paul Murphy** MP
Secretary of State for Northern Ireland	Rt Hon **Peter Mandelson** MP
Secretary of State for Defence	Rt Hon **Geoffrey Hoon** MP
Chief Secretary to the Treasury	Rt Hon **Andrew Smith** MP
Minister of State, Department of the Environment, Transport and the Regions (Minister for Transport)†	Rt Hon **Lord Macdonald of Tradeston** CBE
Captain of the Gentlemen-at-Arms, Government Chief Whip (Lords)†	Rt Hon **Lord Carter**
Law Officers:	
Attorney General	Rt Hon **Lord Williams of Mostyn** QC MP
Solicitor General	**Ross Cranston** QC MP
Advocate General for Scotland	Dr **Lynda Clark** QC MP

*The Minister is appointed as Lord Privy Seal.
†Not Members of the Cabinet, but will attend Cabinet Meetings.

Departmental Ministers

MINISTRY OF AGRICULTURE, FISHERIES AND FOOD

Minister of Agriculture, Fisheries and Food	Rt Hon **Nick Brown** MP
Minister of State	Rt Hon **Joyce Quin** MP
Minister of State	**Baroness Hayman**
Parliamentary Secretary	**Elliot Morley** MP

CABINET OFFICE

Minister for the Cabinet Office‡	Rt Hon Dr **Marjorie Mowlam** MP
Minister of State	**Lord Falconer of Thoroton** QC
Minister of State	Rt Hon **Ian McCartney** MP
Parliamentary Secretary	**Graham Stringer** MP
Leader of the House of Lords and Minister for Women†	Rt Hon **Baroness Jay of Paddington**

DEPARTMENT FOR CULTURE, MEDIA AND SPORT

Secretary of State	Rt Hon **Chris Smith** MP
Parliamentary Under-Secretary of State	**Janet Anderson** MP
Parliamentary Under-Secretary of State	**Kate Hoey** MP
Parliamentary Under-Secretary of State	Rt Hon **Alan Howarth** CBE MP

MINISTRY OF DEFENCE

Secretary of State	Rt Hon **Geoffrey Hoon** MP
Minister of State	**John Spellar** MP
Minister of State	**Baroness Symons of Vernham Dean**
Parliamentary Under-Secretary of State	Dr **Lewis Moonie** MP

DEPARTMENT FOR EDUCATION AND EMPLOYMENT

Secretary of State	Rt Hon **David Blunkett** MP
Minister of State	Rt Hon **Tessa Jowell** MP
Minister of State	Rt Hon **Estelle Morris** MP
Minister of State	**Baroness Blackstone**
Parliamentary Under-Secretary of State	**Malcolm Wicks** MP
Parliamentary Under-Secretary of State	**Margaret Hodge** MBE MP
Parliamentary Under-Secretary of State	**Jacqui Smith** MP
Parliamentary Under-Secretary of State	**Michael Wills** MP

DEPARTMENT OF THE ENVIRONMENT, TRANSPORT AND THE REGIONS

Deputy Prime Minister and Secretary of State	Rt Hon **John Prescott** MP
Minister of State (Transport)§	Rt Hon **Lord Macdonald of Tradeston** CBE
Minister of State	Rt Hon **Michael Meacher** MP
Minister of State	Rt Hon **Hilary Armstrong** MP
Minister of State	**Nick Raynsford** MP
Parliamentary Under-Secretary of State	**Chris Mullin** MP
Parliamentary Under-Secretary of State	**Keith Hill** MP
Parliamentary Under-Secretary of State	**Lord Whitty**
Parliamentary Under-Secretary of State	**Beverley Hughes** MP

†This Minister is appointed as Lord Privy Seal.
‡The Minister is appointed as Chancellor of the Duchy of Lancaster.
§Not a Member of the Cabinet but attends Cabinet Meetings.

FOREIGN AND COMMONWEALTH OFFICE

Secretary of State	Rt Hon **Robin Cook** MP
Minister of State	**Peter Hain** MP
Minister of State	**John Battle** MP
Minister of State	**Keith Vaz** MP
Parliamentary Under-Secretary of State	**Baroness Scotland of Asthal** QC

DEPARTMENT OF HEALTH

Secretary of State	Rt Hon **Alan Milburn** MP
Minister of State	Rt Hon **John Denham** MP
Minister of State	**John Hutton** MP
Parliamentary Under-Secretary of State	**Lord Hunt of Kings Heath** OBE
Parliamentary Under-Secretary of State	**Yvette Cooper** MP
Parliamentary Under-Secretary of State	**Gisela Stuart** MP

HOME OFFICE

Secretary of State	Rt Hon **Jack Straw** MP
Minister of State	Rt Hon **Paul Boateng** MP
Minister of State	**Charles Clarke** MP
Minister of State	**Barbara Roche** MP
Parliamentary Under-Secretary of State	**Mike O'Brien** MP
Parliamentary Under-Secretary of State	**Lord Bassam of Brighton**

DEPARTMENT FOR INTERNATIONAL DEVELOPMENT

Secretary of State	Rt Hon **Clare Short** MP
Parliamentary Under-Secretary of State	**George Foulkes** MP

LAW OFFICERS' DEPARTMENT

Attorney General	Rt Hon **Lord Williams of Mostyn** QC
Solicitor General	**Ross Cranston** QC MP

LORD CHANCELLOR'S DEPARTMENT

Lord Chancellor	Rt Hon **Lord Irvine of Lairg** QC
Parliamentary Secretary	**David Lock** MP
Parliamentary Secretary	**Jane Kennedy** MP

NORTHERN IRELAND OFFICE

Secretary of State	Rt Hon **Peter Mandelson** MP
Minister of State	Rt Hon **Adam Ingram** MP
Parliamentary Under-Secretary of State	**George Howarth** MP

PRIVY COUNCIL OFFICE

President of the Council and Leader of the House of Commons	Rt Hon **Margaret Beckett** MP
Parliamentary Secretary	**Paddy Tipping** MP

SCOTLAND OFFICE

Secretary of State	Rt Hon Dr **John Reid** MP
Minister of State	**Brian Wilson** MP
Advocate General	Dr **Lynda Clark** QC MP

DEPARTMENT OF SOCIAL SECURITY

Secretary of State	Rt Hon **Alistair Darling** MP
Minister of State	Rt Hon **Jeff Rooker** MP
Parliamentary Under-Secretary of State	Rt Hon **Baroness Hollis of Heigham**
Parliamentary Under-Secretary of State	**Angela Eagle** MP
Parliamentary Under-Secretary of State	**Hugh Bayley** MP

DEPARTMENT OF TRADE AND INDUSTRY

Secretary of State	Rt Hon **Stephen Byers** MP
Minister of State	Rt Hon **Helen Liddell** MP
Minister of State	Rt Hon **Richard Caborn** MP
Minister of State	**Patricia Hewitt** MP
Parliamentary Under-Secretary of State	Dr **Kim Howells** MP
Parliamentary Under-Secretary of State	**Alan Johnson** MP
Parliamentary Under-Secretary of State (Minister for Science)*	**Lord Sainsbury of Turville**

HM TREASURY

Prime Minister, First Lord of the Treasury and Minister for the Civil Service	Rt Hon **Tony Blair** MP
Chancellor of the Exchequer	Rt Hon **Gordon Brown** MP
Chief Secretary to the Treasury	Rt Hon **Andrew Smith** MP
Paymaster General	**Dawn Primarolo** MP
Financial Secretary	**Stephen Timms** MP
Economic Secretary	**Melanie Johnson** MP

THE WALES OFFICE

Secretary of State	Rt Hon **Paul Murphy** MP
Parliamentary Under-Secretary of State	**David Hanson** MP

*Unpaid

Alphabetical List of Ministers

Ainsworth, Robert	Whip
Allen, Graham	Whip
Amos, Baroness	Whip
Anderson, Janet	Parliamentary Under-Secretary of State, Department for Culture Media and Sport
Armstrong, Hilary	Minister of State, Department of the Environment, Transport and the Regions
Bach, Lord	Whip
Bassam, Lord	Parliamentary Under-Secretary of State, Home Office
Battle, John	Minister of State, Foreign and Commonwealth Office
Bayley, Hugh	Parliamentary Under-Secretary of State, Department of Social Security
Beckett, Margaret	President of the Council and Leader of the House of Commons
Betts, Clive	Whip
Blackstone, Baroness	Minister of State, Department for Education and Employment
Blair, Tony	Prime Minister, First Lord of the Treasury and Minister for Civil Service
Blunkett, David	Secretary of State for Education and Employment
Boateng, Paul	Minister of State, Home Office and Deputy Home Secretary
Bradley, Keith	Deputy Chief Whip
Brown, Gordon	Chancellor of the Exchequer
Brown, Nick	Minister of Agriculture, Fisheries and Food
Byers, Stephen	Secretary of State for Trade and Industry
Burlison, Lord	Whip
Caborn, Richard	Minister of State, Department of Trade and Industry
Carter, Lord	Chief Whip
Clark, Lynda	Advocate General for Scotland
Clarke, Charles	Minister of State, Home Office
Clelland, David	Assistant Whip
Cook, Robin	Foreign Secretary
Cooper, Yvette	Parliamentary Under-Secretary of State, Department of Health
Cranston, Ross	Solicitor General
Darling, Alistair	Secretary of State for Social Security
Denham, John	Minister of State, Department of Health
Dowd, James	Whip
Eagle, Angela	Parliamentary Under-Secretary of State, Department of Social Security
Falconer of Thoroton, Lord	Minister of State, Cabinet Office
Farrington of Ribbleton, Baroness	Whip
Foulkes, George	Parliamentary Under-Secretary of State, Department for International Development
Hain, Peter	Minister of State, Foreign and Commonwealth Office
Hall, Michael	Assistant Whip
Hanson, David	Parliamentary Under-Secretary of State, Wales Office
Hayman, Baroness	Minister of State, Ministry of Agriculture, Fisheries and Food
Hewitt, Patricia	Minister of State, Department of Trade and Industry
Hill, Keith	Parliamentary Under-Secretary of State, Department of the Environment, Transport and the Regions
Hodge, Margaret	Parliamentary Under-Secretary of State, Department for Education and Employment
Hoey, Kate	Minister for Sport (Parliamentary Under-Secretary of State, Department for Culture, Media and Sport)

Hollis, Baroness	Parliamentary Under-Secretary of State, Department of Social Security
Hoon, Geoffrey	Secretary of State for Defence
Howarth, Alan	Parliamentary Under-Secretary of State, Department for Culture, Media and Sport
Howarth, George	Parliamentary Under-Secretary of State, Northern Ireland Office
Howells, Kim	Parliamentary Under-Secretary of State, Department of Trade and Industry
Hughes, Beverley	Parliamentary Under-Secretary of State, Department of the Environment, Transport and the Regions
Hughes, Kevin	Assistant Whip
Hunt of Kings Heath, Lord	Parliamentary Under-Secretary of State, Department of Health
Hutton, John	Minister of State, Department of Health
Ingram, Adam	Minister of State, Northern Ireland Office
Irvine of Lairg, Lord	Lord Chancellor
Jamieson, David	Whip
Jay of Paddington, Baroness	Lord Privy Seal, Leader of the House of Lords and Minister for Women
Johnson, Alan	Parliamentary Under-Secretary of State, Department of Trade and Industry
Johnson, Melanie	Economic Secretary, HM Treasury
Jowell, Tessa	Minister of State, Department for Education and Employment
Kennedy, Jane	Parliamentary Secretary, Lord Chancellor's Department
Liddell, Helen	Minister of State, Department of Trade and Industry
Lock, David	Parliamentary Secretary, Lord Chancellor's Department
McAvoy, Thomas	Whip
McCartney, Ian	Minister of State, Cabinet Office
Macdonald of Tradeston Lord	Minister of Transport (Minister of State, Department of the Environment, Transport and the Regions)
McGuire, Anne	Assistant Whip
McIntosh of Haringey, Lord	Deputy Chief Whip
McNulty, Tony	Assistant Whip
Mandelson, Peter	Secretary of State for Northern Ireland
Meacher, Michael	Minister of State, Department of the Environment, Transport and the Regions
Milburn, Alan	Secretary of State for Health
Moonie, Dr Lewis	Parliamentary Under-Secretary of State, Ministry of Defence
Morley, Elliot	Parliamentary Secretary, Ministry of Agriculture, Fisheries and Food
Morris, Estelle	Minister of State, Department for Education and Employment
Mowlam, Marjorie	Minister for the Cabinet Office and Chancellor of the Duchy of Lancaster
Murphy, Paul	Secretary of State for Wales
Mullin, Chris	Parliamentary Under-Secretary of State, Department of the Environment, Transport and the Regions
O'Brien, Mike	Parliamentary Under-Secretary of State, Home Office
Pope, Greg	Whip
Prescott, John	Deputy Prime Minister; Secretary of State for the Environment, Transport and the Regions
Primarolo, Dawn	Paymaster General, HM Treasury
Quin, Joyce	Minister of State, Ministry of Agriculture, Fisheries and Food
Ramsay of Cartvale, Baroness	Whip
Raynsford, Nick	Parliamentary Under-Secretary of State, Department of Environment, Transport and the Regions

Reid, John	Secretary of State for Scotland
Roche, Barbara	Minister of State, Home Office
Rooker, Jeff	Minister of State, Department of Social Security
Sainsbury of Turville, Lord	Minister for Science, (Parliamentary Under-Secretary of State, Department of Trade and Industry)
Scotland, Baroness	Parliamentary Under-Secretary of State, Foreign and Commonwealth Office
Short, Clare	Secretary of State for International Development
Smith, Andrew	Chief Secretary, HM Treasury
Smith, Chris	Secretary of State for Culture, Media and Sport
Smith, Jacqui	Parliamentary Under-Secretary of State, Department for Education and Employment
Spellar, John	Minister of State, Ministry of Defence
Straw, Jack	Home Secretary
Stringer, Graham	Parliamentary Secretary, Cabinet Office
Stuart, Gisela	Parliamentary Under-Secretary of State, Department of Health
Sutcliffe, Gerry	Assistant Whip
Symons of Vernham Dean, Baroness	Minister of State, Ministry of Defence
Taylor, Ann	Chief Whip
Timms, Stephen	Financial Secretary, HM Treasury
Tipping, Paddy	Parliamentary Secretary, Privy Council Office
Touhig, Don	Assistant Whip
Vaz, Keith	Minister of State, Foreign and Commonwealth Office
Whitty, Lord	Parliamentary Under-Secretary of State, Department of the Environment, Transport and Regions
Wicks, Malcolm	Parliamentary Under-Secretary of State, Department for Education and Employment
Williams of Mostyn, Lord	Attorney General
Wills, Michael	Parliamentary Under-Secretary of State, Department for Education and Employment
Wilson, Brian	Minister of State, Scotland Office

Ministerial Responsibilities

MINISTRY OF AGRICULTURE, FISHERIES AND FOOD

Minister of Agriculture, Fisheries and Food (Rt Hon **Nick Brown** MP)
Has overall responsibility for all Departmental issues. He will normally represent the UK at EU Council of Agricultural Ministers.
Principal Private Secretary: Andrew Slade *Tel:* 020 7238 5339 *Fax:* 020 7238 5727 (Main Fax for Ministers) *Fax:* 020 7238 5727 *Private Secretaries:* Fiona James, Andy Gregory
Tel: 020 7238 6200 *Assistant Private Secretaries:* Kerry Thompson *Tel:* 020 7238 5343

Minister of State and Deputy Minister of Agriculture, Fisheries and Food (Rt Hon **Joyce Quin** MP)
Deputising for the Minister on EU agricultural policy issues; Responsibility for post-devolution agricultural policy and its implementation in England. Government policy on EU enlargement and CAP reform and euro changeover plan; external trade policy and export promotion; regional policy and organisation; food and drinks industry and marketing (including taking forward the food chain initiative with industry); competition issues; spokesperson in the Commons on food safety and Food Standards Agency issues.
Private Secretary: Teresa Hart *Tel:* 020 7238 5404 *Fax:* 020 7238 5976
Assistant Private Secretary: Claire Rapley *Tel:* 020 7238 6034

Minster of State (Lords) (**Baroness Hayman**)
Responsibility for food safety; food standards; meat hygiene; animal health (including BSE, Pet Travel Scheme and TB in cattle); pesticide safety; veterinary medicines, plant health; research and genetic modification.
Private Secretary: Vic Platten *Tel:* 020 7238 5379 *Fax:* 020 7238 5867
Assistant Private Secretary: Richard Hopley *Tel:* 020 7238 6603

Parliamentary Secretary (Commons) (Minister for Fisheries and the Countryside) (**Elliot Morley** MP)
Responsibility for countryside matters; forestry; farm animal welfare; Departmental Green Minister. Normally represents the UK at meetings of the EU Council of Fisheries Ministers.
E-mail: parlsecc@sec.maff.gov.uk
Private Secretary: Mark Livesey *Tel:* 020 7238 5421 *Fax:* 020 7238 5996
Assistant Private Secretary: Nicola Beacham

Spokespersons in the House of Lords: Baroness Hayman, Lord Carter.

CABINET OFFICE

Minister for the Cabinet Office (Rt Hon Dr **Mo Mowlam** MP)
Responsibility for oversight of the departmental work of Cabinet Office Ministers, including particular responsibilities for inter-departmental co-ordination on social exclusion, biotechnology, anti-drugs policy, regulation, rural affairs and equality, and overall leadership of the Modernising Government programme, and discharges, on a day-to-day basis, the responsibilities of the Miniser for the Civil Service.
E-mail: mmowlam@cabinet-office.x.gsi.gov.uk
Principal Private Secretary: Dr John Fuller *Tel:* 020 7270 0330 *Fax:* 020 7270 0196
Assistant Private Secretary: (Diary) Tracey Temple *Tel:* 020 7270 0225

Minister of State (**Lord Falconer of Thoroton** QC)
Works with Dr Mowlam on taking forward work on the coherent formulation and implementation of policy across government; Works with Dr Mowlam on preparation of the Government's Annual Report and on monitoring the overall performance of the Government; Answers in the House of Lords for the full range of responsibilities of the Minister for the Cabinet Office; Specific regulatory issues as remitted to him, including transposition of EU directives into UK law; Sole shareholder, on behalf of the Government, of the New Millennium Experience Company, responsible for the Millennium Dome and the related national programme; and the Active Community (with the Minister of State in the Home Office, the Rt Hon Paul Boateng MP), a programme to promote and encourage the giving of time to community involvement.
E-mail: cfalconer@cabinet-office.x.gsi.gov.uk
Private Secretary: Mark Langdale *Tel:* 020 7270 0012/0013 *Fax:* 020 7270 1257

Minister of State (Rt Hon **Ian McCartney** MP)

Responsibility for Responsiveness and quality of public services and electronic government within the Modernising Government agenda; Cabinet Office Agencies; Creation of Office of Government Commerce; Works with Dr Mowlam in co-ordinating the anti-drugs policy; Sponsor Minister for (CITU) project on lessons learned from big Government IT projects; Sponsor Minister for (PIU) project on seizure and pursuit of criminal assets; and Co-ordinating the Government's arrangements for the 2002 Commonwealth Games.

E-mail: imccartney@cabinet-office.x.gsi.gov.uk

Private Secretary: Dr Christian Turner *Tel:* 020 7270 0411 *Fax:* 020 7270 1171

Parliamentary Secretary (**Graham Stringer** MP)

Responsibility for Regulatory burdens, including the Bill to amend the Deregulation and Contracting Out Act, and enforcement; Public appointments/NDPBs (creation of, and appointment to, quangos); Issues relating to the Ombudsman (including review of 'joined-up' Ombudsmen); Specific day-to-day civil service management issues such as pensions, TUPE; Oversees the wider public sector workstream of modernising government; supports Dr Mowlam and Mr McCartney in spreading the message to frontline deliverers; Departmental management, including Ministerial ownership of relevant PSA targets; and Departmental role on specific committees: Green Minister, Euro Minister.

E-mail: gstringer@cabinet-office.x.gsi.gov.uk

Private Secretary: Mark Holmes *Tel:* 020 7270 0652/0645 *Fax:* 020 7270 0655

Assistant Private Secretary: Neil Massingham

Leader of the House of Lords and Minister for Women (Lord Privy Seal)

(Rt Hon **Baroness Jay of Paddington**)

The Leader of the House of Lords is responsible for the arrangement of Government business in the House and has a responsibility to the House itself to advise it on procedural matters and other difficulties as they arise; she is also Minister for Women with responsibility for the representation and promotion of women's issues across Government. In this capacity she sits on a number of Cabinet Committees – chairing the Cabinet sub-committee on Women's Issues. In relation to the devolved administrations she retains this responsibility in all subject areas which are not devolved.

Principal Private Secretary: William Connon *Tel:* 020 7270 0501 (Cabinet Office) 020 7219 3200 (House of Lords) *Fax:* 020 7270 0491 (Cabinet Office) 020 7219 3051 (House of Lords)

E-mail: wconnon@cabinet-office.gsi.gov.uk

Spokesmen in the House of Lords: Lord Falconer of Thoroton, Lord Burlison; Spokespersons for Women's Issues: Baroness Jay, Baroness Amos.

OFFICES OF THE CHANCELLOR OF THE DUCHY OF LANCASTER

Chancellor of the Duchy of Lancaster (Rt Hon Dr **Mo Mowlam** MP)

Responsible to The Queen for the general administration of the Duchy of Lancaster, in which she is supported by the Duchy of Lancaster Office.

Principal Private Secretary: Dr John Fuller *Tel:* 020 7270 0330 *Fax:* 020 7270 0196

Private Secretary: Miles Beale *Tel:* 020 7270 1261

See also Cabinet Office

DEPARTMENT FOR CULTURE, MEDIA AND SPORT

Secretary of State for Culture, Media and Sport (Rt Hon **Chris Smith** MP)

Responsibility for Departmental strategy, expenditure and organisation; National Lottery policy; Public appointments; Chairman of the Millennium Commission; The Millennium.

E-mail: chris.smith@culture.gov.uk

Principal Private Secretary: Fergus Muir *Tel:* 020 7211 6243 *Fax:* 020 7211 6249

E-mail: fergus.muir@culture.gov.uk

Private Secretary: Paul Blaker *Tel:* 020 7211 6975

Parliamentary Under-Secretary of State (Minister for Tourism, Film and Broadcasting) (**Janet Anderson** MP)
Responsibility for Tourism; Broadcasting, Film and the Press; The creative industries (including the music industry); The Millennium; Regional and local authority policy issues; Women's Issues; Green Issues.
E-mail: janet.anderson@culture.gov.uk
Private Secretary: Tom Owen-Edmunds *Tel:* 020 7211 6303 *Fax:* 020 7211 6546
E-mail: tom.owen-edmunds@culture.gov.uk
Assistant Private Secretary: Suzanne Bullock *Tel:* 020 7211 6305

Parliamentary Under-Secretary of State (Minister for Sport) (**Kate Hoey** MP)
Responsibility for sport; support for the Secretary of State on the National Lottery; Social policy, access and equal opportunities.
E-mail: kate.hoey@culture.gov.uk
Private Secretary: Simon Cooper *Tel:* 020 7211 6246 *Fax:* 020 7211 6546
E-mail: simon.cooper@culture.gov.uk
Assistant Private Secretary: Philip Chamberlain *Tel:* 020 7211 6247

Parliamentary Under-Secretary of State (Minister for the Arts) (Rt Hon **Alan Howarth** CBE MP)
Responsibility for European and international matters; The arts, the crafts, music and the Government Art Collection; Museums and galleries and libraries; The built heritage, the Royal estate, architecture and design; DCMS interest in information technology, training and education.
E-mail: alan.howarth@culture.gov.uk
Private Secretary: Steven Harding *Tel:* 020 7211 6252 *Fax:* 020 7211 6309
E-mail: steven.harding@culture.gov.uk
Assistant Private Secretary: Sean Kenny *Diary Secretary:* Julia Bradford
Spokesman in the House of Lords: Lord McIntosh of Haringey.

MINISTRY OF DEFENCE

Secretary of State for Defence (Rt Hon **Geoffrey Hoon** MP)
Has overall responsibility for the work of the Ministry.
Private Secretary: Julian Miller *Tel:* 020 7218 2111 *Fax:* 020 7218 7140

Minister of State for the Armed Forces (**John Spellar** MP)
Responsibility for defence policy and planning, including: strategy including nuclear policy; size and shape of the Services (excluding equipment projects); Defence budget issues (including efficiency/asset use); arms control and disarmament; NATO, WEU; United Nations, OSCE; visiting forces. Operations, including: overseas commitments and garrisons; Northern Ireland; military aid to the civil authorities; UN peacekeeping; disaster relief; military assistance overseas; nuclear accident response; MoD Police operations. Service personnel policy, including: armed forces pay; equal opportunities, training and education, Defence medical services; reserves and cadets, veterans, Gulf veterans' illness; compensation policy. Operational sustainability; public presentation of defence.
Private Secretary: Daniel Applegate *Tel:* 020 7218 6385 *Fax:* 020 7218 6542

Minister of State for Defence Procurement (**Baroness Symons of Vernham Dean**)
Responsibility for procurement, including: forward equipment programme (including logistics strategy); project approval (including equipment capability upgrades); equipment collaboration; nuclear procurement (including safety and disposal); defence industrial questions; contracts policy. Science and technology strategy and research, including: Defence Evaluation Research Agency (DERA); civil use of defence research. Defence exports and disposals; intelligence and security policy; public-private partnerships*; all matters concerning Defence in the House of Lords.
*Decisions on specific projects and individual Agencies will be handled by the Minister with responsibility for the area concerned.
Private Secretary: David Hatcher *Tel:* 020 7218 6621 *Fax:* 020 7218 6625

Parliamentary Under-Secretary of State (Dr **Lewis Moonie** MP)
   Responsibility for service personnel casework; civilian and MoD Police personnel policy and casework; market testing*. Defence estate and works, including: service housing; heritage and historic buildings. Regulatory issues, including: environmental matters; health and safety policy. Claims casework; public service matters, including: Service First, the new Charter programme; open Government; non-departmental public bodies; low flying; hydrographic and meteorological offices; service museums; visits by Peers and MPs/Armed Forces Parliamentary Scheme; Procurement matters in the House of Commons; Defence Diversification.
   *Decisions on specific projects and individual Agencies will be handled by the Minister with responsibility for the area concerned.
   Private Secretary: Andrew Dwyer *Tel:* 020 7218 2452 *Fax:* 020 7218 7610
   Spokespersons in the House of Lords: Baroness Symons, Lord Burlison.

DEPUTY PRIME MINISTER AND SECRETARY OF STATE FOR THE ENVIRONMENT, TRANSPORT AND THE REGIONS

John Prescott, MP has combined his cross-Governmental role as Deputy Prime Minister, which includes chairing a number of key Cabinet Committees and representing the Prime Minister at home and abroad, with the post of Secretary of State for the Environment, Transport and the Regions.

DEPARTMENT FOR EDUCATION AND EMPLOYMENT

Secretary of State for Education and Employment (Rt Hon **David Blunkett** MP)
   Has overall responsibility for the Department, its policies and strategy; finance and public expenditure; major appointments.
   Principal Private Secretary: Mike Wardle *Tel:* 020 7925 5829 *Fax:* 020 7925 6995
   E-mail: mike-ps.wardle@dfee.gov.uk
   Private Secretaries: Kevin Rennie *Tel:* 020 7925 5928, Tina Sawyer *Tel:* 020 7925 5180, Lindsay Brown *Tel:* 020 7925 5303, Kim Sibley *Tel:* 020 7925 5206

Minister of State (Minister for Employment, Welfare to Work and Equal Opportunities) (Rt Hon **Tessa Jowell** MP)
   Responsibility for employment and the labour market; Employment Zones; Employment Service performance and programmes; New Deal (including an overview of the New Deal for Lone Parents and the New Deal for Disabled People, together with the inter-relationship with childcare) (MH*); labour market statistics; Welfare Reform, including the 'ONE' Service; Job Seekers' Allowance; employability and competitiveness – Skills Task Force and training (Malcolm Wicks and Michael Wills*); relationships with employers, including small and medium enterprises (Michael Wills*); Performance and Innovation Unit: rural economies; EU and international relations (employment and social affairs) policy; regional and urban policy (Malcolm Wicks and Michael Wills*); competitiveness (Malcolm Wicks*); overview of equal opportunities, EOC and pay gap; economic issues (DB*); social inclusion†; women's issues, including the Ministerial Sub-committee on Women's Issues; Government Spokesperson in the House of Commons on Women's Issues; attends meetings of the Sure Start Ministerial Group in a personal capacity.
   †Tessa Jowell will be the lead minister working with other ministers when proposals fall within their responsibilities.
   Private Secretary: Daniel Jefferson *Tel:* 020 7925 6255 *Fax:* 020 7925 6996
   E-mail: daniel.jefferson@dfee.gov.uk

Minister of State (Minister for School Standards) (Rt Hon **Estelle Morris** MP)
   Responsibility for school standards; Standards and Effectiveness Unit; specialist schools; beacon schools; independent schools; literacy and numeracy strategy; follow-through from National Year of Reading and implementation of Maths Year 2000; excellence in cities; gifted and talented children; liaison with and responsibility for OFSTED; Education Action Zones; class sizes; education business links; National Leadership College; teacher and headteacher supply, training and appraisal; liaison with and responsibility for the Teacher Training Agency; teachers' pay and conditions and reform of teaching profession (DB*); teacher misconduct; overview of national curriculum review (JS*); overview of 5 to 16 admissions and school organisation policy (JS*); school organisation and admissions casework (split territorially with JS); Local Education

Authorities including intervention, the new code and fair funding; schools' recurrent funding; education interest in the Millennium Dome; overview of early years (MH*); implementation of Social Exclusion Unit report on exclusion (TB*).

Private Secretary: Nick Carson *Tel:* 020 7925 5870 *Fax:* 020 7925 5151
E-mail: nick.carson@dfee.gov.uk

Minister of State (Minister for Education and Employment) (Lords) (**Baroness Blackstone**)
Responsibility for education and employment policy, equal opportunities and early years issues in the House of Lords; lifelong learning policy (Malcolm Wicks*); University for Industry and Learning Direct (Michael Wills*); overview of higher education, including science education and relations with the DTI; further education and training (Malcolm Wicks*); student support and the Student Loans Company; individual learning accounts (Malcolm Wicks*); 'Learning to Succeed', review of post-16 provision of education and training (Malcolm Wicks*); overview of national targets for education and training; basic skills; overview of adult education; prison education and related issues; qualifications and examinations and Qualifications and Curriculum Authority (EM*); Modern Apprenticeships and National Traineeships (Malcolm Wicks and where appropriate Michael Wills*); Investors in People; public service reform; European Union and international relations (education); social exclusion including implementation with Malcolm Wicks of 'bridging the gap' (EM and Malcolm Wicks*).

Private Secretary: Matthew Hopkinson *Tel:* 020 7925 6243 *Fax:* 020 7925 5011
E-mail: matthew.hopkinson@dfee.gov.uk

Parliamentary Under-Secretary of State (Lifelong Learning) (**Malcolm Wicks** MP)
Responsibility for lifelong learning; higher and further education, adult education and basic skills (including quality and addressing failure) (TB*); 'Learning to Succeed', review of post-16 provision and the follow through from the Learning Age green paper; overview of youth policy (JS*); development of the new Youth Support Service (ConneXions) together with the further development of National Traineeships (Foundation Apprenticeships) and Modern Apprenticeships (TB*); careers service and adult guidance; co-ordination between TECs, further education and local authorities on post-16 education and training; teachers' pensions; development of broad social policy objectives and overview of government wide inclusion agenda (including family policy, working with Margaret Hodge); National Training Organisations; employability and competitiveness – skills agenda (TJ and Michael Wills*); Individual Learning Accounts development and implementation (TB*); overview of public private partnerships/PFI (JS*); support for New Deal and economic issues (TJ*); analytical services and internal and external research; neighbourhood support fund (TB*); regeneration (other than regional policy and urban policy) (TJ*).

Private Secretary: Steve Bartlett *Tel:* 020 7925 6341 *Fax:* 020 7925 6921
E-mail: steve.bartlett@dfee.gov.uk

Parliamentary Under-Secretary of State (Employment and Equal Opportunities)
(**Margaret Hodge** MBE MP)
Responsibility for employment including the New Deal for Lone Parents (TJ*); New Deal for disabled people (TJ*); family friendly issues; equal opportunities issues, EOC (TJ*); age discrimination; disability rights (and the Disability Rights Commission); work permits; early years education, childcare (EM*) and the implementation of Sure Start (DB and TJ*); day care services; volunteering policy and millennium volunteers (DB*); regulatory burdens.

Private Secretary: Sue Kennett *Tel:* 020 7925 6951 *Fax:* 020 7925 6994
E-mail: sue.kennett@dfee.gov.uk

Parliamentary Under-Secretary of State (School Standards) (**Jacqui Smith** MP)
Responsibility for school standards; family literacy and role of parents in supporting and benefiting from school provision; special educational needs, including post-16 and the work of the National Advisory Group on SEN; schools' capital and schools' public private partnerships/PFI; national curriculum review (personal, social and health education and citizenship and democracy (EM*); the development of high quality content and software for school education (Michael Wills*); study support (and relationship to the New Opportunities Fund); role of and relationship with school governors; General Teaching Council; 14 to 19 issues (TB*); overview of 5 to 16 – admissions and school organisation policy (EM*); school organisation and admissions case work (territorially split) (EM*); rural schools, including closures; reducing bureaucracy; implementation of new school structure including foundation schools; wind up of the Funding Agency for Schools; drugs

education; youth support for young people in school education (Malcolm Wicks*); pupil welfare and school security; ethnic minority achievement grant (formerly section 11) and cross-departmental and cross-Government groups on ethnic minority education issues, including work with the Home Office; achievement of targets on exclusion, truancy and anti-bullying/discipline policy; equality issues in education (including gender); school transport and related cross-departmental issues; green issues, rural issues and the environment.
Private Secretary: Karen Lumley *Tel:* 020 7925 6391 *Fax:* 020 7925 6688
E-mail: karen.lumley@dfee.gov.uk

Parliamentary Under-Secretary of State (**Michael Wills** MP)
Responsibility for ICT in education and employment; National Grid for Learning; University for Industry and Learning Direct (TB*); broadcasting – including the development of world-class digital, satellite and home-based learning; overcoming exclusion in the information age – the gap between the haves and have nots; relationships with employers, including small and medium enterprises (TJ*); employability and competitiveness – Skills Task Force and skills development (TJ*); constitutional reform; regional policy; Regional Development Agencies; departmental efficiency and effectiveness (including budgetary issues) (DB*); completion of work on prevention of problems arising from the millennium bug; workforce development.
Private Secretary: Jenny Grundy *Tel:* 020 7925 6823 *E-mail:* jenny.grundy@dfee.gov.uk
Diary Secretary: Cathy Hare *Tel:* 020 7925 6821

Spokespersons in the House of Lords: Baroness Blackstone, Lord Bach.
*Denotes 'working with'.

DEPARTMENT OF THE ENVIRONMENT, TRANSPORT AND THE REGIONS

Deputy Prime Minister and Secretary of State for the Environment, Transport and the Regions (Rt Hon **John Prescott** MP)
Has responsibility for the overall direction of the Department and its agencies and has overall responsibility for the regions in England and London.
E-mail: john_prescott@detr.gsi.gov.uk
Principal Private Secretary: Peter Unwin *Tel:* 020 7944 4394 *Fax:* 020 7944 4399

Minister of State (Minister for Transport) (Rt Hon **Lord Macdonald of Tradeston** CBE)
Responsibility for Integrated transport strategy; Aviation; Railways; Shipping; Buses; Congestion and workplace charging, National roads; Local transport plans; London Transport; Environmental impacts of transport; Road safety.
E-mail: gus_macdonald@detr.gsi.gov.uk
Private Secretary: Seth Davis *Tel:* 020 7944 4483 *Fax:* 020 7944 4492

Minister of State (Minister for the Environment) (Rt Hon **Michael Meacher** MP)
Responsibility for sustainable development strategy; Environmental protection; Countryside and wildlife; Water; Health and safety; Waste, National waste strategy; Climate change; Energy efficiency.
E-mail: michael_meacher@detr.gsi.gov.uk
Private Secretary: Colin Bird *Tel:* 020 7944 4494 *Fax:* 020 7944 4499

Minister of State (Minister for Local Government and Regions) (Rt Hon **Hilary Armstrong** MP)
Responsibility for strategy for regional and local government; Local government; English regions; Regeneration; Social exclusion; Modernising government.
E-mail: hilary_armstrong@detr.gsi.gov.uk
Private Secretary: Tom Wechsler *Tel:* 020 7944 4488 *Fax:* 020 7944 4489

Minister of State (Minister for Housing, Planning and Construction) (**Nick Raynsford** MP)
Responsibility for housing and planning strategy; Planning; Housing; Construction.
E-mail: nick_raynsford@detr.gsi.gov.uk
Private Secretary: Matt Leach *Tel:* 020 7944 4344 *Fax:* 020 7944 4539

Parliamentary Under-Secretary of State (**Chris Mullin** MP)
Responsibility for aviation; Housing – HMO Licensing, Gypsies, ROSA and RAPS, Research, Private sector renewal and HATs; Water; Coastal policy; Waste – Implementation of strategy at local level; Countryside and wildlife; Trees, Zoos, CITEs, SSSIs, Access; Science and technology policy.
E-mail: chris_mullin@detr.gsi.gov.uk
Private Secretary: Chris Brain *Tel:* 020 7944 4324 *Fax:* 020 7944 4359

Parliamentary Under-Secretary of State (**Keith Hill** MP)
Responsibility for railways; Light rail, buses, taxis, cycling, walking, mobility; London; Local transport plans; Local roads; Marine and shipping; Maritime and Coastguard Agency; Freight policy; Environmental protection issues at local level; Transport aspects of social exclusion.
E-mail: keith_hill@detr.gsi.gov.uk
Private Secretary: Katharine Braddick *Tel:* 020 7944 4403 *Fax:* 020 7944 4521

Parliamentary Under-Secretary of State (**Lord Whitty**)
Responsibility for climate change, energy efficiency; Trunk roads; Road safety; Vehicle safety and environment; Highways Agency and DVO Agencies; British Waterways; Health and safety; European policy; Modernising government.
E-mail: larry_whitty@detr.gsi.gov.uk
Private Secretary: Jenni Borg *Tel:* 020 7944 4536 *Fax:* 020 7944 4538

Parliamentary Under-Secretary of State (**Beverley Hughes** MP)
Responsibility for local government; Planning; Regeneration; Regions; Construction; Tourism; Ordnance Survey; Green Minister.
E-mail: beverley_hughes@detr.gsi.gov.uk
Private Secretary: Rory O'Donnell *Tel:* 020 7944 4334 *Fax:* 020 7944 4339

Spokespersons in the House of Lords: Lord Macdonald, Lord Whitty, Baroness Farrington (Local Government).

FOREIGN AND COMMONWEALTH OFFICE

Secretary of State for Foreign and Commonwealth Affairs (Rt Hon **Robin Cook** MP)
Administration issues including honours, royal matters and the overall responsibility for the work of the department.
Private Secretary: Sherard Cowper-Coles *Tel:* 020 7270 2059 *Fax:* 020 7270 2144

Minister of State for Europe (**Keith Vaz** MP)
European Union Command: European Union Department (Internal), European Union Department (External), European Union Department (Bilateral), Common Foreign and Security Policy Department, Devolved Administrations Department; Wider Europe Command: Central and North West European Department, Eastern Department, Southern European Department; Deputy Political Director Command, Eastern Adriatic Department; (Most of) International Security Command: Security Policy Department, OSCE/Council of Europe Department; Migration and Visa Department.
Private Secretary: James Morrison *Tel:* 020 7270 3367 *Fax:* 020 7270 2988

Minister of State (**Peter Hain** MP)
Africa Command: Africa Department (Equatorial), Africa Department (Southern), Commonwealth Co-ordination Department; (Part of) Asia Command: South Asian Department; Middle East and North Africa Command: Middle East Department, Near East and North Africa Department; Global Issues Command: Environmental Policy Department, United Nations Department, Human Rights Policy Department, Aviation and Maritime Department; (Part of) International Security Command: Non-Proliferation Department; Chief Economist and Economic Relations Department; (Part of) Public Services Command.
Private Secretary: Robin Gwynn *Tel:* 020 7270 2090 *Fax:* 020 7270 3731

Minister of State (**John Battle** MP)
British Trade International; Invest in Britain Bureau (IBB); (Part of) Asia Command: South-East Asia Department, North-East Asia and Pacific Department, China and Hong Kong Department; (Part of) Americas Command: Latin America and Caribbean Department (Latin America only), Overseas Territories Department (Falklands and South Georgia only); Counter-Terrorism Policy Department; Drugs/International Crime Department; FCO Services Organisation: Technical Group, Estates Group, Support Group, Information Management Group, Consultancy Group, Resource Management Group, Conferences and Visits Group.
Private Secretary: Hugo Shorter *Tel:* 020 7270 2129 *Fax:* 020 7270 3539

Parliamentary Under-Secretary of State (**Baroness Scotland of Asthal** QC)
(Most of) Americas Command: Latin America and Caribbean Department (Caribbean only), North America Department, Overseas Territories Department (not Falklands and South Georgia); (Most of) Public Services Command: Consular Division, Cultural Relations Department, Information Department; Records and Historical Services; Personnel Command; Resources Command: Financial Policy Department, Resource Planning Department, Internal Audit Department, Financial Compliance Unit, Purchasing Directorate; Central Administration: Change Management Unit, Estates Strategy Unit, Security Strategy Unit, IT Strategy Unit.
Private Secretary: David Cairns *Tel:* 020 7270 2173 *Fax:* 020 7270 2148
Spokespersons in the House of Lords: Baroness Scotland, Baroness Ramsay.

DEPARTMENT OF HEALTH

Secretary of State for Health (Rt Hon **Alan Milburn** MP)
Overall responsibility for the work of the Department. Also has particular responsibility for: NHS finance – CSR preparation and follow-up; NHS resource allocation; NHS central budgets; performance monitoring; management costs and NHS efficiency; PFI and NHS capital; NHS Estates; strategic communications.
Principal Private Secretary: Janet Grauberg *Tel:* 020 7210 5157
E-mail: janet.grauberg@doh.gsi.gov.uk
Private Secretaries: Heather Rogers, Stephen Waring
Tel: 020 7210 5158/5540 *Fax:* 020 7210 5410

Minister of State (Rt Hon **John Denham** MP)
Responsibility for NHS strategy and planning; NHS structure/organisation; policy on service reconfiguration and mergers; commissioning; waiting times and lists; clinical quality including National Institute for Clinical Excellence (NICE) and Commissions for Health Improvement (CHI); primary care; general medical services; GP walk-in centres; human resources in the NHS; NHS pay and conditions; NHS Pensions Agency; medical training and education; medical workforce planning; equal opportunities; race equality; regional NHS casework for London; London Regional appointments; London Regional reconfiguration and mergers casework.
Private Secretary: Trish Fretten *Tel:* 020 7210 5103 *Fax:* 020 7210 5823
E-mail: trish.fretten@doh.gsi.gov.uk
Assistant Private Secretaries: Helen Kelman, James Skelly

Minister of State (**John Hutton** MP)
Responsibility for PSS resources; services for people with mental illness, special hospitals; homeless mentally ill; child and adolescent mental health services; Road Traffic (NHS Charges) Act; adult social services; services for elderly people (including NHS continuing care); long-term care; service for carers; NHS/PSS interface; Health Action Zones (HAZs); disabilities (including people with sensory and learning disabilities); children's services; adoption and fostering; child protection; Children Act 1989; children's residential care; children's secure units/juvenile offenders; voluntary sector (including Section 64 grant scheme); family issues; statistics; regional NHS casework for Northern and Yorkshire.
Private Secretary: James Adedeji *Tel:* 020 7210 5564 *Fax:* 020 7210 5548
E-mail: james.adedeji@doh.gsi.gov.uk
Assistant Private Secretaries: Bill Jobson, Anna McDevitt

Parliamentary Under-Secretary of State (Lords) (**Lord Hunt of Kings Heath** OBE)
Responsibility for health services development; Pharmaceutical industry (including Pharmaceutical Price Regulation Schemes (PPRS)); pharmaceutical services (including Prescribing and Drugs Bill); Medicines (including licensing); renal services; NSF for diabetes; prison health care; community pharmacy; nursing strategy (including recruitment and retention); professions allied to medicine; transplants; blood; research and development; spreading good practice; medical devices; procurement and NHS Supplies; general dental services; general optical services; counter-fraud services; defence medical services; contingency planning (civil defence); departmental management (including agencies); Regional casework for Eastern and North West.
Private Secretary: Emma De Zoete *Tel:* 020 7210 5826 *Fax:* 020 7210 5066
Assistant Private Secretaries: Sue Cartwright, Lee McGill

Parliamentary Under-Secretary of State (Minister for Public Health) (**Yvette Cooper** MP)

Ministerial responsibility for: public health, health promotion, prevention of ill-health, health inequalities, sure start, cancer, coronary heart disease, smoking, nutrition, alcohol, child health, maternity, infertility, health visiting, abortion, sexual health, HIV/AIDS, BSE, CJD, ethical issues, cloning, genetics and biotechnology, environment and health, radiation, fluoridation of water, vaccinations, communicable disease, regional casework for west Midlands and Trent

Private Secretary: Paul Macnaught *Tel:* 020 7210 5113 *Fax:* 020 7210 5534

E-mail: paul.macnaught@doh.gsi.gov.uk

Assistant Private Secretaries: Marsali Craig, Dominic Hardy

Parliamentary Under-Secretary of State (Minister for Health) (**Gisela Stuart** MP)

Responsibility for NHS Direct; Information Technology; Confidentiality; Finance, Drug Misuse; Food and Food Standards Agency; EU Health Council; World Health Organisation (WHO); Council of Europe; International Business; Independent Health Care Sector; SWRO Regional Casework; Winter Planning; Emergency Services; Critical Care; Complaints; NHS Charter; CHCs; Clinical Negligence; SERO Regional Casework.

Private Secretary: Kevin Holton *Tel:* 020 7210 5325 *Fax:* 020 7210 5616

Assistant Private Secretary: Jon Orr *Tel:* 020 7210 5328 *E-mail:* jon.orr@doh.gsi.gov.uk

Deputy Assistant Secretary: Daniel Scheffer *Tel:* 020 7210 5538

Spokesmen in the House of Lords: Lord Hunt of Kings Heath, Lord Burlison.

HOME OFFICE

Secretary of State for the Home Department (Rt Hon **Jack Straw** MP)

Overall responsibility for the work of the Department; royal matters; security; Public Expenditure Survey; emergency and terrorism issues.

E-mail: Jack.Straw@homeoffice.gsi.gov.uk

Principal Private Secretary: Ms Hilary Jackson *Tel:* 020 7273 4647 *Fax:* 020 7273 3965

Minister of State and Deputy Home Secretary (Rt Hon **Paul Boateng** MP)

Responsibility for Prisons; Probation; Coroners; Family policy; Active Community; Mentally disordered offenders.

E-mail: Paul.Boateng@homeoffice.gsi.gov.uk

Private Secretary: Simon Hayes *Tel:* 020 7273 3458 *Fax:* 020 7273 4090

Minister of State (**Charles Clarke** MP)

Responsibility for criminal policy; Crime reduction; Police policy; Organised and international crime, including IOCA Bill and Terrorism Bill.

E-mail: Charles.Clarke@homeoffice.gsi.gov.uk

Private Secretary: Jacquie Russell *Tel:* 020 7273 4606 *Fax:* 020 7273 2936

Minister of State (**Barbara Roche** MP)

Responsibility for immigration and asylum; Nationality; Passport Agency; EU matters.

E-mail: Barbara.Roche@homeoffice.gsi.gov.uk

Private Secretary: Cathy Hume *Tel:* 020 7273 2742 *Fax:* 020 7273 2043

Parliamentary Under-Secretary of State (**Mike O'Brien** MP)

Responsibility for constitutional issues; freedom of information; Fire and emergency planning; Race relations; Animal welfare; Liquor licensing; Gambling law; Data protection; Elections; Human rights.

E-mail: Mike.O'Brien@homeoffice.gsi.gov.uk

Private Secretary: Lee Bailey *Tel:* 020 7273 2500 *Fax:* 020 7273 2565

Parliamentary Under-Secretary of State (**Lord Bassam of Brighton**)

Responsibility for prisons and probation, supporting Paul Boateng; The Metropolitan Police, supporting the Home Secretary; Policy on police discipline, police complaints and police training in support of Charles Clarke; Measures to combat football hooliganism; Judicial co-operation and extradition; alleged wrongful convictions; bribery and corruption; obscenity and video classification; Channel Islands and Isle of Man. Responsible for all Home Office business in the House of Lords.

E-mail: Lord.Bassamofbrighton@homeoffice.gsi.gov.uk

Private Secretary: Paul Morrison *Tel:* 020 7273 2741 *Fax:* 020 7273 3094

Spokesmen in the House of Lords: Lord Bassam, Lord Bach.

DEPARTMENT FOR INTERNATIONAL DEVELOPMENT

Secretary of State for International Development (Rt Hon **Clare Short** MP)

Overall responsibility for the work of the Department; overseas development; certain overseas pensions.

Private Secretary: Chris Austin *Tel:* 020 7917 0419 *Fax:* 020 7917 0634
E-mail: c.austin@dfid.gov.uk

Parliamentary Under-Secretary of State (**George Foulkes** MP)

Assists the Secretary of State in her duties.

Private Secretary: Christine Atkinson *Tel:* 020 7917 0621 *Fax:* 020 7917 0634
E-mail: c.atkinson@dfid.gov.uk

Spokesperson in the House of Lords: Baroness Amos.

LAW OFFICERS' DEPARTMENTS

Attorney General (Rt Hon **Lord Williams of Mostyn** QC)

Has overall responsibility for the work of the Departments under his superintendence (the Treasury Solicitor's Department, the Crown Prosecution Service, the Serious Fraud Office and the Legal Secretariat to the Law Officers); has a specific statutory duty to superintend the discharge of their duties by the Director of Public Prosecutions (who heads the Crown Prosecution Service) and the Director of the Serious Fraud Office; oversees the functions of the Director of Public Prosecutions for Northern Ireland; is the Government's principal legal adviser; deals with questions of law arising on Bills, and with issues of legal policy; is concerned with all major international and domestic litigation involving the Government; has specific responsibilities for the enforcement of the criminal law.

Private Secretary: Rupert Cazalet *Tel:* 020 7271 2405 *Fax:* 020 7271 2432

Solicitor General (**Ross Cranston** QC MP)

Is responsible for such matters as the Attorney General delegates to him from time to time; presently takes the lead in the conduct of civil litigation and advice on civil law matters, including charity and family issues; proposed claims for public interest immunity; vexatious litigants; questions of European Community and international law.

Private Secretary: Rupert Cazalet *Tel:* 020 7271 2405 *Fax:* 020 7271 2432

LORD CHANCELLOR'S DEPARTMENT

Lord High Chancellor (Rt Hon **Lord Irvine of Lairg** QC)

The Lord Chancellor is responsible for promoting general reforms in the civil law, for the administration of the Supreme Court (Court of Appeal, High Court and Crown Court) and county courts in England and Wales. He also has ministerial responsibility for the locally administered Magistrates' Courts. He is responsible for advising the Crown on the appointment of judges and certain other officers and is himself responsible for the appointment of Masters and Registrars of the High Court and District Judges and magistrates. He is responsible for ensuring that letters patent and other formal documents are passed in the proper form under the Great Seal of the Realm, of which he is the custodian. The work in connection with this is carried out under his direction in the Office of the Clerk of the Crown in Chancery. He is also responsible for Legal Aid and has overall responsibility for the Public Record Office, HM Land Registry, the Public Trust Office and the Court Service, and the Northern Ireland Court Service.

Principal Private Secretary: Ms D Matthews *Tel:* 020 7219 6097 020 7219 4785 *Fax:* 020 7219 4711

Parliamentary Secretary (**David Lock** MP)

Contributes to all major policy decisions and is jointly responsible for the development of the Community Legal Service as Lead Minister. He is responsible for Legal Aid and Legal Services (including the Legal Aid Board); Community Legal Service; Civil Justice; Civil Law Development (including the Law Commission); Northern Ireland Court Service; International Policy; Public Record Office; Legal Services Ombudsman; Statutory Publications Office. Oral parliamentary questions are shared between the two Parliamentary Secretaries.

E-mail: dlock@lcdh.gsi.gov.uk
Private Secretary: Mel Charles *Tel:* 020 7210 8685 *Fax:* 020 7210 1472

Parliamentary Secretary (**Jane Kennedy** MP)

Contributes to all major policy decisions and is jointly responsible for the development of the Community Legal Service. She is responsible for Criminal Policy; Magistrates' Courts; Court Service; Family Policy; Human Rights; Administrative Justice; Devolution Issues; Public Trust Office; Land Registry; Immigration and Asylum Policy; Official Solicitor's Department; Council on Tribunals. Oral parliamentary questions are shared between the two Parliamentary Secretaries.

E-mail: jkennedy@lcdh.gsi.gov.uk

Private Secretary: Robert Moore *Tel:* 020 7210 8562 *Fax:* 020 7210 8620

Spokesmen in the House of Lords: Lord Irvine, Lord Bach.

LORD PRIVY SEAL
See Cabinet Office

NORTHERN IRELAND OFFICE

Secretary of State for Northern Ireland (Rt Hon **Peter Mandelson** MP)

Has responsibility for the work of the Northern Ireland Office matters not devolved to the Assembly. These include matters such as policing, security policy, prisons, criminal justice, international relations, taxation, national insurance, regulation of financial services and the regulation of telecommunications and broadcasting. The Secretary of State will represent Northern Ireland's interest in the United Kingdom Cabinet. Also responsible for the offices of the First and Deputy First Minister.

Private Secretary, Tel: 020 7210 6461 (London) 028 9052 8110/8107 (Belfast) *Fax:* 020 7210 0246 (London) 028 9052 8201 (Belfast)

Minister of State and Deputy to the Secretary of State (Rt Hon **Adam Ingram** MP)

Responsible for Security, Policing, Criminal Justice, Prisons, Victims and Financial and Personnel Issues (NIO).

Private Secretary, Tel: 020 7210 6498 (London) 028 9052 8127 (Belfast) *Fax:* 020 7210 6449 (London) 028 9052 8202 (Belfast)

Parliamentary Under-Secretary of State (**George Howarth** MP)

Responsible for Political Development, Relations with Devolved Institutions (including British Irish Council Members), Information Policy, Europe/Constitutional Issues, Equality and Human rights issues and Community Relations, Non-security legislative issues, legislative support on Patten.

Private Secretary, Tel: 020 7210 6488 (London) 028 9052 8128 (Belfast) *Fax:* 020 7210 6449 (London) 028 9052 8202 (Belfast)

Spokesperson in the House of Lords: Baroness Farrington of Ribbleton.

PRIVY COUNCIL OFFICE
www.privy-council.org.uk

President of the Council and Leader of the House of Commons (Rt Hon **Margaret Beckett** MP)

Responsible for the work of the Privy Council Office and, as Leader of the House of Commons, for the arrangement of Government business in the Commons and for planning and supervising the Government's legislative programme. She chairs the Ministerial Committees on the Queen's Speeches and Future Legislation, Legislation, Food Safety, and Health Strategy. Together with the Minister for the Cabinet Office, she acts as a spokesperson for the Government. She sits on a number of other Cabinet Committees and sub-committees.

Principal Private Secretary: Rupert Holderness *Tel:* 020 7210 1025 *Fax:* 020 7210 1075

Parliamentary Secretary (**Paddy Tipping** MP)

As Deputy Leader of the House of Commons, assists the President of the Council with her duties in supervising and arranging the Government's business in the Commons. He is also responsible for overseeing the effects of the Millennium date change problem.

Private Secretary: Fiona Butcher *Tel:* 020 7210 1021 *Fax:* 020 7210 1073

Assistant Private Secretary: Frances Slee *Tel:* 020 7210 1022

SCOTLAND OFFICE

Secretary of State for Scotland (Rt Hon Dr **John Reid** MP)
The main functions of the Secretary of State for Scotland are to represent Scottish interests within the UK Parliament in matters reserved to the UK Government, to ensure that the reserved policies of the UK Government are presented effectively in Scotland and to promote the devolution settlement for Scotland provided by the Scotland Act 1998.
E-mail: scottishsecretary@scotland.gsi.gov.uk
Principal Private Secretary: Jane Colquhoun *Tel:* 020 7270 6740 (London) 0131-244 9022 (Edinburgh) *Fax:* 020 7270 6815 (London) 0131-244 9028 (Edinburgh)
E-mail: ps/secretaryofstate@scotland.gsi.gov.uk

Minister of State (**Brian Wilson** MP)
Private Secretary: Fiona Hesling *Tel:* 020 7270 6806 (London) 0131-244 9031 (Edinburgh)
Fax: 020 7270 6703 (London) 0131-244 9028 (Edinburgh) *E-mail:* ps/mrwilson@scotland.gsi.gov.uk

Advocate General for Scotland (Dr **Lynda Clark** QC MP)
The Advocate General is a Law Officer and adviser to the UK Government on legal and constitutional matters in Scotland. Her office provides legal services to UK Departments in Scotland.
Private Secretary: Claire Keggie *Tel:* 020 7270 6720 (London) 0131-244 9033 (Edinburgh)
Fax: 020 7270 6813 (London) 0131-244 9028 (Edinburgh)
E-mail: ps/advocategeneral@scotland.gsi.gov.uk *Legal Secretary:* George Duke *Tel:* 020 7270 6810

Spokesperson in the House of Lords: Baroness Ramsay.

DEPARTMENT OF SOCIAL SECURITY

Secretary of State for Social Security (Rt Hon **Alistair Darling** MP)
Has overall responsibility for all Social Security matters; public expenditure issues; handling of all major issues.
Principal Private Secretary: Neil Couling *Tel:* 020 7238 0654 *Fax:* 020 7238 0661
Private Secretaries: Dan Coughlin *Tel:* 020 7238 0656 David Eatock *Tel:* 020 7238 0655
Assistant Private Secretary: Jo Littleton *Tel:* 020 7238 0657

Minister of State for Social Security (Rt Hon **Jeff Rooker** MP)
Deputy to the Secretary of State across the board (including operations); management of legislation in the Commons; pensions review, state pensions, occupational and personal pensions, National Insurance contributions review; older people; long-term care policy development; fraud/methods of payment.
Private Secretary: Denise Whitehead *Tel:* 020 7238 0671 *Fax:* 020 7238 0675
Assistant Private Secretary: Robert Sanguinazzi *Tel:* 020 7238 0672

Parliamentary Under-Secretary of State (Rt Hon **Baroness Hollis of Heigham**)
Responsibility for family policy; Child Benefit and One Parent Benefit; lone parents; child support; Child Support Agency; industrial injuries; compensation recovery; war pensions; War Pensions Agency; management of legislation in the Lords; Citizen's Charter.
Private Secretary: Mary Curran *Tel:* 020 7238 0678 *Fax:* 020 7238 0682
Assistant Private Secretaries: Judith Hartley *Tel:* 020 7238 0679 Michael Coombs
Tel: 020 7238 0681

Parliamentary Under-Secretary of State (**Angela Eagle** MP)
Responsibility for Jobseeker's Allowance/Welfare to Work; Income Support; Family Credit; Housing Benefit; Council Tax Benefit; poverty/low income; social exclusion; Benefits Agency; active modern service; decision-making and appeals; Social Fund; Widows Benefit.
Private Secretary: Chris Jennings *Tel:* 020 7238 0690 *Fax:* 020 7238 0845
Assistant Private Secretaries: Deborah Topping *Tel:* 020 7238 0693 Stefan Penney
Tel: 020 7238 0691 *Diary Secretary:* Martyn Henderson *Tel:* 020 7238 0692

Parliamentary Under-Secretary of State (**Hugh Bayley** MP)
Responsibility for Anti-poverty strategy, income support, Incapacity Benefit; Disability Living Allowance; Attendance Allowance; Motability; carers; Invalid Care Allowance; vaccine damage; deregulation; Statutory Sick and Maternity Pay; War Pensions; management of Department of Social Security headquarters; DSS green issues; devolution issues; Independent Living Fund.
Private Secretary: Tricia Griffiths *Tel:* 020 7238 0684 *Fax:* 020 7238 0687
Assistant Private Secretaries: James Newman *Tel:* 020 7238 0685 Ms Chris McCoy *Tel:* 020 7238 0686

Spokespersons in the House of Lords: Baroness Hollis, Baroness Amos.

DEPARTMENT OF TRADE AND INDUSTRY

Secretary of State for Trade and Industry (Rt Hon **Stephen Byers** MP)
Overall responsibility for the DTI, its agencies and Export Credits Guarantee Department (ECGD). Cabinet Minister responsible for science.
E-mail: tlo.byers@tlo.dti.gov.uk
Principal Private Secretary: Bernadette Kelly *Tel:* 020 7215 5621 *Fax:* 020 7215 5468
Private Secretaries: Dr Brooke Hoskins *Tel:* 020 7215 5622 Damian Nussbaum *Tel:* 020 7215 5623

Minister of State for Energy and Competitiveness in Europe (Rt Hon **Helen Liddell** MP)
Responsible for energy including sponsorship of the oil and gas industries, European Single Market, economic reform and enlargement, and business preparation for the Euro.
E-mail: tlo.liddell@tlo.dti.gov.uk
Senior Private Secretary: Richard Riley *Tel:* 020 7215 5109 *Fax:* 020 7215 5645

Minister for Trade (Rt Hon **Richard Caborn** MP)
Responsible for trade policy, Export Credits Guarantee Department (ECGD), British Trade International, inward investment and regional policy and export projects.
E-mail: tlo.caborn@tlo.dti.gov.uk *Private Secretary:* Graeme Cornell *Tel:* 020 7215 5501

Minister of State, Minister for Small Business and e-Commerce (**Patricia Hewitt** MP)
Responsible for small firms, e-commerce and the information society, industry (supported by Alan Johnson), environment, Radiocommunications Agency.
E-mail: tlo.hewitt@tlo.dti.gov.uk *Private Secretary:* Gaynor Jeffrey *Tel:* 020 7215 5144
Assistant Private Secretary: Joanna Smith

Parliamentary Under-Secretary of State for Consumers and Corporate Affairs (Dr **Kim Howells** MP)
Responsible for competition, consumer affairs, company law, corporate governance, company investigations, Insolvency Service, Patent Office, Companies House, NWML, Export Licensing.
E-mail: tlo.howells@tlo.dti.gov.uk
Private Secretary: Gareth Maybury *Tel:* 020 7215 5568 *Fax:* 020 7215 5560

Parliamentary Under-Secretary of State for Competitiveness (**Alan Johnson** MP)
Responsible for industry (with Patricia Hewitt). Responsibility for hemicals and biotechnology (CB), Engineering Industries Directorate (EID); Employment relations and Post Office.
E-mail: tlo.johnson@tlo.dti.gov.uk *Private Secretary:* Simon Lancaster *Tel:* 020 7215 6202

Parliamentary Under-Secretary of State for Science and Innovation (**Lord Sainsbury of Turville**)
Responsible for science, Research Councils, innovation, design and space.
E-mail: sainsbury.tlo@tlo.dti.gov.uk
Private Secretary: Beccy Eggleton *Tel:* 020 7215 5624 *Fax:* 020 7215 5410

Spokesmen in the House of Lords: Lord Sainsbury of Turville, Lord McIntosh of Haringey.

TREASURY

Prime Minister (Rt Hon **Tony Blair** MP)
First Lord of the Treasury.

Chancellor of the Exchequer (Rt Hon **Gordon Brown** MP)
As Second Lord is its Ministerial head and has overall responsibility for the work of the Treasury.
Principal Private Secretary: Tom Scholar *Tel:* 020 7270 5004 *Fax:* 020 7270 4580
Private Secretaries: James Papps, Nicholas Joicey

Chief Secretary (Rt Hon **Andrew Smith** MP)
Responsibility for public expenditure planning and control (including local authority and nationalised industry finance); Value for money in the public services, including Public Service Agreements; Presentations of economic policy and economic briefings; Welfare reform; Public sector pay, including parliamentary pay, allowances and superannuation; Devolution; Strategic oversight of banking, financial services and insurance; PSX (Public services and expenditure), QFL (Forward Legislation), LG (local government), HS (home and social affairs) and EA (economic affairs) committees; Departmental Investment Strategies including Capital Modernisation/fund and Invest to Save budget; Public/Private Partnerships including Private Finance initiative; Procurement Policy; Resource Accounting and Budgeting.
Private Secretary: Deborah Nickerson *Tel:* 020 7270 4339 *Fax:* 020 7451 7600
E-mail: deborah.nickerson@hm-treasury.gov.uk

Paymaster General (**Dawn Primarolo** MP)
Responsibility for Inland Revenue, Customs and Excise and the Treasury and with overall responsibility for tax and the Finance Bill, personal taxation, NI contributions, tax credits, business taxation, including corporation tax, capital gains tax, inheritance tax, VAT; European and International tax issues.
Private Secretary: Sarah Knight *Tel:* 020 7270 4349 *Fax:* 020 7270 5179
E-mail: sarah.knight@hm-treasury.gov.uk

Financial Secretary (**Stephen Timms** MP)
Responsibility for Growth, with responsibility for the growth unit and productivity agenda; Small firms and venture capital; Science, Research and Development; Welfare to Work issues; Competition and deregulation policy; Export Credit; Customs and Excise taxes, except VAT and road fuel; North Sea Taxation; Support to paymaster General on the Finance Bill; Parliamentary financial business, PAC, NAO; LEG Committee (Current Legislation); Support to the Chief Secretary on the Financial Service Markets Bill.
Private Secretary: Chris Martin *Tel:* 020 7270 4340 *Fax:* 020 7270 5131
E-mail: chris.martin@hm-treasury.gov.uk

Economic Secretary (**Melanie Johnson** MP)
Responsibility for Banking, financial services and insurance and support to the Chief Secretary on the Finance Services and Markets Bill; Foreign exchange reserves and debt management policy; Support to the Chancellor on EU and International issues; Responsibility for National Savings, the Debt Management Office, National Investment and Loans Office, Office of National Statistics, Royal Mint and the Government Actuary's Department; Environmental issues including 'green' taxes and other environmental economic instruments; Taxation of company cars and road fuel; Vehicle excise duty; Financial services tax issues (eg ISA, stamp duty, pensions); Support to the Paymaster General on the Finance Bill; ESOPs; Treasury interest in general accountancy issues; Support to the Chief Secretary on Resource Accounting and Budgeting; Charities and Charity taxation; Women's issues.
Private Secretary: Jo-Anne Daniels *Tel:* 020 7270 4350 *Fax:* 020 7270 5419

Spokesman in the House of Lords: Lord McIntosh of Haringey.

THE WALES OFFICE
(Office of the Secretary of State for Wales)

Secretary of State for Wales (Rt Hon **Paul Murphy** MP)
The Office of the Secretary of State has responsibility for UK-wide policy. The Secretary of State is also responsible for industry; Economic development; Agriculture, transport and planning issues.
Principal Private Secretary: Simon Morris *Tel:* 020 7270 0550
E-mail: simon.morris@wales.gsi.gov.uk
Assistant Private Secretary: Ms Cherie Jones *Tel:* 020 7270 0538 *Fax:* 020 7270 0568

Parliamentary Under-Secretary of State (**David Hanson** MP)
Responsibility for education; Health; Local government; Environment.
Private Secretary: Joanna Salway *Tel:* 020 7270 0569 *E-mail:* jo.salway@wales.gsi.gov.uk *Head of Office of the Secretary of State for Wales:* Alison Jackson *Tel:* 020 7270 0558
Fax: 020 7270 0588

Spokesperson in the House of Lords: Baroness Farrington.

Ministerial salaries

Figures are as set on 1 April 2000 and are in £s.
* including MP's salary of £48,371
† Some ministers do not draw the full salary to which they are entitled.

	Ministerial salary		Total salary*	
	Actual	Entitlement†	Actual	Entitlement†
House of Commons				
Prime Minister	64,580	110,287	112,951	158,658
Cabinet Minister	48,516	66,172	96,887	114,543
Government Chief Whip	48,516	66,172	96,887	114,543
Minister of State	34,326		82,697	
Parliamentary Under Secretary of State	26,053		74,424	
Solicitor General	57,656		106,027	
Advocate General	57,656		106,027	
Government Deputy Chief Whip	34,326		82,697	
Government Whip	22,090		70,461	
Assistant Government Whip	22,090		70,461	
Leader of the Opposition	60,659		109,030	
Opposition Chief Whip	34,326		82,697	
Deputy Chief Opposition Whip	22,090		70,461	
Assistant Opposition Whip	22,090		70,461	
Speaker	66,172		114,543	
Deputy Speaker (Chairman of Ways and Means)	34,326		82,697	
Deputy Speakers	30,168		78,539	
House of Lords				
Cabinet Minister	72,729	85,983		
Minister of State	66,294			
Parliamentary Under Secretary of State	57,244			
Lord Chancellor	167,760			
Attorney General	90,125			
Government Chief Whip	66,294			
Government Deputy Chief Whip	57,244			
Government Whip	52,645			
Leader of the Opposition	57,244			
Opposition Chief Whip	52,645			
Chairman of Committees	66,294			
Principal Deputy Chairman of Committees	61,773			

Government Whips

HOUSE OF LORDS

Chief Whip (Captain of the Honourable Corps of the Gentlemen-at-Arms)	Rt Hon **Lord Carter**
Deputy Chief Whip (Captain of The Queen's Bodyguard of the Yeoman of the Guard)	**Lord McIntosh of Haringey**
Lord in Waiting	**Lord Burlison** DL
Lord in Waiting	**Lord Bach**
Baronesses in Waiting:	**Baroness Farrington of Ribbleton, Baroness Ramsay of Cartvale, The Baroness Amos**

HOUSE OF COMMONS

Chief Whip (Parliamentary Secretary to the Treasury)	Rt Hon **Ann Taylor** MP
Deputy Chief Whip (Treasurer of HM Household)	**Keith Bradley** MP
Whips	
(Comptroller of HM Household) *Pairing Whip*	**Tommy McAvoy** MP
(Vice-Chamberlain of HM Household) *HM Treasury, East Midlands*	**Graham Allen** MP
(Lords Commissioners of HM Treasury) *Culture, Media and Sport, Northern Ireland, London Bill, London*	**Jim Dowd** MP
Environment, Transport and the Regions, West Midlands	**Bob Ainsworth** MP
Health, South East, South West	**David Jamieson** MP
Education and Employment, Committee Whip, Eastern	**Clive Betts** MP
Trade and Industry, North West	**Greg Pope** MP
Assistant Whips	
Defence, International Development, North East	**David Clelland** MP
Social Security, West Yorkshire	**Kevin Hughes** MP
Home Affairs, North West	**Mike Hall** MP
Scotland, Agriculture	**Anne McGuire** MP
Cabinet Office, South Yorkshire	**Gerry Sutcliffe** MP
Foreign Affairs, London	**Tony McNulty** MP
Wales	**Don Touhig** MP

Parliamentary Private Secretaries

THE PRIME MINISTER
Rt Hon Tony Blair MP   Bruce Grocott MP

AGRICULTURE, FISHERIES AND FOOD
Rt Hon Nick Brown MP   Ruth Kelly MP
Rt Hon Joyce Quin MP   Brian Jenkins MP
Baroness Hayman   Bob Blizzard MP

CABINET OFFICE
Minister for the Cabinet Office and
Chancellor of the Duchy of Lancaster
Rt Hon Dr Mo Mowlam MP   Margaret Moran MP
Rt Hon Ian McCartney MP   Frank Doran MP
Lord Falconer of Thoroton QC   Christopher Leslie MP

CULTURE, MEDIA AND SPORT
Rt Hon Chris Smith MP   Fiona Mactaggart MP

DEFENCE
Rt Hon Geoffrey Hoon MP   Sylvia Heal MP
John Spellar MP   David Watts MP
Baroness Symons of Vernham Dean   Gillian Merron MP

EDUCATION AND EMPLOYMENT
Rt Hon David Blunkett MP   Jean Corston MP
                                        Alan Whitehead MP
Rt Hon Tessa Jowel MP (Employment)   Jeff Ennis MP
Rt Hon Estelle Morris MP (Education)   Rachel Squire MP
Baroness Blackstone   Alan Whitehead MP

ENVIRONMENT, TRANSPORT AND THE REGIONS
Rt Hon John Prescott MP   John Heppell MP
   (Deputy Prime Minister)
Rt Hon Lord Macdonald of Tradeston   Phil Woolas MP
   (Transport)
Rt Hon Michael Meacher MP (Environment) Terry Rooney MP
Rt Hon Hilary Armstrong MP   Sally Keeble MP
Nick Raynsford MP   Phil Hope MP

FOREIGN AND COMMONWEALTH OFFICE
Rt Hon Robin Cook MP   Ken Purchase MP
Keith Vaz MP   ⎧ Dennis MacShane MP
Peter Hain MP   ⎨ Caroline Flint MP
John Battle MP   ⎩ Rosemary McKenna CBE MP

HEALTH
Rt Hon Alan Milburn MP   Jim Fitzpatrick MP
Rt Hon John Denham MP   Paul Goggins MP
John Hutton MP   Maria Eagle MP

HOME OFFICE
Rt Hon Jack Straw MP
Rt Hon Paul Boateng MP
Charles Clarke MP
Barbara Roche MP

Colin Pickthall MP
Angela Smith MP
Gareth R Thomas MP
Tom Levitt MP

INTERNATIONAL DEVELOPMENT
Rt Hon Clare Short MP

Dennis Turner MP

LAW OFFICERS
Attorney General: Rt Hon Lord Williams
    of Mostyn QC
Solicitor General: Ross Cranston QC MP

} Michael Jabez Foster MP

LEADER OF THE HOUSE
Lords: and Minister for Women
Rt Hon Baroness Jay of Paddington
Commons: Rt Hon Margaret Beckett MP

Eric Martlew MP
Ivor Caplin MP

LORD CHANCELLOR'S DEPARTMENT
Rt Hon Lord Irvine of Lairg QC

Bridget Prentice MP
Paul Clark MP

NORTHERN IRELAND OFFICE
Rt Hon Peter Mandelson MP
Rt Hon Adam Ingram MP

Helen Jackson MP
Desmond Browne MP

SCOTLAND OFFICE
Rt Hon Dr John Reid MP
Brian Wilson MP

Frank Roy MP
Sandra Osborne MP

SOCIAL SECURITY
Rt Hon Alistair Darling MP
Rt Hon Jeff Rooker MP

Ann Coffey MP
Richard Burden MP

TRADE AND INDUSTRY
Rt Hon Stephen Byers MP
Rt Hon Helen Liddell MP
Rt Hon Richard Caborn MP
Patricia Hewitt MP

Ivan Lewis MP
Derek Twigg MP
Ben Chapman MP
Anne Campbell MP

TREASURY
Rt Hon Gordon Brown MP
Rt Hon Andrew Smith MP
Dawn Primarolo MP (Paymaster General)
Stephen Timms MP

John Healey MP
Joan Ryan MP
Chris Pond MP
Vernon Coaker MP

WALES OFFICE
Rt Hon Paul Murphy MP

Nick Ainger MP

Special Advisers

THE PRIME MINISTER
Rt Hon Tony Blair MP

Policy Unit: David Miliband (Head of Unit), Andrew Adonis, Brian Hackland, Robert Hill, Peter Hyman, Roger Liddle, Liz Lloyd, Geoffrey Norris, Carey Oppenheim, James Purnell, Ed Richards, Derek Scott

AGRICULTURE, FISHERIES AND FOOD
Rt Hon Nick Brown MP

Kieran Simpson
Jack Thurston

CABINET OFFICE
Minister for the Cabinet Office and
Chancellor of the Duchy of Lancaster
Rt Hon Dr Mo Mowlam MP

Nigel Warner
Andrew Lappin

CHIEF WHIP'S OFFICE
Rt Hon Ann Taylor MP

Ian McKenzie
Sue Jackson

CULTURE, MEDIA AND SPORT
Rt Hon Chris Smith MP

Andy Burnham
Ruth MacKenzie

DEFENCE
Rt Hon Geoffrey Hoon MP

Alasdair McGowan
Andrew Hood

EDUCATION AND EMPLOYMENT
Rt Hon David Blunkett MP

Conor Ryan
Tom Engel
Nick Pearce
Leala Padmanabhan

ENVIRONMENT, TRANSPORT AND THE REGIONS
Rt Hon John Prescott MP

Joe Irvin
Joan Hammell

Rt Hon Hilary Armstrong MP
Chris Mullin MP
Rt Hon Lord Macdonald of Tradeston

David Wilson
Paul Hackett
Adrian Long

FOREIGN AND COMMONWEALTH OFFICE
Rt Hon Robin Cook MP

David Clark
Michael Williams
David Mathieson

HEALTH
Rt Hon Alan Milburn MP

Simon Stevens
Darren Murphy

HOME OFFICE
Rt Hon Jack Straw MP

Ed Owen
Justin Russell

INTERNATIONAL DEVELOPMENT
Rt Hon Clare Short MP   David Mepham
                                         Susannah Cox

LEADER OF THE HOUSE
Lords:
Rt Hon Baroness Jay of Paddington   Clare Cozens
                                         Ms Jo Gibbons
Commons: Rt Hon Margaret Beckett MP   Nicci Collins
                                         Sheila Watson

LORD CHANCELLOR
Rt Hon Lord Irvine of Lairg QC   Garry Hart

NORTHERN IRELAND OFFICE
Rt Hon Peter Mandelson MP   To be confirmed

SCOTLAND OFFICE
Rt Hon Dr John Reid MP   Richard Olszewski
                                         Mike Elrick
                                         David Whilton

SCOTTISH EXECUTIVE
First Minister's Office   Neil Gillam
                                         Sharon Ward

SOCIAL SECURITY
Rt Hon Alistair Darling MP   Andrew Maugham
                                         Elsbeth Johnson

TRADE AND INDUSTRY
Rt Hon Stephen Byers MP   Dan Corry
                                         Ms Jo Moore

TREASURY
Rt Hon Gordon Brown MP   Ed Balls (Chief Senior Economic Adviser)
                                         Ian Austin
                                         Sue Nye
                                         Chris Wales
Rt Hon Andrew Smith MP   Edward Milliband
                                         Paul Andrew

WALES OFFICE
Rt Hon Paul Murphy MP   Andrew Bold
                                         Adrian McMenamin

NATIONAL ASSEMBLY FOR WALES
First Secretary's Office   Kevin Brennan
    Special Advisers to the Cabinet   Paul Griffiths
                                         Dr Mark Drakeford
                                         Dr Rachel Jones
                                         Graham Vilder

Ministerial Committees of the Cabinet

Cabinet Committees are established by the Prime Minister to enable the Cabinet to deal more efficiently with the large volume of government business.

All Cabinet Committees are chaired by the Prime Minister or a senior Cabinet minister and will have a number of Cabinet ministers as members. Some are permanent Committees while others are set up to deal with particular issues as they arise.

Cabinet Committees carry out the bulk of Cabinet work and the decisions they take have the authority of full Cabinet. If a Committee cannot agree on an issue it will be sent to the full Cabinet for a final decision.

Some Cabinet Committees have Sub-Committees which do not usually take final decisions on policy, but can enable important discussion of those issues which range across government departments.

Economic Affairs

Chancellor of the Exchequer *(Chair)*
Deputy Prime Minister and Secretary of State for the Environment, Transport and the Regions
Secretary of State for the Home Department
Secretary of State for Education and Employment
President of the Council and Leader of the House of Commons
Chief Whip
Secretary of State for Culture, Media and Sport
Minister for the Cabinet Office and Chancellor of the Duchy of Lancaster
Secretary of State for Social Security
Minister of Agriculture, Fisheries and Food
Secretary of State for Trade and Industry
Secretary of State for Health
Secretary of State for Scotland
Secretary of State for Wales
Secretary of State for Northern Ireland
Chief Secretary, HM Treasury
Minister for Transport
Minister of State, Cabinet Office

Other Ministers are invited to attend for items in which they have a departmental interest. The Chief Scientific Adviser attends for issues relating to science and technology

Terms of Reference
To consider issues relating to the Government's economic policies

Energy Policy Sub-Committee

Chancellor of the Exchequer *(Chair)*
Deputy Prime Minister and Secretary of State for the Environment, Transport and the Regions
Secretary of State for Trade and Industry
Financial Secretary, HM Treasury
Minister of State, Foreign and Commonwealth Office
Minister of State, Cabinet Office
Minister of State, Department of Trade and Industry
Minister of State, Scotland Office
Parliamentary Under-Secretary of State, Wales Office

Terms of Reference
To consider the principles and objectives which should underlie Great Britain's energy strategy; and make recommendations for an energy strategy to the Ministerial Committee on Economic Affairs

Productivity and Competitiveness Sub-Committee

Chancellor of the Exchequer *(Chair)*
Deputy Prime Minister and Secretary of State for the Environment, Transport and the Regions
Secretary of State for the Home Department
Secretary of State for Education and Employment
Secretary of State for Culture, Media and Sport
Minister for the Cabinet Office and Chancellor of the Duchy of Lancaster
Minister of Agriculture, Fisheries and Food
Secretary of State for Trade and Industry
Secretary of State for Scotland
Secretary of State for Wales
Secretary of State for Northern Ireland
Chief Secretary, HM Treasury
Minister of State, Foreign and Commonwealth Office
Minister of State, Cabinet Office

Terms of Reference

To consider measures to improve the productivity and competitiveness of the United Kingdom economy

Welfare to Work Sub-Committee

Chancellor of the Exchequer *(Chair)*
Secretary of State for Education and Employment
Secretary of State for Social Security
Secretary of State for Scotland
Secretary of State for Wales
Secretary of State for Northern Ireland
Chief Secretary, HM Treasury
Minister of State, Department of the Environment, Transport and the Regions
Financial Secretary, HM Treasury
Minister of State, Home Office
Minister of State, Department for Education and Employment
Minister of State, Cabinet Office

The Secretary of State for Health also receives papers. Other Ministers are invited to attend for items in which they have a departmental interest

Terms of Reference

To develop policies to get people from welfare to work and to report as necessary to the Ministerial Committee on Economic Affairs

Public Services and Public Expenditure

Chancellor of the Exchequer *(Chair)*
Lord Chancellor
President of the Council and Leader of the House of Commons
Chief Whip
Minister for the Cabinet Office and Chancellor of the Duchy of Lancaster
Secretary of State for Social Security
Lord Privy Seal, Leader of the House of Lords and Minister for Women
Chief Secretary, HM Treasury
Minister of State, Cabinet Office

Other Ministers are invited to attend for matters in which they have a departmental interest

Terms of Reference

To monitor progress against public service agreements, to review public expenditure allocations and make recommendations to the Cabinet

The Environment

Deputy Prime Minister and Secretary of State for the Environment, Transport and the Regions
 (Chair)
Chancellor of the Exchequer
Secretary of State for Foreign and Commonwealth Affairs
President of the Council and Leader of the House of Commons
Chief Whip
Secretary of State for Culture, Media and Sport
Minister for the Cabinet Office and Chancellor of the Duchy of Lancaster
Secretary of State for International Development
Minister of Agriculture, Fisheries and Food
Secretary of State for Trade and Industry
Secretary of State for Health
Secretary of State for Scotland
Secretary of State for Wales
Secretary of State for Northern Ireland
Chief Secretary, HM Treasury
Minister for Transport
Minister of State, Department of the Environment, Transport and the Regions

The Secretary of State for Social Security and the Secretary of State for Education and Employment also receive papers. They and other Ministers are invited to attend as necessary. The Chief Scientific Adviser attends for issues relating to science and technology

Terms of Reference
To consider environmental policies and to co-ordinate those on sustainable development

Local Government

Deputy Prime Minister and Secretary of State for the Environment, Transport and the Regions
 (Chair)
Chancellor of the Exchequer
Lord Chancellor
Secretary of State for the Home Department
Secretary of State for Education and Employment
President of the Council and Leader of the House of Commons
Chief Whip
Secretary of State for Culture, Media and Sport
Minister for the Cabinet Office and Chancellor of the Duchy of Lancaster
Secretary of State for Social Security
Secretary of State for Trade and Industry
Secretary of State for Health
Secretary of State for Wales
Chief Secretary, HM Treasury
Minister for Transport
Minister of State, Department of the Environment, Transport and the Regions
Minister of State, Cabinet Office

Other Ministers are invited to attend for items in which they have a departmental interest

Terms of Reference
To consider issues affecting local government, including the annual allocation of resources

London Sub-Committee

Deputy Prime Minister and Secretary of State for the Environment, Transport and the Regions *(Chair)*
Minister for Transport
Paymaster General, HM Treasury
Minister of State, Department for Education and Employment
Minister of State, Cabinet Office
Minister of State, Department of Health
Parliamentary Under-Secretary of State, Department of the Environment, Transport and the Regions
Parliamentary Under-Secretary of State, Home Office
Parliamentary Under-Secretary of State, Department for Culture, Media and Sport
Parliamentary Under-Secretary of State, Department of Social Security
Parliamentary Under-Secretary of State, Department of Trade and Industry

Terms of Reference
To co-ordinate the Government's policies on London, and report as necessary to the Ministerial
Committee on Local Government and the Ministerial Committee on Devolution Policy

Biotechnology and Genetic Modification Group

Minister for the Cabinet Office and Chancellor of the Duchy of Lancaster *(Chair)*
Minister of State, Department of the Environment, Transport and the Regions
Minister of State, Foreign and Commonwealth Office
Minister of State, Cabinet Office
Minister of State, Ministry of Agriculture, Fisheries and Food
Minister of State, Department of Trade and Industry
Minister of State, Scotland Office
Economic Secretary, HM Treasury
Parliamentary Under-Secretary of State, Home Office
Parliamentary Under-Secretary of State, Department for International Development
Parliamentary Under-Secretary of State, Department of Trade and Industry
Parliamentary Under-Secretary, Department of Health
Parliamentary Under-Secretary of State, Wales Office
Parliamentary Under-Secretary of State, Northern Ireland Office

The Chief Scientific Adviser also attends

Terms of Reference
To consider issues relating to biotechnology, in particular those arising from genetic modification

Better Government Group

Minister for the Cabinet Office and Chancellor of the Duchy of Lancaster *(Chair)*
Secretary of State for the Home Department
Secretary of State for Education and Employment
Secretary of State for Social Security
Lord Privy Seal, Leader of the House of Lords and Minister for Women
Secretary of State for Trade and Industry
Secretary of State for Health
Secretary of State for Wales
Chief Secretary, HM Treasury
Minister of State, Department of the Environment, Transport and the Regions
Minister of State, Foreign and Commonwealth Office
Minister of State, Cabinet Office
Minister of State, Cabinet Office
Minister of State, Scotland Office
Minister of State, Northern Ireland Office
Parliamentary Under-Secretary of State, Lord Chancellor's Department
Parliamentary Under-Secretary of State, Department for Culture, Media and Sport

Terms of Reference
To develop the Government's programme for improving the quality, coherence and responsiveness of
public services and to oversee its implementation

Health Performance and Expenditure

Prime Minister *(Chair)*
Chancellor of the Exchequer
Secretary of State for Social Security
Lord Privy Seal, Leader of the House of Lords and Minister for Women
Secretary of State for Health
Chief Secretary, HM Treasury
Minister of State, Cabinet Office

Outside experts will be invited to attend as necessary

Terms of Reference
To consider proposals for improving the performance of the National Health Service in England, taking account of the scope for improved inspection, information and management systems; and to agree a revised Public Service Agreement for the Department of Health

Home and Social Affairs

Deputy Prime Minister and Secretary of State for the Environment, Transport and the Regions *(Chair)*
Chancellor of the Exchequer
Lord Chancellor
Secretary of State for the Home Department
Secretary of State for Education and Employment
President of the Council and Leader of the House of Commons
Chief Whip
Secretary of State for Culture, Media and Sport
Minister for the Cabinet Office and Chancellor of the Duchy of Lancaster
Secretary of State for Social Security
Minister of Agriculture, Fisheries and Food
Lord Privy Seal, Leader of the House of Lords and Minister for Women
Secretary of State for Trade and Industry
Secretary of State for Health
Secretary of State for Scotland
Secretary of State for Wales
Secretary of State for Northern Ireland
Chief Secretary, HM Treasury
Minister for Transport
Minister of State, Cabinet Office

The Attorney General, Advocate General and Chief Government Whip in the Lords also receive papers. They and others are invited to attend as necessary

Terms of Reference
To consider issues of home and social policy

Health Strategy Sub-Committee

President of the Council and Leader of the House of Commons *(Chair)*
Secretary of State for International Development
Secretary of State for Health
Minister of State, Department of the Environment, Transport and the Regions
Minister of State, Home Office
Minister of State, Department for Education and Employment
Minister of State, Ministry of Agriculture, Fisheries and Food
Parliamentary Under-Secretary of State, Department of the Environment, Transport and the Regions
Economic Secretary, HM Treasury
Parliamentary Under-Secretary of State, Department of Social Security
Parliamentary Under-Secretary of State, Department of Trade and Industry

The Chief Medical Officer is in attendance. The Secretary of State for Wales also receives papers and is invited to attend as necessary. Other Ministers are invited to attend for items in which they have a departmental interest

Terms of Reference
To oversee the development, implementation and monitoring of the Government's health strategy; and to report as necessary to the Ministerial Committee on Home and Social Affairs

Drug Misuse Sub-Committee

Minister for the Cabinet Office and Chancellor of the Duchy of Lancaster *(Chair)*
Secretary of State for International Development
Solicitor General
Paymaster General, HM Treasury
Minister of State, Foreign and Commonwealth Office
Minister of State, Home Office
Minister of State, Cabinet Office
Minister of State, Department of Health
Minister of State, Scotland Office
Minister of State, Northern Ireland Office
Minister of State, Ministry of Defence
Parliamentary Under-Secretary of State, Department for Education and Employment
Parliamentary Under-Secretary of State, Department for Culture, Media and Sport
Parliamentary Under-Secretary of State, Wales Office

The Parliamentary Under-Secretary of State, Department of the Environment, Transport and the Regions also receives papers and may be invited to attend as appropriate

Terms of Reference
To co-ordinate the Government's national and international policies for tackling drugs misuse, and report as necessary to the Ministerial Committee on Home and Social Affairs

Women's Issues Sub-Committee

Lord Privy Seal, Leader of the House of Lords and Minister for Women *(Chair)*
Minister for the Cabinet Office and Chancellor of the Duchy of Lancaster
Secretary of State for International Development
Minister of State, Home Office
Minister of State, Department for Education and Employment
Minister of State, Scotland Office
Parliamentary Under-Secretary of State, Department of the Environment, Transport and the Regions
Economic Secretary, HM Treasury
Parliamentary Under-Secretary of State, Department of Social Security
Parliamentary Under-Secretary of State, Department of Trade and Industry
Parliamentary Under-Secretary of State, Department of Health
Parliamentary Under-Secretary of State, Wales Office
Parliamentary Under-Secretary of State, Northern Ireland Office

Terms of Reference
To review and develop the Government's policy and strategy on issues of special concern to women; to oversee their implementation; and to report as necessary to the Ministerial Committee on Home and Social Affairs

Legislative Programme

President of the Council and Leader of the House of Commons *(Chair)*
Deputy Prime Minister and Secretary of State for the Environment, Transport and the Regions
Lord Chancellor
Chief Whip
Lord Privy Seal, Leader of the House of Lords and Minister for Women
Secretary of State for Scotland
Secretary of State for Wales
Secretary of State for Northern Ireland
Chief Secretary, HM Treasury
Attorney General
Advocate General
Minister of State, Home Office
Minister of State, Cabinet Office
Lords Chief Whip
Parliamentary Secretary, Privy Council Office

The Minister of State, Foreign and Commonwealth Office, receives papers for the examination of draft Bills

Terms of Reference
To prepare and submit to Cabinet drafts of the Queen's speeches to Parliament and proposals for the legislative programme; to monitor the progress of Bills in preparation and during their passage through Parliament; to review the programme as necessary; to examine all draft Bills; to consider the Parliamentary handling of Government Bills; European Community documents, and Private Members' business, and such other related matters as may be necessary; and to keep under review the Goverment's policy in relation to issues of Parliamentary procedures

Crime Reduction and Youth Justice Group
Secretary of State for the Home Department *(Chair)*
Lord Privy Seal, Leader of the House of Lords and Minister for Women
Chief Secretary, HM Treasury
Solicitor General
Minister of State, Home Office
Minister of State, Cabinet Office
Minister of State, Cabinet Office
Minister of State, Department of Health
Minister of State, Scotland Office
Parliamentary Under-Secretary of State, Department of the Environment, Transport and the Regions
Parliamentary Under-Secretary, Lord Chancellor's Department
Parliamentary Under-Secretary of State, Department for Education and Employment
Parliamentary Under-Secretary of State, Department for Culture, Media and Sport
Parliamentary Under-Secretary of State, Wales Office

The Secretary of State for Northern Ireland also receives papers, and may attend or be represented as necessary

Terms of Reference
To oversee the Government's programme to reduce crime and the reform of youth justice and to make recommendations to the Ministerial Committee on Home and Social Affairs

Rural Affairs Group
Minister for the Cabinet Office and Chancellor of the Duchy of Lancaster *(Chair)*
Secretary of State for the Home Department
Secretary of State for Education and Employment
Secretary of State for Culture, Media and Sport
Minister of State, Agriculture, Fisheries and Food
Secretary of State for Trade and Industry
Secretary of State for Health
Chief Secretary, HM Treasury
Minister of State, Department of the Environment, Transport and the Regions

Terms of Reference
To co-ordinate the Government's policies affecting Rural Areas

Civil Contingencies
Secretary of State for the Home Department *(Chair)*

Representatives of Government departments, including the Cabinet Office and Treasury, and Number 10, as necessary depending on the contingency

Terms of Reference
To co-ordinate the preparation of plans for ensuring in an emergency the supplies and services essential to the life of the community; to keep these plans under regular review; to supervise their prompt and effective implementation in specific emergencies; and to report as necessary to the appropriate ministerial committee

Constitutional Reform Policy

Prime Minister *(Chair)*
Deputy Prime Minister and Secretary of State for the Environment, Transport and the Regions
Chancellor of the Exchequer
Secretary of State for Foreign and Commonwealth Affairs
Lord Chancellor
Secretary of State for the Home Department
President of the Council and Leader of the House of Commons
Chief Whip
Minister for the Cabinet Office and Chancellor of the Duchy of Lancaster
Lord Privy Seal, Leader of the House of Lords and Minister for Women
Secretary of State for Scotland
Secretary of State for Wales
Secretary of State for Northern Ireland

Other Ministers may be invited to attend as necessary

Terms of Reference
To consider strategic issues relating to the Government's constitutional reform policies

Incorporation of the European Convention of Human Rights Sub-Committee

Lord Chancellor *(Chair)*
Deputy Prime Minister and Secretary of State for the Environment, Transport and the Regions
Secretary of State for Foreign and Commonwealth Affairs
Secretary of State for the Home Department
Secretary of State for Education and Employment
President of the Council and Leader of the House of Commons
Chief Whip
Secretary of State for Culture, Media and Sport
Secretary of State for Social Security
Lord Privy Seal, Leader of the House of Lords and Minister for Women
Secretary of State for Health
Secretary of State for Scotland
Secretary of State for Wales
Secretary of State for Northern Ireland
Secretary of State for Defence
Chief Secretary, HM Treasury
Attorney General
Advocate General

Other Ministers are invited to attend for items in which they have a departmental interest. The Minister of State, Cabinet Office receives papers

Terms of Reference
To consider policy and other issues arising from the Government's decision to legislate for the incorporation of ECHR into UK law and to promote and oversee progress of the relevant legislation through Parliament and its subsequent implementation, and to report as necessary to the Ministerial Committee on Constitutional Reform Policy

Freedom of Information Sub-Committee

Lord Chancellor *(Chair)*
Chancellor of the Exchequer
Secretary of State for Foreign and Commonwealth Affairs
Secretary of State for the Home Department
Secretary of State for Education and Employment
President of the Council and Leader of the House of Commons
Chief Whip
Secretary of State for Culture, Media and Sport

Minister for the Cabinet Office and Chancellor of the Duchy of Lancaster
Secretary of State for International Development
Secretary of State for Social Security
Minister of Agriculture, Fisheries and Food
Lord Privy Seal, Leader of the House of Lords and Minister for Women
Secretary of State for Trade and Industry
Secretary of State for Health
Secretary of State for Scotland
Secretary of State for Wales
Secretary of State for Northern Ireland
Secretary of State for Defence
Attorney General
Advocate General
Minister for Transport
Minister of State, Cabinet Office

Other Ministers are invited to attend for items in which they have a departmental interest

Terms of Reference
To consider policy and other issues arising from the Government's decision to legislate on freedom of information; to promote and oversee progress of the relevant legislation through Parliament and its subsequent implementation; and to report as necessary to the Ministerial Committee on Constitutional Reform Policy

Reform of the House of Lords Sub-Committee

Lord Chancellor *(Chair)*
Secretary of State for the Home Department
President of the Council and Leader of the House of Commons
Chief Whip
Minister for the Cabinet Office and Chancellor of the Duchy of Lancaster
Lord Privy Seal, Leader of the House of Lords and Minister for Women
Attorney General
Lords Chief Whip
Minister of State, Cabinet Office

Parliamentary Secretary, Privy Council Office also attends. Other Ministers are invited to attend as necessary

Terms of Reference
To consider policy and other issues arising from the Government's plans for reform of the House of Lords and to make recommendations to the Ministerial Committee on Constitutional Reform Policy

Devolution Policy Committee

Lord Chancellor *(Chair)*
Deputy Prime Minister and Secretary of State for the Environment, Transport and the Regions
Secretary of State for Foreign and Commonwealth Affairs
Secretary of State for the Home Department
Secretary of State for Education and Employment
President of the Council and Leader of the House of Commons
Chief Whip
Secretary of State for Culture, Media and Sport
Secretary of State for Social Security
Minister of Agriculture, Fisheries and Food
Lord Privy Seal, Leader of the House of Lords and Minister for Women
Secretary of State for Trade and Industry
Secretary of State for Health
Secretary of State for Scotland
Secretary of State for Wales

Secretary of State for Northern Ireland
Chief Secretary, HM Treasury
Attorney General
Advocate General
Minister of State, Cabinet Office
Lords Chief Whip

Other Ministers are invited for items in which they have departmental interest

Terms of Reference
To consider policy and other issues arising from the Government's policies for devolution to Scotland, Wales and Northern Ireland and the regions of England and to promote and oversee progress of the relevant legislation through Parliament and its subsequent implementation

Liberal Democratic Party Joint Consultative Committee

The Committee will be chaired by the Prime Minister

Other Ministers are invited to attend for relevant items

Terms of Reference
To consider policy issues of joint interest to the Government and the Liberal Democrats

Defence and Overseas Policy

Prime Minister *(Chair)*
Deputy Prime Minister and Secretary of State for the Environment, Transport and the Regions
Chancellor of the Exchequer
Secretary of State for Foreign and Commonwealth Affairs
Secretary of State for Trade and Industry
Secretary of State for Defence

The Chief of the Defence Staff attends as required, as will the Chiefs of Staff when necessary. Others are invited to attend as necessary

Terms of Reference
To keep under review the Government's defence and overseas policy

Northern Ireland

Prime Minister *(Chair)*
Chancellor of the Exchequer
Secretary of State for Foreign and Commonwealth Affairs
Secretary of State for the Home Department
Secretary of State for Northern Ireland
Secretary of State for Defence

Terms of Reference
To oversee the Government's policy on Northern Ireland issues and relations with the Republic of Ireland on these matters

Intelligence Services

Prime Minister *(Chair)*
Deputy Prime Minister and Secretary of State for the Environment, Transport and the Regions
Chancellor of the Exchequer
Secretary of State for Foreign and Commonwealth Affairs
Secretary of State for the Home Department
Secretary of State for Defence

Terms of Reference
To keep under review policy on the security and intelligence services

Restructuring of the European Aerospace and Defence Industry Group

Secretary of State for Trade and Industry *(Chair)*
Secretary of State for Defence
Financial Secretary, HM Treasury
Minister of State, Foreign and Commonwealth Office
Parliamentary Under-Secretary of State, Department of Trade and Industry

Terms of Reference

To develop Government policy and co-ordinate related activity in promoting the restructuring of the European aerospace and defence industry

European Issues Sub-Committee

Secretary of State for Foreign and Commonwealth Affairs *(Chair)*
Deputy Prime Minister and Secretary of State for the Environment, Transport and the Regions
Chancellor of the Exchequer
Secretary of State for the Home Department
Secretary of State for Education and Employment
President of the Council and Leader of the House of Commons
Chief Whip
Minister for the Cabinet Office and Chancellor of the Duchy of Lancaster
Secretary of State for International Development
Minister of Agriculture, Fisheries and Food
Lord Privy Seal, Leader of the House of Lords and Minister for Women
Secretary of State for Trade and Industry
Secretary of State for Scotland
Secretary of State for Wales
Secretary of State for Northern Ireland
Secretary of State for Defence
Attorney General
Minister of State, Foreign and Commonwealth Office
Minister for Energy and Competitiveness in Europe, Department of Trade and Industry

Other Ministers are invited to attend as the nature of the business requires. The United Kingdom's Permanent Representative to the European Union is also in attendance

Terms of Reference

To consider questions relating to the United Kingdom's membership of the European Union and to report as necessary to the Ministerial Committee on Defence and Overseas Policy

European Trade Issues Sub-Committee

Secretary of State for Foreign and Commonwealth Affairs *(Chair)*
Chancellor of the Exchequer
Secretary of State for International Development
Minister of Agriculture, Fisheries and Food
Secretary of State for Trade and Industry

Other Ministers will be invited to attend as the nature of the business requires. The United Kingdom's Permanent Representative to the European Union is also in attendance

Terms of Reference

To consider questions relating to European Union trade policy issues and to report as necessary to the Ministerial Sub-Committee on European issues

THE OPPOSITION

CONSERVATIVES (Official opposition)

Shadow Cabinet

Leader of the Opposition	Rt Hon **William Hague** MP
Shadow Secretary of State for Foreign and Commonwealth Affairs	Rt Hon **Francis Maude** MP
Shadow Chancellor of the Exchequer	Rt Hon **Michael Portillo** MP
Party Chairman	Rt Hon **Michael Ancram** QC MP
Shadow Home Secretary	Rt Hon **Ann Widdecombe** MP
Shadow Secretary of State for Trade and Industry	Rt Hon **David Heathcoat-Amory** MP
Shadow Secretary of State for Defence	**Iain Duncan Smith** MP
Shadow Leader of the House of Lords	Rt Hon **Lord Strathclyde**
Shadow Secretary of State for Northern Ireland	Rt Hon **Andrew Mackay** MP
Shadow Secretary of State for the Environment, Transport and the Regions	**Archie Norman** MP
Shadow Secretary of State for Social Security	**David Willetts** MP
Shadow Secretary of State for Health	Dr **Liam Fox** MP
Shadow Secretary of State for Culture, Media and Sport	**Peter Ainsworth** MP
Shadow Secretary of State for International Development	**Gary Streeter** MP
Shadow Minister of Agriculture, Fisheries and Food	**Tim Yeo** MP
Shadow Leader of the House of Commons and Constitutional Affairs	**Angela Browning** MP
Shadow Secretary of State for Education and Employment	**Theresa May** MP
Shadow Minister for the Cabinet Office and Policy Renewal	**Andrew Lansley** CBE MP
Shadow Minister for Transport	Hon **Bernard Jenkin** MP
Shadow Chief Secretary to the Treasury	**Oliver Letwin** MP
Opposition Chief Whip (Commons)	Rt Hon **James Arbuthnot** MP
Opposition Chief Whip (Lords)	**Lord Henley**

Law Officers and Lord Chancellor's Department

Shadow Attorney General	**Edward Garnier** QC MP*
Shadow Lord Chancellor	Rt Hon **Lord Kingsland** TD QC

* Not a member of the Shadow Cabinet but attends all meetings

Opposition Front Bench Team

Leader of the Opposition   Rt Hon **William Hague** MP

Agriculture, Fisheries and Food
Shadow Minister   **Tim Yeo** MP
Front Bench Spokespeople   **James Paice** MP
                                             Malcolm Moss MP
Lords   **Baroness Byford** DBE
                                             Lord Glentoran CBE

Cabinet Office
Shadow Minister for the Cabinet Office
  (Policy Renewal) and Shadow Chancellor
  of the Duchy of Lancaster   **Andrew Lansley** CBE MP
Front Bench Spokespeople
  Drugs misuse policy   **Ann Winterton** MP
Lords   Rt Hon **Lord MacKay of Ardbrecknish**
                                             Lord Henley

Culture, Media and Sport
Shadow Secretary of State   **Peter Ainsworth** MP
Front Bench Spokespeople   **John Greenway** MP
Lords   **Baroness Anelay** DBE

Defence
Shadow Secretary of State   **Iain Duncan Smith** MP
Front Bench Spokespeople   **Quentin Davies** MP
                                             Robert Key MP
Lords   **Lord Burnham**
                                             Earl Attlee

Education and Employment
Shadow Secretary of State   **Theresa May** MP
  (also Shadow Cabinet Spokesperson for
    Women's Issues)
Front Bench Spokespeople
  (also for People with Disabilities)   **Tim Boswell** MP
                                             James Clappison MP
                                             John Hayes MP
Lords
  Education   Rt Hon **Baroness Blatch** CBE
  Employment   **Baroness Miller of Hendon** MBE

Environment, Transport and the Regions
Shadow Secretary of State   **Archie Norman** MP
Shadow Minister for Transport   Hon **Bernard Jenkin** MP
Front Bench Spokespeople   **Damian Green** MP
                                             Nigel Waterson MP
                                             Robert Syms MP

  Regions, Urban Regeneration, Housing
    and Poverty   **Timothy Loughton** MP
Lords   **Lord Brabazon**
  Local Government   **Lord Dixon-Smith**
  Transport   **Earl Attlee**

Foreign and Commonwealth Office

Shadow Secretary of State	
Europe	Rt Hon **Francis Maude** MP
Front Bench Spokespeople	**Richard Spring** MP
	Cheryl Gillan MP
Lords	Rt Hon **Lord Howell of Guildford**
	Baroness Rawlings

Health

Shadow Secretary of State	Dr **Liam Fox** MP
Front Bench Spokespeople	**Philip Hammond** MP
(also for Women's Issues, reporting to	**Caroline Spelman** MP
Theresa May at DfEE)	
Lords	**Earl Howe**
	Lord McColl CBE

Home Affairs

Shadow Secretary of State	Rt Hon **Ann Widdecombe** MP
Front Bench Spokespeople	**David Lidington** MP
	Oliver Heald MP
(also for Lord Chancellor's Department)	**Nick Hawkins** MP
	John Bercow MP
Lords	Rt Hon **Lord Cope**
	Viscount Astor

International Development

Shadow Secretary of State	**Gary Streeter** MP
Front Bench Spokesperson	**Cheryl Gillan** MP
Lords	**Baroness Rawlings**

Law Officers' and Lord Chancellor's Department

Shadow Attorney General	**Edward Garnier** QC MP
Shadow Lord Chancellor	Rt Hon **Lord Kingsland** TD QC
Front Bench Spokespeople	**Nick Hawkins** MP
Lords	**Baroness Buscombe**

Northern Ireland

Shadow Secretary of State	Rt Hon **Andrew Mackay** MP
Front Bench Spokesperson	**John M Taylor** MP
Lords	**Lord Glentoran** CBE
	Rt Hon **Lord Cope**

Social Security

Shadow Secretary of State	**David Willetts** MP
Front Bench Spokespeople	**Eric Pickles** MP
	Jacqui Lait MP
Lords	Rt Hon **Lord Higgins** KBE
	Baroness Buscombe

Shadow Leader of the House of Commons and Constitutional Affairs

Angela Browning MP

Front Bench Spokespeople Spokesmen for Scotland **Dominic Grieve** MP
Eleanor Laing MP
Spokesmen for Wales **Nigel Evans** MP
Robert Walter MP

Shadow Leader of the House of Lords and Constitutional Affairs

Rt Hon **Lord Strathclyde**

Deputy Shadow Leader and
Spokesman for Scotland Rt Hon **Lord Mackay of Ardbrecknish**
Front Bench Spokesman for Wales Rt Hon **Lord Roberts**

Trade and Industry

Shadow Secretary of State Rt Hon **David Heathcoat-Amory** MP
Front Bench Spokespeople **Alan Duncan** MP
Nick Gibb MP
Richard Page MP
Lords Rt Hon **Lord MacKay of Ardbrecknish**
Baroness Miller of Hendon MBE
Baroness Buscombe

Treasury

Shadow Chancellor of the Exchequer Rt Hon **Michael Portillo** MP
Shadow Chief Secretary **Oliver Letwin** MP
Front Bench Spokespeople **Richard Ottaway** MP
Howard Flight MP
Lords **Lord Saatchi**
Rt Hon **Lord Kingsland** TD QC

Opposition Whips

House of Commons

Chief Whip Rt Hon **James Arbuthnot** MP
Deputy Chief Whip **Patrick McLoughlin** MP
Pairing Whip: Northern Ireland **James Cran** MP

Foreign Office; Leader of the House;
Private Members' Bills **Stephen Day** MP
Home Office; International Development **Keith Simpson** MP
Treasury; Health **Peter Luff** MP
Environment, Transport and the Regions; Wales **Geoffrey Clifton-Brown** MP
Social Security; Scotland **Peter Atkinson** MP
Education and Employment; Defence **John Randall** MP
Agriculture; Culture, Media and Sport; Legal **Owen Paterson** MP
Trade and Industry; Cabinet Office **Graham Brady** MP

House of Lords

Chief Whip **Lord Henley**
Deputy Chief Whip **Lord Burnham**
Whips **Lord Luke**
Baroness Seccombe DBE
Viscount Bridgeman
Lord Astor of Hever
Lord Northbrook
Earl of Northesk
Baroness Hanham CBE

LIBERAL DEMOCRATS

Shadow Cabinet

Leader	Rt Hon **Charles Kennedy** MP
Deputy Leader	Rt Hon **Alan Beith** MP
Chief Whip and Shadow Leader of the House	**Paul Tyler** MP
Agriculture, Rural Affairs and Fisheries	**Colin Breed** MP
Constitution, Culture and Sport	Rt Hon **Robert Maclennan** MP
Economy	**Matthew Taylor** MP
Education and Employment	**Phil Willis** MP
Environment, Transport, the Regions and Social Justice	**Don Foster** MP
Transport	**Michael Moore** MP
Foreign Affairs and Defence	Rt Hon **Menzies Campbell** MP
International Development	Dr **Jenny Tonge** MP
Health	**Nick Harvey** MP
Home and Legal Affairs	**Simon Hughes** MP
Scotland	**Jim Wallace** MP
Social Security	Prof **Steve Webb** MP
Trade and Industry	Dr **Vincent Cable** MP
Wales	**Richard Livsey** MP

Whips

Chief Whip	**Paul Tyler** MP
Deputy Chief Whip	**Andrew Stunell** MP
	Tom Brake MP
	Sir **Robert Smith** MP
	Adrian Sanders MP
	Bob Russell MP

Spokespeople

* Shadow Cabinet member

Agriculture, Rural Affairs and Fisheries	**Colin Breed** MP*
	David Heath MP
Fisheries	**Andrew George** MP
Constitution, Culture and Sport	Rt Hon **Robert Maclennan** MP*
Tourism	**Ronnie Fearn** MP
Sport	**Bob Russell** MP
Economy	**Matthew Taylor** MP*
	Edward Davey MP
Education and Employment	**Phil Willis** MP*
Employment and childcare and IT	**Richard Allan** MP
Higher education and women	Dr **Evan Harris** MP
Environment, Transport, the Regions and Social Justice	**Don Foster** MP*
	Tom Brake MP
	Adrian Sanders MP
Transport	**Michael Moore** MP*
Planning	**Mike Hancock** MP
Energy	**Andrew Stunell** MP
Foreign Affairs and Defence	Rt Hon **Menzies Campbell** QC MP*
Europe	**Mark Oaten** MP
Defence	**Paul Keetch** MP
International development	Dr **Jenny Tonge** MP*
Health	**Nick Harvey** MP*
	Dr **Peter Brand** MP

Home and Legal Affairs	**Simon Hughes** MP*
Home affairs	**Jackie Ballard** MP
Legal affairs	**John Burnett** MP
Northern Ireland and youth	**Lembit Öpik** MP
Scotland	**Jim Wallace** QC MP*
	Ray Mitchie MP
	Sir **Robert Smith** MP
Social Security	Prof **Steve Webb** MP*
	Andrew George MP
Pensions	**Paul Burstow** MP
Trade and Industry	Dr **Vincent Cable** MP*
Consumer affairs and broadcasting	**Norman Baker** MP
Small businesss	**Brian Cotter** MP
Wales	**Richard Livsey** MP*

ULSTER UNIONIST PARTY

Spokespeople

Leader; Constitutional Affairs	Rt Hon **David Trimble** MP
Deputy Leader; Foreign Affairs, International Development	Rt Hon **John D Taylor** MP
Chief Whip; Shadow Leader of the House; Education and Employment	**Roy Beggs** MP
Environment, Transport and Regional Affairs	**Jeffrey Donaldson** MP
Defence, Trade and Industry	**Ken Maginnis** MP
Home Affairs, Cabinet Office, Treasury	**William Ross** MP
Health, Social Security, Youth and Women's Issues	**Martin Smyth** MP
Agriculture, Local Government	**William Thompson** MP
Culture, Media and Sport (including Community Relations)	**Cecil Walker** MP

NB: Subject to the necessary adjustment after the South Antrim by-election, this allocation of responsibility will continue until the end of this Parliament.

SCOTTISH NATIONAL PARTY

National Convenor	**John Swinney** MP MSP
Parliamentary Leader (Westminster); Chief Whip	**Alasdair Morgan** MP MSP

PLAID CYMRU – THE PARTY OF WALES

Spokespeople

Leader; Health; Agriculture; Foreign Affairs; Defence	**Ieuan Wyn Jones** MP AM
Constitutional Matters; Treasury and Economy; Trade and Industry; Social Security; Disability	Rt Hon **Dafydd Wigley** MP AM
Whip; Parliamentary Leader; Housing; Home Affairs; Local Government; Tourism; Northern Ireland	**Elfyn Llwyd** MP
Environment and the Regions, Transport; Education and Employment; Culture, Media and Sport; Energy	**Simon Thomas** MP

Select Committees (as at mid-October 2000)

The current structure of Select Committees was established in 1979 with the aim of "improving the scrutiny of the expenditure, administration and policy of the main government departments and certain public bodies". The range of inquiries has grown dramatically over the years and tends to reflect matters of current concern and occasional controversy.

Each Department of State is shadowed by a Select Committee. In addition to the 16 departmentally-related select committees there are a number of domestic committees which concern themselves with the day-to-day running of the House, such as the services committee and the broadcasting committee. More recently the work of the Standards and Privileges Committee has come to the forefront with its scrutiny of allegations of misconduct made against individual MPs.

AGRICULTURE
7 Millbank, London SW1P 3JA
Telephone: 020 7219 6194

Members: (11) David Curry (Chairman); David Borrow; David Drew; Alan Hurst; Michael Jack; Paul Marsden; Austin Mitchell; Lembit Öpik; Owen Paterson; Mark Todd; George Turner

Officers: Ms Lynn Gardner (Clerk); Mr Richard Kelly (Specialist Assistant); Mr Mark Oxborough (Committee Assistant); Ms Anne Woolhouse (Secretary)

JOINT COMMITTEE ON CONSOLIDATION OF BILLS ETC
Public Bill Offices, House of Lords/House of Commons, London SW1A 0AA
Telephone: 020 7219 3153/3256

Members: (21) Lord Clyde (Chairman); Lord Campbell of Alloway; Lord Christopher; Viscount Colville of Culross; Earl Dundee; Baroness Fookes; Lord Hobhouse of Woodborough; Lord Janner of Braunstone; Baroness Mallalieu; Lord Phillips of Sudbury; Lord Razzall; Lord Strabolgi; Tony Clarke; Patrick Hall; Robert Marshall-Andrews; James Plaskitt; Laurence Robertson; Adrian Sanders; George Turner; Andrew Tyrie; Brian White

Officers: Mr Fox (Clerk Commons); Mr Ollard (Clerk Lords)

CULTURE, MEDIA AND SPORT
7 Millbank, London SW1P 3JA
Telephone: 020 7219 6188

Members: (11) Gerald Kaufman (Chairman); David Faber; Ronnie Fearn; Christopher Fraser; Llin Golding; Alan Keen; Julie Kirkbride; John Maxton; Diana Organ; Claire Ward; Derek Wyatt

Officers: Mr Colin Lee (Clerk); Mr Richard Cooke (Assistant Clerk); Mrs Nicole Mulloy (Committee Assistant); Mrs Amanda Waller (Secretary)

DEFENCE
Committee Office, House of Commons, London SW1A 0AA
Telephone: 020 7219 5745

Members: (11) Bruce George (Chairman); Julian Brazier; Jamie Cann; Harry Cohen; Mike Gapes; Mike Hancock; Stephen Hepburn; Jimmy Hood; Julian Lewis; Laura Moffatt; Peter Viggers

Officers: Mr Paul Evans (Clerk); Mr Simon Fiander (Audit Adviser); Carol Oxborough (Assistant Clerk); Ms Liz Partridge (Committee Assistant); Mrs Karen Watling (Secretary)

DEREGULATION

7 Millbank, London SW1P 3JA
Telephone: 020 7219 2833

Members: (18) Peter Pike (Chair); Russell Brown; David Chaytor; Brian Cotter; John Cryer; Teresa Gorman; Andy King; Ashok Kumar; Jacqui Lait; Andrew Love; John McDonnell; Denis Murphy; Doug Naysmith; John Randall; William Ross; Anthony Steen; Ian Stewart; Brian White

Officers: Mrs Susan Craig (Clerk); Mr John Vaux (Adviser); Kemi Alagbala (Adviser); Mr Brian Dye (Committee Assistant); Miss Susan Ramsay (Secretary)

EDUCATION AND EMPLOYMENT

7 Millbank, London SW1P 3JA
Telephone: 020 7219 6181

Members: (17) Candy Atherton; Charlotte Atkins; Graham Brady; Valerie Davey; Derek Foster (Chairman (Employment); Michael John Foster; Evan Harris; Helen Jones; Judy Mallaber; Gordon Marsden; Patrick Nicholls; Stephen O'Brien; Ian Pearson; Nicholas St Aubyn; Barry Sheerman (Chairman (Education); Stephen Twigg; Phil Willis

Officers: Mr Liam Laurence Smyth (Clerk); Mr Tom Healey (Assistant Clerk); Mr Eamon Lally (Specialist Assistant); Mr Robert Rees (Specialist Assistant); Mr Darren Hackett (Committee Assistant); Mr Richard Dawson (Committee Assistant); Ms Pam Morris (Secretary); Miss Claire Halls (Secretary)

EDUCATION AND EMPLOYMENT (EDUCATION SUB-COMMITTEE)

7 Millbank, London SW1P 3JA
Telephone: 020 7219 6181

Members: (10) Barry Sheerman (Chairman); Charlotte Atkins; Valerie Davey; Derek Foster; Michael John Foster; Evan Harris; Helen Jones; Gordon Marsden; Stephen O'Brien; Nicholas St Aubyn

Officers: Mr Matthew Hamlyn (Clerk); Mr Robert Rees (Specialist Assistant); Mr Richard Dawson (Committee Assistant); Miss Claire Halls (Secretary)

EDUCATION AND EMPLOYMENT (EMPLOYMENT SUB-COMMITTEE)

7 Millbank, London SW1P 3JA
Telephone: 020 7219 6181

Members: (8) Derek Foster (Chairman); Candy Atherton; Graham Brady; Judy Mallaber; Patrick Nicholls; Ian Pearson; Barry Sheerman; Stephen Twigg

Officers: Mr Tom Healey (Clerk); Mr Eamon Lally (Specialist Assistant); Mr Darren Hackett (Committee Assistant); Ms Pam Morris (Secretary)

ENVIRONMENTAL AUDIT

7 Millbank, London SW1P 3JA
Telephone: 020 7219 6150

Members: (16) John Horam (Chairman); Richard Body; Helen Brinton; David Chaytor; Neil Gerrard; Dominic Grieve; Jon Owen Jones; Paul Keetch; Tim Loughton; Michael Meacher (Ex-officio member); Christine Russell; Malcolm Savidge; Phil Sawford; Jonathan Shaw; Simon Thomas; Joan Walley

Officers: Mr Fergus Reid (Clerk); Mr Eric Lewis (Specialist Assistant); Ms Emma Downing (Specialist Assistant); Ms Tracy Herd (Committee Assistant); Jane Cooper (Secretary)

ENVIRONMENT, TRANSPORT AND REGIONAL AFFAIRS

7 Millbank, London SW1P 3JA
Telephone: 020 7219 4972

Members: (17) Hilary Benn; Andrew Bennett (Chairman (Environment); Crispin Blunt; Thomas Brake; Christine Butler; John Cummings; Jeffrey Donaldson; Brian Donohoe; Gwyneth Dunwoody (Chairman (Transport); Louise Ellman; Teresa Gorman; James Gray; Stephen Ladyman; Anne McIntosh; William O'Brien; Bill Olner; George Stevenson

Officers: Dr David Harrison (Clerk); Mr Gavin Devine (Clerk); Mr Huw Yardley (Clerk); Katie Smith (Specialist Assistant); Mr Kevin Lee (Specialist Assistant); Mr Dave Taylor (Specialist Assistant); Miss Frances Allingham (Committee Assistant); Miss Jackie Recardo (Committee Assistant); Leslie Young (Secretary); Miss Susan Morrison (Secretary)

ENVIRONMENT, TRANSPORT AND REGIONAL AFFAIRS (ENVIRONMENT SUB-COMMITTEE)

7 Millbank, London SW1P 3JA
Telephone: 020 7219 1353

Members: (11) Andrew Bennett (Chairman); Hilary Benn; Crispen Blunt; Thomas Brake; Christine Butler; John Cummings; Brian Donohoe; Gwyneth Dunwoody; Louise Ellman; James Gray; Bill Olner

Officers: Dr David Harrison (Clerk); Mr Hugh Yardley (Clerk); Katie Smith (Specialist Assistant); Mr David Taylor (Specialist Assistant); Miss Jackie Recardo (Committee Assistant); Miss Susan Morrison (Secretary)

ENVIRONMENT, TRANSPORT AND REGIONAL AFFAIRS (TRANSPORT SUB-COMMITTEE)

7 Millbank, London SW1P 3JA
Telephone: 020 7219 6263

Members: (11) Gwyneth Dunwoody (Chairman); Andrew Bennett; Jeffrey Donaldson; Brian Donohoe; Teresa Gorman; James Gray; Stephen Ladyman; Anne McIntosh; William O'Brien; Bill Olner; George Stevenson

Officers: Mr Gavin Devine (Clerk); Mr Kevin Lee (Specialist Assistant); Miss Frances Allingham (Committee Assistant); Miss Leslie Young (Secretary)

EUROPEAN SCRUTINY

7 Millbank, London SW1P 3JA
Telephone: 020 7219 5465

Members: (16) Jimmy Hood (Chairman); Ben Bradshaw; Colin Breed; Roger Casale; William Cash; Michael Connarty; Jim Dobbin; Margaret Ewing; Patrick Hall; Jenny Jones; James Marshall; Nick Palmer; Owen Paterson; Bill Rammell; Laurence Robertson; Anthony Steen

Officers: Mrs Elizabeth Flood (Clerk); Mrs Susan Craig (Clerk Adviser); Miss Josephine Eldred (Clerk Adviser); Mr David Griffiths (Clerk Adviser); Ms Rosemary Melling (Clerk Adviser); Mr Clive Wilson (Clerk Adviser); Ms Karen McLelland (Committee Assistant); Ms Keely Bishop (Secretary); Miss Susan Ramsey (Secretary); Miss Fiona Mearns (Secretary); Ms Alison Ross (Secretary); Ms Melanie Grant (Secretary)

FOREIGN AFFAIRS

Committee Office, House of Commons, London SW1A 0AA
Telephone: 020 7219 6394

Members: (12) Donald Anderson (Chairman); Diane Abbott; David Chidgey; Peter Emery; Norman Godman; Eric Illsley; Andrew Mackinlay; David Madel; Ted Rowlands; John Stanley; Phyllis Starkey; David Wilshire

Officers: Mr Paul Silk (Clerk); Ms Tabitha Brufal (Assistant Clerk); Mr Daniel Thornton (Committee Specialist); Mr James Davies (Committee Assistant); Ana Ferreira (Office Clerk); Mrs Sheryl Bertasius (Secretary)

HEALTH

7 Millbank, London SW1P 3JA
Telephone: 020 7219 6182

Members: (10) David Hinchliffe (Chairman); David Amess; John Austin; Peter Brand; Simon Burns; Eileen Gordon; John Gunnell; Stephen Hesford; Howard Stoate; Robert Syms

Officers: Mr John Benger (Clerk); Mr Tim Goldsmith (Second Clerk); Ms Suzanne O'Leary (Specialist Assistant); Mr Frank McShane (Committee Assistant); Ms Alex Richards (Secretary)

HOME AFFAIRS

7 Millbank, London SW1P 3JA
Telephone: 020 7219 3276

Members: (11) Robin Corbett (Chairman); Ian Cawsey; Janet Dean; Michael Fabricant; Gerald Howarth; Martin Linton; Humfrey Malins; Bob Russell; Marsha Singh; Paul Stinchcombe; David Winnick

Officers: Mr Andrew Kennon (Clerk); Mr Martyn Atkins (Assistant Clerk); Mr Steve Barrett (Committee Assistant); Miss Elizabeth Booth (Secretary)

INTERNATIONAL DEVELOPMENT

7 Millbank, London SW1P 3JA
Telephone: 020 7219 1223

Members: (11) Bowen Wells (Chairman); Ann Clwyd; Tony Colman; Barbara Follett; Nigel Jones; Piara Khabra; Oona King; Tess Kingham; Andrew Robathan; Andrew Rowe; Tony Worthington

Officers: Mr Yusef Azad (Clerk); Miss Janet Hughes (Assistant Clerk); Mr William Benson (Specialist Assistant); Mr Ian Thomson (Committee Assistant); Sam Hill (Secretary)

LIAISON

Committee Office, House of Commons, London SW1A 0AA
Telephone: 020 7219 6432

Members: (33) Robert Sheldon (Chairman); Richard Allan; Donald Anderson; Stuart Bell; Andrew Bennett; Peter Brooke; Sydney Chapman; Michael Clark; Eric Clarke; Robin Corbett; David Curry; David Davis; Gwyneth Dunwoody; Derek Foster; Bruce George; David Hinchliffe; Jimmy Hood; John Horam; Martyn Jones; Gerald Kaufman; Archy Kirkwood; John McWilliam; David Marshall; Martin O'Neill; Peter Pike; Giles Radice; Marion Roe; Barry Sheerman; David Tredinnick; Dennis Turner; Bowen Wells; Nicholas Winterton; Tony Wright

Officers: Mr Charles Winnifrith (Clerk); Ms Annie Power (Secretary)

MODERNISATION OF THE HOUSE OF COMMONS
Committee Office, House of Commons, London SW1A 0AA
Telephone: 020 7219 5978

Members: (15) Margaret Beckett (Chairman); Ivor Caplin; Ann Coffey; Peter Emery; Lorna Fitzsimons; Helen Jackson; Peter Pike; Gordon Prentice; Richard Shepherd; Clive Soley; Andrew Stunell; David Taylor; Paul Tyler; Nicholas Winterton; George Young

Officers: Mr Charles Winnifrith (Clerk); Mr Alan Sandall (Clerk); Carolyn Wilson (Committee Assistant); Ms Louise Sargent (Secretary)

NORTHERN IRELAND AFFAIRS
7 Millbank, London SW1P 3JA
Telephone: 020 7219 2172

Members: (13) Peter Brooke (Chairman); Harry Barnes; Roy Beggs; Colin Burgon; Tony Clarke; John Grogan; Andrew Hunter; Stephen McCabe; Edward McGrady; Nick Palmer; Stephen Pound; Peter Robinson; William Thompson

Officers: Dr Christopher Ward (Clerk); Mr Andrew Hubner (Committee Assistant); Ms Yvonne Platt (Secretary)

JOINT COMMITTEE ON PARLIAMENTARY PRIVILEGE
Journal Office, House of Commons, London SW1A 0AA
Telephone: 020 7219 3316

Members: (12) Lord Nicholls of Birkenhead (Chairman); Lord Archer of Sandwell; Lord Mayhew of Twysden; Lord Merlyn Rees; Lord Waddington; Lord Wigoder; Joe Benton; Patrick Cormack; Bill Michie; Ann Taylor; Paul Tyler; Alan Williams

Officers: Mr Jim Hastings (Clerk); Ms Louise Sargent (Secretary)

PROCEDURE
Journal Office, House of Commons, London SW1A 0AA
Telephone: 020 7219 3318

Members: (14) Nicholas Winterton (Chairman); Tony Banks; Alan Beith; Paul Beresford; Colin Burgon; Keith Darvill; David Drew; Clive Efford; Lorna Fitzsimons; Eric Forth; Barry Gardiner; Nigel Griffiths; Eric Illsley; Andrew Stunell

Officers: Dr Robin James (Clerk); Shona McGlashan (Assistant Clerk); Ms Carolyn Wilson (Committee Assistant); Ms Louise Sargent (Secretary)

PUBLIC ACCOUNTS
7 Millbank, London SW1P 3JA
Telephone: 020 7219 5708

Members: (15) David Davis (Chairman); Alan Campbell; David Curry; Ian Davidson; Geraint Davies; Barry Gardiner; Nigel Griffiths; Edward Leigh; Andrew Love; Jim Murphy; David Rendel; Gerry Steinberg; Stephen Timms; Charles Wardle; Alan Williams

Officers: Mr Ken Brown (Clerk); Miss Susan Monaghan (Committee Assistant); Miss Ronnie Jefferson (Secretary)

PUBLIC ADMINISTRATION
7 Millbank, London SW1P 3JA
Telephone: 020 7219 5730

Members: (11) Tony Wright (Chairman); Ronnie Campbell; David Lepper; John McFall; Mark Oaten; John Townend; Michael Trend; Neil Turner; Andrew Tyrie; Brian White; Anthony D Wright

Officers: Ms Alda Barry (Clerk); Ms Clare Genis (Committee Assistant); Miss Julie Storey (Secretary)

SCIENCE AND TECHNOLOGY

7 Millbank, London SW1P 3JA
Telephone: 020 7219 2794

Members: (11) Michael Clark (Chairman); Paddy Ashdown; Claire Curtis-Thomas; Ian Gibson; Brian Iddon; Robert Jackson; Lynne Jones; Ashok Kumar; Ian Taylor; Desmond Turner; Alan W Williams

Officers: Ms Jessica Mulley (Clerk); Mr Guy Rickett (Committee Specialist); Mrs Leonie Nugent (Committee Assistant); Ms Anna Browning (Secretary)

SCOTTISH AFFAIRS

Committee Office, House of Commons, London SW1A 0AA
Telephone: 020 7219 6295

Members: (11) David Marshall (Chairman); Irene Adams; Peter Atkinson; Anne Begg; Russell Brown; Eric Clarke; Mohammed Sarwar; Robert Smith; Desmond Swayne; Bill Tynan; Andrew Welsh

Officers: Mr John Whatley (Clerk); Ms Jane Appleton (Committee Assistant); Ms Julie Storey (Secretary)

SELECTION

Committee Office, House of Commons, London SW1A 0AA
Telephone: 020 7219 3250

Members: (9) John McWilliam (Chairman); Charlotte Atkins; Clive Betts; Keith Bradley; Karen Buck; James Cran; Philip Hope; Patrick McLoughlin; Paul Tyler

Officers: Ms Elizabeth Payne (Clerk)

SOCIAL SECURITY

7 Millbank, London SW1P 3JA
Telephone: 020 7219 5833

Members: (11) Archy Kirkwood (Chairman); Karen Buck; David Crausby; Andrew Dismore; Joan Humble; Andy King; Edward Leigh; Doug Naysmith; Laurence Robertson; Desmond Swayne; Gareth Thomas

Officers: Mr Philip Moon (Clerk); Ms Janet Allbeson (Committee Specialist); Mrs Diane Nelson (Committee Assistant); Ms Mandy Sullivan (Secretary)

STANDARDS AND PRIVILEGES

Committee Office, House of Commons, London SW1A 0AA
Telephone: 020 7219 6615

Members: (11) Robert Sheldon (Chairman); Martin Bell; Peter Bottomley; Malcolm Bruce; Dale Campbell-Savours; Eric Forth; Michael Foster; Tom Levitt; Terry Lewis; Shona McIsaac; Alan Williams

Officers: Mr Alan Sandall (Clerk); Mr Stephen Mark (Assistant Clerk); Miss Lisa Hasell (Secretary)

JOINT COMMITTEE ON STATUTORY INSTRUMENTS

Ways and Means Office, House of Commons, London SW1A 0AA
Telephone: 020 7219 3773

Members: (14) Lord Greenway; Lord Hardy of Wath; Earl Onslow; Lord Skelmersdale; Lord Thomas of Gresford; Lord Vivian; Lord Walker of Doncaster; David Tredinnick (Chairman); Andrew Bennett; Harold Best; Dominic Grieve; Ivan Henderson; William Ross; Brian White

Officers: Mr Mike Hennessy (Clerk); Mr Simon Burton (Clerk); Ms Michelle Owens (Secretary); Jane Lander (Secretary)

TRADE AND INDUSTRY

7 Millbank, London SW1P 3JA
Telephone: 020 7219 5777

Members: (11) Martin O'Neill (Chairman); Tony Baldry; Roger Berry; John Butterfill; Christopher Chope; James Cunningham; Lindsay Hoyle; Bob Laxton; Alasdair Morgan; Linda Perham; Helen Southworth

Officers: Mr David Natzler (Clerk); Charlotte Littleboy (Assistant Clerk); Ms Julia Gleig (Committee Specialist); Mr Tony Catinella (Committee Assistant); Mrs Alison Game (Secretary)

TREASURY

7 Millbank, London SW1P 3JA
Telephone: 020 7219 5768

Members: (12) Giles Radice (Chairman); Nigel Beard; Elizabeth Blackman; Jim Cousins; Edward Davey; Michael Fallon; David Kidney; James Plaskitt; David Ruffley; Brian Sedgemore; Michael Spicer; Teddy Taylor

Officers: Mr Simon Patrick (Clerk); Mr Mark Egan (Assistant Clerk); Mr Jonathan Lepper (Specialist Assistant); Mr Timothy Jarrett (Committee Specialist); Miss Jane Fox (Secretary); Ms Lisette Andrews (Secretary)

TREASURY (TREASURY SUB-COMMITTEE)

7 Millbank, London SW1P 3JA

Members: (12) Michael Spicer (Chairman); Nigel Beard; Elizabeth Blackman; Jim Cousins; Edward Davey; Michael Fallon; David Kidney; James Plaskitt; Giles Radice; David Ruffley; Brian Sedgemore; Teddy Taylor

Officers: Mr Mark Egan (Clerk); Mr Jonathan Lepper (Committee Specialist); Miss Jane Fox (Committee Assistant); Ms Lisette Andrews (Secretary)

WELSH AFFAIRS

7 Millbank, London SW1P 3JA
Telephone: 020 7219 6189

Members: (11) Martyn Jones (Chairman); Martin Caton; Huw Edwards; Julian Lewis; Richard Livsey; Elfyn Llwyd; Julie Morgan; Owen Paterson; Chris Ruane; John Smith; Betty Williams

Officers: Ms Philippa Helme (Clerk); Mr Paul Derrett (Committee Assistant); Ms Carys Thomas (Secretary)

Domestic Committees

ACCOMMODATION AND WORKS

Committee Office, House of Commons, London SW1A 0AA
Telephone: 020 7219 2471

Members: (9) Sydney Chapman (Chairman); Keith Bradley; Colin Burgon; David Chidgey; Patrick Cormack; David Jamieson; Linda Perham; Raymond Powell; Sydney Rapson

Officers: Mr Mike Clark (Clerk); Miss Jo-Ann Crowder (Secretary)

ADMINISTRATION

Committee Office, House of Commons, London SW1A 0AA
Telephone: 020 7219 3299

Members: (9) Marion Roe (Chairman); David Crausby; Hilton Dawson; Stephen Day; Mike Hall; Fabian Hamilton; Stephen Hepburn; Nicholas Palmer; William Ross

Officers: Mr Mike Clark (Clerk); Mrs Helen Agnew (Secretary); Mrs Karen Georgiou (Secretary)

BROADCASTING

Committee Office, House of Commons, London SW1A 0AA
Telephone: 020 7219 3275

Members: (11) Eric Clarke (Chairman); Norman Baker; Geoffrey Clifton-Brown; Roger Gale; Barry Gardiner; Eileen Gordon; Kelvin Hopkins; David Lepper; Stephen Pound; Jonathan Sayeed; Shaun Woodward

Officers: Mr Mike Clark (Clerk); Ms Lynda Young (Secretary)

CATERING

Committee Office, House of Commons, London SW1A 0AA
Telephone: 020 7219 3299

Members: (9) Dennis Turner (Chairman); Gerald Bermingham; Janet Dean; Michael Fabricant; Lindsay Hoyle; Julie Kirkbride; John Marek; Bob Russell; Gerry Steinberg

Officers: Mrs Davies (Clerk); Mrs Helen Agnew (Secretary); Mrs Karen Georgiou (Secretary)

FINANCE AND SERVICES

Committee Office, House of Commons, London SW1A 0AA
Telephone: 020 7219 3299

Members: (11) Stuart Bell (Chairman); Richard Allan; Keith Bradley; Sydney Chapman; Eric Clarke; Thomas McAvoy; Patrick McLoughlin; Marion Roe; Dennis Turner; Paul Tyler; David Watts

Officers: Dr Malcolm Jack (Clerk); Mrs Karen Georgiou (Secretary); Mrs Helen Agnew (Secretary)

INFORMATION

Committee Office, House of Commons, London SW1A 0AA
Telephone: 020 7219 2471

Members: (9) Richard Allan (Chairman); Ian Bruce; Tim Collins; Michael Connarty; Neil Gerrard; Andrew Miller; Gwyn Prosser; Philip Sawford; Ian Stewart

Officers: Mrs Davies (Clerk); Miss Jo-Ann Crowder (Secretary)

Internal Committees

CHAIRMEN'S PANEL

Public Bill Office, House of Commons, London SW1A 0AA
Telephone: 020 7219 3257

Members: (31) Alan Haselhurst (Chairman of Ways and Means); Michael Martin (First Deputy Chairman of Ways and Means); Michael Lord (Second Deputy Chairman of Ways and Means); Irene Adams; Joe Benton; John Butterfill; Michael Clark; Frank Cook; John Cummings; Jim Cunningham; Gwyneth Dunwoody; Roger Gale; Mike Hancock; Jimmy Hood; Eric Illsley; Barry Jones; Ashok Kumar; John McWilliam; David Madel; Humfrey Malins; John Maxton; Ray Michie; Bill O'Brien; Edward O'Hara; Bill Olner; Marion Roe; Jonathan Sayeed; George Stevenson; Bowen Wells; Andrew Welsh; Nicholas Winterton

Officers: Helen Irwin (Clerk)

COURT OF REFEREES

Public Bill Office, House of Commons, London SW1A 0AA
Telephone: 020 7219 3257

Members: (10) Alan Haselhurst (Chairman of Ways and Means); Michael Martin (First Deputy Chairman of Ways and Means); Michael Lord (Second Deputy Chairman of Ways and Means); Peter Atkinson; John Butterfill; William Etherington; Archy Kirkwood; Alan Meale; Ernest Ross; Dennis Turner

Officers: Helen Irwin (Clerk)

STANDING ORDERS

Ways & Means Office, House of Commons, London SW1A 0AA
Telephone: 020 7219 3771

Members: (11) Alan Haselhurst (Chairman of Ways and Means); Michael Martin (First Deputy Chairman of Ways and Means); Michael Lord (Second Deputy Chairman of Ways and Means); Clive Efford; Llin Golding; Brian Jenkins; Helen Jones; William O'Brien; Ernest Ross; Andrew Stunell; Nicholas Winterton

Officers: Mr Mike Hennessy (Clerk)

UNOPPOSED BILLS (PANEL)

Ways & Means Office, House of Commons, London SW1A 0AA
Telephone: 020 7219 3771

Members: (20) Alan Haselhurst (Chairman of Ways and Means); Michael Martin (First Deputy Chairman of Ways and Means); Michael Lord (Second Deputy Chairman of Ways and Means); John Austin; Nigel Beard; Peter Bottomley; Helen Brinton; John Butterfill; Philip Hammond; Brian Jenkins; Helen Jones; Andrew Mackinlay; David Marshall; John McDonnell; Sydney Rapson; Nicholas St Aubyn; Andrew Stunell; Jon Trickett; Robert Walter; Ann Winterton

Officers: Mr Mike Hennessy (Clerk)

European Standing Committees

There are three European Standing Committees to consider such documents as are referred to them by the European Legislation Committee, Committee A, B and C. Each committee has 13 Members who are appointed by the Committee of Selection for the whole session of Parliament. The Chairman is appointed by the Speaker on an ad hoc basis. Any Member may attend and speak in a sitting of a Committee but cannot vote. Following Committee debate, the Scrutiny process is completed by the Government moving a motion in the House, which is usually (but need not be) the same as that agreed by the Committee. This is not debatable, and amendments may be tabled and, if selected by the Speaker, voted on.

EUROPEAN STANDING COMMITTEE A

Members: (13) David Chaytor, Janet Dean, Jim Dobbin, Michael J Foster, Dr Ian Gibson, Christopher Gill, Owen Paterson, Lawrie Quinn, Sir Robert Smith, George Stevenson, William Thompson, Peter Viggers, Dr Rudi Vis

EUROPEAN STANDING COMMITTEE B

Members: (13) Jackie Ballard, Paul Clark, Eileen Gordon, Jane Griffiths, Fabian Hamilton, Kelvin Hopkins, David Lepper, Dr Nick Palmer, Bill Rammell, William Ross, Robert Walter, Sir Ray Whitney, John Wilkinson

EUROPEAN STANDING COMMITTEE C

Members (13) Norman Baker, David Borrow, David Crausby, Keith Darvill, Dr Evan Harris, Ivan Henderson, Stephen Hesford, Michael Jack, Dr Stephen Ladyman, Tim Loughton, Anne McIntosh, Geraldine Smith, Anthony Wright

Officers and Officials

The House of Commons Commission

Tel 020 7219 3299

The House of Commons Commission is responsible for the employment of all staff in the six departments of the House. It consists of the Speaker (as Chair), the Leader of the House, a Member nominated by the Leader of the Opposition, and three backbenchers: one from the government side, one from the main opposition party and one from another party.

Members
The Speaker
Rt Hon Margaret Beckett MP (Leader of the House)
Archy Kirkwood MP (Liberal Democrat)
Rt Hon Eric Forth MP (Conservative)
Stuart Bell MP (Labour)
Angela Browning MP (Conservative)
Secretary to the Commission: Dr Malcolm Jack

SPEAKER AND THE CHAIRMAN OF WAYS AND MEANS

The Speaker is the presiding officer of the Commons, whose main responsibility is to maintain order in debates and apply the rules and traditions of the House. The Chairman of Ways and Means is the principal deputy Speaker.

The Speaker	Rt Hon **Michael Martin** MP
Chairman of Ways and Means	Rt Hon Sir **Alan Haselhurst** MP
First Deputy Chairman	Vacant
Second Deputy Chairman	**Michael Lord** MP

Speaker's Secretary: Nicolas Bevan CB   *Speaker's Chaplain:* Rev Canon Robert Wright
Secretary to the Chairman of Ways and Means: Mike Hennessy

DEPARTMENT OF THE CLERK OF THE HOUSE

The Clerk of the House is the Speaker's principal adviser on the practice and procedure of Parliament and is also the Accounting Officer for the House of Commons' Votes and Chairman of the Board of Management. The Clerk's Department provides professional and administrative services related to the proceedings of the House.

Clerk of the House: William McKay CB

Head of Office of the Clerk: Dr Richard Ware
Private Secretary: Sarah Davies

Clerk Assistant: George Cubie
Clerk of Committees: Charles Winnifrith CB
Clerk of Legislation: Roger Sands

Principal Clerks
James Hastings CB (Journal Office)
Douglas Millar (Table Office)
Malcolm Jack PhD (Domestic Committees)
Robert Wilson (Overseas Office)
William Proctor (Clerk of Delegated Legislation)
Helen Irwin (Clerk of Bills, Examiner of Petitions for Private Bills, Taxing Officer)
Jacqy Sharpe (Select Committees)
Frank Cranmer (Select Committees)
Robert Rogers (Select Committees)
Supervisor of Parliamentary Broadcasting: Barbara Long

Legal Services Office
Speaker's Counsel and Head of Office: John Vaux
Counsel for Legislation: A D Preston
Counsel for European Legislation: M Carpenter
Assistant Counsel: A Akbar
Assistant Counsel: P Brooksbank

Deputy Principal Clerks
Alda Barry (Clerk of Public Administration Committee)
Christopher Ward PhD (Clerk of Northern Ireland Affairs Committee)
David Doig (Registrar of Members' Interests)
Alan Sandall (Clerk of Standards and Privileges Committee)
David Natzler (Clerk of Trade and Industry Committee)
Paul Silk (Clerk of Foreign Affairs Committee)
Andrew Kennon (Clerk of Home Affairs Committee)
Liam Laurence Smyth (Clerk of Education and Employment Committee)
Simon Patrick (Clerk of the Treasury Committee)
Dorian Gerhold (Clerk of European Scrutiny Committee)
Crispin Poyser (Public Bill Office)
David Harrison PhD (Clerk of Environment, Transport and Regional Affairs Committee)
Stephen Priestley (Public Bill Office)
Alastair Doherty (Table Office)
Paul Evans (Clerk of Defence Committee)
Roger Phillips (Table Office)
Robin James PhD (Journal Office (Clerk of Procedure Committee))
Philippa Helme (Clerk of Welsh Affairs Committee)
David Lloyd (Public Bill Office)
John Benger DPhil (Clerk of Health Committee)
Nicholas Walker (Public Bill Office)
Matthew Hamlyn (Table Office)
Elizabeth Flood (Clerk of European Scrutiny Committee)
Paul Seaward DPhil (Journal Office)
Yusef Azad (Clerk of International Development Committee)
Colin Lee (Clerk of Culture, Media and Sport Committee)

Senior Clerks
Christopher Stanton (National Parliament Office, Brussels)
Christopher Shaw (Table Office)
Lynn Gardner (Clerk of Agriculture Committee)
Kennedy Brown OBE (Clerk of Public Accounts Committee)
Fergus Reid (Clerk of Environmental Audit Committee)
Michael Hennessy (Secretary to Chairman of Ways and Means)
Gavin Devine (Clerk of Transport Sub-Committee)
Phillip Moon (Clerk of Social Security Committee)
Michael Clark (Clerk of Administration, Accommodation and Works and Broadcasting Committees)
Jessica Mulley (Clerk of Employment Sub-Committee)
Thomas Healey (Clerk of the Science and Technology Committee)
Sarah Davies (Private Secretary to Clerk of the House)
John Whatley (Clerk of Scottish Affairs Committee)
Kenneth Fox (Public Bill Office)
James Rhys (Delegation Secretary, European Office)
Susan Craig (Clerk of De-regulation Committee)
Elizabeth Payne (Private Bill Office)
Shona McGlashan (Journal Office)
Carol Oxborough (Second Clerk, Defence Committee)
Thomas Goldsmith (Second Clerk, Health and Social Security Committee)
Huw Yardley (Clerk of Environment Sub-Committee)

Office of the Editorial Supervisor of the Vote
Editorial Supervisor of the Vote: Bernard Tidball
Deputy Editorial Supervisor of the Vote: Lynn Lewis
Personnel and Establishments Officer: Susan Pamphlett

Vote Office
Responsible for providing all parliamentary papers and for the Parliamentary Bookshop
Deliverer: John Collins
Deputy Deliverers: Frank Hallett (Production), Owen Sweeney (Parliamentary), Alexander Powell
(Development)

DEPARTMENT OF THE SERJEANT AT ARMS

Responsible for Order: Security and Ceremonial; Accommodation; Works and Communications

Serjeant at Arms: Michael Cummins
Personal Assistant: Vanessa Green
Deputy Serjeant at Arms: Muir Morton
Personal Assistant and Office Manager: Mary Healey
Assistant Serjeants at Arms: Philip Wright, James Robertson, Mark Harvey
Clerk in Charge and Accommodation Co-ordinator: Judy Scott Thomson
Finance Manager: Stephanie Peterson
Information Systems Manager: Julia Carthew
Safety Manager: Ronald Bentley
Accommodation Rationalisation Manager: Jill Pay (acting)
Admission Order Office: Silvia Warren
Principal Doorkeeper: Trevor Dann
Head Office Keeper: Brendon Mulvihill (acting)
Pass Office Manager: Malcolm Coombs

Parliamentary Works Directorate
Director of Works: Henry Webber
Deputy Director of Works: Leslie Brantingham
Project Sponsor: Andy Makepeace
Deputy Director, Contracts and Procurement: Ian Carr
Manager, Building Project Branch: John Stone
Principal Engineer: Chris Hillier JP
Works Manager: Lester Benjamin
Furnishing Manager: Graham Goode

Parliamentary Communications Directorate
Director of Communications: Chris Gilbert
Communications Manager: Matthew Taylor
Telecommunications Manager: Dr Gareth Williams

General Services
Head of Security: Supt Gregory Roylance
Postmaster: Lawrence Ward

DEPARTMENT OF THE LIBRARY

020 7219 4272
Fax: 020 7219 5839
E-mail: hcinfo@parliament.uk
Librarian: Priscilla Baines BLitt (020 7219 3635)
Director of Human Resources: Keith Cuninghame
Director of Library Resources: Jane Wainwright FIInfSc
Director of Parliamentary and Reference Services: Bob Twigger
Director of Research Services: Robert Clements
Director of Information Systems: Betty McInnes

Heads of Section: Dr Chris Pond, Carole Andrews, Julie Lourie, Christopher Barclay, Jane Fiddick, Christine Gillie, Gillian Allen, Richard Cracknell

Senior Library Clerks: Fiona Poole, Timothy Edmonds, Oonagh Gay, Dr Donna Gore, Barry Winetrobe, Mary Baber, Aileen Walker, Helen Holden, Philippa Carling, Kim Greener, Pat Strickland, Vaughne Miller, Mick Hillyard, Jo Roll, Wendy Wilson, Steve Wise, Edward Wood, Dr Paul Bowers PhD, Antony Seely, Dr Grahame Danby, Bryn Morgan, Lorraine Conway, Christopher Blair PhD, Chris Sear, Felicity Whittle, Mark Oakes, Andrew Presland, Keith Parry (acting)

House of Commons Information Office

Written or telephone enquiries about all aspects of the work and history of the House of Commons are answered by the Information Office: Telephone inquiries: 020 7219 4272.
E-mail: hcinfo@parliament.uk
Website: www.parliament.uk

DEPARTMENT OF FINANCE AND ADMINISTRATION

Responsible for central support services and members' pay and allowances

Director's Office

Director of Finance and Administration: Andrew Walker
Director's Assistant: Michael Page
Head of Special Resources Team: Rachel Harrison

Fees Office

(MPs' pay and allowances)
Director of Operations: Archie Cameron
Assistant Director of Operations: Gill Crowther
Head of Personnel and Pensions: Neil Crawley
Operations Development Manager: Merielle Morris

Personnel Policy Directorate

Director: Brian Wilson
Members' Pay, Allowances and Pensions Policy: Mike Fletcher
Human Resources Strategy: Heather Wood
Pay and Communications: Jane Leverton
Head of Occupational Health, Safety and Welfare Services: Janice Tofts
Occupational Health Manager: Maggie Mainland

Finance Policy Directorate

(Staff pay and running costs of House)
Director of Finance Policy: Michael Barram
Finance Accountant: Norma Norman
Management Accountant: Peter Lamb
Manpower Planning Assistant: Jane Hough
Financial Accountant: Kym Bigwood
Systems Accountant: Sarah Dearson

Information Systems Service

Head of ISS: Peter Skerratt
Operations Manager: Steve Judd

Internal Review Services Directorate

Director of Internal Review Services: Richard Russell
Review Manager: Bob Castle
Senior Auditor: Diane Hill

DEPARTMENT OF THE OFFICIAL REPORT

020 7219 4786 and 5290
Production of Hansard: verbatim report of proceedings in the Chamber and Standing Committees
Editor: Ian Church
Deputy Editor (House): Bill Garland
Deputy Editor (Personnel, Finance and Administration): Lorraine Sutherland
Deputy Editor (Committees): Catherine Fogarty
Principal Assistant Editors

Vivian Widgery	Clare Hanly
Kate Stewart	Mark Watson
Paul Hadlow	Annie Browne
Jenny Dall	Deborah Jones

REFRESHMENT DEPARTMENT

Catering services
Director's Office: 020 7219 3686
Fax: 020 7219 4988
Director of Catering Services: Sue Harrison
Operations Manager: Robert Gibbs 020 7219 0355 *Fax:* 020 7219 4988

PARLIAMENTARY COMMISSIONER FOR STANDARDS

House of Commons, London SW1A 0AA
020 7219 0320   Fax 020 7219 0490
E-mail: filkine@parliament.uk
Parliamentary Commissioner for Standards: Ms Elizabeth Filkin
Registrar of Members' Interests: David Doig

The Commissioner has responsibility for the operation of the Register of Members' Interests; advising Members of Parliament and the Select Committee on Standards and Privileges on questions of propriety; and receiving, and if she thinks fit, investigating complaints about the conduct of Members.

PARLIAMENTARY OFFICE OF SCIENCE AND TECHNOLOGY (POST)

7 Millbank, London SW1P 3JA
020 7219 2848   Fax 020 7219 2849
E-mail: coped@parliament.uk
Website: www.parliament.uk/post/home.htm

Chairman: Dr Ian Gibson MP
Vice-Chairman: Lord Flowers
Director: Prof David Cope
POST Board Members: (Lords) The Earl of Erroll, Lord Oxburgh, Prof Lord Winston, *(Commons)* Richard Allan MP, Dr Michael Clark MP, Anne Campbell MP, Michael Connarty MP, Paul Flynn MP, Dr Ashok Kumar MP, Dr Phyllis Starkey MP, Caroline Spelman MP, Ian Taylor MP

POST is an independent office within Parliament, and is administratively part of the House of Commons. It is an office run by its Board and analyses issues of interest to Parliament on matters of science and technology and also provides assistance to Select Committees in both Houses.

SHORTHAND WRITER TO THE HOUSE

Responsible for verbatim reports of public hearings of Select Committees and Private Bill Committees
Shorthand Writer to the House: Pat Woolgar

General Election 1997

HANDBOOK

OF

HOUSE *of* COMMONS

PROCEDURE

2nd Edition 1999

This book is an essential reference work for anyone who needs to understand the procedures of the House of Commons.

Its author, a Clerk in the Commons with almost two decades' experience of working in the House, has completely revised his original guide to the procedures of the House. It describes the House, its organisation, rules and privileges; the business of the House and its committees; the role of the Speaker and chairmen; the timetables of Parliaments, sessions, weeks and days; question time; the rules of debate, procedures for bills, statutory instruments and European legislation; and the functions and procedures of the Select Committees of the House.

Also included is an extensive glossary of jargon of parliamentary procedure, and many figures and tables which summarise essential information and illustrate the text; and Standing Orders.

Vacher Dod Publishing Limited
PO Box 3700, Westminster, London SW1P 4WU
Tel: 020 7828 7256   Fax: 020 7828 7269
E-mail: politics@vacherdod.co.uk
Website: www.politicallinks.co.uk

POLLING RESULTS

Parties with seats in the House of Commons:

Lab: Labour
Lab/Co-op: Labour Co-operative
Con: Conservative
Lib Dem: Liberal Democrat
PC: Plaid Cymru
SNP: Scottish National Party

UUP: Ulster Unionist Party
DUP: Democratic Unionist Party
SDLP: Social Democratic and Labour Party
SF: Sinn Fein
UKU: United Kingdom Unionist

21st Cent: 21st Century Independent Foresters; **ACA:** Anti-Child Abuse; Anti-corruption Candidate; **Albion:** Albion Party; **Alt LD:** Alternative Liberal Democrat; **ANP:** All Night Party; **Anti-maj:** Anti-majority Democracy; **AS:** Anti-Sleaze; **AS Lab:** Anti-Sleaze Labour; **Bart's:** Independent Save Bart's Candidate; **BDP:** British Democratic Party; **Beanus:** Space Age Super Hero from Planet Beanus; **Beaut:** Independently Beautiful Party; **Bert:** Bertie's Party; **BFAIR:** British Freedom and Individual Rights; **BHMBCM:** Black Haired Medium Build Caucasian Male; **B Ind:** Beaconsfield Independent: Unity Through Electoral Reform; **BIPF:** British Isles People First Party; **BNP:** British National Party; **Bypass:** Newbury Bypass Stop Construction Now; **Byro:** Lord Byro versus the Scallywag Tories; **Care:** Care in the Community; **CASC:** Conservatives Against the Single Currency; **CFSS:** Country, Field and Shooting Sports; **Ch D:** Christian Democrat; **Choice:** People's Choice; **Ch Nat:** Christian Nationalist; **Ch P:** Christian Party; **Ch U:** Christian Unity; **Comm Brit:** Communist Party of Britain; **Comm Lge:** Communist League; **Constit:** Constitutionalist; **Consult:** Independent Democracy Means Consulting the People; **CRP:** Community Representative Party; **CSSPP:** Common Sense Sick of Politicians Party; **Cvty:** Conservatory; **Dem:** Democratic Party; **D Nat:** Democratic Nationalist; **Dream:** Rainbow Dream Ticket Party; **Dynamic:** First Dynamic Party; **EDP:** English Democratic Party; **Embryo:** Anti-Abortion, Euthanasia, Embryo Experiments; **EUP:** European Unity Party; **Fair:** Building a Fair Society; **FDP:** Fancy Dress Party; **Fellowship:** Fellowship Party for Peace and Justice; **FEP:** Full Employment Party; **FP:** Freedom Party; The Fourth Party; **Glow:** Glow Bowling Party; **Green:** Green Party; **Green Ref:** Green Party for Euro Referendum; **GRLNSP:** Green Referendum Lawless Naturally Street Party; **Hemp:** Hemp Coalition; **Home Rule:** British Home Rule; **HR:** Human Rights '97; **Hum:** Humanist Party; **IAC:** Independent Anti-Corruption in Government/TGWU; **Ind:** Independent; **Ind AFE:** Independent Against a Federal Europe; **Ind BB:** Independent Back to Basics; **Ind C:** Independent Conservative; **Ind CRP:** Independent Conservative Referendum Party; **Ind Dean:** Independent Royal Forest of Dean; **Ind Dem:** Independent Democrat; **Ind ECR:** Independent English Conservative and Referendum; **Ind F:** Independent Forester; **Ind Green:** Independent Green: Your Children's Future; **Ind Hum:** English Independent Humanist Party; **Ind Isl:** Island Independent; **Ind JRP:** Justice and Renewal Independent Party; **Ind Lab:** Independent Labour; **Ind No:** Independent No to Europe; **Ind OAP:** Independent Old Age Pensioner; **IZB:** Islam Zinda Baad Platform; **JP:** Justice Party; **Juice:** Juice Party; **KBF:** Keep Britain Free and Independent Party; **Lab Change:** Labour Time for Change Candidate; **LC:** Loyal Conservative; **LCP:** Legalise Cannabis Party; **LGR:** Local Government Reform; **Lib:** Liberal; **Loc C:** Local Conservative; **Loc Ind:** Local Independent; **Logic:** Logic Party Truth Only Allowed; **Loony:** Monster Raving Loony Party; **Mal:** Mal Voice of the People Party; **Meb Ker:** Mebyon Kernow; **Miss M:** Miss Moneypenny's Glamorous One Party; **Mongolian:** Mongolian Barbeque Great Place to Party; **MRAC:** Multi-racial Anti-corruption Alliance; **Musician:** Musician; **Nat Dem:** National Democrat; **New Way:** New Millennium New Way Hemp Candidate; **NF:** National Front; **NIFT:** Former Captain NI Football Team; **NIP:** Northern Ireland Party; **N I Women:** Northern Ireland Women's Coalition; **N Lab:** New Labour; **NLP:** Natural Law Party; **NLPC:** New Labour Party Candidate; **None:** None of the Above Parties; **NPC:** Non-party Conservative; **O Lab:** Old Labour; **Pacifist:** Pacifist for Peace, Justice, Co-operation, Environment; **Party Heart:** Heart 106.2 Alien Party; **PAYR:** Protecting All Your Rights Locally Effectively; **PEC:** Pro-European Conservative Party; **PF:** Pathfinders; **PLP:** People's Labour Party; **Plymouth:** Plymouth First Group; **PP:** People's Party; **PPP:** People's Party Party; **ProLife:** ProLife Alliamce; **PUP:** Progressive Unionist Party; **RA:** Residents' Association; **Rain Isl:** Rainbow Connection Your Island Candidate; **Rain Ref:** Rainbow Referendum; **R Alt:** Radical Alternative; **Ref:** Referendum Party; **Ren Dem:** Renaissance Democrat; **Rep GB:** Republican Party of Great Britain; **Rights:** Charter for Basic Rights; **Rizz:** Rizz Party; **R Lab:** Real Labour Party; **Ronnie:** Ronnie the Rhino Party; **Route 66:** Route 66 Posse Party; **Scrapit:** Scrapit Stop Avon Ring Road Now; **SCU:** Scottish Conservative Unofficial; **SEP:** Socialist Equality Party;

SFDC: Stratford First Democratic Conservative; **SG:** Sub-genius Party; **Shields:** Pro Interests of South Shields People; **SIP:** Sheffield Independent Party; **SLI:** Scottish Labour Independent; **Slough:** People in Slough Shunning Useless Politicians; **SLU:** Scottish Labour Unofficial; **Soc:** Socialist Party; **Soc Dem:** Social Democrat; **Soc Lab:** Socialist Labour Party; **Spts All:** Sportsman's Alliance: Anything but Mellor; **SS:** Scottish Socialist Alliance; **Stan:** Happiness Stan's Freedom to Party; **Teddy:** Teddy Bear Alliance Party; **Third:** Third Way; **Top:** Top Choice Liberal Democrat; **UA:** Universal Alliance; **UKIP:** UK Independence Party; **UKPP:** UK Pensioners' Party; **UKU:** United Kingdom Unionist; **Value:** Value Party; **WCCC:** West Cheshire College in Crisis Party; **Wessex Reg:** Wessex Regionalist; **Whig:** Whig Party; **WP:** Workers' Party; **WRP:** Workers' Revolutionary Party

ABERAVON

		%
*Morris, J. (Lab)	25,650	71.3
McConville, R. (LD)	4,079	11.3
Harper, P. (Con)	2,835	7.9
Cockwell, P. (PC)	2,088	5.8
David, P. (Ref)	970	2.7
Beany, C. (Beanus)	341	0.9
Lab majority	21,571	59.98%
Electorate	50,025	
Total Vote	35,963	Poll 71.9%

*Member of last parliament
Lab Hold (2.7% Swing from LD to Lab)

ABERDEEN CENTRAL

		%
Doran, F. (Lab)	17,745	49.8
Wisely, J. (Con)	6,944	19.5
Topping, B. (SNP)	5,767	16.2
Brown, J. (LD)	4,714	13.2
Farquharson, J. (Ref)	446	1.3
Lab majority	10,801	30.33%
Electorate	54,257	
Total Vote	35,616	Poll 65.6%

Lab Gain (8% Swing from Con to Lab)

ABERDEEN NORTH

		%
Savidge, M. (Lab)	18,389	47.9
Adam, B. (SNP)	8,379	21.8
Gifford, J. (Con)	5,763	15.0
Rumbles, M. (LD)	5,421	14.1
McKenzie, A. (Ref)	463	1.2
Lab majority	10,010	26.06%
Electorate	54,302	
Total Vote	38,415	Poll 70.7%

Lab Hold (6.7% Swing from SNP to Lab)

ABERDEEN SOUTH

		%
Begg, A. (Lab)	15,541	35.3
Stephen, N. (LD)	12,176	27.6
*Robertson, R. (Con)	11,621	26.4
Towers, J. (SNP)	4,299	9.8
Wharton, R. (Ref)	425	1.0
Lab majority	3,365	7.64%
Electorate	60,490	
Total Vote	44,062	Poll 72.8%

*Member of last parliament
Lab Gain (11.2% Swing from Con to Lab)

AIRDRIE AND SHOTTS

		%
*Liddell, H. (Lab)	25,460	61.8
Robertson, K. (SNP)	10,048	24.4
Brook, N. (Con)	3,660	8.9
Wolseley, R. (LD)	1,719	4.2
Semple, C. (Ref)	294	0.7
Lab majority	15,412	37.43%
Electorate	57,673	
Total Vote	41,181	Poll 71.4%

*Member of last parliament
Lab Hold (3.5% Swing from Lab to SNP)

ALDERSHOT

		%
Howarth, G. (Con)	23,119	42.7
Collett, A. (LD)	16,498	30.5
Bridgeman, T. (Lab)	13,057	24.1
Howe, J. (UKIP)	794	1.5
Pendragon, A. (Ind)	361	0.7
Stevens, D. (BNP)	322	0.6
Con majority	6,621	12.23%
Electorate	76,189	
Total Vote	54,151	Poll 71.1%

Con Hold (9.7% Swing from Con to LD)

ALDRIDGE-BROWNHILLS

		%
*Shepherd, R. (Con)	21,856	47.1
Toth, J. (Lab)	19,330	41.7
Downic, C. (LD)	5,184	11.2
Con majority	2,526	5.45%
Electorate	62,441	
Total Vote	46,370	Poll 74.3%

*Member of last parliament
Con Hold (7.8% Swing from Con to Lab)

ALTRINCHAM AND SALE WEST

		%
Brady, G. (Con)	22,348	43.2
Baugh, J. (Lab)	20,843	40.3
Ramsbottom, M. (LD)	6,535	12.6
Landes, A. (Ref)	1,348	2.6
Stephens, J. (Pro-Life)	313	0.6
Mrozinski, R. (UKIP)	270	0.5
Renwick, J. (NLP)	125	0.2
Con majority	1,505	2.91%
Electorate	70,625	
Total Vote	51,782	Poll 73.3%

Con Hold (12.6% Swing from Con to Lab)

ALYN AND DEESIDE

		%
*Jones, B. (Lab)	25,955	61.9
Roberts, T. (Con)	9,552	22.8
Burnham, E. (LD)	4,076	9.7
Jones, M. (Ref)	1,627	3.9
Hills, S. (PC)	738	1.8
Lab majority	16,403	39.11%
Electorate	58,091	
Total Vote	41,948	Poll 72.2%

*Member of last parliament
Lab Hold (12.5% Swing from Con to Lab)

AMBER VALLEY

		%
Mallaber, J. (Lab)	29,943	54.7
*Oppenheim, P. (Con)	18,330	33.5
Shelley, R. (LD)	4,219	7.7
McGibbon, I. (Ref)	2,283	4.2
Lab majority	11,613	21.20%
Electorate	72,005	
Total Vote	54,775	Poll 76%

*Member of last parliament
Lab Gain (11.7% Swing from Con to Lab)

ANGUS

		%
*Welsh, A. (SNP)	20,792	48.3
Leslie, S. (Con)	10,603	24.6
Taylor, C. (Lab)	6,733	15.6
Speirs, R. (LD)	4,065	9.4
Taylor, B. (Ref)	883	2.0
SNP majority	10,189	23.65%
Electorate	59,708	
Total Vote	43,076	Poll 72.1%

*Member of last parliament
SNP Hold (11.3% Swing from Con to SNP)

ARGYLL AND BUTE

		%
*Michie, R. (LD)	14,359	40.2
MacCormick, N. (SNP)	8,278	23.2
Leishman, R. (Con)	6,774	19.0
Syed, A. (Lab)	5,596	15.7
Stewart, M. (Ref)	713	2.0
LD majority	6,081	17.02%
Electorate	49,451	
Total Vote	35,720	Poll 72%

*Member of last parliament
LD Hold (3% Swing from SNP to LD)

ARUNDEL AND SOUTH DOWNS

		%
Flight, H. (Con)	27,251	53.1
Goss, J. (LD)	13,216	25.7
Black, R. (Lab)	9,376	18.3
Herbert, J. (UKIP)	1,494	2.9
Con majority 14,035		27.34%
Electorate	67,641	
Total Vote	51,337	Poll 75.9%

Con Hold (5.2% Swing from Con to LD)

ASHFIELD

		%
*Hoon, G. (Lab)	32,979	65.2
Simmonds, M. (Con)	10,251	20.3
Smith, W. (LD)	4,882	9.6
Betts, M. (Ref)	1,896	3.7
Belshaw, S. (BNP)	595	1.2
Lab majority 22,728		44.91%
Electorate	72,269	
Total Vote	50,603	Poll 70%

*Member of last parliament
Lab Hold (11.3% Swing from Con to Lab)

ASHFORD

		%
Green, D. (Con)	22,899	41.4
Ennals, J. (Lab)	17,544	31.7
Williams, J. (LD)	10,901	19.7
Cruden, C. (Ref)	3,201	5.8
Boden, R. (Green)	660	1.2
Tyrell, S. (NLP)	89	0.2
Con majority 5,355		9.66%
Electorate	74,149	
Total Vote	55,294	Poll 74.6%

Con Hold (12.5% Swing from Con to Lab)

ASHTON UNDER LYNE

		%
*Sheldon, R. (Lab)	31,919	67.5
Mayson, R. (Con)	8,954	18.9
Pickstone, T. (LD)	4,603	9.7
Clapham, L. (Ref)	1,346	2.8
Cymbal, P. (Loony)	458	1.0
Lab majority 22,965		48.57%
Electorate	72,206	
Total Vote	47,280	Poll 65.4%

*Member of last parliament
Lab Hold (10.2% Swing from Con to Lab)

AYLESBURY

		%
*Lidington, D. (Con)	25,426	44.2
Bowles, S. (LD)	17,007	29.5
Langridge, R. (Lab)	12,759	22.2
John, M. (Ref)	2,196	3.8
Sheaff, L. (NLP)	166	0.3
Con majority 8,419		14.63%
Electorate	79,047	
Total Vote	57,554	Poll 72.8%

*Member of last parliament
Con Hold (7.5% Swing from Con to LD)

AYR

		%
Osborne, S. (Lab)	21,679	48.4
*Gallie, P. (Con)	15,136	33.8
Blackford, I. (SNP)	5,625	12.6
Hamblen, C. (LD)	2,116	4.7
Enos, J. (Ref)	200	0.4
Lab majority 6,543		14.62%
Electorate	55,829	
Total Vote	44,756	Poll 80.2%

*Member of last parliament
Lab Gain (5.2% Swing from Con to Lab)

BANBURY

		%
*Baldry, T. (Con)	25,076	42.9
Peperell, H. (Lab)	20,339	34.8
Bearder, C. (LD)	9,761	16.7
Ager, J. (Ref)	2,245	3.8
Cotton, B. (Green)	530	0.9
King, L. (UKIP)	364	0.6
Pearson, I. (NLP)	131	0.2
Con majority 4,737		8.10%
Electorate	77,456	
Total Vote	58,446	Poll 75.1%

*Member of last parliament
Con Hold (9.9% Swing from Con to Lab)

BANFF AND BUCHAN

		%
*Salmond, A. (SNP)	22,409	55.8
Bell-Frain, W. (Con)	9,564	23.8
Harris, M. (Lab)	4,747	11.8
Fletcher, N. (LD)	2,398	6.0
Buchan, A. (Ref)	1,060	2.6
SNP majority 12,845		31.97%
Electorate	58,493	
Total Vote	40,178	Poll 68.7%

*Member of last parliament
SNP Hold (7.9% Swing from Con to SNP)

BARKING

		%
*Hodge, M. (Lab)	21,698	65.8
Langford, K. (Con)	5,802	17.6
Marsh, M. (LD)	3,128	9.5
Taylor, C. (Ref)	1,283	3.9
Tolman, M. (BNP)	894	2.7
Mearns, D. (Pro-Life)	159	0.5
Lab majority 15,896		48.22%
Electorate	53,682	
Total Vote	32,964	Poll 61.4%

*Member of last parliament
Lab Hold (14.9% Swing from Con to Lab)

BARNSLEY CENTRAL

		%
*Illsley, E. (Lab)	28,090	77.0
Gutteridge, S. (Con)	3,589	9.8
Finlay, D. (LD)	3,481	9.5
Walsh, J. (Ref)	1,325	3.6
Lab majority 24,501		67.15%
Electorate	61,133	
Total Vote	36,485	Poll 59.7%

*Member of last parliament
Lab Hold (7.5% Swing from Con to Lab)

BARNSLEY EAST AND MEXBOROUGH

		%
*Ennis, J. (Lab)	31,699	73.1
Ellison, J. (Con)	4,936	11.4
Willis, D. (LD)	4,489	10.4
Capstick, K. (SLP)	1,213	2.8
Miles, A. (Ref)	797	1.8
Hyland, J. (SEP)	201	0.5
Lab majority 26,763		61.76%
Electorate	67,840	
Total Vote	43,335	Poll 63.9%

*Member of last parliament
Lab Hold (3.1% Swing from Con to Lab)

BARNSLEY WEST AND PENISTONE

		%
*Clapham, M. (Lab)	25,017	59.3
Watkins, P. (Con)	7,750	18.4
Knight, W. (LD)	7,613	18.0
Miles, J. (Ref)	1,828	4.3
Lab majority 17,267		40.91%
Electorate	64,894	
Total Vote	42,208	Poll 65%

*Member of last parliament
Lab Hold (5.3% Swing from Con to Lab)

BARROW AND FURNESS

		%
*Hutton, J. (Lab)	27,630	57.3
Hunt, R. (Con)	13,133	27.2
Metcalfe, A. (LD)	4,264	8.8
Hamezeian, J. (PLP)	1,995	4.1
Mitchell, D. (Ref)	1,208	2.5
Lab majority 14,497		30.06%
Electorate	66,960	
Total Vote	48,230	Poll 72%

*Member of last parliament
Lab Hold (11.8% Swing from Con to Lab)

BASILDON

		%
Smith, A. (Lab/Co-op)	29,646	55.8
Baron, J. (Con)	16,366	30.8
Granshaw, L. (LD)	4,608	8.7
Robinson, C. (Ref)	2,462	4.6
Lab/Co-op majority 13,280		25.02%
Electorate	73,989	
Total Vote	53,082	Poll 71.6%

Lab/Co-op Gain (14.7% Swing from Con to Lab)

BASINGSTOKE

		%
*Hunter, A. (Con)	24,751	43.3
Lickley, N. (Lab)	22,354	39.1
Rimmer, M. (LD)	9,714	17.0
Selim, E. (Ind)	310	0.5
Con majority 2,397		4.20%
Electorate	77,035	
Total Vote	57,129	Poll 73.8%

*Member of last parliament
Con Hold (12.1% Swing from Con to Lab)

BASSETLAW

		%
*Ashton, J. (Lab)	29,298	61.0
Cleasby, M. (Con)	11,838	24.8
Kerrigan, M. (LD)	4,950	10.3
Graham, R. (Ref)	1,838	3.9
Lab majority 17,460		36.43%
Electorate	68,101	
Total Vote	47,924	Poll 70.5%

*Member of last parliament
Lab Hold (8.9% Swing from Con to Lab)

BATH

		%
*Foster, D. (LD)	26,169	48.5
McNair, A. (Con)	16,850	31.2
Bush, T. (Lab)	8,828	16.4
Cook, A. (Ref)	1,192	2.2
Scrase, R. (Green)	580	1.1
Sandell, P. (UKIP)	315	0.6
Pullen, N. (NLP)	55	0.1
LD majority 9,319		17.26%
Electorate	70,815	
Total Vote	53,989	Poll 75.5%

*Member of last parliament
LD Hold (6.9% Swing from Con to LD)

BATLEY AND SPEN %
Wood, M. (Lab)	23,213	49.4
*Peacock, E. (Con)	17,072	36.4
Pinnock, K. (LD)	4,133	8.8
Wood, E. (Ref)	1,691	3.6
Smith, R. (BNP)	472	1.0
Lord, C. (Green)	384	0.8
Lab majority	6,141	13.08%
Electorate	64,209	
Total Vote	46,965	Poll 73.1%

*Member of last parliament
Lab Gain (7.4% Swing from Con to Lab)

BATTERSEA %
Linton, M. (Lab)	24,047	50.7
*Bowis, J. (Con)	18,687	39.4
Keaveney, P. (LD)	3,482	7.3
Slater, M. (Ref)	804	1.7
Banks, A. (UKIP)	250	0.5
Marshall, J.		
(Dream)	127	0.3
Lab majority	5,360	11.31%
Electorate	66,928	
Total Vote	47,397	Poll 69%

*Member of last parliament
Lab Gain (10.2% Swing from Con to Lab)

BEACONSFIELD %
Grieve, D. (Con)	24,709	49.2
Mapp, P. (LD)	10,722	21.4
Hudson, A. (Lab)	10,063	20.0
Lloyd, H. (Ref)	2,197	4.4
Story, C. (IndCon)	1,434	2.9
Cooke, C. (UKIP)	451	0.9
Duval, G. (Pro-Life)	286	0.6
Dyball, T. (NLP)	193	0.4
Matthews, R. (Ind)	146	0.3
Con majority	13,987	27.86%
Electorate	68,959	
Total Vote	50,201	Poll 70.8%

Con Hold (8.2% Swing from Con to LD)

BECKENHAM %
*Merchant, P. (Con)	23,084	42.5
Hughes, R. (Lab)	18,131	33.4
Vetterlein, R. (LD)	9,858	18.1
Mead, L. (Ref)	1,663	3.1
Rimmer, P. (Lib)	720	1.3
Pratt, C. (UKIP)	506	0.9
McAuley, J. (NF)	388	0.7
Con majority	4,953	9.11%
Electorate	72,807	
Total Vote	54,350	Poll 74%

*Member of last parliament
Con Hold (15% Swing from Con to Lab)

BEDFORD %
Hall, P. (Lab)	24,774	50.6
Blackman, R. (Con)	16,474	33.7
Noyce, C. (LD)	6,044	12.3
Conquest, P. (Ref)	1,503	3.1
Saunders, P. (NLP)	149	0.3
Lab majority	8,300	16.96%
Electorate	66,560	
Total Vote	48,944	Poll 73.5%

Lab Gain (13% Swing from Con to Lab)

BELFAST EAST %
*Robinson, P. (DUP)	16,640	42.6
Empey, R. (UUP)	9,886	25.3
Hendron, J. (APNI)	9,288	23.8
Dines, S. (Con)	928	2.4
Corr, D. (SF)	810	2.1
Lewsley, P. (SDLP)	629	1.6
Dougan, D. (Ind)	541	1.4
Bell, J. (Workers)	237	0.6
Collins, D. (NLP)	70	0.2
DUP majority	6,754	17.31%
Electorate	61,744	
Total Vote	39,029	Poll 63.2%

*Member of last parliament
DUP Hold (0% Swing from to)

BELFAST NORTH %
*Walker, C. (UUP)	21,478	51.8
Maginness, A. (SDLP)	8,454	20.4
Kelly, G. (SF)	8,375	20.2
Campbell, T. (APNI)	2,221	5.4
Emerson, P. (Green)	539	1.3
Treanor, P. (Workers)	297	0.7
Gribben, A. (NLP)	88	0.2
UUP majority	13,024	31.42%
Electorate	64,577	
Total Vote	41,452	Poll 64.2%

*Member of last parliament
UUP Hold (1.2% Swing from UUP to SDLP)

BELFAST SOUTH %
*Smyth, M. (UUP)	14,201	36.0
McDonald, A. (SDLP)	9,601	24.3
Ervine, D. (PUP)	5,687	14.4
McBride, S. (APNI)	5,112	12.9
Hayes, S. (SF)	2,019	5.1
Campbell, A. (Women)	1,204	3.0
Boal, M. (Con)	962	2.4
Cusack, N. (Lab)	292	0.7
Lynn, P. (Workers)	286	0.7
Anderson, J. (NLP)	120	0.3
UUP majority	4,600	11.65%
Electorate	63,439	
Total Vote	39,484	Poll 62.2%

*Member of last parliament
UUP Hold (13.4% Swing from UUP to SDLP)

BELFAST WEST %
Adams, G. (SF)	25,662	55.9
*Hendron, J. (SDLP)	17,753	38.7
Parkinson, F. (UUP)	1,556	3.4
Lowry, J. (Workers)	721	1.6
Kennedy, L. (HR)	102	0.2
Daly, M. (NLP)	91	0.2
SF majority	7,909	17.24%
Electorate	61,785	
Total Vote	45,885	Poll 74.3%

*Member of last parliament
SF Gain (9.7% Swing from SDLP to SF)

BERWICK-UPON-TWEED %
*Beith, A. (LD)	19,007	45.5
Brannen, P. (Lab)	10,965	26.2
Herbert, N. (Con)	10,056	24.1
Lambton, N. (Ref)	1,423	3.4
Dodds, I. (UKIP)	352	0.8
LD majority	8,042	19.24%
Electorate	56,428	
Total Vote	41,803	Poll 74%

*Member of last parliament
LD Hold (1.1% Swing from LD to Lab)

BETHNAL GREEN AND BOW %
King, O. (Lab)	20,697	46.3
Choudhury, K. (Con)	9,412	21.1
Islam, S. (LD)	5,361	12.0
King, D. (BNP)	3,350	7.5
Milsom, T. (Lib)	2,963	6.6
Osman, S.		
(Real Labour)	1,117	2.5
Petter, S. (Green)	812	1.8
Abdullah, M. (Ref)	557	1.2
Hamid, A. (SLP)	413	0.9
Lab majority	11,285	25.26%
Electorate	73,008	
Total Vote	44,682	Poll 61.2%

Lab Hold (5.9% Swing from Lab to Con)

BEVERLEY AND HOLDERNESS %
*Cran, J. (Con)	21,629	41.2
O'Neill, N. (Lab)	20,418	38.9
Melling, J. (LD)	9,689	18.4
Barley, D. (UKIP)	695	1.3
Withers, S. (NLP)	111	0.2
Con majority	1,211	2.30%
Electorate	71,916	
Total Vote	52,542	Poll 72.9%

*Member of last parliament
Con Hold (16.1% Swing from Con to Lab)

BEXHILL AND BATTLE %
*Wardle, C. (Con)	23,570	48.1
Field, K. (LD)	12,470	25.5
Beckwith, R. (Lab)	8,866	18.1
Thompson, V. (Ref)	3,302	6.7
Pankhurst, J. (UKIP)	786	1.6
Con majority	11,100	22.66%
Electorate	65,584	
Total Vote	48,994	Poll 74.3%

*Member of last parliament
Con Hold (4.4% Swing from Con to LD)

BEXLEYHEATH AND CRAYFORD %
Beard, N. (Lab)	21,942	45.5
*Evennett, D. (Con)	18,527	38.4
Montford, F. (LD)	5,391	11.2
Thomas, B. (Ref)	1,551	3.2
Smith, P. (BNP)	429	0.9
Jenner, W. (UKIP)	383	0.8
Lab majority	3,415	7.08%
Electorate	63,334	
Total Vote	48,223	Poll 76.1%

*Member of last parliament
Lab Gain (15% Swing from Con to Lab)

BILLERICAY %
*Gorman, T. (Con)	22,033	39.8
Richards, P. (Lab)	20,677	37.3
Williams, G. (LD)	8,763	15.8
Hughes, B. (LoyalCon)	3,377	6.1

Buchanan, J.
(Pro-Life)　　　　570　1.0
Con majority　1,356　　2.45%
Electorate　　76,550
Total Vote　　55,420　Poll 72.1%
*Member of last parliament
Con Hold (17.6% Swing from Con to Lab)

BIRKENHEAD　　　　　　%
*Field, F. (Lab)　　27,825　70.8
Crosby, A. (Con)　　5,982　15.2
Wood, R. (LD)　　　3,548　9.0
Cullen, M. (SLP)　　1,168　3.0
Evans, R. (Ref)　　　800　2.0
Lab majority　21,843　　55.56%
Electorate　　59,782
Total Vote　　39,323　Poll 65.8%
*Member of last parliament
Lab Hold (8.5% Swing from Con to Lab)

BIRMINGHAM EDGBASTON %
Stuart, G. (Lab)　　23,554　48.6
Marshall, A. (Con)　18,712　38.6
Gallagher, J. (LD)　4,691　9.7
Oakton, J. (Ref)　　1,065　2.2
Campbell, D. (BDP)　　443　0.9
Lab majority　4,842　　9.99%
Electorate　　70,204
Total Vote　　48,465　Poll 69%
Lab Gain (10% Swing from Con to Lab)

BIRMINGHAM ERDINGTON %
*Corbett, R. (Lab)　23,764　58.8
Tomkins, A. (Con)　11,107　27.5
Garrett, I. (LD)　　4,112　10.2
Cable, G. (Ref)　　1,424　3.5
Lab majority　12,657　　31.32%
Electorate　　66,380
Total Vote　　40,407　Poll 60.9%
*Member of last parliament
Lab Hold (7.3% Swing from Con to Lab)

BIRMINGHAM HALL
GREEN　　　　　　　%
McCabe, S. (Lab)　22,372　53.5
*Hargreaves, A.
(Con)　　　　　13,952　33.4
Dow, C. (LD)　　　4,034　9.6
Bennett, P. (Ref)　1,461　3.5
Lab majority　8,420　　20.13%
Electorate　　58,767
Total Vote　　41,819　Poll 71.2%
*Member of last parliament
Lab Gain (14% Swing from Con to Lab)

BIRMINGHAM HODGE
HILL　　　　　　　%
*Davis, T. (Lab)　22,398　65.6
Grant, E. (Con)　　8,198　24.0
Thomas, H. (LD)　2,891　8.5
Johnson, P. (UKIP)　660　1.9
Lab majority　14,200　　41.58%
Electorate　　56,086
Total Vote　　34,147　Poll 60.9%
*Member of last parliament
Lab Hold (12.1% Swing from Con to Lab)

BIRMINGHAM LADYWOOD %
*Short, C. (Lab)　28,134　74.1
Vara, S. (Con)　　5,052　13.3
Marwa, S. (LD)　3,020　8.0
Gurney, R. (Ref)　1,086　2.9
Carmichael, A.
(Nat Dem)　　　685　1.8
Lab majority　23,082　　60.78%
Electorate　　70,813
Total Vote　　37,977　Poll 54.2%
*Member of last parliament
Lab Hold (4.9% Swing from Con to Lab)

BIRMINGHAM
NORTHFIELD　　　　%
*Burden, R. (Lab)　22,316　57.4
Blumenthal, A.
(Con)　　　　　10,873　28.0
Ashall, M. (LD)　4,078　10.5
Gent, D. (Ref)　　1,243　3.2
Axon, K. (BNP)　　337　0.9
Lab majority　11,443　　29.46%
Electorate　　56,842
Total Vote　　38,847　Poll 68.3%
*Member of last parliament
Lab Hold (13% Swing from Con to Lab)

BIRMINGHAM PERRY
BARR　　　　　　　%
*Rooker, J. (Lab)　28,921　63.0
Dunnett, A. (Con)　9,964　21.7
Hassall, R. (LD)　4,523　9.9
Mahmood, S. (Ref)　843　1.8
Baxter, W. (Lib)　　718　1.6
Windridge, L. (BNP)　544　1.2
Panesar, A. (4th Party)　374　0.8
Lab majority　18,957　　41.31%
Electorate　　71,031
Total Vote　　45,887　Poll 64.6%
*Member of last parliament
Lab Hold (13.4% Swing from Con to Lab)

BIRMINGHAM SELLY OAK %
*Jones, L. (Lab)　28,121　55.6
Green, G. (Con)　14,033　27.8
Osborne, D. (LD)　6,121　12.1
Marshall, L. (Ref)　1,520　3.0
Gardner, G. (Pro-Life)　417　0.8
Sherriff-Knowles, P.
(Loony)　　　　253　0.5
Meads, H. (NLP)　　85　0.2
Lab majority　14,088　　27.87%
Electorate　　72,049
Total Vote　　50,550　Poll 70.2%
*Member of last parliament
Lab Hold (12.1% Swing from Con to Lab)

BIRMINGHAM SPARKBROOK
AND SMALL HEATH　%
*Godsiff, R. (Lab)　26,841　64.3
Hardeman, K. (Con)　7,315　17.5
Harmer, R. (LD)　3,889　9.3
Clawley, A. (Green)　959　2.3
Dooley, R. (Ref)　　737　1.8
Patel, P. (4th Party)　538　1.3
Syed, R. (Rights)　513　1.2

Bi, S. (Ind)　　　490　1.2
Wren, C. (SLP)　　483　1.2
Lab majority　19,526　　46.75%
Electorate　　73,130
Total Vote　　41,765　Poll 57.1%
*Member of last parliament
Lab Hold (4.6% Swing from Con to Lab)

BIRMINGHAM YARDLEY　%
*Morris, E. (Lab)　17,778　47.0
Hemming, J. (LD)　12,463　33.0
Jobson, A. (Con)　6,736　17.8
Livingston, D.
(Ref)　　　　　646　1.7
Ware, A. (UKIP)　　164　0.4
Lab majority　5,315　　14.07%
Electorate　　53,058
Total Vote　　37,787　Poll 71.2%
*Member of last parliament
Lab Hold (4.7% Swing from LD to Lab)

BISHOP AUCKLAND　　%
*Foster, D. (Lab)　30,359　65.9
Fergus, J. (Con)　9,295　20.2
Ashworth, L. (LD)　4,293　9.3
Blacker, D. (Ref)　2,104　4.6
Lab majority　21,064　　45.74%
Electorate　　66,754
Total Vote　　46,051　Poll 69%
*Member of last parliament
Lab Hold (15.5% Swing from Con to Lab)

BLABY　　　　　　　%
*Robathan, A.
(Con)　　　　　24,564　45.8
Willmott, R. (Lab)　18,090　33.8
Welsh, G. (LD)　8,001　14.9
Harrison, R. (Ref)　2,018　3.8
Peacock, J. (BNP)　523　1.0
Stokes, T. (Ind)　　397　0.7
Con majority　6,474　　12.08%
Electorate　　70,471
Total Vote　　53,593　Poll 75.9%
*Member of last parliament
Con Hold (11.5% Swing from Con to Lab)

BLACKBURN　　　　　%
*Straw, J. (Lab)　26,141　55.0
Sidhu, S. (Con)　11,690　24.6
Fenn, S. (LD)　4,990　10.5
Bradshaw, D.
(Ref)　　　　　1,892　4.0
Wingfield, T.
(Nat Dem)　　　671　1.4
Drummond, H. (SLP)　637　1.3
Field, R. (Green)　608　1.3
Carmichael-Grimshaw,
M. (KBFIP)　　　506　1.1
Batchelor, W.
(Common Sense)　362　0.8
Lab majority　14,451　　30.43%
Electorate　　73,058
Total Vote　　47,497　Poll 65%
*Member of last parliament
Lab Hold (9.7% Swing from Con to Lab)

BLACKPOOL NORTH AND FLEETWOOD

	%
Humble, J. (Lab)	28,051	52.2
*Elletson, H. (Con)	19,105	35.5
Hill, B. (LD)	4,600	8.6
Stacey, K. (Ref)	1,704	3.2
Ellis, J. (BNP)	288	0.5
Lab majority	8,946	16.64%
Electorate	74,989	
Total Vote	53,748	Poll 71.6%

*Member of last parliament
Lab Gain (14.4% Swing from Con to Lab)

BLACKPOOL SOUTH

	%
Marsden, G. (Lab)	29,282	57.0
Booth, R. (Con)	17,666	34.4
Holt, D. (LD)	4,392	8.6
Lab majority	11,616	22.63%
Electorate	75,720	
Total Vote	51,340	Poll 67.7%

Lab Gain (11.6% Swing from Con to Lab)

BLAENAU GWENT

	%
*Smith, L. (Lab)	31,493	79.5
Layton, G. (LD)	3,458	8.7
Williams, M. (Con)	2,607	6.6
Criddle, J. (PC)	2,072	5.2
Lab majority	28,035	70.74%
Electorate	54,800	
Total Vote	39,630	Poll 72.3%

*Member of last parliament
Lab Hold (0.9% Swing from Lab to LD)

BLAYDON

	%
*McWilliam, J. (Lab)	27,535	60.0
Maughan, P. (LD)	10,930	23.8
Watson, M. (Con)	6,048	13.2
Rook, R. (IndLab)	1,412	3.1
Lab majority	16,605	36.16%
Electorate	64,699	
Total Vote	45,925	Poll 71%

*Member of last parliament
Lab Hold (2.1% Swing from LD to Lab)

BLYTH VALLEY

	%
*Campbell, R. (Lab)	27,276	64.2
Lamb, A. (LD)	9,540	22.5
Musgrave, B. (Con)	5,666	13.3
Lab majority	17,736	41.75%
Electorate	61,761	
Total Vote	42,482	Poll 68.7%

*Member of last parliament
Lab Hold (12.7% Swing from LD to Lab)

BOGNOR REGIS AND LITTLEHAMPTON

	%
Gibb, N. (Con)	20,537	44.2
Nash, R. (Lab)	13,216	28.5
Walsh, J. (LD)	11,153	24.0
Stride, G. (UKIP)	1,537	3.3
Con majority	7,321	15.76%
Electorate	66,480	
Total Vote	46,443	Poll 69.6%

Con Hold (13.8% Swing from Con to Lab)

BOLSOVER

	%
*Skinner, D. (Lab)	35,073	74.0
Harwood, R. (Con)	7,924	16.7
Cox, I. (LD)	4,417	9.3
Lab majority	27,149	57.26%
Electorate	66,476	
Total Vote	47,414	Poll 71.3%

*Member of last parliament
Lab Hold (9% Swing from Con to Lab)

BOLTON NORTH EAST

	%
Crausby, D. (Lab)	27,621	56.1
Wilson, R. (Con)	14,952	30.4
Critchley, E. (LD)	4,862	9.9
Staniforth, D. (Ref)	1,096	2.2
Kelly, W. (SLP)	676	1.4
Lab majority	12,669	25.75%
Electorate	67,930	
Total Vote	49,207	Poll 72.4%

Lab Win (10.2% Swing from Con to Lab)

BOLTON SOUTH EAST

	%
Iddon, B. (Lab)	29,856	68.9
Carter, P. (Con)	8,545	19.7
Harasiwka, F. (LD)	3,805	8.8
Pickering, W. (Ref)	973	2.2
Walch, L. (NLP)	170	0.4
Lab majority	21,311	49.16%
Electorate	66,459	
Total Vote	43,349	Poll 65.2%

Lab Hold (11.8% Swing from Con to Lab)

BOLTON WEST

	%
Kelly, R. (Lab)	24,342	49.5
*Sackville, T. (Con)	17,270	35.1
Ronson, B. (LD)	5,309	10.8
Kelly, D. (SLP)	1,374	2.8
Frankl-Slater, G. (Ref)	865	1.8
Lab majority	7,072	14.39%
Electorate	63,535	
Total Vote	49,160	Poll 77.4%

*Member of last parliament
Lab Gain (11.3% Swing from Con to Lab)

BOOTLE

	%
*Benton, J. (Lab)	31,668	82.9
Matthews, R. (Con)	3,247	8.5
Reid, K. (LD)	2,191	5.7
Elliot, J. (Ref)	571	1.5
Glover, P. (SLP)	420	1.1
Cohen, S. (NLP)	126	0.3
Lab majority	28,421	74.36%
Electorate	57,284	
Total Vote	38,223	Poll 66.7%

*Member of last parliament
Lab Hold (6% Swing from Con to Lab)

BOSTON AND SKEGNESS

	%
*Body, Sir R. (Con)	19,750	42.4
McCauley, P. (Lab)	19,103	41.0
Dodsworth, J. (LD)	7,721	16.6
Con majority	647	1.39%
Electorate	67,623	
Total Vote	46,574	Poll 68.9%

*Member of last parliament
Con Hold (10.6% Swing from Con to Lab)

BOSWORTH

	%
*Tredinnick, D. (Con)	21,189	40.6
Furlong, A. (Lab)	20,162	38.7
Ellis, J. (LD)	9,281	17.8
Halborg, S. (Ref)	1,521	2.9
Con majority	1,027	1.97%
Electorate	68,113	
Total Vote	52,153	Poll 76.6%

*Member of last parliament
Con Hold (11.7% Swing from Con to Lab)

BOURNEMOUTH EAST

	%
*Atkinson, D. (Con)	17,997	41.4
Eyre, D. (LD)	13,651	31.4
Stevens, J. (Lab)	9,181	21.1
Musgrave-Scott, A. (Ref)	1,808	4.2
Bennet, K. (UKIP)	791	1.8
Con majority	4,346	10.01%
Electorate	61,862	
Total Vote	43,428	Poll 70.2%

*Member of last parliament
Con Hold (7.2% Swing from Con to LD)

BOURNEMOUTH WEST

	%
*Butterfill, J. (Con)	17,115	41.7
Dover, J. (LD)	11,405	27.8
Gritt, D. (Lab)	10,093	24.6
Mills, R. (Ref)	1,910	4.7
Tooley, L. (UKIP)	281	0.7
Morse, J. (BNP)	165	0.4
Springham, A. (NLP)	103	0.3
Con majority	5,710	13.90%
Electorate	62,028	
Total Vote	41,072	Poll 66.2%

*Member of last parliament
Con Hold (5.6% Swing from Con to LD)

BRACKNELL

	%
*Mackay, A. (Con)	27,983	47.4
Snelgrove, A. (Lab)	17,596	29.8
Hilliar, A. (LD)	9,122	15.4
Tompkins, J. (New Labour)	1,909	3.2
Cairns, W. (Ref)	1,636	2.8
Boxall, L. (UKIP)	569	1.0
Roberts, D. (Pro-Life)	276	0.5
Con majority	10,387	17.58%
Electorate	79,292	
Total Vote	59,091	Poll 74.5%

*Member of last parliament
Con Hold (11.3% Swing from Con to Lab)

BRADFORD NORTH

	%
*Rooney, T. (Lab)	23,493	56.1
Skinner, R. (Con)	10,723	25.6
Browne, T. (LD)	6,083	14.5
Wheatley, H. (Ref)	1,227	2.9
Beckett, W. (Loony)	369	0.9
Lab majority	12,770	30.48%
Electorate	66,228	
Total Vote	41,895	Poll 63.1%

*Member of last parliament
Lab Hold (7.4% Swing from Con to Lab)

BRADFORD SOUTH

		%
*Sutcliffe, G. (Lab)	25,558	56.7
Hawkesworth, A.		
(Con)	12,622	28.0
Wilson-Fletcher, A.		
(LD)	5,093	11.3
Kershaw, M. (Ref)	1,785	4.0
Lab majority	12,936	28.71%
Electorate	68,391	
Total Vote	45,058	Poll 65.8%

*Member of last parliament

Lab Hold (9.7% Swing from Con to Lab)

BRADFORD WEST

		%
Singh, M. (Lab)	18,932	41.5
Riaz, M. (Con)	15,055	33.0
Wright, H. (LD)	6,737	14.8
Khan, A. (SLP)	1,551	3.4
Royston, C. (Ref)	1,348	3.0
Robinson, J. (Green)	861	1.9
Osborn, G. (BNP)	839	1.8
Shah, S. (Soc)	245	0.5
Lab majority	3,877	8.51%
Electorate	71,961	
Total Vote	45,568	Poll 62.9%

Lab Hold (5.5% Swing from Lab to Con)

BRAINTREE

		%
Hurst, A. (Lab)	23,729	42.7
*Newton, T. (Con)	22,278	40.1
Ellis, T. (LD)	6,418	11.5
Westcott, N. (Ref)	2,165	3.9
Abbott, J. (Green)	712	1.3
Nolan, M. (New Way)	274	0.5
Lab majority	1,451	2.61%
Electorate	72,772	
Total Vote	55,576	Poll 76.1%

*Member of last parliament

Lab Gain (12.9% Swing from Con to Lab)

BRECON AND RADNORSHIRE

		%
Livsey, R. (LD)	17,516	40.8
*Evans, J. (Con)	12,419	29.0
Mann, C. (Lab)	11,424	26.6
Phillips, L. (Ref)	900	2.1
Cornelius, S. (PC)	622	1.5
LD majority	5,097	11.89%
Electorate	52,142	
Total Vote	42,881	Poll 82.2%

*Member of last parliament

LD Gain (6.1% Swing from Con to LD)

BRENT EAST

		%
*Livingstone, K. (Lab)	23,748	67.3
Francois, M. (Con)	7,866	22.3
Hunter, I. (LD)	2,751	7.8
Keable, S. (SLP)	466	1.3
Shanks, A. (Pro-Life)	218	0.6
Warrilow, C. (Dream)	120	0.3
Jenkin, N. (NLP)	103	0.3
Lab majority	15,882	45.03%
Electorate	53,548	
Total Vote	35,272	Poll 65.9%

*Member of last parliament

Lab Hold (14.4% Swing from Con to Lab)

BRENT NORTH

		%
Gardiner, B. (Lab)	19,343	50.7
*Boyson, R. (Con)	15,324	40.1
Lorber, P. (LD)	3,104	8.1
Davids, T. (NLP)	204	0.5
Clark, G. (Dream)	199	0.5
Lab majority	4,019	10.53%
Electorate	54,149	
Total Vote	38,174	Poll 70.5%

*Member of last parliament

Lab Gain (18.8% Swing from Con to Lab)

BRENT SOUTH

		%
*Boateng, P. (Lab)	25,180	73.0
Jackson, S. (Con)	5,489	15.9
Brazil, J. (LD)	2,670	7.7
Phythian, J. (Ref)	497	1.4
Edler, D. (Green)	389	1.1
Howard, C.		
(Dream)	175	0.5
Mahaldar, A. (NLP)	98	0.3
Lab majority	19,691	57.08%
Electorate	53,505	
Total Vote	34,498	Poll 64.5%

*Member of last parliament

Lab Hold (15.3% Swing from Con to Lab)

BRENTFORD AND ISLEWORTH

		%
Keen, A. (Lab)	32,249	57.4
*Deva, N. (Con)	17,825	31.8
Hartwell, G. (LD)	4,613	8.2
Bradley, J. (Green)	687	1.2
Simmerson, B.		
(UKIP)	614	1.1
Ahmed, M. (NLP)	147	0.3
Lab majority	14,424	25.70%
Electorate	79,058	
Total Vote	56,135	Poll 69.5%

*Member of last parliament

Lab Gain (14.3% Swing from Con to Lab)

BRENTWOOD AND ONGAR

		%
*Pickles, E. (Con)	23,031	45.4
Bottomley, E. (LD)	13,341	26.3
Young, M. (Lab)	11,231	22.1
Kilmartin, A. (Ref)	2,658	5.2
Mills, D. (UKIP)	465	0.9
Con majority	9,690	19.10%
Electorate	66,005	
Total Vote	50,726	Poll 76.9%

*Member of last parliament

Con Hold (4% Swing from Con to LD)

BRIDGEND

		%
*Griffiths, W. (Lab)	25,115	58.1
Davies, D. (Con)	9,867	22.8
McKinlay, A. (LD)	4,968	11.5
Greaves, T. (Ref)	1,662	3.8
Watkins, D. (PC)	1,649	3.8
Lab majority	15,248	35.25%
Electorate	59,721	
Total Vote	43,261	Poll 72.3%

*Member of last parliament

Lab Hold (9.8% Swing from Con to Lab)

BRIDGWATER

		%
*King, T. (Con)	20,174	36.9
Hoban, M. (LD)	18,378	33.6
Lavers, R. (Lab)	13,519	24.8
Evens, F. (Ref)	2,551	4.7
Con majority	1,796	3.29%
Electorate	73,038	
Total Vote	54,622	Poll 74.6%

*Member of last parliament

Con Hold (6.9% Swing from Con to LD)

BRIGG AND GOOLE

		%
Cawsey, I. (Lab)	23,493	50.2
Stewart, D. (Con)	17,104	36.5
Hardy, M. (LD)	4,692	10.0
Rigby, D. (Ref)	1,513	3.2
Lab majority	6,389	13.65%
Electorate	63,648	
Total Vote	46,802	Poll 73.5%

Lab Gain (13.9% Swing from Con to Lab)

BRIGHTON KEMPTOWN

		%
Turner, D. (Lab)	21,479	46.6
*Bowden, Sir A.		
(Con)	17,945	39.2
Gray, C. (LD)	4,478	9.8
Inman, D. (Ref)	1,526	3.3
Williams, H. (SLP)	316	0.7
Bowler, J. (NLP)	172	0.4
Newman, L. (Loony)	123	0.3
Darlow, R. (Dream)	93	0.2
Lab majority	3,534	7.66%
Electorate	65,147	
Total Vote	46,132	Poll 70.4%

*Member of last parliament

Lab Gain (13.6% Swing from Con to Lab)

BRIGHTON PAVILION

		%
Lepper, D.		
(Lab/Co-op)	26,737	54.6
*Spencer, Sir D. (Con)	13,556	27.9
Blanshard, K. (LD)	4,644	9.5
Stocken, P. (Ref)	1,304	2.6
West, P. (Green)	1,249	2.5
Huggett, R. (IndCon)	1,098	2.2
Stevens, P. (UKIP)	179	0.4
Dobbs, B. (Sub-Genius)	125	0.3
Card, A. (Dream)	59	0.1
Lab/Co-op majority	13,181	26.9%
Electorate	66,431	
Total Vote	48,951	Poll 73.7%

*Member of last parliament

Lab/Co-op Gain (16% Swing from Con to Lab)

BRISTOL EAST

		%
*Corston, J. (Lab)	27,418	56.9
Vaizey, E. (Con)	11,259	23.4
Tyzack, P. (LD)	7,121	14.8
Philp, G. (Ref)	1,479	3.1
Williams, P. (SLP)	766	1.6
McLaggan, J. (NLP)	158	0.3
Lab majority	16,159	33.52%
Electorate	68,990	
Total Vote	48,201	Poll 69.7%

*Member of last parliament

Lab Hold (11.9% Swing from Con to Lab)

BRISTOL NORTH WEST

		%
Naysmith, D.		
(Lab/Co-op)	27,575	49.9
*Stern, M. (Con)	16,193	29.3
Parry, I. (LD)	7,263	13.1
Horton, C. (IndLab)	1,718	3.1
Quintanilla, J. (Ref)	1,609	2.9
Shorter, G. (SLP)	482	0.9
Parnell, S. (BNP)	265	0.5
Leighton, T. (NLP)	140	0.3
Lab/Co-op		
majority	11,382	20.60%
Electorate	75,009	
Total Vote	55,245	Poll 73.3%

*Member of last parliament
Lab Hold (7.1% Swing from Con to Lab)

BRISTOL SOUTH

		%
*Primarolo, D. (Lab)	29,890	59.9
Roe, M. (Con)	10,562	21.2
Williams, S. (LD)	6,691	13.4
Guy, D. (Ref)	1,486	3.0
Boxall, J. (Green)	722	1.4
Marshall, I. (Soc)	355	0.7
Taylor, L.		
(Go Bowling)	153	0.3
Lab majority	19,328	38.77%
Electorate	72,393	
Total Vote	49,859	Poll 68.7%

*Member of last parliament
Lab Hold (12.3% Swing from Con to Lab)

BRISTOL WEST

		%
Davey, V. (Lab)	22,068	35.2
*Waldegrave, W. (Con)	20,575	32.8
Boney, C. (LD)	17,551	28.0
Beauchamp, R. (Ref)	1,304	2.1
Quinnell, J. (Green)	852	1.4
Nurse, R. (SLP)	244	0.4
Brierley, J. (NLP)	47	0.1
Lab majority	1,493	2.38%
Electorate	84,870	
Total Vote	62,641	Poll 72.7%

*Member of last parliament
Lab Gain (12.1% Swing from Con to Lab)

BROMLEY AND CHISLEHURST

		%
*Forth, E. (Con)	24,428	46.3
Yeldham, R. (Lab)	13,310	25.2
Booth, P. (LD)	12,530	23.8
Bryant, R. (UKIP)	1,176	2.2
Speed, F. (Green)	640	1.2
Stoneman, M. (NF)	369	0.7
Aitman, G. (Lib)	285	0.5
Con majority	11,118	21.08%
Electorate	71,104	
Total Vote	52,738	Poll 73.6%

*Member of last parliament
Con Hold (11.8% Swing from Con to Lab)

BROMSGROVE

		%
Kirkbride, J. (Con)	24,620	47.2
McDonald, P. (Lab)	19,725	37.8
Davy, J. (LD)	6,200	11.9
Winsor, D. (Ref)	1,411	2.7
Wetton, B. (UKIP)	251	0.5

		%
Con majority	4,895	9.38%
Electorate	67,744	
Total Vote	52,207	Poll 77.1%

Con Hold (7% Swing from Con to Lab)

BROXBOURNE

		%
*Roe, M. (Con)	22,952	48.9
Coleman, B. (Lab)	16,299	34.7
Davies, J. (LD)	5,310	11.3
Millward, D. (Ref)	1,633	3.5
Bruce, D. (BNP)	610	1.3
Cheetham, B.		
(Third Way)	172	0.4
Con majority	6,653	14.16%
Electorate	66,720	
Total Vote	46,976	Poll 70.4%

*Member of last parliament
Con Hold (13.4% Swing from Con to Lab)

BROXTOWE

		%
Palmer, N. (Lab)	27,343	47.0
*Lester, J. (Con)	21,768	37.4
Miller, T. (LD)	6,934	11.9
Tucker, R. (Ref)	2,092	3.6
Lab majority	5,575	9.59%
Electorate	74,144	
Total Vote	58,137	Poll 78.4%

*Member of last parliament
Lab Gain (12.9% Swing from Con to Lab)

BUCKINGHAM

		%
Bercow, J. (Con)	24,594	49.8
Lehmann, R. (Lab)	12,208	24.7
Stuart, N. (LD)	12,175	24.6
Clements, G. (NLP)	421	0.9
Con majority	12,386	25.07%
Electorate	62,945	
Total Vote	49,398	Poll 78.5%

Con Hold (10.6% Swing from Con to Lab)

BURNLEY

		%
*Pike, P. (Lab)	26,210	57.9
Wiggin, W. (Con)	9,148	20.2
Birtwistle, G. (LD)	7,877	17.4
Oakley, R. (Ref)	2,010	4.4
Lab majority	17,062	37.71%
Electorate	67,582	
Total Vote	45,245	Poll 66.9%

*Member of last parliament
Lab Hold (7.7% Swing from Con to Lab)

BURTON

		%
Dean, J. (Lab)	27,810	51.0
*Lawrence, I. (Con)	21,480	39.4
Fletcher, D. (LD)	4,617	8.5
Sharp, K. (Nat Dem)	604	1.1
Lab majority	6,330	11.61%
Electorate	72,601	
Total Vote	54,511	Poll 75.1%

*Member of last parliament
Lab Gain (9.3% Swing from Con to Lab)

BURY NORTH

		%
Chaytor, D. (Lab)	28,523	51.8
*Burt, A. (Con)	20,657	37.5
Kenyon, N. (LD)	4,536	8.2
Hallewell, R. (Ref)	1,337	2.4

		%
Lab majority	7,866	14.29%
Electorate	70,515	
Total Vote	55,053	Poll 78.1%

*Member of last parliament
Lab Gain (11.2% Swing from Con to Lab)

BURY SOUTH

		%
Lewis, I. (Lab)	28,658	56.9
*Sumberg, D. (Con)	16,277	32.3
D'Albert, V. (LD)	4,227	8.4
Slater, B. (Ref)	1,216	2.4
Lab majority	12,381	24.6%
Electorate	66,568	
Total Vote	50,378	Poll 75.7%

*Member of last parliament
Lab Gain (13.2% Swing from Con to Lab)

BURY ST EDMUNDS

		%
Ruffley, D. (Con)	21,290	38.3
Ereira, M. (Lab)	20,922	37.7
Cooper, D. (LD)	10,102	18.2
McWhirter, I. (Ref)	2,939	5.3
Lillis, J. (NLP)	272	0.5
Con majority	368	0.66%
Electorate	74,017	
Total Vote	55,525	Poll 75%

Con Hold (9.6% Swing from Con to Lab)

CAERNARFON

		%
*Wigley, D. (PC)	17,616	51.0
Williams, E. (Lab)	10,167	29.5
Williams, E. (Con)	4,230	12.3
MacQueen, J. (LD)	1,686	4.9
Collins, C. (Ref)	811	2.4
PC majority	7,449	21.5%
Electorate	46,815	
Total Vote	34,510	Poll 73.7%

*Member of last parliament
PC Hold (10.6% Swing from PC to Lab)

CAERPHILLY

		%
*Davies, R. (Lab)	30,697	67.8
Harris, H. (Con)	4,858	10.7
Whittle, L. (PC)	4,383	9.7
Ferguson, A. (LD)	3,724	8.2
Morgan, M. (Ref)	1,337	3.0
Williams, C. (Pro Life)	270	0.6
Lab majority	25,839	57.08%
Electorate	64,621	
Total Vote	45,269	Poll 70%

*Member of last parliament
Lab Hold (5.8% Swing from Con to Lab)

CAITHNESS, SUTHERLAND AND EASTER ROSS

		%
*Maclennan, R. (LD)	10,381	35.6
Hendry, J. (Lab)	8,122	27.8
Harper, E. (SNP)	6,710	23.0
Miers, T. (Con)	3,148	10.8
Ryder, C. (Ref)	369	1.3
Martin, J. (Green)	230	0.8
Carr, M. (UKIP)	212	0.7
LD majority	2,259	7.74%
Electorate	41,566	
Total Vote	29,172	Poll 70%

*Member of last parliament
LD Hold (10.5% Swing from LD to Lab)

CALDER VALLEY

		%
McCafferty, C. (Lab)	26,050	46.1
*Thompson, Sir D.		
(Con)	19,795	35.1
Pearson, S. (LD)	8,322	14.7
Mellor, A. (Ref)	1,380	2.4
Smith, V. (Green)	488	0.9
Jackson, C. (BNP)	431	0.8
Lab majority	6,255	11.08%
Electorate	74,901	
Total Vote	56,466	Poll 75.4%

*Member of last parliament
Lab Gain (9.5% Swing from Con to Lab)

CAMBERWELL AND PECKHAM

		%
*Harman, H. (Lab)	19,734	69.5
Humphreys, M. (Con)	3,383	11.9
Williams, N. (LD)	3,198	11.3
China, N. (Ref)	692	2.4
Ruddock, A. (SLP)	685	2.4
Williams, G. (Lib)	443	1.6
Barker, J. (Soc)	233	0.8
Eames, C. (WRP)	106	0.4
Lab majority	16,351	57.42%
Electorate	50,214	
Total Vote	28,474	Poll 55.6%

*Member of last parliament
Lab Hold (10.7% Swing from Con to Lab)

CAMBRIDGE

		%
*Campbell, A. (Lab)	27,436	53.4
Platt, D. (Con)	13,299	25.9
Heathcock, G. (LD)	8,287	16.1
Burrows, W. (Ref)	1,262	2.5
Wright, M. (Green)	654	1.3
Johnstone, A. (Pro-Life)	191	0.4
Athow, R.		
(Workers Rev)	107	0.2
Gladwin, M. (NLP)	103	0.2
Lab majority	14,137	27.54%
Electorate	71,669	
Total Vote	51,339	Poll 69.2%

*Member of last parliament
Lab Hold (13.2% Swing from Con to Lab)

CANNOCK CHASE

		%
*Wright, T. (Lab)	28,705	54.8
Backhouse, J. (Con)	14,227	27.2
Kirby, R. (LD)	4,537	8.7
Froggatt, P. (Ref)	1,663	3.2
Hurley, W.		
(New Labour)	1,615	3.1
Conroy, M. (SLP)	1,120	2.1
Hartshorne, M.		
(Loony)	499	1.0
Lab majority	14,478	27.65%
Electorate	72,362	
Total Vote	52,366	Poll 72.4%

*Member of last parliament
Lab Hold (8.4% Swing from Con to Lab)

CANTERBURY

		%
*Brazier, J. (Con)	20,913	38.6
Hall, C. (Lab)	16,949	31.3
Vye, M. (LD)	12,854	23.8
Osborne, J. (Ref)	2,460	4.5

Meaden, G. (Green)	588	1.1
Moore, J. (UKIP)	281	0.5
Pringle, A. (NLP)	64	0.1
Con majority	3,964	7.33%
Electorate	74,548	
Total Vote	54,109	Poll 72.6%

*Member of last parliament
Con Hold (13.8% Swing from Con to Lab)

CARDIFF CENTRAL

		%
*Jones, J. (Lab/Co-op)	18,464	43.7
Randerson, J. (LD)	10,541	24.9
Melding, D. (Con)	8,470	20.0
Burns, T. (SLP)	2,230	5.3
Vernon, W. (PC)	1,504	3.6
Lloyd, N. (Ref)	760	1.8
James, C. (Loony)	204	0.5
Hobbs, A. (NLP)	80	0.2
Lab/Co-op		
majority	7,923	18.75%
Electorate	60,354	
Total Vote	42,253	Poll 68.9%

*Member of last parliament
Lab/Co-op Hold (0.9% Swing from Lab to LD)

CARDIFF NORTH

		%
Morgan, J. (Lab)	24,460	50.4
*Jones, G. (Con)	16,334	33.7
Rowland, R. (LD)	5,294	10.9
Palfrey, C. (PC)	1,201	2.5
Litchfield, E. (Ref)	1,199	2.5
Lab majority	8,126	16.76%
Electorate	60,430	
Total Vote	48,488	Poll 79.7%

*Member of last parliament
Lab Gain (11.5% Swing from Con to Lab)

CARDIFF SOUTH AND PENARTH

		%
*Michael, A.		
(Lab/Co-op)	22,647	53.4
Roberts, C. (Con)	8,786	20.7
Wakefield, S. (LD)	3,964	9.3
Foreman, J.		
(New Labour)	3,942	9.3
Haswell, D. (PC)	1,356	3.2
Morgan, P. (Ref)	1,211	2.9
Shepherd, M. (Soc)	344	0.8
Caves, B. (NLP)	170	0.4
Lab/Co-op		
majority	13,861	32.74%
Electorate	61,838	
Total Vote	42,420	Poll 68.6%

*Member of last parliament
Lab/Co-op Hold (5.4% Swing from Con to Lab)

CARDIFF WEST

		%
*Morgan, R. (Lab)	24,297	60.3
Hoare, S. (Con)	8,669	21.5
Gasson, J. (LD)	4,366	10.8
Carr, G. (PC)	1,949	4.8
Johns, T. (Ref)	996	2.5
Lab majority	15,628	38.80%
Electorate	58,198	
Total Vote	40,277	Poll 68.9%

*Member of last parliament
Lab Hold (9.2% Swing from Con to Lab)

CARLISLE

		%
*Martlew, E. (Lab)	25,031	57.4
Lawrence, R. (Con)	12,641	29.0
Mayho, C. (LD)	4,576	10.5
Fraser, A. (Ref)	1,233	2.8
Stevens, W. (NLP)	126	0.3
Lab majority	12,390	28.41%
Electorate	59,917	
Total Vote	43,607	Poll 72.7%

*Member of last parliament
Lab Hold (12.2% Swing from Con to Lab)

CARMARTHEN EAST AND DINEFWR

		%
*Williams, A. (Lab)	17,907	42.9
Thomas, R. (PC)	14,457	34.6
Hayward, E. (Con)	5,022	12.0
Hughes, J. (LD)	3,150	7.5
Humphries-Evans, I.		
(Ref)	1,196	2.9
Lab majority	3,450	8.27%
Electorate	53,079	
Total Vote	41,732	Poll 78.6%

*Member of last parliament
Lab Hold (2.1% Swing from Lab to PC)

CARMARTHEN WEST AND PEMBROKESHIRE SOUTH %

*Ainger, N. (Lab)	20,956	49.1
Williams, O. (Con)	11,335	26.6
Llewellyn, D. (PC)	5,402	12.7
Evans, K. (LD)	3,516	8.2
Poirrier, J. (Ref)	1,432	3.4
Lab majority	9,621	22.56%
Electorate	55,724	
Total Vote	42,641	Poll 76.4%

*Member of last parliament
Lab Hold (9.8% Swing from Con to Lab)

CARRICK, CUMNOCK AND DOON VALLEY %

*Foulkes, G.		
(Lab/Co-op)	29,398	59.8
Marshall, A. (Con)	8,336	17.0
Hutchison, C. (SNP)	8,190	16.7
Young, D. (LD)	2,613	5.3
Higgins, J. (Ref)	634	1.3
Lab/Co-op		
majority	21,062	42.83%
Electorate	65,593	
Total Vote	49,171	Poll 75%

*Member of last parliament
Lab/Co-op Hold (7.2% Swing from Con to Lab)

CARSHALTON AND WALLINGTON

		%
Brake, T. (LD)	18,490	38.2
*Forman, N. (Con)	16,223	33.5
Theobald, A. (Lab)	11,565	23.9
Storey, J. (Ref)	1,289	2.7
Hickson, P. (Green)	377	0.8
Ritchie, G. (BNP)	261	0.5
Povey, L. (UKIP)	218	0.5
LD majority	2,267	4.68%
Electorate	66,038	
Total Vote	48,423	Poll 73.3%

*Member of last parliament
LD Gain (11.8% Swing from Con to LD)

CASTLE POINT %
Butler, C. (Lab) 20,605 42.4
*Spink, R. (Con) 19,462 40.1
Baker, M. (LD) 4,477 9.2
Maulkin, H. (Ref) 2,700 5.6
Kendall, L. (Consult) 1,301 2.7
Lab majority 1,143 2.30%
Electorate 67,146
Total Vote 48,545 Poll 72.3%
*Member of last parliament
Lab Gain (16.9% Swing from Con to Lab)

CENTRAL FIFE %
*McLeish, H. (Lab) 23,912 58.7
Marwick, T. (SNP) 10,199 25.0
Rees-Mogg, J. (Con) 3,669 9.0
Laird, R. (LD) 2,610 6.4
Scrymgeour-
Wedderburn, J. (Ref) 375 0.9
Lab majority 13,713 33.64%
Electorate 58,315
Total Vote 40,765 Poll 69.8%
*Member of last parliament
Lab Hold (3.9% Swing from SNP to Lab)

**CENTRAL SUFFOLK AND
NORTH IPSWICH** %
*Lord, M. (Con) 22,493 42.6
Jones, C. (Lab) 18,955 35.9
Goldspink, M. (LD) 10,886 20.6
Bennell, S. (Ind) 489 0.9
Con majority 3,538 6.70%
Electorate 70,222
Total Vote 52,823 Poll 75.2%
*Member of last parliament
Con Hold (14.2% Swing from Con to Lab)

CEREDIGION %
*Dafis, C. (PC) 16,728 41.6
Harris, R. (Lab) 9,767 24.3
Davies, D. (LD) 6,616 16.5
Aubel, F. (Con) 5,983 14.9
Leaney, C. (Ref) 1,092 2.7
PC majority 6,961 17.32%
Electorate 54,378
Total Vote 40,186 Poll 73.7%
*Member of last parliament
PC Hold (2.5% Swing from Lab to PC)

CHARNWOOD %
*Dorrell, S. (Con) 26,110 46.5
Knaggs, D. (Lab) 20,210 36.0
Wilson, R. (LD) 7,224 12.9
Meechan, H. (Ref) 2,104 3.7
Palmer, M. (BNP) 525 0.9
Con majority 5,900 10.50%
Electorate 72,692
Total Vote 56,173 Poll 77.2%
*Member of last parliament
Con Hold (14.2% Swing from Con to Lab)

**CHATHAM AND
AYLESFORD** %
Shaw, J. (Lab) 21,191 43.1
Knox-Johnston, R.
(Con) 18,401 37.4
Murray, R. (LD) 7,389 15.0

Riddle, K. (Ref) 1,538 3.1
Harding, A. (UKIP) 493 1.0
Martel, T. (NLP) 149 0.3
Lab majority 2,790 5.68%
Electorate 69,172
Total Vote 49,161 Poll 70.8%
Lab Gain (15.1% Swing from Con to Lab)

CHEADLE %
*Day, S. (Con) 22,944 43.7
Calton, P. (LD) 19,755 37.7
Diggett, P. (Lab) 8,253 15.7
Brook, A. (Ref) 1,511 2.9
Con majority 3,189 6.08%
Electorate 67,627
Total Vote 52,463 Poll 77.3%
*Member of last parliament
Con Hold (11% Swing from Con to LD)

CHELMSFORD WEST %
*Burns, S. (Con) 23,781 40.6
Bracken, M. (LD) 17,090 29.2
Chad, R. (Lab) 15,436 26.4
Smith, T. (Ref) 1,536 2.6
Rumens, G. (Green) 411 0.7
Levin, M. (UKIP) 323 0.6
Con majority 6,691 11.42%
Electorate 76,086
Total Vote 58,577 Poll 76.9%
*Member of last parliament
Con Hold (7.2% Swing from Con to LD)

CHELTENHAM %
*Jones, N. (LD) 24,877 49.5
Todman, W. (Con) 18,232 36.2
Leach, B. (Lab) 5,100 10.1
Powell, A. (Ref) 1,065 2.1
Hanks, K. (Loony) 375 0.7
Cook, G. (UKIP) 302 0.6
Harriss, A.
(Pro-Life) 245 0.5
Brighouse, S. (NLP) 107 0.2
LD majority 6,645 13.21%
Electorate 67,950
Total Vote 50,303 Poll 74%
*Member of last parliament
LD Hold (4.9% Swing from Con to LD)

**CHESHAM AND
AMERSHAM** %
*Gillan, C. (Con) 26,298 50.4
Brand, M. (LD) 12,439 23.8
Farrelly, C. (Lab) 10,240 19.6
Andrews, P. (Ref) 2,528 4.8
Shilson, C. (UKIP) 618 1.2
Godfrey, H. (NLP) 74 0.1
Con majority 13,859 26.55%
Electorate 69,244
Total Vote 52,197 Poll 73.7%
*Member of last parliament
Con Hold (6.2% Swing from Con to LD)

CHESTERFIELD %
*Benn, T. (Lab) 26,105 50.8
Rogers, T. (LD) 20,330 39.6
Potter, M. (Con) 4,752 9.2

Scarth, N. (Ind OAP) 202 0.4
Lab majority 5,775 11.24%
Electorate 72,472
Total Vote 51,389 Poll 70.9%
*Member of last parliament
Lab Hold (0.1% Swing from Lab to LD)

CHICHESTER %
Tyrie, A. (Con) 25,895 46.4
Gardiner, P. (LD) 16,161 29.0
Smith, C. (Lab) 9,605 17.2
Denny, D. (Ref) 3,318 5.9
Rix, J. (UKIP) 800 1.4
Con majority 9,734 17.45%
Electorate 74,489
Total Vote 55,779 Poll 74.6%
Con Hold (7.6% Swing from Con to LD)

**CHINGFORD AND
WOODFORD GREEN** %
*Duncan Smith, I.
(Con) 21,109 47.5
Hutchinson, T. (Lab) 15,395 34.6
Seeff, G. (LD) 6,885 15.5
Gould, A. (BNP) 1,059 2.4
Con majority 5,714 12.86%
Electorate 62,904
Total Vote 44,448 Poll 70.7%
*Member of last parliament
Con Hold (13.8% Swing from Con to Lab)

CHIPPING BARNET %
*Chapman, S. (Con) 21,317 43.0
Cooke, G. (Lab) 20,282 40.9
Hooker, S. (LD) 6,121 12.3
Ribekow, V. (Ref) 1,190 2.4
Miskin, B. (Loony) 253 0.5
Scallan, B. (Pro-Life) 243 0.5
Derksen, D. (NLP) 159 0.3
Con majority 1,035 2.09%
Electorate 69,049
Total Vote 49,565 Poll 70.9%
*Member of last parliament
Con Hold (14.1% Swing from Con to Lab)

CHORLEY %
Hoyle, L. (Lab) 30,607 53.0
*Dover, D. (Con) 20,737 35.9
Jones, S. (LD) 4,900 8.5
Heaton, A. (Ref) 1,319 2.3
Leadbetter, P. (NLP) 143 0.2
Lab majority 9,870 17.10%
Electorate 74,387
Total Vote 57,706 Poll 77.6%
*Member of last parliament
Lab Gain (10.6% Swing from Con to Lab)

CHRISTCHURCH %
Chope, C. (Con) 26,095 46.4
*Maddock, D. (LD) 23,930 42.6
Mannan, C. (Lab) 3,884 6.9
Spencer, R. (Ref) 1,684 3.0
Dickinson, R. (UKIP) 606 1.1
Con majority 2,165 3.85%
Electorate 71,488
Total Vote 56,199 Poll 78.6%
*Member of last parliament
Con ReGain (18.3% Swing from Con to LD)

CITIES OF LONDON AND WESTMINSTER

		%
*Brooke, P. (Con)	18,981	47.3
Green, K. (Lab)	14,100	35.1
Dumigan, M. (LD)	4,933	12.3
Walters, A. (Ref)	1,161	2.9
Wharton, P. (Barts)	266	0.7
Merton, C. (UKIP)	215	0.5
Johnson, R. (NLP)	176	0.4
Walsh, N. (Loony)	138	0.3
Webster, G. (Hemp)	112	0.3
Sadowitz, J. (Dream)	73	0.2
Con majority 4,881		12.16%
Electorate	69,047	
Total Vote	40,155	Poll 58.2%

*Member of last parliament
Con Hold (11.5% Swing from Con to Lab)

CITY OF CHESTER

		%
Russell, C. (Lab)	29,806	53.0
*Brandreth, G. (Con)	19,253	34.2
Simpson, D. (LD)	5,353	9.5
Mullan, R. (Ref)	1,487	2.6
Sanderson, I. (Loony)	204	0.4
Johnson, W. (WCCC)	154	0.3
Lab majority 10,553		18.76%
Electorate	71,730	
Total Vote	56,257	Poll 78.1%

*Member of last parliament
Lab Gain (11.4% Swing from Con to Lab)

CITY OF DURHAM

		%
*Steinberg, G. (Lab)	31,102	63.3
Chalk, R. (Con)	8,598	17.5
Martin, N. (LD)	7,499	15.3
Robson, M. (Ref)	1,723	3.5
Kember, P. (NLP)	213	0.4
Lab majority 22,504		45.80%
Electorate	69,340	
Total Vote	49,135	Poll 70.9%

*Member of last parliament
Lab Hold (8.1% Swing from Con to Lab)

CITY OF YORK

		%
*Bayley, H. (Lab)	34,956	59.9
Mallett, S. (Con)	14,433	24.7
Waller, A. (LD)	6,537	11.2
Sheppard, J. (Ref)	1,083	1.9
Hill, M. (Green)	880	1.5
Wegener, E. (UKIP)	319	0.5
Lightfoot, A. (Chr Nat)	137	0.2
Lab majority 20,523		35.18%
Electorate	79,383	
Total Vote	58,345	Poll 73.2%

*Member of last parliament
Lab Hold (12.6% Swing from Con to Lab)

CLEETHORPES

		%
McIsaac, S. (Lab)	26,058	51.6
*Brown, M. (Con)	16,882	33.4
Melton, K. (LD)	5,746	11.4
Berry, J. (Ref)	1,787	3.5
Lab majority 9,176		18.18%
Electorate	68,763	
Total Vote	50,473	Poll 73.4%

*Member of last parliament
Lab Gain (15.1% Swing from Con to Lab)

CLWYD SOUTH

		%
*Jones, M. (Lab)	22,901	58.1
Johnson, B. (Con)	9,091	23.1
Chadwick, A. (LD)	3,684	9.4
Williams, G. (PC)	2,500	6.3
Lewis, A. (Ref)	1,207	3.1
Lab majority 13,810		35.07%
Electorate	53,495	
Total Vote	39,383	Poll 73.6%

*Member of last parliament
Lab Hold (7.8% Swing from Con to Lab)

CLWYD WEST

		%
Thomas, G. (Lab)	14,918	37.1
*Richards, R. (Con)	13,070	32.5
Williams, E. (PC)	5,421	13.5
Williams, W. (LD)	5,151	12.8
Bennett-Collins, H. (Ref)	1,114	2.8
Neal, D. (Conserv)	583	1.4
Lab majority 1,848		4.59%
Electorate	53,467	
Total Vote	40,257	Poll 75.2%

*Member of last parliament
Lab Gain (11.1% Swing from Con to Lab)

CLYDEBANK AND MILNGAVIE

		%
*Worthington, A. (Lab)	21,583	55.2
Yuill, J. (SNP)	8,263	21.1
Morgan, N. (Con)	4,885	12.5
Moody, K. (LD)	4,086	10.5
Sanderson, J. (Ref)	269	0.7
Lab majority 13,320		34.08%
Electorate	52,092	
Total Vote	39,086	Poll 75%

*Member of last parliament
Lab Hold (1.1% Swing from SNP to Lab)

CLYDESDALE

		%
*Hood, J. (Lab)	23,859	52.5
Doig, A. (SNP)	10,050	22.1
Izatt, M. (Con)	7,396	16.3
Grieve, S. (LD)	3,796	8.4
Smith, K. (BNP)	311	0.7
Lab majority 13,809		30.41%
Electorate	63,428	
Total Vote	45,412	Poll 71.6%

*Member of last parliament
Lab Hold (4.4% Swing from SNP to Lab)

COATBRIDGE AND CHRYSTON

		%
*Clarke, T. (Lab)	25,694	68.3
Nugent, B. (SNP)	6,402	17.0
Wauchope, P. (Con)	3,216	8.6
Daly, M. (LD)	2,048	5.4
Bowsley, B. (Ref)	249	0.7
Lab majority 19,292		51.30%
Electorate	52,024	
Total Vote	37,609	Poll 72.3%

*Member of last parliament
Lab Hold (3.1% Swing from SNP to Lab)

COLCHESTER

		%
Russell, R. (LD)	17,886	34.4
Shakespeare, S. (Con)	16,305	31.4
Green, R. (Lab)	15,891	30.5
Hazell, J. (Ref)	1,776	3.4
Basker, L. (NLP)	148	0.3
LD majority 1,581		3.04%
Electorate	74,743	
Total Vote	52,006	Poll 69.6%

LD Gain (6.2% Swing from Con to LD)

COLNE VALLEY

		%
Mountford, K. (Lab)	23,285	41.3
*Riddick, G. (Con)	18,445	32.7
Priestley, N. (LD)	12,755	22.6
Brooke, A. (SLP)	759	1.3
Cooper, A. (Green)	493	0.9
Nunn, J. (UKIP)	478	0.8
Staniforth, M. (Loony)	196	0.3
Lab majority 4,840		8.58%
Electorate	73,338	
Total Vote	56,411	Poll 76.8%

*Member of last parliament
Lab Gain (10.4% Swing from Con to Lab)

CONGLETON

		%
*Winterton, A. (Con)	22,012	41.2
Walmsley, J. (LD)	15,882	29.7
Scholey, F. (Lab)	14,713	27.5
Lockett, J. (UKIP)	811	1.5
Con majority 6,130		11.48%
Electorate	68,873	
Total Vote	53,418	Poll 77.4%

*Member of last parliament
Con Hold (2.7% Swing from Con to LD)

CONWY

		%
Williams, B. (Lab)	14,561	35.0
Roberts, R. (LD)	12,965	31.2
Jones, D. (Con)	10,085	24.3
Davies, R. (PC)	2,844	6.8
Barham, A. (Ref)	760	1.8
Bradley, R. (Alt LD)	250	0.6
Hughes, D. (NLP)	95	0.2
Lab majority 1,596		3.84%
Electorate	55,092	
Total Vote	41,560	Poll 75.3%

Lab Gain (9.4% Swing from Con to Lab)

COPELAND

		%
*Cunningham, J. (Lab)	24,077	58.2
Cumpsty, A. (Con)	12,081	29.2
Putnam, R. (LD)	3,814	9.2
Johnston, C. (Ref)	1,036	2.5
Hanratty, G. (Pro-Life)	389	0.9
Lab majority 11,996		29.0%
Electorate	54,263	
Total Vote	41,397	Poll 76.3%

*Member of last parliament
Lab Hold (11.8% Swing from Con to Lab)

CORBY

		%
Hope, P. (Lab/Co-op)	29,888	55.4
*Powell, W. (Con)	18,028	33.4
Hankinson, I. (LD)	4,045	7.5
Riley-Smith, S. (Ref)	1,356	2.5
Gillman, I. (UKIP)	507	0.9
Bence, J. (NLP)	133	0.2
Lab/Co-op majority 11,860		21.98%
Electorate	69,252	
Total Vote	53,957	Poll 77.7%

*Member of last parliament
Lab Gain (11.3% Swing from Con to Lab)

COTSWOLD %
*Clifton-Brown, G.
  (Con)   23,698 46.4
Gayler, D. (LD)   11,733 23.0
Elwell, D. (Lab)   11,608 22.7
Lowe, R. (Ref)   3,393   6.6
Michael, V. (Green)   560   1.1
Brighouse, H. (NLP)   129   0.3
  Con majority 11,965   23.41%
  Electorate   67,333
  Total Vote   51,121 Poll 75.9%
*Member of last parliament
Con Hold (1.2% Swing from LD to Con)

COVENTRY NORTH EAST %
*Ainsworth, B.
  (Lab)   31,856 66.2
Burnett, M. (Con)   9,287 19.3
Sewards, G. (LD)   3,866   8.0
Brown, N. (Lib)   1,181   2.5
Hurrell, R. (Ref)   1,125   2.3
Khamis, H. (SLP)   597   1.2
Sidwell, C. (Dream)   173   0.4
  Lab majority 22,569   46.94%
  Electorate   74,274
  Total Vote   48,085 Poll 64.4%
*Member of last parliament
Lab Hold (12.7% Swing from Con to Lab)

COVENTRY NORTH WEST %
*Robinson, G. (Lab)   30,901 56.9
Bartlett, P. (Con)   14,300 26.3
Penlington, N. (LD)   5,690 10.5
Butler, D. (Ref)   1,269   2.3
Spencer, D. (SLP)   940   1.7
Wheway, R. (Lib)   687   1.3
Mills, P. (Pro-Life)   359   0.7
Francis, L. (Dream)   176   0.3
  Lab majority 16,601   30.56%
  Electorate   76,439
  Total Vote   54,322 Poll 70.7%
*Member of last parliament
Lab Hold (8.1% Swing from Con to Lab)

COVENTRY SOUTH %
*Cunningham, J.
  (Lab)   25,511 50.9
Ivey, P. (Con)   14,558 29.0
Macdonald, G. (LD)   4,617   9.2
Nellist, D. (Soc)   3,262   6.5
Garratt, P. (Ref)   943   1.9
Jenking, R. (Lib)   725   1.4
Astbury, J. (BNP)   328   0.7
Bradshaw, A. (Dream)   180   0.4
  Lab majority 10,953   21.85%
  Electorate   71,826
  Total Vote   50,124 Poll 68.7%
*Member of last parliament
Lab Gain (13.5% Swing from Con to Lab)

CRAWLEY %
Moffatt, L. (Lab)   27,750 55.0
Crabb, J. (Con)   16,043 31.8
De Souza, H. (LD)   4,141   8.2
Walters, R. (Ref)   1,931   3.8
Saunders, E. (UKIP)   322   0.6
Khan, A. (Justice)   230   0.5

  Lab majority 11,707   23.22%
  Electorate   69,040
  Total Vote   50,417 Poll 72.5%
Lab Gain (13.4% Swing from Con to Lab)

CREWE AND NANTWICH %
*Dunwoody, G. (Lab) 29,460 58.2
Loveridge, M. (Con) 13,662 27.0
Cannon, D. (LD)   5,940 11.7
Astbury, P. (Ref)   1,543   3.0
  Lab majority 15,798   31.22%
  Electorate   68,694
  Total Vote   50,605 Poll 73.5%
*Member of last parliament
Lab Hold (11.3% Swing from Con to Lab)

CROSBY %
Curtis-Tansley, C.
  (Lab)   22,549 51.1
*Thornton, M. (Con)   15,367 34.8
McVey, P. (LD)   5,080 11.5
Gauld, J. (Ref)   813   1.8
Marks, J. (Lib)   233   0.5
Hite, W. (NLP)   99   0.2
  Lab majority 7,182   16.27%
  Electorate   57,190
  Total Vote   44,141 Poll 77.2%
*Member of last parliament
Lab Gain (18.2% Swing from Con to Lab)

CROYDON CENTRAL %
Davies, G. (Lab)   25,432 45.6
*Congdon, D. (Con)   21,535 38.6
Schlich, G. (LD)   6,061 10.9
Cook, C. (Ref)   1,886   3.4
Barnsley, M. (Green)   595   1.1
Woollcott, J. (UKIP)   290   0.5
  Lab majority 3,897   6.98%
  Electorate   80,152
  Total Vote   55,799 Poll 69.6%
*Member of last parliament
Lab Gain (15.5% Swing from Con to Lab)

CROYDON NORTH %
*Wicks, M. (Lab)   32,672 62.2
Martin, I. (Con)   14,274 27.2
Morris, M. (LD)   4,066   7.7
Billis, R. (Ref)   1,155   2.2
Feisenberger, J.
  (UKIP)   396   0.8
  Lab majority 18,398   35.00%
  Electorate   77,063
  Total Vote   52,563 Poll 68.2%
*Member of last parliament
Lab Gain (17.6% Swing from Con to Lab)

CROYDON SOUTH %
*Ottaway, R. (Con)   25,649 47.3
Burling, C. (Lab)   13,719 25.3
Gauge, S. (LD)   11,441 21.1
Barber, T. (Ref)   2,631   4.9
Ferguson, P. (BNP)   354   0.7
Harker, A. (UKIP)   309   0.6
Samuel, M.
  (People's Choice)   96   0.2
  Con majority 11,930   22.01%
  Electorate   73,787
  Total Vote   54,199 Poll 73.5%
*Member of last parliament
Con Hold (11.7% Swing from Con to Lab)

**CUMBERNAULD AND
  KILSYTH** %
McKenna, R. (Lab)   21,141 58.7
Barrie, C. (SNP)   10,013 27.8
Sewell, I. (Con)   2,441   6.8
Biggam, J. (LD)   1,368   3.8
Kara, J. (Pro-Life)   609   1.7
McEwan, K. (ScotSoc)   345   1.0
Cook, P. (Ref)   107   0.3
  Lab majority 11,128   30.89%
  Electorate   40,032
  Total Vote   36,024 Poll 75%
Lab Hold (2.9% Swing from SNP to Lab)

CUNNINGHAME NORTH %
*Wilson, B. (Lab)   20,686 50.3
Mitchell, M. (Con)   9,647 23.5
Nicoll, K. (SNP)   7,584 18.4
Freel, K. (LD)   2,271   5.5
McDaid, L. (SLP)   501   1.2
Winton, I. (Ref)   440   1.1
  Lab majority 11,039   26.84%
  Electorate   54,526
  Total Vote   41,129 Poll 74.1%
*Member of last parliament
Lab Hold (10% Swing from Con to Lab)

CUNNINGHAME SOUTH %
*Donohoe, B. (Lab)   22,233 62.7
Burgess, M. (SNP)   7,364 20.8
Paterson, P. (Con)   3,571 10.1
Watson, E. (LD)   1,604   4.5
Edwin, K. (SLP)   494   1.4
Martlew, A. (Ref)   178   0.5
  Lab majority 14,869   41.95%
  Electorate   49,543
  Total Vote   35,444 Poll 71.5%
*Member of last parliament
Lab Hold (6.6% Swing from SNP to Lab)

CYNON VALLEY %
*Clwyd, A. (Lab)   23,307 69.7
Davies, A. (PC)   3,552 10.6
Price, H. (LD)   3,459 10.3
Smith, A. (Con)   2,262   6.8
John, G. (Ref)   844   2.5
  Lab majority 19,755   59.10%
  Electorate   48,286
  Total Vote   33,424 Poll 69.2%
*Member of last parliament
Lab Hold (0.5% Swing from PC to Lab)

DAGENHAM %
*Church, J. (Lab)   23,759 65.7
Fairrie, J. (Con)   6,705 18.5
Dobrashian, T. (LD)   2,704   7.5
Kraft, S. (Ref)   1,411   3.9
Binding, W. (BNP)   900   2.5
Dawson, R. (Ind)   349   1.0
Hipperson, M.
  (Nat Dem)   183   0.5
Goble, K. (Pro-Life)   152   0.4
  Lab majority 17,054   47.16%
  Electorate   58,573
  Total Vote   36,163 Poll 61.7%
*Member of last parliament
Lab Hold (16.2% Swing from Con to Lab)

DARLINGTON

		%
*Milburn, A. (Lab)	29,658	61.6
Scrope, P. (Con)	13,633	28.3
Boxell, L. (LD)	3,483	7.2
Blakey, M. (Ref)	1,399	2.9
Lab majority 16,025		33.27%
Electorate 65,140		
Total Vote 48,173	Poll 74%	

*Member of last parliament
Lab Hold (14.1% Swing from Con to Lab)

DARTFORD

		%
Stoate, H. (Lab)	25,278	48.6
*Dunn, B. (Con)	20,950	40.3
Webb, D. (LD)	4,872	9.4
McHale, P. (BNP)	424	0.8
Homden, P. (Fancy)	287	0.6
Pollitt, J. (ChriDem)	228	0.4
Lab majority 4,328		8.32%
Electorate 69,726		
Total Vote 52,039	Poll 74.6%	

*Member of last parliament
Lab Gain (11.5% Swing from Con to Lab)

DAVENTRY

		%
*Boswell, T. (Con)	28,615	46.3
Ritchie, K. (Lab)	21,237	34.4
Gordon, J. (LD)	9,233	15.0
Russocki, B. (Ref)	2,018	3.3
Mahoney, B. (UKIP)	443	0.7
France, R. (NLP)	204	0.3
Con majority 7,378		11.95%
Electorate 80,151		
Total Vote 61,750	Poll 76.8%	

*Member of last parliament
Con Hold (11% Swing from Con to Lab)

DELYN

		%
*Hanson, D. (Lab)	23,300	58.4
Lumley, K. (Con)	10,607	26.0
Lloyd, D. (LD)	4,160	10.2
Drake, A. (PC)	1,558	3.8
Soutter, E. (Ref)	1,117	2.7
Lab majority 12,693		31.20%
Electorate 53,693		
Total Vote 40,742	Poll 75.9%	

*Member of last parliament
Lab Hold (12% Swing from Con to Lab)

DENTON AND REDDISH

		%
*Bennett, A. (Lab)	30,137	65.4
Nutt, B. (Con)	9,826	21.3
Donaldson, I. (LD)	6,121	13.3
Lab majority 20,311		44.07%
Electorate 68,866		
Total Vote 46,084	Poll 66.8%	

*Member of last parliament
Lab Hold (12.5% Swing from Con to Lab)

DERBY NORTH

		%
Laxton, R. (Lab)	29,844	53.2
*Knight, G. (Con)	19,229	34.3
Charlesworth, R. (LD)	5,059	9.0
Reynolds, P. (Ref)	1,816	3.2
Waters, J. (Pro-Life)	195	0.3
Lab majority 10,615		18.91%
Electorate 76,116		
Total Vote 56,143	Poll 73.5%	

*Member of last parliament
Lab Gain (13.2% Swing from Con to Lab)

DERBY SOUTH

		%
*Beckett, M. (Lab)	29,154	56.3
Arain, J. (Con)	13,048	25.2
Beckett, J. (LD)	7,438	14.4
Browne, J. (Ref)	1,862	3.6
Evans, R. (Nat Dem)	317	0.6
Lab majority 16,106		31.08%
Electorate 76,386		
Total Vote 51,819	Poll 67.6%	

*Member of last parliament
Lab Hold (11.8% Swing from Con to Lab)

DEVIZES

		%
*Ancram, M. (Con)	25,710	42.8
Vickers, A. (LD)	15,928	26.5
Jeffrey, F. (Lab)	14,551	24.2
Goldsmith, J. (Ref)	3,021	5.0
Oram, S. (UKIP)	622	1.0
Haysom, S. (NLP)	204	0.3
Con majority 9,782		16.29%
Electorate 80,383		
Total Vote 60,036	Poll 74.4%	

*Member of last parliament
Con Hold (2.1% Swing from Con to LD)

DEWSBURY

		%
*Taylor, A. (Lab)	21,286	49.4
McCormick, P. (Con)	12,963	30.1
Hill, K. (LD)	4,422	10.3
Taylor, F. (BNP)	2,232	5.2
Goff, W. (Ref)	1,019	2.4
Daniel, D. (IndLab)	770	1.8
McCourtie, I. (Green)	383	0.9
Lab majority 8,323		19.32%
Electorate 61,523		
Total Vote 43,075	Poll 70%	

*Member of last parliament
Lab Hold (6% Swing from Con to Lab)

DON VALLEY

		%
Flint, C. (Lab)	25,376	58.3
Gledhill, C. (Con)	10,717	24.6
Johnston, P. (LD)	4,238	9.7
Davies, P. (Ref)	1,379	3.2
Ball, N. (SLP)	1,024	2.4
Platt, S. (Green)	493	1.1
Johnson, C. (Pro-Life)	330	0.8
Lab majority 14,659		33.65%
Electorate 65,643		
Total Vote 43,557	Poll 66.3%	

Lab Hold (9.9% Swing from Con to Lab)

DONCASTER CENTRAL

		%
Winterton, R. (Lab)	26,961	62.1
Turtle, D. (Con)	9,105	21.0
Tarry, S. (LD)	4,091	9.4
Cliff, M. (Ref)	1,273	2.9
Kenny, M. (SLP)	854	2.0
Redden, J. (Pro-Life)	694	1.6
Davies, P. (UKIP)	462	1.1
Lab majority 17,856		41.10%
Electorate 67,965		
Total Vote 43,440	Poll 63.8%	

Lab Hold (10.1% Swing from Con to Lab)

DONCASTER NORTH

		%
*Hughes, K. (Lab)	27,843	69.8
Kennerley, P. (Con)	5,906	14.8
Cook, M. (LD)	3,369	8.4
Thornton, R. (Ref)	1,589	4.0
Swan, N. (Anti-Sleaze Lab)	1,181	3.0
Lab majority 21,937		55.00%
Electorate 63,019		
Total Vote 39,888	Poll 63.3%	

*Member of last parliament
Lab Hold (6.4% Swing from Con to Lab)

DOVER

		%
Prosser, G. (Lab)	29,535	54.5
*Shaw, D. (Con)	17,796	32.8
Corney, M. (LD)	4,302	7.9
Anderson, S. (Ref)	2,124	3.9
Hyde, C. (UKIP)	443	0.8
Lab majority 11,739		21.66%
Electorate 68,669		
Total Vote 54,200	Poll 78.6%	

*Member of last parliament
Lab Gain (11.6% Swing from Con to Lab)

DUDLEY NORTH

		%
Cranston, R. (Lab)	24,471	51.2
MacNamara, C. (Con)	15,014	31.4
Lewis, G. (LD)	3,939	8.2
Atherton, M. (SLP)	2,155	4.5
Bavester, S. (Ref)	1,201	2.5
Cartwright, G. (NF)	559	1.2
Darby, S. (Nat Dem)	469	1.0
Lab majority 9,457		19.78%
Electorate 68,835		
Total Vote 47,808	Poll 69.3%	

Lab Hold (9% Swing from Con to Lab)

DUDLEY SOUTH

		%
*Pearson, I. (Lab)	27,124	56.6
Simpson, G. (Con)	14,097	29.4
Burt, R. (LD)	5,214	10.9
Birch, C. (Ref)	1,467	3.1
Lab majority 13,027		27.20%
Electorate 66,731		
Total Vote 47,902	Poll 71.7%	

*Member of last parliament
Lab Hold (11% Swing from Con to Lab)

DULWICH AND WEST NORWOOD

		%
*Jowell, T. (Lab)	27,807	61.0
Gough, R. (Con)	11,038	24.2
Kramer, S. (LD)	4,916	10.8
Coles, B. (Ref)	897	2.0
Goldie, A. (Lib)	587	1.3
Goodman, D. (Dream)	173	0.4
Pike, E. (UKIP)	159	0.3
Captain Rizz (Rizz)	38	0.1
Lab majority 16,769		36.79%
Electorate 69,655		
Total Vote 45,615	Poll 65.5%	

*Member of last parliament
Lab Hold (16.6% Swing from Con to Lab)

DUMBARTON		%
*McFall, J.		
(Lab/Co-op)	20,470	49.6
Mackechnie, B.		
(SNP)	9,587	23.2
Ramsay, P. (Con)	7,283	17.6
Reid, A. (LD)	3,144	7.6
Robertson, L.		
(ScotSoc)	283	0.7
Dempster, G. (Ref)	255	0.6
Lancaster, R. (UKIP)	242	0.6
Lab/Co-op		
majority	10,883	26.37%
Electorate	56,229	
Total Vote	41,264	Poll 73.4%

*Member of last parliament
Lab Hold (0.6% Swing from SNP to Lab)

DUMFRIES		%
Brown, R. (Lab)	23,528	47.5
Stevenson, S. (Con)	13,885	28.0
Higgins, R. (SNP)	5,977	12.1
Wallace, N. (LD)	5,487	11.1
Parker, D. (Ref)	533	1.1
Hunter, E. (NLP)	117	0.2
Lab majority	9,643	19.47%
Electorate	62,759	
Total Vote	49,527	Poll 78.9%

Lab Gain (16.5% Swing from Con to Lab)

DUNDEE EAST		
*McAllion, J. (Lab)	20,718	51.1
Robison, S. (SNP)	10,757	26.5
Mackie, B. (Con)	6,397	15.8
Saluja, G. (LD)	1,677	4.1
Galloway, T. (Ref)	601	1.5
Duke, H. (ScotSoc)	232	0.6
MacKenzie, E. (NLP)	146	0.4
Lab majority	9,961	24.58%
Electorate	58,388	
Total Vote	40,528	Poll 69.4%

*Member of last parliament
Lab Hold (6.2% Swing from SNP to Lab)

DUNDEE WEST		%
*Ross, E. (Lab)	20,875	53.8
Dorward, J. (SNP)	9,016	23.2
Powrie, N. (Con)	5,105	13.2
Dick, E. (LD)	2,972	7.7
Ward, M. (ScotSoc)	428	1.1
MacMillan, J. (Ref)	411	1.1
Lab majority	11,859	30.56%
Electorate	57,346	
Total Vote	38,807	Poll 67.7%

*Member of last parliament
Lab Hold (3.7% Swing from SNP to Lab)

DUNFERMLINE EAST		%
*Brown, G. (Lab)	24,441	66.8
Ramage, J. (SNP)	5,690	15.6
Mitchell QC, I. (Con)	3,656	10.0
Tolson, J. (LD)	2,164	5.9
Dunsmore, T. (Ref)	632	1.7
Lab majority	18,751	51.26%
Electorate	52,072	
Total Vote	36,583	Poll 70.3%

*Member of last parliament
Lab Hold (1.6% Swing from SNP to Lab)

DUNFERMLINE WEST		%
*Squire, R. (Lab)	19,338	53.1
Lloyd, J. (SNP)	6,984	19.2
Harris, E. (LD)	4,963	13.6
Newton, K. (Con)	4,606	12.6
Bain, J. (Ref)	543	1.5
Lab majority	12,354	33.91%
Electorate	52,467	
Total Vote	36,434	Poll 69.4%

*Member of last parliament
Lab Hold (6.1% Swing from SNP to Lab)

DURHAM NORTH		%
*Radice, G. (Lab)	33,142	70.3
Hardy, M. (Con)	6,843	14.5
Moore, B. (LD)	5,225	11.1
Parkin, I. (Ref)	1,958	4.2
Lab majority	26,299	55.76%
Electorate	67,891	
Total Vote	47,168	Poll 69.4%

*Member of last parliament
Lab Hold (10.4% Swing from Con to Lab)

EALING NORTH		%
Pound, S. (Lab)	29,904	53.7
*Greenway, H. (Con)	20,744	37.2
Gupta, A. (LD)	3,887	6.8
Slysz, G. (UKIP)	689	1.2
Seibe, A. (Green)	502	0.9
Lab majority	9,160	16.44%
Electorate	78,144	
Total Vote	55,726	Poll 72.3%

*Member of last parliament
Lab Gain (16.0% Swing from Con to Lab)

EALING SOUTHALL		%
*Khabra, P. (Lab)	32,791	60.0
Penrose, J. (Con)	11,368	20.8
Thomson, N. (LD)	5,687	10.4
Brar, H. (SLP)	2,107	3.9
Goodwin, N. (Green)	934	1.7
Cherry, D. (Ref)	854	1.6
Klepacka, K. (Pro-Life)	473	0.9
Mead, R. (UKIP)	428	0.8
Lab majority	21,423	39.21%
Electorate	81,704	
Total Vote	54,642	Poll 65.7%

*Member of last parliament
Lab Hold (15.1% Swing from Con to Lab)

EALING, ACTON AND SHEPHERD'S BUSH		%
*Soley, C. (Lab)	28,052	58.4
Yerolemou, B. (Con)	12,405	25.8
Mitchell, A. (LD)	5,163	10.7
Winn, C. (Ref)	637	1.3
Gilbert, J. (SLP)	635	1.3
Gomm, J. (UKIP)	385	0.8
Danon, P. (Pro-Life)	265	0.6
Beasley, C. (Glow)	209	0.4
Edwards, W. (Christian)	163	0.3
Turner, K. (NLP)	150	0.3
Lab majority	15,647	32.55%
Electorate	72,078	
Total Vote	48,064	Poll 64%

*Member of last parliament
Lab Hold (12.8% Swing from Con to Lab)

EASINGTON		%
*Cummings, J. (Lab)	33,600	80.2
Hollands, J. (Con)	3,588	8.6
Heppell, J. (LD)	3,025	7.2
Pulfrey, R. (Ref)	1,179	2.8
Colborn, S. (Socialist)	503	1.2
Lab majority	30,012	71.64%
Electorate	62,518	
Total Vote	41,895	Poll 67%

*Member of last parliament
Lab Hold (7.8% Swing from Con to Lab)

EAST ANTRIM		%
*Beggs, R. (UUP)	13,318	38.8
Neeson, S. (APNI)	6,929	20.2
McKee, J. (DUP)	6,682	19.5
Dick, T. (Con)	2,334	6.8
Donaldson, B. (PUP)	1,757	5.1
O'Connor, D. (SDLP)	1,576	4.6
Mason, R. (Ind)	1,145	3.3
McAuley, C. (SF)	543	1.6
McCann, M. (NLP)	69	0.2
UUP majority	6,389	18.60%
Electorate	58,963	
Total Vote	34,353	Poll 58.3%

*Member of last parliament
UUP Hold (0.1% Swing from APNI to UUP)

EAST DEVON		%
*Emery, Sir P. (Con)	22,797	43.4
Trethewey, R. (LD)	15,308	29.1
Siantonas, A. (Lab)	9,292	17.7
Dixon, W. (Ref)	3,200	6.1
Halliwell, G. (Lib)	1,363	2.6
Giffard, C. (UKIP)	459	0.9
Needs, G. (Nat Dem)	131	0.2
Con majority	7,489	14.25%
Electorate	69,094	
Total Vote	52,550	Poll 75.9%

*Member of last parliament
Con Hold (5.6% Swing from Con to LD)

EAST HAM		%
*Timms, S. (Lab)	25,779	64.6
Bray, A. (Con)	6,421	16.1
Khan, I. (SLP)	2,697	6.8
Sole, M. (LD)	2,599	6.5
Smith, C. (BNP)	1,258	3.2
McCann, J. (Ref)	845	2.1
Hardy, G. (Nat Dem)	290	0.7
Lab majority	19,358	48.53%
Electorate	65,591	
Total Vote	39,889	Poll 60.3%

*Member of last parliament
Lab Hold (13.3% Swing from Con to Lab)

EAST HAMPSHIRE		%
*Mates, M. (Con)	27,927	48.0
Booker, R. (LD)	16,337	28.1
Hoyle, R. (Lab)	9,945	17.1
Hayter, J. (Ref)	2,757	4.7
Foster, I. (Green)	649	1.1
Coles, S. (UKIP)	513	0.9
Con majority	11,590	19.94%
Electorate	76,604	
Total Vote	58,128	Poll 75.8%

*Member of last parliament
Con Hold (6.6% Swing from Con to LD)

EAST KILBRIDE %
*Ingram, A. (Lab) 27,584 56.5
Gebbie, G. (SNP) 10,200 20.9
Herbertson, C. (Con) 5,863 12.0
Philbrick, K. (LD) 3,527 7.2
Deighan, J. (Pro-Life) 1,170 2.4
Gray, J. (Ref) 306 0.6
Gilmour, E. (NLP) 146 0.3
Lab majority 17,384 35.63%
Electorate 65,229
Total Vote 48,796 Poll 74.8%
*Member of last parliament
Lab Hold (5.9% Swing from SNP to Lab)

EAST LONDONDERRY %
*Ross, W. (UUP) 13,558 35.6
Campbell, G. (DUP) 9,764 25.6
Docherty, A. (SDLP) 8,273 21.7
O'Kane, M. (SF) 3,463 9.1
Boyle, Y. (APNI) 2,427 6.4
Holmes, J. (Con) 436 1.1
Gallen, C. (NLP) 100 0.3
Anderson, I. (Nat Dem) 81 0.2
UUP majority 3,794 9.96%
Electorate 58,831
Total Vote 38,102 Poll 64.8%
*Member of last parliament
UUP Hold (0% Swing from to)

EAST LOTHIAN %
*Home Robertson, J.
(Lab) 22,881 52.7
Fraser, M. (Con) 8,660 19.9
McCarthy, D. (SNP) 6,825 15.7
MacAskill, A. (LD) 4,575 10.5
Nash, N. (Ref) 491 1.1
Lab majority 14,221 32.74%
Electorate 57,441
Total Vote 43,432 Poll 75.6%
*Member of last parliament
Lab Hold (8.7% Swing from Con to Lab)

EAST SURREY %
*Ainsworth, P. (Con) 27,389 50.1
Ford, B. (LD) 12,296 22.5
Ross, D. (Lab) 11,573 21.2
Sydney, M. (Ref) 2,656 4.9
Stone, A. (UKIP) 569 1.0
Bartrum, S. (NLP) 173 0.3
Con majority 15,093 27.61%
Electorate 72,852
Total Vote 54,656 Poll 74.6%
*Member of last parliament
Con Hold (3.3% Swing from Con to LD)

EAST WORTHING AND
SHOREHAM %
Loughton, T. (Con) 20,864 40.5
King, M. (LD) 15,766 30.6
Williams, M. (Lab) 12,335 23.9
McCulloch, J. (Ref) 1,683 3.3
Jarvis, R. (UKIP) 921 1.8
Con majority 5,098 9.89%
Electorate 70,771
Total Vote 51,569 Poll 72.9%
Con Hold (3.9% Swing from Con to LD)

EASTBOURNE %
*Waterson, N. (Con) 22,183 42.1
Berry, C. (LD) 20,189 38.3
Lines, D. (Lab) 6,576 12.5
Lowe, T. (Ref) 2,724 5.2
Williamson, M. (Lib) 741 1.4
Dawkins, J. (UKIP) 254 0.5
Con majority 1,994 3.79%
Electorate 72,347
Total Vote 52,667 Poll 72.8%
*Member of last parliament
Con Hold (4% Swing from Con to LD)

EASTLEIGH %
*Chidgey, D. (LD) 19,453 35.1
Reid, S. (Con) 18,699 33.7
Lloyd, A. (Lab) 14,883 26.8
Eldridge, V. (Ref) 2,013 3.6
Robinson, P.
(UKIP) 446 0.8
LD majority 754 1.36%
Electorate 72,155
Total Vote 55,494 Poll 76.6%
*Member of last parliament
LD Win (11.3% Swing from Con to LD)

EASTWOOD %
Murphy, J. (Lab) 20,766 39.7
Cullen, P. (Con) 17,530 33.5
Yates, D. (SNP) 6,826 13.1
Mason, C. (LD) 6,110 11.7
Miller, D. (Ref) 497 1.0
Tayan, M. (Pro-Life) 393 0.8
McPherson, D.
(UKIP) 130 0.2
Lab majority 3,236 6.19%
Electorate 66,697
Total Vote 52,252 Poll 78.2%
Lab Gain (14.3% Swing from Con to Lab)

ECCLES %
Stewart, I. (Lab) 30,468 66.7
Barker, G. (Con) 8,552 18.7
Boyd, R. (LD) 4,905 10.7
de Roeck, J. (Ref) 1,765 3.9
Lab majority 21,916 47.97%
Electorate 69,645
Total Vote 45,690 Poll 65.6%
Lab Hold (10.7% Swing from Con to Lab)

EDDISBURY %
*Goodlad, A. (Con) 21,027 42.5
Hanson, M. (Lab) 19,842 40.1
Reaper, D. (LD) 6,540 13.2
Napier, N. (Ref) 2,041 4.1
Con majority 1,185 2.40%
Electorate 65,256
Total Vote 49,450 Poll 75.6%
*Member of last parliament
Con Hold (9.6% Swing from Con to Lab)

EDINBURGH CENTRAL %
*Darling, A. (Lab) 20,125 47.1
Scott-Hayward, M.
(Con) 9,055 21.2
Hyslop, F. (SNP) 6,750 15.8

Utting, K. (LD) 5,605 13.1
Hendry, L. (Green) 607 1.4
Skinner, A. (Ref) 495 1.2
Benson, M. (Ind Dem) 98 0.2
Lab majority 11,070 25.90%
Electorate 63,695
Total Vote 42,735 Poll 67.1%
*Member of last parliament
Lab Hold (8.4% Swing from Con to Lab)

EDINBURGH EAST AND
MUSSELBURGH %
*Strang, G. (Lab) 22,564 53.6
White, D. (SNP) 8,034 19.1
Ward, K. (Con) 6,483 15.4
MacKellar, C. (LD) 4,511 10.7
Sibbet, J. (Ref) 526 1.2
Lab majority 14,530 34.50%
Electorate 59,648
Total Vote 42,118 Poll 70.6%
*Member of last parliament
Lab Hold (3.9% Swing from SNP to Lab)

EDINBURGH NORTH AND
LEITH %
*Chisholm, M. (Lab) 19,209 46.9
Dana, A. (SNP) 8,231 20.1
Stewart, E. (Con) 7,312 17.9
Campbell, H. (LD) 5,335 13.0
Graham, S. (Ref) 441 1.1
Brown, G. (ScotSoc) 320 0.8
Douglas-Reid, P.
(NLP) 97 0.2
Lab majority 10,978 26.81%
Electorate 61,617
Total Vote 40,945 Poll 66.5%
*Member of last parliament
Lab Hold (6.1% Swing from SNP to Lab)

EDINBURGH PENTLANDS %
Clark, L. (Lab) 19,675 43.0
*Rifkind, M. (Con) 14,813 32.4
Gibb, S. (SNP) 5,952 13.0
Dawe, J. (LD) 4,575 10.0
McDonald, M. (Ref) 422 0.9
Harper, R. (Green) 224 0.5
McConnachie, A.
(UKIP) 81 0.2
Lab majority 4,862 10.63%
Electorate 59,635
Total Vote 45,742 Poll 76.7%
*Member of last parliament
Lab Gain (9.8% Swing from Con to Lab)

EDINBURGH SOUTH %
*Griffiths, N. (Lab) 20,993 46.8
Smith, E. (Con) 9,541 21.3
Pringle, M. (LD) 7,911 17.6
Hargreaves, J. (SNP) 5,791 12.9
McLean, I. (Ref) 504 1.1
Dunn, B. (NLP) 98 0.2
Lab majority 11,452 25.54%
Electorate 62,467
Total Vote 44,838 Poll 71.8%
*Member of last parliament
Lab Hold (8.1% Swing from Con to Lab)

EDINBURGH WEST

		%
Gorrie, D. (LD)	20,578	43.2
*Douglas-Hamilton,		
J. (Con)	13,325	28.0
Hinds, L. (Lab)	8,948	18.8
Sutherland, G. (SNP)	4,210	8.8
Elphick, S. (Ref)	277	0.6
Coombes, P. (Lib)	263	0.6
Jack, A. (AntiSleaze)	30	0.1
LD majority	7,253	15.23%
Electorate	61,133	
Total Vote	47,631	Poll 77.9%

*Member of last parliament
LD Gain (11.8% Swing from Con to LD)

EDMONTON

		%
Love, A.		
(Lab/Co-op)	27,029	60.3
*Twinn, I. (Con)	13,557	30.2
Wiseman, A. (LD)	2,847	6.3
Wright, J. (Ref)	708	1.6
Cowd, B. (BNP)	437	1.0
Weald, P. (UKIP)	260	0.6
Lab/Co-op		
majority	13,472	30.05%
Electorate	63,718	
Total Vote	44,838	Poll 70.4%

*Member of last parliament
Lab/Co-op Gain (15.6% Swing from Con to Lab)

ELLESMERE PORT AND NESTON

		%
*Miller, A. (Lab)	31,310	59.6
Turnbull, L. (Con)	15,275	29.1
Pemberton, J. (LD)	4,673	8.9
Rodden, C. (Ref)	1,305	2.5
Lab majority	16,036	30.51%
Electorate	67,573	
Total Vote	52,563	Poll 77.6%

*Member of last parliament
Lab Hold (12.4% Swing from Con to Lab)

ELMET

		%
Burgon, C. (Lab)	28,348	52.4
*Batiste, S. (Con)	19,569	36.2
Jennings, B. (LD)	4,691	8.7
Zawadski, C. (Ref)	1,487	2.7
Lab majority	8,779	16.23%
Electorate	70,423	
Total Vote	54,095	Poll 76.7%

*Member of last parliament
Lab Gain (10.9% Swing from Con to Lab)

ELTHAM

		%
Efford, C. (Lab)	23,710	54.6
Blackwood, C. (Con)	13,528	31.2
Taylor, A. (LD)	3,701	8.5
Clark, M. (Ref)	1,414	3.3
Middleton, H. (Lib)	584	1.3
Hitches, W. (BNP)	491	1.1
Lab majority	10,182	23.45%
Electorate	57,358	
Total Vote	43,428	Poll 75.2%

Lab Gain (13.6% Swing from Con to Lab)

ENFIELD NORTH

		%
Ryan, J. (Lab)	24,148	50.7
Field, M. (Con)	17,326	36.4
Hopkins, M. (LD)	4,264	8.9
Ellingham, R. (Ref)	857	1.8
Griffin, J. (BNP)	590	1.2
O'Ware, J. (UKIP)	484	1.0
Lab majority	6,822	14.31%
Electorate	67,748	
Total Vote	47,669	Poll 70.4%

Lab Gain (16.1% Swing from Con to Lab)

ENFIELD SOUTHGATE

		%
Twigg, S. (Lab)	20,570	44.2
*Portillo, M. (Con)	19,137	41.1
Browne, J. (LD)	4,966	10.7
Luard, N. (Ref)	1,342	2.9
Storkey, A.		
(Christ Dem)	289	0.6
Malakouna, A.		
(Mal Voice)	229	0.5
Lab majority	1,433	3.08%
Electorate	65,796	
Total Vote	46,533	Poll 70.7%

*Member of last parliament
Lab Gain (17.4% Swing from Con to Lab)

EPPING FOREST

		%
Laing, E. (Con)	24,117	45.5
Murray, S. (Lab)	18,865	35.6
Robinson, S. (LD)	7,074	13.3
Berry, J. (Ref)	2,208	4.2
Henderson, P. (BNP)	743	1.4
Con majority	5,252	9.91%
Electorate	72,795	
Total Vote	53,007	Poll 72.8%

Con Hold (13.6% Swing from Con to Lab)

EPSOM AND EWELL

		%
*Hamilton, A. (Con)	24,717	45.6
Woodford, P. (Lab)	13,192	24.3
Vincent, J. (LD)	12,380	22.8
MacDonald, C.		
(Ref)	2,355	4.3
Green, H. (UKIP)	544	1.0
Charlton, H. (Green)	527	1.0
Weeks, K. (Pro-Life)	466	0.9
Con majority	11,525	21.27%
Electorate	73,322	
Total Vote	54,181	Poll 74%

*Member of last parliament
Con Hold (12.4% Swing from Con to Lab)

EREWASH

		%
Blackman, E. (Lab)	31,196	51.7
*Knight, A. (Con)	22,061	36.6
Garnett, M. (LD)	5,181	8.6
Stagg, S. (Ref)	1,404	2.3
Simmons, M.		
(SLP)	496	0.8
Lab majority	9,135	15.14%
Electorate	77,402	
Total Vote	60,338	Poll 77.8%

*Member of last parliament
Lab Gain (12.1% Swing from Con to Lab)

ERITH AND THAMESMEAD

		%
*Austin-Walker, J.		
(Lab)	25,812	62.1
Zahawi, N. (Con)	8,388	20.2
Grigg, A. (LD)	5,001	12.0
Flunder, J. (Ref)	1,394	3.4
Dooley, V. (BNP)	718	1.7
Jackson, M. (UKIP)	274	0.7
Lab majority	17,424	41.90%
Electorate	62,887	
Total Vote	41,587	Poll 66%

*Member of last parliament
Lab Hold (15.3% Swing from Con to Lab)

ESHER AND WALTON

		%
*Taylor, I. (Con)	26,747	49.8
Reay, J. (Lab)	12,219	22.8
Miles, G. (LD)	10,937	20.4
Cruickshank, A.		
(Ref)	2,904	5.4
Collignon, B.		
(UKIP)	558	1.0
Kay, S. (Dream)	302	0.6
Con majority	14,528	27.07%
Electorate	72,382	
Total Vote	53,667	Poll 74.3%

*Member of last parliament
Con Hold (8.1% Swing from Con to Lab)

EXETER

		%
Bradshaw, B. (Lab)	29,398	47.5
Rogers, A. (Con)	17,693	28.6
Brewer, D. (LD)	11,148	18.0
Morrish, D. (Lib)	2,062	3.3
Edwards, P. (Green)	643	1.0
Haynes, C. (UKIP)	638	1.0
Meakin, J. (Pensioners)	282	0.5
Lab majority	11,705	18.92%
Electorate	79,154	
Total Vote	61,864	Poll 77.6%

Lab Gain (11.9% Swing from Con to Lab)

FALKIRK EAST

		%
*Connarty, M. (Lab)	23,344	56.1
Brown, K. (SNP)	9,959	23.9
Nicol, M. (Con)	5,813	14.0
Spillane, R. (LD)	2,153	5.2
Mowbray, S. (Ref)	325	0.8
Lab majority	13,385	32.18%
Electorate	56,792	
Total Vote	41,594	Poll 73.2%

*Member of last parliament
Lab Hold (8.2% Swing from SNP to Lab)

FALKIRK WEST

		%
*Canavan, D. (Lab)	22,772	60.01
Alexander, D.		
(SNP)	8,989	23.4
Buchanan, C. (Con)	4,639	12.1
Houston, D. (LD)	1,970	5.1
Lab majority	13,783	35.92%
Electorate	52,850	
Total Vote	38,370	Poll 72.6%

*Member of last parliament
Lab Hold (4% Swing from SNP to Lab)

FALMOUTH AND CAMBORNE

		%
Atherton, C. (Lab)	18,151	33.8
*Coe, S. (Con)	15,463	28.8
Jones, T. (LD)	13,512	25.2
de Savary, P. (Ref)	3,534	6.6
Geach, J. (Ind Lab)	1,691	3.2
Holmes, P. (Lib)	527	1.0
Smith, R. (UKIP)	355	0.7
Lewarne, R. (MK)	238	0.4
Glitter, G. (Loony)	161	0.3
Lab majority	2,688	5.01%
Electorate	71,383	
Total Vote	53,632	Poll 75.1%

*Member of last parliament
Lab Gain (6.4% Swing from Con to Lab)

FAREHAM

		%
*Lloyd, Sir P. (Con)	24,436	46.8
Prior, M. (Lab)	14,078	27.0
Hill, G. (LD)	10,234	19.6
Markham, W. (Ref)	2,914	5.6
O'Brian, W. (Ind)	515	1.0
Con majority	10,358	19.85%
Electorate	68,787	
Total Vote	52,177	Poll 75.9%

*Member of last parliament
Con Hold (13% Swing from Con to Lab)

FAVERSHAM AND MID KENT

		%
*Rowe, A. (Con)	22,016	44.4
Stewart, A. (Lab)	17,843	36.0
Parmenter, B. (LD)	6,138	12.4
Birley, R. (Ref)	2,073	4.2
Davidson, N. (Loony)	511	1.0
Cunningham, M. (UKIP)	431	0.9
Currer, D. (Green)	380	0.8
Morgan, C. (Street)	115	0.2
Pollard, N. (NLP)	99	0.2
Con majority	4,173	8.41%
Electorate	67,490	
Total Vote	49,606	Poll 73.3%

*Member of last parliament
Con Hold (13.9% Swing from Con to Lab)

FELTHAM AND HESTON
*Keen, A.

		%
(Lab/Co-op)	27,836	60.0
Ground, R. (Con)	12,563	26.7
Penning, C. (LD)	4,264	9.2
Stubbs, R. (Ref)	1,099	2.4
Church, R. (BNP)	682	1.5
Fawcett, D. (NLP)	177	0.4
Lab/Co-op majority	15,273	32.76%
Electorate	71,093	
Total Vote	46,621	Poll 65.6%

*Member of last parliament
Lab/Co-op Hold (15.4% Swing from Con to Lab)

FERMANAGH AND SOUTH TYRONE

		%
*Maginnis, K. (UUP)	24,862	51.5
McHugh, G. (SF)	11,174	23.1
Gallagher, T. (SDLP)	11,060	22.9
Farry, S. (APNI)	977	2.0
Gillan, S. (NLP)	217	0.4
UUP majority	13,688	28.35%
Electorate	64,600	
Total Vote	48,290	Poll 74.8%

*Member of last parliament
UUP Hold (2.4% Swing from UUP to SF)

FINCHLEY AND GOLDERS GREEN

		%
Vis, R. (Lab)	23,180	46.1
*Marshall, J. (Con)	19,991	39.7
Davies, J. (LD)	5,670	11.3
Shaw, G. (Ref)	684	1.4
Gunstock, A. (Green)	576	1.1
Barraclough, D. (UKIP)	205	0.4
Lab majority	3,189	6.34%
Electorate	72,225	
Total Vote	50,306	Poll 68.2%

*Member of last parliament
Lab Gain (15.1% Swing from Con to Lab)

FOLKESTONE AND HYTHE

		%
*Howard, M. (Con)	20,313	39.0
Laws, D. (LD)	13,981	26.9
Doherty, P. (Lab)	12,939	24.9
Aspinall, J. (Ref)	4,188	8.0
Baker, J. (UKIP)	378	0.7
Segal, E. (Soc)	182	0.3
Saint, R. (Field Sport)	69	0.1
Con majority	6,332	12.17%
Electorate	71,153	
Total Vote	52,050	Poll 72.7%

*Member of last parliament
Con Hold (2.4% Swing from Con to LD)

FOREST OF DEAN

		%
Organ, D. (Lab)	24,203	48.2
*Marland, P. (Con)	17,860	35.6
Lynch, A. (LD)	6,165	12.3
Hopkins, J. (Ref)	1,624	3.2
Morgan, G. (Ind)	218	0.4
Palmer, C. (21stCent)	80	0.2
Porter, S. (IndForest)	34	0.1
Lab majority	6,343	12.64%
Electorate	63,465	
Total Vote	50,184	Poll 79.1%

*Member of last parliament
Lab Gain (5.6% Swing from Con to Lab)

FOYLE

		%
*Hume, J. (SDLP)	25,109	52.5
McLaughlin, M. (SF)	11,445	23.9
Hay, W. (DUP)	10,290	21.5
Bell, E. (APNI)	817	1.7
Brennan, D. (NLP)	154	0.3
SDLP majority	13,664	28.58%
Electorate	67,620	
Total Vote	47,815	Poll 70.7%

*Member of last parliament
SDLP Hold (4% Swing from SDLP to SF)

FYLDE

		%
*Jack, M. (Con)	25,443	48.9
Garrett, J. (Lab)	16,480	31.7
Greene, W. (LD)	7,609	14.6
Britton, D. (Ref)	2,372	4.6
Kerwin, T. (NLP)	163	0.3
Con majority	8,963	17.21%
Electorate	71,385	
Total Vote	52,067	Poll 72.8%

*Member of last parliament
Con Hold (12.2% Swing from Con to Lab)

GAINSBOROUGH

		%
*Leigh, E. (Con)	20,593	43.1
Taylor, P. (Lab)	13,767	28.8
Taylor, N. (LD)	13,436	28.1
Con majority	6,826	14.28%
Electorate	63,106	
Total Vote	47,796	Poll 74.6%

*Member of last parliament
Con Hold (9.1% Swing from Con to Lab)

GALLOWAY AND UPPER NITHSDALE

		%
Morgan, A. (SNP)	18,449	43.9
*Lang, I. (Con)	12,825	30.5
Clark, K. (Lab)	6,861	16.3
McKerchar, J. (LD)	2,700	6.4
Wood, R. (Ind)	566	1.3
Kennedy, A. (Ref)	428	1.0
Smith, J. (UKIP)	189	0.4
SNP majority	5,624	13.38%
Electorate	52,751	
Total Vote	42,018	Poll 79.7%

*Member of last parliament
SNP Gain (9.5% Swing from Con to SNP)

GATESHEAD EAST AND WASHINGTON WEST

		%
*Quin, J. (Lab)	31,047	72.1
Burns, J. (Con)	6,097	14.2
Ord, A. (LD)	4,622	10.7
Daley, M. (Ref)	1,315	3.1
Lab majority	24,950	57.91%
Electorate	64,114	
Total Vote	43,081	Poll 67.2%

*Member of last parliament
Lab Hold (13.8% Swing from Con to Lab)

GEDLING

		%
Coaker, V. (Lab)	24,390	46.8
*Mitchell, A. (Con)	20,588	39.5
Poynter, R. (LD)	5,180	9.9
Connor, J. (Ref)	2,006	3.8
Lab majority	3,802	7.29%
Electorate	68,820	
Total Vote	52,164	Poll 75.6%

*Member of last parliament
Lab Gain (13% Swing from Con to Lab)

GILLINGHAM

		%
Clark, P. (Lab)	20,187	39.8
*Couchman, J. (Con)	18,207	35.9
Sayer, R. (LD)	9,649	19.0
Cann, G. (Ref)	1,492	2.9
MacKinlay, C. (UKIP)	590	1.2
Robinson, D. (Loony)	305	0.6
Jury, C. (BNP)	195	0.4
Duguay, G. (NLP)	58	0.1
Lab majority	1,980	3.91%
Electorate	70,389	
Total Vote	50,683	Poll 72%

*Member of last parliament
Lab Gain (16% Swing from Con to Lab)

GLASGOW ANNIESLAND %
*Dewar, D. (Lab)	20,951	61.8
Wilson, W. (SNP)	5,797	17.1
Brocklehurst, R.		
(Con)	3,881	11.5
McGinty, C. (LD)	2,453	7.2
Majid, A. (Pro-Life)	374	1.1
Bonnar, B. (ScotSoc)	229	0.7
Milligan, A. (UKIP)	86	0.3
McKay, G. (Ref)	84	0.2
Pringle, T. (NLP)	24	0.1
Lab majority 15,154		44.73%
Electorate 52,955		
Total Vote 33,879 Poll 63.8%		

*Member of last parliament
Lab Hold (4.3% Swing from SNP to Lab)

GLASGOW BAILLIESTON %
*Wray, J. (Lab)	20,925	65.7
Thomson, P. (SNP)	6,085	19.1
Kelly, M. (Con)	2,468	7.7
Rainger, S. (LD)	1,217	3.8
McVicar, J. (ScotSoc)	970	3.0
McClafferty, J. (Ref)	188	0.6
Lab majority 14,840		46.59%
Electorate 51,152		
Total Vote 31,853 Poll 62.2%		

*Member of last parliament
Lab Hold (3% Swing from SNP to Lab)

GLASGOW CATHCART %
*Maxton, J. (Lab)	19,158	57.4
Whitehead, M. (SNP)	6,193	18.5
Muir, A. (Con)	4,248	12.7
Dick, G. (LD)	2,302	6.9
Indyk, Z. (Pro-Life)	687	2.1
Stevenson, R.		
(ScotSoc)	458	1.4
Haldane, S. (Ref)	344	1.0
Lab majority 12,965		38.83%
Electorate 49,312		
Total Vote 33,390 Poll 67.7%		

*Member of last parliament
Lab Hold (4.3% Swing from SNP to Lab)

GLASGOW GOVAN %
Sarwar, M. (Lab)	14,216	44.1
Sturgeon, N. (SNP)	11,302	35.1
Thomas, W. (Con)	2,839	8.8
Stewart, R. (LD)	1,918	5.9
McCombes, A.		
(ScotSoc)	755	2.3
Paton, P. (Ind)	325	1.0
Badar, I. (IndLab)	319	1.0
Abbassi, Z. (IndCon)	221	0.7
MacDonald, K. (Ref)	201	0.6
White, J. (BNP)	149	0.5
Lab majority 2,914		9.04%
Electorate 49,836		
Total Vote 32,245 Poll 64.7%		

Lab Hold (3.2% Swing from Lab to SNP)

GLASGOW KELVIN %
*Galloway, G. (Lab)	16,643	51.0
White, S. (SNP)	6,978	21.4
Buchanan, E. (LD)	4,629	14.2
McPhie, D. (Con)	3,539	10.8

Green, A. (Scot Soc)	386	1.2
Grigor, R. (Ref)	282	0.9
Vanni, V. (SPGB)	102	0.3
Stidolph, G. (NLP)	95	0.3
Lab majority 9,665		29.60%
Electorate 57,438		
Total Vote 32,654 Poll 56.1%		

*Member of last parliament
Lab Hold (1% Swing from SNP to Lab)

GLASGOW MARYHILL %
*Fyfe, M. (Lab)	19,301	64.9
Wailes, J. (SNP)	5,037	16.9
Attwooll, E. (LD)	2,119	7.1
Baldwin, S. (Con)	1,747	5.9
Blair, L. (NLP)	651	2.2
Baker, M. (Scot Soc)	409	1.4
Hanif, J. (Pro-Life)	344	1.2
Paterson, R. (Ref)	77	0.3
Johnstone, S. (SEP)	36	0.1
Lab majority 14,264		47.99%
Electorate 52,523		
Total Vote 29,721 Poll 56.4%		

*Member of last parliament
Lab Hold (2.4% Swing from SNP to Lab)

GLASGOW POLLOK %
*Davidson, I.		
(Lab/Co-op)	19,653	59.9
Logan, D. (SNP)	5,862	17.9
Sheridan, T.		
(Scot Soc)	3,639	11.1
Hamilton, E. (Con)	1,979	6.0
Jago, D. (LD)	1,137	3.5
Gott, M. (Pro-Life)	380	1.2
Haldane, D. (Ref)	152	0.5
Lab/Co-op		
majority 13,791		42.04%
Electorate 49,284		
Total Vote 32,802 Poll 66.5%		

*Member of last parliament
Lab/Co-op Hold (8.6% Swing from SNP to Lab)

GLASGOW RUTHERGLEN %
*McAvoy, T.		
(Lab/Co-op)	20,430	57.5
Gray, I. (SNP)	5,423	15.3
Brown, R. (LD)	5,167	14.5
Campbell-Bannerman,		
D. (Con)	3,288	9.3
Easton, G. (IndLab)	812	2.3
Kane, R. (ScotSoc)	251	0.7
Kerr, J. (Ref)	150	0.4
Lab/Co-op		
majority 15,007		42.25%
Electorate 50,646		
Total Vote 35,521 Poll 70.1%		

*Member of last parliament
Lab/Co-op Hold (2.2% Swing from SNP to Lab)

GLASGOW SHETTLESTON %
*Marshall, D. (Lab)	19,616	73.2
Hanif, H. (SNP)	3,748	14.0
Simpson, C. (Con)	1,484	5.5
Hiles, K. (LD)	1,061	4.0

McVicar, C. (Scot Soc)	482	1.8
Currie, R. (BNP)	191	0.7
Montguire, T. (Ref)	151	0.6
Graham, A. (WRP)	80	0.3
Lab majority 15,868		59.18%
Electorate 47,990		
Total Vote 26,813 Poll 54.6%		

*Member of last parliament
Lab Hold (4.9% Swing from SNP to Lab)

GLASGOW SPRINGBURN %
*Martin, M. (Lab)	22,534	71.4
Brady, J. (SNP)	5,208	16.5
Holdsworth, M. (Con)	1,893	6.0
Alexander, J. (LD)	1,349	4.3
Lawson, J. (Scot Soc)	407	1.3
Keating, A. (Ref)	186	0.6
Lab majority 17,326		54.87%
Electorate 53,473		
Total Vote 31,577 Poll 58.9%		

*Member of last parliament
Lab Hold (4.9% Swing from SNP to Lab)

GLOUCESTER %
Kingham, T. (Lab)	28,943	50.0
*French, D. (Con)	20,684	35.7
Munisamy, P. (LD)	6,069	10.5
Reid, A. (Ref)	1,482	2.6
Harris, A. (UKIP)	455	0.8
Hamilton, M. (NLP)	281	0.5
Lab majority 8,259		14.26%
Electorate 78,682		
Total Vote 57,914 Poll 73.6%		

*Member of last parliament
Lab Gain (11.5% Swing from Con to Lab)

GORDON %
*Bruce, M. (LD)	17,999	42.6
Porter, J. (Con)	11,002	26.0
Lochhead, R. (SNP)	8,435	20.0
Kirkhill, L. (Lab)	4,350	10.3
Pidcock, F. (Ref)	459	1.1
LD majority 6,997		16.56%
Electorate 58,767		
Total Vote 42,245 Poll 71.9%		

*Member of last parliament
LD Win (18.7% Swing from Con to LD)

GOSPORT %
*Viggers, P. (Con)	21,085	43.6
Gray, I. (Lab)	14,827	30.7
Hogg, S. (LD)	9,479	19.6
Blowers, A. (Ref)	2,538	5.2
Ettie, P. (Ind)	426	0.9
Con majority 6,258		12.94%
Electorate 68,830		
Total Vote 48,355 Poll 70.3%		

*Member of last parliament
Con Hold (15.8% Swing from Con to Lab)

GOWER %
Caton, M. (Lab)	23,313	53.8
Cairns, A. (Con)	10,306	23.8
Evans, H. (LD)	5,624	13.0
Williams, D. (PC)	2,226	5.1
Lewis, R. (Ref)	1,745	4.0
Popham, A. (Freedom)	122	0.3

Lab majority 13,007   30.01%
Electorate 57,691
Total Vote 43,336 Poll 74.9%
Lab Hold (7.5% Swing from Con to Lab)

GRANTHAM AND STAMFORD %
*Davies, Q. (Con) 22,672 42.8
Denning, P. (Lab) 19,980 37.7
Sellick, J. (LD) 6,612 12.5
Swain, M. (Ref) 2,721 5.1
Charlesworth, M.
  (UKIP) 556 1.0
Clark, R. (Pro-Life) 314 0.6
Harper, I. (NLP) 115 0.2
Con majority 2,692 5.08%
Electorate 72,310
Total Vote 52,970 Poll 73.3%
*Member of last parliament
Con Hold (13.3% Swing from Con to Lab)

GRAVESHAM %
Pond, C. (Lab) 26,460 49.7
*Arnold, J. (Con) 20,681 38.8
Canet, J. (LD) 4,128 7.8
Curtis, P. (Ref) 1,441 2.7
Leyshon, A. (Ind) 414 0.8
Palmer, D. (NLP) 129 0.2
Lab majority 5,779 10.85%
Electorate 69,234
Total Vote 53,253 Poll 76.7%
*Member of last parliament
Lab Gain (10% Swing from Con to Lab)

GREAT GRIMSBY %
*Mitchell, A. (Lab) 25,765 59.8
Godson, D. (Con) 9,521 22.1
De Freitas, A.
  (LD) 7,810 18.1
Lab majority 16,244 37.69%
Electorate 65,043
Total Vote 43,096 Poll 66.1%
*Member of last parliament
Lab Hold (11.5% Swing from Con to Lab)

GREAT YARMOUTH %
*Wright, T. (Lab) 26,084 53.4
Carttiss, M. (Con) 17,416 35.6
Wood, D. (LD) 5,381 11.0
Lab majority 8,668 17.73%
Electorate 68,625
Total Vote 48,881 Poll 71.1%
*Member of last parliament
Lab Gain (13.9% Swing from Con to Lab)

GREENOCK AND INVERCLYDE %
*Godman, N. (Lab) 19,480 56.2
Goodall, B. (SNP) 6,440 18.6
Ackland, R. (LD) 4,791 13.8
Swire, H. (Con) 3,976 11.5
Lab majority 13,040 37.59%
Electorate 48,818
Total Vote 34,687 Poll 71.1%
*Member of last parliament
Lab Hold (3.5% Swing from SNP to Lab)

GREENWICH AND WOOLWICH %
*Raynsford, N. (Lab) 25,630 63.4
Mitchell, M. (Con) 7,502 18.6
Luxton, C. (LD) 5,049 12.5
Ellison, D. (Ref) 1,670 4.1
Mallone, R.
  (Fellowship) 428 1.1
Martin-Eagle, D.
  (Constit) 124 0.3
Lab majority 18,128 44.87%
Electorate 61,352
Total Vote 40,403 Poll 64.9%
*Member of last parliament
Lab Hold (9.3% Swing from Con to Lab)

GUILDFORD %
St Aubyn, N. (Con) 24,230 42.5
Sharp, M. (LD) 19,439 34.1
Burns, J. (Lab) 9,945 17.5
Gore, J. (Ref) 2,650 4.7
McWhirter, R. (UKIP) 400 0.7
Morris, J. (Pacifist) 294 0.5
Con majority 4,791 8.41%
Electorate 75,541
Total Vote 56,958 Poll 75.4%
Con Hold (7.1% Swing from Con to LD)

HACKNEY NORTH AND STOKE NEWINGTON %
*Abbott, D. (Lab) 21,110 65.2
Lavender, M. (Con) 5,483 16.9
Taylor, D. (LD) 3,306 10.2
Chong, Y. (Green) 1,395 4.3
Maxwell, B. (Ref) 544 1.7
Tolson, D. (None) 368 1.1
Lovebucket, L.
  (Rainbow Ref) 176 0.5
Lab majority 15,627 48.26%
Electorate 62,045
Total Vote 32,382 Poll 51.2%
*Member of last parliament
Lab Hold (8.7% Swing from Con to Lab)

HACKNEY SOUTH AND SHOREDITCH %
*Sedgemore, B. (Lab) 20,048 59.4
Pantling, M. (LD) 5,068 15.0
O'Leary, C. (Con) 4,494 13.3
Betts, T. (New Labour) 2,436 7.2
Franklin, R. (Ref) 613 1.8
Callow, G. (BNP) 531 1.6
Goldman, M. (Comm) 298 0.9
Goldberg, M. (NLP) 145 0.4
Rogers, W. (WRP) 139 0.4
Lab majority 14,980 44.36%
Electorate 61,728
Total Vote 33,772 Poll 54%
*Member of last parliament
Lab Hold (3% Swing from LD to Lab)

HALESOWEN AND ROWLEY REGIS %
Heal, S. (Lab) 26,366 54.1
Kennedy, J. (Con) 16,029 32.9
Todd, E. (LD) 4,169 8.5
White, P. (Ref) 1,244 2.6

Needs, K. (Nat Dem) 592 1.2
Weller, T. (Green) 361 0.7
Lab majority 10,337 21.20%
Electorate 66,245
Total Vote 48,761 Poll 73.6%
Lab Gain (10.7% Swing from Con to Lab)

HALIFAX %
*Mahon, A. (Lab) 27,465 54.3
Light, R. (Con) 16,253 32.1
Waller, E. (LD) 6,059 12.0
Whitaker, C. (UKIP) 779 1.5
Lab majority 11,212 22.18%
Electorate 71,701
Total Vote 50,556 Poll 70.5%
*Member of last parliament
Lab Hold (10.7% Swing from Con to Lab)

HALTEMPRICE AND HOWDEN %
*Davis, D. (Con) 21,809 44.0
Wallis, D. (LD) 14,295 28.8
McManus, G. (Lab) 11,701 23.6
Pearson, T. (Ref) 1,370 2.8
Bloom, G. (UKIP) 301 0.6
Strevens, B. (NLP) 74 0.1
Con majority 7,514 15.16%
Electorate 65,602
Total Vote 49,550 Poll 75.4%
*Member of last parliament
Con Hold (9.5% Swing from Con to LD)

HALTON %
Twigg, J. (Lab) 31,497 70.9
Balmer, P. (Con) 7,847 17.7
Jones, J. (LD) 3,263 7.3
Atkins, R. (Ref) 1,036 2.3
Proffitt, D. (Lib) 600 1.4
Alley, J. (Republican) 196 0.4
Lab majority 23,650 53.22%
Electorate 64,987
Total Vote 44,439 Poll 68.4%
Lab Hold (11.9% Swing from Con to Lab)

HAMILTON NORTH AND BELLSHILL %
*Reid, J. (Lab) 24,322 64.0
Matheson, M. (SNP) 7,255 19.1
McIntosh, G. (Con) 3,944 10.4
Legg, K. (LD) 1,924 5.1
Conn, R. (Ref) 554 1.5
Lab majority 17,067 44.91%
Electorate 53,607
Total Vote 37,999 Poll 70.9%
*Member of last parliament
Lab Hold (3.2% Swing from SNP to Lab)

HAMILTON SOUTH %
*Robertson, G. (Lab) 21,709 65.6
Black, I. (SNP) 5,831 17.6
Kilgour, R. (Con) 2,858 8.6
Pitts, N. (LD) 1,693 5.1
Gunn, C. (Pro-Life) 684 2.1
Brown, S. (Ref) 316 1.0
Lab majority 15,878 47.98%
Electorate 46,562
Total Vote 33,091 Poll 71.1%
*Member of last parliament
Lab Hold (5.7% Swing from SNP to Lab)

HAMMERSMITH AND FULHAM

		%
Coleman, I. (Lab)	25,262	46.8
*Carrington, M. (Con)	21,420	39.6
Sugden, A. (LD)	4,728	8.8
Bremner, M. (Ref)	1,023	1.9
Johnson-Smith, W. (New Labour)	695	1.3
Streeter, E. (Green)	562	1.0
Roberts, G. (UKIP)	183	0.3
Phillips, A. (NLP)	79	0.1
Elston, A. (Care)	74	0.1
Lab majority	3,842	7.11%
Electorate	78,637	
Total Vote	54,026	Poll 68.7%

*Member of last parliament
Lab Gain (10.1% Swing from Con to Lab)

HAMPSTEAD AND HIGHGATE

		%
*Jackson, G. (Lab)	25,275	57.4
Gibson, E. (Con)	11,991	27.2
Fox, B. (LD)	5,481	12.4
Siddique, M. (Ref)	667	1.5
Leslie, J. (NLP)	147	0.3
Carroll, R. (Dream)	141	0.3
Prince, P. (UKIP)	123	0.3
Harris, R. (Humanist)	105	0.2
Rizz, C. (Rizz)	101	0.2
Lab majority	13,284	30.24%
Electorate	64,889	
Total Vote	44,031	Poll 67.9%

*Member of last parliament
Lab Hold (12.4% Swing from Con to Lab)

HARBOROUGH

		%
*Garnier, E. (Con)	22,170	41.8
Cox, M. (LD)	15,646	29.5
Holden, N. (Lab)	13,332	25.2
Wright, N. (Ref)	1,859	3.5
Con majority	6,524	12.31%
Electorate	70,424	
Total Vote	53,007	Poll 75.3%

*Member of last parliament
Con Hold (3% Swing from Con to LD)

HARLOW

		%
Rammell, B. (Lab)	25,861	54.1
*Hayes, J. (Con)	15,347	32.1
Spenceley, L. (LD)	4,523	9.5
Wells, M. (Ref)	1,422	3.0
Batten, G. (UKIP)	340	0.7
Bowles, J. (BNP)	319	0.7
Lab majority	10,514	21.99%
Electorate	64,072	
Total Vote	47,812	Poll 74.4%

*Member of last parliament
Lab Gain (12.6% Swing from Con to Lab)

HARROGATE AND KNARESBOROUGH

		%
Willis, P. (LD)	24,558	51.5
*Lamont, N. (Con)	18,322	38.5
Boyce, B. (Lab)	4,151	8.7
Blackburn, J. (IndCon)	614	1.3

LD majority	6,236	13.09%
Electorate	65,155	
Total Vote	47,645	Poll 72.9%

*Member of last parliament
LD Gain (15.7% Swing from Con to LD)

HARROW EAST

		%
McNulty, T. (Lab)	29,923	52.5
*Dykes, H. (Con)	20,189	35.4
Sharma, B. (LD)	4,697	8.2
Casey, B. (Ref)	1,537	2.7
Scholefield, A. (UKIP)	464	0.8
Planton, A. (NLP)	171	0.3
Lab majority	9,734	17 09%
Electorate	79,846	
Total Vote	56,981	Poll 71.4%

*Member of last parliament
Lab Gain (18.1% Swing from Con to Lab)

HARROW WEST

		%
Thomas, G. (Lab)	21,811	41.5
*Hughes, R. (Con)	20,571	39.2
Nandhra, P. (LD)	8,127	15.5
Crossman, H. (Ref)	1,997	3.8
Lab majority	1,240	2.36%
Electorate	72,005	
Total Vote	52,506	Poll 72.2%

*Member of last parliament
Lab Gain (17.5% Swing from Con to Lab)

HARTLEPOOL

		%
*Mandelson, P. (Lab)	26,997	60.7
Horsley, M. (Con)	9,489	21.3
Clark, R. (LD)	6,248	14.1
Henderson, M. (Ref)	1,718	3.9
Lab majority	17,508	39.39%
Electorate	67,712	
Total Vote	44,452	Poll 65.6%

*Member of last parliament
Lab Hold (11.2% Swing from Con to Lab)

HARWICH

		%
Henderson, I. (Lab)	20,740	38.8
*Sproat, I. (Con)	19,524	36.5
Elvin, A. (LD)	7,037	13.1
Titford, J. (Ref)	4,923	9.2
Knight, R. (Community)	1,290	2.4
Lab majority	1,216	2.27%
Electorate	75,775	
Total Vote	53,514	Poll 70.5%

*Member of last parliament
Lab Gain (14.6% Swing from Con to Lab)

HASTINGS AND RYE

		%
Foster, M. (Lab)	16,867	34.4
*Lait, J. (Con)	14,307	29.2
Palmer, M. (LD)	13,717	28.0
McGovern, C. (Ref)	2,511	5.1
Amstad, J. (Lib)	1,046	2.1
Andrews, W. (UKIP)	472	1.0
Tiverton, D. (Loony)	149	0.3
Lab majority	2,560	5.22%
Electorate	70,388	
Total Vote	49,069	Poll 69.7%

*Member of last parliament
Lab Gain (18.5% Swing from Con to Lab)

HAVANT

		%
*Willetts, D. (Con)	19,204	39.7
Armstrong, L. (Lab)	15,475	32.0
Kooner, M. (LD)	10,806	22.4
Green, A. (Ref)	2,395	5.0
Atwal, M. (People-1st)	442	0.9
Con majority	3,729	7.72%
Electorate	68,420	
Total Vote	48,322	Poll 70.4%

*Member of last parliament
Con Hold (12.7% Swing from Con to Lab)

HAYES AND HARLINGTON %

McDonnell, J. (Lab)	25,458	62.0
Retter, A. (Con)	11,167	27.2
Little, A. (LD)	3,049	7.4
Page, F. (Ref)	778	1.9
Hutchins, G. (NF)	504	1.2
Farrow, D. (AllNight)	135	0.3
Lab majority	14,291	34.78%
Electorate	56,829	
Total Vote	41,091	Poll 72.3%

Lab Gain (17.4% Swing from Con to Lab)

HAZEL GROVE

		%
Stunell, A. (LD)	26,883	54.5
Murphy, B. (Con)	15,069	30.5
Lewis, J. (Lab)	5,882	11.9
Stanyer, J. (Ref)	1,055	2.1
Black, G. (UKIP)	268	0.5
Firkin-Flood, D. (Humanist)	183	0.4
LD majority	11,814	23.94%
Electorate	63,694	
Total Vote	49,340	Poll 77.3%

LD Gain (12.8% Swing from Con to LD)

HEMEL HEMPSTEAD

		%
McWalter, T. (Lab/Co-op)	25,175	45.7
*Jones, R. (Con)	21,539	39.1
Lindsley, P. (LD)	6,789	12.3
Such, P. (Ref)	1,327	2.4
Harding, D. (NLP)	262	0.5
Lab/Co-op majority	3,636	6.60%
Electorate	71,468	
Total Vote	55,092	Poll 76.7%

*Member of last parliament
Lab/Co-op Gain (12% Swing from Con to Lab)

HEMSWORTH

		%
*Trickett, J. (Lab)	32,088	70.6
Hazell, N. (Con)	8,096	17.8
Kirby, J. (LD)	4,033	8.9
Irvine, D. (Ref)	1,260	2.8
Lab majority	23,992	52.76%
Electorate	66,964	
Total Vote	45,477	Poll 67.9%

*Member of last parliament
Lab Hold (7.4% Swing from Con to Lab)

HENDON

		%
Dismore, A. (Lab)	24,683	49.3
*Gorst, Sir J. (Con)	18,528	37.0
Casey, W. (LD)	5,427	10.8
Rabbow, S. (Ref)	978	2.0
Wright, B. (UKIP)	267	0.5
Taylor, S. (WRP)	153	0.3
Lab majority	6,155	12.30%
Electorate	76,195	
Total Vote	50,036	Poll 64.6%

*Member of last parliament
Lab Gain (16.2% Swing from Con to Lab)

HENLEY

		%
*Heseltine, M. (Con)	23,908	46.4
Horton, T. (LD)	12,741	24.7
Enright, D. (Lab)	11,700	22.7
Sainsbury, S. (Ref)	2,299	4.5
Miles, S. (Green)	514	1.0
Barlow, N. (NLP)	221	0.4
Hibbert, T. (Whig)	160	0.3
Con majority	11,167	21.67%
Electorate	66,424	
Total Vote	51,543	Poll 77.6%

*Member of last parliament
Con Hold (7.2% Swing from Con to LD)

HEREFORD

		%
Keetch, P. (LD)	25,198	47.9
*Shepherd, C. (Con)	18,550	35.3
Chappell, A. (Lab)	6,596	12.6
Easton, C. (Ref)	2,209	4.2
LD majority	6,648	12.65%
Electorate	69,864	
Total Vote	52,553	Poll 75.2%

*Member of last parliament
LD Gain (9.2% Swing from Con to LD)

HERTFORD AND STORTFORD
%

*Wells, B. (Con)	24,027	44.0
Speller, S. (Lab)	17,142	31.4
Wood, M. (LD)	9,679	17.7
Page Croft, H. (Ref)	2,105	3.9
Smalley, B. (UKIP)	1,233	2.3
Franey, M. (Pro-Life)	259	0.5
Molloy, D. (Logic)	126	0.2
Con majority	6,885	12.62%
Electorate	71,759	
Total Vote	54,571	Poll 75.6%

*Member of last parliament
Con Hold (13.5% Swing from Con to Lab)

HERTSMERE

		%
*Clappison, J. (Con)	22,305	44.3
Kelly, B. (Lab)	19,230	38.2
Gray, A. (LD)	6,466	12.8
Marlow, J. (Ref)	1,703	3.4
Saunders, R. (UKIP)	453	0.9
Kahn, N. (NLP)	191	0.4
Con majority	3,075	6.11%
Electorate	68,011	
Total Vote	50,348	Poll 73.4%

*Member of last parliament
Con Hold (15% Swing from Con to Lab)

HEXHAM

		%
*Atkinson, P. (Con)	17,701	38.8
McMinn, I. (Lab)	17,479	38.3
Carr, P. (LD)	7,959	17.4
Waddell, R. (Ref)	1,362	3.0
Lott, D. (UKIP)	1,170	2.6
Con majority	222	0.49%
Electorate	58,914	
Total Vote	45,671	Poll 77.5%

*Member of last parliament
Con Hold (13.9% Swing from Con to Lab)

HEYWOOD AND MIDDLETON
%

Dobbin, J. (Lab/Co-op)	29,179	57.7
Grigg, E. (Con)	11,637	23.0
Clayton, D. (LD)	7,908	15.6
West, C. (Ref)	1,076	2.1
Burke, P. (Lib)	750	1.5
Lab/Co-op majority	17,542	34.70%
Electorate	73,898	
Total Vote	50,550	Poll 68.3%

Lab Hold (9.9% Swing from Con to Lab)

HIGH PEAK

		%
Levitt, T. (Lab)	29,052	50.8
*Hendry, C. (Con)	20,261	35.5
Barber, S. (LD)	6,420	11.2
Hanson-Orr, C. (Ref)	1,420	2.5
Lab majority	8,791	15.38%
Electorate	72,315	
Total Vote	57,153	Poll 78.9%

*Member of last parliament
Lab Gain (11.7% Swing from Con to Lab)

HITCHIN AND HARPENDEN %

*Lilley, P. (Con)	24,038	45.9
Sanderson, R. (Lab)	17,367	33.1
White, C. (LD)	10,515	20.1
Cooke, D. (NLP)	290	0.6
Horton, J. (Soc)	217	0.4
Con majority	6,671	12.72%
Electorate	67,219	
Total Vote	52,427	Poll 78%

*Member of last parliament
Con Hold (15.4% Swing from Con to Lab)

HOLBORN AND ST PANCRAS
%

*Dobson, F. (Lab)	24,707	65.0
Smith, J. (Con)	6,804	17.9
McGuinness, J. (LD)	4,750	12.5
Carr, J. (Ref)	790	2.1
Bedding, T. (NLP)	191	0.5
Smith, S. (Justice)	173	0.5
Conway, B. (WRP)	171	0.4
Rosenthal, M. (Dream)	157	0.4
Rice-Evans, P. (EU Party)	140	0.4
Quintavalle, B. (Pro-Life)	114	0.3
Lab majority	17,903	47.12%
Electorate	63,037	
Total Vote	37,997	Poll 57.2%

*Member of last parliament
Lab Hold (10.5% Swing from Con to Lab)

HORNCHURCH

		%
Cryer, J. (Lab)	22,066	50.2
*Squire, R. (Con)	16,386	37.3
Martins, R. (LD)	3,446	7.8
Khilkoff-Boulding, R. (Ref)	1,595	3.6
Trueman, J. (Third Way)	259	0.6
Sowerby, J. (Pro-Life)	189	0.4
Lab majority	5,680	12.93%
Electorate	60,775	
Total Vote	43,941	Poll 72.2%

*Member of last parliament
Lab Gain (16% Swing from Con to Lab)

HORNSEY AND WOOD GREEN
%

*Roche, B. (Lab)	31,792	61.7
Hart, H. (Con)	11,293	21.9
Featherstone, L. (LD)	5,794	11.3
Jago, H. (Green)	1,214	2.4
Miller, R. (Ref)	808	1.6
Sikorski, P. (SLP)	586	1.1
Lab majority	20,499	39.81%
Electorate	74,537	
Total Vote	51,487	Poll 66.9%

*Member of last parliament
Lab Hold (15.3% Swing from Con to Lab)

HORSHAM

		%
Maude, F. (Con)	29,015	50.8
Millson, M. (LD)	14,153	24.8
Walsh, M. (Lab)	10,691	18.7
Grant, R. (Ref)	2,281	4.0
Miller, H. (UKIP)	819	1.4
Corbould, M. (FullEmp)	206	0.4
Con majority	14,862	26.00%
Electorate	75,432	
Total Vote	57,165	Poll 75.8%

Con Hold (6.8% Swing from Con to LD)

HOUGHTON AND WASHINGTON EAST
%

Kemp, F. (Lab)	31,946	76.4
Booth, P. (Con)	5,391	12.9
Miller, K. (LD)	3,209	7.7
Joseph, C. (Ref)	1,277	3.1
Lab majority	26,555	63.49%
Electorate	67,343	
Total Vote	41,823	Poll 62.1%

Lab Hold (9.1% Swing from Con to Lab)

HOVE

		%
Caplin, I. (Lab)	21,458	44.6
Guy, R. (Con)	17,499	36.4
Pearce, T. (LD)	4,645	9.7
Field, S. (Ref)	1,931	4.0
Furness, J. (IndCon)	1,735	3.6
Mulligan, P. (Green)	644	1.3
Vause, J. (UKIP)	209	0.4
Lab majority	3,959	8.23%
Electorate	69,016	
Total Vote	48,121	Poll 69.7%

Lab Gain (16.4% Swing from Con to Lab)

HUDDERSFIELD

		%
*Sheerman, B. (Lab/Co-op)	25,171	56.5
Forrow, B. (Con)	9,323	20.9
Beever, G. (LD)	7,642	17.2
McNulty, P. (Ref)	1,480	3.3
Phillips, J. (Green)	938	2.1
Lab/Co-op majority	15,848	35.57%
Electorate	65,824	
Total Vote	44,554	Poll 67.5%

*Member of last parliament
Lab/Co-op Hold (10.4% Swing from Con to Lab)

HULL EAST

		%
*Prescott, J. (Lab)	28,870	71.3
West, A. (Con)	5,552	13.7
Wastling, J. (LD)	3,965	9.8
Rogers, G. (Ref)	1,788	4.4
Nolan, M. (Pro-Life)	190	0.5
Whitley, D. (NLP)	121	0.3
Lab majority	23,318	57.60%
Electorate	68,733	
Total Vote	40,486	Poll 58.9%

*Member of last parliament
Lab Hold (9.2% Swing from Con to Lab)

HULL NORTH

		%
*McNamara, K. (Lab)	25,542	65.8
Lee, D. (Con)	5,837	15.0
Nolan, D. (LD)	5,667	14.6
Scott, A. (Ref)	1,533	4.0
Brotheridge, T. (NLP)	215	0.6
Lab majority	19,705	50.79%
Electorate	68,106	
Total Vote	38,794	Poll 57%

*Member of last parliament
Lab Hold (9.2% Swing from Con to Lab)

HULL WEST AND HESSLE

		%
Johnson, A. (Lab)	22,520	58.7
Tress, R. (LD)	6,995	18.2
Moore, C. (Con)	6,933	18.1
Bate, R. (Ref)	1,596	4.2
Franklin, B. (NLP)	310	0.8
Lab majority	15,525	40.48%
Electorate	65,840	
Total Vote	38,354	Poll 58.2%

Lab Hold (3.1% Swing from LD to Lab)

HUNTINGDON

		%
*Major, J. (Con)	31,501	55.3
Reece, J. (Lab)	13,361	23.5
Owen, M. (LD)	8,390	14.7
Bellamy, D. (Ref)	3,114	5.5
Coyne, C. (UKIP)	331	0.6
Hufford, V. (ChriDem)	177	0.3
Robertson, D. (Ind)	89	0.2
Con majority	18,140	31.85%
Electorate	76,094	
Total Vote	56,963	Poll 74.9%

*Member of last parliament
Con Hold (6.8% Swing from Con to Lab)

HYNDBURN

		%
*Pope, G. (Lab)	26,831	55.6
Britcliffe, P. (Con)	15,383	31.9
Jones, L. (LD)	4,141	8.6
Congdon, P. (Ref)	1,627	3.4
Brown, J. (Anti-Corruption)	290	0.6
Lab majority	11,448	23.72%
Electorate	66,806	
Total Vote	48,272	Poll 72.3%

*Member of last parliament
Lab Hold (10% Swing from Con to Lab)

ILFORD NORTH

		%
Perham, L. (Lab)	23,135	47.4
*Bendall, V. (Con)	19,911	40.8
Dean, A. (LD)	5,049	10.3
Wilson, P. (BNP)	750	1.5
Lab majority	3,224	6.60%
Electorate	68,218	
Total Vote	48,845	Poll 71.6%

*Member of last parliament
Lab Gain (17.3% Swing from Con to Lab)

ILFORD SOUTH

		%
*Gapes, M. (Lab/Co-op)	29,273	58.5
Thorne, N. (Con)	15,073	30.1
Khan, A. (LD)	3,152	6.3
Hodges, D. (Ref)	1,073	2.1
Ramsay, B. (SLP)	868	1.7
Owens, A. (BNP)	580	1.2
Lab/Co-op majority	14,200	28.39%
Electorate	72,104	
Total Vote	50,019	Poll 69.4%

*Member of last parliament
Lab/Co-op Win (16.6% Swing from Con to Lab)

INVERNESS EAST, NAIRN AND LOCHABER

		%
Stewart, D. (Lab)	16,187	33.9
Ewing, F. (SNP)	13,848	29.0
Gallagher, S. (LD)	8,364	17.5
Scanlon, M. (Con)	8,355	17.5
Wall, W. (Ref)	436	0.9
Falconer, M. (Green)	354	0.7
Hart, D. (Christian)	224	0.5
Lab majority	2,339	4.90%
Electorate	65,701	
Total Vote	47,768	Poll 72.5%

Lab Gain (9.9% Swing from LD to Lab)

IPSWICH

		%
*Cann, J. (Lab)	25,484	52.7
Castle, S. (Con)	15,048	31.1
Roberts, N. (LD)	5,881	12.2
Agnew, T. (Ref)	1,637	3.4
Vinyard, W. (UKIP)	208	0.4
Caplan, E. (NLP)	107	0.2
Lab majority	10,436	21.59%
Electorate	68.064	
Total Vote	48,365	Poll 71.1%

*Member of last parliament
Lab Hold (10.5% Swing from Con to Lab)

ISLE OF WIGHT

		%
Brand, P. (LD)	31,274	42.7
Turner, A. (Con)	24,868	34.0
Gardiner, D. (Lab)	9,646	13.2
Bristow, T. (Ref)	4,734	6.5
Turner, M. (UKIP)	1,072	1.5
Rees, H. (Ind)	848	1.2
Scivier, P. (Green)	544	0.7
Daly, C. (NLP)	87	0.1
Eveleigh, J. (Rainbow)	86	0.1
LD majority	6,406	8.76%
Electorate	101,680	
Total Vote		Poll 71.7%

LD Gain (5.5% Swing from Con to LD)

ISLINGTON NORTH

		%
*Corbyn, J. (Lab)	24,834	69.3
Kempton, J. (LD)	4,879	13.6
Fawthrop, S. (Con)	4,631	12.9
Ashby, C. (Green)	1,516	4.2
Lab majority	19,955	55.65%
Electorate	57,385	
Total Vote	35,860	Poll 61.4%

*Member of last parliament
Lab Hold (6.7% Swing from LD to Lab)

ISLINGTON SOUTH AND FINSBURY

		%
*Smith, C. (Lab)	22,079	62.5
Ludford, S. (LD)	7,516	21.3
Berens, D. (Con)	4,587	13.0
Bryett, J. (Ref)	741	2.1
Laws, A. (ACA)	171	0.5
Creese, M. (NLP)	121	0.3
Basarik, E. (Ind)	101	0.3
Lab majority	14,563	41.24%
Electorate	55,468	
Total Vote	35,316	Poll 60.1%

*Member of last parliament
Lab Hold (6.6% Swing from LD to Lab)

ISLWYN

		%
*Touhig, D. (Lab/Co-op)	26,995	74.2
Worker, C. (LD)	3,064	8.4
Walters, D. (Con)	2,864	7.9
Jones, D. (PC)	2,272	6.2
Monaghian, S. (Ref)	1,209	3.3
Lab/Co-op majority	23,931	65.74%
Electorate	50,540	
Total Vote	36,404	Poll 71.9%

*Member of last parliament
Lab/Co-op Hold (1.5% Swing from Lab to LD)

JARROW

		%
Hepburn, S. (Lab)	28,497	64.9
Allatt, M. (Con)	6,564	14.9
Stone, T. (LD)	4,865	11.1
Le Blond, A. (IndLab)	2,538	5.8
Mailer, P. (Ref)	1,034	2.4
Bisset, J. (Socialist)	444	1.0
Lab majority	21,933	49.91%
Electorate	63,828	
Total Vote	43,942	Poll 68.8%

Lab Hold (5.4% Swing from Con to Lab)

KEIGHLEY

		%
Cryer, A. (Lab)	26,039	50.6
*Waller, G. (Con)	18,907	36.7
Doyle, M. (LD)	5,064	9.8
Carpenter, C. (Ref)	1,470	2.9
Lab majority	7,132	13.85%
Electorate	67,231	
Total Vote	51,480	Poll 76.3%

*Member of last parliament
Lab Gain (10.2% Swing from Con to Lab)

KENSINGTON AND CHELSEA

		%
Clark, A. (Con)	19,887	53.6
Atkinson, J. (Lab)	10,368	28.0
Woodthorpe Browne, R. (LD)	5,668	15.3
Ellis-Jones, A. (UKIP)	540	1.5
Bear, E. (Teddy)	218	0.6
Oliver, G. (Pensioners)	176	0.5
Hamza, S. (NLP)	122	0.3
Sullivan, P. (Dream)	65	0.2
Parliament, P. (Heart)	44	0.1
Con majority	9,519	25.67%
Electorate	67,786	
Total Vote	37,088	Poll 49.6%

Con Hold (12.9% Swing from Con to Lab)

KETTERING

		%
Sawford, P. (Lab)	24,650	43.3
*Freeman, R. (Con)	24,461	42.9
Aron, R. (LD)	6,098	10.7
Smith, A. (Ref)	1,551	2.7
Le Carpentier, R. (NLP)	197	0.3
Lab majority	189	0.33%
Electorate	75,153	
Total Vote	56,957	Poll 75.5%

*Member of last parliament
Lab Gain (10.6% Swing from Con to Lab)

KILMARNOCK AND LOUDOUN

		%
Browne, D. (Lab)	23,621	49.8
Neil, A. (SNP)	16,365	34.5
Taylor, D. (Con)	5,125	10.8
Stewart, J. (LD)	1,891	4.0
Sneddon, W. (Ref)	284	0.6
Gilmour, W. (NLP)	123	0.3
Lab majority	7,256	15.31%
Electorate	61,376	
Total Vote	47,409	Poll 77.2%

Lab Hold (0.6% Swing from SNP to Lab)

KINGSTON AND SURBITON

		%
Davey, E. (LD)	20,411	36.7
*Tracey, R. (Con)	20,355	36.6
Griffin, S. (Lab)	12,811	23.0
Tchiprout, G. (Ref)	1,470	2.6
Burns, A. (UKIP)	418	0.8
Port, C. (Dream)	100	0.2
Leighton, M. (NLP)	100	0.2
LD majority	56	0.10%
Electorate	73,879	
Total Vote	55,665	Poll 75.3%

*Member of last parliament
LD Gain (13.6% Swing from Con to LD)

KINGSWOOD

		%
*Berry, R. (Lab)	32,181	53.7
Howard, J. (Con)	17,928	29.9
Pinkerton, J. (LD)	7,672	12.8
Reather, A. (Ref)	1,463	2.4
Hart, P. (BNP)	290	0.5
Harding, A. (NLP)	238	0.4
Nicolson, A. (Scrappit)	115	0.2
Lab majority	14,253	23.80%
Electorate	77,026	
Total Vote	59,887	Poll 77.7%

*Member of last parliament
Lab Win (14.5% Swing from Con to Lab)

KIRKCALDY

		%
*Moonie, L. (Lab/Co-op)	18,730	53.6
Hosie, S. (SNP)	8,020	22.9
Black, C. (Con)	4,779	13.7
Mainland, J. (LD)	3,031	8.7
Baxter, V. (Ref)	413	1.2
Lab/Co-op majority	10,710	30.62%
Electorate	52,186	
Total Vote	34,973	Poll 66.9%

*Member of last parliament
Lab/Co-op Hold (3.8% Swing from SNP to Lab)

KNOWSLEY NORTH AND SEFTON EAST

		%
*Howarth, G. (Lab)	34,747	69.9
Doran, C. (Con)	8,600	17.3
Bamber, D. (LD)	5,499	11.1
Jones, C. (SLP)	857	1.7
Lab majority	26,147	52.61%
Electorate	70,918	
Total Vote	49,703	Poll 70.1%

*Member of last parliament
Lab Hold (12.5% Swing from Con to Lab)

KNOWSLEY SOUTH

		%
*O'Hara, E. (Lab)	36,695	77.1
Robertson, G. (Con)	5,987	12.6
Mainey, C. (LD)	3,954	8.3
Wright, A. (Ref)	954	2.0
Lab majority	30,708	64.53%
Electorate	70,532	
Total Vote	47,590	Poll 67.5%

*Member of last parliament
Lab Hold (7.8% Swing from Con to Lab)

LAGAN VALLEY

		%
Donaldson, J. (UUP)	24,560	55.4
Close, S. (APNI)	7,635	17.2
Poots, E. (DUP)	6,005	13.6
Kelly, D. (SDLP)	3,436	7.8
Sexton, S. (Con)	1,212	2.7
Ramsey, S. (SF)	1,110	2.5
McCarthy, F. (Workers)	203	0.5
Finlay, H. (NLP)	149	0.3
UUP majority	16,925	38.20%
Electorate	71,225	
Total Vote	44,310	Poll 62.2%

UUP Hold (8.5% Swing from UUP to APNI)

LANCASTER AND WYRE

		%
Dawson, T. (Lab)	25,173	42.8
*Mans, K. (Con)	23,878	40.6
Humberstone, J. (LD)	6,802	11.6
Ivell, V. (Ref)	1,516	2.6
Barry, J. (Green)	795	1.4
Whittaker, J. (UKIP)	698	1.2
Lab majority	1,295	2.20%
Electorate	78,168	
Total Vote	58,862	Poll 74.9%

*Member of last parliament
Lab Gain (10.6% Swing from Con to Lab)

LEEDS CENTRAL

		%
*Fatchett, D. (Lab)	25,766	69.6
Wild, W. (Con)	5,077	13.7
Freeman, D. (LD)	4,164	11.3
Myers, P. (Ref)	1,042	2.8
Rix, M. (SLP)	656	1.8
Hill, C. (Soc)	304	0.8
Lab majority	20,689	55.90%
Electorate	67,664	
Total Vote	37,009	Poll 54.2%

*Member of last parliament
Lab Hold (7.3% Swing from Con to Lab)

LEEDS EAST

		%
*Mudie, G. (Lab)	24,151	67.5
Emsley, J. (Con)	6,685	18.7
Kirk, M. (LD)	3,689	10.3
Parrish, L. (Ref)	1,267	3.5
Lab majority	17,466	48.80%
Electorate	56,963	
Total Vote	35,792	Poll 62.8%

*Member of last parliament
Lab Hold (9.7% Swing from Con to Lab)

LEEDS NORTH EAST

		%
Hamilton, F. (Lab)	22,368	49.2
*Kirkhope, T. (Con)	15,409	33.9
Winlow, B. (LD)	6,318	13.9
Rose, I. (Ref)	946	2.1
Egan, J. (SLP)	468	1.0
Lab majority	6,959	15.29%
Electorate	63,185	
Total Vote	45,509	Poll 71.8%

*Member of last parliament
Lab Gain (11.9% Swing from Con to Lab)

LEEDS NORTH WEST

		%
Best, H. (Lab)	19,694	39.9
*Hampson, K. (Con)	15,850	32.1
Pearce, B. (LD)	11,689	23.7
Emmett, S. (Ref)	1,325	2.7
Lamb, R. (SLP)	335	0.7
Toone, R. (ProLife)	251	0.5
Duffy, D. (Ronnie)	232	0.5
Lab majority	3,844	7.79%
Electorate	69,972	
Total Vote	49,376	Poll 69.7%

*Member of last parliament
Lab Gain (11.8% Swing from Con to Lab)

LEEDS WEST

		%
*Battle, J. (Lab)	26,819	66.7
Whelan, J. (Con)	7,048	17.5
Amor, N. (LD)	3,622	9.0
Finley, B. (Ref)	1,210	3.0
Blackburn, D. (Green)	896	2.2
Nowosielski, N. (Lib)	625	1.6
Lab majority 19,771		49.16%
Electorate	63,965	
Total Vote	40,220	Poll 62.7%

*Member of last parliament
Lab Hold (10.1% Swing from Con to Lab)

LEICESTER EAST

		%
*Vaz, K. (Lab)	29,083	65.5
Milton, S. (Con)	10,661	24.0
Matabudul, J. (LD)	3,105	7.0
Iwaniw, P. (Ref)	1,015	2.3
Singh Sidhu, S. (SLP)	436	1.0
Slack, N. (Glow)	102	0.2
Lab majority 18,422		41.49%
Electorate	64,012	
Total Vote	44,402	Poll 69.1%

*Member of last parliament
Lab Hold (9.4% Swing from Con to Lab)

LEICESTER SOUTH

		%
*Marshall, J. (Lab)	27,914	58.0
Heaton-Harris, C. (Con)	11,421	23.7
Coles, B. (LD)	6,654	13.8
Hancock, J. (Ref)	1,184	2.5
Dooher, J. (SLP)	634	1.3
Sills, K. (Nat Dem)	307	0.6
Lab majority 16,493		34.28%
Electorate	71,750	
Total Vote	48,114	Poll 66.3%

*Member of last parliament
Lab Hold (8.3% Swing from Con to Lab)

LEICESTER WEST

		%
Hewitt, P. (Lab)	22,580	55.2
Thomas, R. (Con)	9,716	23.7
Jones, M. (LD)	5,795	14.2
Shooter, W. (Ref)	970	2.4
Forse, G. (Green)	586	1.4
Roberts, D. (SLP)	452	1.1
Nicholls, J. (Soc)	327	0.8
Belshaw, A. (BNP)	302	0.7
Potter, C. (Nat Dem)	186	0.5
Lab majority 12,864		31.44%
Electorate	64,570	
Total Vote	40,914	Poll 63.1%

Lab Hold (11.6% Swing from Con to Lab)

LEIGH

		%
*Cunliffe, L. (Lab)	31,652	68.9
Young, E. (Con)	7,156	15.6
Hough, P. (LD)	5,163	11.2
Constable, R. (Ref)	1,949	4.2
Lab majority 24,496		53.34%
Electorate	69,908	
Total Vote	45,920	Poll 65.7%

Lab Hold (10.7% Swing from Con to Lab)

LEOMINSTER

		%
*Temple-Morris, P. (Con)	22,888	45.3
James, T. (LD)	14,053	27.8
Westwood, R. (Lab)	8,831	17.5
Parkin, A. (Ref)	2,815	5.6
Norman, F. (Green)	1,086	2.1
Chamings, R. (UKIP)	588	1.2
Haycock, J. (BNP)	292	0.6
Con majority 8,835		17.48%
Electorate	65,993	
Total Vote	50,553	Poll 76.6%

*Member of last parliament
Con Hold (5.5% Swing from Con to LD)

LEWES

		%
Baker, N. (LD)	21,250	43.2
*Rathbone, T. (Con)	19,950	40.6
Patton, M. (Lab)	5,232	10.6
Butler, L. (Ref)	2,481	5.0
Harvey, J. (UKIP)	256	0.5
LD majority 1,300		2.64%
Electorate	64,340	
Total Vote	49,169	Poll 76.4%

*Member of last parliament
LD Gain (7.4% Swing from Con to LD)

LEWISHAM DEPTFORD

		%
*Ruddock, J. (Lab)	23,827	70.8
Kimm, I. (Con)	4,949	14.7
Appiah, K. (LD)	3,004	8.9
Mulrenan, J. (SLP)	996	3.0
Shepherd, S. (Ref)	868	2.6
Lab majority 18,878		56.11%
Electorate	58,141	
Total Vote	33,644	Poll 57.9%

*Member of last parliament
Lab Hold (11.6% Swing from Con to Lab)

LEWISHAM EAST

		%
*Prentice, B. (Lab)	21,821	58.3
Hollobone, P. (Con)	9,694	25.9
Buxton, D. (LD)	4,178	11.2
Drury, S. (Ref)	910	2.4
Croucher, R. (NF)	431	1.2
White, P. (Lib)	277	0.7
Rizz, C. (Dream)	97	0.3
Lab majority 12,127		32.50%
Electorate	56,333	
Total Vote	37,408	Poll 66.4%

*Member of last parliament
Lab Hold (14.9% Swing from Con to Lab)

LEWISHAM WEST

		%
*Dowd, J. (Lab)	23,273	62.0
Whelan, C. (Con)	8,956	23.8
McGrath, K. (LD)	3,672	9.8
Leese, A. (Ref)	1,098	2.9
Long, N. (SLP)	398	1.1
Oram, E. (Lib)	167	0.4
Lab majority 14,317		38.11%
Electorate	58,659	
Total Vote	37,564	Poll 64%

*Member of last parliament
Lab Hold (17% Swing from Con to Lab)

LEYTON AND WANSTEAD

		%
*Cohen, H. (Lab)	23,922	60.8
Vaudry, R. (Con)	8,736	22.2
Anglin, C. (LD)	5,920	15.1
Duffy, S. (Pro-Life)	488	1.2
Mian, A. (Ind)	256	0.7
Lab majority 15,186		38.62%
Electorate	62,176	
Total Vote	39,322	Poll 63.2%

*Member of last parliament
Lab Hold (11.8% Swing from Con to Lab)

LICHFIELD

		%
*Fabricant, M. (Con)	20,853	42.9
Woodward, S. (Lab)	20,615	42.4
Bennion, R. (LD)	5,473	11.3
Seward, G. (Ref)	1,652	3.4
Con majority 238		0.49%
Electorate	62,720	
Total Vote	48,593	Poll 77.5%

*Member of last parliament
Con Hold (10% Swing from Con to Lab)

LINCOLN

		%
Merron, G. (Lab)	25,563	54.9
Brown, A. (Con)	14,433	31.0
Gabriel, L. (LD)	5,048	10.8
Ivory, J. (Ref)	1,329	2.9
Myers, A. (NLP)	175	0.4
Lab majority 11,130		23.91%
Electorate	65,485	
Total Vote	46,548	Poll 70.9%

Lab Win (11% Swing from Con to Lab)

LINLITHGOW

		%
*Dalyell, T. (Lab)	21,469	54.1
MacAskill, K. (SNP)	10,631	26.8
Kerr, T. (Con)	4,964	12.5
Duncan, A. (LD)	2,331	5.9
Plomer, K. (Ref)	259	0.7
Lab majority 10,838		27.33%
Electorate	53,706	
Total Vote	39,654	Poll 73.8%

*Member of last parliament
Lab Hold (4.1% Swing from SNP to Lab)

LIVERPOOL GARSTON

		%
Eagle, M. (Lab)	26,667	61.3
Clucas, F. (LD)	8,250	19.0
Gordon-Johnson, N. (Con)	6,819	15.7
Dunne, F. (Ref)	833	1.9
Copeland, G. (Lib)	666	1.5
Parsons, J. (NLP)	127	0.3
Nolan, S. (SEP)	120	0.3
Lab majority 18,417		42.36%
Electorate	66,755	
Total Vote	43,482	Poll 65.1%

Lab Hold (6.4% Swing from LD to Lab)

LIVERPOOL RIVERSIDE

		%
Ellman, L. (Lab/Co-op)	26,858	70.4
Fraenkel, B. (LD)	5,059	13.3
Sparrow, D. (Con)	3,635	9.5
Wilson, C. (Soc)	776	2.0
Green, D. (Lib)	594	1.6

Skelly, G. (Ref)   586   1.5
Nielsen, H. (ProLife)   277   0.7
Braid, D. (MRAC)   179   0.5
Gay, G. (NLP)   171   0.4
Lab/Co-op
majority   21,799   57.16%
Electorate   73,429
Total Vote   38,135 Poll 51.6%
Lab Hold (3.6% Swing from LD to Lab)

LIVERPOOL WALTON   %
*Kilfoyle, P. (Lab)   31,516   78.4
Roberts, R. (LD)   4,478   11.1
Kotecha, M. (Con)   2,551   6.3
Grundy, C. (Ref)   620   1.5
Mahmood, L. (Soc)   444   1.1
Williams, H. (Lib)   352   0.9
Mearns, V.
(Pro-Life)   246   0.6
Lab majority   27,038   67.33%
Electorate   67,527
Total Vote   40,207 Poll 59.5%
*Member of last parliament
Lab Hold (3.4% Swing from LD to Lab)

LIVERPOOL WAVERTREE   %
*Kennedy, J. (Lab)   29,592   64.4
Kemp, R. (LD)   9,891   21.5
Malthouse, C. (Con)   4,944   10.8
Worthington, P. (Ref)   576   1.3
McCullough, K. (Lib)   391   0.9
Kingsley, R.
(Pro-Life)   346   0.8
Corkhill, C. (WRP)   178   0.4
Lab majority   19,701   42.90%
Electorate   73,063
Total Vote   45,918 Poll 62.8%
*Member of last parliament
Lab Hold (18.2% Swing from LD to Lab)

LIVERPOOL WEST DERBY   %
*Wareing, R. (Lab)   30,002   71.2
Radford, S. (Lib)   4,037   9.6
Hines, A. (LD)   3,805   9.0
Morgan, N. (Con)   3,656   8.7
Forest, P. (Ref)   657   1.6
Lab majority   25,965   61.59%
Electorate   68,682
Total Vote   42,157 Poll 61.3%
*Member of last parliament
Lab Hold (0% Swing from to)

LIVINGSTON   %
*Cook, R. (Lab)   23,510   54.9
Johnston, P. (SNP)   11,763   27.5
Craigie Halkett, H.
(Con)   4,028   9.4
Hawthorn, E. (LD)   2,876   6.7
Campbell, H. (Ref)   444   1.0
Culbert, M.
(SPGB)   213   0.5
Lab majority   11,747   27.42%
Electorate   60,296
Total Vote   42,834 Poll 70.9%
*Member of last parliament
Lab Hold (3.8% Swing from SNP to Lab)

LLANELLI   %
*Davies, D. (Lab)   23,851   57.9
Phillips, M. (PC)   7,812   19.0
Hayes, A. (Con)   5,003   12.1
Burree, N. (LD)   3,788   9.2
Willock, J. (SLP)   757   1.8
Lab majority   16,039   38.92%
Electorate   58,323
Total Vote   41,211 Poll 70.7%
*Member of last parliament
Lab Hold (0.1% Swing from PC to Lab)

LOUGHBOROUGH   %
Reed, A. (Lab/Co-op) 25,448   48.6
Andrew, K. (Con)   19,736   37.7
Brass, D. (LD)   6,190   11.8
Gupta, R. (Ref)   991   1.9
Lab/Co-op
majority   5,712   10.91%
Electorate   68,945
Total Vote   52,365 Poll 75.5%
Lab Gain (8.9% Swing from Con to Lab)

LOUTH AND HORNCASTLE %
*Tapsell, Sir P. (Con)   21,699   43.4
Hough, J. (Lab)   14,799   29.6
Martin, F. (LD)   12,207   24.4
Robinson, R. (Green) 1,248   2.5
Con majority   6,900   13.81%
Electorate   68,824
Total Vote   49,953 Poll 72.4%
*Member of last parliament
Con Hold (12.6% Swing from Con to Lab)

LUDLOW   %
*Gill, C. (Con)   19,633   42.4
Huffer, I. (LD)   13,724   29.7
O'Kane, N. (Lab)   11,745   25.4
Andrewes, T. (Green)   798   1.7
Freeman-Keel, E.
(UKIP)   385   0.8
Con majority   5,909   12.77%
Electorate   61,267
Total Vote   46,285 Poll 75.5%
*Member of last parliament
Con Hold (6.6% Swing from Con to LD)

LUTON NORTH   %
Hopkins, K. (Lab)   25,860   54.6
Senior, D. (Con)   16,234   34.3
Newbound, K. (LD)   4,299   9.1
Brown, C. (UKIP)   689   1.5
Custance, A. (NLP)   250   0.5
Lab majority   9,626   20.34%
Electorate   64,618
Total Vote   47,332 Poll 73.2%
Lab Gain (17.2% Swing from Con to Lab)

LUTON SOUTH   %
Moran, M. (Lab)   26,428   54.8
*Bright, Sir G. (Con)   15,109   31.4
Fitchett, K. (LD)   4,610   9.6
Jacobs, C. (Ref)   1,205   2.5
Lawman, C. (UKIP)   390   0.8
Scheimann, M. (Green)   356   0.7
Perrin, C. (NLP)   86   0.2
Lab majority   11,319   23.49%

Electorate   68,395
Total Vote   48,184 Poll 70.4%
*Member of last parliament
Lab Gain (12.3% Swing from Con to Lab)

MACCLESFIELD   %
*Winterton, N. (Con) 26,888   49.6
Jackson, J. (Lab)   18,234   33.6
Flynn, M. (LD)   9,075   16.7
Con majority   8,654   15.97%
Electorate   72,049
Total Vote   54,197 Poll 74.9%
*Member of last parliament
Con Hold (8.6% Swing from Con to Lab)

MAIDENHEAD   %
May, T. (Con)   25,344   49.8
Ketteringham, A. (LD) 13,363   26.3
Robson, D. (Lab)   9,205   18.1
Taverner, C. (Ref)   1,638   3.2
Munkley, D. (Lib)   896   1.8
Spiers, N. (UKIP)   277   0.5
Ardley, K. (Glow)   166   0.3
Con majority   11,981   23.54%
Electorate   67,302
Total Vote   50,889 Poll 75.6%
Con Hold (4.1% Swing from Con to LD)

MAIDSTONE AND THE
WEALD   %
*Widdecombe, A.
(Con)   23,657   44.1
Morgan, J. (Lab)   14,054   26.2
Nelson, J. (LD)   11,986   22.4
Hopkins, S. (Ref)   1,998   3.7
Cleator, M. (SLP)   979   1.8
Kemp, P. (Green)   480   0.9
Owen, R. (UKIP)   339   0.6
Oldbury, J. (NLP)   115   0.2
Con majority   9,603   17.91%
Electorate   72,466
Total Vote   53,608 Poll 73.7%
*Member of last parliament
Con Hold (12.9% Swing from Con to Lab)

MAKERFIELD   %
*McCartney, I. (Lab) 33,119   73.6
Winstanley, M. (Con) 6,942   15.4
Hubbard, B. (LD)   3,743   8.3
Seed, A. (Ref)   1,210   2.7
Lab majority   26,177   58.15%
Electorate   67,358
Total Vote   45,014 Poll 66.8%
*Member of last parliament
Lab Hold (9.6% Swing from Con to Lab)

MALDON AND CHELMSFORD
EAST   %
*Whittingdale, J.
(Con)   24,524   48.7
Freeman, K. (Lab)   14,485   28.7
Pooley, G. (LD)   9,758   19.4
Overy-Owen, L. (UKIP) 935   1.9
Burgess, E. (Green)   685   1.4
Con majority   10,039   19.92%
Electorate   66,184
Total Vote   50,387 Poll 76%
*Member of last parliament
Con Hold (15.6% Swing from Con to Lab)

MANCHESTER BLACKLEY %
Stringer, G. (Lab)	25,042	70.0
Barclay, S. (Con)	5,454	15.3
Wheale, S. (LD)	3,937	11.0
Stanyer, P. (Ref)	1,323	3.7
Lab majority	19,588	54.78%
Electorate	62,227	
Total Vote	35,756	Poll 57.3%

Lab Hold (9.3% Swing from Con to Lab)

MANCHESTER CENTRAL %
*Lloyd, T. (Lab)	23,803	71.0
Firth, A. (LD)	4,121	12.3
McIlwaine, S. (Con)	3,964	11.8
Rafferty, F. (SLP)	810	2.4
Maxwell, B. (Ref)	742	2.2
Rigby, T. (Comm)	97	0.3
Lab majority	19,682	58.69%
Electorate	63,815	
Total Vote	33,537	Poll 52%

*Member of last parliament
Lab Hold (0.3% Swing from LD to Lab)

MANCHESTER GORTON %
*Kaufman, G. (Lab)	23,704	65.3
Pearcey, J. (LD)	6,362	17.5
Senior, G. (Con)	4,249	11.7
Hartley, K. (Ref)	812	2.2
Fitz-Gibbon, S. (Green)	683	1.9
Wongsam, T. (SLP)	501	1.4
Lab majority	17,342	47.76%
Electorate	64,349	
Total Vote	36,311	Poll 55.8%

*Member of last parliament
Lab Hold (0.3% Swing from Lab to LD)

MANCHESTER WITHINGTON %
*Bradley, K. (Lab)	27,103	61.6
Smith, J. (Con)	8,522	19.4
Zalzala, Y. (LD)	6,000	13.6
Sheppard, M. (Ref)	1,079	2.5
Caldwell, S. (Pro-Life)	614	1.4
White, J. (Soc)	376	0.9
Kingston, S. (Dream)	181	0.4
Gaskell, M. (NLP)	152	0.3
Lab majority	18,581	42.20%
Electorate	66,116	
Total Vote	44,027	Poll 66%

*Member of last parliament
Lab Hold (10.4% Swing from Con to Lab)

MANSFIELD %
*Meale, A. (Lab)	30,556	64.4
Frost, T. (Con)	10,038	21.2
Smith, P. (LD)	5,244	11.1
Bogusz, J. (Ref)	1,588	3.3
Lab majority	20,518	43.26%
Electorate	67,057	
Total Vote	47,426	Poll 70.6%

*Member of last parliament
Lab Hold (11% Swing from Con to Lab)

MEDWAY %
Marshall-Andrews, R. (Lab)	21,858	48.9
*Fenner, Dame P. (Con)	16,504	36.9

Roberts, R. (LD)	4,555	10.2
Main, J. (Ref)	1,420	3.2
Radlett, S. (UKIP)	405	0.9
Lab majority	5,354	11.97%
Electorate	61,736	
Total Vote	44,742	Poll 72.2%

*Member of last parliament
Lab Gain (14.9% Swing from Con to Lab)

MEIRIONNYDD NANT CONWY %
*Llwyd, E. (PC)	12,465	50.7
Rees, H. (Lab)	5,660	23.0
Quin, J. (Con)	3,922	16.0
Feeley, R. (LD)	1,719	7.0
Hodge, P. (Ref)	809	3.3
PC majority	6,805	27.69%
Electorate	32,345	
Total Vote	24,575	Poll 76%

*Member of last parliament
PC Hold (1.3% Swing from Lab to PC)

MERIDEN %
Spelman, C. (Con)	22,997	42.0
Seymour-Smith, B. (Lab)	22,415	41.0
Dupont, A. (LD)	7,098	13.0
Gilbert, P. (Ref)	2,208	4.0
Con majority	582	1.06%
Electorate	76,287	
Total Vote	54,718	Poll 71.6%

Con Hold (11.6% Swing from Con to Lab)

MERTHYR TYDFIL AND RHYMNEY %
*Rowlands, T. (Lab)	30,012	76.7
Anstey, D. (LD)	2,926	7.5
Morgan, J. (Con)	2,508	6.4
Cox, A. (PC)	2,344	6.0
Cowdell, A. (IndLab)	691	1.8
Hutchings, R. (Ref)	660	1.7
Lab majority	27,086	69.20%
Electorate	56,507	
Total Vote	39,141	Poll 69.2%

*Member of last parliament
Lab Hold (4.5% Swing from LD to Lab)

MID BEDFORDSHIRE %
Sayeed, J. (Con)	24,176	46.0
Mallett, N. (Lab)	17,086	32.5
Hill, T. (LD)	8,823	16.8
Marler, S. (Ref)	2,257	4.3
Lorys, M. (NLP)	174	0.3
Con majority	7,090	13.50%
Electorate	66,979	
Total Vote	52,516	Poll 78.3%

Con Hold (14.6% Swing from Con to Lab)

MID DORSET AND POOLE NORTH %
Fraser, C. (Con)	20,632	40.7
Leaman, A. (LD)	19,951	39.3
Collis, D. (Lab)	8,014	15.8
Nabarro, D. (Ref)	2,136	4.2
Con majority	681	1.34%
Electorate	67,049	
Total Vote	50,733	Poll 75.7%

Con Hold (5.4% Swing from Con to LD)

MID NORFOLK %
Simpson, K. (Con)	22,739	39.6
Zeichner, D. (Lab)	21,403	37.3
Frary, S. (LD)	8,617	15.0
Holder, N. (Ref)	3,229	5.6
Park, T. (Green)	1,254	2.2
Parker, B. (NLP)	215	0.4
Con majority	1,336	2.33%
Electorate	75,311	
Total Vote	57,457	Poll 76.1%

Con Hold (13.1% Swing from Con to Lab)

MID SUSSEX %
*Soames, N. (Con)	23,231	43.5
Collins, M. (LD)	16,377	30.6
Hamilton, M. (Lab)	9,969	18.6
Large, T. (Ref)	3,146	5.9
Barnett, J. (UKIP)	606	1.1
Tudway, E. (Ind JRP)	134	0.3
Con majority	6,854	12.82%
Electorate	68,784	
Total Vote	53,463	Poll 77.7%

*Member of last parliament
Con Hold (8.9% Swing from Con to LD)

MID ULSTER %
McGuiness, M. (SF)	20,294	40.1
*McCrea, W. (DUP)	18,411	36.3
Haughey, D. (SDLP)	11,205	22.1
Bogues, E. (APNI)	460	0.9
Donnelly, M. (Workers)	238	0.5
Murray, M. (NLP)	61	0.1
SF majority	1,883	3.72%
Electorate	58,836	
Total Vote	50,669	Poll 86.1%

*Member of last parliament
SF Gain (10.3% Swing from DUP to SF)

MID WORCESTERSHIRE %
*Luff, P. (Con)	24,092	47.4
Smith, D. (Lab)	14,680	28.9
Barwick, D. (LD)	9,458	18.6
Watson, T. (Ref)	1,780	3.5
Ingles, D. (UKIP)	646	1.3
Dyer, A. (NLP)	163	0.3
Con majority	9,412	18.52%
Electorate	68,381	
Total Vote	50,819	Poll 74.3%

*Member of last parliament
Con Hold (9.4% Swing from Con to Lab)

MIDDLESBROUGH %
*Bell, S. (Lab)	32,925	71.4
Benham, L. (Con)	7,907	17.2
Charlesworth, A. (LD)	3,934	8.5
Edwards, R. (Ref)	1,331	2.9
Lab majority	25,018	54.27%
Electorate	70,931	
Total Vote	46,097	Poll 64.8%

*Member of last parliament
Lab Hold (11.5% Swing from Con to Lab)

MIDDLESBROUGH SOUTH AND EAST CLEVELAND %

Kumar, A. (Lab)	29,319	54.7
*Bates, M. (Con)	18,712	34.9
Garrett, H. (LD)	4,004	7.5
Batchelor, R. (Ref)	1,552	2.9
Lab majority	10,607	19.79%
Electorate	70,481	
Total Vote	53,587	Poll 75.9%

*Member of last parliament
Lab Gain (11.1% Swing from Con to Lab)

MIDLOTHIAN %

*Clarke, E. (Lab)	18,861	53.5
Millar, L. (SNP)	8,991	25.5
Harper, A. (Con)	3,842	10.9
Pinnock, R. (LD)	3,235	9.2
Docking, K. (Ref)	320	0.9
Lab majority	9,870	28.00%
Electorate	47,552	
Total Vote	35,249	Poll 74%

*Member of last parliament
Lab Hold (1.5% Swing from SNP to Lab)

MILTON KEYNES NORTH EAST %

White, B. (Lab)	20,201	39.4
*Butler, P. (Con)	19,961	39.0
Mabbutt, G. (LD)	8,907	17.4
Phillips, M. (Ref)	1,492	2.9
Francis, A. (Green)	576	1.1
Simson, M. (NLP)	99	0.2
Lab majority	240	0.47%
Electorate	70,395	
Total Vote	51,236	Poll 72.8%

*Member of last parliament
Lab Gain (14.2% Swing from Con to Lab)

MILTON KEYNES SOUTH WEST %

Starkey, P. (Lab)	27,298	53.8
*Legg, B. (Con)	17,006	33.6
Jones, P. (LD)	6,065	12.0
Kelly, H. (NLP)	389	0.8
Lab majority	10,292	20.28%
Electorate	71,070	
Total Vote	50,758	Poll 71.4%

*Member of last parliament
Lab Gain (14.6% Swing from Con to Lab)

MITCHAM AND MORDEN %

McDonagh, S. (Lab)	27,984	58.4
*Rumbold, Dame A. (Con)	14,243	29.7
Harris, N. (LD)	3,632	7.6
Isaacs, P. (Ref)	810	1.7
Miller, L. (BNP)	521	1.1
Walsh, T. (Green)	415	0.9
Vaikuntha Vasan, K. (Ind)	144	0.3
Barrett, J. (UKIP)	117	0.2
Dixon, N. (Anti-Corr)	80	0.2
Lab majority	13,741	28.66%
Electorate	65,385	
Total Vote	47,946	Poll 72.4%

*Member of last parliament
Lab Gain (16% Swing from Con to Lab)

MOLE VALLEY %

*Beresford, Sir P. (Con)	26,178	48.0
Cooksey, S. (LD)	15,957	29.3
Payne, C. (Lab)	8,057	14.8
Taber, N. (Ref)	2,424	4.4
Burley, R. (Ind Con Ref)	1,276	2.3
Cameron, I. (UKIP)	435	0.8
Thomas, J. (NLP)	197	0.4
Con majority	10,221	18.75%
Electorate	69,140	
Total Vote	54,524	Poll 78.9%

*Member of last parliament
Con Hold (7% Swing from Con to LD)

MONMOUTH %

Edwards, H. (Lab)	23,404	47.7
*Evans, R. (Con)	19,226	39.2
Williams, M. (LD)	4,689	9.6
Warry, N. (Ref)	1,190	2.4
Cotton, A. (PC)	516	1.1
Lab majority	4,178	8.52%
Electorate	60,703	
Total Vote	49,025	Poll 80.8%

*Member of last parliament
Lab Gain (7.4% Swing from Con to Lab)

MONTGOMERYSHIRE %

Opik, L. (LD)	14,647	45.9
Davies, G. (Con)	8,344	26.1
Davies, A. (Lab)	6,109	19.1
Jones, H. (PC)	1,608	5.0
Bufton, J. (Ref)	879	2.8
Walker, S. (Green)	338	1.1
LD majority	6,303	19.74%
Electorate	42,618	
Total Vote	31,925	Poll 74.9%

LD Hold (2% Swing from Con to LD)

MORAY %

*Ewing, M. (SNP)	16,529	41.6
Findlay, A. (Con)	10,963	27.6
Macdonald, L. (Lab)	7,886	19.8
Storr, D. (LD)	3,548	8.9
Meiklejohn, P. (Ref)	840	2.1
SNP majority	5,566	14.00%
Electorate	58,302	
Total Vote	39,766	Poll 68%

*Member of last parliament
SNP Hold (3.5% Swing from Con to SNP)

MORECAMBE AND LUNESDALE %

Smith, G. (Lab)	24,061	48.9
*Lennox-Boyd, Sir M. (Con)	18,096	36.7
Greenwell, J. (LD)	5,614	11.4
Ogilvie, I. (Ref)	1,313	2.7
Walne, D. (NLP)	165	0.3
Lab majority	5,965	12.11%
Electorate	68,013	
Total Vote	49,249	Poll 72.3%

*Member of last parliament
Lab Gain (16% Swing from Con to Lab)

MORLEY AND ROTHWELL %

*Gunnell, J. (Lab)	26,836	58.5
Barraclough, A. (Con)	12,086	26.3
Galdas, M. (LD)	5,087	11.1
Mitchell Innes, D. (Ref)	1,359	3.0
Wood, R. (BNP)	381	0.8
Sammon, P. (Pro-Life)	148	0.3
Lab majority	14,750	32.14%
Electorate	68,385	
Total Vote	45,897	Poll 67.1%

*Member of last parliament
Lab Hold (9.8% Swing from Con to Lab)

MOTHERWELL AND WISHAW %

Roy, F. (Lab)	21,020	57.4
McGuigan, J. (SNP)	8,229	22.5
Dickson, S. (Con)	4,024	11.0
Mackie, A. (LD)	2,331	6.4
Herriot, C. (SLP)	797	2.2
Russell, T. (Ref)	218	0.6
Lab majority	12,791	34.93%
Electorate	52,252	
Total Vote	36,619	Poll 70.1%

Lab Hold (0.1% Swing from Lab to SNP)

NEATH %

*Hain, P. (Lab)	30,324	73.5
Evans, D. (Con)	3,583	8.7
Jones, T. (PC)	3,344	8.1
Little, F. (LD)	2,597	6.3
Morris, P. (Ref)	975	2.4
Marks, H. (Cannabis)	420	1.0
Lab majority	26,741	64.84%
Electorate	55,425	
Total Vote	41,243	Poll 74.3%

*Member of last parliament
Lab Hold (6% Swing from Con to Lab)

NEW FOREST EAST %

Lewis, J. (Con)	21,053	42.9
Dawson, G. (LD)	15,838	32.3
Goodfellow, A. (Lab)	12,161	24.8
Con majority	5,215	10.63%
Electorate	65,717	
Total Vote	49,052	Poll 74.4%

Con Hold (4.5% Swing from Con to LD)

NEW FOREST WEST %

Swayne, D. (Con)	25,149	50.6
Hale, R. (LD)	13,817	27.8
Griffiths, D. (Lab)	7,092	14.3
Elliott, M. (Ref)	2,150	4.3
Holmes, M. (UKIP)	1,542	3.1
Con majority	11,332	22.78%
Electorate	66,522	
Total Vote	49,750	Poll 74.5%

Con Hold (3.7% Swing from Con to LD)

NEWARK %

Jones, F. (Lab)	23,496	45.2
*Alexander, R. (Con)	20,480	39.4
Harris, P. (LD)	5,960	11.5
Creedy, G. (Ref)	2,035	3.9
Lab majority	3,016	5.80%
Electorate	69,763	
Total Vote	51,971	Poll 74.4%

*Member of last parliament
Lab Gain (10.2% Swing from Con to Lab)

NEWBURY %
*Rendel, D. (LD)	29,887	52.9
Benyon, R. (Con)	21,370	37.8
Hannon, P. (Lab)	3,107	5.5
Snook, T. (Ref)	992	1.8
Stark, R. (Green)	644	1.1
Tubb, R. (UKIP)	302	0.5
Howse, K. (SLP)	174	0.3
LD majority	8,517	15.1%
Electorate	73,680	
Total Vote	56,476	Poll 76.7%

*Member of last parliament
LD Hold (17% Swing from Con to LD)

NEWCASTLE UPON TYNE
CENTRAL %
*Cousins, J. (Lab)	27,272	59.2
Newmark, B.		
(Con)	10,792	23.4
Berry, R. (LD)	6,911	15.0
Coxon, C. (Ref)	1,113	2.4
Lab majority	16,480	35.76%
Electorate	69,781	
Total Vote	46,088	Poll 65.3%

*Member of last parliament
Lab Hold (9.8% Swing from Con to Lab)

NEWCASTLE UPON TYNE
EAST AND WALLSEND %
*Brown, N. (Lab)	29,607	71.2
Middleton, J. (Con)	5,796	13.9
Morgan, G. (LD)	4,415	10.6
Cossins, P. (Ref)	966	2.3
Carpenter, B. (SLP)	642	1.5
Levy, M. (Comm)	163	0.4
Lab majority	23,811	57.25%
Electorate	63,272	
Total Vote	41,589	Poll 65.5%

*Member of last parliament
Lab Hold (11.3% Swing from Con to Lab)

NEWCASTLE UPON TYNE
NORTH %
*Henderson, D.		
(Lab)	28,125	62.2
White, G. (Con)	8,793	19.4
Allen, P. (LD)	6,578	14.5
Chipchase, D. (Ref)	1,733	3.8
Lab majority	19,332	42.74%
Electorate	65,357	
Total Vote	45,229	Poll 69.1%

*Member of last parliament
Lab Hold (12.6% Swing from Con to Lab)

NEWCASTLE-UNDER-LYME %
*Golding, L. (Lab)	27,743	56.5
Hayes, M. (Con)	10,537	21.4
Studd, R. (LD)	6,858	14.0
Suttle, K. (Ref)	1,510	3.1
Mountford, S.		
(Lib)	1,399	2.8
Bell, B. (SLP)	1,082	2.2
Lab majority	17,206	35.02%
Electorate	66,686	
Total Vote	49,129	Poll 73.7%

*Member of last parliament
Lab Hold (8.3% Swing from Con to Lab)

NEWPORT EAST %
*Howarth, A. (Lab)	21,481	57.7
Evans, D. (Con)	7,958	21.4
Cameron, A. (LD)	3,880	10.4
Scargill, A. (SLP)	1,951	5.2
Davis, G. (Ref)	1,267	3.4
Holland, C. (PC)	721	1.9
Lab majority	13,523	36.30%
Electorate	50,997	
Total Vote	37,258	Poll 73.1%

*Member of last parliament
Lab Hold (6.3% Swing from Con to Lab)

NEWPORT WEST %
*Flynn, P. (Lab)	24,331	60.5
Clarke, P. (Con)	9,794	24.4
Wilson, S. (LD)	3,907	9.7
Thompsett, C. (Ref)	1,199	3.0
Jackson, H. (PC)	648	1.6
Moelwyn Hughes, H.		
(UKIP)	323	0.8
Lab majority	14,537	36.16%
Electorate	53,914	
Total Vote	40,202	Poll 74.6%

*Member of last parliament
Lab Hold (9.5% Swing from Con to Lab)

NEWRY AND ARMAGH %
*Mallon, S. (SDLP)	22,904	43.0
Kennedy, D. (UUP)	18,015	33.8
McNamee, P. (SF)	11,218	21.1
Whitcroft, P. (APNI)	1,015	1.9
Evans, D. (NLP)	123	0.2
SDLP majority	4,889	9.18%
Electorate	70,652	
Total Vote	53,275	Poll 75.4%

*Member of last parliament
SDLP Hold (1.9% Swing from SDLP to UUP)

NORMANTON %
*O'Brien, B. (Lab)	26,046	60.6
Bulmer, F. (Con)	10,153	23.6
Ridgway, D. (LD)	5,347	12.4
Shuttleworth, K.		
(Ref)	1,458	3.4
Lab majority	15,893	36.96%
Electorate	62,980	
Total Vote	43,004	Poll 68.3%

*Member of last parliament
Lab Hold (10.7% Swing from Con to Lab)

NORTH ANTRIM %
*Paisley, I. (DUP)	21,495	46.5
Leslie, J. (UUP)	10,921	23.6
Farren, S. (SDLP)	7,333	15.9
McCarry, J. (SF)	2,896	6.3
Alderdice, D.		
(APNI)	2,845	6.2
Hinds, B. (Women)	580	1.3
Wright, J. (NLP)	116	0.3
DUP majority	10,574	22.89%
Electorate	72,411	
Total Vote	46,186	Poll 63.8%

*Member of last parliament
DUP Hold (5% Swing from DUP to UUP)

NORTH CORNWALL %
*Tyler, P. (LD)	31,100	53.2
Linacre, N. (Con)	17,253	29.5
Lindo, A. (Lab)	5,523	9.4
Odam, F. (Ref)	3,636	6.2
Bolitho, J. (MK)	645	1.1
Winfield, R. (Lib)	186	0.3
Cresswell, N.		
(NLP)	152	0.3
LD majority	13,847	23.78%
Electorate	80,076	
Total Vote	58,495	Poll 72.9%

*Member of last parliament
LD Hold (10.3% Swing from Con to LD)

NORTH DEVON %
*Harvey, N. (LD)	27,824	50.8
Ashworth, R. (Con)	21,643	39.5
Brenton, E. (Lab)	5,347	9.8
LD majority	6,181	11.3%
Electorate	70,350	
Total Vote	54,814	Poll 77.9%

*Member of last parliament
LD Hold (5% Swing from Con to LD)

NORTH DORSET %
Walter, R. (Con)	23,294	44.3
Yates, P. (LD)	20,548	39.1
Fitzmaurice, J. (Lab)	5,380	10.2
Evans, M. (Ref)	2,564	4.9
Wheeler, D. (UKIP)	801	1.5
Con majority	2,746	5.22%
Electorate	68,923	
Total Vote	52,587	Poll 76.3%

Con Hold (6.9% Swing from Con to LD)

NORTH DOWN %
*McCartney, R.		
(UKU)	12,817	35.1
McFarland, A.		
(UUP)	11,368	31.1
Napier, O. (APNI)	7,554	20.7
Fee, A. (Con)	1,810	5.0
Farrell, M. (SDLP)	1,602	4.4
Morrice, J. (Women)	1,240	3.4
Mullins, T. (NLP)	108	0.3
Mooney, R.		
(NI Party)	67	0.2
UKU majority	1,449	3.96%
Electorate	63,010	
Total Vote	36,566	Poll 58%

*Member of last parliament
UKU Hold (0% Swing from to)

NORTH EAST
BEDFORDSHIRE %
*Lyell, Sir N. (Con)	22,311	44.3
Lehal, J. (Lab)	16,428	32.6
Bristow, P. (LD)	7,179	14.2
Taylor, J. (Ref)	2,490	4.9
Foley, F. (IndCon)	1,842	3.7
Bence, B. (NLP)	138	0.3
Con majority	5,883	11.68%
Electorate	64,743	
Total Vote	50,388	Poll 77.6%

*Member of last parliament
Con Hold (13.8% Swing from Con to Lab)

NORTH EAST CAMBRIDGESHIRE %
*Moss, M. (Con)	23,855	43.0
Bucknor, V. (Lab)	18,754	33.8
Nash, A. (LD)	9,070	16.4
Bacon, M. (Ref)	2,636	4.8
Bennett, C. (SLP)	851	1.5
Leighton, L. (NLP)	259	0.5
Con majority	5,101	9.20%
Electorate	76,056	
Total Vote	55,425	Poll 72.8%

*Member of last parliament
Con Hold (15.4% Swing from Con to Lab)

NORTH EAST DERBYSHIRE %
*Barnes, H. (Lab)	31,425	60.5
Elliott, S. (Con)	13,104	25.2
Hardy, S. (LD)	7,450	14.3
Lab majority	18,321	35.25%
Electorate	72,653	
Total Vote	51,979	Poll 72.6%

*Member of last parliament
Lab Hold (12.3% Swing from Con to Lab)

NORTH EAST FIFE %
*Campbell, M. (LD)	21,432	51.2
Bruce, A. (Con)	11,076	26.5
Welsh, C. (SNP)	4,545	10.9
Milne, C. (Lab)	4,301	10.3
Stewart, W. (Ref)	485	1.2
LD majority	10,356	24.75%
Electorate	58,794	
Total Vote	41,839	Poll 70.6%

*Member of last parliament
LD Hold (8.4% Swing from Con to LD)

NORTH EAST HAMPSHIRE %
*Arbuthnot, J. (Con)	26,017	50.9
Mann, I. (LD)	11,619	22.7
Dare, P. (Lab)	8,203	16.0
Rees, D. (Ref)	2,420	4.7
Jessavala, K. (Ind)	2,400	4.7
Berry, C. (UKIP)	452	0.9
Con majority	14,398	28.17%
Electorate	69,111	
Total Vote	51,111	Poll 73.6%

*Member of last parliament
Con Hold (5.4% Swing from Con to LD)

NORTH EAST HERTFORDSHIRE %
*Heald, O. (Con)	21,712	41.8
Gibbons, I. (Lab)	18,624	35.8
Jarvis, S. (LD)	9,493	18.3
Grose, J. (Ref)	2,166	4.2
Con majority	3,088	5.94%
Electorate	67,161	
Total Vote	51,995	Poll 77.4%

*Member of last parliament
Con Hold (12.2% Swing from Con to Lab)

NORTH ESSEX %
*Jenkin, B. (Con)	22,480	43.9
Young, T. (Lab)	17,004	33.2
Phillips, A. (LD)	10,028	19.6
Lord, R. (UKIP)	1,202	2.3

Ransome, S. (Green)	495	1.0
Con majority	5,476	10.69%
Electorate	68,008	
Total Vote	51,209	Poll 75.3%

*Member of last parliament
Con Hold (14% Swing from Con to Lab)

NORTH NORFOLK %
Prior, D. (Con)	21,456	36.5
Lamb, N. (LD)	20,163	34.4
Cullingham, M. (Lab)	14,736	25.1
Allen, J. (Ref)	2,458	4.2
Con majority	1,293	2.20%
Electorate	77,113	
Total Vote	58,813	Poll 76.2%

Con Hold (9.5% Swing from Con to LD)

NORTH SHROPSHIRE %
Paterson, O. (Con)	20,730	40.2
Lucas, I. (Lab)	18,535	36.0
Stevens, J. (LD)	10,489	20.4
Allen, D. (Ref)	1,764	3.4
Con majority	2,195	4.26%
Electorate	70,852	
Total Vote	51,518	Poll 72.7%

Con Hold (10.2% Swing from Con to Lab)

NORTH SOUTHWARK AND BERMONDSEY %
*Hughes, S. (LD)	19,831	48.6
Fraser, J. (Lab)	16,444	40.3
Shapps, G. (Con)	2,835	6.9
Davidson, M. (BNP)	713	1.7
Newton, B. (Ref)	545	1.3
Grant, I. (Comm)	175	0.4
Munday, J. (Lib)	157	0.4
Yngvisson, I. (Nat Dem)	95	0.2
LD majority	3,387	8.30%
Electorate	65,598	
Total Vote	40,795	Poll 60.9%

*Member of last parliament
LD Hold (4.3% Swing from LD to Lab)

NORTH TAYSIDE %
Swinney, J. (SNP)	20,447	44.8
*Walker, B. (Con)	16,287	35.7
McFatridge, I. (Lab)	5,141	11.3
Regent, P. (LD)	3,716	8.2
SNP majority	4,160	9.12%
Electorate	61,398	
Total Vote	45,591	Poll 74.3%

*Member of last parliament
SNP Gain (8.4% Swing from Con to SNP)

NORTH THANET %
*Gale, R. (Con)	21,586	44.1
Johnson, I. (Lab)	18,820	38.4
Kendrick, P. (LD)	5,576	11.4
Chambers, M. (Ref)	2,535	5.2
Haines, J. (UKIP)	438	0.9
Con majority	2,766	5.65%
Electorate	71,112	
Total Vote	48,955	Poll 68.8%

*Member of last parliament
Con Hold (14% Swing from Con to Lab)

NORTH TYNESIDE %
*Byers, S. (Lab)	32,810	72.7
McIntyre, M. (Con)	6,167	13.7
Mulvenna, T. (LD)	4,762	10.6
Rollings, M. (Ref)	1,382	3.1
Lab majority	26,643	59.05%
Electorate	66,449	
Total Vote	45,121	Poll 67.8%

*Member of last parliament
Lab Hold (12.1% Swing from Con to Lab)

NORTH WARWICKSHIRE %
*O'Brien, M. (Lab)	31,669	58.4
Hammond, S. (Con)	16,902	31.2
Powell, W. (LD)	4,040	7.4
Mole, R. (Ref)	917	1.7
Cooke, C. (UKIP)	533	1.0
Moorcroft, I. (Bert)	178	0.3
Lab majority	14,767	27.23%
Electorate	72,602	
Total Vote	54,239	Poll 74.6%

*Member of last parliament
Lab Hold (12.4% Swing from Con to Lab)

NORTH WEST CAMBRIDGESHIRE %
*Mawhinney, B. (Con)	23,488	48.1
Steptoe, L. (Lab)	15,734	32.2
McCoy, B. (LD)	7,388	15.1
Watt, A. (Ref)	1,939	4.0
Wyatt, W. (UKIP)	269	0.6
Con majority	7,754	15.88%
Electorate	65,791	
Total Vote	48,818	Poll 74.2%

*Member of last parliament
Con Hold (10.3% Swing from Con to Lab)

NORTH WEST DURHAM %
*Armstrong, H. (Lab)	31,855	68.8
St John Howe, L. (Con)	7,101	15.3
Gillings, A. (LD)	4,991	10.8
Atkinson, R. (Ref)	2,372	5.1
Lab majority	24,754	53.44%
Electorate	67,156	
Total Vote	46,319	Poll 69%

*Member of last parliament
Lab Hold (11.4% Swing from Con to Lab)

NORTH WEST HAMPSHIRE %
*Young, Sir G. (Con)	24,730	45.2
Fleming, C. (LD)	13,179	24.1
Mumford, M. (Lab)	12,900	23.6
Callaghan, P. (Ref)	1,533	2.8
Rolt, T. (UKIP)	1,383	2.5
Baxter, B. (Green)	486	0.9
Anscomb, H. (No Bypass)	231	0.4
Dodd, B. (Ind)	225	0.4
Con majority	11,551	21.13%
Electorate	73,222	
Total Vote	54,667	Poll 74.4%

*Member of last parliament
Con Hold (4.5% Swing from Con to LD)

NORTH WEST
LEICESTERSHIRE   %
Taylor, D.
  (Lab/Co-op)   29,332   56.4
Goodwill, R. (Con)   16,113   31.0
Heptinstall, S. (LD)   4,492   8.6
Abney-Hastings, M.
  (Ref)   2,088   4.0
  Lab/Co-op
    majority   13,219   25.41%
  Electorate   65,069
  Total Vote   52,025 Poll 79.8%
Lab Gain (13.5% Swing from Con to Lab)

NORTH WEST NORFOLK   %
Turner, G. (Lab)   25,250   43.8
*Bellingham, H.
  (Con)   23,911   41.5
Knowles, E. (LD)   5,513   9.6
Percival, R. (Ref)   2,923   5.1
  Lab majority   1,339   2.32%
  Electorate   77,083
  Total Vote   57,597 Poll 74.6%
*Member of last parliament
Lab Gain (10.4% Swing from Con to Lab)

NORTH WILTSHIRE   %
Gray, J. (Con)   25,390   43.8
Cordon, S. (LD)   21,915   37.8
Knowles, N. (Lab)   8,261   14.2
Purves, M. (Ref)   1,774   3.1
Wood, A. (UKIP)   410   0.7
Forsyth, J. (NLP)   263   0.5
  Con majority   3,475   5.99%
  Electorate   77,237
  Total Vote   58,013 Poll 74.6%
Con Hold (9.3% Swing from Con to LD)

NORTHAMPTON NORTH   %
Keeble, S. (Lab)   27,247   52.7
*Marlow, T. (Con)   17,247   33.4
Dunbar, L. (LD)   6,579   12.7
Torbica, D. (UKIP)   464   0.9
Spivack, B. (NLP)   161   0.3
  Lab majority   10,000   19.34%
  Electorate   73,664
  Total Vote   51,698 Poll 69.9%
*Member of last parliament
Lab Gain (13.3% Swing from Con to Lab)

NORTHAMPTON SOUTH   %
Clarke, T. (Lab)   24,214   42.4
*Morris, M. (Con)   23,470   41.1
Worgan, A. (LD)   6,316   11.1
Petrie, C. (Ref)   1,405   2.5
Clark, D. (UKIP)   1,159   2.0
Woollcombe, G. (NLP)   541   0.9
  Lab majority   744   1.30%
  Electorate   79,384
  Total Vote   57,105 Poll 71.7%
*Member of last parliament
Lab Gain (13.4% Swing from Con to Lab)

NORTHAVON   %
Webb, S. (LD)   26,500   42.0
*Cope, Sir J. (Con)   24,363   39.0
Stone, R. (Lab)   9,767   15.6

Parfitt, J. (Ref)   1,900   3.0
  LD majority   2,137   3.42%
  Electorate   78,943
  Total Vote   62,530 Poll 79.1%
*Member of last parliament
LD Gain (10.4% Swing from Con to LD)

NORWICH NORTH   %
Gibson, I. (Lab)   27,346   49.7
Kinghorn, R. (Con)   17,876   32.5
Young, P. (LD)   6,951   12.6
Bailey-Smith, T. (Ref) 1,777   3.2
Marks, H. (Cannabis)   512   0.9
Hood, J. (SLP)   495   0.9
Mills, D. (NLP)   100   0.2
  Lab majority   9,470   17.20%
  Electorate   72,521
  Total Vote   55,057 Poll 75.7%
Lab Gain (10.6% Swing from Con to Lab)

NORWICH SOUTH   %
Clarke, C. (Lab)   26,267   51.7
Khanbhai, B. (Con)   12,028   23.7
Aalders-Dunthorne,
  A. (LD)   9,457   18.6
Holdsworth, D. (Ref)   1,464   2.9
Marks, H. (LCP)   765   1.5
Holmes, A. (Green)   736   1.4
Parsons, B. (NLP)   84   0.2
  Lab majority   14,239   28.03%
  Electorate   70,009
  Total Vote   50,801 Poll 72.6%
Lab Hold (10.1% Swing from Con to Lab)

NOTTINGHAM EAST   %
*Heppell, J. (Lab)   24,755   62.3
Raca, A. (Con)   9,336   23.5
Mulloy, K. (LD)   4,008   10.1
Brown, B. (Ref)   1,645   4.1
  Lab majority   15,419   38.80%
  Electorate   65,581
  Total Vote   39,744 Poll 60.2%
*Member of last parliament
Lab Hold (11.3% Swing from Con to Lab)

NOTTINGHAM NORTH   %
*Allen, G. (Lab)   27,203   65.7
Shaw, G (Con)   8,402   20.3
Oliver, R. (LD)   3,301   8.0
Neal, J. (Ref)   1,858   4.5
Belfield, A. (Soc)   637   1.5
  Lab majority   18,801   45.41%
  Electorate   65,698
  Total Vote   41,401 Poll 62.9%
*Member of last parliament
Lab Hold (12.4% Swing from Con to Lab)

NOTTINGHAM SOUTH   %
*Simpson, A. (Lab)   26,825   55.3
Kirsch, B. (Con)   13,461   27.7
Long, G. (LD)   6,265   12.9
Thompson, k. (Ref)   1,523   3.1
Edwards, S. (Nat Dem)   446   0.9
  Lab majority   13,364   27.54%
  Electorate   72,418
  Total Vote   48,520 Poll 66.6%
*Member of last parliament
Lab Hold (10.8% Swing from Con to Lab)

NUNEATON   %
*Olner, B. (Lab)   30,080   56.2
Blunt, R. (Con)   16,540   30.9
Cockings, R. (LD)   4,732   8.8
English, R. (Ref)   1,533   2.9
Bray, D. (LocInd)   390   0.7
Everitt, P. (UKIP)   238   0.4
  Lab majority   13,540   25.30%
  Electorate   72,032
  Total Vote   53,513 Poll 74.2%
*Member of last parliament
Lab Hold (11.3% Swing from Con to Lab)

OCHIL   %
*O'Neill, M. (Lab)   19,707   45.0
Reid, G. (SNP)   15,055   34.4
Hogarth, A. (Con)   6,383   14.6
Watters, A. (LD)   2,262   5.2
White, D. (Ref)   210   0.5
Macdonald, I.
  (Dem Nat)   104   0.2
Sullivan, M. (NLP)   65   0.1
  Lab majority   4,652   10.62%
  Electorate   56,572
  Total Vote   43,786 Poll 76.9%
*Member of last parliament
Lab Hold (3.2% Swing from Lab to SNP)

OGMORE   %
*Powell, R. (Lab)   28,163   74.0
Unwin, D. (Con)   3,716   9.8
Williams, K. (LD)   3,510   9.2
Rogers, J. (PC)   2,679   7.0
  Lab majority   24,447   64.22%
  Electorate   52,078
  Total Vote   38,068 Poll 73.1%
*Member of last parliament
Lab Hold (3.8% Swing from Con to Lab)

OLD BEXLEY AND SIDCUP   %
*Heath, Sir E. (Con)   21,608   42.0
Justham, R. (Lab)   18,039   35.1
King, I. (LD)   8,284   16.1
Reading, B. (Ref)   2,457   4.8
Bullen, C. (UKIP)   489   1.0
Tyndall, V. (BNP)   415   0.8
Stephens, R. (NLP)   99   0.2
  Con majority   3,569   6.94%
  Electorate   68,044
  Total Vote   51,391 Poll 75.5%
*Member of last parliament
Con Hold (14.1% Swing from Con to Lab)

OLDHAM EAST AND
SADDLEWORTH   %
Woolas, P. (Lab)   22,546   41.7
*Davies, C. (LD)   19,157   35.4
Hudson, J. (Con)   10,666   19.7
Findley, D. (Ref)   1,116   2.1
Smith, I. (SLP)   470   0.9
Dalling, I. (NLP)   146   0.3
  Lab majority   3,389   6.26%
  Electorate   73,189
  Total Vote   54,101 Poll 73.9%
*Member of last parliament
Lab Gain (13.6% Swing from Con to Lab)

OLDHAM WEST AND ROYTON

		%
*Meacher, M. (Lab)	26,894	58.8
Lord, J. (Con)	10,693	23.4
Cohen, H. (LD)	5,434	11.9
Choudhury, G. (SLP)	1,311	2.9
Etherden, P. (Ref)	1,157	2.5
Dalling, S. (NLP)	249	0.5
Lab majority 16,201		35.42%
Electorate 69,203		
Total Vote 45,738	Poll 66.1%	

*Member of last parliament
Lab Hold (12.2% Swing from Con to Lab)

ORKNEY AND SHETLAND

		%
*Wallace, J. (LD)	10,743	52.0
Paton, J. (Lab)	3,775	18.3
Ross, W. (SNP)	2,624	12.7
Anderson, H. (Con)	2,527	12.2
Adamson, F. (Ref)	820	4.0
Wharton, C. (Artist)	116	0.6
Robertson, A. (Ind)	60	0.3
LD majority 6,968		33.72%
Electorate 32,291		
Total Vote 20,665	Poll 63.9%	

*Member of last parliament
LD Hold (3.6% Swing from Lab to LD)

ORPINGTON

		%
*Horam, J. (Con)	24,417	40.6
Maines, C. (LD)	21,465	35.7
Polydorou, S. (Lab)	10,753	17.9
Clark, D. (Ref)	2,316	3.8
Carver, J. (UKIP)	526	0.9
Almond, R. (Lib)	494	0.8
Wilton, N. (Pro-Life)	191	0.3
Con majority 2,952		4.91%
Electorate 78,749		
Total Vote 60,162	Poll 76.4%	

*Member of last parliament
Con Hold (11% Swing from Con to LD)

OXFORD EAST

		%
*Smith, A. (Lab)	27,205	56.8
Djanogly, J. (Con)	10,540	22.0
Kershaw, G. (LD)	7,038	14.7
Young, M. (Ref)	1,391	2.9
Simmons, C. (Green)	975	2.0
Harper-Jones, D. (Pro-Life)	318	0.7
Gardner, P. (UKIP)	234	0.5
Thompson, J. (NLP)	108	0.2
Mylvaganam, P. (Anti-Maj)	68	0.1
Lab majority 16,665		34.81%
Electorate 69,339		
Total Vote 47,877	Poll 69%	

*Member of last parliament
Lab Hold (9.1% Swing from Con to Lab)

OXFORD WEST AND ABINGDON

		%
Harris, E. (LD)	26,268	42.9
Harris, L. (Con)	19,983	32.7
Brown, S. (Lab)	12,361	20.2
Eustace, G. (Ref)	1,258	2.1
Woodin, M. (Green)	691	1.1

Buckton, R. (UKIP)	258	0.4
Hodge, L. (Pro-Life)	238	0.4
Wilson, A. (NLP)	91	0.1
Rose, J. (Local Govt)	48	0.1
LD majority 6,285		10.27%
Electorate 79,329		
Total Vote 61,196	Poll 77.1%	

LD Gain (10.3% Swing from Con to LD)

PAISLEY NORTH

		%
*Adams, I. (Lab)	20,295	59.5
Mackay, I. (SNP)	7,481	21.9
Brookes, K. (Con)	3,267	9.6
Jelfs, A. (LD)	2,365	6.9
Graham, R. (Pro-Life)	531	1.6
Mathew, E. (Ref)	196	0.6
Lab majority 12,814		37.54%
Electorate 49,725		
Total Vote 34,135	Poll 68.5%	

*Member of last parliament
Lab Hold (4.6% Swing from SNP to Lab)

PAISLEY SOUTH

		%
*McMaster, G. (Lab/Co-op)	21,482	57.5
Martin, B. (SNP)	8,732	23.4
McCartin, E. (LD)	3,500	9.4
Reid, R. (Con)	3,237	8.7
Lardner, J. (Ref)	254	0.7
Clerkin, S. (ScotSoc)	146	0.4
Lab/Co-op majority 12,750		34.14%
Electorate 54,040		
Total Vote 37,351	Poll 69.5%	

*Member of last parliament
Lab Hold (3.9% Swing from SNP to Lab)

PENDLE

		%
*Prentice, G. (Lab)	25,059	53.3
Midgley, J. (Con)	14,235	30.3
Greaves, T. (LD)	5,460	11.6
Hockney, D. (Ref)	2,281	4.8
Lab majority 10,824		23.01%
Electorate 63,049		
Total Vote 47,035	Poll 74.5%	

*Member of last parliament
Lab Hold (9.5% Swing from Con to Lab)

PENRITH AND THE BORDER

		%
*Maclean, D. (Con)	23,300	47.6
Walker, K. (LD)	13,067	26.7
Meling, M. (Lab)	10,576	21.6
Pope, C. (Ref)	2,018	4.1
Con majority 10,233		20.90%
Electorate 66,496		
Total Vote 48,961	Poll 73.6%	

*Member of last parliament
Con Hold (4.4% Swing from Con to LD)

PERTH

		%
*Cunningham, R. (SNP)	16,209	36.4
Godfrey, J. (Con)	13,068	29.3
Alexander, D. (Lab)	11,036	24.8
Brodie, C. (LD)	3,583	8.0

MacAuley, R. (Ref)	366	0.8
Henderson, M. (UKIP)	289	0.6
SNP majority 3,141		7.05%
Electorate 60,313		
Total Vote 44,551	Poll 73.9%	

*Member of last parliament
SNP Gain (6.6% Swing from Con to SNP)

PETERBOROUGH

		%
Brinton, H. (Lab)	24,365	50.3
Foster, J. (Con)	17,042	35.2
Howarth, D. (LD)	5,170	10.7
Slater, P. (Ref)	924	1.9
Brettell, C. (NLP)	334	0.7
Linskey, J. (UKIP)	317	0.7
Goldspink, S. (Pro-Life)	275	0.6
Lab majority 7,323		15.12%
Electorate 65,926		
Total Vote 48,427	Poll 72.8%	

Lab Gain (13.4% Swing from Con to Lab)

PLYMOUTH DEVONPORT

		%
*Jamieson, D. (Lab)	31,629	60.9
Johnson, A. (Con)	12,562	24.1
Copus, R. (LD)	5,570	10.7
Norsworthy, C. (Ref)	1,486	2.9
Farrand, C. (UKIP)	478	0.9
Ebbs, S. (Nat Dem)	238	0.5
Lab majority 19,067		36.69%
Electorate 74,483		
Total Vote 51,963	Poll 69.8%	

*Member of last parliament
Lab Hold (12.7% Swing from Con to Lab)

PLYMOUTH SUTTON

		%
Gilroy, L. (Lab/Co-op)	23,881	50.1
Crisp, A. (Con)	14,441	30.3
Melia, S. (LD)	6,613	13.9
Hanbury, T. (Ref)	1,654	3.5
Bullock, R. (UKIP)	499	1.0
Kelway, K. (Plymouth)	396	0.8
Lyons, F. (NLP)	168	0.4
Lab/Co-op majority 9,440		19.81%
Electorate 70,666		
Total Vote 47,652	Poll 67%	

Lab/Co-op Gain (10.9% Swing from Con to Lab)

PONTEFRACT AND CASTLEFORD

		%
Cooper, Y. (Lab)	31,339	75.7
Flook, A. (Con)	5,614	13.6
Paxton, W. (LD)	3,042	7.3
Wood, R. (Ref)	1,401	3.4
Lab majority 25,725		62.14%
Electorate 62,350		
Total Vote 41,396	Poll 66.4%	

Lab Hold (6.6% Swing from Con to Lab)

PONTYPRIDD

		%
*Howells, K. (Lab)	29,290	.63.9
Howells, N. (LD)	6,161	13.5
Cowen, J. (Con)	5,910	12.9
Llewelyn, O. (PC)	2,977	6.5
Wood, J. (Ref)	874	1.9
Skelly, P. (SLP)	380	0.8
Griffiths, R. (Comm)	178	0.4
Moore, A. (NLP)	85	0.2
Lab majority 23,129		50.44%
Electorate 64,185		
Total Vote 45,855	Poll 71.4%	

*Member of last parliament
Lab Hold (0.9% Swing from Lab to LD)

POOLE

		%
Syms, R. (Con)	19,726	42.1
Tetlow, A. (LD)	14,428	30.9
White, H. (Lab)	10,100	21.6
Riddington, J. (Ref)	1,932	4.1
Tyler, P. (UKIP)	487	1.0
Rosta, J. (NLP)	137	0.3
Con majority 5,298		11.32%
Electorate 66,078		
Total Vote 46,810	Poll 70.8%	

Con Hold (7.2% Swing from Con to LD)

POPLAR AND CANNING TOWN

		%
Fitzpatrick, J. (Lab)	24,807	63.2
Steinberg, B. (Con)	5,892	15.0
Ludlow, J. (LD)	4,072	10.4
Tyndall, J. (BNP)	2,849	7.3
Hare, I. (Ref)	1,091	2.8
Joseph, J. (SLP)	557	1.4
Lab majority 18,915		48.17%
Electorate 67,172		
Total Vote 39,268	Poll 58.5%	

Lab Hold (11.3% Swing from Con to Lab)

PORTSMOUTH NORTH

		%
Rapson, S. (Lab)	21,339	47.1
*Griffiths, P. (Con)	17,016	37.6
Sollitt, S. (LD)	4,788	10.6
Evelegh, S. (Ref)	1,757	3.9
Coe, P. (UKIP)	298	0.7
Bex, C. (Wessex Reg)	72	0.2
Lab majority 4,323		9.55%
Electorate 64,539		
Total Vote 45,270	Poll 70.1%	

*Member of last parliament
Lab Gain (13.5% Swing from Con to Lab)

PORTSMOUTH SOUTH

		%
Hancock, M. (LD)	20,421	39.5
*Martin, D. (Con)	16,094	31.1
Burnett, A. (Lab)	13,086	25.3
Trim, C. (Ref)	1,629	3.2
Thompson, J. (Lib)	184	0.4
Evans, J. (UKIP)	141	0.3
Treend, W. (NLP)	140	0.3
LD majority 4,327		8.37%
Electorate 80,514		
Total Vote 51,695	Poll 63.8%	

*Member of last parliament
LD Gain (4.4% Swing from Con to LD)

PRESELI PEMBROKESHIRE

		%
Lawrence, J. (Lab)	20,477	48.3
Buckland, R. (Con)	11,741	27.7
Clarke, J. (LD)	5,527	13.0
Jones, A. (PC)	2,683	6.3
Berry, D. (Ref)	1,574	3.7
Cato, M. (Green)	401	0.9
Lab majority 8,736		20.60%
Electorate 54,088		
Total Vote 42,403	Poll 78.2%	

Lab Gain (11% Swing from Con to Lab)

PRESTON

		%
*Wise, A. (Lab)	29,220	60.8
Gray, P. (Con)	10,540	21.9
Chadwick, W. (LD)	7,045	14.7
Porter, J. (Ref)	924	1.9
Ashforth, J. (NLP)	345	0.7
Lab majority 18,680		38.86%
Electorate 72,933		
Total Vote 48,074	Poll 65.7%	

*Member of last parliament
Lab Hold (9% Swing from Con to Lab)

PUDSEY

		%
Truswell, P. (Lab)	25,370	48.1
Bone, P. (Con)	19,163	36.3
Brown, J. (LD)	7,375	14.0
Crabtree, D. (Ref)	823	1.6
Lab majority 6,207		11.77%
Electorate 70,922		
Total Vote 52,731	Poll 74.3%	

Lab Gain (13.2% Swing from Con to Lab)

PUTNEY

		%
Colman, A. (Lab)	20,084	45.7
*Mellor, D. (Con)	17,108	38.9
Pyne, R. (LD)	4,739	10.8
Goldsmith, J. (Ref)	1,518	3.5
Jamieson, W. (UKIP)	233	0.5
Beige, L. (Stan)	101	0.2
Yardley, M. (Spts All)	90	0.2
Small, J. (NLP)	66	0.2
Poole, A. (Beaut)	49	0.1
Van Braam, D. (Ren Dem)	7	0.0
Lab majority 2,976		6.76%
Electorate 60,176		
Total Vote 43,995	Poll 71.4%	

*Member of last parliament
Lab Gain (11.2% Swing from Con to Lab)

RAYLEIGH

		%
*Clark, M. (Con)	25,516	49.7
Ellis, R. (Lab)	14,832	28.9
Cumberland, S. (LD)	10,137	19.8
Farmer, A. (Lib)	829	1.6
Con majority 10,684		20.82%
Electorate 68,737		
Total Vote 51,314	Poll 74.7%	

*Member of last parliament
Con Hold (12.7% Swing from Con to Lab)

READING EAST

		%
Griffiths, J. (Lab)	21,461	42.7
*Watts, J. (Con)	17,666	35.2

Samuel, R. (LD)	9,307	18.5
Harmer, P. (Ref)	1,042	2.1
Buckley, J. (NLP)	254	0.5
Thornton, A. (UKIP)	252	0.5
Packer, B. (BNP)	238	0.5
Lab majority 3,795		7.56%
Electorate 71,586		
Total Vote 50,220	Poll 70.2%	

*Member of last parliament
Lab Gain (13.9% Swing from Con to Lab)

READING WEST

		%
Salter, M. (Lab)	21,841	45.1
Bennett, N. (Con)	18,844	38.9
Tomlin, D. (LD)	6,153	12.7
Brown, S. (Ref)	976	2.0
Dell, I. (BNP)	320	0.7
Black, D. (UKIP)	255	0.5
Lab majority 2,997		6.19%
Electorate 69,073		
Total Vote 48,389	Poll 70.1%	

Lab Gain (15% Swing from Con to Lab)

REDCAR

		%
*Mowlam, M. (Lab)	32,975	67.3
Isaacs, A. (Con)	11,308	23.1
Benbow, J. (LD)	4,679	9.6
Lab majority 21,667		44.25%
Electorate 68,965		
Total Vote 48,962	Poll 71.0%	

*Member of last parliament
Lab Hold (12.3% Swing from Con to Lab)

REDDITCH

		%
Smith, J. (Lab)	22,280	49.8
McIntyre, A. (Con)	16,155	36.1
Hall, M. (LD)	4,935	11.0
Cox, R. (Ref)	1,151	2.6
Davis, P. (NLP)	227	0.5
Lab majority 6,125		13.69%
Electorate 60,841		
Total Vote 44,748	Poll 73.5%	

Lab Gain (10.2% Swing from Con to Lab)

REGENT'S PARK AND KENSINGTON NORTH

		%
Buck, K. (Lab)	28,367	59.9
McGuinness, P. (Con)	13,710	29.0
Gasson, E. (LD)	4,041	8.5
Dangoor, S. (Ref)	867	1.8
Hinde, J. (NLP)	192	0.4
Sadowitz, D. (Dream)	167	0.4
Lab majority 14,657		30.96%
Electorate 73,752		
Total Vote 47,344	Poll 64.2%	

Lab Hold (11.8% Swing from Con to Lab)

REIGATE

		%
Blunt, C. (Con)	21,123	43.8
Howard, A. (Lab)	13,382	27.8
Samuel, P. (LD)	9,615	20.0
*Gardiner, G. (Ref)	3,352	7.0
Higgs, R. (Loc Ind)	412	0.9
Smith, S. (UKIP)	290	0.6
Con majority 7,741		16.07%
Electorate 64,750		
Total Vote 48,174	Poll 73.8%	

*Member of last parliament
Con Re-gain (12% Swing from Lab to Con)

RHONDDA
		%
*Rogers, A. (Lab)	30,381	74.5
Wood, L. (PC)	5,450	13.4
Berman, R. (LD)	2,307	5.7
Whiting, S. (Con)	1,551	3.8
Gardener, S. (Ref)	658	1.6
Jakeway, K. (Green)	460	1.1
Lab majority	24,931	61.09%
Electorate	57,105	
Total Vote	40,807	Poll 71.5%

*Member of last parliament
Lab Hold (0.8% Swing from Lab to PC)

RIBBLE VALLEY
		%
*Evans, N. (Con)	26,702	46.7
Carr, M. (LD)	20,062	35.1
Johnstone, M. (Lab)	9,013	15.8
Parkinson, J. (Ref)	1,297	2.3
Holmes, N. (NLP)	147	0.3
Con majority	6,640	11.60%
Electorate	72,664	
Total Vote	57,221	Poll 78.5%

*Member of last parliament
Con Hold (1.4% Swing from Con to LD)

RICHMOND (YORKS)
		%
*Hague, W. (Con)	23,326	48.9
Merritt, S. (Lab)	13,275	27.8
Harvey, J. (LD)	8,773	18.4
Bentley, A. (Ref)	2,367	5.0
Con majority	10,051	21.05%
Electorate	65,058	
Total Vote	47,741	Poll 73.4%

*Member of last parliament
Con Hold (13.9% Swing from Con to Lab)

RICHMOND PARK
		%
Tonge, J. (LD)	25,393	44.7
*Hanley, J. (Con)	22,442	39.5
Jenkins, S. (Lab)	7,172	12.6
Pugh, J. (Ref)	1,467	2.6
Beaupre, D. (Loony)	204	0.4
D'Arcy, B. (NLP)	102	0.2
Davies, P. (Dream)	73	0.1
LD majority	2,951	5.19%
Electorate	71,572	
Total Vote	56,853	Poll 77.3%

*Member of last parliament
LD Gain (9.7% Swing from Con to LD)

ROCHDALE
		%
Fitzsimons, L. (Lab)	23,758	49.4
*Lynne, L. (LD)	19,213	40.0
Turnberg, M. (Con)	4,237	8.8
Bergin, G. (BNP)	653	1.4
Salim, M. (Islam)	221	0.5
Lab majority	4,545	9.45%
Electorate	68,529	
Total Vote	48,082	Poll 70%

*Member of last parliament
Lab Gain (4.8% Swing from LD to Lab)

ROCHFORD AND SOUTHEND EAST
		%
*Taylor, T. (Con)	22,683	48.7
Smith, N. (Lab)	18,458	39.7
Smith, P. (LD)	4,387	9.4

Lynch, B. (Lib)	1,007	2.2
Con majority	4,225	9.08%
Electorate	72,848	
Total Vote	46,535	Poll 63.6%

*Member of last parliament
Con Hold (11.2% Swing from Con to Lab)

ROMFORD
		%
Gordon, E. (Lab)	18,187	43.2
*Neubert, Sir M. (Con)	17,538	41.6
Meyer, N. (LD)	3,341	7.9
Ward, S. (Ref)	1,431	3.4
Hurlstone, T. (Lib)	1,100	2.6
Carey, M. (BNP)	522	1.2
Lab majority	649	1.54%
Electorate	59,611	
Total Vote	42,119	Poll 70.5%

*Member of last parliament
Lab Gain (15.6% Swing from Con to Lab)

ROMSEY
		%
*Colvin, M. (Con)	23,834	46.0
Cooper, M. (LD)	15,249	29.4
Ford, J. (Lab)	9,623	18.6
Sked, A. (UKIP)	1,824	3.5
Wigley, M. (Ref)	1,291	2.5
Con majority	8,585	16.57%
Electorate	67,306	
Total Vote	51,821	Poll 76.4%

*Member of last parliament
Con Hold (11.8% Swing from Con to LD)

ROSS, SKYE AND INVERNESS WEST
		%
*Kennedy, C. (LD)	15,472	38.7
Munro, D. (Lab)	11,453	28.7
Paterson, M. (SNP)	7,821	19.6
MacLeod, M. (Con)	4,368	10.9
Durance, A. (Ref)	535	1.3
Hopkins, A. (Green)	306	0.8
LD majority	4,019	10.06%
Electorate	55,639	
Total Vote	39,955	Poll 71.6%

*Member of last parliament
LD Hold (4.9% Swing from LD to Lab)

ROSSENDALE AND DARWEN
		%
*Anderson, J. (Lab)	27,470	53.6
Buzzard, P. (Con)	16,521	32.3
Dunning, B. (LD)	5,435	10.6
Newstead, R. (Ref)	1,108	2.2
Wearden, A. (BNP)	674	1.3
Lab majority	10,949	21.38%
Electorate	69,749	
Total Vote	51,208	Poll 73.4%

*Member of last parliament
Lab Hold (10.6% Swing from Con to Lab)

ROTHER VALLEY
		%
*Barron, K. (Lab)	31,184	67.6
Stanbury, S. (Con)	7,699	16.7
Burgess, S. (LD)	5,342	11.6
Cook, S. (Ref)	1,932	4.2
Lab majority	23,485	50.88%

Electorate	68,622	
Total Vote	46,157	Poll 67.2%

*Member of last parliament
Lab Hold (8.6% Swing from Con to Lab)

ROTHERHAM
		%
*MacShane, D. (Lab)	26,852	71.3
Gordon, S. (Con)	5,383	14.3
Wildgoose, D. (LD)	3,919	10.4
Hollebone, R. (Ref)	1,132	3.0
Neal, F. (Pro-Life)	364	1.0
Lab majority	21,469	57.02%
Electorate	59,895	
Total Vote	37,650	Poll 62.8%

*Member of last parliament
Lab Hold (8.4% Swing from Con to Lab)

ROXBURGH AND BERWICKSHIRE
		%
*Kirkwood, A. (LD)	16,243	46.5
Younger, D. (Con)	8,337	23.9
Eadie, H. (Lab)	5,226	15.0
Balfour, M. (SNP)	3,959	11.3
Curtis, J. (Ref)	922	2.6
Neilson, P. (UKIP)	202	0.6
Lucas, D. (NLP)	42	0.1
LD majority	7,906	22.63%
Electorate	47,259	
Total Vote	34,931	Poll 73.8%

*Member of last parliament
LD Hold (5.2% Swing from Con to LD)

RUGBY AND KENILWORTH
		%
King, A. (Lab)	26,356	43.1
*Pawsey, J. (Con)	25,861	42.3
Roodhouse, J. (LD)	8,737	14.3
Twite, M. (NLP)	251	0.4
Lab majority	495	0.81%
Electorate	79,384	
Total Vote	61,205	Poll 77.1%

*Member of last parliament
Lab Gain (10.6% Swing from Con to Lab)

RUISLIP NORTHWOOD
		%
*Wilkinson, J. (Con)	22,526	50.2
Barker, P. (Lab)	14,732	32.9
Edwards, C. (LD)	7,279	16.2
Griffin, C. (NLP)	296	0.7
Con majority	7,794	17.38%
Electorate	60,393	
Total Vote	44,833	Poll 74.2%

*Member of last parliament
Con Hold (12.8% Swing from Con to Lab)

RUNNYMEDE AND WEYBRIDGE
		%
Hammond, P. (Con)	25,051	48.6
Peacock, I. (Lab)	15,176	29.4
Taylor, G. (LD)	8,397	16.3
Rolt, P. (Ref)	2,150	4.2
Slater, S. (UKIP)	625	1.2
Sleeman, J. (NLP)	162	0.3
Con majority	9,875	19.15%
Electorate	72,177	
Total Vote	51,561	Poll 71.5%

Con Hold (13.1% Swing from Con to Lab)

RUSHCLIFFE %
*Clarke, K. (Con) 27,558 44.4
Pettitt, J. (Lab) 22,503 36.2
Boote, S. (LD) 8,851 14.3
Chadd, S. (Ref) 2,682 4.3
Moore, J. (UKIP) 403 0.6
Miszewska, A. (NLP) 115 0.2
Con majority 5,055 8.14%
Electorate 78,735
Total Vote 62,112 Poll 78.9%
*Member of last parliament
Con Hold (11.5% Swing from Con to Lab)

RUTLAND AND MELTON %
*Duncan, A. (Con) 24,107 45.8
Meads, J. (Lab) 15,271 29.0
Lee, K. (LD) 10,112 19.2
King, R. (Ref) 2,317 4.4
Abbott, J. (UKIP) 823 1.6
Con majority 8,836 16.79%
Electorate 70,150
Total Vote 52,630 Poll 74.9%
*Member of last parliament
Con Hold (14.5% Swing from Con to Lab)

RYEDALE %
*Greenway, J. (Con) 21,351 43.8
Orrell, J. (LD) 16,293 33.4
Hiles, A. (Lab) 8,762 18.0
Mackfall, J. (Ref) 1,460 3.0
Feaster, S. (UKIP) 917 1.9
Con majority 5,058 10.37%
Electorate 65,215
Total Vote 48,783 Poll 74.7%
*Member of last parliament
Con Hold (7.5% Swing from Con to LD)

SAFFRON WALDEN %
*Haselhurst, Sir A.
(Con) 25,871 45.3
Caton, M. (LD) 15,298 26.8
Fincken, M. (Lab) 12,275 21.5
Glover, R. (Ref) 2,308 4.0
Evans, I. (UKIP) 658 1.2
Tyler, R. (Ind) 486 0.9
Edwards, C. (NLP) 154 0.3
Con majority 10,573 18.53%
Electorate 74,097
Total Vote 57,050 Poll 76.6%
*Member of last parliament
Con Hold (4.7% Swing from Con to Lab)

SALFORD %
Blears, H. (Lab) 22,848 69.0
Bishop, E. (Con) 5,779 17.4
Owen, N. (LD) 3,407 10.3
Cumpsty, R. (Ref) 926 2.8
Herman, S. (NLP) 162 0.5
Lab majority 17,069 51.53%
Electorate 58,610
Total Vote 33,122 Poll 56.3%
Lab Hold (9.5% Swing from Con to Lab)

SALISBURY %
*Key, R. (Con) 25,012 42.9
Emmerson-Peirce,
Y. (LD) 18,736 32.2

Rogers, R. (Lab) 10,242 17.6
Farage, N. (UKIP) 3,332 5.7
Soutar, H. (Green) 623 1.1
Holmes, W. (Ind) 184 0.3
Haysom, S. (NLP) 110 0.2
Con majority 6,276 10.78%
Electorate 78,973
Total Vote 58,239 Poll 73.7%
*Member of last parliament
Con Hold (2% Swing from Con to LD)

**SCARBOROUGH AND
WHITBY** %
Quinn, L. (Lab) 24,791 45.6
*Sykes, J. (Con) 19,667 36.2
Allinson, M. (LD) 7,672 14.1
Murray, S. (Ref) 2,191 4.0
Lab majority 5,124 9.43%
Electorate 75,862
Total Vote 54,321 Poll 71.6%
*Member of last parliament
Lab Gain (14.7% Swing from Con to Lab)

SCUNTHORPE %
*Morley, E. (Lab) 25,107 60.4
Fisher, M. (Con) 10,934 26.3
Smith, G. (LD) 3,497 8.4
Smith, P. (Ref) 1,637 3.9
Hopper, B. (SLP) 399 1.0
Lab majority 14,173 34.09%
Electorate 60,393
Total Vote 41,574 Poll 68.8%
*Member of last parliament
Lab Hold (7.9% Swing from Con to Lab)

SEDGEFIELD %
*Blair, T. (Lab) 33,526 71.2
Pitman, E. (Con) 8,383 17.8
Beadle, R. (LD) 3,050 6.5
Hall, M. (Ref) 1,683 3.6
Gibson, B. (SLP) 474 1.0
Lab majority 25,143 53.36%
Electorate 64,923
Total Vote 47,116 Poll 72.6%
*Member of last parliament
Lab Hold (9.6% Swing from Con to Lab)

SELBY %
Grogan, J. (Lab) 25,838 45.9
Hind, K. (Con) 22,002 39.1
Batty, T. (LD) 6,778 12.0
Walker, D. (Ref) 1,162 2.1
Spence, P. (UKIP) 536 1.0
Lab majority 3,836 6.81%
Electorate 75,141
Total Vote 56,316 Poll 74.9%
Lab Gain (11.1% Swing from Con to Lab)

SEVENOAKS %
Fallon, M. (Con) 22,776 45.4
Hayes, J. (Lab) 12,315 24.6
Walshe, R. (LD) 12,086 24.1
Large, N. (Ref) 2,138 4.3
Lawrence, M. (Green) 443 0.9
Ellis, M. (Path) 244 0.5
Hankey, A. (NLP) 147 0.3

Con majority 10,461 20.86%
Electorate 66,474
Total Vote 50,149 Poll 75.4%
Con Hold (10.3% Swing from Con to Lab)

SHEFFIELD ATTERCLIFFE %
*Betts, C. (Lab) 28,937 65.3
Doyle, N. (Con) 7,119 16.1
Smith, A. (LD) 6,973 15.7
Brown, J. (Ref) 1,289 2.9
Lab majority 21,818 49.23%
Electorate 68,548
Total Vote 44,318 Poll 64.7%
*Member of last parliament
Lab Hold (9% Swing from Con to Lab)

SHEFFIELD BRIGHTSIDE %
*Blunkett, D. (Lab) 24,901 73.5
Butler, F. (LD) 4,947 14.6
Buckwell, C. (Con) 2,850 8.4
Farnsworth, B. (Ref) 624 1.8
Davidson, P. (SLP) 482 1.4
Scott, R. (NLP) 61 0.2
Lab majority 19,954 58.92%
Electorate 58,930
Total Vote 33,865 Poll 57.5%
*Member of last parliament
Lab Hold (0.5% Swing from LD to Lab)

SHEFFIELD CENTRAL %
*Caborn, R. (Lab) 23,179 63.6
Qadar, A. (LD) 6,273 17.2
Hess, M. (Con) 4,341 11.9
D'Agorne, A. (Green) 954 2.6
Brownlow, A. (Ref) 863 2.4
Douglas, K. (Soc) 466 1.3
Aitken, M. (Pro-Life) 280 0.8
Driver, M. (WRP) 63 0.2
Lab majority 16,906 46.42%
Electorate 68,667
Total Vote 36,419 Poll 53%
*Member of last parliament
Lab Hold (2.8% Swing from LD to Lab)

SHEFFIELD HALLAM %
Allan, R. (LD) 23,345 51.3
*Patnick, I. (Con) 15,074 33.1
Conquest, S. (Lab) 6,147 13.5
Davidson, I. (Ref) 788 1.7
Booler, P. (SIP) 125 0.3
LD majority 8,271 18.19%
Electorate 62,834
Total Vote 45,479 Poll 72.4%
*Member of last parliament
LD Gain (18.5% Swing from Con to LD)

SHEFFIELD HEELEY %
*Michie, B. (Lab) 26,274 60.7
Davison, R. (LD) 9,196 21.3
Harthman, J. (Con) 6,767 15.6
Mawson, D. (Ref) 1,029 2.4
Lab majority 17,078 39.47%
Electorate 66,599
Total Vote 43,266 Poll 65%
*Member of last parliament
Lab Hold (1.1% Swing from LD to Lab)

SHEFFIELD
HILLSBOROUGH %
*Jackson, H. (Lab)   30,150 56.9
Dunworth, A. (LD)   13,699 25.8
Nuttall, D. (Con)   7,707 14.5
Rusling, J. (Ref)   1,468 2.8

Lab majority 16,451   31.03%
Electorate   74,642
Total Vote   53,024   Poll 71%
*Member of last parliament
Lab Hold (9.6% Swing from LD to Lab)

SHERWOOD %
*Tipping, P. (Lab)   33,071 58.5
Spencer, R. (Con)   16,259 28.8
Moult, B. (LD)   4,889 8.6
Slack, L. (Ref)   1,882 3.3
Ballard, P. (BNP)   432 0.8

Lab majority 16,812   29.74%
Electorate   74,788
Total Vote   56,533   Poll 75.5%
*Member of last parliament
Lab Hold (12.5% Swing from Con to Lab)

SHIPLEY %
Leslie, C. (Lab)   22,962 43.4
*Fox, Sir M. (Con)   19,966 37.8
Cole, J. (LD)   7,984 15.1
Ellams, S. (Ref)   1,960 3.7

Lab majority 2,996   5.67%
Electorate   69,281
Total Vote   52,872   Poll 76.1%
*Member of last parliament
Lab Gain (13.8% Swing from Con to Lab)

SHREWSBURY AND
ATCHAM %
Marsden, P. (Lab)   20,484 37.0
*Conway, D. (Con)   18,814 34.0
Woolland, A. (LD)   13,838 25.0
Barker, D. (Ref)   1,346 2.4
Rowlands, D. (UKIP)   477 0.9
Dignan, A. (Farming)   257 0.5
Williams, A. (People's)   128 0.2

Lab majority 1,670   3.02%
Electorate   73,542
Total Vote   55,344   Poll 75.3%
*Member of last parliament
Lab Gain (11.4% Swing from Con to Lab)

SITTINGBOURNE AND
SHEPPEY %
Wyatt, D. (Lab)   18,723 40.6
*Moate, Sir R. (Con)   16,794 36.4
Truelove, R. (LD)   8,447 18.3
Moull, P. (Ref)   1,082 2.3
Driver, C. (Loony)   644 1.4
Risi, N. (UKIP)   472 1.0

Lab majority 1,929   4.18%
Electorate   63,850
Total Vote   46,162   Poll 72.3%
*Member of last parliament
Lab Gain (14.5% Swing from Con to Lab)

SKIPTON AND RIPON %
*Curry, D. (Con)   25,294 46.5
Mould, T. (LD)   13,674 25.2
Marchant, R. (Lab)   12,171 22.4

Holdsworth, N. (Ref)   3,212 5.9

Con majority 11,620   21.38%
Electorate   72,042
Total Vote   54,351   Poll 75.4%
*Member of last parliament
Con Hold (4.6% Swing from Con to LD)

SLEAFORD AND NORTH
HYKEHAM %
*Hogg, D. (Con)   23,358 43.9
Harriss, S. (Lab)   18,235 34.3
Marriott, J. (LD)   8,063 15.2
Clery, P. (Ref)   2,942 5.5
Overton, R. (Ind)   578 1.1

Con majority 5,123   9.63%
Electorate   71,486
Total Vote   53,176   Poll 74.2%
*Member of last parliament
Con Hold (13.4% Swing from Con to Lab)

SLOUGH %
Mactaggart, F. (Lab)   27,029 56.6
Buscombe, P. (Con)   13,958 29.2
Bushill, C. (LD)   3,509 7.4
Bradshaw, A. (Lib)   1,835 3.8
Sharkey, T. (Ref)   1,124 2.4
Whitmore, P. (Slough)   277 0.6

Lab majority 13,071   27.64%
Electorate   70,283
Total Vote   47,732   Poll 67.9%
Lab Win (13.7% Swing from Con to Lab)

SOLIHULL %
*Taylor, J. (Con)   26,299 44.6
Southcombe, M. (LD) 14,902 25.3
Harris, R. (Lab)   14,334 24.3
Nattrass, M. (Ref)   2,748 4.7
Caffery, J. (Pro-Life)   623 1.1

Con majority 11,397   19.35%
Electorate   78,898
Total Vote   58,906   Poll 74.4%
*Member of last parliament
Con Hold (10.3% Swing from Con to LD)

SOMERTON AND FROME %
Heath, D. (LD)   22,684 39.5
*Robinson, M. (Con)   22,554 39.3
Ashford, R. (Lab)   9,385 16.3
Rodwell, R. (Ref)   2,449 4.3
Gadd, R. (UKIP)   331 0.6

LD majority 130   0.23%
Electorate   73,988
Total Vote   57,403   Poll 77.4%
*Member of last parliament
LD Gain (3.7% Swing from Con to LD)

SOUTH ANTRIM %
*Forsythe, C. (UUP)   23,108 57.5
McClelland, D.
    (SDLP)   6,497 16.2
Ford, D. (APNI)   4,668 11.6
Smyth, H. (PUP)   3,490 8.7
Cushnahan, H. (SF)   2,229 5.5
Briggs, B. (NLP)   203 0.5

UUP majority 16,611   41.33%
Electorate   69,414
Total Vote   40,195   Poll 57.9%
*Member of last parliament
UUP Hold (8.2% Swing from UUP to
SDLP)

SOUTH CAMBRIDGESHIRE %
Lansley, A. (Con)   22,572 42.0
Quinlan, J. (LD)   13,860 25.8
Gray, T. (Lab)   13,485 25.1
Page, R. (Ref)   3,300 6.1
Norman, D. (UKIP)   298 0.6
Chalmers, F. (NLP)   168 0.3

Con majority 8,712   16.23%
Electorate   69,850
Total Vote   53,683   Poll 76.1%
Con Hold (8.7% Swing from Con to LD)

SOUTH DERBYSHIRE %
Todd, M. (Lab)   32,709 54.5
*Currie, E. (Con)   18,742 31.3
Renold, R. (LD)   5,408 9.0
North, R. (Ref)   2,491 4.2
Crompton, I.
    (UKIP)   617 1.0

Lab majority 13,967   23.29%
Electorate   76,672
Total Vote   59,967   Poll 78.2%
*Member of last parliament
Lab Gain (13.2% Swing from Con to Lab)

SOUTH DORSET %
*Bruce, I. (Con)   17,755 36.1
Knight, J. (Lab)   17,678 35.9
Plummer, M. (LD)   9,936 20.2
McAndrew, P. (Ref)   2,791 5.7
Shakesby, M.
    (UKIP)   861 1.8
Napper, G. (NLP)   161 0.3

Con majority 77   0.16%
Electorate   66,318
Total Vote   49,182   Poll 74%
*Member of last parliament
Con Hold (15% Swing from Con to Lab)

SOUTH DOWN %
*McGrady, E.
    (SDLP)   26,181 52.9
Nesbitt, D. (UUP)   16,248 32.8
Murphy, M. (SF)   5,127 10.4
Crozier, J. (APNI)   1,711 3.5
McKeon, R. (NLP)   219 0.4

SDLP majority 9,933   20.07%
Electorate   69,855
Total Vote   49,486   Poll 70.8%
*Member of last parliament
SDLP Hold (0.3% Swing from SDLP to
UUP)

SOUTH EAST
CAMBRIDGESHIRE %
*Paice, J. (Con)   24,397 42.9
Collinson, R. (Lab)   15,048 26.5
Brinton, S. (LD)   14,246 25.1
Howlett, J. (Ref)   2,838 5.0
Lam, K. (Fair)   167 0.3
While, P. (NLP)   111 0.2

Con majority 9,349   16.46%
Electorate   75,666
Total Vote   56,807   Poll 74.8%
*Member of last parliament
Con Hold (10.8% Swing from Con to Lab)

SOUTH EAST CORNWALL   %
Breed, C. (LD)   27,044   47.1
Lightfoot, W. (Con)   20,564   35.8
Kirk, D. (Lab)   7,358   12.8
Wonnacott, J. (UKIP)   1,428   2.5
Dunbar, P. (MK)   573   1.0
Weights, B. (Lib)   268   0.5
Hartley, M. (NLP)   197   0.3
LD majority   6,480   11.28%
Electorate   75,825
Total Vote   57,432   Poll 75.5%
LD Gain (12.1% Swing from Con to LD)

SOUTH HOLLAND AND THE DEEPINGS   %
Hayes, J. (Con)   24,691   49.3
Lewis, J. (Lab)   16,700   33.3
Millen, P. (LD)   7,836   15.6
Erwood, G. (Non-party)   902   1.8
Con majority   7,991   15.94%
Electorate   69,642
Total Vote   50,129   Poll 71.8%
Con Hold (8.5% Swing from Con to Lab)

SOUTH NORFOLK   %
*MacGregor, J. (Con) 24,935   40.2
Hacker, B. (LD)   17,557   28.3
Ross, J. (Lab)   16,188   26.1
Bateson, P. (Ref)   2,533   4.1
Ross-Wagenknecht,
  S. (Green)   484   0.8
Boddy, A. (UKIP)   400   0.6
Con majority   7,378   11.88%
Electorate   79,239
Total Vote   62,097   Poll 78.4%
*Member of last parliament
Con Hold (6.8% Swing from Con to LD)

SOUTH RIBBLE   %
Borrow, D. (Lab)   25,856   46.8
*Atkins, R. (Con)   20,772   37.6
Farron, T. (LD)   5,879   10.6
Adams, M. (Ref)   1,475   2.7
Ashton, N. (Lib)   1,127   2.0
Leadbetter, J. (NLP)   122   0.2
Lab majority   5,084   9.20%
Electorate   71,670
Total Vote   55,231   Poll 77.1%
*Member of last parliament
Lab Gain (12.1% Swing from Con to Lab)

SOUTH SHIELDS   %
*Clark, D. (Lab)   27,834   71.4
Hoban, M. (Con)   5,681   14.6
Ord, D. (LD)   3,429   8.8
Lorraine, A. (Ref)   1,660   4.3
Wilburn, I. (Shields)   374   1.0
Lab majority   22,153   56.83%
Electorate   62,261
Total Vote   38,978   Poll 62.6%
*Member of last parliament
Lab Hold (11.2% Swing from Con to Lab)

SOUTH STAFFORDSHIRE   %
*Cormack, P. (Con)   25,568   50.0
LeMaistre, J. (Lab)   17,747   34.7
Calder, J. (LD)   5,797   11.3

Carnell, P. (Ref)   2,002   3.9
Con majority   7,821   15.30%
Electorate   68,896
Total Vote   51,114   Poll 74.2%
*Member of last parliament
Con Hold (9% Swing from Con to Lab)

SOUTH SUFFOLK   %
*Yeo, T. (Con)   19,402   37.3
Bishop, P. (Lab)   15,227   29.3
Pollard, A. (LD)   14,395   27.7
de Chair, S. (Ref)   2,740   5.3
Holland, A. (NLP)   211   0.4
Con majority   4,175   8.03%
Electorate   67,323
Total Vote   51,975   Poll 77.2%
*Member of last parliament
Con Hold (10.7% Swing from Con to Lab)

SOUTH SWINDON   %
Drown, J. (Lab)   23,943   46.8
*Coombs, S. (Con)   18,298   35.8
Pajak, S. (LD)   7,371   14.4
McIntosh, D. (Ref)   1,273   2.5
Charman, R.
  (Route 66)   181   0.4
Buscombe, K. (NLP)   96   0.2
Lab majority   5,645   11.03%
Electorate   70,207
Total Vote   51,162   Poll 72.9%
*Member of last parliament
Lab Gain (14.6% Swing from Con to Lab)

SOUTH THANET   %
Ladyman, S. (Lab)   20,777   46.2
*Aitken, J. (Con)   17,899   39.8
Hewitt-Silk, B. (LD)   5,263   11.7
Crook, C. (UKIP)   631   1.4
Wheatley, D. (Green)   418   0.9
Lab majority   2,878   6.40%
Electorate   62,792
Total Vote   44,988   Poll 71.6%
*Member of last parliament
Lab Gain (15% Swing from Con to Lab)

SOUTH WEST BEDFORDSHIRE   %
*Madel, Sir D. (Con)   21,534   40.7
Date, A. (Lab)   21,402   40.5
Owen, S. (LD)   7,559   14.3
Hill, R. (Ref)   1,761   3.3
Wise, T. (UKIP)   446   0.8
Le Carpentier, A.
  (NLP)   162   0.3
Con majority   132   0.25%
Electorate   69,781
Total Vote   52,864   Poll 75.2%
*Member of last parliament
Con Hold (15.1% Swing from Con to Lab)

SOUTH WEST DEVON   %
*Streeter, G. (Con)   22,659   42.9
Mavin, C. (Lab)   15,262   28.9
Baldry, K. (LD)   12,542   23.8
Sadler, R. (Ref)   1,668   3.2
King, H. (UKIP)   491   0.9
Hyde, J. (NLP)   159   0.3

Con majority   7,397   14.0%
Electorate   69,293
Total Vote   52,781   Poll 76.2%
*Member of last parliament
Con Hold (13.9% Swing from Con to Lab)

SOUTH WEST HERTFORDSHIRE   %
*Page, R. (Con)   25,462   46.0
Wilson, M. (Lab)   15,441   27.9
Shaw, A. (LD)   12,381   22.3
Millward, T. (Ref)   1,853   3.3
Adamson, C. (NLP)   274   0.5
Con majority   10,021   18.08%
Electorate   71,671
Total Vote   55,411   Poll 76.8%
*Member of last parliament
Con Hold (11.8% Swing from Con to Lab)

SOUTH WEST NORFOLK   %
*Shephard, G. (Con)   24,694   42.0
Heffernan, A. (Lab)   22,230   37.8
Buckton, D. (LD)   8,178   13.9
Hoare, R. (Ref)   3,694   6.3
Con majority   2,464   4.19%
Electorate   80,236
Total Vote   58,796   Poll 73.2%
*Member of last parliament
Con Hold (11.8% Swing from Con to Lab)

SOUTH WEST SURREY   %
*Bottomley, V. (Con)   25,165   44.6
Sherlock, N. (LD)   22,471   39.8
Leicester, M. (Lab)   5,333   9.4
Clementson, J. (Ref)   2,830   5.0
Kirby, P. (UKIP)   401   0.7
Quintavalle, J.
  (Pro-Life)   258   0.5
Con majority   2,694   4.77%
Electorate   72,350
Total Vote   56,458   Poll 78%
*Member of last parliament
Con Hold (10.1% Swing from Con to LD)

SOUTHAMPTON ITCHEN   %
*Denham, J. (Lab)   29,498   54.8
Fleet, P. (Con)   15,289   28.4
Harrison, D. (LD)   6,289   11.7
Clegg, J. (Ref)   1,660   3.1
Rose, K. (SLP)   628   1.2
Hoar, C. (UKIP)   172   0.3
Marsh, G. (Soc)   113   0.2
Barry, R. (NLP)   110   0.2
McDermott, F.
  (Pro-Life)   99   0.2
Lab majority   14,209   26.38%
Electorate   76,869
Total Vote   53,858   Poll 70.6%
*Member of last parliament
Lab Hold (12.3% Swing from Con to Lab)

SOUTHAMPTON TEST   %
Whitehead, A. (Lab) 28,396   54.1
*Hill, Sir J. (Con)   14,712   28.1
Dowden, A. (LD)   7,171   13.7
Day, P. (Ref)   1,397   2.7
Marks, H. (Cannabis)   388   0.7

McCabe, A. (UKIP) 219 0.4
Taylor, P. (Glow) 81 0.2
Sinel, J. (NLP) 77 0.1
Lab majority 13,684 26.09%
Electorate 72,983
Total Vote 52,441 Poll 71.2%
*Member of last parliament
Lab Win (10.5% Swing from Con to Lab)

SOUTHEND WEST %
*Amess, D. (Con) 18,029 38.8
Stimson, N. (LD) 15,414 33.1
Harley, A. (Lab) 10,600 22.8
Webster, C. (Ref) 1,734 3.7
Lee, B. (UKIP) 636 1.4
Warburton, P. (NLP) 101 0.2
Con majority 2,615 5.62%
Electorate 66,493
Total Vote 46,514 Poll 69.8%
*Member of last parliament
Con Hold (9.1% Swing from Con to LD)

SOUTHPORT %
Fearn, R. (LD) 24,346 48.1
*Banks, M. (Con) 18,186 35.9
Norman, S. (Lab) 6,129 12.1
Buckle, F. (Ref) 1,368 2.7
Ashton, S. (Lib) 386 0.8
Lines, E. (NLP) 93 0.2
Middleton, M.
(Nat Dem) 92 0.2
LD majority 6,160 12.17%
Electorate 70,194
Total Vote 50,600 Poll 72.1%
*Member of last parliament
LD Gain (8.9% Swing from Con to LD)

SPELTHORNE %
*Wilshire, D. (Con) 23,306 44.9
Dibble, K. (Lab) 19,833 38.2
Glynn, E. (LD) 6,821 13.1
Coleman, B. (Ref) 1,495 2.9
Fowler, J. (UKIP) 462 0.9
Con majority 3,473 6.69%
Electorate 70,562
Total Vote 51,917 Poll 73.6%
*Member of last parliament
Con Hold (14.5% Swing from Con to Lab)

ST ALBANS %
Pollard, K. (Lab) 21,338 42.0
Rutley, D. (Con) 16,879 33.2
Rowlands, A. (LD) 10,692 21.0
Warrilow, J. (Ref) 1,619 3.2
Craigen, S. (Dream) 166 0.3
Docker, I. (NLP) 111 0.2
Lab majority 4,459 8.78%
Electorate 65,560
Total Vote 50,805 Poll 77.5%
Lab Gain (14.7% Swing from Con to Lab)

ST HELENS NORTH %
Watts, D. (Lab) 31,953 64.9
Walker, P. (Con) 8,536 17.3
Beirne, J. (LD) 6,270 12.7
Johnson, D. (Ref) 1,276 2.6

Waugh, R. (SLP) 833 1.7
Rudin, R. (UKIP) 363 0.7
Lab majority 23,417 47.57%
Electorate 71,380
Total Vote 49,231 Poll 69%
Lab Hold (9.1% Swing from Con to Lab)

ST HELENS SOUTH %
*Bermingham, G.
(Lab) 30,367 68.6
Russell, M. (Con) 6,628 15.0
Spencer, B. (LD) 5,919 13.4
Holdaway, W. (Ref) 1,165 2.6
Jump, H. (NLP) 179 0.4
Lab majority 23,739 53.64%
Electorate 66,526
Total Vote 44,258 Poll 66.5%
*Member of last parliament
Lab Hold (8.5% Swing from Con to Lab)

ST IVES %
George, A. (LD) 23,966 44.5
Rogers, W. (Con) 16,796 31.2
Fegan, C. (Lab) 8,184 15.2
Faulkner, M. (Ref) 3,714 6.9
Garnier, P. (UKIP) 567 1.1
Stephens, G. (Lib) 425 0.8
Lippiatt, K. (Radical) 178 0.3
Hitchins, W. (Male) 71 0.1
LD majority 7,170 13.30%
Electorate 71,680
Total Vote 53,901 Poll 75%
LD Gain (8.1% Swing from Con to LD)

STAFFORD %
Kidney, D. (Lab) 24,606 47.5
Cameron, D. (Con) 20,292 39.2
Hornby, P. (LD) 5,480 10.6
Culley, S. (Ref) 1,146 2.2
May, A. (Loony) 248 0.5
Lab majority 4,314 8.33%
Electorate 67,555
Total Vote 51,772 Poll 76.6%
Lab Gain (10.7% Swing from Con to Lab)

**STAFFORDSHIRE
MOORLANDS** %
Atkins, C. (Lab) 26,686 52.2
Ashworth, A. (Con) 16,637 32.5
Jebb, C. (LD) 6,191 12.1
Stanworth, D. (Ref) 1,603 3.1
Lab majority 10,049 19.66%
Electorate 66,095
Total Vote 51,117 Poll 77.3%
Lab Win (8.7% Swing from Con to Lab)

STALYBRIDGE AND HYDE %
*Pendry, T. (Lab) 25,363 58.9
de Bois, N. (Con) 10,557 24.5
Cross, M. (LD) 5,169 12.0
Clapham, R. (Ref) 1,992 4.6
Lab majority 14,806 34.37%
Electorate 65,468
Total Vote 43,081 Poll 65.7%
*Member of last parliament
Lab Hold (9.3% Swing from Con to Lab)

STEVENAGE %
Follett, B. (Lab) 28,440 55.3
*Wood, T. (Con) 16,858 32.8
Wilcock, A. (LD) 4,588 8.9
Coburn, J. (Ref) 1,194 2.3
Bundy, D. (Pro-Life) 196 0.4
Calcraft, A. (NLP) 110 0.2
Lab majority 11,582 22.54%
Electorate 66,889
Total Vote 51,386 Poll 76.8%
*Member of last parliament
Lab Gain (13.9% Swing from Con to Lab)

STIRLING %
McGuire, A. (Lab) 20,382 47.4
*Forsyth, M. (Con) 13,971 32.5
Dow, E. (SNP) 5,752 13.4
Tough, A. (LD) 2,675 6.2
McMurdo, W.
(UKIP) 154 0.4
Olsen, E. (Value) 24 0.1
Lab majority 6,411 14.92%
Electorate 52,491
Total Vote 42,958 Poll 81.8%
*Member of last parliament
Lab Gain (7.7% Swing from Con to Lab)

STOCKPORT %
*Coffey, A. (Lab) 29,338 62.9
Fitzsimmons, S.
(Con) 10,426 22.3
Roberts, S. (LD) 4,951 10.6
Morley-Scott, W.
(Ref) 1,280 2.7
Southern, G. (SLP) 255 0.5
Newitt, C. (Loony) 213 0.5
Dronsfield, C. (Ind) 206 0.4
Lab majority 18,912 40.52%
Electorate 65,232
Total Vote 46,669 Poll 71.3%
*Member of last parliament
Lab Hold (15.2% Swing from Con to Lab)

STOCKTON NORTH %
*Cook, F. (Lab) 29,726 66.8
Johnston, B. (Con) 8,369 18.8
Fletcher, S. (LD) 4,816 10.8
McConnell, K.
(Ref) 1,563 3.5
Lab majority 21,357 48.02%
Electorate 64,380
Total Vote 44,474 Poll 69%
*Member of last parliament
Lab Hold (13.5% Swing from Con to Lab)

STOCKTON SOUTH %
Taylor, D. (Lab) 28,790 55.2
*Devlin, T. (Con) 17,205 33.0
Monck, L. (LD) 4,721 9.1
Horner, J. (Ref) 1,400 2.7
Lab majority 11,585 22.66%
Electorate 68,470
Total Vote 52,116 Poll 76.1%
*Member of last parliament
Lab Gain (15.8% Swing from Con to Lab)

STOKE-ON-TRENT CENTRAL

		%
*Fisher, M. (Lab)	26,662	66.2
Jones, D. (Con)	6,738	16.7
Fordham, E. (LD)	4,809	11.9
Stanyer, P. (Ref)	1,071	2.7
Coleman, M. (BNP)	606	1.5
Oborski, F. (Lib)	359	0.9
Lab majority	19,924	49.51%
Electorate	64,113	
Total Vote	40,245	Poll 62.5%

*Member of last parliament
Lab Hold (9.7% Swing from Con to Lab)

STOKE-ON-TRENT NORTH

		%
*Walley, J. (Lab)	25,190	65.1
Day, C. (Con)	7,798	20.2
Jebb, H. (LD)	4,141	10.7
Tobin, J. (Ref)	1,537	4.0
Lab majority	17,392	44.98%
Electorate	59,030	
Total Vote	38,666	Poll 65.4%

*Member of last parliament
Lab Hold (11.9% Swing from Con to Lab)

STOKE-ON-TRENT SOUTH

		%
*Stevenson, G. (Lab)	28,645	62.0
Scott, S. (Con)	10,342	22.4
Barnett, P. (LD)	4,710	10.2
Adams, R. (Ref)	1,103	2.4
Micklem, A. (Lib)	580	1.3
Batkin, S. (BNP)	568	1.2
Lawrence, B. (Nat Dem)	288	0.6
Lab majority	18,303	39.59%
Electorate	69,968	
Total Vote	46,236	Poll 66%

*Member of last parliament
Lab Hold (13.3% Swing from Con to Lab)

STONE

		%
*Cash, W. (Con)	24,859	46.8
Wakefield, J. (Lab)	21,041	39.6
Stamp, B. (LD)	6,392	12.0
Winfield, A. (Lib)	545	1.0
Grice, D. (NLP)	237	0.4
Con majority	3,818	7.19%
Electorate	68,242	
Total Vote	53,074	Poll 77.8%

*Member of last parliament
Con Hold (10% Swing from Con to Lab)

STOURBRIDGE

		%
Shipley, D. (Lab)	23,452	47.2
*Hawksley, W. (Con)	17,807	35.8
Bramall, C. (LD)	7,123	14.3
Quick, P. (Ref)	1,319	2.7
Lab majority	5,645	11.36%
Electorate	64,966	
Total Vote	49,701	Poll 76.4%

*Member of last parliament
Lab Gain (11% Swing from Con to Lab)

STRANGFORD

		%
*Taylor, J. (UUP)	18,431	44.3
Robinson, I. (DUP)	12,579	30.2
McCarthy, K. (APNI)	5,467	13.1

STRATFORD-ON-AVON

		%
O'Reilly, P. (SDLP)	2,775	6.7
Chalk, G. (Con)	1,743	4.2
O Fachtna, G. (SF)	503	1.2
Mullins, S. (NLP)	121	0.3
UUP majority	5,852	14.06%
Electorate	69,980	
Total Vote	41,619	Poll 59.5%

*Member of last parliament
UUP Hold (7.6% Swing from UUP to DUP)

STRATFORD-ON-AVON

		%
Maples, J. (Con)	29,967	48.3
Juned, S. (LD)	15,861	25.5
Stacey, S. (Lab)	12,754	20.5
Hilton, A. (Ref)	2,064	3.3
Spilsbury, J. (UKIP)	556	0.9
Brewster, J. (NLP)	307	0.5
Marcus, S. (SFDC)	306	0.5
Miller, S. (ProLife)	284	0.5
Con majority	14,106	22.72%
Electorate	81,434	
Total Vote	62,099	Poll 76.3%

Con Re-gain (5.2% Swing from Con to LD)

STRATHKELVIN AND BEARSDEN

		%
*Galbraith, S. (Lab)	26,278	52.9
McCormick, G. (SNP)	9,986	20.1
Sharpe, D. (Con)	8,111	16.3
Morrison, J. (LD)	4,843	9.7
Wilson, D. (Ref)	339	0.7
Fisher, C. (NLP)	155	0.3
Lab majority	16,292	32.8%
Electorate	62,974	
Total Vote	49,712	Poll 78.9%

*Member of last parliament
Lab Hold (9.6% Swing from Con to Lab)

STREATHAM

		%
*Hill, K. (Lab)	28,181	62.8
Noad, E. (Con)	9,758	21.7
O'Brien, R. (LD)	6,082	13.6
Wall, J. (Ref)	864	1.9
Lab majority	18,423	41.04%
Electorate	74,509	
Total Vote	44,885	Poll 59%

*Member of last parliament
Lab Hold (15% Swing from Con to Lab)

STRETFORD AND URMSTON

		%
Hughes, B. (Lab)	28,480	58.5
Gregory, J. (Con)	14,840	30.5
Bridges, J. (LD)	3,978	8.2
Dore, C. (Ref)	1,397	2.9
Lab majority	13,640	28.01%
Electorate	69,913	
Total Vote	48,695	Poll 69.7%

Lab Hold (9.9% Swing from Con to Lab)

STROUD

		%
Drew, D. (Lab/Co-op)	26,170	42.7
*Knapman, R. (Con)	23,260	37.9
Hodgkinson, P. (LD)	9,502	15.5
Marjoram, J. (Green)	2,415	3.9

Lab/Co-op		
majority	2,910	4.74%
Electorate	77,494	
Total Vote	61,347	Poll 78.8%

*Member of last parliament
Lab/Co-op Gain (10.8% Swing from Con to Lab)

SUFFOLK COASTAL

		%
*Gummer, J. (Con)	21,696	38.6
Campbell, M. (Lab)	18,442	32.8
Jones, A. (LD)	12,036	21.4
Caulfield, S. (Ref)	3,416	6.1
Slade, T. (Green)	514	0.9
Kaplan, F. (NLP)	152	0.3
Con majority	3,254	5.78%
Electorate	74,219	
Total Vote	56,256	Poll 75.8%

*Member of last parliament
Con Hold (11.7% Swing from Con to Lab)

SUNDERLAND NORTH

		%
*Etherington, W. (Lab)	26,067	68.2
Selous, A. (Con)	6,370	16.7
Pryke, G. (LD)	3,973	10.4
Nicholson, M. (Ref)	1,394	3.6
Newby, K. (Loony)	409	1.1
Lab majority	19,697	51.55%
Electorate	64,711	
Total Vote	38,213	Poll 59.1%

*Member of last parliament
Lab Hold (9.9% Swing from Con to Lab)

SUNDERLAND SOUTH

		%
*Mullin, C. (Lab)	27,174	68.1
Schofield, T. (Con)	7,536	18.9
Lennox, J. (LD)	4,606	11.5
Wilkinson, A. (UKIP)	609	1.5
Lab majority	19,638	49.19%
Electorate	67,937	
Total Vote	39,925	Poll 58.8%

*Member of last parliament
Lab Hold (10.5% Swing from Con to Lab)

SURREY HEATH

		%
*Hawkins, N. (Con)	28,231	51.6
Newman, D. (LD)	11,944	21.8
Jones, S. (Lab)	11,511	21.0
Gale, J. (Ref)	2,385	4.4
Squire, M. (UKIP)	653	1.2
Con majority	16,287	29.76%
Electorate	73,813	
Total Vote	54,724	Poll 74.1%

*Member of last parliament
Con Hold (5.4% Swing from Con to LD)

SUTTON AND CHEAM

		%
Burstow, P. (LD)	19,919	42.3
*Maitland, O. (Con)	17,822	37.8
Allison, M. (Lab)	7,280	15.5
Atkinson, P. (Ref)	1,784	3.8
McKie, S. (UKIP)	191	0.4
Wright, D. (NLP)	96	0.2
LD majority	2,097	4.45%
Electorate	62,785	
Total Vote	47,092	Poll 75.1%

*Member of last parliament
LD Gain (12.9% Swing from Con to LD)

SUTTON COLDFIELD

		%
*Fowler, N. (Con)	27,373	52.2
York, A. (Lab)	12,488	23.8
Whorwood, J. (LD)	10,139	19.3
Hope, D. (Ref)	2,401	4.6
Con majority 14,885		28.41%
Electorate	71,864	
Total Vote	52,401	Poll 72.9%

*Member of last parliament
Con Hold (10.9% Swing from Con to Lab)

SWANSEA EAST

		%
*Anderson, D. (Lab)	29,151	75.4
Dibble, C. (Con)	3,582	9.3
Jones, E. (LD)	3,440	8.9
Pooley, M. (PC)	1,308	3.4
Maggs, C. (Ref)	904	2.3
Job, R. (Soc)	289	0.7
Lab majority 25,569		66.11%
Electorate	57,373	
Total Vote	38,674	Poll 67.2%

*Member of last parliament
Lab Hold (6.8% Swing from Con to Lab)

SWANSEA WEST

		%
*Williams, A. (Lab)	22,748	56.2
Baker, A. (Con)	8,289	20.5
Newbury, J. (LD)	5,872	14.5
Lloyd, D. (PC)	2,675	6.6
Proctor, D. (SLP)	885	2.2
Lab majority 14,459		35.73%
Electorate	58,703	
Total Vote	40,469	Poll 68.2%

*Member of last parliament
Lab Hold (7.1% Swing from Con to Lab)

SWINDON NORTH

		%
Wills, M. (Lab)	24,029	49.8
Opperman, G. (Con)	16,341	33.9
Evemy, M. (LD)	6,237	12.9
Goldsmith, G. (Ref)	1,533	3.2
Fisken, A. (NLP)	130	0.3
Lab majority 7,688		15.93%
Electorate	65,535	
Total Vote	48,270	Poll 73.6%

Lab Hold (7.1% Swing from Con to Lab)

TAMWORTH

		%
*Jenkins, B. (Lab)	25,808	51.8
Lightbown, A. (Con)	18,312	36.7
Pinkett, J. (LD)	4,025	8.1
Livesey, D. (Ref)	1,163	2.3
Lamb, C. (UKIP)	369	0.7
Twelvetrees, C. (Lib)	177	0.4
Lab majority 7,496		15.04%
Electorate	67,205	
Total Vote	49,854	Poll 74.2%

*Member of last parliament
Lab Win (12.6% Swing from Con to Lab)

TATTON

		%
Bell, M. (Ind)	29,354	60.2
*Hamilton, N. (Con)	18,277	37.5
Hill, S. (Ind)	295	0.6
Kinsey, S. (Ind)	187	0.4
Penhaul, B. (Miss M)	128	0.3

Muir, J. (Albion)	126	0.3
Kennedy, M. (NLP)	123	0.3
Bishop, D. (Byro)	116	0.2
Nicholas, R. (Ind)	113	0.2
Price, J. (Juice)	73	0.1
Ind majority 11,077		22.70%
Electorate	63,822	
Total Vote	48,792	Poll 76.5%

*Member of last parliament
Ind Gain

TAUNTON

		%
Ballard, J. (LD)	26,064	42.7
*Nicholson, D.		
(Con)	23,621	38.7
Lisgo, E. (Lab)	8,248	13.5
Ahern, B. (Ref)	2,760	4.5
Andrews, L. (BNP)	318	0.5
LD majority 2,443		4.00%
Electorate	79,783	
Total Vote	61,011	Poll 76.5%

*Member of last parliament
LD Gain (4.6% Swing from Con to LD)

TEIGNBRIDGE

		%
*Nicholls, P. (Con)	24,679	39.2
Younger-Ross, R.		
(LD)	24,398	38.8
Dann, S. (Lab)	11,311	18.0
Stokes, S. (UKIP)	1,601	2.5
Banwell, N. (Green)	817	1.3
Golding, L. (Dream)	139	0.2
Con majority 281		0.45%
Electorate	81,667	
Total Vote	62,945	Poll 76.9%

*Member of last parliament
Con Hold (7.3% Swing from Con to LD)

TELFORD

		%
*Grocott, B. (Lab)	21,456	57.8
Gentry, B. (Con)	10,166	27.4
Green, N. (LD)	4,371	11.8
Morris, C. (Ref)	1,119	3.0
Lab majority 11,290		30.42%
Electorate	56,558	
Total Vote	37,112	Poll 65.6%

*Member of last parliament
Lab Hold (5.5% Swing from Con to Lab)

TEWKESBURY

		%
Robertson, L. (Con)	23,859	45.8
Sewell, J. (LD)	14,625	28.0
Tustin, K. (Lab)	13,665	26.2
Con majority 9,234		17.71%
Electorate	68,208	
Total Vote	52,149	Poll 76.5%

Con Hold (0.5% Swing from Con to LD)

THURROCK

		%
*MacKinlay, A. (Lab)	29,896	63.3
Rosindell, A. (Con)	12,640	26.8
White, J. (LD)	3,843	8.1
Compobassi, P. (UKIP)	833	1.8
Lab majority 17,256		36.55%
Electorate	71,600	
Total Vote	47,212	Poll 65.8%

*Member of last parliament
Lab Hold (17.2% Swing from Con to Lab)

TIVERTON AND HONITON

		%
*Browning, A. (Con)	24,438	41.3
Barnard, J. (LD)	22,785	38.5
King, J. (Lab)	7,598	12.8
Lowings, S. (Ref)	2,952	5.0
Roach, J. (Lib)	635	1.1
McIvor, E. (Green)	485	0.8
Charles, D. (Nat Dem)	236	0.4
Con majority 1,653		2.80%
Electorate	75,744	
Total Vote	59,129	Poll 77.9%

*Member of last parliament
Con Hold (8.4% Swing from Con to LD)

TONBRIDGE AND MALLING

		%
*Stanley, J. (Con)	23,640	48.0
Withstandley, B.		
(Lab)	13,410	27.2
Brown, K. (LD)	9,467	19.2
Scrivener, J. (Ref)	2,005	4.1
Bullen, B. (UKIP)	502	1.0
Valente, G. (NLP)	205	0.4
Con majority 10,230		20.78%
Electorate	64,798	
Total Vote	49,229	Poll 75.6%

*Member of last parliament
Con Hold (11.5% Swing from Con to Lab)

TOOTING

		%
*Cox, T. (Lab)	27,516	59.7
Hutchings, J. (Con)	12,505	27.1
James, S. (LD)	4,320	9.4
Husband, A. (Ref)	829	1.8
Rattray, J. (Green)	527	1.1
Boddington, P. (BFAIR)	161	0.3
Koene, J. (Rights)	94	0.2
Bailey-Bond, D. (Dream)	83	0.2
Miller, P. (NLP)	70	0.2
Lab majority 15,011		32.56%
Electorate	66,653	
Total Vote	46,105	Poll 67.9%

*Member of last parliament
Lab Hold (12.3% Swing from Con to Lab)

TORBAY

		%
Sanders, A. (LD)	21,094	39.6
*Allason, R. (Con)	21,082	39.5
Morey, M. (Lab)	7,923	14.9
Booth, G. (UKIP)	1,962	3.7
Cowling, B. (Lib)	1,161	2.2
Wild, P. (Dream)	100	0.2
LD majority 12		0.02%
Electorate	72,258	
Total Vote	53,322	Poll 73.8%

*Member of last parliament
LD Gain (5.1% Swing from Con to LD)

TORFAEN

		%
*Murphy, P. (Lab)	29,863	69.1
Parish, N. (Con)	5,327	12.3
Gray, J. (LD)	5,249	12.1
Holler, D. (Ref)	1,245	2.9
Gough, R. (PC)	1,042	2.4
Coghill, R. (Green)	519	1.2
Lab majority 24,536		56.74%
Electorate	60,343	
Total Vote	43,245	Poll 71.6%

*Member of last parliament
Lab Hold (6.4% Swing from Con to Lab)

TORRIDGE AND WEST
DEVON		%
Burnett, J. (LD)	24,744	41.8
Liddell-Grainger, I.		
(Con)	22,787	38.5
Brenton, D. (Lab)	7,319	12.4
Lea, R. (Ref)	1,946	3.3
Jackson, M. (UKIP)	1,841	3.1
Pithouse, M. (Lib)	508	0.9
LD majority	1,957	3.31%
Electorate	75,919	
Total Vote	59,145	Poll 77.7%

LD Gain (4.4% Swing from Con to LD)

TOTNES		%
*Steen, A. (Con)	19,637	36.5
Chave, R. (LD)	18,760	34.9
Ellery, V. (Lab)	8,796	16.4
Cook, P. (Ref)	2,552	4.7
Venmore, C.		
(Loc C)	2,369	4.4
Thomas, H. (UKIP)	999	1.9
Pratt, A. (Green)	548	1.0
Golding, J. (Dream)	108	0.2
Con majority	877	1.63%
Electorate	70,473	
Total Vote	53,769	Poll 76%

*Member of last parliament

Con Hold (6.8% Swing from Con to LD)

TOTTENHAM		%
*Grant, B. (Lab)	26,121	69.3
Scantlebury, A.		
(Con)	5,921	15.7
Hughes, N. (LD)	4,064	10.8
Budge, P. (Green)	1,059	2.8
Tay, L. (Pro-Life)	210	0.6
Anglin, C. (WRP)	181	0.5
Kent, T. (SEP)	148	0.4
Lab majority	20,200	53.58%
Electorate	66,173	
Total Vote	37,704	Poll 55%

*Member of last parliament

Lab Hold (13.4% Swing from Con to Lab)

TRURO AND ST AUSTELL		%
*Taylor, M. (LD)	27,502	48.5
Badcock, N. (Con)	15,001	26.4
Dooley, M. (Lab)	8,697	15.3
Hearn, C. (Ref)	3,682	6.5
Haithwaite, A. (UKIP)	506	1.0
Robinson, D. (Green)	482	0.8
Hicks, D. (MK)	450	0.8
Yelland, L. (PP)	240	0.4
Boland, P. (NLP)	117	0.2
LD majority	12,501	22.03%
Electorate	76,824	
Total Vote	56,747	Poll 73.9%

*Member of last parliament

LD Hold (4.9% Swing from Con to LD)

TUNBRIDGE WELLS		%
*Norman, A. (Con)	21,853	45.2
Clayton, A. (LD)	14,347	29.7
Warner, P. (Lab)	9,879	20.4
Macpherson, T. (Ref)	1,858	3.8
Anderson-Smart, M.		
(UKIP)	264	0.5
Levy, P. (NLP)	153	0.3

Con majority	7,506	15.52%
Electorate	65,259	
Total Vote	48,354	Poll 74.1%

*Member of last parliament

Con Hold (5% Swing from Con to LD)

TWEEDDALE, ETTRICK AND
LAUDERDALE		%
Moore, M. (LD)	12,178	31.2
Geddes, K. (Lab)	10,689	27.4
Jack, A. (Con)	8,623	22.1
Goldie, I. (SNP)	6,671	17.1
Mowbray, C. (Ref)	406	1.0
Hein, J. (Lib)	387	1.0
Paterson, D. (NLP)	47	0.1
LD majority	1,489	3.8%
Electorate	50,891	
Total Vote	39,001	Poll 76.6%

LD Hold (7.4% Swing from LD to Lab)

TWICKENHAM		%
Cable, V. (LD)	26,237	45.1
*Jessel, T. (Con)	21,956	37.8
Tutchell, E. (Lab)	9,065	15.6
Harrison, M.		
(IndECR)	589	1.0
Haggar, T. (Dream)	155	0.3
Hardy, A. (NLP)	142	0.2
LD majority	4,281	7.36%
Electorate	73,281	
Total Vote	58,144	Poll 78.1%

*Member of last parliament

LD Gain (8.8% Swing from Con to LD)

TYNE BRIDGE		%
*Clelland, D. (Lab)	26,767	76.8
Lee, A. (Con)	3,861	11.1
Wallace, M. (LD)	2,785	8.0
Oswald, G. (Ref)	919	2.6
Brunskill, E. (Soc)	518	1.5
Lab majority	22,906	65.73%
Electorate	61,058	
Total Vote	34,850	Poll 57.1%

*Member of last parliament

Lab Hold (10.5% Swing from Con to Lab)

TYNEMOUTH		%
Campbell, A. (Lab)	28,318	55.4
Callanan, M. (Con)	17,045	33.3
Duffield, A. (LD)	4,509	8.8
Rook, C. (Ref)	819	1.6
Rogers, F. (UKIP)	462	0.9
Lab majority	11,273	22.04%
Electorate	66,341	
Total Vote	51,153	Poll 77%

Lab Gain (14.2% Swing from Con to Lab)

UPMINSTER		%
Darvill, K. (Lab)	19,085	46.2
*Bonsor, N. (Con)	16,315	39.5
Peskett, P. (LD)	3,919	9.5
Murray, T. (Ref)	2,000	4.8
Lab majority	2,770	6.70%
Electorate	57,149	
Total Vote	41,319	Poll 72.1%

*Member of last parliament

Lab Gain (15.4% Swing from Con to Lab)

UPPER BANN		%
*Trimble, D. (UUP)	20,836	43.6
Rodgers, B. (SDLP)	11,584	24.2
O'Hagan, B. (SF)	5,773	12.1
Carrick, M. (DUP)	5,482	11.5
Ramsey, W. (APNI)	3,017	6.3
French, T. (Workers)	554	1.2
Price, B. (Con)	433	0.9
Lyons, J. (NLP)	108	0.2
UUP majority	9,252	19.36%
Electorate	70,398	
Total Vote	47,787	Poll 67.9%

*Member of last parliament

UUP Hold (8.1% Swing from UUP to SDLP)

UXBRIDGE		%
*Shersby, M. (Con)	18,095	43.6
Williams, D. (Lab)	17,371	41.8
Malyan, A. (LD)	4,528	10.9
Aird, G. (Ref)	1,153	2.8
Leonard, J. (Soc)	398	1.0
Con majority	724	1.74%
Electorate	57,497	
Total Vote	41,545	Poll 72.3%

*Member of last parliament

Con Hold (12.8% Swing from Con to Lab)

VALE OF CLWYD		%
Ruane, C. (Lab)	20,617	52.7
Edwards, D. (Con)	11,662	29.8
Munford, D. (LD)	3,425	8.8
Kensler, G. (PC)	2,301	5.9
Vickers, S. (Ref)	834	2.1
Cooke, S. (UKIP)	293	0.7
Lab majority	8,955	22.88%
Electorate	52,418	
Total Vote	39,132	Poll 74.6%

Lab Gain (13.9% Swing from Con to Lab)

VALE OF GLAMORGAN		%
Smith, J. (Lab)	29,054	53.9
*Sweeney, W. (Con)	18,522	34.4
Campbell, S. (LD)	4,945	9.2
Corp, M. (PC)	1,393	2.6
Lab majority	10,532	19.53%
Electorate	67,213	
Total Vote	53,914	Poll 80%

*Member of last parliament

Lab Gain (9.8% Swing from Con to Lab)

VALE OF YORK		%
McIntosh, A. (Con)	23,815	44.7
Carter, M. (Lab)	14,094	26.5
Hall, C. (LD)	12,656	23.8
Fairclough, C. (Ref)	2,503	4.7
Pelton, T. (SDP)	197	0.4
Con majority	9,721	18.25%
Electorate	70,077	
Total Vote	53,265	Poll 76%

Con Hold (15.6% Swing from Con to Lab)

VAUXHALL		%
*Hoey, K. (Lab)	24,920	63.8
Kerr, K. (LD)	6,260	16.0
Bacon, R. (Con)	5,942	15.2
Driver, I. (SLP)	983	2.5

Collins, W. (Green) 864 2.2
Headicar, R. (Socialist) 97 0.2
Lab majority 18,660 47.77%
Electorate 70,402
Total Vote 39,066 Poll 53.5%
*Member of last parliament
Lab Hold (3.1% Swing from LD to Lab)

WAKEFIELD %
*Hinchliffe, D. (Lab) 28,977 57.4
Peacock, J. (Con) 14,373 28.5
Dale, D. (LD) 5,656 11.2
Shires, S. (Ref) 1,480 2.9
Lab majority 14,604 28.93%
Electorate 73,210
Total Vote 50,486 Poll 69%
*Member of last parliament
Lab Hold (10.6% Swing from Con to Lab)

WALLASEY %
*Eagle, A. (Lab) 30,264 64.6
Wilcock, M. (Con) 11,190 23.9
Reisdorf, P. (LD) 3,899 8.3
Hayes, R. (Ref) 1,490 3.2
Lab majority 19,074 40.72%
Electorate 67,714
Total Vote 46,843 Poll 73.5%
*Member of last parliament
Lab Hold (16.8% Swing from Con to Lab)

WALSALL NORTH %
*Winnick, D. (Lab) 24,517 56.6
Bird, M. (Con) 11,929 27.5
O'Brien, T. (LD) 4,050 9.4
Bennett, D. (Ref) 1,430 3.3
Pitt, M. (Ind) 911 2.1
Humphries, A. (NF) 465 1.1
Lab majority 12,588 29.07%
Electorate 67,587
Total Vote 43,302 Poll 64.1%
*Member of last parliament
Lab Hold (10.9% Swing from Con to Lab)

WALSALL SOUTH %
*George, B. (Lab) 25,024 57.9
Leek, L. (Con) 13,712 31.7
Harris, H. (LD) 2,698 6.2
Dent, T. (Ref) 1,662 3.8
Meads, L. (NLP) 149 0.3
Lab majority 11,312 26.16%
Electorate 64,221
Total Vote 43,245 Poll 67.3%
*Member of last parliament
Lab Hold (9.9% Swing from Con to Lab)

WALTHAMSTOW %
*Gerrard, N. (Lab) 25,287 63.1
Andrew, J. (Con) 8,138 20.3
Jackson, J. (LD) 5,491 13.7
Hargreaves, G. (Ref) 1,139 2.8
Lab majority 17,149 42.81%
Electorate 63,818
Total Vote 40,055 Poll 62.8%
*Member of last parliament
Lab Hold (17.9% Swing from Con to Lab)

WANSBECK %
Murphy, D. (Lab) 29,569 65.5
Thompson, A. (LD) 7,202 15.9
Green, P. (Con) 6,299 13.9
Gompertz, P. (Ref) 1,146 2.5
Best, N. (Green) 956 2.1
Lab majority 22,367 49.5%
Electorate 62,998
Total Vote 45,172 Poll 71.7%
Lab Hold (2.5% Swing from LD to Lab)

WANSDYKE %
Norris, D. (Lab) 24,117 44.1
Prisk, M. (Con) 19,318 35.3
Manning, J. (LD) 9,205 16.8
Clinton, K. (Ref) 1,327 2.4
Hunt, T. (UKIP) 438 0.8
House, P. (Loony) 225 0.4
Lincoln, S. (NLP) 92 0.2
Lab majority 4,799 8.77%
Electorate 69,032
Total Vote 54,722 Poll 79.1%
Lab Gain (14.4% Swing from Con to Lab)

WANTAGE %
*Jackson, R. (Con) 22,311 39.8
Wilson, C. (Lab) 16,222 28.9
Riley, J. (LD) 14,862 26.5
Rising, S. (Ref) 1,549 2.8
Kennet, M. (Green) 640 1.1
Tolstoy, N. (UKIP) 465 0.8
Con majority 6,089 10.86%
Electorate 71,657
Total Vote 56,049 Poll 78.2%
*Member of last parliament
Con Hold (11.9% Swing from Con to Lab)

WARLEY %
*Spellar, J. (Lab) 24,813 63.8
Pincher, C. (Con) 9,362 24.1
Pursehouse, J. (LD) 3,777 9.7
Gamre, K. (Ref) 941 2.4
Lab majority 15,451 39.73%
Electorate 59,758
Total Vote 38,893 Poll 64.9%
*Member of last parliament
Lab Hold (10.5% Swing from Con to Lab)

WARRINGTON NORTH %
Jones, H. (Lab) 31,827 62.1
Lacey, R. (Con) 12,300 24.0
Greenhalgh, I. (LD) 5,308 10.4
Smith, A. (Ref) 1,816 3.5
Lab majority 19,527 38.10%
Electorate 72,694
Total Vote 51,251 Poll 70.5%
Lab Hold (9.9% Swing from Con to Lab)

WARRINGTON SOUTH %
Southworth, H. (Lab) 28,721 52.1
Grayling, C. (Con) 17,914 32.5
Walker, P. (LD) 7,199 13.1
Kelley, G. (Ref) 1,082 2.0
Ross, S. (NLP) 166 0.3
Lab majority 10,807 19.62%
Electorate 72,262
Total Vote 55,082 Poll 76.2%
Lab Win (12.3% Swing from Con to Lab)

WARWICK AND LEAMINGTON %
Plaskitt, J. (Lab) 26,747 44.5
*Smith, D. (Con) 23,349 38.9
Hicks, N. (LD) 7,133 11.9
Davis, V. (Ref) 1,484 2.5
Baptie, P. (Green) 764 1.3
Warwick, G. (UKIP) 306 0.5
Gibbs, M. (EDP) 183 0.3
McCarthy, R. (NLP) 125 0.2
Lab majority 3,398 5.65%
Electorate 79,374
Total Vote 60,091 Poll 75.2%
*Member of last parliament
Lab Gain (12% Swing from Con to Lab)

WATFORD %
Ward, C. (Lab) 25,019 45.3
Gordon, R. (Con) 19,227 34.8
Canning, A. (LD) 9,272 16.8
Roe, P. (Ref) 1,484 2.7
Davis, L. (NLP) 234 0.4
Lab majority 5,792 10.49%
Electorate 74,015
Total Vote 55,236 Poll 74.6%
Lab Gain (12.3% Swing from Con to Lab)

WAVENEY %
Blizzard, R. (Lab) 31,486 56.0
*Porter, D. (Con) 19,393 34.5
Thomas, C. (LD) 5,054 9.0
Clark, N. (Ind) 318 0.6
Lab majority 12,093 21.50%
Electorate 75,266
Total Vote 56,251 Poll 74.6%
*Member of last parliament
Lab Gain (14.4% Swing from Con to Lab)

WEALDEN %
*Johnson Smith, G. (Con) 29,417 49.8
Skinner, M. (LD) 15,213 25.7
Levine, N. (Lab) 10,185 17.2
Taplin, B. (Ref) 3,527 6.0
English, M. (UKIP) 569 1.0
Cragg, P. (NLP) 188 0.3
Con majority 14,204 24.03%
Electorate 79,519
Total Vote 59,099 Poll 74.3%
*Member of last parliament
Con Hold (5.3% Swing from Con to LD)

WEAVER VALE %
*Hall, M. (Lab) 27,244 56.4
Byrne, J. (Con) 13,796 28.6
Griffiths, T. (LD) 5,949 12.3
Cockfield, R. (Ref) 1,312 2.7
Lab majority 13,448 27.84%
Electorate 66,011
Total Vote 48,301 Poll 73%
*Member of last parliament
Lab Hold (7.4% Swing from Con to Lab)

WELLINGBOROUGH %
Stinchcombe, P.
  (Lab) 24,854 44.2
*Fry, P. (Con) 24,667 43.8
Smith, P. (LD) 5,279 9.4
Ellwood, A. (UKIP) 1,192 2.1
Lorys, A. (NLP) 297 0.5
Lab majority 187 0.33%
Electorate 74,955
Total Vote 56,289 Poll 74.8%
*Member of last parliament
Lab Gain (9.9% Swing from Con to Lab)

WELLS %
*Heathcoat-Amory,
  D. (Con) 22,208 39.4
Gold, P. (LD) 21,680 38.5
Eavis, M. (Lab) 10,204 18.1
Phelps, P. (Ref) 2,196 3.9
Royse, L. (NLP) 92 0.1
Con majority 528 0.94%
Electorate 72,178
Total Vote 56,380 Poll 77.8%
*Member of last parliament
Con Hold (5.3% Swing from Con to LD)

WELWYN HATFIELD %
Johnson, M. (Lab) 24,936 47.1
*Evans, D. (Con) 19,341 36.5
Schwartz, R. (LD) 7,161 13.5
Cox, V. (WelHat) 1,263 2.4
Harrold, H. (Pro-Life) 267 0.5
Lab majority 5,595 10.56%
Electorate 67,395
Total Vote 52,968 Poll 78.6%
*Member of last parliament
Lab Gain (11% Swing from Con to Lab)

WENTWORTH %
Healey, J. (Lab) 30,225 72.3
Hamer, K. (Con) 6,266 15.0
Charters, J. (LD) 3,867 9.3
Battley, A. (Ref) 1,423 3.4
Lab majority 23,959 57.34%
Electorate 63,951
Total Vote 41,781 Poll 65.3%
Lab Hold (5.3% Swing from Con to Lab)

WEST ABERDEENSHIRE AND
KINCARDINE %
Smith, Sir R. (LD) 17,742 41.1
*Kynoch, G. (Con) 15,080 34.9
Mowatt, J. (SNP) 5,639 13.0
Khan, Q. (Lab) 3,923 9.1
Ball, S. (Ref) 805 1.9
LD majority 2,662 6.16%
Electorate 59,123
Total Vote 43,189 Poll 73%
*Member of last parliament
LD Gain (8.3% Swing from Con to LD)

WEST BROMWICH EAST %
*Snape, P. (Lab) 23,710 57.2
Matsell, B. (Con) 10,126 24.4
Smith, M. (LD) 6,179 14.9
Mulley, G. (Ref) 1,472 3.5

Lab majority 13,584 32.74%
Electorate 63,401
Total Vote 41,487 Poll 65.4%
*Member of last parliament
Lab Hold (11.4% Swing from Con to Lab)

WEST BROMWICH WEST %
*Boothroyd, B.
  (Speaker) 23,969 65.3
Silvester, R. (Ind Lab) 8,546 23.3
Edwards, S.
  (Nat Dem) 4,181 11.4
Speaker
  majority 15,423 42.03%
Electorate 67,496
Total Vote 36,696 Poll 54.3%
*Member of last parliament
Speaker Hold (0% Swing from to)

WEST DERBYSHIRE %
*McLoughlin, P. (Con) 23,945 42.1
Clamp, S. (Lab) 19,060 33.5
Seeley, C. (LD) 9,940 17.5
Gouriet, J. (Ref) 2,499 4.4
Meynell, G. (IndGreen) 593 1.0
Price, H. (UKIP) 484 0.9
Delves, N. (Loony) 281 0.5
Kyslun, M. (Ind) 81 0.1
Con majority 4,885 8.59%
Electorate 72,716
Total Vote 56,883 Poll 78.1%
*Member of last parliament
Con Hold (11.6% Swing from Con to Lab)

WEST DORSET %
Letwin, O. (Con) 22,036 41.1
Legg, R. (LD) 20,196 37.7
Bygraves, R. (Lab) 9,491 17.7
Jenkins, P. (UKIP) 1,590 3.0
Griffiths, M. (NLP) 239 0.4
Con majority 1,840 3.44%
Electorate 70,369
Total Vote 53,552 Poll 76%
Con Hold (5.6% Swing from Con to LD)

WEST HAM %
*Banks, T. (Lab) 24,531 72.9
MacGregor, M. (Con) 5,037 15.0
McDonough, S. (LD) 2,479 7.4
Francis, K. (BNP) 1,198 3.6
Jug, T. (Loony) 300 0.9
Rainbow, J. (Dream) 116 0.3
Lab majority 19,494 57.91%
Electorate 57,058
Total Vote 33,661 Poll 58.4%
*Member of last parliament
Lab Hold (15% Swing from Con to Lab)

WEST LANCASHIRE %
*Pickthall, C. (Lab) 33,022 60.3
Varley, C. (Con) 15,903 29.1
Wood, A. (LD) 3,938 7.2
Carter, M. (Ref) 1,025 1.9
Collins, J. (UKIP) 449 0.8
Hill, D. (Home Rule) 392 0.7
Lab majority 17,119 31.28%
Electorate 73,175
Total Vote 54,729 Poll 74.8%
*Member of last parliament
Lab Hold (12.1% Swing from Con to Lab)

WEST RENFREWSHIRE %
*Graham, T. (Lab) 18,525 46.6
Campbell, C. (SNP) 10,546 26.5
Cormack, C. (Con) 7,387 18.6
MacPherson, B.
  (LD) 3,045 7.7
Lindsay, S. (Ref) 283 0.7
Lab majority 7,979 20.05%
Electorate 52,348
Total Vote 39,786 Poll 75.9%
*Member of last parliament
Lab Hold (1.1% Swing from Lab to SNP)

WEST SUFFOLK %
*Spring, R. (Con) 20,081 40.9
Jeffreys, M. (Lab) 18,214 37.1
Graves, A. (LD) 6,892 14.0
Carver, J. (Ref) 3,724 7.6
Shearer, A. (NLP) 171 0.3
Con majority 1,867 3.80%
Electorate 68,638
Total Vote 49,082 Poll 71.5%
*Member of last parliament
Con Hold (13% Swing from Con to Lab)

WEST TYRONE %
Thompson, W.
  (UUP) 16,003 34.6
Byrne, J. (SDLP) 14,842 32.1
Doherty, P. (SF) 14,280 30.9
Gormley, A. (APNI) 829 1.8
Owens, T. (Workers) 230 0.5
Johnstone, R. (NLP) 91 0.2
UUP majority 1,161 2.51%
Electorate 58,168
Total Vote 46,275 Poll 79.6%
UUP Gain (0% Swing from to)

WEST WORCESTERSHIRE %
*Spicer, M. (Con) 22,223 45.0
Hadley, M. (LD) 18,377 37.2
Stone, N. (Lab) 7,738 15.7
Cameron, S.
  (Green) 1,006 2.0
Con majority 3,846 7.79%
Electorate 64,712
Total Vote 49,344 Poll 76.3%
*Member of last parliament
Con Hold (8.8% Swing from Con to LD)

WESTBURY %
*Faber, D. (Con) 23,037 40.6
Miller, J. (LD) 16,969 29.9
Small, K. (Lab) 11,969 21.1
Hawkins, G. (Lib) 1,956 3.4
Hawkings-Byass, N.
  (Ref) 1,909 3.4
Westbury, R.
  (UKIP) 771 1.4
Haysom, C. (NLP) 140 0.2
Con majority 6,068 10.69%
Electorate 74,301
Total Vote 56,751 Poll 76.2%
*Member of last parliament
Con Hold (3.8% Swing from Con to LD)

WESTERN ISLES

		%
*MacDonald, C. (Lab)	8,955	55.6
Gillies, A. (SNP)	5,379	33.4
McGrigor, J. (Con)	1,071	6.6
Mitchison, N. (LD)	495	3.1
Lionel, R. (Ref)	206	1.3
Lab majority	3,576	22.20%
Electorate	22,983	
Total Vote	16,106	Poll 70.1%

*Member of last parliament

Lab Hold (5.8% Swing from SNP to Lab)

WESTMORLAND AND LONSDALE

		%
Collins, T. (Con)	21,463	42.3
Collins, S. (LD)	16,942	33.4
Harding, J. (Lab)	10,452	20.6
Smith, M. (Ref)	1,924	3.8
Con majority	4,521	8.90%
Electorate	68,389	
Total Vote	50,781	Poll 74.3%

Con Hold (10.3% Swing from Con to LD)

WESTON-SUPER-MARE

		%
Cotter, B. (LD)	21,407	40.1
Daly, M. (Con)	20,133	37.7
Kraft, D. (Lab)	9,557	17.9
Sewell, T. (Ref)	2,280	4.3
LD majority	1,274	2.39%
Electorate	72,445	
Total Vote	53,377	Poll 73.7%

LD Gain (6% Swing from Con to LD)

WIGAN

		%
*Stott, R. (Lab)	30,043	68.6
Loveday, M. (Con)	7,400	16.9
Beswick, T. (LD)	4,390	10.0
Bradborne, A. (Ref)	1,450	3.3
Maile, C. (Green)	442	1.0
Aycliffe, W. (NLP)	94	0.2
Lab majority	22,643	51.67%
Electorate	64,689	
Total Vote	43,819	Poll 67.7%

*Member of last parliament

Lab Hold (8.2% Swing from Con to Lab)

WIMBLEDON

		%
Casale, R. (Lab)	20,674	42.8
*Goodson-Wickes, C. (Con)	17,684	36.6
Willott, A. (LD)	8,014	16.6
Abid, H. (Ref)	993	2.1
Thacker, R. (Green)	474	1.0
Davies, S. (Pro-Life)	346	0.7
Kirby, M. (Mongolian)	112	0.2
Stacey, G. (Dream)	47	0.1
Lab majority	2,990	6.18%
Electorate	64,070	
Total Vote	48,344	Poll 73.3%

*Member of last parliament

Lab Gain (17.9% Swing from Con to Lab)

WINCHESTER

		%
Oaten, M. (LD)	26,100	42.0
*Malone, G. (Con)	26,098	42.0
Davies, P. (Lab)	6,528	10.6
Strand, P. (Ref)	1,598	2.6

Huggett, R. (Top)	640	1.0
Rumsey, D. (UKIP)	476	0.8
Stockton, P. (Loony)	307	0.5
Browne, J. (Ind AFE)	307	0.5
LD majority	2	0.00%
Electorate	78,884	
Total Vote	62,054	Poll

*Member of last parliament

LD Hold (0.0% Swing from Con to LD)

WINDSOR

		%
*Trend, M. (Con)	24,476	48.2
Fox, C. (LD)	14,559	28.7
Williams, A. (Lab)	9,287	18.3
McDermott, J. (Ref)	1,676	3.3
Bradshaw, P. (Lib)	388	0.8
Bigg, E. (UKIP)	302	0.6
Parr, R. (Dynamic)	93	0.2
Con majority	9,917	19.53%
Electorate	69,132	
Total Vote	50,781	Poll 73.5%

*Member of last parliament

Con Hold (3.8% Swing from Con to LD)

WIRRAL SOUTH

		%
*Chapman, B. (Lab)	24,499	50.9
Byrom, L. (Con)	17,495	36.4
Gilchrist, P. (LD)	5,018	10.4
Wilcox, D. (Ref)	768	1.6
Nielsen, J. (Pro-Life)	264	0.5
Mead, G. (NLP)	51	0.1
Lab majority	7,004	14.56%
Electorate	59,372	
Total Vote	48,095	Poll 81%

*Member of last parliament

Lab Hold (15.4% Swing from Con to Lab)

WIRRAL WEST

		%
Hesford, S. (Lab)	21,035	44.9
*Hunt, D. (Con)	18,297	39.0
Thornton, J. (LD)	5,945	12.7
Wharton, D. (Ref)	1,613	3.4
Lab majority	2,738	5.84%
Electorate	60,908	
Total Vote	46,890	Poll 77%

*Member of last parliament

Lab Gain (13.8% Swing from Con to Lab)

WITNEY

		%
Woodward, S. (Con)	24,282	43.1
Hollingsworth, A. (Lab)	17,254	30.6
Lawrence, A. (LD)	11,202	19.9
Brown, G. (Ref)	2,262	4.0
Montgomery, M. (UKIP)	765	1.4
Chaple-Perrie, S. (Green)	636	1.1
Con majority	7,028	12.46%
Electorate	73,520	
Total Vote	56,401	Poll 76.7%

Con Hold (13.6% Swing from Con to Lab)

WOKING

		%
Malins, H. (Con)	19,553	38.4
Goldenberg, P. (LD)	13,875	27.3
Hanson, K. (Lab)	10,695	21.0

Bell, H. (IndCon)	3,933	7.7
Skeate, C. (Ref)	2,209	4.3
Harvey, M. (UKIP)	512	1.0
Sleeman, D. (NLP)	137	0.3
Con majority	5,678	11.15%
Electorate	70,053	
Total Vote	50,914	Poll 72.7%

Con Hold (10.4% Swing from Con to LD)

WOKINGHAM

		%
*Redwood, J. (Con)	25,086	50.1
Longton, R. (LD)	15,721	31.4
Colling, P. (Lab)	8,424	16.8
Owen, P. (Loony)	877	1.8
Con majority	9,365	18.69%
Electorate	66,161	
Total Vote	50,108	Poll 75%

*Member of last parliament

Con Hold (8.7% Swing from Con to LD)

WOLVERHAMPTON NORTH EAST

		%
*Purchase, K. (Lab/Co-op)	24,534	59.3
Harvey, D. (Con)	11,547	27.9
Niblett, B. (LD)	2,214	5.3
Hallmark, C. (Lib)	1,560	3.8
Muchall, A. (Ref)	1,192	2.9
Wingfield, M. (Nat Dem)	356	0.9
Lab/Co-op majority	12,987	31.37%
Electorate	61,642	
Total Vote	41,403	Poll 67%

*Member of last parliament

Lab/Co-op Hold (11.9% Swing from Con to Lab)

WOLVERHAMPTON SOUTH EAST

		%
*Turner, D. (Lab/Co-op)	22,202	63.7
Hanbury, W. (Con)	7,020	20.2
Whitehouse, R. (LD)	3,292	9.5
Stevenson-Platt, T. (Ref)	980	2.8
Worth, N. (SLP)	689	2.0
Bullman, K. (Lib)	647	1.9
Lab/Co-op majority	15,182	43.59%
Electorate	54,291	
Total Vote	34,830	Poll 64.1%

*Member of last parliament

Lab/Co-op Hold (9.3% Swing from Con to Lab)

WOLVERHAMPTON SOUTH WEST

		%
Jones, J. (Lab)	24,657	50.4
*Budgen, N. (Con)	19,539	39.9
Green, M. (LD)	4,012	8.2
Hyde, M. (Lib)	713	1.5
Lab majority	5,118	10.46%
Electorate	67,482	
Total Vote	48,921	Poll 72%

*Member of last parliament

Lab Gain (9.9% Swing from Con to Lab)

WOODSPRING %
*Fox, L. (Con)   24,425 44.4
Kirsen, N. (LD)   16,691 30.4
Sander, D. (Lab)   11,377 20.7
Hughes, R. (Ref)   1,641   3.0
Lawson, R. (Green)   667   1.2
Glover, A. (Ind)   101   0.2
Mears, M. (NLP)   52   0.1
  Con majority   7,734   14.00%
  Electorate   69,964
  Total Vote   54,954 Poll 78.5%
*Member of last parliament
Con Hold (3.8% Swing from Con to LD)

WORCESTER %
Foster, M. (Lab)   25,848 50.1
Bourne, N. (Con)   18,423 35.7
Chandler, P. (LD)   6,462 12.5
Wood, P. (UKIP)   886   1.7
  Lab majority   7,425   14.38%
  Electorate   69,234
  Total Vote   51,619 Poll 74.6%
Lab Gain (10% Swing from Con to Lab)

WORKINGTON %
*Campbell-Savours,
  D. (Lab)   31,717 64.2
Blunden, R. (Con)   12,061 24.4
Roberts, P. (LD)   3,967   8.0
Donnan, G. (Ref)   1,412   2.9
Austin, C. (UniAll)   217   0.4
  Lab majority 19,656   39.81%
  Electorate   65,766
  Total Vote   49,374 Poll 75.1%
*Member of last parliament
Lab Hold (11% Swing from Con to Lab)

WORSLEY %
*Lewis, T. (Lab)   29,083 62.2
Garrido, D. (Con)   11,342 24.2
Bleakley, R. (LD)   6,356 13.6
  Lab majority 17,741   37.92%
  Electorate   68,978
  Total Vote   46,781 Poll 67.8%
*Member of last parliament
Lab Hold (8.1% Swing from Con to Lab)

WORTHING WEST %
*Bottomley, P. (Con)   23,733 46.1
Hare, C. (LD)   16,020 31.1
Adams, J. (Lab)   8,347 16.2
John, N. (Ref)   2,313   4.5
Cross, T. (UKIP)   1,029   2.0
  Con majority   7,713   14.99%
  Electorate   71,329
  Total Vote   51,442 Poll 71.8%
*Member of last parliament
Con Hold (9.6% Swing from Con to LD)

THE WREKIN %
Bradley, P. (Lab)   21,243 46.9
Bruinvels, P. (Con)   18,218 40.2
Jenkins, I. (LD)   5,807 12.8
  Lab majority   3,025   6.68%
  Electorate   59,126
  Total Vote   45,268 Poll 76.5%
Lab Gain (11.3% Swing from Con to Lab)

WREXHAM %
*Marek, J. (Lab)   20,450 56.1
Andrew, S. (Con)   8,688 23.9
Thomas, A. (LD)   4,833 13.3
Cronk, J. (Ref)   1,195   3.3
Plant, J. (PC)   1,170   3.2
Low, N. (NLP)   86   0.2
  Lab majority 11,762   32.29%
  Electorate   50,741
  Total Vote   36,422 Poll 71.8%
*Member of last parliament
Lab Hold (7.4% Swing from Con to Lab)

WYCOMBE %
*Whitney, R. (Con)   20,890 39.9
Bryant, C. (Lab)   18,520 35.4
Bensilum, P. (LD)   9,678 18.5
Fulford, A. (Ref)   2,394   4.6
Laker, J. (Green)   716   1.4
Heath, M. (NLP)   121   0.2
  Con majority   2,370   4.53%
  Electorate   73,589
  Total Vote   52,319 Poll 71.1%
*Member of last parliament
Con Hold (13.6% Swing from Con to Lab)

WYRE FOREST %
Lock, D. (Lab)   26,843 48.8
*Coombs, A. (Con)   19,897 36.1
Cropp, D. (LD)   4,377   8.0
Till, W. (Ref)   1,956   3.6
Harvey, C. (Lib)   1,670   3.0
Millington, A. (UKIP)   312   0.6
  Lab majority   6,946   12.62%
  Electorate   73,063
  Total Vote   55,055 Poll 75.4%
*Member of last parliament
Lab Gain (14.4% Swing from Con to Lab)

WYTHENSHAWE AND
** SALE EAST** %
Goggins, P. (Lab)   26,448 58.1
Fleming, P. (Con)   11,429 25.1
Tucker, V. (LD)   5,639 12.4
Stanyer, B. (Ref)   1,060   2.3
Flannery, J. (SLP)   957   2.1
  Lab majority 15,019   32.98%
  Electorate   71,986
  Total Vote   45,533 Poll 63.2%
Lab Hold (9.2% Swing from Con to Lab)

YEOVIL %
*Ashdown, P. (LD)   26,349 48.7
Cambrook, N.
  (Con)   14,946 27.7
Conway, P. (Lab)   8,053 14.9
Beveridge, J. (Ref)   3,574   6.6
Taylor, D. (Green)   728   1.3
Archer, J.
  (Musician)   306   0.6
Hudson, C. (Dream)   97   0.2
  LD majority   11,403   21.10%
  Electorate   74,165
  Total Vote   54,053 Poll 72.7%
*Member of last parliament
LD Hold (3.2% Swing from Con to LD)

YNYS MON %
*Jones, I. (PC)   15,756 39.5
Edwards, O. (Lab)   13,275 33.2
Owen, G. (Con)   8,569 21.5
Burnham, D. (LD)   1,537   3.8
Gray Morris, R.
  (Ref)   793   2.0
  PC majority   2,481   6.21%
  Electorate   52,952
  Total Vote   39,930 Poll 75.4%
*Member of last parliament
PC Hold (3.7% Swing from PC to Lab)

YORKSHIRE EAST %
*Townend, J. (Con)   20,904 42.7
Male, I. (Lab)   17,567 35.9
Leadley, D. (LD)   9,070 18.5
Allerston, R.
  (SDP)   1,049   2.1
Cooper, M.
  (Nat Dem)   381   0.8
  Con majority   3,337   6.81%
  Electorate   69,409
  Total Vote   48,971 Poll 70.5%
*Member of last parliament
Con Hold (8.7% Swing from Con to Lab)

State of the Parties

	1997 General Election	1992 General Election
Labour Party	418*	270
Conservative Party	165	336
Liberal Democrats	46	20
Ulster Unionist Party	10	9
Scottish Nationalist Party	6	3
Plaid Cymru	4	4
Social Democratic and and Labour Party	3	4
Democratic Unionist Party	2	3
Sinn Fein	2	0
Independent	1	0
UK Unionist	1	0
UPUP	0	1
The Speaker	1	1
Total	**659**	**651**

*Includes 26 Labour/Co-operative MPs

Votes Cast by party

England, Scotland and Wales (GB)

Lab	13,551,381
Con	9,590,565
Lib Dem	5,243,322
SNP	620,434
PC	161,030
Ref	810,778
UKIP	106,019
NLP	30,165
Green	65,997
SocLab	52,516
Liberal	45,166
Ind Con	12,153
Ind Lab	18,497
BNP	35,393
New Lab	10,597

ScotSoc	9,740
SocP	9,486
Comm	911
Loony	7,906
Nat Front	2,716
Rainbow	3,745
MK	1,906
Others	421,292

Northern Ireland:

UUP	258,349
DUP	107,348
SDLP	190,814
Sinn Fein	126,921
APNI	62,972
PUP	10,928
Others	44,358

GB Vote Share

Lab	45%
Con	31%
Lib Dem	17%
Others	7%

Northern Ireland Vote Share

UUP	32.7%
SDLP	24.1%
SF	16.1%
DUP	13.6%
APNI	8.0%
Con	1.2%
Others	4.4%

Geographical Whereabouts

Aberavon	South Wales	Bognor Regis and	
Airdrie and Shotts	North Lanarkshire	Littlehampton	West Sussex
Aldershot	Hampshire	Bolsover	Derbyshire
Aldridge-Brownhills	West Midlands	Bolton North East	Greater Manchester
Altrincham and Sale		Bolton South East	Greater Manchester
West	Greater Manchester	Bolton West	Greater Manchester
Alyn and Deeside	Flintshire	Bootle	Merseyside
Amber Valley	Derbyshire	Boston and	
Angus	East Scotland	Skegness	Lincolnshire
Antrim, East	Northern Ireland	Bosworth	Leicestershire
Antrim, North	Northern Ireland	Bracknell	Berkshire
Antrim, South	Northern Ireland	Braintree	Essex
Argyll and Bute	West Scotland	Brecon and	
Arundel and South		Radnorshire	Powys
Downs	West Sussex	Brent East	North London
Ashfield	Nottinghamshire	Brent North	North London
Ashford	Kent	Brent South	North London
Ashton under Lyne	Greater Manchester	Brentford and	
Aylesbury	Buckinghamshire	Isleworth	West London
Ayr	South Ayrshire	Brentwood and	
Banbury	Oxfordshire	Ongar	Essex
Banff and Buchan	Aberdeenshire	Bridgend	South Wales
Barking	East London	Bridgwater	Somerset
Barnsley Central	South Yorkshire	Brigg and Goole	Lincolnshire
Barnsley East and		Bromley and	
Mexborough	South Yorkshire	Chislehurst	Kent
Barnsley West and		Bromsgrove	Worcestershire
Penistone	South Yorkshire	Broxbourne	Hertfordshire
Barrow and		Broxtowe	Nottinghamshire
Furness	Cumbria	Burnley	Lancashire
Basildon	Essex	Burton	Staffordshire
Basingstoke	Hampshire	Bury North	Greater Manchester
Bassetlaw	Nottinghamshire	Bury South	Greater Manchester
Bath	Somerset	Bury St Edmunds	Suffolk
Batley and Spen	West Yorkshire	Caernarfon	Gwynedd
Battersea	South London	Caerphilly	South Wales
Beaconsfield	Buckinghamshire	Caithness, Sutherland	
Beckenham	Kent	and Easter Ross	Highland
Berwick-upon-Tweed	Northumberland	Calder Valley	West Yorkshire
Bethnal Green and		Camberwell and	
Bow	East London	Peckham	South London
Beverley and		Cannock Chase	Staffordshire
Holderness	East Yorkshire	Carmarthen East	
Bexhill and Battle	East Sussex	and Dinefwr	Carmarthenshire
Bexleyheath and		Carmarthen West	
Crayford	South London	and South	
Billericay	Essex	Pembrokeshire	South West Wales
Birkenhead	Merseyside	Carrick, Cumnock	
Bishop Auckland	County Durham	and Doon Valley	Ayrshire
Blaby	Leicestershire	Carshalton and	
Blackburn	Lancashire	Wallington	South London
Blaenau Gwent	South Wales	Castle Point	Essex
Blaydon	Tyne and Wear	Ceredigion	West Wales
Blyth Valley	Northumberland	Charnwood	Leicestershire

Chatham and	
Aylesford	Kent
Cheadle	Greater Manchester
Chelmsford West	Essex
Cheltenham	Gloucestershire
Chesham and	
Amersham	Buckinghamshire
Chesterfield	Derbyshire
Chichester	West Sussex
Chingford and	
Woodford Green	Essex
Chipping Barnet	North London
Chorley	Lancashire
Christchurch	Dorset
Cleethorpes	Lincolnshire
Clwyd South	North Wales
Clwyd West	North Wales
Clydebank and	
Milngavie	Dunbartonshire
Clydesdale	South Lanarkshire
Coatbridge and	
Chryston	Central Scotland
Colchester	Essex
Colne Valley	West Yorkshire
Congleton	Cheshire
Conwy	North Wales
Copeland	Cumbria
Corby	Northamptonshire
Cotswold	Gloucestershire
Crawley	West Sussex
Crewe and Nantwich	Cheshire
Crosby	Merseyside
Cumbernauld and	
Kilsyth	North Lanarkshire
Cunninghame North	North Ayrshire
Cunninghame South	North Ayrshire
Cynon Valley	South Wales
Dagenham	Essex
Darlington	County Durham
Dartford	Kent
Daventry	Northamptonshire
Delyn	Flintshire
Denton and Reddish	Greater Manchester
Devizes	Wiltshire
Dewsbury	West Yorkshire
Don Valley	South Yorkshire
Down, North	Northern Ireland
Down, South	Northern Ireland
Dudley North	West Midlands
Dudley South	West Midlands
Dulwich and West	
Norwood	South London
Dunfermline East	Fife
Dunfermline West	Fife
Ealing North	West London
Ealing Southall	West London

Ealing, Acton and	
Shepherd's Bush	West London
Easington	County Durham
East Ham	East London
East Kilbride	South Lanarkshire
East Lothian	South East Scotland
Eastbourne	East Sussex
Eastleigh	Hampshire
Eastwood	East Renfrewshire
Eccles	Greater Manchester
Eddisbury	Cheshire
Edmonton	North London
Ellesmere Port and	
Neston	Cheshire
Elmet	West Yorkshire
Eltham	South London
Enfield North	North London
Enfield Southgate	North London
Epping Forest	Essex
Epsom and Ewell	Surrey
Erewash	Derbyshire
Erith and	
Thamesmead	South London
Esher and Walton	Surrey
Exeter	Devon
Falkirk East	Central Scotland
Falkirk West	Central Scotland
Falmouth and	
Camborne	Cornwall
Fareham	Hampshire
Feltham and	
Heston	West London
Fermanagh and	
South Tyrone	Northern Ireland
Finchley and	
Golders Green	North London
Folkestone and	
Hythe	Kent
Forest of Dean	Gloucestershire
Foyle	Northern Ireland
Fylde	Lancashire
Gainsborough	Lincolnshire
Galloway and Upper	
Nithsdale	Dumfries and Galloway
Gateshead East and	
Washington West	Tyne and Wear
Gedling	Nottinghamshire
Gillingham	Kent
Gordon	North Eastern Scotland
Gosport	Hampshire
Gower	South Wales
Grantham and	
Stamford	Lincolnshire
Gravesham	Kent
Great Grimsby	Lincolnshire
Great Yarmouth	Norfolk

Greenock and Inverclyde	West Scotland
Greenwich and Woolwich	South East London
Guildford	Surrey
Hackney North and Stoke Newington	North London
Hackney South and Shoreditch	North London
Halesowen and Rowley Regis	West Midlands
Halifax	West Yorkshire
Haltemprice and Howden	East Yorkshire
Halton	Cheshire
Hamilton North and Bellshill	Lanarkshire
Hamilton South	South Lanarkshire
Hammersmith and Fulham	West London
Hampstead and Highgate	North London
Harborough	Leicestershire
Harlow	Essex
Harrogate and Knaresborough	North Yorkshire
Harrow East	Middlesex
Harrow West	Middlesex
Hartlepool	County Durham
Harwich	Essex
Hastings and Rye	East Sussex
Havant	Hampshire
Hayes and Harlington	Middlesex
Hazel Grove	Greater Manchester
Hemel Hempstead	Hertfordshire
Hemsworth	West Yorkshire
Hendon	North London
Henley	Oxfordshire
Hertsmere	Hertfordshire
Hexham	Northumberland
Heywood and Middleton	Greater Manchester
High Peak	Derbyshire
Hitchin and Harpenden	Hertfordshire
Holborn and St Pancras	Central London
Hornchurch	Essex
Hornsey and Wood Green	North London
Horsham	West Sussex
Houghton and Washington East	Tyne and Wear
Hove	East Sussex
Huddersfield	West Yorkshire
Huntingdon	Cambridgeshire
Hyndburn	Lancashire
Ilford North	Essex
Ilford South	Essex
Inverness East, Nairn and Lochaber	Highland
Ipswich	Suffolk
Islington North	North London
Islington South and Finsbury	Central London
Islwyn	South Wales
Jarrow	Tyne and Wear
Keighley	West Yorkshire
Kettering	Northamptonshire
Kilmarnock and Loudoun	East Ayrshire
Kingston and Surbiton	South West London
Kingswood	Gloucestershire
Kirkcaldy	Fife
Knowsley North and Sefton East	Merseyside
Knowsley South	Merseyside
Lagan Valley	Northern Ireland
Leigh	Greater Manchester
Leominster	Herefordshire
Lewes	East Sussex
Lewisham Deptford	South East London
Lewisham East	South East London
Lewisham West	South East London
Leyton and Wanstead	East London
Lichfield	Staffordshire
Linlithgow	West Lothian
Livingston	West Lothian
Llanelli	Carmarthenshire
Londonderry, East	Northern Ireland
Loughborough	Leicestershire
Louth and Horncastle	Lincolnshire
Ludlow	Shropshire
Luton North	Bedforshire
Luton South	Bedforshire
Macclesfield	Cheshire
Maidenhead	Berkshire
Maidstone and The Weald	Kent
Makerfield	Greater Manchester
Maldon and Chelmsford East	Essex
Mansfield	Nottinghamshire
Medway	Kent
Meirionnydd Nant Conwy	North Wales
Meriden	West Midlands

Merthyr Tydfil and Rhymney	South Wales
Middlesbrough	North Yorkshire
Middlesbrough South and East Cleveland	North Yorkshire
Midlothian	South East Scotland
Milton Keynes North East	Buckinghamshire
Milton Keynes South West	Buckinghamshire
Mitcham and Morden	South West London
Mole Valley	Surrey
Monmouth	South East Wales
Montgomeryshire	Powys
Moray	North Eastern Scotland
Morecambe and Lunesdale	Lancashire
Morley and Rothwell	West Yorkshire
Motherwell and Wishaw	North Lanarkshire
Neath	South Wales
New Forest East	Hampshire
New Forest West	Hampshire
Newark	Nottinghamshire
Newbury	Berkshire
Newcastle-under-Lyme	Staffordshire
Newport East	South Wales
Newport West	South Wales
Newry and Armagh	Northern Ireland
Normanton	West Yorkshire
Northavon	Gloucestershire
Nuneaton	Warwickshire
Ochil	Eastern Central Scotland
Ogmore	South Wales
Old Bexley and Sidcup	South London
Oldham East and Saddleworth	Greater Manchester
Oldham West and Royton	Greater Manchester
Orpington	Kent
Paisley North	Renfrewshire
Paisley South	Renfrewshire
Pendle	Lancashire
Penrith and The Border	Cumbria
Perth	Central Scotland
Peterborough	Cambridgeshire
Pontefract and Castleford	West Yorkshire
Pontypridd	South Wales
Poole	Dorset
Poplar and Canning Town	East London
Preston	Lancashire

Pudsey	West Yorkshire
Putney	South West London
Rayleigh	Essex
Redcar	North Yorkshire
Redditch	Worcestershire
Regent's Park and Kensington North	North London
Reigate	Surrey
Rhondda	South Wales
Ribble Valley	Lancashire
Ribble, South	Lancashire
Richmond Park	South West London
Rochdale	Greater Manchester
Rochford and Southend East	Essex
Romford	Essex
Romsey	Hampshire
Ross, Skye and Inverness West	Highland
Rossendale and Darwen	Lancashire
Rother Valley	South Yorkshire
Rotherham	South Yorkshire
Roxburgh and Berwickshire	Scottish Borders
Rugby and Kenilworth	Warwickshire
Ruislip Northwood	Middlesex
Runnymede and Weybridge	Surrey
Rushcliffe	Nottinghamshire
Ryedale	North Yorkshire
Saffron Walden	Essex
Salford	Greater Manchester
Salisbury	Wiltshire
Scarborough and Whitby	North Yorkshire
Scunthorpe	East Riding of Yorkshire
Sedgefield	County Durham
Selby	North Yorkshire
Sevenoaks	Kent
Sherwood	Nottinghamshire
Shipley	West Yorkshire
Shrewsbury and Atcham	Shropshire
Sittingbourne and Sheppey	Kent
Skipton and Ripon	North Yorkshire
Sleaford and North Hykeham	Lincolnshire
Slough	Berkshire
Solihull	West Midlands
Somerton and Frome	Somerset
South Holland and The Deepings	Lincolnshire
South Shields	Tyne and Wear

Southend West	Essex
Southport	Merseyside
Southwark and Bermondsey, North	South London
Spelthorne	Surrey
St Albans	Hertfordshire
St Helens North	Merseyside
St Helens South	Merseyside
St Ives	Cornwall
Stalybridge and Hyde	Greater Manchester
Stevenage	Hertfordshire
Stirling	Central Scotland
Stockport	Greater Manchester
Stockton North	County Durham
Stockton South	County Durham
Stone	Staffordshire
Stourbridge	West Midlands
Strangford	Northern Ireland
Stratford-on-Avon	Warwickshire
Strathkelvin and Bearsden	East Dunbartonshire
Streatham	South London
Stretford and Urmston	Greater Manchester
Stroud	Gloucestershire
Sunderland North	Tyne and Wear
Sunderland South	Tyne and Wear
Surrey Heath	Surrey
Sutton and Cheam	Surrey
Sutton Coldfield	West Midlands
Swindon, North	Wiltshire
Swindon, South	Wiltshire
Tamworth	Staffordshire
Tatton	Cheshire
Taunton	Somerset
Tayside, North	Central East Scotland
Teignbridge	Devon
Telford	Shropshire
Tewkesbury	Gloucestershire
Thanet, North	Kent
Thanet, South	Kent
Thurrock	Essex
Tiverton and Honiton	Devon
Tonbridge and Malling	Kent
Tooting	South London
Torbay	Devon
Torfaen	South Wales
Totnes	Devon
Tottenham	North London
Truro and St Austell	Cornwall
Tunbridge Wells	Kent
Tweeddale, Ettrick and Lauderdale	South East Scotland
Twickenham	South West London
Tyne Bridge	Tyne and Wear
Tynemouth	Tyne and Wear

Tyneside, North	Tyne and Wear
Tyrone, West	Northern Ireland
Upminster	Essex
Upper Bann	Northern Ireland
Uxbridge	Middlesex
Vale of Clwyd	North Wales
Vale of Glamorgan	South Wales
Vauxhall	South London
Wakefield	West Yorkshire
Wallasey	Merseyside
Walsall North	West Midlands
Walsall South	West Midlands
Walthamstow	East London
Wansbeck	Northumberland
Wansdyke	Somerset
Wantage	Oxfordshire
Warley	West Midlands
Warrington North	Cheshire
Warrington South	Cheshire
Watford	Hertfordshire
Waveney	Suffolk
Wealden	East Sussex
Weaver Vale	Cheshire
Wellingborough	Northamptonshire
Wells	Somerset
Welwyn Hatfield	Hertfordshire
Wentworth	South Yorkshire
West Bromwich East	West Midlands
West Bromwich West	West Midlands
West Ham	East London
Westbury	Wiltshire
Westmorland and Lonsdale	Cumbria
Weston-Super-Mare	Somerset
Wigan	Greater Manchester
Wimbledon	South West London
Winchester	Hampshire
Windsor	Berkshire
Wirral South	Merseyside
Wirral West	Merseyside
Witney	Oxfordshire
Woking	Surrey
Wokingham	Berkshire
Woodspring	Somerset
Workington	Cumbria
Worsley	Greater Manchester
Worthing East and Shoreham	West Sussex
Worthing West	West Sussex
Wrekin, The	Shropshire
Wycombe	Buckinghamshire
Wyre Forest	Worcestershire
Wythenshawe and Sale East	Greater Manchester
Yeovil	Somerset
Ynys Môn	Anglesey

By-elections since 1997 General Election

DEATHS SINCE 1997 GENERAL ELECTION

		Died
Sir **Michael Shersby**	Uxbridge – Conservative	8 May 1997
Gordon McMaster	Paisley South – Labour/Co-operative	28 July 1997
Rt Hon **Derek Fatchett**	Leeds Central – Labour	9 May 1999
Roger Stott	Wigan – Labour	8 August 1999
Rt Hon **Alan Clark**	Kensington and Chelsea – Conservative	5 September 1999
Michael Colvin	Romsey – Conservative	24 February 2000
Bernie Grant	Tottenham – Labour	9 April 2000
Clifford Forsythe	Antrim South – UUP	27 April 2000
Audrey Wise	Preston – Labour	2 September 2000
Rt Hon **Donald Dewar**	Glasgow Anniesland – Labour	11 October 2000

RESIGNATIONS SINCE 1997 GENERAL ELECTION

Piers Merchant	Beckenham	Conservative
Sir **Alastair Goodlad**	Eddisbury	Conservative
George Robertson	Hamilton South	Labour
Cynog Dafis	Ceredigion	Plaid Cymru
Betty Boothroyd	West Bromwich West	Speaker
Dennis Canavan	Falkirk West	MPFW

UXBRIDGE

31 July 1997 due to the death of the Conservative MP Sir Michael Shersby

Con John Randall	16,288
Lab Andrew Slaughter	12,522
Lib Dem Keith Kerr	1,792

Monster Raving Loony Party David Sutch 396, Socialist Party Julia Leonard 259, British National Party Frances Taylor 205, National Democrat Ian Anderson 157, National Front John McCauley 110, Original Liberal Party Henry Middleton 69, UK Independence Party James Feisenberger 39, Rainbow Ronnie Carroll 30

Con majority 3,766 – Con hold
Electorate 57,733 – Total vote 31,867 – Poll 55.2% – 5.04% swing from Lab to Con

PAISLEY SOUTH

6 November 1997 due to the death of the Labour/Co-op MP Gordon McMaster

Lab Douglas Alexander	10,346
SNP I Blackford	7,615
Lib Dem E McCartin	2,582

Con S Laidlaw 1,643, Pro-Life J Deigham 578, Scot Soc F Curran 306, Scot Ind Lab C McLauchlan 155, SLP C Herriot 153, NLP K Blair 57

Lab majority 2,731 – Lab hold
Electorate 54,573 – Total vote 23,435 – Poll 42.94%

BECKENHAM
20 November 1997 due to the resignation of the Conservative MP Piers Merchant

Con	Jacqui Lait	13,162
Lab	Bob Hughes	11,935
Lib Dem	Rosemary Vetterlein	5,864

Lib P Rimmer 330, NF J Mcauley 267, New Brit/Ref L Mead 237, SFP T Campion 69,
NLP J Small 44

Con majority 1,227 – Con hold
Electorate 74,019 – Total vote 31,908 – Poll 43.57%

WINCHESTER
20 November 1997 due to challenge of two-vote victory at General Election of 1 May 1997

Lib Dem	Mark Oaten	37,006
Con	Gerry Malone	15,450
Lab	Patrick Davies	944

Ref/UKI/ALL R Page 521, Loony D Sutch 316, Lit Dem MHTW R Huggett 59, NLP R Barry 48,
Euro Con R Everest 40

Lib Dem majority 21,556 – Lib Dem hold
Electorate 79,121 – Total vote 54,384 – Poll 68.7%

LEEDS CENTRAL
10 June 1999 due to the death of the Labour MP Rt Hon Derek Fatchett

Lab	Hilary Benn	6,361
Lib Dem	Peter Wild	4,068
Con	William Edward Wild	1,618

Green David Blackburn 478, UKI Raymond Northgreaves 353, Left Alliance Chris Hill 258,
Equal Parenting Campaign Julian Fitzgerald 51

Lab majority 2,293 – Lab hold
Electorate 67,569 – Total vote 13,457 – Poll 19.6%

EDDISBURY
22 July 1999 due to the resignation of the Conservative MP Rt Hon Sir Alastair Goodlad

Con	Stephen O'Brien	15,465
Lab	Margaret Hanson	13,859
Lib Dem	Paul Roberts	4,757

Monster Raving Loony Alan Hope 238, Ind Europe Con Roger Everest 98,
Natural Law Dina Grice 80

Con majority 1,606 – Con hold
Electorate 67,086 – Total vote 34,497 – Poll 51.42%

WIGAN
23 September 1999 due to the death of the Labour MP Roger Stott

Lab	Neil Turner	9,641
Con	Thomas Peet	2,912
Lib Dem	Jonathan Rule	2,148

UK Independence John Whittaker 834, Socialist Labour William Kelly 240, Green Christopher
Maile 190, National Democrat Resistance Stephen Ebbs 100, Natural Law Paul Davis 64,
Reverend David Braid 58

Lab majority 6,729 – Lab hold
Electorate 64,755 – Total vote 16,187 – Poll 25.0%

HAMILTON SOUTH

23 September 1999 due to the elevation to the House of Lords of the Labour MP Rt Hon George Robertson

Lab	Bill Tynan	7,172
SNP	Annabelle Ewing	6,616
SSP	Shareen Blackall	1,847
Con	Charles Ferguson	1,406

Accies Stephen Mungall 1,075, SLD Marilyne MacLaren 634, ProLife Monica Burns 257, Socialist Labour Tom Dewar 238, Scottish Unionist James Reid 113, UK Independence Alistair McConnachie 61, Natural Law George Stidolph 18, Status Quo John Drummond Moray 17

Lab majority 556 – Lab hold
Electorate 47,081 – Total vote 19,485 – Poll 41.4%

KENSINGTON AND CHELSEA

25 November 1999 due to the death of the Conservative MP Rt Hon Alan Clark

Con	Rt Hon Michael Portillo	11,004
Lab	John Atkinson	4,298
Lib Dem	Robert Browne	1,831

Pro Europe Conservative John Stevens 740, UK Independence Nicholas Hockney 450, Green Hugo Charlton 446, Democratic Charles Burford 182, Legalise Cannabis Alliance Colin Paisley 141, Living Will Legislation Michael Irwin 97, UK Pensioners George Oliver 75, Referendum Stephen Scott-Fawcett 57, Daily & Sunday Sport Louise Hodges 48, Natural Law Gerard Valente 35, People's Net Dream Ticket Lisa Lovebuckett 26, Independent Environmentalist Stop Climate Change John Davies 24, Equal Parenting Peter May 24, Official Monster Raving Loony Alan Hope 20, Stop Tobacco Companies Farming Our Children Tony Samuelsondotcom 15

Con majority 6,706 – Con hold
Electorate 65,752 – Total vote 19,513 – Poll 29.68%

CEREDIGION

3 February 2000 due to the resignation of the Plaid Cymru MP Cynog Dafis, AM

PC	Simon Thomas	10,716
Lib Dem	Mark Williams	5,768
Con	Paul Davies	4,138
Lab	Maria Battle	3,612

UKIP John Bufton 487, Ind Green John B Davies 289, Wales Martin Shipton 55

PC majority 4,948 – PC hold
Electorate 54,463 – Total vote 25,065 – Poll 46.02%

ROMSEY

4 May 2000 due to the death of the Conservative MP Michael Colvin

Lib Dem	Sandra Gidley	19,571
Con	Timothy Palmer	16,260
Lab	Andrew Howard	1,451

UKIP Garry Rankin-Moore 901, Legalise Cannabis Alliance Derrick Large 417, Independent Thomas Lamont 109

Lib Dem majority 3,311 – Lib Dem gain from Conservatives
Electorate 69,858 – Total vote 38,709 – Poll 55.41%

TOTTENHAM
22 June 2000 due to the death of the Labour MP Bernie Grant

Lab David Lammy		8,785
Lib Dem Duncan Hames		3,139
Con Jane Ellison		2,634

London Soc Weyman Bennett 885, Green Peter Budge 606, Reform 2000 Erol Basarik 177, UK Ind Ashwinkumar Tanna 136, Ind C Derek De Braam 55

Lab majority 5,646 – Lab hold
Electorate 64,554 – Total vote 16,417 – Poll 25.43%

SOUTH ANTRIM
21 September 2000 due to death of UUP MP Clifford Forsythe

DUP William McCrea		11,601
UUP David Burnside		10,779
SDLP Donovan McClelland		3,496

Sinn Fein Martin Meehan 2,611, Alliance David Ford 2,031, NLP David Collins 49

DUP majority 822 – DUP gain from UUP
Electorate 71,047 – Total vote 30,567 – Poll 43.02%

PRESTON
By-election pending due to death of Labour MP Audrey Wise on 2 September 2000

GLASGOW ANNIESLAND
By-election pending due to death of Labour MP Donald Dewar on 11 October 2000

WEST BROMWICH WEST
By-election pending due to resignation of Speaker Betty Boothroyd

Electoral Dates

The Representation of the People Act 1983 sets out the timetable for parliamentary elections. In the case of a General Election, the last day for the delivery of nomination papers is the sixth day after the date of the proclamation summoning the new Parliament, and the poll is held in every constituency on the eleventh day after the last day for delivery of nomination papers. In the case of a by-election, the last day for the delivery of nomination papers is fixed by the Returning Officer and must be not earlier than the third day after the date of publication of the notice of election nor later than the seventh day after that on which the writ is received. Polling takes place on the day fixed by the Returning Officer, which is not earlier than the ninth nor later than the eleventh day after the last day for delivery of nomination papers. In calculating these dates, a Sunday, a Saturday, Christmas Eve, Christmas Day, Maundy Thursday, Good Friday, a bank holiday and a day appointed for public thanksgiving or mourning are disregarded.

Thus the whole process from the last sitting of the old Parliament to the State Opening of the new took just over seven weeks in 1992 and almost six weeks in 1997.

Parliamentary Franchise

A person resident in the United Kingdom on the annual qualifying date (10 October) (15 September in Northern Ireland) is entitled to be entered on the register of electors if he or she is (a) a British or other Commonwealth citizen or a citizen of the Republic of Ireland, and
(b) is at least 18 years of age (or will become 18 during the currency of the register) and is not otherwise disqualified. Under the Representation of the People Act 1985, certain British citizens resident abroad may also vote in parliamentary elections.

Since 1999 hereditary peers, who were previously barred from voting in general elections, have been allowed to do so if they no longer sit in the Lords.

Parliamentary Candidates

A candidate must be at least 21 years old. Since 1999 hereditary peers who no longer sit in the House of Lords have been allowed to stand as candidates for the Commons.

Each candidate must deposit £500 with the Returning Officer at the time of nomination. This sum is returned when he has taken the oath, if elected, or if he is not elected but has polled 5% of the number of votes polled, otherwise the deposit is forefeited.

The maximum expenditure which may be incurred by a candidate is £4965 plus, in a county constituency, 5.6p and, in a borough constituency, 4.2p for every entry in the Register of Electors to be used at the election (as first published). These figures are approximately quadrupled in the case of a by-election.

The Returning Officer's expenses are paid by the Treasury.

Number of Voters

In October 1999 there was a total of 44,388,885 names on the parliamentary electoral register of the United Kingdom. This is broken down as follows: England 36,947,525; Scotland 4,011,450; Wales 2,227,571; and Northern Ireland 1,202,339.

House of Lords

Membership

Since the passing of the House of Lords Act, 1999, the majority of members, over 500, are life peers. In addition, there is a minority of life peers who are Lords of Appeal in Ordinary.

The Archbishops of Canterbury and York and the Bishops of London, Durham and Winchester are ex-officio members of the Lords, while the remaining 21 Bishops who are members sit by rotation according to seniority; these are known as Lords Spiritual.

Ninety hereditary peers still sit by virtue of election by their fellow peers. In addition, some 19 hereditary peers have been created life peers.

There are two hereditary office holders who are members of the House under the House of Lords Act, 1999· the Duke of Norfolk as Earl Marshal, and the Marquess of Cholmondeley as Lord Great Chamberlain.

Summary
(at 24 October 2000)

Archbishops	2	Bishops	24
Dukes	2	Barons/Lords	512
Marquesses	1	Baronesses	110
Earls & Countesses	28	Lady	1
Viscounts	17	*Total*	696

Women Peers by Succession	4 (ie 1 Countess, 2 Baronesses and 1 Lady)
Women Life Peers	108
Hereditary Peers who have received Life Peerages	19

Party Allegiance

Conservative	232	Liberal Democrat	63
Cross-Bencher	164	Others*	29
Labour	200	Peers on Leave of Absence	4

*Includes Lords Spiritual and those peers who have not declared any party affiliation.

House of Lords Appointments Commission

The Appointments Commission is a non-statutory advisory non-departmental public body. It has two main functions: to make recommendations for non-political peers; and to vet for propriety all nominations for peerages, including those from the political parties. The latter task has hitherto been carried out by the Political Honours Scrutiny Committee.

Chairman:
Lord Stevenson of Coddenham CBE
Independent Members: Angela Sarkis CBE,
Dame Deirdre Hine DBE, Felicity Huston
Members nominated by the political parties:
Rt Hon Baroness Dean of Thornton-le-Fylde
(Labour), Rt Hon Lord Hurd of Westwell
CH CBE *(Conservative)*, Lord Dholakia
OBE DL *(Liberal Democrat)*

Secretary to the Commission: J K Barron
Address: House of Lords Appointments
Commission, 35 Great Smith Street, London
SW1P 3BQ
Telephone: 020 7276 2604; GTN 276 2604
General enquiries Telephone: 020 7276 2580

PEERS' BIOGRAPHIES

A

LORD ABERDARE   Conservative

ABERDARE (4th Baron, UK), Morys George Lyndhurst Bruce; cr. 1873. Born 16 June 1919. Son of 3rd Baron, GBE. Succeeded his father 1957; educated Winchester; New College, Oxford (MA). Married 1946, Maud Helen Sarah, daughter of late Sir John Dashwood, 10th Bt, CVO (4 sons). *Armed Forces:* Major, Welsh Guards 1939–46. *Councils, Public Bodies:* DL, Dyfed 1985. *Career:* Chairman: Albany Life Assurance Co Ltd 1975–92, Metlife (UK) Ltd 1986–92. *House of Lords:* Minister of State, Department of Health and Social Security 1970–74; Minister without Portfolio 1974; Chairman of Committees, House of Lords 1976–92; A Deputy Speaker of the House of Lords 1976–; A Deputy Chairman of Committees 1992–; An elected hereditary peer 1999–. *Select Committees:* Chairman, Select Committee on Broadcasting 1978–92. *Other:* President, Welsh National Council of YMCAs; Former President, National Association of Leagues of Hospital Friends; President: Kidney Research Unit for Wales Foundation, The Queen's Club 1993–96. Hon. LLD, University of Wales 1985. *Trusts, etc:* Chairman, The Football Trust 1979–98. *Honours:* Prior for Wales, Order of St John 1957–88; Bailiff Grand Cross, Order of St John 1974; PC 1974; KBE 1984. *Publications: The Story of Tennis* (1959); *The Willis Faber Book of Tennis and Rackets* (1980). *Recreations:* Real tennis. *Sportsclubs:* All England Lawn Tennis, Jesters, Queens. *Clubs:* Lansdowne, MCC, Boodle's. *Address:* Rt Hon the Lord Aberdare, KBE, DL, 26 Crown Lodge, 12 Elystan Street, London, SW3 3PP *Tel:* 020 7581 0825 *Tel:* House of Lords 020 7219 6925.

LORD ACKNER   Cross-Bencher

ACKNER (Life Baron), Desmond James Conrad Ackner; cr. 1986. Born 18 September 1920. Son of late Dr Conrad Ackner; educated Highgate School; Clare College, Cambridge (MA). Married August 24, 1946, Joan Spence, née Evans (1 son 2 daughters). *Armed Forces:* Served in RA 1941–42; Admiralty Naval Law branch 1942–45. *Career:* Called to Bar, Middle Temple 1945; QC 1961; Recorder of Swindon 1962–71; Judge of Courts of Appeal, Jersey and Guernsey 1967–71; Member, General Council of the Bar 1957–61, 1963–70, Treasurer 1964–66, Vice-Chairman 1966–68, Chairman 1968–70; Judge of High Court of Justice, Queen's Bench Division 1971–80; A Lord Justice of Appeal 1980–86; A Lord of Appeal in Ordinary 1986–92. *Select Committees:* Member, House of Lords Select Committees on: Murder and Life Imprisonment 1988–89, Science and Technology Subcommittee on Digital Images as Evidence 1997–98. *Other:* President, Senate of the Four Inns of Court 1983–84; Deputy Treasurer, Middle Temple 1983, Treasurer 1984; President, Society of Sussex Downsmen 1993–96, Vice-President 1996–. Hon. Fellow, Clare College 1984. *Miscellaneous:* Member, British Council 1991–; President, Arbitration Appeal Panel of the Securities and Futures Authority 1993–; Appeal Commissioner, Personal Investment Authority 1994–; Director, City Disputes Panel 1994–98. *Honours:* Kt 1971; PC 1980. *Special Interests:* Law, Alternative Dispute Resolutions. *Recreations:* Gardening, swimming, theatre. *Name, Style and Title:* Raised to the peerage as Baron Ackner, of Sutton in the County of West Sussex 1986. *Address:* Rt Hon the Lord Ackner, House of Lords, London, SW1A 0PW *Tel:* 020 7219 3295; 4 Pump Court, Temple, London, EC4Y 7AN *Tel:* 020 7353 2656; Frivermill, 151 Grosvenor Road, London SW1V 3JN *Tel:* 020 7821 8068; The Flat, Lobs House, South Road, Liphook, Hampshire, GH30 7HS.

LORD ACTON — Labour

ACTON (4th Baron, UK), Richard Gerald Lyon-Dalberg-Acton; cr. 1869; (Life) Baron Acton of Bridgnorth 2000; 11th Bt of Aldenham (E) 1644. Born 30 July 1941. Son of 3rd Baron, CMG, MBE, TD and late Hon. Daphne Strutt, daughter of 4th Baron Rayleigh, DL. Succeeded his father 1989; educated St George's College, Salisbury, Rhodesia; Trinity College, Oxford (MA History 1963). Married 1st, 1965, Hilary Juliet Sarah Cookson (died 1973) (1 son), married 2nd, 1974, Judith, daughter of Hon. Sir Garfield Todd (marriage dissolved 1987), married 3rd, 1988, Patricia Nassif. *Career:* Management trainee, Amalgamated Packaging Industries Ltd 1964–66; Coutts and Co. Bankers, London 1967–74, Director 1970–74; Called to Bar, Inner Temple 1976; Practising Barrister 1977–81; A Senior Law Officer, Ministry of Justice, Legal and Parliamentary Affairs, Harare, Zimbabwe 1981–85; Currently writer in anthologies, academic journals and magazines. *International Bodies:* Member, Commonwealth Parliamentary Association. *Other:* Patron: MIND Jubilee Appeal 1996–, The Mulberry Bush School 1998–; Sponsor, British Defence and Aid Fund for Southern Africa 1980–94; Vice-Patron, 2000 Appeal British School of Osteopathy 1999–; Member, Oxford Brookes University Court 1999–. *Trusts, etc:* Vice-Patron, APEX Trust 1995–. *Publications:* Co-author *To Go Free: A Treasury of Iowa's Legal Heritage,* 1995 (Benjamin F. Shambaugh Award 1996); *A Brit Among the Hawkeyes,* 1998. *Special Interests:* Foreign Affairs, Commonwealth, Anglo-American Relations, Southern Africa, Mental Health, Penal Affairs and Policy. *Recreations:* Reading, travel. *Name, Style and Title:* Created a life peer as Baron Acton of Bridgnorth, of Aldenham in the County of Shropshire 2000. *Address:* The Lord Acton, 152 Whitehall Court, London, SW1A 2EL *Tel:* 020 7839 3077 *Fax:* 020 7839 3077; 100 Red Oak Lane, SE Cedar Rapids, Iowa 52403, USA.

LORD ADDINGTON — Liberal Democrat

ADDINGTON (6th Baron, UK), Dominic Bryce Hubbard; cr. 1887. Born 24 August 1963. Son of 5th Baron. Succeeded his father 1982; educated The Hewett School, Norwich; Aberdeen University (MA 1988). *House of Lords:* An elected hereditary peer 1999–. *Spokesman:* Party Spokesman on Disability 1994–. *Other:* Vice-President, British Dyslexia Association. *Trusts, etc:* With Apex Trust as fund raiser 1990–. *Special Interests:* Education, Environment, Prison Reform. *Recreations:* Rugby football. *Clubs:* National Liberal. *Address:* The Lord Addington, 9–11 Chalk Hill Road, Norwich, NR1 1SL.

LORD AHMED — Labour

AHMED (Life Baron), Nazir Ahmed; cr. 1998. Born 24 April 1957. Son of late Haji Sain Mohammed and Rashem Bibi; educated Spurley Hey Comprehensive School, Rotherham; Thomas Rotherham College, Rotherham; Sheffield Hallam University (BA Public Administration). Married 1974, Sakina Bibi (2 sons 1 daughter). *Trades Union:* Member, USDAW. *Councils, Public Bodies:* Councillor, Rotherham Metropolitan Borough Council 1990–; JP, Rotherham 1992. *Career:* Company Director; Business Development Manager, Kilnhurst Business Park; Non-Executive Chairman, Halal World Plc. *Select Committees:* Member, Library and Computers Sub-Committee, House of Lords Offices Committee 2000–. *International Bodies:* Member: IPU, CPA. *International Bodies (General):* Member, Kashmir Policy Group; Patron: Kashmiri Journalist Association Mirpur, Jammu and Kashmir Human Rights Commission, Mirpur Friendship Association. *Party Groups (General):* Chairman, South Yorkshire Labour Party; Vice-Chairman, South Yorkshire Euro-constituency Party. *Other:* Founder, British Muslim Councillors Forum; Patron: Kashmiri and Pakistani Professional Association, British Hujjaj Association, Young Pakistani Doctors' Association, SARC Foundation. *Special Interests:* Human Rights, Kashmiri Right of Self Determination, Conflict resolution, Race Relations, Relations with Muslim countries. *Recreations:* Volleyball. *Name, Style and Title:* Raised to the peerage as Baron Ahmed, of Rotherham in the County of South Yorkshire 1998. *Address:* The Lord Ahmed, House of Lords, London, SW1A 0PW.

LORD ALDERDICE   Liberal Democrat

ALDERDICE (Life Baron), John Thomas Alderdice; cr. 1996. Born 28 March 1955. Son of Reverend David Alderdice and Annie Margaret Helena, née Shields; educated Ballymena Academy; Queen's University, Belfast (MB, BCh, BAO). Married July 30, 1977, Joan Margaret Hill (2 sons 1 daughter). *Trades Union:* British Medical Association. *Councils, Public Bodies:* Councillor, Belfast City Council 1989–97; Member, Belfast Education and Library Board 1993–97. *Career:* Consultant Psychotherapist, Eastern Health and Social Services Board 1988–; Hon. Lecturer, Faculty of Medicine, Queen's University, Belfast 1991–99, Hon. Senior Lecturer 1999; Executive Medical Director, South and East Belfast Health and Social Services Trust 1993–97.
International Bodies: Associate Member, British-Irish Inter-Parliamentary Body; Member, Commonwealth Parliamentary Association. *Party Groups (General):* Executive Committee, Alliance Party 1984–98, Chairman, Policy Committee 1985–87; Vice-Chairman, Alliance Party March 1987-October 1987, Party Leader 1987–98; Executive Committee, European Liberal Democrat and Reform Party 1987–, Treasurer 1995–99, Vice-President 1999–; Candidate (NI) in European Parliament Election 1989; Leader, Alliance Delegation at Inter-Party and Inter-Governmental Talks on the Future of Northern Ireland 1991–98; Vice-President, Liberal International 1992–99, Bureau Member 1996–; Chairman, Liberal International Human Rights Committee 1999–. *Other:* Member: Northern Ireland Institute of Human Relations, Association for Psychoanalytic Psychotherapy. Hon. Fellow, Royal College of Physicians of Ireland Hon. Professor, Faculty of Medicine, University of San Marcos, Peru. *Trusts, etc:* Trustee, Ulster Museum 1993–97. *Miscellaneous:* Contested Belfast East (Alliance Party) 1987 and 1992 General Elections; Leader, Alliance Delegation, Forum for Peace and Reconciliation, Dublin Castle 1994–97; Member, Northern Ireland Forum 1996–98; Leader, Alliance Delegation to Northern Ireland Multiparty Talks 1996–98; Elected to the Northern Ireland Assembly (as one of the members for Belfast East) 1998–; Speaker of the Northern Ireland Assembly 1998–. Fellow: Ulster Medical Society, Royal Academy of Medicine of Ireland, FRCPsych; Hon. Fellow, Royal College of Physicians of Ireland 1997. *Publications:* Various professional articles on Eating Disorders, Psychotherapy and Ethics, many political papers and articles. *Special Interests:* Northern Ireland, Psychoanalysis and Political Conflict Resolution, Mental Health. *Recreations:* Reading, music, gastronomy. *Clubs:* National Liberal, Ulster Reform (Belfast). *Name, Style and Title:* Raised to the peerage as Baron Alderdice, of Knock in the City of Belfast 1996. *Address:* The Lord Alderdice, 55 Knock Road, Belfast, BT5 6LB *Tel:* 028 9079 3097; The Speaker's Office, Parliament Buildings, Stormont, Belfast, BT4 3XX *E-Mail:* alderdicej@parliament.uk.

LORD ALDINGTON   Conservative

ALDINGTON (1st Baron, UK), Toby Austin Richard William Low; cr. 1962; (Life) Baron Low 1999. Born 25 May 1914. Son of late Colonel Stuart Low, DSO; educated Winchester; New College, Oxford (BA, MA). Married 1947, Mrs Felicite Ann Araminta Bowman, née MacMichael (1 son 2 daughters). *Armed Forces:* Joined the Rangers KRRC as a Territorial, served in the Middle East, Italy, appointed Brigadier General Staff of 5th Corps of the 8th Army 1944; Hon. Col, 268 LAA Regt RA (TA) 1947–59. *Councils, Public Bodies:* DL, Kent 1973. *Career:* Barrister (Middle Temple) 1939; Chairman, Grindlays Bank Ltd 1963–76; Chairman, General Electric Co. Ltd 1964–68, Deputy Chairman 1968–84; Chairman: Sun Alliance and London Insurance Ltd 1971–1985, National Nuclear Corporation 1973–1980, Westland plc 1977–85. *House of Commons:* MP (Conservative) for Blackpool North 1945–62; Parliamentary Secretary to Ministry of Supply 1951–54; Minister of State, Board of Trade 1954–57. *Select Committees:* Chairman: House of Lords Select Committee on Overseas Trade 1984–85, Sub-Committee A House of Lords European Communities Select Committee 1989–92. *Party Groups (General):* Deputy Chairman, Conservative Party Organisation 1959–63. *Other:* Warden, Winchester College 1979–87, Fellow 1972–87; Chairman, Leeds Castle Foundation 1984–94. Hon. Fellow, New College, Oxford 1976. *Trusts, etc:* Brain Research Trust: Chairman 1972–87, President 1987–; Kent Foundation: Member 1986–, Chairman 1986–94. *Miscellaneous:* Chairman: Institute of Neurology Management Committee 1962–86, Port of London

Authority 1971–77, General Advisory Council BBC 1971–78, Governing Bodies Association 1983–89, Independent Schools Joint Council 1986–89; President, British Standards Institution 1986–89.*Honours:* DSO 1941; CBE (Mil) 1945; TD 1950; PC 1954; KCMG 1957. *Recreations:* Golf, gardening. *Sportsclubs:* Royal St George's GC, Royal and Ancient GC. *Clubs:* Carlton. *Name, Style and Title:* Created a life peer as Baron Low, of Bispham in the County of Lancashire 1999.*Address:* Rt Hon the Lord Aldington, KCMG, CBE, DSO, TD, DL, Knoll Farm, Aldington, Ashford, Kent, TN25 7BY *Tel:* 01233 720292.

LORD ALEXANDER OF WEEDON   Conservative

ALEXANDER OF WEEDON (Life Baron), Robert Scott Alexander; cr. 1988. Born 5 September 1936. Son of late Samuel James Alexander and Hannah May Alexander; educated Brighton College; King's College, Cambridge (MA). Married 3rd, 1985, Marie Anderson (2 sons 1 daughter from 1st marriage). *Career:* Called to the Bar, Middle Temple 1961, Bencher 1979; QC (NSW Australia) 1983; Vice-Chairman, Bar Council 1984–85, Chairman 1985–86; Judge of the Courts of Appeal of Jersey and Guernsey 1985–88; Chairman: Panel on Takeovers and Mergers 1987–89, National Westminster Bank plc 1989–99; Non-Executive Director: RTZ Corporation plc 1991–96, International Stock Exchange of the UK and Republic of Ireland 1991–93; Deputy Chairman, Securities and Investments Board 1994–96; Member, Government's Panel on Sustainable Development 1994–. *Chancellor:* Chancellor, Exeter University 1998–. *Select Committees:* Chairman: Delegated Powers Scrutiny Committee, House of Lords 1995–97, Select Committee on Delegated Powers and Deregulation 1997–. *Other:* Governor, Wycombe Abbey School 1986–92; Chairman, Council of Justice; Chairman, Foundation Board, Royal Shakespeare Company. Four honorary law doctorates. *Trusts, etc:* Trustee, National Gallery 1986–93; Chairman, Trustees of Crisis 1988–96. *Miscellaneous:* Member, Independent Commission on Voting Reform 1998; Chairman, Inquiry into Tonnage Tax 1999. *Publications: The Voice of the People: A Constitution for Tomorrow,* 1997. *Special Interests:* Law, Legal Profession, City, Arts. *Recreations:* Tennis, theatre, gardening. *Clubs:* Garrick. *Name, Style and Title:* Raised to the peerage as Baron Alexander of Weedon, of Newcastle-under-Lyme in the County of Staffordshire 1988. *Address:* The Lord Alexander of Weedon, QC, House of Lords, London, SW1A 0PW *Tel:* 020 7219 3000.

LORD ALLEN OF ABBEYDALE   Cross-Bencher

ALLEN OF ABBEYDALE (Life Baron), Philip Allen; cr. 1976. Born 8 July 1912. Son of late Arthur Allen; educated King Edward VII School, Sheffield; Queens' College, Cambridge (MA). Married 1938, Marjorie Brenda Coe. *Career:* Entered Home Office 1934; Served in Offices of War Cabinet 1943–44; Deputy Secretary, Ministry of Housing and Local Government 1955–60; Deputy Under-Secretary of State, Home Office 1960–62; Second Secretary, HM Treasury 1963–66; Permanent Under-Secretary of State, Home Office 1966–72; Chief Counting Officer, EEC Referendum 1975. *Select Committees:* Chairman, Select Committee on a Bill of Rights 1977–78. *Other:* Chairman, Council of Royal Holloway and Bedford New College, London University 1985–92, Visitor 1992–97; Chairman: National Council of Social Service 1973–77, MENCAP 1982–88. Hon. Fellow: Queens' College, Cambridge, Royal Holloway and Bedford New College. *Miscellaneous:* Chairman, Occupational Pensions Board 1973–78; Member: Security Commission 1973–91, Royal Commission on Standards of Conduct in Public Life, Royal Commission on Compensation for Personal Injury, Tribunal of Inquiry into Crown Agents; Chairman, Gaming Board 1977–85. *Honours:* CB 1954; KCB 1964; GCB 1970. *Name, Style and Title:* Raised to the peerage as Baron Allen of Abbeydale, of the City of Sheffield 1976. *Address:* The Lord Allen of Abbeydale, GCB, Holly Lodge, Middle Hill, Englefield Green, Surrey, TW20 0JP *Tel:* 01784 432291.

VISCOUNT ALLENBY OF MEGIDDO   Cross-Bencher

ALLENBY OF MEGIDDO (3rd Viscount, UK), Michael Jaffray Hynman Allenby; cr. 1919. Born 20 April 1931. Son of 2nd Viscount. Succeeded his father 1984; educated Eton; RMA, Sandhurst. Married July 29, 1965, Sara Margaret, daughter of Lieutenant-Colonel Peter Milner Wiggin (1 son). *Armed Forces:* Commissioned August 3, 1951, 11th Hussars as 2nd Lieutenant; Served Malaya and Cyprus, as ADC to Governor 1956–58; Brigade Major, 51 Brigade, Hong Kong 1967–70; Commanded The Royal Yeomanry (TA) 1974–77; GSO1 Instructor, Nigerian Staff College, Kaduna, Nigeria 1977–79. *Career:* Director, Quickrest Ltd 1987–91. *House of Lords:* A Deputy Speaker of the House of Lords; A Deputy Chairman of Committees 1997–; An elected hereditary peer 1999–. *Select Committees:* Member, Select Committee on House of Lords' Offices 1997–99; Procedure Commiteee 1999–. *Other:* Chairman, The International League for The Protection of Horses 1997–99, Vice-President 1999–. *Special Interests:* Defence, Animal Welfare. *Recreations:* Horses, sailing. *Clubs:* Naval and Military. *Address:* The Viscount Allenby of Megiddo, House of Lords, London, SW1A 0PW.

LORD ALLI   Labour

ALLI (Life Baron), Waheed Alli; cr. 1998. Born 16 November 1964; educated Norbury Manor School, South London. *Career:* Director, Atomic TV Poland 1992–98; Founder Joint Managing Director, Planet 24 Television; Managing Director, Planet 24 Products Ltd; Numerous directorships of radio, television and entertainment companies; Director: Carlton Television 1999–; Managing Director, Carlton Productions 1999–. *Other:* Member: Panel 2000, Creative Industries Task Force, Board of the Teacher Training Agency. *Name, Style and Title:* Raised to the peerage as Baron Alli, of Norbury in the London Borough of Croydon 1998. *Address:* The Lord Alli, House of Lords, London, SW1A 0PW.

LORD ALTON OF LIVERPOOL   Cross-Bencher

ALTON OF LIVERPOOL (Life Baron), David Patrick Paul Alton; cr. 1997. Born 15 March 1951. Son of late Frederick Alton, car worker with Ford Motor Company, and Bridget Mulroe; educated Edmund Campion School, Hornchurch; Christ's College of Education, Liverpool; St Andrews University. Married 1988, Elizabeth Bell (3 sons 1 daughter). *Councils, Public Bodies:* Elected at 21 as a city councillor to Liverpool City Council 1972–80 (Chairman, Housing Committee and Deputy Leader of Council 1978); Councillor, Merseyside County Council 1973–77. *Career:* Teacher 1972–74, then with children with special needs 1974–79; Local Government 1972–80, including Deputy Leader of Liverpool City Council; Professor of Citizenship, Liverpool John Moores University 1997–. *House of Commons:* Contested Liverpool Edge Hill February and October 1974; MP for Liverpool Edge Hill 1979–83, and for Liverpool Mossley Hill 1983–97 (Liberal 1979–88, Liberal Democrat 1988–97); Parliamentary Chairman, Council for Education in the Commonwealth 1983–87. *Whip (Commons):* Liberal Chief Whip 1985–87. *Spokesman (Commons):* Former Liberal Spokesman in Parliament on Home Affairs and Environment; Alliance Spokesman, Northern Ireland 1987–88. *International Bodies:* Member: IPU, CPA. *International Bodies (General):* Member: IPU, CPA. *Party Groups (General):* Former National President, National League of Young Liberals; Chairman: Liberal Policy Committee 1981–83, Candidates Committee 1984–87. *Other:* President, Liverpool Old People's Hostels Association; Sponsor, Jubilee Campaign; National Vice-President, LIFE; Vice-President, Liverpool YMCA; Member, Royal Society for the Protection of Birds; Founder member: Jubilee Campaign 1987, Epiphany Group 1989, Movement for Christian Democracy 1990; President, Liverpool Branch, NSPCC; Chairman: Merseyside Council for Voluntary Service, Liverpool Royal Hospital Forget-Me-Not Cancer Appeal; Member, Wavertree Society; Unremunerated Director, The Catholic Central Library. *Trusts, etc:* Trustee of the Charity, Crisis; Patron, Belfast Trust.

Miscellaneous: Visiting Fellowship, St Andrews University (School of Philosophy and Public Affairs and St Mary's College). *Publications: What Kind of Country,* 1987; *Whose Choice Anyway – the Right to Life,* 1988; *Faith in Britain,* 1991; *Signs of Contradiction,* 1996; *Life After Death,* 1997; *Citizen Virtues,* 1998. *Special Interests:* Abortion, Environment, Housing, Inner Cities, Refugees, Human Rights, Northern Ireland, Citizenship. *Recreations:* Walking, reading, theatre. *Name, Style and Title:* Raised to the peerage as Baron Alton of Liverpool, of Mossley Hill in the County of Merseyside 1997. *Address:* The Lord Alton of Liverpool, House of Lords, London, SW1A 0PW *E-Mail:* d.alton@livjm.ac.uk.

BARONESS AMOS — Labour

AMOS (Life Baroness), Valerie Ann Amos; cr. 1997. Born 13 March 1954. Daughter of Michael and Eunice Amos; educated Townley Grammar School for Girls; Warwick University (BA Sociology); Birmingham University (MA Cultural Studies); University of East Anglia (doctoral research). *Career:* With London Boroughs: Lambeth 1981–82, Camden 1983–85, Hackney 1985–89, Head of Training, Head of Management Services; Chief Executive, Equal Opportunities Commission 1989–94; Director, Amos Fraser Bernard 1995–98. *Whip:* A Baroness in Waiting (Government Whip) 1998–. *Spokesman:* Spokesperson on: Social Security 1998–, International Development 1998–, Women's Issues 1998–. *Select Committees:* Co-opted Member, Select Committee on European Communities Sub-Committee F (Social Affairs, Education and Home Affairs) 1997–98. *Other:* Council Member, Institute of Employment Studies 1993–98; Chairman, Board of Governors, Royal College of Nursing Institute 1994–98; Director, Hampstead Theatre 1995–98. Honorary professorship; two honorary doctorates. *Trusts, etc:* Deputy Chairman, Runnymede Trust 1990–98; Trustee, Institute of Public Policy Research 1994–98; Non-Executive Director, UCLH Trust; Chairman, Afiya Trust 1996–98; Trustee: VSO 1997–98, Project Hope 1997–98. *Name, Style and Title:* Raised to the peerage as Baroness Amos, of Brondesbury in the London Borough of Brent 1997. *Address:* The Baroness Amos, House of Lords, London, SW1A 0PW *Tel:* 020 7219 4120 *E-Mail:* amosv@parliament.uk.

LORD AMPTHILL — Cross-Bencher

AMPTHILL (4th Baron, UK), Geoffrey Denis Erskine Russell; cr. 1881. Born 15 October 1921. Son of 3rd Baron, CBE. Succeeded his father 1973; educated Stowe. Married 1st, 1946, Susan Mary, daughter of late Hon. Charles Winn (2 sons 1 daughter and 1 son deceased) (marriage dissolved 1971), married 2nd, 1972, Elisabeth Anne Marie, daughter of late Claude Henri Gustave Mallon (marriage dissolved 1987). *Armed Forces:* Irish Guards 1941–46, Captain 1944. *Career:* General Manager, Fortnum & Mason 1947–51; Chairman, New Providence Hotel Co. Ltd; Managing Director, theatre owning and producing companies 1953–71; Director, Dualvest plc 1980–1987; Director, United Newspapers plc 1981–96, Deputy Chairman 1991–96; Director, Express Newspapers plc 1985–98, Deputy Chairman 1989–98; Chairman, London's Helicopter Emergency Service 1992–97. *House of Lords:* Deputy Chairman of Committees, House of Lords 1980–92, 1997–, Chairman 1992–94; A Deputy Speaker of the House of Lords 1982–; An elected hereditary peer 1999–. *Select Committees:* Member or Chairman, Select Committees on Offices, Finance and Administration 1979–94; Chairman, Refreshment Sub-Committee 1980–92; Chairman, Select Committees on: Channel Tunnel Bill 1987–88, Rail Link Bill 1996; Member, Delegated Powers and Deregulation 1997–. *Other:* Formerly Director, Leeds Castle Foundation. *Honours:* CBE 1986; PC 1995. *Address:* Rt Hon the Lord Ampthill, CBE, 6 North Court, Great Peter Street, London, SW1P 3LL *Tel:* 020 7233 0133 *Fax:* 020 7233 0122.

BARONESS ANDREWS — Labour

ANDREWS (Life Baroness), Elizabeth Kay Andrews; cr. 2000. Born 16 May 1943; educated University of Wales (BA, MA); Sussex University (DPhil). (Marriage dissolved). *Career:* Fellow, Science Policy Research Unit 1968–70; Parliamentary clerk 1970–85; Policy adviser to Neil Kinnock as Leader of the Opposition 1985–92; Director, Education Extra 1992–. *Other:* Member, Education Panel, The Arts Council. *Honours:* OBE 1998. Fellow, Royal Society of Arts. *Publications:* Articles and books on science and education policy, social policy and out of school learning. *Special Interests:* Education social policy, international development, the arts, science policy. *Name, Style and Title:* Raised to the peerage as Baroness Andrews, of Southover in the County of East Sussex 2000. *Address:* The Baroness Andrews, OBE, Education Extra, 17 Old Ford Road, Bethnal Green, London, E2 9PL *Tel:* 020 8709 9900 *E-Mail:* k.andrews@education_extra.org.uk.

BARONESS ANELAY OF ST JOHNS — Conservative

ANELAY OF ST JOHNS (Life Baroness) Joyce Anne Anelay; cr. 1996. Born 17 July 1947. Daughter of late Stanley Charles Clarke and of Annette Marjorie Clarke; educated Enfield County School; Bristol University (BA History); London University Institute of Education (CertEd); Brunel University (MA Public and Social Administration). Married 1970, Richard Alfred Anelay, QC. *Councils, Public Bodies:* JP, NW Surrey 1985–97. *Career:* Teacher, St David's School, Ashford, Middlesex 1969–74. *Whip:* An Opposition Whip 1997–98. *Spokesman:* An Opposition Spokeswoman on: Agriculture 1997–98, Culture, Media and Sport December 1998–, Home Affairs 1997–98, Social Security 1997–99. *Select Committees:* Co-opted Member, Select Committee on European Communities Sub-Committee E (Law and Institutions) 1997–98; Member, Select Committee on Procedure 1997–. *Party Groups (General):* Chairman, SE Area Conservative Womens' Committee 1987–90; Member, National Union Executive Committee of the Conservative Party 1987–97, Vice-Chairman, SE Area Executive Committee 1990–93; Chairman, Women's National Committee 1993–96, Vice-President, National Union 1996–97. *Other:* Voluntary Adviser, Woking Citizens' Advice Bureau 1976–85, Chairman 1988–93, President 1996–; Chairman, Governors, Hermitage First and Middle Schools 1981–88. Hon. DSocSci, Brunel 1997. *Miscellaneous:* Member: Social Security Appeal Tribunal 1983–96, Social Security Advisory Committee for Great Britain and Northern Ireland 1989–96, Women's National Commission 1991–94, Child Support Appeal Tribunal 1993–96, Patron: Tourism For All Consortium 1999–, Restaurant Association of Great Britain 1999–. *Honours:* OBE 1990; DBE 1995. FRSA. *Special Interests:* Social Security, Home Affairs. *Recreations:* Golf, reading. *Sportsclubs:* Woking Golf. *Name, Style and Title:* Raised to the peerage as Baroness Anelay of St Johns, of St Johns in the County of Surrey 1996. *Address:* The Baroness Anelay of St Johns, DBE, House of Lords, London, SW1A 0PW *E-Mail:* anelayj@parliament.uk.

LORD ARCHER OF SANDWELL — Labour

ARCHER OF SANDWELL (Life Baron), Peter Kingsley Archer; cr. 1992. Born 20 November 1926. Son of late Cyril Kingsley Archer and May Archer; educated Wednesbury Boys' High School; London School of Economics (LLM 1950); University College, London (BA philosophy 1952). Married August 7, 1954, Margaret Irene, daughter of late Sydney John Smith (1 son). *Career:* Called to the Bar, Gray's Inn 1952, Bencher 1974, QC, Recorder of the Crown Court 1981–98. *House of Commons:* Contested Hendon South 1959 and Brierley Hill 1964 General Elections; MP (Labour) for Rowley Regis and Tipton 1966–74; PPS to Attorney-General 1967–70; MP (Labour) for Warley West 1974–92; Solicitor General 1974–79; Member, Shadow Cabinet 1981–87. *Spokesman (Commons):* Opposition Front Bench Spokesman on: Legal Affairs 1979–82, Trade, Prices and Consumer Protection 1982–83, Northern Ireland 1983–87. *Spokesman:* An Opposition Spokesman on Foreign Affairs 1992–97. *Select Committees:* Member, Select Committees on: European Affairs (Sub-Committee E) 1993–96, the Scrutiny of Delegated Powers, Delegated Powers and Deregulation 1997–99, Parliamentary Privilege (Joint Committee) 1999–, Chairman, Select Committee on Freedom of Information Bill 1999–. *Party Groups (General):* Chairman, Society of Labour Lawyers 1971–74, 1980–93; President, Fabian Society 1993–; Joint President, Society of Labour Lawyers 1993–;

Member, Labour Party Departmental Committees for: Home Affairs, Foreign Affairs, Defence. *Other:* Chairman, Amnesty International (British Section) 1971–74; President: Methodist Homes for the Aged 1993–, World Disarmament Campaign 1994–, UNA (London Region) 1999–2000. *Trusts, etc:* President, One World Trust. *Miscellaneous:* Chairman: Council on Tribunals 1992–99, Enemy Property Compensation Panel, Member, Intelligence and Security Committee. *Honours:* PC 1977. Freeman: Metropolitan Borough of Sandwell, State of Maryland. *Publications: The Queen's Courts; Communism and the Law; The International Protection of Human Rights;* Co-author *Freedom at Stake; Purpose in Socialism;* Editor, *Social Welfare and the Citizen;* Editor, *More Law Reform Now. Special Interests:* Human Rights, Law Reform, Northern Ireland, World Government, Conservation, Third World. *Recreations:* Music, writing, gardening. *Name, Style and Title:* Raised to the peerage as Baron Archer of Sandwell, of Sandwell in the County of West Midlands 1992. *Address:* Rt Hon the Lord Archer of Sandwell, QC, Highcroft, Hill View Road, Wraysbury, Staines, Middlesex, TW19 5EQ.

LORD ARCHER OF WESTON-SUPER-MARE   Non-Affiliated

ARCHER OF WESTON-SUPER-MARE (Life Baron), Jeffrey Howard Archer; cr. 1992. Born 15 April 1940. Son of late William Archer and of Lola Archer; educated Wellington School, Somerset; Brasenose College, Oxford. Married 1966, Mary Doreen (Dr Mary Archer), daughter of late Harold Norman Weeden (2 sons). *Councils, Public Bodies:* Councillor, GLC for Havering 1966–70. *Career:* Athletics Blues 1963–65; Gymnastics Blue 1963; Represented Great Britain in athletics 1966; Author, Playright and Auctioneer. *House of Commons:* MP (Conservative) for Louth 1969–74. *Party Groups (General):* Deputy Chairman, Conservative Party 1985–86; President, Conservative Party London Clubs 1998–99. *Publications:* Plays: *Beyond Reasonable Doubt,* 1987; *Exclusive,* 1990; Novels/short stories: *Not a Penny More, Not a Penny Less,* 1975; *Shall We Tell the President?* 1977; *Kane and Abel,* 1979; *A Quiver Full of Arrows (short stories),* 1980; *The Prodigal Daughter,* 1982; *First Among Equals,* 1984; *A Matter of Honour,* 1986; *A Twist in the Tale* (short stories) 1988; *As the Crow Flies,* 1991; *Honour Among Thieves,* 1993; *Twelve Red Herrings (short stories),* 1994; *The Fourth Estate,* 1996; *Collected Short Stories,* 1997; *The Eleventh Commandment,* 1998; *To Cut a Long Story Short,* 2000. *Recreations:* Theatre, cricket, auctioneering, art. *Sportsclubs:* President, Somerset AAA 1973–99; Vice-President, Cambridge City RFU; President, World Snooker Association 1997–99. *Clubs:* MCC. *Name, Style and Title:* Raised to the peerage as Baron Archer of Weston-super-Mare, of Mark in the County of Somerset 1992. *Address:* The Lord Archer of Weston-super-Mare, The Penthouse, 93 Albert Embankment, London, SE1 7TY; The Old Vicarage, Grantchester, Cambridge, CB3 9ND *E-Mail:* jeffrey.archer@jeffreyarcher.co.uk.

LORD ARMSTRONG OF ILMINSTER   Cross-Bencher

ARMSTRONG OF ILMINSTER (Life Baron), Robert Temple Armstrong; cr. 1988. Born 30 March 1927. Son of late Sir Thomas Armstrong, musician and late Hester Muriel, née Draper; educated Dragon School; Eton (King's Scholar); Christ Church, Oxford (Scholar) (Classical Mods 1947, Literae Humaniores 1949). Married 1st, 1953, Serena Mary Benedicta, daughter of late Sir Roger Chance, 3rd Bt, MC (2 daughters) (marriage dissolved 1985, she died 1994), married 2nd, 1985, (Mary) Patricia Carlow. *Career:* Assistant Principal, HM Treasury 1950–55; Private Secretary to: Reginald Maudling as Economic Secretary to the Treasury 1953–54, Rab Butler as Chancellor of the Exchequer 1954–55; Principal, Treasury 1955–57; Secretary, Radcliffe Committee on Working of Monetary System 1957–59; Returned to Treasury as Principal 1959–64; Secretary, Armitage Committee on Pay of Postmen 1964; Assistant Secretary: Cabinet Office 1964–66, Treasury 1967–68; Principal Private Secretary to Roy Jenkins as Chancellor of the Exchequer 1968; Under-Secretary (Home Finance), Treasury 1968–70; Principal Private Secretary to Prime Minister 1970–75; Home Office: Deputy Under Secretary of State, 1975–77, Permanent Under Secretary of State 1977–79; Secretary of the Cabinet 1979–87; Head of the Home Civil Service 1981–87; Director various companies 1988–97; Director, Royal Opera House 1988–93; Chairman: Biotechnology Investments Ltd 1989–2000, Bristol and West plc (formerly Building Society) 1993–97; Forensic Investigative Associates plc 1997–; Director, Bank of Ireland 1997–; Chairman, 3i Bioscience Investment Trust plc 2000–.

Chancellor: Chancellor, Hull University 1994–. *Select Committees:* Member, Select Committee on European Union, Sub-Committee A (Economic and Financial Affairs, Trade and External Relations) 2000–. Honorary doctorate. *Trusts, etc:* Fellow of Eton College 1979–94; Member: RUW Trust 1958–, Rhodes Trust 1975–97, Pilgrim Trust 1987–; Chairman: Board of Trustees, V & A Museum 1988–98, Hestercombe Gardens Trust 1996–, Board of Governors, Royal Northern College of Music 2000–. *Miscellaneous:* Hon. Student, Christ Church, Oxford 1985; Hon. Bencher, Inner Temple 1985. *Honours:* CB 1974; CVO 1975; KCB 1978; GCB 1983. Freeman, City of London. Honorary Member, Salters' Company. *Special Interests:* Arts, museums and galleries. *Recreations:* music. *Clubs:* Brooks's, Garrick. *Name, Style and Title:* Raised to the peerage as Baron Armstrong of Ilminster, of Ashill in the County of Somerset 1988. *Address:* The Lord Armstrong of Ilminster, GCB, CVO, House of Lords, London, SW1A 0PW.

EARL OF ARRAN   Conservative

ARRAN (9th Earl of, I), Arthur Desmond Colquhoun Gore; cr. 1762; 9th Viscount Sudley and Baron Saunders (I) 1758; 5th Baron Sudley (UK) 1884; 11th Bt of Castle Gore (I) 1662. Born 14 July 1938. Son of 8th Earl. Succeeded his father 1983. Sits as Baron Sudley; educated Eton; Balliol College, Oxford (MA English Literature). Married 1974, Eleanor Van Cutsem (2 daughters). *Armed Forces:* Served Grenadier Guards, National Service, Commissioned. *Career:* Assistant Manager *Daily Mail* 1972–73; Managing Director, Clark Nelson 1973–74; Assistant General Manager, *Daily Express* and *Sunday Express* June-November 1974; Director, Waterstone & Co Ltd 1984–87; Parliamentary Consultant to the Waste Industry 1995–; Non-Executive Director: HMV (EMI) 1995–98, SWEL (the Economy and Inward Investment of the West Country), Bonham's (Auctioneers) 1998. *House of Lords:* Parliamentary Under-Secretary of State for: The Armed Forces, Ministry of Defence 1989–92, Northern Ireland Office 1992–94, Department of the Environment January-July 1994; An elected hereditary peer 1999–. *Whip:* A Lord in Waiting (Government Whip) 1987–89; Captain of the Queen's Bodyguard of the Yeomen of the Guard (Government Deputy Chief Whip) July 1994-January 1995. *Spokesman:* Spokesman for: The Home Office, DES and DHSS 1987–89, Department of the Environment 1988–89. *Other:* Co-Chairman, Children's Country Holidays Fund. *Special Interests:* Media, Charity, Sport, Foreign Affairs. *Recreations:* Tennis, golf, croquet, shooting and gardening. *Clubs:* Turf, Beefsteak, Pratt's, White's, Annabels. *Address:* Earl of Arran, House of Lords, London, SW1A 0PW.

LORD ASHCROFT   Conservative

ASHCROFT (Life Baron), Michael Anthony Ashcroft; cr. 2000. *Career:* Company Director; Chairman, Carlisle Holdings Ltd; Former Belize Ambassador to the UN. *Party Groups (General):* Senior Party Treasurer, Conservative Party 1998–. *Honours:* KCMG 2000. *Name, Style and Title:* Raised to the peerage as Baron Ashcroft, of Chichester in the County of West Sussex 2000. *Address:* The Lord Ashcroft, KCMG, Conservative Party, 32 Smith Square, London, SW1P 3HH *Tel:* 020 7222 9000 *Fax:* 020 7222 1135 *E-Mail:* Website: www.tory.org.uk.

LORD ASHLEY OF STOKE   Labour

ASHLEY OF STOKE (Life Baron), Jack Ashley; cr. 1992. Born 6 December 1922. Son of late Jack Ashley; educated St Patrick's Elementary School, Widnes; Ruskin College, Oxford (Diploma economics and political science); Gonville and Caius College, Cambridge (BA economics) (President of Union). Married December 15, 1951, Pauline Crispin (3 daughters). *Trades Union:* Shop steward convenor 1946. *Councils, Public Bodies:* Councillor, Widnes Borough Council 1945–47. *Career:* Labourer and crane driver 1935–46; BBC Radio Producer 1951–57; Commonwealth Fund Fellow 1955; BBC Senior Television Producer 1957–66. *House of Commons:* Contested Finchley 1951; MP (Labour) for Stoke-on-Trent South 1966–92; PPS: to Secretary of State for Economic Affairs 1967–70, to Secretary of State for Health and Social Security 1974–79. *Chancellor:* Chancellor, Staffordshire University 1993–. *Party Groups (General):* Member, Labour Party National Executive Committee 1976–78. *Other:* Member, General Advisory Council, BBC 1967–69;

President: Royal College of Speech and Language Therapists 1995–, Royal National Institute for Deaf, Defeating Deafness, British Tinnitus Association. *Awards Granted: Spectator* and *Oldie*, Campaigner of the Year. Twelve honorary degrees. *Honours:* CH 1975; PC 1979. Stoke on Trent. *Publications: Journey into Silence* (autobiography) 1973; *Acts of Defiance*, 1992. *Special Interests:* Disability, Health, Medical Drugs, Poverty, Disadvantaged, Hong Kong, China. *Sportsclubs:* Patron, Widnes Rugby League Club. *Name, Style and Title:* Raised to the peerage as Baron Ashley of Stoke, of Widnes in the County of Cheshire 1992. *Address:* Rt Hon the Lord Ashley of Stoke, CH, House of Lords, London, SW1A 0PW.

BARONESS ASHTON OF UPHOLLAND — Labour

ASHTON OF UPHOLLAND (Life Baroness), Catherine Margaret Ashton; cr. 1999. Born 20 March 1956. Daughter of late Harold and Clare Ashton; educated Upholland Grammar School; Bedford College, London University (BSc 1977). Married 1988, Peter Jon, son of Michael and Pippa Kellner (1 son, 1 daughter, 1 stepson, 2 stepdaughters). *Councils, Public Bodies:* Chairman, East and North Herts Health Authority 1998–. *Career:* Administrative Officer, CND 1977–79; The Coverdale Organisation 1979–81; Central Council for Education and Training in Social Work 1981–83; Director of Community Development and Public Affairs, Business in the Community 1983–89; Public Policy Adviser 1989–, seconded by London First to Home Office 1998–99; Adviser, BE Foundation 2000–; Director, YouGov.com 2000–. *International Bodies (General):* Member, British American Parliamentary Group. *Other:* Advisory Board Member, "Can Do" Network; Vice President, National Council for One Parent Families. *Trusts, etc:* Trustee, Verulamium Museum 2000–. *Special Interests:* Policy Implementation. *Recreations:* Swimming, theatre, "retail therapy". *Clubs:* Royal Commonwealth Society. *Name, Style and Title:* Raised to the peerage as Baroness Ashton of Upholland, of St Albans in the County of Hertfordshire 1999. *Address:* The Baroness Ashton of Upholland, House of Lords, London, SW1A 0PW; East and North Herts Health Authority, Charter House, Parkway, Welwyn Garden City *Tel:* 01707 390855.

VISCOUNT ASTOR — Conservative

ASTOR (4th Viscount, UK), William Waldorf Astor; cr. 1917; 4th Baron Astor (UK) 1916. Born 27 December 1951. Son of 3rd Viscount and Hon. Sarah Katharine Elinor Norton, daughter of 6th Baron Grantley. Succeeded his father 1966; educated Eton. Married January 14, 1976, Mrs Annabel Sheffield, daughter of Timothy Jones (2 sons 1 daughter). *Career:* Citibank, New York 1970–72; Observer, USA 1972; Westminster Press 1973–74; Director: UK and US Property and Investment Companies 1974–84, Blakeney Hotels and Cliveden Hotels 1984–90; Director: Chorion Plc 1996–, Prestbury Plc 1996–, Jupiter European Investment Trust 1996–. *House of Lords:* Parliamentary Under-Secretary of State: Department of Social Security 1993–94, Department of National Heritage 1994–95; An elected hereditary peer 1999–. *Whip:* A Lord in Waiting (Government Whip) 1990–93. *Spokesman:* Spokesman for: Department of Environment 1990–91, Home Office 1991–92, Department of National Heritage 1992–93; An Opposition Spokesman for: Home Office 1997–, Education and Employment 1999–. *Trusts, etc:* Trustee, Stanley Spencer Gallery, Cookham. *Clubs:* White's, Turf. *Address:* The Viscount Astor, Ginge Manor, Nr Wantage, Oxfordshire, OX12 8QT *Tel:* 01235 833228.

LORD ASTOR OF HEVER — Conservative

ASTOR OF HEVER (3rd Baron, UK), John Jacob Astor; cr. 1956. Born 16 June 1946. Son of 2nd Baron, and late Lady Irene Haig, daughter of Field Marshal 1st Earl Haig, KT, GCB, OM, GCVO, KCIE. Succeeded his father 1984; educated Eton. Married 1st, July 18, 1970, Fiona Harvey (3 daughters) (marriage dissolved 1990), married 2nd, 1990, Hon. Elizabeth Mackintosh, daughter of 2nd Viscount Mackintosh of Halifax, OBE, BEM (1 son 1 daughter). *Armed Forces:* Lieutenant, The Life Guards 1966–70. *Councils, Public Bodies:* DL Kent 1996–. *Career:* Managing Director: Honon et Cie 1982–, Astor France SARL 1989–; President, Astor Enterprises Inc. 1986–. *House of Lords:* An elected hereditary peer 1999–. *Whip:* An Opposition Whip

(Health/Social Security) December 1998–. *Select Committees:* Member, Personal Bills Committee, Finance and Staff Sub-Committee. *Party Groups:* Member of Executive, Association of Conservative Peers 1996–98. *Other:* President, Sevenoaks Westminster Patrons Club 1991–; Governor, Cobham Hall School 1992–96; President: Earl Haig Branch, Royal British Legion 1994–, Kent Federation of Amenity Societies 1995–, Motorsport Industry Association 1995–, RoSPA 1996–99, RoSPA Advanced Drivers Association 1997–, CPRE Kent; Patron, Aquarian Opera 1999–. *Trusts, etc:* Trustee: Astor of Hever Trust 1986–, Astor Foundation 1988–, Rochester Cathedral Trust 1988–; Patron, Edenbridge Music and Arts Trust 1989–; Trustee, Canterbury Cathedral Trust 1992–; Patron: Bridge Trust 1993–, Kent Youth Trust 1994–; President, Eden Valley Museum Trust 1998–. *Honours:* Chairman, Council of the Order of St John for Kent 1987–97. Member, Goldsmiths' Company. *Special Interests:* France, Motor Industry, Defence. *Clubs:* White's, Riviera Golf (France). *Address:* The Lord Astor of Hever, DL, House of Lords, London, SW1A 0PW *Tel:* 020 7219 5475 *E-Mail:* astorjj@parliament.uk.

LORD ATTENBOROUGH — Labour

ATTENBOROUGH (Life Baron), Richard Samuel Attenborough; cr. 1993. Born 29 August 1923. Son of late Frederick Attenborough; educated Wyggeston Grammar School, Leicester; Leverhulme scholarship to Royal Academy of Dramatic Art. Married 1945, Sheila Sim (1 son 2 daughters). *Armed Forces:* Served RAF 1943–46. *Career:* Actor, producer and director; Appeared in a number of productions on the London stage including: *Brighton Rock* 1943, *The Mousetrap* 1952–54, *The Rape of the Belt* 1957–58; Film appearances include: *In Which We Serve, Brighton Rock, London Belongs to Me, The Guinea Pig, Morning Departure, The Ship That Died of Shame, I'm Alright Jack, The League of Gentlemen, The Angry Silence* (also co-produced),
The Dock Brief, The Great Escape, Seance On a Wet Afternoon (also produced, BAFTA Award), *Guns at Batasi* (BAFTA Award), *The Flight of the Phoenix, The Sand Pebbles* (Hollywood Golden Globe), *Dr Dolittle* (Hollywood Golden Globe), *10 Rillington Place, The Chess Players, Jurassic Park, Miracle on 34th Street, Lost World, Elizabeth I*; Produced: *Whistle Down the Wind, The L-Shaped Room*; Directed: *Young Winston* (Hollywood Golden Globe), *A Bridge Too Far, Magic, A Chorus Line*; Produced and directed: *Oh! What a Lovely War* (BAFTA Award, Hollywood Golden Globe), *Gandhi* (8 Oscars, 5 BAFTA Awards, 5 Hollywood Golden Globes), *Cry Freedom, Chaplin, Shadowlands* (BAFTA Award); *In Love and War; Grey Owl*; Chairman, Capital Radio 1972–92, Life President 1992–; Chairman: Goldcrest Films and Television Ltd 1982–87, Channel Four Television 1987–92, Deputy Chairman 1980–86. *Chancellor:* Pro-Chancellor, Sussex University 1970–, Chancellor 1998–. *Other:* Member, chair, president numerous organisations in arts, theatre, film including: Chairman, Royal Academy of Dramatic Art 1970–, Mem. Council 1963–; President, Muscular Dystrophy Group of Great Britain 1971–, Vice-President 1962–71; President, The Gandhi Foundation 1983–, Patron, Goodwill Ambassador for Unicef 1987–; Chairman, European Script Fund 1988–96, Hon. President 1996–; President, Combined Theatrical Charities Appeals Council 1988–, Chairman 1964–88; President, Arts for Health 1989–; Patron, Richard Attenborough Centre for Disability and the Arts, Leicester University 1990–; President, National Film and TV School 1997–, Governor 1970–81. *Awards Granted: Evening Standard* Film Award, 40 years service to British Cinema 1983; Martin Luther King Jr Peace Prize 1983; European Film Awards Award of Merit for Humanitarianism in Film Making 1988; Shakespeare Prize for Outstanding Contribution to European Culture 1992; Praemium Imperiale 1998. Ten honorary doctorates and fellowships. *Trusts, etc:* President, The Actors' Charitable Trust 1988–, Chairman 1956–88; Trustee: King George V Fund for Actors and Actresses 1973–, Help a London Child 1975–, Tate Gallery 1976–82 and 1994–96; Chairman, UK Trustees Waterford-Kamhlaba School Swaziland 1976–, Governor 1987–; Trustee: Motability 1977–, Tate Foundation 1986–. *Honours:* CBE 1967; Kt 1976; Padma Bhushan, India 1983; Commandeur, Ordre des Arts et des Lettres, France 1985; Chevalier, Legion d'Honneur, France 1988. Fellow: BAFTA 1983, BFI 1992. Freeman, City of Leicester 1990. *Publications: In Search of Gandhi*, 1982; *Richard Attenborough's Chorus Line* (with Diana Carter) 1986; *Cry Freedom, A Pictorial Record*, 1987. *Special Interests:* Arts, Education, Disability, Underdeveloped Countries. *Recreations:* Collecting paintings and sculpture, listening to music, watching football and reading the newspapers. *Sportsclubs:* Director, Chelsea Football Club 1969–82, Life Vice-President 1993–. *Clubs:* Garrick, Beefsteak. *Name, Style and Title:* Raised to the peerage as Baron Attenborough, of Richmond upon Thames in the London Borough of Richmond upon Thames 1993. *Address:* The Lord Attenborough, CBE, Old Friars, Richmond Green, Richmond upon Thames, Surrey, TW9 1NH *Tel:* 020 8940 7234.

EARL ATTLEE   Conservative

ATTLEE (3rd Earl, UK), John Richard Attlee; cr. 1955; Viscount Prestwood. Born 3 October 1956. Son of 2nd Earl. Succeeded his father 1991; educated Stowe. Married July 31, 1993, Celia Jane Plummer. *Armed Forces:* Major, Territorial Army, Officer Commanding 150 Recovery Company, REME (V) 1998–. *Career:* President, The Heavy Transport Association 1994–; British Direct Aid: In-Country Director (Rwanda) 1995–96. *House of Lords:* An elected hereditary peer 1999–. *Whip:* An Opposition Whip 1997–99. *Spokesman:* An Opposition Spokesman for: Defence June-Oct 1997, Environment, Transport and the Regions (Transport) June-Oct 1997, Northern Ireland June-Oct 1997, December 1998-June 1999, Defence 1998 , Trade and Industry 1998–99, Transport 1999–. *Trusts, etc:* Trustee, Attlee Foundation. *Special Interests:* Engineering, Defence, Transport, Overseas Aid and Development. *Address:* The Earl Attlee, House of Lords, London, SW1A 0PW *E-Mail:* attleej@parliament.uk.

LORD AVEBURY   Liberal Democrat

AVEBURY (4th Baron, UK), Eric Reginald Lubbock; cr. 1900; 7th Bt of Lamas (UK) 1806. Born 29 September 1928. Son of late Hon. Maurice Lubbock, youngest son of 1st Baron, PC, DL, and late Hon. Mary Katharine Adelaide Stanley, daughter of 5th Baron Stanley of Alderley, KCMG, DL. Succeeded his cousin 1971; educated Upper Canada College, Toronto; Harrow; Balliol College, Oxford (BA). Married 1953, Kina Maria, daughter of late Count Joseph O'Kelly de Gallagh, KM (2 sons 1 daughter) (marriage dissolved 1983), married 2nd, 1985, Lindsay Stewart (1 son). *Armed Forces:* Second Lieutenant, Welsh Guards 1949–51. *Career:* With Rolls-Royce (Aero-engine division) 1951–53; Production Engineering Ltd (Management consultant) 1955–60; Charterhouse Group 1960–62; Director, C.L. Projects Ltd. *House of Commons:* MP (Liberal) for Orpington 1962–70. *Whip (Commons):* A former Whip. *House of Lords:* An elected hereditary peer 1999–. *Spokesman:* Spokesman on: Race Relations and Immigration 1971–83, Foreign and Commonwealth Affairs 1998–. *Other:* President: Fluoridation Society 1972–84, Conservation Society 1973–81, London Bach Society, Steinitz Bach Players 1984–98; Patron: Angulinala, Buddhist Prison Chaplaincy 1990–, Kurdish Human Rights Project 1993–, British Campaign for East Timor 1994–. *Miscellaneous:* Member: Speaker's Conference on Electoral Law 1963–65, Royal Commission on Standards of Conduct in Public Life 1975–76. *Honours:* Hilal-i-Quaid-i-Azam (Pakistan) 1990. MInstMechE; FBCS; CEng. *Publications: The Energy Crisis – Growth, Stability or Collapse*, 1973; *Alcohol – Politics and Practicalities*, 1981; *Authority and Accountability*, 1986; *Desolated and Profaned*, 1992; *A Desolation called Peace*, 1993; *Iran: The Subjection of Women*, 1995; *Iran: State of Terror*, 1996. *Address:* The Lord Avebury, 26 Flodden Road, London, SE5 9LH *Tel:* 020 7274 4617 *Fax:* 020 7738 7864 *E-Mail:* ericavebury@hotmail.com.

B

LORD BACH   Labour

BACH (Life Baron), William Stephen Goulden Bach; cr. 1998. Born 25 December 1946. Son of late Stephen Bach, CBE, and late Joan Bach; educated Westminster School; New College, Oxford (BA 1968). Married 1984, Caroline Jones (1 daughter plus 2 children from previous marriage). *Trades Union:* Member, TGWU 1977–. *Councils, Public Bodies:* Leicester City Council: Councillor 1976–87, Chief Whip, Labour Group 1981–83, Councillor, Lutterworth Town Council 1991–99; Mayor, Lutterworth 1993–94; Harborough District Council: Councillor 1995–99, Chair, Contracts Services Committee 1995–97; Chief Whip, Labour Group 1995–98. *Career:* Called to the Bar, Middle Temple 1972, Tenant Barristers' Chambers 1975–, Head of

Chambers 1996–99; Joint Head of Chambers 1999–; Served on a number of circuit and local court and bar committees over many years. *Whip:* A Lord in Waiting (Government Whip) 1999–. *Select Committees:* Member, European Communities Sub Committee E (Laws and Institutions) 1998–99. *Party Groups (General):* Executive Committee Member, Society of Labour Lawyers; Elected Member, Labour Party: National Policy Forum 1998–99, Economic Policy Commission 1998–99; Member: Co-operative Party, Fabian Society; Chair and Co-Founder, Society of Labour Lawyers, East Midlands; Chair: Harborough District Labour Party 1989–95, Northants and Blaby Euro Constituency GC 1992–99. *Other:* Council Member, Leicester University 1980–99; Court Member, 1980–. *Miscellaneous:* Contested (Labour): Gainsborough 1979, Sherwood 1983 and 1987 General Elections. *Special Interests:* Crime and Criminal Justice, Local Government, USA Affairs, Sport. *Recreations:* Playing and watching football and cricket, supporting Leicester City FC, American crime writing. *Sportsclubs:* Leicester City FC, Leicestershire CCC; Founder Member and President, Walcote Cricket Club. *Name, Style and Title:* Raised to the peerage as Baron Bach, of Lutterworth in the County of Leicestershire 1998. *Address:* The Lord Bach, House of Lords, London, SW1A 0PW *Tel:* 020 7222 2597 *Tel:* 0116–252 7710.

LORD BAGRI   Conservative

BAGRI (Life Baron), Raj Kumar Bagri; cr. 1997. Born 24 August 1930. Son of late Sohan Lal Bagri. Married 1954, Usha Maheshwary (1 son 1 daughter). *Career:* Founder and Chairman, Metdist Group 1970–; Chairman, The London Metal Exchange Limited 1993–, Director 1983, Vice-Chairman 1990. *Other:* Member: Advisory Committee of The Prince's Youth Business Trust, Governing Body of School of Oriental and African Studies; Chairman, Bagri Foundation. Two honorary doctorates. *Trusts, etc:* Chairman, Trustees of The Rajiv Gandhi (UK) Foundation; Trustee, Sangam. *Honours:* CBE 1995. *Recreations:* Fine art, classical music, antiques. *Clubs:* MCC. *Name, Style and Title:* Raised to the peerage as Baron Bagri, of Regent's Park in the City of Westminster 1997. *Address:* The Lord Bagri, CBE, 80 Cannon Street, London, EC4N 6EJ.

LORD BAKER OF DORKING   Conservative

BAKER OF DORKING (Life Baron), Kenneth Wilfred Baker; cr. 1997. Born 3 November 1934. Son of late Wilfred Michael Baker, OBE; educated St Paul's School; Magdalen College, Oxford (Secretary of Union). Married 1963, Mary Elizabeth Gray-Muir (1 son 2 daughters). *Armed Forces:* National Service 1953–55 (Lieutenant in Gunners). *Councils, Public Bodies:* Councillor, Twickenham Borough Council 1960–62. *House of Commons:* Contested Poplar 1964, Acton 1966; MP (Conservative) for Acton 1968–70, St Marylebone 1970–83 and for Mole Valley June 1983–97; PPS to Minister of State, Department of Employment 1970–72; Parliamentary Secretary, Civil Service Department 1972–74; Minister of State for Industry and Information Technology 1981–84; Minister for Local Government 1984–85; Secretary of State: for The Environment 1985–86, for Education and Science 1986–89; Chancellor of the Duchy of Lancaster 1989–90; Secretary of State for the Home Department 1990–92. *Party Groups (General):* Chairman, Conservative Party 1989–90. *Other:* Chairman: Hansard Society 1978–81, Museum of British History 1995–. Hon. Degree, Richmond College, The American University in London. *Honours:* PC 1984; CH 1992. *Publications: London Lines; I Have No Gun But I Can Spit; The Faber Book of English History in Verse; Unauthorised Versions: Poems and their Parodies; The Faber Book of Conservatism; The Turbulent Years: My Life in Politics,* 1993; *The Prime Ministers – An Irreverent Political History in Cartoons,* 1995; *Kings and Queens: An Irreverent Cartoon History of the British Monarchy,* 1996; *The Faber Book of War Poetry,* 1996; *Childrens English History in Verse,* 2000; *The Faber Book of Landscape Poetry,* 2000. *Special Interests:* Education, History, Information Technology. *Recreations:* Collecting books, collecting political cartoons. *Clubs:* Carlton, Athenaeum, Garrick. *Name, Style and Title:* Raised to the peerage as Baron Baker of Dorking, of Iford in the County of East Sussex 1997. *Address:* Rt Hon the Lord Baker of Dorking, CH, House of Lords, London, SW1A 0PW.

EARL BALDWIN OF BEWDLEY   Cross-Bencher

BALDWIN OF BEWDLEY (4th Earl, UK), Edward Alfred Alexander Baldwin; cr. 1937; Viscount Corvedale. Born 3 January 1938. Son of 3rd Earl and late Joan Elspeth, née Tomes. Succeeded his father 1976; educated Eton; Trinity College, Cambridge (MA, CertEd). Married 1970, Sarah, daughter of Evan James (3 sons). *Armed Forces:* National Service 1956–58, 2nd Lieutenant, Intelligence Corps 1957–58. *Career:* Schoolmaster 1970–77; Education Officer 1978–87. *House of Lords:* An elected hereditary peer 1999–. *Select Committees:* Co-opted Member, Select Committee on Science and Technology Sub-Committee I (Complementary and Alternative Medicine) 2000–. *Miscellaneous:* Chairman, British Acupuncture Accreditation Board 1990–98; Former Member, Research Council for Complementary Medicine. *Special Interests:* Complementary Medicine, Environment, Education. *Recreations:* Mountains, tennis, music. *Clubs:* MCC. *Address:* The Earl Baldwin of Bewdley, Manor Farm House, Godstow Road, Upper Wolvercote, Oxford, OX2 8AJ *Tel:* 01865 552683 *Fax:* 01865 552683.

LORD BARBER   Conservative

BARBER (Life Baron), Anthony Perrinott Lysberg Barber; cr. 1974. Born 4 July 1920. Son of late John Barber, CBE, Company director of Doncaster; educated Retford Grammar School; Oriel College, Oxford (MA). Married 1st, September 5, 1950, Jean Patricia (died 1983), daughter of Milton Asquith (2 daughters), married 2nd, September 8, 1989, Mrs Rosemary Surgenor, daughter of late Canon Youens. *Armed Forces:* Served 1939–45, Commissioned Army, seconded RAF pilot (mentioned in despatches) (P.O.W. 1942–45) (Germany). *Councils, Public Bodies:* DL, West Yorkshire 1987. *Career:* Called to the Bar, Inner Temple 1948; Chairman, Standard Chartered Bank plc. 1974–87; Director, BP 1979–88. *House of Commons:* Contested Doncaster 1950; MP (Conservative) for: Doncaster 1951–64, Altrincham and Sale 1965–74; PPS, Air Ministry 1952; PPS to Rt Hon. Harold Macmillan, Prime Minister 1958; Economic Secretary to the Treasury 1959–62; Financial Secretary to Treasury 1962–63; Minister of Health and member of the Cabinet 1963–64; Chancellor of the Duchy of Lancaster and member of the Cabinet June-July 1970; Chancellor of the Exchequer 1970–74. *Whip (Commons):* Government Whip 1955; Lord Commissioner HM Treasury (Government Whip) 1957–58. *Party Groups (General):* Chairman, Conservative Party 1967–70. *Other:* Member, Falkland Islands Enquiry (Franks Committee) 1982; British Member, Eminent Persons Group on South Africa 1986; Chairman, RAF Benevolent Fund 1991–96. Hon. Fellow, Oriel College 1973. *Honours:* TD, PC 1963. *Publications:* Memoirs: *Taking the Tide. Clubs:* Carlton, Royal Air Force. *Name, Style and Title:* Raised to the peerage as Baron Barber, of Wentbridge in the County of West Yorkshire 1974. *Address:* Rt Hon the Lord Barber, TD, DL, House of Lords, London, SW1A 0PW.

LORD BARBER OF TEWKESBURY   Cross-Bencher

BARBER OF TEWKESBURY (Life Baron), Derek Coates Barber; cr. 1992. Born 17 June 1918. Son of late Thomas Smith-Barber; educated Royal Agricultural College, Cirencester. Married 1st, (dissolved 1981), married 2nd, 1983, Rosemary Jennifer, daughter of late Lieutenant-Commander Randolph Brougham Pearson, RN. *Armed Forces:* Served in Second World War (invalided). *Councils, Public Bodies:* Councillor, Cheltenham Rural District Council 1948–52. *Career:* Farmer in Gloucestershire; Various posts, Ministry of Agriculture, Fisheries and Food 1946–72; Environment consultant to Humberts, Chartered Surveyors 1972–93. *Select Committees:* Member, House of Lords Select Committees on: European Communities, Sub-Committee D (Food and Agriculture) 1993–96, Sustainable Development 1994–95. *Other:* Chairman, Royal Society for the Protection of Birds 1976–81, Vice-President 1981–, President 1990–91; President, Gloucestershire Naturalists' Society 1981–; Vice-President, Ornithological Society of the Middle East 1987–97; President: Royal Agricultural Society of England 1991–92, British Pig Association 1995–97. *Awards Granted:* Bledisloe Gold Medal for distinguished service to UK agriculture 1967; RSPB Gold Medal 1982;

RASE Gold Medal for services to agriculture 1991; Massey-Ferguson Award for Services to agriculture. Hon. DSc, Bradford University 1986. *Trusts, etc:* Council Member, British Trust for Ornithology 1987–90; President: Rare Breeds Survival Trust 1991–95 and 1997–99, The Hawk and Owl Trust 1991–96. *Miscellaneous:* Chairman: BBC Central Agricultural Advisory Committee 1974–80, Countryside Commission 1981–91; Member, Ordnance Survey Advisory Board 1982–85; Chairman: Booker Countryside Advisory Board 1990–96, The National Forest Advisory Board 1991–94. *Honours:* Kt 1984. Hon. Fellow, Royal Agricultural Society of England 1986; Fellow: Royal Agricultural Societies (FRAgS) 1991, Institute of Agricultural Management (FIAgrM) 1992. *Publications:* Joint Author of books on agriculture as well as contributing to journals on farming and wildlife. *Special Interests:* Farming, Forestry, Environment. *Recreations:* Birds, farming. *Clubs:* Farmers'. *Name, Style and Title:* Raised to the peerage as Baron Barber of Tewkesbury, of Gotherington in the County of Gloucestershire 1992. *Address:* The Lord Barber of Tewkesbury, Chough House, Gretton Road, Gotherington, Gloucestershire, GL52 4QU *Tel:* 01242 673908.

BARONESS BARKER   Liberal Democrat

BARKER (Life Baroness); Elizabeth Jean Barker; cr. 1999. Born 31 January 1961; educated Dalziel High School, Motherwell, Lanarkshire, Scotland; Broadway School, Oldham, Lancashire; Southampton University (BSc(SocSci) Psychology). *Trades Union:* Member, ACCTS. *Career:* Age Concern England; Project Co-ordinator, Opportunities for Volunteering Programme 1983–88, Grants Officer 1988–92, Field Officer based in London 1992–; Management Consultant to Age Concern organisations in eight London Boroughs. *Party Groups (General):* Joined Liberal Party 1979; Member, Union of Liberal Students 1979–83, Chair 1982–83; Member: Liberal Party National Executive 1982–83, Liberator Collective which produces *Liberator* magazine 1983–96, Liberal Assembly Committee 1984–, Federal Policy Committee 1997–; Chair, Liberal Democrat Federal Conference Committee 1997–; Member: The Future of Social Services Policy Working Group, Freedom and Fairness for Women Policy Working Group; Working Group – An Age of Opportunity. *Trusts, etc:* Trustee, Andy Lawson Memorial Fund. *Special Interests:* Health, Social Services, Ageing, Poverty, Civil Liberties, Governance of the UK. *Name, Style and Title:* Raised to the peerage as Baroness Barker, of Anagach in Highland 1999. *Address:* The Baroness Barker, c/o Liberal Democrat Whips Office, House of Lords, London, SW1A 0PW.

LORD BARNETT   Labour

BARNETT (Life Baron), Joel Barnett; cr. 1983. Born 14 October 1923. Son of late Louis and Ettie Barnett; educated Elementary school; Manchester Central High School; Correspondence course, qualified as Accountant. Married 1949, Lilian Goldstone (1 daughter). *Armed Forces:* RASC 1939–45. *Councils, Public Bodies:* Councillor, Prestwich Council 1956–59; JP, Manchester Bench 1960. *Career:* Accountant; Senior Partner, J. C. Allen & Co (now Hacker Young) until 1974; Vice-Chairman, BBC 1986–93; Chairman, British Screen Finance Ltd 1986–97; Member, International Advisory Board of Unisys Inc. 1989–96; Chairman: Education Broadcasting Services Trust Ltd 1993–, Origin (UK) Ltd 1996–, Mercury Recycling Ltd 1996–, Helping Hands plc 1997–98; Previously Chairman and Director for a number of public limited companies. *House of Commons:* Contested (Labour) Runcorn 1959; MP (Labour) for Heywood and Royton 1964–83; Chief Secretary to the Treasury 1974–79; Member of Cabinet, February 1977–79. *Spokesman (Commons):* Official Opposition Spokesman on Financial and Economic matters 1970–74. *Spokesman:* Official Front Bench Spokesman on Treasury Affairs in House of Lords 1983–86. *Select Committees:* Chairman, Sub-Committee A of European Communities Select Committee (Economic and Financial Affairs, Trade and External Relations) 1995–97, 1997–98; Member, Select Committees on: European Communities 1997–, Monetary Policy of the Bank of England 1998–. *Party Groups (General):* Member, Fabian Society. *Other:* Chairman, Hansard Society 1984–90; President, Royal Institute of Public Administration (RIPA) 1988–91; Chairman, Mansfield 2010 1993–97. Hon. LLD, Strathclyde University 1983; Hon. Fellow, Birkbeck College, London University. *Trusts, etc:* Trustee: Victoria and Albert Museum 1983–97,

Open University Foundation 1995–. *Miscellaneous:* Chairman, Building Society Ombudsman Council 1986–96. *Honours:* PC 1975. FACCA. *Publications: Inside the Treasury*, 1982. *Recreations:* Walking, reading, theatre, good food, watching Manchester United. *Name, Style and Title:* Raised to the peerage as Baron Barnett, of Heywood and Royton in Greater Manchester 1983. *Address:* Rt Hon the Lord Barnett, 7 Hillingdon Road, Whitefield, Manchester, M45 7QQ; House of Lords, London, SW1A 0PW *Tel:* House of Lords 020 7219 5440.

LORD BASSAM OF BRIGHTON — Labour

BASSAM OF BRIGHTON (Life Baron), (John) Steven Bassam; cr. 1997. Born 11 June 1953. Son of late Sydney Stevens and of Enid Bassam; educated Secondary Modern School; Sussex University (BA history 1975), Kent University (MA social work 1979). *Trades Union:* Member, UNISON. *Councils, Public Bodies:* Councillor, Brighton and Hove Council 1983, subsequently Deputy Leader of Labour Group, Leader of Unitary Council 1996–99; Head of Environmental Health and Consumer Issues, Local Government Association 1997–99. *Career:* Social Worker, East Sussex County Council 1976–77; Legal Adviser, North Lewisham Law Centre 1979–88; Former Consultant Advisor, KPMG Capital. *House of Lords:* Parliamentary Under-Secretary of State, Home Office 1999–. *Miscellaneous:* Contested Brighton Kemptown (Lab) 1987. *Recreations:* Cricket, walking. *Sportsclubs:* Preston Village Cricket Club. *Name, Style and Title:* Raised to the peerage as Baron Bassam of Brighton, of Brighton in the County of East Sussex 1997. *Address:* The Lord Bassam of Brighton, House of Lords, London, SW1A 0PW; Longstone, 25 Church Place, Brighton, BN2 5JN.

BISHOP OF BATH AND WELLS — Non-Affiliated

BATH AND WELLS (77th Bishop of), James Lawton Thompson. Born 11 August 1936. Son of Bernard and Marjorie Thompson; educated Dean Close School, Cheltenham; Emmanuel College, Cambridge (MA 1971). Married 1965, Sally Patricia Stallworthy (1 son 1 daughter). *Armed Forces:* Second Lieutenant, 3rd Royal Tank Regiment 1959–61. *Career:* Deacon 1966; Curate, East Ham 1966–68; Chaplain, Cuddesdon College, Oxford 1968–71; Rector of Thamesmead and Ecumenical Team Leader 1971–78; Suffragan, then Area, Bishop of Stepney 1978–91; Chairman: London Diocesan Board for Social Responsibility 1978–96, Committee for Relations with People of Other Faiths, British Council of Churches 1983–89; Member, House of Bishops, General Synod of the Church of England 1983–; Chairman, Urban Studies Centre, then Urban Learning Foundation 1985–91; Co-Chairman, Interfaith Network (UK) 1987–92; Chairman: Church at Work, London 1989–91, Social Policy Committee, Board of Social Responsibility 1990–97; Bishop of Bath and Wells 1991–; Took his seat in the House of Lords 1997. *Other:* Member, NFU; Chairman: Tower Hamlets Association for Racial Justice, Auschwitz Exhibition 1983, The Children's Society 1997–; President, Royal Bath and West of England Show 1997–98; Co-President, English Churches Housing Group. *Awards Granted:* (Jointly) Sir Sigmund Sternberg Award for Christian-Jewish Relations 1987; Founding Society Award 1995. Five honorary doctorates/fellowships. *Miscellaneous:* Visitor, Wadham College, Oxford 1992. FCA 1959. *Publications: Halfway: Reflections in Midlife,* 1986; *The Lord's Song,* 1990; *Stepney Calling,* 1991; *Why God?,* 1997. *Recreations:* Riding, painting, sport. *Clubs:* Farmers'. *Address:* Rt Rev the Lord Bishop of Bath and Wells, The Palace, Wells, Somerset, BA5 2PD *Tel:* 01749 672341 *E-Mail:* bishop@bathwells.anglican.org.

Dod *on* Line
An Electronic Directory without rival . . .
Peers' biographies and photographs available with daily updates *via* the internet
For a *free* trial, call Oliver Cox on 020 7828 7256

LORD BAUER   Conservative

BAUER (Life Baron), Peter Thomas Bauer; cr. 1983. Born 6 November 1915. Son of late Aladar Bauer; educated Scolae Piae, Budapest, Hungary; Gonville and Caius College, Cambridge (MA). *Career:* Fellow, Gonville and Caius College 1946–60, 1968–; Smuts Reader, Cambridge University 1956–60; Professor of Economics, London School of Economics (University of London) 1960–1983, Emeritus Professor 1983–. *Publications:* Author of several books and articles on economic subjects. *Clubs:* Garrick, Beefsteak. *Name, Style and Title:* Raised to the peerage as Baron Bauer, of Market Ward in the City of Cambridge 1983. *Address:* Professor the Lord Bauer, House of Lords, London, SW1A 0PW.

LORD BEAUMONT OF WHITLEY   Green Party

BEAUMONT OF WHITLEY (Life Baron), Timothy Wentworth Beaumont; cr. 1967. Born 22 November 1928. Son of late Major Michael Wentworth Beaumont, TD, DL, MP and Hon. Faith Pease, daughter of 1st Baron Gainford, PC, DL; educated Gordonstoun; Christ Church, Oxford (MA); Westcott House, Cambridge. Married June 13, 1955, Mary Rose, daughter of Lieutenant-Colonel Charles Edward Wauchope, MC (1 son 2 daughters and 1 son deceased). *Trades Union:* Member, NUJ 1970–80. *Career:* Ordained 1955; Assistant Chaplain, Hong Kong Cathedral 1955–57; Vicar of Christchurch, Kowloon Tong, Hong Kong 1957–59; Owner of various periodicals including: *Time & Tide*, 1960–62, *New Christian*, 1965–70; Chairman, Studio Vista Ltd. (book publishers) 1963–68; Member, Parliamentary Assembly Council of Europe and Western European Union 1974–78; Leader, British Liberal Delegation 1977–78; Vice-Chairman, Council of Europe Liberal Group 1977–78; Vicar of St Philip's and St Luke's churches, Kew 1986–91; Joint Organiser, Southwark Diocese Spiritual Direction Course 1994–96. *Spokesman:* Liberal Party Spokesman on the Arts, Education, the Environment 1983–86; Liberal Democrat Party Spokesman on Conservation and Countryside 1993–99; Green Party Spokesman on Agriculture 2000–. *Select Committees:* Member, Select Committee on Sustainable Development 1994–95; Co-opted Member, Select Committee on European Communities Sub-Committee C (Environment, Public Health and Consumer Protection) 1997–; Member, Ecclesiastical Committee 1997–. *Party Groups (General):* Hon. Treasurer, Liberal Party 1965–66; Chairman, Liberal Party 1967–68, President 1969–70; Editor, *New Outlook* 1972–74; Chairman: Liberal Party Education Panel 1972–74, Liberal Party General Election Committee 1974; Co-ordinator, The Green Alliance 1978–80; Director of Policy Promotion, Liberal Party 1980–82; Member, Liberal Democrat Party National Policy Committee 1992–95. *Other:* Chairman, Institute of Research into Mental Retardation 1972–74; President, British Federation of Film Societies 1974–79. *Awards Granted:* Green Futures Award for Lifetime Service to the Green Movement 2000. *Publications: Where shall I put my Cross? exercising Christian responsibility in politics,* 1987; *The End of the Yellow Brick Road: Ways and Means to the Sustainable Society,* 1997. *Special Interests:* Ecological Economics, Poverty, Environment. *Name, Style and Title:* Raised to the peerage as Baron Beaumont of Whitley, of Child's Hill in the County of Greater London 1967. *Address:* The Lord Beaumont of Whitley, 40 Elms Road, London, SW4 9EX *Tel:* Home: 020 7498 8664; House of Lords, London, SW1A 0PW *Tel:* House of Lords 020 7219 3121.

LORD BELL   Conservative

BELL (Life Baron), Timothy John Leigh Bell; cr. 1998. Born 18 October 1941. Son of late Arthur Bell and of Greta Bell; educated Queen Elizabeth's Grammar School, Barnet, Herts. Married 1988, Virginia Wallis Hornbrook (1 son 1 daughter). *Career:* ABC Television 1959–61; Colman Prentis and Varley 1961–63; Hobson Bates 1963–66; Geers Gross 1966–70; Managing Director, Saatchi and Saatchi 1970–75; Chairman and Managing Director, Saatchi and Saatchi Compton 1975–85; Group Chief Executive, Lowe Howard-Spink Campbell Ewald 1985–87; Deputy Chairman, Lowe Hoard-Spink and Bell 1987–89; Chairman, Lowe Bell Communications 1987–; Chairman, Chime Communications plc 1994–. *Other:* Member: Public Relations Committee,

Greater London Fund for the Blind 1979–86, Council, Royal Opera House 1982–85; Chairman, Charity Projects 1984–93, President 1993–; Member: Public Affairs, World Wide Fund for Nature 1985–88, Council, School of Communication Arts 1985–87; Director, Centre for Policy Studies 1989–92; Chairman, Conservative Party Keep the œ Campaign 1999–. *Miscellaneous:* Governor, British Film Institute 1983–86; Special Adviser: to Chairman, National Coal Board 1984–86, to South Bank Board 1985–86. *Honours:* Kt 1990. FIPA. *Special Interests:* Golf, Music. *Sportsclubs:* Prince Edward Yacht Club Sydney, RAC. *Name, Style and Title:* Raised to the peerage as Baron Bell, of Belgravia in the City of Westminster 1998. *Address:* The Lord Bell, Office: 7 Hertford Street, London, W1Y 7DY.

LORD BELLWIN   Conservative

BELLWIN (Life Baron), Irwin Norman Bellow; cr. 1979. Born 7 February 1923. Son of late Abraham and Leah Bellow; educated Leeds Grammar School; Leeds University (LLB). Married November 15, 1948, Doreen Barbara, daughter of Myer Saperia (1 son 2 daughters). *Councils, Public Bodies:* Councillor, Leeds City Council 1965–79; JP, City of Leeds 1969; Leader of Leeds City Council 1975–79; DL, West Yorkshire 1991–. *House of Lords:* Department of the Environment: Parliamentary Under-Secretary of State 1979–83, Minister of State for Local Government 1983–1984. *Other:* Former Vice-President, International New Towns Association; Vice-Chairman, Board of Governors, Leeds Grammar School. *Trusts, etc:* Chairman, North Hull Housing Action Trust 1993–99. *Miscellaneous:* Member, Commission for the New Towns 1985–95; Vice-Chairman, Association of Metropolitan Authorities 1976–79. Past Master, Guild of World Traders in London 1990. *Recreations:* Golf (President Moor Allerton Golf Club, Leeds). *Name, Style and Title:* Raised to the peerage as Baron Bellwin, of the City of Leeds 1979. *Address:* The Lord Bellwin, DL, JP, Woodside Lodge, Ling Lane, Scarcroft, Leeds, West Yorkshire, LS14 3HX.

LORD BELSTEAD   Conservative

BELSTEAD (2nd Baron, UK), John Julian Ganzoni; cr. 1938; (Life) Baron Ganzoni 1999; 2nd Bt of Ipswich (UK) 1929. Born 30 September 1932. Son of 1st Baron, DL. Succeeded his father 1958; educated Eton; Christ Church, Oxford. *Councils, Public Bodies:* JP for Borough of Ipswich 1962; DL, Suffolk 1979–94, Lord Lieutenant 1994–; Chairman, The Parole Board 1992–97. *House of Lords:* Parliamentary Under-Secretary of State: Department of Education and Science 1970–1973, Northern Ireland Office 1973–74, Home Office 1979–82; Minister of State: Foreign and Commonwealth Office 1982–83, Ministry of Agriculture, Fisheries and Food 1983–87, Department of Environment 1987–88; Deputy Leader of House of Lords 1983–87; Lord Privy Seal and Leader of the House of Lords 1987–90; Paymaster General and Deputy to the Secretary of State for Northern Ireland 1990–92. *Spokesman:* Government Spokesman on: Trade and Industry 1982–84, Employment 1984–85, Arts and Civil Service 1985–87. *Other:* Chairman, Association of Governing Bodies of Public Schools 1974–79. *Honours:* PC 1983. *Sportsclubs:* All England Lawn Tennis. *Clubs:* MCC, Boodle's. *Name, Style and Title:* Created a life peer as Baron Ganzoni, of Ipswich in the County of Suffolk 1999. *Address:* Rt Hon the Lord Belstead, House of Lords, London, SW1A 0PW.

LORD BERKELEY   Labour

BERKELEY (18th Baron, E), Anthony Fitzhardinge Gueterbock; cr. 1421; (Life) Baron Gueterbock 2000. Born 20 September 1939. Son of late Brigadier Ernest Adolphus Leopold Gueterbock, and late Hon. Cynthia Ella Gueterbock. Succeeded his aunt, Mary Lalle Foley, Baroness Berkeley (17th in line) 1992; educated Eton; Trinity College, Cambridge (MA). Married 1st, July 10, 1965, Diana Christine (Dido) Townsend (2 sons 1 daughter); married 2nd, 1999, Rosalind Julia Georgia Clarke. *Career:* Civil Engineer; Public Affairs Manager, Eurotunnel 1987–; Chairman, The Piggyback Consortium. *Whip:* Opposition Whip 1996–97. *Spokesman:* Opposition Spokesman on Transport 1996–97. *Select Committees:* Member, European Communities Committee 1997–; Co-opted Member, Select Committee on European Communities Sub-Committee B (Energy, Industry and Transport) 1997–. *Other:* Vice-President, Federation of Economic Development Authorities. *Honours:* OBE 1989. MICE. *Special Interests:* Transport. *Recreations:* Sailing, skiing. *Name, Style and Title:* Created a life peer as Baron Gueterbock, of Cranford in the London Borough of Hillingdon 2000. *Address:* The Lord Berkeley, OBE, House of Lords, London, SW1A 0PW.

BERNSTEIN OF CRAIGWEIL (Life Baron), Alexander Bernstein; cr. 2000. Born 15 March 1936. Son of late Cecil Bernstein and of Myra Bernstein; educated Stowe School; St John's College, Cambridge. Married 1st, 1962, Vanessa Anne Mills (1 son 1 daughter) (marriage dissolved 1993); married 2nd, 1995, Angela Mary Serota. *Career:* Director, Granada Group plc 1964–96, Chairman 1979–96; Director, Waddington Galleries 1966–; Joint managing director, Granada Television 1971–75. *Other:* Member of Court: Salford University 1976–87, Manchester University 1983–98; Chairman: Royal Exchange Theatre 1983–94, Old Vic Theatre Trust 1998–; Member, National Theatre Development Council 1996–98. Hon DLitt, Salford 1981; Hon LLD, Manchester 1996. *Trusts, etc:* Trustee: Granada Foundation 1968–, Charitable Foundation 1996–, Trusthouse. *Recreations:* Modern art, skiing, gardening. *Name, Style and Title:* Raised to the peerage as Baron Bernstein of Craigweil, of Craigweil in the County of West Sussex 2000. *Address:* The Lord Bernstein of Craigweil, House of Lords, London, SW1A 0PW.

BIFFEN (Life Baron) (William) John Biffen; cr. 1997. Born 3 November 1930. Son of late Victor W. Biffen; educated Dr Morgan's Grammar School, Bridgwater; Jesus College, Cambridge (BA). Married November 2, 1979, Mrs Sarah Wood née Drew (1 step son 1 step daughter). *Councils, Public Bodies:* DL, Shropshire 1993–. *Career:* Tube Investments Ltd. 1953–60; Economist Intelligence Unit 1960–61; Member Board: Glynwed International 1987–, Rockware Group 1988–91, J. Bibby & Sons 1988–97; Barlow International plc 1997–. *House of Commons:* Contested (Conservative) Coventry East 1959; MP (Conservative) for Oswestry By-election 1961–83 and for Shropshire North 1983–97; Chief Secretary to the Treasury 1979–81; Secretary of State for Trade 1981–82; Lord President of the Council 1982–83; Leader of the House of Commons 1982–87; Lord Privy Seal 1983–87. *Party Groups (General):* Vice-Chairman, Federation of University Conservative and Unionist Associations. *Trusts, etc:* London Clinic. *Honours:* PC 1979. *Publications:* Author of *Inside the House of Commons*, 1989. *Name, Style and Title:* Raised to the peerage as Baron Biffen, of Tanat in the County of Shropshire 1997. *Address:* Rt Hon the Lord Biffen, DL, House of Lords, London, SW1A 0PW.

BILLINGHAM (Life Baroness), Angela Theodora Billingham; cr. 2000. Born 31 July 1939. Daughter of late Theodore and Eva Case; educated Aylesbury Grammar School; College of Education (London); Department of Education, Oxford University (MEd). Married August 17, 1962, Peter Billingham (died 1992) (2 daughters). *Trades Union:* Member: NUT, GMB. *Councils, Public Bodies:* Councillor: Banbury Borough Council 1970–74, Cherwell District Council 1974–84: Leader of Labour Group; Mayor of Banbury 1976; JP 1976–; Councillor, Oxfordshire County Council 1993–94. *Career:* Teacher 1960–90; Examiner for Education Board 1990–95; MEP for Northamptonshire and Blaby 1994–99: Former Rapporteur on: Postal Services, Strategy for Motor Fuel Emission, Services of General Interest (Public Services); Former Chief Whip, Socialist Group. *Miscellaneous:* Former Member, Sports Council; Contested Banbury 1992 general election; Chair, Banbury and District Sport for the Disabled; Member, Special Olympics. *Special Interests:* Europe, Education, Health, Sport. *Recreations:* Family, tennis, cinema, bridge, gardening. *Sportsclubs:* Former Captain, Oxfordshire County Tennis Team; Member, Cumberland Lawn Tennis and Squash Club. *Name, Style and Title:* Raised to the peerage as Baroness Billingham, of Banbury in the County of Oxfordshire 2000. *Address:* The Baroness Billingham, House of Lords, London, SW1A 0PW.

LORD BINGHAM OF CORNHILL   Cross-Bencher

BINGHAM OF CORNHILL (Life Baron), Thomas Henry Bingham; cr. 1996. Born 13 October 1933. Son of late Dr Thomas Bingham and Dr Catherine Bingham; educated Sedbergh; Balliol College, Oxford (MA, Gibbs Scholar in Modern History 1956). Married 1963, Elizabeth, daughter of late Peter Loxley (2 sons 1 daughter). *Armed Forces:* 2nd Lieutenant, Royal Ulster Rifles 1952–54; London Irish Rifles (TA) 1954–59. *Career:* Called to the Bar, Gray's Inn 1959, Bencher 1979; Standing Junior Counsel to Department of Employment 1968–72; QC 1972; A Recorder of the Crown Court 1975–80; Leader, Investigation into the supply of petroleum products to Rhodesia 1977–78; Judge of the High Court of Justice, Queen's Bench Division and Judge of the Commercial Court 1980–86; A Lord Justice of Appeal 1986–92; Chairman: King's Fund Working Parties into Statutory Registration of Osteopaths and Chiropractors 1989–93, Inquiry into the Supervision of the Bank of Credit and Commerce 1991–92; Interceptions Commissioner 1992–94; Master of the Rolls 1992–96; Lord Chief Justice of England and Wales 1996–2000; Senior Lord of Appeal in Ordinary 2000–; Member, Lord Chancellor's Law Reform Committee. *Other:* Governor, Sedbergh 1978–88; Chairman, Council of Legal Education 1982–86; Fellow, Winchester 1983–93; Governor, Atlantic College 1984–89; Visitor, Balliol College, Oxford 1986–; Advisory Council, Centre for Commercial Law Studies, Queen Mary and Westfield College, London University 1989–92; Visitor, Royal Postgraduate Medical School 1989–99; Advisory Council on Public Records 1992–96; President, British Records Association 1992–96; Visitor, Nuffield College, Oxford 1992–96; Royal Commission of Historical Manuscripts 1994–; Visitor: Darwin College, Cambridge 1996, Templeton College, Oxford 1996–. Six honorary doctorates; Three honorary fellowships, including Balliol College, Oxford. *Trusts, etc:* Trustee, Pilgrim Trust 1991–; Magna Carta Trust 1992–96. *Miscellaneous:* Hon. Bencher, Inn of Court, Northern Ireland 1993. *Honours:* Kt 1980, PC 1986. *Publications:* Assistant Editor, *Chitty on Contracts* (22nd edition), 1961. *Clubs:* Athenaeum. *Name, Style and Title:* Raised to the peerage as Baron Bingham of Cornhill 1996. *Address:* Rt Hon the Lord Bingham of Cornhill, House of Lords, London, SW1A 0PW.

BISHOP OF BIRMINGHAM   Non-Affiliated

BIRMINGHAM (7th Bishop of), Mark Santer. Born 29 December 1936. Son of late Rev. Canon Eric Arthur Robert Santer and late Phyllis Clare Barlow; educated Marlborough; Queens' College, Cambridge; Westcott House, Cambridge. Married 1st, 1964, Henriette Cornelia Weststrate (died 1994) (1 son 2 daughters); married 2nd, 1997, Sabine Boehmig Bird. *Career:* Deacon 1963; Assistant Curate, Cuddesdon 1963–67; Tutor, Cuddesdon Theological College 1963–67; Priest 1964; Fellow and Dean of Clare College, Cambridge 1967–72; University Assistant Lecturer in Divinity 1968–72; Principal, Westcott House, Cambridge 1973–81; Hon. Canon, Winchester Cathedral 1978–81; Bishop of Kensington 1981–87; Co-Chairman, Anglican Roman Catholic International Commission 1983–; Bishop of Birmingham 1987–; Took his seat in the House of Lords 1994. *Other:* Member, Council of NACRO 1985–98; Chairman, NACRO Young Offenders' Committee 1987–97; Non-executive director, University Hospital Birmingham NHS Trust 1998–. Five honorary fellowships/doctorates. *Miscellaneous:* Chairman, Anglican-Roman Catholic International Commission 1983–98. *Publications:* (contributor) *The Phenomenon of Christian Belief*, 1970; (jointly) *Documents in Early Christian Thought*, 1975; *Their Lord and Ours*, 1982; (contributor) *The Church and the State*, 1984; (contributor) *Dropping the Bomb*, 1985; (contributor) *Reconciling Memories*, 1988, 1998. *Address:* Rt Rev the Lord Bishop of Birmingham, Bishop's Croft, Old Church Road, Harborne, Birmingham, B17 0BG *Tel:* 0121–427 1163 *Fax:* 0121–426 1322.

Visit the Vacher Dod Website . . .
www.politicallinks.co.uk

LORD BIRT — Non-Affiliated

BIRT (Life Baron), John Birt; cr. 2000. Born 10 December 1944. Son of Leo and Ida Birt; educated St Mary's College, Liverpool; St Catherine's College, Oxford (MA). Married 1965, Jane Frances Lake (1 son 1 daughter). *Career:* Producer, Nice Time 1968–69; Joint Editor, World in Action 1969–70; Producer, The Frost Programme 1971–72; Executive Producer, Weekend World 1972–74; London Weekend Television: Head of Current Affairs 1974–77, Controller of Features and Current Affairs 1977–81, Director of Programmes 1981–87; BBC: Deputy Director-General 1987–92, Director-General 1992-March 2000. *Other:* Member, Wilton Park Academic Council 1980–83; Vice-President, Royal Television Society 1994 (Fellow 1989). *Awards Granted:* Emmy Award, US National Academy of Television, Arts and Sciences 1995. Hon. Fellow, St Catherine's College, Oxford 1992; Hon. DLitt: Liverpool John Moores 1992, City University 1998.*Miscellaneous:* Visiting Fellow, Nuffield College, Oxford 1991–99.*Honours:* Kt 1998. *Name, Style and Title:* Raised to the peerage as Baron Birt, of Liverpool in the County of Merseyside 2000.*Address:* The Lord Birt, House of Lords, London, SW1A 0PW.

BISHOP OF BLACKBURN — Non-Affiliated

BLACKBURN (7th Bishop of), Alan David Chesters. Born 26 August 1937. Son of Herbert and Catherine Chesters; educated Elland Grammar School, West Yorkshire; St Chad's College, Durham University (BA Modern History); St Catherine's College, Oxford (BA Theology, MA). Married 1975, Jennie Garrett (1 son). *Career:* Curate of St Anne's, Wandsworth 1962–66; Chaplain and Head of Religious Education, Tiffin School, Kingston-upon-Thames 1966–72; Director of Education and Rector of Brancepeth, Diocese of Durham 1972–84; Honorary Canon, Durham Cathedral 1975–84; Member: General Synod of the Church of England 1975, Standing Committee 1985–89, 1990–95; A Church Commissioner 1982–98, Member, Board of Governors 1984–89, 1992–98; Archdeacon of Halifax 1985–89; Bishop of Blackburn 1989–; Chairman, Higher Education Funding Council for England Church Colleges Committee 1993–99; President, Woodard Corporation 1994–99; Member: The Countryside Agency 1999–; The Countryside Commission 1995–99, Took his seat in the House of Lords 1995. *Other:* Chairman, Governors of The University College of St Martin's, Lancaster 1990–; Chairman, Council of St Stephen's House, Oxford 1994–; President, Relate Lancashire 1997; Governor, Elmslie School, Blackpool; Member, Corporation Board, Blackburn College; Chairman, Church of England Board of Education and Council, National Society 1999–. *Special Interests:* Education, Countryside, Transport. *Recreations:* Railways, hill walking, reading. *Address:* Rt Rev the Lord Bishop of Blackburn, Bishop's House, Ribchester Road, Blackburn, Lancashire, BB1 9EF.

BARONESS BLACKSTONE — Labour

BLACKSTONE (Life Baroness), Tessa Ann Vosper Blackstone; cr. 1987. Born 27 September 1942. Daughter of late Geoffrey Blackstone, CBE, GM, and of Joanna (née Vosper); educated Ware Grammar School; LSE (BScSoc, PhD). Married 1963, Tom Evans (1 son 1 daughter) (marriage dissolved 1975, he died 1985). *Career:* Associate Lecturer, Enfield College 1965–66; Assistant Lecturer then Lecturer, Department of Social Administration, LSE 1966–75; Fellow, Centre for Studies in Social Policy 1972–74; Adviser, Central Policy Review Staff, Cabinet Office 1975–78; Professor of Educational Administration, University of London Institute of Education 1978–83; Deputy Education Officer (Resources), Inner London Education Authority 1983–86; Fellow, Policy Studies Institute 1987; Master, Birkbeck College, London University October 1987–97. *House of Lords:* Minister of State, Department for Education and Employment (Minister for Education and Employment) (Lords) 1997–. *Spokesman:* Opposition Spokesman on: Education and Science 1988–96, Treasury Matters 1990–91; Principal Opposition Spokesman on Education and Science 1990–92; Opposition Spokesman on Trade and Industry 1992–96; Principal Opposition Spokesman on Foreign Affairs 1992–97. *Other:* Chairman and Founder Member, Institute for Public Policy Research 1988–97;

Member of Board, Royal Opera House 1987–97, Chairman, Ballet Board 1991–97. Seven honorary doctorates. *Trusts, etc:* Member, Board of Trustees, The Natural History Museum 1992–97. *Miscellaneous:* Chairman, General Advisory Council of BBC 1987–91. *Publications: A Fair Start,* 1971; Co-author *Inside the Think Tank: Advising the Cabinet* 1971–84, 1988; *Prison and Penal Reform,* 1982; *The Academic Labour Market,* 1974 (co-author); Co-author *Educational Policy and Educational Inequality,* 1982, *Disadvantage and Education,* 1982, *Response to Adversity,* 1983, *Race Relations in Britain,* 1998. *Special Interests:* Education, Social Policy, Foreign Affairs, Arts. *Recreations:* Tennis, walking, ballet, opera, cinema. *Name, Style and Title:* Raised to the peerage as Baroness Blackstone, of Stoke Newington in the County of Greater London 1987. *Address:* The Baroness Blackstone, Department for Education and Employment, Sanctuary Buildings, Great Smith Street, London, SW1P 3BT *Tel:* 020 7925 6242 *Fax:* 020 7925 5011.

LORD BLACKWELL   Conservative

BLACKWELL (Life Baron), Norman Roy Blackwell; cr. 1997. Born 29 July 1952. Son of Albert and Frances Blackwell; educated Latymer Upper School, Hammersmith; Royal Academy of Music (Junior Exhibitioner); Trinity College, Cambridge (MA); Wharton Business School, University of Pennsylvania (AM, MBA, PhD 1976). Married 1974, Brenda Clucas (3 sons 2 daughters). *Career:* Plessey Company 1976–78; Partner, McKinsey & Co 1978–95, Partner 1984; Special Adviser, Prime Minister's Policy Unit 1986–87, Head 1995–97; Director, Group Development, NatWest Group 1997–2000; Director, Dixons Group 2000–; Chairman, Centre for Policy Studies 2000–; Special Adviser, KPMG Corporate Finance 2000–. *Recreations:* Classical music, walking. *Clubs:* Carlton, Royal Automobile. *Name, Style and Title:* Raised to the peerage as Baron Blackwell, of Woodcote in the County of Surrey 1997. *Address:* The Lord Blackwell, House of Lords, London, SW1A 0PW *Tel:* 020 7694 3724.

LORD BLAKE   Conservative

BLAKE (Life Baron), Robert Norman William Blake; cr. 1971. Born 23 December 1916. Son of late William Joseph Blake and late Norah Lindley, née Daynes; educated King Edward VI School, Norwich; Magdalen College, Oxford. Married August 22, 1953, Patricia Mary (died 1995), eldest daughter of late Thomas Richard Waters and Cicelie Bowyer Howlett (3 daughters). *Armed Forces:* Served Royal Artillery 1939–46 (despatches 1944); POW Italy 1942–44, escaped 1944. *Councils, Public Bodies:* Councillor (Conservative), Oxford City Council 1957–64; JP, Oxford City 1964–85. *Career:* Student and Tutor in Politics, Christ Church, Oxford 1947–68; Provost, The Queen's College, Oxford 1968–87; A Pro Vice-Chancellor of Oxford 1971–87; A Director of Channel Four Television 1983–87. *Party Groups:* Member, Association of Conservative Peers 1971–. *Other:* High Steward, Westminster Abbey 1989–99. Hon. Student, Christ Church, Oxford 1977; Hon. Fellow: The Queen's College, Oxford 1987, Pembroke College, Cambridge 1992. *Trusts, etc:* Trustee, British Museum 1978–88; Rhodes Trustee 1971–87, Chairman 1983–87; Beit Trustee 1973–99. *Miscellaneous:* Member, Royal Commission on Historical Manuscripts 1975–97, Chairman 1982–89. Fellow, British Academy 1967. Member: Dyers' Company 1947–, Prime Warden 1976–77. *Publications:* Several books including: *The Unknown Prime Minister, Bonar Law,* 1955; *Disraeli,* 1966; *The Conservative Party from Peel to Churchill,* 1970 (re-issued as *Peel to Thatcher,* 1985 and *Peel to Major,* 1997); *A History of Rhodesia,* 1977; *The Decline of Power 1915–64,* 1985; *Winston Churchill, a Pocket Biography,* 1998. *Special Interests:* Electoral Reform, Education, Foreign Affairs. *Recreations:* Writing and reading. *Clubs:* Vincent's (Oxford), United Oxford and Cambridge University, Brooks's, Beefsteak, Pratt's, Norfolk (Norwich). *Name, Style and Title:* Raised to the peerage as Baron Blake, of Braydeston in the County of Norfolk 1971. *Address:* The Lord Blake, Riverview House, Brundall, Norfolk, NR13 5LA *Tel:* 01603 712133.

LORD BLAKER
Conservative

BLAKER (Life Baron), Peter Allan Renshaw Blaker; cr. 1994. Born 4 October 1922. Son of late Cedric Blaker, CBE, MC, ED and Louisa Douglas Chapple; educated Shrewsbury; Toronto University (BA Classics); New College, Oxford (MA Jurisprudence). Married October 24, 1953, Jennifer, daughter of late Sir Pierson Dixon, GCMG, CB (1 son 2 daughters). *Armed Forces:* Served with Argyll and Sutherland Highlanders of Canada 1942–46 (wounded; Captain). *Career:* Admitted a Solicitor 1948; Called to the Bar, Lincoln's Inn 1952; HM Foreign Service 1953–64, serving in Cambodia, Canada, the UN and London; Private Secretary to the Minister of State, Foreign Office 1962–64, attended the signing of the Nuclear Test Ban Treaty, Moscow 1963; Chairman, Royal Ordnance Factories 1972–74. *House of Commons:* MP (Conservative), Blackpool South 1964–92; PPS to Chancellor of the Exchequer 1970–72; Parliamentary Under-Secretary of State: Army, Ministry of Defence 1972–74, Foreign and Commonwealth Office 1974; Minister of State: FCO 1979–81, Armed Forces, MoD 1981–83. *Whip (Commons):* An Opposition Whip 1966–67. *International Bodies (Commons):* Hon. Secretary, Franco-British Parliamentary Relations Committee 1975–79. *Party Groups (General):* Vice-President, Conservative Foreign and Commonwealth Council 1983–92, Patron 1992–. *Other:* Chairman of Governors, Welbeck College 1972–74; Member of Council: Britain-Russia Centre (formerly GB-USSR Ass) 1974–78 and 1992–, Vice-Chair 1983–92; Royal Institute for International Affairs (Chatham House) 1977–79, 1986–90; Arms Control 1983–92; Freedom Association 1984–97. *Trusts, etc:* Trustee, Institute for Negotiation and Conciliation 1984–92. *Miscellaneous:* Vice-Chairman, Peace Through NATO 1983–93; Member: Public Accounts Commission 1987–92, Intelligence and Security Committee 1996–97. *Honours:* PC 1983; KCMG 1983. *Publications: Coping with the Soviet Union*, 1977; *Small is Dangerous: micro states in a macro world*, 1984. *Special Interests:* Foreign Affairs, Commonwealth, Defence, Tourism. *Recreations:* Opera, tennis, sailing. *Name, Style and Title:* Raised to the peerage as Baron Blaker, of Blackpool in the County of Lancashire and of Lindfield in the County of West Sussex 1994. *Address:* Rt Hon the Lord Blaker, KCMG, House of Lords, London, SW1A 0PW.

BARONESS BLATCH
Conservative

BLATCH (Life Baroness), Emily May Blatch; cr. 1987. Born 24 July 1937. Daughter of late Stephen and Sarah Triggs; educated Prenton Girls School, Birkenhead. Married September 7, 1963, John Richard, AFC, son of late George Henry Blatch (1 son 1 twin son and daughter and 1 son deceased). *Armed Forces:* Women's Royal Air Force, Air Traffic Control 1955–59. *Councils, Public Bodies:* Councillor, Cambridgeshire County Council 1977–89, Leader 1981–85; Member, Peterborough Development Corporation 1984–88. *Career:* Air Traffic Control (Civilian) 1959–63. *House of Lords:* Parliamentary Under-Secretary of State, Department of Environment 1990–91; Minister of State (Heritage) 1991–92; Minister of State: Department for Education 1992–94; Home Office 1994–97; Shadow Minister for Education 1997–. *Whip:* A Baroness in Waiting (Government Whip) January-September 1990. *Spokesman:* A Spokeswoman on Education and Employment 1998–. *Party Groups:* Member, Association of Conservative Peers. *Other:* President, Probation Managers Association; Vice President, Local Government Association; Member, European Economic and Social Committee 1986–87; President, National Benevolent Institute 1988–; National Vice-President, Alzheimers Disease Society; Patron: Macmillan Nurses, Cathedral Camps, English Schools Orchestra, Huntingdon Male Voice Choir; Member: Air League Council, Air Cadet Council. Rotarian Paul Harris Fellow 1992; Hon. LLD, Teesside University 1997. *Trusts, etc:* Trustee: Dorman Museum, RAF Museum. *Honours:* CBE 1983; PC 1993. FRSA 1985. *Special Interests:* Local Government Management, Education, Anglo-American Relations. *Recreations:* Family, music, theatre. *Clubs:* Royal Air Force. *Name, Style and Title:* Raised to the peerage as Baroness Blatch, of Hinchingbrooke, in the County of Cambridgeshire 1987. *Address:* Rt Hon the Baroness Blatch, CBE, House of Lords, London, SW1A 0PW *E-Mail:* blatche@parliament.uk.

LORD BLEASE Labour

BLEASE (Life Baron), William John Blease; cr. 1978. Born 28 May 1914. Son of late William John Blease; educated Public Elementary School; Technical College, Belfast; National Council Labour Colleges; Workers Educational Associations (student and voluntary executive member). Married July 14, 1939, Sarah Evelyn Caldwell (died 1995) (3 sons 1 daughter). *Trades Union:* Divisional Councillor, Union Shop Workers 1948–59; Northern Ireland Officer, Irish Congress of Trade Unions 1959–75. *Councils, Public Bodies:* JP, County Borough of Belfast 1974–. *Career:* Apprentice to Provision Trade 1930; Branch Manager Co-op. 1939. *Whip:* An Opposition Whip 1979–84. *Spokesman:* Opposition Spokesman on Northern Ireland 1979–83. *Backbench Committees:* Parliamentary Labour Party, Northern Ireland Committee Member. *International Bodies:* Member: British-Irish Inter-Parliamentary Body 1990–, CPA, IPU. *Other:* President, Northern Ireland Hospice 1980–85, Vice-President 1985–95, Patron 1995–; Member, Board of Governors, St MacNissi's College 1981–91; President: Northern Ireland Care and Resettlement of Offenders (NICRO) 1982–84, Northern Ireland Festival of Youth Society 1982–84, Belfast East Group for Disabled 1983–88; Patron, Northern Ireland Widows' Association 1985–90; Member, Board of Co-operative Development Agency Northern Ireland 1987–91, Patron 1991–2000; President, Belfast Housing Aid 1988–95; Member of Management Board, Rathgael Child Care and Youth Treatment Centre 1989–93; Patron, Action Cancer 1994–; Joint President, Northern Ireland Forum on Industrial Relations (NIFIR) 1994–; Hon. President, Institute of Management (Belfast Branch) 1995–; Duke of Edinburgh Award, Northern Ireland and Honorary Member 1979–. *Awards Granted:* New Ireland University Peace Trophy 1971–74; Ford Foundation Travel Award, USA 1958. Hon. DLitt, New University of Ulster 1972; Hon. LLD, Queen's University Belfast 1982. *Trusts, etc:* Trustee, Belfast Charitable Trust for Integrated Education 1984–88; Member, Board of Trustees, TSB Foundation (Northern Ireland) 1986–94. *Miscellaneous:* Northern Ireland Economic Council 1964–75; Member, Independent Broadcasting Authority 1974–79; Research Fellow, New University of Ulster (NUU) 1976–78; Member, Standing Commission on Human Rights 1977–79; Rapporteur to EEC on Cross Border Communications Study on Londonderry-Donegal 1978–79; Chairman, Community Service Order Committee 1979–80. Fellow, British Institute of Management 1981. *Publications:* Encyclopaedia of Labour Law Vol 1, *The Trade Union – Movement in Northern Ireland. Recreations:* Gardening, Reading. *Name, Style and Title:* Raised to the peerage as Baron Blease, of Cromac in the City of Belfast 1978. *Address:* The Lord Blease, House of Lords, London, SW1A 0PW.

VISCOUNT BLEDISLOE Cross-Bencher

BLEDISLOE (3rd Viscount, UK), Christopher Hiley Ludlow Bathurst; cr. 1935; 3rd Baron Bledisloe (UK) 1918. Born 24 June 1934. Son of 2nd Viscount, QC. Succeeded his father 1979; educated Eton; Trinity College, Oxford. Married 1962, Elizabeth Mary Thompson (2 sons 1 daughter) (marriage dissolved 1986). *Armed Forces:* 2nd Lieutenant, 11th Hussars (PAO) 1954–55. *Career:* Called to Bar Gray's Inn 1959; QC 1978; Director, Portsmouth & Sunderland Newspapers plc. *House of Lords:* An elected hereditary peer 1999–. *Select Committees:* Member, Select Committee on European Union 1999–. *Trusts, etc:* Trustee, Equitas. *Clubs:* Garrick. *Address:* The Viscount Bledisloe, QC, Lydney Park, Gloucestershire, GL15 6BT *Tel:* 01594 842566; Fountain Court, Temple, London, EC4Y 9DH *Tel:* 020 7583 3335; 44 Sussex Street, London, SW1V 4RH *Tel:* 020 7630 6300.

Dod *on* Line
An Electronic Directory without rival . . .
Peers' biographies and photographs available with daily updates *via* the internet
For a *free* trial, call Oliver Cox on 020 7828 7256

BARONESS BLOOD   Cross-Bencher

BLOOD (Life Baroness), May Blood; cr. 1999. Born 26 May 1938. Daughter of late William and Mary Blood; educated Linfield Secondary, Belfast. *Trades Union:* Member, TGWU. *Career:* Cutting Supervisor, Blackstaff Mill 1952–90; Community Worker, Gt Shankill Partnership 1990–. *International Bodies (General):* Citizen's Global Circle, Boston. Two honorary doctorates from Northern Ireland. *Trusts, etc:* Groundwork Northern Ireland. *Miscellaneous:* Member: Independent Industrial Tribunals, Labour Relations Agency. *Honours:* MBE 1996. *Special Interests:* Women's Issues, Low Pay, Working Class Issues, Family, Children. *Recreations:* Reading, gardening. *Name, Style and Title:* Raised to the peerage as Baroness Blood, of Blackwatertown in the County of Armagh 1999. *Address:* The Baroness Blood, MBE, 7 Blackmountain Place, Belfast, BT13 3TT *Tel:* 028 9032 6514; Alessie Centre, 60 Shankhill Road, Belfast, BT13 2BD *Tel:* 028 9087 4000 *Fax:* 028 9087 4009.

LORD BLYTH OF ROWINGTON   Conservative

BLYTH OF ROWINGTON (Life Baron), James Blyth; cr. 1995. Born 8 May 1940. Son of Daniel and Jane Blyth; educated Spiers School; Glasgow University (MA). Married 1967, Pamela Anne Campbell Dixon (1 daughter and 1 son deceased). *Career:* Mobil Oil Company 1963–69; General Foods Ltd 1969–71; Mars Ltd 1971–74; General Manager: Lucas Batteries Ltd 1974–77, Lucas Aerospace Ltd 1977–81; Head of Defence Sales, Ministry of Defence 1981–85; Non-executive Director, Imperial Group plc 1984–86; Managing Director, Plessey Electronic Systems 1985–86; Chief Executive, The Plessey Co plc 1986–87; Non-executive Director, Cadbury-Schweppes plc 1986–90; Director and Chief Executive, The Boots Company plc 1987–, Deputy Chairman 1994–98, Chairman 1998–2000–; Non-executive Director: British Aerospace 1990–94, Anixter Inc 1995–; Director: NatWest Group 1998–2000, Diageo plc 1999–, Chairman 2000–. *Other:* Governor, London Business School 1987–96. Hon. LLD, Nottingham University 1992; Hon. Fellow, London Business School 1997. *Miscellaneous:* Chairman, Advisory panel on Citizen's Charter 1991–97. *Honours:* Kt 1985. FRAeS. Liveryman, Coachmakers' and Coach Harness Makers' Company. *Recreations:* Skiing, tennis, paintings, theatre. *Sportsclubs:* The Queen's Club. *Clubs:* East India, Devonshire, Sports and Public Schools, Royal Automobile. *Name, Style and Title:* Raised to the peerage as Baron Blyth of Rowington, of Rowington in the County of Warwickshire 1995. *Address:* The Lord Blyth of Rowington, Diageo plc, 8 Henrietta Place, London, W1G 0LZ *E-Mail:* chairmans.office@diageo.com.

LORD BOARDMAN   Conservative

BOARDMAN (Life Baron), Thomas Gray Boardman; cr. 1980. Born 12 January 1919. Son of late John Clayton Boardman and late Janet Boardman (née Houston); educated Bromsgrove. Married 1948, Norah Mary Deirdre, daughter of late Hubert Gough and widow of John Chaworth-Musters (2 sons 1 daughter). *Armed Forces:* Served Northants Yeomanry 1939–45, 1947–56, Commanding 1954–56. *Councils, Public Bodies:* DL, Northants 1977–; High Sheriff, Northants 1979; One of HM Lieutenants for the City of London 1990–. *Career:* Qualified as a Solicitor 1947; Director, Chamberlain Phipps Ltd 1958–72, Chairman 1968–72; Director, Allied Breweries Ltd 1968–72, 1974–77, Vice-Chairman 1975–76; Director, Steetley plc 1975–83, Chairman 1978–83; Director, National Westminster Bank plc 1979, Chairman 1983–89; Director, MEPC plc 1980–89; Chairman, Committee of London and Scottish Banks 1987–89; Advisory Board, L.E.K. 1990–97; Chairman, Heron International NV 1993–95. *House of Commons:* Contested Leicester South West 1964 and 1966 general elections; MP (Conservative): Leicester South West 1967 by-election–February 1974, Leicester South February-September 1974; Minister for Industry, Department of Trade and Industry 1972–74; Chief Secretary to Treasury 1974. *Select Committees:* Member, Sub-Committee A of House of Lords Select Committee on European Communities 1991–94, Co-opted Member 1997–2000.

Party Groups: Member, Executive Association of Conservative Peers 1981–84, 1991–95.*Party Groups (General):* Honorary Treasurer, Conservative Party 1981–82. *Other:* President, Association of British Chambers of Commerce 1977–80. Two honorary doctorates. *Trusts, etc:* Chairman, Appeal for Prince's Youth Business Trust (PYBT) 1987–90, Trustee 1989–93.*Honours:* MC 1944; TD 1952. Freeman, City of London. *Special Interests:* Finance, Trade and Industry.*Recreations:* Riding, hunting. *Clubs:* Cavalry and Guards. *Name, Style and Title:* Raised to the peerage as Baron Boardman, of Welford in the County of Northampton 1980. *Address:* The Lord Boardman, MC, TD, DL, The Manor House, Welford, Northampton, NN6 6HX *Tel:* 01858 575235; 29 Tufton Court, Tufton Street, London, SW1P 3QH *Tel:* 020 7222 6793.

LORD BORRIE   Labour

BORRIE (Life Baron), Gordon Johnson Borrie; cr. 1995. Born 13 March 1931. Son of Stanley Borrie; educated John Bright Grammar School, Llandudno; Manchester University (LLB, LLM). Married 1960, Dorene, daughter of Herbert Toland. *Armed Forces:* National Service with Army Legal Services, HQ British Commonwealth Forces in Korea 1952–54. *Career:* Barrister-at-Law and Harmsworth Scholar of the Middle Temple; Called to the Bar, Middle Temple 1952, Bencher 1980; Practiced as a barrister in London 1954–57; Lecturer and later Senior Lecturer, College of Law 1957–64; Birmingham University: Senior Lecturer in Law 1965–68, Professor of English Law and Director, Institute of Judicial Administration 1969–76, Dean of Faculty of Law 1974–76, Hon. Professor of Law 1989–; Member: Parole Board for England and Wales 1971–74, CNAA Legal Studies Board 1971–76; Member, Equal Opportunities Commission 1975–76; Director General of Fair Trading 1976–92; Director: Woolwich Building Society 1992–2000, Three Valleys Water 1992–, Chairman, Commission on Social Justice 1992–94; Director: Mirror Group 1993–99, TeleWest 1994–; Chairman, Direct Marketing Auditing 1997–; Director, General Utilities 1998–; Chairman, Accountancy Foundation 2000–. *Select Committees:* Member: European Union Committee 1997–, Select Committee on European Union Sub-Committee E (Law and Institutions) 1996–. *Other:* Governor, Birmingham College of Commerce 1966–70; Member: Circuit Advisory Committee, Birmingham Group of Courts 1972–74, Council, Consumers' Association 1972–75, Consumer Protection Advisory Committee 1973–76; Vice-President, Institute of Trading Standards Administration 1985–92 and 1997–, President 1992–97; Patron, Public Concern at Work; Jubilee Patron, MIND; Access to Justice Advisory Board, NSPCC; President, Money Advice Trust. Six honorary law doctorates. *Miscellaneous:* Contested (Labour): Croydon North East 1955, Ilford South 1959 General Elections. *Honours:* Kt 1982. Fellow: Chartered Institute of Arbitrators, Royal Society of Arts. *Publications: Commercial Law*, 1962; *The Consumer, Society and the Law*, 1963 (with Professor A. L. Diamond); *Law of Contempt*, 1973 (with N. V. Lowe); *The Development of Consumer Law and Policy* (Hamlyn Lectures) 1984. *Recreations:* Gastronomy, playing the piano, travel. *Clubs:* Garrick, Reform. *Name, Style and Title:* Raised to the peerage as Baron Borrie, of Abbots Morton in the County of Hereford and Worcester 1995. *Address:* The Lord Borrie, QC, Manor Farm, Abbots Morton, Worcestershire, WR7 4NA *Tel:* 01386 792330; 4 Brick Court, Temple, London, EC4Y 9AD *Tel:* 020 7353 4434.

LORD BOSTON OF FAVERSHAM   Cross-Bencher

BOSTON OF FAVERSHAM (Life Baron), Terence George Boston; cr. 1976. Born 21 March 1930. Son of late George Thomas and Kate Boston; educated Woolwich Polytechnic School; King's College, London University. Married April 3, 1962, Margaret Joyce Head. *Armed Forces:* Commissioned RAF; National Service 1950–52. *Career:* BBC News Sub-editor 1957–60; Senior Producer, Current Affairs 1960–64; Called to the Bar, Inner Temple 1960; UK Delegate, UN General Assembly 1976–78; QC 1981; Chairman: TVS Entertainment plc 1980–90, TVS Television Ltd 1986–90, TVS Music Ltd 1983–90. *House of Commons:* Contested Wokingham 1955 and 1959 general elections; MP (Labour) for Kent, Faversham division 1964–70; PPS: to Minister of Public Building and Works 1964–66, to Minister of Power 1966–68, to Minister of Transport 1968–69. *Whip (Commons):* Assistant Government Whip 1969–70. *House of Lords:* Minister of State, Home Office 1979; Deputy Chairman of Committees, House of Lords 1991–92; Principal Deputy

Chairman of Committees 1992–94, Chairman of Committees 1994–97, 1997–; A Deputy Speaker of the House of Lords. *Spokesman:* Opposition Spokesman: Home Office Affairs 1979–84, Defence 1984–86. *Select Committees:* Member, Select Committee on Bill of Rights 1977–78; Member: Joint Select Committee on Statutory Instruments 1986–92, Select Committee on the Committee work of the House of Lords 1991–92; Chairman: Select Committee on the European Communities 1992–94, Select Committee on House of Lords' Offices 1994–97, 1997–; and other Domestic Select Committees of the House of Lords. *Party Groups (General):* Member: National Committee Young Socialists (then Labour League of Youth) 1949–51, Executive Committee, International Union of Socialist Youth 1950. *Miscellaneous:* A Lords' Member, Parliamentary Broadcasting Unit Limited 1994–97, 1997–. *Publications:* Joint Author of *Do We Needs A Bill of Rights?*. *Recreations:* Fell-walking, opera. *Name, Style and Title:* Raised to the peerage as Baron Boston of Faversham, of Faversham in the County of Kent 1976. *Address:* The Lord Boston of Faversham, QC, House of Lords, London, SW1A 0PW.

LORD BOWNESS — Conservative

BOWNESS (Life Baron), Peter Spencer Bowness; cr. 1996. Born 19 May 1943. Son of late Hubert Bowness and of Doreen Bowness; educated Whitgift School, Croydon; Law Society School of Law, College of Law. Married 1st, 1969 (1 daughter) (marriage dissolved 1983); married 2nd, 1984, Mrs Patricia Jane Cook (1 stepson). *Armed Forces:* Hon. Colonel, 151 (Greater London) Transport Regiment, Royal Corps of Transport (Volunteers) 1988–93. *Councils, Public Bodies:* Councillor, London Borough of Croydon 1968–98, Leader 1976–94, Mayor 1979–80; Deputy Chairman, Association of Metropolitan Authorities 1978–80; Chairman, London Boroughs Association 1978–94; DL, Greater London 1981–; Member: Audit Commission 1983–95, London Residuary Body 1985–93, National Training Task Force 1989–92. *Career:* Admitted Solicitor 1966; Partner, Weightman Sadler, Solicitors, Purley, Surrey 1970–. *House of Lords:* House of Lords representative to Convention to Draft an EU Charter of Fundamental Rights. *Spokesman:* An Opposition Spokesman on Environment, Transport and the Regions (Local Government) 1997–98. *Select Committees:* Chairman, Joint Committee on Draft Local Government (Organisation and Standards) Bill 1999. *International Bodies:* Member, IPU. *International Bodies (General):* Member: UK Delegation to Congress of Regional and Local Authorities of Europe (Council of Europe) 1990–98, UK Delegation to the Committee of the Regions of the EU (COR) 1994–98; Member of the Bureau and of Transport and Telecommunications Commission and of Institutional Affairs Commission (COR) 1994–98; Vice-President, European People's Party Group COR 1994–98. *Other:* Governor, Whitgift Foundation 1982–96; Member, Royal Society for the Protection of Birds. *Honours:* CBE 1981; Kt 1987. Freeman, City of London 1984. *Special Interests:* Local Government, Europe, London. *Recreations:* Travel, theatre. *Name, Style and Title:* Raised to the peerage as Baron Bowness, of Warlingham in the County of Surrey and of Croydon in the London Borough of Croydon 1996. *Address:* The Lord Bowness, CBE, DL, 1 The Exchange, Purley Road, Purley, Surrey, CR8 2YY *Tel:* 020 8660 6455 *Fax:* 020 8668 3250 *E-Mail:* bowness@globalnet.co.uk.

LORD BRABAZON OF TARA — Conservative

BRABAZON OF TARA (3rd Baron, UK), Ivon Anthony Moore-Brabazon; cr. 1942. Born 20 December 1946. Son of 2nd Baron, CBE. Succeeded his father 1974; educated Harrow. Married September 8, 1979, Harriet Frances de Courcy Hamilton (1 son 1 daughter). *Councils, Public Bodies:* DL, Isle of Wight 1993–. *Career:* Member, Stock Exchange 1972–84; Director: Aurigny Aviation Holdings Ltd, Exxtor Group CI Ltd. *House of Lords:* Parliamentary Under-Secretary of State, Department of Transport 1986–89; Minister of State: Foreign and Commonwealth Office 1989–90, Department of Transport 1990–92; An elected hereditary peer 1999–. *Whip:* Government Whip (Lord in Waiting) 1984–86. *Spokesman:* House of Lords Spokesman on: Transport 1984–85, Trade and Industry, Treasury and Energy 1985–86; Opposition Spokesman on Environment, Transport and the Regions (Transport) 1998–. *Select Committees:* Member: House of Lords European Communities Sub-Committee B 1993–97, Select Committee on the Public Service 1996–97, Select Committee on House of Lords' Offices 1997–. *Other:* President, United Kingdom Warehousing Association 1992–;

Deputy Chairman, Foundation for Sport and the Arts 1992–; Council Member, Shipwrecked Mariners' Society 1993–; President, Natural Gas Vehicles Association 1995–97; Deputy President, Institute of the Motor Industry 1997–98, President 1998–; President, British International Freight Association 1997–98. *Trusts, etc:* Trustee, Medical Commission on Accident Prevention. *Miscellaneous:* Director, Parliamentary Council for Transport Safety. Fellow, Institute of the Motor Industry 1997–. *Special Interests:* Transport. *Recreations:* Sailing, golf. *Clubs:* White's, Royal Yacht Squadron (Cowes). *Address:* The Lord Brabazon of Tara, DL, House of Lords, London, SW1A 0PW *E-Mail:* brabazoni@parliament.uk.

BISHOP OF BRADFORD — Non-Affiliated

BRADFORD (8th Bishop of), David James Smith. Born 14 July 1935. Son of Stanley and Gwendolen Smith; educated Hertford Grammar School; King's College, London (Theology). Married 1961, Mary Hunter Moult (1 son 1 daughter). *Armed Forces:* National Service, Royal Artillery 1953–55. *Career:* Assistant Curate: All Saints, Gosforth 1959–62, St Francis, High Heaton 1962–64, Long Benton 1964–68; Vicar: Longhirst with Hebron 1968–75, St Mary, Monkseaton 1975–81; Archdeacon of Lindisfarne 1981–87; Vicar, Felton 1982–83; Bishop Suffragan of Maidstone 1987–92; Bishop to HM Forces 1990–92; Bishop of Bradford 1992–; Took his seat in the House of Lords 1997. Fellow, King's College London 1999. *Recreations:* Fell-walking, reading novels. *Clubs:* Bradford. *Address:* Rt Rev the Lord Bishop of Bradford, Bishopscroft, Ashwell Road, Bradford, West Yorkshire, BD9 4AU *Tel:* 01274 545414 *Fax:* 01274 544831 *E-Mail:* bishbrad@nildram.co.uk.

LORD BRADSHAW — Liberal Democrat

BRADSHAW (Life Baron), William Peter Bradshaw; cr. 1999. Born 9 September 1936. Son of late Leonard Charles and Ivy Doris Bradshaw; educated Slough Grammar School; Reading University (BA 1957, MA 1960). Married November 30, 1957, Jill, daughter of James and Florence Hayward (1 son 1 daughter). *Armed Forces:* National Service 1957–59. *Councils, Public Bodies:* Councillor, Oxfordshire County Council 1993; Member, Thames Valley Police Authority 1993–95 and 1997–, Vice-Chairman 1999; Member: Commission for Integrated Transport, British Railways Board (Shadow Strategic Rail Authority). *Career:* Management Trainee, British Rail Western Region 1959; Various Appointments, London and West of England Division; Division Manager, Liverpool 1973; Chief Operating Manager, London Midland Region Crewe 1976; Deputy General Manager, LM Region 1977; Chief Operations Manager, BR Headquarters 1978; Director, Policy Unit 1980; General Manager, Western Region BR 1983–85; Professor of Transport Management, University of Salford 1986–92; Chairman, Ulsterbus and Citybus Ltd Belfast 1987–93; Special Adviser to Transport Select Committee of the House of Commons 1992–97. *Select Committees:* European Union, Sub-Committee B (Energy Industry and Transport). *Trusts, etc:* Trustee, Oxford Preservation Trust. FCIT. *Publications:* Many chapters and articles on transport issues. *Special Interests:* Transport, Environment, Planning, Police. *Recreations:* Growing hardy perennial plants, playing member of a brass band. *Clubs:* National Liberal. *Name, Style and Title:* Raised to the peerage as Baron Bradshaw, of Wallingford in the County of Oxfordshire 1999. *Address:* Professor the Lord Bradshaw, House of Lords, London, SW1A 0PW.

LORD BRAGG — Labour

BRAGG (Life Baron), Melvyn Bragg; cr. 1998. Born 6 October 1939. Son of Stanley and Mary Ethel Bragg; educated Nelson-Thomlinson Grammar School, Wigton; Wadham College, Oxford (MA). Married 1st, 1961, Marie-Elisabeth Roche (died 1971) (1 daughter); married 2nd, 1973, Catherine Mary Haste (1 son 1 daughter). *Career:* BBC Radio and TV Producer 1961–67; Novelist 1964–; Writer and Broadcaster 1967–; Presenter, BBC TV series: *2nd House* 1973–77, *Read All About It* 1976–77; Presenter and Editor: *The South Bank Show* for ITV 1978–, *Start the Week* for Radio 4 1988–98; Controller of Arts, London Weekend Television 1990–, Head of Arts 1982–90; Chairman, Border Television 1990–95, Deputy Chairman 1985–90; Governor, London School of Economics 1997; *In Our Time* for Radio 4 1998–. *Chancellor:* Chancellor, Leeds University 1999–. *Other:* Member, Arts Council; Chairman, Literature Panel of Arts Council 1977–80; President: Cumbrians for Peace 1982–, Northern Arts 1983–87, National Campaign for the Arts 1986–. *Awards Granted:* RTS Gold Medal; John Llewllyn-Rhys Memorial Award; PEN Awards for Fiction; Richard Dimbleby Award for Outstanding Contribution to Television 1987; Ivor Novello Award for Best Musical *The Hired Man* 1985; Numerous prizes for *The South Bank Show* including a record three Prix Italia's; TRIC Award: Radio Programme of the Year for *Start the Week* 1990, Radio Personality of the Year for *Start the Week* 1991; WHS Literary Award for *The Soldier's Return*. Eight honorary doctorates, four honorary fellowships. Fellow: Royal Society of Literature, Royal Television Society. *Publications: For Want of a Nail*, 1965; *The Second Inheritance*, 1966; *Without a City Wall*, 1968; *The Hired Man*, 1969; *A Place in England*, 1970; *The Nerve*, 1971; *Josh Lawton*, 1972; *The Silken Net*, 1974; *A Christmas Child*, 1976; *Speak for England*, 1976; *Mardi Gras*, (musical) 1976; *Orion*, (TV play) 1977; *Autumn Manoeuvres*, 1978; *Kingdom Come*, 1980; *Love and Glory*, 1983; *Land of the Lakes*, 1983; *Laurence Olivier*, 1984; *The Hired Man*, (musical) 1984; *The Maid of Buttermere*, 1987; *Rich: The Life of Richard Burton*, 1988; *A Time to Dance*, 1990; *Crystal Rooms*, 1992; *King Lear in New York*, (play) 1992; *The Seventh Seal: a study of Ingmar Bergman*, 1993; *Credo*, 1996; *On Giants' Shoulders*, 1998; *The Soldier's Return*, 1999; Screenplays: *Isadora*; *Jesus Christ Superstar*, *Clouds of Glory* (with Ken Russell). *Recreations:* Walking, books. *Clubs:* Garrick. *Name, Style and Title:* Raised to the peerage as Baron Bragg, of Wigton in the County of Cumbria 1998. *Address:* The Lord Bragg, 12 Hampstead Hill Gardens, London, NW3 2PL.

LORD BRAMALL — Cross-Bencher

BRAMALL (Life Baron), Edwin Noel Westby Bramall; cr. 1987. Born 18 December 1923. Son of late Major Edmund Haselden Bramall and late Katharine Bridget Bramall, née Westby; educated Eton; Army Staff College; Imperial Defence College. Married 1949, Dorothy Avril Wentworth, daughter of late Brigadier Henry Albemarle Vernon, DSO (1 son 1 daughter). *Armed Forces:* Joined Army in ranks 1942; Commissioned into KRRC 1943; Served in North West Europe 1944–45; Occupation of Japan 1946–47; Instructor, School of Infantry 1949–51; PSC 1952; GS02 Div HQ and Company Commander, Middle East 1953–58; Instructor, Army Staff College 1958–61; Brevet Leiutenant Colonel 1961; On staff of Lord Mountbatten with special responsibilty for reorganisation of MOD 1963–64; CO, 2 Green Jackets KRRC, Malaysia, during Indonesian confrontation 1965–66; Commander, 5th Airportable BDE 1967–69; IDC 1970; GOC, 1st Division BAOR 1971–73; Lt Gen. 1973; Commander, British Forces, Hong Kong 1973–76; Colonel Commandant, 3rd Battalion Royal Green Jackets 1973–84; General 1976; Commander-in-Chief, UK Land Forces 1976–78; Colonel, 2nd Goorkas 1976–86; Vice-Chief of Defence Staff (Personnel and Logistics) 1978–79; Chief of the General Staff 1979–82; ADC (General) 1979–82; Field Marshal 1982; Chief of the Defence Staff 1982–85. *Councils, Public Bodies:* Lord Lieutenant, Greater London 1986–98; JP 1986. *Other:* Vice-President, SSAFA 1985–; President: Greater London TAVRA 1986–98, Gurkha Brigade Association 1987–97, London Playing Fields Society 1990–, Greater London Association of Disabled People 1986–98, Age Concern Greater London 1986–, Not Forgotten Association 1985–, Order of St John 1986–98. *Trusts, etc:* Trustee, Imperial War Museum 1983–, Chairman 1990–98. *Miscellaneous:* Member, Council of Radley College 1985–. *Honours:* MC 1945; OBE (Mil) 1965; GCB (Mil) 1979; KG 1990; K St J 1986. Freeman, City of London. Hon. Member, The Skinner's Company.

Publications: Co-Author: *The Chiefs – The Story of the UK Chiefs of Staff. Special Interests:* Defence, Hong Kong, Foreign Affairs, Education. *Recreations:* Cricket, painting, shooting, travel. *Sportsclubs:* I Zingari, Free Foresters, St Evedoc Golf Club. *Clubs:* Travellers', Army and Navy, Pratt's, MCC (President 1988–89), (Hon Life Vice President 1997–). *Name, Style and Title:* Raised to the peerage as Baron Bramall, of Bushfield in the County of Hampshire 1987. *Address:* Field Marshal The Lord Bramall, KG, GCB, OBE, MC, JP, House of Lords, London, SW1A 0PW.

LORD BRENNAN   Labour

BRENNAN (Life Baron), Daniel Joseph Brennan; cr. 2000. Born 19 March 1942. Son of late Daniel and Mary Brennan; educated St Bede's Grammar School, Bradford; Manchester University (LLB). Married 1968, Pilar, daughter of late Luis Sanchez Hernandez (4 sons). *Career:* Called to the Bar, Gray's Inn 1967 (Bencher 1993); Crown Court Recorder 1982–; QC 1985; Member, Criminal Injuries Compensation Board 1989–97; Vice-Chairman, General Council of the Bar 1998, Chairman 1999. FRSA. *Publications: Provisional Damages*, 1986; General editor *Personal Injury Manual*, 1997; General editor *Bullen and Leake on Pleadings*, 2000. *Name, Style and Title:* Raised to the peerage as Baron Brennan, of Bibury in the Country of Gloucestershire 2000. *Address:* The Lord Brennan, QC, (chambers), 39 Essex Street, London, WC2R 3AT *Tel:* 020 7832 1111.

LORD BRETT   Labour

BRETT (Life Baron), William Henry Brett; cr. 1999. Born 6 March 1942. Son of late William and Mary Brett; educated Radcliffe Secondary Technical College. Married 1st, 1961, Jean Valerie (marriage dissolved 1986) (1 son 1 daughter); married 2nd, 1994, Janet Winters (2 daughters). *Trades Union:* Member: APEX 1960–99, IPMS 1974–. *Councils, Public Bodies:* Councillor, London Borough of Lewisham 1964–68. *Career:* Various Administrative Positions, British Rail 1958–64; Administrative Assistant, Transport Salaried Staffs Association 1965–67; North West Organiser, National Union of Bank Employees 1966–68; Divisional Officer, Association of Scientific Technical and Managerial Staffs 1968–74; Institution of Professionals, Managers and Specialists: Assistant General Secretary 1980–89, General Secretary 1989–99; Member: Executive Committee, Public Services International 1989–99, General Council, Trades Union Congress 1989–99; Member, Governing Body, International Labour Organisation (Geneva) 1992–; Vice-Chairman, ILO 1993–; Chair, Worker Group, ILO 1993–. FRSA. *Publications: International Labour in the 21st Century,* 1994. *Special Interests:* Human Rights, Development, Economics, Labour Issues. *Recreations:* Reading, walking. *Clubs:* Lydd War Memorial Institute. *Name, Style and Title:* Raised to the peerage as Baron Brett, of Lydd in the County of Kent 1999. *Address:* The Lord Brett, Sycamore House, 2 Mill Road, Lydd, Romney Marsh, Kent, TN29 9EP *Tel:* 01797 321597 *Fax:* 01797 322148 *E-Mail:* brett4571@aol.com.

LORD BRIDGE OF HARWICH   Cross-Bencher

BRIDGE OF HARWICH (Life Baron), Nigel Cyprian Bridge; cr. 1980. Born 26 February 1917. Son of late Commander C. D. C. Bridge, RN; educated Marlborough. Married 1944, Margaret Swinbank (1 son 2 daughters). *Armed Forces:* Army Service 1940–46, Commissioned KRRC 1941. *Career:* Called to the Bar, Inner Temple 1947, Bencher 1964, Treasurer 1986; Junior Counsel to Treasury (Common Law) 1964–68; Judge of High Court, Queen's Bench Division 1968–75; Presiding Judge, Western Circuit 1972–74; A Lord Justice of Appeal 1975–80; A Lord of Appeal in Ordinary 1980–92. *Select Committees:* Chairman, Ecclesiastical Committee (Joint Committee of both Houses of Parliament) 1981–92. Hon. Fellow: American College of Trial Lawyers 1984, Wolfson College, Cambridge 1989. *Miscellaneous:* Member, Security Commission 1977–85, Chairman 1982–85; Chairman, Church of England Synodical Government Review 1993–97. *Honours:* Kt 1968; PC 1975. *Name, Style and Title:* Raised to the peerage as Baron Bridge of Harwich, of Harwich in the County of Essex 1980. *Address:* Rt Hon the Lord Bridge of Harwich, House of Lords, London, SW1A 0PW.

VISCOUNT BRIDGEMAN — Conservative

BRIDGEMAN (3rd Viscount, UK), Robin John Orlando Bridgeman; cr. 1929. Born 5 December 1930. Son of late Brigadier Hon. Geoffrey Bridgeman, MC, FRCS, second son of 1st Viscount, PC. Succeeded his uncle 1982; educated Eton. Married 1966, Victoria Harriet Lucy Turton (4 sons). *Armed Forces:* 2nd Lieutenant, The Rifle Brigade 1950–51. *Career:* Chartered Accountant; Partner, Henderson Crosthwaite and Co., Stockbrokers 1973–86; Director: Guinness Mahon and Co. Ltd 1988–90, Nestor-BNA plc 1988–. *House of Lords:* An elected hereditary peer 1999–. *Whip:* An Opposition Whip (Home Office, Legal Affairs) December 1998–. *Select Committees:* Former Member: Joint Committee on Statutory Instruments, European Communities, Sub-Committee C (Environment, Public Health and Consumer Protection). *Other:* Chairman, Friends of Lambeth Palace Library; Treasurer, New England Company. *Trusts, etc:* Special Trustee, Hammersmith and Queen Charlotte's Hospital Authority 1992–2000; Treasurer, Florence Nightingale Aid in Sickness Trust; Chairman, Hospital of St John and St Elizabeth; Trustee, Music at Winchester. *Honours:* Knight of Malta. CA. *Special Interests:* Health, Social Services, Environment, Home Affairs, Local Government. *Recreations:* Gardening, music, shooting, skiing. *Clubs:* Beefsteak, MCC, Pitt. *Address:* The Viscount Bridgeman, 19 Chepstow Road, London, W2 5BP *Tel:* 020 7727 4065.

LORD BRIDGES — Cross-Bencher

BRIDGES (2nd Baron, UK), Thomas Edward Bridges; cr. 1957. Born 27 November 1927. Son of 1st Baron, KG, PC, GCB, GCVO, MC, and late Hon. Katharine Dianthe Farrer, daughter of 2nd Baron Farrer. Succeeded his father 1969; educated Eton; New College, Oxford (MA). Married 1953, Rachel Mary, daughter of late Sir Henry Noel Bunbury, KCB (2 sons 1 daughter). *Armed Forces:* Commissioned in Royal Signals 1946–48. *Councils, Public Bodies:* Vice-President, Council for National Parks 2000–. *Career:* Entered HM Foreign Service 1951; Served in Bonn, Berlin, Rio de Janeiro, Athens and Moscow, Private Secretary (Overseas Affairs) to the Prime Minister 1972–74; Minister (Commercial) at British Embassy, Washington, DC 1976–79; Deputy Secretary, Foreign and Commonwealth Office 1979–82; HM Ambassador to Italy 1983–87; Independent Board Member, Securities and Futures Authority Ltd 1989–97. *House of Lords:* An elected hereditary peer 1999–. *Select Committees:* Member, Select Committee on the European Communities 1988–92, 1994–98. *Other:* Chairman, UK National Committee for UNICEF 1989–97; Chairman, British-Italian Society 1991–97, Hon. Vice-President 1998–; President, Dolmetsch Foundation. *Trusts, etc:* Trustee, Rayne Foundation. *Honours:* GCMG 1988. FRSA. *Clubs:* Athenaeum. *Address:* The Lord Bridges, GCMG, 56 Church Street, Orford, Woodbridge, Suffolk, IP12 2NT.

LORD BRIGGS — Cross-Bencher

BRIGGS (Life Baron), Asa Briggs; cr. 1976. Born 7 May 1921. Son of late William Walker Briggs; educated Keighley Grammar School; Sidney Sussex College, Cambridge (MA). Married 1955, Susan Anne Banwell (2 sons 2 daughters). *Career:* Professor of Modern History, Leeds University 1955–61; Sussex University: Professor of History, 1961–76, Vice-Chancellor, 1967–76; Provost, Worcester College, Oxford 1976–91. *Chancellor:* Chancellor, Open University 1979–94. *Other:* President: Social History Society, Victorian Society, Ephemera Society. *Trusts, etc:* Trustee, Glyndebourne Arts Trust 1966–91; Member, Civic Trust 1976–86. *Miscellaneous:* Chairman: Committee on Nursing 1970–72, Advisory Board Redundant Churches 1983–88, Commonwealth of Learning Board 1988–93. Fellow, British Academy; American Academy of Arts and Sciences. Member, Spectacle Makers Company. *Publications:* Various historical works including six volumes on history of British broadcasting. *Special Interests:* Education, Social Policy. *Recreations:* Travel. *Clubs:* Beefsteak, United Oxford and Cambridge University. *Name, Style and Title:* Raised to the peerage as Baron Briggs, of Lewes in the County of East Sussex 1976. *Address:* The Lord Briggs, The Caprons, Keere Street, Lewes, East Sussex, BN7 1TY *Tel:* 01273 474704.

LORD BRIGHTMAN   Cross-Bencher

BRIGHTMAN (Life Baron), John Anson Brightman; cr. 1982. Born 20 June 1911. Son of late William Henry Brightman; educated Marlborough; St John's College, Cambridge. Married 1945, Roxane, daughter of late Gerasimo Ambatielo (1 son). *Armed Forces:* Able seaman, merchant navy 1939–40; RNVR (Lieutenant-Commander) 1940–46; Anti-submarine warfare base, Tobermory; North Atlantic and Mediterranean convoys; Royal Naval Staff College, Greenwich; Assistant Naval Attaché, Ankara; Staff, South East Asia Command. *Career:* Called to the Bar, Lincoln's Inn 1932; Member, General Council of the Bar 1956–60, 1966–70; QC 1961; Bencher of Lincoln's Inn 1966; Attorney General of the Duchy of Lancaster 1969–70; Judge of the High Court of Justice, Chancery Division 1970–79; Judge of National Industrial Relations Court 1971–74; Lord Justice of Court of Appeal 1979–82; A Lord of Appeal in Ordinary 1982–86. *Select Committees:* Chairman: Select Committee on British Waterways 1991–92, Special Standing Committee on Property Law 1994, Special Public Bill Committeee on Private International Law 1995, Special Public Bill Committeee on Family Homes and Domestic Violence 1995; Member, Ecclesiastical Committee 1997–. *Other:* Chairman, Tancred's Foundation 1982–96. Honorary Fellow, St John's College, Cambridge 1982. *Miscellaneous:* Member, Tax Law Review Committee's Working Party on Parliamentary Procedures for the enactment of Rewritten Tax Law 1996. *Honours:* Kt 1970; PC 1979. FRGS 1993. *Publications: Historical Sites in Franz Josef Land,* 1997. *Special Interests:* Charity Law, Abortion, High Arctic. *Recreations:* Arctic travel, cross country skiing, mountain trekking. *Sportsclubs:* Bar Yacht. *Name, Style and Title:* Raised to the peerage as Baron Brightman, of Ibthorpe in the County of Hampshire 1982. *Address:* Rt Hon the Lord Brightman, 30 Onslow Gardens, London, SW7 3AH *Tel:* 020 7584 8488 *Fax:* 020 7584 8488; House of Lords, London, SW1A 0PW *Tel:* House of Lords 020 7219 2034; Ibthorpe, Nr Hurstbourne Tarrant, Hampshire, SP11 0BY *Tel:* 01264 736280 *Fax:* 01264 736280.

BARONESS BRIGSTOCKE   Conservative

BRIGSTOCKE (Life Baroness), Heather Renwick Brigstocke; cr. 1990. Born 2 September 1929. Daughter of late Squadron-Leader J. R. Brown, DFC and Mrs. M. J. C. Brown; educated Abbey School, Reading; Girton College, Cambridge (MA). Married 1st, August 16, 1952, Geoffrey Brigstocke (died 1974) (3 sons 1 daughter); married 2nd, January 22, 2000, The Rt Hon. the Lord Griffiths, MC (*qv*). *Career:* Classics Mistress, Francis Holland School, London 1951–53; Part-time Classics Mistress, Godolphin and Latymer School 1954–60; Part-time Latin Teacher, National Cathedral School, Washington DC 1962–64; Headmistress, Francis Holland School London 1965–74; High Mistress, St. Paul's Girls' School 1974–89; Non-Executive Director, London Weekend Television 1982–90, Member, Programme Advisory Board 1990–93; Independent National Director, Times Newspapers Holdings 1990–; Non exec director, Burberry's 1993–96; Associate director, Great Universal Stores 1993–96. *Select Committees:* Former Member, House of Lords Library Sub-Committee. *Other:* Past and present senior posts in numerous organisations, especially educational establishments, including: Governor: Imperial College of Science, Technology and Medicine 1991–99; Member, European Cultural Foundation (UK Committee) 1992–99; Chairman, English Speaking Union 1993–99. *Trusts, etc:* Trustee: National Gallery 1975–82, Kennedy Memorial Trust 1980–85, City Technology Colleges Trust 1987–; Chairman: Thames LWT Telethon Trust 1990, The Menerva Educational Trust 1991–93; Council Member, National Literacy Trust 1993–; Trustee, The Great Britain Sasakawa Foundation 1994–. *Miscellaneous:* Member, Modern Foreign Languages Working Group 1989–90; Commissioner, Museums and Galleries Commission 1992–2000; Hon. Bencher, The Inner Temple 1992–. *Honours:* CBE 2000. *Special Interests:* Education, Health, Broadcasting, Museums and Galleries. *Name, Style and Title:* Raised to the peerage as Baroness Brigstocke, of Kensington in the Royal Borough of Kensington and Chelsea 1990. *Address:* The Baroness Brigstocke, CBE, House of Lords, London, SW1A 0PW *Tel:* House of Lords 020 7219 3000.

BISHOP OF BRISTOL   Non-Affiliated

BRISTOL (54th Bishop of), Barry Rogerson. Born 25 July 1936. Son of late Eric Rogerson, and of Olive Rogerson; educated Magnus Grammar School, Newark, Notts; Leeds University (BA); Wells Theological College. Married December 28, 1961, Olga, daughter of late Wilfred Gibson, and of May Gibson (2 daughters). *Armed Forces:* National Service, RAF (Radar) 1955–57. *Career:* Bank Clerk, Midland Bank 1952–57; Deaconed; Curate, St. Hilda with St. Thomas, South Shields (diocese of Durham; priested 1963) 1962–65; Curate, St. Nicholas, Bishopwearmouth 1965–67; Lecturer, Lichfield Theological College 1967–71, Vice-Principal 1971–72; Lecturer, Salisbury and Wells Theological College 1972–75; Team Rector, St. Thomas, Wednesfield (diocese of Lichfield) 1975–79; Chairman, Melanesian Mission 1979–; Honorary Canon, Lichfield Cathedral 1979–85; Suffragan Bishop of Wolverhampton 1979–85; Bishop of Bristol 1985–; Chairman, Advisory Board of Ministry, General Synod of Church of England 1987–93; Member, World Council of Churches Faith and Order Commission 1987–98 and Central Committee 1991–; Took his seat in the House of Lords 1990; President, Churches Together in Britain and Ireland (CTBI) 1999–. Hon. LLD, Bristol. *Special Interests:* Homeless, Housing, Vocational Education. *Recreations:* Cinema, stained glass, photography, sailing. *Clubs:* Commonwealth Trust. *Address:* Rt Rev the Lord Bishop of Bristol, Bishop's House, Clifton Hill, Clifton, Bristol, BS8 1BW *Tel:* 0117–973 0222 *Fax:* 0117–923 9670.

LORD BRITTAN OF SPENNITHORNE   Conservative

BRITTAN OF SPENNITHORNE (Life Baron), Leon Brittan; cr. 2000. Born 25 September 1939. Son of late Dr Joseph Brittan and Mrs Rebecca Brittan; educated Haberdashers' Aske's School; Trinity College, Cambridge (MA) (President of Cambridge Union); Yale University, USA (Henry Fellow). Married December 23, 1980, Diana Peterson (2 step-daughters).*Career:* Called to the Bar, Inner Temple 1962; QC 1978; Bencher 1983; European Commission: Member 1989–99, Vice President 1989–93 and 1995–99; Vice-Chairman, UBS Warburg 2000–; Consultant, Herbert Smith 2000–; Advisory Director, Unilever 2000–; Distinguished Visiting Scholar, Yale University 2000–. *House of Commons:* Contested North Kensington 1966 and 1970; MP (Conservative) for Cleveland and Whitby February 1974–83 and for Richmond, North Yorkshire 1983–88; Minister of State, Home Office 1979–81; Chief Secretary to HM Treasury 1981–83; Home Secretary 1983–85; Secretary of State for Trade and Industry 1985–86. *Spokesman (Commons):* Opposition Spokesman on: Devolution 1976–79, Employment 1978–79. *Chancellor:* Chancellor, University of Teesside 1993–. *Party Groups (General):* Chairman, Bow Group 1966–68; Editor, *Crossbow* 1966–68; Chairman, Society of Conservative Lawyers 1986–88. Seven honorary doctorates from England and Korea. *Honours:* PC 1981; Kt 1989. *Publications: Defence and Arms Control in a Changing Era,* 1988; *European Competition Policy,* 1992; *The Europe We Need,* 1994; *A Diet of Brussels,* 2000; has contributed to various Conservative pamphlets. *Recreations:* Opera, art, cricket, walking. *Clubs:* Carlton, MCC, White's, Pratt's. *Name, Style and Title:* Raised to the peerage as Baron Brittan of Spennithorne, of Spennithorne in the County of North Yorkshire 2000.*Address:* Rt Hon the Lord Brittan of Spennithorne, QC, House of Lords, London, SW1A 0PW.

LORD BROOKE OF ALVERTHORPE   Labour

BROOKE OF ALVERTHORPE (Life Baron), Clive Brooke; cr. 1997. Born 21 June 1942. Son of John and Mary Brooke; educated Thornes House School, Wakefield. Married 1967, Lorna Hopkin Roberts. *Trades Union:* Member, Public and Commercial Services Union (PCS). *Career:* Inland Revenue Staff Federation: Assistant Secretary 1964–82, Deputy General Secretary 1982–88, General Secretary 1988–95; Joint General Secretary, Public Services Tax and Commerce Union 1996–98; Member, TUC: General Council 1989–96, Executive Committee 1993–96. *Select Committees:* Chairman, Select Committee on European Communities Sub-Committee B (Energy, Industry and Transport); Member, Select Committee on European Union 1999–. *Backbench Committees:* Member, Labour Departmental Committees for: Defence, Home Affairs, Education and Employment, Cabinet Office.*International Bodies:* Member: IPA, CPA.

Party Groups (General): Member: Labour Party, Fabian Society. *Other:* Patron: Learning Through Life Foundation, Community Initiatives Foundation; Council Member, Institute for Employment Studies; Chairman, Unions 21. *Trusts, etc:* Trustee: Community Service Volunteers 1989–, Duke of Edinburgh's Study Conference 1993–, Institute for Public Policy Research, London Dorchester Committee Trust. *Miscellaneous:* Member: House of Commons Speaker's Commission on Citizenship 1988, Pensions Compensation Board 1996–, Council of Churches for Britain and Ireland Enquiry into Unemployment and the Future of Work 1995–97. FRSA. *Special Interests:* Employment, Education, Community Care. *Recreations:* Travel, community services, politics, church affairs, reading, walking. *Name, Style and Title:* Raised to the peerage as Baron Brooke of Alverthorpe, of Alverthorpe in the County of West Yorkshire 1997. *Address:* The Lord Brooke of Alverthorpe, House of Lords, London, SW1A 0PW *Tel:* 020 7219 5353.

VISCOUNT BROOKEBOROUGH   Cross-Bencher

BROOKEBOROUGH (3rd Viscount, UK), Alan Henry Brooke; cr. 1952; 7th Bt of Cole Brooke (UK) 1822. Born 30 June 1952. Son of 2nd Viscount, PC. Succeeded his father 1987; educated Harrow; Millfield; Royal Agricultural College, Cirencester. Married April 12, 1980, Janet Elizabeth Cooke.*Armed Forces:* Commission, 17th/21st Lancers 1971; Transferred to: Ulster Defence Regiment 1977, Royal Irish Regiment 1992; Lieutenant-Colonel 1993; Hon. Colonel, 4th/5th Battalion, The Royal Irish Rangers 1997–. *Councils, Public Bodies:* DL, Co. Fermanagh 1987–; High Sheriff, Co. Fermanagh 1995. *Career:* Non-Executive Director: Green Park Health Care Trust 1993–, Basel International (Jersey); A Personal Lord in Waiting to HM The Queen 1997–. *House of Lords:* An elected hereditary peer 1999–. *Select Committees:* Member, Select Committee on European Communities: Sub-Committee D (Agriculture and Food) 1989–93, 1994–97; Sub-Committee B (Energy, Industry and Transport) 1998–. *Other:* Vice-President, Somme Association 1990–; President, Army Benevolent Fund, Northern Ireland 1995–.*Trusts, etc:* Fellow, Industry and Parliament Trust. *Special Interests:* Northern Ireland, Agriculture, Tourism, Defence, Health. *Recreations:* Shooting, fishing, gardening, sailing. *Clubs:* Cavalry and Guards, Pratt's. *Address:* The Viscount Brookeborough, DL, Colebrooke, Brookeborough, Enniskillen, Co. Fermanagh, BT94 4DW *Tel:* 01365 53402.

LORD BROOKES   Cross-Bencher

BROOKES (Life Baron), Raymond Percival Brookes; cr. 1976. Born 10 April 1909. Son of late William Brookes; educated Kenrick Technical College, West Bromwich. Married 1937, Florence Sharman (1 son). *Career:* Group Chairman and Chief Executive, Guest, Keen & Nettlefolds Ltd. 1965–74, now Life President. *Other:* President, Society of Motor Manufacturers and Traders Ltd. 1974–75; Member, Court of Governors, University of Birmingham 1966–75; A Vice-President, Engineering Employers' Federation 1967–75. *Honours:* Kt 1971. *Name, Style and Title:* Raised to the peerage as Baron Brookes, of West Bromwich in the County of West Midlands 1976. *Address:* The Lord Brookes, Mallards, Santon, Isle of Man, IM4 1EH.

LORD BROOKMAN   Labour

BROOKMAN (Life Baron), David Keith Brookman; cr. 1998. Born 3 January 1937. Son of George Henry Brookman, MM and Blodwin Brookman; educated Nantyglo Grammar School, Gwent. Married 1958, Patricia Worthington (3 daughters). *Trades Union:* Member: Educational Advisory Committee for Wales 1976–82, Trades Union Congress 1992–99; Chairman, Trades Union Congress: Steel Committee (UK) 1998–99, European Coal and Steel Committee (ECCC) 1992–; International Metal Workers (IMF); President, Iron and Steel Non-Ferrous Department 1992–99. *Armed Forces:* National Service, RAF 1955–57. *Career:* Steel worker, Richard Thomas and Baldwin, Ebbw Vale 1953–55, 1957–73; Iron and Steel Trades Confederation: Organiser 1973–85, Assistant General Secretary 1985–93, General Secretary 1993–99; Board Member, British Steel (Industry) 1993–. *International Bodies (General):* Honorary Secretary, International Metalworkers' Federation (British Section) 1993–99: President, International Metalworkers' Federation, Iron, Steel and Non-Ferrous Metals Department 1993–99. *Party Groups (General):* Labour Party: Member: Executive Committee, Wales 1982–85, National Constitutional Committee 1987–91, NEC 1991–92.*Other:* Governor, Gwent College of Higher Education 1980–84. *Trusts, etc:* Trustee, Julian Melchett Trust 1985–95.

Miscellaneous: Member: Joint Industrial Council for Slag Industry 1985–93, British Steel Joint Accident Prevention Advisory Committee 1985–93, British Steel Advisory Committee on Education and Training 1986–93, Executive Council, European Metalworkers Federation 1985–95; Member, National T.U. Steel Co-ordinating Committee 1991–, Chairman 1993–; Member, European Coal and Steel Community Consultative Committee 1993–; Joint Secretary: British Steel Strip Trade Board 1993–98, British Steel Joint Standing Committee 1993–98, British Steel European Works Council 1996–99. *Recreations:* Cricket, rugby, reading, keep-fit, golf. *Sportsclubs:* Harrington Common Golf Club. *Clubs:* Reform. *Name, Style and Title:* Raised to the peerage as Baron Brookman, of Ebbw Vale in the County of Gwent 1998. *Address:* The Lord Brookman, 4 Bassett Close, Redbourn, Hertfordshire, AL3 2JY *Tel:* 01582 792066 (Home).

LORD BROOKS OF TREMORFA   Labour

BROOKS OF TREMORFA (Life Baron), John Edward Brooks; cr. 1979. Born 12 April 1927. Son of Edward George Brooks; educated Elementary schools; Coleg Harlech. Married 1st, 1948 (1 son 1 daughter) (marriage dissolved 1956), married 2nd, 1958, Margaret Pringle (2 sons). *Councils, Public Bodies:* Councillor, South Glamorgan County Council 1973–93, Leader 1973–77, 1986–92, Chairman 1981–82; Member, Cardiff Bay Development Corporation 1987–, currently Deputy Chairman; DL, South Glamorgan 1994–. *Spokesman:* Opposition Defence Spokesman 1980–81. *Select Committees:* Former Member, Joint Committee on Statutory Instruments. *Party Groups (General):* Secretary, Cardiff South East Labour Party 1966–; Parliamentary Agent to James Callaghan MP 1970 and 1979 general elections; Chairman, Labour Party, Wales 1978–79. *Other:* Steward, British Boxing Board of Control 1986–, Vice-Chairman 1999–; Chairman: Welsh Sports Hall of Fame 1988–, Sportsmatch Wales 1992–. *Miscellaneous:* Contested Barry (Labour) February and October 1974 General Elections. *Recreations:* Reading, most sports. *Name, Style and Title:* Raised to the peerage as Baron Brooks of Tremorfa, of Tremorfa in the County of Glamorgan 1979. *Address:* The Lord Brooks of Tremorfa, DL, 46 Kennerleigh Road, Rumney, Cardiff, CF3 9BJ *Tel:* 01222 791848.

LORD BROUGHAM AND VAUX   Conservative

BROUGHAM AND VAUX (5th Baron, UK), Michael John Brougham; cr. 1860. Born 2 August 1938. Son of 4th Baron. Succeeded his father 1967; educated Lycée Jaccard, Lausanne; Millfield School; Northampton Institute of Agriculture. Married 1st, 1963, Olivia Susan, daughter of late Rear-Admiral Gordon T. S. Gray, CB, DSC (1 daughter) (marriage dissolved 1967); married 2nd, January 17, 1969, Catherine Gulliver (1 son) (marriage dissolved 1981 and who died 1986). *House of Lords:* A Deputy Chairman of Committees, House of Lords 1993–97, 1997–; A Deputy Speaker House of Lords 1995–; An elected hereditary peer 1999–. *Select Committees:* Member, Select Committees on: House of Lords' Offices 1997–99, Hybrid Instruments, Procedure. *Backbench Committees:* Vice-Chairman, Association of Conservative Peers 1998–. *Other:* President, Royal Society for the Prevention of Accidents 1986–89; Chairman: The Tax Payers' Society 1989–91, European Secure Vehicle Alliance 1992–; President, National Health Safety Groups Council 1994–. *Honours:* CBE 1995. *Special Interests:* Road Safety, Transport, Motor Industry, Aviation. *Recreations:* Photography, bridge, shooting. *Address:* The Lord Brougham and Vaux, CBE, 11 Westminster Gardens, Marsham Street, London, SW1P 4JA.

LORD BROWNE-WILKINSON   Cross-Bencher

BROWNE-WILKINSON (Life Baron), Nicolas Christopher Henry Browne-Wilkinson; cr. 1991. Born 30 March 1930. Son of late Canon A. R. Browne-Wilkinson; educated Lancing; Magdalen College, Oxford (BA). Married 1st, 1955, Ursula de Lacy Bacon (died 1987) (3 sons 2 daughters), married 2nd, 1990, Mrs Hilary Tuckwell. *Career:* Called to the Bar, Lincoln's Inn 1953, Bencher 1977; Junior Counsel: to Registrar of Restrictive Trading Agreements 1964–66, to Attorney-General in Charity Matters 1966–72, in bankruptcy to Department of Trade and Industry 1966–72; QC 1972; A Judge of the Courts of Appeal of Jersey and Guernsey 1976–77; A Judge of the High Court, Chancery Division 1977–83; President, Employment Appeal Tribunal 1981–83; A Lord Justice of Appeal 1983–85; President, Senate of the Inns of Court and the Bar 1984–86; Vice-Chancellor of the Supreme Court 1985–91; A Lord of Appeal in Ordinary 1991–; Senior Law Lord 1998–2000. *Party Groups:* Vice-Chairman, Association of Conservative Peers 1998–. Hon. Fellow: St Edward Hall, Oxford 1987, Magdalen College, Oxford 1993. *Recreations:* Gardening, music. *Name, Style and Title:* Raised to the peerage as Baron Browne-Wilkinson, of Camden in the London Borough of Camden 1991. *Address:* Rt Hon the Lord Browne-Wilkinson, House of Lords, London, SW1A 0PW.

LORD BRUCE OF DONINGTON   Labour

BRUCE OF DONINGTON (Life Baron), Donald William Trevor Bruce; cr. 1974. Born 3 October 1912. Son of late W. T. Bruce; educated The Grammar School, Donington, Lincolnshire. Married 1st, 1939, Joan Butcher (1 son 2 daughters and 1 daughter deceased) (marriage dissolved 1980), married 2nd, 1981, Mrs Cyrena Shaw Heard. *Armed Forces:* Served Royal Signals 1939; Major 1942; General Staff 1943–45. *Career:* Chartered Accountant; Economist; Member, European Parliament 1975–79. *House of Commons:* MP (Labour), Portsmouth North Division 1945–50; PPS to Minister of Health 1945–50; Contested The Wrekin 1959. *Spokesman:* Opposition Spokesman on: Trade and Industry 1985–88, The Treasury 1979–85, 1988–90. *Select Committees:* Member: House of Lords Select Committee on the European Community 1982–97, Select Committee on House of Lords' Offices 1997–. *Miscellaneous:* Specialist on EU matters 1990–. FCA. *Publications:* Co-author *The State of the Nation,* 1998. *Special Interests:* Finance, Industry, Economic Policy, European Union. *Recreations:* Swimming. *Name, Style and Title:* Raised to the peerage as Baron Bruce of Donington, of Rickmansworth in the County of Hertfordshire 1974. *Address:* The Lord Bruce of Donington, 2 Bloomsbury Street, London, WC1B 3ST *Tel:* 020 7413 5100.

LORD BULLOCK   Cross-Bencher

BULLOCK (Life Baron), Alan Louis Charles Bullock; cr. 1976. Born 13 December 1914. Son of late Rev. Frank Bullock; educated Bradford Grammar School; Wadham College, Oxford. Married 1940, Hilda Handy (3 sons 1 daughter and 1 daughter deceased). *Career:* Fellow, Dean and Tutor in Modern History, New College Oxford 1945–52; Founding Master, St. Catherine's College, Oxford 1960–80; Vice-Chancellor, Oxford University 1969–73. *Other:* Foreign Member, American Academy of Arts and Sciences; Chairman, Friends of the Ashmolean Museum. Five honorary doctorates. *Miscellaneous:* Chairman, National Advisory Council on the Training and Supply of Teachers 1963–65. *Honours:* Kt 1972; Chevalier, Legion D'Honneur (France) 1970; Commander's Cross of the Order of Merit (Germany) 1995. FBA 1967. *Publications: Hitler, A Study in Tyranny; The Liberal Tradition; The Life and Times of Ernest Bevin; Hitler and Stalin: Parallel Lives,* and other Works. *Name, Style and Title:* Raised to the peerage as Baron Bullock, of Leafield in the County of Oxfordshire 1976. *Address:* The Lord Bullock, St. Catherine's College, Oxford, OX1 3UJ.

Visit the Vacher Dod Website . . .
www.politicallinks.co.uk

LORD BURLISON   Labour

BURLISON (Life Baron), Thomas Henry Burlison; cr. 1997. Born 23 May 1936. Son of Robert and Georgina Burlison; educated Edmondsley, Co. Durham. Married 1981, Valerie Stephenson (2 sons 1 daughter). *Trades Union:* Member, GMB. *Armed Forces:* RAF 1959–61. *Councils, Public Bodies:* DL, Tyne and Wear 1997–. *Career:* Panel Beater 1951–57; Professional Footballer 1953–65; General and Municipal Workers' Union, then General, Municipal, Boilermakers and Allied Trades Union, later GMB: Regional Officer 1965–78, Regional Secretary 1978–91, Deputy General Secretary 1991–. *Whip:* Government Whip (Lord in Waiting) 1999–. *Spokesman:* Spokesman on: Cabinet Office 1999–, Defence 1999–, Home Office 1999–. *Party Groups (General):* Treasurer, Labour Party 1992–96. *Miscellaneous:* Honorary President, Hartlepool United F.C. *Recreations:* Gardening. *Name, Style and Title:* Raised to the peerage as Baron Burlison, of Rowlands Gill in the County of Tyne and Wear 1997. *Address:* The Lord Burlison, DL, High Point, West Highhorse Close, Rowlands Gill, Tyne and Wear, NE39 1AL.

LORD BURNHAM   Conservative

BURNHAM (6th Baron), Hugh John Frederick Lawson; cr. 1903; 6th Bt of Hall Barn and Peterborough Court (UK) 1892. Born 15 August 1931. Son of Major-General 4th Baron, CB, DSO, MC, TD, DL. Succeeded his brother 1993; educated Eton; Balliol College, Oxford (MA). Married 1955, Hilary Hunter (1 son 2 daughters). *Armed Forces:* Late Scots Guards. *Career: Daily Telegraph* 1954–86, Deputy Managing Director 1984–86. *House of Lords:* A Deputy Speaker 1995–; A Deputy Chairman of Committees 1995–; An elected hereditary peer 1999–. *Whip:* Opposition Deputy Chief Whip 1997–. *Spokesman:* Opposition Spokesman on Defence 1997–. *Select Committees:* Member: Hybrid Instruments Committee 1996–, Select Committee on Procedure 1997–. *Other:* Director General, King George's Fund for Sailors 1988–93; A Younger Brother of Trinity House 1998. *Miscellaneous:* Provincial Grand Master, Buckinghamshire Freemasons; A Lords' Member, Parliamentary Broadcasting Unit 2000–. *Special Interests:* Freemasonry. *Recreations:* Horse racing, shooting, sailing. *Clubs:* Pratt's, Royal Yacht Squadron (Cowes), Royal Ocean Racing. *Address:* The Lord Burnham, Woodlands Farm, Burnham Road, Beaconsfield, Buckinghamshire, HP9 2SF.

LORD BURNS   Cross-Bencher

BURNS (Life Baron), Terence Burns; cr. 1998. Born 13 March 1944. Son of Patrick and Doris Burns; educated Houghton-le-Spring Grammar School; Manchester University (BA Economics). Married 1969, Anne Elizabeth Powell (1 son 2 daughters). *Career:* London Business School: Research posts 1965–70, Lecturer in Economics 1970–74, Senior Lecturer 1974–79, Director, LBS Centre for Economic Forecasting 1976–79, Professor of Economics 1979, Fellow 1989; Member, HM Treasury Academic Panel 1976–79; Chief Economic Adviser to the Treasury and Head of the Government Economic Service 1980–91; Visiting Fellow, Nuffield College, Oxford 1989–97; Permanent Secretary, HM Treasury 1991–98; Visiting Professor, Durham University 1995–; Non-Executive Director: Legal and General Group plc 1999–, Pearson plc 1999–, The British Law Company plc 2000–. *Select Committees:* Member, Select Committee on Monetary Policy of the Bank of England 1998–; Chairman, Financial Services and Markets Joint Committee 1999. *Other:* Vice-President, Society of Business Economists 1985–98, President 1998–; Vice-President, Royal Economic Society 1992–; Board Member, Manchester Business School 1992–98; Non-executive Director, Queens Park Rangers FC 1996–; Governor: Royal Academy of Music 1998–, National Institute of Economic and Social Research. Four honorary degrees. *Miscellaneous:* Member: Scottish Fee Support Review, 1998–2000, The Hansard Society Commission on the Scrutiny Role of Parliament 1999–; Chairman, The Committee of Inquiry into Hunting with Dogs in England and Wales 2000.

Honours: Kt 1983; GCB 1995. Fellow, London Business School 1989–. *Publications: The Interpretation and Use of Economic Predictions* (*Proceedings of the Royal Society*, London, A 407), 1986; *The UK Government's Financial Strategy* (*Keynes and Economic Policy*), 1988. *Recreations:* Watching football, music, golf. *Sportsclubs:* Ealing Golf, Royal St George's Golf; President, Civil Service Golf Society. *Clubs:* Reform. *Name, Style and Title:* Raised to the peerage as Baron Burns, of Pitshanger in the London Borough of Ealing 1998. *Address:* The Lord Burns, GCB, House of Lords, London, SW1A 0PW *E-Mail:* burnst@parliament.uk.

BARONESS BUSCOMBE   Conservative

BUSCOMBE (Life Baroness), Peta Jane Buscombe; cr. 1998. Born 12 March 1954; educated Hinchley Wood School, Hinchley Wood, Surrey, Rosebery Grammar School, Epsom, Surrey; Inns of Court School of Law. Married 1980, Philip John Buscombe (twin sons, 1 daughter). *Councils, Public Bodies:* Councillor, South Oxfordshire District Council 1995–99. *Career:* Former Corporate Lawyer; Barrister-at-Law; Called to the Bar, Inner Temple 1977. *Spokesman:* Opposition Spokeswoman for: Law Officers and Lord Chancellor's Department 1999–, Social Security 1999–, Trade and Industry 1999–. *International Bodies:* Member, IPU. *Party Groups (General):* A Vice-Chairman, The Conservative Party 1997–99;
President, Slough Conservative Association 1997–. *Miscellaneous:* Contested (Conservative) Slough 1997 General Election. *Special Interests:* Education, Law and Order, Trade and Industry. *Recreations:* Gardening, boating, swimming, tennis, theatre, cinema. *Sportsclubs:* Rock Sailing. *Clubs:* Carlton, Sloane. *Name, Style and Title:* Raised to the peerage as Baroness Buscombe, of Goring in the County of Oxfordshire 1998. *Address:* The Baroness Buscombe, House of Lords, London, SW1A 0PW *E-Mail:* buscombep@parliament.uk.

LORD BUTLER OF BROCKWELL   Non-Affiliated

BUTLER OF BROCKWELL (Life Baron) (Frederick Edward) Robin Butler; cr. 1998. Born 3 January 1938. Son of late Bernard and Nora Butler; educated Harrow School; University College, Oxford (BA Lit. Hum. 1961, MA). Married 1962, Gillian Lois Galley (1 son 2 daughters). *Career:* Joined HM Treasury 1961; Private Secretary to Financial Secretary to Treasury 1964–65; Secretary, Budget Committee 1965–69; Seconded to Cabinet Office as Member, Central Policy Review Staff 1971–72; Private Secretary: to Rt Hon. Edward Heath, MP 1972–74, to Rt Hon. Harold Wilson, MP 1974–75; Returned to HM Treasury as Assistant Secretary, General Expenditure Intelligence Division 1975; Under Secretary, General Expenditure Policy
Group 1977–80; Principal Establishment Officer 1980–82; Principal Private Secretary to Margaret Thatcher as Prime Minister 1982–85; Second Permanent Secretary, Public Expenditure, HM Treasury 1985–87; Secretary of the Cabinet and Head of the Home Civil Service 1988–98; Master, University College, Oxford 1998–. *Other:* Governor, Harrow School 1975–91, Chairman of Governors 1988–91; Chairman of Governors, Dulwich College 1997–. *Hon. Degrees:* Cranfield University, Exeter University, Aston University, London University. *Miscellaneous:* Member, Royal Commission on the Reform of the House of Lords 1999. *Honours:* CVO 1986; KCB 1988; GCB 1992. Hon. Member, The Salters' Company. *Recreations:* Competitive games. *Sportsclubs:* President, Oxford University Rugby Football Member: Royal Lytham and St Anne's Golf, Fritford Heath Golf, St Enodoc Golf, Dulwich and Sydenham Hill Golf. *Clubs:* Athenaeum, Brooks's, Beefsteak, Anglo-Belgian, MCC. *Name, Style and Title:* Raised to the peerage as Baron Butler of Brockwell, of Herne Hill in the London Borough of Lambeth 1998. *Address:* The Lord Butler of Brockwell, GCB, CVO, University College, Oxford, OX1 4BH *E-Mail:* lord.butler@univ.coll.ox.ac.uk.

LORD BUTTERWORTH   Conservative

BUTTERWORTH (Life Baron), John Blackstock Butterworth; cr. 1985. Born 13 March 1918. Son of late John William Butterworth; educated Queen Elizabeth's Grammar School, Mansfield; The Queen's College, Oxford (MA). Married 1948, Doris Crawford Elder (1 son 2 daughters). *Armed Forces:* Served Royal Artillery 1939–46. *Councils, Public Bodies:* JP: Oxford 1962–63, Coventry 1963–88; DL, West Midlands 1974–. *Career:* New College, Oxford: Fellow 1946–63, Bursar 1956–63; Barrister-at-law, Lincolns Inn 1947; First Vice-Chancellor, Warwick University 1963–85. *Select Committees:* Frequent Member: Sub-Committees of Select Committee on Science and Technology, Sub-Committee A of Select Committee on European Communities. *Other:* Governor, Royal Shakespeare Theatre 1964–, Honorary Emeritus Governor 1999–; Chairman, Inter-University Council for Higher Education Overseas 1968–77; Board Member, British Council 1981–85; Member, Foundation for Science and Technology 1989–, Chairman 1990–97, President 1997–. Hon. DCL (Sierra Leone); Hon. DSc (Aston); Hon. LLD (Warwick). *Trusts, etc:* Managing Trustee, Nuffield Foundation 1964–85, Ordinary Trustee 1985–. *Miscellaneous:* Member: Royal Commission on Working of Tribunals of Inquiry (Act) 1921 1966, Inter-governmental Committee on Law of Contempt in relation to Tribunals of Inquiry 1968, Committee on University Efficiency 1986; Croham Committee on the Review of the UGC 1987; Hon. Bencher, Lincolns Inn 1988. *Honours:* CBE 1982. *Special Interests:* Education, Industry, Industrial Relations, Overseas Aid and Development. *Name, Style and Title:* Raised to the peerage as Baron Butterworth, of Warwick in the County of Warwickshire 1985. *Address:* The Lord Butterworth, CBE, DL, The Barn, Barton, Guiting Power, Gloucestershire, GL54 5US *Tel:* 01451 850297 *Fax:* 01451 850108; 727 Nell Gwynn House, Sloane Avenue, London, SW3 3AX *Tel:* 020 7581 4838 *Fax:* 020 7823 9388.

LORD BUXTON OF ALSA   Conservative

BUXTON OF ALSA (Life Baron), Aubrey Leland Oakes Buxton; cr. 1978. Born 15 July 1918. Son of late Leland Wilberforce Buxton; educated Ampleforth; Trinity College, Cambridge. Married 1st, 1946, Pamela Birkin (died 1983) (2 sons 4 daughters), married 2nd, July 16, 1988, Mrs Kathleen Peterson. *Armed Forces:* Served RA 1939–45; In Burma 1942–45. *Councils, Public Bodies:* High Sheriff, Essex 1972; DL, Essex 1975–85. *Career:* Extra Equerry to HRH the Duke of Edinburgh 1964–97; Member, Countryside Commission 1968–72; Member, Royal Commission on Pollution 1970–75; Chairman: Independent Television News Ltd 1980–86, Oxford Scientific Films Ltd 1982–86; Member, Nature Conservancy Council 1984–86; Chairman: Anglia Television Group 1986–88, Survival Anglia 1986–92. *Other:* Treasurer, Zoological Society 1976–83; President, Falkland Islands Foundation 1990–96. *Trusts, etc:* A Trustee of the British Museum (Natural History) 1971–73; British Trustee, World Wildlife Fund; Trustee, Wildfowl Trust. *Honours:* MC 1943; KCVO 1996. *Recreations:* Travel, natural history, painting, sport. *Clubs:* White's. *Name, Style and Title:* Raised to the peerage as Baron Buxton of Alsa, of Stiffkey in the County of Norfolk 1978. *Address:* The Lord Buxton of Alsa, KCVO, MC, Old Hall Farm, Stiffkey, Norfolk, NR23 1QJ *Tel:* 01328 830351.

BARONESS BYFORD Conservative

BYFORD (Life Baroness), Hazel Byford; cr. 1996. Born 14 January 1941. Daughter of late Sir Cyril Osborne, Conservative MP for Louth 1945–69, and Lady Osborne; educated St Leonard's School, St Andrews; Moulton Agricultural College, Northampton. Married 1962, C. Barrie Byford (1 daughter and 1 son deceased). *Career:* Farmer. *Whip:* An Opposition Whip 1997–98. *Spokesman:* Opposition Spokesman on: Agriculture December 1998–, Environment, Transport and the Regions (Rural Affairs) December 1998–. *Party Groups (General):* Chairman, National Committee, Conservative Women 1990–93; Vice-President, National Union of Conservative and Unionist Associations 1993–95, President 1996–97. *Other:* WRVS Leicestershire 1961–96, County Organiser 1972–76; Member: CLA, NFU. *Miscellaneous:* Member: Transport Users' Consultative Committee 1989–94, Rail Users' Consultative Committee 1994–95. *Honours:* DBE 1994. *Recreations:* Golf, reading, bridge. *Clubs:* Farmers'. *Name, Style and Title:* Raised to the peerage as Baroness Byford, of Rothley in the County of Leicestershire 1996. *Address:* The Baroness Byford, DBE, House of Lords, London, SW1A 0PW *E-Mail:* byfordh@Parliament.uk.

C

EARL OF CAITHNESS Conservative

CAITHNESS (20th Earl of, S), Malcolm Ian Sinclair; cr. 1455; Lord Berriedale; 15th Bt of Canisbay (NS) 1631. Born 3 November 1948. Son of 19th Earl, CVO, CBE, DSO. Succeeded his father 1965; educated Marlborough; Royal Agricultural College, Cirencester. Married January 9, 1975, Diana Caroline Coke (died 1994) (1 son 1 daughter). *Career:* Savills 1972–78; Brown and Mumford 1978–80; Director of various companies 1980–84; Director: Victoria Soames Ltd, Residential Property Consultants, and other companies. *House of Lords:* Parliamentary Under-Secretary of State, Department of Transport 1985–86; Minister of State: Home Office 1986–88, Department of Environment 1988–89; Paymaster General and Treasury Minister 1989–90; Minister of State: Foreign and Commonwealth Office 1990–92, for Aviation and Shipping, Department of Transport 1992–94; An elected hereditary peer 1999–. *Whip:* Government Whip (Lord in Waiting) 1984–85. *Spokesman:* A Government Spokesman for DHSS 1984–85; A Government Spokesman on Scotland 1984–86. *Select Committees:* Member, Select Committee on House of Lords' Offices 1997–. *Honours:* PC 1990. FRICS. *Address:* Rt Hon the Earl of Caithness, House of Lords, London, SW1A 0PW.

LORD CALLAGHAN OF CARDIFF Labour

CALLAGHAN OF CARDIFF (Life Baron), Leonard James Callaghan; cr. 1987. Born 27 March 1912. Son of late James Callaghan, RN, and Charlotte, née Cundy; educated Portsmouth Northern Secondary School. Married 1938, Audrey Elizabeth Moulton (1 son 2 daughters). *Trades Union:* Member, GMBU; Hon. Member, NUM (South Wales); Life Member, IRSF. *Armed Forces:* Served with Royal Navy during World War II. *Career:* Inland Revenue 1929–36; Assistant Secretary, Inland Revenue Staff Federation 1936–50; Consultant to Police Federations of England, Wales and Scotland 1955–64. *House of Commons:* MP (Labour) for South Cardiff 1945–50, for Cardiff South East 1950–83, and for Cardiff South and Penarth 1983–87; Parliamentary Secretary, Ministry of Transport 1947–50; Parliamentary and Financial Secretary to the Admiralty 1950–51; Chancellor of the Exchequer 1964–67; Secretary of State for the Home Department from 1967–1970; Foreign and Commonwealth Secretary 1974–76; Prime Minister and First Lord of the Treasury 1976–79; Leader of the Opposition 1979–80. *International Bodies (General):* Member, The Interaction Council.

Party Groups (General): Member, National Executive Labour Party 1957–80, Treasurer 1967–76, Chairman 1973. *Other:* Chairman, Advisory Committee on Protection of the Sea 1952–63, President 1963–; President: United Kingdom Pilots Association 1963–76, International Maritime Pilots Association 1971–76, University College of Wales, Swansea 1986–95; Joint President, Royal Institute of International Affairs (Chatham House); President, Cardiff Community Housing Association. *Awards Granted:* Hubert H. Humphrey International Award 1978. Hon. Fellow, Nuffield College, Oxford 1967 and three other universities; honorary doctorates from nine universities in UK, India and Japan. *Trusts, etc:* Member: British Museum Development Trust Council, Cambridge Commonwealth Trust, Pegasus Trust, Inner Temple. *Miscellaneous:* Visiting Fellow, Nuffield College, Oxford 1956–67; Hon. Bencher, Inner Temple 1976. *Honours:* PC 1964; Grand Cross First Class of the Order of Merit of the Federal Republic of Germany 1979; KG 1987; Order of the Nile, Egypt. Hon. Freeman: City of Cardiff 1975, City of Sheffield 1979, City of Portsmouth 1991, City of Swansea 1993. *Publications: A House Divided: the dilemma of Northern Ireland,* 1973; *Time and Chance* (autobiography) 1987. *Special Interests:* Agriculture, Farming. *Clubs:* Athenaeum. *Name, Style and Title:* Raised to the peerage as Baron Callaghan of Cardiff, of the City of Cardiff in the County of South Glamorgan 1987. *Address:* Rt Hon the Lord Callaghan of Cardiff, KG, House of Lords, London, SW1A 0PW *Tel:* 020 7219 5802.

LORD CAMERON OF LOCHBROOM — Cross-Bencher

CAMERON OF LOCHBROOM (Life Baron), Kenneth John Cameron; cr. 1984. Born 11 June 1931. Son of late Hon. Lord Cameron, KT, DSC; educated The Edinburgh Academy; Corpus Christi, Oxford (MA); Edinburgh University (LLB). Married August 8, 1964, Jean Pamela, daughter of late Colonel Granville Murray, RA (2 daughters). *Armed Forces:* Served RNVR 1950–62; Commissioned 1951. *Career:* Called to the Scottish Bar 1958; QC (Scot) 1972; Advocate Depute 1981–84; Senator, College of Justice in Scotland 1989–. *House of Lords:* Lord Advocate 1984–89. *Miscellaneous:* President, Pensions Appeal Tribunal (Scotland) 1976–84; Chairman, Royal Fine Art Commission for Scotland 1995–. *Special Interests:* Law, Local Government, Arts. *Recreations:* Fishing, music, sailing. *Clubs:* Scottish Arts (Edinburgh), New (Edinburgh). *Name, Style and Title:* Raised to the peerage as Baron Cameron of Lochbroom, of Lochbroom in the District of Ross and Cromarty 1984. *Address:* Rt Hon the Lord Cameron of Lochbroom, Court of Session, Parliament Square, Edinburgh, EH1 1RF *Tel:* 0131–225 2595.

LORD CAMPBELL OF ALLOWAY — Conservative

CAMPBELL OF ALLOWAY (Life Baron), Alan Robertson Campbell; cr. 1981. Born 24 May 1917. Son of late John Kenneth Campbell and Juliet Pinner; educated Aldenham; Ecole des Sciences Politiques, Paris; Trinity Hall, Cambridge (MA). Married 1957, Vivien de Kantzow. *Armed Forces:* Second Lieutenant (Royal Artillery Supplementary Reserve), BEF 1939–40; PoW Colditz 1940–45. *Career:* Called to the Bar, Inner Temple 1939; QC 1965; Bencher 1972; Recorder of the Crown Court 1976–89. *Select Committees:* Member: House of Lords Committee for Privileges 1982–2000, House of Lords Select Committee on Murder and Life Imprisonment 1988–89, Ecclesiastical Committee 2000–, Joint Select Committee on Consolidation of Bills 1999–. *Party Groups:* Member, Association of Conservative Peers. *International Bodies (General):* Consultant to Council of Europe on Industrial Espionage 1965–74. *Party Groups (General):* Chairman, Legal Research Committee of Society of Conservative Lawyers 1968–80; Co-Patron, Inns of Court School of Law Conservatives 1996–. *Other:* Member, Management Committee of UK Association for European Law 1975–89; Vice-President, Association des Juristes Franco-Britanniques 1989–91; President, Colditz Association 1978–. *Miscellaneous:* Member: Law Advisory Panel of British Council 1974–79, Scottish Peers' Association. *Honours:* ERD 1996. *Publications:* Co-author *Restrictive Trade Practices and Monopolies,* 1956, 2nd edn 1966, Supplements 1 and 2 1965; *Restrictive Trading Agreements in the Common Market,* 1964, Supplement 1965; *Common Market Law,* vols 1 and 2 1969, vol 3 1973, Supplement 1975; *Industrial Relations Act,* 1971; *EC Competition Law,* 1980; *Trade Unions and the Individual,* 1980. *Special Interests:* Industrial Relations, European Union, Restrictive Trade Practices and Monopolies, Constitutional Affairs. *Clubs:* Beefsteak, Carlton, Pratt's. *Name, Style and Title:* Raised to the peerage as Baron Campbell of Alloway, of Ayr in the District of Kyle and Carrick 1981. *Address:* The Lord Campbell of Alloway, ERD, QC, 2 King's Bench Walk, Temple, London, EC4 7DE.

LORD CAMPBELL OF CROY   Conservative

CAMPBELL OF CROY (Life Baron), Gordon Thomas Calthrop Campbell; cr. 1974. Born 8 June 1921. Son of late Major-General J. A. Campbell, DSO and Bar; educated Wellington. Married 1949, Nicola Madan (2 sons 1 daughter). *Armed Forces:* Served Regular Army 1939–46; Major, 15th Scottish Division 1942 (MC 1944 and Bar 1945); Wounded and disabled 1945. *Councils, Public Bodies:* DL, Nairn 1985–98; Vice-Lord Lieutenant of Nairn 1988–98. *Career:* HM Foreign Service 1946–57; Foreign Office 1946–49; UK Permanent Mission UN 1949–52; Private Secretary to the Secretary to the Cabinet 1954–56; British Embassy, Vienna 1956–57; Partner, Holme Rose Farms and Estate; Consultant to Chevron Corporation 1975–94; Chairman, Stoic Insurance Services 1980–93; Director, Alliance and Leicester Building Society 1985–92, Chairman of its Scottish Board to 1994; In retirement, lecturing to the Armed Forces in the UK and abroad on Second World War battles. *House of Commons:* MP (Conservative), Moray and Nairn 1959–74; Under-Secretary of State for Scotland 1963–64; Secretary of State for Scotland 1970–74. *Whip (Commons):* Assistant Government Whip 1961–62; Government Whip (Lord Commissioner of HM Treasury) and Scottish Whip 1962–63. *Spokesman (Commons):* Opposition Front Bench Spokesman on: Defence 1966–68, Scotland (Shadow Cabinet) 1969–70. *Spokesman:* Opposition Front Bench Spokesman on many subjects 1975–79. *Select Committees:* Member, and co-opted to its sub-committees at other times, Select Committee on the European Communities 1975–93; Co-opted to Sub-Committee, Select Committee on Science and Technology 1989–92; Member, Select Committee on Delegated Powers 1993–95. *Other:* Vice-President and Acting Chairman, Advisory Committee on Pollution of the Sea 1980–82, Chairman 1987–89; Chairman for Scotland of the International Year of Disabled People 1981; Office-bearer in several organisations for the disabled; President, Anglo-Austrian Society 1991–. *Trusts, etc:* Trustee, Thomson Foundation 1980–. *Miscellaneous:* Chairman, Scottish Council of Independent Schools 1976–80. *Honours:* MC 1944 and Bar 1945; PC 1970; Gold Grand Cross With Star (Austria). First Fellow, Nuffield Provincial Hospitals Trust, Queen Elizabeth The Queen Mother Fellowship 1980. *Publications: Disablement in the UK, Problems and Prospects,* 1981. *Special Interests:* Foreign Affairs, Defence, Environment, Consumer Affairs. *Recreations:* Music, natural history. *Name, Style and Title:* Raised to the peerage as Baron Campbell of Croy, of Croy in the County of Nairn 1974. *Address:* Rt Hon the Lord Campbell of Croy, MC, Holme Rose, Cawdor, Nairnshire, IV12 5XT *Tel:* 01667 493223; House of Lords, London, SW1A 0PW *Tel:* 020 7219 5353 *Fax:* 020 7219 5979.

ARCHBISHOP OF CANTERBURY   Non-Affiliated

CANTERBURY (103rd Archbishop of), George Leonard Carey. Born 13 November 1935. Son of late George and Ruby Carey; educated Bifrons School, Barking; King's College, London (PhD); London College of Divinity (ALCD, BD, MTh). Married June 25, 1960, Eileen Harmsworth Hood (2 sons 2 daughters). *Career:* Curate of St Mary's, Islington 1962–66; Lecturer: Oakhill Theological College 1966–70, St John's College, Nottingham; Occasional teacher at Nottingham University 1970–75; Vicar of St Nicholas Church, Durham 1975–82; Principal, Trinity Theological College, Bristol 1982–87; Bishop of Bath and Wells 1987–91; Archbishop of Canterbury 1991–; Entered the House of Lords 1991. *International Bodies (General):* President, Worldwide Anglican Communion. *Honours:* PC 1991. Freeman: City of London, Bath, Wells. Honorary Liveryman, The Scriveners' Company. *Publications: I Believe in Man,* 1975; *God Incarnate,* 1976; Co-author *The Great Acquittal,* 1980; *The Meeting of the Waters,* 1985; *The Church in the Market Place,* 1984; *The Gate of Glory,* 1986; *The Message of the Bible,* 1986; *The Great God Robbery,* 1989; *I Believe,* 1991; *Sharing a Vision,* 1993; *Spiritual Journey,* 1994; Co-author *My Journey, Your Journey,* 1996; *Canterbury Letters to the Future,* 1998; *Jesus 2000,* 1999. *Recreations:* Family life, music, poetry, reading, walking. *Clubs:* Athenaeum, Nobodies. *Address:* Most Rev and Rt Hon the Lord Archbishop of Canterbury, Lambeth Palace, London, SE1 7JU *Tel:* 020 7928 8282; Old Palace, Canterbury, Kent, CT1 2EE.

LORD CARLILE OF BERRIEW — Liberal Democrat

CARLILE OF BERRIEW (Life Baron), Alexander Charles Carlile; cr. 1999. Born 12 February 1948. Son of Dr Erwin Falik; educated Epsom College; King's College, London University (LLB, AKC 1969); Council of Legal Education. Married October 19, 1968, Frances Soley (3 daughters). *Career:* Called to the Bar, Gray's Inn 1970, Bencher 1992; QC 1984; A Recorder of the Crown Court 1986–; Deputy High Court Judge; Honorary Recorder of the City of Hereford 1996–. *House of Commons:* Contested (Lib) Flint East, February 1974 and 1979; MP (Lib) for Montgomery 1983–88, (Lib Dem) 1988–97. *Spokesman (Commons):* Liberal Spokesman on Home Affairs, Law 1985–88; Former Alliance Spokesman on Legal Affairs 1987; SLD Spokesman on Foreign Affairs 1988–89; Liberal Democrat Spokesman on: Legal Affairs 1989–90, Trade and Industry 1990–92, Wales 1992–97, Employment 1992–94, Health 1994–95, Justice, Home Affairs and Immigration 1995–97. *Party Groups (General):* Chairman, Welsh Liberal Party 1980–82; Leader, Welsh Liberal Democrat Party 1992–97; President, Liberal Democrats Wales 1997–99. *Other:* Patron, National Depression Campaign. *Trusts, etc:* Fellow, Industry and Parliament Trust; Trustee: Nuffield Trust, Hope House Childrens' Hospice; Council Member and Trustee, NACRO. *Miscellaneous:* Lay Member, General Medical Council 1989–99; Member, Advisory Council on Public Records 1989–95; Non-Executive Director, Wynnstay and Clwyd Farmers plc. Fellow, Institute of Advanced Legal Studies. *Publications:* Various Articles. *Special Interests:* Home Affairs, Agriculture, Legal Affairs, United Nations, Central and Eastern Europe, Arts, Wales, Mental Health, Medical Profession. *Recreations:* Family, politics, theatre, food, Association Football. *Clubs:* Athenaeum. *Name, Style and Title:* Raised to the peerage as Baron Carlile of Berriew, of Berriew in the County of Powys 1999. *Address:* The Lord Carlile of Berriew, QC, 9–12 Bell Yard, London, WC2A 2LF *E-Mail:* accqc@compuserve.com.

LORD CARLISLE OF BUCKLOW — Conservative

CARLISLE OF BUCKLOW (Life Baron), Mark Carlisle; cr. 1987. Born 7 July 1929. Son of late Philip and Mary Carlisle; educated Radley; Manchester University (LLB 1953). Married 1959, Sandra Joyce Des Voeux (1 daughter). *Armed Forces:* National service as 2nd Lieutenant, Royal Army Education Corps 1948–50. *Councils, Public Bodies:* DL, Cheshire 1983–. *Career:* Called to the Bar Gray's Inn 1953, Entrance Scholar Junior; Northern Circuit; Practised in Manchester from February 1954; Member of Bar Council 1966–70; QC 1971; Recorder 1976–98; Chairman, Criminal Injuries Compensation Board 1989–2000; A Judge of the Courts of Appeal of Jersey and Guernsey 1990–99; Chairman, Manchester and London Investment Trust plc 1997–. *House of Commons:* Contested (Conservative) St. Helens 1958 and 1959; MP (Conservative) for Runcorn 1964–83; Under-Secretary of State, Home Office 1970–72; Minister of State, Home Office 1972–74; Secretary of State for Education and Science 1979–81; MP (Conservative) for Warrington South 1983–87. *International Bodies (General):* Hon. Treasurer, Commonwealth Parliamentary Association 1982–85, Vice-Chairman (UK Branch) 1985–87. *Party Groups (General):* Chairman: Federation of University Conservative and Union Associations 1953–54, Society of Conservative Lawyers 1996–. *Trusts, etc:* Trustee, The Foundation for Children with Leukaemia; Chairman, The Drugwatch Trust. *Miscellaneous:* Member: Home Office Advisory Council on the Penal System 1966–70, BBC Advisory Council 1975–79; Chairman: Parole Review Committee 1987–88, Prime Minister's Advisory Committee on Business Appointments for Crown Servants 1988–1998, Commonwealth Observer Group to the Elections in Lesotho 1993. *Honours:* PC 1979. *Special Interests:* Penal Affairs and Policy, Education, Law, Human Rights. *Recreations:* Golf. *Clubs:* Garrick, St James' (Manchester). *Name, Style and Title:* Raised to the peerage as Baron Carlisle of Bucklow, of Mobberley in the County of Cheshire 1987. *Address:* Rt Hon the Lord Carlisle of Bucklow, QC, DL, 3 Holt Gardens, Blakeley Lane, Mobberley, Cheshire, WA16 7LH; Office: Queen Elizabeth Buildings, Temple, London, EC4Y 9BS *Tel:* 020 7583 5766.

LORD CARMICHAEL OF KELVINGROVE   Labour

CARMICHAEL OF KELVINGROVE (Life Baron), Neil George Carmichael; cr 1983. Son of late James Carmichael; educated Estbank Academy; Royal College of Science and Technology, Glasgow. Married 1948, Catherine McIntosh Rankin (1 daughter) (marriage dissolved). *Councils, Public Bodies:* A Glasgow City Councillor 1962–63. *Career:* Employed by Gas Board in Planning Department. *House of Commons:* MP (Labour) for Glasgow Woodside 1962–74; Joint Parliamentary Under-Secretary, Ministry of Transport 1967–1969; Joint Parliamentary Secretary, Ministry of Technology 1969–70; MP (Labour) for Glasgow Kelvingrove 1974–83; Under-Secretary of State: Department of Environment 1974–75, Department of Industry 1975–1976. *Spokesman:* Opposition Front Bench Spokesman on: Transport 1987–97, Scotland 1987–97. *Name, Style and Title:* Raised to the peerage as Baron Carmichael of Kelvingrove, of Camlachie in the District of the City of Glasgow 1983. *Address:* The Lord Carmichael of Kelvingrove, 53 Partickhill Road, Glasgow, G11 5AB.

EARL OF CARNARVON   Cross-Bencher

CARNARVON (7th Earl of, GB), Henry George Reginald Molyneux Herbert; cr. 1793; Baron Porchester (GB) 1780. Born 19 January 1924. Son of 6th Earl. Succeeded his father 1987; educated Eton; Royal Agricultural College, Cirencester (McClelland Gold Medal). Married 1956, Jean Margaret Wallop (2 sons 1 daughter). *Armed Forces:* Lieutenant, Royal Horse Guards 1943–47; Hon. Colonel, Hampshire Fortress Regiment Royal Engineers (TA) 1963–67. *Councils, Public Bodies:* Councillor, Hampshire County Council 1954–65, County Alderman 1965–74; Member: Hampshire Agricultural Executive 1955–65, Andover Town Development Committee 1960–65, Basingstoke Town Development Committee 1960–74; DL, Hants 1965–; Chairman, New Hampshire County Council 1974–77; Hon Alderman, Hampshire County Council 1999. *Career:* Racing Manager to Her Majesty the Queen 1969–; Chairman: Newbury Racecourse plc 1985–98, Serplan 1989–. *House of Lords:* An elected hereditary peer 1999–. *Select Committees:* Chairman, House of Lords Select Committee on the Croydon Tramlink Bill November 1992-January 1993; Member, Joint Select Committee on Draft Local Government (Organisation and Standards) Bill 1999. *Other:* Verderer of the New Forest 1961–65; Chairman, Thoroughbred Breeders' Association 1964–66, President 1969–74, 1986–91; President: Amateur Riders Association 1970–76, Hampshire Association for the Care of the Blind (Sight-Concern Hampshire) 1975–. Hon. Fellow, Portsmouth Polytechnic 1976; Hon. DSc, Reading University 1980. *Trusts, etc:* Chairman, Basingstoke Sports Trust 1970–82, President 1983–86; President, Hampshire and the Isle of Wight Naturalists Trusts 1987–; Chairman, North Hampshire Hospital Fund. *Miscellaneous:* Member, Nature Conservancy 1953–66; Chairman and founding member, Game Research Association 1960–67, became Game Conservancy 1967, Vice-President 1967; Member, Sports Council, Chairman, Planning Committee 1965–70, Member, Forestry Commission 1967–70; Chairman, South East Economic Planning Council 1971–79; Vice-Chairman, County Councils Association 1972–79; Chairman: Agricultural Research Council 1978–83, Standing Conference on Countryside Sports 1978–; London and South East Regional Planning Conference 1989–; Member: Horseracing Betting Levy Board, National Stud Advisory Panel. *Honours:* KBE 1976; KCVO 1982. Hon RICS. *Publications:* A Study of Exmoor, 1977 Co-author Second Chamber, 1995. *Special Interests:* Horse Racing. *Recreations:* Gardening. *Sportsclubs:* Member, Jockey Club 1964–; Member, Hampshire Cricket Club 1966–, President 1966–68; Hon. Member, South Wales Hunts Cricket Club. *Clubs:* White's, Portland. *Address:* The Earl of Carnarvon, KCVO, KBE, DL, Milford Lake House, Burghclere, Newbury, Berkshire, RG20 9EL *Tel:* 01635 253387.

Visit the Vacher Dod Website...
www.politicallinks.co.uk

BARONESS CARNEGY OF LOUR
Conservative

CARNEGY OF LOUR (Life Baroness), Elizabeth Patricia Carnegy of Lour; cr. 1982. Born 28 April 1925. Daughter of late Lieutenant-Colonel U. E. C. Carnegy of Lour, DSO, MC, DL, and of late Violet Carnegy, MBE; educated Downham School, Essex. *Councils, Public Bodies:* Co-opted Education Committee, Angus County Council 1967–75; Honorary Sheriff 1969–84; Councillor, Tayside Regional Council 1974–82; Convener, Education Committee 1976–82; DL, Angus 1988–; Chairman, Tayside Committee on Medical Research Ethics 1990–93. *Career:* Farmer 1956–89. *Select Committees:* Member: House of Lords European Communities Select Committee 1993–96, Sub-committee D (Agriculture and Food) 1990–93, Sub-committee E (Law and Institutions) 1993–97. *Party Groups:* Member, Association of Conservative Peers, Vice-Chairman 1990–94. *Other:* Served Cavendish Laboratory, Cambridge 1943–46; Girl Guides Association: Training Advisor, Scotland 1958–62, Commonwealth HQ 1963–65, President for Scotland 1979–89; Formerly Member, Visiting Committee Noranside Borstal Institution; Member, Council and Finance Committee of Open University 1984–96; Honorary President, Scottish Library Association 1989–92, Honorary Member 1996–; Member of Court, St Andrews University 1991–96. Hon. LLD: University of Dundee 1991, University of St Andrews 1997; Hon. DrUniv, Open University 1998. *Trusts, etc:* Member, Administration Council, Royal Jubilee Trusts 1984–88. *Miscellaneous:* Chairman, Working Party on Professional Training in Community Education Scotland 1975–77; Commissioner, Manpower Services Commission 1979–82; Member, Scottish Council for Tertiary Education 1979–84; Chairman, Manpower Services Commission Committee for Scotland 1980–83; Member, Scottish Economic Council 1980–93; Former Chairman, Scottish Council for Education 1981–88; Hon. Fellow, Scottish Community Education Council 1993. FRSA; Hon. Fellow, Scottish Community Education Council. *Special Interests:* Education, European Union, Local Government, Scottish Affairs, Agriculture, Countryside, Medical Research Ethics, Constitution, Health Service, Social Security. *Clubs:* Lansdowne, New (Edinburgh). *Name, Style and Title:* Raised to the peerage as Baroness Carnegy of Lour, of Lour in the District of Angus 1982. *Address:* The Baroness Carnegy of Lour, DL, Lour, Forfar, Angus, DD8 2 LR *Tel:* 01307 820237.

LORD CARR OF HADLEY
Conservative

CARR OF HADLEY (Life Baron), (Leonard) Robert Carr; cr. 1976. Born 11 November 1916. Son of late Ralph Edward Carr; educated Westminster School; Gonville and Caius College, Cambridge (MA). Married 1943, Joan Kathleen Twining (2 daughters and 1 son deceased). *Career:* Director, John Dale Ltd 1948–55, Chairman 1958–63, 1965–70; Member, London Board Scottish Union and National Insurance Co. 1958–63; Director, S. Hoffnung & Co. 1958–63, 1965–70, 1974–80; Deputy Chairman, Metal Closures Group Ltd 1960–63, 1965–70, Director 1965–70; Director, Securicor Ltd and Security Services Ltd 1961–63, 1965–70, 1974–85; Member, Norwich Union Insurance Group (London Advisory Board) 1965–70, 1974–76; Director, SGB Group Ltd 1974–86; Member of Council, CBI 1976–78; Director, Prudential Assurance Co. 1976–85, Chairman 1980–85; Chairman, CBI Education and Training Committee 1977–82; Director, Cadbury Schweppes Ltd 1979–87; Director, Prudential Corporation 1979–89, Chairman 1980–85; Chairman, CBI Special Programme Unit 1981–84; Chairman, Business in the Community 1984–87; Advisory Director: P. A. Strategy Partners 1985–87, Lek Partnership 1987–95. *House of Commons:* MP (Conservative) for: Mitcham 1950–74, Sutton Carshalton 1974–76; PPS to Rt Hon. Anthony Eden as: Secretary of State for Foreign Affairs 1951–55, Prime Minister 1955; Parliamentary Secretary, Ministry of Labour 1955–58; Secretary for Technical Co-operation 1963–64; Secretary of State for Employment 1970–72; Lord President of the Council and Leader of the House of Commons 1972; Home Secretary 1972–74. *Spokesman (Commons):* Opposition Spokesman on: Aviation 1965–67, Labour 1967–70, Treasury 1974–75. *Spokesman:* Opposition Spokesman on Economics, Industrial and Home Affairs 1976–79. *Select Committees:* Member, House of Lords Select Committee on the European Communities 1990–93. *Other:* Governor: St Mary's Hospital 1954–55, 1958–63, Imperial College of Science and Technology 1959–63, 1976–87; Vice-President, Birmingham Settlement; Vice-President, CORDA (Coronary Artery

Disease Research Association). Fellow, Imperial College 1985. *Honours:* PC 1963. Fellow, Institute of Metallurgists 1957; Companion: British Institute of Management, Institute of Personel Management. *Publications:* Co-author: *One Nation*, 1950, *Change is our Ally*, 1954, *The Responsible Society*, 1958, *One Europe*, 1965. *Recreations:* Lawn tennis, music, gardening. *Sportsclubs:* President, Surrey County Cricket Club 1985–86; Vice-President, All England Lawn Tennis Club 1990–. *Clubs:* Brooks's, MCC. *Name, Style and Title:* Raised to the peerage as Baron Carr of Hadley, of Monken Hadley in the County of Greater London 1976. *Address:* Rt Hon the Lord Carr of Hadley, 14 North Court, Great Peter Street, London, SW1P 3LL.

LORD CARRINGTON   Conservative

CARRINGTON (6th Baron, I), Peter Alexander Rupert Carington; cr. 1796; 6th Baron Carrington (GB) 1797; (Life) Baron Carington of Upton 1999. Born 6 June 1919. Son of 5th Baron, DL, and late Hon. Sybil Marion Colville, daughter of 2nd Viscount Colville of Culross. Succeeded his father 1938; educated Eton; RMC, Sandhurst. Married April 25, 1942, Iona, daughter of late Lieutenant-Colonel Sir Francis McClean, AFC (1 son 2 daughters). *Armed Forces:* Major, Grenadier Guards, served North West Europe 1940–46. *Councils, Public Bodies:* JP, Bucks 1948; DL, Bucks 1951. *Career:* UK High Commissioner in Australia 1956–59; Chairman, GEC 1983–84; Secretary-General, NATO 1984–88; Chairman, Christies International plc 1988–93; Director, The Telegraph plc 1990–96; Chairman, EC Peace Conference on Yugoslavia 1991–92. *Chancellor:* Chancellor, Reading University 1992–. *House of Lords:* Joint Parliamentary Secretary, Ministry of Agriculture and Fisheries 1951–54; Parliamentary Secretary, Ministry of Defence 1954–56; First Lord of the Admiralty 1959–63; Minister without Portfolio and Leader of the House of Lords October 1963-October 1964; Leader of Opposition, House of Lords 1964–70, 1974–79; Secretary of State for Defence 1970–74; Minister of Aviation Supply 1971–74; Secretary of State for: Energy January-February 1974, Foreign and Commonwealth Affairs 1979–82. *Whip:* Opposition Whip, House of Lords 1947–51. *Party Groups (General):* Chairman, Conservative Party 1972–74. *Other:* President, The Pilgrims 1983–; Elder Brother, Trinity House 1984; President, VSO 1993–98. Hon. LLD, Cambridge 1981; Hon. Fellow, St Antony's College, Oxford 1982, plus 12 honorary degrees from universities in the United Kingdom and abroad. *Trusts, etc:* Trustee, Cambridge Commonwealth Trust 1982–; Chairman of Trustees, Victoria and Albert Museum 1983–88; Trustee, Winston Churchill Memorial Trust. *Miscellaneous:* Hon. Bencher of the Middle Temple 1983–; Chancellor of the Order of St Michael and St George 1984–94; Chancellor of the Most Noble Order of the Garter 1994–. *Honours:* MC 1945; PC 1959; CH 1983; KG 1985; GCMG 1988. *Publications: Reflect on Things Past* (autobiography) 1988. *Clubs:* Pratt's, White's. *Name, Style and Title:* Created a life peer as Baron Carington of Upton, of Upton in the County of Nottinghamshire 1999. *Address:* Rt Hon the Lord Carrington, KG, GCMG, CH, MC, DL, The Manor House, Bledlow, Princes Risborough, Buckinghamshire, HP27 9PB *Tel:* 01844 343499; 32A Ovington Square, London, SW3 1LR *Tel:* 020 7584 1476 *Fax:* 020 7823 9051.

LORD CARTER   Labour

CARTER (Life Baron), Denis Victor Carter; cr. 1987. Born 17 January 1932. Son of late Albert and Annie Carter; educated Xaverian College, Brighton; East Sussex College of Agriculture 1954–55; Essex College of Agriculture (Queens Prize of the Royal Agricultural Society of England and Fream Memorial Prize) 1955–57; Worcester College, Oxford (BLitt 1976). Married August 3, 1957, Teresa Mary, daughter of late Cecil and Elsie Greengoe (1 daughter and 1 son deceased). *Armed Forces:* National Service, Egypt 1950–52. *Councils, Public Bodies:* Member, Northfield Committee of enquiry into ownership and occupancy of agricultural land 1977–79; JP 1966–70. *Career:* Audit Clerk 1949–50, 1953; Farmworker 1953–54; Agricultural education 1954–57; Founder and Director, Agricultural Accounting and Management Co. (AKC Ltd) 1957–97; Director: United Oilseeds Marketing Ltd 1972–97, W.E. and D.T. Cave Ltd 1976–97; Partner, Drayton Farms 1976–97; Executive Producer, Link Television programme for people with disabilities 1988–97. *House of Lords:* A Deputy Chairman of Committees 1997–; A Deputy Speaker 1999–. *Whip:* Opposition Whip 1987–92; Deputy Opposition Chief Whip 1990–92; Captain of the Honourable Corps of the Gentlemen at Arms (Government Chief Whip) 1997–. *Spokesman:* Spokesman on: Agriculture 1987–97, Social Security 1988–97, Health (Community Care) 1989–97. *Select Committees:* Member: House of Lords Select Committee on European Communities, Sub-Committee D 1987–92, Select Committee on House of Lords' Offices 1997–, Select Committee on House of Lords' Procedure 1997–. *Other:* Member, Council of Royal Agricultural Society of England 1994–97. Honorary doctorate, Essex University. *Trusts, etc:* Trustee: Farmers' Club 1985–97, Rural Housing Trust 1991–97, John Arlott Memorial Trust 1993–97. *Miscellaneous:* Contested (Labour) Basingstoke 1970; MAFF Senior Research Fellowship in Agricultural Marketing, Oxford 1970–72; Member, Central Council for Agricultural and Horticultural Co-operation 1977–80; Chairman: BBC Central Agricultural Advisory Committee 1985–89, UK Co-operative Council 1993–97. *Honours:* PC 1997. Fellow, Institute of Agricultural Management 1992–; Fellow in Business Administration, Royal Agricultural College Fellow, Royal Agricultural Societies. *Special Interests:* Agriculture, Rural Affairs, Disability, Community Care, Health, Football. *Recreations:* Walking, reading, supporting Southampton FC. *Clubs:* Farmers' (Chairman 1982). *Name, Style and Title:* Raised to the peerage as Baron Carter, of Devizes in the County of Wiltshire 1987. *Address:* Rt Hon the Lord Carter, House of Lords, London, SW1A 0PW *Tel:* 020 7219 3131.

CARVER (Life Baron), Richard Michael Power Carver; cr. 1977. Born 24 April 1915. Son of late Harold Power Carver and Anne, née Wellesley; educated Winchester; RMC, Sandhurst. Married November 22, 1947, Edith, daughter of late Lieutenant-Colonel Sir Henry Lowry-Corry, MC (2 sons 2 daughters). *Armed Forces:* Comd., 4th Armd Bde 1944–47; Deputy Chief of Staff, E. Africa 1954–55; Chief of Staff, E. Africa 1955–56; Director Army Plans 1958–59; Comd, 6th Bde 1960–62; GOC, 3rd Divn 1962–64; Director, Army Staff Duties 1964–66; Comd, Far East Land Forces 1966–67; Commander-in-Chief, Far East 1967–69; GOC in C, Southern Command 1969–71; Chief of General Staff 1971–73; Chief of Defence Staff 1973–76; Field Marshal 1973. *Select Committees:* Member, House of Lords Select Committee on Science and Technology 1985–92. *Other:* Vice-Councillor, Cancer Research Campaign; President, Army Records Society. Hon DLitt, Southampton University 1991. *Honours:* MC 1941; DSO and Bar 1943; CBE (Mil) 1945; GCB (Mil) 1970. *Publications: El Alamein,* 1962; *Tobruk,* 1964; *Harding of Petherton,* 1978; *The Apostles of Mobility,* 1979; *War Since 1945,* 1980; *A Policy for Peace,* 1982; *The Seven Ages of the British Army,* 1984; *Dilemmas of the Desert War,* 1986; *Twentieth Century Warriors,* 1987; *Out of Step,* 1989; *Tightrope Walking,* 1992; *Britain's Army in the Twentieth Century,* 1998; *The National Army Museum Book of the Boer War,* 1999; Editor: *The War Lords,* 1976, *Letters of A Victorian Army Officer: Edward Wellesley: 1840–1854,* 1995. *Special Interests:* Defence, Science and Technology. *Recreations:* Gardening. *Clubs:* Anglo-Belgian, Cavalry and Guards. *Name, Style and Title:* Raised to the peerage as Baron Carver, of Shackleford in the County of Surrey 1977. *Address:* Field Marshal The Lord Carver, GCB (Mil), CBE (Mil), DSO, MC, Wood End House, Wickham, Nr Fareham, Hampshire, PO17 6JZ *Tel:* 01329 832143.

CASTLE OF BLACKBURN (Life Baroness), Barbara Anne Castle; cr. 1990. Born 6 October 1910. Daughter of late Frank and Annie Betts; educated Bradford Girls' Grammar School; St. Hugh's College, Oxford (BA politics, philosophy and economics 1931). Married 1944, Edward Cyril Castle (later created life peer as Baron Castle, died 1979). *Trades Union:* Shop Assisants' Union 1932; Life member, NUJ. *Councils, Public Bodies:* Councillor, St. Pancras Borough Council 1937–45; Member, Metropolitan Water Board 1940–45. *Career:* Assistant Editor, *Town and County Councillor* 1936–40; Administrative Officer, Ministry of Food 1941–44; Housing Correspondent and Forces Adviser, Daily Mirror 1944–45; MEP (Labour) for: Greater Manchester North, European Parliament 1979–84, Greater Manchester West 1984–89; Leader, British Labour Group 1979–85; Vice-Chairman, Socialist Group, European Parliament 1979–86. *House of Commons:* MP (Labour) for: Blackburn 1945–50, Blackburn East 1950–55, Blackburn 1955–79; Minister of Overseas Development 1964–65; Minister of Transport 1965–68; First Secretary of State and Secretary of State for

Employment and Productivity 1968–70; Secretary of State for Social Services 1974–76. *Party Groups (General):* Member, National Executive Committee of Labour Party 1950–85; Vice-Chairman, Labour Party 1957–58, Chairman 1958–59. Hon. Fellow, St. Hugh's College, Oxford 1966; 11 honorary doctorates and fellowships. *Miscellaneous:* Co-Chairman, Women's National Commission 1975–76. *Honours:* PC 1964; Cross of Order of Merit of the Federal Republic of Germany 1990. Freeman, City of Bradford 1997. *Publications: The Castle Diaries 1964–70,* 1980, *1974–76,* 1984; *Sylvia and Christabel Pankhurst* 1987; *Fighting all the Way,* 1993. *Recreations:* Poetry, walking. *Name, Style and Title:* Raised to the peerage as Baroness Castle of Blackburn, of Ibstone in the County of Buckinghamshire 1990. *Address:* Rt Hon the Baroness Castle of Blackburn, House of Lords, London, SW1A 0PW.

LORD CAVENDISH OF FURNESS   Conservative

CAVENDISH OF FURNESS (Life Baron), Richard Hugh Cavendish; cr. 1990. Born 2 November 1941. Son of late Captain Richard Edward Osborne Cavendish, DL; educated Eton. Married 1970, Grania Mary, daughter of Brigadier Toby St. George Caulfeild, CBE (1 son 2 daughters). *Councils, Public Bodies:* Councillor, Cumbria County Council 1985–90; High Sheriff of Cumbria 1978; DL, Cumbria 1988. *Career:* International merchanting and banking in London 1961–71; Chairman, Holker Estate Group of Companies 1971–; Commissioner for the Historic Buildings and Monuments Commission (English Heritage) 1992–98; Director, UK Nirex Ltd 1993–99. *Whip:* A Lord in Waiting (Government Whip) 1990–92. *Select Committees:* Member, Select Committee on: the Croydon Tramlink Bill 1992–93, the European Union Sub-Committee B (Energy, Industry and Transport). *Party Groups:* Member, Association of Conservative Peers. *Party Groups (General):* Chairman, Morecambe and Lonsdale Conservative Association 1975–78. *Other:* Chairman of Governors, St. Anne's School, Windermere 1983–89; Chairman, Lancashire and Cumbria Foundation for Medical Research 1994–. Fellow, Royal Society of Arts 1988. Liveryman, Fishmongers' Company. *Special Interests:* Education, Environment, Local Issues, Industry, Foreign Affairs, Drug and Alcohol Rehabilitation, Agriculture, Forestry. *Recreations:* Gardening, National Hunt racing, shooting, reading, travel. *Clubs:* Brooks's, White's, Pratt's, Beefsteak. *Name, Style and Title:* Raised to the peerage as Baron Cavendish of Furness, of Cartmel in the County of Cumbria 1990. *Address:* The Lord Cavendish of Furness, DL, Holker Hall, Cark-in-Cartmel, Cumbria, LA11 7PL *Tel:* 01539 558220 *Tel:* Office: 01539 558123 *Fax:* 01539 558776 *E-Mail:* cavendish@holker.co.uk.

LORD CHADLINGTON   Conservative

CHADLINGTON (Life Baron), Peter Selwyn Gummer; cr. 1996. Born 24 August 1942. Son of late Canon Selwyn Gummer and late Sybille (née Mason); educated King's School, Rochester, Kent; Selwyn College, Cambridge (BA, MA). Married 1982, Lucy Rachel, daughter of A. Ponsonby Dudley-Hill (1 son 3 daughters). *Career:* Portsmouth and Sunderland Newspaper Group Ltd 1964–65; Viyella International 1965–66; Hodgkinson and Partners 1966–67; Industrial and Commercial Finance Corporation 1967–74; Chairman, Shandwick International plc 1974–2000; Non-Executive Director: CIA Group plc 1990–94, Halifax Building Society 1994–; Chairman, International Public Relations 1998–2000; Director, Black Box Music Ltd 1999–; Director, Walbrook Club 2000–. *Select Committees:* Member, Select Committee on the European Union Sub-Committee B (Energy, Industry and Transport). *Other:* Chairman, Royal Opera House 1996–97; Council Member, Cheltenham Ladies College 1998–; Chairman, Action on Addiction 2000–. Honorary Fellow, Bournemouth University 1999–. *Trusts, etc:* Chairman, Understanding Industry Trust 1991–95; Trustee, Atlantic Partnership 1999–; Board of Trustees, American University 1999–. *Miscellaneous:* Member: NHS Policy Board 1991–95, Arts Council of England 1991–96; Chairman, National Lottery Advisory Board for Arts and Film 1994–96; Non-Executive Director, Oxford Resources 1999–; Non-Executive Chairman, guideforlife.com 2000–. FRSA; FIPR. Freeman, City of London. *Publications:* Various articles and booklets on public relations. *Recreations:* Opera, rugby, cricket. *Clubs:* Garrick, MCC, Carlton. *Name, Style and Title:* Raised to the peerage as Baron Chadlington, of Dean in the County of Oxfordshire 1996. *Address:* The Lord Chadlington, House of Lords, London, SW1A 0PW, *Tel:* 020 7408 2232.

LORD CHALFONT
Cross-Bencher

CHALFONT (Life Baron), Alun Arthur Gwynne Jones; cr. 1964. Born 5 December 1919. Son of late Arthur Gwynne Jones; educated West Monmouth School; School of Slavonic Studies, London University. Married November 6, 1948, Mona, daughter of late Harry Douglas Mitchell (1 daughter deceased). *Armed Forces:* Commissioned as 2nd Lieutenant in South Wales Borderers 1940; Served in Burma and afterwards in Cyprus, Malaya and East Africa; Has held various intelligence appointments; Graduate of: Army Staff College 1950, Joint Service Staff College 1958; Resigned commission as Brevet Lieutenant-Colonel in 1961 upon appointment as Defence Correspondent of *The Times*; Hon. Colonel, University of Wales Officer Training Corps 1992–95. *Career:* Director: Shandwick plc 1979–94, IBM (UK) 1983–90, Lazard Bros & Co Ltd 1983–91; Chairman, Vickers Shipbuilding and Engineering Ltd 1987–95; Deputy Chairman, Independent Broadcasting Authority 1989–90; Chairman, Radio Authority 1991–95; Chairman, Marlborough Stirling 1994–99; Director, Television Corporation 1996–; Chairman, Southern Mining Corp 1997–99. *House of Lords:* Minister of State for Foreign Affairs 1964–70. *Spokesman:* Opposition Spokesman on Defence and Foreign Affairs 1970–73. *International Bodies (General):* President: Hispanic and Luso Brazilian Council 1972–79, European Atlantic Group 1983–90. *Other:* President: Llangollen International Music Festival 1978–87, RNID 1980–87, Freedom in Sport 1982–88; Member: Royal Academy of Morocco, Pilgrims Society. *Honours:* MC 1957; OBE (Mil) 1961; PC 1964; Grand Officer, Order of the Southern Cross (Brazil) 1976. FRSA. Freeman, City of London. Member, Paviors' Company. *Publications:* Several books including: *The Great Commanders*, 1973; *Montgomery of Alamein*, 1976; *Waterloo: A Battle of Three Armies*, 1979; *Star Wars*, 1985; *Defence of the Realm*, 1987; *By God's Will*, 1989; *The Shadow of My Hand*, 2000. *Special Interests:* Defence, Foreign Affairs. *Recreations:* Music. *Sportsclubs:* London Welsh RFC, Llanelli RFC. *Clubs:* MCC, Garrick, City Livery. *Name, Style and Title:* Raised to the peerage as Baron Chalfont, of Llantarnam, in the County of Monmouth 1964. *Address:* Rt Hon the Lord Chalfont, OBE, MC, House of Lords, London, SW1A 0PW.

BARONESS CHALKER OF WALLASEY
Conservative

CHALKER OF WALLASEY (Life Baroness), Lynda Chalker; cr. 1992. Born 29 April 1942. Daughter of late Sidney Henry James Bates, and late Marjorie Kathleen Randell; educated Roedean; Heidelberg University; London University; Central London Polytechnic. Married 1st 1967, Eric Robert Chalker (marriage dissolved 1973), married 2nd, December 10, 1981, Clive Landa. *Armed Forces:* Hon. Colonel, Royal Logistic Corps (156 Transport Regiment NW). *Career:* Formerly executive director, International Market Research company; Independent Consultant on Africa and Development 1997–. *House of Commons:* MP (Conservative) for Wallasey February 1974–92; Parliamentary Under-Secretary of State, Department of Health and Social Security 1979–82; Parliamentary Under-Secretary of State, Department of Transport 1982–83; Minister of State 1983–86; Minister of State, Foreign and Commonwealth Office with special responsibility for: Europe, International trade, Economic relations, Personnel 1986–89, Sub-Saharan Africa and The Commonwealth 1986–97; Deputy to Foreign Secretary 1987–97. *Spokesman (Commons):* Opposition spokesman on Social Services 1976–79. *House of Lords:* Minister of Overseas Development and Minister for Africa and Commonwealth in Foreign and Commonwealth Office 1989–97. *Party Groups (General):* National Vice-Chairman, Young Conservatives 1970–71. *Other:* President and Chairman, Board of Management of London School of Hygiene and Tropical Medicine. Seven honorary degrees. *Miscellaneous:* Member, BBC Advisory Committee 1974–79. *Honours:* PC 1987. Fellow, Royal Statistical Society. *Publications:* *Police in Retreat*, 1968; *Unhappy Families*, 1972; *We're Richer than We Think*, 1978; *Africa – Turning the Tide*, 1989. *Special Interests:* Voluntary Sector, European Co-operation, Africa, Overseas Aid and Development, Trade, Transport. *Recreations:* Theatre, cooking, gardening, jazz. *Name, Style and Title:* Raised to the peerage as Baroness Chalker of Wallasey, of Leigh-on-Sea in the County of Essex 1992. *Address:* Rt Hon the Baroness Chalker of Wallasey, House of Lords, London, SW1A 0PW *Tel:* House of Lords 020 7219 3000.

VISCOUNT CHANDOS   Labour

CHANDOS (3rd Viscount, UK), Thomas Orlando Lyttelton; cr. 1954; (Life) Baron Lyttelton of Aldershot 2000. Born 12 February 1953. Son of 2nd Viscount. Succeeded his father 1980; educated Eton; Worcester College, Oxford (BA). Married October 19, 1985, Arabella Sarah Bailey (2 sons 1 daughter). *Career:* Director: Kleinwort Benson 1985–93, Botts & Company Limited 1993–98, Capital and Regional Properties plc 1993–, Cine-UK Limited 1995–, Video Networks Limited 1996–; Chairman: Lopex plc 1997–, Mediakey plc 1998–. *Spokesman:* Formerly SDP Spokesman on Finance and Trade; Opposition Spokesman on Treasury and Economic Affairs 1995–97. *Other:* Director, English National Opera 1995–; Governor, National Film and Television School 1996–. *Trusts, etc:* Trustee: 21st Century Learning Initiative 1995–, Education Low-Priced Sponsored Texts 1996–. *Name, Style and Title:* Created a life peer as Baron Lyttelton of Aldershot, of Aldershot in the County of Hampshire 2000. *Address:* The Viscount Chandos, Video Networks Ltd, 5th Floor, 29 Queen Anne's Gate, London, SW1H 9BU *E-Mail:* tomc@videonetworks.com.

LORD CHAPPLE   Cross-Bencher

CHAPPLE (Life Baron), Francis Joseph Chapple; cr. 1985. Born 1921. Son of late Frank Chapple; educated Elementary School. Married 1st 1944, Joan (died 1994), daughter of James Nicholls (2 sons); married 2nd 1999, Phyllis, daughter of Wilfred Luck. *Trades Union:* Member, Electrical Trade Union 1937–83; Shop Steward and Branch Official; General Secretary, Electrical, Electronic, Telecommunication and Plumbing Union 1966–84; Member, General Council of the TUC 1971–83, Chairman 1982–83, Gold Badge of Congress 1983. *Select Committees:* Member, Select Committee on Sustainable Development 1994–95. *Miscellaneous:* Member: Royal Commission on Environmental Pollution 1973–77, Horserace Totalisator Board 1976–90, NEDC 1979–83. *Publications: Sparks Fly* (autobiography) 1984. *Recreations:* Pigeon racing. *Name, Style and Title:* Raised to the peerage as Baron Chapple, of Hoxton in Greater London 1985. *Address:* The Lord Chapple, House of Lords, London, SW1A 0PW.

BISHOP OF CHELMSFORD   Non-Affiliated

CHELMSFORD (Bishop of), John Freeman Perry. Born 15 June 1935. Son of Richard and Elsie Perry; educated Mill Hill School, London; London College of Divinity; St John's College, Nottingham (Licentiate in Theology 1974); Westminster College, Oxford (MPhil 1986). Married 1959, Gay Valerie Brown (3 sons 2 daughters). *Armed Forces:* National Service, Royal Corps of Signals 1953–55. *Career:* Assistant Curate: Christ Church, Woking, Surrey 1959–62, Christ Church, Chorleywood, Herts 1962–63; Vicar, St Andrew's, Chorleywood 1963–77; Rural Dean of Rickmanworth 1972–77; Warden, Lee Abbey, Lynton, North Devon 1977–89; Rural Dean of Shirwell 1980–84; Suffragan Bishop of Southampton 1989–96; Hon Canon, Winchester Cathedral 1989–96; Bishop of Chelmsford 1996–; took his seat in the House of Lords 2000. *Trusts, etc:* Chairman, Burrswood Trustees. *Publications: Effective Christian Leadership,* 1983. *Special Interests:* Healing, Healthcare. *Recreations:* Walking, sport, travel, classical music, film reviews. *Address:* Rt Rev the Lord Bishop of Chelmsford, Bishopscourt, Margaretting, Ingatestone, Essex, CM4 0HD *E-Mail:* bishopscourt@chelmsford.anglican.org.

BISHOP OF CHICHESTER — Non-Affiliated

CHICHESTER (77th Bishop of), Eric Waldram Kemp. Born 27 April 1915. Son of late Tom and Florence Kemp; educated Brigg Grammar School; Exeter College, Oxford (MA); St Stephen's House, Oxford (DD). Married 1953, Leslie Patricia Kirk (1 son 4 daughters). *Career:* Curate of St Luke, Southampton 1939–41; Librarian, Pusey House, Oxford 1941–46; Chaplain, Christ Church, Oxford 1943–46; Chaplain, Fellow and Lecturer at Exeter College, Oxford 1946–69; Proctor in Convocation 1949–69; Prebendary of Caistor in Lincoln Cathedral 1954–; Chaplain to HM Queen 1967–69; Dean of Worcester 1969–74; Bishop of Chichester 1974–; Took his seat in the House of Lords November 1979. Two honorary doctorates. *Miscellaneous:* Chanoine d'Honneur (Honorary Canon), Chartres Cathedral 1998. FRHistS. *Publications: Canonization and Authority in the Western Church,* 1948; *Norman Powell Williams,* 1954; *An Introduction to Canon Law in the Church of England,* 1957; *The Life and Letters of Kenneth Escott Kirk, Bishop of Oxford 1937–1954,* 1959; *Counsel and Consent: Aspects of the Government of the Church,* 1961; *The Anglican Methodist Conversations,* 1964; Editor *Man: Fallen and Free,* 1969; *Square Words in a Round World,* 1980. *Recreations:* Music, history. *Clubs:* National Liberal (President 1994–). *Address:* Rt Rev the Lord Bishop of Chichester, DD, The Palace, Chichester, West Sussex, PO19 1PY *Tel:* 01243 782161 *Fax:* 01243 531332 *E-Mail:* bishopchi@diochi.freeserve.co.uk.

LORD CHILVER — Conservative

CHILVER (Life Baron), Amos Henry Chilver; cr. 1987. Born 30 October 1926. Son of late Amos Henry Chilver; educated Southend High School; Bristol University. Married 1959, Claudia Grigson (3 sons 2 daughters). *Councils, Public Bodies:* Chairman, Milton Keynes Development Corporation 1983–92. *Career:* Railway Engineer 1947–48; Research Assistant, then Assistant Lecturer, then Lecturer, Bristol University 1948–54; Demonstrator then Lecturer, Cambridge University 1954–61; Professor Civil Engineering, UCL 1961–69; Vice-Chancellor, Cranfield Institute of Technology 1970–89; Chairman, English China Clays plc 1989–95; Non-executive Director: ICI 1990–93, Zeneca 1993–95; Chairman, RJB Mining 1993–97. Fellow, Corpus Christi College, Cambridge 1958–61. *Miscellaneous:* Chairman, Universities Funding Council 1988–91. *Special Interests:* Education, Industry, Environment. *Clubs:* Athenaeum, United Oxford and Cambridge University. *Name, Style and Title:* Raised to the peerage as Baron Chilver, of Cranfield in the County of Bedfordshire 1987. *Address:* The Lord Chilver, FRS, English China Clays plc, 125 Wood Street, London, EC2V 7AQ *Tel:* 020 7696 9229.

LORD CHITNIS — Cross-Bencher

CHITNIS (Life Baron), Pratap Chidamber Chitnis; cr. 1977. Born 1 May 1936. Son of late Dr Chidamber N. Chitnis; educated Stonyhurst College; Birmingham University (BA); University of Kansas (MA). Married October 24, 1964, Anne Brand (1 son deceased). *Career:* Administration Assistant, National Coal Board 1958–59; Secretary, The Joseph Rowntree Social Service Trust 1969–75, Chief Executive and Director, 1975–88; Member, Community Relations Commission 1970–77; Member, BBC Asian Programme Advice Committee 1972–77, Chairman 1979–83; Chairman, Refugee Action 1981–86; Chairman, British Refugee Council 1986–89. *Party Groups (General):* Liberal Party Organisation: Local Government Officer 1960–62, Agent, Orpington By-election 1962, Training Officer 1962–64, Press Officer 1964–66; Head, Liberal Party Organisation 1966–69. *Name, Style and Title:* Raised to the peerage as Baron Chitnis, of Ryedale in the County of North Yorkshire 1977. *Address:* The Lord Chitnis, House of Lords, London, SW1A 0PW.

MARQUESS OF CHOLMONDELEY — Cross-Bencher

CHOLMONDELEY (7th Marquess of, UK), David George Philip Cholmondeley; cr. 1815; 10th Earl of Cholmondeley (E) 1706; 7th Earl of Rocksavage (UK) 1815; 10th Viscount Malpas (E) 1706; 11th Viscount Cholmondeley (I) 1661; 10th Baron Cholmondeley (E) 1689; 10th Baron Newburgh (GB) 1716; 10th Baron Newborough (I) 1715. Born 27 June 1960. Son of 6th Marquess, GCVO, MC, DL. Succeeded his father 1990; educated Eton; Sorbonne. *Career:* A film maker; A Page of Honour to HM The Queen 1974–76; Joint Hereditary Lord Great Chamberlain of England (acting for the reign of Queen Elizabeth II) since 1990. *Recreations:* Music, tennis, travel. *Clubs:* White's, Vanderbilt, Champney's, Cercle de l'Union Interallée (Paris).
Address: Most Hon the Marquess of Cholmondeley, Office: 10 St. James's Place, London, SW1A 1PE
Tel: 020 7408 0418; House of Lords, London, SW1A 0PW; Cholmondeley Castle, Malpas, Cheshire, SY14 8AH.

LORD CHRISTOPHER — Labour

CHRISTOPHER (Life Baron), Anthony (Tony) Martin Grosvenor Christopher; cr. 1998. Born 25 April 1925. Son of late George and Helen Christopher; educated Cheltenham Grammar School; Westminster College of Commerce. Married 1962, Adela Joy Thompson. *Trades Union:* Member, TUC General Council 1976–89, Chairman 1988–89; Member, TUC Committees: Economic Committee 1977–89, Education Committee 1977–85, International Committee 1982–89, Finance and General Purposes Committee 1983–89, Education and Training Committee 1985–86, Employment and Organisation Committees 1985–89. *Armed Forces:* RAF 1944–48. *Career:* Articled Pupil, Agricultural Valuers, Gloucester 1941–44; Inland Revenue 1948–57; Inland Revenue Staff Federation: Assistant Secretary 1957–60, Assistant General Secretary 1960–74, Joint General Secretary 1975, General Secretary 1976–88; Chairman, TU Fund Managers Ltd 1983, Director 1981–; Industrial and Public Affairs Consultant 1988–. *Select Committees:* Member, Select Committees on: European Communities Sub-Committee D (Agriculture, Fisheries and Food) 1999–, Joint Committee on Consolidation of Bills 2000–. *International Bodies (General):* Members' Auditor, International Confederation of Free Trades Unions 1984–. *Trusts, etc:* Trustee: NACRO 1956–98, Trades Union Unit Trust Charitable Trust 1981–, Commonwealth Trades Union Council Charitable Trust 1985–89, Save The Children Fund 1985–90; Trustee, Institute for Public Policy Research 1989–94, Treasurer 1990–94. *Miscellaneous:* Member, Council, NACRO 1956–98, Chairman 1973–98; Director, Civil Service Building Society 1958–87, Chairman 1978–87; Member: Inner London Probation and After-care Committee 1966–79, Tax Reform Committee 1974–70, Royal Commission on Distribution of Income and Wealth 1978–79, Independent Broadcasting Authority 1978–83; Chairman, Tyre Industry Economic Development Council 1983–86; Member: Council of Institute of Manpower Studies 1984–89, Economic and Social Research Council 1985–88; Vice-President, Building Societies Association 1985–90; Director, Birmingham Midshires Building Society 1987–88; Member: General Medical Council 1989–94, Audit Commission 1989–95, Broadcasting Complaints Commission 1989–97; Former member of several other committees, inquiries and working parties. *Honours:* CBE 1984. FRSA 1989. *Publications:* Co-author: *Policy for Poverty*, 1970; *The Wealth Report*, 1979; *The Wealth Report 2*, 1982. *Special Interests:* Agriculture, Financial Services, Pensions, Penal Affairs and Policy, Economics, Industry. *Recreations:* Gardening. *Clubs:* Beefsteak, Wig and Pen, Royal Automobile. *Name, Style and Title:* Raised to the peerage as Baron Christopher, of Leckhampton in the County of Gloucestershire 1998. *Address:* The Lord Christopher, CBE, TU Fund Managers Ltd, Congress House, Great Russell Street, London, WC1B 3LQ.

Dod *on* Line
An Electronic Directory without rival ...

Peers' biographies and photographs available with daily updates *via* the internet

For a *free* trial, call Oliver Cox on 020 7828 7256

LORD CLARK OF KEMPSTON — Conservative

CLARK OF KEMPSTON (Life Baron), William Gibson Haig Clark; cr. 1992. Born 18 October 1917. Son of late Hugh Clark; educated London. Married August 28, 1944, Irene Dorothy Rands (2 sons and 1 son and 1 daughter deceased). *Armed Forces:* Served in Army in UK and India 1941–46, Major. *Councils, Public Bodies:* Councillor, Wandsworth Borough Council 1949–53. *House of Commons:* Contested (Conservative) Northampton 1955 General Election; MP (Conservative) for: Nottingham South 1959–66, Surrey East 1970–74, Croydon South 1974–92. *Spokesman (Commons):* Front Bench Spokesman on Trade, Finance and Economics 1964–66. *Select Committees:* Former Member, Procedure Committee. *Party Groups (General):* Chairman: Clapham Conservative Association 1949–52, Mid-Bedforshire Conservative Association 1956–59; Joint Treasurer, Conservative Party 1974–75; Deputy Chairman, Conservative Party 1975–77. *Other:* Hon. National Director, £2 million Carrington Appeal 1967; Chairman, Anglo-Austrian Society 1983–98, Patron 1998–; President, The City Group for Smaller Companies (Cisco) 1993–98. *Trusts, etc:* Fellow, Industry and Parliament Trust; Trustee, Carlton Club. *Honours:* Kt 1980; Order of the Golden Fleece (Austria) 1989; PC 1990; Grand Decoration of Honour in Gold with Star (Austria) 1994. Member, Chartered Association of Certified Accountants 1941. Freeman, City of London. *Special Interests:* Finance, Industry, Trade and Industry, Housing, Cane Sugar, Insurance. *Recreations:* Reading. *Clubs:* Buck's, Carlton. *Name, Style and Title:* Raised to the peerage as Baron Clark of Kempston, of Kempston in the County of Bedfordshire 1992. *Address:* Rt Hon the Lord Clark of Kempston, The Clock House, Box End, Bedford, MK43 8RT *Tel:* 01234 852361; 3 Barton Street, London, SW1P 3NG *Tel:* 020 7222 5759.

LORD CLARKE OF HAMPSTEAD — Labour

CLARKE OF HAMPSTEAD (Life Baron), Anthony James Clarke; cr. 1998. Born 17 April 1932. Son of Henry Walter and Elizabeth Clarke; educated St Dominics Roman Catholic School, Kentish Town; Ruskin College, Oxford. Married 1954, Josephine Ena Turner (1 son and 1 daughter). *Trades Union:* UPW: Committee Member 1953, Branch Secretary 1962–69; Member: London Trades Council 1965–69 (EC Member 1967–68), TUC Disputes Panel 1972–93, TUC SE Regional Council 1974–79, London Council of Post Office Unions 1975–79, Midlands Council of Post Office Unions 1975–79. *Armed Forces:* National Service, Royal Signals 1950–52; TA and Army Emergency Reserve 1952–68. *Councils, Public Bodies:* Councillor, London Borough of Camden 1971–78. *Career:* Post Office: Telegraph Boy, Postman, Postman Higher Grade (Sorter); Full-time Trade Union Officer, UPW 1979–93; Editor, UPW journal (*The Post*) 1979; Deputy General Secretary, UPW 1981–93. *International Bodies (General):* Organiser and Lecturer, Postal and Telegraph International (PTTI) in Malaysia and India. *Party Groups (General):* Member: Hampstead Labour Party 1954–86, Executive Committee, Labour Friends of Israel 1972–, Labour Party National Executive Committee 1983, St Albans Labour Party 1986–98, Chair, The Labour Party 1992–93; Governor, Westminster Foundation for Democracy 1992–98. *Other:* Governor, Quentin Kynaston Comprehensive School (ILEA) 1973–78; Executive Committee Member, Camden Committee for Community Relations 1974–81; Chairman, Camden Council of Social Services 1978–87; Management Committee Member: Hampstead Old Peoples' Homes, Newstead Old Peoples' Home. *Trusts, etc:* Trustee, Post Office Pension Funds 1991–97; Founder Member and Trustee, One World Action. *Miscellaneous:* Contested (Labour) Camden Hampstead February and October 1974 General Elections. *Honours:* Knight of St Gregory (Papal Order) 1994; CBE 1998. *Special Interests:* Overseas Aid and Development, Industrial Relations. *Recreations:* Arsenal FC, *The Archers*, reading. *Name, Style and Title:* Raised to the peerage as Baron Clarke of Hampstead, of Hampstead in the London Borough of Camden 1998. *Address:* The Lord Clarke of Hampstead, CBE, House of Lords, London, SW1A 0PW.

LORD CLEDWYN OF PENRHOS   Labour

CLEDWYN OF PENRHOS (Life Baron), Cledwyn Hughes; cr. 1979. Born 14 September 1916. Son of late Rev. Henry David Hughes, Presbyterian Minister, and Emily Hughes; educated Holyhead Grammar School; University College of Wales, Aberystwyth (LLB 1937); Law Society. Married June 19, 1949, Jean Beatrice, daughter of Captain Jesse Hughes and Sarah Hughes, of Holyhead (1 son 1 daughter). *Armed Forces:* Served RAF (Flight/Lieutenant 1940–46). *Councils, Public Bodies:* Councillor, Anglesey County Council 1946–53, Alderman 1973. *Career:* Solicitor, qualified 1940 admitted January 1946; Consultant and Former Partner, T. R. Evans, Hughes & Co, Holyhead; Acting Clerk, Holyhead UDC to 1949; Anglesey County Council 1946–53. *House of Commons:* Contested Anglesey 1945 and 1950; MP (Labour) Anglesey 1951–79; Minister of State, Commonwealth Relations 1964–1966; Secretary of State for Wales 1966–68; Minister of Agriculture, Fisheries and Food 1968–70. *Spokesman (Commons):* Opposition Spokesman on Housing and Local Government 1959–64; Opposition Spokesman on Agriculture 1970–72. *Party Groups (Commons):* Chairman, Parliamentary Labour Party 1974–79. *Chancellor:* Pro-Chancellor, University of Wales 1985–95. *House of Lords:* Deputy Leader of the Opposition 1981–82; Leader of the Opposition 1982–92. *Spokesman:* Opposition Spokesman on: Agriculture, The Civil Service 1983–88, Foreign Affairs, Welsh Affairs 1983–92. *Select Committees:* Chairman, Select Committee on Agriculture, Food and Consumer Affairs 1980–82; Member, Select Committee on Privileges. *Party Groups (General):* Member of Labour Party since 1938; Vice-Chairman, Parliamentary Labour Party 1974–75, Chairman 1975–79. *Other:* President: University College of Wales, Aberstwyth 1976–84, University of Wales, Bangor 1995–2000. Five honorary doctorates/fellowships. *Miscellaneous:* Represented British Government at Kenya Republic celebrations 1964; Leader, UK delegation to The Gambia Independence celebrations 1965; Prime Minister's Envoy to Southern Africa 1978; Chairman, Welsh Committee on Economic Affairs 1982–84; President, Assembly of Welsh Counties 1990–; Member: Political Honours Scrutiny Committee 1992–99, Bardic Circle of the Royal National Eisteddfod of Wales. *Honours:* PC 1966; CH 1977. Hon. Freeman: Borough of Beaumaris 1972, Isle of Anglesey 1976. *Publications: Conditions on the Island of St Helena,* 1958. *Special Interests:* Welsh Literature, Welsh Sport. *Clubs:* Travellers'. *Name, Style and Title:* Raised to the peerage as Baron Cledwyn of Penrhos, of Holyhead in the Isle of Anglesey 1979. *Address:* Rt Hon the Lord Cledwyn of Penrhos, CH, Penmorfa, Trearddur, Holyhead, Gwynedd *Tel:* 01407 860544; House of Lords, London, SW1A 0PW *Tel:* House of Lords 020 7219 3236.

LORD CLEMENT-JONES   Liberal Democrat

CLEMENT-JONES (Life Baron), Timothy Francis Clement-Jones; cr. 1998. Born 26 October 1949. Son of late Maurice Llewelyn Clement-Jones; educated Haileybury; Trinity College, Cambridge (BA Economics and Law). Married 1st, June 14, 1973, Dr Vicky Yip (died 1987); married 2nd, July 15, 1994, Jean Whiteside (1 son). *Career:* Solicitor; Head of Legal Services, London Weekend Television 1980–83; Legal Director, Grand Metropolitan Retailing 1984–86; Group Company Secretary and Legal Adviser, Kingfisher plc 1986–95; Chairman, Environmental Context Ltd 1997–; Head of DLA Upstream, the public affairs practice of DLA 1999–. *Spokesman:* Liberal Democrat Spokesman on Health 1998–. *Party Groups (General):* Chairman: Association of Liberal Lawyers 1981–86, Liberal Democrat Party Federal Finance Committee 1991–98; Director, Liberal Democrat Campaign for the European Parliamentary Elections 1994; Member, Liberal Democrat National Executive; Chairman, Liberal Democrat London 2000 Mayoral and Assembly Campaign. *Other:* Former Chairman and Director, Crime Concern; Former Member, Council of the London Lighthouse; Former Director, Brixton City Challenge. *Trusts, etc:* Trustee: Cancer BACUP, Lambeth Crime Prevention Trust. *Honours:* CBE 1988. *Recreations:* Travelling, eating, talking, reading, walking. *Clubs:* Royal Automobile, National Liberal. *Name, Style and Title:* Raised to the peerage as Baron Clement-Jones, of Clapham in the London Borough of Lambeth 1998. *Address:* The Lord Clement-Jones, CBE, House of Lords, London, SW1A 0PW.

LORD CLINTON-DAVIS   Labour

CLINTON-DAVIS (Life Baron), Stanley Clinton Clinton-Davis; cr. 1990. Born 6 December 1928. Son of Sidney and Lily Davis; educated Hackney Down School, Mercer's School; King's College, London University (LLB 1950). Married 1954, Frances Jane Lucas (1 son 3 daughters). *Councils, Public Bodies:* Councillor, London Borough of Hackney 1959–71, Mayor 1968–69. *Career:* Admitted solicitor 1953; President, UN Selection Committee for the Sasakawa Environment Project 1989–97; Consultant on European law and affairs with S. J. Berwin & Co. solicitors 1989–. *House of Commons:* Contested (Labour): Portsmouth, Langstone in 1955, Yarmouth in 1959 and 1964 General Elections; MP (Labour) for Hackney Central 1970–83; Parliamentary Under-Secretary of State, Department of Trade 1974–79. *Spokesman (Commons):* Opposition Spokesman on: Trade, prices and consumer protection 1979–81, Foreign affairs 1981–83. *House of Lords:* Minister of State, Department of Trade and Industry (Minister for Trade) 1997–98. *Spokesman:* Opposition Spokesman on Transport in the House of Lords 1990–97; Supporting Spokesman on: Trade and Industry 1990–96, Foreign Affairs 1990–97. *International Bodies:* Member, Parliamentary Assembly of the Council of Europe and the Assembly of the Western European Union 2000–. *International Bodies (General):* Member, Royal Institute for International Affairs. *Party Groups (General):* Member, Executive Council, National Association of Labour Student Organisations 1949–50; Joint President, Society of Labour Lawyers. *Other:* President, Hackney Branch, Multiple Sclerosis Society; Patron, Hackney Association for the Disabled; President, UK Pilots (Marine); President: Institute of Travel Management, British Airline Pilots Association, Aviation Environment Federation; Vice-President, Chartered Institute of Environmental Health; Chairman, Europe 21. *Awards Granted:* Awarded first medal by Eurogroup for Animal Welfare 1988. Fellow, Queen Mary and Westfield College; Holds an Hon. Doctorate at the Polytechnic University of Bucharest; Hon. ACA Degree. *Trusts, etc:* Trustee, Bernt Carlsson Trust 1989–. *Miscellaneous:* Member, Commission of the European Communities 1985–89; Chair, Advisory Committee on Pollution of the Sea 1984–85, 1989–97; Member: Council of Justice, Council of British Maritime League 1989–; Chair, Refugee Council 1989–97; Former President, Association of Municipal Authorities (AMA); Member, Advisory Panel of CIS Environ Trust. *Honours:* Grand Cross, Order of Leopold II (Belgium) for services to the EC 1990; PC 1998. Fellow, Chartered Institution of Water and Environmental Management. *Publications:* Joint Author of a Report in a British Parliamentary Delegation in 1982, *Good Neighbours? Nicaragua, Central America and the United States. Special Interests:* Transport, Environment, Foreign Affairs, Law, Civil Liberties. *Recreations:* Association football, golf, political biographies. *Sportsclubs:* Hendon Golf Club. *Clubs:* Royal Overseas League. *Name, Style and Title:* Raised to the peerage as Baron Clinton-Davis, of Hackney in the London Borough of Hackney 1990. *Address:* Rt Hon the Lord Clinton-Davis, House of Lords, London, SW1A 0PW.

LORD CLYDE   Cross-Bencher

CLYDE (Life Baron), James John Clyde; cr. 1996. Born 29 January 1932. Son of late Rt Hon. Lord Clyde; educated Edinburgh Academy; Corpus Christi College, Oxford (BA); Edinburgh University (LLB). Married 1963, Ann Clunie Hoblyn (2 sons). *Armed Forces:* National Service 1954–56. *Career:* Called to the Scottish Bar 1959; QC (Scot) 1971; Advocate-Depute 1973–74; Chancellor to the Bishop of Argyll and the Isles 1972–85; A Judge of the Courts of Appeal of Jersey and Guernsey 1979–85; A Senator of the College of Justice in Scotland 1985–96; A Lord of Appeal in Ordinary 1996–; Elected as Honorary Master of the Bench of the Middle Temple 1996. *Select Committees:* Chairman, Joint Select Committee on Consolidation of Bills 1998–. *Other:* Director, Edinburgh Academy 1979–88; Vice-President, Royal Blind Asylum and School 1987–; Hon. President, Scottish Young Lawyers' Association 1988–97; Governor, Napier Polytechnic 1989–93; Chairman, Governors, St George's School for Girls 1989–97; Assessor to the Chancellor of Edinburgh University and Vice-Chairman of Court 1989–97. DUniv, Heriot-Watt 1991; DLitt, Napier University 1995; Hon. Fellow Corpus Christi College, Oxford 1996 DUniv, Edinburgh University 1997. *Trusts, etc:* Trustee: St Mary's Music School 1976–92, National Library of Scotland 1977–93; Chairman, Special Trustees of St Mary's Hospital, Paddington 1997–99; Chairman, Statute Law Society 2000–.

Miscellaneous: Contested (Conservative) Dundee East February 1974; Chairman: Medical Appeal Tribunal 1974–85, Committee of Investigation for Scotland on Agricultural Marketing 1984–85, Scottish Valuation Advisory Council 1987–96, Member 1972–96, European Institute 1990–97, Orkney Children Inquiry 1991–92. *Honours:* PC 1996. *Publications:* Co-editor *Armour on Valuation,* 5th ed. 1985; Co-author *Judicial Review,* 2000. *Recreations:* Music, gardening. *Clubs:* New (Edinburgh). *Name, Style and Title:* Raised to the peerage as Baron Clyde, of Briglands in Perthshire and Kinross 1996. *Address:* Rt Hon the Lord Clyde, 12 Dublin Street, Edinburgh, EH1 3PP *Tel:* 0131–556 7114; House of Lords, London, SW1A 0PW.

LORD COBBOLD   Cross-Bencher

COBBOLD (2nd Baron, UK), David Antony Fromanteel Lytton Cobbold; cr. 1960. Born 14 July 1937. Son of 1st Baron, KG, PC, GCVO, DL, and Lady Hermione Bulwer-Lytton, daughter of 2nd Earl of Lytton, KG, PC, GCSI, GCIE, DL. Succeeded his father 1987; educated Eton; Trinity College, Cambridge (BA Moral Sciences). Married 1961, Christine Elizabeth, daughter of late Sir Dennis Stucley, 5th Bt (3 sons 1 daughter). *Armed Forces:* Pilot Officer, RAF 1955–57. *Councils, Public Bodies:* DL, Hertfordshire 1993–. *Career:* Bank of London and South America 1962–72; Chairman and Managing Director, Lytton Enterprises Ltd 1971–; Treasurer, Finance for Industry Ltd 1974–79; Manager, Treasury Division BP Finance International 1979–87; Director: 39 Production Co. Ltd 1987–99, Hill Samuel Bank Ltd 1988–89; Head of Treasury and Financial Markets, TSB England and Wales plc and Hill Samuel Bank Ltd 1988–89; Managing Director, Gaiacorp UK Ltd 1989–94; Director: Close Brothers Group plc 1993–, Stevenage Leisure Ltd 1998–. *House of Lords:* An elected hereditary peer 2000–. *Other:* Hon. Treasurer, Historic Houses Association 1988–97; Member, Association for Monetary Union in Europe 1991–; President, University of Hertfordshire Development Committee 1991–; Member, Board of Governors, University of Hertfordshire 1993–; Governor, European Union of Historic Houses Association 1993–97. *Trusts, etc:* Chairman, Stevenage Community Trust 1991–; Trustee, Pilgrim Trust 1993–; Director: Shuttleworth Trust 1998–, English Sinfonia Ltd 1998–. *Miscellaneous:* Assumed by deed poll the additional surname of Lytton before his patronymic; Contested: (Liberal) Bishop Auckland October 1974 General Election, Hertfordshire European Parliamentary Election 1979. Fellow, Association of Corporate Treasurers 1983–. *Special Interests:* China, European Monetary Union, Historic Buildings. *Address:* The Lord Cobbold, DL, Knebworth House, Knebworth, Hertfordshire, SG3 6PY *Tel:* 01438 812661 *Fax:* 01438 811908 *E-Mail:* lordcobbold@knebworthhouse.com.

LORD COCKFIELD   Conservative

COCKFIELD (Life Baron), Francis Arthur Cockfield; cr. 1978. Born 28 September 1916. Son of Lieutenant Charles Francis Cockfield, killed in the battle of the Somme 1916; educated Dover Grammar School; London School of Economics (LLB, BSc Economics). Married 1970, Aileen Monica Mudie (died 1992). *Career:* Called to the Bar, Inner Temple, 1942; HM Customs and Excise 1933; Estate Duty Office 1935; Secretaries' Office Board of Inland Revenue 1938, Assistant Secretary 1945; Director, Statistics and Intelligence 1945–52; Commissioner of Inland Revenue 1951–52; Finance Director, Boots Pure Drug Co. 1953–61, Managing Director and Chairman of Executive Committee 1961–67 (retired); Member, NEDC 1962–64, 1982–83; Adviser on Taxation Policy to Chancellor of the Exchequer 1970–73; Chairman, Price Commission 1973–77; Vice-President, Commission of the European Communities 1985–89; Adviser, Peat Marwick McLintock 1989–93. *House of Lords:* Minister of State, Treasury, June 1979–82; Secretary of State for Trade 1982–1983; Chancellor of the Duchy of Lancaster 1983–84. *Spokesman:* Government Spokesman on Trade and Industry and for the Treasury 1983–84. *Other:* Member, County Governors, Nottingham University 1963–67. Hon. Fellow, LSE 1972–; four honorary doctorates. *Honours:* Kt 1974; PC 1982; Grand Cross, Order of Leopold II (Belgium). President, The Royal Statistical Society 1968–69. *Publications: The European Union: Creating the Single Market,* 1994. *Name, Style and Title:* Raised to the peerage as Baron Cockfield, of Dover in the County of Kent 1978. *Address:* Rt Hon the Lord Cockfield, House of Lords, London, SW1A 0PW.

LORD COCKS OF HARTCLIFFE   Labour

COCKS OF HARTCLIFFE (Life Baron), Michael Francis Lovell Cocks; cr 1987. Born 19 August 1929. Son of late Dr H. F. Lovell Cocks; educated Bristol University. Married 1st, 1954, Janet Macfarlane (2 sons 2 daughters), married 2nd, 1979, Valerie Davis. *Career:* Various posts in education from 1954; Lecturer, Bristol Polytechnic 1968. *House of Commons:* Contested (Labour): Bristol West 1959, South Gloucestershire 1964, 1966; MP (Labour) for Bristol South 1970–87. *Whip (Commons):* Chief Whip April 1976–79. *House of Lords:* Deputy Speaker of the House of Lords 1990–; Deputy Chairman of Committees 1997–. *Party Groups (General):* President, Bristol Borough Labour Party 1961–63. *Miscellaneous:* Vice-Chairman, BBC 1993–98. *Name, Style and Title:* Raised to the peerage as Baron Cocks of Hartcliffe, of Chinnor in the County of Oxfordshire 1987. *Address:* Rt Hon the Lord Cocks of Hartcliffe, House of Lords, London, SW1A 0PW.

LORD COE   Conservative

COE (Life Baron), Sebastian Newbold Coe; cr. 2000. Born 29 September 1956. Son of Peter and Angela Coe; educated Tapton Secondary Modern School, Sheffield; Abbeydale Grange School; Loughborough University (BSc Economics and Social History). Married 1990, Nicola McIrvine (2 sons 2 daughters). *Career:* Athlete; Sports Council: Member 1983–89, Vice-Chairman 1986–89; Member: Athletes and Medical Commission, International Olympic Committee, Health Education Authority 1987–92; Associate Member, Academy of Sport (France) 1982; Steward, British Boxing Board of Control 1994–; Company director; President, Amateur Athletics Association 2000–. *House of Commons:* Member for Falmouth and Camborne 1992–97; PPS: to Roger Freeman: as Minister of State for Defence Procurement 1994–95, as Chancellor of the Duchy of Lancaster and Minister of Public Service 1995–96, to Nicholas Soames as Minister of State for the Armed Forces 1994–95, to Michael Heseltine as First Secretary of State and Deputy Prime Minister 1995–96; Private Secretary to William Hague as Leader of the Opposition 1997–. *Whip (Commons):* Assistant Government Whip 1996–97. *Awards Granted:* Has won gold and silver medals at the Moscow Olympic Games 1980 and Los Angeles Olympic Games 1984; European Champion for 800m Stuttgart, 1986; Set nine world records; Holder still of 800m world record; BBC Sport Personality of the Year 1979; Sportswriters' Sportsman of the Year: 1979, 1980, 1981, 1984. Hon. DSc, Hull University 1988; Hon. LLD, Sheffield University. *Honours:* MBE 1982; OBE 1990. *Special Interests:* Health, Foreign Affairs, Education, Environment, Economy, The Voluntary Movement. *Recreations:* Jazz, theatre, reading. *Clubs:* Carlton, East India. *Name, Style and Title:* Raised to the peerage as Baron Coe, of Ranmore in the County of Surrey 2000. *Address:* The Lord Coe, OBE, House of Lords, London, SW1A 0PW.

BARONESS COHEN OF PIMLICO   Labour

COHEN OF PIMLICO (Life Baroness), Janet Cohen; cr. 2000. Born 4 July 1940. Daughter of late George Edric Neel and of Mary Isabel Neel; educated South Hampstead High Shool; Newnham College, Cambridge (BA law 1962) (Associate Fellow 1988–91). Married 1971, James Lionel Cohen (2 sons 1 daughter). *Career:* Articled clerk, Frere Cholmeley 1963–65; admitted solicitor 1965; Consultant: ABT Associates, USA 1965–67, John Laing Construction 1968–69; Department of Trade and Industry: principal 1969–78, assistant secretary 1978–82; Assistant director, Charterhouse Bank Ltd 1982–88, Director 1988–; Chairman, Café Pelican Ltd 1984–90; Director, Yorkshire Building Society 1991–94, Vice-Chairman 1994–99; Non-executive director, BPP Holdings 1994–2001; Director: Waddington plc 1994–97, London and Manchester Assurance 1997–98, United Assurance 1999–2000. *Other:* Member, Sheffield Development Corporation 1993–97; Governor, BBC 1994–99. Hon DLitt, Humberside 1995. *Miscellaneous:* Member: Schools Examination and Assessment Council 1990–93, Sheffield Development Corporation 1993–97; A Governor, BBC 1994–99. *Publications:* As Janet Neel: *Death's Bright Angel*, 1988; *Death on Site*, 1989; *Death of a Partner*, 1991; *Death among the Dons*, 1993; *A Timely Death*, 1999; *To Die For*, 1998; *O Gentle Death*, 2000; As Janet Cohen: *The Highest Bidder*, 1992; *Children of a Harsh Winter*, 1994. *Recreations:* Restaurants, writing. *Clubs:* Reform. *Name, Style and Title:* Raised to the peerage as Baroness Cohen of Pimlico, in the City of Westminster 2000. *Address:* The Baroness Cohen of Pimlico, 20 Morpeth Mansions, Morpeth Terrace, London, SW1P 1ER.

VISCOUNT COLVILLE OF CULROSS — Cross-Bencher

COLVILLE OF CULROSS (4th Viscount, UK), John Mark Alexander Colville; cr. 1902; 13th Lord Colville of Culross (S) 1604; 4th Baron Colville of Culross (UK) 1885. Born 19 July 1933. Son of 3rd Viscount, DL. Succeeded his father, who was killed on active service, 1945; educated Rugby; New College, Oxford (BA 1957, MA 1963). Married 1st, 1958, Mary Elizabeth Webb-Bowen (4 sons) (marriage dissolved 1973), married 2nd, 1974, Margaret Birgitta, Viscountess Davidson, daughter of late Major-General C. H. Norton, CB, CBE, DSO (1 son). *Armed Forces:* Lieutenant, Grenadier Guards (RARO). *Career:* Called to the Bar, Lincoln's Inn 1960; QC 1978; UK Representative, UN Commission on Human Rights 1980–83; Special Rapporteur on Guatemala 1983–87; Chairman, Mental Health Act Commission 1983–87; Bencher 1986; Chairman, Parole Board for England and Wales 1988–92; Recorder 1990–93; Judge, South Eastern Circuit 1993–99; Member, UN Human Rights Committee 1996–2000. *House of Lords:* Minister of State, Home Office 1972–74; An elected hereditary peer 1999–. *Select Committees:* Member: Joint Select Committee on Consolidation of Bills 1998–, Liaison Committee. Hon. Fellow, New College, Oxford 1997; Hon. DCL, University of East Anglia 1998. *Miscellaneous:* Member, Queen's Bodyguard for Scotland, Royal Company of Archers. *Address:* The Viscount Colville of Culross, The Manor House, West Lexham, King's Lynn, Norfolk, PE32 2QN.

LORD COLWYN — Conservative

COLWYN (3rd Baron, UK), (Ian) Anthony Hamilton-Smith; cr. 1917; 3rd Bt of Colwyn Bay (UK) 1912. Born 1 January 1942. Son of 2nd Baron. Succeeded his father 1966; educated Cheltenham College; St Bartholomew's Hospital and Royal Dental Hospital, London University (BDS (London University 1966, LDS, RCS (England) 1966). Married 1st, May 30, 1964, Sonia Jane Morgan (1 son 1 daughter) (marriage dissolved 1977), married 2nd, 1977, Nicola Jeanne, daughter of Arthur Tyers (2 daughters). *Trades Union:* Member, Musicians' Union. *Career:* Dental Practice; Chairman, Dental Protection Ltd. 1995–; Non-Executive Director: Medical Protection Society, Project Hope; Bandleader, Lord Colwyn Organisation; Chairman, RAW FM (Radio). *House of Lords:* An elected hereditary peer 1999–. *Select Committees:* Member, Select Committees on: Medical Ethics 1993–97, Finance and Staff 1997–, Administration and Works 1997–, House of Lords' Offices 1997–; Chairman, Refreshment Sub-Committee 1997–; Co-opted Member, Select Committee on Science and Technology Sub-Committee I (Complementary and Alternative Medicine) 2000–. *International Bodies (General):* Director, Project Hope (UK). *Party Groups (General):* Member, Conservative Medical Society. *Other:* President: Natural Medicines Society 1988–, Huntington's Disease Association 1991–98, Society for Advancement of Anaesthesia in Dentistry 1993–98, Arterial Health Foundation 1993–, Metropolitan Branch, British Dental Association 1994–95; Council Member, Medical Protection Society 1994–. *Trusts, etc:* Member, Eastman Research Institute Trust. *Honours:* CBE 1989. Member, Royal Society of Medicine; Fellow, Institute of Directors. *Publications:* Various articles on Anaesthesia in Dentistry. *Special Interests:* Broadcasting, Health, Alternative Medicine, Arts. *Recreations:* Bandleader, music, riparian pursuits. *Sportsclubs:* Cheltenham Rugby, Colwyn Bay Rugby. *Address:* The Lord Colwyn, CBE, 53 Wimpole Street, London, W1M 7DF *Tel:* 020 7935 6809 *E-Mail:* colwyna@parliament.uk.

LORD CONSTANTINE OF STANMORE — Conservative

CONSTANTINE OF STANMORE (Life Baron), Theodore Constantine; cr. 1981. Born 15 March 1910. Son of late Leonard Constantine; educated Acton College, London. Married May 2, 1935, Sylvia Mary (died 1990), daughter of late Wallace Legge-Pointing (1 son 1 daughter). *Armed Forces:* Served Royal Auxiliary Air Force, Fighter Command 1939–45 (Air Efficiency Award 1945). *Councils, Public Bodies:* High Sheriff, Greater London 1967; DL, Greater London 1967. *Career:* Secretary to Managing Director, Calders Ltd 1926–28; Personal Assistant to Managing Director, Pedestros Ltd 1928–31; Administration Manager, A.T. Betts & Co Ltd 1931–34; General Manager, Allen and Hanburys (Acoustic Division) 1934–39; Director, Allen and

Hanburys (Acoustics) Ltd 1945–50; Chief Executive, Bonochord Ltd 1950–63; Deputy Chairman, Henry C. Stephens Ltd 1964–66; Chairman: Waterman Pen Co. Ltd 1966–68, Anscon Ltd 1966–, London Private Health Group plc 1981–85, Health Care Services plc 1985; Director, Stratstone Ltd 1985–92. *Party Groups (General):* Chairman, National Union Conservative Party 1968, President 1980; Work for Conservative party as constituency Chairman, area Chairman, Member National Executive Committee, Policy Committee, National Advisory Committee on publicity. *Trusts, etc:* Trustee, Sir John Wolstenholme Charity 1962–89. *Honours:* AE 1945; CBE 1956; Kt 1964. Freeman, City of London 1949. Master, Worshipful Company of Coachmakers 1975. *Recreations:* Reading, walking, watching motor racing. *Clubs:* Carlton. *Name, Style and Title:* Raised to the peerage as Baron Constantine of Stanmore, of Stanmore in Greater London 1981. *Address:* The Lord Constantine of Stanmore, CBE, AE, DL, House of Lords, London, SW1A 0PW.

LORD COOKE OF ISLANDREAGH   Ulster Unionist/Cross-Bencher

COOKE OF ISLANDREAGH (Life Baron), Victor Alexander Cooke; cr. 1992. Born 18 October 1920. Son of Victor and Alice Cooke; educated Marlborough College; Trinity College, Cambridge (MA). Married 1951, Alison Sheila Casement (2 sons 1 daughter). *Armed Forces:* Engineer Officer, Royal Navy 1940–46. *Councils, Public Bodies:* DL, Co. Antrim 1970–96. *Career:* Henry R. Ayton Ltd, Belfast 1946–89, Chairman 1970–89; Chairman: Belfast Savings Bank 1963, Springvale EPS 1964–; Chairman, Harland & Wolff Ltd 1980–81, Director 1970–87; Director, Northern Ireland Airports 1970–85; Senator, Parliament of Northern Ireland 1960–68. *Miscellaneous:* Member, Northern Ireland Economic Council 1974–78; A Belfast Harbour Commissioner 1968–79; A Commissioner of Irish Lights 1983–96, Chairman 1990–92; Member, The Foyle, Carlingford and Irish Lights Commission, North/South Ministerial Council 2000–. CEng; FIMechE. *Special Interests:* Manufacturing Industries, Energy, Maritime Affairs. *Recreations:* Sailing, shooting. *Name, Style and Title:* Raised to the peerage as Baron Cooke of Islandreagh, of Islandreagh in the County of Antrim 1992. *Address:* The Lord Cooke of Islandreagh, OBE, House of Lords, London, SW1A 0PW.

LORD COOKE OF THORNDON   Cross-Bencher

COOKE OF THORNDON (Life Baron), Robin Brunskill Cooke; cr. 1996. Born 9 May 1926. Son of late Hon. Philip Brunskill Cooke, MC, Judge of the Supreme Court of New Zealand, and of Valmai Digby Gore; educated Wanganui Collegiate School, New Zealand; Victoria University College, Wellington, New Zealand (LLM); Clare College, Cambridge; Gonville and Caius College, Cambridge (MA, PhD). Married 1952, Phyllis Annette Miller (3 sons). *Career:* Travelling Scholarship in Law, New Zealand 1950; Fellow, Gonville and Caius College, Cambridge 1952–56; Called to the Bar, Inner Temple 1954; Practised at New Zealand Bar 1955–72; QC 1964; Chairman, Commission of Inquiry into Housing 1970–71; Judge of the Supreme Court 1972; President, Court of Appeal of: Western Samoa 1982, 1994, 1995, Cook Islands 1981, 1982; Appointed a Judge of the Supreme Court of Fiji and sat at its inaugural session in November 1995; Administrator, Government of New Zealand for periods in 1986, 1992, 1993 and 1995; Judge, Court of Appeal of New Zealand 1976–86, President 1986–96; Member, Advisory Board, Centre for Independence of Judges and Lawyers 1989; Commission Member representing New Zealand, International Commission of Jurists 1993–; A Lord of Appeal 1996–; Overseas Judge: Court of Final Appeal of Hong Kong 1997–, Court of Appeal Kiribati 1999–. *Other:* Special Status Member, The American Law Institute 1993–; Life Member, Lawasia; Patron, Wellington Cricket Association, New Zealand. *Awards Granted:* Yorke Prize, University of Cambridge 1954. Hon. Fellow, Gonville and Caius College, Cambridge 1982; Hon. LLD: Victoria University of Wellington 1989, Cambridge University 1990; Hon. DCL, Oxford University 1991. *Miscellaneous:* Hon. Bencher, Inner Temple 1985; Visiting Fellow, All Souls, Oxford 1990; Hon. Fellow, New Zealand Legal Research Foundation 1993–; Distinguished Visiting Fellow, Victoria University of Wellington 1998–. *Honours:* PC 1977; Kt 1977; KBE 1986. *Publications: Portrait of a Profession* (Centennial Book of New Zealand Law Society), 1969 (editor); *The Laws of New Zealand,* Editor-in-Chief 1990–; Sultan Azlan Shah Lecture, Malaysia 1990;

Peter Allan Memorial Lecture, Hong Kong 1994; *Turning Points of the Common Law* (Hamlyn Lectures), 1996; Has contributed many articles in law journals and papers at international law conferences. *Recreations:* Theatre, cricket, *The Times* crossword. *Sportsclubs:* Wellington Golf (NZ). *Clubs:* United Oxford and Cambridge University, Wellington (NZ). *Name, Style and Title:* Raised to the peerage as Baron Cooke of Thorndon, of Wellington in New Zealand and of Cambridge in the County of Cambridgeshire 1996. *Address:* Rt Hon the Lord Cooke of Thorndon, KBE, 4 Homewood Crescent, Karori, Wellington 6005, New Zealand; Lords of Appeal Corridor, House of Lords, London, SW1A 0PW *E-Mail:* ddensem@attglobal.net.

LORD COPE OF BERKELEY — Conservative

COPE OF BERKELEY (Life Baron), John Ambrose Cope; cr. 1997. Born 13 May 1937. Son of late George Cope, MC, FRIBA; educated Oakham School, Rutland. Married March 29, 1969, Djemila Payne (2 daughters).*Armed Forces:* National Service (Commissioned RA) 1955–57, subsequently TA. *Career:* Chartered Accountant; Worked for the Conservative Party, Westminster 1965–70. *House of Commons:* Contested Woolwich East 1970; MP (Conservative) for Gloucestershire South February 1974–83 and for Northavon 1983–97; Minister of State for: Employment with special responsibility for Small Firms 1987–89, Northern Ireland Office 1989–90; Paymaster General, HM Treasury 1992–94. *Whip (Commons):* Government Whip 1979–1981; Government Whip (Lord Commissioner to the Treasury) 1981–83; Deputy Chief Whip (Treasurer, Her Majesty's Household) 1983–87.*Spokesman:* Opposition Spokesman on: Northern Ireland 1997–, the Home Office 1998–. *International Bodies (General):* Member, UK Parliamentary Delegation to Council of Europe and Western European Union 1995–97. *Party Groups (General):* Conservative Party: Deputy Chairman 1990–92, Hon. Joint Treasurer 1991–92. *Other:* Commissioner, Royal Hospital Chelsea 1992–94; Deputy Chairman, Small Business Bureau; Patron, Friends of Spafford Children's Centre of Jerusalem. *Trusts, etc:* Patron, The Vigilant Trust. *Honours:* PC 1988; Kt 1991. FCA. *Clubs:* Carlton, Beefsteak, Tudor House (Chipping Sodbury). *Name, Style and Title:* Raised to the peerage as Baron Cope of Berkeley, of Berkeley in the County of Gloucestershire 1997. *Address:* Rt Hon the Lord Cope of Berkeley, House of Lords, London, SW1A 0PW *E-Mail:* copej@parliament.uk.

EARL OF COURTOWN — Conservative

COURTOWN (9th Earl of, I), James Patrick Montagu Burgoyne Winthrop Stopford; cr. 1762; Viscount Stopford; 9th Baron Courtown (I) 1758; 8th Baron Saltersford (GB) 1796. Born 19 March 1954. Son of 8th Earl, OBE, TD. Succeeded his father 1975. Sits as Baron Saltersford; educated Eton; Berkshire College of Agriculture; Royal Agricultural College, Cirencester. Married July 6, 1985, Elisabeth Dunnett (1 son 1 daughter). *Career:* Land Agent: Bruton Knowles, Gloucester 1987–90, John German, Shrewsbury 1990–93.*House of Lords:* An elected hereditary peer 1999–. *Whip:* Government Whip 1999–; Opposition Whip 1997–2000.*Spokesman:* Former Government Spokesman for the Home Office, Scotland and Transport. *Select Committees:* Member, Select Committee on Bodmin Moor Commons Bill 1994. ARICS.*Special Interests:* Agriculture, Environment, Property. *Recreations:* Fishing, shooting, skiing. *Address:* The Earl of Courtown, House of Lords, London, SW1A 0PW.

LORD COWDREY OF TONBRIDGE
Conservative

COWDREY OF TONBRIDGE (Life Baron), Michael Colin Cowdrey; cr. 1997. Born 24 December 1932. Son of Ernest and Kathleen Cowdrey; educated Tonbridge; Brasenose College, Oxford. Married 1st, 1956, Penelope Susan Chiesman (3 sons 1 daughter) (marriage dissolved 1985); married 2nd, 1985, Lady Herries of Terregles, daughter of 16th Duke of Norfolk, KG. *Armed Forces:* RAF, National Service. *Career:* A cricketer; 117 appearances for England 1954–75, Captain on 23 occasions, 11 Overseas Tours, 107 centuries in first-class cricket, of which 22 were Test centuries, on retirement in 1975, held record for most runs and most catches in Test matches; Chairman: International Cricket Conference 1986–87, International Cricket Council 1989–93; Director, Bilton plc; Consultant, Barclays Bank plc. Hon. Fellow, Durham University. *Trusts, etc:* Member, Council of Winston Churchill Memorial Trust 1969–88. *Honours:* CBE 1972; Kt 1992. Freeman, City of London 1962. Master, Skinners' Company 1985. *Publications: Cricket Today,* 1961; *Time for Reflection,* 1962; *Tackle Cricket This Way, 1969;* The Incomparable Game, 1970; MCC: The Autobiography of a Cricketer, 1976. *Recreations:* Golf. *Sportsclubs:* President, Lords Taverners; West Sussex Golf Club, Kent County Cricket Club, I Zingari. *Clubs:* MCC, Boodle's, Royal and Ancient Golf. *Name, Style and Title:* Raised to the peerage as Baron Cowdrey of Tonbridge, of Tonbridge in the County of Kent 1997. *Address:* The Lord Cowdrey of Tonbridge, CBE, Angmering Park, Littlehampton, West Sussex, BN16 4EX *Tel:* 01903 871423.

BARONESS COX
Conservative

COX (Life Baroness), Caroline Anne Cox; cr. 1983. Born 6 July 1937. Daughter of late Robert John McNeill Love, FRCS, FACS, and late Dorothy Ida Borland; educated Channing School, Highgate, London; London University (external student, (BSc(Soc), MSc(Econ); London Hospital (SRN). Married January 10, 1959, Dr Murray Newall Cox (died 1997), son of late Rev. Roland Cox (2 sons 1 daughter). *Career:* Staff Nurse, Edgware General Hospital 1960; Polytechnic of North London: Lecturer, Senior Lecturer and Principal Lecturer, 1969–74, Head, Department of Sociology 1975–77; Director, Nursing Education Research Unit, Chelsea College, London University 1977–84; Fellow, Royal College of Nursing, Vice-President, 1990–. *Chancellor:* Chancellor, Bournemouth University 1992–. *House of Lords:* A Deputy Speaker of the House of Lords 1986–; A Deputy Chairman of Committees 1986–. *Whip:* A Baroness in Waiting (Government Whip) April-August 1985. *Other:* Chairman, Parental Alliance for Choice in Education; Council of Management, St Christopher's Hospice 1986–92; Standing Conference on Women's Organisations, Institute of Administrative Management; Vice-President, Girl Guides Association; Patron: Medical Aid for Poland Fund, Physicians for Human Rights, UK; Non-executive Director: Andrei Sakarov Foundation; Board of Management/President, Christian Solidarity Worldwide. *Awards Granted:* Wilberforce Award 1995. 12 honorary doctorates and fellowships. *Trusts, etc:* President, Tushinskaya Children's Hospital Trust; Trustee: MERLIN (Medical Emergency Relief International), Siberian Medical University, The Nuffield Trust, Lambeth Health Care Trust, The Trusthouse Charitable Foundation. *Honours:* Commander Cross of the Order of Merit of the Republic of Poland 1990. SRN; FRCN; Hon. FRCS 1997. *Publications:* Former Co-editor, International Journal of Nursing Studies; Author of numerous publications on education and health care, including: *A Sociology of Medical Practice,* (edited jointly) 1975; *The Right to Learn,* 1982; *Sociology: A Guide for Nurses, Midwives and Health Visitors,* 1983; Editor, *Trajectories of Despair: Misdiagnosis and Maltreatment of Soviet Orphans,* 1991; Co-author with John Eibner (CSI): *Ethnic Cleansing in Progress: War in Nagorno Karabakh,* 1993; *Made to Care: The Case for Residential and Village Communities for People with a Mental Handicap,* (jointly) 1995; Co-author *Remorse: The Most Dreadful Sentiment* in *Remorse and Reparation,* Ed. Murray Cox, 1998. *Special Interests:* Human Rights, Humanitarian Aid, Education, Health, Nursing. *Recreations:* Squash, campanology, hill walking. *Sportsclubs:* Axis Squash, Northwood; Cumberland Lawn Tennis. *Clubs:* Royal Over-Seas League. *Name, Style and Title:* Raised to the peerage as Baroness Cox, of Queensbury in Greater London 1983. *Address:* The Baroness Cox, House of Lords, London, SW1A 0PW *Tel:* 020 8204 7336 *Fax:* 020 8204 5661 *E-Mail:* cox@ertnet.demon.co.uk.

LORD CRAIG OF RADLEY

CRAIG OF RADLEY (Life Baron), David Brownrigg Craig; cr. 1991. Born 17 September 1929. Son of late Major Francis Brownrigg Craig and Hannah Olivia (Olive) Craig; educated Radley College; Lincoln College, Oxford (BA pure maths 1951, MA). Married March 12, 1955, June, daughter of late Charles James Derenburg (1 son 1 daughter). *Armed Forces:* Commissioned into RAF 1951; Served as Qualified Flying Instructor on Meteors and as Hunter Pilot in Fighter Command; CO, No. 35 Squadron 1963–65; Military Assistant to Chief of the Defence Staff 1965–68; Group Captain 1968; Station CO, RAF College, Cranwell 1968–70; ADC to HM The Queen 1969–71; Director, Plans and Operations, HQ Far East Command 1970–71; OC, RAF Akrotiri (Cyprus) 1972–73; Assistant Chief of Air Staff (Operations) Ministry of Defence 1975–78; Air Officer Commanding No 1 Group 1978–80; Vice-Chief of Air Staff 1980–82; Air Officer Commanding-in-Chief Strike Command and Commander-in-Chief UK Air Forces 1982–85; Chief of the Air Staff 1985–88; Air ADC to HM The Queen 1985–88; Marshal of the Royal Air Force 1988; Chief of the Defence Staff 1988–91. *House of Lords:* Convenor of the Cross-Bench Peers December 1999–. *Select Committees:* Member: Select Committee on Science and Technology 1993–98, House of Lords Offices Committee 2000–, Finance and Staff Sub-Committee, House of Lords Offices Committee 2000–, Administration and Works Sub-Committee 2000–. Hon. Fellow, Lincoln College, Oxford 1984; Hon. DSc, Cranfield Institute of Technology 1988. *Honours:* OBE (Mil) 1967; CB 1978; KCB 1981; GCB (Mil) 1984. FRAeS. *Special Interests:* Defence. *Recreations:* Golf, fishing, shooting, woodwork. *Clubs:* Royal Air Force. *Name, Style and Title:* Raised to the peerage as Baron Craig of Radley, of Helhoughton in the County of Norfolk 1991. *Address:* Marshal of the Royal Air Force The Lord Craig of Radley, GCB (Mil), OBE (Mil), House of Lords, London, SW1A 0PW *E-Mail:* craigd@parliament.uk.

VISCOUNT CRAIGAVON

CRAIGAVON (3rd Viscount, UK), Janric Fraser Craig; cr. 1927; 3rd Bt of Craigavon (UK) 1918. Born 9 June 1944. Son of 2nd Viscount. Succeeded his father 1974; educated Eton; London University (BA, BSc). *Career:* A Chartered Accountant. *House of Lords:* An elected hereditary peer 1999–. *Select Committees:* Member, Hybrid Instruments Committee 1993–97, 1999–. *Other:* Member, Executive Committee Anglo-Austrian Society. *Trusts, etc:* Former Trustee now Advisor, Progress Educational Trust. *Honours:* Commander of the Order of the Lion (Finland) 1998; Commander of the Royal Order of the Polar Star (Sweden) 1999. *Address:* The Viscount Craigavon, 54 Westminster Mansions, 1 Little Smith Street, London, SW1P 3DQ *Tel:* 020 7222 1949.

VISCOUNT CRANBORNE

CRANBORNE (Viscount, E), Robert Michael James Gascoyne-Cecil; cr. 1604; (Life) Baron Gascoyne-Cecil 1999. Born 30 September 1946. Son of 6th Marquess of Salisbury, DL; educated Eton; Christ Church, Oxford. Married 1970, Hannah Ann, daughter of late Lieutenant-Colonel William Joseph Stirling (2 sons 3 daughters). *Councils, Public Bodies:* DL, Dorset 1987–. *House of Commons:* MP (Conservative) for Dorset South 1979–87. *House of Lords:* Parliamentary Under-Secretary of State for Defence, Ministry of Defence 1992–94; Lord Privy Seal and Leader of the House of Lords 1994–97; Member, Shadow Cabinet 1997–98; Leader of the Opposition in the House of Lords 1997–98. *Spokesman:* An Opposition Spokesman on the Public Service 1997–98. *Select Committees:* Member, Ecclesiastical Committee 2000–. *Miscellaneous:* Holds courtesy title of Viscount Cranborne (E) 1604; Heir to marquessate; Summoned to the Upper House in his father's barony of Cecil, of Essendon in the County of Rutland, by a Writ in Acceleration 1992. *Honours:* PC 1994. *Clubs:* White's, Pratt's, Beefsteak. *Name, Style and Title:* Created a life peer as Baron Gascoyne-Cecil, of Essendon in the County of Rutland 1999. *Address:* Rt Hon the Viscount Cranborne, DL, House of Lords, London, SW1A 0PW.

LORD CRATHORNE   Conservative

CRATHORNE (2nd Baron, UK), (Charles) James Dugdale; cr. 1959; 2nd Bt of Crathorne (UK) 1945. Born 12 September 1939. Son of 1st Baron, PC, TD. Succeeded his father 1977; educated Eton; Trinity College, Cambridge. Married January 8, 1970, Sylvia Mary, daughter of late Brigadier Arthur Montgomery, OBE, TD (1 son 2 daughters). *Councils, Public Bodies:* DL, County of Cleveland 1983–96; DL, County of North Yorkshire 1996–98, Lord Lieutenant 1999–; JP 1999–. *Career:* Impressionist Painting department, Sotheby & Co. 1963–66; Assistant to President, Parke-Bernet Galleries, New York 1966–69; Independent Fine Art Consultancy, James Dugdale & Associates 1969–; Lecture tours to the USA 1969–; Director, Blakeney Hotels Ltd 1979–96; Lecture series *Aspects of England*, in Metropolitan Museum, New York 1981; Australian Bicentennial Lecture Tour 1988; Director: Woodhouse Securities Ltd 1988–99, Cliveden plc 1996–99, Cliveden Ltd 1999–. *House of Lords:* An elected hereditary peer 1999–. *Party Groups (General):* Member, Conservative Advisory Group on Arts and Heritage 1988–99. *Other:* Council, RSA 1982–88; Editorial Board of the House Magazine 1983–; Member, University Court of the University of Leeds 1985–97; Executive Committee, Georgian Group 1985–, Chairman 1990–99; Governor, Queen Margarets School York Ltd. 1986–99; President: Yarm Civic Society 1987–, Cleveland Family History Society 1988–, Cleveland Sea Cadets 1988–; Hambleton District of CPRE 1988–; Patron, Cleveland Community Foundation 1990–; Deputy Chairman, Joint Committee of National Amenity Societies 1993–96, Chairman 1996–99; President, Cleveland and North Yorkshire Magistrates' Association 1997–; Vice-President: The Public Monuments and Sculpture Association 1997–, Yorkshire and Humberside TAVRA 1999–; President, North Yorkshire County Scout Council 1999–; Patron, British Red Cross North Yorkshire Branch 1999–. *Trusts, etc:* Trustee, Georgian Theatre Royal, Richmond, Yorkshire 1970–; Trustee, Captain Cook Birthplace Museum Trust 1978–, Chairman 1993–; Yorkshire Regional Committee, National Trust 1988–94; Vice-President, Cleveland Wildlife Trust 1989–; Patron, Attingham Trust for the Study of the British Country House 1990–; Trustee, National Heritage Memorial Fund 1992–95. *Honours:* KStJ 1999. FRSA 1972. *Publications:* Articles in *The Connoisseur* and *Apollo*; *Edouard Vuillard*, 1967; *Cliveden, the Place and the People*, 1995; *The Royal Crescent Book of Bath*, 1998; Co-Author: *Tennant's Stalk*, 1973; *A Present from Crathorne*, 1989; Co-Photographer *Parliament in Pictures*, 1999. *Special Interests:* Visual and Performing Arts, Country Houses. *Recreations:* Photography, jazz, collecting, country pursuits, travel with the family. *Address:* The Lord Crathorne, Crathorne House, Yarm, North Yorkshire, TS15 0AT *Tel:* 01642 700431 *Fax:* 01642 700632; House of Lords, London, SW1A 0PW *Tel:* 020 7219 5224 *Fax:* 020 7219 2772.

EARL OF CRAWFORD AND BALCARRES   Conservative

CRAWFORD (29th Earl of, S), cr. 1398, AND BALCARRES (12th Earl of, S), cr. 1651; Robert Alexander Lindsay; Lord Lindsay of Crawford before 1143. Lord Lindsay (S) 1633; Lord Balniel (S) 1651; 5th Baron Wigan (UK) 1826; (Life) Baron Balniel 1974. Born 5 March 1927. Son of 28th Earl, KT, GBE. Succeeded his father 1975; educated Eton; Trinity College, Cambridge. Married 1949, Ruth Beatrice, daughter of Leo Meyer-Bechtler (2 sons 2 daughters). *Armed Forces:* Served with Grenadier Guards 1945–48. *Councils, Public Bodies:* DL, Fife. *Career:* A Director, National Westminster Bank 1975–89; Vice-Chairman, Sun Alliance & London Insurance 1975–91; First Commissioner of the Crown Estate 1980–85; Chairman, Royal Commission on the Ancient and Historical Monuments of Scotland 1985–95; Chairman, Board of the National Library of Scotland 1991–2000; Lord Chamberlain to HM Queen Elizabeth the Queen Mother 1992–. *House of Commons:* MP (Conservative) for: Hertford 1955–74, Welwyn and Hatfield March-October 1974; PPS: to Financial Secretary to The Treasury 1955–56, to Minister of Housing and Local Government 1956–59; Minister of State for Defence 1970–72, Minister of State, Foreign and Commonwealth Affairs 1972–74. *Spokesman (Commons):* Principal Opposition Front Bench Spokesman on Health and Social Security 1967–70. *Miscellaneous:* Premier Earl of Scotland on Union Roll; Head of the House of Lindsay. *Honours:* PC 1972; KT 1996. *Name, Style and Title:* Created a life peer as Baron Balniel, of Pitcorthie in the County of Fife 1974. *Address:* Rt Hon the Earl of Crawford and Balcarres, KT, DL, House of Lords, London, SW1A 0PW.

BARONESS CRAWLEY   Labour

CRAWLEY (Life Baroness), Christine Mary Crawley; cr. 1998. Born 9 January 1950; educated Notre Dame Catholic Secondary Girls School, Plymouth; Digby Stuart Training College, Roehampton. Married (1 son 2 daughters). *Trades Union:* Member: MSF, UNISON. *Councils, Public Bodies:* Former Town and District Councillor in South Oxfordshire. *Career:* Former Teacher and Youth Theatre Leader; MEP for Birmingham East 1984–99, Chair: Women's National Commission, West Midlands Regional Cultural Consortium. *Select Committees:* Member: European Select Committee, Europan Communities Committee Sub-Committee A (Economic and Financial Affairs, Trade and External Relations) 2000–. *Party Groups (General):* Member: Fabian Society, Co-operative Party, Labour Movement in Europe; Deputy Leader, EP Labour Party in charge of links with the Labour Government in UK 1994–98; Member, Socialist Group Bureau in European Parliament. *Other:* Member, Amnesty International. *Miscellaneous:* Contested Staffordshire South East 1983 General Election; Chair, Regional Cultural Consortium – West Midlands. Fellow, Royal Society of Arts. *Publications:* Contributions to a number of publications including *Changing States – Labour Agenda for Europe*; Articles on women's rights and equality policy. *Special Interests:* Women's Rights, Equal Opportunities, Economics and Monetary Union, European Union. *Recreations:* Latin American literature, amateur dramatics, attending local football matches in Birmingham. *Name, Style and Title:* Raised to the peerage as Baroness Crawley, of Edgbaston in the County of West Midlands 1998. *Address:* The Baroness Crawley, House of Lords, London, SW1A 0PW *E-Mail:* ccrawley@enterprise.net.

LORD CRICKHOWELL   Conservative

CRICKHOWELL (Life Baron), Roger Nicholas Edwards; cr. 1987. Born 25 February 1934. Son of late Ralph Edwards, CBE, FSA; educated Westminster School; Trinity College, Cambridge. Married 1963, Ankaret Healing (1 son 2 daughters). *Armed Forces:* National Service, (Second Lieutenant) Royal Welch Fusiliers; Lieutenant, TA. *Career:* Member of Lloyds 1963–; Chairman: ITNET Plc, HTV Group Ltd; Director, Anglesey Mining plc; Former Director: William Brandts Ltd and Associated Companies, A. L. Sturge Holdings Ltd, PA International & Sturge Underwriting Agency Ltd, Associated British Ports Holdings plc, Globtik Tankers Ltd; Chairman: National Rivers Authority Advisory Committee 1988–89, National Rivers Authority 1989–96. *House of Commons:* MP (Conservative) for Pembroke 1970–87; Secretary of State for Wales, May 1979–87. *Other:* Member, Committee of the AA 1988–98; President: Cardiff University of Wales 1988–98, South East Wales Arts Association 1988–94. Hon. Fellow, Cardiff University of Wales. *Trusts, etc:* Chairman, Cardiff Bay Opera House Trust 1993–97. *Honours:* PC 1979. Member, Fishmongers' Company. *Publications: Opera House Lottery – Zaha Hadid and The Cardiff Bay Project*, 1997; *Westminster, Wales and Water*, 1999. *Special Interests:* Environment, Economic Policy, Urban Policies, Arts. *Clubs:* Brooks's, Cardiff and County (Cardiff). *Name, Style and Title:* Raised to the peerage as Baron Crickhowell, of Pont Esgob in the Black Mountains and County of Powys 1987. *Address:* Rt Hon the Lord Crickhowell, 4 Henning St, London, SW11 3DR; Pont Esgob Mill, Fforest Coalpit, Nr Abergavenny, Gwent, NP7 7LS *E-Mail:* ncrickhowell@cs.com.

LORD CROHAM   Cross-Bencher

CROHAM (Life Baron), Douglas Albert Vivian Allen; cr. 1978. Born 15 December 1917. Son of Albert John Allen (killed in action 1918); educated Wallington County Grammar School for Boys; London School of Economics. Married August 16, 1941, Sybil Eileen (died 1994), daughter of late John Marco Allegro (2 sons 1 daughter). *Trades Union:* Member, First Division Association (FDA). *Armed Forces:* Served Royal Artillery 1940–45. *Career:* Joined Home Civil Service, Board of Trade 1939; Treasury 1948, Assistant Secretary 1949–58; Under-Secretary, Ministry of Health 1958–60; Treasury 1960–64; Third Secretary 1962; Department of Economic Affairs 1964–68, Permanent Secretary 1966–68; Permanent Secretary, Treasury 1968–74; Permanent Secretary, Civil Service Department and Head of Home Civil Service 1974–77; Chairman: British National Oil Corporation 1982–86, Guinness Peat Group plc 1982–87, Trinity Insurance Ltd 1987–92. *Select Committees:* Member, Select Committee on the Public Service 1996–97.

Other: President, Institute for Fiscal Studies 1978–92; Chairman, Anglo-German Foundation 1982–98; President, British Institute of Energy Economics 1986–94; Vice-President, Anglo-German Association; Governor: London School of Economics, Wallington County Grammar School. Hon. DSocSc, Southampton University. *Miscellaneous:* Member, Institute of Directors; Companion, Institute of Management. *Honours:* CB 1963; KCB 1967; GCB 1973. Fellow, Royal Society of Arts. *Special Interests:* Finance, Economic Policy, Energy. *Recreations:* Woodwork, Bridge. *Clubs:* Reform, Civil Service. *Name, Style and Title:* Raised to the peerage as Baron Croham, of the London Borough of Croydon 1978. *Address:* The Lord Croham, GCB, 9 Manor Way, South Croydon, Surrey, CR2 7BT *Tel:* 020 8688 0496.

LORD CUCKNEY   Conservative

CUCKNEY (Life Baron), John (Graham) Cuckney; cr. 1995. Born 12 July 1925. Son of late Air Vice-Marshal E. J. Cuckney, CB, CBE, DSC and Bar, and Lilian, née Williams; educated Shrewsbury; St Andrews University (MA). Married 2nd, 1960, Muriel, daughter of late Walter Scott Boyd. *Armed Forces:* War service with Royal Northumberland Fusiliers, King's African Rifles, followed by attachment to War Office (Civil Assistant General Staff) until 1957. *Career:* Director, Lazard Brothers & Co. 1964–70, 1988–90; Independent Member, Railway Policy Review Committee 1966–67; Chairman, Mersey Docks and Harbour Board 1970–72; Chief Executive (Second Permanent Secretary), Property Services Agency, DoE 1972–74; Senior Crown Agent and Chairman, Crown Agents for Overseas Governments and Administrations 1974–78; Chairman: International Military Services (an MoD company) 1974–85, EDC for Building 1976–80, Port of London Authority 1977–79, Thomas Cook Group Ltd 1978–88; Director, Midland Bank plc 1978–88; Council, British Executive Service Overseas 1981–84; Chairman: Brooke Bond Group plc 1981–84, International Maritime Bureau of International Chamber of Commerce 1981–85, John Brown plc 1983–86, Westland Group 1985–89; Deputy Chairman, TI Group plc 1985–90; Chairman, Royal Insurance Holdings plc 1985–94; Director: Brixton Estate plc 1985–96, SBAC 1986–89; Chairman: 3i Group plc 1987–92, Understanding Industry Trust 1988–91, NEDC Working Party on European Public Purchasing 1990–92; Vice-Chairman, Glaxo Wellcome plc 1990–95; Adviser to the Secretary of State for Social Security on the Maxwell pensions affair and founder Chairman of the Maxwell Pensioners' Trust 1992–95; Controller, ROH Development Land Trust 1993–96; Chairman, The Orion Publishing Group Ltd 1994–97. *Select Committees:* Member, Select Committees on: Science and Technology Sub-Committee II on the Innovation Exploitation Barrier 1996–97, Public Service 1996–97, Monetary Policy of the Bank of England 2000–. *Other:* Governor, Centre for International Briefing, Farnham Castle 1974–84; Elder Brother of Trinity House 1980–; Vice-President, Liverpool School of Tropical Medicine 1985–93. Hon. DSc, Bath 1991; Hon. LLD, St Andrews 1993. *Trusts, etc:* Trustee, RAF Museum 1987–99. *Honours:* Kt 1978. Freeman, City of London 1977. *Special Interests:* City, Economic Policy. *Clubs:* Athenaeum. *Name, Style and Title:* Raised to the peerage as Baron Cuckney, of Millbank in the City of Westminster 1995. *Address:* The Lord Cuckney, House of Lords, London, SW1A 0PW.

BARONESS CUMBERLEGE   Conservative

CUMBERLEGE (Life Baroness), Julia Frances Cumberlege; cr. 1990. Born 27 January 1943. Daughter of late Dr. L. U. Camm; educated Convent of the Sacred Heart, Tunbridge Wells. Married 1961, Patrick Cumberlege (3 sons). *Councils, Public Bodies:* Chairman, Brighton Health Authority 1981–88; Councillor, Lewes District Council 1966–79, Leader 1977–78; Councillor, East Sussex County Council 1974–85, Chairman, Social Services Committee 1979–82; Chairman, South West Thames Regional Health Authority 1988–92; JP, East Sussex 1973–85; DL, East Sussex 1986–; Vice-Lord Lieutenant 1992; Chairman, St George's Medical School Council 2000–. *Career:* Executive Director, MJM Healthcare Solutions 1997–. *House of Lords:* Joint Parliamentary Under-Secretary of State, Department of Health 1992–97. *Spokesman:* An Opposition Spokeswoman on Health 1997. *Other:* Vice-President: Royal College of Nursing 1989–, Pre-School Playgroups Association 1989–91; Council Member: Brighton Polytechnic 1987–89, St George's Medical School 1988–92; Governor, Chailey Heritage School and Hospital 1982–88, Patron 1996–;

President: Age Concern Sussex 1993–, Sussex Care for the Carers 1996–. *DUniv:* Surrey University 1990, Brighton University 1994. *Trusts, etc:* Trustee, Chailey Heritage, Cancer Link. *Miscellaneous:* Council Member, National Association of Health Authorities 1982–88, Vice-Chairman 1984–87, Chairman 1987–88; Member, Press Council 1984–90; Chairman, Review of Community Nursing for England 1985; Member: DHSS Expert Advisory Group on AIDS 1987–89, NHS Policy Board for England 1989–; Council Member, UK Central Council for Nursing, Midwifery and Health Visiting 1989–92; Chairman, Review of Maternity Services for England 1993. *Honours:* CBE 1985. Fellow, Royal Society of Arts 1989. *Special Interests:* Local Government, Health Service, Media, Education. *Recreations:* Other people's gardens, bicycling. *Clubs:* Royal Society of Medicine. *Name, Style and Title:* Raised to the peerage as Baroness Cumberlege, of Newick in the County of East Sussex 1990.*Address:* The Baroness Cumberlege, CBE, DL, Snells Cottage, The Green, Newick, Lewes, East Sussex, BN8 4LA *Tel:* 01825 722154 *E-Mail:* cumberlegej@parliament.uk.

LORD CURRIE OF MARYLEBONE   Labour

CURRIE OF MARYLEBONE (Life Baron), David Anthony Currie; cr. 1996. Born 9 December 1946. Son of late Kennedy Currie and of Marjorie Currie; educated Battersea Grammar School; Manchester University (BSc Maths); Birmingham University (MSoc Sci Econs); London University (PhD Economics). Married 1st, 1975, Shaziye Gazioglu (2 sons) (marriage dissolved 1992); married 2nd, 1995, Angela Mary Piers Dumas (1 son). *Career:* Economist, Hoare Govett 1971–72; Lecturer, Reader and Professor of Economics, Queen Mary College, London University 1972–88; Visiting Scholar, International Monetary Fund 1987; London Business School: Professor of Economics 1988–, Research Dean 1989–92, Governor 1989–95, Deputy Principal 1992–95, Deputy Dean, External Relations 1999–; Director, Joseph Rowntree Reform Trust 1991–; Director, International Schools of Business Management 1992–95; Visiting Professor, European University Institute 1992–95; Director, Charter 88 1994–98; Director, Solar Energy Group Holdings 1999–; Member, Terra Firma, Advisory Board of Nomura Private Finance Group 2000–. *International Bodies (General):* Council Member of Britain in Europe and the European Policy Forum. *Other:* Member, Royal Economic Society. Honorary fellowship and doctorate. *Trusts, etc:* Trustee and Director, New Policy Network Foundation. *Miscellaneous:* Research Fellow, Centre for Economic Policy Research 1983–; Houblon-Norman Resident Fellow, Bank of England 1985–86; Member: Retail Price Index Advisory Committee 1992–95, Treasury's Panel of Independent Forecasters 1992–95, Management Board OFGEM 1999–. FRSA. *Publications: Advances in Monetary Economics,* 1985; Co-author: *The Operation and Regulation of Financial Markets,* 1986, *Macroeconomic Interactions Between North and South,* 1988, *Rules, Reputation and Macroeconomic Policy Co-ordination,* 1993, *EMUs Problems in the Transition to a Single European Currency,* 1995, *North-South Linkages and International Macroeconomic Policy,* 1995; *The Pros and Cons of EMU,* 1997; *Will the Euro Work?,* 1998; Articles in journals. *Special Interests:* Economic Policy, Education, Constitutional Reform. *Recreations:* Music, literature, swimming. *Name, Style and Title:* Raised to the peerage as Baron Currie of Marylebone, of Marylebone in the City of Westminster 1996. *Address:* Professor the Lord Currie of Marylebone, London Business School, Sussex Place, London, NW1 4SA *Tel:* 020 7262 5050 *E-Mail:* dcurrie@london.edu.

D

LORD DACRE OF GLANTON — Conservative

DACRE OF GLANTON (Life Baron), Hugh Redwald Trevor-Roper; cr. 1979. Born 15 January 1914. Son of late Dr Bertie W. E. Trevor-Roper; educated Charterhouse School; Christ Church, Oxford. Married October 4, 1954, Lady Alexandra Howard-Johnston (died 1997), daughter of Field Marshal 1st Earl Haig, KT, GCB, OM. *Armed Forces:* Served in Army Intelligence Corps (Major) 1939–45. *Career:* Student of Christ Church, Oxford 1946–57; Regius Professor of Modern History, Oxford 1957–80; Director, Times Newspapers Ltd 1974–88; Master of Peterhouse, Cambridge 1980–87. *Miscellaneous:* Junior Research Fellow, Merton College, Oxford 1937. *Publications:* Several works, including: *Archbishop Laud*; *The Last Days of Hitler*; *The Rise of Christian Europe*; *Religion, The Reformation and Social Change*; *Princes and Artists*; *A Hidden Life*; *Renaissance Essays*; *Catholics, Anglicans and Puritans*; *From Counter-Reformation to Glorious Revolution*. *Clubs:* Beefsteak, Garrick. *Name, Style and Title:* Raised to the peerage as Baron Dacre of Glanton, of Glanton in the County of Northumberland 1979. *Address:* The Lord Dacre of Glanton, The Old Rectory, Didcot, Oxon, OX11 7EB.

LORD DAHRENDORF — Liberal Democrat

DAHRENDORF (Life Baron), Ralf Dahrendorf; cr. 1993. Born 1 May 1929. Son of late Gustav Dahrendorf and of Lina Dahrendorf; educated in Hamburg and Berlin; Postgraduate studies at London School of Economics 1952–54 (Leverhulme Research Scholar 1953–54, PhD 1956). Married 1980, Mrs Ellen de Kadt, née Krug. *Career:* Fellow at Center for Advanced Study in the Behavioural Sciences, Palo Alto, USA 1957–58; Professor of Sociology: Hamburg 1957–60, Tubingen 1960–64, Konstanz 1966–69; Parliamentary Secretary of State, Federal German Ministry of Foreign Affairs 1969–70; Member, EEC, Brussels 1970–74; Director, London School of Economics 1974–84, Governor 1986–; Professor of Social Science, Konstanz University 1984–86; Non-Exec Director, Glaxo Holdings plc 1984–92; Visiting Professor at several European and North American Universities; Visiting Scholar, Russell Sage Foundation, New York 1986–87; Warden, St Antony's College, Oxford 1987–97; Chairman, Newspaper Publishing plc 1992–93; Non-Executive Director, Bank Gesellschaft Berlin 1996–. *Select Committees:* Member, Select Committee on Delegated Powers and Deregulation 1997–; Co-opted Member, Select Committee on European Communities Sub-Committee A (Economic and Financial Affairs, Trade and External Relations) 1997–99. *Other:* Chairman, Council for Charitable Support 1995–. Hon. Fellow, London School of Economics 1970; Fellow, St Antony's College, Oxford 1976; Holder of twenty-five Honorary Degrees from Universities in Great Britain, Ireland, Belgium, Italy, Malta, the United States, Canada, Argentina, Israel and France and Bulgaria. *Trusts, etc:* Trustee: Ford Foundation 1976–88, Charities Aid Foundation. *Miscellaneous:* Adopted British nationality 1988; Member: Hansard Society Commission on Electoral Reform 1975–76, Royal Commission on Legal Services 1976–79, Committee to Review Functioning of Financial Institutions 1977–80. *Honours:* Holder of decorations from Senegal, Germany, Luxembourg, Austria, Belgium and Spain; KBE 1982. FBA 1977; FRSA 1977; Hon. FRCS 1982. Freeman, City of London 1998. *Publications:* Several works on philosophy, sociology and politics, including:*Marx in Perspective*, 1953; *Class and Class Conflict*, 1959; *Society and Democracy in Germany*, 1966; *Essays on the Theory of Society*, 1968; *The New Liberty*, 1975; *On Britain*, 1982; *Law and Order*, 1985; *The Modern Social Conflict*, 1988; *Reflections on the Revolution in Europe*, 1990; *A History of the London School of Economics and Political Science 1895–1995*, 1995; *After 1989*, 1997; many of which have been translated into several European and Asian languages. *Clubs:* Reform, Garrick. *Name, Style and Title:* Raised to the peerage as Baron Dahrendorf, of Clare Market in the City of Westminster 1993. *Address:* The Lord Dahrendorf, KBE, FBA, Bankgesellschaft Berlin (UK) plc, 1 Crown Court, Cheapside, London, EC2V 6JP *Tel:* 020 7572 6100 *Fax:* 020 7572 6256.

BARONESS DARCY DE KNAYTH   Cross-Bencher

DARCY DE KNAYTH (Baroness, 18th in line, E), Davina Marcia Ingrams; cr. 1332. Born 10 July 1938. Daughter of 17th Baron (Viscount Clive), son of 4th Earl of Powis. Succeeded her father, who was killed in action, March 1943; educated St. Mary's School, Wantage, Oxfordshire; Italy; Sorbonne, Paris. Married 1960, Rupert George Ingrams (died 1964), son of late Leonard Ingrams (1 son 2 daughters). *House of Lords:* An elected hereditary peer 1999–. *Select Committees:* Member: House of Lords European Committees Sub-Committee C 1985–88, House of Lords Select Committee on murder and life imprisonment 1988–89, Refreshment Sub-Committee, House of Lords Offices Committee 2000–. *Other:* President, SKILL (National Bureau for Students with Disabilities); Member, Joint Committee on Mobility for Disabled People (JCMDP); Member, IPSEA (Independent Panel on Special Education Advice); Council Member, Grange Centre for People with Disabilities; President, Windsor and Maidenhead District Sports Association for Disabled People. *Miscellaneous:* Former Member, Independent Broadcasting Authority General Advisory Council. *Honours:* DBE 1996. *Special Interests:* Disability. *Recreations:* Theatre, cinema. *Sportsclubs:* Stoke Paraplegic Athletics, Windsor, Ascot, Maidenhead and District Sports Association for Disabled People. *Address:* The Baroness Darcy de Knayth, DBE, Camley Corner, Stubbings, Maidenhead, Berkshire, SL6 6QW *Tel:* 01628 822935.

BARONESS DAVID   Labour

DAVID (Life Baroness), Nora Ratcliff David; cr. 1978. Born 23 September 1913. Daughter of late George Blockley Blakesley, JP; educated Ashby-De-La-Zouch Girls' Grammar School; St. Felix School, Southwold; Newnham College, Cambridge (MA 1935). Married August 18, 1935, Richard William David, CBE (died 1993) (2 sons 2 daughters). *Councils, Public Bodies:* Councillor: Cambridge City Council 1964–67, 1968–74, Cambridgeshire County Council 1974–78; Member of Board, Peterborough Development Corporation 1976–78; JP, Cambridge City 1965–. *Whip:* Baroness-in-Waiting (Government Whip) November 1978–79; Opposition Whip 1979–85; Opposition Deputy Chief Whip 1983–87. *Spokesman:* Spokesman for Education 1979–85; Opposition Spokesman on: the Environment 1985–87, Education 1987–97. *Select Committees:* Member: Select Committee on European Communities 1990–94, Sub-Committee on Social and Consumer Affairs 1989–94, Sub-Committee on Agriculture 1993–97, Administration and Works Committee, Refreshment Committee. *International Bodies (General):* Member: CPA, IPU. Hon. Fellow: Newnham College, Cambridge 1986, Anglia Polytechnic University 1989; Hon. DLitt, Staffordshire University 1995. *Special Interests:* Education, Environment, Home Affairs, Children. *Recreations:* Walking, swimming, theatre, travel. *Name, Style and Title:* Raised to the peerage as Baroness David, of Romsey in the City of Cambridge 1978. *Address:* The Baroness David, 50 Highsett, Cambridge, CB2 1NZ *Tel:* 01223 350376; Cove, New Polzeath, Cornwall, PL27 6UF *Tel:* 01208 863310; House of Lords, London, SW1A 0PW *Tel:* House of Lords 020 7219 3159.

LORD DAVIES OF COITY   Labour

DAVIES OF COITY (Life Baron), (David) Garfield Davies; cr. 1997. Born 24 June 1935. Son of late David and Lizzie Davies; educated Heolgam Secondary Modern School; Bridgend Technical College (part-time). Married 1960, Marian Jones (4 daughters). *Trades Union:* Member, TUC General Council 1986–97, Chairman, International Committee 1992–94; Spokesperson on International Affairs 1994–97; Member: Executive Board, International Confederation of Free Trade Unions 1992–97, Executive Committee, European Trade Union Confederation 1992–97; Governor, Birmingham College of Food, Tourism and Creative Studies 1995–99. *Armed Forces:* RAF 1956–58. *Councils, Public Bodies:* Parish Councillor 1963–69; Councillor, Penybont RDC 1966–69; JP, Ipswich 1972–78. *Career:* Junior Operative, Electrial Apprentice and Electrician, British Steel Corporation, Port Talbot 1950–69; USDAW: Area Organiser, Ipswich 1969–73, Deputy Division Officer,

London/Ipswich 1973–78, National Officer, Manchester 1978–85, General Secretary 1986–97. *International Bodies (General):* Member: IPU, CPU, British-American Parliamentary Group. *Miscellaneous:* Member, Employment Appeal Tribunal. *Honours:* CBE 1996. *Special Interests:* Health Service, Education, Industrial Relations. *Recreations:* Most sport, swimming, jogging, family, reading, golf. *Sportsclubs:* Lancashire CCC, Stockport County AFC. *Clubs:* Reform. *Name, Style and Title:* Raised to the peerage as Baron Davies of Coity, of Penybont in the County of Mid Glamorgan 1997. *Address:* The Lord Davies of Coity, CBE, 64 Dairyground Road, Bramhall, Stockport, Cheshire, SK7 2QW *Tel:* 0161–439 9548.

LORD DAVIES OF OLDHAM   Labour

DAVIES OF OLDHAM (Life Baron), Bryan Davies; cr. 1997. Born 9 November 1939. Son of late George and Beryl Davies; educated Redditch High School, Worcs; University College, London (BA History); Institute of Education (PGCE Education (Distinction); London School of Economics (BSc Economics). Married 1963, Monica Shearing (2 sons 1 daughter). *Trades Union:* Divisional Executive Officer, NATFHE 1967–74; Member, TGWU 1979–. *Career:* Teacher, Latymer School 1962–65; Lecturer, Middlesex Polytechnic, Enfield 1965–74; Secretary, Parliamentary Labour Party and Shadow Cabinet 1979–92. *House of Commons:* Contested Norfolk Central 1966 and Newport West 1983; MP (Labour) for Enfield North 1974–1979 and for Oldham Central and Royton 1992–97. *Whip (Commons):* Assistant Government Whip 1978–79. *Spokesman (Commons):* Opposition Spokesman on: Education 1993–95, Education and Employment 1995–97. *Backbench Committees:* Member, Education, Transport and Economic Affairs Committees 1997–. *Other:* President, Royal Society for the Prevention of Accidents (RoSPA) 1999–. Honorary Doctorate, Middlesex University 1996. *Miscellaneous:* Member, Medical Research Council 1977–79; Chairman, Further Education Funding Council 1998–. *Special Interests:* Economic Policy, Employment, Training, Education, Arts, Transport. *Recreations:* Sport, literature. *Name, Style and Title:* Raised to the peerage as Baron Davies of Oldham, of Broxbourne in the County of Hertfordshire 1997. *Address:* The Lord Davies of Oldham, House of Lords, London, SW1A 0PW *Tel:* 020 7219 4103 *Fax:* 01992 300166.

LORD DEAN OF HARPTREE   Conservative

DEAN OF HARPTREE (Life Baron), (Arthur) Paul Dean; cr. 1993. Born 14 September 1924. Son of late Arthur Percival Dean and of Jessie Margaret Dean; educated Ellesmere College, Shropshire; Exeter College, Oxford (MA, BLitt). Married 1st, 1957, Doris Ellen Webb (died 1979), married 2nd, April 8, 1980, Mrs Peggy Parker. *Armed Forces:* Served War of 1939–45, Captain, Welsh Guards, ADC to Commander, 1st British Corps in Germany. *Career:* Farmer 1950–56; Resident Tutor, Swinton Conservative College 1957; Conservative Research Department 1957–64, Assistant Director 1962–64; Member, Commonwealth Parliamentary Association, UK Branch Executive Committee 1975–92; Former Director: Charterhouse Pensions Ltd, Watney, Mann and Truman Holdings Ltd, Grand Metropolitan Brewing, Foods, Leisure and Retailing Ltd. *House of Commons:* Contested (Conservative) Pontefract 1962 By-Election; MP (Conservative): Somerset North 1964–83, Woodspring 1983–92; Parliamentary Under-Secretary of State, Department of Health and Social Security 1970–74; Deputy Chairman of Ways and Means and Deputy Speaker 1982–92. *Spokesman (Commons):* A Front Bench Spokesman on Health and Social Security 1969–70. *House of Lords:* A Deputy Speaker of the House of Lords 1995–; A Deputy Chairman of Committees 1997–. *Select Committees:* Member, Select Committees on: Procedure 1995, Delegated Legislation 1995–97, Delegated Powers and Deregulation 1997–. *Party Groups:* Member Executive Committee, Association of Conservative Peers 1995–. *Honours:* Kt 1985; PC 1991. *Special Interests:* Constitutional Affairs, Health, Social Security. *Recreations:* Fishing, walking, gardening. *Clubs:* United Oxford and Cambridge University. *Name, Style and Title:* Raised to the peerage as Baron Dean of Harptree, of Wedmore in the County of Somerset 1993. *Address:* Rt Hon the Lord Dean of Harptree, Archer's Wyck, Knightcott, Banwell, Weston-Super-Mare, BS29 6HS; House of Lords, London, SW1A 0PW.

BARONESS DEAN OF THORNTON-LE-FYLDE   Labour

DEAN OF THORNTON-LE-FYLDE (Life Baroness), Brenda McDowall; cr. 1993. Born 29 April 1943. Daughter of Hugh and Lillian Dean; educated St Andrew's Junior School, Eccles; Stretford High School for Girls. Married 1988, Keith Desmond McDowall, CBE (2 step-daughters). *Trades Union:* Member: TUC General Council 1985–92, Graphical, Paper and Media Union 1959–. *Career:* SOGAT, Administrative Secretary 1959–72, Assistant Secretary, Manchester Branch 1972–76, Secretary 1976–83, Member, National Executive Council 1977–83, President, SOGAT '82 1983–85, General-Secretary 1985–91; Deputy General Secretary, Graphical, Paper and Media Union 1991–92. *Whip:* An Opposition Whip 1996–97. *Spokesman:* An Opposition Spokesperson on: Employment 1994–96, National Heritage 1996–97. *Select Committees:* Co-opted Member, Select Committee on European Communities Sub-Committee B (Energy, Industry and Transport) 1995–97, 1997–98. *Other:* Council Member: Association for Business Sponsorship of the Arts 1990–96, City University 1991–96; Governor, Ditchley Foundation 1992–; Member, Board of Council, London School of Economics 1994–99; Member of Council, Open University 1995–98. Six honorary degrees. *Trusts, etc:* Non-Executive Board Member, University College London Hospitals NHS Trust 1993–98; Trustee: Industry and Parliament Trust, Inveresk plc Pension Fund 1996–, The Prince's Foundation 1999–. *Miscellaneous:* Co-Chairman, Women's National Commission 1985–87; Member: Printing and Publishing Training Board 1974–82, Supplementary Benefits Commission 1976–80, Price Commission 1977–79, Occupational Pensions Board 1983–87, General Advisory Council, BBC 1984–88, NEDC 1989–92, Employment Appeal Tribunal 1991–93; Member, Independent Committee for Supervision of Telephone Information Services 1991–93, Chairman 1993–; Non-Executive Director, Inveresk plc 1993–96; Member: Armed Forces Pay Review Body 1993–94, Press Complaints Commission 1993–98, Broadcasting Complaints Commission 1993–94; Non-Executive Director: Chamberlain Phipps plc 1994–, Takecare plc 1995–98; Member, Committee of Inquiry into Future of Higher Education 1996–97; Chairman, Housing Corporation 1997–; Member: Royal Commission on the Reform of the House of Lords 1999, House of Lords Appointments Commission 2000–. *Honours:* PC 1998. FRSA. *Special Interests:* Industry, Media, Arts Sponsorship, Women's Issues, Telecommunications, Pensions, Housing. *Recreations:* Sailing, family, theatre, cooking. *Sportsclubs:* Royal Cornwall Yacht. *Clubs:* Reform. *Name, Style and Title:* Raised to the peerage as Baroness Dean of Thornton-le-Fylde, of Eccles in the County of Greater Manchester 1993. *Address:* Rt Hon the Baroness Dean of Thornton-le-Fylde, House of Lords, London, SW1A 0PW.

LORD DEARING   Cross-Bencher

DEARING (Life Baron), Ronald Ernest Dearing; cr. 1998. Born 27 July 1930. Son of late E. H. A. Dearing; educated Doncaster Grammar School; Hull University (BSc Economics); London Business School (Sloan Fellow). Married 1954, Margaret Patricia Riley (2 daughters). *Armed Forces:* RAF 1949–51. *Career:* Ministry of Labour and National Service 1946–49; Ministry of Power 1949–62; HM Treasury 1962–64; Ministry of Power, Ministry of Technology, Department of Trade and Industry 1965–72; Regional Director, Northern Region, DTI 1972–74; Under-Secretary, DTI later Department of Industry 1972–75, Deputy Secretary 1975–80; Deputy Chairman, Post Office Corporation 1980–81, Chairman 1981–87; Chairman: CNAA 1987–88, County Durham Development Company 1987–90; Chairman: Polytechnics and Colleges Funding Council 1988–93, Northern Development Company 1990–94; Non-Executive Director, Ericsson Ltd 1991–94; Chairman: Council of National Academic Awards 1986–88, Polytechnic Colleges Funding Council 1998–91, Universities' Funding Council 1991–93, High Education Funding Council for England 1992–93, Camelot Group 1993–95, Financial Reporting Council 1983–94, School Curriculum and Assessment Authority 1993–96; Non Executive Director, SDX plc 1995–98; Chairman: National Committee of Enquiry into Higher Education 1996–97, Write Away 1996–99; University for Industry 1998–2000. *Chancellor:* Chancellor, Nottingham University 1993–. *Other:* Member: Council Industrial Society 1985–98, Governing Council London Business School 1985–89; Chairman, Accounting Standards Review Committee 1987–88; Member, Council, Durham University 1988–91;

Chairman: Financial Reporting Council 1989–94, London Education Business Partnership 1989–92, Northern Sinfonia Appeals Committee 1993–94; President, Institute of Direct Marketing 1994–98; Member, Council Melbourne University 1997–99. *Awards Granted:* Gold Medal of British Institute of Management 1994. Twelve honorary doctorates and fellowships. *Honours:* CB 1979; Kt 1984. Hon. FEng 1992. Freeman, City of London 1982. *Publications: The National Curriculum and its Assessment,* 1993; *Review of Qualifications for 16–19 Year Olds,* 1996. *Special Interests:* Education, Post Office. *Recreations:* Gardening, DIY. *Clubs:* Athenaeum. *Name, Style and Title:* Raised to the peerage as Baron Dearing, of Kingston upon Hull in the County of the East Riding of Yorkshire 1998. *Address:* The Lord Dearing, CB, House of Lords, London, SW1A 0PW.

LORD DEEDES — Conservative

DEEDES (Life Baron), William Francis Deedes; cr. 1986. Born 1 June 1913. Son of late William Herbert Deedes; educated Harrow. Married November 21, 1942, Evelyn Hilary Branfoot (1 son 3 daughters and 1 son deceased). *Armed Forces:* Served with 12th KRRC 1939–44. *Councils, Public Bodies:* DL, Kent 1962. *Career:* Journalist with the *Morning Post* and *Daily Telegraph* 1931–; Editor, *The Daily Telegraph* 1974–86. *House of Commons:* MP (Conservative) for Ashford 1950–74; Parliamentary Secretary, Ministry of Housing and Local Government 1954–55; Parliamentary Under-Secretary of State, Home Office 1955–57; Minister without Portfolio 1962–64. *Party Groups (Commons):* Chairman, One Nation Group 1970–74. *Other:* Trustee: CARE International UK, African Medical and Research Foundation (AmREF); Member, Mines Advisory Group (MAE). Hon. DCL, University of Kent. *Honours:* MC 1944; PC 1962; KBE 1999. *Publications: The Drugs Epidemic,* 1970. *Special Interests:* Race Relations, Agriculture, Media, Home Office Affairs, Overseas Aid and Development. *Recreations:* Golf. *Clubs:* Carlton, Beefsteak, Royal and Ancient (St Andrews). *Name, Style and Title:* Raised to the peerage as Baron Deedes, of Aldington in the County of Kent 1986. *Address:* Rt Hon the Lord Deedes, KBE, MC, DL, New Hayters, Aldington, Kent, TN25 7DT *Tel:* 01233 720269 *Tel:* Office: 020 7538 5000.

BARONESS DELACOURT-SMITH OF ALTERYN — Labour

DELACOURT-SMITH OF ALTERYN (Life Baroness), Margaret Delacourt-Smith; cr. 1974. Born 5 April 1916. Daughter of late F. J. Hando, of Newport, Monmouth; educated Newport High School for Girls; St Anne's College, Oxford (MA). Married 1st, 1939, Charles Smith, later Baron Delacourt-Smith, PC (died 1972) (1 son 2 daughters), married 2nd, 1978, Professor Charles Blackton. *Name, Style and Title:* Raised to the peerage as Baroness Delacourt-Smith of Alteryn, of Alteryn in the County of Gwent 1974. *Address:* The Baroness Delacourt-Smith of Alteryn, House of Lords, London, SW1A 0PW.

LORD DENHAM — Conservative

DENHAM (2nd Baron, UK), Bertram Stanley Mitford Bowyer; cr. 1937; 10th Bt of Denham (E) 1660; 2nd Bt of Weston Underwood (UK) 1933. Born 3 October 1927. Son of 1st Baron, MC. Succeeded his father 1948; educated Eton; King's College, Cambridge (BA English Literature). Married February 14, 1956, Jean, eldest daughter of late Kenneth McCorquodale, MC, TD (3 sons 1 daughter). *House of Lords:* An elected hereditary peer 1999–. *Whip:* Government Whip Lord in Waiting 1961–64, 1970–71; Opposition Whip 1964–70; Deputy Chief Whip (Captain of the Queen's Bodyguard of Yeomen of the Guard) 1972–74; Opposition Deputy Chief Whip 1974–78; Opposition Chief Whip 1978–79; Government Chief Whip (Captain of the Honourable Corps of Gentlemen at Arms) 1979–91. *Miscellaneous:* Member, Countryside Commission 1993–99; A Extra Lord in Waiting to HM The Queen 1998–. *Honours:* PC 1981; KBE 1991. *Publications: The Man Who Lost His Shadow,* 1979; *Two Thyrdes,* 1983; *Foxhunt,* 1988; *Black Rod,* 1997. *Clubs:* White's, Pratt's, Garrick, Beefsteak. *Address:* Rt Hon the Lord Denham, KBE, The Laundry Cottage, Weston Underwood, Olney, Buckinghamshire, MK46 5JZ *Tel:* 01234 711535.

BARONESS DENTON OF WAKEFIELD   Conservative

DENTON OF WAKEFIELD (Life Baroness), Jean Denton; cr. 1991. Born 29 December 1935. Daughter of late Charles and Kathleen Moss; educated Rothwell Grammar School; London School of Economics (BSc Econ). Married 1958, Dr Anthony Denton, CBE (marriage dissolved 1974). *Councils, Public Bodies:* Deputy Chairman, Black Country Development Corporation 1987–92. *Career:* Procter and Gamble 1959–61; EIU 1961–64; IPC 1964–66; Racing/rally driver 1969–72; Managing Director, Herondrive 1980–85; External Affairs Director, Austin-Rover 1985–86; Director, Ordnance Survey 1985–88; Director: British Nuclear Fuels 1987–92, Burson-Marsteller 1987–92, London and Edinburgh Insurance Group 1989 92; Director, Triplex Lloyd plc 1990–92; Director: Eureka! 1991–92, North West Television 1991–92; Managing Director, Burson-Marstellar Europe 1997–. *House of Lords:* Parliamentary Under-Secretary of State: for Consumer Affairs and Small Firms, Department of Trade and Industry 1992–93, at Department of Environment 1993–94, at Northern Ireland Office (Minister for Economy, Agriculture and Women's Issues) 1994–97. *Whip:* A Baroness in Waiting (Government Whip) 1991–92. *Spokesman:* An Opposition Spokeswoman on: Northern Ireland 1997, Trade and Industry 1997, 1998–. *Party Groups (General):* President, Wakefield Conservative Association 1994–. *Other:* President: FORUM UK 1989–, Women on the Move against Cancer 1979–; Governor, LSE 1982–92. Hon. DLitt, Bradford University 1993; Hon. Doctor of Humanities, King's College, Pennsylvania 1994. *Trusts, etc:* Trustee, Brooklands Museum 1987–89. *Miscellaneous:* Director, Interim Advisory Committee on School Teachers' Pay and Conditions 1989, 1990, 1991; Director, NHS Policy Board 1991–92; Co-Chairman, Women's National Commission 1992–95. *Honours:* CBE 1990. FCIM. *Special Interests:* Motor Industry, Retail Industry, Transport, Northern Ireland, Women's Issues. *Recreations:* Talking Shop, USA. *Sportsclubs:* British Women's Racing Drivers. *Name, Style and Title:* Raised to the peerage as Baroness Denton of Wakefield, of Wakefield in the County of West Yorkshire 1991. *Address:* The Baroness Denton of Wakefield, CBE, House of Lords, London, SW1A 0PW *Tel:* House of Lords 020 7219 3000.

BISHOP OF DERBY   Non-Affiliated

DERBY (6th Bishop of), Jonathan Sansbury Bailey. Born 24 February 1940. Son of late Walter Bailey, and of Audrey Sansbury Bailey; educated Quarry Bank High School, Liverpool; Trinity College, Cambridge (MA). Married 1965, Rev Susan Bennett-Jones (3 sons). *Career:* Assistant Curate: Sutton, St Helens, Lancashire 1965–68, St Paul, Warrington 1968–71; Warden, Marrick Priory 1971–76; Vicar of Wetherby, West Yorkshire 1976–82; Archdeacon of Southend and Bishop's Officer for Industry and Commerce, Diocese of Chelmsford 1982–92; Suffragan Bishop of Dunwich 1992–95; Bishop of Derby 1995–; Clerk of the Closet to HM the Queen 1996–; Took his seat in the House of Lords 1999. *Recreations:* Theatre, music, beekeeping, carpentry. *Clubs:* United Oxford and Cambridge University. *Address:* Rt Rev the Lord Bishop of Derby, Bishop's Office, Derby Church House, Full Street, Derby, DE1 3DR *Tel:* 01332 346744 *Fax:* 01332 295810.

LORD DESAI   Labour

DESAI (Life Baron), Meghnad Jagdishchandra Desai; cr. 1991. Born 10 July 1940. Son of late Jagdishchandra and Mandakini Desai; educated University of Bombay (BA, MA); University of Pennsylvania (PhD). Married June 27, 1970, Gail Graham Wilson (1 son 2 daughters) (separated 1995). *Trades Union:* Member, AUT. *Councils, Public Bodies:* Chair, Management Committee, City Roads. *Career:* Associate specialist, Department of Agricultural Economics, University of California, Berkeley, California 1963–65; London School of Economics: Lecturer in Economics 1965–77, Senior Lecturer 1977–80, Reader 1980–83, Professor 1983–, Convenor, Economics Department 1987–90, Head, Development Studies Institute 1990–95, Director, Centre for the Study of Global Governance 1992–. *Whip:* Opposition Whip 1991–94. *Spokesman:* Opposition Spokesman on:

Health 1991–93, Treasury and Economic Affairs 1992–93. *Select Committees:* Member: Science and Technology 1993–94, European Affairs Sub Committee A 1995–97; Co-opted Member, Select Committee on European Communities Sub-Committee A (Economic and Financial Affairs, Trade and External Relations) 1997–. *International Bodies:* Member, Executive Committee, IPU British Group 1995–. *Other:* Member: One World Action; Association of University Teachers. Four honorary doctorates. *Trusts, etc:* Member: Sir Ernest Cassel Trust, Tribune Newspaper; Chair of Trustees, Training for Life. *Miscellaneous:* Member, Marshall Aid Commission until 1998. FRSA. *Publications:* Author of several publications on economics. *Special Interests:* Economic Policy, Education, Development. *Recreations:* Reading, writing, cricket. *Clubs:* Reform. *Name, Style and Title:* Raised to peerage as Baron Desai, of St Clement Danes in the City of Westminster 1991. *Address:* Professor the Lord Desai, London School of Economics, Houghton Street, Aldwych, London, WC2A 2AE *Tel:* 020 7955 7489; 606 Collingwood House, Dolphin Square, London, SW1V 3NF *Tel:* 020 7798 8673 *E-Mail:* m.desai@lse.ac.uk.

LORD DHOLAKIA   Liberal Democrat

DHOLAKIA (Life Baron), Navnit Dholakia; cr. 1997. Born 4 March 1937. Son of Permananddas Mulji Dholakia and Shantabai Permananddas Dholakia; educated Indian Public Schools in Moshi, Arusha, Tabora and Morogoro in Tanzania; Institute of Science, Bhavnagar, Gujarat, India; Brighton Technical College. Married 1967, Ann McLuskie (2 daughters). *Councils, Public Bodies:* Councillor, County Borough of Brighton 1961–64; JP, Mid Sussex 1978; Member, Sussex Police Authority 1991–94; DL, West Sussex 1999–. *Career:* Medical Laboratory Technician, Southlands Hospital, Shoreham-by-Sea 1960–66; Development Officer, National Committee for Commonwealth Immigrants 1966–68; Senior Development Officer, Community Relations Commission 1968–74, Principal Officer and Secretary 1974–76; Principal Fieldwork, Administration and Liaison Officer, Commission for Racial Equality 1976–78, Principal Officer, Management 1978–81, Head, Administration of Justice Section 1984–94; Member, Police Complaints Authority 1994–98. *Whip:* Liberal Democrat Party Whip October 1998–. *Spokesman:* A Liberal Democrat Spokesman on Home Affairs October 1998–. *Select Committees:* Co-opted Member, European Communities Sub-Committee F (Social Affairs, Education and Home Affairs) 1997–; House of Lords Offices Committee. *Party Groups (General):* Chairman: Brighton Young Liberals 1959–62, Brighton Liberal Association 1962–64; Secretary, Race and Community Relations Panel, Liberal Party 1969–74; Member, Federal Policy and Federal Executive Committee of the Liberal Democrats 1996–97; President, Liberal Democrat Party 2000–. *Other:* Member, Lord Hunt's Committee on Immigration and Youth Service 1967–69; Secretary, Race and Community Relations Panel, Liberal Party 1969–74; Member, Board of Visitors, HM Prison Lewes 1978–95; Council Member, National Association of Care and Resettlement of Offenders 1984–, Chairman 1998–; Member, Home Office Inter-departmental Committee on Racial Attacks and Harassment 1987–92; Chairman, Race Issues Advisory Committee of the National Association of Care and Resettlement of Offenders 1989–; Member, Ethnic Minority Advisory Committee of the Judicial Studies Board 1992–96; Council Member: The Howard League of Penal Reform 1992–, Save The Children Fund; Editorial Board, The Howard Journal of Criminology 1993–; Member: Lord Carlisle's Committee on Parole Systems Review, Home Secretary's Race Forum 1999–; Vice Chairman, Policy Research Institute on Aging and Ethnicity. *Trusts, etc:* Trustee, Mental Health Foundation 1997–. *Miscellaneous:* Member: Governing Body, Commonwealth Institute 1999–, House of Lords Appointments Commission 2000–. *Honours:* OBE 1994. *Publications:* Various articles on criminal justice matters. *Recreations:* Photography, travel, gardening, cooking exotic dishes. *Name, Style and Title:* Raised to the peerage as Baron Dholakia, of Waltham Brooks in the County of West Sussex 1997. *Address:* The Lord Dholakia, OBE, DL, 76 Penland Road, Haywards Heath, West Sussex, RH16 1PH *Tel:* 01444 450065 *Fax:* 01444 450065 *E-Mail:* dholakian@parliament.uk.

Visit the Vacher Dod Website . . .
www.politicallinks.co.uk

LORD DIAMOND   Labour

DIAMOND (Life Baron), John Diamond; cr. 1970. Born 30 April 1907. Son of late Rev. Solomon Diamond; educated Leeds Grammar School. Married (2 sons 2 daughters). *Career:* Practised as Chartered Accountant from 1931–64 Managing Director, Capital and Provincial News Theatres 1951–57. *House of Commons:* MP (Labour): Manchester, Blackley division 1945–51, (contested Manchester, Blackley 1955), Gloucester 1957–70; PPS to Minister of Works 1946; Chief Secretary to the Treasury 1964–70; Cabinet Minister 1968–70. *House of Lords:* Principal Deputy Chairman Committees, House of Lords 1974. *Party Groups (General):* Hon. Treasurer, Fabian Society 1950–64; Trustee, Social Democratic Party 1981 82; Leader of SDP in the House of Lords 1982–88. *Other:* Council Member, London Philharmonic Orchestra 1972–74. Hon. LLD, Leeds 1978. *Trusts, etc:* Director, Sadler's Wells Trust 1957–64; Chairman of Trustees, Industry and Parliament Trust 1977–82. *Miscellaneous:* Member, General Nursing Council (Chairman of Financial and General Purposes Committee) 1947–53; Hon. Treasurer, The European Movement 1973–74; Chairman, Royal Commission on Distribution of Income and Wealth 1974–79; Chairman, Civil Service Advisory Committee on Business Appointments 1975–88. *Honours:* PC 1965. FCA. *Publications: Public Expenditure in Practice,* 1975; Co-author *Socialism The British Way,* 1948. *Recreations:* Music, gardening, classical languages. *Name, Style and Title:* Raised to the peerage as Baron Diamond, of the City of Gloucester 1970. *Address:* Rt Hon the Lord Diamond, Aynhoe, Doggetts Wood Lane, Chalfont St. Giles, Buckinghamshire, HP8 4TH *Tel:* 01494 763229.

LORD DIXON   Labour

DIXON (Life Baron), Donald Dixon; cr. 1997. Born 6 March 1929. Son of late Albert Dixon, shipyard worker; educated Ellison Street Elementary School, Jarrow. Married Doreen Morad (1 son 1 daughter). *Trades Union:* Member, GMWU and Branch Secretary. *Armed Forces:* Royal Engineers 1947–49. *Councils, Public Bodies:* Councillor: Jarrow Borough Council 1963–74, South Tyneside Metropolitan District Council 1974–81; DL, Tyne and Wear 1997–. *Career:* Previously shipyard worker. *House of Commons:* MP (Labour) for Jarrow May 1979–97. *Whip (Commons):* Opposition Deputy Chief Whip 1987–96. *Select Committees:* Member, House of Lords' Offices Committee. *Party Groups (General):* Joined Labour Party 1950; Former Chairman, Northern Group Labour MPs; Member, Local Co-operative Group. *Honours:* PC 1996. Freeman: Jarrow 1972, South Tyneside 1997. *Special Interests:* Trade Unions, Ships and Shipbuilding, Maritime Affairs, Housing, Transport, Social Services. *Recreations:* Football, reading, boxing. *Clubs:* Jarrow Ex-Servicemen's, Jarrow Labour. *Name, Style and Title:* Raised to the peerage as Baron Dixon, of Jarrow in the County of Tyne and Wear 1997. *Address:* Rt Hon the Lord Dixon, DL, 1 Hillcrest, Jarrow, Tyne and Wear, NE32 4DP *Tel:* 0191–489 7635.

LORD DIXON-SMITH   Conservative

DIXON-SMITH (Life Baron), Robert William Dixon-Smith; cr. 1993. Born 30 September 1934. Son of late Dixon and Alice Winifred Smith; educated Oundle; Writtle Agricultural College, Essex. Married February 13, 1960, Georgina Janet, daughter of George and Kathleen Cook (1 son 1 daughter). *Armed Forces:* Second Lieutenant, King's Dragoon Guards (National Service) 1956–57. *Councils, Public Bodies:* Councillor, Essex County Council 1965–93, Chairman 1986–89; DL, Essex 1986. *Career:* Farmer. *Spokesman:* An Opposition Spokesman on Environment, Transport and the Regions (Local Government) December 1998–. *Select Committees:* Member, Select Committees on: Science and Technology 1994–97, European Communities 1994–97. *Other:* Governor, Writtle Agricultural College 1967–94, Chairman 1973–85; Chairman, Governors of Anglia Polytechnic University 1993–94 (formerly Anglia Polytechnic), Governor 1973–. Honorary Doctorate, Anglia Polytechnic University; Fellow, Writtle College. *Miscellaneous:* Member, Association of County Councils 1983–93, Chairman 1992–93. Liveryman, Farmers' Company 1990. *Special Interests:* Agriculture, Environment, Transport. *Recreations:* Country sports, golf. *Name, Style and Title:* Raised to the peerage as Baron Dixon-Smith, of Bocking in the County of Essex 1993. *Address:* The Lord Dixon-Smith, DL, Home: Lyons Hall, Braintree, Essex, CM7 9SH *Tel:* 01376 326834; Office: Houchins, Coggeshall, Colchester, Essex, CO6 1RT *Tel:* 01376 561448.

LORD DONALDSON OF LYMINGTON
Cross-Bencher

DONALDSON OF LYMINGTON (Life Baron), John Francis Donaldson; cr. 1988. Born 6 October 1920. Son of late Malcolm Donaldson, FRCS, FRCOG; educated Charterhouse; Trinity College, Cambridge (MA 1949, MA (Oxon) 1982). Married 1945, Dorothy Mary (Dame Mary Donaldson, GBE), daughter of late Reginald George Gale Warwick (1 son 2 daughters). *Armed Forces:* Commissioned, Royal Signals 1941; Served with: Guards Armoured Divisional Signals in UK and North West Europe 1942–45, Military Government, Schleswig-Holstein 1945–46. *Councils, Public Bodies:* Councillor, Croydon Borough Council 1949–53. *Career:* Called to Bar, Middle Temple 1946; Harmsworth Law Scholar 1946; Bencher 1966; Member, General Council of the Bar 1956–61; QC 1961; Judge of the High Court, Queen's Bench Division 1966–79; President, National Industrial Relations Court 1971–74; A Lord Justice of Appeal 1979–82; Master of the Rolls 1982–92. *Other:* Hon. Member, Association of Average Adjusters 1966, Chairman 1981; President, British Maritime Law Association 1979–95, Vice-President 1969–78; President, British Insurance Law Association 1979–81, Deputy President 1978–79; Governor, Sutton's Hospital in Charterhouse 1981–84; Visitor: UCL 1982–92, Nuffield College, Oxford 1982–92, London Business School 1986–92; President, Council, Inns of Court 1987–90; Hon. Life Member, The Law Society 1994. *Awards Granted:* Silver Medal Thomas Gray Memorial Trust 1995. Hon. Fellow, Trinity College, Cambridge 1983; Four honorary doctorates. *Miscellaneous:* Chairman: Financial Law Panel 1993–, Inquiry into pollution from merchant shipping 1993–94, Lord Donaldson's Assessment (Derbyshire) 1995; Chairman, Review of: Salvage and Intervention Command and Control 1997–98, Four Year Strategy for HM Coastguard 1999. *Honours:* Kt 1966; PC 1979. Fellow, Chartered Institute of Arbitrators 1980, President 1980–83. City of London. Honorary Freeman, Drapers Company 1994; Honorary Liveryman 2000. *Special Interests:* Law and the Administration of Justice, Maritime Safety. *Recreations:* Sailing. *Sportsclubs:* Royal Lymington Yacht; Royal Cruising Club. *Name, Style and Title:* Raised to the peerage as Baron Donaldson of Lymington, of Lymington in the County of Hampshire 1988. *Address:* Rt Hon the Lord Donaldson of Lymington, House of Lords, London, SW1A 0PW *Tel:* Home: 020 7588 6610.

LORD DONOUGHUE
Labour

DONOUGHUE (Life Baron), Bernard Donoughue; cr. 1985. Born 8 September 1934. Son of late Thomas Joseph Donoughue; educated Campbell Secondary Modern School, Northampton; Northampton Grammar School; Lincoln College and Nuffield College, Oxford (MA, DPhil); Harvard University, USA. Married November 26, 1959, Carol Ruth Goodman (2 sons 2 daughters) (marriage dissolved 1989). *Trades Union:* Member, GMBW. *Career:* Editorial Staff, *The Economist* 1959–60; Senior Research Officer, Political and Economic Planning Institute 1960–63; Senior Lecturer, London School of Economics 1963–74; Senior Policy Adviser to the Prime Minister 1974–79; Development Director, Economist Intelligence Unit 1979–81; Assistant Editor, *The Times* 1981–82; Head of Research and Investment Policy, Grieveson Grant and Co. 1982–86; Head of International Research and Director, Kleinwort Grieveson Securities Ltd 1986–88; Executive Vice-Chairman, LBI 1988–91; Director, Towcester Racecourse Ltd 1992–97; Visiting Professor of Government LSE 2000–. *House of Lords:* Parliamentary Secretary (Lords), Ministry of Agriculture, Fisheries and Food (Minister for Farming and the Food Industry) 1997–99. *Spokesman:* Opposition Spokesman on: Energy 1991–92, Treasury Affairs 1991–92, National Heritage 1992–97. *Other:* Chairman Executive, London Symphony Orchestra 1979–91, Patron 1989–95; Member, LSE Court of Governors 1997; Consultant Member, House Industry Confederation 1999–; Chairman: British Housing Board Committee on VAT 2000–, Committee on House Welfare. Hon. Fellow, Lincoln College, Oxford; Hon. LLD, Leicester; Hon. Fellow, LSE. *Trusts, etc:* Member: Dorneywood Trust, Victoria Country History of Northamptonshire. *Miscellaneous:* Member: Sports Council 1965–71, Commission of Enquiry into Association Football 1966–68, London Arts Board 1992–97. FRHS. *Publications:* Books on history and politics including: *Trade Unions in a Changing Society,* 1963; *British Politics and the American Revolution,* 1964; *The People into Parliament,* 1966; *Herbert Morrison,* 1973; *Prime Minister,* 1987. *Special Interests:* Arts, Finance, Sport. *Recreations:* Music, theatre, sport. *Sportsclubs:* Houses of Parliament Cricket Club. *Clubs:* Pratt's, Farmers', 1795. *Name, Style and Title:* Raised to the peerage as Baron Donoughue, of Ashton in the County of Northamptonshire 1985. *Address:* The Lord Donoughue, House of Lords, London, SW1A 0PW *Tel:* Home: 020 7730 7332.

DORMAND OF EASINGTON (Life Baron), John Donkin Dormand; cr. 1987. Born 27 August 1919. Son of late Bernard and Mary Dormand; educated Wellfield Grammar School; Bede College, Durham University; Loughborough College; St Peter's College, Oxford; Harvard University. Married December 26, 1963, Mrs Doris Robinson, daughter of Thomas Pearson (1 step-son 1 step-daughter). *Trades Union:* Member: APEX (GMB), NUT. *Career:* Teacher 1940–48; Education Adviser 1948–52, 1959–63; Education Officer, NCB 1957–59; Education Officer, Easington Rural District Council 1963–70. *House of Commons:* MP (Labour) for Easington 1970–87. *Whip (Commons):* Assistant Government Whip 1974, Government Whip (Lord Commissioner of HM Treasury) 1974–79; Opposition Whip 1979–81. *House of Lords:* Labour Peers' Representative on Parliamentary Committee (Shadow Cabinet) 1994–97. *Select Committees:* Former Member: Select Committee on Nationalised Industries 1970–73, Select Committee on Committee Structure of House of Lords June-December (chairman) 1991; House of Lords Liaison Committee 1992–97, Procedure Committee. *Backbench Committees:* Education, Trade and Industry, Sport. *Party Groups (General):* Chairman, Parliamentary Labour Party 1981–87. *Awards Granted:* Fulbright Scholar, Harvard University, USA. Hon. Fellow, St Peter's College, Oxford. *Special Interests:* Education, Coal Industry, Regional Policy, Local Government, Tourism, Film Industry. *Recreations:* Music, sport, films. *Sportsclubs:* Houghton Rugby Union Club, Burmoor Cricket Club, Durham County Cricket Club, Durham County Rugby Union Club. *Clubs:* Peterlee Labour, Easington Workmen's. *Name, Style and Title:* Raised to the peerage as Baron Dormand of Easington, of Easington in the County of Durham 1987. *Address:* The Lord Dormand of Easington, House of Lords, London, SW1A 0PW *Tel:* House of Lords 020 7219 5419.

DUBS (Life Baron), Alfred Dubs; cr. 1994. Born 5 December 1932. Born 1932; educated London School of Economics (BSc Econ). Married (1 son 1 daughter). *Trades Union:* Member, TGWU. *Councils, Public Bodies:* Councillor, Westminster City Council 1971–78; Chairman, Westminster Community Relations Council 1972–77; Member, Kensington, Chelsea and Westminster Area Health Authority 1975–78; Non-Executive Director, Pathfinder NHS Trust 1995–97. *Career:* Formerly a local government officer; Director, Refugee Council 1988–95; Member, Broadcasting Standards Council 1988–94, Deputy Chairman 1994–97. *House of Commons:* Contested (Labour): Cities of London and Westminster 1970, Hertfordshire South February and October 1974 general elections; MP (Labour) for: Battersea South 1979–83, Battersea 1983–87; contested Battersea 1987 and 1992 general elections. *Spokesman (Commons):* Opposition Front Bench Spokesman on Home Affairs 1983–87. *House of Lords:* Parliamentary Under-Secretary of State, Northern Ireland Office (Minister for Environment and Agriculture) 1997–99. *Whip:* Opposition Whip 1995–97. *Spokesman:* Opposition Spokesman on: The Environment (Health and Safety) 1996–97, Energy 1996–97. *Select Committees:* Member, Select Committees on: Relations between Central and Local Government 1995–96, European Community 1996–97. *Party Groups (General):* Member, The Co-operative Party; Chairman, Fabian Society 1993–94. *Other:* Chairman, Liberty 1990–92. *Trusts, etc:* Trustee: Action Aid 1989–97, Immigration Advisory Service 1992–97. *Publications: Lobbying: An Insider's Guide to the Parliamentary Process,* 1989. *Special Interests:* Civil Liberties, Penal Reform, Race Relations, Immigration, Health Service, Ireland, Human Rights. *Recreations:* Walking in the Lake District. *Name, Style and Title:* Raised to the peerage as Baron Dubs, of Battersea in the London Borough of Wandsworth 1994. *Address:* The Lord Dubs, House of Lords, London, SW1A 0PW.

EARL OF DUNDEE — Conservative

DUNDEE (12th Earl of, S), Alexander Henry Scrymgeour; cr. 1660; Viscount Dudhope (S) 1641; Lord Scrymgeour (S) 1641; Lord Inverkeithing (S) 1660; Baron Glassary (UK) 1954. Born 5 June 1949. Son of 11th Earl, PC, DL. Succeeded his father 1983; educated Eton; St Andrews University. Married July 19, 1979, Siobhan Mary Llewellyn (1 son 3 daughters). *House of Lords:* An elected hereditary peer 1999–. *Whip:* Government Whip 1986–89. *Select Committees:* Member, Select Committees on: European Communities Sub-Committee F (Social Affairs, Education and Home Affairs) 1997–, Joint Committee on Consolidation of Bills 2000–. *International Bodies (General):* Substitute, UK Delegation to Council of Europe and Western European Union; Representative, UK Delegation to Organisation for Security and Co-operation in Europe. *Miscellaneous:* Hereditary Royal Standard Bearer for Scotland; Page of Honour to HM The Queen 1964–65; Contested (Conservative) Hamilton By-election 1978. *Clubs:* White's, New (Edinburgh). *Address:* The Earl of Dundee, Farm Office, Birkhill, Cupar, Fife, KY15 4QP *Tel:* 01826 24200.

BARONESS DUNN — Cross-Bencher

DUNN (Life Baroness), Lydia Dunn; cr. 1990. Born 29 February 1940. Daughter of late Yen Chuen Yih Dunn and Bessie Dunn; educated St Paul's Convent School, Hong Kong; College of the Holy Names, Oakland, California; University of California, Berkeley, California. Married April 2, 1988, Michael Thomas, CMG, QC. *Career:* Member, Legislative Council, Hong Kong 1976–88, Senior Member 1985–88; Director: John Swire & Sons (HK) Ltd 1978–, Mass Transit Railway Corporation 1979–85; Chairman: Special Committee on Land Supply 1981–83, Prince Philip Dental Hospital 1981–87; Director, Hong Kong & Shanghai Banking Corporation Ltd 1981–96, Deputy Chairman 1992–96; Director: Swire Pacific Ltd 1981–, Kowloon Canton Railway Corporation 1982–84; Member, Hong Kong Executive Council 1982–95; Senior Member 1988–95; Chairman, Hong Kong Trade Development Council 1983–91; Deputy Chairman, Executive Committee, Commonwealth Parliamentary Association, Hong Kong Branch 1985–88; Director, Cathay Pacific Airways Ltd 1985–97; Director, HSBC Holdings plc 1990, Non-Executive Deputy Chairman 1992–; Director: Volvo AB 1991–93, Christies International plc 1996–98; Executive Director, John Swire & Sons Ltd 1996–; Director, The General Electric Company plc 1997–; Adviser to Board, Cathay Pacific Airways Ltd 1997–; Christies Fine Art Limited 1998–2000. *Other:* Member: General Committee, Federation of Hong Kong Industries 1978–83, World Wildlife Fund Hong Kong 1982–85, Hong Kong/Japan Business Co-operation Committee 1983–87, Hong Kong/US Economic Co-operation Committee 1984–93, The International Council of the Asia Society 1986–96, Hong Kong Association, United Kingdom 1991. *Awards Granted:* Prime Minister of Japan's Trade Award 1987; *To Peace and Commerce* Award, USA Secretary of Commerce 1988. Hon. LLD: Chinese University of Hong Kong 1984, Hong Kong University 1991, University of British Columbia, Canada 1991, University of Leeds 1994; Hon. DSc, University of Buckingham 1995. *Trusts, etc:* Industry Committee of the Animal Health Trust 1996–. *Miscellaneous:* Member: Governing Body Commonwealth Institute 1999–; Executive Council Hong Kong 1982–95. *Honours:* OBE 1978; CBE 1983; DBE 1989. Fellow: Institute of Directors 1989–, The Royal Society for the Encouragement of Arts, Manufacturers and Commerce 1989–. *Publications: In the Kingdom of the Blind,* 1983. *Recreations:* Art, antiques. *Clubs:* Hong Kong, Hong Kong Jockey. *Name, Style and Title:* Raised to the peerage as Baroness Dunn, of Hong Kong Island in Hong Kong and of Knightsbridge in the Royal Borough of Kensington and Chelsea 1990. *Address:* The Baroness Dunn, DBE, John Swire and Sons Ltd, Swire House, 59 Buckingham Gate, London, SW1E 6AJ *Tel:* 020 7834 7717.

BISHOP OF DURHAM   Non-Affiliated

DURHAM (93rd Bishop of), Anthony Michael Arnold Turnbull. Born 27 December 1935. Son of late George and late Adeline Turnbull; educated Ilkley Grammar School; Keble College, Oxford (MA); St John's College, Durham (Dip. Theology). Married 1963, Brenda Susan Merchant (1 son 2 daughters). *Career:* Deacon 1960; Priest 1961; Curate: Middleton 1960–61, Luton 1961–65; Domestic Chaplain to Archbishop of York 1965–69; Rector of Heslington and Chaplain to York University 1969–76; Member, General Synod of the Church of England 1970–75, 1987–; Chief Secretary, Church Army 1976–84; Examining Chaplain to the Bishop of Norwich 1982–84; Archdeacon of Rochester, also Canon Residentiary of Rochester Cathedral and Chairman Diocesan Board for Mission and Unity 1984–88; Bishop of Rochester 1988–94; Member, Board of Church Commissioners 1989–98, Vice-Chairman, Central Board of Finance, C of E 1990–98; Member, Archbishop's Commission on Cathedrals 1992–94; Bishop of Durham 1994–; Took his seat in the House of Lords 1994; Chairman, Archbishop's Commission on Organisation of C of E 1994–95; Visitor, University of Durham; Member, Archbishops' Council, Chairman, Ministry Division. *Other:* Chairman: College of Preachers 1990–98, Bible Reading Fellowship 1990–94, Partnership for World Mission 1991–94; Member, Court of Governors, University of Greenwich 1992–94. DLitt (Hon. Causa). *Publications: God's Front Line,* 1979; *Parish Evangelism,* 1980; *Learning to Pray,* 1981. *Special Interests:* Housing, Employment, Overseas Aid and Development. *Recreations:* Cricket, family life. *Sportsclubs:* Member, Durham CCC. *Clubs:* Athenaeum, MCC. *Address:* Rt Rev the Lord Bishop of Durham, Auckland Castle, Bishop Auckland, Co. Durham, DL14 7NR *Tel:* 01388 602576 *E-Mail:* bishop.of.durham@durham.anglican.org.

E

LORD EAMES   Cross-Bencher

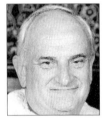

EAMES (Life Baron), Robert Henry Alexander Eames; cr. 1995. Born 27 April 1937. Son of William and Mary Eames; educated Belfast Royal Academy; Methodist College, Belfast; Queen's University, Belfast (LLB, PhD); Trinity College, Dublin. Married 1966, Ann Christine Daly (2 sons). *Career:* Research Scholar and Tutor, Faculty of Laws, Queen's University 1960–63; Curate Assistant, Bangor Parish Church 1963–66; Rector of St Dorothea's, Belfast 1966–74; Examining Chaplain to the Bishop of Down 1973; Rector of St Mark's, Dundela 1974–75; Bishop of Derry and Raphoe 1975–80; Bishop of Down and Dromore 1980–86; Archbishop of Armagh and Primate of All Ireland 1986–; Select Preacher, Oxford University 1987; Chairman: Commission on Communion and Women in the Episcopate 1988–, Commission on Inter-Anglican Relations 1988–; Select Preacher, University of Cambridge 1990; Chairman, Inter-Anglican Theological and Doctrinal Commission 1991; Select Preacher, University of Edinburgh 1993; Chairman, Inter-Anglican Finance Committee 1997–. *International Bodies (General):* Member, Anglican International Consultative Council. *Other:* Governor, Church Army 1985–; Chairman: Board of Governors, Royal School, Armagh, Armagh Observatory and Planetarium. Seven honorary doctorates from British and Irish universities. *Miscellaneous:* Hon. Bencher, Lincoln's Inn 1998. *Publications: A Form of Worship for Teenagers,* 1965; *The Quiet Revolution – Irish Disestablishment,* 1970; *Through Suffering,* 1973; *Thinking through Lent,* 1978; *Through Lent,* 1984; *Chains to be Broken,* 1992. *Special Interests:* Northern Ireland, Social Issues, Community Care, Broadcasting. *Recreations:* Sailing, Rugby Union. *Clubs:* Kildare Street and University (Dublin). *Name, Style and Title:* Raised to the peerage as Baron Eames, of Armagh in the County of Armagh 1995. *Address:* Most Rev the Lord Eames, Lord Archbishop of Armagh and Primate of All Ireland, The See House, Cathedral Close, Armagh, Co. Armagh, BT61 7EE *Tel:* 01861 522851 *Fax:* 01861 527823.

LORD EATWELL Labour

EATWELL (Life Baron), John Leonard Eatwell; cr. 1992. Born 2 February 1945. Son of late Harold Jack Eatwell, and late Mary Eatwell; educated Headlands Grammar School, Swindon; Queens' College, Cambridge (BA 1967, MA 1971); Harvard University (PhD 1975). Married April 24, 1970, Hélène Seppain (2 sons 1 daughter). *Trades Union:* Member, Association of University Teachers. *Career:* Teaching Fellow, Graduate School of Arts and Sciences, Harvard University 1968–69; Research Fellow, Queens' College, Cambridge 1969–70; Fellow of Trinity College, Cambridge 1970–96; Assistant Lecturer, Faculty of Economics and Politics, Cambridge University 1975–77, Lecturer 1977–; Visiting Professor of Economics, New School for Social Research, New York 1982–96; Economic Adviser to Neil Kinnock as Leader of the Labour Party 1985–92; Trustee and Secretary, Institute for Public Policy Research 1988–97, Chairman 1997–; Director, Securities and Futures Authority 1997–; President, Queens' College, Cambridge 1997–; Chairman, British Screen 1997–2000; Member, Board of Directors of the Royal Opera House 1998–. *Spokesman:* An Opposition Spokesman on: Trade and Industry 1992–96, Treasury and Economic Affairs 1992–93; Principal Opposition Spokesman on Treasury and Economic Affairs 1993–97. *Select Committees:* Member, Joint Committee on the Financial Services and Markets Bill, 1999–. *Other:* Chairman: Crusaid, the national fundraiser for AIDS 1993–98, Commercial Radio Companies Association 2000–. *Trusts, etc:* Governor, Contemporary Dance Trust 1991–95; Director, Arts Theatre Trust, Cambridge 1991–98. *Publications:* Co-author *An Introduction to Modern Economics*, 1973; *Whatever happened to Britain?*, 1982; Co-author *Keynes's Economics and the Theory of Value and Distribution*, 1983; *The New Palgrave: A Dictionary of Economics*, 4 vols, 1987; *The New Palgrave Dictionary of Money and Finance*, 3 vols, 1992; Editor *Global Unemployment: Loss of Jobs in the '90s*, 1996; Co-author *Not Just Another Accession: The Political Economy of EU Enlargement to the East*, 1997; *Understanding Globalisation: The Nation-State, Democracy and Economic Policies in the New Epoch*, 1998; *Global Finance at Risk: The Case for International Regulation*, 2000; *Hard Budgets and Soft States: Social Policy Choices in Central and Eastern Europe*, 2000; Articles in scientific journals and other collected works. *Special Interests:* Economics, Trade and Industry, Arts. *Recreations:* Classical and contemporary dance, rugby union football. *Sportsclubs:* Lords and Commons RUFC. *Clubs:* Harvard Club of New York City. *Name, Style and Title:* Raised to the peerage as Baron Eatwell, of Stratton St Margaret in the County of Wiltshire 1992. *Address:* The Lord Eatwell, The President's Lodge, Queens' College, Cambridge, CB3 9ET *Tel:* 01223 335532 *Fax:* 01223 335555 *E-Mail:* president@quns.cam.ac.uk.

VISCOUNTESS ECCLES Conservative

ECCLES OF MOULTON (Life Baroness), Diana Catherine Eccles; cr. 1990. Born 4 October 1933. Daughter of late Raymond and Margaret Sturge; educated St. James's School, West Malvern; Open University (BA 1979). Married January 29, 1955, Hon. John Dawson Eccles (Now 2nd Viscount Eccles, CBE) (1 son 3 daughters). *Councils, Public Bodies:* Member, Teesside Urban Development Corporation 1987–98; Chairman: Ealing District Health Authority 1988–93, Ealing, Hammersmith and Hounslow Health Authority 1993–2000; DL, North Yorkshire 1998–. *Career:* Voluntary work, Middlesbrough Community Council 1955–58; Partner in graphic design business 1963–77; Member, North Eastern Electricity Board 1974–85; Vice-Chairman, National Council for Voluntary Organisations 1981–87; Lay Member, Durham University Council 1981–, Vice-Chairman 1985–; Chairman, Tyne Tees Television Programme Consultative Council 1982–84; Member: Advisory Council on Energy Conservation (Department of Energy) 1982–84, Widdicombe Inquiry into Local Government 1985–86, Home Office Advisory Panel on Licences for Experimental Community Radio 1985–86, British Rail Eastern Board 1986–92; Director: Tyne Tees Television 1986–94, J. Sainsbury plc 1986–95, Yorkshire Electricity Group plc 1990–97; Member, Unrelated Live Transplant Regulatory Authority 1990–99; Director: National and Provincial Building Society 1991–96, Times Newspapers Holdings Ltd 1998–, Opera North 1998–. Hon. DCL, Durham 1995. *Trusts, etc:* Trustee: Charities Aid Foundation 1982–89, York Minster Trust Fund; Member, British Heart Foundation. *Name, Style and Title:* Raised to the peerage as Baroness Eccles of Moulton, of Moulton in the County of North Yorkshire 1990. *Address:* The Viscountess Eccles, Lady Eccles of Moulton, DL, 5 St John's House, 30 Smith Square, London, SW1P 3HF *Tel:* 020 7222 4040; Moulton Hall, Richmond, North Yorkshire, DL10 6QH *Tel:* 01325 377227.

LORD EDEN OF WINTON   Conservative

EDEN OF WINTON (Life Baron), John Benedict Eden; cr 1983; 9th Bt of West Auckland (E) 1672; 7th Bt of Maryland (GB) 1776. Born 15 September 1925. Son of Sir Timothy Eden, 8th and 6th Bt; educated Eton; St Paul's School, USA. Married 1st, January 28, 1958, Belinda Jane, daughter of late Sir John Pascoe (2 sons 2 daughters) (marriage dissolved 1974), married 2nd, 1977, Margaret Ann, Viscountess Strathallan, daughter of late Robin Gordon. *Armed Forces:* Served British and Indian Armies 1943–47; Lieutenant, Rifle Brigade, seconded to 2nd King Edward's Own Goorkha Rifles and the Gilgit Scouts. *Career:* Former Chairman of various plcs; Chairman, Lady Eden's School Ltd; Member, Timken Company International Advisory Board. *House of Commons:* Contested Paddington North 1953 by-election; MP (Conservative) for Bournemouth West 1954–83; Minister of State, Ministry of Technology June-October 1970; Minister for Industry 1970–72; Minister of Posts and Telecommunications 1972–74. *Spokesman (Commons):* Former opposition Spokesman on Defence (RAF) and Power. *International Bodies (Commons):* Former Member: WEU, NATO Parliamentarians, Council of Europe. *Party Groups (General):* President, Wessex Area Council, National Union of Conservative and Unionist Associations 1974–77; Hon. Life Vice-President, Association of Conservative Clubs Ltd. *Other:* President, Independent Schools Association 1969–71; Chairman, The British Lebanese Association 1990–98; Vice-President, International Tree Foundation to 1998. *Trusts, etc:* Chairman, The Royal Armouries Board of Trustees 1986–94. *Honours:* PC 1972. Hon. Freeman: Annapolis, Maryland, USA 1976, Bournemouth 1984. *Clubs:* Boodle's, Pratt's. *Name, Style and Title:* Raised to the peerage as Baron Eden of Winton, of Rushyford in the County of Durham 1983. *Address:* Rt Hon the Lord Eden of Winton, 41 Victoria Road, London, W8 5RH *E-Mail:* lordeden@clara.net.

LORD ELDER   Labour

ELDER (Life Baron), Thomas Murray Elder; cr. 1999. Born 9 May 1950; educated Kirkcaldy High School; Edinburgh University (MA Economic History). *Career:* Bank of England 1972–80; Labour Party Scotland 1984–92, General Secretary 1988–92; Chief of Staff to Rt Hon. John Smith, MP 1992–94; Special Adviser, Scottish Office 1997–99. *House of Commons:* Contested (Labour) Ross, Cromarty and Skye 1983 general election. *Select Committees:* Member, Select Committee on Monetary Policy of the Bank of England 2000–. *Recreations:* Walking, reading, opera. *Name, Style and Title:* Raised to the peerage as Baron Elder, of Kirkcaldy in Fife 1999. *Address:* The Lord Elder, House of Lords, London, SW1A 0PW.

LORD ELIS-THOMAS   Cross-Bencher

ELIS-THOMAS (Life Baron), Dafydd Elis Elis-Thomas; cr. 1992. Born 18 October 1946; educated Ysgol Dyffryn Conwy; University College of Wales (PhD). Married 1st, 1970, Elen M. Williams (3 sons) (marriage dissolved), married 2nd, December 29, 1993, Mair Parry Jones. *Career:* Tutor in Welsh Studies, Coleg Harlech 1971–74; Has subsequently taught at: The University College of North Wales, Bangor, Aberystwyth, Cardiff, The Open University; Has been a broadcaster on BBC Wales, HTV, S4C, Radio Wales; Consultant to 1999: S4C, The Welsh Development Agency, The Rural Initiative Programme, The Assembly of European Regions, The Government of Catalonia; Chairman, Screen Wales; Director and Deputy Chairman, Cynefin Environmental; Director and Chairman, New Media Agency; Director: Oriel Mostyn, National Botanical Gardens, MFM Marcher. *House of Commons:* Contested Conway 1970; MP (Plaid Cymru) for: Meirionnydd February 1974–83, Meirionnydd Nant Conwy 1974–92. *Select Committees:* Member: Select Committee on European Communities 1997–98, Select Committee on European Communities Sub-Committee C (Environment, Public Health and Consumer Protection) 1997–98. *Party Groups (General):* President, Plaid Cymru 1984–91. *Other:* President, Hay-on-Wye Literature Festival; Vice-President –1999: Ramblers Association in Wales –1999, Snowdonia National Park Society –1999, Abbeyfield –1999.*Trusts, etc:* Trustee –1999: Big Issue Foundation –1999, Theatr Bara Caws –1999; Patron, Prince of Wales Trust – Bro; Member, Wales Committee of National Trust. *Miscellaneous:* Member –1999: Welsh Arts Council –1999, Welsh Film Council –1999, Welsh Film Board –1999, BBC General Consultative Council –1999;

Chairman, Welsh Language Board 1993–96, 1996–99; Fellow, International Centre for Intercultural Studies, Institute of Education, London; AM for the Constituency of Meirionnydd Nant Conwy since May 6, 1999 (contested the seat as Dafydd Elis-Thomas); Presiding Officer (The Speaker) National Assembly for Wales May 1999–, Surname changed from Thomas to Elis-Thomas by deed poll 1992. *Recreations:* Welsh literature and art, music, theatre, films, hill and mountain walking, swimming, jogging. *Name, Style and Title:* Raised to the peerage as Baron Elis-Thomas, of Nant Conwy in the County of Gwynedd 1992. *Address:* The Lord Elis-Thomas, AM, 3 Lon Warfield, Caernarfon, Gwynedd, LL55 1LA; Pen y Ceunant, Betws y Coed, Conwy, LL24 0SL; Tŷ Glyndŵr, Heol Glyndŵr, Dolgellau, Gwynedd, LL40 1BD *E-Mail:* dafydd.elis-thomas@wales.gsi.gov.uk.

BARONESS ELLES   Conservative

ELLES (Life Baroness), Diana Louie Elles; cr. 1972. Born 19 July 1921. Daughter of late Colonel Stewart Newcombe, DSO; educated Private Schools, London, Paris, Florence; London University (BA). Married August 14, 1945, Neil Patrick Moncrieff Elles (1 son 1 daughter). *Armed Forces:* Served in WAAF 1941–45; Flight Officer 1944. *Career:* Called to the Bar, Lincoln's Inn, 1956; Voluntary Care Committee Worker, Kennington 1956–72; UK delegate, United Nations General Assembly 1972; Member, UN Sub-Commission for Prevention of Discrimination and Protection of Minorities 1973–74; International Chairman, European Union of Women 1973–79; UK delegate to European Parliament 1973–75; UN Special Rapporteur on Human Rights 1975–79; Member for Thames Valley in the European Parliament 1979–89; Vice-President, European Parliament 1982–1987; Group Spokesman, Political Affairs Northern Ireland 1980–1987; Chairman, European Parliament Legal Affairs Committee 1987–89. *Spokesman:* Opposition Spokesman in House of Lords 1975–79. *Select Committees:* Member: House of Lords European Communities Select Committee 1989–94, Ad Hoc Sub-Committee on 1996 Inter-Governmental Conference 1995–97, Sub-Committee E on Law and Institutions 1994–97, Co-opted Member 1997–99. *International Bodies (General):* Member: International Bar Association, International Law Association, IPU. *Party Groups (General):* Chairman, Conservative Party International Office 1973–78. *Other:* Council Member, Royal Institute of International Affairs 1977–86; Governor, British Institute Florence 1986–96, Chairman, Board of Governors 1994–96, Life Governor 1996–; Governor, Reading University 1986–96. *Trusts, etc:* Trustee: Industry and Parliament Trust 1985–96, Caldecott Community 1990–97. *Miscellaneous:* Hon. Bencher, Lincoln's Inn 1993. *Publications: UN Human Rights of Non-Citizens*, 1984; Contribution to: *Legal Issues of the Maastricht Treaty*, 1995, *European and World Trade Law*, 1996; *Procedural Aspects of Competition Law*, 1975; articles on EC law. *Name, Style and Title:* Raised to the peerage as Baroness Elles, of the City of Westminster 1972. *Address:* The Baroness Elles, 75 Ashley Gardens, London, SW1P 1HG *Tel:* House of Lords 020 7219 3149; Villa Fontana, Ponte del Giglio, Lucca, Italy.

LORD ELLIOTT OF MORPETH   Conservative

ELLIOTT OF MORPETH (Life Baron), Robert William Elliott; cr. 1985. Born 11 December 1920. Son of late Richard Elliott; educated Edward VI Grammar School, Morpeth. Married June 16, 1956, Catherine Jane Morpeth (1 son 4 daughters inc twins). *Councils, Public Bodies:* DL, Northumberland 1985. *Career:* Chairman, Newcastle and Gateshead Water Company 1983–93; Non-Executive Director, T. Cowie 1987–95; Chairman, United Artists Communications (North East) 1995–; Vice-Chairman, Lyonaisse UK; Former Chairman, Metro Radio Group; Former Director: Port of Tyne Authority, Ferguson Industrial Holdings plc, Corporate Trade Finance plc, Sino French Holdings (Hong Kong). *House of Commons:* Contested (Conservative): Morpeth by-election 1954, General Election 1955; MP (Conservative) for Newcastle upon Tyne North 1957–83; PPS to: Joint Parliamentary Secretaries, Ministry of Transport and Civil Aviation 1958–59, Under-Secretary, Home Office 1959–60, Minister of State, Home Office 1960–61, Secretary for Technical Co-operation 1961–63. *Whip (Commons):* Assistant Government Whip 1963–64; Opposition Whip 1964; Government Whip (Comptroller of HM Household) June-September 1970. *House of Lords:* A Deputy Speaker of the House of Lords 1992–; A Deputy Chairman of Committees 1997–. *Party Groups (General):* Vice-Chairman, Conservative Party Organisation 1970–74. *Other:* President, Water Companies Association 1975–92; Chairman, Tyneside Save The Children. *Honours:* Kt 1974. *Special Interests:* Regional Policy. *Recreations:* Country life, family. *Clubs:* Northern Counties (Newcastle upon Tyne). *Name, Style and Title:* Raised to the peerage as Baron Elliott of Morpeth, of Morpeth in the County of Northumberland and of the City of Newcastle-upon-Tyne 1985. *Address:* The Lord Elliott of Morpeth, DL, No 3 Apartment, Hindley Hall, Stocksfield, Northumberland, NE43 7RY *Tel:* 01434 684777 *Tel:* 020 7730 7619.

LORD ELTON   Conservative

ELTON (2nd Baron, UK), Rodney Elton; cr. 1934. Born 2 March 1930. Son of 1st Baron. Succeeded his father 1973; educated Eton; New College, Oxford (MA). Married 1st, 1958, Anne Frances Tilney (1 son 3 daughters) (marriage dissolved 1979), married 2nd, August 24, 1979, Richenda, CVO, daughter of late Sir Hugh Gurney, KCMG, MVO. *Armed Forces:* Late 2nd Lieutenant, The Queens Bays; Late Captain, Queen's Own Warwickshire and Worcestershire Yeomanry; Late Major, Leicestershire and Derbyshire Yeomanry. *Career:* Farming 1957–73; Assistant Mastership (History): Loughborough Grammar School 1962–67, Fairham Comprehensive School for Boys 1967–69; Lecturer, Bishop Lonsdale College of Education 1969–72; Director: Overseas Exhibitions Ltd 1977–79, Building Trades Exhibition Ltd 1977–79; Director and Deputy Chairman, Andry Montgomery Ltd 1987–; Licencesd Lay Minister, Church of England 1998–; Founded the DIVERT Trust 1993; Chairman, Quality Standards Committee, City and Guilds of London Institute 1999–. *House of Lords:* Parliamentary Under-Secretary of State for Northern Ireland 1979–81; Parliamentary Under-Secretary of State: Department of Health and Social Security September 1981–82, Home Office 1982–84; Minister of State: Home Office 1984–85, Department of the Environment 1985–86; A Deputy Chairman of Committees 1997–; A Deputy Speaker 1999–; An elected hereditary peer (office holder) 1999–. *Whip:* Opposition Whip 1974–76. *Spokesman:* An Opposition Spokesman 1976–79. *Select Committees:* Member, Select Committee on the Scrutiny of Delegated Powers 1994–97. *Party Groups:* Deputy Chairman, Association of Conservative Peers 1988–93. *Other:* Chairman, Intermediate Treatment Fund 1990–93; Vice-President, Institute of Trading Standards Administration. *Trusts, etc:* Trustee: The Airey Neave Trust 1991–96, City Parochial Foundation and Trust for London 1991–97; Chairman, DIVERT Trust 1993–96, President 1999–. *Miscellaneous:* Contested (Conservative) Loughborough division of Leicestershire 1966 and 1970 General Elections; Member, Boyd Commission (South Rhodesia Independence Elections) 1979; Chairman, Financial Intermediaries Managers & Brokers Regulatory Association 1987–90; Member, Panel on Takeovers and Mergers 1988–90; Chairman, Inquiry into Discipline in Schools (The Elton Report) 1988. *Honours:* TD 1970. *Special Interests:* Juvenile Justice. *Recreations:* Painting. *Clubs:* Beefsteak, Pratt's, Cavalry and Guards. *Address:* The Lord Elton, TD, House of Lords, London, SW1A 0PW.

LORD ELYSTAN-MORGAN   Cross-Bencher

ELYSTAN-MORGAN (Life Baron), Dafydd Elystan Elystan-Morgan; cr. 1981. Born 7 December 1932. Son of late Dewi Morgan, Journalist; educated Ardwyn Grammar School; University of Wales, Aberystwyth LLB(Hons.). Married November 14, 1959, Alwen Roberts (1 son 1 daughter). *Career:* Called to the Bar 1971 (Gray's Inn); Partner in North Wales firm of solicitors 1958–68; Recorder of the Wales and Chester Circuit 1983–1987; Judge of the Wales and Chester Circuit 1987–. *House of Commons:* MP (Labour) for Cardigan 1966–74; Joint Under-Secretary of State, Home Office April 1968–70. *Spokesman (Commons):* Deputy Opposition Spokesman: Home Affairs 1970–72, Welsh Affairs 1972–74. *Spokesman:* Opposition Spokesman on Home Affairs and Legal Affairs 1983–87. *Party Groups (General):* Chairman, Welsh Parliamentary Party 1964, 1974. *Miscellaneous:* President, Association of Welsh Local Authorities 1970–74. *Name, Style and Title:* Raised to the peerage as Baron Elystan-Morgan, of Aberteifi in the County of Dyfed 1981. *Address:* His Honour Judge The Lord Elystan-Morgan, Carreg Afon, Dolau, Bow Street, Dyfed.

BARONESS EMERTON   Cross-Bencher

EMERTON (Life Baroness), Audrey Caroline Emerton; cr. 1997. Born 10 September 1935. Daughter of late George Emerton, and of Lily Emerton; educated Tunbridge Wells Grammar School; St George's Hospital; Battersea College of Technology. *Councils, Public Bodies:* DL, Kent 1992–. *Career:* Senior Tutor, St George's Hospital, London SW1 1965–68; County Nursing Officer, St John Ambulance, Kent 1967–85, County Commissioner 1985–88; Principal Nursing Officer, Education, Bromley Hospital Management Committee 1968–70; Chief Nursing Officer, Tunbridge Wells and Leybourne Hospital Management Committee 1970–73; Regional Nursing Officer, SE Thames RHA 1973–91; Chief Nursing Officer, St John Ambulance 1988–96,

Chairman, Medical Board 1993–96; Vice-Chairman, Brighton Health Care NHS Trust 1993–94, Chairman 1994–; Chief Officer, Care in the Community, St John Ambulance 1996–; Chief Commander, St John Ambulance 1998–. *Other:* President, Association of Nurse Administrators 1979–82; Chairman, English National Board for Nursing, Midwifery and Health Visiting 1983–85; Chairman, United Kingdom Central Council for Nursing, Midwifery and Health Visiting 1985–93; Hon. Vice-President, Royal College of Nursing 1994–; Member, Court of the University of Sussex 1996–98; Lay Member, General Medical Council 1996–. Hon. DCL, Kent University 1989; Hon. DUniv, University of Central England in Birmingham 1997; Hon. DSc, University of Brighton 1997. *Trusts, etc:* Trustee, Kent Community Housing Trust 1993–98. *Honours:* CStJ 1978; DBE 1989; DStJ 1993. Fellow, Royal Society of Arts; Member, Royal Society of Medicine. *Name, Style and Title:* Raised to the peerage as Baroness Emerton, of Tunbridge Wells in the County of Kent and of Clerkenwell in the London Borough of Islington 1997. *Address:* The Baroness Emerton, DBE, DL, St John Ambulance HQ, 1 Grosvenor Crescent, London, SW1X 7EF.

LORD EMSLIE — Cross-Bencher

EMSLIE (Life Baron), George Carlyle Emslie; cr. 1980; MBE (Mil) 1946. Born 6 December 1919. Son of late Alexander Emslie, Insurance Manager; educated The High School of Glasgow; Glasgow University (MA, LLB). Married October 2, 1942, Lilias Ann Mailer (died 1998), daughter of late Robert Hannington (3 sons). *Armed Forces:* Served with Argyll & Sutherland Highlanders in Middle East, Italy and Greece and as Brigade Major 1939–45. *Career:* Advocate 1948; Advocate Depute 1955; QC (Scotland) 1957; Sheriff of Perth and Angus 1963–66; Dean of the Faculty of Advocates 1965–70; Senator (Lord Emslie) of the College of Justice 1970–72; Lord Justice-General and Lord President of the Court of Session 1972–89. Hon. LLD, Glasgow 1973. *Trusts, etc:* Trustee, National Library of Scotland 1965–, Vice-Chairman 1975–. *Miscellaneous:* Member, Scottish Committee, Council on Tribunals 1962–70; Chairman, Scottish Agricultural Wages Board 1969–73; Hon. Bencher: Inner Temple 1974, Inn of Court, Northern Ireland. *Honours:* MBE (Mil) 1946; PC 1972. FRSE 1987. *Recreations:* Golf, walking, reading, the piano. *Sportsclubs:* The Honourable Company of Edinburgh Golfers. *Clubs:* New (Edinburgh). *Name, Style and Title:* Raised to the peerage as Baron Emslie, of Potterton in the district of Gordon 1980. *Address:* Rt Hon the Lord Emslie, MBE, LLB, FRSE, 47 Heriot Row, Edinburgh, EH3 6EX *Tel:* 0131–225 3657.

EARL OF ERROLL — Cross-Bencher

ERROLL (24th Earl of, S), Merlin Sereld Victor Gilbert Hay; cr. 1452. 25th Lord Hay (S) 1429, 24th Lord Slains (S) 1452; 12th Bt of Moncreiffe of that Ilk (NS) 1685; 28th Hereditary Lord High Constable of Scotland, 1314; 32nd Chief of The Hays since 1160 (Celtic Title) Mac Garadh Mhor. Born 20 April 1948. Son of Sir Iain Moncreiffe of that Ilk, 11th Bt and Diana Denyse, Countess of Erroll (23rd in line). Succeeded his mother to the earldom 1978 and his father to the baronetcy 1985; educated Eton; Trinity College, Cambridge. Married 1982, Isabelle Jacqueline Laline, daughter of late Major Thomas Astell, MC (changed surname from Hohler and assumed name and arms of Astell by Royal Licence 1978), and of late Mrs Astell (2 sons 2 daughters). *Armed Forces:* TA 1975–90; Hon. Colonel, RMPTA 1992–97. *Career:* Hayway Partners (Marketing) 1991–; Computer Consultant until 1993; Group Director Applications and Development, Girovend Holdings plc 1993–94; Chairman, CRC Ltd 1995–. *House of Lords:* An elected hereditary peer 1999–. *Select Committees:* Member, Library and Computers Sub-Committee 1999–; Board Member of Parliamentary Office of Science and Technology 2000–. *Miscellaneous:* Page to the Lord Lyon 1956; Lieutenant, Atholl Highlanders 1974; Member, Queens Body Guard for Scotland, Royal Company of Archers; Member, Parliamentary Office of Science and Technology (POST) 2000–. *Honours:* OStJ 1977. Freeman, City of London. Member, Court of Assistant of Fishmongers' Company, Prime Warden 2000–01. *Special Interests:* Defence, Technology, Scotland, Environment. *Recreations:* Skiing, climbing. *Clubs:* White's, Pratt's, Puffin's (Edinburgh). *Address:* The Earl of Erroll, Woodbury Hall, Everton, Sandy, Bedfordshire, SG19 2HR *Tel:* 01767 650251 *E-Mail:* errollm@parliament.uk.

LORD EVANS OF PARKSIDE   Labour

EVANS OF PARKSIDE (Life Baron), John Evans; cr. 1997. Born 19 October 1930. Son of late James and Margaret Evans; educated Jarrow Central School. Married June 6, 1959, Joan, daughter of late Thomas Slater (2 sons 1 daughter). *Trades Union:* Joined AEU 1951. *Armed Forces:* Royal Engineers 1949–50. *Councils, Public Bodies:* Hebburn Urban District Council: Councillor 1962–74, Chairman 1972–73, Leader 1969–74; Councillor, South Tyneside Metropolitan District Council 1973–74. *Career:* Tyneside Shipyard Worker. *House of Commons:* MP (Labour) for Newton February 1974–83 and for St. Helens North 1983–97; PPS to Leader of Opposition 1980–83; Shadow Employment Minister 1983–87. *Whip (Commons):* Government Whip 1978–1979; Opposition Whip 1979–80. *Select Committees:* Member, Administration and Works Sub-Committee, House of Lords Offices Committee 2000–. *International Bodies (General):* UK Member, European Parliament 1975–78; Chairman, European Parliament Policy and Transport Committee 1976–78. *Party Groups (General):* Joined Labour Party 1954; Political Secretary, National Union of Labour and Socialist Clubs; Member, National Executive Committee of the Labour Party 1982–96; Labour Party: Vice-Chairman 1990–91, Chairman 1991–92. Freeman, Metropolitan Borough of St Helens 1997. *Special Interests:* Employment, Energy, Transport, Manufacturing Industries, Industrial Relations, Licensed Trade. *Recreations:* Gardening, watching Rugby League and Association Football. *Name, Style and Title:* Raised to the peerage as Baron Evans of Parkside, of St Helens in the County of Merseyside 1997. *Address:* The Lord Evans of Parkside, 6 Kirkby Road, Culcheth, Warrington, Cheshire, WA3 4BS.

LORD EVANS OF TEMPLE GUITING   Labour

EVANS OF TEMPLE GUITING (Life Baron), Matthew Evans; cr. 2000. Born 7 August 1941. Son of late George Ewart Evans and Florence Ellen Evans; educated Friends' School, Saffron Walden; LSE (BSc economics). Married 1st, 1966, Elizabeth Mead (2 sons) (marriage dissolved 1991); married 2nd, 1991, Caroline Michel (2 sons 1 daughter). *Career:* Bookselling 1963–64; Faber & Faber Ltd 1964–, Managing Director 1972–93, Chairman 1981–; Director, Which? Ltd 1997–. *Other:* Governor, BFI 1982–97 (Vice-Chairman 1996–97); Member: Council, Publishers Association 1978–84, Franco-British Society 1981–; Chairman: National Book League 1982–84, English Stage Company 1984–90. Hon. DLitt, Sunderland. *Miscellaneous:* Member, Literary Advisory Panel, British Council 1986–97; Chairman, Library and Information Commission 1995–; Member: Arts Council National Lottery Advisory Panel 1997–, University for Industry Advisory Group 1997, Sir Richard Eyre's Working Group on Royal Opera House 1997, Arts and Humanities Research Board 1998–; Chairman, Museums, Libraries and Archives Council 2000–. *Honours:* CBE 1998. FRSA 1990; Hon FRCA 1999; Hon FLA 1999. *Clubs:* Groucho. *Name, Style and Title:* Raised to the peerage as Baron Evans of Temple Guiting, of Temple Guiting in the County of Gloucestershire 2000. *Address:* The Lord Evans of Temple Guiting, CBE, Faber & Faber Ltd, 3 Queen Square, London, WC1N 3AU *E-Mail:* matthewe@faber.co.uk.

LORD EVANS OF WATFORD   Labour

EVANS OF WATFORD (Life Baron), David Charles Evans; cr. 1998. Born 30 November 1942. Son of Arthur Charles Evans and Phyllis Connie Evans; educated Hampden Secondary School; Watford College of Technology. Married May 7, 1966, June Scaldwell (1 son 1 daughter). *Trades Union:* GPMU. *Career:* Apprentice Printer, Stone and Cox Ltd 1957; Has worked for various printers as Sales Executive and Sales Director; Chairman, Centurion Press Group and subsidiary companies in the United Kingdom, The Netherlands and the USA; Chairman: Personnel Publications Ltd, Indigo Publishing Ltd, Centurion Publishing Ltd. *House of Lords:* Departmental Liaison Peer for the DTI 1999–. *Select Committees:* Member, Library and Computers Sub-Committee, House of Lords Offices Committee 2000–. *Other:* Life Governor, Imperial Cancer Research Fund; Chairman, CT Spiral Scanner Appeal, Watford Hospital; Member of Benevolent

Committee, The Royal British Legion. *Miscellaneous:* Assisted in the creation of the One World group (now One World Action); Lecturer, on a voluntary basis, for the Postal Telegraph and Telephone International in trade union studies and media public relations; Non-executive Director of Hendon Museum Enterprises Ltd. Fellow: Chartered Institute of Marketing, Institute of Directors. Member, Worshipful Company of Marketors. *Special Interests:* Industrial Relations, Current Affairs, Education, Voluntary Sector. *Recreations:* Theatre, the arts, reading, travel. *Clubs:* Mortons. *Name, Style and Title:* Raised to the peerage as Baron Evans of Watford, of Chipperfield in the County of Hertfordshire 1998. *Address:* The Lord Evans of Watford, House of Lords, London, SW1A 0PW *Tel:* 01923 891001 (Office) *E-Mail:* lordevans@centurion.co.uk.

LORD EWING OF KIRKFORD   Labour

EWING OF KIRKFORD (Life Baron), Harry Ewing; cr. 1992. Born 20 January 1931. Son of late William Ewing; educated Beath High School, Cowdenbeath. Married July 10, 1954, Margaret Greenhill (1 son 1 daughter). *Trades Union:* Active Trade Unionist, AUEW, Member No. 1 District Council 1958–61; Holder of various offices within Union of Post Office Workers 1962–71. *Armed Forces:* RAF 1949–51. *Councils, Public Bodies:* DL, Fife 1995–. *House of Commons:* Contested (Labour) East Fife in 1970 General Election; MP (Labour) for: Stirling and Falkirk 1971–74, Stirling, Falkirk and Grangemouth 1974–83, Falkirk East 1983–92; Parliamentary Under-Secretary of State, Scottish Office (with special responsibility for Devolution matters) 1974–79.
Spokesman (Commons): Opposition Front Bench Spokesman on: Scotland 1979–84, Trade and Industry 1984–85, Scotland 1985–87. *Spokesman:* An Opposition Spokesman on: Scottish Office Affairs 1992–96, Transport 1993–96, Energy 1994–95. *International Bodies (General):* Member: Council of Europe 1987–92, Western European Union 1987–92. *Party Groups (General):* Has held many local and national positions in the Co-operative Movement. *Other:* Chairman, Scottish Disability Foundation 1992–; Non-executive Director, Kirkcaldy Acute Hospitals NHS Trust 1994–96; Chairman, Fife Healthcare NHS Trust 1996–98. Hon. DU, University of Stirling 1998. *Miscellaneous:* Joint Chairman, Scottish Constitutional Convention 1990–96; Chairman, Ewing Enquiry into the availability of housing for wheelchair disabled in Scotland November 1993, report published April 1994. *Special Interests:* Health, Social Services. *Recreations:* Gardening, bowls. *Name, Style and Title:* Raised to the peerage as Baron Ewing of Kirkford, of Cowdenbeath in the District of Dunfermline 1992. *Address:* The Lord Ewing of Kirkford, DL, Gowanbank, 45 Glenlyon Road, Leven, Fife, KY8 4AA *Tel:* 01333 426123.

LORD EZRA   Liberal Democrat

EZRA (Life Baron), Derek Ezra; cr. 1983. Born 23 February 1919. Son of late David Ezra; educated Monmouth School; Magdalene College, Cambridge. Married 1950, Julia Elizabeth Wilkins. *Armed Forces:* Army Service 1939–47. *Career:* Various positions in Marketing Department, National Coal Board 1947–60; Director General of Marketing, NCB 1960–65, Board Member 1965–67, Deputy Chairman 1967–71; Chairman: NCB 1971–82, Energy and Technical Services Group plc, AHS-Emstar plc, Sheffield Heat & Power Ltd; Director, Aran Energy plc; Chairman, Throgmorton Trust 1985–90; Director: Solvay SA 1979–89, Redland plc 1981–89; Member, International Advisory Board: Banca del Lavoro 1981–, Creditanstalt Bankverein 1981–91; Member: Advisory Board, Petrofina SA 1981–90, Advisory Committee, Energy International SA 1975–90.
Spokesman: Former Liberal Democrat spokesman on economic affairs in the House of Lords; Spokesman on: Energy 1998–, Rural Affairs 1999–. *Select Committees:* Member, Select Committee on Monetary Policy of the Bank of England 1998–. *Other:* Former President, Coal Industry Society. *Miscellaneous:* Former President, British Standards Institution; President, Institute of Trading Standards Administration 1987–92; Former President, Keep Britain Tidy Group; Patron (Past President), Neighbourhood Energy Action; President, Combustion Engineering Association. *Honours:* MBE (Mil) 1945; Kt 1974. *Publications: Coal and Energy*, 1978; *The Energy Debate*, 1983. *Name, Style and Title:* Raised to the peerage as Baron Ezra, of Horsham in the County of West Sussex 1983. *Address:* The Lord Ezra, MBE, House of Lords, London, SW1A 0PW *Tel:* House of Lords 020 7219 3180.

F

FALCONER OF THOROTON (Life Baron), Charles Leslie Falconer; cr. 1997. Born 19 November 1951. Son of John Leslie Falconer and of late Anne Mansel Falconer; educated Trinity College, Glenalmond; Queens' College, Cambridge. Married 1985, Marianna Catherine Thoroton, daughter of late Sir David Hildyard, KCMG, DFC (3 sons 1 daughter). *Career:* Called to the Bar, Inner Temple 1974; QC 1991. *House of Lords:* Solicitor General 1997–98; Minister of State, Cabinet Office 1998–. *Miscellaneous:* Elected Master, Bench of the Inner Temple 1997. *Name, Style and Title:* Raised to the peerage as Baron Falconer of Thoroton, of Thoroton in the County of Nottinghamshire 1997. *Address:* The Lord Falconer of Thoroton, QC, Cabinet Office, 70 Whitehall, London, SW1A 2AS *E-Mail:* cfalconer@cabinet-office.x.gsi.gov.uk.

FALKENDER (Life Baroness), Marcia Matilda Falkender; cr. 1974. Born 10 March 1932. Daughter of late Harry Field; educated Northampton High School for Girls; Queen Mary College, London University (BA Hons, History). Married December 1, 1955, George Edmund Charles Williams (marriage dissolved 1961). *Career:* Secretary to General Secretary Labour Party HQ 1955–56; Private Secretary to Rt Hon. Harold Wilson 1956–64; Political Secretary to Rt Hon. Harold Wilson and head of his Political Office 1964–76; Columnist, *Mail on Sunday* 1983–88; Local Director, Cheltenham and Gloucester Building Society, Peckham; Director: South London Investment Mortgage Corporation 1986–91, Canvasback Productions 1988–91, Regent (GM) Laboratories 1996–. *Other:* Lay Governor, Queen Mary and Westfield College, London University 1987–93. *Trusts, etc:* Formerly President, UN Unifem UK Trust; Trustee: The Silver Trust 1986–, Women Aid. *Miscellaneous:* Member: Film Industry Working Party 1975, British Screen Advisory Council 1985–, Film Industry Action Committee 1977–. *Publications: Inside No. 10*, 1972; *Perspective on Downing Street*, 1983. *Special Interests:* Exports, Health, Breast Cancer, British Film Industry. *Recreations:* Films. *Clubs:* Reform. *Name, Style and Title:* Raised to the peerage as Baroness Falkender, of West Haddon in the County of Northamptonshire 1974. *Address:* The Baroness Falkender, CBE, 3 Wyndham Mews, Upper Montagu Street, London, W1H 1RS *Tel:* 020 7402 8570 *Fax:* 020 7402 3407.

FALKLAND (15th Viscount of, S), Lucius Edward William Plantagenet Cary; cr. 1620; Lord Cary. Born 8 May 1935. Son of 14th Viscount. Succeeded his father 1984; educated Wellington College. Married 1st, 1962, Caroline Butler (1 son 2 daughters and 1 daughter deceased) (marriage dissolved 1990), married 2nd, September 12, 1990, Nicole Mackey (1 son). *Armed Forces:* Late 2nd Lieutenant, 8th Hussars. *Career:* Formerly: Journalist, Theatrical agent, Chartered shipbroker; Chief executive, C. T. Bowring Trading (Holdings) Ltd; Marketing consultant 1980–. *House of Lords:* An elected hereditary peer 1999–; Deputy Chairman of Committees 2000–. *Whip:* Liberal Democrat Deputy Whip 1988–. *Spokesman:* Party Spokesman on: National Heritage 1995–97, Culture, Media and Sport 1997–. *Select Committees:* Member: House of Lords Select Committee on Overseas Trade 1984–85, Select Committee on House of Lords' Offices 1997–, Refreshment Sub-Committee, House of Lords Offices Committee 2000–. *Miscellaneous:* Chairman, Motorcycle Industry Theft Action Group 1991–. *Special Interests:* Developing World, Film Industry, Alcohol and Drug Addiction, Transport, Motorcycle Industry. *Recreations:* Golf, cinema, motorcycling. *Sportsclubs:* Sunningdale Golf. *Clubs:* Brooks's. *Address:* The Viscount of Falkland, House of Lords, London, SW1A 0PW *Tel:* House of Lords 020 7219 3230.

LORD FANSHAWE OF RICHMOND   Conservative

FANSHAWE OF RICHMOND (Life Baron), Anthony Henry Fanshawe Royle; cr. 1983. Born 27 March 1927. Son of late Sir Lancelot Royle, KBE; educated Harrow; RMA, Sandhurst. Married 1957, Shirley Worthington (2 daughters). *Armed Forces:* Captain, The Life Guards 1945–48; 21st Special Air Service Regiment (TA) 1948–51. *Career:* Director, Brooke Bond Liebig plc 1974–84; Director, Wilkinson Sword Ltd 1974–86, Chairman 1980–83; Director, Sedgwick Group 1984–, Chairman 1993–97; Director: Westland Group plc 1985–94, TI Group plc 1990–2000, Xerox UK Ltd 1988–, Pratt & Whitney Europe Advisory Board 1993–. *House of Commons:* Contested (Conservative): St Pancras North 1955, Torrington 1958; MP (Conservative) for Richmond 1959–83; PPS to: Secretary of State for Air 1960–62, Minister of Aviation 1962–64; Member, UK Delegation to Council of Europe and WEU 1965; Parliamentary Under-Secretary of State for Foreign and Commonwealth Affairs 1970–74. *Whip (Commons):* Opposition Whip 1967–70. *Party Groups (General):* Vice-Chairman, Conservative Party Organisation 1979–84; Chairman, Conservative Party International Office 1979–84. *Trusts, etc:* Trustee, National Army Museum 1975–. *Honours:* KCMG 1974; Most Esteemed Family Order of the State of Brunei (1st Class) 1974. *Special Interests:* Foreign Affairs, Defence, Arts, Aviation. *Clubs:* Brooks's, White's, Pratt's. *Name, Style and Title:* Raised to the peerage as Baron Fanshawe of Richmond, of South Cerney in the County of Gloucestershire 1983. *Address:* The Lord Fanshawe of Richmond, KCMG, The Chapter Manor, South Cerney, Gloucestershire, GL7 5TN.

BARONESS FARRINGTON OF RIBBLETON   Labour

FARRINGTON OF RIBBLETON (Life Baroness), Josephine Farrington; cr. 1994. Born 29 June 1940. Daughter of late Ernest Joseph Cayless, and of Dorothy Cayless. Married April 16, 1960, Michael James Farrington (3 sons). *Councils, Public Bodies:* Councillor: Preston Borough Council 1973–76, Lancashire County Council 1977–; Chairman, Education Committee 1981–91; Chairman of County Council 1992–93. *Career:* Member, Council of Europe Standing Conference of Local and Regional Authorities 1981–94 and of new Congress; Chairman, Culture, Education, Media and Sport Committee 1988–94; International observer at local elections in Poland, Ukraine and Albania; Member, Committee of the Regions – EU; Chairman, Education and Training 1994; Currently Chairman, Association of County Councils; Service as: Education Spokesperson, Chairman of Policy Committee, Labour Group Deputy and Leader; Has served on Burnham Primary and Secondary and Further Education Committees; Member, National Advisory Body for Public Sector Higher Education. *Whip:* Opposition Whip 1995–97; Government Whip 1997–. *Spokesman:* A Spokeswoman on: Environment, Transport and the Regions 1997–, Northern Ireland 1997–. *Awards Granted:* UK Woman of Europe 1994. *Miscellaneous:* Contested (Labour) Lancashire West 1983 general election. *Recreations:* Reading. *Name, Style and Title:* Raised to the peerage as Baroness Farrington of Ribbleton, of Fulwood in the County of Lancashire 1994. *Address:* The Baroness Farrington of Ribbleton, House of Lords, London, SW1A 0PW.

LORD FAULKNER OF WORCESTER   Labour

FAULKNER OF WORCESTER (Life Baron), Richard Oliver Faulkner; cr. 1999. Born 22 March 1946. Son of late Harold and Mabel Faulkner; educated Merchant Taylors' School, Northwood; Worcester College, Oxford (BA philosophy, politics and economics, MA). Married 1968, Susan, daughter of late Donald Heyes (2 daughters). *Trades Union:* Member: RMT, NUJ. *Councils, Public Bodies:* Councillor, Merton Borough Council 1971–78. *Career:* Research Assistant and Journalist, Labour Party 1967–69; Public Relations Officer, Construction Industry Training Board 1969–70; Editor, *Steel News* 1971; Account Director, F J Lyons (Public Relations) Ltd 1971–73; Director, PPR International 1973–76; Government Relations Adviser to various companies, unions, councils and bodies 1973–99; Co-Founder, Parliamentary Journal *The House Magazine*; Communications Adviser to Leader of the Opposition and Labour Party (unpaid) in general elections 1987, 1992, 1997; Communications Adviser to the Bishop at Lambeth 1990; Deputy Chairman, Citigate Westminster 1997–99 (Joint Managing Director, Westminster Communications Group 1989–97);

Director, Cardiff Millennium Stadium plc 1997–; Strategy Adviser: Littlewoods Leisure 1999–, Financial Services Authority 1999–, Incepta Group plc 1999–. *House of Lords:* Departmental Liaison Peer, Department of the Environment, Transport and the Regions. *Select Committees:* Member, Select Committee on European Communities Sub-Committee B (Energy, Industry and Transport). *International Bodies:* Member, CPA IPU. *Other:* Member: Football League Enquiry into Membership Schemes 1984, Sports Council 1986–88, Anti-hooliganism Committee 1987–90; Chairman: Women's Football Association 1988–91, Sports Grounds Initiative 1995–2000; Director, Brighton and Hove Albion Football Club 1997–; Former Director, Wimbledon and Crystal Palace Football Clubs; Vice-Chairman, Transport 2000 Ltd 1986–99; Chairman, Worcester College Appeal Campaign 1996–; Vice-Chairman, Football Task Force 1997–99; Patron, Roy Castle Lung Cancer Foundation 1999–; Member, Court of University of Luton 1999–; Patron, The TERRE Foundation. *Trusts, etc:* Trustee, Football Trust 1979–82, Secretary 1983–86, First Deputy Chairman 1986–98; Trustee, Foundation for Sport and the Arts 2000–. *Miscellaneous:* Contested (Labour) Devizes 1970, February 1974, Monmouth October 1974, Huddersfield West 1979. MIPR. *Special Interests:* Transport, Sport, Human Rights. *Recreations:* Travelling by railway, collecting Lloyd George memorabilia, tinplate trains, watching Association Football. *Clubs:* Reform. *Name, Style and Title:* Raised to the peerage as Baron Faulkner of Worcester, of Wimbledon in the London Borough of Merton 1999. *Address:* The Lord Faulkner of Worcester, House of Lords, London, SW1A 0PW *Tel:* 020 7219 8503 *Tel:* 020 7219 8503 (Voice Mail) *E-Mail:* faulknerro@parliament.uk; faulknerro@hotmail.com.

LORD FELDMAN   Conservative

FELDMAN (Life Baron), Basil Feldman; cr. 1996. Born 23 September 1926. Son of late Philip and Tilly Feldman; educated Grocers' School; SE London Technical College. Married 1952, Gita Julius (2 sons 1 daughter). *Career:* Chairman, Martlet Services Group Ltd 1973–81; Member, Post Office Users' National Council 1978–81; Chairman, The Clothing Little Neddy 1978–85; Underwriting Member of Lloyds 1979–97; Chairman: Solport Ltd 1980–85, Better Made in Britain 1983–; A Director, The Young Entrepreneurs Fund 1985–94; Member, English Tourist Board 1986–96; Chairman: The Quality Mark 1987–92, Shopping Hours Reform Council 1988–94, Better Business Opportunities 1990–98, Market Opportunities Advisory Group, Department of Trade and Industry 1991–93. *Party Groups (General):* Deputy Chairman, National Union of Conservative and Unionist Associations, Greater London Area 1975–78, Chairman 1978–81, President 1981–85, Vice President 1985–; Vice Chairman, National Union of the Conservative Party 1982–85, Chairman 1985–86, Vice-President 1986–; Member, National Union Executive Committee 1975–, Chairman 1991–96; Joint National Chairman, Conservative Party's Impact 80s Campaign 1982–87; Vice-President, Greater London Young Conservatives 1975–77; Has held various other posts within the Conservative Party including Party Treasurer 1996–. *Other:* Governor, Sports Aid Foundation 1990–; Founder/Chairman, The London Arts Season 1993–96; Chairman: The Festival of Arts and Culture 1995, Conservative National Golf Tournament Charitable Settlement. *Miscellaneous:* Adopted Member: GLC Housing Management Committee 1973–77, GLC Arts Board 1976–81. *Honours:* Kt 1982. FRSA 1987. Freeman, City of London 1983. *Publications:* Several publications, booklets and pamphlets for the Conservative Party; *Constituency Campaigning,* 1977; *Some Thoughts on Job Creation,* (for NEDO) 1984. *Special Interests:* Industry, Arts, Construction Industry, Retail Industry, Import Substitution, Tourism, Sport. *Recreations:* Golf, tennis, theatre, opera, travel. *Clubs:* Carlton. *Name, Style and Title:* Raised to the peerage as Baron Feldman, of Frognal in the London Borough of Camden 1996. *Address:* The Lord Feldman, House of Lords, London, SW1A 0PW.

LORD FELLOWES — Cross-Bencher

FELLOWES (Life Baron), Robert Fellowes; cr. 1999. Born 11 December 1941. Son of late Sir William Fellowes, KCVO and Lady Fellowes; educated Eton. Married April 20, 1978, Lady Jane Spencer, daughter of 8th Earl Spencer, LVO, and Hon. Mrs Shand Kydd (1 son 2 daughters). *Armed Forces:* Short Service Commission, Scots Guards 1960–63. *Career:* Director, Allen Harvey & Ross Ltd 1968–77; Assistant Private Secretary to HM The Queen 1977–86, Deputy Private Secretary 1986–90, Private Secretary 1990–99; Vice-Chairman, Barclays Private Banking 1999–2000, Chairman 2000–; Director: South African Breweries 1999–, Getmapping.com 2000–. *Other:* Vice-Chairman, Commonwealth Institute 2000–. *Honours:* LVO 1983; CB 1987; KCVO 1989; PC 1990; KCB 1991; GCVO 1996; GCB 1998; QSO 1999. Liveryman, Goldsmith's Company. *Recreations:* Golf, watching cricket, reading, shooting. *Clubs:* White's, Pratt's, MCC, Royal Overseas League. *Name, Style and Title:* Raised to the peerage as Baron Fellowes, of Shotesham in the County of Norfolk 1999. *Address:* Rt Hon the Lord Fellowes, GCB, GCVO, QSO, House of Lords, London, SW1A 0PW.

EARL FERRERS — Conservative

FERRERS (13th Earl, GB), Robert Washington Shirley; cr. 1711; Viscount Tamworth; 19th Bt of Staunton Harold (E) 1611. Born 8 June 1929. Son of 12th Earl. Succeeded his father 1954; educated Winchester College; Magdalene College, Cambridge (MA). Married July 21, 1951, Annabel Mary Carr (2 sons 3 daughters). *Armed Forces:* Coldstream Guards, Malaya 1949. *Councils, Public Bodies:* DL, Norfolk 1983. *Career:* Trustee, East Anglian Trustee Savings Bank 1957–75; Trustee, Trustee Savings Bank of Eastern England 1975–79, Chairman 1977–79; Member, Central Board Trustee Savings Bank 1977–79; Director: Central Trustee Savings Bank Ltd 1978–79, TSB Trustcard Ltd 1978–79; Director, Norwich Union Insurance Group 1975–79, 1983–88; Director, Economic Forestry Group plc 1985–88. *House of Lords:* Parliamentary Secretary to Ministry of Agriculture, Fisheries and Food 1974; Member, Armitage Committee on Political Activities of Civil Servants 1976; Joint Deputy Leader of the Opposition, House of Lords 1976–79; Minister of State, Ministry of Agriculture, Fisheries and Food 1979–83; Deputy Leader of the House of Lords 1979–83; Minister of State, Home Office 1988–94; Deputy Leader of the House of Lords 1988–97; Minister of State, Department of Trade and Industry (Minister for Small Firms and Consumer Affairs) 1994–95; Minister of State, Department of the Environment (Minister for the Environment and Countryside) 1995–97; An elected hereditary peer 1999–. *Whip:* Opposition Whip 1964–67; Government Whip (Lord in Waiting) 1962–64, 1971–74. *Other:* Member, Council of Hurstpierpoint College 1959–68; High Steward, Norwich Cathedral 1979–; Member, Council of Food from Britain 1985–88. *Trusts, etc:* Director, The Chatham Historic Dockyard Trust 1984–88. *Miscellaneous:* Chairman: Royal Commission on Historical Monuments (England) 1984–88, British Agricultural Export Council 1984–88. *Honours:* PC 1982. *Recreations:* Shooting, music, travel. *Clubs:* Beefsteak. *Address:* Rt Hon the Earl Ferrers, DL, Ditchingham Hall, Bungay, Suffolk, NR35 2LE *Tel:* 01508 482250.

LORD FILKIN — Labour

FILKIN (Life Baron), David Geoffrey Nigel Filkin; cr. 1999. Born 1 July 1944. Son of late Donald Geoffrey and Winifred Filkin; educated King Edward VI School, Birmingham; Clare College, Cambridge (MA History 1966); Manchester University (DipTP); Birmingham University (post graduate study). Married 1974, Elizabeth Tompkins (3 daughters) (marriage dissolved 1994). *Career:* Teacher on VSO, Ghana 1966–67; Town Planner, Redditch Development Corporation (New Town) 1969–72; Manager, Brent Housing Aid Centre, London Borough of Brent 1972–75; Deputy Chief Executive, Merseyside Improved Housing 1975–79; Borough Housing Officer, Ellesmere Port and Neston Borough Council 1979–82; Director of Housing, London Borough of Greenwich 1982–88; Chief Executive, Reading Borough Council 1988–91;

Secretary, Association of District Councils 1991–97; Local Government Adviser to Joseph Rowntree Foundation 1997–; Director, New Local Government Network 1997–; Policy Analyst and Writer 1997–. *Honours:* CBE 1997. *Publications: Best Value for the Public; Political Leadership of Best Value; Partnerships for Best Value; Modernising Local Government; Starting to Modernise; Achieving Best Value. Special Interests:* Policy Development, Policy Implementation, Housing, West Africa, Southern Africa. *Recreations:* Music, walking, swimming, singing, church. *Name, Style and Title:* Raised to the peerage as Baron Filkin, of Pimlico in the City of Westminster 1999. *Address:* The Lord Filkin, CBE, House of Lords, London, SW1A 0PW *E-Mail:* gfilkin1@aol.com.

BARONESS FISHER OF REDNAL   Labour

FISHER OF REDNAL (Life Baroness), Doris Mary Fisher; cr. 1974. Born 13 September 1919. Daughter of late Frederick Satchwell, BEM; educated Birmingham Schools; Fircroft College. Married July 1, 1939, Joseph Fisher (died 1978) (2 daughters). *Councils, Public Bodies:* Councillor, Birmingham City Council 1952–74; Past Chairman of its Housing Committee; JP, Birmingham 1961; Formerly Member, Warrington New Town Development Corporation; Member, New Towns Staff Commission 1976–79. *Career:* Member, European Parliament 1975–79. *House of Commons:* Contested Birmingham Ladywood 1969 by-election; MP (Labour) for Birmingham, Ladywood 1970–74. *Whip:* Opposition Whip 1983–84. *Spokesman:* Opposition Spokesman on the Environment 1983–84. *Party Groups (General):* National President, Women's Co-op Guild 1961–62. *Other:* Chairman, Baskerville Special School 1981–89; Warden, Birmingham Assay Office 1981–89; President, Birmingham Royal Institute of Blind (now Focus) 1982–; Member, Hallmarking Council 1989–94; President, Motability Midlands 1989–95; Governor, Hunters Hill Special School, Bromsgrove; President, The British Fluoridation Society 1993–; Midland Area Chairman: NSPCC 1993 , Macmillan Nurses 1995 ; Patron, St Basil's Young Homeless, Birmingham. Formerly Member, General Medical Council. Hon. Doctor, University of Central England, Birmingham 1998. *Special Interests:* Housing, Local Government. *Recreations:* Swimming. *Name, Style and Title:* Raised to the peerage as Baroness Fisher of Rednal, of Rednal in the City of Birmingham 1974. *Address:* The Baroness Fisher of Rednal, 60 Jacoby Place, Priory Road, Edgbaston, Birmingham, B5 7UW.

LORD FITT   Independent Socialist

FITT (Life Baron), Gerard Fitt; cr. 1983. Born 9 April 1926. Son of late George Fitt; educated in Belfast. Married November 5, 1947, Susan Doherty (died 1996) (5 daughters and 1 daughter deceased). *Councils, Public Bodies:* Councillor, Dock Ward, Belfast Corporation 1958. *Career:* Merchant Seaman 1941–53; Member (Irish Labour) Parliament of Northern Ireland, Dock Division of Belfast 1962–72; Member (SDLP), North Belfast, Northern Ireland Assembly 1973–75; Deputy Chief Executive of the Northern Ireland Executive 1974. *House of Commons:* MP for Belfast West as: Republican Labour 1966–70, SDLP 1970–79, Socialist 1979–83. *Name, Style and Title:* Raised to the peerage as Baron Fitt, of Bell's Hill in the County of Down 1983. *Address:* The Lord Fitt, House of Lords, London, SW1A 0PW.

BARONESS FLATHER   Conservative

FLATHER (Life Baroness), Shreela Flather; cr. 1990. Daughter of Aftab and Krishna Rai; educated University College, London (LLB). Married, Gary Denis Flather, OBE, QC, son of late Denis Flather and Joan Flather (2 sons).*Councils, Public Bodies:* JP, Maidenhead 1971–90 (Crown Supplemental List); Councillor, Royal Borough of Windsor and Maidenhead 1976–91, Deputy Mayor 1985–86, Mayor 1986–87; DL, Berkshire 1994–. *Career:* Called to the Bar, Inner Temple 1962; Infant teacher, ILEA 1965–67; Teacher of English as second language, Altwood Comprehensive School, Maidenhead 1968–74; Teacher of English as second language, Broadmoor Hospital 1974–78; Member, Committee of Management, Servite Houses Ltd 1987–94; UK Member, Economic and Social Committee European Community 1987–90; Director, Meridian Broadcasting (MAI) Ltd 1990–; Chairman, Alcohol Education and Research Council 1995–; Director: Marie Stopes International 1996–, Cable Corporation 1997–2000; Fellow, University College, London.

Select Committees: Former Member: European Communities Sub-Committee C, Select Committee on Medical Ethics. *Party Groups (General):* Member, Conservative Women's National Committee 1978–88; Member, Anglo-Asian Conservative Society 1979–83; Resigned the Conservative Whip December 1998, rejoined November 1999. *Other:* Senior posts in numerous organisations involved in refugee, community, carer, race relations and prison work, including Member: Commission for Racial Equality 1980–86, Social Security Advisory Committee 1987–90; Vice-Chairman, The Refugee Council 1991–94; Governor, Commonwealth Institute 1993–98; Joint President, Family Planning Association 1995–98; Resigned the Conservative Whip December 1998, rejoined November 1999. *Awards Granted: Asian Who's Who* Asian of the Year 1996. Hon. DUniv, Open University 1994. *Trusts, etc:* Trustee: Hillingdon Hospital 1990–98, Rajiv Gandhi (UK) Foundation 1993–; Member: Council of the Winston Churchill Memorial Trust 1993–, Council of St George's House, Windsor Castle 1996–, Council of University College London 2000–. *Miscellaneous:* Member, BBC South and East Regional Advisory Council 1987–89. *Special Interests:* Race Relations, European Union. *Recreations:* Reading, cinema, travel. *Name, Style and Title:* Raised to the peerage as Baroness Flather, of Windsor and Maidenhead in the Royal County of Berkshire 1990. *Address:* The Baroness Flather, JP, DL, FRSA, Triveni, Ascot Road, Maidenhead, Berkshire, SL6 2HT *Tel:* 01628 625408.

LORD FLOWERS   Cross-Bencher

FLOWERS (Life Baron), Brian Hilton Flowers; cr. 1979. Born 13 September 1924. Son of late Rev. Harold Joseph Flowers; educated Bishop Gore Grammar School, Swansea; Gonville and Caius College, Cambridge (MA); Birmingham University (DSc). Married October 26, 1951, Mary Frances, eldest daughter of late Sir Leonard F. Behrens, CBE (2 step-sons). *Career:* Anglo-Canadian Atomic Energy Project (Tube Alloys) 1944–46; Research in nuclear physics and atomic energy at Atomic Energy Research Establishment (AERE), Harwell 1946–50; Department of mathematical physics, Birmingham University 1950–52; Head of theoretical physics division, AERE, Harwell 1952–58; Manchester University: Professor of theoretical physics 1958–61, Langworthy Professor of physics 1961–72; Chairman, Science Research Council 1967–73; London University: Rector, Imperial College 1973–85, Vice-Chancellor 1985–90. *Chancellor:* Chancellor, Manchester University 1994–. *Select Committees:* Member, House of Lords Select Committee on Science and Technology 1980–93, 1994–97, Chairman 1989–93, Co-opted Member 2000–; Member, Select Committees on: Science and Technology Sub-Committee II (Aircraft Cabin Environment) 2000–, Science and Technology Sub-Committee IIA (Human Genetic Databases) 2000–. *Other:* Chairman: Computer Board for Universities and Research Council 1966–70, Member, Atomic Energy Authority 1971–81; President, Institute of Physics 1972–74; Chairman, Royal Commission on Environmental Pollution 1973–76; President: European Science Foundation 1974–80, National Society for Clean Air 1977–79; Chairman: Commission on Energy and the Environment 1978–81, University of London Working Party on future of medical and dental teaching resources 1979–80, Committee of Vice-Chancellors and Principals for 1983–85; Member of Council, Academia Europaea 1988–91; Member of Council and Vice-Chairman, Royal Postgraduate Medical School 1990–97; Member of Management Board, London School of Hygiene and Tropical Medicine 1991–95, Chairman 1994–95; Governor, Middlesex University 1992–; Chairman, Committee of Enquiry into the Academic Year 1992–93. 15 honorary doctorates; 3 honorary university fellowships. *Trusts, etc:* Managing Trustee, Nuffield Foundation 1982–98, Chairman 1987–98. *Miscellaneous:* Vice-Chairman, Parliamentary Office of Science and Technology (POST) 1998–. *Honours:* Kt 1969; Officier de la Légion d'Honneur (France), 1981. FRS 1961. *Publications:* Co-author *Properties of Matter*, 1970; *An Introduction to Numerical Methods C++*, 1995; Contributions to scientific periodicals on scientific structure of atomic nucleus, nuclear reations, science policy, energy and the environment. *Special Interests:* Higher Education, Science and Technology, Environment. *Recreations:* Music, walking, gardening, computing. *Name, Style and Title:* Raised to the peerage as Baron Flowers, of Queen's Gate in the City of Westminster 1979. *Address:* The Lord Flowers, FRS, 53 Athenaeum Road, London, N20 9AL *Tel:* 020 8446 5993 *E-Mail:* fofqg@clumsies.demon.co.uk.

BARONESS FOOKES   Conservative

FOOKES (Life Baroness), Janet Evelyn Fookes; cr. 1997. Born 21 February 1936. Daughter of late Lewis Aylmer Fookes, retired company director, and late Evelyn Margery (née Holmes); educated Hastings and St. Leonards Ladies' College; Hastings High School for Girls; Royal Holloway College, London University (BA 1957). *Councils, Public Bodies:* County Borough of Hastings: Councillor 1960–61, 1963–70, Chairman, Education Committee 1967–70; Member, Council of Stonham Housing Association 1980–92. *Career:* School Teacher 1958–70. *House of Commons:* MP (Conservative) for Merton and Morden 1970–74, and for Plymouth Drake 1974–97; Deputy Speaker and Second Deputy Chairman of Ways and Means 1992–97; Sponsored as Private Member's Bill: Sexual Offences Act 1985, Dangerous Dogs Act 1989. *Select Committees:* Member, Joint Select Committee on Consolidation of Bills 2000–. *Other:* Member: Commonwealth War Graves Commission 1987–97, Council of Management, College of St Mark and St John 1989–, Royal Horticultural Society, National Art Collections Fund. DLitt, University of Plymouth (hc); Hon. Fellow, Royal Holloway College. *Trusts, etc:* Fellow, Industry and Parliament Trust. *Honours:* DBE 1989. *Special Interests:* Penal Affairs and Policy, Mental Health, Defence, Animal Welfare, Equal Opportunities, Housing. *Recreations:* Keep fit exercises, swimming, gardening, theatre, Yoga. *Sportsclubs:* Westminster Gymnasium. *Name, Style and Title:* Raised to the peerage as Baroness Fookes, of Plymouth in the County of Devon 1997. *Address:* The Baroness Fookes, DBE, House of Lords, London, SW1A 0PW.

LORD FORSYTH OF DRUMLEAN   Conservative

FORSYTH OF DRUMLEAN (Life Baron), Michael Bruce Forsyth; cr. 1999. Born 16 October 1954. Son of John T. Forsyth; educated Arbroath High School; St Andrews University (MA). Married 1977, Susan Jane, daughter of John B. Clough (1 son 2 daughters). *Councils, Public Bodies:* Councillor, Westminster City Council 1978–83. *Career:* Former Company Director; Director, Robert Fleming & Co Ltd 1997–. *House of Commons:* MP (Conservative) for Stirling 1983–97; PPS to the Foreign Secretary 1986–87; Parliamentary Under-Secretary of State, Scottish Office 1987–90; Minister of State at: Scottish Office with responsibility for Health, Education, Social Work and Sport 1990–92, Department of Employment 1992–94, Home Office 1994–95; Secretary of State for Scotland 1995–97. *Select Committees:* Member, Select Committee on Monetary Policy of the Bank of England 2000–. *Party Groups (General):* President, St Andrews University Conservative Association 1973–76; Member, Executive Committee National Union of Conservative and Unionist Associations 1975–77; Chairman: Federation of Conservative Students 1976–77, Scottish Conservative Party 1989–90. *Other:* Patron, Craighalbent Centre for Children with motor impairments; Member: Development Board, National Portrait Gallery, Commission on Strengthening Parliament 1999–2000, Council Member Aims. *Awards Granted:* Highland Park/*The Spectator* Parliamentarian of the Year 1996; Member to Watch 1993. *Miscellaneous:* Vice-President, Students' Representative Council, St Andrew's University 1974–75. *Honours:* PC 1995; Kt 1997. *Publications:* Various Pamphlets on Privatisation and Local Government. *Special Interests:* Local Government, Privatisation, Economics, Health Care, Mental Handicap, Environment, Constitution. *Recreations:* Mountaineering, photography, gardening, fishing, astronomy. *Name, Style and Title:* Raised to the peerage as Baron Forsyth of Drumlean, of Drumlean in Stirling 1999. *Address:* Rt Hon the Lord Forsyth of Drumlean, House of Lords, London, SW1A 0PW.

LORD FORTE   Conservative

FORTE (Life Baron), Charles Forte; cr. 1982. Born 26 November 1908. Son of late Rocco Giovanni Forte; educated Alloa Academy; Dumfries College; Mamiani, Rome. Married 1943, Irene Chierico (1 son 5 daughters). *Career:* Former Honorary Consul-General for San Marino; Chief Executive, Forte plc 1971–78, Deputy Chairman 1970–78, Executive Chairman 1979–92, President 1992–96; Member, London Tourist Board. *Honours:* Kt 1970. *Publications: Forte* (autobiography). *Clubs:* Carlton, Royal Thames Yacht. *Name, Style and Title:* Raised to the peerage as Baron Forte, of Ripley in the County of Surrey 1982. *Address:* The Lord Forte, House of Lords, London, SW1A 0PW *Tel:* 020 7235 6244.

LORD FOSTER OF THAMES BANK   Cross-Bencher

FOSTER OF THAMES BANK (Life Baron), Norman Robert Foster; cr. 1999. Born 1 June 1935. Son of late Robert and Lily Foster; educated Burnage Grammar School; Manchester University School of Architecture (DipArch, CertTP 1961); Yale University School of Architecture (MArch); Henry Fellowship and Guest Fellow, Jonathan Edward College, Yale School of Architecture. Married 1st, 1964, Wendy Ann Cheeseman (4 sons) (died 1989), married 2nd, September 20, 1996, Dr Elena Ochoa (1 daughter). *Armed Forces:* National Service, Royal Air Force 1953–55. *Career:* Private Practice, Team Four 1963–67; Foster Associate, later Foster and Partners (Chairman) 1967–; Collaboration with Richard Buckminster Fuller 1968–83; RIBA Visiting Board of Education and External Examiner 1971–73; Vice-President, Architectural Association 1974; Consultant Architect to University of East Anglia 1978–87; Trustee, Architecture Foundation 1991–99; Hon. Professor, University of Buenos Aires 1997; Visiting Professor, Urban Research, Bartlett School of Architecture, London 1998. *Other:* Member, The Norman Foster Foundation; Council Member: Architectural Association, London 1969–71, Royal College of Art, London 1981. *Awards Granted:* RIBA Silver Medal; Heywood Medal; Builders Association Scholarship; Manchester Society of Architects Bronze Medal; Walpamur Design Prize; Batsford Essay Prize; RIBA Royal Gold Medal 1983; Japan Design Foundation Award 1987; Gorsse Kunstpreis Award, Akademie der Kunst, Berlin 1989; The Chicago Architecture Award 1990; Academie d'Architecture, France Gold Medal 1991; Mies van der Rohe Pavilion Award 1991; Arnold W Brunner Memorial Prize, American Academy and Institute of Arts and Letters 1992; American Institute of Atechitects Gold Medal 1994; Universidad Internacional 'Menendez Pelayo' Santander, Spain Gold Medal 1995; MIPIM Man of the Year Award 1996; The 'Building' Award Construction Personality of the Year Award 1996; Premi a la millor tasca de promoció international de Barcelona Award 1997; Chartered Society of Designers Silver Medal 1997; Prince Phillip Designers Prize 1997; Berliner Zeitung Kultur-preis 1998; German-British Forum Special Prize 1998; Pritzker Architecture Prize – 21st Laureate 1999; Walpole Medal of Excellence 1999; Le Prix Européen de l'Architecture de la Fondation Européene de la Culture Pro Europa 1999; Special Prize 4th International Biennal of Architecture, São Paolo 1999. Ten honorary degrees and fellowships. *Honours:* Kt 1990; Officer of the Order of the Arts and Letters – Ministry of Culture, France 1994; Order of North Rhine Westphalia 1995; OM 1997; Commander's Cross of the Order of Merit of the Federal Republic of Germany 1999. RIBA 1965; FCSD 1975; IBM Fellow Aspen Conf 1980; RA 1983; Hon. BDA 1983: Hon. FAIA 1980; Member, International Academy of Atechitecture, Sofia, Bulgaria 1988; RDI 1988; Member, French Order of Architects 1989; Associate, Academie Royale de Belgique 1990; Hon. Fellow, Kent Institute of Art and Design 1994; Member, Department of Architecture Akademie der Künste 1994; Foreign Member, Royal Academy of Fine Arts Sweden 1995; Hon.FEng 1995; Member, European Academy of Sciences and Art 1996; Foreign Hon. Member, American Academy of Arts and Sciences 1996; Hon. Fellowship of the Royal Incorporation of Architects in Scotland 2000. *Publications: Buildings and Projects: Foster Associates Volumes 1, 2, 3, 4,* 1989–96; *Norman Foster Sketches,* 1992; *Sir Norman Foster* 1997; *Norman Foster: Selected and Current Works,* 1997; *Rebuilding The Reichstag,* 1999; *On Foster.Foster On,* 2000. *Recreations:* Flying, skiing, running. *Clubs:* Athenaeum, The China Club, Hong Kong. *Name, Style and Title:* Raised to the peerage as Baron Foster of Thames Bank, of Reddish in the County of Greater Manchester 1999. *Address:* The Lord Foster of Thames Bank, OM, Foster and Partners, Riverside Three, 22 Hester Road, London, SW11 4AN *Tel:* 020 7738 0455 *Fax:* 020 7738 1107/8 *E-Mail:* enquiries@fosterandpartners.com.

LORD FRASER OF CARMYLLIE   Conservative

FRASER OF CARMYLLIE (Life Baron), Peter Lovat Fraser; cr. 1989. Born 29 May 1945. Son of late George Robson Fraser, Church of Scotland Minister; educated Loretto; Gonville and Caius College, Cambridge (BA, LLM); Edinburgh University. Married July 26, 1969, Fiona Macdonald Mair (1 son 2 daughters). *Career:* Called to the Scottish Bar 1969–; Lecturer in Constitutional Law, Heriot Watt University 1972–74; Standing Junior Counsel in Scotland to Foreign and Commonwealth Office 1979; QC (Scot) 1982 Solicitor General for Scotland 1982–89; Chairman, International Petroleum Exchange 1999–. *House of Commons:* Contested (Conservative) Aberdeen North October 1974 General Election; MP (Conservative) for: Angus South 1979–83, Angus East 1983–87; PPS to the Rt Hon. George Younger MP, Secretary of State for Scotland 1981–82. *House of Lords:* Lord Advocate 1989–92; Minister of State: Scottish Office 1992–95, Department of Trade and Industry 1995–97; Deputy Leader of the Opposition 1997–98. *Spokesman:* An Opposition Spokesman on Trade and Industry 1997–98. *Select Committees:* Member: Select Committee on House of Lords' Offices 1997–98; Select Committee European Union (Sub Committee E) 1999–. *Party Groups (General):* Chairman, Scottish Conservative Lawyers Reform Group 1976. Hon. Professor of Law, Dundee University. *Trusts, etc:* Fellow, Industry and Parliament Trust. *Miscellaneous:* Hon. Bencher of Lincoln's Inn 1989. *Honours:* PC 1989. *Recreations:* Skiing, golf. *Name, Style and Title:* Raised to the peerage as Baron Fraser of Carmyllie, of Carmyllie in the District of Angus 1989. *Address:* Rt Hon the Lord Fraser of Carmyllie, QC, Slade House, Carmyllie, by Arbroath, Angus, DD11 2RE *E-Mail:* lordfraser@hotmail.

LORD FREEMAN   Conservative

FREEMAN (Life Baron), Roger Norman Freeman; cr. 1997; PC 1993. Born 27 May 1942. Son of Norman James Freeman, CBE; educated Whitgift School; Balliol College, Oxford (BA philosophy, politics and economics 1964). Married February 15, 1969, Jennifer Margaret Watson (1 son 1 daughter). *Career:* Managing Director, Bow Publications Ltd 1968–69; Executive Director, Lehman Bros 1969–86; Director, Martini & Rossi UK Ltd and Baltic Leasing Group plc to May 1986; Partner, Pricewaterhouse Cooper, Corporate Finance Division 1997–98, Adviser 1999–; Chairman, Thomson – CSF Racal PLC 1999–. *House of Commons:* Contested Don Valley 1979; MP (Conservative) for Kettering 1983–97; Parliamentary Under-Secretary of State: for the Armed Forces 1986–88, at the Department of Health 1988–90; Minister of State for: Public Transport, Department of Transport 1990–94, Defence Procurement, Ministry of Defence 1994–95; Chancellor of the Duchy of Lancaster and Cabinet Minister for Public Service 1995–97. *Party Groups (General):* President, Oxford University Conservative Association 1964; Treasurer, Bow Group 1967–68; Chief Financial Officer, Conservative Central Office 1984–86; Vice-Chairman, Conservative Party July-December 1997; Special Adviser on Candidates, Conservative Party December 1998–. *Other:* President: Council of the Reserve Forces and Cadets Association 1999–, British International Freight Association 1999–. *Honours:* PC 1993. Fellow, Institute of Chartered Accountants, England and Wales. *Clubs:* Carlton, Kennel, Royal Aeronautical Society. *Name, Style and Title:* Raised to the peerage as Baron Freeman, of Dingley in the County of Northamptonshire 1997. *Address:* Rt Hon the Lord Freeman, House of Lords, London, SW1A 0PW.

LORD FREYBERG   Cross-Bencher

FREYBERG (3rd Baron, UK), Valerian Bernard Freyberg; cr. 1951. Born 15 December 1970. Son of Colonel 2nd Baron, OBE, MC, and Ivry Perronelle Katharine, daughter of Cyril Harrower Guild. Succeeded his father 1993; educated Eton; Camberwell College of Arts. *Career:* Sculptor. *House of Lords:* An elected hereditary peer 1999–. *Select Committees:* Former Member, House of Lords Library and Computers Sub-Committee until 1999; Member, House of Lords Offices Sub-Committee: Advisory Panel on Works of Art 2000–. *Special Interests:* Visual Arts. *Recreations:* Beekeeping, music. *Address:* The Lord Freyberg, House of Lords, London, SW1A 0PW *E-Mail:* freybergv@parliament.uk.

LORD FYFE OF FAIRFIELD
Labour

FYFE OF FAIRFIELD (Life Baron), George Lennox Fyfe; cr. 2000. Born 10 April 1941. Son of George and Elizabeth Fyfe; educated Alloa Academy; Co-operative College, Loughborough. Married 1965, Ann Clark Asquith (died 1999) (1 daughter). *Councils, Public Bodies:* JP, Perthshire 1972–75. *Career:* General manager, Kirriemuir Co-operative Society 1966–68; Regional manager, Scottish Co-operative Society 1968–72; Group general manager, CWS 1972–75; Chief executive, Leicestershire Co-operative Society 1975–95; Director, Shoefayre Ltd 1981–, Chairman 1984–; Director, CWS 1981–, Vice-Chairman 1986–89, Chairman 1989–; Director: Co-operative Insurance Society Ltd 1982–, Central TV-East 1983–92; Co-operative Bank plc: Director 1986, Deputy Chairman 1996–; Chief executive, Midlands Co-operative Society 1995–. *Miscellaneous:* Member, East Midlands Economic Planning Council 1976–79. Companion, Institute of Management. *Recreations:* History, reading, music, classic cars. *Name, Style and Title:* Raised to the peerage as Baron Fyfe of Fairfield, of Sauchie in Clackmannanshire 2000. *Address:* The Lord Fyfe of Fairfield, The Byre, off Main Street, Little Stretton, Leicestershire, LE2 2FS.

G

BARONESS GALE
Labour

GALE (Life Baroness), Anita Gale; cr. 1999. Born 28 November 1940. Daughter of late Arthur Gale, coalminer and late Lilian Gale, housewife; educated Treherbert Secondary Modern School; Pontypridd Technical College 1970–73; University College of Wales, Cardiff (BSc Econ politics 1976). Married 1959, Morcom Holmes (marriage dissolved 1983) (2 daughters). *Trades Union:* Shop Steward, Tailors and Garment Workers' Union 1966–69; Chair, National Union of Labour Organisers 1988–90; Labour Organiser, branch of GMB, Branch Chair 1990–99 ; Equalities Officer 1994–99.*Career:* Sewing machinist, clothing factory 1956–57; Shop assistant 1957–59; Sewing machinist 1965–69; Women's Officer and Assistant Organiser, Wales Labour Party 1976–84; General Secretary, Wales Labour Party 1984–99. *International Bodies (General):* IPU. *Party Groups (General):* Member, Labour Women's Network National Committee; Vice-Chairman, Labour Animal Welfare Society. *Other:* Member: Ramblers Association, Christian Socialist Movement, H. S. Chapman Society. *Special Interests:* Animal Welfare, Women's Issues, Children's Rights. *Recreations:* Swimming, walking, gardening. *Name, Style and Title:* Raised to the peerage as Baroness Gale, of Blaenrhondda in the County of Mid Glamorgan 1999. *Address:* The Baroness Gale, House of Lords, London, SW1A 0PW *Tel:* 020 7219 8511.

LORD GALLACHER
Labour/Co-operative

GALLACHER (Life Baron), John Gallacher; cr. 1983. Born 7 May 1920. Son of late William Gallacher; educated St Patrick's High School, Dumbarton; Co-operative College, Loughborough 1946–48. Married June 28, 1947, Freda Vivian, daughter of late Alfred Chittenden (1 son). *Trades Union:* Member, National Association of Co-operative Officials.*Armed Forces:* RAF 1940–45. *Career:* Chartered Secretary; President, Enfield Highway Co-operative Society 1954–68; Secretary, International Co-operative Alliance 1964–68; Sectional Secretary, Co-operative Union 1968–73; Parliamentary Secretary, Co-operative Union 1973–83. *Whip:* Opposition Whip 1985–92. *Spokesman:* Opposition Front Bench Spokesman on Agriculture, Food, Forestry and Fisheries 1987–97. *Select Committees:* Chairman, Sub-Committee on Common Agricultural Policy and Fisheries 1984–87; Co-opted Member, Select Committee on European Communities Sub-Committee D (Agriculture, Fisheries and Food) 1997–. *International Bodies (General):* Member, Economic and Social Committee of the European Communities 1978–82. *Party Groups (General):* Member, Co-operative Party. *Other:* President, Institute of Meat 1983–86. Hon. Freeman, The Worshipful Company of Butchers. *Special Interests:* European Union. *Name, Style and Title:* Raised to the peerage as Baron Gallacher, of Enfield in Greater London 1983. *Address:* The Lord Gallacher, House of Lords, London, SW1A 0PW.

BARONESS GARDNER OF PARKES   Conservative

GARDNER OF PARKES (Life Baroness), Rachel Trixie Anne Gardner; cr. 1981. Born 17 July 1927. Daughter of late Hon. J. J. Gregory McGirr and late Rachel McGirr, OBE, LC; educated Monte Sant Angelo College, North Sydney; East Sydney Technical College; Sydney University (BDS 1954); Cordon Bleu de Paris (Diplome 1956). Married 1956, Kevin Anthony, son of late George Gardner and of late Rita Gardner, of Sydney, Australia (3 daughters). *Councils, Public Bodies:* Councillor, Westminster City Council 1968–78; Lady Mayoress of Westminster 1987–88; Member, Westminster, Kensington and Chelsea Area Health Authority 1974–81; JP, North Westminster 1971–97 Councillor, GLC for: Havering 1970–73, Enfield-Southgate 1977–86; Vice-Chairman, North East Thames Regional Health Authority 1990–94. *Career:* Came to UK 1954; Dentist in General Practice 1955–90; British Chairman, European Union of Women 1978–82; UK representative on the UN Status of Women Commission 1982–88; Director: Gateway Building Society 1987–88, Woolwich Building Society 1988–93; Chairman (UK), Plan International 1989–; Chairman, Royal Free Hampstead NHS Trust 1994–97. *House of Lords:* A Deputy Chairman of Committees 1999–; A Deputy Speaker 1999–. *International Bodies:* Elected Member, Executive of Inter-Parliamentary Union to 1997. *Other:* Governor: National Heart Hospital 1974–90, Eastman Dental Hospital 1971–80; Hon. President, War Widows' Association of Great Britain 1984–87; President, British Fluoridation Society 1990–93; Chairman, The Cook Society 1996. DU, Middlesex 1997. *Trusts, etc:* Chairman, Suzy Lamplugh Trust 1993–96. *Miscellaneous:* Member, Inner London Executive Council NHS 1966–71; Standing Dental Advisory Committee for England and Wales 1968–76; Contested (Conservative) Blackburn 1970, North Cornwall February 1974 General Elections; Chairman, London Canals' Consultative Committee 1970–73; Member, Inland Waterways Amenity Advisory Council 1971–74; Member, Industrial Tribunal Panel for London 1974–97; Department of Employment's Advisory Committee on Women's Employment 1980–89; North Thames Gas Consumer Council 1980–82; Elected to General Dental Council 1984–86, 1987–91; Member, London Electricity Board 1984–90; Trustee, Parliamentary Advisory Council on Transport Safety 1992–98; Vice-President, National House Building Council 1992–. Former Fellow, Institute of Directors. Freeman, City of London 1992. *Special Interests:* Transport, Housing, Health, Planning, Energy. *Recreations:* Family life, gardening, needlework, travel. *Name, Style and Title:* Raised to the peerage as Baroness Gardner of Parkes, of Southgate in Greater London and of Parkes in the State of New South Wales and Commonwealth of Australia 1981. *Address:* The Baroness Gardner of Parkes, House of Lords, London, SW1A 0PW *E-Mail:* gardnert@parliament.uk.

LORD GAREL-JONES   Conservative

GAREL-JONES (Life Baron), (William Armand Thomas) Tristan Garel-Jones; cr. 1997. Born 28 February 1941. Son of Bernard Garel-Jones; educated The King's School, Canterbury; Madrid University. Married 1966, Catalina Garrigues (4 sons 1 daughter). *Career:* In business on the Continent 1960–70; Merchant banker 1971–74; Managing Director, UBS Warburg. *House of Commons:* Personal Assistant to Michael Roberts, MP at Cardiff North in February 1970 General Election; Contested Caernarvon February 1974, and Watford October 1974 General Elections; Personal Assistant to Rt Hon. Lord Thorneycroft 1978–79; MP (Conservative) for Watford 1979–97; PPS to Barney Hayhoe, MP, as Minister of State, Civil Service Department March 1981–82; Minister of State, Foreign and Commonwealth Office 1990–93. *Whip (Commons):* Assistant Government Whip 1982–83; Government Whip 1983–89: Lord Commissioner of the Treasury 1983–86, Vice-Chamberlain, HM Household 1986–88, Comptroller, HM Household 1988–89; Deputy Chief Whip (Treasurer, HM Household) 1989–90. *Honours:* PC 1992. *Recreations:* Book collecting. *Clubs:* Beefsteak. *Name, Style and Title:* Raised to the peerage as Baron Garel-Jones, of Watford in the County of Hertfordshire 1997. *Address:* Rt Hon the Lord Garel-Jones, House of Lords, London, SW1A 0PW.

GAVRON (Life Baron), Robert Gavron; cr. 1999. Born 13 September 1930. Son of Nathaniel and Leah Gavron; educated Leighton Park School; St Peter's College, Oxford (MA). Married 1st, 1955, Hannah Fyvel (died 1965) (2 sons); married 2nd, 1967, Nicolette Coates (2 daughters) (marriage dissolved 1987); married 3rd, 1989, Katharine Gardiner, née Macnair. *Armed Forces:* RAEC, National Service 1949–50. *Career:* Called to the Bar, Middle Temple 1955; Founded St Ives Group 1964, Director 1964–98, Chairman 1964–93; Director: Octopus Publishing plc 1975–87, Electra Management plc 1981–92; Proprietor, The Carcanet Press Ltd 1983–; Chairman: Folio Society Ltd 1982–, National Gallery Publications Ltd 1996–98, Guardian Media Group plc 1997–2000. *Select Committees:* Member, House of Lords Offices Sub-Committee: Advisory Panel on Works of Art 2000–. *Other:* Chairman, Open College of the Arts 1991–96; Director, Royal Opera House 1992–98; Governor, LSE 1997–. Hon. Fellow, St Peter's College, Oxford 1992; Hon. PhD, Thames Valley University 1997. *Trusts, etc:* Trustee: National Gallery 1994–, Scott Trust 1997–2000; Chairman of Trustees, Robert Gavron Charitable Trust. *Honours:* CBE 1990. Hon. Fellow: Royal College of Art 1990, Royal Society of Literature 1996. *Publications:* (jointly) *The Entrepreneurial Society*, 1998. *Clubs:* Groucho, MCC. *Name, Style and Title:* Raised to the peerage as Baron Gavron, of Highgate in the London Borough of Camden 1999. *Address:* The Lord Gavron, CBE, 44 Eagle Street, London, WC1R 4FS *Tel:* 020 7400 4300.

GEDDES (3rd Baron, UK), Euan Michael Ross Geddes; cr. 1942. Born 3 September 1937. Son of 2nd Baron, KBE, DL. Succeeded his father 1975; educated Rugby; Gonville and Caius College, Cambridge (MA); Harvard Business School. Married 1st, May 7, 1966, Gillian (died 1995), daughter of late William Arthur Butler (1 son 1 daughter), married 2nd, 1996, Susan Margaret Hunter, daughter of late George Harold Carter. *Armed Forces:* Royal Navy 1956–58; Lieutenant-Commander, RNR (Rtd). *Career:* Chairman: Trinity College London, Chrome Castle Ltd; Director: Pacific Chartered Capital Management Limited, Trinity College of Music and other Companies. *House of Lords:* An elected hereditary peer 1999–; A Deputy Chairman of Committees 2000–. *Select Committees:* Member: House of Lords European Select Committee 1994–, Sub-Committee A 1985–90; Member, Sub-Committee B 1990–94, 1995–, Chairman 1996–99; Member: Science and Technology Sub-Committee 1 1990–92, Refreshment Sub-Committee, House of Lords Offices Committee 2000–. *Party Groups:* Member, Executive of Association of Conservative Peers 1999–. Hon. FTCL. *Special Interests:* Shipping, Anglo-Chinese Relations, Hong Kong, South East Asia, Immigration, Energy, Transport, Industry. *Recreations:* Golf, music, bridge, gardening, skiing. *Sportsclubs:* Aldeburgh Golf, Hong Kong Golf. *Clubs:* Brooks's, Hong Kong, Noblemen and Gentlemen's Catch. *Address:* The Lord Geddes, House of Lords, London, SW1A 0PW *Tel:* 01379 388001.

GERAINT (Life Baron), Geraint Wyn Howells; cr. 1992. Born 15 April 1925. Son of late David and Mary Howells; educated Ardwyn Grammar School, Aberystwyth. Married September 7, 1957, Mary Olwen Hughes, née Griffiths (2 daughters). *Career:* Farmer; Vice-Chairman, British Wool Marketing Board 1971–83; Chairman, Wool Producers of Wales 1977–87. *House of Commons:* MP (Liberal) for: Cardigan 1974–83, Ceredigion and Pembroke North 1983–92 (Liberal Democrat 1989–92). *Spokesman (Commons):* Spokesman on: Welsh Affairs 1985–87, Agriculture 1987–92. *House of Lords:* A Deputy Speaker of the House of Lords; A Deputy Chairman of Committees 1997–. *Spokesman:* Spokesman on Welsh Rural Affairs. *Other:* Past President, Royal Welsh Show, Builth Wells, Powys; Chairman, Bronglais Hospital Cancer Appeal Fund, Aberystwyth. *Miscellaneous:* An Extra Lord in Waiting to HM The Queen 1998–. FRAgS. *Special Interests:* Agriculture, Wales, Devolution of Power, Language and Culture, Rural Affairs, Third World. *Recreations:* Rugby, walking. *Sportsclubs:* London Welsh RFC Ltd, Aberstwyth Football Club. *Clubs:* National Liberal, St David's (London), London Welsh. *Name, Style and Title:* Raised to the peerage as Baron Geraint, of Ponterwyd in the County of Dyfed 1992. *Address:* The Lord Geraint, Glennydd, Ponterwyd, Sir Aberteifi, SY23 3LB *Tel:* 01970 85258.

LORD GIBSON   Cross-Bencher

GIBSON (Life Baron), Richard Patrick Tallentyre Gibson; cr. 1975. Born 5 February 1916. Son of late Thornely Carbutt Gibson and of Elizabeth, née Coit; educated Eton; Magdalen College, Oxford. Married July 14, 1945, Elisabeth Dione, daughter of late Hon. Clive Pearson (4 sons). *Armed Forces:* Served Middlesex Yeomanry 1939–46 (North Africa 1940–41; POW 1941–43; Special Operations Executive 1943–45); Political Intelligence Department, Foreign Office 1945–46. *Career:* London Stock Exchange 1937; Director, Whitehall Securities Corporation 1948–60; Director, S. Pearson & Son 1960–88, Chairman 1978–83; Chairman, Pearson Longman 1967–79; Director, Whitehall Securities Corporation 1973–83. *Other:* Chairman, Arts Council of Great Britain 1972–77. Hon. Fellow, Magdalen College, Oxford; Hon. Degrees: Reading University, Keele University. *Trusts, etc:* Chairman, National Trust 1977–86. *Special Interests:* Arts, Heritage, Environment, Media. *Recreations:* Architecture, music, gardening. *Clubs:* Brooks's, Garrick. *Name, Style and Title:* Raised to the peerage as Baron Gibson, of Penn's Rocks in the County of East Sussex 1975. *Address:* The Lord Gibson, Penn's Rocks, Groombridge, East Sussex, TN3 9PA.

BARONESS GIBSON OF MARKET RASEN   Labour

GIBSON OF MARKET RASEN (Life Baroness), Anne Gibson; cr. 2000. Born 10 December 1940. Daughter of Harry and Jessie Tasker; educated Market Rasen Junior School; Caistor Grammar School, Lincolnshire; Chelmsford College of Further Education; Essex University (BA government). Married 1st, 1962, John Donald Gibson (1 daughter); married 2nd, 1988, John Bartell (1 stepdaughter). *Trades Union:* Member, MSF. *Career:* Secretary 1956–59; bank cashier 1959–62; organiser, Saffron Walden Labour Party 1966–70; *House Magazine* 1976–77; assistant secretary, Organisation and Industrial Relations Department, TUC 1977–87; national secretary, MSF 1987–2000. *Backbench Committees:* Member, Labour Party Departmental Committee for Environment, Transport and the Regions. *Party Groups:* Member, PLP Women's Committee. *Party Groups (General):* Member: Labour Animal Welfare Society, Fawcett Society, Fabian Society, Labour Party National Constitutional Committee 1997–2000. *Other:* Chair, EC Committee on Violence at Work; Member: Occupational Health and Safety Committee, EC Committee on Health and Safety, Bilbao Agency. *Trusts, etc:* Member, Emily Pankhurst Trust. *Miscellaneous:* Member: TUC General Council 1989–2000, Equal Opportunities Commission 1991–98, Department of Employment Advisory Group for Older Workers 1993–96, Health and Safety Commission 1996–2000. *Honours:* OBE 1998. *Publications:* Numerous pamphlets including: *Women and Trade Unions, Trade Union and Race Relations, People with disabilities and Trade Unions, Lesbian and Gay Rights in the Workplace, Equal Opportunities in the 1990's, Violence at Work, Sexual Harassment at Work: a trade union guide, Guide to the Equal Pay Act, Guide to the Sex Discrimination Act.* *Special Interests:* Industrial Relations, Equality Issues, Women's Issues, Health and Safety at Work, Adoption. *Recreations:* Embroidery, reading, theatre. *Name, Style and Title:* Raised to the peerage as Baroness Gibson of Market Rasen, of Market Rasen in the County of Lincolnshire 2000. *Address:* The Baroness Gibson of Market Rasen, OBE, House of Lords, London, SW1A 0PW.

LORD GIBSON-WATT   Conservative

GIBSON-WATT (Life Baron), James David Gibson-Watt; cr 1979. Born 11 September 1918. Son of late Major James Miller Gibson-Watt, DL, JP; educated Eton; Trinity College, Cambridge (BA). Married 1942, Diana (died August 3, 2000), daughter of late Sir Charles Hambro, KBE, MC (2 sons 2 daughters and 1 son deceased). *Armed Forces:* Major, Welsh Guards during 2nd World War. *Councils, Public Bodies:* DL, Powys 1968–97. *House of Commons:* Contested Brecon and Radnor 1950 and 1951; MP (Conservative) for Hereford 1956–October 1974; Minister of State, Welsh Office 1970–74. *Whip (Commons):* A Lord Commissioner of the Treasury (Government Whip) 1959–61. *Other:* Chairman, Council of Royal Welsh Agricultural Society 1977–93;

Chairman, Timber Growers United Kingdom 1987–90, currently Hon. President. *Miscellaneous:* Member, Historic Buildings Council, Wales 1975–80; A Forestry Commissioner 1976–86; Chairman, Council on Tribunals 1980–86. *Honours:* MC 1943 and 2 Bars; PC 1974. *Recreations:* Fishing, forestry. *Clubs:* Boodle's, Army and Navy. *Name, Style and Title:* Raised to the peerage as Baron Gibson-Watt, of the Wye in the District of Radnor 1979. *Address:* Rt Hon the Lord Gibson-Watt, MC, Doldowlod, Llandrindod Wells, Powys, LD1 6HF *Tel:* 01597 89208.

LORD GILBERT — Labour

GILBERT (Life Baron), John William Gilbert; cr. 1997. Born 5 April 1927. Son of Stanley Gilbert; educated Merchant Taylors' School, Northwood, Middlesex; St John's College, Oxford; New York University (PhD). Married 1963, Jean Ross Skinner (2 daughters from previous marriage). *Trades Union:* Member, GMB 1951–. *Armed Forces:* 1st Lieutenant, Royal Navy 1946–48. *Career:* Chartered Accountant (Canada). *House of Commons:* Contested: Ludlow 1966, Dudley 1968; MP for: Dudley 1970–74, Dudley East 1974–97; Financial Secretary to the Treasury 1974–75; Minister for Transport 1975–76; Minister of State for Defence 1976–79. *House of Lords:* Minister of State for Defence Procurement, Ministry of Defence 1997–99. Hon. LLD, Wake Forest (S. Carolina) 1983. *Miscellaneous:* Member, Committee on Intelligence and Security 1994–97. *Honours:* PC 1978. FRGS. *Special Interests:* Defence, Foreign Affairs, Economic Policy, Conservation, Transport, Amnesty International. *Clubs:* Reform. *Name, Style and Title:* Raised to the peerage as Baron Gilbert, of Dudley in the County of West Midlands 1997. *Address:* Rt Hon the Lord Gilbert, House of Lords, London, SW1A 0PW.

LORD GILMOUR OF CRAIGMILLAR — Conservative

GILMOUR OF CRAIGMILLAR (Life Baron), Ian Hedworth John Little Gilmour; cr. 1992; 3rd Bt of Liberton and Craigmillar (UK) 1926. Born 8 July 1926. Son of Sir John Little Gilmour, 2nd Bt. Succeeded his father 1977; educated Eton; Balliol College, Oxford. Married 1951, Lady Caroline Margaret Montagu-Douglas-Scott, youngest daughter of 8th Duke of Buccleuch and Queensberry, KT, GCVO, PC (4 sons 1 daughter). *Armed Forces:* Served with Grenadier Guards 1944–47; 2nd Lieutenant 1945. *Career:* Called to the Bar, Inner Temple 1952; Editor, *The Spectator* 1954–59; Chairman, Conservative Research Department 1974–75. *House of Commons:* MP (Conservative) for: Norfolk Central 1962–74, Chesham and Amersham 1974–92; PPS to Rt Hon. Quintin Hogg, MP 1963–64; Parliamentary Under-Secretary of State for the Army, Ministry of Defence 1970–71; Minister of State for: Defence Procurement 1971–72, Defence 1972–74; Secretary of State for Defence 1974; Lord Privy Seal 1979–81. Hon. DU, Essex 1995. *Honours:* PC 1973. *Publications: The Body Politic,* 1969; *Inside Right: A Study of Conservatism,* 1977; *Britain Can Work,* 1983; *Riot, Risings and Revolution,* 1992; *Dancing with Dogma,* 1992; Co-author *Whatever Happened to the Tories,* 1997. *Clubs:* Pratt's, White's, MCC. *Name, Style and Title:* Raised to the peerage as Baron Gilmour of Craigmillar, of Craigmillar in the District of the City of Edinburgh 1992. *Address:* Rt Hon the Lord Gilmour of Craigmillar, The Ferry House, Park Road, Old Isleworth, Middlesex, TW7 6BD *Tel:* 020 8560 6769.

LORD GLADWIN OF CLEE — Labour

GLADWIN OF CLEE (Life Baron), Derek Oliver Gladwin; cr. 1994. Born 6 June 1930. Son of late Albert and Ethel Gladwin; educated Wintringham Grammar School; Ruskin College, Oxford (MA); London School of Economics. Married 1956, Ruth Ann Pinion (1 son). *Councils, Public Bodies:* JP, Surrey 1969. *Career:* British Railways, Grimsby 1946–52; Fishing industry, Grimsby 1952–56; General and Municipal Workers' Union: Regional Officer 1956–63, National Industrial Officer 1963–70, Regional Secretary (Southern Region) 1970–90; Board Member: Post Office 1972–94, British Aerospace 1977–91; Member, Employment Appeal Tribunal 1992–. *Whip:* An Opposition Whip 1995–97. *Select Committees:* Member, Select Committees on:

Broadcasting 1995–97, Procedure 1997–. *International Bodies:* Member, NATO Parliamentary Assembly 1997. *Party Groups (General):* Chairman, Labour Party Conference Arrangements Committee 1974–90. *Other:* Chairman, Governing Council, Ruskin College, Oxford 1979–99; Governor, Kingston University 1998–; President, Holiday Care Service 1998–; Honorary President, Ruskin College, Oxford 1999–. Hon MA (Oxon 1978). *Trusts, etc:* Trustee, Diabetes UK 1995–. *Miscellaneous:* Visiting Fellow, Nuffield College, Oxford (MA) 1978–86; Member, Armed Forces Pay Review Body 1998–. *Honours:* OBE 1977; CBE 1979. *Special Interests:* Industrial Relations, Employment Law, Tourism, Industry. *Name, Style and Title:* Raised to the peerage as Baron Gladwin of Clee, of Great Grimsby in the County of Humberside 1994. *Address:* The Lord Gladwin of Clee, CBE, 2 Friars Rise, Woking, Surrey, GU22 7JL *Tel:* 01483 714591.

LORD GLENAMARA   Labour

GLENAMARA (Life Baron), Edward Watson Short; cr. 1977. Born 17 December 1912. Son of late Charles Short; educated Bede College, Durham. Married 1941, Jennie Sewell (1 son 1 daughter). *Armed Forces:* Served 1939–45 War as Captain, DLI. *Councils, Public Bodies:* Former Councillor, Newcastle City Council, Leader of Labour Group 1948. *Career:* Chairman, Cable and Wireless Ltd 1976–80. *House of Commons:* MP (Labour) for Newcastle upon Tyne Central 1951–76; Postmaster General 1966–68; Secretary of State for Education and Science 1968–70; Lord President of the Council and Leader of the House of Commons 1974-April 1976. *Whip (Commons):* Opposition Assistant Whip 1955; Deputy Opposition Chief Whip 1962; Chief Whip 1964–66 *Spokesman (Commons):* Opposition Spokesman on Education 1970–72. *Chancellor:* Chancellor, University of Northumbria at Newcastle upon Tyne 1984–. *Select Committees:* Member: Privileges Committee 1985–, Ecclesiastical Committee 1997–. *Party Groups (General):* Deputy Leader Labour Party April 1972-December 1976. *Other:* President, Finchale Abbey Training College for the Disabled 1985–. Seven honorary doctorates and fellowships. *Honours:* PC 1964; CH 1976. Fellow, College of Preceptors. *Publications: The Story of the Durham Light Infantry; The Infantry Instructor; Education in a Changing World; Birth to Five; I Knew my Place; Whip to Wilson.* *Recreations:* Painting. *Name, Style and Title:* Raised to the peerage as Baron Glenamara, of Glenridding in the County of Cumbria 1977. *Address:* Rt Hon the Lord Glenamara, CH, House of Lords, London, SW1A 0PW.

LORD GLENARTHUR   Conservative

GLENARTHUR (4th Baron, UK), Simon Mark Arthur; cr. 1918; 4th Bt of Carlung (UK) 1903. Born 7 October 1944. Son of 3rd Baron, OBE, DL. Succeeded his father 1976; educated Eton. Married November 12, 1969, Susan Barry (1 son 1 daughter). *Armed Forces:* Commissioned 10th Royal Hussars (PWO) 1963; ADC to High Commissioner, Aden 1964–65; Captain 1970; Major 1973; Retired 1975; Major, The Royal Hussars TAVR 1976–80. *Councils, Public Bodies:* DL, Aberdeenshire 1988. *Career:* Captain, British Airways Helicopters Ltd 1976–82; Director: Aberdeen and Texas Corporate Finance Ltd 1977–82, ABTEX Computer Systems Ltd 1979–82; Senior Executive Hanson plc 1989–96; Deputy Chairman, Hanson Pacific Ltd 1994–98; Director, Whirly Bird Services Ltd 1995–; Consultant, British Aerospace 1989–99; President, National Council for Civil Protection 1991–; Chairman, British Helicopter Advisory Board 1992–; Director, Lewis Group plc 1993–94; Consultant, Chevron UK Ltd 1994–97; Director, Millennium Chemicals Inc 1996–; Consultant: Hanson plc 1996–99, Imperial Tobacco Group plc 1996–98; Chairman: European Helicopter Association 1996–, International Federation of Helicopter Associations 1997–. *House of Lords:* Parliamentary Under-Secretary of State: DHSS 1983–85, Home Office 1985–86; Minister of State: Scottish Office 1986–87, Foreign and Commonwealth Office 1987–89; An elected hereditary peer 1999–. *Whip:* A Lord in Waiting (Government Whip) 1982–83. *Spokesman:* Government Spokesman for: the Treasury 1982–85, Home Office, Employment and Industry 1982–83; A Government Spokesman on Defence 1983–89. *Other:* Council Member, The Air League 1994–; Member, National Employers Liaison Committee for HM Reserve Forces 1996–. *Trusts, etc:* Chairman, St Mary's Hospital, Paddington, NHS Trust 1991–98; Scottish Patron, The Butler Trust 1994–; A Special Trustee, St Mary's Hospital, Paddington 1991–. *Miscellaneous:* Member (Brigadier) of the Queen's Bodyguard for Scotland

(Royal Company of Archers). Member, Chartered Institute of Transport 1978, Fellow 1999; Fellow, Royal Aeronautical Society 1992. Freeman, City of London 1996. Freeman, Guild of Air Pilots and Air Navigators 1992, Liveryman 1996. *Special Interests:* Aviation, Foreign Affairs, Defence, Penal Affairs and Policy, Health, Scotland. *Recreations:* Field sports, gardening, choral singing, antique barometers. *Clubs:* Cavalry and Guards, Pratt's. *Address:* The Lord Glenarthur, DL, PO Box 11012, Banchory, Kincardineshire, AB31 6ZJ *Tel:* 01330 844467 *Fax:* 01330 844465 *E-Mail:* glenarth@rsc.co.uk; glenarthurs@parliament.uk.

LORD GLENTORAN — Conservative

GLENTORAN (3rd Baron, UK), (Thomas) Robin Valerian Dixon; cr. 1939; 5th Bt of Ballymenoch (UK) 1903. Born 21 April 1935. Son of 2nd Baron, PC, KBE, and late Lady Diana Wellesley, daughter of 3rd Earl Cowley. Succeeded his father 1995; educated Eton; Grenoble University, France. Married 1st, January 12, 1959, Rona Colville (3 sons) (marriage dissolved 1975), married 2nd, January 2, 1979, Alwyn Mason (marriage dissolved 1988), married 3rd, January 3, 1990, Mrs Margaret Rainey. *Armed Forces:* Grenadier Guards 1954–66, retired as Major. *Councils, Public Bodies:* DL, Co. Antrim 1995. *Career:* Managing Director, Redland (NI) Ltd 1971–95, Chairman 1995–98; Chairman, Roofing Industry Alliance 1997–. *House of Lords:* An elected hereditary peer 1999–. *Spokesman:* An Opposition Spokesman for Northern Ireland 1999–, Ariculture 2000–. *International Bodies:* Associate Member, British/Irish Parliamentary Body. *Other:* Member, The Sports Council for Northern Ireland 1980–87; Founder Chairman, The Ulster Games Foundation 1983–90; Commissioner, Irish Lighthouse Service 1986–; President, British Bobsleigh Association 1987–; Chairman, Northern Ireland Tall Ships Council 1987; Regional Chairman, The British Field Sports Society 1990–; Chairman: Positively Belfast 1992–96, Growing a Green Economy (reporting to Minister for the Environment, Northern Ireland Office) 1993–95; Member, The Millennium Commission 1994–; Chairman, Northern Ireland Classic Gold Promotions 1996–; Hon. President: Chartered Institute of Marketing, Northern Ireland 1996–, The Institute of Roofing 1996–; Member, Countryside Alliance. *Miscellaneous:* Won Olympic Gold Medal (Bobsleigh) 1964. *Honours:* MBE 1969; CBE 1992. Liveryman, Worshipful Company of Tylers and Bricklayers. *Special Interests:* Sport, Environment, Northern Ireland, Army, Maritime Affairs. *Recreations:* Sailing, golf, travel, music, arts. *Sportsclubs:* Royal Portrush Golf, Aloha Golf, Irish Cruising, Soto Grande Golf Club. *Clubs:* Royal Cruising, Carlton, Royal Yacht Squadron (Cowes). *Address:* The Lord Glentoran, CBE, DL, Drumadarragh House, Ballyclare, Co. Antrim, BT39 0TA *Tel:* 019603 40222; 17 Redcliffe Street, London, SW10 9DR *Tel:* 020 7370 7190 *Fax:* 020 7341 0023 *E-Mail:* rg@glentoran.demon.co.uk (Home); glentoran@parliament.uk (Office).

BISHOP OF GLOUCESTER — Non-Affiliated

GLOUCESTER (39th Bishop of), David Edward Bentley. Born 7 August 1935. Son of William and Florence Bentley; educated Great Yarmouth Grammar School; Leeds University (BA English); Westcott House, Cambridge. Married 1962, Clarice Lahmers (2 sons 2 daughters). *Armed Forces:* Second Lieutenant, 5th Regiment, Royal Horse Artillery. *Career:* Deacon 1960; Priest 1961; Curate: St Ambrose, Bristol 1960–62, Holy Trinity with St Mary, Guildford 1962–66; Rector: Headley, Bordon 1966–73, Esher 1973–86; Rural Dean of Emly 1977–82; Chairman: Guildford Diocesan House of Clergy 1977–86, Guildford Diocesan Council of Social Responsibility 1980–86; Hon. Canon, Guildford Cathedral 1980; Member, various church committees on recruitment and selection 1987–; Warden, Community of All Hallows, Ditchingham 1989–93; Bishop of Gloucester 1993–; Took his seat in the House of Lords 1998. *Recreations:* Music, cricket, theatre, family. *Sportsclubs:* Vice President, Gloucestershire CCC. *Clubs:* MCC. *Address:* Rt Rev the Lord Bishop of Gloucester, Bishopscourt, Pitt Street, Gloucester, GL1 2BQ *Tel:* 01452 524598 *E-Mail:* bshpglos@star.co.uk.

LORD GOFF OF CHIEVELEY   Cross-Bencher

GOFF OF CHIEVELEY (Life Baron), Robert Lionel Archibald Goff; cr. 1986. Born 12 November 1926. Son of late Lieutenant Colonel L. T. Goff; educated Eton; New College, Oxford (MA 1953, DCL 1972). Married 1953, Sarah Cousins (1 son 2 daughters and 1 son deceased). *Armed Forces:* Served Scots Guards 1945–48. *Career:* Fellow and Tutor, Lincoln College, Oxford 1951–55; Called to Bar, Inner Temple 1951; Bencher 1975; QC 1967; In practice at the Bar 1956–75; Member, General Council of the Bar 1971–74; A Recorder 1974–75; Judge of the High Court, Queen's Bench Division 1975–82; Judge i/c Commercial Court 1979–81; A Lord Justice of Appeal 1982–86; A Lord of Appeal in Ordinary 1986–98; Second Senior Law Lord 1994–96; Senior Law Lord 1996–98. *Select Committees:* Chairman, Sub-Committee E, House of Lords Select Committee on European Communities 1986–88. *Other:* Chairman, Council of Legal Education 1975–82; President, Chartered Institute of Arbitrators 1986–91; Chairman, Court of London University 1986–91; President, New College Society; High Steward, Oxford University; Chairman: British Institute of International and Comparative Law, Oxford Institute of European and Comparative Law. Hon. Fellow: Lincoln College, Oxford 1983, New College, Oxford 1986; Five honorary degrees. *Honours:* Kt 1975; PC 1982. FBA 1987. *Publications:* Co-author *The Law of Restitution. Name, Style and Title:* Raised to the peerage as Baron Goff of Chieveley, of Chieveley in the Royal County of Berkshire 1986. *Address:* Rt Hon the Lord Goff of Chieveley, FBA, House of Lords, London, SW1A 0PW.

LORD GOLDSMITH   Labour

GOLDSMITH (Life Baron), Peter Henry Goldsmith; cr. 1999. Born 5 January 1950. Son of late Sydney Elland Goldsmith, and of Myra Nurick; educated Quarry Bank High School, Liverpool; Gonville and Caius College, Cambridge (MA); University College, London (LLM 1972). Married December 22, 1974, Joy, daughter of Alan and Joan Elterman (3 sons 1 daughter). *Career:* Called to the Bar, Gray's Inn 1972; In Practice 1972–; QC 1987; A Recorder of the Crown Court 1991–; Chairman, Bar Council of England and Wales 1995; Member, Paris Bar (Avocat a la Cour) 1997. *International Bodies (General):* Prime Minister's Representative on Convention for a Charter of Fundamental Rights of the EU 1999–. *Other:* Executive Committee Member, Great Britain China Centre 1996–; Council Member, Public Concern at Work 1996–99. *Miscellaneous:* Chairman, Bar Council International Relations Committee 1996–; Member, Financial Reporting Review Panel 1995–, Chairman 1997–2000; Chairman, IBA Standing Committee on Globalisation 1996–98; Founder and Chairman, Bar Pro Bono Unit 1996–; Co-Chairman, IBA Human Pro Rights Institute 1998–; Various Offices held in International Law Organizations. *Name, Style and Title:* Raised to the peerage as Baron Goldsmith, of Allerton in the County of Merseyside 1999. *Address:* The Lord Goldsmith, QC, House of Lords, London, SW1A 0PW; Fountain Court Chambers, Fountain Court, Temple, London, EC4 *Tel:* 020 7583 3335 *Fax:* 020 7353 0329 *E-Mail:* PHgoldsmith_QC@compuserve.com.

LORD GOODHART   Liberal Democrat

GOODHART (Life Baron), William (Howard) Goodhart; cr. 1997. Born 18 January 1933. Son of late Professor Arthur Goodhart, Hon. KBE, QC, FBA; educated Eton; Trinity College, Cambridge (Scholar, MA); Harvard Law School (Commonwealth Fund Fellow, LLM). Married May 21, 1966, Hon. Celia McClare Herbert, daughter of 2nd Baron Hemingford (1 son 2 daughters). *Armed Forces:* Second Lieutenant, Oxford and Bucks Light Infantry 1951–53 (National Service). *Career:* Called to the Bar, Lincoln's Inn 1957, QC 1979–; Bencher 1986–; Director, Bar Mutual Indemnity Fund Ltd 1988–97. *Spokesman:* Liberal Democrat Spokesman on the Lord Chancellor's Department 2000–. *Select Committees:* Co-opted Member, Select Committees on European Communities Sub-Committee E 1997–; Member, Select Committees on: Delegated Powers and Deregulation 1998–, European Communities 1998–, Freedom of Information Bill 1999. *International Bodies (General):* Member, International Commission of Jurists 1993–, Executive Committee 1995–;

Committee Officer, Human Rights Institute 1995–2000. *Party Groups (General):* Chairman: SDP Council Arrangements Committee 1982–88, Liberal Democrat Conference Committee 1988–91, Liberal Democrat Lawyers Association 1988–91; Member, Liberal Democrat Policy Committee 1988, Vice-Chairman 1995–97. *Other:* Justice: Member of Council 1972–, Vice-Chairman, Executive Committee 1978–88, Chairman, Executive Committee 1988–94; Member: Trust Law Committee 1994–, Tax Law Review Committee 1994–; Vice-Chairman of Council 1999–; Council Member, Royal Institute of International Affairs, 1999–. *Trusts, etc:* Trustee, Airey Neave Trust 1999–. *Miscellaneous:* Contested: Kensington (SDP) 1983, (SDP/Alliance) 1987, (Lib Dem) July 1988, Oxford West and Abingdon (Lib Dem) 1992; Member: Council of Legal Education 1986–92, Conveyancing Standing Committee, Law Commission 1987–89; Has led reporting missions on human rights to Hong Kong 1991, Kashmir 1993, Israel and the West Bank 1994, Kenya 1996 and Sri Lanka 1997; Member, Committee on Standards in Public Life 1997–. *Honours:* Kt 1989. *Publications: Specific Performance,* 1986 (2nd ed. 1996) (with Professor Gareth Jones); Has contributed to *Halsbury's Laws of England;* also articles in legal journals. *Special Interests:* Human Rights. *Recreations:* Walking, skiing. *Clubs:* Brooks's, Century Association (New York). *Name, Style and Title:* Raised to the peerage as Baron Goodhart, of Youlbury in the County of Oxfordshire 1997. *Address:* The Lord Goodhart, QC, 11 Clarence Terrace, London, NW1 4RD *Tel:* 020 7262 1319 *Fax:* 020 7723 5851; Youlbury House, Boars Hill, Oxford, OX1 5HH *Tel:* 01865 735477 *E-Mail:* goodhartw@parliament.uk.

LORD GORDON OF STRATHBLANE   Labour

GORDON OF STRATHBLANE (Life Baron), James Stuart Gordon; cr. 1997. Born 17 May 1936. Son of late James and Elsie Gordon, née Riach; educated St Aloysius' College, Glasgow; Glasgow University (MA Hons). Married, 1971, Margaret Anne Stevenson (2 sons 1 daughter). *Career:* Political Editor, STV 1965–73; Managing Director, Radio Clyde 1973–96; Chief Executive, Scottish Radio Holdings 1991–96, Chairman 1996–; Vice-Chairman, Melody Radio 1991–97; Director: Clydeport Holdings 1992–98, Johnston Press plc 1996–, AIM Trust plc 1996–; Chairman, Scottish Tourist Board 1998–. *Other:* Member, Scottish Development Agency 1981–90; Chairman, Scottish Exhibition Centre 1983–89; Member: Court of University of Glasgow 1984–97, Committee of Enquiry into Teachers' Pay and Conditions 1986, Scottish Advisory Board, BP 1990–; Member, Scottish Tourist Board 1997–, Chairman 1998–; Chair, Advisory Group on Listed Events 1997–98; Board Member, British Tourist Authority 1999–. Hon. DLitt, Glasgow Caledonian 1994; DUniv, Glasgow University 1998. *Trusts, etc:* Trustee: National Galleries of Scotland 1998–, John Smith Memorial Trust 1995–. *Miscellaneous:* Contested East Renfrewshire (Lab) 1964 General Election; Member, Committee on Funding of the BBC 1998–99. *Honours:* CBE 1984. *Recreations:* Skiing, walking, genealogy, golf. *Sportsclubs:* Buchanan Castle Golf, Prestwick Golf. *Clubs:* New (Edinburgh), Glasgow Art. *Name, Style and Title:* Raised to the peerage as Baron Gordon of Strathblane, of Deil's Craig in Stirling 1997. *Address:* The Lord Gordon of Strathblane, CBE, Deil's Craig, Strathblane, Glasgow, G63 9ET *Tel:* 0141–565 2202 *Fax:* 0141–565 2322 *E-Mail:* james.gordon@srh.co.uk.

VISCOUNT GOSCHEN   Conservative

GOSCHEN (4th Viscount, UK), Giles John Harry Goschen; cr. 1900. Born 16 November 1965. Son of 3rd Viscount, KBE. Succeeded his father 1977; educated Eton. Married February 23, 1991, Sarah Penelope Horsnail (1 daughter). *Career:* Deutsche Bank 1997–. *House of Lords:* Parliamentary Under-Secretary of State, Department of Transport 1994–97; An elected hereditary peer 1999–. *Whip:* Government Whip 1992–94. *Spokesman:* Government Spokesman for Environment, Employment, Social Security, Transport and Trade and Industry 1992–94; Opposition Spokesman on Environment, Transport and the Regions (Transport) 1997. *Clubs:* Air Squadron, Pratt's. *Address:* The Viscount Goschen, House of Lords, London, SW1A 0PW.

BARONESS GOUDIE   Labour

GOUDIE (Life Baroness), Mary Teresa Goudie; cr. 1998. Born 2 September 1946. Daughter of Martin and Hannah Brick; educated Our Lady of The Visitation, Greenford; Our Lady of St Anselm, Hayes. Married 1969, James Goudie, QC (2 sons). *Trades Union:* Member: APEX, GMB. *Councils, Public Bodies:* Councillor, London Borough of Brent 1971–78, Chairman, Housing and Planning Committees, Deputy Whip. *Career:* Assistant Director, Brent People's Housing Association 1980–87; Director: The Hansard Society for Parliamentary Government 1985–89, *The House Magazine* (weekly journal of the Houses of Parliament and the Parliamentary Information Unit) 1989–90; Public Affairs Manager, World Wide Fund for Nature (UK) 1990–95; Independent Public Affairs Consultant 1995–. *Select Committees:* Co-opted Member – European Select Committee, Sub-Committee E, Law and Institutions 1998–. *International Bodies (General):* Member: Labour Movement in Europe, Inter-Parliamentary Union, British-American Parliamentary Group. *Party Groups (General):* Secretary, Labour Solidarity Campaign 1980–84; Member: Society of Labour Lawyers, Fabian Society, Smith Institute. *Other:* Chair, Family Courts' Consortium; Secretary, Industry Forum Scotland; Community Service Volunteers, Scotland. *Trusts, etc:* Trustee, Tower Hamlets Old People's Trust; Patron, National Childbirth Trust. *Special Interests:* Europe, Ireland, Scotland, Regional Development, Home Affairs, Children, Charity Law, Machinery of Government. *Recreations:* Family, travelling, gardening, food and wine, art. *Clubs:* Reform. *Name, Style and Title:* Raised to the peerage as Baroness Goudie, of Roundwood in the London Borough of Brent 1998. *Address:* The Baroness Goudie, House of Lords, London, SW1A 0PW.

BARONESS GOULD OF POTTERNEWTON   Labour

GOULD OF POTTERNEWTON (Life Baroness), Joyce Brenda Gould; cr. 1993. Born 29 October 1932. Daughter of late Sydney and Fanny Manson; educated Roundhay High School for Girls; Bradford Technical College. Married 1952, Kevin Gould (1 daughter) (separated). *Trades Union:* Member: TGWU, GMW. *Career:* Pharmaceutical Dispenser 1952–65; Organiser, Pioneer Women 1965; Clerical Worker 1966–69; Worked for the Labour Party 1969–93; Assistant Regional Organiser 1969–75; Secretary, National Joint Committee of Working Women's Organisations 1975–85; Assistant National Agent and Chief Women's Officer 1975–85; Director of Organisation, Labour Party 1985–93. *Whip:* Opposition Whip 1994–97; Government Whip (Social Security, Health and Women) May-December 1997. *Spokesman:* Opposition Spokesperson on: Citizen's Charter 1994–96, Women 1996–97. *Select Committees:* Former Member: Select Committee on Finance and Staffing, European Select Committee, Sub-Committee C (Environmental Affairs). *Backbench Committees:* Vice-Chairperson, Labour Party Departmental Committee for Women; Member, Labour Party Departmental Committees for: Health, Social Security. *International Bodies (General):* Vice-President, Socialist International Women 1978–85; Member: Council of Europe and Education and Cultural Committee 1993–95, WEU and Parliamentary and Public Relations Committee, CPA, IPU. *Party Groups (General):* Member: Regional Women's Advisory Committee, National Labour Women's Committee, Plant Committee on Electoral Systems; Chair, Computing for Labour; Member: Fabian Society, Labour Electoral Reform Association, Bevan Society, Labour Heritage, Arts for Labour. *Other:* Secretary: National Joint Committee of Working Women, Yorkshire National Council for Civil Liberties; Committee Member, Campaign Against Racial Discrimination; Executive Member, Joint Committee Against Racism; Member, Management Committee, Grand Theatre, Leeds; Senior posts various charities; Member: Fawcett Society, Hansard Society, Howard League, Yorkshire Society; Council Member, Constitution Unit. Hon. Degree, Bradford University 1997. *Trusts, etc:* Chair and Trustee, Mary MacArthur Holiday Trust; Trustee and Director: Diarama Arts, Studio Upstairs, Yigol Allon Trust; Trustee and Fellow, Industry and Parliamentary Trust. *Miscellaneous:* Executive Member, Women's National Commission; Member: Department of Employment Women's Advisory Committee, Home Office Committee on Electoral Matters, Commission on Conduct of Referendums, Independent Commission on Electoral System 1997–98. *Publications:* Include *Women and Health* (editor);

pamphlets on Feminism, Socialism and Sexism, Women's Right to Work, Violence in Society; articles and reports on Women's Rights, Electoral systems – their practices and procedures. *Special Interests:* Women's Equality, Constitutional Affairs, Electoral Affairs, Race Relations, Population and Development, Disabled. *Recreations:* Theatre, cinema, reading. *Name, Style and Title:* Raised to the peerage as Baroness Gould of Potternewton, of Leeds in the County of West Yorkshire 1993. *Address:* The Baroness Gould of Potternewton, Flat 1, 5 Foulser Road, London, SW17 8UE *Tel:* 020 8672 0641 *Fax:* 020 8672 0641; 6 St Johns Mews, Bristol Road, Brighton, BN2 1BN *Tel:* 01273 607474.

LORD GRABINER — Labour

GRABINER (Life Baron), Anthony Stephen Grabiner; cr. 1999. Born 21 March 1945. Son of late Ralph and Freda Grabiner (née Cohen); educated Central Foundation Boys' Grammar School, London EC2; LSE; London University (LLB 1966, LLM 1967); Lincoln's Inn (Hardwicke Scholar 1966, Droop Scholar 1968). Married 1983, Jane, daughter of Dr Benjamin Portnoy (3 sons 1 daughter). *Career:* Called to the Bar, Lincoln's Inn 1968; Standing Junior Counsel to Department of Trade, Export Credits Guarantee Department 1976–81; Junior Counsel to the Crown 1978–81; QC 1981; Bencher 1989; Recorder of the Crown Court 1990–; Deputy High Court Judge 1994–. *Other:* Member, Court of Governors, LSE 1991–, Vice-Chairman 1993–98, Chairman 1998–. *Publications:* Co-editor, *Sutton and Shannon on Contract,* 7th edition 1970; Contributor, *Banking Documents to Encyclopedia of Forms and Precedents,* 5th edition 1986; *The Informal Economy* (March 2000) Report to Chancellor of the Exchequer. *Special Interests:* Law Reform, Commercial and Intellectual Property Law, Higher Education. *Recreations:* Golf, theatre, reading. *Sportsclubs:* Hendon Golf. *Clubs:* Garrick, Royal Automobile, MCC. *Name, Style and Title:* Raised to the peerage as Baron Grabiner, of Aldwych in the City of Westminster 1999. *Address:* The Lord Grabiner, QC, 1 Essex Court, Temple, London, EC4Y 9AR *Tel:* 020 7583 2000 *Fax:* 020 7583 0118; House of Lords, London, SW1A 0PW *E-Mail:* jhuxley@oeclaw.co.uk.

LORD GRAHAM OF EDMONTON — Labour

GRAHAM OF EDMONTON (Life Baron), Thomas Edward Graham; cr. 1983. Born 26 March 1925. Son of late Thomas Edward Graham; educated Elementary School; WEA Co-operative College; Open University (BA). Married 1950, Margaret Golding (2 sons). *Trades Union:* Member, National Association of Co-operative Officials. *Armed Forces:* Corporal, Royal Marines 1943–46. *Councils, Public Bodies:* Labour Leader, Enfield Borough Council 1961–68; Chairman, Housing and Redevelopment Committee 1961–68. *Career:* Various posts within the Co-operative Movement 1939–74. *House of Commons:* Contested (Labour and Co-operative) Enfield West in 1966; MP (Labour and Co-operative) for Enfield, Edmonton 1974–83; PPS to Minister of State, Department of Prices and Consumer Affairs 1974–76. *Whip (Commons):* Government Whip (Lord Commissioner of the Treasury) 1976–79. *Spokesman (Commons):* Spokesman on the Environment 1981–83. *House of Lords:* A Deputy Speaker of the House of Lords; A Deputy Chairman of Committees 1997–. *Whip:* Opposition Whip 1983–90, Opposition Chief Whip 1990–97. *Spokesman:* Opposition Front Bench Spokesman on the Environment, Northern Ireland and Defence 1983–90; Former Opposition Spokesman on National Heritage (Tourism). *Select Committees:* Former Member of several select committees including Privileges, Procedure and Selection. *Backbench Committees:* Member, Refreshments Committee 1990–. *Party Groups:* Chair, Labour Peers Group. *Party Groups (General):* Member, Co-operative Party. *Other:* President, Institute of Meat. Hon. Degree of Master of Open University 1989. *Honours:* PC 1998. Fellow: Institute of British Management, Royal Society of Arts. Freeman, Worshipful Company of Butchers. *Special Interests:* Local Government, Consumer Affairs, Environment. *Name, Style and Title:* Raised to the peerage as Baron Graham of Edmonton, of Edmonton in Greater London 1983. *Address:* Rt Hon the Lord Graham of Edmonton, 2 Clerks Piece, Loughton, Essex, IG10 1NR; House of Lords, London, SW1A 0PW *Tel:* House of Lords 020 7219 6704.

LORD GRAY OF CONTIN   Conservative

GRAY OF CONTIN (Life Baron), James Hector Northey Hamish Gray; cr. 1983. Born 28 June 1927. Son of late James Northey Gray, JP, and late Mrs M. E. Gray; educated Inverness Royal Academy. Married September 11, 1953, Judith W. Brydon (2 sons 1 daughter). *Armed Forces:* Served Queens Own Cameron Highlanders 1945–48. *Councils, Public Bodies:* Served Highland Chamber of Commerce 1963–70; Inverness Town Council 1965–70; DL, Lochaber, Inverness, Badenoch and Strathspey 1989–96, Vice-Lord Lieutenant 1994–96; Lord Lieutenant of Inverness 1996–; JP, Inverness 1996–. *Career:* Company Director 1950–70; Business and Parliamentary Consultant 1987–; Non-Executive Director 1995–. *House of Commons:* MP (Conservative) Ross and Cromarty 1970–83; Successfully piloted Education Scotland (Mentally Handicapped) Bill through Parliament 1974; Minister of State for Energy 1979–83. *Whip (Commons):* Assistant Government Whip 1971–73; Government Whip (Lord Commissioner of the Treasury) 1973–74; Opposition Whip 1974–75. *Spokesman (Commons):* Opposition Spokesman on Energy 1975–79. *House of Lords:* Minister of State, Scottish Office 1983–86. *Spokesman:* A Government Spokesman on Employment 1983–84; Principal Government Spokesman on Energy 1984–86. *Select Committees:* Member, Select Committees on: Channel Tunnel 1986–87, Relations between Central and Local Government 1995–96. *International Bodies (General):* President, British Romanian Chamber of Commerce 1999–. *Other:* Hon. President: National Charities, Energy Action Scotland 1987–97; Hon. Vice-President: Neighbourhood Energy Action 1987–98, National Energy Action 1987–98. *Honours:* PC 1982. *Recreations:* Golf, cricket, walking, gardening, reading. *Name, Style and Title:* Raised to the peerage as Baron Gray of Contin, of Contin in the District of Ross and Cromarty 1983. *Address:* Rt Hon the Lord Gray of Contin, House of Lords, London, SW1A 0PW.

LORD GREAVES   Liberal Democrat

GREAVES (Life Baron), Anthony Robert Greaves; cr. 2000. Born 27 July 1942. Son of late Geoffrey Lawrence Greaves and of Moyra Louise Greaves; educated Queen Elizabeth Grammar School, Wakefield; Hertford College, Oxford (BA geography 1963). Married 1968, Heather Ann Baxter (2 children). *Councils, Public Bodies:* Councillor: Colne Borough Council 1971–74, Pendle Borough Council 1973–98, Lancashire County Council 1973–97. *Career:* Teacher; Lecturer; Organising Secretary, Association of Liberal Councillors; Manager, Liberal Party Publications; Book Dealer; Assistant to Chris Davies, MEP. *Miscellaneous:* Contested Nelson and Colne February and October 1974, Pendle 1997 general elections. *Publications:* Co-author *Merger: The Inside Story. Recreations:* Climbing, mountaineering, botany, cycling. *Name, Style and Title:* Raised to the peerage as Baron Greaves, of Pendle in the County of Lancashire 2000. *Address:* The Lord Greaves, 3 Hartington Street, Winewall, Colne, Lancashire, BB8 6XB *Tel:* 01282 864346 *E-Mail:* tonygreaves@cix.co.uk.

LORD GREENE OF HARROW WEALD   Labour

GREENE OF HARROW WEALD (Life Baron), Sidney Francis Greene; cr. 1974. Born 12 February 1910. Son of late Frank Greene; educated elementary schools. Married 1936, Masel Elizabeth Carter (3 daughters). *Trades Union:* General Secretary, National Union of Railwaymen 1957–75; Member, General Council of TUC 1957–75. *Councils, Public Bodies:* JP, London 1941–65. *Career:* Joined Railway Service 1924; Director: Bank of England 1970–78, RTZ Corporation 1975–80, Times Newspapers 1975–82. *Miscellaneous:* Member, National Economic Development Council 1962–75. *Name, Style and Title:* Raised to the peerage as Baron Greene of Harrow Weald, of Harrow in the County of Greater London 1974. *Address:* The Lord Greene of Harrow Weald, CBE, 26 Kynaston Wood, Boxtree Road, Harrow Weald, Middlesex, HA3 6UA.

BARONESS GREENGROSS   Cross-Bencher

GREENGROSS (Life Baroness), Sally Ralea Greengross; cr. 2000. Born 29 June 1935; educated Brighton and Hove High School; LSE. Married Sir Alan Greengross (1 son 3 daughters). *Career:* Formerly a linguist, executive in industry, lecturer and researcher; Age Concern England: Assistant Director 1977–82, Deputy Director 1982–87, Director-General (formerly Director) 1987–; Vice-President (Europe), International Federation on Ageing 1987–, (Secretary General 1982–87); Joint Chairman, Age Concern Institute of Gerontology, King's College London 1987–; Vice-President, Research Institute for the Care of the Elderly 1987–. *International Bodies (General):* Member, Advisory Council, European Movement 1992–; Independent Member, UN and WHO Networks on Ageing 1983–. *Other:* President, Action on Elder Abuse 1994–; Vice-President, EXTEND 1996. Hon. DLitt, Ulster 1994; DUniv, Kingston 1996. *Trusts, etc:* Trustee, British Association of Domiciliary Care Officers 1989–. *Miscellaneous:* Past and current member several advisory bodies concerned with the elderly. *Honours:* OBE 1993. FRSH 1994; FRSA 1994. *Publications:* Consultant, *Journal of Educational Gerontology,* 1987–; Editor, *Ageing: an adventure in living,* 1985; has edited and contributed to other publications on ageing issues and social policy. *Recreations:* Countryside, music. *Clubs:* Reform, Hurlingham. *Name, Style and Title:* Raised to the peerage as Baroness Greengross, of Notting Hill in the Royal Borough of Kensington and Chelsea 2000. *Address:* The Baroness Greengross, OBE, 9 Dawson Place, London, W2 4TD *Tel:* 020 7229 1939.

LORD GREENHILL OF HARROW   Cross-Bencher

GREENHILL OF HARROW (Life Baron), Denis Arthur Greenhill; cr. 1974. Born 7 November 1913. Son of late James and Susie Greenhill; educated Bishops Stortford College, Herts; Christ Church, Oxford (Hon. Student). Married June 4, 1941, Angela, daughter of late William McCulloch (1 son and 1 son deceased). *Armed Forces:* Royal Engineers 1939–45. *Career:* Apprentice, London North Eastern Railway 1935–39; Diplomatic Service, Sofia, Washington, NATO delegation Paris, Singapore 1946–73; Permanent Under-Secretary. Foreign and Commonwealth Office 1969–73; Government Director, British Petroleum 1973–78; Director, Leyland International 1977–82; Director, S. G. Warburg & Co. 1974–86, Adviser 1986–95; Director: BAT Industries 1974–83, Hawker Siddeley Group 1974–84, Clerical Medical Association 1974–86, Wellcome Foundation 1974–85. *Select Committees:* Member, House of Lords Select Committee on Overseas Trade 1985; Member, European Select Committee and Sub-Committee 1985–87; Former Chairman, House of Lords Select Committee on King's Cross Private Bill. *Other:* Governor, BUPA 1978–84; Chairman, King's College Hospital Medical School 1976–83; Member, Rayne Foundation; Former Chairman of the Governing Body, School of Oriental and African Studies, London University 1978–85; Governor, Wellington College 1974–83; President: Royal Society of Asian Affairs 1976–84, Anglo-Finnish Society 1981–84. *Miscellaneous:* Governor, BBC 1973–78; Member, Security Commission.*Honours:* OBE (Mil) 1941; CMG 1960; KCMG 1967; GCMG 1972; Grand Cross Order of the Finnish Lion 1984. Fellow, King's College, London. *Publications: More by Accident* (memoir) 1992. *Clubs:* Travellers'. *Name, Style and Title:* Raised to the peerage as Baron Greenhill of Harrow, of the Royal Borough of Kensington and Chelsea 1974. *Address:* The Lord Greenhill of Harrow, GCMG, OBE, 25 Hamilton House, Vicarage Gate, London, W8 4HL *Tel:* 020 7937 8362.

LORD GREENWAY   Cross-Bencher

GREENWAY (4th Baron, UK), Ambrose Charles Drexel Greenway; cr. 1927; 4th Bt of Stanbridge Earls (UK) 1919. Born 21 May 1941. Son of 3rd Baron. Succeeded his father 1975; educated Winchester. Married October 26, 1985, Mrs Rosalynne Peta Schenk, née Fradgley. *Career:* Marine Photographer. *House of Lords:* An elected hereditary peer 1999–. *Other:* Younger Brother, Trinity House 1987; Chairman, The Marine Society 1994–; Vice-President, Sail Training Association 1995–. *Publications: Soviet Merchant Ships,* 1976; *Comecon Merchant Ships,* 1978; *A Century of Cross-Channel Passenger Ferries,* 1981; *A Century of North Sea Passenger Steamers,* 1986. *Special Interests:* Shipping, Marine Industry. *Recreations:* Sailing. *Clubs:* House of Lords Yacht. *Address:* The Lord Greenway, House of Lords, London, SW1A 0PW.

LORD GREGSON   Labour

GREGSON (Life Baron), John Gregson; cr. 1975. Born 29 January 1924. Son of late John Gregson. *Councils, Public Bodies:* DL, County of Greater Manchester 1979. *Career:* Joined Fairey Engineering 1939, Board Member 1966, Managing Director 1978–94, retired as Non-Executive Director, Fairey Holding 1994; Non-Executive Director: British Steel plc 1976–94, Otto-Simon Carves Ltd 1995, Innvotech Ltd. *Select Committees:* Member, House of Lords Select Committees on: Science and Technology 1980–97, Sustainable Development 1994–97. *Party Groups (General):* President, Labour Finance and Industry Group. *Other:* Former Vice-President, Association of Metropolitan Authorities; Member, National Rivers Authority 1991–95; Member Council, University of Manchester Institute of Science and Technology; President, Defence Manufacturers Association 1984–; Chairman, Waste Management Industry Training and Advisory Board; Member, Court of: UMIST, University of Manchester. Four honorary doctorates. Hon. Fellow: Royal Academy of Engineering, Institute of Civil Engineers 1987; AMCT; CIMgt. *Recreations:* Mountaineering, ski-ing, sailing, gardening. *Name, Style and Title:* Raised to the peerage as Baron Gregson, of Stockport in the County of Greater Manchester 1975. *Address:* The Lord Gregson, DL, 12 Rosemont Road, Richmond, Surrey, TW10 6QL.

LORD GRENFELL   Labour

GRENFELL (3rd Baron, UK), Julian Pascoe Francis St Leger Grenfell; cr. 1902; (Life) Baron Grenfell of Kilvey 2000. Born 23 May 1935. Son of 2nd Baron, CBE, TD. Succeeded his father 1976; educated Eton; King's College, Cambridge 1959 (President of the Union 1959). Married 1st, 1961, Loretta Reali, of Florence, Italy (1 daughter) (marriage dissolved 1970), married 2nd, 1970, Gabrielle Raab, of Berlin, Germany (2 daughters) (marriage dissolved 1987), married 3rd, June 3, 1987, Mrs Elizabeth Porter, of Richmond, Virginia (marriage dissolved 1992), married 4th, October 4, 1993, Mrs Dagmar Langbehn Debreil, daughter of Dr Carl Langbehn, of Berlin, Germany. *Armed Forces:* 2nd Lieutenant, KRRC (60th Rifles) 1954–56; Captain, Queen's Royal Rifles, TA 1963. *Career:* Television Reporter, ATV Ltd 1960–63; With World Bank: Washington DC 1965–69, Paris 1969–74; Representative of the World Bank to the United Nations 1974–81; Senior Adviser, The World Bank, Washington, DC 1983–90; Head of External Affairs, European Office of the World Bank 1990–95. *Select Committees:* Sub-Committee A, European Union Committee: Member 1996–99, Chairman 1999, Member 2000–; Member, Select Committee on European Union 1999, 2000–. *International Bodies:* Member, UK Delegation to the Parliamentary Assemblies of the Council of Europe and Western European Union 1997–99. *Other:* Member, Council, Worldaware. *Publications: Margot* (novel), 1987. *Special Interests:* European Affairs, Economic Policy, Overseas Development. *Recreations:* Walking, reading. *Clubs:* Royal Green Jackets. *Name, Style and Title:* Created a life peer as Baron Grenfell of Kilvey, of Kilvey in the County of Swansea 2000. *Address:* The Lord Grenfell, House of Lords, London, SW1A 0PW.

LORD GRIFFITHS   Cross-Bencher

GRIFFITHS (Life Baron), William Hugh Griffiths; cr. 1985. Born 26 September 1923. Son of late Sir Hugh Griffiths, CBE; educated Charterhouse; St John's College, Cambridge. Married 1st, 1949, Evelyn Krefting (died March 1998) (1 son 3 daughters); married 2nd, January 22, 2000, The Baroness Brigstocke (*qv*). *Armed Forces:* Commissioned Welsh Guards 1942. *Career:* Called to the Bar, Inner Temple 1949; QC 1964; Recorder of: Margate 1962–64, Cambridge 1964–70; A Judge of the High Court of Justice, Queen's Bench Division 1971–80; A Lord Justice of Appeal 1980–85; A Lord of Appeal in Ordinary 1985–93. *Other:* President, Bar Association for Commerce, Finance and Industry. *Miscellaneous:* Chairman, Security Commission 1985–92. *Honours:* MC 1944; Kt 1971; PC 1980. *Clubs:* Garrick, MCC, Royal and Ancient (St Andrews). *Name, Style and Title:* Raised to the peerage as Baron Griffiths, of Govilon in the County of Gwent 1985. *Address:* Rt Hon the Lord Griffiths, MC, House of Lords, London, SW1A 0PW.

LORD GRIFFITHS OF FFORESTFACH — Conservative

GRIFFITHS OF FFORESTFACH (Life Baron), Brian Griffiths; cr. 1991. Born 27 December 1941. Son of Ivor Winston and Phyllis Griffiths; educated Dynevor Grammar School; London School of Economics. Married September 18, 1965, Rachel Jane, daughter of Howard and Ruth Jones (1 son 2 daughters). *Career:* Lecturer, London School of Economics 1965–76; Professor of Banking and Director of Centre, Banking and International Finance The City University 1977–82; Dean, Business School The City University 1983–85; Director, Bank of England 1983–85; Head, Prime Minister's Policy Unit and Special Adviser to The Rt Hon. Margaret Thatcher MP 1985–90; Director: Thorn EMI 1990–96, Herman Miller Inc. 1991–, Times Newspapers Ltd 1991–; Chairman, Schools Examinations and Assessment Council 1991–93; International Adviser, Goldman Sachs 1991–; Vice-Chairman, Goldman Sachs (Europe); Director: Servicemaster 1992–, HTV 1992–93, Telewest 1995–98, English, Welsh, Scottish Railway 1996–; Chairman: Trillium 1998–, Westminster Health Care 1999–. *Select Committees:* Member, Select Committee on the European Union, Sub-Committee F (Social Affairs, Education and Home Affairs). Freeman, City of London. *Publications:* Several books on economics including: *The Creation of Wealth*, 1984; *Morality and the Market Place*, 1989. *Special Interests:* Economic Policy, Education, Broadcasting, Social Policy. *Clubs:* Garrick. *Name, Style and Title:* Raised to the peerage as Baron Griffiths of Fforestfach, of Fforestfach in the County of West Glamorgan 1991. *Address:* The Lord Griffiths of Fforestfach, House of Lords, London, SW1A 0PW.

BISHOP OF GUILDFORD — Non-Affiliated

GUILDFORD (8th Bishop of), John Warren Gladwin. Born 30 May 1942. Son of late Thomas and Muriel Gladwin; educated Hertford Grammar School; Churchill College, Cambridge (BA History and Theology, MA 1969); St John's College, Durham (DipTheol). Married 1981, Lydia Elizabeth Adam. *Career:* Assistant Curate, St John the Baptist, Kirkheaton, Huddersfield 1967–71; Tutor, St John's College, Durham and Hon. Chaplain to Students, St Nicholas Church, Durham 1971–77; Director, Shaftesbury Project on Christian Involvement in Society 1977–82; Secretary, General Synod Board for Social Responsibility 1982–88; Prebendary, St Paul's Cathedral 1984–88; Provost of Sheffield 1988–94; Member, General Synod of the Church of England 1990–; Bishop of Guildford 1994–; Took his seat in the House of Lords 1999. *Other:* President, Church's National Housing Coalition; Chairman, Board of Christian Aid; Member, Archbishop's Council. Freeman, City of London. *Publications: God's People in God's World*, 1979; *The Good of the People*, 1988; *Love and Liberty*, 1998. *Recreations:* Gardening, travel, bee keeping. *Address:* Rt Rev the Lord Bishop of Guildford, Willow Grange, Woking Road, Guildford, Surrey, GU4 7QS *Tel:* 01483 590500 *Fax:* 01483 590501 *E-Mail:* bishop.john@cofeguildford.org.uk; mary.morris@cofeguildford.org.uk (Secretary).

Dod *on* Line
An Electronic Directory without rival . . .
Peers' biographies and photographs
available with daily updates *via* the internet

For a *free* trial, call Oliver Cox on 020 7828 7256

H

LORD HABGOOD   Cross-Bencher

HABGOOD (Life Baron), John Stapylton Habgood; cr. 1995. Born 23 June 1927. Son of late Arthur Henry Habgood, DSO, MB, BCH, and late Vera Chetwynd-Stapylton; educated Eton; King's College, Cambridge (MA, PhD); Cuddesdon Theological College, Oxford. Married 1961, Rosalie Mary Anne Boston (2 sons 2 daughters). *Career:* Demonstrator in Pharmacology, Cambridge University 1950–53; Curate, St Mary Abbots, Kensington 1954–56; Vice-Principal, Westcott House, Cambridge 1956–62; Rector, St John's Church, Jedburgh 1962–67; Principal, Queen's College, Birmingham 1967–73; Bishop of Durham 1973–83; Took his seat in the House of Lords 1973; Archbishop of York 1983–95. *Chancellor:* Pro-Chancellor, York University 1985–90. *Select Committees:* Member, Select Committee on Medical Ethics 1993–94. *International Bodies (General):* Member, World Council of Churches 1983–91. *Other:* Patron, National Family Mediation 1990–; Vice-President, Population Concern 1991–. 10 honorary doctorates from UK and USA; honorary fellow King's College, Cambridge. *Miscellaneous:* Chairman, UK Xenotransplantation Interim Regulatory Authority 1997–; Member, Round Table on Sustainable Development 1997–99.*Honours:* PC 1983. *Publications: Religion and Science*, 1964; *A Working Faith*, 1980; *Church and Nation in a Secular Age*, 1983; *Confessions of a Conservative Liberal*, 1988; *Making Sense*, 1993; *Faith and Uncertainty*, 1997; *Being A Person*, 1998; *Varieties of Unbelief*, 2000. *Special Interests:* Science, Medicine, Ethics. *Recreations:* Travel, DIY, Painting. *Clubs:* Athenaeum. *Name, Style and Title.* Raised to the peerage as Baron Habgood, of Calverton in the County of Buckinghamshire 1995.*Address:* Rt Rev and Rt Hon the Lord Habgood, 18 The Mount, Malton, North Yorkshire, YO17 7ND.

LORD HAILSHAM OF ST MARYLEBONE   Conservative

HAILSHAM OF ST MARYLEBONE (Life Baron), Quintin McGarel Hogg; cr. 1970. Born 9 October 1907. Son of 1st Viscount, PC, KC whom he succeeded in 1950; disclaimed the viscountcy and barony of Hailsham for life; educated Eton; Christ Church, Oxford (MA) (President of the Union 1929). Married 1st, November 12, 1932, Natalie Sullivan (marriage dissolved 1943, she died 1987), married 2nd, April 18, 1944, Mary Evelyn Martin (died 1978) (2 sons 3 daughters), married 3rd, March 1, 1986, Deirdre (died 1998), daughter of late Captain Peter Shannon, and of Mrs Margaret Briscoe. *Armed Forces:* Served overseas with Rifle Brigade 1939–45. *Career:* Called to the Bar, Lincoln's Inn 1932; QC 1953, Bencher 1956, Treasurer 1975; Editor,*Halsbury's Laws of England*, 4th edition 1972–98. *House of Commons:* MP (Conservative) for: Oxford City 1938–50, St. Marylebone 1963–70; Joint Parliamentary Under-Secretary of State for Air April-July 1945; Minister with responsibility for: Sport 1962–64; Unemployment in the North East 1963–64; Higher Education December 1963-February 1964; Secretary of State for Education and Science April-October 1964.*House of Lords:* First Lord of the Admiralty 1956–57; Minister of Education January-September 1957; Deputy Leader of the House of Lords 1957–60, Leader 1960–63; Lord President of the Council 1957–59, 1960–64; Minister for Science and Technology 1959–64; Lord High Chancellor 1970–74, 1979–87; A Former Deputy Speaker of the House of Lords. *Party Groups (General):* Chairman, Conservative Party 1957–59. Fellow, All Souls College 1931; eight honorary doctorates from UK, Canada, USA and India.*Honours:* PC 1956; CH 1974; KG 1988. FRS 1973. *Publications: The Law of Arbitration* 1935; *One Year's Work* 1944; *The Law and Employers' Liability* 1944; *The Times We Live In* 1944; *Making Peace* 1945; *The Left was never Right* 1945; *The Purpose of Parliament* 1946; *Care for Conservatism* 1947; *The Law of Monopolies, Restrictive Practices and Resale Price Maintenance* 1956; *The Conservative Case* 1959; *Interdependence* 1961; *Science and Politics* 1963; *The Devil's Own Song* 1968; *The Door Wherein I Went* 1975; *Elective Dictatorship* 1976; *The Dilemma of Democracy* 1978; *Hamlyn Revisited: the British legal system (Hamlyn Lectures)* 1978; *A Sparrow's Flight* (memoirs) 1990; *On the Constitution* 1992; *Values: Collapse and Cure* 1994. *Recreations:* In recent years, reading and study, formerly mountaineering and walking. *Clubs:* Carlton, Alpine, MCC. *Name, Style and Title:* Raised to the peerage as Baron Hailsham of St Marylebone, of Herstmonceux in the County of Sussex 1970. *Address:* Rt Hon the Lord Hailsham of St Marylebone, KG, CH, FRS, The Corner House, Heathview Gardens, London, SW15 3SZ.

LORD HAMBRO Conservative

HAMBRO (Life Baron), Charles Eric Alexander Hambro; cr. 1994. Born 24 July 1930. Son of late Sir Charles Hambro, KBE, MC and of Pamela, daughter of John and Lady Evelyn Cobbold; educated Eton. Married 1st, July 1, 1954, Rose Evelyn, daughter of late Sir Richard Cotterell, 5th Bt, CBE, TD (2 sons 1 daughter) (marriage dissolved 1976), married 2nd, June 15, 1976, Cherry Felicity, daughter of late Sir John Huggins, GCMG, MC.*Armed Forces:* Served Coldstream Guards 1949–51. *Career:* Joined Hambros Bank Ltd 1952: Managing Director 1957, Deputy Chairman 1965, Chairman 1972–83; Director, Taylor Woodrow 1964–97; Director, Guardian Royal Exchange Assurance 1968–99, Chairman 1988–99; Chairman, Hambros plc 1983–97; Director: Peninsula and Oriental Steamship Company 1987–, General Oriental Investments, San Paolo Bank Holdings 1989–98. *Party Groups (General):* Senior Hon. Treasurer, Conservative Party 1993–97. *Other:* Chairman, Royal National Pension Fund for Nurses 1968. *Trusts, etc:* Trustee, The British Museum 1984–94. Liveryman, Fishmongers' Company. *Recreations:* Shooting, golf. *Sportsclubs:* Swinley Forest Golf. *Clubs:* White's, MCC. *Name, Style and Title:* Raised to the peerage as Baron Hambro, of Dixton and Dumbleton in the County of Gloucestershire 1994. *Address:* The Lord Hambro, Dixton Manor, Gotherington, Cheltenham, Gloucestershire, GL52 4RB *Tel:* 01242 672011; c/o P & O, Schomberg House, 4th Floor, 80 Pall Mall, London, SW1Y 5EJ *Tel:* 020 7321 4478.

LORD HAMLYN Labour

HAMLYN (Life Baron), Paul Bertrand Hamlyn; cr. 1998. Born 12 February 1926. Second son of late Professor Richard Hamburger and Mrs L Hamburger (née Hamburg); educated St Christopher's School, Letchworth, Herts. Married 1st, 1952, Eileen Margaret Watson (1 son 1 daughter) (marriage dissolved 1969); married 2nd, 1970, Mrs Helen Guest. *Career:* Publisher and Company Director; Founded: Books for Pleasure 1949, Prints for Pleasure 1960, Records for Pleasure and Golden Pleasure Books (jointly with Golden Press Inc. New York) 1961, Music for Pleasure (jointly with EMI) 1965, Hamlyn Publishing Group 1968, which he re-purchased from Reed International 1986; Director, IPC 1965–70; Chairman, IPC Books controlling Hamlyn Publishing Group 1965–70; Joint Managing Director, News International Ltd 1970–71; Chairman: Octopus Books 1971, Mandarin Offset (formerly Mandarin Publishers) Hong Kong 1971–97; Founder and Chairman, Octopus Publishing Group 1971–97; Director: News International Ltd 1971–86, Reed Book Publishing 1971–97, Octopus Books International BV (Holland) 1973–86, Octopus Books Ltd 1979–91, TV am 1981–83, Reed International Books 1983–97, Michelin House Development 1985–; Chairman, Heinemann Publishers (Oxford) Ltd (formerly Heinemann Group) 1985–97; Director: Bibendum Restaurant 1986–, Reed International 1987–97, Brandchart 1987–, Chateau de Bagnols 1988–, Michelin House Investment Co 1989–, Reed Elsevier 1993–98, Paul Hamlyn Ventures Ltd 1997, Alice Developments Ltd 1999, Macaw Nominees Ltd 1999. *Chancellor:* Chancellor, Thames Valley University 1993–99. *Awards Granted:* Albert Medal, RSA 1993. Hon. DLitt: Keele 1988, Warwick 1991. *Trusts, etc:* Chairman, Trustees, Public Policy Centre 1985–87. *Honours:* CBE 1993. Hon. FRCSI (Dublin) 1993. *Name, Style and Title:* Raised to the peerage as Baron Hamlyn, of Edgeworth in the County of Gloucestershire 1998. *Address:* The Lord Hamlyn, CBE, 18 Queen Anne's Gate, London, SW1H 9AA *Tel:* 020 7227 3500.

BARONESS HAMWEE Liberal Democrat

HAMWEE (Life Baroness), Sally Rachel Hamwee; cr. 1991. Born 12 January 1947. Daughter of late Alec and Dorothy Hamwee; educated Manchester High School for Girls; Girton College, Cambridge. *Councils, Public Bodies:* Councillor, London Borough of Richmond upon Thames 1978–98; Chair, Planning Committee 1983–87; Vice-Chair, Policy and Resources Committee 1987–91; Chair, London Planning Advisory Committee 1986–94; Member, Greater London Authority 2000–; Deputy Chair of Assembly 2000–01. *Career:* Admitted Solicitor 1972; Currently partner, Clintons Solicitors. *Spokesman:* Liberal Democrat Spokesman on: Local Government 1991–98, Housing and Planning 1993–98, Local Government and Planning 1998–;

Principal Spokesman on Environment, Transport and the Regions 1999–. *Select Committees:* Member, House of Lords Select Committee on Relations between Central and Local Government 1995–96, Joint Select Committee on Draft Local Government and Bill 1999–. *Party Groups (General):* Past President, ALDC (Liberal Democrat Councillors' and Campaigners' Association); Member: National Executive, Liberal Party 1987–88, Federal Executive, Liberal Democrats 1989–91, Federal Policy Committee 1996–98. *Other:* Member of Council, Parents for Children 1977–86; Legal adviser, The Simon Community 1980–; Member of Council, Refuge 1991–; Chair, Xfm Ltd 1996–98; Member of Council, Family Policy Studies Centre; President, Town and Country Planning Association; Member, Joseph Rowntree Foundation Inquiry, Planning for Housing; Member, Advisory Council, London First.*Special Interests:* Local Government, Planning, London, Arts, Media, Housing.*Name, Style and Title:* Raised to the peerage as Baroness Hamwee, of Richmond upon Thames in the London Borough of Richmond upon Thames 1991. *Address:* The Baroness Hamwee, 101A Mortlake High Street, London, SW14 8HQ *Tel:* 020 88/8 1380 *E-Mail:* sally.hamwee@london.gov.uk.

BARONESS HANHAM   Conservative

HANHAM (Life Baroness), Joan Brownlow Hanham; cr. 1999. Born 23 September 1939. Daughter of late Alfred and Mary Spark (née Mitchell); educated Hillcourt School, Dublin. Married 1964, Dr Iain William Ferguson Hanham, FRCP, FRCR (1 son 1 daughter). *Councils, Public Bodies:* Royal Borough of Kensington and Chelsea: Councillor 1970–, Mayor 1983–84, Chairman: Town Planning Committee 1984–86, Social Services Committee 1987–89, Policy and Resources Committee 1989–, Leader of the Council 1989–2000; Chairman, Policy Committee, London Boroughs Association 1991–95; JP: City of London Commission 1984, Inner London Family Proceedings Court 1992. *Whip:* An Opposition Whip 2000–. *International Bodies (General):* Member, Committee of the Regions. *Other:* Director, London First 1996–99; Governor: Sir John Cass Foundation 1996–99, Sir John Cass primary School 1997–99. *Trusts, etc:* Trustee: Commonwealth Institute 1991–, Children's Hospital Trust; Patron, Kensington Housing Trust (Appeal). *Miscellaneous:* Member, Mental Health Act Commission 1983–90; Non-Executive Member, North West Thames Regional Health Authority 1983–94; Chairman, St Mary's Hospital NHS Trust 2000–. *Honours:* CBE 1997. Freeman, City of London 1984. *Special Interests:* Local Government, Health, Justice, Environment. *Recreations:* Music, travel. *Clubs:* Hurlingham. *Name, Style and Title:* Raised to the peerage as Baroness Hanham, of Kensington in the Royal Borough of Kensington and Chelsea 1999. *Address:* Councillor The Baroness Hanham, CBE, The Town Hall, Hornton Street, London, W8 7NX *Tel:* 020 7937 8692 *Fax:* 020 7361 3105.

LORD HANNINGFIELD   Conservative

HANNINGFIELD (Life Baron), Paul Edward Winston White; cr. 1998. Born 16 September 1940. Son of Edward Ernest William White and Irene Joyce Gertrude White (née Williamson; educated King Edward VI Grammar School, Chelmsford; Nuffield Scholarship for Agriculture (research in USA specialising in marketing in farming). *Councils, Public Bodies:* DL Essex 1991–; Essex County Council: Councillor, Stock Area 1970–, various positions from 1973–98 including Chairman of Education Committee, Chairman 1989–92, Leader of the Council 1998–99, Conservative Group Leader. *Career:* A Farmer. *International Bodies (General):* President, Assembly of European Regions Sub-Commission 1990–; Conservative Group Leader, Committee of the Regions, Member 1994–. *Party Groups (General):* Member, Chelmsford Conservative Party Executive 1962–; Chairman: Conservative Party (Stock Area) 1968–75, Conservative Party Eastern Area Local Government Advisory Committee 1995–98, Conservative Party National Local Government Advisory Committee, Conservative Councillors Association Steering Committee; Board Member, Conservative Party representing local government; Member, Conservative Party National Union Executive. *Other:* Member, National Executive, NFU 1965; Association of County Councils: Member 1981–97, Chairman of Education Committee 1989–93, Conservative Leader 1995–97.

Chairman: Council of Local Education Authorities (CLEA) 1990–92; Eastern Region Further Education Funding Council 1992–97; Deputy Chairman and Conservative Group Leader, Local Government Association. *Miscellaneous:* Chairman, Chelmsford Young Farmers 1962; Member, Court of Essex University; Governor, Brentwood School, Essex. *Publications:* Several contributions to local government journals. *Recreations:* Botany, current affairs, travel, food and wine. *Name, Style and Title:* Raised to the peerage as Baron Hanningfield, of Chelmsford in the County of Essex 1998. *Address:* The Lord Hanningfield, DL, House of Lords, London, SW1A 0PW.

LORD HANSON — Conservative

HANSON (Life Baron), James Edward Hanson; cr. 1983. Born 20 January 1922. Son of late Robert Hanson, CBE. Married 1959, Geraldine Kaelin (2 sons 1 step-daughter). *Armed Forces:* Served Duke of Wellington's Regiment (TA) 1939–46. *Career:* Chairman, Hanson plc 1965–97, Chairman Emeritus 1997–; Chairman, Hanson Transport Group Ltd 1965–96, Director 1997–; Former Chairman, Trident Television Ltd 1972–76, 1984–85, Director 1970–85; Director, Hanson Capital Ltd 2000–. *Other:* Member, Court of Patrons, Royal College of Surgeons of England 1991. Hon. LLD, Leeds 1984; Hon. DBA, Huddersfield 1991; Hon. Fellow: St Peter's College, Oxford 1996, Royal College of Radiologists 1998. *Honours:* Kt 1976. Hon. Liveryman, Worshipful Company of Saddlers. *Special Interests:* Industry. *Clubs:* Brooks's, Huddersfield Borough, The Brook (New York), Toronto (Canada). *Name, Style and Title:* Raised to the peerage as Baron Hanson, of Edgerton in the County of West Yorkshire 1983. *Address:* The Lord Hanson, 1 Grosvenor Place, London, SW1X 7JH *Tel:* 020 7245 6996.

LORD HARDIE — Cross-Bencher

HARDIE (Life Baron), Andrew Rutherford Hardie; cr 1997. Born 8 January 1946. Son of Andrew Rutherford and Elizabeth Currie Hardie; educated St Mungo's Primary School, Alloa; St Modan's High School, Stirling; Edinburgh University (MA, LLB). Married 1971, Catherine Storrar Elgin (2 sons 1 daughter). *Career:* Solicitor 1971; Member, Faculty of Advocates 1973; Advocate Depute 1979–83; QC (Scot) 1985 Treasurer, Faculty of Advocates 1989–94, Dean 1994–97; A Senator of the College of Justice in Scotland 2000–; Honorary Bencher, Lincoln's Inn. *House of Lords:* Lord Advocate 1997–2000; Lord Advocate, Scottish Executive 1999–2000. *Honours:* PC 1997. *Special Interests:* Childcare. *Recreations:* Cricket. *Clubs:* Caledonian. *Name, Style and Title:* Raised to the peerage as Baron Hardie, of Blackford in the City of Edinburgh 1997. *Address:* Rt Hon the Lord Hardie, High Court of Justiciary and Court of Session, Parliament House, Parliament Square, Edinburgh, EH1 1RF.

LORD HARDY OF WATH — Labour

HARDY OF WATH (Life Baron), Peter Hardy; cr. 1997. Born 17 July 1931. Son of late Lawrence Hardy, Miner – Underground Official; educated Wath-upon-Dearne Grammar School, South Yorkshire; Westminster College, London; Sheffield University; Leeds University; College of Preceptors. Married July 28, 1954, Margaret Ann Brookes (2 sons). *Trades Union:* Sponsored by NACODS 1983–97; Hon. Life Member, UNISON. *Armed Forces:* RAF 1949–51 and Reserve service; Completed Parliamentary attachment to RAF 1992. *Councils, Public Bodies:* Councillor, Wath-upon-Dearne Urban District Council 1960–70, Chairman 1968; DL, South Yorkshire 1997–. *Career:* Teacher, South Yorkshire 1953–70; Head of Department 1960–70. *House of Commons:* Contested Scarborough and Whitby 1964 and Sheffield Hallam 1966; MP (Labour) for Rother Valley 1970–83 and for Wentworth 1983–97; Sponsored: The Badgers Act 1973, The Conservation of Wild Creatures and Wild Plants Act 1975, The Protection of Birds (Amendment) Act 1976, The Education (Northern Ireland) Act 1978; PPS: to Secretary of State for the Environment 1974–76, to Foreign and Commonwealth Secretary 1976–79. *International Bodies (Commons):*

Member, Delegation to Council of Europe and Western European Union 1976–97, Leader, Labour Delegation 1983–96; Vice-Chairman, Socialist Group of Council of Europe 1983–96; Chairman, Environment Committee 1986–90; Rapporteur Defence Committee WEU and for several Council of Europe Committees. *House of Lords:* Sponsor, Waste Minimisation Bill 1998. *Select Committees:* Member: Ecclesiastical Committee 1997–, Select Committee on Statutory Instruments (Joint Committee) 1997–. *Backbench Committees:* Chairman, Labour Party Departmental Committee for Defence (Lords). *International Bodies:* Hon. Member, Council of European Parliamentary Assembly. *International Bodies (General):* Rapporteur, Committee on Environment, Council of Europe 1977–96; Vice-Chairman, Socialist Group WEU 1979–83; Leader, Labour delegation to Council of Europe and WEU 1983–95; Vice-Chairman, Socialist Group of Council of Europe 1983–95; Chairman, Council of Europe Committee on Environment 1986–89; Leader, Labour delegation to OSCE 1990–97; Rapporteur, Committee on Defence (WEU) 1993–97. *Other:* Member: Council of RSPB 1985–89, Central Executive NSPCC 1986–94; Vice-President, The South Yorkshire Foundation; Hon. Member, The Kennel Club 1992; President, South Yorkshire, North Derbyshire and Peak District Branch, CPRE; President, Air Training Corps Squadron, Rotherham. *Awards Granted:* Green Ribbon Award for Services to Conservation 1997. *Trusts, etc:* Patron, Yorkshire Wildlife Trust; Fellow, Industry and Parliament Trust. *Miscellaneous:* Involved in campaign to improve hedgerow protection for fifteen years. *Publications: Lifetime of Badgers,* 1975. *Special Interests:* Wildlife, Conservation, Foreign Affairs, Home Affairs, Defence, Energy. *Recreations:* Wildlife observation, dogs, occasionally judging dogs. *Clubs:* Kennel. *Name, Style and Title:* Raised to the peerage as Baron Hardy of Wath, of Wath upon Dearne in the County of South Yorkshire 1997. *Address:* The Lord Hardy of Wath, DL, House of Lords, London, SW1A 0PW.

LORD HARRIS OF GREENWICH — Liberal Democrat

HARRIS OF GREENWICH (Life Baron), John Henry Harris; cr. 1974. Born 5 April 1930. Son of late Alfred George Harris and May Harris; educated Pinner County Grammar School, Middlesex. Married 1st, September 1, 1952, Patricia Margaret Alstrom (1 son 1 daughter) (marriage dissolved 1982), married 2nd, March 25, 1983, Angela Smith. *Armed Forces:* National Service in the Directorate of Army Legal Services, The War Office. *Councils, Public Bodies:* Councillor, Harlow Council (Essex) 1957–63, Chairman 1960–61. *Career:* A director of companies; Journalist on newspapers in Bournemouth, Leicester, Glasgow and London; Personal Assistant to Rt Hon. Hugh Gaitskell as Leader of the Opposition 1960–62; Special Assistant to: Foreign Secretary 1964–66, Home Secretary 1966–67, Chancellor of the Exchequer 1967–70; Staff of *The Economist* 1970–74; Member, Executive Committee Britain in Europe Referendum Campaign 1975, Joint Chairman, Publicity Committee; Chairman, Parole Board for England and Wales 1979–82. *House of Lords:* Minister of State, Home Office 1974–79. *Whip:* Liberal Democrat Chief Whip 1994–. *Spokesman:* SDP Spokesman on Home Affairs 1983–88; Liberal Democrat Spokesman on Home Affairs 1988–94. *Select Committees:* Member, House of Lords Select Committees on: Murder and Life Imprisonment 1988–89, The Public Services 1996–97, House of Lords' Offices 1997–. *Party Groups (General):* Director of Publicity, Labour Party 1962–64. *Other:* President, National Association of Senior Probation Officers 1983–93. *Trusts, etc:* Trustee, The Police Foundation, Chairman, Executive Committee. *Honours:* PC 1998. *Special Interests:* Criminal Justice. *Sportsclubs:* Member: Kent CCC, Durham CCC. *Clubs:* MCC, Reform. *Name, Style and Title:* Raised to the peerage as Baron Harris of Greenwich, of Greenwich in the County of Greater London 1974. *Address:* Rt Hon the Lord Harris of Greenwich, House of Lords, London, SW1A 0PW.

LORD HARRIS OF HARINGEY — Labour

HARRIS OF HARINGEY (Life Baron), Jonathan Toby Harris; cr. 1998. Born 11 October 1953. Son of late Professor Harry Harris, FRS and Muriel Harris; educated Haberdashers' Aske's School, Elstree; Trinity College, Cambridge (BA Natural Sciences and Economics) (President of the Union 1974). Married 1979, Ann Sarah Herbert (2 sons 1 daughter). *Trades Union:* Member, MSF. *Councils, Public Bodies:* London Borough of Haringey: Councillor 1978–, Chair, Social Services Committee 1982–87, Leader of the Council 1987–99; Member: London Ambulance Service NHS Trust 1998–, London Pension Fund Authority 1998–, Metropolitan Police Committee 1998–; Member, Greater London Authority for Barnet and Camden 2000–. *Career:* Economics Division, Bank of England 1975–79; Member, Electricity Consumers' Council 1979–86, Director 1983; Director, Association of Community Health Councils for England and Wales 1987–98. *Select Committees:* Member, Finance and Staff Sub-Committee, House of Lords Offices Committee 2000–. *International Bodies (General):* Committee of the Regions of EU: Member 1994–98, Alternate Member 1998–. *Party Groups (General):* Chair: Cambridge University Labour Club 1973, Young Fabian Group 1976–77, Hornsey Labour Party 1978, 1979, 1980; Member: Labour Party National Policy Forum 1992–, Labour Party Local Government Committee 1993–. *Other:* Governor, National Institute for Social Work 1986–94; Board Member, London First 1993–; Executive Council Member, RNIB 1993–94; Member, Court of Middlesex University 1995–. *Trusts, etc:* Trustee: Evening Standard Blitz Memorial Appeal 1995–, Help for Health Trust 1995–, The Learning Agency 1996–; Chair, English National Stadium Trust 1997–. *Miscellaneous:* Deputy Chair, National Fuel Poverty Forum 1981–86; Deputy Chair, AMA 1991, Chair, Social Services Committee 1986–93; Member: London Drug Policy Forum 1990–, National Nursery Examination Board 1992–94, Home Office Advisory Council on Race Relations 1992–97; Chair, Association of London Authorities 1993–95, Deputy Chair 1990–93, Chair, Social Services Committee 1984–88; Chair: Local Government Anti-Poverty Unit 1994–97, Association of London Government 1995–; Member, Joint London Advisory Panel 1996–; Elected to the Greater London Assembly as Member for Brent and Harrow May 4, 2000–. FRSA. Freeman, City of London 1998. *Publications:* Co-author *Why Vote Labour?*, 1979; Contributor to *Economics of Prosperity*, 1980; Co-editor *Energy and Social Policy*, 1983; Contributor to *Rationing in Action*, 1993 and *Whistleblowing in the Health Service: accountability, law and professional practice*, 1994. *Recreations:* Reading, walking. *Name, Style and Title:* Raised to the peerage as Baron Harris of Haringey, of Hornsey in the London Borough of Haringey 1998. *Address:* The Lord Harris of Haringey, 4 Beatrice Road, London, N4 4PD.

LORD HARRIS OF HIGH CROSS — Cross-Bencher

HARRIS OF HIGH CROSS (Life Baron), Ralph Harris; cr. 1979. Born 10 December 1924. Son of late W. H. Harris; educated Tottenham Grammar School; Queens' College, Cambridge (Foundation Scholar) (MA). Married November 5, 1949, Jose Jeffery (1 daughter and 2 sons deceased). *Career:* Lecturer, St Andrew's University 1949–56; Leader writer, Glasgow Herald 1956; General Director, Institute of Economic Affairs 1957–87, Chairman, Institute of Economic Affairs 1987–89, A director, Times Newspapers Holdings Ltd 1988–; Chairman, Bruges Group 1989–91; Founder President, Institute of Economic Affairs 1990–; Joint Chairman, International Centre for Research into Economic Transformation (Moscow) 1990–. *Other:* Member, Political Economy Club; Chairman, FOREST 1989–; President, Mont Pelerin Society 1982–84. *Awards Granted:* Free Enterprise Award 1976. DSc honoris causa, Buckingham University 1984. *Trusts, etc:* Trustee: Wincott Foundation, McWhirter Foundation, Centre for Research into Communist Economies 1984–, Civitas 1999–. *Miscellaneous:* Contested: Kirkcaldy (Liberal Unionist) 1951, Edinburgh Central (Conservative) 1955. *Publications:* Co-author several publications including: *Advertising in a Free Society*; *Hire Purchase in a Free Society*; *Choice in Welfare*; *Over-ruled on Welfare*; *Not from Benevolence*; *End of Government*; *Morality and Markets*; *Challenge of a Radical Reactionary*; *Beyond the Welfare State*; *No Prime Minister!*. *Special Interests:* European Union, Economic Policy, Social Policy, Russia, Eastern Europe. *Recreations:* Word processing, reading, sea swimming. *Name, Style and Title:* Raised to the peerage as Baron Harris of High Cross, of Tottenham in the County of Greater London 1979. *Address:* The Lord Harris of High Cross, 5 Catley Close, Wood Street, Barnet, Hertfordshire, EN5 4SN *Tel:* 020 8449 6212.

LORD HARRIS OF PECKHAM   Conservative

HARRIS OF PECKHAM (Life Baron), Philip Charles Harris; cr. 1996. Born 15 September 1942. Son of Charles Harris, MC and Ruth Harris; educated Streatham Grammar School. Married 1960, Pauline Norma Chumley (3 sons 1 daughter). *Career:* Chairman, Harris Queensway plc 1964–88, Chief Executive 1987–88; Non-executive director: Great Universal Stores 1986–, Fisons plc 1986–94; Chairman: Harris Ventures Ltd 1988–, C. W. Harris Properties 1988–97; Non-executive director, Molyneux Estates 1990–95; Chairman, Carpetright plc 1993–. *Party Groups (General):* Deputy Chairman, Conservative Party Treasurers 1993. *Other:* Member, United Medical and Dental Schools of Guy's and St Thomas's Hospitals, Governor 1983–98; Member, Court of Patrons, Royal College of Gynaecologists 1984–; University of London Court 1990–94, Council Member 1994–96. *Awards Granted:* Hambro Business Man of the Year 1983. Four honorary fellowships; Honorary doctorate. *Trusts, etc:* Chairman, Guy's and Lewisham NHS Trust 1991–93; Deputy Chairman, Lewisham NHS Trust 1991–97. *Honours:* Kt 1985. Hon. Fellow, Royal College of Radiologists 1993. Freeman, City of London 1992. Liveryman, Broderers' Company 1992. *Recreations:* Football, cricket, show jumping, tennis. *Name, Style and Title:* Raised to the peerage of Baron Harris of Peckham, of Peckham in the London Borough of Southwark 1996. *Address:* The Lord Harris of Peckham, Harris Ventures Limited, Philip Harris House, 1A Spur Road, Orpington, Kent, BR6 0AR *Tel:* 01689 875135 *Fax:* 01689 870781.

BARONESS HARRIS OF RICHMOND   Liberal Democrat

HARRIS OF RICHMOND (Life Baroness), Angela Felicity Harris; cr. 1999. Born 4 January 1944. Daughter of late Rev. G H Hamilton Richards and Eva Richards; educated Canon Slade Grammar School, Bolton; Ealing Hotel and Catering College. Married 2nd, 1976, John Philip Roger Harris, son of Philip and Margaret Harris (1 son from previous marriage). *Councils, Public Bodies:* Councillor, Richmond Town Council 1978–81, 1991–99, Mayor 1993–94; Councillor, Richmondshire District Council 1979–89, Chair 1987–88; Councillor, North Yorkshire County Council 1981–, Chair 1991–92; DL, North Yorkshire 1994; JP 1982–98; Non-Executive Director, Northallerton NHS Trust 1990–97; Deputy Chairman, National Association of Police Authorities 1997–; Member, Service Authority of National Crime Squad and Police Negotiating Board. *Select Committees:* Member, European Union Sub-Committee F (Social Affairs, Education and Home Affairs) 2000–. *International Bodies:* Member, British-American Parliamentary Group. *Other:* Patron: Hospice Homecare, Northallerton, Trauma International, Lister House (Royal British Legion), North Yorkshire Neighbourhood Watch Partnership; Member, Court of the University of York 1996–98. *Miscellaneous:* A Liberal Democrat candidate in European Elections 1999. *Special Interests:* Police. *Recreations:* Music, political biographies. *Name, Style and Title:* Raised to the peerage as Baroness Harris of Richmond, of Richmond in the County of North Yorkshire 1999. *Address:* The Baroness Harris of Richmond, DL, House of Lords, London, SW1A 0PW.

LORD HARRISON   Labour

HARRISON (Life Baron), Lyndon Henry Arthur Harrison; cr. 1999. Born 28 September 1947. Son of late Charles and Edith Harrison; educated Oxford School; Warwick University (BA); Sussex University (MA); Keele University (MA). Married October 25, 1980, Hilary Plank (1 son 1 daughter). *Trades Union:* Member, GMB. *Councils, Public Bodies:* Cheshire County Council: Councillor 1981–90, Chairman: Libraries Committee 1982, 1984–89, Tourism Committee 1985–89, Further Education Committee 1984–89. *Career:* Research Officer, UMIST Union, Manchester 1975–78; Union Manager, North East Wales Institute, Clwyd 1978–89; MEP for Cheshire West 1989–94, and for Cheshire West and Wirral 1994–99; Secretary, European Parliamentary Labour Party 1991–94. *House of Lords:* Departmental Liaison Peer for Northern Ireland. *Select Committees:* Member, European Union Select Committee Sub-Committee C (Common Foreign and Security Policy).

International Bodies: Member: British-American Parliamentary Group, IPU. *Miscellaneous:* Deputy Chairman, North West Tourist Board 1986–89; Vice-President, Association of County Councils 1990–97. *Special Interests:* Small Business, Tourism, Monetary Union, Children. *Recreations:* Chess, the arts, sport. *Name, Style and Title:* Raised to the peerage as Baron Harrison, of Chester in the County of Cheshire 1999. *Address:* The Lord Harrison, 3 Newton Lane, Hoole, Chester, Cheshire, CH2 3RB *Tel:* 01244 343428.

LORD HARTWELL   Cross-Bencher

HARTWELL (Life Baron), William Michael Berry; cr. 1968; 3rd Bt of Long Cross (UK) 1921. Born 18 May 1911. Second son of 1st Viscount Camrose, DL. Succeeded his brother to viscountcy, barony, and baronetcy 1995; disclaimed the viscountcy and barony of Camrose for life on March 9, 1995 under the provisions of the Peerage Act, 1963; educated Eton; Christ Church, Oxford (MA philosophy, politics and economics 1933, MA). Married January 7, 1936, Lady Pamela Margaret Elizabeth Smith (died 1982), younger daughter of 1st Earl of Birkenhead, PC, GCSI, KC (2 sons 2 daughters). *Armed Forces:* Second Lieutenant, (City of London Yeomanry) Light Anti-Aircraft Regiment, RA (TA) 1938; Served War of 1939–45 (despatches twice, MBE); Captain and Major 1940, Lieutenant-Colonel 1944. *Career:* Editor, *Sunday Mail,* Glasgow 1934–35; Managing Editor, *Financial Times* 1937–39; Chairman, Amalgamated Press Ltd 1954–59; Chairman and Editor-in-Chief: *The Daily Telegraph* 1954–87, *The Sunday Telegraph* 1961–87; Director, The Daily Telegraph (later The Telegraph plc) 1946–95. *Publications: Party Choice,* 1948; *William Camrose, Giant of Fleet Street,* 1992. *Recreations:* Arboriculture. *Clubs:* White's, Beefsteak, Royal Yacht Squadron (Cowes). *Name, Style and Title:* Raised to the peerage as Baron Hartwell, of Peterborough Court in the City of London 1968. *Address:* The Lord Hartwell, MBE, TD, 18 Cowley Street, London, SW1H 0BH *Tel:* 020 7222 4673; Office: 36 Broadway, London, SW1H 0BH *Tel:* 020 7222 3833; Oving House, Whitchurch, Nr Aylesbury, Bucks, HP22 4HN *Tel:* 01296 641307.

LORD HASKEL   Labour

HASKEL (Life Baron), Simon Haskel; cr. 1993. Born 8 October 1934. Son of late Isaac and Julia Haskel; educated Sedbergh School; Salford College of Advanced Technology. Married June 24, 1962, Carole, daughter of Wilbur Lewis, and late Frances Lewis, of New York (1 son 1 daughter). *Armed Forces:* National Service Commission, Royal Artillery 1959. *Career:* Joined Perrotts Ltd 1961; Chairman, Perrotts Group plc and associated companies 1973–97. *Whip:* An Opposition Whip 1994–97; Government Whip (A Lord in Waiting) 1997–98. *Spokesman:* An Opposition Spokesman on Trade and Industry 1994–97; A Spokesman on: Social Security 1997–98, Trade and Industry 1997–98, the Treasury 1997–98. *Select Committees:* Member, Select Committees on: Science and Technology 1994–97, Science and Technology Sub-Committee II (Science and Society) 1999–2000, Science and Technology Sub-Committee I (Complementary and Alternative Medicine) 2000–, Science and Technology Sub-Committee IIA (Human Genetic Databases) 2000–. *Party Groups (General):* Joined Labour Party 1968; Founder Member, Labour Party Industry 1972 Group, Secretary 1976–81; Secretary, Labour Finance and Industry Group 1982–90, Chairman 1990–96. *Other:* Vice-Chairman, Institute of Jewish Affairs 1993–; Chairman, Thames Concerts Society 1982–90. *Trusts, etc:* Trustee, Lord and Lady Haskel Charitable Foundation. *Miscellaneous:* Member, Joint Committee on Financial Services and Markets Bill. *Special Interests:* Trade and Industry, Science and Technology. *Recreations:* Music, cycling. *Sportsclubs:* Cyclists' Touring, Tandem. *Clubs:* Reform. *Name, Style and Title:* Raised to the peerage as Baron Haskel, of Higher Broughton in the County of Greater Manchester 1993. *Address:* The Lord Haskel, House of Lords, London, SW1A 0PW *E-Mail:* haskel@compuserve.com.

Visit the Vacher Dod Website...

www.politicallinks.co.uk

LORD HASKINS — Labour

HASKINS (Life Baron), Christopher Robin Haskins; cr. 1998. Born 30 May 1937. Son of Robin and Margaret Haskins; educated St Columba's College, Dublin; Trinity College, Dublin (BA). Married 1959, Gilda Horsley (3 sons 2 daughters). *Councils, Public Bodies:* Member, Board of "Yorkshire Forward" Regional Development Agency. *Career:* Ford Motor Company, Dagenham 1960–62; Northern Foods 1962–, Chairman 1986–. *International Bodies (General):* Member: Aspen Institute, Italia. Five honorary doctorates. *Trusts, etc:* Trustee: Runnymede Trust 1989–98, Demos 1993–, Civil Liberties Trust 1997–99, Legal Assistance Trust 1998–. *Miscellaneous:* Member: Commission for Social Justice 1992–94, UK Round Table on Sustainable Development 1995–97, Hampel Committee on Corporate Governance 1996–97, New Deal Task Force 1997–; Chairman, Better Regulation Task Force 1997–. *Special Interests:* Europe. *Name, Style and Title:* Raised to the peerage as Baron Haskins, of Skidby in the County of the East Riding of Yorkshire 1998. *Address:* The Lord Haskins, Quarryside Farm, Skidby, Nr Cottingham, East Yorkshire, HU16 5TG *Tel:* 01482 842692.

LORD HASLAM — Conservative

HASLAM (Life Baron), Robert Haslam; cr. 1990. Born 4 February 1923. Son of late Percy and Mary Haslam; educated Bolton School; Birmingham University (BSc coal mining 1944). Married 1st, June 5, 1947, Joyce (died 1995), daughter of late Frederick Quin (? sons), married 2nd, July 20, 1996, Elizabeth, daughter of late William Norman Pitt, of Hampton, Middlesex, and widow of Hon. Michael David Sieff, CBE. *Career:* Mining Engineer: Manchester Collieries 1944, National Coal Board 1947; Personnel Director, ICI Nobel Division 1960; Commercial Director, ICI Plastics Division 1963, Deputy Chairman 1966; Deputy Chairman, ICI Fibres 1969, Chairman 1971; Director, Main Board ICI plc 1974, Deputy Chairman 1980–83; Chairman, ICI Americas Inc. 1978–81; Director: Imperial Metal Industries Ltd. 1975–77, AECI 1978–79; Non-Exec Director, Cable and Wireless 1982–83; Chairman: Tate and Lyle plc 1983–86, British Steel plc 1983–86; Chairman, Nationalised Industries Chairmen's Group 1985–86; Member, NEDC 1985–89; Director, Bank of England 1985–93; Advisory Director, Unilever plc 1986–93; Chairman: British Coal Corporation 1986–90, Bechtel Ltd 1991–94, Wasserstein Perella & Co Ltd 1991–99, British Occupational Health Research Foundation 1991–, Michael Sieff Foundation 1995–. *Select Committees:* Member: Sub-Committee A of European Communities Committee 1993–97, Select Committee on European Communities 1997–99, Select Committee on European Communities Sub-Committee B (Energy, Industry and Transport) 1997–99. *Other:* Chairman: Council, Manchester Business School 1985–90, Governors of Bolton School 1990–97. Hon. DEng, Birmingham University; Hon. DTech, Brunel University. *Honours:* Kt 1985. Freeman, City of London 1985. *Special Interests:* Energy, Finance, Industry, Industrial Relations, Environment. *Recreations:* Golf, cruising, opera. *Sportsclubs:* Wentworth Golf. *Name, Style and Title:* Raised to the peerage as Baron Haslam, of Bolton in the County of Greater Manchester 1990. *Address:* The Lord Haslam, Tokeneke Lodge, East Drive, Virginia Water, Surrey, GU25 4JY *Tel:* 01344 842553.

LORD HATTERSLEY — Labour

HATTERSLEY (Life Baron), Roy Sydney George Hattersley; cr. 1997. Born 28 December 1932. Son of late Frederick Roy Hattersley; educated Sheffield City Grammar School; Hull University (BSc Economics). Married 1956, Molly Loughran. *Trades Union:* Member, NUJ. *Councils, Public Bodies:* Councillor, Sheffield City Council 1957–65. *House of Commons:* Contested Sutton Coldfield in 1959; MP (Labour) for Birmingham Sparkbrook 1964–97; PPS to Minister of Pensions October 1964-February 1967; Parliamentary Secretary, Ministry of Labour March 1967-March 1968; Parliamentary Under-Secretary of State, Department of Employment and Productivity March 1968-August 1969; Minister of Defence for Administration August 1969–70; Minister of

State, Foreign and Commonwealth Affairs 1974–76; Secretary of State for Prices and Consumer Protection September 1976–79; Deputy Leader, Labour Party 1983–92. *Spokesman (Commons):* Opposition Spokesman on: Defence 1972, Education and Science 1972–74; Principal Opposition Front Bench Spokesman on: the Environment May 1979-December 1980, Home Affairs Dec 1980–83, Treasury and Economic Affairs October 1983–87, Home Affairs June 1987–92. *Party Groups (General):* Joined Labour Party 1949. *Honours:* PC 1975. *Publications: Nelson,* 1974; *Goodbye to Yorkshire,* (essays) 1976; *Politics Apart,* 1982; *Press Gang,* 1983; *A Yorkshire Boyhood,* 1983; *Endpiece Revisited,* (essays) 1985; *Choose Freedom: the future for Democratic Socialism,* 1987; *Economic Priorities for a Labour Government,* 1987; *The Maker's Mark* (novel), 1990; *In that Quiet Earth,* (novel) 1991; *Between Ourselves,* (essays) 1993; *Who Goes Home? Scenes from a Political Life,* 1995; *Fifty Years On,* 1997. *Recreations:* Writing, watching football and cricket. *Clubs:* Garrick. *Name, Style and Title:* Raised to the peerage as Baron Hattersley, of Sparkbrook in the County of West Midlands 1997. *Address:* Rt Hon the Lord Hattersley, House of Lords, London, SW1A 0PW.

LORD HAYHOE   Conservative

HAYHOE (Life Baron), Bernard (Barney) John Hayhoe; cr. 1992. Born 8 August 1925. Son of late Frank and Catherine Hayhoe; educated State schools; Croydon and Borough Polytechnics. Married 1962, Ann Gascoigne, daughter of late Bernard W. Thornton (2 sons 1 daughter). *Career:* Tool Room Apprentice 1941–44; Technical and Engineering appointments in Ministry of Supply and Ministry of Aviation 1944–63; Associate Director, Ariel Foundation 1963–65; Head of Research Section, Conservative Research Department 1965–70; Director: Portman Building Society 1987–96, Abbott Laboratories Inc. 1989–96. *House of Commons:* MP (Conservative) for: Heston and Isleworth 1970–74, Brentford and Isleworth 1974–92; PPS to Lord President of the Council and Leader of the House of Commons 1972–74; Parliamentary Under-Secretary of State for Defence (Army) 1979–81; Minister of State: Civil Service Department January-November 1981, Treasury 1981–85; Minister of State for Health, DHSS 1985–86. *Spokesman (Commons):* An Opposition Spokesman on Employment 1974–79. *Select Committees:* Member, Select Committee on the Public Service 1997–98. *Party Groups:* Member, Association of Conservative Peers Executive Committee 1995–98. *Party Groups (General):* Joint Secretary, Conservative Group for Europe 1970, Vice-Chairman 1973–76; Chairman, The Hansard Society 1991–94. *Other:* Governor, Birkbeck College 1976–79; President, Help The Hospices 1992–98. *Trusts, etc:* Chairman, The Guys and St Thomas' NHS Trust 1993–95; Trustee: The Tablet Trust 1989–, British Brain and Spine Foundation 1992–, Liver Research Trust 1994–. *Honours:* PC 1985; Kt 1987. CEng; FIMechE. *Clubs:* Garrick. *Name, Style and Title:* Raised to the peerage as Baron Hayhoe, of Isleworth in the London Borough of Hounslow 1992. *Address:* Rt Hon the Lord Hayhoe, 20 Wool Road, London, SW20 0HW *Tel:* 020 8947 0037.

BARONESS HAYMAN   Labour

HAYMAN (Life Baroness), Helene Valerie Hayman; cr. 1996. Born 26 March 1949. Daughter of late Maurice and Maude Middleweek; educated Wolverhampton Girls' High School; Newnham College, Cambridge (MA) (President of Union 1969). Married August 30, 1974, Martin Heathcote, son of Ronald and Rosemary Hayman (4 sons). *Councils, Public Bodies:* Member, Bloomsbury Health Authority 1985–88; Vice-Chairman: Bloomsbury Health Authority 1988–90, Bloomsbury and Islington Health Authority 1991–92. *Career:* With Shelter, National Campaign for the Homeless 1969–71; Social Services Department, London Borough of Camden 1971–74; Deputy Director, National Council for One Parent Families 1974; Member, Royal College of Gynaecologists Ethics Committee 1982–97; Member, University College London/University College Hospital Committee on Ethics of Clinical Investigation 1987–97, Vice Chairman 1990–97; Member, Council, University College, London 1992–97; Chairman, Whittington Hospital NHS Trust 1992–97. *House of Commons:* Contested (Labour) Wolverhampton South West, February 1974; MP (Labour) for Welwyn and Hatfield, October 1974–79. *House of Lords:* Parliamentary Under-Secretary of State: Department of the Environment, Transport and the Regions (Minister for Roads) 1997–98, Department of Health 1998–99; Minister of State, Ministry of Agriculture, Fisheries and Food 1999–. *Spokesman:* An Opposition Spokeswoman on Health 1996–97. Two honorary fellowships; Honorary doctorate. *Special Interests:* Health, Education. *Name, Style and Title:* Raised to the peerage as Baroness Hayman, of Dartmouth Park in the London Borough of Camden 1996. *Address:* The Baroness Hayman, House of Lords, London, SW1A 0PW.

LORD HEALEY   Labour

HEALEY (Life Baron), Denis Winston Healey; cr. 1992. Born 30 August 1917. Son of late William Healey; educated Bradford Grammar School; Balliol College, Oxford (BA, MA). Married December 21, 1945, Edna May, daughter of Edward Edmunds (1 son 2 daughters). *Trades Union:* Member, GMB. *Armed Forces:* Served North Africa and Italy in Second World War (mentioned in despatches, MBE), Major RE. *House of Commons:* Contested (Labour) Pudsey and Otley 1945 General Election; MP (Labour) for: South East Leeds 1952–55, Leeds East 1955–92; Member, Shadow Cabinet 1959–64, 1970–74, 1979–87; Secretary of State for Defence 1964–70; Chancellor of the Exchequer 1974–79. *Spokesman (Commons):* Opposition Spokesman on Foreign Affairs 1983–87. *Party Groups (General):* Secretary, International Department, Labour Party 1945–52; Member, Labour Party National Exec Committee 1970–75; Deputy Leader, Labour Party 1980–83. *Other:* President, National Trust Appeal Yorkshire Moors and Dales 1985–95; Member, Council for Global Energy Studies 1990; President, Birkbeck College 1993–99. Hon. Fellow, Balliol College, Oxford 1979; three honorary degrees; Hon. Fellow, Birkbeck College 1999. *Miscellaneous:* Chairman, IMF Interim Committee 1977–79. *Honours:* MBE (Mil) 1945; PC 1964; CH 1979; Grand Cross of Order of Merit (Germany) 1979. Freeman, City of Leeds 1991. *Publications:* Author of several political works and Fabian essays as well as: *Healey's Eye*, 1980; *The Time of My Life*, (autobiography) 1989; *When Shrimps Learn to Whistle* (essays), 1990; *My Secret Planet* (anthology) 1992; *Denis Healey's Yorkshire Dales*, 1995. *Special Interests:* Foreign Affairs, Defence, Arts. *Recreations:* Music, painting photography, gardening. *Name, Style and Title:* Raised to the peerage as Baron Healey, of Riddlesden in the County of West Yorkshire 1992. *Address:* Rt Hon the Lord Healey, CH, MBE, House of Lords, London, SW1A 0PW.

LORD HENLEY   Conservative

HENLEY (8th Baron, I), Oliver Michael Robert Eden; cr. 1799; 6th Baron Northington (UK) 1885. Born 22 November 1953. Son of 7th Baron. Succeeded his father 1977. Sits as Baron Northington; educated Dragon School, Oxford; Clifton College; Durham University. Married October 11, 1984, Caroline Patricia Sharp (3 sons 1 daughter). *Councils, Public Bodies:* County Councillor, Cumbria 1986–89. *Career:* Called to the Bar, Middle Temple 1977. *House of Lords:* Joint Parliamentary Under-Secretary of State: Department of Social Security 1989–93, Department of Employment 1993–94, Ministry of Defence 1994–95; Minister of State, Department of Education and Employment 1995–97; Deputy Speaker 1999–; Deputy Chairman of Committees 1999–; An elected hereditary peer 1999–. *Whip:* Government Whip and Spokesman for Health February-July 1989; Opposition Chief Whip December 1998–. *Spokesman:* An Opposition Spokesman for: Defence 1997, Education and Employment 1997, Treasury 1997–98, Home Affairs 1997–98, Constitutional Affairs December 1998-June 1999, Cabinet Office June 1999–. *Select Committees:* Member, Select Committee on Selection 1999–. *Party Groups (General):* Chairman, Penrith and the Border Conservative Association 1987–89, President 1989–94. *Miscellaneous:* President, Cumbria Association of Local Councils 1981–89. *Clubs:* Brooks's, Pratt's. *Address:* The Lord Henley, Scaleby Castle, Carlisle, Cumbria, CA6 4LN *E-Mail:* henleyo@parliament.uk.

BISHOP OF HEREFORD   Non-Affiliated

HEREFORD (103rd Bishop of), John Keith Oliver. Born 14 April 1935. Son of Walter and Ivy Oliver; educated Westminster School; Gonville and Caius College, Cambridge (MA, MLitt); Westcott House. Married 1961, Meriel Moore (2 sons 1 daughter). *Career:* Assistant Curate, Hilborough Group of Parishes, Norfolk 1964–68; Chaplain and Assistant Master, Eton College 1968–72; Team Rector: South Molton Group of Parishes, Devon 1973–82; Parish of Central Exeter 1982–85; Archdeacon of Sherborne 1985–90; Bishop of Hereford 1990–; Chairman, Advisory Board of Ministry 1993–; Took his seat in the House of Lords 1997. *Spokesman:* Spokesman for the Bench of Bishops on Environmental, Agricultural and Transport Issues.

Other: Chairman, West Midlands Churches' Forum; President, Herefordshire CPRE. *Trusts, etc:* Trustee, Eveson Charitable Trust; President, River Wye Preservation Trust. *Publications: The Church and Social Order,* 1968; Contributions to: *Theology, Crucible. Special Interests:* Transport, Environment. *Recreations:* Railways, music, architecture, motorcycling. *Sportsclubs:* Worcester County Cricket Club. *Clubs:* United Oxford and Cambridge University. *Address:* Rt Rev the Lord Bishop of Hereford, Bishop's House, The Palace, Hereford, HR4 9BN.

LORD HIGGINS   Conservative

HIGGINS (Life Baron), Terence Langley Higgins; cr. 1997. Born 18 January 1928. Son of late Reginald and Rose Higgins; educated Alleyn's School, Dulwich; Gonville and Caius College, Cambridge (MA) (President of Union 1958); Yale University, USA. Married September 30, 1961, Rosalyn Cohen (later QC and DBE) (1 son 1 daughter). *Armed Forces:* Served in the RAF 1946–48. *Councils, Public Bodies:* DL, West Sussex 1988. *Career:* New Zealand Shipping Co., in UK and New Zealand 1948–55; British Olympic Team 1948, 1952; Commonwealth Games Team 1950; Economic Specialist, Unilever Ltd 1958–64; Economic Consultant, Lex Services Group plc 1975–; Director: Warne Wright Group 1976–84, Lex Service Group 1980–92; First Choice Holidays plc (formerly Owners Abroad plc) 1991–97; Chairman and Trustee, Lex Services Pension Fund 1994–. *House of Commons:* MP (Conservative) for Worthing 1964–97; Minister of State, Treasury 1970–72; Financial Secretary, Treasury 1972–74. *Spokesman (Commons):* Conservative Opposition Front Bench Spokesman on Treasury and Economic Affairs 1967–70; Opposition Spokesman on: Treasury and Economic Affairs 1974, Trade 1974–76. *Spokesman:* Principal Opposition Spokesman for Social Security 1997–; Opposition Spokesman for the Treasury 1997–99. *Party Groups (General):* Former Treasurer, Cambridge University Conservative Association. *Other:* Governor: Dulwich College 1980–95, National Institute Economic Social Research 1988–, Alleyn's School, Dulwich 1995–99. *Trusts, etc:* Trustee, Industry and Parliament Trust 1987–92. *Miscellaneous:* Council, Royal Institute of International Affairs 1980–85; Council, Institute of Advanced Motorists 1980–97, Fellow 1997. *Honours:* PC 1979; KBE 1993. Freeman, Worthing 1997. *Special Interests:* Finance, Transport, Sport, Social Security. *Recreations:* Golf. *Sportsclubs:* Royal Blackheath Golf, Worthing Golf, Koninklijke Haagsche Golf. *Clubs:* Hawk's (Cambridge); Reform, Yale Club of London. *Name, Style and Title:* Raised to the peerage as Baron Higgins, of Worthing in the County of West Sussex 1997. *Address:* Rt Hon the Lord Higgins, KBE, DL, House of Lords, London, SW1A 0PW *E-Mail:* higginst@parliament.uk.

LORD HILL-NORTON   Cross-Bencher

HILL-NORTON (Life Baron), Peter John Hill-Norton; cr. 1979. Born 8 February 1915. Son of late Captain Martin John Norton and late Mrs M. B. Gooch; educated Royal Naval Colleges, Dartmouth and Greenwich. Married July 30, 1936, Margaret Eileen Linstow (1 son 1 daughter). *Armed Forces:* Served War 1939–45, Arctic Convoys and NW Approaches; Commander 1948; Captain 1952; Naval Attaché, Argentina, Uruguay and Paraguay 1953–55; Commanded: HMS Decoy 1956–57, HMS Ark Royal 1959–61; Second Sea Lord and Chief of Naval Personnel January-August 1967; Vice-Chief of Naval Staff 1967–68; Commander-in-Chief, Far East 1969–70; First Sea Lord 1970–71; Chief of Defence Staff 1971–73; Chairman, NATO Military Committee 1974–77. *Other:* Friends of Osborne House. *Honours:* CB 1964; KCB 1967; GCB (Mil) 1970. Freeman, City of London 1973. Liveryman, Worshipful Company of Shipwrights. *Publications: No Soft Options,* 1978; *Sea Power,* 1982. *Special Interests:* Defence, UFOs. *Recreations:* Shooting, gardening. *Clubs:* Army and Navy, Royal Navy of 1765. *Name, Style and Title:* Raised to the peerage as Baron Hill-Norton, of South Nutfield in the County of Surrey 1979. *Address:* Admiral of the Fleet The Lord Hill-Norton, CB, KCB, GCB, Cass Cottage, Hyde, Fordingbridge, Hampshire, SP6 2QH.

BARONESS HILTON OF EGGARDON — Labour

HILTON OF EGGARDON (Life Baroness), Jennifer Hilton; cr. 1991. Born 12 January 1936. Daughter of late John Robert Hilton, CMG, and of Margaret Frances Hilton; educated Bedales School, Hampshire; Manchester University (BA Psychology 1970, MA 1971); London University (Diplomas: Criminology, History of Art). *Career:* Joined Metropolitan Police as Constable 1956; Manchester University (Police Scholarship) 1967–71; National Police Staff College, directing staff; Metropolitan Police Management Services 1975–76; Superintendent/Chief Superintendent 1977–83; Senior Command Course, National Staff College 1979; New Scotland Yard 1983–87; North West London, responsible for Complaints/Discipline, Personnel, Community Relations 1987–88; Peel Centre, Hendon, responsible for all Metropolitan Police Training 1988–90; Retired 1990; Member of: ACPOs Executive Committee, Equal Opportunities, Extended Interview Panel, Various Home Office Committees. *House of Lords:* A Trustee, House of Lords Collection Trust 2000–. *Whip:* Opposition Whip 1991–95. *Spokesman:* An Opposition Spokesman on: the Environment 1991–97, Home Affairs 1994–97. *Select Committees:* Member, Environment Sub-Committee of European Union Committee 1991–95, Chairman 1995–97, 2000–; Member: Science and Technology Select Committee 1992–95, Select Committee on European Union 1997–99; Chairman: Select Committee on European Union Sub-Committee C (Environment, Public Health and Consumer Protection) 1997–99, Advisory Panel on Works of Art, Select Committee on European Union Sub-Committee (Common Foreign and Security Policy). *Honours:* QPM 1989. *Publications:* Co-author *The Gentle Arm of the Law*, 1967; *Individual Development and Social Experience*, 1974. *Special Interests:* Environment, Race Relations, Criminal Justice. *Recreations:* Gardening, travel, art. *Name, Style and Title:* Raised to the peerage as Baroness Hilton of Eggardon, of Eggardon in the County of Dorset 1991. *Address:* The Baroness Hilton of Eggardon, QPM, House of Lords, London, SW1A 0PW.

LORD HOBHOUSE OF WOODBOROUGH — Cross-Bencher

HOBHOUSE OF WOODBOROUGH (Life Baron), John Stewart Hobhouse; cr. 1998. Born 31 January 1932; educated Christ Church, Oxford (BCL 1955, MA 1958). Married 1959, Susannah Roskill (2 sons 1 daughter). *Career:* Called to the Bar, Inner Temple 1955; QC 1973; A Judge of the High Court, Queen's Bench Division 1982–93; A Lord Justice of Appeal 1993–98; A Lord of Appeal in Ordinary 1998–. *Select Committees:* Member, Joint Select Committee on Consolidation of Bills 1999–. *Honours:* Kt 1982; PC 1993. *Name, Style and Title:* Raised to the peerage as Baron Hobhouse of Woodborough, of Woodborough in the County of Wiltshire 1998. *Address:* Rt Hon the Lord Hobhouse of Woodborough, House of Lords, London, SW1A 0PW.

LORD HODGSON OF ASTLEY ABBOTTS — Conservative

HODGSON OF ASTLEY ABBOTTS (Life Baron), Robin Granville Hodgson; cr. 2000. Born 25 April 1942. Son of late Henry Edward Hodgson, and of Natalie Beatrice Hodgson; educated Shrewsbury School; Oxford University (BA 1964); Wharton School of Finance, Pennsylvania University (MBA 1969). Married 1982, Fiona Ferelith Allom (3 sons 1 daughter and 1 twin son deceased). *Career:* Investment Banker, New York and Montreal 1964–67; Industry in Birmingham 1969–72; Director: Johnson Brothers & Co Ltd Walsall 1970–, Granville Baird Group 1972– (Group Chief Executive 1979–95, Chairman 1995–), Domnick Hunter plc 1989–, Staffordshire Building Society 1995–2000, Community Hospitals plc 1995–, Securities and Futures Authority 1993–. *House of Commons:* Contested (Conservative) Walsall North, February and October 1974 General Elections; MP for Walsall North November 1976–79. *Party Groups (General):* National Union of Conservative Associations: Member: Executive Committee 1988–98, General Purpose Committee 1990–98, Vice-President 1995–96, Chairman 1996–98; Chairman, National Conservative Convention 1998–2000; Deputy Chairman, Conservative Party 1998–2000. *Trusts, etc:* Trustee: Shrewsbury School, St Peter's College, Oxford. *Miscellaneous:* Member: Council for the Securities Industry 1980–85, Securities and Investment Board 1985–89, West Midlands Industrial Development Board 1989–97.

Honours: CBE 1992. Liveryman, Goldsmith's Company 1983. *Publications: Britain's Home Defence Gamble*, 1978. *Recreations:* Squash, fishing, theatre. *Clubs:* Carlton, Lansdowne. *Name, Style and Title:* Raised to the peerage as Baron Hodgson of Astley Abbotts, of Nash in the County of Shropshire 2000. *Address:* The Lord Hodgson of Astley Abbotts, CBE, 15 Scarsdale Villas, London, W8 6PT *Tel:* 020 7937 2964; Nash Court, Ludlow, Shropshire, SY8 3DG *Tel:* 01584 811677 *E-Mail:* robin@thehodgsons.com; robin.hodgson@granvillebaird.com (Secretary).

LORD HOFFMANN — Cross-Bencher

HOFFMANN (Life Baron), Leonard Hubert Hoffmann; cr. 1995. Born 8 May 1934; educated South African College School, Cape Town; University of Cape Town (BA); The Queen's College, Oxford (Rhodes Scholar, MA, BCL, Vinerian Law Scholar). Married 1957, Gillian Lorna Sterner (2 daughters). *Career:* Advocate of Supreme Court of South Africa 1958–60; Stowell Civil Law Fellow, University College, Oxford 1961–73; Called to the Bar, Gray's Inn 1964; Bencher 1984; Member, Royal Commission on Gambling 1976–78; QC 1977; A Judge of the Courts of Appeal of Jersey and Guernsey 1980–85; Member, Council of Legal Education 1983–92, Chairman 1989–92; A Judge of the High Court of Justice, Chancery Division 1985–92; A Lord Justice of Appeal 1992–95; A Lord of Appeal in Ordinary 1995–. *Select Committees:* Member, Select Committee on European Committees; Chairman, Select Committee on European Communities Sub-Committee E (Law and Institutions) 1997–. *Other:* President, British-German Jurists Association 1991–; Director, English National Opera 1985–90, 1991–94. Hon. Fellow, The Queen's College, Oxford 1992; Hon. DCL: City University 1992, University of the West of England 1995. *Honours:* Kt 1985; PC 1992. *Publications:* Author of *The South African Law of Evidence*, 1963. *Name, Style and Title:* Raised to the peerage as Baron Hoffmann, of Chedworth in the County of Gloucestershire 1995. *Address:* Rt Hon the Lord Hoffmann, House of Lords, London, SW1A 0PW; Surrey Lodge, 23 Keats Grove, London, NW3 2RS.

BARONESS HOGG — Conservative

HOGG (Life Baroness), Sarah Elizabeth Mary Hogg; cr. 1995. Born 14 May 1946. Daughter of late Rt Hon Baron Boyd-Carpenter; educated St Mary's Convent, Ascot; Lady Margaret Hall, Oxford (1st class PPE). Married 1968, Rt Hon. Douglas Martin Hogg, QC, MP (*qv*), son of Rt Hon. Baron Hailsham of St Marylebone (*qv*) (1 son 1 daughter). *Career:* On staff of *The Economist* 1967–81; Literary Editor 1970–77, Economics Editor 1977–81; Economics Editor, *The Sunday Times* 1981–82; Presenter, Channel 4 News 1982–83; Economics Editor and Deputy Executive Editor, Finance and Industry, *The Times* 1984–86; Assistant Editor and Business and City Editor, *The Independent* 1986–89; Economics Editor, *The Daily Telegraph* and *The Sunday Telegraph* 1989–90; Head, Prime Minister's Policy Unit 1990–95; Director: London Broadcasting Company 1982–90, Royal National Theatre 1988–91; London Economics 1995–96, Chairman 1997–99; Foreign and Colonial Smaller Companies Trust 1995–, Chairman 1997–; NPI 1996–99; International Advisory Board, National Westminster Bank 1995–98; Advisory Board, Bankinter 1995–98; Director: The Energy Group 1996–98, GKN 1996–; Director, 3i 1997–, Deputy Chairman 2000–; Director: Scottish Eastern Investment Trust 1998–99, Martin Currie Portfolio Trust 1999–, P&O 1999–. *Select Committees:* Member: House of Lords Select Committee for Science and Technology 1996–99; Select Committee on Monetary Policy of the Bank of England 2000–. *Other:* Governor, Centre for Economic Policy Research 1985–92; Council Member: The Royal Economic Society 1996–, The Institute for Fiscal Studies 1996–, The Hansard Society for Parliamentary Government 1996–, The Lincolnshire Foundation 1996–98; A Governor, BBC 2000–. *Awards Granted:* Wincott Foundation Financial Journalist of the Year 1985. Hon. MA, Open University 1987; Hon. DLitt, Loughborough University 1992; Fellow, Eton College 1996–; Hon. Fellow, Lady Margaret Hall, Oxford. *Trusts, etc:* Trustee, St Mary's School, Ascot. *Publications:* Co-author *Too Close to Call*, 1995. *Name, Style and Title:* Raised to the peerage as Baroness Hogg, of Kettlethorpe in the County of Lincolnshire 1995. *Address:* The Baroness Hogg, House of Lords, London, SW1A 0PW *Tel:* 020 7219 5417 *E-Mail:* hoggs@parliament.uk.

LORD HOGG OF CUMBERNAULD — Labour

HOGG OF CUMBERNAULD (Life Baron), Norman Hogg; cr. 1997. Born 12 March 1938. Son of late Norman Hogg, CBE, DL, LLD, JP and late Mary Hogg; educated Ruthrieston Secondary School, Aberdeen. Married March 28, 1964, Elizabeth McCall, daughter of late John Christie. *Trades Union:* Member: NALGO 1953–67, TGWU 1967–. *Councils, Public Bodies:* Chairman, Bus Appeals Body 2000–. *Career:* Local Government Officer, Aberdeen Corporation 1953–67; District Officer, Scottish District, National and Local Government Officers Association 1967–79. *House of Commons:* MP (Labour) for Dunbartonshire East 1979–83 and for Cumbernauld and Kilsyth 1983–97. *Whip (Commons):* Scottish Labour Whip 1982–83; Opposition Deputy Chief Whip November 1983–87. *Spokesman (Commons):* Front Bench Spokesman on Scottish Affairs 1987–88. *Party Groups (Commons):* Chairman, Scottish Parliamentary Labour Group 1981–82. *Select Committees:* Member, Select Committee on Delegated Powers and Deregulation 1999–. *Party Groups (General):* Member, Fabian Society 1984–. *Other:* Member, Transport Users Consultative Committee for Scotland 1977–79; Hon. President, YMCA Scotland 1998–. Hon LLD, Aberdeen University 1999. *Miscellaneous:* Appointed Lord High Commissioner to the 1998 and 1999 General Assembly of the Church of Scotland 1997. *Special Interests:* Public Transport, Local Government, Constitutional Affairs. *Name, Style and Title:* Raised to the peerage as Baron Hogg of Cumbernauld, of Cumbernauld in North Lanarkshire 1997. *Address:* The Lord Hogg of Cumbernauld, House of Lords, London, SW1A 0PW *E-Mail:* normanhoggl@compuserve.com.

LORD HOLDERNESS — Conservative

HOLDERNESS (Life Baron), Richard Frederick Wood; cr. 1979. Born 5 October 1920. Son of 1st Earl of Halifax, KG, PC, OM, GCMG, GCSI, GCIE, TD, and late Lady Dorothy Onslow, CI, DCVO, daughter of 4th Earl of Onslow, PC, GCMG; educated Eton; New College, Oxford. Married April 15, 1947, Diana, daughter of late Colonel E. O. Kellett, DSO, MP and Hon. Mrs William McGowan (1 son 1 daughter). *Armed Forces:* Lieutenant, 60th Rifles 1941–43 (wounded); Hon. Colonel: Queen's Royal Rifles 1962, 4th Battalion, Royal Green Jackets 1967–89. *Councils, Public Bodies:* DL, Humberside 1968. *Career:* Director: Hargreaves Group of Companies until 1986, Lloyds Bank, Yorkshire and Humberside 1980–89; Chairman: Disablement Services Authority 1987–91, Advisory Group on Rehabilitation, Department of Health 1991–96, Wilton 65 Publishing. *House of Commons:* MP (Conservative) for Bridlington 1950–79; PPS to Viscount Amory 1951–55; Joint Parliamentary Secretary to Minister of Pensions and National Insurance 1955–58; Parliamentary Secretary to Minister of Labour 1958–59; Minister of Power 1959–63; Minister of Pensions and National Insurance 1963–64; Ministry for Overseas Development 1970–74. *Select Committees:* Member, Ecclesiastical Committee 1994–97. *Other:* President, Queen Elizabeth's Foundation for Disabled People 1983–96. Hon. LLD: Sheffield University 1962, Leeds University 1978, Hull University 1982. *Honours:* PC 1959. *Recreations:* Gardening, reading. *Name, Style and Title:* Raised to the peerage as Baron Holderness, of Bishop Wilton in the County of Humberside 1979. *Address:* Rt Hon the Lord Holderness, DL, Flat Top House, Bishop Wilton, York, YO42 1RY *Tel:* 01759 368266; 43 Lennox Gardens, London, SW1X 0DF *Tel:* 020 7225 2151.

LORD HOLLICK — Labour

HOLLICK (Life Baron), Clive Richard Hollick; cr. 1991. Born 20 May 1945. Son of late Leslie Hollick, and of Olive Hollick; educated Taunton's School, Southampton; Nottingham University. Married August 27, 1977, Susan, daughter of HE Ulric Cross (3 daughters). *Armed Forces:* University Air Squadron. *Career:* Joined Hambros Bank 1967, Director 1973–96; Managing Director, MAI plc 1974–96; Director, Mills and Allen Ltd. 1975–89; Chairman, Shepperton Studios Ltd. 1976–84; Member, National Bus Company 1984–91; Director: Logica plc 1987–91, Avenir Havas Media SA (France) 1988–92, National Opinion Polls Ltd. 1989–97, Satellite Information Services 1990–94; Chairman, Meridian Broadcasting 1991–96; Director, British Aerospace 1992–97;

Member, Financial Law Panel 1993–97; Director, Anglia Television 1994–97; Member, Commission on Public Policy and British Business 1995–97; Director, United Broadcasting and Entertainment Ltd 1995–; Chief Executive, United News and Media plc 1996–; Special Adviser to President of the Board of Trade 1997–98; Director Express Newspapers plc 1998–, TRW Inc 2000–. *Select Committees:* Member, Science and Technology Sub-Committee I, Information Superhighway 1995–96. *Other:* Governor, London School of Economics and Political Science 1997–. Hon. LLD, Nottingham University 1993. *Trusts, etc:* Founding Trustee, Institute for Public Policy Research 1988. *Special Interests:* Business, Economic Policy, Constitutional Affairs, Transport. *Recreations:* Reading, countryside, cinema, theatre, tennis. *Name, Style and Title:* Raised to the peerage as Baron Hollick, of Notting Hill in the Royal Borough of Kensington and Chelsea 1991. *Address:* The Lord Hollick, United News and Media plc, Ludgate House, 245 Blackfriars Road, London, SE1 9UY.

BARONESS HOLLIS OF HEIGHAM   Labour

HOLLIS OF HEIGHAM (Life Baroness), Patricia Lesley Hollis; cr. 1990. Born 24 May 1941. Daughter of late H. L. G. Wells, of Norwich; educated Plympton Grammar School; Cambridge University (BA, MA); University of California and Columbia University, New York (Harkness Fellow 1962–64); Nuffield College, Oxford (MA, DPhil). Married September 18, 1965, Professor James Martin Hollis, FBA (died 1998), son of Hugh Mark Noel Hollis (2 sons). *Trades Union:* Member, AUT. *Councils, Public Bodies:* Councillor, Norwich City Council 1968–91, Leader 1983–88; Councillor, Norfolk County Council 1981–85; Member: East Anglian Planning Council 1975–79, Regional Health Authority 1979–83; DL, Norfolk 1994–. *Career:* Lecturer, then Reader and former Dean, University of East Anglia; Founder-director, Radio Broadland 1983–97. *House of Lords:* Parliamentary Under-Secretary of State, Department of Social Security 1997–. *Whip:* Opposition Whip 1990–95. *Spokesman:* Opposition Spokesman on Environment and Social Security 1990–97. *Other:* Patron: Chatterbox, Norwich, Norfolk Millenium Carers, Norfolk Rural Art. Two honorary doctorates; Honorary fellowship. *Trusts, etc:* Patron, St Martin's Housing Trust. *Miscellaneous:* Contested (Labour) Great Yarmouth February and October 1974, 1979 General Elections; National Commissioner, English Heritage 1988–91; Member, Press Council 1988–90; Former Vice-President: Association of District Councils, Association of Metropolitan Authorities, Environmental Health Officers, National Federation of Housing Associations. *Honours:* PC 1999. Fellow, Royal Historical Society. *Publications: The Pauper Press,* 1970; *Class and Class Conflict 1815–50,* 1973; *Pressure from Without,* 1974; *Women in Public, 1850–1900,* 1979; *Robert Lowry, Radical and Chartist,* 1979; *Ladies Elect: women in English Local Government 1865–1914,* 1987; *Jennie Lee: a Life,* 1997. *Special Interests:* Local Government, Education, Media, Heritage, Health. *Recreations:* Boating, singing, domesticity. *Name, Style and Title:* Raised to the peerage as Baroness Hollis of Heigham, of Heigham in the City of Norwich 1990. *Address:* Rt Hon the Baroness Hollis of Heigham, DL, 30 Park Lane, Norwich, Norfolk, NR2 3EE *Tel:* 01603 621990.

LORD HOLME OF CHELTENHAM   Liberal Democrat

HOLME OF CHELTENHAM (Life Baron), Richard Gordon Holme; cr. 1990. Born 27 May 1936. Son of late Jack Richard Holme; educated Royal Masonic School, Bushey, Hertfordshire; St. John's College, Oxford. Married 1958, Kay Mary Powell (2 sons 2 daughters). *Armed Forces:* Commissioned, 10th Gurkha Rifles 1954. *Career:* Marketing Trainee and Manager, Unilever 1959–63; Marketing Director, Penguin Books Ltd. 1963–65; Chairman, BPC Publishing 1967–69; Executive Vice-President, CRM Inc 1970–74; Chairman: Threadneedle Publishing Group 1988–98, Hollis Directories 1989–98, DPR Publishing Ltd 1993–98, Brassey's Ltd 1995–98; Director, RTZ Corporation plc (now RioTinto plc) 1995–98; CRA Ltd (now RioTinto Ltd) 1996–98; Deputy Chairman, Independent Television Commission 1999; Chairman, Broadcasting Standards Commission 1999–2000. Chancellor, University of Greenwich 1998–. *Spokesman:* Liberal Democrat Spokesman on Northern Ireland 1991–99. *Party Groups (General):* President, The Liberal Party 1980–81; Vice-Chairman, Policy Committee, Liberal Democrat Party 1989–. *Other:* Chairman, English College Foundation in Prague 1991–; Board Member, Campaign for Oxford 1990–; Council Member, Cheltenham Ladies College 1994–, Chairman, College Council 1998–. Hon. Fellow, St John's College, Oxford.

Miscellaneous: Contested (Liberal): East Grinstead 1964 and By-election 1965, Braintree 1974, Cheltenham 1983, 1987; Director, National Committee for Electoral Reform 1975–85; Member of Council, The Hansard Society 1979–, Vice-Chairman 1990–; Chairman: Constitutional Reform Centre 1985–92, ICC Environment Commission 1999–. *Honours:* CBE 1983; PC 2000. *Special Interests:* Constitutional Reform, Industry, Environment, Foreign Affairs, Broadcasting. *Recreations:* Walking, opera, collecting books. *Clubs:* Brooks's, Reform. *Name, Style and Title:* Raised to the peerage as Baron Holme of Cheltenham, of Cheltenham in the County of Gloucestershire 1990. *Address:* Rt Hon the Lord Holme of Cheltenham, CBE, House of Lords, London, SW1A 0PW.

EARL OF HOME   Conservative

HOME (15th Earl of, S), David Alexander Cospatrick Douglas-Home; cr. 1604; Lord Dunglass; 20th Lord Home (S) 1473; 5th Baron Douglas (UK) 1875. Born 20 November 1943. Son of 14th Earl, KT, PC, DL, who disclaimed the earldom for life on October 23, 1963 under the provisions of the Peerage Act, October 1963, and who was subsequently raised to the peerage as a life peer as Baron Home of the Hirsel 1974. Succeeded his father 1995; educated Eton; Christ Church, Oxford (BA 1966). Married 1972, Jane Margaret, younger daughter of Colonel John Francis Williams-Wynne, CBE, DSO (1 son 2 daughters). *Career:* Director, Douglas and Angus Estates 1966–, Chairman 1995–; Director: Morgan Grenfell & Co. Ltd. 1974–99, Arab-British Chamber of Commerce 1975–84; Director, Morgan Grenfell (Asia) Ltd. 1978–82, Deputy Chairman 1979–82; Director: Arab Bank Investment Co. 1979–87, Agricultural Mortgage Corporation plc 1979–93; Director, Tandem Group plc (formerly EFG plc) 1981–96, Chairman 1993–96; Chairman: Morgan Grenfell Export Services 1984–98, Morgan Grenfell (Scotland) 1986–98, Committee for Middle East Trade 1986–92, Morgan Grenfell International Ltd 1987–98; Director: Deutsche Morgan Grenfell Hong Kong Ltd (name changed from Morgan Grenfell Asia (Hong Kong) Ltd May 1996) 1989–99, Deutsche Morgan Grenfell Asia Holdings Pte Ltd (name changed from Morgan Grenfell Asia Holdings Pte Ltd May 1996) 1989–99, K & N Kenanga Holdings Bhd 1993–99; Non-Executive Director, Grosvenor Estate Holdings 1993–; Director: Kenanga DMG Futures Sdn Bhd 1995–99 (name changed to Kenanga Deutsche Futures Sdn Bhd September 1998–), Deutsche Morgan Grenfell Group plc 1996–99; Chairman, Coutts and Company 1999–. *House of Lords:* An elected hereditary peer 1999–. *Spokesman:* Opposition Front Bench Spokesman on: Trade 1997–98, the Treasury 1997–98. *Other:* Governor: Ditchley Foundation 1977–, Commonwealth Institute 1988–98; Council Member: Royal Agricultural Society of England 1990–, Glenalmond College 1995–. *Trusts, etc:* Trustee: Grosvenor Estate 1993–, The Royal Agricultural Society of England 1999–. *Miscellaneous:* Member, Export Guarantee Advisory Council, ECGD 1988–93. *Honours:* CBE 1991; CVO 1997. Fellow, Chartered Institute of Bankers 1999–. *Special Interests:* Foreign Affairs, Scottish Affairs, Industry, Agriculture. *Recreations:* Outdoor sports. *Clubs:* Turf, Caledonian Westminster Business. *Address:* The Earl of Home, CVO, CBE, 99 Dovehouse Street, London, SW3 6JZ *Tel:* 020 7352 9060; The Hirsel, Coldstream, Berwickshire, TD12 4LP *Tel:* 01890 882345; Castlemains, Douglas, Lanarkshire, ML11 0RX *Tel:* 01555 851241.

BARONESS HOOPER   Conservative

HOOPER (Life Baroness), Gloria Dorothy Hooper; cr. 1985. Born 25 May 1939. Daughter of late Frederick Hooper; educated La Sainte Union Convent; Royal Ballet School; Southampton University (BA Law); Universidad Central, Ecuador (Rotary Foundation Fellow). *Career:* Assistant to Chief Registrar, John Lewis Partnership; Editor, Current Law, Sweet & Maxwell, Law Publishers; Information Officer, Winchester City Council; Assistant Solicitor, Taylor and Humbert; Legal Adviser, Slater Walker France S.A.; Partner, Taylor Garrett 1974–84; Member, European Parliament (Conservative) for Liverpool 1979–84; Vice-Chairman, European Parliament's Committee on Environment, Public Health and Consumer Protection; Deputy Chief Whip, European Democratic Group; Member, Delegation to Council of Europe and Western European Union 1992–97. *House of Lords:* Parliamentary Under-Secretary of State, Department of: Education and Science 1987–88, Energy 1988–89, Health 1989–92; A Deputy Speaker of the House of Lords 1993–; A Deputy Chairman of Committees 1993–; PPS (Lords) to William Hague as Leader of the Opposition 1999–.

Whip: Government Whip 1985–87. *Party Groups:* Member, Association of Conservative Peers. *International Bodies (General):* Member: IPU, CPA. *Other:* Member, The Law Society; General Governor, British Nutrition Foundation; President: British Educational Equipment and Supplies Association, Canning House (Hispanic and Luso Brazilian Council), Waste Watch, European Foundation For Heritage Skills. *Trusts, etc:* Trustee/Governor: English Speaking Union, Royal Academy of Dancing, Centre for International Briefing, Royal Ballet, Centre for Global Energy Studies, National Museums and Galleries of Merseyside; Fellow and Trustee, Industry and Parliament Trust. *Honours:* Order of Francisco de Miranda (Venezuela). Fellow: Royal Geographical Society, RSA. *Special Interests:* European Union, Latin America, Inner Cities. *Recreations:* Theatre, travel. *Name, Style and Title:* Raised to the peerage as Baroness Hooper, of Liverpool and St James's in the City of Westminster 1985. *Address:* The Baroness Hooper, House of Lords, London, SW1A 0PW.

LORD HOOSON — Liberal Democrat

HOOSON (Life Baron), Hugh Emlyn Hooson; cr. 1979. Born 26 March 1925. Son of late Hugh Hooson, farmer and Elsie Hooson; educated Denbigh Grammar School; University College of Wales, Aberystwyth (BA law 1948); Gray's Inn. Married 1950, Shirley Margaret Wynne, daughter of late Sir George Hamer, CBE (2 daughters). *Armed Forces:* Royal Navy 1943–46. *Career:* Called to the Bar, Gray's Inn 1949; Deputy Chairman: Flintshire Quarter Sessions 1960–72, Merioneth Quarter Sessions 1960–67, Chairman 1967–72; Bencher, Gray's Inn 1968; Recorder of Merthyr Tydfil 1971; Recorder of Swansea July 1971; Elected Leader of Wales and Chester Circuit 1971–74, Treasurer 1986; Recorder of Crown Courts 1972–91; Non-executive Director, Laura Ashley plc 1985–95, Chairman: Severn River Crossing plc 1991–2000 Laura Ashley plc 1995–96. *House of Commons:* MP (Liberal) for Montgomeryshire 1962–79. *Spokesman (Commons):* Spokesman for Defence, Foreign Affairs, Home Affairs, Legal Affairs, Agriculture and Welsh Affairs 1962–79. *International Bodies (Commons):* British Delegate to the Atlantic Assembly (formerly NATO Parliamentarians) 1962–79; Member, Political Committee of North Atlantic Assembly 1962–79, Vice-Chairman 1975–79; Raporteur, Working Party on East-West Relations 1974–79. *Spokesman:* Liberal Democrat Spokesman on Welsh Affairs 1996–98; Former Spokesman on Legal Affairs, Agriculture and European Affairs. *International Bodies (General):* European and International Affairs. *Party Groups (General):* Leader, Welsh Liberal Party 1966–79; President, Welsh Liberal Party 1983–86. *Other:* President: Royal National Eisteddfod of Wales, Newtown 1965, Llangollen International Eisteddfod 1987–93, Wales International 1995–98. Hon. Professorial Fellow, University College of Wales, Aberystwyth 1971–. *Trusts, etc:* Chairman, Trustees of Laura Ashley Foundation 1986–97. *Special Interests:* Law, Constitutional Affairs, Agriculture, Defence, Wales, Europe, International Affairs. *Recreations:* Music, theatre, reading, walking, farming. *Name, Style and Title:* Raised to the peerage as Baron Hooson, of Montgomery in the County of Powys and Colomendy in the County of Clwyd 1979. *Address:* The Lord Hooson, QC, Summerfield Park, Llanidloes, Powys *Tel:* 01686 412298; House of Lords, London, SW1A 0PW *Tel:* House of Lords 020 7219 5226.

LORD HOPE OF CRAIGHEAD — Cross-Bencher

HOPE OF CRAIGHEAD (Life Baron), James Arthur David Hope; cr. 1995. Born 27 June 1938. Son of late Arthur Henry Cecil Hope, OBE, WS; educated Edinburgh Academy; Rugby School; St John's College, Cambridge (Scholarship 1956, BA 1962, MA 1978); Edinburgh University (LLB 1965). Married 1966, Katharine Mary, daughter of late W. Mark Kerr, WS (twin sons 1 daughter). *Armed Forces:* National Service, Seaforth Highlanders 1957–59. *Career:* Admitted Faculty of Advocates 1965; Standing Junior Counsel in Scotland to Board of Inland Revenue 1974–78; Advocate-Depute 1978–82; QC (Scotland) 1978; Legal Chairman, Pensions Appeal Tribunal 1985–86; Chairman, Medical Appeal Tribunals 1985–86; Dean, Faculty of Advocates 1986–89; Lord Justice General of Scotland and Lord President of the Court of Session 1989–96; A Lord of Appeal in Ordinary 1996–. *Chancellor:* Chancellor, Strathclyde University 1998–. *Select Committees:* Member, Select Committee on European Communities 1998–; Chairman, Sub-Committee E (Law and Institutions) 1998–. *Other:* President, The Stair Society 1993–; Council Member, Commonwealth Magistrates' and Judges' Association 1998–; President, International Criminal Law Association 2000–.

Hon. LLD: Aberdeen 1991, Strathclyde 1993, Edinburgh 1995; Hon. Fellow, St John's College, Cambridge 1995. *Trusts, etc:* Board of Trustees, National Library of Scotland 1989–1996; Member, University of Strathclyde Charitable Foundation 1998–. *Miscellaneous:* Hon. Bencher: Gray's Inn 1989, Inn of Court of Northern Ireland 1995. *Honours:* PC 1989. *Publications:* Co-editor *Gloag and Henderson's Introduction to the Law of Scotland; Armour on Value for Rating;* Co-author *The Rent (Scotland) Act, 1984,* 1986; Contributor *Stair Memorial Encyclopaedia of Scots Law. Recreations:* Walking, ornithology, music. *Clubs:* New (Edinburgh). *Name, Style and Title:* Raised to the peerage as Baron Hope of Craighead, of Bamff in the District of Perth and Kinross 1995. *Address:* Rt Hon the Lord Hope of Craighead, 34 India Street, Edinburgh, EH3 6HB *Tel:* 0131–225 8245 *Fax:* 0131–225 8245; Law Lords Corridor, House of Lords, London, SW1A 0PW *Tel:* 020 7219 3202 *Fax:* 020 7219 3202 *E-Mail:* craighead@dial.pipex.com (home); hopejad@parliament.uk (House of Lords).

EARL HOWE   Conservative

HOWE (7th Earl, UK), Frederick Richard Penn Curzon; cr. 1821; 8th Viscount Curzon (UK) 1802; 9th Baron Howe (GB) 1788; 8th Baron Curzon (GB) 1794. Born 29 January 1951. Son of late Commander Chambré George William Penn Curzon, RN, grandson of 3rd Earl, GCVO, CB, and of late Mrs Jane Victoria Curzon (née Fergusson). Succeeded his kinsman 1984; educated Rugby; Christ Church, Oxford (MA Literae Humaniores). Married March 26, 1983, Elizabeth Helen, DL, daughter of Captain Burleigh Edward St Lawrence Stuart (1 son ss3 daughters). *Trades Union:* Member, NFU. *Career:* Arable and Dairy Farmer; Director: Adam & Company plc 1987–90, Provident Life Association Ltd 1988–91, Barclays Bank plc 1973–87, Senior Manager 1984–87; Chairman, LAPADA 1999–. *House of Lords:* Parliamentary Secretary, Ministry of Agriculture, Fisheries and Food 1992–95; Parliamentary Under-Secretary of State, Ministry of Defence 1995–97; An elected hereditary peer 1999–. *Whip:* Government Whip (A Lord in Waiting) 1991–92. *Spokesman:* An Opposition Spokesman on: Defence May-October 1997, Health October 1997–. *Other:* Governor, King William IV Naval Foundation 1984–; Vice-President, National Society for Epilepsy 1984–86, President 1986–; President: Chilterns Branch RNLI 1985–, South Bucks Association for the Disabled 1984–; Member, RNLI Committee of Management 1997–; Patron, Demand. *Trusts, etc:* Governor, The Trident Trust 1985–; Trustee: Milton's Cottage 1986, Sir William Borlase's Grammar School, Merlow 1998–. *Miscellaneous:* President, CPRE (Penn Country Branch) 1986–92. Associate, Chartered Institute of Bankers 1976–. *Special Interests:* Agriculture, Penal Affairs and Policy, Finance. *Recreations:* Gardening, music, writing. *Address:* The Earl Howe, House of Lords, London, SW1A 0PW *E-Mail:* howef@parliament.uk.

LORD HOWE OF ABERAVON   Conservative

HOWE OF ABERAVON (Life Baron), (Richard Edward) Geoffrey Howe; cr. 1992. Born 20 December 1926. Son of late Benjamin Edward Howe, of Port Talbot, Glamorgan; educated Winchester; Trinity Hall, Cambridge (Scholar, MA, LLB). Married August 29, 1953, Elspeth Rosamund, CBE, daughter of late Philip Morton Shand (1 son 2 daughters). *Armed Forces:* Lieutenant, Royal Signals 1945–48; Seconded to E African Signals 1947–48. *Career:* Called to the Bar, Middle Temple 1952, Bencher 1969, Reader 1993; Deputy Chairman, Glamorgan Quarter Sessions 1966–70; Director: AGB Research Group 1974–79, Sun Alliance and Insurance Group 1974–79, EMI Ltd 1976–79, BICC plc 1991–97, Glaxo Wellcome 1991–96; Chairman, Framlington Russian Investment Fund 1994–; Special Adviser on European and International Affairs to law firm of Jones, Day, Reavis and Pogue; International Advisory Councils of: J. P. Morgan & Co., Stanford University's Institute for International Studies; Visitor at the School of Oriental and African Studies, University of London 1991–; Fuji International European Advisory Board 1996–; Carlyle European Advisory Board 1996–. *House of Commons:* Contested (Conservative) Aberavon in 1955 and 1959 General Elections; MP (Conservative) for: Bebington 1964–66, Reigate 1970–74, Surrey East 1974–92; Solicitor-General 1970–72; Minister for Trade and Consumer Affairs, Department of Trade and Industry 1972–74; Chancellor of the Exchequer 1979–83; Secretary of State for Foreign and Commonwealth Affairs 1983–89; Lord President of the Council, Leader of the House of Commons and Deputy Prime Minister 1989–90.

Spokesman (Commons): Opposition Spokesman on: Social Services 1974–75, Treasury and Economic Affairs 1975–79. *International Bodies (General):* Chairman, Interim Committee International Monetary Fund 1982–83. *Party Groups (General):* Chairman: Cambridge University Conservative Association 1951, Bow Group 1955; Managing Director, Crossbow 1957–60, Editor 1960–62. *Other:* Member, General Council of the Bar 1957–61; Visitor, School of Oriental and African Studies 1991–; President: Great Britain-China Centre 1992–, The Academy of Experts 1996–. *Awards Granted:* Joseph Bech Memorial Prize, Luxembourg 1993. Hon. Fellow, Trinity Hall, Cambridge 1992; two honorary doctorates, two honorary fellowships. *Trusts, etc:* Trustee, Thomson Foundation 1991–. *Miscellaneous:* President, Consumers' Association 1993–. *Honours:* Kt 1970; PC 1972; Grand Cross of the Order of Merit of the Federal Republic of Germany 1992; CH 1996. Freeman, Borough of Port Talbot 1992. *Publications: Conflict of Loyalty,* 1994; Various political pamphlets for the Bow Group and Conservative Political Centre. *Clubs:* Athenaeum, Garrick. *Name, Style and Title:* Raised to the peerage as Baron Howe of Aberavon, of Tandridge in the County of Surrey 1992. *Address:* Rt Hon the Lord Howe of Aberavon, Kt, CH, QC, House of Lords, London, SW1A 0PW *Tel:* 020 7219 6986.

LORD HOWELL OF GUILDFORD   Conservative

HOWELL OF GUILDFORD (Life Baron), David Arthur Russell Howell; cr. 1997. Born 18 January 1936. Son of late Arthur Howell, retired Army Officer and Businessman; educated Eton; King's College, Cambridge (BA 1959, MA). Married August 10, 1967, Davina Wallace (1 son 2 daughters). *Armed Forces:* Second Lieutenant, 2nd Btn Coldstream Guards 1954–56. *Career:* Treasury 1959–60; Leader writer, *Daily Telegraph* 1960–64; Director: Monks Investment Trust plc, John Laing (Investment) plc; Advisory Director, UBS-Warburg 1997–2000. *House of Commons:* Contested (Conservative) Dudley 1964; MP (Conservative) for Guildford 1966–97; Parliamentary Secretary, Civil Service Department 1970–72; Parliamentary Under-Secretary of State at: Department of Employment 1971–72, Northern Ireland Office March-November 1972; Minister of State: Northern Ireland Office 1972–74, Department of Energy 1974; Secretary of State for: Energy 1979–81, Transport 1981–83. *Whip (Commons):* Lord Commissioner of the Treasury (Government Whip) 1970–71. *Spokesman:* Opposition Spokesman on Foreign and Commonwealth Affairs 2000–. *Select Committees:* Member: Select Committee on European Communities Sub-Committee B (Energy, Industry and Transport) 1997–99, Select Committee on European Communities 1999–2000. *International Bodies (General):* Member, Trilateral Commission. *Party Groups (General):* Chairman, Bow Group 1962; Editor, "Crossbow" 1962–64; Director, Conservative Political Centre 1964–66. *Other:* Member: Royal Institute of International Affairs (Chatham House), Development Council and Trustee, Shakespeare Globe Theatre. *Miscellaneous:* Visiting Fellow, Nuffield College, Oxford; Chairman, UK-Japan 21st Century Group. *Honours:* PC 1979. Liveryman, Clothworkers' Company. *Publications:* Co-author *Principles in Practice,* 1960; *The Conservative Opportunity,* 1965; *Freedom and Capital,* 1981; *Blind Victory: a study in income, wealth and power,* 1986; *The Edge of Now,* 2000. *Special Interests:* Economics, International Finance, Energy, Oil, Foreign Affairs. *Recreations:* Writing, travel, golf, do-it-yourself. *Clubs:* Buck's, Beefsteak. *Name, Style and Title:* Raised to the peerage as Baron Howell of Guildford, of Penton Mewsey in the County of Hampshire 1997. *Address:* Rt Hon the Lord Howell of Guildford, House of Lords, London, SW1A 0PW *Tel:* 020 7219 5415 *E-Mail:* howelld@parliament.uk.

BARONESS HOWELLS OF ST DAVIDS   Labour

HOWELLS OF ST DAVIDS (Life Baroness), Rosalind Patricia-Anne Howells; cr 1999. Born 10 January 1931; educated St Joseph's Convent, Grenada; South West London College; City University, Washington DC. Married 1955, John Charles Howells (2 daughters). *Career:* Former Community and Equal Opportunities Worker, with Moonshot Youth Club, Community Industry, then to Greenwich Racial Equality Council as Equal Opportunities Director until retirement. *Other:* Chair, Lewisham Racial Equality Council; Ex-Chair: Charlton Consortium, Carnival Liaison Committee, Greater London Action on Race Equality; Director, Smithville Associates; President, Grenada Convent Past Pupils Association; Patron: Grenada Arts Council, Mediation Service; Member, Court of Governors, University of Greenwich; Former Vice-Chair, London Voluntary Services Council;

Has served on various committees including: Advisory Committee to the Home Secretary, Commonwealth Countries League, Greenwich Police/Community Consultative Group. *Awards Granted:* Hansib Publications Award; The Voice Newspaper Community Award. Hon. DUniv, Greenwich 1998. *Trusts, etc:* Trustee: West Indian Standing Conference, Museum of Ethnic Arts, Women of the Year Committee, Stephen Lawrence Charitable Trust, City Parochial Foundation. *Miscellaneous:* Has been an active campaigner for justice in the field of race relations: The New Cross Fire, Roland Adams Campaign, Stephen Lawrence Family Campaign, SUS Campaign. *Honours:* OBE 1993. *Special Interests:* Community Relations. *Recreations:* Food, music of all kinds, cricket, football. *Name, Style and Title:* Raised to the peerage as Baroness Howells of St Davids, of Charlton in the London Borough of Greenwich 1999. *Address:* The Baroness Howells of St Davids, OBE, House of Lords, London, SW1A 0PW *Tel:* 020 8852 9808 *Fax:* 020 8297 1975.

LORD HOWIE OF TROON   Labour

HOWIE OF TROON (Life Baron), William Howie; cr. 1978. Born 2 March 1924. Son of late Peter Howie; educated Marr College, Troon; Royal Technical College, Glasgow (BSc civil engineering 1944). Married March 24, 1951, Mairi, daughter of late John Sanderson (2 daughters 2 sons). *Trades Union:* Life Member, NUJ. *Career:* Civil Engineer; Journalist and Publisher; Director: Internal Relations of Thomas Telford Ltd 1976–95, Seto 1996–; Consultant, George S Hall Ltd 1999–. *House of Commons:* Contested Cities of London and Westminster 1959; MP (Labour) for Luton 1963–70. *Chancellor:* Pro-Chancellor, City University 1984–91. *Select Committees:* Member of House of Lords Select Committees on Science and Technology 1992–95, 1997–, the European Communities 1995–97; Co-opted Member, Select Committee on European Communities Sub-Committee B (Energy, Industry and Transport) 1997–98; Member, Select Committee on Science and Technology: Sub-Committee II (Science and Society) 1999–2000, Sub-Committee I (Complementary and Alternative Medicine) 2000. *Other:* Member: Council of Institution of Civil Engineers 1965–68, Council of City University 1968–91; Vice-President, Periodical Publishers Association. *Awards Granted:* Institution of Civil Engineers Garth Watson Medal. Hon. DSc, City University; Hon. LLD, Strathclyde. *Trusts, etc:* Fellow, Industry and Parliamentary Trust. *Miscellaneous:* Member, Committee of Inquiry into Engineering Profession 1977–79. Fellow, Institution of Civil Engineers; Member, Society of Engineers and Scientists (France). *Publications:* Co-author *Public Sector Purchasing,* 1968; *Trade Unions and the Professional Engineer,* 1977; *Trade Unions in Construction,* 1981; Co-author *Thames Tunnel to Channel Tunnel,* 1987. *Special Interests:* Construction Industry, Professional Engineers, Higher Education. *Name, Style and Title:* Raised to the peerage as Baron Howie of Troon, of Troon, Kyle and Carrick 1978. *Address:* The Lord Howie of Troon, 34 Temple Fortune Lane, London, NW11 7UL *Tel:* 020 8455 0492.

LORD HOYLE   Labour

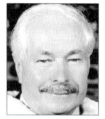

HOYLE (Life Baron), (Eric) Douglas Harvey Hoyle; cr. 1997. Born 17 February 1930. Son of late William Hoyle; educated Adlington School; Horwich Technical College. Married December 20, 1952, Pauline Spencer (died 1991) (1 son). *Trades Union:* Vice-President, ASTMS 1972–74, President 1977–81, Vice-President 1981–85, President 1985–88; Merged with TASS 1988; Joint President, MSF 1988–90, President 1990–91. *Councils, Public Bodies:* JP 1958; Former Member, North West Regional Health Authority. *Career:* British Rail 1945–51; AEI 1951–53; Sales Engineer, C. Weston Ltd, Salford 1953–74; Chairman, Warrington Rugby League plc 1999–. *House of Commons:* Contested (Labour) Clitheroe 1964, Nelson and Colne 1970 and February 1974 general elections; MP (Labour) for: Nelson and Colne October 1974–79, Warrington 1981–83, Warrington North 1983–97. *Party Groups (Commons):* Member, Labour Party National Executive 1978–82, 1983–85; Chairman, Parliamentary Labour Party 1992–97. *Whip:* Government Whip 1997–99. *Spokesman:* A Spokesman on: Defence 1997–99, Home Office 1997–99, Agriculture 1997–99. *Special Interests:* Trade, Employment, Industrial Relations, Health, Immigration, Arts. *Recreations:* Cricket, theatre, cinema, sport. *Sportsclubs:* President: Chorley Rugby League Club 1989–96, Warrington Rugby League Supporters Club 1990–, Adlington Cricket Club 1994–. *Name, Style and Title:* Raised to the peerage as Baron Hoyle, of Warrington in the County of Cheshire 1997. *Address:* The Lord Hoyle, JP, 30 Ashfield Road, Anderton, Nr Chorley, Lancashire, PR6 9PN; House of Lords, London, SW1A 0PW.

LORD HUGHES OF WOODSIDE   Labour

HUGHES OF WOODSIDE (Life Baron), Robert Hughes; cr. 1997. Born 3 January 1932; educated Robert Gordon's College, Aberdeen; Benoni High School, Transvaal; Pietermaritzburgh Technical College, Natal. Married 1957, Ina Margaret Miller (2 sons 3 daughters). *Trades Union:* Member, AEF. *Councils, Public Bodies:* Councillor, Aberdeen Town Council 1962–71; Former Member, North East Scotland Regional Hospital Board. *Career:* Emigrated to South Africa 1947; Returned UK 1954; Draughtsman. *House of Commons:* Contested North Angus and Mearns 1959; MP (Labour) for Aberdeen North 1970–97; Parliamentary Under-Secretary of State, Scottish Office March 1974–75; Piloted the Rating (Disabled Persons) Act 1978 to Statute as Private Members Bill. *Spokesman (Commons):* Front Bench Opposition Spokesman on Transport November 1981–83; Opposition Spokesman on: Agriculture, Fisheries and Food 1983–84, Transport 1984–88. *Party Groups (Commons):* Vice-Chairman, Tribune Group of MPs 1984–85. *Party Groups (General):* Chairman, Aberdeen City Labour Party 1963–69. *Other:* Founder Member, CND; Vice-Chairman, Anti-Apartheid Movement 1976, Chairman 1977–94; Chairman, Action for Southern Africa (ACTSA) 1994–. *Miscellaneous:* Member, General Medical Council 1976–81. *Special Interests:* Anti-Apartheid Work, Agriculture, Fishing Industry, Transport, Health Service, Overseas Aid and Development. *Recreations:* Fishing, golf. *Name, Style and Title:* Raised to the peerage as Baron Hughes of Woodside, of Woodside in the City of Aberdeen 1997. *Address:* The Lord Hughes of Woodside, House of Lords, London, SW1A 0PW.

LORD HUNT OF CHESTERTON   Labour

HUNT OF CHESTERTON (Life Baron), Julian Charles Roland Hunt; cr. 2000. Born 5 September 1941. Son of Roland Charles Hunt, CMG; educated Westminster School; Trinity College, Cambridge (BA 1963, PhD 1967); Warwick University. Married 1965, Marylla Ellen Shephard (1 son 2 daughters). *Trades Union:* Member, AUT. *Councils, Public Bodies:* Councillor, Cambridge City Council 1971–74, Leader Labour Group 1972. *Career:* Post-doctoral research, Cornell University, USA 1967; Research officer, Central Electricity Research Laboratories 1968–70; Cambridge University: Fellow 1966–, Senior research fellow 1998–99; Trinity College: Lecturer in applied mathematics and in engineering 1970–78, Reader in fluid mechanics 1978–90, Professor 1990–92, Hon Professor 1992–; Visiting Professor: Colorado State University, USA 1980, National Center for Atmospheric Research, Boulder, Colorado, USA 1983; Founder Director, Cambridge Environmental Research Ltd 1986–91, Director 1997–; Chief Executive, Meteorological Office 1992–97; Visiting Scientist, Cerfacs, Toulouse, France 1997, 1998; Visiting Professor: Arizona State University, USA 1997–98, Stanford University, USA 1998; Professor in climate modelling, University College, London 1999–. Six honorary doctorates from England, France and Sweden. *Miscellaneous:* Member: Management board, European Research Community for Flow Turbulence and Combustion 1988–95, Executive council, World Meteorological Organisation 1992–97; President, Institute of Mathematics and its Applications 1993–95; Member of Council, Royal Society 1998–. *Honours:* CB 1998. FRS 1989. *Publications:* Articles in mathematical and scientific publications. *Name, Style and Title:* Raised to the peerage as Baron Hunt of Chesterton, of Chesterton in the County of Cambridgeshire 2000. *Address:* Professor the Lord Hunt of Chesterton, CB, FRS, Department of Space and Climate Physics, University College, Gower Street, London, WC1E 6BT *E-Mail:* jcrh@mssl.ucl.ac.uk; l.clemente@ucl.ac.uk (Secretary).

LORD HUNT OF KINGS HEATH   Labour

HUNT OF KINGS HEATH (Life Baron), Philip Alexander Hunt; cr. 1997. Born 19 May 1949. Son of late Rev. Philip Hunt and Muriel Hunt; educated City of Oxford High School; Oxford School; Leeds University (BA). Married 1st, 1974 (dissolved) (1 daughter); married 2nd, 1988, Selina Ruth Stewart (3 sons 1 daughter). *Trades Union:* Member, Unison. *Councils, Public Bodies:* Councillor, Oxford City Council 1973–79; Member, Oxfordshire Area Health Authority 1975–77; Councillor, Birmingham City Council 1980–82. *Career:* Oxford Regional Hospital Board 1972–74; Nuffield Orthopaedic Centre 1974–75; Secretary, Edgware/Hendon Community Health Council 1975–78; National Association of Health Authorities: Assistant Secretary 1978–79,

Assistant Director 1979–84, Director 1984–90; Director, National Association of Health Authorities and Trusts 1990–96; Chief Executive, NHS Confederation 1996–97. *House of Lords:* Parliamentary Under-Secretary of State, Department of Health 1999–. *Whip:* Government Whip (A Lord in Waiting) 1998–99. *Spokesman:* A Spokesman on: Education and Employment 1998–99, Health 1998–. *Select Committees:* Member, Joint Select Committee on Consolidation of Bills 1998. *International Bodies (General):* Council, International Hospital Federation 1986–91. *Other:* Council, Association for Public Health 1992, Co-Chairman 1994–98; President, Family Planning Association 1997–98. *Honours:* OBE 1993. *Special Interests:* Devolution, Transport, Environment. *Recreations:* Cycling, swimming, supporting Birmingham City FC, music. *Sportsclubs:* Warwickshire CCC. *Name, Style and Title:* Raised to the peerage as Baron Hunt of Kings Heath, of Birmingham in the County of West Midlands 1997. *Address:* The Lord Hunt of Kings Heath, OBE, House of Lords, London, SW1A 0PW.

LORD HUNT OF TANWORTH · Cross-Bencher

HUNT OF TANWORTH (Life Baron), John Joseph Benedict Hunt; cr. 1980. Born 23 October 1919. Son of late Major A. L. Hunt; educated Downside; Magdalene College, Cambridge. Married 1st, 1941, Hon. Magdalen Robinson (died 1971), daughter of 1st Baron Robinson (2 sons and 1 daughter deceased), married 2nd, 1973, Lady Madeleine Frances, daughter of late Sir William Hume, CMG, FRCP, and widow of Sir John Charles, KCB, FRCP. *Armed Forces:* Served Royal Naval Volunteer Reserve 1940–45. *Career:* Entered Home Civil Service 1946; Dominions Office 1946; Private Secretary to Parliamentary Under-Secretary 1947; Second Secretary, UK High Commission Ceylon 1948–50; Private Secretary to Secretary of Cabinet and Permanent Secretary to Treasury and Head of Civil Service 1956–58; Assistant Secretary, Commonwealth Relations Office 1958; Cabinet Office 1960; HM Treasury 1962–67; Deputy Secretary 1968; First Civil Service Commissioner, Civil Service Department 1968–71; Third Secretary, Treasury 1971–72; Second Permanent Secretary, Cabinet Office 1972–73; Secretary of the Cabinet 1973–79; Chairman, Banque Nationale de Paris plc 1980–97; Director, IBM (UK) Ltd 1980–90; Advisory Director, Unilever 1980–90; Director, Prudential Corporation plc 1980–92, Chairman: Disasters Emergency Committee 1981–89, Inquiry into Cable Expansion and Broadcasting Policy 1982, Tablet Publishing Co. Ltd 1984–96, Director 1984–99, Prudential Corporation plc 1985–90, European Policy Forum 1992–98, Council 1992–. *Select Committees:* Member, Sub-Committee A of House of Lords European Communities Committee 1992–95, Chairman 1993–97; Member, House of Lords European Communities Committee 1993–96; Chairman, House of Lords Select Committee on Central and Local Government Relations 1995–96. *Other:* Chairman, Ditchley Foundation 1983–91; President, The Local Government Association 1997–. Hon. Fellow, Magdalene College, Cambridge 1977. *Honours:* CB 1968; KCB 1973; GCB 1977; Officier, Légion d'Honneur (France) 1987; Knight Commander with Star of the Order of Pius IX 1997. *Recreations:* Gardening. *Name, Style and Title:* Raised to the peerage as Baron Hunt of Tanworth, of Stratford-on-Avon in the County of Warwickshire 1980. *Address:* The Lord Hunt of Tanworth, GCB, 8 Wool Road, London, SW20 0HW *Tel:* 020 8947 7640 *Fax:* 020 8947 4879.

LORD HUNT OF WIRRAL · Conservative

HUNT OF WIRRAL (Life Baron), David James Fletcher Hunt; cr. 1997. Born 21 May 1942. Son of late Alan Nathaniel Hunt, OBE, Shipping Agent and late Jessie Edna Ellis Hunt; educated Liverpool College; Montpellier University, France; Bristol University; Guildford College of Law (LLB). Married June 2, 1973, Paddy, daughter of late Roger, and Margery Orchard (2 sons 2 daughters). *Career:* Solicitor; Senior Partner, Beachcroft Wansbroughs; Director, BET Omnibus Services Ltd 1980–81. *House of Commons:* Contested Bristol South 1970 and Kingswood 1974; MP (Conservative) for Wirral 1976–83 and for Wirral West 1983–97; PPS: to Secretary of State for Trade 1979–81, to Secretary of State for Defence 1981; Parliamentary Under-Secretary of State, Department of Energy 1984–87; Minister of State, Department of the Environment (Minister for Local Government and Inner Cities) 1989–90; Secretary of State: for Wales 1990–93, for Employment 1993–94; Chancellor of the Duchy of Lancaster and Minister for Public Service and Science 1994–95.

Whip (Commons): Assistant Government Whip 1981–83; Government Whip (Lord Commissioner of the Treasury) 1983–84; Deputy Government Chief Whip (Treasurer of Her Majesty's Household) 1987–89. *Spokesman (Commons):* Spokesman for Shipping and Shipbuilding 1977–79. *Select Committees:* Member, Offices Committee 1999–, European Communities Committee, Sub-Committee E, Law and Institutions 1999–. *Party Groups (General):* Chairman, Bristol University Conservative Association 1964–65; National Vice-Chairman, Federation of Conservative Students 1965–66; Chairman: Bristol City CPC 1965–68, Bristol Federation of Young Conservatives; Member: General Purposes Committee, National Union Executive 1967–76, 1983–89; Vice-Chairman, Bristol Conservative Association 1970; Chairman, National Young Conservatives 1972–73; Vice-Chairman, National Union 1974–76; Vice-President, European Conservative and Christian Democratic Youth Community; Vice-Chairman, Conservative Party 1983–84; President, Tory Reform Group 1991–97. *Other:* Member, Government Advisory Committee on Pop Festivals; Governor: European Youth Foundation at Strasbourg 1972–75, English Speaking Union 1998–. *Trusts, etc:* Trustee, Holocaust Educational Trust; President: Hoylake Cottage Hospital Trust, Arrowe Park Sick Children's Fund. *Miscellaneous:* Chairman, British Youth Council 1971–74; Member, South West Economic Planning Council 1972–76; Chairman, National Youth Study Group on Young People and Politics; President, British Youth Council 1978–80. *Honours:* MBE 1973; PC 1990. *Recreations:* Cricket, walking. *Clubs:* Hurlingham. *Name, Style and Title:* Raised to the peerage as Baron Hunt of Wirral, of Wirral in the County of Merseyside 1997. *Address:* Rt Hon the Lord Hunt of Wirral, MBE, Senior Partner, Beachcroft Wansbroughs, 100 Fetter Lane, London, EC4A 1BN *E-Mail:* lordhunt@bwlaw.co.uk.

LORD HURD OF WESTWELL   Conservative

HURD OF WESTWELL (Life Baron), Douglas Richard Hurd; cr. 1997. Born 8 March 1930. Son of late Baron Hurd (Life Peer); educated Eton; Trinity College, Cambridge (President, Cambridge Union 1952). Married 1st, November 10, 1960, Tatiana, daughter of Arthur Benedict Eyre, MBE (3 sons) (marriage dissolved 1982), married 2nd, May 7, 1982, Judith, daughter of Sidney Smart (1 son 1 daughter). *Armed Forces:* 2nd Lieutenant, Royal Artillery 1948–49. *Career:* HM Foreign Service, Peking; UN, Rome 1952–66; Conservative Research Department 1966–68; Deputy Chairman, Natwest Markets 1995–98; Chairman, British Invisibles 1997–2000; Deputy Chairman, Coutts & Co 1998–. *House of Commons:* MP (Conservative) for Mid Oxon 1974–83 and for Witney 1983–97; Political Secretary to Edward Heath MP 1968–74; Minister of State for: Foreign and Commonwealth Office 1979–83, Home Office 1983–84; Secretary of State for: Northern Ireland 1984–85, The Home Department 1985–89, Foreign and Commonwealth Affairs 1989–95; Contested Leadership of the Conservative Party November 1990. *Spokesman (Commons):* Opposition Spokesman on Europe 1976–79. *Trusts, etc:* Trustee, Prayer Book Society 1989–; Chairman, Prison Reform Trust 1997–. *Miscellaneous:* A Vice-President, The Falkland Islands Association 1996–2000, President 2000–; Member: The Constitutional Commission 1998–99, Royal Commission on the Reform of the House of Lords 1999; High Steward, Westminster Abbey 1999–, House of Lords Appointments Commission 2000–. *Honours:* CBE 1974; PC 1982; CH 1996. *Publications: The Arrow War*, 1967; *Truth Game*, 1972; *Vote to Kill*, 1975; *An End to Promises*, 1979; Co-author *Send Him Victorious*, 1968; *The Smile on the Face of the Tiger*, 1969; *Scotch on the Rocks*, 1971; *War Without Frontiers*, 1982; Co-author *Palace of Enchantments*, 1985; *The Search for Peace*, 1997; *The Shape of Ice*, 1998; *Ten Minutes to Turn the Devil*, 1999. *Recreations:* Writing novels. *Clubs:* Beefsteak, Travellers', Pratt's. *Name, Style and Title:* Raised to the peerage as Baron Hurd of Westwell, of Westwell in the County of Oxfordshire 1997. *Address:* Rt Hon the Lord Hurd of Westwell, CH, CBE, House of Lords, London, SW1A 0PW *Tel:* 020 7219 3000.

Dod *on* Line
An Electronic Directory without rival . . .
Peers' biographies and photographs available with daily updates *via* the internet

For a *free* trial, call Oliver Cox on 020 7828 7256

LORD HUSSEY OF NORTH BRADLEY   Cross-Bencher

HUSSEY OF NORTH BRADLEY (Life Baron) Marmaduke James Hussey; cr. 1996. Born 29 August 1923. Son of late Eric Robert James Husssey, CMG, and of Mrs Christine Hussey; educated Rugby; Trinity College, Oxford (Scholar, MA). Married April 25, 1959, Lady Susan Waldegrave, DCVO, daughter of 12th Earl Waldegrave, KG, GCVO, TD, DL (1 son 1 daughter). *Armed Forces:* Served World War II, with Grenadier Guards in Italy (wounded). *Career:* Associated Newspapers 1949, Director 1964; Managing Director, Harmsworth Publications 1967–70; Thomson Organisation Executive Board 1971; Chief Executive and Managing Director, Times Newspapers Ltd 1971–80, Director 1982–86; Director, Colonial Mutual Group 1982 96; Joint Chairman, Great Western Radio 1985–86; Director, William Collins plc 1985–89, MAID plc 1996–; Chairman: Ruffer Investment Management 1996–, Casweb Ltd. *Select Committees:* Member: Select Committee on European Communities 1997–, Select Committee on European Communities Sub-Committee A (Economic and Financial Affairs, Trade and External Relations) 1997–. *Other:* Member: Board of British Council 1983–96, Government Working Party on Artificial Limb and Appliance Centres in England 1984–86; Chairman: Royal Marsden Hospital 1985–98, BBC 1986–96; Member, Management and Education Committees, King Edward's Hospital Fund for London 1987–; President, Royal Bath and West of England Society 1990–91; Chairman, King's Fund London Committee 1996; President, Iris Fund for Prevention of Blindness 1998–; Various positions held in these charities: BLESMA, British Legion, Cheshire Homes,. Hon. Fellow, Trinity College, Oxford 1989. *Trusts, etc:* Trustee: Rhodes Trust 1972–91, Royal Academic Trust 1988–97. *Clubs:* Brooks's. *Name, Style and Title:* Raised to the peerage as Baron Hussey of North Bradley, of North Bradley in the County of Wiltshire 1996. *Address:* The Lord Hussey of North Bradley, Flat 15, 47 Courtfield Road, London, SW7 4DB *Tel:* 020 7370 1414; Waldegrave House, Chewton Mendip, near Bath, Somerset, BA3 4PD *Tel:* 01761 241289.

LORD HUTCHINSON OF LULLINGTON   Liberal Democrat

HUTCHINSON OF LULLINGTON (Life Baron), Jeremy Nicolas Hutchinson; cr. 1978. Born 28 March 1915. Son of late St John Hutchinson, KC; educated Stowe; Magdalen College, Oxford (MA). Married 1st, 1940, Dame Peggy Ashcroft, DBE (1 son 1 daughter) (marriage dissolved 1966, she died 1991), married 2nd, 1966, June Osborn. *Armed Forces:* RNVR 1939–46. *Career:* Called to the Bar, Middle Temple 1939; QC 1961; Bencher 1963; Recorder of Bath 1962–72; Recorder of Crown Court 1973–76; Professor of Law, Royal Academy of Arts 1988–. *Spokesman:* Liberal Democrat Spokesman on the Arts, Penal Affairs 1983–92. *Trusts, etc:* Trustee, Tate Gallery 1977–80, Chairman 1980–84. *Miscellaneous:* Member: Committee on Immigration Appeals 1966–68, Committee on Identi-fication Procedures 1974–76; Vice-Chairman, Arts Council of Great Britain 1976–78. *Clubs:* MCC. *Name, Style and Title:* Raised to the peerage as Baron Hutchinson of Lullington, of Lullington in the County of East Sussex 1978. *Address:* The Lord Hutchinson of Lullington, QC, House of Lords, London, SW1A 0PW.

LORD HUTTON   Cross-Bencher

HUTTON (Life Baron), James Brian Edward Hutton; cr. 1997. Born 29 June 1931. Son of late James and Mabel Hutton; educated Shrewsbury; Balliol College, Oxford (BA Jurisprudence); Queen's University, Belfast. Married 1975, Mary Gillian Murland (died 2000) (2 daughters). *Career:* Called to Northern Ireland Bar 1954; Junior Counsel to Attorney-General for Northern Ireland 1969; QC (NI) 1970; Called to English Bar 1972; Legal Adviser to Ministry of Home Affairs (NI) 1973; Senior Crown Counsel in NI 1973–79; Member, Joint Law Enforcement Commission 1974; Bencher, Inn of Court of Northern Ireland 1974; Judge of the High Court of Justice (NI) 1979–88; Lord Chief Justice of Northern Ireland 1988–97; Lord of Appeal in Ordinary 1997–. *Other:* President, Northern Ireland Association for Mental Health 1983–90; Visitor of the University of Ulster 1999–. Hon. Fellow, Balliol College, Oxford 1988; Hon. LLD, Queen's University, Belfast 1992. *Miscellaneous:* Deputy Chairman, Boundary Commission (NI) 1985–88; Hon. Bencher: Inner Temple 1988, King's Inn, Dublin 1988. *Honours:* PC 1988; Kt 1988. *Name, Style and Title:* Raised to the peerage as Baron Hutton, of Bresagh in the County of Down 1997. *Address:* Rt Hon the Lord Hutton, House of Lords, London, SW1A 0PW.

LORD HYLTON   Cross-Bencher

HYLTON (5th Baron), Raymond Hervey Jolliffe; cr. 1866; 5th Bt of Merstham (UK) 1821. Born 13 June 1932. Son of 4th Baron. Succeeded his father 1967; educated Eton; Trinity College, Oxford (MA). Married June 29, 1966, Joanna, daughter of late Andrew de Bertodano (4 sons 1 daughter). *Armed Forces:* National Service, commissioned Coldstream Guards. *Councils, Public Bodies:* DL, Somerset 1975–90; Councillor, Frome RDC 1968–72. *Career:* Assistant Private Secretary to the Governor-General of Canada 1960–62. *House of Lords:* Private Members Bills: Sexual Offences (Amendment) Bill, Overseas Domestic Workers (Protection) Bill; An elected hereditary peer 1999–. *International Bodies (General):* Chairman, MICOM – Moldova Initiatives Committee of Management 1994. *Other:* Associated in various capacities since 1962 with: Abbeyfield Society, Catholic Housing Aid Society, The London Housing Aid Centre, National Federation of Housing Associations, Age Concern, L'Arche Ltd, Royal MENCAP, Foundation for Alternatives, Christian College for Adult Education, Mendip Wansdyke Local Enterprise Group, Hugh of Witham Foundation, Action around Bethlehem Children with Disability (ABCD); President, Northern Ireland Association for Care and Resettlement of Offenders 1988–; Housing Associations Charitable Trust,. Hon. DSc, Southampton University 1994. *Trusts, etc:* Associated in various capacities since 1962 with: Acorn Christian Healing Trust; Chairman, St Francis and St Sergius Trust Fund (for the churches and youth in Russia) 1993–. ARICS 1960. *Special Interests:* Northern Ireland, Housing, British-Irish Relations, Human Rights, Prisons, Penal Affairs and Policy, Middle East, Europe, Former Soviet Union, Conflict Resolution. *Clubs:* Lansdowne. *Address:* The Lord Hylton, House of Lords, London, SW1A 0PW *Tel:* Messages: 020 7219 5353 *Fax:* 020 7219 5979.

BARONESS HYLTON-FOSTER   Cross-Bencher

HYLTON-FOSTER (Life Baroness), Audrey Pellew Hylton-Foster; cr. 1965. Born 19 May 1908. Daughter of late 1st Viscount Ruffside, PC, DL, Speaker of the House of Commons 1943–51 and late Viscountess Ruffside; educated St George's, Ascot; Ivy House, Wimbledon. Married December 22, 1931, Rt Hon. Sir Harry Hylton-Foster, QC, MP (died 1965), Speaker of the House of Commons 1959–65. *House of Lords:* Former Member of all Sub-Committees of the House of Lords by virtue of her position as Convenor of the Cross-Bench Peers 1974–95. *Party Groups (General):* Member, Cross-Bench Parliamentary Group 1965–. *Other:* Director, Chelsea Division, County of London Branch, British Red Cross Society 1950–60; President, County of London Branch, BRCS 1960–74; Member, Executive Committee BRCS 1966–76; President and Chairman, The London Branch BRCS 1974–83; Member, Council of BRCS 1977–81, Patron, London Branch; Member, National BRCS HQ consultative panel 1984; President, Prevention of Blindness Research Fund 1965–76, Patron 1976–; Vice-President Dorking and District: Rifle Club, Preservation Society. *Awards Granted:* BRCS Queen's Badge of Honour. *Honours:* DBE 1990. *Special Interests:* Social Welfare, Environment. *Recreations:* Fishing, gardening. *Name, Style and Title:* Raised to the peerage as Baroness Hylton-Foster, of the City of Westminster 1965. *Address:* The Baroness Hylton-Foster, DBE, The Coach House, Tanhurst, Leith Hill, Holmbury St. Mary, Dorking, Surrey, RH5 6LU *Tel:* 01306 711975 *Tel:* 020 7584 2889 *Tel:* House of Lords 020 7219 3209.

I

IMBERT (Life Baron), Peter Michael Imbert; cr. 1999. Born 27 April 1933. Son of late William Henry Imbert, and of Frances May (née Hodge); educated Harvey's Grammar School, Folkestone; Holborn College of Law, Languages and Commerce. Married 1956, Iris Dove (1 son 2 daughters).*Councils, Public Bodies:* DL, Greater London 1994–98, Lord Lieutenant 1998–; JP 1998. *Career:* Joined Metropolitan Police 1953; Metropolitan Police Anti-Terrorist Squad 1973–75; Police negotiator at Balcombe Street siege December 1975; Assistant Chief Constable, Surrey Constabulary 1976, Deputy Chief Constable 1977; Chief Constable, Thames Valley Police 1979–85; Secretary, National Crime Committee-ACPO Council 1980–83, Chairman 1983–85; Deputy Commissioner, Metropolitan Police 1985–87, Commissioner 1987–93; Leader, International Criminal Justice Delegation to Russia 1993; Visiting International Fellow, Australian Police Staff College 1994 and 1997; Has lectured on terrorism and siege situations in UK, Europe, Australia and Canada; Chairman, Capital Eye Security 1997–. *Other:* President, Richmond Horse Show 1993–; Governor, Harvey's Grammar School 1994–. Hon. DLitt, Reading University 1987. *Trusts, etc:* Trustee, Queen Elizabeth Foundation of St Catharine's 1988–; Chairman, Surrey CCC Youth Trust 1993–96. *Miscellaneous:* Member: General Advisory Council, BBC 1980–87, Criminal Justice Consultative Committee 1992–93, Ministerial Advisory Group, Royal Parks 1993–, Public Policy Committee, RAC 1993–, Mental Health Foundation, Committee of Inquiry into Care in the Community for the Severely Mentally Ill 1994. *Honours:* QPM 1980; Kt 1988. CIMgt (CBIM 1982). *Recreations:* Bridge, golf, grandchildren. *Name, Style and Title:* Raised to the peerage as Baron Imbert, of New Romney in the County of Kent 1999. *Address:* The Lord Imbert, QPM, The Lieutenancy Office, 18th Floor, City Hall, PO Box 240, Victoria Street, London, SW1E 6QP.

INGE (Life Baron), Peter (Anthony) Inge; cr. 1997. Born 5 August 1935. Son of late Raymond and Grace Inge; educated Summer Fields; Wrekin College; RMA, Sandhurst. Married 1960, Letitia Marion Beryl, daughter of late Trevor Thornton-Berry (2 daughters). *Armed Forces:* Regular Army Officer with Service of 43 years; Commissioned Green Howards 1956; Served Hong Kong, Malaya, Germany, Libya and UK; ADC to GOC, 4 Division 1960–61; Adjutant, 1 Green Howards 1963–64; Student, Staff College 1966; Ministry of Defence 1967–69; Company Commander, 1 Green Howards 1969–70; Student, Joint Services Staff College 1971; BM, 11 Armoured Brigade 1972; Instructor, Staff College 1973–74; CO, 1 Green Howards 1974–76; Commandant, Junior Division, Staff College 1977–79; Commander, Task Force C/4 Armoured Brigade 1980–81; Chief of Staff, HQ 1 (BR) Corps 1982–83; Colonel, The Green Howards 1982–94; GOC, NE District and Commander 2nd Infantry Division 1984–86; Director General, Logistic Policy (Army), Ministry of Defence 1986–87; Commander, 1st (Br) Corps 1987–89; Colonel Commandant, Royal Military Police 1987–92; Commander, Northern Army Group and C-in-C, BAOR 1989–92; ADC General to HM The Queen 1991–94; Chief of the General Staff 1992–94; Field Marshal 1994; Chief of the Defence Staff 1994–97; Constable, HM Tower of London 1996–. *Councils, Public Bodies:* DL, North Yorkshire 1994. *Select Committees:* Member, Select Committee Sub-Committee C European Union.*International Bodies (General):* Member, International Institute for Strategic Studies. *Other:* Commissioner Royal Hospital, Chelsea; President, Army Benevolent Fund. Hon. DCL, University of Newcastle upon Tyne.*Trusts, etc:* Chairman, Windsor Leadership Trust; St George's House; Royal Armouries; Deputy Chairman, Historic Royal Palaces. *Honours:* KCB 1988; GCB (Mil) 1992. Freeman, City of London. Liveryman, Fan Makers' Company. *Special Interests:* Defence. *Recreations:* Cricket, walking, music, reading. *Clubs:* Boodle's, Beefsteak, Army and Navy, MCC. *Name, Style and Title:* Raised to the peerage as Baron Inge, of Richmond in the County of North Yorkshire 1997. *Address:* Field Marshal The Lord Inge, GCB, DL, House of Lords, London, SW1A 0PW.

LORD INGLEWOOD Conservative

INGLEWOOD (2nd Baron, UK), (William) Richard Fletcher-Vane; cr. 1964. Born 31 July 1951. Son of 1st Baron, TD, DL. Succeeded his father 1989; educated Eton; Trinity College, Cambridge (MA); Cumbria College of Agriculture and Forestry. Married August 29, 1986, Cressida, daughter of late Desmond Pemberton-Pigott, CMG (1 son 2 daughters). *Councils, Public Bodies:* Member, Lake District Special Planning Board 1984–90; Chairman, Development Control Committee 1985–89; Member, North West Water Authority 1987–89; DL, Cumbria 1993. *Career:* Called to the Bar, Lincoln's Inn 1975; MEP (Conservative) for Cumbria and Lancashire North 1989–94; British Conservative Group spokesman, Legal Affairs Committee, European Parliament 1989–94, 1999–; Chief Whip, British Conservative Section of EPP Group 1994; MEP (Conservative) for North West Region 1999–: leader NW Conservative MEPs 1999–; Vice-President, EP-China Delegation. *House of Lords:* Parliamentary Under-Secretary of State, Department of National Heritage 1995–97; An elected hereditary peer 1999–. *Whip:* Government Whip (A Lord in Waiting) 1994–95; Government Deputy Chief Whip (Captain of HM Bodyguard of the Yeomen of the Guard) January-July 1995. *Spokesman:* An Opposition Spokesman: on National Heritage 1997, on Culture, Media and Sport 1997–98. *Miscellaneous:* Contested (Conservative), Houghton and Washington 1983 General Election; Contested (Conservative), Durham 1984 European Election. ARICS. Liveryman, Skinners' Company. *Special Interests:* Rural Affairs, Agriculture, Environment, Europe, Local Government, Regional Policy, Legal Affairs, Media, Arts. *Clubs:* Travellers', Pratt's. *Address:* The Lord Inglewood, MEP, DL, Hutton-in-the-Forest, Penrith, Cumbria, CA11 9TH *Tel:* 017684 84500 *Fax:* 017684 84571.

LORD INGROW Conservative

INGROW (Life Baron), John Aked Taylor; cr. 1983. Born 15 August 1917. Son of late Percy Taylor; educated Shrewsbury School. Married October 11, 1949, Barbara Mary (died 1998), daughter of late Percy Wright Stirk (2 daughters). *Armed Forces:* Served Overseas in 1939–45 War, DWR and Royal Signals (Major). *Councils, Public Bodies:* Councillor, Keighley Town Council 1946–67; JP, Keighley 1949; Mayor, Keighley 1956–57; DL, West Yorks 1971–76; Vice Lord-Lieutenant, West Yorks 1976–85; Lord-Lieutenant, West Yorks 1985–92. *Career:* Chairman and Managing Director, Timothy Taylor & Co. Ltd 1954–95, Life President 1995–; General Commissioner of Income Taxes 1965–92. *Party Groups (General):* Chairman: Keighley Conservative Association 1952–56, 1957–67, Yorkshire Area Conservatives 1966–71, Executive Committee, National Union 1971–76. *Other:* Member, Magistrates' Association Council 1957–86, Hon. Treasurer 1976–86; Member, Court of University of Leeds 1986–. Hon. D, University of Bradford 1990. *Honours:* TD 1951; OBE 1960; Kt 1972; KStJ 1986. *Name, Style and Title:* Raised to the peerage as Baron Ingrow, of Keighley in the County of West Yorkshire 1983. *Address:* The Lord Ingrow, OBE, TD, Fieldhead, Keighley, West Yorkshire, BD20 6LP *Tel:* 01535 603895.

LORD IRVINE OF LAIRG Labour

IRVINE OF LAIRG (Life Baron), Alexander Andrew Mackay Irvine; cr. 1987. Born 23 June 1940. Son of Alexander and Margaret Christina Irvine; educated Inverness Royal Academy, Hutchesons' Boys' Grammar School, Glasgow; Glasgow University (MA, LLB); Christ's College, Cambridge (Scholar, BA, LLB). Married 1974, Alison Mary McNair (2 sons). *Career:* University Lecturer, London School of Economics 1965–69; Called to the Bar, Inner Temple 1967; QC 1978; Head, 11 King's Bench Walk Chambers 1981–97; Bencher of the Inner Temple, 1985; Recorder 1985–88; Deputy High Court Judge 1987–97. *House of Lords:* Shadow Lord Chancellor 1992–97; Lord Chancellor 1997–. *Spokesman:* Shadow Spokesman on Legal Affairs and Home Affairs 1987–92. *Select Committees:* Member, Select Committees on: House of Lords' Offices 1997–, Procedure 1997–. *International Bodies:* Joint President: British-American Parliamentary Group, CPA, IPU.

International Bodies (General): Vice-Patron, World Federation of Mental Health. *Other:* President, Magistrates Association; Chairman, Glasgow 2001 Committee; Member, Committee of the Slade School of Fine Art 1990–. *Awards Granted:* George and Thomas Hutcheson Award 1998. Hon. Fellow, Christ's College, Cambridge 1996; Hon. LLD, Glasgow 1997. *Trusts, etc:* Foundation Trustee, Whitechapel Art Gallery 1990–97; Trustee: John Smith Memorial Trust 1992–97, Hunterian Collection 1997–; Joint President, Industry and Parliament Trust. *Miscellaneous:* Contested (Labour) Hendon North, General Election 1970; Church Commissioner; Hon. Bencher, Inn of Court of Northern Ireland 1998. *Honours:* PC 1997. Hon. Fellow, Society for Advanced Legal Studies; Fellow, US College of Trial Lawyers 1998–. *Special Interests:* Legal Affairs, Home Affairs, Constitutional Affairs. *Recreations:* Collecting paintings, travel, reading, cinema and theatre. *Clubs:* Garrick. *Name, Style and Title:* Raised to the peerage as Baron Irvine of Lairg, of Lairg in the District of Sutherland 1987. *Address:* Rt Hon the Lord Irvine of Lairg, House of Lords, London, SW1A 0PW.

LORD ISLWYN   Labour

ISLWYN (Life Baron), Royston John (Roy) Hughes; cr. 1997. Born 9 June 1925. Son of late John Hughes, Miner; educated Ruskin College, Oxford. Married June 10, 1957, Marion, daughter of John Appleyard (3 daughters). *Trades Union:* Has held numerous offices in TGWU from 1959; Chairman, Parliamentary Group TGWU 1968–69, 1979–82. *Armed Forces:* Served 2nd Btn, Welch Regiment. *Councils, Public Bodies:* Coventry City Councillor 1962–66; DL, Gwent 1992–. *House of Commons:* MP (Labour) for Newport 1966–83 and for Newport East 1983–97. *Spokesman (Commons):* Front Bench Spokesman on Welsh Affairs 1984–88. *International Bodies (General):* Member, Executive British Group, Inter Parliamentary Union 1986–92, Treasurer 1991; Member, Council of Europe 1990–97. *Party Groups (General):* Secretary, Coventry Borough Labour Party 1962–66; Chairman, Welsh Parliamentary Party 1969–70. *Miscellaneous:* Chairman, Welsh Grand Committee 1982–84, 1990–97; Spokesman, Pensioners' Convention 1998–. *Special Interests:* Steel, Motor Industry, Sport, Road Programme, International Affairs. *Recreations:* Rugby, soccer, cricket, gardening. *Sportsclubs:* Vice-President: Crawshay's (Wales) Rugby XV 1991–, Glamorgan County Cricket Club. *Name, Style and Title:* Raised to the peerage as Baron Islwyn, of Casnewydd in the County of Gwent 1997. *Address:* The Lord Islwyn, DL, Chapel Field, Chapel Lane, Abergavenny, Gwent, NP7 7BT *Tel:* 01873 856502.

J

LORD JACOBS   Liberal Democrat

JACOBS (Life Baron) (David) Anthony Jacobs; cr. 1997. Born November 1931. Son of Ridley and Ella Jacobs; educated Clifton College; London University (BCom). Married 1954, Evelyn Felicity Patchett (1 son 1 daughter). *Career:* Chairman: Nig Securities Group 1957–72, Tricoville Group 1961–90, 1992–94, British School of Motoring 1973–90. *House of Lords:* Member of Liberal Democrat Party. *Select Committees:* Member, House of Lords Offices Sub-Committee: Advisory Panel on Works of Art 2000–. *Party Groups (General):* Joint Treasurer, Liberal Party 1984–87; Vice-President, Social and Liberal Democrats 1988, Member, Federal Executive 1988. *Other:* Chairman, Board of Governors, Haifa University, Israel. *Miscellaneous:* Crown Estate Paving Commissioner. *Honours:* Kt 1988. FCA. *Recreations:* Golf, reading, theatre, opera, travel. *Sportsclubs:* Coombe Hill Golf (Surrey). *Name, Style and Title:* Raised to the peerage as Baron Jacobs, of Belgravia in the City of Westminster 1997. *Address:* The Lord Jacobs, FCA, 9 Nottingham Terrace, London, NW1 4QB *Tel:* 020 7486 6323.

BARONESS JAMES OF HOLLAND PARK — Conservative

JAMES OF HOLLAND PARK (Life Baroness), Phyllis Dorothy James; cr. 1991. Born 3 August 1920. Daughter of late Sydney and Dorothy James; educated Cambridge High School for Girls. Married August 8, 1941, Connor Bantry White (died 1964) (2 daughters). *Councils, Public Bodies:* JP, Willesden and Inner London 1979–84. *Career:* Administrator, National Health Service 1949–68; Civil Servant: appointed Principal, Home Office 1968, Police Department 1968–72, Criminal Policy Department 1972–79; A Governor, BBC 1988–93; Member, Arts Council 1988–92, Chairman, Literature Advisory Panel 1988–92; Board Member, British Council 1988–93. *Other:* Chairman: Booker Panel of Judges 1987, Society of Authors 1984–86; President, Society of Authors 1997–; Member, Liturgical Commission, Church of England; Vice-President, Prayer Book Society. Seven honorary doctorates, two honorary fellowships. *Honours:* OBE 1983. Fellow, Royal Society of Literature 1987; FRSA. *Publications:* As P.D. James: *Cover her Face*, 1962; *A Mind to Murder*, 1963; *Unnatural Causes*, 1967; *Shroud for a Nightingale*, 1971; *The Maul and the Pear Tree* (with T.A. Critchley), 1971; *An Unsuitable Job for a Woman*, 1972; *The Black Tower*, 1975; *Death of an Expert Witness*, 1977; *Innocent Blood*, 1980; *The Skull Beneath the Skin*, 1982; *A Taste for Death*, 1986; *Devices and Desires*, 1989; *The Children of Men*, 1992; *Original Sin*, 1994; *A Certain Justice*, 1997; *Time to be in Earnest*, 1999; *Death in Holy Orders*, 2001. *Special Interests:* Literature, Arts, Criminal Justice, Broadcasting. *Recreations:* Reading, exploring churches, walking by the sea. *Clubs:* Detection. *Name, Style and Title:* Raised to the peerage as Baroness James of Holland Park, of Southwold in the County of Suffolk 1991. *Address:* The Baroness James of Holland Park, OBE, c/o Greene and Heaton Ltd, 37 Goldhawk Road, London, W12 8QQ.

LORD JANNER OF BRAUNSTONE — Labour

JANNER OF BRAUNSTONE (Life Baron), Greville Ewan Janner; cr. 1997. Born 11 July 1928. Son of late Baron Janner (Life Peer) and late Lady Janner, CBE; educated St Paul's School; Trinity Hall, Cambridge (MA); Harvard Post-Graduate Law School, USA. Married July 6, 1955, Myra Sheink (died 1996) (1 son 2 daughters). *Trades Union:* Member, NUJ (London Freelance Branch); Hon. Member, NUM, Leicester. *Armed Forces:* National Service 1946–48, RA, BAOR, War Crimes Investigator. *Career:* Former President, Cambridge Union; Called to the Bar, Middle Temple 1954; QC 1971; Non-executive director, Ladbroke plc 1986–95; Chairman, JSB Group and Effective Presentational Skills 1987–97; President, REACH (Retired Executives' Action Clearing House) 1989–. *House of Commons:* Contested Wimbledon 1955; MP (Labour) for Leicester North-West 1970–74, and for Leicester West 1974–97. *Select Committees:* Member, Joint Select Committee on Consolidation of Bills 1998–. *Party Groups (General):* Former Chairman, Cambridge University Labour Club; International Secretary, National Association of Labour Students 1952; Labour Friends of: Israel, India. *Other:* President: Board of Deputies of British Jews 1979–85, Commonwealth Jewish Council 1982–; Founder/President, Interparliamentary Council Against Anti-Semitism 1985–; Vice-President, World Jewish Congress 1991–; Founder and President, Maimonides Foundation 1995–; Vice-President: Association of Jewish Ex-Servicemen, Association for Jewish Youth. Hon. PhD, Haifa University; Hon. LLD, De Montfort University. *Trusts, etc:* Chairman: Holocaust Educational Trust, Lord Forte Charitable Trust. Fellow, Institute of Personnel Management and Development. Freeman, City of London. *Publications:* Many books including: *Janner's Complete Speechmaker* (6th Edition); *One Hand Alone Cannot Clap*, 1998. *Special Interests:* Employment Law, Industrial Relations, Jewish Causes, Human Rights, Consumer Protection, Commonwealth, India, Middle East. *Recreations:* Swimming, member of the Magic Circle and International Brotherhood of Magicians, languages. *Name, Style and Title:* Raised to the peerage as Baron Janner of Braunstone, of Leicester in the County of Leicestershire 1997. *Address:* The Lord Janner of Braunstone, QC, House of Lords, London, SW1A 0PW.

LORD JAUNCEY OF TULLICHETTLE   Cross-Bencher

JAUNCEY OF TULLICHETTLE (Life Baron), Charles Eliot Jauncey; cr. 1988. Born 8 May 1925. Son of late Captain John Henry Jauncey, DSO, RN; educated Radley; Christ Church, Oxford; Glasgow University. Married 1st, 1948, Jean Graham (2 sons 1 daughter) (divorced 1969), married 2nd, 1973, Elizabeth Ballingal (divorced 1977), married 3rd, 1977, Camilla Cathcart (1 daughter). *Armed Forces:* Served in War 1943–46, Sub-Lieutenant RNVR. *Career:* Advocate, Scottish Bar 1949; Standing Junior Counsel to Admiralty 1954; QC (Scotland) 1963; Kintyre Pursuivant of Arms 1955–71; Sheriff Principal of Fife and Kinross 1971–74; Judge of the Courts of Appeal of Jersey and Guernsey 1972–79; A Senator of the College of Justice in Scotland 1979–88; A Lord of Appeal in Ordinary 1988–96. *Miscellaneous:* Member: Queen's Body Guard for Scotland, Royal Company of Archers 1951, Historic Buildings Council for Scotland 1972–92. *Honours:* PC 1998. *Recreations:* Shooting, fishing, genealogy, bicycling. *Clubs:* Royal (Perth). *Name, Style and Title:* Raised to the peerage as Baron Jauncey of Tullichettle, of Comrie in the District of Perth and Kinross 1988. *Address:* Rt Hon the Lord Jauncey of Tullichettle, Tullichettle, Comrie, Crieff, Perthshire, PH6 2HU.

BARONESS JAY OF PADDINGTON   Labour

JAY OF PADDINGTON (Life Baroness), Margaret Ann Jay; cr. 1992. Born 18 November 1939. Daughter of Rt Hon. Baron Callaghan of Cardiff, KG (*qv*); educated Blackheath High School; Somerville College, Oxford (BA philosophy, politics and economics). Married 1st, 1961, Hon. Peter Jay, son of late Baron Jay, PC (1 son 2 daughters) (marriage dissolved 1986), married 2nd, 1994, Professor Michael W. Adler, CBE. *Trades Union:* Member, NUJ. *Councils, Public Bodies:* Member, Kensington and Chelsea and Westminster Health Authority 1993–97; Former Member, Central Research and Development Committee for the NHS. *Career:* Various production posts with BBC Television in current affairs and further education 1965–77; A Former Reporter for: BBC Television's *Panorama*, Thames Television's *This Week*; Founder Director, The National AIDS Trust 1988–92; Non-Executive Director: Carlton Television to 1997, Scottish Power to 1997. *House of Lords:* Minister of State, Department of Health 1997–98; Deputy Leader, House of Lords 1997–98; Leader of the House of Lords and Minister for Women (Lord Privy Seal) 1998–. *Whip:* An Opposition Whip 1992–95. *Spokesman:* An Opposition Spokesman on Health 1992–97, Principal Opposition Spokesman 1995–97. *Select Committees:* Member: House of Lords Select Committee on Medical Ethics 1993–94, Select Committee on House of Lords' Offices 1997–. *Other:* Former Chairman: National Association of League of Hospital Friends, North Thames Regional Committee for Research and Development in the NHS; Former Member of Council, The Overseas Development Institute; Former Governor, South Bank University; Former Member, Governing Board: Queen Charlotte's Maternity Hospital, Chelsea Hospital for Women. *Honours:* PC 1998. *Publications: How Rich Can We Get?*, 1972; *Battered – The Story of Child Abuse* (joint author), 1986. *Special Interests:* Health, Overseas Aid and Development, Media, Broadcasting. *Name, Style and Title:* Raised to the peerage as Baroness Jay of Paddington, of Paddington in the City of Westminster 1992. *Address:* Rt Hon the Baroness Jay of Paddington, House of Lords, London, SW1A 0PW.

BARONESS JEGER   Labour

JEGER (Life Baroness), Lena May Jeger; cr. 1979. Born 19 November 1915. Daughter of late Charles and Alice Chivers, of Yorkley, Gloucestershire; educated Southgate County School; Birkbeck College (BA (London), Hon Fellow 1994). Married 1948, Dr Santo Jeger (died 1953), formerly MP for Holborn and St Pancras South. *Trades Union:* Life Member NUJ. *Councils, Public Bodies:* Councillor: St Pancras Borough Council 1945–59, London County Council 1951–54. *Career:* Formerly employed at the Ministry of Information and Foreign Office; Assistant editor in Moscow of *British Ally,* a newspaper published by the British Government for issue in the Soviet Union; Staff writer on *The Guardian* 1959–64; UK representative on the Status of Women Commission of UN 1967; Member, Consultative Assembly of the Council of Europe and of Western European Union 1969–71. *House of Commons:* MP (Labour) for Holborn and St Pancras South 1953–59, 1964–79; Chairman, Government's Working Party on Sewage Disposal 1969–70.*Spokesman:* Opposition Spokesman on: Health 1983–86, Social Security 1983–90.*International Bodies:* Member of: CPA, IPU. *Party Groups (General):* Member, National Executive Committee of the Labour Party 1960–61, 1968–80; Chairman, Labour Party 1979–80. *Name, Style and Title:* Raised to the peerage as Baroness Jeger, of St Pancras in the County of Greater London 1979. *Address:* The Baroness Jeger, 9 Cumberland Terrace, Regents Park, London, NW1 4HS.

EARL JELLICOE   Conservative

JELLICOE (2nd Earl, UK), George Patrick John Rushworth Jellicoe; cr. 1925; Viscount Brocas; Viscount Jellicoe (UK) 1918; (Life) Baron Jellicoe of Southampton 1999. Born 4 April 1918. Son of Admiral of the Fleet 1st Earl, GCB, OM, GCVO. Succeeded his father 1935; educated Winchester; Trinity College, Cambridge (Exhibitioner, 1st Class Hons History). Married 1st, 1944, Patricia Christine O'Kane (2 sons 2 daughters) (marriage dissolved 1966), married 2nd, 1966, Philippa, daughter of late Philip Dunne (1 son 2 daughters). *Armed Forces:* Served in Middle East 1941–45 (despatches thrice, DSO, MC), No 8 Commando, Coldstream Guards, SAS and SBS, Lieutenant-Colonel. *Career:* HM Foreign Service 1947–58, serving in Washington, Brussels and Baghdad (Deputy Secretary General, The Baghdad Pact); Chairman: Greece Fund 1988–94, European Capital 1991–95; Director, Tate & Lyle plc 1973–93, Chairman 1978–83; Director, Sothebys 1973–93; Chairman: Davy Corporation 1985–90, Booker Tate 1988–91; Director: Smiths Industries 1973–86, S. G. Warburg 1964–70, 1973–88, Morgan Crucible 1974–88; President, East European Trade Council, Chairman 1986–90; Chairman, British Overseas Trade Board 1983–86. *Chancellor:* Chancellor, Southampton University 1984–95. *House of Lords:* Joint Parliamentary Secretary, Ministry of Housing and Local Government 1961–62; Minister of State, Home Office 1962–63; First Lord of the Admiralty 1963–64; Minister of Defence for the Royal Navy April-October 1964; Deputy Leader of Opposition in the House of Lords 1967–70; Lord Privy Seal, Leader of the House of Lords and Minister for the Civil Service Department 1970–73. *Whip:* Government Whip (A Lord in Waiting) January-June 1961. *Select Committees:* Former Chairman, Select Committee on Committees. *Other:* Chairman, Council, King's College, London 1977–84; President, London Chamber of Commerce and Industry 1979–82; Chairman, Medical Research Council 1982–90; President: British Heart Foundation 1992–95, Royal Geographical Society 1993–97, The Geographical Club 1993–97, SAS Regimental Association 1996–. Hon. Degrees: Kings College, London, Southampton University, University of Southampton, Long Island, USA.*Trusts, etc:* President, Kennet and Avon Canal Trust 1987–94. *Honours:* DSO 1942; MC 1944; PC 1963; KBE 1986; French Legion d'Honneur; Croix de Guerre; Greek Order of Honour; Greek War Cross. Hon. Fellow, Royal Scottish Geographical Society 1997; FRS. Freeman, City of Athens. Member, Mercers' Company. *Special Interests:* Foreign Affairs, Education, Environment, Arts. *Recreations:* Skiing, travel. *Sportsclubs:* Ski Club of Great Britain. *Clubs:* Brooks's, Special Forces. *Name, Style and Title:* Created a life peer as Baron Jellicoe of Southampton, of Southampton in the County of Hampshire 1999. *Address:* Rt Hon the Earl Jellicoe, KBE, DSO, MC, FRS, Tidcombe Manor, Tidcombe, Nr Marlborough, Wiltshire, SN8 3SL *Tel:* 01264 731225 *Fax:* 01264 731418; 97 Onslow Square, London, SW7 3LU *Tel:* 020 7584 1551.

LORD JENKIN OF RODING   Conservative

JENKIN OF RODING (Life Baron), Charles Patrick Fleeming Jenkin; cr. 1987. Born 7 September 1926. Son of late Charles Jenkin, Industrial Chemist; educated Clifton College; Jesus College, Cambridge. Married 1952, Alison Monica Graham (2 sons 2 daughters). *Armed Forces:* Served in the Cameron Highlanders, including service abroad 1945–48. *Councils, Public Bodies:* Councillor, Hornsey Borough Council 1960–63. *Career:* Went to the Middle Temple as a Harmsworth Scholar; Called to the Bar 1952; A Barrister, practised at the Bar 1952–57; Employed by The Distillers Co. Ltd 1957–70; Adviser, Andersen Consulting, Management Consultants 1985–96; Member, UK Advisory Board, National Economic Research Associates Inc. 1985–98; Chairman, Target Finland Ltd 1987–96; Director, Friends Provident Life Office, Chairman 1988–98; Member, Supervisory Board, Achmea Holding NV (Netherlands) 1992–98; UK Co-Chairman, UK-Japan 2000 Group 1986–90, Board Member 1990–99; Non-Executive Director, Crystalate Holdings plc 1987–90, Chairman 1988–90; Chairman, Lamco Paper Sales Ltd 1987–93; Adviser, Sumitomo Trust and Banking Co. Ltd 1989–; Member, International Advisory Board, Marsh and McLennan Group of Companies (US) 1993–99; Adviser, Thames Estuary Airport Co. Ltd. 1992–; Senior Vice-President, World Congress on Urban Growth and the Environment (Hong Kong) 1992–94. *House of Commons:* MP (Conservative) for Wanstead and Woodford 1964–87; Financial Secretary to the Treasury 1970–72; Chief Secretary to the Treasury 1972–74; Mininster for Energy 1974; Secretary of State for: Social Services 1979–81, Industry September 1981–83, the Environment 1983–85. *Spokesman (Commons):* Opposition Spokesman on Treasury, Trade and Economic Affairs October 1965; An Opposition Front Bench Spokesman for the Treasury 1967–70; Member, Shadow Cabinet and Opposition Spokesman on: Energy 1974–76, Social Services 1976–79. *Select Committees:* Member: House of Lords Offices Committee and Finance and Staffing Sub-Committee 1991–94, House of Lords Select Committee on Sustainable Development 1994–95, Select Committee on Science and Technology 1997–; Chairman, Select Committee on Science and Technology Sub-Committee II (Science and Society) 1999–2000; Member, Select Committees on: Science and Technology Sub-Committee II (Aircraft Cabin Environment) 2000–, Science and Technology Sub-Committee IIA (Human Genetic Databases) 2000–. *Party Groups:* Executive Committee Member, ACP 1996–2000. *International Bodies (General):* Member: CPA, IPU. *Party Groups (General):* Member, Bow Group from 1951; President: Conservative Greater London Area Education Committee 1967–80, Conservative Greater London Area CPC Committee 1981–83, National CPC Committee 1982–85; Vice-President, Greater London Area Conservatives 1987–89, President 1989–93; President, Saffron Walden Constituency Conservative Association 1994–. *Other:* Member, London Council of Social Service 1963–67; Governor, Westfield College (London University) 1964–70; President, Old Cliftonian Society 1987–89; Council Member, Guide Dogs for the Blind Association 1987–97; Council Member, UK Council for Economic and Environmental Development 1987–; Vice-President: National Association of Local Councils 1987–97; Association of Metropolitan Authorities 1987–97; President, British Urban Regeneration Association 1990–96; Chairman, Visual Handicap Group 1991–98; Council Member, Imperial Cancer Research Fund 1991–93, Deputy Chairman 1994–97; President: London Boroughs Association 1993–95, Clifton College, Bristol 1993–99; Member, International Advisory Board, Nijenrode University (Netherlands) 1994–99; Joint President, Association of London Government 1995–; Vice-President, Foundation for Science and Technology 1996–97, Chairman 1997–; Vice-President, Local Government Association 1997–. Fellow, Queen Mary and Westfield College 1991–; Hon. LLD, South Bank University, London 1995. *Trusts, etc:* Chairman, Westfield College Trust 1989–2000; Patron: Stort Trust 1991–, Redbridge Community Trust 1992–95, St Clare Hospice Trust 1992–; Chairman, Forest Healthcare NHS Trust 1992–97; Trustee: Monteverdi Choir and Orchestra 1992–, Conservative Agents Superannuation Fund 1992–2000; Patron, London North-East Community Foundation 1995–. *Honours:* PC 1973. Freeman, City of London 1985; Hon. Freeman, London Borough of Redbridge 1988. *Special Interests:* Economic Policy, Industry, Science, Technology, Health, Disabled, Energy, Housing, Planning, Financial Services. *Recreations:* Gardening, DIY, bricklaying, sailing, music. *Clubs:* West Essex Conservative Club. *Name, Style and Title:* Raised to the peerage as Baron Jenkin of Roding, of Wanstead and Woodford in Greater London 1987. *Address:* Rt Hon the Lord Jenkin of Roding, House of Lords, London, SW1A 0PW *Tel:* 020 7219 6966 *Fax:* 020 7219 0759 *E-Mail:* jenkinp@parliament.uk.

LORD JENKINS OF HILLHEAD   Liberal Democrat

JENKINS OF HILLHEAD (Life Baron), Roy Harris Jenkins; cr. 1987. Born 11 November 1920. Son of late Arthur Jenkins, MP for Pontypool 1935–46; educated Abersychan Grammar School; Balliol College, Oxford. Married 1945, Dame (Mary) Jennifer, DBE, daughter of late Sir Parker Morris (2 sons 1 daughter). *Armed Forces:* Served War of 1939–45; RA 1942–46; Captain 1944–46. *Career:* Member, Staff of Industrial and Commercial Finance Corporation Ltd 1946–48; Director, Financial Operations, John Lewis Partnership 1962–64; Director, Morgan Grenfell Holdings Ltd 1981–82; President, European Commission 1977–81; Chairman, Independent Commission on the Voting System 1998. *House of Commons:* Contested (Labour) Solihull division of Warwickshire at General Election 1945; MP (Labour): Central Southwark 1948–50, Stechford, Birmingham 1950–76; PPS to Secretary of State for Commonwealth Relations 1949–50; Minister of Aviation 1964–65; Home Secretary 1965–67; Chancellor of the Exchequer 1967–70; Home Secretary 1974–76; MP (SDP) Glasgow Hillhead 1983–87. *Spokesman (Commons):* Senior Spokesman of the Social Democrat Party 1983. *Chancellor:* Chancellor, Oxford University 1987–. *Spokesman:* Treasury Spokesman for the Alliance 1987. *Party Groups:* Leader, Liberal Democrat Peers 1988–97. *Party Groups (General):* Chairman, Oxford University Democratic Socialist Club; Member, Executive Committee of Fabian Society 1949–61; Chairman, Fabian Society 1957–58; Deputy Leader, Labour Party 1970–72; Member, Joint Leadership Social Democratic Party 1981–82; Elected Leader July 1982-June 83. *Other:* Secretary and Librarian, Oxford Union Society; Member, Committee of Management, Society of Authors 1956–60; President, Royal Society of Literature 1988–. *Awards Granted:* Charlemagne Prize 1972; Robert Schuman Prize 1972; Prix Bentinck 1978. Hon. Fellow, Balliol College, Oxford 1968; Hon. DCL, Oxford 1973; 30 honorary degrees from the United Kingdom, Italy, Barbados, Belgium, Ireland, USA. *Trusts, etc:* Trustee, Pilgrim Trust 1973–98. *Miscellaneous:* Governor, British Film Institute 1955–58; President, UWIST 1975–81. *Honours:* PC 1964; Order of European Merit (Luxembourg) 1976; Grand Cross, Order of Charles III (Spain) 1980; Order of Merit (Italy) 1990; Ordem do Infante Dom Henrique of Portugal 1993; OM 1993; Légion d'Honneur (France) 1999. Hon. Foreign Member, American Academic Arts and Sciences 1973; Honorary Fellow, British Academy 1993. Freeman, City of Brussels 1980. Liveryman, Goldsmiths' Company 1965. *Publications:* Editor *Purpose and Policy* (a volume of the Prime Minister's Speeches), 1947; *Mr Attlee: An Interim Biography*, 1948; *Pursuit of Progress*, 1953; *Mr Balfour's Poodle*, 1954; *Sir Charles Dilke: A Victorian Tragedy*, 1958; *The Labour Case* (Penguin Special), 1959; *Asquith*, 1964; *Essays and Speeches*, 1967; *Afternoon on the Potomac*, 1972; *What Matters Now*, 1972; *Nine Men of Power*, 1975; *Partnership of Principle*, 1985; *Truman*, 1986; *Baldwin*, 1987; *Gallery of Twentieth Century Portraits*, 1988; *European Diary*, 1989; *A Life at the Centre*, 1991; *Portraits and Miniatures*, 1993; *Gladstone*, 1995; *The Chancellors*, 1998. *Clubs:* Athenaeum, Beefsteak, Brooks's, Pratt's, Reform, United Oxford and Cambridge University. *Name, Style and Title:* Raised to the peerage as Baron Jenkins of Hillhead, of Pontypool in the County of Gwent 1987. *Address:* Rt Hon the Lord Jenkins of Hillhead, OM, 2 Kensington Park Gardens, London, W11 3HB; St Amand's House, East Hendred, Oxfordshire, OX12 8LF *E-Mail:* Macphersong@parliament.uk.

LORD JENKINS OF PUTNEY   Labour

JENKINS OF PUTNEY (Life Baron), Hugh Gater Jenkins; cr. 1981. Born 27 July 1908. Son of late Joseph Walter Jenkins, Dairyman and late Florence Gater; educated Enfield Grammar School. Married 1st, 1936, Marie Crosbie (died 1989), married 2nd, 1991, Helena Maria Pavlidis (died 1994). *Trades Union:* Trade Unionist since 1930; Member: Prudential Staff Union 1930–40, MSF 1947–, Actors Equity 1948–. *Armed Forces:* Flight-Lieutenant, Royal Air Force during World War II. *Councils, Public Bodies:* London County Councillor 1958–64, Member, Town Planning Committee. *Career:* Prudential Assurance Company 1930–40, Assistant-Superintendent 1935–40; Research and Publicity Officer, National Union of Bank Employees 1946–50; Former Editor, *The Bank Officer;* Assistant General Secretary, Actors' Equity to 1964. *House of Commons:* Contested (Labour) Enfield West 1950, Mitcham 1955; MP (Labour) for Wandsworth, Putney division October 15, 1964–79; Minister for the Arts 1974–76. *Spokesman (Commons):* Spokesman for the Arts 1973–74; Former Member, Public Records Committee. *Party Groups (Commons):* Member, Tribune Group.

International Bodies (Commons): Member: CPA, IPU. *Spokesman:* Spokesman on the Arts 1981–83. *International Bodies:* Member: CPA, IPU. *International Bodies (General):* Member, British-American Security Information Committee. *Party Groups (General):* Member, London Labour Party Executive Committee; Chairman, Victory For Socialism; Vice-Chairman, Labour Action For Peace.*Other:* Former Chairman, now Vice-President, Campaign for Nuclear Disarmament. *Trusts, etc:* President, Theatres Trust. *Miscellaneous:* Life-President, Theatres Advisory Council; Former Member: The Arts Council, The National Theatre Board. *Publications: The Culture Gap*, 1980; *Rank and File*, 1981; As well as radio plays (BBC Radio Four), various pamphlets and contributions to journals and newspapers. *Special Interests:* Disarmament, Arts, Trade Unions, Media, Nuclear Disarmament. *Recreations:* Avoiding retirement, writing, listening, talking, viewing, reading, concert and theatre-going.*Name, Style and Title:* Raised to the peerage as Baron Jenkins of Putney, of Wandsworth in Greater London 1981.*Address:* The Lord Jenkins of Putney, House of Lords, London, SW1A 0PW *Tel:* House of Lords 020 7219 6706 *Tel:* 020 8788 0371.

LORD JOFFE   Cross-Bencher

JOFFE (Life Baron), Joel Goodman Joffe; cr. 2000. Born 12 May 1932. Son of Abraham and Dena Joffe; educated Marist Brothers' College, Johannesburg, South Africa; University of Witwatersrand (BCom, LLB). Married 1962, Vanetta Pretorius (3 daughters). *Career:* Admitted Solicitor, Johannesburg 1956; Called to the Bar, South Africa 1962; Human Rights lawyer 1958–65; Director and secretary, Abbey Life Assurance Company 1965–70; Director, Joint Managing Director and Deputy Chairman, Allied Dunbar, Life Assurance Company 1971–91; Chairman, Swindon Private Hospital 1982–87; Oxfam: Hon. Secretary 1982–85, Executive Committee Chairman 1985–93, Chairman 1995–. *Other:* Chairman: Swindon Health Authority 1988–93, Swindon and Marlborough NHS Trust 1993–95. Two honorary doctorates.*Trusts, etc:* Trustee of: Chair, Allied Dunbar Charitable Trust 1974–93, Action for Disability and Development 1984–98, Oxfam 1979–, Canon Collins Educational Trust for Southern Africa 1985–, Legal Assistance Trust for Southern Africa 1995–, International Alert 1994–2000, The Smith Institute 1999–. *Miscellaneous:* Member, Royal Commission on Long Term Care for the Elderly 1997–98, Special Adviser to the South African Minister of Transport 1997–98. *Honours:* CBE 1999. *Publications: The Rivonia Trial*, 1995. *Special Interests:* Human Rights, Developing World, Financial Services, Consumer Protection.*Recreations:* Tennis, skiing. *Clubs:* Royal Commonwealth Society.*Name, Style and Title:* Raised to the peerage as Baron Joffe, of Liddington in the County of Wiltshire 2000. *Address:* The Lord Joffe, CBE, Liddington Manor, Liddington, Swindon, Wiltshire, SN4 0HD *Tel:* 01793 790203 *Fax:* 01793 791144.

LORD JOHNSTON OF ROCKPORT   Conservative

JOHNSTON OF ROCKPORT (Life Baron), Charles Collier Johnston; cr. 1987. Born 4 March 1915. Son of Captain Charles Moore Johnston (killed, Somme, 1916) and late Muriel Florence Mellon; educated Tonbridge. Married 1st, June 15, 1939, Audrey Boyes, only daughter of late Edgar Monk (2 sons), married 2nd, September 1, 1981, Mrs Yvonne Shearman, daughter of late Reginald and Dora Marley. *Armed Forces:* Commissioned 1938, Territorial; RA 1939–46; Retired as Major. *Career:* Managing Director, Standtex International Ltd 1948–76, Chairman 1951–77; Chairman: Thames & Kennet Marina Ltd 1982–94, James Burn International 1986–, Standtex Holdings Ltd 1983. *Party Groups (General):* Chairman, Macclesfield Constituency Conservative Association 1961–65; Hon. Treasurer, North West Conservatives, Member, Conservative Board of Finance 1965–71; Chairman, North West Area Conservatives 1971–76; A Vice-President, National Union of Conservative and Unionist Associations, Executive Committee 1965–87, Chairman 1976–81, President 1986–87; Joint Hon. Treasurer, Conservative Party 1984–87; National Chairman, Conservative Friends of Israel 1983–86. *Miscellaneous:* An official observer at 1980 elections, Zimbabwe (Boyd Commission). *Honours:* Kt 1973. *Recreations:* Gardening, Spectator Sports. *Name, Style and Title:* Raised to the peerage as Baron Johnston of Rockport, of Caversham in the Royal County of Berkshire 1987.*Address:* The Lord Johnston of Rockport, TD, The Dower House, Marston, Devizes, Wiltshire, SN10 5SN *Tel:* 01380 725782 *Tel:* 020 7730 3557.

LORD JOPLING Conservative

JOPLING (Life Baron), (Thomas) Michael Jopling; cr. 1997. Born 10 December 1930. Son of late Mark Jopling; educated Cheltenham College; King's College, Newcastle upon Tyne (BSc Agriculture). Married April 1958, Gail, daughter of late Ernest Dickinson (2 sons). *Councils, Public Bodies:* Councillor, Thirsk Rural District Council for six years; DL: Cumbria 1991–97, North Yorkshire 1998–. *Career:* Farmer, farms 500 acres. *House of Commons:* Contested (Conservative) Wakefield at 1959 General Election; MP (Conservative) for Westmorland 1964–83 and for Westmorland and Lonsdale 1983–97; Sponsored Private Member's Bill on Parish Councils 1969; PPS to the Minister of Agriculture, Fisheries and Food June 1970–71; Shadow Cabinet 1975–76; Minister of Agriculture, Fisheries and Food 1983–87; Sponsored Private Member's Bills on: Children's Seat Belts 1990, Antarctica 1994. *Whip (Commons):* Assistant Whip 1971–73; Lord Commissioner of the Treasury (Government Whip) 1973–74; Parliamentary Secretary to the Treasury (Chief Whip) 1979–83. *Spokesman (Commons):* Front Bench Spokesman on Agriculture 1974–79. *Select Committees:* Former Co-opted Member, Select Committee on European Communities Sub-Committee D (Agriculture, Fisheries and Food) 1997–99; Member, Select Committee on European Union 1999–; Sub-Committee C (Common Foreign and Security) 1999–. *Party Groups:* Committee Member, Association of Conservative Peers 1997–. *International Bodies (General):* Executive Committee, UK Branch of CPA 1974–79, 1987–97, Vice-Chairman 1977–78 Executive, CPA HQ 1988–89; UK Delegate, North Atlantic Assembly 1987–97; Leader of UK Delegation, OSCE Parliamentary Assembly 1991–97; Delegate 2000–. *Other:* Member, National Council of NFU 1962–65; President, Auto Cycle Union 1990–. Hon. DCL, Newcastle 1992. *Trusts, etc:* Fellow, Industry and Parliament Trust. *Honours:* PC 1979. Member, Farmers Company. *Clubs:* Beefsteak, Buck's, Royal Automobile. *Name, Style and Title:* Raised to the peerage as Baron Jopling, of Ainderby Quernhow in the County of North Yorkshire 1997. *Address:* Rt Hon the Lord Jopling, DL, Ainderby Hall, Thirsk, North Yorkshire, YO7 4HZ.

LORD JORDAN Labour

JORDAN (Life Baron), William Brian Jordan; cr. 2000. Born 28 January 1936. Son of Walter and Alice Jordan; educated Secondary Modern School, Birmingham. Married 1958, Jean Ann Livesey (3 daughters). *Trades Union:* Member of: AEEU England, FGTB Belgium. *Councils, Public Bodies:* Board Member, English Partnerships. *Career:* Convenor of shop stewards, Guest, Keen and Nettlefold 1966; full time AUEW divisional organiser 1976; President, AEU, then AEEU 1986–95; Member, TUC General Council 1986–95; General Secretary, ICFTU (International Confederation of Free Trade Unions) 1995–. *International Bodies (General):* President: European Metal Workers Federation 1986–95, International Metal Workers Federation 1986–95. *Other:* Governor: LSE 1987–, Manchester Business School 1987–92, BBC 1988–98. DUniv, Central England 1993; Hon. DSc, Cranfield 1995. *Miscellaneous:* Member: NEDC 1986–92, Engineering Industry Training Board 1986–91, Council, Industrial Society 1987–. *Honours:* CBE 1992. *Recreations:* Reading, watching football. *Name, Style and Title:* Raised to the peerage as Baron Jordan, of Bournville in the County of West Midlands 2000. *Address:* The Lord Jordan, CBE, House of Lords, London, SW1A 0PW; ICFTU (International Confederation of Free Trade Unions), Boulevard du Roi Albert II, 5, B–1210 Brussels, Belgium.

LORD JUDD Labour

JUDD (Life Baron), Frank Ashcroft Judd; cr. 1991. Born 28 March 1935. Son of late Charles Judd, CBE, and late Helen Judd, JP; educated City of London School; London School of Economics (BSc Economics). Married 1961, Christine Elizabeth Willington (2 daughters). *Trades Union:* Member: MSF, GMB. *Armed Forces:* Short Service Commission, RAF 1957–59. *Career:* General Secretary, International Voluntary Service 1960–66; Associate Director, International Defence and Aid Fund for Southern Africa 1979–80; Director, Voluntary Service Overseas 1980–85; Director, Oxfam 1985–91; Chairman, International Council of Voluntary Agencies 1985–90; Non-Executive Director, Portsmouth Harbour Renaissance; Senior Fellow (professional) Saferworld;

Consultant (professional) to De Montfort University on international and community action issues.*House of Commons:* Contested (Labour): Sutton and Cheam 1959 General Election, Portsmouth West 1964 General Election; MP (Labour) for: Portsmouth West 1966–74, Portsmouth North 1974–79; PPS to: Minister of Housing 1967–70, Leader of Opposition 1970–72; Parliamentary Under-Secretary of State (Navy) Ministry of Defence 1974–76; Minister of State: Overseas Development 1976–77, Foreign and Commonwealth Office 1977–79. *Spokesman (Commons):* Opposition Defence Spokesman (Navy) 1972–74. *International Bodies (Commons):* Member, Parliamentary Delegation to Council of Europe and WEU 1969–72. *Spokesman:* An Opposition Spokesman on Foreign Affairs 1991–92; Principal Opposition Spokesman on: Development and Co-operation 1992–97, Education 1992–94; An Opposition Spokesman on Defence 1995–97. *Select Committees:* Co-opted Member, Select Committee on European Communities Sub-Committee D (Environment, Agriculture, Public Health and Consumer Protection) 1997–. *International Bodies:* Member, Parliamentary Delegation to Council of Europe and WEU 1997–2000; Chair. Refugee Sub-Committee, Council of Europe 1998–, British-American Parliamentary Group, Parliamentary University Group; All Party Parliamentary Group for: World Government, on Citzenship; Rapporteur and Chair, Ad Hoc Committee on Chechnya of the Council of Euorpe 1999–. *International Bodies (General):* Member, Commission on Global Governance. *Party Groups (General):* Member, Labour Party since 1951; Member, Fabian Society, former Chair; Member, Christian Socialist Movement. *Other:* President, YMCA (England); Governor: London School of Economics, Lancaster University, Vice-President: Intermediate Technology Group, Council for National Parks; Member: Royal Institute for International Affairs, Oxfam Association; Chair, Social Responsibility Forum of Churches Together in Cumbria and North Lancashire. Five honorary doctorates/fellowships. *Trusts, etc:* Trustee: Overseas Development Institute, Global Education Trust, Beryl Le Poer Power Trust (Royal Institute of International Affairs); Trustee, World Humanity Action Trust; Member, North West Regional Committee of the National Trust. *Miscellaneous:* Member British Council,. FRSA. Freeman, City of Portsmouth 1995. *Publications:* Co-author: *Radical Future,* 1967; *Purpose in Socialism,* 1973; Also various articles on current affairs. *Special Interests:* Foreign Affairs, Third World, Defence, Education, Refugees, Migration, Race Relations, Penal Affairs and Policy.*Recreations:* Walking, family holidays. *Clubs:* Royal Commonwealth Society. *Name, Style and Title:* Raised to the peerage as Baron Judd, of Portsea in the County of Hampshire 1991. *Address:* The Lord Judd, House of Lords, London, SW1A 0PW.

K

KEITH OF CASTLEACRE (Life Baron), Kenneth Alexander Keith; cr.1980. Born 30 August 1916. Son of late Edward Charles Keith; educated Rugby. Married 1st, 1946, Lady Ariel Olivia Winifred Baird (1 son 1 daughter) (divorced 1958), married 2nd, 1962, Mrs Nancy Hayward (divorced 1972, she died 1990), married 3rd, 1973, Mrs Marie Hanbury. *Armed Forces:* 2nd Lieutenant, Welsh Guards 1939; Lieutenant-Colonel 1945; Served in North Africa, Italy, France and Germany; (despatches, Croix de Guerre with Silver Star). *Career:* Trained as a chartered accountant; Merchant Banker; Assistant to Director General, Political Intelligence Department, Foreign Office 1945–46; Director: Philip Hill and Partners 1947–51, Eagle Star Insurance Co. 1955–75; Vice-Chairman, BEA 1964–71; Member, NEDC 1964–71; Chairman, Economic Planning Council for East Anglia 1965–70; Director, National Provincial Bank 1967–69; Chairman, Hill Samuel Group Ltd 1970–80; Director, British Airways 1971–72; Chairman, Philip Hill Investment Trust Ltd 1972–87; Chairman and Chief Executive, Rolls-Royce Ltd 1972–80; Member, CBI/NEDC Liaison Committee 1974–78, Vice-Chairman, Beecham Group Ltd 1974–87, Director, Standard Telephones & Cables Ltd 1977–89, Member, National Defence Industries Council to January 1980; Chairman, Standard Telephones & Cables Ltd 1985–1989; Chairman, Beecham Group Ltd 1986–87; Member: SBAC, Defence Industries Council. *Other:* Vice-President, Engineering Employers' Federation to January 1980; Governor, National Institute of Economic and Social Research; President, British Standards Institute 1989–94. Hon. Companion, Royal Aeronautical Society 1979.*Recreations:* Shooting, golf. *Clubs:* White's, Links (New York). *Name, Style and Title:* Raised to the peerage as Baron Keith of Castleacre, of Swaffham in the County of Norfolk 1980. *Address:* The Lord Keith of Castleacre, 9 Eaton Square, London, SW1W 9DB *Tel:* 020 7730 4000; The Wicken House, Castle Acre, Norfolk, PE32 2BP*Tel:* 01760 755225.

LORD KEITH OF KINKEL — Cross-Bencher

KEITH OF KINKEL (Life Baron), Henry Shanks Keith; cr. 1977. Born 7 February 1922. Son of late Rt Hon. Baron Keith of Avonholm; educated Edinburgh Academy; Magdalen College, Oxford (MA); Edinburgh University (LLB). Married 1955, Alison Hope Alan Brown, MA, JP (4 sons 1 daughter).*Armed Forces:* Served Second World War Scots Guards (mentioned in despatches). *Career:* Advocate, Scottish Bar 1950; Barrister, Gray's Inn 1951; QC (Scot) 1962; Sheriff, Roxburgh, Berwick and Selkirk 1970–71; Senator, College of Justice in Scotland with judicial title of Lord Keith 1971–77; Bencher, Gray's Inn 1976; Deputy Chairman, Parliamentary Boundary Commission for Scotland 1976; A Lord of Appeal in Ordinary 1977–96; Chairman, Committee on the Powers of the Revenue Departments 1980–84. Hon. Fellow, Magdalen College, Oxford 1978. *Honours:* PC 1976; GBE 1997. *Clubs:* Flyfishers'. *Name, Style and Title:* Raised to the peerage as Baron Keith of Kinkel, of Strathtummel in the District of Perth and Kinross 1977. *Address:* Rt Hon the Lord Keith of Kinkel, GBE, House of Lords, London, SW1A 0PW.

LORD KELVEDON — Conservative

KELVEDON (Life Baron), (Henry) Paul Guinness Channon; cr. 1997. Born 9 October 1935. Son of late Sir Henry Channon, MP and of late Lady Honor Svejdar, daughter of 2nd Earl of Iveagh, KG, CB, CMG; educated Eton; Christ Church, Oxford. Married 1963, Mrs Ingrid Olivia Georgia Guinness, daughter of late Major Guy Wyndham, MC (1 son 1 daughter, 1 daughter deceased). *Armed Forces:* 2nd Lieutenant, Royal Horse Guards (The Blues) 1955–56. *House of Commons:* MP (Conservative) for Southend West 1959–97; PPS: to Minister of Power 1959–60, to Home Secretary 1960–62, to First Secretary of State July 1962, to Foreign Secretary 1963–64; Joint Parliamentary Secretary to the Minister of Housing and Local Government June-October 1970; Joint Parliamentary Under-Secretary of State, Department of the Environment 1970–72; Minister of State for Northern Ireland 1972; Minister for Housing and Construction 1972–74; Minister of State, Civil Service Department 1979–81; Minister for: The Arts 1981–83, Trade 1983–86; Secretary of State for: Trade and Industry 1986–87, Transport 1987–89. *Spokesman (Commons):* Opposition Spokesman on: Arts and Amenities 1967–70; Price and Consumer Affairs February-November 1974, The Environment 1974–75. *International Bodies (General):* Deputy Leader, Conservative Group on Council of Europe 1976–79. *Miscellaneous:* Chairman, British Association for Central and Eastern Europe 1992–.*Honours:* PC 1980. *Clubs:* White's, Buck's. *Name, Style and Title:* Raised to the peerage as Baron Kelvedon, of Ongar in the County of Essex 1997. *Address:* Rt Hon the Lord Kelvedon, House of Lords, London, SW1A 0PW.

BARONESS KENNEDY OF THE SHAWS — Labour

KENNEDY OF THE SHAWS (Life Baroness), Helena Ann Kennedy; cr. 1997. Born 12 May 1950. Daughter of late Joshua Kennedy and of Mary Kennedy; educated Holyrood Secondary School, Glasgow; Council of Legal Education. Partner 1977–84, Roger Iain Mitchell (1 son); married 1986, Dr Iain Louis Hutchison (1 son 1 daughter). *Career:* Called to the Bar, Gray's Inn 1972; Established Chambers at: Garden Court 1974, Tooks Court 1984, Doughty Street 1990. *Chancellor:* Chancellor, Oxford Brookes University 1994–. *Other:* Member: National Board, Women's Legal Defence Fund 1989–91, Council, Howard League for Penal Reform 1989–, Bar Council 1990–93, Committee, Association of Women Barristers 1991–92, Hampstead Theatre Board. *Awards Granted:* Women's Network Award for her work on women and justice 1992; UK Woman of Europe Award 1995; National Federation of Women's Institutes Making a World of Difference Award Institutes for her work on equal rights 1996; The Times Newspaper (Joint) Lifetime Achievement Award 1997. 11 honorary law doctorates. *Miscellaneous:* Board Member, City Limits Magazine 1982–84; Chairman, Haldane Society 1983–86, Vice-President 1986–; Broadcaster: First female moderator, Hypotheticals (Granada) on surrogate motherhood and artificial insemination; Presenter: Heart of the Matter, BBC 1987, Putting Women in the Picture, BBC2 1987, Time Gentlemen Please, BBC Scotland 1994; Has also presented many other television programmes; Board Member: New Statesman 1990–96, Counsel Magazine 1990–; Chairman, Charter '88 1992–97; Chairman, Standing Committee for Youth Justice, NACRO 1993–; British Council's Law Advisory Committee; Advisory Board, International Centre for Prison Studies;

Advisor on Steering Group, University College London's Diploma in Forensic Psycho-Therapy; Chair, London International Festival of Theatre; Chairman, British Council 1998–. Fellow, Royal Society of Arts; Hon. Fellow, Institute of Advanced Legal Studies 1997. *Publications:* Co-author: *The Bar on Trial*, 1978, *Child Abuse Within the Family*, 1984, *Balancing Acts*, 1989; *Eve was Framed*, 1992; Leader of enquiry into health, environmental and safety aspects of Atomic Weapons Establishment *Secrecy Versus Safety*, 1994; *Learning Works* Official report for the FEFC on widening participation in Further Education, 1997; *Inquiry into Violence in Penal Institutions for Young People*, report published 1995; Lectures; Has contributed articles on law, civil liberties and women. *Recreations:* Theatre, spending time with family and friends. *Name, Style and Title:* Raised to the peerage as Baroness Kennedy of The Shaws, of Cathcart in the City of Glasgow 1997. *Address:* The Baroness Kennedy of The Shaws, QC, c/o Hilary Hard, 12 Athelstan Close, Harold Wood, Essex, RM3 0QJ.

LORD KILPATRICK OF KINCRAIG   Cross-Bencher

KILPATRICK OF KINCRAIG (Life Baron), Robert Kilpatrick; cr. 1996. Born 29 July 1926. Son of late Robert Kilpatrick; educated Buckhaven High School; Edinburgh University (MB, ChB 1949, MD 1960) (Ettles Scholar, Leslie Gold Medallist). Married 1950, Elizabeth Gibson Page Forbes (2 sons 1 daughter). *Career:* Medical Registrar, Edinburgh 1951–54; Sheffield University: Lecturer 1955–66, Professor of Clinical Pharmacology and Therapeutics 1966–75; Dean, Faculty of Medicine 1971–74; Member, General Medical Council 1972–76, 1979–, President 1989–95; Chairman, Society of Endocrinology 1975–78; Chairman, Advisory Committee on Pesticides 1975–87; Leicester University 1975 89: Dean, Faculty of Medicine 1975–89, Professor and Head of Department of Clinical Pharmacology and Therapeutics 1975–83, Professor of Medicine 1984–89; President, British Medical Association 1997–98. Dr hc Edinburgh 1987; Hon. LLD, Dundee 1992; Hon. DSc: Hull 1994, Leicester 1994; Hon. LLD, Sheffield 1995. *Honours:* CBE 1979; Kt 1986. FRCP (Ed) 1963; FRCP 1975; FRCPGlas 1991; Hon. FRCS, 1995; Hon. FRCP, Dublin 1995; Hon. FRCS, Edinburgh 1996; Hon. RC Path. 1996; FRSE 1998. *Publications:* Several articles in medical and scientific journals. *Special Interests:* Health, Education, Professional Self-Regulation. *Recreations:* Golf. *Clubs:* Royal and Ancient (St Andrews), New (Edinburgh). *Name, Style and Title:* Raised to the peerage as Baron Kilpatrick of Kincraig, of Dysart in the District of Kirkcaldy 1996. *Address:* The Lord Kilpatrick of Kincraig, CBE, 12 Wester Coates Gardens, Edinburgh, EH12 5LT.

LORD KIMBALL   Conservative

KIMBALL (Life Baron), Marcus Richard Kimball; cr. 1985. Born 18 October 1928. Son of late Major Lawrence Kimball; educated Eton; Trinity College, Cambridge. Married March 15, 1956, June Mary, eldest daughter of Montagu Fenwick (2 daughters). *Armed Forces:* Captain, Leicestershire and Derbyshire Yeomanry (TA). *Councils, Public Bodies:* Member, Rutland County Council 1955–62; DL, Leicestershire 1984–97, Rutland 1997–. *Career:* Director, The Royal Trust Bank 1970–93; Elected to the Council of Lloyd's of London 1982–90; Chairman, South East Assured Tenancies plc 1989–96; Chairman, British Greyhound Racing Fund Ltd 1993–96. *House of Commons:* Contested (Conservative) Derby South 1955; MP (Conservative) for Gainsborough 1956–83. *Select Committees:* Member of: Liaison Committee 1998–, Procedure Committee 1999–. *Party Groups (General):* Chairman, East Midlands Area Young Conservatives 1954–58. *Other:* Privy Council Representative, Royal College of Veterinary Surgeons 1969–82; Chairman: British Field Sports Society 1966–82, Firearms Consultation Committee 1989–94; President: National Light Horse Breeding Society 1990–, Olympia International Show Jumping Championship 1991–; President, British Field Sports Society 1996–98, Deputy President 1998–. *Trusts, etc:* Chairman, University of Cambridge Veterinary School Trust 1989–97. *Honours:* Kt 1981. Hon. Associate, Royal College of Veterinary Surgeons 1982. *Special Interests:* Finance, Agriculture. *Recreations:* Fishing, hunting, shooting. *Clubs:* White's, Pratt's. *Name, Style and Title:* Raised to the peerage as Baron Kimball, of Easton in the County of Leicestershire 1985. *Address:* The Lord Kimball, DL, Great Easton Manor, Market Harborough, Leicestershire, LE16 8TB *Tel:* 01536 770333 *Fax:* 01536 770453.

LORD KING OF WARTNABY — Conservative

KING OF WARTNABY (Life Baron), John Leonard King; cr. 1983. Son of late Albert John King. Married 1st, 1941, Lorna Sykes (died 1969) (3 sons 1 daughter), married 2nd, 1970, Hon. Isabel Monckton. *Career:* Founded: Whitehouse Industries Ltd 1945, Ferrybridge Industries Ltd; Chairman, Pollard Ball & Roller Bearing Co Ltd 1961–69; Babcock International Group plc (firstly Babcock and Wilcox Ltd, secondly Babcock International plc, thirdly FKI Babcock plc and fourthly Babcock International Group plc) 1970–, President 1994–; Dennis Motor Holdings Ltd 1970–72; NEDC Finance Committee, Review Board for Government Contracts 1975–78; SKF (UK) Ltd 1976–89; British Nuclear Associates Ltd 1978–89; British Airways 1981–93, President 1993–; Numerous directorships, especially in aviation companies, in USA and UK; Member: Advisory Committee, Optima Fund Management LP, USA, Advisory Council, Westinghouse Electric Europe. *Other:* Chairman, British Olympics Appeal Committee 1975–78; MacMillan Appeal for Continuing Care (Cancer Relief) 1977–78; Alexandra Rose Day 1980–85; Committee Member, Ranfurly Library Service; MFH Badsworth Foxhounds 1949–58; Duke of Rutlands Foxhounds (Belvoir) 1958–72, Chairman 1972–; President: Brooklands Club, British Show Jumping Association. Hon. Dr Hum., Gardner-Webb College (USA) 1980; Hon. Dr of Science, Cranfield Institute of Technology; Hon. City and Guilds Insignia Award in Technology. *Trusts, etc:* Trustee: Royal Opera House Trust, Liver Research Unit, Blenheim Foundation; Advisory Council, Prince's Youth Business Trust. *Honours:* Kt 1979; Commander of the Royal Order of the Polar Star (Sweden) 1983. ARAeS 1982 (President Heathrow Branch); FCIT 1982; FBIM; Companion, Royal Aeronautical Society 1985–87. Freedom, City of London 1984. *Clubs:* White's, Pratt's, The Brook (New York). *Name, Style and Title:* Raised to the peerage as Baron King of Wartnaby, of Wartnaby in the County of Leicestershire 1983. *Address:* The Lord King of Wartnaby, Wartnaby, Melton Mowbray, Leicestershire, LE14 3HY.

LORD KING OF WEST BROMWICH — Labour

KING OF WEST BROMWICH (Life Baron), Tarsem King; cr. 1999. Born 24 April 1937. Son of Ujagar Singh, and Dalip Kaur; educated Khalsa High School, Dosanjh, Kalan, Punjab, India; Punjab University, India (BA Exam); National Foundry College, Wolverhampton (Diploma in Foundry Technology and Management); Aston University, Birmingham (Post Graduate Diploma in Management Studies); Teacher Training College, Wolverhampton (Teachers' Certificate); Essex University (MSc Statistics and Operational Research). Married 1957, Mrs Mohinder Kaur, daughter of Gurdev Singh and Satwant Kaur (1 son). *Trades Union:* Member, NUT. *Councils, Public Bodies:* Councillor, Sandwell Metropolitan Borough Council 1979–, Deputy Mayor, 1982–83, Deputy Leader 1992–97, Leader 1997–; JP, West Bromwich 1987–. *Career:* Laboratory Assistant, Coneygre Foundry 1960–62; Foundry Trainee, Birmid Group of Companies 1964–65; Teacher, Churchfields School, West Bromwich 1968–74; Deputy Head, Mathematics Department, Great Barr School, Birmingham 1974–90; Managing Director, Sandwell Polybags Ltd 1990–. *Select Committees:* Member: Hybrid Instruments Committee 1999–, Select Committee on European Union, Sub-Committee F (Social Affairs, Education and Home Affairs) 2000–. *Party Groups (General):* National Policy Forum Member, West Midlands Constituency Labour Party; Co-operative Party Sponsored Councillor; Secretary, West Bromwich Ward Branch Labour Party; Treasurer: Sandwell Local Government Committee, Executive Member, West Bromwich East GC; Member, SEA. *Other:* Member: Black Country Joint Advisory Group, Black Country Consortium; Vice-Chair: Faith in Sandwell Organisation, Director, Smethwick Asian Sheltered and Residential Association; Vice-President, West Bromwich and District YMCA; Vice-Chair, West Midlands Joint Committee. *Trusts, etc:* Member, South Staffordshire Water Company Charitable Trust. *Miscellaneous:* Represents Sandwell in: West Midlands Local Goverment Association, West Midlands Regional Chamber. MSc; CEd; DipFTM; DMS; MBIM. *Special Interests:* Local Government, Education, Small Businesses. *Recreations:* Reading, music. *Name, Style and Title:* Raised to the peerage as Baron King of West Bromwich, of West Bromwich in the County of West Midlands 1999. *Address:* Councillor The Lord King of West Bromwich, Sandwell MBC, Leader's Office, Sandwell Council House, PO Box 2374, Oldbury, West Midlands, B69 3DE *Tel:* 0121–569 3045 *Fax:* 0121–569 3051; 27 Roebuck Lane, West Bromwich, B70 6QP.

LORD KINGSDOWN Cross-Bencher

KINGSDOWN (Life Baron), Robert (Robin) Leigh-Pemberton; cr. 1993. Born 5 January 1927. Son of late Robert Douglas Leigh-Pemberton, MBE, MC; educated St Peter's Court, Broadstairs; Eton; Trinity College, Oxford (MA). Married 1953, Rosemary Davina, OBE, daughter of late Lieutenant-Colonel D. W. A. W. Forbes, MC and late Dowager Marchioness of Exeter (4 sons and 1 son deceased). *Armed Forces:* Served Grenadier Guards 1945–48; Hon. Colonel: Kent and Sharpshooters Yeomanry Squadron 1979–92, 265 (Kent and County of London Yeomanry) Signal Squadron (V) 1979–92, 5th Volunteer Battalion, The Queen's Regiment 1987–93. *Councils, Public Bodies:* Councillor, Kent County Council 1961–77, Chairman 1972–75; JP, Kent 1961–75; DL, Kent 1970–72, Vice-Lord-Lieutenant 1972–82, Lord Lieutenant 1982–. *Career:* Called to Bar, Inner Temple 1954; Director, National Westminster Bank 1972–83, Deputy Chairman 1974–77, Chairman 1977–83; Director, Birmid Qualcast 1966–83, Chairman 1975–77; Director, University Life Assurance Society 1967–78; Member, South East Planning Council 1972–74; Director, Redland Ltd 1972–83; Member: Prime Minister's Committee on Local Government Rules of Conduct 1973–74, Medway Ports Authority 1974–76, Committee on Police Pay 1977–79; Director, Equitable Life Assurance Society 1979–83; Member, National Economic Development Council 1982–92, Governor, Bank of England 1983–93; Non-Executive Director: Hambros plc 1993–98, Glaxo Wellcome plc 1993–96, Redland plc 1993–98, Foreign and Colonial Investment Trust 1993–98. *Chancellor:* Pro-Chancellor, University of Kent 1977–83. *Other:* Seneschal, Canterbury Cathedral 1983–; Governor, Ditchley Foundation 1987–. Hon. DCL, Kent 1983; Hon. Fellow, Trinity College, Oxford 1984; Hon. DLitt: City 1988, Loughborough 1990. *Trusts, etc:* Trustee, Glyndebourne Arts Trust 1971–83. *Miscellaneous:* Hon. Bencher, Inner Temple 1983. *Honours:* PC 1987; KG 1994. FRSA 1977; FBIM 1977. Liveryman, Mercers' Company. *Recreations:* Country life, The Arts. *Sportsclubs:* Kent County Cricket, Royal St George Golf (Sandwich). *Clubs:* Brooks's, Cavalry and Guards. *Name, Style and Title:* Raised to the peerage as Baron Kingsdown, of Pemberton in the County of Lancashire 1993. *Address:* Rt Hon the Lord Kingsdown, KG, Lieutenancy Office, County Hall, Maidstone, Kent, ME14 1XQ *E-Mail:* gill.herriot@kent.gov.uk.

LORD KINGSLAND Conservative

KINGSLAND (Life Baron), Christopher James Prout; cr. 1994. Born 1 January 1942. Son of late Frank Yabsley Prout, MC and Bar, and of Doris Lucy Prout (née Osborne); educated Sevenoaks School; Manchester University (BA); The Queen's College, Oxford (Scholar, BPhil, DPhil). *Armed Forces:* TA Officer (Major); OU OTC 1966–74; 16/5 The Queen's Royal Lancers 1974–82; 3rd Armoured Division 1982–88; RARO 1988–. *Councils, Public Bodies:* DL, Shropshire 1997–. *Career:* English Speaking Union Fellow, Columbia University, New York 1963–64; Leverhulme Fellow and Lecturer in Law, Sussex University 1969–79; Staff Member, IBRD (UN) Washington DC 1966–69; Barrister-at-Law, Called to the Bar Middle Temple 1972, QC 1988, Bencher 1996; Recorder of the Crown Court (Wales and Chester Circuit) 1997–. *House of Lords:* Shadow Lord Chancellor 1997–. *Select Committees:* Chairman, Select Committee on European Communities Sub-Committee F 1996–97. *Other:* President, Shropshire and West Midlands Agricultural Show 1993. *Awards Granted:* Grande Medaille de la Ville de Paris 1988; Schuman Medal 1995. *Miscellaneous:* MEP (Conservative) for Shropshire and Stafford 1979–94; Deputy Whip, European Democratic Group (EDG) 1979–82; Chief Whip, EDG 1983–87; Chairman, Parliamentary Committee, Legal Affairs 1987; Leader, Conservative MEPs 1987–94; Chairman and Leader, EDG 1987–92; Vice-Chairman, European People's Party Parliamentary Group 1992–94; Contested Herefordshire and Shropshire in 1994 European Elections. *Honours:* TD 1987; Kt 1990; PC 1994. Master, Shrewsbury Drapers Company 1995. *Publications: Market Socialism in Yugoslavia,* 1985; (contributed) Vols 8, 51 and 52, *Halsbury's Law of England* (4th ed.); Miscellaneous lectures, pamphlets, chapters and articles. *Recreations:* Boating, gardening, musical comedy, the turf. *Clubs:* White's, Pratt's, Beefsteak, Royal Ocean Racing, Royal Yacht Squadron (Cowes). *Name, Style and Title:* Raised to the peerage as Baron Kingsland, of Shrewsbury in the County of Shropshire 1994. *Address:* Rt Hon the Lord Kingsland, TD, QC, DL, House of Lords, London SW1A 0PW *Tel:* 020 7353 5835.

LORD KIRKHAM — Conservative

KIRKHAM (Life Baron), Graham Kirkham; cr. 1999. Born 14 December 1944. Son of Tom and Elsie Kirkham; educated Maltby Grammar School. Married 1965, Pauline Fisher (1 son and 1 daughter). *Career:* Executive Chairman, DFS Furniture Company Plc, Founded Company in 1969, Listed on UK Stock Exchange 1993. *Party Groups (General):* Chairman, Conservative Party Treasurers 1997. *Other:* Member: Duke of Edinburgh's Award Scheme, Duke of Edinburgh's International Award Scheme, Chairman, Joint Funding Board; Member, Blue Cross; Patron, War on Cancer. Hon. Member, Emmanuel College, Cambridge 1995 Hon. Doctorate, Bradford University 1997. *Trusts, etc:* Trustee, Outward Bound Trust; Member: Animal Health Trust (Hon. Fellow 1997), The Prince's Youth Business Trust. *Honours:* Kt 1995. *Name, Style and Title:* Raised to the peerage as Baron Kirkham, of Old Cantley in the County of South Yorkshire 1999. *Address:* The Lord Kirkham, DFS Furniture Co Ltd, Bentley Moor Lane, Adwick-le-Street, Doncaster, DN6 7BD.

LORD KIRKHILL — Labour

KIRKHILL (Life Baron), John Farquharson Smith; cr. 1975. Born 7 May 1930. Son of late Alexander Findlay Smith and Ann Farquharson. Married 1965, Frances Mary Walker Reid. *Career:* Lord Provost, Aberdeen 1971–75; Chairman, North of Scotland Hydro-Electric Board 1979–82. *House of Lords:* Minister of State, Scottish Office 1975–78. *International Bodies (General):* Member, Assemblies of the Council of Europe and of WEU 1987–; Chairman, Legal Affairs and Human Rights Committee of the Parliamentary Assembly of the Council of Europe 1991–95. Hon. LLD, Aberdeen University 1974. *Name, Style and Title:* Raised to the peerage as Baron Kirkhill, in the District of the City of Aberdeen 1975. *Address:* The Lord Kirkhill, 3 Rubislaw Den North, Aberdeen, AB15 4AL.

BARONESS KNIGHT OF COLLINGTREE — Conservative

KNIGHT OF COLLINGTREE (Life Baroness) (Joan Christabel) Jill Knight; cr. 1997. Born 9 July 1927. Daughter of late A. E. Christie; educated King Edward Grammar School, Birmingham. Married June 14, 1947, James Montague Knight (died 1986) (2 sons). *Councils, Public Bodies:* Councillor, Northampton County Borough Council 1956–66. *Career:* Director: Computeach International Ltd 1985–, Heckett Multiserv plc 1999–. *House of Commons:* Contested Northampton 1959 and 1964; MP (Conservative) for Birmingham Edgbaston 1966–97. *Select Committees:* European Union Sub-Committee F (Social Affairs, Education and Home Affairs) 2000–. *International Bodies:* Member, Parliamentary Assembly of the Council of Europe and the Assembly of the Western European Union 1977–88, 1999–; Chairman: WEU Relations with Parliaments Committee 1984–88, Member again 1999–; British IPU 1994–97. *Other:* National Chairman, Lifeline 1974–84; Vice-President, Townswomen's Guilds 1989–95. Hon. DSc, Aston University 1998. *Honours:* MBE (New Year's Honours) 1964; DBE 1985. San Francisco. *Publications:* About the House, 1995. *Special Interests:* Health, Social Security, Childcare, Industry, Council of Europe and Western European Union. *Recreations:* Antique collecting, tapestry work, singing, theatre, cooking. *Name, Style and Title:* Raised to the peerage as Baroness Knight of Collingtree, of Collingtree in the County of Northamptonshire 1997. *Address:* The Baroness Knight of Collingtree, DBE, House of Lords, London, SW1A 0PW.

Visit the Vacher Dod Website . . .

www.politicallinks.co.uk

LORD KNIGHTS   Cross-Bencher

KNIGHTS (Life Baron), Philip Douglas Knights; cr. 1987. Born 3 October 1920. Son of late Thomas James Knights, market gardener and late Ethel Ginn, schoolteacher; educated East Grinstead County School; King's School, Grantham; Police Staff College. Married June 23, 1945, Jean, daughter of late James Burman. *Armed Forces:* RAF 1943–45. *Councils, Public Bodies:* DL, West Midlands 1985. *Career:* Police Cadet, Lincolnshire Constabulary 1937; Seconded to the Home Office in 1946; Superintendent 1955; Chief Superintendent 1957; Assistant Chief Constable, Birmingham 1959; Deputy Commandant, Police Staff College, Bramshill 1962–66; Deputy Chief Constable, Birmingham 1970; Chief Constable, Sheffield and Rotherham Constabulary 1972, responsible for Police Force of the newly created County of South Yorkshire 1974; Chief Constable, West Midlands Police 1975–85; Member, Departmental Committee, chaired by Lord Devlin, which reported in 1976 on Identification Procedures; Formerly Adviser, Police and Fire Committee of the Association of Municipal Authorities; Vice-President, Association of Metropolitan Authorities. *Other:* Past President, Association of Chief Police Officers; Member: Council of Aston University 1985–98, Council of Cambridge Institute of Criminology 1986–. Hon. DSc, Aston University 1996. *Trusts, etc:* Trustee, Police Foundation 1979–98. *Honours:* QPM 1964; OBE 1971; CBE 1976; Kt 1980. Companion, British Institute of Management 1977. *Special Interests:* Law and Order, Police, Inner Cities, Local Government. *Recreations:* Gardening, reading, travel, sport. *Sportsclubs:* Vice-President, Warwickshire County Cricket Club. *Clubs:* Royal Over-Seas League. *Name, Style and Title:* Raised to the peerage as Baron Knights, of Edgbaston in the County of West Midlands 1987. *Address:* The Lord Knights, CBE, QPM, CIMgt, DL, 11 Antringham Gardens, Edgbaston, Birmingham, B15 3QL *Tel:* 0121-455 0057.

L

LORD LAING OF DUNPHAIL   Conservative

LAING OF DUNPHAIL (Life Baron), Hector Laing; cr. 1991. Born 12 May 1923. Son of late Hector Laing and Margaret Norris Grant; educated Loretto School; Jesus College, Cambridge. Married April 1, 1950, Marian Clare, daughter of late Major-General Sir John Laurie, 6th Bt, CBE, DSO (3 sons). *Armed Forces:* Served Scots Guards 1942–47 Captain (American Bronze Star, mentioned in despatches). *Career:* Director, McVitie and Price 1947, Chairman 1963; Director, United Biscuits 1953, Managing Director 1964; Chairman, United Biscuits (Holdings) plc 1972–90, Life President 1990–; Director, Bank of England 1973–91; Chairman: Food and Drink Industries Council 1977–79, City and Industrial Liaison Council 1985–90; Director: Grocery Manufacturers of America 1984–90, Exxon Corporation Inc 1984–94. *Party Groups (General):* Joint Treasurer, Conservative Party 1988–93. *Other:* Governor, Wycombe Abbey School 1981–93; Chairman, Scottish Business in the Community 1982–90; President, Goodwill 1983–92; Joint Chairman, The Per Cent Club 1986–90; Chairman, Business in the Community 1987–92; President, The Weston Spirit 1989–95; Member, Advisory Board, Phillips Son and Neale 1990–93; President, Trident 1992–95. Hon. Doctorates: Stirling University 1984, Heriot-Watt University 1986; Hon. Fellow, Jesus College, Cambridge 1988. *Trusts, etc:* Chairman of Trustees, The Lambeth Fund 1983–; Trustee, Royal Botanic Gardens Kew Foundation 1990–. *Recreations:* Walking, gardening. *Clubs:* White's, Boodle's. *Name, Style and Title:* Raised to the peerage as Baron Laing of Dunphail, of Dunphail in the County of Moray 1991. *Address:* The Lord Laing of Dunphail, High Meadows, Gerrards Cross, Buckinghamshire, SL9 8ST *Tel:* 01753 882437.

LORD LAIRD   Cross-Bencher/Ulster Unionist

LAIRD (Life Baron), John Dunn Laird; cr. 1999. Born 23 April 1944. Son of late Dr Norman D Laird, OBE, sometime Northern Ireland MP, and of late Councillor Mrs Margaret Laird; educated Royal Belfast Academical Institution. Married, Caroline Ethel, daughter of William and Mary Ferguson (1 son 1 daughter). *Career:* Bank Official 1963–67; Bank Inspector 1967–68; Computer Programmer 1968–73; PR Consultant 1973–76; Chairman, John Laird Public Relations 1976–; Visiting Professor of Public Relations, University of Ulster. *Party Groups (General):* Member, Ulster Unionist Party. *Other:* Governor, Royal Belfast Academical Institution. *Miscellaneous:* MP for St Annes, Belfast, Northern Ireland Parliament 1970–73; Member for West Belfast: Northern Ireland Assembly 1973–75, Northern Ireland Convention 1975–76; Member, Ulster-Scots Agency, North/South Ministerial Council 2000–; Chairman of the Ulster/Scots Agency. Fellow, Institute of Public Relations 1991. *Publications:* Videos: *Trolley Bus Day in Belfast*, 1992, *Swansong of Steam in Ulster*, 1994, *Twilight of Steam in Ulster* 1995. *Special Interests:* Transport, Dyslexia, Ulster Scots Activity. *Recreations:* Local history, railways, cricket. *Name, Style and Title:* Raised to the peerage as Baron Laird, of Artigarvan in the County of Tyrone 1999. *Address:* The Lord Laird, 104 Holywood Road, Belfast, BT4 1ND *Tel:* 028 9047 1282 *Fax:* 028 9065 6022.

LORD LAMING   Cross-Bencher

LAMING (Life Baron), William Herbert Laming; cr. 1998. Born 19 July 1936. Son of William and Lillian Laming; educated Durham University (Applied Social Sciences); Rainer House; LSE. Married July 21, 1962, Aileen Margaret Pollard. *Councils, Public Bodies:* DL, Hertfordshire 1999–. *Career:* Nottingham Probation Service: Probation Officer 1961–66, Senior Probation Officer 1966–68; Assistant Chief Probation Officer, Nottingham City and County Probation Service 1968–71; Hertfordshire County Council Social Services: Deputy Director 1971–75, Director 1975–91; Chief Inspector, Social Services Inspectorate, Department of Health 1991–98. *Other:* President, Association of Directors of Social Services 1982–83. Hon. DSc, University of Hertfordshire 1997; Hon. DSc, University of Durham 1999. *Honours:* CBE 1985; Kt 1996. Freeman, City of London 1996. *Publications: Lessons from America: the balance of services in social care*, 1985. *Name, Style and Title:* Raised to the peerage as Baron Laming, of Tewin in the County of Hertfordshire 1998. *Address:* The Lord Laming, CBE, DL, 1 Firs Walk, Tewin Wood, Welwyn, Hertfordshire, AL6 0NY *Tel:* 01438 798574.

LORD LAMONT OF LERWICK   Conservative

LAMONT OF LERWICK (Life Baron), Norman Stewart Hughson Lamont; cr. 1998. Born 8 May 1942. Son of late Daniel Lamont; educated Loretto School (Scholar); Fitzwilliam College, Cambridge (BA 1965) (President of Union 1964). Married September 18, 1971, Rosemary White (marriage dissolved 1999) (1 son 1 daughter). *Career:* N. M. Rothschild & Sons Ltd 1968–79, Director 1993–95; Director, Balli plc 1995–; Adviser, The Monsanto Company 1995–99; Chairman: Indonesia Fund 1994–, East European Food Fund 1994–, Archipelago Fund 1994–; Director Jupiter European Investment Trust 1994–. *House of Commons:* Contested Kingston-upon-Hull East 1970 General Election; MP (Conservative) for Kingston-upon-Thames 1972–97; PPS to Norman St John Stevas, MP, as Minister for the Arts 1974; Parliamentary Under-Secretary of State, Department of Energy 1979–81; Minister of State, Department of Trade and Industry 1981–85; Minister for Defence Procurement, Ministry of Defence 1985–86; Financial Secretary to HM Treasury 1986–89; Chief Secretary to HM Treasury 1989–90; Chancellor of the Exchequer 1990–93; Contested Harrogate and Knaresborough 1997 General Election. *Spokesman (Commons):* Opposition Spokesman on: Prices and Consumer Affairs 1975–76, Industry 1976–79. *Select Committees:* Member: Select Committee on European Union 1999–, Europan Communities Committee Sub-Committee A (Economic and Financial Affairs, Trade and External Relations). *Party Groups (General):* Chairman, Bow Group 1971–72; Vice-President, Bruges Group 1994–. *Honours:* PC 1986. *Publications: Sovereign Britain*, 1995; *In Office*, 1999. *Special Interests:* Economics, European Union, Foreign Affairs. *Recreations:* Theatre, history, ornithology. *Clubs:* Garrick, Beefsteak. *Name, Style and Title:* Raised to the peerage as Baron Lamont of Lerwick, of Lerwick in the Shetland Islands 1998. *Address:* Rt Hon the Lord Lamont of Lerwick, Balli Group plc, 5 Stanhope Gate, London, SW1Y 5LA.

LORD LANE — Cross-Bencher

LANE (Life Baron), Geoffrey Dawson Lane; cr. 1979. Born 17 July 1918. Son of late Percy Albert Lane and late Mary Lane (née Dawson); educated Shrewsbury; Trinity College, Cambridge (1st Class Hons Classical Tripos and Law Tripos Parts 1 and 2). Married January 25, 1944, Jan, daughter of Donald Macdonald (1 son). *Armed Forces:* Served in RAF 1939–45. *Career:* Called to the Bar, Gray's Inn 1946; QC 1962; Bencher 1966; Recorder of Bedford 1963–66; A Judge of the High Court of Justice, Queen's Bench Division 1966–74; A Lord Justice of Appeal 1974–79; A Lord of Appeal in Ordinary 1979–80; Lord Chief Justice of England 1980–92; Elected an Honorary Master of the Bench of the Inner Temple July 1980. Hon. DCL, Cambridge; Hon. Fellow, Trinity College, Cambridge. *Trusts, etc:* Former Member, Prison Reform Trust. *Honours:* AFC 1943, Kt 1966, PC 1974. *Name, Style and Title:* Raised to the peerage as Baron Lane, of St Ippollitts in the County of Hertfordshire 1979. *Address:* Rt Hon the Lord Lane, AFC, c/o Child & Co., 1 Fleet Street, London, EC4Y 1BD.

LORD LANE OF HORSELL — Conservative

LANE OF HORSELL (Life Baron), Peter Stewart Lane; cr. 1990. Born 29 January 1925. Son of late Leonard George Lane; educated Sherborne. Married 1951, Doris Florence Botsford (died 1969) (2 daughters). *Armed Forces:* Sub-Lieutenant, RNVR 1943–46. *Councils, Public Bodies:* JP, Surrey. *Career:* Senior Partner, BDO Binder Hamlyn, Chartered Accountants 1979–92; Chairman, Brent International 1985–95; Deputy Chairman, More O'Ferrall 1985–97; Deputy Chairman, Automated Security (Holdings) 1992–94, Chairman 1994–96; Director, Attwoods 1992–94, Chairman 1994. *Select Committees:* Member, Select Committees on: the Public Service 1996–, House of Lords' Offices 1997–98. *Party Groups (General):* National Union of Conservative Associations: Vice-President 1984–, Chairman 1983–84, Chairman Executive Committee 1986–91. *Trusts, etc:* Governor, Nuffield Nursing Homes Trust 1985–96, Chairman 1993–96; Trustee, Chatham Historic Dockyard Trust 1992–. *Honours:* Kt 1984. FCA. Freeman, City of London. *Publications:* Co-author *Maw on Corporate Governance*, 1994. *Clubs:* Boodle's, MCC, Beefsteak. *Name, Style and Title:* Raised to the peerage as Baron Lane of Horsell, of Woking in the County of Surrey 1990. *Address:* The Lord Lane of Horsell, Rossmore, Pond Road, Woking, Surrey, GU22 0JY.

LORD LANG OF MONKTON — Conservative

LANG OF MONKTON (Life Baron), Ian Bruce Lang; cr. 1997. Born 27 June 1940. Son of late James Lang, DSC; educated Lathallan School, Montrose; Rugby School; Sidney Sussex College, Cambridge (BA). Married 1971, Sandra Montgomerie (2 daughters). *Councils, Public Bodies:* DL, Ayrshire and Arran 1998–. *Career:* Non-Executive Director: European Telecom plc, Marsh and Mclennan Companies Inc, Murray TMT plc, Second Scottish National Trust plc, and other companies. *House of Commons:* Contested Ayrshire Central 1970 and Glasgow Pollok in February 1974 General Elections; MP (Conservative) for Galloway 1979–83 and for Galloway and Upper Nithsdale 1983–97; Parliamentary Under-Secretary of State: at Department of Employment 1986, at Scottish Office 1986–87; Minister of State, Scottish Office 1987–90; Secretary of State for Scotland 1990–95; President of the Board of Trade and Secretary of State for Trade and Industry 1995–97. *Whip (Commons):* Assistant Government Whip 1981–83; Lord Commissioner of HM Treasury (Government Whip) 1983–86. *Party Groups (General):* Hon. President, Scottish Young Conservatives 1982–84; Vice-Chairman, Scottish Conservative Party 1983–87. *Other:* A Governor, Rugby School 1997–; President, The Association for the Protection of Rural Scotland 1998–; Chairman, Patron of the National Galleries of Scotland 1999–. *Miscellaneous:* Member, Queen's Bodyguard for Scotland, Royal Company of Archers 1974. *Honours:* Officer of the Order of St John 1974; PC 1990. *Sportsclubs:* Prestwick Golf Club. *Clubs:* Pratt's. *Name, Style and Title:* Raised to the peerage as Baron Lang of Monkton, of Merrick and the Rhinns of Kells in Dumfries and Galloway 1997. *Address:* Rt Hon the Lord Lang of Monkton, DL, House of Lords, London, SW1A 0PW.

LORD LAWSON OF BLABY — Conservative

LAWSON OF BLABY (Life Baron), Nigel Lawson; cr. 1992. Born 11 March 1932. Son of late Ralph Lawson and late Elisabeth Lawson (née Davis); educated Westminster School; Christ Church, Oxford (Scholar, first class hons PPE). Married 1st, 1955, Vanessa Mary Salmon (1 son 2 daughters and 1 daughter deceased) (marriage dissolved 1980, she died 1985), married 2nd, 1980, Thérèse Mary Maclear (1 son 1 daughter). *Armed Forces:* Served Royal Navy 1954–56. *Career:* A former journalist; Member, editorial staff, *Financial Times* 1956–60; City Editor, *Sunday Telegraph* 1961–63; Special Assistant to Rt Hon. Sir Alec Douglas-Home, KT, MP then Prime Minister 1963–64; *Financial Times* columnist and BBC broadcaster 1965; Editor, *The Spectator* 1966–70; Chairman, Central Europe Trust (CET) 1990–; Director, Barclays Bank plc 1990–98. *House of Commons:* Contested (Conservative) Eton and Slough in 1970 General Election; MP (Conservative) for Blaby February 1974–92; Financial Secretary to the Treasury 1979–81; Secretary of State for Energy 1981–83; Chancellor of the Exchequer 1983–89. *Whip (Commons):* An Opposition Whip 1976–77. *Spokesman (Commons):* Opposition Spokesman on Treasury and Economic Affairs 1977–79. Hon. Student, Christ Church, Oxford 1996. *Miscellaneous:* President, British Insititute of Energy Economics 1995–. *Honours:* PC 1981. *Publications:* Co-author: *The Power Game*, 1976; *The View from Number 11: Memoirs of a Tory Radical*, 1992; Co-author *The Nigel Lawson Diet Book*, 1996. *Clubs:* Garrick, Pratt's. *Name, Style and Title:* Raised to the peerage as Baron Lawson of Blaby, of Newnham in the County of Northamptonshire 1992. *Address:* Rt Hon the Lord Lawson of Blaby, House of Lords, London, SW1A 0PW.

LORD LAYARD — Labour

LAYARD (Life Baron) (Peter) Richard Grenville Layard; cr. 2000. Born 15 March 1934. Son of Dr John Layard and Doris Layard; educated Eton; King's College, Cambridge (BA); London School of Economics (MSc Econ). Married 1991, Molly Meacher. *Career:* History master London secondary schools 1959–61; Senior Research Officer, Robbins Committee on Higher Education 1961–63; London School of Economics: Deputy Director, Higher Education Research Unit 1964–74; Lecturer in Economics 1968–75; Reader in Economics of Labour 1975–80; Head, Centre for Labour Economics 1974–90; Professor of Economics 1980–; Director, Centre for Economic Performance 1990–; Economic Consultant to the Russian Government 1991–97; Consultant, Department for Education and Employment 1997–. *Other:* Member, UGC 1985–89; Chairman, Employment Institute 1987–92. *Publications:* Co-author: *The Causes of Graduate Unemployment in India*, 1969; *The Impact of Robbins: Expansion in Higher Education*, 1969; *Qualified Manpower and Economic Performance: An Inter-Plant Study in the Electrical Engineering Industry*, 1971; Editor, *Cost-Benefit Analysis*, 1973, 2nd ed 1994; Co-author: *Microeconomic Theory*, 1978; *The Causes of Poverty*, 1978; Author of: *Jobs, Less Inflation*, 1982; *How to Beat Unemployment*, 1986; Co-author: *Handbook of Labour Economics*, 1986; *The Performance of the British Economy*, 1988; *Unemployment: Macroeconomic Performance and the Labour Market*, 1991; *Reform in Eastern European*, 1991; *East-West Migration: the alternatives*, 1992; *Post-Communist Russia: pain and progress*, 1993; *Macroeconomics: a test for Russia*, 1994; Co-author *The Coming Russian Boom*, 1996; Author of: *What Labour Can Do*, 1997; *Tackling Unemployment*, 1999; *Tackling Inequality*, 1999. *Recreations:* Walking, tennis, the clarinet. *Name, Style and Title:* Raised to the peerage as Baron Layard, of Highgate in the London Borough of Haringey 2000. *Address:* Professor the Lord Layard, 45 Cholmeley Park, London, N6 5EL *Tel:* 020 7955 7281.

Dod *on* Line
An Electronic Directory without rival …
Peerss' biographies and photographs available with daily updates *via* the internet
For a *free* trial, call Oliver Cox on 020 7828 7256

LEA OF CRONDALL (Life Baron), David Edward Lea; cr. 1999. Born 2 November 1937. Son of late Edward and Lilian Lea; educated Farnham Grammar School; Christ's College, Cambridge (MA 1961). *Trades Union:* Member, T&GWU 1962–. *Armed Forces:* National Service, Royal Horse Artillery 1955–57. *Career:* Economist Intelligence Unit 1961–63; Trades Union Congress: Research/Economic Department 1964–67, Assistant Secretary, Economic and Social Affairs 1968–70, Head, Economic and Social Affairs 1970–77, Assistant General Secretary 1978–99. *Select Committees:* Member, Europan Communities Committee Sub-Committee A (Economic and Financial Affairs, Trade and External Relations) 2000–; Joint Committee on Statutory Instruments 2000–. *Other:* Chair, Farnham Roads Action. *Trusts, etc:* Trustee, Employment Policy Institute 1982–2000. *Miscellaneous:* Member: DTI Inward Investment Mission in Japan 1974, Channel Tunnel Advisory Committee 1974–75, Bullock Committee on Industrial Democracy 1975–77, Royal Commission on the Distribution of Income and Wealth 1975–79, Delors Committee on Economic and Social Concepts in the Community 1977–79, Energy Commission 1977–79, UN Commission on Transnational Corporations 1977–82, NEDC Committee on Finance for Industry 1978–82, Led TUC Mission to Study Employment and Technology in the USA 1980; Chair, ETUC Economic Committee 1980–90; Vice-President, ETUC 1997–98; Member, Franco-British Council 1982–99; Governor, National Institute of Economic and Social Research; Editorial Board Member, New Economy (IPPR) 1991–99; Member, Retail Prices Index Advisory Committee 1985–99; Secretary, TUC Nuclear Energy Review Body 1986–88; Member: Kreisky Commission on Employment Issues in Europe 1987–89, Tripartite Mission EU, Japan 1990, European TUC Executive Committee and Steering Group 1991–99, European Social Dialogue Joint Steering Committee 1992–, UK Delegation Earth Summit, Rio 1992; Secretary, TUC Task Force on Representation at Work 1994–99; Member, Round Table on Sustainable Development (sub Group of the Round Table) 1995–99; Chair, Sub-Group on Sustainable Business – A Stakeholder Approach (sub Group of the Round Table) 1997–98; Member: Trade Union and Sustainable Development Advisory Committee 1998–99, Advisory Committee on Vehicle Emissions 1998–99, EU High Level Group on Benchmarking 1998–99, Treasury Advisory Committee on EMU 1998–99, Central Arbitration Committee 2000–. *Honours:* OBE 1968. *Publications: Trade Unionism,* 1966; *Industrial Democracy,* 1974; *Trade Unions and Multinational Companies. Recreations:* Tennis, music, theatre, skiing. *Sportsclubs:* Bourne Club, Farnham, Lords/Commons Tennis and Ski Club. *Name, Style and Title:* Raised to the peerage as Baron Lea of Crondall, of Crondall in the County of Hampshire 1999.*Address:* The Lord Lea of Crondall, OBE, South Court, Crondall, Nr Farnham, Surrey, GU10 5QF *Tel:* 01252 850711 *Fax:* 01252 850711; 17 Ormonde Mansions, 106 Southampton Row, London, WC1B 4BP *Tel:* 020 7405 6237 *E-Mail:* lead@parliament.uk.

LESTER OF HERNE HILL (Life Baron), Anthony Paul Lester; cr. 1993. Born 3 July 1936. Son of late Harry Lester, and of Kate Lester; educated City of London School; Trinity College, Cambridge (MA); Harvard Law School (LLM). Married 1971, Catherine Elizabeth Debora Wassey (1 son 1 daughter). *Armed Forces:* 2nd Lieutenant, Royal Artillery 1955–57 (National Service). *Career:* Called to Bar, Lincoln's Inn 1963; QC 1975, QC (NI) 1984; Bencher 1985; Called to Bar of Northern Ireland 1984; Irish Bar 1983; Special Adviser to: Home Secretary 1974–76, Special Adviser to Standing Advisory Commission on Human Rights in Northern Ireland 1975–77; Hon. Visiting Professor, University College London 1983–; A Recorder of the Crown Court 1987–93. *Select Committees:* Member, House of Lords Procedure Committee 1995–97; Member, European Communities Select Committee Sub-Committees E: Law and Institutions 1995–97, 1999–, 1996 Inter-Governmental Conference 1995–97; Member, Select Committee on European Communities Sub-Committee F (Social Affairs, Education and Home Affairs) 1997–99. *Party Groups (General):* A founder member of the Social Democrat Party; President, Liberal Democrat Lawyers' Association.*Other:* President, Interights (The International Centre for the Legal Protection of Human Rights) 1991–; Governor, British Institute of Human Rights; Board of Governors, James Allen's Girls' School 1987–93;

Member, Executive Committee and Council of Justice; Executive Committee, European Roma Rights Center, Co-Chair 1998–; Member, Board of Directors, Salzburg Seminar; Governor, Westminster School 1998–. *Awards Granted:* Liberty Human Rights Lawyer of the Year Award 1997. Hon. DUniv, The Open University; Hon. DLitt: University of Ulster, University of South Bank; Hon. Life Fellow, University College London 1998. Member, American Law Institute 1985–; Hon. Fellow, Society for Advanced Legal Studies 1998–. *Publications: Justice in the American South,* (Amnesty International) 1964; Co-editor *Shawcross and Beaumont on Air Law,* 3rd edition 1964; Co-author*Race and Law,* 1972; Numerous articles on human rights law and constitutional reform; Contributor to other legal publications; Editor-in-Chief, *Butterworths Human Rights Cases;* Member, Editorial Board of *Public Law;* Consultant Editor and Contributor, *Halsbury's Laws of England,* 4th edition, reissued 1996, title on 'Constitutional Law and Human Rights'; Co-editor *Butterworths Human Rights Law and Practice,* 1999. *Special Interests:* Human Rights, Constitutional Reform, Law Reform, Equality and Non-Discrimination, Media, European Political Integration. *Recreations:* Walking, golf, sailing, watercolours. *Name, Style and Title:* Raised to the peerage as Baron Lester of Herne Hill, of Herne Hill in the London Borough of Southwark 1993. *Address:* The Lord Lester of Herne Hill, QC, Odysseus Trust, 18–20 Outer Temple, 222 Strand, London, WC2 1BA *E-Mail:* lestera@parliament.uk.

LORD LEVENE OF PORTSOKEN   Cross-Bencher

LEVENE OF PORTSOKEN (Life Baron), Peter Keith Levene; cr. 1997. Born 8 December 1941. Son of late Maurice and Rose Levene; educated City of London School; Manchester University (BA Econ). Married 1966, Wendy Fraiman (2 sons 1 daughter). *Armed Forces:* Hon. Col. Comdt, Royal Logistic Corps 1993–. *Councils, Public Bodies:* Member (Candlewick Ward), Court of Common Council, City of London 1983–84, Alderman (Portsoken Ward) 1984–; JP, City of London 1984–; Sheriff, City of London 1995–96; Lord Mayor of London 1998–99. *Career:* Joined United Scientific Holdings 1963, Managing Director 1968–85, Chairman 1982–85; Member, SE Asia Trade Advisory Group 1979–83; Council Member, Defence Manufacturers' Association 1982–85, Chairman 1984–85; Personal Adviser to the Secretary of State for Defence 1984; Chief of Defence Procurement, Ministry of Defence 1985–91; UK National Armaments Director 1988–91; Chairman, European National Armaments Directors 1989–90; Personal Adviser to Secretary of State for the Environment 1991–92, Chairman, Docklands Light Railway Ltd 1991–94; Deputy Chairman, Wasserstein Perella & Co Ltd 1991–94; Personal Adviser to Chancellor of the Exchequer on Competition and Purchasing 1992; Member, Citizen's Charter Advisory Panel 1992–93; Personal Adviser to the President of the Board of Trade 1992–95; Adviser to the Prime Minister on Efficiency and Effectiveness 1992–97; Chairman and Chief Executive, Canary Wharf Ltd 1993–96; Senior Adviser, Morgan Stanley & Co Ltd 1996–98; Chairman: Bankers Trust International plc 1998–99, Investment Banking Europe Deutsche Bank 1999–. *Chancellor:* Chancellor, City University 1998–99. *Other:* Governor, City of London School for Girls 1984–85; Member, Board of Management, London Homes for the Elderly 1984–93, Chairman 1990–93; Governor, City of London School 1986–. Fellow, Queen Mary and Westfield College 1995; Hon. DSc, City University 1998. *Trusts, etc:* Chairman, Bevis Marks Trust. *Honours:* KBE 1989; OStJ 1996; Commandeur, Ordre National du Merite (France) 1996; Knight Commander Order of Merit (Germany) 1998; Middle Cross Order of Merit (Hungary) 1999. CIMgt; FCIT; FCIPS. Liveryman, Carmen's Company 1984–, Master 1992–93; Liveryman, Information Technologists 1992–. *Recreations:* Ski-ing, watching football, travel. *Clubs:* Guildhall, City Livery, Royal Automobile. *Name, Style and Title:* Raised to the peerage as Baron Levene of Portsoken, of Portsoken in the City of London 1997. *Address:* The Lord Levene of Portsoken, KBE, House of Lords, London, SW1A 0PW *E-Mail:* peter.k.levene@db.com.

LEVY (Life Baron), Michael Abraham Levy; cr. 1997. Born 11 July 1944. Son of Samuel and Annie Levy; educated Hackney Downs Grammar School. Married 1967, Gilda Altbach (1 son 1 daughter). *Career:* Lubbock Fine (Chartered Accountants) 1961–66; Principal, M. Levy & Co. 1966–69; Partner, Wagner Prager Levy & Partners 1969–73; Chairman, Magnet Group of Companies 1973–88; Vice-Chairman: Phonographic Performance Ltd 1979–84, British Phonographic Industry Ltd 1984–87; Chairman: D & J Securities Ltd 1988–92, M & G Records Ltd 1992–97, Chase Music Ltd (formerly M & G Music Ltd) 1992–, Wireart Ltd 1992–. *Other:* National Campaign Chairman, United Joint Israel Appeal 1982–85, Vice-President 1994–; Member, World Board of Governors of the Jewish Agency 1990–95; Governor, Jewish Free School 1990–95, Hon. President 1995–; Chairman, Jewish Care 1991–97, President 1998–; World Chairman, Youth Aliyah Committee of Jewish Agency Board of Governors 1991–95; Chairman: Chief Rabbinate Awards for Excellence 1992–, Foundation for Education 1993–, Jewish Care Community Foundation 1995–; Member: World Commission on Israel-Diaspora Relations 1995–, International Board of Governors of the Peres Centre for Peace 1997–; Patron, Ben Uri Art Society 1997–; Member: Advisory Council to the Foreign Policy Centre 1997–, Foreign and Commonwealth Office Panel 2000 1998–; President, Community Service Volunteers 1998–; Member, National Council for Voluntary Organisations Advisory Committee 1998–; Member, Community Legal Service Champions Panel 1999–; Patron, Save A Child's Heart Foundation 2000–; Director, Israel Britain and the Commonwealth Association 2000–. *Awards Granted:* B'nai B'rith First Lodge Award 1994; Friends of the Hebrew University of Jerusalem Scopus Award 1998. Honorary Doctorate, Middlesex University 1999. *Trusts, etc.* Member, Keren Hayesod World Board of Trustees 1991–95; Patron, Prostate Cancer Charitable Trust 1997–; Trustee, Holocaust Education Trust 1998–; Patron, Friends of Israel Educational Trust 1998–. *Miscellaneous:* Chairman, British Music Industry Awards Committee 1992–95; Patron, British Music Industry Awards 1995–. FCA 1966. *Special Interests:* Voluntary Sector, Social Welfare, Education, Middle East Peace Process. *Recreations:* Tennis, swimming. *Name, Style and Title:* Raised to the peerage as Baron Levy, of Mill Hill in the London Borough of Barnet 1997. *Address:* The Lord Levy, House of Lords, London, SW1A 0PW *E-Mail:* ml@lmalvy.demon.co.uk.

LEWIS OF NEWNHAM (Life Baron), Jack Lewis; cr. 1989. Born 13 February 1928. Son of late Robert Lewis; educated Barrow Grammar School; London University (BSc 1949, DSc 1961); Nottingham University (PhD 1952); Manchester University (MSc 1964); Sidney Sussex College, Cambridge (MA 1970, ScD 1977). Married 1951, Elfreida Mabel, daughter of Frank Lamb (1 son 1 daughter). *Career:* Lecturer: Sheffield University 1954–56, Imperial College, London 1956–57; Lecturer/Reader, University College, London 1957–61; Professor of Chemistry: Manchester University 1961–67, University College, London 1967–70, Cambridge University 1970–95; Member, Cambridge University 1970–; First Warden, Robinson College, Cambridge 1975–; Member, Council of SERC 1979–84; Member, Council, Royal Society 1982–84, 1996–98, Vice-President 1983–84; Chairman, Visiting Committee, Cranfield Institute of Technology 1982–92; Chairman, Royal Commission on Environmental Pollution 1986–92; President, Royal Society of Chemistry 1986–88; Science Representative for UK on NATO Science Committee 1986–98; Director, The BOC Foundation 1990–; Member, Council, Royal Society of Chemistry 1992–95, 1996–98; President, National Society for Clean Air and Environmental Protection 1993–95; Chairman, ESART Board 1998–. *Select Committees:* Member: Science and Technology Sub-Committee II 1990–91, 1995–97, European Communities Sub-Committee F 1991–92, Science and Technology Sub-Committee I 1992–93, European Communities Sub-Committee C 1993–95 (Chairman), European Communities Sub-Committee B 1995–97; Co-opted Member, Select Committee on European Communities: Sub-Committee B (Energy, Industry and Transport) 1997–, Sub-Committee C 1997–; Member, Science and Technology Sub-Committee II (Aircraft Cabin Environment) 2000–. *Other:* Patron, Student Community Action Development Unit 1985–; Foreign Member: American Academy of Arts and Sciences 1983, American Philosophical Society 1994, Accademia Nazionale dei Lincei, Italy 1995, Polish Academy of Arts and Sciences 1996–;

Hon. Member, Society of Chemical Industry 1996; Chairman, The Leys School Governors 1997–; President, Arthritis Research Campaign 1998–; Hon. Fellow, Royal Society of Chemistry 1998–. Hon. Fellow, Sidney Sussex College, Fellow 1970–77; 18 honorary doctorates from the UK, Canada, Hong Kong, France and Ireland; 3 honorary university fellowships. *Trusts, etc:* Chairman, Executive Committee of the Cambridge Overseas Trust 1988–; Trustee: Kennedy Memorial Trust 1989–99, Croucher Foundation 1989–98. *Miscellaneous:* Hon. President, Environmental Industries Commission 1996–; Chairman, Standing Committee on Structural Safety 1998–. *Honours:* FRS 1973, Kt 1982; Chevalier dans l'Ordre des Palmes Académiques; Commander Cross of the Order of Merit of the Republic of Poland. Fellow, Indian National Science Academy 1985; Foreign Associate, National Academy of Sciences, USA 1987; Foreign Fellow, Bangladesh Academy of Sciences 1992; FRSA. *Publications:* Some 850 papers and review articles. *Special Interests:* Education, Environment. *Recreations:* Music, walking. *Clubs:* Royal Over-Seas League, United Oxford and Cambridge University. *Name, Style and Title:* Raised to the peerage as Baron Lewis of Newnham, of Newnham in the County of Cambridgeshire 1989. *Address:* Professor the Lord Lewis of Newnham, FRS, Robinson College, Grange Road, Cambridge, CB3 9AN *Tel:* 01223 339120 *E-Mail:* jl219@cam.ac.uk.

BISHOP OF LICHFIELD — Non-Affiliated

LICHFIELD (97th Bishop of), Keith Norman Sutton. Born 23 June 1934. Son of late Norman and Irene Sutton; educated Battersea Grammar School; Jesus College, Cambridge; Ridley Hall, Cambridge. Married June 8, 1963, Edith Mary Jean, daughter of Dr Henry and late Mrs Anne Geldard (3 sons 1 daughter). *Career:* Curate, St Andrew's, Plymouth 1959–62; Chaplain, St John's College, Cambridge 1962–67; Tutor and Chaplain, Bishop Tucker College, Mukono, Uganda 1968–73; Principal, Ridley Hall, Cambridge 1973–78; Suffragan Bishop of Kingston-upon-Thames 1978–84; Governing Body Member, St John's College, Durham 1986–94; President, Queen's College, Birmingham 1986–94; Diocesan Bishop of Lichfield 1984–; Entered the House of Lords 1989; Chairman: General Synod Board for Mission and Unity 1989–91, General Synod Board of Mission 1991–94; Episcopal Visitor, Simon of Cyrene Theological Institute, London 1992–98. Hon. D Keele University 1992; Hon. DLit, Wolverhampton University 1994. *Publications: The People of God,* (SPCK) 1984; Articles in: *The Times, The Guardian, Church Times* etc. *Special Interests:* Foreign Affairs, Africa, Overseas Aid and Development, Urban regeneration. *Recreations:* Russian literature, walking, Baroque music. *Address:* Rt Rev the Lord Bishop of Lichfield, Bishop's House, 22 The Close, Lichfield, Staffordshire, WS13 7LG *Tel:* 01543 306000 *Fax:* 01543 306009.

BISHOP OF LINCOLN — Non-Affiliated

LINCOLN (70th Bishop of), Robert Maynard Hardy. Born 5 October 1936. Son of Harold and Monica Hardy; educated Queen Elizabeth Grammar School, Wakefield; Clare College, Cambridge (MA). Married 1970, Isobel Mary, daughter of Charles and Ella Burch (2 sons 1 daughter). *Career:* Deacon 1962; Priest 1963; Assistant Curate, All Saints and Martyrs, Langley, Manchester 1962–65; Vicar of All Saints, Borehamwood 1972–75; Priest-in-charge, Apsley Guise 1975; Course Director, St Albans Diocese Ministerial Training Scheme 1975; Incumbent of United Benefice of Apsley Guise with Husborne Crawley and Ridgmont 1980; Bishop of Suffragan of Maidstone 1980–86; Bishop to HM Prisons 1985–; Bishop of Lincoln 1987–; Entered the House of Lords 1993. Fellow and Chaplain, Selwyn College, Cambridge 1965–72, Hon. Fellow 1986; Hon. DD, Hull University 1993. *Recreations:* Walking, gardening, reading. *Address:* Rt Rev the Lord Bishop of Lincoln, Bishop's House, Eastgate, Lincoln, LN2 1QQ *Tel:* 01522 534701 *E-Mail:* bishlincoln@claranet.co.uk.

Visit the Vacher Dod Website . . .
www.politicallinks.co.uk

EARL OF LINDSAY   Conservative

LINDSAY (16th Earl of, S), James Randolph Lindesay-Bethune; cr. 1633; Viscount Garnock (S) 1703; Lord Lindsay of the Byres (S) 1445; Lord Parbroath (S) 1633; Lord Kilbirnie, Kingsburn and Drumry (S) 1703. Born 19 November 1955. Son of 15th Earl and Hon. Mary-Clare Douglas Scott Montagu, daughter of 2nd Baron Montagu of Beaulieu, KCIE, CSI, DL. Succeeded his father 1989; educated Eton; Edinburgh University (MA); University of California, Davis. Married March 2, 1982, Diana Mary, daughter of Major Nigel Chamberlayne-Macdonald, LVO, OBE (2 sons 3 daughters inc. twins). *Career:* Vice-President, International Tree Foundation 1993–95, President 1995–; Chairman, Assured British Meat Ltd (ABM) 1997 ; Deputy Chairman, Scottish Salmon Growers Association Ltd (SSGA) 1997–98, Chairman 1998–99; Chairman, Scottish Quality Salmon 1999–; Board Member, Cairngorms Partnership 1998–; Non-Executive Director, UA Group plc 1998–; Chairman: UA Properties Ltd 1999–, UA Forestry Ltd 1999–. *House of Lords:* Parliamentary Under-Secretary of State, Scottish Office 1995–97; An elected hereditary peer 1999–. *Whip:* A Lord-in-Waiting (Government Whip) January-July 1995. *Spokesman:* An Opposition Spokesman on Agriculture, Fisheries and Food, Environment, Transport and the Regions (Green Issues) June-October 1997. *Select Committees:* Member: European Communities Sub-Committee C (Environment and Social Affairs) 1993–95, 1997–98, Select Committee on Sustainable Development 1994–95. *International Bodies:* Inter-Parliamentary Union Committee on Environment 1993–95, Vice-Chairman 1994–95. *Other:* Chairman: Landscape Foundation 1992–95, RSPB Scotland 1998–; Council Member, RSPB (UK) 1998–. *Awards Granted:* Green Ribbon Political Award 1995. *Trusts, etc:* Member, Advisory Panel, Railway Heritage Trust 1990–. *Miscellaneous:* Member: Advisory Council World Resource Foundation 1994–99, Secretary of State's Advisory Group on Sustainable Development 1998–99, UK Round Table on Sustainable Development Sub-Group: Sustainability – Devolved and Regional Dimensions 1998–99, ScottishPower Environment Forum 1998–. Hon. Fellow, Institute of Wastes Management (IWM) 1998–; Associateship of Royal Agricultural Societies (ARAgS). *Publications:* Co-author *Garden Ornament,* 1989; *Trellis,* 1991. *Special Interests:* Environment, Transport, Energy, Waste Management. *Clubs:* New (Edinburgh). *Address:* The Earl of Lindsay, Lahill, Upper Largo, Fife, KY8 6JE *Tel:* 01333 360251.

BARONESS LINKLATER OF BUTTERSTONE   Liberal Democrat

LINKLATER OF BUTTERSTONE (Life Baroness), Veronica Linklater; cr. 1997. Born 15 April 1943. Daughter of Lieutenant-Colonel Archibald Michael Lyle, OBE, JP, DL and late Hon. Elizabeth Sinclair, daughter of 1st Viscount Thurso, KT, PC, CMG; educated Cranborne Chase School; Sussex University; London University (DipSoc). Married 1967, Magnus Duncan Linklater, son of late Eric Robert Linklater, CBE, TD (2 sons 1 daughter). *Career:* Social Worker (Childcare Officer); Social Administrator. *Other:* Founder and Chairman, The New School, Butterstone Ltd; President, The Society of Friends of Dunkeld Cathedral; Patron, The Airborne Initiative (Scotland) Ltd; Member, The Beattie Committee on post-school provision for young people with special needs 1998–99; Vice-Chairman, Pushkin Prizes, Scotland. *Trusts, etc:* Member: The Butler Trust, The Esmée Fairbairn Charitable Trust, The Maggie Keswick Jencks Cancer Caring Trust; Patron: The Sutherland Trust, University of the Highlands and Islands, Liberating Scots Trust, The Sutherland Trust. *Miscellaneous:* Contested (Lib Dem) Perth and Kinross By-election 1995. *Special Interests:* Education, Youth Affairs, Penal Affairs and Policy. *Recreations:* Music, theatre, reading. *Name, Style and Title:* Raised to the peerage as Baroness Linklater of Butterstone, of Riemore in Perth and Kinross 1997. *Address:* The Baroness Linklater of Butterstone, 5 Drummond Place, Edinburgh, EH3 6PH *Tel:* 0131–557 5705.

Dod *on* Line
An Electronic Directory without rival . . .
Peers' biographies and photographs available with daily updates *via* the internet
For a *free* trial, call Oliver Cox on 020 7828 7256

LIPSEY (Life Baron), David Lawrence Lipsey; cr. 1999. Born 21 April 1948. Son of late Lawrence Lipsey, and of Penlope Lipsey; educated Bryanston School; Magdalen College, Oxford (BA philosophy, politics and economics 1970). Married 1982 (1 daughter, 2 stepsons). *Career:* Research Assistant, GMWU 1970–72; Political Adviser to Rt Hon. Anthony Crosland (in Opposition, DoE and FCO) 1972–77; Adviser to 10 Downing Street 1977–79; Journalist, *New Society* 1979–80, Editor 1986–88; Journalist, then Economics Editor, *Sunday Times* 1980–86; Founder/Deputy Editor, *Sunday Correspondent* 1988–90; Associate (Acting Deputy Editor) *Times* 1990–92; Journalist, Political Editor, Public Policy Editor, *Economist* 1992–99; Public Interest Director, Personal Investment Authority 1994–2000; Non-Executive Director, The Tote; Member of Council, Advertising Standards Authority; Director, Political Quarterly; International Advisory Board, Angus Reid Group. *Party Groups (General):* Secretary, Streatham Labour Party 1970–72; Chair, Fabian Society 1982–83. *Other:* Advisory Council: Constitution Unit, Centre for Research into Election and Social Trends. *Miscellaneous:* Member: Jenkins Commission on Electoral Reform 1998; Royal Commission on Long-term Care of the Elderly 1998–99, Davies Panel on BBC Licence Fee 1999. *Publications: Labour and Land*, 1972; *The Socialist Agenda*, Editor 1981; *The Name of the Rose*, 1992; *The Secret Treasury*, 2000. *Special Interests:* Horse Racing, Financial Regulation, Electoral Reform, Broadcasting, Machinery of Government, Psephology. *Recreations:* Golf, racing, opera, swimming. *Sportsclubs:* Wimbledon Park Golf Club, South London Swimming Club. *Name, Style and Title:* Raised to the peerage as Baron Lipsey, of Tooting Bec in the London Borough of Wandsworth 1999. *Address:* The Lord Lipsey, 94 Drewstead Road, London, SW16 1AG *Tel:* 020 8677 7446 *Fax:* 020 8677 7446 *E-Mail:* david.lipsey@btinernet.com.

LISTOWEL (6th Earl of, I), Francis Michael Hare; cr. 1822; 6th Viscount Ennismore and Listowel (I) 1816; 6th Baron Ennismore (I) 1800; 4th Baron Hare (UK) 1869. Born 28 June 1964. Son of 5th Earl, PC, GCMG. Succeeded his father 1997. Sits as Baron Hare; educated Westminster School; Queen Mary and Westfield College, University of London. *House of Lords:* An elected hereditary peer 1999–. *Select Committees:* Member, Library and Computers Sub-Committee, House of Lords Offices Committee 2000–. *Special Interests:* Young Under-privileged, Constitutional Affairs. *Recreations:* Singing, music, art. *Clubs:* Reform. *Address:* The Earl of Listowel, House of Lords, London, SW1A 0PW *E-Mail:* listowelf@parliament.uk.

LIVERPOOL (5th Earl of, UK), Edward Peter Bertram Savile Foljambe; cr. 1905; Viscount Hawkesbury; 5th Baron Hawkesbury (UK) 1893. Born 14 November 1944. Son of Captain Peter George William Savile Foljambe. Succeeded his great-uncle 1969; educated Shrewsbury; Perugia University, Italy. Married 1st, January 29, 1970, Lady Juliana Noel (2 sons) (divorced 1994), married 2nd, May 26, 1995, Comtesse Marie-Ange de Pierredon. *Career:* Managing Director, Melbourns Brewery Ltd, Stamford, Lincolnshire 1971–76, Joint Chairman and Managing Director 1977–87; Director: Hilstone Developments Ltd 1986–91, Hart Hambleton plc 1986–92, Rutland Properties Ltd 1987–, J. W. Cameron & Co. Ltd 1987–91; Chairman and Managing Director, Maxador Ltd 1987–. *House of Lords:* An elected hereditary peer 1999–. *Recreations:* Flying, golf, shooting. *Clubs:* Turf, Pratt's, Air Squadron. *Address:* The Earl of Liverpool, House of Lords, London, SW1A 0PW.

LORD LLOYD OF BERWICK   Cross-Bencher

LLOYD OF BERWICK (Life Baron), Anthony John Leslie Lloyd; cr. 1993. Born 9 May 1929. Son of late Edward John Boydell Lloyd; educated Eton; Trinity College, Cambridge (BA Classics and law). Married 1960, Jane Helen Violet Shelford. *Armed Forces:* Served Coldstream Guards (National Service) 1948. *Councils, Public Bodies:* DL, East Sussex 1983–. *Career:* Called to Bar, Inner Temple 1955; QC 1967; Bencher 1976; Attorney-General to Prince of Wales 1969–77; Judge of the High Court of Justice, Queen's Bench Division 1978–84; A Lord Justice of Appeal 1984–93; Vice-Chairman, Security Commission 1985–92, Chairman 1992–99; A Lord of Appeal in Ordinary 1993–98; Treasurer, Inner Temple 1999–. *Other:* Director, Royal Academy of Music 1979–98; Vice-President, Corporation of the Sons of the Clergy 1996–. Choate Fellow, Harvard 1952; Fellow Peterhouse 1953; Hon. Fellow, Peterhouse 1981. *Trusts, etc:* Trustee, Glyndebourne Arts Trust 1973–, Chairman 1975–94. *Honours:* Kt 1978; PC 1984. Hon. FRAM 1985. Hon. Member, Salters' Company 1988–, Master 2000–. *Recreations:* Music, carpentry. *Clubs:* Brooks's. *Name, Style and Title:* Raised to the peerage as Baron Lloyd of Berwick, of Ludlay in the County of East Sussex 1993. *Address:* Rt Hon the Lord Lloyd of Berwick, DL, House of Lords, London, SW1A 0PW.

BARONESS LLOYD OF HIGHBURY   Cross-Bencher

LLOYD OF HIGHBURY (Life Baroness), June Kathleen Lloyd; cr. 1996. Born 1 January 1928. Daughter of late Arthur Cresswell Lloyd, MBE, and late Lucy Bevan Lloyd; educated Royal School, Bath; Bristol University (MD); Durham University (DPH). *Career:* Junior hospital appointments in Bristol, Oxford and Newcastle 1951–57; Resident Fellow and Lecturer on Child Health, University of Birmingham 1958–65; Senior Lecturer, Reader in Paediatrics, Institute of Child Health 1965–73; Professor of Paediatrics, London University 1973–75; Professor of Child Health, St George's Medical School, London University 1975–85; Visiting Examiner in Paediatrics in Universities in the UK and abroad; Nuffield Professor of Child Health, British Postgraduate Medical Federation, London University 1985–92, currently Emeritus Professor; Past Chairman, Department of Health Advisory Committee on Gene Therapy. *International Bodies (General):* Member of Paediatric Associations in: Finland, France, Switzerland, Germany, USA, Sri Lanka, Australia. *Other:* Member, Royal College of Physicians, London 1982–85, 1986–88; President, British Paediatric Association 1988–91. Hon. DSc: Bristol 1991, Birmingham 1993. *Honours:* DBE 1990. *Publications:* Several articles in scientific journals. *Recreations:* Cooking, gardening, walking. *Name, Style and Title:* Raised to the peerage as Baroness Lloyd of Highbury, of Highbury in the London Borough of Islington 1996. *Address:* The Baroness Lloyd of Highbury, DBE, House of Lords, London, SW1A 0PW.

LORD LLOYD-WEBBER   Conservative

LLOYD-WEBBER (Life Baron), Andrew Lloyd Webber; cr. 1997. Born 22 March 1948. Son of late William Southcombe Lloyd Webber, CBE, FRCM, FRCO, and late Jean Hermione Johnstone; educated Westminster School; Magdalen College, Oxford; Royal College of Music. Married 1st, 1971, Sarah Jane Tudor (1 son 1 daughter) (marriage dissolved 1983), married 2nd, 1984, Sarah Brightman (marriage dissolved 1990), married 3rd, 1991, Madeleine Astrid Gurdon (2 sons, 1 daughter). *Career:* Composer: Variations (based on A minor Caprice No 24 by Paganini) 1977, symphonic version 1986, Joseph and the Amazing Technicolour Dreamcoat (with lyrics by Timothy Rice) 1968, Jesus Christ Superstar (with lyrics by Timothy Rice) 1970, Gumshoe (film score) 1971, The Odessa File (film score) 1974, Jeeves (with lyrics by Alan Ayckbourn) 1975, Evita (with lyrics by Timothy Rice) 1976, Tell Me On a Sunday 1980, Cats (with lyrics by T. S. Eliot) 1981, Starlight Express 1984, Requiem Mass 1985, The Phantom of the Opera (with lyrics by Charles Hart and Richard Stilgoe) 1986, Aspects of Love (with lyrics by Don Black and Charles Hart) 1989, Sunset Boulevard (with lyrics by Don Black and Christopher Hampton) 1993, By Jeeves (with lyrics by Alan Ayckbourn) 1996, Whistle Down The Wind (with lyrics by Jim Steinman) 1996, Evita (film score) 1996;

The Beautiful Game (with lyrics by Ben Elton) 2000. *Select Committees:* Member, Offices Sub-Committee: Advisory Panel on Works of Art 2000–. *Awards Granted:* Star on the Hollywood Walk of Fame 1993; The American Society of Composers, Authors and Publishers Triple Play Award 'First recipient'; Tony Awards; Drama Desk Awards; Grammy Awards; Five Laurence Olivier Awards; Praemium Imperial Award for Music 1995; Richard Rodger's Award for contributions/excellence to/in Musical Theatre 1996; Oscar and Golden Globe for best original song "You must love me' from Evita the movie. *Trusts, etc:* Member, Open Churches Trust. *Honours:* Kt 1992. FRCM 1988. *Publications: Evita,* (with Tim Rice); *Cats the book of the musical,* 1981; *Joseph and the Amazing Technicolor Dreamcoat,* 1982; *The Complete Phantom of the Opera,* 1987; *The Complete Aspects of Love,* 1989; *Sunset Boulevard: From Movie to Musical,* 1993. *Special Interests:* Art, Architecture. *Recreations:* Architecture, art, food and wine. *Clubs:* Marc's. *Name, Style and Title:* Raised to the peerage as Baron Lloyd-Webber, of Sydmonton in the County of Hampshire 1997. *Address:* The Lord Lloyd-Webber, 22 Tower Street, London, WC2H 9NS.

BARONESS LOCKWOOD   Labour

LOCKWOOD (Life Baroness), Betty Lockwood; cr. 1978. Born 22 January 1924. Daughter of late Arthur Lockwood; educated East Borough Girls School, Dewsbury; Ruskin College, Oxford. Married 1978, Lieutenant-Colonel Cedric Hall (died 1988). *Councils, Public Bodies:* Member, Leeds Development Corporation 1988–95; DL, West Yorkshire 1987. *Career:* Assistant Agent, Reading 1948–50; Secretary-Agent, Gillingham Labour Party 1950–52; Yorkshire Regional Women's Officer, Labour Party 1952–67; Chief Woman Officer and Assistant National Agent, Labour Party 1967–75; Chairman, Equal Opportunities Commission 1975–83; Chairman, European Advisory Committee on Equal Opportunities for Women and Men 1982–83; Member, Council of Advertising Standards Authority 1983–92; Member, Council of Europe and WEU 1992–94. *Chancellor:* Pro-Chancellor, Bradford University 1987–97, Chancellor 1997–. *House of Lords:* A Deputy Speaker of the House of Lords 1990–; A Deputy Chairman of Committees 1997–. *Select Committees:* Member, House of Lords Select Committees: Science and Technology 1983–89, European Communities 1985–93; Chairman, Sub-Committee on Social and Community Affairs 1990–93. *Other:* President, Birkbeck College, University of London 1983–89; Member of Council: University of Bradford 1983–, University of Leeds 1985–91; President, Hillcroft College 1987–94; Chairman, National Coal Mining Museum for England 1995–. Hon. DLitt, Bradford 1981; Hon. Dr of Law, Strathclyde University 1985; Hon. Fellow: UMIST 1986, Birkbeck College, University of London 1987; Hon. Dr of University Leeds Metropolitan University 1999. *Trusts, etc:* Fellow, Industry and Parliament Trust. Hon. Fellow: UMIST 1986, Birkbeck College 1987. *Special Interests:* Sex Equality, Education, Industrial Training, Training, Industry. *Recreations:* Enjoying the Yorkshire Dales. *Clubs:* Soroptimist International. *Name, Style and Title:* Raised to the peerage as Baroness Lockwood, of Dewsbury in the County of West Yorkshire 1978. *Address:* The Baroness Lockwood, DL, 6 Sycamore Drive, Addingham, Nr Ilkley, West Yorkshire, LS29 0NY *Tel:* 01943 831098.

LORD LOFTHOUSE OF PONTEFRACT   Labour

LOFTHOUSE OF PONTEFRACT (Life Baron), Geoffrey Lofthouse; cr. 1997. Born 18 December 1925. Son of late Ernest Lofthouse; educated Featherstone Secondary School; Leeds University (day release). Married April 20, 1946, Sarah (died 1985), daughter of Joesh Thomas Onions (1 daughter). *Trades Union:* Member, NUM. *Councils, Public Bodies:* JP Pontefract 1970; Pontefract Borough Council: Councillor 1962–74, Leader of Council, Mayor of Pontefract 1967–68; Wakefield Metropolitan District Council: Councillor 1973–79, First Chairman, Chairman: Housing Committee, Wakefield Area Health Authority 1998–. *Career:* Personnel Manager, NCB Fryston 1970–78. *House of Commons:* MP (Labour) for Pontefract and Castleford 1978 By-election–97; First Deputy Chairman, Ways and Means 1992–97. *House of Lords:* A Deputy Chairman of Committees 1999–. *Party Groups (General):* Vice-President, Wakefield District Labour Party. *Other:* Member: Division Education Executive Committee, All Governing/Managing Bodies of Pontefract Schools; Chairman: Primary Schools' Managers, Pontefract Carleton High School Governing Body;

Patron, Heartlink. *Honours:* Knighted 1995. Fellow, Institute of Personnel Development 1984–. *Publications: A Very Miner MP* (Autobiography), 1986 *From Coal Sack to Woolsack*(Autobiography), 1999. *Special Interests:* Housing, Industrial Relations, Energy, Local Government, Human Rights. *Recreations:* Rugby League and cricket. *Sportsclubs:* Vice-President, Featherstone Rovers RLFC; President, British Amateur Rugby League Association; Vice-Chairman, Policy Making Board of Rugby Football League. *Name, Style and Title:* Raised to the peerage as Baron Lofthouse of Pontefract, of Pontefract in the County of West Yorkshire 1997.*Address:* The Lord Lofthouse of Pontefract, 67 Carleton Crest, Pontefract, West Yorkshire, WF8 2QR *Tel:* 01977 704275.

BISHOP OF LONDON   Non-Affiliated

LONDON (132nd Bishop of), Richard John Carew Chartres. Born 11 July 1947. Son of late Richard Chartres and of Charlotte Chartres; educated Hertford Grammar School; Trinity College, Cambridge (MA); Cuddesdon Theological College, Oxford; Lincoln Theological College (BD (Lambeth). Married 1982, Caroline Mary McLintock (2 sons 2 daughters). *Career:* Deacon 1973; Priest 1974; Assistant Curate, St Andrew's, Bedford 1973–75; Bishop's Domestic Chaplain, St Albans 1975–80; Archbishop of Canterbury's Chaplain 1980–84; Vicar, St Stephen with St John, Westminster 1984–92; Director of Ordinands for the London Area 1985–92; Gresham Professor of Divinity 1986–92; Area Bishop of Stepney 1992–95; Prelate of the Most Excellent Order of the British Empire 1995–; Bishop of London 1995–; Took his seat in the House of Lords 1996; Dean of HM Chapels Royal 1996–. *Other:* Member: The Court of the City University, The Ecclesiological Society; Chairman, Church Heritage Forum; Bencher of the Middle Temple; Ecclesiastical Patron, The Prayer Book Society; Chaplain to the Order of St John. Hon. DD: London, City, Brunel Universities; Hon. DLitt, Guildhall London. *Trusts, etc:* Member: St Ethelburga's Centre for Reconciliation and Peace, St Catherine's Foundation, St Andrew's Trust. *Honours:* PC 1996. FSA, 1999. Freeman, City of London. Liveryman, Merchant Taylors' Company; Hon. Freeman: Weavers' Company, Leathersellers' Company, Drapers' Company, Woolmen Company. *Publications: A Brief History of Gresham College,* 1997. *Special Interests:* London, Environment. *Recreations:* Family. *Clubs:* Garrick. *Address:* Rt Rev and Rt Hon the Lord Bishop of London, The Old Deanery, Dean's Court, London, EC4V 5AA *Tel:* 020 7248 6233 *E-Mail:* bishop@londin.clara.co.uk.

EARL OF LONGFORD   Labour

LONGFORD (7th Earl of, I), Francis Aungier Pakenham; cr. 1785; Baron Longford (I) 1756; 6th Baron Silchester (UK) 1821; 1st Baron Pakenham (UK) 1945; (Life) Baron Pakenham of Cowley 1999. Born 5 December 1905. Son of late 5th Earl, KP, MVO, and Lady Mary Julia Child Villiers. Succeeded his brother 1961. Sits as Baron Pakenham; educated Eton; New College, Oxford (MA Modern Greats 1934). Married November 3, 1931, Elizabeth Harman (4 sons 3 daughters and 1 daughter deceased). *Armed Forces:* Served with Oxford and Bucks. Yeomanry (TA) May 1939-May 1940; Member, Oxford Home Guard 1940–45. *Career:* Former Tutor, Christ Church, Oxford, Member, Governing Body; Member, Conservative Party Economic Research Department 1930–32; Chief Assistant to Sir William Beveridge 1941–44; Chairman, National Bank Ltd 1955–63; Chairman, National Youth Employment Council 1968–71; Chairman, Sidgwick and Jackson Ltd Publishers 1970–80. *House of Lords:* A Lord in Waiting to HM King George VI 1945–46; Parliamentary Under-Secretary of State for War 1946–47; Chancellor of the Duchy of Lancaster 1947–48; Minister of Civil Aviation 1948–51; First Lord of the Admiralty May-October 1951; Lord Privy Seal 1964–65, 1966–68; Leader of the House of Lords 1964–68; Secretary of State for the Colonies December 1965-April 1966. *Party Groups (General):* Joined Labour Party 1936. *Other:* Joint Founder, New Bridge for Ex-Prisoners 1956. *Honours:* PC 1948; KG 1971. *Publications:* Several books including: *A History of the House of Lords,* 1988; *Suffering and Hope,* 1990; *Punishment and the Punished,* 1991; *Prisoner or Patient,* 1992; *Young Offenders,* 1993; *Avowed Intent* (memoir), 1994. *Name, Style and Title:* Created a life peer as Baron Pakenham of Cowley, of Cowley in the County of Oxfordshire 1999.*Address:* Rt Hon the Earl of Longford, KG, Bernhurst, Hurst Green, East Sussex, TN19 7QN*Tel:* 01580 860248; 18 Chesil Court, Chelsea Manor Street, London, SW3 5QP.

LORD LOVELL-DAVIS   Labour

LOVELL-DAVIS (Life Baron), Peter Lovell Lovell-Davis; cr. 1974. Born 8 July 1924. Son of late William Lovell-Davis, Accountant; educated King Edward VI Grammar School, Stratford-upon-Avon; Jesus College, Oxford (MA). Married July 29, 1950, Jean, daughter of late Peter Foster Graham (1 son 1 daughter). *Armed Forces:* RAF Flight/Lieutenant Pilot 1943–47. *Councils, Public Bodies:* Member, Islington District Health Authority 1982–85. *Career:* Managing Director, Central Press Features Ltd; Director of other newspaper and printing companies 1950–70; Chairman: Features Syndicate Ltd, Davis and Harrison Visual Productions Ltd 1970–74; Member, London Consortium 1977–87; Board Member, Commonwealth Development Corporation 1978–84; Chairman, Lee Cooper Licensing Services Ltd 1983–90; Chairman, Pettifor, Morrow and Associates 1986–99. *House of Lords:* Parliamentary Under-Secretary of State for Energy 1975–76. *Whip:* Government Whip (A Lord in Waiting) 1974–75. *Spokesman:* Spokesman for Energy 1974–76. *Select Committees:* Former Member, Select Committee on European Communities; Former Chairman, Sub-Committee Report on Energy Conservation. *Party Groups (General):* Voluntary Adviser on publicity to the Labour Party and Government Departments 1962–74. *Other:* Vice-President, Youth Hostels Association 1977–. *Trusts, etc:* Trustee: Academic Centre of the Whittington Hospital, Highgate 1980–, The Museum of the Port of London and Docklands 1985–98. *Special Interests:* Health, European Union, Media, Energy. *Recreations:* Aviation, bird-watching, industrial archaeology, inland waterways, walking, music. *Name, Style and Title:* Raised to the peerage as Baron Lovell-Davis, of Highgate in the County of Greater London 1974. *Address:* The Lord Lovell-Davis, 80 North Road, Highgate, London, N6 4AA *Tel:* 020 8348 3919 *E-Mail:* ploved@dircon.co.uk.

LORD LUCAS OF CRUDWELL AND DINGWALL   Conservative

LUCAS OF CRUDWELL (11th Baron, E) cr. 1663, and DINGWALL (de facto 8th Lord, 14th but for the attainder) (S) 1609; Ralph Matthew Palmer. Born 7 June 1951. Son of late Major Hon. Robert Jocelyn Palmer, MC, and Anne Rosemary, Baroness Lucas of Crudwell (10th in line). Succeeded his mother 1991; educated Eton; Balliol College, Oxford (BA Physics). Married 1st 1978, Clarissa Marie Lockett (1 son 1 daughter) (marriage dissolved 1995), married 2nd 1995, Amanda Atha (died 2000). *Career:* Articles with various firms now part of Arthur Andersen 1972–76; With S. G. Warburg & Co. Ltd 1976–88; Director of various companies. *House of Lords:* An elected hereditary peer 1999–. *Whip:* A Lord in Waiting (Government Whip) 1994–97. *Spokesman:* A Spokesman for: the Department of Education 1994–95, Department of Social Security and the Welsh Office 1994–97, the Ministry of Agriculture, Fisheries and Food and Department of the Environment 1995–97; An Opposition Spokesman on: Agriculture, Fisheries and Food 1997, Constitutional Affairs, Scotland and Wales (Wales) 1997, Environment, Transport and the Regions (Environment) 1997, International Development 1997–98. *Miscellaneous:* A Co-heir to the Barony of Butler. FCA. Liveryman, Mercers' Company. *Special Interests:* Education, Trade and Industry, Finance. *Address:* The Lord Lucas of Crudwell and Dingwall, House of Lords, London, SW1A 0PW *Tel:* 020 7219 4177 *E-Mail:* lucas@dingwall.demon.co.uk.

LORD LUCE   Cross-Bencher

LUCE (Life Baron), Richard Napier Luce; cr. 2000. Born 14 October 1936. Son of late Sir William Luce; educated Wellington College, Berkshire; Christ's College, Cambridge (history). Married April 5, 1961, Rose Nicholson (2 sons). *Councils, Public Bodies:* DL, West Sussex 1991–. *Career:* National service 1955–57; Overseas Civil Service, Kenya 1961–63; Marketing manager: Gallaher Ltd 1963–65, Spirella 1965–67; Director, National Innovations Centre 1967–71; Vice-president, Institute of Patentees and Inventors 1974–79; Non-executive director, European Advisory Board, Corning Glass International SA 1976–79; Chair, Courtenay Stewart International Limited 1975–79; Non-executive director: Booker Tate 1991–96, Meridian Broadcasting 1991–97; Vice-chancellor, Buckingham University 1992–96; Governor and Commander-in-chief, Gibraltar 1997–2000; Lord Chamberlain of the Queen's Household 2000–. *House of Commons:* Contested Hitchin 1970; Conservative MP for West Sussex, Arundel and Shoreham

1971–74 and for Shoreham 1974–92; PPS to Minister for Trade and Consumer Affairs 1972–74; Opposition Whip 1974–75; Parliamentary Under-Secretary of State for Foreign and Commonwealth Affairs 1979–81; Minister of State, Foreign and Commonwealth Office 1981–82 (resigned April 1982 on Falklands issue); Minister of State, Foreign and Commonwealth Office 1983–85; Minister for Arts (Minister of State, Privy Council Office) 1985–90. *Spokesman (Commons):* Opposition spokesman for Foreign and Commonwealth Affairs 1977–79. *International Bodies (General):* Atlantic Council of UK 1991–96; Chair, Commonwealth Foundation 1992–96. *Other:* President, Voluntary Art Network 1993–; Member court of governors, Royal Shakespeare Theatre 1994–. *Trusts, etc:* Trustee, Geographers' A-Z Map Trust 1993–. *Honours:* PC 1986; Kt 1991; GCVO 2000. *Recreations:* Walking, reading, tennis. *Name, Style and Title:* Raised to the peerage as Baron Luce, of Adur in the County of West Sussex 2000. *Address:* Rt Hon The Lord Luce, DL, GCVO, Lord Chamberlain, Buckingham Palace, London SW1A 1AA *Tel:* 020 7930 4832.

BARONESS LUDFORD   Liberal Democrat

LUDFORD (Life Baroness), Sarah Ann Ludford; cr. 1997. Born 14 March 1951. Daughter of Joseph Campbell Ludford and Valerie Kathleen Ludford (née Skinner); educated Portsmouth High School for Girls; London School of Economics (BSc (Econ) International History, MSc (Econ) European Studies); Inns of Court School of Law. Married, Stephen Hitchins. *Councils, Public Bodies:* Councillor, London Borough of Islington 1991–. *Career:* Department of the Environment 1972–73; Independent Broadcasting Authority 1973–75; Called to the Bar, Gray's Inn 1979; European Commission, Brussels 1977–78 and 1979–85; Lloyds of London 1985–87; American Express Europe 1987–90; Freelance European Consultant 1990–; Elected a Liberal Democrat MEP for the London Region 1999–. *Spokesman:* A Spokesman on Foreign and Commonwealth Affairs 1998–. *International Bodies (General):* Member: European Movement Management Board, European Liberal Democrat and Reform Party (ELDR). *Party Groups (General):* Vice-Chair, Liberal Democrat Federal Policy Committee. *Miscellaneous:* Member, Royal Institute of International Affairs (Chatham House); Contested (Lib Dem) European Elections: Hampshire East and Wight 1984, London Central 1989 and 1994, Islington North 1992, Islington South and Finsbury 1997. *Special Interests:* Europe, Local Government, Social Issues, Health, Economic Policy. *Recreations:* Theatre, ballet, gardening. *Clubs:* National Liberal. *Name, Style and Title:* Raised to the peerage as Baroness Ludford, of Clerkenwell in the London Borough of Islington 1997. *Address:* The Baroness Ludford, MEP, 70 St Peter's Street, London, N1 8JS.

LORD LUKE   Conservative

LUKE (3rd Baron, UK), Arthur Charles St John Lawson Johnston; cr. 1929. Born 13 January 1933. Son of 2nd Baron. Succeeded his father 1996; educated Eton; Trinity College, Cambridge (BA). Married 1st, August 6, 1959, Silvia Maria Roigt (1 son 2 daughters) (divorced 1971), married 2nd, 1971, Sarah Louise Hearne, OBE (1 son). *Councils, Public Bodies:* A County Councillor for Bedfordshire 1965–70; High Sheriff, Bedfordshire 1969–70; DL, Bedfordshire 1989. *Career:* Fine Art Dealer. *House of Lords:* An elected hereditary peer 1999–. *Whip:* An Opposition Whip 1997–. *Spokesman:* Spokesman for: Agriculture, Culture, Media and Sport. *Other:* President, National Association of Warehouse-keepers 1962–78; Member, Court of Corporation of Sons of the Clergy 1980–; Commander, St John's Ambulance Brigade, Bedfordshire 1983–90; President, International Association of Book Keepers 1997–. *Honours:* KStJ. Freeman, City of London. Junior Warden, Drapers' Company 1993, Member of Court 1993–, Second Master Warden 1999–. *Special Interests:* Art, Heritage, Church Affairs, Military History, River Thames, Tourism, Defence. *Recreations:* Watching cricket, shooting, fishing, watching motor sports. *Clubs:* MCC. *Address:* The Lord Luke, Odell Manor, Bedfordshire, MK43 7BB *Tel:* 01234 720416 *Fax:* 01234 721311 *Tel:* House of Lords: 020 7219 3703 *E-Mail:* rupes@currantbun.com.

LORD LYELL — Conservative

LYELL (3rd Baron), Charles Lyell; cr. 1914; 3rd Bt of Kinnordy (UK) 1894. Born 27 March 1939. Son of 2nd Baron, VC. Succeeded his father, who was killed in action, 1943; educated Eton; Christ Church, Oxford. *Armed Forces:* 2nd Lieutenant Scots Guards 1957–59. *Councils, Public Bodies:* DL, Angus 1988. *Career:* Chartered Accountant. *House of Lords:* Parliamentary Under-Secretary of State for Northern Ireland 1984–89; A Deputy Speaker of the House of Lords; A Deputy Chairman of Committees 1997–; An elected hereditary peer 1999–. *Whip:* Opposition Whip 1974–79; A Lord in Waiting (Government Whip) 1979–1984. *Spokesman:* A Government Spokesman on: Health and Social Security, The Treasury 1982, Scotland 1982–84, Foreign Office Affairs 1983–84. *International Bodies (General):* Member: North Atlantic Assembly 1973–79, UK Delegation to North Atlantic Assembly 1994–97. *Miscellaneous:* Member, Queen's Bodyguard for Scotland, Royal Company of Archers. *Sportsclubs:* Chairman, Lords and Commons Ski Club 1990–93. *Clubs:* Turf, White's. *Address:* The Lord Lyell, DL, 20 Petersham Mews, London, SW7 5NR *Tel:* 020 7584 9419; Kinnordy, Kirriemuir *Tel:* 01575 572848; Angus, DD8 5ER.

M

LORD McALPINE OF WEST GREEN — Independent Conservative

McALPINE OF WEST GREEN (Life Baron), Robert Alistair McAlpine; cr. 1984. Born 14 May 1942. Son of late Baron McAlpine of Moffat (Life Peer); educated Stowe. Married 1st, 1964, Sarah Alexandra Baron (2 daughters) (divorced 1979), married 2nd, 1980, Romilly Hobbs (1 daughter). *Career:* Joined Sir Robert McAlpine and Sons Ltd 1958, Director 1963–95; Treasurer, European League for Economic Co-operation 1974–75, Vice-President 1975–; Director, ICA 1972–73; Member, Arts Council of GB 1981–82. *Party Groups (General):* Hon. Treasurer, European Democratic Union 1978–88; Hon. Treasurer, Conservative and Unionist Party 1975–90, jointly 1981–90, Deputy Chairman 1979–83. *Other:* Vice-President, Friends Ashmolean Museum 1969–; Greater London Arts Association 1971–77; Vice-Chairman, Contemporary Arts Society 1973–80; President, British Waterfowl Association 1978–81, Patron since 1981; Member, Council, English Stage Co. 1973–75; Governor: Polytechnic of the South Bank 1981–82, Stowe School 1981–83; President, Medical College of St. Bartholomew's Hospital 1993–. *Trusts, etc:* Trustee, Royal Opera House Trust 1974–80. *Miscellaneous:* Chairman, The Referendum Movement 1997. *Publications: The Servant*, 1992; *Journal of a Collector*, 1994; *Letters to a Young Politician*, 1995; *Once a Jolly Bagman*, 1997; *The New Machiavelli*, 1997; *Collecting and Display*, 1998; *Bagman to Swagman*, 1999. *Recreations:* The arts, horticulture, aviculture, agriculture. *Clubs:* Garrick, Pratt's. *Name, Style and Title:* Raised to the peerage as Baron McAlpine of West Green, of West Green in the County of Hampshire 1984. *Address:* The Lord McAlpine of West Green, Sir Robert McAlpine & Sons Ltd, 40 Bernard Street, London, WC1N 1LE.

LORD MACAULAY OF BRAGAR — Labour

MACAULAY OF BRAGAR (Life Baron), Donald Macaulay; cr. 1989. Born 14 November 1933. Son of late John and Henrietta Macaulay; educated Hermitage School, Helensburgh; Clydebank High School; Glasgow University (MA, LLB). Married March 26, 1962, Mary Morrison (2 daughters). *Armed Forces:* National Service, RASC 1958–60. *Councils, Public Bodies:* Member, Bryden Committee on Identification following Devlin Report. *Career:* Solicitor 1960–62; Called to Scottish Bar 1963; Advocate Depute (Crown Prosecutor) 1967–70, 1973–76; Standing Junior Counsel to Highlands and Islands Development Board; Chairman, SACRO 1993–96; Chairman, Supreme Court Legal Aid Committee; Member, Central Legal Aid Committee both during 1970s; Member, Criminal

Injuries Compensation Board; Scottish Chairman, Committee for Abolition of Paybeds in NHS; Founder Member and former Chairman, Advocates' Criminal Law Group. *Spokesman:* Former Opposition Spokesman on Scottish Legal Affairs. *Select Committees:* Member, Select Committees on: Computers, Crofting. *Miscellaneous:* Contested (Labour) Inverness 1970 General Election. *Special Interests:* Scottish Law, Education, Local Government, Sport, Theatre. *Recreations:* Art, music, theatre, football, golf, running. *Sportsclubs:* Royal Musselburgh Golf. *Clubs:* Edinburgh Press, College Club, University of Glasgow. *Name, Style and Title:* Raised to the peerage as Baron Macaulay of Bragar, of Bragar in the County of Ross and Cromarty 1989. *Address:* The Lord Macaulay of Bragar, QC, Belmont, 2 South Morton Street, Edinburgh, EH15 2NB *Tel:* 0131–669 6419; Advocates' Library, Parliament House, Edinburgh *E-Mail:* macaulayd@parliament.uk.

LORD McCARTHY   Labour

McCARTHY (Life Baron), William Edward John McCarthy; cr. 1976. Born 30 July 1925. Son of Edward McCarthy; educated Holloway County School; Ruskin College, Oxford; Merton College, Oxford; Nuffield College, Oxford (MA, DPhil). Married January 18, 1956, Margaret, daughter of Percy and Anne Godfrey. *Trades Union:* Member, Association of University Teachers. *Career:* Research Director, Royal Commission on Trade Union & Employers Associations 1965–68; Fellow, Nuffield College 1969–; Chairman, Railway National Staff Tribunal 1974–85; Member, ACAS Arbitrational Panel 1975–; Associate Fellow, Templeton College 1980–; Member, Civil Service Arbitration Tribunal 1994–; Formerly Special Commissioner, Equal Opportunities Commission; Member, TUC's Independent Review Committee; Chairman, TUC Working Party on new National Daily; Former Director, Harland and Wolff, Belfast. *Spokesman:* Front Bench Spokesman on Employment 1979–97. *Select Committees:* Member, Select Committee on Unemployment 1980–82. *Party Groups:* Member, Labour Peers Trade and Industry Group. *Party Groups (General):* Member: Labour Party Job Creation Group, Labour Party Education and Employment Group, Labour Party Culture, Media and Sport Committee. *Other:* Member, Society for Theatre Research. *Miscellaneous:* Research Fellow, Nuffield College 1959–63. Fellow, Institute of Personnel and Development 1989. *Publications:* Numerous books and articles on industrial relations and labour economics. *Recreations:* Theatre, ballet, gardening, theatrical history, opera. *Clubs:* Reform. *Name, Style and Title:* Raised to the peerage as Baron McCarthy, of Headington in the City of Oxford 1976. *Address:* The Lord McCarthy, Nuffield College, Oxford, OX1 1NF *Tel:* 01865 278554; House of Lords, London, SW1A 0PW *Tel:* House of Lords 020 7219 3214.

LORD McCLUSKEY   Cross-Bencher

McCLUSKEY (Life Baron), John Herbert McCluskey; cr. 1976. Born 12 June 1929. Son of late Francis John McCluskey and Margaret McCluskey (née Doonan); educated St Bede's College, Manchester; Holy Cross Academy, Edinburgh; Edinburgh University (Harry Dalgety Bursar 1948, Vans Dunlop Scholar). Married December 28, 1956, Ruth, daughter of Aaron Friedland (2 sons 1 daughter). *Armed Forces:* Royal Air Force 1952–54 (Sword of Honour, Spitalgate OCTU 1953). *Career:* Admitted to Faculty of Advocates 1955; QC (Scot) 1967; Sheriff Principal of Dumfries and Galloway 1973–74; Senator of the College of Justice in Scotland 1984–; Reith Lecturer 1986. *House of Lords:* Solicitor-General for Scotland 1974–79. *Spokesman:* Opposition Spokesman on Scottish Legal Affairs 1979–84. *International Bodies (General):* Vice-Chairman: International Bar Association, IBA Human Rights Institute. *Other:* Chairman: Scottish Association for Mental Health 1985–94, Fairbridge in Scotland 1995–97. Hon. LLD, Dundee 1989. *Trusts, etc:* Chair, John Smith Memorial Trust. *Publications: Law, Justice and Democracy*, 1987; *Criminal Appeals*, 1992, 2nd edition 2000. *Special Interests:* Mental Health. *Recreations:* Tennis, swimming. *Sportsclubs:* Edinburgh Sports. *Clubs:* Royal Air Force. *Name, Style and Title:* Raised to the peerage as Baron McCluskey, of Churchhill in the District of the City of Edinburgh 1976. *Address:* The Lord McCluskey, Parliament House, Edinburgh, EH1 1RQ *Tel:* 0131–225 2595.

LORD McCOLL OF DULWICH   Conservative

McCOLL OF DULWICH (Life Baron), Ian McColl; cr. 1989. Born 6 January 1933. Son of late Frederick and Winifred McColl; educated Hutchesons' Grammar School, Glasgow; St Paul's School, London (Foundation Scholarship in Classics); University of London (MS). Married 1960, Dr Jean Lennox, daughter of late Arthur James McNair, FRCS, FRCOG (1 son 2 daughters). *Career:* Consultant surgeon and Sub Dean, St Bartholomew's Hospital 1967–71; Professor and Director of Surgery, Guy's Hospital 1971–98; Professor of Surgery, University of London 1971–; Consultant Surgeon to the Army 1980–98; Chairman, Government Working Party on Artificial Limbs and Wheelchair Service 1984–86; Vice-Chairman, Disablement Services Authority 1987–91; Chairman, Department of Surgery of the United Medical Schools of Guy's and St Thomas' Hospital 1988–92. *House of Lords:* PPS (Lords) to the Prime Minister 1994–97; A Deputy Speaker of the House of Lords 1994–97, 1998–; A Deputy Chairman of Committees 1994–97, 1998–. *Spokesman:* Opposition Spokesman on Health 1997–. *Select Committees:* Former Member, House of Lords Select Committees on: European Communities, Sub-Committee F (Environment), Medical Ethics 1993–94; Member, Select Committees on: Science and Technology Sub-Committee II (Aircraft Cabin Environment) 2000–, Science and Technology Sub-Committee IIA (Human Genetic Databases) 2000–. *Backbench Committees:* Member, Backbench Committee on Disablement. *International Bodies:* Member, Executive Committee, CPA UK Branch 1999–. *International Bodies (General):* Member, International Board of Mercy Ships. *Other:* Chairman, U.K. Board of Mercy Ships; Governor-at-large for England, Board of Governors, American College of Surgeons 1982–86; President, Mildmay Mission Hospital 1985–; Member of Council, Royal College of Surgeons 1986–94; President: Society of Minimally Invasive Surgery 1991–94, National Association of Limbless Disabled 1992–; Vice-President, John Groom's Association for Disabled People 1992–; President: The Hospital Saving Association 1994–, Association of Endoscopic Surgery of Great Britain and Ireland, Leprosy Mission 1996–. *Awards Granted:* George and Thomas Hutchesons Award 2000. *Miscellaneous:* Research Fellow, Harvard Medical School 1967. *Honours:* CBE 1997. FRCS; FRCSE; FACS. Master, Worshipful Company of Barbers. *Publications: Intestinal Absorption in Man*, 1976; *NHS Data Book*, 1984; *Government Report on Artificial Limb and Appliance Centre Service*, 1986; As well as articles in medical journals. *Special Interests:* Disability, Higher Education, Health Service, Forestry, Medicine, Health. *Recreations:* Forestry. *Sportsclubs:* Palace of Westminster. *Clubs:* Royal College of Surgeons. *Name, Style and Title:* Raised to the peerage as Baron McColl of Dulwich, of Bermondsey in the London Borough of Southwark 1989. *Address:* Professor the Lord McColl of Dulwich, CBE, House of Lords, London, SW1A 0PW *E-Mail:* mccolli@parliament.uk.

LORD McCONNELL   Ulster Unionist - sits as a Cross-Bencher

McCONNELL (Life Baron), Robert William Brian McConnell; cr. 1995. Born 25 November 1922. Son of late Alfred McConnell; educated Sedbergh School; Queen's University, Belfast (BA, LLB). Married 1951, Sylvia Elizabeth Joyce Agnew (2 sons 1 daughter). *Career:* Called to the Bar of Northern Ireland 1948; MP (U) for South Antrim in the Northern Ireland Parliament 1951–68; Deputy Chairman, Ways and Means 1962; Held various posts in the Government and Parliament of Northern Ireland 1963–68; Parliamentary Secretary to Ministry of Health and Local Government 1963–64; Minister of Home Affairs 1964–66; Minister of State, Ministry of Development 1966–67; Leader of the House of Commons 1967–68; President, Industrial Court of Northern Ireland 1968–81; Social Security (formerly National Insurance) Commissioner for Northern Ireland 1968–87. *Select Committees:* Former Member, European Select Committee and Sub-Committee A. *Other:* President, European Movement in Northern Ireland 1992–95, Vice-Chairman 1987–92. *Honours:* PC (NI) 1964. Freeman, City of London 1971. *Clubs:* Ulster Reform (Belfast), Farmers'. *Name, Style and Title:* Raised to the peerage as Baron McConnell, of Lisburn in the County of Antrim 1995. *Address:* Rt Hon the Lord McConnell, 50A Glenavy Road, Knocknadona, Lisburn, Co. Antrim, BT28 3UT *Tel:* 01846 663432.

LORD MACDONALD OF TRADESTON   Labour

MACDONALD OF TRADESTON (Life Baron), Angus John Macdonald; cr. 1998. Born 20 August 1940. Son of late Colin and Jean Macdonald; educated Allan Glen's School, Glasgow; Apprenticeship, Marine engineer. Married 1963, Theresa McQuaid (2 daughters). *Career:* Marine Fitter 1955–63; Circulation Manager, *Tribune* 1964–65; Feature Writer, *The Scotsman* 1965–67; Granada Television: Reporter/Editor/Executive Producer: *World in Action* 1967–75, Successively Head of Current Affairs/Regional Programmes/Features 1975–82, Programme Presenter: Right to Reply, Union World, Party Conferences; Chairman: Scottish Media Group plc 1996–97 (Director of Programmes 1985–90, Managing Director 1990–96), Taylor and Francis plc 1997–98; Board Member, Bank of Scotland. *House of Lords:* Parliamentary Under-Secretary of State, Scottish Office (Minister of Business and Industry) 1998–99; Minister of State for Transport, Department of the Environment, Transport and the Regions (Minister for Transport) 1999–. *Spokesman:* Spokesman on the Scottish Office 1998–99. *Other:* Chairman: Edinburgh International Television Festival 1976, ITV Broadcasting Board 1992–94, Edinburgh Film Festival 1994–96; Member, Press and Broadcasting Advisory Committee, Ministry of Defence 1994–95; Vice-President, Royal Television Society 1994–98; Chairman, Cairngorms Partnership 1997–98; Board Member: Scottish Enterprise, British Film Institute. *Awards Granted:* BAFTA Award, Best Factual Television (*World in Action*) 1973; BAFTA Scotland Lifetime Achievement Award 1997–; Scottish Business Elite 'Corporate Leader of the Year' and 'Chairman of the Year' 1997. DUniv, Stirling 1992; DLit: Napier 1997, Robert Gordon 1998. *Honours:* CBE 1997; PC 1999. *Publications: The Documentary Idea and Television Today,* 1977; *Camera: Victorian eyewitness,* 1979 *Clubs:* Royal Automobile, Groucho. *Name, Style and Title:* Raised to the peerage as Baron Macdonald of Tradeston, of Tradeston in the County of Glasgow 1998. *Address:* Rt Hon the Lord Macdonald of Tradeston, CBE, House of Lords, London, SW1A 0PW.

LORD MACFARLANE OF BEARSDEN   Conservative

MACFARLANE OF BEARSDEN (Life Baron), Norman Somerville Macfarlane; cr. 1991. Born 5 March 1926. Son of late Daniel Robertson Macfarlane; educated High School of Glasgow. Married 1953, Marguerite Campbell (1 son 4 daughters). *Armed Forces:* Served in Palestine with RA 1945–47. *Councils, Public Bodies:* DL, Dumbartonshire 1993. *Career:* Founded N. S. Macfarlane & Co. Ltd. 1949, becoming Macfarlane Group (Clansman) plc 1973, Managing Director 1973–90, Chairman 1973–98, Honorary Life President 1998; Member, Council CBI Scotland 1975–81; Chairman, The Time Art Society plc 1976–98; Underwriting Member, Lloyd's 1978–99; Member, Board of Scottish Development Agency 1979–87; Member, Royal Fine Art Commission for Scotland 1980–82; Director, Edinburgh Fund Managers plc 1980–97; Chairman, Glasgow Development Agency (Formerly Glasgow Section) 1985–92; Director, Clydesdale Bank plc 1980–96, Deputy Chairman 1993–96; Director, General Accident Fire & Life Assurance Corporation 1984–96; Chairman, Amercian Trust plc 1984–97; Chairman, United Distillers UK plc 1989–96, Hon. Life President 1996–; Joint Deputy Chairman, Guinness plc 1989–92, Chairman 1987–89; Lord High Commissioner to the General Assembly of the Church of Scotland 1992, 1993 and 1997. *Other:* President: Stationers Association of Great Britain and Ireland 1965, Royal Glasgow Institute of the Fine Arts 1976–87; Director, Scottish National Orchestra 1977–82; Member, Court of the University of Glasgow 1979–87; Vice-Chairman, Scottish Ballet 1983–87; Hon. President, Chas Rennie McIntosh Society 1988–; President, High School of Glasgow 1992–; Patron, Scottish Licensed Trade Association (SLTA) 1992–; Regent, Royal College of Surgeons of Edinburgh 1997–. Seven honorary doctorates/fellowships. *Trusts, etc:* Trustee: National Heritage Memorial Fund 1984–97, National Galleries of Scotland 1986–97. *Honours:* Kt 1983; KT 1996. Hon. FRIAS 1984; Hon. RSA 1987; Hon. RGI 1987; Hon. SCOTVEC 1991; Hon. FRCPS (Glasgow) 1992. *Special Interests:* The arts. *Recreations:* Golf, Sport. *Sportsclubs:* Glasgow Golf, North Berwick Golf. *Clubs:* Royal Scottish Automobile (Glasgow), New (Edinburgh). *Name, Style and Title:* Raised to the peerage as Baron Macfarlane of Bearsden, in the District of Bearsden and Milngavie 1991. *Address:* The Lord Macfarlane of Bearsden, KT, DL, FRSE, Macfarlane Group (Clansman) plc, 21 Newton Place, Glasgow, G3 7PY.

BARONESS McFARLANE OF LLANDAFF   Cross-Bencher

McFARLANE OF LLANDAFF (Life Baroness), Jean Kennedy McFarlane; cr. 1979. Born 1 April 1926. Daughter of late Dr James McFarlane; educated Howell's School, Llandaff; Bedford and Birkbeck Colleges, London University (MA, BSc(Soc), HV Tut Cert). *Career:* Staff Nurse, St. Bartholomew's Hospital, London 1950–51; Health Visitor, Cardiff City 1953–59; Tutor, Royal College of Nursing, London 1960–62; Education Officer, Royal College of Nursing, Birmingham 1962–66; Research Project Leader, Royal College of Nursing, London 1967–69; Director of Education, Royal College of Nursing, London 1969–71; Senior Lecturer in Nursing, University of Manchester 1971–74; Professor and Head of Department of Nursing, University of Manchester 1974–88; Member: General Synod, Church of England 1990–, General Synod Review of Synodical Government Group 1993–. *Select Committees:* Member: Priorities in Medical Research 1987–88, Medical Ethics 1993–97. Hon. MSc, Manchester; Hon. DSc, Ulster. *Miscellaneous:* Member: Royal Commission on NHS 1976–79, Commonwealth War Graves Commission 1983–88. FRCN; SRN; SCM. *Special Interests:* Health, Education. *Name, Style and Title:* Raised to the peerage as Baroness McFarlane of Llandaff, of Llandaff in the County of South Glamorgan 1979. *Address:* The Baroness McFarlane of Llandaff, 5 Dovercourt Avenue, Heaton Mersey, Stockport, SK4 3QB *Tel:* 0161–432 8367.

LORD McINTOSH OF HARINGEY   Labour

McINTOSH OF HARINGEY (Life Baron), Andrew Robert McIntosh; cr. 1983. Born 30 April 1933. Son of late Professor Albert William McIntosh, OBE, and late Jenny McIntosh (née Britton); educated Royal Grammar School, High Wycombe; Jesus College, Oxford; Ohio State University. Married May 15, 1962, Mrs Naomi Ellen Kelly, daughter of late Tom Sargant, OBE, and Marie Cerny (née Hlouskova) (2 sons). *Councils, Public Bodies:* Councillor: Borough of Hornsey 1963–64, London Borough of Haringey 1964–68; Councillor, Greater London Council 1973–83, Leader of the Opposition 1980–81. *Career:* Market Research Society: Editor of Journal 1963–67, Chairman 1972–73, President 1995–98; Managing Director, IFF Research Ltd 1965–81, Chairman 1981–88, Deputy Chairman 1988–97; Principal (Honorary), Working Men's College, London 1988–97. *House of Lords:* Deputy Leader of the Opposition 1992–97; A Deputy Chairman of Committees 1997–; A Deputy Speaker 1999–. *Whip:* Captain of HM Bodyguard of the Yeomen of the Guard (Deputy Chief Whip) 1997–. *Spokesman:* Opposition Spokesman on: Education and Science 1985–87, The Environment 1987–92, Home Affairs 1992–97; A Spokesman on: Legal Affairs 1997–98, the Treasury 1997–, Trade and Industry 1998–. *Party Groups (General):* Chairman, Fabian Society 1985–86. *Miscellaneous:* Chairman, Association for Neighbourhood Councils 1974–80. *Recreations:* Cooking, reading, music. *Name, Style and Title:* Raised to the peerage as Baron McIntosh of Haringey, of Haringey in the County of Greater London 1983. *Address:* The Lord McIntosh of Haringey, 27 Hurst Avenue, London, N6 5TX *Tel:* 020 8340 1496 *Fax:* 020 8348 4641; House of Lords, London, SW1A 0PW *Tel:* House of Lords 020 7219 3126/6782 *Fax:* 020 7219 6837 *E-Mail:* mcintoshar@parliament.uk.

BARONESS McINTOSH OF HUDNALL   Labour

McINTOSH OF HUDNALL (Life Baroness), Genista Mary McIntosh; cr. 1999. Born 23 September 1946. Daughter of late Geoffrey Tandy, and of Maire Tandy; educated Hemel Hempstead Grammar School; York University (BA Philosophy and Sociology 1968). Married 1971, Neil Scott Wishart McIntosh (1 son 1 daughter) (marriage dissolved 1990). *Career:* Press Secretary, York Festival of Arts 1968–69; Royal Shakespeare Company: Casting Director 1972–77, Planning Controller 1977–84, Senior Administrator 1986–90, Associate Producer 1990; Executive Director, Royal National Theatre 1990-January 1997 and October 1997–; Chief Executive, Royal Opera House, Covent Garden 1997; Board Member: The Roundhouse Trust, Welsh National Opera. *Select Committees:* Member, House of Lords Offices Sub-Committee: Advisory Panel on Works of Art 2000–. Hon. DUniv, University of York 1998. *Trusts, etc:* Trustee, National Endowment for Science, Technology and Arts; Member, Peggy Ramsay Foundation; Patron, Helena Kennedy Bursary Scheme. *Miscellaneous:* Member, British Council Drama and Dance Advisory Committee. FRSA. *Special Interests:* Arts, Public Health, Prison Reform, Education. *Recreations:* Gardening, music. *Name, Style and Title:* Raised to the peerage as Baroness McIntosh of Hudnall, of Hampstead in the London Borough of Camden 1999. *Address:* The Baroness McIntosh of Hudnall, Royal National Theatre, Upper Ground, London, SE1 9PX *Tel:* 020 7452 3347 *Fax:* 020 7452 3350.

LORD MACKAY OF ARDBRECKNISH   Conservative

MACKAY OF ARDBRECKNISH (Life Baron), John Jackson MacKay; cr. 1991. Born 15 November 1938. Son of late Jackson MacKay; educated Dunoon and Campbeltown Grammar Schools; Glasgow University (BSc); Jordanhill College of Education. Married 1961, Sheena, daughter of late James Wagner (2 sons 1 daughter). *Councils, Public Bodies:* Councillor, Oban Town Council and Burgh Treasurer 1969–74; Member, Argyll Water Board 1970–74; JP, City of Glasgow; DL, City of Glasgow 1997. *Career:* Principal mathematics teacher, Oban High School 1972–79; Chief Executive, Scottish Conservative Central Office 1987–90; Chairman, Sea Fish Industry Authority 1990–93. *House of Commons.* Contested (Conservative): Western Isles in February 1974, Argyll in October 1974 General Elections; MP (Conservative): Argyll 1979–83, Argyll and Bute 1983–87; Parliamentary Under-Secretary of State, Scottish Office 1982–87. *House of Lords:* Parliamentary Under-Secretary of State, Department of Transport January-July 1994; Minister of State, Department of Social Security 1994–97; Deputy Leader of the Opposition December 1998–. *Whip:* Government Whip (A Lord in Waiting) 1993–94. *Spokesman:* An Opposition Spokesman for: Treasury 1997–98, Constitutional Affairs and Scotland 1997–, Education and Employment (Employment) December 1998-June 1999, Cabinet Office June 1999–, Trade and Industry June 1999–. *Select Committees:* Former Member: Select Committee on the European Communities, Sub-Committee B of EC Committee, Delegated Powers Scrutiny Committee; Member, Select Committee on House of Lords' Offices 1998–. *Awards Granted:* Channel 4 and House Award 'Peer of 1998' 1999. *Honours:* PC 1996. *Recreations:* Fishing. *Clubs:* Royal Scottish Automobile (Glasgow). *Name, Style and Title:* Raised to the peerage as Baron MacKay of Ardbrecknish, of Tayvallich in the District of Argyll and Bute 1991. *Address:* Rt Hon the Lord MacKay of Ardbrecknish, DL, Innishail, 51 Springkell Drive, Pollokshields, Glasgow, G41 4EZ *E-Mail:* mackayj@parliament.uk.

LORD MACKAY OF CLASHFERN   Conservative

MACKAY OF CLASHFERN (Life Baron), James Peter Hymers Mackay; cr. 1979. Born 2 July 1927. Son of late James Mackay, Railwayman; educated George Heriot's School; Edinburgh University; Trinity College, Cambridge. Married 1958, Elizabeth Gunn Hymers (1 son 2 daughters).*Career:* Lecturer in Mathematics, St Andrews 1948–50; Advocate 1955; QC (Scotland) 1965; Sheriff Principal, Renfrew and Argyll 1972–74; Vice-Dean, Faculty of Advocates 1973–76, Dean of Faculty 1976–79; Director, Stenhouse Holdings Ltd 1976–78; Part-time Member, Scottish Law Commission 1976–79; Member, Insurance Brokers' Registration Council 1978–79; Senator of the College of Justice in Scotland 1984–85; Lord of Appeal in Ordinary 1985–87; Editor, *Halsbury's Laws of England* 1998–. *Chancellor:* Chancellor, Heriot-Watt University 1991–. *House of Lords:* Lord Advocate 1979–84; Lord High Chancellor 1987–97.*Spokesman:* Government Spokesman on Legal Affairs in Scotland 1983–84. *Other:* Elder Brother, Trinity House. Hon. Fellow: Trinity College, Cambridge, Girton College, Cambridge; and other Universities' Honorary Degrees. *Miscellaneous:* Chairman, The Constitutional Commission 1998–99. *Honours:* PC 1979; KT 1997. Hon. Fellow: Royal College of Surgeons of Edinburgh 1989, Royal Society of Edinburgh, RICE, Royal College of Physicians Edinburgh 1990, Royal College of Obstetrics and gynecology, Chartered Institute of Taxation. Hon. Freeman, Woolman's Company. *Clubs:* New (Edinburgh), Caledonian, Athenaeum. *Name, Style and Title:* Raised to the peerage as Baron Mackay of Clashfern, of Eddrachillis in the District of Sutherland 1979. *Address:* Rt Hon the Lord Mackay of Clashfern, KT, House of Lords, London, SW1A 0PW *Tel:* 020 7219 3000.

LORD MACKAY OF DRUMADOON
Cross-Bencher

MACKAY OF DRUMADOON (Life Baron), Donald Sage Mackay; cr. 1995. Born 30 January 1946. Son of late Rev. Donald George Mackintosh Mackay and late Jean Margaret Mackay; educated George Watson's Boys' College, Edinburgh; Edinburgh University (LLB 1966, LLM 1968); University of Virginia (LLM 1969). Married 1979, Lesley Ann Waugh (1 son 2 daughters). *Career:* Law apprentice 1969–71; Solicitor with Allan McDougall & Co., SSC, Edinburgh 1971–76; Called to the Scottish Bar 1976; Advocate Depute 1982–85; QC (Scot) 1987–; Member, Criminal Injuries Compensation Board 1989–95; Solicitor-General for Scotland 1995; A Senator of the College of Justice in Scotland 2000–. *House of Lords:* Lord Advocate 1995–97.
Spokesman: A Government Spokesman on Legal Affairs and for the Home and Scottish Offices 1995–97; An Opposition Spokesman on: Constitutional Affairs, Scotland 1997–2000, Home Affairs 1997–2000, Lord Advocate's Department 1997–99. *Honours:* PC 1996. *Recreations:* Golf, gardening, Isle of Arran. *Sportsclubs:* Commons and Lords Rugby Club, Shiskine Golf and Tennis Club. *Clubs:* Western (Glasgow). *Name, Style and Title:* Raised to the peerage as Baron Mackay of Drumadoon, of Blackwaterfoot in the District of Cunninghame 1995. *Address:* Rt Hon the Lord Mackay of Drumadoon, Parliament House, Edinburgh, EH1 1RF *Tel:* 0131–225 2595 *Fax:* 0131–240 6711; 39 Hermitage Gardens, Edinburgh, EH10 6AZ *Tel:* 0131–447 1412 *Fax:* 0131–447 9863.

LORD MACKENZIE OF CULKEIN
Labour

MACKENZIE OF CULKEIN (Life Baron), Hector Uisdean MacKenzie; cr. 1999. Born 25 February 1940. Son of late George MacKenzie, principal lighthouse keeper, and late Williamina Budge, née Sutherland; educated Isle of Erraid Public School, Argyll; Aird Public School, Isle of Lewis; Nicolson Institute, Stornoway; Portree High School, Skye; Leverndale School of Nursing, Glasgow; West Cumberland School of Nursing, Whitehaven. Married March 2, 1961, Anna, daughter of late George and Sarah Morrison (1 son 3 daughters) (marriage dissolved 1991). *Trades Union:* Member, UNISON. *Armed Forces:* Sergeant, 1st Cadet Btn Queen's Own Cameron Highlanders. *Career:* Student Nurse, Leverndale Hospital 1958–61; Assistant Lighthouse Keeper, Clyde Lighthouses Trust 1961–64; West Cumberland Hospital: Student Nurse 1964–66, Staff Nurse 1966–69; Confederation of Health Service Employees: Assistant Regional Secretary 1969, Regional Secretary, Yorkshire and East Midlands 1970–74, National Officer 1974–83, Assistant General Secretary 1983–87, General Secretary 1987–93; Associate General Secretary, UNISON 1993–2000; Company Secretary, UIA Insurance ltd 1996–2000; President, TUC 1998–99; Senior Vice-President, TUC 1999–2000. *International Bodies (General):* First Substitute Member, World Executive of Public Services International 1987–2000; British-American Parliamentary Group; Inter-Parliamentary Union (British Group). *Party Groups (General):* Member: Labour Party Policy Forum, Labour Party Policy Commission on Health. *Other:* Governor Member, RNLI; Hon. Secretary, Wallington Branch, RNLI; Governor Member, Marine Society; Member, RSPB. *Awards Granted:* Lindsay Robertson Gold Medal for Nurse of the Year 1966. *Trusts, etc:* Member, National Trust for Scotland. RGN; RMN. *Publications:* Various articles in Nursing and Specialist Health Service Press. *Special Interests:* Health, Nursing, Defence, Aviation, Maritime Affairs, Land Reform. *Recreations:* Reading, Celtic music, shinty, aviation. *Clubs:* St Elpheges, Wallington. *Name, Style and Title:* Raised to the peerage as Baron MacKenzie of Culkein, of Assynt in Highland 1999. *Address:* The Lord MacKenzie of Culkein, House of Lords, London, SW1A 0PW *Tel:* 020 7219 8515 *Fax:* 020 7219 5979.

LORD MACKENZIE OF FRAMWELLGATE — Labour

MACKENZIE OF FRAMWELLGATE (Life Baron), Brian Mackenzie; cr. 1998. Born 21 March 1943. Son of Frederick Mackenzie and Lucy Mackenzie (née Ward); educated Eastbourne Boys' School, Darlington; London University (LLB); FBI National Academy, Quantico, USA (Graduate). Married March 6, 1965, Jean Seed (2 Sons). *Trades Union:* Former Member, Police Federation of England and Wales; Former National President, Police Superintendents' Association; Member, National Association of Retired Police Officers (NARPO). *Career:* Former Chief Superintendent, Durham Constabulary. *Party Groups:* Chair, Labour Home Affairs Committee. *International Bodies (General):* Member: FBI National Academy Associates, International Association of Chiefs of Police. *Other:* President, Association of Police Superintendents of England and Wales 1995–98; Patron, Kid Scape; Joint-President, Security Industry Council (JSIC). *Miscellaneous:* Honorary Billetmaster, City of Durham. *Honours:* OBE 1998. *Special Interests:* Police, Home Affairs, Legal Affairs. *Recreations:* Herpetology, after-dinner speaking, swimming, fitness, singing. *Clubs:* Dunelm, Durham City. *Name, Style and Title:* Raised to the peerage as Baron Mackenzie of Framwellgate, of Durham in the County of Durham 1998. *Address:* The Lord Mackenzie of Framwellgate, OBE, House of Lords, London, SW1A 0PW *E-Mail:* mackenzieb@parliament.uk.

LORD MACKIE OF BENSHIE — Liberal Democrat

MACKIE OF BENSHIE (Life Baron), George Yull Mackie; cr. 1974. Born 10 July 1919. Son of late Maitland Mackie, OBE, LLD, of North Ythsie, Tarves; educated Aberdeen Grammar School; Aberdeen University. Married 1st, 1944, Lindsay Sharp (died 1985) (3 daughters and 1 son deceased), married 2nd, 1988, Mrs Jacqueline Lane, daughter of late Colonel Marcel Rauch, and widow of Andrew Lane. *Trades Union:* Member, NFU. *Armed Forces:* Served with RAF 1940–46; Squadron-Leader 1944; DSO 1944; DFC 1944; Air Staff 1944–45. *Career:* Farming in Angus for 45 years; Formerly Chairman: Perth and Angus Fruit Growers Ltd, Caithness Glass Ltd; Rector, Dundee University 1980–83; Member Council of Europe and WEU 1986. *House of Commons:* Contested (Liberal) South Angus 1959; MP (Liberal) Caithness and Sutherland 1964–66. *Whip (Commons):* Scottish Whip 1964–66. *Spokesman (Commons):* Spokesman on Economic Affairs 1964–66. *Spokesman:* Former Liberal Democrat Party Spokesman on Agriculture and Scottish Affairs until 2000. *Select Committees:* Member, European Union Committee: Sub-Committee D 1975–95, Sub-Committee C 1998–99, Sub-Committee D (Environment, Agriculture, Public Health and Consumer Protection) 2000–. *International Bodies:* Executive Committee Member, IPU British Group; Member, CPA. *Party Groups (General):* Former Chairman, Scottish Liberal Party; President, Scottish Liberal Party 1983–88. *Other:* Member, Scottish Farmers Union; Former President, Royal Agricultural and Highlands Society, currently Vice-President. Hon. LLD, Dundee University 1982. *Honours:* DSO 1944; DFC 1944; CBE 1971. *Special Interests:* Agriculture. *Recreations:* Golf, social life. *Clubs:* Garrick, Farmers', Royal Air Force. *Name, Style and Title:* Raised to the peerage as Baron Mackie of Benshie, of Kirriemuir in the County of Angus 1974. *Address:* The Lord Mackie of Benshie, CBE, DSO, DFC, Benshie Cottage, Oathlaw, By Forfar, Angus, DD8 3PQ *Tel:* 01307 850376; House of Lords, London, SW1A 0PW *Tel:* House of Lords 020 7219 3179.

LORD MACLAURIN OF KNEBWORTH — Conservative

MACLAURIN OF KNEBWORTH (Life Baron), Ian Charter MacLaurin; cr. 1996. Born 30 March 1937. Son of late Arthur George and Evelina Florence MacLaurin; educated Malvern College. Married 1961, Ann Margaret Collar (died 1999) (1 son 2 daughters). *Armed Forces:* National Service, RAF Flight Command 1956–58. *Councils, Public Bodies:* DL, Hertfordshire 1992–. *Career:* Tesco plc: Joined 1959, Director 1970, Managing Director 1973–85, Deputy Chairman 1983–85, Chairman 1985–97; Director, Enterprise Oil 1984–90; Non-Executive Director: National Westminster Bank plc 1990–96, Gleneagles Hotels plc 1992–97, Vodafone Group plc 1997– (Chairman 1998–), Whitbread plc 1997–. *Chancellor:* Chancellor, University of Hertfordshire 1996–. *Other:*

Chairman, Food Policy Group, Retail Consortium 1980–84; Committee Member, MCC 1986–; President, Institute of Grocery Distribution 1989–92; Governor and Member of Council, Malvern College. Hon. DPhil, Stirling 1987; Hon. LLD, University of Hertfordshire; Hon. Fellow, University of Wales. *Trusts, etc:* Trustee, Royal Opera House Trust 1992. *Miscellaneous:* Former Chairman, UK Sports Council, resigned 1997; Chairman, England and Wales Cricket Board (formerly Test and County Cricket Board) 1996–. *Honours:* Kt 1989. FRSA 1986; FIM 1987; Hon. FCGI 1992. Freeman, City of London 1981. Liveryman, The Carmen's Company 1982–. *Publications: Tiger by the Tail. Recreations:* Golf. *Sportsclubs:* President, Brocket Hall Golf. *Clubs:* MCC, Harry's Bar. *Name, Style and Title:* Raised to the peerage as Baron MacLaurin of Knebworth, of Knebworth in the County of Hertfordshire 1996. *Address:* The Lord MacLaurin of Knebworth, DL, 14 Great College Street, London, SW1P 3RX *Tel:* 020 7233 2203 *Fax:* 020 7233 0438.

LORD McNALLY — Liberal Democrat

McNALLY (Life Baron), Tom McNally; cr. 1995. Born 20 February 1943. Son of late John and Elizabeth McNally; educated College of St Joseph, Blackpool; University College, London (BSc Economics) (President, Students Union 1965–66). Married 1st, 1970, Eileen Powell (marriage dissolved 1990), married 2nd, 1990, Juliet Lamy Hutchinson (2 sons 1 daughter). *Trades Union:* Vice-President, National Union of Students 1966–67. *Career:* Political Adviser to: Secretary of State for Foreign and Commonwealth Affairs 1974–76, Prime Minister 1976–79; Public Affairs Adviser, GEC 1983–84; Director-General, Retail Consortium, Director, British Retailers Association 1985–87; Head of Public Affairs, Hill & Knowlton 1987–93; Head of Public Affairs, Shandwick 1993–96, Vice-Chairman 1996–. *House of Commons:* MP (Labour 1979–81, SDP 1981–83) for Stockport South; Contested (SDP) Stockport in 1983 General Election. *Spokesman (Commons):* SDP Spokesman on Education and Sport 1981–83. *Spokesman:* Spokesman on: Broadcasting and Trade and Industry 1996–97, Home Affairs 1998–. *Select Committees:* Member: Select Committee on Public Service 1996–97; Select Committee on Freedom of Information 1999. *Party Groups (General):* Assistant General Secretary, The Fabian Society 1966–67; Labour Party Researcher 1967–68; International Secretary, Labour Party 1969–74. *Other:* Member, Institute of Public Relations (MIPR); President, British Radio and Electronic Equipment Manufacturers Association (BREMA). Fellow, University College, London 1995. *Trusts, etc:* Trustee of Verulamium Museum, St Albans; Fellow of Parliament Industry Trust 1981. FIPR 2000. *Special Interests:* Trade and Industry, Broadcasting, Retail Industry, Tourism, Leisure Industries, Foreign Affairs. *Recreations:* Playing and watching sport, reading political biographies. *Clubs:* National Liberal. *Name, Style and Title:* Raised to the peerage as Baron McNally, of Blackpool in the County of Lancashire 1995. *Address:* The Lord McNally, House of Lords, London, SW1A 0PW *E-Mail:* tmcnally@shandwick.com.

BARONESS MADDOCK — Liberal Democrat

MADDOCK (Life Baroness), Diana Maddock; cr. 1997. Born 19 May 1945. Daughter of late Reginald Derbyshire, former Senior Scientific Officer, AERE, Harwell, and of Margaret Evans; educated Shenstone Training College; Portsmouth Polytechnic (CertEd, Postgraduate linguistics diploma). Married July 23, 1966, Robert Frank Maddock (2 daughters). *Councils, Public Bodies:* Portswood Ward, Southampton City Council: Councillor 1984–93, Leader, Liberal Democrat Group. *Career:* Teacher: Weston Park Girls' School, Southampton 1966–69, Extra-Mural Department, Stockholm University 1969–72, Sholing Girls' School, Southampton 1972–73, Anglo-Continental School of English, Bournemouth 1973–76, Greylands School of English (part time) 1990–91. *House of Commons:* Contested Southampton Test in 1992 General Election; MP (Liberal Democrat) for Christchurch By-election 1993–97; Sponsored as Private Member's Bill, Home Energy Conservation Act 1995. *Spokesman (Commons):* Liberal Democrat Spokeswoman on: Housing, Women's Issues and Family Policy 1994–97. *Spokesman:* Liberal Democrat Spokesperson on Housing 1998–. *Party Groups (General):* President, Liberal Democrat Party 1998–2000. *Other:* President, National Housing Forum 1997–; Vice-President, National Housing Federation 1997–; President, Dorset Victim Support 1997–; Board Member, Western Challenge Housing Association 1997–99;

Member, Board of Corporation, Brockenhurst College. *Trusts, etc:* Trustee: National Energy Foundation, Community Development Foundation. *Miscellaneous:* Member, Standing Committees for: Finance Bill 1994, Housing Bill 1996. *Special Interests:* Education, Local Government, Housing, Environment. *Recreations:* Theatre, music, reading, travel. *Clubs:* National Liberal. *Name, Style and Title:* Raised to the peerage as Baroness Maddock, of Christchurch in the County of Dorset 1997. *Address:* The Baroness Maddock, House of Lords, London, SW1A 0PW.

BARONESS MALLALIEU — Labour

MALLALIEU (Life Baroness), Ann Mallalieu; cr. 1991. Born 27 November 1945. Daughter of late Sir William Mallalieu and Lady Mallalieu; educated Holton Park Girls' Grammar School; Newnham College, Cambridge (MA, LLM). Married 1979, Timothy Felix Harold Cassel (2 daughters). *Career:* Called to the Bar, Inner Temple 1970; Elected Member, General Council of the Bar 1973–75; A Recorder 1985–94; Bencher 1992. *Spokesman:* Opposition Spokesman on: Home Affairs 1992–97, Legal Affairs 1992–97. *Select Committees:* Member, Joint Select Committee on Consolidation of Bills 1998–. *Party Groups (General):* Member, Society of Labour Lawyers; Chairman, Leave Country Sports Alone Labour Support Campaign. *Other:* President, Countryside Alliance May 1998–. Hon. Fellow, Newnham College, Cambridge 1992. *Trusts, etc:* Chairman, Suzy Lamplugh Trust 1996–. *Miscellaneous:* Chairman, Council of the Ombudsman for Corporate Estate Agents 1993–. *Special Interests:* Law, Home Affairs, Agriculture, Environment. *Recreations:* Hunting, poetry, sheep, fishing. *Name, Style and Title:* Raised to the peerage as Baroness Mallalieu, of Studdridge in the County of Buckinghamshire 1991. *Address:* The Baroness Mallalieu, QC, House of Lords, London, SW1A 0PW.

BISHOP OF MANCHESTER — Non-Affiliated

MANCHESTER (10th Bishop of), Christopher John Mayfield. Born 18 December 1935. Son of Dr Roger Mayfield and Muriel Mayfield; educated Sedbergh School; Gonville and Caius College, Cambridge (MA 1961); Linacre House, Oxford (DipTheology); Cranfield Institute of Technology (MSc 1993). Married 1962, Caroline Ann Roberts (2 sons 1 daughter). *Armed Forces:* Served as Commissioned Officer, Education Branch, RAF 1957–61. *Career:* Deacon 1963; Priest 1964; Curate of St Martin-in-the-Bull Ring, Birmingham 1963–67; Lecturer at St Martin's, Birmingham 1967–71; Chaplain at Children's Hospital, Birmingham 1967–71; Vicar of: Luton 1971–80, East Hyde 1971–76; Rural Dean of Luton 1974–79; Archdeacon of Bedford 1979–85; Bishop Suffragan of Wolverhampton 1985–93; Bishop of Manchester 1993–; Took his seat in the House of Lords 1998. *Recreations:* Walking, gardening, family. *Clubs:* St James's Club, Manchester. *Address:* Rt Rev the Lord Bishop of Manchester, Bishopscourt, Bury New Road, Manchester, M7 4LE *Tel:* 0161–792 2096 *E-Mail:* bishop@bishopscourtman.free-online.co.uk.

LORD MANCROFT — Conservative

MANCROFT (3rd Baron, UK), Benjamin Lloyd Stormont Mancroft; cr. 1937; 3rd Bt of Mancroft (UK) 1932. Born 16 May 1957. Son of 2nd Baron, KBE, TD and of late Diana, only daughter of late Lieutenant-Colonel Horace Lloyd, DSO. Succeeded his father 1987; educated Eton. Married September 20, 1990, Emma, eldest daughter of Thomas and Gabriel Peart (2 sons 1 daughter). *Career:* Chairman: Inter Lotto (UK) Ltd 1995–, Scratch-n-Win Lotteries Ltd 1995–98; Non-executive director St Martin's Magazines plc. *House of Lords:* An elected hereditary peer 1999–. *Select Committees:* Member: Select Committee on Broadcasting 1992–94, House of Lords Offices Sub-Committee: Advisory Panel on Works of Art 2000–; Procedure Committee 2000–. *Party Groups:* Member, Executive Association of Conservative Peers 1989–94, 1999–. *Party Groups (General):* Member, Executive of National Union of Conservative Associations 1989–94. *Other:* Joint Master, Vale of White Horse Fox Hounds 1987–89; Chairman, Addiction Recovery Foundation 1989–;

Director, Phoenix House Housing Association 1991–96, Vice-Chairman 1992–96; Deputy Chairman, British Field Sports Society 1992–97; Chairman, Drug and Alcohol Foundation 1994–; President, Alliance of Independent Retailers 1996–; Director, Countryside Alliance 1997–. *Trusts, etc:* Patron, Sick Dentists' Trust 1991–; Board Member, Mentor Foundation; Patron, Osteopathic Centre for Children. *Special Interests:* Drug Addiction, Alcoholism, Rural Affairs. *Recreations:* Hunting, stalking, shooting, fishing. *Clubs:* Pratt's. *Address:* The Lord Mancroft, House of Lords, London, SW1A 0PW; 36 Dover Street, London, W1X 3RB *E-Mail:* mancroft@iluk.co.uk.

COUNTESS OF MAR   ·Cross-Bencher

MAR (Countess of, 31st in line, S), Margaret of Mar; cr. 1114, precedence 1404; Lady Garioch (24th in line, S) 1320. Born 19 September 1940. Daughter of 30th Earl. Succeeded her father 1975; educated Kenya High School for Girls, Nairobi; Lewes County Grammar School for Girls. Married 1st, 1959, Edwin Noel Artiss (1 daughter) (marriage dissolved 1976), married 2nd, 1976, John Salton (marriage dissolved 1981), married 3rd, 1982, John Jenkin, MA, (Cantab) FRCO, LRAM, ARCM. *Trades Union:* President, Association of Members of the Immigration Appeal Tribunal. *Career:* Civil Service Clerical Officer 1959–63; PO/BT Sales Superintendent 1969–82. *House of Lords:* A Deputy Chairman of Committees 1997–; A Deputy Speaker 1999–; An elected hereditary peer 1999–. *Select Committees:* Co-opted Member, Select Committee on European Communities Sub-Committee C (Environment, Public Health and Consumer Protection) 1997–99.*Other:* Lay Governor, The King's School, Gloucester 1984–87; Patron, Dispensing Doctors Association 1985–96; Lay Member, Immigration Appeal Tribunal 1985–; Member, English Advisory Committee for Telecommunications 1985–86; Patron, Worcester Branch National Back Pain Association 1987–89; President, Avanti 1987–89; Chairman, Employer-led Endorsed Care Training Steering Committee 1988–; Patron, Worcestershire Mobile Disabled Group 1989–; President, Elderly Accommodation Counsel 1993–; Member, British Red Cross 1994–; Patron, Gulf Veterans' Association 1995–; Member, OP Information Network 1995–; Chairman, Environmental Medicine Foundation 1996–; Member, Specialist Cheesemakers Association; Patron: BRAME 2000–, 25% ME Group 2000–; Chairman, Honest Food 2000–. *Awards Granted:* Laurent Perrier/Country Life Parliamentarian of the Year 1996; BBC Wildlife Magazine Green Ribbon Award 1997; Spectator 'Peer of the Year' 1997. *Miscellaneous:* Holder of the Premier Earldom of Scotland; Recognised in the surname "of Mar" by warrant of the Court of the Lord Lyon 1967, when she abandoned her second Christian name of Alison. *Special Interests:* Health Service, Social Security, Agriculture, Environment, Pesticides, Food standards. *Recreations:* Gardening, goat keeping, reading. *Clubs:* Farmers'. *Address:* The Countess of Mar, St Michael's Farm, Great Witley, Worcester, WR6 6JB *Tel:* 01299 896608.

EARL OF MAR AND KELLIE   Scottish Liberal Democrat

MAR (14th Earl of, S); cr. 1565, AND KELLIE (16th Earl of, S); cr. 1619, James Thorne Erskine; 16th Viscount Fentoun (S) 1606; 19th Lord Erskine (S) 1429; 16th Lord Erskine of Dirleton (S) 1604; 16th Lord Dirleton (S) 1606; (Life) Baron Erskine of Alloa Tower 2000. Born 10 March 1949. Son of 13th Earl. Succeeded his father 1993; educated Eton; Moray House College of Education (Diploma in Social Work, Diploma in Youth and Community Work); Inverness College (Certificate in Building). Married 1974, Mrs Mary Irene Mooney, daughter of Dougal McD. Kirk (1 step-son 4 step-daughters).*Trades Union:* NALGO 1973–76. *Armed Forces:* RAuxAF Pilot Officer 1979–82, Flying Officer 1982–86; Royal Naval Auxiliary Service 1986–88. *Councils, Public Bodies:* DL, Clackmannan 1991–. *Career:* Community Service Volunteer, York 1967–68; Youth Worker, Craigmillar 1971–73; Senior Social Worker, Sheffield District Council 1973–76; Social Worker: Grampian Regional Council 1976–78, Highland Regional Council 1978–87, HM Prison, Inverness 1979–81; Youth Worker, Merkinch Centre 1982; Community Service Offenders Supervisor, Inverness 1983–87; Slater, Kincardine 1989–91; Project Worker, SACRO 1991–93; Canoe builder 1993–; Estate worker 1993–. *House of Lords:* Chairman, Strathclyde Tram Inquiry 1996; Commissioner, Burrell Collection (Lending) Inquiry 1997. *Spokesman:* A Liberal Democrat Spokesman on Scotland 2000–. *Select Committees:* Member, Select Committee on Transfer of Crofting Estates (Scotland) Bill 1996.

Other: Hon. Vice-President, Scottish Canoe Association. *Miscellaneous:* Premier Viscount of Scotland; Hereditary Keeper of Stirling Castle; Page of Honour to HM the Queen 1962, 1963 (Order of Thistle page); Contested the Scottish Parliamentary Constituency of Ochil, May 6, 1999. Liveryman, Cordwainers' Company 1965. *Special Interests:* Scotland, Prisons, Probation, Social Policy, Devolution. *Recreations:* Canoeing, hillwalking, cycling, Alloa Tower, boat building. *Clubs:* Farmers'. *Name, Style and Title:* Created a life peer as Baron Erskine of Alloa Tower, of Alloa in Clackmannanshire 2000. *Address:* The Earl of Mar and Kellie, DL, Hilton Farm, Alloa, Clackmannan, FK10 3PS.

LORD MARLESFORD   Conservative

MARLESFORD (Life Baron), Mark Shuldham Schreiber; cr. 1991. Born 11 September 1931. Son of late John Shuldham Schreiber, AE, DL; educated Eton; Trinity College, Cambridge. Married 1969, Gabriella Federica, daughter of Count Teodoro Veglio di Castelletto d'Uzzone (2 daughters). *Armed Forces:* National Service, Coldstream Guards, 2nd Lieutenant 1950–51. *Councils, Public Bodies:* Councillor, East Suffolk County Council 1968–70; DL, Suffolk 1991–. *Career:* Fisons Ltd 1957–63; Conservative Research Department 1963–70; Special Adviser to HM Government 1970–74; Special Adviser to Leader of the Opposition 1974–75; Editorial consultant, *The Economist* 1974–91; Member: Countryside Commission 1980–92, Rural Development Commission 1985–93; Director, Eastern Group plc 1990–96; Adviser to Mitsubishi Corporation International NV 1990–; An independent national director of Times Newspaper Holdings 1991–; Adviser to Board of John Swire and Sons Ltd 1992–; Chairman, Council for the Protection of Rural England 1993–98. *Other:* President: Suffolk ACRE 1995–, Suffolk Preservation Society 1997–. *Special Interests:* Hong Kong, China, Conservation. *Recreations:* Planting trees and hedges, collecting minerals. *Clubs:* Pratt's. *Name, Style and Title:* Raised to the peerage as Baron Marlesford, of Marlesford in the County of Suffolk 1991. *Address:* The Lord Marlesford, DL, Marlesford Hall, Woodbridge, Suffolk, IP13 0AU *E-Mail:* marlesford@parliament.uk.

LORD MARSH   Cross-Bencher

MARSH (Life Baron), Richard William Marsh; cr. 1981. Born 14 March 1928. Son of late William Marsh; educated Jennings School, Swindon; Ruskin College, Oxford. Married 1st, 1950, Evelyn Mary Andrews (2 sons) (marriage dissolved 1973); married 2nd, 1973, Caroline Dutton (died 1975); married 3rd, June 25, 1979, Hon. Felicity McFadzean. *Trades Union:* Health Services Officer, National Union of Public Employees 1951–59. *Career:* Chairman: British Rail Board 1970–75, Newspaper Publishers Association 1975–, Allied Investments Ltd 1977–81, British Iron and Steel Consumers Council 1977–82, Strategy International Ltd 1978–84; Director, European Board Imperial Life of Canada 1980–; Chairman: Lee Cooper Group plc 1982–88, Mannington Management Services Ltd 1981–; Deputy Chairman, TV-AM Ltd 1981, Chairman 1982; Chairman, China & Eastern Investment Co. 1987–96; Executive Chairman: Laurentian Holding Company, Laurentian Life 1989–95; Chairman, British Industry Committee on South Africa Ltd 1989–95; Chairman, British Income and Growth Trust Ltd 1993–; Director, Imperial Life of Canada (Canada) 1995–. *House of Commons:* MP (Labour) for Greenwich 1959–70; Parliamentary Secretary, Ministry of Labour 1964–65; Joint Parliamentary Secretary, Ministry of Technology 1965–66; Minister of Power 1966–68; Minister of Transport 1968–70. *Select Committees:* Member, Select Committee on: European Communities 1997–, European Communities Sub-Committee B (Energy, Industry and Transport) 1997–. *Trusts, etc:* Chairman, Special Trustees of Guy's Hospital 1982–96. *Honours:* PC 1966; Kt 1976. FCIT; FInstD; FInstM. *Special Interests:* Industry, Economic Policy, Financial Services, Far East. *Name, Style and Title:* Raised to the peerage as Baron Marsh, of Mannington in the County of Wiltshire 1981. *Address:* Rt Hon the Lord Marsh, House of Lords, London, SW1A 0PW.

LORD MARSHALL OF KNIGHTSBRIDGE   Cross-Bencher

MARSHALL OF KNIGHTSBRIDGE (Life Baron), Colin Marsh Marshall; cr. 1998. Born 16 November 1933. Son of Marsh and Florence Marshall; educated University College School, Hampstead. Married 1958, Janet Cracknell (1 daughter). *Career:* Orient Steam Navigation Co 1951–58; Hertz Corporation in USA, Canada, Mexico, UK, Netherlands, Belgium 1958–64; Avis Inc 1964–79: President and Chief Executive Officer 1976–79; Norton Simon Inc 1979–81; Sears Holdings Ltd 1981–83; Director: British Airways Helicopters Limited 1983–86, BEA Airtours Limited 1983–87; Chairman, British Airways Associated Companies Limited 1983–97; British Airways 1983–: Chief Exective 1983–95, Deputy Chairman 1989–93, Chairman 1993–; Chairman: British Caledonian Airways Limited 1988–91, British Caledonian Group plc 1988–97; Director, several banking and airline companies; Deputy Chairman, British Telecommunications plc 1996–; Chairman: Inchcape plc 1996–2000, Invensys plc 1998–. *Other:* Member, British Tourist Authority 1986–1993; Vice-Chairman, World Travel and Tourism Council 1990–99; Governor, Ashridge Management College 1991–99; President, Chartered Institute of Marketing 1991–96; Deputy Chairman, London First 1993–98; Chairman: International Advisory Board British American Business Council 1994–96, London First Centre 1994–98; President: CBI 1996–98, Commonwealth Youth Exchange Council 1998–; Chairman, London Development Partnership 1998–2000; Chairman, Britain in Europe 1999–. Eleven honorary doctorates. *Trusts, etc:* Trustee, RAF Museum; The Conference Board since June 1996. *Honours:* Kt 1987. FCIT; FCIM. Freeman, City of London. Liveryman: Company of Information Technologists, Guild of Airline Pilots and Navigators. *Recreations:* Tennis. *Sportsclubs:* Queen's. *Clubs:* Royal Automobile. *Name, Style and Title:* Raised to the peerage as Baron Marshall of Knightsbridge, of Knightsbridge in the City of Westminster 1998. *Address:* The Lord Marshall of Knightsbridge, Chairman, British Airways plc, Berkeley Square House, Berkeley Square, London, W1J 6BA *E-Mail:* anne.p.hensman@british-airways.com.

BARONESS MASHAM OF ILTON   Cross-Bencher

MASHAM OF ILTON (Life Baroness), Susan Lilian Primrose Cunliffe-Lister; cr. 1970. Born 14 April 1935. Daughter of late Major Sir Ronald Sinclair, 8th Bt, TD, DL; educated Heathfield School, Ascot; London Polytechnic. Married December 8, 1959, Lord Masham, now 2nd Earl of Swinton (1 son 1 daughter both adopted). *Councils, Public Bodies:* Member: Peterlee and Newton Aycliffe Corporation 1973–85; Yorkshire Regional Health Authority 1982–90; DL, North Yorkshire 1991–; Member, North Yorkshire Family Health Service Authority 1990–96. *Career:* Has made career in voluntary social work. *Select Committees:* Member, Select Committee on Science and Technology Sub-Committee on Resistance to Anti-Microbial Agents 1997–. *Other:* President, North Yorkshire Red Cross 1963–88, Patron 1989–; Former and current president, patron, chair, member of numerous charities, especially in areas of health and disability. Six honorary degrees. *Trusts, etc:* Council Member, Winston Churchill Trust 1980–; Patron: International Spinal Research Trust, Northern Counties Trust for People Living with HIV/AIDS; Chairman, Stonham Memorial Trust. *Miscellaneous:* Chairman: Home Office Crime Prevention Working Group on Young People and Alcohol 1987, Howard League Inquiry into Girls in Prison. Hon. Fellowship: RCGP 1981, Chartered Society of Physiotherapy 1996. Freedom, Borough of Harrogate 1989. *Publications: The World Walks By. Special Interests:* Health, Disability, Penal Affairs and Policy, Drug Abuse. *Recreations:* Breeding Highland ponies, gardening, swimming. *Name, Style and Title:* Raised to the peerage as Baroness Masham of Ilton, of Masham in the North Riding of the County of Yorkshire 1970. *Address:* The Countess of Swinton, Baroness Masham of Ilton, DL, Dykes Hill House, Masham, Nr Ripon, North Yorkshire, HG4 4NS *Tel:* 01765 689241 *Fax:* 01765 688184; 46 Westminster Gardens, Marsham Street, London, SW1P 4JG *Tel:* 020 7834 0700.

LORD MASON OF BARNSLEY Labour

MASON OF BARNSLEY (Life Baron), Roy Mason; cr. 1987. Born 18 April 1924. Son of late Joseph Mason, miner; educated Carlton and Royston Elementary Schools; London School of Economics (TUC Scholarship). Married October 20, 1945, Marjorie, daughter of Ernest Sowden (2 daughters). *Trades Union:* Member, Yorkshire Miners' Council 1949–53; Chairman, Parliamentary Triple Alliance of Miners, Railway and Steel Union MPs 1979–80. *Armed Forces:* Flight Sergeant, Air Force Cadets, Royston Flight, Barnsley. *Councils, Public Bodies:* DL, South Yorkshire 1992–. *Career:* Coal Miner 1938–53; Member, Council of Europe and Western European Union 1973. *House of Commons:* Labour candidate for Bridlington 1951 53; MP (Labour) for: Barnsley 1953–83, Barnsley Central 1983–87; Minister of State (Shipping), Board of Trade 1964–67; Minister of Defence Equipment 1967–1968; Postmaster General April-June 1968; Minister of Power 1968–69; President, Board of Trade 1969–70; Secretary of State for: Defence 1974–76, Northern Ireland 1976–79. *Spokesman (Commons):* Opposition Spokesman on Defence and Post Office Affairs 1960–64; Principal Opposition Spokesman on Board of Trade Affairs 1970–74; Principal Opposition Spokesman on Agriculture, Fisheries and Food 1979–81. *Party Groups (Commons):* Chairman: Yorkshire Group of Labour MPs 1970–74, 1981–84, Miners' Group of MPs 1973–74, 1980–81. *International Bodies (Commons):* Member, Council of Europe 1970–71. *Other:* President, Yorkshire Salmon and Trout Association, Member, National Council; President, Yorkshire Water Colour Society; Vice-President, South Yorkshire Foundation (Charity); Chairman, Barnsley Business and Innovation Centre Ltd; Member, National Council of The Scouts Association. DUniv, Hallam University, Sheffield. *Trusts, etc:* Chairman, Prince's Youth Business Trust, South Yorkshire. *Miscellaneous:* Member: National Rivers Authority Advisory Committee 1988, National Rivers Authority 1989–92; President, Lords and Commons Pipe and Cigar Club. *Honours:* PC 1968. *Publications: Paying the Price* (autobiography), 1999. *Special Interests:* Coal Industry, Human Rights, Northern Ireland, Defence, Anti-Pollution Matters. *Recreations:* Fly-fishing, golf, tie designing (cravatology), specialist philately. *Sportsclubs:* President, Lords and Commons Fly Fishing Club. *Name, Style and Title:* Raised to the peerage as Baron Mason of Barnsley, of Barnsley in South Yorkshire 1987. *Address:* Rt Hon the Lord Mason of Barnsley, DL, 12 Victoria Avenue, Barnsley, South Yorkshire, S70 2BH.

BARONESS MASSEY OF DARWEN Labour

MASSEY OF DARWEN (Life Baroness), Doreen Elizabeth Massey; cr. 1999. Born 5 September 1938. Daughter of late Jack and Mary Ann Hall (née Sharrock); educated Darwen Grammar School; Birmingham University (BA French 1961, DipEd 1962); London University (MA Health Education 1985). Married February 26, 1966, Dr Leslie Massey, son of James and Annie Massey (2 sons 1 daughter). *Trades Union:* Former Member: NUT, MSF. *Career:* Graduate Service Overseas, Gabon 1962–63; Teacher: South Hackney School 1964–67, Springside School, Philadelphia 1967–69; Running Community Playgroup 1970–77, Teacher/Head of Year/Senior Teacher, Walsingham School, London 1979–83; Adviser in Personal, Social and Health Education, Inner London Education Authority 1983–85; Director of Training, Family Planning Association 1981–89; Director of Young People's Programme, Health Education Authority 1985–87; Director, FPA 1989–94; Independent Consultant in Health Education 1994–. *Select Committees:* Member, Ecclesiastical Committee 2000–. *Other:* Member: Book Advisory Centres, Family Planning Association, Opera North, English National Opera, Royal Shakespeare Company, Sex Education Forum. *Trusts, etc:* Advisory Council for Alcohol and Drug Education; Trust for the Study of Adolescence. FRSA. *Publications: Teaching About HIV/AIDS*, 1988; Co-author *Sex Education Factpack*, 1988; *Sex Education: Why, What and How*, 1988; Editor *The Sex Education Source Book*, 1995; *Lovers' Guide Encyclopaedia*, 1996; articles on health education in a variety of journals. *Special Interests:* Education, Health, International Development, Children and Young People. *Recreations:* Theatre, opera, reading, walking, yoga, travel, sports. *Name, Style and Title:* Raised to the peerage as Baroness Massey of Darwen, of Darwen in the County of Lancashire 1999. *Address:* The Baroness Massey of Darwen, 66 Lessar Avenue, London, SW4 9HQ *Tel:* 020 8673 5436 *Fax:* 020 8673 7734 *E-Mail:* dem@healthskills.demon.co.uk.

LORD MAYHEW OF TWYSDEN — Conservative

MAYHEW OF TWYSDEN (Life Baron), Patrick Barnabas Burke Mayhew; cr. 1997. Born 11 September 1929. Son of late A. G. H. Mayhew, MC, and the late Sheila Mayhew (née Roche); educated Tonbridge; Balliol College, Oxford (BA jurisprudence 1953, MA). Married April 15, 1963, Jean Elizabeth, OBE, daughter of John Gurney (4 sons). *Armed Forces:* Served in 4th/7th Royal Dragoon Guards National Service; Army Emergency Reserve (Captain). *Career:* Called to the Bar by Middle Temple 1955; QC 1972; Bencher 1976; Reader 2000. *House of Commons:* Contested (Conservative) Camberwell-Dulwich 1970; MP (Conservative) for Tunbridge Wells 1974–97; Parliamentary Under Secretary of State, Department of Employment 1979–81; Minister of State, Home Office 1981–83; Solicitor-General 1983–87; Attorney General 1987–92; Secretary of State for Northern Ireland 1992–97. *Select Committees:* Member, Select Committees on: Deregulation and Devolved Legislation 1997–, Parliamentary Privilege (Joint Committee) 1997–99. *Party Groups:* Executive Member, Association Conservative Peers 1998–. *Trusts, etc:* President, The Airey Neave Trust 1997–; Trustee, Rochester Cathedral Appeal 1985–. *Honours:* Kt 1983; PC 1986. Liveryman, Worshipful Company of Skinners 1954–. *Clubs:* Pratt's, Beefsteak, Garrick, Tunbridge Wells Constitutional. *Name, Style and Title:* Raised to the peerage as Baron Mayhew of Twysden, of Kilndown in the County of Kent 1997. *Address:* Rt Hon the Lord Mayhew of Twysden, QC, House of Lords, London, SW1A 0PW.

LORD MERLYN-REES — Labour

MERLYN-REES (Life Baron), Merlyn Merlyn-Rees; cr. 1992. Born 18 December 1920. Son of late L. D. Rees; educated Harrow Weald Grammar School; Goldsmiths' College (President, Students' Union 1940); London School of Economics (BSc MSc Economics). Married December 26, 1949, Colleen Faith Cleveley (3 sons). *Armed Forces:* Served RAF 1941–46; Demobilised as Squadron-Leader. *Councils, Public Bodies:* Member, Committee to examine Section 2 of Official Secrets Act 1971; Member, Franks' Committee of Enquiry on Falkland Islands 1982. *Career:* Economics and History teacher, Harrow Weald Grammar School 1949–60; Lecturer in Economics, Luton College of Technology 1962–63. *House of Commons:* Contested (Labour) Harrow East in: General Elections 1955, 1959, By-election 1959; MP (Labour) for: Leeds South 1963–83, Morley and South Leeds 1983–92; PPS to Chancellor of the Exchequer 1964–65; Parliamentary Under-Secretary of State: Ministry of Defence, for the Army 1965–66, for the Royal Air Force 1966–68, Home Office 1968–70; Member, Shadow Cabinet 1972–74; Secretary of State for Northern Ireland 1974–76; Home Secretary 1976–79. *Spokesman (Commons):* Opposition Front Bench Spokesman for Northern Ireland 1972; Principal Front Bench Spokesman on: Home Affairs 1979–80, Energy 1980–82, Industry and Employment Co-ordination 1982–83. *Chancellor:* Chancellor, University of Glamorgan 1993–. *Select Committees:* Member, Select Committees on: the Civil Service 1996–97, Delegated Powers and Deregulation 1997–, Public Service 1997–, Parliamentary Privilege (Joint Committee) 1997–. *International Bodies (General):* Member: CPA, IPU, British American Parliamentary Group. *Party Groups (General):* Organiser, Festival of Labour 1960–62. Hon. LLD, Wales 1987; Fellow, Polytechnic of Wales 1989; Hon. LLD, Leeds 1992. *Miscellaneous:* Assumed the surname of Merlyn-Rees in lieu of his patronymic 1992; President, Video Standards Council 1990–. *Honours:* PC 1974. *Publications: The Public Sector in the Mixed Economy,* 1973; *Northern Ireland: A Personal Perspective,* 1985. *Special Interests:* Housing, Education, Penal Reform. *Recreations:* Reading, theatre. *Name, Style and Title:* Raised to the peerage as Baron Merlyn-Rees, of Morley and South Leeds in the County of West Yorkshire and of Cilfynydd in the County of Mid Glamorgan 1992. *Address:* Rt Hon the Lord Merlyn-Rees, House of Lords, London, SW1A 0PW.

LORD METHUEN   Liberal Democrat

METHUEN (7th Baron), Robert Alexander Holt Methuen; cr. 1838. Born 22 July 1931. Son of 5th Baron. Succeeded his brother 1994; educated Shrewsbury; Trinity College, Cambridge. Married 1st, May 10, 1958, Mary Catherine Jane, daughter of late Venerable Charles Hooper, Archdeacon of Ipswich (2 daughters) (marriage dissolved 1993), married 2nd, January 8, 1994, Margrit Andrea, daughter of Friedrich Karl Ernst Hadwiger, of Vienna, Austria. *Career:* Design Engineer, Westinghouse Brake and Signal Company 1957–67; Computer Systems Engineer: IBM UK Ltd 1968–75, Rolls-Royce plc 1975–94; Retired. *House of Lords:* A Deputy Chairman of Committees 1999–; An elected hereditary peer 1999–. *Spokesman:* Spokesman for Transport. *Select Committees:* Member: European Communities Sub-Committee B (Energy, Industry and Transport) 1995–99, Channel Tunnel Rail Link 1996, Administration and Works Sub-Committee 1997–, Science and Technology 1999–; Science and Technology Sub-Committee II (Aircraft Cabin Environment) 2000 . *Trusts, etc:* Patron, Lady Margaret Hungerford Charity. *Recreations:* Walking, horse trekking, industrial archaeology. *Address:* The Lord Methuen, House of Lords, London, SW1A 0PW.

BARONESS MILLER OF CHILTHORNE DOMER   Liberal Democrat

MILLER OF CHILTHORNE DOMER (Life Baroness), Susan Elisabeth Miller; cr. 1998. Born 1 January 1954. Daughter of Frederick Oliver Meddows Taylor and Norah Langham; educated Sidcot School, Winscombe, Somerset; Oxford Polytechnic. Married April 12, 1980 (marriage dissolved 1998) (2 daughters). *Councils, Public Bodies:* Councillor: Chilthorne Domer Parish Council 1987, South Somerset District Council 1991–, Leader 1996–98; Councillor, Somerset County Council 1997–. *Career:* In publishing: David & Charles, Weidenfeld & Nicolson, Penguin Books 1975–79; Bookshop Owner 1979–89. *Spokesman:* Liberal Democrat Spokesman on Agriculture and Rural Affairs 1999–. *Select Committees:* Member, European Communities Sub Committee D (Agriculture, Fisheries and Food). *International Bodies (General):* Member, IPU. *Miscellaneous:* Member, Rural Commission Steering Group; Chair, Local Government Association International Panel,. *Recreations:* Walking, reading, friends. *Name, Style and Title:* Raised to the peerage as Baroness Miller of Chilthorne Domer, of Chilthorne Domer in the County of Somerset 1998. *Address:* The Baroness Miller of Chilthorne Domer, House of Lords, London, SW1A 0PW *Tel:* 020 7219 6042 *E-Mail:* millers@parliament.uk.

BARONESS MILLER OF HENDON   Conservative

MILLER OF HENDON (Life Baroness), Doreen Miller; cr. 1993. Born 13 June 1933. Daughter of Bernard and Hetty Feldman; educated Brondesbury and Kilburn High School; London School of Economics. Married September 1, 1955, Henry Lewis Miller, son of Ben and Eva Miller (3 sons). *Councils, Public Bodies:* JP, Brent 1971; Chairman, Barnet Family Health Services Authority 1990–94. *Whip:* Government Whip (A Baroness in Waiting) 1994–97; An Opposition Whip 1997–99. *Spokesman:* Spokeswoman on: Health 1995–97, Education and Employment 1996–97, Trade and Industry 1996–97, Office of Public Service 1996, Environment 1996–97; An Opposition Spokeswoman on: Environment, Transport and the Regions 1997–2000, DTI 1997–, Employment 2000–. *Party Groups (General):* Greater London Area Conservative and Unionist Associations: Joint Treasurer 1990–93, Chairman 1993–96, President 1996–98; Member, Conservative Board of Finance and its Training and Fund Raising Sub-Committees 1990–93; President, Hampstead and Highgate Womens' Committee 1993–96; Member, Conservative Womens' National and General Purposes Committees 1993–96, Patron 1996–; President, Greenwich and Woolwich Conservative Association 1996–; Patron: Eltham and Woolwich Conservative Association 1996–, Hackney North Conservative Association 1996–, North Thanet Conservative Association 1996–, Hendon Conservative Association 2000–. *Other:* National Chairman and Executive Director, 300 Group 1985–88; Chairman, Women into Public Life Campaign 1986–92; Human Rights Adviser, Soroptomist International 1987–90; Chairman, National Association of Leagues of Hospital and Community Friends 1997–. *Trusts, etc:* Patron, Minerva Educational Trust.

Miscellaneous: Contested (Conservative): London South Inner, European Parliamentary elections 1984, ILEA 1986; Non-Executive Director, Crown Agents 1990–94; Member, Monopolies and Mergers Commission 1992–93. *Honours:* MBE, 1989. Fellow, Institute of Marketing; FRSA. *Special Interests:* Women's Issues, Health, Law and Order, Small Businesses. *Recreations:* Reading, football, politics. *Clubs:* Carlton. *Name, Style and Title:* Raised to the peerage as Baroness Miller of Hendon, of Gore in the London Borough of Barnet 1993. *Address:* The Baroness Miller of Hendon, MBE, House of Lords, London, SW1A 0PW *Tel:* 020 7219 3164 *E-Mail:* hlmillerandco@compuserve.com; dm@hlmanddm.freeserve.co.uk.

LORD MILLETT — Cross-Bencher

MILLETT (Life Baron), Peter Julian Millett; cr. 1998. Born 23 June 1932. Son of late Denis Millett and Adele Millett; educated Harrow; Trinity Hall, Cambridge (Scholar, MA). Married 1959, Ann Mireille, daughter of late David Harris (2 sons and 1 son deceased). *Armed Forces:* Flying Officer, RAF, National Service 1955–57. *Career:* Called to the Bar: Middle Temple 1955, Lincoln's Inn 1959 (Bencher 1960), Singapore 1976, Hong Kong 1979; At Chancery Bar 1958–86; Examiner and Lecturer in Practical Conveyancing, Council of Legal Education 1962–76; Junior Counsel to Department of Trade and Industry in Chancery matters 1967–73; Member, General Council of the Bar 1971–75; Outside Member, Law Commission on working party on co-ownership of the matrimonial home 1972–73; QC 1973; Member, Department of Trade Insolvency Law Review Committee 1977–82; A Judge of the High Court of Justice 1986–94; A Lord Justice of Appeal 1994–98; A Lord of Appeal in Ordinary 1998–; Non-Permanent Judge of the Court of Final Appeal, Hong Kong 2000–. *Other:* President, West London Synagogue of British Jews 1991–95. Hon. Fellow, Trinity Hall, Cambridge; honorary doctorate. *Honours:* Kt 1986; PC 1994. *Publications:* Has contributed to several legal publications including *Halsbury's Law of England*; Editor in Chief, *Encyclopaedia of Forms and Precedents. Recreations:* Philately, bridge, *The Times* crossword. *Clubs:* Home House. *Name, Style and Title:* Raised to the peerage as Baron Millett, of St Marylebone in the City of Westminster 1998. *Address:* Rt Hon the Lord Millett, House of Lords, London, SW1A 0PW.

LORD MILNER OF LEEDS — Labour

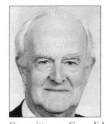

MILNER OF LEEDS (2nd Baron, UK), Arthur James Michael Milner; cr. 1951. Born 12 September 1923. Son of 1st Baron, PC, MC, TD, DL. Succeeded his father 1967; educated Oundle; Trinity Hall, Cambridge (MA). Married March 31, 1951, Sheila Margaret Hartley (died 2000) (1 son 1 daughter and 1 daughter deceased). *Armed Forces:* RAF short course, Trinity Hall, Cambridge 1942; RAF 1942–46, Flight-Lieutenant; 609 (West Riding) Squadron, RAuxAF 1947–52, Flight-Lieutenant. *Career:* Admitted Solicitor 1951; Former Partner, Milners Curry & Gaskell; Consultant, Gregory Rowcliffe and Milners 1988–99. *House of Lords:* An elected hereditary peer 1999–. *Whip:* Opposition Whip 1971–74. *Select Committees:* Member: Joint Committee on Consolidation Bills 1982–92, Select Committee on Channel Rail Link Bill 1996, Several Private Bill Committees 1990–93. *Other:* Member, Pilgrims Society. Member, Clothworkers' Company. *Clubs:* Royal Air Force. *Address:* The Lord Milner of Leeds, AE, 2 The Inner Court, Old Church Street, London, SW3 5BY *Tel:* 020 7352 7588; 1 Bedford Row, London, WC1R 4BZ *Tel:* 020 7242 0631.

LORD MISHCON — Labour

MISHCON (Life Baron), Victor Mishcon; cr. 1978. Born 14 August 1915. Son of late Rabbi Arnold Mishcon; educated City of London School. Married 1976, Joan Estelle Monty (2 sons 1 daughter by former marriage). *Armed Forces:* Served HM Forces during Second World War. *Councils, Public Bodies:* Councillor, Lambeth Borough Council 1945–49, Chairman, Finance Committee; Councillor, LCC 1946–65, Chairman 1954–55; Councillor, GLC, Chairman, General Purposes Committe; Member, ILEA 1964–67; DL, Greater London 1954. *Career:* A Solicitor, Former Senior Partner and now Consultant to Mishcon De Reya; Member: National Theatre Board 1965–90, South Bank Theatre Board 1966–67; Vice-President, Board of Deputies of British Jews 1967–73, Vice-Chairman, Council of Christians and Jews 1976–77; Former Member, various Government Committees. *Spokesman:* Principal Opposition Spokesman on: Home Affairs 1983–90, Legal Affairs 1990–93. Hon. LLD, Birmingham University 1991; Hon. Fellow, University College, London 1993. *Miscellaneous:* Contested (Labour): North West Leeds 1950, Bath 1951, Gravesend 1955, 1959 General Elections. *Honours:* Commander, Royal Swedish Order of North Star 1954; Star of Ethiopia 1954; QC (Hon) 1992; Star of Jordan 1995. *Name, Style and Title:* Raised to the peerage as Baron Mishcon, of Lambeth in the County of Greater London 1978. *Address:* The Lord Mishcon, QC, DL, 21 Southampton Row, London, WC1B 5HS.

LORD MITCHELL — Labour

MITCHELL (Life Baron), Parry Andrew Mitchell; cr. 2000. Born 6 May 1943. Son of Leon and Rose Mitchell; educated Christ's College Grammar School, London; London University (BSc Economics); Graduate School of Business, Columbia University, New York (MBA). Married 1st (marriage dissolved) (1 daughter); married 2nd, Hannah Lowy (twin sons). *Career:* Information technology entrepreneur; Founder, Syscap plc. *Trusts, etc:* Mitchell Charitable Trust. *Special Interests:* Information Technology, Small Business. *Recreations:* Scuba diving, theatre, jazz, opera. *Clubs:* RAC, Groucho, Players' (New York). *Name, Style and Title:* Raised to the peerage as Baron Mitchell, of Hampstead in the London Borough of Camden 2000. *Address:* The Lord Mitchell, House of Lords, London, SW1A 0PW *E-Mail:* parrym@mac.com.

LORD MOLLOY — Labour

MOLLOY (Life Baron), William John Molloy; cr. 1981. Born 26 October 1918. Son of late William John Molloy; educated St Thomas's Council School, Swansea; University College of Wales, Swansea. Married 1945, Eva Mary Lewis (died 1980) (1 daughter). *Armed Forces:* TA 1938; Served Field Company Royal Engineers 1939–46. *Councils, Public Bodies:* Leader, Fulham Borough Council 1956–66. *Career:* Foreign Office, Whitley Council Departmental Staff-Side Chairman 1946–52; Trade Union Lecturer; Former Editor *Civil Service Review*; Member, Assemblies Council of Europe (Chairman, Health Services Committee) and Western European Union 1969–73; Member, European Parliament 1975–78; Member, Executive Committee IPU; Member, CPA. *House of Commons:* MP (Labour) Ealing North 1964–79; PPS to Minister of Post and Telecommunications 1969–70. *Other:* Patron, Metropolitan Area Royal British Legion; National Vice-President, Royal British Legion; Vice-President, Greenford Branch Royal British Legion; Elected to RGS Council 1981. Hon. Fellow 1986. Fellow: Royal Geographical Society, World Association Arts and Sciences (elected 1985); Hon. Associate, British Vetinerary Association 1988. *Special Interests:* Health Service, Foreign Affairs, Commonwealth, Commerce, Industry. *Recreations:* Music, collecting dictionaries. *Name, Style and Title:* Raised to the peerage as Baron Molloy, of Ealing in Greater London 1981. *Address:* The Lord Molloy, 2A Uneeda Drive, Greenford, Middlesex, UB6 8QB; House of Lords, London, SW1A 0PW *Tel:* House of Lords 020 7219 6710.

LORD MOLYNEAUX OF KILLEAD — Cross-Bencher

MOLYNEAUX OF KILLEAD (Life Baron), James Henry Molyneaux; cr. 1997. Born 27 August 1920. Son of late William Molyneaux; educated Aldergrove School, Co. Antrim. *Armed Forces:* RAF 1941–46. *Councils, Public Bodies:* JP, Co. Antrim 1957–86; Antrim County Councillor 1964–73. *House of Commons:* MP (UUP) for Antrim South 1970–83 and for Lagan Valley 1983–97. *Spokesman (Commons):* Spokesman, Treasury 1995–97. *Spokesman:* Spokesman on Northern Ireland. *Party Groups (General):* Hon. Secretary, South Antrim Unionist Association 1964–70; Former Chairman, Antrim division Unionist Association; Leader: United Ulster Unionist Coalition 1974–77, Ulster Unionist Parliamentary Party 1974–95, Ulster Unionist Party 1979–95. *Other:* Vice-Chairman, Eastern Special Care Hospital Committee 1966–73; Chairman: Antrim Mental Health Branch 1967–70, Crumlin Branch, Royal British Legion; Sovereign Grand Master, British Commonwealth Royal Black Institution; A Vice-President, Federation of Economic Development Authorities. *Honours:* PC 1983; KBE 1996. *Special Interests:* Constitutional Affairs, Mental Health, Local Government. *Recreations:* Gardening, music. *Name, Style and Title:* Raised to the peerage as Baron Molyneaux of Killead, of Killead in the County of Antrim 1997. *Address:* Rt Hon the Lord Molyneaux of Killead, KBE, House of Lords, London, SW1A 0PW.

LORD MONRO OF LANGHOLM — Conservative

MONRO OF LANGHOLM (Life Baron), Hector Seymour Peter Monro; cr. 1997. Born 4 October 1922. Son of late Captain Alastair Monro, Queens Own Cameron Highlanders; educated Canford School; King's College, Cambridge. Married 1st, March 4, 1949, Elizabeth Anne Welch (died 1994) (2 sons); married 2nd, December 23, 1994, Mrs Doris Kaestner, of Baltimore, Maryland, USA. *Armed Forces:* Served RAF 1941–46; RAuxAF 1947–54; Hon. Air Commodore 1982–2000; Hon. Inspector General RAuxAF 1989–2000. *Councils, Public Bodies:* Councillor, Dumfries County Council 1952–67; JP Dumfries 1972–; DL, Dumfriesshire 1973. *House of Commons:* MP (Conservative) for Dumfries 1964–97; Parliamentary Under-Secretary of State: for Scotland 1971–74, at Department of Environment and Minister for Sport 1979–81; Joint Parliamentary Under-Secretary of State, Scottish Office 1992–95. *Whip (Commons):* Government Whip 1967–70; Government Whip (Lord Commissioner of the Treasury) 1970–71. *Spokesman (Commons):* Opposition Spokesman on: Scottish Affairs 1974–75 Sport 1974–79. *Party Groups (General):* Chairman, Dumfriesshire Conservative Association 1958–63. *Other:* Chairman, Dumfries and Galloway Police Committee; Area Executive, NFU; Member, Nature Conservancy Council 1982–91; President: Auto Cycle Union 1983–90, National Small-bore Rifle Association 1987–92. *Miscellaneous:* Member, Queen's Bodyguard for Scotland, Royal Company of Archers. *Honours:* AE 1953; Knighted 1981; PC 1995. FRAGS. *Special Interests:* Scotland, Agriculture, Aviation, Defence, Sport, Recreation, Heritage. *Recreations:* Sport, flying, shooting, music. *Sportsclubs:* Scottish Rugby Union: Member 1957–77, Vice-President 1975, President 1976–77. *Clubs:* MCC, Royal Scottish Automobile (Glasgow), Royal Air Force, Royal and Ancient (St Andrews). *Name, Style and Title:* Raised to the peerage as Baron Monro of Langholm, of Westerkirk in Dumfries and Galloway 1997. *Address:* Rt Hon the Lord Monro of Langholm, AE, DL, Williamwood, Kirtlebridge, Lockerbie, Dumfries, DG11 3LU.

LORD MONSON — Cross-Bencher

MONSON (11th Baron, GB), John Monson; cr. 1728; 15th Bt of Carlton (E) 1611. Born 3 May 1932. Son of 10th Baron. Succeeded his father 1958; educated Eton; Trinity College, Cambridge (BA). Married 1955, Emma Devas (3 sons). *House of Lords:* An elected hereditary peer 1999–. *Select Committees:* Member, Administration and Works Sub-Committee, House of Lords Offices Committee 2000–. *Other:* President, Society for Individual Freedom. *Address:* The Lord Monson, The Manor House, South Carlton, Nr Lincoln, LN1 2RN *Tel:* 01522 730263.

MONTAGU OF BEAULIEU (3rd Baron, UK), Edward John Barrington Douglas-Scott-Montagu; cr. 1885. Born 20 October 1926. Son of 2nd Baron, KCIE, CSI, DL. Succeeded his father 1929; educated St Peter's Court, Broadstairs; Ridley College; St Catharines, Ontario; Eton; New College, Oxford. Married 1st, April 11, 1959, Belinda Crossley (1 son 1 daughter) (marriage dissolved 1974), married 2nd, 1974, Fiona Herbert (1 son). *Armed Forces:* Lieutenant, Grenadier Guards 1945–48. *Career:* Author, Museum Founder, Stately Home Owner; Founded Montagu Motor Museum 1952, which became the National Motor Museum 1972; Founder and Editor, *Veteran and Vintage Magazine* 1956–79; President, Fédération Internationale des Voitures Anciennes 1980–83; Development Commissioner 1980–84; First Chairman, Historic Buildings and Monuments Commission (English Heritage) 1984–92; Chairman: Report on Britain's Historic Buildings: A Policy for their Future Use, English Tourist Board's Committee of Enquiry publishing Britain's Zoos. *House of Lords:* An elected hereditary peer 1999–. *International Bodies (General):* Member, Commission Historique Internationale de FIA (Federation Internationale de l'Automobile). *Other:* President, Southern Tourist Board; President Emeritus, Tourism Society; President, United Kingdom Vineyards Association; Chancellor, Wine Guild UK; President: Historic Commercial Vehicle Society, Disabled Drivers Motor Club, Millennium Institute of Journalists; First President: Historic Houses Association 1973–78, European Union of Historic Houses Associations 1978–81; President: Museums Association 1982–84, Federation of British Historic Vehicle Clubs 1988–. Hon. DTech. FRSA; FMA; Hon. RICS; FMI; FIMI; FIPR. *Publications: More Equal than Others*; *Gilt and the Gingerbread*; *Jaguar: A Biography*; *Daimler Century*, 1995, *Wheels Within Wheels*, 2000; and many other motoring books and books on motoring history and historic houses. *Special Interests:* Heritage, Museums and Galleries, Road Transport, Motor Industry, Tourism. *Recreations:* Water and field sports, theatre, cinema, music. *Sportsclubs:* Commodore, Beaulieu River Sailing Club. *Clubs:* Vice-Commodore, House of Lords Yacht, RAC, Beefsteak. *Address:* The Lord Montagu of Beaulieu, Palace House, Beaulieu, Brockenhurst, Hampshire, SO42 7ZN *Tel:* 01590 612345 *Fax:* 01590 612623; Flat 11, Wyndham House, Bryanston Square, London, W1H 2DS *Tel:* 020 7262 2603 *Fax:* 020 7724 3262 *Tel:* 01590 614701 (direct) *E-Mail:* lord.montague@beaulieu.com.uk.

MONTROSE (8th Duke of, S), James Graham; cr. 1707; Marquess of Montrose (S) 1644; Marquess of Graham and Buchanan (S) 1707; Earl of Montrose (S) 1505; Earl of Kincardine (S) 1707; Earl Graham (GB) 1722; Viscount Dundaff (S) 1707; Lord Graham (S) 1445; Lord Aberuthven, Mugdock and Fintrie (S) 1707; Baron Graham (GB) 1722; 12th Bt of Braco (NS) 1625. Born 6 April 1935. Son of 7th Duke and late Isobel Veronica, daughter of late Lieutenant-Colonel Thomas Sellar, CMG, DSO. Succeeded his father 1992; educated Loretto. Married 1970, Catherine Elizabeth MacDonnell, daughter of late Captain Norman Andrew Thomson Young, of Ottawa, Canada (2 sons 1 daughter). *Councils, Public Bodies:* Chairman, Buchanan Community Council 1982–93. *House of Lords:* An elected hereditary peer 1999–. *International Bodies:* Member: CPA, IPU. *Other:* Member: Council of Scottish National Farmers Union 1981–90, Royal Scottish Pipers Society, Royal Highland and Agricultural Society, President 1997–98. *Miscellaneous:* Member, Queen's Bodyguard for Scotland (Royal Company of Archers) 1965–, Brigadier 1986–; Hereditary Sheriff, Dunbartonshire; Vice-Chairman, Secretary of State's Working Party for Loch Lomond and the Trossachs. *Honours:* OStJ 1978. *Special Interests:* Europe, Agriculture, Rural Affairs. *Address:* His Grace the Duke of Montrose, Auchmar, Drymen, Glasgow, G63 0AG.

Visit the Vacher Dod Website . . .

www.politicallinks.co.uk

LORD MOORE OF LOWER MARSH   Conservative

MOORE OF LOWER MARSH (Life Baron), John Edward Michael Moore; cr. 1992. Born 26 November 1937. Son of late Edward Moore; educated Licensed Victuallers' School, Slough; London School of Economics (BSc Econ). Married June 23, 1962, Sheila Sarah Tillotson (2 sons 1 daughter). *Armed Forces:* National Service with Royal Sussex Regiment in Korea 1955–57, Commissioned. *Councils, Public Bodies:* Councillor, London Borough of Merton 1971–74. *Career:* Chairman, Dean Witter (International) Ltd 1975–79, Director 1968–79; Advisory Board Member, Marvin and Palmer Inc. 1989–; Director, Monitor Inc. 1990–, Chairman, European Executive Committee; Member, Advisory Board, Sir Alexander Gibb & Co. 1990–95; Chairman, Credit Suisse Asset Management 1992–2000; Director: Swiss American NY Inc 1992–96, GTECH 1993–, Blue Circle Industries plc 1993–, Camelot Holdings plc 1993–98; Director, Rolls-Royce plc 1994–, Deputy Chairman 1996–; Supervisory Board Member, ITT Automotive Europe GMBH, Germany 1994–97; Director: Central European Growth Fund Ltd 1995–2000, BEA (NY) 1996–98, TIG Holdings Inc (NY) 1997–99, PCP (Zurich) 1999–. *House of Commons:* MP (Conservative) Croydon Central February 1974–92; Parliamentary Under-Secretary of State for Energy 1979–83; Economic Secretary to the Treasury June–October 1983; Financial Secretary to the Treasury 1983–86; Secretary of State for: Transport 1986–87, Social Services 1987–88, Social Security 1988–89. *Party Groups (General):* Chairman, Conservative Association, LSE 1958; Chairman, Stepney Green Conservative Association 1968; Vice-Chairman, Conservative Party with responsibility for Youth 1975–79. *Other:* President, Student Union, LSE 1959–60; Member, Court of Governors, LSE 1977–; Council Member, Institute of Directors 1991–99. *Trusts, etc:* Chairman, Energy Savings Trust 1992–95, President 1995–. *Honours:* PC 1986. *Clubs:* Royal Automobile, Institute of Directors. *Name, Style and Title:* Raised to the peerage as Baron Moore of Lower Marsh, of Lower Marsh in the London Borough of Lambeth 1992. *Address:* Rt Hon the Lord Moore of Lower Marsh, House of Lords, London, SW1A 0PW.

LORD MOORE OF WOLVERCOTE   Cross-Bencher

MOORE OF WOLVERCOTE (Life Baron), Philip Brian Cecil Moore; cr. 1986. Born 6 April 1921. Son of late Cecil Moore, ICS; educated Dragon School; Cheltenham College; Brasenose College, Oxford (Classical Exhibitioner 1940). Married 1945, Joan Ursula Greenop (2 daughters). *Armed Forces:* RAF Bomber Command, POW 1942–45. *Career:* Entered Home Civil Service 1947; Assistant Private Secretary to First Lord of the Admiralty 1950–51; Principal Private Secretary to First Lord of the Admiralty 1957–58; Deputy UK Commissioner and Deputy British High Commissioner, Singapore 1961–65; Chief of Public Relations, Ministry of Defence 1965–66; Assistant Private Secretary to HM The Queen 1966–72, Deputy Private Secretary 1972–77, Private Secretary 1977–86; A Permanent Lord-in-Waiting to HM The Queen 1990–. Hon. Fellow, Brasenose College, Oxford. *Honours:* CMG 1966; CB 1973; KCVO 1976; PC 1977; KCB 1980; GCVO 1983; GCB 1985; QSO 1986. *Special Interests:* Foreign Affairs, Commonwealth, Defence, Church Affairs. *Recreations:* Golf, shooting, fishing. *Clubs:* MCC. *Name, Style and Title:* Raised to the peerage as Baron Moore of Wolvercote, of Wolvercote in the City of Oxford 1986. *Address:* Rt Hon the Lord Moore of Wolvercote, GCB, GCVO, CMG, QSO, Hampton Court Palace, East Molesey, Surrey, KT8 9AU *Tel:* 020 7943 4695.

LORD MORAN   Cross-Bencher

MORAN (2nd Baron, UK), (Richard) John McMoran Wilson; cr. 1943. Born 22 September 1924. Son of 1st Baron, MC, MD, FRCP, and late Dorothy, MBE, daughter of late Samuel Dufton. Succeeded his father 1977; educated Eton; King's College, Cambridge. Married 1948, Shirley Rowntree, daughter of George James Harris, MC, of Bossall Hall, York (2 sons 1 daughter). *Armed Forces:* Served RNVR 1943–45; Ordinary Seaman, HMS Belfast 1943; Sub-Lieutenant, Motor Torpedo Boats and HM Destroyer Oribi 1944–45. *Career:* Foreign Office 1945; Served in Ankara, Tel Aviv, Rio de Janeiro, Washington and South Africa; Head of West African Department, Foreign Office 1968–73; Concurrently non-resident Ambassador to Chad 1970–73; Ambassador to: Hungary 1973–76, Portugal 1976–81; High Commissioner to Canada 1981–84. *House of Lords:* An elected hereditary peer 1999–.

Select Committees: Member: Industry Sub-Committee of European Communities Committee 1984–86, Environmental Sub-Committee of European Communities Committee 1986–91, Sub-Committee of the Science and Technology Committee on the Scientific Base of the Nature Conservancy Council 1990, Agriculture Sub-Committee of European Communities Committee 1991–95, Sub-Committee of the Science and Technology Committee on Fish Stocks 1995, Sub-Committee on the 1996 Inter-Governmental Conference 1995–97; Co-opted Member, Select Committee on European Communities Sub-Committee D (Agriculture, Fisheries and Food) 1997–2000. *Other:* Chairman, Wildlife and Countryside Link 1990–95; Council Member, RSPB 1992–94, Vice-President 1996–97; President, Welsh Salmon and Trout Angling Association 1988–95; Chairman, Salmon and Trout Association 1997–2000, Executive Vice-President 2000–. *Trusts, etc:* Vice-Chairman, Atlantic Salmon Trust 1988–95; President, Radnorshire Wildlife Trust 1994–. *Miscellaneous:* Chairman, National Rivers Authority Regional Fisheries Advisory Committee for the Welsh Region 1989–94. *Honours:* CMG 1970; KCMG 1981; Grand Cross Order of the Infante, Portugal 1978. *Publications:* C.B. *– A Life of Sir Henry Campbell-Bannerman*, 1973 (Whitbread Award for Biography); *Fairfax*, 1985. *Recreations:* Fly-fishing, bird-watching. *Clubs:* Flyfishers' (President 1987–88). *Address:* The Lord Moran, KCMG, House of Lords, London, SW1A 0PW.

LORD MORGAN   Labour

MORGAN (Life Baron), Kenneth Owen Morgan; cr. 2000. Born 16 May 1934. Son of late David and Margaret Morgan; educated Aberdyfi Council School; University College School, Hampstead; Oriel College, Oxford (BA 1955, MA, DPhil 1958, DLitt 1985). Married January 4, 1973, Jane Keeler (died 1992) (1 son 1 daughter). *Trades Union:* Member, AUT to 1995. *Career:* Lecturer, later Senior Lecturer in History, University College of Wales, Swansea 1958–66, Visiting Fellow, Columbia University 1962–63; Visiting Professor 1965; Fellow and Praelector, Modern History and Politics, The Queen's College, Oxford 1966–89; Neale Lecturer, University College, London 1986; Principal, then Vice-Chancellor, University College of Wales, Aberystwyth and Professor in the University of Wales 1989–95, Senior Vice-Chancellor 1993–95, Emeritus Professor 1999; BBC (Wales) Lecturer 1995; Prothero Lecturer, Royal Historical Society 1996; Visiting Professor, Witwatersrand 1997, 1998 and 2000. *International Bodies:* Life member, British-American Parliamentary Group 2000. *Other:* Vice-President, Hon Secretary, Cymmrodarion Llafur, International Eisteddfod of Llangollen. Hon. Fellow: Swansea 1985, The Queen's College, Oxford 1992, Cardiff 1997; Hon. DLitt: Wales 1997, Glamorgan 1997; Hon. Fellow, Carmarthen 1998. *Miscellaneous:* Editor, *Welsh History Review* 1961–; Member: Board of Celtic Studies 1972–, Council, Royal Historical Society 1983–86, Council, National Library of Wales 1991–95. FRHistS 1964; FBA 1983. *Publications: Wales in British Politics*, 1963; *David Lloyd George: Welsh radical as world statesman*, 1963; *Freedom or Sacrilege?*, 1967; *Keir Hardie*, 1967; *The Age of Lloyd George*, 1971; Editor *Lloyd George Family Letters*, 1973; *Lloyd George*, 1974; *Keir Hardie, Radical and Socialist*, 1975; *Consensus and Disunity*, 1979; Co-author *Portrait of a Progressive*, 1980; *Rebirth of a Nation: Wales 1880–1980*, 1981; *David Lloyd George*, 1981; *Labour in Power, 1945–1951*, 1984; Editor *The Oxford Illustrated History of Britain*, 1984; *Labour People*, 1987; Editor *The Oxford History of Britain*, 1988; *The Red Dragon and the Red Flag*, 1989; *The People's Peace*, 1990, new edn 1999; *Modern Wales: politics, places and people*, 1995; *Britain and Europe*, 1995; Editor *The Young Oxford History of Britain and Ireland*, 1996; *Callaghan: a life*, 1997; Co-editor *Crime, Protest and Police in Modern British Society*, 1999; *The Twentieth Century*, 2000; author and editor of other works, as well as articles and reviews. *Special Interests:* Education, Europe, Foreign Affairs, Constitutional Reform, Civil Liberties. *Recreations:* Music, travel, sport (cricket), architectural history. *Clubs:* Reform. *Name, Style and Title:* Raised to the peerage as Baron Morgan, of Aberdyfi in the County of Gwynedd 2000. *Address:* Professor the Lord Morgan, The Croft, 63 Millwood End, Long Hanborough, Witney, Oxfordshire, OX8 8BP *E-Mail:* k.morgan@online.rednet.co.uk.

LORD MORRIS OF CASTLEMORRIS **LORD MORRIS OF CASTLEMORRIS** Labour

MORRIS OF CASTLEMORRIS (Life Baron), Brian Robert Morris; cr. 1990. Born 4 December 1930. Son of late Capt. William Robert Morris and of Ellen Elizabeth Morris (née Shelley); educated Cardiff High School; Worcester College, Oxford (MA, DPhil). Married 1955, Sandra, daughter of late Percival Samuel James (1 son 1 daughter). *Trades Union:* Member, AUT 1954–91. *Armed Forces:* Served, Welch Regiment, National Service 1949–51; TA 1951–56. *Career:* Fellow, Shakespeare Institute, Birmingham University 1956–58; Assistant Lecturer, Reading University 1958–60, Lecturer 1960–65; General Editor, New Mermaid Dramatists 1964–86; Lecturer, York University 1965–67; Senior Lecturer 1967–71; Member, Archbishops' Council on Evangelism 1971–75; Professor of English Literature, Sheffield University 1971–80; General Editor, New Arden Shakespeare 1974–82; Member, Museum and Galleries Commission 1975, Chairman 1985–90, Member, Yr Academi Gymreig 1979–; Council Member, Poetry Society 1980–90, Vice-President 1990–; Director, British Library Board 1980–91; Council Member, National Library of Wales 1981–91; Member: Welsh Arts Council 1983–86, Welsh Advisory Committee, British Council 1983–91; Vice-President, Council for National Parks 1985–; Member, Anthony Panizzi Foundation 1987–91; Broadcaster, scriptwriter and presenter of television programmes. *Whip:* Opposition Whip 1990–92; Deputy Opposition Chief Whip, House of Lords 1992–97. *Spokesman:* An Opposition Spokesman on: Home Office matters 1990–92, Citizen's Charter 1992–94, National Heritage 1992–96, Welsh Affairs 1992–97, Northern Ireland 1994–97, Principal Spokesman on: Education 1994–97, Education and Employment 1994–97; Former Front Bench Spokesman on: Arts and Heritage, Libraries, Broadcasting, Energy and Science. *Select Committees:* Former Member, Select Committees on: Liaison 1997–99, Offices, Advisory Panel on Works of Art. *Other:* Member, Council of Yorkshire Arts Association 1973–81; Vice-President, Museums Association 1985–88; Principal, St. David's University College, Lampeter and Pro-Vice-Chancellor of the University of Wales 1980–91; Chairman of Council, The Prince of Wales's Institute of Architecture 1993–97; President, Brontë Society 1996–; Vice-President: Prayer Book Society 1990–, The Arkwright Society 1992–; Director, Middleton Botanic Garden (now known as the Botanic Garden of Wales) 1994–97; Member, Advisory Board of the Botanic Garden of Wales 1997–. Hon. LittD, Sheffield 1991; Hon. LLD, Wales 1992. *Trusts, etc:* Trustee, National Portrait Gallery 1977–, Vice-Chairman of Trustees 1993–; Trustee, National Heritage Memorial Fund 1980–91; President, Welsh Historic Gardens Trust 1990–; Trustee: Museum of Empire and Commonwealth Trust 1991–, Campaign for the Protection of Rural Wales 1991–, National Heritage 1993–. Freeman, Fulton County, Georgia, USA. *Publications:* Author/editor of several books on poetry as well as plays, also contributor to journals. *Recreations:* Music, mountains, museums. *Clubs:* Athenaeum. *Name, Style and Title:* Raised to the peerage as Baron Morris of Castlemorris, of St. Dogmaels in the County of Dyfed 1990. *Address:* The Lord Morris of Castlemorris, The Old Hall, Foolow, Eyam, Hope Valley, Derbyshire, S32 5QR *Tel:* 01433 631186 *Fax:* 01433 631186.

LORD MORRIS OF MANCHESTER **LORD MORRIS OF MANCHESTER** Labour

MORRIS OF MANCHESTER (Life Baron), Alfred Morris; cr. 1997. Born 23 March 1928. Son of late George Henry Morris and late Jessie Morris (née Murphy); educated Manchester Elementary School; Matriculated by means of evening school tuition; Ruskin College, Oxford 1949–50; St Catherine's College, Oxford 1950–53 (MA); Department of Education, University of Manchester 1953–54 (DipEd). Married September 30, 1950, Irene, daughter of Abel and Esther Jones (2 sons 2 daughters). *Trades Union:* Member, GMB. *Armed Forces:* Served in the army, mainly in the Middle East 1946–48. *Career:* Manchester Schoolteacher and Lecturer 1954–56; Industrial Relations Officer, Electricity Supply Industry 1956–64. *House of Commons:* Contested Liverpool, Garston 1951 and Manchester Wythenshawe 1959; MP (Labour/Co-operative) for Manchester Wythenshawe 1964–97; PPS: to Minister of Agriculture, Fisheries and Food 1964–1967, to Leader of the House of Commons 1968–70; Parliamentary Under-Secretary of State, Department of Health and Social Security with special responsibility for the Disabled 1974–79; UK's first Minister for Disabled People; Promoted three Acts of Parliament as Private Member: Chronically Sick and Disabled Persons Act 1970, Food and Drugs (Milk) Act 1970, Police Act 1972. *Spokesman (Commons):* Opposition Front Bench

Spokesman on the Social Services 1970–74; Principal Opposition Front Bench Spokesman for the Disabled 1979–92. *International Bodies (Commons):* Treasurer, IPU British Group 1968–74; Joint-Treasurer, British-American Parliamentary Group 1983–97; Chairman, ANZAC Group of MPs and Peers 1972–97, President 1997. *International Bodies:* Member, Executive Committee, CPA UK Branch 1999–. *International Bodies (General):* British representative, UN advisory Council on the International Year of Disabled People; Chairman, World Planning Group appointed to draft *Charter for the 1980's* and *Charter for the New Millennium* for disabled people world-wide; Life Patron, Rehabilitation International. *Party Groups (General):* Former National Chairman, Labour League of Youth; Chairman, Parliamentary Cooperative Group 1970–71, 1983–85; President, Co-operative Congress 1995–96. *Other:* Member, General Advisory Council, BBC 1968–74, 1979–97; Vice-President, Rehab UK 1995–; President: Society of Chiropodists and Pediatrists 1997; Haemophilia Society 1999–. *Awards Granted:* First-ever recipient, Field Marshal Lord Harding Award for outstanding services to disabled people 1971; Louis Braille Memorial Award of the National Federation of the Blind for distinguished services to blind people 1971; Paul Harris Fellow, Rotary International; Earl of Snowdon Award for expanding the rights of disabled people 1997; Automobile Association Award for work of immeasurable value to disabled road users 1998. Hon. Fellow, Manchester Metropolitan University 1990; Hon. MA, University of Salford 1997; Hon. LLD, University of Manchester 1998. *Trusts, etc:* Chairman, Managing Trustees, Parliamentary Contributory Pension Scheme and House of Commons Members' Fund 1983–97; Trustee of many charities for disabled people. *Honours:* PC 1979; Queen's Service Order (QSO) awarded by Government of New Zealand 1989; Order of Australia (AO) 1991. Hon. Associate, British Veterinary Association; Hon. Fellow, Association of Building Engineers 2000. *Publications: Human Relations in Industry,* 1963; *The Growth of Parliamentary Scrutiny by Committee,* 1971; *VAT: A Tax on the Consumer,* 1972; Contributor to numerous books on the problems and needs of disabled people. *Special Interests:* Disability, Co-operative Movement, Regional Development, Airport Policy, Science and Technology. *Recreations:* Tennis, gardening, chess, snooker. *Name, Style and Title:* Raised to the peeerage as Baron Morris of Manchester, of Manchester in the County of Greater Manchester 1997. *Address:* Rt Hon the Lord Morris of Manchester, AO, QSO, 20 Hitherwood Drive, London, SE19 1XB.

LORD MOWBRAY AND STOURTON   Conservative

MOWBRAY (26th Baron, E), Charles Edward Stourton; cr. 1283; 27th Baron SEGRAVE (E) 1283; 23rd Baron STOURTON (E) 1448. Born 11 March 1923. Son of 25th Baron, MC, Premier Baron of England. Succeeded his father 1965; educated Ampleforth; Christ Church, Oxford. Married 1st, June 28, 1952, Hon. Jane de Yarburgh-Bateson (died 1998), daughter of 5th Baron Deramore (2 sons); married 2nd, February 1999, Joan, Lady Holland, daughter of late Captain Herbert Edmund Street, 20th Hussars, and widow of Sir Guy Holland, 3rd Bt. *Armed Forces:* Served as Lieutenant, 2nd Armoured Battalion Grenadier Guards 1943–45; Wounded in France 1944; Invalided. *Councils, Public Bodies:* Councillor, Niddesdale RDC 1954–61. *Career:* Director, Securicor (Scotland) Ltd 1964–70; Chairman, Government Picture Buying Committee 1972–74; Director: EIRC Holdings Ltd (Jersey), EIRC (Ghana) Ltd, GDC (Ghana) Ltd 1980, EIRC Canada Inc. 1980–, Ghadeco (UK) Ltd 1986–; Chairman, Thames Estuary Airport Company Ltd 1993–; Member, Parliamentary Delegation to Bicentennial Celebrations in Washington DC. *House of Lords:* An elected hereditary peer 1999–. *Whip:* Opposition Whip 1967–70, 1974–78; Deputy Chief Opposition Whip 1978–79; Government Whip (A Lord in Waiting) 1970–74, 1979–80. *Spokesman:* Spokesman for Department of the Environment 1970–74; Spokesman for Departments of Environment and Transport and Arts 1979–80. *Select Committees:* Member, House of Lords Select Committee for Privileges 1992–99. *Other:* Patron, Normandy Veterans Association Tayside and Mearns Branch. *Awards Granted:* Recipient, 1976 Bicentennial Year Award of Baronial Order of Magna Carta (USA). *Trusts, etc:* Trustee, College of Arms Trust 1975–. *Honours:* CBE 1982; Knight of Sovereign and Military Order of Malta. *Clubs:* Turf, White's, Pratt's. *Address:* The Lord Mowbray and Stourton, CBE, 23 Warwick Square, London, SW1V 2AB; Marcus, By Forfar, Angus, DD8 3QH *Tel:* 01307 850219.

LORD MOYNIHAN — Conservative

MOYNIHAN (4th Baron, UK), Colin Berkeley Moynihan; cr. 1929; 4th Bt of Carr Manor (UK) 1922. Born 13 September 1955. Son of 2nd Baron, OBE, TD. Succeeded his half-brother (who died in 1991) in 1997; educated Monmouth School (Music Scholar); University College, Oxford (BA philosophy, politics and economics 1977, MA 1982) (President of the Union). Married 1992, Gaynor-Louise, daughter of Paul Metcalf (2 sons 1 daughter). *Councils, Public Bodies:* Director, Canterbury Festival 1999–. *Career:* Personal Assistant to Chairman, Tate and Lyle Ltd 1978–80; Manager, Tate and Lyle Agribusiness 1980–82; Chief Executive, Ridgways Tea and Coffee Merchants 1982–83; Chairman 1983–87; Chairman, CMA Consultants 1993–; Managing Director, Independent Power Corporation plc 1996–; Chairman, Consort Resources group of companies 2000–; Director, Rowan group of companies. *House of Commons:* MP (Conservative) for Lewisham East 1983–92; Chairman, Trade and Industry Standing Committee 1983–87; PPS: to Minister of Health 1985, to Paymaster-General 1985–87; Parliamentary Under-Secretary of State: at Department of Environment (Minister for Sport) 1987–90, at Department of Energy 1990–92. *House of Lords:* An elected hereditary peer 1999–. *Spokesman:* Senior Opposition Spokesman on Foreign and Commonwealth Affairs 1997–2000. *Party Groups (General):* Member, The Bow Group 1978–92. *Other:* Governor, Sports Aid Foundation (London and South East) 1980–82. *Awards Granted:* Oxford Double Blue, Rowing and Boxing 1976 and 1977; World Gold Medal for Lightweight Rowing, International Rowing Federation 1978; Olympic Silver Medal for Rowing 1980; World Silver Medal for Rowing 1981. *Miscellaneous:* Member, Sports Council 1982–85; The succession to the barony was in dispute between 1991 and 1997, when the present baron was recognised as the lawful holder of the peerage by decision of the House of Lords. Freeman, City of London 1978. Liveryman, Worshipful Company of Haberdashers 1981. *Special Interests:* Foreign Affairs, Trade and Industry, Sport, Inner Cities, Refugees, Overseas Aid and Development. *Recreations:* Reading, sport, music. *Sportsclubs:* London Rowing, Leander Rowing. *Clubs:* Brooks's, Vincent's (Oxford). *Address:* The Lord Moynihan, House of Lords, London, SW1A 0PW *E-Mail:* cbm@dial.pipex.com.

LORD MOYOLA — Conservative

MOYOLA (Life Baron), James Dawson Chichester-Clark; cr. 1971. Born 12 February 1923. Son of late Captain James Jackson Chichester-Clark, DSO, RN; educated Eton. Married March 14, 1959, Mrs Moyra Maud Haughton, daughter of late Brigadier Arthur De Burgh Morris, CBE, DSO (1 stepson 2 daughters). *Armed Forces:* Served Irish Guards 1942–60; Wounded Anzio 1944; ADC to Governor-General of Canada 1947–49; Staff College, Camberley 1956; Retired from Irish Guards as Major 1960. *Councils, Public Bodies:* DL, Co Londonderry 1954. *Career:* MP (UU) for South Londonderry, Northern Ireland Parliament 1960; Assistant Whip 1963; Chief Whip 1963–66; Leader of House and Chief Whip 1966–67; Minister of Agriculture 1967–69; Prime Minister of Northern Ireland 1969–71. *Honours:* PC (NI) 1966. *Special Interests:* Agriculture, Northern Ireland. *Recreations:* Fishing, gardening, dendrology, shooting. *Name, Style and Title:* Raised to the peerage as Baron Moyola, of Castledawson in the County of Londonderry 1971. *Address:* Rt Hon the Lord Moyola, DL, Moyola Park, Castledawson, Co. Londonderry, BT45 8ED.

LORD MURRAY OF EPPING FOREST — Labour

MURRAY OF EPPING FOREST (Life Baron), Lionel Murray; cr. 1985. Born 2 August 1922; educated State Schools; Queen Mary College, University of London; New College, Oxford. Married September 22, 1945, Heather Woolf (2 sons 2 daughters). *Armed Forces:* Wartime service with King's Shropshire Light Infantry. *Career:* TUC 1947–84, General Secretary 1973–84. *Other:* President, Friends of Epping Forest; Vice-President: Wesley's Chapel, National Youth Theatre; Patron, St Clare's Hospice. Hon. Fellow, New College, Oxford 1975; six honorary doctorates/fellowships. *Trusts, etc:* President, Friends of Ironbridge Museum Trust: Trustee, NUMAST; Patron, Winged Fellowship Trust. *Honours:* OBE 1966; PC 1976. *Special Interests:* Children, Homeless, Disability. *Recreations:* Theatre, music, looking at Epping Forest. *Name, Style and Title:* Raised to the peerage as Baron Murray of Epping Forest, of Telford in the County of Shropshire 1985. *Address:* Rt Hon the Lord Murray of Epping Forest, OBE, 29 The Crescent, Loughton, Essex, IG10 4PY *Tel:* Home: 020 8508 4425.

LORD MURTON OF LINDSIFARNE   Conservative

MURTON OF LINDISFARNE (Life Baron), (Henry) Oscar Murton; cr. 1979. Born 8 May 1914. Son of late H. E. C. Murton; educated Uppingham. Married 1st, May 1939, Constance Frances Connell (died 1977) (1 son and 1 daughter deceased 1986), married 2nd, April 1979, Pauline Teresa, youngest daughter of late Thomas Keenan, JP, of Johannesburg. *Armed Forces:* Commissioned TA 1934 in Royal Northumberland Fusiliers; General Staff 1939–46; A Lieutenant-Colonel. *Councils, Public Bodies:* Councillor, Poole Borough Council 1961–64; Member, Herrison (Dorchester) Hospital Management Committee until 1974; JP, Borough of Poole 1963, latterly Supplemental List Inner London. *Career:* Managing Director, Private Limited Company with Department Stores NE England 1949–57. *House of Commons:* MP (Conservative) for Poole 1964–79; Introduced Highways (Amendment) Act 1965, PPS to Minister of Local Government and Development 1970–71; Deputy Chairman, Ways and Means 1973–76; Chairman, Ways and Means and the Deputy Speaker House of Commons 1976–79. *Whip (Commons):* Assistant Government Whip 1971; Government Whip (Lord Commissioner to the Treasury) 1972–73. *House of Lords:* A Deputy Chairman of Committees House of Lords 1981–; A Deputy Speaker since 1983; Introduced Access to Neighbouring Land Act 1992. *Select Committees:* Member, Joint Select Committee of Lords and Commons on Private Bill Procedure 1987–88. *Party Groups (General):* President, Poole Conservative Association 1983–95. *Other:* Chancellor, Primrose League 1983–88. *Honours:* OBE (Mil) 1946; PC 1976. Freeman, City of London. Freeman, Wax Chandlers Company; Past-Master, Clockmakers Company. *Special Interests:* Defence. *Recreations:* Sailing, painting. *Name, Style and Title:* Raised to the peerage as Baron Murton of Lindisfarne, of Hexham in the County of Northumberland 1979. *Address:* Rt Hon the Lord Murton of Lindisfarne, OBE, TD, 49 Carlisle Mansions, Carlisle Place, London, SW1P 1HY *Tel:* 020 7834 8226.

LORD MUSTILL   Cross-Bencher

MUSTILL (Life Baron), Michael John Mustill; cr. 1992. Born 10 May 1931. Son of late Clement William and Marion Mustill; educated Oundle; St John's College, Cambridge (LLD 1992). Married 1st, 1960, Beryl Davies (marriage dissolved 1983), married 2nd, 1991, Mrs Caroline Phillips (2 sons 1 step-daughter). *Armed Forces:* Served Royal Artillery 1949–51. *Career:* Called to the Bar, Gray's Inn 1955; Bencher 1976; QC 1968; Deputy Chairman, Hampshire Quarter Sessions 1971; Chairman, Civil Service Appeal Tribunal 1971–78; A Recorder of the Crown Court 1972–78; Judge of the High Court, Queen's Bench Division 1978–85; Presiding Judge, NE Circuit 1981–84; Chairman: Judicial Studies Board 1985–89, Departmental Committee on Law of Arbitration 1985–90; A Lord Justice of Appeal 1985–92; A Lord of Appeal in Ordinary 1992–97. *Select Committees:* Member, House of Lords Select Committee on Medical Ethics 1993–. *Honours:* Kt 1978; PC 1985. FBA. *Publications:* Author of several legal works as well as articles in legal journals. *Name, Style and Title:* Raised to the peerage as Baron Mustill, of Pateley Bridge in the County of North Yorkshire 1992. *Address:* Rt Hon the Lord Mustill, Essex Court Chambers, 24 Lincoln's Inn Fields, London, WC2A 3ED.

N

LORD NASEBY   Conservative

NASEBY (Life Baron), Michael Wolfgang Laurence Morris; cr. 1997. Born 25 November 1936. Son of late C. L. Morris, FRIBA; educated Bedford School; St Catharine's College, Cambridge (MA 1960). Married September 3, 1960, Ann, daughter of late Percy Appleby (2 sons 1 daughter). *Armed Forces:* National Service Pilot (RAF and NATO wings). *Councils, Public Bodies:* London Borough of Islington: Councillor 1968–74, Leader 1969–71, Alderman 1971–74. *Career:* Marketing Manager, Reckitt and Colman Group 1960–64; Director: Service Advertising 1964–71, Benton & Bowles Ltd 1971–81. *House of Commons:* Contested Islington North 1966; MP (Conservative) for Northampton South 1974–97; PPS to Minister of State, Northern Ireland 1979–81; Chairman, Ways and Means and Deputy Speaker 1992–97. *International Bodies (General):* Member, Council of Europe and Western European Union 1983–91.

Other: Chairman, Progressive Supranuclear Palsy Charity; Chairman of Governors, Bedford School. *Trusts, etc:* Chairman, Northamptonshire Victoria County History Trust. *Honours:* PC 1994. *Publications: Helping The Exporter,* 1967; Co-author *Marketing Below The Line,* 1970; *The Disaster of Direct Labour,* 1978. *Special Interests:* Energy, Health Service, Food and Nutrition, Exports, South East Asia, Marketing, Parliamentary Procedure, National Lottery. *Recreations:* Golf (Past Captain Parliamentary Golfing Society), cricket, tennis, shooting, forestry, budgerigars. *Sportsclubs:* John O'Gaunt Golf, Port Stanley Golf, All England Lawn Tennis, Royal St George's Golf, Lords Taverners, Northamptonshire County Cricket (Committee). *Clubs:* Carlton, Northampton Town and Country, MCC. *Name, Style and Title:* Raised to the peerage as Baron Naseby, of Sandy in the County of Bedfordshire 1997. *Address:* Rt Hon the Lord Naseby, Caesar's Camp, Sandy, Bedfordshire, SG19 2AD.

LORD NEILL OF BLADEN — Cross-Bencher

NEILL OF BLADEN (Life Baron), Francis Patrick Neill; cr. 1997. Born 8 August 1926. Son of late Sir Thomas Neill, JP, and late Lady (Annie) Neill; educated Highgate School; Magdalen College, Oxford (BA, MA); All Souls College, Oxford (BCL). Married 1954, Caroline Susan, daughter of late Sir Piers Debenham, 2nd Bt (4 sons 2 daughters). *Armed Forces:* Served Rifle Brigade 1944–47 (Captain); GSO III (Training) British Troops, Egypt 1947. *Career:* Fellow, All Souls, Oxford 1950–77, Sub-Warden 1972–74, Warden 1977–95; Called to the Bar, Gray's Inn 1951, QC 1966, Bencher 1971, Vice-Treasurer 1989, Treasurer 1990; Lecturer in Air Law, LSE 1955–58; Member, Bar Council 1967–71, Vice-Chairman 1973–74, Chairman 1974–75; Chairman, Senate of the Inns of Court and the Bar 1974–75; A Recorder of the Crown Court 1975–78; A Judge of the Courts of Appeal of Jersey and Guernsey 1977–94; Chairman: Press Council 1978–83, Council for the Securities Industry 1978–85; Chairman, Justice – All Souls Committee for Review of Administrative Law 1978–87; Hon. Professor of Legal Ethics, Birmingham University 1983–84; Vice-Chancellor, Oxford University 1985–89; Chairman, DTI Committee of Inquiry into Regulatory Arrangements at Lloyd's 1986–87; Vice-Chairman, Committee of Vice-Chancellors and Principals of the Universities of the United Kingdom 1987–90; Independent National Director, Times Newspaper Holdings 1988–97; Chairman: Feltrum Loss Review Committee at Lloyd's 1991–92, Committee on Standards in Public Life 1997–; Visitor, Buckingham University 1997–. Hon. Fellow, All Souls College 1995; Magdalen College, Oxford 1988, Three honorary law doctorates. *Honours:* Kt 1983. *Publications: Administrative Justice: some necessary reforms,* 1988. *Recreations:* Music, forestry. *Clubs:* Athenaeum, Garrick, Beefsteak. *Name, Style and Title:* Raised to the peerage as Baron Neill of Bladen, of Briantspuddle in the County of Dorset 1997. *Address:* The Lord Neill of Bladen, QC, 1 Hare Court, Temple, London, EC4Y 7BE.

LORD NEWBY — Liberal Democrat

NEWBY (Life Baron), Richard Mark Newby; cr 1997. Born 14 February 1953. Son of Frank and Kathleen Newby; educated Rothwell Grammar School; St Catherine's College, Oxford (MA). Married 1978, Ailsa Ballantyne Thomson (2 sons). *Career:* HM Customs and Excise: Administration Trainee 1974; Private Secretary to Permanent Secretary 1977–79; Principal, Planning Unit 1979–81; Secretary, SDP Parliamentary Committee 1981; Joined SDP Headquarters staff 1981; National Secretary, SDP 1983–88, Executive 1988–90; Director, Corporate Affairs, Rosehaugh plc 1991; Director, Matrix Communications Consultancy Ltd 1992–99; Chair: Reform Publications Ltd 1993–, Centre for Reform Management Committee; Director, Flagship Group Ltd 1999–; Chief of Staff to Charles Kennedy, MP 1999–. *Spokesman:* A Liberal Democrat Spokesman for: Trade and Industry 1998–, The Treasury 1998–. *Select Committees:* Member, Select Committee on Monetary Policy of the Bank of England 1998–. *Party Groups (General):* Deputy Chairman, Liberal Democrat General Election Team 1995–97. *Trusts, etc:* Trustee: Allachy Trust, Aviation Health Institute. *Honours:* OBE 1990. *Special Interests:* Europe, Regional Development. *Recreations:* Football, cricket. *Clubs:* Reform, MCC. *Name, Style and Title:* Raised to the peerage as Baron Newby, of Rothwell in the County of West Yorkshire 1997. *Address:* The Lord Newby, OBE, 4 Rockwells Gardens, Dulwich Wood Park, London, SE19 1HW *Tel:* 020 8244 5675.

LORD NEWTON OF BRAINTREE   Conservative

NEWTON OF BRAINTREE (Life Baron), Antony Harold Newton; cr. 1997. Born 29 August 1937. Son of late Harold Newton; educated Friend's School, Saffron Walden; Trinity College, Oxford. Married 1st, August 25, 1962, Janet Huxley (2 daughters) (divorced 1986), married 2nd, September 26, 1986, Mrs Patricia Gilthorpe (1 stepson 2 stepdaughters). *Career:* President, Oxford Union Society 1959; Debating tour in US 1960; Conservative Research Department 1961–74; Head, Economic Section 1965–70; Assistant Director 1970–74. *House of Commons:* Contested Sheffield Brightside 1970; MP (Conservative) for Braintree 1974–97; Parliamentary Under-Secretary of State, Department of Health and Social Security 1982–84; Minister for the Disabled 1983; Minister of State for Social Security and the Disabled 1983–86; Minister for Health 1986–88; Chancellor of the Duchy of Lancaster (Minister of Trade and Industry) 1988–89; Secretary of State for Social Security 1989–92; Lord President of the Council and Leader of the House of Commons 1992–97. *Whip (Commons):* Assistant Government Whip 1979–81; Government Whip 1981–82. *Party Groups (General):* President, Oxford University Conservative Association 1958; Secretary, Bow Group 1962–64. *Honours:* OBE 1972; PC 1988. *Special Interests:* Tax, Social Security, Pensions, Disability, Health, Social Services. *Name, Style and Title:* Raised to the peerage as Baron Newton of Braintree, of Coggeshall in the County of Essex 1997. *Address:* Rt Hon the Lord Newton of Braintree, OBE, House of Lords, London, SW1A 0PW.

LORD NICHOLLS OF BIRKENHEAD   Cross-Bencher

NICHOLLS OF BIRKENHEAD (Life Baron), Donald James Nicholls; cr. 1994. Born 25 January 1933. Son of late William Greenhow Nicholls; educated Birkenhead School; Liverpool University (LLB); Trinity Hall, Cambridge (BA Law Tripos, LLB). Married 1960, Jennifer Mary Thomas (2 sons 1 daughter). *Career:* Called to the Bar, Middle Temple 1958; Bencher 1981, Treasurer 1997; In practice, Chancery Bar 1958–83; QC 1974; Judge of the High Court of Justice, Chancery Division 1983–86; A Lord Justice of Appeal 1986–91; Vice-Chancellor of the Supreme Court 1991–94; A Lord of Appeal in Ordinary 1994–; Member, Senate of Inns of Court and the Bar 1974–76; Chairman, Lord Chancellor's Advisory Committee on Legal Education and Conduct 1996–97. *Select Committees:* Chairman, Select Committee on Parliamentary Privilege (Joint Committee) 1997–99. *Other:* President, Birkenhead School 1986–; Patron, Cayman Islands Law School 1994–. Hon. Fellow, Trinity Hall, Cambridge 1986; Hon. LLD, Liverpool University 1987. *Honours:* Kt 1983; PC 1986. *Recreations:* Walking, history, music. *Clubs:* Athenaeum (Trustee). *Name, Style and Title:* Raised to the peerage as Baron Nicholls of Birkenhead, of Stoke D'Abernon in the County of Surrey 1994. *Address:* Rt Hon the Lord Nicholls of Birkenhead, House of Lords, London, SW1A 0PW.

BARONESS NICHOLSON OF WINTERBOURNE   Liberal Democrat

NICHOLSON OF WINTERBOURNE (Life Baroness), Emma Harriet Nicholson; cr. 1997. Born 16 October 1941. Daughter of late Sir Godfrey Nicholson, 1st and last Bt and late Lady Katharine Lindsay, daughter of 27th Earl of Crawford, KT, PC; educated Portsdown Lodge School, Bexhill; St Mary's School, Wantage; The Royal Academy of Music (LRAM, ARCM). Married May 9, 1987, Sir Michael Harris Caine (died 1999), son of late Sir Sidney Caine, KCMG (2 step-children and 1 ward/foster son). *Career:* ICL 1961–64; Computer Consultant, John Tyzack and Partners 1964–69; McLintock Mann and Whinney Murray 1969–74; Save the Children Fund 1974–85, Director of Fundraising 1977–85; Visiting Fellow, St Antony's College, Oxford 1995–96, Senior Associate Member 1997–98, 1998–99; MEP for the South East Region 1999–; Whip, Liberal Democrat Party 1999–; Vice Chair, Foreign Affairs, Human Rights, Common Security and Defence Policy Committee 1999–. *House of Commons:* Contested Blyth 1979; MP for Devon West and Torridge 1987–97; Resigned from the Conservative Party December 1995 and joined the Liberal Democrats; PPS to Michael Jack, MP, as Minister of State: at Home Office 1992–93, at Ministry of Agriculture, Fisheries and Food 1993–95, at The Treasury 1995. *Spokesman (Commons):* Liberal Democrat Spokesman on Overseas Development and Human Rights 1996–97. *Party Groups (Commons):* Former Treasurer, Positive European Group (Conservative). *Spokesman:* Member, Liberal Democrat Foreign Affairs Team; Front Bench Spokesperson on Data Protection 1998. *International Bodies (General):* Treasurer, Positive European Group; Alternate Member, UK Delegation to WEU and Council of Europe 1990–92; Former Member, European Union of Women; Official Observer, Commonwealth Secretariat team for Zambian General Election 1991. *Party Groups (General):* Vice-Chairman, Conservative Party with special responsibility for women 1983–87; Member, Liberal Democrat Parliamentary Foreign Affairs Team 1996. *Other:* Patron, senior positions in over 50 charities, especially those concerned with disability, particularly deafness and blindness, including: Co-founder, now patron Cities in Schools 1990–; Founder and president, AMAR Appeal (aid to Iraqui Marsh Arabs) 1991–; Founder chair, now patron Blind in Business 1992–; Co-Chairman, UNA Advisory Group UNESCO, International Year of the Disabled, Chairman, UNA 1998–2000. Hon. Doctorate, University of North London. *Trusts, etc:* Trustee, chair, fellow, member nine trusts, particularly ones concerned with disability, including: Founder chair and trustee, ADAPT (Access for Disabled People to Arts Premises Today). *Miscellaneous:* Member: European Standing Committee A, Standing Committee on Statutory Instruments; Liberal Democrat Prospective European Parliament Candidate for the South-East Region 1999. LRAM; ARCM; FRSA. Freeman, Worshipful Company of Information Technologists. *Publications: Why Does the West Forget?,* 1993; *Secret Society – Inside and Outside the Conservative Party,* 1996; as well as various articles and pamphlets. *Special Interests:* European Union, Information Technology, Human Rights, Education, Health, Foreign Affairs, Intellectual Property, Farming, Defence, Iraq, Iran, Kuwait, Islamic World, Children, Refugees/Displaced People, Freedom of Information. *Recreations:* Music, chess, walking, reading. *Clubs:* Reform, The National Liberal Club. *Name, Style and Title:* Raised to the peerage as Baroness Nicholson of Winterbourne, of Winterbourne in the Royal County of Berkshire 1997. *Address:* The Baroness Nicholson of Winterbourne, MEP, House of Lords, London, SW1A 0PW.

LORD NICKSON   Cross-Bencher

NICKSON (Life Baron), David Wigley Nickson; cr. 1994. Born 27 November 1929. Son of late Geoffrey Wigley Nickson and of late Janet Mary Dobie; educated Eton; RMA, Sandhurst. Married 1952, Helen Louise Cockcraft (3 daughters). *Armed Forces:* Commissioned Coldstream Guards 1949–54. *Councils, Public Bodies:* DL, Stirling and Falkirk 1982–97, Vice-Lieutenant 1997–. *Career:* Joined William Collins Sons & Co. Ltd publishers 1954, Director 1961–85, Joint Managing Director 1967, Vice-Chairman 1976–83, Group Managing Director 1979–82; Director, Scottish United Investors plc 1970–83; Director, General Accident Fire and Life Assurance Corporation plc 1971–98, Deputy Chairman 1993–98; Member, Scottish Committee, Design Council 1978–81; Chairman, CBI in Scotland 1979–81; Member, Scottish Economic Council 1980–95; Director, Clydesdale Bank plc 1981–89, 1990–98, Deputy Chairman 1990–91, Chairman 1991–98; Director, Scottish & Newcastle Breweries plc 1981–95, Deputy Chairman 1982–83, Chairman 1983–89; Chairman, Pan Books Ltd 1982; Director, Radio Clyde plc 1982–85; Chairman, Countryside Commission for Scotland 1983–85; Director, Edinburgh Investment Trust plc 1983–94; Member, NEDC 1985–88; President, CBI 1986–88; Director, Hambro's plc 1989–98; Chairman: Senior Salaries Review Body 1989–95, Scottish Development Agency 1989–92; Director, National Australia Bank Ltd 1991–96; Chairman, Scottish Enterprise 1992–94. *Chancellor:* Chancellor, Glasgow Caledonian University 1993–. *Other:* Vice-Chairman, Association of Scottish District Salmon Fishery Boards 1989–92, President 1996–; Chairman, Scottish Advisory Committee, Imperial Cancer Research Fund 1994–, Life Governor. DUniversity: Stirling University 1986, Napier University 1991, Paisley University 1992; Hon. Dr., Glasgow Caledonian University 1993. *Trusts, etc:* Atlantic Salmon Trust: Member, Council of Management 1982–, Chairman 1989–95, Vice-President 1995–; Trustee: Prince's Youth Business Trust 1987–90, Game Conservancy 1988–91, Princess Royal's Trust for Carers 1990–94. *Miscellaneous:* Brigadier, Queen's Body Guard for Scotland, The Royal Company of Archers; Chairman, Secretary of State for Scotland's Scottish Salmon Strategy Task Force 1996–; Independent Adviser, Secretary of State for Scotland's Appointments Committee 1996–99. *Honours:* CBE 1981; KBE 1987. CIMgt; FRSE 1987. Freeman, City of London. Hon. Freeman, Fishmongers' Company 1999–. *Recreations:* Fishing, shooting, birdwatching. *Clubs:* Boodle's, MCC, Flyfishers'. *Name, Style and Title:* Raised to the peerage as Baron Nickson, of Renagour in the District of Stirling 1994. *Address:* The Lord Nickson, KBE, House of Lords, London, SW1A 0PW.

BARONESS NICOL — Labour

NICOL (Life Baroness), Olive Mary Wendy Nicol; cr. 1982. Born 21 March 1923. Daughter of late James and Harriet Rowe-Hunter; educated Cahir School, Ireland. Married December 18, 1947, Alexander Douglas Ian Nicol (2 sons 1 daughter). *Councils, Public Bodies:* JP, Cambridge Bench 1972–86; Cambridge City Council 1972–82, Deputy Mayor 1974, Chairman, Environment Committee 1978–82. *Career:* Inland Revenue 1942–44; Admiralty 1944–48; United Charities 1967–86; Supplementary Benefits Tribunal 1976–78; Co-operative Board 1976–85, President 1981–85 Careers Service Consultative Panel 1978–81. *House of Lords:* Member, Opposition Front Bench Environment Team with responsibility for Green issues 1983–92; Deputy Speaker, House of Lords 1995–; Deputy Chairman of Committees 1997–. *Whip:* Opposition Whip 1983–87; Opposition Deputy Chief Whip 1987–89. *Spokesman:* Opposition Spokesman on Energy 1988–89. *Select Committees:* Member, Select Committees on: European Communities 1986–91, Science and Technology 1990–93, Environment and Social Affairs Sub-Committee of EC Committee 1993–95, Sustainable Development 1994–95; Member, Ecclesiastical Committee 1990–96; Member, Select Committees on: House of Lords' Offices 1997–, Offices Library and Computers Sub-Committee until 2000, Science and Technology Sub-Committee on Management of Nuclear Waste 1998–99. *Party Groups:* Member, Labour Party Departmental Committees for: Agriculture, Environment. *Party Groups (General):* Member, Co-operative Party. *Other:* Various School Governing Bodies and other public service areas, including Granta Housing Association; Council Member, RSPB 1989–94; Vice-President: Marine Conservation Society, Vice-President, Youth Hostels Association, RSPB, Council for National Parks. *Miscellaneous:* Member, Lord Chancellor's Advisory Committee 1982–88; Vice-President: Council for National Parks 1995–, Association of Municipal Authorities, Association of District Councils; Board Member, Parliamentary Office of Science and Technology (POST) 1998–2000. FRGS 1990. *Special Interests:* Commerce, Conservation, Environment, Energy, Forestry. *Recreations:* Reading, walking, gardening. *Name, Style and Title:* Raised to the peerage as Baroness Nicol, of Newnham in the County of Cambridge 1982. *Address:* Baroness Nicol, 39 Granchester Road, Newnham, Cambridge, CB3 9ED *Tel:* 01223 323733; House of Lords, London, SW1A 0PW *Tel:* House of Lords 020 7219 6705.

BARONESS NOAKES — Conservative

NOAKES (Life Baroness), Sheila Valerie Noakes; cr. 2000. Born 23 June 1949. Daughter of Albert and Iris Masters; educated Eltham Hill Grammar School; Bristol University (LLB). Married 1985, Colin Barry Noakes. *Councils, Public Bodies:* Member: Inland Revenue Management Board 1992–99, NHS Policy Board 1992–95, Chancellor of the Exchequer's Private Finance Panel 1993–97; Commissioner, Public Works Loan Board 1995–; Member, Public Services Productivity Panel 1998–2000. *Career:* Joined Peat Marwick Mitchell & Co 1970, Partner KPMG (formerly Peat Marwick Mitchell & Co, then KPMG Peat Marwick) 1983–2000, adviser 2000–; seconded to HM Treasury 1979–81; seconded to Department of Health, as Director of Finance, NHS Management Executive 1988–91; a Director, Bank of England 1994–, senior non-executive director 1998–. *Other:* Governor: London Business School 1998–, Marlborough College 2000–, Eastbourne College 2000–; Member: Board of Companions, Institute of Management; Council, Institute of Chartered Accountants of England and Wales 1987–, President 1999–2000. Hon. DBA, London Guildhall University 1999; Hon. LLD, Bristol University 2000. *Trusts, etc:* Trustee, Reuters Founders Share Co 1998–. *Honours:* DBE 1996. FCA; CIMgt; ATII. Freeman, City of London. Member, Court of Assistants, Worshipful Company of Chartered Accountants. *Special Interests:* Health, Public finance, Public service management, Horse-racing, Rural issues. *Recreations:* Ski-ing, horse racing, opera, early classical music. *Clubs:* Farmers'. *Name, Style and Title:* Raised to the peerage as Baroness Noakes, of Goudhurst in the County of Kent 2000. *Address:* The Baroness Noakes, DBE, Church House, Goudhurst, Kent, TN17 1AJ.

LORD NOLAN

NOLAN (Life Baron), Michael Patrick Nolan; cr. 1994. Born 10 September 1928. Son of James Thomas Nolan; educated Ampleforth; Wadham College, Oxford. Married 1953, Margaret, daughter of Alfred Noyes, CBE (1 son 4 daughters). *Armed Forces:* Served Royal Artillery 1947–49; TA 1949–55. *Career:* Called to the Bar, Middle Temple 1953; Bencher 1975; QC 1968; Member, Bar Council 1973–74; Member, Sandilands Committee on Inflation Accounting 1973–75; Called to the Bar, Northern Ireland 1974; QC (Northern Ireland) 1974; Member, Senate of Inns of Court and Bar 1974–81, Treasurer 1977–79; A Recorder of the Crown Court 1975–82; Judge, High Court of Justice, Queen's Bench Division 1982–91; Presiding Judge, Western Circuit 1985–88; A Lord Justice of Appeal 1991–94; A Lord of Appeal in Ordinary 1994–98; Chairman, Committee on Standards in Public Life 1994–97; Commissioner, Interception of Communications Act 1985, 1994–2000. *Chancellor:* Chancellor, Essex University 1997–. *Other:* Member, Governing Body, Convent of the Sacred Heart, Woldingham 1973–83; Chairman, Board of Institute of Advanced Legal Studies 1994–2000. Hon. Fellow, Wadham College, Oxford 1992; six honorary doctorates.*Honours:* Kt 1982; PC 1991. *Clubs:* Army and Navy, MCC, Boodle's. *Name, Style and Title:* Raised to the peerage as Baron Nolan, of Brasted in the County of Kent 1994. *Address:* Rt Hon the Lord Nolan, House of Lords, London, SW1A 0PW.

DUKE OF NORFOLK

NORFOLK (17th Duke of, E), Miles Francis Stapleton Fitzalan-Howard; cr. 1483; Earl of Arundel (E) 1139/1289; Earl of Surrey (E) 1483; Earl of Norfolk (E) 1644; Baron Beaumont (E) 1309; Baron Maltravers (E) 1330; Baron FitzAlan, Clun, and Oswaldestre (E) 1627; Baron Howard of Glossop (UK) 1869. Born 21 July 1915. Son of 3rd Baron Howard of Glossop, MBE, great grandson of 13th Duke, KG, and Mona Josephine Tempest, OBE, Baroness Beaumont (11th in line). Succeeded his mother 1971, his father 1972 and his cousin to the dukedom in 1975; educated Ampleforth; Christ Church, Oxford (MA 1937). Married July 4, 1949, Anne Mary Theresa, CBE, daughter of late Wing Commander Gerald Constable-Maxwell, MC, DFC, AFC (2 sons 3 daughters). *Armed Forces:* 2nd Lieutenant, Grenadier Guards 1937; Served War of 1939–45 France, North Africa, Sicily, Italy (despatches, MC), NW Europe; Commanded 2nd Battalion Grenadier Guards 1955–57; Appointed Head, British Military Mission to Russian Forces in Germany 1957–59; Commanded 70 Brigade KAR 1961–63; GOC, 1 Division 1963–65, Major-General; Director: Management and Support Intelligence MoD 1965–66, Service Intelligence MoD 1966–67; Retired 1967. *Councils, Public Bodies:* DL, West Sussex, 1977. *Career:* Chairman, Arundel Castle Trustees Ltd; Former Director, Robert Fleming Holdings Ltd. *Other:* President, Building Societies Association 1982–86. Hon. Fellow, St Edmund's College, Cambridge 1983–. *Miscellaneous:* Earl Marshal and Hereditary Marshal and Chief Butler of England; Premier Duke and Earl of England; Hon. Student, Christ Church, Oxford 1983–; Hon. Bencher, Inner Temple 1984. *Honours:* MC 1944; CBE (Mil) 1960; CB 1966; Knight of the Sovereign Order of Malta; Knight Grand Cross of the Order of Pius IX 1977; KG 1983; GCVO 1986. Prime Warden, Fishmongers' Livery Co. 1985–86. *Address:* Major-General His Grace the Duke of Norfolk, KG, GCVO, CB, CBE, MC, DL, Arundel Castle, Arundel, West Sussex, BN18 9AB; Carlton Towers, Goole, Yorkshire, DN14 9LZ; Bacres House, Hambleden, Henley-on-Thames, Oxfordshire, RG9 6RY; 61 Clabon Mews, London, SW1X 0EQ *Tel:* 020 7584 3430.

LORD NORTHBOURNE Cross-Bencher

NORTHBOURNE (5th Baron, UK), Christopher George Walter James; cr. 1884; 6th Bt of Langley Hall (GB) 1791. Born 18 February 1926. Son of 4th Baron. Succeeded his father 1982; educated Eton; Magdalen College, Oxford (MA). Married 1959, Marie Sygne, daughter of Henri Claudel, of Chatou-sur-Seine, France (3 sons 1 daughter). *Councils, Public Bodies:* DL Kent 1996–. *Career:* Farmer and Businessman in the UK and Overseas; Chairman, Betteshanger Farms Ltd; Director: Plantation and General Investment plc to 1995, Center Parks plc to 1995. *House of Lords:* An elected hereditary peer 1999–. *Spokesman:* Independent Spokesman on Education and Children especially disadvantaged and excluded children. *Select Committees:* Formei Member, Select Committee on European Communities Sub-Committees C and D. *International Bodies:* Member, Anglo French Parliamentary Group. *Other:* Deputy Chairman, Toynbee Hall; Chairman: Parenting Support Forum, Stepney Childrens Fund; Governor, Wye College. *Trusts, etc:* Trustee, Caldecott Community/Toynbee Hall. FRICS. *Special Interests:* Agriculture, Horticulture, Education, Disadvantaged and Excluded Children, Family. *Recreations:* Painting, sailing, gardening. *Clubs:* Brooks's, Royal Yacht Squadron (Cowes), House of Lords Yacht Club. *Address:* The Lord Northbourne, DL, 11 Eaton Place, London, SW1X 8BN *Tel:* 020 7235 6790 *Tel:* Office 020 7235 6224 *Fax:* Office 020 7235 6224; Coldharbour, Northbourne, Deal, Kent, CT14 0LP *Tel:* 01304 611277 *Fax:* 01304 611128.

LORD NORTHBROOK Conservative

NORTHBROOK (6th Baron, UK), Francis Thomas Baring; cr. 1866; 8th Bt of The City of London (GB) 1793. Born 21 February 1954. Son of 5th Baron. Succeeded his father 1990; educated Winchester; Bristol University (BA). Married 1987, Amelia Taylor (3 daughters). *Career:* Trainee Accountant, Dixon Wilson & Co. 1976–80; Baring Bros & Co. Ltd 1981–89; Senior Investment Manager, Taylor Young Investment Management Ltd 1990–93; Investment Fund Manager, Smith and Williamson 1993–95; Managing Director, Cabincity Ltd 1995–; Director, Mars Asset Management 1996–. *House of Lords:* An elected hereditary peer 1999–. *Whip:* An Opposition Whip 1999–. *Trusts, etc:* Trustee, Winchester Medical Trust. *Special Interests:* City, Agriculture, Foreign Affairs. *Recreations:* Cricket, Skiing, Shooting. *Clubs:* White's. *Address:* The Lord Northbrook, House of Lords, London, SW1A 0PW.

EARL OF NORTHESK Conservative

NORTHESK (14th Earl of, S), David John MacRae Carnegie; cr. 1647; 14th Lord Rosehill and Inglismaldie (S) 1639. Born 3 November 1954. Son of 13th Earl. Succeeded his father 1994; educated Eton; University College, London. Married 1979, Jacqueline Reid (1 son 3 daughters). *Career:* Landowner; Estate manager; Company director. *House of Lords:* An elected hereditary peer 1999–. *Whip:* An Opposition Whip 1999–. *Select Committees:* Member, Select Committee on House of Lords' Offices 1997–. *Special Interests:* Agriculture, Conservation, Heritage. *Address:* The Earl of Northesk, House of Lords, London, SW1A 0PW.

LORD NORTHFIELD Labour

NORTHFIELD (Life Baron), (William) Donald Chapman; cr. 1975. Born 25 November 1923; educated Barnsley Grammar School; Emmanuel College, Cambridge (MA Econ, Senior Scholar). *Councils, Public Bodies:* Cambridge City Councillor 1945–47; Chairman: HM Development Commissioners 1974–80, Telford Development Corporation 1975–87, Northfield Committee of Enquiry into Ownership and Occupancy of Agricultural land 1977–79. *Career:* A Company director; Special Adviser to ECC Commission on Environmental Policy 1981–85; Chairman, Consortium Developments Ltd 1986–92; Director, Wembley Stadium plc 1985–88. *House of Commons:* MP (Labour) for Birmingham Northfield 1951–70. *Party Groups (General):* General Secretary, Fabian Society 1949–53; Formerly Hon. Secretary, Cambridge Trades Council and Labour Party. *Other:* A Vice-President, Federation of Economic Development Authorities. G. Gibbon Fellow, Nuffield College, Oxford 1971–73. *Recreations:* Swimming, travel. *Name, Style and Title:* Raised to the peerage as Baron Northfield, of Telford in the County of Shropshire 1975. *Address:* The Lord Northfield, House of Lords, London, SW1A 0PW.

BARONESS NORTHOVER — Liberal Democrat

NORTHOVER (Life Baroness), Lindsay Patricia Northover; cr. 2000. Born 21 August 1954. Daughter of Charles and Patricia Granshaw; educated Brighton and Hove High School; St Anne's College, Oxford (Modern history BA Hons 1976, MA 1978); Bryn Mawr College, Pennsylvania University, USA (History and philosophy of science MA 1978, PhD 1981). Married 1988, John Northover (2 sons 1 daughter). *Trades Union:* Former member of AUT. *Councils, Public Bodies:* Former member Camden and Islington Family Practitioner Committee. *Career:* Research Fellow: University College London and St Mark's Hospital 1980–83, St Thomas's Medical School, London 1983–84; Lecturer, University College 1984–91. *House of Lords:* Member of Liberal Democrats Health Team. *Party Groups (General):* Chair: SDP Health and Social Welfare Association 1987–88, Liberal Democrats' Parliamentary Candidates Association 1988–91, Women Liberal Democrats 1992–95. *Awards Granted:* St Anne's College Exhibition 1973; Herbert Plumer Bursary for postgraduate study overseas 1976; English-speaking Union Fellowship 1976–77; Mrs Giles Whiting Fellowship in the Humanities 1979–80. *Trusts, etc:* Trustee, Bryn Mawr College Association, Great Britain. *Miscellaneous:* Contested Welwyn Hatfield 1983 and 1987 general elections; Contested Basildon in 1997 general election. *Publications:* Various academic publications. *Name, Style and Title:* Raised to the peerage as Baroness Northover, of Cissbury in the County of West Sussex 2000. *Address:* The Baroness Northover, House of Lords, London, SW1A 0PW *E-Mail:* lnorthover@cix.co.uk.

LORD NORTON OF LOUTH — Conservative

NORTON OF LOUTH (Life Baron), Philip Norton; cr. 1998. Born 5 March 1951. Youngest son of late George E. Norton, and of Ena D. Norton; educated King Edward VI Grammar School, Louth; Sheffield University (BA, PhD) (Nalgo Prize); University of Pennsylvania (MA) (Thouron Scholar). *Councils, Public Bodies:* Chairman, Standards Committee, Kingston-upon-Hull City Council 1999–. *Career:* Hull University: Lecturer 1977–82, Senior Lecturer 1982–84, Reader 1984–86, Professor of Government 1986–, Director, Centre of Legislative Studies 1992–. *Select Committees:* Member, Select Committee on European Union Sub-Committee E (Law and Institutions) 1999–. *Party Groups (General):* Vice-President, Political Studies Association 1999–; Chairman, Conservative Academic Group 2000–. *Other:* Council Member, Hansard Society–; Executive Committee Member: Study of Parliament Group 1981–93, Political Studies Association 1983–89; Member, Society and Politics Research Development Group, Economic and Social Research Council 1987–90; Associate Editor, *Political Studies* 1987–93; Governor, King Edward VI Grammar School 1988–, Warden 1990–93; President: British Politics Group (USA) 1988–90, Politics Association 1993–; Co-chair, Research Committee of Legislative Specialists, International Political Science Association 1994–; Editor, *The Journal of Legislative Studies* 1995–; Chairman, Commission to Strengthen Parliament 1999–. *Trusts, etc:* Trustee, History of Parliament Trust 1999–. FRSA 1995. *Publications:* Author or editor: *Dissension in the House of Commons 1945–74*, 1975; *Conservative Dissidents*, 1978; *Dissension in the House of Commons 1974–79*, 1980; *The Commons in Perspective*, 1981; *Conservatives and Conservatism*, (co-author) 1981; *The Constitution in Flux*, 1982; *Law and Order and British Politics*, 1984; *The British Polity*, 1984 (4th edition 2000); *Parliament in the 1980s*, 1985; *The Political Science of British Politics*, (joint editor) 1986; *Legislature*, 1990; *Parliaments in Western Europe*, 1990; *New Directions in British Politics?*, 1991; *Politics UK*, (with others) 1990 (4th edition 2000); *Parliamentary Questions*, (joint editor) 1993; *Back from Westminster*, (joint author) 1993; *Does Parliament Matter?*, 1993; *National Parliaments and the European Union*, 1996; *The New Parliaments of Central and Eastern Europe*, (joint editor) 1996; *The Conservative Party*, 1996; *Legislatures and Legislators*, 1998; *Governments and Parliaments in Western Europe*, 1998; *Parliaments and Pressure Groups in Western Europe*, 1998; *Parliaments in Asia*, 1999. *Special Interests:* Constitutional Affairs, Parliamentary Affairs, Legislatures, British Politics, American Politics. *Recreations:* Table-tennis, walking, writing. *Clubs:* Royal Overseas League, Royal Commonwealth Society. *Name, Style and Title:* Raised to the peerage as Baron Norton of Louth, of Louth in the County of Lincolnshire 1998. *Address:* Professor the Lord Norton of Louth, Department of Politics, University of Hull, HU6 7RX *Tel:* 01482 465863 *Fax:* 01482 466208 *E-Mail:* p.norton@pol-as.hull.ac.uk.

O

LORD OAKESHOTT OF SEAGROVE BAY   Liberal Democrat

OAKESHOTT OF SEAGROVE BAY (Life Baron), Matthew Alan Oakeshott; cr. 2000. Born 10 January 1947. Son of Keith Robertson Oakeshott CMG and Eva Jill Oakeshott; educated Charterhouse School (Senior Foundation Scholar); University and Nuffield Colleges, Oxford (BA philosophy, politics and economics 1968, MA). Married 1976, Dr Phillipa Poulton (2 sons 1 daughter). *Councils, Public Bodies:* Former Oxford City Councillor, Vice-Chairman, Finance Committee. *Career:* Founder Director, OLIM Ltd; Former ODI/Nuffield Fellow, Kenya Ministry of Finance and Economic Planning 1968–70 Former special adviser to Roy Jenkins 1972–76; Former Director, Warburg Investment Management 1976–81, Former Manager, Courtaulds Pension Fund 1981–85; Investment Director, Value and Income Trust plc 1986–. *Party Groups (General):* Former Member: SDP National Committee, National Economic Policy Committee. *Miscellaneous:* Contested Horsham and Crawley (Labour) October 1974 and (Alliance) 1983 Cambridge general elections. *Publications:* Chapter in *By-Elections in British Politics. Special Interests:* Economic policy, Housing, Transport, Overseas development. *Recreations:* Music, elections, supporting Arsenal FC. *Name, Style and Title:* Raised to the peerage as Baron Oakeshott of Seagrove Bay, of Seagrove Bay in the County of the Isle of Wight 2000. *Address:* The Lord Oakeshott of Seagrove Bay, House of Lords, London, SW1A 0PW.

BARONESS O'CATHAIN   Conservative

O'CATHAIN (Life Baroness), Detta O'Cathain; cr. 1991. Born 3 February 1938. Daughter of late Caoimhghin and Margaret O'Cathain; educated Laurel Hill, Limerick; University College, Dublin (BA Economics, English and French). Married June 4, 1968, William Ernest John Bishop, son of late William and Clara Bishop. *Career:* Assistant Economist, Aer Lingus 1959–66; Group Economist, Tarmac 1966–69; Economic Adviser to Chairman, Rootes Motors/Chrysler 1969–72; Senior Economist, Carrington Viyella 1972; Economic Adviser, British Leyland 1973–74, Director, Market Planning 1974–76; Corporate Planning Executive, Unigate plc 1976–81; Head of Strategic Planning, Milk Marketing Board 1981–83, Director and General Manager 1984–85, Managing Director 1985–88; Managing Director, Barbican Centre 1990–95; Non-executive director: Midland Bank plc 1984–93, Tesco plc 1985–2000, Sears plc 1987–94, British Airways plc 1993–, BET plc 1994–96, BNP/Paribas (UK) 1995–, Thistle Hotels plc 1996–, South East Water plc 1997–, Allders plc 2000–, William Baird plc 2000–. *Select Committees:* Former Member, Public Service Select Committee 1996–97; Member, Select Committees on: Monetary Policy of the Bank of England 1998–, European Communities Sub Committee B (Energy, Industry and Transport) 1998–, European Union 1999–. *Other:* Member, Council of Industrial Society 1986–92; Past President, Agricultural Section of the British Association for the Advancement of Science; Former Member: Design Council, Engineering Council; President, Chartered Institute of Marketing 1998–. *Honours:* OBE 1983; Commander: Royal Norwegian Order 1993, Order of the Lion of Finland 1994. Fellow: Royal Society of Arts 1986, Chartered Institute of Marketing 1987. Freeman, City of London. *Special Interests:* Arts, Agriculture, Industry, Commerce, Banking, Retail Industry, Disabled, Economic Policy. *Recreations:* Music, reading, swimming, walking, gardening. *Name, Style and Title:* Raised to the peerage as Baroness O'Cathain, of The Barbican in the City of London 1991. *Address:* The Baroness O'Cathain, OBE, Eglantine, Tower House Gardens, Arundel, West Sussex, BN18 9RU *Tel:* 01903 883775; 121 Shakespeare Tower, Barbican, London, EC2Y 8DR *Tel:* 020 7638 6443 *E-Mail:* ocathaind@parliament.uk.

Visit the Vacher Dod Website . . .
www.politicallinks.co.uk

LORD OLIVER OF AYLMERTON   Cross-Bencher

OLIVER OF AYLMERTON (Life Baron), Peter Raymond Oliver; cr. 1986. Born 7 March 1921. Son of late David Thomas Oliver, LLM, LLD; educated Leys School, Cambridge; Trinity Hall, Cambridge (Scholar). Married 1st, July 4, 1945, Mary Chichester (died 1985), daughter of late Sir Eric Keightley Rideal, MBE, FRS (1 son 1 daughter), married 2nd, January 6, 1987, Wendy Anne, widow of I. L. Lloyd Jones. *Armed Forces:* Military Service, 12th Battalion RTR 1941–45. *Career:* Called to the Bar, Lincoln's Inn 1948; QC 1965; Bencher, Lincoln's Inn 1973; Judge of the High Court 1974–80; Member, Restrictive Practices Court 1976–80; Chairman, Review Body on Chancery Division 1979–81; Lord Justice of Appeal 1980–86; A Lord of Appeal in Ordinary 1986–92. *Select Committees:* Chairman, Sub-Committee E (Law and Institutions) of Select Committee on the European Communities 1989–91. *Honours:* Kt 1974; PC 1980. *Recreations:* Gardening, music. *Name, Style and Title:* Raised to the peerage as Baron Oliver of Aylmerton, of Aylmerton in the County of Norfolk 1986. *Address:* Rt Hon the Lord Oliver of Aylmerton, House of Lords, London, SW1A 0PW.

BARONESS O'NEILL OF BENGARVE   Cross-Bencher

O'NEILL OF BENGARVE (Life Baroness), Onora Sylvia O'Neill; cr. 1999. Born 23 August 1941. Daughter of late Hon. Sir Con O'Neill, GCMG and Lady Garvey, neé Pritchard and widow of Sir Terence Garvey, KCMG; educated St Paul's Girls' School; Somerville College, Oxford (BA, MA); Harvard University (PhD). Married January 19, 1963, Edward John Nell (2 sons) (marriage dissolved 1976). *Career:* Assistant, then Associate Professor, Barnard College, Columbia University 1970–77; University of Essex: Lecturer 1977–78, Senior Lecturer 1978–83, Reader 1983–87, Professor of Philosophy 1987–92; Principal, Newnham College, Cambridge 1992–. *International Bodies (General):* Fellow, Wissenschaftskolleg, Berlin 1989–90; Foreign Hon. Member, American Academy of Arts and Sciences 1993; Fellow, Academic Advisory Board 1996–. *Other:* Chairman, Nuffield Foundation 1998–. Hon. Fellow, Somerville College, Oxford 1993; Hon. DLitt, University of East Anglia 1995; Hon. Degree, University of Essex 1996; Hon. LLD, Nottingham 1999. *Miscellaneous:* President, Aristotelian Society 1988–89; Member, Animal Procedures Committee 1990–94; Member, Nuffield Council on Bioethics 1991–98, Chairman 1996–98; Member, Human Genetics Advisory Commission 1996–. *Honours:* CBE 1995. FBA 1993. *Publications: Acting on Principle*, 1976, *Faces of Hunger*, 1986; *Constructions of Reason*, 1989, *Towards Justice and Virtue*, 1996; Numerous articles on philosophy in learned journals. *Name, Style and Title:* Raised to the peerage as Baroness O'Neill of Bengarve, of The Braid in the County of Antrim 1999. *Address:* The Baroness O'Neill of Bengarve, CBE, FBA, Newnham College, Cambridge, CB3 9DF *Tel:* 01223 335821.

EARL OF ONSLOW   Conservative

ONSLOW (7th Earl of, UK), Michael William Coplestone Dillon Onslow; cr. 1801; Viscount Cranley; 10th Baron Onslow (GB) 1716; Baron Cranley (GB) 1776; 11th Bt of West Clandon (E) 1660. Born 28 February 1938. Son of 6th Earl. Succeeded his father 1971; educated Eton; Sorbonne. Married 1964, Robin Lindsay Bullard (1 son 2 daughters). *Career:* A Farmer. *House of Lords:* An elected hereditary peer 1999–. *Clubs:* Beefsteak, White's. *Address:* The Earl of Onslow, Temple Court, Clandon Park, Guildford, Surrey, GU4 7RQ.

LORD ONSLOW OF WOKING Conservative

ONSLOW OF WOKING (Life Baron), Cranley Gordon Douglas Onslow; cr. 1997. Born 8 June 1926; educated Harrow; Oriel College, Oxford; Geneva University. Married May 7, 1955, Lady June Hay (1 son 3 daughters). *Armed Forces:* Served Royal Armoured Corps (Lieutenant 7th Hussars) 1944–48. *Councils, Public Bodies:* Councillor, Kent County Council 1961–64. *Career:* HM Foreign Service 1951–60, serving in Burma 1953–56. *House of Commons:* MP (Conservative) for Woking 1964–97; Parliamentary Under-Secretary of State, Aerospace and Shipping, Department of Trade and Industry 1972–74; Minister of State, Foreign and Commonwealth Office April 1982-June 1983. *Spokesman (Commons):* Opposition Spokesman on: Health and Social Security 1974–75, Defence 1975–76. *Honours:* PC 1988; KCMG 1993. *Special Interests:* Aviation, Defence, Conservation. *Recreations:* Fishing, shooting. *Clubs:* Beefsteak, Travellers'. *Name, Style and Title:* Raised to the peerage as Baron Onslow of Woking, of Woking in the County of Surrey 1997. *Address:* Rt Hon the Lord Onslow of Woking, KCMG, House of Lords, London, SW1A 0PW.

BARONESS OPPENHEIM-BARNES Conservative

OPPENHEIM-BARNES (Life Baroness), Sally Oppenheim-Barnes; cr. 1989. Born 26 July 1930. Daughter of late Mark Viner; educated Sheffield High School; Lowther College, North Wales. Married 1st, 1949, Henry Oppenheim (died 1980) (1 son 2 daughters), married 2nd, July 5, 1984, John Barnes. *Career:* A Non-Executive Director, The Boots Co. plc 1981–93; Chairman, National Consumer Council 1987–89; Director, Fleming High Income Trust plc 1989–97; Non-Executive Director, HFC Bank plc 1990–98; Former Vice-President, South Wales and West Fire Liaison Panel. *House of Commons:* MP (Conservative) for Gloucester 1970–87; Member of the Shadow Cabinet 1975–79; Minister of State for Consumer Affairs 1979–82. *Spokesman (Commons):* Opposition Spokesman on Prices and Consumer Protection 1974–79. *Party Groups (General):* President, Conservative Club of Gloucester 1970. *Other:* Former National Vice-President, National Mobile Homes Residents' Association; Vice-President, National Union of Townswomen's Guilds 1973–79; Former Vice-President, Western Centre of Public Health Inspectors; Former President, National Waterways Trust to 1990. *Honours:* PC 1979. *Special Interests:* Consumer Affairs. *Recreations:* Bridge, tennis. *Sportsclubs:* Vanderbilt Racquet Club. *Clubs:* House of Lords Bridge Club. *Name, Style and Title:* Raised to the peerage as Baroness Oppenheim-Barnes, of Gloucester in the County of Gloucestershire 1989. *Address:* Rt Hon the Baroness Oppenheim-Barnes, House of Lords, London, SW1A 0PW.

LORD ORME Labour

ORME (Life Baron), Stanley Orme; cr. 1997. Born 5 April 1923. Son of Sherwood Orme; educated Elementary school; Part-time Technical; NCLC; WEA. Married 1951, Irene Mary, daughter of Vernon F. Harris. *Trades Union:* Member, AEEU. *Armed Forces:* Served in RAF 1942–47, Warrant Officer, Air-Bomber Navigator. *Councils, Public Bodies:* Councillor, Sale Borough Council 1958–64. *Career:* Skilled Engineer. *House of Commons:* Contested Stockport South 1959; MP (Labour) for Salford West 1964–83 and for Salford East 1983–97; Minister of State: for Northern Ireland 1974–76, for Department of Health and Social Security April-September 1976; Minister for Social Security and Member of the Cabinet 1976–79. *Spokesman (Commons):* Principal Opposition Front Bench Spokesman on: Health and Social Security 1979–80, Industry 1980–83, Energy 1983–87. *International Bodies (General):* Member: IPU, CPA. *Party Groups (General):* Joined Labour Party 1944; Chairman, AEEU Parliamentary Group of Labour Members 1976–96; Chairman, Parliamentary Labour Party 1987–92. *Other:* Hon. President, The Lotteries Council. Hon. DSc, University of Salford 1985. *Honours:* PC 1974. *Recreations:* Walking, jazz, opera, reading American literature, supporting Manchester United Football Club and Lancashire County Cricket Club. *Name, Style and Title:* Raised to the peerage as Baron Orme, of Salford in the County of Greater Manchester 1997. *Address:* Rt Hon the Lord Orme, 8 Northwood Grove, Sale, Cheshire, M33 3DZ.

LORD OWEN
An Independent Social Democrat/Sits as a Cross-Bencher

OWEN (Life Baron), David Anthony Llewellyn Owen; cr. 1992. Born 2 July 1938. Son of late Dr John Owen, General Practitioner and Alderman Molly Owen; educated Bradfield College; Sidney Sussex College, Cambridge (MA, BChir); St Thomas's Hospital, London (MB). Married 1968, Deborah, daughter of late Kyril Schabert, of New York, USA (2 sons 1 daughter). *Career:* Various house appointments, St Thomas's Hospital 1962–64; Neurological and Psychiatric Registrar 1964–66; Non-Executive Director: New Crane Publishing 1992–, Coats Viyella 1994–; Executive Chairman, Middlesex Holdings plc 1995–; Director: Deborah Owen Ltd 1972–, Center for International Health and Cooperation 1995–, Abbott Laboratories plc 1996–, New Europe 1999–; Non-executive Deputy Chairman, Europe-Steel (Inc) 2000–. *House of Commons:* Contested (Labour) Torrington 1964 General Election; MP (Labour) for Plymouth Sutton 1966–74; MP for Plymouth Devonport 1974–92 (Labour 1974–81, SDP 1981–92); PPS to Minister of Defence (Administration) 1966–68; Parliamentary Under-Secretary of State for Defence (Royal Navy) 1968–70; Parliamentary Under-Secretary of State, Department of Health and Social Security 1974, Minister of State 1974–76; Minister of State, Foreign Office 1976–77; Secretary of State for Foreign and Commonwealth Affairs 1977–79. *Spokesman (Commons):* Opposition Spokesman on Defence 1970–72; Principal Opposition Spokesman on Energy 1979–80. *Chancellor:* Chancellor, Liverpool University 1996–. *Party Groups (General):* One of the founders of the Social Democratic Party, Formally launched March 26 1981; Chairman, Parliamentary Committee 1981–82; Deputy Leader of the Party 1982–83, Leader 1983–87, Resigned over merger with Liberal Party; Re-elected SDP Leader 1988–92. *Other:* Patron, Social Market Foundation. *Miscellaneous:* Research Fellow, Medical Unit 1966–68; Member: Palme Commission on Disarmament and Security Issues 1980–89, Independent Commission on International Humanitarian Issues 1983–88; EU Co-Chairman, International Conference on former Yugoslavia 1992–95, Carnegie Commission on Preventing Deadly Conflict 1994–99; Eminent Persons Group on curbing illicit traffic in small arms and light weapons 1999–. *Honours:* PC 1976; CH 1994. *Publications: A Unified Health Service,* 1968; *The Politics of Defence,* 1972; *In Sickness and in Health,* 1976; *Human Rights,* 1978; *Face the Future,* 1981; *A Future that will Work,* 1984; *A United Kingdom,* 1986; *Personally Speaking* (to Kenneth Harris), 1987; *Our NHS,* 1988; *Time to Declare* (autobiography) 1991; *Seven Ages* (an anthology of poetry) 1992; *Balkan Odyssey,* 1995. *Special Interests:* International affairs (foreign and defence). *Recreations:* Sailing. *Name, Style and Title:* Raised to the peerage as Baron Owen, of the City of Plymouth 1992. *Address:* Rt Hon the Lord Owen, PC, CH, House of Lords, London, SW1A 0PW; 78 Narrow Street, London, E14 8BP *Tel:* 020 7987 5441 *E-Mail:* lordowen@nildram.co.uk.

LORD OXBURGH
Cross-Bencher

OXBURGH (Life Baron), Ernest Ronald Oxburgh; cr. 1999. Born 2 November 1934. Son of Ernest Oxburgh and Violet Oxburgh (née Bugden); educated Liverpool Institute; Oxford University (BA 1957, MA 1960); Princeton University, USA (PhD 1960). Married, Ursula Mary Brown (1 son 2 daughter). *Career:* Oxford University: Departmental Demonstrator, 1960–61, Lecturer in Geology 1962–78, Fellow, St Edmund Hall 1964–78, Emeritus Fellow 1978; Visiting Professor: California Institute of Technology 1967–68 (Fairchild Fellow 1995–96), Stanford and Cornell Universities 1973–74; Cambridge University: Professor of Mineralogy and Petrology 1978–91, Head of Department of Earth Sciences 1980–88, Fellow of Trinity Hall 1978–82, President, Queens' College 1982–89, Professorial Fellow 1989–91; Chief Scientific Adviser, Ministry of Defence 1988–93; Rector, Imperial College of Science, Technology and Medicine 1993–2001. *Select Committees:* Member, Select Committees on: Science and Technology 1999–, Science and Technology Sub-Committee II (Science and Society) 1999–2000, Science and Technology Sub-Committee II (Aircraft Cabin Environment) 2000–; Chairman, Select Committee on Science and Technology Sub-Committee IIA (Human Genetic Databases) 2000–. *International Bodies (General):* Member: Conseil National De La Science, France, Conseil D'Administration Ecole Polytechnique, France. *Other:* President, European Union of Geosciences 1985–87; Member, National Committee of Inquiry into Higher Education (Dearing Committee) 1996–97; Member of Geological and Scientific Academies and Societies in USA, Germany, Austria and Venezuela; President, Geological Society 1999–2001. *Awards Granted:* Bigsby Medal,

Geological Society 1979. Hon. Fellow: Trinity Hall, Cambridge 1982, University College, Oxford 1983, St Edmund Hall, Oxford 1986; Queen's College Cambridge 1992; six honorary doctorates. *Trusts, etc:* Council Member, Winston Churchill Memorial Trust 1995–; Trustee, Natural History Museum 1993, Chairman of Trustees 1999–. *Miscellaneous:* Member, Parliamentary Office of Science and Technology (POST) 2000–. *Honours:* KBE 1992; Officier, Ordre des Palmes Académiques (France) 1995. FRS 1978, Hon FIMechE 1993, Hon FCGI 1996, Hon FREng 2000. *Publications:* Has contributed to a number of geological, defence and scientific journals. *Clubs:* Athenaeum. *Name, Style and Title:* Raised to the peerage as Baron Oxburgh, of Liverpool in the County of Merseyside 1999. *Address:* The Lord Oxburgh, KBE, FRS, Rector, Imperial College of Science, Technology and Medicine, Exhibition Road, London, SW7 2AZ *E-Mail:* rector@ic.ac.uk.

BISHOP OF OXFORD — Non-Affiliated

OXFORD (41st Bishop of), Richard Douglas Harries. Born 2 June 1936. Son of late Brigadier W. D. J. Harries, CBE; educated Wellington College; RMA, Sandhurst; Selwyn College, Cambridge (MA 1965); Cuddesdon College, Oxford. Married 1963, Josephine Bottomley, MB, BChir, DCH (1 son 1 daughter). *Armed Forces:* Lieutenant, Royal Corps of Signals 1955–58. *Career:* Curate, Hampstead Parish Church 1963–69; Chaplain, Westfield College 1966–69; Lecturer, Wells Theological College 1969–72; Vicar, All Saints, Fulham 1972–81; Dean, King's College, London 1981–87; Bishop of Oxford 1987–; Took his seat in the House of Lords December 1993. *House of Lords:* Convenor of Bench of Bishops. *Select Committees:* Member, Select Committee on House of Lords' Offices 1997–. *International Bodies (General):* Member, Anglican Consultative Council; Consultant, Anglican Peace and Justice Network. *Other:* General Ordination examiner in Christian Ethics 1972–76; Director, Post Ordination Training, Kensington Jurisdiction 1973–79; Chairman, Southwark Ordination Course 1982–87; President, Johnson Society 1988–89. Hon. DD, University of London; Hon. Fellow, Selwyn College Cambridge. *Miscellaneous:* Vice-Chairman: Council for Christian Action 1979–87, Council for Arms Control 1982–87; Member, Home Office Advisory Committee for reform of sexual offences law 1981–85; Chairman: Board of Social Responsibility for the Church of England, Council of Christians and Jews; Board Member, Christian Aid; Member, Royal Commission on the Reform of the House of Lords 1999. Fellow: King's College, London, Royal Society of Literature. *Publications: Prayers of Hope,* 1975; *Turning to Prayer,* 1978; *Prayers of Grief and Glory,* 1979; *Being a Christian,* 1981; *Should Christians Support Guerillas?* 1982; *The Authority of Divine Love,* 1983; *Praying Round the Clock,* 1983; *Prayer and the Pursuit of Happiness,* 1985; *Morning Has Broken,* 1985; *Christianity and War in a Nuclear Age,* 1986; *C. S. Lewis: the man and his God,* 1987; *Christ is Risen,* 1988; *Is There a Gospel for the Rich,* 1992; *Art and the Beauty of God,* 1993; *The Real God: A Response to Anthony Freeman,* 1994; *Questioning Belief,* 1995; *A Gallery of Reflections – The Nativity in Art,* 1995; *Two Cheers For Secularism,* (ed. with Sidney Brichto) 1998; *In The Gladness of Today,* 2000; Has edited and contributed to other Christian publications as well as articles in the press and periodicals. *Special Interests:* Overseas Aid and Development, Poverty, Housing, Business Ethics, Arts, Arms Control, Moral Issues. *Recreations:* Theatre, literature, sport. *Address:* Rt Rev the Lord Bishop of Oxford, FKC, DD, FRSL, Diocesan Church House, North Hinksey, Oxford, OX2 0NB *Tel:* 01865 208222 *E-Mail:* bishopoxon@dch.oxford.anglican.org.

VISCOUNT OF OXFUIRD — Conservative

OXFUIRD (13th Viscount of, S), George Hubbard Makgill; cr. 1651; Lord Makgill of Cousland; 13th Bt of Cranston Riddell (NS) 1627. Born 7 January 1934. Son of late Squadron-Leader Richard James Robert Haldane Makgill, AFC. Succeeded his uncle 1986; educated Wanganui Collegiate School, Wanganui, New Zealand. Married 1st, 1967, Alison Campbell Jensen (3 sons) (marriage dissolved 1977), married 2nd, 1980, Venetia Cunitia Mary Steward (1 son). *Armed Forces:* Royal Air Force 1954; Commission G. D. Branch. *Career:* Department of Civil Engineering, Wellington, New Zealand 1952; Ford Motor Company 1958, Lansing Ltd 1964; Export Area Manager 1976; External Affairs Manager, Lansing Linde Ltd 1988–93. *House of Lords:* A Deputy Speaker of the House of Lords 1990–; A Deputy Chairman of Committees 1990–;

An elected hereditary peer 1999–. *Select Committees:* Former Member: Joint Committee on Statutory Instruments, Personal Bills Committee 1992–94, Offices Committee 1995–97; Member, Hybrid Bills Committee 1996–. *Party Groups:* Member, Executive of the Association of Conservative Peers 1991–, Deputy Chairman 1993–98. *Other:* President: World Travel Market Council, Institute of Supervision and Management. *Trusts, etc:* Member, Understanding Industry Trust. *Miscellaneous:* Committee for British Postal Equipment Exports 1967. *Honours:* CBE 1997. MIMH. *Special Interests:* Industry, Exports. *Recreations:* Fishing, gardening, racing, shooting. *Clubs:* Caledonian. *Address:* The Viscount of Oxfuird, CBE, House of Lords, London, SW1A 0PW.

P

LORD PALMER — Cross-Bencher

PALMER (4th Baron), Adrian Bailie Nottage Palmer; cr. 1933; 4th Bt of Grosvenor Crescent (UK) 1916. Born 8 October 1951. Son of late Colonel Hon. Sir Gordon Palmer, KCVO, OBE, TD, youngest son of 2nd Baron. Succeeded his uncle 1990; educated Eton; Edinburgh University. Married 1977, Cornelia Dorothy Katharine, daughter of Rohan Wadham, DFC (2 sons 1 daughter). *Career:* Served as an apprentice with Huntley and Palmers Ltd; Sales manager in Southern Belgium and Luxembourg for three years; Scottish Representative to the European Landowning Organisation 1986–92; A Farmer. *House of Lords:* An elected hereditary peer 1999–. *Select Committees:* Member: Advisory Panel on Works of Art, Refreshment Committee until 2000, Select Committee on European Union, Sub-Committee D (Environment, Agriculture, Public Health and Consumer Protection) 2000–. *Other:* Vice-Chairman, Historic Houses Association for Scotland 1993–94, Chairman 1994–99; Member: Executive Council of Historic Houses Association 1981–99, Council of Scottish Landowners Federation 1986–92; Secretary, Royal Caledonian Hunt 1989–; President, Palm Tree Silk Co (St Lucia). *Trusts, etc:* Chairman, Country Sports Defence Trust 1994–. *Miscellaneous:* Member, Queen's Bodyguard for Scotland (The Royal Company of Archers) 1990–96. *Special Interests:* Agriculture, Environment, Heritage, Media. *Recreations:* Hunting, shooting, gardening. *Clubs:* New (Edinburgh), MCC, Pratt's. *Address:* The Lord Palmer, Manderston, Duns, Berwickshire, TD11 3PP *Tel:* 01361 883450 *Fax:* 01361 882010 *E-Mail:* palmer@manderston.demon.co.uk.

LORD PALUMBO — Conservative

PALUMBO (Life Baron), Peter Garth Palumbo; cr. 1991. Born 20 July 1935. Son of late Rudolph Palumbo and of Elsie Palumbo; educated Eton; Worcester College, Oxford (MA). Married 1st, 1959, Denia Wigram (died 1986) (1 son 2 daughters), married 2nd, 1986, Hayat Morowa (1 son 2 daughters). *Chancellor:* Chancellor, University of Portsmouth 1992–. *Other:* Governor, London School of Economics and Political Science 1976–94; Chairman: Tate Gallery Foundation 1986–87, Serpentine Gallery 1994–; Member of Council, Royal Albert Hall 1995–99; Governor, The Royal Shakespeare Theatre 1995–2000. Hon. DLitt, Portsmouth University 1993. *Trusts, etc:* Trustee: Mies van der Rohe Archive 1977–, Tate Gallery 1978–85, Whitechapel Arts Gallery Foundation 1981–87; Trustee and Hon. Treasurer, Writers and Scholars Educational Trust 1984–99; Chairman, Painshill Park Trust Appeal 1986–96; Trustee: The Natural History Museum 1994–, The Design Museum 1995–. *Miscellaneous:* Chairman, Arts Council of Great Britain 1989–94. *Honours:* National Order of the Southern Cross (Federal Republic of Brazil). Hon. FRIBA; Hon. FFB 1994; Hon. FIStructE 1994. Liveryman, Salters' Company. *Recreations:* Music, travel, gardening, reading. *Clubs:* White's, Pratt's, Athenaeum, Knickerbocker (New York), Garrick. *Name, Style and Title:* Raised to the peerage as Baron Palumbo, of Walbrook in the City of London 1991. *Address:* The Lord Palumbo, Bagnor Manor, Bagnor, Newbury, Berkshire, RG20 8AG *Tel:* 01635 40930; *Office:*, Vestry House, Laurence Poutney Hill, London, EC4R 0EH *Tel:* 020 7626 9236.

LORD PAREKH   Labour

PAREKH (Life Baron), Bhikhu Chhotalal Parekh; cr. 2000. Born 4 January 1935. Son of Chhotalal and Gajaraben Parekh; educated HDS High School, Amalsad 1943–50; Bombay University (BA 1954, MA 1956); London University (PhD 1966). Married 1959, Pramila Dalal (3 sons). *Career:* Tutor, LSE 1962–63; Assistant Lecturer, Glasgow University 1963–64; Hull University: Lecturer, Senior Lecturer and Reader 1964–82, Professor of Political Theory 1982–. *International Bodies (General):* Founding Member and Past President, Research Committee on Political Philosophy of International Political Science Association. *Awards Granted:* British Asian of the Year 1991; BBC's Special Lifetime Achievement Award for Asians 1999. *Hon. Doctorates:* Leeds Metropolitan University, University of Lincolnshire and Humberside. *Trusts, etc:* Trustee: Runnymede Trust 1986–, Gandhi Foundation 1988 (Vice-President 1996–), Anne Frank Educational Trust 1992–. *Miscellaneous:* Visiting Professor, University of British Columbia, Canada 1967–68; Visiting Professor: Concordia University 1974–75, McGill University 1976–77; Member, Rampton/Swann Committee of Inquiry into Educational Problems of Ethnic Minority Children 1978–82; Vice-Chancellor, University of Baroda 1981–84; Council Member, Policy Studies Institute 1985–90; Deputy Chairman, Commission for Racial Equality 1985–90; Vice-President, UK Council for Overseas Students Affairs 1989–; Council Member, Institute for Public Policy Records 1990–96; Visiting Professor: Harvard University 1996, Institute of Advanced Study, Vienna 1997, University of Pompeu Fabra, Barcelona 1997, University of Pennsylvania 1998; Chairman, Commission on Future of Multi-Ethnic Britain 1998–. FRSA 1988; Fellow, Academy of the Learned Societies in Social Sciences (FALSSS). *Publications: Politics and Experience,* 1968; *Dissent and Disorder,* 1971; *The Morality of Politics,* 1972; *Knowledge and Belief in Politics,* 1973; *Bentham's Political Thought,* 1973; *Colour, Culture and Consciousness,* 1974; *Jeremy Bentham: ten critical essays,* 1974; *The Concept of Socialism,* 1975; *Hannah Arendt and the Search for a new Political Philosophy,* 1981; *Karl's Marx's Theory of Ideology,* 1982; *Contemporary Political Thinkers,* 1982; *Political Discourse,* 1986; *Gandhi's Political Philosophy,* 1989; *Colonialism, Tradition and Reform,* 1989; *Jeremy Bentham: critical assessments,* (4 volumes) 1993; *The Decolonisation of Imagination,* 1995; *Crisis and Change in Contemporary India,* 1995; *Gandhi,* 1996; *Rethinking Multiculturalism,* 2000; articles in various learned journals. *Special Interests:* Race relations, Higher education, Ethnic conflicts, Global justice, International trade. *Recreations:* Reading, music, walking. *Clubs:* Royal Society of Arts. *Name, Style and Title:* Raised to the peerage as Baron Parekh, of Kingston upon Hull in the East Riding of Yorkshire 2000. *Address:* Professor the Lord Parekh, 211 Victoria Avenue, Hull, HU5 3EF *E-Mail:* profparekh@hullvictoria.freeserve.co.uk.

BARONESS PARK OF MONMOUTH   Conservative

PARK OF MONMOUTH (Life Baroness), Daphne Margaret Sybil Désirée Park; cr. 1990. Born 1 September 1921. Daughter of late John Alexander and Doreen Gwynneth Park; educated Rosa Bassett School, Streatham; Somerville College, Oxford (BA Modern Languages); Newnham College, Cambridge (CCK Russian). *Armed Forces:* Served WTS (FANY) 1943–48; Allied Commission, Austria 1946–48. *Councils, Public Bodies:* Member, Sheffield Development Corporation Board 1989–92. *Career:* Entered Foreign Office 1948; Member, UK delegation to NATO 1952; Second Secretary, British Embassy, Moscow 1954–56; FO 1956–59; Consul and First Secretary, Leopoldville 1959–61; FO 1961–63; High Commission, Lusaka 1964–67; FO 1967–69; Consul-General, Hanoi 1969–70; Hon. Research Fellow, University of Kent 1971–72; Chargé d'Affaires a.i. British Embassy, Ulan Bator, Mongolia April-June 1972; FCO 1973–79; Principal, Somerville College, Oxford 1980–89; Governor, BBC 1982–87; Member, British Library Board 1983–89; Chairman, Lord Chancellor's Advisory Committee on Legal Aid 1984–90; Pro-Vice Chancellor, University of Oxford 1985–89; Chairman, Royal Commission on the Historical Monuments of England 1989–94. *Select Committees:* Member, European Communities, Sub-Committee C: (Environment, Public Health and Education) 1994–97, (Common Foreign and Security Policy) 2000–. *Other:* Member, Royal Asiatic Society; Governor, Ditchley Foundation; Member, Forum UK 1994–96; President, Society for the Promotion of the Training of Women 1994–. Hon. LLD: Bristol 1988, Mount Holyoke College 1993. *Trusts, etc:* Director, Zoo Development Trust 1989–90; Trustee: Jardine Educational Trust to 1998, Royal Armouries Development Trust 1991–92, Great Britain-Sasakawa

Foundation 1994–, Lucy Faithfull Travel Scholarship Fund. *Honours:* OBE 1960; CMG 1971. Fellow: Chatham House (RIIA), RSA. *Special Interests:* Higher Education, Foreign Affairs, Defence, Heritage, Northern Ireland. *Recreations:* Good talk, politics and difficult places. *Clubs:* Naval and Military, Commonwealth Trust, Special Forces, United Oxford and Cambridge University. *Name, Style and Title:* Raised to the peerage as Baroness Park of Monmouth, of Broadway in the County of Hereford and Worcester 1990. *Address:* The Baroness Park of Monmouth, CMG, OBE, House of Lords, London, SW1A 0PW.

LORD PARKINSON — Conservative

PARKINSON (Life Baron), Cecil Edward Parkinson; cr. 1992. Born 1 September 1931. Son of Sydney Parkinson; educated Royal Grammar School, Lancaster; Emmanuel College, Cambridge (MA). Married 1957, Ann Mary Jarvis (3 daughters). *Career:* Chartered Accountant; Company director. *House of Commons:* MP (Conservative) for: Enfield West 1970–74, Hertfordshire South 1974–83, Hertsmere 1983–92; PPS to Minister for Aerospace and Shipping, Department of Trade and Industry 1972–74; Minister for Trade, Department of Trade 1979–81; Paymaster General 1981–83; Chancellor, Duchy of Lancaster 1982–83; Secretary of State for: Trade and Industry June-October 1983, Energy 1987–89, Transport 1989–90; Member, Shadow Cabinet 1997–98. *Whip (Commons):* Assistant Government Whip 1974; Opposition Whip 1974–79. *Spokesman (Commons):* Spokesman on Trade 1976–79. *Party Groups (General):* Chairman, Conservative Party 1981–83 and 1997–98. *Publications: Right at the Centre: An Autobiography,* 1992. *Recreations:* Reading, golf, skiing. *Clubs:* Beefsteak, Garrick, Pratt's, Hawks (Cambridge). *Name, Style and Title:* Raised to the peerage as Baron Parkinson, of Carnforth in the County of Lancashire 1992. *Address:* Rt Hon the Lord Parkinson, House of Lords, London, SW1A 0PW.

LORD PARRY — Labour

PARRY (Life Baron), Gordon Samuel David Parry; cr. 1975. Born 30 November 1925. Son of late Rev. Thomas Lewis Parry; educated Trinity College, Carmarthen; Liverpool University (diploma advanced education). Married August 4, 1948, Glenys Catherine Incledon (1 daughter). *Trades Union:* Member, NUT 1945. *Councils, Public Bodies:* Councillor, Neyland (Dyfed) Urban District Council 1948–65; DL, Dyfed 1993–. *Career:* Assistant teacher various schools 1945–52; Housemaster, County Secondary School, Haverfordwest 1952–62, 1963–67; Institute of Education, Liverpool University 1962–63; Warden, Pembrokeshire Teachers' Centre 1967–76; Milford Docks Co: chair 1984–91, president 1991–; Chairman: Milford Leisure Co. 1984–, Taylor Plan Services 1988–97; Director, Seacon 1990–97; Chairman, Clean World International 1991–; Director, Marriott UK 1997–98. *Other:* Past and present president, chair numerous charities and organisations, especially in areas of physically and mentally handicapped and choirs. Hon. Fellow: James Cook University, Australia, Trinity College, Carmarthen, University of Glamorgan; Awarded Hon. Doctorate of Education, Swansea Institute of Higher Education 1992; Fellow, Pembrokeshire College 1996. *Miscellaneous:* Member: Welsh Independent TV Authority, Welsh Independent Broadcasting Authority, General Advisory Council, IBA, Welsh Development Agency, Welsh Arts Council, Schools Council for Wales; Chairman, The Wales Tourist Board; Member, British Tourist Authority 1978–84; Chairman, British Cleaning Council; Member: Board of British Rail, Western Region 1982–83, BBC Advisory Council and of its Council for Wales. Fellow: Tourism Society, Royal Society of Arts, British Institute of Cleaning Science, Hotel and Catering and Institutional Management Association; Hon. Fellow, Institute of Wastes Management. Hon. Freedom: Niagara, New York, USA 1981; Dallas, Texas, USA 1982; Macon, Georgia, USA 1985; Myrtle Beach, North Carolina, USA 1985; Burgess (Hon. Freeman), Guild of Freemen of Haverford West, Pembrokeshire 1998. *Publications: A Legacy For Life,* 1996. *Special Interests:* Tourism, Wales, North American Matters, Australia. *Recreations:* Watching the Welsh Rugby XV win, travelling, reading and writing. *Sportsclubs:* Neyland Yacht Club, Neyland RFC. *Name, Style and Title:* Raised to the peerage as Baron Parry, of Neyland in the County of Dyfed 1975. *Address:* The Lord Parry, DL, Willowmead, 52 Portlion, Llangwm, Pembrokeshire, Dyfed, SA62 4JT *Tel:* 01646 600667 *Tel:* Office: 01437 751294.

LORD PATEL   Cross-Bencher

PATEL (Life Baron), Narendra Babubhai Patel; cr. 1999. Born 11 May 1938.
Son of Babubhai and Lalita Patel; educated Government Secondary School,
Dar Es Salaam, Tanzania; Harrow High School; St Andrews University (MB
ChB 1964). Married 1970, Dr Helen Dally (twin sons 1 daughter). *Career:*
Consultant Obstetrician, Ninewells Hospital, Dundee; Honorary Professor,
University of Dundee. *Select Committees:* Member, Select Committees on:
Science and Technology Sub-Committee II (Aircraft Cabin Environment)
2000–, Science and Technology Sub-Committee IIA (Human Genetic
Databases) 2000–. *International Bodies (General):* Member, International
Federation of Obstetricians and Gynaecologists; Member, European Board,
College of Obstetricians and Gynaecologists; President Elect, European Association of Obstetrics and
Gynaecology. *Other:* Past President, Royal College of Obstetricians; Past Chairman, Academy of Medical
Royal Colleges. Hon. DSc; Hon. Degrees from: Australia and New Zealand, South Africa, USA, Canada,
India, Sri Lanka, Finland, Argentina, Italy, Germany; Royal College of Surgery, Medicine, Anesthetics.
Miscellaneous: Chairman, Clinical Standards Board of Scotland 1999–. *Honours:* Kt 1997. Hon. FRCS
(Eng); Hon. FRCS (Edinburgh); Hon. FRCP (Edinburgh); Hon. FRCP (Glasgow); Hon. FRCAnest; Hon.
DSc FMedSci; MBClB; FACOG; FSOGC; FRCOG; FRSE; PRACOG; PSLCOG; PSACOG; PFCOG.
Publications: Author of publications in the areas of Maternal/Fetal medicine, epidemiology, obstetrics,
gynaecology, etc. *Special Interests:* Women's Health, Higher Education, Regulation of Medicine, Ethnic
Minority Issues, Standards in Medicine. *Name, Style and Title:* Raised to the peerage as Baron Patel, of
Dunkeld in Perth and Kinross 1999. *Address:* The Lord Patel, House of Lords, London, SW1A 0PW
E-Mail: npatel@sol.co.uk.

LORD PATEL OF BLACKBURN   Labour

PATEL OF BLACKBURN (Life Baron), Adam Hafejee Patel; cr. 2000. Born 7 June 1940. Son of late
Hafejee Ismail Patel and of Aman Hafejee Patel; educated The Pioneer High School, Bharuch, Gujarat,
India; MS Baroda University, India (Bachelor of Commerce). Married May 10, 1964, Ayesha (4 sons
4 daughters). *Career:* Retired Managing Director, clothing manufacturing company; Director: East
Lancashire Training Enterprise Council, Enterprise plc. *International Bodies:* Member, CPA. *Other:*
Former President, Lancashire Council of Mosques; Vice-President, Blackburn Community Relations
Council; Counsellor, Muslim Council of Britain. *Awards Granted:* Honorary Fellowship, Bolton Institute.
Special Interests: Community and Social Work, Education, Race Relations, Economy and Regeneration.
Recreations: Gardening, watching football and cricket. *Sportsclubs:* Blackburn Rovers Football Club.
Name, Style and Title: Raised to the peerage as Baron Patel of Blackburn, of Langho in the County of
Lancashire 2000. *Address:* The Lord Patel of Blackburn, House of Lords, London, SW1A 0PW.

LORD PATTEN   Conservative

PATTEN (Life Baron), John Haggitt Charles Patten; cr. 1997. Born 17 July
1945. Son of late Jack Patten; educated Wimbledon College; Sidney Sussex
College, Cambridge (MA, PhD). Married July 4, 1978, Louise Alexandra
Virginia Charlotte, daughter of late John Rowe (1 daughter). *Councils, Public
Bodies:* Oxford City Councillor 1973–76. *Career:* Oxford University:
University Teacher 1969–79, Fellow and Tutor, Hertford College 1972–81,
Supernumary Fellow, Hertford College 1981–94; Editor (with Lord Blake) *The
Conservative Opportunity;* Investment Banker and Company Director. *House
of Commons:* MP (Conservative) for Oxford 1979–83 and for Oxford West and
Abingdon 1983–97; PPS to the Ministers of State at the Home Office 1980;
Parliamentary Under-Secretary of State for: Northern Ireland 1981–83, Health 1983–85; Minister of State
for: Housing, Urban Affairs and Construction, Department of Environment 1985–87, Home Office
1987–92; Secretary of State for Education 1992–94. Hon. Fellow, Harris Manchester College, Oxford.
Honours: PC 1990. Liveryman, Drapers' Company. *Publications: Things to Come: The Tories in the 21st
Century,* 1995, and other volumes. *Recreations:* Talking with my wife and daughter. *Name, Style and
Title:* Raised to the peerage as Baron Patten, of Wincanton in the County of Somerset 1997. *Address:*
Rt Hon the Lord Patten, House of Lords, London, SW1A 0PW.

LORD PAUL   Labour

PAUL (Life Baron), Swraj Paul; cr. 1996. Born 18 February 1931. Son of late Payare Paul and of Mongwati Paul; educated Punjab University (BSc); Massachusetts Institute of Technology (BSc, MSc Mechanical Engineering). Married 1956, Aruna Vij (3 sons 1 daughter and 1 daughter deceased). *Councils, Public Bodies:* Member, London Development Agency 2000–. *Career:* Partner in family firm in India, Apeejay Surrendra Group 1953; Came to the UK in 1966, establishing first business Natural Gas Tubes Ltd; Caparo Group Ltd formed in 1978; Chairman: Caparo Group Ltd 1978–; Caparo Industries plc 1981–; Caparo Inc. USA 1988–. *Chancellor:* Pro-Chancellor, Thames Valley University 1998–; Chancellor, Wolverhampton University 1999–. *Select Committees:* Member, Select Committees on: European Communities Sub-Committee B (Energy, Industry and Transport) 1997–, Monetary Policy of the Bank of England 1998–. *International Bodies:* Member, Parliamentarians for Global Action. *Other:* Past President, BISPA (British Iron and Steel Producers Association) 1994–95; Vice-President, Engineering Employers Federation. *Awards Granted:* Corporate Leadership Award, MIT 1987. Six honorary doctorates from England, Switzerland and USA. *Trusts, etc:* Founder and Chairman, Ambika Paul Foundation. *Honours:* Padma Bhushan (Government of India) 1983. Freeman, City of London 1998. *Publications: Indira Gandhi*, 1984; *Beyond Boundaries*, 1998. *Sportsclubs:* Royal Calcutta Turf, Royal Calcutta Golf, Cricket of India (Bombay). *Clubs:* MCC, Royal Automobile. *Name, Style and Title:* Raised to the peerage as Baron Paul, of Marylebone in the City of Westminster 1996. *Address:* The Lord Paul, Caparo Group Ltd, Caparo House, 103 Baker Street, London, W1U 6LN *Tel:* 020 7486 1417.

LORD PEARSON OF RANNOCH   Conservative

PEARSON OF RANNOCH (Life Baron), Malcolm Everard MacLaren Pearson; cr. 1990. Born 20 July 1942. Son of late Colonel John MacLaren Pearson; educated Eton. Married 1st, 1965, Francesca Frua de Angeli (1 daughter) (marriage dissolved 1970); married 2nd, 1977, Hon. Mary Charteris (2 daughters) (marriage dissolved 1995); married 3rd, 1997, Caroline, daughter of Major Hugh Launcelot St Vincent Rose. *Career:* Founded Pearson Webb Springbett (PWS) Group of reinsurance brokers 1964, currently Chairman. *Select Committees:* Member, House of Lords Select Committee on the European Communities and Sub-Committee on Social Affairs and the Environment 1992–96. *Other:* Hon. President, RESCARE (The National Society for Mentally Handicapped People in Residential Care) 1994–; Patron, British Society of Chinese Herbal Medicine Practitioners. Hon. LLD from CNAA 1992. *Trusts, etc:* Founded Rannoch Trust 1984. *Miscellaneous:* Member, Council for National Academic Awards 1983–93, Hon. Treasurer 1986–93. *Special Interests:* European Union, Mental Handicap, Education, Scottish Highlands. *Recreations:* Stalking, shooting, fishing, golf. *Sportsclubs:* Swinley Forest Golf. *Clubs:* White's. *Name, Style and Title:* Raised to the peerage as Baron Pearson of Rannoch, of Bridge of Gaur in the District of Perth and Kinross 1990. *Address:* The Lord Pearson of Rannoch, House of Lords, London, SW1A 0PW; Office: PWS Holdings plc, 52 Minories, London, EC3N 1JJ *Tel:* 020 7480 6622.

EARL PEEL — Conservative

PEEL (3rd Earl, UK), William James Robert Peel; cr. 1929. 4th Viscount Peel (UK) 1895; Viscount Clanfield (UK) 1929; 8th Bt of Drayton Manor (GB) 1800. Born 3 October 1947. Son of 2nd Earl. Succeeded his father 1969; educated Ampleforth College; Tours University, France; Royal Agricultural College, Cirencester. Married 1st, March 28, 1973, Veronica Naomi, daughter of Major Alastair Timpson, MC (1 son 1 daughter) (marriage dissolved 1987), married 2nd, April 15, 1989, Hon. Mrs. Charlotte Hambro, daughter of late Lord Soames, CH, GCMG, GCVO, CBE, PC, and of Lady Soames (1 daughter). *Councils, Public Bodies:* DL, North Yorkshire 1998–. *House of Lords:* An elected hereditary peer 1999– *Other:* Former member, Yorkshire Dales National Parks Committee; Chairman, North of England Grouse Research Project 1979–96; Member, The Moorland Association Executive Committee 1988–; President, Gun Trade Association. *Trusts, etc:* President, Yorkshire Wildlife Trust. *Miscellaneous:* President, The Game Conservancy; Council Member, Nature Conservancy Council 1989–95. Member, Council of the Duchy of Cornwall 1993–; Lord Warden of the Stannaries, Duchy of Cornwall 1994–; Vice-Chairman, Standing Committee on Country Sports. *Recreations:* Shooting, cricket, photography, ornithology. *Clubs:* White's. *Address:* The Earl Peel, DL, Eelmire, Masham, Ripon, HG4 4PF *Tel:* 01465 688801 *Fax:* 01465 688802.

BARONESS PERRY OF SOUTHWARK — Conservative

PERRY OF SOUTHWARK (Life Baroness), Pauline Perry; cr. 1991. Born 15 October 1931. Daughter of late John and Elizabeth Welch; educated Wolverhampton Girls' High School; Girton College, Cambridge (MA). Married July 26, 1952, George Perry, son of late Percy and Edith Perry (3 sons 1 daughter). *Career:* University lecturer, journalist and teacher 1952–70; Has worked in USA, Canada and at Universities of Exeter and Oxford; HM Inspector, Department of Education and Science 1970–74; Staff Inspector, HM Inspectorate, responsible for: teacher training 1975–78 higher education 1978–81; Chief Inspector, HM Inspectorate, responsible for advice to Ministers on general higher education, research, LEA finance, teacher training and international relations 1981–86; Vice-Chancellor and Chief Executive, South Bank Polytechnic/University 1987–93; Chairman, South Bank University Enterprises Ltd 1989–93; Member, Board of Directors, Greater London Enterprise 1990–91; Director, South Bank Arts Centre 1991–94; President, Lucy Cavendish College, Cambridge University 1994–; Member, Economic and Social Research Council. *Chancellor:* Pro-Chancellor, Surrey University. *Select Committees:* Member, House of Lords Select Committees on: Science and Technology 1992–97, Scrutiny of Delegated Powers 1993–97, Relations between Central and Local Government 1995–96. *Party Groups:* Member, Association of Conservative Peers 1991–; President, Cambridge City Conservative Association 1998–. *International Bodies:* Member, IPU. *International Bodies (General):* British Council Committee on International Co-operation in Higher Education 1989–96 Chair, DTI Export Group for Education and Training 1993–98; Member, Overseas Projects Board, DTI 1993–98. *Other:* Rector's Warden, Southwark Cathedral 1990–94; Member of the Court, Bath University 1991–98; Vice-President, City and Guilds of London Institute 1994–99; Member, Board of Patrons of the Royal Society Appeal 1996–; Chairman, Friends of Southwark Cathedral 1996–; Governor (Board Member), English Speaking Union 1997–; Member: British-Thai Business Group, Partnership Korea, Indo-British Partnership 1997–99, UK-Korea Forum for the Future 1999–; Patron: British Youth Opera, Women's Engineering Society. Thirteen honorary doctorates and fellowships. *Trusts, etc:* Member: Cambridge Foundation, Alzheimer's Research Trust, Southwark Cathedral Millennium Project; Non-Executive Board Member, Addenbrooke's NHS Trust 1999–. *Miscellaneous:* Member: British Council's Committee on International Co-operation in Higher Education 1987–96, Economic and Social Research Council 1988–91; Academic Adviser, Home Office, Police Training Council 1990–92; Chairman, DTI Committee for Education and Training Exports 1993–98; Member, Citizen's Charter Advisory Panel 1993–97; Chairman, Charter Mark Judging Panel 1997–. Hon. Fellow: College of Preceptors 1987, Royal Society of Arts 1988; City and Guilds London Institute 1999; Member, Institute of Directors; Companion, Institute of Management. Freedom, City of London 1991. Liveryman, Worshipful Company of Bakers. *Publications:* Has published three books, chapters in ten other books and a wide variety of articles in educational journals and in the national press, and has participated in international seminars and study visits on education. *Special Interests:* Education, International Affairs. *Recreations:* Gardening, walking, listening to music, French countryside, food and literature. *Clubs:* Institute of Directors. *Name, Style and Title:* Raised to the peerage as Baroness Perry of Southwark, of Charlbury in the County of Oxfordshire 1991. *Address:* The Baroness Perry of Southwark, Lucy Cavendish College, Lady Margaret Road, Cambridge, CB3 0BU *Tel:* Office: 01223 332192 *E-Mail:* pp204@cam.ac.uk.

LORD PERRY OF WALTON — Liberal Democrat

PERRY OF WALTON (Life Baron), Walter Laing Macdonald Perry; cr. 1979. Born 16 June 1921. Son of late Fletcher Perry; educated Ayr Academy; Dundee High School; St Andrews University (MB, ChB 1943, MD 1948, DSc 1958). Married 1st, 1946, Anne Elizabeth Grant (3 sons) (marriage dissolved 1971), married 2nd, 1971, Catherine Hilda, daughter of late Ambrose Crawley (2 sons 1 daughter). *Armed Forces:* Medical Officer, RAF 1946–47. *Career:* Medical Officer, Colonial Medical Service, Nigeria 1944–46; Member of Staff, Medical Research Council 1947–52; Director, Department of Biological Standards, National Institute for Medical Research 1952–58; Professor of Pharmacology, Edinburgh University 1958–68, Vice-Principal 1967–68; Vice-Chancellor, The Open University 1969–81; Formerly Senior Consultant to United Nations University; President, Videotel International; Former Member, Board of Editors Encyclopaedia Britannica; Hon. Director, International Centre for Distance Learning. *Spokesman:* SDP Spokesman on Education, Health and Social Security 1983–91. *Select Committees:* Member, Select Committees on: Science and Technology 1985–90, 1992–97, 1997–, Science and Technology Sub-Committee II (Science and Society) 1999–2000, Science and Technology Sub-Committee IIA (Human Genetic Databases) 2000–. *Party Groups:* Deputy Leader, Social Democratic Peers 1981–83, 1988–89. *Other:* President, Research Defence Society. Fellow: Open University, University College, London; Holder of ten Hon. Degrees from Universities in UK, Asia, Australia, Canada and USA. *Honours:* OBE 1957; Kt 1974. FRS 1985; FRCP; FRCPE; FRSE. *Publications: Open University*, 1976. *Recreations:* Music, golf. *Clubs:* Scottish Arts (Edinburgh). *Name, Style and Title:* Raised to the peerage as Baron Perry of Walton, of Walton in the County of Buckinghamshire 1979. *Address:* The Lord Perry of Walton, OBE, FRS, The Open University, 10 Drumsheugh Gardens, Edinburgh, EH3 7QJ *Tel:* 0131–226 3851; Glenholm, 2 Cramond Road South, Davidson's Mains, Edinburgh, EH4 6AD *Tel:* 0131–336 3666.

LORD PESTON — Labour

PESTON (Life Baron), Maurice Harry Peston; cr. 1987. Born 19 March 1931. Son of late Abraham and Yetta Peston; educated Belle Vue High School, Bradford; Hackney Downs School; London School of Economics (BSc Economics); Princeton. Married 1958, Helen Conroy (2 sons 1 daughter). *Career:* Scientific and Senior Scientific Officer, Army Operations Research Group 1954–57; Assistant Lecturer, Lecturer, Reader in Economics, London School of Economics 1957–65; Economic Adviser, HM Treasury 1962–64; Professor of Economics, Queen Mary College, London University 1965–88, Emeritus Professor 1988–; Editor, Applied Economics 1972–; Special Adviser to Secretary of State for: Education and Science 1974–75, Prices 1976–79; Chairman: Pools Panel 1991–94, National Foundation for Education Research 1991–97, Office of Health Economics 1991–. *Chancellor:* Pro-Chancellor, Gyosei International College. *Spokesman:* Opposition Spokesman on: Energy 1987–97, Education and Science 1987–97, Treasury 1990–92, Trade and Industry 1992–97. *Select Committees:* Chairman, Select Committee on Monetary Policy of the Bank of England 1998–. *Other:* Member, Council Royal Pharmaceutical Society of Great Britain 1986–96. Hon. DEd, University of East London 1984; Hon. Fellow: Portsmouth University 1987, Queen Mary and Westfield College 1992, London School of Economics 1995. *Miscellaneous:* Member, CNNA 1967–73, Chairman, Economics Board; Member, SSRC 1976–79, Chairman, Economics Board. Hon. Member, Royal Pharmaceutical Society of Great Britain 1996. *Publications: Elementary Matrices for Economics*, 1969; *Public Goods and the Public Sector*, 1972; *Theory of Macroeconomic Policy*, 1974; *Whatever Happened to Macroeconomics?*, 1980; *The British Economy*, 1982. *Name, Style and Title:* Raised to the peerage as Baron Peston, of Mile End in Greater London 1987. *Address:* The Lord Peston, House of Lords, London, SW1A 0PW *E-Mail:* pestonhh@parliament.uk.

LORD PEYTON OF YEOVIL   Conservative

PEYTON OF YEOVIL (Life Baron), John Wynne William Peyton; cr. 1983. Born 13 February 1919. Son of late Ivor Eliot Peyton; educated Eton; Trinity College, Oxford. Married 1st, 1947, Diana Clinch (1 son 1 daughter and 1 son deceased) (marriage dissolved 1966), married 2nd, July 27, 1966, Mrs Mary Cobbold, daughter of late Colonel Hon. Humphrey Wyndham, MC. *Armed Forces:* Served 1939–45 with 15/19 Hussars (POW Germany). *Career:* Called to the Bar, Inner Temple June 1945; Chairman, Texas Instruments 1974–90; Non-Executive Chairman, British Alcan Aluminium 1987–91, President 1991–97. *House of Commons:* Contested (Conservative) Bristol Central 1950; MP (Conservative) for Yeovil 1951–1983; Parliamentary Secretary to Ministry of Power 1962–64; Minister of Transport June-October 1970; Minister of Transport Industries 1970–74. *Other:* Treasurer, The Zoological Society of London 1984–91. *Honours:* PC 1970. *Publications: Without Benefit of Laundry,* 1997. *Clubs:* Boodle's, Pratt's, Beefsteak. *Name, Style and Title:* Raised to the peerage as Baron Peyton of Yeovil, of Yeovil in the County of Somerset 1983. *Address:* Rt Hon the Lord Peyton of Yeovil, 6 Temple West Mews, West Square, London, SE11 4TJ *Tel:* 020 7582 3611; The Old Malt House, Hinton St George, Somerset, TA17 8SE *Tel:* 01460 73618.

LORD PHILLIPS OF SUDBURY   Liberal Democrat

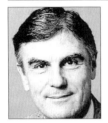

PHILLIPS OF SUDBURY (Life Baron), Andrew Wyndham Phillips; cr. 1998. Born 15 March 1939; educated Sudbury, Culford, Uppingham; Trinity Hall, Cambridge (BA economics and law). Married 1968, Penelope Ann Bennett (1 son 2 daughters). *Career:* Solicitor 1964; Established own practice, Bates, Wells & Braithwaite 1970; Director of several commercial companies including DP Mann Ltd; Chairman, Gough Hotels; Freelance Journalist and Broadcaster. *Select Committees:* Member, Joint Select Committee on Consolidation of Bills 2000–. *Party Groups (General):* Member, Society of Liberal Democrat Lawyers 1996–. *Other:* Governor, Contemporary Applied Arts; Co-Founder and Chairman, Legal Action Group 1971; Initiated: Lawyers in the Community Scheme 1987; President, Solicitors Pro Bono Group 1996; Chairman, Citizenship Foundation 1989–; Member: Charter 88 from inception until 1994, National Lottery Charities Board 1994–96. *Trusts, etc:* Trustee of: Scott Trust (owner of Guardian/Observer), Gainsborough House and other charities. *Miscellaneous:* Contested: Harwich (Lab) 1970, expelled as Lab candidate for North Norfolk 1973, Saffron Walden By-election (Lib) 1977 and General Election (Lib) 1979, North East Essex Euro-election (Lib) 1979, Gainsborough (Lib/All) 1983. *Honours:* OBE 1996. *Publications: The Living Law, Charitable Status – A Practical Handbook, Justice Beyond Reach;* Co-author: *Charity Investment – Law and Practice.* Name, Style and Title: Raised to the peerage as Baron Phillips of Sudbury, of Sudbury in the County of Suffolk 1998. *Address:* The Lord Phillips of Sudbury, OBE, House of Lords, London, SW1A 0PW.

LORD PHILLIPS OF WORTH MATRAVERS   Cross-Bencher

PHILLIPS OF WORTH MATRAVERS (Life Baron), Nicholas Addison Phillips; cr. 1999. Born 21 January 1938; educated Bryanston School; King's College, Cambridge (BA law 1961, MA). Married 1972, Christylle Marie-Thérèse Rouffiac (née Doreau) (2 daughters and 1 step-son 1 step-daughter). *Armed Forces:* National Service with Royal Navy, commissioned RNVR 1956–58. *Career:* Called to the Bar, Middle Temple (Harmsworth Scholar) 1962; In practice at the Bar 1962–87; Junior Counsel to the Ministry of Defence and to Treasury in Admiralty matters 1973–78; QC 1978; Member, Panel of Wreck Commissioners 1979; A Recorder 1982–87; A Judge of the High Court of Justice (Queen's Bench Division) 1987–95; Chairman, Law Advisory Committee, British Council 1991–97; Chairman, Council of Legal Education 1992–97; Vice-President, British Maritime Law Association 1993–; A Lord Justice of Appeal 1995–98; A Lord of Appeal in Ordinary 1999–2000; Master of the Rolls 2000–. *Other:* Governor, Bryanston School 1975–, Chairman of Governors 1981–. Hon. LLD, Exeter 1998. *Honours:* Kt 1987; PC 1995. *Recreations:* Sea, mountains. *Clubs:* Brooks's. *Name, Style and Title:* Raised to the peerage as Baron Phillips of Worth Matravers, of Belsize Park in the London Borough of Camden 1999. *Address:* Rt Hon the Lord Phillips of Worth Matravers, House of Lords, London, SW1A 0PW.

BARONESS PIKE — Conservative

PIKE (Life Baroness), Irene Mervyn Pike; cr. 1974. Born 16 September 1918. Daughter of late Samuel Pike, and late Alice Goodhead; educated Hunmanby Hall, East Yorks; Reading University (BA). *Armed Forces:* Served in WAAF 1941–46. *Career:* Managing Director, Clokie and Co. Ltd 1946–60; Director, Watts, Blake, Bearne 1964–89. *House of Commons:* Contested (Conservative): Pontefract (Yorkshire) 1951, Leek (Staffordshire) 1955; MP (Conservative) for Melton 1956–74; Assistant Postmaster-General 1959–63; Joint Parliamentary Under-Secretary of State, Home Office 1963–64. *Other:* National Chairman, WRVS 1974–81. *Miscellaneous:* Chairman, Broadcasting Complaints Commission 1981–85. *Honours:* DBE 1981. *Recreations:* Gardening, reading, walking. *Name, Style and Title:* Raised to the peerage as Baroness Pike, of Melton in the County of Leicestershire 1974. *Address:* The Baroness Pike, DBE, Hownam, Nr Kelso, Roxburgh, TD5 8AL.

LORD PILKINGTON OF OXENFORD — Conservative

PILKINGTON OF OXENFORD (Life Baron), Peter Pilkington; cr. 1996. Born 5 September 1933. Son of late Frank and Doris Pilkington; educated Dame Allans School, Newcastle upon Tyne; Jesus College, Cambridge (MA). Married 1966, Helen Wilson (died 1997) (2 daughters). *Trades Union:* Member, National Association of Head Teachers. *Career:* Schoolmaster, Tanganyika 1955–57; Ordained 1959; Curate in Bakewell, Derbyshire 1959–62; Schoolmaster, Eton College 1962–75, Master in College 1965–75; Headmaster, The King's School, Canterbury 1975–86; High Master, St Paul's School 1986–92; Hon. Canon of Canterbury Cathedral 1975–90, currently Canon Emeritus; Member, Parole Board 1990–95; Chairman, Broadcasting Complaints Commission 1992–96. *Spokesman:* An Opposition Spokesman on Education and Employment 1997–98. *Select Committees:* Co-opted Member, Select Committee on European Communities Sub-Committee F (Social Affairs, Education and Home Affairs) 1997–; Member, Ecclesiastical Committee 1997–. *Clubs:* Beefsteak, Garrick. *Name, Style and Title:* Raised to the peerage as Baron Pilkington of Oxenford, of West Dowlish in the County of Somerset 1996. *Address:* Rev Canon the Lord Pilkington of Oxenford, Oxenford House, Nr Ilminster, Somerset, TA19 OPP *Tel:* 01460 52813.

BARONESS PITKEATHLEY — Labour

PITKEATHLEY (Life Baroness), Jill Elizabeth Pitkeathley; cr. 1997. Born 4 January 1940. Daughter of Roland and May Bisson; educated Ladies' College, Guernsey; Bristol University (BA Economics). Married 1961, W. Pitkeathley (1 son 1 daughter) (marriage dissolved 1978). *Career:* Social Worker 1961–68; Voluntary Service Co-ordinator, West Berkshire Health Authority 1970–83; National Consumer Council 1983–86; Director, National Council for Carers 1986 until merger with Association of Carers 1988; Adviser to Griffith's Review of Community Care 1986–88; Chief Executive, Carers National Association 1988–98; Vice-President, Community Council for Berkshire 1990–98, President 1998–. *Other:* Patron: Bracknell CVS, National Centre for Volunteering, National Institute for Social Work. *Miscellaneous:* Chair, New Opportunities Fund 1998–. *Honours:* OBE 1993. Hon. RCGP. *Publications:* When I Went Home, 1978; *Mobilising Voluntary Resources,* 1984; *Supporting Volunteers,* 1985; *It's my duty, isn't it?,* 1989; *Age Gap Relationships,* 1996 (with David Emerson); *Only Child,* 1994 (with David Emerson). *Recreations:* Gardening, grand-children, writing. *Name, Style and Title:* Raised to the peerage as Baroness Pitkeathley, of Caversham in the Royal County of Berkshire 1997. *Address:* The Baroness Pitkeathley, OBE, House of Lords, London, SW1A 0PW *E-Mail:* pitkeathleyj@parliament.uk.

LORD PLANT OF HIGHFIELD   Labour

PLANT OF HIGHFIELD (Life Baron), Raymond Plant; cr. 1992. Born 19 March 1945. Son of late Stanley Plant and of Marjorie Plant; educated Havelock School, Grimsby; King's College, London (BA); Hull University (PhD). Married 1967, Katherine Sylvia Dixon (3 sons). *Career:* Lecturer, then Senior Lecturer in Philosophy, Manchester University 1967–79; Has lectured on philosophy in several universities 1981–91; Professor of Politics, Southampton University 1979–94; Master, St Catherine's College, Oxford 1994–. *Chancellor:* Pro-Chancellor, Southampton University 1996–. *Spokesman:* Opposition Spokesman on Home Affairs 1992–96. *Select Committees:* Member, House of Lords Select Committee on Relations between Central and Local Government 1995–96. *Party Groups (General):* Chairman, Labour Party Commission on Electoral Systems 1991–. *Other:* President, National Council for Voluntary Organisations (NCVO) 1998–. Hon. DLitt: Hull University, London Guildhall; Hon. ACA Degree. FRSA 1992. *Publications:* A contributor to *The Times*; *Hegel*, 1974; *Community and Ideology*, 1974; *Political Philosophy and Social Welfare*, 1981; *Philosophy, Politics and Citizenship*, 1984; *Conservative Capitalism in Britain and the United States: a critical appraisal*, 1988; *Modern Political Thought*, 1991. *Recreations:* Music, opera, reading. *Name, Style and Title:* Raised to the peerage as Baron Plant of Highfield, of Weelsby in the County of Humberside 1992. *Address:* Professor the Lord Plant of Highfield, Master's Lodgings, St Catherine's College, Oxford, OX1 3UJ.

BARONESS PLATT OF WRITTLE   Conservative

PLATT OF WRITTLE (Life Baroness), Beryl Catherine Platt; cr. 1981. Born 18 April 1923. Daughter of late Ernest and Dorothy Myatt; educated Westcliff High School for Girls; Girton College, Cambridge (MA). Married October 22, 1949, Stewart Sydney, son of late Sydney Rowland Platt (1 son 1 daughter). *Councils, Public Bodies:* Councillor, Chelmsford RDC 1959–74; Essex County Council 1965–83; Alderman 1964–74; Chairman, Education Committee 1971–80; Vice-Chairman, County Council 1980–83; DL, County of Essex 1983. *Career:* Technical Assistant: Hawker Aircraft 1943–46, British European Airways 1946–49; Chairman, Equal Opportunities Commission 1983–88. *Chancellor:* First Chancellor, Middlesex University 1993–2000. *Select Committees:* Member, House of Lords Select Committees on: Murder and Life Imprisonment 1988–89, Science and Technology 1982–85, 1990–94, 1996–, Relations between Central and Local Government 1995–96, Science and Technology Sub-Committee II (Science and Society) 1999–2000, Sub-Committee II (Aircraft Cabin Environment) 2000–. *Party Groups:* Member, Association of Conservative Peers. *International Bodies (General):* Member: European Communities Advisory Committee on Equal Opportunities for Women and Men 1983–98; UK Delegation to Narobi for UN Decade for Women World Conference 1985–. *Other:* Member of court four universities since 1964; Member numerous organisations concerned with higher education, science, engineering, including: Foundation for Science and Technology 1989–, Member of Council 1991–97; Patron: Women into Science and Engineering 1995, Women in Banking and Finance until 2000, and local charities. *Awards Granted:* City and Guilds of London Insignia Award 1988. 16 honorary doctorates and fellowships. *Trusts, etc:* Trustee, Homerton College 1970–81. *Honours:* CBE 1978. Hon. FIMechE; Hon. FInst of Training and Development; Hon. Fellowship,: Royal Aeronautical Society 1994, Royal College of Preceptors 1986; Fellow, Fellowship of Engineering (FEng) (now Royal Academy of Engineering) 1987; European Engineer (EurIng) 1987; Hon. Fellow: Women's Engineering Society 1989, Smallpiece Trust 1989; Fellow, Institution of Gas Engineers 1990; Hon. Fellow: Institute of Civil Engineers 1991, Institute of Structural Engineers 1991; Companion: Institute of Energy, Institute of Personnel Development 1995. Freeman, City of London 1988. Liveryman, Worshipful Company of Engineers 1988, Assistant to the Court 1996. *Special Interests:* Education, Women's Opportunities in Engineering, Local Government. *Recreations:* Reading, swimming for pleasure, cookery. *Clubs:* United Oxford and Cambridge University. *Name, Style and Title:* Raised to the peerage as Baroness Platt of Writtle, of Writtle in the County of Essex 1981. *Address:* The Baroness Platt of Writtle, CBE, DL, House of Lords, London, SW1A 0PW.

LORD PLOWDEN   Cross-Bencher

PLOWDEN (Life Baron), Edwin Noel Plowden; cr. 1959. Born 6 January 1907. Son of late Roger H. Plowden; educated Switzerland; Pembroke College, Cambridge. Married 1933, Dame Bridget Horatia Richmond (died 2000) (2 sons 1 daughter and 1 daughter deceased). *Career:* Temporary Civil Servant, Ministry of Economic Warfare 1939–40; Ministry of Aircraft Production 1940–46; Chief Executive and Member, Aircraft Supply Council 1945–46; Director, Commercial Union Assurance Co. Ltd 1946–78; Cabinet Office 1947; Treasury, as Chief Planning Officer and Chairman, Economic Planning Board 1947–53; Vice-Chairman, Temporary Council Committee NATO 1951–52; Chairman Designate, UK Atomic Energy Authority 1953–54, Chairman 1954–59; Chairman, Committee of Enquiry, Treasury Control of Public Expenditure 1959–61; Director, National Westminster Bank Ltd 1960–77; Chairman, Committee of Enquiry, Organization of Representational Services Overseas 1963–64; Chairman, Committee of Enquiry, Aircraft Industry 1964–65; Chairman, London Graduate School of Business Studies 1964–76, President 1976–90; Chairman, Standing Advisory Committee on Pay of Higher Civil Service 1968–70; Member, Civil Service College Advisory Council 1970–76; Chairman: Committee of Enquiry into Structure of Electricity Supply Industry 1974–75, Enquiry into CBI's Aims and Organisation 1974–75, Police Complaints Board 1976–81, CBI Companies Committee 1976–80, Equity Capital for Industry Ltd 1976–82; Member, Ford European Advisory Council 1976–83; Chairman, Tube Investments Ltd 1963–76, President 1976–90; Deputy Chairman, Committee of Inquiry on the Police 1977–79; Vice-Chairman, CBI Presidents Committee 1977–80; Member, Top Salaries Review Body 1977–81, Chairman 1981–89; Chairman, Police Negotiating Board 1979–82; Member, International Advisory Board Southeast Bank NA Miami 1982–86. Hon. Fellow, Pembroke College, Cambridge 1958; Three honorary doctorates. *Miscellaneous:* Visiting Fellow, Nuffield College 1956–64. *Honours:* KBE 1946; KCB 1951; GBE 1987. *Publications: An Industrialist in the Treasury: the post war years.* Clubs: Brooks's. *Name, Style and Title:* Raised to the peerage as Baron Plowden, of Plowden in the County of Salop 1959. *Address:* The Lord Plowden, GBE, KCB, Martels Manor, Dunmow, Essex, CM6 1NB *Tel:* 01371 872141.

LORD PLUMB   Conservative

PLUMB (Life Baron), Charles Henry Plumb; cr. 1987. Born 27 March 1925. Son of late Charles Plumb; educated King Edward VI School, Nuneaton. Married 1947, Marjorie Dorothy Dunn (1 son 2 daughters). *Councils, Public Bodies:* DL, Warwick 1977. *Career:* Member, Council, NFU 1959, Vice-President 1964–65, Deputy President 1966–69, President 1970–79; Member, Duke of Northumberland's Committee of Enquiry, Foot and Mouth Disease 1967–68; President, Comité des Organisations Professionnelles Agricoles de la CEE (COPA) 1975–77; Chairman, British Agricultural Council 1975–79; Non-Executive Director, Lloyds Bank, United Biscuits, Fisons 1979–94; MEP (Conservative) for Cotswolds 1979–99; Chairman, EP Agricultural Committee 1979–82; Chairman (Conservative) EDG, EP 1982–87, 1994–99; President, European Parliament 1987–89; Co-President, EU-ACP Joint Assembly 1994–99; Chairman, Agricultural Mortgage Corporation 1994–95. *Chancellor:* Chancellor, Coventry University. *International Bodies (General):* President, International Federation of Agricultural Producers 1979–82; Chairman: International Agricultural Training Programme 1987–, International Policy Council on Agriculture, Food and Trade 1987–. *Other:* Member Council, NFU 1959, Vice-President 1964–65, Deputy President 1966–69, President 1970–79; President, Royal Agricultural Society of England 1977; Deputy to HRH The Prince of Wales 1978. Hon. Fellow, Wye College 1995; Four honorary doctorates. *Trusts, etc:* Henry Plumb Trust. *Honours:* Kt 1973; Knight Commander's Cross of the Order of Merit, Federal Republic of Germany 1976; Ordén de Merito, Portugal 1987; Order of Merit, Luxembourg 1988; Grand Cross of the Order of Civil Merit, Spain 1989; Grand Order of the Phoenix, Greece 1997; Medal Mediterraneum, European Institute, Florence. Court Member, Farmers' Company; Hon. Liveryman, Worshipful Company of Fruiterers. *Clubs:* St Stephen's Constitutional. *Name, Style and Title:* Raised to the peerage as Baron Plumb, of Coleshill in the County of Warwickshire 1987. *Address:* The Lord Plumb, DL, Maxstoke, Coleshill, Warwickshire, B46 2QJ *Tel:* 01675 463133 *Fax:* 01675 464156 *E-Mail:* plumbh@parliament.uk.

PLUMMER OF ST MARYLEBONE (Life Baron), (Arthur) Desmond Herne Plummer; cr. 1981. Born 25 May 1914. Son of late Arthur Herne and Janet Plummer, née McCormick; educated Hurstpierpoint College; College of Estate Management. Married 1941, Pat Holloway (died 1998) (1 daughter). *Armed Forces:* Served Royal Engineers 1939–46, field and staff. *Councils, Public Bodies:* Councillor, St Marylebone Borough Council 1952–65, Mayor 1958–59; London County Council for St Marylebone 1960–65; Inner London Education Authority 1964–76; Greater London Council for: Cities of London and Westminster 1964–73, St Marylebone 1973–76; Leader of GLC Opposition 1966–67, 1973–74; Leader of Council 1967–73; JP 1958; DL, Greater London 1970. *Career:* Executive Committee British Section of International Union of Local Authorities 1967–74; Deputy Chairman, National Employers' Mutual General Insurance Association 1973–86; Chairman, National Stud 1975–82; Chairman, National Employers' Life Assurance Association 1983–88; Chairman, Portman Building Society 1983–90, President 1990–. *Party Groups:* Member, Association of Conservative Peers. *Other:* President, Metropolitan Association of Building Societies 1983–89; Member Court, University of London 1967–77. Hon. FFAS 1966. *Miscellaneous:* Member: South Bank Theatre Board 1964–74, Standing Conference on South East Planning 1967–74, Transport Co-ordinating Council for London 1967–69, Local Authority Conditions of Service Advisory Board 1967–71; Chairman, Horserace Betting Levy Board 1974–82. *Honours:* TD 1950; Kt 1971; KStJ 1986. FRSA; FRICS; Hon. FFAS. The Worshipful Company of Tin Plate Workers Alias Wireworkers of London. *Publications: Time For Change in Greater London*, 1958; *Report to London*, 1970. *Sportsclubs:* Otter Swimming Club. *Clubs:* Carlton, MCC, Royal Automobile. *Name, Style and Title:* Raised to the peerage as Baron Plummer of St Marylebone, of the City of Westminster 1981. *Address:* The Lord Plummer of St Marylebone, TD, DL, 4 The Lane, Marlborough Place, London, NW8 0PN *E-Mail:* plumerne@clara.co.uk.

PONSONBY OF SHULBREDE (4th Baron), Frederick Matthew Thomas Ponsonby; cr. 1930; (Life) Baron Ponsonby of Roehampton 2000. Born 27 October 1958. Son of 3rd Baron. Succeeded his father 1990; educated Holland Park Comprehensive School; University College, Cardiff; Imperial College, London. *Councils, Public Bodies:* Councillor, London Borough of Wandsworth 1990–94. *Spokesman:* An Opposition Spokesman on Education 1992–97. *Select Committees:* Member, Select Committees on: European Communities Sub-Committee C 1997–98, Science and Technology 1998–99, Science and Technology Sub-Committee II (Science and Society) 1999. *International Bodies (General):* Delegate to: Council of Europe 1997–, Western European Union 1997–. FIMM. *Name, Style and Title:* Created a life peer as Baron Ponsonby of Roehampton, of Shulbrede in the County of West Sussex 2000. *Address:* The Lord Ponsonby of Shulbrede, House of Lords, London, SW1A 0PW.

PORTER OF LUDDENHAM (Life Baron), George Porter; cr. 1990. Born 6 December 1920. Son of late John and Alice Porter; educated Thorne Grammar School; Leeds University (BSc 1941); Emmanuel College, Cambridge (MA, PhD, ScD). Married August 12, 1949, Stella Jean, daughter of late Colonel George Brooke (2 sons). *Armed Forces:* Served RNVR, Radar Officer 1941–45. *Career:* Demonstrator in Physical Chemistry, Cambridge University 1949–52; Assistant Director of Research in Physical Chemistry, Cambridge University; Assistant Director, British Rayon Research Association 1954–55; Professor of Physical Chemistry, Firth Professor and Head of Department of Chemistry, Sheffield University 1955–66; Director, The Royal Institution 1966–87, Emeritus Professor 1988–; Visiting Professor, Department of Chemistry, Univesity College, London 1978–89; President, Royal Society 1985–90; Chairman, Centre for Photomolecular Sciences, Imperial College, London 1986–; Professor of Photochemistry, Department of Pure and Applied Biology,

Imperial College 1986–. *Chancellor:* Chancellor, Leicester University 1986–95. *Select Committees:* Member, House of Lords Select Committee on Science and Technology 1990–94, 1995–99. *Other:* Member: BBC Science Consultative Group 1967–75, Cabinet Office Advisory Council on Science and Technology (ACOST) 1987–91. *Awards Granted:* Nobel Prize (joint) for Chemistry 1967; Royal Society: Davy Medal 1971, Rumford Medal 1978; Royal Society of Chemistry: Faraday Medal 1981, Copley Medal 1992. Fellow, Emmanuel College 1952–54; Research Professor and Fellow, Imperial College, London 1987–; Hon. Doctorates of 34 universities in UK and abroad, including: DSc Oxford, DSc London, LLD Cambridge. *Trusts, etc:* Trustee, British Museum 1972–74. *Miscellaneous:* President, The Research and Development Society 1977–82. *Honours:* Kt 1972; OM 1989. FRS 1960. Master, Salters' Company 1993–94. *Publications: Chemistry for the Modern World,* 1962; *Chemistry in Microtime,* 1997; as well as scientific papers for Royal Society, Faraday Society etc. *Special Interests:* Education, Science. *Recreations:* Sailing. *Clubs:* Athenaeum. *Name, Style and Title:* Raised to the peerage as Baron Porter of Luddenham, of Luddenham in the County of Kent 1990. *Address:* Professor the Lord Porter of Luddenham, OM, FRS, Departments of Chemistry and Biochemistry, Imperial College, London, SW7 2AY *Tel:* 020 7594 5785 *E-Mail:* gporter@ic.ac.uk.

BISHOP OF PORTSMOUTH   Non-Affiliated

PORTSMOUTH (Bishop of), Kenneth William Stevenson. Born 9 November 1949. Son of Frederik and Margrete Stevenson; educated Edinburgh Academy; Edinburgh University (MA 1970); Southampton University (PhD 1975); Manchester University (DD 1987). Married 1970, Sarah Glover (1 son 3 daughters). *Career:* Ordained Deacon 1973; Priest 1974–; Assistant Curate, Grantham with Manthorpe 1973–76; Lecturer, Boston 1976–80; Part-time Lecturer, Lincoln Theological College 1975–80; Chaplain and Lecturer, Manchester University 1980–86; Team Vicar 1980–82; Team Rector, Whitworth, Manchester 1982–86; Visiting Professor, University of Notre Dame, Indiana, USA 1983; Rector, Holy Trinity and St Mary's, Guildford 1986–95; Secretary, Anglo-Nordic Baltic Theological Conference, 1986–97 Member: Church of England Liturgical Commission 1986–96, Faith and Order Advisory Group 1991–96, Church of England Doctrine Commission 1996–; Bishop of Portsmouth 1995–; Chairman, Anglo-Nordic-Baltic Theological Conference 1997–; Vice-Chairman, Church of England Porvoo Panel; Took his seat in the House of Lords 1999. Fellow, Royal Historical Society 1990. *Publications:* include: *Nuptial Blessing,* 1982; *Eucharist and Offering,* 1986; *Jerusalem Revisited,* 1988; *The First Rites,* 1989; *Covenant of Grace Renewed,* 1994; Co-author *The Mystery of the Eucharist in the Anglican Tradition,* 1995; *The Mystery of Baptism in the Anglican Tradition,* 1998; *All the Company of Heaven,* 1998; *Abba, Father: Using the Lord's Prayer,* 2000 Contributor to: *Theology, Scottish Journal of Theology, La Maison Dieu;* Reviewer in: *Theology, Journal of Theological Studies; Church Times; Expository Times. Recreations:* Historical biographies, thrillers, walking, butterflies, piano, horn. *Address:* Rt Rev the Lord Bishop of Portsmouth, Bishopgrove, 26 Osborn Road, Fareham, Hampshire, PO16 7DQ *Tel:* 01329 280247 *Fax:* 01329 231538 *E-Mail:* bishports@clara.co.uk.

LORD POWELL OF BAYSWATER   Cross-Bencher

POWELL OF BAYSWATER (Life Baron), Charles David Powell; cr. 2000. Born 6 June 1941. Son of Air Vice Marshal John Powell, OBE; educated King's School, Canterbury; New College, Oxford (BA). Married 1964, Carla Bonnardi (2 sons). *Career:* Entered Diplomatic Service 1963; Third Secretary, Foreign Office 1963–65; Second Secretary, Helsinki 1965–67; Foreign and Commonwealth Office 1968–71; First Secretary and Private Secretary to HM Ambassador, Washington 1971–74; First Secretary, Bonn 1974–77; Foreign and Commonwealth Office 1977–80 (Counsellor 1979, Special Counsellor for Rhodesia negotiations 1979–80); Counsellor, Office of UK Permanent Representative to European Communities 1980–83; Private Secretary to the Prime Minister, The Rt Hon. Margaret Thatcher, MP 1983–91; Director: Jardine Matheson Holdings and associated companies 1991–, National Westminster Bank 1991–2000, J Rothschild Name Company 1992–, Said Holdings 1993–, Arjo-Wiggins Appleton 1993–2000, Louis-Vuitton-Moet-Hennessy 1995–, British Mediterranean Airways 1997–; International Advisory Board: Textron Corporation, Rolls Royce,

GEMS, Barrick Gold, Hicks Muse. *Trusts, etc:* Trustee, Aspen Institute 1995–; Chairman, Trustees of Said Business School Oxford. *Miscellaneous:* President, China-Britain Business Council 1990–; Chairman, Singapore British Business Council 1994–. *Honours:* KCMG 1990. *Special Interests:* Foreign Affairs, Defence, Intelligence, Trade. *Recreations:* Walking. *Clubs:* Turf. *Name, Style and Title:* Raised to the peerage as Baron Powell of Bayswater, of Canterbury in the County of Kent 2000. *Address:* The Lord Powell of Bayswater, KCMG, c/o Matheson & Company Ltd, 3 Lombard Street, London, EC3V 9AQ.

BARONESS PRASHAR   Cross-Bencher

PRASHAR (Life Baroness), Usha Kumari Prashar; cr. 1999. Born 29 June 1948. Daughter of late Naurhia Lal and Durga Devi Prashar; educated Duchess Gloucester School, Nairobi, Kenya; Wakefield Girls' High School, Yorkshire; Leeds University (BA 1970); Glasgow University (DipSocAdmin 1971). Married July 21, 1973, Vijay Kumar Sharma. *Career:* Conciliation Officer, Race Relations Board 1971–75; Director, Runnymede Trust 1976–84; Fellow, Policy Studies Institute 1984–86; Director, National Council of Voluntary Organisations 1986–91; Part-time Civil Service Commissioner 1991–96; Chairman, Parole Board of England and Wales 1997–2000; First Civil Service Commissioners 2000–. *Chancellor:* Chancellor, De Montfort University. *International Bodies (General):* Board Member, Salzburg Seminar. *Other:* Patron: Sickle Cell Society 1986–, Elfrida Rathbone Society 1988–; Hon. Vice-President, Council for Overseas Student Affairs 1986–; Governor, De Montfort University 1996–. Hon. Fellow, Goldsmith's College, London University; Six honorary doctorates. *Trusts, etc:* Deputy Chairman, National Literacy Trust; Trustee, Camelot Foundation; Management Board King's Fund; Trustee, Ethnic Minority Foundation. *Miscellaneous:* Member: Arts Council of Great Britain 1979–81, Study Commission on the Family 1980–83, Social Security Advisory Committee 1980–83, Executive Committee, Child Poverty Action Group 1984–85, London Food Commission 1984–90, BBC Educational Broadcasting Council 1987–89, Solicitor's Complaints Bureau 1989–90, Royal Commission on Criminal Justice 1991–93, Lord Chancellor's Advisory Committee on Legal Education and Conduct 1991–97, Board of Energy Saving Trust 1992–98, Arts Council of England 1994–97; Non-Executive Director, Channel Four 1992–98; Deputy Chairman, National Literacy Trust 1992–. *Honours:* CBE 1994. FRSA. *Publications:* Has contributed to several publications on health and race relations. *Recreations:* Golf, music, art, reading. *Sportsclubs:* Foxhills Golf Club. *Clubs:* Reform, Royal Commonwealth Society. *Name, Style and Title:* Raised to the peerage as Baroness Prashar, of Runnymede in the County of Surrey 1999. *Address:* The Baroness Prashar, CBE, First Civil Service Commissioner, 35 Great Smith Street, London, SW1P 3BQ *Tel:* 020 7276 2601.

LORD PRENTICE   Conservative

PRENTICE (Life Baron), Reginald Ernest Prentice; cr. 1992. Born 16 July 1923. Son of late Ernest and Elizabeth Prentice; educated Whitgift School; London School of Economics (BSc Economics). Married 1948, Joan Godwin (1 daughter). *Trades Union:* Member of staff, TGWU 1950–57. *Armed Forces:* Served RA 1942–46; Commissioned 1943; Served Italy and Austria 1944–46. *Councils, Public Bodies:* Councillor, Borough of Croydon 1949–55; Alderman, GLC 1970–71; JP, Croydon 1961. *Career:* Temporary civil servant 1940–42; Company Director and Consultant; Consultant, Aid-Call plc 1981–98; Director, EW Fact pl 1992–98. *House of Commons:* MP (Labour): East Ham North 1957–74, Newham North East 1974–77; Resigned from Labour Party and joined Conservative Party 1977; MP (Conservative): Newham North East 1977–79, Daventry 1979–87; Minister of State, Department of Education and Science 1964–66; Minister of Public Building and Works 1966–67; Minister of Overseas Development 1967–69, 1975–76; Secretary of State for Education and Science 1974–75; Minister of State for Social Security, DHSS 1979–81. *Spokesman (Commons):* Opposition Spokesman on Employment 1972–74. *Party Groups (General):* Member, Executive Committee, National Union of Conservative Associations 1988–90; President, Devizes Constituency Conservative Association 1989–. *Honours:* PC 1966; Kt 1987. *Publications:* Co-author *Social Welfare and the Citizen,* 1957; *Right Turn,* 1978. *Special Interests:* Industrial Relations, Foreign Affairs. *Recreations:* Walking. *Name, Style and Title:* Raised to the peerage as Baron Prentice, of Daventry in the County of Northamptonshire 1992.*Address:* Rt Hon the Lord Prentice, Wansdyke, Church Lane, Mildenhall, Marlborough, Wiltshire, SN8 2LU.

LORD PRIOR
Conservative

PRIOR (Life Baron), James Michael Leathes Prior; cr. 1987. Born 11 October 1927. Son of late Charles Bolingbroke Leathes Prior, JP; educated Charterhouse; Pembroke College, Cambridge. Married January 30, 1954, Jane Primrose Gifford, daughter of late Air Vice-Marshal O. G. W. G. Lywood, CB, CBE (3 sons 1 daughter). *Armed Forces:* Commissioned in Army 1946; Served in India and Germany. *Career:* Farmer and Land Agent 1950; Chairman: The General Electric Company plc 1984–98, Allders Ltd 1984–94; Director, United Biscuits plc 1990–94; Member: Tenneco Europe Ltd (Advisory Committee) to 1998, American International (Advisory Council); Chairman: East Anglia Radio plc 1992–95, African Cargo Handling Ltd 1998–; Deputy Chairman, MSI Cellular Investments BV 2000–. *House of Commons:* MP (Conservative) for: Lowestoft 1959–83, Waveney 1983–87; PPS to the: President of the Board of Trade 1962–63, Minister of Power 1963–64, Leader of the Opposition 1965–70; Minister of Agriculture, Fisheries and Food 1970–72; Lord President and Leader of the House 1972–74; Secretary of State for: Employment 1979–81, Northern Ireland 1981–1984. *Spokesman (Commons):* Conservative Spokesman on Employment 1974–79. *Chancellor:* Chancellor, Anglia Polytechnic University 1993–99. *International Bodies (General):* Chairman, Arab-British Chamber of Commerce 1996–. *Party Groups (General):* Vice-Chairman, Conservative Party 1965, Deputy Chairman 1972–74. *Other:* Chairman: Royal Veterinary College 1990–99, Wishing Well Appeal (Great Ormond Street Childrens' Hospital) 1999–. Hon. Fellow, Pembroke College, Cambridge; Hon. Doctorate: Anglia Polytechnic University, Stafford University. *Trusts, etc:* Chairman: Industry and Parliament Trust 1990–94, NAC Rural Housing Trust 1990–99, London Playing Fields Society 1998–; Chairman, Special Trustees, Wishing Well Appeal (Great Ormond Street Childrens' Hospital). *Miscellaneous:* Chairman: Council for Industry and Higher Education 1985–92, Archbishops' Commission on Rural Areas. *Honours:* PC 1970. *Publications:* A Balance of Power, 1986. *Clubs:* Garrick, MCC. *Name, Style and Title:* Raised to the peerage as Baron Prior, of Brampton in the County of Suffolk 1987. *Address:* Rt Hon the Lord Prior, House of Lords, London, SW1A 0PW.

LORD PRYS-DAVIES
Labour

PRYS-DAVIES (Life Baron), Gwilym Prys-Davies; cr 1982. Born 8 December 1923. Son of late William Davies; educated Tywyn School, Gwynedd; University College of Wales, Aberystwyth (LLB, LLM law). Married August 30, 1951, Llinos, daughter of Abraham and Olwen Evans (3 daughters). *Career:* Solicitor; Consultant and formerly Partner, Morgan Bruce & Hardwickes, Cardiff and Pontypridd; Chairman, Welsh Hospitals Board 1968–74; Special Adviser to Secretary of State for Wales 1974–78; Member, Economic and Social Committee, EEC 1978–82. *Spokesman:* Opposition Front Bench Spokesman on: Health 1983–87, Welsh Office 1987–97, Northern Ireland 1982–93. *Select Committees:* Member, House of Lords Select Committees on: Murder and Life Imprisonment 1988–89, Parochial Charities (Neighbourhood Trusts Bill and the Small Charities Bill) 1983–84, Relations between Central and Local Government 1995–96; Member: Joint Committee on Statutory Instruments 1993–99; Select Committee on Delegated Powers and Deregulation 1999–. *International Bodies:* Member, British-Irish Parliamentary Body 1990–97. *Other:* President, University of Wales, Swansea 1997–. Hon. Fellow: University College of Wales, Aberystwyth, Trinity College, Carmarthen, University of Wales Institute, Cardiff; Hon. LLD (Wales). *Name, Style and Title:* Raised to the peerage as Baron Prys-Davies, of Llanegryn in the County of Gwynedd 1982. *Address:* The Lord Prys-Davies, Lluest, 78 Church Road, Tonteg, Pontypridd, Mid Glamorgan, CF38 1EN *Tel:* 01443 202462 *Tel:* Office: 01443 402233.

LORD PUTTNAM   Labour

PUTTNAM (Life Baron), David Terence Puttnam; cr. 1997. Born 25 February 1941. Son of late Leonard and Marie Puttnam; educated Minchenden Grammar School, London; City and Guilds 1958–62. Married 1961, Patricia Jones (1 son 1 daughter). *Trades Union:* Member, BECTU. *Career:* Advertising 1958–68; Film Production 1968–; Producer of films including:*Bugsy Malone*, 1976 (four BAFTA Awards), *Midnight Express*, 1978 (two Academy Awards, three BAFTA Awards), *Chariots of Fire*, 1981 (four Academy Awards, three BAFTA Awards including awards for best film), *Local Hero*, 1982 (two BAFTA Awards); *The Killing Fields*, 1984 (three Academy Awards, seven nominations: eight BAFTA Awards including Best Film); *The Mission,* 1986 (Palme D'Or, Cannes, one Academy Award, seven nominations; three BAFTA Awards);*Memphis Belle*, 1990, as well as several others; Chairman, Enigma Productions Ltd 1978–; Director: National Film Finance Corporation 1980–85, Anglia Television Group 1982–99; Chairman and Chief Executive Officer, Columbia Pictures 1986–88; Village Roadshow plc 1988–99. *Chancellor:* Chancellor, University of Sunderland. *International Bodies (General):* Fellow, World Economic Forum, Davos, Switzerland. *Other:* Governor, National Film and Television School 1974–, Chairman 1988–96; Vice-President, BAFTA 1993–; Chairman, National Museum of Photography, Film and Television 1996–97; Member, Court of Governors: The London School of Economics 1997–, The London Institute 1997–; Member: Academic Board Bristol University, Arts and Humanities Research Board. *Awards Granted:* Michael Balcon Award for outstanding contribution to British Film Industry, BAFTA 1982; Benjamin Franklin Award, RSA 1996; The Crystal Award presented by The World Economic Forum 1997. Seventeen honorary doctorates and fellowships. *Trusts, etc:* Trustee: Tate Gallery 1986–93, Science Museum 1996–. *Miscellaneous:* Visiting Professor, Bristol University 1983–97; Visiting Lecturer, London School of Economics 1997–; President, CPRE 1985–92, Vice-President 1997–; Member: British Screen Advisory Council 1988–98, British Film Commission 1992–98, Arts Council Lottery Panel 1995–97; Vice-President, Royal Geographical Society 1997–99; Member, Government's Education Standards Task Force 1997–; Chairman: National Endowment for Science, Technology and Arts 1998–, General Teaching Council 1999–. *Honours:* CBE 1983; Chevalier 1985; Officier de l'Ordre des Arts and des Lettres (France) 1992; Kt 1995. FRGS; FRSA; FRPS; FCGI; Fellow: Royal Society of Arts, Royal Geographical Society, The British Film Institute. *Publications:* Contributor *The Third Age of Broadcasting*, 1982; Co-author *Rural England*, 1988; *A Submission to the EC Think Tank on Audio-Visual Policy*, 1994; *The Creative Imagination* in 'What Needs to Change', 1996; *The Undeclared War*, 1997. *Recreations:* Reading, cinema, landscape. *Clubs:* Chelsea Arts, MCC, Athenaeum. *Name, Style and Title:* Raised to the peerage as Baron Puttnam, of Queensgate in the Royal Borough of Kensington and Chelsea 1997. *Address:* The Lord Puttnam, CBE, Enigma Productions Ltd, 29a Tufton Street, London, SW1P 3QL *Tel:* 020 7222 5757 *Fax:* 020 7222 5858 *E-Mail:* puttnam@enigma.co.uk.

LORD PYM   Conservative

PYM (Life Baron), Francis Leslie Pym; cr. 1987. Born 13 February 1922. Son of late Leslie Ruthven Pym, JP, MP, and late Iris Rosalind (née Orde); educated Eton; Magdalene College, Cambridge. Married June 25, 1949, Valerie Fortune, née Daglish (2 sons 2 daughters). *Armed Forces:* Captain, 9th Lancers; Served in Africa and Italy, MC 1945. *Councils, Public Bodies:* Councillor, Herefordshire County Council 1958–61; DL, Cambridgeshire 1973–. *Career:* Director, Christie Brockbank Shipton Ltd; Chairman, Diamond Cable Communications. *House of Commons:* Contested (Conservative) Rhondda West 1959; MP (Conservative) for: Cambridgeshire 1961–83, Cambridgeshire South East 1983–87; PPS to the Chancellor of the Exchequer 1962; Secretary of State for Northern Ireland 1973–74; Secretary of State for Defence 1979–1981; Chancellor of the Duchy of Lancaster, Paymaster General and Leader of the House of Commons 1981; Lord President of the Council and Leader of the House of Commons 1981–82; Secretary of State for Foreign and Commonwealth Affairs 1982–83. *Whip (Commons):* Assistant Government Whip 1962–64; Opposition Whip 1964–67; Deputy Chief Whip for the Opposition 1967–70; Parliamentary Secretary to the Treasury and Government Chief Whip 1970–73. *Spokesman (Commons):* Opposition Spokesman on: Northern Ireland and Agriculture 1974, Agriculture, Fisheries and Food 1974–76, House of Commons Affairs and on Devolution 1976–78, Foreign and Commonwealth Affairs 1978–79. *Other:* Member, Liverpool University Council 1949–53; President, Atlantic Treaty Association 1985–88; Chairman, English Speaking Union 1987–92. Hon. Fellow, Magdalene College, Cambridge 1979. *Trusts, etc:* Chairman, The St Andrew's (Ecumenical) Trust until 1998. *Honours:* MC 1945; PC 1970. *Publications: The Politics of Consent,* 1984; *Sentimental Journey: tracing an outline of family history,* 1998. *Special Interests:* Foreign Affairs, Defence, Rural Affairs, Parliamentary Affairs. *Clubs:* Buck's. *Name, Style and Title:* Raised to the peerage as Baron Pym, of Sandy in the County of Bedfordshire 1987. *Address:* Rt Hon the Lord Pym, MC, DL, Everton Park, Sandy, Bedfordshire, SG19 2DE.

Q

LORD QUINTON — Conservative

QUINTON (Life Baron), Anthony Meredith Quinton; cr. 1983. Born 25 March 1925. Son of late Surgeon-Captain Richard Frith Quinton, RN; educated Stowe School; Christ Church, Oxford. Married August 2, 1952, Marcelle Wegier (1 son 1 daughter). *Armed Forces:* Served RAF 1943–46; Flying Officer and Navigator. *Career:* Delegate, Oxford University Press 1970–76; Fellow: All Souls College, Oxford 1949–55, New College 1955–78, Winchester College 1970–85; President, Trinity College, Oxford 1978–87; Fellow, Member, Arts Council 1979–81; Chairman, British Library Board 1985–90; Emeritus Fellow, New College, Oxford; Former Vice-Chairman, Encyclopaedia Britannica Board of Editors. *Other:* Governor, Stowe School 1963–84, Chairman of Governors 1969–75; President: Aristotelian Society 1975–76, Royal Institute of Philosophy 1990–; Chairman, Kennedy Memorial Foundation 1990–95. Hon DHum Lit, New York University USA; Hon DHum, Ball State University USA. *Trusts, etc:* Wolfson Foundation; Radcliffe Trusts. *Honours:* Order of Leopold II (Belgium) 1984; FBA. *Publications: Political Philosophy* (editor) 1967; *The Nature of Things,* 1973; *Utilitarian Ethics,* 1973, 1990; *The Politics of Imperfection,* 1978; *Francis Bacon,* 1980; *Thoughts and Thinkers,* 1982; *From Wodehouse to Wittgenstein,* 1998. *Special Interests:* Education, Arts, Media. *Clubs:* Garrick, Beefsteak, Brooks's. *Name, Style and Title:* Raised to the peerage as Baron Quinton, of Holywell in the City of Oxford and County of Oxfordshire 1983. *Address:* The Lord Quinton, FBA, A11 Albany, Piccadilly, London, W1V 9RD *Tel:* 020 7287 8686.

LORD QUIRK — Cross-Bencher

QUIRK (Life Baron), Charles Randolph Quirk; cr. 1994. Born 12 July 1920. Son of late Thomas and Amy Randolph Quirk; educated Douglas High School, Isle of Man; University College, London (MA, PhD, DLitt); Yale University. Married 1st, 1946, Jean, daughter of Ellis Gauntlett Williams (2 sons) (marriage dissolved 1979, she died 1995), married 2nd, 1984, Gabriele, daughter of Judge Helmut Stein. *Armed Forces:* Served RAF 1940–45. *Career:* Lecturer in English, University College, London 1947–54; Commonwealth Fund Fellow, Yale University and University of Michigan 1951–52; Reader in English Language and Literature, Durham University 1954–58, Professor 1958–60 and at London University 1960–68; Quain Professor of English Language and Literature, University College, London 1968–81; Chairman, Committee of Enquiry in Speech Therapy Services 1969–72; Member of Senate, London University 1970–85; Governor, British Institute of Recorded Sound 1975–80; Member, BBC Archives Committee 1975–81; Vice-Chancellor, London University 1981–85; President, Institute of Linguistics 1982–86; Member, Board of British Council 1983–91; Chairman, Anglo-Spanish Foundation 1983–85; Chairman, British Library Advisory Committee 1984–97; Member, RADA Council 1985–; President, British Academy 1985–89; Trustee, City Technology Colleges 1986–98; President, College of Speech Therapists 1987–91; Trustee, Wolfson Foundation 1987–; Royal Commissioner, 1851 Exhibition 1987–95; President, North of England Educational Conference 1989. *Select Committees:* Member, Select Committee on Science and Technology Sub-Committee II (Science and Society) 1999–2000; Sub-Committee I (Complementary and Alternative Medicine) 2000–.

Other: Member: Linguistic Society of America, Modern Language Association, Philological Society. *Awards Granted:* Jubilee Medal, Institute of Linguistics 1973. Hon. LLD, DLitt, DSc. from universities in the United Kingdom, USA and Europe; Jubilee Medal, Institute of Linguistics 1973; Foreign Fellow, Royal Belgian Academy of Science 1975; Hon. Fellow: Imperial College 1985, Queen Mary College 1986, Goldsmiths' College 1987; Foreign Fellow, Royal Swedish Academy 1987; Member, Academia Europaea 1988; Hon. Fellow, King's College 1990; Foreign Fellow: Finnish Academy of Science 1991, American Academy of Arts and Sciences 1995. *Honours:* CBE 1975; Kt 1985. FBA 1975. *Publications:* Co-author of several works on the English Language, notably *A Comprehensive Grammar of the English Language,* 1985; Solely: *The Concessive Relation in Old English Poetry,* 1954; *Essays on the English Language – Medieval and Modern,* 1968; *The English Language and Images of Matter,* 1972; *The Linguist and the English Language,* 1974; *Style and Communication in the English Language,* 1984; *Words at Work – Lectures on Textual Structures,* 1986; *Grammatical and Lexical Variance in English,* 1995; Has contributed to conference proceedings and learned journals. *Special Interests:* Education, Public Communication, Health, Speech Pathology, Broadcasting, Media. *Clubs:* Athenaeum. *Name, Style and Title:* Raised to the peerage as Baron Quirk, of Bloomsbury in the London Borough of Camden 1994. *Address:* Professor the Lord Quirk, CBE, FBA, University College London, Gower Street, London, WC1E 6BT *Tel:* 020 7679 2938 *Fax:* 020 7916 2054.

R

BARONESS RAMSAY OF CARTVALE   Labour

RAMSAY OF CARTVALE (Life Baroness), Meta Ramsay; cr. 1996. Born 12 July 1936. Daughter of Alexander Ramsay and Sheila Ramsay (née Jackson); educated Battlefield Primary School; Hutchesons' Girls' Grammar School, Glasgow; Glasgow University (MA, MEd); Graduate Institute for International Affairs, Geneva. *Trades Union:* Member, GMB. *Councils, Public Bodies:* Member, Lewisham Community Health Council 1992–94. *Career:* HM Diplomatic Service 1969–91; Foreign Policy Adviser to late Rt Hon. John Smith, MP, Leader of the Labour Party 1992–94; Special Adviser to Rt Hon. John Cunningham, MP, Shadow Secretary of State for Trade and Industry 1994–95. *Whip:* A Baroness in Waiting (Government Whip) December 1997–. *Spokesman:* A Spokeswoman on: Culture, Media and Sport 1997–98, Health 1997–98, Scotland 1997–, Foreign Affairs and Europe 1998–. *Select Committees:* Member: Select Committee on European Communities 1997, Select Committee on European Communities Sub-Committee F (Social Affairs, Education and Home Affairs) 1997. *International Bodies:* Member, British Delegation to the Parliamentary Assembly of OSCE 1997. *Party Groups (General):* Member: Labour Party, Fabian Society, Co-operative Party, Labour Finance and Industry Group, Labour Movement in Europe. *Other:* President, Scottish Union of Students 1959–60; Chair, Atlantic Council of the United Kingdom 1997; Member: RIIA, Institute for Jewish Policy Research, 300 Group; Chair, Board of Governors, Fairlawn Primary School, Forest Hill, South London until 1997. Hon. DLitt, University of Bradford. *Miscellaneous:* Honorary Visiting Research Fellow in Peace Studies, Bradford University; Member, Intelligence and Security Committee 1997. FRSA. *Recreations:* Theatre, opera, ballet. *Clubs:* University Women's, Reform, Royal Scottish Automobile (Glasgow). *Name, Style and Title:* Raised to the peerage as Baroness Ramsay of Cartvale, of Langside in the City of Glasgow 1996. *Address:* The Baroness Ramsay of Cartvale, House of Lords, London, SW1A 0PW.

LORD RANDALL OF ST BUDEAUX   Labour

RANDALL OF ST BUDEAUX (Life Baron), Stuart Jeffrey Randall; cr. 1997. Born 22 June 1938. Son of late Charles Randall; educated University College of Wales, Cardiff. Married August 22, 1963, Gillian Michael (3 daughters). *Career:* Electrical fitter apprentice, HM Dockyard, Devonport 1953–58; Systems engineer: English Electric Computers, Radio Corporation of America, USA 1963–66; Project leader, Marconi Automation 1966–68; Consultant, Inter-Bank Research Organisation 1968–71; Manager: British Steel Corporation 1971–76, British Leyland 1976–80; Consultant, Nexos Office Systems 1980–82; Manager, Plessey Communications Systems Ltd 1982–83. *House of Commons:* Contested Worcestershire South October 1974; Contested Midlands West European Parliament election 1979; MP (Labour) for Hull West 1983–97; PPS to the Roy Hattersley as Deputy Leader of the Labour Party and Shadow Chancellor of the Exchequer 1984–85. *Spokesman (Commons):* Opposition Front Bench Spokesman on: Agriculture 1985–87, Home Affairs 1987–92. *Select Committees:* Member, Select Committee on European Communities Sub-Committee A (Economic and Financial Affairs, Trade and External Relations) 1997–. *Special Interests:* Information Technology. *Recreations:* Sailing, walking, flying. *Name, Style and Title:* Raised to the peerage as Baron Randall of St Budeaux, of St Budeaux in the County of Devon 1997. *Address:* The Lord Randall of St Budeaux, House of Lords, London, SW1A 0PW.

BARONESS RAWLINGS   Conservative

RAWLINGS (Life Baroness), Patricia Elizabeth Rawlings; cr. 1994. Born 27 January 1939. Daughter of late Louis Rawlings and of Mary Rawlings (née Boas de Winter); educated Oak Hall, Haslemere, Surrey; Le Manoir, Lausanne, Switzerland; Florence University; University College, London (BA Hons); London School of Economics (Postgraduate diploma (International Relations). Married 1962, Sir David Wolfson (created Baron Wolfson of Sunningdale,*qv*) (marriage dissolved 1967). *Career:* Director: California Dress Company 1969–82, Rheims and Laurent, French Fine Art Auctioneers 1969–71; Member, Peace through NATO Council 1985–88; Member, British Video Classification Council 1986–89; Special Adviser, Department of the Environment 1987–88; MEP (Conservative) for Essex South West 1989–94; Group Deputy Whip; Former Vice-President, Delegation for Relations with Albania, Bulgaria and Romania; Former Member, Delegation for Relations with USA; Board Member, British Association for Central and Eastern Europe 1994–. *Whip:* An Opposition Whip 1997–98. *Spokesman:* An Opposition Spokeswoman on: Culture, Media and Sport 1997–98, Foreign and Commonwealth Affairs December 1998–, International Development December 1998–. *Select Committees:* Member, House of Lords Offices Sub-Committee: Advisory Panel on Works of Art 2000–. *International Bodies (General):* Governor, American University in Bulgaria. *Party Groups (General):* Member, Conservative Women's National Committee 1983–88. *Other:* Member, LCC Children's Care Committee 1959–61; Member, British Red Cross Society 1964–, Chairman Appeals, London Branch (National Badge of Honour 1981), Hon. Vice-President 1988–; Director, English Chamber Orchestra and Music Society 1980–; Member, British Council 1997–; Council Member, NACF; Member: RIIA, IISS, Advisory Council, The Prince's Youth Baroness Trust; Chairman of Council, King's College, London. *Awards Granted:* British Red Cross National Badge of Honour 1987. Hon. DLitt, University of Buckingham. *Miscellaneous:* Contested (Conservative): Sheffield Central 1983, Doncaster Central 1987 General Elections; Contested Essex West and Hertfordshire East in 1994 European Parliamentary Elections. *Honours:* Order of the Rose (Silver) Bulgaria 1991; Grand Official, Order of the Southern Cross, Republic of Brazil 1997. *Special Interests:* International Affairs, Culture, Heritage, Broadcasting. *Recreations:* Music, art, architecture, gardening, travel, skiing, golf. *Clubs:* Honorary Secretary, Grillions, Royal West Norfolk, Queen's. *Name, Style and Title:* Raised to the peerage as Baroness Rawlings, of Burnham Westgate in the County of Norfolk 1994. *Address:* The Baroness Rawlings, House of Lords, London, SW1A 0PW.

LORD RAWLINSON OF EWELL   Conservative

RAWLINSON OF EWELL (Life Baron), Peter Anthony Grayson Rawlinson; cr. 1978. Born 26 June 1919. Son of late Lieutenant-Colonel A. R. Rawlinson, OBE; educated Downside; Christ's College, Cambridge (Exhibitioner 1938). Married 1st, 1940, Haidee Kavanagh (3 daughters) (marriage dissolved and annulled by Sacred Rota, Rome 1954), married 2nd, 1954, Elaine, daughter of late Vincent Dominguez of Newport, RI, USA (2 sons 1 daughter). *Armed Forces:* Irish Guards, Major, mentioned in despatches 1939–46. *Career:* Called to the Bar, Inner Temple 1946; Queens Counsel 1959; Bencher, Inner Temple 1962; QC (NI) 1972; Treasurer 1984; Recorder, Salisbury 1960–62; Chairman of the Bar 1975–76; Leader, Western Circuit 1975–82, Recorder, Kingston-upon-Thames 1975; President, Senate of Inns of Court and the Bar 1986–87. *House of Commons:* MP (Conservative) for Epsom and Ewell 1955–78; Solicitor General 1962–64; Attorney General 1970–74. *Spokesman (Commons):* Conservative Spokesman on Law 1967–70. *Select Committees:* Member, Select Committee on Euthanasia. *Other:* President, Senate of Inns of Court and the Bar 1986–87. Hon. Fellow, Christ's College, Cambridge 1981. *Honours:* Kt 1962; PC 1964. Hon. Member, Americans' Bar Association; Hon. Fellow, American College Trial Lawyers. *Publications:* War Poems and Poetry, 1943; Public Duty and Personal Faith – the example of Thomas More, 1978; A Price Too High (autobiography) 1989; The Jesuit Factor, 1990; The Colombia Syndicate (novel) 1991; Hatred and Contempt (novel) 1992; His Brother's Keeper (novel) 1993; Indictment for Murder, (novel) 1994; The Caverel Claim, (novel) 1998. *Recreations:* Painting. *Clubs:* White's, MCC, Royal Automobile (Vice-President). *Name, Style and Title:* Raised to the peerage as Baron Rawlinson of Ewell, of Ewell in the County of Surrey 1978. *Address:* Rt Hon the Lord Rawlinson of Ewell, QC, House of Lords, London, SW1A 0PW.

LORD RAYNE   Cross-Bencher

RAYNE (Life Baron), Max Rayne; cr. 1976. Born 8 February 1918. Son of late Phillip and Deborah Rayne; educated Central Foundation School, London; University College, London. Married 1st, 1941, Margaret Marco (1 son 2 daughters) (marriage dissolved 1960), married 2nd, 1965, Lady Jane Vane-Tempest-Stewart, daughter of 8th Marquess of Londonderry, DL (2 sons 2 daughters). *Armed Forces:* Served RAF 1940–45. *Career:* Chairman, London Merchant Securities 1960–2000; Deputy Chairman, British Lion Films 1967–72; Director, Housing Corporation (1974) Ltd 1974–78 Chairman, Westpool Investment Trust 1980–; Non-executive Director, First Leisure Corporation plc 1995–99, Deputy Chairman 1984–92, Chairman 1992–95; Life President, London Merchant Securities 2000–. *Other:* Governor: St Thomas's Hospital 1962–74, Royal Ballet School 1966–79, Yehudi Menuhin School 1966–87, Malvern College 1966–, Centre for Environmental Studies 1967–73; Member: General Council, King Edward VII's Hospital Fund for London 1966–98, Council, St Thomas's Hospital Medical School 1965–82, Council of Governors, United Medical Schools of Guy's and St Thomas' Hospitals 1982–89; Hon. Vice-President, Jewish Care 1966–; Chairman, National Theatre Board 1971–88; Founder Patron, The Rayne Foundation 1962–; Vice-President, Yehudi Menuhin School 1987–; RADA Council 1973–; Founder Member, Motability 1979–96 (Life Vice-President 1996). Eight honorary university fellowships; honorary doctorate. *Trusts, etc:* Special Trustee, St Thomas's Hospital 1974–92; Chairman, London Festival Ballet Trust 1967–75. *Honours:* Kt 1969; Officier, Legion d'Honneur 1987; Chevalier 1973. Hon. Fellow: Royal College of Psychiatrists 1977, Royal College of Physicians 1992. *Name, Style and Title:* Raised to the peerage as Baron Rayne, of Prince's Meadow in the County of Greater London 1976. *Address:* The Lord Rayne, 33 Robert Adam Street, London, W1M 5AH *Tel:* 020 7935 3555.

Visit the Vacher Dod Website . . .
www.politicallinks.co.uk

LORD RAZZALL   Liberal Democrat

RAZZALL (Life Baron), Edward Timothy Razzall; cr. 1997. Born 12 June 1943. Son of Leonard Humphrey Razzall; educated St Paul's School; Worcester College, Oxford (BA). Married 1982, Deirdre Bourke (1 son 1 daughter from previous marriage). *Councils, Public Bodies:* Councillor, Mortlake Ward, London Borough of Richmond 1974–; Deputy Leader, Richmond Council 1983–96. *Career:* Teaching Associate, North Western University, Chicago, USA 1965–66; Frere Cholmeley Bischoff, solicitors 1966–96, Partner 1973–96; Partner, Argonaut Associates 1996–; Director, Cala plc 1973–99; Chairman, Abaco Investments plc 1974–90; Director: Star Mining Corporation NL 1993–, Chairman, C&B Publishing plc 1997–; Delancey Estates plc 1999–. *Spokesman:* Liberal Democrat Spokesman on Trade and Industry 1998–. *Select Committees:* Member, Joint Select Committee on Consolidation of Bills 1998–. *Party Groups (General):* Treasurer: Liberal Party 1986–87, Liberal Democrats 1987–; President, Association of Liberal Democrat Councillors 1990–95; Chairman, Liberal Democrats General Election Campaign 1999–. *Honours:* CBE 1993. *Recreations:* Sport, food and wine. *Clubs:* National Liberal, MCC. *Name, Style and Title:* Raised to the peerage as Baron Razzall, of Mortlake in the London Borough of Richmond 1997. *Address:* The Lord Razzall, CBE, House of Lords, London, SW1A 0PW *Tel:* 020 7976 1233 *E-Mail:* argonaut@easynet.co.uk.

LORD REA   Labour

REA (3rd Baron, UK), John Nicolas Rea; cr. 1937; 3rd Bt of Eskdale (UK) 1935. Born 6 June 1928. Son of late Hon. James Russell Rea. Succeeded his uncle 1981; educated Dartington Hall School; Belmont Hill School, Massachusetts, USA; Dauntsey's School; Christ's College, Cambridge (MA, MD); University College Hospital, London (DObst, DCH, DPH). Married 1st, March 24, 1951, Elizabeth Robinson (4 sons 2 daughters) (divorced 1991), married 2nd, December 16, 1991, Judith Mary Powell. *Trades Union:* Member, MSF. *Armed Forces:* Acting Sergeant, Suffolk Regiment, National Service 1946–48. *Career:* Junior Hospital Posts 1954–57; Research Fellow in Paediatrics in Ibadan and Lagos, Nigeria 1962–65; Lecturer in Social Medicine, St Thomas' Hospital Medical School, London 1966–68; General Practitioner, North London 1957–62, 1968–93. *House of Lords:* An elected hereditary peer 1999–. *Spokesman:* Opposition Spokesman on Health and International Development 1992–97. *Select Committees:* Member, Select Committees on: Science and Technology 1987–88, 1997–, Science and Technology Sub-Committee I (Complementary and Alternative Medicine) 2000–, Science and Technology Sub-Committee IIA (Human Genetic Databases) 2000–. *International Bodies:* Member: IPU, CPA. *Trusts, etc:* Member: Action Research, Healthlink Worldwide, Back Care, Mary Ward Centre, Medicinal Cannabis Centre. FRCGP. *Publications:* Papers in Medical Journals. *Special Interests:* Health, Food and Nutrition, Third World, Arms Control, Human Rights. *Recreations:* Music (bassoon), outdoor activities. *Clubs:* Royal Society of Medicine. *Address:* The Lord Rea, 11 Anson Road, London, N7 0RB *Tel:* 020 7607 0546 *Fax:* 020 7687 1219 *Tel:* Office: 020 7267 4411.

LORD REAY   Conservative

REAY (14th Lord, S), Hugh William Mackay; cr. 1628; 14th Bt of Far (NS) 1627; 7th Baron Mackay Van Ophemert (Netherlands) 1822. Born 19 July 1937. Son of 13th Lord. Succeeded his father 1963; educated Eton; Christ Church, Oxford. Married 1st, September 14, 1964, Hon. Annabel Therese Fraser (2 sons 1 daughter) (divorced 1978), married 2nd, June 20, 1980, Hon. Victoria Isabella Warrender (2 daughters). *Career:* Member: European Parliament 1973–79, Council of Europe and WEU 1979–86. *House of Lords:* Joint Parliamentary Under-Secretary of State, Department of Trade and Industry 1991–92; An elected hereditary peer 1999–. *Whip:* Government Whip 1989–91. *Spokesman:* Former Spokesman for Department of Environment, Home Office, Foreign and Commonwealth Office and Ministry of Defence and Welsh Office. *Select Committees:* Member, European Select Committee 1993–97, 1997–; Chairman, Select Committee on European Communities Sub-Committee D (Agriculture, Fisheries and Food) 1997–. *Miscellaneous:* Chief of Clan Mackay. *Address:* The Lord Reay, House of Lords, London, SW1A 0PW.

LORD REDESDALE   Liberal Democrat

REDESDALE (6th Baron, UK), Rupert Bertram Mitford; cr. 1902; (Life) Baron Mitford 2000. Born 18 July 1967. Son of 5th Baron. Succeeded his father 1991; educated Highgate School, London; Newcastle University (BA archaeology). Married October 10, 1998, Helen Shipsey. *Spokesman:* Liberal Democrat Spokesman on: Overseas Development 1994–99, Northern Ireland 1999, Tourism 2000–. *Select Committees:* Member: House of Lords Select Committee on Science and Technology 1993–97, Sub-Committee II 1994–97. *Other:* Member, Court of Newcastle University 1993–; Council Member, Institute of Advanced Motorists 1994–. *Special Interests:* Environment, Archaeology, Development. *Recreations:* Caving, climbing, skiing. *Name, Style and Title:* Created a life peer as Baron Mitford, of Redesdale in the County of Northumberland 2000. *Address:* The Lord Redesdale, 2 St Mark's Square, London, NW1 7TP *Tel:* 020 7722 1965.

LORD REES   Conservative

REES (Life Baron), Peter Wynford Innes Rees; cr. 1987. Born 9 December 1926. Son of late Major-General T. W. Rees, IA; educated Stowe; Christ Church, Oxford. Married December 15, 1969, Mrs Anthea Wendell, née Hyslop. *Armed Forces:* Served with Scots Guards 1945–48. *Career:* Called to the Bar, Inner Temple 1953; QC 1969; Practised Oxford Circuit, Bencher, Inner Temple 1976; Former Chairman and Director of companies. *House of Commons:* Contested (Conservative): Abertillery 1964, 1965, Liverpool, West Derby 1966 General Elections; MP (Conservative) for: Dover 1970–74, Dover and Deal 1974–83, Dover 1983–87; PPS to Solicitor General 1972–73; Minister of State, HM Treasury 1979–81; Minister for Trade 1981–83; Chief Secretary, HM Treasury 1983–85. *Miscellaneous:* Member: Court and Council of the Museum of Wales until 1997, Museums and Galleries Commission 1988–97. *Honours:* PC 1983. Liveryman, Clockmakers Company. *Clubs:* Boodle's, Beefsteak, White's, Pratt's. *Name, Style and Title:* Raised to the peerage as Baron Rees, of Goytre in the County of Gwent 1987. *Address:* Rt Hon the Lord Rees, QC, Goytre Hall, Nantyderry, Abergavenny, Gwent, NP7 9DL; 39 Headfort Place, London, SW1X 7DE.

LORD REES-MOGG   Cross-Bencher

REES-MOGG (Life Baron), William Rees-Mogg; cr. 1988. Born 14 July 1928. Son of late Edmund Fletcher Rees-Mogg; educated Charterhouse; Balliol College, Oxford. Married 1962, Gillian Morris (2 sons 3 daughters). *Trades Union:* Institute of Journalists. *Armed Forces:* RAF (National Service) 1946–48. *Councils, Public Bodies:* High Sheriff, Somerset 1978. *Career: Financial Times* 1952–60, Chief Leader Writer 1955–60, Assistant Editor 1957–60; *Sunday Times* City Editor 1960–61, Political and Economic Editor 1961–63, Deputy Editor 1964–67; Editor, *The Times* 1967–81; Member, Executive Board Times Newspapers 1968–81; Director, *The Times* Ltd 1968–81; Vice-Chairman, Board of Governors BBC 1981–86; Chairman and Proprietor, Pickering and Chatto (Publishers) Ltd 1981–; Chairman, Arts Council of Great Britain 1982–89; Chairman, Sidgwick and Jackson Ltd 1985–88; Director, M & G 1988–92; Chairman, Broadcasting Standards Council 1988–93; Chairman: American Trading Company Ltd 1992–, International Business Communications plc (now Informa plc) 1993–99, Fleet Street Publications Ltd 1995–; Director: General Electric Company 1981–97, J. Rothschild Investment Management Ltd 1987–96, St James's Place Capital plc 1990–96, The Private Bank and Trust Company 1993–, Private Financial Holdings Ltd 1995–, Value Realisation Trust plc 1996–99. *Party Groups (General):* Vice-Chairman, Conservative Party's National Advisory Committee on Political Education 1961–63. Hon. LLD, Bath. *Miscellaneous:* Contested (Conservative) Chester-le-Street, Co. Durham: 1956 (By-election), General Election 1959; Visiting Fellow, Nuffield College, Oxford 1968–72. *Honours:* Kt 1981. *Publications: The Reigning Error*, 1974; *An Humblier Heaven* 1977. *Recreations:* Collecting. *Clubs:* Garrick. *Name, Style and Title:* Raised to the the peerage as Baron Rees-Mogg, of Hinton Blewitt in the County of Avon 1988. *Address:* The Lord Rees-Mogg, 17 Pall Mall, London, SW1Y 5NB *Tel:* Office: 020 7242 2241.

BARONESS RENDELL OF BABERGH   Labour

RENDELL OF BABERGH (Life Baroness), Ruth Barbara Rendell; cr. 1997. Born 17 February 1930. Daughter of Arthur and Ebba Grasemann. Married 1950, Donald Rendell (divorced 1975, re-married 1977) (died 1999) (1 son). *Career:* Author and crime novelist 1964–. *Awards Granted:* Arts Council National Book Award for Genre Fiction, 1981; *Sunday Times* Award for Literary Excellence, 1990; Crime Writers' Association Gold Dagger (4 times) and Diamond Dagger; Mystery Writers of America three Edgar Allan Poe Awards. Hon. DLitt: University of Bowling Green (Ohio), University of Essex, University of East Anglia; Hon. MLitt, University of East London. *Honours:* CBE 1996. FRSL. *Publications: From Doon with Death,* 1964; *To Fear a Painted Devil,* 1965; *Vanity Dies Hard,* 1966; *A New Lease of Death,* 1967; *Wolf to the Slaughter,* 1967; *The Secret House of Death,* 1968; *The Best Man to Die,* 1969; *A Guilty Thing Surprised,* 1970; *One Across Two Down,* 1971; *No More Dying Then,* 1972; *Some Die and Some Lie,* 1973; *The Face of Trespass,* 1974; *Shake Hands for Ever,* 1975; *A Demon in my View,* 1976; *A Judgement in Stone,* 1977; *A Sleeping Life,* 1978; *Make Death Love Me,* 1979; *The Lake of Darkness,* 1980; *Put on by Cunning,* 1981; *Master of the Moor,* 1982; *The Speaker of Mandarin,* 1983; *The Killing Doll,* 1984; *The Tree of Hands,* 1984; *An Unkindness of Ravens,* 1985; *Live Flesh,* 1986; *Heartstones,* 1987; *Talking to Strange Men,* 1987; (Editor) *A Warning to the Curious – The Ghost Stories of M. R. James,* 1987; *The Veiled One,* 1988; *The Bridesmaid,* 1989; *Ruth Rendell's Suffolk,* 1989; (with Colin Ward) *Undermining the Central Line,* 1989; *Going Wrong,* 1990; *Kissing the Gunner's Daughter,* 1992; *The Crocodile Bird,* 1993; *Simisola,* 1994; (Editor) *The Reason Why,* 1995; Short Stories: *The Fallen Curtain,* 1976; *Means of Evil,* 1979; *The Fever Tree,* 1982; *The New Girl Friend,* 1985; *Collected Short Stories,* 1987; *The Copper Peacock,* 1991; *Blood Linen,* 1995; *Road Rage,* 1997; As Barbara Vine: *A Dark-Adapted Eye,* 1986; *A Fatal Inversion,* 1987; *The House of Stairs,* 1988; *Gallowglass,* 1990; *King Solomon's Carpet,* 1991; *Asta's Book,* 1993; *No Night is Too Long,* 1994; *The Brimstone Wedding,* 1996; *The Chimney Sweeper's Boy,* 1998. *Recreations:* Reading, walking, opera. *Clubs:* Groucho. *Name, Style and Title:* Raised to the peerage as Baroness Rendell of Babergh, of Aldeburgh in the County of Suffolk 1997. *Address:* The Baroness Rendell of Babergh, CBE, House of Lords, London, SW1A 0PW; 11 Maida Avenue, Little Venice, London, W2 1SR.

LORD RENFREW OF KAIMSTHORN   Conservative

RENFREW OF KAIMSTHORN (Life Baron), (Andrew) Colin Renfrew; cr. 1991. Born 25 July 1937. Son of late Archibald and Helena Renfrew; educated St Albans School; St John's College, Cambridge (Exhibitioner, BA Archaeology and Anthropology, MA, PhD, ScD); British School of Archaeology, Athens. Married 1965, Jane Margaret, daughter of Ven. Walter Ewbank (2 sons 1 daughter). *Armed Forces:* National Service with RAF 1956–58. *Career:* Sheffield University: Lecturer in Prehistory and Archaeology 1965–70, Senior Lecturer 1970–72, Reader 1972; Professor of Archaeology, Southampton University 1972–81; Visiting Lecturer, University of California 1967; Has lectured on archaeology in numerous British and American Universities; Has excavated in Greece and the United Kingdom; Chairman, Hampshire Archaeological Committee 1974–81; Member: Ancient Monuments Board for England 1974–84, Royal Commission for Historical Monuments (England) 1977–87; Disney Professor of Archaeology, Cambridge University 1981–; A Vice-President, Royal Archaeological Institute 1982–85; Member: Historical Buildings and Monuments Commission for England 1984–86, Ancient Monuments Advisory Committee 1984–, UK National Commission for UNESCO 1984–86; Master, Jesus College, Cambridge 1986–97, Fellow 1986–; Director, McDonald Institute for Archaeological Research 1990–; A Trustee, British Museum 1991–2000. *Select Committees:* Member, House of Lords European Communities Select Committee, Sub-Committee A 1993–96; Chairman, Library and Computing Sub-Committee 1995–; Member: Select Committee on House of Lords' Offices 1995–, Administration and Works Sub-Committee 1995–, Finance and Staff Sub-Committee 1995–. *International Bodies (General):* Foreign Associate, National Academy of Sciences of the USA; Corresponding Member of the Austrian Academy of Sciences. Hon. DLitt, Sheffield 1987; Hon. Doctorate, Athens 1991; Hon. DLitt, Southampton 1995. *Miscellaneous:* Contested (Conservative) Sheffield Brightside 1968 by-election; Board Member, Parliamentary Office of Science and Technology (POST) 1997–98.

FSA; FSA (Scotland); FBA 1980. Freeman, City of London. *Publications: The Emergence of Civilisation*, 1972; *The Explanation of Culture Change*, 1973 (editor); *Before Civilisation*, 1973; *British Prehistory, a New Outline*, 1974 (editor); *Investigations in Orkney*, 1979; *Problems in European Prehistory*, 1979; *An Island Polity*, 1982; *Approaches to Social Archaeology*, 1984; *The Prehistory of Orkney*, 1985; *The Archaeology of Cult*, 1985; *Archaeology and Language*, 1987; *The Cycladic Spirit*, 1991; *Loot, Legitimacy and Ownership: the Ethical Crisis in Archaeology*, 2000 Has also collaborated with other authors on archaeological subjects, as well as contributions to archaeological journals. *Special Interests:* National Heritage, Arts, Museums and Galleries, Education, Foreign Affairs. *Recreations:* Contemporary Art. *Clubs:* Athenaeum, United Oxford and Cambridge University. *Name, Style and Title:* Raised to the peerage as Baron Renfrew of Kaimsthorn, of Hurlet in the District of Renfrew 1991. *Address:* Professor the Lord Renfrew of Kaimsthorn, FBA, FSA, McDonald Institute for Archaeological Research, Downing Street, Cambridge, CB2 3ER *Tel:* 01223 333521.

LORD RENNARD   Liberal Democrat

RENNARD (Life Baron), Christopher John Rennard; cr. 1999. Born 8 July 1960. Son of late Cecil and Jean Rennard; educated Liverpool Blue Coat School; Liverpool University (BA Hons 1982). Married 1989, Ann McTegart. *Trades Union:* Member, GMBATU. *Career:* Liberal Party Agent, Liverpool, Mossley Hill 1982–84; Liberal Party Regional Agent, East Midlands 1984–88; Social and Liberal Democrats Election Co-Ordinator 1988–89; Director of Campaigns and Elections, Liberal Democrats 1989–. *International Bodies (General):* Member: IPU, CPA. *Other:* Member, Amnesty International. *Honours:* MBE 1989. *Publications: Winning Local Elections*, 1988; *The Campaign Manual*, 1995. *Recreations:* Cooking, wine, France. *Name, Style and Title:* Raised to the peerage as Baron Rennard, of Wavertree in the County of Merseyside 1999. *Address:* The Lord Rennard, MBE, Liberal Democrat Party, 4 Cowley Street, London, SW1P 3NB *Tel:* 020 7222 7999 *Fax:* 020 7233 3140 *E-Mail:* chrisrennard@cix.co.uk.

LORD RENTON   Conservative

RENTON (Life Baron), David Lockhart-Mure Renton; cr. 1979. Born 12 August 1908. Son of late Dr Maurice Waugh Renton and Eszma Olivia Renton; educated Oundle; University College, Oxford (MA, BCL). Married July 17, 1947, Claire Cicely (died 1986), daughter of late Walter Duncan (3 daughters). *Armed Forces:* Major RA; Served 1939–45 (overseas 1942–45). *Councils, Public Bodies:* DL: Huntingdonshire 1962, Huntingdonshire and Peterborough 1964, Cambridgeshire 1974. *Career:* Called to the Bar, Lincoln's Inn 1933; QC 1954; Bencher of Lincoln's Inn 1962; Treasurer 1979; Recorder: Rochester 1963–68, Guildford 1968–71. *House of Commons:* MP for Huntingdonshire 1945–79 (National Liberal 1945–50, National Liberal and Conservative 1951–66, Conservative 1966–79); Parliamentary Secretary: Ministry of Fuel and Power December 1955–57, Ministry of Power 1957–58; Joint Parliamentary Under-Secretary of State, Home Office 1958–61; Minister of State 1961–62. *Party Groups (Commons):* Chairman, Conservative Transport 1953–55. *House of Lords:* A Deputy Speaker House of Lords 1982–88. *Select Committees:* Member, Committee for Privileges 1975–79. *International Bodies (General):* Delegate to Council of Europe 1951 and 1952. *Party Groups (General):* Patron, Huntingdon Conservative Association 1979–. *Other:* President, Conservation Society 1971–72; Chairman, MENCAP 1978–82, President 1982–88; President, Statute Law Society 1980–; Patron: National Law Library, Design and Manufacture for Disability, Greater London Association for the Disabled, Ravenswood Foundation, Royal British Legion, Huntingdonshire. Hon. Fellow, University College, Oxford 1990–. *Miscellaneous:* Royal Commission on the Constitution 1971–74; Chairman, Committee on Preparation of Legislation 1973–75; Vice-Chairman, Council of Legal Education 1968–73; President, National Council for Civil Protection 1980–91. *Honours:* PC 1962; KBE 1964; TD. *Publications:* Various Legal and Political Articles; Various Obituaries. *Special Interests:* Drafting of Legislation, Mental Handicap, Environment, Law and Order, Trade Union Law, Devolution, European Legislation, Armed Forces. *Recreations:* Gardening, outdoor sports and games. *Sportsclubs:* Vice-President, Huntingdonshire Cricket Club 1959–. *Clubs:* Carlton, Pratt's. *Name, Style and Title:* Raised to the peerage as Baron Renton, of Huntingdon in the County of Cambridgeshire 1979. *Address:* Rt Hon the Lord Renton, KBE, QC, TD, DL, 16 Old Buildings, Lincoln's Inn, London, WC2A 3TL *Tel:* 020 7242 8986; Moat House, Abbots Ripton, Huntingdon, Cambridgeshire, PE18 2PE *Tel:* 01487 773227.

LORD RENTON OF MOUNT HARRY — Conservative

RENTON OF MOUNT HARRY (Life Baron), (Ronald) Timothy Renton; cr. 1997. Born 28 May 1932. Son of late R. K. D. Renton, CBE; educated Eton (Kings Scholar); Magdalen College, Oxford (Roberts Gawen Scholar) (MA Modern History). Married April 2, 1960, Alice, daughter of late Sir James Fergusson, 8th Bt of Kilkerran (2 sons 3 daughters). *Trades Union:* Member, APEX 1977–90. *Councils, Public Bodies:* Member, Council of Sussex University 2000–. *Career:* C. Tennant Sons & Co. Ltd, Canada 1957–62; Managing Director, Tennant Trading Ltd 1964–71; Director: Silvermines Ltd 1966–84, ANZ Banking Group Ltd 1969–76, J. H. Vavasseur & Co. Ltd 1971–74; Director, Fleming Continental European Investment Trust 1992–, Chairman 1999–. *House of Commons:* Contested (Conservative) Sheffield Park 1970; MP (Conservative) for Sussex Mid 1974–97; PPS: to Chief Secretary to the Treasury 1979–81, to Secretary of State for Trade January-May 1981, to Chancellor of the Exchequer, Rt Hon. Sir Geoffrey Howe, QC, MP January-June 1983; Parliamentary Under-Secretary of State, at Foreign and Commonwealth Office 1984–85; Minister of State: at Foreign and Commonwealth Office 1985–87, at Home Office 1987–89; Government Chief Whip 1989–90; Minister of State, Privy Council Office (Minister for the Arts) 1990–92. *Whip (Commons):* Government Chief Whip 1989–90. *Select Committees:* Member: Select Committee on European Communities 1997–, Europan Communities Committee Sub-Committee A (Economic and Financial Affairs, Trade and External Relations) 2000–. *Party Groups (General):* President, Conservative Trade Unionists 1980–84. *Other:* President: Roedean School 1997–, Federation of Sussex Amenity Societies 2000–. *Trusts, etc:* Fellow, Industry and Parliament Trust. *Miscellaneous:* Member, Know How Fund Advisory Board 1992–; Vice-Chairman, British Council 1992–97, Board Member 1997–99; Chairman: Outside Art Archive and Collection 1993–99; Sussex Downs Conservation Board 1997–. *Honours:* PC 1989. *Publications: The Dangerous Edge,* 1994; *Hostage to Fortune,* 1997; Articles published in journals and newspapers. *Special Interests:* Arts, Privatisation, Financial Institutions, Conservation. *Recreations:* Writing, mucking about in boats, arguing about operatic tenors, touring France on a bicycle. *Clubs:* Garrick, Grillions. *Name, Style and Title:* Raised to the peerage as Baron Renton of Mount Harry, of Offham in the County of East Sussex 1997. *Address:* Rt Hon the Lord Renton of Mount Harry, House of Lords, London, SW1A 0PW *E-Mail:* rentont@parliament.uk.

LORD RENWICK OF CLIFTON — Labour

RENWICK OF CLIFTON (Life Baron), Robin William Renwick; cr. 1997. Born 13 December 1937. Son of late Richard Renwick and of Clarice Renwick; educated St Paul's School; Jesus College, Cambridge; University of Paris (Sorbonne). Married 1965, Annie Colette Giudicelli (1 son 1 daughter). *Armed Forces:* Army Service 1956–58. *Career:* Entered Foreign Service 1963; Dakar 1963–64; FO 1964–66; New Delhi 1966–70; Private Secretary to Minister of State, FCO 1970–72; First Secretary, Paris 1972–76; Counsellor, Cabinet Office 1976–78; Rhodesia Department, FCO 1978–80; Political Adviser to Governor of Rhodesia 1980; Head of Chancery, Washington 1981–84; Assistant Under-Secretary of State, FCO 1984–87; Ambassador to: South Africa 1987–91, USA 1991–95; Deputy Chairman, Robert Fleming Holdings Ltd 1999–; Chairman: Fluor Daniel 1996–, Robert Fleming Holdings (S.A.) Ltd 2000–; Director: Compagnie Financiere Richemont AG 1995–, British Airways plc 1996–, Fluor Corporation 1997–, Canal Plus 1997–, Billiton plc 1997–, South African Breweries 1999–. Hon. Fellow, Jesus College 1992; Hon. DLitt: University of the Witwatersrand, South Africa 1990, College of William and Mary, USA 1993, Oglethorpe University 1995. *Trusts, etc:* Trustee, The Economist 1996–. *Miscellaneous:* Visiting Fellow, Center for International Affairs, Harvard University 1980–81. *Honours:* CMG 1980; KCMG 1988. FRSA. *Publications: Economic Sanctions,* 1981; *Fighting with Allies,* 1996; *Unconventional Diplomacy,* 1997. *Recreations:* Tennis, trout fishing. *Clubs:* Brooks's, Hurlingham, Travellers'. *Name, Style and Title:* Raised to the peerage as Baron Renwick of Clifton, of Chelsea in the Royal Borough of Kensington and Chelsea 1997. *Address:* The Lord Renwick of Clifton, KCMG, Robert Fleming & Co Ltd, 25 Copthall Avenue, London, EC2R 7DR *E-Mail:* lord.renwick@flemings.com.

LORD RICHARD   Labour

RICHARD (Life Baron), Ivor Seward Richard; cr. 1990. Born 30 May 1932. Son of Seward Thomas Richard; educated St. Michael's School, Bryn, Llanelly; Cheltenham College; Pembroke College, Oxford (Wightwick Scholar, BA Jurisprudence 1953). Married 1st, 1956, Geraldine Moore (1 son) (marriage dissolved 1962), married 2nd, June 2, 1962, Alison Mary Imrie (1 son 1 daughter) (marriage dissolved), married 3rd, September 1, 1989, Janet Jones (1 son). *Career:* Called to the Bar, Inner Temple 1955; Bencher 1985; Practised in London 1955–74; QC 1971; UK Permanent Representative to UN 1974–79; Member, EEC Commission 1981–85; Chairman, World Trade Centre Wales Ltd 1985–97; Director, WMC Communications Ltd 1999–. *House of Commons:* Contested (Labour) South Kensington General Election 1959; MP (Labour) Barons Court 1964–74; PPS to Secretary of State for Defence 1966–67; Parliamentary Under-Secretary of State (Army) Ministry of Defence 1969–70. *Spokesman (Commons):* Opposition Spokesman, Broadcasting, Posts and Telecommunications 1970–71; Deputy Spokesman on Foreign Affairs 1971–74. *House of Lords:* Leader of the Opposition in the House of Lords 1992–97; Lord Privy Seal and Leader of the House of Lords 1997–98. *Spokesman:* An Opposition Spokesman on: Home Office affairs 1990–92, The Civil Service 1992–97, European Affairs 1992–97, The Treasury and Economic Affairs 1992–93. *Select Committees:* Former Member, Select Committees on: House of Lords' Offices 1997–98, Finance and Staff Sub-Committee, Liaison, Privileges, Procedure, Selection. Hon. Fellow, Pembroke College, Oxford 1981. *Honours:* PC 1993. *Publications:* Co-author *Europe or the Open Sea*, 1971; *We, the British*, 1983; Co-author *Unfinished Business – the Reform of the House of Lords*, 1999; as well as articles in political journals. *Recreations:* Music, talking. *Name, Style and Title:* Raised to the peerage as Baron Richard, of Ammanford in the County of Dyfed 1990. *Address:* Rt Hon the Lord Richard, QC, House of Lords, London, SW1A 0PW.

LORD RICHARDSON   Cross-Bencher

RICHARDSON (Life Baron), John Samuel Richardson; cr. 1979; 1st Bt of Eccleshall (UK) 1963. Born 16 June 1910. Son of late John Watson Richardson, solicitor, killed in action 1917; educated Charterhouse; Trinity College, Cambridge; St Thomas's Hospital (MB, BChir, MD, MRCP). Married 1933, Sybil Angela Stephanie Trist (2 daughters). *Armed Forces:* RAMC, medical specialist – Major and Lieutenant-Colonel August 1939-November 1945. *Career:* Qualified 1935; Junior posts at St Thomas's Hospital until 1939; Deputy, Medical Unit at St Thomas's Hospital 1945–47, Physician 1947–75; Consulting Physician for Metropolitan Police 1957–80; Consulting Physician to Army 1964–75; President, International Society for Internal Medicine 1966–70; Chairman, Joint Consultants Committee 1967–72; President: Royal Society of Medicine 1969–71, BMA 1970–71, GMC 1973–80. *International Bodies (General):* President, International Society for Internal Medicine. *Awards Granted:* Gold Medal, BMA 1982. Hon. Fellow: Kings College, London, Trinity College, Cambridge; Six honorary doctorates. *Miscellaneous:* Hon. Bencher, Gray's Inn. *Honours:* LVO 1943; Kt 1960; CStJ. FRCP; FRCPE; Hon. FRCPI; Hon. FRCS; Hon. FRCPSG; Hon. FRCPsych; Hon. FRPharm Soc. Member: Cutlers, Society of Apothecaries. *Publications: The Practice of Medicine*, 2nd ed. 1960; *Connective Tissue Disorders*, 1963. *Recreations:* Living in the country. *Name, Style and Title:* Raised to the peerage as Baron Richardson, of Lee in the County of Devon 1979. *Address:* The Lord Richardson, LVO, FRCP, Windcutter, Lee, Nr Ilfracombe, Devon, EX34 8LW *Tel:* 01271 863198.

Visit the Vacher Dod Website . . .
www.politicallinks.co.uk

BARONESS RICHARDSON OF CALOW   Cross-Bencher

RICHARDSON OF CALOW (Life Baroness), Kathleen Margaret Richardson; cr. 1998. Born 24 February 1938. Daughter of Francis William and Margaret Fountain; educated St Helena School, Chesterfield; Stockwell College; Wesley Deaconess College; Wesley House, Cambridge. Married 1964, Ian David Godfrey Richardson (3 daughters). *Career:* First Woman President of the Methodist Conference 1992–93; Moderator, Free Churches Council 1995–99; President, Churches Together In England 1995–99. *Select Committees:* Member, Administration and Works Sub-Committee, House of Lords Offices Committee 2000–. Three honorary doctorates. *Trusts, etc:* Citizen Organising Foundation. *Honours:* OBE 1994. *Special Interests:* Church Affairs, Inter Faith Relations. *Recreations:* Reading, needlework. *Name, Style and Title:* Raised to the peerage as Baroness Richardson of Calow, of Calow in the County of Derbyshire 1998. *Address:* The Reverend Baroness Richardson of Calow, OBE, House of Lords, London, SW1A 0PW *E-Mail:* richardsonk@parliament.uk.

LORD RICHARDSON OF DUNTISBOURNE   Cross-Bencher

RICHARDSON OF DUNTISBOURNE (Life Baron), Gordon William Humphreys Richardson, cr. 1983. Born 25 November 1915. Son of late John Robert and Nellie Richardson; educated Nottingham High School; Gonville and Caius College, Cambridge (MA, LLB). Married January 18, 1941, Margaret Alison, elder daughter of late Very Rev. Hugh Richard Lawrie Sheppard, Canon and Precentor of St Paul's Cathedral (1 son 1 daughter). *Armed Forces:* Commissioned South Notts Hussars Yeomanry 1939; Staff College, Camberley 1941; Served until 1946. *Councils, Public Bodies:* One of HM Lieutenants, City of London 1974–; DL, Gloucestershire 1983–. *Career:* Called to the Bar, Gray's Inn 1946; Member, Bar Council 1951–55; With Industrial & Commercial Finance Corporation 1955–57; Director, J. Henry Schroder & Co Ltd 1957, Deputy Chairman 1960–62, Chairman 1962–72; Member, Company Law Amendment Committee 1959–62; Chairman: Committee on Turnover Taxation 1963–64, Schroders Ltd 1966–73; Director, Bank of England 1967–83, Governor 1973–83; Chairman, Schroders Incorporated 1968–73; Member, NEDC 1971–73, 1980–83; Chairman, Industrial Development Advisory Board 1972–73; Director, Bank for International Settlements 1973–93, Vice-Chairman 1985–88, 1991–93; Member, Morgan Stanley Advisory Board 1984–; Chairman, Group of Thirty 1985–91, Honorary Chairman 1991–; Chairman, Morgan Stanley International Incorporated 1986–95; Chairman, International Advisory Board Chemical Bank, New York 1986–96; Vice-Chairman, The Chase Manhattan Corporation International Advisory Council 1996–98, Chairman Emeritus 1998–. *Other:* High Steward, Westminster Cathedral 1985–89; Deputy High Steward, University of Cambridge 1982–. Hon. LLD, Cambridge; Hon. Fellow: Wolfson College, Cambridge, Gonville and Caius College, Cambridge; Hon. DSc: City University, Aston University; Hon. DCL, University of East Anglia. *Trusts, etc:* Trustee, Pilgrim Trust, Chairman 1984–89. *Miscellaneous:* Hon. Bencher, Gray's Inn. *Honours:* MBE 1944; PC 1976; TD 1979; KG 1983. Freeman, City of London 1975. Liveryman, Mercers' Company. *Clubs:* Brooks's, Pratt's. *Name, Style and Title:* Raised to the peerage as Baron Richardson of Duntisbourne, of Duntisbourne in the County of Gloucestershire 1983. *Address:* Rt Hon the Lord Richardson of Duntisbourne, KG, MBE, TD, DL, c/o Morgan Stanley UK Group, 25 Cabot Square, Canary Wharf, London, E14 4QA *E-Mail:* gordonlord.richardson@msdw.com; gillian.gaff@msdw.com.

LORD RIX   Cross-Bencher

RIX (Life Baron), Brian Norman Roger Rix; cr. 1992. Born 27 January 1924. Son of late Herbert and Fanny Rix; educated Bootham School, York. Married 1949, Elspet Jeans, daughter of late James MacGregor-Gray (Elspet Gray, actress) (2 sons 2 daughters). *Trades Union:* Life Member, British Actors' Equity Association. *Armed Forces:* Served in RAF and as Bevin Boy. *Councils, Public Bodies:* DL, Greater London 1987–88, 1997–, Vice-Lord-Lieutenant 1988–97. *Career:* Actor 1942–; Actor Manager 1947–77 (mostly at the Whitehall Theatre and Garrick Theatre, London). *Chancellor:* Chancellor, University of East London. *Select Committees:* Former Co-opted Member, Select Committee on European Communities Member, Sub-Committee F (Social Affairs, Education and Home Affairs) 1997–. *Other:* Chairman, Friends of Normansfield 1973–;

Secretary-General, MENCAP (Royal Society for Mentally Handicapped Children and Adults) 1980–87, Chairman 1988–98, President 1998–; Founder and Governor, Mencap City Foundation 1984, Chairman 1988–; Chairman: Libertas Group of Charities 1988–, Mencap City Insurance Services (now MCIS Ltd) 1993–; Life Vice-President, Radio Society of Great Britain. *Awards Granted:* Evian Health Award 1988; RNID Communicator of the Year Award 1990; *The Spectator* Campaigner of the Year Award 1999. Eight honorary degrees and fellowships. *Trusts, etc:* Chairman, Family Charities Ethical Trust Advisory Panel 1994–. *Miscellaneous:* Member, Arts Council 1986–93; Chairman: Drama Panel 1986–93, Monitoring Committee, Arts and Disabled People 1988–93, Independent Development Council for People with Mental Handicap 1981–86. *Honours:* CBE 1977; Kt 1986. Hon. FRSM, Hon. FRCPsch. *Publications: My Farce from My Elbow* (autobiography) 1975; *Farce about Face* (autobiography) 1989; *Tour de Farce* (history of theatre touring) 1992; *Life in the Farce Lane*, 1995 (history of farce); Editor and Contributor, *Gullible's Travels* 1996. *Special Interests:* Arts, Disability, Theatre, Voluntary Sector, Charities, Cricket. *Recreations:* Cricket, amateur radio, gardening. *Sportsclubs:* Yorkshire County Cricket. *Clubs:* Garrick, MCC. *Name, Style and Title:* Raised to the peerage as Baron Rix, of Whitehall in the City of Westminster and of Hornsea in Yorkshire 1992. *Address:* The Lord Rix, CBE, DL, 8 Ellerton Road, Wimbledon Common, London, SW20 0EP *Tel:* 020 8879 7748.

LORD ROBERTS OF CONWY   Conservative

ROBERTS OF CONWY (Life Baron), (Ieuan) Wyn Pritchard Roberts; cr. 1997. Born 10 July 1930. Son of late Rev. Evan Pritchard Roberts; educated Beaumaris County School; Harrow School; University College, Oxford (MA). Married 1956, Enid Grace Williams (3 sons). *Armed Forces:* Intelligence Corps 1948–49. *Career:* Sub-Editor, *Liverpool Daily Post* 1952–54; News Assistant, BBC 1954–57; Executive: TWW Ltd 1957–68, Harlech TV Ltd 1968–69. *House of Commons:* MP (Conservative) for Conwy 1970–97; PPS to Secretary of State for Wales 1970–74; Parliamentary Under-Secretary of State, Welsh Office 1979–87; Minister of State, Welsh Office 1987–94. *Spokesman (Commons):* Conservative Spokesman on Welsh Affairs 1974–79. *Spokesman:* Front Bench Spokesman on Welsh Affairs 1997–. *International Bodies:* Life Member, CPA. *Party Groups (General):* President, Welsh Conservative Clubs. *Other:* Member, Royal National Eisteddfod Gorsedd of Bards; President, University of Wales College of Medicine. Hon. Fellow, University Colleges of Wales, Bangor and Aberystwyth. *Honours:* Knighted 1990; PC 1991. *Special Interests:* Education, Health, Training, Tourism, Small Businesses, Transport, Economics, Conservation. *Recreations:* Fishing, walking. *Clubs:* Savile, Cardiff and County (Cardiff). *Name, Style and Title:* Raised to the peerage as Baron Roberts of Conwy, of Talyfan in the County of Gwynedd 1997. *Address:* Rt Hon the Lord Roberts of Conwy, House of Lords, London, SW1A 0PW *E-Mail:* robertsw@parliament.uk.

LORD ROBERTSON OF PORT ELLEN   Cross-Bencher

ROBERTSON OF PORT ELLEN (Life Baron), George Islay MacNeill Robertson; cr. 1999. Born 12 April 1946. Son of George P. Robertson, Police Inspector, and late Marion Robertson; educated Dunoon Grammar School, Argyll; Dundee University (MA 1968). Married June 1, 1970, Sandra, daughter of James U. Wallace (2 sons 1 daughter). *Career:* Research Assistant, Tayside Study, Economics Group 1968–69; Scottish Organiser, GMWU 1969–78; Governor, Scottish Police College 1974–78; Board Member, Scottish Development Agency 1976–78; Secretary-General, North Atlantic Treaty Organisation (NATO) 1999–. *House of Commons:* MP (Lab) for Hamilton from By-election May 1978–1997, and for Hamilton South from May 1, 1997-August 24, 1999; PPS to Secretary of State for Social Services February-May 1979; Shadow Secretary of State for Scotland 1993–97; Secretary of State for Defence 1997–99. *Spokesman (Commons):* Opposition Front Bench Spokesman on: Scotland 1979–80, Defence 1980–81, Foreign and Commonwealth Affairs 1981–93, European and Community Affairs 1985–93. *Party Groups (Commons):* Chairman, Scottish Labour Party 1977–78. *House of Lords:* Secretary of State for Defence August-October 1999. *International Bodies (General):* Member, Steering Committee, British German Königswinter Committee 1985–92; Joint Vice-Chairman, British-American Parliamentary Group 1996–99. *Other:* Council, Royal Institute of International Affairs 1985–91; Vice-President, Raleigh International 1984–;

Chairman, Seatbelt Survivors Club; Governor, Ditchley Foundation 1990–; Council, British Executive Service Overseas 1991–97; Vice-Chairman, Westminster Foundation for Democracy 1992–94. Two honorary doctorates. *Trusts, etc:* Fellow, Industry and Parliament Trust. *Miscellaneous:* Vice-Chairman, British Council 1985–94. *Honours:* Commanders Cross of the Order of Merit (Federal Republic of Germany) 1991; PC 1997. FRSA, 1999. *Special Interests:* Foreign Affairs, Car Safety, Defence, Industrial Relations, Lighting, Scotland, European Union. *Recreations:* Photography, golf, reading. *Name, Style and Title:* Raised to the peerage as Baron Robertson of Port Ellen, of Islay in Argyll and Bute 1999. *Address:* Rt Hon the Lord Robertson of Port Ellen, House of Lords, London, SW1A 0PW.

BISHOP OF ROCHESTER — Non-Affiliated

ROCHESTER (106th Bishop of), Michael Nazir-Ali. Born 19 August 1949. Son of James and Patience Nazir-Ali; educated St Paul's School and St Patrick's College, Karachi; University of Karachi (BA Economics and Sociology 1970); Fitzwilliam College and Ridley Hall, Cambridge (MLitt 1976); St Edmund Hall, Oxford (BLitt 1974, MLitt 1981); Australian College of Theology, University of New South Wales (PhD) with Centre for World Religions, Harvard 1983. Married 1972, Valerie Cree (2 sons). *Career:* Assistant: Christ Church, Cambridge 1970–72, St Ebbe's, Oxford 1972–74; Burney Lecturer in Islam, Cambridge 1973–74; Assistant Curate, Holy Sepulchre Cambridge 1974–76; Tutorial Supervisor in Theology, University of Cambridge 1974–76; Tutor, then Senior Tutor, Karachi Theological College 1976–81; Associate Priest, Holy Trinity Cathedral, Karachi 1976–79; Priest-in-Charge, St Andrew's, Akhtar Colony, Karachi 1979–81; Provost of Lahore Cathedral 1981–84; Bishop of Raiwind, Pakistan 1984–86; Assistant to Archbishop of Canterbury, Co-ordinator of Studies and Editor for the Lambeth Conference 1986–89; Director-in-Residence, Oxford Centre for Mission Studies 1986–89; Member, Board of Christian Aid 1987–96; Secretary, Archbishop's Commission on Communion and Women in the Episcopate (Eames' Commission) 1988–; General Secretary, Church Missionary Society 1989–94; Member, Anglican-Roman Catholic International Commission 1991–; Member, Board of Mission of the General Synod of the Church of England 1991–; Chairman, Church of England Mission Theology Advisory Group 1992–; Canon Theologian, Leicester Cathedral 1992–94; Bishop of Rochester 1994–; Visiting Professor, University of Greenwich 1996–; Took his seat in the House of Lords 1999; Chairman, Trinity College, Bristol. *International Bodies (General):* World Council of Chruches. *Awards Granted:* Oxford Society Award for Graduate Studies 1972–73; Cambridge Burnley Award 1974–75. Fellow, St Edmund Hall, Oxford 1998–. *Trusts, etc:* Trustee: Traidcraft 1986–89, Mission Enterprise–1994, Trinity College Bristol 1996–, Church of England Newspaper 1998–; Adviser to: Diocesan Trust 1994–, Layton Rahimtoola Trust 1999–. *Miscellaneous:* Member, Human Fertilisation and Embryology Authority 1998–, Chairman, Ethics Committee 1998–. *Publications: Islam: a Christian perspective,* 1983; *Frontiers in Muslim-Christian Encounter,* 1987; *Martyrs and Magistrates: toleration and trial in Islam,* 1989; *From Everywhere to Everywhere: a World-View of Christian Mission,* 1990; *Mission and Dialogue,* 1995; *The Mystery of Faith,* 1995; *Citizens and Exiles: Christian Faith in a plural world,* 1998; Has edited various Lambeth Conference papers and reports as well as contributing articles for journals. *Special Interests:* Sufism, Middle Eastern History and Politics. *Recreations:* Cricket, hockey, detective novels, humour and poetry, writing fiction and poetry, table-tennis, Persian poetry. *Sportsclubs:* Kent Brothers. *Clubs:* Nikaean. *Address:* Rt Rev the Lord Bishop of Rochester, Bishopscourt, Rochester, Kent, ME1 1TS *Tel:* 01634 842721 *E-Mail:* bchaplain@clara.net; bishops.secretary@rochester.anglican.org.

LORD RODGER OF EARLSFERRY — Cross-Bencher

RODGER OF EARLSFERRY (Life Baron), Alan Ferguson Rodger; cr. 1992. Born 18 September 1944. Son of late Professor Thomas Ferguson Rodger and Jean Margaret Smith Chalmers; educated Kelvinside Academy, Glasgow; Glasgow University (MA, LLB); New College, Oxford (MA, DPhil, DCL). *Career:* Member, Faculty of Advocates 1974, Clerk of Faculty 1976–79; QC (Scot) 1985; Advocate Depute 1985–88; Home Advocate Depute 1986–88; Maccabaean Lecturer, British Academy 1991; Solicitor-General for Scotland 1989–92; A Senator of the College of Justice 1995–96; President of the Court of Session and Lord Justice General of Scotland 1996–. *House of Lords:* Lord Advocate 1992–95. *Other:* Hon. Member, Society of Public Teachers of Law.

Fellow, New College, Oxford 1970–72; Two honorary doctorates. *Miscellaneous:* Junior Research Fellow, Balliol College, Oxford 1969–70, Honorary Fellow 1999; Member, Mental Welfare Commission for Scotland 1981–84; Hon. Bencher, Lincoln's Inn 1992. *Honours:* PC 1992. FBA 1991; FRSE 1992. *Publications:* Author of several publications and articles on legal matters. *Recreations:* Walking. *Clubs:* Athenaeum. *Name, Style and Title:* Raised to the peerage as Baron Rodger of Earlsferry, of Earlsferry in the District of North East Fife 1992. *Address:* Rt Hon the Lord Rodger of Earlsferry, FBA, House of Lords, London, SW1A 0PW.

LORD RODGERS OF QUARRY BANK   Liberal Democrat

RODGERS OF QUARRY BANK (Life Baron), William Thomas Rodgers; cr. 1992. Born 28 October 1928. Son of William and Gertrude Rodgers, educated Sudley Road Council School; Quarry Bank High School, Liverpool; Magdalen College, Oxford. Married 1955, Silvia, daughter of Hirsch Szulman (3 daughters). *Armed Forces:* National Service 1947–48. *Councils, Public Bodies:* Borough Councillor, St Marylebone 1958–62. *Career:* General Secretary: The Fabian Society 1953–60, Publishing 1960–64, 1970–72; Director-General, Royal Institute of British Architects 1987–94; Chairman, Advertising Standards Authority 1995–. *House of Commons:* Contested (Labour) Bristol West 1957; MP (Labour) Stockton-on-Tees 1962–74; Parliamentary Under-Secretary of State: Department of Economic Affairs 1964–67, Foreign Office 1967–68; Leader, UK Delegation to the Council of Europe and WEU 1967–68; Minister of State: Board of Trade 1968–69, Treasury 1969–70; Chairman, Expenditure Committee on Trade and Industry 1971–74; MP (Labour) Teeside, Stockton 1974–81; Minister of State, Ministry of Defence 1974–76; Secretary of State for Transport 1976–79; Elected to Shadow Cabinet (Labour) 1979 and 1980; MP (SDP) Teeside, Stockton 1981–83; Contested: (SDP) Stockton North 1983, (SDP/Alliance) Milton Keynes 1987. *Spokesman (Commons):* Opposition (Shadow) Defence Secretary 1979–80. *Spokesman:* Liberal Democrat Spokesman on Home Office Affairs 1994–97. *Select Committees:* Former Member: Sub-Committee on Declaration and Registration of Interests, Select Committee on the Public Service. *Party Groups:* Leader, Liberal Democrat Peers 1998–. *Party Groups (General):* General Secretary, Fabian Society 1953–60; A joint founder, Social Democratic Party 1981, Vice-President 1982–87. *Honours:* PC 1975. Hon. FRIBA; Hon. FIStructE. *Publications: Hugh Gaitskell 1906–1963,* (editor) 1964; *The People into Parliament,* (jointly) 1966; *The Politics of Change,* 1982; *Government and Industry,* (editor) 1986; *Fourth Among Equals,* 2000. *Clubs:* Garrick. *Name, Style and Title:* Raised to the peerage as Baron Rodgers of Quarry Bank, of Kentish Town in the London Borough of Camden 1992. *Address:* Rt Hon the Lord Rodgers of Quarry Bank, 43 North Road, London, N6 4BE *Tel:* 020 8341 2434.

LORD ROGAN   Cross-Bencher

ROGAN (Life Baron), Dennis Robert David Rogan; cr. 1999. Born 30 June 1942. Son of late Robert Henderson Rogan; educated The Wallace High School; Belfast Institute of Technology; The Open University (BA). Married August 7, 1968, Lorna Elizabeth Colgan (2 sons). *Councils, Public Bodies:* Chairman, Lisburn Unit of Management Health Board 1984–85. *Career:* Moygashel Ltd 1960–69; William Ewart & Sons Ltd 1969–72; Lamont Holdings plc 1972–78; Dennis Rogan Assoc 1978–, currently Managing Director; Associated Processors Ltd 1985–, currently Chairman; Communications Ltd 1996–, currently Chairman; Northern Ireland Events Company 1996–, currently Director; Patron, The Somme Association 1999–. *Party Groups (General):* Chairman: Ulster Young Unionist Council 1968–69, South Belfast Constituency Association 1992–96, Ulster Unionist Party 1996–. *Special Interests:* Northern Ireland, Trade and Industry, Defence. *Recreations:* Rugby football, oriental carpets, gardening. *Clubs:* Ulster Reform, Belfast. *Name, Style and Title:* Raised to the peerage as Baron Rogan, of Lower Iveagh in the County of Down 1999. *Address:* The Lord Rogan, 31 Notting Hill, Malone Road, Belfast, BT9 5NS *Tel:* 028 9066 2468; House of Lords, London, SW1A 0PW.

LORD ROGERS OF RIVERSIDE   Labour

ROGERS OF RIVERSIDE (Life Baron), Richard George Rogers; cr. 1996. Born 23 July 1933. Son of Dada Geiringer and Nino Rogers; educated Architectural Association (AA Dipl); Yale University (MArch, Fulbright, Edward D. Stone and Yale Scholar); RIBA. Married 1st, 1961, Su Brumwell (3 sons); married 2nd, 1973, Ruth Elias (2 sons). *Career:* Team 4 1963–67; Richard & Su Rogers 1968–70; Piano + Rogers 1970–78; Visiting Professor to Yale and UCL 1978; Chairman, Richard Rogers Architects Ltd 1978–; Gave the BBC Reith Lectures entitled 'Cities for a Small Planet' 1995; Has been involved in masterplans for many city centres, including Shanghai, Berlin, Palma and London; Has designed buildings including: the Centre Georges Pompidou in Paris (with Renzo Piano), Lloyds of London, the European Court of Human Rights in Strasbourg, Kabuki-Cho Tower in Tokyo, Channel 4 Headquarters in London, Millennium Dome in Greenwich, Law Courts in Bordeaux, Lloyds Registry of Shipping in London; Current projects include: National Assembly of Wales, Cardiff; Barajas Airport, Madrid; Terminal 5, Heathrow Airport, London; Antwerp Law Courts. *Other:* Director, River Cafe; Member, United Nations Architects' Committee. *Awards Granted:* BSC Award 1975; RIBA Regional Awards (Commendation) 1975; Financial Times Industrial Architecture Award 1975, Architecture at Work Award (Commendation) 1983; Royal Gold Medal for Architecture 1985; Friend of Barcelona 1997; Thomas Jefferson Memorial Foundation Medal in Architecture 1999; Japan Art Association Praemium Imperiale Award for Architecture. Five honorary degrees from British and Czech universities. *Trusts, etc:* Chairman: Board of Trustees, Tate Gallery 1984–88, National Tenants Resource Centre 1991–, Architecture Foundation 1991–. *Miscellaneous:* Vice-Chairman, Arts Council of England 1994–96; Chairman, Government's Urban Task Force 1997–99. *Honours:* Kt 1991; Chevalier de la Legion d'Honneur (France); Officier des Arts et des Lettres 1995. Hon. Fellow: Royal Academy of Art, The Hague, American Institute of Architects, Tokyo Society of Architects and Building Engineers 1996; Fellow, Royal Society for the Arts 1996; Academician, International Academy of Architecture; Royal Academician, Royal Academy of London. *Publications: Richard Rogers + Architects,* 1985; *A + U: Richard Rogers 1978–88,* 1988; *Architecture: A Modern View,* 1990; (jointly) *A New London,* 1992; *Richard Rogers,* 1995; *Cities for a Small Planet,* 1997; *Towards an Urban Renaissance (Urban Task Force),* 1999; *Richard Rogers, Complete Works,* Vol 1, 1999; *Paying for an Urban Renaissance,* 2000. *Special Interests:* Sustainable Built Environment, Arts. *Recreations:* Friends, food, art, architecture, travel. *Name, Style and Title:* Raised to the peerage as Baron Rogers of Riverside, of Chelsea in the Royal Borough of Kensington and Chelsea 1996.*Address:* The Lord Rogers of Riverside, Thames Wharf, Rainville Road, London, W6 9HA *Tel:* 020 7385 1235 *Fax:* 020 7385 8409 *E-Mail:* jo.m@richardrogers.co.uk.

LORD ROLL OF IPSDEN   Cross-Bencher

ROLL OF IPSDEN (Life Baron), Eric Roll; cr. 1977. Born 1 December 1907. Son of late Mathias Roll, Banker; educated on the Continent; Birmingham University. Married 1934, Winifred Taylor (died 1998) (2 daughters). *Career:* Professor of Economics, University College, Hull 1935–46; Entered Civil Service 1941; Under-Secretary, Treasury 1948; Deputy Head, UK delegation to NATO 1952; Under-Secretary, Ministry of Agriculture, Fisheries and Food 1953–57; Executive Director, International Sugar Council 1957–59; Economic Minister and Head of UK Treasury delegation Washington and UK Executive Director International Monetary Fund and World Bank 1963–64; Permanent Under-Secretary of State, Department of Economic Affairs 1964–66; Hon. Chairman, Book Development Council 1967–; Director: Times Newspapers Ltd 1967–80, Bank of England 1968–77; Chairman (later Joint Chairman), S. G. Warburg & Co. Ltd 1974–86; Director, Times Newspapers Holdings Ltd 1980–83; President, S. G. Warburg Group plc 1986–95; Senior Advisor, UBS Warburg 1995–. *Chancellor:* Chancellor, Southampton University 1974–84. *Select Committees:* Former Member, Subcommittee A of Select Committee on European Community; Member, Select Committee on Monetary Policy of the Bank of England 1999–. Hon. DSc, Hull 1967; Hon. DSocSci, Birmingham 1967; Hon. LLD, Southampton 1974; Hon. Fellow, LSE. *Trusts, etc:* Chairman, Daiwa Anglo-Japanese Foundation. *Honours:* CMG 1947; CB 1956; KCMG 1962; Grosses Goldene Ehrenzeichen Mit Stern (Austria) 1979; First Class Order of the Dannebrog (Denmark) 1981; Officer Legion D'Honneur (France) 1984;

Order of the Sacred Treasure (First Class) (Japan) 1993; Grand Cross of the Order of Merit of the Republic of Italy 2000. *Publications: An Early Experiment in Industrial Organisation,* 1930; *Spotlight on Germany,* 1933; *About Money,* 1935; *Crowded Hours,* 1985; *A History of Economic Thought,* 1995 (fifth edition); *Where Did We Go Wrong?,* 1996; *Where Are We Going,* 2000. *Special Interests:* Economics, Finance. *Recreations:* Reading, music. *Clubs:* Brooks's. *Name, Style and Title:* Raised to the peerage as Baron Roll of Ipsden, of Ipsden in the County of Oxfordshire 1977. *Address:* The Lord Roll of Ipsden, KCMG, CB, UBS Warburg, 1 Finsbury Avenue, London, EC2M 2PP *E-Mail:* lorderic.roll@ubsw.com.

LORD ROPER — Liberal Democrat

ROPER (Life Baron), John Francis Hodgkess Roper; cr. 2000. Born 10 September 1935. Son of late Rev. Frederick Mabor Hodgkess Roper, and of Ellen Frances Roper; educated William Hulme's Grammar School, Manchester; Reading School; Magdalen College, Oxford; University of Chicago. Married 1959, Valerie Hope Edwards (1 daughter). *Armed Forces:* Commissioned RNVR (National Service) 1954–56. *Career:* Harkness Fellow, Commonwealth Fund 1959–61; Research Fellow in Economic Statistics, Manchester University 1961; Assistant Lecturer in Economics 1962–64, Lecturer 1964–70, Faculty Tutor 1968–70; Director: CWS 1969–74, Co-op Insurance Society 1973–74; RIIA: Editor of *International Affairs* 1983–88, Head of International Security Programme 1985–88 and 1989–90, Head of WEU Institute for Security Studies, Paris 1990–95; Visiting Professor, College of Europe, Bruges 1997–. *House of Commons:* Contested (Labour) High Peak, Derbyshire 1964 General Election; MP Farnworth 1970–83 (Labour and Co-operative 1970–81 and SDP 1981–83); PPS to Minister of State, Department of Industry 1978–79; Contested (SDP) Worsley 1983 General Election. *Spokesman (Commons):* Opposition Spokesman on Defence 1979–81. *International Bodies (General):* Council of Europe: Consultant 1965–6, Member, Consultative Assembly 1973–80, Chairman, Committee on Culture and Education 1979–80; President, General Council, UNA 1972–78; Member, WEU Assembly 1973–80; Chairman, Committee on Defence Questions and Armaments, WEU 1977–80. *Party Groups (General):* Hon. Treasurer, Fabian Society 1976–81; Chairman: Labour Committee for Europe 1976–80, GB/East Europe Centre 1987–90. *Other:* Vice-President, Manchester Statistical Society 1971–; Member, Council, Institute for Fiscal Studies 1975–90. *Trusts, etc:* Trustee, History of Parliament Trust 1974–84. *Publications: Towards Regional Co-operatives,* 1967; *The Teaching of Economics at University Level,* 1970; *The Future of British Defence Policy,* 1985; editor (with others) of publications on European Defence. *Clubs:* United Oxford and Cambridge University. *Name, Style and Title:* Raised to the peerage as Baron Roper, of Thorney Island in the City of Westminster 2000. *Address:* The Lord Roper, 21 Gladstone Court, 97 Regency Street, London, SW1P 4AL *Tel:* 020 7976 6220.

EARL OF ROSSLYN — Cross-Bencher

ROSSLYN (7th Earl of, UK), Peter St Clair-Erskine; cr. 1801; 7th Baron Loughborough (GB) 1795; 11th Bt of Alva (NS) 1666. Born 31 March 1958. Son of 6th Earl. Succeeded his father 1977; educated Eton; Bristol University. Married 1982, Helen Watters (2 sons 2 daughters). *Career:* Metropolitan Police 1980–. *House of Lords:* An elected hereditary peer 1999–. *Trusts, etc:* Trustee, Dunimarle Museum. *Recreations:* Church music, piano, opera. *Clubs:* White's. *Address:* The Earl of Rosslyn, House of Lords, London, SW1A 0PW.

ROTHERWICK (3rd Baron), (Herbert) Robin Cayzer; cr. 1939; 3rd Bt of Tylney (UK) 1924. Born 12 March 1954. Son of 2nd Baron. Succeeded his father 1996; educated Harrow; RMA, Sandhurst; Royal Agricultural College, Cirencester (Diploma in Agriculture). Married 1st, 1982, Sara Jane, only daughter of Robert James McAlpine (2 sons 1 daughter) (marriage dissolved 1994); married 2nd, June 21, 2000, Tania Jane, daughter of Christopher Fox. *Armed Forces:* Former Acting Captain, The Life Guards. *Career:* Aviation, Agriculture and Conservation. *House of Lords:* An elected hereditary peer 1999–. *International Bodies (General):* Council of Europe. *Other:* Member, Executive Committee of the Popular Flying Association; President, General Aviation Awareness Council. *Trusts, etc:* Industry and Parliamentary Trust. *Miscellaneous:* Heir presumptive to baronetcy of his kinsman Sir James Cayzer, 5th Bt of Gartmore. *Special Interests:* Defence, Aviation, Agriculture. *Recreations:* Aviation, equitation, conservation. *Clubs:* White's. *Address:* The Lord Rotherwick, Cornbury Park, Charlbury, Oxford, OX7 3EH *E-Mail:* rr@cpark.co.uk.

RUSSELL (5th Earl), Conrad Sebastian Robert Russell; cr. 1861; Viscount Amberley. Born 15 April 1937. Son of 3rd Earl, OM, FRS. Succeeded his half-brother 1987; educated Eton; Merton College, Oxford (BA 1958, MA 1962). Married 1962, Elizabeth Sanders (2 sons). *Career:* Bedford College, London University 1960–74: History lecturer 1960–74, Reader 1974–79; Professor of history, Yale University, USA 1979–84; Astor Professor of British history, University College, London 1984–89; Professor of history, King's College London 1990–. *House of Lords:* An elected hereditary peer 1999–. *Spokesman:* Liberal Democrat Spokesman on Social Security 1990–. *Awards Granted:* Highland Park/*Spectator.* Peer of the Year Award 1996. *Miscellaneous:* President of the Electoral Reform Society 1997–. FBA. *Publications: The Crisis of Parliaments: English History 1509–1660,* 1971; *Parliaments and English Politics 1621–1629,* 1979; *The Causes of the English Civil War,* 1990; *The Fall of the British Monarchies,* 1991; *An Intelligent Person's Guide to Liberalism,* 1999. *Address:* Professor the Earl Russell, FBA, Dept of History, King's College, Strand, London, WC2R 2LS.

RUSSELL-JOHNSTON (Life Baron), David Russell Russell-Johnston; cr. 1997. Born 28 July 1932. Son of late David Knox Johnston; educated Carbost Public School, Isle of Skye; Portree Secondary School, Skye; Edinburgh University (MA History); Moray House College of Education. Married 1967, Joan Graham, daughter of Donald Menzies (3 sons). *Armed Forces:* Commissioned service Intelligence Corps (National Service) 1958–59. *Career:* History Teacher, Liberton Secondary School Edinburgh 1961–63; Member, European Parliament 1973–75, 1976–79. *House of Commons:* MP (Liberal 1964–88, Liberal Democrat 1988–97) for Inverness 1964–83 and for Inverness, Nairn and Lochaber 1983–97. *Spokesman (Commons):* Liberal Spokesman on: Scotland 1985–87, Foreign and Commonwealth Affairs 1970–75, 1979–85, 1987–88, EEC 1986–88; Alliance Spokesman on Scotland and EEC affairs 1987–88; SLD Spokesman on Foreign and Commonwealth Affairs 1988–89; Liberal Democrat Spokesman on: European Community Affairs 1988, Europe Affairs and East-West relations 1989–94, Central and Eastern Europe 1994–97. *International Bodies (General):* Member, WEU and Representative to Council of Europe 1984–86, 1987–; President: Council of Europe Liberal, Democratic and Reform Group 1994–99, Sub-Committee on Youth and Sport 1992–94; Vice-President: European Liberal, Democratic and Reform Parties 1990–92, Liberal International 1994–; President, Committee on Culture and Education 1995–99; Vice-President, WEU Defence Committee; Vice Chairman: WEU Parliamentary and Public Relations Committee, WEU Liberal, Democratic and Reformers' Group; President, Parliamentary Assembly of the Council of Europe 1999–. *Party Groups (General):* President, Edinburgh University Liberal Club 1956–57, Vice-President 1960–61; Member, Scottish Liberal Party Executive 1961–; Research Assistant, Scottish Liberal Party 1963–64; Vice-Chairman, Scottish Liberal Party 1965–70, Chairman 1970–74, Leader 1974–88;

President, Scottish Liberal Democrats 1988–94; Deputy Leader: SLD 1988–89, Liberal Democrats 1989–92. *Other:* Member, Governing Body, Know How Fund for Poland; Vice-Chairman, Westminster Foundation for Democracy; Parliamentary Spokesman, Scottish National Federation for the Welfare of the Blind 1967–; Parliamentary Representative, RNIB 1977. *Trusts, etc:* Trustee, National Life Story Collection. *Miscellaneous:* Member, Royal Commission on Local Government in Scotland 1966–69. *Honours:* Knighted 1985. *Publications: Highland Development; To Be A Liberal; Scottish Liberal Party Speeches,* (2 vols). *Special Interests:* Foreign Affairs, Commonwealth, European Union, East-West Relations, Scottish Affairs, Human Rights, Blind People, Light Rail Transport. *Recreations:* Reading, photography, shinty (Vice-Chief, Camanachd Association 1987–90). *Name, Style and Title:* Raised to the peerage as Baron Russell-Johnston, of Minginish in Highland 1997. *Address:* The Lord Russell-Johnston, House of Lords, London, SW1A 0PW.

LORD RYDER OF EATON HASTINGS   Cross-Bencher

RYDER OF EATON HASTINGS (Life Baron), Sydney Thomas Franklin Ryder; cr. 1975. Born 16 September 1916. Son of late John Ryder; educated Ealing County Grammar School. Married 1950, Eileen Dodds (1 son 1 daughter). *Career:* Editor *Stock Exchange Gazette* 1950–60; Joint Managing Director 1960–61, Managing Director, Kelly Iliffe Holdings & Associated Press Ltd 1961–63; Director, IPC 1963–70; Chief Executive, Reed International 1963, Chairman and Chief Executive 1968–75; President, National Materials Handling Centre 1970–77; Board Member, British Gas Corporation 1973–78; Member, National Economic Development Council 1975–77; Chairman, National Enterprise Board 1975–77. *Other:* Vice-President, Royal Society for the Prevention of Accidents. Formerly Fellow and Deputy Chairman, British Institute of Management. *Name, Style and Title:* Raised to the peerage as Baron Ryder of Eaton Hastings, of Eaton Hastings in the County of Oxfordshire 1975. *Address:* The Lord Ryder of Eaton Hastings, Eaton House, Curly Hill, Ilkley, West Yorkshire.

BARONESS RYDER OF WARSAW   Cross-Bencher

RYDER OF WARSAW (Life Baroness), Sue Ryder; cr. 1979. Born 3 July 1923. Daughter of late Charles Ryder; educated Benenden School, Kent. Married April 5, 1959, Group-Captain Leonard Cheshire (died 1992) (1 son 1 daughter). *Armed Forces:* Served war of 1939–45 with FANY and Special Operations Executive. *Other:* Founder and Social Worker, Sue Ryder Foundation for the Sick and Disabled of all age groups; Co-founder, Ryder Cheshire Foundation; Founder, International Sue Ryder Foundation for the Relief of Suffering of all Age Groups. Seven honorary doctorates. *Trusts, etc:* President, Leonard Cheshire; Trustee: National Memorial Arboretum, The Depaul Trust. *Honours:* OBE 1957; Polonia Restituta (Poland) 1965; Medal of Yugoslav Flag with Gold Wreath and Diploma by Marshall Tito 1971; Golden Order of Merit – Polish People's Republic 1976; CMG 1976; Polish Order of the Smile 1981; Pro Ecclesia et Pontifice Award 1982; Commander's Cross of the Order of Polonia Restituta 1992; Order of Merit from the President of Poland 1992; Silver Cross of the Czech Parachutists 1996; Polish Humanitarian Award 1996; Ecclesiae Populoque Servitium Praestanti, awarded by Cardinal Glemp of Poland 1996. *Publications: And The Morrow Is Theirs,* 1975; *Child Of My Love,* 1986 (new edition 1997). *Special Interests:* Architecture, Building. *Recreations:* Listening to classical music while driving trucks and other vehicles. *Clubs:* SOE. *Name, Style and Title:* Raised to the peerage as Baroness Ryder of Warsaw, of Warsaw in Poland and of Cavendish in the County of Suffolk 1979. *Address:* The Baroness Ryder of Warsaw, CMG, OBE, PO Box 5259, Sue Ryder Home, Cavendish, Sudbury, Suffolk, CO10 8AN *Tel:* 01787 280653 *Fax:* 01787 280548.

LORD RYDER OF WENSUM — Conservative

RYDER OF WENSUM (Life Baron), Richard Ryder; cr. 1997. Born 4 February 1949. Son of Stephen Ryder, DL, farmer; educated Radley; Magdalene College, Cambridge. Married 1981, Caroline, MBE, daughter of late Sir David Stephens, KCB, CVO (1 daughter, 1 son deceased). *Career:* Former journalist; Partner in family business in Suffolk; Political Secretary to Rt Hon. Mrs Margaret Thatcher 1975–81; Chairman, Eastern Counties Radio 1997–. *House of Commons:* Contested Gateshead East February and October 1974; MP (Conservative) for Norfolk Mid 1983–97; Former PPS to Financial Secretary to the Treasury; PPS to Foreign Secretary 1983–86; Parliamentary Secretary, Ministry of Agriculture, Fisheries and Food 1988–89; Economic Secretary, HM Treasury 1989–90; Paymaster-General July-November 1990. *Whip (Commons):* Government Whip 1986–88; Government Chief Whip (Parliamentary Secretary to HM Treasury) 1990–95. *Other:* Former Vice-Chairman, Eastern Region Council for Sport and Recreation. *Honours:* OBE 1981; PC 1990. *Name, Style and Title:* Raised to the peerage as Baron Ryder of Wensum, of Wensum in the County of Norfolk 1997. *Address:* Rt Hon the Lord Ryder of Wensum, OBE, House of Lords, London, SW1A 0PW.

S

LORD SAATCHI — Conservative

SAATCHI (Life Baron), Maurice Saatchi; cr. 1996. Born 21 June 1946. Son of Nathan and Daisy Saatchi; educated London School of Economics (BSc Economics). Married 1984, Josephine Hart (1 son 1 step-son). *Career:* Co-Founder, Saatchi & Saatchi 1970, Chairman 1985–94; Partner, M & C Saatchi Agency 1995–. *Spokesman:* Opposition Spokesman for the Treasury 1999–. *Other:* Governor, London School of Economics; Council Member, Royal College of Art. *Name, Style and Title:* Raised to the peerage as Baron Saatchi, of Staplefield in the County of West Sussex 1996. *Address:* The Lord Saatchi, M & C Saatchi Agency, 36 Golden Square, London, W1R 4EE *Tel:* 020 7543 4500 *E-Mail:* maurices@mcsaatchi.com.

LORD SAINSBURY OF PRESTON CANDOVER — Conservative

SAINSBURY OF PRESTON CANDOVER (Life Baron), John Davan Sainsbury; cr. 1989. Born 2 November 1927. Son of late Lord Sainsbury (Life Peer); educated Stowe; Worcester College, Oxford. Married 1963, Anya Eltenton (2 sons 1 daughter). *Armed Forces:* Served Life Guards 1945–48. *Career:* Joined J. Sainsbury 1950 in buying departments, Director 1958, Vice-Chairman 1967, Chairman and Chief Executive 1969–92, President 1992–; Director, Royal Opera House, Covent Garden 1969–85, Chairman 1987–91; Director, The Economist 1972–80; Joint Hon. Treasurer, European Movement 1972–75; Member of Council, British Retail Consortium 1975–79, President 1993–97; President's Committee CBI 1982–84. *Other:* Governor, Royal Ballet School 1965–76, 1987–91; Chairman, Council of Friends of Covent Garden 1969–81; Chairman, Royal Ballet Governors 1995–, Governor 1987–; Chairman, Benesh Institute of Choreology 1986–87; Member, Contemporary Arts Society 1958–, Hon. Secretary 1965–71, Vice-Chairman 1971–74, Vice-President 1984; Associate, Victoria and Albert Museum 1976–85; President, Sparsholt College, Hampshire 1993–. *Awards Granted:* Awarded the Albert Medal, Royal Society of Arts 1989. Hon. Fellow, Worcester College, Oxford 1982; Hon. DSc Economics (London) 1985; Hon. DLitt, South Bank University 1992; Hon. LLD, Bristol University 1993. *Trusts, etc:* Director, Royal Opera House Trust 1974–84, 1987–; Chairman, Trustees of Dulwich Picture Gallery 1994–; Trustee: National Gallery 1976–83, Westminster Abbey Trust 1977–83, Tate Gallery 1982–83, Rhodes Trust 1984–98. *Honours:* Kt 1980; Honorary Bencher, Inner Temple 1985; KG 1992. Fellow, Institute of Grocery Distribution 1973–; Hon. FRIBA 1993. *Special Interests:* Commerce, Arts. *Clubs:* Garrick, Beefsteak. *Name, Style and Title:* Raised to the peerage as Baron Sainsbury of Preston Candover, of Preston Candover in the County of Hampshire 1989. *Address:* The Lord Sainsbury of Preston Candover, KG, Stamford House, Stamford Street, London, SE1 9LL *Tel:* 020 7695 6663 *E-Mail:* Offjds@tao.j-sainsbury.co.uk.

LORD SAINSBURY OF TURVILLE   Labour

SAINSBURY OF TURVILLE (Life Baron), David John Sainsbury; cr 1997. Born 24 October 1940. Son of late Sir Robert Sainsbury; educated King's College, Cambridge (BA); Columbia University, New York (MBA). Married 1973, Susan Carole Reid (3 daughters). *Career:* Joined J. Sainsbury plc 1963: Finance Director 1973–90, Deputy Chairman 1988–92, Chairman and Chief Executive 1992–98. *House of Lords:* Parliamentary Under-Secretary of State, Department of Trade and Industry (Minister for Science) 1998–. *Other:* Member, Committee of Review of the Post Office (Carter Committee) 1975–77; Member, Governing Body, London Business School 1985, Chairman 1991–98. Four honorary doctorates; Hon FFng 1994. *Trusts, etc:* Trustee, Social Democratic Party 1982–90. *Miscellaneous:* Visiting Fellow, Nuffield College, Oxford 1987–95. *Publications: Government and Industry: a new partnership*, 1981; Co-author *Wealth Creation and Jobs*, 1987. *Name, Style and Title:* Raised to the peerage as Baron Sainsbury of Turville, of Turville in the County of Buckinghamshire 1997. *Address:* The Lord Sainsbury of Turville, House of Lords, London, SW1A 0PW *Tel:* 020 7215 5624 *E-Mail:* tlo.sainsbury@tlo.dti.gov.uk.

BISHOP OF ST ALBANS   Non-Affiliated

ST ALBANS (Bishop of), Christopher William Herbert. Born 7 January 1944. Son of Walter Meredith Herbert and Hilda Lucy Dibben; educated Monmouth School; St David's College, Lampeter (BA); Bristol University (PGCE); Wells Theological College; currently studying for MPhil at Leicester University. Married 1968, Janet Elizabeth Turner (2 sons). *Career:* Assistant Curate, Tupsley, Hereford 1967–71; Assistant Master, Bishop's School, Hereford 1967–71; Diocese of Hereford: Adviser in Religious Education 1971–76, Director of Education 1976–81; Vicar, St Thomas on The Bourne, Farnham, Surrey 1981–90; Archdeacon of Dorking 1990–95; Director of Post Ordination Training, Diocese of Guildford 1984–90; Hon. Canon of Guildford 1990–95; Bishop of St Albans 1995–; Took his seat in the House of Lords 1999–. FRSA. *Publications: The New Creation*, 1971; *A Place to Dream*, 1976; *St Paul's: A Place to Dream*, 1981; *The Edge of Wonder*, 1981; *Listening to Children*, 1983; *On the Road*, 1984; *Be Thou My Vision*, 1985; *This Most Amazing Day*, 1986; *The Question of Jesus*, 1987; *Alive to God*, 1987; *Ways into Prayer*, 1987; *Help in your Bereavement*, 1988; *Prayers for Children*, 1993; *Pocket Prayers*, 1993; *The Prayer Garden*, 1994; *Words of Comfort*, 1994; *Pocket Prayers for Children*, 1999. *Special Interests:* Education, National Health Service (Hospital Chaplaincy). *Recreations:* Walking, cycling, gardening, reading, art history of fifteenth century northern Europe. *Address:* Rt Rev the Lord Bishop of St Albans, Abbey Gate House, St Albans, Hertfordshire, AL3 4HD *Tel:* 01727 853305.

LORD ST JOHN OF BLETSO   Cross-Bencher

ST JOHN OF BLETSO (21st Baron, E), Anthony Tudor St John; cr. 1558; 18th Bt of Bletso (E) 1660. Born 16 May 1957. Son of 20th Baron, TD. Succeeded his father 1978; educated Diocesan College, Cape Town; University of Cape Town (BSocSc 1977, BA (Law) 1979, BProc (Law) 1982, LLM (London University) 1983). Married September 16, 1994, Dr Helen Jane Westlake, daughter of Michael Westlake (2 sons 2 daughters). *Career:* Solicitor; Attorney in South Africa 1983–85; Oil Analyst/Stockbroker, County Natwest 1985–88; Consultant to Merrill Lynch 1988–; Chairman, Eurotrust International 1993–; Managing Director, Globix 1997–. *House of Lords:* An elected hereditary peer 1999–. *Select Committees:* Former Member, Select Committee on European Communities Sub-Committee A (Economic and Financial Affairs, Trade and External Relations) 1997–; Member, Library and Computers Sub-Committee 1998–2000. *International Bodies (General):* Chairman of Governing Board of Certification International. *Trusts, etc:* Trustee: TVE (Television for the Environment), TUSK, SAN Foundation. *Miscellaneous:* A Extra Lord in Waiting to HM The Queen 1999–. *Special Interests:* Foreign Affairs, Finance, Legal Affairs, Sport. *Recreations:* Ski-ing, golf, windsurfing, tennis. *Sportsclubs:* Wisley Golf. *Clubs:* Hurlingham. *Address:* The Lord St John of Bletso, House of Lords, London, SW1A 0PW; Woodlands, Llanishen, Nr Chepstow, Gwent, NP6 6QQ *E-Mail:* asj@enterprise.net.

LORD ST JOHN OF FAWSLEY — Conservative

ST JOHN OF FAWSLEY (Life Baron), Norman Anthony Francis St John-Stevas; cr. 1987. Born 18 May 1929. Son of late Stephen S. Stevas and late Kitty St John-O'Connor; educated Ratcliffe College, Leicester; Fitzwilliam College, Cambridge (MA Law 1950, Yorke Prize 1957) (President, Cambridge Union 1950); Christ Church, Oxford (BCL 1954); Yale University, USA (Blackstone and Harmsworth Scholar 1952). *Career:* An author and barrister; Called to the Bar, Middle Temple 1952; Tutored in jurisprudence: King's College, London, Christ Church and Merton, Oxford 1953–57; Political correspondent, *The Economist* 1959; Editor, *Dublin Review* 1961; Chairman, Royal Fine Arts Commission July 1985–; Master of Emmanuel College, Cambridge 1991–. *House of Commons:* Contested (Conservative) Dagenham General Election 1951; MP (Conservative) for Chelmsford 1964–87; Chancellor of the Duchy of Lancaster and Leader of the House of Commons 1979–1981. *Spokesman (Commons):* Conservative Spokesman on Education and the Arts 1975–79. Fellow, Yale Law School 1960. Fellow, Royal Society of Literature 1966.*Publications:* include *Obscenity and the Law*, 1956; *Walter Bagehot*, 1959; *Life, Death and the Law*, 1961; *The Right to Life*, 1963; *The Collected Works of Walter Bagehot*, in fifteen volumes 1965–86; *The Agonising Choice*, 1971. *Clubs:* Garrick, White's, Pratt's. *Name, Style and Title:* Raised to the peerage as Baron St John of Fawsley, of Preston Capes in the County of Northamptonshire 1987. *Address:* Rt Hon the Lord St John of Fawsley, The Old Rectory, Preston Capes, Daventry, Northamptonshire, NN11 6TE.

BISHOP OF SALISBURY — Non-Affiliated

SALISBURY (77th Bishop of), David Staffurth Stancliffe. Born 1 October 1942. Son of late Very Rev. Michael Staffurth Stancliffe; educated Westminster School; Trinity College, Oxford (MA); Cuddesdon Theological College. Married 1965, Sarah Loveday Smith (1 son 2 daughters). *Career:* Assistant Curate, St Bartholomew's, Armley, Leeds 1967–70; Chaplain to Clifton College, Bristol 1970–77; Canon Residentiary of Portsmouth Cathedral, Diocesan Director of Ordinands and Lay Ministry Adviser 1977–82; Provost of Portsmouth 1982–93; Member, General Synod 1985–; Member, Liturgical Commission 1986, Chairman 1993–; Member, Cathedral's Fabric Commission 1991–; Bishop of Salisbury 1993–; Took his seat in the House of Lords 1998. *Other:* President, Council of Marlborough College 1994–. DLitt, Portsmouth University 1993; Hon. Fellow, St Chad's College, Durham 2000. *Recreations:* Old music, Italy. *Address:* Rt Rev the Lord Bishop of Salisbury, South Canonry, 71 The Close, Salisbury, Wiltshire, SP1 2ER *Tel:* 01722 334031 *E-Mail:* dsarum@eluk.co.uk.

LADY SALTOUN OF ABERNETHY — Cross-Bencher

SALTOUN OF ABERNETHY (Lady, 20th in line, S), Flora Marjory Fraser; cr. 1445. Born 18 October 1930. Daughter of 19th Lord, MC. Succeeded her father 1979; educated St Mary's School, Wantage. Married October 6, 1956, Captain Alexander Ramsay of Mar, DL, only son of late Admiral Hon. Sir Alexander Ramsay, GCVO, KCB, DSO, and Lady Patricia Ramsay, CI (3 daughters). *House of Lords:* An elected hereditary peer 1999–. *Select Committees:* Member, House of Lords Offices Sub-Committee: Advisory Panel on Works of Art 2000–. *Awards Granted:* Cordon Bleu Diploma in Cookery 1950. *Miscellaneous:* Member, Standing Council of Scottish Chiefs; Chief of the Name of Fraser. *Special Interests:* Scottish Affairs, Defence. *Address:* The Lady Saltoun of Abernethy, House of Lords, London, SW1A 0PW.

Visit the Vacher Dod Website . . .
www.politicallinks.co.uk

LORD SANDBERG   Liberal Democrat

SANDBERG (Life Baron), Michael Graham Ruddock Sandberg; cr. 1997. Born 31 May 1927. Son of Gerald and Ethel Sandberg; educated St Edward's School, Oxford. Married 1954, Carmel Mary Donnelly (2 sons 2 daughters). *Armed Forces:* 6th Lancers (Indian Army) and First King's Dragoon Guards 1945. *Career:* Joined Hong Kong and Shanghai Banking Corporation 1949, Chairman 1977–86. *Select Committees:* Member, Select Committee on European Communities Sub-Committee B (Energy, Industry and Transport) 1999–. *International Bodies (General):* The Commonwealth Party Association; The British Council Associate Parliamentary Group; The Inter-Parliamentary Union British Group. *Other:* Member, Executive Council, Hong Kong 1978–86; Treasurer, University of Hong Kong 1977–86. Hon. LLD, Hong Kong 1984. *Honours:* OBE 1977; CBE 1982; Kt 1986. FCIB; FRSA 1983. Freeman, City of London. Liveryman, Clockmakers' Company. *Recreations:* Horse racing, bridge, cricket, horology. *Sportsclubs:* President, Surrey County Cricket Club 1988. *Clubs:* Cavalry and Guards, Portland, White's, MCC. *Name, Style and Title:* Raised to the peerage as Baron Sandberg, of Passfield in the County of Hampshire 1997. *Address:* The Lord Sandberg, CBE, 100 Piccadilly, London, W1V 9FN.

LORD SANDERSON OF BOWDEN   Conservative

SANDERSON OF BOWDEN (Life Baron), Charles Russell Sanderson; cr. 1985. Born 30 April 1933. Son of late Charles Plummer Sanderson; educated St Mary's School, Melrose; Glenalmond College; Bradford Technical College; Scottish College of Textiles. Married July 5, 1958, Elizabeth, daughter of late Donald Alfred Macaulay (1 son 2 daughters and 1 son deceased). *Armed Forces:* Commissioned Royal Signals 1952. *Councils, Public Bodies:* DL, Roxburgh, Ettrick and Lauderdale 1990–. *Career:* Partner, Charles P. Sanderson, Wool and Yarn Merchants 1958–87; Director: Johnston of Elgin 1980–87, Illingworth Morris 1982–87; Chairman: Edinburgh Financial Trust plc 1983–87; Director, Clydesdale Bank plc 1986–87, 1994–, Deputy Chairman 1996–99, Chairman 1999–; Chairman, Hawick Cashmere Co. 1991–; Director, Scottish Mortgage and Trust plc 1991–, Chairman 1993–; Director: Woolcombers plc 1992–95, Edinburgh Woollen Mills 1992–97, United Auctions Ltd 1992–99, Watson-Philip plc 1993–99, Morrison Construction 1995–. *House of Lords:* Minister of State, Scottish Office 1987–90. *Party Groups:* Vice-Chairman, Scottish Peers Association 1996, Chairman 1998–2000. *Party Groups (General):* President, Scottish Conservative and Unionist Association 1977–79; Vice-President, National Union of Conservative and Unionist Associations 1979–81; Chairman, National Union Executive Committee 1981–86; Chairman, Scottish Conservative Party 1990–93. *Other:* Chairman, Eildon Housing Association 1976–82; Member, Scottish Council of Independent Schools 1984–87; Chairman, Council of Glenalmond College 1994–2000; Member of Court, Napier University, Edinburgh 1994–. *Honours:* Kt 1981. Liveryman, The Worshipful Company of Framework Knitters. *Special Interests:* Industry, Textile Industry, Small Businesses, Scottish Affairs, Housing, Transport. *Recreations:* Golf, fishing. *Sportsclubs:* Hon. Company of Edinburgh Golfers. *Clubs:* Caledonian. *Name, Style and Title:* Raised to the peerage as Baron Sanderson of Bowden, of Melrose in the District of Ettrick and Lauderdale 1985. *Address:* The Lord Sanderson of Bowden, DL, Becketts Field, Bowden, Melrose, Borders, TD6 0ST *Tel:* 01835 822736; Office: The Square, Bowden, Melrose, Borders, TD6 0ST *Tel:* 01835 822271 *Fax:* 01835 823272.

EARL OF SANDWICH   Cross-Bencher

SANDWICH (11th Earl of, E), John Edward Hollister Montagu; cr. 1660; Viscount Hinchingbrooke and Baron Montagu. Born 11 April 1943. Son of Victor Montagu, 10th Earl, formerly Viscount Hinchingbrooke MP, who disclaimed the earldom and other honours for life on July 24, 1964 under the terms of the Peerage Act, 1963. Succeeded his father 1995; educated Eton; Trinity College, Cambridge (MA history and modern language Tripos); OU Course in European Studies 1973. Married July 1, 1968, (Susan) Caroline, daughter of late Canon Perceval Hayman (2 sons 1 daughter). *Trades Union:* Former member NUJ. *Career:* Assistant Editor, The Bodley Head 1966–68; Editor, India Tourism Development Corporation 1968–69; Christian Aid: Information Officer 1974–85, Research Officer 1985–86;

Joint owner/administrator, Mapperton Estate, Dorset 1982–; Consultant, CARE Britain 1987–93; Editor, Save the Children 1990–92. *House of Lords:* An elected hereditary peer 1999–. *Select Committees:* Member, Standing Orders (Private Bills) Committee 2000–. *Other:* Governor, Beaminster School, Dorset 1996–; Council, Anti-Slavery International 1997–; Vice-President, Worldaware 1997–; Board, Christian Aid 1999–. *Trusts, etc:* Managing Trustee, St Francis School, Dorset 1987–92; TSW Telethon Trustee 1987–93; Trustee, Britain-Afghanistan Trust 1994–98. *Miscellaneous:* President, Samuel Pepys Club. *Publications:* Author or Editor of: *The Book of the World,* 1971; *Prospects for Africa,* 1988; *Prospects for Africa's Children,* 1990; *Children at Crisis Point,* 1992; Co-author *Hinch: A Celebration,* 1997. *Special Interests:* Overseas Aid and Development, International Affairs, National Heritage. *Recreations:* Walking, tennis, sailing, ski-ing. *Address:* The Earl of Sandwich, House of Lords, London, SW1A 0PW.

LORD SAVILLE OF NEWDIGATE — Cross-Bencher

SAVILLE OF NEWDIGATE (Life Baron), Mark Oliver Saville; cr. 1997. Born 20 March 1936. Son of Kenneth and Olivia Saville; educated Rye Grammar School; Brasenose College, Oxford (BA, BCL). Married 1961, Jill Gray (2 sons). *Armed Forces:* Second Lieutenant, Royal Sussex Regiment 1954–56. *Career:* Oxford University 1956–60, Vinerian Scholar 1960; Called to the Bar, Middle Temple 1962, Bencher 1963; QC 1975; Judge of the High Court, Queen's Bench Division 1985–93; A Lord Justice of Appeal 1994–97; A Lord of Appeal in Ordinary 1997–. *Select Committees:* Member, Joint Select Committee on Consolidation of Bills 1998–. Hon. LLD, Guildhall University 1997; Hon. Fellow, Brasenose College, Oxford 1998. *Honours:* Kt 1985; PC 1994. *Recreations:* Sailing, flying. *Name, Style and Title:* Raised to the peerage as Baron Saville of Newdigate, of Newdigate in the County of Surrey 1997. *Address:* Rt Hon the Lord Saville of Newdigate, House of Lords, London, SW1A 0PW.

LORD SAWYER — Labour

SAWYER (Life Baron), Lawrence Sawyer; cr. 1998. Born 12 May 1943; educated Dodmire School; Wastbourne School; Darlington Technical School. *Trades Union:* Member, UNISON. *Career:* Engineering apprentice, Robert Stephenson and Hawthorne 1958–63; Engineering inspector, Lockhead Brakes, Leamington Spa 1963–65; Engineering inspection and work study officer, Cummins Engines, Darlington 1965–71; NUPE Officer 1971–75, Northern Regional Officer 1975–81, Deputy General Secretary, NUPE/UNISON 1981–94; General Secretary, The Labour Party 1994–98; Director: Reed Executive 1998–, Britannia Building Society 1999–; Chairman, Notting Hill Housing Association 1999–; Visiting Professor, Cranfield Business School 1999–; Business consultant. *Party Groups (General):* Labour Party: Member, National Executive 1982–94, 1998–, Party Chairman 1992; Chairman, Labour Home Policy Committee 1994–98. *Other:* Member: Post Office Advisory Board 1997–99, Nurses' and Midwives' Whitley Council 1997–99, NJIC for Low Paid Manual Workers 1997–99. *Miscellaneous:* Board Member, Investors in People UK 1999–. *Recreations:* Antiquarian book dealer and collector. *Clubs:* Royal Commonwealth Society, Royal Overseas League. *Name, Style and Title:* Raised to the peerage as Baron Sawyer, of Darlington in the County of Durham 1998. *Address:* The Lord Sawyer, House of Lords, London, SW1A 0PW.

LORD SCANLON — Labour

SCANLON (Life Baron), Hugh Parr Scanlon; cr. 1979. Born 26 October 1913. Son of late Hugh Scanlon; educated Stretford Elementary School; National Council of Labour Colleges (NCLC). Married 1943, Nora Markey (2 daughters). *Trades Union:* Divisional Organiser, AEU Manchester 1947–63, Member, Executive Council 1963–67; President, Amalgamated Union of Engineering Workers 1968–78; Member, TUC General Council 1968–78; President, European Metal Workers Federation 1974–78. Hon. DCL, Kent University 1988. *Miscellaneous:* Member, British Gas Corporation 1976–82; Chairman, Engineering Industry Training Board 1975–82. *Recreations:* Golf, gardening. *Name, Style and Title:* Raised to the peerage as Baron Scanlon, of Davyhulme in the County of Greater Manchester 1979. *Address:* The Lord Scanlon, 23 Seven Stones Drive, Broadstairs, Kent, CT10 1TW.

LORD SCARMAN Cross-Bencher

SCARMAN (Life Baron), Leslie George Scarman; cr. 1977. Born 29 July 1911. Son of late George Charles Scarman, Lloyds Underwriter; educated Radley College; Brasenose College, Oxford (BA mods and greats). Married 1947, Ruth, daughter of late Clement Wright, ICS (1 adopted son). *Armed Forces:* RAFVR 1940–45. *Career:* Called to the Bar, Middle Temple 1936; QC 1957; Judge of the High Court of Justice, Probate, Divorce and Admiralty Division 1961–72; Chairman, Law Commission 1965–72; Lord Justice of Appeal 1972–77; President, Senate of Inns of Court and Bar 1976–79; Lord of Appeal in Ordinary 1977–86. *Chancellor:* Chancellor, Warwick University 1977–89. *Other:* Member, Charter 88. 12 honorary law doctorates from British and German universities. *Honours:* OBE (Mil) 1944; Order of Battle Merit (Russia) 1945; Kt 1961; PC 1972. *Publications: English Law: The New Dimension,* 1974. *Special Interests:* Law Reform, Constitutional Reform, Homeless, Human Rights, Education. *Recreations:* History, music, walking. *Clubs:* Royal Air Force, RAC, Garrick. *Name, Style and Title:* Raised to the peerage as Baron Scarman, of Quatt in the county of Shropshire 1977. *Address:* Rt Hon the Lord Scarman, OBE, House of Lords, London, SW1A 0PW *Tel:* House of Lords 020 7219 3202.

BARONESS SCOTLAND OF ASTHAL Labour

SCOTLAND OF ASTHAL (Life Baroness), Patricia Janet Scotland; cr. 1997; educated London University (LLB). Married 1985, Richard Mawhinney (2 sons). *Career:* Called to the Bar, Middle Temple 1977; Member, Antigua Bar. *House of Lords:* Parliamentary Under-Secretary of State, Foreign and Commonwealth Office 1999–. *Miscellaneous:* Former Member, Commission for Racial Equality; Member, Millenium Commission 1994–. *Name, Style and Title:* Raised to the peerage as Baroness Scotland of Asthal, of Asthal in the County of Oxfordshire 1997. *Address:* The Baroness Scotland of Asthal, QC, 1 Gray's Inn Square, London, WC1R 5AG.

LORD SCOTT OF FOSCOTE Cross-Bencher

SCOTT OF FOSCOTE (Life Baron), Richard Rashleigh Folliott Scott; cr. 2000. Born 2 October 1934. Son of Lieutenant-Colonel C. W. F. Scott, 2/9th Gurkha Rifles and Katharine Scott; educated Michaelhouse College, Natal, South Africa; Cape Town University (BA); Trinity College, Cambridge (BA, LLB). Married 1959, Rima Elisa Ripoll (2 sons 2 daughters). *Career:* Called to the Bar, Inner Temple 1959, Bencher 1981; In practice, Chancery Bar 1960–83; QC 1975; Duchy and County Palatine of Lancaster: Attorney General 1980–83, Vice-Chancellor 1987–91; Chairman of the Bar 1982–83; Hon. Member: American Bar Association 1983, Canadian Bar Association 1983; Judge of the High Court of Justice, Chancery Division 1983–91; A Lord Justice of Appeal 1991–94; Inquiry into defence related exports to Iraq and related prosecutions 1992–96; Vice-Chancellor of the Supreme Court 1994–2000; Head of Civil Justice 1995–2000; A Lord of Appeal in Ordinary 2000–. Two Hon LLDs. *Honours:* Kt 1983; PC 1991. *Publications:* Articles in legal journals. *Recreations:* Tennis, bridge) hunting (foxhounds and bloodhounds). *Sportsclubs:* Vanderbilt Racquet. *Clubs:* Hawks (Cambridge). *Name, Style and Title:* Raised to the peerage as Baron Scott of Foscote, of Foscote in the County of Buckinghamshire 2000. *Address:* Rt Hon the Lord Scott of Foscote, House of Lords, London, SW1A 0PW.

BARONESS SCOTT OF NEEDHAM MARKET — Liberal Democrat

SCOTT OF NEEDHAM MARKET (Life Baroness), Rosalind Carol Scott; cr. 2000. Born 10 August 1957. Daughter of Kenneth Vincent and Carol Leadbeater; educated Whitby Grammar School; Kent School; University of East Anglia (BA). Married (1 son 1 daughter). *Councils, Public Bodies:* Councillor: Mid Suffolk District Council 1991–94, Suffolk County Council 1993–, former Vice-Chairman, Leader of the Liberal Democrat Group; Vice-Chairman, Transport Committee, Local Government Association. *International Bodies:* IPU. *International Bodies (General):* Member: EU Committee of the Regions, Council of European Municipalities and Regions, Congress of Local and Regional Authorities in Europe. *Trusts, etc:* Hon. President East Coast Sailing Trust; Patron MacClea Wheelchair Trust. *Special Interests:* Transport. *Recreations:* Walking, political biography. *Clubs:* Royal Commonwealth Society. *Name, Style and Title:* Raised to the peerage as Baroness Scott of Needham Market, of Needham Market in the County of Suffolk 2000. *Address:* The Baroness Scott of Needham Market, House of Lords, London, SW1A 0PW.

BARONESS SECCOMBE — Conservative

SECCOMBE (Life Baroness), Joan Anna Dalziel Seccombe; cr. 1991. Born 3 May 1930. Daughter of late Robert John Owen, and of Olive Barlow Owen; educated St Martin's, Solihull. Married July 15, 1950, Henry Laurence, son of late Herbert Stanley Seccombe (2 sons). *Councils, Public Bodies:* JP, Solihull 1968–2000, Chairman of Bench 1981–84; Councillor, West Midlands County Council 1977–81, Chairman, Trading Standards Committee 1979–81. *Whip:* An Opposition Whip: Environment 1997–2000; Education, Northern Ireland 1997–. *Select Committees:* Member, House of Lords Committees on: Offices 1992–94, 1998–, Broadcasting 1994–97, Personal Bills 1994–97; Member, Sub-Committees on: Administration and Works 1992–94, Finance and Staff 1994–97. *Party Groups (General):* Chairman, West Midlands Conservative Women's Committee 1975–78; Chairman, Conservative Women's National Committee 1981–84; Chairman, National Union of Conservative and Unionist Associations 1987–88, Vice-Chairman 1984–87, Member of Executive 1975–97; Chairman, Conservative Party Annual Conference, Blackpool 1987; Vice-Chairman, Conservative Party with special responsibility for Women 1987–97. *Other:* A Vice-President, Institute of Trading Standards Administration 1992–; Governor, Nuffield Hospitals 1988–, Deputy Chairman 1993–. *Trusts, etc:* Chairman, Trustees of Nuffield Hospitals Pension Scheme. *Miscellaneous:* Chairman, Lord Chancellor's Advisory Committee 1975–93; Member, Heart of England Tourist Board 1977–81, Chairman, Marketing Sub-committee 1979–81; Member, Women's National Commission 1984–90. *Honours:* DBE, 1984. *Special Interests:* Women's Issues, Family. *Recreations:* Golf, ski-ing, embroidery. *Sportsclubs:* President, St Enedoc Golf Club. *Name, Style and Title:* Raised to the peerage as Baroness Seccombe, of Kineton in the County of Warwickshire 1991. *Address:* The Baroness Seccombe, DBE, JP, Linden Cottage, The Green, Little Kineton, Warwickshire, CV35 0DJ *Tel:* 01926 640562 *Fax:* 01926 640308 *E-Mail:* seccombej@parliament.uk.

LORD SEFTON OF GARSTON — Labour

SEFTON OF GARSTON (Life Baron), William Henry Sefton; cr. 1978. Born 5 August 1915. Son of late George Sefton; educated Duncombe Road School, Liverpool. Married 1940, Phyllis Kerr. *Councils, Public Bodies:* Councillor, Liverpool City Council, Leader 1964; Chairman and Leader, Merseyside County Council 1974–77; Chairman, Runcorn Development Corporation 1974–81; Chairman, North West Economic Planning Council 1975–89. *Select Committees:* Member, House of Lords Select Committee on Relations between Central and Local Government 1995–96. *Name, Style and Title:* Raised to the peerage as Baron Sefton of Garston, of Garston in the County of Merseyside 1978. *Address:* The Lord Sefton of Garston, House of Lords, London, SW1A 0PW.

EARL OF SELBOURNE — Conservative

SELBORNE (4th Earl of, UK), John Roundell Palmer; cr. 1882; Viscount Wolmer; 4th Baron Selborne (UK) 1872. Born 24 March 1940. Son of Captain Viscount Wolmer (died on active service 1942), son of 3rd Earl, PC, CH. Succeeded his grandfather 1971; educated Eton; Christ Church, Oxford. Married 1969, Joanna Van Antwerp, daughter of Evan James (3 sons 1 daughter). *Councils, Public Bodies:* DL, Hampshire 1982. *Career:* Member, Apple and Pear Development Council 1969–73; Chairman: Hops Marketing Board 1978–82, Agricultural and Food Research Council 1982–89; Chairman, Joint Nature Conservation Committee 1991–97; Member, NEDC Food Sector Group 1991–92; Member, Royal Commission on Environmental Pollution 1993–98; Director: Lloyd's Bank Plc 1994–95, Lloyds TSB Group Plc 1995–. *Chancellor:* Chancellor, Southampton University 1996–. *House of Lords:* An elected hereditary peer 1999–. *Select Committees:* Chairman, Sub-Committee D, European Communities Select Committee 1991–93, and 1999–; Member, Select Committee on Science and Technology 1992–97, Chairman 1993–97; Co-opted Member, Select Committee on European Communities Sub-Committee (Environment, Public House and Consumer Protection) 1998; Member, Select Committees on: Science and Technology Sub-Committee I (Non-Food Crops) 1999, European Union 1999–. *Other:* President: Royal Agricultural Society of England 1987–88, Royal Institute of Public Health and Hygiene 1991–97; A Vice-President, Foundation for Science and Technology; President, Royal Geographical Society (with the Institute of British Geographers) 1997–2000. Five honorary doctorates. *Honours:* KBE 1987. FRS 1991. Master, Mercers' Company 1989. *Special Interests:* Science, Agriculture, Education, Conservation. *Clubs:* Brooks's, Farmers'. *Address:* The Earl of Selborne, KBE, FRS, DL, Temple Manor, Selborne, Alton, Hampshire, GU34 3LR.

LORD SELKIRK OF DOUGLAS — Conservative

SELKIRK OF DOUGLAS (Life Baron), James Alexander Douglas-Hamilton; cr. 1997. Born 31 July 1942. Son of 14th Duke of Hamilton and Brandon, KT, PC, GCVO, AFC, DL, and Lady Elizabeth Percy, OBE, DL, daughter of 8th Duke of Northumberland, KG, CBE, MVO; educated Eton; Balliol College, Oxford (MA Modern History) (Oxford Boxing Blue 1961, President, Oxford Union Society Summer 1964); Edinburgh University (LLB Scots Law). Married August 24, 1974, Hon. Susan Buchan, daughter of 2nd Baron Tweedsmuir, CBE, and late Baroness Tweedsmuir of Belhelvie, PC (4 sons including twins). *Armed Forces:* Captain, Cameronians RARO 1961–66; Captain, 2nd Btn Lowland Volunteers, TAVR 1971–73; Hon. Air Commodore No 2 (City of Edinburgh), Maritime Headquarters Unit 1994. *Councils, Public Bodies:* Councillor: Murrayfield-Cramond Ward 1972–74, Murrayfield District 1974. *Career:* Scots Advocate and Interim Procurator Fiscal Depute at Scottish Bar 1968–72; QC 1996. *House of Commons:* MP (Conservative) for Edinburgh West 1974–97; PPS to Rt Hon. Malcolm Rifkind: as Minister of State, Foreign Office 1983–85, as Secretary of State for Scotland 1986–87; Parliamentary Under-Secretary of State, Scottish Office: Minister for Home Affairs and Environment 1987–92, Minister for Education and Housing 1992–95; Minister of State (Minister for Health and Home Affairs) 1995–97. *Whip (Commons):* Scottish Conservative Whip 1976–79; Government Whip and Lord Commissioner of the Treasury 1979–81. *International Bodies (General):* President, International Rescue Corps 1995–. *Party Groups (General):* President, Oxford University Conservative Association Winter 1963. *Other:* Hon. President, Scottish Boxing Association 1975–98; President: Royal Commonweath Society in Scotland 1979–87, Scottish National Council, UN Association 1981–87. *Trusts, etc:* Trustee, Selkirk Charitable Trust. *Miscellaneous:* Disclaimed the Earldom of Selkirk, November 1994; Member, Royal Company of Archers, the Queen's Bodyguard for Scotland; Contested Edinburgh West constituency 1997, elected as a list MSP for the Region of Lothians since May 6, 1999 (contested the seat as Lord James Douglas-Hamilton); Scottish Parliament: Member, Parliamentary Bureau 1999–; Business Manager (Chief Whip of the Conservative Group) 1999–. *Honours:* PC 1996. *Publications:* Author of: *Motive for a Mission: The Story Behind Hess's Flight to Britain,* 1971; *The Air Battle for Malta: The Diaries of a Fighter Pilot,* 1981; *Roof of the World: Man's First Flight over Everest,* 1983; *The Truth About Rudolph Hess,* 1993. *Special Interests:* Foreign Affairs, Defence, Scottish Affairs, Law Reform, Conservation, Arts, Housing, Health, Education, Local Government, Environment, Heritage. *Recreations:* Golf, boxing, forestry, debating, history. *Clubs:* Pratt's, New (Edinburgh). *Name, Style and Title:* Raised to the peerage as Baron Selkirk of Douglas, of Cramond in the City of Edinburgh 1997. *Address:* Rt Hon the Lord Selkirk of Douglas, MSP, House of Lords, London, SW1A 0PW.

LORD SELSDON   Conservative

SELSDON (3rd Baron, UK), Malcolm McEacharn Mitchell-Thomson; cr. 1932; 4th Bt of Polmood (UK) 1900. Born 27 October 1937. Son of 2nd Baron, DSC. Succeeded his father 1963; educated Winchester College. Married 1st, 1965, Patricia Anne Smith (1 son) (divorced), married 2nd, 1995, Gabrielle Williams. *Armed Forces:* Served in the Royal Navy 1956–58, Sub-Lieutenant RNR. *Career:* Merchant Banker, Midland Bank Group, Public Finance Adviser 1979–90; Delegate, Council of Europe and Western European Union 1972–78; Member, British Overseas Trade Board 1983–86; Chairman, Committee for Middle East Trade (COMET) 1979–86; Member, East European Trade Council 1983–87. *House of Lords:* An elected hereditary peer 1999–. *Other:* President, British Exporters' Association 1992–. *Miscellaneous:* Chairman, Greater London and South East Council for Sport and Recreation 1977–83. *Special Interests:* Trade and Industry, Foreign Affairs, Defence, Economic Policy. *Recreations:* Ski-ing, sailing, tennis, lawn tennis. *Clubs:* MCC. *Address:* The Lord Selsdon, House of Lords, London, SW1A 0PW.

BARONESS SEROTA   Labour

SEROTA (Life Baroness), Beatrice Serota; cr. 1967. Born 15 October 1919. Daughter of Alexander Katz; educated John Howard School; London School of Economics (BSc Economics). Married December 27, 1942, Stanley Serota (1 son 1 daughter). *Councils, Public Bodies:* JP, Inner London Area; Councillor, Hampstead Borough Council 1945–49; Councillor, LCC for Brixton 1954–65, Chairman, Children's Committee 1958–65; Councillor, GLC for Lambeth 1964–67; Chief Whip (GLC) and Vice-Chairman, Inner London Education Committee 1964–67; Member: Longford Committee on Crime – a Challenge to us all 1964, Latey Committee on Age of Majority 1965–66, Seebohm Committee on Organization of the Local Authority Personal Social Services 1966–68. *Career:* Assistant Principal, Ministry of Fuel and Power 1941–46; Member: Advisory Council on Child Care and Central Training Council in Child Care 1958–68, Advisory Council on Treatment of Offenders 1960–64, Royal Commission on Penal System 1964–66; Member, Advisory Council on the Penal System 1966–78, Chairman 1976–78; Member, Community Relations Commission 1971–77; Founder Chairman, Commission for Local Administration in England, Local Commissioner for Greater London and the South-East (Local Government Ombudsman) 1974–82; Member, BBC Complaints Commission 1975–77; Governor, BBC 1977–82. *House of Lords:* Minister of State (Health), Department of Health and Social Security 1969–70; A Deputy Speaker, House of Lords 1985–; A Deputy Chairman of Committees 1985–; Principal Deputy Chairman of Committees 1986–92. *Whip:* Baroness-in-waiting (Government Whip) 1968–69. *Spokesman:* Opposition Spokesperson on Health 1970–73. *Select Committees:* Member, Select Committee on Sport and Leisure 1972–73; Chairman, House of Lords Select Committee on the European Communities 1986–92; Member, Select Committee on the Public Service 1996–97. Hon. DLitt, Loughborough; Hon. Fellow, LSE. *Honours:* DBE 1992. *Recreations:* Gardening, needlepoint, collecting shells. *Name, Style and Title:* Raised to the peerage as Baroness Serota, of Hampstead in Greater London 1967. *Address:* The Baroness Serota, DBE, The Coach House, 15 Lyndhurst Terrace, London, NW3 5QA.

LORD SEWEL   Labour

SEWEL (Life Baron), John Buttifant Sewel; cr. 1996. Born 15 January 1946. Son of late Leonard Sewel, and of Hilda Ivy Sewel; educated Hanson Boys' Grammar School, Bradford; Durham University (BA); University College of Wales, Swansea (MSc Economics); Aberdeen University (PhD). Married, 2nd, 1987, Leonora Mary Harding (1 son 1 daughter from previous marriage). *Councils, Public Bodies:* Councillor, Aberdeen City Council 1974–84, Leader 1977–80. *Career:* Aberdeen University 1969–: successively research fellow, lecturer, senior lecturer, Dean, Faculty of Economic and Social Sciences 1989–94, Vice-Principal and Dean, Faculty of Social Sciences and Law 1995–97, Professor and Vice Principal 1999–. *House of Lords:* Parliamentary Under-Secretary of State, Scottish Office (Minister for Agriculture, the Environment and Fisheries) 1997–99.

Spokesman: Opposition Spokesman on Scotland 1996–97. *Miscellaneous:* President, Convention of Scottish Local Authorities 1982–84; Member: Accounts Commission for Scotland 1987–97, Scottish Constitutional Commission 1994–95. *Publications:* Books and learned articles mainly on politics and development in Scotland. *Special Interests:* Scotland, Local Government, Public Finance. *Recreations:* Hill walking, skiing. *Name, Style and Title:* Raised to the peerage as Baron Sewel, of Gilcomstoun in the District of the City of Aberdeen 1996. *Address:* The Lord Sewel, CBE, Birklands, Raemoir, Banchory, Kincardineshire, AB31 3QU *Tel:* 01330 844545.

LORD SHARMAN   Liberal Democrat

SHARMAN (Life Baron), Colin Morven Sharman; cr. 1999. Born 19 February 1943. Son of Colonel Terence John Sharman; educated Bishops Wordsworth School, Salisbury, Wiltshire. Married 1966, Angela Timmins (1 son 1 daughter). *Career:* Qualified as a Chartered Accountant 1965; Peat Marwick Mitchell, later KPMG Peat Marwick, then KPMG 1966–99: Partner 1973, Senior Partner (National Marketing and Industry Groups) 1987–90, UK Senior Partner 1994–98, Chairman, KPMG International 1998–99; Director: UKAEA, AEA Technology; Chairman: Le Gavroche Ltd, Aegis Group Plc. *Select Committees:* Member, Europan Communities Committee Sub-Committee A (Economic and Financial Affairs, Trade and External Relations) 2000–. *Other:* Member: Council, CBI, Appeal Committee, Golden Jubilee Appeal, National Association of Almshouses, Industry Society. Hon. Doctorate, Cranfield School of Management 1998. *Miscellaneous:* Companion, British Institute of Management; Member: Council of the CBI, Industrial Society, Association of Business Sponsorship of the Arts, Advisory Board of the George Washington Institute for Management, Hon. Member, Securities Institute; Chairman: Audit Committee, DTI Foresight Crime Prevention Panel. *Honours:* OBE 1979. FCA; CIMgt. Liveryman, Company of Gunmakers 1992. *Recreations:* Shooting, sailing, opera, food and wine. *Sportsclubs:* Bembridge Sailing. *Clubs:* Flyfishers', Reform. *Name, Style and Title:* Raised to the peerage as Baron Sharman, of Redlynch in the County of Wiltshire 1999. *Address:* The Lord Sharman, OBE, KPMG, 8 Salisbury Square, London, EC4Y 8BB.

BARONESS SHARP OF GUILDFORD   Liberal Democrat

SHARP OF GUILDFORD (Life Baroness), Margaret Lucy Sharp; cr. 1998. Born 21 November 1938. Daughter of Osmund Hailstone and Sydney Mary Ellen Hailstone; educated Tonbridge Girls' Grammar School; Newnham College, Cambridge. Married March 24, 1962. *Trades Union:* Member, Association of University Teachers. *Career:* Assistant Principal, Board of Trade and Industry 1960–63; Lecturer, LSE 1964–72; Economic Advisor, NEDO 1977–81; Sussex University: Research Fellow 1981–84, Senior Research Fellow 1984–92, Director, ESRC Research Centre 1992–99, Visiting Fellow 2000–. *Spokesman:* Liberal Democrat Spokesman on: Higher Education 2000–, Education 2000–. *Select Committees:* Member, Select Committee on European Communities Sub Committee A (Economic and Financial Affairs, Trade and External Relations) 1998–. *International Bodies (General):* IPU. *Party Groups (General):* Founder Member: Social Democrat Party 1981, Liberal Democrats 1988; Member, Liberal Democrat Federal Policy Committee 1992–, Vice-Chair 1995–96, 1998–99. *Other:* Governor, Stoke Hill School, Guildford; Local Council Member, Guildford High School; Executive Committee Member, Save British Science 1988–97; Editorial Board Member, *Political Quarterly* 1987–97; Member: Charter 88, Howard League. *Trusts, etc:* Trustee, Nancy Seear Trust. *Miscellaneous:* Contested Guildford Constituency: for SDP/All 1983 and 1987, for Lib Dems 1992 and 1997. Fellow, Royal Economic Society. *Publications: The State, the Enterprise and the Individual,* 1974; Editor *Europe and the New Technologies,* 1985; Co-author *Managing Change in British Industry,* 1986; Co-editor *Strategies for New Technologies,* 1987; *Technology and the Future of Europe,* 1992; Co-author *Technology Policy in the European Union,* 1998; plus numerous articles, book chapters etc in learned journals on issues relating to science and technology policy. *Special Interests:* Economic Policy, Industrial Issues, Science and Technology, Higher Education. *Recreations:* Reading, walking, theatre and concert going. *Name, Style and Title:* Raised to the peerage as Baroness Sharp of Guildford, of Guildford in the County of Surrey 1998. *Address:* The Baroness Sharp of Guildford, House of Lords, London, SW1A 0PW *E-Mail:* m.l.sharp@sussex.ac.uk.

BARONESS SHARPLES   Conservative

SHARPLES (Life Baroness), Pamela Sharples; cr. 1973. Born 11 February 1923. Daughter of late Lieutenant-Commander K. W. Newall, RN (Retired); educated Southover Manor, Lewes; Florence. Married 1st, July 12, 1946, Major Richard C. Sharples, OBE, MC (later Sir Richard Sharples, KCMG, OBE, MC, Governor of Bermuda, assassinated 1973) (2 sons 2 daughters), married 2nd, August 13, 1977, Patrick D. de Laszlo (died 1980), married 3rd, December 24, 1983, Robert Douglas Swan (died 1995). *Armed Forces:* WAAF 1941–46. *Career:* Director, TVS 1982–93; A Former Publican. *Trusts, etc:* Member, Wessex Medical Trust 1997–2000. *Miscellaneous:* Member, Review Body on Armed Services Pay 1979–81. *Special Interests:* Small Businesses, Cheque-Book Journalism, Prisoners' Wives, Pet Quarantine. *Recreations:* Tennis, golf, walking, gardening, fishing. *Sportsclubs:* Royal Cape Golf, Rushmoor Golf. *Clubs:* Mid-Ocean Bermuda. *Name, Style and Title:* Raised to the peerage as Baroness Sharples, of Chawton in the County of Hampshire 1973.*Address:* The Baroness Sharples, Well Cottage, Higher Coombe, Shaftesbury, Dorset, SP7 9LR *Tel:* 01747 852971; 60 Westminster Gardens, London, SW1P 4JG *Tel:* 020 7821 1875.

LORD SHAW OF NORTHSTEAD   Conservative

SHAW OF NORTHSTEAD (Life Baron), Michael Norman Shaw; cr. 1994. Born 9 October 1920. Son of late Norman Shaw, FCA; educated Sedbergh. Married April 25, 1951, Joan Mary Louise, daughter of late Sir Alfred Mowat, DSO, OBE, MC, DL, 2nd and last Bt (3 sons). *Councils, Public Bodies:* JP, Dewsbury 1953; DL, West Yorkshire 1977. *Career:* Chartered Accountant; Member, UK Delegation to the European Parliament 1974–79. *House of Commons:* MP (Conservative) for: Brighouse and Spenborough 1960 (By-election)–1964, Scarborough and Whitby 1966–74, Scarborough 1974–92; PPS to: Minister of Labour 1962–63, Secretary of State for Trade and Industry 1970–72, Chancellor of the Duchy of Lancaster 1972–74. *Select Committees:* Co-opted Member, Select Committee on European Communities Sub-Committee A (Economic and Financial Affairs, Trade and External Relations) 1997–. *Honours:* Kt 1982. ACA 1945; FCA 1952. *Recreations:* Golf, opera, music. *Clubs:* Carlton. *Name, Style and Title:* Raised to the peerage as Baron Shaw of Northstead, of Liversedge in the County of West Yorkshire 1994.*Address:* The Lord Shaw of Northstead, DL, Duxbury Hall, Liversedge, West Yorkshire, WF15 7NR *Tel:* 01924 402270.

LORD SHAWCROSS   Cross-Bencher

SHAWCROSS (Life Baron), Hartley William Shawcross; cr. 1959. Born 4 February 1902. Son of late John Shawcross, MA; educated Dulwich College; Geneva University. Married 1st, May 24, 1929, Alberta Shyvers (died 1943), married 2nd, September 21, 1944, Joan Mather (died 1974) (2 sons 1 daughter). *Career:* Called to the Bar, Gray's Inn 1925; Bencher 1939; Chairman, Enemy Aliens' Tribunal 1939–40; QC 1939; Regional Commissioner 1940–45; Chief Prosecutor for UK before International Military Tribunal, Nuremberg 1945–46; Director: Shell Petroleum Co. 1958, Shell Transport and Trading Co. 1962–72; Recorder of Salford 1942–45; Chairman: General Council of the Bar 1952–57, Medical Research Council 1961–65, Royal Commission on the Press 1962, Upjohn Ltd 1967–76; Special Adviser, Morgan Guaranty Trust Co. of New York 1968–93; Former Director: EMI Ltd, Hawker-Siddeley Group Ltd, Caffyns Ltd, Morgan et Cie SA, Morgan et Cie International SA; Director, Times Newspapers Ltd 1968–74; Chairman: City Panel on Take Overs and Mergers 1968–80, Thames Television Ltd 1970–74, European Enterprises Development SA 1970–78, The Press Council 1974–78, London and Continental Bank Ltd 1970–80; Consultant to public companies. *House of Commons:* MP (Labour) for St Helens 1945–58; Attorney-General 1945–51; President, Board of Trade April-October 1951 with Cabinet rank. *Chancellor:* Chancellor, University of Sussex 1965–86. *Other:* Chairman of Governors, Dulwich College and Alleyn's School 1958–72; Member, Court of London University 1956–78; Chairman, International Chamber of Commerce Committee on Unethical Practices. Hon. LLD: Bristol, Liverpool, Sussex, Hull, Columbia USA, Michigan USA, Lehigh USA,

New Brunswick Canada, London 1978 Universities. *Honours:* Kt 1945; PC 1946; GBE 1974. Hon. Fellow: Royal College of Obstetricians and Gynaecologists 1978, Royal College of Surgeons 1980. *Publications: Life Sentence* (Autobiography), 1994. *Special Interests:* City, Foreign Affairs. *Recreations:* Sailing. *Clubs:* Pratt's, Garrick, Royal Yacht Squadron (Cowes). *Name, Style and Title:* Raised to the peerage as Baron Shawcross, of Friston in the County of Sussex 1959. *Address:* Rt Hon the Lord Shawcross, GBE, QC, Friston Place, East Dean, Nr Eastbourne, East Sussex, BN20 0AH *Tel:* 01323 422206; Office: 60 Victoria Embankment, London, EC4Y 0JP *Tel:* 020 7325 5127.

LORD SHEPHERD   Labour

SHEPHERD (2nd Baron, UK), Malcolm Newton Shepherd; cr. 1946; (Life) Baron Shepherd of Spalding 1999. Born 27 September 1918 Son of 1st Baron, PC. Succeeded his father 1954; educated Friends' School, Saffron Walden. Married November 15, 1941, Allison Redmond (died 1998) (2 sons). *Armed Forces:* Served as Lieutenant, RASC 1939–45 war in North Africa, Sicily and Italy. *Career:* Deputy Chairman, Sterling Group of Companies 1976–86; Director, Sun Hung Kai Securities 1977–86; Chairman, National Bus Co. 1979–84; President, Centre European De L'Enterprise Publique 1985–; Member of Council, European Security Forum 1990–; Chairman: Cheque Point International Ltd, Ceko Banka Cheque Point Prague. *House of Lords:* Minister of State for Foreign and Commonwealth Affairs 1967–70; Deputy Leader Opposition 1970–74; Lord Privy Seal and Leader of House of Lords 1974–76. *Whip:* Opposition Whip 1959–64; Opposition Chief Whip 1964; Government Chief Whip (Captain of the Gentlemen-at-Arms) 1964–67. *Select Committees:* Former Member, Select Committee Channel Tunnel; Chairman: Lords Select Committee on Procedure 1976, European Communities Sub-Committee on Energy and Transport Research 1986–90; Former Member: European Communities Sub-Committee A (Finance and Economics Affairs) 1990–97, Delegated Powers Scrutiny Committee, House of Lords. *International Bodies (General):* Member, NATO Party Conferences 1962–64. *Party Groups (General):* Deputy Leader, Labour Peers 1967–70. *Other:* President, Institute of Road Transport Engineers 1987–. *Miscellaneous:* Deputy Chairman, Erroll Committee Home Office Licencing Laws 1971–72; Chairman, Civil Service Pay Research Unit Board 1978–81; Chairman: Medical Research Council 1978–82, Packaging Council 1978–82. *Honours:* PC 1965. FCIT 1986; FIRTE 1986. *Recreations:* Golf. *Name, Style and Title:* Created a life peer as Baron Shepherd of Spalding, of Spalding in the County of Lincolnshire 1999. *Address:* Rt Hon the Lord Shepherd, 29 Kennington Palace Court, London, SE11 5UL.

LORD SHEPPARD OF DIDGEMERE   Conservative

SHEPPARD OF DIDGEMERE (Life Baron), Allen John George Sheppard; cr. 1994. Born 25 December 1932. Son of late John and Lily Sheppard; educated Ilford County School; London School of Economics (BSc Econ). Married 1st, 1959, Peggy Jones (marriage dissolved 1980), married 2nd, 1980, Mary Stewart. *Career:* Ford Motor Company 1958–68; Rootes/Chrysler 1968–71; British Leyland 1971–75; Grand Metropolitan plc 1975–96, Group Managing Director 1982–86, Chief Executive 1986–93, Chairman 1987–96; Chairman: UBM Group 1981–85, Mallinson-Denny Group 1985–87; Director, Meyer International plc 1989–92, Deputy Chairman 1992–94; Non-executive Director, Bowater plc 1994–95; Non-executive Chairman: Bright Reasons Group plc 1995–96, Group Trust plc 1994–, McBride plc 1995–, Unipart Group 1996–; Non-executive Chairman, GB Railways plc 1996–; Director, High-Point Rendel Group plc 1997–; Non-executive Chairman, Oneclicker plc 1999–; Director: Gladstone plc 1999–, Nyne plc 2000–. *Chancellor:* Chancellor, Middlesex University 2000–. *Party Groups (General):* Member, Board of Management, Conservative Party 1993–98. *Other:* Governor, London School of Economics 1989–; Deputy Chairman, International Business Leaders' Forum 1990–96; Chairman: Advisory Board, British-American Chamber of Commerce 1991–94, London First 1992–; Board of Governors, Blue Cross; Vice-President: United Response, Brewers and Licensed Retailers Association, Business in the Community; Board Member: Central London Partnership, East London Business Alliance, London Business Board. *Awards Granted:* Institute of Management Gold Medal 1993; Marketing Society International Hall of Fame Award 1994; British-American Chamber of Commerce Trans-Atlantic Business Award 1995. Six honorary doctorates.

Trusts, etc: Chairman: Board of Trustees, Prince's Youth Business Trust 1990–94, Administrative Council, Prince of Wales' Trusts 1995–98; Executive Committee, Animal Health Trust. *Miscellaneous:* Part-time Member, British Rail Board 1985–90. *Honours:* Kt 1990; KCVO 1998. FCIM; FCMA; FCIS; ATII; FRSA. *Publications: Your Business Matters,* 1958; *Maximum Leadership,* 1995. *Recreations:* Gardens, reading, red setter dogs. *Clubs:* Athenaeum. *Name, Style and Title:* Raised to the peerage as Baron Sheppard of Didgemere, of Roydon in the County of Essex 1994. *Address:* The Lord Sheppard of Didgemere, KCVO, House of Lords, London, SW1A 0PW *E-Mail:* lord_allen_sheppard@unipart.co.uk.

LORD SHEPPARD OF LIVERPOOL   Labour

SHEPPARD OF LIVERPOOL (Life Baron), David Stuart Sheppard; cr. 1998. Born 6 March 1929. Son of late Stuart Morton Winter Sheppard and late Barbara Sheppard; educated Sherborne School; Trinity Hall, Cambridge (MA); Ridley Hall Theological College. Married 1957, Grace Isaac (1 daughter).*Armed Forces:* 2nd Lieut, Royal Sussex Regiment, National Service 1947–49. *Career:* Assistant Curate, St Mary's, Islington 1955–57; Warden, Mayflower Family Centre, Canning Town 1957–69; Chairman, Evangelical Urban Training Project 1968–75; Bishop Suffragan of Woolwich 1969–75; Chairman, Martin Luther King Foundation 1970–75; Bishop of Liverpool 1975–97; Chairman Area Manpower Board, Manpower Services Commission 1976–83; A Lord Spiritual 1980–97; National President, Family Service Units 1987–97; Chairman: Central Religious Advisory Committee for BBC and IBA 1989–93, General Synod Board for Social Responsibility 1991–96, Churches' Enquiry in to Unemployment and the Failure of Work 1995–97. Seven honorary doctorates. *Miscellaneous:* Cricket: Cambridge University 1950–52, Captain 1952, Sussex 1947–62, Captain 1953, England (played 22 times) 1950–63, Captain 1954. Freeman, City of Liverpool 1995 (jointly with late Archbishop Derek Worlock). *Publications: Parson's Pitch,* 1964; *Built as a City,* 1974; *Bias to the Poor,* 1983; Co-author: *Better Together,* 1988, *Christ in the Wilderness,* 1990, *With Hope in our Hearts,* 1994. *Special Interests:* Urban Policies, Race Relations, Unemployment, Future of Work, Youth Work. *Recreations:* Family, reading, music, painting, visiting gardens, following cricket. *Sportsclubs:* Vice-President: Sussex County Cricket Club, Lancashire County Cricket Club. *Clubs:* MCC. *Name, Style and Title:* Raised to the peerage as Baron Sheppard of Liverpool, of West Kirby in the County of Merseyside 1998. *Address:* Rt Rev the Lord Sheppard of Liverpool, Ambledown, 11 Melloncroft Drive, West Kirby, Merseyside, CH48 2JA.

LORD SHORE OF STEPNEY   Labour

SHORE OF STEPNEY (Life Baron), Peter David Shore; cr. 1997. Born 20 May 1924; educated Quarry Bank Grammar School, Liverpool; King's College, Cambridge. Married 1948, Elizabeth Catherine Wrong (Dr Elizabeth Catherine Shore, CB) (1 son 2 daughters, and 1 son deceased). *Trades Union:* Member, TGWU. *Armed Forces:* Flying Officer, RAF 1943–46. *Career:* Head of Research Department, Labour Party 1959–64. *House of Commons:* Contested (Labour): St Ives, Cornwall 1950, Halifax 1959; MP (Labour) for Stepney 1964–74, for Stepney and Poplar 1974–83, and for Bethnal Green and Stepney 1983–97; PPS to the Prime Minister 1965–1966; Joint Parliamentary Secretary, Ministry of Technology 1966–1967; Joint Parliamentary Under-Secretary, Department of Economic Affairs 1967; Secretary of State for Economic Affairs 1967–1969; Minister without Portfolio October 1969–70; Deputy Leader of the House of Commons 1969–70; Secretary of State for: Trade 1974–1976, The Environment 1976–1979; Shadow Leader of the House of Commons 1984–87. *Spokesman (Commons):* Member, Shadow Cabinet and Opposition Spokesman on Europe 1971–74; Principal Opposition Front Bench Spokesman on: Foreign and Commonwealth Affairs 1979–1980, Treasury and Economic Affairs 1980–83; Shadow Leader of the House and Opposition Front Bench Spokesman on Trade and Industry 1983–84. *Select Committees:* Member, Sub-Committee C of Select Committee on European Affairs 1999–. *International Bodies (General):* British/American Parliamentary Group Executive Committee; Chairman, British/Bangladesh. *Party Groups (General):* Joined Labour Party 1948; Member, Fabian Society; Chairman, Labour Euro-Safeguards Campaign. Hon. Fellow, Queen Mary and Westfield College London. *Honours:* PC 1967. Borough of Tower Hamlets 2000. *Publications: Entitled to Know,* 1966; *Leading the Left,* 1993; *Separate Ways: the Heart of Britain,* 2000. *Special Interests:* Europe (Anti-Federalist), Unemployment, Race Relations, Home Affairs, Middle East. *Recreations:* Reading, swimming, opera. *Name, Style and Title:* Raised to the peerage as Baron Shore of Stepney, of Stepney in the London Borough of Tower Hamlets 1997. *Address:* Rt Hon the Lord Shore of Stepney, 23 Dryburgh Road, London, SW15 1BN *Fax:* 020 8788 1071.

EARL OF SHREWSBURY AND WATERFORD   Cross-Bencher

SHREWSBURY (22nd Earl of, E), cr. 1442, AND WATERFORD (22nd Earl of, I), cr. 1446; Charles Henry John Benedict Crofton Chetwynd Chetwynd-Talbot; Earl Talbot and Viscount Ingestre (GB) 1784; Baron Talbot (GB) 1733. Born 18 December 1952. Son of 21st Earl. Succeeded his father 1980; educated Harrow. Married 1974, Deborah, daughter of Noel Hutchinson (2 sons 1 daughter). *Councils, Public Bodies:* DL, Staffordshire 1994–. *Career:* Landowner and Farmer; Joint Deputy Chairman, Britannia Building Society 1987–92; Director, Richmount Enterprise Zone Trust 1988–94; Chairman, Firearms Consultative Committee 1994–99; President and National Executive Director, British Institute of Innkeeping 1996–98; Director: PMI Limited 1996–98, Banafix Limited 1996–98, Minibusplus 1997–. *Chancellor:* Chancellor, Wolverhampton University 1993–99. *House of Lords:* An elected hereditary peer 1999–. *Other:* President, Building Societies Association 1993–97. Hon. LLD, Wolverhampton University 1994. *Miscellaneous:* Premier Earl on Rolls of both England and Ireland; Hereditary Lord High Steward of Ireland. Member: Worshipful Company of Blacksmiths, Worshipful Company of Weavers. *Special Interests:* Transport, Agriculture, Environment, Construction Industry, Property, West Midlands, Mineral Extraction. *Recreations:* Shooting, fishing. *Clubs:* Farmers'. *Address:* The Earl of Shrewsbury and Waterford, DL, Wanfield Hall, Kingstone, Uttoxeter, Staffordshire, ST14 8QT *Tel:* 01889 500275 *E-Mail:* shrewsburyestates@quista.net.

LORD SHUTT OF GREETLAND   Liberal Democrat

SHUTT OF GREETLAND (Life Baron), David Trevor Shutt; cr. 2000. Born 16 March 1942. Son of late Edward Angus Shutt and of Ruth Satterthwaite Shutt (née Berry); educated Pudsey Grammar School. Married June 12, 1965, Margaret (2 sons 1 daughter). *Councils, Public Bodies:* Mayor of Calderdale 1982–83 Member: Policy and Resources, Education, Town Planning and Environment Committees for several years, West Yorkshire Passenger Transport Authority 1987–90, Yorkshire Regional Assembly 1998–; Councillor, Calderdale MBC 1973–90, 1995–, Leader, Liberal Democrat Group 1979–82, 1995–2000. *Career:* Chartered Accountant; Articled clerk: Smithson Blackburn and Company, Leeds 1959–66, Bousfield Waite and Company, Halifax 1967–70; Partner, Bousfield Waite and Company, Halifax 1970–94; Consultant 1994; Former Director: Pluto Press Ltd, New Society Ltd, *New Society*, Statesman and Nation Publishing Company Ltd, *New Statesman*, Gerald Duckworth and Co. Ltd, Job Ownership Ltd, Bradford Community Radio *Pennine Radio*. *Other:* Chairman, Board of Governors, The Brooksbank School, Elland; Former Board Member, DEMOS. *Awards Granted:* Citoyen d'Honneur de la Ville de Riorges (France) 1983; Paul Harris Fellow 1999. *Trusts, etc:* Trustee: Joseph Rowntree Charitable Trust, The Irish Peace Institute, Joseph Rowntree Reform Trust Ltd; Treasurer, Institute for Citizenship Studies; Chairman and founder, Calderdale Community Foundation 1990–99. *Miscellaneous:* Contested Sowerby and later Calder Valley (Lib/Lib.All) 1970, Feb 1974, 1979, 1983, 1987, 1992 and Pudsey (LibDem) 1992. *Honours:* OBE 1992. FCA. Freeman, Metropolitan Borough of Calderdale 2000. *Publications:* A couple of pamphlets. *Special Interests:* Member of the Society of Friends (Quakers). *Recreations:* Travel, Transport. *Name, Style and Title:* Raised to the peerage as Baron Shutt of Greetland, of Greetland and Stainland in the County of West Yorkshire 2000. *Address:* The Lord Shutt of Greetland, OBE, FCA, 197 Saddleworth Road, Greetland, Halifax, HX4 8LZ *Tel:* 01422 375276 *Fax:* 01422 310707 *E-Mail:* shutt@jrrt.org.uk.

Visit the Vacher Dod Website . . .
www.politicallinks.co.uk

LORD SIEFF OF BRIMPTON   Conservative

SIEFF OF BRIMPTON (Life Baron), Marcus Joseph Sieff; cr. 1980. Born 2 July 1913. Son of late Baron Sieff (Life Baron); educated Manchester Grammar; St Paul's; Corpus Christi College, Cambridge (MA). Married 1st, 1937, Rosalie Fromson (1 son) (marriage dissolved 1947), married 2nd, 1951, Elsie Florence Gosen (marriage dissolved 1953), married 3rd, 1956, Brenda Mary Beith (1 daughter) (marriage dissolved 1962), married 4th, 1963, Mrs Pauline Lily Moretzki (died 1997), daughter of Friedrich Spatz (1 daughter). *Armed Forces:* Served with Royal Artillery 1939–45. *Career:* Joined Marks and Spencer plc 1935, Assistant Managing Director 1963, Vice-Chairman 1965, Joint Managing Director 1967, Deputy Chairman 1971, Chairman and Managing Director 1972–84, President 1984, Hon. President 1985; Chairman, First International Bank of Israel Financial Trust Ltd 1983–94. *Other:* President, Anglo-Israel Chamber of Commerce 1975. *Awards Granted:* Hambro Award, Businessman of the Year 1976. Five honorary doctorates. *Trusts, etc:* A Trustee, National Portrait Gallery 1986–92. *Miscellaneous:* Member, BNEC 1965–71, Chairman, Export Committee for Israel 1965–68. *Honours:* OBE (Mil) 1944; Kt 1971; Hon. Master, Bench of the Inner Temple 1987. Hon. FRCS 1984. *Name, Style and Title:* Raised to the peerage as Baron Sieff of Brimpton, of Brimpton in the Royal County of Berkshire 1980. *Address:* The Lord Sieff of Brimpton, OBE.

VISCOUNT SIMON   Labour

SIMON (3rd Viscount), Jan David Simon; cr. 1940. Born 20 July 1940. Son of 2nd Viscount, CMG. Succeeded his father 1993; educated Westminster School; School of Navigation, Southampton University; Sydney Technical College. Married 1969, Mary Elizabeth, daughter of late John J Burns, of Sydney, New South Wales (1 daughter). *House of Lords:* A Deputy Chairman of Committees 1998–; A Deputy Speaker 1999–; An elected hereditary peer 1999–. *Select Committees:* Member, Select Committees on: Dangerous Dogs (Amendment) Bill 1995–96, London Local Authorities Bill 1998, House of Lords Procedure 1999–. *Special Interests:* Disability, Motor Industry, Police, Road Safety, Science and Technology, Aviation. *Clubs:* Oriental. *Address:* The Viscount Simon, House of Lords, London, SW1A 0PW *E-Mail:* simonj@parliament.uk.

LORD SIMON OF GLAISDALE   Cross-Bencher

SIMON OF GLAISDALE (Life Baron), Jocelyn Edward Salis Simon; cr. 1971. Born 15 January 1911. Son of late Frank Cecil Simon; educated Gresham's School, Holt; Trinity Hall, Cambridge 1934. Married 1st, 1934, Gwendolen Helen Evans (died 1937), married 2nd, 1948, Fay Elizabeth Leicester, daughter of Brigadier H. G. A. Pearson (3 sons). *Armed Forces:* Served War World II; Commissioned Royal Tank Regiment 1939; Madagascar 1942 (despatches); Burma 1944. *Councils, Public Bodies:* DL, North Yorkshire 1973–. *Career:* Called to the Bar, Middle Temple 1934; Bencher 1958; KC 1951; President, Probate, Divorce and Admiralty Division of High Court of Justice 1962–71; Lord of Appeal in Ordinary 1971–77. *House of Commons:* MP (Conservative) for Middlesbrough West 1951–62; Joint Parliamentary Under-Secretary, Home Office 1957–58; Financial Secretary, HM Treasury 1958–59; Solicitor-General 1959–62. *Party Groups (Commons):* Member, One-Nation Group. *Select Committees:* Former Chairman, Joint Select Committee on Consolidation Bill. *Other:* Elder Brother, Trinity House. Docteur-en-Droit Hon, Laval University, Quebec; LLD Hon. Cambridge University. *Miscellaneous:* Member, Royal Commission on Law relating to Mental Illness and Mental Deficiency 1954–57. *Honours:* Kt 1959; PC 1961. *Publications: Change is our Ally* (part), 1954; *The Church and the Law of Nullity of Marriage* (part), 1955. *Name, Style and Title:* Raised to the peerage as Baron Simon of Glaisdale, of Glaisdale in the North Riding of the County of Yorkshire 1971. *Address:* Rt Hon the Lord Simon of Glaisdale, DL, House of Lords, London, SW1A 0PW.

LORD SIMON OF HIGHBURY   Labour

SIMON OF HIGHBURY (Life Baron), David Alec Gwyn Simon; cr. 1997. Born 24 July 1939. Son of late Roger Simon; educated Christ's Hospital, Horsham; Gonville and Caius College, Cambridge (MA Hons); INSEAD (MBA). Married 1st, 1964, Hanne Mohn (2 sons) (marriage dissolved 1987); married 2nd, 1992, Sarah Roderick Smith. *Career:* Joined The British Petroleum Co plc 1961; Marketing Co-ordinator, European Region 1975–80; Director, BP Oil UK and Chairman, National Benzole Company 1980–82; Managing Director, BP Oil International 1982–85; Managing Director 1986–95; Chief Operating Officer 1990–92; Deputy Chairman 1990–95; Chief Group Executive 1992–95; Chairman 1995–97; Non-executive Director, Grand Metropolitan plc 1989–97; Member, Advisory Board, Deutsche Bank 1991–97; Non-executive Director, RTZ Corporation plc 1995–97; Member: International Advisory Council, Allianz AG Holding 1993–97, Court of Bank of England 1995–97. *House of Lords:* Minister of State, at both the Treasury and Department of Trade and Industry (Minister for Trade and Competitiveness in Europe) 1997–99. *Spokesman:* Spokesman for Department of Trade and Industry 1997–99. Hon. DSc Economics, Hull 1990; Hon. DU, North London 1995; Hon. DSc Economics, Bath 1997. *Miscellaneous:* Member: Sports Council 1988–92, 1994–95, President's Committee, CBI 1992–97, European Round Table 1993–97, Vice-Chairman 1995–97, European Union Competitive Advisory Group 1995–97, International Council, INSEAD; Adviser, European Commission President 1999–. *Honours:* CBE 1991; Kt 1995. Liveryman: Tallow Chandlers, Carmen. *Recreations:* Golf, books, music. *Sportsclubs:* Highgate Golf, Royal West Norfolk Golf, Hunstanton Golf. *Clubs:* Brooks's, Athenaeum. *Name, Style and Title:* Raised to the peerage as Baron Simon of Highbury, of Canonbury in the London Borough of Islington 1997. *Address:* The Lord Simon of Highbury, CBE, House of Lords, London, SW1A 0PW.

LORD SIMPSON OF DUNKELD   Labour

SIMPSON OF DUNKELD (Life Baron), George Simpson; cr. 1997. Born 2 July 1942. Son of late William and Elizabeth Simpson; educated Morgan Academy, Dundee; Dundee Institute of Technology. Married 1964, Eva Chalmers (1 son 1 daughter). *Career:* Senior Accountant, Gas Industry, Scotland 1962–69; Central Audit Manager, British Leyland 1969–73; Financial Controller, Leyland Bus and Truck Division 1973–76; Director of Accounting, Leyland Cars 1976–78; Finance and Systems Director, Leyland Trucks 1978–80; Managing Director: Coventry Climax Ltd 1980–83, Freight Rover Ltd 1983–86; Chief Executive Officer, Leyland DAF 1986–88; Rover Group: Managing Director 1989–91, Chief Executive 1991–92, Chairman 1991–94; Deputy Chief Executive, British Aerospace 1992–94; Director 1990–94; Chairman, Ballast Nedam Construction Ltd 1992–94; Member, Supervisory Board and Non-Executive Director: Pilkington plc 1992–99, Northern Venture Capital 1992–, Pro Share 1992–94; Chairman, Arlington Securities 1993–94; Chief Executive, Lucas Industries plc 1994–96; Non-Executive Director, ICI plc 1995–; Chief Executive, General Electric Company plc (now Marconi plc) 1996–; Non-Executive Director, Nestlé SA 1999–; Industrial Professor at Warwick University; Governor, London Business School; Board of Institute for Manufacturing. *International Bodies (General):* Governor, Economic Forum; Member, European Round Table. *Other:* Member, Executive Committee, Society of Motor Manufacturers and Traders 1986–, Vice-President 1986–95, President 1995–96. Hon. Degrees: Warwick University, Abertay University, Aston University. ACIS; FCCA; FIMI; FCIT. Liveryman, Worshipful Company of Coachmakers. *Recreations:* Golf, squash, watching rugby. *Sportsclubs:* Royal Birkdale, Gleneagles Golf, New Zealand Golf, Kenilworth Rugby Football, Pine Valley Golf Club. *Name, Style and Title:* Raised to the peerage as Baron Simpson of Dunkeld, of Dunkeld in Perth and Kinross 1997. *Address:* The Lord Simpson of Dunkeld, Marconi plc, 1 Bruton Street, London, W1J 6AQ *Tel:* 020 7493 8484 *E-Mail:* lord.simpson@marconi.com.

LORD SKELMERSDALE — Conservative

SKELMERSDALE (7th Baron, UK), Roger Bootle-Wilbraham; cr. 1828. Born 2 April 1945. Son of Brigadier 6th Baron and late Ann Quilter. Succeeded his father 1973; educated Eton; Lord Wandsworth College, Odiham, Hampshire; Somerset Farm Institute; Hadlow College of Agriculture and Horticulture. Married February 5, 1972, Christine Joan Morgan (1 son 1 daughter). *Career:* Horticulturist; Managing Director, Broadleigh Nurseries Ltd 1973–81, Director 1991–; Parliamentary Affairs Adviser 1992–. *House of Lords:* Parliamentary Under-Secretary of State: Department of the Environment 1986–87, Department of Health and Social Security 1987–88, Department of Social Security 1988–89, Northern Ireland Office 1989–90; Deputy Chairman of Committees 1991–95, 1997–; Deputy Speaker 1994–; An elected hereditary peer 1999–. *Whip:* Government Whip 1981–86. *Spokesman:* Former Government Spokesman on: Environment, Transport, Foreign Affairs, Energy, Agriculture, Post Office. *Select Committees:* Member: Sub-Committee F of European Select Committee (Environment) 1975–81, Sub-Committee B European Energy Transport and Industry; Co-opted Member, Select Committee on European Communities Sub-Committee B (Energy, Industry and Transport) 1997–; Member, Joint Committee on Statutory Instruments 1998–. *Other:* Vice-Chairman, Co-En-Co (Council for Environmental Conservation) 1979–81; President, British Naturalists Association 1979–95; Governor, Castle School, Taunton 1992–96; Chairman of Council, The Stroke Association 1993–; President, Somerset Opera 1980–. *Trusts, etc:* President, Somerset Trust for Nature Conservation 1980–. Fellow, Linnaen Society. Liveryman, Worshipful Company of Gardeners. *Special Interests:* Horticulture, Post Office, Energy, Environment, Privatised Utilities. *Recreations:* Bridge, gardening, reading, walking. *Address:* The Lord Skelmersdale, House of Lords, London, SW1A 0PW *Tel:* House of Lords 020 7219 3224.

LORD SKIDELSKY — Conservative

SKIDELSKY (Life Baron), Robert Jacob Alexander Skidelsky; cr. 1991. Born 25 April 1939. Son of late Boris Skidelsky and Galia, née Sapelkin; educated Brighton College; Jesus College, Oxford (BA modern history 1961). Married 1970, Augusta, daughter of late Humphrey Hope and of Elisabeth Hope (2 sons 1 daughter). *Trades Union:* AUT. *Councils, Public Bodies:* Member: Lord Chancellor's Advisory Council on Public Records 1987–92, School Examinations and Assessment Council 1992–93. *Career:* Research Fellow, Nuffield College, Oxford 1965–68; Associate Professor, School of Advanced International Studies, Johns Hopkins University, Washington DC 1970–76; Head of the Department of History, Philosophy and European Studies, Polytechnic of North London 1976–78; Professor of International Studies, Warwick University 1978–90, Professor of Political Economy 1990–. *Spokesman:* Opposition Spokesman on: Culture, Media and Sport 1997–98, the Treasury 1998–99. *Select Committees:* Member, House of Lords Select Committees on: The European Communities 1991–94, Sustainable Development 1994–97. *International Bodies:* Member, Inter-Parliamentary Union. *Other:* Chairman: Social Market Foundation 1991–, Hands Off Reading Campaign 1994–97; Governor: Portsmouth University 1994–97, Brighton College 1998–. *Awards Granted:* Wolfson Prize for History 1992. Hon. DLitt, University of Buckingham; Hon. Fellow, Jesus College, Oxford 1997. *Trusts, etc:* Chairman, Charleston Trust 1987–92; Trustee: Humanitas 1991, Manhattan Institute 1993–, The Hon. Dorothy Burns Will Trust 2000–. Fellow: Royal Historical Society 1973, Royal Society of Literature 1978, British Academy 1994. Freeman, Knocksville, Tennessee, USA 1998. *Publications:* Include: *Politicians and the Slump*, 1967; *English Progressive Schools*, 1969; *Oswald Mosley*, 1975; *John Maynard Keynes*, Vol. 1, 1983, Vol. 2, 1992, Vol. 3, 2000; *The World After Communism*, 1995. *Special Interests:* Education, Economic Policy, Europe, Transition Economies, Hong Kong, Arts. *Recreations:* Opera, listening to music, tennis, table tennis, good conversation. *Clubs:* Grillion. *Name, Style and Title:* Raised to the peerage as Baron Skidelsky, of Tilton in the County of East Sussex 1991. *Address:* Professor the Lord Skidelsky, Tilton House, Firle, East Sussex, BN8 6LL.

VISCOUNT SLIM   Cross-Bencher

SLIM (2nd Viscount, UK), John Douglas Slim; cr. 1960. Born 20 July 1927. Son of Field Marshal 1st Viscount, KG, GCB, GCMG, GCVO, GBE, DSO, MC. Succeeded his father 1970; educated Prince of Wales Royal Indian Military College, Dehra Dun. Married July 18, 1958, Elisabeth, daughter of late Arthur Rawdon Spinney, CBE (2 sons 1 daughter). *Armed Forces:* Served: Indian Army 6th Gurkha Rifles 1944, Argyll and Sutherland Highlanders 1948, Special Air Service; Staff College Camberley 1961; Joint Services Staff College 1964; Retired from Army 1972. *Councils, Public Bodies:* DL, Greater London 1988. *Career:* Chairman, Peek plc 1976–91, Deputy Chairman 1991–; Director, Trailfinders Ltd, and other companies. *House of Lords:* An elected hereditary peer 1999–. *Select Committees:* Member, Select Committee on House of Lords' Offices 1997–99. *Other:* President, Burma Star Association 1971; Vice-President, Britain-Australia Society; Vice-Chairman, Arab-British Chamber of Commerce 1977–96. *Honours:* OBE (Mil) 1973. Fellow, Royal Geographical Society 1983. Master, The Clothworkers' Company 1995–96. *Clubs:* White's, Special Forces. *Address:* The Viscount Slim, OBE, DL, House of Lords, London, SW1A 0PW.

LORD SLYNN OF HADLEY   Cross-Bencher

SLYNN OF HADLEY (Life Baron), Gordon Slynn; cr. 1992. Born 17 February 1930. Son of late John Slynn and of Edith Slynn; educated Sandbach School, Cheshire; Goldsmiths' College; Trinity College, Cambridge (Senior Scholar, MA, LLM). Married 1962, Odile Marie Henriette Boutin. *Armed Forces:* Commissioned RAF 1951–54. *Career:* Called to the Bar, Gray's Inn 1956, Bencher 1970, Treasurer 1988; Junior Counsel, Ministry of Labour 1967–68; Junior Counsel to the Treasury (Common Law) 1968–74; Recorder of Hereford 1971; A Recorder and Hon. Recorder of Hereford 1972–76; QC 1974; Leading Counsel to the Treasury 1974–76; A Judge of the High Court of Justice, Queen's Bench Division 1976–81; President, Employment Appeal Tribunal 1978–81; An Advocate-General of the Court of Justice of the European Communities 1981–88, Visiting Professor in Law: University of Durham 1981–88, Cornell University 1983, King's College, London 1985–90, 1995–, National University of India 1992–; Judge 1988–91; A Lord of Appeal in Ordinary 1992–. *Select Committees:* Member, European Communities Select Committee 1992–97; Chairman: Sub-Committee E 1992–95, Select Committee on Public Service 1996–97. *International Bodies (General):* Chairman, Executive Council, International Law Association 1988–; Hon. Vice-President, Union Internationale des Avocats. *Other:* Visitor, Mansfield College, Oxford. 15 honorary doctorates from UK, Australia, India, Argentina, USA; two honorary fellowships. *Miscellaneous:* Deputy Chief Steward of Hereford 1977–78, Chief Steward 1978–. *Honours:* Kt 1976; PC 1992. FCIArb; FKC. Freeman, City of Hereford. Master, Broderers' Company 1994–95. *Publications:* Has contributed to *Halsbury's Laws of England* as well as lectures published in legal journals. *Clubs:* Beefsteak, Garrick, Athenaeum. *Name, Style and Title:* Raised to the peerage as Baron Slynn of Hadley, of Eggington in the County of Bedfordshire 1992. *Address:* Rt Hon the Lord Slynn of Hadley, House of Lords, London, SW1A 0PW.

LORD SMITH OF CLIFTON   Liberal Democrat

SMITH OF CLIFTON (Life Baron), Trevor Arthur Smith; cr. 1997. Born 14 June 1937. Son of late Arthur Smith, and of Vera Smith; educated Hounslow College; Chiswick Polytechnic; LSE (BSc Economics 1958). Married 1st, 1960, Brenda Eustace (2 sons) (marriage dissolved 1973); married 2nd, 1979, Julia Bullock (1 daughter). *Councils, Public Bodies:* Member, Tower Hamlets District Health Authority 1987–91; Non-Executive Director, North Yorkshire Regional Health Authority 2000–. *Career:* Schoolteacher, LCC 1958–59; Temporary Assistant Lecturer, Exeter University 1959–60; Research Officer, Acton Society Trust 1960–62; Lecturer in Politics, Hull University 1962–67; Visiting Associate Professor, California State University, Los Angeles 1969; Queen Mary College, later Queen Mary and Westfield College, London: Head of Department 1972–85, Dean of Social Studies 1979–82, Pro-Principal 1983–87, Lecturer, Senior Lecturer, Professor in Political

Studies 1983–91, Senior Pro-Principal 1987–89, Senior Vice-Principal 1989–91; Director: Job Ownership Ltd 1978–85, New Society Ltd 1986–88; Member, Senate, London University 1987–91; Director, Statesman and Nation Publishing Company Ltd 1988–90, Chairman 1990; Director, Gerald Duckworth & Co 1990–95; Vice-Chancellor and Hon. Professor, University of Ulster 1991–99; Visiting Professor of Politics, York 1999–, Portsmouth Universities 2000–. *Spokesman:* Liberal Democrat Spokesman on Northern Ireland 2000–. *Select Committees:* Science and Technology Sub-Committee on Complementary and Alternative Medicine 1999–2000. *Party Groups (General):* Member, Liberal Party Executive 1958–59. *Other:* Governor: St John Cass and Redcoats School 1979–94, University of Haifa 1985–91; Chairman, Political Studies Association of UK 1988–89, Vice-President 1989–91 and 1993–, President 1991–93; Vice-Chairman, Board of Governors, Princess Alexandra and Newnham College of Nursing and Midwifery 1990–91; Deputy President, Institute of Citizenship Studies 1992–; Member, UK Socrates Council 1993–99, Chairman 1996–99; Member: Administrative Board, International Association of Universities 1995–96, Editorial Board, Government and Opposition 1995–, Board, A Taste of Ulster 1996–99. Hon. LLD: Dublin 1992, Hull 1993, Belfast 1995, NUI 1996; Hon. DHL, Alabama 1998. *Trusts, etc:* Trustee, Joseph Rowntree Reform Trust 1975–, Chairman 1987–99; Trustee: Acton Society Trust 1975–87, Employment Institute 1987–92; President, Belfast Civic Trust 1995–99. *Honours:* Kt 1996. FRHistS; CIMgt (CBIM 1992); FICPD. *Publications:* Co-author: *Training Managers*, 1962, *Town Councillors*, 1964; *Town and County Hall*, 1966; *Anti-Politics: consensus and reform*, 1972; *The Politics of the Corporate Economy*, 1979; Co-author *The Fixers*, 1996; Various articles and papers, book reviews and broadcasts. *Special Interests:* Northern Ireland, Health, Transport (aircraft), Higher Education, Constitutional Reform. *Recreations:* Water colour painting. *Clubs:* Reform. *Name, Style and Title:* Raised to the peerage as Baron Smith of Clifton, of Mountsandel in the County of Londonderry 1997. *Address:* Professor the Lord Smith of Clifton, House of Lords, London, SW1A 0PW *Tel:* 020 7219 5353 *Fax:* 020 7219 5979 *E-Mail:* sirtas@cocoon.co.uk.

BARONESS SMITH OF GILMOREHILL — Labour

SMITH OF GILMOREHILL (Life Baroness), Elizabeth Margaret Smith; cr. 1995. Born 4 June 1940. Daughter of late Frederick William Moncrieff Bennett, and of late Elizabeth Waters Irvine Shanks; educated Hutchesons' Girls' Grammar School, Glasgow; Glasgow University (MA 1962). Married July 5, 1967, Rt Hon. John Smith, MP (died 1994), MP for Lanarkshire North 1970–83 and for Monklands East 1983–94, Leader of the Labour Party 1992–94 (3 daughters). *Councils, Public Bodies:* DL, City of Edinburgh 1996. *Career:* Chairman, Lamda Development Board; BP Advisory Board for Scotland; Non-executive director Deutsche Bank, Scotland. *Chancellor:* Chancellor, Birbeck College. *Spokesman:* Opposition Spokeswoman on National Heritage (Tourism) 1996–97. *Backbench Committees:* Member, Labour Party Departmental Committee for Foreign Affairs. *International Bodies:* Executive Committee Member, IPU British Group. *International Bodies (General):* Member: Britain-Russia Centre, British Association for Central and Eastern Europe. *Other:* Member: British Heart Foundation, English Speaking Union, Russo-British Chamber of Commerce, Centre for European Reform; President, Scottish Opera; Chairman, Edinburgh Festival Fringe; Board Member: Edinburgh International Festival –1999, BACEE; Council Member, Britain in Europe Campaign. Hon. LLD, University of Glasgow. *Trusts, etc:* Member: Future of Europe Trust, John Smith Memorial Trust, Know How Fund Advisory Board –1999; Trustee, Hakluyt Foundation. *Miscellaneous:* Member: Press Complaints Commission 1995–, BP Scottish Advisory Board. *Special Interests:* Arts, Russia, Former Soviet Union. *Name, Style and Title:* Raised to the peerage as Baroness Smith of Gilmorehill, of Gilmorehill in the District of the City of Glasgow, 1995. *Address:* The Baroness Smith of Gilmorehill, DL, House of Lords, London, SW1A 0PW.

LORD SMITH OF LEIGH Labour

SMITH OF LEIGH (Life Baron), Peter Richard Charles Smith; cr. 1999. Born 24 July 1945. Son of Ronald and Kathleen Smith; educated Bolton School; London School of Economics (BSc Economics 1967); Garnett College, London University (CertEd(FE) 1969); Salford University (MSc Urban Studies 1983). Married January 5, 1968, Joy Lesley, daughter of James and Dorothy Booth (1 daughter). *Trades Union:* Member, NATFHE. *Councils, Public Bodies:* Wigan Metropolitan Borough Council: Councillor 1978–, Chairman, Finance Committee 1982–91, Leader of Council 1991–. *Career:* Lecturer: Walbrook College, London 1969–74, Manchester College of Art and Technology 1974–91, part-time 1991–. *Miscellaneous.* Member: Association of Metropolitan Authorities Policy Committee 1991–97, Local Government Association Policy and Strategy Committee 1997–; Vice-Chair, Special Interest Group for Municipal Authorities 1997–; Member, Improvement and Development Agency 1999–; Chair: North West Regional Assembly 1999–2000, Association of Greater Manchester Authorities 2000–. *Special Interests:* Local Government, Regionalism, Airport Policy. *Recreations:* Gardening, sport, jazz. *Clubs:* Hindley Green Labour. *Name, Style and Title:* Raised to the peerage as Baron Smith of Leigh, of Wigan in the County of Greater Manchester 1999. *Address:* The Lord Smith of Leigh, Town Hall, Library Street, Wigan, WN1 1YN *Tel:* 01942 827001 *Fax:* 01942 827365; Mysevin, Old Hall Mill Lane, Atherton, Manchester, M46 0RG *Tel:* 01942 676127 *Fax:* 01942 676127 *E-Mail:* leader@wiganmbc.gov.uk.

EARL OF SNOWDON Cross-Bencher

SNOWDON (1st Earl of, UK), Antony Charles Robert Armstrong-Jones; cr. 1961; Viscount Linley; (Life) Baron Armstrong-Jones 1999. Born 7 March 1930. Son of late Ronald Owen Lloyd Armstrong-Jones, MBE, QC, DL, and late Anne, Countess of Rosse; educated Eton; Jesus College, Cambridge (architecture, 2 years, no degree). Married 1st, May 6, 1960, HRH The Princess Margaret, CI, GCVO (1 son 1 daughter) (marriage dissolved 1978), married 2nd, December 15, 1978, Mrs Lucy Lindsay-Hogg (1 daughter). *Trades Union:* Member, NUJ. *Career:* Constable of Caernarfon Castle, Wales 1963–; Artistic Adviser to the: *Sunday Times* and Sunday Times Publications Ltd 1962–90, *Daily Telegraph* Magazine 1990–95; Consultative Adviser to the Design Council, London 1962–87; Editorial Adviser to Design Magazine 1962–87; President for England, International Year for Disabled People 1981; Public Appearances 1991; Television Films: 'Don't Count the Candles' 1968 (2 Hollywood EMMY Awards); 'Love of a Kind' 1969; 'Born To Be Small' 1971 (Chicago Hugo Awards); 'Happy Being Happy' 1973; 'Mary Kingsley' 1975; 'Burke and Wills' 1975; 'Peter, Tina and Steve' 1977; 'Snowdon on Camera' (BAFTA nomination) 1981; Exhibitions: Photocall 1957, Assignments 1972, Serendipity 1989; Designer of: Snowdon Aviary for London Zoo 1965 (Listed Grade II* starred 1998), Mobile chair for disabled people (The Chairmobile) 1972. *Other:* President: Contemporary Art Society for Wales, Welsh Theatre Company; Member of Council, National Fund for Research into Crippling Diseases; Patron: National Youth Theatre 1962–87, Metropolitan Union of YMCAs, British Water Ski Federation, Welsh National Rowing Club, Physically Handicapped and Able Bodied, Circle of Guide Dog Owners; Started Snowdon award scheme for further education of disabled students 1981; Patron: Polio Plus 1988, British Disabled Water Ski Association; Provost, Royal College of Art. Hon. LLD: Bradford University 1989, Bath University 1989, Portsmouth University 1993. *Trusts, etc:* President, Civic Trust for Wales. *Miscellaneous:* Member, Prince of Wales Advisory Group on Disability. *Honours:* GCVO 1969. Senior Fellow, Royal College of Art 1986; Fellow: Manchester College of Art and Design; Chartered Society of Designers (London), Royal Photographic Society (London), Royal Society of Arts; FRSA, RDI. Liveryman, The Cloth Workers' Company. *Publications: Malta* (in collaboration with Sacheverell Sitwell) 1958; *London,* 1958; *Assignments,* 1972; *A View of Venice,* 1972; *Integrating the disabled -The Snowdon Report,* 1976; *Inchcape Review,* 1977; *Personal View,* 1979; *Private View* (in collaboration with John Russell and Bryan Robertson) 1965; *Pride of the Shires* (with John Oaksey) 1979; *Tasmania Essay,* 1981; *Sittings,* 1983; *Israel – A First View,* 1986; *My Wales* (with Viscount Tonypandy) 1986; *Stills,* 1987; *Personal Appearances,* 1992; *Wild Flowers,* 1995; *Snowdon On Stage,* 1996; *Wild Fruit,* 1997; *London Sight Unseen,* 1999. *Special Interests:* Art and Design. *Recreations:* Photography. *Sportsclubs:* Leander (Henley-on-Thames), Hawks. *Clubs:* Buck's. *Name, Style and Title:* Created a life peer as Baron Armstrong-Jones, of Nymans in the County of West Sussex 1999. *Address:* The Earl of Snowdon, GCVO, 22 Launceston Place, London, W8 5RL.

LORD SOULSBY OF SWAFFHAM PRIOR   Conservative

SOULSBY OF SWAFFHAM PRIOR (Life Baron), Ernest Jackson Lawson Soulsby; cr. 1990. Born 23 June 1926. Son of late William George Lawson Soulsby; educated Queen Elizabeth Grammar School, Penrith; Edinburgh University (MRCVS veterinary medicine 1948, DVSM 1949, PhD immunology 1952); Cambridge University (MA 1954). Married 1st 1950, Margaret Macdonald (1 son 1 daughter), married 2nd, 1962, Georgina Elizabeth Annette Williams. *Career:* Veterinary Officer, City of Edinburgh 1949–52; Lecturer in: Clinical Parasitology, Bristol University 1952–54, Animal Pathology, Cambridge University 1954–63; Professor of: Parasitology, University of Pennsylvania 1964–78, Animal Pathology, Cambridge University 1978–93, Emeritus Professor 1993–; Ford Foundation Visiting Professor, University of Ibadan 1964; Member, EEC Advisory Committee on Veterinary Training 1981–86; Expert Adviser to several UN Agencies and overseas governments 1963–; Member, Veterinary Advisory Committee Horserace Betting Levy Board 1984, Chairman 1985–98; Member, Agriculture and Food Research Council 1984–88; Chairman, Animal Research Grants Board 1986–89; Member, Home Office Animal Procedures Committee 1987–95; Chairman: Ethics Committee, British Veterinary Association 1994–, Companion Animal Welfare Council 1998–. *Select Committees:* Member: Sub-Committee F of European Communities 1990–92, Sub-Committee II, Select Committee for Science and Technology 1993–97, Select Committee for Science and Technology 1995–2000; Chairman, Sub-Committee I of Select Committee for Science and Technology 1997–98; Member, Sub-Committee I 1999–. *International Bodies (General):* Advisory, General Parasitology, World Health Organisation, Geneva; Trustee, Windward Islands Research and Education Funds 1999–. *Party Groups (General):* Member, Association of Conservative Peers. *Other:* Council Member, Royal College of Veterinary Surgeons 1978–92, President 1984, Senior Vice-President 1985; Hon. Member, Parasitology Societies in Germany, Mexico, Argentina, UK and USA; Corresponding Member, Academic Royale de Médicine de Belgique; President, Pet Advisory Committee 1996–; Patron: Veterinary Benevolent Fund, Fund for the Replacement of Animals in Medical Research; President, Royal Society of Medicine 1998–2000. *Awards Granted:* R. N. Chaudhury Gold Medal, Calcutta School of Tropical Medicine 1976; Behring-Bilharz Prize, Cairo 1977; Ludwig-Schunk Prize, Justus Liebig University, Germany 1979; Mussemmeir Medal, Humboldt University, Berlin 1991; Centaur Award 1999 (Brit. Vet. Assn). Hon. AM, University of Pennsylvania 1975; Hon. DSc, University of Pennsylvania 1984; Hon. DVMS, University of Edinburgh 1991; Hon. DVM, University of Leon 1993; Emeritus Fellow, Wolfson College, Cambridge 1993–; Hon. DSc, University of Peradeniya, Sri Lanka. *Miscellaneous:* Member, Home Office Committee of Inquiry into *Hunting with Dogs* 2000–. FRCVS; Hon. Fellow, Royal Society of Medicine 1996; Fellow, Institute Medical Sciences 1998. Freeman, City of London. Member, Worshipful Company of Farriers. *Publications:* Include: *Textbook of Veterinary Clinical Parasitology,* 1965; *Biology of Parasites,* 1966; *Reaction of the Host to Parasitism,* 1968; *Immune Response to Parasitic Infections,* 1987; *Zoonoses,* 1998; As well as other works, articles in journals of parasitology, immunology and pathology. *Special Interests:* Higher Education, Environment, Agriculture, Animal Welfare, Foreign Affairs. *Recreations:* Gardening, travel. *Clubs:* Farmers', United Oxford and Cambridge University. *Name, Style and Title:* Raised to the peerage as Baron Soulsby of Swaffham Prior, of Swaffham Prior in the County of Cambridgeshire 1990. *Address:* The Lord Soulsby of Swaffham Prior, House of Lords, London, SW1A 0PW.

BISHOP OF SOUTHWARK   Non-Affiliated

SOUTHWARK (9th Bishop of), Thomas Frederick Butler. Born 5 March 1940. Son of late Thomas and Elsie Butler; educated King Edward's Grammar School, Fiveways, Birmingham; Leeds University (BSc, MSc, PhD). Married 1964, Barbara Joan Clark (1 son 1 daughter). *Career:* College of the Resurrection, Mirfield 1962–64; Curate: St Augustine's, Wisbech 1964–66, St Saviour's, Folkestone 1966–68; Lecturer and Chaplain, University of Zambia 1968–73; Acting Dean of Holy Cross Cathedral, Lusaka, Zambia 1973; Chaplain to University of Kent at Canterbury 1973–80; Six Preacher, Canterbury Cathedral 1979–84; Archdeacon of Northolt 1980–85; Area Bishop of Willesden 1985–91; Bishop of Leicester 1991–98; Chairman, Board of Mission, General Synod of the Church of England 1995–; Took his seat in the House of Lords 1996;

Bishop of Southwark 1998–. *Select Committees:* Former Member, Select Committee on Science and Technology Sub-Committee on Digital Images as Evidence. Hon. LLD: Leicester University, De Montfort University; Hon. DSc, Loughborough University. *Publications:* Co-author: *Just Mission, Just Spirituality in a World of Faiths. Special Interests:* Science, Technology, Education, Development. *Recreations:* Reading, mountain walking, marathon running. *Address:* Rt Rev the Lord Bishop of Southwark, Bishop's House, 38 Tooting Bec Gardens, Streatham, London, SW16 1QZ *Tel:* 020 8769 3256 *Fax:* 020 8769 4126 *E-Mail:* bishops.house@dswark.org.uk.

LORD STALLARD   Labour

STALLARD (Life Baron), Albert William Stallard; cr. 1983. Born 5 November 1921. Son of late Frederick and Agnes Stallard, née Jupp; educated Low Waters School; Hamilton Academy. Married July 29, 1944, Julia Murphy (1 son 1 daughter). *Trades Union:* Member, AUEW (AUEW Order of Merit 1968). *Councils, Public Bodies:* Councillor, St Pancras 1953–59, Alderman 1962–65; Councillor, Camden 1965–71, Alderman 1971–78. *Career:* Precision Engineer 1937–65; Technical Training Officer 1965–70. *House of Commons:* MP (Labour) for: St Pancras North 1970–1974, St Pancras North division of Camden 1974–1983; PPS to: Minister of Agriculture 1974–75, Minister of Housing 1975–76. *Whip (Commons):* Assistant Government Whip 1976–78, Government Whip (Lord Commissioner HM Treasury) 1978–79. *Spokesman:* A former Opposition Front Bench Spokesman on Environment and on Social Security. *Other:* Vice-President, Camden Association for Mental Health; Chairman and Member, Camden Town Disablement Advisory Committee 1951–. *Miscellaneous:* Formerly Member, Institution of Training Officers. *Special Interests:* Education, Social Services, Health, Housing, Northern Ireland, Cyprus. *Recreations:* Photography, chess, reading. *Name, Style and Title:* Raised to the peerage as Baron Stallard, of St Pancras in the London Borough of Camden 1983. *Address:* The Lord Stallard, Flat 2, 2 Belmont Street, Chalk Farm Road, London, NW1 8HH; House of Lords, London, SW1A 0PW *Tel:* House of Lords 020 7219 3225.

LORD STEEL OF AIKWOOD   Liberal Democrat

STEEL OF AIKWOOD (Life Baron), David Martin Scott Steel; cr. 1997. Born 31 March 1938. Son of Very Rev. Dr David Steel, Moderator of the General Assembly of the Church of Scotland 1974–75; educated Prince of Wales School, Nairobi; George Watson's College; Edinburgh University (MA 1960, LLB 1962). Married October 26, 1962, Judith MacGregor (2 sons 1 daughter). *Councils, Public Bodies:* DL, Roxburgh, Ettrick and Lauderdale 1990. *Career:* Broadcaster; Journalist; President, Edinburgh University Students' Representative Council 1961; BBC Television interviewer in Scotland 1964–65; Rector, University of Edinburgh 1982–85. *House of Commons:* Contested (Liberal) Roxburgh, Selkirk and Peebles October 1964; MP (Liberal) for Roxburgh, Selkirk and Peebles 1965 By-election–83, and for Tweeddale, Ettrick and Lauderdale 1983–97 (as Liberal Democrat 1988–97); Sponsor, Abortion Act 1967. *Whip (Commons):* Liberal Chief Whip 1970–74. *Spokesman (Commons):* Liberal Democrat Convenor and Spokesman on Foreign Affairs and Overseas Development 1989–94. *Party Groups:* Deputy Leader, Liberal Democrat Peers 1997–99. *International Bodies (General):* President, Liberal International 1992–94. *Party Groups (General):* President, Edinburgh University Liberal Club 1960; Assistant Secretary, Scottish Liberal Party 1962–64; Leader, Liberal Party 1976–88; Joint Founder, Social and Liberal Democrats 1988. *Other:* Past President, Anti-Apartheid Movement in GB; Chairman, Scottish Advisory Council of Shelter 1968–72; Vice-President, Countryside Alliance 1998–99. Four honorary doctorates. *Miscellaneous:* Visiting Fellow, Yale University 1987; MSP for the Region of Lothians since May 6, 1999 (stood as Sir David Steel); Presiding Officer of the Scottish Parliament May 1999–. *Honours:* PC 1977; KBE 1990; Commander's Cross of the Order of Merit (Germany) 1992. Freeman: Tweeddale 1987, Ettrick and Lauderdale 1989. *Publications: No Entry, A House Divided*; Editor *Partners in One Nation*; *David Steel's Border Country*; Co-author *Mary Stuart's Scotland*; *Against Goliath*, 1989. *Special Interests:* International Democracy. *Recreations:* Angling, classic car rallying. *Clubs:* National Liberal, Galashiels Liberal. *Name, Style and Title:* Raised to the Peerage as Baron Steel of Aikwood, of Ettrick Forest in The Scottish Borders 1997. *Address:* Rt Hon the Lord Steel of Aikwood, KBE, DL, MSP, Scottish Parliament, Edinburgh, EH99 1SP.

LORD STERLING OF PLAISTOW   Conservative

STERLING OF PLAISTOW (Life Baron), Jeffrey Maurice Sterling; cr. 1991. Born 27 December 1934. Son of late Harry and Alice Sterling; educated Reigate Grammar School; Preston Manor County School; Guildhall School of Music. Married June 14, 1985, Dorothy Ann, daughter of Ronald Smith (1 daughter). *Armed Forces:* Honorary Captain, Royal Naval Reserve 1991. *Career:* Paul Schweder and Co. (Stock Exchange) 1955–57; G. Eberstadt & Co. 1957–62; Financial Director, General Guarantee Corporation 1962–64; Managing Director, Gula Investments Ltd 1964–69; Chairman, Sterling Guarantee Trust plc 1969, merging with P & O 1985; Board Member, British Airways 1979–82; Chairman, The Peninsular and Oriental Steam Navigation Company 1983–; Special Adviser to: Secretary of State for Industry 1982–83, Secretary of State for Trade and Industry 1983–90; President, General Council of British Shipping 1990–91; President, European Community Shipowners' Associations 1992–94. *Other:* Chairman, Organisation Committee, World ORT Union 1969–73, Member: Executive 1966–, Technical Services 1974–; Vice-President, British ORT 1978–; Deputy Chairman and Hon. Treasurer, London Celebrations Committee, Queen's Silver Jubilee 1975–83; Chairman, Young Vic Company 1975–83; Chairman, Motability 1994–, Vice-Chairman 1977–94, Chairman of Executive 1977–; Chairman of Governors, Royal Ballet School 1983–99; Governor, Royal Ballet 1986–99; Elder Brother, Trinity House 1991. Hon. D (Business Administration), Nottingham Trent University 1995; Hon. DCL, Durham University 1996. *Honours:* Kt 1985; CBE 1977; KStJ 1998. Hon. Fellow: Institute of Marine Engineers 1991, Institute of Chartered Shipbrokers 1992; Hon. Member, Royal Institute of Chartered Surveyors 1993; Fellow, Incorporated Society of Valuers and Auctioneers 1995; Hon. Fellow, Royal Institute of Naval Architects 1997. Freeman, City of London. *Special Interests:* Shipping, Construction Industry, Economics, Disability, Arts, Music. *Recreations:* Music, swimming, tennis. *Clubs:* Carlton, Garrick, Hurlingham. *Name, Style and Title:* Raised to the peerage as Baron Sterling of Plaistow, of Pall Mall in the City of Westminster 1991. *Address:* The Lord Sterling of Plaistow, CBE, The Peninsular and Oriental Steam Navigation Company, 79 Pall Mall, London, SW1Y 5EJ *Tel:* 020 7930 4343.

BARONESS STERN   Cross-Bencher

STERN (Life Baroness) Vivien Helen Stern; cr. 1999. Born 25 September 1941. Daughter of Frederick Stern and Renate Mills; educated Kent College, Pembury, Kent; Bristol University (BA, MLitt, CertEd). *Career:* Lecturer in Education 1970; Community Relations Commission 1970–77; Director, NACRO 1977–96; Visiting Fellow, Nuffield College Oxford 1984–91; Secretary-General, Penal Reform International 1989–; Senior Research Fellow, International Centre for Prison Studies, King's College London 1997–. *Select Committees:* Member, Select Committee on European Union 2000–. *Other:* Patron, Clean Break; Board Member: Association for Prevention of Torture, Geneva 1993–2000, Eisenhower Foundation, Washington 1993–; President, The New Bridge Law Advisory Committee, British Council. Hon. LLD: Bristol 1990, Oxford Brookes 1996; Hon. Fellow, LSE 1996. *Trusts, etc:* Patron, Prisoners Education Trust. *Miscellaneous:* Member: Special Programmes Board, Manpower Services Commission 1980–82, Youth Training Board 1982–88, General Advisory Council, IBA 1982–87, Committee on the Prison Disciplinary System 1984–85, Advisory Council, PSI 1993–96. *Honours:* CBE 1992. *Publications: Bricks of Shame,* 1987; *Imprisoned by Our Prisons,* 1989; *Deprived of their Liberty, a report for Caribbean Rights,* 1990; *The Future of the Voluntary Sector and the Pressure Groups in Prison after Woolf,* 1994; *A Sin Against the Future: imprisonment in the world,* 1998; *Alternatives to Prison in Developing Countries,* 1999; Editor *Sentenced to Die: The Problems of TB in Prisons in Eastern Europe and Central Asia,* 2000. *Special Interests:* Criminal Justice, Foreign Affairs, Human Rights, International Development. *Name, Style and Title:* Raised to the peerage as Baroness Stern, of Vauxhall in the London Borough of Lambeth 1999. *Address:* The Baroness Stern, CBE, International Centre for Prison Studies, School of Law, King's College London, 8th Floor, 75–79 York Road, London, SE1 7AW *Tel:* 020 7401 2559 *Fax:* 020 7401 2577 *E-Mail:* icps@kcl.ac.uk.

LORD STEVENS OF LUDGATE — Conservative

STEVENS OF LUDGATE (Life Baron), David Robert Stevens; cr. 1987. Born 26 May 1936. Son of late A. Edwin Stevens, CBE and of Kathleen James; educated Stowe; Sidney Sussex College, Cambridge. Married 1st, May 1961, Patricia Rose (1 son 1 daughter) (marriage dissolved 1971), married 2nd, 1977, Mrs Melissa Sadoff, née Milicevic (died 1989), married 3rd, January 20, 1990, Mrs Meriza Giori, née Dzienciolsky. *Armed Forces:* Second Lieutenant, Royal Artillery, National Service 1954–56. *Career:* Management Trainee, Elliot Automation 1959; Hill Samuel Securities 1959–68; Drayton Group 1968–74; Chairman: City and Foreign (Renamed in 1987 Alexander Proudfoot) 1976–95, Drayton Far East 1976–93, English and International 1976–89, Consolidated Venture 1979–93, Drayton Consolidated 1980–92, Drayton Japan 1980–88; Chairman and Chief Executive, MIM Britannia Ltd (formerly Montagu Investment Management Ltd) 1980–89, Chairman only 1989–93; Chairman, United Newspapers plc 1981–95, United News and Media plc 1995–99, Director 1974–; Chairman, Express Newspapers plc 1985–98; Deputy Chairman, Britannia Arrow Holdings plc 1987–89; Chairman: Invesco MIM plc (formerly Britannia Arrow Holdings) 1989–93, Premier Asset Mangement 1997–, Express National Newspapers Limited 1998–99, The Personal Number Company 1998–. Hon. Fellow, Sidney Sussex College, Cambridge. *Miscellaneous:* Chairman, EDC for Civil Engineering 1984–86. *Honours:* Grand Official Order of the Southern Cross (Brazil). *Recreations:* Gardening, golf. *Sportsclubs:* Sunningdale Golf, Swinley Forest Golf. *Clubs:* White's. *Name, Style and Title:* Raised to the peerage as Baron Stevens of Ludgate, of Ludgate in the City of London 1987. *Address:* The Lord Stevens of Ludgate, 22 Cheyne Gardens, London, SW3 5QT.

LORD STEVENSON OF CODDENHAM — Cross-Bencher

STEVENSON OF CODDENHAM (Life Baron), Henry Dennistoun Stevenson; cr. 1999. Born 19 July 1945. Son of late Alexander and Sylvia Stevenson (née Ingleby); educated Trinity College, Glenalmond; King's College, Cambridge (MA). Married 1972, Charlotte Susan Vanneck (4 sons). *Career:* Chairman: SRU Group of Companies 1972–96, Sinfonia 21; Numerous non-executive directorships. *House of Lords:* Chairman, House of Lords Appointments Commission 2000–. *Other:* Chairman, National Association of Youth Clubs 1973–81; Governor: London School of Economics 1996–, London Business School 1996–. *Trusts, etc:* Chairman, Trustees, Tate Gallery 1988–98; Member, Tate Gallery Foundation 1998–2000. *Miscellaneous:* Chairman: Government Working Party on role of voluntary movements and youth in the environment 1971, Newton Aycliffe and Peterlee New Town Development Corporation 1971–80, Independent Advisory Committee on Pop Festivals 1972–76; Director, National Building Agency 1977–81; Adviser on Agricultural Marketing to the Minister of Agriculture 1979–83; Director, London Docklands Development Corporation 1981–88; Chairman, Intermediate Technology Development Group 1983–90; Member: Panel on Takeovers and Mergers 1992–, Board, British Council 1996–; Hon. Member, The Royal Society of Musicians of Great Britain 1998–. *Honours:* CBE 1981; Kt 1998. *Publications: Stevenson Commission Information and Communications Technology in UK Schools Report,* 1997. *Clubs:* Brooks's, MCC. *Name, Style and Title:* Raised to the peerage as Baron Stevenson of Coddenham, of Coddenham in the County of Suffolk 1999. *Address:* The Lord Stevenson of Coddenham, CBE, Little Tufton House, 3 Dean Trench Street, London, SW1P 3HB *E-Mail:* dennis@maxima.demon.co.uk.

Dod *on* Line
An Electronic Directory without rival . . .

Peers' biographies and photographs
available with daily updates *via* the internet

For a *free* trial, call Oliver Cox on 020 7828 7256

LORD STEWARTBY — Conservative

STEWARTBY (Life Baron), (Bernard Harold) Ian Halley Stewart; cr. 1992. Born 10 August 1935. Son of Professor Harold Stewart, CBE, MD, DL, KStJ, FRSE; educated Haileybury; Jesus College, Cambridge (MA, DLitt 1978). Married October 8, 1966, Deborah Charlotte, JP, daughter of Hon. William Buchan (now 3rd Baron Tweedsmuir, *qv*) (1 son 2 daughters). *Armed Forces:* Served RNVR 1954–56; Lieutenant-Commander RNR. *Career:* Brown Shipley & Co. Ltd 1960–83, Director 1971–83; Chairman, The Throgmorton Trust plc 1990–; Deputy Chairman, Standard Chartered plc 1993–; Director, Financial Services Authority 1993–97; Deputy Chairman: Amlin plc 1995–, Portman Building Society 1999–. *House of Commons:* Contested (Conservative) North Hammersmith 1970 General Election; MP (Conservative) for: Hitchin 1974–83, Hertfordshire North 1983–92; PPS to Chancellor of the Exchequer 1979–83; Parliamentary Under-Secretary of State (Procurement) Ministry of Defence January-October 1983; Economic Secretary to the Treasury 1983–87; Minister of State: Armed Forces, MoD 1987–88, Northern Ireland Office 1988–89. *Spokesman (Commons):* Opposition Spokesman on the Banking Bill 1978–79. *Party Groups (General):* Chairman, Bow Group Economic Standing Committee 1978–83. *Other:* Life Governor, Haileybury 1977; County Vice-President, St John's Ambulance Brigade for Hertfordshire 1978–; Director, British Numismatic Society 1965–75. *Awards Granted:* Royal Numismatic Society Medal 1996. Hon. Fellow, Jesus College, Cambridge 1994. *Trusts, etc:* Trustee, Sir Halley Stewart Trust 1978–. *Miscellaneous:* Chairman, Treasure Valuation Committee 1996–. *Honours:* RD 1972; PC 1989; Kt 1991; KStJ 1992. FSA (Council Member 1974–76); FBA 1981; FRSE 1986. *Publications: The Scottish Coinage,* 1955, 1967; *Scottish Mints,* 1971; Co-author: *Studies in Numismatic Method,* 1983, *Coinage in Tenth Century England,* 1989. *Special Interests:* Financial Markets, Tax, Charities, Foreign Affairs, Defence. *Recreations:* Archaeology, tennis, cricket. *Sportsclubs:* Lords and Commons Cricket Club. *Clubs:* New (Edinburgh), Beefsteak, MCC, Hawks (Cambridge), Royal Automobile. *Name, Style and Title:* Raised to the peerage as Baron Stewartby, of Portmoak in the District of Perth and Kinross 1992. *Address:* Rt Hon the Lord Stewartby, RD, FBA, House of Lords, London, SW1A 0PW.

LORD STEYN — Cross-Bencher

STEYN (Life Baron), Johan van Zyl Steyn; cr. 1995. Born 15 August 1932; educated Jan van Riebeeck School, Cape Town, South Africa; University of Stellenbosch, South Africa (BA, LLB); University College, Oxford (Rhodes Scholar). Married Susan Lewis (2 sons and 2 daughters from previous marriage; 1 step-son and 1 step-daughter). *Career:* Commenced practice at the South African Bar 1958, English Bar 1973; QC 1979; Bencher, Lincoln's Inn 1985; Judge of the High Court, Queen's Bench Division 1985–91; Chairman, Race Relations Committee of the Bar 1987–88; A Presiding Judge, Northern Circuit 1989–91; President, British Insurance Law Association 1992–94; A Lord Justice of Appeal 1992–95; Chairman, Advisory Council, Centre for Commercial Law Studies, Queen Mary and Westfield College, London 1993–94; Chairman, Lord Chancellor's Advisory Committee on Legal Aid and Conduct 1994–96; A Lord of Appeal in Ordinary 1995–. Hon. LLD, Queen Mary and Westfield College, London; Hon. LLD, UAE. *Honours:* Kt 1985; PC 1992. Hon. Member, American Law Institute. *Name, Style and Title:* Raised to the peerage as Baron Steyn, of Swafield in the County of Norfolk 1995. *Address:* Rt Hon the Lord Steyn, House of Lords, London, SW1A 0PW.

LORD STODART OF LEASTON — Non-Affiliated

STODART OF LEASTON (Life Baron), (James) Anthony Stodart; cr. 1981. Born 6 June 1916. Son of late Colonel Thomas Stodart, CIE; educated Wellington. Married September 12, 1940, Hazel Jean Usher (died 1995). *Career:* Farmer since 1934; Executive Committee, East Lothian NFU 1948–51; Chairman, Agricultural Credit Corporation 1975–87; Chairman: Committee of Enquiry into Local Government in Scotland 1980, Manpower Review of Veterinary Profession in UK 1984–85. *House of Commons:* Contested: (Liberal) Berwick and East Lothian 1950, (Conservative) Midlothian and Peebles 1951, 1955; MP (Conservative) for Edinburgh West 1959–74; Joint Under-Secretary of State for Scotland 1963–1964; Parliamentary Secretary, Ministry of Agriculture, Fisheries and Food 1970–72, Minister of State 1972–74.

Spokesman (Commons): Spokesman on Agriculture and Scottish Affairs 1966–69. *Select Committees:* Member, European Union Sub-Committee D (Agriculture, Fisheries and Food) 1988–97. *Other:* Hon. President, Edinburgh University Agricultural Society 1952. *Honours:* PC 1974. *Special Interests:* Agriculture, Fishing Industry, Local Government. *Recreations:* Music, vintage films. *Sportsclubs:* Hon. Company of Edinburgh Golfers. *Clubs:* Cavalry and Guards, New (Edinburgh). *Name, Style and Title:* Raised to the peerage as Baron Stodart of Leaston, of Humbie in the District of East Lothian 1981. *Address:* Rt Hon the Lord Stodart of Leaston, Lorimers, North Berwick, East Lothian, EH39 4NG *Tel:* 01620 892457; Leaston, Humbie, East Lothian, EH36 5PD *Tel:* 01875 833213.

LORD STODDART OF SWINDON   Labour

STODDART OF SWINDON (Life Baron), David Leonard Stoddart; cr. 1983. Born 4 May 1926. Son of late Arthur L. Stoddart, Coal Miner; educated St Clement Danes and Henley Grammar Schools. Married 2nd, June 24, 1961, Jennifer Percival-Alwyn (2 sons) (1 daughter by previous marriage). *Trades Union:* Trade Unions: EETPU (now AEEU) 1953–, NALGO 1951–70. *Councils, Public Bodies:* Councillor, Reading County Borough Council 1954–72; Leader of Labour Group on Council 1962–72; Leader of Council 1967–72; Served at various times as Chairman of Housing, Transport and Finance and General Purposes Committees and as a member of various Boards inc. Thames Valley Water Board and Police Authority. *Career:* Power Station Clerical Worker 1951–70. *House of Commons:* Contested (Labour) Newbury 1959, 1964; MP (Labour) for Swindon 1970–83; PPS to Minister for Housing and Construction 1974–75. *Whip (Commons):* Assistant Government Whip 1975–77; Government Whip (Lord Commissioner of the Treasury) 1976–77. *Spokesman (Commons):* Junior Opposition Front Bench Spokesman on Industry 1982–83. *Whip:* Opposition Whip 1983–88. *Spokesman:* Opposition Front Bench Spokesman in House of Lords on Energy 1983–88. *Other:* Member, Court and Council of Reading University 1964–68; Treasurer, Anzac Group 1985–; Chairman: Campaign for an Independent Britain 1989–, Anti-Maastrich Alliance 1991–; Founder Member, Global Britain. *Miscellaneous:* Member, National Joint Council for the Electricity Supply Industry 1967–70. *Special Interests:* Commonwealth, Economic Policy, Energy, European Union, Housing, Industry, Local Government, Transport. *Name, Style and Title:* Raised to the peerage as Baron Stoddart of Swindon, of Reading in the Royal County of Berkshire 1983. *Address:* The Lord Stoddart of Swindon, 'Sintra', 37A Bath Road, Reading, Berkshire, RG1 6HL *Tel:* 0118–957 6726.

LORD STOKES   Cross-Bencher

STOKES (Life Baron), Donald Gresham Stokes; cr. 1969. Born 22 March 1914. Son of late Harry Potts Stokes; educated Blundell's School; Harris Institute of Technology, Preston. Married 1st, 1939, Laura Elizabeth Courteney (died 1995), daughter of late Frederick C. Lamb (1 son), married 2nd, 2000, Patricia June Pascal. *Armed Forces:* Served War 1939–45, REME, Lieutenant-Colonel. *Councils, Public Bodies:* DL, Lancs 1968. *Career:* Commenced Student Apprenticeship, Leyland Motors Ltd 1930; Re-joined Leyland as Exports Manager 1946, General Sales and Service Manager 1950, Director 1954; Managing Director, The Leyland Motor Corporation 1963, Chairman 1967. Chairman and Chief Executive: British Leyland (UK) Ltd, British Leyland International and subsidiary companies 1968–75; President, British Leyland Limited 1975–79; Consultant to Leyland Vehicles Ltd 1979–81; Director, District Bank Limited 1964–69; President, Motor Industry Research Association 1966; Chairman, Electronics Committee of the NEDC 1966–68; Director, London Weekend Television Limited 1967–71; Deputy Chairman, Industrial Reorganisation Corporation 1969–71; Director, National Westminster Bank 1969–81; Member, CBI Council; President, EDC for the Motor Manufacturing Industry 1969–; Chairman, British Arabian Advisory Co. Ltd 1977–85; Chairman, Two Counties Radio Ltd 1979–84, 1990–, President 1994–; Director: GWR Group 1990–94, Opus Public Relations Ltd 1979–84, KBH Communications Ltd 1985–96; Chairman, Jack Barclay Ltd 1980–90; Director, Scottish and Universal Investments Ltd 1980–92; Chairman: Dovercourt Motor Co. Ltd 1980–90, Dutton-Forshaw Motor Group Ltd 1981–91, Beherman Auto-Transports NV (Belgium) 1982–89. *Other:* President: SMMT Council 1961–2, The Institution of Mechanical Engineers 1972, The University of Manchester Institute of Science and Technology 1968–76. Four honorary doctorates.

Trusts, etc: Chairman, Nuffield Trust for the Forces of the Crown 1971–96. *Honours:* TD 1945; Officier de l'Ordre de la Couronne (Belgium) 1964; Kt 1965; Commandeur de l'Ordre de Leopold II (Belgium) 1972. FEng; FIMechE; MSAE; FIMI; FCIT; FICE; FIRTE; Fellow, Institute of Road Transport Engineers 1968, President 1982. Liveryman, Worshipful Company of Carmen. *Recreations:* Sailing. *Sportsclubs:* Commodore, Royal Motor Yacht Club, Poole 1979–81. *Clubs:* Army and Navy, Royal Motor Yacht Club. *Name, Style and Title:* Raised to the peerage as Baron Stokes, of Leyland in the County Palatine of Lancaster 1969. *Address:* The Lord Stokes, TD, Kt, DL, Branksome Cliff, Westminster Road, Poole, Dorset, BH13 6JW *Tel:* 01202 763088.

LORD STONE OF BLACKHEATH — Labour

STONE OF BLACKHEATH (Life Baron), Andrew Zelig Stone; cr. 1997. Born 7 September 1942. Son of Sydney and Louise Stone; educated Cardiff High School. Married 1973, Vivienne Wendy Lee (1 son 2 daughters). *Career:* Marks and Spencer plc: Management Trainee 1966, Merchandise Manager 1973, Personal Assistant to Chairman 1978–80, Divisional Director 1986, Menswear 1986, Children's Wear 1990, Director 1990–, Joint Managing Director 1994–2000. *Select Committees:* Member, Refreshment Sub-Committee, House of Lords Offices Committee 2000–. *Other:* Chairman, British Overseas Trade Board for Israel 1991–99. Two honorary degrees. *Trusts, etc:* Trustee, Jewish Association of Business Ethics. *Miscellaneous:* Governor, Weizmann Institute Foundation 1993–; Patron, Interalia Institute of Arts and Science; Council Member, Arts and Business; Member, National Advisory Committee for Creative and Cultural Education; President, British Overseas Trade Board for Israel. FRSA. *Special Interests:* Middle East, Arts, Science, Conflict Resolution. *Recreations:* Reading, walking, thinking. *Name, Style and Title:* Raised to the peerage as Baron Stone of Blackheath, of Blackheath in the London Borough of Greenwich 1997. *Address:* The Lord Stone of Blackheath, House of Lords, London, SW1A 0PW *Tel:* 020 7935 4422 *E-Mail:* stonea@parliament.uk.

LORD STRABOLGI — Labour

STRABOLGI (11th Baron, E), David Montague de Burgh Kenworthy; cr. 1318. Born 1 November 1914. Son of Lieutenant-Commander Joseph Montague Kenworthy, RN, MP, later 10th Baron, and Doris Whitley, only child of late Sir Frederick Whitley-Thomson, MP. Succeeded his father 1953. A Co-heir to the baronies of Cobham and Burgh; educated Gresham's School, Holt; Chelsea School of Art. Married June 3, 1961, Doreen Margaret, daughter of late Alexander Morgan. *Armed Forces:* Served BEF 1939–40; MEF 1940–45, Lieutenant-Colonel, RAOC. *Career:* Member, Parliamentary delegations to: Russia 1954, France 1981, 1983, 1985; Director, Bolton Building Society 1958–74, 1979–87, Deputy Chairman 1983–85, Chairman 1986–87; Member, British Section Franco-British Council 1981–98; President, Franco-British Society 1999. *House of Lords:* PPS to the Lord Shackleton, KG, Lord Privy Seal and the Leader of the House of Lords 1969–70; A Deputy Speaker House of Lords and Deputy Chairman of Committees 1986–; An Extra Lord in Waiting to HM The Queen 1998–; An elected hereditary peer 1999–. *Whip:* Opposition Whip 1970–74; Captain of the Queen's Bodyguard of the Yeomen of the Guard and Deputy Chief Whip, House of Lords 1974–79. *Spokesman:* Opposition Front Bench Spokesman on the Arts 1979–85. *Select Committees:* Member: Select Committee for Privileges 1987–, Joint Committee (with Commons) on Consolidation Bills 1987–97, 1998–, Personal Bills Committee 1987–97, Ecclesiastical Committee 1991–97, 1997–, Select Committee on Procedure of the House 1993–97, 1998–. *Party Groups (General):* Vice-Chairman, Labour Party Films Group 1968–70. *Honours:* Officier de la Légion d'Honneur 1981. Freeman, City of London. *Special Interests:* Environment, National Heritage, France, Venice. *Recreations:* French art and literature. *Clubs:* Reform. *Address:* The Lord Strabolgi, House of Lords, London, SW1A 0PW.

BARONESS STRANGE   Cross-Bencher

STRANGE (Baroness, 16th in line, E), Jean Cherry Drummond of Megginch; cr. 1628. Born 17 December 1928. Daughter of 15th Baron and late Violet Margaret Florence Buchanan-Jardine; educated Oxenfoord Castle School; St Andrews University (MA 1951); Cambridge University. Married June 2, 1952, Captain Humphrey ap Evans, MC, who assumed the name of Drummond of Megginch by decree of the Lord Lyon, 1966 (3 sons 3 daughters). *House of Lords:* An elected hereditary peer 1999–. *Party Groups:* Member, Executive Committee Association of Conservative Peers 1991–94. *International Bodies:* Member, Parliamentary Delegation, Bangladesh 1990; Delegate, Inter-Parliamentary Union Conference, Ottawa 1993; Member, Parliamentary Delegation: Bulgaria 1998, Isle of Man 1999, Kazakhstan 1999, Ikraine 2000; Executive Committee IPU 1999; Member: IPU Executive Committee 1999–, CPA. *Party Groups (General):* Chairman, Glencarse Junior Unionists 1947–52. *Other:* President, War Widows Association of Great Britain 1990–; Member: Age Concern, Scottish Peers Association. *Miscellaneous:* The barony was in abeyance from 1982–86, when terminated in favour of the present peer. FSA (Scotland); Hon. FIMarE. *Publications: Love from Belinda; Lalage in Love; Creatures Great and Small; Love is For Ever; The Remarkable Life of Victoria Drummond – Marine Engineer. Special Interests:* Defence, Foreign Affairs, Children, Countryside, Arts. *Address:* The Baroness Strange, Megginch Castle, Errol, Perthshire, PH2 7SW *Tel:* 01821 642222.

LORD STRATHCLYDE   Conservative

STRATHCLYDE (2nd Baron), Thomas Galbraith; cr. 1955. Born 22 February 1960. Son of late Hon. Sir Thomas Galbraith, KBE, MP, eldest son of 1st Baron, PC. Succeeded his grandfather 1985; educated Wellington; University of East Anglia; University of Aix-en-Provence. Married June 27, 1992, Jane Skinner (3 daughters). *Career:* Lloyd's Insurance Broker; Bain Clarkson Ltd 1982–88. *House of Lords:* Parliamentary Under-Secretary of State: Department of Employment (Minister for Tourism) 1989–90, Department of Environment July-Sept 1990, Scottish Office (Minister for Agriculture and Fisheries) 1990–92; Joint Parliamentary Under-Secretary of State, Department of Environment 1992–93; Joint Parliamentary Under-Secretary of State for Consumer Affairs and Small Firms, Department of Trade and Industry 1993–94, Minister of State January-July 1994; Member, Shadow Cabinet 1997–; A Former Deputy Speaker of the House of Lords; A Former Deputy Chairman of Committees; Leader of the Opposition in the House of Lords December 1998–; An elected hereditary peer 1999–. *Whip:* Government Whip (A Lord in Waiting) 1988–89; Government Chief Whip (Captain of the Honourable Corps of the Gentlemen-at-Arms) 1994–97; Opposition Chief Whip in the House of Lords 1997–98. *Spokesman:* Government Spokesman for DTI, Treasury and Scotland 1988–89; Opposition Spokesman on Constitutional Affairs December 1998–. *Awards Granted:* Peer of 2000, Channel 4 and *The House* Magazine 2000. *Miscellaneous:* Contested (Conservative) European Elections for Merseyside East 1984; Chairman, Commission on the Future Structure of the Scottish Conservative and Unionist Party 1997–98. *Honours:* PC 1995. *Address:* Rt Hon the Lord Strathclyde, House of Lords, London, SW1A 0PW *Tel:* House of Lords 020 7219 5353.

LORD SWINFEN   Conservative

SWINFEN (3rd Baron, UK), Roger Mynors Swinfen Eady; cr. 1919. Born 14 December 1938. Son of 2nd Baron. Succeeded his father 1977; educated Westminster; RMA, Sandhurst. Married 1962, Patricia Anne, daughter of late Frank Blackmore (1 son 3 daughters). *Armed Forces:* Lieutenant, The Royal Scots (The Royal Regiment). *Councils, Public Bodies:* JP, Kent 1983–85. *House of Lords:* An elected hereditary peer 1999–. *Select Committees:* Member: Select Committee on Greater Manchester Bill 1979, House of Lords European Communities Sub-Committee C 1990–94. *Other:* President, South East Region British Sports Association for the Disabled; Patron: Disablement Income Group 1988–, 1 in 8 Group 1996, Labrador Rescue South East 1996; Hon. President, Britain Bangladesh Friendship Association. *Trusts, etc:* Fellow, Industry and Parliament Trust 1983–. *Miscellaneous:* Chairman, Parliamentary Working Party on Video Violence and Children 1982–85; Member, Direct Mail Services Standards Board 1983–97. ARICS 1970. Liveryman, Worshipfull Company of Drapers. *Special Interests:* Disability. *Recreations:* Gardening, painting, reading history. *Address:* The Lord Swinfen, House of Lords, London, SW1A 0PW.

BARONESS SYMONS OF VERNHAM DEAN — Labour

SYMONS OF VERNHAM DEAN (Life Baroness), Elizabeth Conway Symons; cr. 1996. Born 14 April 1951. Daughter of Ernest Vize and Elizabeth Megan Symons; educated Putney High School for Girls; Girton College, Cambridge (MA). *Career:* Research, Girton College, Cambridge 1972–74; Administration Trainee, Department of the Environment 1974–77; Inland Revenue Staff Federation: Assistant Secretary 1977–78, Deputy General Secretary 1978–89; General Secretary, Association of First Division Civil Servants 1989–97. *House of Lords:* Parliamentary Under-Secretary of State, Foreign and Commonwealth Office 1997–99; Minister of State for Defence Procurement, Ministry of Defence 1999–. *Other:* Former Member: General Council, TUC, Council, RIPA, Governor, Polytechnic of North London 1989–94; Member: Executive Council, Campaign for Freedom of Information 1989–97, Hansard Society Council 1992–97, Advisory Council, Civil Service College 1992–97; Governor, London Business School 1993–97; Member: Council, Industrial Society 1994–97, Council, Open University 1994–97. *Miscellaneous:* Hon. Associate, National Council of Women 1989; Member, Employment Appeal Tribunal 1995–97. FRSA. *Recreations:* Reading, gardening. *Name, Style and Title:* Raised to the peerage as Baroness Symons of Vernham Dean, of Vernham Dean in the County of Hampshire 1996. *Address:* The Baroness Symons of Vernham Dean, House of Lords, London, SW1A 0PW.

T

LORD TANLAW — Cross-Bencher

TANLAW (Life Baron), Simon Brooke Mackay; cr. 1971. Born 30 March 1934. Son of late 2nd Earl of Inchcape; educated Eton; Trinity College, Cambridge (MA 1966). Married 1st, April 1, 1959, Joanna Susan Hirsch (1 son 2 daughters and 1 son deceased), married 2nd, May 5, 1976, Rina Siew Yong, daughter of late Tiong Cha Tan (1 son 1 daughter). *Armed Forces:* Served as 2nd Lieutenant, XII Royal Lancers, Malaya. *Career:* Worked in Inchcape Group of Companies India and Far East 1960–66, Managing Director 1967–71, Director 1971–92; Chairman and Managing Director, Fandstan Group of Companies 1973–; Member, Executive Committee of the Great Britain-China Centre 1981–88. *Whip (Commons):* Deputy Whip, Liberal Party 1971–83. *Select Committees:* Member, European Communities Committee Sub-Committee F (Energy Transport, Research and Technology) 1980–83. *Other:* Chairman, Building Committee, University College at Buckingham 1973–77, Council of Management 1973–; Member, Court of Governors, London School of Economics 1980–96; President, Sarawak Association 1973–75, 1997–; Hon. Treasurer, Scottish Peers Association 1979–86. Hon. DUniversity, University of Buckingham 1983. *Miscellaneous:* Contested Galloway 1959, 1960 and 1964 as Liberal candidate; Member, Lord Chancellor's Inner London Advisory Committee on Justices of the Peace 1972–83. Fellow, British Horological Institute. Member: Worshipful Company of Fishmongers, Worshipful Company of Clockmakers. *Publications:* In the *Horological Journal: The Case for a British Astro-Physical Masterclock, Spacetime and Horology GMT or UTC for the Millennium?*. *Special Interests:* Time, Space. *Recreations:* Fishing, horology. *Clubs:* White's, Oriental, Puffin's (Edinburgh). *Name, Style and Title:* Raised to the peerage as Baron Tanlaw, of Tanlawhill in the County of Dumfries 1971. *Address:* The Lord Tanlaw, 31 Brompton Square, London, SW3 2AE; Tanlawhill, Eskdalemuir, by Langholm, Dumfriesshire, DG13 0PQ *E-Mail:* tanlaws@parliament.uk.

Dod *on* Line
An Electronic Directory without rival …
Peers' biographies and photographs available with daily updates *via* the internet
For a *free* trial, call Oliver Cox on 020 7828 7256

LORD TAVERNE   Liberal Democrat

TAVERNE (Life Baron), Dick Taverne; cr. 1996. Born 18 October 1928. Son of late Dr N. J. M. Taverne and of Mrs L. V. Taverne; educated Charterhouse; Balliol College, Oxford (First in Greats). Married 1955, Janice Hennessey (2 daughters). *Career:* Called to the Bar, Middle Temple 1954; QC 1965; Director, Institute for Fiscal Studies 1970–79, Director-General 1979–81, Chairman 1981–83; Director, Axa Equity and Law 1972–, Chairman 1997–; Director, BOC Group 1975–95; Member, International Independent Review Body to review workings of the European Commission 1979; Chairman, Public Policy Centre 1983–87; Director, PRIMA Europe Ltd 1987–, Chairman 1991–93, President 1993–98; Chairman, OLIM Investment Trust 1989–99; Deputy Chairman: Central European Growth Fund, Industrial Finance Group 1995–. *House of Commons:* Contested Wandsworth, Putney (Labour) 1959 General Election; MP (Labour) for Lincoln, March 1962-October 1972, resigned; Parliamentary Under-Secretary of State, Home Office 1966–68; Minister of State, HM Treasury 1968–69; Financial Secretary, HM Treasury 1969–70; MP (Democratic Labour) for Lincoln, March 1973-September 1974; Contested (SDP): Southwark, Peckham, October 1982, Dulwich 1983. *Spokesman:* Liberal Democrat Spokesman on Treasury Issues 1998–. *Select Committees:* Member, Select Committee on Monetary Policy of the Bank of England 2000–. *Party Groups (General):* Member: National Committee, Social Democratic Party 1981–87; Federal Policy Committee, Liberal Democrats 1989–90. *Other:* Chairman: Council of Alcohol and Drug Abuse Prevention and Treatment Ltd, Advisory Board of Oxford Centre for the Environment, Ethics and Society. *Publications: The Future of the Left: Lincoln and after,* 1974; *The Pension Time Bomb in Europe,* 1995; *Pensions in Europe,* 1997; *Qualified Majority Voting,* 1997; *Tax and the Euro,* 1999; *Can Europe Pay for its Pensions,* 2000. *Special Interests:* European Union, Pensions, Welfare, Corporate Governance, Science and Technology, Crime and Drugs, Tax, Economic Policy.*Recreations:* Sailing. *Sportsclubs:* Cruising Association. *Name, Style and Title:* Raised to the peerage as Baron Taverne, of Pimlico in the City of Westminster 1996. *Address:* The Lord Taverne, QC, 60 Cambridge Street, London, SW1V 4QQ.

LORD TAYLOR OF BLACKBURN   Labour

TAYLOR OF BLACKBURN (Life Baron), Thomas Taylor; cr. 1978. Born 10 June 1929. Son of James Taylor; educated Blakey Moor Elementary School. Married September 23, 1950, Kathleen Nurton (1 son). *Councils, Public Bodies:* Councillor, Blackburn Council 1954–76, Leader of Council until 1976; JP, Blackburn 1960; DL, Lancashire 1994–. *Career:* Former Deputy Director, Central Lancashire Family and Community Project; Chairman: Bygone Times Ltd, Grove Properties Ltd, Canatxx Energy Ventures Limited, Chameleon Educational Systems Limited; Director of other companies; Consultant, Shorrock Security Systems Ltd; Adviser: BAe, BAe Sema, EDS, Omega Investment Research Limited. *Chancellor:* Deputy Pro-Chancellor, Lancaster University 1961–95. *Select Committees:* Member: Select Committee on Science and Technology 1987–92, House of Lords' Offices Committee 1993–97. *Party Groups:* Member, Labour North West Group. *International Bodies:* Member, CPA 1978–. *Other:* Past President, Association of Education Committees; Member of Council, University of Lancaster 1961–95; President, Free Church Council 1962–63; Chairman, Electricity Consumers Council for North West 1977–80; Member, Norweb Board; Vice-President, The Association of Lancastrians in London. Hon. LLD, Lancaster 1996. *Trusts, etc:* Patron, Lancashire Wildlife Trust. *Miscellaneous:* Past Chairman of several Government Committees of Enquiry. *Honours:* OBE 1969; CBE 1974. FRGS 1994. Freeman, Borough of Blackburn 1992. *Special Interests:* Education, North West, Railways, Commonwealth, Energy, Local Government. *Recreations:* Gardening, radio, books, music. *Name, Style and Title:* Raised to the peerage as Baron Taylor of Blackburn, of Blackburn in the County of Lancaster 1978. *Address:* The Lord Taylor of Blackburn, CBE, JP, DL, 9 Woodview, Cherry Tree, Blackburn, Lancashire, BB2 5LL *Tel:* 01254 209571; House of Lords, London, SW1A 0PW *Tel:* House of Lords 020 7219 5130.

LORD TAYLOR OF GRYFE — Labour

TAYLOR OF GRYFE (Life Baron), Thomas Johnston Taylor; cr. 1968. Born 27 April 1912. Son of late John Taylor; educated Bellahouston Academy, Glasgow. Married 1943, Isobel Wands (2 daughters). *Councils, Public Bodies:* DL, Renfrewshire 1970. *Career:* Former President, Scottish Co-operative Wholesale Society; Executive Committee, Scottish Council (Development & Industry); Former Chairman: Forestry Commission, Economic Forestry Group; Former Director, British Railways Board; Director: British Railways Property Board, Scottish Metropolitan Property Co. Ltd, Whiteways, Laidlaw & Co; Former Chairman, Morgan Grenfell (Scotland) Ltd; Member, Advisory Board Morgan Grenfell Ltd. *Other:* Chairman, Scottish Peers Association 1989–91. Hon. LLD, Strathclyde 1974. *Trusts, etc:* Chairman, Edith and Isaac Wolfson (Scotland) Trust 1972–90; Trustee, Dulverton Trust 1980–. *Honours:* Commanders Cross of the Order of Merit of the Federal Republic of Germany. Fellow: Royal Society (Edinburgh), Royal Society of Arts. *Special Interests:* Finance, Industry, Forestry, Transport. *Recreations:* Golf, theatre. *Sportsclubs:* Royal and Ancient Golf Club. *Clubs:* Caledonian, Royal and Ancient (St Andrews). *Name, Style and Title:* Raised to the peerage as Baron Taylor of Gryfe, of Bridge of Weir in the County of Renfrewshire 1968. *Address:* The Lord Taylor of Gryfe, DL, Glentyan, 33 Seagate, Kingsbarns, Fife, KY16 8SR *Tel:* 01334 880430.

LORD TAYLOR OF WARWICK — Conservative

TAYLOR OF WARWICK (Life Baron), John David Beckett Taylor; cr. 1996. Born 21 September 1952. Son of late Derief Taylor, professional cricketer, and Mrs Enid Taylor, nurse; educated Moseley Church of England School, Birmingham; Moseley Grammar School (Head Pupil); Keele University (BA Law); Gray's Inn, Inns of Court School of Law, Honorary Doctorate. Married, 1981, Dr Katherine Taylor (1 son 2 daughters). *Trades Union:* Member, NUJ. *Councils, Public Bodies:* Councillor, Solihull Borough Council 1986–91; Member: North West Thames Regional Health Authority 1992–93, Greater London Further Education Funding Council 1992–95; Vice-President, British Board of Film Classification 1998–; Member, The Independent Football Commission 2000–. *Career:* Barrister-at-Law, called Gray's Inn 1978; Television and radio presenter, writer and company director 1992. *House of Lords:* Introduced the Criminal Evidence (Amendment) Bill on February 10, 1997, which came into force March 1997 as the Criminal Evidence (Amendment) Act 1997. *Party Groups:* Member, Association of Conservative Peers. *International Bodies:* Member: CPU, IPU. *Other:* Life Patron, West Indian Senior Citizens Association (WISCA); Patron, Parents Need Children Adoption Charity; Executive Committee Member, Sickle Cell Anaemia Relief Charity; Member: Royal Television Society, Radio Academy; Vice-President, National Small Business Bureau; President, African Caribbean Westminster Business Initiative; Barker, Variety Club of Great Britain. *Awards Granted:* Gray's Inn Advocacy Prize 1978. *Trusts, etc:* Member, Industry and Parliament Trust. *Miscellaneous:* Contested (Conservative) Cheltenham 1992 General Election; Member, Institute of Directors; Vice-President, British Board of Film Classification 1998–. City of London 1998. *Special Interests:* Law, Broadcasting, Film. *Recreations:* Singing, soccer and cricket, spending time with my family. *Sportsclubs:* Aston Villa Football Club; President, Ilford Town Football Club. *Name, Style and Title:* Raised to the peerage as Baron Taylor of Warwick, of Warwick in the County of Warwickshire 1996. *Address:* The Lord Taylor of Warwick, House of Lords, London, SW1A 0PW *E-Mail:* taylorjdb@parliament.uk; www.lordtaylor.org; www.warwickconsulting.com.

LORD TEBBIT   Conservative

TEBBIT (Life Baron), Norman Beresford Tebbit; cr. 1992. Born 29 March 1931. Son of late Leonard Albert Tebbit; educated Edmonton County Grammar School. Married September 29, 1956, Margaret Elizabeth Daines (2 sons 1 daughter). *Trades Union:* Member, BALPA. *Armed Forces:* RAF Pilot, 1949–51, Commissioned; Served RAuxAF 604 Squadron 1952–55. *Career:* Journalist 1947–49; Publicist and Publisher 1951–53; Airline Pilot 1953–70; Assistant Director of Information, National Federation of Building Trades Employers 1975–79; A Political Commentator on Sky Television's Target programme 1989–98; Columnist: *Sun* newspaper 1995–97, *The Mail on Sunday* 1997–; Company Director: Sears Holdings plc 1987–99, British Telecom 1987–96, BET 1987–96, Spectator (1828) Ltd 1989–, Onix Ltd 1990–92. *House of Commons:* Contested (Conservative) South West Islington 1967–69; MP (Conservative) for: Epping 1970–74, Chingford 1974–92; PPS to Minister of State, Department of Employment 1972–73; Parliamentary Under-Secretary of State, Department of Trade 1979–81; Minister of State for Industry January-September 1981; Secretary of State for Employment 1981–83; Secretary of State for Trade and Industry and President of the Board of Trade 1983–85; Chancellor of the Duchy of Lancaster 1985–87. *Party Groups (General):* Held various offices in: YC organisation 1946–55, Hemel Hempstead Conservative Association 1960–67; Chairman, Conservative Party 1985–87. *Other:* Chairman: The Nuffield Ortholics Appeal, Nuffield Orthopaedic Appeal; Council Member and Past President of The Air League. *Miscellaneous:* Air Line Transport Pilots Licence; Flight Navigators Licence; Former office holder with BALPA (British Airline Pilots' Association). *Honours:* PC 1981; CH 1987. Liveryman, Guild of Air Pilots and Air Navigators. *Publications: Upwardly Mobile,* 1988; *Unfinished Business,* 1991. *Recreations:* Gardening. *Clubs:* Royal Air Force, Beefsteak, The Other Club. *Name, Style and Title:* Raised to the peerage as Baron Tebbit, of Chingford in the London Borough of Waltham Forest 1992. *Address:* Rt Hon the Lord Tebbit, CH, House of Lords, London, SW1A 0PW.

LORD TEMPLEMAN   Cross-Bencher

TEMPLEMAN (Life Baron), Sydney William Templeman; cr. 1982. Born 3 March 1920. Son of late Herbert William Templeman; educated Southall Grammar School; St John's College, Cambridge. Married 1st, January 19, 1946, Margaret Rowles (died 1988) (2 sons); married 2nd, December 12, 1996, Mrs Sheila Edworthy. *Armed Forces:* Served Second World War 1939–45; Commissioned 4/1st Gurkha Rifles 1941; NW Frontier 1942; Arakan 1943; Imphal 1944 (despatches, Hon. Major); Burma 1945. *Career:* Called to the Bar, Middle Temple and Lincoln's Inn 1947; Member, Bar Council 1961–65; Attorney-General of the Duchy of Lancaster 1970–72; A Judge of the High Court of Justice, Chancery Division 1972–78; President, Senate of the Inns of Court and the Bar 1974–76; Member, Royal Commission on Legal Services 1976–79; A Lord Justice of Appeal 1978–82; A Lord of Appeal in Ordinary 1982–94; Treasurer, Middle Temple 1987; Chairman, Ecclesiastical Committee 1992–. *Select Committees:* Member, Ecclesiastical Committee 1997–. Hon. Fellow, St John's College, Cambridge 1982; Six honorary doctorates. *Honours:* MBE (Mil) 1946; Kt 1972; PC 1978. *Name, Style and Title:* Raised to the peerage as Baron Templeman, of White Lackington in the County of Somerset 1982. *Address:* Rt Hon the Lord Templeman, MBE, 'Mellowstone', 1 Rosebank Crescent, Exeter, Devon, EX4 6EJ *Tel:* 01392 275428.

VISCOUNT TENBY   Cross-Bencher

TENBY (3rd Viscount, UK), William Lloyd-George; cr. 1957. Born 7 November 1927. Son of 1st Viscount, PC, TD. Succeeded his brother 1983; educated Eastbourne College; St Catharine's College, Cambridge (Late Exhibitioner) BA. Married April 23, 1955, Ursula Diana Ethel, daughter of late Lieutenant-Colonel Henry Edward Medlicott, DSO (1 son 2 daughters). *Councils, Public Bodies:* Former JP, Hampshire, North East Hants Bench, retired 1997; Member, Hampshire Police Authority 1985–94. *Career:* Editorial Assistant, Herbert Jenkins Ltd 1951–54; Advertisement Department, Associated Newspapers 1954–57; Group Advertising Manager, United Dominions Trust Ltd 1957–74; P.R. Adviser to Chairman, Kleinwort Benson Ltd 1974–87;

Consultant, Williams Lea Group 1985–93; Director, Ugland International plc 1993–95. *House of Lords:* An elected hereditary peer 1999–. *Select Committees:* Former Member: Finance and Building Sub-Committee, Committee on Procedure; Member: Select Committee on Selection, Refreshment Sub-Committee, House of Lords Offices Committee 2000–. *Backbench Committees:* Member, Backbench Sub-Committees: on Smoking, on Broadcasting. *Trusts, etc:* Chairman Trustees, Byways Residential Home. *Miscellaneous:* President, Hampshire CPRE. *Special Interests:* Communications Industry, Magistracy, Railways, Environment. *Recreations:* Ornithology, music, reading. *Address:* The Viscount Tenby, The White House, Dippenhall Street, Crondall, Nr Farnham, Surrey, GU10 5PE *Tel:* 01252 850592 (Home) *Fax:* 01252 850913 (Home) *Tel:* 020 7219 5403 (Office).

BARONESS THATCHER   Conservative

THATCHER (Life Baroness), Margaret Hilda Thatcher; cr. 1992. Born 13 October 1925. Daughter of late Alfred Roberts; educated Kesteven and Grantham High School; Somerville College, Oxford (MA, BSc). Married, 1951, Denis Thatcher, MBE, TD (created Sir Denis Thatcher, 1st Bt 1991) (twin son and daughter). *Career:* Research Chemist 1947–51; Called to the Bar, Lincoln's Inn 1954. *House of Commons:* Contested (Conservative) Dartford in 1950, 1951 General Elections under her maiden name of Roberts; MP (Conservative) for Finchley 1959–92; Joint Parliamentary Secretary, Ministry of Pensions and National Insurance 1961–64; Shadow Minster of: Transport 1968–69, Education 1969–70; Secretary of State for Education and Science 1970–74; Leader of the Opposition 1975–79; Prime Minister, First Lord of the Treasury and Minister for the Civil Service 1979–90. *Spokesman (Commons):* Opposition Front Bench Spokesman on: Pensions and National Insurance 1964, Housing and Land 1965–66, The Treasury 1966–67; Chief Opposition Front Bench Spokesman on Power and Member of the Shadow Cabinet 1967; Opposition Treasury Spokesman 1974. *Chancellor:* Chancellor, Buckingham University 1992–98; Chancellor, College of William and Mary, Williamsburg, Virginia 1993–. *Party Groups (General):* Leader of Conservative and Unionist Party 1975–90. Hon. Doctorates: Louisiana State University 1993, Mendeleyev University, Moscow 1993. *Miscellaneous:* Hon. Bencher 1975; Elected Honorary Master of the Bench of Gray's Inn 1983; Hon. President, The Bruges Group 1991–. *Honours:* PC 1970; OM 1990; LG 1995; Presidential Medal of Freedom (USA) 1991; Order of Good Hope (South Africa) 1991; Order of the White Lion (First Class) (Czech Republic) 1999. FRS 1983. Freedom, London Borough of Barnet 1980; Hon. Freedom: Falkland Islands 1983, City of London 1989; Freeman, City of Westminster 1991. Hon. Freeman, Worshipful Company of Grocers 1980. *Recreations:* Music, reading. *Clubs:* Carlton. *Name, Style and Title:* Raised to the peerage as Baroness Thatcher, of Kesteven in the County of Lincolnshire 1992. *Address:* Rt Hon the Baroness Thatcher, LG, OM, FRS, House of Lords, London, SW1A 0PW.

LORD THOMAS OF GRESFORD   Liberal Democrat

THOMAS OF GRESFORD (Life Baron), (Donald) Martin Thomas; cr. 1996. Born 13 March 1937. Son of late Hywel Thomas and of Olwen Thomas; educated Grove Park Grammar School, Wrexham; Peterhouse, Cambridge (MA, LLB). Married 1961, Nan Thomas (née Kerr) (3 sons 1 daughter). *Career:* Solicitor, Wrexham 1961–66; Lecturer in Law 1966–68; QC 1979; Called to the Bar, Gray's Inn 1967, Bencher 1989; Barrister, Wales and Chester Circuit 1968–; Deputy Circuit Judge 1974–76; Recorder of the Crown Court 1976–; Deputy High Court Judge 1985–. *Spokesman:* Liberal Democrat Spokesman on Welsh Affairs. *Party Groups (General):* Vice-Chairman, Welsh Liberal Party 1967–69, Chairman 1969–74; President: Wrexham Liberal Association 1975–, Welsh Liberal Party 1977, 1978, 1979, Welsh Liberal Democrats 1993, Vice-President 1991–93. *Other:* Chairman, Marcher Sound 1991–2000, Vice-Chairman 1983–91. *Miscellaneous:* Contested (Liberal): West Flintshire 1964, 1966, 1970, Wrexham February and October 1974, 1979, 1983, 1987; Member, Criminal Injury Compensation Board 1985–93. *Honours:* OBE 1982. *Special Interests:* Hong Kong, China. *Recreations:* Rugby football, rowing, golf, music, fishing. *Sportsclubs:* Wrexham Rugby. *Clubs:* Reform, Western (Glasgow). *Name, Style and Title:* Raised to the peerage as Baron Thomas of Gresford, of Gresford in the County Borough of Wrexham 1996. *Address:* The Lord Thomas of Gresford, OBE, QC, Glasfryn, Gresford, Wrexham, LL12 8RG *E-Mail:* thomasm@parliament.uk.

LORD THOMAS OF GWYDIR   Conservative

THOMAS OF GWYDIR (Life Baron), Peter John Mitchell Thomas; cr. 1987. Born 31 July 1920. Son of late David Thomas, Solicitor; educated Epworth College, Rhyl; Jesus College, Oxford (MA). Married December 20, 1947, Frances Elizabeth Tessa (died 1985), daughter of late Basil Dean, CBE, theatrical producer and late Lady Mercy Greville (2 sons 2 daughters). *Armed Forces:* War Service in RAF (POW Germany 1941–45). *Career:* Called to the Bar, Middle Temple 1947; QC 1965; Master of the Bench 1971, Emeritus 1991; Deputy Chairman, Cheshire Quarter Sessions 1966–70; Denbighshire Quarter Sessions 1968–70; Recorder of Crown Courts 1974–88; An Arbitrator, International Chamber of Commerce Courts of Arbitration, Paris 1974–88.

House of Commons: MP (Conservative) for: Conway 1951–66, Hendon South 1970–87; PPS to Solicitor-General 1954–59; Parliamentary Secretary to Ministry of Labour 1959–61; Parliamentary Under-Secretary of State, Foreign Office 1961–63; Minister of State for Foreign Affairs 1963–64; Secretary of State for Wales and Member of the Cabinet June 1970–74. *Spokesman (Commons):* Opposition Frontbench Spokesman on Foreign Affairs and Law 1964–66. *Party Groups (General):* Chairman, Conservative Party 1970–72; President, National Union of Conservative and Unionist Association 1974–76; National President, Conservative Friends of Israel 1984–91. *Honours:* PC 1964. *Special Interests:* Foreign Affairs. *Clubs:* Carlton. *Name, Style and Title:* Raised to the peerage as Baron Thomas of Gwydir, of Llanrwst in the County of Gwynedd 1987 *Address:* Rt Hon the Lord Thomas of Gwydir, PC, QC, 37 Chester Way, London, SE11 4UR *Tel:* 020 7735 6047; Millicent Cottage, Elstead, Surrey, GU8 6HD *Tel:* 01252 702052.

LORD THOMAS OF MACCLESFIELD   Labour

THOMAS OF MACCLESFIELD (Life Baron), Terence James Thomas; cr. 1997. Born 19 October 1937. Son of late William Emrys Thomas, and of Mildred Evelyn Thomas; educated Queen Elizabeth Grammar School, Carmarthen; School of Management, Bath University (Postgraduate Diploma). Married 1963, Lynda Stevens (3 sons). *Career:* National Provincial Bank (later National Westminster) 1962–71; Market Research Manager, later National Sales Manager, The Joint Credit Card Company 1971–73; Marketing Manager, The Co-operative Bank plc 1973–77, Assistant General Manager, later Joint General Manager 1977–83, General Manager, Customer Services 1984–87, Executive Director 1984–88, Managing Director 1988–; Visiting Professor,

Stirling University 1988–91; Various Company Directorships including: Unity Trust Bank plc 1983–95, Co-operative Commercial Ltd 1985–87, Co-operative City Investments Ltd 1988–90, Vector Investments Ltd 1992–95 (Chairman), Stanley Leisure Organisation plc 1994–98, Venture Technic (Cheshire) Ltd (Chairman), FI Group Shareholders Trust (Chairman); Rathbone CI 1997–98; Capita Group 1997–98; Chairman, The North West Development Agency 1998–. *Select Committees:* Member, Select Committees on: European Affairs, Monetary Policy of the Bank of England 1998–. *International Bodies (General):* President, International Co-operative Banking Association (ICBA) 1988–95; A Lords' Member, Parliamentary Broadcasting Unit 2000–. *Other:* Chief Examiner, Chartered Institute of Bankers 1983–85; Trustee, Board of UNICEF 1998; President, Society for Co-operative Studies; Chairman: North West Partnership, East Manchester Partnership, Sustainability North West; Fellow and Member, General Council of the Institute of Bankers; Member: British Invisibles European Committee (Bank of England appointment), The Parliamentary Reneweable and Sustainable Energy Group (PRASEG), Court of Governors, UMIST 1996–; Patron, Northern Friends of ARMS (Multiple Sclerosis Therapy Centre); Appeal Chairman, City of Manchester and District Macmillan Nurse Appeal. *Awards Granted:* Mancunian of the Year 1998. Hon. DLitt, University of Salford 1996; Hon. Dr Business Administration, Manchester Metropolitan University 1998; Hon. Degree Business Management, Manchester Federal School of Business and Management. *Trusts, etc:* Patron, Macclesfield Museums Trust. *Honours:* CBE 1997. FCIB; CIMgt; MCIM. *Clubs:* Reform. *Name, Style and Title:* Raised to the peerage as Baron Thomas of Macclesfield, of Prestbury in the County of Cheshire 1997. *Address:* The Lord Thomas of Macclesfield, CBE, House of Lords, London, SW1A 0PW.

LORD THOMAS OF SWYNNERTON — Liberal Democrat

THOMAS OF SWYNNERTON (Life Baron), Hugh Swynnerton Thomas; cr. 1981. Born 21 October 1931. Son of late Hugh Whitelegge Thomas, and of Margery Swynnerton; educated Sherborne; Queens' College, Cambridge; The Sorbonne. Married May 5, 1961, Hon. Vanessa Jebb, daughter of 1st Baron Gladwyn, GCMG, GCVO, CB (2 sons 1 daughter). *Career:* Professor of History, Reading University 1966–76; Chairman, Centre for Policy Studies 1979–90; King Juan Carlos I Professor of Spanish Civilisation, New York University 1995–96; Professor, University Professors' Programme, Boston University, USA 1996–. *Awards Granted:* Somerset Maughan Prize 1962; Arts Council Prize for History 1980. *Trusts, etc:* Trustee, Fondacion Medinaceli. *Honours:* Order of Isabel la Católica (Spain); Order of the Aztec Eagle (Mexico). *Publications: The Spanish Civil War,* 1961, 1976; *The Suez Affair,* 1967; *Cuba or The Pursuit of Freedom,* 1971; *John Strachey,* 1973; *Goya and the Third of May,* 1973; *An Unfinished History of the World,* 1979; *Havannah!,* 1984; *Armed Truce,* 1986; *Ever Closer Union: Britain's Destiny in Europe,* 1991; *The Conquest of Mexico,* 1993; *The Slave Trade,* 1997; *The Future of Europe,* 1997. *Clubs:* Athenaeum, Beefsteak. *Name, Style and Title:* Raised to the peerage as Baron Thomas of Swynnerton, of Notting Hill in Greater London 1981. *Address:* The Lord Thomas of Swynnerton, 29 Ladbroke Grove, London, W11 3BB *Tel:* 020 7727–2288.

BARONESS THOMAS OF WALLISWOOD — Liberal Democrat

THOMAS OF WALLISWOOD (Life Baroness), Susan Petronella Thomas; cr. 1994. Born 20 December 1935. Daughter of John Arrow, and of Mrs Ebba Fordham; educated Cranborne Chase; Lady Margaret Hall, Oxford University (BA history 1967). Married 1958, David Churchill Thomas, CMG (1 son 2 daughters) (separated). *Councils, Public Bodies:* Councillor, Surrey County Council 1985–97, Vice-Chairman 1993–96, Chairman 1996–97; Chairman of Highways and Transport Committee 1993–96; Former Surrey County Representative, Association of County Councils; Former Member, East Surrey Community Health Council; Non-executive Director, East Surrey Hospital and Community Healthcare Trust 1992–96; DL, Surrey 1996; Member, Surrey Probation Committee 1997–. *Career:* National Economic Development Office 1971–74; Chief Executive, British Clothing Industries, Council for Europe 1974–78. *Spokesman:* Liberal Democrat Spokesman on Transport 1994–. *Select Committees:* Member: Select Committee on House of Lords' Offices 1997–, Hybrid Instruments Committee 2000–. *International Bodies (General):* Member, IPU. *Party Groups (General):* Has served on many Liberal and Liberal Democrat policy committees; Former President, Women Liberal Democrats; Member, Liberal International 1999–. *Other:* School Governor 1985–94. *Miscellaneous:* Contested (Liberal Alliance) Mole Valley in 1983, 1987 General Elections; Contested (Liberal Democrat) Surrey 1994 European Parliament Election. *Honours:* OBE 1989. *Recreations:* Gardening, reading, ballet, theatre, travel. *Name, Style and Title:* Raised to the peerage as Baroness Thomas of Walliswood, of Dorking in the County of Surrey 1994. *Address:* The Baroness Thomas of Walliswood, OBE, DL, House of Lords, London, SW1A 0PW.

LORD THOMSON OF MONIFIETH — Liberal Democrat

THOMSON OF MONIFIETH (Life Baron), George Morgan Thomson; cr. 1977. Born 16 January 1921. Son of late James Thomson, of Dundee; educated Grove Academy, Broughty Ferry. Married December 23, 1948, Grace, daughter of Cunningham Jenkins (2 daughters). *Trades Union:* Member, NUJ. *Armed Forces:* RAF 1941–46. *Councils, Public Bodies:* DL, Kent 1992–98. *Career:* Journalist and Former Editor of "Forward"; Joint Chairman, Council for Education in the Commonwealth 1960–64; Chairman, David Davies Institute of International Affairs 1971–77; UK Commissioner for Regional Policy to EEC Brussels 1973–77; Chairman, British Council European Movement 1977–79; Chairman, Advertising Standards Authority 1977–80; First Crown Estate Commissioner 1977–80; Chairman, Independent Broadcasting Authority 1981–88; Deputy Chairman, Woolwich Building Society 1988–91; Member, Committee on Standards in Public Life 1994–97. *House of Commons:* Contested (Labour) Glasgow Hillhead Division 1950;

MP (Labour) Dundee East 1952–72; Minister of State, Foreign Office 1964–66; Chancellor of the Duchy of Lancaster 1966–67; Secretary of State for Commonwealth Affairs 1967–68; Minister without Portfolio 1968-October 1969; Chancellor of the Duchy of Lancaster and Deputy Foreign Secretary 1969–70; Shadow Defence Minister 1970–72. *Spokesman (Commons):* Spokesman on Colonial Affairs 1957–64. *Chancellor:* Chancellor, Heriot-Watt University 1977–91. *Spokesman:* Liberal Democrat Party Spokesman on Broadcasting and Foreign Affairs in the House of Lords 1989–97. *Select Committees:* Chairman, Lords Select Committee on Broadcasting 1993–97. *Party Groups (General):* Chairman, Labour Committee for Europe 1972–73. *Other:* Chairman: Franco-British Council 1977–80, Centre European Agricultural Institute 1978–82; European Television and Film Forum 1989–91. Two Scottish honorary doctorates. *Trusts, etc:* Trustee, Thomson Foundation 1978–; Trustee, Leeds Castle Foundation 1978–, Chairman 1994–; Pilgrim Trustee 1977–97; President, History of Advertising Trust 1985–99. *Miscellaneous:* A Lords' Member, Parliamentary Broadcasting Unit 1993–. *Honours:* PC 1966; KT 1981 FRS Edinburgh; Fellow of the Royal Television Society. Freeman: Monfieth 1967, Dundee 1973. *Recreations:* Swimming, cycling. *Name, Style and Title:* Raised to the peerage as Baron Thomson of Monifieth, of Monifieth in the District of the City of Dundee 1977. *Address:* Rt Hon the Lord Thomson of Monifieth, KT, Leeds Castle Foundation, Maidstone, Kent, ME17 1PL *Tel:* 01622 880656; House of Lords, London, SW1A 0PW *Tel:* House of Lords 020 7219 6718.

THORNTON (Life Baroness), Dorothea Glenys Thornton; cr. 1998. Born 16 October 1952. Daughter of Peter and Jean Thornton, of Bradford, West Yorkshire; educated Thornton Secondary School, Bradford; LSE (BSc Economics 1976). Married February 1977, John Carr (1 son 1 daughter). *Trades Union:* Member, GMB. *Career:* Former General Secretary, Fabian Society; Former Public Affairs Adviser, CWS; Freelance Public Affairs Consultant. *Select Committees:* Member: Select Committee on European Communities Sub Committee C (Environment, Public Health and Consumer Protection) 1999–2000, Special Joint (both Houses) Select Committee on Local Government Legislation on Elected Mayors 1999; Member, European Union Sub-Committee D (Environment, Agriculture, Public Health and Consumer Protection) 2000–. *Party Groups (General):* Chairman, The Greater London Labour Party 1986–91. RSA. *Special Interests:* Children, London, Media. *Recreations:* Canoeing, hill-walking, *Star Trek. Name, Style and Title:* Raised to the peerage as Baroness Thornton, of Manningham in the County of West Yorkshire 1998. *Address:* The Baroness Thornton, House of Lords, London, SW1A 0PW *E-Mail:* thorntong@parliament.uk.

TOMBS (Life Baron), Francis Leonard Tombs; cr. 1990. Born 17 May 1924. Son of late Joseph and Jane Tombs; educated Elmore Green School, Walsall; Birmingham College of Technology (BSc). Married February 26, 1949, Marjorie, daughter of Albert Evans (3 daughters). *Career:* GEC 1939–45; Birmingham Corporation 1946–47; British Electricity Authority, Midlands, then Central Electricity Authority, Merseyside and North Wales 1948–57; General Manager, GEC, Erith 1958–67; Director and General Manager, James Howden and Co., Glasgow 1967–68; Successively Director of Engineering, Deputy Chairman and Chairman, South of Scotland Electricity Board 1969–77; Chairman, The Electricity Council 1977–80; Chairman: The Weir Group 1981–83, Turner and Newall 1982–89; Director: N M Rothschild & Sons Ltd 1981–94, Shell UK 1983–94; Chairman, Rolls-Royce plc 1985–92, Director 1982–92. *Chancellor:* Chancellor, Strathclyde University 1991–98. *Select Committees:* Member, House of Lords Select Committee on Science and Technology 1992–94, 1997–; Chairman, House of Lords Select Committee on Sustainable Development 1994–95; Chairman, Sub Committee II (Management of Nuclear Waste) 1998–99; Member, Select Committee on Science and Technology Sub-Committee II (Science and Society) 1999–2000. *Other:* Chairman, The Molecule Theatre of Science 1985–92, President 1992–94. 14 honorary doctorates from

British and Polish universities. *Trusts, etc:* Chairman, Brooklands Museum Trust 1994–. *Honours:* Kt 1978. FEng 1977; Hon. FIChemE 1985; Hon. FICE 1986; Hon. FIProdE 1986; Hon. FIMechE 1989; Hon. FIEE 1991; Hon. FRAeS 1995. City of London. Liveryman, Goldsmiths' Company 1981–, Prime Warden 1994–95. *Special Interests:* Science, Technology, Engineering. *Recreations:* Golf, music. *Name, Style and Title:* Raised to the peerage as Baron Tombs, of Brailes in the County of Warwickshire 1990. *Address:* The Lord Tombs, FEng, House of Lords, London, SW1A 0PW; Honington Lodge, Honington, Shipston-on-Stour, Warwickshire, CV36 5AA *Tel:* 01608 661437.

LORD TOMLINSON   Labour

TOMLINSON (Life Baron), John Edward Tomlinson; cr. 1998. Born 1 August 1939. Son of Frederick and Doris Tomlinson; educated Westminster City School; Co-operative College, Loughborough; Brunel University; Warwick University (MA). *Trades Union:* Member, TGWU. *Career:* Sometime Senior Lecturer in Industrial Relations and Management, Solihull College of Technology; Head of Research for AUEW 1968–70; MEP for Birmingham West 1984–99: Socialist Group Spokesman on: Budgetary Control Committee 1984–99. *House of Commons:* MP (Lab) for Meriden 1974–79; PPS to the Prime Minister 1975–76; Parliamentary Under-Secretary of State, Foreign and Commonwealth Office 1976–79; Parliamentary Secretary, Ministry of Overseas Development 1977–79. *Select Committees:* Member, Select Committee on European Communities 1998–; Chairman, Europan Communities Committee Sub-Committee A (Economic and Financial Affairs, Trade and External Relations) 2000–. *Other:* Vice-President, The Hansard Society; President, British Fluoridation Society. *Trusts, etc:* Trustee, Industry and Parliament Trust. *Special Interests:* Finance, Europe, International Development, Foreign Policy. *Recreations:* Walking, reading, sport. *Clubs:* West Bromwich Labour. *Name, Style and Title:* Raised to the peerage as Baron Tomlinson, of Walsall in the County of West Midlands 1998. *Address:* The Lord Tomlinson, House of Lords, London, SW1A 0PW.

LORD TOPE   Liberal Democrat

TOPE (Life Baron), Graham Norman Tope; cr. 1994. Born 30 November 1943. Son of late Leslie Tope; educated Whitgift School, South Croydon. Married July 22, 1972, Margaret East (2 sons). *Armed Forces:* London Scottish TA 1962–64. *Councils, Public Bodies:* London Borough of Sutton: Councillor 1974–, Leader of the Liberal (later Liberal Democrat) Group 1974–99, Leader of Opposition 1984–86, Leader of the Council 1986–99; Member, Greater London Authority 2000–. *Career:* Former Company Secretary and Insurance Manager; Deputy General Secretary, Voluntary Action Camden 1975–90; Chairman, Community Investors Ltd 1995–98. *House of Commons:* MP (Liberal) Sutton and Cheam December 1972-February 1974; Contested (Liberal) Sutton and Cheam February and October 1974. *Spokesman (Commons):* Spokesman on The Environment and Northern Ireland 1973–74. *Whip:* Assistant Whip 1998–. *Spokesman:* Liberal Democrat Party Spokesman on Education 1994–. *Select Committees:* Member, House of Lords Select Committee on Relations between Central and Local Government 1995–96. *International Bodies:* EU Committee of the Regions: Member 1994–, Vice-Chair, UK Delegation 1996–, Bureau Member 1996–; President (Leader), ELDR (Liberal) Group 1998–; Member, Council of Europe, Congress of Local and Regional Authorities in Europe 1996–. *Party Groups (General):* Vice-Chairman, National League of Young Liberals 1971–73, President 1973–75; Member, Liberal Party National Council 1970–76; Executive Committee of London Liberal Party 1981–84; President, London Liberal Democrats 1991–. *Miscellaneous:* Member, London Boroughs Association Policy and Finance Committee 1986–95, Chair 1994–95; Member, Association of London Goverment Leaders' Committee 1995–; Deputy Leader of Opposition, Association of Metropolitan Authorities 1995–97; Member, London Fire and Civil Defence Authority 1995–97; Vice-President, Local Government Association 1997–; Vice-Chair, Association of London Government 1997–; Elected an Additional Member of the Greater London Assembly May 4, 2000–. *Honours:* CBE 1991. Freeman, City of London 1998. Member, Needle Makers Company. *Publications:* Co-author of *Liberals and the Community*, 1974. *Special Interests:* Local Government, Education, Environment, Europe. *Name, Style and Title:* Raised to the peerage as Baron Tope, of Sutton in the London Borough of Sutton 1994. *Address:* The Lord Tope, CBE, 88 The Gallop, Sutton, Surrey, SM2 5SA *Tel:* 020 8770 7269 *Fax:* 020 8770 7269; House of Lords, London, SW1A 0PW *Tel:* House of Lords 020 8219 3098 *E-Mail:* Grahamtope.sutton@dial.pipex.com.

LORD TORDOFF   Liberal Democrat

TORDOFF (Life Baron), Geoffrey Johnson Tordoff; cr. 1981. Born 11 October 1928. Son of late Stanley Acomb Tordoff; educated Manchester Grammar School; Manchester University. Married October 22, 1953, Mary Patricia, daughter of late Thomas Swarbrick (2 sons 3 daughters). *Career:* Former: Marketing Executive, Shell Chemicals, Public Affairs Manager (Chemicals), Shell UK; Hon. President, British Youth Council 1986–92; Chairman, Middle East Committee, Refugee Council 1990–94; Member, Press Complaints Commission 1995–. *House of Lords:* Principal Deputy Chairman of Committees 1994–; A Deputy Speaker of the House of Lords. *Whip:* Deputy Whip 1983–84; Chief Whip 1984–88; Liberal Democrat Chief Whip 1988–94.

Spokesman: Liberal Democrat Transport Spokesman 1988–94. *Select Committees:* Chairman, Select Committee on the European Communities 1994–; Member, Select Committee on House of Lords' Offices 1997–. *Party Groups (General):* Chairman: Liberal Party Assembly Committee 1974–76, Liberal Party 1976–79, Liberal Party Campaigns and Elections Committee 1980–82; President, Liberal Party 1983–84. *Miscellaneous:* Contested (Liberal): Northwich 1964, Knutsford 1966, 1970 General Elections. *Special Interests:* Foreign Affairs, Europe. *Clubs:* National Liberal. *Name, Style and Title:* Raised to the peerage as Baron Tordoff, of Knutsford in the County of Cheshire 1981. *Address:* The Lord Tordoff, House of Lords, London, SW1A 0PW *Tel:* House of Lords 020 7219 6613 *E-Mail:* tordoffg@parliament.uk.

LORD TREFGARNE   Conservative

TREFGARNE (2nd Baron, UK), David Garro Trefgarne; cr. 1947. Born 31 March 1941. Son of 1st Baron. Succeeded his father 1960; educated Haileybury; Princeton University, USA. Married November 9, 1968, Hon. Rosalie Lane, daughter of Baron Lane of Horsell (*qv*) (2 sons 1 daughter). *Career:* Non-Exec Director, Siebe plc 1991–98; Chairman, Engineering and Marine Training Authority (EMTA) 1994–. *House of Lords:* Parliamentary Under-Secretary of State: Department of Trade 1980–81, Foreign and Commonwealth Office 1981–82, Department of Health and Social Security 1982–83, for the Armed Forces June 1983–85; Minister of State: for Defence Support 1985–86, for Defence Procurement 1986–89, Department of Trade and Industry (Minister for Trade) 1989–90; An elected hereditary peer 1999–. *Whip:* Opposition Whip 1977–1979; A Lord in Waiting (Government Whip) 1979–80. *Party Groups:* Treasurer, Association of Conservative Peers 1997–2000, Chairman 2000–. *Other:* President: Mechanical and Metal Trades Confederation (METCOM) 1990–, Governor, Guildford School of Acting 1992–; Life Governor and Member of Council, Haileybury 1993–; Hon. President, British Association of Aviation Consultants 1993–; Vice-Chairman, Army Cadet Force 1993–. *Awards Granted:* Royal Aero Club Bronze Medal 1963. *Trusts, etc:* Member, Mary Rose Trust. *Honours:* PC 1989. *Special Interests:* Aviation. *Recreations:* Photography. *Clubs:* White's. *Address:* Rt Hon the Lord Trefgarne, House of Lords, London, SW1A 0PW.

LORD TROTMAN   Non-Affiliated

TROTMAN (Life Baron), Alexander James Trotman; cr. 1999. Born 22 July 1933. Son of late Charles and Agnes Trotman; educated Boroughmuir School, Edinburgh; Michigan State University, USA (MBA). Married 1963, Valerie Anne Edgar. *Armed Forces:* Flying Officer Navigator, Royal Air Force 1951–55. *Career:* Ford 1955–98: Various positions Ford of Britain 1955–67; Director, Car Product Planning, Ford Europe 1967–69; Positions in Car Product Planning and Sales Planning Departments, Ford US 1969–75; Chief Car Planning Manager, Ford Motor Co 1975–79; Vice-President, European Truck Operations 1979–83; President: Ford Asia Pacific 1983–84, Ford of Europe 1984–88; Executive Vice-President, North American Automotive Operations 1989–93; President, Ford Automotive Group 1993; Chairman and Chief Executive Officer, Ford Motor Company 1993–98; Director: IBM Corporation 1996–, New York Stock Exchange 1996–, ICI UK 1997–. Hon. Doctorate, University of Edinburgh. *Trusts, etc:* Trustee, Shakespeare Globe Trust. *Honours:* Kt 1996. *Clubs:* Royal Air Force. *Name, Style and Title:* Raised to the peerage as Baron Trotman, of Osmotherley in the County of North Yorkshire 1999. *Address:* The Lord Trotman, Kt, House of Lords, London, SW1A 0PW.

BARONESS TRUMPINGTON   Conservative

TRUMPINGTON (Life Baroness), Jean Alys Barker; cr. 1980. Born 23 October 1922. Daughter of late Major Arthur Edward Campbell-Harris, MC and of Doris Marie Robson; educated privately in England and France. Married March 18, 1954, William Alan Barker (died 1988) (1 son). *Armed Forces:* Landgirl to the Rt Hon. David Lloyd George, MP, at Churt 1939–41; Naval Intelligence at Bletchley Park 1941–45. *Councils, Public Bodies:* Cambridge City Councillor 1963–73, Hon. City Councillor (Cambridge) 1975; Mayor of Cambridge 1971–72, Deputy Mayor 1972–73; Cambridgeshire County Councillor 1973–75; JP, Cambridgeshire 1972–82; South Westminster. *Career:* European Central Inland Transport Organization (in London and Paris) 1946–49; Secretary to the Viscount Hinchingbrooke, MP 1949–52; Copywriter in Advertising Agency, New York City 1952–54; Member: Board of Visitors of HM Prison, Pentonville 1975–81, Mental Health Review Tribunal 1975–1981; General Commissioner of Taxes 1975–83; United Kingdom representative to the United Nations Status of Women Commission 1979–81. *House of Lords:* Parliamentary Under-Secretary of State for Health and Social Security 1985–87; Parliamentary Secretary, Ministry of Agriculture, Fisheries and Food 1987–89; Minister of State 1989–92. *Whip:* Baroness in Waiting (Government Whip) 1983–1985, 1992–97. *Spokesman:* A Former Government Spokesman for: The Foreign Commonwealth Office 1983–85, Home Office 1983–85, Office of Public Service 1996–97, Department of National Heritage. *International Bodies (General):* Vice-President, International League for the Protection of Horses 1990–99. *Party Groups (General):* Chairman, Cambridge City Conservative Association 1969–71. *Other:* Member, Airline Users Committee 1973–80, Deputy Chairman 1977, Chairman 1979–80; President, Association of Heads of Independent Schools 1980–90; Steward, Folkestone Racecourse 1980–92. Hon. Fellow, Lucy Cavendish College, Cambridge 1980. *Trusts, etc:* Member, Council and Executive Committee of the Animal Health Trust 1981–87. *Miscellaneous:* A Extra Baroness in Waiting to HM The Queen 1998–. *Honours:* PC 1992. Hon. Fellow, Royal College of Pathologists; Hon. Associate, Royal College of Veterinary Surgeons 1994; Hon. Member, British Veterinary Association. *Recreations:* Antiques, bridge, cookery, golf, needlepoint, racing. *Clubs:* Grillions, Farmers'. *Name, Style and Title:* Raised to the peerage as Baroness Trumpington, of Sandwich in the County of Kent 1980. *Address:* Rt Hon the Baroness Trumpington, House of Lords, London, SW1A 0PW.

LORD TUGENDHAT   Conservative

TUGENDHAT (Life Baron), Christopher Samuel Tugendhat; cr. 1993. Born 23 February 1937. Son of late Dr Georg Tugendhat and Mrs Mairé Tugendhat; educated Ampleforth College; Gonville and Caius College, Cambridge. Married 1967, Julia Dobson (2 sons). *Armed Forces:* National Service 1955–57; Second Lieutenant, Essex Regiment 1956–57. *Career:* Journalist with *The Financial Times* 1960–70; Director: Sunningdale Oils 1971–76, Phillips Petroleum International (UK) Ltd 1972–76, EEC Commission: Member 1977–85, A Vice-President 1981–85; Director: National Westminster Bank 1985–91, The BOC Group 1985–96; Chairman, Civil Aviation Authority 1986–91; Director, Commercial Union Assurance 1988–91; Deputy Chairman, National Westminster Bank 1990–91; Director: LWT (Holdings) plc 1991–94, Eurotunnel plc 1991–; Chairman: Abbey National plc 1991–, Blue Circle Industries plc 1996–; Non-executive Director, Rio Tinto plc 1997–. *House of Commons:* MP (Conservative): Cities of London and Westminster 1970–74, City of London and Westminster South 1974–76. *Spokesman (Commons):* Deputy Spokesman on: Employment 1975, Foreign Affairs 1975–76. *Chancellor:* Chancellor, Bath University 1998–. *Other:* Chairman, The Royal Institute for International Affairs (Chatham House) 1986–95; Governor, Council of Ditchley Foundation 1986–; Chairman: Construction Industry Trust for Youth 1997, European Policy Forum 1997; Member, National Portrait Gallery Advisory Committee. Hon. LLD, Bath University 1998. *Honours:* Kt 1990. Freeman, City of London. *Publications: Oil: the biggest business,* 1968; *The Multinationals,* 1971; *Making Sense of Europe,* 1986; Co-author *Options for British Foreign Policy in the 1990s,* 1988. *Recreations:* Family, reading, conversation. *Clubs:* Athenaeum, Anglo-Belgian. *Name, Style and Title:* Raised to the peerage as Baron Tugendhat, of Widdington in the County of Essex 1993. *Address:* The Lord Tugendhat, 35 Westbourne Park Road, London, W2 5QD *E-Mail:* christopher.tugendhat@abbeynational.co.uk.

LORD TURNBERG   Labour

TURNBERG (Life Baron), Leslie Arnold Turnberg; cr. 2000. Born 22 March 1934. Son of Hyman and Dora Turnberg; educated Stand Grammar School, Whitefield; Manchester University (MB, ChB 1957, MD 1966). Married 1968, Edna Barme (1 son 1 daughter). *Career:* Junior medical posts: Manchester Jewish Hospital, Northern Hospital, Ancoats Hospital, Manchester Royal Infirmary 1957–61 and 1964–66; Registrar, UCH 1961–64; Lecturer, Royal Free Hospital 1967; Research Fellow, University of Texas South-Western Medical School, Dallas, Texas 1968; Manchester University: Lecturer, then Senior Lecturer 1968–73, Dean, Faculty of Medicine 1986–89, Professor of Medicine 1973–97; Chairman: Conference of Medical Royal Colleges 1994–96, Specialist Training Authority 1996–98, Public Health Laboratory Service Board 1997–, Health Quality Service 1999–. *Select Committees:* Co-opted Member, Select Committee on Science and Technology Sub-Committee IIA (Human Genetic Databases) 2000–. *Other:* Member: Salford Health Authority 1974–81 and 1990–92, North West Regional Health Authority 1986–89; Member of Council, Royal College of Physicians 1989–92, President 1992–97; Member, Medical Council on Alcoholism 1997–; President: Medical Protection Society 1997–, British Society of Gastroenterology 1999–2000. Hon DSc: Salford 1996, Manchester 1998, Imperial College, London 2000. *Honours:* Kt 1994. MRCP 1961; FRCP 1973; FRCPE 1993; FRCP(I) 1993; Hon. Fellow: Academy of Medicine, Singapore 1994, College of Medicine, South Africa 1994; FRCPSGlas 1994; FCPPak 1994; Hong Kong Coll of Physns 1995; FRAustCP 1995; FRCS 1996; FRCOphth 1996; FRCObsGyna 1996; FRCPsych 1997; Malaysia Coll of Med 1997; FMedSci 1998. *Publications:* Author of publications on intestinal research and clinical gastroenterology. *Special Interests:* Health Service, Medical Care. *Recreations:* Reading, antiquarian books, Chinese ceramics, walking. *Name, Style and Title:* Raised to the peerage as Baron Turnberg, of Cheadle in the County of Cheshire 2000. *Address:* The Lord Turnberg, 47 Belsize Court, Lyndhurst Gardens, London, NW3 5QP.

BARONESS TURNER OF CAMDEN   Labour

TURNER OF CAMDEN (Life Baroness), Muriel Turner; cr. 1985. Born 18 September 1927. Daughter of Edward Price. Married 1955, Wing-Commander Reginald Turner (died 1995). *Trades Union:* Assistant General Secretary, Association of Scientific, Technical and Managerial Staffs 1970–87; Member, TUC General Council 1980–87. *House of Lords:* Deputy Chairman of Committees 1997–. *Spokesman:* Opposition Spokesman on: Social Security 1987–96, Employment 1987–96. *Select Committees:* Former Member, European Select Committee (Consumer Affairs); Co-opted Member, Select Committee on European Communities Sub-Committee F (Social Affairs, Education and Home Affairs) 1997–; Member, Select Committee on House of Lords' Offices 1997–98. *Other:* Council Member, Save The Children Fund 1991–98. Hon. LLD, Leicester University 1991. *Miscellaneous:* Member: Equal Opportunities Commission 1982–88, Occupational Pensions Board 1977–93; Chair, PIA Ombudsman Council 1994–97. *Special Interests:* Employment, Social Security, Pensions. *Recreations:* Reading, music. *Clubs:* RAF. *Name, Style and Title:* Raised to the peerage as Baroness Turner of Camden, of Camden in Greater London 1985. *Address:* The Baroness Turner of Camden, 87 Canfield Gardens, London, NW6 3EA *Tel:* 020 7624 3561.

Dod *on* Line
An Electronic Directory without rival . . .

Peers' biographies and photographs
available with daily updates *via* the internet

For a *free* trial, call Oliver Cox on 020 7828 7256

U

UDDIN (Life Baroness), Pola Manzila Uddin; cr. 1998. Born 1959; educated Plashet School for Girls, Newham; University of North London (Diploma in Social Work). Married 1976, Komar Uddin (4 sons 1 daughter). *Councils, Public Bodies:* Councillor, London Borough of Tower Hamlets 1990–98, Deputy Leader of Council 1994–96; Vice-Chair: Policy and Resources Committee, Finance Committee; Member: Education Committee 1990–98, Social Services Committee to 1998. *Career:* Administrator 1976–79; Youth and Community Worker, YWCA 1980–82; Liaison Officer, Tower Hamlets Social Services 1982–84; Manager: Tower Hamlets Womens' Health Project 1984–88, Asian Family Counselling Services 1989–90; Policy Officer, Domestic Violence 1990–91; Newham Social Services: Social Worker 1993–96; Manager 1996–97; Local Government Adviser 1998–. *Select Committees:* European Select Committee. *Other:* Member: British Council of Churches/Board of Social Responsibility, Community Health Council 1982–86, Joint Health and Social Services Consultative Council 1985–88, Race Equality Council; Health Authority Board Member, EOP Implementation Committee; School Governor 1990–98. *Trusts, etc:* Trustee: St Katherine's and Shadwell Trust 1990–95, Toynbee Hall. *Special Interests:* Education, Health, Children, Local Government, Equal Opportunities, Disability, Foreign and Commonwealth Affairs. *Recreations:* Family, community work. *Name, Style and Title:* Raised to the peerage as Baroness Uddin, of Bethnal Green in the London Borough of Tower Hamlets 1998. *Address:* The Baroness Uddin, House of Lords, London, SW1A 0PW *E-Mail:* uddinm@parliament.uk.

V

VARLEY (Life Baron), Eric Graham Varley; cr. 1990. Born 11 August 1932. Son of late Frank Varley; educated Chesterfield Technical College; Ruskin College, Oxford; Sheffield University (extra mural studies). Married 1955, Marjorie Turner (1 son). *Trades Union:* Branch Secretary, NUM 1955–64, Member, Area Executive Committee, Derbyshire 1956–64. *Councils, Public Bodies:* DL, Derbyshire 1989. *Career:* Craftsman in mining industry 1947–64; Chairman and Chief Executive, Coalite Group 1984–89; A Regional Director, Lloyds Bank plc 1987–91; Director: Cuthelco Ltd 1989–99, Laxgate Ltd 1991–92; Member, Thyssen (UK) Ltd Advisory Board 1991–98. *House of Commons:* MP (Labour) for Chesterfield 1964–84; PPS to Harold Wilson as Prime Minister 1968–69; Minister of State, Ministry of Technology 1969–70; Secretary of State for: Energy 1974–75, Industry 1975–79. *Whip (Commons):* Assistant Government Whip 1967–68. *Spokesman (Commons):* Principal Opposition Spokesman on Employment 1979–83. *Select Committees:* Former Member: House of Lords European Communities Select Committee, Sub-committee A. *Party Groups (General):* Chairman, Trade Union Group of Labour MPs 1971–74; Treasurer, Labour Party 1981–83. *Other:* Vice President, Ashgate Hospital Chesterfield. *Miscellaneous:* Visiting Fellow, Nuffield College 1981–83. *Honours:* PC, 1974. *Recreations:* Reading, gardening, music, sport. *Name, Style and Title:* Raised to the peerage as Baron Varley, of Chesterfield in the County of Derbyshire 1990. *Address:* Rt Hon the Lord Varley, DL, House of Lords, London, SW1A 0PW.

Visit the Vacher Dod Website ...
www.politicallinks.co.uk

LORD VINCENT OF COLESHILL   Cross-Bencher

VINCENT OF COLESHILL (Life Baron), Richard Frederick Vincent; cr. 1996. Born 23 August 1931. Son of late Frederick Vincent and Frances Elizabeth (née Coleshill); educated Aldenham School; Royal Military College of Science. Married, 1955, Jean, daughter of late Kenneth Stewart (1 son 1 daughter and 1 son deceased). *Armed Forces:* Commissioned, Royal Artillery, National Service 1951, Germany 1951–55, Gunnery Staff 1959; Radar Research Establishment, Malvern 1960–61; BAOR 1962, Technical Staff Training 1963–64; Staff College 1965; Commonwealth Brigade, Malaysia 1966–68; Ministry of Defence 1968–70; Commanded 12th Light Air Defence Regiment, Germany, UK and Northern Ireland 1970 72; Instructor, Staff College 1972–73; Greenlands Staff College, Henley 1974; Military Director of Studies, Royal Military College of Science 1974–75; Commanded 19th Airportable Brigade 1975–77; Royal College of Defence Studies 1978; Deputy Military Secretary 1979–80; Commandant, Royal Military College of Science 1980–83; Colonel Commandant, REME 1981–87; Hon. Colonel 100 (Yeomanry) Field Regiment RA (TA) 1982–91; Master General of the Ordnance, Ministry of Defence 1983–87; Colonel Commandant, RA 1983– Hon. Colonel 12th Air Defence Regiment 1987–91; Vice-Chief, Defence Staff 1987–91, Chief 1991–92; Chairman, Military Committee, NATO 1993–96; Master Gunner, St James's Park 1996–. *Career:* Director: Vickers Defence Systems 1996–, Royal Artillery Museums Ltd; Chairman: Imperial College of Science, Technology and Medicine 1996–, Hunting Defence Ltd 1996–, Hunting Engineering Ltd 1998–, Hunting – BRAE 1998. *Chancellor:* Chancellor, Cranfield University 1998–. *International Bodies (General):* Member, The Pilgrims. *Other:* Past and present member, president, chair numerous organisations, especially those concerned with military, education and sport, including: Vice-President, Defence Manufacturers Association 1996–2000, President 2000–; Chairman, Imperial College of Science, Technology and Medicine 1996–; President Elect, DMA 2000–. Hon. DSc, Cranfield 1985; Fellow, Imperial College of Science, Technology and Medicine 1996; Hon. Fellow, City and Guilds of London Institute. *Miscellaneous:* Visiting Fellow, Australian College of Defence and Strategic Studies 1995–; Member, Commission on Britain and Europe (Royal Institute of International Affairs) 1996–98; Adviser to Secretary of State on The Strategic Defence Review 1997–98. *Honours:* DSO 1972; KCB 1984; GBE 1990; Jordanian Order of Military Merit 1992; Commander, US Legion of Merit 1993. FRAeS 1990; FIMechE 1990; FIC 1996. Freeman, City of London 1992. Member, The Guild of Freemen of the City of London; Freeman, Worshipful Company of Wheelwrights 1997. *Publications:* Has contributed to military journals and publications. *Clubs:* Army and Navy, Royal Scots, Grillions. *Name, Style and Title:* Raised to the peerage as Baron Vincent of Coleshill, of Shrivenham in the County of Oxfordshire 1996. *Address:* Field Marshal The Lord Vincent of Coleshill, GBE, KCB, DSO, c/o The Midland Bank, The Commons, High Street, Shaftesbury, Dorset, SP7 8JX.

LORD VINSON   Conservative

VINSON (Life Baron), Nigel Vinson; cr. 1985. Born 27 January 1931. Son of late Ronald Vinson, farmer; educated Nautical College, Pangbourne. Married 1972, Yvonne, daughter of Dr Olaf Collin (3 daughters). *Armed Forces:* Lieutenant, Queen's Royal Regiment 1948–50. *Councils, Public Bodies:* DL, Northumberland 1990. *Career:* Founder, Plastic Coatings Ltd 1952; Director, Sugar Board 1968–75; Member: Crafts Advisory Committee 1971–77, Design Council 1973–80; Director, British Airports Authority 1973–; Co-Founder, Centre for Policy Studies 1974–80; Member: CBI Grand Council 1975–, President's Committee 1979–83; Deputy Chairman, CBI Smaller Firms Council 1979–84; Chairman, The Rural Development Commission 1980–90; Director, Barclays Bank UK 1982–87; Member, Industry Year Steering Committee, Royal Society of Arts, Chairman 1985; Deputy Chairman, Electra Investment Trust 1990–98. *Select Committees:* Former Member, Select Committee on Pollution; Member, Select Committee on Monetary Policy of the Bank of England 1998–. *Other:* Hon. Director, Queen's Silver Jubilee Appeal 1976–78; Member, Northumbrian National Parks and Countryside Committee 1977–87; President, Industrial Participation Association 1979–90; Member, Foundation of Science and Technology 1991–96. *Awards Granted:* Queen's Award to Industry 1971.

Trusts, etc: Member, Regional Committee, National Trust 1977–84; Chairman, Trustees of Institute of Economic Affairs 1988–95; Trustee, St George's House, Windsor 1990–96. *Honours:* LVO 1979. CBIM; FRSA. *Publications: Personal Pensions for All. Special Interests:* Small Businesses, De-Regulation, Tax, Pensions. *Recreations:* Objets d'art, farming, horses. *Clubs:* Boodle's. *Name, Style and Title:* Raised to the peerage as Baron Vinson, of Roddam Dene in the County of Northumberland 1985. *Address:* The Lord Vinson, LVO, DL, 34 Kynance Mews, London, SW7 4QR *Tel:* 01668 217230.

LORD VIVIAN — Conservative

VIVIAN (6th Baron), Nicholas Crespigny Laurence Vivian; cr. 1841; 6th Bt of Truro (UK) 1828. Born 11 December 1935. Son of 5th Baron. Succeeded his father 1991; educated Eton; Madrid University. Married 1st, 1960, Catherine Joyce, daughter of late James Kenneth Hope, CBE, DL (1 son 1 daughter) (marriage dissolved 1972), married 2nd, 1972, Carol, daughter of late Frederick Alan Martineau, MBE (2 daughters). *Armed Forces:* Commissioned 3rd Carabiniers (Prince of Wales's Dragoon Guards) 1955; Royal Scots Dragoon Guards (Carabiniers and Greys) 1971; Commanded Independent Squadron, Royal Scots Dragoon Guards 1973; Principal Staff Officer to Commander British Contingent, UNFICYP 1975–76; Lieutenant Colonel, Commanding Officer, 16th/5th The Queen's Royal Lancers 1976–79; MoD Defence Intelligence Staff 1979–81; Colonel, General Staff Officer, Future Anti-Armour Study, MoD 1982–84; Chief of Staff and Deputy Commander, Land Forces, Cyprus 1984–87; Brigadier; Commander, British Communication Zone (North West Europe, Netherlands, Belgium and North West France) 1987–90; Retired in rank of Brigadier 1990. *House of Lords:* An elected hereditary peer 1999–. *Select Committees:* Member, Joint Committee on Statutory Instruments 1997–. *Party Groups:* Deputy Chairman, Association of Conservative Peers. *International Bodies (General):* Member, RUSI. *Other:* Commissioner, Royal Hospital, Chelsea. *Trusts, etc:* Special Trustee: Westminster and Roehampton Hospitals, Chelsea and Westminster Hospital; Commissioner Royal Hospital 1994–2000. *Special Interests:* Defence, United Nations, Drug Abuse, Terrorism, Cyprus, Cornwall. *Recreations:* Travel. *Clubs:* White's, Cavalry and Guards. *Address:* The Lord Vivian, House of Lords, London, SW1A 0PW.

W

LORD WADDINGTON — Conservative

WADDINGTON (Life Baron), David Charles Waddington; cr. 1990. Born 2 August 1929. Son of late Charles Waddington, JP; educated Sedbergh; Hertford College, Oxford. Married December 20, 1958, Gillian Rosemary, daughter of late Alan Green, CBE (3 sons 2 daughters). *Armed Forces:* Second Lieutenant, 12th Royal Lancers 1951–53; Captain, Duke of Lancaster's Yeomanry 1953–60. *Councils, Public Bodies:* DL, Lancashire 1991–. *Career:* Called to Bar, Gray's Inn 1951; QC 1971; Bencher 1985; Recorder of the Crown Court 1972; Governor and Commander-in-Chief, Bermuda 1992–97. *House of Commons:* Contested (Conservative): Farnworth 1955, Nelson and Colne 1964, Heywood and Royton 1966; MP (Conservative) for: Nelson and Colne 1968–74, Clitheroe 1979–83, Ribble Valley 1983–90; Parliamentary Under-Secretary of State, Department of Employment 1981–83; Minister of State, Home Office 1983–87; Secretary of State for the Home Department 1989–90. *Whip (Commons):* Government Whip (Lord Commissioner of HM Treasury) 1979–81; Government Chief Whip (Parliamentary Secretary to HM Treasury) 1987–89. *House of Lords:* Lord Privy Seal and Leader of the House of Lords 1990–92. *Select Committees:* Member, Select Committees on: Parliamentary Privilege (Joint Committee) 1997–98, Delegated Powers and Deregulation 1999–. *Party Groups (General):* President, Oxford University Conservative Association 1950; Chairman, Clitheroe Constituency Young Conservatives 1953. Honorary Fellow, Hertford College, Oxford. *Miscellaneous:* President: Hertford Society 1997–, East Lancashire Scout Council 1997–; Vice-Chairman, Bermuda Society 1999–. *Honours:* PC 1987; GCVO 1994. *Special Interests:* Legal Affairs, Textile Industry, Lancashire. *Recreations:* Sailing. *Name, Style and Title:* Raised to the peerage as Baron Waddington, of Read in the County of Lancashire 1990. *Address:* Rt Hon the Lord Waddington, GCVO, DL, QC, House of Lords, London, SW1A 0PW; Stable House, Sabden, Nr Clitheroe, Lancashire, BB7 9HP *E-Mail:* waddingtond@parliament.uk.

LORD WADE OF CHORLTON   Conservative

WADE OF CHORLTON (Life Baron), William Oulton Wade; cr. 1990. Born 24 December 1932. Son of late Samuel Norman Wade, farmer, and late Joan Ferris Wade (née Wild); educated Birkenhead School; Queen's University, Belfast. Married May 9, 1959, Gillian Margaret, daughter of Desmond Leete, of Buxton, Derbyshire (1 son 1 daughter). *Councils, Public Bodies:* JP, Cheshire 1965; Councillor, Cheshire County Council 1973–77.*Career:* Farmer and Cheesemaster; Chairman, Cheese Export Council 1982–84; Member, Food From Britain Export Council 1984–88; Chairman: William Wild and Son (Mollington) Ltd, Enterprise Business Solutions; Director: Murray Vernon Holdings Ltd, Murray Vernon Limited, Cartmel PR Limited, John Wilman Ltd; Chairman, NIMTECH; President, Campus Ventures Ltd. *Select Committees:* Member, European Committee D 1997–2000; Former Member: Science and Technology Committee Biotechnology Sub-Committee 1993, Committee on Relationship between Central and Local Government 1995–96; Member, Select Committees on: Science and Technology Sub-Committee II (Aircraft Cabin Environment) 2000–, Science and Technology Select Committee 2000–. *International Bodies (General):* UK Representative to The International Business Advisory Council (IBAC) of UNIDO. *Party Groups (General):* Chairman, North West Area Conservative Association 1976–81; Member, National Union Executive Committee 1975–90; Joint Hon. Treasurer, Conservative Party 1982–90. *Other:* President: CHPA, Federation of Economic Development Authorities. *Trusts, etc:* Chairman: Cheshire Historic Churches Trust 1993–, Chester Heritage Trust 1994–, The Christie Hospital Against Cancer Centenary Appeal. *Miscellaneous:* Chairman, Rural Economy Group. *Honours:* Kt 1982. Freeman, City of London 1980. Member, Worshipful Company of Farmers. *Special Interests:* Food Industry, Agriculture, Industry, Transport, Planning, Technology. *Recreations:* Shooting, reading, farming. *Clubs:* The City (Chester), Chester Grosvenor, St James Manchester. *Name, Style and Title:* Raised to the peerage as Baron Wade of Chorlton, of Chester in the County of Cheshire 1990.*Address:* The Lord Wade of Chorlton, House of Lords, London, SW1A 0PW.

BISHOP OF WAKEFIELD   Non-Affiliated

WAKEFIELD (11th Bishop of), Nigel Simeon McCulloch. Born 17 January 1942. Born Crosby, Liverpool. Son of late Pilot Officer Kenneth McCulloch, RAFVR, and of Audrey McCulloch; educated Liverpool College; Selwyn College, Cambridge (Kitchener Scholar, BA 1964, MA 1969); Cuddesdon College, Oxford. Married 1974, Celia Hume, daughter of Canon H. L. Townshend (2 daughters). *Career:* Ordained 1966; Curate of Ellesmere Port 1966–70; Chaplain of Christ's College, Cambridge 1970–73; Director of Theological Studies, Christ's College, Cambridge 1970–75; Diocesan Missioner, Norwich Diocese 1973–78; Rector of St Thomas' and St Edmund's, Salisbury 1978–86; Archdeacon of Sarum 1979–86; Prebendary of: Ogbourne, Salisbury Cathedral 1979–86, Wanstrow, Wells Cathedral 1986–92; Bishop Suffragan of Taunton 1986–92; Canon Emeritus, Salisbury Cathedral 1989; Member, House of Bishops, General Synod of Church of England 1990–; Bishop of Wakefield 1992–; Chairman: Church of England Communications Unit 1993–99, Church of England Mission, Evangelism and Renewal Committee 1990–99; Took his seat in the House of Lords 1997; Lord High Almoner to HM The Queen 1997–. *Other:* Council Member, Royal School of Church Music 1984–; Chaplain, St John Council: Somerset 1987–91, West and South Yorkshire 1991–; Chairman, Somerset County Scout Association 1988–92; President: Central Yorkshire Scouts 1992–, CALCB 1997–2000. *Trusts, etc:* Chairman, Sandford St Martin Trust 1999–. *Publications:* A Gospel to Proclaim, 1992; Barriers to Belief, 1995. *Special Interests:* Broadcasting and Communications. *Recreations:* Music, walking in the Lake District. *Clubs:* Athenaeum. *Address:* Rt Rev the Lord Bishop of Wakefield, Bishop's Lodge, Woodthorpe Lane, Wakefield, West Yorkshire, WF2 6JL *E-Mail:* bishop.wakefield@wakefield.anglican.org.

LORD WAKEHAM — Conservative

WAKEHAM (Life Baron), John Wakeham; cr. 1992. Born 22 June 1932. Son of late Major Walter John Wakeham; educated Charterhouse. Married 1st, September 9, 1965, Anne Roberta Bailey (died 1984), (2 sons), married 2nd, July 19, 1985, Alison Ward, MBE, daughter of Venerable Edwin Ward, LVO (1 son). *Armed Forces:* National Service 1955–57, commissioned Royal Artillery. *Councils, Public Bodies:* JP, Inner London 1972; DL, Hampshire 1997. *Career:* Non-Executive Director: Azurix Corporation 1991–, Bristol and West plc 1994–, Enron Corporation 1994–; N. M. Rothschild & Sons 1995–; Chairman: Genner Holdings 1994–, Kalon 1995–, Vosper Thorneycroft 1995–, Press Complaints Commission 1995–, Michael Page Group 1995–97, President 1997–, British Horseracing Board 1996–98; Non-Executive Director, Rothschilds Continuation Holdings AG (Switzerland) 1999–. *House of Commons:* Contested (Conservative): Coventry East 1966, Putney 1970 General Elections; MP (Conservative) for: Maldon 1974–83, South Colchester and Maldon 1983–92; Parliamentary Under-Secretary of State, Department of Industry 1981–82; Minister of State, HM Treasury 1982–83; Lord Privy Seal and Leader of the House of Commons 1987–88; Lord President of the Council and Leader of the House of Commons 1988–89; Secretary of State for Energy 1989–92; Given additional responsibility for co-ordinating the development of the presentation of Government policies 1990–92. *Whip (Commons):* Assistant Government Whip 1979–81; Government Whip (Lord Commissioner of HM Treasury) 1981; Government Chief Whip (Parliamentary Secretary to the Treasury) 1983–87. *Chancellor:* Chancellor, Brunel University 1997–. *House of Lords:* Lord Privy Seal and Leader of the House of Lords 1992–94. *Party Groups (General):* Chairman, Carlton Club 1992–98. *Other:* Member, Governing Body, Charterhouse 1986–; Governor, Sutton's Hospital, Charterhouse 1992–; Governor, St Swithun's School 1994–; President: GamCare 1997–, Brendoncare Foundation 1998–, Printers' Charitable Corporation 1998–; Chairman: Alexandra Rose Day 1998–, Cothill House 1998–. Hon. PhD, Anglia Polytechnic University 1992; Hon. DUniv, Brunel University 1998. *Trusts, etc:* Trustee, HMS Warrior 1860 1997; Trustee and Committee of Management, RNLI 1995–. *Miscellaneous:* Chairman, Royal Commission on the Reform of the House of Lords 1999. *Honours:* PC 1983. FCA. *Recreations:* Sailing, farming, racing, reading. *Clubs:* Buck's, Carlton, St Stephen's Constitutional, Garrick, Royal Yacht Squadron (Cowes). *Name, Style and Title:* Raised to the peerage as Baron Wakeham, of Maldon in the County of Essex 1992. *Address:* Rt Hon the Lord Wakeham, DL, House of Lords, London, SW1A 0PW *Tel:* House of Lords 020 7219 3162.

LORD WALDEGRAVE OF NORTH HILL — Conservative

WALDEGRAVE OF NORTH HILL (Life Baron), William Arthur Waldegrave; cr. 1999. Born 15 August 1946. Son of 12th Earl Waldegrave, KG, GCVO, TD, DL; educated Eton; Corpus Christi College, Oxford (Open Scholar, BA literae humaniores) (President of Union); Harvard University. Married July 25, 1977, Caroline Burrows, OBE (1 son 3 daughters). *Councils, Public Bodies:* JP, Inner London Juvenile Court 1975–79. *Career:* Member: Central Policy Review Staff, Cabinet Office 1971–73, Political Staff at 10 Downing Street 1973–74; Leader of Opposition's Office 1974–75; With GEC Ltd 1975–81; Director: Bristol and West plc (formerly Bristol and West Building Society) 1997–, Waldegrave Farms Ltd, Henry Sotherans Ltd; Director, Corporate Finance, Dresdner Kleinwort Benson 1998–. *House of Commons:* MP (Conservative) for Bristol West 1979–97; Parliamentary Under-Secretary of State at: Department of Education and Science 1981–83, Department of Environment 1983–85; Minister of State for: Department of the Environment 1985–86, Environment Countryside and Planning 1986–87, Housing and Planning 1987–88, Foreign and Commonwealth Office 1988–90; Secretary of State for Health 1990–92; Chancellor of the Duchy of Lancaster and Minister for Public Service and Science 1992–94; Minister of Agriculture, Fisheries and Food 1994–95; Chief Secretary to HM Treasury 1995–97. Fellow, All Souls, Oxford 1971–86, 1999–; Hon. Fellow, Corpus Christi College, Oxford. *Trusts, etc:* Trustee, Rhodes Trust 1992–; Chairman, Bristol Cathedral Trust. *Honours:* PC 1990. Liveryman, The Merchant Taylors' Company. *Publications:* The Binding of Leviathan, 1978. *Clubs:* Beefsteak, Pratt's, Clifton (Bristol). *Name, Style and Title:* Raised to the peerage as Baron Waldegrave of North Hill, of Chewton Mendip in the County of Somerset 1999. *Address:* Rt Hon the Lord Waldegrave of North Hill, 66 Palace Gardens Terrace, London, W8 4RR.

LORD WALKER OF DONCASTER   Labour

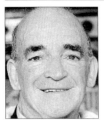

WALKER OF DONCASTER (Life Baron), Harold Walker; cr. 1997. Born 12 July 1927. Son of late Harold Walker; educated Manchester College of Technology; NCLC. Married 1st, 1956, Barbara Hague (died 1981) (1 daughter), married 2nd, 1984, Mary Griffin. *Trades Union:* Former Chairman of stewards and convener, AEU. *Armed Forces:* Served Fleet Air Arm 1946–48. *Councils, Public Bodies:* DL, South Yorkshire 1997–. *Career:* Toolmaker; Industrial Administrator; Political and Trade Union Lecturer/Tutor. *House of Commons:* MP (Labour) for Doncaster 1964–83 and for Doncaster Central 1983–97; Parliamentary Under-Secretary of State, Department of Employment and Productivity 1968–70; Parliamentary Under-Secretary of State for Employment 1974–76; Minister of State for Employment 1976–79; Chairman, Ways and Means and Deputy Speaker 1983–92. *Whip (Commons):* Assistant Government Whip April 1967–68. *Spokesman (Commons):* Front Bench (Opposition) Spokesman on Employment 1970–74; Opposition Front Bench Spokesman on Employment 1979–83. *Select Committees:* Member, Joint Select Committee on Statutory Instruments 1998–. *Other:* President: St John's Hospice Appeal, Doncaster Multiple Sclerosis, Doncaster Mencap, Doncaster and District Punjab Association. *Trusts, etc:* President, Doncaster Cancer Detection Trust. *Honours:* PC 1979; Knighted 1992. Freeman, Doncaster 1998. *Special Interests:* Industrial Relations, Health and Safety at Work, Manpower Policy. *Name, Style and Title:* Raised to the peerage as Baron Walker of Doncaster, of Audenshaw in the County of Greater Manchester 1997. *Address:* Rt Hon the Lord Walker of Doncaster, DL, House of Lords, London, SW1A 0PW.

LORD WALKER OF WORCESTER   Conservative

WALKER OF WORCESTER (Life Baron), Peter Edward Walker; cr. 1992. Born 25 March 1932. Son of late Sydney Walker; educated Latymer Upper School. Married February 22, 1969, Tessa Pout (3 sons 2 daughters). *Career:* Non-Executive Director: Smith New Court 1990–95, British Gas plc 1990–96, Tate & Lyle 1990–, Chairman: English Partnerships 1992–98, Cornhill Insurance plc 1992–; Non-Executive Director, Liffe 1995–; Chairman, Kleinwort Benson Group plc 1996–98; Vice-Chairman, Dresdner Kleinwort Benson 1998–. *House of Commons:* Contested (Conservative) Dartford in 1955, 1959 General Elections; MP (Conservative) for Worcester 1961–92; PPS to Rt Hon. Selwyn Lloyd, MP 1963–64; Minister of Housing and Local Government June-October 1970; Secretary of State for: The Environment 1970–72, Trade and Industry 1972–74; Minister of Agriculture, Fisheries and Food 1979–83; Secretary of State for: Energy 1983–87, Wales 1987–90. *Spokesman (Commons):* Opposition Front Bench Spokesman on: Finance and Economics 1964–66, Transport 1966–68, Local Government, Housing and Land 1968–70; Opposition Spokesman on: Trade, Industry and Consumer Affairs February-June 1974, Defence 1974–75. *Party Groups (General):* Member, National Executive Committee of Conservative Party 1956–62; National Chairman, Young Conservatives 1968–70. *Honours:* MBE 1960; PC 1970; Commander's Cross of the Order of Merit (Germany) 1994; Chilean Order of Bernardo O'Higgins, Degree Gran Oficial 1995. *Publications: The Ascent of Britain,* 1977; *Trust the People,* 1987; *Staying Power,* 1991. *Clubs:* Carlton. *Name, Style and Title:* Raised to the peerage as Baron Walker of Worcester, of Abbots Morton in the County of Hereford and Worcester 1992. *Address:* Rt Hon the Lord Walker of Worcester, MBE, Abbots Morton Manor, Gooms Hill, Abbots Morton, Worcester, WR7 4LT.

LORD WALLACE OF COSLANY   Labour

WALLACE OF COSLANY (Life Baron), George Douglas Wallace; cr. 1974. Born 18 April 1906. Son of late George Wallace; educated Cheltenham Central School. Married March 28, 1932, Vera Randall (1 son 1 daughter). *Trades Union:* Member, TGWU. *Armed Forces:* Sergeant, RAF 1941–45. *Councils, Public Bodies:* Councillor: Chislehurst, Sidcup UDC 1937–45, Kent County Council 1952–57. *House of Commons:* MP (Labour) for: Chislehurst 1945–50, Norwich North 1964–74; Contested (Labour): Chislehurst 1951, 1955, Norwich South 1959; PPS to: Lord President of Council 1964–66, Secretary of State for Commonwealth Affairs 1966–67, Minister of State, Housing and Local Government 1967–68. *Whip (Commons):* Assistant Government Whip 1947–50. *International Bodies (Commons):* Member, UK delegation to IPU Conference, Stockholm 1949;

Delegate to: CPA Conference, Ottawa 1966, IPU Conference, Delhi 1969. *Whip:* A Lord in Waiting (Government Whip) 1977–79; Opposition Whip 1979–84. *Spokesman:* Opposition Spokesman on Health, Social Security 1983–84. *Party Groups (General):* Joined Labour Party 1935. *Other:* President, Radio Society of Gt Britain 1977; Formerly President, London Society of Recreational Gardeners; President, League of Friends, Queen Mary's Hospital, Sidcup 1980–. *Miscellaneous:* A Commissioner, Commonwealth War Graves Commission 1970–86. *Recreations:* Amateur radio, gardening. *Sportsclubs:* President, Norwich City London Supporters. *Name, Style and Title:* Raised to the peerage as Baron Wallace of Coslany, of Coslany in the City of Norwich 1974. *Address:* The Lord Wallace of Coslany, 44 Shuttle Close, Sidcup, Kent, DA15 8EP *Tel:* 020 8300 3634; House of Lords, London, SW1A 0PW *Tel:* House of Lords 020 7219 5408.

LORD WALLACE OF SALTAIRE — Liberal Democrat

WALLACE OF SALTAIRE (Life Baron), William John Lawrence Wallace; cr. 1995. Born 12 March 1941. Son of late William Edward Wallace and late Mary Agnes Tricks; educated Westminster Abbey Choir School; St Edward's School, Oxford; King's College, Cambridge (BA History 1962); Cornell University, USA (PhD Government 1968); Nuffield College, Oxford. Married August 24, 1968, Helen Sarah, daughter of late Edward Rushworth (1 son 1 daughter). *Career:* Lecturer in Government, Manchester University 1967–77; Director of Studies, Royal Institute of International Affairs 1978–90; Walter F. Hallstein Fellow, St Antony's College, Oxford 1990–95; London School of Economics 1995–: international relations reader 1995–99; Professor 1999–. *Spokesman:* Liberal Democrat Spokesman on: Defence 1997–, Foreign and Commonwealth Affairs 1998–. *Select Committees:* Member, Select Committee on European Communities 1997–2000; Chairman, Select Committee on European Communities Sub-Committee F (Social Affairs, Education and Home Affairs) 1997–2000; Member, Ecclesiastical Committee 1997–. Doctorate hc, Université Libre de Bruxelles 1992. *Honours:* Chevalier, Ordre pour le Mérite (France) 1995. *Publications: The Foreign Policy Process in Britain,* 1977; *The Transformation of Europe,* 1990; *The Dynamics of European Integration,* 1990; *Regional Integration – The West European Experience,* 1994; *Policy-making in the European Union,* with Helen Wallace 1996, 2000. *Special Interests:* Foreign Affairs, Defence, Europe, Constitutional Affairs. *Recreations:* Swimming, walking, gardening. *Sportsclubs:* Sattaire Tennis Club. *Name, Style and Title:* Raised to the peerage as Baron Wallace of Saltaire, of Shipley in the County of West Yorkshire 1995. *Address:* The Lord Wallace of Saltaire, House of Lords, London, SW1A 0PW.

BARONESS WALMSLEY — Liberal Democrat

WALMSLEY (Life Baroness), Joan Margaret Walmsley; cr. 2000. Born 12 April 1943. Daughter of Leo and Monica Watson; educated Notre Dame High School, Liverpool; Liverpool University; Manchester Metropolitan University. Married, Christopher Walmsley (deceased) (1 son 1 daughter 1 stepson 2 stepdaughters). *Career:* Cytologist, Christie Hospital, Manchester 1965–67; Teacher, Buxton College, Derbyshire 1979–86; Public Relations Consultant 1987–. *Party Groups (General):* Secretary, Association of Liberal Democrat Councillors' Standing Committee; Member, Liberal Democrats Federal Conference Committee. *Miscellaneous:* Contested (Liberal Democrat) Leeds South and Morley 1992 and Congleton 1997 General Election. *Recreations:* Music, theatre, gardening, good company. *Name, Style and Title:* Raised to the peerage as Baroness Walmsley, of West Derby in the County of Merseyside 2000. *Address:* The Baroness Walmsley, House of Lords, London, SW1A 0PW *E-Mail:* walmsleyj@parliament.uk.

LORD WALPOLE
Cross-Bencher

WALPOLE (10th Baron, GB), Robert (Robin) Horatio Walpole; cr 1723; 8th Baron Walpole of Wolterton (GB) 1756. Born 8 December 1938. Son of 9th Baron, TD. Succeeded his father 1989; educated Eton; King's College, Cambridge (MA, DipAgric). Married 1st, 1962, Judith Schofield (2 sons 2 daughters) (divorced 1979), married 2nd, 1980, Laurel Celia Ball (2 sons 1 daughter). *Councils, Public Bodies:* Councillor, Norfolk County Council 1970–81; Variously Chairman: Highways, Library and Recreation, Planning and Transportation, Norfolk Joint Museums Committees; JP, Norfolk 1972. *House of Lords:* An elected hereditary peer 1999–. *Select Committees:* Member: Agriculture Sub-Committee of European Communities Committee 1991–94, Environment Sub-Committee of European Communities Committee 1995–97, Select Committee on European Communities 1997–, Select Committee on European Communities Sub-Committee C (Environment, Public Health and Consumer Protection) 1997–. *Other:* Chairman: Area Museums Service for South East England 1976–79, Norwich School of Art 1977–87; Chairman, Textile Conservation Centre 1981–88, President 1988; Member: CPRE, RSPB. Hon. Fellow, St Mary's University College, Strawberry Hill 1997. *Miscellaneous:* Chairman, East Anglian Tourist Board 1982–88. *Special Interests:* Agriculture, Arts, Tourism, Conservation. *Address:* The Lord Walpole, Mannington Hall, Norwich, Norfolk, NR11 7BB *Tel:* 01263 587763 *E-Mail:* walpolerh@parliament.uk.

LORD WALTON OF DETCHANT
Cross-Bencher

WALTON OF DETCHANT (Life Baron), John Nicholas Walton; cr. 1989. Born 16 September 1922. Son of late Herbert and Eleanor Walton; educated Alderman Wraith Grammar School, Spennymoor, Co. Durham; Medical School, King's College, Newcastle upon Tyne (Durham University) (MB, BS, MD, DSc, MA Oxon). Married August 31, 1946, Mary Elizabeth, daughter of Joseph Bell Harrison (1 son 2 daughters). *Armed Forces:* Service in RAMC 1947–49; Colonel (late RAMC) and Officer Commanding 1 (N) General Hospital (TA) 1963–66; Hon. Colonel 1968–73. *Career:* Nuffield Foundation Fellow in Neurology, Massachusetts General Hospital, Boston USA 1953–54; King's College Travelling Fellow in Medicine, National Hospital, London 1954–55; First Assistant in Neurology, King's College and Royal Infirmary, Newcastle 1956–58; Consultant Neurologist, Newcastle General Hospital 1958–83; Lecturer in Neurology, Newcastle University 1966–68; Director, Muscular Dystrophy Group Research Laboratories, Newcastle General Hospital 1965–83; Professor of Neurology, Newcastle University 1968–83; Dean of Medicine, Newcastle University 1971–81; Warden, Green College, Oxford 1983–89. *Select Committees:* Member, House of Lords Select Committees on: Science and Technology 1992–96, 1997–, Medical Ethics 1993–94, Science and Technology Sub-Committee IIA (Human Genetic Databases) 2000–. *Other:* Chairman, Muscular Dystrophy Group of Great Britain and Northern Ireland 1971–95; Member: General Medical Council 1971–79, President 1982–89; Medical Research Council 1974–78; President: British Medical Association 1980–82, Royal Society of Medicine 1984–86, Association of British Neurologists 1987–88; First Vice-President, World Federation of Neurology 1987–89, President 1989–97. Nine honorary degrees from British, Italian and Thai universities. *Honours:* TD 1962; Kt 1979. FRCP; Hon. FRCPEd; Hon. FRCPC; Hon. FRCPsych; Hon. FRCPath; Hon. FRCPCH; FMedSci; Hon. Fellow, Institute of Education, London. Hon. Freeman, Newcastle upon Tyne 1980; Freeman, City of London 1981. *Publications:* Several medical titles including: *Essentials of Neurology*, 1961; *Disorders of Voluntary Muscle*, 1964; *The Spice of Life* (autobiography), 1993; as well as numerous chapters in books and articles in scientific journals. *Special Interests:* Medicine, Health, Science, Education. *Recreations:* Golf, cricket, reading, music, opera. *Sportsclubs:* President, Bamburgh Castle Golf Club. *Clubs:* Athenaeum, United Oxford and Cambridge University, Royal Society of Medicine, MCC. *Name, Style and Title:* Raised to the peerage as Baron Walton of Detchant, of Detchant in the County of Northumberland 1989. *Address:* The Lord Walton of Detchant, TD, 13 Norham Gardens, Oxford, OX2 6PS *Tel:* Office: 01865 512492 *Fax:* 01865 512495.

LORD WARNER   Labour

WARNER (Life Baron), Norman Reginald Warner; cr. 1998. Born 8 September 1940. Son of Albert and Laura Warner; educated Dulwich College; University of California, Berkeley (MPH) (Harkness Fellowship 1971–73). Married 1st, 1961, Anne Lesley Lawrence (1 son 1 daughter) (marriage dissolved 1981); married 2nd, 1990, Suzanne Elizabeth Reeve (1 son). *Councils, Public Bodies:* Chairman, City and East London FHSA 1991–94. *Career:* Joined Ministry of Health 1959; Assistant Private Secretary: to Minister of Health 1967–68, to Secretary of State for Social Services 1968–69; Executive Councils Division, Department of Health and Social Security 1969–71; NHS Reorganisation, DHSS 1973–74; Principal Private Secretary to Secretary of State for Social Services 1974–76; Supplementary Benefits Division 1976–78; Management Services, DHSS 1979–81; Regional Controller, Wales and South Western Region, DHSS 1981–83; Gwilym Gibbon Fellow, Nuffield College, Oxford 1983–84; Under-Secretary, Supplementary Benefits Division, DHSS 1984–85; Director of Social Services, Kent County Council 1985–91; Managing Director, Warner Consultancy and Training Services Ltd 1991–97; Senior Policy Adviser to the Home Secretary 1997–; Chairman, Youth Justice Board for England and Wales 1998–. *Other:* Member, Carers National Association 1991–94; Member, Royal Philanthropic Society 1991–, Chairman 1993–98; Chairman: Expert Panel for UK Harkness Fellowships 1994–97, Residential Forum, in Association with National Institute for Social Work 1994–97. *Trusts, etc:* Trustee: Leonard Cheshire Foundation 1994–96, MacIntyre Care 1994–97. *Miscellaneous:* Chairman, National Inquiry into Selection, Development and Management of Staff in Children's Homes 1991–92; Member, Local Government Commission 1995–96. Manhatten Fellow, USA 1971–72; Gwilym Gibbon Fellow, Nuffield College, Oxford 1984. *Publications:* Editor, *Commissioning Community Alternatives in European Social and Health Care*, 1993; several articles in specialised journals. *Special Interests:* Law and Order, Children, Social and Health Care. *Recreations:* Reading, cinema, theatre, exercise, travel. *Sportsclubs:* Surrey Cricket Club. *Name, Style and Title:* Raised to the peerage as Baron Warner, of Brockley in the London Borough of Lewisham 1998. *Address:* The Lord Warner, House of Lords, London, SW1A 0HA.

BARONESS WARNOCK   Cross-Bencher

WARNOCK (Life Baroness), Helen Mary Warnock; cr. 1985. Born 14 April 1924. Daughter of late Archibald Edward Wilson; educated St Swithun's, Winchester; Lady Margaret Hall, Oxford (MA, BPhil). Married 1949, Sir Geoffrey James Warnock (died 1995) (2 sons 3 daughters). *Career:* Fellow and Tutor in Philosophy, St Hugh's College, Oxford 1952–66, Headmistress, Oxford High School 1966–72; Chairman, Committee of Inquiry into Special Education 1974–78; Member, Royal Commission on Environmental Pollution 1979–84; Chairman, Committee of Inquiry on Human Fertility and Embryology 1982–84; Mistress, Girton College, Cambridge 1985–91; Gifford Lecturer, Glasgow University 1991–92; Visiting Professor, Gresham College 2000–01. *Select Committees:* Member, House of Lords Select Committees on: Medical Ethics 1993–94, Dangerous Dogs 1996. *Other:* President, British Dyslexia Association. *Awards Granted:* Albert Medalist, Royal Society of Arts 1998. 13 honorary degrees from UK and Australia; 5 honorary university fellowships. *Trusts, etc:* Director, Girls' Public Dayschool Trust; Trustee, National Primary Trust. *Miscellaneous:* Research Fellow, St Hugh's College, Oxford 1972–84; Hon. Bencher, Gray's Inn. *Honours:* DBE 1984. Fellow, College of Teachers (formerly College of Preceptors); Hon. FRCM; Hon. Fellow: Royal Society of Physicians, Scotland, British Academy 2000. *Publications:* Author of books on ethics and education and philosophy of mind. *Special Interests:* Education, Broadcasting, Medicine, Environment. *Recreations:* Music, gardening. *Name, Style and Title:* Raised to the peerage as Baroness Warnock, of Weeke in the City of Winchester 1985. *Address:* The Baroness Warnock, DBE, 3 Church Street, Great Bedwyn, Marlborough, Wiltshire, SN8 3PE.

BARONESS WARWICK OF UNDERCLIFFE   Labour

WARWICK OF UNDERCLIFFE (Life Baroness), Diana Warwick; cr. 1999. Born 16 July 1945. Daughter of Jack and Olive Warwick; educated St Joseph's College, Bradford; Bedford College, University of London (BA Hons). Married 1969, Sean Bowes Young, son of Terence Young and Dorothea Bennet. *Career:* Technical Assistant to General Secretary, NUT 1969–72; Assistant Secretary, Civil and Public Services Association 1972–83; General Secretary, Association of University Teachers 1983–92; Chief Executive: Westminster Foundation for Democracy 1992–95, Committee of Vice-Chancellors and Principals 1995–. *Select Committees:* Member, Science and Technology Sub-Committee II (Aircraft Cabin Environment) 2000–. *International Bodies (General):* Member: RIIA, IPU, CPA, British American Parliamentary Group. *Other:* Chairman, Voluntary Service Overseas 1994–. Hon. DLitt: Bradford University 1993, Open University 1998. *Trusts, etc:* Trustee: Royal Anniversary Trust 1991–93, St Catherine's Foundation, Windsor 1996–. *Miscellaneous:* Member: Board, British Council 1985–95, Employment Appeal Tribunal 1987–99, Executive and Council, Industrial Society 1987–, TUC General Council 1989–92, Council, Duke of Edinburgh's Seventh Commonwealth Study Conference 1991, Neill Committee on Standards in Public Life 1994–99, OST Technology Foresight Steering Group 1997–, Commonwealth Institute 1988–95. FRSA 1984. *Recreations:* Theatre, opera, looking at pictures. *Name, Style and Title:* Raised to the peerage as Baroness Warwick of Undercliffe, of Undercliffe in the County of West Yorkshire 1999 *Address:* The Baroness Warwick of Undercliffe, Committee of Vice-Chancellors and Principals, Woburn House, 20 Tavistock Square, London, WC1H 9HQ *Tel:* 020 7419 5402 *Fax:* 020 7380 0137 *E-Mail:* diana.warwick@cvcp.ac.uk.

LORD WATSON OF INVERGOWRIE   Labour

WATSON OF INVERGOWRIE (Life Baron), Michael Goodall Watson; cr. 1997. Born 1 May 1949. Son of late Clarke and Senga Watson; educated Invergowrie Primary School, Dundee; Dundee High School; Heriot-Watt University, Edinburgh (BA Economics and Industrial Relations 1974). Married October 31, 1986, Lorraine Therese McManus (separated). *Trades Union:* Member, Manufacturing, Science and Finance Union (formerly ASTMS) 1975–. *Career:* Development Officer, WEA East Midlands District 1974–77; MSF: Full-time official 1977–89, Industrial Officer 1977–79, Regional Officer based in Glasgow 1979–89; Visiting Research Fellow, Department of Government, University of Strathclyde 1993–; Director, PS Communication Consultants Ltd, Edinburgh 1997–99. *House of Commons:* MP (Labour) for Glasgow Central 1989–97. *Select Committees:* Member, Select Committee on European Communities Sub-Committee F (Social Policy) 1997–98. *Party Groups:* Member, Parliamentary Labour Party: Education and Employment Group, Foreign Affairs Group, Overseas Development Group. *Party Groups (General):* Member, Labour Party Scottish Executive Committee 1987–90. *Other:* Member: Board of Management, Volunteer Centre, Scotland 1994–; Scottish Youth Theatre 1998–. Hon. LLD, University of Abertay Dundee 1998. *Miscellaneous:* MSP for the Constituency of Glasgow Cathcart since May 6, 1999 (contested the seat as Mike Watson); Scottish Parliament Committees: Convener, Finance Committee 1999–; Member, Social Inclusion, Housing and Voluntary Sector Committee 1999–. *Publications: Rags to Riches: The Official History of Dundee United FC*, 1985; *The Tannadice Encyclopedia*, 1997. *Special Interests:* Scottish Parliament, Higher Education, Employment Law, Overseas Aid and Development, Foreign Affairs. *Recreations:* Supporting Dundee United FC, running, reading, especially political biographies. *Name, Style and Title:* Raised to the peerage as Baron Watson of Invergowrie, of Invergowrie in Perth and Kinross 1997. *Address:* The Lord Watson of Invergowrie, MSP, House of Lords, London, SW1A 0PW *E-Mail:* watsonm@parliament.uk; mike.watson.msp@scottish.parliament.uk.

Visit the Vacher Dod Website . . .
www.politicallinks.co.uk

LORD WATSON OF RICHMOND — Liberal Democrat

WATSON OF RICHMOND (Life Baron), Alan John Watson; cr. 1999. Born 3 February 1941. Son of Rev. John William Watson and Edna Mary (née Peters); educated Diocesan College, Cape Town, South Africa; Kingswood School, Bath; Jesus College, Cambridge (Open Scholar in History 1959, State Scholar 1959, MA) (Vice-President, Cambridge Union). Married 1965, Karen Lederer (2 sons). *Career:* Research Assistant, Cambridge University 1962–64; BBC 1965–66; Reporter, BBC TV, The Money Programme 1966–68; Chief Public Affairs Commentator, London Weekend Television 1969–70; Reporter, Panorama, BBC TV 1971–74; Presenter, The Money Programme 1974–75; Head of TV, Radio, Audio-Visual Division, EEC, and Editor, European Community Newsreel Service to Lomé Convention Countries 1975–79; Director, Charles Barker City Ltd 1980–85, Chief Executive 1980–83; Deputy Chairman, Sterling Public Relations 1985–86; Chairman: City and Corporate Counsel Ltd 1987–94, Threadneedle Publishing Group 1987–94, Corporate Vision Ltd 1989–98, Corporate Television Networks 1992–; Member, Y&R Partnership Board; Chairman: Burson-Marsteller UK 1994–, Burson-Marsteller Europe 1996–. *Spokesman:* A Liberal Democrat Spokesman on Foreign and Commonwealth Affairs (Europe) 2000–. *Select Committees:* Member, Select Committee on European Union, Sub-Committee C (Common Foreign and Security Policy) 2000–. *International Bodies (General):* Chairman, British-German Association 1992–2000; Vice-Chairman, The European Movement 1995–; Chairman, English Speaking Union 2000–; President, British-German Association 2000–; Member, High Level EU-Romania Group 2000–. *Party Groups (General):* Former President, Cambridge University Liberal Club; Chairman, Liberal Party Parliamentary Association 1982–84; Member, Liberal Party National Executive 1982–86; President, Liberal Party 1984–85. *Other:* Chairman of Governors, Westminster College, Oxford 1988–94; President, Heathrow Association for Control of Aircraft Noise 1992–95; Prince of Wales Business Leaders Forum 1996–. Hon. Doctorate, St Lawrence University. *Miscellaneous:* Contested Richmond, Surrey (Liberal) 1974 and 1979, Richmond and Barnes (Liberal/Aliance) 1983 and 1987 General Elections Member, Executive Board UNICEF 1985–92; Presenter: BBC 1 1990, Channel 4 1992; Visiting Fellow, Louvanium International Business Centre, Brussels 1990–95; Visiting Erasmus Professor in European Studies, Louvain University 1990; Hon. Professor, German Studies, Birmingham University 1997–; Trustee, Humboldt University; Chairman, Chemistry Appeal Advisory Board, Cambridge. *Honours:* CBE 1985; Order of Merit (Germany) 1995. FRSA; FIPR; FIVCA. *Publications: Europe at risk,* 1972; *The Germans: who are they now?,* 1992; *Thatcher and Kohl: old rivalries revisited,* 1996. *Special Interests:* European History, South Africa. *Recreations:* Boating, wines, foreign travel, art. *Clubs:* Brooks's, Royal Automobile, Kennel, House of Lords Yacht. *Name, Style and Title:* Raised to the peerage as Baron Watson of Richmond, of Richmond in the London Borough of Richmond upon Thames 1999. *Address:* The Lord Watson of Richmond, CBE, Cholmondeley House, 3 Cholmondeley Walk, Richmond upon Thames, Surrey, TW9 1NS; Somerset Lodge, Nunney, Somerset, BA11 4NP *E-Mail:* alan_watson@uk.bm.com.

VISCOUNT WAVERLEY — Cross-Bencher

WAVERLEY (3rd Viscount, UK), John Desmond Forbes Anderson; cr. 1952. Born 31 October 1949. Son of 2nd Viscount. Succeeded his father 1990; educated Malvern. Married January 4, 1994, HE Dr Ursula Barrow (1 son). *Career:* Landscape Contractor (Europe/Middle East) 1975–85; Publishers' Agent (Latin America/Africa) 1985–93; Emerging Markets Support 1993–. *House of Lords:* An elected hereditary peer 1999–. *International Bodies:* Member, Executive Committee, Commonwealth Parliamentary Association 1994–95; Member, Inter-Parliamentary Union; Parliamentary visits to: Japan, Falkland Islands, Bangladesh, Kashmir, Belize, Nigeria, Ghana, Burundi; Observer, 1994 San José X Ministerial Conference (EU/Central America); Aid Programme Evaluation, Nepal; Commonwealth Observer, Bangladesh General Elections 1996. *Other:* Member, Royal Institute of International Affairs. *Honours:* Order of San Carlos (Grand Cross) Colombia 1998. Companion, Institute of Export. *Special Interests:* Britain's Export Performance, Foreign Affairs, Commonwealth, Overseas Aid and Development, Conflict Resolution. *Recreations:* Golf, scuba diving, walking, travel. *Sportsclubs:* Rye Golf. *Address:* The Viscount Waverley, House of Lords, London, SW1A 0PW *Tel:* 020 7219 3000 *E-Mail:* waverley@int-affairs.com.

LORD WEATHERILL Cross-Bencher

WEATHERILL (Life Baron), (Bruce) Bernard Weatherill; cr. 1992. Born 25 November 1920. Son of late Bernard Weatherill and Gertrude Weatherill (née Creak); educated Malvern College. Married 1949, Lyn Eatwell (2 sons 1 daughter). *Armed Forces:* Commissioned 1940 in 4/7 Royal Dragoon Guards; Transferred to 19th King George V's Own Lancers (Indian Army) 1941–46; Served Burma and North-West Europe. *Councils, Public Bodies:* DL, Kent 1992. *Career:* Employed in family business of Bernard Weatherill Ltd, Tailors, of Savile Row, London, W1 1946–70, President of the Company 1992. *House of Commons:* MP (Conservative) for Croydon North East 1964–83, and as an Independent 1983–92; Chairman of Ways and Means and Deputy Speaker 1979–83; Speaker 1983–92. *Whip (Commons):* Opposition Whip 1967–70; Government Whip 1970–73 (Lord Commissioner of HM Treasury 1970–71, Vice-Chamberlain, HM Household 1971–72, Comptroller, HM Household 1972–73); Deputy Chief Whip (Treasurer, HM Household) 1973–74; Opposition Deputy Chief Whip 1974–79. *House of Lords:* Alternate Convenor of the Cross-Bench Peers 1993–95, Convenor 1995–99. *Select Committees:* Former Member, House of Lords Offices Committee; Member, Select Committees on: Offices, Finance and Staff, Administration and Works, Liaison Privileges, Procedure, Selection; Member, Ecclesiastical Committee 2000–. *International Bodies:* Vice-President: Commonwealth Parliamentary Association, Intra-Parliamentary Union. *Other:* Chairman, Commonwealth Speakers and Presiding Officers 1986–88; High Bailiff of Westminster Abbey and Searcher of the Sanctuary 1989–99; Chairman, Industry and Churches Forum; President: The Institute for Citizenship, Kent County Scout Association. Hon. DCL: University of Kent, University of William and Mary USA, University of Denver, Colorado USA, Open University 1993. *Trusts, etc:* Chairman, Industry and Parliamentary Trust 1993–; Trustee: The Prince's Trust, Prince's Youth Business Trust. *Miscellaneous:* Hon. Bencher of Lincoln's Inn. *Honours:* PC 1980; KStJ 1992; Vice-Chancellor, Order of St John of Jerusalem; Hilal-i-Pakistan 1993. Freeman: City of London 1949, Borough of Croydon 1983. Member: Gold and Silver Wyre Drawers, Merchant Taylors, Blacksmiths. *Publications:* Acorns To Oaks, (a policy for small businesses) 1967. *Recreations:* Tennis, Golf. *Sportsclubs:* President, Lucifer Golfing Society 1992; Tandridge Golf. *Clubs:* Cavalry and Guards, Reform. *Name, Style and Title:* Raised to the peerage as Baron Weatherill, of North East Croydon in the London Borough of Croydon 1992. *Address:* Rt Hon the Lord Weatherill, DL, Emmetts House, Ide Hill, Kent, TN14 6BA; House of Lords, London, SW1A 0PW *Tel:* House of Lords 020 7219 2224.

LORD WEDDERBURN OF CHARLTON Labour

WEDDERBURN OF CHARLTON (Life Baron), Kenneth William Wedderburn; cr. 1977. Born 13 April 1927. Son of late Herbert J. Wedderburn; educated Aske's Hatcham Boys School; Whitgift School, Croydon; Queens' College, Cambridge (MA, LLB). Married 1st, 1951, Nina, daughter of Dr M. Salaman (1 son 2 daughters) (marriage dissolved 1962), married 2nd, 1962, Mrs Dorothy Cole (marriage dissolved 1969), married 3rd, 1969, Frances, daughter of Basil Knight (1 son). *Trades Union:* Member, Association of University Teachers. *Armed Forces:* Served RAF 1949–51. *Career:* Fellow of Clare College, Cambridge and University Lecturer in Law 1952–64; Called to the Bar, Middle Temple 1953; Cassel Professor of Commercial Law, London University (London School of Economics) 1964–92, Emeritus Professor 1992–; Visiting Professor, Harvard Law School 1969–70; General Editor, Modern Law Review 1971–88; QC 1990. *Spokesman:* Deputy Opposition Front Bench Spokesman on Employment 1980–92. *Select Committees:* Co-opted Member, Select Committee on European Communities Sub-Committee E (Law and Institutions) 1997–. *Party Groups (General):* Editorial Board, International Labour Law Reports 1975–. *Other:* Chairman, London and Provincial Theatre Councils 1973–93; Hon. President, Industrial Law Society 1997–. *Awards Granted:* Chancellor's Medal for English Law 1949. Hon. Dottore Giur, University Pavia; Hon. Dottore Econ, University Siena; Hon. Doctor of Laws, University of Stockholm; Hon. Fellow: Clare College, Cambridge 1997–, London School of Economics 1999–. *Miscellaneous:* Chairman, TUC Independent Review Committee 1976–. FBA 1980. *Publications:* Employment Rights in Britain and Europe, 1991; Labour Law and Freedom, 1995; The Worker and The Law, 1986. *Special Interests:* Industrial Relations, Employment Law, Company Law, Education. *Recreations:* Charlton Athletic Football Club. *Name, Style and Title:* Raised to the peerage as Baron Wedderburn of Charlton, of Highgate in the County of Greater London 1977. *Address:* Professor the Lord Wedderburn of Charlton, QC, FBA, Chambers: 1 Verulam Buildings, Gray's Inn, London, WC1R 5LQ *Tel:* 020 7831 0801; 29 Woodside Avenue, Highgate, London, N6 4SP *Tel:* 020 8444 8472.

LORD WEIDENFELD   Cross-Bencher

WEIDENFELD (Life Baron), (Arthur) George Weidenfeld; cr. 1976. Born 13 September 1919. Son of late Max Weidenfeld; educated Piaristen Gymnasium, Vienna; Vienna University (Diplomatic Academy, Vienna). Married 1st, 1952, Jane Sieff (1 daughter), married 2nd, 1956, Mrs Barbara Connolly (marriage dissolved 1961, she died 1996), married 3rd, 1966, Mrs Sandra Meyer (marriage dissolved 1976), married 4th, July 14, 1992, Annabelle, daughter of late Commander Nicholas Whitestone, RN. *Career:* BBC Monitoring Service 1939–42; News Commentator, BBC Empire and North American Service 1942–46; Columnist, *News Chronicle* 1943–44; Political Adviser and Chief of Cabinet to President Weizmann of Israel 1949–50; Chairman, Weidenfeld and Nicolson Ltd, Publishers; Director, Hollinger Group of Companies; Chairman, Cheyne Capital Management Limited. *Spokesman:* SDP Spokesman on Foreign Affairs, the Arts, Broadcasting 1983–90. *Other:* Chairman, Board of Governors, Ben Gurion University of the Negev, Beer-Sheva, Israel; Governor: Weizmann Institute of Science, Tel Aviv University, Bezalel Academy of Art, Jerusalem, Jerusalem Foundation; Board Member, English National Opera 1988–98; Member, South Bank Board; Vice-President, Oxford University Development Programme; Board Member, Diplomatic Academy, Vienna 1997–; Consultant, Bertelsmann Foundation; Trustee, Quandt Stiftung, Bad Homburg. *Awards Granted:* Charlemagne Medal. Hon. PhD, Ben Gurion University of the Negev 1984; Hon. MA, Oxon 1992; Hon. Fellow: St Peter's College, Oxford, St Anne's College, Oxford; Hon. Senator (Ehrensenator), Bonn University; Magister, Diplomatic College, Vienna University. *Trusts, etc:* Trustee Emeritus, Aspen Foundation; Former Trustee, National Portrait Gallery. *Honours:* Kt 1969; Chevalier de l'Ordre National de la Legion d'Honneur; Golden Knight's Cross with Star of the Austrian Order of Merit; Knight Commander's Cross (Badge and Star) of the Order of Merit of Germany 1991. City of London; City of San Francisco; Jerusalem. *Recreations:* Travel, opera. *Clubs:* Garrick, Athenaeum. *Name, Style and Title:* Raised to the peerage as Baron Weidenfeld, of Chelsea in the County of Greater London 1976. *Address:* The Lord Weidenfeld, Orion House, 5 Upper St Martin's Lane, London, WC2H 9EA *Tel:* 020 7240 3444.

LORD WEINSTOCK   Cross-Bencher

WEINSTOCK (Life Baron), Arnold Weinstock; cr. 1980. Born 29 July 1924. Son of late Simon Weinstock; educated Albion Road Central School, London; London University (BSc statistics 1945). Married 1949, Netta, daughter of late Sir Michael Sobell (1 daughter and 1 son deceased). *Career:* Junior Administrative Officer, Admiralty 1944–47; Joined Radio & Allied (Holdings) Ltd 1954; When it merged with the General Electric Co. Ltd in 1961, appointed director of GEC, MD January 1963–96, Chairman Emeritus 1996–; Director, Rolls-Royce (1971) Ltd 1971–73. 11 honorary doctorates; 2 honorary university fellowships. *Trusts, etc:* Trustee, British Museum 1985–96. *Honours:* Kt 1970; Hon. Master of the Bench of Gray's Inn 1982; Officier, Legion d'Honneur (France) 1991; Commendatore of the Order of Merit (Italy) 1991. Liveryman, Company of Information Technologists. *Recreations:* Racing, bloodstock, classical music. *Name, Style and Title:* Raised to the peerage as Baron Weinstock, of Bowden in the County of Wiltshire 1980. *Address:* The Lord Weinstock, 1 Bruton Street, London, W1X 8AQ *Tel:* 020 7493 8484.

LORD WHADDON   Labour

WHADDON (Life Baron), John Derek Page; cr. 1978. Born 14 August 1927. Son of late John Page; educated St Bedes College, Manchester; BSc Sociology London External. Married 1st, December 4, 1948, Catherine Audrey Halls (died 1979) (1 son 1 daughter), married 2nd, 1981, Mrs Angela Rixon. *Career:* Sales Manager, Carnegies of Welwyn 1960–62; Director, Cambridge Chemical Co Ltd 1962–; Member, East Anglia Economic Planning Council until 1980; Director, Microautomatics Ltd 1981–87; Member, Lloyds 1981–94; Former Member, COSIRA Board; Director, Rindalbourne Ltd 1983–89; Chairman: Daltrade Ltd 1984–, Skorimpex-Rind Ltd 1985–, Britpol Ltd 1989–90, Crag Group Ltd 1996–. *House of Commons:* MP (Labour) for King's Lynn 1964–70. *Select Committees:* Former Member, House of Lords Select Committee on Science and Technology. *Other:* Patron, International Piano Festival, Warsaw. *Honours:* Golden Insignia of Order of Merit (Poland) 1989. *Special Interests:* Eastern Europe. *Recreations:* Private pilot. *Clubs:* Reform. *Name, Style and Title:* Raised to the peerage as Baron Whaddon, of Whaddon in the County of Cambridgeshire 1978. *Address:* The Lord Whaddon, The Old Vicarage, Whaddon, Royston, Hertfordshire *Tel:* 01223 207209.

BARONESS WHITAKER — Labour

WHITAKER (Life Baroness), Janet Alison Whitaker; cr. 1999. Born 1936. Daughter of Allan Harrison Stewart and Ella, née Saunders; educated Nottingham High School for Girls; Girton College, Cambridge (BA); Bryn Mawr College, USA (MA); Harvard University, USA (Radcliffe Fellow). Married, December 18, 1964, Ben Whitaker, son of late Sir John Whitaker, 2nd Bt, CB, CBE, DL, JP (2 sons 1 daughter). *Trades Union:* Member, FDA. *Councils, Public Bodies:* Non-Executive Director, Tavistock and Portman NHS Trust; Chair, Working Men's College for Men and Women; Member, Employment Tribunals. *Career:* André Deutsch (Publishers) 1961–66; Health and Safety Executive 1974–88; Department of Education and Employment 1988–96. *House of Lords:* International Development Liaison Peer. *Select Committees:* Select Committee on the European Union Sub-Committee F (Education, Employment and Home Affairs). *International Bodies:* Member: IPU, CPA. *Other:* Member: Camden Racial Equality Council, SOS Sahel Population Concern, ACORD Gender Committee, Society of Labour Lawyers, Fabian Society, British Humanist Association. *Trusts, etc:* Trustee, Runnymede Trust. FRSA. *Special Interests:* Race Relations, International Development, Further Education. *Recreations:* Travel, walking, art, music, reading. *Clubs:* Reform. *Name, Style and Title:* Raised to the peerage as Baroness Whitaker, of Beeston in the County of Nottinghamshire 1999. *Address:* The Baroness Whitaker, House of Lords, London, SW1A 0PW.

LORD WHITTY — Labour

WHITTY (Life Baron), John Lawrence Whitty; cr. 1996. Born 15 June 1943. Son of late Frederick James and Kathleen May Whitty; educated Latymer Upper School; St John's College, Cambridge (BA Economics). Married 1st, 1969, Tanya Margaret Gibson (2 sons) (marriage dissolved 1986); married 2nd, 1993, Angela Forrester. *Trades Union:* Member, GMB. *Career:* Hawker Siddeley Aviation 1960–62; Ministry of Aviation Technology 1965–70; Trades Union Congress 1970–73; General, Municipal, Boilermakers and Allied Trade Union 1973–85; The Labour Party: General Secretary 1985–94, European Co-ordinator 1994–. *House of Lords:* Parliamentary Under-Secretary of State, Department of the Environment, Transport and the Regions (Minister for Roads and Road Safety) 1998–. *Whip:* A Lord in Waiting (Government Whip) 1997–98. *Spokesman:* Spokesman on European Affairs, International Development, Foreign and Commonwealth Affairs, Education and Employment 1997–98. *Party Groups (General):* Member, Fabian Society. *Other:* Member, Friends of the Earth. *Recreations:* Theatre, cinema, swimming. *Name, Style and Title:* Raised to the peerage as Baron Whitty, of Camberwell in the London Borough of Southwark 1996. *Address:* The Lord Whitty, 33 Gilbert House, Churchill Gardens, London, SW1V 3HN; 61 Bimport, Shaftesbury, Dorset, SP7 8AZ.

LORD WIGODER — Liberal Democrat

WIGODER (Life Baron), Basil Thomas Wigoder; cr. 1974. Born 12 February 1921. Son of late Dr Philip Wigoder; educated Manchester Grammar School; Oriel College, Oxford (MA) (President, Oxford Union 1946). Married August 30, 1948, Yoland, daughter of Ben Levinson (3 sons 1 daughter). *Armed Forces:* RA 1942–45. *Career:* Called to the Bar, Grays Inn 1946; QC 1966; General Council of the Bar 1970–74; A Recorder of the Crown Court 1972–84; Master of the Bench, Gray's Inn 1972; Chairman, Health Services Board 1977–80; Member, Council on Tribunals 1980; Chairman, BUPA 1981–92; Treasurer, Gray's Inn 1989. *Whip:* Liberal Chief Whip 1976–85. *Spokesman:* Liberal Party Spokesman on Home Affairs and Law 1983–88. *Select Committees:* Former Member: Consolidation Bills Joint Committee, Delegated Powers Scrutiny Committee, Member: Select Committee on European Communities Sub-Committee E (Law and Institutions) 1997–, Joint Committee on Parliamentary Privilege 1997–, Committee for Privileges, Sub-Committee on Lords' Interests. *Party Groups (General):* Chairman, Liberal Party Executive 1963–65. *Special Interests:* Home Office Affairs, Health Service. *Recreations:* Cricket. *Clubs:* National Liberal, MCC. *Name, Style and Title:* Raised to the peerage as Baron Wigoder, of Cheetham in the City of Manchester 1974. *Address:* The Lord Wigoder, QC, House of Lords, London, SW1A 0PW *Tel:* House of Lords 020 7219 3115.

LORD WILBERFORCE   Cross-Bencher

WILBERFORCE (Life Baron), Richard Orme Wilberforce; cr. 1964. Born 11 March 1907. Son of late Samuel Wilberforce; educated Winchester; New College, Oxford. Married July 10, 1947, Yvette, daughter of late Roger Lenoan (1 son 1 daughter). *Armed Forces:* Served in the 1939–45 War in Norway, France and Germany, Hon. Brigadier; Under-Secretary, Control Office, Germany and Austria 1946–47. *Career:* Called to the Bar, Middle Temple 1932; QC 1954; Bencher 1961; A Judge of the High Court (Chancery division) 1961–64; A Lord of Appeal in Ordinary 1964–82. *Chancellor:* Chancellor, Hull University 1978–94. *International Bodies (General):* Patron, International Law Association; Hon. Member, American Society of International Law; Member, Permanent Court of Arbitration 1964–87; Chairman Executive Council, International Law Association 1967–90; President, Federation Internationale du Droit Européen 1978. *Other:* High Steward, Oxford University 1967–90; Joint President, Anti-Slavery International; Vice-President, Royal College of Music. Fellow, All Souls College, Oxford 1932; Four honorary doctorates. *Miscellaneous:* Hon. Member, Faculty of Advocates, Scotland. *Honours:* OBE (Mil) 1944; Bronze Star, USA 1944; CMG 1956; Kt 1961; PC 1964; Grand Cross of St Jean de Penafort, Spain 1970. Hon. Companion, Royal Aeronautical Society; Hon. FRCM. *Publications: The Law of Restrictive Trade Practices.* Clubs: Athenaeum, Oxford and Cambridge University. *Name, Style and Title:* Raised to the peerage as Baron Wilberforce, of the City and County of Kingston-upon-Hull 1964. *Address:* Rt Hon the Lord Wilberforce, CMG, OBE, 8 Cambridge Place, London, W8 5PB.

BARONESS WILCOX   Conservative

WILCOX (Life Baroness), Judith Ann Wilcox; cr. 1996. Born 31 October 1940. Daughter of John and Elsie Freeman; educated St Dunstan's Abbey, Devon; St Mary's Convent, Wantage; Plymouth University. Married 1st, 1961, Keith Davenport (1 son), (marriage dissolved 1986), married 2nd, 1986, Sir Malcom George Wilcox, CBE (died 1986). *Career:* Management of family business in Devon 1969–79; Founder/Financial Director, Capstan Fisheries Ltd, Devon 1979–84; Founder/Chairman, Channel Foods Ltd, Cornwall 1984–89; President Directeur-General, Pecheries de la Morinie, Boulogne-sur-Mer, France 1989–91; Chairman, National Consumer Council 1990–96; Chairman, Morinie et Cie, Boulogne-sur-Mere, France 1991–94; Board Member, Automobile Association 1991–; Member (non-executive), Inland Revenue Board 1992–95; Member, Prime Minister's Advisory Panel to Citizen's Charter Unit 1992–97; Commissioner, Local Government Commission 1992–95; Chairman, Citizen's Charter Complaints Task Force 1993–95; Board Member, Port of London Authority 1993–2000, Vice-Chairman 2000–; Director: Cadbury Schweppes plc 1997–, Director, Carpetright plc 1997–. *Select Committees:* Member: Select Committee on European Communities Sub-Committee C (Environment, Public Health and Consumer Protection) 1997–, Ecclesiastical Committee 1997–, Select Committee on Science and Technology Sub-Committee II (Science and Society) 1999–2000, Select Committee on Science and Technology Sub-Committee IIA (Human Genetic Databases) 2000–; Chairman, Select Committee on Science and Technology Sub-Committee II (Aircraft Cabin Environment) 2000–. *Other:* Member: Council of Institute of Directors 1991–98, General Advisory Council of the BBC 1996, Lord Chancellor's Review of the Court of Appeal 1996–97, Tax Law Review Committee 1996–, Governing Body of Institute of Food Research 1996–; President: National Federation of Consumer Groups 1996–, Institute of Trading Standards Administration (ITSA) 1996–. FIMgt; FRSA. Freeman, City of London. Hon. Member, Fishmongers' Company 1998. *Special Interests:* Fishing Industry, Mariculture, Consumer Affairs, Environment. *Recreations:* Sailing, birdwatching, flyfishing, calligraphy. *Sportsclubs:* St Mawes Sailing. *Name, Style and Title:* Raised to the peerage as Baroness Wilcox, of Plymouth in the County of Devon 1996. *Address:* The Baroness Wilcox, 17 Great College Street, London, SW1P 3RX *E-Mail:* wilcoxj@parliament.uk.

BARONESS WILKINS   Labour

WILKINS (Life Baroness), Rosalie Catherine Wilkins; cr. 1999. Born 6 May 1946. Daughter of late Eric Frederick and Marjorie Phyllis Elizabeth Wilkins; educated Dr Challoner's Grammar School, Amersham; St Helen's School, Northwood, Middlesex; Manchester University (BA 1969). *Career:* PA to Director, Central Council for the Disabled 1971–74; Information Officer, MIND (National Association for Mental Health) 1974–78; Researcher/ Presenter, The Link Programme (magazine programme for disabled people), ATV Network/Central Television 1975–88; Freelance Video and Documentary Producer 1988–96; Information Officer, National Centre for Independent Living 1997–99. *Awards Granted:* The Snowdon Award 1983. *Trusts, etc.* Trustee: Graeae Theatre Company, HAFAD (Hammersmith and Fulham Action for Disability). *Publications:* Contributing Author to *Able Lives – Women's Experience of Paralysis*, 1989. *Special Interests:* Disability. *Recreations:* Friends, gardening, theatre. *Name, Style and Title:* Raised to the peerage as Baroness Wilkins, of Chesham Bois in the County of Buckinghamshire 1999. *Address:* The Baroness Wilkins, House of Lords, London, SW1A 0PW *Tel:* 020 7381 1227 *Fax:* 020 7381 1227 *E-Mail:* roswilkins@compuserve.com.

BARONESS WILLIAMS OF CROSBY   Liberal Democrat

WILLIAMS OF CROSBY (Life Baroness), Shirley Vivian Teresa Brittain Williams; cr. 1993. Born 27 July 1930. Daughter of late Professor Sir George Catlin, and late Mrs Catlin (Vera Brittain); educated Schools in Great Britain and the United States; Somerville College, Oxford (Scholar, MA); Columbia University, New York (Fulbright Scholarship). Married 1st, 1955, Professor Sir Bernard Arthur Owen Williams, FBA, son of late Owen Williams, OBE (1 daughter) (marriage dissolved 1974), married 2nd, 1987, Professor Richard Elliott Neustadt (1 stepson deceased, 1 stepdaughter). *Trades Union:* Member, NUGMW 1960–. *Career:* Journalist: *Daily Mirror* 1952–54, *Financial Times* 1954–58; General Secretary, Fabian Society 1960–64; Fellow, Institute of Politics, Harvard University 1979–80, Acting Director 1987–88; Professor of Elective Politics, John F. Kennedy School of Government, Harvard University 1988–2000; Lectureships: Pick Lecturer, Chicago University, Godkin Lecturer, Harvard University, Janeway Lecturer, Princeton University, Regents Lecturer, University of California at Berkeley, Rede Lecturer, Darwin Lecturer, Cambridge University, Dainton Lecturer, British Library, Gresham Lecturer, Corporation of London; Associate, Center for European Studies, Harvard; Belfer Center for Science and International Affairs. *House of Commons:* Contested: (Labour) Harwich 1954, 1955, Southampton Test 1959, (SDP) Crosby 1983, (SDP/Alliance) Cambridge 1987; MP: (Labour) Hitchin 1964–74, Hertford and Stevenage 1974–79, (SDP) Crosby 1981–83; PPS to Minister of Health 1964–66; Parliamentary Secretary, Ministry of Labour 1966–67; Minister of State: Department of Education and Science 1967–69, Home Office 1969–70; Secretary of State for: Prices and Consumer Protection 1974–76, Education and Science 1976–79; Paymaster General 1976–79. *Spokesman (Commons):* Opposition Spokesman on: Social Services 1970–71, Home Affairs 1971–73, Prices and Consumer Protection 1973–74. *Spokesman:* Spokesman on Foreign and Commonwealth Affairs 1998–. *Select Committees:* Member: Select Committee on European Communities 1997–99, Select Committee on European Communities Sub-Committee A (Economic and Financial Affairs, Trade and External Relations) 1997–99. *Party Groups:* Deputy Leader, Liberal Democrat Peers in the House of Lords 1999–. *International Bodies (General):* International Advisory Committee Member, Council on Foreign Relations, USA; President, British-Russian Society and East-West Centre; Board Member, Moscow School of Political Studies; Co-Chairman, Anglo-Dutch Society; Board Member, European Movement; Council Member, Britain in Europe. *Party Groups (General):* Joined the Labour Party 1946; General Secretary, Fabian Society 1960–64, Chairman 1980–81; Member, Labour Party National Executive Committee 1970–81; Co-founder, Social Democratic Party 1981, President 1982–88. *Other:* Director, Turing Institute, Glasgow 1985–90; Board Member, Rand Corporation, Europe 1993–; Governor, Ditchley Foundation 1994–. *Awards Granted:* Silver Medal, Royal Society of Arts. Hon. Fellow: Somerville College, Oxford 1970, Newnham College, Cambridge 1977; Seven honorary doctorates from British, Belgian and US universities. *Trusts, etc:* Trustee, Century Foundation, New York 1976–. *Miscellaneous:* Visiting Fellow, Nuffield College, Oxford 1967–75;

Member, Advisory Committee on Business Appointments 1999–. *Honours:* PC 1974; Grand Cross (second class), Federal Republic of Germany. *Publications: Politics is for People*, 1981; *Jobs for the 1980s*; *Youth Without Work*, 1981; Co-author *Unemployment and Growth in the Western Economies*, 1984; *A Job to Live*, 1985; *Snakes and Ladders*, 1996. *Recreations:* Music, hill-walking, poetry. *Clubs:* The Other Club. *Name, Style and Title:* Raised to the peerage as Baroness Williams of Crosby, of Stevenage in the County of Hertfordshire 1993. *Address:* Rt Hon the Baroness Williams of Crosby, House of Lords, London, SW1A 0PW.

LORD WILLIAMS OF ELVEL — Labour

WILLIAMS OF ELVEL (Life Baron), Charles Cuthbert Powell Williams; cr. 1985. Born 9 February 1933. Son of late Dr N. P. Williams, DD, Lady Margaret Professor of Divinity at Oxford, and Mrs Muriel de Lérisson Williams, née Cazenove; educated Westminster; Christ Church, Oxford (MA); London School of Economics. Married March 1, 1975, Jane Gillian, DL, daughter of late Lieutenant-Colonel Gervase Portal (1 stepson). *Armed Forces:* National Service 1955–57, Subaltern KRRC (60th Rifles) HQ Battalion (Winchester) and Derna (Libya). *Career:* British Petroleum Co. Ltd 1958–61; Bank of London and Montreal 1964–66; Eurofinance SA Paris 1966–70; Baring Bros & Co. Ltd 1970–77, Managing Director 1971–77; Chairman, Price Commission 1977–79; Managing Director: Henry Ansbacher & Co. Ltd 1979–82, Henry Ansbacher Holdings 1982–85; Director, Mirror Group Newspapers plc 1985–92. *Spokesman:* Opposition Front Bench Spokesman on: Trade and Industry 1987–92, Defence 1990–97, the Environment 1992–97. *Select Committees:* Member: Ecclesiastical Committee 1997–, Select Committee on European Union 1999–. *Party Groups:* Deputy Leader of the Opposition in the House of Lords 1989–92. *Other:* Chairman, Academy of St Martin-in-the-Fields 1988; President, Campaign for the Protection of Rural Wales 1989–95, Immediate Past President and Vice-President 1995–; A Vice-President, Federation of Economic Development Authorities. *Trusts, etc:* A Busby Trustee, Westminster School 1989–99. *Honours:* CBE 1980. *Publications: The Last Great Frenchman: a life of General de Gaulle*, 1993; *Bradman: an Australian Hero*, 1996; *Adenauer: the Father of the New Germany*, 2000. *Special Interests:* Banking, Finance, Environment. *Clubs:* MCC. *Name, Style and Title:* Raised to the peerage as Baron Williams of Elvel, of Llansantffraed in Elvel in the County of Powys 1985. *Address:* The Lord Williams of Elvel, CBE, House of Lords, London, SW1A 0PW *Tel:* 020 7581 1783 *Tel:* Wales: 01591 823235 *E-Mail:* williamssc@parliament.uk.

LORD WILLIAMS OF MOSTYN — Labour

WILLIAMS OF MOSTYN (Life Baron), Gareth Wyn Williams; cr. 1992. Born 5 February 1941. Son of late Albert and Selina Williams; educated Rhyl Grammar School; Queens' College, Cambridge (Open Scholar History, LLM, MA). Married 1st, 1962, Pauline Clarke (1 son 2 daughters) (marriage dissolved), married 2nd, 1994, Veena Maya Russell (1 daughter). *Career:* Called to the Bar, Gray's Inn 1965; QC 1978; A Recorder of the Crown Court 1978–97; Deputy High Court Judge 1986–97; Member, Bar Council 1986–92; Leader of the Wales and Chester Circuit 1987–89; Bar Council: Vice-Chairman 1991–92, Chairman 1992–93; Fellow, University College of Wales, Aberystwyth 1993–; Hon. Professor, School of Sociology and Social Policy, University College of North Wales 1994; Visiting Professor, City University, London 1994–95; Fellow, University College of Wales, Bangor 1996. *Chancellor:* Pro-Chancellor, University of Wales 1994–. *House of Lords:* Parliamentary Under-Secretary of State, Home Office (Minister for Constitutional Issues) 1997–98; Minister of State, Home Office (Minister for Prisons and Probation) 1998–99; Deputy Leader of the House of Lords 1998–; Attorney-General 1999–. *Spokesman:* An Opposition Spokesman on: Legal Affairs 1992–97, Northern Ireland 1993–97, Wales 1995–96. *Other:* President: Commonwealth and Ethnic Bar Association 1993–97, Prisoners' Rights 1993–97, Welsh College of Music and Drama 1993–. *Trusts, etc:* Trustee: NSPCC 1993–97, Council of Justice 1993–97. *Honours:* PC 1999. Hon. Fellow, Institute of Advanced Legal Studies 1997–. *Special Interests:* Law, Foreign Affairs, Europe. *Name, Style and Title:* Raised to the peerage as Baron Williams of Mostyn, of Great Tew in the County of Oxfordshire 1992. *Address:* Rt Hon the Lord Williams of Mostyn, QC, House of Lords, London, SW1A 0PW.

LORD WILLIAMSON OF HORTON   Cross-Bencher

WILLIAMSON OF HORTON (Life Baron), David Francis Williamson; cr. 1999. Born 8 May 1934. Son of late Samuel and Marie Williamson; educated Tonbridge School; Exeter College, Oxford (MA). Married 1961, Patricia Margaret Smith (2 sons). *Armed Forces:* Second Lieutenant, Royal Signals 1956–58. *Career:* Joined Ministry of Agriculture, Fisheries and Food 1958; Private Secretary to Permanent Secretary and to successive Parliamentary Secretaries 1960–62; HM Diplomatic Service as First Secretary (Agriculture and Food) Geneva, for Kennedy Round Trade Negotiations 1965–67; Principal Private Secretary to successive Ministers of Agriculture, Fisheries and Food 1967–70; Head of Milk and Milk Products Division, Marketing Policy Division and Food Policy Division 1970–74; Under-Secretary, General Agricultural Policy Group 1974–76, EEC Group 1976–77; Deputy Director-General, Agriculture, European Commission 1977–83; Deputy Secretary, Cabinet Office 1983–87; Secretary-General, Commission of the European Communities 1987–97; Visiting Professor, Bath University 1997–; Non-Executive Director, Whitbread plc 1998–. *Select Committees:* Member, Select Committee on Science and Technology Sub-Committee I (Non-Food Crops) 1999–; Member, European Union Committee Sub-Committee C (Foreign and Security Policy) 1999–. *Other:* President, University Association for Contemporary European Studies; Co-Chairman, Europe 21; Member, Wessex Regional Committee, National Trust. Four honorary doctorates. *Honours:* CB 1984; Knight Commander's Cross of the Order of Merit (Germany) 1991; GCMG 1998; Commander Grand Cross of the Royal Order of the Polar Star (Sweden) 1998; Commander Légion d'Honneur (France) 1999. *Name, Style and Title:* Raised to the peerage as Baron Williamson of Horton, of Horton in the County of Somerset 1999. *Address:* The Lord Williamson of Horton, GCMG, CB, Thatchcroft, Broadway, Ilminster, Somerset, TA19 9QZ.

LORD WILLOUGHBY DE BROKE   Conservative

WILLOUGHBY DE BROKE (21st Baron, E), Leopold David Verney; cr. 1491. Born 14 September 1938. Son of 20th Baron, MC, AFC. Succeeded his father 1986; educated Le Rosey, Switzerland; New College, Oxford. Married May 1, 1965, Petra, daughter of late Colonel Sir John Aird, 3rd Bt, MVO, MC (3 sons) (marriage dissolved 1989). *Councils, Public Bodies:* DL, Warwickshire 1999–. *Career:* Member, Council, Anglo-Hong Kong Trust 1989–; Chairman: St Martin's Magazines 1992–, SM Theatre ltd 1992–; President, Heart of England Tourist Board. *House of Lords:* An elected hereditary peer 1999–. *Select Committees:* Member: Select Committee on European Communities 1997–, Select Committee on European Communities Sub-Committee D (Agriculture, Fisheries and Food) 1997–. *Party Groups (General):* Vice-President, Conservatives Against a Federal Europe (CAFE) 1997–. *Other:* Patron, Warwickshire Association of Boys' Clubs 1990–; Governor, Royal Shakespeare Theatre 1992–. FRSA; FRGS. *Special Interests:* Hong Kong, Tibet, Europe. *Sportsclubs:* All England Lawn Tennis. *Clubs:* White's. *Address:* The Lord Willoughby de Broke, DL, Ditchford Farm, Moreton in Marsh, Gloucestershire, GL56 9RD *Tel:* 01608 661990 *E-Mail:* willoughbyl@parliament.uk.

LORD WILSON OF TILLYORN   Cross-Bencher

WILSON OF TILLYORN (Life Baron), David Clive Wilson; cr. 1992. Born 14 February 1935. Son of late Rev. William Skinner Wilson and late Enid Wilson; educated Trinity College, Glenalmond; Keble College, Oxford (Scholar, MA, PhD (London) 1973). Married 1967, Natasha, daughter of late Bernard Gustav Alexander (2 sons). *Armed Forces:* National Service, The Black Watch 1953–55. *Career:* Entered Foreign Service 1958; Served Vientiane, Laos 1959–60; Language Student, Hong Kong 1960–62; First Secretary, Peking Embassy 1963–65; FCO 1965–68; Resigned 1968; Editor, China Quarterly 1968–74; Visiting Scholar, Columbia University, New York 1972; Rejoined Diplomatic Service 1974; Cabinet Office 1974–77; Political Adviser, Hong Kong 1977–81; FCO: Head of Southern European Department 1981–84, Assistant Under-Secretary of State 1984–87; Governor and Commander-in-Chief, Hong Kong 1987–92; Chairman: Scottish Hydro

Electric plc 1993–98 (now Scottish and Southern Energy plc 1998–). *Chancellor:* Chancellor, University of Aberdeen 1997–. *Select Committees:* Chairman, Select Committee on Revised Red Deer Act (Scotland) 1996. *Other:* President, Bhutan Society of the UK; Member: Oxford University Expedition to Somaliland 1957, British Mount Kongur Expedition (North West China) 1981; President: Hong Kong Society, Hong Kong Association; Vice-President, Royal Scotish Geographical Society; Member, Royal Society for Asian Affairs; Chairman of Council, Glenalmond College 2000–. Hon. LLD, Aberdeen University 1990; Hon. DLitt, Sydney University 1991; Hon. LLD: University of Abertay, Dundee 1995, Chinese University of Hong Kong 1996. *Trusts, etc:* Member, Hopetown House Preservation Trust 1993–98; Trustee, Scotland's Churches Trust 1999–; Trustee, Museums of Scotland 1999–; Carnegie Trust for the Universities of Scotland 2000–. *Miscellaneous:* Member, Board of British Council 1993–; Chairman, Scottish Committee of the British Council 1993–; Member of Council, CBI Scotland; Vice-Chairman Scottish Peers Association 1998–2000, Chairman 2000–; Member, Advisory Committee on Public Appointments 2000–. *Honours:* CMG 1985; KCMG 1987; KStJ 1987; GCMG 1991. FRSE; FRGS. *Special Interests:* Hong Kong, East and South-East Asia, Scottish Affairs. *Recreations:* Mountaineering, reading. *Clubs:* Alpine, New (Edinburgh). *Name, Style and Title:* Raised to the peerage as Baron Wilson of Tillyorn, of Finzean in the District of Kincardine and Deeside and of Fanling in Hong Kong 1992. *Address:* The Lord Wilson of Tillyorn, GCMG, House of Lords, London, SW1A 0PW; Scottish and Southern Energy plc, 10 Dunkeld Road, Perth, PH15 5WA *Tel:* 01738 455200.

BISHOP OF WINCHESTER   Non-Affiliated

WINCHESTER (96th Bishop of), Michael Charles Scott-Joynt. Born 15 March 1943. Son of The Revd A. G. and Mrs D. B. M. Scott-Joynt; educated Bradfield College; King's College, Cambridge (MA); Cuddesdon Theological College. Married 1965, Louise White (2 sons 1 daughter). *Career:* Deacon 1967; Priest 1968; Curate, Cuddesdon 1967–70; Tutor, Cuddesdon College 1967–71, Chaplain 1971–72; Team Vicar, Newbury 1972–75; Priest-in-charge: Caversfield 1975–79, Bicester 1975–79, Bucknell 1976–79; Rural Dean of Bicester and Islip 1976–81; Rector, Bicester Area Team Ministry 1979–81; Canon Residentiary of St Albans 1982–87; Director, Ordinands and In-Service Training, Diocese of St Albans 1982–87; Suffragan Bishop of Stafford 1987–95; Bishop of Winchester 1995–; Prelate of the Most Noble Order of the Garter 1995–; Took his seat in the House of Lords 1996. *Special Interests:* Education, Local Government, Poverty, Welfare, Eastern Germany, Malaysia, Pensioners' Issues, Uganda, Rwanda. *Address:* Rt Rev the Lord Bishop of Winchester, Wolvesey, Winchester, Hampshire, SO23 9ND *Tel:* 01962 854050 *E-Mail:* michael.scott-joynt@dial.pipex.com.

LORD WINDLESHAM   Conservative

WINDLESHAM (3rd Baron, UK), David James George Hennessy; cr. 1937; (Life) Baron Hennessy 1999; 3rd Bt of Winchester (UK) 1927. Born 28 January 1932. Son of 2nd Baron. Succeeded his father 1962; educated Ampleforth; Trinity College, Oxford (MA); Brasenose College, Oxford (DLitt). Married 1965, Prudence Glynn (died 1986) (1 son 1 daughter). *Councils, Public Bodies:* Councillor, Westminster City Council 1958–62. *Career:* ATV Network: Managing Director 1974–81, Joint Managing Director 1974, Chairman 1981; Trustee, British Museum 1981–96, Chairman 1986–96; Chairman, The Parole Board 1982–88; Member, Museums and Galleries Commission 1984–86; Director, W. H. Smith Group plc 1986–95; Principal, Brasenose College, Oxford 1989–; Weinberg/Goldman, Sachs Visiting Professor, Princeton University 1997. *House of Lords:* Minister of State, Home Office 1970–72; Minister of State for Northern Ireland 1972–73; Lord Privy Seal and Leader of the House of Lords 1973–74; Leader of the Opposition 1974. *Select Committees:* Member, House of Lords Select Committee on Murder and Life Imprisonment 1988–89. *Party Groups (General):* Chairman, Bow Group 1959–60, 1962–63. *Other:* Vice-President, Royal Television Society 1977–82; Joint Deputy Chairman, Queen's Silver Jubilee Appeal 1977; President, Victim Support 1992–; Chairman, Oxford Society 1985–88. Hon. Fellow, Trinity College, Oxford 1982. *Trusts, etc:* Deputy Chairman, Royal Jubilee Trust 1977–80; Chairman, Oxford Preservation Trust 1979–89; Trustee: The Royal Collection 1993–2000, Community Service Volunteers. *Miscellaneous:* Visiting Fellow, All Souls College,

Oxford 1986; Hon. Bencher, Inner Temple 1999–. *Honours:* PC 1973; CVO 1981. *Publications: Communication and Political Power*, 1966; *Politics in Practice*, 1975; *Broadcasting in a Free Society*, 1980; *Responses to Crime*, Vol 1, 1987, Vol 2, 1993, Vol 3, 1996; *Politics, Punishment, and Populism*, 1998; Co-author *The Windlesham/Rampton Report on Death on the Rock*, 1989. *Clubs:* Brooks's. *Name, Style and Title:* Created a life peer as Baron Hennessy, of Windlesham in the County of Surrey 1999. *Address:* Rt Hon the Lord Windlesham, CVO, House of Lords, London, SW1A 0PW.

LORD WINSTON   Labour

WINSTON (Life Baron), Robert Maurice Lipson Winston; cr. 1995. Born 15 July 1940. Son of late Laurence Winston, and of Ruth Winston-Fox, MBE; educated St Paul's School; London Hospital Medical College, London University (MB, BS 1964). Married 1973, Lira Helen Feigenbaum (2 sons 1 daughter). *Career:* Wellcome Research Senior Lecturer, Institute of Obstetrics and Gynaecology 1974–78; Has held other posts in the United Kingdom, Belgium and USA; Consultant Obstetrician and Gynaecologist: Hammersmith Hospital 1978–; Presenter, *Your Life in their Hands*, BBC TV 1979–87; Past Dean, Institute of Obstetrics and Gynaecology, RPMS, London; Past Chairman, British Fertility Society; Professor of Fertility Studies, Institute of Obstetrics and Gynaecology, Royal Postgraduate Medical School, London University 1987–97; Imperial College, London; Presenter: *Making Babies*, BBC TV 1995, *The Human Body*, BBC TV 1998, *Secret Life of Twins*, BBC TV 1999; *The Superhuman*, BBC TV 2000. *Select Committees:* Member, Select Committee on Science and Technology 1996–, Chairman 1998–; Sub-Committee II (Cannabis) 1998; Member, Select Committees on: Science and Technology Sub-Committee II (Science and Society) 1999–2000, Science and Technology Sub-Committee II (Aircraft Cabin Environment) 2000–, Science and Technology Sub-Committee IIA (Human Genetic Databases) 2000–. *Other:* Member: Council of Imperial Cancer Research Fund; Board of Lyric Theatre, Hammersmith. *Awards Granted:* Cedric Carter Medal, Clinical Genetics Society 1993; Victor Bonney Triennial Prize, Royal College of Surgeons of England 1993; Gold Medal, Royal Society for Promotion of Health 1998; Michael Faraday Gold Medal, The Royal Society 1999. Hon. Fellow, Queen Mary Westfield College. *Miscellaneous:* Member, Parliamentary Office of Science and Technology (POST) 1998–. MRCS; LRCP; FRCOG 1983; FRSA; FScMed. *Publications: Reversibility of Sterilization*, 1978; Co-author *Tubal Infertility*, 1981; *Infertility, a Sympathetic Approach*, 1987; *The IVF Revolution*, 1999; *The Superhuman*, 2000; As well as over 250 papers in scientific journals on human and experimental reproduction. *Special Interests:* Health, Science and Technology, Education, Arts. *Recreations:* Theatre, broadcasting, music, wine. *Clubs:* Athenaeum. *Name, Style and Title:* Raised to the peerage as Baron Winston, of Hammersmith in the London Borough of Hammersmith and Fulham 1995. *Address:* Professor the Lord Winston, 11 Denman Drive, London, NW11 6RE *Tel:* 020 8455 7475 *E-Mail:* rwinston@globalnet.co.uk.

LORD WOLFSON   Conservative

WOLFSON (Life Baron), Leonard Gordon Wolfson; cr. 1985; 2nd Bt of St Marylebone (UK) 1962. Born 11 November 1927. Son of late Sir Isaac Wolfson, 1st Bt, and late Lady Edith Wolfson. Succeeded his father to the baronetcy 1991; educated King's School, Worcester. Married 1st, 1949, Ruth Sterling (4 daughters) (marriage dissolved 1991), married 2nd, September 1, 1991, Mrs Estelle Jackson (1 step son, 1 step daughter). *Career:* Founder Trustee, Wolfson Foundation 1955–; Chairman: Wolfson Foundation 1972–, Burberry's Ltd 1978–96, Great Universal Stores 1981–96. *Other:* President, Jewish Welfare Board 1972–82. Hon. Phd, Tel Aviv 1971; Hon. DCL, Oxon 1972; 14 honorary doctorates from British and Israeli universities; Honorary fellowships of five Oxbridge colleges, including Wolfson College, Oxford and Wolfson College, Cambridge and six other honorary university fellowships. *Trusts, etc:* Trustee, Imperial War Museum 1988–94. *Honours:* Kt 1977. Hon. FRCP 1977; Hon. FBA 1986; Hon. FRCS 1988; Hon. Member, Royal College of Surgeons, Edinburgh 1997; Hon. Fellow, Royal College of Engineering 1997. *Recreations:* History, economics. *Name, Style and Title:* Raised to the peerage as Baron Wolfson, of Marylebone in the City of Westminster 1985. *Address:* The Lord Wolfson, House of Lords, London, SW1A 0PW.

LORD WOLFSON OF SUNNINGDALE   Conservative

WOLFSON OF SUNNINGDALE (Life Baron), David Wolfson; cr. 1991. Born 9 November 1935. Son of late Charles and Hylda Wolfson; educated Clifton College; Trinity College, Cambridge (MA); Stanford University, California, USA (MBA). Married 1st, 1962, Patricia Rawlings (created Baroness Rawlings, *qv*) (marriage dissolved 1967), married 2nd, 1967, Susan Davis (2 sons 1 daughter). *Career:* Director, Great Universal Stores 1973–78, 1993–2000, Chairman 1996–2000; Secretary to Shadow Cabinet 1978–79; Chief of Staff, Political Office, 10 Downing Street 1979–85; Chairman, Alexon Group plc 1982–86; Chairman, Next plc 1990–98. Hon. Fellow, Hughes Hall, Cambridge 1989. *Honours:* Kt 1984. Hon. FRCR; Hon. FRCOG. *Special Interests:* Health. *Recreations:* Golf, bridge. *Sportsclubs:* Sunningdale Golf, Woburn Golf, Trevose Golf. *Clubs:* Portland. *Name, Style and Title:* Raised to the peerage as Baron Wolfson of Sunningdale, of Trevose in the County of Cornwall 1991. *Address:* The Lord Wolfson of Sunningdale, Kt, The Great Universal Stores plc, Leconfield House, London, W1Y 7FL *Tel:* 020 7495 0070 *Fax:* 020 7495 1567; 1 Portobello Studios, Haydens Place, London, W11 1LY *Tel:* 020 7792 2200 *Fax:* 020 7792 4400.

LORD WOOLF   Cross-Bencher

WOOLF (Life Baron), Harry Kenneth Woolf; cr. 1992. Born 2 May 1933. Son of late Alexander and Leah Woolf; educated Fettes College; University College, London (LLB). Married 1961, Marguerite, daughter of late George and Victoria Sassoon (3 sons). *Armed Forces:* Commissioned (National Service) 15/19th Royal Hussars 1954; Seconded to Army Legal Services 1954; Captain 1955. *Career:* Called to Bar, Inner Temple 1954, Bencher 1976; Started Practice at Bar 1956; A Recorder of the Crown Court 1972–79; Junior Counsel, Inland Revenue 1973–74; First Treasury Junior Counsel (Common Law) 1974–79; A Judge of the High Court of Justice, Queen's Bench Division 1979–86; Presiding Judge, South Eastern Circuit 1981–84; Member, Senate, Inns of Court and Bar 1981–85; Member, Board of Management, Institute of Advanced Legal Studies 1985–93; Chairman, Lord Chancellor's Advisory Committee on Legal Education 1986–90; A Lord Justice of Appeal 1986–92; Chairman, Board of Management, Institute of Advanced Legal Studies 1986–93; Held inquiry into prison disturbances 1990, part II with Judge Tumim, report 1991; A Lord of Appeal in Ordinary 1992–96; Held inquiry into Access to Justice 1994–96 (interim report 1995, final report and rules 1996); Master of the Rolls 1996–2000; Chairman, Advisory Committee on Public Records 1996; Visitor: University College, London 1996, Nuffield College, Oxford 1996–2000; Downing College, Cambridge 2000–; Lord Chief Justice of England and Wales 2000. *Chancellor:* Pro Chancellor, London University 1994–. *House of Lords:* Cross Bencher. *Other:* President: Association of Law Teachers 1985–89, South West London Magistrates Association 1987–92, Central Council of Jewish Social Services 1989–99; Mogen Dovid Adom 1995–; Governor, Oxford Centre of Hebrew Studies 1990–93 (Emeritus). Fellow, University College, London 1981; Hon. Fellow, Leeds Municipal University. *Trusts, etc:* Chairman: Butler Trust 1992–96, President 1996–, St Mary's Hospital Special Trustees 1993–97. *Honours:* Kt 1979; PC 1986. FBA. Honorary Liveryman of the Drapers' Company. *Publications:* Protection of the public: A New Challenge (Hamlyn lecture) 1990; Co-author: *Zamir and Woolf: The Declaratory Judgement* 2nd edition, 1993, *De Smith, Woolf and Jowell,* 5th edition 1995, *Principles of Judicial Review. Clubs:* Garrick, Royal Automobile. *Name, Style and Title:* Raised to the peerage as Baron Woolf, of Barnes in the London Borough of Richmond 1992. *Address:* Rt Hon the Lord Woolf, Royal Courts of Justice, Strand, WC2A 2LL.

LORD WOOLMER OF LEEDS — Labour

WOOLMER OF LEEDS (Life Baron), Kenneth John Woolmer; cr. 1999. Born 25 April 1940. Son of late Joseph Woolmer; educated Kettering Grammar School; Leeds University (BA Economics). Married September 23, 1961, Janice Chambers (3 sons). *Trades Union:* Member, AUT. *Councils, Public Bodies:* Councillor, Leeds County Borough Council 1970–74, Deputy Leader 1972–74; Councillor, Leeds Metropolitan District Council 1973–78; Councillor, West Yorkshire Metropolitan County Council 1973–80, Deputy Leader 1973–75, Leader 1975–77, Leader of the Opposition 1977–79; Chairman, Planning and Transportation Committee of Association of Metropolitan Authorities 1974–77. *Career:* Research Fellow, University of the West Indies 1961–62; Teacher, Friern Road Secondary Modern School, London 1963; Lecturer: Leeds University (Economics) 1963–66, University of Ahmadu Bello, Nigeria 1966–68, Leeds University 1968–79; Principal, Halton Gill Associates 1979–96; University of Leeds, Leeds University Business School: Director of MBA Programmes 1991–97, Dean of External Relations 1997, Dean of Business School 1997–. *House of Commons:* MP (Labour) for Batley and Morley 1979–83; Contested Batley and Spen (Labour) 1983 and 1987. *Spokesman (Commons):* Front Bench Opposition Spokesman on: Trade, Aviation, Shipping, Film Industry 1981–82, Prices and Consumer Protection 1982. *Party Groups (Commons):* Chairman, PLP Finance and Economic Committee 1980–81, Vice-Chairman 1981–82. *Other:* Director, Leeds United AFC 1991–96. *Miscellaneous:* Former Parliamentary Adviser, Inland Revenue Staff Federation. *Recreations:* Football, cricket. *Sportsclubs:* Leeds United AFC supporter, Yorkshire CCC supporter. *Name, Style and Title:* Raised to the peerage as Baron Woolmer of Leeds, of Leeds in the County of West Yorkshire 1999. *Address:* The Lord Woolmer of Leeds, 8 Ancaster Crescent, Leeds, LS16 5HS *E-Mail:* kjw@lubs.leeds.ac.uk.

LORD WRIGHT OF RICHMOND — Cross-Bencher

WRIGHT OF RICHMOND (Life Baron), Patrick Richard Henry Wright; cr. 1994. Born 28 June 1931. Son of late Herbert Wright and of Rachel Wright; educated Marlborough; Merton College, Oxford (MA). Married 1958, Virginia Anne Gaffney (2 sons 1 daughter). *Armed Forces:* Served Royal Artillery 1950–51. *Career:* Entered Diplomatic Service 1955; Middle East Centre for Arabic Studies 1956–57; Third Secretary, Beirut Embassy 1958–60; Private Secretary and later First Secretary, Washington DC Embassy 1960–65; Private Secretary to Permanent Under-Secretary, Foreign Office 1965–67; First Secretary and Head of Chancery, Cairo Embassy 1967–70; Deputy Political Resident, Bahrain 1971–72; Head of Middle East Department, FCO 1972–74; Private Secretary (Overseas Affairs) to Prime Minister 1974–77; Ambassador to: Luxembourg 1977–79; Syria 1979–81; Deputy Under-Secretary of State, FCO 1982–84; Ambassador to Saudi Arabia 1984–86; Permanent Under-Secretary of State and Head of the Diplomatic Service 1986–91; Director: Barclays Bank plc 1991–96, British Petroleum Co. (now BP Amoco) 1991–, De La Rue 1991–2000, Unilever 1991–99, BAA 1992–98; Member, Security Commission 1993–. *Other:* Member, Council of Royal Institute of International Affairs 1992–99, Chairman 1995–99; Member of Council: Atlantic College 1993–, Royal College of Music 1991–; Governor: Ditchley Foundation 1986–, Wellington College 1991–; Registrar, OStJ 1991–95, Director of Overseas Relations 1995–97; Vice-President, Home-Start UK 1991–. Hon. Fellow, Merton College, Oxford 1987. *Trusts, etc:* Trustee, Home-Start International 1999–. *Honours:* CMG 1978; KCMG 1984; GCMG 1989; KStJ 1990. FRCM 1994. *Special Interests:* Foreign Affairs, Commonwealth. *Recreations:* Music, philately, travel. *Clubs:* United Oxford and Cambridge University. *Name, Style and Title:* Raised to the peerage as Baron Wright of Richmond, of Richmond upon Thames in the London Borough of Richmond upon Thames, 1994. *Address:* The Lord Wright of Richmond, GCMG, House of Lords, London, SW1A 0PW.

Visit the Vacher Dod Website . . .
www.politicallinks.co.uk

Y

ARCHBISHOP OF YORK   Non-Affiliated

YORK (96th Archbishop of), David Michael Hope. Born 14 April 1940. Son of late Jack and Florence Hope; educated Queen Elizabeth Grammar School, Wakefield; Nottingham University (BA); St Stephen's House; Linacre College, Oxford (DPhil). *Career:* Curate, St John, Tuebrook, Liverpool 1965–67, 1968–70; Chaplain, Church of the Resurrection, Bucharest 1967–68; Vicar, St Andrew, Orford, Warrington 1970–74; Principal, St Stephen's House, Oxford 1974–82; Vicar, All Saints, Margaret Street, London W1 1982–85; Diocesan Bishop of Wakefield 1985–91; Took his seat in the House of Lords 1990; Prelate of the Most Excellent Order of the British Empire 1991–95; Bishop of London 1991–95; Archbishop of York 1995–. Hon. LLD CNAA; Hon. DD, Nottingham University. *Honours:* PC 1991; KCVO 1995. *Publications: The Leonine Sacramentary, The Living Gospel, Friendship with God. Special Interests:* Eastern Europe, Inner Cities, Africa. *Recreations:* Music, fell walking, photography. *Clubs:* Athenaeum. *Address:* Most Rev and Rt Hon the Lord Archbishop of York, KCVO, Bishopthorpe, York, North Yorkshire, YO23 2GE *Tel:* 01904 707021 *E-Mail:* office@bishopthorpe.u_net.com.

BARONESS YOUNG   Conservative

YOUNG (Life Baroness), Janet Mary Young; cr. 1971. Born 23 October 1926. Daughter of John Norman Leonard Baker; educated Dragon School Oxford; Headington School and in the USA; St Anne's College, Oxford (MA). Married July 15, 1950, Geoffrey Tyndale Young (3 daughters). *Councils, Public Bodies:* Councillor, Oxford City Council 1957; Alderman and Leader of the Conservative Group on the Council 1967; DL, Oxfordshire 1989–; A Vice-President, Association of District Councils 1990–96. *Career:* Director, UK Provident Institution 1975; Member, British Railways Western Region Advisory Board 1977; Co-Chairman, Women's National Commission 1979–83; Director, National Westminster Bank 1987–96; Non-Executive Director, Marks & Spencer 1987–97; Chairman, Independent Schools Joint Council 1989–92, 1994–97. *Chancellor:* Chancellor, University of Greenwich 1993–98. *House of Lords:* Parliamentary Under-Secretary of State, Department of the Environment 1973–74; Minister of State, Department of Education and Science 1979–81; Chancellor of the Duchy of Lancaster and Leader of the House of Lords 1981–82; Minister in charge of: Civil Service Department 1981, Management and Personnel Office, November 1981–83; Lord Privy Seal and Leader of the House 1982–83; Minister of State, Foreign and Commonwealth Office 1983–87. *Whip:* Government Whip 1972–73. *Spokesman:* Government Spokesman for Wales 1982. *Select Committees:* Member, Ecclesiastical Committee 2000–. *Party Groups:* President, Association of Conservative Peers 1995–. *Party Groups (General):* A Vice-Chairman, Conservative Party Organization 1975–83, Deputy Chairman 1977–79. *Other:* President: The West India Committee 1987–95, The Coba Initiative; Member, Council of Royal Albert Hall, London 1988–, Vice-President 1996; Chairman, Governing Bodies of Girls Schools 1989–94, Vice-Chairman 1994–99; Member, Council of Management, Ditchley Foundation 1990–; Member of Court, Cranfield University 1991–; Chairman, Council of Headington School 1992–; Patron, Family and Youth Concern 1996–. Hon. Fellow, St. Anne's College, Oxford; Hon. DCL, Mt. Holyoke College, USA; Hon. DUniv, Greenwich. *Trusts, etc:* Trustee: Lucy Cavendish College, Cambridge 1992–97, Dorneywood Trust 1992–; Patron, Family Education Trust 1997–. *Honours:* PC 1981. Hon. Fellow, Institution of Civil Engineers. *Special Interests:* Family, Children, Education, Caribbean. *Recreations:* Music. *Clubs:* University Women's. *Name, Style and Title:* Raised to the peerage as Baroness Young, of Farnworth in the County Palatine of Lancaster 1971. Recreation: Music. *Address:* Rt Hon the Baroness Young, DL, House of Lords, London, SW1A 0PW.

LORD YOUNG OF DARTINGTON — Labour

YOUNG OF DARTINGTON (Life Baron), Michael Young; cr. 1978. Born 9 August 1915. Son of late Gibson Young, musician, and Edith Young, WEA tutor; educated Dartington Hall School; University of London. Married 1st, 1945, Joan Lawson (2 sons 1 daughter), married 2nd, 1960, Sasha Moorsom (died 1993) (1 son 1 daughter), married 3rd, November 5, 1995, Dorit Uhlemann (1 daughter). *Trades Union:* Former Member, TGWU. *Career:* Director, Political and Economic Planning 1941–45; Secretary, Labour Party Research Department 1945–51; Director, Institute of Community Studies 1953–; A Sociologist; Member, Central Advisory Council for Education 1963–66; Founder President, Consumers' Association 1965–, Member, National Economic Development Council 1975–78. *Other:* President, National Extension College 1970–; Chairman, Tawney Society 1982–84; President, College of Health 1983–. *Awards Granted:* Albert Medal, RSA. 11 honorary degrees and fellowships. *Trusts, etc:* Trustee, Dartington Hall 1942–92. Hon. FBA. *Publications: The Rise of the Meritocracy; The Elmhirsts of Dartington – The Creation of an Utopian Community; The Metronomic Society – Natural Rhythms and Human Timetables; Life After Work*; Co-author: *Family and Kinship in East London, A Good Death – Conversations with East Londoners. Name, Style and Title:* Raised to the peerage as Baron Young of Dartington, of Dartington in the County of Devon 1978. *Address:* The Lord Young of Dartington, 18 Victoria Park Square, London, E2 9PF.

LORD YOUNG OF GRAFFHAM — Conservative

YOUNG OF GRAFFHAM (Life Baron), David Ivor Young; cr. 1984. Born 27 February 1932. Son of late Joseph Young; educated Christ's College, Finchley; University College, London (LLB). Married 1956, Lita Marianne Shaw (2 daughters). *Councils, Public Bodies:* DL, West Sussex 1999–. *Career:* Solicitor 1956; Executive, Great Universal Stores 1956–61; Chairman: Eldonwall Ltd 1961–75, Manufacturers Hanover Property Services Ltd 1974–84; Industrial Adviser/Special Adviser, Department of Industry 1979–82; Chairman, Manpower Services Commission 1982–84; Executive Chairman, Cable and Wireless plc 1990–95; Director, Salomon Inc 1990–94; Chairman, Young Associates Ltd 1996–; Currently Chairman of several companies, including: Autohit plc, Inter Digital Networks Ltd, Pixology Ltd. *House of Lords:* Cabinet Minister without Portfolio 1984–85; Secretary of State for: Employment 1985–87, Trade and Industry 1987–89. *Party Groups (General):* Deputy Chairman, Conservative Party 1989–90. *Other:* President, Institute of Directors 1993–; Chairman of Council, University College, London 1995; Chairman: Chichester Festival Theatre Productions Company Ltd, West Sussex Economic Forum. *Honours:* PC 1984. *Publications: The Enterprise Years,* 1990. *Recreations:* Fishing, photography. *Clubs:* Savile. *Name, Style and Title:* Raised to the peerage as Baron Young of Graffham, of Graffham in the County of West Sussex 1984. *Address:* Rt Hon the Lord Young of Graffham, DL, Young Associates Ltd, Harcourt House, 19 Cavendish Square, London, W1M 9AB *Tel:* 020 7447 8800 *E-Mail:* young@youngassoc.com.

BARONESS YOUNG OF OLD SCONE — Labour

YOUNG OF OLD SCONE (Life Baroness), Barbara Scott Young; cr. 1997. Born 8 April 1948. Daughter of late George Young and of Mary Young; educated Perth Academy; Edinburgh University (MA Classics 1970); Strathclyde University (DipSocSci, DipHSM 1971). *Career:* Sector Administrator, Glasgow Health Board 1973–78; Director of Planning and Development, St Thomas' Health District 1978–79; District General Administrator, NW District, Kensington and Chelsea and Westminster Area Health Authority 1979–82; District Administrator, Haringey Health Authority 1982–85; District General Manager: Paddington and North Kensington HA 1985–88, Parkside HA 1988–91; Chief Executive, Royal Society for the Protection of Birds 1991–98; Chairman, English Nature 1998–; Vice-Chairman, BBC 1998–; Non-Executive Director, Anglian Water 1998–. *Select Committees:* Member, Select Committee on European Communities Sub-Committee D (Agriculture, Fisheries and Food) 1998–.

Other: Member: Committee, King's Fund Institute 1986–90, Delegacy, St Mary's Hospital Medical School 1991–94, World Council, Birdlife International 1994–98, Vice President 1999–; Vice-President, Flora and Fauna International 1998–; Council Member, Forum for the Future 1999–. DUniv, Stirling 1995; Hon. DSc: University of Hertfordshire 1997, Cranfield University 1998. *Trusts, etc:* Trustee, National Council for Voluntary Organisations 1994–98. *Miscellaneous:* Member, BBC General Advisory Council 1985–88; President, Institute of Health Services Management 1987–88; Patron, Institute of Ecological and Environment Management 1993– Member: Committee of Secretary of State for the Environment's Going for Green Initiative 1994–96, UK Round Table on Sustainability 1995–, Commission on the Future of the Voluntary Sector 1995–97, Committee on the Public Understanding of Science 1996–97. *Recreations:* Cinema, gardening. *Name, Style and Title:* Raised to the peerage as Baroness Young of Old Scone, of Old Scone in Perth and Kinross 1997. *Address:* The Baroness Young of Old Scone, House of Lords, London, SW1A 0PW.

VISCOUNT YOUNGER OF LECKIE   Conservative

YOUNGER OF LECKIE (4th Viscount, UK), George Kenneth Hotson Younger; cr. 1923; (Life) Baron Younger of Prestwick 1992; 4th Bt of Leckie (UK) 1911. Born 22 September 1931. Son of 3rd Viscount, OBE, TD. Succeeded his father 1997; educated Winchester; New College, Oxford. Married 1954, Diana Tuck (3 sons 1 daughter). *Armed Forces:* Served Argyll and Sutherland Highlanders 1950–65. *Councils, Public Bodies:* DL, Stirlingshire 1968–. *Career:* Director: George Younger & Son Ltd 1958–68, Maclachlans Ltd 1968–70, Tennant Caledonian Breweries Ltd 1977–79, The Royal Bank of Scotland Group plc (Chairman) 1989, The Royal Bank of Scotland plc (Chairman) 1989, Murray Ventures plc (Chairman) 1989–98, Murray Income Trust plc (Chairman) 1989–99, Murray International Trust plc (Chairman) 1989, Murray Smaller Markets Trust plc (Now known as Murray Global Return) (Chairman) 1989, Siemens Plessey Electronic Systems Limited (Chairman) 1990–98; Chairman, Speed plc 1992–98; Banco Santander, SA (Now known as Banco Santander Central Hispano) 1991, PIK Holdings Limited (Chairman) 1991–98, Quality Scotland Foundation 1992, Quality Scotland Education Trust 1992, Scottish Partnership in Electronics for Effective Distribution Limited (Chairman) 1992–98, Scottish Council Development and Industry 1992, The New Atherton Investment Corporation Limited 1993–95, New Harrison Trust Limited 1993–95, Scottish Equitable Policyholders' Trust Limited 1993–98, Scottish Equitable Holdings Limited 1993–98, Scottish Equitable plc 1993–98; Murray Johnstone Holdings Limited 1993, Scottish Equitable Life Assurance Society 1994, Scottish European Educational Trust 1994, The Fleming Mercantile Investment Trust plc 1994, Alliance Logistics Limited 1994–99, Orangefield Investments Limited (Chairman) 1994, Royal Armouries' Board of Trustees (Chairman) 1994, European Children's Trust Limited (Now known as TECT Ltd) 1995. *House of Commons:* Contested (U) North Lanarkshire 1959 General Election; MP (Conservative) for Ayr 1964–92; Parliamentary Under-Secretary of State for Development, Scottish Office 1970–74; Minister of State for Defence, January–March 1974; Secretary of State for: Scotland 1979–86, Defence 1986–89. *Whip (Commons):* Scottish Conservative Whip 1965–67. *Chancellor:* Chancellor, Napier University 1993–. *Party Groups (General):* Deputy Chairman, Conservative Party in Scotland 1967–70, Chairman 1974–75; President, National Union of Conservative and Unionist Associations 1988. *Other:* Former Governor, Royal Scottish Academy of Music; Director, The Romanian Orphanage Trust (Now known as The European Childrens' Trust Ltd) (Chairman) 1990–99; Chairman, Royal Anniversary Trust 1990–; President, Council of the Territorial Auxiliary and Volunteer Reserve Associations 1993–. Fellow, New College, Oxford 1992–; Six honorary doctorates. *Miscellaneous:* Brigadier, The Queen's Bodyguard for Scotland (The Royal Company of Archers). *Honours:* TD 1964; PC 1979; KCVO 1993; KT 1995. *Special Interests:* Arts, Small Businesses. *Recreations:* Music, tennis, sailing, golf. *Clubs:* Caledonian, Highland Brigade. *Name, Style and Title:* Created a life peer as Baron Younger of Prestwick, of Ayr in the District of Kyle and Carrick 1992. *Address:* Rt Hon Viscount Younger of Leckie, KT, KCVO, TD, DL, House of Lords, London, SW1A 0PW.

Peers' Special Interests

Abortion
Alton of Liverpool, L.
Brightman, L.

Adoption
Gibson of Market Rasen, B.

Africa
Chalker of Wallasey, B.
Lichfield, Bp.
York, Abp.

Ageing
Barker, B.

Agriculture
Brookeborough, V.
Callaghan of Cardiff, L.
Carlile of Berriew, L.
Carnegy of Lour, B.
Carter, L.
Cavendish of Furness, L.
Christopher, L.
Courtown, E.
Deedes, L.
Dixon-Smith, L.
Geraint, L.
Home, E.
Hooson, L.
Howe, E.
Hughes of Woodside, L.
Inglewood, L.
Kimball, L.
Mackie of Benshie, L.
Mallalieu, B.
Mar, C.
Monro of Langholm, L.
Montrose, D.
Moyola, L.
Northbourne, L.
Northbrook, L.
Northesk, E.
O'Cathain, B.
Palmer, L.
Rotherwick, L.
Selborne, E.
Shrewsbury and Waterford, E.
Soulsby of Swaffham Prior, L.
Stodart of Leaston, L.
Wade of Chorlton, L.
Walpole, L.

Airport Policy
Morris of Manchester, L.
Smith of Leigh, L.

Alcoholism
Falkland, V.
Mancroft, L.

Alternative Dispute Resolutions
Ackner, L.

American Politics
Norton of Louth, L.

Amnesty International
Gilbert, L.

Anglo-American Relations
Acton, L.
Blatch, B.

Anglo-Chinese Relations
Geddes, L.

Animal Welfare
Allenby of Megiddo, V.
Fookes, B.
Gale, B.
Soulsby of Swaffham Prior, L.

Anti-Apartheid Work
Hughes of Woodside, L.

Anti-Pollution Matters
Mason of Barnsley, L.

Archaeology
Redesdale, L.

Architecture
Lloyd-Webber, L.
Ryder of Warsaw, B.

Armed Forces
Renton, L.

Arms Control
Oxford, Bp.
Rea, L.

Army
Glentoran, L.

Art
Lloyd-Webber, L.
Luke, L.
Snowdon, E.

Arts
Alexander of Weedon, L.
Andrews, B.
Armstrong of Ilminster, L.
Attenborough, L.
Blackstone, B.
Cameron of Lochbroom, L.
Carlile of Berriew, L.
Colwyn, L.
Crickhowell, L.
Davies of Oldham, L.
Dean of Thornton-le-Fylde, B.
Donoughue, L.
Eatwell, L.
Fanshawe of Richmond, L.
Feldman, L.
Gibson, L.
Hamwee, B.
Healey, L.
Hoyle, L.
Inglewood, L.
James of Holland Park, B.
Jellicoe, E.
Jenkins of Putney, L.
MacFarlane of Bearsen, L.
McIntosh of Hudnall, B.
O'Cathain, B.
Oxford, Bp.
Quinton, L.
Renfrew of Kaimsthorn, L.
Renton of Mount Harry, L.
Rix, L.
Rogers of Riverside, L.
Sainsbury of Preston
  Candover, L.
Selkirk of Douglas, L.
Skidelsky, L.
Smith of Gilmorehill, B.
Sterling of Plaistow, L.
Stone of Blackheath, L.
Strange, B.
Walpole, L.
Winston, L.
Younger of Leckie, V.

Arts Sponsorship
Dean of Thornton-le-Fylde, B.

Australia
Parry, L.

Aviation
Brougham and Vaux, L.
Fanshawe of Richmond, L.

Glenarthur, L.
MacKenzie of Culkein, L.
Monro of Langholm, L.
Onslow of Woking, L.
Rotherwick, L.
Simon, L.
Trefgarne, L.

Banking
O'Cathain, B.
Williams of Elvel, L.

Blind People
Russell-Johnston, L.

Breast Cancer
Falkender, B.

**Britain's Export
  Performance**
Waverley, V.

British Film Industry
Falkender, B.

British Politics
Norton of Louth, L.

British-Irish Relations
Hylton, L.

Broadcasting
Brigstocke, B.
Colwyn, L.
Eames, L.
Griffiths of Fforestfach, L.
Holme of Cheltenham, L.
James of Holland Park, B.
Jay of Paddington, B.
Lipsey, L.
McNally, L.
Quirk, L.
Rawlings, B.
Taylor of Warwick, L.
Wakefield, Bp.
Warnock, B.

Building
Ryder of Warsaw, B.

Business
Hollick, L.

Business Ethics
Oxford, Bp.

Cane Sugar
Clark of Kempston, L.

Car Safety
Robertson of Port Ellen, L.

Caribbean
Young, B.

Central and Eastern Europe
Carlile of Berriew, L.

Charities
Arran, E.
Rix, L.
Stewartby, L.

Charity Law
Brightman, L.
Goudie, B.

Cheque-Book Journalism
Sharples, B.

Childcare
Hardie, L.
Knight of Collingtree, B.

Children
Blood, B.
David, B.
Gale, B.
Goudie, B.
Harrison, L.
Massey of Darwen, B.
Murray of Epping Forest, L.
Nicholson of Winterbourne, B.
Strange, B.
Thornton, B.
Uddin, B.
Warner, L.
Young, B.

China
Ashley of Stoke, L.
Cobbold, L.
Marlesford, L.
Thomas of Gresford, L.

Church Affairs
Luke, L.
Moore of Wolvercote, L.
Richardson of Calow, B.

Citizenship
Alton of Liverpool, L.

City
Alexander of Weedon, L.
Cuckney, L.
Northbrook, L.
Shawcross, L.

Civil Liberties
Barker, B.
Clinton-Davis, L.
Dubs, L.
Morgan, L.

Co-operative Movement
Morris of Manchester, L.

Coal Industry
Dormand of Easington, L.
Mason of Barnsley, L.

Commerce
Molloy, L.
Nicol, B.
O'Cathain, B.
Sainsbury of Preston
  Candover, L.

**Commercial and Intellectual
  Property Law**
Grabiner, L.

Commonwealth
Acton, L.
Blaker, L.
Janner of Braunstone, L.
Molloy, L.
Moore of Wolvercote, L.
Russell-Johnston, L.
Stoddart of Swindon, L.
Taylor of Blackburn, L.
Waverley, V.
Wright of Richmond, L.

Communications Industry
Tenby, V.
Wakefield, Bp.

**Community and Social
  Work**
Patel of Blackburn, L.

Community Care
Brooke of Alverthorpe, L.
Carter, L.
Eames, L.

Community Relations
Howells of St Davids, B.

Company Law
Wedderburn of Charlton, L.

Complementary Medicine
Colwyn, L.
Baldwin of Bewdley, E.

Conflict Resolution
Ahmed, L.
Hylton, L.
Stone of Blackheath, L.
Waverley, V.

Conservation
Archer of Sandwell, L.
Gilbert, L.
Hardy of Wath, L.
Marlesford, L.
Nicol, B.
Northesk, E.
Onslow of Woking, L.
Renton of Mount Harry, L.
Roberts of Conwy, L.
Selborne, E.
Selkirk of Douglas, L.
Walpole, L.

Constitutional Affairs
Campbell of Alloway, L.
Carnegy of Lour, B.
Dean of Harptree, L.
Forsyth of Drumlean, L.
Gould of Potternewton, B.
Hogg of Cumbernauld, L.
Hollick, L.
Hooson, L.
Irvine of Lairg, L.
Listowel, E.
Molyneaux of Killead, L.
Norton of Louth, L.
Wallace of Saltaire, L.

Constitutional Reform
Currie of Marylebone, L.
Holme of Cheltenham, L.
Lester of Herne Hill, L.
Morgan, L.
Scarman, L.
Smith of Clifton, L.

Construction Industry
Feldman, L.
Howie of Troon, L.

Shrewsbury and Waterford, E.
Sterling of Plaistow, L.

Consumer Affairs
Campbell of Croy, L.
Graham of Edmonton, L.
Janner of Braunstone, L.
Joffe, L.
Oppenheim-Barnes, B.
Wilcox, B.

Cornwall
Vivian, L.

Corporate Governance
Taverne, L.

**Council of Europe and
    Western European Union**
Knight of Collingtree, B.

Country Houses
Crathorne, L.

Countryside
Blackburn, Bp.
Carnegy of Lour, B.
Strange, B.

Cricket
Rix, L.

Crime and Criminal Justice
Bach, L.

Crime
Taverne, L.

Criminal Justice
Harris of Greenwich, L.
Hilton of Eggardon, B.
James of Holland Park, B.
Stern, B.

Culture
Geraint, L.
Rawlings, B.

Current Affairs
Evans of Watford, L.

Cyprus
Stallard, L.
Vivian, L.

De-Regulation
Vinson, L.

Defence
Allenby of Megiddo, V.
Astor of Hever, L.
Attlee, E.
Blaker, L.
Bramall, L.
Brookeborough, V.
Campbell of Croy, L.
Carver, L.
Chalfont, L.
Craig of Radley, L.
Erroll, E.
Fanshawe of Richmond, L.
Fookes, B.
Gilbert, L.
Glenarthur, L.
Hardy of Wath, L.
Healey, L.
Hill-Norton, L.
Hooson, L.
Inge, L.
Judd, L.
Luke, L.
MacKenzie of Culkein, L.
Mason of Barnsley, L.
Monro of Langholm, L.
Moore of Wolvercote, L.
Murton of Lindisfarne, L.
Nicholson of Winterbourne, B.
Onslow of Woking, L.
Park of Monmouth, B.
Powell of Bayswater, L.
Pym, L.
Robertson of Port Ellen, L.
Rogan, L.
Rotherwick, L.
Saltoun of Abernethy, Ly.
Selkirk of Douglas, L.
Selsdon, L.
Stewartby, L.
Strange, B.
Vivian, L.
Wallace of Saltaire, L.

Developing World
Falkland, V.
Joffe, L.

Development
Brett, L.
Desai, L.
Redesdale, L.
Southwark, Bp.

Devolution
Hunt of Kings Heath, L.
Mar and Kellie, E.
Renton, L.

Devolution of Power
Geraint, L.

Disability
Ashley of Stoke, L.
Attenborough, L.
Carter, L.
Darcy de Knayth, B.
McColl of Dulwich, L.
Masham of Ilton, B.
Morris of Manchester, L.
Murray of Epping Forest, L.
Newton of Braintree, L.
Rix, L.
Simon, L.
Sterling of Plaistow, L.
Swinfen, L.
Uddin, B.
Wilkins, B.

Disabled
Gould of Potternewton, B.
Jenkin of Roding, L.
O'Cathain, B.

Disadvantaged
Ashley of Stoke, L.

Disadvantaged and Excluded Children
Northbourne, L.

Disarmament
Jenkins of Putney, L.

Drafting of Legislation
Renton, L.

Drug Addiction
Cavendish of Furness, L.
Falkland, V.
Mancroft, L.
Masham of Ilton, B.
Taverne, L.
Vivian, L.

Dyslexia
Laird, L.

East and South-East Asia
Wilson of Tillyorn, L.

East-West Relations
Russell-Johnston, L.

Eastern Europe
Harris of High Cross, L.
Whaddon, L.
York, Abp.

Eastern Germany
Winchester, Bp.

Ecological Economics
Beaumont of Whitley, L.

Economic Policy
Bruce of Donington, L.
Crickhowell, L.
Croham, L.
Cuckney, L.
Currie of Marylebone, L.
Davies of Oldham, L.
Desai, L.
Gilbert, L.
Grenfell, L.
Griffiths of Fforestfach, L.
Harris of High Cross, L.
Hollick, L.
Jenkin of Roding, L.
Ludford, B.
Marsh, L.
Oakeshott of Seagrove Bay, L.
O'Cathain, B.
Selsdon, L.
Sharp of Guildford, B.
Skidelsky, L.
Stoddart of Swindon, L.
Taverne, L.

Economics
Brett, L.
Christopher, L.
Eatwell, L.
Forsyth of Drumlean, L.
Howell of Guildford, L.
Lamont of Lerwick, L.
Roberts of Conwy, L.
Roll of Ipsden, L.
Sterling of Plaistow, L.

Economy
Coe, L.

Economy and Regeneration
Patel of Blackburn, L.

Education
Addington, L.
Attenborough, L.
Baker of Dorking, L.
Baldwin of Bewdley, E.
Billingham, B.
Blackburn, Bp.
Blackstone, B.
Blake, L.
Blatch, B.
Bramall, L.
Briggs, L.
Brigstocke, B.
Brooke of Alverthorpe, L.
Buscombe, B.
Butterworth, L.
Carlisle of Bucklow, L.
Carnegy of Lour, B.
Cavendish of Furness, L.
Chilver, L.
Coe, L.
Cox, B.
Cumberlege, B.
Currie of Marylebone, L.
David, B.
Davies of Coity, L.
Davies of Oldham, L.
Dearing, L.
Desai, L.
Dormand of Easington, L.
Evans of Watford, L.
Griffiths of Fforestfach, L.
Hayman, B.
Hollis of Heigham, B.
Jellicoe, E.
Judd, L.
Kilpatrick of Kincraig, L.
King of West Bromwich, L.
Levy, L.
Lewis of Newnham, L.
Linklater of Butterstone, B.
Lockwood, B.
Lucas of Crudwell and Dingwall, L.
Macaulay of Bragar, L.
McFarlane of Llandaff, B.
McIntosh of Hudnall, B.
Maddock, B.
Massey of Darwen, B.
Merlyn-Rees, L.
Morgan, L.
Nicholson of Winterbourne, B.
Northbourne, L.
Patel of Blackburn, L.
Pearson of Rannoch, L.
Perry of Southwark, B.

Education *continued*
Platt of Writtle, B.
Porter of Luddenham, L.
Quinton, L.
Quirk, L.
Renfrew of Kaimsthorn, L.
Roberts of Conwy, L.
St Albans, Bp.
Scarman, L.
Selborne, E.
Selkirk of Douglas, L.
Skidelsky, L.
Southwark, Bp.
Stallard, L.
Taylor of Blackburn, L.
Tope, L.
Uddin, B.
Walton of Detchant, L.
Warnock, B.
Wedderburn of Charlton, L.
Winchester, Bp.
Winston, L.
Young, B.

Education Social Policy
Andrews, B.

Electoral Affairs
Gould of Potternewton, B.

Electoral Reform
Blake, L.
Lipsey, L.

Employment
Brooke of Alverthorpe, L.
Davies of Oldham, L.
Durham, Bp.
Evans of Parkside, L.
Hoyle, L.
Sheppard of Liverpool, L.
Shore of Stepney, L.
Turner of Camden, B.

Employment Law
Gladwin of Clee, L.
Janner of Braunstone, L.
Watson of Invergowrie, L.
Wedderburn of Charlton, L.

Energy
Cooke of Islandreagh, L.
Croham, L.
Evans of Parkside, L.
Gardner of Parkes, B.
Geddes, L.
Hardy of Wath, L.

Haslam, L.
Howell of Guildford, L.
Jenkin of Roding, L.
Lindsay, E.
Lofthouse of Pontefract, L.
Lovell-Davis, L.
Naseby, L.
Nicol, B.
Skelmersdale, L.
Stoddart of Swindon, L.
Taylor of Blackburn, L.

Engineering
Attlee, E.
Tombs, L.

Environment
Addington, L.
Alton of Liverpool, L.
Baldwin of Bewdley, E.
Barber of Tewkesbury, L.
Beaumont of Whitley, L.
Bradshaw, L.
Bridgeman, V.
Campbell of Croy, L.
Cavendish of Furness, L.
Chilver, L.
Clinton-Davis, L.
Coe, L.
Courtown, E.
Crickhowell, L.
David, B.
Dixon-Smith, L.
Erroll, E.
Flowers, L.
Forsyth of Drumlean, L.
Gibson, L.
Glentoran, L.
Graham of Edmonton, L.
Hanham, B.
Haslam, L.
Hereford, Bp.
Hilton of Eggardon, B.
Holme of Cheltenham, L.
Hunt of Kings Heath, L.
Hylton-Foster, B.
Inglewood, L.
Jellicoe, E.
Lewis of Newnham, L.
Lindsay, E.
London, Bp.
Maddock, B.
Mallalieu, B.
Mar, C.
Nicol, B.
Palmer, L.

Redesdale, L.
Renton, L.
Selkirk of Douglas, L.
Shrewsbury and Waterford, E.
Skelmersdale, L.
Soulsby of Swaffham Prior, L.
Strabolgi, L.
Tenby, V.
Tope, L.
Warnock, B.
Wilcox, B.
Williams of Elvel, L.

Equal Opportunities
Crawley, B.
Fookes, B.
Gibson of Market Rasen, B.
Lester of Herne Hill, L.
Uddin, B.

Ethics
Habgood, L.

Ethnic Conflicts
Parekh, L.

Ethnic Minority Issues
Patel, L.

Europe
Billingham, B.
Bowness, L.
Goudie, B.
Haskins, L.
Hooson, L.
Hylton, L.
Inglewood, L.
Ludford, B.
Montrose, D.
Morgan, L.
Newby, L.
Shore of Stepney, L.
Skidelsky, L.
Tomlinson, L.
Tope, L.
Tordoff, L.
Wallace of Saltaire, L.
Williams of Mostyn, L.
Willoughby de Broke, L.

European Affairs
Grenfell, L.

European Co-operation
Chalker of Wallasey, B.

European History
Watson of Richmond, L.

European Legislation
Renton, L.

European Monetary Union
Cobbold, L.
Crawley, B.
Harrison, L.

European Political Integration
Lester of Herne Hill, L.

European Union
Bruce of Donington, L.
Campbell of Alloway, L.
Carnegy of Lour, B.
Crawley, B.
Flather, B.
Gallacher, L.
Harris of High Cross, L.
Hooper, B.
Lamont of Lerwick, L.
Lovell-Davis, L.
Nicholson of Winterbourne, B.
Pearson of Rannoch, L.
Robertson of Port Ellen, L.
Russell-Johnston, L.
Stoddart of Swindon, L.
Taverne, L.

Exports
Falkender, B.
Naseby, L.
Oxfuird, V.

Family
Blood, B.
Northbourne, L.
Seccombe, B.
Young, B.

Far East
Marsh, L.

Farming
Barber of Tewkesbury, L.
Callaghan of Cardiff, L.
Nicholson of Winterbourne, B.

Film Industry
Dormand of Easington, L.
Falkland, V.
Taylor of Warwick, L.

Finance
Boardman, L.
Bruce of Donington, L.
Clark of Kempston, L.
Croham, L.
Donoughue, L.
Haslam, L.
Higgins, L.
Howe, E.
Kimball, L.
Lucas of Crudwell and Dingwall, L.
Roll of Ipsden, L.
St John of Bletso, L.
Taylor of Gryfe, L.
Tomlinson, L.
Williams of Elvel, L.

Financial Institutions
Renton of Mount Harry, L.

Financial Markets
Stewartby, L.

Financial Regulation
Lipsey, L.

Financial Services
Christopher, L.
Jenkin of Roding, L.
Joffe, L.
Marsh, L.

Fishing Industry
Hughes of Woodside, L.
Stodart of Leaston, L.
Wilcox, B.

Food and Nutrition
Naseby, L.
Rea, L.

Food Industry
Wade of Chorlton, L.

Food Standards
Mar, C.

Football
Carter, L.

Foreign Affairs
Acton, L.
Arran, E.
Blackstone, B.
Blake, L.

Blaker, L.
Bramall, L.
Campbell of Croy, L.
Cavendish of Furness, L.
Chalfont, L.
Clinton-Davis, L.
Coe, L.
Fanshawe of Richmond, L.
Gilbert, L.
Glenarthur, L.
Hardy of Wath, L.
Healey, L.
Holme of Cheltenham, L.
Home, E.
Howell of Guildford, L.
Jellicoe, E.
Judd, L.
Lamont of Lerwick, L.
Lichfield, Bp.
McNally, L.
Molloy, L.
Moore of Wolvercote, L.
Morgan, L.
Moynihan, L.
Nicholson of Winterbourne, B.
Northbrook, L.
Park of Monmouth, B.
Powell of Bayswater, L.
Prentice, L.
Pym, L.
Renfrew of Kaimsthorn, L.
Robertson of Port Ellen, L.
Russell-Johnston, L.
St John of Bletso, L.
Selkirk of Douglas, L.
Selsdon, L.
Shawcross, L.
Soulsby of Swaffham Prior, L.
Stern, B.
Stewartby, L.
Strange, B.
Thomas of Gwydir, L.
Tomlinson, L.
Tordoff, L.
Uddin, B.
Wallace of Saltaire, L.
Watson of Invergowrie, L.
Waverley, V.
Williams of Mostyn, L.
Wright of Richmond, L.

Forestry
Barber of Tewkesbury, L.
Cavendish of Furness, L.
McColl of Dulwich, L.
Nicol, B.
Taylor of Gryfe, L.

Former Soviet Union
Hylton, L.
Smith of Gilmorehill, B.

France
Astor of Hever, L.
Strabolgi, L.

Freedom of Information
Nicholson of Winterbourne, B.

Freemasonry
Burnham, L.

Further Education
Whitaker, B.

Future of Work
Sheppard of Liverpool, L.

Global Justice
Parekh, L.

Golf
Bell, L.

Governance of the UK
Barker, B.

Healing
Chelmsford, Bp.

Health
Ashley of Stoke, L.
Barker, B.
Billingham, B.
Bridgeman, V.
Brigstocke, B.
Brookeborough, V.
Carter, L.
Coe, L.
Colwyn, L.
Cox, B.
Dean of Harptree, L.
Ewing of Kirkford, L.
Falkender, B.
Gardner of Parkes, B.
Glenarthur, L.
Hanham, B.
Hayman, B.
Hollis of Heigham, B.
Hoyle, L.
Jay of Paddington, B.
Jenkin of Roding, L.
Kilpatrick of Kincraig, L.
Knight of Collingtree, B.

Lovell-Davis, L.
Ludford, B.
McColl of Dulwich, L.
McFarlane of Llandaff, B.
MacKenzie of Culkein, L.
Masham of Ilton, B.
Massey of Darwen, B.
Miller of Hendon, B.
Newton of Braintree, L.
Nicholson of Winterbourne, B.
Noakes, B.
Quirk, L.
Rea, L.
Roberts of Conwy, L.
Selkirk of Douglas, L.
Smith of Clifton, L.
Stallard, L.
Uddin, B.
Walton of Detchant, L.
Winston, L.
Wolfson of Sunningdale, L.

Health and Safety at Work
Gibson of Market Rasen, B.
Walker of Doncaster, L.

Health Care
Chelmsford, Bp.
Forsyth of Drumlean, L.

Health Service
Carnegy of Lour, B.
Cumberlege, B.
Davies of Coity, L.
Dubs, L.
Hughes of Woodside, L.
McColl of Dulwich, L.
Mar, C.
Molloy, L.
Naseby, L.
Turnberg, L.
Wigoder, L.

Heritage
Gibson, L.
Hollis of Heigham, B.
Luke, L.
Monro of Langholm, L.
Montagu of Beaulieu, L.
Northesk, E.
Palmer, L.
Park of Monmouth, B.
Rawlings, B.
Selkirk of Douglas, L.

High Arctic
Brightman, L.

Higher Education
Flowers, L.
Grabiner, L.
Howie of Troon, L.
McColl of Dulwich, L.
Parekh, L.
Park of Monmouth, B.
Patel, L.
Sharp of Guildford, B.
Smith of Clifton, L.
Soulsby of Swaffham Prior, L.
Watson of Invergowrie, L.

Historic Buildings
Cobbold, L.

History
Baker of Dorking, L.

Home Affairs
Anelay of St Johns, B.
Bridgeman, V.
Carlile of Berriew, L.
David, B.
Deedes, L.
Goudie, B.
Hardy of Wath, L.
Irvine of Lairg, L.
Mackenzie of Framwellgate,
    L.
Mallalieu, B.
Shore of Stepney, L.
Wigoder, L.

Homeless
Bristol, Bp.
Murray of Epping Forest, L.
Scarman, L.

Hong Kong
Ashley of Stoke, L.
Bramall, L.
Geddes, L.
Marlesford, L.
Skidelsky, L.
Thomas of Gresford, L.
Willoughby de Broke, L.
Wilson of Tillyorn, L.

Horse-racing
Carnarvon, E.
Lipsey, L.
Noakes, B.

Horticulture
Northbourne, L.
Skelmersdale, L.

Housing
Alton of Liverpool, L.
Bristol, Bp.
Clark of Kempston, L.
Dean of Thornton-le-Fylde, B.
Dixon, L.
Durham, Bp.
Filkin, L.
Fisher of Rednal, B.
Fookes, B.
Gardner of Parkes, B.
Hamwee, B.
Hylton, L.
Jenkin of Roding, L.
Lofthouse of Pontefract, L.
Maddock, B.
Merlyn-Rees, L.
Oakeshott of Seagrove Bay, L.
Oxford, Bp.
Sanderson of Bowden, L.
Selkirk of Douglas, L.
Stallard, L.
Stoddart of Swindon, L.

Human Rights
Ahmed, L.
Alton of Liverpool, L.
Archer of Sandwell, L.
Brett, L.
Carlisle of Bucklow, L.
Cox, B.
Dubs, L.
Faulkner of Worcester, L.
Goodhart, L.
Hylton, L.
Janner of Braunstone, L.
Joffe, L.
Lester of Herne Hill, L.
Lofthouse of Pontefract, L.
Mason of Barnsley, L.
Nicholson of Winterbourne, B.
Rea, L.
Russell-Johnston, L.
Scarman, L.
Stern, B.

Humanitarian Aid
Cox, B.

Immigration
Dubs, L.
Geddes, L.
Hoyle, L.

Import Substitution
Feldman, L.

India
Janner of Braunstone, L.

Industrial Relations
Butterworth, L.
Campbell of Alloway, L.
Clarke of Hampstead, L.
Davies of Coity, L.
Evans of Parkside, L.
Evans of Watford, L.
Gibson of Market Rasen, B.
Gladwin of Clee, L.
Haslam, L.
Hoyle, L.
Janner of Braunstone, L.
Lofthouse of Pontefract, L.
Prentice, L.
Robertson of Port Ellen, L.
Walker of Doncaster, L.
Wedderburn of Charlton, L.

Industrial Training
Lockwood, B.

Industry
Bruce of Donington, L.
Butterworth, L.
Cavendish of Furness, L.
Chilver, L.
Christopher, L.
Clark of Kempston, L.
Dean of Thornton-le-Fylde, B.
Feldman, L.
Geddes, L.
Gladwin of Clee, L.
Hanson, L.
Haslam, L.
Holme of Cheltenham, L.
Home, E.
Jenkin of Roding, L.
Knight of Collingtree, B.
Lockwood, B.
Marsh, L.
Molloy, L.
O'Cathain, B.
Oxfuird, V.
Sanderson of Bowden, L.
Sharp of Guildford, B.
Stoddart of Swindon, L.
Taylor of Gryfe, L.
Wade of Chorlton, L.

Information Technology
Baker of Dorking, L.
Mitchell, L.
Nicholson of Winterbourne, B.
Randall of St Budeaux, L.

Inner Cities
Alton of Liverpool, L.
Hooper, B.
Knights, L.
Moynihan, L.
York, Abp.

Insurance
Clark of Kempston, L.

Intellectual Property
Nicholson of Winterbourne, B.

Intelligence
Powell of Bayswater, L.

Inter Faith Relations
Richardson of Calow, B.

International Affairs
Hooson, L.
Islwyn, L.
Owen, L.
Perry of Southwark, B.
Rawlings, B.
Sandwich, E.

International Democracy
Steel of Aikwood, L.

International Development
Andrews, B.
Massey of Darwen, B.
Stern, B.
Tomlinson, L.
Whitaker, B.

International Finance
Howell of Guildford, L.

Iran
Nicholson of Winterbourne, B.

Iraq
Nicholson of Winterbourne, B.

Ireland
Dubs, L.
Goudie, B.

Islamic World
Nicholson of Winterbourne, B.

Jewish Causes
Janner of Braunstone, L.

Justice
Hanham, B.

Juvenile Justice
Elton, L.

Kashmiri Right of Self-Determination
Ahmed, L.

Kuwait
Nicholson of Winterbourne, B.

Labour Issues
Brett, L.

Lancashire
Waddington, L.

Land Reform
MacKenzie of Culkein, L.

Latin America
Hooper, B.

Law
Ackner, L.
Alexander of Weedon, L.
Cameron of Lochbroom, L.
Carlisle of Bucklow, L.
Clinton-Davis, L.
Donaldson of Lymington, L.
Hooson, L.
Mallalieu, B.
Taylor of Warwick, L.
Williams of Mostyn, L.

Law and Order
Buscombe, B.
Knights, L.
Miller of Hendon, B.
Renton, L.
Warner, L.

Law Reform
Archer of Sandwell, L.
Grabiner, L.
Lester of Herne Hill, L.
Scarman, L.
Selkirk of Douglas, L.

Legal Affairs
Carlile of Berriew, L.
Inglewood, L.
Irvine of Lairg, L.

Mackenzie of Framwellgate, L.
St John of Bletso, L.
Waddington, L.

Legal Profession
Alexander of Weedon, L.

Legislatures
Norton of Louth, L.

Leisure Industries
McNally, L.

Licensed Trade
Evans of Parkside, L.

Light Rail Transport
Russell-Johnston, L.

Lighting
Robertson of Port Ellen, L.

Literature
James of Holland Park, B.

Local Government
Bach, L.
Blatch, B.
Bowness, L.
Bridgeman, V.
Cameron of Lochbroom, L.
Carnegy of Lour, B.
Cumberlege, B.
Dormand of Easington, L.
Fisher of Rednal, B.
Forsyth of Drumlean, L.
Graham of Edmonton, L.
Hamwee, B.
Hanham, B.
Hogg of Cumbernauld, L.
Hollis of Heigham, B.
Inglewood, L.
King of West Bromwich, L.
Knights, L.
Lofthouse of Pontefract, L.
Ludford, B.
Macaulay of Bragar, L.
Maddock, B.
Molyneaux of Killead, L.
Platt of Writtle, B.
Selkirk of Douglas, L.
Sewel, L.
Smith of Leigh, L.
Stodart of Leaston, L.
Stoddart of Swindon, L.

Taylor of Blackburn, L.
Tope, L.
Uddin, B.
Winchester, Bp.

Local Issues
Cavendish of Furness, L.

London
Bowness, L.
Hamwee, B.
London, Bp.
Thornton, B.

Low Pay
Blood, B.

Machinery of Government
Goudie, B.
Lipsey, L.

Magistracy
Tenby, V.

Malaysia
Winchester, Bp.

Manpower Policy
Walker of Doncaster, L.

Manufacturing Industries
Cooke of Islandreagh, L.
Evans of Parkside, L.

Marine Industry
Greenway, L.
Wilcox, B.

Maritime Affairs
Cooke of Islandreagh, L.
Dixon, L.
Glentoran, L.
MacKenzie of Culkein, L.

Maritime Safety
Donaldson of Lymington, L.

Marketing
Naseby, L.

Media
Arran, E.
Cumberlege, B.
Dean of Thornton-le-Fylde, B.
Deedes, L.
Gibson, L.

Hamwee, B.
Hollis of Heigham, B.
Inglewood, L.
Jay of Paddington, B.
Jenkins of Putney, L.
Lester of Herne Hill, L.
Lovell-Davis, L.
Palmer, L.
Quinton, L.
Quirk, L.
Thornton, B.

Medical Care
Turnberg, L.

Medical Drugs
Ashley of Stoke, L.

Medical Profession
Carlile of Berriew, L.

Medical Research Ethics
Carnegy of Lour, B.

Medicine
Habgood, L.
McColl of Dulwich, L.
Walton of Detchant, L.
Warnock, B.

Member of the Society of Friends (Quakers)
Shutt of Greetland, L.

Mental Handicap
Forsyth of Drumlean, L.
Pearson of Rannoch, L.
Renton, L.

Mental Health
Acton, L.
Alderdice, L.
Carlile of Berriew, L.
Fookes, B.
McCluskey, L.
Molyneaux of Killead, L.

Middle East
Hylton, L.
Janner of Braunstone, L.
Levy, L.
Shore of Stepney, L.
Stone of Blackheath, L.

Middle Eastern History and Politics
Rochester, Bp.

Migration
Judd, L.

Military History
Luke, L.

Mineral Extraction
Shrewsbury and Waterford, E.

Moral Issues
Oxford, Bp.

Motor Industry
Astor of Hever, L.
Brougham and Vaux, L.
Denton of Wakefield, B.
Islwyn, L.
Montagu of Beaulieu, L.
Simon, L.

Motorcycle Industry
Falkland, V.

Museums and Galleries
Armstrong of Ilminster, L.
Brigstocke, B.
Montagu of Beaulieu, L.
Renfrew of Kaimsthorn, L.

Music
Bell, L.
Sterling of Plaistow, L.

National Health Service (Hospital Chaplaincy)
St Albans, Bp.

National Heritage
Renfrew of Kaimsthorn, L.
Sandwich, E.
Strabolgi, L.

National Lottery
Naseby, L.

North American Matters
Parry, L.

North West
Taylor of Blackburn, L.

Northern Ireland
Alderdice, L.
Alton of Liverpool, L.
Archer of Sandwell, L.
Brookeborough, V.

Denton of Wakefield, B.
Eames, L.
Glentoran, L.
Hylton, L.
Mason of Barnsley, L.
Moyola, L.
Park of Monmouth, B.
Rogan, L.
Smith of Clifton, L.
Stallard, L.

Nuclear Disarmament
Jenkins of Putney, L.

Nursing
Cox, B.
MacKenzie of Culkein, L.

Oil
Howell of Guildford, L.

Overseas Aid and Development
Attlee, E.
Butterworth, L.
Chalker of Wallasey, B.
Clarke of Hampstead, L.
Deedes, L.
Durham, Bp.
Hughes of Woodside, L.
Jay of Paddington, B.
Lichfield, Bp.
Moynihan, L.
Oxford, Bp.
Sandwich, E.
Watson of Invergowrie, L.
Waverley, V.

Overseas Development
Grenfell, L.
Oakeshott of Seagrove Bay, L.

Parliamentary Affairs
Norton of Louth, L.
Pym, L.

Parliamentary Procedure
Naseby, L.

Penal Affairs and Policy
Acton, L.
Carlisle of Bucklow, L.
Christopher, L.
Fookes, B.
Glenarthur, L.

Penal Affairs and Policy
continued
Howe, E.
Hylton, L.
Judd, L.
Linklater of Butterstone, B.
Masham of Ilton, B.

Penal Reform
Dubs, L.
Merlyn-Rees, L.

Pensioners' Issues
Winchester, Bp.

Pensions
Christopher, L.
Dean of Thornton-le-Fylde, B.
Newton of Braintree, L.
Taverne, L.
Turner of Camden, B.
Vinson, L.

Pesticides
Mar, C.

Pet Quarantine
Sharples, B.

Planning
Bradshaw, L.
Gardner of Parkes, B.
Hamwee, B.
Jenkin of Roding, L.
Wade of Chorlton, L.

Police
Bradshaw, L.
Harris of Richmond, B.
Knights, L.
Mackenzie of Framwellgate, L
Simon, L.

Policy Development
Filkin, L.

Policy Implementation
Ashton of Upholland, B.
Filkin, L.

Population and Development
Gould of Potternewton, B.

Post Office
Dearing, L.
Skelmersdale, L.

Poverty
Ashley of Stoke, L.
Barker, B.
Beaumont of Whitley, L.
Oxford, Bp.
Winchester, Bp.

Prison Reform
Addington, L.
Hylton, L.
McIntosh of Hudnall, B.
Mar and Kellie, E.

Prisoners' Wives
Sharples, B.

Privatisation
Forsyth of Drumlean, L.
Renton of Mount Harry, L.

Privatised Utilities
Skelmersdale, L.

Probation
Mar and Kellie, E.

Professional Engineers
Howie of Troon, L.

Professional Self-Regulation
Kilpatrick of Kincraig, L.

Property
Courtown, E.
Shrewsbury and Waterford, E.

Psephology
Lipsey, L.

Psychoanalysis and Political Conflict Resolution
Alderdice, L.

Public Communication
Quirk, L.

Public Finance
Noakes, B.
Sewel, L.

Public Health
McIntosh of Hudnall, B.

Public Service Management
Noakes, B.

Public Transport
Hogg of Cumbernauld, L.

Race Relations
Ahmed, L.
Deedes, L.
Dubs, L.
Flather, B.
Gould of Potternewton, B.
Hilton of Eggardon, B.
Judd, L.
Parekh, L.
Patel of Blackburn, L.
Sheppard of Liverpool, L.
Shore of Stepney, L.
Whitaker, B.

Railways
Taylor of Blackburn, L.
Tenby, V.

Recreation
Monro of Langholm, L.

Refugees
Alton of Liverpool, L.
Judd, L.
Moynihan, L.
Nicholson of Winterbourne, B.

Regional Development
Goudie, B.
Morris of Manchester, L.
Newby, L.

Regional Policy
Dormand of Easington, L.
Elliott of Morpeth, L.
Inglewood, L.

Regionalism
Smith of Leigh, L.

Regulation of Medicine
Patel, L.

Relations with Muslim countries
Ahmed, L.

Restrictive Trade Practices and Monopolies
Campbell of Alloway, L.

Retail Industry
Denton of Wakefield, B.
Feldman, L.
McNally, L.
O'Cathain, B.

River Thames
Luke, L.

Road Programme
Islwyn, L.

Road Safety
Brougham and Vaux, L.
Simon, L.

Road Transport
Montagu of Beaulieu, L.

Rural Affairs
Carter, L.
Geraint, L.
Inglewood, L.
Mancroft, L.
Montrose, D.
Noakes, B.
Pym, L.

Russia
Harris of High Cross, L.
Smith of Gilmorehill, B.

Rwanda
Winchester, Bp.

Science
Andrews, B.
Habgood, L.
Jenkin of Roding, L.
Porter of Luddenham, L.
Selborne, E.
Southwark, Bp.
Stone of Blackheath, L.
Tombs, L.
Walton of Detchant, L.

Science and Technology
Carver, L.
Flowers, L.
Haskel, L.
Morris of Manchester, L.
Sharp of Guildford, B.
Simon, L.
Taverne, L.
Winston, L.

Scotland
Erroll, E.
Glenarthur, L.
Goudie, B.
Mar and Kellie, E.
Monro of Langholm, L.
Robertson of Port Ellen, L.
Sewel, L.

Scottish Affairs
Carnegy of Lour, B.
Home, E.
Russell-Johnston, L.
Saltoun of Abernethy, Ly.
Sanderson of Bowden, L.
Selkirk of Douglas, L.
Wilson of Tillyorn, L.

Scottish Highlands
Pearson of Rannoch, L.

Scottish Law
Macaulay of Bragar, L.

Scottish Parliament
Watson of Invergowrie, L.

Sex Equality
Lockwood, B.

Shipping
Geddes, L.
Greenway, L.
Sterling of Plaistow, L.

Ships and Shipbuilding
Dixon, L.

Small Businesses
Harrison, L.
King of West Bromwich, L.
Miller of Hendon, B.
Mitchell, L.
Roberts of Conwy, L.
Sanderson of Bowden, L.
Sharples, B.
Vinson, L.
Younger of Leckie, V.

Social and Health Care
Warner, L.

Social Policy
Blackstone, B.
Briggs, L.
Eames, L.

Griffiths of Fforestfach, L.
Harris of High Cross, L.
Ludford, B.
Mar and Kellie, E.

Social Security
Anelay of St Johns, B.
Barker, B.
Bridgeman, V.
Carnegy of Lour, B.
Dean of Harptree, L.
Dixon, L.
Ewing of Kirkford, L.
Higgins, L.
Knight of Collingtree, B.
Mar, C.
Newton of Braintree, L.
Stallard, L.
Turner of Camden, B.

Social Welfare
Hylton-Foster, B.
Levy, L.

South Africa
Watson of Richmond, L.

South East Asia
Geddes, L.
Naseby, L.

Southern Africa
Acton, L.
Filkin, L.

Space
Tanlaw, L.

Speech Pathology
Quirk, L.

Sport
Arran, E.
Bach, L.
Billingham, B.
Donoughue, L.
Faulkner of Worcester, L.
Feldman, L.
Glentoran, L.
Higgins, L.
Islwyn, L.
Macaulay of Bragar, L.
Monro of Langholm, L.
Moynihan, L.
St John of Bletso, L.

Standards in Medicine
Patel, L.

Steel
Islwyn, L.

Sufism
Rochester, Bp.

**Sustainable Built
  Environment**
Rogers of Riverside, L.

Tax
Newton of Braintree, L.
Stewartby, L.
Taverne, L.
Vinson, L.

Technology
Erroll, E.
Jenkin of Roding, L.
Southwark, Bp.
Tombs, L.
Wade of Chorlton, L.

Telecommunications
Dean of Thornton-le-Fylde, B.

Terrorism
Vivian, L.

Textile Industry
Sanderson of Bowden, L.
Waddington, L.

Theatre
Macaulay of Bragar, L.
Rix, L.

Third World
Archer of Sandwell, L.
Geraint, L.
Judd, L.
Rea, L.

Tibet
Willoughby de Broke, L.

Time
Tanlaw, L.

Tourism
Blaker, L.
Brookeborough, V.
Dormand of Easington, L.

Feldman, L.
Gladwin of Clee, L.
Harrison, L.
Luke, L.
McNally, L.
Montagu of Beaulieu, L.
Parry, L.
Roberts of Conwy, L.
Walpole, L.

Trade and Industry
Boardman, L.
Buscombe, B.
Chalker of Wallasey, B.
Clark of Kempston, L.
Eatwell, L.
Haskel, L.
Hoyle, L.
Lucas of Crudwell and
   Dingwall, L.
McNally, L.
Moynihan, L.
Parekh, L.
Powell of Bayswater, L.
Rogan, L.
Selsdon, L.

Trade Unions
Dixon, L.
Jenkins of Putney, L.
Renton, L.

Training
Davies of Oldham, L.
Lockwood, B.
Roberts of Conwy, L.

Transition Economies
Skidelsky, L.

Transport
Attlee, E.
Berkeley, L.
Blackburn, Bp.
Brabazon of Tara, L.
Bradshaw, L.
Brougham and Vaux, L.
Chalker of Wallasey, B.
Clinton-Davis, L.
Davies of Oldham, L.
Denton of Wakefield, B.
Dixon, L.
Dixon-Smith, L.
Evans of Parkside, L.
Falkland, V.
Faulkner of Worcester, L.

Gardner of Parkes, B.
Geddes, L.
Gilbert, L.
Hereford, Bp.
Higgins, L.
Hollick, L.
Hughes of Woodside, L.
Hunt of Kings Heath, L.
Laird, L.
Lindsay, E.
Oakeshott of Seagrove Bay, L.
Roberts of Conwy, L.
Sanderson of Bowden, L.
Scott of Needham Market, B.
Shrewsbury and Waterford, E.
Smith of Clifton, L.
Stoddart of Swindon, L.
Taylor of Gryfe, L.
Wade of Chorlton, L.

UFOs
Hill-Norton, L.

Uganda
Winchester, Bp.

Ulster Scots Activity
Laird, L.

Underdeveloped Countries
Attenborough, L.

United Nations
Carlile of Berriew, L.
Vivian, L.

Urban Policies
Crickhowell, L.
Sheppard of Liverpool, L.

Urban regeneration
Lichfield, Bp.

USA Affairs
Bach, L.

Venice
Strabolgi, L.

Visual Arts
Crathorne, L.
Freyberg, L.

Vocational Education
Bristol, Bp.

Voluntary Sector
Chalker of Wallasey, B.
Coe, L.
Evans of Watford, L.
Levy, L.
Rix, L.

Wales
Carlile of Berriew, L.
Geraint, L.
Hooson, L.
Parry, L.

Waste Management
Lindsay, E.

Welfare
Taverne, L.
Winchester, Bp.

Welsh Literature
Cledwyn of Penrhos, L.

Welsh Sport
Cledwyn of Penrhos, L.

West Africa
Filkin, L.

West Midlands
Shrewsbury and Waterford,
E.

Wildlife
Hardy of Wath, L.

Women's Health
Patel, L.

Women's Issues
Blood, B.
Crawley, B.
Dean of Thornton-le-Fylde, B.
Denton of Wakefield, B.
Gale, B.

Gibson of Market Rasen,
B.
Gould of Potternewton, B.
Miller of Hendon, B.
Seccombe, B.

**Women's Opportunities in
Engineering**
Platt of Writtle, B.

Working Class Issues
Blood, B.

World Government
Archer of Sandwell, L.

Young Under-privileged
Listowel, E.

Youth Affairs
Linklater of Butterstone, B.
Sheppard of Liverpool, L.

Members who are Hereditary Peers

Those who have also received life peerages are given in bold. Peers of Ireland are marked*, with their British honours in parenthesis.
There are two hereditary office holders, Duke of Norfolk (Earl Marshal), and Marquess of Cholmondeley (Lord Great Chamberlain)

Aberdare, L.
Acton, L. (LP **B. Acton of Bridgnorth**, 2000)
Addington, L.
Aldington, L, (LP **B. Low**, 1999)
Allenby of Megiddo, V.
Ampthill, L.
Arran, E.* (B. Sudley)
Astor of Hever, L.
Astor, V.
Attlee, E.
Avebury, L.
Baldwin of Bewdley, E.
Belstead, L. (LP **B. Ganzoni**, 1999)
Berkeley, L. (LP **B. Gueterbock**, 2000)
Bledisloe, V.
Brabazon of Tara, L.
Bridgeman, V.
Bridges, L.
Brookeborough, V.
Brougham and Vaux, L.
Burnham, L.
Caithness, E.
Carnarvon, E.
Carrington, L.
    (LP **B. Carington of Upton**, 1999)
Chandos, V.
    (LP **B. Lyttelton of Aldershot**, 2000)
Cholmondeley, M.
Cobbold, L.
Colville of Culross, V.
Colwyn, L.
Courtown, E.* (B. Saltersford)
Craigavon, V.
Cranborne, V. (LP **B. Gascoyne-Cecil**, 1999)
Crathorne, L.
Crawford and Balcarres, E. (LP **B. Balniel**, 1974)
Darcy de Knayth, B.
Denham, L.
Dundee, E.
Elton, L.
Erroll, E.
Falkland, V.
Ferrers, E.
Freyberg, L.
Geddes, L.
Glenarthur, L.
Glentoran, L.
Goschen, V.
Greenway, L.

Grenfell, L. (LP **B. Grenfell of Kilvey**, 2000)
Henley, L.* (B. Northington)
Home, E.
Howe, E.
Hylton, L.
Inglewood, L.
Jellicoe, E.
    (LP **B. Jellicoe of Southampton**, 1999)
Lindsay, E.
Listowel, E.* (B. Hare)
Liverpool, E.
Longford, E.*
    (LP **B. Pakenham of Cowley**, 1999)
Lucas of Crudwell, L.
Luke, L.
Lyell, L.
Mancroft, L.
Mar, C.
Mar and Kellie, E.
    (LP **B. Erskine of Alloa Tower**, 2000)
Methuen, L.
Milner of Leeds, L.
Monson, L.
Montagu of Beaulieu, L.
Montrose, D.
Moran, L.
Mowbray and Stourton, L.
Moynihan, L.
Norfolk, D.
Northbourne, L.
Northbrook, L.
Northesk, E.
Onslow, E.
Oxfuird, V.
Palmer, L.
Peel, E.
Ponsonby of Shulbrede, L.
    (LP **B. Ponsonby of Roehampton**, 2000)
Rea, L.
Reay, L.
Redesdale, L. (LP **B. Mitford**, 2000)
Rosslyn, E.
Rotherwick, L.
Russell, E.
St John of Bletso, L.
Saltoun of Abernethy, Lady
Sandwich, E.
Selborne, E.
Selsdon, L.

Shepherd, L.
(LP **B. Shepherd of Spalding**, 1999)
Shrewsbury and Waterford, E.
Simon, V.
Skelmersdale, L.
Slim, V.
Snowdon, E. (LP **B. Armstrong-Jones**, 1999)
Strabolgi, L.
Strange, B.
Strathclyde, L.

Swinfen, L.
Tenby, V.
Trefgarne, L.
Vivian, L.
Walpole, L.
Waverley, V.
Willoughby de Broke, L.
Windlesham, L. (LP **B. Hennessy**, 1999)
Younger of Leckie, V.
    (LP **B. Younger of Prestwich**, 1992)

Hereditary Peers' Election Results 27/28 October 1999

At the elections held on 27/28 October 1999 for 15 hereditary peers ready to serve as Deputy Speakers and other office holders, in accordance with the provisions of the House of Lords Bill and Standing Order 9(2)(ii), the candidates received the following number of votes:

Candidate	Votes	Place	Candidate	Votes	Place
C. Mar	570	1st	L. Colwyn	488	9th
L. Strabolgi	558	2nd	V. Oxfuird	482	10th
L. Elton	558	3rd	L. Reay	471	11th
L. Lyell	547	4th	L. Geddes	461	12th
L. Skelmersdale	544	5th	V. Simon	453	13th
L. Aberdare	530	6th	L. Methuen	421	14th
L. Brougham and Vaux	525	7th	L. Ampthill	418	15th
V. Falkland	519	8th			

3/4 November 1999

At the elections held on 3/4 November 1999 for 75 hereditary peers elected by the hereditary peers in their party or group, in accordance with the provisions of the House of Lords Bill and Standing Order 9(2)(i), the candidates received the following number of votes:

CONSERVATIVE PEERS

Candidate	Votes	Place	Candidate	Votes	Place
E. Ferrers	190	1st	V. Bridgeman	125	23rd
L. Strathclyde	174	2nd	L. Luke	124	24th
L. Trefgarne	173	3rd	E. Lindsay	116	25th
L. Denham	169	4th	L. Lucas of Crudwell		
L. Mancroft	168	5th	and Dingwall	115	26th
E. Howe	165	6th	L. Montagu of Beaulieu	113	27th
L. Brabazon of Tara	165	7th	E. Home	113	28th
E. Caithness	161	8th	L. Glentoran	104	29th
L. Henley	160	9th	E. Onslow	99	30th
L. Glenarthur	157	10th	L. Crathorne	97	31st
L. Astor of Hever	151	11th	L. Willoughby de Broke	96	32nd
V. Astor	146	12th	L. Inglewood	95	33rd
E. Courtown	143	13th	L. Northbrook	95	34th
E. Peel	142	14th	L. Swinfen	95	35th
L. Moynihan	137	15th	E. Shrewsbury	95	36th
E. Attlee	135	16th	L. Selsdon	94	37th
V. Goschen	132	17th	E. Liverpool	93	38th
D. Montrose	127	18th	E. Arran	90	39th
L. Burnham	127	19th	E. Dundee	90	40th
L. Vivian	126	20th	L. Mowbray and Stourton	88	41st
E. Northesk	126	21st	L. Rotherwick	88	42nd
E. Selborne	125	22nd			

CROSSBENCH PEERS

Candidate	Votes	Place	Candidate	Votes	Place
B. Darcy de Knathy	85	1st	E. Carnarvon	58	17th
L. Freyberg	82	2nd	E. Listowel	58	18th
L. St John of Bletso	81	3rd	L. Moran	57	19th
L. Northbourne	78	4th	B. Strange	53	20th
E. Sandwich	78	5th	E. Erroll	52	21st
V. Allenby of Megiddo	75	6th	L. Walpole	52	22nd
V. Tenby	74	7th	V. Craigavon	51	23rd
L. Palmer	72	8th	B. Wharton*	48	24th
V. Slim	72	9th	V. Colville of Culross	47	25th
V. Bledisloe	70	10th	V. Waverley	47	26th
L. Monson	70	11th	L. Greenway	47	27th
V. Brookeborough	68	12th	E. Rosslyn	45	28th
L. Bridges	68	13th	L. Cobbold*	43	29th
Lady Saltoun of Abernethy	64	14th			
L. Hylton	64	15th	* Lord Cobbold replaced the late		
E. Baldwin of Bewdley	63	16th	Baroness Wharton		

LABOUR PEERS

Candidate	Votes	Place	Candidate	Votes	Place
L. Milner of Leeds	8	1st	L. Rea	7	2nd

LIBERAL DEMOCRAT PEERS

Candidate	Votes	Place	Candidate	Votes	Place
E. Russell	17	1st	L. Addington	10	3rd
L. Avebury	13	2nd			

Bishops

By ancient usage the two Anglican archbishops and the bishops of London, Durham and Winchester automatically have seats in the House of Lords. Since the mid-nineteenth century the number of bishops in the House (known as lords spiritual as opposed to lords temporal) has been limited to 26. The remaining diocesan bishops qualify for membership according to seniority, the longest serving bishop outside the Lords succeeding to a vacancy among the lords spiritual.

ARCHBISHOPS (2) AND DIOCESAN BISHOPS (3) EX OFFICIO

Most Rev. George Leonard Carey	Canterbury
Most Rev. David Michael Hope	York
Rt Rev. Richard John Carew Chartres	London
Rt Rev. Anthony Michael Arnold Turnbull	Durham
Rt Rev. Michael Charles Scott-Joynt	Winchester

BISHOPS IN ORDER OF SENIORITY (21)

		Elected
Rt Rev. Eric Waldram Kemp*	Chichester	1974
Rt Rev. Keith Norman Sutton	Lichfield	1984
Rt Rev. Barry Rogerson	Bristol	1985
Rt Rev. Robert Maynard Hardy	Lincoln	1987
Rt Rev. Richard Douglas Harries	Oxford	1987
Rt Rev. Mark Santer	Birmingham	1987
Rt Rev. Alan David Chesters	Blackburn	1989
Rt Rev. John Keith Oliver	Hereford	1990
Rt Rev. Thomas Frederick Butler	Southwark	1991

*retires 31 January 2001

Rt Rev. James Lawton Thompson	Bath and Wells	1991
Rt Rev. Nigel Simeon McCulloch	Wakefield	1992
Rt Rev. David John Smith	Bradford	1992
Rt Rev. Christopher John Mayfield	Manchester	1993
Rt Rev. David Staffurth Stancliffe	Salisbury	1993
Rt Rev. David Edward Bentley	Gloucester	1993
Rt Rev. Michael James Nazir-Ali	Rochester	1994
Rt Rev. John Warren Gladwin	Guildford	1994
Rt Rev. Kenneth William Stevenson	Portsmouth	1995
Rt Rev. Jonathan Sansbury Bailey	Derby	1995
Rt Rev. Christopher William Herbert	St Albans	1995
Rt Rev. John Freeman Perry	Chelmsford	1996

DIOCESAN BISHOPS WITHOUT SEATS

Elected

Rt Rev. Ian Patrick Martyn Cundy	Peterborough	1996
Rt Rev. Peter Robert Forster	Chester	1996
Rt Rev. John Hubert Richard Lewis	St Edmundsbury and Ipswich	1997
Rt Rev. William Ind	Truro	1997
Rt Rev. Peter Selby	Worcester	1997
Rt Rev. John Martin Wharton	Newcastle	1997
Rt Rev. John Nicholls	Sheffield	1997
Rt Rev. Colin James Bennetts	Coventry	1997
Rt Rev. James Stuart Jones	Liverpool	1998
Rt Rev. Timothy John Stevens	Leicester	1999
Rt Rev. George Henry Cassidy	Southwell	1999
Rt Rev. Graham Richard James	Norwich	1999
Rt Rev. Michael Laurence Langrish	Exeter	2000
Rt Rev. John Richard Packer	Ripon and Leeds	2000
Rt Rev. Anthony John Russell	Ely	2000
Rt Rev. Graham Geoffrey Dow	Carlisle	2000

BISHOPS NOT ELIGIBLE TO HAVE A SEAT

Appointed

| Rt Rev. Noel Debroy Jones | Sodor and Man | 1989 |
| Rt Rev. John William Hind | Europe | 1993 |

Peerages created January to October 2000

Baron Acton of Bridgnorth (Richard Gerald, Baron Acton)	17 April
Baroness Andrews (Elizabeth Kay Andrews OBE)	9 May
Baron Ashcroft (Sir Michael Ashcroft)	24 October
Baron Bernstein of Craigweil (Alexander Bernstein Esq)	15 May
Baroness Billingham (Angela Theodora Billingham)	2 May
Baron Birt (Sir John Birt Kt)	11 February
Baron Brennan (Daniel Joseph Brennan Esq QC)	2 May
Baron Brittan of Spennithorne (Rt Hon Sir Leon Brittan Kt QC)	9 February
Baron Coe (Sebastian Newbold Coe Esq OBE)	16 May
Baroness Cohen of Pimlico (Janet Cohen)	3 May
Baron Erskine of Alloa Tower (James Thorne, Earl of Mar and Kellie)	19 April
Baron Evans of Temple Guiting (Matthew Evans Esq CBE)	11 May
Baron Fyfe of Fairfield (George Lennox Fyfe Esq)	16 May
Baroness Gibson of Market Rasen (Anne Gibson OBE)	9 May
Baron Greaves (Anthony Robert Greaves Esq)	4 May
Baroness Greengross (Sally Ralea Greengross OBE)	10 February
Baron Grenfell of Kilvey (Julian Pascoe Francis St Leger, Baron Grenfell)	17 April
Baron Gueterbock (Anthony Fitzhardinge, Baron Berkeley OBE)	18 April
Baron Hodgson of Astley Abbotts (Robin Granville Hodgson Esq CBE)	7 June
Baron Hunt of Chesterton (Julian Charles Roland Hunt Esq CB FRS)	5 May
Baron Joffe (Joel Goodman Joffe CBE)	16 February
Baron Jordan (William Brian Jordan Esq CBE)	5 June
Baron Layard (Peter Richard Grenville Layard Esq)	3 May
Baron Luce (Sir Richard Napier Luce)	2 October
Baron Lyttelton of Aldershot (Thomas Orlando, Viscount Chandos)	19 April
Baron Mitchell (Parry Andrew Mitchell Esq)	10 May
Baron Mitford (Rupert Bertram, Baron Redesdale)	18 April
Baron Morgan (Kenneth Owen Morgan Esq)	12 June
Baroness Noakes (Dame Sheila Valerie Masters DBE)	7 June
Baroness Northover (Dr Lindsay Patricia Granshaw, Mrs Northover)	1 May
Baron Oakeshott of Seagrove Bay (Matthew Alan Oakeshott Esq)	1 May
Baron Parekh (Bikhu Chhotalal Parekh Esq)	10 May
Baron Patel of Blackburn (Adam Hafejee Patel Esq)	14 February
Baron Ponsonby of Roehampton (Frederick Matthew Thomas, Baron Ponsonby of Shulbrede)	19 April
Baron Powell of Bayswater (Sir Charles David Powell KCMG)	15 February
Baron Roper (John Francis Hodgkess Roper Esq)	12 May
Baron Scott of Foscote (Rt Hon Sir Richard Rashleigh Folliott Scott Kt)	17 July
Baroness Scott of Needham Market (Mrs Rosalind Carol Scott)	11 May
Baron Shutt of Greetland (David Trevor Shutt Esq OBE)	12 May
Baron Turnberg (Sir Leslie Arnold Turnberg Kt)	4 May
Baroness Walmsley (Joan Margaret Walmsley)	15 May

Peerage pending
Betty Boothroyd

Obituaries

JANUARY–OCTOBER 2000

Annan (Life Baron); d. 21 February
Braine of Wheatley (Life Baron); d. 5 January
Brooke of Ystradfellte (Life Baroness); d. 1 September
Butterfield (Life Baron); d. 22 July
Coggan (Life Baron); d. 17 May
Erroll of Hale (1st Baron, UK) (Life Baron Erroll of Kilmun); d. 14 September
Harmar-Nicholls (Life Baron); d. 15 September
Henderson of Brompton (Life Baron); d. 13 January
Mackenzie-Stuart (Life Baron); d. 1 April
MacLehose of Beoch (Life Baron); d. 27 May
Runcie (Life Baron); d. 11 July
Wharton (Baroness, 11th in line, E); d. 15 May

Lords who are members of other assemblies

Lord Alderdice	Northern Ireland Assembly
Lord Bethell	European Parliament
Lord Elis-Thomas	National Assembly for Wales
Baroness Hamwee	Greater London Assembly
Lord Harris of Haringey	Greater London Assembly
Lord Inglewood	European Parliament
Baroness Ludford	European Parliament
Baroness Nicholson of Winterbourne	European Parliament
Lord Selkirk of Douglas	Scottish Parliament
Lord Steel of Aikwood	Scottish Parliament
Lord Tope	Greater London Assembly
Lord Watson of Invergowrie	Scottish Parliament

Women members

Women were first admitted into the House of Lords by the Life Peerage Act, 1958. At October 2000, there were 107 women who had received life peerages. Women peers by succession (indicated with an asterisk) were not admitted into the Upper House until 1963. At August 1, 2000, there were four, all of whom were elected by their fellow hereditary peers.

Amos, B.   1997
Andrews, B.   2000
Anelay of St Johns, B.   1996
Ashton of Upholland, B.   1999
Barker, B.   1999
Billingham, B.   2000
Blackstone, B.   1987
Blatch, B.   1987
Blood, B.   1999
Brigstocke, B.   1990
Buscombe, B.   1998
Byford, B.   1996
Carnegy of Lour, B.   1982
Castle of Blackburn, B.   1990
Chalker of Wallasey, B.   1992
Cohen of Pimlico, B.   2000
Cox, B.   1983
Crawley, B.   1998
Cumberlege, B.   1990

*Darcy de Knayth, B. (E)   1332
David, B.   1978
Dean of Thornton-le-Fylde, B.   1993
Delacourt-Smith of Alteryn, B.   1974
Denton of Wakefield, B.   1991
Dunn, B.   1990
Eccles of Moulton, B.   1990
Elles, B.   1972
Emerton, B.   1997
Falkender, B.   1974
Farrington of Ribbleton, B.   1994
Fisher of Rednal, B.   1974
Flather, B.   1990
Fookes, B.   1997
Gale, B.   1999
Gardner of Parkes, B.   1981
Gibson of Market Rasen, B.   2000
Goudie, B.   1998
Gould of Potternewton, B.   1993

Greengross, B.   2000
Hamwee, B.   1991
Hanham, B.   1999
Harris of Richmond, B.   1999
Hayman, B.   1996
Hilton of Eggardon, B.   1991
Hogg, B.   1995
Hollis of Heigham, B.   1990
Hooper, B.   1985
Howells of St Davids, B.   1999
Hylton-Foster, B.   1965
James of Holland Park, B.   1991
Jay of Paddington, B.   1992
Jeger, B.   1979
Kennedy of The Shaws, B.   1997
Knight of Collingtree, B.   1997
Linklater of Butterstone, B.   1997
Lloyd of Highbury, B.   1996
Lockwood, B.   1978
Ludford, B.   1997
McFarlane of Llandaff, B.   1979
McIntosh of Hudnall, B.   1999
Maddock, B.   1997
Mallalieu, B.   1991
*Mar, C. (S)   1114/1404
Masham of Ilton, B.   1970
Massey of Darwen, B.   1999
Miller of Chilthorne Domer, B.   1998
Miller of Hendon, B.   1993
Nicholson of Winterbourne, B.   1997
Nicol, B.   1982
Noakes, B.   2000
Northover, B.   2000
O'Cathain, B.   1991
O'Neill of Bengarve, B.   1999
Oppenheim-Barnes, B.   1989
Park of Monmouth, B.   1990

Perry of Southwark, B.   1991
Pike, B.   1974
Pitkeathley, B.   1997
Platt of Writtle, B.   1981
Prashar, B.   1999
Ramsay of Cartvale, B.   1996
Rawlings, B.   1994
Rendell of Babergh, B.   1997
Richardson of Calow, B.   1998
Ryder of Warsaw, B.   1979
*Saltoun of Abernethy, Ly. (S)   1445
Scotland of Asthal, B.   1997
Scott of Needham Market, B.   2000
Seccombe, B.   1991
Serota, B.   1967
Sharp of Guildford, B.   1998
Sharples, B.   1973
Smith of Gilmorehill, B.   1995
Stern, B.   1999
*Strange, B. (E)   1628
Symons of Vernham Dean, B.   1996
Thatcher, B.   1992
Thomas of Walliswood, B.   1994
Thornton, B.   1998
Trumpington, B.   1980
Turner of Camden, B.   1985
Uddin, B.   1998
Walmsley, B.   2000
Warnock, B.   1985
Warwick of Undercliffe, B.   1999
Whitaker, B.   1999
Wilcox, B.   1996
Wilkins, B.   1999
Williams of Crosby, B.   1993
Young, B.   1971
Young of Old Scone, B.   1997

Whips and Spokesmen

GOVERNMENT SPOKESMEN

Lord Privy Seal, Leader of the House and Minister for Women	Rt Hon **Baroness Jay of Paddington**
Deputy Leader	**Lord Williams of Mostyn**
Agriculture	**Baroness Hayman** Rt Hon **Lord Carter**
Attorney-General	**Lord Williams of Mostyn**
Cabinet Office	**Lord Falconer of Thoroton** QC **Lord Burlison**
Culture, Media and Sport	**Lord McIntosh of Haringey**
Defence	**Baroness Symons of Vernham Dean** **Lord Burlison**
Education and Employment	**Baroness Blackstone** **Lord Bach**
Environment, Transport and the Regions	Rt Hon **Lord Macdonald of Tradeston** **Lord Whitty** **Baroness Farrington of Ribbleton** *(Local Government)*
Foreign and Commonwealth Office	**Baroness Scotland of Asthal** **Baroness Ramsay of Cartvale**
Health	**Lord Hunt of Kings Heath** **Lord Burlison**
Home Office	**Lord Bassam of Brighton** **Lord Bach**
International Development	**Baroness Amos**
Legal Affairs	Rt Hon **Lord Irvine of Lairg**
Lord Chancellor's Department	Rt Hon **Lord Irvine of Lairg** **Lord Bach**
Northern Ireland	**Baroness Farrington of Ribbleton** **Lord Falconer**
Scotland Office	**Baroness Ramsay of Cartvale**
Social Security	Rt Hon **Baroness Hollis of Heigham** **Baroness Amos**
Trade and Industry	**Lord Sainsbury of Turville** **Lord McIntosh of Haringey**
Treasury	**Lord McIntosh of Haringey**
Wales Office	**Baroness Farrington of Ribbleton**
Women's Issues	Rt Hon **Baroness Jay of Paddington** **Baroness Amos**

OPPOSITION WHIPS AND SPOKESMEN

Leader of the Opposition	Rt Hon **Lord Strathclyde**
Deputy Leader of the Opposition	Rt Hon **Lord Mackay of Ardbrecknish**
Chief Whip	**Lord Henley**
Deputy Chief Whip	**Lord Burnham**
Whips	**Baroness Hanham** **Baroness Seccombe** **Lord Luke** **Viscount Bridgeman** **Lord Astor of Hever** **Earl of Northesk** **Lord Northbrook**

Agriculture | **Baroness Byford**
Lord Glentoran
Whip | **Lord Luke**
Constitutional Affairs | Rt Hon **Lord Strathclyde**
(Deputy Leader and Scotland) | Rt Hon **Lord Mackay of Ardbrecknish**
Wales | **Lord Henley**
Whip | **Earl of Northesk**
Culture, Media and Sport | **Baroness Anelay of St Johns**
Whip | **Lord Luke**
Defence | **Lord Burnham**
Earl Attlee
Whip | **Lord Northbrook**
Education and Employment
Education | Rt Hon **Baroness Blatch**
Employment | **Baroness Miller of Hendon**
Employment | **Viscount Astor**
Whip | **Baroness Seccombe**
Environment, Transport and the Regions | **Lord Brabazon of Tara**
Local Government | **Lord Dixon Smith**
Transport | **Earl Attlee**
Whip | **Baroness Hanham**
Foreign and Commonwealth Office | Rt Hon **Lord Howell of Guildford**
Baroness Rawlings
Whip | **Earl of Northesk**
Health | **Earl Howe**
Lord McColl of Dulwich
Whip | **Lord Astor of Hever**
Home Office | Rt Hon **Lord Cope of Berkeley**
Viscount Astor
Whip | **Viscount Bridgeman**
International Development | **Baroness Rawlings**
Whip | **Earl of Northesk**
Legal Affairs
(Shadow Lord Chancellor) | Rt Hon **Lord Kingsland** QC
Baroness Buscombe
Whip | **Viscount Bridgeman**
Northern Ireland | **Lord Glentoran**
Rt Hon **Lord Cope of Berkeley**
Whip | **Baroness Seccombe**
Scotland | Rt Hon **Lord Mackay of Ardbrecknish**
Whip | **Baroness Hanham**
Social Security | Rt Hon **Lord Higgins**
Baroness Buscombe
Whip | **Lord Astor of Hever**
Trade and Industry | Rt Hon **Lord Mackay of Ardbrecknish**
Baroness Miller of Hendon
Baroness Buscombe
Whip | **Lord Northbrook**
Treasury | **Lord Saatchi**
Rt Hon **Lord Kingsland** QC
Whip | **Earl of Northesk**
Wales | Rt Hon **Lord Roberts of Conwy**
Whip | **Baroness Hanham**

LIBERAL DEMOCRAT WHIPS AND SPOKESMEN

Leader	Rt Hon **Lord Rodgers of Quarry Bank**
Deputy Leader	Rt Hon **Baroness Williams of Crosby**
Chief Whip	Rt Hon **Lord Harris of Greenwich**
Deputy Whip	**Viscount of Falkland**
Assistant Whip	**Lord Dholakia**
Agriculture and Rural Affairs	**Baroness Miller of Chilthorne Domer**
Culture, Media and Sport	**Viscount of Falkland**
Media	Rt Hon **Lord Thomson of Monifieth**
Sport	**Lord Addington**
Tourism	**Lord Redesdale**
Defence	**Lord Wallace of Saltaire**
Education and Employment	**Lord Tope**
Higher Education	**Baroness Sharp of Guildford**
Environment, Transport and the Regions	**Baroness Hamwee**
Local Government and Planning	**Baroness Hamwee**
Housing	**Baroness Maddock**
Transport	**Baroness Thomas of Walliswood**
	Lord Methuen
Foreign and Commonwealth Affairs and International Development	Rt Hon **Baroness Williams of Crosby**
	Lord Wallace of Saltaire
	Lord Avebury
Europe	**Lord Watson of Richmond**
Health	**Lord Clement-Jones**
Home Office	**Lord McNally**
	Lord Thomas of Gresford
	Lord Dholakia
Lord Chancellor's Department	**Lord Goodhart**
Northern Ireland	**Lord Smith of Clifton**
Scotland	**Lord Mackie of Benshie**
	Earl of Mar and Kellie
Social Security	**Earl Russell**
	Lord Goodhart
Disability	**Lord Addington**
Trade and Industry	**Lord Razzall**
Energy	**Lord Ezra**
	Lord Newby
Treasury	**Lord Taverne**
	Lord Newby
Wales	**Lord Thomas of Gresford**
	Lord Hooson
	Lord Geraint

Lord Lester of Herne Hill, Lord Thomas of Gresford and Lord Goodhart assist spokesmen on legal matters.

Speaker and deputies

LORD CHANCELLOR
(*ex officio* Speaker)

The Lord Chancellor presides over the deliberations of the House, except when it is in Committee.
Lord Chancellor: Lord Irvine of Lairg.

DEPUTY SPEAKERS

Several Lords are appointed by the Crown by Commission under the Great Seal to act as Speaker of the House of Lords in the absence of the Lord Chancellor. Deputy Chairmen may also act as Speaker. In the event of none of these Lords being present, the House may on Motion appoint its own Speaker.

Aberdare, *L.*
Allenby of Megiddo, *V.*
Ampthill, *L.*
Boston of Faversham, *L.*
Brougham and Vaux, *L.*
Burnham, *L.*
Carter, *L.*
Cocks of Hartcliffe, *L.*
Cox, *B.*
Dean of Harptree, *L.*
Elliott of Morpeth, *L.*
Elton, *L.*
Graham of Edmonton, *L.*
Henley, *L.*
Hooper, *B.*
Lockwood, *B.*
Lyell, *L.*
McColl of Dulwich, *L.*
McIntosh of Haringey, *L.*
Mar, *C.*
Murton of Lindisfarne, *L.*
Nicol, *B.*
Oxfuird, *V.*
Serota, *B.*
Simon, *V.*
Skelmersdale, *L.*
Strabolgi, *L.*
Tordoff, *L.*
Turner of Camden, *B.*

CHAIRMAN AND DEPUTY CHAIRMEN

At the beginning of every session, or whenever a vacancy occurs, Lords are appointed by the House to fill the offices of Chairman and Principal Deputy Chairman of Committees. The Chairman takes the Chair in all Committees of the Whole House and is also chairman ex-officio of all committees of the House unless the House otherwise directs. In addition to his duties in the House, he exercises a general supervision and control over Provisional Order Confirmation Bills, Private Bills and Hybrid Instruments. He is also the first of the Deputy Speakers, appointed by Commission. The Principal Deputy Chairman of Committees, in addition to assisting the Chairman in his duties, is appointed to act as Chairman of the European Communities Committee. Other Deputy Chairmen may also take the Chair in Committees of the Whole House.

Chairman of Committees: Lord Boston of
  Faversham.
Principal Deputy Chairman of Committees:
  Lord Tordoff.
Panel of Deputy Chairmen:
Aberdare, *L.*
Allenby of Megiddo, *V.*
Ampthill, *L.*
Brougham and Vaux, *L.*
Burnham, *L.*
Carter, *L.*
Cocks of Hartcliffe, *L.*
Cox, *B.*
Dean of Harptree, *L.*
Elliott of Morpeth, *L.*
Elton, *L.*
Falkland, *V.*
Gardner of Parkes, *B.*
Geddes, *L.*
Graham of Edmonton, *L.*
Henley, *L.*
Hooper, *B.*
Lockwood, *B.*
Lofthouse of Pontefract, *L.*
Lyell, *L.*
McColl of Dulwich, *L.*
McIntosh of Haringey, *L.*
Mar, *C.*
Methuen, *L.*
Murton of Lindisfarne, *L.*
Nicol, *B.*
Oxfuird, *V.*
Serota, *B.*
Simon, *V.*
Skelmersdale, *L.*
Strabolgi, *L.*
Turner of Camden, *B.*

LORDS OF APPEAL

†*Lord of Appeal in Ordinary.*
†Bingham of Cornhill, *L. (Senior Lord of Appeal in Ordinary)*
Browne-Wilkinson, *L.*
  Cameron of Lochbroom, *L.*
†Clyde, *L.*
  Cooke of Thorndon, *L.*
  Goff of Chieveley, *L.*
  Hardie, *L.*
†Hobhouse of Woodborough, *L.*
†Hoffmann, *L.*
†Hope of Craighead, *L.*
†Hutton, *L.*
  Irvine of Lairg, *L. (Lord Chancellor)*
  Jauncey of Tullichettle, *L.*
  Lloyd of Berwick, *L.*
  McCluskey, *L.*
  Mackay of Clashfern, *L.*
†Millett, *L.*
  Mustill, *L.*
†Nicholls of Birkenhead, *L.*
  Nolan, *L.*
†Phillips of Worth Matravers, *L.*
  Rodger of Earlsferry, *L.*
†Saville of Newdigate, *L.*
†Scott of Foscote, *L.*
†Slynn of Hadley, *L.*
†Steyn, *L.*
  Woolf, *L. (Lord Chief Justice)*

Note: Lords of Appeal who, having attained the age of 75, are no longer eligible to hear appeals, are excluded from this list.

Select Committees

BANK OF ENGLAND MONETARY POLICY COMMITTEE

Chairman: Lord Peston.
Members: Lord Barnett, Lord Burns, Lord Cuckney, Lord Elder, Lord Forsyth of Drumlean, Baroness Hogg, Lord Newby, Baroness O'Cathain, Lord Paul, Lord Roll of Ipsden, Lord Taverne.
Clerk: S. P. Burton.

CONSOLIDATION BILLS: JOINT COMMITTEE

The function of this Committee is to consider Consolidation Bills and report them with or without amendment to the House. These Bills fall into five categories:

(*a*) Consolidation Bills, whether public or private, which are limited to re-enacting existing law;
(*b*) Statute Law Revision Bills, which are limited to repeal of obsolete, spent, unnecessary or superseded enactments;
(*c*) Bills presented under the Consolidation of Enactments (Procedure) Act 1949, which include corrections and minor improvements to the existing law;
(*d*) Bills to consolidate any enactments with amendments to give effect to recommendations made by the Law Commissions;
(*e*) Bills prepared by the Law Commissions to promote the reform of the Statute Law by the repeal of enactments which are no longer of practical utility.

The committee consists of 24 members, 12 from each House, appointed on the recommendation of the Lord Chancellor and the Speaker respectively. The Committee appoints its own chairman.

Chairman: Lord Clyde.
Lords' Members: Lord Campbell of Alloway, Lord Christopher, Viscount Colville of Culross, Earl of Dundee, Baroness Fookes, Lord Hobhouse of Woodborough, Lord Janner of Braunstone, Baroness Mallalieu, Lord Phillips of Sudbury, Lord Razzall, Lord Strabolgi.
Clerk: Rhodri Walters.

DELEGATED POWERS AND DEREGULATION COMMITTEE

The duty of this Committee is to report whether the provisions of any bill inappropriately delegate legislative power; to report on documents laid before Parliament under section 3(3) of the Deregulation and Contracting Out Act 1994 and on draft orders laid under section 1(4) of that Act; and to perform, in respect of such documents and orders, the functions performed in respect of other instruments by the Joint Committee on Statutory Instruments.

Chairman: Lord Alexander of Weedon.
Members: Lord Ampthill, Lord Dahrendorf, Lord Goodhart, Lord Hogg of Cumbernauld, Lord Mayhew of Twysden, Lord Merlyn-Rees, Lord Prys-Davies, Lord Waddington.
Clerk: Dr Philippa Tudor.
Counsel: Sir James Nursaw.

EUROPEAN UNION COMMITTEE

Chairman: Lord Tordoff.

Members: Viscount Bledisloe, Lord Borrie,
Viscount Brookeborough, Lord Brooke of
Alverthorpe, Baroness Crawley, Lord
Goodhart, Lord Grenfell, Lord Hope of
Craighead, Lord Hussey of North Bradley,
Lord Jopling, Lord Lamont of Lerwick,
Baroness O'Cathain, Earl of Selborne,
Baroness Stern, Lord Tomlinson, Lord
Wallace of Saltaire, Lord Williams of Elvel,
Lord Willoughby de Broke.

Clerk: Tom Mohan.
Legal Adviser: Dr C. S. Kerse.

*Members of Sub-Committees with asterisks (*)
after their names are co-opted members, i.e. they
are not members of the main committee*

Sub-committee A

ECONOMIC AND FINANCIAL AFFAIRS, TRADE AND
EXTERNAL RELATIONS

Chairman: Lord Tomlinson.

Members: Lord Armstrong of Ilminster*,
Baroness Crawley, Lord Grenfell, Lord
Hussey of North Bradley, Lord Lamont of
Lerwick, Lord Lea of Crondall*, Lord
Randall of St Budeaux*, Lord Renton of
Mount Harry*, Lord Sharman*, Baroness
Sharp of Guildford*, Lord Shaw of
Northstead*.

Clerk: Dr E. A. Hopkins.

Sub-committee B

ENERGY, INDUSTRY AND TRANSPORT

Chairman: Lord Brooke of Alverthorpe.

Members: Lord Bradshaw*, Viscount
Brookeborough, Lord Cavendish of Furness*,
Lord Chadlington*, Lord Faulkner of
Worcester*, Lord Marsh*, Baroness
O'Cathain, Lord Paul*, Lord Sandberg*,
Lord Skelmersdale*, Lord Woolmer of
Leeds*.

Clerk: P. F. M. Wogan.

Sub-committee C

COMMON FOREIGN AND SECURITY POLICY

Chairman: Baroness Hilton of Eggardon.

Members: Lord Harrison*, Lord Inge*, Lord
Jopling, Baroness Park of Monmouth*, Lord
Shore of Stepney*, Lord Watson of
Richmond*, Lord Williams of Elvel, Lord
Williamson of Horton*.

Clerk: D. J. Batt.

Sub-committee D

ENVIRONMENT, AGRICULTURE, PUBLIC HEALTH AND
CONSUMER PROTECTION

Chairman: Earl of Selborne.

Members: Lord Christopher*, Lord Judd*, Lord
Lewis of Newnham*, Lord Mackie of
Benshie*, Baroness Miller of Chilthorne
Domer*, Lord Palmer*, Lord Perry of
Walton*, Baroness Thornton*, Baroness
Wilcox*, Lord Willoughby de Broke,
Baroness Young of Old Scone*.

Clerk. T. E. Radice.

Sub-committee E

LAW AND INSTITUTIONS

Chairman: Lord Hope of Craighead.

Members: Viscount Bledisloe, Lord Borrie,
Lord Fraser of Carmyllie*, Lord Goodhart,
Baroness Goudie*, Lord Hunt of Wirral*,
Lord Lester of Herne Hill*, Lord Norton of
Louth+, Lord Plant of Highfield*, Lord
Wedderburn of Charlton*, Lord Wigoder*.

Clerk: S. P. Burton.
Legal Adviser: Dr C. S. Kerse.

Sub-committee F:

SOCIAL AFFAIRS, EDUCATION AND HOME AFFAIRS

Chairman: Lord Wallace of Saltaire.

Members: Lord Bridges*, Lord Dholakia*,
Lord Griffiths of Fforestfach*, Baroness
Harris of Richmond*, Lord King of West
Bromwich*, Baroness Knight of
Collingtree*, Lord Pilkington of Oxenford*,
Lord Rix*, Baroness Stern*, Baroness Turner
of Camden*, Baroness Whitaker*.

Clerk: Dr C. Johnson.

HOUSE OF LORDS OFFICES

Chairman: Lord Boston of Faversham

Members: Earl of Caithness, Lord Carter, Lord
Chalfont, Lord Colwyn, Lord Craig of
Radley, Lord Dholakia, Lord Dixon, Lord
Elton, Lord Gilbert, Lord Harris of
Greenwich, Lord Henley, Baroness Hilton of
Eggardon, Lord Hunt of Wirral, Lord Irvine
of Lairg, Baroness Jay of Paddington, Lord
Laming, Lord Mackay of Ardbrecknish, Lord
Marsh, Bishop of Oxford, Lord Renfrew of
Kaimsthorn, Lord Rodgers of Quarry Bank,
Baroness Seccombe, Baroness Serota, Lord
Strathclyde, Baroness Thomas of
Walliswood, Lord Tordoff, Lord Williams of
Mostyn, with the Clerk of the Parliaments
and the Gentleman Usher of the Black Rod.

Clerk: J. A. Vaughan.

ADMINISTRATION AND WORKS SUB-COMMITTEE
Chairman: Lord Boston of Faversham.
Members: Lord Carter, Lord Colwyn, Lord
 Craig of Radley, Baroness David, Lord Evans
 of Parkside, Lord Harris of Greenwich, Lord
 Henley, Baroness Hilton of Eggardon, Lord
 Methuen, Lord Monson, Baroness Rawlings,
 Lord Renfrew of Kaimsthorn, Baroness
 Richardson of Calow, with the Clerk of the
 Parliaments and the Gentleman Usher of the
 Black Rod.
Clerk: J. A. Vaughan.

ADVISORY PANEL ON WORKS OF ART
Chairman: Baroness Hilton of Eggardon.
Members: Lord Freyberg, Lord Gavron, Lord
 Jacobs, Lord Lloyd-Webber, Baroness
 McIntosh of Hudnall, Lord Mancroft, Lord
 Palmer, Baroness Rawlings, Lady Saltoun of
 Abernethy, with the Clerk of the Parliaments.
Clerk: J. A. Vaughan.

FINANCE AND STAFF SUB-COMMITTEE
Chairman: Lord Boston of Faversham.
Members: Lord Astor of Hever, Lord Colwyn,
 Lord Craig of Radley, Lord Gladwin of Clee,
 Lord Harris of Greenwich, Lord Harris of
 Haringey, Baroness Jay of Paddington, Lord
 Renfrew of Kaimsthorn, Lord Rodgers of
 Quarry Bank, Lord Williams of Elvel, with
 the Clerk of the Parliaments.
Clerk: Edward Ollard.

LIBRARY AND COMPUTERS
SUB-COMMITTEE
Chairman: Lord Renfrew of Kaimsthorn.
Members: Lord Ahmed, Lord Avebury, Lord
 Butterworth, Earl of Erroll, Lord Evans of
 Watford, Lord Hoffman, Earl of Listowel,
 Lord McIntosh of Haringey, Baroness Nicol,
 Earl of Northesk, Baroness Platt of Writtle,
 Baroness Rendell of Babergh, with the Clerk
 of the Parliaments.
Clerk: T. E. Radice.

REFRESHMENT SUB-COMMITTEE
Chairman: Lord Colwyn.
Members: Lord Burnham, Lord Carter,
 Baroness Darcy de Knayth, Baroness David,
 Viscount of Falkland, Lord Geddes, Lord
 Graham of Edmonton, Lord Harris of
 Greenwich, Lord Stone of Blackheath,
 Viscount Tenby, with the Clerk of the
 Parliaments.
Clerk: Edward Ollard.

HYBRID INSTRUMENTS COMMITTEE

The function of the Committee is to consider
Hybrid Instruments against which Petitions have
been presented and to recommend to the House
what action should be taken in each case.

Chairman: Lord Boston of Faversham.
Members: Lord Brougham and Vaux, Lord
 Burnham, Earl of Courtown, Viscount
 Craigavon, Lord King of West Bromwich,
 Baroness Thomas of Walliswood, Baroness
 Wilkins.
Clerk: Dr Philippa Tudor.

LIAISON COMMITTEE

The duties of this Committee are to advise the
House on the resources required for select
committee work and to allocate resources
between select committees; to review the select
committee work of the House; to consider
requests for *ad hoc* committees and report to the
House with recommendations; to ensure
effective coordination between the two Houses;
and to consider the availability of Lords to serve
on committees.

Chairman: Lord Boston of Faversham.
Members: Lord Clinton-Davis, Viscount
 Colville of Culross, Lord Craig of Radley,
 Baroness Jay of Paddington, Lord Kimball,
 Baroness Pitkeathley, Lord Rodgers of
 Quarry Bank, Lord Strathclyde, Lord
 Wigoder, Baroness Young.
Clerk: David Beamish.

PERSONAL BILLS COMMITTEE

The duties of the Committee are to examine
Petitions for Personal Bills and the provisions of
such Bills and consider whether the objects of
the Bill are proper to be enacted by a Personal
Bill; and if so, to see whether the provisions of
the Bill are proper for carrying its purposes into
effect, and to make any amendments, either of
substance or drafting to the draft Bill for this
purpose.

Chairman: Lord Boston of Faversham.
Members: Lord Astor of Hever, Lord Hogg of
 Cumbernauld, Lord Sandberg, Lord
 Templeman, Lord Wilberforce.
Clerk: Dr Philippa Tudor.

PRIVILEGES, COMMITTEE FOR

The House refers to this Committee questions regarding its privileges and claims of peerage and of precedence. In any claim of peerage, the Committee may not sit unless four Lords of Appeal are present. In certain circumstances claims to Irish Peerages are also referred to the Committee.

Chairman: Lord Boston of Faversham.
Members: Lord Allen of Abbeydale, Lord Carter, Lord Cledwyn of Penrhos, Viscount Cranborne, Lord Glenamara, Lord Henley, Baroness Jay of Paddington, Lord Mackay of Clashfern, Lord Marsh, Lord Mayhew of Twysden, Lord Rodgers of Quarry Bank, Lord Strabolgi, Lord Strathclyde, Lord Weatherill, Lord Wigoder, together with any four Lords of Appeal.
Clerk: Mr Brendan Keith.
Clerk (Peerage Claims): James Vallance White.

SUB-COMMITTEE ON LORDS' INTERESTS

By resolutions of 7 November 1995, Lords are required to register consultancies, or similar arrangements, involving payment or other incentives or reward for providing Parliamentary advice or services, and financial interests in businesses involved in Parliamentary lobbying on behalf of clients; and are debarred for speaking, voting or lobbying in respect of such interests. They may also register other particulars relating to matters which they consider may affect the public perception of the way in which they discharge their Parliamentary duties.
Chairman: Lord Nolan.
Members: Earl Ferrers, Baroness Serota, Lord Wigoder, together with any two other Lords of Appeal.
Clerk to the Sub-Committee and Registrar of Lords' Interests: James Vallance White

PROCEDURE COMMITTEE

Chairman: Lord Boston of Faversham.
Members: Viscount Allenby of Megiddo, Baroness Anelay of St Johns, Viscount Bledisloe, Lord Burlison, Lord Burnham, Earl of Caithness, Lord Carter, Lord Clarke of Hampstead, Lord Craig of Radley, Lord Denham, Earl Ferrers, Baroness Gould of Potternewton, Baroness Hamwee, Lord Harris of Greenwich, Lord Henley, Lord Irvine of Lairg, Baroness Jay of Paddington, Lord Kimball, Baroness Lockwood, Lord Mackay of Ardbrecknish, Lord Mancroft, Lord Rodgers of Quarry Bank, Lord Shepherd, Viscount Simon, Lord Skelmersdale, Lord Strabolgi, Lord Strathclyde, Lord Tordoff, Lord Williams of Mostyn, with the Clerk of the Parliaments.
Clerk: Brendan Keith.

SCIENCE AND TECHNOLOGY COMMITTEE

Chairman: Lord Winston.
Members: Lord Flowers*, Lord Haskel, Lord Howie of Troon, Lord Jenkin of Roding, Lord McColl of Dulwich, Lord Methuen, Lord Oxburgh, Lord Patel, Lord Perry of Walton, Baroness Platt of Writtle, Lord Quirk, Lord Rea, Lord Tombs, Lord Wade of Chorlton, Lord Walton of Detchant, Baroness Warwick of Undercliffe, Baroness Wilcox.
Clerk: Andrew Makower.

SUB COMMITTEE I
Complementary and Alternative Medicine
Chairman: Lord Walton of Detchant.
Members: Earl Baldwin of Bewdley*, Lord Colwyn*, Lord Haskel, Lord Howie of Troon, Lord Perry of Walton, Lord Quirk, Lord Rea, Lord Smith of Clifton*, Lord Soulsby of Swaffham Prior*, Lord Tombs.
Clerk: Miss C. K. S. K. Mawson.

SUB COMMITTEE II
Aircraft Cabin Environment
Chairman: Baroness Wilcox.
Members: Lord Flowers, Lord Jenkin of Roding, Lord Lewis of Newnham*, Lord McColl of Dulwich, Lord Methuen, Lord Oxburgh, Lord Patel, Baroness Platt of Writtle, Lord Wade of Chorlton, Baroness Warwick of Undercliffe, Lord Winston.
Clerk: E. R. Morgan.

SUB COMMITTEE IIA
Genetic Databases
Chairman: Lord Oxburgh.
Members: Lord Flowers, Lord Haskel, Lord Jenkin of Roding, Lord McColl of Dulwich, Lord Patel, Lord Perry of Walton, Lord Rea, Lord Turnberg*, Lord Wade of Chorlton, Lord Walton of Detchant, Baroness Wilcox, Lord Winston.
Clerk: E. R. Morgan

SELECTION, COMMITTEE OF

The main function of the Committee is to select Lords to form each Select Committee of the House, and the Lords members of Joint Committees. It also selects and proposes to the House the panel of Lords to act as Deputy Chairmen of Committees for each session.

Chairman: Lord Boston of Faversham.
Members: Lord Burnham, Lord Carter, Lord Craig of Radley, Lord Harris of Greenwich, Lord Henley, Baroness Jay of Paddington, Lord McIntosh of Haringey, Lord Rodgers of Quarry Bank, Lord Strathclyde, Viscount Tenby.
Clerk: J. A. Vaughan.

STANDING ORDERS (PRIVATE BILLS) COMMITTEE

The function of this Committee is to consider cases referred to them on a report from the Examiners of Petitions for Private Bills, who certify whether in the case of a particular Private Bill the Standing Orders have, or have not, been complied with and report the circumstances in cases where they have not. The Committee then consider whether, in such cases, the Standing Orders ought, or ought not, to be dispensed with and, if so, on what conditions.

The parties either appear in person or are represented by their parliamentary agents. Counsel are not heard.

Chairman: Lord Boston of Faversham.
Members: Baroness Ashton of Upholland, Lord Brett, Viscount Bridgeman, Lord Brougham and Vaux, Viscount of Falkland, Earl of Liverpool, Earl of Sandwich.
Clerk: Dr Philippa Tudor.

STATUTORY INSTRUMENTS: JOINT COMMITTEE

This Joint Committee of seven members from each House scrutinises nearly all Statutory Instruments to ensure they comply with relevant requirements.

Chairman: D. Tredinnick MP.
Lords' Members: Lord Greenway, Lord Hardy of Wath, Earl of Onslow, Lord Skelmersdale, Lord Thomas of Gresford, Lord Vivian, Lord Walker of Doncaster.
Clerk (Lords): Miss L. J. Mouland.

HOUSE OF LORDS COLLECTION TRUST

The Trust is a registered charity whose aim (in brief) is to establish a collection of works of art, books etc. which will enhance public awareness and understanding of the British political system past and present, placing particular emphasis on the role of the House of Lords and its members.

Trustees

Baroness Jay of Paddington *(Chairman)*	The Clerk of the Parliaments
Lord Boston of Faversham	The Clerk of the Records
Baroness Hilton of Eggardon	

Secretary: J. A. Vaughan.

LORDS' MEMBERS OF BRITISH–IRISH INTER-PARLIAMENTARY BODY

Lord Alderdice (associate member), Lord Blease, Lord Glentoran, Lord Lester of Herne Hill (associate member), Lord Lyell (associate member), Lord Merlyn-Rees, Baroness O'Cathain (associate member).
British Clerk to the Body: F. A. Cranmer.

LORDS MEMBERS OF INTERNATIONAL ASSEMBLIES

United Kingdom delegation to the North Atlantic Assembly.

Representatives
Lord Gladwin of Clee
Lord Sewel

Secretary: J. D. W. Rhys.

Parliamentary Assembly of the Council of Europe and the Assembly of Western European Union.

Representatives	*Substitutes*
Lord Clinton-Davis	Lord Judd
Lord Kirkhill	Lord Lucas of Crudwell
Baroness Knight of Collingtree	
Lord Ponsonby of Shulbrede	
Lord Russell-Johnston	

Secretary: C. A. Shaw.

Parliamentary Assembly of the Organisation for Security and Co-operation in Europe.

Representative	*Substitute*
Viscount Montgomery of Alamein	Lord Jopling
Baroness Hilton of Eggardon	

Secretary: C. A. Shaw.

ECCLESIASTICAL COMMITTEE: JOINT COMMITTEE (LORDS' MEMBERS)

Lord Beaumont of Whitley, Lord Brightman, Lord Campbell of Alloway, Viscount Cranborne, Lord Glenamara, Lord Hardy of Wath, Baroness Massey of Darwen, Lord Pilkington of Oxenford, Lord Strabolgi, Lord Templeman, Lord Wallace of Saltaire, Lord Weatherill, Baroness Wilcox, Lord Williams of Elvel, Baroness Young.
Secretary: Rhodri Walters.

PARLIAMENTARY BROADCASTING UNIT LTD (PARBUL) (LORDS' MEMBERS)

Lord Boston of Faversham, Lord Burnham, Lord Thomson of Monifieth, Lord Morris of Castle Morris.

Principal Officers and Officials

Lord Chancellor:
  Rt Hon the Lord Irvine of Lairg QC

DEPARTMENT OF CHAIRMAN OF COMMITTEES

Chairman of Committees:
  Lord Boston of Faversham QC
Principal Deputy Chairman of Committees:
  Lord Tordoff
Counsel to the Chairman of Committees:
  Sir James Nursaw KCB QC, Dr C S Kerse,
  D W Saunders CB

DEPARTMENT OF CLERK OF THE PARLIAMENTS

Clerk of the Parliaments: Michael Davies
Clerk Assistant and Clerk of Legislation:
  Paul Hayter LVO
Reading Clerk and Principal Finance Officer:
  Michael Pownall
Fourth Clerk at the Table (Judicial) and Clerk of the Judicial Office, and Registrar of Lords' Interests: James Vallance White CB
Clerk of the Journals: Brendan Keith
Clerk of Committees and Clerk of the Overseas Office: David Beamish
Establishment Officer: Edward Ollard
Clerk of Private Bills: Dr Philippa Tudor DPhil
Clerk of Public Bills: Rhodri Walters DPhil
Clerks of Select Committees: Andrew Makower,
  Tom Mohan, S P Burton
Legal Assistant, European Union Committee:
  Ms L Gibson
Examiners of Petitions for Private Bills:
  Dr Philippa Tudor, W J Proctor
Taxing Officer (Private Bills):
  Dr Philippa Tudor

Judicial Taxing Officer:
  James Vallance White CB
Clerk of the Records: Stephen Ellison
Assistant Clerks of the Records: D L Prior,
  Ms C Shenton DPhil
Records Manager: J Whiting
Librarian: D L Jones; *Deputy Librarian:*
  Dr P G Davis
Senior Library Clerk: Miss I L Victory
Legal Library Executive: G R Dymond
Senior Information Officer:
  Miss M L Morgan
Staff Adviser: D A W Dunn ISO
Director of Works: H P Webber
Editor of the Official Report: Mary Villiers
  OBE; *Deputy Editor:* Mrs C J Boden

DEPARTMENT OF GENTLEMAN USHER OF THE BLACK ROD

Gentleman Usher and Serjeant at Arms:
  General Sir Edward Jones KCB CBE
Yeoman Usher and Deputy Serjeant at Arms:
  Brigadier Hedley Duncan MBE
Administration Officer: Brig A J McD Clark
Assistant Serjeant at Arms: Miss J Rowe
Staff Superintendent:
  Major A M Charlesworth BEM
Principal Doorkeeper: R M Skelton

Clerk of the Crown in Chancery:
  Sir Hayden Phillips KCB
Deputy Clerk of the Crown:
  Michael Huebner CB

REFRESHMENT DEPARTMENT

Superintendent: A D O Bibbiani
Banqueting Manager: R J Ellwood

Parliamentary Terms and Procedures

Terms relate to the House of Commons unless otherwise specified.
For further details see *Handbook of House of Commons Procedure* by Paul Evans (Vacher Dod Publishing 1999). References in bold italics have entries of their own.

accounting officer: person, usually the permanent secretary of a government department, responsible for accounting to parliament for the expenditure of money voted by parliament for the public service

act of parliament: *bill* having completed its parliamentary progress, been given *Royal Assent* and become part of the statute law

adjournment motion: technically a motion to bring to a conclusion a sitting of the House or a committee, but often used as a procedural device for enabling a debate to take place without having come to a conclusion

adjournment debate: debate on an *adjournment motion* (see also *daily adjournment*)

allocation of time motion: see *guillotine*

allotted days: days allotted to debate a *bill* under a *guillotine*, also the 20 days allotted each session as *opposition* days

all-party group: unofficial group of MPs and peers which acts as a focus of cross-party discussion of a particular topic. 'Registered groups' admit outsiders as members as well as MPs and peers

ambit: description of the scope of expenditure covered by a *vote* (see also *appropriation* and *estimates*)

amendment: proposal to change the terms of a *motion* or to alter a *bill*

appropriation: allocation of money by parliament to specified purposes. The Appropriation Accounts are the *Comptroller and Auditor General*'s audited accounts showing that money has been spent in accordance with Parliament's instructions (see also *Consolidated Fund*, *Estimates*)

back bench: back benches are where MPs who are not government Ministers or official opposition *shadows* sit in the Chamber, hence *back bencher*, an MP who holds no official position in government or in his or her party and who is therefore not bound by the convention of collective responsibility

ballot: draw to determine precedence for *private members' bills*. There are no secret ballots provided for in the House's proceedings

Bar of the House: line across the floor of the Chamber which marks its formal threshold: the Bar is also marked by a rail (now invariably retracted) to which, in former times, *strangers* might be summoned to address the House or to be arraigned before it

bill: proposal for legislation formally presented to either House of Parliament

Black Rod: Gentleman Usher of the Black Rod, a member of the royal household, who summons the Commons to the Lords at the opening and closing of *sessions*

board of management: executive body of the permanent service of the House

book entry: entry in the *Votes and Proceedings* which records as a procedural event something which occurred without any actual proceedings taking place on the floor of the House

breach of privilege: abuse of a privilege of Parliament or an attempt to impede or frustrate the House or MP in the exercise of one of its privileges

budget resolutions: series of financial resolutions, passed by the House at the conclusion of the debate on the *budget statement*, on which the *Finance Bill* is founded

budget statement: annual statement (usually in March) by the Chancellor of the Exchequer setting out the government's tax and spending plans for the forthcoming financial year: at the end of the five-day debate on the budget, the *budget resolutions* are passed and the *Finance Bill* introduced

business committee: committee, chaired by the *Chairman of Ways and Means*, appointed by the *Speaker*, to work out in detail the *timetable* for a bill subject to a *guillotine*

business motion: motion proposing to regulate the time available to the House for consideration of a specified item of business at a specified sitting (see *ten o'clock motions*)

business question: private notice question (PNQ) asked each Thursday after questions in reply to which the *Leader of the House* announces the main items of business to be taken on each sitting day for the next week or so

business sub-committee: sub-committee of a *standing committee*, appointed by the *Speaker* to work out in detail a *timetable* for a bill before the standing committee to which a *guillotine* has been applied

by-election: election in a single constituency to fill a vacancy created between *general elections* by the death, resignation or *disqualification*, etc. of an MP

C&AG: see *Comptroller and Auditor General*

Cabinet: inner circle of the government consisting of ministers in charge of government departments and certain other ministers, presided over by the Prime Minister

Chairman of Committees (Lords): chairman of every Select Committee in the Lords unless another chairman is appointed; also principal deputy Speaker and Chair of Committees of the Whole House

Chairman of Ways and Means: first deputy Speaker, with particular responsibilities for *private business* and *committees of the whole House*

Chairmen's Panel: body of MPs appointed by the *Speaker* from among whom are chosen the chairmen of each *standing committee*

Chiltern Hundreds: mythical 'office of profit under the Crown' to which MPs are appointed when wishing to resign their seats by disqualifying themselves from membership of the House (see *disqualification*): the Stewardship of the Manor of Northstead is also used for this purpose

Clandestine Outlawries Bill: bill presented *proforma* on the first day of each session

Class: largest of the sub-divisions of the *Estimates*; usually representing the overall spread of a single government department's public spending

Clause: individual articles of *bills*. When a bill becomes an *act*, the clauses are called sections

Clerk Assistant: second *Clerk at the Table*, and first deputy to the *Clerk of the House*

Clerks at the Table: senior clerks in the *Clerk of the House's* Department who sit at the *Table* of the House

Clerk of Bills: principal clerk responsible for public and private bills

Clerk of Legislation: Principal Clerk in charge of the *Legislation Service* of the House

Clerk of the House: principal permanent officer and also the *accounting officer* for the House of Commons *votes*

Clerk of the Parliaments: principal permanent officer of the House of Lords and the accounting officer for the House of Lords *votes*

closure: procedural device for bringing a debate to a conclusion

code of conduct: guide to MPs on questions relating to declarations in the *Register of Members' Interests*, the rule against paid advocacy, the deposit of copies of contracts of employment and other matters relating to financial relationships with outside persons and bodies

command paper: government publication (more often than not a *White Paper*) presented to Parliament by 'command of Her Majesty'

Commissioner for Standards: officer of the House appointed to supervise the *Register of Members' Interests*, to advise MPs on the interpretation of the *code of conduct* and to assist the *Committee on Standards and Privileges* in its work

committal: act of sending a *bill* to a committee of one kind or another after it has received a *second reading*

committee: see *committee of the whole House, joint committee, select committee, standing committee.*

Committee of Selection: committee which appoints MPs to *standing committees* and proposes MPs to the *departmental select committees* and the *domestic committees*

Committee on Standards and Privileges: select committee which investigates allegations of *breaches of privilege, contempts* and, with the assistance of the *Commissioner for Standards*, matters relating to the *code of conduct*, in particular complaints about MPs in relation to outside financial interests and related matters

committee of the Whole House: committee of all MPs to take the committee stage of a *bill*

Comptroller and Auditor General: officer of the House responsible for running the National Audit Office and for assisting the *Public Accounts Committee* in their scrutiny of public expenditure

consideration: more formal title for the *report stage* of a bill

Consolidated Fund: general fund into which almost all government receipts (in the form of taxes, duties, etc.) are paid and out of which almost all government expenditure is met

consolidation bill: *bill* which consolidates much of the existing law on a particular subject into one convenient statute: because such bills do not (except within strict and very narrow limits) change the law, they are subject to special procedures distinct from the general procedures applying to *public bills*

constituency: geographical area represented by one MP (currently 659). Every 10 to 15 years constituency boundaries are altered on the recommendation of the Boundary Commissions, which are responsible for ensuring that constituency size throughout each country of the United Kingdom is as equal as possible

contempt: disobedience to, or defiance of, an order of the House, or some other insult to the House or its dignity or a *breach of privilege*

crown prerogative: actions which the executive may take without the sanction of Parliament: they include *prorogation* and *dissolution* of Parliament, the grant of honours, the declaration of war and, in some circumstances, the making of treaties with foreign governments

daily adjournment: half-hour debate at the end of each day's *sitting* at which a *backbench* MP has the opportunity to raise a matter with a Minister

debates: any formal discussion of any *motion* in either House of Parliament. More commonly applied to discussions not related to legislative or financial business

delegated legislation: legislation made by Ministers under powers granted to them in Acts of Parliament, usually by means of *statutory instrument*

departmental reports: reports on government departments' activities and financial performance presented to Parliament each February, often forming the basis of *departmental Select Committees* enquiries

departmental select committees: select committees which oversee the work of government departments

Deputy Chairmen: First and Second Deputy Chairmen of Ways and Means, who with the *Chairman of Ways and Means* share with the *Speaker* the duties of presiding over the House

despatch box: two despatch boxes at either side of the *Table*, at the far end from the Speaker's Chair, which serve as lecterns for those leading debate (or answering questions) from the government and official opposition *front benches*

dilatory motion: motion for the adjournment of debate or for the adjournment of the House or a standing committee moved for the purpose of superseding the business in hand

disqualification: MPs may not hold 'offices of profit under the Crown', though ministers (up to a maximum of 95) are exempt from disqualification on those grounds; be civil servants, police officers, members of the armed forces, judges (though not everyone commonly described as a judge falls within this disqualification) and members of non-Commonwealth overseas legislatures; be ordained ministers and priests of the Church of England, the Church of Ireland, the Church of Scotland and the Roman Catholic Church; be ineligible to vote in a general election, sentenced prisoners, persons detained under the Mental Health Act 1983 or bankrupts. MPs may also be disqualified after an election if their candidature or conduct of an election is found to have been in breach of electoral law. The following are disqualified from membership of the House of Lords: aliens; those under 21; bankrupts; peers convicted of treason

dissolution: on the advice of the prime minister, the Queen may at any time dissolve Parliament, thereby initiating a general election

division: means by which the House or one of its committees ascertains the number of MPs for and against a proposition before it when the Chair's opinion as to which side is in the majority on a *Question* is challenged

division bell area: area from within which it is deemed possible to reach the *division lobbies* within the period from the ringing of the *division bells* to the closing of the lobby doors during a *division*

division bells: bells in the House and its precincts and outbuildings, and elsewhere (such as pubs and restaurants and the private homes of members) within the *division bell area*, which are rung to summon MPs to vote in a *division*

division lobbies: the lobbies along either side of the Chamber through which MPs pass to register their votes in a *division*

domestic committees: *select committees* concerned with the running of the House

dropped order: when, for instance, the *member in charge* of a bill does not name a new day for it to be set down for one of its stages after a stage has been completed or adjourned on any day, the order for that stage becomes a dropped order and the bill enters a sort of procedural limbo where it remains unless the member in charge revives it (which he or she can do by means of a *book entry*)

dummy bill: when a *bill* is presented to the House by a member he or she hands to the *Clerk at the Table* a folded card on which the short and long titles of the bill and the names of any supporters (up to a maximum of 12, including the *member in charge*) are written, together with other details. These dummy bills are prepared by the *Public Bill Office*. Usually the bill is properly printed and published shortly afterwards, but in the case of *private members' bills*, they sometimes never have an existence beyond this dummy form

early day motions (EDM): expressions of opinion by MPs on almost any subject published in the form of motions printed in the *Notice Paper* part of the *Vote Bundle*, to which other MPs may add their names to indicate support

Ecclesiastical Committee: statutory committee of members of both Houses which considers Church of England *Measures*

EDM: see *early day motions*

effective orders: that part of the *Order Paper* which includes the items of business actually to be taken at a sitting, so called to distinguish it from the *remaining orders*

electoral system: relative majority or first past the post method. The country is divided into *constituencies* each represented by one MP. Electors choose just one candidate. No order of priority is expressed among candidates. The candidate with the greatest number of votes is the winner. Elections take place at least every five years. An earlier general election may take place if the prime minister advises the Queen to dissolve Parliament

emergency debate: debates granted by the Speaker. Other emergency debates may occur in both Houses when government business managers re-arrange the parliamentary timetable at short notice because of a widespread desire that a particular debate should take place

Erskine May: Erskine May's *Treatise on the Law, Privileges, Proceedings and Usage of Parliament*, first published by the then *Clerk of the House*, Thomas Erskine May in 1844 and revised by his successors ever since: it is acknowledged as the authoritative text book on the law and practice of both Houses of Parliament: the latest edition is the 22nd, edited by Limon and McKay (Butterworths, London 1997)

Estimates: form in which the government presents, for approval by the Commons, its requests for the sums needed to cover recurring public expenditure

Estimates days: three days in each session set aside for consideration of the Estimates, in practice used for debate on one or more select committee reports chosen by the *Liaison Committee*

European Union: in the Commons, documents are examined by the Scrutiny Committee on European Legislation, which reports its opinion on the legal and political importance of each, recommends which documents should be considered by a European *Standing Committee* and considers any other issue arising from a document or group of documents. In the House of Lords, European Union proposals are scrutinised by the Select Committee on the European Union. This Committee has at present six Sub-Committees covering the different areas of EU activity

Examiner of Petitions: officer of the House with responsibility for examining certain matters relating to private bills and hybrid bills for compliance with the standing orders relating to *private business*; there is an equivalent officer in the House of Lords who joins in this examination

exempted business: business which, under standing orders or under a specific order of the House, may be carried on after the *moment of interruption*

Father of the House: longest continuously serving MP

Finance Bill: annual bill, founded on the *budget resolutions*, which embodies the government's statutory power to levy most taxes and duties, and which may include other provisions relating to taxes management

financial privilege: Commons' right to approve proposals for taxation or for government expenditure, not shared with the Lords

financial resolutions: collective term for *money resolutions*, *ways and means resolutions*, and *supply resolutions*

first reading: formal first stage of a *bill*'s progress, which occurs without debate or vote after it has been introduced to the House

forthwith: *Question* on which there can be no debate; as soon as it is moved the Chair must immediately put it to the House or committee for decision: although there can be no debate there may be a *division*. Many Questions which are put forthwith are also *exempted business*

front bench: where Ministers and their official opposition *shadows* sit in the Chamber, hence *frontbencher* or *frontbench spokesman* (the government front bench is also known as the *Treasury bench*)

general election: nation-wide election in all constituencies; must be held at least every five years

Green Paper: document published for consultative purposes before the final formulation of policy

guillotine: order which limits the time available to debate any stage or stages of a bill

Hansard: colloquial name for the *Official Report*, the publications containing the accurate and full (though not strictly verbatim as often claimed) reports of what is said and done in the debates and committees in both houses of Parliament

health service commissioners: officer of the House who acts as the ombudsman for the NHS who also holds the office of Parliamentary Commissioner for Administration (PCA) and who reports to the Public Administration select committee: although there are separate commissioners for England, Wales and Scotland, the posts are held by the same person

House of Commons Commission: executive body of MPs responsible for the running of the House It consists of the Speaker (Chairman), the Leader of the House, an MP appointed by the Leader of the Opposition and three other non-ministerial MPs appointed by the House. It is responsible (with a few exceptions) for the appointment, pay and conditions of the House's staff and also prepares estimates of the expenses of the House

Information Office: office which answers enquiries from the public about the work of Parliament; its telephone number in the Commons is 020 7219 4272 and in the Lords 020 7219 3107

instruction: after *committal* of a bill, the House may give an instruction to any committee to which it is committed to do certain things that the committee might not otherwise be empowered to do

joint committees: committees which include members of both Houses. There are two permanent joint committees, the Joint Committee on Statutory Instruments (JCSI) and the Joint Committee on Consolidation, etc. Bills. The standing orders also provide for the Joint Committee on Tax Simplification Bills: the House may commit other kinds of *bill* to a joint committee or establish a joint committee to inquire into and report upon some specific matter

Journal Office: office of the Clerk's Department responsible, among other duties, for the preparation of the *Votes and Proceedings*, the oversight of *Public Petitions*, and the preparation of the *Journals* of the House

Journals: authoritative record of the decisions of the House

law commissions: prepare proposals for reform of the law and also for its rationalisation by means of *consolidation bills* and statute law repeal bills

Law Lords (Lords of Appeal): The House of Lords is the ultimate court of appeal in the United Kingdom (except in Scottish criminal cases). The Lords of Appeal consist of the Lord Chancellor and a maximum of 12 Lords of Appeal in Ordinary, three constituting a quorum, and Lords who hold or have held high judicial office. Appeals are normally heard by five Lords of Appeal sitting as an Appellate Committee, but judgments are delivered at judicial sittings of the House

Leader of the House: Cabinet Minister responsible for the management of the House and its business, but distinct from the *usual channels*. *Ex officio* member of the *House of Commons Commission* and also has responsibility for the cabinet committees dealing with the management of the government's legislative programme

leader of the opposition: leader of the second largest party in the House, paid a ministerial salary and appointed to the Privy Council. Has certain well-entrenched conventional rights to initiate certain kinds of business, in particular to move a motion of no confidence in the government

leave: there are a number of types of proceeding which may only be done *by leave of the House* (or a committee). These include to speak more than once to a Question other than in committee, to withdraw a motion before the House or a committee and to move certain types of motion. Generally leave must be unanimous

Liaison Committee: select committee of chairmen of other select committees, which has certain powers and duties in relation to the proceedings of the House, as well as a more informal role exercising oversight of the work, and as an advocate of the interests, of select committees in general

lobby correspondents: certain representatives (about 150) of the various news media who may enter the *Members' Lobby* when the House is sitting and who enjoy certain other privileges of access to areas of the Palace otherwise closed to people apart from members and permanent staff. They also subscribe to a code of conduct relating to the disclosure of the sources of their information (hence the expression 'on lobby terms')

lobby group: any group organised to influence opinion among MPs, peers and others. Firms of professional lobbyists, sometimes known as parliamentary consultants, also exist

Lords Amendments: amendments proposed by the Lords to a *bill* which has been passed by the Commons

Lord Chancellor: Lord Keeper of the Great Seal and also Speaker of the House of Lords. It is his duty ordinarily to attend as Speaker, to sit on the Woolsack and to preside over the deliberations of the House, except when it is in Committee. He puts the Question on all Motions which are submitted to the House, but he has no power either to maintain order or to act in any way as the representative or mouthpiece of the House, unless the House confers the necessary authority upon him. He is responsible for the recall of the House during a period of adjournment. The Lord Chancellor is a member of the Government and like other Peers he may take part in debate and vote

Lords Commissioners: Peers appointed by the Queen to deliver her *proclamation* proroguing Parliament and her *royal assent* to acts agreed just before *prorogation*

Lords Spiritual: Anglican Archbishops of Canterbury and York, the Bishops of London, Durham and Winchester and 21 other diocesan bishops of the Church of England according to their seniority of appointment to diocesan sees are members of the House of Lords and are collectively known as the Lords Spiritual. On retirement, a bishop ceases to be a member of the House of Lords but he is entitled to sit on the steps of the Throne and use the facilities of the House

Loyal Address: motion moved in reply to the *Queen's Speech* on which the debate on the Queen's Speech takes place

Mace: symbol of the Crown's authority in Parliament displayed on the *Table* whenever the House is in session

maiden speech: first speech delivered by an MP after election to the House. By convention it includes a tribute to his or her predecessor, an encomium to his or her constituency, and avoids controversy (though this latter tradition shows signs of dying out). Also, by tradition, it is heard without interruption from other members

manuscript amendment: amendment of which no *notice* has been given, which is presented to the Chair during debate in manuscript or typescript form, and only selected in very rare circumstances

Measure: legislative proposal of the General Synod of the Church of England

Member in charge: MP who introduces a bill to the House, and has certain prerogatives in relation to that bill. In the case of a government bill, any Minister (including a *Whip*) may exercise the rights of the member in charge

Members' lobby: area immediately outside the Chamber generally reserved to MPs and *lobby correspondents* and staff of the House when the House is sitting; the Peers' Lobby is the equivalent in the Lords

Minister: member of the government, entitled to receive a ministerial salary: for procedural purposes, the members of the government (including *Whips*) are each regarded as being able to act on behalf of any other Minister

Minister of State: minister within a government department, not usually of Cabinet rank

moment of interruption: time set by standing orders at which the main business of a day's sitting normally ends (10 pm on Mondays to Wednesdays, 7 pm on Thursdays and 2.30 pm on Fridays) after which business may be taken only if it is *exempted business* or unopposed business. The concept has recently been extended to sittings of the grand committees

money bill: bill concerned exclusively with raising or spending public money and which, under the terms of the *Parliament Acts*, cannot be amended by the Lords

money resolution: *resolution* of the House, agreed on a motion which may be moved only by a *Minister*, authorising the provisions of a *bill* which entail novel forms of public expenditure

motions: with the exception of occasions like question time and ministerial statements, most proceedings or debates in Parliament are based on motions: for example, 'That the Bill be read a Second Time', 'That the Amendment be made' or 'That this House has no confidence in Her Majesty's Government'. The motion is proposed or 'made' by a member, is 'put' from the Chair, normally debated and then decided by the House, on a **division** if necessary

naming: device for disciplining an MP who persistently defies the authority of the Chair in the House, which immediately causes a motion to be moved to suspend the member from the service of the House

National Audit Office: office under the direction of the *Comptroller and Auditor General* which audits the expenditure of government departments

Northstead, Manor of: see *Chiltern Hundreds.*

Notice Paper: blue pages of the *Vote Bundle* include the Notice Papers for notices of questions, notices of motions for future days, notices of *early day motions* and notices of amendments to bills

official opposition: party with the second largest number of MPs, with certain privileges by long standing convention (such as the right of its official spokesmen and spokeswomen to sit on the *front bench* and to address the House from the *despatch box*) as well as certain rights under the standing orders (to initiate debate on the majority of *opposition days*) and by statute (such as for certain of its officers to receive ministerial salaries)

Official Report: see *Hansard.*

ombudsman: see *Parliamentary Commissioner for Administration.*

opposition days: 20 days each session set aside under standing orders on which the opposition parties have the right to choose the business for debate

oral question: see *parliamentary questions.*

order: when the House agrees a motion that something should happen (such as a bill being set down for a second reading or for consideration) it becomes an order of the House. Other examples of orders might be the outcome of a *business motion* or a *guillotine* (see also *resolution*). The word is also commonly used in a parliamentary context to connote procedural regularity (as in the expression 'in order') or to correct parliamentary behaviour (as in the Chair's call of "Order, order", which is also used as a form of oral procedural 'punctuation')

Order Book: daily publication divided into two parts: Part 1 lists all questions for written answer on that day, Part 2 lists all outstanding parliamentary questions for oral or written answer on future days, and other motions and notices for future days

Order Paper: paper published each sitting day (except the first day of a *session*), which lists the business of the House for that day, as well as questions for oral or written answer to be asked that day, questions for written answer that day which have not previously appeared in print, and certain other items such as committee notices, *remaining orders* and lists of future business

other business: business of the House which is neither *private business* nor *public business*, when there is no *question* before the House for decision, principally covering question time and ministerial statements

Outlawries Bill: see *Clandestine Outlawries Bill.*

PAC: see *Public Accounts Committee.*

Pairing: unofficial system under which two MPs, one from each of the two major parties, agree to be absent from the Chamber from particular votes or for agreed periods of time. In this way the government's majority is not affected by absences

Papers, moving for: in the House of Lords a common method of initiating a general debate is for a peer to call attention to a matter 'and to move for papers'. Since this is a debating device, the motion is generally withdrawn at the conclusion of the debate

Parliament Acts: Parliament Act 1911 as amended and supplemented by the Parliament Act 1949 which restrict the powers of the Lords to amend *money bills* or delay other *bills* agreed by the Commons

Parliamentary Commissioner for Administration: officer of the House who investigates complaints of maladministration in the public service, commonly known as the ombudsman. His work is watched over by the Public Administration Committee (see *health service commissioners*)

Parliamentary Commissioner for Standards: officer responsible for maintaining and monitoring the operations of the *Register of Members' Interests*; and receiving and investigating complaints about the conduct of MPs and reporting findings to the Committee on Standards and Privileges

Parliamentary Counsel: lawyers employed by the government to draft bills which the government intends to present to Parliament

Parliamentary Private Secretary (PPS): backbench MPs from the government party who are chosen by individual cabinet ministers and ministers of state to assist them in their parliamentary duties. They are not paid a salary and are not ministers, though they are not supposed to vote against government policy

parliamentary question: question addressed (generally) to a Minister for answer orally on the floor of the House or in writing in *Hansard*

Parliamentary Secretary: junior minister in Ministry of Agriculture, Fisheries and Food, Cabinet Office, Lord Chancellor's Department and Privy Council Office

Parliamentary Under Secretary (of State): junior minister in most departments of state

periodic adjournment: formal name for one of the House's recesses

PCA: see *Parliamentary Commissioner for Administration.*

PNQ: see *private notice question.*

PQ: see *parliamentary question.*

point of order: properly, a request by an MP to the Chair for elucidation of, or a ruling on, a question of procedure, but frequently misused by MPs who do not have the floor of the House or of a committee to interrupt proceedings for other purposes

prayers: prayers conducted by the *Speaker's Chaplain* in the Commons and by a bishop in the Lords at the beginning of each sitting. The term is also used colloquially to describe a motion to annul a *statutory instrument* subject to negative resolution procedure and to designate the final paragraph of a *public petition*

prerogative: see *Crown prerogative.*

press gallery: gallery of the Chamber above and behind the Speaker's Chair reserved to accredited representatives of the various news media, also used more generally to describe the large area outside and behind this gallery given over to the use of journalists etc and also to describe collectively the accredited members of the press gallery (see also *lobby correspondents*)

previous question: procedural device for superseding debate, now generally disregarded in favour of the *closure*

private bill: bill to confer upon individuals, or more commonly corporate bodies of one kind or another, powers in excess of the general law

private business: business of the House for the most part relating directly or indirectly to *private bills*

private Member's bill: *bill* introduced to the House by an MP who is not a *minister*

private notice question: oral parliamentary question asked without published *notice* relating to an urgent and important matter (see also *business question*)

privilege: privilege enjoyed by the House collectively or MPs individually in excess of the general law which enables it or them to fulfil the functions and duties of the House

Privy Counsellor: Member of the Queen's Privy Council, the body of senior royal advisers which in former times was something equivalent to the *Cabinet*, membership of which is now conferred automatically on Cabinet Ministers and certain senior judges; it is also by convention granted to the leaders of parties of any size in the Commons and is occasionally conferred as a mark of honour on senior back benchers. The Council retains certain judicial functions and residual executive functions. Membership is for life, unless withdrawn

Procedure Committee: *select committee* appointed to consider proposals for the reform of House of Commons procedures

programme: order made by the House after agreement through the *usual channels* after a *bill*'s *second reading* to *timetable* the subsequent proceedings on that bill

prorogation: end of a *session*

Public Accounts Commission: board of the *National Audit Office*

Public Accounts Committee: *select committee* responsible for ensuring propriety, efficiency, economy and effectiveness in the spending of public money

Public Bill Office: office within the *Legislation Service* of the *Clerk of the House*'s department responsible for the management of legislation and for clerking the *standing committees* of the House

public gallery: gallery of the Chamber in which *strangers* may sit to observe its proceedings, also known as Strangers' Gallery; each committee room has an area open to the public

public petition: petition to the House for redress of a grievance or other relief

Queen's Speech: speech read by the Queen from her throne in the House of Lords on the first day of each session setting out, among other matters, details of the government's proposed legislative programme

question: see *parliamentary question*.

Question: the matter before the House or a committee awaiting decision at any time

question time: period from around 2.30 to 3.30 pm on Mondays to Wednesdays and from 11.30 am to 12.30 pm on Thursdays set aside for *parliamentary questions* to be asked and answered orally on the floor of the House

reasoned amendment: amendment proposed to the motion to give a *bill* a *second* or *reading*

Recall of parliament: both Houses have procedures allowing them to be recalled during an adjournment. The normal method is for the Lord Chancellor (or in his absence, the Lord Chairman) and the Speaker respectively to call the House together on a day earlier than that to which it has been adjourned. The initiative for requesting a recall of Parliament rests with the Government, who inform the Speaker and Lord Chancellor of their belief that the public interest requires a recall. Parliament must also meet within five days if the reserve forces are mobilised, or if a state of emergency is proclaimed

recess: strictly, period when the House is prorogued; now used to refer to the House's holiday adjournments

Register of Members' Interests: annual register in which MPs record their outside financial interests and the receipt of gifts, free travel, etc; it is updated regularly and made available to the public in updated form on application to the *Registrar of Members' Interests*

Registrar of Members' Interests: officer of the House responsible for the maintenance of the *Register of Members' Interests* and for giving advice (along with the *Commissioner for Standards*) about declarations made in it; a member of the Speaker's Office

report stage: stage of a *bill*'s progress between its being reported from committee and its *third reading*, at which further detailed amendments may be made

resolution: motion agreed by the House (unless it is an *order*)

return: answer or response to an address from the House

royal assent: Queen's assent to a *bill* agreed to by both Houses of Parliament, the final act which makes that bill an Act of Parliament

Salisbury Convention: convention that the Lords do not reject at second reading any government legislation which carries out a manifesto commitment and which has been passed by the House of Commons, named after an understanding reached between the Conservative opposition in the Lords (led by the then Marquis of Salisbury) and the Labour government in 1945

second reading: first stage at which a *bill* is debated and voted on

Secretary of State: Cabinet Minister who heads a major department of state

select committees: committees established by the House to inquire into particular matters or subject areas and to report back their findings and recommendations

senior member: MP with longest *continuous* service in the House, also known as the *Father of the House*; on a *select committee* the senior member on that committee names the time of its first meeting. At present the Father of the House is Sir Edward Heath, prime minister from 1970-74, who was first elected in 1950

Serjeant at Arms: officer of the House responsible for security, housekeeping functions and the maintenance and repair of the physical infrastructure of the buildings. Each House has a Serjeant at Arms, appointed by the Crown. In the Lords, the Serjeant is also the Gentleman Usher of the *Black Rod*

session: period between the state opening of Parliament and its prorogation or dissolution, generally a year running from November to November, but often altered by the timing of general elections

sessional orders: traditional orders passed on the first day of a *session*; also any *order* made by the House explicitly framed to have effect for a session (for example, those specifying the dates during a session for private members' bill Fridays and non-sitting Fridays)

shadow: official Opposition MPs with responsibility for presenting in and out of Parliament opposition policies relating to government departments, hence 'Shadow Home Secretary' etc (also called *frontbench spokesmen or spokeswomen*)

shuffle: process by which the *parliamentary questions* for oral answer are randomly sorted to determine which Members' questions will be printed on the *Order Paper* on any given day, and in what order

sitting: single meeting of the House or one of its committees

sittings in Westminster Hall: 'parallel chamber' of the House of Commons which meets in the Grand Committee Room off Westminster Hall

Speaker: impartial presiding officer of the House. The Lord Chancellor is *ex officio* Speaker of the House of Lords

standing committee: committee to which the House delegates the task of debating certain matters such as *bills*, *delegated legislation*, proposals for European legislation, etc.

standing orders: rules formulated by the House to regulate its own proceedings

Statements: Ministerial announcement in Parliament of a new policy initiative or views on some important matter. Most statements are made in the Commons and repeated, if requested by the Opposition, in the Lords. In both Houses statements are normally taken after question time. A statement will not be repeated in the other House until after it has been delivered in the House in which is originates. After delivery, there follows a period of comment and questions from the Opposition spokesmen and backbenchers

state opening: occasion on the first day of each *session* on which the Queen usually attends in the House of Lords to deliver the *Queen's Speech*

statutory instruments: form in which most *delegated legislation* is made

strangers: traditional appellation for anyone who is not a MP, officer or official of the House, hence *Strangers' Gallery* etc.

Strangers' Gallery: more traditional name for the *public gallery*

supplementary question: oral question asked as a separate but supplementary question to one which has appeared on the *Order Paper* and has been asked during *question time*

supply resolution: one of the *resolutions* on which the *Consolidated Fund* bills are founded

ten o'clock motion: motion, moved by a Minister, to suspend the operation of the *moment of interruption*

Test Roll: document signed by each MP after taking the oath or affirming after being elected to the House

third reading: final stage of a whole *bill*'s passage through the House, though Lords Amendments to the bill may subsequently be considered

timetable: term variously applied: *guillotine* motions are sometimes described as timetable motions; under the proposals of the *modernisation committee* the House has begun to use *programme* motions to timetable a bill's proceedings at the outset of their progress. Many bills are also subject to an informal timetable agreed between the *usual channels*, especially during their standing committee stages. In essence, a timetable for a bill fixes the points at which various stages of its consideration will be completed

usual channels: colloquial name for the discussions which take place between the *Whips*

Vote: most significant of the sub-divisions of the *Estimates*; the House's agreement to a Vote, together with its *ambit*, represents the detailed *appropriation* of public money to the public service by Parliament

Votes and Proceedings: daily minute of the House's proceedings

Vote Bundle: papers published each day on which the House sits, including among other things the *Order Paper*, the *remaining orders*, the *Votes and Proceedings*, and the *notice papers*

Vote Office: distribution centre for all parliamentary papers

ways and means resolution: *resolution* authorising a charge on the people, that is, for the most part, taxes and duties: the *Finance Bill* is founded on ways and means resolutions. The Lords may reject, but cannot modify those parts of the bill which are founded on Ways and Means Resolutions

Whips: officers of each party in the House with particular responsibilities for party management and organisation of the business of the House and its committees. Also announcement of business circulated weekly among members of a party, indicating by underlining the importance attached to attendance at particular business: a 'three-line' whip amounts to compulsion

White Paper: *command paper* embodying some statement of government policy, often including proposals for legislation

writ: issue of a writ is the formal process for initiating a by-election

Political Parties

LABOUR PARTY

Millbank Tower, Millbank,
London SW1P 4GT
020 7802 1000 Fax 020 7802 1234
E-mail: labour-party@geo2.poptel.org.uk
Website: www.labour.org.uk

Chair: Maggie Jones
Vice-Chair: Margaret Wall
Leader: Rt Hon Tony Blair MP
Deputy Leader: Rt Hon John Prescott MP
General Secretary: Margaret McDonagh
Treasurer: Margaret Prosser

National Executive Committee 2000–01

Division I – Trade Unions

John Gibbins – Amalgamated Engineering and
Electrical Union (AEEU)
Cath Speight – Amalgamated Engineering and
Electrical Union (AEEU)
Mike Griffiths – Graphical, Paper, Media Union
(GPMU)
John Hannett – Union of Shop, Distributive and
Allied Workers (USDAW)
Vernon Hince – Rail, Maritime and Transport
Union (RMT)
Derek Hodgson – Communication Workers
Union (CWU)
Diana Holland – Transport and General
Workers Union (TGWU)
Maggie Jones – UNISON
Steve Pickering – General Municipal,
Boilermakers Union (GMB)
Anne Picking – UNISON
Mary Turner – General Municipal,
Boilermakers Union (GMB)
Margaret Wall – Manufacturing Science
Finance Union (MSF)

Division II – Socialist Societies

Dianne Hayter

Division III – Constituency Labour Parties

Ann Black, Shahid Malik, Tony Robinson,
Christine Shawcroft, Lord Sawyer,
Ruth Turner

Division IV – Local Government

Sir Jeremy Beecham, Sally Powell

Division V – Parliamentary Labour Party/European Parliamentary Labour Party

Clive Soley MP; Helen Jackson MP;
Dennis Skinner MP

Division VI – Government

Rt Hon Hilary Armstrong MP; Rt Hon Ian
McCartney MP; Rt Hon Mo Mowlam MP

Treasurer: Margaret Prosser
Youth Representative Claire McCarthy
Ex-officio:
Rt Hon Tony Blair MP; Rt Hon John Prescott
MP; Margaret McDonagh; Simon Murphy
MEP

Parliamentary Office – House of Commons

Secretary: Alan Haworth (020 7219 4266)
Administrator: Vacant (020 7219 4552)
Senior Committee Officer: Catherine Jackson
(020 7219 5278)
Committee Officers:
Liz Djilali (020 7219 5277)
Fiona Twycross (020 7219 5953)
Press Officer: Beverley Priest (020 7219 2458)

CO-OPERATIVE PARTY

77 Weston Street, London SE1 3SD
020 7357 0230 Fax 020 7407 4476
E-mail: p.hunt@co-op-party.org.uk

Chair: Gareth R Thomas MP
Vice-Chair: Jeanette Timmins
Chair of Parliamentary Group: Andy Love MP
National Secretary: Peter Hunt
The Co-operative Party is not affiliated to the
Labour Party at national level, but its candidates
stand as joint candidates of both parties and are
badged 'Labour/Co-operative'.

CONSERVATIVE AND UNIONIST PARTY

32 Smith Square
London SW1P 3HH
020 7222 9000 Fax 020 7222 1135
Website: www.tory.org.uk

Chairman: Rt Hon Michael Ancram QC MP
Deputy Chairman and Chief Executive:
Hon David Prior MP
Senior Vice-Chairman: Tim Collins CBE MP
Vice-Chairman (Wales): Nigel Evans MP

Vice-Chairman (Cultural Unit, Network and Conservative Future): Steve Norris
Senior Party Treasurer: Lord Ashcroft
Head of News and Media: Amanda Platell

LIBERAL DEMOCRATS

4 Cowley Street
London SW1P 3NB
020 7222 7999 Fax 020 7799 2170
E-mail: libdems@cix.co.uk
Website: www.libdems.org.uk

Leader: Rt Hon Charles Kennedy MP
President: Lord Dholakia
Vice-Presidents:
  Paul Farthing (England)
  Lembit Öpik MP (Wales)
  Ian Yuill (Scotland)
Chief Executive: Hugh Rickard
Director of Campaigns: Lord Rennard MBE
Director of Policy: Dr Richard Grayson
Head of Policy Unit: Christian Moon
Policy Officer: Helen Belcher
Director of Marketing, Fundraising and Members' Services: David Loxton
Press Office
Director of Communications: David Walter
Director of Press and Broadcasting:
  Elizabeth Peplow
Press and Broadcasting Officers: Lissa Cook, Johanna Howitt, Vanessa Buckle, Andy McGuffie, Ruwan Kodikara
Press Assistant: Vacant
E-mail: ldpressoffice@cix.co.uk
Conference and Events Organiser:
  Penny McCormack
Financial Controller: Nigel Bliss
Head of International Office: Karla Hatrick
Regional Press Officer: Andrea Kinnear
Head of Administration and Personnel:
  Elizabeth Johnson
Information Officer: Stephen Thornton

Parliamentary Office – House of Commons

Secretary: Ben Williams (020 7219 5654)
Parliamentary Assistant: David Oliver
  (020 7219 1415)
Fax: 020 7219 5894
E-mail: libdemcommons@cix.co.uk

ULSTER UNIONIST PARTY (UUP)

3 Glengall Street
Belfast BT12 5AE
028 9032 4601 Fax 028 9024 6738
E-mail: uup@uup.org
Website: www.uup.org

Patron: Rt Hon the
  Lord Molyneaux of Killead KBE
President:
Leader: Rt Hon David Trimble MP MLA
Chairman of the Executive Committee:
  Lord Rogan of Lower Iveagh
Vice-Chairman of the Executive Committee:
  James Cooper
Vice-Presidents:
  Ken Maginnis MP
  Jim Nicholson MEP
  Sir Reg Empey OBE MLA
  Jeffrey Donaldson MP
Hon Secs:
  Rev Martin Smyth MP
  Dermot Nesbitt MLA
  Cllr Jim Rodgers
  Mrs Arlene Foster
Hon Treasurer: Jack Allen OBE
Asst Hon Treasurer:
  Mrs May Steele MBE JP
Whip: Cllr Roy Beggs MP
General Secretary: David Boyd

SCOTTISH NATIONAL PARTY (SNP)

6 North Charlotte Street
Edinburgh EH2 4JH
0131-226 3661 Fax 0131-225 9597
E-mail:snp.hq@snp.org
Website: www.snp.org

President: Winnie Ewing MSP
Parliamentary Leader:
  Alasdair Morgan MP MSP
Chief Whip: Alasdair Morgan MP MSP
National Convenor:
  John Swinney MP MSP
National Secretary: Stewart Hosie
Acting National Treasurer:
  Kenneth MacAskill MSP
Director of Organisation and Headquarters:
  Allison Hunter
Communications Manager: Kevin Pringle
Director of Administration: Irene White

PLAID CYMRU – THE PARTY OF WALES (PC)

Tý Gwynfor, 18 Park Grove, Cardiff CF10 3BN
029 2064 6000 Fax 029 2064 6001
E-mail: post@plaidcymru.org
Website: www.plaidcymru.org

President: Ieuan Wyn Jones MP AM
Chair: Elin Jones
Treasurer: Jeff Canning
Chief Executive: Karl Davies
Press Officer: Anna Brychan

SOCIAL DEMOCRATIC AND LABOUR PARTY (SDLP)

Northern Ireland

121 Ormeau Road, Belfast BT7 1SH
028 9024 7700 Fax 028 9023 6699
E-mail: sdlp@indigo.ie
Website: www.sdlp.ie/

Leader: John Hume MP MEP MLA
Deputy Leader: Séamus Mallon MP MLA
Chief Whip: Eddie McGrady MP MLA
Chairperson: Jim Lennon
Vice-Chairpersons:
  Mary McKeown
  Sean McKee
Treasurer: Jonathan Stephenson
Assistant Treasurer: Justin McCamphill
International Secretary: Denis Haughey MLA
General Secretary: Gerry Cosgrove

MLA – Member of Legislative Assembly

ULSTER DEMOCRATIC UNIONIST PARTY (DUP)

91 Dundela Avenue
Belfast BT4 3BU
028 9047 1155 Fax 028 9047 1797
E-mail: info@dup.org.uk
Website: www.dup.org.uk

Leader: Rev Dr Ian Paisley MP MEP MLA
Deputy Leader: Ald Peter Robinson MP MLA
Chairman: Cllr Maurice Morrow MLA
Vice-Chair: Cllr William May
Vice-Chair: Ald Iris Robinson MLA
Party Secretary: Ald Nigel Dodds MLA
Treasurer: Ald Gregory Campbell MLA
Director of Communications:
  St Clair McAlister
Chief Executive: Allan Ewart

UK UNIONIST PARTY (UKUP)

10 Hamilton Road, Bangor
Co Down BT20 4LE
028 9127 2994 Fax 028 9146 5037
E-mail: info@ukup.org
Website: www.ukup.org

Leader: Robert McCartney QC MP MLA
Deputy Leader: David Vance
Chairman: Nelson Wharton
Secretary: Flora Henderson
Treasurer: Anne Moore
Special Adviser: Tom Sheridan

SINN FEIN (SF)

44 Parnell Square, Dublin 1
+353 1 8726932/8726100
Fax +353 1 8733441/8783595
E-mail: sinnfein@iol.ie
Website: www.sinnfein.ie

Press Officer: Miss Dawn Doyle

Parliamentary Press Gallery

The Parliamentary Lobby Journalists are those journalists authorised to work in Parliament. There are about 120 British and Irish journalists who are allowed access to the Members' Lobby of the House of Commons. A further 50 or so foreign correspondents also have access to the Lobby. Members of the Lobby are marked with an asterisk

Tel 020 7219 4700; for individual desk numbers prefix 020 7219 in most cases.

Press Gallery Chairman	Trevor Kavanagh 6144
Vice-Chairman	
Hon. Secretary	John Deans 6140/6561
Hon. Treasurer	Rodney Foster 7973 6160
Gallery Secretary	Stella Thomas 4395
Gallery Superintendents	5371
Lobby Journalists' Chairman	John Sergeant
Lobby Journalists' Vice Chairman	Colin Brown 6580
Press Bar	4284
Press Dining Room	6406/4393/4240

NATIONAL DAILY NEWSPAPERS

The Daily Telegraph
*George Jones 5719
*Ben Brogan 3688
3685 (admin)
*Andrew Sparrow 3689
*Rachel Sylvester 4960
*Sarah Womack 4054
*Andy McSmith 3687

The Financial Times
Brian Groom 4380
*Andrew Parker 3680
*Robert Shrimsley 6892
*Rosemary Bennett 6142
*Chris Adams

The Independent
*Andy Grice 4665
*Don Macintyre 5285
*Fran Abrams 4392
Sarah Schaefer 4392
Simon Carr
*Paul Waugh 4392
*Marie Woolf

The Guardian
Hugo Young 020 7278 2332
Jonathan Freedland 020 7278 2332
*Michael White 6143
*David Hencke 6769
Simon Hoggart 6738
*Patrick Wintour 3681
*Nick Watt 6831

The Times
*Peter Riddell 4751
Matthew Parris 5284
Jill Sherman 6543
*Phil Webster 5241
*James Landale 5284
*Roland Watson 5284
*Tom Baldwin 6543
Andrew Pierce

The Express
*Anthony Bevins 3389
*Alison Little 3387/3389
*Kirsty Walker 6743/6149
*Patrick O'Flynn 6764

Daily Mail
*David Hughes 3679
*John Deans 6140
*Paul Eastham 3683
*Graeme Wilson 6561
Quentin Letts 0616
Gill Watmough (admin) 6894
*Michael Clarke

The Mirror
*Peter MacMahon 4379
*Nigel Morris 6733
*James Hardy 4377
*Oona Blackman 4379
Paul Routledge 4377

The Daily Star

The Sun
*Trevor Kavanagh 6144
*George Pascoe-Watson 3337
*Mike Lea 0141
*Paul Gilfeather 4683
Chris Davis 7782-4087

Morning Star
*Mike Ambrose 4681

SUNDAY NEWSPAPERS

The Sunday Times
*Michael Jones 5397
*Michael Prescott 5397
*Eben Black
Nicholas Rufford

The Sunday Telegraph
*Joe Murphy 0615
Matthew D'Ancona
*David Cracknell 6116

The Observer
*Andrew Rawnsley 7713-4286
*Kamal Ahmed
*Gaby Hinsliff 6687

The Sunday Express
*Jon Craig 5596
*Peter Oborne 5596
Richard Whitely 6149
*Julia Hartley-Brewer

Sunday Mirror
*Chris Buckland 6733
*Chris MacLaughlan

The Independent on Sunday
*Colin Brown 6580
Steve Richards
*Jo Dillon

The Mail on Sunday
*Simon Walters
*Mark Fox
*Jonathan Oliver

The People
*Nigel Nelson 4377

News of the World
*Ian Kirby 6768
*Keith Gladdis

Scotland on Sunday
*Francis Elliott 6763

Sunday Mercury
*Gerri Peev

Sunday Post

Sunday Mail

Sunday Business
*Steve Bevan

Newcastle Sunday Sun
*Ian Hernon 5396

Wales on Sunday
*Julia Langdon

Birmingham Sunday Mercury
*Richard Williamson

Sunday Herald
*Iain Watson

REGIONAL PRESS

Evening Standard
*Charles Reiss 5718
*Patrick Hennessy 0052
*Joanne Revill 4680
*Ben Leapman 4281
*Peter Kellner

The Scotsman
*Jenny Percival 4682
*Jon Hibbs

Glasgow Herald
*Mike Settle 0156
Jim McKillop 7405-2121
Roy Rogers 7405-2121
*Catherine McLeod 6147
*Deborah Summers

Glasgow Evening Times
*5396

Aberdeen Press and Journal
*David Perry 4390

Dundee Courier
*Gordon Campbell, OBE 3338
*Steve Bargeton 01382-23131

Daily Record
3336
*Dave King
*David Thompson

Aberdeen Evening Express
Middlesbrough Evening Gazette
*Bill Doult 4388

Edinburgh Evening News
Bolton Evening News
Lancashire Evening Telegraph
4391
*Bill Jacobs
Ian Swanson

Cambridgeshire Evening News
Worcester Evening News
Yorkshire Evening News
3385
*Nick Cecil

Stoke Evening Sentinel
Plymouth Evening News
Torquay Herald Express
Gloucestershire Echo
Gloucestershire Citizen
*Bob Podmore 3682

Nottingham Post
Leicester Mercury
Lincolnshire Echo
*Kristiina Cooper 0875

Hull Daily Mail
Grimsby Telegraph
South Wales Evening Post
Derby Evening Telegraph
Scunthorpe Telegraph
*Kirsty Buchanon 4691

Derby Telegraph
*Bob Podmore 3682

Manchester Evening News
*Ian Craig 6672
*Ian Wylie 6672

Birmingham Post
*Jason Beattie 3765
John Lewis 4700

East Anglian Daily Times
*Graham Dines 4700

Coventry Evening Telegraph
*Paul Dale 4700

Portsmouth and Sunderland News
*Brian Brady 6539

Eastern Daily Press
*Chris Fisher 3384
*Ian Collins 3384/3339

Liverpool Daily Post
*David Rose 3383

The Newcastle Journal
*Paul Linford 4389

Yorkshire Post
*Sarah Neville 3674/222 1137

Northern Echo
*Brendan Carlin

Western Daily Press
*Matthew George 3673

Western Morning News
*Andrew Porter

Western Mail
South Wales News
*Nike Speed 4382
*Leslie Able

Birmingham Mail
*Shaun Connolly 4277

Bristol Evening Post
Oldham Chronicle
Carlisle News and Star
North West Evening Mail
*Rob Merrick 5287

Liverpool Echo
*Ian Hernon 6723

Shropshire Express
*

Southern Daily Echo
South Wales Argus
Bournemouth Daily Echo
Dorset Evening Echo

Wolverhampton Express & Star
Shropshire Star
*John Hipwood 3381
*Ben Bevington 3381

Yorkshire Evening Post
Sheffield Star
Lancashire Evening Post
*Hugh Lawrence 6766

Belfast Telegraph
*Des McCartan 6725

South Wales Echo
*Richard Hazelwood 6146

Irish Independent
*Bernard Purcell 4700

Irish Press
*Aiden Hennigan 4700

Irish Times
*Frank Millar 4700

Belfast Newsletter
*Mervyn Pauley 4700
*Donna Carton

MAGAZINES

Spectator
*Bruce Anderson 3689

New Statesman/Society
*Jacqueline Ashley 6564

Tribune
*Hugh Macpherson 4700

The Economist
*Adam Raphael 7830-7047
*Peter David

Punch
Jerry Hayes

Marketing News
4700

The House Magazine
7233-1388

AFX News
*Frank Prenesti 4700

Bridge News
*Christopherson Davison
*David Robinson 0618
Stephen Ball

Dow-Jones
*Rupert Cooke 4700

Gallery News
*Robert Gibson 2908

AGENCIES

Reuters
*5389
*Michael Peacock 5380
*Brian Williams 5380
*Edna Fernandez
*Dominic Evans
*Cheryl Juckes

Bloomberg News
*David Healy 2035
Andrew Atkinson

Central Press
*Matthew George 3385
*Nick Cecil 3385

Press Association (PA News)
Trevor Mason 4299/4288
*James Lyons
*Jon Smith
Chris Mead 4299/4282
Nigel Williams 4299/4282
*Chris Moncrieff 4299
*Gavin Cordon
Jackie Storer 4282
*Andrew Woodcock 4282
David Roberts
Benjamin Davies
Martin Evans
*Bob Roberts
Dominic Hayes
*Amanda Brown
Catherine Chattaway
*John Deane
Sarah Westcott

Robinson's Parliamentary News Agency
*Mike Peters 4283
*Julian Robinson 4283

Newspoint Agency
4279
4279
*Simon Page 6148
*Mike Steele 4278
*Malcolm MacMillan 4279
*David Bearfield 4279
William Pickering

BROADCASTING

Independent Radio News
7799-2360
*Peter Murphy
*Peter Russell
*Kevin Murphy
*Roland Buerk

IRN Scotland
*Gordon Campbell 3338

Israel Radio
*Jerry Lewis 0452

London Weekend TV (LWT)
4700
Dollan Cannell
Charles Harrison
David Mapstone

Channel One TV
Stephen Punter 4700

HTV – Wales
*Max Perkins 4278

HTV – West
Bob Constantine 3673
*Jo Kiernan

London News Radio
*Max Cotton 4700

Tyne Tees TV
*Gerry Foley 6739

RTE – Irish Broadcasting
*Brian O'Connell 4700

Ulster TV
*Ken Reid 5381

Welsh Fourth Channel
*Vaughan Roderick 4700
*Beth Kilfoil 4700

Yorkshire TV
*David Harrison 6720
Richard Whiteley 6720

West Country TV
*John Ray 7976-0831
*Deborah Geraghty
Angus Walker

Scottish TV
Bernard Ponsonby 6724
*Rae Stewart 6724
*Michael Crow 6724

Granada TV
*Mark Lyons 6891
*Benedict Fitzgerald 6891
Rob McLoughlin

London News Network
*Clare Rewcastle 4700

Southern Radio
*Brian Shallcross 6729

Meridian
*Emma Hutchinson
*Alan Clark 6729

Grampian TV
*Michael Crow 6148

Central TV
*Peter Hayes 3765
*Simon Mares 4681
Zoe Cummings
Vivienne Read

Anglia TV
*Phil Hornby

Border TV
*Simon Page 6148

Sky TV
*Rachel Ward 7976-7120
*Adam Boulton 7976-7120
*John Ray 7976-7120
*Peter Spencer 7976-7120
*Paul Bromley 7976-7120

GM-TV
*Rachel Ward 3678
*Sue Jameson
William Runcon

Carlton TV
*Ed Boyle 4700
*Angus Walker 4700

Channel 5 News
*Andrew Bell 4700
*Vincent Dowd

BBC

National Correspondents
020 7973 6057/6044/6010
*Andrew Marr (Political Editor – 7973 6010)
*Jon Devitt (World Service)
*Guto Harri
*Laura Trevelyan
*Nick Robinson (News 24)
*Mark Mardell (7973 6072)
*Nick Jones   *Carolyn Quinn
*John Kampfner   *Carole Walker
*John Pienaar
*Tim Franks
  (Political
  Correspondent)
*Jonathan Beale
*Martha Kearney

Regional Correspondents
020 7973 6170
*Mark Simpson (North West)
Shaun Ley (South East)
*Bruce Parker (South)
*Paul Cannon (West)
Paul Rowley
Bruce Parker (South)
Chris Rogers (South West)
Paul Cannon (West)
*Rosy Billington (Northern Ireland)
*Luke Waltone (North East)
John Hess (East Midlands)
Patrick Burns (West Midlands)
Jim Hancock (Manchester)
Deborah McGurran (East)
Peter Lugg (North)
*Sean Curran
*Nick Assinder (BBC Online)

Other BBC Correspondents
David Cornock (Wales) 7973 6240
Mike Fairbairn (Parliamentary) 7973 6058
David Porter (Scotland) 7973 6185

ITN
3334/4387
*John Sergeant (Political Editor)
*Graham Forrester
Julie Hulme
Anne Lingley
*John Ray
*Lauren Taylor
*Jo Andrews
Lucy Manning

Channel 4
3334/4387
*Elinor Goodman
*Gary Gibbon
Adam Bandermark 7430-4935
7430 4909
Andrew Brown
*Oliver King

Parliamentary Agents

Parliamentary Agents provide general information on Parliament to both individuals and firms, fully reporting on progress of Bills. There are two types of Agent, those registered to propose and oppose bills on behalf of their clients and those who only oppose Bills.

The Register of authorised Parliamentary Agents is kept in the Private Bills Office of the House of Commons. Generally associated with the legal profession, Agents carry out their duties under the rules, originally laid down by the Speaker in 1837, of both the Houses of Parliament.

One or more of the Partners of the firms listed below are authorised to practise as Parliamentary Agents.

BIRCHAM DYSON BELL
1 Dean Farrar Street, Westminster
London SW1H 0DY
020 7222 8044
Fax: 020 7630 1280
E-mail: ppl@bdb-law.co.uk
Partners: Ian McCulloch, Paul Thompson,
    Nicholas Brown, Robert Owen,
    David Mundy, Jonathan Bracken

LEWIN GREGORY & CO
1 The Sanctuary, Westminster
London SW1P 3JT
020 7222 5381
Fax: 020 7222 4646
E-mail: enquiries@1thesanctuary.com
Partners: Joe Durkin, Patrick Cronin,
    Graham Fountain, Peter Lane, Monica Peto,
    Philip Sergeant

REES & FRERES
1 The Sanctuary, Westminster
London SW1P 3JT
020 7222 5381
Fax: 020 7222 4646
E-mail: enquiries@1thesanctuary.com
Partners: Joe Durkin, Peter Beesley,
    Patrick Cronin, Andrew Davies,
    Michael Fletcher, Graham Fountain,
    Peter Lane, Monica Peto, Ziggy Reisman,
    Nicholas Richens, Peter Robinson,
    Philip Sergeant, Julia Taplin, Keith Wallace

SHARPE PRITCHARD
Elizabeth House, Fulwood Place
London WC1V 6HG
020 7222 3551
Fax: 020 7222 1451
E-mail: parliamentary@sharpepritchard.co.uk
Paliamentary Agents: Alastair Lewis,
    Michael Pritchard (Consultant)

VIZARD OLDHAM
42 Bedford Row
London WC1R 4JL
020 7663 2222
Fax: 020 7663 2226
E-mail: ron.perry@vizold.co.uk
Partner: Ron Perry

WINCKWORTH SHERWOOD
35 Great Peter Street, Westminster
London SW1P 3LR
DX 2312 Victoria
020 7593 5000
Fax: 020 7593 5199
E-mail: cmvine@winckworths.co.uk
Parliamentary Agents (Partners): Alison Gorlov,
    Chris Vine, Paul Irving, Stephen Wiggs

HISTORICAL INFORMATION

Parliaments of the 20th and 21st centuries

Assembled	Dissolved	Length			Ministries	Took Office	
		yrs.	m.	d.			
VICTORIA							
Dec. 3, 1900	Jan. 8, 1906	5	1	5	⌠ Salisbury (C)	Dec.	6, 1900
					⌡ Balfour (C)	July	12, 1902
EDWARD VII							
Feb. 13, 1906	Jan. 10, 1910	3	10	28	⌠ C. Bannerman (L)	Dec.	5, 1905
					⌡ Asquith (L)	April	5, 1908
Feb. 15, 1910	Nov. 28, 1910		9	13	Asquith (L)	Feb.	15, 1910
GEORGE V							
Jan. 31, 1911	Nov. 25, 1918	7	9	25	⌠ Asquith (L)	May	25, 1915
Feb. 4, 1919	Oct. 25, 1922	3	8	21	⦃ Lloyd George (L)	Dec.	6, 1916
					⌡ Coalition		
Nov. 20, 1922	Nov. 16, 1923		11	27	A. Bonar Law (C)	Oct.	23, 1922
Jan. 8, 1924	Oct. 9, 1924		9	1	J. R. MacDonald (Lab.)	Jan.	22, 1924
Dec. 2, 1924	May 10, 1929	4	5	8	S. Baldwin (C)	Nov.	4, 1924
June 25, 1929	Oct. 7, 1931	2	3	12	J. R. MacDonald (Lab.)	June	5, 1929
					⌠ J. R. MacDonald	Aug.	24, 1931
Nov. 3, 1931	Oct. 25, 1935	3	11	22	⦃ (Nat. Govt.)		
					⌡ S. Baldwin		
Nov. 26, 1935					S. Baldwin	June	7, 1935
					(Nat. Govt.)		
EDWARD VIII					N. Chamberlain	May	28, 1937
					(Nat. Govt.)		
GEORGE VI	June 15, 1945	9	6	20	W. Churchill	May	10, 1940
					(Nat. Govt.)		
Aug. 1, 1945	Feb. 3, 1950	4	6	2	C. R. Attlee (Lab.)	July	26, 1945
Mar. 1, 1950	Oct. 5, 1951	1	7	4	C. R. Attlee (Lab.)	Feb.	25, 1950
Oct. 31, 1951	May 6, 1955	3	6	6	⌠ W. Churchill (C)	Oct.	26, 1951
					⌡ A. Eden (C)		
ELIZABETH II					A. Eden (C)	Apr.	6, 1955
June 7, 1955	Sept. 18, 1959	4	3	11	⌠ H. Macmillan (C)	Jan.	10, 1957
					⌡ H. Macmillan (C)	Oct.	9, 1959
Oct. 20, 1959	Sept. 25, 1964	4	11	5	A. Douglas-Home (C)	Oct.	9, 1963
Oct. 27, 1964	Mar. 10, 1966	1	4	11	⌠ H. Wilson (Lab.)	Oct.	16, 1964
Apr. 18, 1966	May 29, 1970	4	1	11	⌡ H. Wilson (Lab.)	Apr.	1, 1966
June 29, 1970	Feb. 8, 1974	3	7	10	E. R. G. Heath (C)	June	19, 1970
Mar. 6, 1974	Sept. 20, 1974		6	14	H. Wilson (Lab.)	Mar.	4, 1974
					(Minority Govt.)		
Oct. 22, 1974	April 7, 1979	4	5	15	⌠ H. Wilson (Lab.)	Oct.	11, 1974
					⌡ J. Callaghan (Lab.)	Apr.	5, 1976
May 9, 1979	May 13, 1983	4	0	4	Mrs M. Thatcher (C)	May	3, 1979
June 15, 1983	May 18, 1987	3	11	3	Mrs M. Thatcher (C)	June	9, 1983
June 17, 1987	Mar. 16, 1992	4	8	28	⌠ Mrs M. Thatcher (C)	June	11, 1987
					⌡ J. Major (C)	Nov.	28, 1990
April 27, 1992	April 8, 1997	4	11	19	J. Major (C)	April	10, 1992
May 7, 1997					T. Blair (Lab.)	May	1, 1997

Size of the House of Commons since 1801

With the Union of Great Britain and Ireland in 1801 the number of members of Parliament of the United Kingdom was fixed at 658. This number was adhered to by the Reform Act, 1832. In 1885 the total was increased to 670, and by the Act of 1918 to 707. With the creation of the Irish Free State in 1922, the Irish representation was reduced to 13 members from Ulster, making the membership of the House of Commons 615. In 1945, owing to the division of large Constituencies, the number was increased by 25 to 640. Under the Act of 1948 the number was decreased to 625. Under the Orders passed in 1954 and 1955 the number was increased to 630. As the result of redistribution and boundary changes, the total number of MPs elected at the 1979 General Election was 635. The House of Commons (Redistribution of Seats) Act 1979 and the Boundary Commission reports of 1983 resulted in an increase of 15 seats after the 1983 Election. The size of the House of Commons up until the 1992 General Election was 650 members. At the 1992 Election, 651 Members were elected, an extra seat having been created for Milton Keynes. Reports from the Boundary Commission caused an increase to 659 at the 1997 Election.

General Election Majorities since the Reform Act

(NB *In certain cases, such as the election of* 1910, *the Government party had a working arrangement with other parties, which ensured them a majority in the House*)

1832	Lib.	300	1923	Con.	No majority
1835	Lib.	108	1924	Con.	223
1837	Lib.	40	1929	Lab.	No majority
1841	Con.	78	1931	Nat. Govt.	493
1847	Lib.	2	1935	Nat. Govt.	249
1852	Con.	8	1945	Lab.	146
1857	Lib.	92	1950	Lab.	5
1859	Lib.	40	1951	Con.	17
1865	Lib.	62	1955	Con.	58
1868	Lib.	106	1959	Con.	100
1874	Con.	52	1964	Lab.	4
1880	Lib.	176	1966	Lab.	96
1885	Lib.	No majority	1970	Con.	30
1886	Unionist	120	1974	(Feb.) Lab.	No majority
1892	Lib.	No majority	1974	(Oct.) Lab.	3
1895	Unionist	152	(3 over all parties, 42 over Cons.)		
1900	Unionist	135	1979	Con.	43
1906	Lib.	130	1983	Con.	144
1910	(Jan.) Lib.	No majority	1987	Con.	101
1910	(Dec.) Lib.	No majority	1992	Con.	21
1918	Coalition	249	1997	Lab.	177
1922	Con.	75			

Long Parliaments

The longest lived Parliaments in English history have been the Elizabethan Parliament of 1572–83, the Long Parliament of 1640–53, and the Cavalier Parliament of 1661–79. The First World War Parliament met on 31 January 1911, and was dissolved on 25 November 1918. That of the Second met 26 November 1935, and was dissolved 15 June 1945.

Prime Ministers since 1721

1721–42	Sir Robert Walpole (Whig)
1742–43	Spencer Compton (Whig)
1743–54	Henry Pelham (Whig)
1754–56	Duke of Newcastle (Whig)
1756–57	Duke of Devonshire (Whig)
1757–62	Duke of Newcastle (Whig)
1762–63	Earl of Bute (Tory)
1763–65	George Grenville (Whig)
1765–66	Marquess of Rockingham (Whig)
1766–67	William Pitt (the Elder) (Whig)
1767–70	Duke of Grafton (Whig)
1770–82	Lord North (Tory)
1782	Marquess of Rockingham (Whig)
1782–83	Earl of Shelburne (Whig)
1783	Duke of Portland (Coalition)
1783–1801	William Pitt (the Younger) (Tory)
1801–04	Henry Addington (Tory)
1804–06	William Pitt (the Younger) (Tory)
1806–07	Lord Grenville (Whig)
1807–09	Duke of Portland (Tory)
1809–12	Spencer Perceval (Tory)
1812–27	Earl of Liverpool (Tory)
1827	George Canning (Tory)
1827–28	Viscount Goderich (Tory)
1828–30	Duke of Wellington (Tory)
1830–34	Earl Grey (Whig)
1834	Viscount Melbourne (Whig)
1834–35	Sir Robert Peel (Tory)
1835–41	Viscount Melbourne (Whig)
1841–46	Sir Robert Peel (Tory)
1846–52	Lord John Russell (Whig)
1852	Earl of Derby (Con)
1852–55	Earl of Aberdeen (Coalition)
1855–58	Viscount Palmerston (Lib)
1858–59	Earl of Derby (Con)
1859–65	Viscount Palmerston (Lib)
1865–66	Earl Russell (Lib)
1866–68	Earl of Derby (Con)
1868	Benjamin Disraeli (Con)
1868–74	William Gladstone (Lib)
1874–80	Benjamin Disraeli (Con)
1880–85	William Gladstone (Lib)
1885–86	Marquess of Salisbury (Con)
1886	William Gladstone (Lib)
1886–92	Marquess of Salisbury (Con)
1892–94	William Gladstone (Lib)
1894–95	Earl of Rosebery (Lib)
1895–1902	Marquess of Salisbury (Con)
1902–05	Arthur Balfour (Con)
1905–08	Sir Henry Campbell-Bannerman (Lib)
1908–16	Herbert Asquith (Lib)
1916–22	David Lloyd George (Coalition)
1922–23	Andrew Bonar Law (Con)
1923–24	Stanley Baldwin (Con)
1924	Ramsay MacDonald (Lab)
1924–29	Stanley Baldwin (Con)
1929–35	Ramsay MacDonald (Lab)
1935–37	Stanley Baldwin (Nat Govt)
1937–40	Neville Chamberlain (Nat Govt)
1940–45	Winston Churchill (Coalition)
1945–51	Clement Attlee (Lab)
1951–55	Winston Churchill (Con)
1955–57	Sir Anthony Eden (Con)
1957–63	Harold Macmillan (Con)
1963–64	Sir Alec Douglas-Home (Con)
1964–70	Harold Wilson (Lab)
1970–74	Edward Heath (Con)
1974–76	Harold Wilson (Lab)
1976–79	James Callaghan (Lab)
1979–90	Margaret Thatcher (Con)
1990–97	John Major (Con)
1997–	Tony Blair (Lab)

VACHER'S PARLIAMENTARY COMPANION

Published continuously since 1832 and updated quarterly

Opening with comprehensive details of the Government, the new look quarterly *Vacher's* pocket book continues with the Cabinet Office, Ministerial Responsibilities, Permanent Secretaries and Opposition Spokesmen, MPs' contact directory, Constituency results and By-elections, Select Committees and Political Parties' Organisations followed by the House of Lords. New sections on the Scottish Parliament, the National Assembly for Wales, Northern Ireland Assembly and the Greater London Assembly are treated with the same thoroughness of detail. Then follow sections on Government Departments, Senior Civil Servants and UK MEPs – all designed for speed and handiness.

Vacher Dod Publishing Limited
PO Box 3700, Westminster, London SW1P 4WU
Tel: 020 7828 7256   Fax: 020 7828 7269
E-mail: politics@vacherdod.co.uk
Website: www.politicallinks.co.uk

GOVERNMENT AND PUBLIC OFFICES

GOVERNMENT DEPARTMENTS

Permanent Secretaries

AGRICULTURE, FISHERIES AND FOOD
Permanent Secretary   Brian Bender CB

CABINET OFFICE
Secretary of the Cabinet and
Head of the Home Civil Service   Sir Richard Wilson KCB
Permanent Secretary   Mavis McDonald

CULTURE, MEDIA AND SPORT   Robin Young

DEFENCE
Permanent Under-Secretary   Kevin Tebbit CMG
Second Permanent Under-Secretary   Roger Jackling CBE

EDUCATION AND EMPLOYMENT   Sir Michael Bichard KCB

ENVIRONMENT,
TRANSPORT AND THE REGIONS   Sir Richard Mottram KCB

FOREIGN AND COMMONWEALTH OFFICE
Permanent Under-Secretary of State
and Head of HM Diplomatic Service   Sir John Kerr KCMG

HEALTH   Nigel Crisp

HOME OFFICE   Sir David Omand KCB

INTERNATIONAL DEVELOPMENT   Sir John Vereker KCB

LORD CHANCELLOR'S DEPARTMENT   Sir Hayden Phillips KCB

NORTHERN IRELAND OFFICE
Permanent Under-Secretary of State   Joe Pilling CB
Second Permanent Under-Secretary of State
and Head of NICS   Gerry Loughran

SCOTTISH EXECUTIVE   Muir Russell

SOCIAL SECURITY   Rachel Lomax

TRADE AND INDUSTRY   Sir Michael Scholar KCB

TREASURY   Sir Andrew Turnbull KCB CVO

NATIONAL ASSEMBLY FOR WALES   Jon Shortridge

Ministry of Agriculture, Fisheries and Food

Nobel House, 17 Smith Square,
London SW1P 3JR (LNH)
020 7238 3000 *Fax:* 020 7238 6591
MAFF Helpline (Public Enquiries)
0645 335577
E-mail: helpline@inf.maff.gsi.gov.uk
Website: www.maff.gov.uk/maffhome.htm

OTHER HEADQUARTERS ADDRESSES

Ergon House, c/o 17 Smith Square,
London SW1P 3JR (LER)
020 7238 3000 *Fax:* 020 7238 6591

Eastbury House, 30-34 Albert Embankment,
London SE1 7TL (LEA)
020 7238 6000 *Fax:* 020 7238 6616

Foss House, 1-2 Peasholme Green, Kings Pool,
York YO1 7PX (YKF)
01904 641000

Government Buildings, Epsom Road, Guildford,
Surrey GU1 2LD (GUI)
01483 568121 *Fax:* 01483 37396

1a Page Street, London SW1P 4PQ (LPS)
020 7904 6000

55 Whitehall, London SW1A 2EY (L55W)
020 7238 6000 *Fax:* 020 7270 8721

Whitehall Place, London SW1A 2HH (LWP)
020 7238 6000 *Fax:* 020 7270 8721

White House Lane, Huntingdon Road,
Cambridge CB3 0LE (CWL)
01223 277151 *Fax:* 01223 342386

19-29 Woburn Place, London WC1H 0LU
(LWO)
020 7273 3000

Responsible for Government policies on agriculture, horticulture and fisheries in England. In association with the other Agriculture Departments in the UK and the Intervention Board Executive Agency it is responsible for negotiations in the European Community on the Common Agricultural and Common Fisheries Policies and for Single European Market questions which relate to its agricultural, fisheries and food responsibilities. The Ministry exercises responsibilities for the protection and the enhancement of the countryside and the marine environment, for flood and coastal defence and for other rural issues. It is the licensing authority for veterinary medicines and the registration authority for pesticides. It administers policies relating to control of animal, plant and fish diseases. It provides scientific, technical and professional services and advice to farmers, growers and ancillary industries, and it commissions research to assist in the formulation and assessment of policy and to underpin applied research and development work done by industry.

Minister:
  Rt Hon Nick Brown MP
Parliamentary Private Secretary:
  Ruth Kelly MP
Special Advisers: Kieran Simpson,
  Jack Thurston
Minister of State and Deputy Minister:
  Rt Hon Joyce Quin MP
Parliamentary Private Secretary:
  Brian Jenkins MP
Minister of State (Lords): Baroness Hayman
Parliamentary Private Secretary:
  Bob Blizzard MP
Parliamentary Secretary (Commons):
  Elliot Morley MP

Spokespersons in the House of Lords:
Baroness Hayman, Lord Carter

Permanent Secretary: Brian Bender CB
Priv Sec: Lloyd Burdett
Parliamentary Branch (for all MAFF Ministers)
020 7238 5456
Parliamentary Clerk: Christine Dix
*Head of Agricultural Crops and Commodities
  Directorate:* Kate Timms CB
*Head of Animal Health and Environment
  Directorate:* Jenny Bacon CB
Head of Fisheries Department:
  Stephen Wentworth
Based at LNH
Chief Scientist:
  David Shannon PhD BAgr DMS (LPS)
Legal Adviser and Solicitor:
  Kathyrn Morton (L55W)

AGRICULTURAL CROPS AND
COMMODITIES DIRECTORATE
European Union and International Policy Group
*Head of European Union and International
  Policy Group:* Andy Lebrecht
Heads of Division: David Dawson, Tom Eddy
  (LWP)

AGRICULTURAL GROUP
Head of Agricultural Group: David Hunter
Heads of Division: Henry Brown,
    Richard Cowan, Gavin Rose, Andrew Kuyk,
    Alan Taylor
Based at LWP
George Noble (LEA)
Andrew Perrins (YKF)
Sarah Hendry (YKF)
David Boreham (CWL)

FOOD INDUSTRY COMPETITIVENESS AND
CONSUMERS
*Head of Food Industry Competitiveness and
    Consumers:* John Robbs
Heads of Division: David Orchard,
    Jane Rabagliati, Judy Allfrey
Ann Waters
Based at LWP
Alison Blackburn (LNH)
Jim Park (LEA)

REGIONAL SERVICES AND DEFENCE
GROUP
Head of Regional Services and Defence Group:
    Jane Brown (LWP)
Head of Division: Janet Purnell (LWP)
Head of Unit: David Putley (LNH)

REGIONAL SERVICE CENTRE DIRECTORS

ANGLIA REGION
Bedfordshire, Cambridgeshire, Essex,
Hertfordshire, Norfolk and Suffolk
Block B, Government Buildings
Brooklands Avenue, Cambridge CB2 2DR
01223 462727 *Fax:* 01223 455652
Martin Edwards

NORTHERN REGION
Cumbria, Lancashire, Northumberland
and Tyne and Wear
Eden Bridge House, Lowther Street
Carlisle, Cumbria CA3 8DX
01228 523400 *Fax:* 01228 640205
Ian Pearson

EAST MIDLANDS REGION
Derbyshire, Leicestershire, Lincolnshire,
Northamptonshire and Nottinghamshire
Block 7, Government Buildings,
Chalfont Drive, Nottingham NG8 3SN
0115-929 1191 *Fax:* 0115-929 4886
Graham Norbury

SOUTH EAST REGION
Berkshire, Buckinghamshire, Hampshire,
Isle of Wight, Kent, Greater London,
Oxfordshire, Surrey and Sussex (East
and West)
Block A, Government Buildings
Coley Park, Reading, Berks RG1 6DT
0118-958 1222 *Fax:* 0118-939 2399
Virginia Silvester

SOUTH WEST REGION
Cornwall, Devon and Isles of Scilly
Clyst House, Winslade Park,
Clyst St Mary, Exeter, Devon EX5 1DY
01392 447400 *Fax:* 01392 266000
Mike Highman

NORTH EAST REGION
Cleveland, Durham, Humberside and Yorkshire
(North, South and West)
Government Buildings, Crosby Road
Northallerton, North Yorkshire DL6 1AD
01609 773751 *Fax:* 01609 780179
Peter Watson

SOUTH MERCIA REGION
Hereford and Worcester,
Gloucestershire, Warwickshire and
West Midlands
Block C, Government Buildings
Whittington Road, Worcester WR5 2LQ
01905 763355 *Fax:* 01905 763180
Brinley Davies

NORTH MERCIA REGION
Cheshire, Merseyside, Greater Manchester,
Shropshire and Staffordshire
Electra Way, Crew Business Park,
Crewe CW1 6GJ
01270 754000 *Fax:* 01270 669494
Tony Percival *(acting)*

WESSEX REGION
Avon, Dorset, Somerset and Wiltshire
Block 3, Government Buildings
Burghill Road, Westbury-on-Trym
Bristol BS10 6NJ
0117-959 1000 *Fax:* 0117-950 5392
Carole Deakins *(acting)*

ANIMAL HEALTH AND ENVIRONMENT
DIRECTORATE

Chief Veterinary Officer: Jim Scudamore
Deputy Chief Veterinary Officer (Policy):
    Richard Cawthorne
Heads of Division: Robin Bell, David Pritchard,
    Debbie Reynolds, Danny Matthews,
    Fred Landeg

Deputy Chief Veterinary Officer (Services):
   Martin Atkinson
Head of Division: Betty Phillip
Heads of Veterinary Services: John Cross (West),
   Richard Drummond (North),
   Gareth Jones (East)
Assistant Chief Veterinary Officer (Scotland):
   Leslie Gardener
Head of Veterinary Services (Scotland):
   Derick McIntosh
Assistant Chief Veterinary Officer (Wales):
   Tony Edwards
Based at LPS

ANIMAL HEALTH GROUP
Head of Animal Health: Neil Thornton
Heads of Division: Valerie Smith,
   Roy Hathaway, Peter Nash
Catherine Harrold
Based at LPS

ENVIRONMENT GROUP

Head of Environment Group: Dudley Coates
Heads of Division: John Osmond,
   Lindsay Cornish, Peter Cleasby, John Osmond
Based at LNH

ECONOMICS AND STATISTICS GROUP

Head of Economics and Statistics:
   David Thompson
Heads of Division: Peter Muriel, Nigel Atkinson
Howard Fearn
Based at LWP
Stuart Platt
Peter Helm
Based at YKF

FISHERIES GROUP

Fisheries Secretary: Stephen Wentworth
Heads of Division: Peter Boyling, Sue Brown,
   Ivor Llewelyn
Barry Edwards
Chief Inspector, Sea Fisheries Inspectorate:
   George Ellson
Based at LNH

LEGAL DEPARTMENT

Legal Adviser and Solicitor: Kathryn Morton
Prin Asst Solicitors: Catherine Crisham,
   David Pearson
Heads of Division: Charles Allen, Ian Corbett,
   Peter Davis, Nigel Lambert, Susan Spence,
   Mayur Patel, Colin Gregory, Anne Werbicki
Chief Investigation Officer: Jan Panting
Based at L55W

CHIEF SCIENTIST GROUP

Chief Scientist: David Shannon PhD DMS
Heads of Division:
   Dr John Sherlock PhD FRSC CChem FIFST,
   Dr Ken MacOwan PhD MRCVS,
   Dr Tony Burne
Based at LPS

ESTABLISHMENTS GROUP

Director of Establishments: Roger Saunderson
   (LNH)
Heads of Division: Tony Nickson (LEA),
   Bronwen Jones (LNH), Teresa Newell (LNH)
Acting Director of IT: Shaun Soper
Heads of Division: David Brown, Peter Barber
Acting Head of Division: Alan Hill
Based at GUI

FINANCE GROUP

Prin Finance Officer: Paul Elliott (LWP)
Heads of Division: David Rabey (LWO),
   Brian Harding (LWP)
Head of Unit: Vivien Bodnar (LWP)
*Director of Audit Consultancy and Management
   Services:* David Fisher FCCA (LWO)
Head of Resource Management Division:
   Julie Flint (YKF)

CHANGE MANAGEMENT UNIT
Head of Unit: David Rossington
Based at LWP

AGENCY OWNERSHIP UNIT
Head of Unit: Dr Mike Tas (LWP)

COMMUNICATIONS DIRECTORATE
Director of Communications: Robert Lowson
   (LNH)

TRANSMISSIBLE SPONGIFORM ENCEPHALOPATHIES
RESEARCH AND SURVEILLANCE UNIT
Head of Unit: Dr Mandy Bailey (LEA)

Executive Agencies: Central Science
Laboratory (CSL); Centre for Environment,
Fisheries and Aquaculture Science (CEFAS);
Farming and Rural Conservation Agency
(FRCA); Intervention Board; Pesticides Safety
Directorate (PSD); Veterinary Laboratories
Agency (VLA); Veterinary Medicines
Directorate (VMD)

Cabinet Office

10 Downing Street, London SW1A 2AA
Tel: Direct Line from 020 7930 4433
Website: www.number—10.gov.uk

To help the Prime Minister and Ministers collectively to reach and implement decisions on policy, modernise Government, improve public services. Responsible for the civil service.

The Prime Minister: Rt Hon Tony Blair MP

Details of the Prime Minister's staff may be found under Prime Minister's Office in this Section.

70 Whitehall, London SW1A 2AS
020 7270 0400 *Fax:* 020 7270 0196
Website: www.cabinet-office.gov.uk

Minister for the Cabinet Office:
    Rt Hon Dr Mo Mowlam MP
Parliamentary Private Secretary:
    Margaret Moran MP
Special Advisers: Nigel Warner, Andrew Lappin

Minister of State:
    Lord Falconer of Thoroton QC
Parliamentary Private Secretary:
    Christopher Leslie MP

Minister of State: Rt Hon Ian McCartney MP
Parliamentary Private Secretary:
    Frank Doran MP

Parliamentary Secretary: Graham Stringer MP

Parliamentary Clerk: Selvin Brown

Leader of the House of Lords and Minister for Women (Lord Privy Seal):
    Rt Hon Baroness Jay of Paddington
Parliamentary Private Secretary:
    Eric Martlew MP
Special Advisers: Clare Cozens, Jo Gibbons
    (020 7270 1294 Fax: 020 7270 0491)

Admin Officer: Tracey Goddard

Spokesmen in the House of Lords: Lord Falconer, Lord Burlison; Spokespersons for Women's Issues: Baroness Jay, Baroness Amos

Secretary of the Cabinet and Head of the Home Civil Service:
    Sir Richard Wilson KCB
Permanent Secretary: Mavis McDonald
    020 7270 0003

SECRETARIATS
70 Whitehall, London SW1A 2AS
020 7270 3000
Economic and Domestic Secretariat:
    Sumaantra Chakrabarti, Lindsey Bell,
    Paul Britton

Defence and Overseas Affairs Secretariat:
    Tom McKane
Joint Intelligence Organisation: Peter Ricketts,
    Jon Day
European Secretariat: Stephen Wall,
    Martin Donnelly, M Roberts
Constitution Secretariat: Jonathan Tross,
    Judith Simpson, Rosemary Jeffreys

CENTRAL SECRETARIAT
020 7276 2455 *Fax:* 020 7270 1860
E-mail: open.co.wh@gtnet.gov.uk
Director: Siona Phippard

PUBLIC SERVICE DELIVERY
4 Matthew Parker Street, London SW1H 9NL

REGULATORY IMPACT UNIT
35 Great Smith Street, London SW1P 3BQ
E-mail: plewis@cabinet-office.x.gsi.gov.uk
Director: Philip Wynn-Owen
Fax: 020 7276 2151

WOMEN'S UNIT
10 Great George Street, London SW1P 3AE
Minister for Women: Rt Hon Baroness Jay
Director: Fiona Reynolds

CENTRAL IT UNIT
53 Parliament Street, London SW1
020 7238 2015 GTN 238 2015
Fax: 020 7238 2006 GTN 238 2006
E-mail: citu@citu.gov.uk
Website: www@citu.gov.uk
Director: David Cooke

GOVERNMENT DIRECT TEAM
Mark Gladwyn, Ian White, Jeremy Crump,
    Paul Waller, Anne Steward

MODERNISING PUBLIC SERVICES GROUP
Admiralty Arch, The Mall, London SW1A 2WH
Fax: 020 7276 1484
E-mail: servicefirst@gtnet.gov.uk
Website: www.servicefirst.gov.uk
Director: Jonathan Stephens

CIVIL SERVICE MANAGEMENT MATTERS

CIVIL SERVICE CORPORATE MANAGEMENT
COMMAND
Admiralty Arch, The Mall, London SW1A 2WH
E-mail: cseg@gtnet.gov.uk
Head of Unit: Brian Fox CB

RECRUITMENT AND DEVELOPMENT OF PEOPLE
GROUP
Admiralty Arch, The Mall, London SW1A 2WH
Fax: 020 7276 1616
Director: John Barker

PERFORMANCE MANAGEMENT GROUP
Admiralty Arch, The Mall, London SW1A 2WH
Director: Sally Hinkley CBE

CENTRE FOR MANAGEMENT AND POLICY STUDIES
Admiralty Arch, The Mall, London SW1A 2WH
Director-General: Prof Ronald Amann
Corporate Development and Training Director:
  Robert Green
Business Director: Peter Tebby

GOVERNMENT INFORMATION AND
COMMUNICATIONS SERVICE
Head of Communications: Mike Granatt

INFORMATION DIVISION/PRESS OFFICE
70 Whitehall, London SW1A 2AS
020 7270 0516
E-mail: pmartin@cabinet-office.gov.uk
Director of Information: Paul Martin

UK ANTI-DRUGS CO-ORDINATION UNIT
4 Matthew Parker Street, London SW1H 9NL
020 7270 5776
Head of Unit: Sue Killan
UK Anti-Drugs Co-ordinator: Keith Hellawell
Deputy Anti-Drugs Co-ordinator: Michael Trace

CORPORATE RESOURCES AND SERVICES GROUP
Queen Anne's Chambers, 28 Broadway
London SW1H 9JS
Director: Peter Wardle

Executive Agencies: Central Office of
Information (COI); Government Car and
Despatch Agency (GCDA)

Crown Office

25 Chambers Street, Edinburgh
EH1 1LA, Scotland
0131-226 2626 *Fax:* 0131-226 6910
E-mail: co.isunit@dial.pipex.com

The Law Officers for Scotland are the Lord
Advocate and the Solicitor General for Scotland.
The Lord Advocate's Department is responsible
for drafting Scottish legislation, for providing
legal advice to other departments on Scottish
questions and for assistance to the Law Officers
for Scotland in certain of their legal duties.

Lord Advocate: Rt Hon Colin Boyd QC
Solicitor General for Scotland: Neil Davidson QC
*Private Secretary to Lord Advocate and Solicitor
  General for Scotland:* J A Gibbons

Crown Agent: Andrew Normand
Deputy Crown Agent: Frank Crowe
Assistant Solicitors: M J Bell, J Brisbane,
  Mrs J E Cameron, Miss E C Munro,
  Mrs G M Watt
Head of Practice and Quality Review: G Napier
Senior Deputes: B M Logan, C B McClory,
  Dr A N Brown
Legal Assistant to the Crown Agent:
  Miss M A M McLaughlin
Principal Deputes: Miss S C Barrie, I G Bradley,
  A Brown, Miss D F Bruce, Miss C E S
  Bryden, Mrs S M Burns, W C Craig,
  Mrs A M Di Rollo, K W Donnelly,
  Ms C M D Duncan, J A Dunn,
  Miss C R Frame, A S D Laing, J T Logue,
  M M MacLeod, A Miller, Miss M R Paterson,
  S Pattison, B Robertson, Ms K A Stewart,
  Ms A B Swarbrick, Miss M B Watson

Department for Culture, Media and Sport

2–4 Cockspur Street, London SW1Y 5DH
020 7211 6200 *Fax:* 020 7211 6032
E-mail: enquiries@culture.gsi.gov.uk
Website: www.culture.gsi.gov.uk

Responsible for Government policies on arts and
libraries, broadcasting and the press; sports,
including the safety of sports grounds; tourism
and heritage; film policy; the export licensing of
antiques; the National Lottery; volunteering and
charities; museums and galleries.

Secretary of State: Rt Hon Chris Smith MP
Parliamentary Private Secretary: Fiona
  Mactaggart MP
Special Advisers:
  020 7211 6101 *Fax:* 020 7211 6249
  Andy Burnham
  E-mail: andy.burnham@culture.gsi.gov.uk
  Ruth MacKenzie
  E-mail: ruth.mackenzie@culture.gsi.gov.uk
*Parliamentary Under-Secretart of State
  (Minister for Tourism, Film and
  Broadcasting):* Janet Anderson MP
*Parliamentary Under-Secretary of State
  (Minister for Sport):* Kate Hoey MP
*Parliamentary Under-Secretary of State
  (Minister for the Arts):*
  Alan Howarth CBE MP

Spokesman in the House of Lords: Lord
McIntosh of Haringey

Permanent Secretary: Robin Young
E-mail: robin.young@culture.gov.uk

Corporate Services Group
Head of Group: Nicholas Kroll
Director of Finance: Andy Mclellan
Head of Personnel and Central Services
  Division: Ruth Siemaszko
Head of National Lottery Division: Jon Zeff
Head of Accounts: Kathy Hosker
Head of Internal Audit: David Rix
Head of Economics: Dr Stephen Creigh-Tyte
Head of Central Appointments Unit:
  Stuart Roberts

Creative Industries, Media and Broadcasting Group
Head of Group: Andrew Ramsay
Head of Media Division: Michael Seeney
Head of Broadcasting Policy Division:
  Diana Kahn
Head of Creative Industries Unit: Allan Ferries

Museums, Galleries, Libraries and Heritage Group
Head of Group: Alexandra Stewart
Head of Buildings, Monuments and Sites
  Division: Nigel Pittman
Head of Museums and Galleries Division:
  Hugh Corner
Head of Libraries, Information and Archives
  Division: Janet Evans
Head of Government Art Collection:
  Penny Johnson

Strategy and Communications Group
Director of Strategy and Communications:
  Paul Bolt
Departmental Secretariat: Shaun Cove
  (Secretary to the Management Board)
Statistics and Social Policy Unit: Paul Allin
Head of News: Vacant
Head of Publicity and Communications:
  Graham Newsom

Education, Training, Arts and Sports Group
Head of Group: Philippa Drew
Head of Sports and Recreation Division:
  Harry Reeves
Head of Arts Division: William Nye
Head of Education and Training Unit:
  Tony Dyer

Regions, Tourism, Millennium and International Group
Head of Group: Brian Leonard
Head of Local, Regional and International
  Division: Paul Douglas
Head of Tourism Division: Simon Broadley
Head of Millennium Unit: Clare Pillman

Legal Adviser
Isabel Letwin
DCMS Legal Advisers, 28 Broadway,
London SW1
020 7210 3278 *Fax:* 020 7210 3448

Parliamentary and Correspondence Unit
Manager: Simon Stephenson 020 7211 6288
Ministerial Support Unit
Vacant 020 7211 6253

Executive Agency: Royal Parks

Ministry of Defence
FOR SECURITY REASONS, CERTAIN
DEPARTMENTS NOT PUBLISHED
Main Building, Whitehall,
London SW1A 2HB
Switchboard 020 7218 9000
Parliamentary Section 020 7218 6169
E-mail: public@ministers.mod.uk
for all Ministers
Website: www.mod.uk

Responsible for the control, administration, equipment and support of the armed forces.

Secretary of State:
  Rt Hon Geoffrey Hoon MP
Parliamentary Private Secretary:
  Sylvia Heal MP
Special Advisers: Alasdair McGowan,
  Andrew Hood

Minister of State for the Armed Forces:
  John Spellar MP
Parliamentary Private Secretary:
  David Watts MP

Minister of State for Defence Procurement:
  Baroness Symons of Vernham Dean
Parliamentary Private Secretary:
  Gillian Merron MP

Parliamentary Under-Secretary of State:
  Dr Lewis Moonie MP

Spokespersons in the House of Lords: Baroness
Symons, Lord Burlison

Permanent Under-Secretary:
  Kevin Tebbit CMG 020 7218 2839
Second Permanent Under-Secretary:
  Roger Jackling CBE

DIRECTOR GENERAL CORPORATE
COMMUNICATIONS
Public Enquiry Office
0870 607 4455

Director-General of Corporate
  Communications: John Pitt-Brooke
  (020 7218 0546)

Director of Corporate Services: Chris Williams
(020 7218 6181)
Director of News: Martin Howard
(020 7218 2717)
Head of Communication Planning: Nick Gurr
Director Corporate Communications (Navy):
Cdre Hugh Edleston RN (020 7218 7906)
Director Corporate Communications (Army):
Brig Sebastian Roberts OBE (020 7218 2500)
Director Corporate Communications (RAF):
Air Cdre David Walker (020 7218 3559)
Director News/Chief Press Officer:
Simon Wren (020 7218 7950)
*Defence Press and Broadcasting Advisory
Committee Secretary:*
Rear Adm Nick Wilkinson (020 7218 3820)

CENTRAL STAFFS
Vice-Chief of the Defence Staff:
Adm Sir Peter Abbott KCB (until May 2001);
Air Chief Marshal Sir Anthony Bagnall (from
May 2001)
*Deputy Chief of the Defence Staff (Equipment
Capability):* Vice-Adm Sir Jeremy Blackham
KCB
Capability Manager (Strategic/Deployment):
Rear Adm R G J Ward
*Directorate of Science (Strategic/Deployment
and Strike):* Dr John Jones
Capability Manager (Manoeuvre):
Maj Gen John Russell-Jones OBE
Directorate of Science (Manoeuvre):
Dr Ian Sharp
Capability Manager (Strike): Air Vice-Marshal
Steve Nicholl CBE AFC FRAeS
Deputy Chief of the Defence Staff (Personnel):
Air Marshal Malcolm Pledger OBE AFC
FRAeS
Assistant Chief of Defence Staff (Programmes):
Maj Gen John Kiszely MC
*Assistant Under-Secretary of State (Service
Personnel):* Barry Miller
Surgeon General:
Lt Gen Robert Menzies OBE QHS
Chief of Staff to Surgeon General:
Rear Adm Christopher Stanford
Principal Finance Officer: Colin Balmer
Director-General (Resources and Plans):
Trevor Woolley
Director-General (Equipment): Nick Witney
Director-General (Financial Management):
David Jones
Assistant Under-Secretary of State:
Chris Sandars

Defence Services Secretary: J R E Sinfield
Directorate of Reserve Forces and Cadets:
Brig Richard Holmes
*Deputy Chief of the Defence Staff
(Commitments):* Maj Gen A D Pigott CBE
*Assistant Chief of the Defence Staff
(Operations):* Rear Adm Simon Moore
*Assistant Under Secretary of State (Home and
Overseas):* Simon Webb
Gulf Veterans' Illnesses Unit: Christopher Baker
Chief of the Defence Staff (Logistics):
Gen Sir Sam Cowan KCB CBE
Policy Director: Richard Hatfield
*Assistant Under-Secretary of State (Service
Personnel):* Desmond Bowen
NATO European Policy Group:
Brig Jim Dutton
Assistant Chief of the Defence Staff (Policy):
Maj Gen J G Reith CB
Director of Defence Policy: Patrick Turner
*Deputy Under Secretary of State (Civilian
Management):* Michael Legge
*Assistant Under Secretary of State (Civilian
Management):* Brian Taylor
*Assistant Under Secretary (Security and
Support):* (Security – name withheld)
Legal Adviser: Martin Hemming
*Director-General Information and
Communications Services:* Andrew Sleigh
*Joint Service Command and Staff College
(Bracknell):* Air Vice-Marshal B K Burridge

CHIEFS OF STAFF
Chief of the Defence Staff:
General Sir Charles Guthrie GCB LVO OBE
ADC Gen (until February 2001); Admiral Sir
Michael Boyce GCB CBE (from February
2001)
Chief of Naval Staff and First Sea Lord:
Adm Sir Michael Boyce GCB CBE (until
February 2001); Adm Sir Nigel Essenhigh
(from February 2001)
Assistant Chief of the Naval Staff:
Rear Adm J M Burnett-Nugent CBE
Chief of the General Staff: Gen Sir Michael
Walker GCB CMG ADC Gen
Assistant Chief of the General Staff:
Maj Gen Kevin O'Donohue CBE
Director-General Development and Doctrine:
Maj Gen Christopher Elliott KCB
Chief of the Air Staff:
Air Chief Marshal Sir Peter Squire
Assistant Chief of the Air Staff:
Air Vice-Marshal Philip Sturley MBE

British-American Community Relations: Air
Marshal Sir John Kemball (rtd) KCB CBE
Chief Executive, National Air Traffic Services:
William Semple
Directorate of Airspace Policy:
Air Vice-Marshal J R D Arscott

DEFENCE INTELLIGENCE STAFF
Chief of Defence Intelligence:
Vice-Admiral Sir Alan West KCB DSC
*Director Intelligence Programmes and
Resources:* P I Bailey
*Director Defence Intelligence Secretariat and
Communications Information Sytems:*
C A Younger
*Deputy Chief of Defence Intelligence
Defence Intelligence Analysis Staff:* A J Cragg
Director Regional Assessments:
Brig N J Cottam OBE
Director Intelligence Global Issue:
J M Cunningham
Director Intelligence Scientific and Technical:
P H West
*Director General Intelligence and Geographic
Resources:* Air Vice-Marshal J C French CBE

DEFENCE SCIENTIFIC STAFF
Chief Scientific Adviser:
Prof Sir Keith O'Nions FRS
*Deputy Under-Secretary of State (Science and
Technology):* Graham Jordan

SECOND SEA LORD/COMMANDER-IN-CHIEF
NAVAL HOME COMMAND
*Second Sea Lord/Commander-in-Chief Naval
Home Command:*
Vice-Adm Sir Peter Spencer ADC
*Director-General Naval Personnel Strategy and
Plans:* Rear Adm Peter Dunt
Flag Officer Training and Recruiting:
Rear Adm John Chadwick
Medical Director-General (Naval):
Surg Rear Adm I L Jenkins

CINC FLEET (INCLUDING CGRM)
Commander in Chief Fleet – Cincfleet:
Adm Nigel Essenhigh KCB; to be replaced by
Vice-Adm Sir Alan West
Deputy Commander Fleet and Chief of Staff:
Vice-Adm F Malbon
*Chief of Staff Operations and Flag Officer
Submarines:* Rear Adm R P Stevens OBE
Flag Officer Surface Flotilla:
Rear Adm I A Forbes CBE
Commander UK Task Group:
Rear Adm S R Meyer

Flag Officer Naval Aviation:
Rear Adm I R Henderson CBE
Commandant-General Royal Marines:
Maj Gen R H Fulton
Flag Officer, Sea Training:
Rear Adm Alexander Backus
Commodore Royal Fleet Auxiliary:
Commodore P J Lannin RFA

ADJUTANT GENERAL'S DEPARTMENT
Headquarters Adjutant General
(Personnel and Training Command)
Adjutant General:
Lt Gen Timothy Granville Chapman
Chief of Staff to the Adjutant General:
Maj Gen Peter Currie
*Director-General Army Training and
Recruiting:* Maj Gen A M D Palmer CBE
Directorate General Army Medical Services:
Maj Gen R C Menzies
Director-General Development and Doctrine:
Maj-Gen C L Elliot
Directorate of Army Legal Services:
Maj Gen G Risius
Military Secretary: Maj Gen Alastair Irwin CBE
HQ Advisory: Brig P J Bryant
Headquarters Army Personnel Centre:
Maj Gen David Burden CBE
*Directorate of Individual Training Policy
(Army):* Brig J P Weller
Royal Military Academy Sandhurst:
Maj Gen A G Denaro CBE
Royal Military College of Science:
Maj Gen J C B Sutherell CBE ADC

CINCLAND
Commander-in-Chief Land Command:
General Sir Mike Jackson
Deputy Commander-in-Chief Land Command:
Lt Gen J F Deverell KCB OBE
Chief of Staff Headquarters Land Command:
Maj Gen F R Viggers MBE
*Deputy Chief of Staff Headquarters Land
Command:* Maj Gen Peter Chambers

STRIKE COMMAND
Commander-in-Chief (Strike Command): Air
Chief Marshal Sir Anthony Bagnall KCB
OBE ADC FRAeS
Deputy Commander-in-Chief (Strike Command):
Air Marshal Sir Timothy Jenner KCB FRAeS
Deputy Chief of Staff (Operations):
Air Vice-Marshal N Sudborough
*Air Officer (Logistcs and CIS) (Strike
Command):* Air Vice-Marshal P J Scott

Air Officer Administration (Strike Command):
Air Vice-Marshal A G Burton OBE
Command Secretariat (Strike Command):
C J Wright
Air Officer Commanding 1 Group:
Air Vice-Marshal P Harris AFC FRAeS
Air Officer Commanding 2 Group:
Air Vice-Marshal K D Filbey CBE
Air Officer Commanding 3 Group:
(Joint Force 2000):
Rear Adm I R Henderson CBE

HEADQUARTERS LOGISTIC COMMAND (RAF)
DISBANDED 31 MARCH 2000
SEA DEFENCE LOGISTICS ORGANISATION

PERSONNEL AND TRAINING COMMAND (RAF)
Air Member for Personnel Commander in Chief:
Air Marshal John Day KCB OBE FRAeS
Air Officer Commanding and Commandant
RAF College Cranwell: Air Vice-Marshal
Bill Rimmer OBE MA FRAeS
Directorate General Medical Services:
Air Vice-Marshal C J Sharples QHP MS
FFOM MRCS LRCP DArmed MRAeS
Clinical Director: Air Cdre D J Rainford MBE
MB BS FRCP MRCS
Directorate of RAF Legal Services:
Air Vice-Marshal J Weeden LLB
Command Secretary: L D Kyle

Executive Agencies: Armed Forces Personnel Administration Agency (AFPAA); Army Base Repair Organisation (ABRO); Army Personnel Centre (APC); Army Training and Recruiting Agency (ATRA); British Forces Post Office (BFPO); Defence Analytical Services Agency (DASA); Defence Aviation Repair Agency (DARA); Defence Bills Agency (DBA), Defence Clothing and Textiles Agency (DCTA); Defence Communication Services Agency (DCSA); Defence Dental Agency (DDA); Defence Estates (DE); Defence Evaluation and Research Agency (DERA); Defence Geographic and Imagery Intelligence Agency (DGIA); Defence Housing Executive (DHE); Defence Intelligence and Security Centre (DISC); Defence Medical Training Organisation (DMTO); Defence Procurement Agency (DPA); Defence Secondary Care Agency (DSCA); Defence Storage and Distribution Agency (DSDA); Defence Transport and Movements Agency (DTMA); Defence Vetting Agency (DVA); Disposal Sales Agency (DSA); Duke of York's Royal Military School (DYRMS); Logistic Information Systems Agency (LISA); Medical Supplies Agency (MSA); Meteoro-logical Office; Ministry of Defence Police Agency (MDP); Naval Bases and Supply Agency (NBSA); Naval Manning Agency (NMA); Naval Recruiting and Training Agency (NRTA); Pay and Personnel Agency (PPA), Queen Victoria School (QVS); RAF Personnel Management Agency (RAFPMA); RAF Training Group Defence Agency (RAF TGDA); Service Children's Education (SCE); Ships Support Agency (SSA); UK Hydrographic Office (UKHO)

Department for Education and Employment

Sanctuary Buildings, Great Smith Street,
London SW1P 3BT

Caxton House, Tothill Street,
London SW1H 9NA

Moorfoot, Sheffield S1 4PQ

East Lane, Runcorn WA7 2DN

Mowden Hall, Staindrop Road,
Darlington DL3 9BG

Press Office: 020 7925 5106
Information Office: 020 7925 5189
Main switchboard: 0870 0012345
Website: www.dfee.gov.uk
E-mail: dfee.ministers@dfee.gov.uk for all ministers

Responsible for ensuring that all young people reach 16 equipped for lifelong learning, work and citizenship; developing in everyone a commitment to lifelong learning; helping people wihout a job into work.

Secretary of State:
Rt Hon David Blunkett MP
Parliamentary Private Secretaries:
Jean Corston MP,
Alan Whitehead MP
Special Advisers: Conor Ryan, Tom Engel,
Nick Pearce, Leala Padmanabhan
Minister of State (Minister for Employment,
Welfare to Work and Equal Opportunities):
Rt Hon Tessa Jowell MP
Parliamentary Private Secretary: Jeff Ennis MP
Minister of State (Minister for School
Standards): Rt Hon Estelle Morris MP
Parliamentary Private Secretary:
Rachel Squire MP
Minister of State (Minister for Education and
Employment (Lords):
Baroness Blackstone

Parliamentary Private Secretary:
Alan Whitehead MP

*Parliamentary Under-Secretary of State
(Lifelong Learning):* Malcolm Wicks MP

*Parliamentary Under-Secretary of State
(Employment and Equal Opportunities):*
Margaret Hodge MBE MP

*Parliamentary Under-Secretary of State (School
Standards):* Jacqueline Smith MP

Parliamentary Under-Secretary of State:
Michael Wills MP

Spokespersons in the House of Lords: Baroness
Blackstone, Lord Bach

Permanent Secretary: Sir Michael Bichard KCB
Parliamentary Clerk: John Major

CORPORATE SERVICES AND DEVELOPMENT DIRECTORATE
Director: Hilary Douglas
Divisional Managers
Training and Development Division:
Jim Gordon
Information Systems Division: Ray Hinchcliffe
Leadership and Change Division:
Graham Archer
Personnel Division: Mike Ship
Facilities Management: Les Webb
Procurement and Contracting: Paul Neill
Equal Opportunities Unit: Nick Parker *(acting)*

FINANCE AND ANALYTICAL SERVICES DIRECTORATE
Director-General: Peter Shaw CB
Director Analytical Services: Denis Allnutt
Divisional Managers
*Analytical Services – Equal Opportunities and
Research Programme:* Richard Bartholomew
*Analytical Services – Employability and Adult
Learning:* Bob Butcher
*Analytical Services – Qualifications, Pupil
Assessment and IT Support:* Malcolm Britton
*Analytical Services – Youth and Further
Education:* John Elliott
*Analytical Services – Higher Education
Evaluation Strategy and International:*
Simon Field
*Analytical Services – Schools, Teachers and
Resources:* Audrey Brown
Efficiency: Rob Wye
Financial Accounting: Peter Connor
Programmes: Carol Hunter
Planning and Expenditure: Susanna Todd
Capital Investment: Stephen Burt
Internal Audit: Neville Thirtle

SCHOOLS DIRECTORATE
Director-General: David Normington CB
*Director School Organisation and Funding
Group:* Helen Williams
Divisional Managers
School and LEA Funding: Andrew Wye
*Schools Admissions Organisation and
Governance:* Caroline Macready
LEA Support: Elizabeth Wylie
Schools Capital and Buildings: Ken Beeton
Architects and Building: Mukund Patel
Director Teachers Group: Peter Makeham
Divisional Managers
Teacher Development: Richard Harrison
School Leadership: Christina Bienkowska
School Teachers' Pay and Policy:
Anne Jackson
Teachers Standards and Pensions: Penny Jones
Teacher Supply and Training: Graham Holley
Director, Pupils Support and Inclusion Group:
Rob Smith
Divisional Managers
Special Educational Needs: Chris Wells
School Plus: Anne-Marie Lawlor,
Ms Susan Johnson
Pupil Support and Independent Schools:
Michael D Phipps
School Inclusion: Barnaby Shaw
Early Years: Alan Cranston
Head of Standards and Effectiveness Unit:
Prof Michael Barber
Divisional Managers
Pupil Standards: Sandy Adamson
LEA Improvement: Sheila Scales
School Improvement: Stephen Crowne
Diversity and Best Practice: Jane Benham
Excellence in Cities Unit: Chris Wormald
*Director, Curriculum and Communications
Group:* Imogen Wilde
Divisional Managers
Curriculum: Ian Berry
Schools Communications: Stuart Edwards
Parents and Performance: Nick Baxter
NGFL – National Grid for Learning Division:
Doug Brown
ICT Strategy Unit: Dick Palmer
Sure Start Unit: Naomi Eisenstadt

LIFELONG LEARNING DIRECTORATE
Director-General: Nick Stuart
Director-General: Roger Dawe
Director: John Hedger
Millennium Volunteers: Anne Weinstock
Quality and Financial Assurance: Susan Orr
Resources and Budget Management:
Paul Holme

Director, Learning Quality and Delivery Group:
Peter Lauener
Divisional Managers
LSC Implementation: Jim Reid
LSC/ALI Information and Business Systems:
Michael Stock
LSC Policy Structure and Appointments:
Peter Mucklow
Post-16 Legislation: Andrew McCully
Post-16 Implementation: Peter Houten
Director, Adult Learning Group: Derek Grover
Divisional Managers
Basic Skills Unit: Vacant
BSA Quinquennial Review: Peter Thorpe
Individuals Learning: Tim Down
Lifelong Learning and Technologies:
Jeanette Pugh
National Training Organisations: John Fuller
Skills Unit: John Temple
Workplace Learning: Linda Ammon
Director, Higher Education Group: Nick Sanders
Divisional Managers
HE Funding and Organisation Division:
Michael Hipkins
Student Support 1 Division: Neil Flint
Student Support 2 Division: Berverly Evans
HE Quality and Employability Division:
Paul Cohen
Director, Qualifications: Rob Hull
Divisional Managers
Qualifications for Work Division: John West
School and College Qualifications Division:
Celia Johnson
Review of Support for Adult Learning:
Michael Stark
Director, Further Education and Youth Training:
David Forrester
Divisional Managers
Connexions Unit: Claire Tyler
FE Funding and Organisation: Stephen Hillier
FE and 16-19 Student Support: Trevor Fellowes
Partnership Skills and Young People:
Alan Davies
Standards, Quality and Access: Alan Clarke
Youth Support Service Implementation:
Steve Geary

EMPLOYMENT, EQUALITY AND
INTERNATIONAL RELATIONS
DIRECTORATE
Director-General: Clive Tucker

The Directorate is the main link for the
Department to:
the Employment Service;
the Commission for Racial Equality;
Investors in People UK;
the Basic Skills Agency;

the National Council for the Employment of
Disabled People;
the Equal Opportunities Commission;
the new National Disabilities Council;
the Management Charter Initiative;
the National Council for Education Technology.

New Deal for Young People.
Fax: 020 7925 5091
Enquiry Point: 020 7925 6943
Director, Employment Policy:
Michael J Richardson
Divisional Managers
Economy and Labour Market: Bill Wells
Sructural Unemployment Policy: Jeremy Moore
Welfare to Work: Chris Barnham
Adult Disadvantage Policy Division: Eric Galvin
Learning and Work Bank Project: Neil Atkinson
DfEE/ES New Agency Division: Mike Daly
Director, Opportunity and Diversity Group:
Shirley Trundle
Divisional Managers
Overseas Labour: Martyn Craske
Disability Policy: Liz Tillett
Child Care Unit: Caroline Slocock
Sex and Race Equality: Jenny Eastabrook
Director, International: Clive Tucker
Divisional Managers
International Relations: Marie Niven
European Union: Win Harris
European Social Fund: Elaine Trewartha
New Deal Task Force Secretariat: Gay Stratton

STRATEGY AND COMMUNICATIONS
DIRECTORATE
Director: Peter Wanless
Communications and Knowledge Management
Division: Caroline Bicknell
Divisional Managers
Speeches and General Briefing: Vacant
Strategy: Vacant
Media Relations: Julia Simpson
Media Relations: Trevor Cook
Publicity: John Ross
Welfare to Work: Yasmin Diamond
Regional Policy Division: Gordon McKenzie

LEGAL ADVISER'S OFFICE
Legal Adviser: Donald Macrae
Divisional Managers
Schools: Simon Harker
Post 16: Francis Clarke
HE, Teachers and Support Directorates:
Alan Preston
Equality and External: Deborah Collins
Standards and Effectiveness: Patrick Kilgarriff

Executive Agency: Employment Service

Department of the Environment, Transport and the Regions

The Department of the Environment, Transport and the Regions is mainly based in 3 Central London locations:

Eland House
Bressenden Place, London SW1E 5DU
020 7944 3000

Ashdown House
123 Victoria Street, London SW1E 6DE
020 7944 3000

Great Minster House
76 Marsham Street, London SW1P 4DR
020 7944 3000
Website: www.detr.gov.uk

To protect and improve the environment, and to integrate the environment with other policies across government and in international fora.

To offer everyone the opportunity of a decent home.

To promote efficient and integrated transport services across different modes and reduce road traffic growth.

To deliver regulatory and other transport services to the public and industry.

To enhance opportunity in rural areas, improve enjoyment of the countryside and conserve and manage wildlife resources.

To create a fair and efficient land use planning system.

To promote a system of elected local government in England.

To promote economic development and social cohesion throughout England through effective regional action and integrated local regeneration programmes.

To ensure an efficient market in the construction industry.

To improve health and safety by reducing risks from work activity, travel and the environment.

Deputy Prime Minister and Secretary of State:
  Rt Hon John Prescott MP
Parliamentary Private Secretary:
  John Heppell MP
Special Advisers: Joe Irvin, Joan Hammell
Minister of State (Minister for Transport):
  Rt Hon Lord Macdonald of Tradeston CBE
Parliamentary Private Secretary:
  Phil Woolas MP
Special Adviser: Adrian Long

Minister of State (Minister for the Environment):
  Rt Hon Michael Meacher MP
Parliamentary Private Secretary:
  Terry Rooney MP
*Minister of State (Minister for Local
  Government and Regions):*
  Rt Hon Hilary Armstrong MP
Parliamentary Private Secretary:
  Sally Keeble MP
Special Adviser: David Wilson
*Minister of State (Minister for Housing,
  Planning and Construction):*
  Nick Raynsford MP
Parliamentary Private Secretary:
  Phil Hope MP
Parliamentary Under-Secretary of State:
  Chris Mullin MP
Special Adviser: Paul Hackett
Parliamentary Under-Secretary of State:
  Keith Hill, MP
Parliamentary Under-Secretary of State:
  Lord Whitty
Parliamentary Under-Secretary of State:
  Beverley Hughes MP
Parliamentary Clerk: Paul Davies

Spokespersons in the House of Lords: Lord Macdonald, Lord Whitty, Baroness Farrington (Local Government)

Permanent Secretary:
  Sir Richard Mottram KCB

Parliamentary Branch:
(Ministers) 020 7944 3019
Ministerial Correspondence Section:
020 7944 3085

DIRECTORATE OF COMMUNICATION
Director: Alun Evans
*Deputy Director (Marketing and Corporate
  Communication):* Charles Skinner
Deputy Director (Media Centre): Jane Groom

ENVIRONMENTAL PROTECTION GROUP
Director-General: Dinah Nichols CB

ENERGY, ENVIRONMENT AND WASTE
DIRECTORATE
Director: Phillip Ward
Leslie Packer, David Vincent, Bob Ryder,
  Terence Ilott, Duncan Prior, Sue Ellis,
  Simon Hewitt

ENVIRONMENT: RISKS AND ATMOSPHERE
Director: Henry Derwent
Martin Williams, Peter Hinchcliffe, Pete Betts,
  Martin Hurst, Richard Wood

ENVIRONMENT PROTECTION STRATEGY
DIRECTORATE
Director: Andrew Burchell
Robin Wilson, Hilary Hillier, John Adams,
  Sheila McCabe, Joan Bailey, James Bradley,
  Patricia Hayes

WATER AND LAND DIRECTORATE
Director: Alan Davis
Michael Rouse, Alan Simcock, Stuart Hoggan,
  Rodney Anderson

FINANCE GROUP
Director and Principal Finance Officer:
  John Ballard
Alan Beard, Campbell Arnott, Ken Arnold,
  Peter McCarthy, Andrew Lean

URBAN AND RURAL POLICY, HOUSING
AND CONSTRUCTION
Director-General: Genie Turton CB

HOUSING
Director: Michael Gahagan CB
Hilary Chipping, Philip Cox, Bruce Oelman,
  Michael Faulkner, Richard Horsman,
  Martin Jones, Judith Littlewood CBE,
  Nick Murphy, Bert Provan

CONSTRUCTION DIRECTORATE
Director: John Hobson
Paul Everall, John Stambollouian,
  Nigel Dorling, Bob Davies

ROUGH SLEEPERS' UNIT
Director: Louise Casey

WILDLIFE AND COUNTRYSIDE DIRECTORATE
Director: Sophia Lambert
Susan Carter, Roger Pritchard, Chris Braun,
  Henry Cleary

REGENERATION DIRECTORATE
Director: Paul Evans
John Roberts, Jon Bright, Lisette Simcock,
  Paul Houston

LEGAL GROUP
Director-General: David Hogg CB

COUNTRYSIDE, PLANNING AND TRANSPORT
Director: Sandra Unerman
Nigel Lefton, Gloria Hedley-Dent,
  Richard Lines, Alan Jones, Judith-
  Anne MacKenzie, Hussein Kaya,
  David Ingham

COMMERCIAL, ENVIRONMENT, HOUSING AND
LOCAL GOVERNMENT
Director: Christopher Muttukumaru
John Comber, Pamela Conlon,
  Donatella Phillips, Dudley Aries,
  David Jordan, Neil Thomas, John Wright

ENVIRONMENT (INTERNATIONAL AND EU)
Director: Patrick Széll
Alistair McGlone

LEGISLATIVE UNIT
Director: Allan Roberts

LOCAL AND REGIONAL GOVERNMENT
GROUP
Director-General: Philip Wood CB

LOCAL GOVERNMENT DIRECTORATE
Director: Andrew Whetnall
Paul Rowsell, Richard Footitt, Tony Redpath,
  Terry Crossley

LOCAL GOVERNMENT FINANCE POLICY
DIRECTORATE
Director: Mark Lambirth
Richard Gibson, Ian Scotter, Meg Green,
  Pam Williams, Stephen Claughton

TRANSPORT STRATEGY
Director-General: Willy Rickett
Director: Diane Phillips CB
Iain Todd, Bronwyn Hill, Lucy Robinson,
  Daniel Hulls

MOBILITY AND INCLUSION UNIT
Divisional Manager: Ann Frye

PLANNING DIRECTORATE
Director: Jeff Jacobs
Lester Hicks, Mike Ash, Jeff Channing,
  Alan Oliver, Martin Leigh-Pollitt,
  Christopher Bowden

ROADS AND TRAFFIC DIRECTORATE
Director: Dennis Roberts
Neil McDonald, Mike Talbot, Tom Worsley,
  Roger Donachie

INTEGRATED AND LOCAL TRANSPORT
Director: Richard Bird
Edward Neve, Mike Walsh, Kevin Lloyd,
    Andrew Whybrow, Peter Capell

ROAD SAFETY AND ENVIRONMENT
Director: John Plowman
Roger Peal, Malcolm Fendick, Richard Jones,
    Tim Carter, Martin Brasher

RAILWAYS, AVIATION LOGISTICS AND
MARITIME
Director-General: David Rowlands CB

RAILWAYS
Director: Bob Linnard
Peter Thomas, Stuart Connolly, Alison Munro,
    Mark Coulshed

LOGISTICS AND MARITIME TRANSPORT
Director: Brian Wadsworth
Rear Adm John Lang, Mike Hughes,
    Angela Moss, David Liston-Jones,
    Stephen Reeves, Frank Wall, David Cooke,
    David Rowe, Clive Young, Thomas Allan

AVIATION
Director: Roy Griffins
Tony Baker, Mike Smethers, Michael Fawcett,
    Elizabeth Duthie, Michael Mann,
    Ian McBrayne, David McMillan
Ken Smart CBE

LONDON UNDERGROUND TASK FORCE GROUP
Director: Mike Fuhr
Richard Bennett, Ian Jordan, Beth Ann Bostock

TRANSPORT SECURITY
Director: David Lord
William Gillan

REGIONAL CO-ORDINATION UNIT
Director-General: Rob Smith
Regional Co-ordination Directorate
Director: Andrew Wells
Mike Ross
Bob Dinwiddy
Jan Scoones

STRATEGY AND CORPORATE SERVICES
GROUP
Director-General: Richard Dudding
Directors: Ian Harris, Gareth Jones, Ray Long

HUMAN RESOURCES
Director: Hazel Parker-Brown
Mike Bailey, Sandy Bishop, Eddie Gibbons,
    Peter Walton

CENTRAL STRATEGY (AND CHIEF SCIENTIST)
Director: David Fisk CBE
John Stevens, Alan Apling, Graham Pendlebury,
    John Grubb, Ian Heawood

CHIEF ECONOMIST
Director: Chris Riley
Elizabeth Cleary, Nigel Campbell

Executive Agencies: Driver and Vehicle
Licensing Agency (DVLA); Driving Standards
Agency (DSA); Highways Agency; Maritime
and Coastguard Agency (MCA); Ordnance
Survey; Planning Inspectorate (PINS); Queen
Elizabeth II Conference Centre; The Rent
Service (TRS); Vehicle Certification Agency
(VCA); Vehicle Inspectorate (VI)

Export Credits Guarantee Department

PO Box 2200
2 Exchange Tower,
Harbour Exchange Square,
London E14 9GS
020 7512 7000 *Fax:* 020 7512 7649
Telex: 290350 ECGD HQ G
Website: www.ecgd.gov.uk

Its main role is to assist the export of UK capital
and project-related goods by providing exporters
with insurance against the commercial and political risks of not being paid by their buyers.
ECGD also guarantees the repayment of bank
loans to overseas borrowers which finance the
purchase of UK goods and services and insures
UK investors against the political risks of not
receiving earnings from their overseas investments. ECGD reinsurance is available for private
sector insurers who cover the export of UK
goods sold on credit terms of less than two years.

MINISTERS
Secretary of State for Trade and Industry:
    Rt Hon Stephen Byers MP
Minister for Trade: Rt Hon Richard Caborn MP
Chief Executive: Vivian Brown

STRATEGY AND COMMUNICATIONS
Director: John Ormerod

UNDERWRITING GROUP
Group Director: John Weiss
Directors: Steve Dodgson, Roger Gotts,
    Chris Leeds, Mike Pentecost, Gordon Welsh

ASSET MANAGEMENT GROUP
Group Director: Victor Lunn-Rockliffe
Directors: Ross Lethbridge, John Snowdon, Linda Woods

RESOURCE MANAGEMENT GROUP
Group Director and Principal Establishment and Finance Officer: Tom Jaffray
Directors: Pat Callaghan, Graham Cassell, Jimmy Croall, Richard Healey, Ruth Kaufman, Paul Radford, Eric Walsby

LEGAL BRANCH
ECGD General Counsel: Nicholas Ridley

EXPORT GUARANTEES ADVISORY COUNCIL
Chairman: D H A Harrison CBE

Foreign and Commonwealth Office HM Diplomatic Service

Whitehall, London SW1A 2AH
020 7270 1500
Consular/Travel Advice: 020 7238 4503/4
Media Section Information:
E-mail: newmedia@info.mail.fco.gov.uk
Website: www.fco.gov.uk

Telegraphic address: Prodrome, London
Telex: 297711 (a/b PRDRME G)

Provides, mainly through diplomatic missions, the means of communication between Her Majesty's Government and other governments and international organisations in the field of international relations. It is responsible for alerting the Government to the implications of developments overseas; for protecting British interests overseas; for protecting British citizens abroad; for explaining British policies to, and cultivating friendly relations with, Governments overseas and for the discharge of British responsibilities to the overseas territories.

Secretary of State (Foreign Secretary):
Rt Hon Robin Cook MP
Parliamentary Private Secretary:
Ken Purchase MP
Special Advisers: David Clark,
David Mathieson, Michael Williams

Minister of State: Peter Hain MP

Minister of State: John Battle MP

Minister of State for Europe: Keith Vaz MP

Parliamentary Under-Secretary of State:
Baroness Scotland of Asthal QC

Parliamentary Private Secretaries to the Ministers: Denis MacShane MP, Rosemary McKenna MP, Caroline Flint MP

Spokespersons in the House of Lords: Baroness Scotland, Baroness Ramsay

Permanent Under-Secretary and Head of HM Diplomatic Service: Sir John Kerr KCMG
Chief Executive British Trade International:
Sir David Wright KCMG LVO
Deputy Under-Secretaries of State
Christopher Hum CMG (Chief Clerk)
Colin Budd CMG (Director for EU and Economic Affairs)
Stephen Wright CMG
Emyr Jones Parry CMG (Political Director)
Peter Westmacott CMG LVO
Michael Wood CMG (Legal Adviser)
Directors
Mike Lyall Grant (Africa and the Commonwealth)
Vacant (Wider Europe)
Kim Darroch (European Union)
R E Dibble (General Services)
Tony Brenton (Global Issues)
William Ehrman (International Security)
Alan Goulty (Middle East and North Africa)
David Hall (Overseas Trade)
Denise Holt (Personnel)
Charles Crawford CMG (Deputy Political Director)
David Reddaway (Public Services)
Peter Collecott (Resources)
Rosalind Marsden (Asia Pacific)
Richard Wilkinson (Americas)

HEADS OF DEPARTMENTS
African (Equatorial): Frank Baker
African (Southern): Neil Chrimes
Aviation and Maritime: Norman Ling
Diplomatic Service Families Association:
Agnes Budd
Central North and West European:
Sir John Ramsden
Change Management Unit: Sheena Matthews
China and Hong Kong: Tony Sprake
Commonwealth Co-ordination: Colin Bright
Common Foreign and Security Policy:
Colin Roberts
Conference and Visits (Acting Head):
James Clark
Consular Division: James Watt
Counter Terrorism Policy Department:
Keith Bloomfield
Cultural Relations: Dr Michael Reilly

DS Whitley Council (TUS): P May
Drugs and International Crime: Michael Ryder
Eastern Adriatic Dept: Stephen Wordsworth
Eastern: Vacant
Economic Relations: Creon Butler
Environment, Science and Energy: John Ashton
Estates Command: Boyd McCleary
European Unit (Bilateral):
    Jeremy Cresswell CVO
European Union (External): Simon Featherstone
European Union (Internal): James Bevan
Financial Compliance Dept: Mike Purves
Financial Policy: Mike Brown
Government Hospitality Fund:
    Robert Alexanders
Human Rights Policy: Dr Carolyn Browne
Information: Peter Dun
Information Systems Division: Nigel Stickells
Internal Audit: Roger Elias
Invest in Britain Bureau: Andrew Fraser
Joint Export Promotion Directorate.
    Ian Fletcher
Latin America and Caribbean: John Dew
Legal Adviser: Michael Wood, CMG
Information Management Group:
    John Thompson MBE
Management Consultancy Services: Vivien Life
Middle East: William Patey
Joint Entry Clearance Unit (JECU):
    Robert Brinkley
National Audit Office: John Pearce
Near East and North Africa:
    Christopher Prentice
News: Vacant
Non-Proliferation: Paul Hare
North America: Philip Priestley CBE
North East Asia and Pacific: Peter Carter
Overseas Territories: John White
*Organisation for Security and Co-operation in
    Europe:* Alan Huckle
*Parliamentary Relations and Devolution
    Department:* Mark Hutton
Prosper: Colin J Edgerton OBE
Personnel Management: Peter Jones
Personnel Services: Richard Fell
Personnel Policy Unit: Scott Wightman
Policy Planning Staff: Richard Clarke
Protocol: Kathryn Colvin
Purchasing Directorate: Michael Gower
Research Analysts: Stuart Jack, Richard Lavers
Resource Planning: Martin Williamson
Security: Tom Duggin
Security Policy: Adam Thomson
Services, Planning and Resources Dept:
    Joan Link
South Asian: Stephen Evans

Records and Historical Department:
    Heather Yasamee
South-East Asian: Robert Gordon
Southern European: Jeremy Hill
Support Services: Michael Carr
United Nations: Stephen Pattison
Whitehall Liaison Department: Lyn Parker

Executive Agency: Wilton Park

Government Offices for the Regions

The Government Offices for the Regions were established in April 1994. There are 9 Government Offices, which combine the former regional offices of the Departments of the Environment, Transport and the Regions, (previously Department of Environment and Transport), Trade and Industry and Education and Employment (previously the Employment Department). The offices deliver Government programmes, such as Technology Development and Training and Enterprise. They are also responsible for planning and transport issues. Each Government Office is headed by a Regional Director who is accountable to the Secretary of States of all the Government Departments.

REGIONAL CO-ORDINATION UNIT
2nd Floor, Riverwalk House
157-161 Millbank, London SW1P 4RR
020 7217 3595 *Fax:* 020 7217 3590

The purposes of the unit are to: consider Government initiatives with a regional or local dimension; promote closer links between government activity in the regions and the centre; and to provide operational support to the Government Offices for the Regions. The Unit is an inter-Departmental one, reporting from 1 April 2001 at official level to the Permanent Secretary, DETR. Lord Falconer, Cabinet Office Minister, has day to day ministerial responsibility for the unit, reporting to the Deputy Prime Minister.

Director-General: Rob Smith
Director: Andrew Wells
Divisional Managers:
RCU Operations: Jan Scoones
    (Secretariat; personnel and pay policy, finance and IT)
RCU Development: Bob Dinwiddy
    (Area-based initiative co-ordination, cross-departmental integration)
RCU Transition: Mike Ross
    (Finance review of Government Offices and pay and personnel review of Government Offices)

EAST OF ENGLAND
Building A, Westbrook Centre
Milton Road, Cambridge CB4 1YG
01223 346700 *Fax:* 01223 346701
E-mail:
customerservices.goe@go-regions.gsi.gov.uk
Website: www.go-east.gov.uk

Victory House, Vision Park, Histon
Cambridge CB4 9ZR
01223 202000 *Fax:* 01223 202020

Heron House, 49–53 Goldington Road
Bedford MK40 3LL
01234 796332 *Fax:* 01234 796230

Regional Director (Westbrook Centre):
  Alan Riddell
  E-mail: ariddell.goe@go-regions.gsi.gov.uk
Director Strategy and Resources (Westbrook Centre): Chris Beesley
  E-mail: cbeesley.goe@go-regions.gsi.gov.uk
Director Economic Development (Westbrook Centre): Martin Oldham
  E-mail: moldham.goe@go-regions.gsi.gov.uk
Director Skills and Enterprise (Victory House):
  John Street
  E-mail: jstreet.goe@go-regions.gsi.gov.uk
Director Planning and Transport (Heron House): Caroline Bowdler
  E-mail: cbowdler.goe@go-regions.gsi.gov.uk
Director Housing, Regeneration and Environment (Heron House): Chris Dunabin
  E-mail: cdunabin.goe@go-regions.gsi.gov.uk

EAST MIDLANDS
The Belgrave Centre, Stanley Place,
Talbot Street, Nottingham NG1 5GG
0115-971 9971 *Fax:* 0115-971 2404
E-mail: enquiries.goem@go-regions.gov.uk
Website: www.go-em.gov.uk

Regional Director: Dennis Morrison
Director Environment and Community Development: Dr Stephen Kennett
Director, Corporate Affairs: Robert Smith
Director Competitiveness and European Policy:
  Roger Poole
Director Skills and Enterprise: Scott McIntyre
Director, Regional Crime Reduction:
  Stephen Brookes

LONDON
Riverwalk House, 157–161 Millbank
London SW1P 4RR
020 7217 3456 *Fax:* 020 7217 3450
E-mail:
enquiries-london.gol@go-regions.gov.uk
Website: www.go-london.gov.uk

Acting Joint Regional Directors: John Owen,
  Joyce Bridges
GLA Liaison, Environment and Corporate Directorate: Joyce Bridges
Skills, Education and Regeneration Directorate:
  John Owen
Division Head Corporate: Corinne Lyons
Division Head London Government and Europe Programmes: Sarah Ebanja
Head of Division, London Co-ordination and Environment: Andrew Melville
Division Head of Trade and Industry:
  Ken Timmins
Division Head of Skills and Education:
  Andrew Sargent
Heads of Divisions for Government/GLA Unit:
  Sandra Webber, Jane Anderson
Home Office Liaison: Bertie Mann

NORTH EAST
Wellbar House, Gallowgate,
Newcastle upon Tyne NE1 4TD
0191-201 3300 *Fax:* 0191-202 3998
E-mail: general.enquiries.gone@go-regions.gsi.gov.uk
Website: www.go-ne.gov.uk

Regional Director: Dr Bob Dobbie CB
Director Education, Skills, Enterprise and Regeneration: Miss Denise Caudle
Director Europe, Industry, Trade and Technology: Tony Dell
Director Planning Environment and Transport:
  Jim Darlington
Director Strategy and Resources:
  Mrs Diana Pearce

NORTH WEST
Sunley Tower, Piccadilly Plaza
Manchester M1 4BE
0161-952 4000 *Fax:* 0161-952 4099
Website: www.go-nw.gov.uk

Washington House, New Bailey Street,
Manchester M3 5ER
0161-952 4000 *Fax:* 0161-952 4169

Cunard Building, Pier Head
Liverpool L3 1QB
0151-224 6300 *Fax:* 0151-224 6470

Regional Director: Keith Barnes
Director, Corporate Services: David Hopewell
Director, Environment and Planning and Strategy: Eira Hughes
Director, Housing and Transport: Peter Styche
Director, Business and Europe:
  Dr David Higham

Director, Europe: Ian Jamieson
Director, Europe (Merseyside): John Flamson
Director, Skills and Enterprise: David Duff
Director, Operations: Mike Hill
Director, New Business: Nigel Burke
Director, Regional Crime: David Smith

SOUTH WEST
Bristol: The Pithay, Bristol BS1 2PB
0117-900 1700 *Fax:* 0117-900 1900
Website: www.gosw.gov.uk

Plymouth: Mast House, Shepherds Wharf
24 Sutton Road, Plymouth PL4 0HJ
01752 635000 *Fax:* 01752 227647

Regional Director: Jane Henderson
Director Environment and Regeneration:
    Celia Carrington
Director Competitiveness and Skills:
    Thoss Shearer
Director Devon and Cornwall (Plymouth):
    Richard Bayly
Director Corporate Services: Malcolm Davey

SOUTH EAST
Bridge House, 1 Walnut Tree Close
Guildford, Surrey GU1 4GA
01483 882255 *Fax:* 01483 882259
E-mail: [firstinitialandsurname].gose@
go-regions.gov.uk

Regional Director: David Saunders
Area Director, Hants/IoW: Colin Byrne
Area Director, Berks/Oxon/Bucks: Nick Wilson
Area Director, Surrey/E Sussex/W Sussex:
    David Andrews
Area Director, Kent: Andrew Campbell
Director, Regional Strategy Team:
    Charlotte Dixon
Director, Finance and Corporate Management:
    Peter Craggs
Director, Crime and Reduction: Hugh Marriage

WEST MIDLANDS
77 Paradise Circus Queensway
Birmingham B1 2DT
0121-212 5050 *Fax:* 0121-212 1010
Website: www.go-wm.gov.uk
GTN: 6177 5050

Regional Director: David Ritchie
    (*E-mail:* jwilkes.gowm@go-regions.gov.uk)
Director of Business and Learning Division:
    David Way
    (*E-mail:* dway.gowm@go-regions.gov.uk)
Director of Local Government Division:
    Philippa Holland
    (*E-mail:* pholland.gowm@go-regions.gov.uk)

*Director of Corporate Affairs and Europe
    Division:* Chris Marsh
    (*E-mail:* cmarsh.gowm@go-regions.gov.uk)

YORKSHIRE AND THE HUMBER
PO Box 213, City House,
New Station Street, Leeds LS1 4US
0113-280 0600 *Fax:* 0113-233 8301

Regional Director: Felicity Everiss
    (*E-mail:* feveriss.goyh@go-regions.gov.uk)
Director Strategy and Europe: Greg Dyche
    (*E-mail:* gdyche.goyh@go-regions.gov.uk)
Director Planning and Transport: John Jarvis
    (*E-mail:* jjarvis.goyh@go-regions.gov.uk)
Director Business Enterprise and Skills:
    Simon Perryman
    (*E-mail:* sperryman.goyh@go-regions.gov.uk)
Operations Director: Nick Best
    (*E-mail:* nbest.goyh@go-regions.gov.uk)
Director Regeneration: Margaret Jackson
    (*E-mail:* mjackson.goyh@go-regions.gov.uk)
Director Personnel and Resources:
    Martin Doxey
    (*E-mail:* mdoxey.goyh@go-regions.gov.uk)

Department of Health

Richmond House, 79 Whitehall
London SW1A 2NL
020 7210 3000 *Fax:* 020 7210 5523
Website: www.doh.gov.uk

Skipton House, 80 London Road
London SE1 6LH
020 7972 2000

Wellington House,
133–155 Waterloo Road,
London SE1 8UG
020 7972 2000

Quarry House, Quarry Hill,
Leeds LS2 7UE
0113-254 5000

Hannibal House, Elephant and Castle,
London SE1 6TE
020 7972 2000
(non MDA Staff)

Hannibal House, Elephant and Castle,
London SE1 6YA
020 7972 8000
(MDA Staff)

Market Towers, 1 Nine Elms Lane,
London SW8 5NQ
020 7273 3000

Eileen House
80–94 Newington Causeway,
London SE1 6EF
020 7972 2000

Regional Offices

Eastern Regional Office
6–12 Capital Drive, Linford Wood,
Milton Keynes MK14 6QP
01908 844400

London Regional Office
40 Eastbourne Terrace,
London W2 3QR
020 7725 5300

North West Regional Office
930–932 Birchwood Boulevard,
Millennium Park, Birchwood,
Warrington WA3 7QN
0192-570 4000

Northern and Yorkshire Regional Office
John Snow House,
Durham University Science Park,
Durham DH1 3YG
0191-301 1300

South East Regional Office
40 Eastbourne Terrace,
London W2 3QR
020 7725 2500

South and West Regional Office
Westward House, Lime Kiln Close,
Stoke Gifford, Bristol BS34 8SR
0117-984 1750

Trent Regional Office
Fullwood House, Old Fullwood Road,
Sheffield S10 3TH
0114-263 0300

West Midlands Regional Office
Bartholomew House, 142 Hagley Road,
Edgbaston, Birmingham B16 9PA
0121-224 4600

Social Services Inspectorate
40 Berkeley Square, Clifton, Bristol BS8 1HU
0117-941 6501

2nd Floor, John Rothschild House, Castle Quay,
Castle Boulevard, Nottingham NG7 1FW
0115-959 7500

Ladywood House, 45/46 Stephenson Street,
Birmingham B2 4DH
0121-606 4360

Tyne Bridge Tower, Church Street, Gateshead,
Tyne and Wear NE8 2DU
0191-490 3400

West Point, 501 Chester Road, Old Trafford,
Manchester M16 9HU
0161-876 2400

National Cancer Services
St Thomas's Hospital, Lambeth Palace Road,
London SE1 7EH
020 7928 9292

NHS Purchases and Supplies Agency
Foxbridge Way, Normanton,
West Yorkshire WF6 1TL
01924 328700

80 Lightfoot Street, Chester CH2 3AD
01244 586700

Millennium House, 30 Junction Road,
Sheffield S11 8XB
0114-267 6004

Premier House, 60 Caversham Road,
Reading, Berkshire RG1 7EB
0118-980 8600

Clipper House, 62-66 London Street,
Reading, Berkshire RG1 4SQ
0118-980 8032

Responsible for:
– supporting activity at national level to protect, promote and improve the nation's health.
– providing comprehensive medical care for all those who need it.
– securing responsive social care and child protection.

Richmond House
Secretary of State and Chairman of the NHS Policy Board: Rt Hon Alan Milburn MP
Parliamentary Private Secretary: Jim Fitzpatrick MP
Special Advisers: Darren Murphy, Simon Stevens (020 7210 5942)
Minister of State: Rt Hon John Denham MP
Parliamentary Private Secretary: Paul Goggins MP
Minister of State: John Hutton MP
Parliamentary Private Secretary: Maria Eagle MP
Parliamentary Under-Secretary of State (Lords): Lord Hunt of Kings Heath OBE
Parliamentary Under-Secretary of State (Minister for Public Health): Yvette Cooper, MP
Parliamentary Under-Secretary of State (Minister for Health): Gisela Stuart MP

Parliamentary Clerk: Jeremy Mean
Private Office Manager: Simon Stephenson

Spokesmen in the House of Lords: Lord Hunt of Kings Heath, Lord Burlison

Permanent Secretary: Nigel Crisp
Priv Sec: Helen Causley
Asst Priv Sec: Ruth Wetterstad

Chief Medical Officer: Prof Liam Donaldson
Priv Sec: Rachel Dickson
Asst Priv Sec: Tasneem Baloch

Deputy Chief Medical Officers: Dr Pat Troop, Dr Sheila Adam

Director of National Cancer Services:
   Prof Michael Richards MA MD FRCP
   (Based at St Thomas's Hospital)

Chief Executive, NHS Management Executive:
   Nigel Crisp
Deputy Chief Executive: Neil McKay
   Priv Sec: Zoe Lawrence

Ministerial Correspondence Unit:
020 7210 5615

REGIONAL CHAIRMAN'S MEETING
Chairman: Rt Hon Alan Milburn MP
Board Members:
Rt Hon John Denham MP
John Hutton, MP
Lord Hunt of Kings Heath OBE
Yvette Cooper MP
Gisela Stuart MP
Nigel Crisp
Zahida Manzoor
Ian Mills
Janet Trotter OBE
Rosie Varley
Sir William Wells
Clive Wilkinson
Prof Joan Higgins
Dr Peter Barrett
Secretariat: Chris Walker, Simon Stevens, Darren Murphy, Janet Grauberg
Regional Directors also attend

NATIONAL HEALTH SERVICE EXECUTIVE
BOARD
Chair: Nigel Crisp
Headquarters Directors:
Dr Sheila Adam
Prof J Pattison
Ron Kerr CBE
Sarah Mullally
Colin Reeves CBE
Hugh Taylor
Prof Liam Donaldson
Helen McCallum
Aidan Halligan
Peter Addison-Child (observer)

Regional Directors:
John Bacon (acting)
Stephen Day
Peter Garland
Peter Houghton
Tony Laurance
David Nicholson *(acting)*
Barbara Stocking CBE
Robert Tinston
Secretariat: Chris Walker, Zoe Lawrence

COMMUNICATIONS DIRECTORATE
Richmond House, Skipton House and Quarry House
Director of Communications:
   Helen McCallum
Chief Press Officer: Laurence Knight
Head of Business Management:
   Carol Hulkes
Deputy Director of Campaigns:
   Wyn Roberts
Deputy Director of Media Relations:
   Sian Jarvis
Deputy Director Corporate Communications:
   Peter Addison-Child

CORPORATE MANAGEMENT DIRECTORATE
Richmond House
Group Head: Alice Perkins
Private Secretary: Andrew Cooper

ORGANISATIONAL DEVELOPMENT BRANCH
Richmond House
Branch Head: Fran Spencer

PERSONNEL SERVICES
Director of Personnel: Flora Goldhill
Skipton House

INTERNATIONAL AND CONSTITUTIONAL BRANCH
Branch Head: Nick Boyd

MPI – MEDICINES, PHARMACY AND INDUSTRY DIVISION
Head of MPI: Andy McKeon
MPI – PPB PHARMACY AND PRESCRIBING
Branch Head: Kevin Guinness
PHARMACY
Acting Chief Pharmacist: Jeannette Howe
MPI – PPRS
Pharmaceutical Price Regulation Scheme (PPRS); EC pharmaceutical pricing.
Branch Head: Mike Brownlee

MPI – IB INDUSTRY BRANCH
Sponsorship branch for pharmaceutical and health industries
Branch Head: John Middleton

INFORMATION SERVICES DIVISION
Skipton House
Director: Dr Andrew Holt

RACE EQUALITY UNIT
Joint Heads of Unit (Job Share):
  Barry Mussenden, Lydia Yee

SOCIAL CARE GROUP (SCG)
Wellington House
Head of Social Care Policy: David Walden
Chief Inspector: Denise Platt, CBE

SOCIAL CARE REGIONS
  Northern: Paul Brearley
  Central: John Cypher
  Southern: Fran McCabe
  London: Jo Cleary
INSPECTION DIVISION
Head of Inspection Division: Averil Nottage
  North West: Bill Riddell
  North East: John Fraser
  West: Richard Balfe
  South: Lynda Hoare
  East: Alan Jones
Inspection Resource Group: Jenny Owen
Joint Review Group:
Project Director: Dr Andrew Webster

PUBLIC HEALTH DIVISION
Wellington House

Division Head: Prof Donald Nutbeam

PH – DCMO
Policy on Communicable Diseases for the Corporate Management of the Public Health Group

Deputy Chief Medical Officer: Dr Pat Troop
  (Public Health)

PH – TPU TEENAGE PREGNANCY UNIT
Head of Unit: Cathy Hamlyn

PH1 – HEALTH STRATEGY BRANCH
The branch contains the Central Health Monitoring Unit and the Ethnic Minority Health Unit

Acting Branch Head: Nick Dean

PH2 – CORONARY HEART DISEASE AND STROKE PREVENTION BRANCH
Branch Head: Imogen Sharp

PH3 – SUBSTANCE MISUSE BRANCH
Head of Branch: Mohammed Haroon

PH4 – SEXUAL HEALTH – GENETICS BRANCH
Branch Head: Marcia Fry

PH5 – ENVIRONMENT AND HEALTH BRANCH
Branch Head: Vacant

PH6 – COMMUNICABLE DISEASE BRANCH
Branch Head: Dr Elizabeth Smales

PH7 – CORPORATE MANAGEMENT BRANCH
Branch Head: Andy Smith

MEDICAL EDITORIAL UNIT
Eileen House
Ed Davis

HM INSPECTOR OF ANATOMY
Wellington House
Dr Jeremy Metters

PLANNING DIRECTORATE
Richmond House and Quarry House
Planning, analytical services, information and IT

Director of Planning: Vacant
Head of Planning: Penny Dash
Chief Economic Adviser: Clive Smee CB
Director of Statistics: Dr John Fox
Head of Information Policy Unit: Dr Peter Drury

PLANNING DIVISION
Section Head: Patrick Hennessy

OPERATIONAL PLANNING BRANCH
Section Branch Head: Patrick Hennessy

STRATEGIC PLANNING BRANCH
Branch Head: Richard Walsh

ECONOMICS AND OPERATIONAL RESEARCH DIVISION
Skipton House and Quarry House
Chief Economic Adviser: Clive Smee CB
Economic support to the NHS Executive
(EOR1 – Quarry House)
Senior Economic Adviser: Nick York (EOR1)
Economic Support to the wider Department and NHS Executive in London
(EOR3 – Skipton House)

Senior Economic Adviser:
  Dr Simon Harding (EOR3)
Operational Research/ Management Science
support to the NHS Executive in Leeds
(EOR2 – Quarry House)
Head of Operational Research:
  Dr Geoff Royston
Operational Research/Management Science
support in London
(EOR4 – Skipton House)
Head of Operational Research: Andre Hare

STATISTICS DIVISION
Skipton House
Director of Statistics: Dr John Fox
Deputy Director: Greg Phillpotts

NURSING SERVICES
Richmond House and Quarry House
All aspects of nursing, midwifery and health
visiting
Chief Nursing Officer and Director of Nursing;
  Private Office London and Leeds:
  Sarah Mullally

Richmond House
Assistant Chief Nursing Officer (NUR-PS):
  Gillian Stephens BSc(Econ) RGN RHV

Quarry House
Assistant Chief Nursing Officer – Clinical
  Practice: Liz Fradd
Assistant Chief Nursing Officer – Corporate
  Management: David Moore

Richmond House
QUAL – NHS Quality Management
Branch Head: Julian Brookes *(acting)*

NUR – QC
Citizens' Charter; Patients' Charter; NHS
performance tables; patient partnership and
public involvement; volunteering; community
health councils; Health Information Service;
liaison with Health Service Commissioner;
development of complaints policy; NHS indemnity for clinical negligence

Acting Branch Head: Duncan Innes

RESEARCH AND DEVELOPMENT
DIVISION
Richmond House and Skipton House
Director of Research and Development:
  Prof Sir John Pattison
Deputy Director of Research and Development:
  Dr Christopher Henshall

OPERATIONS DIRECTORATE
Director of Operations: Ron Kerr, CBE

HUMAN RESOURCES DIVISION
Quarry House
Director of Human Resources: Hugh Taylor CB

HEALTH SERVICES DIRECTORATE
Director of Health Services: Dr Sheila Adam
Deputy Director: Vacant

HEALTH SERVICES DIRECTORATE – 2
Hospital Development Policy: policy on blood,
pathology and ambulance services, NBA, blood
policy and safety, pathology policy, ambulance
and patient transport services, emergency and
elective surgical care and anaesthesia, transplantation, renal, hepatic, general medicine

Acting Branch Head: Dr Mike McGovern

HEALTH SERVICES DIRECTORATE – 3
Women's and Children's Health Services

Branch Head: Kathryn Tyson

HEALTH SERVICES DIRECTORATE – 4
Policy and services for people with mental health
problems

Joint Heads of Mental Health Services Branch:
  Antony Sheehan, John Mahoney

HEALTH SERVICES DIRECTORATE – 5
Mental health legislation branch, Mental Health
Review Tribunal Secretariat

Branch Head: Andrea Humphrey

HEALTH SERVICES DIRECTORATE – 6
NHS services for older people including older
people with mental health problems
Branch Head: Almas Mithani

HEALTH SERVICES DIRECTORATE – 7
Physical and Sensory Disabilities; Clinical and
professional advice related to therapy and other
professions allied to medicine and psychogeri-
atric medicine. AIDS/HIV National Strategy

Branch Head: Mark Davies

HEALTH SERVICES DIRECTORATE – 8
Development and co-ordination of HSD's contribution to equal opportunities and race equality in
service delivery. Development and implementation of the National Service Framework for
Diabetes

Branch Head: Dr Gillian Chapman

HSD – PUBLIC HEALTH DEVELOPMENT UNIT – PHDU
Head: Vacant

HSD – CHD CARDIAC SERVICES
Branch Head: Heather Gwynn

HSD – CMC
Corporate Management and Commissioning

Head of Corporate Management and Commissioning: Linda Percival

HSD – CLINICAL SERVICES MODERNISATION TEAM
Section Head: Dr Val Day

HSD – CT
Cancer Team

Head of Cancer Services Policy Team: Helen Shirley-Quirk

HSD – MENTAL HEALTH ACT COMMISSION
Acting Chief Executives: Paul Hampshire, Cheryl Robinson

HSD – PRISON HEALTH TASK FORCE
Head: John Boyington

HSD – PRISON HEALTH CARE POLICY UNIT
Head: Dr Felicity Harvey

HSD – PRIMARY CARE DIVISION
Acting Head: Mike Farrar

HSD – PC – DOS
Dental and Optical Services Branch
Branch Head: Helen Robinson

HSD – PC – WIT
White Paper Implementation Team
Head of Team: Mike Farrar

HSD – PC – GMS
General Medical Services
Branch Head: Mike Farrar

FINANCE AND PERFORMANCE DIVISION
Quarry House and Richmond House

Director of Finance and Performance: Colin Reeves CBE

FINANCE AND PERFORMANCE DIVISION A
Public expenditure on health and personal social services

Deputy Director of Finance: Bill McCarthy

FINANCE AND PERFORMANCE DIVISION B
Health Authority and Trust financial allocations, plans and monitoring, NHS Trust financial management, private finance initiative and NHS financial development

Deputy Director of Finance: Christine Daws
Acting Deputy Director of Finance: Malcolm Harris CBE

DIRECTORATE OF COUNTER FRAUD SERVICES
Director: Jim Gee

REGIONAL OFFICES

EASTERN REGIONAL OFFICE
Chairman: Rosie Varley
Regional Director: Peter Houghton

LONDON REGIONAL OFFICE
Chairman: Ian Mills
Regional Director: John Bacon (acting)

NORTH WEST REGIONAL OFFICE
Chairman: Prof Joan Higgins
Regional Director: Robert Tinston

NORTHERN AND YORKSHIRE REGIONAL OFFICE
Chair: Zahida Manzoor
Regional Director: Peter Garland

SOUTH EAST REGIONAL OFFICE
Chairman: Sir William Wells
Regional Director: Barbara Stocking CBE

SOUTH AND WEST REGIONAL OFFICE
Chair: Janet Trotter OBE
Regional Director: Tony Laurence

TRENT REGIONAL OFFICE
Chairman: Dr Peter Barrett
Acting Regional Director: David Nicholson

WEST MIDLANDS REGIONAL OFFICE
Chairman: Clive Wilkinson
Regional Director: Stephen Day

SOLICITOR'S OFFICE
Solicitor: Marilynne Morgan CB
New Court

HEALTH AND PERSONAL SOCIAL SERVICES
MATTERS (OTHER THAN NATIONAL HEALTH
SERVICE SUPERANNUATION)
Director of Legal Services: Greer Kerrigan
Asst Directors: Ken Baublys, David Dunleavy,
Sue Edwards, Anita James, Peter Milledge,
Ron Powell, Rachel Sandby-Thomas,
Mary Trefgarne, Sandra Walker

Executive Agencies: Medical Devices Agency
(MDA); Medicines Control Agency (MCA);
NHS Estates (NHSE); NHS Pensions Agency
(NHSPA); NHS Purchasing and Supply Agency
(NHSPASA)

Home Office

50 Queen Anne's Gate,
London SW1H 9AT
020 7273 4000 *Fax:* 020 7273 3965
Gen Fax: 020 7273 2190
E-mail: gen.ho@gtnet.gov.uk
Website: www.homeoffice.gov.uk/

Responsible for:
– reduction in crime and in the fear of crime; and
 the maintenance of public safety and good
 order.
– delivery of justice through investigation, prosecution, trial and sentencing, and through
 support for victims.
– prevention of terrorism, reduction in other
 organised and international crime, and protection against threats to national security.
– execution of the sentences of the courts.
– regulation of entry to and settlement in the UK
 and facilitation of travel by UK citizens.
– reduction in the incidence of fire and related
 death, injury and damage, and ensuring the
 safety of the public through civil protection.

Secretary of State (Home Secretary):
 Rt Hon Jack Straw MP
Parliamentary Private Secretary:
 Colin Pickthall MP
Special Advisers: Justin Russell (020 7273 2713),
 Ed Owen (020 7273 2852 Fax: 020 7273 2745)

Minister of State and Deputy Home Secretary:
 Rt Hon Paul Boateng MP
Parliamentary Private Secretary:
 Angela Smith MP

Minister of State: Charles Clarke MP
Parliamentary Private Secretary:
 Gareth R Thomas MP

Minister of State: Barbara Roche MP
Parliamentary Private Secretary:
 Tom Levitt MP

Parliamentary Under-Secretary of State:
 Mike O'Brien MP
Parliamentary Clerk: Ms Diane Caddle
Parliamentary Under-Secretary of State:
 Lord Bassam of Brighton

Spokesmen in the House of Lords: Lord Bassam,
Lord Bach

Permanent Under-Secretary:
 Sir David Omand KCB
 Fax: 020 7273 2972
Directors
Policing and Crime Reduction Group:
 John Lyon
Corporate Resources Directorate:
 Lynda Lockyer
Criminal Policy Group: John Halliday CB
Criminal Policy Group: Sue Street
Policing and Crime Reduction Group:
 Jim Daniell
Planning, Finance and Performance Group:
 Robert Fulton
Communications Directorate: Brian Butler
Research, Development and Statistics:
 Prof Paul Wiles
Corporate Development Directorate:
 Dr David Pepper
*Constitutional and Community Policy
 Directorate:* Carolyn Sinclair
Fire and Emergency Planning Directorate:
 Charles Everett

Director-General, HM Prison Service:
 Martin Narey
*Director-General, Immigration and Nationality
 Directorate:* Stephen Boys-Smith
Organised and International Crime Directorate:
 John Warne CB

Advisers
Legal Adviser: David Seymour
*Chief Medical Officer (at Department of Health
 and Social Security):*
 Prof Liam Donaldson QHP

DIRECTORATES

COMMUNICATION DIRECTORATE
50 Queen Anne's Gate, London SW1H 9AT
020 7273 4000
Director, Communications (Head of News):
 Brian Butler
Head of Publicity and Corporate Services:
 Anne Nash

CONSTITUTIONAL AND COMMUNITY POLICY
DIRECTORATE
50 Queen Anne's Gate, London SW1H 9AT
020 7273 4000
Director: Carolyn Sinclair
Mrs P G Catto, Trevor Cobley, E Grant,
    L Hughes, Ms S Marshall, M de Pulford,
    Paul Regan, N Varney, G White, C Young
Gaming Board for Great Britain: T J Kavanagh*
    (Secretary to the Board)
*Based at Berkshire House,
168/173 High Holborn, London WC1V 7AA

ANIMALS (SCIENTIFIC PROCEDURE)
INSPECTORATE
Chief Inspector: Dr J Richmond

CORPORATE DEVELOPMENT DIRECTORATE
50 Queen Anne's Gate, London SW1H 9AT
020 7273 4000
Director: Dr David Pepper
Tony Edwards, Ms S Rae, T Williams

CORPORATE RESOURCES DIRECTORATE
Grenadier House, 99/105 Horseferry Road,
London SW1P 2DD
020 7273 4000
Director: Lynda Lockyer
Elizabeth Moody, D J McDonough, J G Jones,
    Ms D Loudon, Ms F Spencer, S Wharton,
    C Welsh

CRIMINAL POLICY GROUP
50 Queen Anne's Gate,
London SW1H 9AT
020 7273 4000
Director, Criminal Justice Policy:
    John Halliday CB
Director, Sentencing and Correctional Policy:
    Sue Street
Ms S Atkins, Mike Boyle, Ian Chisholm,
    Ms G Fletcher-Cooke, Michael Lewer,
    G H Marriage OBE, A Norbury, J Powls,
    P Pugh, Christine Stewart, N Warner,
    Howard Webber* Mrs T Burnhams,
    Ms J Furniss, Mrs D Grice, Ms S Grimshaw,
    Mrs A Johnstone, Dr Dilys Jones,
    A D Macfarlane, Ms L Rogerson
*Based at Morley House,
26/30 Holborn Viaduct, London EC1A 2JQ

HM INSPECTORATE OF PROBATION
Chief Insp: Sir Graham Smith, CBE
Asst Chief Insp: J Kuipers

FIRE AND EMERGENCY PLANNING
DIRECTORATE
Horseferry House, Dean Ryle Street,
London SW1P 2AW
020 7273 4000
Director: Charles Everett
Dr David Peace, Peter Davies, Eddie Guy CBE,
    Peter Jones
Marketing Group Manager: R Smith*
T Lewis

*Based at The Hawkhills, Easingwold,
York YO6 3EG

HM FIRE SERVICE INSPECTORATE
Chief Insp: Graham Meldrum CBE QFSM
    DUniv FIFireE CIMgt

IMMIGRATION AND NATIONALITY DIRECTORATE
Apollo House, 40 Wellesley Road,
Croydon, Surrey CR9 3RR
020 8760 plus ext
Director-General: Stephen Boys-Smith
Deputy Director-General – Operations:
    Dr Chris Mace
Deputy Dir-General – Policy: Peter Wrench
Directors: Jim Acton, Mrs M Bishop,
    Stephen Calvard, B Eagle, Chris Hudson,
    Jonathan Potts, Aileen Simkins,
    Alan Underwood, Bob Whalley
Director (Enforcement): Ian Boon
Director (Ports): P Higgins
C Harbin, D Roberts
36 Wellesley Road, Croydon CR9 3RR
†Based at 50 Queen Anne's Gate
London SW1H 9AT
‡Based at India Buildings
3rd Floor, Water Street, Liverpool L2 0QN

EUROPEAN AND INTERNATIONAL UNIT
50 Queen Anne's Gate, London SW1H 9AT
020 7273 4000
Lesley Pallett

LEGAL ADVISER'S BRANCH
50 Queen Anne's Gate, London SW1H 9AT
020 7273 4000
Deputy Leg Advs: Sally Evans, Tim Middleton

ORGANISED AND INTERNATIONAL CRIME
DIRECTORATE
50 Queen Anne's Gate, London SW1H 9AT
020 7273 4000
Director: John Warne CB
Godfrey Stadlen, Peter Storr, Brian Paterson

PRISONS OMBUDSMEN
Ashley House, 2 Monck Street,
London SW1P 2BQ
Ombudsmen: Stephen Shaw
See Ombudsmen and Consumer Protection

PLANNING, FINANCE AND PERFORMANCE GROUP
50 Queen Anne's Gate, London SW1H 9AT
020 7273 4000
Director: Robert Fulton
R Scotland, Colin Harnett, Allan Mortimer,
Les Haugh, Colin Allars
R B Woodland

POLICING AND CRIME REDUCTION GROUP
50 Queen Anne's Gate, London SW1H 9AT
020 7273 4000
Directors: Jim Daniell, John Lyon
J Duke-Evans, A Cory**, R Kornicki
R A Ginman*, S Wells**, C Byrne,
Jim Nicholson, Vic Hogg, Paul Pugh,
Vic Clayton, Vivienne Dews, Steve Trimmins,
John Thompson, Ian McDonald,
Brian Coleman
**Based at Horseferry House

HM INSPECTORATE OF CONSTABULARY
50 Queen Anne's Gate,
London SW1H 9AT
020 7273 4000
HM Chief Inspector:
David O'Dowd, CBE, QPM

RESEARCH, DEVELOPMENT AND STATISTICS
DIRECTORATE
50 Queen Anne's Gate,
London SW1H 9AT
020 7273 4000
Director: Prof Paul Wiles
Chris Lewis, David Moxon, Peter Ward*,
Mrs Carole Willis
G Barclay, Ms M Colledge, P Collier, Mrs P
Dowdeswell, David Faulks, Mike Koudra,
Mrs C L Lehman, Mrs P Mayhew, OBE,
R Price, R Walmsley, Barry Webb, Dr J Youell
*Based at Abell House, John Islip Street,
London SW1P 4LH

PERFORMANCE AND STRATEGY UNIT (PSU) (PART
OF PFPG)
50 Queen Anne's Gate,
London SW1H 9AT
020 7273 4000
Head of Unit: Collin Allars

HM INSPECTORATE OF PRISONS
50 Queen Anne's Gate,
London SW1H 9AT
020 7273 4000
HM Chief Inspector of Prisons:
Sir David Ramsbotham
HM Deputy Chief Inspector of Prisons:
Colin Allen

Executive Agencies: Fire Service College;
Forensic Science Service; HM Prison Service;
UK Passport Agency

Department for International Development

94 Victoria Street, London SW1E 5JL
020 7917 7000 *Fax:* 020 7917 0016
GTN: 3535 7000

Abercrombie House, Eaglesham Road,
East Kilbride, Glasgow G75 8EA
01355 844000 *GTN:* 7243 1000
Public Enquiry Point: 0845 3004100
E-mail: enquiry@dfid.gov.uk
Website: www.dfid.gov.uk

Responsible for managing Britain's bilateral and
multilateral development projects in poorer
countries and for ensuring that Government policies which affect developing countries take
account of developing country issues.

Secretary of State: Rt Hon Clare Short MP
Parliamentary Private Secretary:
Dennis Turner MP
Special Advisers: David Mepham,
Susannah Cox

Parliamentary Under-Secretary of State:
George Foulkes MP

Head of Parliamentary Unit: Ian Ruff
Parliamentary Assistant: Craig French

Spokesperson in the House of Lords:
Baroness Amos

Permanent Secretary: Sir John Vereker KCB

Director-General Programmes: Barrie Ireton
Director-General Resources:
Richard Manning CB
Principal Finance Officer: Peter Freeman

AFRICA DIVISION
Director: Graham Stegman
AFRICA POLICY AND ECONOMICS DEPARTMENT
Head of Unit: Owen Barder
AFRICA, GREATER HORN AND CO-ORDINATION
DEPARTMENT
Head of Department: Tim Craddock
WEST AND NORTH AFRICA DEPARTMENT
Head of Department: Brian Thomson
DFID EASTERN AFRICA (NAIROBI)
Kenya.
Head of Division: Mark Lowcock
DFID EASTERN AFRICA (TANZANIA)
Head of Division: Caroline Sergeant
DFID EASTERN AFRICA (UGANDA)
Head of Division: Mike Hammond

DFID Central Africa (Harare)
Malawi, Mozambique, Zambia, Zimbabwe.
Head of Division: John Winter

DFID Southern Africa (Pretoria)
Head of Division: Sam Sharpe

DFID Nigeria
Head: Paul Spray

ASIA AND PACIFIC DIVISION
Director: Martin Dinham

DFID Nepal (Katmandu)
Head of Department: Sue Wardell

DFID Pacific (Suva)
Head of Department: Jackie Creighton

Eastern Asia and Pacific Department
Head of Department: Sarah Smith

DFID India
India, Bhutan.
Head of Department:
    Robert Graham-Harrison

Western Asia Department
Iraq, Jordan, Pakistan, Yemen, Occupied Territories; regional programmes.
Head of Department: Margaret Vowles

DFID South East Asia (Bangkok)
Head of Division: Mark Mallalieu

DFID Bangladesh (Dhaka)
Head of Department: Paul Ackroyd

INTERNATIONAL DIVISION
Director: Tony Faint

European Union Department
Head of Department: Anthony Smith

United Nations and Commonwealth Department
Head of Department: Michael Mosselmans

International Financial Institutions Department
World Bank Group; IBRD/IMF Development Committee: Asian Development Bank/Fund; African Development Bank/Fund; Caribbean Development Bank; Inter-American Development Bank; debt, IMF and export credits.
Head of Department: Margaret Cund

Conflict and Humanitarian Affairs Department
Head of Department and Senior Humanitarian Adviser: Dr Mukesh Kapila

WESTERN HEMISPHERE AND EASTERN EUROPEAN DIVISION
Director: John Kerby

Central and South Eastern Europe Department
Head of Department: Simon Ray

Eastern Europe and Central Asia Department
Head of Department: Matthew Wyatt

Western Hemisphere and Eastern Europe Economics Department
Acting Head of Department: Tracey Lane

UK Representative at The European Bank for Reconstruction and Development
Head of Unit: Michael McCulloch

Latin America, Caribbean and Atlantic Department
Head of Department: Alex Archbold

DFID Caribbean
Head of Division: Desmond Curran

EDUCATION DEPARTMENT
Chief Education Adviser: Myra Harrison

INFRASTRUCTURE AND URBAN DEVELOPMENT DEPARTMENT
Chief Engineering Adviser: John Hodges

HEALTH AND POPULATION DEPARTMENT
Chief Health and Population Adviser:
    Dr Julian Lobb-Levyt

RURAL LIVELIHOODS AND ENVIRONMENT DIVISION
Director, Production Capacity & Environment and Chief Natural Resources Adviser:
    Andrew Bennett

ENVIRONMENT POLICY DEPARTMENT
Head of Department: Adrian Davis

RURAL LIVELIHOOD DEPARTMENT
Head of Department: Michael Scott

ECONOMICS, STATISTICS AND ENTERPRISE DEVELOPMENT DIVISION
Chief Economist: Adrian Wood

Asia, Regional Economics and Policy Department
Head of Department: Peter Grant

Africa Economics Department
Head of Department: Peter Landymore

Economics Policy and Research Department
Head of Department: Peter Landymore

INTERNATIONAL ECONOMIC POLICY DEPARTMENT
Head of Department: John Roberts

ENTERPRISE DEVELOPMENT GROUP
Chief Enterprise Development Adviser:
  David Stanton

GOVERNANCE DEPARTMENT
Chief Governance Adviser: Roger Wilson

STATISTICS DEPARTMENT
Chief Statistician: Tony Williams

AID POLICY DEPARTMENT
Head of Department: David Sands Smith

FINANCE DEPARTMENT
Head of Department: Kevin Sparkhall

ACCOUNTS DEPARTMENT
Head of Department: Mike Smithson

BUSINESS PARTNERSHIPS DEPARTMENT
Head of Department: Rosemary Stevenson

SOCIAL DEVELOPMENT DEPARTMENT
Chief Social Development Adviser:
  Dr Michael Schultz

MEDICAL AND WELFARE DEPARTMENT
Head of Department: Elaine Kennedy

INTERNAL AUDIT UNIT
Head of Department: Roger Elias

EVALUATION DEPARTMENT
Ex-post evaluation of aid activities.
Head of Department: Colin Kirk

HUMAN RESOURCES DIVISION
Head of Division: Dave Fish

HUMAN RESOURCES OPERATIONS DEPARTMENT
Head of Department: John Anning

HUMAN RESOURCES POLICY DEPARTMENT
Head of Department: Dave Richards

PROCUREMENT DEPARTMENT
Head of Department: Stephen Chard

CIVIL SOCIETY DEPARTMENT
Head of Department: Stephen Chard

OVERSEAS PENSIONS DEPARTMENT
Head of Department: Peter Brough

INFORMATION SYSTEMS AND SERVICES
DEPARTMENT
Head of Department: David Gillett

INFORMATION DEPARTMENT/LIBRARY
Head of Department: Richard Calvert

LIBRARY
Enquiries: 01355 843599/843246
GTN: 7243 35993246

Law Officers' Departments

Attorney General's Chambers,
9 Buckingham Gate, London SW1E 6JP
020 7271 2400 *Fax:* 020 7271 2432
E-mail: islo@gtnet.gov.uk

Overall responsibility for the work of the Treasury Solicitor's Department, the Crown Prosecution Service, the Serious Fraud Office and the Legal Secretariat to the Law Officers.

The Attorney General is the Government's principal legal adviser; deals with questions of law arising on Bills, and with issues of legal policy; is concerned with all major international and domestic litigation involving the Government; and has specific responsibilities for the enforcement of the criminal law.

The Director of Public Prosecution for Northern Ireland is also responsible to the Attorney General.

Attorney General:
  Rt Hon Lord Williams of Mostyn QC

Solicitor General: Ross Cranston QC MP
Parliamentary Private Secretary:
  Michael Jabez Foster MP

Legal Secretary to the Law Officers:
  David Brummell
Deputy Legal Secretary: Stephen Parkinson

Executive Agency: Treasury Solicitor's Department

Lord Chancellor's Department

House of Lords, London SW1A 0PW
020 7219 6097/4785 *Fax:* 020 7219 4711
Website: www.open.gov.uk/lcd

Responsible for promoting general reforms in the civil law, for the procedure of the civil courts and for the administration of the Supreme Court (Court of Appeal, High Court and Crown Court) and county courts in England and Wales. The Lord Chancellor also has ministerial responsibility for the locally administered Magistrates' Courts and is responsible for advising the Crown on the appointment of judges and certain other officers and is personally responsible for the appointment of Masters and Registrars of the High Court and District Judges and magistrates. He is also responsible for Legal Aid and has overall responsibility for the Public Record Office, HM Land Registry, the Public Trust Office and the Court Service, and the Northern Ireland Court Service.

Lord Chancellor:
  Rt Hon Lord Irvine of Lairg QC
Parliamentary Private Secretaries:
  Bridget Prentice MP, Paul Clark MP
Special Adviser: Garry Hart

Spokesmen in the House of Lords: Lord Irvine,
Lord Bach
Parliamentary Clerk: Alexander Clark

Selborne House, 54/60 Victoria Street
London SW1E 6QW
020 7210 8500 *Fax:* 020 7210 0647
Parliamentary Secretaries:
David Lock MP
Jane Kennedy MP
Permanent Secretary: Sir Hayden Phillips KCB

CROWN OFFICE
House of Lords
Clerk of the Crown in Chancery:
  Sir Hayden Phillips KCB
Deputy Clerk of the Crown in Chancery:
  Michael Huebner CB
Clerk of the Chamber: C I P Denyer

POLICY GROUP
Selborne House, 54/60 Victoria Street,
London SW1E 6QW
020 7210 8719
Director-General: Joan MacNaughton
Heads of Divisions:
Director, Civil Justice and Legal Services:
  Alan Cogbill
Director, Criminal Justice Group:
  Mark Ormerod
Civil Justice Division: John Tanner
Legal Services Development Division:
  Peter Harris
Civil Law Development Division: Hugh Burns
Legal Aid: Head of Legal Aid Division:
  Derek Hill
Community Legal Services Division:
  Colin Myerscough
Public and Private Rights Directorate:
  Ms Amanda Finlay
Family Policy Division: Maggy Pigot,
  Judith Killick
Administrative Justice Division: Bryan Wells
Magistrates' Courts IT Division: Peter White

Magistrates' Courts Division: Ms Sally Field
Policy Group Secretariat: Mrs Kerry Allen
Social Policy Unit: Mrs Jackie Brown
Human Rights and Constitution Division:
  Ms C Collins, Ms K Di Lorenzo
Criminal Courts Review: Michael Kron

Criminal Justice: Paul Stockton
Children and Family Court Advisory Services:
  David Lye

JUDICIAL GROUP
Selborne House, 54/60 Victoria Street,
London SW1E 6QW
020 7210 8928
Director-General: Michael Huebner CB
Director: Elizabeth Grimsey
David Staff, David Gladwell,
  Stephen Humphreys, Mrs C Pulford,
  Malcolm Watts

LEGAL ADVISER'S GROUP
3rd Floor, Southside, 105 Victoria Street,
London SW1E 6QT
020 7210 0712 *Fax:* 020 7210 0748
E-mail: cleitao@lcdhq.gsi.gov.uk
Legal Adviser: Paul Jenkins
Michael Collon, Alasdair Wallace, Peter Fish

CORPORATE SERVICES GROUP
Selborne House, 54/60 Victoria Street,
London SW1E 6QW
020 7210 8503 *Fax:* 020 7210 8752
Director: Jenny Rowe
Heads of Divisions
Richard Atkinson, Bruce Eadie, Keith Garrett,
  Dominic Hartley, Andrew Maultby, Alan Pay,
  Alan Rummins, Ray Sams, Stephen Smith

COMMUNICATIONS GROUP
Selborne House, 54-60 Victoria Street,
London SW1E 6QW
Press enquiries (24 hours):
020 7210 8512 *Fax:* 020 7210 8633
Director of Communications:
  Allan Percival LVO
E-mail: apercival@lcdhq.gsi.gov.uk
Chief Press Officer: Mike Wicksteed
E-mail: mwicksteed@lcd.gsi.gov.uk

MAGISTRATES' COURT SERVICES INSPECTORATE
Christopher Chivers

ECCLESIASTICAL PATRONAGE
No. 10 Downing Street, London SW1
020 7930 4433
Secretary for Ecclesiastical Patronage:
  Nick Wheeler
Asst Sec for Ecclesiastical Patronage:
  N C Wheeler

Executive Agencies: Court Service; HM Land
Registry; Public Record Office (PRO); Public
Trust Office (PTO)

NORTHERN IRELAND COURT SERVICE
Windsor House, Bedford Street,
Belfast BT2 7LT
028 9032 8594 *Fax:* 028 9043 9110
Director General
Maintenance of Courts' Charter, customer service and communications

OPERATIONS
Administrative support for Supreme Court of Judicature, Northern Ireland (comprising Court of Appeal, High Court and Crown Court), county courts, magistrates' courts, the Enforcement of Judgments Office, coroners' courts and Offices of the Social Security and Child Support Commissioners
Director

POLICY AND LEGISLATION
Formulation and implementation of policy initiatives, including those for legal aid; preparation and drafting of primary and secondary legislation; secretarial support to Court Rules Committees, Advisory Committees and Judicial Studies Board for Northern Ireland; provision of legal services and strategic control and monitoring of legal aid expenditure and administration
Director

CORPORATE SERVICES
Human Resources, Resource Management, Procurement, Judicial Appointments, Internal Audit
Director

Northern Ireland Office

NB: SECURITY RESTRICTIONS

11 Millbank, Whitehall, London SW1 4PN
020 7210 3000 *Fax:* 020 7210 0249

Castle Buildings, Belfast BT4 3SG
028 9052 0700 *Fax:* 028 9052 8195
E-mail: press.nio@nics.gov.uk
Website: www.nio.gov.uk

Overall responsibility for the government of Northern Ireland.

The Secretary of State is directly responsible for political and constitutional matters, security policy, broad economic questions and other major policy issues, while such matters as agriculture, economic development, education, environment, finance and personnel, and health and social services are the responsibility of the Northern Ireland Assembly.

Secretary of State:
  Rt Hon Peter Mandelson MP
Parliamentary Private Secretary:
  Helen Jackson MP
Minister of State: Rt Hon Adam Ingram MP
Parliamentary Private Secretary:
  Desmond Browne MP
Parliamentary Under-Secretary of State:
  George Howarth MP

Spokespeople in the House of Lords: Baroness Farrington of Ribbleton, Lord Falconer

Permanent Under-Secretary: Joe Pilling CB

Parliamentary Branch for all Ministers
020 7210 6551

NORTHERN IRELAND CIVIL SERVICE
Central Secretariat
Parliament Buildings, Belfast BT4 8SG
028 9052 0700
Head of NICS and Second Permanent Under-Secretary of State: Gerry Loughran

PERMANENT SECRETARIES OF THE NORTHERN IRELAND EXECUTIVE
Department of Agriculture and Rural Development: Peter Small
Department of Culture, Arts and Leisure: Dr Aideen McGinley
Department of Education: Nigel Hamilton
Department of Enterprise, Trade and Investment: Bruce Robinson
Department of Environment: Stephen Quinn
Department of Finance and Personnel: Pat Carvill
Department of Health, Social Services and Public Safety: Clive Gowdy
Department of Higher and Further Education, Training and Employment: Alan Shannon
Department of Regional Development: Ronnie Spence
Department of Social Development: John Hunter

Executive Agencies: Compensation Agency; Forensic Science Northern Ireland (FSNI); NI Prison Service (NIPS)

Prime Minister's Office

10 Downing Street, London SW1A 2AA
Telephone: Direct line from 020 7270 3000
Press Office: 020 7270 3000
Website: www.number—10.gov.uk

Prime Minister and First Lord of the Treasury and Minister for the Civil Service:
  Rt Hon Tony Blair MP
Chief of Staff: Jonathan Powell

Principal Private Secretary to the Prime
  Minister: Jeremy Heywood
Parliamentary Private Secretary:
  Bruce Grocott MP
Private Secretary Foreign Affairs:
  John Sawers CMG
Private Secretaries to Prime Minister:
  Simon Virley (Economic Affairs), Clare
  Sumner (Parliamentary Affairs), David North
  (Home Affairs), Anna Wechsberg (Assistant
  on Overseas Affairs), Michael Tatham
  (Assistant Overseas Affairs), Magi Cleaver
  (Assistant Overseas Affairs),
  Julian Braithwaite (Speechwriter)
Personal Assistant to Prime Minister:
  Kate Garvey (Diary)
Secretary for Appointments: William Chapman
Special Assistant for Presentation and Planning:
  Anji Hunter
Policy Unit Special Advisers: David Miliband
  (Head of Unit)
  Andrew Adonis, Jim Gallagher, Brian Hackland,
  Robert Hill, Peter Hyman, Roger Liddle, Liz
  Lloyd, Geof Mulgan, Geoffrey Norris, Carey
  Oppenheim, James Purnell, Ed Richards,
  Derek Scott
Chief Press Secretary: Alastair Campbell
Deputy Press Secretary: Godric Smith
Senior Manager of Strategic Communications
  Unit: James Humphreys
Executive Secretary: Ms Pat Dixon
Political Secretary: Sally Morgan
Political Office: John Cruddas,
  Michael Stephenson, Faz Hakim,
  Caroline Adams, Gill Christopher-Chambers,
  Angela Goodchild
Parliamentary Clerk: Clive Barbour

Privy Council Office

2 Carlton Gardens, London SW1Y 5AA
020 7210 1033 *Fax:* 020 7210 1071
E-mail: jlindsay@cabinet-office.x.gsi.gov.uk
Website: www.privy-council.org.uk

Responsible for numerous formalities and
appointments relating to Crown and government
business.
  The President of the Council and Leader of the
House of Commons is responsible for supervising the Government's legislative programme
and upholding the rights and privileges of the
House.
  The Leader of the House of Lords is responsible for the arrangement of Government business in the House and has a responsibility to the
House itself to advise it on procedural matters
and other difficulties as they arise.

PRIVY COUNCIL OFFICE
Clerk of the Council: Alex Galloway
Deputy Clerk: Graham Donald
Senior Clerk: Miss Meriel McCullagh

JUDICIAL COMMITTEE OF THE PRIVY
COUNCIL
Downing Street, London SW1A 2AJ
020 7270 0483 *Fax:* 020 7270 0460
Website: www.privy-council.org.uk
Registrar of the Privy Council: J A C Watherston
Chief Clerk: F G Hart
Second Clerk: S Condon

OFFICE OF PRESIDENT OF THE COUNCIL
Privy Council Office, Regency Building,
2 Carlton Gardens, London SW1Y 5AA
020 7210 1025/020 7219 4040
President of the Council and Leader of the
  House of Commons:
  Rt Hon Margaret Beckett MP
Parliamentary Private Secretary:
  Ivor Caplin MP
Special Advisers: Sheila Watson, Nicci Collins
Parliamentary Secretary: Paddy Tipping MP
Business Co-ordination Unit:
Head of Unit: Mark Savigar (020 7210 1063)

HM Procurator General and Treasury Solicitor

Queen Anne's Chambers
28 Broadway, London SW1H 9JS
020 7210 3000 *Fax:* 020 7222 6006

Provides litigation and advisory services to
Government departments and other publicly
funded bodies in England and Wales. Also
administers estates of people who die intestate
with no known kin.

HM Procurator-General and Treasury Solicitor:
  Juliet Wheldon
Deputy Treasury Solicitor: Anthony Inglese
Treasury Legal Adviser: Mark Blythe CB
R N Ricks, M Thomas, D Brummell, D Macrae
Mrs L Addison, R Aitken, Mrs D Babar,
  P Bennett, J R J Braggins, J Burnet,
  F D W Clarke, Mrs V Collett, J E Collins,
  Mrs D Collins, S T Harker, M J Hemming,
  C House, Miss R Jeffreys, L John-Charles,
  J Jones, P Kilgarreff, A D Lawton,
  A Leithead, Mrs I G Letwin, B McKay,
  P R Messer, Miss F Nash, Ms L Nicoll,
  D Palmer, A Perrett, R J Phillips, A Ridout,
  A J Sandal, E B Solomons, Miss J V Stokes

Scotland Office

Dover House, Whitehall,
London SW1A 2AU
020 7270 6754 *Fax:* 020 7270 6812
E-mail: scottishsecretary@scotland.gsi.gov.uk
Website: www.scottishsecretary.gov.uk

Parliamentary Branch for all Ministers:
020 7270 6727

The Secretary of State for Scotland represents Scottish interests in the UK Government in matters such as the constitution, foreign affairs, defence, the civil service, financial and economic matters, national security, immigration and nationality, misuse of drugs, trade and industry, energy (eg electricity, coal, oil and gas, nuclear energy), many aspects of transport (eg railways), social security, employment, abortion, genetics, surrogacy, medicines, broadcasting and equal opportunities.

Secretary of State: Rt Hon Dr John Reid MP
Parliamentary Private Secretary: Frank Roy MP
Special Advisers:
   Richard Olszewski (020 7270 6779),
   Mike Elrick (020 7270 6807)

Minister of State: Brian Wilson MP
Parliamentary Private Secretary:
   Sandra Osborne MP

Advocate General for Scotland:
   Dr Lynda Clark QC MP
Legal Secretary to the Advocate General:
   George Duke (020 7270 6810)

Spokesperson in the House of Lords:
Baroness Ramsay

Scotland Office Management Group
Head of Department: Ian Gordon
   (020 7270 6742)
*Head of Division: Parliamentary and
   Constitutional (London):* Eric Ferguson
   (020 7270 6800)
   E-mail: eric.ferguson@scotland.gov.uk
*Head of Division: Home and Social
   (Edinburgh):* Stuart MacDonald
   (0141-242 5946)
*Head of Division: Economy and Industry
   (Glasgow):* Ian Hooper (0141-242 5965)
Head of Finance and Administration:
   Norman Kernohan (Edinburgh)
   (0131-244 9001)
Office of the Solicitor to the Advocate General
Solicitor: Hugh Macdiarmid (Edinburgh)
   (0131-244 1634)

Department of Social Security

Richmond House, 79 Whitehall
London SW1A 2NS
020 7238 0800
E-mail: ministers@ms41.dss.gov.uk
Website: www.dss.gov.uk

Adelphi
1–11 John Adam Street
London WC2N 6HT
020 7962 8000

Benefits Agency, Quarry House,
Quarry Hill, Leeds LS2 7UH
0113-232 4000

Central Office DSS
Newcastle upon Tyne NE98 1YX
0191-213 5000

New Court, 48 Carey Street
London WC2A 2LS
020 7962 8000

North Fylde Central Offices,
Norcross, Blackpool, Lancs FY5 3TA
01253 856123

Parliamentary Branch for all Ministers
020 7238 0715

Responsible for the social security system in England, Wales and Scotland. The system includes cash benefits for sick and disabled people, Job Seekers Allowance, Retirement Pensions, War Pensions, Family Credit, Child Benefit, and Child Support, The Social Fund, Income Support, Housing Benefit, Community Charge Benefit and the collection and assessment of National Insurance contributions.

Secretary of State: Rt Hon Alistair Darling MP
Parliamentary Private Secretary: Ann Coffey MP
Special Advisers: Andrew Maugham,
   Elsbeth Johnson
Minister of State: Rt Hon Jeff Rooker MP
Parliamentary Private Secretary:
   Richard Burden MP

Parliamentary Under-Secretary of State:
   Rt Hon Baroness Hollis of Heigham

Parliamentary Under-Secretary of State:
   Angela Eagle MP

Parliamentary Under-Secretary of State:
   Hugh Bayley MP
Parliamentary Clerk: Tim Elms

Spokespersons in the House of Lords: Baroness Hollis, Baroness Amos

Permanent Secretary: Rachel Lomax
(*E-mail:* rlomax@rch001.dss.gov.uk)

ANALYTICAL SERVICES DIVISION (ASD)
The Adelphi
Director: David Stanton CB
020 7962 8611 *Fax:* 020 7962 8795
E-mail: d.stanton@ms42.drs.gov.uk

CORPORATE SERVICES DIRECTORATE
Adelphi, Richmond House, Quarry House, North Fylde
Corporate Services Director: Stephen Hickey

COMMUNICATIONS DIRECTORATE
Richmond House
Director of Communications: Simon MacDowall

OFFICE OF CHIEF MEDICAL ADVISER
MEDICAL POLICY AND CORPORATE
MEDICAL GROUP
Adelphi
020 7962 8000
Chief Medical Adviser and Medical Director:
  Dr Mansel Aylward

MEDICAL POLICY MANAGERS
State Incapacity Benefits. Decision Making and Appeals.
Medical Policy Manager: Dr Philip Sawney
  (Adelphi)

Disability and Carer Benefits: Disability Living Allowance, Attendance Allowance, Disability Living Allowance Advisory Board. NHS Pensions Agency.
Medical Policy Adviser: Dr Roger Thomas
  (Adelphi)

Chief Medical Officer's Representative to Lord Chancellor's Department and Appeals Service.

European Union of Medical Advisers in Social Security (UEMASS).
Medical Policy Manager: Dr Paul Stidolph
  (Adelphi)

Contractorisation of Medical Services (IMPACT Project). Contract Monitoring. Medical Quality Issues. Vaccine Damage Payments. Disability Handbook. Accreditation Issues. Faculty of Occupational Medicine. Professional Development.
Medical Policy Manager: Dr Moira Henderson
  (Adelphi)

War Pensions Policy.
Medical Policy Manager: Dr Anne Braidwood
  (Norcross)

LAW AND SPECIAL POLICY GROUP
New Court
Solicitor: Marilynne Morgan CB
E-mail: mmorgan@nct001.dss.gov.uk

SOL A
Director of Legal Services: John Catlin
Assistant Directors of Legal Services
SOL Prosecutions: Sue Edwards
Commercial Branch: Ronald Powell
SOL Litigation: Anita James

WORKING AGE CLIENT GROUP
Group Director: Ursula Brennan
Directors
Strategy and Stewardship: Robert Devereux
Change: Stephen Hewitt
Benefit Fraud Inspectorate: Chris Bull

PENSIONS AND CHILDREN CLIENT GROUP
Group Director: Paul Gray
Directors
Pensions Strategy and Stewardship:
  Steve Heminsley
Pensions Specification and Change:
  Hilary Reynolds
Children: Helen Ghosh
Disability Extra Costs Benefits: Don Brereton

FRAUD STRATEGY PROJECTS
Policy Manager: Brendan O'Gorman

DEVOLUTION OF CONSTITUTIONAL REFORM
Policy Manager: John Griffiths

WELFARE REFORM UNIT
Policy Director: Alan Woods

PENSION PROVISION GROUP
Policy Manager: Guy Fiegehen

INCAPACITY BENEFITS
Policy Manager: Lesley Richards

WELFARE TO WORK
Policy Manager: Jeremy Groombridge

Executive Agencies: Appeals Service (AS); Benefits Agency (BA); Child Support Agency (CSA); War Pensions Agency

Department of Trade and Industry

1 Victoria Street, London SW1H 0ET
020 7215 5000 *Fax:* 020 7222 0613
Minicom: 020 7215 6740
Website: www.dti.gov.uk

Parliamentary Branch for all Ministers:
020 7215 6630

Responsibilities include industrial sponsorship, trade policy, inward investment, export promotion, energy policy, science and technology, consumer and investor protection, corporate government, industrial relations, company law, support for small and medium-sized industries, e-commerce and the information society.

DTI incorporates the Office of Science and Technology, whose aim is to develop and co-ordinate, transdepartmentally, Government policy on science, engineering and technology. The Head of OST is also the Chief Scientific Adviser to the Government, with direct access to the Prime Minister.

Secretary of State: Rt Hon Stephen Byers MP
Parliamentary Private Secretary: Ivan Lewis MP
Special Advisers: Dan Corry, Jo Moore

Minister of State for Energy and Competitiveness in Europe:
Rt Hon Helen Liddell MP
Parliamentary Private Secretary:
Derek Twigg MP

Minister for Trade: Rt Hon Richard Caborn MP
Parliamentary Private Secretary:
Ben Chapman MP

Minister of State (Minister for Small Business and E-Commerce): Patricia Hewitt MP
Parliamentary Private Secretary:
Anne Campbell MP

Parliamentary Under-Secretary of State for Consumers and Corporate Affairs:
Dr Kim Howells MP

Parliamentary Under-Secretary of State for Competitiveness: Alan Johnson MP

Parliamentary Under-Secretary of State for Science and Innovation:
Lord Sainsbury of Turville

Spokesmen in the House of Lords: Lord Sainsbury of Turville, Lord McIntosh of Haringey

British Trade International Board Chairmen:
Rt Hon Richard Caborn MP, John Battle MP
Chief Executive, British Trade International:
Sir David Wright KCMG LVO
Permanent Secretary: Sir Michael Scholar KCB
Parliamentary Clerk: Tim Williams
Chief Scientific Adviser to the Government and Head of Office of Science and Technology:
Prof David King ScD FRS
Director-General, Research Councils:
Dr John Taylor OBE

TRADE POLICY GROUP
151 Buckingham Palace Road,
London SW1W 9SS

Director-General: Richard Carden
Director Trade Policy: Charles Bridge
Director New Issues and Services; EC Trade Policy Competence: Charles Bridge
Director Trade Facilitation and Import Policy:
Alec Berry
Director International Economics:
Christopher Moir
Director European Policy: John Alty
Director Emu and Enlargement:
Tim Abraham CMG
Director Export Control and Non-proliferation:
Susan Haird
Director Export Control Organisation:
Susan Haird
Director Non-proliferation: John Neve

BRITISH TRADE INTERNATIONAL
(including Trade Partners UK, Invest UK)
Kingsgate House, 66–74 Victoria Street,
London SW1E 6SW
020 7215 5000
Website: www.tradepartners.gov.uk

Joint Board Chairmen:
Rt Hon Richard Caborn MP, John Battle MP
Chief Executive: Sir David Wright KCMG LVO
Deputy Chief Executive: David Hall

CENTRAL SERVICES GROUP
Group Director: David Hall
Director, Personnel and Finance:
Bronwen Northmore
Director, Knowledge Management Services:
Mike Cohen
Director, Overseas Market Services: Clive Stitt

REGIONAL GROUP
Group Director: Ian Jones
Director, Regions: Barbara Phillips

INTERNATIONAL GROUP
Group Director: Quinton Quayle
Director, Middle East and Africa:
   Suresh Khanna CBE
Director, Asia Pacific: Vincent Fean
Director, Europe: Keith Levinson
Director, Americas: Mike Mowlam

BUSINESS GROUP
Group Director: David Warren
Director, Infrastructure and Power:
   Graham Atkinson
*Director, Services, Sectors, Overseas Aid,
   Finance and Investment:* Robin Lamb
Director, Sectoral Partnership: Pauline Davies
*Director, International Business Schemes and
   Engineering:* Brian Gallagher
Director, Oil and Gas Business Group:
   Ken Forrest

STRATEGY AND COMMUNICATIONS GROUP
Group Director: Stephen Lyle Smythe
Head, Policy: Steve Loach
Head, Performance: Louise Rickitt
Head, Communications: Leigh Jackson
Head, Planning: Jan Titcombe

INVEST UK
Chief Executive: Vacant
Director, Operations: Alistair Morgan
Director, International: David Cockerham

BUSINESS COMPETITIVENESS GROUP
151 Buckingham Palace Road
London SW1W 9SS
020 7215 5000

Director-General: Jonathan Spencer
*Director Space and Director-General British
   National Space Centre:* Dr Colin Hicks
Director IS – Innovation Services: Mandy Mayer
*Deputy Director-General Space Technology,
   Chairman BNSC and Space Technology
   Advisory Board:* Dr David Leadbeater
*Director Space Applications and
   Transportation:* Paula Freedman
Director Chemicals and Biotechnology:
   Derek Davis
Director Chemicals: Dr David Jennings
Director Biotechnology: Dr Monica Darnbrough
Director Engineering Industries: Mike O'Shea
*Director, Aerospace and Defence Industries
   Policy:* John Hunt
*Director, Aerospace and Defence Industries
   Technology and Assessment:* David Way

*Director Mechanical and Electrical Engineering
   Industries:* Hugh Brown
*Director Automotive Components and
   Technology:* Iain Cameron
Director Motor Vehicles: John Dennis
Director Metals, Minerals and Shipbuilding:
   Erica Zimmer
Director Innovation Services:
   Robert Foster
Assistant Director Innovation Policy:
   Gillian Hunter
*Director Technology Economics Statistics and
   Evaluation:* John Barber
Director Standards and Technical Regulations:
   David Reed
Director National Measurement System:
   Sheiley Ian Charick
Director Future and Innovation Unit:
   John Reynolds
Director Environment: Alistair Keddie
*Director Consumer Goods, Business and Postal
   Services:* Derek Davis
Director Posts, Director Post Office Reform:
   Judy Britton
*Director Consumer Goods/Materials, Consumer
   and Business Services:* Brian Hopson
*Head of Communications and Information
   Industries:* Bill Macintyre
Director UK Communications Policy:
   David Lumley
Director Technology Policy and Innovation:
   Christopher Holmes
Director Content and Applications:
   Chris Matthews
Director Industrial Sponsorship Support Unit:
   Martin Berry
Director Industry Economics and Statistics:
   Nicholas Owen

ENERGY GROUP
1 Victoria Street, London SW1H 0ET
020 7215 5000

Director-General: Anna Walker
Deputy Director-General: Neil Hirst
*Energy Policy Technology, Analysis and Coal
Director Coal:* Peter Mason
Director Energy Utilities Technologies:
   Ian Fletcher
Director Energy Technologies:
   Godfrey Bevan
Chief Engineering Inspector: Peter Fenwick

Director Energy Policy and Analysis Unit:
  Nigel Peace
Director, BNFL Public Private Partnership Team: John Rhodes
Director Economics: Adrian Gault
Energy Head, Energy Statistics: Dissemination and Analysis: Chris Bryant
Director Nuclear Industries:
  Helen Leiser
Director UKAEA, Nuclear Decommissioning and Fusion: Peter Hayes
Director Euratom, Nuclear Safety, Security and Emergency Planning: Patrick Robinson
Director Oil and Gas: Geoff Dart
Director International Economics, Oil, Taxation, Downstream Oil and Gas Markets and Policy: Geoffrey Riggs
Director Hydrocarbons Exploration and Licensing: John Brooks CBE
Director Oil and Gas Development and Production: Simon Toole
Director Reform of Energy Regulation Team (RER): Keith Long

REGIONAL ENTERPRISE AND INNOVATION
1 Victoria Street, London SW1H 0ET

Director-General: Mark Gibson
Deputy Director-General Regions:
  Paul McIntyre
Director Regional Policy: David Smith
Director Regional European Funds:
  Keith Masson
Director Regional Assistance:
  Andrew Steele
Director Central Directorate: David Evans

SMALL BUSINESS SERVICE (SBS)
Chief Executive, : David Irwin
Deputy Chief Executive: Peter Waller
Deputy Director-General: Paul McIntyre
Director Local Network: Haf Merrifield
Director National Services: Ken Poulter
Director Corporate Service:
  Richard Allpress
Director Research and Development:
  Pat Jackson
Director Regulatory Issues: John Hobday
Director Policy and Communications:
  Matthew Cocks

CORPORATE AND CONSUMER AFFAIRS GROUP
1 Victoria Street, London SW1H 0ET
020 7215 5000

Director-General: Dr Catherine Bell
Director Employment Relations: Stephen Hadrill
Director, Consumer Affairs: Jonathan Rees
Deputy Director Consumer Safety Strategy and Safety: Geoff Dessent
Director, Competition Policy:
  Rolande Anderson
Director Consumer Policy: Dr Anne Eggington
Director Anti-Competitive Practices Policy:
  Jonathan May
Director EU and International Competition Policy: David Miner
Assistant Director EU Competition Policy:
  Neil Feinson
Director Enterprise Unit: Mark Higson
Director Employee Involvement, EU and Partnership and Working Time:
  Dr Elizabeth Baker
Director Special Employment Rights and Fairness at Work: Jonathan Startup
Director National Minimum Wage: Nicola Carter
Director Employment Market Analysis and Research: Mark Beatson
Director Employment Rights and Tribunals:
  Nicola Carter
Director Parental Leave Review: Janice Munday
Director Company Law and Investigations:
  Richard Rogers
Director Company Law Reform: Robert Burns
Director Financial Reporting Policy:
  John Grewe
Director of Investigations and Inspector of Companies: Grahame Harp

LEGAL SERVICES GROUP
10 Victoria Street, London SW1H 0NN
020 7215 5000

The Solicitor and Director-General:
  David Nissen, CB
Director Legal Services A: John Stanley
Director Legal Services B: Philip Bovey
Director Legal Services C:
  Alex Brett-Holt
Director Legal Services D: Tessa Dunstan

RESOURCES AND SERVICES GROUP
1 Victoria Street, London SW1H 0ET
020 7215 5000

Director-General: Jonathan Phillips
Director Staff Personnel Operations:
  Rob Wright

*Director Information Management and Process
Engineering:* Dick Wheeler
Director Estates and Facilities Management:
Michael Coolican
Director Internal Audit: Roger Louth
Director Finance and Resource Management:
Edmund Hosker
Director Finance: Alan Wright
Director Resource Management:
Hugh Savill
Director Resource Accounting: Keith Hills
Director Knowledge Management Unit:
Tim Soane

OFFICE OF SCIENCE AND TECHNOLOGY
Albany House, 94–98 Petty France
London SW1H 9ST
020 7271 2000

*Chief Scientific Adviser and Head of Office of
Science and Technology:*
Prof David King ScD FRS
*Director Transdepartmental Science and
Technology:* Jo Durning
Director International Science and Technology:
Dr Miles Parker
Director LINK: Alan Wootton
Director Foresight: Julie Carney
Director Science in Government:
Mrs Pat Sellers
Director-General Research Councils:
Dr John Taylor OBE FRS FEng
Director Science and Engineering Base:
Dr Martin Earwicker
Director Research Councils:
Frances Saunders
Director Projects: Richard King
Director Finance and Central Issues:
Keith Root

CENTRAL FUNCTIONS AND THE MINISTERIAL
ORGANISATION
1 Victoria Street, London SW1H 0ET
020 7215 5000

Chief Economic Adviser: David Coates CB
Chief Adviser on Statistics: Janet Dougharty
*Director, Strategy and Competitiveness, Central
Directorate:* David Evans
Director, Competitiveness Unit:
Sarah Chambers
Director, Enterprise Unit: Mark Higson
Director, Future and Innovation Unit:
John Reynolds

COMMUNICATIONS
*Director Publicity and Internal
Communications:* Peter Burke
Director of News: Iain Hepplewhite
Deputy Director News: Colin Seabrook
Director Publicity: Peter Burke

Executive Agencies: Companies House;
Employment Tribunals Service (ETS); Insol-
vency Service; National Weights and Measures
Laboratory (NWML); Patent Office; Radio-
communications Agency (RA); Small Business
Service

HM Treasury

Treasury Chambers, Parliament Street,
London SW1P 3AG
020 7270 5000 *Fax:* 020 7270 5653
E-mail:
firstname.surname@hm-treasury.gov.uk
Website: www.hm-treasury.gov.uk

Parliamentary Branch (for all Ministers)
020 7270 5005/07/5183
Ministerial Correspondence (for all Ministers)
020 7270 5163

Responsible for formulating and implementing
government financial and economic policy.

The Prime Minister has the title of First Lord of
the Treasury, and the government whips in both
Houses of Parliament and the Leader of the
House of Lords are all officially part of HM
Treasury. They do not, however, play a part in
the day-to-day life of the departmental Treasury
which is headed by the Chancellor of the
Exchequer.

Chancellor of the Exchequer:
Rt Hon Gordon Brown MP
Parliamentary Private Secretary:
John Healey MP
Chief Senior Economic Adviser: Ed Balls
(020 7270 4941)
Special Advisers: Ian Austin, Sue Nye,
Chris Wales

Chief Secretary: Rt Hon Andrew Smith MP
Parliamentary Private Secretary: Joan Ryan MP
Special Advisers: Paul Andrew (020 7270 5027),
Edward Milliband

Paymaster General: Dawn Primarolo MP
Parliamentary Private Secretary:
Chris Pond MP

Financial Secretary: Stephen Timms MP
Parliamentary Private Secretary:
Vernon Coaker MP

Economic Secretary: Melanie Johnson MP

Spokesman in the House of Lords:
Lord McIntosh of Haringey

Parliamentary Clerk: David S Martin

DIRECTORATE MANAGEMENT
Permanent Secretary:
Sir Andrew Turnbull KCB CVO

MACROECONOMIC POLICY AND INTERNATIONAL
FINANCE
Managing Director: Gus O'Donnell, CB
Directors: Jonathan Taylor**, Jon Cunliffe,
Ivan Rogers

BUDGET AND PUBLIC FINANCES
Managing Director: Robert Culpin
Managing Director: Colin Mowl
Nick Macpherson

PUBLIC SERVICES
Managing Director: John Gieve CB
Directors: Joe Grice*, Gill Noble CB,
Adam Sharples, Lucy De Groot

FINANCIAL MANAGEMENT, REPORTING AND
AUDIT
Managing Director: Andrew Likierman**
Director: Brian Glicksman*

FINANCE REGULATION AND INDUSTRY
Managing Director: Sir Steven Robson KCB
Directors: Harry Bush CB, Robin Fellgett

*combined director and head of standing team
**head of cross-directorate standing team

CORPORATE SERVICES AND DEVELOPMENT
Managing Director: Hilary Douglas
Non-Executive Director: Margaret Exley

Heads of Directorate Standing Teams:
Sam Beckett, Richard Bent, Rob Brightwell,
Alastair Bridges, Peter Brook, Simon Brooks,
Richard Brown, Harry Bush CB, Chris Butler,
Ian Carruthers, Peter Curwen,
Melanie Dawes, David Deaton,
Jonathan De Berker, Paula Diggle,
John Dodds, Tim Dowse, Ros Dunn,
Michael Ellam, Donald Franklin, Alex Gibbs,
Brian Glicksman, Mike Glycopantis,
Dilwyn Griffiths, Joseph Halligan,
Jim Hibberd, Nicholas Holgate, Helen John,
Anne-Marie Jones, Peter Kane, Chris Kelly,
Andrew Kilpatrick, John Kingman,

David Lawton, Andrew Lewis, David Loweth,
Clive Maxwell, Paul Mills, Sarah Mullen,
Graham Parker, Paul Pegler, Dave Ramsden,
James Richardson, Mike Richardson,
Allen Ritchie, Kevin Ross, Philip Rutnam,
Peter Schofield, Tom Scholar, Adam Sharples,
Michael Swan, Ian Taylor, Ric Todd,
Helen Tuffs, Ian Walker, Mike Williams,
Paul Williams
Treasury Representative Abroad:
Stephen Pickford

OFFICE OF GOVERNMENT COMMERCE
Fleetbank House, 2-6 Salisbury Square,
London EC4Y 8AE
Fax: 020 7211 1358
Chief Executive: Peter Gershon CBE
020 7211 1350
Deputy Chief Executive: Brian Rigby
020 7211 1310
Executive Manager: Alexandra Turnock
020 7211 1311
Assistant to Executive Manager: Lucy Stares
020 7211 1327

Executive Agencies: The Buying Agency;
Central Computer and Telecommunications
Agency (CCTA); National Savings (NS); Office
for National Statistics (ONS); Royal Mint; UK
Debt Management Office (DMO)

The Wales Office
OFFICE OF THE SECRETARY OF STATE
FOR WALES
Gwydyr House, Whitehall,
London SW1A 2ER
020 7270 0549 *GTN:* 1208
Fax: 020 7270 0568
Website: www.walesoffice.gov.uk

The National Assembly for Wales
Cardiff Bay, Cardiff CF99 1NA
029 2082 5111
Website: www.wales.gov.uk

New Crown Building, Cathays Park,
Cardiff CF10 3NQ
029 2082 5111 *GTN:* 1208
Telex: 498228
Fax enquiries should be made through
the switchboard

Parliamentary Branch for all Ministers:
020 7270 0554

The Secretary of State represents Wales in the Cabinet and is responsible for defence and foreign affairs, justice, police and prison systems, taxation and social security benefits and macro-economic policy. The National Assembly for Wales implements Government policies in Wales including health, the environment, transport and agriculture, housing, local government and planning.

Secretary of State:
  Rt Hon Paul Murphy MP
Parliamentary Private Secretary:
  Nick Ainger MP
Special Advisers: Hywel Francis,
  Adrian McMenamin

Parliamentary Under-Secretary of State:
  David Hanson MP

Head of Office of the Secretary of State for Wales: Alison Jackson
Parliamentary Clerk: Michael Williams

Spokesperson in the House of Lords:
Baroness Farrington

INFORMATION DIVISION
Director of News: Pat Wilson

FINANCE AND ADMINISTRATION
Head of Finance and Administration:
  John Williams

POLICY GROUP 1
Head of Group: Anne Morrice
Responsibility for: Industry and Training; Agriculture; Transport, Planning and Environment

POLICY GROUP 2
Head of Group: Sarah Canning
Responsibility for: Education; Health; Local Government, Housing and Social Services

NON-MINISTERIAL DEPARTMENTS

Non-Ministerial Government Departments are headed by office-holders, boards or Commissioners with specific statutory responsibilities.

Building Societies Commission

25 The North Colonnade, Canary Wharf,
London E14 5HS
020 7676 1000

First Commissioner and Chairman:
Geoffrey Fitchew CMG
Deputy Chairman: Carol Sergeant
Commissioners: Sir James Birrell,
Nigel Fox-Bassett, Shaun Mundy,
Jeremy Palmer, Graham Sunderland,
Jock Worsley
Secretary: Graham Johnson
Legal Adviser: Chris Stallard

Charity Commission

Harmsworth House, 13-15 Bouverie Street,
London EC4Y 8DP
0870 333 0123 *Fax:* 020 7674 2310
E-mail:
feedback@charity-commission.gov.uk
Website: www.charity-commission.gov.uk

Responsible for the registration and supervision of registered charities in England and Wales.

Chief Commissioner: John Stoker
Director of Operations: Simon Gillespie
Director of Resources: Bill Richardson
Director of Policy: Richard Carter
Regional Operations Manager:
Christina Parry

2nd Floor, 20 Kings Parade,
Queens Dock, Liverpool L3 4DQ
0870 333 0123 *Fax:* 0151-703 1555
Regional Operations Manager:
Neil Peterson

Woodfield House, Tangier, Taunton
Somerset TA1 4BL
0870 333 0123 *Fax:* 01823 345003
Regional Operations Manager:
Ceinwen Thorne

Crown Estate

16 Carlton House Terrace,
London SW1Y 5AH
020 7210 4377 *Fax:* 020 7930 8187
E-mail: pr@crownestate.co.uk
Website: www.crownestate.co.uk

Manages the Crown Estate, land and landed property which remains part of the hereditary possessions of the Sovereign. It is not a government department but neither is it part of the private estate of the reigning monarch.

First Commissioner and Chairman (part-time):
Sir Denys Henderson Kt
Second Commissioner and Chief Executive:
Sir Christopher Howes KCVO CB
Commissioner and Director of Finance and Administration: Roger Bright
Director of Urban Estates: Tony Bickmore
Legal Adviser: David Harris

Crown Prosecution Service

Headquarters, 50 Ludgate Hill,
London EC4M 7EX
020 7796 8000 *Fax:* 020 7796 8650
E-mail: enquiries@cps.gov.uk
Website: www.cps.gov.uk

The Crown Prosecution Service is responsible for the independent review and conduct of criminal proceedings instituted by police forces in England and Wales (with the exception of cases conducted by the Serious Fraud Office and certain minor offences).

Director of Public Prosecutions:
David Calvert-Smith, QC
Chief Executive: Mark Addison
*Chief Inspector: Stephen Wooler
Director, Business Information Systems:
Lonny Carey
Director, Casework: Chris Newell
Director, Finance: John Graham
Director, Human Resources: Indi Seehra
Director, Policy: Garry Patten
Head of Communications: Lyn Salisbury
Head of Management Audit Services:
Bob Capstick
*Legislation is before Parliament which will create the Inspectorate as an independent statutory body

HM Customs and Excise

New King's Beam House,
22 Upper Ground, London SE1 9PJ
020 7620 1313 *Fax:* 020 7865 5048
Website:
www.open.gov.uk/customs/c&ehome.htm

Collects and administers taxes and duties, mainly on consumer expenditure (indirect taxation), including Value Added Tax (VAT), excise duties on hydrocarbon oils, tobacco products, alcoholic drinks, betting and gaming and Insurance Premium Tax and Air Passenger Duty and the landfill tax. It also collects customs duties and agricultural levies on behalf of the EU.

Customs' other main responsibility is the enforcement of import prohibitions and restrictions on drugs, firearms, indecent material and endangered species.

Ministers: Chancellor of the Exchequer:
 Rt Hon Gordon Brown MP
 Paymaster General: Dawn Primarolo MP

THE BOARD
Chairman: Richard Broadbent (020 7865 5001)
Priv Sec: Donna Morris

Commissioners:
 Mike Eland (020 7865 5405)
 Mike Hanson (020 7865 5019)
 Alex Fraser (020 7865 4817)
 Richard Allen (020 7865 5933),
 Mike Norgrove (020 7865 5978),
 Martin Brown (020 7865 5016),
 Terry Byrne (020 7865 5025),
 Ray McAfee (020 7865 5445),

Director, Policy: Mike Eland
Director, Strategy: Michael Hanson
Director, Enforcement: Terry Byrne
Director, Logistics: Alex Fraser
Director, Outfield: Ray McAfee
Director, Delivery: Mike Norgrove
Director, Human Resources: Richard Allen
Head of Tax Practice: Martin Brown
Solicitor: David Pickup

Executive Agencies: HM Customs and Excise Executive Units

Estyn: Her Majesty's Inspectorate for Education and Training in Wales

Phase 1, Government Buildings,
Tŷ Glas Road, Llanishen, Cardiff CF14 5FQ
029 2032 7291 *Fax:* 029 2075 8182
or *Secure Fax* 029 2076 5201

Responsible for standards and quality in education and training in Wales through independent inspection and advice.

HM Chief Inspector: Susan Lewis
Head of Inspection Division – Pre-16 and Early Years Education: Mike Haines
Head of Inspection Division – Post-16 and Training: Elizabeth Kidd
Head of Policy, Planning and Corporate Services: Shan Howells

Food Standards Agency

London Headquarters, Hannibal House,
PO Box 30080, London SE1 6YA
020 7238 6550 *Fax:* 020 7238 6330
E-mail: helpline@foodstandards.gsi.gov.uk
Website: www.foodstandards.gov.uk

Responsible for all aspects of food safety and standards throughout the UK.

Chairman: Prof Sir John Krebs
Deputy Chair: Suzi Leather
Chief Executive: Geoffrey Podger

Executive Agency: Meat Hygiene Service

Forestry Commission

231 Corstorphine Road,
Edinburgh EH12 7AT
0131-334 0303 *Fax:* 0131-334 3047
E-mail: enquiries@forestry.gsi.gov.uk
Website: www.forestry.gov.uk

Responsible for forestry policy in Great Britain.

Chairman: Sir Peter Hutchison Bt CBE
Director-General and Deputy Chairman:
 David Bills
Chief Executive Forest Enterprise:
 Dr Bob McIntosh
Secretary to the Commissioners: Frank Strang

SECRETARIAT
Head of Secretariat: Frank Strang
Policy Support: Peter Edwards
Communications: Colin Morton

CORPORATE SERVICES
Head of Corporate Services: Duncan Macniven
Head of Policy Practice: Tim Rollinson
Head of Country Services: Roger Herbert
Chief Conservators:
 England (Cambridge): Paul Hill-Tout
 Scotland (Edinburgh): David Henderson-Howat
 Wales (Aberystwyth): Simon Hewitt

Executive Agencies: Forest Enterprise; Forest Research

Friendly Societies Commission

25 The North Colonnade, Canary Wharf,
London E14 5HS
020 7676 1000

Chairman: Martin Roberts
Commissioners: Felipe da Rocha, Sarah Brown,
Tony Geddes, Brian Richardson,
Patricia Triggs
Secretary: Janice Erskine
Legal Adviser: John Wylde

Inland Revenue

Somerset House, Strand,
London WC2R 1LB
020 7438 6622 *Fax:* 020 7438 6494
Website: www.open.gov.uk/inrev/

Administers and collects income tax, corporation
tax, capital gains tax, stamp duty, inheritance tax,
petroleum revenue tax and National Insurance
Contributions, and advises the Chancellor of the
Exchequer on tax policy.

Ministers: Chancellor of the Exchequer:
Rt Hon Gordon Brown MP
Paymaster General: Dawn Primarolo MP

THE BOARD
Chairman: Nick Montagu CB
Deputy Chairmen: Tim Flesher, Ann Chant
Director General: Dave Hartnett
Chief Executive VOA: Michael Johns CB

Head Office Directors
Human Resources: Alexa Walker
International: Gabs Makhlouf
Capital and Savings: Marjorie Williams
Financial Institutions: Stephen Jones
Cross Cutting Policy Unit: Robin Martin
Business Tax: Jenny Williams
Business and Management Services:
John Yard CBE
Personal Tax: Tony Orhnail
Finance: John Gant
Tax Law Rewrite: Neil Munro
Business Operations: Vacant
Director Analytical Services Division:
Reginald Ward
Senior Economic Adviser: William McNie
NICO – National Insurance Contribution Office:
Director: Bridget Woodley (Executive Office)

Executive Agencies: Valuation Office; 26 Inland
Revenue Executive Units

National Investment and Loans Office

1 King Charles Street, London SW1A 2AP
020 7270 3861 *Fax:* 020 7270 1651
E-mail: firstname.secondname@nilo.gov.uk
Website: www.nilo.gov.uk

Provides common office services to the National
Debt Office, the Public Works Loan Board and
the Office of HM Paymaster General.
Current role is mainly the investment of a series
of Government funds (National Insurance Fund,
National Savings and the National Lottery).
The Public Works Loan Board considers loan
applications from local authorities and other prescribed bodies and, where loans are made, to col-
lect the repayments.

Director: Ian Peattie

NATIONAL DEBT OFFICE
020 7270 3868 *Fax:* 020 7270 3860
Website: www.national-debt-office.gov.uk
Comptroller General: Ian Peattie
Assistant Comptroller General: Alex Lawrie

PUBLIC WORKS LOAN BOARD
020 7270 3874 *Fax:* 020 7270 3860
Website: www.pwlb.gov.uk
Chairman: Anthony Loehnis CMG
Deputy Chairman: Vera Di Palma OBE
Secretary: Ian Peattie
Assistant Secretary: Mark Frankel

OFFICE OF HM PAYMASTER GENERAL
020 7270 1652 *Fax:* 020 7270 3863
Website: www.opg.gov.uk
Paymaster General: Dawn Primarolo MP
Assistant Paymaster General: Ian Peattie
Head of Banking: Lee Palmer
Banking Manager: Peter Harris

Office for Standards in Education

Alexandra House, 33 Kingsway
London WC2B 6SE
020 7421 6800 *Fax:* 020 7421 6707
E-mail: geninfo@ofsted.gov.uk
Website: www.ofsted.gov.uk

Inspects initial teacher training, local education
authorities, independent schools and LEA-
funded youth and adult education.

HM Chief Inspector: Chris Woodhead
Directors of Inspection:
Michael Tomlinson, CBE, David Taylor

Director of Policy, Planning and Resources:
Judith Phillips, CBE
Head of Research, Analysis and International:
Christine Agambar
Head of School Improvement:
Elizabeth Passmore OBE
Head of Secondary: Mike Raleigh
Head of Primary: Keith Lloyd
Head of Nursery: Dorian Bradley
Head of SEN: Chris Marshall
Head of Post Compulsory: Stephen Grix
Head of Contracts: Clive Bramley
Head of Teacher Education: Cliff Gould
Head of Personnel Management: Andrew White
Head of IT: Mike Worthy
*Head of Communications, Media and Public
Relations:* Jonathan Lawson
Head of Accommodation: Keith Francis
Head of Inspection Quality: Peter Matthews
Head of Curriculum Advice and Inspection:
Brian McCafferty
Head of LEA Reviews: David Singleton
Head of Finance: Peter Jolly
Heads of Corporate Services: Roger Knight,
Jos Parsons

Office for the Regulation of Electricity and Gas

Brookmount Buildings, 42 Fountain Street,
Belfast BT1 5EE
028 9031 1575 *Fax:* 028 9031 1740
E-mail: ofreg@nics.gov.uk
Website: ofreg.nics.gov.uk/

OFREG is the joint regulatory authority for the electricity and natural gas industries in Northern Ireland. It is responsible for promoting competition in the generation and supply of electricity; promoting the development of the natural gas industry, and regulating certain electricity and gas prices.

Director-General of Electricity Supply NI:
Director-General of Gas NI: Douglas McIldoon
*Deputy Director-General of
Electricity Supply NI:*
Deputy Director-General of Gas NI: Vacant

Office of Fair Trading

Fleetbank House, 2–6 Salisbury Square,
London EC4Y 8JX
020 7211 8000 *Fax:* 020 7211 8800
E-mail: enquiries@oft.gov.uk
Website: www.oft.gov.uk

Has responsibility to keep all commercial activities under review, to identify behaviour that adversely affects the consumer or damages competition;

– has the power to take regulatory enforcement action to protect the interests of consumers;
– has the power among other things, to make references to the Competition Commission and impose penalties on companies.

Director-General: John Vickers
Director of Consumer Affairs: Caroline Banks
E-mail: caroline.banks@oft.gov.uk
Director of Competition Policy: Margaret Bloom
E-mail: margaret.bloom@oft.gov.uk
Legal Director: Pat Edwards
E-mail: pat.edwards@oft.gov.uk
Director of Information: Dermod Hill
E-mail: dermod.hill@oft.gov.uk
Director of Resources and Services:
Rosemary Heyhoe
E-mail: rosemary.heyhoe@oft.gov.uk

Office of Gas and Electricity Markets

9 Millbank, London SW1P 3GE
020 7901 7000 *Fax:* 020 7901 7066
Website: www.ofgem.gov.uk

Responsible for regulating the gas and electricity markets and protecting customers' interests. It also encourages competition in both markets.

Director-General: Callum McCarthy
*Deputy Director-General, Regulation and
Financial Affairs:* Richard Morse
*Deputy Director-General, Competition and
Trading Arrangements:*
Dr Eileen Marshall CBE
*Deputy Director-General, Customers and
Supply:* John Neilson
Chief Operating Officer: Gill Whittington
Director, Public Affairs: Sarah Harrison
General Counsel: Charles Bankes

Office of Telecommunications

50 Ludgate Hill, London EC4M 7JJ
020 7634 8700 *Fax:* 020 7634 8943
E-mail: infocent.oftel@gtnet.gov.uk
Website: www.oftel.gov.uk

Independent regulator of the UK telecommunications industry operating in the interests of telecommunications customers.

Director-General: David Edmonds
Director of Operations: Anne Lambert
Director of Regulatory Policy: Christopher Kenny
Director of Compliance: Keith Long
Director of Technology: Peter Walker
Director of Strategy and Forecasting: Alan Bell
Director of Business Support: David Smith
Director of Communications: Duncan Stroud

Office of the International Rail Regulator

1 Waterhouse Square, 138–142 Holborn,
London EC1N 2TQ
020 7282 2000 *Fax:* 020 7282 2040
E-mail: orr@dial.pipex.com
Website: www.rail-reg.gov.uk
International Rail Regulator: Tom Winsor
Head of Communications: Sue Daniels

Office of the Rail Regulator

1 Waterhouse Square, 138–142 Holborn,
London EC1N 2TQ
020 7282 2000 *Fax:* 020 7282 2040
E-mail: orr@dial.pipex.com
Website: www.rail-reg.gov.uk

Independent regulatory body. Functions include licensing operators and protecting the interests of rail users.

Rail Regulator: Tom Winsor
Director of Strategy, Planning and
 Communications: Keith Webb
Director, Railway Network Group:
 Michael Beswick
Director, Operator Regulation: Melanie Leech
Chief Economist: Paul Plummer
Chief Legal Adviser: Sally Barrett-Williams
Head of Communications: Sue Daniels

Office of Water Services

Centre City Tower, 7 Hill Street,
Birmingham B5 4UA
0121-625 1300 *Fax:* 0121-625 1400
E-mail: enquiries@ofwat.gsi.gov.uk
Website: www.open.gov.uk/ofwat/

Responsible for regulating the water and sewerage industry in England and Wales, protecting customers, facilitating competition and promoting economy and efficiency.

Director General: Philip Fletcher
Director of Costs and Performance, and Chief
 Engineer: Dr Bill Emery
Director of Tariffs and Consumer Affairs:
 Michael Saunders
Director of Operations: Roger Dunshea
Legal Adviser: Allan Merry
Head of External Relations: Julia Havard
Parliamentary Affairs and Briefing Officer:
 Ingrid Olsen
Head of Consumer Representation Division:
 Roy Wardle

Registry of Friendly Societies

Victory House, 30–34 Kingsway,
London WC2B 6ES
020 7663 5025 *Fax:* 020 7663 5059

Provides a public registry for mutual organisations registered under the Building Societies Act 1986, Friendly Societies Acts 1974 and 1992 and the Industrial and Provident Societies Act 1965. The Chief Registrar is responsible for the supervision of credit unions, and advises the Government on issues affecting them.

Chief Registrar: Geoffrey Fitchew CMG
Assistant Registrars: Sallie Eden,
 Eric Engstrom, Nigel Fawcett, Shaun Mundy
Assistant Registrar: James Craig
 (Registry of Friendly Societies (Scotland),
 58 Frederick Street, Edinburgh EH2 1NB)

Shadow Strategic Rail Authority

55 Victoria Street, London SW1H 0EU
020 7654 6000 *Fax:* 020 7654 6010
E-mail: secretariat@sra.gov.uk
Website: www.sra.gov.uk

Monitors and manages the passenger train franchises operating on the national railway network in Great Britain, and seeks to strategically direct the growth of passenger and freight rail transport.

Chairman: Sir Alastair Morton
Chief Executive and Director of Passenger Rail
 Franchising: Mike Grant
Executive Director, Franchise Management:
 Nick Newton
Executive Director, Finance: Martin McGann
Executive Director, External Relations:
 Chris Austin
The Solicitor: Terence Jenner
Freight Director: Julia Clarke
Chief Economist: Bob Stannard
Head of Secretariat: James McArthur Watson
Head of Public Affairs: Paul McKie

EXECUTIVE AGENCIES

The Next Steps concept, launched in 1988 to modernise and improve the management of government services, entailed setting up executive agencies to perform specific administrative functions of government departments.

The establishment of agencies was largely completed by 2000, by which time over three-quarters of civil servants were working in some 130 executive agencies and four government bodies, the Crown Prosecution Service, HM Customs and Excise, Inland Revenue and the Serious Fraud Office, which work on Next Step lines.

Agencies' chief executives are directly responsible to the minister heading the relevant government department, who sets policy, budget and targets and is responsible to parliament for the agency.

ABRO

Monxton Road, Andover,
Hampshire SP11 8HT
01264 383295 *Fax:* 01264 383144

Provides an equipment repair and refurbishment service for the armed services.

Chief Executive: Jim Drew CBE
Deputy Chief Executive: Dr Les Salmon
Commercial Director: Alan Lewis
Production Director: Graham Benjamin
Department: Defence
Launched: 1/4/93

Appeals Service

4th Floor, Whittington House
19-30 Alfred Place
London WC1E 7LW
020 7712 2600 *Fax:* 020 7712 2650
Website: www. appeals-service.gov.uk

Chief Executive: Neil Ward
Finance Director: Alex Maddocks
Operational Policy Director: Emma Churchill
Department: Social Security
Launched: 3/4/00

Armed Forces Personnel Administration Agency

Building 182, RAF Innsworth,
Gloucester GL3 1HW
01452 712612 ext 7347 *Fax:* 01452 510887

Provides the data and systems for the payment of all service personnel (including pensions), and supports the Armed Forces personnel management function.

Chief Executive: Terence Lord
Deputy Chief Executive and Director Strategy:
    Commodore Trevor Spires
Director Development: Brigadier Richard Leighton
Director Operations:
    Air Commodore Paul Thomas, MBE
Director Personnel and Finance: Charles Boyle
EDS Account Director: Barry Cooke
Department: Defence
Launched: 1/4/97

Army Personnel Centre

Kentigern House, 65 Brown Street,
Glasgow G2 8EX
0141-224 2070 *Fax:* 0141-224 3555

Task is to man the Army, manage the careers of Army personnel and to provide Army pay, personnel and pensions administration.

Military Secretary/Chief Executive:
    Major General Alistair Irwin CBE
Deputy Military Secretary:
    Brigadier Mark Elcomb, OBE
Director Personnel Administration:
    Brigadier Malcolm Duncan
APC Secretary: Dr Alec Stevenson
Department: Defence
Launched: 2/12/96

Army Training and Recruiting Agency

Trenchard Lines, Upavon, Pewsey,
Wiltshire SN9 6BE
01980 615024 *Fax:* 01980 615300
E-mail: hqatra@gtnet.gov.uk

Provides manpower trained in the individual skills required to sustain the Army's military effectiveness.

Chief Executive:
    Major General Anthony Palmer, CBE
Deputy Chief Executive: Martyn Piper
*Chief of Staff Directorate of Individual Training
    Policy (Army):* Brigadier Roy Wilde
Head of Policy, Strategy and Communications:
    Colonel Tom Richardson
Head of Operations and Plans:
    Colonel John Durance
Head of Resources, Programmes and Finance:
    John Thornton
Agency Secretary: David Simpson
Head of Commerce and Estates: Brian Court
Department: Defence
Launched: 1/4/97

Benefits Agency

Quarry House, Quarry Hill
Leeds LS2 7UA
0113-232 4000
Customer Helpline 0113-232 4143
E-mail: baadmin@baadmin.demon.co.uk
Website: www.dss.gov.uk
Details of Agency local offices available on
website

The Benefits Agency is responsible for administering claims and payments of social security
benefits.

Chief Executive: Alexis Cleveland
Pensions Director for Strategy, Stewardship and
Delivery: Steve Heminsley
Director of Field Operations (North):
Charlie MacKinnon
Director of Field Operations (South): Tony Edge
Department: Social Security
Launched: 2/4/91

British Forces Post Office

Inglis Barracks, Mill Hill, London NW7 1PX
020 8818 6315 *Fax:* 020 8818 6309
E-mail: bfpo@compuserve.com

Provides postal and courier services.

Chief Executive: Brigadier Barry Cash
Deputy Chief Executive/Head Policy and
Strategy: Colonel George McGarr OBE
Head Postal and Courier Services/Operations:
Colonel Don Kent
Department: Defence
Launched: 1/7/92 as DPCSA
Re-launched: 1/7/99 as BFPO

Business Development Service

Craigantlet Buildings, Stoney Road,
Belfast BT4 3SX
028 9052 0444 *Fax:* 028 9052 7447
E-mail: bds@nics.gov.uk
Website: www.nics.gov.uk/bds/

Provides business support services to Northern
Ireland departments, their executive agencies
and the wider public sector.

Chief Executive: Ken Millar
Department: Finance and Personnel
(Northern Ireland)
Launched: 1/10/96

The Buying Agency

Royal Liver Building, Pier Head,
Liverpool L3 1PE
0151-227 4262 *Fax:* 0151-227 3315
Procurement Advice
0151-224 2242/3
E-mail: marketing@tba.gov.uk
Website: www.open.gov.uk/tba/tbahome.htm

TBA provides a high quality, professional procurement service to government, public sector
organisations and their private sector contractors.

Chief Executive: Stephen Sage
Finance Director: Alan Philips
Human Resource Director: Keith Pope
Commercial Director: Dr Clare Poulter
Operations Director: Kevin Cahill
Department: Office of Government
Commerce (HM Treasury)
Launched: 31/10/91

Cadw/Welsh Historic Monuments

Crown Buildings,
Cathays Park, Cardiff CF10 3NQ
029 2050 0200 *Fax:* 029 2082 6375
E-mail: lorraine.griffiths@wales.gsi.gov.uk
Website: www.cadw.wales.gov.uk

Maintains and preserves the built heritage of
Wales and presents those monuments in the care
of the National Assembly for Wales to the public.

Chief Executive: Thomas Cassidy
Director of Policy and Administration: Vacant
Chief Architect: Douglas Hogg
Chief Inspector: Richard Avent
Head of Presentation: Andrew Hood
Head of Corporate Services: Jeffrey Jenkins
Responsible Assembly Members:
First Secretary and Sue Essex AM
Launched 2/4/91

Central Computer and Telecommunications Agency

Rosebery Court, St Andrew's Business Park,
Norwich NR7 0HS
01603 704567 *Fax:* 01603 704817
E-mail: info@ccta.gsi.gov.uk
Website: www.ccta.gov.uk

Provides information technology expertise to
public sector organisations.

Chief Executive: Bob Assirati
Department: Office of Government
Commerce (HM Treasury)
Launched: 1/4/96

Central Office of Information

Hercules Road, London SE1 7DU
020 7928 2345 *Fax:* 020 7928 5037
Website: www.coi.gov.uk

Provides consultancy, procurement and project management services to central government for publicity and provides specialist services in certain areas.

Chief Executive: Carol Fisher
Group Directors,
  Establishment and Finance: Keith Williamson
  Marketing Communications: Peter Buchanan
  Publications: Michael Reid
  Films, Radio Events: Sally Whetton
  Client Services: Ian Hamilton
  Regional Network: Rob Haslam
Network Office Directors,
  East: Richard Humphries
  North East: Lynn Taylor
  North West: Eileen Jones
  Yorkshire and Humberside: Wendy Miller
  Midlands West: Brent Garner
  Midlands East: Peter Smith
  South East: Virginia Burdon
  South West: Peter Whitbread
Department: The Central Office of Information is a separate Government Department reporting directly to the Minister for the Cabinet Office
Launched: 5/4/90

Central Science Laboratory

Sand Hutton, York YO41 1LZ
01904 462000 *Fax:* 01904 462111
E-mail: science@csl.gov.uk
Website: www.csl.gov.uk

Provides a wide range of scientific services including:
– plant health
– the authenticity, chemical and microbiological safety and nutritional value of the food supply
– pesticide safety, including monitoring of residues in food
– veterinary drug residues
– the control of pests and diseases of growing and stored foodstuffs
– wildlife management, and
– the impact of food production on the environment and the consumer.

Chief Executive: Prof Peter Stanley
Research Director (Agriculture and Environment): Prof Tony Hardy

Research Director (Food): Prof John Gilbert
Commercial Director: Dr Robert Bolton
Finance and Procurement Director:
  Richard Shaw
Corporate Services Director: Dr Helen Crews
Department: Agriculture, Fisheries and Food
Launched: 1/4/92

Centre for Environment, Fisheries and Aquaculture Science

Lowestoft Laboratory, Pakefield Road
Lowestoft, Suffolk NR33 0HT
01502 562244 *Fax:* 01502 513865
E-mail: marketing@cefas.co.uk
Website: www.cefas.co.uk

Provides scientific research, assessment and advice in fisheries management, environmental protection, and fish health, hygiene and aquaculture.

Chief Executive: Dr Peter Greig-Smith
Deputy to the Chief Executive and Chief Fisheries Science Adviser to MAFF:
  Dr Joe W Horwood
Department: Agriculture, Fisheries and Food
Launched: 1/4/97

Child Support Agency

Room 158A, Longbenton,
Newcastle upon Tyne NE98 1YX
E-mail: csa-chief-execs-office@
new100.dss.gsi.gov.uk
Website: www.gov.dss.uk/csa

Assesses, collects and, where necessary, enforces Child Support maintenance.

Chief Executive: Doug Smith
  0191-225 9151
Deputy Chief Executive: Mike Isaac
  0191-225 7699
Child Support Reform Programme Director:
  Vince Gaskell 0191-225 5151
Director of Operations: John Lutton
  0191-225 9292
Resources Director: Mick Davison
  0191-225 7508
Director of Support Services: Paul Hedley
  0191-225 5329
Director of Operations Strategy and Customer Relations: Marietta Di Ciacca 0191-225 9497
Department: Social Security
Launched: 5/4/93

Companies House

Crown Way, Cardiff CF14 3UZ
029 2038 8588 *Fax:* 029 2038 0900
E-mail: enquiries@companieshouse.gov.uk
Website: www.companieshouse.gov.uk

Registers companies and collects statutory documents and returns and makes information available to the public.

Chief Executive and Registrar of Companies for England and Wales: John Holden
Director of Operations: Jeanne Spinks
Director of Information Technology: Mark Pacey
Director of Finance: Jack Mansfield
Director of Policy and Planning: Liz Carter

LONDON INFORMATION CENTRE
Companies House
21 Bloomsbury Street, London WC1B 3XD
029 2038 8588 *Fax:* 029 2038 0900

COMPANIES HOUSE
37 Castle Terrace, Edinburgh EH1 2EB
0131-535 5800 *Fax:* 0131-535 5820
Registrar for Scotland: Jim Henderson

Department: Trade and Industry
Launched: 3/10/88

Compensation Agency

Royston House, 34 Upper Queen Street
Belfast BT1 6FD
028 9024 9944 *Fax:* 028 9024 6956
E-mail: comp-agency@nics.gov.uk
Website: www.nics.gov.uk/ca

Administers the criminal injuries and criminal damage compensation schemes and pays compensation under the emergency provisions legislation.

Chief Executive: Frank W Brannigan
Head of Operations: Norman Mills
Department: Northern Ireland Office
Launched: 1/4/92

Construction Service

Churchill House, Victoria Square
Belfast BT1 4QW
028 9025 0250 *Fax:* 028 9025 0333
Business Enquiries: 028 9025 0283
E-mail: info.cs.doe@nics.gov.uk
Website: www.doeni.gov.uk/const.htm

Provides a professional design, maintenance and advisory service to government departments, agencies and other public bodies covering a wide range of construction industry disciplines.

Acting Chief Executive: Billy Walker
Department: Finance and Personnel (Northern Ireland)
Launched: 1/4/96

Court Service

Southside, 105 Victoria Street,
London SW1E 6QT
020 7210 1672 *Fax:* 020 7210 1797
E-mail: cust.ser.cs@gtnet.gov.uk
Website: www.courtservice.gov.uk

Provides administrative support to the Court of Appeal, High Court, Crown Court, County courts and some tribunals in England and Wales.

Chief Executive: Ian Magee
Department: Lord Chancellor's
Launched: 3/4/95
For full details of the Court Service see Judiciary

HM Customs and Excise

The Board of HM Customs and Excise – see also Non-Ministerial Government Departments
New King's Beam House
22 Upper Ground, London SE1 9PJ
020 7620 1313 *Fax:* 020 7865 5048
Website:
www.open.gov.uk/customs/c&ehome.htm

Chairman: Richard Broadbent

CYMRU (WALES) COLLECTION
Collector: Carole Upshaw
HM Customs and Excise
Portcullis House, 21 Cowbridge Road East
Cardiff CF1 9SS
029 2038 6000 *Fax:* 029 2038 6033

EAST MIDLANDS COLLECTION
Collector: Arthur Durrant
HM Customs and Excise
Bowman House, 100/102 Talbot Street
Nottingham NG1 5NF
0115-971 2100 *Fax:* 0115-971 2235

EASTERN COLLECTION
Collector: John Hendry
HM Customs and Excise, Haven House
17 Lower Brook Street, Ipswich IP4 1DN
01473 235700 *Fax:* 01473 235922

LONDON COLLECTION
Collector: Jim Maclean
HM Customs and Excise, Dorset House,
Stamford Street, London SE1 9PY
020 7928 3344 *Fax:* 020 7202 4216

LONDON INTERNATIONAL COLLECTION
Collector: Mike Hill
HM Customs and Excise, Custom House
Nettleton Road, North Side,
Heathrow Airport London, Hounslow
Middlesex TW6 2LA
020 8910 3600 *Fax:* 020 8910 3616

NORTH WEST COLLECTION
Collector: Tony Allen
HM Customs and Excise, 1st Floor
Queen's Dock, Liverpool L74 4AG
0151-703 8000 *Fax:* 0151-703 1355

NORTHERN IRELAND COLLECTION
Collector: Bill Logan
HM Customs and Excise, Custom House,
Custom House Square, Belfast BT1 3ET
028 9056 2600 *Fax:* 028 9056 2976

SCOTLAND COLLECTION
Collector: Ian Mackay
HM Customs and Excise, 44 York Place
Edinburgh EH1 3JW
0131-469 2000 *Fax:* 0131-469 7333

SOUTH EAST (CENTRAL) COLLECTION
Collector: Martin Peach
HM Customs and Excise, Eaton Court
104-112 Oxford Road, Reading RG1 7FU
0118-964 4200 *Fax:* 0118-964 4093

SOUTH EAST COLLECTION
Collector: Jerry Tullberg
HM Customs and Excise
Priory Court, St Johns Road
Dover, Kent CT17 9SH
01304 206789 *Fax:* 01304 224420

SOUTH WEST COLLECTION
Collector: Hugh Burnard
HM Customs and Excise, Froomsgate House,
Rupert Street, Bristol BS1 2QP
0117-900 2000 *Fax:* 0117-922 1723

WEST MIDLANDS COLLECTION
Collector: David Garlick
HM Customs and Excise,
Two Broadway, Broad Street, Fiveways,
Birmingham B15 1BG
0121-697 4000 *Fax:* 0121-697 4002

YORKSHIRE, HUMBER AND NORTH EAST
COLLECTION
Collector: Hugh Peden
HM Customs and Excise
Peter Bennett House, Redvers Close
West Park Ring Road, Leeds LS16 6RQ
0113-389 4200 *Fax:* 0113-389 4490

Launched: 1/4/91

Defence Analytical Services Agency

Ministry of Defence, Room 112,
Northumberland House,
Northumberland Avenue, London WC2N 5BP
020 7218 0729 *Fax:* 020 7218 5203
E-mail: info@dasa.mod.uk
Website: www.dasa.mod.uk

Provides services including compilation of manpower, financial and logistical statistics, a manpower planning and forecasting service to the Armed Services. It also provides project-based consultancy services to Ministers and senior officials.

Chief Executive: Colin Youngson
Director (Information Services and Logistics):
    Glen Watson
Head of Business Services: Sue Johnston
Department: Defence
Launched: 1/7/92

Defence Aviation Repair Agency

DARA Head Office, St Athan, Barry,
Vale of Glamorgan CF62 4WA
01446 798439 *Fax:* 01446 798187
Website: www.dara.mod.uk

Provides repair, maintenance, modification and overhaul facility for aircraft and aerosystems of the UK Armed Forces.

DARA also provides aircraft storage services, marine gas turbine engine repair and overhaul, and complementary support services for the logistics supply chain and UK Armed Forces operations.

Chief Executive: Stephen Hill, OBE
Deputy Chief Executive:
    Air Commodore Peter Dye
Finance Director: David Roberts
Commercial Director: Ron Jones
Information Systems Director:
    Captain Paul Bishop, RN
Human Resources Director:
    Bernard Galton
Contracts Director: Bob Allen-Burns
Corporate Development Director:
    Andy Hamilton
Department: Defence
Launched: 1/4/99

Defence Bills Agency

Ministry of Defence, Mersey House,
Drury Lane, Liverpool L2 7PX
Fax: 0151-242 2470
E-mail: cao.dba@gtnet.gov.uk
Website: www.defencebills.gov.uk

Provides bill payment, debt collection and associated management information services for MoD.

Chief Executive: Iain Elrick 0151-242 2234
Department: Defence
Launched: 1/1/96

Defence Clothing and Textiles Agency

Skimmingdish Lane, Caversfield,
Oxfordshire OX6 9TS
01869 875501 *Fax:* 01869 875509
E-mail: dcta@dial.pipex.com
Website: www.mod.uk

Supplies uniforms, clothing, textiles, common user items and engineer stores required by the Armed Forces.

Chief Executive: Brigadier Michael Roycroft
Product Director: Group Captain Dave Bernard
Deputy Product Director/Science Adviser:
   Dr Claire Millard
Director Business Management: John Deas
*Director Quality and Product Support Division/
   Research and Technology (DES):* Alan Beattie
Finance Director: Bob Dixson
Contracts Director: Neil Manners
Department: Defence
Launched: 22/11/94

Defence Communication Services Agency

HQ DCSA, Basil Hill Site,
Corsham, Wiltshire SN13 9NR
01225 814785 *Fax:* 01225 814966
E-mail: ce@dcsa.mod.uk

Manages world-wide communications and information transfer services for the Ministry of Defence and Armed Forces.

Chief Executive:
   Major General Tony Raper, CBE
Deputy Chief Executive:
   Air Commodore Ian Kane
Director Operations:
   Commodore Pat Tyrrell, OBE

Director Resources: Norman Swanney
*Director Communication and Information
   Systems:* Brigadier Howard Ham, CBE
Department: Defence
Launched: 1/4/98
Joined Defence Logistics Organisation 1/4/00

Defence Dental Agency

Ministry of Defence, Headquarters DDA
RAF Halton, Aylesbury
Buckinghamshire HP22 5PG
01296 623535 ext 6103
Fax: 01296 626535 ext 6251
E-mail: dda@hqdda.demon.co.uk

Provides dental treatment to service personnel, entitled dependants and other entitled civilians.

Chief Executive:
   Air Vice-Marshal Ian McIntyre
*Director Clinical Services (Director Naval
   Dental Services):*
   Surgeon Commodore (D) John Hargraves
*Director Corporate Planning (Director Army
   Dental Services):* Brigadier John Gamon
Director of Dental Services (RAF):
   Air Commodore Richard Butler
Head of Finance and Secretariat:
   John Knight
Department: Defence
Launched: 1/3/96

Defence Estates

DE Head Office, Blakemore Drive,
Sutton Coldfield, West Midlands B75 7RL
0121-311 3850 *Fax:* 0121-311 2100
E-mail: de_hq@dial.pipex.com
Website: www.defence-estates.mod.uk

Chief Executive: Ian Andrews, CBE, TD
Operations Director: Alan Threadgold
Finance Director: Stephen Dolan
Commercial Director: Ted Pearson
Personnel Director: Stephen Harmer
   (Waterbeach 01223 255051)
Estates Director: Allan Baillie
Projects Director: Howard Lawrence
Quality Director: Clive Cain
Senior Military Officer:
   Colonel Guy Kershaw
Agency Secretary: Hugh Kernohan
Department: Defence
**Launched as Defence Estate Organisation:
   18/3/97**
Re-launched as Defence Estates: 29/3/99

Defence Evaluation and Research Agency

DERA, Ively Road, Farnborough,
Hampshire GU14 0LX
01252 393300 *Fax:* 01252 393399
E-mail: centralenquiries@dera.gov.uk
Website: www.dera.gov.uk

Provides non-nuclear research for the MoD, government departments and other customers.

Chief Executive: Sir John Chisholm
Finance Director and MD Business Services:
    Stephen Park
Technical Director: Dr Adrian Mears
Director, Corporate Affairs: Elizabeth Peace
MD Defence Programmes: John Mabberley
MD Through Life Support: Dr Mike Goodfellow
MD Future Systems Technology:
    Dr David Anderson
MD Sensors and Electronics:
    Dr Derek Barnes
MD Knowledge and Information Systems:
    Andrew Middleton
MD Security: Bill Clifford
Director, Corporate Development:
    David Steeds
Director, Marketing: Fiona Driscoll
Senior Military Officer:
    Commodore Richard Pelly
Department: Defence
Launched: 1/4/95

Defence Geographic and Imagery Intelligence Agency

Headquarters, Watson Building, Elmwood
Avenue, Feltham, Middlesex TW13 7AH
020 8818 2422 *Fax:* 020 8818 2246

Chief Executive: Brigadier Peter Walker
Director Plans and Systems:
    Group Captain Ian Denholm
Director Resources: Pam Titchmarsh
Commander Geographic Engineer Group:
    Colonel Nick Rigby
*Officer Commanding Joint Air Reconnaissance
Intelligence Centre:*
    Group Captain Martin Hallam
Director Defence Geographic Centre:
    Maggie Jacobs
Director Finance: Lisa Boulton
Department: Defence
Launched: 01/04/00

Defence Housing Executive

St Christopher House, Southwark Street,
London SE1 0TD
020 7305 2035 *Fax:* 020 7305 2564

Provides a housing service to Service families across mainland UK, including allocation, maintenance and construction.

Chief Executive: John Wilson
Director Housing: Wendy Jarvis
Director Services Liaison:
    Brigadier Christopher Price, CBE
Director Finance and Secretariat:
    Ashley Adams
Department: Defence
Launched: 1/4/99

Defence Intelligence and Security Centre

Chicksands, Shefford,
Bedfordshire SG17 5PR
01462 752228 *Fax:* 01462 752291
E-mail: ync30@dial.pipex.com

Trains authorised personnel in the intelligence, security and information support disciplines while maintaining an operational capability.

Chief Executive: Brigadier Chris Holtom
Chief of Staff/Deputy Chief Executive:
    Group Captain John Gimblett
Department: Defence
Launched: 1/10/96

Defence Medical Training Organisation

Building 87, Fort Blockhouse, Gosport,
Hampshire PO12 2AB
023 9276 5223 *Fax:* 023 9276 5501
E-mail: hq.dmto@dial.pipex.com

Trains specialist defence medical personnel and provides medical services training for other service personnel in all three services.

Chief Executive: Brigadier Ronnie Brown
Department: Defence
Launched: 1/4/97

Defence Procurement Agency

Abbey Wood, Bristol BS34 8JH
0117-913 0000
Website: www.mod.uk/dpa

Procures new equipment for the Armed Forces in response to approved requirements and provides other procurement related services to its customers in and beyond the Ministry of Defence.

Chief of Defence Procurement and Chief Executive: Sir Robert Walmsley, KCB
Deputy Chief Executive: David Gould

EXECUTIVE DIRECTORS
Executive Director 1: Ian Fauset
Executive Director 2:
Major General Peter Gilchrist
Executive Director 3:
Air Vice Marshal Peter Thornton
Executive Director 4:
Rear Admiral Nigel Guild
Executive Director 5: Stan Porter
Executive Director 6: Susan Scholefield
Engineering Adviser to the Board:
Major General Liam Curran
Department: Defence
Launched: 1/4/99

Defence Secondary Care Agency

St Christopher House, Southwark Street, London SE1 0TD
020 7305 6190 *Fax:* 020 7305 6043
E-mail: mikeblac@dsca.gov.uk
Website: www.open.gov.uk/dsca/

Provides deployable, trained Service medical staff to supply medical care and support to the Armed Forces in exercises and military operations and works very closely with the NHS.

Chief Executive: John Tuckett
Director of Personnel and Services:
Air Commodore Warwick Pike
Director of Corporate Development:
Maggie Somekh
Director of Finance and Management Information: Kathy Makin
Department: Defence
Launched: 30/4/96

Defence Storage and Distribution Agency

Ploughley Road, Lower Arncott, Bicester, Oxfordshire OX25 2LD
01869 256804 *Fax:* 01869 256860
E-mail: ce@dsda.org.uk

Store, maintains and distributes stock to the three armed services, the Procurement Agency, other government departments, MoD administrative and training units and other authorities including NATO allies, Commonwealth and foreign governments, defence contractors and other agencies.

Chief Executive: Brigadier Peter Foxton, CBE
Deputy Chief Executive: Paul Clasper
Director Plans: Group Captain Don Cannon
Director Storage: Colonel Harry O'Hare, OBE
Director Distribution: Colonel Nigel Lloyd
Department: Defence
Launched: 1/4/99

Defence Transport and Movements Agency

Headquarters Defence Logistics Organisation (Andover), Monxton Road, Andover, Hampshire SP11 8HT
01264 383766 *Fax:* 01264 382881

Provides defence and other authorised users with agreed transport and movements services to meet their world-wide requirements in peace, crisis and war.

Chief Executive: Air Commodore Peter Whalley
Department: Defence
Launched: 1/4/99

Defence Vetting Agency

Imphal Barracks, Fulford Road, York YO10 4AS
01904 662444 *Fax:* 01904 665820
E-mail: ce.dva@mod.uk

Grants and maintains security clearances for armed forces personnel, MoD staff, defence industry employees and untertakes investigation work for other government departments.

Chief Executive: Michael Wilson
Head of Corporate Services: Clive Hodgeon
Personnel Manager: Jim Simmonds
Department: Defence
Launched: 1/4/97

Disposal Sales Agency

6 Hercules Road, London SE1 7DJ
020 7261 8836 *Fax:* 020 7261 8696
E-mail: disposalsales@dial.pipex.com
Website: www.disposalsales.agency.mod.uk

Sells surplus equipment and stockholdings from the public sector as a whole.

Chief Executive: Sym Taylor, CBE
Agency Administrator: Joan Lyons
Department: Defence
Launched: 1/10/94

Driver and Vehicle Licensing Agency

Longview Road, Morriston
Swansea SA6 7JL
01792 782341 *Fax:* 01792 782793
E-mail: dvla@gtnet.gov.uk
Website: www.dvla.gov.uk

Principal responsibilities are the registration and licensing of drivers in Great Britain and the registration and licensing of vehicles, together with the collection and enforcement of vehicle excise duty in the UK.

Chief Executive: Clive Bennett
Director of Operations: Richard Ley
Director of External and Corporate Services: Trevor Horton
Director of Development: Graham Pritchard
Department: Environment, Transport and the Regions
Launched: 2/4/90

Driver and Vehicle Licensing Northern Ireland

County Hall, Castlerock Road, Coleraine,
County Londonderry BT51 3HS
028 7034 1249 *Fax:* 028 7034 1424
E-mail: dvlni@doeni.gov.uk
Website: www.doeni.gov.uk/dvlni

Issues driving licences to appropriately qualified drivers, and registers and licenses vehicles in Northern Ireland and collects and enforces vehicle excise duty.

Chief Executive: Brendan Magee
Director of Development: Trevor Evans
Director of Vehicle Licensing: Aileen Gault
Director of Driver Licensing and Corporate Services: George Dillon
Director of Finance: Lucia O'Connor
Department: Environment (Northern Ireland)
Launched: 2/8/93

Driver and Vehicle Testing Agency

Balmoral Road, Belfast BT12 6QL
028 9068 1831 *Fax:* 028 9066 5520
E-mail: dvta@nics.gov.uk
Website: www.doeni.gov.uk/dvta

Tests drivers and vehicles in Northern Ireland.

Chief Executive: Brian Watson
Director of Operations: Trevor Hassin
Director of Human Resources: Marianne Cuthbertson
Director of Technical Policy and Legislation: Alastair Peoples
Director of Administration: Stanley Duncan
Director of Finance: Colin Berry
Department: Environment (Northern Ireland)
Launched: 1/4/92

Driving Standards Agency

Stanley House, 56 Talbot Street,
Nottingham NG1 5GU
0115-901 2500 *Fax:* 0115-901 2540
E-mail: customer.service@dsa.gsi.gov.uk
Website: www.driving-tests.co.uk

Driver testing for cars, motorcycles, lorries and buses and supervision of car and lorry driving instructors and approved training bodies for motorcyclists in Great Britain.

Chief Executive: Gary Austin
Finance Director: Laraine Manley
Acting Operations Director: Brian Gilhooley
Acting IT Director: Gordon Court
Chief Driving Examiner: Robin Cummins
Commercial Director: Christine Morris
Registrar of Approved Driving Instructors: Mike Ambrose
Head of Policy: Paul Butler
Department: Environment, Transport and the Regions
Launched: 2/4/90

Duke of York's Royal Military School

Dover, Kent CT15 5EQ
01304 245024 *Fax:* 01304 245019
E-mail: duke@easynet.co.uk

Provides boarding school secondary education for the children of serving and retired Service personnel.

Headmaster and Chief Executive:
John Cummings, MA
Deputy Headmasters: Terry Porter, Alan Bisby
Bursar: Lt Col Roger Say
Department: Defence
Launched: 1/4/92

Employment Service

Level 6, Caxton House,
Tothill Street, London SW1H 9NA
020 7273 3000 *Fax:* 020 7273 6143
Steel City House, West Street,
Sheffield S1 2GQ
0870 001 0171 *Fax:* 0114-259 5003
E-mail: erb.es@gtnet.gov.uk
Website: www.employmentservice.co.uk

Administers Jobseekers' Allowance and facilities for finding jobs for the unemployed.

Board
Chief Executive: Leigh Lewis, CB
Director, Jobcentre Services: Clare Dodgson
Director, Human Resources: Kevin White
Director, Welfare to Work Delivery:
Richard Foster
Director, Finance, Commercial and Corporate
Services: Mark Neale
Non-Executive Members:
Lucy De Groot,
Chief Executive Bristol City Council
Richard Dykes,
Managing Director of Royal Mail
Heads of Division
Commercial Policy: Rob Wormald
Corporate Governance: Irene Morrison
Employer and Marketing Services:
Simon Norton
Estates and National Contracts: Julian Capell
Finance: Rob Booth *(acting)*
IT Partnership: Bob Harris
Jobcentre Performance: Pat Hughes
Jobseeker Disability Services: Paul Keen
Jobseeker Mainstream Services:
Matthew Nicholas
Joint Planning and Operations: John Myers
Personnel: Gill Adey
Product Development: Gordon Macnair
Occupational Psychology: Mary Dalgleish
Research and Development: Jenny Dibden
Training and Development: Jon Ashe
Head of Timebound Projects
HR Partnership: Malcolm Rennard
Modernising ES Programme: Sandra Newton
Regional Directors
East Mids and Eastern: Diana Ross *(acting)*

London and South East: Stephen Holt, OBE
Northern: Vincent Robinson
North West: Lee Brown
South West: Ken Pascoe, CBE
West Midlands: Rosemary Thew
Yorkshire and the Humber: Roger Lasko
Office for Scotland Alan Brown
Office for Wales: Sheelagh Keyse
Department: Education and Employment
Launched: 2/4/90

Employment Tribunals Service

19-29 Woburn Place, London WC1H 0LU
020 7273 8512 *Fax:* 020 7273 8670

Provides administrative support to the employment tribunals and to the Employment Appeal Tribunal (EAT).

Chief Executive: Roger Heathcote
Director of Operations, Employment Tribunals:
Martin Wilson
Registrar EAT: Veronica Selio, OBE
Director of Finance and Planning: Steve Loach
Director of Personnel: Gerard Oates
Director of Information Technology: Jeremy Ilic
Director of Estates: Alastair Scott
Department: Trade and Industry
Launched: 1/4/97

Environment and Heritage Service

Commonwealth House, 35 Castle Street,
Belfast BT1 1GU
028 9054 6533 *Fax:* 028 9054 6660
E-mail: ca@doeni.gov.uk
Website: www.ehsni.gov.uk

Protects and conserves the natural and built environment and promotes its appreciation for the benefit of present and future generations.

Acting Chief Executive: Jim Lamont
028 9054 6570
Director of Natural Heritage: Dr John Faulkner
028 9054 6571
Director of Environmental Protection:
Jim Lamont 028 9054 6614
Director of Built Heritage:
Nick Brannon 028 9054 3024
Acting Director of Corporate Affairs:
Liam Gibson 028 9054 6620
Department: Environment (Northern
Ireland)
Launched: 1/4/96

Farming and Rural Conservation Agency

Nobel House, 17 Smith Square
London SW1P 3JR
020 7238 5432 *Fax:* 020 7238 5588
E-mail: frca.genenq@maff.gsi.gov.uk
Website: www.maff.gov.uk/aboutmaf/
agency/frca/frca.htm

Promotes integration of farming and conservation, environmental protection, rural land use and the rural economy.

Chief Executive: Sarah Nason
(020 7238 5960 *Fax:* 020 7238 5372)
Resources Director: Eddie Routledge
(020 7238 6597 *Fax:* 020 7238 5588)
Director, Eastern Region: Clive Whitworth
(01223 455907 *Fax:* 01223 455829)
Director, Northern Region: Mike Silverwood
(0113-230 3900 *Fax:* 0113-230 3963)
Director, Western Region: David Sisson
(0117-959 1000 *Fax:* 0117-959 0463)
Director, Wales: Jeff Robinson
(029 2058 6101 *Fax:* 029 2058 6763)
**Department: Agriculture, Fisheries and Food
and the National Assembly for Wales**
Launched: 1/4/97

Fire Service College

Moreton-in-Marsh,
Gloucestershire GL56 0RH
01608 650831 *Fax:* 01608 651788
E-mail: enquiries@fireservicecollege.ac.uk
Website: www.fireservicecollege.ac.uk

Provides a wide range of specialist fire related and management and finance training for fire officers. It also provides training for commerce and industry, and for students from overseas fire brigades.

Chief Executive and Commandant:
Terry Glossop OStJ QFSM
E-mail: tglossop@fireservicecollege.ac.uk
Director, Sales and Marketing: Julie Tew
Department: Home Office
Launched: 1/4/92

Fisheries Research Services

Marine Laboratory, PO Box 101
Victoria Road, Aberdeen AB11 9DB
01224 876544 *Fax:* 01224 295511
E-mail: heaths@marlab.ac.uk
Website: www.marlab.ac.uk

Provides expert scientific and technical advice and information on marine and freshwater fisheries, on aquaculture, and on the protection of the aquatic environment and its wildlife.

Director: Prof Anthony Hawkins CBE
Deputy Director: Dr John Davies
Aquatic Environment Programme:
Dr Colin Moffat
Fisheries Management: Dr Robin Cook
Aquaculture and Aquatic Animal Health:
Dr Ron Stagg
Freshwater Fisheries Laboratory:
Dr Richard Shelton
**Department: Scottish Executive Rural Affairs
Department**
Launched: 1/4/97

Forensic Science Northern Ireland

151 Belfast Road, Carrickfergus,
Co Antrim BT38 8PL
028 9036 1888 *Fax:* 028 9036 1900
E-mail: forensic.science@fsni.gov.uk
Website: www.fsni.gov.uk

Provides scientific support in the investigation of crime and expert evidence to the courts in Northern Ireland.

Chief Executive: Dr Richard W Adams
Department: Northern Ireland Office
Launched: 1/9/95

Forensic Science Service

Priory House, Gooch Street North,
Birmingham B5 6QQ
0121-607 6800 *Fax:* 0121-666 7327
Website: www.fss.org.uk

Provides scientific support in the investigation of crime and expert evidence to the courts in Great Britain.

Chief Executive: Dr Janet Thompson CB
(London)
Director of Quality and Head of Profession:
Mike Loveland
Chief Scientist: Dr Bob Bramley

Service Delivery Director (Operations and DNA): Dr Dave Werrett
Director of Research and Service Development: Trevor Howitt
Marketing Director: Gary Pugh (London)
Customer Relations Director: Phil Jones

CORPORATE OFFICE
109 Lambeth Road, London SE1 7LP
020 7230 6700 *Fax:* 020 7230 6253
Department: Home Office
Launched: 1/4/91

Forest Enterprise

231 Corstorphine Road
Edinburgh EH12 7AT
0131-334 0303 *Fax:* 0131-334 3047
E-mail: carol.finlayson@forestry.gsi.gov.uk
Website: www.forestry.gsi.gov.uk

Manages the national forest.

Chief Executive: Dr Bob McIntosh
Heads of Divisions:
  Forest Planning: Wilma Harper
  Forest Enterprise Personnel:
    Iain Miller
  Forest Operations: Ian Forshaw
  Estate Management: Peter Ranken
  Corporate Services: Keith Gliddon
  Environment and Communications:
    Alan Stevenson
Territorial Directors:
  Forest Enterprise England (Bristol):
    Geoff Hatfield
  Forest Enterprise Wales (Aberystwyth):
    Bob Farmer
  *Forest Enterprise Scotland (North)
    (Inverness):* Hugh Insley
  *Forest Enterprise Scotland (South)
    (Dumfries):* Mike Lofthouse
Department: Forestry Commission
Launched: 1/4/96

Forest Research

Northern Research Station, Roslin,
Midlothian EH25 9SY
0131-445 2176 *Fax:* 0131-445 5124
E-mail: forest.research@forestry.gsi.gov.uk
Website: www.forestry.gov.uk/forest-research

Provides research, development, surveys and technical services to the forest industry.

Chief Executive: Jim Dewar
Chief Research Officer:
  Dr Peter Freer-Smith
Alice Holt Lodge, Wrecclesham,
Farnham, Surrey GU10 4LH
01420 22255 *Fax:* 01420 23653
Department: Forestry Commission
Launched: 1/4/97

Forest Service

Dundonald House, Upper Newtownards Road,
Belfast BT4 3SB
028 9052 4480 *Fax:* 028 9052 4570
E-mail: forest.customer@dardni.gov.uk
Website: www.dani.gov.uk/forestry/

Sustainable management of Northern Ireland forests and the development of afforestation.

Chief Executive: Malcolm Beatty
Director, Operations: Ken Ellis
Director, Policy and Standards: Pat Hunter Blair
Director, Corporate Services: Brian O'Hara
**Department: Agriculture and Rural
  Development (Northern Ireland)**
Launched: 1/4/98

Government Car and Despatch Agency

46 Ponton Road, London SW8 5AX
020 7217 3821 *Fax:* 020 7217 3875
E-mail: gcda@compuserve.com

Provides secure transport and mail services to central government.

Chief Executive: Nick Matheson
Operations Director: Jerry Doyle
Department: Cabinet Office
Launched: 1/4/97

Government Purchasing Agency

Rosepark House, Upper Newtownards Road,
Belfast BT4 3NR
028 9052 6560 *Fax:* 028 9052 6440
Website: www.gpa-ni.gov.uk
E-mail: tara.cunningham@gpa-ni.gov.uk

Establishes on behalf of customers effective contracts for the procurement of goods and services.

Chief Executive: David Court
**Department: Finance and Personnel
  (Northern Ireland)**
Launched: 1/4/96

Health Estates

Stoney Road, Dundonald,
Belfast BT16 1US
028 9052 0025 *Fax:* 028 9052 3900
E-mail: health.estates@dhssps.gov.uk
Website:
www.dhssni.gov.uk/hpss/health_estates

Provides policy, advice, guidance and support on
estate matters at strategic and operational levels
to the various bodies charged with responsibility
for the Health and Social Services estate in
Northern Ireland.

Chief Executive: Ronnie Browne
**Department: Health, Social Services and
Public Safety (Northern Ireland)**
Launched: 2/10/95

Highways Agency

St Christopher House, Southwark Street
London SE1 0TE
Information Line: 08457 504030
Enquiries: 08459 556575
E-mail: ha_info@highways.gsi.gov.uk
Website: www.highways.gov.uk

Responsible for maintaining, operating and
improving the trunk road network.

Chief Executive: Tim Matthews
Director, Network and Customer Services:
Peter Nutt
Director, Project Services: David York
Director, Quality Services: John Kerman
Director, Finance Services: Jon Seddon
Acting Director, Human Resource Services:
Ginny Clarke
**Department: Environment, Transport and
the Regions**
Launched 1/4/94

Historic Scotland

Longmore House, Salisbury Place,
Edinburgh EH9 1SH
0131-668 8600 *Fax:* 0131-668 8699
Website: www.historic-scotland.gov.uk

Protects and promotes public understanding and
enjoyment of Scotland's ancient monuments and
archaeological sites and landscapes, historic buildings, parks, gardens and designed landscapes.

Director and Chief Executive:
Graeme N Munro
Directors: Frank Lawrie, Ingval Maxwell,
Brian Naylor, Brian O'Neil, Leslie Wilson

Chief Inspector of Historic Buildings:
Richard Emerson
Chief Inspector of Ancient Monuments:
David Breeze
Department: Scottish Executive
Launched: 1/4/91

Industrial Research and Technology Unit

17 Antrim Road, Lisburn, BT28 3AL
028 9262 3000 *Fax:* 028 9267 6054
E-mail: info@irtu.detini.gov.uk
Website: www.irtu-ni.gov.uk

Responsible for spearheading the drive for competitiveness in NI companies through innovation, R&D, use of technology and technology
transfer.

Chief Executive: Jim Wolstencroft
**Department: Enterprise, Trade and
Investment (Northern Ireland)**
Launched: 3/4/95

Inland Revenue

The Board of Inland Revenue – see also Non-
Ministerial Government Departments

26 EXECUTIVE OFFICES

INLAND REVENUE EAST
Director: Stephen Banyard
Churchgate, New Road
Peterborough PE1 1TD
01733 754321 *Fax:* 01733 755003
E-mail: stephen.banyard@ir.gsi.gov.uk

INLAND REVENUE LONDON
Director: Roy Massingale
New Court, Carey Street,
London WC2A 2JE
020 7324 1229 *Fax:* 020 7324 1076
E-mail: roy.massingale@ir.gsi.gov.uk

INLAND REVENUE NORTHERN ENGLAND
Director: Geoff Lunn
Dunedin House, Columbia Drive,
Stockton-on-Tees TS17 6QZ
01642 637700 *Fax:* 01642 605328
The Triad, Stanley Road, Bootle,
Merseyside L75 2DD
0151-300 3000 *Fax:* 0151-300 3750
Concept House, 5 Young Street
Sheffield S1 4LF
0114-296 9801 *Fax:* 0114-296 9797

INLAND REVENUE NORTHERN IRELAND
Director: David Hinstridge
Dorchester House,
52–58 Great Victoria Street, Belfast BT2 7QE
028 9050 5050 *Fax:* 028 9050 5058
E-mail: david.hinstridge@ir.gsi.gov.uk

INLAND REVENUE SCOTLAND
Director: Ian Gerrie
Clarendon House, 114–116 George Street
Edinburgh EH2 4LH
0131-473 4100 *Fax:* 0131-473 9118
E-mail: ian.gerrie@ir.gsi.gov.uk

INLAND REVENUE SOUTH EAST AND SOUTH WEST
Director: Tony Sleeman
Dukes Court, Duke Street, Woking,
Surrey GU21 5XR
01483 264402 *Fax:* 01483 264410
E-mail: anthony.sleeman@ir.gsi.gov.uk

INLAND REVENUE WALES AND MIDLANDS
Director: J Harra
Phase II Building, Tŷ Glas
Llanishen, Cardiff CF14 5TS
029 2032 6600 *Fax:* 029 2075 5730

ACCOUNTS OFFICE (CUMBERNAULD)
Director: A Geddes, OBE
Inland Revenue, St Mungo's Road
Cumbernauld, Glasgow G70 5TR
01236 783600 *Fax:* 01236 725959
E-mail: andrew.geddes@ir.gsi.gov.uk

ACCOUNTS OFFICE (SHIPLEY)
Director: R Jack Warner
Inland Revenue, Victoria Street, Shipley, West
Yorkshire BD98 8AA
01274 539590 *Fax:* 01274 580385
E-mail: jack.warner@ir.gsi.gov.uk

CAPITAL TAXES OFFICE
Director: Ed McKeegan
Inland Revenue, Ferrers House,
PO Box 38, Castle Meadow Road,
Nottingham NG2 1BB
0115-974 3043 *Fax:* 0115-974 3041

ENFORCEMENT OFFICE
Director: David Ellis
Inland Revenue, Durrington Bridge House
Barrington Road, Worthing
West Sussex BN12 4SE
01903 701011 *Fax:* 01903 701401
E-mail: david.r.ellis@ir.gsi.gov.uk

FINANCIAL ACCOUNTING OFFICE
Director: Mary McLeish
Inland Revenue, South Block
Barrington Road, Worthing
West Sussex BN12 4XH
01903 509015 *Fax:* 01903 509107

FINANCIAL INTERMEDIARIES AND CLAIMS
OFFICE
Director: John Johnston
Inland Revenue, St Johns House
Merton Road, Bootle, Merseyside L69 9BB
0151-472 6010 *Fax:* 0151-944 1254
E-mail: john.johnston@ir.gsi.gov.uk

INTERNAL AUDIT OFFICE
Director: Norman Buckley
Inland Revenue, 22 Kingsway,
London WC2B 6NR
020 7438 7280 *Fax:* 020 7438 7197
E-mail: norman.buckley@ir.gsi.gov.uk

LARGE BUSINESS OFFICE
Director: Stephen Jones
Inland Revenue, 22 Kingsway,
London WC2B 6NR
020 7438 7977 *Fax:* 020 7438 6633
E-mail: stephen.jones@ir.gsi.gov.uk

NATIONAL INSURANCE CONTRIBUTIONS OFFICE
Director: Bridget Woodley
Benton Park Road, Longbenton,
Newcastle upon Tyne, NE98 1ZZ
0191-225 5187 *Fax:* 0191-225 3328

OIL TAXATION OFFICE
Director: Bob Mountain
Inland Revenue, Melbourne House
Aldwych, London WC2B 4LL
020 7438 6908 *Fax:* 020 7438 6910
E-mail: bob.mountain@ir.gsi.gov.uk

PENSION SCHEMES OFFICE
Director: Geoff Nield
Inland Revenue, Yorke House
PO Box 62, Castle Meadow Road
Nottingham NG2 1BG
0115-974 1599 *Fax:* 0115-974 1651
E-mail: geoff.nield@ir.gsi.gov.uk

SOLICITOR'S OFFICE
Solicitor: Philip Ridd
Inland Revenue, East Wing
Somerset House, Strand
London WC2R 1LB
020 7438 6538 *Fax:* 020 7438 6653
E-mail: philip.ridd@ir.gsi.gov.uk

SPECIAL COMPLIANCE OFFICE
Director: John Middleton
Inland Revenue, Angel Court
199 Borough High Street, London SE1 1HZ
020 7234 3701 *Fax:* 020 7234 3730
E-mail: john.middleton@ir.gsi.gov.uk

STAMP OFFICE
Director: Linda Martin
Inland Revenue, Ground Floor
Ferrers House, PO Box 38,
Castle Meadow Road,
Nottingham NG2 1BB
0115-974 2604 *Fax:* 0115-974 2507

TAX CREDIT OFFICE
Director: William Carr
Inland Revenue, St Mary's House,
St Mary's Street, Preston PR1 4AT
01772 235552 *Fax:* 01772 235553
E-mail: bill.carr@ir.gsi.gov.uk

TRAINING OFFICE
Director: Lin Hinnigan
Inland Revenue Training Office,
Lawress Hall, Riseholme Park,
Lincoln LN2 2BJ
01522 561710 *Fax:* 01522 561850
E-mail: lin.hinnigan@ir.gsi.gov.uk

Launched: 1/4/92

Insolvency Service

PO Box 203, 21 Bloomsbury Street
London WC1B 3QW
020 7637 1110 *Fax:* 020 7636 4709
Website: www.insolvency.gov.uk

Administers and investigates the affairs of bankrupts and companies in compulsory liquidation, deals with the disqualification of directors in all corporate failures, regulates insolvency practitioners and their professional bodies, provides banking and investment services for bankruptcy and liquidation estates, and advises ministers on insolvency policy issues.

The Insolvency Service also has responsibility in Scotland for disqualifications, insolvency practitioner regulation and certain aspects of corporate insolvency policy.

Inspector General and Agency Chief Executive:
Peter Joyce, CB
Deputy Inspector Generals: Desmond Flynn,
Les Cramp
Director of Policy/Technical: Eamon Murphy
Director of Enforcement: Patrick Chillery
*Director of Finance, Planning and Corporate
Resources:* Lesley Beech
Director of Human Resources: Terry Hart
Director of Banking and Audit: Jim Curtois
Department: Trade & Industry
Launched: 21/3/90

Intervention Board

PO Box 69, Reading RG1 3YD
0118-958 3626 *Fax:* 0118-953 1370
Website: www.ib-uk.gov.uk
E-mail: chief.ib.kh@gtnet.gov.uk

Responsible for the implementation of EU regulations covering the market support arrangements of the Common Agriculture Policy.

Chairman: Ian Kent
Chief Executive: George Trevelyan
Secretary: Alison Couch
Operations Directorate:
Hugh MacKinnon
Corporate Services Division: Alison Parker
Finance Division: Geoffrey Trantham
Legal Division: Philip Kent
Operations Newcastle: John Bradbury
Operations Reading: Alec Sutton
Procurement and Supply: Nick Rogers
**Department: The Intervention Board is a
separate Government Department
reporting directly to the four Agriculture
Ministers.**
Launched: 1/4/90

Land Registers of Northern Ireland

Lincoln Building, 27–45 Great Victoria
Street, Belfast BT2 7SL
028 9025 1515 *Fax:* 028 9025 1550
E-mail: customer.information@lrni.gov.uk
Website: www.lrni.gov.uk

Maintains and develops a unified and reliable system of land registration in Northern Ireland.

Registrar of Titles/Chief Executive:
Arthur Moir
**Department: Finance and Personnel
(Northern Ireland)**
Launched: 1/4/96

HM Land Registry

Lincoln's Inn Fields, London WC2A 3PH
020 7917 8888 *Fax:* 020 7955 0110
E-mail: hmlr@landreg.gov.uk
Website: www.landreg.gov.uk

Maintains and develops a unified and reliable system of land registration in England and Wales.

Chief Land Registrar and Chief Executive:
Peter Collis

Management Board:
  Solicitor to HM Land Registry:
    Christopher West
  Director of Corporate Services: Ted Beardsall
  Director of Practice and Legal Services:
    Joe Timothy
  Director of Operations: Andy Howarth
  Director of Information Technology: Peter Smith
  Director of Finance: Heather Jackson
  Director of Facilities: Paul Laker
  Land Registrar Agency Case Review Team:
    Mike Westcott Rudd
  Director of Communications: Alan Pemberton
Department: The Land Registry is a separate Government Department reporting directly to the Lord Chancellor
Launched: 2/7/90

Logistic Information Systems Agency

HQ DLO, Monxton Road, Andover,
Hampshire SP11 8HT
01264 382745 *Fax:* 01264 382820
E-mail: hq.lisa@gtnet.gov.uk

Responsible for the army's IS strategy; Information systems consultancy; Development and operation of logistic information systems.

Chief Executive: Brigadier Paul Flanagan
Director Programme Management:
  Adrian Withey
Department: Defence
Launched: 21/11/94

Maritime and Coastguard Agency

Spring Place, 105 Commercial Road
Southampton SO15 1EG
023 8032 9100 *Fax:* 023 8032 9298
E-mail: infoline@swan.mcagency.org.uk
Website: www.mcga.gov.uk

Responsible for marine safety; aims to minimise loss of life amongst seafarers and coastal users; to respond to maritime emergencies 24hrs a day; and to minimise the risk of pollution of the marine environment from ships and where pollution occurs, minimise the impact on UK interests.

Chief Executive: Maurice Storey
Maritime Operations Director: John Astbury
Maritime Safety and Pollution Prevention
  Director: Alan Cubbin
Corporate Services Director: Dave Lawrence
Department: Environment, Transport and the Regions
Launched: 1/4/98

Meat Hygiene Service

Foss House, Kings Pool
1–2 Peasholme Green, York YO1 7PX
01904 455501 *Fax:* 01904 455502
E-mail: enquire@mhs.maff.gsi.gov.uk

Veterinary supervision and meat inspection in licensed fresh meat establishments.

Chief Executive: Johnston McNeill
Director of Operations: Peter Soul
  01904 455520 *Fax:* 01904 455502
Department: Food Standards Agency
Launched: 1/4/95

Medical Devices Agency

Hannibal House, Elephant and Castle
London SE1 6TQ
020 7972 8000 *Fax:* 020 7972 8108
E-mail: mail@medical-devices.gov.uk
Website: www.medical-devices.gov.uk

Endures that medical devices and equipment meet appropriate standards of safety, quality and performance and that they comply with relevant Directives of the EU.

Chief Executive: Dr David Jefferys
Department: Health
Launched: 27/9/94

Medical Supplies Agency

Drummond Barracks, Ludgershall
Andover, Hampshire SP11 9RU
01264 798603 *Fax:* 01264 798676
E-mail: postmaster@msa.mod.uk

Provides medical, dental and veterinary material, blood and blood products, trained personnel and technical and logistic support to the armed forces.

Chief Executive: Brian Nimick
Director of Customer and Technical Services:
  Graham North
Director of Operational Support:
  Lt Col Sam Johnston
Director of Management Services:
  Jeremy Baines
Department: Defence
Launched: 1/3/96

Medicines Control Agency

Market Towers, 1 Nine Elms Lane
London SW8 5NQ
020 7273 0000 *Fax:* 020 7273 0353
E-mail: info@mca.gov.uk
Website:
www.open.gov.uk/mca/mcahome.htm

Controls medicine through a system of licensing, monitoring, inspection, and enforcement of standards which ensure that medicines marketed in the UK meet rigorous standards of safety, quality and efficacy.

Chief Executive: Dr Keith Jones, CB
Department: Health
Launched: 11/7/91

Meteorological Office

London Road, Bracknell
Berkshire RG12 2SZ
01344 420242 (switchboard)
Fax: 01344 854412
0845 3000 300 (customer centre)
E-mail: dchardy@email.meto.gov.uk
Website: www.met-office.gov.uk

Responsible for provision of meteorological services to the Armed Forces and civil aviation, shipping, emergency services, media, commerce, industry and the public, and for undertaking research related to meteorology and climate.

Chief Executive: Peter Ewins
Chief Scientist: Prof Paul Mason, FRS
Company Secretary: Martin Sands
Finance Director: Philip Mabe
Business Director: Roger Hunt
Forecasting Director: Colin Flood
Managing Director, Commercial Division: Stephen Lawrenson
Technical Director: Dr Jim Caughey
Acting Director Numerical Weather Prediction: Dr Alan Dickinson
Director Climate Research: Prof Alan Thorpe
Director Information Technology: John Ponting
Director Relocation: Steve Noyes
Department: Defence
Launched: 2/4/90

Ministry of Defence Police Agency

Wethersfield, Braintree
Essex CM7 4AZ
01371 854000 *Fax:* 01371 854060

Responsible for the prevention, detection and investigation of crime within the MoD and Crown Estate.

Chief Constable/Chief Executive: Lloyd Clarke
Deputy Chief Constable: Anthony Comben
Agency Secretary and Director of Finance and Administration: Paul Crowther
Assistant Chief Constable (Personnel and Training): Barry Smith
Assistant Chief Constable (Territorial Operations): Richard Miles
Assistant Chief Constable (Support): David Ray
Department: Defence
Launched: 1/4/96

National Archives of Scotland (formerly Scottish Record Office)

HM General Register House,
Edinburgh EH1 3YY
0131-535 1314 *Fax:* 0131-535 1360
E-mail: enquiries@nas.gov.uk
Website: www.nas.gov.uk

Responsible for preserving the public records of Scotland and other records which have been transmitted to it, and for making them available for public inspection.

Keeper: Patrick Cadell; George MacKenzie from January 2001
Deputy Keeper: Peter Anderson
Responsible Minister: First Minister, Scottish Parliament
Launched: 1/4/93

National Savings

375 Kensington High Street, London W14 8SD
020 7348 9200
E-mail: via website
Website: www.nationalsavings.co.uk

Government savings organisation.

Chief Executive: Peter Bareau
Sourcing Director: Jeannie Bevan
Commercial Director: Gill Cattanach
Finance Director: Richard Douglas
Personnel Director: Scott Speedie
Department: National Savings is a separate Government Department reporting directly to the Chancellor of the Exchequer
Launched: 1/7/96

National Weights and Measures Laboratory

Stanton Avenue, Teddington,
Middlesex TW11 0JZ
020 8943 7272 *Fax:* 020 8943 7270
E-mail: info@nwml.dti.gov.uk
Website: www.nwml.gov.uk

Administers weights and measures legislation; regulation and certification of equipment in use for trade; EU Directives on measuring instruments; equipment testing, calibration and training services.

Chief Executive: Dr Seton Bennett
Department: Trade & Industry
Launched: 18/4/89

Naval Bases and Supply Agency

(TO BE MERGED WITH SHIPS SUPPORT AGENCY FROM APRIL 2001)

Ministry of Defence, Ensleigh,
Bath BA1 5AB
01225 467854 *Fax:* 01225 468307

Provides engineering, supply naval personnel and other support services to the Fleet and other customers.

Chief Executive:
    Rear Admiral Brian Perowne
Deputy Chief Executive: Malcolm Westgate
Naval Base Commander, Clyde:
    Rear Admiral Derek Anthony
Naval Base Commander, Devonport:
    Commodore Paul Boissiere
Naval Base Commander, Portsmouth:
    Commodore Steve Graham, OBE
Director, Commercial: Stewart Yeo
*Director, Business Development, Finance and
    Plans:* Keith Earley
Director, Base Support:
    Captain Peter Horsted, RN
Director Defence Munitions: Alan Blair
Non-Executive Board Member:
    Alan Howell
Department: Defence
Launched: 11/12/96

Naval Manning Agency

Victory Building, HM Naval Base
Portsmouth, Hampshire PO1 3LS
023 9272 7400 *Fax:* 023 9272 7413

Ensures that sufficient naval manpower is available in trained strength and effectively deployed at all times.

Chief Executive:
    Rear Admiral Jeremy de Halpert
Department: Defence
Launched: 1/7/96

Naval Recruiting and Training Agency

Room 041, Victory Building
HM Naval Base, Portsmouth,
Hampshire PO1 3LS
023 9272 7600 *Fax:* 023 9272 7613

Primarily involved in providing and maintaining a pool of suitably trained manpower for deployment in the Naval Service.

Chief Executive:
    Rear Admiral John Chadwick
Deputy Chief Executive/Training Director:
    Commodore Simon Goodall ADC
Director Naval Recruiting:
    Commodore Julian Williams
Director of Naval Reserves:
    Captain John Rimington, RN
Projects Director: Captain John Rees, RN
Commercial Director: Peter Clark
Finance Director: Malcolm Heritage-Owen
Department: Defence
Launched: 1/4/95

NHS Estates

Department of Health, 1 Trevelyan Square,
Boar Lane, Leeds LS1 6AE
0113-254 7000 *Fax:* 0113-254 7299
E-mail: nhs.estates@doh.gov.uk
Website: www.nhsestates.gov.uk

Property advisers and consultants for the management and development of the National Health Service estate.

Chief Executive: Kate Priestley
*Executive Director of Business Development and
    Modernisation:* David Lawrence
Executive Finance Director: Tim Straughan
*Executive Director of Policy and Performance
    Management:* Peter Wearmouth
Chief Engineer: John Parkin
Department: Health
Launched: 1/4/91

NHS Pensions Agency

Hesketh House, 200–220 Broadway
Fleetwood, Lancashire FY7 8LG
01253 774774 *Fax:* 01253 774860
E-mail: acowan@nhspa.gov.uk
Website: www.nhspa.gov.uk

Administers the NHS Occupational Pension
Scheme.

Chief Executive: Alec Cowan
Resource and Development Director:
  Nigel Holden
Information Systems Director: Bill McCallum
Department: Health
Launched: 20/11/92

NHS Purchasing and Supply Agency

Headquarters: Premier House,
60 Caversham Road, Reading RG1 7EB
0118-980 8600 *Fax:* 0118-980 8650
Website: www.pasa.doh.gov.uk

Purchasing Offices:
80 Lightfoot Street, Chester CH2 3AD

Foxbridge Way, Normanton, West Yorkshire
WF6 1TL
Chief Executive: Duncan Eaton
Department: Health
Launched: 1/4/00

Northern Ireland Child Support Agency

Great Northern Tower
17 Great Victoria Street, Belfast BT2 7AD
028 9089 6666 *Fax:* 028 9089 6850
E-mail: customerservices.csa@dsdni.gov.uk
Website:
www.dhssni.gov.uk/childsupportagency

Assesses, collects and enforces child maintenance in Northern Ireland.

Chief Executive: Gerry Keenan
Department: Social Development (Northern
  Ireland)
Launched: 5/4/93

Northern Ireland Prison Service

Dundonald House, Upper Newtownards
Road, Belfast BT4 3SU
028 9052 2922 *Fax:* 028 9052 5100
Press Office: 028 9052 5354/5139
Fax: 028 9052 5100
E-mail: info@niprisonservice.gov.uk
Website: www.niprisonservice.gov.uk

Provides prison services in Northern Ireland.

Director-General: Robin Halward
Department: Northern Ireland Office
Launched: 3/4/95

Northern Ireland Statistics and Research Agency

McAuley House, 2–14 Castle Street,
Belfast BT1 1SA
028 9034 8100 *Fax:* 028 9034 8106
E-mail: edgar.jardine@dfpni.gov.uk
Website: www.nisra.gov.uk

Provides Government in Northern Ireland with a
statistical and research service to support decision making; informs debate in Parliament and
the wider community about social and economic
issues; and registers key life events.

Chief Executive: Edgar Jardine
Registrar General: Dr Norman Caven
Head of Corporate Affairs: Dr Gerry Mulligan
Department: Finance and Personnel
  (Northern Ireland)
Launched: 1/4/96

Office for National Statistics

Headquarters
1 Drummond Gate, London SW1V 2QQ
020 7533 5888 *Fax:* 020 7533 6261
E-mail: info@ons.gov.uk
Website: www.ons.gov.uk

Government Buildings, Cardiff Road
Newport, Gwent NP9 1XG
01633 815696 *Fax:* 01633 812343

Segensworth Road, Titchfield, Fareham
Hampshire PO15 5RR
01329 842511

Smedley Hydro, Trafalgar Road
Birkdale, Southport, Lancashire PR8 2HH
01704 569824

East Lane, Runcorn, Cheshire WA7 2DN
01928 715151

Somerford Road, Christchurch
Dorset BH23 3QA
01202 486154

ONS provides government at all levels with a statistical service to support the formulation and monitoring of economic and social policies, informs Parliament and the citizen about the state of the nation and performance of government.

Chief Executive: Len Cook
Directors: Alan Goldsmith (Principal Finance Officer), John Kidgell, Susan Linacre, John Pullinger
Principal Establishment Officer: Eryl Williams
Head of Information: Ian Scott
Parliamentary Clerks: Ghazala Maynard, John Bailey
Department: The Office for National Statistics is a separate Government Department reporting directly to the Chancellor of the Exchequer
Launched: 1/4/96

Ordnance Survey

Romsey Road, Southampton,
Hampshire SO16 4GU
023 8079 2000 *Fax:* 023 8079 2452
E-mail: enquiries@ordsvy.co.uk
Website: www.ordnancesurvey.gov.uk

Carries out official topographic surveying and mapping of Great Britain and produces a wide range of maps and computer data products for Government, business, administrative, educational and leisure use.

Director General: Vanessa Lawrence
Director of Strategic Operations: Vacant
Director of Data Collection: Ian Logan
Director of Product Development: Steve Erskine
Senior Press Officer: Philip Round
Department: Ordnance Survey is a separate Government Department reporting directly to the Secretary of State for the Environment, Transport and the Regions
Launched: 1/5/90

Ordnance Survey of Northern Ireland

Colby House, Stranmillis Court
Belfast BT9 5BJ
028 9025 5755 *Fax:* 028 9025 5700
E-mail: osni@nics.gov.uk
Website: www.osni.gov.uk/

The official survey and cartographic organisation for Northern Ireland.

Chief Executive: Michael Cory
Department: Culture, Arts and Leisure (Northern Ireland)
Launched: 1/4/92

Patent Office

Concept House, Cardiff Road,
Newport NP10 8QQ
01633 814000 *Fax:* 01633 814444
E-mail: enquiries@patent.gov.uk
Website: www.patent.gov.uk

Grants patents and trade marks, registers designs, and formulates policy on intellectual property.

Chief Executive: Alison Brimelow
Director Patents and Designs: Ron Marchant
Director Trade Marks: Peter Lawrence
Director Intellectual Property Policy: Graham Jenkins
Director Copyright: Anthony Murphy
Secretary: Claire Clancy
Financial Controller: Julian Thompson
Department: Trade & Industry
Launched: 1/3/90

Pay and Personnel Agency

Ministry of Defence, Warminster Road,
Bath BA1 5AA
01225 828105 *Fax:* 01225 828728

Provides a central payroll service to MoD and other departments.

Chief Executive: Mike Rowe
Deputy Chief Executive: David Wealthall
Director Corporate Services: Val Hudspeth
Department: Defence
Launched: 1/2/96

Pesticides Safety Directorate

Mallard House, Kings Pool
3 Peasholme Green, York YO1 7PX
01904 640500 *Fax:* 01904 455733
E-mail: psd.information@psd.maff.gsi.gov.uk
Website: www.maff.gov.uk/aboutmaff/agency/psd/psdhome.htm

Controls the sale, supply and use of pesticides.

Chief Executive: Dr Kerr Wilson
Director (Policy): John Bainton
Director of Finance: Kathryn Dyson
Director (Approvals): Dr David Martin
Deputy Director (Approvals): Richard Davis
Department: Agriculture, Fisheries and Food
Launched: 1/4/93

Planning Inspectorate

Tollgate House, Houlton Street
Bristol BS2 9DJ
Cathays Park, Cardiff CF1 3NQ
01225 825007 *Fax:* 01225 825150
E-mail: enquiries.pins@gtnet.gov.uk
Website: www.open.gov.uk/pi/pihome.htm

Appeals and other casework under Planning, Housing, Environment, Highways, Transport and Works Legislation. Also provision of Inspectors to hold local inquiries into objections to local authority plans, and administration of the Lord Chancellor's Panel of Independent Inspectors.

Chief Planning Inspector (Chief Executive):
    Chris Shepley
    0117-987 8963 *Fax:* 0117-987 8408
Deputy Chief Planning Inspector:
    David Hanchet
    0117-987 8961 *Fax:* 0117-987 8408
Directors
Highways, Rights of Way: Brian Dodd
Rights of Way: 0117-987 8895
Highways: 0117-987 8905/8907
Enforcement Casework: Rhys Davies
    0117-987 8916/8917 *Fax:* 0117-987 8782
All Welsh Office Appeals and Casework:
    Rhys Davies
    (based at Cardiff Office) 01225 825 3861
Structure and Local Plans: Brian Dodd
    0117-987 8895
Planning Appeals Administration:
    Graham Saunders
    0117-987 8727 *Fax:* 0117-987 8335
Finance and Management Services:
    Marion Headicar
    0117-987 8391 *Fax:* 0117-987 8335
Departments: Environment, Transport and the Regions and the National Assembly for Wales
Launched: 1/4/92

Planning Service

Clarence Court, 10-18 Adelaide Street
Belfast BT2 8GB
028 9054 0651 *Fax:* 028 9054 0662
E-mail: planning.service.hq@nics.gov.uk
Website: www.doeni.gov.uk/planning/index.htm

Implements the Government's policies and strategy for town and country planning in Northern Ireland.

Chief Executive: Hugh McKay
Director of Corporate Services: Cynthia Smith
Director of Professional Services: John Cleland
Professional Services Manager: Hilary Heslip
Department: Environment (Northern Ireland)
Launched: 1/4/96

HM Prison Service

Cleland House, Page Street,
London SW1P 4LN
020 7217 6000 (enquiries)
Fax: 020 7217 6403
Website: www.hmprisonservice.gov.uk

Provides prison services in England and Wales, both directly and through contractors.

Management Board
Director-General: Martin Narey
Deputy Director-General: Phil Wheatley
Director of Security: Brodie Clark
Director of Prison Health Policy Unit:
    Felicity Harvey
Director of Regimes: Ken Sutton
Director of Finance: Julian Le Vay
Director of Personnel: Gareth Hadley
Director of High Security Prisons:
    Peter Atherton
Director of Corporate Affairs: Clare Pelham
Prison Service Non-Executive Directors of the
    Strategy Board for Correctional Services:
    Sir Duncan Nichol, CBE
    Rosemary Thomson, CBE
    Patrick Carter
    Richard Rosser
Secretary and Head of Secretariat:
    Clare Checksfield

AREA MANAGERS

EAST MIDLANDS (NORTH)
Enquiries: 020 7217 2893
Area Manager: David Waplington

EAST MIDLANDS (SOUTH)
Enquiries: 020 7217 6711
Area Manager: Mitch Egan

EASTERN
Enquiries: 01603 431279
Area Manager: Michael Spurr
c/o HMP/YOI Norwich, Knox Road, Norwich,
    Norfolk NR1 4LU

KENT, SURREY AND SUSSEX (SOUTH EAST)
Enquiries: 020 7217 6137
Area Manager: Tom Murtagh

LANCASHIRE AND CUMBRIA (NORTH WEST)
Enquiries: 01925 764404
Area Manager: Tony Fitzpatrick
c/o Oakwood House, Yew Tree Court,
    Warrington Road, Risley, Warrington

LONDON
Enquiries: 020 7217 2893
Area Manager: Adrian Smith

MANCHESTER, MERSEY AND CHESHIRE (NORTH
WEST)
Enquiries: 020 7217 6424
Area Manager: Ian Lockwood

NORTH EAST
Enquiries: 020 7217 6640
Area Manager: Ray Mitchell

SOUTH WEST
Enquiries: 020 7217 6925
Area Manager: Jerry Petherick
c/o Eastwood Park, 7-8 Church Avenue
Falfield, Wotton under Edge
Gloucestershire GL12 8BQ

THAMES VALLEY AND HAMPSHIRE (SOUTH EAST)
Enquiries: 020 7217 6588
Area Manager: Sarah Payne

WALES
Enquiries: 020 7217 6925
Area Manager: John May

WEST MIDLANDS
Enquiries: 020 7217 6589
Area Manager: Bryan Payling

YORKSHIRE AND HUMBERSIDE
Enquiries: 020 7217 6288
Area Manager: Peter Earnshaw

DIRECTORATE OF HIGH SECURITY PRISONS
Enquiries: 020 7217 2888
Director and Area Manager: Peter Atherton

AREA MANAGER FOR WOMEN'S PRISONS
Enquiries:
Operational Manager: Niall Clifford

Department: Home Office
Launched: 1/4/93

Property Advisers to the Civil Estate

Trevelyan House, Great Peter Street
London SW1P 2BY
General Enquiries: 020 7271 2833
Fax: 020 7271 2715
E-mail: enquiries@property.gsi.gov.uk
Website: www.property.gov.uk

PACE is responsible for promoting co-operation between Departments in the management of their property assets.

Chief Executive: Vivien Bodnar
Department: Office of Government
    Commerce (HM Treasury)
Launched: 1/4/96

Public Record Office

Ruskin Avenue, Kew, Richmond
Surrey TW9 4DU
020 8876 3444 *Fax:* 020 8878 8905
E-mail: enquiry@pro.gov.uk
Website: www.pro.gov.uk

Houses the national archives of England and Wales and the UK, that is, records created by the actions of central government and the courts of law. Its responsibilities include ensuring the selection of records which should be permanently preserved, their preservation and their use by the public.

Keeper of Public Records and Chief Executive:
    Sarah Tyacke, CB
Director of Public Services:
    Dr Elizabeth Hallam-Smith
Director of Government, Information and
    Corporate Services: Dr Duncan Simpson
Department: The Public Record Office is a
    separate Government Department
    reporting directly to the Lord Chancellor
Launched: 1/4/92

Public Record Office of Northern Ireland

66 Balmoral Avenue, Belfast BT9 6NY
028 9025 1318 *Fax:* 028 9025 5999
E-mail: proni@doeni.gov.uk
Website: http://proni.nics.gov.uk/index.htm

Identifies and preserves Northern Ireland's archival heritage and ensures public access to that heritage which fully meets Open Government standards.

Chief Executive: Dr Gerry Slater
Department: Culture, Arts and Leisure
    (Northern Ireland)
Launched: 3/4/95

Public Trust Office

MENTAL HEALTH AND TRUST DIVISIONS
Stewart House, 24 Kingsway
London WC2B 6JX
020 7664 7000 *Fax:* 020 7664 7705
E-mail: enquiries@publictrust.gov.uk
Website: www.publictrust.gov.uk

COURT FUNDS OFFICE
22 Kingsway, London WC2B 6LE
020 7947 6000

Looks after the private assets and financial affairs of members of the public who are suffering from mental disorder, those involved with trusts where the Public Trustee is executor of trust, those involved in civil actions in the courts and those interested in some institutional funds.

*Acting Chief Executive and Accountant General
   of the Supreme Court:* Nick Smedley
Acting Public Trustee: Jill Martin
Department: Lord Chancellor's
Launched: 1/7/94

Queen Elizabeth II Conference Centre

Broad Sanctuary, London SW1P 3EE
020 7222 5000 *Fax:* 020 7798 4200
E-mail: gillp@qeiicc.co.uk
Website: www.qeiicc.co.uk

Provides conference and banqueting facilities for government and commercial use on a national and international scale.

Chief Executive: Marcus Buck CBE
Commercial Director: Gill Price
Department: Environment, Transport and
**   the Regions**
Launched: 6/7/86

Queen Victoria School

Dunblane, Perthshire FK15 0JY
01786 822288 *Fax:* 0131-310 2926
E-mail: enquiries@qvs.org.uk
Website: www.qvs.org.uk

Provides secondary boarding education for the children of Scottish service personnel.

Headmaster and Chief Executive:
   Brian Raine
Deputy Head: Colin Philson
Assistant Head: Alice Hainey
Department: Defence
Launched: 1/4/92

Radiocommunications Agency

Wyndham House, 189 Marsh Wall,
London E14 9SX
020 7211 0211 *Fax:* 020 7211 0507
E-mail: library@ra.gsi.gov.uk
Website: www.radio.gov.uk

Responsible for the management of the civil radio spectrum in the UK. It also represents UK radio interests internationally.

Chief Executive: David Hendon
Spectrum Policy Director: Mike Goddard
Spectrum Services Director: Hazel Canter
Customer Services Director: Barry Maxwell
Corporate Services and Facilities Director:
   Chris de Grouchy
Department: Trade and Industry
Launched: 2/4/90

RAF Personnel Management Agency

RAF Innsworth, Gloucester GL3 1EZ
01452 712612 Ext 7849
Fax: 01452 712612 Ext 7309
Website: www.raf.mod.uk/ptc/pma

Provides personnel to meet the RAF's worldwide manpower commitments and manages individuals' careers.

Air Secretary and Chief Executive:
   Air Vice-Marshal Ian Stewart, CB, AFC
*Director of Personnel Management Agency
   (Officers and Airmen Aircrew):*
   Air Commodore Andrew Neal, AFC
*Director of Personnel Management Agency
   (Airmen and Reserve Forces):*
   Air Commodore Rod Brumpton
*Director of Personnel Management Agency
   (Policy):* Air Commodore Andy Collier, CBE
Personnel Management Agency Air Secretary 1:
   Air Commodore (Retired) Bob Arnott, CBE
Personnel Management Agency (Casework):
   Group Captain Ray Innes, OBE
Personnel Management Agency (Secretary):
   Alan Cowpe
Department: Defence
Launched: 2/2/97

RAF Training Group Defence Agency

Royal Air Force Innsworth, Gloucester,
Gloucestershire GL3 1EZ
01452 712612 Ext 5312 *Fax:* 01452 510825
E-mail: ca@tgda.gov.uk
Website: www.tgda.gov.uk

Responsible for the recruitment and selection of all Royal Air Force personnel and for RAF non-operational training.

Chief Executive: Air Vice-Marshal Ian Corbitt
Director of Training:
   Air Commodore Chris Chambers
Director of Corporate Development:
   Air Commodore Dil Williams
Department: Defence
Launched: 1/4/94

Rate Collection Agency

Oxford House, 49–55 Chichester Street,
Belfast BT1 4HH
028 9025 2252 *Fax:* 028 9025 2113
E-mail: rca@doeni.gov.uk
Website: www.dfpni.gov.uk/rca/

Collects rates and administers the Housing Benefit Scheme for owner-occupiers.

Chief Executive: Arthur Scott
Department: Finance and Personnel
   (Northern Ireland)
Launched: 1/4/91

Registers of Scotland

Meadowbank House, 153 London Road,
Edinburgh EH8 7AU
0131-659 6111 Ext 3293
Fax: 0131-459 1221
E-mail: keeper@ros.gov.uk
Website: www.ros.gov.uk

Maintains registers of land etc. in Scotland.

Chief Executive: Alan W Ramage
Deputy Keeper: Alistair Rennie
Managing Director: Frank Manson
Director of Legal Services: Ian Davis
Responsible Minister: First Minister, Scottish
   Parliament
Launched: 6/4/90

The Rent Service

1st Floor, Clifton House, 87-113 Euston Road,
London NW1 2RA
020 7554 2451 *Fax:* 020 7554 2490

Chief Executive: Steve Williams
Finance Director: Charlotte Copeland
Operations Support Director:
   Rebecca Lawrence
Personnel Director: Mark Merka-Richards
Regional Director, North: Jane Durkin
Regional Director, South: Alan Corcoran
Regional Director, Midlands and Eastern:
   Janet Butler
Regional Director, London: Melvyn Beck
Department: Environment, Transport and
   the Regions
Launched: 1/10/99

Rivers Agency

Hydebank, 4 Hospital Road,
Belfast BT8 8JP
028 9025 3355 *Fax:* 028 9025 3455
E-mail: rivers@dard.gov.uk

Maintains watercourses, flood and sea defences in Northern Ireland.

Chief Executive: John Hagan
Department: Agriculture and Rural
   Development (Northern Ireland)
Launched: 1/10/96

Roads Service

Clarence Court, 10–18 Adelaide Street
Belfast BT2 8GB
028 9054 0540 *Fax:* 028 9054 0024
E-mail: roads@drdni.gov.uk
Website: www.drdni.gov.uk/roads

Responsible for the road network in Northern Ireland.

Chief Executive: Colin James
Director of Corporate Services: Jim Carlisle
Director of Network and Customer Services:
   Grahame Fraser
Department: Regional Development
   (Northern Ireland)
Launched: 1/4/96

Royal Mint

Llantrisant, Pontyclun, CF72 8YT
01443 222111 *Fax:* 01443 623185
7 Grosvenor Gardens, London SW1W 0BD
020 7592 8601 *Fax:* 020 7592 8634
E-mail: ldosker@royalmint.gov.uk
Website: www.royalmint.com

The manufacture and distribution of UK and overseas coins (circulating and commemorative); medals and seals.

Chief Executive: Roger Holmes
Director of Finance: Graham Davies
Director of Sales: Keith Cottrell
Director of Collector Coin: Alan Wallace
Director of Engineering Services: Geoff Payne
Department: The Royal Mint is a separate Government Department reporting directly to the Chancellor of the Exchequer
Launched: 1/4/90

Royal Parks

The Old Police House, Hyde Park,
London W2 2UH
020 7298 2000 *Fax:* 020 7298 2005
Website: www.open.gov.uk/rp/rphome.htm

Manages and polices the Royal Parks in London – St James's Park, Green Park, Hyde Park, Kensington Gardens, Regent's Park, Primrose Hill, Greenwich Park, Richmond Park and Bushy Park. It also manages and polices a number of other areas.

Chief Executive: William Weston
Chief Officer, Royal Parks Constabulary:
   Walter Ross OBE
Department: Culture, Media and Sport
Launched: 1/4/93

Scottish Agricultural Science Agency

82 Craigs Road, East Craigs,
Edinburgh EH12 8NJ
0131-244 8890 *Fax:* 0131-244 8940
E-mail: library@sasa.gov.uk
Website: www.sasa.gov.uk

Provides Government, primarily the Scottish Executive, with expert scientific information and advice on agricultural and horticultural crops and aspects of the environment.

Director: Dr Robert Hay
Deputy Director: Simon Cooper
Head of Administration: Shelagh Quinn
Department: Scottish Executive Rural Affairs Department
Launched: 1/4/92

Scottish Court Service

Hayweight House, 23 Lauriston Street
Edinburgh EH3 9DQ
0131-229 9200 *Fax:* 0131-221 6895
E-mail: enquiries@scotcourts.gov.uk
Website: www.scotcourts.gov.uk

Responsible for the provision and maintenance of Court Houses, and for ensuring the supply of trained staff and of administrative and organisational services, to support the judiciary, in the Supreme and Sheriff Courts in Scotland.

Chief Executive: John Ewing
Deputy Chief Executive and Area Director West:
   Ian Scott
Head of Operations and Policy Unit:
   Eric Cumming
Head of Resources and Efficiency Unit:
   Nicola Bennett
Director of Personnel and Development Unit:
   Alan Swift
Head of Property and Services Unit:
   Gillian Jewel
Department: Scottish Executive Justice Department
Launched: 3/4/95

Scottish Fisheries Protection Agency

Pentland House, 47 Robb's Loan
Edinburgh EH14 1TY
0131-244 6059 *Fax:* 0131-244 6086
E-mail: sfpa.agency@.so003.scotoff.gov.uk
Website: www.scotland.gov.uk

Enforces UK, EU and international fisheries law and regulations in Scottish waters and ports.

Chief Executive: Paul Du Vivier
Director of Corporate Strategy and Resources:
   John Roddin
Director, Operations: Robert Walker
Marine Superintendent: Captain Alan Brown
Department: Scottish Executive Rural Affairs Department
Launched: 12/4/91

Scottish Prison Service

Headquarters, Calton House
5 Redheughs Rigg, Edinburgh EH12 9HW
0131-244 8745 *Fax:* 0131-244 8774
Website: www.sps.gov.uk

Provides prison services in Scotland.

Chief Executive: Tony Cameron
Director of Custody: John Durno
Area Director (North and East): Peter Withers
Area Director (South and West): Mike Duffy
Director of Human Resources: Peter Russell
Director of Finance and Information Systems:
   William Pretswell
Deputy Director of Custody: David Croft
Deputy Director of Regime Services and
   Supplies: John McNeill
Deputy Director of Estates and Building
   Division: David Bentley
Department: Scottish Executive Justice
   Department
Launched: 1/4/93

Scottish Public Pensions Agency

St Margaret's House, 151 London Road
Edinburgh EH8 7TG
Teachers Scheme Helpline: 0131-244 3586
NHS Scheme Helpline: 0131-244 3585
Fax: 0131-244 3334

Responsible for the pension arrangements of
employees of the NHS and teaching service.

Chief Executive: Ralph Garden
Policy Director: Gavin Mowat
Human Resources Director and STSS Manager:
   Murray McDermott
NHS Scheme Manager: Gordon Taylor
Department: Scottish Executive
Launched: 1/4/93

Service Children's Education

BFPO 40
00 49 2161 908 + Ext 2372
Fax: 00 49 2161 908 + Ext 2396
E-mail: tutor4@bfgnet.com

Provides an education service for the dependent
children of service personnel and UK based
civilian support staff residing overseas.

Chief Executive Officer: David Wadsworth
Assistant Chief Executive (Operations):
   Paul S Niedzwiedzki

Assistant Chief Executive (Corporate Affairs):
   Linda Moore-Rosindell
Assistant Chief Executive (Quality Assurance):
   Judith Morris
Department: Defence
Launched: 1/4/96

Ships Support Agency

(TO BE MERGED WITH NAVAL BASES AND SUPPLY
AGENCY FROM APRIL 2001)

B Block, Foxhill, Bath BA5 5AB
01225 883935 *Fax:* 01225 884313
E-mail: ssasresla2asec@navynet.gtnet.gov.uk

Defines and directs the materiel support of the
Royal Navy's ships and submarines.

Director-General Equipment Support (Sea) and
   Chief Executive Ships Support Agency:
   John Coles
Director Resources: Andy McClelland
Director Operations Equipment: Fred Edwards
Director Operations Platform: Mike Frowde
Director Support Chain: Pat Montague
Director Technical: Roy Cummings
Director Business Development: Tony Rossi
Director Commercial: John Hall
Frigates IPT/TL: John Chapman
Submarine Support IPT/TL:
   Commodore Tim Chittenden
Strategic Systems IPT/TL:
   Commodore Mike Holmes
Superintendent Ships (Devonport):
   Commodore David Hall
Department: Defence
Launched: 11/12/96

Small Business Service

1 Victoria Street, London SW1H 0ET
020 7215 5363 *Fax:* 020 7215 2773
E-mail: enquiries@sbs.gsi.gov.uk
Website: www. businessadviceonline.org

Chief Executive: David Irwin
Deputy Chief Executive: Peter Waller
Department: Trade and Industry
Launched: 1/4/00

Social Security Agency

Churchill House, Victoria Square,
Belfast BT1 4SS
028 9056 9100 *Fax:* 028 9056 9178
E-mail: ssa@nics.gov.uk
Website: http://ssa.nics.gov.uk

Delivers a wide range of social security benefits
and services. It also provides processing services
for the Benefits Agency in Great Britain.

Chief Executive: Chris Thompson
Director of Operations: Barney McGahan
Director of Benefit Security: David McCurry
Director of Business Development: Peter Gray
Director of Finance and Support: John Deery
Director of Personnel and Planning:
  Frank Duffy
Non-Executive Director: Andrew Smith
**Department: Social Development (Northern
  Ireland)**
Launched: 1/7/91

Student Awards Agency for Scotland

Gyleview House, 3 Redheughs Rigg
Edinburgh EH12 9HH
0131-476 8212 *Fax:* 0131-244 5887
E-mail: saas.geu@scotland.gov.uk
Website: www.student-support-saas.gov.uk

Administers student awards and other related services for Scottish domiciled students in full-time higher education.

Chief Executive: David Stephen
**Department: Scottish Executive Education
  and Lifelong Learning Department**
Launched: 5/4/94

Training and Employment Agency

Adelaide House, 39-49 Adelaide Street,
Belfast BT2 8FD
028 9025 7777 *Fax:* 028 9025 7778
E-mail: info.tea@nics.gov.uk
Website: www.tea-ni.org/

Administration of employment and training services in Northern Ireland.

Chief Executive: Ian Walters
*Director New Deal Development and Support
  Division:* Roy Gamble
Director Skills and Industry Division: Tom Scott
Director Regional Operations Division:
  Adrian Arbuthnot
**Department: Higher and Further Education,
  Training and Employment (Northern
  Ireland)**
Launched: 2/4/90

Treasury Solicitor's Department

Queen Anne's Chambers, 28 Broadway,
London SW1H 9JS
020 7210 3079 *Fax:* 020 7210 3004
E-mail: tsol.tsd.qac@gtnet.gov.uk
Website: www.open.gov.uk/tsd/tsdhome.htm

Provides litigation and advisory services to government departments and other publicly funded bodies in England and Wales. Also administers estates of people who die intestate with no known kin.

Chief Executive: Juliet Wheldon CB QC
**Department: The Treasury Solicitor's
  Department is a separate Government
  Department reporting directly to the
  Attorney General**
Launched: 1/4/96
For full details of Treasury Solicitor's Department – see Government Departments

UK Passport Agency

Clive House, Petty France,
London SW1H 9HD
020 7271 8881 *Fax:* 020 7271 8897
Website: www.passport.gov.uk

Chiefly concerned with issuing and servicing UK passports to British nationals who are resident in the UK.

Chief Executive: Bernard Herdan
*Deputy Chief Executive and Director of
  Operations:* Kevin Sheehan
Department: Home Office
Launched: 2/4/91

United Kingdom Debt Management Office

Cheapside House, 138 Cheapside,
London EC2V 6BB
020 7862 6500 *Fax:* 020 7862 6509
E-mail: firstname.surname@dmo.gov.uk
Website: www.dmo.gov.uk

Responsible for administering the Government's debt management policy of minimising its financing costs over the long term, taking account of risk, and to manage the aggregate cash needs of the Exchequer in the most cost-effective way.

Chief Executive: Mike Williams 020 7862 6533
Markets: Jo Whelan 020 7862 6531
Business Services: Bob Tobin 020 7862 6515
Department: HM Treasury
Launched: 1/4/98

United Kingdom Hydrographic Office

Admiralty Way, Taunton
Somerset TA1 2DN
01823 337900 *Fax:* 01823 284077
E-mail: firstname.surname@ukho.gov.uk
Website: www.ukho.gov.uk

Produces charts and navigational publications for the Royal Navy and other customers at home and abroad.

Hydrographer/Chief Executive:
    Rear Admiral John P Clarke, CB, LVO, MBE
Director of Production: Vic Jenkins
Director of Finance: Bill Burgess
Deputy Director Defence Services:
    William Salmon
Director of Marketing: Bob Moss
Director Planning: Nick Beadle
Director of Human Resources: Steve Parnell
Department: Defence
Launched: 6/4/90

Valuation and Lands Agency

Queen's Court,
56–66 Upper Queen Street,
Belfast BT1 6FD
028 9025 0700 *Fax:* 028 9054 3800
E-mail: bobby.stranaghan@dfpni.gov.uk
Website: http://vla.nics.gov.uk

Responsible for maintenance of the Valuation List for rating purposes in Northern Ireland and, periodically, the preparation of a new Valuation List; provision of a valuation, estate management and property data service to the public sector.

Chief Executive and Commissioner of Valuation:
    Nigel Woods
Assistant Commissioner: David Rainey
Assistant Commissioner: Brian McClure
Department: Finance and Personnel
    (Northern Ireland)
Launched: 1/4/93

Valuation Office

New Court, Carey Street,
London WC2A 2JE
020 7506 1700 *Fax:* 020 7506 1998
E-mail: custserv.voa@gtnet.gov.uk
Website: www.voa.gov.uk

Provides land and buildings valuation service to government departments, other public bodies and a number of local authorities throughout Great Britain.

Ministers: Chancellor of the Exchequer,
    Paymaster General
Chief Executive: Michael Johns CB
Deputy Chief Executive: John Ebdon
Director of Professional and Customer Services:
    Tony Prior
Director of Business Resources:
    Anne Wheatcroft
Director Finance, Planning and Strategy:
    John Keelby
Director of Financial Operations: David Cruden
Director of Business Development:
    Richard Dales
Director of Corporate Communications:
    Angela McKenna
Director of Modernisation: Bruce Jones
Chief Valuer, Scotland: Allan Ainslie
Chief Valuer, Wales: Peter Clement
Department: Inland Revenue
Launched: 30/9/91

Vehicle Certification Agency

1 The Eastgate Office Centre
Eastgate Road, Bristol BS5 6XX
0117-951 5151 *Fax:* 0117-952 4103
E-mail: enquiries@vca.gov.uk
Website: www.vca.gov.uk

Tests and certificates vehicles and their components to UK and international standards.

Chief Executive: Derek Harvey
Deputy Chief Executive: Peter Nicholl
Department: Environment, Transport and
    the Regions
Launched: 2/4/90

Vehicle Inspectorate

Berkeley House, Croydon Street
Bristol BS5 0DA
0117-954 3200 *Fax:* 0117-954 3212
E-mail: enquiries@via.gov.uk
Website: www.via.gov.uk

Checks vehicles and drivers at the roadside and other enforcement checks and through the annual testing of all vehicles.

Chief Executive: Maurice Newey
Product Strategy and Policy Director:
    Hugh Edwards
Operations Director: Bob Tatchell
Process Director: Jeff Belt
Department: Environment, Transport and
    the Regions
Launched: 1/8/88

Veterinary Laboratories Agency

Woodham Lane, New Haw, Addlestone,
Surrey KT15 3NB
01932 341111 *Fax:* 01932 347046
E-mail: enquiries@vla.maff.gsi.gov.uk
Website: www.maff.gov.uk/vla

Provides specialist veterinary advice to MAFF based on sound investigation and surveillance, laboratory testing, research and development. It also offers this service to other government departments and the private sector.

Chief Executive: Dr Steve Edwards
Research Director: Dr John Morris
Director of Surveillance and Laboratory Services: Roger Hancock
Department: Agriculture, Fisheries and Food
Launched: 1/10/95

Veterinary Medicines Directorate

Woodham Lane, New Haw, Addlestone,
Surrey KT15 3LS
01932 336911 *Fax:* 01932 336618
E-mail: postbk@vmd.maff.gov.uk
Website: www.vmd.gov.uk

Assesses applications for veterinary medicines, issues authorisations and monitors suspected adverse reactions and the presence of residues of veterinary medicines in meat and animal products. Advises Ministers on policy for veterinary medicines.

Director and Chief Executive: Dr Michael Rutter
Director of Licensing: Steve Dean
Director of Policy: Ray Anderson
VMD Secretary and Head of Business Unit: John FitzGerald
Department: Agriculture, Fisheries and Food
Launched: 2/4/90

War Pensions Agency

Norcross, Blackpool, Lancashire FY5 3WP
Freephone: 0800 169 2277
Textphone: 0800 169 3458
Fax: 01253 330561
E-mail: warpensions@gtnet.gov.uk
Website: www.dss.gov.uk/wpa/index.htm

Responsible for the assessment and payment of war pensions, the War Pensions Welfare Offices and the Ilford Park Polish Home in Devon.

Chief Executive: Gordon Hextall
Director of Operations: Alan Burnham
Director of Finance and Personnel: Stuart Munslow
Medical Director: Dr Paul Kitchen
Head of IPPH and Welfare: Sue Turner
Department: Social Security
Launched: 1/4/94

Water Service

Northland House, 3–5 Frederick Street
Belfast BT1 2NR
028 9024 4711 *Fax:* 028 9035 4888
E-mail: water.service@nics.gov.uk
Website: www.waterni.gov.uk

Provides water and sewerage services in Northern Ireland.

Chief Executive: Robert C Martin
Director of Corporate Services: Robin Mussen
Director of Operations: John Kelly
Director of Development: John McMillen
Director of Finance: David Carson
Technical Director: Harry Thompson
Department: Regional Development (Northern Ireland)
Launched: 1/4/96

Wilton Park

Wiston House, Steyning,
Sussex BN44 3DZ
01903 815020 *Fax:* 01903 815931
E-mail: wilton@pavilion.co.uk

Arranges and runs conferences on international affairs for politicians, officials, academics and others from around the world. Also hosts conferences for public and private sector customers.

Chief Executive: Colin Jennings
Manager, Wiston House Conference Centre: Roger Barr
Director, Wilton Park Conferences: Dr Richard Latter
Department: Foreign and Commonwealth Office
Launched: 1/9/91

OMBUDSMEN AND COMPLAINT-HANDLING BODIES

Ombudsmen deal with complaints about the public or private sector bodies within their jurisdiction. Ombudsman services are free. The majority of Ombudsman schemes are set up by statute. Others are voluntary, non-statutory schemes set up on the initiative of the service sectors concerned. In most schemes there are individual Ombudsmen.

All the schemes listed below, other than the European Ombudsman, are recognised or associate members of the British and Irish Ombudsman Association. To be recognised they have to meet four key criteria: independence from the organisations the Ombudsman has the power to investigate; effectiveness; fairness; and public accountability.

Further information about Ombudsmen is available on the Association's Website: www.intervid.co.uk/bioa or from the Secretary, British and Irish Ombudsman Association, 24 Paget Gardens, Chislehurst, Kent BR7 5RX, *Tel/Fax:* 020 8467 7455, *E-mail:* g.d.a@btinternet.com, *Website:* www.bioa.org.uk. For information about an individual scheme contact the appropriate scheme direct.

Adjudicator's Office

Haymarket House, 28 Haymarket,
London SW1Y 4SP
020 7930 2292 *Fax:* 020 7930 2298
E-mail: adjudicators@gtnet.gov.uk
Website: www.open.gov.uk/adjoff/aodemo1.htm

The Adjudicator investigates complaints from people and businesses against the Inland Revenue (including the Valuation Office Agency) and Customs and Excise.

The Adjudicator: Dame Barbara Mills, DBE, QC
Head of Office: Charlie Gordon

Assembly Ombudsman and Commissioner for Complaints – Northern Ireland

Progressive House, 33 Wellington Place,
Belfast BT1 6HN
028 9023 3821 *Fax:* 028 9023 4912
Free call Information Service: 0800 343424
E-mail: ombudsman@ni-ombudsman.org.uk
Website: www.ni-ombudsman.org.uk

The Ombudsman investigates complaints from those who think they have been unfairly treated by a government department or other public body. Included are matters relating to the Code of Practice on Access to Government Information duties in relation to Health Services and matters in the Public Service.

Ombudsman: Tom Frawley
Deputy Ombudsman: John MacQuarrie

Banking Ombudsman, Office of the

South Quay Plaza, 183 Marsh Wall,
London E14 9SR
020 7404 9944 *Fax:* 020 7405 5052
E-mail: banking.ombudsman@obo.org.uk
Website: www.obo.org.uk

To be merged into the Financial Ombudsman Service in mid 2001.

Chairman of the Council: Sir David Calcutt, QC
Principal Ombudsman: David Thomas
Ombudsmen: Jane Hingston, Sue Wrigley
Divisional Administrator: Brenda Costello

Broadcasting Standards Commission

7 The Sanctuary, London SW1P 3JS
020 7808 1000 *Fax:* 020 7233 0397
E-mail: bsc@bsc.org.uk
Website: www.bsc.org.uk

The Broadcasting Standards Commission is the statutory body for standards and fairness in broadcasting.

Chairman: Vacant
Deputy Chair: Lady Suzanne Warner
Commissioners: David Boulton,
    Dame Fiona Caldicott, DBE, Uday Dholakia,
    Geoff Elliott, Strachan Heppell, CB,
    Rev Rose Hudson-Wilkin, Sally O'Sullivan,
    Maggie Redfern, Sioned Wyn Thomas
Director: Stephen Whittle
Deputy Director: Norman McLean

Building Societies Ombudsman, Office of the

South Quay Plaza, 183 Marsh Wall,
London E14 9SR
020 7964 1000 *Fax:* 020 7964 1001
E-mail via:
rachel.fagg@financial-ombudsman.org.uk
DX: 141280, Isle of Dogs 3

To be merged into the Financial Ombudsman Service in mid 2001.

Ombudsman: Roger Yeomans
Registrar to the Council: Barbara Cheney

Complaints Adjudicator for Companies House

PO Box 2, Fakenham, Norfolk NR21 0RS

Adjudicator: Bill Thomas

Complaints Commissioner to the General Council of the Bar

Northumberland House,
303-306 High Holborn, London WC1V 7JZ
020 7440 4000 *Fax:* 020 7440 4001
E-mail: laycommissioner@barcouncil.org.uk
Website: www.barcouncil.org.uk

Complaints Commissioner:
   Michael Scott, CB, CBE, DSO

Estate Agents, Ombudsman for

Beckett House, 4 Bridge Street
Salisbury, Wiltshire SP1 2LX
01722 333306 *Fax:* 01722 332296
E-mail: admin@oea.co.uk
Website: www.oea.co.uk

Ombudsman: Stephen Carr-Smith

European Ombudsman

1 avenue du Président Robert Schuman,
BP 403, 67001 Strasbourg Cedex, France
00 33 3 88 17 23 13
Fax: 00 33 3 88 17 90 62
E-mail: euro-ombudsman@europarl.eu.int
Website: www.euro-ombudsman.eu.int

The European Ombudsman is empowered to receive complaints from any citizen of the European Union concerning instances of maladministration in the activities of the EU institutions or bodies.

Ombudsman: Jacob Söderman

Financial Ombudsman Service

South Quay Plaza, 183 Marsh Wall,
London E14 9SR
020 7964 1000 *Fax:* 020 7964 1001
E-mail:
enquiries@financial-ombudsman.org.uk
Website: www.financial-ombudsman.org.uk

From mid 2001, the Financial Ombudsman Service will bring the current eight financial services ombudsman schemes under one roof. These are: The Banking Ombudsman, The Building Societies Ombudsman, The Investment Ombudsman, The Insurance Ombudsman, The PIA Ombudsman, The Personal Insurance Arbitration Service, The SFA Complaints Bureau and the FSA Direct Regulation Complaints Unit.

Chief Ombudsman: Walter Merricks
Principal Ombudsmen: David Thomas,
   Tony Boorman, Jane Whittles
Chief Operating Officer: Ian Marshall
Head of Communications: David Cresswell

Funeral Ombudsman Scheme

Fifth Floor, 26-28 Bedford Row,
London WC1R 4HE
020 7430 1112 *Fax:* 020 7430 1012
E-mail: fos@dircon.co.uk
Website: funeralombudsman.org.uk

Chairman of the Council: John Hosker
Ombudsman: Prof Geoffrey Woodroffe
Scheme Manager: Regina Weston

Health Service Ombudsman for England

Millbank Tower, Millbank,
London SW1P 4QP
0845 015 4033 *Fax:* 020 7217 4940
E-mail: ohsc-enqu@online.rednet.co.uk
Text telephone: 020 7217 4066
Website: www.ombudsman.org.uk

Health Service Ombudsman: Michael Buckley
Deputy Health Service Commissioner:
   Hilary Scott

Health Service Ombudsman for Scotland

28 Thistle Street, Edinburgh EH2 1EN
0845 601 0456 *Fax:* 0131-226 4447
Website: www.ombudsman.org.uk

Health Service Ombudsman: Michael Buckley
Investigations Manager: George Keil

Health Service Ombudsman for Wales

5th Floor, Capital Tower,
Greyfriars Road, Cardiff CF10 3AG
0845 601 0987 *Fax:* 029 2022 6909
Website: www.ombudsman.org.uk

Health Service Ombudsman: Michael Buckley
Investigations Manager: Stan Drummond

Housing Association Ombudsman for Scotland

2 Belford Road, Edinburgh EH4 3BL
0131-220 0599 *Fax:* 0131-220 0577

Ombudsman: Barney Crockett

Independent Case Examiner

PO Box 155, Chester CH99 9SA
0151-801 8800 *Fax:* 0151-801 8801
Minicom: 0151-801 8888
Local call rate number: 0845 606 0777
E-mail: ice@ukgov.demon.co.uk
Website: www.ind-case-exam.org.uk

PO Box 1245, Belfast BT2 7DF

Independent Case Examiner: Anne Parker
Office Manager: Phil Latus

Independent Complaints Reviewer

Newspaper House (First Floor),
8-16 Great New Street, London EC4A 3EU
020 7583 1172 *Fax:* 020 7583 1173
DX461 London Chancery Lane
E-mail: icr@icrev.demon.co.uk
Website:
www.icrev.demon.co.uk/icrbook.htm

The ICR investigates complaints about HM Land Registry, the Charity Commission and the Public Record Office.

Independent Complaints Reviewer: Jodi Berg

Independent Housing Ombudsman Scheme

Norman House, 105–109 Strand,
London WC2R 0AA
020 7836 3630 *Fax:* 020 7836 3900
Lo-call Tel: 0345 125973
E-mail: ombudsman@ihos.org.uk
Website: www.ihos.org.uk

IHO deals with complaints against social landlords registered with the Housing Corporation, and other landlords who have volunteered to join the scheme. IHO is also managing a pilot scheme to resolve disputes about rent deposits in the private sector.

Chair: Kate Lampard
Ombudsman: Roger Jefferies
General Manager and Company Secretary:
    Lawrence Greenberg

Insurance Ombudsman Bureau

South Quay Plaza, 183 Marsh Wall,
London E14 9SR
020 7964 1000 *Fax:* 020 7964 1001
Enquiries: 0845 600 6666
E-mail: complaint@theiob.org.uk
Website: www.theiob.org.uk

To be merged into the Financial Ombudsman Service in mid 2001.

Chairman of the Council: Maurice Healy
Principal Ombudsman: Tony Boorman
Ombudsmen: Reidy Flynn, Steve Lilley,
    Michael Lovegrove

Investment Ombudsman, Office of the

South Quay Plaza, 183 Marsh Wall,
London E14 9SR
020 7796 3065

To be merged into the Financial Ombudsman Service in mid 2001.

Investment Ombudsman: Peter Dean, CBE
Executive Director: Ronald Bennett

Lay Observer for Northern Ireland

Lancashire House, 1st Floor,
5 Linenhall Street, Belfast BT2 8AA
028 9054 2900 *Fax:* 028 9054 2909

The Lay Observer is an independent non-legal person appointed to monitor the nature of complaints against solicitors made to the Law Society and to report on the manner in which the Law Society handles them.

Lay Observer: Prof Vincent Mageean, OBE

Legal Services Ombudsman, Office of the

22 Oxford Court, Oxford Street,
Manchester M2 3WQ
Local call rate: 0845 601 0794
0161-236 9532 *Fax:* 0161-236 2651
E-mail: enquiries.olso@gtnet.gov.uk
Website: www.olso.org

Ombudsman: Ann Abraham

Local Administration In England, Commission for

Chairman of the Commission and Local
  Government Ombudsman for London:
  Edward Osmotherly, CB
Secretary to the Commission: Nigel Karney
21 Queen Anne's Gate, London SW1H 9BU
020 7915 3210 *Fax:* 020 7233 0396

Local Government Ombudsman for Southern
  England (except London), East Anglia, the
  South West and most of Central England:
  Jerry White
The Oaks, No 2 Westwood Way, Westwood
Business Park, Coventry CV4 8JB
024 7669 5999 *Fax:* 024 7669 5902

Vice-Chairman and Local Government
  Ombudsman for Birmingham, Shropshire,
  Staffordshire, Cheshire, Derbyshire,
  Nottinghamshire, Lincolnshire and the North
  of England: Patricia Thomas
Beverley House, 17 Shipton Road,
York YO30 5FZ
01904 663200 *Fax:* 01904 663269

Adviceline: 0845 602 1983
Website: www.open.gov.uk/lgo

Local Administration in Scotland, Commissioner for

23 Walker Street, Edinburgh EH3 7HX
0131-225 5300 *Fax:* 0131-225 9495
Website: www.ombudslgscot.org.uk

Handles complaints of administrative shortcoming against local authorities in Scotland and housing complaints against Scottish Homes.

Commissioner (Ombudsman): Ian Smith
Deputy Commissioner and Secretary:
  Janice Renton

Local Administration in Wales, Commission for

Derwen House, Court Road, Bridgend,
CF31 1BN
01656 661325 *Fax:* 01656 658317
E-mail: enquiries@ombudsman-wales.org
Website: www.ombudsman-wales.org

Local Commissioner (Ombudsman):
  Elwyn Moseley
Secretary to the Commission: David Bowen
Parliamentary Commissioner (ex officio):
  Michael Buckley

Office for the Supervision of Solicitors

Victoria Court, 8 Dormer Place,
Leamington Spa, Warwickshire CV32 5AE
01926 820082 *Fax:* 01926 431435
Website: www.lawsociety.org.uk

Director: Jim Wagstaffe

Parliamentary Commissioner for Administration, Office of the

Millbank Tower, Millbank,
London SW1P 4QP
0845 015 4033 *Fax:* 020 7217 4160
E-mail: opca-enqu@ombudsman.org.uk
Website: www.ombudsman.org.uk

The Parliamentary Commissioner for Administration (the Parliamentary Ombudsman) is independent of Government and is an officer of Parliament. He investigates complaints referred to him by MPs from members of the public about maladministration by or on behalf of government departments and certain non-departmental public bodies. He also investigates complaints referred by MPs alleging that access to official information has been wrongly refused under the Code of Practice on Access to Government Information 1994.

Parliamentary Commissioner for Administration: Michael Buckley
Deputy Parliamentary Commissioner for Administration: Alan Watson

Pensions Ombudsman

6th Floor, 11 Belgrave Road,
London SW1V 1RB
020 7834 9144 *Fax:* 020 7821 0065

Primarily complaints investigated relate to alleged maladministration of occupational pension schemes. Personal pension complaints would normally be dealt with only if outside the jurisdiction of The Personal Investment Authority (PIA).

Pensions Ombudsman: Dr Julian Farrand

Personal Investment Authority Ombudsman Bureau

South Quay Plaza, 183 Marsh Wall,
London E14 9SR
020 7216 0016 *Fax:* 020 7712 8742

To be merged into the Financial Ombudsman Service in mid 2001.

Principal Ombudsman: Jane Whittles
Ombudsmen: Richard Prior, Philip Roberts, Chris Tilson
Press and Information Officer: Iris Baker

Police Complaints Authority

10 Great George Street,
London SW1P 3AE
020 7273 6450 *Fax:* 020 7273 6401
E-mail: info@pca.gov.uk
Website: www.pca.gov.uk

Chairman: Sir Alistair Graham
Deputy Chairman: Molly Meacher

Police Ombudsman for Northern Ireland

New Cathedral Buildings, St Anne's Square,
11 Church Street, Belfast BT1 1PG
028 9082 8600
E-mail: nuala.o'loan@belfast.org.uk

The office of Police Ombudsman must investigate complaints against the police where it is alleged that the conduct of a police officer may have caused death or serious injury and may investigate less serious complaints or refer them to the Chief Constable to investigate.

Police Ombudsman: Nuala O'Loan

Press Complaints Commission

1 Salisbury Square, London EC4Y 8JB
020 7353 1248 *Fax:* 020 7353 8355
Help-line: 020 7353 3732
Scottish Helpline: 0131-220 6652
E-mail: pcc@pcc.org.uk
Website: www.pcc.org.uk

Chairman: Rt Hon Lord Wakeham, FCA
Director: Guy Black
PR Officer: Luke Chauveau

Prisons Ombudsman

Ashley House, 2 Monck Street
London SW1P 2BQ
020 7276 2876 *Fax:* 020 7276 2860
E-mail:
prisons.ombudsman@homeoffice.gsi.gov.uk
Website:
www.homeoffice.gov.uk/prisons/prisomb.htm

The Prisons Ombudsman considers complaints submitted by individual prisoners who have failed to obtain satisfaction from the Prison Service requests and complaints system.

Prisons Ombudsman: Stephen Shaw

Public Appointments, Office of the Commission for

3rd Floor 35 Great Smith Street,
London SW1P 3BQ
020 7256 2625 *Fax:* 020 7256 2633
E-mail: ocpa@gtnet.gov.uk
Website: www.ocpa.gov.uk

The Commissioner for Public Appointments is independent of government. Her role is to monitor, regulate and provide advice on ministerial appointments to the boards of executive and advisory non-departmental public bodies, NHS bodies, public corporations and nationalised industries. In addition, the three regulatory posts for gas and electricity, water and telecommunications also fall within her remit. She has the right to investigate complaints.

Commissioner: Dame Rennie Fritchie DBE

Scottish Legal Services Ombudsman

Mulberry House, 16 Picardy Place,
Edinburgh EH1 3JT
0131-556 5574 *Fax:* 0131-556 1519
E-mail: complaints@scot-legal-ombud.org.uk
Website: www.scot-legal-ombud.org.uk

Ombudsman: Linda Costelloe-Baker

Scottish Parliamentary Commissioner for Administration

28 Thistle Street, Edinburgh EH2 1EN
0845 601 0456 *Fax:* 0131-226 4447
Website: www.ombudsman.org.uk

The Scottish Parliamentary Commissioner investigates complaints by members of the Scottish Parliament about injustice resulting from maladministration by the Scottish Executive, the Parliamentary corporation and a range of bodies involved in devolved Scottish affairs. He can also look at complaints that individuals have been refused information to which they are entitled under the Code of Practice on Access to Scottish Executive Information.

Parliamentary Commissioner for
    Administration: Michael Buckley
Investigations Manager: George Keil

Waterways Ombudsman

PO Box 406, Haywards Heath,
West Sussex RH17 5GF
Tel/Fax: 01273 832624

The independent Waterways Ombudsman investigates and resolves complaints of maladministration against British Waterways.

Ombudsman: Stephen Edell

Welsh Administration Ombudsman

5th Floor, Capital Tower, Greyfriars Road,
Cardiff CF10 3AG
0845 601 0987 *Fax:* 029 2022 6909
Website: www.ombudsman.org.uk

The Welsh Administration Ombudsman investigates complaints about injustice resulting from maladministration by the National Assembly for Wales or certain public bodies involved in devolved Welsh affairs. He can also look at complaints that individuals have been refused information to which they are entitled under the Code of Practice on Public Access to Information adopted by the National Assembly.

Parliamentary Commissioner for
    Administration: Michael Buckley
Investigations Manager: Stan Drummond

PRIVY COUNSELLORS

Privy Counsellors historically advised the monarch. The title is now largely honorary; it is given automatically to all cabinet members and the Speaker, the archbishops of Canterbury and York and the bishop of London and to holders of certain judicial appointments. Leaders of the main political parties are conventionally nominated. Other members from the UK and Commonwealth are appointed on the prime minister's recommendation.

Privy Counsellors are given precedence over other MPs by the Speaker in the House of Commons. The appointment is for life and holders are addressed as 'Right Honourable'.

HRH The Duke of Edinburgh
HRH The Prince of Wales
Lord Aberdare
Lord Ackner
Earl of Airlie
Lord Aldington
Sir William Aldous
Ezekiel Alebua
Michael Alison
Lord Ampthill
Michael Ancram
Hon Douglas Anthony
James Arbuthnot
Lord Archer of Sandwell
Hilary Armstrong
Sir John Arnold
Hon Owen Arthur
Sir Paddy Ashdown
Lord Ashley of Stoke
Sir Robert Atkins
Sir Robin Auld
Lord Baker of Dorking
Lord Barber
Lord Barnett
Margaret Beckett
Alan Beith
Sir Roy Beldam
Lord Belstead
Tony Benn
Sir Frederic Bennett
Lord Biffen
Lord Bingham of Cornhill
Hon William Birch
*Sir Gordon Bisson
Tony Blair
Lord Blaker
Hon Peter Blanchard
Baroness Blatch
David Blunkett
Paul Boateng
James Bolger
Albert Booth
Betty Boothroyd
Robert Boscawen
Virginia Bottomley

Colin Boyd
Sir Rhodes Boyson
Sir Nicholas Brathwaite
Lord Bridge of Harwich
Lord Brightman
Lord Brittan of Spennithorne
Sir Henry Brooke
Peter Brooke
Gordon Brown
Nicholas Brown
Sir Simon Brown
Sir Stephen Brown
Lord Browne-Wilkinson
Sir Adam Butler
Dame Elizabeth Butler-Sloss
Sir Richard Buxton
Stephen Byers
Richard Caborn
Earl of Caithness
Lord Callaghan of Cardiff
Lord Cameron of Lochbroom
Lord Camoys
Menzies Campbell
Sir William Campbell
Lord Campbell of Croy
Most Rev the Lord Archbishop of Canterbury
Lord Carlisle of Bucklow
Lord Carr of Hadley
Lord Carrington
Sir Robert Carswell
Lord Carter
*Hon Sir Maurice Casey
Baroness Castle of Blackburn
Sir John Chadwick
Lord Chalfont
Baroness Chalker of Wallasey
Hon Sir Julius Chan
Sir Christopher Chataway
David Clark
Helen Clark
Lord Clark of Kempston
Sir Anthony Clarke
Kenneth Clarke
Thomas Clarke
Lord Cledwyn of Penrhos

Lord Clinton-Davis
Lord Clyde
Lord Cockfield
Lord Cocks of Hartcliffe
Fraser Colman
Sir John Compton
John Concannon
Robin Cook
Lord Cooke of Thorndon
Sir Frank Cooper
Lord Cope of Berkeley
Sir Frederick Corfield
Lord Coulsfield
Sir Zelman Cowen
Sir Percy Cradock
Viscount Cranborne
Earl of Crawford & Balcarres
Hon Wyatt Creech
Lord Crickhowell
Sir David Croom-Johnson
Lord Cullen
Jack Cunningham
David Curry
Alistair Darling
Denzil Davies
Ron Davies
David Davis
Terence Davis
*Hon Sir Ronald Davison
Lord Dean of Harptree
Baroness Dean of Thornton-le-Fylde
Lord Deedes
Lord Denham
John Denham
Duke of Devonshire
Lord Diamond
Sir Brian Dillon
Lord Dixon
Frank Dobson
Lord Donaldson of Lymington
Stephen Dorrell
*Sir William Douglas
Sir Edward Du Cann
Sir Robin Dunn
Paul East
Lord Eden of Winton
Timothy Eggar
*Sir Thomas Eichelbaum
The Hon Dame Sian Elias
Sir Peter Emery
Lord Emslie
Manuel Esquivel
Sir Anthony Evans
Sir Edward Eveleigh
Sir Donald Farquharson
Lord Fellowes

Earl Ferrers
Frank Field
*Sir Vincent Floissac
Michael Foot
Lord Forsyth of Drumlean
Eric Forth
Derek Foster
Sir Norman Fowler
Sir Marcus Fox
Sir Michael Fox
Hon Malcolm Fraser
Lord Fraser of Carmyllie
John Freeman
Lord Freeman
Reginald Freeson
Lord Garel-Jones
*Hon Thomas Gault
Edward George
* Telford Georges
*Hon Sir Harry Gibbs
Sir Peter Gibson
Sir Ralph Gibson
Lord Gibson-Watt
Lord Gilbert
Lord Gilmour of Craigmillar
Lord Glenamara
Sir Iain Glidewell
Lord Goff of Chieveley
Sir Alastair Goodlad
Hon Sir John Gorton
Earl of Gowrie
Lord Graham of Edmonton
Hon Sir Douglas Graham
Lord Gray of Contin
Lord Griffiths
John Selwyn Gummer
Lord Habgood
William Hague
Lord Hailsham of St Marylebone
Dame Brenda Hale
Sir Archibald Hamilton
Jeremy Hanley
Lord Hardie
Sir Michael Hardie Boys
Harriet Harman
Lord Harris of Greenwich
Walter Harrison
Sir Alan Haselhurst
Lord Hattersley
Lord Hayhoe
Lord Healey
Sir Edward Heath
David Heathcote-Amory
Sir Denis Henry
Hon John Henry
Michael Heseltine

Sir William Heseltine
Lord Hesketh
Lord Higgins
Sir David Hirst
Lord Hobhouse of Woodborough
Lord Hoffmann
Douglas Hogg
Lord Holderness
Baroness Hollis of Heigham
Lord Holme of Cheltenham
Geoffrey Hoon
Lord Hope of Craighead
Sir Peter Hordern
Michael Howard
Alan Howarth
Lord Howe of Aberavon
Lord Howell of Guildford
Lord Hunt of Wirral
Jonathan Hunt
Lord Hurd of Westwall
Sir Michael Hutchison
Lord Hutton
Hubert Ingraham
Adam Ingram
Lord Irvine of Lairg
John Michael Jack
Sir Robin Janvrin
Lord Jauncey of Tullichettle
Baroness Jay of Paddington
Earl Jellicoe
Lord Jenkin of Roding
Lord Jenkins of Hillhead
Sir Geoffrey Johnson Smith
Aubrey Jones
Stephen Barry Jones
Lord Jopling
Tessa Jowell
Sir Igor Judge
Hon Sir Anerood Jugnauth
Gerald Kaufman
Sir John Kay
Lord Keith of Kinkel
Hon Sir Kenneth Keith
Sir Basil Kelly
Lord Kelvedon
Hon Sir Peter Kenilorea
Charles Kennedy
Sir Paul Kennedy
Sir Michael Kerr
Thomas King
Lord Kingsdown
Lord Kingsland
Lord Kirkwood
Neil Kinnock
Gregory Knight
Lord Lamont of Lerwick

Lord Lane
Lord Lang of Monkton
David Lange
Hon Kamuta Latasi
Sir David Latham
Hon Toaripi Lauti
Sir John Laws
Lord Lawson of Blaby
Sir Frederick Lawton
Sir Andrew Leggatt
Rev Graham Leonard
Helen Liddell
Peter Lilley
Lord Lloyd of Berwick
Sir Peter Lloyd
Rt Rev Lord Bishop of London
Earl of Longford
Hon Allan Louisy
Lord Luce
Sir Nicholas Lyell
Dickson Mabon
Sir John MacDermott
Lord Macdonald of Tradeston
John MacGregor
Hon Duncan MacIntyre
Lord Mackay of Ardbrecknish
Lord Mackay of Clashfern
Andrew Mackay
David Maclean
Robert Maclennan
John Major
Sir Jonathan Mance
Peter Mandelson
Sir Charles Mantell
Hon Ratu Sir Kamisese Mara
Lord Marsh
Michael Martin
Lord Mason of Barnsley
Francis Maude
Sir Brian Mawhinney
Sir Anthony May
Lord Mayhew of Twysden
*Hon Sir Thaddeus McCarthy
Ian McCartney
Sir Liam McCollum
Sir Anthony McCowan
*Hon Ian McKay
Hon Donald McKinnon
*Sir Duncan McMullin
Michael Meacher
Sir Robert Megarry
David Mellor
Lord Merlyn-Rees
Alun Michael
Alan Milburn
Bruce Millan

Lord Millett
Lord Milligan
Hon James Mitchell
Lord Molyneaux of Killead
Lord Monro of Langholm
Lord Moore of Lower Marsh
Lord Moore of Wolvercote
Michael Moore
Rhodri Morgan
Lord Morris of Manchester
Charles Morris
Estelle Morris
John Morris
Sir Robert Morritt
Marjorie Mowlam
Roland Moyle
Sir John Mummery
Paul Murphy
Sir Donald Murray
Lord Murray
Lord Murray of Epping Forest
Lord Murton of Lindisfarne
Lord Mustill
Sir Patrick Nairne
Sir Rabbie Namaliu
Lord Naseby
Sir Richard Needham
Sir Brian Neill
Lord Newton of Braintree
Lord Nicholls of Birkenhead
Sir Michael Nicholson
Lord Nolan
Sir John Nott
Sir Martin Nourse
Gordon Oakes
Sir Patrick O'Connor
Turlough O'Donnell
Francis O'Flynn
Sir Angus Ogilvy
Lord Oliver of Aylmerton
Lord Onslow of Woking
Baroness Oppenheim-Barnes
Lord Orme
Sir Philip Otton
Lord Owen
Hon Bikenibeu Paeniu
Sir Michael Palliser
Sir Geoffrey Palmer
Sir Jonathan Parker
Sir Roger Parker
Lord Parkinson
Chris Patten
Lord Patten
Percival Patterson
Sir Geoffrey Pattie
Earl of Perth

Hon Winston Peters
Lord Peyton of Yeovil
Lord Phillips of Worth Matravers
Sir Malcolm Pill
Michael Portillo
Sir Mark Potter
Lord Prentice
John Prescott
Hon George Price
Lord Prior
Lord Prosser
Sir Tomasi Puapua
Sir Francis Purchas
Lord Pym
Joyce Quin
Giles Radice
Sir Timothy Raison
James Ramsden
Lord Rawlinson of Ewell
John Redwood
Lord Rees
John Reid
Lord Renton
Lord Renton of Mount Harry
Lord Richard
*Hon Sir Ivor Richardson
Lord Richardson of Duntisbourne
Sir Malcolm Rifkind
Sir Bernard Rix
Lord Roberts of Conwy
Lord Robertson of Port Ellen
Sir John Roch
Lord Rodger of Earlsferry
Lord Rodgers of Quarry Bank
Jeffrey Rooker
Sir Christopher Rose
Lord Ross
Dame Angela Rumbold
Sir Patrick Russell
Lord Ryder of Wensum
Sir Timothy Sainsbury
Erskine Sandiford
Lord Saville of Newdigate
Lord Scarman
Sir Konrad Schiemann
Sir Nicholas Scott
Lord Scott of Foscote
Hon Edward Seaga
Sir Stephen Sedley
Lord Selkirk of Douglas
Lord Shawcross
Hon Hugh Shearer
Robert Sheldon
Gillian Shephard
Lord Shepherd
Lord Shore of Stepney

Hon Jennifer Shipley
Clare Short
Hon Kennedy Simmonds
Lord Simon of Glaisdale
Hon Ian Sinclair
Sir Christopher Slade
Lord Slynn of Hadley
Andrew Smith
Chris Smith
Hon Sir Michael Somare
*Hon Sir Edward Somers
Lord St John of Fawsley
Sir John Stanley
Sir Christopher Staughton
Lord Steel of Aikwood
Sir Ninian Stephen
Lord Stewartby
Lord Steyn
Lord Stodart of Leaston
Gavin Strang
Lord Strathclyde
Jack Straw
Sir Murray Stuart-Smith
Lord Sutherland
Hon Sir Brian Talboys
Ann Taylor
Lord Tebbit
Lord Templeman
Baroness Thatcher
Lord Thomas of Gwydir
Hon Edmund Thomas
Sir Swinton Thomas
Lord Thomson of Monifieth
Jeremy Thorpe
Sir Mathew Thorpe
Hon Andrew Tipping
Robert Tizard

Lord Trefgarne
David Trimble
Baroness Trumpington
Sir Simon Tuckey
Viscount Ullswater
Hon Simon Upton
Lord Varley
Lord Waddington
Sir John Waite
Lord Wakeham
Lord Waldegrave of North Hill
Lord Walker of Doncaster
Lord Walker of Worcester
Sir Robert Walker
Sir Mark Waller
Sir Alan Ward
Sir Tasker Watkins
Lord Weatherill
Sir John Wheeler
Ann Widdecombe
Dafydd Wigley
Lord Wilberforce
Alan Williams
Baroness Williams of Crosby
Lord Williams of Mostyn
Lord Windlesham
Hon Paias Wingti
Hon Reginald Withers
*Hon Sir Owen Woodhouse
Lord Woolf
Lord Wylie
Most Rev Lord Archbishop of York
Baroness Young
Lord Young of Graffham
Sir George Young
Viscount Younger of Leckie
*Edward Zacca

* Judges from the Commonwealth, members of the Judicial Committee – see Privy Council Office.

DEVOLVED PARLIAMENT AND ASSEMBLIES

Two important new books from Vacher Dod

THE SCOTTISH PARLIAMENT

and

THE NATIONAL ASSEMBLY FOR WALES
CYNULLIAD CENEDLAETHOL CYMRU

*Members' Biographies and Photographs,
Historical Background, Election Results,
Structure and Functions, Contact Directories*

Vacher Dod Publishing Limited
PO Box 3700, Westminster, London SW1P 4WU
Tel: 020 7828 7256   Fax: 020 7828 7269
E-mail: politics@vacherdod.co.uk
Website: www.politicallinks.co.uk

SCOTTISH PARLIAMENT

George IV Bridge, Edinburgh EH99 1SP
0131-348 5000   *General Enquiries:* 0845 278 1999
Public Information: E-mail: sp.info@scottish.parliament.uk
Presiding Officer: E-mail: presiding.officer@scottish.parliament.uk
Website:
www.scottish.parliament.uk
E-mails:
sp.media@scottish.parliament.uk (Media enquiries)
scottish.ministers@scotland.gov.uk
education.service@scottish.parliament.uk
chamber.office@scottish.parliament.uk (Debating chamber)
committee.office@scottish.parliament.uk
petitions@scottish.parliament.uk
presiding.officer@scottish.parliament.uk
webmaster@scottish.parliament.uk

Election 6 May 1999
1 July 1999 Official Opening by HM The Queen
Winter recess: 21 December – 7 January 2001

Future elections are to be held every four years.

ELECTORAL SYSTEM

The election was conducted using a method combining the traditional first past the post system and a form of proportional representation called the Additional Member System. Each voter cast two votes. One vote was for one of 73 constituency members, based on the Westminster parliament constituencies. The second went towards the election of 56 regional members, seven for each of the eight regions used in the European Parliament elections. These seats ensure that each party's representation in the Parliament reflects its overall share of the vote.

POWERS AND RESPONSIBILITIES

The Parliament has administrative and legislative powers relating to Scotland in the following areas:

agriculture	law and order
economic development	local government
education	social work
environment	transport
health	

It can vary the basic rate of income tax in Scotland by 3p in the £.

Westminster retains responsibility for:

defence	national finance and economics
employment	social security
international relations	

The interests of Scotland in the United Kingdom Government are represented by the Secretary of State for Scotland and the Westminster Parliament allocates a budget to the Scottish Parliament.

OPERATION/PROCEDURES

The First Minister is elected by Members and appoints Ministers from among Members to be responsible for specific areas of policy. The First Minister, Ministers and the Law Officers, the Lord Advocate and the Solicitor General for Scotland (who do not have to be Members), make up the Scottish Executive. The Cabinet consists of all these except the Solicitor General.

The Parliament appoints a Presiding Officer and deputy from among its members, to oversee debates, advise on procedure in a similar role to the Speaker of the House of Commons.

Committees made up of members of the Parliament consider in detail various policy areas.

Parliament will sit for 30 to 33 weeks a year, fitting in with school holidays, and will work normal business hours.

STATE OF THE PARTIES (October 2000)

	Constituency MSPs	Regional MSPs	Total MSPs
Scottish Labour Party*	51	3	54
(includes Scottish Labour/Co-operative Party)			
Scottish National Party	7	28	35
Scottish Conservative and Unionist Party	1	18	19
Scottish Liberal Democrats	12	5	17
Scottish Green Party	0	1	1
Scottish Socialist Party	0	1	1
MSP for Falkirk West	1	0	1
	73	56	129*

* By-election pending in Glasgow Anniesland due to death of Donald Dewar on 11 October

Members (MSPs)

Lab	Labour Party
SNP	Scottish National Party
Con	Conservative
Lib Dem	Liberal Democrats
Green	Green Party
SSP	Scottish Socialist Party
MSPFW	MSP for Falkirk West

	Party	Constituency/Region*	Majority
ADAM Brian	SNP	North East Scotland*	
AITKEN Bill	Con	Glasgow*	
ALEXANDER Wendy	Lab	Paisley North	4,616
Minister for Communities			
BAILLIE Jackie	Lab	Dumbarton	4,758
Deputy Minister for Communities (Social Inclusion, Equality and the Voluntary Section)			
BARRIE Scott	Lab	Dunfermline West	5,021
BOYACK Sarah	Lab	Edinburgh Central	4,626
Minister for Transport and the Environment			
BRANKIN Rhona	Lab/Co-op	Midlothian	5,525
Deputy Minister for Children and Education (Culture and Sport)			
BROWN Robert	Lib Dem	Glasgow*	
CAMPBELL Colin	SNP	West of Scotland*	
CANAVAN Dennis	MSPFW	Falkirk West	12,192
†CHISHOLM Malcolm	Lab	Edinburgh North and Leith	7,736
CRAIGIE Cathie	Lab	Cumbernauld and Kilsyth	4,259
CRAWFORD Bruce	SNP	Mid Scotland and Fife*	
†CUNNINGHAM Roseanna	SNP	Perth	2,027
CURRAN Margaret	Lab	Glasgow Baillieston	3,072

DAVIDSON David	Con	North East Scotland*	
DEACON Susan	Lab	Edinburgh East and Musselburgh	6,714
Minister for Health and Community Care			
‡DOUGLAS-HAMILTON			
Rt Hon Lord James	Con	Lothian*	
EADIE Helen	Lab/Co-op	Dunfermline East	8,699
ELDER Dorothy-Grace	SNP	Glasgow*	
EWING Fergus	SNP	Inverness East, Nairn and Lochaber	441
†EWING Margaret	SNP	Moray	4,129
EWING Winifred	SNP	Highlands and Islands*	
FABIANI Linda	SNP	Central Scotland*	
FERGUSON Patricia	Lab	Glasgow Maryhill	4,326
FERGUSSON Alex	Con	South of Scotland*	
FINNIE Ross	Lib Dem	West of Scotland*	
Minister for Rural Affairs			
†GALBRAITH Sam	Lab	Strathkelvin and Bearsden	12,121
Minister for Children and Education			
GALLIE Phil	Con	South of Scotland*	
GIBSON Kenneth	SNP	Glasgow*	
GILLON Karen	Lab	Clydesdale	3,880
GODMAN Trish	Lab	West Renfrewshire	2,893
GOLDIE Annabel	Con	West of Scotland*	
†GORRIE Donald OBE	Lib Dem	Central Scotland*	
GRAHAME Christine	SNP	South of Scotland*	
GRANT Rhoda	Lab	Highlands and Islands*	
GRAY Iain	Lab	Edinburgh Pentlands	2,885
Deputy Minister for Health and Community Care (Community Care)			
HAMILTON Duncan	SNP	Highlands and Islands*	
HARDING Keith	Con	Mid Scotland and Fife*	
HARPER Robin	Green	Lothian*	
HENRY Hugh	Lab	Paisley South	4,495
†HOME ROBERTSON John	Lab	East Lothian	10,946
Deputy Minister for Rural Affairs (Fisheries)			
HUGHES Janis	Lab	Glasgow Rutherglen	7,287
HYSLOP Fiona	SNP	Lothian*	
INGRAM Adam	SNP	South of Scotland*	
JACKSON Gordon	Lab	Glasgow Govan	1,756
JACKSON Sylvia	Lab	Stirling	3,981
JAMIESON Cathy	Lab/Co-op	Carrick, Cumnock and Doon Valley	8,803
JAMIESON Margaret	Lab	Kilmarnock and Loudoun	2,760
JENKINS Ian	Lib Dem	Tweeddale, Ettrick and Lauderdale	4,478
JOHNSTON Nick	Con	Mid Scotland and Fife*	
JOHNSTONE Alex	Con	North East Scotland*	
KERR Andy	Lab	East Kilbride	6,499
LAMONT Johann	Lab/Co-op	Glasgow Pollok	4,642
LIVINGSTONE Marilyn	Lab/Co-op	Kirkcaldy	4,475
LOCHHEAD Richard	SNP	North East Scotland*	
LYON George	Lib Dem	Argyll and Bute	2,057
†McALLION John	Lab	Dundee East	2,854
MacASKILL Kenny	SNP	Lothian*	
McAVEETY Frank	Lab/Co-op	Glasgow Shettleston	5,467
Deputy Minister for Communities (Local Government)			
McCABE Tom	Lab	Hamilton South	7,176
Minister for Parliament (Chief Whip)			
McCONNELL Jack	Lab	Motherwell and Wishaw	5,046
Minister for Finance			

MACDONALD Lewis	Lab	Aberdeen Central	2,696
MacDONALD Margo	SNP	Lothian*	
McGRIGOR Jamie	Con	Highlands and Islands*	
McGUGAN Irene	SNP	North East Scotland*	
MACINTOSH Kenneth	Lab	Eastwood	2,125
McINTOSH Lyndsay	Con	Central Scotland*	
MacKAY Angus	Lab	Edinburgh South	5,424
Deputy Minister for Justice			
MacLEAN Kate	Lab	Dundee West	121
†McLEISH Henry	Lab	Central Fife	8,675
Interim First Minister			
McLEOD Fiona	SNP	West of Scotland*	
McLETCHIE David	Con	Lothian*	
McMAHON Michael	Lab	Hamilton North and Bellshill	5,606
MACMILLAN Maureen	Lab	Highlands and Islands*	
McNEIL Duncan	Lab	Greenock and Inverclyde	4,313
McNEILL Pauline	Lab	Glasgow Kelvin	4,408
McNULTY Des	Lab	Clydebank and Milngavie	4,710
MARTIN Paul	Lab	Glasgow Springburn	7,893
MARWICK Tricia	SNP	Mid Scotland and Fife*	
MATHESON Michael	SNP	Central Scotland*	
MONTEITH Brian	Con	Mid Scotland and Fife*	
†MORGAN Alasdair	SNP	Galloway and Upper Nithsdale	3,201
MORRISON Alasdair	Lab	Western Isles (Eilean Siar)	2,093
Deputy Minister for Enterprise and Lifelong Learning (Highlands and Islands and Gaelic)			
MULDOON Bristow	Lab	Livingston	3,904
MULLIGAN Mary	Lab	Linlithgow	2,928
MUNDELL David	Con	South of Scotland*	
MUNRO John Farquhar	Lib Dem	Ross, Skye and Inverness West	1,539
MURRAY Elaine	Lab	Dumfries	3,654
NEIL Alex	SNP	Central Scotland*	
OLDFATHER Irene	Lab	Cunninghame South	6,541
PATERSON Gil	SNP	Central Scotland*	
PEACOCK Peter	Lab	Highlands and Islands*	
Deputy Minister for Children and Education			
PEATTIE Cathy	Lab	Falkirk East	4,139
QUINAN Lloyd	SNP	West of Scotland*	
RADCLIFFE Nora	Lib Dem	Gordon	4,195
RAFFAN Keith	Lib Dem	Mid Scotland and Fife*	
REID George	SNP	Mid Scotland and Fife*	
Deputy Presiding Officer			
ROBISON Shona	SNP	North East Scotland*	
ROBSON Euan	Lib Dem	Roxburgh and Berwickshire	3,585
RUMBLES Mike	Lib Dem	West Aberdeenshire and Kincardine	2,289
RUSSELL Michael	SNP	South of Scotland*	
†SALMOND Alex	SNP	Banff and Buchan	11,292
SCANLON Mary	Con	Highlands and Islands*	
SCOTT John	Con	Ayr	3,344
SCOTT Tavish	Lib Dem	Shetland	3,194
SHERIDAN Tommy	SSP	Glasgow*	
SIMPSON Richard	Lab	Ochil	1,303
SMITH Elaine	Lab	Coatbridge and Chryston	10,404
SMITH Iain	Lib Dem	North East Fife	5,064
Deputy Minister for Parliament (Deputy Chief Whip)			
SMITH Margaret	Lib Dem	Edinburgh West	4,583
‡STEEL Rt Hon Sir David KBE	Lib Dem	Lothian*	
Presiding Officer			
STEPHEN Nicol	Lib Dem	Aberdeen South	1,760
Deputy Minister for Enterprises and Lifelong Learning			

STONE Jamie	Lib Dem	Caithness, Sutherland and Easter Ross	4,391
STURGEON Nicola	SNP	Glasgow*	
†SWINNEY John	SNP	North Tayside	4,192
THOMSON Elaine	Lab	Aberdeen North	398
TOSH Murray	Con	South of Scotland*	
ULLRICH Kay	SNP	West of Scotland*	
WALLACE Ben	Con	North East Scotland*	
†WALLACE Jim QC	Lib Dem	Orkney	4,619
Deputy First Minister and Minister for Justice			
‡WATSON Mike	Lab	Glasgow Cathcart	5,374
†WELSH Andrew	SNP	Angus	8,901
WHITE Sandra	SNP	Glasgow*	
WHITEFIELD Karen	Lab	Airdrie and Shotts	8,985
WILSON Allan	Lab	Cunninghame North	4,796
WILSON Andrew	SNP	Central Scotland*	
YOUNG John	Con	West of Scotland*	

† *Also a Member of the House of Commons*
‡ *Also a Member of the House of Lords*

MSPs representing the regions

Central Scotland
FABIANI Linda	SNP
GORRIE Donald	Lib Dem
McINTOSH Lyndsay	Con
MATHESON Michael	SNP
NEIL Alex	SNP
PATERSON Gil	SNP
WILSON Andrew	SNP

Glasgow
AITKEN Bill	Con
BROWN Robert	Lib Dem
ELDER Dorothy-Grace	SNP
GIBSON Kenneth	SNP
SHERIDAN Tommy	SSP
STURGEON Nicola	SNP
WHITE Sandra	SNP

Highlands and Islands
EWING Winifred	SNP
GRANT Rhoda	Lab
HAMILTON Duncan	SNP
McGRIGOR Jamie	Con
MACMILLAN Maureen	Lab
PEACOCK Peter	Lab
SCANLON Mary	Con

Lothians
DOUGLAS-HAMILTON Rt Hon Lord James	Con
HARPER Robin	Green
HYSLOP Fiona	SNP
MacASKILL Kenny	SNP
MacDONALD Margo	SNP
McLETCHIE David	Con
STEEL Rt Hon Sir David	Lib Dem

Mid Scotland and Fife
CRAWFORD Bruce	SNP
HARDING Keith	Con
JOHNSTON Nick	Con
MARWICK Tricia	SNP
MONTEITH Brian	Con
RAFFAN Keith	Lib Dem
REID George	SNP

North East Scotland
ADAM Brian	SNP
DAVIDSON David	Con
JOHNSTONE Alex	Con
LOCHHEAD Richard	SNP
McGUGAN Irene	SNP
ROBISON Shona	SNP
WALLACE Ben	Con

South of Scotland
FERGUSSON Alex	Con
GALLIE Phil	Con
GRAHAME Christine	SNP
INGRAM Adam	SNP
MUNDELL David	Con
RUSSELL Michael	SNP
TOSH Murray	Con

West of Scotland
CAMPBELL Colin	SNP
FINNIE Ross	Lib Dem
GOLDIE Annabel	Con
McLEOD Fiona	SNP
QUINAN Lloyd	SNP
ULLRICH Kay	SNP
YOUNG John	Con

Members by Party

Constituency/Region

SCOTTISH LABOUR PARTY (48)

ALEXANDER Wendy	Paisley North
BAILLIE Jackie	Dumbarton
BARRIE Scott	Dunfermline West
BOYACK Sarah	Edinburgh Central
CHISHOLM Malcolm	Edinburgh North and Leith
CRAIGIE Cathie	Cumbernauld and Kilsyth
CURRAN Margaret	Glasgow Baillieston
DEACON Susan	Edinburgh East and Musselburgh
FERGUSON Patricia	Glasgow Maryhill
GALBRAITH Sam	Strathkelvin and Bearsden
GILLON Karen	Clydesdale
GODMAN Trish	West Renfrewshire
GRANT Rhoda	Highlands and Islands*
GRAY Iain	Edinburgh Pentlands
HENRY Hugh	Paisley South
HOME ROBERTSON John	East Lothian
HUGHES Janis	Glasgow Rutherglen
JACKSON Gordon	Glasgow Govan
JACKSON Sylvia	Stirling
JAMIESON Margaret	Kilmarnock and Loudoun
KERR Andy	East Kilbride
McALLION John	Dundee East
McCABE Tom	Hamilton South
McCONNELL Jack	Motherwell and Wishaw
MACDONALD Lewis	Aberdeen Central
MACINTOSH Kenneth	Eastwood
MacKAY Angus	Edinburgh South
MacLEAN Kate	Dundee West
McLEISH Henry	Central Fife
McMAHON Michael	Hamilton North and Bellshill
MACMILLAN Maureen	Highlands and Islands*
McNEIL Duncan	Greenock and Inverclyde
McNEILL Pauline	Glasgow Kelvin
McNULTY Des	Clydebank and Milngavie
MARTIN Paul	Glasgow Springburn
MORRISON Alasdair	Western Isles (Eilean Siar)
MULDOON Bristow	Livingston
MULLIGAN Mary	Linlithgow
MURRAY Elaine	Dumfries
OLDFATHER Irene	Cunninghame South
PEACOCK Peter	Highlands and Islands*
PEATTIE Cathy	Falkirk East
SIMPSON Richard	Ochil
SMITH Elaine	Coatbridge and Chryston
THOMSON Elaine	Aberdeen North
WATSON Mike	Glasgow Cathcart
WHITEFIELD Karen	Airdrie and Shotts
WILSON Allan	Cunninghame North

SCOTTISH NATIONAL PARTY (35)

ADAM Brian (Joint Deputy Whip)	North East Scotland*
CAMPBELL Colin	West of Scotland*
CRAWFORD Bruce (Chief Whip)	Mid Scotland and Fife*
CUNNINGHAM Roseanna	Perth
ELDER Dorothy-Grace	Glasgow*
EWING Fergus	Inverness East, Nairn and Lochaber
EWING Margaret	Moray
EWING Winifred	Highlands and Islands*
FABIANI Linda	Central Scotland*
GIBSON Kenneth	Glasgow*
GRAHAME Christine	South of Scotland*
HAMILTON Duncan	Highlands and Islands*
HYSLOP Fiona	Lothian*
INGRAM Adam	South of Scotland*
LOCHHEAD Richard	North East Scotland*
MacASKILL Kenny	Lothian*
MacDONALD Margo	Lothian*
McGUGAN Irene	North East Scotland*
McLEOD Fiona	West of Scotland*
MARWICK Tricia	Mid Scotland and Fife*
MATHESON Michael	Central Scotland*
MORGAN Alasdair	Galloway and Upper Nithsdale
NEIL Alex	Central Scotland*
PATERSON Gil	Central Scotland*
QUINAN Lloyd	West of Scotland*
REID George	Mid Scotland and Fife*
ROBISON Shona	North East Scotland*
RUSSELL Michael	South of Scotland*
SALMOND Alex	Banff and Buchan
STURGEON Nicola	Glasgow*
SWINNEY John	North Tayside
ULLRICH Kay	West of Scotland*
WELSH Andrew	Angus
WHITE Sandra (Joint Deputy Whip)	Glasgow*
WILSON Andrew	Central Scotland*

SCOTTISH CONSERVATIVE AND UNIONIST PARTY (19)

AITKEN Bill (Deputy Whip)	Glasgow*
DAVIDSON David	North East Scotland*
DOUGLAS-HAMILTON Rt Hon Lord James (Chief Whip)	Lothian*
FERGUSSON Alex	South of Scotland*
GALLIE Phil	South of Scotland*
GOLDIE Annabel (Deputy Leader)	West of Scotland*
HARDING Keith	Mid Scotland and Fife*
JOHNSTON Nick	Mid Scotland and Fife*
JOHNSTONE Alex	North East Scotland*
McGRIGOR Jamie	Highlands and Islands*
McINTOSH Lyndsay	Central Scotland*
McLETCHIE David (Leader)	Lothian*
MONTEITH Brian	Mid Scotland and Fife*
MUNDELL David	South of Scotland*
SCANLON Mary	Highlands and Islands*
SCOTT John	Ayr
TOSH Murray	South of Scotland*
WALLACE Ben	North East Scotland*
YOUNG John	West of Scotland*

SCOTTISH LIBERAL DEMOCRAT PARTY (17)

BROWN Robert	Glasgow*
FINNIE Ross	West of Scotland*
GORRIE Donald	Central Scotland*
JENKINS Ian	Tweeddale, Ettrick and Lauderdale
LYON George	Argyll and Bute
MUNRO John Farquhar	Ross, Skye and Inverness West
RADCLIFFE Nora	Gordon
RAFFAN Keith	Mid Scotland and Fife*
ROBSON Euan	Roxburgh and Berwickshire
RUMBLES Mike	West Aberdeenshire and Kincardine
SCOTT Tavish	Shetland
SMITH Iain (Business Manager)	North East Fife
SMITH Margaret	Edinburgh West
STEEL Rt Hon Sir David	Lothian*
STEPHEN Nicol	Aberdeen South
STONE Jamie	Caithness, Sutherland and Easter Ross
WALLACE Jim (Leader)	Orkney

SCOTTISH LABOUR/CO-OPERATIVE PARTY (6)

BRANKIN Rhona	Midlothian
EADIE Helen	Dunfermline East
JAMIESON Cathy	Carrick, Cumnock and Doon Valley
LAMONT Johann	Glasgow Pollok
LIVINGSTONE Marilyn	Kirkcaldy
McAVEETY Frank	Glasgow Shettleston

MSP FOR FALKIRK WEST (1)

CANAVAN Dennis	Falkirk West

SCOTTISH GREEN PARTY (1)

HARPER Robin	Lothian*

SCOTTISH SOCIALIST PARTY (1)

SHERIDAN Tommy	Glasgow*

* Region

Women Members

ALEXANDER Wendy	GRAHAME Christine	MULLIGAN Mary
BAILLIE Jackie	GRANT Rhoda	MURRAY Elaine
BOYACK Sarah	HUGHES Janis	OLDFATHER Irene
BRANKIN Rhona	HYSLOP Fiona	PEATTIE Cathy
CRAIGIE Cathie	JACKSON Sylvia	RADCLIFFE Nora
CUNNINGHAM Roseanna	JAMIESON Cathy	ROBISON Shona
CURRAN Margaret	JAMIESON Margaret	SCANLON Mary
DEACON Susan	LAMONT Johann	SMITH Elaine
EADIE Helen	LIVINGSTONE Marilyn	SMITH Margaret
ELDER Dorothy-Grace	MacDONALD Margo	STURGEON Nicola
EWING Margaret	McGUGAN Irene	THOMSON Elaine
EWING Winifred	McINTOSH Lyndsay	ULLRICH Kay
FABIANI Linda	MacLEAN Kate	WHITE Sandra
FERGUSON Patricia	McLEOD Fiona	WHITEFIELD Karen
GILLON Karen	MACMILLAN Maureen	
GODMAN Trish	McNEILL Pauline	
GOLDIE Annabel	MARWICK Tricia	

Regions* and Constituencies

Central Scotland*
Airdrie and Shotts
Coatbridge and Chryston
Cumbernauld and Kilsyth
East Kilbride
Falkirk East
Falkirk West
Hamilton North and Bellshill
Hamilton South
Kilmarnock and Loudoun
Motherwell and Wishaw

Glasgow*
Glasgow Anniesland
Glasgow Baillieston
Glasgow Cathcart
Glasgow Govan
Glasgow Kelvin
Glasgow Maryhill
Glasgow Pollok
Glasgow Rutherglen
Glasgow Shettleston
Glasgow Springburn

Highlands and Islands*
Argyll and Bute
Caithness, Sutherland and Easter Ross
Inverness East, Nairn and Lochaber
Moray
Orkney
Ross, Skye and Inverness West
Shetland
Western Isles (Eilean Siar)

Lothians*
Edinburgh Central
Edinburgh East and Musselburgh
Edinburgh North and Leith
Edinburgh Pentlands
Edinburgh South
Edinburgh West
Linlithgow
Livingston
Midlothian

Mid Scotland and Fife*
Central Fife
Dunfermline East
Dunfermline West
Kirkcaldy
North East Fife
North Tayside
Ochil
Perth
Stirling

North East Scotland*
Aberdeen Central
Aberdeen North
Aberdeen South
Angus
Banff and Buchan
Dundee East
Dundee West
Gordon
West Aberdeenshire and Kincardine

South of Scotland*
Ayr
Carrick, Cumnock and Doon Valley
Clydesdale
Cunninghame South
Dumfries
East Lothian
Galloway and Upper Nithsdale
Roxburgh and Berwickshire
Tweeddale, Ettrick and Lauderdale

West of Scotland*
Clydebank and Milngavie
Cunninghame North
Dumbarton
Eastwood
Greenock and Inverclyde
Paisley North
Paisley South
Strathkelvin and Bearsden
West Renfrewshire

Scottish Government
At the time of going to press a reshuffle was imminent.

THE CABINET (Labour/Liberal Democrat Partnership)

Interim First Minister	**Henry McLeish** MP MSP
Deputy First Minister and Minister for Justice	**Jim Wallace** QC MSP
Deputy Minister for Justice	**Angus MacKay** MSP
Minister for Finance	**Jack McConnell** MSP
Minister for Health and Community Care	**Susan Deacon** MSP
Deputy (Community Care)	**Iain Gray** MSP
Minister for Communities	**Wendy Alexander** MSP
Deputy (Local Government)	**Frank McAveety** MSP
Deputy (Social Inclusion, Equality and the Voluntary Sector)	**Jackie Baillie** MSP
Minister for Transport and the Environment	**Sarah Boyack** MSP
Minister for Enterprise and Lifelong Learning	**Henry McLeish** MSP
Deputy Minister for Enterprise and Lifelong Learning	**Nicol Stephen** MSP
Deputy (Highlands and Islands and Gaelic)	**Alasdair Morrison** MSP
Minister for Rural Affairs	**Ross Finnie** MSP
Deputy Minister for Rural Affairs (Fisheries)	**John Home Robertson** MSP
Minister for Children and Education	**Sam Galbraith** MSP
Deputy (Culture and Sport)	**Rhona Brankin** MSP
Deputy (Children and Education)	**Peter Peacock** MSP
Minister for Parliament (Chief Whip)	**Tom McCabe** MSP
Deputy Minister for Parliament (Deputy Chief Whip)	**Iain Smith** MSP
Law Officers	
Lord Advocate	Rt Hon **Colin Boyd** QC
Deputy (Solicitor General for Scotland)	**Neil Davidson** QC
	(not a member of the Cabinet)

PRINCIPAL OFFICERS AND OFFICIALS

OFFICE OF THE PRESIDING OFFICER

Presiding Officer	Rt Hon Sir **David Steel** KBE MSP
Deputy Presiding Officer	**George Reid** MSP

SCOTTISH PARLIAMENTARY CORPORATE BODY
(responsible for administration)

Robert Brown MSP	**Andrew Welsh** MSP
Des McNulty MSP	**John Young** MSP

Secretary to the SPCB: Huw Williams

PARLIAMENTARY BUREAU
(responsible for all-party business programme and forward planning)

Rt Hon Sir **David Steel** MSP (Presiding Officer)	**Tom McCabe** MSP (Lab)
Rt Hon Lord **James Douglas-Hamilton** MSP (Con)	**Michael Russell** MSP (SNP)
	Iain Smith MSP (Lib Dem)

PRINCIPAL OFFICERS

Clerk/Chief Executive	**Paul Grice**
Legal Adviser	**Ann Nelson**
Director of Clerking and Reporting	**Carol McCracken**
Director of Corporate Services	**Stewart Gilfillan**
Director of Communications	**Lesley Beddie**
Holyrood Project Director	**Alan Ezzi**
Audit Adviser	**Dave Ferguson**
Head of Chamber Office	**Bill Thomson**
Head of Committee Office	**Elizabeth Watson**
Editor of the Official Report	**Henrietta Hales**
Head of Information Systems	**Bethan Hubbard**
Head of Research and Information Service	**Janet Seaton**
Head of Information Technology	**Cathy Watkins**
Head of Security	**Bill Anderson**
Head of Broadcasting	**Alan Smart**
Head of Finance	**Robin Andrews**
Head of Purchasing	**Lynn Garvie**
Head of Personnel	**Ian Macnicol**
Head of Facilities Management	**Charlie Fisher**

Ministerial Responsibilities

The death of First Minister Donald Dewar on 11 October led to the appointment of Henry McLeish, Minister for Enterprise and Lifelong Learning, as interim First Minister. A reshuffle of the following portfolios was imminent at the time of passing for press. For up-to-date information see Addenda, www.politicallinks@vacherdod.co.uk or *Vacher's Parliamentary Companion* December 2000 edition.

Ministers' E-mail: scottish.ministers@scotland.gov.uk

THE FIRST MINISTER

Interim First Minister (**Henry McLeish** MP MSP)
Based at St Andrews House (SAH), Regent Road, Edinburgh EH1 3DG *Tel:* 0131-556 8400

JUSTICE

Deputy First Minister and Minister for Justice (**Jim Wallace** QC MSP)
   With the First Minister, responsible for the development, implementation and presentation of Scottish Executive policies. Responsible for Home Affairs, including civil law and criminal justice, criminal justice social work services, police, fire and emergency planning, prisons and courts, law reform, land reform policy and freedom of information.
   Private Secretary: Michael Kellet *Tel:* 0131-244 4576 (SH) 0131-244 5227 (SAH)
   Fax: 0131-244 2756 *Special Advisers:* Polly McPherson *Tel:* 0131-244 2066
   Sam Ghibaldan *Tel:* 0131-244 2066
Based at St Andrews House (SAH), Regent Road, Edinburgh EH1 3DG *Tel:* 0131-556 8400

Deputy Minister for Justice (**Angus MacKay** MSP)
   Deputy to the Minister for Justice, with particular responsibility for land reform and co-ordination of Executive policy in relation to drugs.
   Private Secretary: Fiona Armstrong *Tel:* 0131-244 4579 *Fax:* 0131-244 2121
   Diary Secretary Samantha Kibble *Tel:* 0131-244 4578
Based at Saughton House (SH), Broomhouse Drive, Edinburgh EH11 3XD *Tel:* 0131-556 8400

CHILDREN AND EDUCATION

Minister for Children and Education (**Sam Galbraith** MSP)
Responsible for pre-school and school education, children and young people, culture and the arts, the built heritage, architecture, sport and lottery funding.
Private Secretary: Gabby Pieraccini *Tel:* 0131-244 7716 *Fax:* 0131-244 7715
Diary Secretary: Gerry Fitzpatrick *Tel:* 0131-244 7850 *Constituency Secretary:* Anne Devine
Tel: 0141-942 9662 *Fax:* 0141-942 9658

Deputy Minister for Children and Education (**Peter Peacock** MSP)
Deputy to the Minister for Children and Education with responsibility for pre-school and school education, children and young people.
Private Secretary: Steven Szymoszowskyj *Tel:* 0131-244 1469 *Fax:* 0131-244 7401
Parliamentary Assistant: Richard Welsh *Tel:* 0131-348 5766 *Fax:* 0131-348 5767
Private and Constituency Secretary: Andrene Maxwell *Tel:* 01349 867650 *Fax:* 01349 867762

Deputy Minister for Culture and Sport (**Rhona Brankin** MSP)
Deputy to the Minister for Children and Education with responsibility for culture and the arts, the built heritage, architecture, sport and lottery funding.
Private Secretary: Fiona McLauchlan *Tel:* 0131-244 7717 *Fax:* 0131-244 7402
Diary Secretary: Angela Rowan *Tel:* 0131-244 7866
Based at Victoria Quay (VQ), Edinburgh EH6 6QQ *Tel:* 0131-556 8400

ENTERPRISE AND LIFELONG LEARNING

Minister for Enterprise and Lifelong Learning (**Henry McLeish** MSP)
Responsible for the economy, business and industry including Scottish Enterprise, Highlands and Islands Enterprise, tourism, trade and inward investment, further and higher education, the science base, lifelong learning, training and the delivery of the New Deal.
Private Secretary: Joan Serafini *Tel:* 0141-242 5475 (MC) *Fax:* 0141-242 5462

Deputy Minister for Enterprise and Lifelong Learning (**Nicol Stephen** MSP)
Deputy to the Minister for Enterprise and Lifelong Learning, with particular responsibility for training further and higher education and the delivery of the New Deal.
Private Secretary: Liz Shea *Tel:* 0141-242 5587 *Fax:* 0141-242 5462/5709

Deputy Minister for Enterprise in the Highlands and Islands and Gaelic (**Alasdair Morrison** MSP)
Deputy to the Minister for Enterprise and Lifelong Learning with responsibility
for Highlands and Islands Enterprise, the University of the Highlands and Islands and tourism, and Gaelic.
Private Secretary: Juliet Grimes *Tel:* 0141-242 5777 *Fax:* 0141-242 5462/5709
Diary Secretary: Wendy Fleming *Tel:* 0141-242 5778
Based at Meridian Court (MC), 5 Cadogan Street, Glasgow G2 6AT
Tel: 0141-248 2855 and 0131-556 8400

FINANCE

Minister for Finance (**Jack McConnell** MSP)
Responsible for the Scottish Budget, including Local Government Finance, and European Structural funds, resource allocation and accounting and for Modernising Government. Assists the First Minister and Deputy First Minister on the development and co-ordination of Executive policy.
Private Secretary: Deborah Smith *Tel:* 0131-244 1558 *Fax:* 0131-244 1555
Based at Victoria Quay (VQ), Edinburgh EH6 6QQ

HEALTH AND COMMUNITY CARE

Minister for Health and Community Care (**Susan Deacon** MSP)
Responsible for health policy, the National Health Service in Scotland, community care, and food safety.
Private Secretary: Karen Jackson *Tel:* 0131-244 4017 *Diary Secretary:* Joanne Ramsay
Tel: 0131-244 2135 *Fax:* 0131-244 3563 *Office Administrator:* Nikki Tongs *Tel:* 0131-244 5135

Deputy Minister for Community Care (**Iain Gray** MSP)
Deputy to the Minister for Health and Community Care with particular responsibility for community care.
Private Secretary: David Thomson *Tel:* 0131-244 2186 *Diary Secretary:* Catherine McGoldrick *Tel:* 0131-244 5131 *Fax:* 0131-244 3563
Based at St Andrew's House (SAH), Regent Road, Edinburgh EH1 3DG *Tel:* 0131-556 8400

LAW OFFICERS*

The Lord Advocate (**Rt Hon Colin Boyd** QC)
Responsible for legal advice to the Scottish Executive; prosecution in the Scottish criminal courts and tribunals.
Private Secretary: Jeff Gibbons *Tel:* 0131-247 2875 E-mail: jeff.gibbons@scotland.gov.uk
Assistant Private Secretary/Diary Secretary: Carol McDivitt *Tel:* 0131-225 5806
Fax: 0131-226 6910

Solicitor-General for Scotland (**Neil Davidson QC**)
Assists the Lord Advocate, with particular responsibility for prosecutions.
Private Secretary: Jeff Gibbons *Tel:* 0131-247 2875
Based at The Crown Office (CO), 25 Chambers Street, Edinburgh EH1 1LA *Tel:* 0131-226 2626
Fax: 0131-226 6910 *E-mail:* co.isunit@dial.pipex.com

PARLIAMENT

Minister for Parliament (**Tom McCabe** MSP)
Responsible for Parliamentary Affairs and the management of Executive business in the Parliament. Labour Business Manager.
Private Secretary: Ian Campbell *Tel:* 0131-348 5573 *Fax:* 0131-348 5564
Assistant Private Secretary: Audrey Snedden *Tel:* 0131-348 5573 *Fax:* 0131-348 5564

Deputy Minister for Parliament (**Iain Smith** MSP)
Deputy to the Minister for Parliament, with particular responsibility for the Parliamentary handling of the legislative programme. Liberal Democrat Business Manager.
Private Secretary: Callum Stanners *Tel:* 0131-348 5816 *Fax:* 0131-348 5564
Temporarily based at Parliament Headquarters (PHQ), George IV Bridge, Edinburgh EH99 1SP
Tel: 0131-556 8400

RURAL AFFAIRS

Minister for Rural Affairs (**Ross Finnie** MSP)
Responsible for policy in relation to rural development including agriculture, fisheries and forestry.
Private Secretary: Shirley Laing *Tel:* 0131-244 4456 *Fax:* 0131-244 4458

Deputy Minister for Rural Affairs (Fisheries) (**John Home Robertson** MSP)
Deputy to the Minister for Rural Affairs with particular responsibility for fisheries, forestry and research. Assists the Minister for Rural Affairs on policy in relation to rural development.
Private Secretary: Stuart McLean *Tel:* 0131-244 4425 *Fax:* 0131-244 4458
Based at Pentland House (PH), 47 Robbs Loan, Edinburgh EH14 1TY *Tel:* 0131-556 8400

COMMUNITIES

Minister for Communities (**Wendy Alexander** MSP)
Responsible for Social Inclusion, local government and housing. Lead responsibility for Executive policy on equality issues and the voluntary sector.
Private Secretary: Nicola Williams *Tel:* 0131-244 7818 *Fax:* 0131-244 7403

Deputy Minister for Local Government (**Frank McAveety** MSP)
Deputy to the Minister for Communities with particular responsibility for local government.
Private Secretary: Al Gibson *Tel:* 0131-244 0228 *Fax:* 0131-244 7403

Deputy Minister for Communities (**Jackie Baillie** MSP)
Deputy to the Minister for Communities with particular responsibility for social inclusion; for co-ordination of Executive policy on equality and the voluntary sector.
Private Secretary: Scott Rogerson *Tel:* 0131-244 5539 *Fax:* 0131-244 7404 *Diary Secretary:* Tracy Rae *Tel:* 0131-244 5538
Based at Victoria Quay (VQ), Edinburgh EH6 6QQ *Tel:* 0131-556 8400

TRANSPORT AND THE ENVIRONMENT
Minister for Transport and the Environment (**Sarah Boyack** MSP)
Responsible for transport and environment including the development of integrated transport policy, natural heritage, sustainable development, the land-use planning system and building control.
Private Secretary: Neil MacLennan *Tel:* 0131-244 0627 *Fax:* 0131-244 7405
Based at Victoria Quay (VQ), Edinburgh EH6 6QQ *Tel:* 0131-556 8400

Committees

Titles and membership are likely to change with the election of the new First Minister. For updated information see *Vacher's Parliamentary Companion* December 2000 edition.

Audit

Convenor: Andrew Welsh
Deputy: Nick Johnston
Brian Adam; Scott Barrie; Cathie Craigie; Annabel Goldie; Margaret Jamieson; Paul Martin; Euan Robson; Karen Whitefield; Andrew Wilson
Clerk Team Leader: Callum Thomson
Senior Assistant Clerk: Anne Peat
Assistant Clerk: Sean Wixted

Education, Culture and Sport

Convenor: Mary Mulligan
Deputy: Cathy Peattie
Cathy Jamieson; Ian Jenkins; Johann Lamont; Kenneth Macintosh; Fiona McLeod; Brian Monteith; Michael Russell; Jamie Stone; Nicola Sturgeon
Clerk Team Leader: Martin Verity (0131-348 5204)
Senior Assistant Clerk: David McLaren
Assistant Clerk: Ian Cowan

Enterprise and Lifelong Learning

Convenor: Alex Neil MSP
Deputy: Annabel Goldie
Fergus Ewing; Nick Johnston; Marilyn Livingstone; George Lyon; Margo MacDonald; Duncan McNeil; Elaine Murray; Elaine Thomson; Allan Wilson
Clerk Team Leader: Simon Watkins (0131-348 5207)
Senior Assistant Clerk: David McLaren

Equal Opportunities

Convenor: Kate MacLean
Deputy: Shona Robison
Malcolm Chisholm; Johann Lamont; Marilyn Livingstone; Jamie McGrigor; Irene McGugan; Michael McMahon; Tricia Marwick; John Munro; Nora Radcliffe; Tommy Sheridan; Elaine Smith
Clerk Team Leader: Lee Bridges (0131-348 5211)
Senior Assistant Clerk: Mary Dinsdale
Assistant Clerk: Alison Campbell

European

Convenor: Hugh Henry
Deputy: Cathy Jamieson
Dennis Canavan; Bruce Crawford; Winnie Ewing; Sylvia Jackson; Margo MacDonald; Maureen Macmillan; David Mundell; Irene Oldfather; Tavish Scott; Ben Wallace; Allan Wilson
Clerk Team Leader: Stephen Imrie (0131-348 5234)
Assistant Clerk: David Simpson

Finance

Convenor: Mike Watson
Deputy: Elaine Thomson
David Davidson; Rhoda Grant; Adam Ingram; George Lyon; Kenneth Macintosh; Keith Raffan; Richard Simpson; John Swinney; Andrew Wilson
Clerk Team Leader: Callum Thomson (0131-348 5205)
Senior Assistant Clerk: Anne Peat
Assistant Clerk: Graeme Elliot

Health and Community Care

Convenor: Margaret Smith
Deputy: Malcolm Chisholm
Dorothy-Grace Elder; Duncan Hamilton; Hugh
    Henry; Margaret Jamieson; Irene Oldfather;
    Mary Scanlon; Richard Simpson;
    Kay Ullrich; Ben Wallace
Clerk Team Leader: Jennifer Smart
    (0131-348 5210)
Senior Assistant Clerk: Irene Fleming

Justice and Home Affairs

Convenor: Alasdair Morgan MSP
Deputy: Gordon Jackson
Scott Barrie; Phil Gallie; Christine Grahame;
    Lyndsay McIntosh; Kate MacLean; Maureen
    Macmillan; Pauline McNeill; Michael
    Matheson; Euan Robson
Clerk Team Leader: Andrew Mylne
    (0131-348 5206)
Senior Assistant Clerk: Alison Taylor
Assistant Clerk: Fiona Groves

Local Government

Convenor: Trish Godman
Deputy: Johann Lamont
Colin Campbell; Kenneth Gibson; Donald
    Gorrie; Keith Harding; Sylvia Jackson;
    Michael McMahon; Bristow Muldoon;
    Gil Paterson; Jamie Stone
Clerk Team Leader: Eugene Windsor
    (0131-348 5208)
Senior Assistant Clerk: Irene Fleming
Assistant Clerk: Craig Harper

Procedures

Convenor: Murray Tosh
Deputy: Janis Hughes
Donald Gorrie; Gordon Jackson; Andy Kerr;
    Gil Paterson; Michael Russell
Clerk Team Leader: John Patterson
    (0131-348 5175)
Senior Assistant Clerk: Mark MacPherson
Remit: To consider and report on: The practice
    and procedures of the Scottish Parliament in
    relation to its public business.

Public Petitions

Convenor: John McAllion
Deputy: Pauline McNeill
Helen Eadie; Christine Grahame; John Scott;
    Margaret Smith; Sandra White
Senior Assistant Clerk: Steve Farrell
    (0131-348 5186)
Remit: To consider and report on: Whether a
    public petition is admissible, and what action
    is to be taken upon the petition.

Rural Affairs

Convenor: Alex Johnstone
Deputy: Alasdair Morgan
Alex Fergusson; Rhoda Grant; Richard Lochhead;
    Irene McGugan; Des McNulty; John Munro;
    Elaine Murray; Cathy Peattie; Mike Rumbles
Clerk Team Leader: Richard Davies
    (0131-348 5209)
Senior Assistant Clerk: Richard Walsh
Assistant Clerk: Tracey Hawe

Social Inclusion, Housing and Voluntary Sector

Convenor: Margaret Curran
Deputy: Fiona Hyslop
Bill Aitken; Robert Brown; Cathie Craigie; John
    McAllion; Alex Neil; Lloyd Quinan; Keith
    Raffan; Mike Watson; Karen Whitefield
Clerk Team Leader: Lee Bridges
    (0131-348 5211)
Senior Assistant Clerk: Mary Dinsdale

Standards

Convenor: Mike Rumbles
Deputy: Tricia Marwick
James Douglas-Hamilton; Patricia Ferguson;
    Karen Gillon; Adam Ingram; Des McNulty
Clerk Team Leader: Samantha Jones
    (0131-348 5213)
Senior Assistant Clerks: Jim Johnston; David Igoe
Remit: To consider and report on: Member's
    conduct

Subordinate Legislation

Convenor: Kenny MacAskill
Deputy: Ian Jenkins
Fergus Ewing; Trish Godman; Ken Mackintosh;
    Bristow Muldoon; David Mundell
Clerk Team Leader: Alasdair Rankin
    (0131-348 5212)
Assistant Clerk: Alistair Fleming
Assistant Clerk: Ruth Cooper

Transport and Environment

Convenor: Andy Kerr
Deputy: Nora Radcliffe
Helen Eadie; Linda Fabiani; Donald Gorrie;
    Robin Harper; Janis Hughes; Cathy Jamieson;
    Kenny MacAskill; Des McNulty; Murray Tosh
Clerk Team Leader: Shelagh McKinlay
    (0131-348 5208)
Senior Assistant Clerk: Richard Walsh
Assistant Clerk: Alistair McFie

*NB: Full Official Report details can be
contacted at:*
Website:
www.scottish.parliament.uk/parl_bus/pab.html

The Scottish Executive – Civil Service

Website: www.scotland.gov.uk

The Scottish Executive is the Government in Scotland for all devolved matters. It is accountable to the Scottish Parliament. The Executive consists of the First Minister plus a team of 12 Scottish Ministers including Law Officers. The statutory powers and duties exercised by UK Ministers in Scotland in relation to devolved matters have been transferred to the Scottish Ministers.

The Scottish Executive consists of six main departments:

Development Department; Education Department; Enterprise and Lifelong Learning Department; Justice Department*; Health Department; Rural Affairs Department – together with Executive Secretariat, Corporate Services and Finance.

Includes Scottish Courts Administration

SCOTTISH EXECUTIVE SECRETARIAT

Senior Management

OFFICE OF THE PERMANENT SECRETARY
(St Andrew's House)

Permanent Secretary: Muir Russell
Private Secretary: Joanna Young
  Tel: 0131-244 4026 and 0131-270 6796 (DH)
Assistant Private Secretary: Stephanie Amice
  Tel: 0131-244 2348 *Fax:* 0131-244 2756
Diary Secretary: Alison Knox
  Tel: 0131-244 4028

POLICY UNIT

Head of Unit: Brian Fitzpatrick
  Tel: 0131-244 5205
Deputy Head of Unit: Vacant
  Tel: 0131-244 2078

RURAL AFFAIRS DEPARTMENT
(Pentland House)

Head: John Graham
Private Secretary: David Brown
  Tel: 0131-244 6022
Assistant Private Secretary: Scott McDowell
  Tel: 0131-244 6023 *Fax:* 0131-244 6116
Senior Management:
Agricultural and Biological Research Group
Head of Group: Andrew Rushworth
Head of Food and Agriculture Group: David Crawley
Heads of Divisions:
Land Use and Rural Policy: Douglas Greig
Plants, Environment and Pollution: Ian Anderson
Agriculture, Food and EU Policy: Jan Polley
CAP Management: Dr Jim Wildgoose
Information Systems: Walter Ferguson
Livestock Policy and Animal Health and Welfare: Stephen Rooke

Economic and Statistics:
  Monica Robertson
Chief Agricultural Officer: Andy Robertson
Assistant Chief Veterinary Officer (MAFF):
  Leslie Gardner
Fisheries Group
Head of Group: Dr Paul Brady
Heads of Divisions:
Sea Fisheries: Derek Feeley
Salmon and Freshwater Fisheries:
  J Hutchison
Inspector: David Dunkley
Fisheries Research Services:
  Prof Tony Hawkins
Environment Group
Head of Group: Nicola Munro
Head of Divisions:
Countryside and Natural Heritage:
  Andrew Dickson
Environment Protection: Bridget Campbell
Air, Climate and Engineering Unit/Chief Water Engineer: Philip Wright
Water Services: Mike Neilson
Ecological Adviser: Dr John Miles OBE
Strategy and Co-ordination:
  Sandy Cameron

Departments

DEVELOPMENT DEPARTMENT
(Victoria Quay)

Head: Kenneth MacKenzie CB
Private Secretary: John Peerless
  Tel: 0131-244 0760
Senior Management:
Housing and Area Regeneration Group
Head of Group: David Befall
Heads of Divisions:
Housing Division 1: John Breslin
Housing Division 2: Richard Grant

Housing Division 3: Geoff Huggins
Area Regeneration: Doreen Mellon
Social Inclusion: Linda Rosborough
Local Government Group
Head of Group: David Middleton
Head of Divisions:
Division 1 – Current Expenditure and
  Government Support: Christie Smith
Division 2 – Local Government Non-Fiancial
  Issues: L Evans
Division 3 – Local Taxation, Value for Money,
  Capital Expenditure: Ainslie McLaughlin
Chief Inquiry Reporter: Richard Hickman
Transport and Planning Group
Head of Group: John Martin
Head of Planning Division: Maureen McGinn
Chief Planner: Jim Mackinnon
Head of Building Control Division:
  Dr Phil Cornish
Senior Economic Adviser: Neil Jackson

HEALTH DEPARTMENT
NHS IN SCOTLAND
(St Andrew's House)

Head of Department and Chief Executive:
  Vacant
Private Secretary: Gill Wylie
  Tel: 0131-244 2410
Assistant Private Secretary: Adam Sinclair
  Tel: 0131-244 2440 *Fax:* 0131-244 2162
Public Health Policy Unit
Chief Medical Officer: Dr Mac Armstrong
Private Secretary: Laura Crooks
  Tel: 0131-244 2317 *Fax:* 0131-244 2835
Deputy Chief Medical Officers:
  Dr Andrew Fraser, Dr Aileen Keel
Chief Dental Officer: Ray Watkins
Chief Pharmacist: Bill Scott
Senior Management:
Finance-Electronic Clinical Communications
  Implementations Directorate
Head of Division: Ken Brewer
Strategy and Performance Management
Director: Godfrey Robson
Heads of Divisions:
Health Gain: Hector MacKenzie
Health Care Policy: Vacant
Performance Management: A Brown
Economics and Information: Alasdair Munro
Primary Care Directorate
Director: Vacant

Heads of Divisions:
Division A: Wilma Dickson
Division B: Dr Hamish Wilson
Senior Medical Officers: Dr Hugh Whyte,
  Dr Liz Jordan
Finance Directorate
Director: John Aldridge
Deputy Director: David Palmer
Estates Division, Building and Estates Adviser:
  Roderick McCallum
Computing and IT Strategy Head:
  Charles Knox
Human Resources Directorate
Director: Gerry Marr
Assistant Directors: Robin Naysmith (Policy),
  Janet McGregor (Strategy and
  Implementation)
Head of Development: E Kelly
Medical Adviser: Dr David Ewing
Director and Chief Nursing Officer:
  Anne Jarvie CBE
Chief Scientist: Graeme Catto
Public Health Policy Unit
Head of Group: G Robson
Head of Divisions:
Division 1: Jim Brown
Division 2: Kay Barton
Community Care: Thea Teale

EDUCATION DEPARTMENT
(Victoria Quay)

Head: John Elvidge
Private Secretary: Johann MacDougall
  Tel: 0131-244 1484
Assistant Private Secretaries: I F Martin
  Tel: 0131-244 1479 Derek Jackson
  Tel: 0131-244 1483 *Fax:* 0131-244 1475
Senior Management:
Schools Group
Head of Group: Michael Ewart
Head of Divisions:
Schools Standards and Improvement:
  Jeane Freeman
Pupil Support: Joan Fraser
Secondary Education – HM Chief Inspector:
  Philip Banks
Curriculum, International and IT:
  Eleanor Emberson
Teacher Education (HMIT): Harvey Stalker
Arts and Culture Heritage: Bob Irvine
Schools – Inspectorate
Douglas Osler, Graham Donaldson,
  Colin MacLean
Social Work Services – Inspectorate
Chief Inspector: Angus Skinner
Chief Education Statistician: Rob Wishart

Children and Young People's Group
Head of Group: Gillian Stewart
Heads of Divisions:
Children and Families: Jane Morgan
Early Education and Childcare: Roma Menlowe
Young People and Looked After Children:
  Gerald McHugh
Head of Sports Policy Unit: John Gilmour
Construction Industry, Chief Architect:
  John Gibbons CBE
Modernising Government: Isabelle Low
Digital Scotland: Vacant

ENTERPRISE AND LIFELONG LEARNING DEPARTMENT
(Meridian Court)

Head: Eddie Frizzell CB
Private Secretary: David Wallace
  Tel: 0141-242 5704
Assistant Private Secretary: Janet Smith
  Tel: 0141-242 5703 *Fax:* 0141-242 5477
Senior Management:
Enterprise and Industrial Affairs
Head of Group: S F Hampson
Head of Business Growth Unit: Ian Howie
Heads of Divisions:
Investment Assistance: Wilson Malone
Enterprise and Industrial Affairs: John Mason
Innovation and Support: Colin Wood
Energy Division: Vacant
Scottish Trade International: Les Brown
Locate in Scotland: David Macdonald
Economic Development, Advice and
  Employment: Mike Foulis
Economic Adviser and Statistician:
  Dr John Rigg
Enterprise Networks and Tourism:
  David Wilson
New Deal and Adult Training:
  Andrew MacLeod
Qualifications and Skills: Alistair Aitken OBE
Lifelong Learning Group
Head of Group: Ed Weeple
Transitions to Work: Kevin Doran
Opportunities for Learning: David Stewart
Higher Education Science and Student Support:
  Lucy Hunter
Further and Adult Education: Colin Reeves

JUSTICE DEPARTMENT
(Saughton House)

Head: Jim Gallagher
Private Secretary: Jackie Knox
  Tel: 0131-244 2791
Assistant Private Secretary: Vacant
  Tel: 0131-244 2122 *Fax:* 0131-244 2121

Senior Management
Police, Fire and Emergenices Group
Head of Group: Colin Baxter
Heads of Divisions:
Adult Offenders and Victim Issues:
  Elizabeth Carmichael
Police Division 1:
Management, Expenditure and Staffing:
  Ian Snedden
Police Division 2:
Training, Information Technology, Crime
  Prevention: John Rowell OBE
Fire Service and Emergency Planning:
  Marion Gunn
Civil and Criminal Law Group
Head of Group: Niall Campbell
Civil Law Division:
  Micheline Brannan
Criminal Justice: Donald Carmichael
Parole and Legal Aid:
  Robin MacEwen
HM Chief Inspector of Prisons:
  Clive Fairweather OBE
HM Chief Inspector of Fire Services:
  Dennis Davis OBE
HM Chief Inspector of Constabulary:
  William Taylor QPM
Central Research Unit:
Chief Research Officer:
  Dr Andrew Scott
Social Work Services Group and Inspectorate:
Chief Inspector of Social Work Services for
  Scotland: Angus Skinner

Courts Group

Civil Justice and International Division
Hayweight House
23 Lauriston Street
Edinburgh EH3 9DQ
Tel: 0131-229 9200
Fax: 0131-221 6895/6894
Judicial Appointments and Finance Division
Head of Division: David Stewart
Private Secretary to Mr Gallagher and
  Mr Stewart: Morag Moore
  Tel: 0131-221 6801
Civil Justice and International Division
Head of Division: Peter Beaton
Private Secretary: Mrs Gerry Kernohan
  Tel: 0131-221 6807

CORPORATE SERVICES

16 Waterloo Place, Edinburgh EH1 3DN
Principal Establishment Officer and Head of
Corporate Services: Agnes Robson
Private Secretary: Carolyn Murdoch
  Tel: 0131-244 3939
Private Secretary (PEO): Caroline Banks
  Tel: 0131-244 4593
Assistant Private Secretary: Steven Feeney
  Tel: 0131-244 3921 *Fax:* 0131-244 3095

Scottish Executive Secretariat

St Andrew's House
Edinburgh EH1 3DG
Enquiries: 0131-556 8400

Senior Management

Head of Executive: Robert Gordon
  CB *Personal Assistant:* Jane McEwan
  Tel: 0131-244 5598
Personal Secretary: Liz Fanning
  Tel: 0131-244 7938 *Fax:* 0131-244 5536

CONSTITUTIONAL POLICY

Head of Division: Michael Lugton
Personal Secretary: Vicky Stewart
  Tel: 0131-244 7661 *Fax:* 0131-244 5599

CABINET SECRETARIAT

Head of Secretariat: Ian Walford
  Tel: 0131-244 5532
Personal Secretary: Tracy Ramsay
  Tel: 0131-244 5533 *Fax:* 0131-244 5599

SOLICITORS
(Victoria Quay)

Tel: 0131-244 0549
Solicitor: Richard Henderson
Deputy Solicitor: Jim Maclean
  Tel: 0131-244 0494
Personal Secretary: Sheena Cooper
  Tel: 0131-244 0495 *Fax:* 0131-244 7417

EXTERNAL RELATIONS DIVISION

Head of Division: Barbara Doig
Personal Secretary: Lisa Nugent
  Tel: 0131-244 7362 *Fax:* 0131-244 7258

OFFICE OF THE CHIEF ECONOMIC ADVISER

Chief Economic Adviser: Dr Andrew Goudie
Personal Secretary: Linda Boag
  Tel: 0131-244 2788 *Fax:* 0131-244 2824

MEDIA AND COMMUNICATIONS GROUP

Provision of advice to Ministers and Scottish Executive Departments on public presentation and policy.
Headquarters: St Andrew's House
Head of New Media and Presentation:
  Roger Williams
Personal Assistant: Kirsten Boag
  Tel: 0131-244 2664 *Fax:* 0131-244 2918
Press Head: Owen Kelly *Tel:* 0131-244 2019
Personal Assistant: Claire McGuigan
  Tel: 0131-244 1716 *Fax:* 0131-244 1778

EQUALITY AND VOLUNTARY ISSUES GROUP

Head of Group: Valerie Macniven
Voluntary Issues Unit
Head of Group: Sheenagh Adams
Personal Secretary to Heads of Group:
  Karen Smith *Tel:* 0131-244 2630
  Fax: 0131-244 2659
Equality Unit
Head of Unit: Yvonne Strachan
Personal Secretary: Angela Gibson
  Tel: 0131-244 5199

OFFICE OF THE SCOTTISH PARLIAMENT COUNSEL
(Victoria Quay)
Tel: 0131-244 1663

First Scottish Parliamentary Counsel:
  John McCluskie, QC
Personal Secretary: Vacant *Tel:* 0131-244 1672
  Fax: 0131-244 1661
Counsel: Gregor Clark, Colin Wilson
Deputes: John Harkness, Madelaine Mackenzie

LEGAL SECRETARIAT TO THE LORD ADVOCATE

Crown Office, 25 Chamber Street,
  Edinburgh EH1 1LA.
Tel: 0131-247 2665
Legal Secretary: Patrick Layden
Deputy Legal Secretary: Malcolm McMillane
Personal Secretary: Janice Elvine
  Tel: 0131-247 2665 *Fax:* 0131-247 2652

EU OFFICE (BRUSSELS)

Scotland House, Rond-Point, Schuman 6,
    Brussels 1040, Belgium.
Tel: +32 2 282 8330
Head: George Calder

FINANCE GROUP

Head of Group: Dr Peter Collings
Senior Personal Secretary: Sylvia Cunningham
    MBE *Tel:* 0131-244 7285
    Fax: 0131-244 7287
Assistant Statistician: Susie Braham
    Tel: 0131-244 7505
Heads of Divisions: Graeme Dickson, John
    Henderson, Alasdair McLeod, David Reid
Head of Audit Unit: Bill Tait
Head of Accountancy Services Unit: Ian Smith

SCOTTISH EXECUTIVE AGENCIES

Fisheries Research Service (FRS); Historic
Scotland; Intervention Board (IB); Scottish
Agricultural Science Agency (SASA); Scottish
Court Service; Scottish Fisheries Protection
Agency (SFPA); Scottish Prison Service (SPS);
Scottish Public Pensions Agency (SPPA);
Student Awards Agency for Scotland (SAAS).
Registers of Scotland and National Archives of
Scotland (NAS) both report directly to the First
Minister.

Source: Scottish Executive Secretariat

Political Parties and Shadow Cabinet Spokespeople

SCOTTISH LABOUR PARTY

John Smith House, 145 Regent Street,
Glasgow G2 4RE
0141-572 6900 Fax 0141-572 2566
E-mail: scotland@new.labour.org
Website: www.scottish.labour.org.uk

General Secretary: Lesley Quinn
Director of Communications: John Scott

SCOTTISH NATIONAL PARTY

6 North Charlotte Street, Edinburgh EH2 4JH
0131-226 3661 Fax 0131-225 9575
E-mail: snp.hq@snp.org
Website: www.snp.org

National Convenor: John Swinney MSP
Senior Vice-Convenor:
    Roseanna Cunningham MSP
Communications Manager: Kevin Pringle
Parliamentary Group Convenor:
    Margaret Ewing MP MSP
Parliamentary Group Secretary:
    Shona Robison MSP

SHADOW CABINET

First Minister: John Swinney MP MSP
Deputy Leader and Justice:
    Roseanna Cunningham MP MSP
Enterprise and Lifelong Learning:
    Kenny MacAskill MSP
Children and Education: Michael Russell MSP
*Social Justice and Housing plus Co-ordination
    of Policy Programme:* Fiona Hyslop MSP
Health and Community Care:
    Nicola Sturgeon MSP

Rural Affairs: Fergus Ewing MSP
Finance: Andrew Wilson MSP
Local Government: Kenny Gibson MSP
Transport and Environment:
    Bruce Crawford MSP
Defence: Colin Campbell MSP
Social Security: Christine Grahame MSP
Business Manager:
    Tricia Marwick MSP
Chief Whip: Kay Ullrich MSP
Europe: Neil MacCormick MEP
*Leader of the Westminster Parliamentary
    Group:* Alasdair Morgan MP MSP

SCOTTISH CONSERVATIVE AND UNIONIST PARTY

83 Princes Street, Edinburgh EH2 2ER
0131-247 6890 Fax 0131-247 6891
Press: 0131-247 6872
E-mail: scuco@scottish.tory.org.uk

Chairman: Raymond Robertson
Leader: David McLetchie MSP
Director: Simon J Turner

Scottish Parliament
0131-348 5000 Fax 0131-348 5940

SHADOW CABINET

Leader: David McLetchie MSP
*Deputy Leader, Economy, Industry and
    Finance:* Annabel Goldie MSP
Chief Whip and Business Manager:
    Rt Hon Lord James Douglas-Hamilton MSP

Home Affairs: Phil Gallie MSP
Education, Arts, Culture and Sport:
Brian Monteith MSP
Transport and Environment: Murray Tosh MSP
Rural Affairs: Alex Johnstone MSP
Health and Social Work: Mary Scanlon MSP
Local Government and Housing:
Keith Harding MSP
Deputies:
Economy, Industry and Finance:
David Davidson MSP,
Nick Johnstone MSP
Homes Affairs: Lyndsay McIntosh MSP
Education: David Mundell MSP
Transport and Environment: John Young MSP
Rural Affairs (Fisheries):
Jamie McGrigor MSP,
Alex Fergusson MSP
Health and Social Work: Ben Wallace MSP
Local Government and Housing, Deputy
Business Manager: Bill Aitken MSP

SCOTTISH LIBERAL DEMOCRATS

4 Clifton Terrace, Edinburgh EH12 5DR
0131-337 2314 Fax 0131-337 3566
E-mail: scotlibdem@cix.co.uk
Website: www.scotlibdems.org.uk
Chief Executive: Kilvert Croft
Party Administrator: Mrs Rae Grant
Scottish Parliament:
Chief of Staff: Willie Rennie
Senior Press Officer: Neil Mackinnon
Tel: 0131-348 5809

PARLIAMENTARY SPOKESPEOPLE

Leader: Jim Wallace QC MP MSP
Communities and Housing: Robert Brown MSP
Local Government; Parliamentary Procedures:
Donald Gorrie OBE MP MSP
Culture, Arts and Sport: Ian Jenkins MSP
Enterprise and Life-Long Learning:
George Lyon MSP
Highlands and Islands and Gaelic:
John Farquhar Munro MSP
Health; Equal Opportunities:
Nora Radcliffe MSP
Finance; Drugs: Keith Raffan MSP
Justice: Euan Robson MSP
Rural Affairs; Convenor of Standards
Committee: Mike Rumbles MSP
Transport, the Environment and Europe:
Tavish Scott MSP
Convenor of Health and Community Care
Committee: Margaret Smith MSP
Children and School Education:
Jamie Stone MSP

WESTMINSTER SPOKESPEOPLE:

Scotland: Sir Robert Smith MP
Parliamentary Group Convenor:
Michael Moore MP

SCOTTISH GREEN PARTY

14 Albany Street, Edinburgh EH1 3QB
0131-478 7896 Fax 0131-478 7896
E-mail: info@scottishgreens.org.uk
Website: www.scottishgreens.org.uk
Council Convenor: Dr Nina Baker
Executive Convenor: Dr Caroline Hoffmann

PRINCIPAL SPOKESPEOPLE

Robin Harper MSP, Dr Eleanor Scott

Scottish Parliament Headquarters, Room 3.09
Robin Harper MSP
0131-348 5927 Fax 0131-348 5972
E-mail:
robin.harper.msp@scottish.parliament.uk
Policy Support Officer: Dr Steve Burgess
Administrative Support Officer:
Alison Johnstone
Lothians Constituency Office
14 Albany Street, Edinburgh EH1 3QB
0131-478 7895 Fax: 0131-478 7891

SCOTTISH SOCIALIST PARTY

73 Robertson Street, Glasgow G2 8QD
0141-221 7714 Fax 0141-221 7715
E-mail: ssv@ndirect.co.uk
Website: www.scottishsocialistparty.org
West of Scotland Organiser: Richie Venton
Convenor: Tommy Sheridan MSP
Scottish Parliament Office: 0131-348 5632
Fax 0131-348 5948
E-mail:
thomas.sheridan.msp@scottish.parliament.uk
Glasgow City Council: 0141-287 3934
Fax 0141-287 3933

MSP FOR FALKIRK WEST

Dennis Canavan MSP
Scottish Parliament:
Member: European Committee
Convenor: Cross-Party Sports Group
Constituency Office, 37 Church Walk, Denny,
Stirlingshire FK6 6DF
01324 825922 Fax 01324 823972
Parliamentary Assistant: Adele Brown
Constituency Secretary: Anne Thomson

Members of the Scottish Parliament
Contact Directory

The Scottish Parliament
George IV Bridge, Edinburgh EH99 1SP
0131-348 5000
(Move to permanent residence at Holyrood in Edinburgh)
General Enquiries: 0845 278 1999
Public Information: E-mail: sp.info@scottish.parliament.uk
Presiding Officer: E-mail: presiding.officer@scottish.parliament.uk
Website: www.scottish.parliament.uk/contact.html
E-mail: scottish.ministers@scotland.gov.uk

ADAM, Brian *(SNP)* – North East Scotland*
   E-mail: brian.adam.msp@scottish.parliament.uk
   Parliamentary Assistant: Stuart Pratt *Tel:* 0131-348 5692 *Fax:* 0131-348 5953
AITKEN, Bill *(Con)* – Glasgow*
   Tel: 0131-348 5642 *E-mail:* bill.aitken.msp@scottish.parliament.uk
   Secretary: Sandra Russell
ALEXANDER, Wendy *(Lab)* – Paisley North
   Tel: 0131-348 5752 *E-mail:* wendy.alexander.msp@scottish.parliament.uk
   Researcher: Gordon MacRae *Tel:* 0131-348 5752
   Private Secretary: Nicola Williams *Tel:* 0131-244 7818 *Fax:* 0131-244 7403
   Constituency contact: Anne-Marie Cooper *Tel:* 0141-561 5800
BAILLIE, Jackie *(Lab)* – Dumbarton
   Tel: 0131-348 5905 *Fax:* 0131-348 5986 *E-mail:* jackie.baillie.msp@scottish.parliament.uk
   Private Secretary: Scott Rogerson *Tel:* 0131-244 5539
   Diary Secretaries: Tracy Rae, Jacqueline D'Archy *Tel:* 0131-244 5538 *Fax:* 0131-244 7404
   Constituency Contact: Jamie Reid *Tel:* 01389 734214 *Fax:* 01389 761498
   E-mail: jamie.reid@scottish.parliament.uk
BARRIE, Scott *(Lab)* – Dunfermline West
   Tel: 0131-348 5849 *E-mail:* scott.barrie.msp@scottish.parliament.uk
   Parliamentary Assistant: Thomas Docherty
BOYACK, Sarah *(Lab)* – Edinburgh Central
   Tel: 0131-348 5751 *Fax:* 0131-348 5974 *E-mail:* sarah.boyack.msp@scottish.parliament.uk
   Parliamentary Assistant: Mrs Jo Eady
   Private Secretary: Neil MacLennan *Tel:* 0131-244 0627 *Fax:* 0131-244 7405
BRANKIN, Rhona *(Lab/Co-op)* – Midlothian
   Tel: 0131-348 5838 *E-mail:* rhona.brankin.msp@scottish.parliament.uk
   Parliamentary Assistant: Simon Tiernan
   Private Secretary: Fiona McLauchlan *Tel:* 0131-244 7717 *Fax:* 0131-244 7402
   Diary Secretary: Angela Rowan *Tel:* 0131-244 7866
BROWN, Robert *(Lib Dem)* – Glasgow*
   E-mail: robert.brown.msp@scottish.parliament.uk
   Parliamentary Assistant: Angela Nixon *Tel:* 0131-348 5792
CAMPBELL, Colin *(SNP)* – West of Scotland*
   Tel: 0131-348 5723 *Fax:* 0131-348 5735 *E-mail:* colin.campbell.msp@scottish.parliament.uk
   Parliamentary Assistant: Johnny Mellor *Tel:* 0131-348 5923 *Fax:* 0131-348 5954
CANAVAN, Dennis *(MSPFW)* – Falkirk West
   E-mail: dennis.canavan.msp@scottish.parliament.uk
   Parliamentary Assistant: Adele Brown *Tel:* 0131-348 5630
   Constituency Secretary: Anne Thomson *Tel:* 01324 825922 *Fax:* 01324 823972
CHISHOLM, Malcolm *(Lab)* – Edinburgh North and Leith
   Tel: 0131-348 5908 *E-mail:* malcolm.chisholm.msp@scottish.parliament.uk
   Researcher: Annette Lamont

CRAIGIE, Cathie *(Lab)* – Cumbernauld and Kilsyth
Tel: 0131-348 5756 *Fax:* 0131-348 5977 *E-mail:* cathie.craigie.msp@scottish.parliament.uk
Parliamentary Assistant: Fiona Stanton
CRAWFORD, Bruce *(SNP)* – Mid Scotland and Fife*
Tel: 0131-348 5686 *E-mail:* bruce.crawford.msp@scottish.parliament.uk
Parliamentary Assistant: David Scott *Tel:* 0131-348 5687 *Fax:* 0131-348 5957
Diary Secretary: Pauline Archibald *Tel:* 0131-348 5704
CUNNINGHAM, Roseanna *(SNP)* – Perth
Tel: 0131-348 5696 *E-mail:* roseanna.cunningham.msp@scottish.parliament.uk
Parliamentary Assistant: John Watts *Tel:* 0131-348 5697 *Fax:* 0131-348 5952
CURRAN, Margaret *(Lab)* – Glasgow Baillieston
Tel: 0131-348 5842 *Fax:* 0131-348 5843 *E-mail:* margaret.curran.msp@scottish.parliament.uk
Parliamentary Assistant: Tel: 0131-348 5843
DAVIDSON, David *(Con)* – North East Scotland*
Tel: 0131-348 5653 *E-mail:* david.davidson.msp@scottish.parliament.uk
Parliamentary Secretary: Liz Cameron *Tel:* 0131-348 5654
DEACON, Susan *(Lab)* – Edinburgh East and Musselburgh
Tel: 0131-348 5753 *Fax:* 0131-348 5973 *E-mail:* susan.deacon.msp@scottish.parliament.uk
Private Secretary: Karen Jackson *Tel:* 0131-244 4017
Diary Secretary: Joanne Ramsay *Tel:* 0131-244 2135 *Fax:* 0131-244 3563
Office Administrator: Nikki Tongs *Tel:* 0131-244 5135 *Fax:* 0131-244 3563
Constituency Assistant: Room 318 PHQ, Edna Milne *Tel:* 0131-348 5753 *Fax:* 0131-348 5973
DOUGLAS-HAMILTON, Rt Hon Lord James *(Con)* – Lothian*
Tel: 0131-348 5660 *E-mail:* james.douglas-hamilton.msp@scottish.parliament.uk
Private Secretary: Margaret Dundas *Tel:* 0131-348 5661 *Fax:* 0131-348 5936
EADIE, Helen *(Lab/Co-op)* – Dunfermline East
E-mail: helen.eadie.msp@scottish.parliament.uk
Parliamentary Assistant: Fiona Yates *Tel:* 0131-348 5749
ELDER, Dorothy-Grace *(SNP)* – Glasgow*
Tel: 0131-348 5682 *E-mail:* dorothy.elder.msp@scottish.parliament.uk
Parliamentary Assistant: Fiona Macauley *Tel:* 0131-348 5683 *Fax:* 0131-348 5944
EWING, Fergus *(SNP)* – Inverness East, Nairn and Lochaber
Tel: 0131-348 5732 *E-mail:* fergus.ewing.msp@scottish.parliament.uk
Parliamentary Assistant: Norman Will (Constituency Secretary)
Tel: 0131-348 5731 *Fax:* 0131-348 5943
EWING, Margaret *(SNP)* – Moray
Tel: 0131-348 5705 *E-mail:* margaret.ewing.msp@scottish.parliament.uk
Parliamentary Assistant: Pauline Archibald *Tel:* 0131-348 5704 *Fax:* 0131-348 5857
EWING, Winifred *(SNP)* – Highlands and Islands*
Tel: 0131-348 5726 *E-mail:* winnie.ewing.msp@scottish.parliament.uk
Parliamentary Assistant: James MacInnes *Tel:* 0131-348 5725 *Fax:* 0131-348 5947
FABIANI, Linda *(SNP)* – Central Scotland*
Tel: 0131-348 5698 *E-mail:* linda.fabiani.msp@scottish.parliament.uk
Parliamentary Assistant: Archie Buchanan *Tel:* 0131-348 5699 *Fax:* 0131-348 5895
FERGUSON, Patricia *(Lab)* – Glasgow Maryhill
Tel: 0131-348 5311 *E-mail:* patricia.ferguson.msp@scottish.parliament.uk
Parliamentary Assistant: Chris Kelly
FERGUSSON, Alex *(Con)* – South of Scotland*
Tel: 0131-348 5636 *E-mail:* alex.fergusson.msp@scottish.parliament.uk
Parliamentary Assistant: Gillian Gillies *Tel:* 0131-348 5638 *Fax:* 0131-348 5932
FINNIE, Ross *(Lib Dem)* – West of Scotland*
Tel: 0131-348 5783 *E-mail:* ross.finnie.msp@scottish.parliament.uk
Parliamentary Assistant: Fora Hird *Tel:* 0131-348 5784 *Fax:* 0131-348 5966
Private Secretary: Shirley Laing

GALBRAITH, Sam *(Lab)* – Strathkelvin and Bearsden
E-mail: sam.galbraith.msp@scottish.parliament.uk
Private Secretary: Gabby Pieraccini *Tel:* 0131-244 7716
Diary Secretary: Gerry Fitzpatrick *Tel:* 0131-244 7850
Constituency Secretary: Anne Devine *Tel:* 0141-942 9662 *Fax:* 0141-942 9658
GALLIE, Phil *(Con)* – South of Scotland*
Tel: 0131-348 5665 *E-mail:* phil.gallie.msp@scottish.parliament.uk
Parliamentary Assistant: Amy Kenyon
GIBSON, Kenneth *(SNP)* – Glasgow*
Tel: 0131-348 5924 *Fax:* 0131-348 5716
E-mail: kenneth.gibson.msp@scottish.parliament.uk
Parliamentary Assistants: Gordon Archer and David Ritchie
Tel: 0131-348 5925 *Fax:* 0131-348 5943
GILLON, Karen *(Lab)* – Clydesdale
Tel: 0131-348 5823 *E-mail:* karen.gillon.msp@scottish.parliament.uk
Parliamentary Assistant: Stuart Clark *Tel:* 0131-348 5822
GODMAN, Trish *(Lab)* – West Renfrewshire
Tel: 0131-348 5837 *E-mail:* trish.godman.msp@scottish.parliament.uk
Researcher: Fiona O'Donnell
GOLDIE, Annabel *(Con)* – West of Scotland*
Tel: 0131-348 5662 *E-mail:* annabel.goldie.msp@scottish.parliament.uk
Secretary: Gillian Cameron
GORRIE, Donald OBE *(Lib Dem)* – Central Scotland*
Tel: 0131-348 5795 *E-mail:* donald.gorrie.msp@scottish.parliament.uk
Parliamentary Assistant: Doreen Nisbet *Tel:* 0131-348 5796 *Fax:* 0131-348 5963
GRAHAME, Christine *(SNP)* – South of Scotland*
Tel: 0131-348 5729 *E-mail:* christine.grahame.msp@scottish.parliament.uk
Parliamentary Assistant: Mark Hirst *Tel:* 0131-348 5730 *Fax:* 0131-348 5945
GRANT, Rhoda *(Lab)* – Highlands and Islands*
ft2:E-mail: rhoda.grant.msp@scottish.parliament.uk
Parliamentary Assistant: Richard Welsh *Tel:* 0131-348 5766 *Fax:* 0131-348 5767
Secretary: Andrene Maxwell
GRAY, Iain *(Lab)* – Edinburgh Pentlands
Tel: 0131-348 5754 *E-mail:* iain.gray.msp@scottish.parliament.uk
Private Secretary: David Thomson *Tel:* 0131-244 2186
Diary Secretary: Catherine McGoldrick *Tel:* 0131-244 5131 *Fax:* 0131-244 3563
Constituency Assistant: Room 3.18 PHQ, John Orton
Tel: 0131-477 4511 *Fax:* 0131-477 2816 (Constituency)
HAMILTON, Duncan *(SNP)* – Highlands and Islands*
Tel: 0131-348 5700 *Fax:* 0131-348 5895 *E-mail:* duncan.hamilton.msp@scottish.parliament.uk
Parliamentary Assistant: Shirley-Anne Somerville *Tel:* 0131-348 5700 *Fax:* 0131-348 5737
E-mail: shirley-anne.somerville@scottish.parliament.uk
HARDING, Keith *(Con)* – Mid Scotland and Fife*
Tel: 0131-348 5643 *E-mail:* keith.harding.msp@scottish.parliament.uk
Parliamentary Assistant: Anne Harding
HARPER, Robin *(Green)* – Lothian*
E-mail: robin.harper.msp@scottish.parliament.uk
Researcher: Steve Burgess
Administrator: Alison Johnstone *Tel:* 0131-348 5927 *Fax:* 0131-348 5972
HENRY, Hugh *(Lab)* – Paisley South
Tel: 0131-348 5928 *E-mail:* hugh.henry.msp@scottish.parliament.uk
Parliamentary Assistant: Dannielle Henry
HOME ROBERTSON, John *(Lab)* – East Lothian
Tel: 0131-348 5839 *E-mail:* john.home-robertson.msp@scottish.parliament.uk
Private Secretary: Stuart McLean *Tel:* 0131-244 4425 *Fax:* 0131-244 4458
Researcher: Simon Tierman

HUGHES, Janis *(Lab)* – Glasgow Rutherglen
Tel: 0131-348 5820 *E-mail:* janis.hughes.msp@scottish.parliament.uk
Parliamentary Assistant: Katie Semple
HYSLOP, Fiona *(SNP)* – Lothian*
Tel: 0131-348 5920 *E-mail:* fiona.hyslop.msp@scottish.parliament.uk
Parliamentary Assistants: Isobel Hutton *Tel:* 0131-348 5921
Fax: 0131-348 5716 Gordon Archer *Tel:* 0131-348 5925
INGRAM, Adam *(SNP)* – South of Scotland*
Tel: 0131-348 5719 *E-mail:* adam.ingram.msp@scottish.parliament.uk
Parliamentary Assistant: Karen Newton *Tel:* 0131-348 5012 *Fax:* 0131-348 5735
JACKSON, Gordon *(Lab)* – Glasgow Govan
Tel: 0131-348 5898 *E-mail:* gordon.jackson.msp@scottish.parliament.uk
JACKSON, Sylvia *(Lab)* – Stirling
Tel: 0131-348 5742 *E-mail:* sylvia.jackson.msp@scottish.parliament.uk
Parliamentary Assistant: Graham Fraser
JAMIESON, Cathy *(Lab/Co-op)* – Carrick, Cumnock and Doon Valley
Tel: 0131-348 5776 *E-mail:* cathy.jamieson.msp@scottish.parliament.uk
Parliamentary Assistant: John Dalzell
Researcher: Jackson Cullinane
JAMIESON, Margaret *(Lab)* – Kilmarnock and Loudoun
Tel: 0131-348 5774 *E-mail:* margaret.jamieson.msp@scottish.parliament.uk
Parliamentary Assistant: Andrew Kerrigan
JENKINS, Ian *(Lib Dem)* – Tweeddale, Ettrick and Lauderdale
Tel: 0131-348 5802 *E-mail:* ian.jenkins.msp@scottish.parliament.uk
Parliamentary Assistant: Rosemary Macdonald *Tel:* 0131-348 5801 *Fax:* 0131-348 5964
JOHNSTON, Nick *(Con)* – Mid Scotland and Fife*
E-mail: nicholas.johnston.msp@scottish.parliament.uk
Parliamentary Assistant: Gail Whitton *Tel:* 0131-348 5645
JOHNSTONE, Alex *(Con)* – North East Scotland*
Tel: 0131-348 5649 *E-mail:* alexander.johnstone.msp@scottish.parliament.uk
Secretary: Liz Cameron *Tel:* 0131-348 5654
KERR, Andy *(Lab)* – East Kilbride
Tel: 0131-348 5902 *E-mail:* andy.kerr.msp@scottish.parliament.uk
Parliamentary Assistant: Sam Harty
LAMONT, Johann *(Lab/Co-op)* – Glasgow Pollok
Tel: 0131-348 5846 *E-mail:* johann.lamont.msp@scottish.parliament.uk
Parliamentary Assistant: Stephen Law
LIVINGSTONE, Marilyn *(Lab/Co-op)* – Kirkcaldy
Tel: 0131-348 5744 *E-mail:* marilyn.livingstone.msp@scottish.parliament.uk
Parliamentary Assistant: Neil Crooks
LOCHHEAD, Richard *(SNP)* – North East Scotland*
Tel: 0131-348 5713 *E-mail:* richard.lochhead.msp@scottish.parliament.uk
Parliamentary Assistant: Jean Pyle *Tel:* 0131-348 5712 *Fax:* 0131-348 5944
LYON, George *(Lib Dem)* – Argyll and Bute
Tel: 0131-348 5787 *E-mail:* george.lyon.msp@scottish.parliament.uk
Parliamentary Assistant: Euan Page *Tel:* 0131-348 5788 *Fax:* 0131-348 5807
McALLION, John *(Lab)* – Dundee East
Tel: 0131-348 5931 *E-mail:* john.mcallion.msp@scottish.parliament.uk
Parliamentary Assistant: Richard McCready *Tel:* 0131-348 5930
MacASKILL, Kenny *(SNP)* – Lothian*
Tel: 0131-348 5722 *E-mail:* kenny.macaskill.msp@scottish.parliament.uk
Parliamentary Assistant: Karen Newton *Tel:* 0131-348 5721 *Fax:* 0131-348 5735
Researcher: Craig Milroy
McAVEETY, Frank *(Lab/Co-op)* – Glasgow Shettleston
Tel: 0131-348 5906 *E-mail:* frank.mcaveety.msp@scottish.parliament.uk
Private Secretary: Al Gibson *Tel:* 0131-244 0228 *Fax:* 0131-244 7403
Constituency Contact: Alex Glass *Tel:* 0141-764 0175

McCABE, Tom *(Lab)* – Hamilton South
  Tel: 0131-348 5830 *E-mail:* tom.mccabe.msp@scottish.parliament.uk
  Private Secretary: Ian Campbell *Tel:* 0131-348 5573 *Fax:* 0131-348 5564
  Assistant Private Secretary: Audrey Snedden *Tel:* 0131-348 5573 *Fax:* 0131-348 5564
  Researcher: Hayley Moncur *Tel:* 01698 454018 *Fax:* 01698 454222
McCONNELL, Jack *(Lab)* – Motherwell and Wishaw
  Tel: 0131-348 5831 *E-mail:* jack.mcconnell.msp@scottish.parliament.uk
  Private Secretary: Deborah Smith *Tel:* 0131-244 1558 *Fax:* 0131-244 1555
  Constituency Personal Secretary: Christina Marshall *Tel:* 0131-348 5831 (VQ)
  Tel: 01698 303040 *Fax:* 01698 303060 (Constituency)
MACDONALD, Lewis *(Lab)* – Aberdeen Central
  Tel: 0131-348 5915 *E-mail:* lewis.macdonald.msp@scottish.parliament.uk
  Parliamentary Assistant: David McIntosh
MacDONALD, Margo *(SNP)* – Lothian*
  Tel: 0131-348 5715 *E-mail:* margo.macdonald.msp@scottish.parliament.uk
  Parliamentary Assistant: Peter Warren *Tel:* 0131-348 5714 *Fax:* 0131-348 5716
McGRIGOR, Jamie *(Con)* – Highlands and Islands*
  Tel: 0131-348 5648 *E-mail:* jamie.mcgrigor.msp@scottish.parliament.uk
  Secretary: Amy Kenyon
McGUGAN, Irene *(SNP)* – North East Scotland*
  Tel: 0131-348 5711 *E-mail:* irene.mcgugan.msp@scottish.parliament.uk
  Parliamentary Assistant: Tel: 0131-348 5710 *Fax:* 0131-348 5944
MACINTOSH, Kenneth *(Lab)* – Eastwood
  Tel: 0131-348 5896 *E-mail:* kenneth.macintosh.msp@scottish.parliament.uk
McINTOSH, Lyndsay *(Con)* – Central Scotland*
  Tel: 0131-348 5639 *E-mail:* lyndsay.mcintosh.msp@scottish.parliament.uk
  Secretary: Sandra Russell *Fax:* 0131-348 5655
MacKAY, Angus *(Lab)* – Edinburgh South
  Tel: 0131-348 5025 *E-mail:* angus.mackay.msp@scottish.parliament.uk
  Private Secretary: Fiona Armstrong *Tel:* 0131-244 4579 *Fax:* 0131-244 2121
  Diary Secretary: Samantha Kibble *Tel:* 0131-244 4578
  Researcher and Constituency Assistant: Gail Birrell *Tel:* 0131-348 5025
MacLEAN, Kate *(Lab)* – Dundee West
  Tel: 0131-348 5758 *E-mail:* kate.maclean.msp@scottish.parliament.uk
  Researcher: Shona Main *Tel:* 0131-348 5757
McLEISH, Henry *(Lab)* – Central Fife
  E-mail: henry.mcleish.msp@scottish.parliament.uk
  Private Secretary: Joan Seratini *Tel:* 0141-242 5475 *Fax:* 0141-242 5462
  Constituency Assistant: Gwen Newall *Tel:* 01592 755540 *Fax:* 01592 610325
McLEOD, Fiona *(SNP)* – West of Scotland*
  Tel: 0131-348 5670
  E-mail: fiona.mcleod.msp@scottish.parliament.uk
  Secretary: Kate Higgins *Tel:* 0131-348 5669 *Fax:* 0131-348 5958
  E-mail: kate.higgins@scottish.parliament.uk
McLETCHIE, David *(Con)* – Lothian*
  E-mail: david.mcletchie.msp@scottish.parliament.uk
  Parliamentary Assistant: Ann Menzies *Tel:* 0131-348 5659 *Fax:* 0131-348 5935
McMAHON, Michael *(Lab)* – Hamilton North and Bellshill
  Tel: 0131-348 5828 *E-mail:* michael.mcmahon.msp@scottish.parliament.uk
  Parliamentary Assistant: Martin Grey
MACMILLAN, Maureen *(Lab)* – Highlands and Islands*
  Tel: 0131-348 5766 *E-mail:* maureen.macmillan.msp@scottish.parliament.uk
  Parliamentary Assistant: Richard Welsh *Tel:* 0131-348 5766 *Fax:* 0131-348 5767
  *Secretary:*Andrene Maxwell
McNEIL, Duncan *(Lab)* – Greenock and Inverclyde
  Tel: 0131-348 5913 *E-mail:* duncan.mcneil.msp@scottish.parliament.uk
  Parliamentary Assistant: Margaret McDade

McNEILL, Pauline *(Lab)* – Glasgow Kelvin
  Tel: 0131-348 5910 *E-mail:* pauline.mcneill.msp@scottish.parliament.uk
  Researcher: Lynn Henderson *Tel:* 0131-348 5909
McNULTY, Des *(Lab)* – Clydebank and Milngavie
  Tel: 0131-348 5918 *E-mail:* des.mcnulty.msp@scottish.parliament.uk
MARTIN, Paul *(Lab)* – Glasgow Springburn
  Tel: 0131-348 5844 *E-mail:* paul.martin.msp@scottish.parliament.uk
MARWICK, Tricia *(SNP)* – Mid Scotland and Fife*
  Tel: 0131-348 5861/5680 *E-mail:* tricia.marwick.msp@scottish.parliament.uk
  Parliamentary Assistant: Craig Milroy *Tel:* 0131-348 5012 *Fax:* 0131-348 5708
MATHESON, Michael *(SNP)* – Central Scotland*
  Tel: 0131-348 5672 *E-mail:* michael.matheson.msp@scottish.parliament.uk
  Parliamentary Assistant: Andrew Maclachlan *Tel:* 0131-348 5671 *Fax:* 0131-348 5958
MONTEITH, Brian *(Con)* – Mid Scotland and Fife*
  Tel: 0131-348 5644 *E-mail:* brian.monteith.msp@scottish.parliament.uk
  Secretary: Amy Kenyon
MORGAN, Alasdair *(SNP)* – Galloway and Upper Nithsdale
  Tel: 0131-348 5728 *E-mail:* alasdair.morgan.msp@scottish.parliament.uk
  Parliamentary Assistant: Malcolm Fleming *Tel:* 0131-348 5727 *Fax:* 0131-348 5945
MORRISON, Alasdair *(Lab)* – Western Isles (Eilean Siar)
  E-mail: alasdair.morrison.msp@scottish.parliament.uk
  Private Secretary: Juliet Grimes *Tel:* 0141-242 5777 *Fax:* 0141-242 5462/5709
  Diary Secretary: Wendy Fleming *Tel:* 0141-242 5778
  Constituency Contact: Ann Ross *Tel:* 01851 704684 *Fax:* 01851 703048
MULDOON, Bristow *(Lab)* – Livingston
  Tel: 0131-348 5760 *E-mail:* bristow.muldoon.msp@scottish.parliament.uk
  Parliamentary Assistant: John Duncan *Tel:* 0131-348 5759
MULLIGAN, Mary *(Lab)* – Linlithgow
  Tel: 0131-348 5779 *E-mail:* mary.mulligan.msp@scottish.parliament.uk
  Parliamentary Assistant: Heather Smart
MUNDELL, David *(Con)* – South of Scotland*
  Tel: 0131-348 5635 *E-mail:* david.mundell.msp@scottish.parliament.uk
  Secretary: Gillian Gillies *Tel:* 0131-348 5638 *Fax:* 0131-348 5932
MUNRO, John Farquhar *(Lib Dem)* – Ross, Skye and Inverness West
  Tel: 0131-348 5793 *E-mail:* john.munro.msp@scottish.parliament.uk
  Parliamentary Researcher: Jamie Paterson *Tel:* 0131-348 5790 *Fax:* 0131-348 5807
MURRAY, Elaine *(Lab)* – Dumfries
  Tel: 0131-348 5768 *E-mail:* elaine.murray.msp@scottish.parliament.uk
NEIL, Alex *(SNP)* – Central Scotland*
  Tel: 0131-348 5703 *E-mail:* alex.neil.msp@scottish.parliament.uk
  Parliamentary Assistant: Luke Cavanagh *Tel:* 0131-348 5702 *Fax:* 0131-348 5716/5895
OLDFATHER, Irene *(Lab)* – Cunninghame South
  Tel: 0131-348 5769 *E-mail:* irene.oldfather.msp@scottish.parliament.uk
PATERSON, Gil *(SNP)* – Central Scotland*
  Tel: 0131-348 5922 *E-mail:* gil.paterson.msp@scottish.parliament.uk
  Parliamentary Assistant: Karen Newton *Tel:* 0131-348 5923/5924 *Fax:* 0131-348 5943/5716
  Researcher: Jane Devine
PEACOCK, Peter *(Lab)* – Highlands and Islands*
  E-mail: peter.peacock.msp@scottish.parliament.uk
  Parliamentary Assistant: Richard Welsh *Tel:* 0131-348 5766 *Fax:* 0131-348 5767
  Secretary: Andrene Maxwell
  Private Secretary: Steven Szymoszowskyj *Tel:* 0131-244 1469 *Fax:* 0131-244 7401
  Constituency Secretary: Andrene Maxwell *Tel:* 01349 867650 *Fax:* 01349 867762
PEATTIE, Cathy *(Lab)* – Falkirk East
  Tel: 0131-348 5746 *E-mail:* cathy.peattie.msp@scottish.parliament.uk
  Parliamentary Assistant: Dave Smith *Tel:* 0131-348 5747

QUINAN, Lloyd *(SNP)* – West of Scotland*
 Tel: 0131-348 5734 *E-mail:* lloyd.quinan.msp@scottish.parliament.uk
 Parliamentary Assistant: Amanda Quinan *Tel:* 0131-348 5733 *Fax:* 0131-348 5735
RADCLIFFE, Nora *(Lib Dem)* – Gordon
 Tel: 0131-348 5804 *E-mail:* nora.radcliffe.msp@scottish.parliament.uk
 Parliamentary Researcher: Barry Cameron *Tel:* 0131-348 5803 *Fax:* 0131-348 5964
RAFFAN, Keith *(Lib Dem)* – Mid Scotland and Fife*
 Tel: 0131-348 5800 *E-mail:* keith.raffan.msp@scottish.parliament.uk
 Parliamentary Assistant: (Vacant) *Tel:* 0131-348 5799 *Fax:* 0131-348 5808
REID, George *(SNP)* – Mid Scotland and Fife*
 Tel: 0131-348 5312 *E-mail:* george.reid.msp@scottish.parliament.uk
 Parliamentary Assistant: Catriona Black and Susan Love
 Tel: 0131-348 5911 *Fax:* 0131-348 5996
ROBISON, Shona *(SNP)* – North East Scotland*
 Tel: 0131-348 5706/5707 *Fax:* 0131-348 5949
 E-mail: shona.robison.msp@scottish.parliament.uk
ROBSON, Euan *(Lib Dem)* – Roxburgh and Berwickshire
 Tel: 0131-348 5806 *E-mail:* euan.robson.msp@scottish.parliament.uk
 Parliamentary Researcher: Fiona Milne *Tel:* 0131-348 5805 *Fax:* 0131-348 5808
RUMBLES, Mike *(Lib Dem)* – West Aberdeenshire and Kincardine
 Tel: 0131-348 5798 *E-mail:* mike.rumbles.msp@scottish.parliament.uk
 Parliamentary Assistant: Bruce Purdon *Tel:* 0131-348 5797 *Fax:* 0131-348 5964
RUSSELL, Michael *(SNP)* – South of Scotland*
 Tel: 0131-348 5678 *E-mail:* michael.russell.msp@scottish.parliament.uk
 Parliamentary Assistant: Dr Alasdair Allan *Tel:* 0131-348 5679 *Fax:* 0131-348 5708
SALMOND, Alex *(SNP)* – Banff and Buchan
 Tel: 0131-348 5739 *E-mail:* alex.salmond.msp@scottish.parliament.uk
 Researchers: Noel Dolan *Tel:* 0131-348 5013
 Sarah Paterson *Tel:* 0131-348 5014 *Fax:* 0131-348 5709
SCANLON, Mary *(Con)* – Highlands and Islands*
 Tel: 0131-348 5650 *E-mail:* mary.scanlon.msp@scottish.parliament.uk
 Researcher: Jennifer Birnie
SCOTT, John *(Con)* – Ayr
 Tel: 0131-348 5664 *E-mail:* john.scott.msp@scottish.parliament.uk
 Private Secretary: Anna Traquair *Tel:* 0131-348 5611 *Fax:* 0131-348 5940
SCOTT, Tavish *(Lib Dem)* – Shetland
 E-mail: tavish.scott.msp@scottish.parliament.uk
 Parliamentary Researcher: Alistair Easton *Tel:* 0131-348 5815 *Fax:* 0131-348 5807
SHERIDAN, Tommy *(SSP)* – Glasgow*
 Tel: 0131-348 5631 *E-mail:* tommy.sheridan.msp@scottish.parliament.uk
 Researchers: Felicity Garvie, Hugh Kerr *Tel:* 0131-348 5632 *Fax:* 0131-348 5946
 Constituency: *Tel:* 0141-221 7714 *Fax:* 0141-221 7715
SIMPSON, Richard *(Lab)* – Ochil
 Tel: 0131-348 5740 *E-mail:* richard.simpson.msp@scottish.parliament.uk
SMITH, Elaine *(Lab)* – Coatbridge and Chryston
 Tel: 0131-348 5824 *Fax:* 0131-348 5834
 E-mail: elaine.smith.msp@scottish.parliament.uk
 Researcher: Joanne Milligan
SMITH, Iain *(Lib Dem)* – North East Fife
 E-mail: iain.smith.msp@scottish.parliament.uk
 Parliamentary Assistant: Callum Irving *Tel:* 0131-348 5817 *Fax:* 0131-348 5962
 Private Secretary: Callum Stanners *Tel:* 0131-348 5816 *Fax:* 0131-348 5564
 Senior Researcher: Matthew Clark
 Constituency Assistant: Niall Dowds *Tel:* 01334 656361 *Fax:* 01334 654045
SMITH, Margaret *(Lib Dem)* – Edinburgh West
 Tel: 0131-348 5785 *E-mail:* margaret.smith.msp@scottish.parliament.uk
 Personal Assistant: Ann Taylor *Tel:* 0131-348 5785 *Fax:* 0131-348 5965

STEEL, Rt Hon Sir David KBE *(Lib Dem)* – Lothian*
Tel: 0131-348 5302 *Fax:* 0131-348 5301 *E-mail:* presiding.officer@scottish.parliament.uk
Private Secretary: Huw Williams
STEPHEN, Nicol *(Lib Dem)* – Aberdeen South
Tel: 0131-348 5818 *E-mail:* nicol.stephen.msp@scottish.parliament.uk
Private Secretary: Liz Shea *Tel:* 0141-242 5587 *Fax:* 0141-242 5462/5709
Constituency Secretary: Vicki Harris *Tel:* 01224 252728 *Fax:* 01224 455678
STONE, Jamie *(Lib Dem)* – Caithness, Sutherland and Easter Ross
Tel: 0131-348 5789 *E-mail:* jamie.stone.msp@scottish.parliament.uk
Parliamentary Researcher: Jamie Paterson *Tel:* 0131-348 5790 *Fax:* 0131-348 5807
STURGEON, Nicola *(SNP)* – Glasgow*
Tel: 0131-348 5695 *E-mail:* nicola.sturgeon.msp@scottish.parliament.uk
Parliamentary Assistant: Hilary Brown *Tel:* 0131-348 5694 *Fax:* 0131-348 5952
SWINNEY, John *(SNP)* – North Tayside
Tel: 0131-348 5718 *E-mail:* john.swinney.msp@scottish.parliament.uk
Parliamentary Assistant: Phil Henderson *Tel:* 0131-348 5717 *Fax:* 0131-348 5946
THOMSON, Elaine *(Lab)* – Aberdeen North
Tel: 0131-348 5917 *Fax:* 0131-348 5979 *E-mail:* elaine.thomson.msp@scottish.parliament.uk
Secretary: Contact Constituency Office *Tel:* 01224 699666
TOSH, Murray *(Con)* – South of Scotland*
Tel: 0131-348 5637 *Fax:* 0131-348 5932 *E-mail:* murray.tosh.msp@scottish.parliament.uk
Researcher: Kevin Ancell
ULLRICH, Kay *(SNP)* – West of Scotland*
Tel: 0131-348 5667 *Fax:* 0131-348 5958 *E-mail:* kay.ullrich.msp@scottish.parliament.uk
Parliamentary Assistant: Campbell Martin *Tel:* 0131-348 5668 *Fax:* 0131-348 5737
WALLACE, Ben *(Con)* – North East Scotland*
Tel: 0131-348 5651 *E-mail:* ben.wallace.msp@scottish.parliament.uk
Secretary: Liz Cameron *Tel:* 0131-348 5654
Researcher: Liza Cooke *Tel:* 0131-348 5652 *Fax:* 0131-348 5934
Press Officer: Marcus Boothe
Constituency Contact: Linda Lawson *Tel:* 01569 762785 *Fax:* 01569 767177
WALLACE, Jim QC *(Lib Dem)* – Orkney
E-mail: jim.wallace.msp@scottish.parliament.uk
Parliamentary Researcher and Constituency Assistant: Alistair Easton
Tel: 0131-348 5815 *Fax:* 0131-348 5807
Private Secretary: Michael Kellet *Tel:* 0131-244 4576 *Fax:* 0131-244 2756
WATSON, Mike *(Lab)* – Glasgow Cathcart
Tel: 0131-348 5840 *E-mail:* mike.watson.msp@scottish.parliament.uk
Parliamentary Assistant: Ann Henderson *Tel:* 0131-348 5841
WELSH, Andrew *(SNP)* – Angus
Tel: 0131-348 5690 *E-mail:* andrew.welsh.msp@scottish.parliament.uk
Parliamentary Assistant: Andrew Hinson *Tel:* 0131-348 5691 *Fax:* 0131-348 5953
WHITE, Sandra *(SNP)* – Glasgow*
Tel: 0131-348 5689 *E-mail:* sandra.white.msp@scottish.parliament.uk
Parliamentary Assistant: Kenny McLean *Tel:* 0131-348 5688 *Fax:* 0131-348 5954
WHITEFIELD, Karen *(Lab)* – Airdrie and Shotts
Tel: 0131-348 5832 *E-mail:* karen.whitefield.msp@scottish.parliament.uk
Parliamentary Assistant: David Fagan *Tel:* 0131-348 5833
WILSON, Allan *(Lab)* – Cunninghame North
Tel: 0131-348 5772 *E-mail:* allan.wilson.msp@scottish.parliament.uk
WILSON, Andrew *(SNP)* – Central Scotland*
Tel: 0131-348 5674 *Fax:* 0131-348 5677 *E-mail:* andrew.wilson.msp@scottish.parliament.uk
Parliamentary Assistant: Stephen Gethins *Tel:* 0131-348 5673 *Fax:* 0131-348 5895
YOUNG, John *(Con)* – West of Scotland*
Tel: 0131-348 5640 *E-mail:* john.young.msp@scottish.parliament.uk
Secretary: Sandra Russell

* *Region*

NATIONAL ASSEMBLY FOR WALES
CYNULLIAD CENEDLAETHOL CYMRU

Cardiff Bay
Cardiff CF99 1NA
029 2082 5111 Cathays Park
E-mail: assembly.info@wales.gsi.gov.uk
Website: www.wales.gov.uk
(To move to new Assembly building at Pier Head, Cardiff in 2001)

Election 6 May 1999
26 May 1999 Official Opening by HM The Queen

Future elections are to be held every four years.

ELECTORAL SYSTEM

The election was conducted using a method combining the traditional first past the post system and a form of proportional representation called the Additional Member System. Each voter cast two votes. One vote was for one of 40 constituency members, based on the Westminster parliament constituencies. The second went towards the election of 20 regional members, four for each of the five regions used in the European Parliament elections. These seats ensure that each party's representation in the Assembly reflects its overall share of the vote.

The Assembly operates a three-day week conducted during normal business hours.

POWERS AND RESPONSIBILITIES

The Assembly decides on its priorities and allocates funds in the following policy areas as they apply to Wales:

agriculture	industry
ancient monuments and historic buildings	local government
culture	social services
economic development	sport and leisure
education and training	tourism
environment	town and country planning
health	transport and roads
highways	Welsh language
housing	

The Assembly does not have powers to enact primary legislation.

The following areas remain the responsibility of Westminster:

broadcasting policy	labour market policy
competition policy	macro-economic policy
defence	National Lottery
fiscal and common markets policy	police service
fire service	prisons
foreign affairs	social security benefits
justice system	taxation

The Secretary of State for Wales represents the interests of Wales in the Cabinet of the UK Government.

COMPOSITION

The Assembly has 60 members elected by universal sufferage.

The members elect the First Secretary, who appoints Assembly Secretaries to be responsible for particular policy areas. The Secretaries and the First Secretary make up the Cabinet, which is responsible to the Assembly.

STATE OF PARTIES (October 2000)

	First past post	*Top up*	*Total seats*
Labour	27	1	28
Plaid Cymru	9	8	17
Conservative	1	8	9
Liberal Democrat	3	3	6
			60 seats

Members (AMs)

Lab	Labour Party
PC	Plaid Cymru
Con	Conservative
Lib Dem	Liberal Democrats
Lab/Co-op	Labour/Co-operative

	Party	*Constituency/Region**	*Majority*
BARRETT Lorraine	Lab/Co-op	Cardiff South and Penarth	6,803
BATES Michael	Lib Dem	Montgomeryshire	5,504
BLACK Peter	Lib Dem	South Wales West*	
BOURNE Nicholas	Con	Mid and West Wales*	
BUTLER Rosemary	Lab	Newport West	4,710
CAIRNS Alun	Con	South Wales West*	
CHAPMAN Christine	Lab/Co-op	Cynon Valley	677
Deputy Assembly Secretary			
DAFIS Cynog	PC	Mid and West Wales*	
DAVIDSON Jane	Lab	Pontypridd	1,575
Minister for Education and Lifelong Learning			
DAVIES Andrew	Lab	Swansea West	1,926
Business Manager			
DAVIES David	Con	Monmouth	2,712
DAVIES Geraint	PC	Rhondda	2,285
DAVIES Glyn	Con	Mid and West Wales*	
DAVIES Janet	PC	South Wales West*	
DAVIES Jocelyn	PC	South Wales East*	
†DAVIES Rt Hon Ron	Lab	Caerphilly	2,861
EDWARDS Dr Richard	Lab	Preseli Pembrokeshire	2,738
‡ELIS-THOMAS Dafydd	PC	Meirionnydd Nant Conwy	8,742
Presiding Officer			
ESSEX Sue	Lab	Cardiff North	2,304
Minister for Environment			
EVANS Delyth	Lab	Mid and West Wales*	
FELD Val	Lab	Swansea East	3,781
GERMAN Michael	Lib Dem	South Wales East*	
Deputy First Minister			
GIBBONS Brian	Lab	Aberavon	6,743
GRAHAM William	Con	South Wales East*	
GREGORY Janice	Lab	Ogmore	4,565

GRIFFITHS John	Lab/Co-op	Newport East	5,111
GWYTHER Christine	Lab	Carmarthen West and South	
		Pembrokeshire	1,492
HALFORD Alison	Lab	Delyn	5,417
HANCOCK Brian	PC	Islwyn	604
HART Edwina MBE	Lab	Gower	3,160
Minister for Finance and Communities			
HUMPHREYS Christine	Lib Dem	North Wales*	
HUTT Jane	Lab	Vale of Glamorgan	926
Minister for Health and Social Services			
JARMAN Pauline	PC	South Wales Central*	
JONES Ann	Lab	Vale of Clwyd	3,341
JONES Carwyn	Lab	Bridgend	4,258
Minister for Rural Affairs			
JONES Elin	PC	Ceredigion	10,249
JONES Gareth OBE	PC	Conwy	114
JONES Helen Mary	PC	Llanelli	688
†JONES Ieuan Wyn	PC	Ynys Môn	9,288
LAW Peter	Lab/Co-op	Blaenau Gwent	10,568
LEWIS Huw	Lab/Co-op	Merthyr Tydfil and Rhymney	4,214
LLOYD Dr David	PC	South Wales West*	
†MAREK Dr John	Lab	Wrexham	6,472
Deputy Presiding Officer			
MELDING David	Con	South Wales Central*	
MIDDLEHURST Tom	Lab	Alyn and Deeside	6,359
MORGAN Jonathan	Con	South Wales Central*	
†MORGAN Rt Hon Rhodri	Lab	Cardiff West	10,859
First Minister			
NEAGLE Lynne	Lab	Torfaen	5,285
PUGH Alun	Lab	Clwyd West	760
Deputy Assembly Secretary			
RANDERSON Jennifer	Lib Dem	Cardiff Central	3,168
RICHARDS Rod	Con	North Wales*	
ROGERS Peter	Con	North Wales*	
RYDER Janet	PC	North Wales*	
SINCLAIR Karen	Lab	Clwyd South	3,685
THOMAS Gwenda	Lab	Neath	2,618
THOMAS Owen John	PC	South Wales Central*	
THOMAS Rhodri	PC	Carmarthen East and Dinefwr	6,980
†WIGLEY Rt Hon Dafydd	PC	Caernarfon	12,273
WILLIAMS Kirsty	Lib Dem	Brecon and Radnorshire	5,852
WILLIAMS Dr Philip	PC	South Wales East*	

† *Also a Member of the House of Commons*
‡ *Also a Member of the House of Lords*

Dod *on* Line
An Electronic Directory without rival . . .

AMs' biographies and photographs
available with daily updates *via* the internet

For a *free* trial, call Oliver Cox on 020 7828 7256

AMs REPRESENTING THE REGIONS

Mid and West Wales
BOURNE Nicholas	Con
DAFIS Cynog	PC
DAVIES Glyn	Con
EVANS Delyth	Lab

North Wales
HUMPHREYS Christine	Lib Dem
RICHARDS Rod	Con
ROGERS Peter	Con
RYDER Janet	PC

South Wales Central
JARMAN Pauline	PC
MELDING David	Con
MORGAN Jonathan	Con
THOMAS Owen John	PC

South Wales East
DAVIES Jocelyn	PC
GERMAN Michael	Lib Dem
GRAHAM William	Con
WILLIAMS Dr Philip	PC

South Wales West
BLACK Peter	Lib Dem
CAIRNS Alun	Con
DAVIES Janet	PC
LLOYD Dr David	PC

MEMBERS BY PARTY

Constituency/Region*

LABOUR PARTY (23)
Labour/Co-operative Party
BUTLER Rosemary	Newport West
DAVIDSON Jane	Pontypridd
DAVIES Andrew	Swansea West
DAVIES Rt Hon Ron	Caerphilly
EDWARDS Dr Richard	Preseli Pembrokeshire
ESSEX Sue	Cardiff North
EVANS Delyth	Mid and West Wales*
FELD Val	Swansea East
GIBBONS Brian	Aberavon
GREGORY Janice	Ogmore
GWYTHER Christine	Carmarthen West and South Pembrokeshire
HALFORD Alison	Delyn
HART Edwina	Gower
HUTT Jane	Vale of Glamorgan
JONES Ann	Vale of Clwyd
JONES Carwyn	Bridgend
MAREK Dr John	Wrexham
MIDDLEHURST Tom	Alyn and Deeside
MORGAN Rt Hon Rhodri	Cardiff West
NEAGLE Lynne	Torfaen
PUGH Alun	Clwyd West
SINCLAIR Karen	Clwyd South
THOMAS Gwenda	Neath

PLAID CYMRU (17)
DAFIS Cynog	Mid and West Wales*
DAVIES Geraint	Rhondda
DAVIES Janet	South Wales West*
DAVIES Jocelyn	South Wales East*
ELIS-THOMAS Dafydd	Meirionnydd Nant Conwy
HANCOCK Brian *(Deputy Whip)*	Islwyn

JARMAN Pauline	South Wales Central*
JONES Elin *Chief Whip)*	Ceredigion
JONES Gareth	Conwy
JONES Helen Mary	Llanelli
JONES Ieuan Wyn *Leader)*	Ynys Môn
LLOYD Dr David	South Wales West*
RYDER Janet	North Wales*
THOMAS Owen John	South Wales Central*
THOMAS Rhodri	Carmarthen East and Dinefwr
WIGLEY Rt Hon Dafydd	Caernarfon
WILLIAMS Dr Philip	South Wales East*

CONSERVATIVE PARTY (9)

BOURNE Nicholas *(Leader)*	Mid and West Wales*
CAIRNS Alun	South Wales West*
DAVIES David *(Chief Whip)*	Monmouth
DAVIES Glyn	Mid and West Wales*
GRAHAM William	South Wales East*
MELDING David	South Wales Central*
MORGAN Jonathan	South Wales Central*
RICHARDS Rod	North Wales*
ROGERS Peter	North Wales*

LIBERAL DEMOCRAT PARTY (6)

BATES Michael	Montgomeryshire
BLACK Peter	South Wales West*
GERMAN Michael *(Leader)*	South Wales East*
HUMPHREYS Christine	North Wales*
RANDERSON Jennifer *(Whip)*	Cardiff Central
WILLIAMS Kirsty	Brecon and Radnorshire

LABOUR/CO-OPERATIVE PARTY (5)

BARRETT Lorraine	Cardiff South and Penarth
CHAPMAN Christine	Cynon Valley
GRIFFITHS John	Newport East
LAW Peter	Blaenau Gwent
LEWIS Huw	Merthyr Tydfil and Rhymney

* Indicates Region

WOMEN MEMBERS

BARRETT Lorraine	HUMPHREYS Christine
BUTLER Rosemary	HUTT Jane
CHAPMAN Christine	JARMAN Pauline
DAVIDSON Jane	JONES Ann
DAVIES Janet	JONES Elin
DAVIES Jocelyn	JONES Helen Mary
ESSEX Sue	NEAGLE Lynne
EVANS Delyth	RANDERSON Jennifer
FELD Val	RYDER Janet
GREGORY Janice	SINCLAIR Karen
GWYTHER Christine	THOMAS Gwenda
HALFORD Alison	WILLIAMS Kirsty
HART Edwina	

Regions* and Constituencies

Mid and West Wales*
Brecon and Radnorshire
Carmarthen East and Dinefwr
Carmarthen West and South Pembrokeshire
Ceredigion
Llanelli
Meirionydd Nant Conwy
Montgomeryshire
Presli Pembrokeshire

North Wales*
Alyn and Deeside
Caernarfon
Clwyd South
Clwyd West
Conwy
Delyn
Vale of Clwyd
Wrexham
Ynys Môn

South Wales Central*
Cardiff Central
Cardiff North
Cardiff South and Penarth

Cardiff West
Cynon Valley
Pontypridd
Rhondda
Vale of Glamorgan

South Wales East*
Blaenau Gwent
Caerphilly
Islwyn
Merthyr Tydfil and Rhymney
Monmouth
Newport East
Newport West
Torfaen

South Wales West*
Aberavon
Bridgend
Gower
Neath
Ogmore
Swansea East
Swansea West

National Assembly for Wales
Cynulliad Cenedlaethol Cymru

First Minister

Presiding Officer
Deputy Presiding Officer

Rt Hon **Rhodri Morgan** AM

Lord Dafydd Elis-Thomas AM
John Marek AM

CABINET (October 2000)
First Minister
Deputy First Minister,
Minister for Economic Development
Business Manager [Whip]
Minister for Finance and Communities
Minister for Education and Lifelong Learning
Minister for Culture and Sport
Minister for Environment
Minister for Rural Affairs
Minister for Health and Social Services

Rhodri Morgan (Labour)

Michael German (Lib Dem)
Andrew Davies (Labour)
Edwina Hart (Labour)
Jane Davidson (Labour)
Jenny Randerson (Lib Dem)
Sue Essex (Labour)
Carwyn Jones (Labour)
Jane Hutt (Labour)

PRINCIPAL OFFICERS AND OFFICIALS
Permanent Secretary
Senior Director, Economic Affairs, Transport,
    Planning and Environment
Senior Director, Social Policy and Local Government
Clerk to the Assembly
Deputy Clerk and Head of Office of Presiding Officer
Counsel General
Director Personnel, Management and
    Business Services
Principal Finance Officer

Jon Shortridge

Derek Jones
George Craig
John Lloyd CB
(Vacant)
Winston Roddick QC

Peter Gregory
David Richards

Ministerial Responsibilities

First Minister (Rt Hon **Rhodri Morgan** AM)
Heading government in Wales; north Wales
E-mail: rhodri.morgan@wales.gsi.gov.uk
Interim Special Adviser: Kevin Brennan
Principal Private Secretary: Anna Coleman *Tel:* 029 2089 8765
E-mail: anna.coleman@wales.gsi.gov.uk *Fax:* 029 2089 8198
Private Secretaries: Rose Stewart *Tel:* 029 2089 8764 *E-mail:* rose.stewart@wales.gsi.gov.uk
Prys Davies *Tel:* 029 2089 8763 *E-mail:* prys.davies@wales.gsi.gov.uk
Diary Secretaries: Beverly Summers *Tel:* 029 2089 8197 *E-mail:* bev.summers@wales.gsi.gov.uk,
Lynne Jones *Tel:* 029 2089 8789

Deputy First Minister and Minister for Economic Development (**Michael German** AM)
Deputises in First Minister's absence. Responsible for all aspects of economic development in
Wales.

Business Manager (**Andrew Davies** AM)
Responsible for management of government business in the Assembly; co-ordinating strategic
development of government corporate policy and implementing 'Putting Wales First' and
'betterwales.com'; for corporate communications and co-ordinating developments in information
and communications technology.
E-mail: andrew.davies@wales.gsi.gov.uk
Private Secretary and Head of Business Unit: Marion Stapleton *Tel:* 029 2089 8772
Fax: 029 2089 8475 *E-mail:* marion.stapleton@wales.gsi.gov.uk
Assistant Private Secretary and Diary Secretary: Siwan Gwyndaf *Tel:* 029 2089 8779
E-mail: siwan.gwyndaf@wales.gsi.gov.uk

Minister for Finance and Communities (**Edwina Hart** AM)
Responsible for government finances, including local government; for social inclusion and
regeneration of the most disadvantaged communities; for the Assembly's relationship with local
government; housing; relations with police authorities and others in achieving community safety.
E-mail: edwina.hart@wales.gsi.gov.uk
Private Secretary: Jo-Ann Bainton *Tel:* 029 2089 8774 *Fax:* 029 2089 8129
E-mail: jo-ann.bainton@wales.gsi.gov.uk

Minister for Education and Lifelong Learning (**Jane Davidson** AM)
Responsible for all aspects of education, training and lifelong learning.

Minister for Culture and Sports (**Jenny Randerson** AM)
Responsible for arts, sports, libraries, museums and Wales' languages.

Minister for Environment (**Sue Essex** AM)
Responsible for environment, planning, transport and sustainable development.
E-mail: sue.essex@wales.gsi.gov.uk
Private Secretary: Sarah Austin *Tel:* 029 2089 8773 *Fax:* 029 2089 8129
E-mail: sarah.austin2@wales.gsi.gov.uk *Diary Secretary:* Angela Williams *Tel:* 029 2089 8472
E-mail: angela.williams@wales.gsi.gov.uk

Minister for Rural Affairs (**Carwyn Jones** AM)
Responsible for development of rural parts of Wales, including agriculture, forestry, fisheries;
development and promotion of food production.
E-mail: carwyn.jones@wales.gsi.gov.uk
Private Secretary: Nicola Britton *Tel:* 029 2089 8769 *Fax:* 029 2089 8129
E-mail: nicola.britton@wales.gsi.gov.uk *Diary Secretary:* Mandy Lewis *Tel:* 029 2089 8452
Fax: 029 2089 8129

Minister for Health and Social Services (**Jane Hutt** AM)
Responsible for all aspects of health and social services in Wales (excluding benefits); Voluntary
sector partnership.
E-mail: jane.hutt@wales.gsi.gov.uk
Private Secretary: Heulwen Evans *Tel:* 029 2089 8783 *Fax:* 029 2089 8129
E-mail: heulwen.evans@wales.gsi.gov.uk *Diary Secretary:* Louise Rees *Tel:* 029 2089 8787
E-mail: louise.rees@wales.gsi.gov.uk

Cabinet Special Advisers
Paul Griffiths
Dr Mark Drakeford
Dr Rachel Jones
Graham Vidler

Executive Agencies
CADW: Welsh Historic Monuments
Farming and Rural Conservation Agency
Intervention Board
Planning Inspectorate

Committees

SUBJECT COMMITTEES

Members are elected onto various subject committees in proportion to their party's representation in the Assembly.

Portfolios in the Cabinet were changed in a reshuffle in mid-October, which will lead to changes in the subject committees which correspond to ministerial responsibilities. Information on the re-organisation of committees was not available at the time of going to press, but will be available in December's *Vacher's Parliamentary Companion.*

STANDING COMMITTEES

Audit

Chair: Janet Davies
Lorraine Barrett; Peter Black; Alun Cairns; Geraint Davies; Jane Davidson; Brian Gibbons; Alison Halford; Dafydd Wigley
Clerk: Andrew George (029 2089 8155)
Deputy Clerk: Julie Bragg (029 2089 8026)
Remit: The role of the Audit Committee is to examine the reports on the accounts of the Assembly and other public bodies prepared by the Auditor General for Wales and to consider reports by the Auditor General for Wales on examinations into the economy, efficiency and effectiveness with which the Assembly has used its resources in discharging its functions.
E-mail: audit.comm@wales.gsi.gov.uk

Equal Opportunities

Chair: Edwina Hart
Lorraine Barrett; Christine Chapman; Glyn Davies; Richard Edwards; Alison Halford; Gareth Jones; Helen Jones; David Melding; Janet Ryder; Kirsty Williams
Clerk: Andrew George (029 2089 8155)
Deputy Clerk: Julie Bragg (029 2089 8026)
E-mail: equality.comm@wales.gsi.gov.uk

European Affairs

Chairman: Rhodri Morgan
Mick Bates; Nick Bourne; Jocelyn Davies; Delyth Evans; Val Feld; Christine Gwyther; Jonathan Morgan; Alun Pugh; Rhodri Thomas; Phil Williams
Clerk: Andrew George (029 2089 8155)
Deputy Clerk: Julie Bragg (029 2089 8026)
E-mail: europe.comm@wales.gsi.gov.uk

Legislation

Chairman: Michael German
Nick Bourne; Jocelyn Davies; Huw Lewis; David Lloyd; John Marek; Lynne Neagle; Karen Sinclair; Owen John Thomas
Clerk: Adrian Green (029 2089 8147)
Deputy Clerk: Julie Owen (029 2089 8018)
Remit: The Legislation Committee is to check that the legislation coming before the Assembly is not defective and that any relevant requirements have been complied with.
E-mail: legislation.comm@wales.gsi.gov.uk

Standards of Conduct

Chairman: David Melding
Janet Davies; Richard Edwards; Val Feld; Janice Gregory; Brian Hancock; Christine Humphreys; Gareth Jones; Gwenda Thomas
Clerk: Barbara Wilson (029 2089 8226)
Deputy Clerk: Julie Grant (029 2089 8228)

REGIONAL COMMITTEES

The four regional committees, for Mid, North, South East and South West Wales, are made up from members for the relevant constituencies and regions and represent the interests of those areas.

The role of the four regional committees is to advise the Assembly on:
- matters affecting the regions;
- the effect of Assembly policies in those regions; and
- the work of public bodies in the regions.

Regional Committees will form a crucial link between the Assembly and local communities.

Mid Wales

Ceredigion and Powys and the area of Gwynedd comprising the former district of Meirionydd

Chairman: Glyn Davies
Mick Bates; Nick Bourne; Cynog Dafis; Dafydd Elis-Thomas; Delyth Evans; Elin Jones; Kirsty Williams
Clerk: Delyth Thomas (029 2089 8164)
Deputy Clerk: Brian Duddridge (029 2089 8154)
E-mail: mwales.regcomm@wales.gsi.gov.uk

North Wales

Conwy, Denbighshire, Flintshire, Isle of Anglesey, Wrexham and the area of Gwynedd made up of the former districts of Arfon and Dwyfor

Chairman: Ann Jones

Dafydd Elis-Thomas; Alison Halford; Christine Humphreys; Gareth Jones; Ieuan Wyn Jones; John Marek; Tom Middlehurst; Alun Pugh; Rod Richards; Peter Rogers; Janet Ryder; Karen Sinclair; Dafydd Wigley

Clerk: Adrian Crompton (029 2089 8264)

Deputy Clerk: Howell Rees

E-mail: nwales.regcomm@wales.gsi.gov.uk

South East Wales

Blaenau Gwent, Bridgend, Caerphilly, Cardiff, Merthyr Tydfil, Monmouthshire, Newport, Rhondda Cynon Taff, Torfaen, The Vale of Glamorgan

Chairman: Jenny Randerson

Lorraine Barrett; Peter Black; Rosemary Butler; Alun Cairns; Christine Chapman; Jane Davidson; David Davies; Geraint Davies; Janet Davies; Jocelyn Davies; Ron Davies; Sue Essex; Michael German; William Graham; Janice Gregory; John Griffiths; Brian Hancock; Jane Hutt; Pauline Jarman; Carwyn Jones; Peter Law; Huw Lewis; David Lloyd; David Melding; Jonathan Morgan; Rhodri Morgan; Lynne Neagle; Owen John Thomas; Phil Williams

Clerk: Martin Stevenson (029 2089 8409)

Deputy Clerk: Phil Mulraney (029 2089 8024)

E-mail: martin.stevenson@wales.gsi.gov.uk

South West Wales

Carmarthenshire, Neath, Port Talbot, Pembrokeshire, Swansea

Chairman: Alun Cairns

Peter Black; Nick Bourne; Cynog Dafis; Andrew Davies; Glyn Davies; Janet Davies; Richard Edwards; Delyth Evans; Val Feld; Brian Gibbons; Christine Gwyther; Edwina Hart; Helen Jones; David Lloyd; Gwenda Thomas; Rhodri Thomas

Clerk: Jane Westlake (029 2089 8149)

Deputy Clerk: Claire Morris (029 2089 8148)

E-mail: swwales.regcomm@wales.gsi.gov.uk

Political Parties and Shadow Assembly Spokespeople

WALES LABOUR PARTY

PLAID LAFUR CYMRU

Transport House, 1 Cathedral Road, Cardiff CF11 9HA
029 2087 7700 Fax 029 2022 1153
E-mail: contact@walesnew.labour.org.uk
Website: www.waleslabourparty.org.uk

General-Secretary: Jessica Morden
Director of Communications: Huw Evans
Press Officer: Jackie Aplin

PLAID CYMRU

THE PARTY OF WALES

Tŷ Gwynfor, 18 Park Grove, Cardiff CF10 3BN
029 2064 6000 Fax 020 2064 6001
E-mail: post@plaidcymru.org
Website: www.plaidcymru.org
Assembly Office: 029 2089 8709

Chief Executive: Karl Davies
Press Officer: Emyr Williams 029 2089 8401

SHADOW CABINET

Leader and Finance Secretary:
Ieuan Wyn Jones MP AM
Business Manager: Jocelyn Davies AM
Chief Whip and Agriculture and Rural Development Secretary: Elin Jones AM

Economic Development Secretary:
Dr Phil Williams AM
Environment, Transport and Planning Secretary: Helen Mary Jones AM
Health and Social Services Secretary:
Dai Lloyd AM
Pre-16 Education Secretary:
Gareth Jones OBE AM
Local Government and Housing Secretary:
Janet Ryder AM
Business Manager: Jocelyn Davies AM

WELSH CONSERVATIVE PARTY

PLAID GEIDWADOL CYMRU

4 Penlline Road, Whitchurch, Cardiff CF14 2XS
029 2061 6031 Fax 029 2061 0544
E-mail: ccowales@callnetuk.com

Chairman: Henri Lloyd Davies
Director: Leigh Jeffes

NATIONAL ASSEMBLY CONSERVATIVE GROUP

Leader: Nick Bourne AM
Economic Development: Alun Cairns AM
Chief Whip; Environment, Transport and Planning; Policy Presentation:
David Davies AM

Finance: Glyn Davies AM
Business Secretary: William Graham AM
Health and Social Services: David Melding AM
Education: Jonathan Morgan AM
Agriculture and the Rural Economy:
  Peter Rogers AM

WELSH LIBERAL DEMOCRATS

DEMOCRATIAID RHYDDFRYDOL CYMRU

Bay View House, 102 Bute Street,
Cardiff CF10 5AD
029 2031 3400 Fax 029 2031 3401
E-mail: ldwales@cix.co.uk
Website: www.libdemwales.org.uk

Chief Executive: Chris Lines
Administrative Officer:
  Helen Northmore-Thomas

ASSEMBLY SPOKESPEOPLE

Leader and Economic Development:
  Michael German AM
Education (under 16) (Whip):
  Jenny Randerson AM
Education (16+) and Environment:
  Christine Humphreys AM
Health and Social Services:
  Kirsty Williams AM
Rural Development: Mike Bates AM
Local Government and Housing:
  Peter Black AM

Assembly Members' Contact Directory

National Assembly for Wales, Cardiff Bay, Cardiff CF99 1NA
029 2082 5111 Cathays Park
E-mail: assembly.info@wales.gsi.gov.uk
Website: www.wales.gov.uk

BARRETT, Lorraine *(Lab/Co-op)* – Cardiff South and Penarth
  Tel: 029 2089 8376 *E-mail:* lorraine.barrett@wales.gsi.gov.uk
  Private Secretary: Barbara Windsor *Tel:* 029 2089 8749
BATES, Mick *(Lib Dem)* – Montgomeryshire
  Tel: 029 2089 8340 *E-mail:* mick.bates@wales.gsi.gov.uk
  Private Secretary: Gavin Cox *Tel:* 029 2089 8737
BLACK, Peter *(Lib Dem)* – South Wales West*
  Tel: 029 2089 8361 *E-mail:* peter.black@wales.gsi.gov.uk
BOURNE, Prof Nicholas *(Con)* – Mid and West Wales*
  Tel: 029 2089 8349 *E-mail:* nicholas.bourne@wales.gsi.gov.uk
BUTLER, Rosemary *(Lab)* – Newport West
  E-mail: rosemary.butler@wales.gsi.gov.uk
  Private Secretary: Sian Mitchell *Tel:* 029 2089 8767 *E-mail:* sian.mitchell@wales.gsi.gov.uk
  E-mail: claire.mcdonald@wales.gsi.gov.uk
CAIRNS, Alun *(Con)* – South Wales West*
  Tel: 029 2089 8331 *E-mail:* alun.cairns@wales.gsi.gov.uk
CHAPMAN, Christine *(Lab/Co-op)* – Cynon Valley
  Tel: 029 2089 8364 *E-mail:* christine.chapman@wales.gsi.gov.uk
  Private Secretary: Linda Devet *Tel:* 029 2089 8366
DAFIS, Cynog *(PC)* – Mid and West Wales*
  Tel: 029 2089 8271 *E-mail:* cynog.dafis@wales.gsi.gov.uk
DAVIDSON, Jane *(Lab)* – Pontypridd
  Tel: 029 2089 8912 *E-mail:* jane.davidson@wales.gsi.gov.uk
DAVIES, Andrew *(Lab)* – Swansea West
  E-mail: andrew.davies@wales.gsi.gov.uk
  Private Secretary and Head of Business Unit: Marion Stapleton *Tel:* 029 2089 8772
  Fax: 029 2089 8475 *E-mail:* marion.stapleton@wales.gsi.gov.uk
  Assistant Private Secretary and Diary Secretary: Siwan Gwindaf *Tel:* 029 2089 8779
  E-mail: siwan.gwindaf@wales.gsi.go.uk
  Constituency Secretary: Ceri Williams *Tel:* 029 2089 8249 *E-mail:* ceri.williams@wales.gsi.gv.uk

DAVIES, David *(Con)* – Monmouth
Tel: 029 2089 8325 *E-mail:* david.davies@wales.gsi.gov.uk
DAVIES, Geraint *(PC)* – Rhondda
Tel: 029 2089 8280 *E-mail:* geraint.davies@wales.gsi.gov.uk
DAVIES, Glyn *(Con)* – Mid and West Wales*
Tel: 029 2089 8337 *E-mail:* glyn.davies.@wales.gsi.gov.uk
DAVIES, Janet *(PC)* – South Wales West*
Tel: 029 2089 8289 *E-mail:* janet.davies.@wales.gsi.gov.uk
DAVIES, Jocelyn *(PC)* – South Wales East*
Tel: 029 2089 8259 *E-mail:* jocelyn.davies@wales.gsi.gov.uk
DAVIES, Rt Hon Ron *(Lab)* – Caerphilly
Tel. 029 2089 8079 *E-mail:* ron.davies@wales.gsi.gov.uk
Private Secretary: Lee Waters *Tel:* 029 2089 8027
EDWARDS, Dr Richard *(Lab)* – Preseli Pembrokeshire
Tel: 029 2089 8298 *E-mail:* richard.edwards@wales.gsi.gov.uk
ELIS-THOMAS Lord, Dafydd *(PC)* – Meirionnydd Nant Conwy
Tel: 029 2089 8911 *E-mail:* dafydd.elis-thomas@wales.gsi.gov.uk
ESSEX, Sue *(Lab)* – Cardiff North
Tel: 029 2089 8391 *E-mail:* sue.essex@wales.gsi.gov.uk
Private Secretary: Sarah Austin *Tel:* 029 2089 8773 *Fax:* 029 2089 8129
E-mail: sarah.austin2@wales.gsi.gov.uk
Diary Secretary: Angela Williams *Tel:* 029 2089 8472 *E-mail:* angela.williams@wales.gsi.gov.uk
EVANS, Delyth *(Lab)* – Mid and West Wales*
Tel: 029 2089 8488
Secretary: Ann Garrard *Tel:* 029 2089 8449
FELD, Val *(Lab)* – Swansea East
Tel: 029 2089 8316 *E-mail:* val.feld@wales.gsi.gov.uk
GERMAN, Michael *(Lib Dem)* – South Wales East*
Tel: 029 2089 8352 *E-mail:* michael.german@wales.gsi.gov.uk
Private Secretary: Michelle Poulter *Tel:* 029 2089 8357
GIBBONS, Brian *(Lab)* – Aberavon
Tel: 029 2089 8382 *E-mail:* brian.gibbons@wales.gsi.gov.uk
GRAHAM, William *(Con)* – South Wales East*
Tel: 029 2089 8346 *E-mail:* william.graham@wales.gsi.gov.uk
GREGORY, Janice *(Lab)* – Ogmore
Tel: 029 2089 8373 *E-mail:* janice.gregory@wales.gsi.gov.uk
Private Secretary: Mike Gregory *Tel:* 029 2089 8374
GRIFFITHS, John *(Lab/Co-op)* – Newport East
Tel: 029 2089 8307 *E-mail:* john.griffiths@wales.gsi.gov.uk
GWYTHER, Christine *(Lab)* – Carmarthen West and
South Pembrokeshire
E-mail: christine.gwyther@wales.gsi.gov.uk
Constituency Assistant: David Bezzina *Tel:* 01297 238306 *Fax:* 01267 220555
E-mail: david.bezzina@wales.gsi.gov.uk
HALFORD, Alison *(Lab)* – Delyn
Tel: 029 2089 8319 *E-mail:* alison.halford@wales.gsi.gov.uk
HANCOCK, Brian *(PC)* – Islwyn
Tel: 029 2089 8292 *E-mail:* brian.hancock@wales.gsi.gov.uk
HART, Edwina MBE *(Lab)* – Gower
E-mail: edwina.hart@wales.gsi.gov.uk
Private Secretary: Jo-Ann Bainton *Tel:* 029 2089 8774 *Fax:* 029 2089 8129
E-mail: jo-ann.bainton@wales.gsi.gov.uk
HUMPHREYS, Christine *(Lib Dem)* – North Wales*
Tel: 029 2089 8343 *E-mail:* christine.humphreys@wales.gsi.gov.uk

HUTT, Jane *(Lab)* – Vale of Glamorgan
E-mail: jane.hutt@wales.gsi.gov.uk
Private Secretary: Heulwen Evans *Tel:* 029 2089 8783 *Fax:* 029 2089 8129
E-mail: heulwen.evans@wales.gsi.gov.uk
Diary Secretary: Louise Rees *Tel:* 029 2089 8787 *E-mail:* louise.rees@wales.gsi.gov.uk
JARMAN, Pauline *(PC)* – South Wales Central*
Tel: 029 2089 8256 *E-mail:* pauline.jarman@wales.gsi.gov.uk
JONES, Ann *(Lab)* – Vale of Clwyd
Tel: 029 2089 8388 *E-mail:* ann.jones@wales.gsi.gov.uk
JONES, Carwyn *(Lab)* – Bridgend
Tel: 029 2089 8301 *Fax:* 029 2089 8302 *E-mail:* carwyn.jones@wales.gsi.gov.uk
Private Secretary: Nicola Britton *Tel:* 029 2089 8769 *Fax:* 029 2089 8129
E-mail: nicola.britton2@wales.gsi.gov.uk
Diary Secretary: Mandy Lewis *Tel:* 029 2089 8452
Researcher: Chris Morgan *Tel:* 029 2089 8300 *Fax:* 029 2089 8299
E-mail: chris.morgan@wales.gsi.gov.uk
Constituency Assistant: Helen Davies *Tel:* 01656 664320 *Fax:* 01656 669349
E-mail: helen.davies@wales.gsi.gov.uk
JONES, Elin *(PC)* – Ceredigion
Tel: 029 2089 8262 *E-mail:* elin.jones@wales.gsi.gov.uk
JONES, Gareth OBE *(PC)* – Conwy
Tel: 029 2089 8253 *E-mail:* gareth.jones@wales.gsi.gov.uk
JONES, Helen Mary *(PC)* – Llanelli
Tel: 029 2089 8274 *E-mail:* helen.jones@wales.gsi.gov.uk
JONES, Ieuan Wyn *(PC)* – Ynys Môn
Tel: 029 2089 8268 *E-mail:* ieuan.wynjones@wales.gsi.gov.uk
Private Secretary: Bethan Jones *Tel:* 029 2089 8023
LAW, Peter *(Lab/Co-op)* – Blaenau Gwent
E-mail: peter.law@wales.gsi.gov.uk
Private Secretary: Susanne Powell *Tel:* 029 2089 8768 *Fax:* 029 2089 8129
E-mail: susanne.powell@wales.gsi.gov.uk
Constituency Secretary: Joanne Thomas *Tel:* 029 2089 8136
E-mail: joanne.thomas@wales.gsi.gov.uk
LEWIS, Huw *(Lab/Co-op)* – Merthyr Tydfil and Rhymney
Tel: 029 2089 8385 *E-mail:* huw.lewis@wales.gsi.gov.uk
LLOYD, Dr David *(PC)* – South Wales West*
Tel: 029 2089 8283 *E-mail:* dai.lloyd@wales.gsi.gov.uk
MAREK, Dr John *(Lab)* – Wrexham
Tel: 029 2089 8313 *E-mail:* john.marek@wales.gsi.gov.uk
Private Secretary: Anne Marek *Tel:* 029 2089 8727
MELDING, David *(Con)* – South Wales Central*
Tel: 029 2089 8328 *E-mail:* david.melding@wales.gsi.gov.uk
MIDDLEHURST, Tom *(Lab)* – Alyn and Deeside
E-mail: tom.middlehurst@wales.gsi.gov.uk
Assembly Assistant: Jayne Bryant *Tel:* 029 2089 8309 *Fax:* 029 2089 8419
E-mail: jayne.bryant@wales.gsi.gov.uk
Constituency Secretary: Linda Lee *Tel:* 01244 823547 *Fax:* 01244 823548
E-mail: linda.lee@wales.gsi.gov.uk
MORGAN, Jonathan *(Con)* – South Wales Central*
Tel: 029 2089 8334 *E-mail:* jonathan.morgan@wales.gsi.gov.uk

MORGAN, Rt Hon Rhodri *(Lab)* – Cardiff West
E-mail: rhodri.morgan@wales.gsi.gov.uk
Interim Special Adviser: Kevin Brennan
Principal Private Secretary: Anna Coleman *Tel:* 029 2089 8765
E-mail: anna.coleman@wales.gsi.gov.uk
Private Secretaries: Rose Stewart *Tel:* 029 2089 8764 *Fax:* 029 2089 8198
E-mail: rose.stewart@wales.gsi.gov.uk
Prys Davies *Tel:* 029 2089 8763 *E-mail:* prys.davies@wales.gsi.gov.uk
Diary Secretaries: Beverly Summers *Tel:* 029 2089 8197 *E-mail:* bev.summers@wales.gsi.gov.uk
Lynne Jones *Tel:* 029 2089 8789
Constituency Secretary: Annabel Harle *Tel:* 029 2089 8773
NEAGLE, Lynne *(Lab)* – Torfaen
Tel: 029 2089 8367 *E-mail:* lynne.neagle@wales.gsi.gov.uk
PUGH, Alun *(Lab)* – Clwyd West
Tel: 029 2089 8370 *Fax:* 029 2089 8371
E-mail: alun.pugh@wales.gov.uk
Research Assistant: Clare Phillips
Constituency Admin Assistant: Delyth Ross *Tel/Fax:* 01745 825855
RANDERSON, Jennifer *(Lib Dem)* – Cardiff Central
Tel: 029 2089 8355 *E-mail:* jenny.randerson@wales.gsi.gov.uk
Private Secretary: Carol Kellaway *Tel:* 029 2089 8742
RICHARDS, Rod *(Con)* – North Wales*
Tel: 029 2089 8394 *E-mail:* rod.richards@wales.gsi.gov.uk
Private Secretary: Beth *Tel:* 029 2089 8755
ROGERS, Peter *(Con)* – North Wales*
Tel: 029 2089 8322 *E-mail:* peter.rogers@wales.gsi.gov.uk
RYDER, Janet *(PC)* – North Wales*
Tel: 029 2089 8250 *E-mail:* janet.ryder@wales.gsi.gov.uk
SINCLAIR, Karen *(Lab)* – Clwyd South
Tel: 029 2089 8304 *E-mail:* karen.sinclair@wales.gsi.gov.uk
THOMAS, Gwenda *(Lab)* – Neath
Tel: 029 2089 8382 *E-mail:* gwenda.thomas@wales.gsi.gov.uk
THOMAS, Owen John *(PC)* – South Wales Central*
Tel: 029 2089 8295 *E-mail:* owen-john.thomas@wales.gsi.gov.uk
THOMAS, Rhodri *(PC)* – Carmarthen East and Dinefwr
Tel: 029 2089 8277 *E-mail:* rhodri.thomas@wales.gsi.gov.uk
WIGLEY, Rt Hon Dafydd *(PC)* – Caernarfon
Tel: 029 2089 8265 *E-mail:* dafydd.wigley@wales.gsi.gov.uk
Constituency Secretary: Gwenda Williams *Tel:* 01286 672076
WILLIAMS, Kirsty *(Lib Dem)* – Brecon and Radnorshire
Tel: 029 2089 8358 *E-mail:* kirsty.williams@wales.gsi.gov.uk
WILLIAMS, Dr Philip *(PC)* – South Wales East*
Tel: 029 2089 8286 *E-mail:* phil.williams@wales.gsi.gov.uk

* *Region*s

NORTHERN IRELAND ASSEMBLY

Parliament Buildings
Stormont
Belfast BT4 3XX
028 9052 1333 Fax 028 9052 1961
E-mail: info.office@niassembly.gov.uk
Website: www.niassembly.gov.uk
Executive's website: www.northernireland.gov.uk

Background

From 1921, Northern Ireland was governed by a devolved parliament under the terms of the Government of Ireland Act 1920 which provided for separate parliaments in the north and south of Ireland. In 1972, the Government at Westminster prorogued the Northern Ireland Parliament and introduced a system of 'Direct Rule'. Various political initiatives attempted to restore some form of devolved government at different times during the following 25 years. Eventually, following the Westminster election of May 1997, a series of talks, under the chairmanship of former US Senator George Mitchell, led to the publication on 10 April 1998 of what has become known as the 'Good Friday' or Belfast Agreement.

The Good Friday Agreement

The governments of the United Kingdom and Ireland, together with a number of the political parties in Northern Ireland, agreed to support a three stranded approach to resolving the historical differences which had provided the context for political instability in Northern Ireland. The three strands provided for arrangements within Northern Ireland; within Ireland north and south; and within the British Isles as a whole. The Agreement was endorsed by referenda in both parts of Ireland in May 1998.

The Assembly

Under Strand One of the Agreement, a new democratic institution was created within Northern Ireland. Elections to this body of 108 members were held in June 1998 and the new Northern Ireland Assembly held its first meeting at Castle Buildings, Stormont on 1 July 1998.

The Assembly is responsible for all 'transferred matters', ie for all public services not 'reserved' or 'excepted' in the Northern Ireland Act 1998, including areas such as taxation, foreign affairs, defence etc. The powers were devolved to the Northern Ireland Assembly on 2 December 1999.

The Assembly has agreed to the structure of the administration after devolution. Ten Departments have been formed out of the original six. Each Department is also 'shadowed' by a Departmental Committee which will scrutinise the policy of the Department and play a role in the initiation and development of legislation. The Assembly has also developed its own Standing Orders.

Ten Ministers and Chairpersons, Deputy Chairpersons and members for the ten Departmental Committees were nominated at an Assembly plenary on 29 November 1999.

New Institutions

On 2 December 1999, the day power was devolved to the Assembly, the following became fully functioning institutions:

North/South Ministerial Council

and its six implementation bodies:

Waterways Ireland
Food Safety Promotion Board
Trade and Business Development Board
Special European Union Programmes Body
Foyle, Carlingford and Irish Lights Commission
North/South Language Body

The British-Irish Council
British-Irish Inter-governmental Conference

STATE OF THE PARTIES (October 2000)

UUP	Ulster Unionist Party	28 seats
SDLP	Social Democratic and Labour Party	24 seats
DUP	Democratic Unionist Party	20 seats
SF	Sinn Fein	18 seats
A	Alliance	*6 seats
NIUP†	Northern Ireland Unionist Party	§3 seats
UUAP‡	United Unionist Assembly Party	3 seats
PUP	Progressive Unionist Party	2 seats
NIWC	Women's Coalition	2 seats
UKUP	UK Unionist Party	1 seat
Ind Un	Independent Unionist	1 seat
		108 seats

18 Constituencies
6 Members per constituency
108 Members

*Includes the Speaker
†Elected as UK Unionist candidates. Formed Northern Ireland Unionist Party 15 January 1999
‡Independents formed United Unionist Assembly Party 21 September 1998
§One member left the NIUP 1 December 1999

Members (MLAs)

	Party	*Constituency*
*ADAMS Gerry	SF	Belfast West
ADAMSON Dr Ian	UUP	Belfast East
AGNEW Fraser	UUAP	Belfast North
‡ALDERDICE Lord	Speaker	Belfast East
The Speaker		
ARMITAGE Pauline	UUP	East Londonderry
ARMSTRONG Billy	UUP	Mid Ulster
ATTWOOD Alex	SDLP	Belfast West
BEGGS Jnr Roy	UUP	East Antrim
BELL Billy	UUP	Lagan Valley
BELL Eileen	A	North Down
BENSON Thomas	UUP	Strangford
BERRY Paul	DUP	Newry and Armagh
BIRNIE Dr Esmond	UUP	Belfast South
BOYD Norman	NIUP	South Antrim
BRADLEY P J	SDLP	South Down
BYRNE Joe	SDLP	West Tyrone

CAMPBELL Gregory	DUP	East Londonderry
Minister for Regional Development		
CARRICK Mervyn	DUP	Upper Bann
CARSON Joan	UUP	Fermanagh and South Tyrone
CLOSE Seamus OBE	A	Lagan Valley
CLYDE Wilson	DUP	South Antrim
COBAIN Fred	UUP	Belfast North
COULTER Rev Robert	UUP	North Antrim
DALLAT John	SDLP	East Londonderry
DAVIS Ivan	UUP	Lagan Valley
De BRÚN Bairbre	SF	Belfast West
Minister of Health, Social Services and Public Safety		
DODDS Nigel OBE	DUP	Belfast North
DOHERTY Arthur	SDLP	East Londonderry
DOHERTY Pat	SF	West Tyrone
DOUGLAS Boyd	UUAP	East Londonderry
DURKAN Mark	SDLP	Foyle
Minister of Finance and Personnel		
EMPEY Sir Reg	UUP	Belfast East
Minister of Enterprise, Trade and Investment		
ERVINE David	PUP	Belfast East
FARREN Dr Sean	SDLP	North Antrim
Minister of Higher and Further Education, Training and Employment		
FEE John	SDLP	Newry and Armagh
FORD David	A	South Antrim
FOSTER Sam	UUP	Fermanagh and South Tyrone
Minister of the Environment		
GALLAGHER Tommy	SDLP	Fermanagh and South Tyrone
GIBSON Oliver	DUP	West Tyrone
GILDERNEW Michelle	SF	Fermanagh and South Tyrone
§GORMAN Sir John CVO CBE	UUP	North Down
Deputy Speaker		
HANNA Carmel	SDLP	Belfast South
HAUGHEY Denis	SDLP	Mid Ulster
Junior Minister		
HAY William	DUP	Foyle
HENDRON Dr Joe	SDLP	Belfast West
HILDITCH David	DUP	East Antrim
*HUME John†	SDLP	Foyle
HUSSEY Derek	UUP	West Tyrone
HUTCHINSON Billy	PUP	Belfast North
HUTCHINSON Roger	Ind Un	East Antrim
KANE Gardiner	DUP	North Antrim
KELLY John	SF	Mid Ulster
KELLY Gerry	SF	Belfast North
KENNEDY Danny	UUP	Newry and Armagh
LESLIE James	UUP	North Antrim
LEWSLEY Patricia	SDLP	Lagan Valley
McCARTHY Kieran	A	Strangford
*McCARTNEY Robert QC	UKUP	North Down
McCLARTY David	UUP	East Londonderry
§McCLELLAND Donovan	SDLP	South Antrim
Deputy Speaker		
*McCREA Rev Dr William	DUP	Mid Ulster
McDONNELL Dr Alasdair	SDLP	Belfast South
McELDUFF Barry	SF	West Tyrone
McFARLAND Alan	UUP	North Down

McGIMPSEY Michael	UUP	Belfast South
Minister of Culture, Arts and Leisure		
*McGRADY Eddie	SDLP	South Down
*McGUINNESS Martin	SF	Mid Ulster
Minister of Education		
McHUGH Gerry	SF	Fermanagh and South Tyrone
McLAUGHLIN Mitchel	SF	Foyle
McMENAMIN Eugene	SDLP	West Tyrone
McNAMEE Pat	SF	Newry and Armagh
McWILLIAMS Prof Monica	NIWC	Belfast South
MAGINNESS Alban	SDLP	Belfast North
*MALLON Séamus	SDLP	Newry and Armagh
Deputy First Minister		
MASKEY Alex	SF	Belfast West
MOLLOY Francie	SF	Mid Ulster
§MORRICE Jane	NIWC	North Down
Deputy Speaker		
MORROW Maurice	DUP	Fermanagh and South Tyrone
Minister for Social Development		
MURPHY Conor	SF	Newry and Armagh
MURPHY Mick	SF	South Down
NEESON Sean	A	East Antrim
NELIS Mary	SF	Foyle
NESBITT Dermot	UUP	South Down
Junior Minister		
O'CONNOR Danny	SDLP	East Antrim
O'HAGAN Dr Dara	SF	Upper Bann
ONEILL Eamon	SDLP	South Down
*PAISLEY Rev Dr Ian†	DUP	North Antrim
PAISLEY Ian Jnr	DUP	North Antrim
POOTS Edwin	DUP	Lagan Valley
RAMSEY Sue	SF	Belfast West
ROBINSON Iris	DUP	Strangford
ROBINSON Ken	UUP	East Antrim
ROBINSON Mark	DUP	Belfast South
*ROBINSON Peter David	DUP	Belfast East
ROCHE Patrick	NIUP	Lagan Valley
RODGERS Brid	SDLP	Upper Bann
Minister of Agriculture and Rural Development		
SAVAGE George	UUP	Upper Bann
SHANNON Jim	DUP	Strangford
SHIPLEY-DALTON Duncan	UUP	South Antrim
*TAYLOR Rt Hon John D	UUP	Strangford
TIERNEY John	SDLP	Foyle
*TRIMBLE Rt Hon David	UUP	Upper Bann
First Minister		
WATSON Denis	UUAP	Upper Bann
WEIR Peter	UUP	North Down
WELLS Jim	DUP	South Down
WILSON Cedric	NIUP	Strangford
WILSON Jim	UUP	South Antrim
WILSON Sammy	DUP	Belfast East

*   *Also a Member of the House of Commons*
†   *Also a Member of the European Parliament*
‡   *Also a Member of the House of Lords*
§   *Deputy Speakers of the Assembly*

MEMBERS BY PARTY

Constitusency

ULSTER UNIONIST PARTY (UUP) (28)

ADAMSON Dr Ian	Belfast East
ARMITAGE Pauline	East Londonderry
ARMSTRONG Billy	Mid Ulster
BEGGS Jnr Roy	East Antrim
BELL Billy	Lagan Valley
BENSON Thomas	Strangford
BIRNIE Dr Esmond	Belfast South
CARSON Joan	Fermanagh and South Tyrone
COBAIN Fred	Belfast North
COULTER Rev Robert	North Antrim
DAVIS Ivan *(Deputy Whip)*	Lagan Valley
EMPEY Sir Reg	Belfast East
FOSTER Sam	Fermanagh and South Tyrone
†GORMAN Sir John	North Down
HUSSEY Derek	West Tyrone
KENNEDY Danny	Newry and Armagh
LESLIE James	North Antrim
McCLARTY David	East Londonderry
McFARLAND Alan	North Down
McGIMPSEY Michael	Belfast South
NESBITT Dermot	South Down
ROBINSON Ken	East Antrim
SAVAGE George	Upper Bann
SHIPLEY-DALTON Duncan	South Antrim
TAYLOR Rt Hon John D *(Deputy Leader)*	Strangford
TRIMBLE Rt Hon David *(Leader)*	Upper Bann
WEIR Peter	North Down
WILSON Jim *(Chief Whip)*	South Antrim

SOCIAL DEMOCRATIC AND LABOUR PARTY (SDLP) (24)

ATTWOOD Alex	Belfast West
BRADLEY P J	South Down
BYRNE Joe	West Tyrone
DALLAT John	East Londonderry
DOHERTY Arthur	East Londonderry
DURKAN Mark	Foyle
FARREN Dr Sean	North Antrim
FEE John	Newry and Armagh
GALLAGHER Tommy	Fermanagh and South Tyrone
HANNA Carmel	Belfast South
HAUGHEY Denis	Mid Ulster
HENDRON Dr Joe	Belfast West
HUME John *(Leader)*	Foyle
LEWSLEY Patricia	Lagan Valley
†McCLELLAND Donovan	South Antrim
McDONNELL Dr Alasdair	Belfast South
McGRADY Eddie *(Chief Whip)*	South Down
McMENAMIN Eugene	West Tyrone
MAGINNESS Alban	Belfast North
MALLON Séamus *(Deputy Leader)*	Newry and Armagh
O'CONNOR Danny	East Antrim
ONEILL Eamon	South Down
RODGERS Brid	Upper Bann
TIERNEY John	Foyle

DEMOCRATIC UNIONIST PARTY (DUP) (20)

BERRY Paul	Newry and Armagh
CAMPBELL Gregory	East Londonderry
CARRICK Mervyn	Upper Bann
CLYDE Wilson	South Antrim
DODDS Nigel *(Chief Whip)*	Belfast North
GIBSON Oliver	West Tyrone
HAY William	Foyle
HILDITCH David	East Antrim
KANE Gardiner	North Antrim
McCREA Rev Dr William	Mid Ulster
MORROW Maurice	Fermanagh and South Tyrone
PAISLEY Rev Dr Ian *(Leader)*	North Antrim
PAISLEY Ian Jnr	North Antrim
POOTS Edwin	Lagan Valley
ROBINSON Iris *(Deputy Whip)*	Strangford
ROBINSON Mark	Belfast South
ROBINSON Peter *(Deputy Leader)*	Belfast East
SHANNON Jim	Strangford
WELLS Jim	South Down
WILSON Sammy	Belfast East

SINN FEIN (SF) (18)

ADAMS Gerry *(President)*	Belfast West
De BRÚN Bairbre	Belfast West
DOHERTY Pat *(Vice-President)*	West Tyrone
GILDERNEW Michelle	Fermanagh and South Tyrone
KELLY John	Mid Ulster
KELLY Gerry	Belfast North
McELDUFF Barry	West Tyrone
McGUINNESS Martin	Mid Ulster
McHUGH Gerry	Fermanagh and South Tyrone
McLAUGHLIN Mitchel	Foyle
McNAMEE Pat	Newry and Armagh
MASKEY Alex *(Joint Chief Whip)*	Belfast West
MOLLOY Francie	Mid Ulster
MURPHY Conor *(Joint Chief Whip)*	Newry and Armagh
MURPHY Mick	South Down
NELIS Mary	Foyle
O'HAGAN Dr Dara	Upper Bann
RAMSEY Sue	Belfast West

ALLIANCE (A) (6)*

BELL Eileen *(President)*	North Down
CLOSE Seamus *(Deputy Leader)*	Lagan Valley
FORD David *(Chief Whip)*	South Antrim
McCARTHY Kieran	Strangford
NEESON Sean *(Leader)*	East Antrim

NORTHERN IRELAND UNIONIST PARTY (NIUP) (3)

BOYD Norman *(Whip)*	South Antrim
ROCHE Patrick *(Deputy Leader)*	Lagan Valley
WILSON Cedric *(Leader)*	Strangford

UNITED UNIONIST ASSEMBLY PARTY (UUAP) (3)

AGNEW Fraser	Belfast North
DOUGLAS Boyd	East Londonderry
WATSON Denis *(Leader)*	Upper Bann

PROGRESSIVE UNIONIST PARTY (PUP) (2)

ERVINE David	Belfast East
HUTCHINSON Billy	Belfast North

NORTHERN IRELAND WOMEN'S COALITION (NIWC) (2)

McWILLIAMS Prof Monica	Belfast South
†MORRICE Jane	North Down

UK UNIONIST PARTY (UKUP) (1)

McCARTNEY Robert QC *(Leader)*	North Down

INDEPENDENT UNIONIST (Ind Un) (1)

HUTCHINSON Roger	East Antrim

*Includes the Speaker of the Northern Ireland Assembly.
†Deputy Speakers of the Northern Ireland Assembly.

WOMEN MEMBERS

ARMITAGE Pauline	McWILLIAMS Prof Monica
BELL Eileen	MORRICE Jane
CARSON Joan	NELIS Mary
De BRÚN Bairbre	O'HAGAN Dr Dara
GILDERNEW Michelle	RAMSEY Sue
HANNA Carmel	ROBINSON Iris
LEWSLEY Patricia	RODGERS Brid

CONSTITUENCIES

EAST ANTRIM	FERMANAGH AND SOUTH TYRONE
NORTH ANTRIM	FOYLE
SOUTH ANTRIM	LAGAN VALLEY
BELFAST EAST	EAST LONDONDERRY
BELFAST NORTH	NEWRY AND ARMAGH
BELFAST SOUTH	STRANGFORD
BELFAST WEST	WEST TYRONE
NORTH DOWN	MID ULSTER
SOUTH DOWN	UPPER BANN

Northern Ireland Assembly

First Minister: Rt Hon David Trimble MLA (UUP)
Deputy First Minister: Séamus Mallon MLA (SDLP)
Speaker: The Lord Alerdice MLA
Deputy Speakers: Sir John Gorman CVO CBE MLA, Donovan McClelland MLA, Jane Morrice MLA

ASSEMBLY COMMISSION

The Commission is responsible for property, staff and services.
Members (6):
Chairman: The Speaker
Eileen Bell MLA, Rev Robert Coulter MLA, John Fee MLA, Dr Dara O'Hagan MLA, Jim Wells MLA
Clerk to the Commission: Tom Evans

PRINCIPAL OFFICERS AND OFFICIALS

The Speaker: The Lord Alderdice, FRCPI, FRCPsych MLA

OFFICE OF THE SPEAKER

Speaker's Special Adviser: Niall Johnston
Speaker's Counsel: Nicolas Hanna, QC
Speaker's Private Secretary: Georgina Campbell 028 9052 1181 Fax: 028 9052 1959

PRINCIPAL OFFICERS

Clerk to the Assembly: Vacant
Deputy Clerk: Vacant
Head of Administration: Gerry Cosgrave
Clerk Assistant: Murray Barnes
Editor of Debates: Alex Elder
Keeper of the House: Peter Waddell
Director of Research and Information: Allan Black
Director of Finance and Personnel: Dennis Millar
Clerk of Bills: Alan Patterson
Clerk of Business: Joe Reynolds
Clerk of Committees: John Torney

NORTHERN IRELAND EXECUTIVE COMMITTEE

First Minister: Rt Hon David Trimble MLA (UUP)
Deputy First Minister: Séamus Mallon MLA (SDLP)
Minister of Agriculture and Rural Development: Brid Rogers MLA (SDLP)
Minister of Culture, Arts and Leisure: Michael McGimpsey MLA (UUP)
Minister of Education: Martin McGuinness MLA (SF)
Minister of Enterprise, Trade and Investment: Sir Reg Empey MLA (UUP)
Minister of the Environment: Sam Foster MLA (UUP)
Minister of Finance and Personnel: Mark Durkan MLA (SDLP)
Minister of Health, Social Services and Public Safety: Bairbre de Brún MLA (SF)
Minister of Higher and Further Education, Training and Employment: Dr Sean Farren MLA (SDLP)
*Minister for Regional Development: Gregory Campbell MLA (DUP)
*Minister for Social Development: Maurice Morrow MLA (DUP)

*The DUP periodically rotates their two portfolios between their members.

Powers
The Secretary of State will retain responsibility for excepted and reserved matters as defined in the Northern Ireland Act 1998. However, it is open to the Secretary of State to lay appropriate legislation at any time following devolution if it appears to him that any reserved matter should become a transferred matter or that any transferred matter should become a reserved matter. This transfer has to have the cross-community support of the Assembly before any legislation can be laid.

Ministerial Responsibilities

OFFICE OF THE FIRST MINISTER AND DEPUTY FIRST MINISTER

First Minister (Rt Hon **David Trimble** MLA – UUP)
Areas of responsibility: Economic Policy Unit; Equality Unit; liaison with NSMC including Secretariat; liaison with BIC; Civic Forum (administrative and other arrangements, including Secretariat support); liaison with Secretary of State (excepted or reserved); European affairs/international matters/Washington Bureau; liaison with IFI; information services; community relations; Executive Committee Secretariat; Legislative Progress Unit; Office of the Legislative Counsel; public appointments policy; visits; honours; freedom of information; victims; Nolan standards; Public Service Office; machinery of government; emergency planning; women's issues; Policy Innovation Unit; cross-departmental co-ordination; Assembly Ombudsmen (liaison and appointment issues).
Principal Private Secretary: David Lavery *Tel:* 028 9052 1799 *Fax:* 028 9052 1118
Private Secretary: Maura Quinn *Chief of Staff:* David Campbell
Economic Adviser: Dr Graham Gudgin *Press Secretary:* David Kerr

Deputy First Minister (**Séamus Mallon** MLA – SDLP)
Areas of responsibility: Economic Policy Unit; Equality Unit; liaison with NSMC including Secretariat; liaison with BIC; Civic Forum (administrative and other arrangements, including Secretariat support); liaison with Secretary of State (excepted or reserved); European affairs/international matters/Washington Bureau; liaison with IFI; information services; community relations; Executive Committee Secretariat; Legislative Progress Unit; Office of the Legislative Counsel; public appointments policy; visits; honours; freedom of information; victims; Nolan standards; Public Service Office; machinery of government; emergency planning; women's issues; Policy Innovation Unit; cross-departmental co-ordination; Assembly Ombudsmen (liaison and appointment issues).
Principal Private Secretary: Peter May *Tel:* 028 9052 1126 *Fax:* 028 9052 1687
Private Secretary: Billy Gamble *Tel:* 028 9052 1012

Joint Junior Ministers (**Denis Haughey** MLA, **Dermot Nesbitt** MLA)
Assists the First Minister and Deputy First Minister in respect of their Department.
Special Advisers Hugh Logue *Tel:* 028 9052 1683 Brian Barrington *Tel:* 028 9052 1732
Colm Larkin *Tel:* 028 9052 1972

AGRICULTURE AND RURAL DEVELOPMENT

Minister of Agriculture and Rural Development (**Bríd Rodgers** MLA – SDLP)
Areas of responsibility: Food, farming and environment policy; agri-food development; science; veterinary matters; science service; rural development; forestry; sea fisheries, rivers.
E-mail: library.dani@nics.gov.uk
Private Secretary: Michael McAvoy *Tel:* 028 9052 4159 *Fax:* 028 9052 4170
Special Adviser: Conall McDevitt *Tel:* 028 9052 4119 *E-mail:* private.office@dardini.gov.uk

CULTURE, ARTS AND LEISURE

Minister of Culture, Arts and Leisure (**Michael McGimpsey** MLA – UUP)
Areas of responsibility: Arts and culture; sport and leisure; libraries; museums; Armagh Planetarium; Ulster Historical Foundation; inland waterways; inland fisheries; Ordnance Survey; Public Record Office; language policy; lottery matters; millennium events and events companies; visitors' amenities.
E-mail: decalni@nics.gov.uk
Private Secretary: Mrs Arlene McCreight *Tel:* 028 9025 8807 *Fax:* 028 9025 8906

EDUCATION

Minister of Education (**Martin McGuinness** MLA – SF)
Areas of responsibility: Schools' funding and administration; special education; school effectiveness; school planning and provision; Schools' Inspectorate; pre-school education; Youth Service; teachers (numbers and remuneration); Education and Library Board appointments.
E-mail: deni@nics.gov.uk
Private Secretary: Conor McFarland *Tel:* 028 9127 9303 *Fax:* 028 9127 9779

ENTERPRISE, TRADE AND INVESTMENT

Minister of Enterprise, Trade and Investment (Sir **Reg Empey** MLA – UUP)
Areas of responsibility: Economic development policy; industry (IDB, LBDU); research and development (IRTU); tourism; Health and Safety Executive; Employment Medical Advisory Service; company regulation; consumer affairs; energy policy; Minerals and Petroleum Unit (including Geological Survey); NICO; company training grant schemes (Company Development Programme and Explorers).
Private Secretary: Kim Burns *Tel:* 028 9052 9208 *Fax:* 028 9052 9545
E-mail: private.office@detini.gov.uk *Assistant Private Secretary:* Marion Magill *Tel:* 028 9052 9208

ENVIRONMENT

Minister of the Environment (**Sam Foster** MLA – UUP)
Areas of responsibility: Planning control; environment and heritage; protection of the countryside; waste management; pollution control; wildlife protection; local government; sustainable development; mineral resources (planning aspects); Driver and Vehicle Testing Agency; road safety; Driver and Vehicle Licensing Agency; transport licensing and enforcement.
E-mail: private.office@doeni.gov.uk
Private Secretary: David Steele *Tel:* 028 9054 1166 *Fax:* 028 9054 0092

FINANCE AND PERSONNEL

Minister of Finance and Personnel (**Mark Durkan** MLA – SDLP)
  Areas of responsibility: Finance; personnel, IT and common services; accommodation; legal services; Business Development Service; Construction Service; Government Purchasing Agency; Land Registers of NI; NI Statistics and Research Agency; Rate Collection Agency; Valuation and Lands Agency; Office of Law Reform.
  E-mail: m.durkan@sdlp.ie; dfpni@nics.gov.uk
  Private Secretary: Alison Ross *Tel:* 028 9185 8170 *Fax:* 028 9185 8282
  E-mail: alison.ross@dfpni.gov.uk

HEALTH, SOCIAL SERVICES AND PUBLIC SAFETY

Minister of Health, Social Services and Public Safety (**Bairbre de Brun** MLA – SF)
  Areas of responsibility: Health; social services; public health and safety; health promotion; Fire Authority.
  E-mail: sinnfein@iol.ie; webmaster@dhsspsni.gov.uk
  Private Secretary: Craig Allen *Tel:* 028 9052 0642 *Fax:* 028 9052 0557
  Special Adviser Leo Grant *Tel:* 028 9052 0500 *Fax:* 028 9052 0557

HIGHER AND FURTHER EDUCATION, TRAINING AND EMPLOYMENT

Minister of Higher and Further Education, Training and Employment (**Dr Sean Farren** MLA – SDLP)
  Areas of responsibility: Higher education; further education, vocational training; employment services; employment law and labour relations; teacher training and teacher education; student support and postgraduate awards; training grants.
  E-mail: farren@sdlp.ie; info.tea@nics.gov.uk
  Private Secretary: Ms Linda Meldrum *Tel:* 028 9025 7777 028 9025 7919
  E-mail: private.office.dhfeteni@nics.gov.uk

REGIONAL DEVELOPMENT

Minister for Regional Development (***Gregory Campbell** MLA – DUP)
  Areas of responsibility: Transport planning; public transport; roads; rail; ports and airports; city visioning; water; strategic planning, energy strategy.
  E-mail: private.office@drdni.gov.uk
  Private Secretary: Sheila McClelland *Tel:* 028 9054 0105 *Fax:* 028 9054 0028
  Special Adviser: Richard Bullick *Tel:* 028 9054 0012

SOCIAL DEVELOPMENT

Minister for Social Development (***Maurice Morrow** MLA – DUP)
  Areas of responsibility: Housing policy; Northern Ireland Housing Executive; voluntary activity; urban renewal; community sector; Laganside Corporation; Rent Assessment Panel; Housing Benefit Review Boards; Social Security Agency; Child Support Agency; Lands Division; Independent Tribunal Service; Office of Social Fund Commissioner; social legislation.
  E-mail: webmaster@dsdni.gov.uk
  Private Secretary: Mark O'Donnell *Tel:* 028 9056 9216 *Fax:* 028 9056 9244
  Special Adviser: Ian Crozier

*Democratic Unionist Party rotate their two portfolios between their members periodically

Executive Agencies
Business Development Service
Construction Service
Driver and Vehicle Licensing Northern Ireland
Driver and Vehicle Testing Agency
Environment and Heritage Service
Forest Service
Government Purchasing Agency
Health Estates
Industrial Research and Technology Unit
Intervention Board
Land Registers of Northern Ireland

Northern Ireland Child Support Agency
Northern Ireland Statistics and Research Agency
Ordnance Survey of Northern Ireland
Planning Service
Public Record Office of Northern Ireland
Rate Collection Agency
Rivers Agency
Roads Service
Social Security Agency
Training and Employment Agency
Valuation and Lands Agency
Water Service

Departmental Committees

Ten Departmental Committees have been established to advise and assist each Northern Ireland Minister in the formulation of policy with respect to matters within his/her responsibilities and to undertake a scrutiny, policy development and consultation role.

Agriculture and Rural Development
Chairman: Rev Dr Ian Paisley
Deputy Chairman: George Savage
William Armstrong, P J Bradley, John Dallat, Boyd Douglas, David Ford, Gardiner Kane, Gerry McHugh, Francie Molloy, Ian Paisley Jr
Clerk: Martin Wilson (028 9052 1785 Fax 028 9052 1939)

Culture, Arts and Leisure
Chairman: Eamon ONeill
Deputy Chair: Mary Nelis
Dr Ian Adamson, Fraser Agnew, Ivan Davis, David Hilditch, Kieran McCarthy, Barry McElduff, Eugene McMenamin, Jim Shannon, Jim Wilson
Clerk: Cathie White (028 9052 1230 Fax 028 9052 1063)

Education
Chairman: Danny Kennedy
Deputy Chairman: Sammy Wilson
Eileen Bell, Thomas Benson, John Fee, Tommy Gallagher, Oliver Gibson, Patricia Lewsley, Barry McElduff, Gerry McHugh, Ken Robinson
Clerk: Gillian Ardis (028 9052 1448 Fax 028 9052 1371)

Enterprise, Trade and Investment
Chairman: Pat Doherty
Deputy Chairman: Sean Neeson
Alex Attwood, Gregory Campbell, Wilson Clyde, Patricia Lewsley, David McClarty, Dr Alasdair McDonnell, Jane Morrice, Dr Dara O'Hagan, Duncan Shipley-Dalton, Jim Wells
Clerk: Cathie White (028 9052 1230 Fax 028 9052 1063)

Environment
Chairman: Rev Dr William McCrea
Deputy Chair: Carmel Hanna
Thomas Benson, Joan Carson, Arthur Doherty, David Ford, James Leslie, Mitchel McLaughlin, Mick Murphy, Edwin Poots, Denis Watson
Clerk: Debbie Pritchard (028 9052 1281 Fax 028 9052 0343)

Finance and Personnel
Chairman: Francie Molloy
Deputy Chairman: James Leslie
Alex Attwood, Billy Bell, Seamus Close, Nigel Dodds, Derek Hussey, Donovan McClelland, Alex Maskey, Peter Robinson, Peter Weir
Clerk: Martin Wilson (028 9052 1785 Fax 028 9052 1939)

Health, Social Services and Public Safety
Chairman: Dr Joe Hendron
Deputy Chairman: Tommy Gallagher
Pauline Armitage, Paul Berry, Robert Coulter, Carmel Hanna, John Kelly, Alan McFarland, Prof Monica McWilliams, Sue Ramsey, Iris Robinson
Clerk: George Martin (028 9052 1786 Fax 028 9052 1939)

Higher and Further Education, Training and Development
Chairman: Dr Esmond Birnie
Deputy Chairman: Mervyn Carrick
Roy Beggs Jnr, Joe Byrne, Joan Carson, John Dallat, William Hay, Roger Hutchinson, John Kelly, Prof Monica McWilliams, Mary Nelis
Clerk: Eileen Sung (028 9052 1272 Fax 028 9052 1433)

Regional Development
Chairman: Alban Maginness
Deputy Chairman: Alan McFarland
P J Bradley, Joe Byrne, David Ervine, William Hay, Roger Hutchinson, Derek Hussey, Pat McNamee, Rt Hon John Taylor, MP, Jim Wells
Clerk: Debbie Pritchard (028 9052 1281 Fax 028 9052 0343)

Social Development
Chairman: Fred Cobain
Deputy Chair: Michelle Gildernew
Sir John Gorman, Billy Hutchinson, Gerry Kelly, David McClarty, Danny O'Connor, Eamon ONeill, Mark Robinson, John Tierney, Sammy Wilson
Clerk: George Martin (028 9052 1786 Fax 028 9052 1939)

Standing Committees

Procedures

Chairman: Conor Murphy
Deputy Chairman: Duncan Shipley-Dalton
Fraser Agnew, Alex Attwood, Tom Benson, Roger Hutchinson, Alban Maginness, David McClarty, Pat McNamee, Maurice Morrow, Sammy Wilson
Clerk: Joe Reynolds (Clerk of Business) (028 9052 1919 Fax 028 9052 1447)

Business

Chairman, The Speaker: Lord Alderdice
Ivan Davis, Nigel Dodds, David Ford, Billy Hutchinson, Dr Alasdair McDonnell, Edward McGrady, Prof Monica McWilliams, Alex Maskey, Conor Murphy, Ian Paisley Jnr, Dennis Watson, Jim Wilson
Clerk: Joe Reynolds (Clerk of Business) (028 9052 1919 Fax 028 9052 1447)

Committee of the Centre

Remit: To examine and report on the following functions carried out in the Office of the First Minister and the Deputy First Minister, and on any other related matters determined by the Assembly.
Economic Policy Unit (excluding Programme of Government); Equality Unit; Civic Forum; European Affairs and International Matters; Community Relations; Public Appointments Policy; Freedom of Information; Victims; Nolan Standards; Public Service Office; Emergency Planning; Women's Issues.
Chairman: Edwin Poots
Deputy Chairman: Oliver Gibson
Roy Beggs Jnr, Eileen Bell, Dr Esmond Birnie, P J Bradley, Fred Cobain, David Ervine, Michelle Gildernew, James Leslie, Patricia Lewsley, Alex Maskey, Dr Alasdair McDonnell, Eugene McMenamin, Conor Murphy, Ken Robinson, James Shannon, John D Taylor.
The Committee will have the power to send for persons and papers.
Clerk: Dr Andrew Peoples (028 9052 1787 Fax 028 9052 1433)

Public Accounts

Chairman: William Bell
Deputy Chair: Sue Ramsey
Pauline Armitage, Roy Beggs Jnr, Mervyn Carrick, Seamus Close, John Dallat, David Hilditch, Jane Morrice, Donovan McCleland, Danny O'Connor
The Committee will have the power to send for persons, papers and records and to report from time to time.
Clerk: Michael Rickard (028 9052 1532 Fax 028 9052 1371)

Standards and Privileges

Chairman: Donovan McCleland
Deputy Chairman: Roy Beggs Jnr
Dr Ian Adamson, Paul Berry, Arthur Doherty, Sir John Gorman, Kieran McCarthy, Pat McNamee, Danny O'Connor, Dr Dara O'Hagan, Edwin Poots, James Wells
Clerk: John Torney (028 9052 1783 Fax 028 9052 1893)

Audit

Chairman: John Dallat
Deputy Chairman: Billy Hutchinson
Derek Hussey, Gerry McHugh, Mark Robinson
Clerk: Ms Eileen Sung (028 9052 1272 Fax 028 9052 1433)

Ad Hoc Committees

Ad Hoc Committees will be established from time to time to deal with specific time-bound terms of reference that the Assembly may set.

Visit the Vacher Dod Website . . .

www.politicallinks.co.uk

Political Parties and Shadow Assembly Spokespeople

ULSTER UNIONIST PARTY
3 Glengall Street, Belfast BT12 5AE
028 9032 4601 Fax 028 9024 6738
E-mail: uup@uup.org
Website: www.uup.org
Leader: Rt Hon David Trimble MP MLA
Deputy Leader:
   Rt Hon John D Taylor MP MLA
Assembly:
028 9052 1327 Fax: 028 9052 1395
Chief Whip: Jim Wilson MLA
028 9052 1544
Press Officer: Philip Robinson
028 9052 1328 Fax 028 9052 1395
Administration Office: 028 9052 1327

SOCIAL DEMOCRATIC AND LABOUR PARTY
121 Ormeau Road, Belfast BT7 1SH
028 9024 7700 Fax 028 9023 6699
E-mail: sdlp@indigo.ie
Website: www.sdlp.ie
Leader: John Hume MP MLA
Deputy Leader:
   Séamus Mallon MP MLA
General Secretary: Gerry Cosgrove
Assembly:
Room 272
028 9052 1319/1649 Fax 028 9052 1329
Assembly Spokespeople:
Agriculture: P J Bradley MLA
Culture, Arts and Leisure:
   Eugene McMenamin MLA
Education and Women's Issues:
   Patricia Lewsley MLA
Enterprise, Trade and Investment:
   Alasdair McDonnell MLA
Environment: Arthur Doherty MLA
Finance and Personnel:
   Donovan McClelland MLA
Further and Higher Education, Training and Employment: John Dallat MLA
Health and Social Services:
   Danny O'Connor MLA
Regional Development: Joe Byrne MLA
Social Development: John Tierney MLA

DEMOCRATIC UNIONIST PARTY
91 Dundela Avenue, Belfast BT4 3BU
028 9047 1155 Fax 028 9047 1797
E-mail: info@dup.org.uk
Website: www.dup.org.uk
Leader: Rev Dr Ian Paisley MP MEP MLA

Deputy Leader: Peter Robinson MP MLA
Assembly:
Room 207
028 9052 1322/1323 Fax: 028 9052 1289
Assembly Spokespeople:
Agriculture and Rural Development: Rev Dr
   Ian Paisley MLA, Ian Paisley Jnr MLA
Agriculture and Rural Development: Finance and Personnel: Gardiner Kane MLA
Culture, Arts and Leisure:
   David Hilditch MLA, Jim Shannon MLA
Enterprise, Trade and Investment:
   Wilson Clyde MLA
Environment: Rev Dr William McCrea MP
   MLA, Edwin Poots MLA
Finance and Personnel: Peter Robinson MP
   MLA, Nigel Dodds MLA
Education; Social Development: Sammy
   Wilson MLA
Health, Social Services and Public Safety:
   Iris Robinson MLA, Paul Berry MLA
Higher and Further Education, Training and Development: Mervyn Carrick MLA
Higher and Further Education, Training and Development; Regional Development:
   William Hay MLA
Social Development: Mark Robinson MLA
Director of Communications:
   St Clair McAlister
Chief Executive: Allan Ewart

SINN FEIN
44 Parnell Square, Dublin 1
+353 1 8726932/8726100
Fax +353 1 8733441/8783595
E-mail: sinnfein@iol.ie
Website: www.sinnfein.ie
President: Gerry Adams MLA
Vice-President: Pat Doherty MLA
Press Officer: Miss Dawn Doyle
Assembly:
028 9052 1470 Fax 028 9052 1474
Assembly Spokespeople:
Agriculture and Rural Development; Education: Gerry McHugh MLA
Agriculture and Rural Development; Finance and Personnel: Francie Molloy MLA
Culture, Arts and Leisure; Higher and Further Education, Training and Employment:
   Mary Nelis MLA
Culture, Arts and Leisure; Education:
   Barry McElduff MLA
Enterprise, Trade and Investment: Pat Doherty
   MLA, Dr Dara O'Hagan MLA

Environment: Mitchel McLaughlin MLA,
Mick Murphy MLA
Finance and Personnel: Alex Maskey MLA
Health, Social Services and Public Safety:
Sue Ramsey MLA
Health, Social Services and Public Safety;
Higher and Further Education, Training and
Employment: John Kelly MLA
Regional Development: Pat McName MLA
Social Development: Michelle Gildernew MLA,
Gerry Kelly MLA

ALLIANCE
88 University Street, Belfast BT7 1HE
028 9032 4274 Fax 028 9033 3147
E-mail: alliance@allianceparty.org
Website: www.allianceparty.org
Chair: Tom Ekin
Leader: Sean Neeson MLA
Hon Treasurer: Stewart Dickson,
Dan McGuinness
General Secretary: Stephen Farry
Assembly:
Assistant to Chief Whip: Pam Tilson
028 9052 1314 Fax 028 9052 1313
E-mail: alliance.party@niassembly.gov.uk
Assembly Spokespeople:
Leader: Enterprise, Trade and Investment;
Regional Development; European; Political
Development: Sean Neeson MLA
Deputy Leader: Finance and Personnel; Social
Development: Séamus Close MLA
Chief Whip: Agriculture and Rural
Development; Environment:
David Ford MLA
Culture, Arts and Leisure; Health and Social
Services: Kieran McCarthy MLA
President: Education; Further Higher
Education and Training and Employment;
Equality and Community Relations:
Eileen Bell MLA

NORTHERN IRELAND UNIONIST PARTY
Room 358, Parliament Buildings, Stormont,
Belfast BT4 3XX
028 9052 1533/1901 Fax 028 9052 1845
Leader: Cedric Wilson MLA
028 9052 1294 Fax 028 9052 1293
Website: www.niup.org
Party Whip: Norman Boyd MLA
028 9052 1733 Fax 028 9052 1754
E-mail: norman.boyd@niassembly.gov.uk
Deputy Leader: Patrick Roche MLA
028 9052 1994 Fax 028 9052 1848
E-mail: patrick.roche@niassembly.gov.uk

UNITED UNIONIST ASSEMBLY PARTY
Room 259, Parliament Buildings, Stormont,
Belfast BT4 3XX
Party Leader: Denis Watson MLA
Assembly:
028 9052 1466 Fax 028 9052 1465

PROGRESSIVE UNIONIST PARTY
182 Shankill Road, Belfast BT13 2BH
028 9032 6233 Fax 028 9024 9602
David Ervine MLA
E-mail: david.crvine@niassembly.gov.uk
Billy Hutchinson, MLA
Assembly:
028 9052 1469 Fax 028 9052 1468

NORTHERN IRELAND WOMEN'S COALITION
50 University Street, Belfast BT7 1HB
028 9023 3100 Fax 028 9024 0021
E-mail: niwc@iol.ie
Website: www.nicw.org
Monica McWilliams MLA
Jane Morrice MLA
Assembly:
028 9052 1463 Fax 028 9052 1461

UK UNIONIST PARTY
10 Hamilton Road, Bangor,
Co Down BT20 4LE
028 9127 2994 Fax 028 9146 5037
E-mail: info@ukup.org
Website: www.ukup.org
Leader: Robert McCartney QC MP MLA
Deputy Leader: David Vance
Chairman: Nelson Wharton
Secretary: Vacant
Treasurer: Anne Moore
Special Adviser: Tom Sheridan
Assembly:
028 9052 1482 Fax 028 9052 1483
E-mail: info@ukup.org
Website: www.ukup.org

INDEPENDENT UNIONIST (Ind Un)
Room 301, Parliament Buildings, Stormont,
Belfast BT4 3XX
028 9052 1743 Fax 028 9052 1752
Mobile: 07767 442989
E-mail: roger.hutchinson@niassembly.gov.uk
Roger Hutchinson MLA
Political Researcher: Karan Spence
Mobile: 07971 753731

GREATER LONDON ASSEMBLY

Romney House
Marsham Street
London SW1P 3PY
020 7983 4000
Fax: 020 7983 4057
E-mails: stateoflondon@london.gov.uk
mayor@london.gov.uk
website: www.london.gov.uk

Background

The Greater London Council replaced the London County Council in 1965. It was abolished by Margaret Thatcher's administration in the Local Government Act, 1985, along with the Metropolitan County Councils. Its last day of operation was 31 March 1986, when its responsibilities were handed over to the individual Greater London borough councils.

In its 1997 general election manifesto the Labour party undertook to hold a referendum to confirm popular demand for a body with responsibility for London, and if so to establish a directly elected strategic authority and mayor. Following Labour's win in the general election a referendum was held in May 1998. 34.1% of the total London electorate voted, with 72% voting in favour of the proposals for the establishment of a Greater London Authority and 28% voting against. This majority of 44% among those who voted constituted about a quarter of the eligible London electorate.

Election

The election for the Mayor and Assembly was held on 4 May 2000, using a system of proportional representation. The turnout was 33.65%.

The Mayor was chosen using the Supplementary Vote system of election, with voters indicating a first and second choice candidate. A candidate receiving more than half the first-choice votes cast would become Mayor.

If no candidate received more than half of first-choice votes the two with the most first-choice votes would go through to a second round and the other candidates would be eliminated. Any second-choice votes from the eliminated candidates' papers for either of the two remaining candidates would be added to their first-round total.

Of the eleven candidates none polled more than half the first-choice votes; in the second round between Ken Livingstone, standing as a independent, and the Conservative Steven Norris, Ken Livingstone won with a total of 57.92 per cent.

The 25 members of the Greater London Assembly (GLA) were elected using the Additional Member System. Once again, the voter had two votes. The first vote was for a candidate in the voter's GLA constituency, of which there are 14, elected in the first-past-the-post system.

The second vote was for the 11 'party list' GLA members. These members were elected according to the number of votes cast for each political party London-wide. The total number of 'party list' votes from each constituency was calculated and places on the Assembly were allocated to the parties in accordance with the proportion of votes they each received. In the event of an elected candidate leaving the GLA, the next candidate on that party's list becomes a GLA member. This has already happened. David Lammy stood as Labour candidate in the Tottenham by-election on 22 June 2000, following the death of Bernie Grant, MP. He was returned to Parliament and has resigned from the GLA. His place has been now taken by Jennette Arnold.

The Greater London Assembly consists of 9 Labour members (6 constituency and 3 London-wide), 9 Conservatives (8 constituency and 1 London-wide), 4 Liberal Democrats (all London-wide) and 3 Greens (all London-wide).

MEMBERS

Constituency

ARBOUR, Tony	Con	South West
BARNES, Richard	Con	Ealing and Hillingdon
BIGGS, John	Lab	City and East
BRAY, Angie	Con	West Central
COLEMAN, Brian	Con	Barnet and Camden
DUVALL, Len	Lab	Greenwich and Lewisham
EVANS, Roger	Con	Havering and Redbridge
GAVRON Nicky	Lab	Enfield and Haringey
HARRIS OF HARINGEY, Lord	Lab	Brent and Harrow
HILLIER, Meg	Lab	North East
HOWLETT, Elizabeth	Con	Merton and Wandsworth
NEILL, Bob	Con	Bexley and Bromley
PELLING, Andrew	Con	Croydon and Sutton
SHAWCROSS, Valerie	Lab	Lambeth and Southwark

London list

ANDERSON, Victor	Green
ARNOLD, Jennette	Lab
BLOOM, Louise	LibDem
FEATHERSTONE, Lynne	LibDem
HAMWEE, Baroness	LibDem
HEATH, Samantha	Lab
JOHNSON, Darren	Green
JONES, Jennifer	Green
OLLERENSHAW, Eric	Con
PHILLIPS, Trevor	Lab
TOPE, Lord	LibDem

Responsibilities

The Greater London Authority was established for the purpose of 'promoting economic and social development in Greater London and the improvement of the environment in Greater London'. It consists of the Mayor, the Deputy Mayor, the 25 Greater London Assembly members and advisers and staff.

It assumed its primary responsibilities on 3 July 2000, with other responsibilities being phased in. (The Mayor takes over responsibility for Trafalgar and Parliament Squares in October 2000 and for London Underground in April 2001). It has responsibility for policy in the following areas: Transport, London's Development, the Metropolitan Police, Fire and Emergency Planning, Environment, Planning, Culture Strategy, Health.

Advisory Cabinet

The Mayor has appointed an Advisory Cabinet, which provides him with advice about policy matters. It includes six GLA members. The following are the current members of the Advisory Cabinet with their portfolios.

Nicky Gavron (Deputy Mayor)	Spatial development and strategic planning.
Toby Harris	Chair, Metropolitan Police Authority
Graham Tope	Human rights and equalities
Valerie Shawcross	Chair, London Fire and Emergency Planning Authority
Darren Johnson	Environment
Glenda Jackson, MP	Homelessness
Diane Abbott, MP	Women and equality
George Barlow	Chair, London Development Agency
Judith Mayhew	City and business
John McDonnell, MP	Consultation and local government
Kumar Murshid	Regeneration
Lee Jasper	Race relations
Richard Stone	Community relations
Sean Baine	London Voluntary Services Council
Caroline Gooding	Disability rights
Yasmin Anwar	Chair, Cultural Strategy Group
Richard Rogers	Urban strategy
Sue Atkinson	Health issues
Rod Robertson	Trade union issues
Lynne Featherstone	Liberal Democrat representative

Committees

A system of committees within the GLA has been established, which are made up exclusively of GLA members. A chair and deputy chair are elected in each committee. There are currently committees for the following areas:

Transport Policy and Spatial Development Policy
Appointments
Transport Operations Scrutiny
Environment
Planning
Affordable Housing Scrutiny
Budget
Standards
Economic Development

Work has begun on the construction of a specially designed Greater London Authority building next to Tower Bridge, on the South Bank of the river, opposite the Tower of London. It is not expected to be ready until 2002.

The Parliamentarian

Journal of the Parliaments of the Commonwealth

provides an authoritative insight into the political, parliamentary and constitutional development of the Commonwealth written by the Parliamentarians and senior officials directly involved in setting policy. Factual reports and expert assessments of important advances in the evolution of political policy and systems of government present a broad picture of the state of democracy in approximately 160 Commonwealth Parliaments and Legislatures. Recent editions have covered:

Summary Report of the 46th Commonwealth Parliamentary Conference

Summary Report of the 20th Small Countries Conference

Nigeria: Is the Transition to Democracy on Track?

Democracy Under the Gun in the Solomon Islands

Keeping Politics in Parliament in Antigua and Barbuda

The "Main Game": Parliament and the Media

Information Technology in Parliament

Parliament and the Judiciary

Changing the Face of British Politics

Self-determination in Jersey

Gibraltar: Determining its Own Destiny

Parliamentarians and the World Trade Organization

Parliament and the Executive: Too Close a Relationship?

Published quarterly by:

The Headquarters Secretariat
Commonwealth Parliamentary Association
Suite 700, Westminster House, 7 Millbank
London SW1P 3JA, United Kingdom
Phone: 020 7799 1460   Fax: 020 7222 6073
E-mail: cpahq.org

Price:

Per Copy: £8 (UK), £9 (world, surface mail). £10 (air mail)
Per Year: £28 (UK), £30 (world, surface mail), £36 (air mail)

JUDICIARY

There are separate legal systems for England and Wales, Scotland and Northern Ireland. The House of Lords is the supreme judicial authority for England and Wales, and is the ultimate Court of Appeal from most courts in Great Britain and Northern Ireland.

LORD HIGH CHANCELLOR OF GREAT BRITAIN
Rt Hon Lord Irvine of Lairg QC

HOUSE OF LORDS
LORDS OF APPEAL IN ORDINARY
(In order of seniority)
Rt Hon Lord Bingham of Cornhill *(Senior Lord of Appeal in Ordinary)*, Rt Hon Lord Slynn of Hadley, Rt Hon Lord Nicholls of Birkenhead, Rt Hon Lord Steyn, Rt Hon Lord Hoffmann, Rt Hon Lord Hope of Craighead, Rt Hon Lord Clyde, Rt Hon Lord Hutton, Rt Hon Lord Saville of Newdigate, Rt Hon Lord Hobhouse of Woodborough, Rt Hon Lord Millett, Rt Hon Lord Scott of Foscote
Clerk of the Parliaments and Registrar:
    J M Davies
Fourth Clerk at the Table (Judicial):
    J A Vallance White CB

Website: www.publications.parliament.uk/pa/ld/ldjudinf.htm

RETIRED LORDS OF APPEAL IN ORDINARY who are eligible to hear appeals
(In order of seniority)
Rt Hon Lord Goff of Chieveley, Rt Hon Lord Mustill, Rt Hon Lord Lloyd of Berwick, Rt Hon Lord Nolan, Rt Hon Lord Browne-Wilkinson

OTHER LORDS OF APPEAL who are eligible to hear appeals
(In order of seniority)
Rt Hon Lord Mackay of Clashfern, Rt Hon Lord McCluskey, Rt Hon Lord Cameron of Lochbroom, Rt Hon Lord Rodger of Earlsferry *(Lord Justice General and Lord President of the Court of Session in Scotland)*, Rt Hon Lord Woolf *(Lord Chief Justice) (a former Lord of Appeal in Ordinary)*, Rt Hon Lord Cooke of Thorndon, Rt Hon Lord Hardie, Rt Hon Lord Phillips of Worth Matravers *(Master of the Rolls) (a former Lord of Appeal in Ordinary)*

RETIRED LORDS OF APPEAL IN ORDINARY who, having attained the age of 75, are no longer eligible to hear appeals (Judicial Pensions and Retirement Act 1993)
(In order of their place in the Roll of the Lords Spiritual and Temporal)
Rt Hon Lord Wilberforce, Rt Hon Lord Simon of Glaisdale, Rt Hon Lord Keith of Kinkel, Rt Hon Lord Scarman OBE, Rt Hon Lord Lane of Horsell, Rt Hon Lord Bridge of Harwich, Rt Hon Lord Brightman, Rt Hon Lord Templeman MBE, Rt Hon Lord Griffiths MC, Rt Hon Lord Ackner, Rt Hon Lord Oliver of Aylmerton, Rt Hon Lord Jauncey of Tullichettle

OTHER LORDS OF APPEAL who, having attained the age of 75, are no longer eligible to hear appeals (Judicial Pensions and Retirement Act 1993)
(In order of their place in the Roll of the Lords Spiritual and Temporal)
Rt Hon Lord Hailsham of Saint Marylebone, Rt Hon Lord Emslie, Rt Hon Lord Donaldson of Lymington

ENGLAND AND WALES
The Supreme Court of Judicature comprises the Court of Appeal, the High Court of Justice and the Crown Court.

COURT OF APPEAL
Rt Hon Lord Phillips *(Master of the Rolls)*
Rt Hon Sir Martin Charles Nourse
Rt Hon Sir Paul Joseph Morrow Kennedy
Rt Hon Sir Simon Denis Brown
Rt Hon Sir Christopher Dudley Roger Rose
Rt Hon Sir John Ormond Roch
Rt Hon Sir Peter Leslie Gibson
Rt Hon Sir Denis Robert Maurice Henry
Rt Hon Sir Swinton Barclay Thomas
Rt Hon Sir Philip Howard Otton
Rt Hon Sir Robin Ernest Auld
Rt Hon Sir Malcolm Thomas Pill
Rt Hon Sir William Aldous
Rt Hon Sir Alan Hylton Ward
Rt Hon Sir Konrad Hermann Theodor Schiemann
Rt Hon Sir Mathew Alexander Thorpe
Rt Hon Sir Mark Howard Potter
Rt Hon Sir Henry Brooke
Rt Hon Sir Igor Judge (senior presiding Judge)
Rt Hon Sir George Mark Waller

Rt Hon Sir John Frank Mummery
Rt Hon Sir Charles Mantell
Rt Hon Sir John Chadwick ED
Rt Hon Sir Robert Walker
Rt Hon Sir Richard Joseph Buxton
Rt Hon Sir Anthony Tristram May
Rt Hon Sir Simon Tuckey
Rt Hon Sir Anthony Clarke
Rt Hon Sir John Grant McKenzie Laws
Rt Hon Sir Stephen John Sedley
Rt Hon Sir Jonathan Hugh Mance
Dame Brenda Marjorie Hale DBE
Rt Hon Sir David Nicholas Ramsay Latham
Rt Hon Sir John William Kay
Rt Hon Sir Bernard Anthony Rix
Hon Dame Mary Howarth Arden DBE OBE
Hon Sir Jonathan Frederic Parker
Hon Sir John Anthony Dyson
Hon Sir David Wolfe Keene
Hon Sir Andrew Centlivres Longmore

HIGH COURT OF JUSTICE

The High Court of Justice, the superior civil
court, is divided into three: the Chancery
Division concerned principally with equity,
bankruptcy and contentious probate; Queen's
Bench Division dealing with commercial and
maritime law, serious personal injury and
medical negligence, breach of contract and
professional negligence and the Family
Division.

CHANCERY DIVISION

Rt Hon Lord Irvine of Lairg
   (Lord High Chancellor)
Rt Hon Sir Andrew Morritt, CVO
   (Vice-Chancellor)
Hon Sir Donald Keith Rattee
Hon Sir Francis Mursell Ferris TD
Hon Sir John Edmund Frederic Lindsay
Hon Sir Edward Christopher Evans-Lombe
Hon Sir Robert Raphael Hayim (Robin) Jacob
Hon Sir William Anthony Blackburne
Hon Sir Gavin Anthony Lightman
Hon Sir Robert John Anderson Carnwath CVO
Hon Sir Colin Percy Farquharson Rimer
Hon Sir Hugh Ian Lang Laddie
Hon Sir Timothy Andrew Wigram Lloyd
Hon Sir David Edmund Neuberger
Hon Sir Andrew Edward Wilson Park
Hon Sir Nicholas Richard Pumfrey
Hon Sir Michael Christopher Campbell Hart
Hon Dame Rafferty

QUEEN'S BENCH DIVISION

Rt Hon Lord Woolf *(Lord Chief Justice of
   England) (President)*
Hon Sir Richard Howard Tucker
Hon Sir Patrick Neville Garland
Hon Sir Michael John Turner
Hon Sir John Downes Alliott
Hon Sir John Arthur Dalziel Owen
Hon Sir Francis Humphrey Potts
Hon Sir Richard George Rougier
Hon Sir Ian Alexander Kennedy
Hon Sir Stuart Neil McKinnon
Hon Sir Thomas Scott Gillespie Baker
Hon Sir Edwin Frank Jowitt
Hon Sir Douglas Dunlop Brown
Hon Sir Michael Morland
Hon Sir Roger John Buckley
Hon Sir Anthony Brian Hidden
Hon Sir John Michael Wright
Hon Sir John Christopher Calthorpe Blofeld
Hon Sir Peter John Cresswell
Hon Dame Ann Marian Ebsworth DBE
Hon Sir Christopher John Holland
Hon Sir Richard Herbert Curtis
Hon Dame Janet Hilary Smith DBE
Hon Sir Anthony David Colman
Hon Sir John Thayne Forbes
Hon Sir Michael Alexander Geddes Sachs
Hon Sir Stephen George Mitchell
Hon Sir Rodger Bell
Hon Sir Michael Guy Vicat Harrison
Hon Dame Anne Heather Steel DBE
Hon Sir William Marcus Gage
Hon Sir Thomas Richard Atkin Morison
Hon Sir Andrew David Collins
Hon Sir Maurice Ralph Kay
Hon Sir Frank Brian Smedley
Hon Sir Anthony Hooper
Hon Sir Alexander Neil Logie Butterfield
Hon Sir George Michael Newman
Hon Sir David Anthony Poole
Hon Sir Martin James Moore-Bick
Hon Sir Gordon Julian Hugh Langley
Hon Sir Roger John Laugharne Thomas
Hon Sir Robert Franklyn Nelson
Hon Sir Roger Grenfell Toulson
Hon Sir Michael John Astill
Hon Sir Alan George Moses
Hon Sir Timothy Edward Walker
Hon Sir David Eady
Hon Sir Jeremy Mirth Sullivan
Hon Sir Stephen Price Richards
Hon Sir David Herbert Penry-Davey
Hon Sir David William Steel
Hon Sir Rodney Conrad Klevan
Hon Sir Charles Gray

Hon Sir Nicolas Dusán Bratza
Hon Sir Michael John Burton
Hon Sir Rupert Matthew Jackson
Dame Heather Carol Hallett DBE
Hon Sir Patrick Elias
Hon Sir Richard Pearson Aikens
Hon Sir Stephen Robert Silber
Hon Sir John Bernard Goldring
Hon Sir Peter Francis Crane
Dame Anne Judith Rafferty DBE
Hon Sir Geoffrey Douglas Grigson
Hon Sir Richard John Hedley Gibbs
Hon Sir Richard Henry Quixano Henriques
Hon Sir Stephen Miles Tomlinson
Hon Sir Stanley Jeffrey Burnton
Hon Sir Andrew Charles Smith
Hon Sir Christopher John Pitchford
Hon Sir Patrick James Hunt

FAMILY DIVISION

Rt Hon Dame Elizabeth Butler-Sloss DBE
Hon Sir Edward Stephen Cazalet DL
Hon Sir Robert Lionel Johnson
Hon Dame Joyanne Winifred Bracewell DBE
Hon Sir Michael Bryan Connell
Hon Sir Jan Peter Singer
Hon Sir Nicholas Alan Roy Wilson
Hon Sir Nicholas Peter Rathbone Wall
Hon Sir Andrew Tristram Hammett Kirkwood
Hon Sir Hugh Peter Derwyn Bennett
Hon Sir Edward James Holman
Dame Mary Claire Hogg DBE
Hon Sir Christopher John Sumner
Hon Sir Anthony Philip Gilson Hughes
Hon Sir Arthur William Hessin Charles
Hon Sir David Roderick Lessiter Bodey
Dame Jill Margaret Black DBE
Hon Sir James Munby QC
Hon Sir Paul James Duke Coleridge

CENTRAL OFFICE OF THE SUPREME COURT

Royal Courts of Justice,
London WC2A 2LL
020 7936 6000
*Senior Master of the Queen's Bench Division
and Queen's Remembrancer:* R L Turner
Masters of the Queen's Bench Division:
   D L Prebble, G H Hodgson, J Trench, M I
   Tennant, P M Miller, N O G Murray, I H Foster,
   G H Rose, P G A Eyrel, J Ungley, L Leslie

SUPREME COURT COSTS OFFICE

Cliffords Inn, Fetter Lane,
London EC4A 1DQ
020 7936 6000
Chief Taxing Master: P T Hurst
Masters: C C Wright, M Ellis, T Seager Berry,
   P R Rogers, D N Pollard, J O'Hare,
   C D N Campbell

CHANCERY CHAMBERS

Royal Courts of Justice,
London WC2A 2LL
020 7936 6000
Chief Master: J I Winegarten
Masters: J A Moncaster, R Bowman, N Bragge,
   T Bowles, N Price

ADMIRALTY AND COMMERCIAL REGISTRY

Royal Courts of Justice,
London WC2A 2LL
020 7936 6000
Registrar: P M Miller

Court of Protection

Stewart House, 24 Kingsway,
London WC2B 6JX
020 7664 7300
Master: D Lush

OFFICIAL SOLICITOR'S DEPARTMENT

81 Chancery Lane, London WC2A 1DD
020 7911 7127
Official Solicitor: L Oates
Deputy Official Solicitor: H J Baker

BANKRUPTCY COURT AND COMPANIES COURT

Thomas More Building
Royal Courts of Justice
Strand, London WC2A 2ZZ
020 7936 6448
Telex 296933 DX 44450 STRAND
Chief Registrar: Mr Registrar Buckley
Registrars: W S James, J A Simmonds,
   P J S Rawson, S Baister, P Jacques

PRINCIPAL REGISTRY OF THE FAMILY DIVISION

1st Avenue House, 42-49 High Holborn,
London WC1V 6NP
Sen District Judge: G B N A Angel
District Judges: B P F Kenworthy-Browne,
   Mrs K T Moorhouse, M J Segal,
   R Conn, Miss I M Plumstead, G J Maple,
   Miss H C Bradley, K J White, M C Berry,
   P A Waller, C E Million, P Cushing,
   S M Bowman, A O S Bassett-Cross,
   R S Harper, G Brasse

ARCHES (COURT OF)

16 Beaumont Street, Oxford OX1 2LZ
01865 297200 Fax 01865 726274
E-mail: lscott@ws-oxford.co.uk
Judge: Right Worshipful Sir John Arthur
   Dalziel Owen
Registrar and Record Keeper: Revd John Rees

CONSISTORY COURT OF LONDON
Registry Chambers, The Old Deanery,
Dean's Court, London EC4V 5AA
020 7593 5110 Fax 020 7248 3221
Chancellor: Sheila Cameron QC
Registrar: Paul Morris
Deputy Registrar: Michael Thatcher

CONSISTORY COURT OF SOUTHWARK
Registry Chambers, The Old Deanery,
Dean's Court, London EC4V 5AA
020 7593 5110 Fax 020 7248 3221
Chancellor: Charles George QC
Registrar: Paul Morris

FACULTY OFFICE
1 The Sanctuary, SW1P 3JT
020 7222 5381 Fax 020 7222 7502
E-mail: faculty.office@1thesanctuary.com
Website: www.facultyoffice.org.uk
Office for Marriage Licences (Special and
Common), Appointment of Notaries Public, etc
Master: Right Worshipful Sir John Arthur
    Dalziel Owen
Registrar: P F B Beesley
Chief Clerk and Sealer: S J Borton
Asst Clerk: S E Turner

VICAR-GENERAL'S OFFICE
16 Beaumont Street, Oxford OX1 2LZ
01865 297200 Fax 01865 726274
E-mail: lscott@ws-oxford.co.uk
Vicar-General: Miss Sheila M Cameron QC
Registrar: Revd John Rees

JUDGE ADVOCATE GENERAL
OF THE FORCES, OFFICE OF THE
(Lord Chancellor's Establishment)
(Joint Service for the Army and
Royal Air Force)
22 Kingsway, London WC2B 6LE
020 7218 8079 Fax 020 7218 8090
Judge Advocate General:
    His Honour Judge J W Rant CB QC
Vice-Judge Advocate General:
    Edmwnd G Moelwyn-Hughes
Assistant Judge Advocates General:
    Judge Advocate M A Hunter, Judge
    Advocate J P Camp, Judge Advocate
    S E Woollam, R C C Seymour, Judge
    Advocate I H Pearson, Judge Advocate
    R G Chapple, Judge Advocate J F T Bayliss
Acting Registrar: Michelle Peachey
Seven Assistant Judge Advocates General
comprise the judicial staff, three of whom are
stationed in the German Federal Republic.

THE COURT SERVICE
Southside, 105 Victoria Street
London SW1E 6QT
020 7210 1672 Fax 020 7219 1797
E-mail: cust.ser.cs@gtnet.gov.uk
Website: www.courtservice.gov.uk
The Court Service provides administrative
support to the Supreme Court of England and
Wales (comprising the Court of Appeal, the
High Court of Justice – including the probate
service – and the Crown Court), county courts
and a number of tribunals. While the outcome
of cases coming before these courts and
tribunals is determined by a judge or judicial
officer, much of the work necessary to enable
these decisions to be made and given effect is
carried out by the staff of the Court Service.
The Court Service does not provide support for
the magistrates' courts, which are supported by
a separate locally administered service.
Chief Executive: Ian Magee
Change Director: Kevin Pogson
Director of Operational Policy:
    Miss Bernadette Kenny
Director of Finance: Peter Commins
Director of Purchasing and Contracts
    Management: Colin Lyne
Director of Information Services Division:
    Ms Annette Vernon
Director of Personnel and Training:
    Ms Helen Dudley
Director of Civil and Family Business:
    John Sills
Director of Crown Court Operations:
    Mark Camley
Director of Tribunals Operations: Simon Smith
Director of Supreme Court Group: Ian Hyams
NB: See Executive Agencies

SUPREME COURT GROUP

Royal Courts of Justice
Strand, London WC2A 2LL
020 7936 6000
Director: I Hyams

Circuit Administrators
Midland and Oxford Circuit:
P Handcock,
The Courts
33 Bull Street, Birmingham B4 6DU
0121-681 3000 Fax 0121-681 3210
North Eastern Circuit:
P J Farmer,
17th Floor West Riding House,
Albion Street, Leeds LS1 5AA
0113-251 1200 Fax 0113-234 0948

Northern Circuit:
R A Vincent,
15 Quay Street
Manchester M60 9PD
0161-833 1005 Fax 0161-832 8596

South Eastern Circuit:
R J Clark,
New Cavendish House
18 Maltravers Street, London WC2R 3EU
020 7936 6000 Fax 020 7936 7230

South Eastern (Provincial Administrator)
J Powell,
1st Floor, Steeple House,
Church Lane, Chelmsford CM1 1NH
01245 257425 Fax 01245 493216

Wales and Chester Circuit:
P Risk,
2nd Floor, Churchill House
Churchill Way, Cardiff CF1 4HH
029 2041 5500 Fax 029 2034 5786

Western Circuit:
D Ryan,
Bridge House
Clifton Down, Bristol BS8 4BN
0117-974 3763 Fax 0117-974 4133

SUPREME COURTS, SCOTLAND
(COURT OF SESSION)

INNER HOUSE
First Division: Rt Hon Lord Rodger of Earlsferry (Lord President), Rt Hon Lord Sutherland, Rt Hon Lord Prosser, Rt Hon Lord Cameron of Lochbroom

Second Division: Rt Hon Lord Cullen (Lord Justice Clerk), Rt Hon Lord Kirkwood, Rt Hon Lord Coulsfield, Rt Hon Lord Milligan

OUTER HOUSE
Hon Lord Marnoch, Hon Lord MacLean, Hon Lord Penrose, Hon Lord Osborne, Hon Lord Abernethy, Hon Lord Johnston, Hon Lord Gill (seconded to the Scottish Law Commission), Hon Lord Hamilton, Hon Lord Dawson, Hon Lord Macfadyen, Hon Lady Cosgrove, Hon Lord Nimmo Smith, Hon Lord Philip, Hon Lord Kingarth, Hon Lord Bonomy, Hon Lord Eassie, Hon Lord Reed, Hon Lord Wheatley, Hon Lady Paton, Hon Lord Carloway, Hon Lord Clarke, Rt Hon Lord Hardie, Rt Hon Lord Mackay of Drumadoon, Hon Lord McEwan

Principal Clerk of Session: J L Anderson, Parliament House, Edinburgh EH1 1RQ

HIGH COURT OF JUSTICIARY
Lord Justice-General: Rt Hon Lord Rodger of Earlsferry

Lord Justice-Clerk: Rt Hon Lord Cullen
The remaining judges of the Court of Session are also Lords Commissioners of Justiciary

Principal Clerk of Justiciary: J L Anderson, Parliament House, Edinburgh EH1 1RQ
0131-225 2595 Fax: 0131-240 6755
Website: www.scotcourts.gov.uk

SUPREME COURT, NORTHERN IRELAND

Royal Courts of Justice, Chichester Street, Belfast BT1 3JF   028 9023 5111
Principal Secretary to the Lord Chief Justice: G W Johnston
(gwjohnston@nicts.dnet.co.uk)
Departments of the Supreme Court
Central Office
Master (Queen's Bench and Appeals): J W Wilson QC
Master (High Court): Mrs D M Kennedy
Chancery Office
Master: R A Ellison
Bankruptcy and Companies Office: *Master:* C W G Redpath
Probate and Matrimonial Office: *Master:* Miss M J McReynolds
Office of Care and Protection: *Master:* F B Hall
Official Solicitor's Office: *Official Solicitor:* Miss B M Donnelly
Taxing Office, Bedford House, Bedford Street, Belfast BT2 7DS. 028 9024 5081
Master: J C Napier

Supreme Court of Judicature of Northern Ireland
The Lord Chief Justice of Northern Ireland: Rt Hon Sir Robert Carswell
Rt Hon Lord Justice Nicholson, Rt Hon Lord Justice McCollum, Rt Hon Lord Justice Campbell, Hon Mr Justice Sheil, Hon Mr Justice Kerr, Hon Mr Justice Higgins, Hon Mr Justice Girvan, Hon Mr Justice Coghlin, Hon Mr Justice Gillen, Hon Mr Justice McLaughlin

THE PRIVY COUNCIL OF NORTHERN IRELAND
By virtue of the Northern Ireland Constitution Act 1973 no further appointments will be made to the Privy Council of Northern Ireland, but existing members will retain their existing style and dignity.
R J Bailie, D W Bleakley, W Craig, J Dobson, Hon Lord Justice Kelly, H V Kirk, W J Long, Lord McConnell, W B McIvor, Lord Moyola, Sir Ivan Neill, Sir Robert Porter, John D Taylor MP MLA, H W West

UK GOVERNMENT REPRESENTATIVES/ OVERSEAS REPRESENTATIVES IN UK

VACHER'S EUROPEAN COMPANION

Accurate and up-to-date • Revised quarterly
Fully indexed

The original European reference book –

covering all the EU institutions, other important European organisations, sources of information, national sections for East and West
European countries. Features include:

- **EU Institutions** – Comprehensive listings of key personnel and how to
  make contact, including fax, e-mail and web addresses.

- **European Countries** – Detailed digests of 30 countries, not just the 15 EU
  member states but also East and Central European applicants. Information
  on governments, elections, political structure, economic and trade activities.

- **Sources of Information** – Documentation, Databases, Legislation and
  European Information Networks.

"With its clear and up-to-date listings [Vacher's European Companion] *has
established its reputation as an essential reference book for all those who need
to keep abreast of developments in the European Parliament and other
institutions"*
Nicole Fontatine, President of the European Parliament

Call now to start your subscription to this essential European reference book

Four issues per annum

Vacher Dod Publishing Limited
PO Box 3700, Westminster, London SW1P 4WU
Tel: 020 7828 7256   Fax: 020 7828 7269
E-mail: politics@vacherdod.co.uk
Website: www.politicallinks.co.uk

HM Lord-Lieutenants

ENGLAND

Bedfordshire	Samuel Charles Whitbread Esq
Berkshire	Philip Lavallin Wroughton Esq
Bristol	James Napier Tidmarsh Esq MBE
Buckinghamshire	Sir Nigel Mobbs
Cambridgeshire	James Gee Pascoe Crowden Esq
Cheshire	William Arthur Bromley-Davenport Esq
Cornwall	Lady Mary Holborow
Cumbria	James Cropper Esq
Derbyshire	John Knollys Bather Esq
Devon	Eric Dancer Esq CBE
Dorset	Captain Michael Fulford-Dobson CVO RN
Durham	Sir Paul Nicholson
East Riding of Yorkshire	Richard Marriott Esq TD
East Sussex	Phyllida Stewart-Roberts OBE
Essex	Lord Braybrooke
Gloucestershire	Henry William George Elwes Esq
Greater London	Lord Imbert QPM
Greater Manchester	Colonel John Bradford Timmins OBE TD
Hampshire	Mary Fagan
Herefordshire	Sir Thomas Dunne KCVO
Hertfordshire	Simon Alexander Bowes Lyon Esq
Isle of Wight	Christopher Donald Jack Bland Esq
Kent	Rt Hon Lord Kingsdown KG
Lancashire	Lord Shuttleworth
Leicestershire	Timothy Gerald Martin Brooks Esq
Lincolnshire	Bridget Cracroft-Eley
Merseyside	Alan William Waterworth Esq
Norfolk	Sir Timothy Colman KG
Northamptonshire	Lady Juliet Margaret Townsend LVO
Northumberland	Sir John Riddell Bt
North Yorkshire	Lord Crathorne
	Lord Gisborough TD *(HM Lieutenant)*
Nottinghamshire	Sir Andrew George Buchanan Bt
Oxfordshire	Hugo Brunner Esq
Rutland	Air Chief Marshal Sir Thomas Kennedy GCB AFC
Shropshire	Algernon Heber-Percy Esq
Somerset	Lady Gass
South Yorkshire	Earl of Scarbrough
Staffordshire	James Appleton Hawley Esq TD
Suffolk	Rt Hon Lord Belstead
Surrey	Sarah Goad
Tyne and Wear	Colonel Sir Ralph Carr-Ellison KCVO TD
Warwickshire	Martin Dunne Esq
West Midlands	Robert Richard Taylor Esq OBE
West Sussex	Hugh Wyatt Esq
West Yorkshire	John Lyles Esq CBE
Wiltshire	Lieutenant-General Sir Maurice Johnston KCB OBE
Worcestershire	Sir Thomas Dunne KCVO

WALES

Clwyd	Sir Erskine William Gladstone Bt KG
Dyfed	Sir David Courtenay Mansel Lewis KCVO
Gwent	Vacant
Gwynedd	Professor Eric Sunderland OBE
Mid Glamorgan	Murray Adams McLaggan Esq
Powys	Hon Shän Legge-Bourke LVO
South Glamorgan	Captain Norman Lloyd-Edwards RD RNR (retired)
West Glamorgan	Robert Cameron Hastie Esq CBE RD

SCOTLAND

The Lord Provosts for the time being of the four City Districts (Aberdeen, Dundee, Edinburgh and Glasgow) are Lord-Lieutenants of those districts ex-officio

Aberdeen City	Lord Provost *ex officio* Margaret Smith
Aberdeenshire (Grampian Region)	Angus Farquharson Esq OBE
Angus (Tayside Region)	Rt Hon Earl of Airlie KT GCVO
Argyll and Bute (Strathclyde Region)	His Grace the Duke of Argyll
Ayrshire and Arran (Strathclyde Region)	Major Richard Henderson TD
Banffshire (Grampian Region)	James Alexander Strachan McPherson Esq CBE
Berwickshire (Borders Region)	Major Alexander Trotter
Caithness (Highland Region)	Major Graham Dunnett TD
Clackmannan (Central Region)	Lieutenant-Colonel Robert Christie Stewart CBE TD
Dumfries (Dumfries and Galloway Region)	Captain Ronald Charles Cunningham-Jardine
Dunbartonshire (Strathclyde Region)	Brigadier Donald David Graeme Hardie TD
Dundee	Lord Provost *ex officio* Helen Wright
East Lothian (Lothian Region)	Major Sir Hew Hamilton-Dalrymple Bt KCVO
Edinburgh	Lord Provost *ex officio* Eric Milligan Esq
Fife	Margaret Dean
Glasgow	Lord Provost *ex officio* Alex Mosson Esq
Inverness (Highland Region)	Rt Hon Lord Gray of Contin
Kincardineshire (Grampian Region)	John Smart Esq
Lanarkshire (Strathclyde Region)	Vacant
Midlothian (Lothian Region)	Captain George Wardlaw Burnet LVO
Moray (Grampian Region)	Air Vice-Marshal George Arthur Chesworth CB OBE DFC
Nairn (Highland Region)	Ewen Brodie Esq
Orkney	George Robert Marwick Esq
Perth and Kinross (Tayside Region)	Sir David Montgomery Bt
Renfrewshire (Strathclyde Region)	Cameron Holdsworth Parker Esq OBE
Ross and Cromarty (Highland Region)	Captain Roderick William Kenneth Stirling of Fairburn TD
Roxburgh, Ettrick and Lauderdale (Borders Region)	Dr June Paterson-Brown CBE
Shetland	John Hamilton Scott Esq
Stewartry of Kirkcudbright (Dumfries and Galloway Region)	Lieutenant-General Sir Norman Arthur KCB
Stirling and Falkirk (Central Region)	Colonel James Stirling of Garden CBE TD
Sutherland (Highland Region)	Major-General David Houston CBE
Tweeddale (Borders Region)	Captain David Younger
Western Isles	Vacant
West Lothian (Lothian Region)	Earl of Morton
Wigtown (Dumfries and Galloway Region)	Major Edward Orr Ewing

NORTHERN IRELAND

Antrim	Lord O'Neill TD
Armagh	Earl of Caledon
Belfast	Lady Carswell OBE
Down	William Joseph Hall Esq
Fermanagh	Earl of Erne
Londonderry	Denis Desmond Esq CBE
Londonderry City	James Thompson Eaton Esq CBE TD
Tyrone	His Grace the Duke of Abercorn KG

Association of Lord-Lieutenants

Chairman	Rt Hon Lord Kingsdown KG
Secretary	Andrew Makower Esq
	(House of Lords, London SW1P 3JY)

Crown Dependencies

The Isle of Man, Jersey and Guernsey are dependencies of the Crown, which is represented by a Lieutenant-Governor. They are internally self-governing, but defence and international affairs, including foreign representation are the responsibility of the UK government.

Isle of Man

Lieutenant-Governor: HE Air Marshal Ian David MacFadyen CB OBE
The President of Tynwald: Hon Noel Q Cringle
*Speaker of the House of Keys:*Hon J David Q Cannan SHK
Chief Minister: Hon Donald James Gelling FInstMM MHK

Population: 71,714
Area: 221 square miles
Capital: Douglas

Clerk to Tynwald: Prof T St John Bates MA LLM

Legislative Buildings, Douglas,
Isle of Man IM1 3PW

01624 685500 Fax 01624 685504
Tynwald (www.tynwald.isle-of-man.org.im)
Government offices: 01624 685685
Isle of Man Government (www.gov.im)

Jersey

*Lieutenant-Governor:*HE General Sir Michael Wilkes KCB CBE
The Bailiff (President of the States Assembly and the Royal Court): Sir Philip Bailhache

Population: 85,150
Area: 45 square miles
Capital: St Helier

The Bailiff's Chambers,
Royal Court House, St Helier,
Jersey, JE1 1DD, Channel Islands

01534 502100 Fax 01534 502199

G H C Coppock MA (Cantab),
Greffier (Clerk) of the States,
Morier House, Halkett Place, St Helier,
Jersey JE1 1DD, Channel Islands

01534 502013 Fax 01534 502098
E-mail: stgreffe@itl.net

Guernsey

*Lieutenant-Governor:*HE Lieutenant General Sir John Foley KCB OBE MC
The Bailiff de V G Carey

Population: 60,000 approx
Area: 24 square miles
Capital: St Peter Port

Alderney, Sark, Herm, Jethou, Brechou and Lihou are included in the Bailiwick.

The Bailiff's Chambers,
The Royal Court House,
Guernsey GY1 2PB, Channel Islands

01481 726161

British Overseas Territories
Governors and Commanders-in-Chief

Anguilla	HE Peter Johnstone *(Governor)*
Bermuda	HE Thorold Masefield CMG *(Governor and Commander-in-Chief)*
British Antarctic Territory	Mr C J B White *(Commissioner)* (Resident in London)
British Indian Ocean Territory	Mr C J B White *(Commissioner)* (Resident in London)
British Virgin Islands	HE Frank Savage CMG LVO OBE *(Governor)*
Cayman Islands	HE Peter Smith CBE *(Governor)*
Falkland Islands	HE Donald Lamont *(Governor)*
Gibraltar	HE David Durie CMG *(Governor and Commander-in-Chief)*
Montserrat	HE Anthony Abbott OBE *(Governor)*
Pitcairn, Henderson, Ducie and Oeno Islands	HE Martin Williams CVO OBE *(Governor)* (Non-resident) see New Zealand – British Embassies and High Commissions Overseas section
St Helena and Dependencies	HE Mr D Hollamby *(Governor and Commander-in-Chief)*
South Georgia and South Sandwich Islands	HE Donald Lamont *(Commissioner)* (Resident in Stanley)
Turks and Caicos Islands	HE Mervyn Jones *(Governor)*

The Commonwealth

Of the 54 member countries of the Commonwealth, Queen Elizabeth II is Head of State of 16 (including the United Kingdom), 33 are republics, and 5 are monarchies with other sovereigns. The Queen remains symbolically Head of the Commonwealth.

Governors-General

In the overseas realms of which she is Queen, Her Majesty is represented by a Governor-General

Antigua and Barbuda
HE Sir James Carlisle KCMG
Prime Minister: Hon Lester B Bird

Australia
HE Sir William Deane AC KBE
Prime Minister: Hon John Howard MP

Bahamas
HE Sir Orville Turnquest KCMG
Prime Minister: Rt Hon Hubert A Ingraham

Barbados
HE Sir Clifford Husbands GCMG
Prime Minister: Rt Hon Owen Arthur

Belize
HE Sir Colville Norbert Young Sr KCMG
Prime Minister: Hon Said Musa

Canada
HE Hon Adrienne Clarkson
Prime Minister: Rt Hon Jean Chretien

Grenada
HE Sir Charles Daniel Williams GCMG QC
Prime Minister: Hon Dr Keith Mitchell

Jamaica
HE Sir Howard Felix Cooke GCMG CD
Prime Minister: Rt Hon P J Patterson QC

New Zealand
HE Rt Hon Sir Michael Hardie Boys GCMG (until March 2001)
Dame Silvia Cartwright (from March 2001)
Prime Minister: Rt Hon Helen Clark

Papua New Guinea
HE Sir Sailas Atopare GCMG
Prime Minister: Hon Sir Mekere Morauta

Solomon Islands
HE Rev John Ini Lapli GCMG
Prime Minister: Hon Manasseh Sogavare

*St Christopher and Nevis
HE Sir Cuthbert M Sebastian GCMG OBE
Prime Minister: Hon Dr Denzil Douglas

*St Lucia
HE Dame Calliopa Pearlette Louisy GCMG
Prime Minister: Dr Hon Kenny D Anthony

*St Vincent and The Grenadines
HE Sir Charles James Antrobus GCMG OBE
Prime Minister: Rt Hon Sir James Fitz Allen Mitchell KCMG

Tuvalu
HE Rt Hon Sir Tomasi Puapua KBE
Prime Minister: Hon Ionatana Ionatana

*Eastern Caribbean States

Republics and other Commonwealth Monarchies
Heads of State and Heads of Government

Bangladesh
President and Head of State: HE Shahabuddin Ahmed
Prime Minister and Head of Government: Hon Sheikh Hasina

Botswana
President and Head of Government: HE Festus G Mogae

Brunei
Sultan and Head of Government: HM Paduka Seri Baginda Sultan Haji Hassanal Bolkiah Mu'izzaddin Waddaulah; Sultan and Yang Di-Pertuan Negara Brunei Darussalam

Cameroon
President and Head of Government: HE Paul Biya

Cyprus
President and Head of Government: HE Glafkos Clerides

Dominica
President and Head of State: HE Vernon Shaw
Prime Minister and Head of Government: Hon Roosevelt Douglas

**Fiji Islands	*President:* HE Ratu Josefa Iloilo
	Prime Minister Laisenia Qarase
The Gambia	*President and Head of Government:* HE Yahya A J J Jammeh
Ghana	*President and Head of Government:* HE Flt Lt (rtd) Jerry J Rawlings
Guyana	*President and Head of Government:* HE Bharrat Jagdeo
India	*President and Head of State:* HE Mr K R Narayanan
	Prime Minister and Head of Government: Hon Atal Bihari Vajpayee
Kenya	*President and Head of Government:* HE Daniel arap Moi CGH
Kiribati	*President and Head of Government:* HE Teburoro Tito
Lesotho	*Head of State:* HM King Letsie III
	Prime Minister and Head of Government: Hon Bethuel Pakalitha Mosisili
Malawi	*President and Head of Government:* HE Bakili Muluzi
Malaysia	*Head of State:* HM Sultan Salahuddin Abdul Aziz Shah *(King of Malaysia)*
	Prime Minister and Head of Government: Hon Datuk Seri Dr Mahathir Mohamad
Maldives	*President and Head of Government:* HE Maumoon Abdul Gayoom GCMG
Malta	*President and Head of State:* HE Professor Guido de Marco
	Prime Minister and Head of Government: Hon Dr Edward Fenech Adami
Mauritius	*President and Head of State:* HE Cassam Uteem GCSK
	Prime Minister and Head of Government: Hon Dr Navinchandra Ramgoolam
Mozambique	*President and Head of State:* HE Joaquim A Chissano
Namibia	*President and Head of Government:* HE Dr Sam Nujoma
Nauru	*President and Head of Government:* HE Bernard Dowiyogo
Nigeria	*President and Head of State:* HE General (Rtd) Olusegun Obasanjo
**Pakistan	*President and Head of State:* HE Rafiq Tarar
	Chief Executive: General Pervaiz Musharraf
Samoa	*Head of State:* HH Malietoa Tanumafili II GCMG CBE
	Prime Minister and Head of Government: Hon Tuilaepa Sailele Malielegaoi
Seychelles	*President and Head of Government:* HE France Albert René
Sierra Leone	*President:* HE Alhaji Dr Ahmed Tejan Kabbah
Singapore	*President and Head of State:* HE Ong Teng Cheong
	Prime Minister and Head of Government: Hon Goh Chok Tong
South Africa	*President and Head of Government:* HE Thabo Mbeki
Sri Lanka	*President and Head of Government:* HE Chandrika Bandaranaike Kumaratunga
Swaziland	*Head of State:* HM King Mswati III
	Prime Minister and Head of Government: Hon Dr Barnabas Dlamini
Tanzania	*President and Head of Government:* HE Benjamin William Mkapa
Tonga	*Head of State:* HM King Taufa'ahau Tupou IV GCMG
	Prime Minister and Head of Government: HRH Prince 'Ulukalala Lavaka Ata
Trinidad and Tobago	*President and Head of State:* HE Mr A N R Robinson
	Prime Minister and Head of Government: Hon Basdeo Panday
Uganda	*President and Head of Government:* HE Yoweri Museveni
Vanuatu	*President and Head of State:* HE Fr John Bani
	Prime Minister and Head of Government: Hon Donald Kalpokas
Western Samoa	– See Samoa
Zambia	*President and Head of Government:* HE Frederick Chiluba
Zimbabwe	*President and Head of Government:* HE Robert Mugabe MP

**These countries are currently suspended from the Councils of the Commonwealth.

British Embassies and High Commissions

AFGHANISTAN
(Post currently vacant)

ALBANIA
British Embassy
Rruga, Skenderbeg 12, Tirana
00 900 355 42 34973 Fax 00 900 355 42 47697
Ambassador: HE Dr Peter January

ALGERIA
British Embassy
Résidence Cassiopée, Bâtiment B, 7 Chemin
des Glycines (B P 08, Alger-Gare 16000)
00 213 2 23 00 92 Fax 00 213 2 23 00 67
Ambassador: HE William Sinton OBE

ANDORRA – see Spain

ANGOLA
British Embassy
Rua Diogo Caõ, 4 (Caixa Postal 1244), Luanda
00 244 2 334582 Fax 00 244 2 333331
E-mail: britemb.ang@ebonet.net
Ambassador: HE Caroline Elmes
Commercial: R Izzard
(Non-resident: Sao Tome)

ANTIGUA & BARBUDA
British High Commission
PO Box 483, Price Waterhouse Centre,
11 Old Parham Road, St John's
00 1 268 462 0008/463 0010
Fax 00 1 268 562 2124
High Commissioner: HE Gordon M Baker
(Resides in Barbados)
Resident High Commissioner:
HE Mrs S Murphy

ARGENTINA
British Embassy
Dr Luis Agote 2141, 1425 Buenos Aires
00 54 11 4803 2222 Fax 00 54 11 4803 1731
Ambassador: HE Sir Robin Christopher KCMG
Commercial: Ms H H Deas – First Secretary

ARMENIA
British Embassy
28 Charents Street, Yerevan
00 3742 151841 Fax 00 3742 151064
Ambassador: HE Timothy Jones

AUSTRALIA
British High Commission
Commonwealth Avenue, Yarralumla, Canberra,
ACT 2600
00 61 2 6270 6666
Fax Chancery 00 61 2 6270 6653
E-mail: bhc.canberra@emb.gov.at
High Commissioner:
HE The Rt Hon. Sir Alastair Goodlad KCMG

AUSTRIA
British Embassy
Jaurèsgasse 12, 1030 Vienna
00 43 1 716130 Fax 00 43 1 71613 2999
E-mail: britem@netway.at
Ambassador: HE Antony Ford CMG

AZERBAIJAN
British Embassy
2 Izmir Street, Baku 370065
00 994 12 975188 Fax 00 994 12 922739
E-mail: office@ukemb.baku.az
Ambassador: HE Andrew Tucker

BAHAMAS
British High Commission
Ansbacher House (3rd Floor), East Street,
PO Box N7516, Nassau
00 1 242 325 7471 Fax 00 1 242 323 3871
High Commissioner: HE Mr P Heigl
Commercial: Ms E J Huggins –
Commercial/Information Officer

BAHRAIN
British Embassy
21 Government Avenue, Manama 306,
PO Box 114, Bahrain
00 973 534404 Fax 00 973 531273
E-mail: britemb@batelco.com.bh
Telegrams: PRODROME, BAHREIN
Ambassador and Consul-General:
HE Mr P Ford
Commercial: Mr K J Shaughnessy –
Second Secretary

BANGLADESH
British High Commission
United Nations Road, Baridhara Dhaka
00 880 2 8822705 Fax 00 880 2 8823 437
High Commissioner:
HE David Carter CVO
Commercial: Mr C Allcorn – Second Secretary

BARBADOS
British High Commission
Lower Collymore Rock (PO Box 676),
Bridgetown
00 61 1 246 430 7800
Fax 00 61 1 246 430 7851
E-mail: britishhc@sunbeach.net
High Commissioner: HE Gordon M Baker
(Non-resident: St Lucia, Grenada, St Kitts &
Nevis, Commonwealth of Dominica, St Vincent
& the Grenadines, Antigua & Barbuda)

BELARUS
British Embassy
37 Karl Marx Street, 220030 Minsk
00 375 172 105920 Fax 00 375 172 292306
Ambassador: HE Iain Kelly

BELGIUM
British Embassy
Rue d'Arlon 85, 1040 Brussels
00 32 2 287 6211 Fax 00 32 2 287 6355
Ambassador: HE David H Colvin CMG
Commercial: Mr D J Currie – First Secretary
Fax 00 32 2 287 6240

BELIZE
British High Commission
PO Box 91 Belmopan, or BFPO 12
00 501 8 22146/7 Fax 00 501 8 22761
E-mail: brithicom@btl.net
High Commissioner: HE Timothy David

BENIN – see Nigeria

BOLIVIA
British Embassy
Avenida Arce 2732 (Casilla 694), La Paz
00 591 2 433424 Fax: 00 591 2 431073
E-mail: ppa@mail.megalink.com
Ambassador: HE Graham Minter LVO
Commercial: Mr E Suarez –
Commercial Officer

BOSNIA AND HERZEGOVINA
8 Tina Ujevica, Sarajevo
00 387 71 444429 Fax 00 387 71 666131
Ambassador: HE Graham Hand
Commercial: Mr C J Poole MBE –
First Secretary

BOTSWANA
British High Commission
Private Bag 0023, Gaborone
E-mail: british@bc.bw
00 267 3 52841/2/3 Fax 00 267 356105
High Commissioner: HE Mr J Wilde

BRAZIL
British Embassy
Setor de Embaixadas Sul, Quadra 801,
Conjunto K, CEP 70.408-900 or
Avenida das Naçoes, Caixa Postal 07-0586,
70359 Brasilia-DF
00 55 61 225-2710 Fax 00 55 61 225 1777
E-mail: britemb@nutecnet.com.br
Ambassador: HE Roger Bone CMG

BRUNEI
British High Commission
2/01, 2nd Floor, Block D,
Komplexs Bangunan Yayasan,
Sultan Haji Hassanal Bolkiah, Jalan Pretty,
PO Box 2197, Bandar Seri Begawan 1921
00 673 2 222231/223121 Fax 00 673 2 234315
High Commissioner: HE Stuart Laing
Commercial: Mr M Y Moon –
Second Secretary

BULGARIA
British Embassy
38 Boulevard Vassil Levski, Sofia
00 359 2980 1220 Fax: 00 359 2980 1229
Ambassador: HE Richard Stagg
Commercial: Mr D Leith – First Secretary

BURKINA FASO – see Cote d'Ivoire

BURMA
British Embassy
80 Strand Road (Box No 638), Rangoon
00 95 1 295300/295309 Fax 00 95 1 289566
Ambassador: HE Dr John Jenkins LVO

BURUNDI – see Rwanda

CAMBODIA
British Embassy
29 Street 75, Phnom Penh
00 855 23 427124 Fax 00 855 23 427125
Ambassador: HE George Edgar until December
2000; Stephen Bridges from December 2000

CAMEROON
British High Commission
Avenue Winston Churchill, BP 547, Yaoundé
00 237 22 05 45/07 96 Fax 00 237 22 01 48
High Commissioner: HE Peter Boon
(Non-resident: Chad, Central African Republic,
Equatorial Guinea, Gabon)

CANADA
British High Commission
80 Elgin Street, Ottawa K1P 5K7
00 1 613 237-1530 Fax 00 1 613 237 7980
Telegraphic address: UKREP OTTAWA
E-mail: bhc@ottawa.mail.fco.gov.uk
High Commissioner:
HE Sir Andrew Burns KCMG
Commercial: Ms E Miller – Third Secretary

CAPE VERDE – see Senegal

**CENTRAL AFRICAN REPUBLIC –
see Cameroon**

CHAD – see Cameroon

CHILE
British Embassy
Av El Bosque 0125, Casilla 72-D or Casilla
16552, Santiago 9
00 56 2 370 3737 Fax 00 56 2 370 4140
E-mail: chancery@santiago.mail.fco.gov.uk
Ambassador: Gregory Faulkner
Commercial: Mr T A Torlot – First Secretary

CHINA
British Embassy
11 Guang Hua Lu, Jian Guo Men Wai,
Peking 100 600
00 86 10 6532 1961 Fax 00 86 10 6532 1937
E-mail: beinfo@public.bta.net.cn
Ambassador:
HE Sir Anthony Galsworthy KCMG
Commercial: Mr C M J Segar – Counsellor

Hong Kong
British Consulate General,
No 1 Supreme Court Road, Central,
Hong Kong (PO Box 528)
00 852 2901 3000 Fax 00 852 2901 3066
Consul-General: Sir James Hodge KCVO CMG
*British Senior Representative to the Sino-British
Joint Liaison:* Mr A Paul CMG

COLOMBIA
British Embassy
Edificio Ing Barings, Carrera 9 No 76-49 Piso
9, Bogotá
00 57 1 317 6690/6310/6321
Fax 00 57 1 317 6298
E-mail: britain@cable.net.co
Ambassador: HE Jeremy Thorp

COMOROS – see Madagascar

CONGO, DEMOCRATIC REPUBLIC OF
British Embassy
Avenue du Roi Baudouin, Kinshasa
00 243 88 46102
E-mail: ambrit@ic.cd
Ambassador: HE James Atkinson
(Non-resident: Congo, Peoples Republic)

CONGO, REPUBLIC OF
Ambassador: HE James Atkinson
(resident in Democratic Republic of Congo)

COSTA RICA
British Embassy
Apartado 815, Edificio Centro Colon,
(11th Floor), San José 1007
00 506 258 20 25 Fax 00 506 233 99 38
E-mail: britemb@sol.racsa.co.cr
Ambassador and Consul-General:
HE Mr P J Spiceley MBE

COTE D'IVOIRE
British Embassy
3rd Floor, Immeuble "Les Harmonies",
Angle Boulevard Carde et Avenue, Dr Jamot,
Plateau, Abidjan
Postal address: 01 BP 2581, Abidjan 01
00 225 226850 Fax 00 225 223221
E-mail: britemb.a@africaonline.co.ci
Ambassador and Consul-General:
HE Haydon Warren-Gash
(Non-resident: Burkina Faso, Niger and
Liberia)
Commercial: Mr F G Geere – First Secretary,
Consul and Deputy Head of Mission

CROATIA
British Embassy
Vlaska, 121, 3rd Floor, PO Box 454,
10000 Zagreb
00 385 1 455 5310 Fax 00 385 1 455 1685
E-mail: british-embassy@zg.tel.hr
Ambassador: HE Nicholas Jarrold
Commercial: Mr G Kirby – First Secretary

CUBA
British Embassy
Calle 34 No. 702/4 entre 7ma Avenida 17,
Miramar, Havana
00 53 7 24 1771/2 Fax 00 53 7 24 8104
E-mail: embrit@ceniai.inf.cu
Ambassador: HE David Ridgway OBE
Commercial: Mr N D Sutcliffe – First Secretary

CYPRUS
British High Commission
Alexander Pallis Street (PO Box 1978), Nicosia
or BFPO 567
00 357 2 861100 Fax 00 357 2 861125
E-mail: infobhc@cylink.com.cy
High Commissioner:
HE Edward Clay CMG
Commercial: Mr W L Ross – First Secretary

CZECH REPUBLIC
British Embassy
Thunovská 14, 11800 Prague 1
00 420 2 5753 0278 Fax 420 2 5753 0285
Ambassador: HE David Broucher
Commercial: Palac Myslbek,
Na Prikope 21, 117 19 Prague 1
00 420 2 2224-0021/2/3
Fax 00 420 2 2224-3625
E-mail: info@britain.cz
Mr M C Day – First Secretary

DENMARK
British Embassy
Kastelsvej 36/38/40, DK-2100 Copenhagen Ø
00 45 35 44 52 00 Fax 00 45 35 44 52 93
E-mail: www.brit-emb@post6.tele.dk
Ambassador: HE Philip Astley CVO
Commercial: Mr F J Martin – First Secretary
Fax 00 45 35 44 52 46

DJIBOUTI – see Ethiopia

DOMINICA – see Barbados

DOMINICAN REPUBLIC
British Embassy
Edificio Corominas Pepin, Ave 27 de Fabrero
No 233, Santo Domingo
00 1 809 472 7111/7905
Ambassador: HE David Ward
(Non-resident: Haiti)

ECUADOR
British Embassy
Citiplaza Building, Naciones Unidas Avenue
and Republica de El Salvador, 14th Floor, PO
Box 17-17-830, Quito
00 593 2 970 800 Fax 00 593 2 970 811
E-mail: britemcom@impsat.net.ec
Ambassador: HE Mr I Gerken LVO

EGYPT
British Embassy
Ahmed Ragheb Street, Garden City, Cairo
00 20 2 354-0850/0852 Fax 00 20 2 354-0859
E-mail: britemb@idsc.gov.eg
Ambassador: HE Graham Boyce CMG
Commercial: Mr D G Reader – First Secretary

EL SALVADOR
British Embassy
Edifio Inter-Inversiones, Paseo General Escalón
4828, PO Box 1591, San Salvador
00 503 263 6527 Fax 00 503 263 6516
Ambassador and Consul-General:
HE Patrick Morgan

EQUATORIAL GUINEA – see Cameroon

ERITREA – see Ethiopia

ESTONIA
British Embassy
Wismari 6, Tallinn 10136
00 372 667 4700 Fax 00 372 667 4755
Ambassador: HE Sarah Squire

ETHIOPIA
British Embassy
Fikre Mariam Abatechan Street, Addis Ababa
00 251 161 2354 Fax 00 251 161 0588
Postal address: PO Box 858
E-mail: b.emb4@telecom.net.et
Ambassador: HE Myles Wickstead
(Non-resident: Eritrea and Djibouti)

FIJI ISLANDS
British High Commission
Victoria House, 47 Gladstone Road, Suva
(PO Box 1355)
00 679 311033 Fax 00 679 301406
E-mail: ukchancery@is.com.fj
High Commissioner: HE Michael Price
(Non-resident: Nauru, Tuvalu and Kiribati)
HE Christopher Haslam – Deputy Head of
Mission and Consul, and non-resident
Ambassador to Micronesia, Marshall Islands,
Palau and Deputy High Commissioner to
Kiribati, Nauru and Tuvalu

FINLAND
British Embassy
Itainen Puistotie 17, 00140 Helsinki
00 358 09 2286 5100 Fax 00 358 09 2286 5284
E-mail: info@ukembassy.fi
Ambassador: HE Alyson Bailes
Commercial: Mr M Towsey – First Secretary

FRANCE
British Embassy
35 rue du Faubourg St Honoré, 75383 Paris
Cedex 08
00 33 1 44 51 31 00 Fax 00 33 1 44 51 34 83
Ambassador:
HE Sir Michael Jay KCMG
Commercial: Mr S Bradley – Counsellor
(Trade, Promotion and Investment)

GABON – see Cameroon

GAMBIA, THE
British High Commission
48 Atlantic Road, Fajara (PO Box 507), Banjul
00 220 4 95133 Fax 00 220 4 96134
E-mail: bhcbanjul@commet.gm
High Commissioner: HE John Perrott

GEORGIA
British Embassy
Metechi Palace Hotel, 380003 Tbilisi
00 995 32 955 497 Fax 00 995 32 001 065
Ambassador: HE Mr Richard Jenkins OBE

GERMANY
British Embassy
Wilhelmstrasse 70, 10117 Berlin
00 49 030 201 84-0 Fax 00 49 030 201 84-277
Ambassador: HE Sir Paul Lever, KCMG
Commercial: Mr D S Schroeder –
First Secretary

GHANA
British High Commission
Osu Link, off Gamel Abdul Nasser Avenue
(PO Box 296), Accra
00 233 21 221665 Fax 00 233 21 7010655
E-mail:
high.commission@accra.mail.fco.gov.uk
High Commissioner:
HE Dr Roderick Pullen
(Non-resident: Togo)
Commercial: Mr M A Ives – First Secretary

GREECE
British Embassy
1 Ploutarchou Street, 106 75 Athens
00 30 1 727 2600 Fax 00 30 1 727 2734
E-mail: britania@hol.gr
Ambassador: HE David Madden CMG
Commercial: Mr G G Thomas – First Secretary

GRENADA
British High Commission
14 Church Street, St Georges
00 1 473 440 3222 Fax 00 1 473 440 4939
E-mail: bhcgrenada@caribsurf.com
High Commissioner: HE Gordon M Baker
(Resides in Barbados)
Resident Acting High Commissioner:
Mr D R Miller

GUATEMALA
British Embassy
Avenida La Reforma 16-00, Zona 10,
Edificio Torre Internacional, Nivel 11,
Guatemala City
00 502 367 5425/29 Fax 00 502 367 5430
E-mail: embassy@inforia.com.gt
Ambassador: HE Andrew Caie

GUINEA – see Senegal

GUINEA-BISSAU – see Senegal

GUYANA
British High Commission
44 Main Street (PO Box 10849), Georgetown
00 592 2 65881 Fax 00 592 2 53555
High Commissioner:
HE Mr Edward Glover MVO
(Non-resident: Suriname)

HAITI – see Dominican Republic

HOLY SEE
British Embassy
91 Via dei Condotti, I-00187 Rome
00 39 6 699 23561 Fax 00 39 6 6994 0684
Ambassador: HE Mr Mark Pellew LVO

HONDURAS
British Embassy
Edificio Palmira, 3er Piso, Colonia Palmira,
PO Box 290, Tegucigalpa
00 504 232 0612 Fax 00 504 232 5480
Ambassador and Consul-General:
HE David Osborne

HUNGARY
British Embassy
Harmincad Utca 6, Budapest 1051
00 36 1 266-2888 Fax 00 36 1 266 0907
E-mail: info@britemb.hu
Ambassador: HE Nigel Thorpe CVO
Commercial: Mr S C Martin – First Secretary

ICELAND
British Embassy
Laufasvegur 31, 101 Reykjavik
(Postal address: PO Box 460, 121 Reykjavik)
00 354 550 5100/2 Fax 00 354 550 5105
E-mail: britemb@centrum.is
Ambassador and Consul-General:
HE James R McCulloch
Commercial: Orn Valdimarsson –
Commercial Officer

INDIA
British High Commission
Chanakyapuri, New Delhi 11000-21
00 91 11 687 2161 Fax 00 91 11 6872882
High Commissioner:
HE Sir Robertson Young KCMG
Commercial: Mr G C Gillham – Counsellor
(Economic and Commercial)
Bombay: Deputy High Commissioner's Office,
Maker Chambers IV, 222 Jamnalal Bajaj Road,
(PO Box 11714) Nariman Point,
Bombay 400 021
00 91 22 283 0517/283 2330
Fax 00 91 22 202 7940
E-mail: bdhcnet@vsnl.com
Deputy High Commissioner:
Mr M C Bates OBE
Commercial: Mr P O D McCoy –
First Secretary

INDONESIA
British Embassy
Jalan M. H. Thamrin 75, Jakarta 10310
00 62 21 315 6264 Fax: 00 62 21 314 6263
Ambassador:
HE Richard Gozney CMG
Commercial: Mr A Godson – Counsellor
(Commercial/Development)

IRAN
British Embassy
143 Ferdowsi Avenue, Tehran 11344,
(PO Box No 11365-4474)
00 98 21 675011 Fax 00 98 21 6708021
Ambassador: HE N W Browne CMG
Commercial: Mr E Jenkinson – First Secretary

IRAQ – No representation

IRELAND
British Embassy
29 Merrion Road, Ballsbridge, Dublin 4
00 353 1 205 3700 Fax 00 353 1 205 3885
E-mail: bembassy@internet-ireland.ie
Ambassador: HE Sir Ivor Roberts KCMG
Commercial: Mr R N J Baker – First Secretary

ISRAEL
British Embassy
192 Hayarkon Street, Tel Aviv 63405
00 972 3 7251222 Fax 00 972 3 524 3313
Ambassador: HE Mr F Cornish CMG LVO
Commercial: Mr I Morrison – First Secretary

ITALY
British Embassy
Via XX Settembre 80a, 00187 Rome
00 39 06 482 5441/5551
Fax 00 39 06 487 3324
Ambassador:
HE John Shepherd CMG
(Non-resident: San Marino)
Commercial: Mr M A Hatfull – Counsellor

IVORY COAST – see Cote D'Ivoire

JAMAICA
British High Commission
PO Box 575, Trafalgar Road, Kingston 10
00 1 876 92 69050 Fax 00 1 876 92 97869
E-mail: bhckingston@cw.com
High Commissioner: HE Antony Smith

JAPAN
British Embassy
No 1 Ichiban-cho, Chiyoda-ku, Tokyo 102-8381
00 81 3 5211 1100 Fax: 00 81 3 5275-3164
E-mail: embassy@tokyo.mail.fco.gov.uk
Ambassador:
HE Sir Stephen Gommersall KCMG
Commercial: Mr P Bateman – Counsellor
Fax 00 81 3 3265 5580

JERUSALEM
British Consulate-General
19 Nashashibi Street, Sheikh Jarrah Quarter
PO Box 19690, East Jerusalem 97200
00 972 2 541 4100 Fax 00 972 2 532 5629
E-mail: britain@palnet.com
Consul General: Mr R A Kealy CMG

JORDAN
British Embassy
(PO Box 87) Abdoun, Amman
00 962 6 5923100 Fax 00 962 6 5923759
Telex: 22209 (a/b 22209 PRODRM JO)
Ambassador: HE Edward Chaplin OBE
Commercial: Mrs D A Dixon –
Second Secretary

KAZAKHSTAN
British Embassy
Ul Furmanova 173, Almaty
00 7 3272 506191/192/229 Fax 00 7 3272
506260
E-mail: british-embassy@kaznet.kz
Ambassador: HE Richard Lewington
(Non-resident: Kyrgyzstan)

KENYA
British High Commission
Upper Hill Road, Nairobi, PO Box 30465
00 254 2 714699 Fax 00 254 2 719082
E-mail: consular@nairobi.mail.fco.gov.uk
High Commissioner:
HE Mr J R James CMG
Commercial: PO Box 30133, Nairobi
Mr J Chandler – First Secretary

KIRIBATI – see Fiji Islands

KOREA
British Embassy
4, Chung-Dong, Chung-Ku, Seoul 100-120
00 82 2 735-7341/3 Fax 00 82 2 725 1738
Ambassador: HE Charles Humfrey, CMG
Commercial: Mr D Brown – First Secretary
Fax 00 82 2 736 6241

KUWAIT
British Embassy
Arabian Gulf Street
Postal address: PO Box 2 Safat, 13001 Safat
00 965 240 3334 Fax 00 965 242 6799
E-mail: britemb@kems.net
Ambassador: HE Richard Muir CMG
Commercial: PO Box 300, Safat, 13001 Safat
Fax 00 965 240 7395
Mr J Clayton – First Secretary

KYRGHYZSTAN – see Kazakhstan

LAOS
British Embassy
PO Box 6626, Vientiane, Laos, PDR
00 856 21 413606 Fax 00 856 21 413607
Ambassador: HE Mr B Smith
(Resides in Thailand)

LATVIA
British Embassy
5 Alunana Iela Street, Riga LV 1010
00 371 7 338126 Fax 00 371 7 338132
E-mail: british.embassy@apollo.lv
Ambassador: HE Stephen Nash CMG

LEBANON
British Embassy
East Beirut: 8th Street, Rabieh
00 961 4 417007/405070 Fax 00 961 4 402032
E-mail: britemb@cyberia.net.lb
Ambassador: HE Richard Kinchen MVO

LESOTHO
British High Commission
PO Box Ms 521, Maseru 100
00 266 313961 Fax 00 266 310120
E-mail: hcmaseru@lesoff.co.za
High Commissioner:
HE Kaye Oliver OBE

LIBERIA – see Cote d'Ivoire

LIBYA
British Embassy
Sharia Uahran 1, PO Box 4206, Tripoli
00 218 21 333 1191/2/3
Fax 00 218 21 444 9121
Ambassador: HE Richard Dalton CMG

LIECHTENSTEIN – see Switzerland

LITHUANIA
British Embassy
2 Antakalnio, 2055 Vilnius
00 370 2 22 20 70 Fax 00 370 2 72 75 79
Ambassador: HE Mr C Robbins

LUXEMBOURG
British Embassy
14 Boulevard Roosevelt, L-2450, Luxembourg
00 352 22 98 64/65/66 Fax 00 352 22 98 67
Ambassador and Consul-General:
HE Gordon Wetherell
Commercial: Mr S Smith – Counsellor
(Resides at Brussels)

MACEDONIA
British Embassy
Dimitrija Chupovski 26 (4th Floor), 9100
Skopje
00 389 91 116 772 Fax 00 389 91 117 005
Ambassador: HE Mr W M L Dickinson OBE

MADAGASCAR
British Embassy
Lot II 1 164 TER, Alarobia-Amboniloa, BP
167, Antananarivo
00 261 2 0 2249378 Fax 00 261 2 0 2249381
E-mail: ukembant@simicro.mg
Ambassador: HE Charles Mochan
(Non-resident: Comoros)
Commercial: Mr M Rakotolehibe –
Commercial Officer

MALAWI
British High Commission
PO Box 30042, Lilongwe 3
00 265 782 400 Fax 00 265 782 657
E-mail: britcom@malawi.net
High Commissioner: HE Mr G Finlayson

MALAYSIA
British High Commission
185 Jalan Ampang, 50450 Kuala Lumpur, or
PO Box 11030, 50732 Kuala Lumpur
00 60 3 2482122 Fax 00 60 3 2447766
E-mail: bhckulcom@app.nasionet.net
High Commissioner: HE Graham Fry
Commercial: Mr H Parkinson CVO OBE –
Counsellor
Fax 00 60 3 2480880

MALDIVES – see Sri Lanka

MALI – see Senegal

MALTA
British High Commission
PO Box 506, 7 St Anne Street, Floriana
00 356 233134 Fax 00 356 233184
E-mail: bhc@vol.net.mt
High Commissioner:
HE Howard Pearce CVO
Commercial: Mr P Tissot – Deputy High
Commissioner and First Secretary
(Commercial/Economic)

MARSHALL ISLANDS – see Fiji Islands
Ambassador:
HE Christopher Haslam (Non-resident)

MAURITANIA – see Morocco

MAURITIUS
British High Commission
Les Cascades Building, Edith Cavell Street,
Port Louis, PO Box 1063
00 230 211 1361 Fax 00 230 211 1369
E-mail: bhc@bow.intnet.mu
High Commissioner: HE David Snoxell
Commercial: Mr J S Taylor – Deputy High
Commissioner and First Secretary
(Commercial)
00 230 208 9850 Fax 00 230 212 1369

MEXICO
British Embassy
Rio Lerma 71, Col Cuauhtémoc,
06500 Mexico City
00 525 207 2089 Fax 00 525 207 7672
E-mail:
infogen@mail.embajdabritanica.com.mx
Ambassador: HE Mr A C Thorpe CMG
Commercial: Mr A C Stephens – First Secretary

MICRONESIA – see Fiji Islands
Ambassador: HE Chistopher Haslam
(Non-resident)

MOLDOVA – see Russian Federation

MONACO
British Consulate-General
33 Boulevard Princesse Charlotte BP 265,
MC98005 Monaco CEDEX
00 377 93 50 99 66
Fax 00 377 93 50 14 47
Consul-General: Mr I Davies
(Resides Marseilles)

MONGOLIA
British Embassy
30 Enkh Taivny Gudamzh (PO Box 703),
Ulaanbaatar 13
00 976 1 458133 Fax 00 976 1 458036
E-mail: britemb@magicnet.mn
Ambassador and Consul-General:
HE Kay Coombs

MOROCCO
British Embassy
17 Boulevard de la Tour Hassan (BP 45), Rabat
00 212 7 72 96 96 Fax 00 212 7 70 45 31
E-mail: britemb@mtds.com
Ambassador: HE Anthony Layden
(Non-resident: Mauritania)

MOZAMBIQUE
British High Commission
Av Vladimir I Lenine 310, Caixa Postal 55,
Maputo
00 258 1 420111 Fax 00 258 1 421666
E-mail: bhc@virconn.com
High Commissioner: HE Robert Dewar
Commercial: Mr D G Harries OBE –
Third Secretary (Commercial/Development)

MYANMAR – see Burma

NAMIBIA
British High Commission
116 Robert Mugabe Avenue, PO Box 22202,
Windhoek 9000
00 264 61 223022 Fax 00 264 61 228895
E-mail: bhc@iwwn.com.na
High Commissioner: HE Mr R H G Davies

NAURU – see Fiji Islands

NEPAL
British Embassy
Lainchaur Kathmandu (PO Box 106)
00 977 1 410583/414588 Fax 00 977 1 411789
E-mail: britemb@wlink.com.np
Ambassador: HE Ronald Nash LVO

NETHERLANDS
British Embassy
Lange Voorhout 10, 2514 ED, The Hague
00 31 70 427 0427 Fax 00 31 70 427 0345
Ambassador:
HE Dame Rosemary Spencer DCMG
Commercial: Miss C Bradley – Counsellor and
Consul-General
Fax 00 31 70 427 0346

NEW ZEALAND
British High Commission
44 Hill Street, Wellington 1
00 64 4 472 6049 Fax 00 64 4 473 4982
E-mail: bhc.wel@xtra.co.nz
High Commissioner:
HE Martin Williams CVO OBE
(Non-resident: Samoa)
(Also Governor of Pitcairn, Henderson, Ducie
& Oeno Islands)
Commercial: Ms R L Foxwell – First Secretary

NICARAGUA
British Embassy
Plaza Churchill, Reparto "Los Robles",
Managua, Apartado A-169, Managua
00 505 2 780014/780887 Fax 00 505 2 784085
Ambassador and Consul-General:
HE Harry Wiles

NIGER – see Cote d'Ivoire

NIGERIA
British High Commission
Shehu Shangari Way (North), Maitama, Abuja
00 234 9 5232010/5232011
Fax 00 234 9 5233552
E-mail: chancery@lagos.mail.fco.gov.uk
High Commissioner:
HE Sir Graham Burton KCMG
(Non-resident: Benin)

NORWAY
British Embassy
Thomas Heftyesgate 8, 0244 Oslo
00 47 23 13 27 00 Fax 00 47 23 13 27 41
Ambassador: HE Richard Dales CMG
Commercial: Mr M Phelan – First Secretary
Fax 00 47 23 13 27 05

OMAN
British Embassy
PO Box 300, Muscat, Postal Code 113
00 968 693077 Fax 00 968 693087
Ambassador: HE Sir Ivan Callan KCVO CMG
Commercial:
Mr R Mackenzie – First Secretary
Fax 00 968 693088

PAKISTAN
British High Commission
Diplomatic Enclave, Ramna 5, PO Box 1122,
Islamabad
00 92 51 822131 Fax 00 92 51 823439
E-mail: bhctrade@isb.comsats.net.pk
High Commissioner:
HE Mr Hilary Synnott CMG
Commercial: Mr M Pakes – First Secretary

PALAU – see Fiji Islands
Ambassador: HE Christopher Haslam
(Non-resident)

PANAMA
British Embassy
Torre Swiss Bank, Calle 53 (Apartado 889)
Zona 1, Panama City
00 507 269-0866 Fax 00 507 223-0730
E-mail: britemb@cwp.net.pa
Ambassador and Consul-General:
HE Glyn Davies

PAPUA NEW GUINEA
British High Commission
PO Box 212, Waigani NCD 131
00 675 3251643/45 Fax 00 675 3253547
E-mail: bhcpng@datec.com.pg
High Commissioner:
HE Mr S Scadden

PARAGUAY
British Embassy
Avenida Boggiani 5848, C/R 16 Boqueron,
Asunción
00 595 21 612611 Fax 00 595 21 605007
E-mail: brembasu@mail.pla.net.py
Ambassador and Consul-General:
HE Andrew George

PERU
British Embassy
Edificio El Pacifico Washington (Piso 12),
Plaza Washington, Avenida Arequipa
(PO Box No 854), Lima 100
00 51 14 33 4738 Fax 00 51 14 33 4735
E-mail: britemb@cosapidata.com.pe
Ambassador: HE Roger Hart CMG
Commercial: Mr D J Kerr – First Secretary

PHILIPPINES
British Embassy
Floors 15–17 LV Locsin Building, 6752 Ayala
Avenue, Cor Makati Avenue, 1226 Makati,
(PO Box 2927 MCPO), Manila
00 63 2 816 7116 Fax 00 63 2 819 7206
Telex: 63282 (a/b 63282 PRODME PN)
E-mail: bremb@skyin.net
Ambassador: HE Alan Collins CMG
Commercial: Mr E J McAvoy – First Secretary
Fax 00 63 2815 815 6233

POLAND
British Embassy
Aleje Roz No 1, 00-556 Warsaw
00 48 22 6281001
Fax 00 48 22 621 7161
E-mail: britemb@it.com.pl
Ambassador: HE Mr J Macgregor CVO
Commercial: Warsaw Corporate Centre,
2nd Floor, Emilii Platter 28 00 688
00 00 48 22 625 3030
Fax 00 00 48 22 625 3472
Mr M H Davenport MBE –
Director of Trade Promotion/Consul-General

PORTUGAL
British Embassy
Rua de São Bernardo 33, 1200 Lisbon
00 351 1 392 40 00 Fax 00 351 1 392 41 83
E-mail: britembassy@mail.telepac.pt
Ambassador:
HE Sir John Holmes KBE CMG CVO
Commercial: Mr P A Sinkinson –
First Secretary

QATAR
British Embassy
PO Box 3, Doha
00 974 421991 Fax 00 974 438692
Ambassador:
HE David Wright OBE
Commercial: 8th Floor, Toyota Tower
00 974 353543 Fax 00 974 356131
E-mail: bembcomm@qatars.net.qa
Mr P Cole – First Secretary and
Deputy Head of Mission

ROMANIA
British Embassy
24 Strada Jules Michelet, 70154 Bucharest
00 40 1 312 0303 Fax 00 40 1 312 0229
Ambassador:
HE Richard Ralph CMG CVO
Commercial: Mr R J Cork – First Secretary
Fax 00 40 1 312 9742

RUSSIAN FEDERATION
British Embassy
Sofiskaya Naberezhnaya 14, Moscow 121099
00 7 095 956 7200 Fax 00 7 095 956 7201
E-mail: britembppas@glas.apc.org
Ambassador: HE Sir Roderic Lyne KBE CMG
(Non-resident: Moldova)
Commercial:
Mr J Dauris – First Secretary

RWANDA
British Embassy
Parcelle No 1131, Boulevard de l'Umuganda,
Kacyira-Sud, BP 576, Kigali
00 250 84098 Fax 00 250 82044
Ambassador: HE Graeme Loten
(Non-resident: Burundi)

ST CHRISTOPHER AND NEVIS
British High Commission
PO Box 483, Price Waterhouse Centre,
11 Old Parham Road, St John's, Antigua
00 1 268 462 0008/9
Fax 00 1 268 462 2806
High Commissioner: HE Gordon M Baker
(Resident in Barbados)
Resident Acting High Commissioner:
Mrs S Murphy

ST LUCIA
British High Commission
NIS Waterfront Building,
2nd Floor (PO Box 227), Castries
00 1 758 45 22484 Fax 00 1 758 45 31543
E-mail: postmaster@castries.mail.fco.gov.uk
High Commissioner: HE Gordon M Baker
(Resident in Barbados)
Resident Acting High Commissioner:
Mr P J Hughes

ST VINCENT AND THE GRENADINES
British High Commission
Granby Street (PO Box 132), Kingstown
00 1 784 457 1701/2
Fax 00 1 784 456 2750
High Commissioner: HE Gordon M Baker
(Resident in Barbados)
Resident Acting High Commissioner:
Mr B Robertson

SAMOA – see New Zealand

SAN MARINO – see Italy

SÃO TOMÉ & PRÍNCIPE – see Angola

SAUDI ARABIA
British Embassy
PO Box 94351, Riyadh 11693
00 966 1 488 0077 Fax 00 966 1 488
2373/0623
E-mail: @riyadh.mail.fco.gov.uk
Ambassador:
HE Derek Plumbly CMG
Commercial: Mr P Parham – Counsellor

SENEGAL
British Embassy
20 Rue du Docteur Guillet (Boîte Postale
6025), Dakar
00 221 823 7392, 823 9971
Fax 00 221 823 2766
E-mail: britemb@telecom—plus.sn
Ambassador: HE Alan Burner
(Non-resident: Cape Verde, Guinea-Bissau,
Mali, Guinea)

SEYCHELLES
British High Commission
Oliaji Trade Centre, PO Box 161, Victoria,
Mahé
00 248 225225/356/396 Fax 00 248 225127
E-mail: bhcsey@seychelles.net
High Commissioner: HE Mr John Yapp

SIERRA LEONE
British High Commission
Spur Road, Freetown
00 232 22 232961 Fax 00 232 22 228169
E-mail: bhc@sierratel.sl
High Commissioner:
HE Alan Jones

SINGAPORE
British High Commission
Tanglin Road, Singapore 247919
00 65 4739333 Fax 00 65 474 1958
E-mail: brit_hc@pacific.net.sg/firecrest
High Commissioner:
HE Alan Hunt CMG
Commercial:
00 65 474 0461 Fax 00 65 475 2320
Mr A J Gooch – Counsellor and
Deputy High Commissioner

SLOVAK REPUBLIC
British Embassy
Panska 16, 811 01 Bratislava
00 421 7 5441 9632 Fax 00 421 7 5441 0002
E-mail: bebra@internet.sk
Ambassador: HE Mr D Lyscom
Commercial: Fax 00 421 7 5441 0003

SLOVENIA
British Embassy
4th Floor, Trg Republike 3, 61000 Ljubljana
00 386 1 200 3910 Fax: 00 386 1 425 0174
E-mail: info@british-embassy.si
Ambassador: HE David A Lloyd OBE

SOLOMON ISLANDS
British High Commission
Telekom House, Mendana Avenue, Honiara
Postal address: PO Box 676
00 677 21705/706 Fax 00 677 21549
E-mail: bhcl@welkam.solomon.com.sb
High Commissioner: HE Alan Waters

SOMALIA – No representation

SOUTH AFRICA
British High Commission
91 Parliament Street, Cape Town 8001
00 27 21 461-7220 Fax 00 27 21 4610017
E-mail: britain@icon.co.za
and at 255 Hill Street,
Arcadia 0083, Pretoria
00 27 12 4831200 Fax 00 27 12 4831302
E-mail: bhc@icon.co.za
High Commissioner:
HE Ann Grant

SPAIN
British Embassy
Calle de Fernando el Santo 16, 28010 Madrid
00 34 91 700 82 00
Fax 00 34 91 700 83 09
Ambassador: HE Peter Torry
(Non-resident: Andorra)
Commercial: Mr J Hawkins – Counsellor

SRI LANKA
British High Commission
190 Galle Road, Kollupitiya (PO Box 1433),
Colombo 3
00 94 1 437336/43 Fax 00 94 1 430308
E-mail: bhc@eureka.lk
High Commissioner:
HE Linda Duffield
(Non-resident: Maldives)
Commercial: Mr A Madeley – First Secretary

SUDAN
British Embassy
off Sharia Al Baladia, Khartoum East
(PO Box No 801)
00 249 11 777105
Fax 00 249 11 776457
E-mail: british@sudanmail.net
Ambassador: HE Richard Makepeace

SURINAME – see Guyana

SWAZILAND
British High Commission
Callers: Allister Miller Street, Mbabane
Postal address: Private Bag, Mbabane
00 268 404 2582 Fax 00 268 404 2585
High Commissioner:
HE Neil Hook MVO

SWEDEN
British Embassy
Skarpögatan 6–8, Box 27819, 115 93
Stockholm
00 46 8 671 9000 Fax 00 46 8 662 9989
Ambassador: HE John Grant CMG
Commercial: Mr P J Mathers LVO – Counsellor

SWITZERLAND
British Embassy
Thunstrasse 50, 3005 Berne
00 41 31 359 77 00 Fax 00 41 31 359 77 01
Ambassador:
HE Christopher Hulse CMG OBE
(Non-resident: Liechtenstein)
Commercial: Miss A J Pring – First Secretary

SYRIA
British Embassy
Kotob Building, 11 Mohammad Kurd Ali
Street, Malki, PO Box 37, Damascus
00 963 11 371 9241 Fax 00 963 11 373 1600
Ambassador: HE Henry Hogger

TAJIKESTAN – see Uzbekistan

TANZANIA
British High Commission
Social Security House, Samora Avenue
(PO Box 9200)
00 255 22 2 117659/64,112953
Fax 00 225 22 2 112952
E-mail: bhc.dar@dar.mail.fco.gov.uk
High Commissioner: HE Bruce Dinwiddy
Commercial: Mr K E Green – Second Secretary

THAILAND
British Embassy
Wireless Road, Bangkok 10330
00 66 2 253-0191 Fax 00 66 2 254 9578
Ambassador:
HE Mr B Smith (Non-resident: Laos)
Commercial: Mr D Wyatt – Counsellor
Fax 00 66 2 255 8619

TOGO – see Ghana

TONGA
British High Commission
PO Box 56, Nuku'alofa
00 676 24285/24395 Fax 00 676 24109
E-mail: britcomt@candw.to
*High Commissioner and Consul for American
Samoa:* HE Brian Connelly

TRINIDAD AND TOBAGO
British High Commission
19 St Clair Avenue, St Clair, Port of Spain
00 1 868 622 2748/9895
Fax 00 1 868 622 4555
E-mail: csbhc@opus.co.h
High Commissioner:
HE Peter Harborne
Commercial: Mr B Nicholas –
Second Secretary

TUNISIA
British Embassy
5 Place de la Victoire, Tunis
00 216 1 341 444 Fax 00 216 1 354 877
E-mail: british.emb@planet.tn
Ambassador and Consul-General:
HE Ivor Rawlinson OBE
Commercial: Mr B J Conley – Second Secretary

TURKEY
British Embassy
Sehit Ersan Caddesi 46/A, Cankaya, Ankara
00 90 312 468 6230 Fax 00 90 312 468 6249
E-mail: britembank@ankara.mail.fco.gov.uk
Ambassador: HE Sir David Logan KCMG
Commercial: Ms J MacPherson – First Secretary
Fax 00 90 312 468 3214

TURKMENISTAN
British Embassy
3rd Floor, Office Building, Ak Altin Plaza
Hotel, Ashgabat
00 993 1 251 0616 Fax 00 993 1 251 0868
E-mail: postmaster@beasb.cat.glasnet.ru
Ambassador: HE Fraser Wilson MBE

TUVALU – see Fiji Islands

UGANDA
British High Commission
10/12 Parliament Avenue, PO Box 7070,
Kampala
00 256 41 257054 Fax 00 256 41 257304
E-mail: bhcinfo@starcom.co.ug
High Commissioner:
HE Tom Phillips CMG
Commercial: Miss H C Rawlins –
Second Secretary

UKRAINE
British Embassy
252025 Kiev Desyatinna 9
00 380 44 462 0011 Fax 00 380 44 462 0013
E-mail: ukembinf@sovam.com
Ambassador: HE Roland Smith CMG
Commercial: Mr R C C Cook – First Secretary

UNITED ARAB EMIRATES
British Embassy
PO Box 248, Abu Dhabi
00 971 2 6326600/6321364
Fax 00 971 2 6318138
Ambassador: HE Patrick Nixon CMG OBE
Commercial: Mr D A Bell –
Commercial Secretary
  Dubai:
  PO Box 65, Dubai
  00 971 4 3971070 Fax 00 971 4 3972153
  Consul-General and Counsellor:
  Mr S P Collis
  Commercial: Mr N E Cole OBE –
  First Secretary/Deputy Head of Mission

UNITED STATES OF AMERICA
British Embassy
3100 Massachusetts Avenue NW,
Washington DC 20008
00 1 202 588 6500 Fax 00 1 202 588 7870
Ambassador:
HE Sir Christopher Meyer KCMG
Trade: Fax 00 1 202 588 7901
Mr N J Westcott – Counsellor
(Trade and Transport)

URUGUAY
British Embassy
Calle Marco Bruto 1073, 11300 Montevideo,
PO Box 16024
00 598 2 6223630/650 Fax 00 598 2 6227815
Ambassador: HE Andrew Murray

UZBEKISTAN
British Embassy
Ul.Gulyamova 67, Tashkent 700000
00 998712 1206822
Ambassador: HE Christopher Ingham
(Non-resident: Tajikistan)

VANUATU
British High Commission
KPMG House, Rue Pasteur, Port Vila, Vanuatu,
PO Box 567
00 678 23100 Fax 00 678 27153
E-mail: bhcvila@vanuatu.com.vu
High Commissioner:
HE Michael Hill

VATICAN CITY – see Holy See

VENEZUELA
British Embassy
Edificio Torre Las Mercedes (Piso 3),
Avenida La Estancia, Chuao, Caracas 1061
(Postal address: Embajada Britanica,
Apartado 1246 Caracas 1010-A)
00 58 2 993 41 11 Fax 00 58 2 993 99 89
E-mail: embcarac@ven.net
Ambassador: HE Dr John Hughes
Commercial: Mr S J Seaman MBE –
First Secretary

VIETNAM
British Embassy
Central Building, 31 Hai Ba Trung, Hanoi
00 84 4 8252510 Fax 00 84 4 8265762
Ambassador: HE Warwick Morris
Commercial: Mr R Lally – Second Secretary

YEMEN
British Embassy
129 Haddah Road, Sana'a
Postal address: PO Box 1287
00 967 1 264081 Fax 00 967 1 263059
Ambassador and Consul-General:
HE Victor Henderson CMG

YUGOSLAVIA, FEDERAL REPUBLIC OF
(Serbia and Montenegro)
British Embassy
Generala Zdanova, 46, 11000 Belgrade
00 381 11 645055/034/043/087
Fax 00 381 11 659651
(Embassy closed, British interests handled by
Brazilian Embassy)

ZAIRE – see Democratic Republic of Congo

ZAMBIA
British High Commission
Independence Avenue (PO Box 50050),
15101, Lusaka
00 260 1 251133 Fax 00 260 1 253798
E-mail: brithc@zamnet.zm
High Commissioner: HE Thomas Young
Commercial: Miss I M Mulvaney –
Second Secretary
Fax 00 260 1 251923

ZIMBABWE
British High Commission
Corner House, Samora Machel Avenue/
Leopold Takawaira Street (PO Box 4490),
Harare
00 263 4 772990 Fax 00 263 4 774617
High Commissioner: HE Peter Longworth
Commercial: Mr D Seddon – First Secretary

Missions and Delegations

United Kingdom Permanent Representation
to the European Union
Avenue d'Auderghem 10, 1040 Brussels,
Belgium
00 32 2 287 82 11 Fax 00 32 2 287 83 98
UK Permanent Representative:
HE Nigel Sheinwald CMG

United Kingdom Delegation to the North
Atlantic Treaty Organisation
NATO, Autoroute Bruxelles – Zavbentem,
Evere, 1110 Brussels, Belgium
00 32 2 707 72 11 Fax 00 32 2 707 75 96
E-mail: ukdelnato@csi.com
UK Permanent Representative on the North
Atlantic Council: HE Sir John Goulden KCMG

United Kingdom Delegation to the Western
European Union
Rue de la Regence 4, Room 301, 1000
Brussels, Belgium
00 32 2 287 63 36 Fax 00 32 2 287 63 37
UK Permanent Representative:
HE Sir John Goulden KCMG

United Kingdom Permanent Representation
to the Conference on Disarmament
37-39 Rue de Vermont, 1211 Geneva 20,
Switzerland
00 41 22 918 23 00 Fax 00 41 22 918 23 44
E-mail: disarm.uk@itu.int
UK Permanent Representative:
HE Mr S I Soutar

United Kingdom Mission to the Office of the
United Nations and other International
Organisations at Geneva
37-39 Rue de Vermont, 1211 Geneva 20,
Switzerland
00 41 22 918 23 00 Fax 00 41 22 918 23 33
E-mail: mission.uk@ties.itu.int
UK Permanent Representative:
HE Simon Fuller CMG

United Kingdom Delegation to the United
Nations Educational, Scientific and Cultural
Organisation (UNESCO)
1 Rue Miollis, 75732 Paris, Cedex 15, France
00 33 01 45 68 27 84 Fax 00 33 01 47 83 27 77
UK Permanent Representative:
HE Mr D L Stanton

United Kingdom Mission to the United Nations
1 Dag Hammarskjold Plaza, 28th Floor, 885 Second Avenue, New York, NY 10017, USA

00 1 212 745 9200 Fax 00 1 212 745 9316/9396/9395

UK Permanent Representative to the UN and UK Representative on the Security Council:
HE Sir Jeremy Greenstock KCMG

United Kingdom Delegation to the Organisation for Economic Co-operation and Development
19 Rue de Franqueville, 75116 Paris, France

0 33 1 45 24 98 28 Fax 0 33 1 45 24 98 37

UK Permanent Representative:
HE Mr C Crabbie CMG

United Kingdom Delegation to the Council of Europe
18 Rue Gottfried, 67000-Strasbourg, France

00 33 3 88 35 00 78 Fax 00 33 3 88 36 74 39

UK Permanent Representative to the Council of Europe: HE Mr A Carter CMG

United Kingdom Delegation to the Organisation for Security and Co-operation in Europe (OSCE) in Vienna
Jaurégasse 12, 1030 Vienna, Austria

00 43 1 716130 Fax 00 43 1 71613 3900

Head of UK Delegation:
HE Mr J R de Fonblanque CMG

United Kingdom Missions to the United Nations in Vienna
Jaurégasse 12, 1030 Vienna, Austria

00 43 1 716130 Fax 00 43 1 71613 4900

UK Permanent Representative:
HE Dr J P G Freeman

London Embassies and High Commissions

AFGHANISTAN
Embassy of the Islamic State of Afghanistan
31 Prince's Gate, London SW7 1QQ
020 7589 8891 Fax 020 7581 3452
Telex: 916641
Ahmad Wali Masud *(Chargé d'Affaires)*

ALBANIA
Embassy of the Republic of Albania
2nd Floor, 24 Buckingham Gate,
London SW1E 6LB
020 7827 8897 Fax 020 7828 8869
Ambassador: HE Agim Besim Fagu

ALGERIA
Embassy of Algeria
54 Holland Park, London W11 3RS
020 7221 7800 Fax 020 7221 0448
Ambassador: Vacant

ANDORRA
Delegation of Andorra
63 Westover Road, London SW18 2RF
020 8874 4806
Ambassador: HE Juli Minoves-Triquel
(Resident in Madrid)

ANGOLA
Embassy of the Republic of Angola
98 Park Lane, London W1Y 3TA
020 7495 1752 Fax 020 7495 1635
Telex: 8813258 EMBAUK G
Ambassador:
HE Senhor Antonio DaCosta Fernandes

ANTIGUA AND BARBUDA
High Commission for Antigua and Barbuda
15 Thayer Street, London W1M 5LD
020 7486 7073 Fax 020 7486 9970
Telex: 814503AK ANTEGA G
High Commissioner:
HE Ronald Sanders, CMG

ARGENTINA
Embassy of the Argentine Republic
65 Brook Street, London W1Y 1YE
020 7318 1300 Fax 020 7318 1301
Ambassador: HE Senor Vicente Berasategui
Commercial: 4th Floor, 65 Brook Street,
London W1Y 1YE
020 7318 1330 Fax 020 7318 1331
Senor Gustavo A Martino – Counsellor
(Economic and Commercial)

ARMENIA
Embassy of the Republic of Armenia
25A Cheniston Gardens, London W8 6TG
020 7938 5435 Fax 020 7938 2595
Ambassador: Vacant
Mr Armen Liloyan *(Chargé d'Affaires)*

AUSTRALIA
Australian High Commission
Australia House, Strand,
London WC2B 4LA
020 7379 4334 Fax 020 7240 5333
High Commissioner: HE Michael L'Estrange
Commercial: Mark Jenkins – Minister
(Commercial)

AUSTRIA
Austrian Embassy
18 Belgrave Mews West,
London SW1X 8HU
020 7235 3731 Fax 020 7344 0292
Ambassador: HE Dr Alexander Christiani
Commercial: Dr Rudolf J Engel – Counsellor
and Trade Commissioner

AZERBAIJAN
Embassy of the Azerbaijan Republic
4 Kensington Court, London W8 5DL
020 7938 5482/3412 Fax 020 7937 1783
Ambassador: HE Mahmud Mamed-Kuliyev

BAHAMAS
High Commission for the Commonwealth of
the Bahamas
10 Chesterfield Street, London W1X 8AH
020 7408 4488 Fax 020 7499 9937
High Commissioner:
HE Basil O'Brien CMG

BAHRAIN
Embassy of the State of Bahrain
98 Gloucester Road, London SW7 4AU
020 7370 5132/3 Fax 020 7370-7773
Telex: 917829
Ambassador:
HE Shaikh Abdul Aziz Mubarak Al Khalifa

BANGLADESH
High Commission for the People's Republic of
Bangladesh
28 Queen's Gate, London SW7 5JA
020 7584 0081 Fax 020 7225 2130
Telex: 918016
High Commissioner: HE A H Mahmood Ali

BARBADOS
Barbados High Commission
1 Great Russell Street, London WC1B 3JY
020 7631 4975 Fax 020 7323 6872
High Commissioner:
HE Peter Patrick Simmons

BELARUS
Embassy of the Republic of Belarus
6 Kensington Court, London W8 5DL
020 7937 3288 Fax 020 7361 0005
Ambassador: HE Valery E Sadokho

BELGIUM
Belgian Embassy
103–105 Eaton Square, London SW1W 9AB
020 7470 3700 Fax 020 7259 6213
Telex: 22823 BELAM G
Ambassador: HE Lode Willems

BELIZE
Belize High Commission
22 Harcourt House, 19 Cavendish Square,
London W1M 9AD
020 7499 9728 Fax 020 7491 4139
Telex: 94082284 BHCOM
High Commissioner: HE Assad Shoman

BENIN
No London Embassy
Embassy of the Republic of Benin
87 Avenue Victor Hugo, 75116 Paris, France
00 45-009882 Fax 00 42-223244
Ambassador:
HE Mons André-Guy Ologoudou
(Resident in Paris)
Honorary Consulate:
Dolphin House, 16 The Broadway,
Stanmore, Middlesex HA7 4DW
020 8954 8800

BOLIVIA
Bolivian Embassy
106 Eaton Square, London SW1W 9AD
020 7235 4248/2557 Fax 020 7235 1286
Telex: 918885 COMBOL G
Ambassador:
HE Senor Jaime Quiroga-Matos

BOSNIA AND HERZEGOVINA
Embassy of the Republic of Bosnia and
Herzegovina
4th Floor, Morley House,
320 Regent Street, London W1R 5AB
020 7255 3758 Fax 020 7255 3760
Ambassador: HE Osman Topcagic

BOTSWANA
Botswana High Commission
6 Stratford Place, London W1N 9AE
020 7499 0031 Fax 020 7495 8595
High Commissioner: HE Roy Blackbeard

BRAZIL
Brazilian Embassy
32 Green Street, Mayfair, London W1Y 4AT
020 7499 0877 Fax 020 7493 5105
Telex: 261157 BRASLO G
Ambassador:
HE Senhor Sergio Silva do Amaral KBE
Commercial: Senhor João de Mendonça Lima
Neto – Counsellor

BRUNEI
Brunei Darussalam High Commission
19–20 Belgrave Square, London SW1X 8PG
020 7581 0521 Fax 020 7235 9717
Telex: 888 369
High Commissioner:
HE Dato Haji Yusof Hamid

BULGARIA
Embassy of the Republic of Bulgaria
186–188 Queen's Gate, London SW7 5HL
020 7584 9400/9433 Fax 020 7584 4948
Ambassador: HE Valentin Dobrev
Commercial: Christo Charenkov – Counsellor
(Commercial/Economic)
020 7581 3144 Fax 020 7589 4875

BURKINA
No London Embassy
Embassy of the Republic of Burkina
16 Place Guy d'Arezzo 16, 1060 Brussels,
Belgium
00 32 2 345 99 12 Fax 00 32 2 345 06 12
Ambassador: Vacant
Monsieur Raymond Balima *(Chargé d'Affaires)*
(Resident in Brussels)
Honorary Consulate:
5 Cinnamon Row, Plantation Wharf,
London SW11 3TW 020 7738 1800

BURMA (Union of Myanmar)
19A Charles Street, Berkeley Square,
London W1X 8ER
020 7499 8841 Fax 020 7629 4169
Telex: 267609 MYANMA G
Ambassador: HE Dr Kyaw Win

BURUNDI
Embassy of the Republic of Burundi
26 Armitage Road, London NW11 8RD
020 8381 4092 Fax 020 8458 8596
Ambassador: HE Jonathas Niyungeko
(Resident in Brussels)

CAMEROON
High Commission of the Republic of Cameroon
84 Holland Park, London W11 3SB
020 7727 0771 Fax 020 7792 9353
Telex: 921880
High Commissioner:
HE Samuel Libock Mbei

CANADA
Canadian High Commission
Macdonald House, 1 Grosvenor Square,
London W1X 0AB
020 7258 6600 Fax 020 7258 6333
High Commissioner: Vacant
Commercial: Tom MacDonald – Minister

CAPE VERDE
No London Embassy
Embassy of the Republic of Cape Verde
Burgemeester Patijnlaan 1930, 2585 CB,
The Hague, Netherlands
00 31 70 355-36-51
Ambassador: HE Julio Vasco de Sousa Lobo
(Resident in The Hague)
Honorary Consulate:
43 Upper Grosvenor Street,
London W1X 9PG 020 7493 4840

CENTRAL AFRICAN REPUBLIC
No London Embassy
Embassy of the Central African Republic
30 rue des Perchamp, 75016 Paris, France
00 42 24 42 56
Ambassador: Vacant (Resident in Paris)

CHAD
No London Embassy
Embassy of the Republic of Chad
Boulevard Lambermont 52, 1030 Brussels,
Belgium
00 32 2 215 19 75
Mons Idriss Adjide *(Chargé d'Affaires)*
(Resident in Brussels)

CHILE
Embassy of Chile
12 Devonshire Street, London W1N 2DS
020 7580 6392 Fax 020 7436 5204
Ambassador: Señor Cristian Barros Melet
Commercial: Señor Marcial Ubilla – Counsellor

CHINA
Embassy of the People's Republic of China
49–51 Portland Place, London W1N 4JL
020 7636 9375/5726
Ambassador: HE Ma Zhengang
Commercial: 13 Leinster Gardens,
London W2 6DP 020 7723 8923

COLOMBIA
Colombian Embassy
Flat 3A, 3 Hans Crescent, London SW1X 0LN
020 7589 9177/5037 Fax 020 7581 1829
Ambassador:
HE Señor Victor Ricardo

CONGO, DEMOCRATIC REPUBLIC OF
Embassy of the Democratic Republic of Congo
26 Chesham Place, London SW1X 8HH
020 7235 6137 Fax 020 7235 9048
Telex: 25651
Henri N'Swana *(Chargé d'Affaires)*

CONGO, REPUBLIC OF
No London Embassy
Embassy of the Republic of Congo
37 bis Rue Paul Valery, 75116 Paris, France
00 1 45 00 60 57
Ambassador: HE Mons Henri Lopes
(Resident in Paris)
Honorary Consulate:
4 Wendle Court, 131–137 Wandsworth Road,
London SW8 2LH 020 7622 0419

COSTA RICA
Costa Rican Embassy
Flat 1, 14 Lancaster Gate, London W2 3LH
020 7706 8844 Fax 020 7706 8655
Ambassador: HE Señor Rodolfo Gutiérrez

COTE D'IVOIRE
Embassy of the Republic of Côte d'Ivoire
2 Upper Belgrave Street, London SW1X 8BJ
020 7235 6991 Fax 020 7259 5320
Telex: 23906 IVORY G
Ambassador: HE Mons Kouadio Adjoumani
Commercial: 2 Upper Belgrave Street,
London SW1X 8BJ 020 7235 6991
Mons Kouame Clement Goli – Attaché

CROATIA
Embassy of the Republic of Croatia
21 Conway Street, London W1P 5HL
020 7387 2022 Fax 020 7387 0310
Ambassador: HE Andrija Kojakovic

CUBA
Embassy of the Republic of Cuba
167 High Holborn, London WC1 6PA
020 7240 2488 Fax 020 7836 2602
Ambassador: Vacant
Commercial:
Elena Blanco Diaz – Counsellor

CYPRUS
Cyprus High Commission
93 Park Street, London W1Y 4ET
020 7499 8272 Fax 020 7491 0691
High Commissioner:
HE Mrs Myrna Y Kleopas
Commercial: 3rd Floor, 29 Princes Street,
London W1R 7RG 020 7629 6288
Andreas Georgiades – Counsellor

CZECH REPUBLIC
Embassy of the Czech Republic
26–30 Kensington Palace Gardens,
London W8 4QY
020 7243 1115 Fax 020 7727 9654
Ambassador: HE Pavel Seifter

DENMARK
Royal Danish Embassy
55 Sloane Street, London SW1X 9SR
020 7333 0200 Fax 020 7333 0270
Ambassador: HE Ole Lønsmann Poulsen
Commercial: Gunner Richard Tetler –
Counsellor

DJIBOUTI
No London Embassy
Embassy of the Republic of Djibouti
26 Rue Emile Mènier, 75116 Paris, France
00 1 47 27 49 22
Ambassador: HE Mons Djama Omar Idleh
(Resident in Paris)

DOMINICA
Office of the High Commissioner for the
Commonwealth of Dominica
1 Collingham Gardens, London SW5 0HW
020 7370 5194/5 Fax 020 7373 8743
Telex: 8813931 DACOM G
High Commissioner: HE George E Williams

DOMINICAN REPUBLIC
Embassy of the Dominican Republic
139 Inverness Terrace, London W2 6JF
020 7727 6285 Fax 020 7727 3693
Ambassador: Vacant

EASTERN CARIBBEAN STATES
see St Christopher and Nevis; St Lucia;
St Vincent and the Grenadines

ECUADOR
Embassy of Ecuador
Flat 3B, 3 Hans Crescent, London SW1X 0LS
020 7584 2648/8084 Fax 020 7823 9701
Telex: 8811087
Ambassador
HE Senor Oswaldo Ramirez-Landazuri

EGYPT
Embassy of the Arab Republic of Egypt
26 South Street, London W1Y 6DD
020 7499 3304/2401 Fax 020 7491 1542
Telex: 23650 BOSTAN G
Ambassador: HE Adel El Gazzar
Commercial: 23 South Street,
London W1Y 6EL
020 7499 3002 Fax 020 7493 8110

EL SALVADOR
Embassy of El Salvador
Tennyson House, 159 Great Portland Street,
London W1N 5FD
020 7436 8282 Fax 020 7436 8181
Ambassador:
HE Senor Mauricio Castro-Aragōn

EQUATORIAL GUINEA
No London Embassy
Embassy of the Republic of Equatorial Guinea
6 Rue Alfred de Vigny, 75008 Paris, France
00 1 47 66 44 33/95 70
Ambassador: HE Lino-Sima Ekua Avomo
(Resident in Paris)

ERITREA
Embassy of the State of Eritrea
96 White Lion Street, London N1 9PF
020 7713 0096 Fax 020 7713 0161
Ambassador: HE Ghirmai Ghebremariam

ESTONIA
Embassy of the Republic of Estonia
16 Hyde Park Gate, London SW7 5DG
020 7589 7690/3428 Fax 020 7589 3430
Ambassador: HE Raul Mälk

ETHIOPIA
Embassy of the Federal Democratic Republic of Ethiopia
17 Prince's Gate, London SW7 1PZ
020 7589 7212/5 Fax 020 7584 7054
Ambassador: HE Dr Beyone Negewo
Commercial: Osman Imam Beshir – Counsellor

FIJI ISLANDS
High Commission of the Fiji Islands
34 Hyde Park Gate, London SW7 5DN
020 7584 3661 Fax 020 7584 2838
High Commissioner: HE Filimone Jitoko
Commercial: Sung Kangwai –
Counsellor 020 7584 3661

FINLAND
The Embassy of Finland
38 Chesham Place, London SW1X 8HW
020 7838 6200 Fax 020 7235 3680
Ambassador: HE Pertti Salolainen
Commercial: 3rd Floor, 30–35 Pall Mall,
London SW1 020 7747 3000
Marcus Moberg – Counsellor

FRANCE
French Embassy
58 Knightsbridge, London SW1X 7JT
020 7201 1000 Fax 020 7201 1004
Telex: 261 95 FRALON
Ambassador:
HE Monsieur Daniel Bernard CMG CBE
Commercial: Mons Philippe O'Quin –
Minister-Counsellor

GABON
Embassy of the Republic of Gabon
27 Elvaston Place, London SW7 5NL
020 7823 9986 Fax 020 7584 0047
Telex: 919418 AMBGAB G
Ambassador:
HE Madame Honorine Dossou-Naki
(Resident in Paris)

GAMBIA, THE
The Gambia High Commission
57 Kensington Court, London W8 5DG
020 7937 6316/7/8 Fax 020 7937 9095
High Commissioner: Vacant
Bala Garba-Jahumpa *(Acting High
Commissioner)*

GEORGIA
Embassy of the Republic of Georgia
3 Hornton Place, London W8 4LZ
020 7937 8233 Fax 020 7938 4108
Ambassador: HE Teimuraz Mamatsashvili

GERMANY
Embassy of the Federal Republic of Germany
23 Belgrave Square, 1 Chesham Place,
London SW1X 8PZ
020 7824 1300 Fax 020 7824 1435
Telex: 21650 AALDN E
Ambassador:
HE Herr Dr Hans-Friedrich von Ploetz

GHANA
Office of the High Commissioner for Ghana
13 Belgrave Square, London SW1X 8PN
020 7235 4142 Fax 020 7245 9552
High Commissioner: HE James Emmanuel
Kwegyir Aggrey-Orleans

GREECE
Embassy of Greece
1A Holland Park, London W11 3TP
020 7229 3850 Fax 020 7229 7221
Telex: 266751 GREEMB G
Ambassador: Vacant
Constantinos Bitsios *(Chargé d'Affaires)*
Commercial: 020 7727 8860
Fax 020 7727 9934

GRENADA
High Commission for Grenada
1 Collingham Gardens, London SW5 0HW
020 7373 7809 Fax 020 7370 7040
High Commissioner: HE Ruth Rouse

GUATEMALA
Embassy of Guatemala
13 Fawcett Street, London SW10 9HN
020 7351 3042 Fax 020 7376 5708
Telex: 926556 GUATEM
Ambassador: Vacant
Dr Magda Lopez Toledo *(Chargé d'Affaires)*

GUINEA
No London Embassy
Embassy of the Republic of Guinea
51 rue de la Faisanderie, 75016 Paris, France
00 1 47 04 81 48
Ambassador HE Mons Ibrahim Sylla
(Resident in Paris)
Honorary Consulate:
20 Upper Grosvenor Street, London W1X 9PB
020 7333 0044

GUINEA-BISSAU

No London Embassy
Embassy of the Republic of Guinea-Bissau
94 rue St Lazare, Paris 9, France
00 1 45 26 18 51
Ambassador: HE Fali Embalo (Resident in
Paris)
Honorary Consulate:
Flat 5, 8 Palace Gate, London W8 5NF
020 7589 5253

GUYANA

High Commission for Guyana
3 Palace Court, Bayswater Road,
London W2 4LP
020 7229 7684-8 Fax 020 7727 9809
High Commissioner:
HE Laleshwar K N Singh

HAITI

Embassy closed 30 March 1987

HOLY SEE

Apostolic Nunciature
54 Parkside, London SW19 5NF
020 8946 1410/7971 Fax 020 8947 2494
Apostolic Nuncio: HE Archbishop Pablo Puente

HONDURAS

Embassy of Honduras
115 Gloucester Place, London W1H 3PJ
020 7486 4880 Fax 020 7486 4550
Telex: 296368
Ambassador:
HE Senor Hernan Antonio Bermudez

HUNGARY

Embassy of the Republic of Hungary
35 Eaton Place, London SW1X 8BY
020 7235 5218 Fax 020 7823 1348
Ambassador: HE Gabor Szentivanyi
Commercial: 46 Eaton Place, London SW1
020 7235 8767
Andras Hirschler – Counsellor (Commercial)

ICELAND

Embassy of Iceland
1 Eaton Terrace, London SW1W 8EY
020 7590 1100 Fax 020 7730 1683
Telex: 918226 ICEMBY G
Ambassador: HE Thorsteinn Pálsson

INDIA

Office of the High Commissioner for India
India House, Aldwych, London WC2B 4NA
020 7836 8484 Fax 020 7836 4331
Telex: 267166 HCILDNG 263581 INDSUPG
24104 INDSUPG
High Commissioner: HE Nareshwar Dayal

INDONESIA

Embassy of the Republic of Indonesia
38 Grosvenor Square, London W1X 9AD
020 7499 7661 Fax 020 7491 4993
Ambassador:
HE Nana Sutresna Sastradidjaja
Commercial: 61 Welbeck Street,
London W1M 7HB
020 7935 1616 Fax 020 7935 0034
Andreas Anugerah – Attaché

IRAN

Embassy of the Islamic Republic of Iran
16 Prince's Gate, London SW7 1PT
020 7225 3000 Fax 020 7589 4440
Ambassador: HE Gholamreza Ansari

IRAQ

Diplomatic Relations broken
February 1991
Iraqi Interests Section: Embassy of the
Hashemite Kingdom of Jordan,
21 Queen's Gate, London SW7 5JG
020 7584 7141 Fax 020 7584 7716
Minister/Head of Interests Section: Dr
Mudhafer Amin

IRELAND

Irish Embassy
17 Grosvenor Place, London SW1X 7HR
020 7235 2171 Fax 020 7245 6961
Telex: 916104
Ambassador: HE Edward Barrington
Commercial: Orla Maher
(Commercial Attaché)

ISRAEL

Embassy of Israel
2 Palace Green, London W8 4QB
020 7957 9500 Fax 020 7957 9555
Ambassador: HE Dror Zeigerman
Commercial: Mrs Ronit Kan – Counsellor

ITALY
Italian Embassy
14 Three Kings Yard, Davies Street,
London W1Y 2EH
020 7312 2200 Fax 020 7312 2230
Telex: 05123520 ITADIPG
Ambassador: HE Signor Luigi Amaduzzi

IVORY COAST – see Côte D'Ivoire

JAMAICA
Jamaican High Commission
1–2 Prince Consort Road, London SW7 2BZ
020 7823 9911 Fax 020 7589 5154
Telex: 263304
High Commissioner:
HE Hon David Muirhead QC

JAPAN
Embassy of Japan
101–104 Piccadilly, London W1V 9FN
020 7465 6500 Fax 020 7491 9348
Ambassador: HE Sadayuki Hayashi
Commercial: Haruhiko Kuramochi – Minister

JORDAN
Embassy of the Hashemite Kingdom of Jordan
6 Upper Phillimore Gardens, London W8 7HB
020 7937 3685 Fax 020 7937 8795
Ambassador: HE Timoor Ghazi Daghistani

KAZAKHSTAN
Embassy of the Republic of Kazakhstan
33 Thurloe Square, London SW7 2DS
020 7581 4646 Fax 020 7584 8481
Ambassador: HE Dr Adil Akhmetov

KENYA
Kenya High Commission
45 Portland Place, London W1N 4AS
020 7636 2371/5 Fax 020 7323 6717
Telex: 262551
High Commissioner: HE Mrs Nancy Kirui
Commercial: D Mbugua – Attaché

KIRIBATI
Kiribati High Commission
c/o Office of the President, PO Box 68,
Bairiki, Tarawa, Kiribati
Acting High Commissioner: Peter T Timeon
(Resident in Tarawa, Kiribati)

KOREA
Embassy of the Republic of Korea
60 Buckingham Gate, London SW1E 6AJ
020 7227 5500 Fax 020 7227 5503
Ambassador: HE Choi Sung-hong
Commercial: Kim Chil-doo – Counsellor

KUWAIT
Embassy of the State of Kuwait
2 Albert Gate, London SW1X 7JU
020 7590 3400 Fax 020 7823 1712
Ambassador:
HE Khaled A A S Al Duwaisan GCVO

KYRGYZ REPUBLIC
Embassy of the Kyrgyz Republic
Ascot House, 119 Crawford Street,
London W1H 1AF
020 7935 1462 Fax 020 7935 7449
Ambassador: HE Mrs Roza Otunbayeva

LAOS
No London Embassy
Embassy of the Lao People's
Democratic Republic
74 Avenue Raymond-Poincaré,
75116 Paris, France
00 1 45 53 02 98 Telex: 00 1 61-07-11
Ambassador: HE Khamphan Simmalavong
(Resident in Paris)

LATVIA
Embassy of the Republic of Latvia
45 Nottingham Place, London W1M 3FE
020 7312 0040 Fax 020 7312 0042
Ambassador: HE Normans Penke

LEBANON
Lebanese Embassy
21 Kensington Palace Gardens,
London W8 4QM
020 7229 7265 Fax 020 7243 1699
Telex: 262048 ALIBAN G
Ambassador: HE Jihad Mortada

LESOTHO
High Commission for the Kingdom of Lesotho
7 Chesham Place, London SW1 8HN
020 7235 5686 Fax 020 7235 5023
Telex: 262995
High Commissioner:
HE Miss Lebohang Ramohlanka

LIBERIA
Embassy of the Republic of Liberia
2 Pembridge Place, London W2 4XB
020 7221 1036
Ambassador: Vacant
Jeff Gongoer Dowana, Senior
(Chargé d'Affaires)

LIBYA
Libyan People's Bureau
61-62 Ennismore Gardens, London SW7 1NH
020 7589 6120
Isa Baruni Edaeki *(Chargé d'Affaires)*

LITHUANIA
Embassy of the Republic of Lithuania
84 Gloucester Place, London W1H 3HN
020 7486 6401 Fax 020 7486 6403
Ambassador: HE Justas Vincas Paleckis

LUXEMBOURG
Embassy of Luxembourg
27 Wilton Crescent, London SW1X 8SD
020 7235 6961 Fax 020 7235 9734
Ambassador: HE Mons Joseph Weyland

MACEDONIA
Embassy of the Republic of Macedonia
Suite 10, 4th Floor, Harcourt House,
19–19A Cavendish Square, London W1M 9AD
020 7499 5152 Fax 020 7499 2864
Ambassador: HE Stevo Crvenkovski

MADAGASCAR
No London Embassy
Embassy of the Republic of Madagascar
4 Avenue Raphael, 75016 Paris, France
00 33 1 45 04 62 11
Ambassador: HE Mons Malala Zo Raolison
(Resident in Paris)
Honorary Consulate:
16 Lanark Mansions, Pennard Road,
London W12 8DT 020 8746 0133

MALAWI
High Commission for the Republic of Malawi
33 Grosvenor Street, London W1X 0DE
020 7491 4172/7 Fax 020 7491 9916
High Commissioner:
HE Mr Bright Mcbin Msaka

MALAYSIA
Malaysian High Commission
45 Belgrave Square, London SW1X 8QT
020 7235 8033 Fax 020 7235 5161
Telex: 262550
High Commissioner:
HE Dato Mohamad Amir bin Jaafar
Commercial Counsellor: Mohd Ghazali Idris

MALDIVES
High Commission of the Republic of Maldives
22 Nottingham Place, London W1M 3FB
020 7224 2135 Fax 020 7224 2157
Adam Hassan *(Acting High Commissioner)*

MALI
No London Embassy
Embassy of the Republic of Mali
Avenue Moliere 487, 1050 Brussels, Belgium
00 32 2 345 74 32
Ambassador: Vacant
Mons Moussa Kouyate *(Chargé d'Affaires)*
(Resident in Brussels)

MALTA
Malta High Commission
Malta House, 36–38 Piccadilly,
London W1P 0PQ
020 7292 4800 Fax 020 7734 1831
Telex: 261102
High Commissioner:
HE Dr George Bonello Dupuis

MAURITANIA
Embassy of the Islamic Republic of Mauritania
140 Bow Common Lane, London E3 4BH
020 8980 4382 Fax 020 8980 2232
Ambassador: HE Dr Diaganna Youssouf

MAURITIUS
Mauritius High Commission
32/33 Elvaston Place, London SW7 5NW
020 7581 0294 Fax 020 7823 8437
High Commissioner:
HE Sir Satcam Boolell, QC

MEXICO
Embassy of Mexico
42 Hertford Street, London W1Y 7TF
020 7499 8586 Fax 020 7495 4035
Ambassador: HE Señor Santiago Oñate
Commercial: 5th Floor Rear,
3 St James's Square, London SW1W 4JU
020 7839 6586 Fax 020 7839 4425

MOLDOVA
No London Embassy
Embassy of the Republic of Moldova
Avenue Emile Max 175, 1040 Brussels,
Belgium
00 322 732 96 59/93 00 Fax 00 322 732 96 60
Ambassador: HE Ion Capatina
(Resident in Brussels)

MONGOLIA
Embassy of Mongolia
7 Kensington Court, London W8 5DL
020 7937 0150
Ambassador: HE Tsedenjavyn Suhbaatar

MOROCCO
Embassy of the Kingdom of Morocco
49 Queen's Gate Gardens, London SW7 5NE
020 7581 5001/4 Fax 020 7225 3862
Telex: 28389
Ambassador: HE Mohammed Belmahi

MOZAMBIQUE
High Commission of the Republic of
Mozambique
21 Fitzroy Square, London W1P 5HJ
020 7383 3800 Fax 020 7383 3801
High Commissioner:
HE Dr Eduardo J B Koloma

MYANMAR – see Burma

NAMIBIA
High Commission of the Republic of Namibia
6 Chandos Street, London W1M 0LQ
020 7636 6244 Fax 020 7637 5694
High Commissioner: HE Mrs Monica Nashandi

NAURU
No London High Commission
Honorary Consulate:
Romshed Courtyard, Under River,
Nr Sevenoaks, Kent TN15 0SD
01732 746016

NEPAL
Royal Nepalese Embassy
12A Kensington Palace Gardens,
London W8 4QU
020 7229 1594 Fax 020 7792 9861
Ambassador: HE Dr Singha B Basnyat

NETHERLANDS
Royal Netherlands Embassy
38 Hyde Park Gate, London SW7 5DP
020 7590 3200 Fax 020 7225 0947
Ambassador:
HE Baron William Bentinck van Schoonheten

NEW ZEALAND
New Zealand High Commission
New Zealand House, Haymarket,
London SW1Y 4TQ
020 7930 8422 Fax 020 7839 4580
High Commissioner:
HE The Rt Hon Paul East QC
Commercial: J N Waugh – Minister

NICARAGUA
The Embassy of Nicaragua
Suite 12, Vicarage House,
58–60 Kensington Church Street,
London W8 4DP
020 7938 2373 Fax: 020 7937 0952
Ambassador:
HE Senora Nora Campos de Lankes

NIGER
No London Embassy
Embassy of the Republic of Niger
154 Rue de Longchamp, 75116 Paris, France
00 33 1 45 04 80 60
Ambassador: HE Madame Mariama Hima
(Resident in Paris)

NIGERIA
High Commission for the Federal Republic of
Nigeria
Nigeria House, 9 Northumberland Avenue,
London WC2N 5BX
020 7839 1244 Fax 020 7839 8746
Telex: 23665/916814/8952931
High Commissioner: HE Prince Bola A. Ajibola

NORWAY
Royal Norwegian Embassy
25 Belgrave Square, London SW1X 8QD
020 7591 5500 Fax 020 7245 6993
Ambassador: HE Tarald Osnes Brautaset
Commercial: Charles House, 5th Floor,
5–11 Lower Regent Street, London SW1
020 7973 0188 Fax 020 7973 0189
Sverre Johan Lindtvedt – Counsellor (Trade)

OMAN
Embassy of the Sultanate of Oman
167 Queen's Gate, London SW7 5HE
020 7225 0001 Fax 020 7589 2505
Ambassador: HE Hussain Ali Abdullatif

PAKISTAN
High Commission for the Islamic Republic of
Pakistan
35–36 Lowndes Square, London SW1X 9JN
020 7664 9200 Fax 020 7664 9299
High Commissioner: Vacant
Javid Iqbal *(Acting High Commissioner)*

PANAMA
Embassy of the Republic of Panama
48 Park Street, London W1Y 3PD
020 7493 4646 Fax 020 7493 4333
Ambassador:
HE Senora Ariadne E Singares Robinson
Commercial: Flat 2, 48 Park Street, London
W1Y 3PD
Salim Kheireddine – Counsellor

PAPUA NEW GUINEA
Papua New Guinea High Commission
3rd Floor, 14 Waterloo Place,
London SW1R 4AR
020 7930 0922/7 Fax 020 7930 0828
Telex: 25827 Kundu G
High Commissioner: HE Sir Kina Bona KBE

PARAGUAY
Embassy of Paraguay
Braemar Lodge, Cornwall Gardens,
London SW7 4AQ
020 7937 1253 Fax 020 7937 5687
Ambassador: HE Senor Raul dos Santos

PERU
Embassy of Peru
52 Sloane Street, London SW1X 9SP
020 7235 1917/2545 Fax 020 7235 4463
Ambassador:
HE Senor Gilbert Chauny De Porturas Hoyle

PHILIPPINES
Embassy of the Philippines
9A Palace Green, London W8 4QE
020 7937 1600 Fax 020 7937 2925
Ambassador: HE Hon. César B Bautista
Commercial: 1a Cumberland House,
Kensington Court Road, London W8
020 7937 1898
Vicente Casim – Commercial Attaché

POLAND
Embassy of the Republic of Poland
47 Portland Place, London W1N 3AG
020 7580 4324/9 Fax 020 7323 4018
Telex: 265691
Ambassador: HE Dr Stanislaw Komorowski
Commercial: 15 Devonshire Street,
London W1N 2AR 020 7580 5481
Piotr Kozerski – Commercial
Counsellor/Minister Plenipotentiary

PORTUGAL
Portuguese Embassy
11 Belgrave Square, London SW1X 8PP
020 7235 5331/4 Fax 020 7245 1287
Telex: 28484
Ambassador: HE Senhor José Gregõrio Faria
Commercial: Senhor Antonio Silva – Counsellor

QATAR
Embassy of the State of Qatar
1 South Audley Street, London W1Y 5DQ
020 7493 2200 Fax 020 7493 2661
Telex: 284 69
Ambassador: Vacant

ROMANIA
Embassy of Romania
4 Palace Green, London W8 4QD
020 7937 9666 Fax 020 7937 8069
Telex: 22232
Ambassador: HE Radu Onofrei

RUSSIA
Embassy of the Russian Federation
13 Kensington Palace Gardens,
London W8 4QX
020 7229 3628/2666/6412 Fax 020 7727 8625
Ambassador: HE Grigory B. Karasin

RWANDA
Embassy of the Republic of Rwanda
Uganda House, 58–59 Trafalgar Square,
London WC2N 5DX
020 7930 2570 Fax 020 7930 2572
Ambassador: Vacant

ST CHRISTOPHER AND NEVIS
High Commission for St Christopher and Nevis
10 Kensington Court, London W8 5DL
020 7937 9522 Fax 020 7937 5514
*High Commissioner:*Vacant
Mrs Shirley Pemberton *(Chargé d'Affaires)*

ST LUCIA
High Commission for St Lucia
10 Kensington Court, London W8 5DL
020 7937 9522 Fax 020 7937 5514
High Commissioner:
HE Emmanuel Cotter MBE

ST VINCENT AND THE GRENADINES
High Commission for St Vincent and the
Grenadines
10 Kensington Court, London W8 5DL
020 7565 2874
High Commissioner: HE Carlyle Dougan QC

SAMOA
No London High Commission
Embassy of the Independent State of Samoa
Avenue Franklin D Roosevelt 123,
1050 Brussels, Belgium
00 32 2 660 84 54 Fax 00 32 2 675 03 36
High Commissioner:
HE Mr Tau'ili'ili U'ili Meredith
(Resident in Brussels)
Honorary Consulate:
18 Northumberland Avenue,
London WC2N 5BJ
020 7930 6733

SAN MARINO
No London Embassy
Consulate:
Flat 51, 162 Sloane Street, London SW1
020 7823 4768

SÃO TOMÉ AND PRÍNCIPE
Embassy of the Democratic Republic of São
Tomé and Príncipé:
Square Montgomery, 175 Avenue de Tervuren,
1150 Brussels, Belgium
00 32 2 734 89 66 Fax 00 32 2 734 88 15
Mons Antonio de Lima Viegas
(Chargé d'Affaires) (Resident in Brussels)

SAUDI ARABIA
Royal Embassy of Saudi Arabia
30 Charles Street, London W1X 7PM
020 7917 3000
Ambassador: HE Dr Ghazi A Algosaibi
Commercial: Mohammed Abdullah
Al-Sheddi – Attaché

SENEGAL
Embassy of the Republic of Senegal
39 Marloes Road, London W8 6LA
020 7937 7237 Fax 020 7938 2546
Ambassador: HE Gabriel Alexandre Sar

SEYCHELLES
High Commission for Seychelles
Box 4PE, 2nd Floor, Eros House, 111 Baker
Street, London W1M 1FE
020 7224 1660 Fax 020 7487 5756
High Commissioner: HE Bertrand Rassool

SIERRA LEONE
Sierra Leone High Commission
Oxford Circus House, 245 Oxford Street,
London W1R 1LF
020 7287 9884 Fax 020 7734 3822
High Commissioner: Vacant
Sulaiman Tejan-Jalloh
(Acting High Commissioner)

SINGAPORE
High Commission for the Republic of Singapore
9 Wilton Crescent, London SW1X 8RW
020 7235 8315 Fax 020 7245 5874
High Commissioner:
HE Professor Pang Eng Fong
Commercial: 5 Chesham Street,
London SW1X 8ND
020 7235 4558 Fax 020 7235 4557
Kheng Hian Philip Ho – First Secretary

SLOVAK REPUBLIC
Embassy of the Slovak Republic
25 Kensington Palace Gardens,
London W8 4QY
020 7243 0803 Fax 020 7727 5824
Ambassador: HE Frantisek Dlhopolcek
Commercial: Michal Vrabel – Counsellor

SLOVENIA
Embassy of the Republic of Slovenia
Suite 1, Cavendish Court,
11 15 Wigmore Street, London W1H 9LA
020 7495 7775 Fax 020 7495 7776
Ambassador: HE Marjan Setinc

SOLOMON ISLANDS
No London High Commission
Embassy of the Solomon Islands
Boulevard Saint Michel, (First Floor),
Box 23, 1040 Brussels, Belgium
00 32 2 732 70 85 Fax 00 32 2 732 68 85
High Commissioner: Robert Sisilo
(Resident in Brussels)

SOMALIA
Embassy closed 2 January 1992

SOUTH AFRICA
High Commission of the Republic of South
Africa
South Africa House, Trafalgar Square,
London WC2N 5DP 020 7451 7299
Fax 020 7451 7284
High Commissioner:
HE Cheryl Ann Carolus

SPAIN
Spanish Embassy
39 Chesham Place, London SW1X 8SB
020 7235 5555/6/7 Fax 020 7235 9905
Telex: 21110/261333
Ambassador:
HE The Marques de Tamarón
Commercial: 66 Chiltern Street,
London W1M 1PR
020 7486 0101 Fax 020 7487 5586
Señor Don Felix Martinez-Burgos, Head of
Commercial Office

SRI LANKA
High Commission for the Democratic Socialist
Republic of Sri Lanka
13 Hyde Park Gardens, London W2 2LU
020 7262 1841/7 Fax 020 7262 7970
High Commissioner: HE Mangala Moonesinghe
Commercial: T G Ariyaratne – Minister

SUDAN
The Embassy of the Republic of the Sudan
3 Cleveland Row, London SW1A 1DD
020 7839 8080 Fax 020 7839 7560
Ambassador: HE Dr Hassan Abdin

SURINAME
No London Embassy
Embassy of the Republic of Suriname
2 Alexander Gogelweg, The Hague 2517JH,
The Netherlands
00 31 70 3650 844
Ambassador:
HE Evert Guillaume Azimullah
(Resident in The Hague)

SWAZILAND
Kingdom of Swaziland High Commission
20 Buckingham Gate, London SW1E 6LB
020 7630 6611 Fax 020 7630 6564
Telex: 28853
High Commissioner:
HE Rev Percy Sipho Mngomezulu

SWEDEN
Embassy of Sweden
11 Montagu Place, London W1H 2AL
020 7917 6400 Fax 020 7724 4174
Telex: 28249
Ambassador: HE Mats Bergquist CMG
Commercial/Trade: 73 Welbeck Street, London
W1M 8AN 020 7935 9601
Jonas Brogardh – Commercial Counsellor and
Trade Commissioner

SWITZERLAND
Embassy of Switzerland
16/18 Montagu Place, London W1H 2BQ
020 7616 6000 Fax 020 7724 7001
Telex 28212
Ambassador: HE Bruno Spinner
Commercial: Herr Jürg Schneeberger –
Counsellor (Commercial)

SYRIA
Embassy of the Syrian Arab Republic
8 Belgrave Square, London SW1X 8PH
020 7245 9012 Fax 020 7235 4621
Ambassador: Vacant
Dr Sami Glaiel *(Chargé d'Affaires)*

TAJIKISTAN
No London Embassy
Honorary Consulate:
33 Ovington Square, London SW3 1LJ
020 7584 5111

TANZANIA
High Commission for the United Republic of
Tanzania
43 Hertford Street, London W1Y 8DB
020 7499 8951/4 Fax 020 7491 9321
Telex: 262504 TANLDN G
High Commissioner:
HE Dr Abdul-Kader A Shareef
Commercial: Simon U R Mlay –
Minister-Counsellor

THAILAND
Royal Thai Embassy
29–30 Queen's Gate, London SW7 5JP
020 7589 2944 Fax 020 7823 9695
Telex: 27661
Ambassador:
HE Vidhya Rayananonda KCVO
Commercial: 11 Hertford Street,
London W1Y 7DX
020 7493 5749 Fax 020 7493 7416
Sanya Sara</>ndh – Minister/Commercial

TOGO
No London Embassy
Embassy of the Republic of Togo
8 rue Alfred-Roll, 75017 Paris, France
00 1 42 80 12 13
Ambassador: Vacant
(Resident in Paris)

TONGA
Tonga High Commission
36 Molyneux Street, London W1H 6AB
020 7724 5828
High Commissioner:
HE Colonel Fetu'utolu Tupou

TRINIDAD AND TOBAGO
Office of the High Commissioner for the
Republic of Trinidad and Tobago
42 Belgrave Square, London SW1X 8NT
020 7245 9351 Fax 020 7823 1065
High Commissioner: Vacant
Mrs Sandra McIntyre-Trotman
(Acting High Commissioner)
Commercial: Candyce Kelshall –
Commercial Attaché

TUNISIA
Tunisian Embassy
29 Prince's Gate, London SW7 1QG
020 7584 8117 Fax 020 7225 2884
Telex: 23736
Ambassador: HE Khemaies Jhinaoui

TURKEY
Turkish Embassy
43 Belgrave Square, London SW1X 8PA
020 7393 0202
Ambassador: HE Korkmaz Haktanir
Commercial: Münir Aksoy –
Counsellor 020 7235 4233/4991

TURKMENISTAN
Embassy of Turkmenistan,
St George's House, 14-17 Wells Street,
London W1P 3FP
020 7255 1071 Fax 020 7323 9184
Ambassador: HE Chary Babaev

TUVALU
No London High Commission
Honorary Consulate:
Tuvalu House, 230 Worple Road,
London SW20 8RH 020 8879 0985

UGANDA
Uganda High Commission
Uganda House, 58/59 Trafalgar Square,
London WC2N 5DX
020 7839 5783 Fax 020 7839 8925
Telex: 915141
High Commissioner: HE Prof George Kirya
(Doyen of the Diplomatic Corps)

UKRAINE
Embassy of Ukraine
60 Holland Park, London W11 3SJ
020 7727 6312 Fax 020 7792 1708
Ambassador: HE Professor Volodymyr
Vassylenko

UNITED ARAB EMIRATES
Embassy of the United Arab Emirates
30 Princes Gate, London SW7 1PT
020 7581 1281 Fax 020 7581 9616
Telex: 918459
Ambassador: HE Easa Sakh Al Gurg CBE
Commercial: 48 Princes Gate, London SW7
020 7589 3434

UNITED STATES OF AMERICA
American Embassy
24 Grosvenor Square, London W1A 1AE
020 7499 9000
Ambassador: HE Philip Lader
Commercial: David Katz – Minister-Counsellor

URUGUAY
Embassy of the Oriental Republic of Uruguay
2nd Floor, 140 Brompton Road,
London SW3 1HY
020 7589 8835 Fax 020 7581 9585
Telex: 264180 URUBRI G
Ambassador:
HE Dr Agustin Espinosa-Lloveras

UZBEKISTAN
Embassy of the Republic of Uzbekistan
41 Holland Park, London W11 2RP
020 7229 7679 Fax 020 7229 7029
Ambassador: HE Alisher Faizullaev

VANUATU
No London High Commission
c/o Department for Foreign Affairs,
Port Vila, Vanuatu
High Commissioner: Vacant
(Residence in Vanuatu)

VENEZUELA
Venezuelan Embassy
1 Cromwell Road, London SW7
020 7584 4206/7 Fax 020 7589 8887
Ambassador: Vacant

VIETNAM
Embassy of the Socialist Republic of Vietnam
12–14 Victoria Road, London W8 5RD
020 7937 1912 Fax 020 7937 6108
Telex: 887361
Ambassador: HE Vuong Thua Phong
Commercial: Dinh Van Hoi – Counsellor

WESTERN SAMOA – see Samoa

YEMEN
Embassy of the Republic of Yemen
57 Cromwell Road, London SW7 2ED
020 7584 6607 Fax 020 7589 3350
Ambassador:
HE Dr Hussain Abdullah Al-Amri

YUGOSLAVIA
Diplomatic relations broken March 25, 1999. A
Yugoslav Interests Section has been established
in the Cyprus High Commission

ZAÏRE – see Democratic Republic of Congo

ZAMBIA
High Commission for the Republic of Zambia
2 Palace Gate, London W8 5NG
020 7589 6655 Fax 020 7581 1353
Telex: 263544
High Commissioner: Vacant

ZIMBABWE
High Commission for the Republic of
Zimbabwe
Zimbabwe House, 429 Strand,
London WC2R 0SA
020 7836 7755 Fax 020 7379 1167
High Commissioner:
HE Mr Simbarashe S Mumbengegwi

EUROPEAN UNION

History

In 1957 France, Germany and Italy joined Belgium, the Netherlands and Luxembourg in setting up the European Economic Community (EEC) and the European Atomic Energy Agency (EAEC) through the Treaties of Rome. The United Kingdom joined this founding group together with Ireland and Denmark in 1973. The European Community continued to expand, in terms both of membership and of the policy areas coming within its competence. In 1981 Greece became the tenth member state followed by Spain and Portugal in 1986. In 1990 the unification of Germany automatically brought the former East German territory within the Community. In 1995 the European Community became the European Union, and was further enlarged with the accession of Austria, Finland and Sweden. In March 1998, accession discussions were launched with Cyprus, Poland, Hungary, the Czech Republic, Slovenia and Estonia. A further six countries opened accession talks to join the European Union in February 2000: Bulgaria, Latvia, Lithuania, Malta, Romania and Slovakia. Turkey is also now accepted as a candidate for membership of the European Union.

The European Union is managed by five institutions:

Council of the European Union

rue de la Loi, 170, 1048 Brussels, Belgium
Tel: 00 32 2 285 6511 *Fax:* 00 32 2 285 7397/7381
Website: ue.eu.int

The 15-member Council of the European Union is the only institution which directly represents the member governments. For major decisions the Foreign Ministers are usually present – at other times the appropriate Ministers according to the subject before the Council. The Presidency rotates every six months. From 1 January 2001 the six-monthly Presidency rotates in the following order: Sweden, Belgium, Spain, Denmark, Greece.

European Commission

rue de la Loi, 200, 1049 Brussels, Belgium
Tel: 00 32 2 299 1111
Website: europa.eu.int/comm/index—en.htm

UK Commissioners: Rt Hon Neil Kinnock, Rt Hon Chris Patten

The European Commission's main powers are those of supervision, initiative and implementation. It proposes Union policies and legislation, supervises the day-to-day running of Union policies and is the 'guardian' of the Treaties and can initiate action against member states which do not comply with Union rules. It also has wide powers of its own in certain sectors such as coal and steel and competition.

Representation of the European Commission in the UK:

London Office: 8 Storey's Gate, London SW1P 3AT
Tel: 020 7973 1992 *Fax:* 020 7973 1900
Website: www.cec.org.uk

Regional Offices
Windsor House, 9/15 Bedford Street, Belfast BT2 7EG
Tel: 028 9024 0708 *Fax:* 028 9024 8241

4 Cathedral Road, Cardiff CF1 9SG
Tel: 029 2037 1631 *Fax:* 029 2039 5489

9 Alva Street, Edinburgh EH2 4PH
Tel: 0131-225 2058 *Fax:* 0131-226 4105

European Parliament

The European Parliament exercises democratic control over the running of the European Union. Its 626 MEPs are elected every five years with the most recent election for the 1999–2004 Parliament having taken place in June 1999. The Parliament meets and debates in public, with plenary sessions taking place in Strasbourg for on average one week in each month except for August. In addition there are mini sessions in Brussels to facilitate contacts with the Commission and the Council. The major working unit of the European Parliament is the specialised committee where much of the legislative scrutiny takes place. The new Parliament has 17 permanent committees. As well as legislative powers, the Parliament also has powers relating to the Budget, to the conclusion of international agreements and general supervisory powers.

United Kingdom Information Office:
2 Queen Anne's Gate, London SW1H 9AA
Tel: 020 7227 4300 *Fax:* 020 7227 4302 *Library Fax:* 020 7227 4301
Website: www.europarl.org.uk

Scotland: 9 Alva Street, Edinburgh EH2 4PH
Tel: 0131-225 2508 *Fax:* 0131-226 4105

PARTY MEMBERSHIP OF UK MEPs

Conservative	36		
Labour	29		
Liberal Democrat	10		
UK Independence Party	2		
Green Party	2		
Scottish National Party	2	**UK MEPs**	
Plaid Cymru	2		
Democratic Unionist Party (DUP)	1	England	71
Social Democratic & Labour (SDLP)	1	Scotland	8
Ulster Unionist Party (UUP)	1	Wales	5
Michael Holmes	1	Northern Ireland	3
Total	**87**	**Total**	**87**

UK MEPs' DIRECTORY

Adam, Gordon   PES   Lab
Member Agriculture and Rural Development Committee
Member Ukraine, Belarus and Moldova Delegation
Substitute Industry, External Trade, Research and Energy Committee
European Parliament, Rue Wiertz, 1047 Brussels, Belgium
Tel: 00 32 2 284 52 02   Fax: 00 32 2 284 92 02

Atkins, Robert   EPP-ED   Con
Vice-chair EU-Cyprus Joint Parliamentary Committee Delegation
Member Regional Policy, Transport and Tourism Committee
Substitute Foreign Affairs, Human Rights, Common Security and Defence Policy Committee
Manor House, Garstang Lancashire PR3 1JA
Tel: 01995 602225   Fax: 01995 605690   E-mail: ratsmep@aol.com
Website: www.sir-robertatkins.org

Attwooll, Elspeth   ELDR   LD
Member Fisheries Committee
Member Regional Policy, Transport and Tourism Committee
Member Canada Delegation
Substitute Employment and Social Affairs Committee
Substitute Environment, Public Health and Consumer Policy Committee
2A Whitton Street, Glasgow G20 0AN, Scotland
Tel: 0141 946 1370   Fax: 0141 945 4056

Balfe, Richard   **PES**   **Lab**
Member Economic and Monetary Affairs Committee
Substitute EU-Turkey Joint Parliamentary Committee Delegation
PHS 8B09, European Parliament, Rue Wiertz, 1047 Brussels, Belgium
Tel: 00 32 2 284 54 06   Fax: 00 32 2 284 94 06   E-mail: rbalfe@europarl.eu.int
Website: www.poptel.org.uk/richard.balfe

Beazley, Christopher   **EPP-ED**   **Con**
Vice-chair Constitutional Affairs Committee
Member EU-Estonia Joint Parliamentary Committee Delegation
Substitute Industry, External Trade, Research and Energy Committee
Substitute EU-Slovenia Joint Parliamentary Committee Delegation
Hertford & Stortford Conservative Association, 4a Swains Mill, Ware, Hertfordshire SG12 9PY
Tel: 01920 462182   Fax: 01920 485805

Bethell, Nicholas (Lord)   **EPP-ED**   **Con**
Vice-chair EU-Poland Joint Parliamentary Committee Delegation
Member Foreign Affairs, Human Rights, Common Security and Defence Policy Committee
Substitute EU-Slovak Republic Joint Parliamentary Committee Delegation
Conservative Central Office, 32 Smith Square, London SW1P 3HH
Tel: 020 7821 1687   E-mail: nikbeth@aol.com

Bowe, David   **PES**   **Lab**
Member Environment, Public Health and Consumer Policy Committee
Member China Delegation
Substitute Industry, External Trade, Research and Energy Committee
2 Blenheim Terrace, Leeds LS2 9JG
Tel: 01132458993   Fax: 01132442742   E-mail: mail@davidbowe.demon.co.uk

Bowis, John   **EPP-ED**   **Con**
Vice-chair Kazakhstan, Kyrgyzstan, Uzbekistan, Tajikistan, Turkmenistan and Mongolia Delegation
Member Environment, Public Health and Consumer Policy Committee
Substitute Development and Co-operation Committee
PO Box 262, New Malden, Surrey KT3 4WJ
Tel: 020 8949 2555   Fax: 020 8395 7463   E-mail: johnbowis@aol.com

Bradbourn, Philip   **EPP-ED**   **Con**
Member Regional Policy, Transport and Tourism Committee
Member EU-Slovenia Joint Parliamentary Committee Delegation
Substitute Legal Affairs and Internal Market Committee
Substitute ECHELON Interception System Temporary Committee
Substitute EU-Malta Joint Parliamentary Committee Delegation
10 Greenfield Crescent, Birmingham B15 3AU
Tel: 0845 606 0239   Fax: 0121 456 5989   Website: www.torymeps.com

Bushill-Matthews, Philip   **EPP-ED**   **Con**
Member Employment and Social Affairs Committee
Member Mashreq and Gulf States Delegation
Member Japan Delegation
Substitute Environment, Public Health and Consumer Policy Committee
Manor House, Leamington Spa, Warwickshire CV33 9HX
Tel: 01926 612476   Fax: 01926 613168   E-mail: bushillm@aol.com   Website: www.torymeps.com

Callanan, Martin   **EPP-ED**   **Con**
Member Regional Policy, Transport and Tourism Committee
Member ACP-EU Joint Assembly
Substitute Economic and Monetary Affairs Committee
22 Osborne Road, Newcastle upon Tyne NE2 2AD
Tel: 0191 240 2600   Fax: 0191 240 2612

Cashman, Michael   **PES**   **Lab**
Member Citizens' Freedoms and Rights, Justice and Home Affairs Committee
Substitute Foreign Affairs, Human Rights, Common Security and Defence Policy Committee

West Midlands Labour Party, 67 Birmingham Road, West Bromwich B70 6PN
Tel: 0121 553 6642   Fax: 0121 553 6603   E-mail: Lp-west-mids@geo2.poptel.org.uk

Chichester, Giles   **EPP-ED**   **Con**
Member Industry, External Trade, Research and Energy Committee
Member Australia and New Zealand Delegation
Substitute Regional Policy, Transport and Tourism Committee

Constituency Office, 48 Queen Street, Exeter EX4 3SR
Tel: 01392 491815   Fax: 01392 491588   E-mail: gileschichestermep@eclipse.co.uk
Website: www.gileschichestermep.org.uk

Clegg, Nicholas   **ELDR**   **LD**
Member Industry, External Trade, Research and Energy Committee
Member South America and MERCOSUR Delegation
Substitute Economic and Monetary Affairs Committee

17-21 High Street, Ruddington, Nottinghamshire NG11 6DT
Tel: 0115 846 0661   Fax: 0115 846 1796   E-mail: ld_eastmidland@cix.co.uk

Corbett, Richard   **PES**   **Lab**
Member Constitutional Affairs Committee
Member ASEAN, South-east Asia and Republic of Korea Delegation
Substitute Economic and Monetary Affairs Committee

2 Blenheim Terrace, Leeds LS2 9JG
Tel: 0113 245 8978   Fax: 0113 245 8992   E-mail: richard@corbett-euro.demon.co.uk
Website: www.corbett-euro.demon.co.uk

Corrie, John   **EPP-ED**   **Con**
Chair ACP-EU Joint Assembly
Member Development and Co-operation Committee
Substitute Budgets Committee

West Midland Region, 10 Greenfield Crescent, Birmingham B15 3AU
Tel: 0845 606 0239   Fax: 0121 456 5989   E-mail: jacorrie@compuserve.com
Website: www.torymeps.com

Davies, Chris   **ELDR**   **LD**
Member Environment, Public Health and Consumer Policy Committee
Member EU-Cyprus Joint Parliamentary Committee Delegation
Substitute Regional Policy, Transport and Tourism Committee
Substitute Petitions Committee

87A Castle Street, Stockport, Lancashire SK3 9AR
Tel: 0161 477 7070   Fax: 0161 477 7007   E-mail: chrisdaviesmep@cix.co.uk

Deva, Nirj   **EPP-ED**   **Con**
Member Development and Co-operation Committee
Member ACP-EU Joint Assembly
Substitute Environment, Public Health and Consumer Policy Committee

169B Kennington Road, London SE11 6SF
Tel: 020 7642 8880   Fax: 020 7642 8879   E-mail: nirjdevamep@hotmail.com

Dover, Densmore   **EPP-ED**   **Con**
Vice-chair EU-Malta Joint Parliamentary Committee Delegation
Member Budgets Committee
Substitute Employment and Social Affairs Committee

166 Furzehill Road, Boreham Wood, Hertfordshire WD6 2DS
Tel: 020 8953 5945   Fax: 020 8386 0840

Duff, Andrew   **ELDR**   **LD**
Vice-chair EU-Turkey Joint Parliamentary Committee Delegation
Member Constitutional Affairs Committee
Substitute Foreign Affairs, Human Rights, Common Security and Defence Policy Committee
Orwell House, Cambridge CB4 0PP
Tel: 01223 566700   Fax: 01223 566698   E-mail: mep@andrewduffmep.org
Website: www.andrewduffmep.org

Elles, James   **EPP-ED**   **Con**
Member Budgets Committee
Member USA Delegation
Substitute Foreign Affairs, Human Rights, Common Security and Defence Policy Committee
Substitute Budgetary Control Committee
ASP 14E153, European Parliament, Rue Wiertz, 1047 Brussels, Belgium
Tel: 00 32 2 284 59 51   Fax: 00 32 2 284 99 51   E-mail: jelles@europarl.eu.int

Evans, Jill   **Green-EFA**   **PC**
Vice-chair Women's Rights and Equal Opportunities Committee
Member Employment and Social Affairs Committee
Member EU-Lithuania Joint Parliamentary Committee Delegation
Substitute Environment, Public Health and Consumer Policy Committee
8 Morfa Lane, Carmarthen SA31 3AX
Tel: 01267 234546   Fax: 01267 234546

Evans, Jonathan   **EPP-ED**   **Con**
Member Economic and Monetary Affairs Committee
Member Petitions Committee
Member Japan Delegation
Substitute Industry, External Trade, Research and Energy Committee
4 Penlline Road, Cardiff CF4 2XS, Wales
Tel: 029 2061 6031   Fax: 029 2061 3539   E-mail: jevans@tory.org

Evans, Robert   **PES**   **Lab**
Vice-chair Citizens' Freedoms and Rights, Justice and Home Affairs Committee
Member ECHELON Interception System Temporary Committee
Member South Asia and SAARC Delegation
Substitute Culture, Youth, Education, Media and Sport Committee
Substitute EU-Romania Joint Parliamentary Committee Delegation
Labour European Office, 16 Charles Square, London N1 6HP
Tel: 020 7253 1782   Fax: 020 7490 2143   Website: www.poptel.org.uk/robert-evans-mep

Farage, Nigel   **EDD**   **UKIP**
Member Economic and Monetary Affairs Committee
Member Fisheries Committee
Member EU-Malta Joint Parliamentary Committee Delegation
74 Holmethorpe Avenue, Redhill, Surrey RH1 2NL
Tel: 01737 780222   Fax: 01737 768590

Ford, Glyn   **PES**   **Lab**
Member Industry, External Trade, Research and Energy Committee
Member Japan Delegation
Substitute Citizens' Freedoms and Rights, Justice and Home Affairs Committee
Substitute ECHELON Interception System Temporary Committee
Southwest Labour Party, 1 Newfoundland Court, Bristol BS2 9AP
Tel: 0117 924 6399   Fax: 0117 924 8599   E-mail: mep@glynford.com   Website: ww.glynford.com

Foster, Jacqueline   **EPP-ED**   **Con**
Member ACP-EU Joint Assembly
Substitute Industry, External Trade, Research and Energy Committee
Substitute Regional Policy, Transport and Tourism Committee

European Parliament, Rue Wiertz, 1047 Brussels, Belgium
Tel: 00 32 2 284 59 57   Fax: 00 32 2 284 99 57   E-mail: jfoster@europarl.eu.int

Gill, Neena   **PES**   **Lab**
Member Budgets Committee
Member ASEAN, South-east Asia and Republic of Korea Delegation
Substitute Industry, External Trade, Research and Energy Committee

West Midlands Labour Party, 67 Birmingham Street, West Bromwich B70 6PN
Tel: 0121 553 6642   Fax: 0121 553 6603

Goodwill, Robert   **EPP-ED**   **Con**
Member Environment, Public Health and Consumer Policy Committee
Member Ukraine, Belarus and Moldova Delegation
Substitute Agriculture and Rural Development Committee

Southwood Farm, York YO6 6QB
Tel: 01653 648459   Fax: 01653 648225   E-mail: r.goodwill@farmline.com

Hannan, Daniel   **EPP-ED**   **Con**
Member Citizens' Freedoms and Rights, Justice and Home Affairs Committee
Member Kazakhstan, Kyrgyzstan, Uzbekistan, Tajikistan, Turkmenistan and Mongolia Delegation
Substitute Budgets Committee
Substitute EU-Estonia Joint Parliamentary Committee Delegation

Conservative Central Office, 32 Smith Square, London SW1P 3HH
Tel: 020 7984 8238   Fax: 020 7984 8207   E-mail: office@hannan.co.uk
Website: www.hannan.co.uk

Harbour, Malcolm   **EPP-ED**   **Con**
Member Legal Affairs and Internal Market Committee
Member Japan Delegation
Substitute Industry, External Trade, Research and Energy Committee

Manor Cottage, Solihull, West Midlands B91 2BL
Tel: 0121 711 3158   Fax: 0121 711 3159   E-mail: manor_cottage@compuserve.com

Heaton-Harris, Christopher   **EPP-ED**   **Con**
Member Budgetary Control Committee
Member Culture, Youth, Education, Media and Sport Committee
Member South Asia and SAARC Delegation
Substitute Budgets Committee

Blaby Conservative Association, 53 Lutterworth Road, Leicester LE8 4DW
Tel: 0116 277 9992   Fax: 0116 277 0098   E-mail: chhmep@netscapeonline.co.uk
Website: www.heatonharris.org.uk

Helmer, Roger   **EPP-ED**   **Con**
Member Environment, Public Health and Consumer Policy Committee
Member ASEAN, South-east Asia and Republic of Korea Delegation
Substitute Employment and Social Affairs Committee

Blaby Conservative Association, 35 Lutterworth Road, Leicester LE8 4DW
Tel: 0116 277 9992   Fax: 0116 278 6664   Website: www.rogerhelmer.org.uk

Holmes, Michael   **EDD**   **Ind**
Member Budgetary Control Committee
Substitute Citizens' Freedoms and Rights, Justice and Home Affairs Committee

European Parliament, Rue Wiertz, 1047 Brussels, Belgium
Tel: 00 32 2 284 57 63   Fax: 00 32 2 284 97 63

Honeyball, Mary   **PES**   **Lab**
Member Regional Policy, Transport and Tourism Committee
Substitute Employment and Social Affairs Committee

ASP 13G258, European Parliament, Rue Wiertz, 1047 Brussels, Belgium
Tel: 00 32 2 284 52 09   Fax: 00 32 2 284 92 09

Howitt, Richard   **PES**   **Lab**
Member Development and Co-operation Committee
Member ACP-EU Joint Assembly
Substitute Employment and Social Affairs Committee

ASP 13G246, European Parliament, Rue Wiertz, 1047 Brussels, Belgium
Tel: 00 32 2 284 54 77   Fax: 00 32 2 284 94 77

Hudghton, Ian   **Green-EFA**   **SNP**
Member Employment and Social Affairs Committee
Member Fisheries Committee
Member EEA Joint Parliamentary Committee Delegation
Substitute Economic and Monetary Affairs Committee

70 Rosemount Place, Aberdeen AB25 2XJ
Tel: 01224 623150   Fax: 01224 623160

Hughes, Stephen   **PES**   **Lab**
Member Employment and Social Affairs Committee
Member Russia Delegation
Substitute Budgets Committee

North East European Constituency Office, Room 4/38, Durham DH1 5UR
Tel: 0191 384 9371   Fax: 0191 384 6100   E-mail: alma@mep.u-net.com
Website: www.daltonet.com/stephenhughesmep

Huhne, Chris   **ELDR**   **LD**
Member Economic and Monetary Affairs Committee
Member Palestinian Legislative Council Delegation
Substitute Development and Co-operation Committee

Liberal Democrat Office European Parliament, 2 Queen Anne's Gate, London SW1H 9AA
Tel: 020 7227 4319   Fax: 020 7233 3959   E-mail: chuhne@dialstart.net
Website: www.chrishuhnemep.org

Hume, John   **PES**   **SDLP**
Member Regional Policy, Transport and Tourism Committee
Substitute Agriculture and Rural Development Committee

5 Bayview Terrace, Derry BT48 7EE, Northern Ireland
Tel: 028 7126 5340   Fax: 028 7136 3423

Inglewood, Lord ((William) Richard Fletcher-Vane)   **EPP-ED**   **Con**
Vice-chair China Delegation
Member Legal Affairs and Internal Market Committee
Substitute Constitutional Affairs Committee

Hutton-in-the-Forest, Penrith, Cumbria CA11 9TH
Tel: 017684 84500   Fax: 017684 84571

Jackson, Caroline   **EPP-ED**   **Con**
Chair Environment, Public Health and Consumer Policy Committee
Member Palestinian Legislative Council Delegation
Substitute Women's Rights and Equal Opportunities Committee

European Office, 14 Bath Road, Swindon SN1 4BA
Tel: 01793 422663   Fax: 01793 422664   E-mail: cj@carolinejackson.demon.co.uk
Website: www.carolinejacksonmep.org.uk

Khanbhai, Bashir   **EPP-ED**   **Con**
Member Development and Co-operation Committee
Member ACP-EU Joint Assembly
Substitute Industry, External Trade, Research and Energy Committee

57 Peninsula Cottage, Wroxham, Norfolk NR12 8RN
Tel: 01603 781480   Fax: 01732 469237   E-mail: bashir@khanbhai.co.uk
Website: www.khanbai.co.uk

Kinnock, Glenys   **PES**   **Lab**
Vice-chair ACP-EU Joint Assembly
Member Development and Co-operation Committee
Substitute Foreign Affairs, Human Rights, Common Security and Defence Policy Committee

Labour European Office, 16 Sachville Avenue, Cardiff, Wales CF14 3NY
Tel: 029 2061 8337   Fax: 029 2061 8226   E-mail: gkinnock@europe-wales.new.labour.org.uk

Kirkhope, Timothy   **EPP-ED**   **Con**
Member Citizens' Freedoms and Rights, Justice and Home Affairs Committee
Member EU-Czech Republic Joint Parliamentary Committee Delegation
Substitute Culture, Youth, Education, Media and Sport Committee
Substitute EEA Joint Parliamentary Committee Delegation

7 Dewar Close, Wetherby LS22 5JR
Tel: 01937 574649   Fax: 01937 574651   E-mail: timothy@leedsne.demon.co.uk
Website: www.kirkhope.org.uk

Lambert, Jean   **Green-EFA**   **Green**
Member Employment and Social Affairs Committee
Member Petitions Committee
Member Russia Delegation
Substitute Citizens' Freedoms and Rights, Justice and Home Affairs Committee
Substitute ECHELON Interception System Temporary Committee

Suites 58, The Hop Exchange, 24 Southwark Street, London SE1 1TY
Tel: 020 7407 62 69   Fax: 020 7234 01 83   E-mail: jeanlambert@greenmeps.org.uk

Lucas, Caroline   **Green-EFA**   **Green**
Vice-chair ACP-EU Joint Assembly
Member Industry, External Trade, Research and Energy Committee
Substitute Regional Policy, Transport and Tourism Committee

Suite 58, Hop Exchange, 24 Southwark Street, London SE1 1TY
Tel: 020 7407 6281   Fax: 020 7233 4008   E-mail: carolinelucas@greenmeps.org.uk

Ludford, Sarah (Baroness)   **ELDR**   **LD**
Member Citizens' Freedoms and Rights, Justice and Home Affairs Committee
Member South-east Europe Delegation
Substitute Foreign Affairs, Human Rights, Common Security and Defence Policy Committee
Substitute EU-Cyprus Joint Parliamentary Committee Delegation

Liberal Democrats, European Parliament Office, 2 Queen Anne's Gate, London SW1H 9AA
Tel: 020 7799 3429

Lynne, Liz   **ELDR**   **LD**
Member Employment and Social Affairs Committee
Member South Asia and SAARC Delegation
Substitute Culture, Youth, Education, Media and Sport Committee

55 Ely Street, Stratford upon Avon CV37 6LN
Tel: 01789 255354   Fax: 01789 268848

McAvan, Linda   **PES**   **Lab**
Member Foreign Affairs, Human Rights, Common Security and Defence Policy Committee
Member EU-Estonia Joint Parliamentary Committee Delegation
Member Ukraine, Belarus and Moldova Delegation
Substitute Regional Policy, Transport and Tourism Committee

Labour Constituency Office, 79 High Street, Wath upon Dearne S63 7QB
Tel: 01708 875665   Fax: 01709 874207   E-mail: linda.mcavan@virgin.net

McCarthy, Arlene   **PES**   **Lab**
Member Legal Affairs and Internal Market Committee
Member South Asia and SAARC Delegation
Substitute Economic and Monetary Affairs Committee

3-5 St John Street, Manchester M3 4DN
Tel: 0161 831 9848   Fax: 0161 831 9849   E-mail: arlene.mccarthy@easynet.co.uk

MacCormick, Neil   **Green-EFA**   **SNP**
Vice-chair ECHELON Interception System Temporary Committee
Member Legal Affairs and Internal Market Committee
Member Japan Delegation
Substitute Constitutional Affairs Committee

Scottish National Party, 6 North Charlotte Street, Edinburgh EH2 4JH
Tel: 0131 225 3497   Fax: 0131 225 3499   E-mail: neil@maccormick.fsnet.co.uk

McMillan-Scott, Edward   **EPP-ED**   **Con**
Chair EEA Joint Parliamentary Committee Delegation
Member Budgets Committee
Substitute Foreign Affairs, Human Rights, Common Security and Defence Policy Committee

Conservatives in the European Parliament, 32 Smith Square, London SW1P 3HH
Tel: 020 7222 1720   Fax: 020 7222 2501

McNally, Eryl   **PES**   **Lab**
Member Industry, External Trade, Research and Energy Committee
Member Women's Rights and Equal Opportunities Committee
Member South America and MERCOSUR Delegation
Substitute Environment, Public Health and Consumer Policy Committee

European Office, 270 St Alban's Road, Watford, Hertfordshire WD24 6PE
Tel: 01923242102   Fax: 01923242063   Website: www.erylmcnallymep.org.uk

Martin, David   **PES**   **Lab**
Member Budgets Committee
Member ACP-EU Joint Assembly
Substitute Development and Co-operation Committee

PO Box 27030, Edinburgh, Scotland EH10 7YP
Tel: 0131 654 1606   Fax: 0131 654 1607   E-mail: david.martin@ccis.org.uk

Miller, Bill   **PES**   **Lab**
Member Legal Affairs and Internal Market Committee
Substitute Economic and Monetary Affairs Committee

PO Box 7212, Glasgow G43 2WN
Tel: 0141 569 7494   Fax: 0141 577 0214   E-mail: bmillermep@aol.com

Moraes, Claude   **PES**   **Lab**
Vice-chair South Africa Delegation
Member Employment and Social Affairs Committee

Labour European Office, 16 Charles Square, London N1 6HP
Tel: 020 7253 9615   Fax: 020 7253 9614   E-mail: cmoraes@europarl.fsnet.co.uk

Morgan, Eluned   **PES**   **Lab**
Member Budgetary Control Committee
Member Central America and Mexico Delegation
Substitute Budgets Committee

Labour European Office, 16 Sachville Avenue, Cardiff CF14 3NY
Tel: 029 2061 8337   Fax: 029 2061 8226   E-mail: emorgan@europe-wales.new.labour.org.uk
Website: www.poptel.org.uk/eluned.morgan.mep

Murphy, Simon   **PES**   **Lab**
Member Economic and Monetary Affairs Committee
Member EU-Slovak Republic Joint Parliamentary Committee Delegation

West Midlands Labour Party, 67 Birmingham Road, West Bromwich B70 6PY
Tel: 0121 553 6642   Fax: 0121 553 6603

Newton Dunn, Bill   **EPP-ED**   **Ind**
Vice-chair Foreign Affairs, Human Rights, Common Security and Defence Policy Committee
Member Israel Delegation
Substitute Citizens' Freedoms and Rights, Justice and Home Affairs Committee
Substitute ECHELON Interception System Temporary Committee

10 Church Lane, Lincoln LN5 0EG
Tel: 0552 810812   Fax: 0552 810812   Website: www.newton-dunn.com

Nicholson, Emma (Baroness)   **ELDR**   **LD**
Vice-chair Foreign Affairs, Human Rights, Common Security and Defence Policy Committee
Member Development and Co-operation Committee
Member ACP-EU Joint Assembly

House of Lords, London SW1A 0PW
Tel: 020 7219 8516

Nicholson, James   **EPP-ED**   **UUP**
Chair Australia and New Zealand Delegation
Member Fisheries Committee
Substitute Agriculture and Rural Development Committee
Substitute Regional Policy, Transport and Tourism Committee

European Office, 3 Glengall Street, Belfast BT12 5AE, Northern Ireland
Tel: 028 9043 9431   Fax: 028 9024 6738

O'Toole, Mo   **PES**   **Lab**
Member Culture, Youth, Education, Media and Sport Committee
Member EU-Poland Joint Parliamentary Committee Delegation
Substitute Industry, External Trade, Research and Energy Committee

7 Palmersville, Great Lime Road, Newcastle upon Tyne NE12 9HN
Tel: 0191 256 6066   Fax: 0191 256 6067   E-mail: botoolemep@aol.com

Paisley, Ian   **NA**   **DUP**
Member Development and Co-operation Committee
Member EU-Estonia Joint Parliamentary Committee Delegation
Substitute Industry, External Trade, Research and Energy Committee

256 Ravenhill Road, Belfast BT6 8GF
Tel: 028 9045 4255   Fax: 028 9045 7783   E-mail: ianrkpaisley@btinternet.com

Parish, Neil   **EPP-ED**   **Con**
Member Agriculture and Rural Development Committee
Member EU-Bulgaria Joint Parliamentary Committee Delegation
Substitute Employment and Social Affairs Committee
Substitute EU-Czech Republic Joint Parliamentary Committee Delegation

16 Northgate, Bridgwater, Somerset TA6 3EU
Tel: 01278 423110   Fax: 01278 431034

Perry, Roy   **EPP-ED**   **Con**
Vice-chair Petitions Committee
Member Culture, Youth, Education, Media and Sport Committee
Member EU-Slovak Republic Joint Parliamentary Committee Delegation

Tarrants Farmhouse, Maurys Lane, Romsey, Hampshire SO51 6DA
Tel: 01794 322472   Fax: 01794 323498   E-mail: royperry@europe.com
Website: www.ourworld.compuserve.com/homepages/wightandhampshiresouth

Provan, James   **EPP-ED**   **Con**
Member Employment and Social Affairs Committee
Member EU-Cyprus Joint Parliamentary Committee Delegation
Substitute Regional Policy, Transport and Tourism Committee

Middle Lodge, near Horsham, West Sussex RH13 7NL
Tel: 01403 733700   Fax: 01403 733588   E-mail: jamesprovan@europarl.tory.org.uk
Website: www.europarl.tory.org.uk

Purvis, John   **EPP-ED**   **Con**
Member Industry, External Trade, Research and Energy Committee
Member Mashreq and Gulf States Delegation
Substitute Economic and Monetary Affairs Committee
Substitute EU-Bulgaria Joint Parliamentary Committee Delegation

Gilmerton, St Andrews KY16 8NB
Tel: 01334 475830   Fax: 01334 477754   E-mail: purvisco@compuserve.com
Website: www.scottishtorymeps.org.uk

Read, Mel   **PES**   **Lab**
Chair USA Delegation
Member Industry, External Trade, Research and Energy Committee
Substitute Legal Affairs and Internal Market Committee

East Midlands Labour MEPs - Regional Centre, 23 Barratt Lane, Nottingham NG9 6AD
Tel: 0115 922 0624   Fax: 0115 922 0621   E-mail: readm@labmeps-emid.fsnet.co.uk
Website: www.labmeps-emids.fsnet.co.uk

Simpson, Brian   **PES**   **Lab**
Vice-chair Switzerland, Iceland and Norway Delegation
Member Regional Policy, Transport and Tourism Committee
Substitute Agriculture and Rural Development Committee
Substitute EU-Poland Joint Parliamentary Committee Delegation

Cheshire East European Office, Gilbert Wakefield House, Warrington WA2 7JQ
Tel: 01925 654074   Fax: 01925 654077   E-mail: briansimpson@lab.u-net.com

Skinner, Peter   **PES**   **Lab**
Member Economic and Monetary Affairs Committee
Member USA Delegation
Substitute Employment and Social Affairs Committee
Substitute Culture, Youth, Education, Media and Sport Committee

99 Kent Road, Dartford, Kent DA1 2AJ
Tel: 01332 281500   Fax: 01332 281553

Stevenson, Struan   **EPP-ED**   **Con**
Member Agriculture and Rural Development Committee
Member China Delegation
Substitute Fisheries Committee

Scottish Conservative and Unionist Central Office, 83 Princes Street, Edinburgh EH2 2ER
Tel: 0131 247 6890   Fax: 0131 247 6891   E-mail: struanmep@aol.com

Stihler, Catherine   **PES**   **Lab**
Member Environment, Public Health and Consumer Policy Committee
Member EU-Hungary Joint Parliamentary Committee Delegation
Substitute Fisheries Committee

Unit 3, Albany Business Centre, Dunfermline KY12 0RN
Tel: 01383 731 890 Fax: 01383 731 835

Stockton, Earl of (Alexander Macmillan)   **EPP-ED**   **Con**
Member Constitutional Affairs Committee
Member ASEAN, South-east Asia and Republic of Korea Delegation
Substitute Culture, Youth, Education, Media and Sport Committee

South West Region European Office, 5 Westfield Park, Bristol BS6 6LT
Tel. 0117 946 7860 Fax: 0117 923 8153 E-mail: alexanderstockton@tory.org

Sturdy, Robert   **EPP-ED**   **Con**
Chair Canada Delegation
Member Agriculture and Rural Development Committee
Substitute Environment, Public Health and Consumer Policy Committee

153 St Neots Road, Cambridge CB3 7QJ
Tel: 01954 211790 Fax: 01954 211786 E-mail: rsturdy@tory.org

Sumberg, David   **EPP-ED**   **Con**
Member Employment and Social Affairs Committee
Member Development and Co-operation Committee
Member USA Delegation
Substitute Foreign Affairs, Human Rights, Common Security and Defence Policy Committee

Northwest Regional Office, 9 Montford Enterprise Centre, Salford M5 2SN
Tel: 0161 745 7880 Fax: 0161 737 1980

Tannock, Charles   **EPP-ED**   **Con**
Member Economic and Monetary Affairs Committee
Member EU-Slovak Republic Joint Parliamentary Committee Delegation
Substitute Environment, Public Health and Consumer Policy Committee
Substitute EU-Hungary Joint Parliamentary Committee Delegation

Conservative Central Office, 32 Smith Square, London SW1P 3HH
Tel: 020 7984 8235/8231 Fax: 020 7984 8292

Titford, Jeffrey   **EDD**   **UKIP**
Member Budgets Committee
Substitute Agriculture and Rural Development Committee
Substitute Regional Policy, Transport and Tourism Committee

Suites 1 and 2, Rochester House, 145 New London Road, Chelmsford, Essex CM2 0QT
Tel: 01245 266466/251651 Fax: 01245 252071 E-mail: ukipeast@globalnet.co.uk
Website: www.ukip.org/htm/eastern_region.html

Titley, Gary   **PES**   **Lab**
Chair EU-Lithuania Joint Parliamentary Committee Delegation
Member Foreign Affairs, Human Rights, Common Security and Defence Policy Committee
Substitute Legal Affairs and Internal Market Committee
Substitute ECHELON Interception System Temporary Committee
Substitute EU-Slovenia Joint Parliamentary Committee Delegation

European Office, 16 Spring Lane, Manchester M26 2TQ
Tel: 0161 724 4008 Fax: 0161 724 4009 E-mail: contact@gary-titley-mep.new.labour.org.uk
Website: www.garytitley.com

Van Orden, Geoffrey   **EPP-ED**   **Con**
Member Foreign Affairs, Human Rights, Common Security and Defence Policy Committee
Member EU-Turkey Joint Parliamentary Committee Delegation
Substitute Employment and Social Affairs Committee

Conservative Regional Office, 88 Rectory Lane, Chelmsford, Essex CM1 1RF
Tel: 01245 345141 Fax: 01245 269757

Villiers, Theresa   **EPP-ED**   **Con**
Member Economic and Monetary Affairs Committee
Member Women's Rights and Equal Opportunities Committee
Member South Asia and SAARC Delegation
Substitute Legal Affairs and Internal Market Committee
Conservative Central Office, 32 Smith Square, London SW1P 3HH
Tel: 020 7984 8227   Fax: 020 7984 8292   E-mail: tvilliers@conservative-party.org.uk

Wallis, Diana   **ELDR**   **LD**
Vice-chair Switzerland, Iceland and Norway Delegation
Member Legal Affairs and Internal Market Committee
Substitute Regional Policy, Transport and Tourism Committee
Substitute EU-Romania Joint Parliamentary Committee Delegation
Land of Green Ginger, Hull HU1 2EA
Tel: 01482 609943   Fax: 01482 609951   E-mail: dianawallismep@cix.co.uk
Website: www.dianawallismep.org.uk

Watson, Graham   **ELDR**   **LD**
Chair Citizens' Freedoms and Rights, Justice and Home Affairs Committee
Member Japan Delegation
Substitute Regional Policy, Transport and Tourism Committee
Bagehot's Foundry, Beard's Yard, Langport, Somerset TA10 9PS
Tel: 01458 259176/252265   Fax: 01458 259174/253174   E-mail: euro_office@cix.co.uk
Website: www.grahamwatsonmep.org

Watts, Mark   **PES**   **Lab**
Vice-chair EU-Malta Joint Parliamentary Committee Delegation
Member Regional Policy, Transport and Tourism Committee
Member Petitions Committee
Substitute Employment and Social Affairs Committee
European Office, 29 Park Road, Sittingbourne, Kent ME10 1DR
Tel: 01795 477880   Fax: 01795 437224   E-mail: mfwatts@aol.com
Website: www2.prestel.co.uk/walters/watts

Whitehead, Philip   **PES**   **Lab**
Member Environment, Public Health and Consumer Policy Committee
Member Culture, Youth, Education, Media and Sport Committee
Member EU-Czech Republic Joint Parliamentary Committee Delegation
Substitute Development and Co-operation Committee
East Midlands Labour MEPs Regional Centre, 23 Barratt Lane, Nottingham NG9 6AD
Tel: 0115 922 0624   Fax: 0115 922 0621   E-mail: whiteheadp@labmeps-emids.fsnet.co.uk
Website: www.labmeps-emids.fsnet.co.uk

Wyn, Eurig   **Green-EFA**   **PC**
Member Culture, Youth, Education, Media and Sport Committee
Member Petitions Committee
Member South Africa Delegation
Substitute Agriculture and Rural Development Committee
Swyddfa Plaid Cymru/Ewrop, Premier House, Llandudno, Conwy LL30 2UU, Wales
Tel: 01492 871 700   Fax: 01492 871 710   E-mail: anna.siddiqi@wales.gsi.gov.uk

Wynn, Terence   **PES**   **Lab**
Chair Budgets Committee
Member Australia and New Zealand Delegation
Lakeside, Alexandra Park, St Helens WA10 3TT
Tel: 01744 451609   Fax: 01744 29832   Website: www.terrywynn.com

Court of Justice of the European Communities

2925 Luxembourg
Tel: 00 352 43031 *Fax:* 00 352 4303 2500 (Press and Information)
Fax: 00 352 4303 2600 (Registry)
Website: www.curia.eu.int/en/index.htm

The Court of Justice of the European Communities and the Court of First Instance rule on questions of Union law, and whether actions by the Commission, the Council of Ministers, member governments and other bodies are compatible with the Treaties.

European Court of Auditors

12 rue Alcide de Gasperi, 1615 Luxembourg
Tel: 00 352 4398 45413 *Fax:* 00 352 4398 46430
Website: www.eca.eu.int

The European Court of Auditors examines all revenue and expenditure accounts of the Union. There are 15 members, one per member state.

Economic and Social Committee

2 rue Ravenstein, 1000 Brussels, Belgium
Tel: 00 32 2 546 9011 *Fax:* 00 32 2 513 4893
Website: www.esc.eu.int

An advisory body of the EU established by the Rome Treaties. It is consulted by the Commission and the Council and may deliver opinions on its own initiative. It has 222 members from the fifteen member states, including 24 from the UK.

Committee of the Regions

rue Belliard, 79, 1040 Brussels, Belgium
Tel: 00 32 2 282 2211 *Fax:* 00 32 2 282 2085
Website: www.cor.eu.int

A consultative assembly of representatives of regional and local authorities such as mayors, county councillors and regional presidents. It began working in 1994. There are 24 members and 24 alternate members from the UK.

European Central Bank

Postfach 160319, 60066 Frankfurt-am-Main, Germany
Tel: 00 49 69 13 440 *Fax:* 00 49 69 13 44 6000 *Website:* www.ecb.int

European Investment Bank

100 Boulevard Konrad Adenauer, 2950 Luxembourg
Tel: 00 352 43791 *Fax:* 00 352 437704
Website: www.eib.org

The EU's financing institution, providing long-term loans for capital investment.

London Office: 68 Pall Mall, London SW1Y 5ES
Tel: 020 7343 1200 *Fax:* 020 7930 9929

Royal Households

HER MAJESTY'S HOUSEHOLD
Buckingham Palace, London SW1A 1AA 020 7930 4832

Private Secretary to HM The Queen: Rt Hon Sir Robin Janvrin KCVO CB

HRH THE PRINCE PHILIP, DUKE OF EDINBURGH
Buckingham Palace, London SW1A 1AA
020 7930 4832

Private Secretary:
Brigadier Miles Hunt-Davis CVO CBE

HM QUEEN ELIZABETH THE QUEEN MOTHER
Clarence House, St James's,
London SW1A 1BA
020 7930 3141

Private Secretary and Comptroller:
Captain Sir Alastair Aird GCVO

HRH THE PRINCE OF WALES
St James's Palace, London SW1A 1BS
020 7930 4832

Private Secretary and Treasurer:
Stephen Lamport Esq CVO

HRH THE DUKE OF YORK
Buckingham Palace, London SW1A 1AA
020 7930 4832

Private Secretary and Treasurer:
Captain Neil Blair LVO RN

TRH THE EARL AND COUNTESS OF WESSEX
Bagshot Park, Bagshot, Surrey GU19 5PL
01276 700843

Private Secretary:
Lieutenant-Colonel Sean O'Dwyer LVO

HRH THE PRINCESS ROYAL
Buckingham Palace, London SW1A 1AA
020 7930 4832

Private Secretary: Colonel Timothy Earl OBE

HRH THE PRINCESS MARGARET COUNTESS OF SNOWDON
Kensington Palace, London W8 4PU
020 7930 3141

Private Secretary and Comptroller:
Rt Hon Viscount Ullswater

HRH PRINCESS ALICE, DUCHESS OF GLOUCESTER AND TRH THE DUKE AND DUCHESS OF GLOUCESTER
Kensington Palace, London W8 4PU
020 7937 6374

Private Secretary, Comptroller and Equerry:
Major Nicholas Barne LVO

TRH THE DUKE AND DUCHESS OF KENT
St James's Palace, London SW1A 1BQ
020 7930 4872

Private Secretary: Nicolas Adamson Esq OBE

TRH PRINCE AND PRINCESS MICHAEL OF KENT
Kensington Palace, London W8 4PU
020 7938 3519

Private Secretary: Nicholas Chance Esq

HRH PRINCESS ALEXANDRA, THE HONOURABLE LADY OGILVY
Buckingham Palace, London SW1A 1AA
020 7930 1860

Private Secretary: Captain Neil Blair LVO RN

Forms of Address

Formal modes of address become less formal every year but there are occasions when a person may want to address someone with strict formality. The first form of address given is that which should always be used on the envelope, the second is the formal salutation and conclusion and the third is the less formal salutation and conclusion. Each is detailed respectively as (1), (2) and (3).

The following points should be noted:–

1. The honorific prefix 'The Right Honourable' is not now generally used for Peers other than Privy Counsellors.

2. The courtesy titles Honourable, Lady and Lord to which sons and daughters of Peers (depending on the rank of their father) are not prefixed by the definite article. These are the practices adopted by the Earl Marshal's Office and that of the Lord Chamberlain of the Household and consequently have been followed here.

3. In the formal mode of address the conclusion '...... Obedient Servant' has been used. This is a matter of choice as it can be 'humble and obedient servant' or simply 'I am, Sir (my Lord or whatever) Yours faithfully'.

4. In all appropriate cases the use of the masculine can be interpreted as including the feminine.

AMBASSADOR—(1) His Excellency Mr., Dr., etc. as appropriate, (Esquire is never used), Ambassador of the Italian Republic, (the name of the Country in full i.e. not The Italian Ambassador). (2) Your Excellency, conclude I am Your Excellency's Obedient Servant. (3) Dear Mr Ambassador, conclude Yours sincerely. A list of Ambassadors is given towards the end of the book. In conversation an Ambassador is addressed as 'Your Excellency', but once is sufficient, thereafter 'Sir' is normal.

AMBASSADOR'S WIFE—(1) As an ordinary married woman. She is not 'Your Excellency' nor 'Ambassadress'.

ARCHBISHOP—(1) The Most Rev. The Lord Archbishop of York. Or, The Most Rev. John Smith, Lord Archbishop of York. (2) Your Grace or My Lord Archbishop, conclude I am Your Grace's Obedient Servant. (3) Dear Archbishop, conclude Yours sincerely. Note: The Archbishops of Canterbury and York are Privy Counsellors and are therefore addressed as The Most Reverend and Right Honourable.

BARON—(1) The Lord Barton. (2) My Lord, conclude I am, My Lord, Your Obedient Servant. (3) Dear Lord Barton, conclude Yours sincerely.

BARONESS IN HER OWN RIGHT OR BARON'S WIFE —(1) The Lady Barton or, in the case of Baronesses in their own right, most prefer to be styled The Baroness Barton (see biographies of Members of the House of Lords). (2) Dear Madam, conclude Yours faithfully. (3) Dear Lady Barton or Dear Baroness Barton, conclude Yours sincerely.

BARONETS—(1) Sir John Smith, Bt. (the abbreviation Bart. is not much used today but is not incorrect). (2) Dear Sir, conclude Yours faithfully. (3) Dear Sir John, conclude Yours sincerely.

BISHOP—(1) The Right Reverend The Lord Bishop of Buxton. Or, The Right Reverend John Smith, Lord Bishop of Buxton. (2) My Lord Bishop, conclude I am, My Lord, Your Obedient Servant. (3) Dear Lord Bishop, Dear Bishop or Dear Bishop of Buxton, conclude Yours sincerely. Note: Bishops suffragan are addressed by courtesy in the same way as diocesan bishops.

COUNTESS—(1) The Countess of Poole. (2) Dear Madam, conclude Yours faithfully. (3) Dear Lady Poole, conclude Yours sincerely.

DAME—(1) Dame Mary Smith, followed by appropriate post-nominal letters (e.g. D.B.E.). (2) Dear Madam, conclude Yours faithfully. (3) Dear Dame Mary, conclude Yours sincerely.

DUCHESS—(1) Her Grace The Duchess of Avon. (2) Your Grace, conclude I am, Your Grace's Obedient Servant. (3) Dear Duchess of Avon, conclude Yours sincerely.

DUKE—(1) His Grace The Duke of Avon. (2) Your Grace, or My Lord Duke, conclude I am, Your Grace's Obedient Servant. (3) Dear Duke of Avon, conclude Yours sincerely.

EARL—(1) The Earl of Hethe. (2) My Lord, conclude I am my Lord Your Obedient Servant. (3) Dear Lord Hethe, conclude Yours sincerely.

GOVERNORS GENERAL, GOVERNORS AND LIEUTENANT GOVERNORS—As for Ambassadors but followed by description of office, such as Governor General and Commander-in-Chief of New Zealand. (3) Dear Governor General, Governor or Lieutenant-Governor, conclude Yours sincerely. The Lieutenant-Governors of Guernsey, Jersey and the Isle of Man enjoy this style. The Governor General of Canada has the style 'The Right Honourable' for life and a Lieutenant-Governor of a Canadian Province is 'His Honour' for life.

JUDGE (LORD JUSTICE OF APPEAL)—(1) The Right Honourable Sir John Smith, as he is invariably a Privy Counsellor and a Knight, or the Right Honourable Lord Justice Smith. (2) My Lord, conclude I am My Lord, Your Obedient Servant. (3) Dear Sir John, conclude Yours sincerely.

JUDGE (JUSTICE OF THE HIGH COURT)—(1) The Honourable Sir John Smith, as he is invariably a Knight, or The Honourable Mr Justice Smith. (2) and (3) as for a Lord Justice of Appeal.

JUDGE (CIRCUIT JUDGE)—(1) His Honour Judge Smith. (2) Your Honour, conclude I have the honour to be Your Honour's Obedient Servant. (3) Dear Sir (or Judge Smith), conclude Yours sincerely.

JUDGE (WOMEN JUDGES)—(1) The Right Honourable Dame Ann Smith, D.B.E. (if a Lord of Appeal), The Honourable Dame Anne Smith, D.B.E. (if a High Court Judge). (2) and (3) as for a male Judge with suitable gender changes.

KNIGHT—(1) Sir John Smith, if a Knight Bachelor there is no post-nominal addition in this respect (Kt., K. Bach., or K.T. is quite wrong) but if a Knight or Knight Grand Cross or Grand Commander of an Order of Chivalry the appropriate post-nominal letters should be added. A Knight may be so addressed when his knighthood is announced, there is now no need to wait for the accolade to have been conferred. (2) Dear Sir, conclude Yours faithfully. (3) Dear Sir John, conclude Yours sincerely.

LORD LIEUTENANT—(1) The normal form of address, followed by, for courtesy, H.M.'s Lord Lieutenant for the County of Newshire. (2) My Lord Lieutenant, conclude I have the honour to be my Lord Lieutenant, Your Obedient Servant. (3) Dear Lord (Sir John or Mr. as appropriate), conclude Yours sincerely.

LORD OF SESSION IN SCOTLAND—(1) The Honourable (or Right Honourable if a Privy Counsellor), Lord Glentie. (2) My Lord, conclude I have the honour to be My Lord, Your Obedient Servant. (3) Dear Lord Glentie, conclude Yours sincerely. Note: The wife of a Lord of Session is styled as the wife of a Baron but her children have no courtesy titles. The Lord Justice General or Lord Justice Clerk is usually so addressed in correspondence, rather than by his juridical title.

MEMBER OF PARLIAMENT—(1) Address according to rank with the addition of the letters M.P. after the name. Privy Counsellors have the prefix 'The Right Honourable'. Letters to Ministers may start Dear Minister or, in the case of the Prime Minister Dear Prime Minister. Members of the Scottish Parliament should have the letters MSP added after their name, e.g. Angus Fraser Esq, MSP Members of the Welsh Assembly should have AM added, e.g. Hugh Jones Esq, AM. Members of the Northern Ireland Assembly should have MLA added.

NORTHERN IRELAND ASSEMBLY—See Member of Parliament.

PRIME MINISTER—see Member of Parliament, also Privy Counsellor.

PRINCE—(1) H.R.H. The Prince Henry of Wales or, if a Duke, H.R.H. The Duke of Kent; the children of the Sovereign use the definite article before Prince (e.g. The Prince Edward). (2) Your Royal Highness or Sir, conclude I have the honour to be Your Royal Highness's Obedient Servant. In conversation address as Your Royal Highness but once is sufficient, thereafter Sir is normal.

PRINCESS—(1) H.R.H. Princess Beatrice of York, or, if the wife of a Royal Duke, H.R.H. The Duchess of Kent; a daughter of the Sovereign uses the definite article before Princess (e.g. The Princess Margaret, Countess of Snowdon). (2) Your Royal Highness or Madam, conclude I have the honour to be Your Royal Highness's Obedient Servant. In conversation address as Your Royal Highness but once is sufficient, thereafter Ma'am (pronounced so as to rhyme with lamb) is normal.

PRIVY COUNSELLOR—(1) The Right Honourable prefixes the name and style except in respect of Marquesses and Dukes when the letters P.C. are placed after the name. The letters follow those indicating membership of Orders of Chivalry. (2) Address according to rank. (See also Member of Parliament).

QUEEN—(1) Her Majesty the Queen, although letters are usually addressed to The Private Secretary to Her Majesty the Queen. (2) Your Majesty or 'May it please your Majesty', conclude I have the honour to be Your Majesty's Obedient Subject. (3) Madam, conclude With my humble duty to Your Majesty. In conversation address as Your Majesty at first thereafter as Ma'am (see Princess).

SCOTTISH MEMBER OF PARLIAMENT—See Member of Parliament.

WALES, MEMBER OF NATIONAL ASSEMBLY—See Member of Parliament.

Recommended Reading

Adonis, A. *Parliament Today*, Manchester University Press, 2nd edition, 1993.

Bagehot, W. *The English Constitution*, Introduction by R. H. S. Crossman. London, Fontana, 1963.

Biffen, John. *Inside the House of Commons*, Grafton, 1989.

Bradshaw, K. A., and Pring, D. A. M. *Parliament and Congress*. Quartet Books, Revised Edition, 1981.

Butler, D. and Kavanagh, D. *The British General Election of 1997*. London, Macmillan, 1997.

Cook, Sir Robert. *The Palace of Westminster*. Burton Skira, 1987.

Crewe, Ivor and Fox A. *British Parliamentary Constituencies: A Statistical Compendium*. London, Faber, 1984.

de Smith, S. A. *Constitutional and Administrative Law*, 8th edn. Penguin, 1998.

Drewry, G. (ed.) *The New Select Committees*. Oxford, 2nd Ed., 1989.

Englefield, D. J. T. *Westminster and Whitehall*. Longman, 1985.

Englefield, D. J. T. (Ed.) *Workings of Westminster*. Dartmouth, 1991.

Evans, Paul. *Handbook of House of Commons Procedure*, 2nd edition, Vacher Dod Publishing, 1999.

Fell, Sir Bryan and Mackenzie, K. R. *The Houses of Parliament: A guide to the Palace of Westminster*, 15th edn. Editor: D. L. Natzler. London, HMSO, 1994.

Franklin, Mark and Norton, Philip (eds.). *Parliamentary Questions*, Oxford, 1993.

Garrett, John, *Westminster—Does Parliament Work?* Gollancz, 1992.

Giddings, Philip and Drewry, Gavin (eds.), *Westminster and Europe*. Macmillan 1995.

Griffith, J. A. G. *Parliamentary Scrutiny of Government Bills*. London, Allen & Unwin, 1974.

Griffith J. A. G. and Ryle M. T., *Parliament*, Sweet and Maxwell, 1989.

Jones, Christopher. *The Great Palace: the Story of Parliament*. London, BBC Books, 1983.

Judge, D. (ed.). *The Politics of Parliamentary Reform*. Heinemann, 1983.

Liaison Select Committee. *The Select Committee System* (HC Paper 92 (1982–83)), HMSO.

McDonald, Oonagh, *Parliament at Work*, Methuen, 1989.

May, Sir T. Erskine. *Parliamentary Practice*, 22nd edn. London, Butterworth, 1997.

Miers, D. and Page, A., *Legislation*, Sweet and Maxwell, 2nd edition 1990.

Norton, Philip. *The Commons in Perspective*, Martin Robertson, 1981.

Norton, Philip, *Legislatures*, Oxford, 1990.

Norton, Philip (ed.), *National Parliaments and the European Union*, Frank Cass, 1996.

Norton, Philip (ed.). *Parliament in the 1980's*. Basil Blackwell, 1985.

Radice, L., Vallance, E. and Willis, V. *Member of Parliament*. London, Macmillan, 1987.

Riddell, P. *Parliament Under Pressure*. London, Gollancz, 1997.

Rush, Michael (ed), *Parliament and Pressure Groups*, Oxford, 1990.

Rush, Michael, *Parliamentary Government in Britain*. Pitman, 1981.

Ryle, M. and Richards, P. *The Commons Under Scrutiny*, Routledge, 1988.

Ryle, M and Griffith, J. *Parliament*, Sweet and Maxwell, 1989.

Shell, Donald. *The House of Lords*, Harvester Wheatsheaf, 2nd edition, 1992.

Shell, Donald and Beamish, David (eds.). *The House of Lords at Work*, Oxford, 1993.

Silk, Paul and Walters, Rhodri. *How Parliament Works*, 4th edn. Longman, 1998.

Walkland, S. A. *The Legislative Process in Great Britain*. London, Allen & Unwin, 1968, and *The House of Commons in the Twentieth Century*. Oxford University Press, 1979.

Parliamentary Papers (including Hansard and the Votes and Proceedings) are available from the Parliamentary Bookshop, or from the Stationery Office. Various fact sheets are also available from the Public Information Offices of both Houses (see Index).

Abbreviations

AC	Companion of the Order of Australia
ACA	Associate, Institute of Chartered Accountants
ACAS	Advisory, Conciliation and Arbitration Service
ACC	Anglican Consultative Council; Association of County Councils
ACCA	Association of Chartered Certified Accountants
ACCAC	Qualifications, Curriculum and Assessment Authority for Wales
ACE	Action for Community Employment
ACF	Army Cadet Force
ACOPS	Advisory Committee on Protection of the Sea
ACP	African/Caribbean/Pacific
ACPO	Association of Chief Police Officers
ACTT	Association of Cinematograph, Television and Allied Technicians
ADC	Aide-de-camp
AE	Air Efficiency Award
AEC	Agriculture Executive Council; Atomic Energy Commission
AEEU	Amalgamated Engineering and Electrical Union
AEF	Amalgamated Union of Engineering and Foundry Workers
AERE	Atomic Energy Research Establishment (Harwell)
AEU	Amalgamated Engineering Union
AFC	Air Force Cross
AFFOR	All Faiths for One Race
AFHQ	Allied Force Headquarters
AFPAA	Armed Forces Personnel Administration Agency
AFPRB	Armed Forces' Pay Review Body
Agric	Agricultural; Agriculture
ai	ad interim
AIB	Associate, Institute of Bankers
AIF	Australian Imperial Forces
AIM	Alternative Investment Market
AM	Assembly Member (National Assembly for Wales)
AMS	Additional Member System; Army Medical Services; Assistant Military Secretary
ANAF	Arab Non-Arab Friendship
ANZAC	Australia and New Zealand All-Party Committee
APACS	Association for Payment Clearing Services
APC	Army Personnel Centre
APEX	Association of Professional, Executive, Clerical and Computer Staff
ARA	Associate, Royal Academy
ARCM	Associate, Royal College of Music
ARCS	Associate, Royal College of Science
ARICS	Professional Associate, Royal Institution of Chartered Surveyors
ASA	Advertising Standards Authority
ASEAN	Association of South East Asian Nations
ASLEF	Associated Society of Locomotive Engineers and Firemen
ASTMS	Association of Scientific, Technical and Management Staffs (now part of MSF, *qv*)
ATII	Associate Member, Incorporated Institute of Taxation
ATRA	Army Training and Recruiting Agency
ATSA	Army Technical Support Agency
AUA	Association of University Administrators
AUC	Air Transport Users Council
AUEW	Amalgamated Union of Engineering Workers
BA	Bachelor of Arts; Benefits Agency
BAA	British Airports Authority
BAFTA	British Academy of Film and Television Arts
BBA	British Board of Agrément
BBC	British Broadcasting Corporation
BBSRC	Biotechnology and Biological Sciences Research Council
BCCI	Bank of Credit and Commerce International
BCE	Boundary Commission for England
BChir	Bachelor of Surgery
BCL	Bachelor of Civil Law
BCom	Bachelor of Commerce
BD	Bachelor of Divinity
BDS	Business Development Service
BECTa	British Educational Communications and Technology agency
BECTU	Broadcasting, Entertainment, Cinematograph and Theatre Union
BEd	Bachelor of Education

BEF	British Equestrian Federation; British Expeditionary Force	CCTA	Central Computer and Telecommunications Agency
BEM	British Empire Medal	CCW	Countryside Council for Wales
BFI	British Film Institute	CD	Canadian Forces Decoration
BFPO	British Forces Post Office	CDA	Co-operative Development Agency
BIC	British-Irish Council	CDC	Commonwealth Development Corporation
BIGC	British-Irish Governmental Conference	CDipAF	Certified Diploma in Accounting and Finance
BLESMA	British Limbless Ex-Servicemen's Association	CDS	Chief of the Defence Staff
BLitt	Bachelor of Literature	CEE	Communauté Economique Européenne
BMA	British Medical Association		
BMus	Bachelor of Music	CEFAS	Centre for Environment, Fisheries and Aquaculture Science
BNAF	British North Africa Force		
BNIF	British Nuclear Industry Forum	CEG	Consumers in Europe Group
BR	British Rail	CEGB	Central Electricity Generating Board
BRB	British Railways Board		
BRC	British Retail Consortium	CEH	Centre for Ecology and Hydrology
BRE	Building Research Establishment	CEng	Chartered Engineer
BSc	Bachelor of Science	CertEd	Certificate of Education
BSI	British Standards Institution	CFB	Communications for Business
Bt	Baronet	CFF	National Funding Formula
BT	British Telecommunication Plc	CH	Companion of Honour
BUPA	British United Provident Association	ChB	Bachelor of Surgery
		CHC	Community Health Council
BWI	British West Indies	CHD	Coronary Heart Disease
C	Conservative	Chev	Chevalier
C-in-C	Commander-in-Chief	ChM	Master of Surgery
CA	Contributions Agency	CI	Imperial Order of the Crown of India
CAA	Civil Aviation Authority		
CABE	Commission for Architecture and the Built Environment	CICA	Criminal Injuries Compensation Authority
CAC	Central Arbitration Committee	CICAP	Criminal Injuries Compensation Appeals Panel
CAFOD	Catholic Aid Fund for Overseas Development	CIE	Companion of the Order of the Indian Empire
Cantab	Cantabrigiensis (of Cambridge)		
CAO	Chief Adjudication Officer	CIMA	Chartered Institute of Management Accountants
Capt	Captain		
CAS	Central Adjudication Services	CIPFA	Chartered Institute of Public Finance and Accountancy
CB	Companion of the Order of the Bath; Chemical and Biotechnology	CIS	Institute of Chartered Secretaries and Administrators
CBC	County Borough Council	CITB	Construction Industry Training Board
CBE	Commander of the Order of the British Empire	CITES	Convention on International Trade in Endangered Species
CBI	Confederation of British Industry	CITU	Central IT Unit
CBIM	Companion, British Institute of Management	CIU	Club and Institute Union
		CLA	Country Landowners' Association
CC	City Council; County Council; Cricket Club	CLP	Constituency Labour Party
		CMG	Companion of the Order of St Michael and St George
CCF	Combined Cadet Force		
CCLRC	Council for the Central Laboratory of the Research Councils	CML	Council of Mortgage Lenders
CCMS	Centre for Coastal and Marine Science	CMPS	Centre for Management and Policy Studies

CNAA	Council for National Academic Awards	DARD	Department of Agriculture and Rural Development
CND	Campaign for Nuclear Disarmament	DASA	Defence Analytical Services Agency
CNT	Commission for the New Towns	DBA	Defence Bills Agency
COHSE	Confederation of Health Service Employees (see Unison)	DBE	Dame Commander of the Order of the British Empire
COI	Central Office of Information	DC	District Council
Con	Conservative	DCB	Dame Commander of the Order of the Bath
COPUS	Committee on the Public Understanding of Science	DCL	Doctor of Civil Law
COSHEP	Committee of Scottish Higher Education Principals	DCM	Distinguished Conduct Medal
		DCMG	Dame Commander of the Order of St Michael and St George
COSLA	Convention of Scottish Local Authorities	DCMS	Department for Culture, Media and Sport
CPA	Commonwealth Parliamentary Association	DCSA	Defence Communication Services Agency
CPAS	Church Pastoral Aid Society	DCTA	Defence Clothing and Textiles Agency
CPC	Conservative Political Centre		
CPRE	Council for the Protection of Rural England	DCVO	Dame Commander of the Royal Victorian Order
CPS	Crown Prosecution Service	DD	Doctor of Divinity
cr	Created	DDA	Defence Dental Agency
CRE	Commission for Racial Equality	DDRB	Review Body on Doctors' and Dentists' Remuneration
CRP	Constitutional Reform Policy		
CRP(EC)	Incorporation of the European Convention of Human Rights	DE	Defence Estates
		DENI	Department of Education for Northern Ireland
CRP(FOI)	Freedom of Information		
CRP(HL)	House of Lords Reform	DERA	Defence Evaluation and Research Agency
CSA	Child Support Agency		
CSC	Civil Service College	DETR	Department of the Environment, Transport and the Regions
CSCE	Conference on Security and Co-operation in Europe		
		DFC	Distinguished Flying Cross
CSI	Committee on the Intelligence Services; Companion of the Order of the Star of India	DfEE	Department for Education and Employment
		DFID	Department for International Development
CSL	Central Science Laboratory		
CST	Council for Science and Technology	DFM	Distinguished Flying Medal
		DGIA	Defence Geographic and Imagery Intelligence Agency
CStJ	Commander, Most Venerable Order of the Hospital of St. John of Jerusalem		
		DHE	Defence Housing Executive
		DHSS	Department of Health and Social Security
CTBI	Churches Together in Britain and Ireland		
		DIEL	Advisory Committee on Telecommunications for Disabled and Elderly People
CVCP	Committee of Vice-Chancellors and Principals of the Universities of the UK		
		DipAgriSci	Diploma in Agricultural Science
CVO	Commander of the Royal Victorian Order	DipEd	Diploma in Education
		DipObst	Diploma in Obstetrics
CVS	Council for Voluntary Service	DISC	Defence Intelligence and Security Centre
CWP	Community Work Programme		
CWS	Co-operative Wholesale Society	DL	Deputy Lieutenant
CWU	Communication Workers Union	DLI	Durham Light Infantry
DANI	Department of Agriculture for Northern Ireland	DLO	Defence Logistics Organisation
		DMO	UK Debt Management Office
DARA	Defence Aviation Repair Agency		

DMS	Diploma in Management Studies
DMTO	Defence Medical Training Organisation
DoH	Department of Health
DOP	Defence and Overseas Policy
DOP(E)	European Issues
DOP(E)(T)	European Trade Issues
DOS	Dental and Optical Services Branch
DP	Devolution Policy
DPA	Defence Procurement Agency
DPH	Diploma in Public Health
DPhil	Doctor of Philosophy
DSA `	Disposal Sales Agency; Driving Standards Agency
DSC	Distinguished Service Cross
DSc	Doctor of Science
DSCA	Defence Secondary Care Agency
DSDA	Defence Storage and Distribution Agency
DSO	Distinguished Service Order
DSS	Department of Social Security
DStJ	Dame of Grace/Dame of Justice, Most Venerable Order of the Hospital of St. John of Jerusalem
DSTJ	Dame of Grace/or Dame of Justice, Order of the Hospital of St John of Jerusalem
DTI	Department of Trade and Industry
DTMA	Defence Transport and Movements Agency
DU	Doctor of the University
DUP	Democratic Unionist Party
DVA	Defence Vetting Agency
DVLA	Driver and Vehicle Licensing Agency
DVLNI	Driver and Vehicle Licensing Northern Ireland
DVTA	Driver and Vehicle Testing Agency
DYRMS	Duke of York's Royal Military School
E	England
EA	Economic Affairs; Environment Agency; Executive Agency
EA(N)	Energy Policy
EA(PC)	Productivity and Competitiveness
EA(WW)	Welfare to Work
EAT	Employment Appeal Tribunal
EC	European Community
ECA	Economic Commission for Africa (UN)
ECCs	Electricity Consumers' Committees
ECE	Economic Commission for Europe (UN)
ECHR	European Convention of Human Rights
ECITB	Engineering Construction Industry Training Board
ECLAC	Economic Commission for Latin America and the Caribbean (UN)
Econ	Economics
EDC	Economic Development Committee
EDG	European Democratic Group
EEC	European Economic Community
EEF	Engineering Employers' Federation
EETPU	Electrical, Electronic Telecommunications and Plumbing Union
EHS	Environment and Heritage Service
EID	Engineering Industries Directorate
ELLID	Employment, Lifelong Learning and International Directorate
EMU	European Monetary Union
ENV	The Environment
EOC	Equal Opportunities Commission
EP	English Partnerships; European Parliament
EPSRC	Engineering and Physical Sciences Research Council
ERD	Emergency Reserve Decoration (Army)
ES	Employment Service
ESCAP	Economic and Social Commission for Asia and the Pacific (UN)
ESCWA	Economic and Social Commission for Western Asia (UN)
ESRC	Economic and Social Research Council
ETS	Employment Tribunals Service
EU	European Union
FANY	First Aid Nursing Yeomanry
FAO	Food and Agriculture Organization of the UN
FAS	Funding Agency for Schools
FBA	Fellow, British Academy
FBIM	Fellow, British Institute of Management
FC	Football Club
FCCA	Fellow, Chartered Association of Certified Accountants
FCIM	Fellow, Chartered Institute of Marketing
FCIT	Fellow, Chartered Institute of Transport
FCO	Foreign and Commonwealth Office
FDA	Association of First Division Civil Servants
FEDA	Federation of Economic Development Authorities
FEFC	Further Education Funding Council
FEFCW	Further Education Funding Council for Wales

FFB	Food from Britain
FHCIMA	Fellow, Hotel, Catering and Institutional Management Association
FICE	Fellow, Institution of Civil Engineers
FICO	Financial Intermediaries and Claims Office
FIEE	Fellow, Institution of Electrical Engineers
FILA	Fellow, Institute of Landscape Architects
FIMechE	Fellow, Institution of Mechanical Engineers
FIMgt	Fellow, Institute of Management
FIMI	Fellow, Institute of the Motor Industry
FIMT	Fellow, Institute of the Motor Trade
FInstM	Fellow, Institute of Marketing
FInstPS	Fellow, Institute of Purchasing and Supply
FIQA	Fellow, Institute of Quality Assurance
FIRTE	Fellow, Institute of Road Transport Engineers
FKC	Fellow, King's College, London
FOI	Freedom of Information
FPC	Family Practitioner Committee
FRAM	Fellow, Royal Academy of Music
FRAME	Fund for the Replacement of Animals in Medical Experiments
FRCA	Farming and Rural Conservation Agency
FRCOG	Fellow, Royal College of Obstetricians and Gynaecologists
FRCP	Fellow, Royal College of Physicians, London
FRCS	Fellow, Royal College of Surgeons of England
FRCVS	Fellow, Royal College of Veterinary Surgeons
FREng	Fellow, Royal Academy (formerly Fellowship) of Engineering
FRGS	Fellow, Royal Geographical Society
FRIBA	Fellow, Royal Institute of British Architects
FRPS	Fellow, Royal Photographic Society
FRS	Fellow, The Royal Society; Fisheries Research Services
FRSA	Fellow, Royal Society of Arts
FRSE	Fellow, The Royal Society of Edinburgh
FSA	Fellow, Society of Antiquaries; Financial Services Authority

FSAA	Fellow, Society of Incorporated Accountants and Auditors
FSB	Federation of Small Businesses
FSNI	Forensic Science Northern Ireland
FSS	Forensic Science Service
GAC	Government Art Collection
GATT	General Agreement on Tariffs and Trade
GB	Great Britain
GBE	Knight or Dame Grand Cross of the Order of the British Empire
GC	George Cross
GCB	Knight or Dame Grand Cross of the Order of the Bath
GCC	Gas Consumers Council
GCCNI	General Consumer Council for Northern Ireland
GCDA	Government Car and Despatch Agency
GCIE	Knight Grand Commander, Order of the Indian Empire
GCMG	Knight or Dame Grand Cross of the Order of St Michael and St George
GCSI	Knight Grand Commander, Order of the Star of India
GCVO	Knight or Dame Grand Cross of the Royal Victorian Order
GDC	General Dental Council
GEST	Grant for Education, Support and Training
GL	Local Government
GL(L)	London
GLA	Greater London Assembly; Greater London Authority
GLC	Greater London Council
GM	Genetic Modification
GMB	General Municipal Boilermakers Union
GMBATU	General, Municipal, Boilermakers and Allied Trades Union (see GMB)
GMP	General Medical Practitioner
GMS	General Medical Services
GMW	General Municipal Boilermakers and Allied Trades Union
GMWU	General Municipal Workers' Union
GOC	General Officer Commanding
GOL	Government Office for London
GP	General Practitioner
GPA	Government Purchasing Agency
GPDST	Girls' Public Day School Trust
GPMU	Graphical, Paper, Media Union
GPO	General Post Office
GSO	General Staff Officer
GSO1	General Staff Officer 1

GTN	Government Telephone Network	IHO	Independent Housing Ombudsman Scheme
HAC	Honourable Artillery Company		
HACC	Heathrow Airport Consultative Committee	IiP	Investor in People
		ILO	International Labour Office (or Organization)
HAT	Housing Action Trusts		
HAZ	Health Action Zones	ILT	Institute of Logistics and Transport
HBLB	Horserace Betting Levy Board	IM	Institute of Management
HE	His (Her) Excellency	IMF	International Monetary Fund (UN)
HEA	Health Education Authority	IMO	International Maritime Organization (UN)
HEFCE	Higher Education Funding Council for England		
		IMRO	Investment Management Regulatory Organisation
HEFCW	Higher Education Funding Council for Wales		
		IN	Northern Ireland
HHEW	Heads of Higher Education Institutions in Wales	Ind	Independent
		INSEAD	Institut Européen d'Administration des Affaires
HIE	Highlands and Islands Enterprise		
HLI	Highland Light Infantry	INSTRAW	International Research and Training Institute for the Advancement of Women (UN)
HM	His (or Her) Majesty (Majesty's)		
HMCI	Her Majesty's Chief Inspector		
HMS	His (or Her) Majesty's Ship	INTERPOL	International Criminal Police Organization
HMT	Her Majesty's Treasury		
HO	Home Office	IOCA	Interception of Communications Act
Hon	Honorary; Honourable		
HQ	Headquarters	IOD	Institute of Directors
HRH	His (or Her) Royal Highness	IPT	Integrated Project Team
HS	Health and Safety; Home and Social Affairs	IPU	Inter-Parliamentary Union
		IR	Inland Revenue
HS(D)	Drug Misuse	IRS	Independent Review Service for The Social Fund
HS(H)	Health Strategy		
HS(W)	Women's Issues	IRTU	Industrial Research and Technology Unit
HSC	Health and Safety Commission		
HSE	Health and Safety Executive	IS	Information Systems
HSH	His (or Her) Serene Highness	ISC	Independent Schools Council
HSW	Health and Safety at Work	ISIS	Independent Schools Information Service
I	Ireland		
IA	Indian Army	ISO	Imperial Service Order
IAEA	International Atomic Energy Agency (UN)	IT	Information Technology
		ITC	Independent Television Commission
IB	Intervention Board		
IBA	Independent Broadcasting Authority	ITSA	Information Technology Services Agency
		ITU	International Telecommunication Union (UN)
ICE	Independent Case Examiner		
ICR	Independent Complaints Reviewer	IUA	International Underwriting Association
ICS	Indian Civil Service; Investors Compensation Scheme		
		IVF	In Vitro Fertilisation
ICT	Information and Communications Technology	IWAAC	Inland Waterways Amenity Advisory Council
IDB	Industrial Development Board		
IDC	Imperial Defence College	JARIC	Joint Air Reconnaissance Intelligence Centre
IDS	InterDespatch Service		
IFAD	International Fund for Agricultural Development (UN)	JCC	Joint Consultative Committee with the Liberal Democrat Party
IFC	International Finance Corporation (UN)	JECU	Joint Entry Clearance Unit
		JNCC	Joint Nature Conservation Committee
IFI	International Fund for Ireland		
IFS	Institute for Fiscal Studies	JP	Justice of the Peace

JSB	Judicial Studies Board		LSE	London School of Economics
JSD	Doctor of Juristic Science		LT	London Transport
KAR	King's African Rifles		LTS	Lands Tribunal for Scotland
KBE	Knight Commander of the Order of the British Empire		LTScotland	Learning and Teaching Scotland
			LVO	Lieutenant of the Royal Victorian Order
KCB	Knight Commander of the Order of the Bath		LWT	London Weekend Television
KCIE	Knight Commander of the Order of the Indian Empire		MA	Master of Arts
			MAFF	Ministry of Agriculture, Fisheries and Food
KCMG	Knight Commander of the Order of St Michael and St George		MB	Bachelor of Medicine
KCSI	Knight Commander of the Order of the Star of India		MBA	Master of Business Administration
			MBC	Metropolitan Borough Council
KCVO	Knight Commander of the Royal Victorian Order		MBE	Member of the Order of the British Empire
KG	Knight of the Order of the Garter		MC	Military Cross
KM	Knight of Malta		MCA	Maritime and Coastguard Agency; Medicines Control Agency
KP	Knight, Order of St Patrick			
KRRC	King's Royal Rifle Corps		MD	Doctor of Medicine
KStJ	Knight of the Most Venerable Order of the Hospital of St John of Jerusalem		mda	Museum Documentation Association
			MDA	Medical Devices Agency
KT	Knight of the Order of the Thistle		MDC	Metropolitan District Council
Kt	Knight Bachelor; knighted		MDP	Ministry of Defence Police Agency
Lab	Labour		ME	Myalgic Encephalomyelitis
Lab Co-op	Labour Co-operative		MEd	Master of Education
LACOTS	Local Authorities Co-ordinating Body on Food and Trading Standards		MELF	Middle East Land Forces
			MEP	Member of the European Parliament
LAO	Lord of Appeal in Ordinary		MFCM	Member, Faculty of Community Medicine
LAPADA	London and Provincial Dealers' Association			
LCC	London County Council (Later GLC)		MHS	Meat Hygiene Service
			MIBiol	Member, Institute of Biology
LDS	Licentiate in Dental Surgery		MICE	Member, Institution of Civil Engineers
LEA	Local Education Authority			
LEDU	Local Enterprise Development Unit		MIMechE	Member, Institution of Mechanical Engineers
LEG	Legislation			
LG	Lady Companion, Order of the Garter		MIMinE	Member, Institution of Mining Engineers
LGA	Local Government Association		MISC	Miscellaneous
LGSM&D	Licentiate, Guildhall School of Music and Drama		MLA	Member of Legislative Assembly (Northern Ireland Assembly)
LHS	Local Management of Schools		MM	Military Medal
Lib Dem	Liberal Democrat		MN	Merchant Navy
LIBiol	Licentiate, Institute of Biology		MO	Medical Officer; Military Operations
LISA	Logistic Information Systems Agency			
			MoD	Ministry of Defence
LLB	Bachelor of Laws		MP	Member of Parliament
LLD	Doctor of Laws		MPH	Master of Public Health
LLM	Master of Laws		MPhil	Master of Philosophy
LRAM	Licentiate, Royal Academy of Music		MRC	Medical Research Council
			MRCGP	Member, Royal College of General Practitioners
LRCP	Licentiate, Royal College of Physicians, London			
			MS	Master of Surgery
LRT	London Regional Transport		MSA	Medical Supplies Agency

MSAE	Member, Society of Automotive Engineers (USA)
MSc	Master of Science
MSC	Manpower Services Commission
MSDA	Military Survey Defence Agency
MSF	Manufacturing Science Finance Union
MSP	Member of Scottish Parliament
MSPFW	MSP for Falkirk West
MVO	Member of the Royal Victorian Order
NA	National Academician (USA)
NAC	National Agriculture Centre
NALGO	National and Local Government Officers' Association (see Unison)
NAO	National Audit Office
NAPRB	Review Body for Nursing Staff, Midwives, Health Visitors and Professions Allied to Medicine
NAS	National Academy of Sciences; National Archives of Scotland
NATFHE	National Association of Teachers in Further and Higher Education
NATO	North Atlantic Treaty Organization
NATS	National Air Traffic Services
NBA	National Blood Authority
NBSA	Naval Bases and Supply Agency
NCB	National Coal Board
NCC	National Consumer Council
NCVQ	National Council for Vocational Qualifications
NDPB	Non-Departmental Public Body
NEC	National Executive Committee
NECC	National Electricity Consumers' Council
NEDC	National Economic Development Council
NERC	Natural Environment Research Council
NFER	National Foundation for Educational Research
NFU	National Farmers' Union
NGO	Non-governmental Organisation
NHBC	National House-Building Council
NHS	National Health Service
NHSPA	NHS Pensions Agency
NHSPASA	NHS Purchasing and Supply Agency
NHSSS	NHS Superannuation Scheme (Scotland)
NIACT	Northern Ireland Advisory Committee on Telecommunications
NIAO	Northern Ireland Audit Office

NIBSC	National Institute for Biological Standards and Control
NICO	National Insurance Contributions Office
NICO	Northern Ireland Company Overseas
NIH	North Irish Horse
NILO	National Investment and Loans Office
NIO	Northern Ireland Office
NIPS	Northern Ireland Prison Service
NISRA	Northern Ireland Statistics and Research Agency
NLCB	National Lottery Charities Board
NLP	Natural Law Party
NMA	Naval Manning Agency
NMRS	National Monuments Record of Scotland
NMS	National Museums of Scotland
NRA	National Rifle Association; National Rivers Authority
NRPB	National Radiological Protection Board
NRTA	Naval Recruiting and Training Agency
NS	National Savings; Nova Scotia
NSMC	North-South Ministerial Council
NUJ	National Union of Journalists
NUM	National Union of Mineworkers
NUPE	National Union of Public Employees (see Unison)
NUR	National Union of Railwaymen
NUT	National Union of Teachers
NVQ	National Vocational Qualification
NWML	National Weights and Measures Laboratory
NY	New York
OAU	Organisation for African Unity
OBE	Officer of the Order of the British Empire
OC	Officer Commanding; Officer, Order of Canada
ODI	Overseas Development Institute
OECD	Organisation for Economic Co-Operation and Development
Ofgem	Office of Gas and Electricity Markets
OFREG	Office for the Regulation of Electricity and Gas
OFSTED	Office for Standards in Education
OFT	Office of Fair Trading
OFTEL	Office of Telecommunications
OFWAT	Office of Water Services
OGC	Office of Government Commerce
OGD	Other Government Departments

OHMCI W	HM Chief Inspector of Schools, Wales	PIA	Personal Investment Authority
		PINS	Planning Inspectorate
OIRR	Office of the International Rail Regulator	PITCOM	Parliamentary Information Technology Committee
OIS	Office Information Systems	PIU	Performance and Innovation Unit
OLA	Other Lords of Appeal	Pl C	Plaid Cymru
O & M	organisation and method	plc	Public Limited Company
OM	Order of Merit	PLP	Parliamentary Labour Party
OME	Office of Manpower Economics	PMB	Private Member's Bill
ONS	Office for National Statistics	PMPA	Public Management and Policy Association
OP	Organo Phosphate Group		
OPA	Oil and Pipelines Agency	PO	Post Office
OPRA	Occupational Pensions Regulatory Authority	POEU	Post Office Engineering Union
		POST	Parliamentary Office of Science and Technology
OPRAF	Office of Passenger Rail Franchising	POUNC	Post Office Users' National Council
OPS	Office of Public Service		
ORR	Office of the Rail Regulator	PoW	Prisoner of War
OS	Ordnance Survey	PPA	Pay and Personnel Agency
OSCE	Organisation on Security and Co-operation in Europe	PPARC	Particle Physics and Astronomy Research Council
OSNI	Ordnance Survey of Northern Ireland	PPB	Professional and Policy Branch
		PPE	Philosophy, Politics and Economics
OSS	Office for the Supervision of Solicitors	PPRS	Pharmaceutical Price Regulatory Scheme
OSSW	Office of the Secretary of State for Wales	PPS	Parliamentary Private Secretary; Political Planning Services
OStJ	Officer of the Most Venerable Order of the Hospital of St John of Jerusalem	PR	Proportional Representation; Public Relations
		PRASEG	Parliamentary Renewable and Sustainable Energy Group
OTC	Officers' Training Corps		
OU	Open University; Oxford University	PRO	Public Record Office
		PRONI	Public Record Office of Northern Ireland
PA	Personal Assistant		
PAC	Public Accounts Committee	PSA	Public Services Agreement
PACE	Property Advisers to the Civil Estate	psc	Graduate of Staff College
		PSD	Pesticides Safety Directorate
PACTS	Parliamentary Advisory Council for Transport Safety	PSI	Policy Studies Institute
		PSX	Public Services and Public Expenditure
PAM	Professions Allied to Medicine		
PAO	Prince Albert's Own	PTO	Public Trust Office
PASEG	Parliamentary Astronomy and Space Environment Group	PWO	Prince of Wales's Own
		QAA	Quality Assurance Agency for Higher Education
PC	Privy Counsellor; Productivity and Competitiveness; Plaid Cymru		
		QC	Queen's Counsel
PCA	Police Complaints Authority	QCA	Qualifications and Curriculum Authority
PCC	Press Complaints Commission		
PE	Procurement Executive	QFL	Queen's Speeches and Future Legislation
PES	Public Expenditure Survey		
PGCE	Post Graduage Certificate of Education	QMG	Quartermaster General
		QPM	Queen's Police Medal
PHAB	Physically Handicapped and Able-bodied	QSO	Queen's Service Order (New Zealand)
PhD	Doctor of Philosophy	QUB	Queen's University, Belfast
PHLS	Public Health Laboratory Service Board	qv	quod vide (which see)
		QVS	Queen Victoria School

RA	Radiocommunications Agency; Royal Academician; Royal Regiment of Artillery	RMN	Registered Mental Nurse
		RMT	Rail, Maritime and Transport Union
RAC	Royal Agricultural College; Royal Automobile Club	RN	Royal Navy
		RNIB	Royal National Institute for the Blind
RACS	Royal Arsenal Co-operative Society	RNLI	Royal National Lifeboat Institution
RAF	Royal Air Force	RNR	Royal Navy Reserve
RAFPMA	RAF Personnel Management Agency	RNVR	Royal Naval Volunteer Reserve
		ROSA	Rent Office Service Agreements
RAFSEE	RAF Signals Engineering Establishment	RPMS	Royal Postgraduate Medical School
		RSC	Royal Society of Chemistry
RAFTGDA	RAF Training Group Defence Agency	RSO	Resident Surgical Officer
		Rt Hon	The Right Honourable
RAFVR	Royal Air Force Volunteer Reserve	Rt Rev	The Right Reverend
RAMC	Royal Army Medical Corps	RUR	Royal Ulster Regiment
RAPC	Royal Army Pay Corps	RUSI	Royal United Services Institute
RAPS	Rent Assessment Panels	RYS	Royal Yacht Squadron
RARO	Regular Army Reserve of Officers	S	Scotland
RASC	Royal Army Service Corps	SA	South Africa; South Australia
RAuxAF	Royal Auxiliary Air Force	SAAS	Student Awards Agency for Scotland
RC	Roman Catholic		
RCA	Rate Collection Agency	SAC	Scottish Arts Council
RCAC	Royal Canadian Armoured Corps	SACOT	Scottish Advisory Committee on Telecommunications
RCAHMS	Royal Commission on the Ancient and Historical Monuments of Scotland	SASA	Scottish Agricultural Science Agency
RCAHMW	Royal Commission on the Ancient and Historical Monuments of Wales	SBAC	Society of British Aerospace Companies
		SCAA	School Curriculum and Assessment Authority
RCT	Royal Corps of Transport		
RCVS	Royal College of Veterinary Surgeons	SCE	Service Children's Education
		SCS	Senior Civil Servant
RD	Royal Naval and Royal Marine Forces Reserve Decoration	SDLP	Social Democratic and Labour Party
RDA	Regional Development Agency	SDP	Social Democratic Party
RDC	Rural Development Commission; Rural District Council	SECS	Scottish Executive Corporate Services
RE	Royal Engineers	SEDD	Scottish Executive Development Department
REME	Royal Electrical and Mechanical Engineers	SEED	Scottish Executive Education Department
Retd LAO	Retired Lord of Appeal in Ordinary	SEEDA	South East of England Development Agency
Rev	Reverend		
RFC	Royal Flying Corps; Rugby Football Club	SEELLD	Scottish Executive Enterprise and Lifelong Learning Department
RGN	Registered General Nurse	SEF	Scottish Executive Finance
RGS	Royal Geographical Society	SEHD	Scottish Executive Health Department
RHG	Royal Horse Guards		
RI	Rhode Island	SEJD	Scottish Executive Justice Department
RICS	Royal Institution of Chartered Surveyors		
		SEO	Society of Education Officers
RIIA	Royal Institute of International Affairs	SEPA	Scottish Environment Protection Agency
RLC	Royal Logistics Corps		
RMC	Royal Military College (now RMA)	SERAD	Scottish Executive Rural Affairs Department

SERC	Science and Engineering Research Council	SSRC	Social Science Research Council
SES	Scottish Executive Secretariat	SSSI	Sites of Special Scientific Interest
SF	Sinn Fein	STRB	School Teachers' Review Body
SFEFC	Scottish Further Education Funding Council	STSS	Scottish Teachers' Superannuation Scheme
SFO	Serious Fraud Office	STV	Single Transferable Vote
SFPA	Scottish Fisheries Protection Agency	SVQ	Scottish Vocational Qualification
SHAC	London Housing Aid Centre	T&AF	Territorial and Auxiliary Forces
SHAEF	Supreme Headquarters, Allied Expeditionary Force	TA	Territorial Army
		TARO	Territorial Army Reserve of Officers
SHAPE	Supreme Headquarters, Allied Powers, Europe	TASS	Technical Administrative and Supervisory Section of MSF (qv)
SHEFC	Scottish Higher Education Funding Council	TAVRA	Territorial Auxiliary and Volunteer Reserve Association
SIs	Statutory Instruments	TBA	The Buying Agency
SITPRO	Simpler Trade Procedures Board	TD	Territorial Efficiency Decoration
SLC	Student Loans Company	TEA	Training and Employment Agency
SLD	Scottish Liberal Democrats; Social and Liberal Democrats	TGO	Timber Growers' Association
		TGWU	Transport and General Workers Union
SMMT	Society of Motor Manufacturers and Traders Ltd	TL	Team Leader
SNH	Scottish Natural Heritage	TOTE	Horserace Totalisator Board
SNP	Scottish National Party	TRS	The Rent Service
SOGAT	Society of Graphical and Allied Trades	TTA	Teacher Training Agency
		TU	Trade Union
SOLACE	Society of Local Authority Chief Executives	TUC	Trades Union Congress
SP	Scottish Parliament	TUPE	Transfer of Undertakings (Protection of Employment Regulation)
SPCB	Scottish Parliament Corporate Body	TV	Television
SPPA	Scottish Public Pensions Agency	UC	University College
SPS	Scottish Prison Service	UCATT	Union of Construction, Allied Trades and Technicians
SPUC	Society for the Protection of the Unborn Child	UCH	University College Hospital (London)
SQA	Scottish Qualifications Authority	UCL	University College London
SRB	Single Regeneration Budget	UDC	Urban Development Corporation; Urban District Council
SRC	Science Research Council; Students' Representative Council	UDUP	Ulster Democratic Unionist Party
SRN	State Registered Nurse	UGC	University Grants Committee
SRO	Supplementary Reserve of Officers	UK	United Kingdom
SS	Saints	UKAEA	United Kingdom Atomic Energy Authority
SSA	Ships Support Agency	UKHO	United Kingdom Hydrographic Office
SSA	Social Security Agency		
SSAC	Social Security Advisory Committee	UK Sport	United Kingdom Sports Council
SSAFA	Soldiers', Sailors' and Airmen's Families Association	UKU	United Kingdom Unionist
		UKUP	United Kingdom Unionist Party
SSC	Solicitor before Supreme Court (Scotland)	ULTRA	Unrelated Live Transplant Regulatory Authority
SSEB	South of Scotland Electricity Board	UMIST	University of Manchester Institute of Science and Technology
SSG	Small Systems Group		
SSP	Scottish Socialist Party	UN	United Nations
SSRA	Shadow Strategic Rail Authority	UNCTAD	United Nations Conference on Trade and Development
SSRB	Review Body on Senior Salaries		

UNDCP	United Nations International Drug Control Programme	US	United States
UNDP	United Nations Development Programme	USA	United States of America
UNEP	United Nations Environment Programme	USDAW	Union of Shop Distributive and Allied Workers
UNESCO	United Nations Educational, Scientific and Cultural Organization	UUP	Ulster Unionist Party
		UUUC	United Ulster Unionist Coalition
UNFICYP	United Nations Force in Cyprus	VC	Victoria Cross
UNFPA	United Nations Population Fund	VCA	Vehicle Certification Agency
UNHCR	United Nations High Commissioner for Refugees	VI	Vehicle Inspectorate
		VLA	Valuation and Lands Agency; Veterinary Laboratories Agency
UNICEF	United Nations Children's Fund	VMD	Veterinary Medicines Directorate
UNICRI	United Nations Inter-Regional Crime and Justice Research Institute	VR	Volunteer Reserve
		VRD	Royal Naval Volunteer Reserve Officers' Decoration
UNIDIR	United Nations Institute for Disarmament Research	WAAF	Women's Auxiliary Air Force
		WDA	Welsh Development Agency
UNIDO	United Nations Industrial Development Organization	WEA	Workers' Educational Association
		WEU	Western European Union
UNISON	(an amalgamation of COHSE, NALGO and NUPE)	WFP	World Food Programme (UN)
		WHO	World Health Organization (UN)
UNITAR	United Nations Institute for Training and Research	WIPO	World Intellectual Property Organization (UN)
		WIT	White Paper Implementation Team
UNOG	United Nations Office at Geneva	WLGA	Welsh Local Government Association
UNRISD	United Nations Research Institute for Social Development	WMO	World Meteorological Organization (UN)
UNRWA	United Nations Relief and Works Agency for Palestine Refugees in the Near East	WNC	Women's National Commission
		WS	Writer to the Signet
		WTO	World Tourism Organization (UN); World Trade Organization
UNU	United Nations University		
UPU	Universal Postal Union (UN)	WW	Welfare to Work
URA	Urban Regeneration Agency	YC	Young Conservative

Government Relations and Parliamentary Consultants' Directory

by *Michael Burrell*

Throughout its long history *Dod's Parliamentary Companion* has taken pride in being right up-to-date. So it is entirely appropriate that these days it includes a Government Relations and Parliamentary Consultants' Directory.

Lobbying is as old as Britain's Parliamentary democracy. The House of Commons was itself established as a lobby aimed at influencing the King. As power shifted Westminster and Whitehall themselves became the target of lobbying by those with grievances. However, the concept of seeking help from professional lobbying consultancies is really a phenomenon of the last quarter of a century.

Few have questioned the right of companies and others to take advice on how best to put a case to the authorities. Where concerns have arisen they have not generally been over the right to lobby itself, but rather over how that lobbying is done and, in particular, over the issue of financial connections between business and MPs. These concerns were part of the reason for setting up the Committee on Standards in Public Life (the Nolan, now the Neill Committee).

The Committee has encouraged Government, Parliament and the lobbying industry to abide by a set of principles. Within Government these are set out in guidance for civil servants. The House of Commons has established rules for itself that are enforced by the Standards Committee. In turn the consultancy world has established a self-regulatory system.

The principal self-regulatory body for the industry is the Association of Professional Political Consultants (APPC). The APPC has a detailed code of conduct, to which member consultancies commit themselves, and it publishes a twice-yearly register of clients, so that everyone can see the advisers and the interests they advise upon. The Association has consistently taken the view that lobbyists and the lobbied should be separate, so the code bars financial connections between consultancies and politicians. Specifically, it makes it impossible for staff to be simultaneously consultants and MPs, peers, Members of the European Parliament, Scottish Parliament, National Assembly for Wales, Northern Ireland Assembly or the Greater London Assembly.

The list reflects the way the industry itself has evolved to reflect the dispersal of power from Westminster to the institutions of the European Union in one direction and to the devolved assemblies in the other. Lobbyists aim to be wherever power lies, for only by doing so can they serve the needs of their clients.

So much for history. But what do lobbyists/public affairs consultancies/Government relations consultancies/Parliamentary consultants actually do?

Perhaps the easiest way to start to explain is to say what they don't do – which is lobby. They don't actually tap legislators or officials on the shoulder and urge them to follow a particular course of action, and they don't do so for the simple reason that it wouldn't work. Politicians and civil servants expect to hear directly from those who are affected by their actions and are generally impatient with intermediaries.

The role that consultancies play is advisory: they advise their clients on how best to put a case: who to contact, when, how, at what length and in what tone of voice. It is accumulated common sense, rather than rocket science, but because it is what consultants do every day of their working lives, the best of them become very skilled in the most effective routes to success, rather as effective lawyers know how best to make a case in court.

Take the who, for example. Many people will start with the assumption that the answer to their political problem will rest with an MP. It may do – in that some of the most successful lobbying campaigns have culminated in private members' legislation. But, to be frank, the key to a particular problem will far more frequently lie within the civil service. So knowing where to go in Whitehall, which departments to approach and at what level will normally be very important. Or very likely, part of the solution will be found in a regulatory body, or some other quango. Or perhaps not in London at all, but in one of the directorates-general of the European Commission in Brussels, or at *cabinet* level there. Or in a committee of the Scottish Parliament. Or somewhere in local government. The possibilities are almost endless, but it is at the heart of a consultant's job to know where to go.

Or take the how. It might be as simple as a telephone call or as complicated as a five-year public inquiry. More often than not, it will involve mapping out a chessboard of different influences and making an assessment of how best to approach each. In some cases that will involve organising one-to-one meetings with officials. Often it will mean setting out the case in writing, clearly, briefly and without deploying jargon. It will almost certainly involve a judgement on when will be the most effective time to act. It may well include a careful judgement of which of a number of possible solutions are most feasible, politically or economically. It could include taking a view on whether securing media exposure for the arguments will help or hinder. Clients look to their consultants for all this and much more besides.

Today's political consultancy world is intensely competitive and, as a result, the quality of the advice on offer is generally high. If you haven't used a consultancy before it probably makes sense to talk to two or three about your issue, so that you can compare different approaches, before making a selection. Having done so, you should find that your consultant will work hard and conscientiously to secure a result. But just one final cautionary note. Just as a lawyers owe a duty to the court, as well as to their client, so political consultants have a duty to the system, as well as to you. That means that should you, inadvertently, ask them to do something inappropriate, they will politely, but firmly, decline. It is part of what you are paying them for.

Michael Burrell is Chairman of the Association of Professional
Political Consultants and of Westminster Strategy

GOVERNMENT RELATIONS AND PARLIAMENTARY CONSULTANTS

ADVANCE COMMUNICATIONS

Advance Communications offers monitoring, counselling and strategic planning services relating to all aspects of the political and government system in the UK and Europe.

Our expertise covers a wide range of policy areas, with particular strengths in healthcare issues.

The company operates from its London based office with affiliates in Strasbourg and Brussels.

A range of businesses and charities of all sizes benefit from sound judgement based on many years' experience in the Government Relations field.

For further information please contact:

Berkeley Greenwood

Advance Communications
3/19 Holmbush Road,
Putney
London
SW15 3LE
Tel: 020 8780 9110
Fax: 020 8789 0795
E-mail:
advance@portcullisresearch.com

APCO
u k

APCO UK, a London based public affairs and strategic communications consultancy, is part of the APCO Worldwide network which provides support to clients whose operating environment is affected by political, regulatory and communications issues. Our expertise includes: Political monitoring, government and media relations, coalition building, grassroots campaigning, corporate positioning, corporate community relations, internal communications and technology services.

Number of UK staff: 46

Senior Directors:
Nick DeLuca, Simon Milton, Rosemary Grogan

For further information about APCO UK or our European offices in Berlin, Brussels, Geneva, Paris and Rome, please contact:

Nick DeLuca, Managing Director
APCO UK
95 New Cavendish Street
London W1W 6XQ
Tel: 020 7526 3600
Fax: 020 7526 3699
E-mail: ndeluca@apcouk.com
Home Page:
http://www.apcouk.com

 association of professional political consultants

BEAUMARK
LONDON • BRUSSELS

Beaumark provides expert public affairs guidance on Westminster, Whitehall and the institutions of the European Union. Beaumark consultants have proven expertise across the political parties and can demonstrate in-depth knowledge of the political process and parliamentary procedure

Consultancy services range from political research and strategic advice through to full political representation and advocacy.

Contact: David Bennett,
Managing Director,
Beaumark Ltd,
14 Great College Street,
London
SW1P 3RX
Tel: 020 7222-1371
Fax: 020 7222-1440
E-mail:
info@beaumark.ndirect.co.uk
Website: www.beaumark.com

Europe Analytica
Av. Livingstone 26 (Bte 3)
B-1000 Brussels,
Belgium
Tel: 0032-2-231-1299
E-mail:
info@europe-analytica.com

 association of professional political consultants

GOVERNMENT RELATIONS AND PARLIAMENTARY CONSULTANTS

For information regarding listings please call:

Jane Smith on

020 7630 7654

or write to:
Vacher Dod Publishing Limited
PO Box 3700, Westminster, London, SW1P 4WU
E-mail: janesmith@vacherdod.co.uk

GCI Political Counsel is the strategic public affairs arm of top-10 PR consultancy GCI. Our team provides a complete range of public affairs services from political monitoring and government relations to issues management, corporate communications and stakeholder dialogue.

The strategies we develop with our clients are based on the realities of modern politics and cover the diverse and complex influences on the political process. We are driven by the business and organisational needs of our clients, not by the process of communications itself.

For a different slant on public affairs, please contact:

Rod Cartwright
Director
GCI London Ltd.
1 Chelsea Manor Gardens
London SW3 5PN

Tel: 020 7349 5015
Fax: 020 7349 5085
E-mail: rcartwright@gciuk.com

Or visit our website at
www.gciuk.com

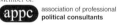
G J W
B S M G   W O R L D W I D E

GJW is Europe's largest specialist public affairs consultancy with offices in London, Edinburgh, Cardiff, Brussels and throughout central and eastern Europe. Now part of BSMG Worldwide, we also work with the group's wide network of offices throughout North America, Europe, and the Far East.

We can assist you in all aspects of your political communications including monitoring, policy analysis, strategic advice and campaigning. And if you need to run a more comprehensive campaign, we can provide an integrated political, media and corporate communications package, all from one agency.

As well as campaigning on broad political issues within the UK we have also developed units specialising in defence, healthcare, competition and regulation, planning and local government, transport and construction and new technologies

GJW is a founder member of the Association of Professional Political Consultants.

For further information contact:
Paul Barnes at
GJW@BSMG Worldwide
110 St Martin's Lane
London WC2N 4DY
Tel: 020 7841 5555
Fax: 020 7841 5777
e-mail: pbarnes@gjw.bsmg.com

 association of professional political consultants

 Government Policy Consultants

Europe's leading Public Affairs consultancy, advising private, public and voluntary organisations on all aspects of public policy communications. Our consultants are organised in specialist units servicing the transport, health, environmental, local government, IT, energy, retailing, broadcast and defence sectors amongst others.

Based in London, Edinburgh, Berlin, Brussels, Paris and with a global network including North America, our staff are drawn from a wide range of political, civil service, European Commission, academic and commercial backgrounds.

As part of the world-wide Omnicom group of companies, we manage strategic communications issues management and crises programmes.

For information please contact:

Caroline Wunnerlich
Managing Director
GPC Brussels
Rue d'Arlon 50
B-1000 Brussels
Tel: (00) 322 285 4604
Fax: (00) 322 230 3165
caroline.wunnerlich@
gpcbrussels.com
www.gpcinternational.com

Peter Bingle
Managing Director
GPC London
4 Millbank
London SW1P 3GP
Tel: 020 7799 1500
Fax: 020 7222 5872
peter.bingle@gpclondon.com

Jane Saren
Managing Director
GPC Scotland
14 Charlotte Square
Edinburgh EH2 4DJ
Tel: 0131-226 2102
Fax: 0131-225 9859
jane.saren@gpcscotland.com

 association of professional political consultants

GRANT BUTLER COOMBER
PUBLIC AFFAIRS

Strategic, Creative and Effective Political and Public Relations

Carl Gibson or Peter Golds
Grant Butler Coomber
Westminster House
Kew Road
Richmond
TW9 2ND
t: 020 8322 1922
f: 020 8322 1923
e: carlg@GBC.co.uk
w: grantbutlercoomber.com

HILL & KNOWLTON

H & K's Public and Corporate Affairs Division offers the full range of political consultancy services covering Whitehall, Westminster and Brussels. It develops strategies to manage issues and to influence policy through the full range of 'opinion formers' including regulators, the media, pressure and interest groups and think tanks.

H & K's services are designed to meet three fundamental client needs: to anticipate policy change; to influence the policy process; and to help clients protect their corporate reputation.

H & K offers a full international public affairs service.

For further information please contact:
Andrew Pharoah
Managing Director
Hill & Knowlton (UK) Ltd
35 Red Lion Square
London WC1R 4SG
Tel: 020 7413 3049
Fax: 020 7413 3113
E-mail:
apharoah@hillandknowlton.com
Website:
www.hillandknowlton.com

appc association of professional
political consultants

KEENE PUBLIC AFFAIRS
CONSULTANTS LIMITED

Established in 1986 as an independent consultancy, we specialise in government relations and public affairs in the UK and Europe.

Through our London office and our European associate, Euralia, we offer a professional, cost-effective service based on a thorough analysis of our clients' needs.

Our services include: Monitoring, research and strategic advice; Assistance in contact-making and campaigning; Government marketing; Public and media relations; Crisis communications and media training; Speech writing; Event and conference organisation.

For further information please contact:
Tony Richards
Managing Director
Keene Public Affairs Consultants
Victory House
99-101 Regent Street
London
W1B 4EZ
Tel: 020 7287 0652
Fax: 020 7494 0493
E-mail:
kpac@keenepa.demon.co.uk

Politics International

Founded in 1991, Politics International now has over thirty staff working from our offices in London, Edinburgh, Cardiff, Belfast and Brussels. Our specialist local solutions network, and community relations advisors, provide grass-roots, local and regional support.

We offer the full range of public affairs and related services and provide a one-stop shop for strategic advice and practical support at all levels. The principles upon which the company was founded include a rigorously ethical approach; in-depth understanding of clients and their priorities; acute awareness of the commercial implications of political and public policy decisions and professionalism.

For more information about how we can help your business please contact:

Andrew Dunlop
Managing Director
Politics International
Greencoat House
Francis Street
London SW1P 1DH
Tel: 020 7592 3800
Fax: 020 7630 7283
E-mail: pi@politicsint.co.uk
Website: www.politicsint.co.uk

 association of professional
political consultants

GOVERNMENT RELATIONS AND PARLIAMENTARY CONSULTANTS

For information regarding listings please call:

Jane Smith on

020 7630 7654

or write to:
Vacher Dod Publishing Limited
PO Box 3700, Westminster, London, SW1P 4WU
E-mail: janesmith@vacherdod.co.uk

GOVERNMENT RELATIONS AND PARLIAMENTARY CONSULTANTS (cont)

PORTCULLIS RESEARCH

Government relations consultants
Policy research • Advice • Lobbying

Understanding Government, informing policy – the true public private partnership

Sound advice depends on good information. Our clients reach better informed business decisions, because they get the best political intelligence.

By understanding and informing the public policy process, clients are enabled to influence out-comes. We aim to achieve clients' commercial objectives through high quality work, ethically conducted.

Advising multi-nationals, blue-chips, Government institutions, trade associations and charities, we provide a full range of Government relations services and skills, including monitoring, research and advocacy in the UK and EU political institutions.

Our clients benefit from a record of solid success across a comprehensive range of policy areas, including:

- financial services
- food & drink
- healthcare & pharmaceuticals
- industrial/environmental
- telecoms
- transport

Contact: **Charles Cockburn**

Portcullis Research
3/19 Holmbush Road
London
SW15 3LE
Tel: 020•8789 2798
Fax: 020•8789 0795
E-mail:
info@portcullisresearch.com
Website:
www.portcullisresearch.com

The PPS Group

The PPS Group comprises 40 public affairs professionals in two companies:

- PPS (Local and Regional) Ltd advises on presenting to local and regional government and community campaigning. Specialist areas include planning and the environment.
- PPS (Public Affairs) Ltd specialises in strategic advice, e-campaigning and public policy analysis in Westminster, Whitehall, Holyrood, Cardiff and Brussels.

For further information see our website www.ppsgroup.co.uk then contact:

Nick Keable
Managing Director
PPS (Local and Regional) Ltd
or
Mark Pendlington
Managing Director
PPS (Public Affairs) Ltd
at
69 Grosvenor Street
London W1X 9DB
020 7629 7377

Daniel Smith
Associate Director
PPS Edinburgh
12 Alva Street
Edinburgh EH2 4QG
0131-226 1951

Keith Butterick
Associate Director
PPS North
66/67 Barton Arcade Chambers
Deansgate
Manchester M3 2BJ
0161-832 2139

Fiona MacIntosh
Associate Director
PPS South West
9 North Court
The Courtyard
Woodlands
Almondsbury
Bristol BS32 4NQ
fiona.macintosh@
ppssouthwest.co.uk

  association of professional political consultants

getting it right

Through the provision of accurate and timely political intelligence and the development of reality based strategies, Profile provides sound political relations and corporate communications advice and undertakes implementation of that advice for companies, organisations and overseas governments.

We work with our clients in establishing coalitions of support for their political message and then advise on the communicating of that message to a political audience. We particularly specialise in community relations, legislative support and campaign and issue management.

Our work covers local and national issues in the UK with our associate in Edinburgh. In addition, we have associates in Brussels, Washington DC, New York and Los Angeles.

For further information please contact:
Susan Eastoe
Director
Profile
31 Great Peter Street
London SW1P 3LR
Tel: 020 7654 5600
Fax: 020 7222 2030
E-mail: eastoes@profilecc.com

ANIMAL WELFARE

ANIMAL DEFENDERS

Educates, creates awareness, and promotes interest in the cause of justice and the suppression of all forms of cruelty to animals; to alleviate suffering, to conserve and protect animals and the environment.

Initiatives include a campaign against use of animals in circuses; to bring permanent circus quarters under regulation such as the Zoo Licensing Act.

Contact Jan Creamer, Director
Animal Defenders
261 Goldhawk Road
London
W12 9PE
Tel: 020 8846 9777
Fax: 020 8846 9712
E-mail:
info@animaldefenders.org.uk
Web:
www.animaldefenders.org.uk

NATIONAL ANTI-VIVISECTION SOCIETY

Provides scientific reports, briefing papers, video and photos from investigations of use of animals in experiments.

Currently campaigning on excessive secrecy of animal research licensing process.

We also fund sophisticated non-animal techniques; projects include breast and lung cancer, cataracts, dental filling toxicity, drugs, cot deaths, safety testing.

Contact Jan Creamer, Director,
National Anti-Vivisection Society
261 Goldhawk Road
London W12 9PE
Tel: 020 8846 9777
Fax: 020 8846 9712
E-mail: info@navs.org.uk
Web: www.navs.org.uk

ARCHITECTS

The Architects Registration Board (ARB) was established by statute in 1997 and is the independent regulator for the architectural profession in the United Kingdom. It has a dual mandate to protect the interests of consumers and to safeguard the reputation of architects by

- maintenance of an accurate register of those entitled to use the title 'architect' and prosecuting title abuse
- working to improve professional standards in education and in practice
- operating an efficient and effective information and complaints service
- managing disciplinary procedures where necessary

Architects Registration Board
8 Weymouth Street
London W1N 3FB
Tel 020 7580 5861
Fax 020 7436 5269
E-mail: info@arb.org.uk
Website: www.arb.org.uk

BANKING AND FINANCE

BRITISH BANKERS' ASSOCIATION

105-108 Old Broad Street
London EC2N 1EX
The British Bankers' Association is the principal trade association for over 300 member banks from more than sixty countries doing banking business in the UK. We provide information on banking matters in the UK, EU and the World.

Website: www.bba.org.uk

Press and General Information
Brian Capon 020 7216 8810

Director of Communications
Simon Pitkeathley 020 7216 8906
simonp@bba.org.uk

Banks & Building Societies
National Training Organisation
Liz Chiswell 020 7216 8900

BUILDING SOCIETIES

Bradford & Bingley

As a leading provider and distributor of financial services with more than 3m customers, Bradford & Bingley Group offers choice and advice from a name people can trust. The Group is developing a national mortgage broking service through its 600 high street sites, its Charcol subsidiary and on the internet through "Charcolonline". Bradford & Bingley is also the largest high street provider of independent financial advice and a prominent estate agency.

Contacts:
Chris Holland, Group Corporate Affairs Manager, on 01274 554709.
Fax 01274 554933; e-mail chris.holland@bbbs-group.co.uk
PO Box 88 Croft Road,
Crossflatts, Bingley,
West Yorkshire BD16 2UA

BUSINESS REPRESENTATION

The Institute of Directors is a non-political business organisation, with 52,000 members worldwide. It helps directors to carry out their leadership responsibilities in creating wealth for the benefit of business and society. The IoD represents members' interests to government and opinion formers, in the areas of small business policy, corporate governance, employment, education and training, taxation, economic policy, environment and regulation.

Contact: Nina Wilkins
Policy Unit,
IoD,
116 Pall Mall,
London SW1Y 5ED
Tel: 020 7451 3280
Fax: 020 7839 2337
E-mail: policy-unit@iod.co.uk

CONSTRUCTION

NATIONAL HOUSE-BUILDING COUNCIL
Buildmark House,
Chiltern Avenue, Chesham,
Bucks HP6 5AP

NHBC is the standard setting and independent regulatory body for the UK house-building industry. It has around 18,000 registered house builders and developers on its register and approximately 1.7 million homes under its Buildmark cover. It has enjoyed over 60 years at the heart of the house-building industry, and is a highly respected authority on housing construction and home buyer protection.

NHBC sets the standards for house-building, monitors homes built to those standards, and then provides its 'Buildmark' cover on around 85 per cent of private sector new homes in the UK. Independent actuaries have confirmed that housing defects are now less than half what they otherwise would have been without NHBC's insistence on raising standards.

Independent of Government, the Governing Council of NHBC represents all those interested in improving the standard of new home construction.
Contact: Derek Hamilton-Knight, Public Affairs Manager
Tel: 01494 434477
Fax: 01494 735201

CABLE COMMUNICATIONS

Telewest Communications plc is a leading digital media and telecoms group. The company has the potential to provide broadband services to approximately 6 million homes and businesses throughout the country. Telewest's 1.6 million residential customers and 61,000 companies have access to multi-channel television, telephony, unmetered Internet access and new digital services through a single, high-speed, always-on, broadband connection. The company is also the largest supplier of basic television channels to the UK multi-channel market and is BBC Worldwide's 50:50 partner in the UKTV joint venture.

For further information and/or advice on policy issues contact:

Charles Wilby
Head of Public Affairs
Tel 020 7299 5324

ENERGY

ScottishPower

Mike Watson
Government Relations Manager
Scottish Power plc
5th Floor
30 Cannon Street
London
EC4M 6XH
Tel: 020 7651 2060
Fax: 020 7651 2062
E-mail: mike.watson@scottish power.plc.uk

Jamie Maxton
Parliamentary Liaison Officer
Scottish Power plc
1 Atlantic Quay
Glasgow
G2 8SP
Tel: 0141 636 4563
Fax: 0141 636 4566
E-mail: jamie.maxton@ scottish power.plc.uk

ENERGY

Lattice

Lattice – the Infrastructure Technology Group – is a family of businesses whose essence is the provision, management and servicing of infrastructure networks. Its principal business is Transco, which owns, operates and develops the main gas transportation system in Great Britain. It is also establishing businesses to provide state-of-the-art infrastructure for the next generation of mobile phones and internet applications. It has property, leasing, technology, as well as other energy and utility services businesses which will be seeking to exploit the unprecedented growth opportunities provided by market liberalisation, competition, the digital revolution and the transforming potential of the internet, not only in Britain but also in other developed countries."

For information on Lattice Group's activities, please contact:

Mish Tullar
Group Head of Public Affairs
Lattice Group
31 Homer Road, Solihull
West Midlands B91 3LT
Tel : 0121 623 2162
Fax : 0121 709 0205
Mobile: 07887832 699

Registered Office:
Lattice Group
130 Jermyn Street
London SW1Y 4UR
www.lattice-group.com

Chris Jamieson
Public Affairs
Corporate Affairs
0121 623 (7592) 2162
chris.jamieson@uktransco.com

ENERGY (cont)

 **National Grid**

National Grid Group plc
Government Affairs
15 Marylebone Road
London NW1 5JD

National Grid owns and operates the electricity transmission system in England and Wales. National Grid also has interests in electricity in the USA, Argentina, Zambia, Australia, and elsewhere in the world, building on our reputation for innovation and the use of hi-tech solutions to increase business efficiency.

National Grid also developed Energis, a major telecoms business. National Grid is now involved in major telecoms start-up businesses in Brazil, Argentina, Chile and Poland.

Chief Executive: David Jones
Group Director, UK and Europe
Roger Urwin

For further information on National Grid's role in managing the electricity system and on our other business activities, please contact our Government Affairs Team:

Judith Ward
Head of Government Affairs
Tel: 020 7312 5744
Fax: 020 7312 5659

Jane Smith
Tel: 020 7312 5746
Fax: 020 7312 5659

E-mail:
govt_affairs@uk.ngrid.com

GOVERNMENT RELATIONS AND PARLIAMENTARY CONSULTANTS

For information regarding listings please call:

Jane Smith on
020 7630 7654

or write to:
Vacher Dod Publishing Limited
PO Box 3700, Westminster,
London, SW1P 4WU
E-mail:
janesmith@vacherdod.co.uk

ENGINEERING

National Training Organisation for Engineering Manufacture

EMTA's mission is to raise the level of skills in the British engineering industry to world-class standards.

Contact us for information as follows:

EMTA
Tel: 020 7222 0464
Fax: 020 7222 3004

NVQs
Tel: 0345 581207

Engineering Careers
Tel: 0800 282167

Visit EMTA on the internet:
http://www.emta.org.uk

EMTA
2 Queen Anne's Gate Buildings
Dartmouth Street
London SW1H 9BP

INSURANCE

ASSOCIATION OF BRITISH INSURERS

ABI is the trade association for insurance companies and represents virtually the whole of the UK insurance company market. The Association represents insurers to Government, Parliament, civil servants and regulatory bodies.

The Association maintains close links with Westminster and Whitehall.

For briefings, information sheets, or help with constituents' queries, contact:

Mary Francis, Director General
Tel: 020 7216 7300
Fax: 020 7216 7302
E-mail: mary.francis@abi.org.uk
or
Stephen Sklaroff,
Deputy Director General
Tel: 020 7216 7400
Fax: 020 7696 8996
E-mail:
stephen.sklaroff@abi.org.uk
Internet: http://www.abi.org.uk

Association of British Insurers
51 Gresham Street
London EC2V 7HQ

The **International Underwriting Association of London** is the research and representational association for companies operating in the wholesale international insurance and reinsurance market centred on London.

For news and information about our members' contribution to UK inward investment and invisible exports, contact:

Marie-Louise Rossi
Chief Executive
Nick Lowe
Government Affairs
Tel: 020 7617 4444
Fax: 020 7617 4440
Website: www.iua.co.uk

LEGAL RESEARCH

MANORIAL SOCIETY OF GREAT BRITAIN

Research into legal title, history, and the holding of auction sales and of Manors and Feudal Baronies. Publishers of *The House of Lords, a thousand years of British tradition*, *The House of Commons, 700 years of British tradition*, *The Monarchy, 1500 Years of British tradition*, and other historical and constitutional books.

Manorial Society of Great Britain
104 Kennington Road
London SE11 6RE

Tel: 020 7735 6633
Fax: 020 7582 7022
E-mail: msgb@manor.net

MORTGAGE LENDERS

Council of Mortgage Lenders

Representative body for mortgage lenders, covering 98% of the market.

3 Savile Row
London W1X 1AF
tel: 020 7437 0075
fax: 020 7434 3791
website: www.cml.org.uk

Director General:
Michael Coogan
Deputy Director General:
Peter Williams
Head of External Affairs:
Sue Anderson

INDEX

Visit the Vacher Dod Website...

www.Politicallinks.co.uk

Political information and biographies updated daily

- TODAY'S BUSINESS
- THIS WEEK'S BUSINESS
- PROGRESS OF GOVERNMENT BILLS
- SELECT COMMITTEES
- DIARY
- HOUSE OF COMMONS
- HOUSE OF LORDS
- SCOTTISH PARLIAMENT

- NATIONAL ASSEMBLY FOR WALES
- NORTHERN IRELAND ASSEMBLY
- GREATER LONDON ASSEMBLY
- EUROPEAN UNION
- GENERAL ELECTION
- STOP PRESS

Vacher Dod Publishing Limited
PO Box 3700, Westminster, London SW1P 4WU
Tel: 020 7828 7256   Fax: 020 7828 7269
E-mail: politics@vacherdod.co.uk
Website: www.politicallinks.co.uk